ILLUSTRATED
ENCYCLOPEDIA

Copyright © 2001 George Philip Limited

George Philip Limited,
an imprint of Octopus Publishing Group
2–4 Heron Quays
Docklands
London
E14 4JP

EDITORS Chris Humphries
Steve Luck
Frances Adlington
Rachel Lawrence

ART EDITOR Mike Brown

PRODUCTION Sally Banner

Reproduction by Dorchester Typesetting

ISBN 0-540-07916-2

A catalogue record for this book is available
from the British Library

Printed in China

Details of other Philip's titles and services can
be found on our website at
www.philips-maps.co.uk

EDITORIAL CREDITS

Prof. A.E. Walsby *University of Bristol*
Prof. K. Simkiss *University of Reading*
Dr I. Hall *Victoria University of Manchester*
Prof. T. Halliday *Open University*
Prof. A.E. Walsby *University of Bristol*
Dr A.S. Bailey *University of Oxford*
Prof. Michael Tooley *University of St Andrews*
Dr Jan Brandts *University of Bristol*
Dr Kevin Thompson *University of Durham*
Prof. S.L. Lightman *University of Bristol*
Prof. Ron Chrisley *University of Sussex*
Prof. John Gribbin *University of Sussex*
Dr P.L. Domone *University College London*
David Miles *Director of The Oxford
Archaeological Unit*
Prof. Martin Pitts *Middlesex University*
Dr P.J. Heather *University College London*
Dr Rick Halpern *University College London*
Dr Jonathan Morris *University College London*
Dr Charles Beresford *University College London*
Prof. Richard Coates *University of Sussex*
Dr Mary Peace *Roehampton Institute, London*
Uma Dinsmore *Goldsmiths College, London*
Dr Derrick Puffet *University of Cambridge*
Dr Allan Griffiths *University College London*
Prof. Brian Barry *London School of Economics
and Political Science*
Prof. Margaret Boden *University of Sussex*
Prof. Colin Gunton *Kings College London*
Bob Peach *The Sports Council*
Peter Astley
Jill Bailey
John Bailie
Richard Brzezinski
Ian Chilvers
Roy Carr
John O.E. Clark
Sean Connolly
Chris Cooper
Mike Darton
Stephanie Driver
Roger Few
Keith Lye
Eddie Mizzi
Paulette Pratt
A.T.H. Rowland-Entwistle
Tom Ruppel
Clint Twist
Keith Wicks
Richard Widdows
John D. Wright

CURRICULUM CONSULTANTS

Duncan Hawley
David J. McHugh
Silvia Newton
Brian Speed
Jane Wheatley

PHILIP'S

ILLUSTRATED
ENCYCLOPEDIA

The *Philip's Illustrated Encyclopedia* has been created as a stimulating reference source for family use. It will be as useful for secondary school or college students as it will be for adult family members. The encyclopedia offers a wealth of factual information about the world and its people, from earliest times to the present, and as such provides answers to thousands of potential questions, while also opening a treasure-chest for browsers. The alphabetically organized entries provide clear, essential information on a vast variety of subjects, from world affairs to science and the arts.

When choosing a single-volume encyclopedia, the most important consideration for the user is the criteria by which the articles have been selected. The *Philip's Illustrated Encyclopedia* has been created with secondary school students particularly in mind. Core subjects (science and technology, English, history, contemporary politics and the humanities) have been given the greatest attention. The articles, compatible with and complementary to what is studied in the classroom, are as up-to-date as possible, and have been written with exceptional clarity so that even complex concepts can be understood by readers as young as thirteen or fourteen.

An encyclopedia, however, must contain more than just a comprehensive coverage of core subjects. Equally full in their treatment are the articles that cover leisure interests, such as sports and popular music, animals and plants, films, and current affairs, making this encyclopedia ideal for home reference as well as an important resource at school or college.

Cross References

The *Philip's Illustrated Encyclopedia* has more than 35,000 individual cross references, indicated by SMALL CAPITAL letters, that take readers from the primary article to all other articles that provide useful related information. For example, contained within the "pancreas" article are cross-references to small intestine, amylase, trypsin, insulin and diabetes.

Alphabetical Order

The order of articles is strictly alphabetical, except that Mc is treated as if it were spelled Mac, and concatenation as if spelled out in full; thus St. is treated as Saint. Articles that share the same main heading follow the basic hierarchy of people, places and things for example:

Washington, Booker T. (Taliaferro)
Washington, Denzel
Washington, George
Washington

Washington, D.C.
Washington, Treaty of

The hierarchy for biographical entries is: saints, popes, emperors, kings and queens, other royalty, non-royalty. However, when popes, emperors and monarchs share the same name, they are collected together by country and then follow in chronological order. Thus Henry I, Henry II, Henry III, etc. (of England) are grouped together, followed by Henry II, Henry III, Henry IV (of France).

Places that share a name are ordered by the alphabetical order of the country. Foreign place names have been anglicized, with the local spelling in parenthesis; for example, Florence (Firenze); Moscow (Moskva).

Alternative Spellings

For Chinese spellings the Pinyin system of transliteration is generally preferred, with cross-references to the Wade-Giles system where appropriate; for example, Peking *See* Beijing. Wade-Giles transliterations have also been retained where they remain in common use; for example, Chiang Kai-shek.

Alternative spellings and names of article titles follow the article title in parenthesis; for example, Dalai Lama (Grand Lama).

International Coverage

The importance of cultures beyond the English-speaking world is deliberately emphasized. In an age when international barriers are being steadily removed, the *Philip's Illustrated Encyclopedia* provides a greater proportion of entries on peoples, cultures, religions and beliefs than any other single-volume encyclopedia.

Science

In keeping with the conventions used in schools and colleges, modern scientific names have been used. For example, information on "acetaldehyde" will be found under "ethanal." Where the modern name used in the article title is less well known than the old name, a cross reference will be found under the old name directing readers to the article; for example, readers looking up formic acid will be directed to the article with the title methanoic acid.

A/a, first letter of the Roman alphabet. It evolved from the ancient Egyptian hieroglyph representing the head of an ox through the Hebrew word aleph, *meaning ox, to the Greek* alpha.

Aachen (Aix-la-Chapelle) City in sw North Rhine-Westphalia, w Germany. It is noted for its hot sulphur baths, used by the Romans and the hottest in N Europe. Aachen was the site of medieval imperial diets and the coronations of the monarchs of the Holy Roman Empire from 1349 to 1531. Industries: machinery, iron and steel, textiles. Pop. (1995) 247,000.

Aalto, Alvar (1898–1976) Finnish architect and furniture designer, famous for his imaginative handling of floor levels and use of natural materials and irregular forms. Aalto's work includes the Sanatorium at Paimio (1931), the Finnish pavilion at the New York International Exhibition (1939), Baker House at the Massachusetts Institute of Technology (1947–49) and Finlandia House, Helsinki (1967–71). *See also* MODERNISM

aardvark Nocturnal, bristly haired mammal of central and S Africa. It lives on termites and ants, which it scoops up with its sticky 30cm (12in) tongue. Length: up to 1.5m (5ft); weight: up to 70kg (154lb). It is the only representative of the order *Tubulidentata*.

Aarhus *See* ÅRHUS

Aaron In the Old Testament, elder brother of MOSES and the founder and first head of the Jewish priesthood. According to the book of Exodus, he led the Israelite tribe of Levi out of slavery in Egypt. Aaron cast a spell that brought ten plagues upon Egypt. He lapsed into idolatry and made a golden calf for the people to worship, but was later restored to divine favour.

Aaron, Hank (Henry Louis) (1934–) US baseball player. He was one of the first African Americans to play in the major leagues when he joined (1954) the Milwaukee Braves. In 1974, Aaron surpassed Babe RUTH's major-league career home run record of 714. In 1976 he retired from playing, having hit a record 755 home runs.

abacus Archaic mathematical tool used since ancient times in the Middle and Far East for addition and subtraction. One form of abacus consists of beads strung on wires and arranged in columns.

abalone (ormer) Gastropod MOLLUSC with a single, flattened spiral shell perforated by a row of respiratory holes. They are found in the shallows of rocky shores. Abalones are eaten and their shells used as ornaments. Length: to 30cm (12in). Family Haliotidae; species include *Haliotis rufescens*.

Abbado, Claudio (1933–) Italian conductor. He was musical director at La Scala, Milan (1972–86), the London Symphony Orchestra (1983–88), Vienna State Opera (1986–91) and the Berlin Philharmonic (1989–2002). He is noted for his interpretations of 20th-century music.

Abbas I (the Great) (1571–1629) Shah of Persia (1588–1629). The outstanding ruler of the SAFAVID dynasty, Abbas restored Persia as a great power, waging war successfully against the invading Uzbeks and Ottoman Turks and recapturing Hormuz from the Portuguese. Tolerant in religion, he encouraged Dutch and English merchants and admitted Christian missionaries. Abbas made ISFAHAN his capital.

Abbas II (1874–1944) Last khedive (Turkish viceroy) of Egypt (1892–1914). Abbas succeeded his father, Tewfik Pasha. He was generally hostile to the British, the dominant power, but he also rejected the nationalists' demands for liberal reform. Deposed when the British established a protectorate, he spent the rest of his life in exile.

Abbasid Muslim CALIPH dynasty (750–1258). They traced their descent from al-Abbas, the uncle of MUHAMMAD, and came to power by defeating the UMAYYADS. In 862, the Abbasids moved the caliphate from Damascus to Baghdad, where it achieved great splendour. From the 10th century, Abbasid caliphs ceased to exercise political power, becoming religious figureheads. After the family's downfall in 1258, following the fall of Baghdad to the Mongols, one member was invited by the Mameluke sultan to Cairo where the dynasty was recognized until the 16th century.

Abbey Theatre Theatre erected on Abbey St, Dublin (1904), by Annie E.F. Horniman to house the Irish National Theatre Society. In 1925, the Abbey became the National Theatre of Ireland. Works by W.B. YEATS, Lady Gregory, J.M. SYNGE and Sean O'CASEY have been introduced here and the theatre is renowned for its support of new writers.

Abd al-Kadir (1808–83) Algerian leader and emir of Mascara. He displaced (1832–39) the French and Turks from N Algeria before launching a holy war against the French. In 1843, Abd al-Kadir was forced into Morocco where he enlisted the support of the sultan. He and his Moroccan forces were defeated at Isly (1844). Abd al-Kadir was imprisoned in France (1847–52).

Abd el-Krim (1882?–1963) Moroccan Berber resistance leader. In 1921 he led the Rif tribes to victory against the Spanish. He continued to gain ground, and by 1925 had advanced into French-held territory. In 1926, he was defeated by a combined French-Spanish force and sent into exile in Réunion. In 1947, he escaped to Egypt and formed a liberation movement. In 1958, King Muhammad V of Morocco proclaimed him a national hero.

abdomen In VERTEBRATES, that portion of the body between the chest and the pelvis containing the abdominal cavity and the abdominal viscera, including most of the digestive organs. In arthropods it is the posterior part of the body, containing the reproductive organs and part of the digestive system.

Abdul Hamid II (1842–1918) Last Ottoman sultan (1876–1909). On his accession, Abdul Hamid suspended

▲ **aardvark** Found throughout much of Africa, the aardvark (*Orycteropus afer*) is a shy, nocturnal animal. Its presence may be detected by its large burrows, dug by the hoof-like claws on its front feet.

Parliament and the new constitution. He concluded the disastrous RUSSO-TURKISH WARS by ceding vast lands to Russia at the Treaty of San Stefano (1878). Abdul Hamid is remembered as the "Great Assassin" for his part in the Armenian massacres (1894–96) – it is estimated that more than 200,000 Armenians were killed in 1896 alone. In 1908, the Young Turks forced him to reimplement the 1876 constitution and he was deposed shortly after.

Abdullah ibn Hussein (1882–1951) King of Jordan (1946–51), son of HUSSEIN IBN ALI of the Hashemite family. In 1921, after aiding Britain in World War I, he became emir of Trans-Jordan. Abdullah lost control of Hejaz to Ibn SAUD. In World War II he resisted the Axis. Abdullah fought against the creation of Israel, annexed Palestinian land, and signed an armistice (1949). He was assassinated in Jerusalem, and Talal ascended the throne.

Abel In the Old Testament (Genesis), the second son of ADAM and EVE. Abel, the primal farmer, was killed by his brother CAIN, the primal hunter, who was jealous that God had rejected his offering but accepted Abel's.

Abel, John Jacob (1857–1938) US biochemist, best known for the first identification (1898) of a hormone, ADRENALINE (epinephrine). He made the discovery after years of studying the chemical composition of body tissue. Abel also isolated amino acids from blood by DIALYSIS, and discovered insulin in crystalline form.

Abelard, Pierre (1079–1142) French philosopher noted for his application of LOGIC in approaching theological questions. In his famous work *Sic et Non*, he attempted to reconcile differences between the Fathers of the Church by using the Aristotelian method of DIALECTIC. His views were condemned by the Council of Sens (1140). Abelard is known for his tragic love for his young pupil Héloise. The affair scandalized his contemporaries. He was castrated and became a monk, while Héloise was forced to enter a convent. These events inspired his work *Historia Calamitatum Mearum*. Abelard and Héloise are buried together at Parclete, Paris.

Aberdeen, George Hamilton Gordon, 4th Earl of (1784–1860) British statesman, prime minister (1852–55). He served as foreign secretary (1828–30) under the Duke of WELLINGTON. As foreign secretary (1841–46) to Sir Robert PEEL, Aberdeen negotiated the Webster–Ashburton and the Oregon Boundary treaties with the USA. He and Peel resigned over the issue of the CORN LAWS. Aberdeen emerged to form the "Aberdeen coalition" ministry. He was swayed into entering the CRIMEAN WAR by Viscount PALMERSTON, but was blamed for the mismanagement of the war and was forced to resign.

Aberdeen Third-largest city in Scotland (after Glasgow and Edinburgh), situated between the rivers Dee (S) and Don (N). Aberdeen is the principal seaport on the NE coast of Scotland. Chartered by William the Lion in 1179, Aberdeen is known as the "Granite City" for its grey granite architecture such as St Machar's Cathedral (1131). Since the 1970s, the exploitation of oil reserves in the North Sea has seen the city develop into a major centre of the British oil industry. Pop. (1994) 195,000.

aberration In astronomy, the apparent slight change of position of a star due to the effect of the Earth's orbital motion and the finite velocity of light. A telescope must be inclined by an angle of up to $c.20°$ to compensate for aberration. The effect was first described by James Bradley in 1729 and was used to prove that the Earth orbits the Sun.

aberration In physics, defect in lens and mirror images arising when the incident light is not at or near the centre of the lens or mirror. **Spherical** aberration occurs when rays falling on the periphery of a lens or mirror are not brought to the same focus as light at the centre; the image is blurred. **Chromatic** aberration occurs when the wavelengths of the dispersed light are not brought to the same focus; the image is falsely coloured.

Abidjan Former capital of the Ivory Coast (and the largest city in W Africa) situated on the Ebrié Lagoon, inland from the Gulf of Guinea. The country's chief port and commercial centre, Abidjan was founded by French colonists at the end of the 19th century. Although it lost capital status to YAMOUSSOUKRO in 1983, it remains Ivory Coast's cultural and economic centre. Industries: textiles, sawmilling. Pop. (1990) 2,500,000.

Abkhazia Autonomous republic on the Black Sea coast of Georgia. The capital is Sukhumi. The area was conquered by the Romans, Byzantines, Arabs and the Turks before becoming a Russian protectorate in 1910. It was made a Soviet republic in 1921 and an autonomous republic within Georgia in 1930. In 1992, after the establishment of an independent Georgia, the Abkhazian parliament unilaterally declared independence. In 1993, Abkhazian forces seized the capital from the Georgian army. In 1995, its independent status was confirmed by a new Georgian constitution. Tobacco, tea, grapes and citrus fruits are the main crops. Area: 8,600sq km (3,320sq mi). Pop. (1990) 537,500.

abolitionists In US history, militant opponents of SLAVERY. Inspired by British evangelicals in the Clapham Sect (in particular William WILBERFORCE), preachers such as Lyman BEECHER launched a moral crusade to end slavery in the United States. In 1831, William Lloyd GARRISON published *The Liberator*, an antislavery journal. In 1833, the American Anti-Slavery Society was formed and within five years such societies boasted more than 250,000 members, mainly from Northern states. In 1840, the Liberty Party was formed by James G. Birney, it advocated direct political action to achieve the emancipation of black slaves. The party attracted the support of escaped slaves, such as Frederick DOUGLASS. The passage of a tough, new FUGITIVE SLAVE LAW (1850) led to increased activity on the UNDERGROUND RAILROAD. An abolitionist novel, *Uncle Tom's Cabin* (1852), by Harriet Beecher STOWE sold more than 300,000 copies in its first year of publication. The militant actions of abolitionists culminated in the raid on the US arsenal at Harper's Ferry, Virginia, led by John BROWN. The bitter antagonism between North and South on the issue of slavery was a major cause of the American CIVIL WAR. In 1863, President Abraham LINCOLN issued the EMANCIPATION PROCLAMATION.

aborigines Strictly, the indigenous inhabitants of a country. The term is used most often in reference to NATIVE AUSTRALIANS.

abortion Termination of pregnancy before a FETUS is sufficiently advanced to survive outside the mother's UTERUS. **Spontaneous** abortion (miscarriage) occurs in $c.20\%$ of apparently normal pregnancies. Miscarriages in the first three months of pregnancy are usually caused by fetal abnormalities. Miscarriages later in pregnancy may be caused by defects in the maternal environment, such as reproductive system disorders. **Induced** or **therapeutic** abortion is the termination of pregnancy by drugs (such as prostaglandins and mifepristone) or surgery (such as vacuum suction and dilation and curettage). The rights of the fetus and the mother's right to choose provoke much political and ethical debate. Induced abortion has been practised since ancient times. In the 19th century, many countries passed stringent antiabortion legislation. In 1869 the Catholic Church prohibited induced abortion under any circumstances and this remains the official Roman Catholic position. In many countries, abortion has been legalized to circumvent the dangers of "backstreet" abortions and provide help in cases where pregnancy may endanger the physical or mental health of the mother. In the UK, abortion was legalized in 1967. Currently, the legal time-limit for an abortion is up to 24 weeks after conception. In the US, the Supreme Court decision in *Roe v. Wade* (1973) made abortion legal during the first six months of pregnancy.

Aboukir (Abukir, Abu Qir) Bay on the Mediterranean coast of Egypt, between Alexandria and the mouth of the Nile. In the Battle of the Nile (1–2 August 1798), Horatio NELSON defeated the French fleet under Breuys. Nelson's victory at Aboukir forced NAPOLEON to abandon his attempt to conquer parts of the British empire.

Abraham (Ibrahim) In the Old Testament, progenitor of the Hebrews and founder of JUDAISM. According to the book of Genesis, Abraham was called on by God to travel with his wife Sarah and nephew LOT from Ur to Haran in NW Mesopotamia, and thence to Canaan. He had a son ISHMAEL by Sarah's maid Hagar, but then at 100 years of age fathered a son ISAAC by Sarah, who was previously barren. God tested his loyalty by demanding he sacrifice Isaac. He is esteemed by Muslims who regard him as the ancestor, through Ishmael, of the Arabs.

abrasion In geology, mechanical wearing down of rock surface by wind, water, glacial movements, tides or currents. Common agents of abrasion are the bed load of streams, rock debris at the base of glaciers, and sand transported by wind or waves. *See also* EROSION

abrasive Hard and rough substance used to shape and polish surfaces. Some abrasives are used as fine powders, others in larger fragments with sharp cutting edges. Brittle materials such as ceramics and glass are machined to shape through the use of abrasives. Most natural abrasives are minerals, such as DIAMOND, GARNET, CORUNDUM, PUMICE, FLINT and QUARTZ. Flint is used in the manufacture of sandpaper. Synthetic abrasives, such as silicon carbide and aluminium oxide, are widely used in industry.

Absalom In the Old Testament, third and favourite son of King DAVID. A youth of uncontrollable arrogance, he murdered his brother Amnon, led a rebellion against David, and was routed. Trapped in flight when his hair became entangled in the branches of an oak, he was killed by David's general Joab.

abscess Collection of pus anywhere in the body, contained in a cavity of inflamed tissue. It is caused by bacterial infection.

absolute zero Temperature at which all parts of a system are at the lowest energy permitted by the laws of QUANTUM MECHANICS; zero on the kelvin temperature scale, which is $-273.15°C$ $(-459.67°F)$. At this temperature the system's ENTROPY is also zero, although the total energy of the system may not be zero.

absorption Taking up chemically or physically of molecules of one substance into another. The absorbed matter permeates all of the absorber. This includes a gas taken in by a liquid and a liquid or gas absorbed by a solid. The process is often utilized commercially, such as the purification of natural gas by the absorption of hydrogen sulphide in aqueous ethanolamine. *See also* ADSORPTION

abstract art Art in which recognizable objects are reduced to schematic marks. Although abstraction was evident in impressionist, neo- and post-impressionist work of the late 19th century, the movement did not become established until the early 20th century. Its most

radical form is called **non-objective** or non-iconic art. In this, the artist creates marks, signs or three-dimensional constructions which have no connection with images or objects in the visible world. There are two main types of non-objective art: **expressionist**, which is fundamentally emotional, spontaneous and personal; and **geometrical**, which works from the premise that geometry is the only discipline precise and universal enough to express our intellectual and emotional longings. Art historians often credit Wassily KANDINSKY with being the first to explore expressionist abstraction in 1910. Kandinsky inspired the BLAUE REITER group and his work helped to pave the way toward ABSTRACT EXPRESSIONISM, ACTION PAINTING and Tachism. Geometrical abstraction found (*c.*1913) its most adept, early exponents in Russia. The pioneers included Kasimir MALEVICH who invented SUPREMATISM and El LISSITZKY, a leading proponent of CONSTRUCTIVISM. The French *Section d'Or* worked in parallel to the Russians. Other individuals who provided landmarks in geometrical abstraction include Piet MONDRIAN, Naum GABO and Ben NICHOLSON; influential movements include De STIJL and concrete art. *See also* BRANCUSI, CONSTANTIN; EXPRESSIONISM

abstract expressionism Mainly US art movement in which the creative process itself is examined and explored. It is neither wholly abstract nor wholly expressionist. The term originally applied to paintings created (1945–55) by about 15 artists from the New York School. Although very different in temperament and style, these individuals shared a fascination with SURREALISM and "psychic automatism" as well as other progressive European styles. Toward the early 1950s, two distinct groups emerged with Willem DE KOONING and Jackson POLLOCK heading the most aggressive trend (loosely known as ACTION PAINTING), which involved dripping or throwing paint on the canvas. Barnett NEWMAN, Ad Reinhardt and Mark ROTHKO were more contemplative.

Absurd, Theatre of the Dramatic and literary critical term developed from the philosophy of Albert CAMUS to describe discordant human experience in an inhuman world. It was first applied in 1961 to describe contemporary drama which depicted the irrationality of life in an unconventional dramatic style. Exponents include Samuel BECKETT, Eugène IONESCO, Jean GENET and Edward ALBEE. Such drama attempts to abandon logical, linguistic processes. The connection between language and meaning is fractured (often by the use of repetition) and characters appear dislocated from their surroundings. Beckett's play *Waiting for Godot* is a classic of the genre.

Abu Bakr (*c.*573–634) First Muslim CALIPH. One of the earliest converts to Islam, Abu Bakr was chief adviser to the Prophet MUHAMMAD. After Muhammad's death he was elected leader of the Muslim community. During his short reign (632–34), he defeated the tribes that had revolted against Muslim rule in Medina after the death of Muhammad and restored them to Islam. By invading the Byzantine Christian provinces of Syria and Palestine and the Iranian province of Iraq, he launched the series of Holy Wars through which the first major expansion of the Islamic world was accomplished.

Abu Dhabi (Abu Zaby) Largest and wealthiest of the seven UNITED ARAB EMIRATES, lying on the S coast of the Persian Gulf. Also the name of its capital city (1995 pop. 928,000), federal capital of the UAE. It has been ruled since the 18th century by the Al-bu-Falah clan of the Bani Yas tribe. There are longstanding frontier disputes with Saudi Arabia and Oman. Since the discovery of oil in the late 1950s, Abu Dhabi's economy has been based almost entirely on crude oil production. Area: 67,340sq km (26,000sq mi). Pop. (1995) 928,360.

Abuja Nigeria's administrative capital since December 1991. The new city was designed by the Japanese architect Kenzo Tange, and work began in 1976. Government offices began moving in the 1980s to relieve pressure on the infrastructure of Lagos. Pop. (1996 est.) 350,000.

Abu Simbel Ancient Egyptian village on the w bank of the River Nile, near the border with Sudan. It is the location of two rock-cut sandstone temples built by Ramses II (c.1292–1225 BC). In a huge operation (1963–66), the temples and statuary were moved further inland. This was to prevent their disappearance under the waters of Lake Nasser, created by the construction of the new High Dam at Aswan.

abyssal Term to describe oceanic features occurring at great depths, usually more than c.3,000m (10,000ft) below sea level. Abyssal **plains** cover c.30% of the Atlantic and nearly 75% of the Pacific ocean floors. They are covered by deposits of biogenic oozes formed by the remains of microscopic plankton and nonbiogenic sediments (red clays). The gradient is less than 1:1000, except for the occasional low, oval-shaped abyssal **hill**. The plains are characterized by stable temperatures from $-1°C$ to $5°C$ ($30°F$ to $41°F$) and the relative lack of currents. The abyssal **zone** is the deepest area of the ocean. It receives no sunlight, so there are no seasons and no plants, but there are many forms of life, such as sponges, crinoids (sea lilies) and brachiopods (lampshells).

acacia (mimosa, wattle) Evergreen shrub and tree widely distributed in tropical and subtropical regions, especially Australia. Acacias have compound leaves made up of many small leaflets, and yellow or white flowers. Height: 1.2–18m (4–59ft). Family Leguminosae; genus *Acacia*.

Académie française Official French literary society, now part of the *Institut de France*. Originating as a private discussion group whose members were persuaded by Cardinal Richelieu to become an official body in 1635, the society is the guardian of the French language and of literary conventions. Past members have included many of the giants of French literature, such as Racine, Voltaire and Hugo.

Academy School of philosophy founded (c.387 BC) by Plato. He met his pupils in a garden outside Athens, said to have belonged to a Greek hero called Academus. Much of the history of the Academy is uncertain, though we know its students included Aristotle, Epicurus and Zeno of Citium. In AD 529 it was closed by Emperor Justinian. *See also* Neoplatonism; scepticism; university

Academy Award *See* Oscar

Acadia (Acadie) Historic region in North America, from which the term Cajun derives. The first French settlement was established in 1605 and the region expanded to include present-day Nova Scotia, New Brunswick, Prince Edward Island and parts of Québec and Maine. The Treaty of Utrecht (1713) ceded the region to the British, who deported (in 1755 and 1758) many Acadians.

acanthus Perennial plant with thistle-like leaves, found in Africa, the Mediterranean region, India and Malaysia. It has lobed, often spiny leaves and white or coloured flower spikes. The pattern of the leaves in a stylized form is a common classical architectural motif.

Acapulco (Acapulco de Juárez) City-port on the sw coast of Mexico. Founded in 1550, Acapulco was for 250 years an important port on the galleon route linking Spain and the Philippines. Now the country's most famous Pacific resort, it is noted for its beautiful scenery, deep-sea fishing and luxurious hotels. Exports: cotton, fruit, hides and tobacco. Pop. (1990) 593,212.

ACAS Acronym for the Advisory, Conciliation and Arbitration Service

acceleration Amount by which the velocity of an object increases in a certain time. It is measured in metres or feet per second per second (m/s^2 or ft/s^2). For example, a stone dropped over a cliff accelerates from zero velocity at a rate of 9.81m (32.2ft) per second per second, this acceleration being due to the pull of Earth's gravity. The rate of acceleration can be found by applying the equation: acceleration = (change in velocity)/(time taken for change). When an object rotates about an axis, its **angular** acceleration is given as the change in angular velocity divided by elapsed time, expressed in radians per second per second (rad/s^2).

accelerator (particle accelerator) In particle physics, machine for increasing the energy of charged particles by increasing their speed with the use of alternating electric fields in an evacuated chamber. Magnetic fields are used to focus the particles into a narrow stable beam and to maintain the required curvature of the beam. As the particle velocity rises a relativistic increase in mass occurs. Accelerators are used mostly in experiments to force high-energy particles to collide with other particles. The way the fragments of particles produced behave following the collision provides physicists with information on the forces found within atoms. In a **linear** accelerator, the particles travel in a straight line, usually accelerated by an electric field. In a **cyclotron**, particles are accelerated in a spiral path between pairs of D-shaped magnets with an alternating voltage between them. In a **synchrocyclotron**, the accelerating voltage is synchronized with the time it takes the particles to make one revolution. A **synchrotron** consists of a large circular tube with magnets to deflect the particles in a curve and radio-frequency fields to accelerate them. The most advanced modern accelerators are **colliders**, in which beams of particles moving in opposite directions are allowed to collide with each other, thus achieving higher energy of interaction. *See also* bubble chamber

acclimatization Adjustment of an organism to a new environment or circumstance. It involves a gradual, natural change in the physiology of an organism, but unlike evolution does not involve genetic change.

accommodation Process by which the eye focuses on objects at various distances. In the human eye, focusing is achieved when the muscles of the ciliary body contract or relax to change the shape (curvature) of the lens and bring light rays into focus on the light-sensitive retina found at the back of the eye.

accordion Musical instrument of the reed organ type. It has an organ-like tone produced by air from the bellows vibrating reeds. It was invented in c.1822 and is widely used in folk music.

Accra Capital and largest city of Ghana, on the Gulf of Guinea. Occupied by the Ga people since the 15th century, Accra became the capital of Britain's Gold Coast colony in 1875. Today, it is a major port and economic centre and the headquarters of the Defence Commission of the Organization of African Unity (OAU). Industries: engineering, timber, textiles, chemicals. The main export is cacao. Pop. (1988 est.) 1,781,000.

accretion Continually growing or building up; a term frequently used to describe certain modes of geological deposition. The term is also used in astronomy to describe the gradual building up of larger celestial bodies from smaller ones by gravitational attraction;

also the accumulation of matter by a star or other celestial object. Accretion is an important factor in the evolution of stars, planets and comets.

accumulator (secondary CELL or storage BATTERY) Voltaic cell (battery) that can be recharged. The commonly used car battery is a lead-acid accumulator.

acetaldehyde *See* ETHANAL

acetate *See* ETHANOATE

acetic acid *See* ETHANOIC ACID

acetone *See* PROPANONE

Achaean League Two confederations of Greek city states formed in the area of the Peloponnese called Achaea (Akkaia). The first, founded in the 5th century BC, lasted for *c*.100 years. The second, founded in 280 BC, warred with Sparta, siding with Rome in 198 BC. In 146 BC Rome subjugated and dissolved the League.

Achaemenids Ruling dynasty of the first Persian empire, which stretched from the River Nile as far E as modern Afghanistan. The dynasty was founded by CYRUS THE GREAT (r.559–529 BC) and named after his ancestor, Achaemenes. DARIUS I (r.521–486 BC) decentralized government administration. The last Achaemenid ruler, DARIUS III (r.336–330 BC), was defeated by ALEXANDER THE GREAT. The dynasty was responsible for the spread of ZOROASTRIANISM throughout Asia and the remains at PERSEPOLIS are testimony to the splendour of PERSIAN ART and architecture at this time.

Achebe, (Albert) Chinua (Chinualumogu) (1930–) Nigerian novelist. His work explores the effects of cultural change in modern Africa. Achebe's highly acclaimed debut novel, *Things Fall Apart* (1958), depicts life in an African village before and after the arrival of missionaries. He received the Nobel Prize for literature in 1989. Other works include *No Longer at Ease* (1960), *Arrow of God* (1964) and *Anthills of the Savannah* (1987).

Acheson, Dean Gooderham (1893–1971) US statesman, secretary of state (1949–53) under Harry S TRUMAN. His desire to stem the growth of communism was fundamental to the establishment of the North Atlantic Treaty Organization (NATO), the ANZUS Pact, the Marshall Plan and the TRUMAN DOCTRINE. Acheson was criticized for his lack of support for the state of Taiwan and his support for US military intervention in South Korea.

Achilles In the Greek epic tradition, a formidable warrior, the most fearless Greek fighter of the Trojan War, and the hero of Homer's *Iliad*. Legend held him invulnerable from weapons because he had been dipped by his mother, Thetis, in the River Styx at birth, except for the heel by which he was held. Achilles sought glory fighting at TROY, but an arrow shot by PARIS struck his heel and killed him.

Achilles tendon Strong band of elastic connective tissue at the back of the ankle. One of the largest tendons in the body, it connects the calf muscles to the heel bone. The spring provided by this tendon is very important in walking, running and jumping.

acid Chemical compound containing hydrogen that can be replaced by a metal or other positive ION to form a SALT. Acids dissociate in water to yield aqueous hydrogen ions (H^+), thus acting as proton donors. The solutions are corrosive, have a sour taste, and have a pH below 7. (The pH scale ranges from 1 for extremely acidic to 14 for extremely basic or alkaline, with 7 being neutral.) **Strong** acids, such as sulphuric acid, are fully dissociated into ions and make good ELECTROLYTES. **Weak** acids, such as ethanoic acid, only partially dissociate. *See also* BASE

acid house Variation of HOUSE MUSIC popular during the late 1980s and early 1990s. Characterized by hypnotic and repetitive synthesized sounds and deep whirling bass lines, acid house was part of an underground resurgence of drugs such as LSD (lysergic acid) and Ecstasy.

acid rain Rain that is highly acidic due to sulphur oxides, nitrogen oxides, hydrocarbons and other air pollutants dissolved in it. Acid rain may have a pH value as low as 2.8. When acid rain falls on the ground, often great distances from its source, it dissolves and liberates heavy metals and aluminium. Acid rain can severely damage both plant and animal life. Certain lakes, for example, have lost all fish and plant life because of acid rain. The major causes of acid rain are motor vehicle emissions, industrial processes and the burning of fossil fuels in power-stations.

Ackroyd, Peter (1949–) English novelist and biographer. Ackroyd's biographies include *T.S. Eliot* (1984), *Dickens* (1990), *Blake* (1996) and *The Life of Thomas More* (1999). His novels are an intriguing blend of history, biography and fiction. *Hawksmoor* (1985) won the Whitbread Prize and *Chatterton* (1987) was shortlisted for the Booker Prize. Other books include *English Music* (1992), *Milton in America* (1997) and *London: The Biography* (2000).

acne Inflammatory disorder of the sebaceous (oil-producing) glands of the SKIN resulting in skin eruptions such as blackheads and infected pimples; it is seen mostly on the face, neck, back and chest. Acne is extremely common in both sexes at PUBERTY, but is usually more pronounced in boys. It does not usually persist beyond early adulthood.

Aconcagua Mountain in the Andes range on the border between Argentina and Chile. The highest peak outside Asia at 6,960m (22,834ft), the snow-capped extinct volcano was first climbed in 1897. The River Aconcagua rises at its NW foot and enters the Pacific N of Valparaiso.

aconite Flowering plant of the genus *Aconitum*. Its roots provide the ALKALOID aconitine, used in medicine; in ancient times it was used as a poison. Species include monkshood and wolfsbane. Family Ranunculaceae.

acorn Fruit of an OAK tree

acoustics Study of SOUND, especially the behaviour of sound waves. Experts apply acoustics in the design of concert and lecture halls, microphones, loudspeakers and musical instruments. Audiologists use acoustics to assess degrees of abnormality in their patients' hearing. *See also* ANECHOIC CHAMBER

▲ **accordion** Invented in the 1820s, the accordion is a reed organ working along the same principle as the mouth organ – that is, a separate reed is provided for each note. Air is forced through the reeds by bellows that form the centre of the instrument. The right hand plays the melody on the keyboard, while the left hand operates the buttons for accompanying chords.

acquired characteristic Feature that develops during the lifetime of an organism. The enlarged muscles of a manual worker are an example of an acquired characteristic. Because they are not genetically controlled, acquired characteristics cannot be passed on to offspring.

Acquired Immune Deficiency Syndrome (AIDS) Fatal disease caused by a RETROVIRUS, called HUMAN IMMUNODEFICIENCY VIRUS (HIV), that mainly attacks T-4 cells (which help the production of ANTIBODIES) and renders the body's IMMUNE SYSTEM incapable of resisting infection. The first diagnosis was made in New York in 1979. In 1983–84 scientists at the Pasteur Institute in France and the National Cancer Institute in the US isolated HIV as the cause of the disease. The virus can remain dormant in infected cells for up to 10 years. Initial AIDS-related complex (ARC) symptoms include severe weight loss and fatigue. It may develop into the AIDS syndrome, characterized by secondary infections, neurological damage and cancers. AIDS is transmitted only by a direct exchange of body fluids. Transmission is most commonly through sexual intercourse, the sharing of contaminated needles by intravenous drug users, and the uterus of infected mothers to their babies. Before effective screening procedures were introduced, many haemophiliacs were infected through transfusions of contaminated blood. In the US and Europe, more than 90% of victims have been homosexual or bisexual men. However, 90% of reported cases are in the developing world, and many victims are heterosexual. Recent combinations of drugs have met with some success in controlling symptoms. By 2000, more than 18.8 million people worldwide had died from AIDS.

acre Unit of area measurement in English-speaking countries, equal to 0.405ha (4,840sq yd).

acropolis Hilltop fortress of an ancient Greek city. The earliest known examples were fortified castles built for the Mycenaean kings, and it was only later that they became symbolic homes of the gods. The most famous one is the Acropolis built in Athens in the 13th century BC; it includes the PARTHENON of the 5th century BC.

acrylic Type of plastic, one of a group of synthetic, short-chain, unsaturated, carboxylic acid derivatives. Variations include hard and transparent, soft and resilient or liquid forms. They are used for moulded structural parts, adhesives and paints.

actinide series Group of radioactive elements with similar chemical properties. Their atomic numbers range from 89 to 103. The most important of the group is URANIUM. Each element is analogous to the corresponding LANTHANIDE SERIES. Those having atomic numbers greater than 92 are called TRANSURANIC ELEMENTS.

actinium (symbol Ac) Radioactive, metallic element, the first of the ACTINIDE SERIES, discovered in 1899 by André Debierne. It is found associated with uranium ores. Ac^{227}, a decay product of U^{235}, emits beta particles (electrons) during disintegration. Properties: at.no. 89; r.d. 10.07 (calc.); m.p. 1,100°C (1,900°F); b.p. 3,200°C (5,800°F); most stable isotope Ac^{227} (half-life 21.8 yr).

action painting Act and result of applying paint spontaneously. A dynamic style, it gained momentum in 1952 when painters such as Willem DE KOONING and Jackson POLLOCK moved away from ABSTRACT EXPRESSIONISM to make pictures with spontaneous gestures, such as dripping and pouring paint onto their canvases. Its purpose is to stimulate vision and to show a record of passing emotions. Other practitioners include Robert MOTHERWELL.

action potential Change that occurs in the electrical potential between the outside and the inside of a nerve fibre or muscle fibre when stimulated by the transmission of a nerve impulse. At rest, the fibre is electrically negative inside and positive outside. When the nerve or muscle is stimulated, the charges are momentarily reversed.

Actium, Battle of (31 BC) Naval battle in which the fleet of Octavian (later Emperor AUGUSTUS) defeated the fleets of Mark ANTONY and CLEOPATRA. Mark Antony's army surrendered a week later, and Octavian became sole ruler of the Roman Empire.

activation energy Smallest amount of energy necessary to make a CHEMICAL REACTION take place. As chemical bonds are broken and formed during a reaction, the energy of the system increases from that of the reactants, reaches a maximum, and then decreases to that of the products. The difference between the energy of the reactants and the maximum is the activation energy. Often this energy has to be supplied to the reaction mixture in the form of heat, although some chemical reactions take place spontaneously.

active transport Energy-requiring process by which molecules or ions are transported across the membranes of living cells against a concentration gradient. It is particularly important in the uptake of food across the gut lining, in the reabsorption of water and salts from the urine in the kidney before excretion, and in the uptake of minerals by the plant root. Active transport enables cells to maintain an internal chemical environment which is of a different composition from that of their surroundings.

act of Congress Statute adopted by the US CONGRESS. It overrides conflicting legislation from any other source, but can be ruled unconstitutional by the SUPREME COURT.

act of Parliament Statute created in Britain when a bill, having passed through several stages in both the HOUSE OF COMMONS and HOUSE OF LORDS, receives the royal assent. An act remains in force until it is repealed by Parliament.

Act of Union *See* UNION, ACTS OF

Actors' Studio Theatre workshop founded (1947) by Elia KAZAN, Cheryl Crawford and Robert Lewis in New York. It became noted for the "method" approach to acting, particularly under Lee STRASBERG. In the early 1960s, it also produced plays on Broadway. An enduring and influential workshop, its eminent members include Marlon BRANDO, Dustin HOFFMAN and Robert DE NIRO.

Acts of the Apostles Book of the New Testament describing the spread of the Gospel of Christ immediately after his death and resurrection. It mainly focuses on St PETER and St PAUL. The book was probably written c.AD 65 by the author of St Luke's gospel.

acupuncture System of medical treatment in which long needles are inserted into the body to assist healing, relieve pain or for anaesthetic purposes. In ancient Chinese philosophy, acupuncture is proposed to restore the balance of YIN AND YANG by freeing the flow of life-energy (*chi*) through pathways (meridians) in the body. A possible scientific explanation is that the needles may activate deep sensory nerves that stimulate the pituitary gland and hypothalamus to produce ENDORPHINS.

Adam In the Old Testament (Genesis 2), first man and progenitor of all mankind, created from dust by God in his own image. He and his wife EVE were cast out of the Garden of EDEN to become mortal after they ate forbidden fruit from the Tree of the Knowledge of Good and Evil. Adam and Eve's sons were SETH, CAIN and ABEL.

Adam, Robert (1728–92) Scottish architect, best known of four brothers who were all architects. Adam was the greatest British architect of the late-18th century and his refined neo-classical style was widely influential. He also excelled as an interior decorator and furniture designer. The Adelphi complex, London, begun in 1768, was his most ambitious project; his interior designs include Kenwood House, London (1767) and Syon House, Middlesex (1762–69). *See also* NEOCLASSICISM

Adams, Ansel (1902–84) US photographer. Concentrating on the scenic grandeur of the West, Adams produced magnificent prints that are widely exhibited and reproduced. A co-founder of the *f*/64 group, he was instrumental in forming museum and university photographic departments and was a celebrated teacher. He wrote the *Basic Photo-Books* series of technical manuals (1968).

Adams, Douglas (1952–) English writer. He first attracted attention with the cult UK radio series *The Hitchhiker's Guide to the Galaxy*, which formed the basis for a sequence of satirical, science fiction novels. Other novels include *Dirk Gently's Holistic Detective Agency* (1987) and *The Long Dark Tea-time of the Soul* (1988).

Adams, Gerry (1948–) Northern Irish politician, president of SINN FEIN (1983–). He was interned (1972–78) by the British for his involvement in the IRISH REPUBLICAN ARMY (IRA), before becoming vice president (1978–83) of Sinn Féin. Adams is seen as a pivotal figure between the "ballot box" and "bullet" factions of the Republican movement. He served (1983–92, 1997–) as a member of parliament for Belfast West, but never took his seat at Westminster. Adams' negotiations with John HUME led to an IRA cease-fire (1994). He headed the Sinn Féin delegation in the 1997 peace talks, and became the first Republican leader to meet a British prime minister since 1921. Following the Dublin Agreement and David TRIMBLE's appointment as first minister, Adams continued to play a pivotal rule in the peace talks and negotiations on the decommissioning of arms.

Adams, Henry Brooks (1838–1918) US historian and writer. A direct descendant of John ADAMS and John Quincy ADAMS, his best-known work is an autobiography, *The Education of Henry Adams* (1907), which is also an ironic analysis of a technological society.

Adams, John (1735–1826) Second US president (1797–1801). Influenced by his radical cousin Samuel ADAMS, he helped draft the DECLARATION OF INDEPENDENCE (1776) and the Treaty of Paris (1783) that ended the AMERICAN REVOLUTION. Adams was George WASHINGTON's vice president (1789–97). His presidency was marked by conflict between the FEDERALIST PARTY, led by Alexander HAMILTON and Thomas JEFFERSON's DEMOCRATIC-REPUBLICAN PARTY. Adams' moderate stance enabled a settlement of the XYZ AFFAIR (1797–98). He reluctantly endorsed the ALIEN AND SEDITION ACTS (1798). Adams was succeeded by Thomas Jefferson.

Adams, John (1947–) US composer. He became interested in electronics, jazz and the music of experimental US composers such as John CAGE and Morton FELDMAN. Most of his output is written in an intentionally accessible minimalist style. In 1989 Adams won a Grammy Award for Best Contemporary Composition for his opera *Nixon in China* (1987).

Adams, John Couch (1819–92) British astronomer. Noting that Uranus' observed path was not in agreement with its calculated orbit, Adams believed that the discrepancies could be accounted for by the gravitational influence of an undiscovered planet. NEPTUNE, as it was subsequently called, was discovered near a position predicted by Urbain LEVERRIER. The honours of predicting the existence of Neptune were shared between Adams and Leverrier. However, it now seems that neither Adams' nor Leverrier's calculations were accurate.

Adams, John Quincy (1767–1848) Sixth US president (1825–29), son of the second president John

ADAMS. He served in his father's administration, before acting (1803–08) as FEDERALIST PARTY member in the US Senate. Adams was secretary of state (1817–24) for James MONROE. He was largely responsible for formulating the MONROE DOCTRINE and negotiating the ADAMS-ONÍS TREATY (1819). Adams became president without an electoral majority, his appointment confirmed by the House of Representatives. His lack of a mandate and non-partisan approach contributed to his electoral defeat by Andrew JACKSON. Adams served in the House of Representatives (1830–48).

Adams, Richard (1920–) English novelist. His novels often feature animals as narrators or central figures. Adams' debut novel, *Watership Down* (1972), was a popular success, and was made into an animated film. Other novels include *Shardik* (1974), *The Plague Dogs* (1977) and *Girl on a Swing* (1980).

Adams, Samuel (1722–1803) American revolutionary leader. As a member and clerk of the Massachusetts legislature (1765–74), he was the chief spokesman for revolution. Adams helped form several radical organizations, led the STAMP ACT protest in 1765, helped plan the BOSTON TEA PARTY of 1773, and was a signatory of the DECLARATION OF INDEPENDENCE (1776). He was a delegate to the CONTINENTAL CONGRESS until 1781.

Adams-Onís Treaty (1819) Agreement between the US and Spain. Negotiated by secretary of state John Quincy ADAMS and Spanish minister Luis de Onís, Spain gave up its land E of the Mississippi River and its claims to the Oregon Territory; the US assumed debts of $5 million and gave up claims to Texas.

Adana City on the River Seyhan, S Turkey; capital of Adana province. Adana served as a Roman military station and was later occupied by the ABBASIDS before coming under the rule of the Ottoman Turks. It lies at the centre of a fertile, cotton-growing region. Industries: agricultural machinery, textiles. Pop. (1995) 167,000.

adaptation Adjustment by a living organism to its surroundings. Animals and plants adapt to changes in

▲ **adaptation** The various honeycreepers of Hawaii in the Pacific evolved from one species of bird now long extinct (centre). Over millions of years the honeycreepers evolved different methods of feeding. This ensured the island's various habitat niches could be exploited, resulting in less competition among the birds and therefore allowing more to survive. The main adaptation was the dramatic change in the shape of the beaks. A few species evolved beaks best suited to feed on nectar (1), others feed purely on insects (2), while some feed on fruit (3) or seeds (4).

their environment through variations in structure, reproduction or organization within communities. Some such changes are temporary (ACCLIMATIZATION), while others may involve changes in the genetic material (DNA) and be inherited by offspring (EVOLUTION). Adaptation is also used to describe a particular characteristic, such as body size, shape, colour, physiology or behaviour, that fits an organism to survive in its environment.

adaptive radiation In biology, the EVOLUTION of different forms of living organisms from a common ancestral stock, as different populations adapt to different environmental conditions or modes of life. Eventually the populations may become so different that they constitute separate species. Examples are the many different kinds of finches in the GALÁPAGOS ISLANDS, which diversified to specialize in different kinds of food, feeding methods and HABITATS. *See also* ADAPTATION

Addams, Jane (1860–1935) US reformer. She shared the 1931 Nobel Peace Prize with Nicholas Murray Butler. In 1889, Addams founded Hull House, Chicago – an early settlement house. She pioneered labour, housing, health and legal reforms, and campaigned for female suffrage, pacifism and the rights of immigrants.

adder Any of several snakes throughout the world, some poisonous and others harmless. The European VIPER (*Vipera berus*) is called an adder in Britain and is the country's only poisonous snake. The puff adder (*Bitis arietans*) is a large African viper, and the death adder (*Acanthophis antarticus*) is a dangerous Australian elapid.

Addington, Henry, 1st Viscount Sidmouth (1757–1844) British statesman, prime minister (1801–04). He entered Parliament in 1783 and served as speaker of the House (1789–1801). Addington succeeded William PITT (THE YOUNGER) as prime minister. His administration was tarnished by the failure of the Treaty of Amiens (1802) with Napoleon I. As home secretary (1812–22) under Lord LIVERPOOL, Addington was criticized for his harsh treatment of the LUDDITES and was widely blamed for the PETERLOO MASSACRE (1819).

Addis Ababa Capital and largest city in Ethiopia, located on a plateau at *c*.2,400m (8,000ft) in the highlands of Shewa province. Addis Ababa was made capital of Ethiopia in 1889. It is the headquarters of the ORGANIZATION OF AFRICAN UNITY (OAU). It is the main centre for the country's vital coffee trade. Industries: food, tanning, textiles, wood products. Pop. (1994 est.) 2,316,000.

Addison, Joseph (1672–1719) English essayist, poet and politician. His poetic celebration of the Duke of MARLBOROUGH's victory at the Battle of BLENHEIM, *The Campaign* (1704), led to a government appointment. Addison is chiefly remembered as a brilliant essayist: his stylish articles were a major reason for the success of the newly-established *Tatler* and *Spectator* periodicals. Addison served as secretary of state (1717–18).

addition reaction CHEMICAL REACTION in which two substances combine to form a third substance, with no other substance being produced. It is most commonly used in ORGANIC CHEMISTRY, particularly by adding a simple molecule across a carbon-carbon double bond in an UNSATURATED COMPOUND. *See also* SUBSTITUTION

Adelaide Capital of the state of SOUTH AUSTRALIA, situated at the mouth of the River Torrens on the Gulf of St Vincent. Founded in 1836 and named after William IV's wife, Adelaide is noted for its churches and fine cathedrals. There are two universities. The port provides facilities for an extensive hinterland and exports wool, fruit, wine and wheat. Industries: oil refining, motor vehicles, electronics, chemicals, textiles. Pop. (1994) 1,076,400.

Aden Commercial capital and largest city of Yemen, historic capital of the Aden Protectorate (1937–67) and the former (southern) People's Democratic Republic of Yemen (1967–90). A seaport city on the Gulf of Aden, 160km (100mi) E of the Red Sea, Aden was an important Roman trading port. With the opening of the SUEZ CANAL in 1869, its importance increased. It was made a British crown colony in 1937; the surrounding territory became the Aden Protectorate. In 1970, Aden became the sole capital of the new People's Democratic Republic of Yemen. When the (northern) Yemen Arab Republic and the (southern) People's Democratic Republic of Yemen combined to form a united Republic of Yemen in 1990, SANA'A became the official capital. Industries: cigarette manufacture, oil and salt refining. Pop. (1995) 562,000.

Adenauer, Konrad (1876–1967) German statesman, first chancellor of the Federal Republic of Germany (1949–63). He was Lord Mayor of Cologne (1917–33) and was twice imprisoned by the Nazis. Adenauer helped to create the Christian Democratic Union (CDU), West Germany's dominant post-war party, and was its leader (1946–66). He led West Germany into NATO (1955) and campaigned for the establishment of the European Economic Community.

adenoids Masses of LYMPH tissue in the upper part of the PHARYNX (throat) behind the NOSE; part of a child's defences against disease, they normally disappear by the age of ten.

adenosine diphosphate (ADP) Nucleotide chemical involved in energy-generating reactions during cell METABOLISM. ADP consists of the PURINE base ADENINE linked to the sugar D-ribose, which in turn carries two phosphate groups. It is formed by the HYDROLYSIS of ADENOSINE TRIPHOSPHATE (ATP) – with the release of energy – or the phosphorylation of adenosine monophosphate (AMP) – which requires the input of energy; both reactions are catalyzed by enzymes.

adenosine triphosphate (ATP) Nucleotide chemical consisting of adenine, D-ribose and three phosphate groups. It is found in all plant and animal cells, and is fundamental in the biochemical reactions required to support life. In animals, during RESPIRATION ATP can be broken down through the process of HYDROLYSIS to form ADENOSINE DIPHOSPHATE (ADP) and phosphate. The reaction, catalyzed by enzymes, yields large amounts of energy that is used either to create more complex molecules or to control an activity such as muscle contraction. Conversely, energy is used up when ATP is indirectly synthesized from ADP and AMP by complex biochemical reactions during the KREBS CYCLE. In plants, ATP is synthesized during PHOTOSYNTHESIS.

adhesion In chemistry, attraction of molecules of one substance to the molecules of another. GUM, GLUE and paste use the property of adhesion to join substances together. *See also* COHESION

adhesion In medicine, fibrous band of connective tissue developing at a site of inflammation or damage; it may bind together adjacent tissues, such as loops of intestine, occasionally causing obstruction.

adipose tissue (fatty tissue) Connective tissue made up of body cells which store large globules of fat.

Adige (Ger. Etsch) Second-longest river (after the PO) in Italy. It rises in the Tyrolean Alps, N Italy, and enters the Adriatic Sea S of Chioggia. A dam supplies hydroelectric power and irrigation. Length: 410km (255mi).

Adi Granth (Hindi, First Book) Principal sacred text of SIKHISM. The preachings of the first five Sikh Gurus were collected by Guru Arjan (1536–1606), the fifth Guru, and the text was expanded by the tenth Guru, GOBIND SINGH. Gobind Singh declared that he was the last Guru and the book was retitled **Granth Sahib** (Hindi, Revered Book).

Adirondack Mountains Circular mountain group located in NE New York state, reaching from Mohawk Valley in the S to the St Lawrence River in the N. There are many gorges, waterfalls and lakes. Much of the area makes up the Adirondack Forest Preserve. Noted for its resorts (including Lake Placid), its highest point is Mount Marcy, 1,629m (5,344 ft).

Adjani, Isabelle (1955–) French actress. In 1972, she became a member of the Comédie Française. Adjani earned an Academy Award nomination for her film debut in François TRUFFAUT's *The Story of Adèle H*. She gained another Oscar nomination for her title role in *Camille Claudel* (1988). Other credits include *Possession* (1981), *Subway* (1985) and *La Reine Margot* (1994).

Adler, Alfred (1870–1937) Austrian psychiatrist. After working with Sigmund FREUD (1902–11), Adler broke away to found his own school of "individual psychology". He believed that striving for social success and power was fundamental in human motivation. According to his theory, individuals develop problems and maladjustments when they cannot surmount feelings of inferiority acquired in childhood. The inferiority complex is often countered by compensation, which involves assertive or aggressive behaviour.

Adler, Felix (1851–1933) US ethical philosopher, b. Germany. Like KANT, Adler stressed the importance of the individual and believed that ETHICS need not be founded on religious or philosophical beliefs. In 1876, he founded the Society for Ethical Culture, the forerunner of the international Ethical Movement. His works include *Creed and Deed* (1877), *The Moral Instruction of Children* (1892) and *An Ethical Philosophy of Life* (1918).

Adonis In Phoenician and Greek myth, a youth of remarkable beauty, loved by PERSEPHONE and APHRODITE. Adonis was gored to death by a boar and during his afterlife Zeus decided that Adonis should spend part of the year with Persephone, queen of the underworld, and part with Aphrodite.

adoption Act of person(s) legally taking as a child one who is not his/her own by birth or law. In Britain, anyone over 21 years of age can legally adopt a child. Married couples must adopt "jointly", unmarried couples may not adopt "jointly". Adoptions are organized either by the social services departments of local authorities or by registered, voluntary agencies such as Barnardo's. An adoption is formally legalized by a High Court (Family Division) order. Usually the child's natural parent/s must consent to the adoption. Once adopted, the child assumes the rights and responsibilities of a natural legitimate offspring. All adoptions in the UK are registered, and once the adopted child reaches adulthood s/he can apply to obtain a full birth certificate.

Adorno, Theodor Wiesengrund (1903–69) German philosopher. He was a leading member of the Frankfurt school of philosophy and served as director (1958–69) of the Frankfurt Institute for Social Research. In 1933 Adorno was forced into exile by the Nazis and his subsequent thought was strongly marked by the rise of fascism. In *Dialectic of the Enlightenment* (1947), he and Max Horkenheimer criticized the tyranny of reason. In *The Jargon of Authenticity* (1965) Adorno attacked the poverty of sociopolitical thought in EXISTENTIALISM. *Negative Dialectics* (1966) provides a general summary of his reworking of MARXISM. Adorno was a perceptive critic and *Philosophy of Modern Music* (1958) is a key work.

adrenal gland One of a pair of small endocrine glands situated on top of the KIDNEYS. They produce many STEROIDS that regulate the blood's salt and water balance and are concerned with the METABOLISM of carbohydrates, proteins and fats, and the HORMONES adrenaline and noradrenaline. *See also* ENDOCRINE SYSTEM

adrenaline (epinephrine) HORMONE secreted by the ADRENAL GLANDS, important in preparing the body's response to stress. It has widespread effects in the body, increasing the strength and rate of heart beat and the rate and depth of breathing, diverting blood from the skin and digestive system to the heart and muscles, and stimulating the release of GLUCOSE from the liver by promoting increased RESPIRATION. Synthetic adrenaline is used medicinally in some situations, especially in the resuscitation of patients in shock or following heart attack.

Adrian IV (*c*.1100–59) Pope (1154–59), b. Nicholas Breakspear, the only English pope. In 1155 he crowned emperor FREDERICK I, Barbarossa.

Adrianople, Battle of (AD 378) Conflict between the Romans and the VISIGOTHS, fought at present-day EDIRNE, Turkey. The Visigoths, led by Fritigern, crushed the Roman army and killed Emperor Valens, paving the way for a full-scale invasion of the Roman Empire.

Adriatic Sea Shallow arm of the Mediterranean Sea, separated from the Ionian Sea by the Strait of Otranto, between Albania and the "heel" of Italy. Lobsters and sardines are the chief catches of local fisheries. Length: *c*.800km (500mi); Max. depth: 1,230m (4,035ft).

adsorption Attraction of a gas or liquid to the surface of a solid or liquid. It involves attraction of molecules, unlike ABSORPTION, which implies incorporation. The amounts adsorbed and the rate of adsorption depend on the structure exposed, the chemical identities and concentrations of the substances involved, and the temperature.

Advaita (Sanskrit, "non-duality") Most influential school of VEDANTA Hinduism, based on the thought of Shankara (AD 788–820). Shankara systematized the teachings of the UPANISHADS (last section of the VEDAS), stressing the indivisibility of BRAHMAN and ATMAN.

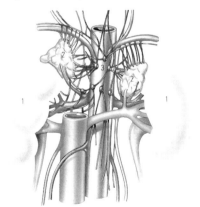

▲ **adrenal gland** Located above the kidneys (1), the two adrenal glands (2) are well supplied with blood entering from the aorta (3). Each gland consists of an outer layer (the cortex) and a central medulla. The cortex produces steroid hormones and hormones involved in maintaining water balance, and small quantities of sex hormones. The medulla produces adrenaline and noradrenalin, both of which prepare the body for an emergency situation.

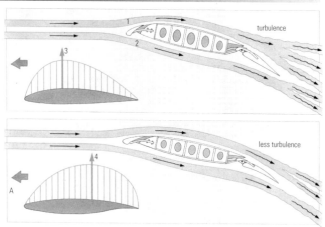

▶ **aerodynamics** As air passing over the top edge of an aerofoil (1) has to travel further than the air flowing beneath it (2), an area of low pressure forms above the wing that generates lift (3). In modern high-lift aerofoils (A), the centre of pressure is further toward the rear of the wing (4). By moving the point of maximum lift backwards, the aerofoil has a more even distribution of lift allowing a plane to fly more slowly without stalling.

Advent (Lat. coming) Liturgical season preceding CHRISTMAS. It begins on the Sunday nearest 30 November (St Andrew's Day). In many countries, observances during Advent include the lighting of candles. Advent refers both to Christ's birth and his coming in glory as judge at the end of history.

Adventists Christians belonging to any of a group of churches whose distinctive belief concerns the imminent Second Coming of Christ. William Miller (1782–1849) formed (1831) the first organized Adventist movement in the United States. Christ's failure to return on dates forecast by Miller led to splits in the movement. The largest group to emerge was the SEVENTH-DAY ADVENTISTS. *See also* MILLENARIANISM

Advisory, Conciliation and Arbitration Service (ACAS) UK governmental organization (established 1975) to promote the improvement of relations between employers and trade unions and provide facilities for the resolution of industrial disputes. A governing council is appointed by the secretary of state for trade and industry.

Aegean civilization (*c*.3000–1100 BC) Bronze Age cultures, chiefly MINOAN and MYCENAEAN, of Greece and the Aegean islands. The artistically brilliant Minoan civilization flourished in Crete, reaching its height between *c*.1700 and 1100 BC, when it was probably overrun by Mycenaens from mainland Greece.

Aegean Sea Part of the Mediterranean Sea between Greece and Turkey, bounded by Crete to the S and connected to the Black Sea and the Sea of Marmara by the Dardanelles and the NE. Oil and natural gas have been discovered in the area, but the principal income is derived from tourism, fishing and crops.

Aelfric (955–1020) Anglo-Saxon monk who composed works of religious instruction. His *Catholic Homilies* (990–92) and *Lives of the Saints* (993–96) were written in rhythmic, alliterative English, to appeal to clergy and laity alike. Aelfric also wrote a Latin/English grammar primer.

Aeneas In Greek mythology, the son of Anchises and Aphrodite. Active in the defence of TROY, he led the Trojans to Italy. The Romans acknowledged Aeneas and his Trojan company as their ancestors. The exploits of Aeneas form the basis of the *Aeneid*, a 12-volume book of poetry written (30–19 BC) by the Roman poet VIRGIL.

Aeolians Ancient Greek people. In *c*.1100 BC, they settled on Lesbos and other islands. They were famous for their music and poetry. The **aeolian harp** is a stringed musical instrument sounded by the wind.

aerial (antenna) Conductor component of radio and television systems for the broadcast and transmission of signals. An aerial's design usually depends on the wavelength of the signal.

aerobic Connected with, or dependent on, the presence of free oxygen or air. An aerobic organism can only survive in the presence of oxygen and depends on it for breaking down glucose and other foods to release energy. This is called aerobic respiration. *See also* ANAEROBIC

aerodynamics Science of gases in motion and the forces acting on objects, such as aircraft, in motion through the air. An aircraft designer must consider four main factors and their interrelationships: **weight** of the aircraft and the load it will carry; **lift** to overcome the pull of gravity; **drag**, or the forces that retard motion; and **thrust**, the driving force. Air resistance (drag) increases as the square of an object's speed and is minimized by streamlining. Engineers use the WIND TUNNEL and computer systems to predict aerodynamic performance.

aerofoil Any shape or surface, such as a wing, tail or propeller blade on an aircraft, that has as its major function the deflection of airflow to produce a pressure differential or LIFT. A typical aerofoil has a leading and trailing edge, and an upper and lower camber.

aeronautics Study of flight and the control of AIRCRAFT involving AERODYNAMICS, aircraft structures and methods of propulsion. Aeronautics started with the study of the BALLOON, which mainly concerned the raising of a load by means of BUOYANCY. It later included the heavier-than-air flight of gliders, planes, helicopters and rockets. A HELICOPTER utilizes LIFT provided by a rotor. Gliders and planes use wings to provide lift, but a minimum forward speed is essential to maintain height. A plane is pulled forward by a propeller, or is pushed by the reaction forces of expanding gases from one or more jet or ROCKET engines. The increased speeds of modern aircraft to supersonic (speeds in excess of that of sound, *c*.1,200km/h or 750mph) and the accompanying shock waves this produces has brought changes in wing and fuselage designs to improve streamlining. While with hypersonic speeds (in excess of five times the speed of sound or Mach 5), the forces involved again change fundamentally requiring further design adjustments.

aeroplane *See* AIRCRAFT

aerosol Suspension of liquid or solid particles in a gas. Fog – millions of tiny water droplets suspended in air – is a liquid-based example; airborne dust or smoke is a solid-based equivalent. Manufactured aerosols are used in products such as deodorants, cosmetics, paints and household sprays. CHLOROFLUOROCARBONS (CFCs) are being phased out as aerosol propellants because they damage the OZONE LAYER.

Aeschylus (525–456 BC) Earliest of the great Greek playwrights. Aeschylus is said to have been responsible for the development of TRAGEDY as a dramatic form through his addition of a second actor, and for his reduction of the role of the chorus. He was also the first to introduce scenery. His best-known work is the trilogy *Oresteia*, which comprises *Agamemnon*, *The Choephori* and *The Eumenides*.

Aesir Primary group of Nordic gods who lived in Asgard. Woden (Odin), Thor (Donar) and Tyr (Tiw), with a few others, were the object of a cult that extended throughout the lands inhabited by Germanic peoples. Secondary to the Aesir was a group of gods known as the Vanir.

Aesop (620–560 BC) Semi-legendary Greek fabulist. He was the reputed creator of numerous short tales about animals, all illustrating human virtues and failings (they are almost certainly written by several people). According to one tradition, Aesop was a former slave.

aesthetic movement Late 19th-century English cult of beauty. It grew out of aestheticism, a philosophy which spread across Europe in reaction to industrialization and UTILITARIANISM. The principal figures of the movement were Aubrey BEARDSLEY, J.M. WHISTLER, Oscar WILDE and Walter Pater.

aesthetics (Gk. *aisthēsis*, perception) Specialized branch of philosophy concerned with the arts. PLATO's classical formulation of art as a mirror of nature was developed by ARISTOTLE in his *Poetics*. As a distinct discipline, aesthetics dates from Alexander Baumgarten's *Reflections on Poetry* (1735). Common problems in aesthetics include a definition of beauty and the ascribing of artistic value. For Plato and Aristotle, beauty was objective, it resided in the object. David HUME argued that the value of art was dependent on subjective perception. In *Critique of Judgement* (1790), Immanuel KANT mediated between the two, arguing that artistic value may be subjective, but it has universal validity in the form of pleasure. Later philosophers, such as George SANTAYANA and Benedetto CROCE, have focused on art as a socially symbolic act.

Afghan hound Tall, hunting dog originating in Egypt (4000–3000 BC) and later established in Afghanistan. It has a long, slender head and jaws; long, hanging ears; and a long, tapered tail with a curve at the end. The thick, silky coat is short and smooth on the back. Height: 61–71cm (24–28in) at shoulder. Weight: 23–27kg (51–60lb).

Afghanistan Republic in S central Asia. Afghanistan is bordered by Turkmenistan, Uzbekistan, Tajikistan, China, Pakistan and Iran. The central highlands make up nearly 75% of total land area and, in the E, reach a height of more than 7,600m (25,000ft). The capital, KABUL, lies in the foothills of the main range, the HINDU KUSH. The River Kabul flows E to the KHYBER PASS border with Pakistan. North of the central highlands are smaller hills and broad plateaux. Southern Afghanistan is mainly lowland, with vast stretches of desert in the SW. **Climate** In winter,

northerly winds bring extremely cold weather to the highlands. Summers are hot and dry. Southern Afghanistan has lower rainfall and higher average temperatures. **Vegetation** Grassland covers much of the N, while the vegetation in the dry S is sparse. Trees are rare, but forests of conifers grow on the mountain slopes. Alder, ash and juniper grow in the valleys. **History** Afghanistan's location on the overland routes between Iran, the Indian subcontinent and Central Asia has encouraged numerous invasions. Its situation, however, has helped to repulse many attacks. In ancient times, Afghanistan was invaded successively by Aryans, Persians, Greeks, Macedonians and warrior armies from central Asia. Buddhism was introduced in the 2nd century BC, and Arab armies brought Islam in the late 7th century. NADIR SHAH extended Persian rule to encompass most of Afghanistan. His successor, AHMAD SHAH, founded the Durrani dynasty and established the first unified state in 1747. In 1818, the dynasty died and Russia and Britain competed for control: Russia sought an outlet to the Indian Ocean, while Britain tried to protect its Indian territories. The first Afghan War (1838–42) was inconclusive. The second Afghan War (1878–80) ended with the accession of Abd ar-Rahman Khan as emir. The dominance of British interests was recognized in the Anglo-Russian Agreement (1907). Following the Third Afghan War, Afghanistan became fully independent under Amanullah (1921). He established an unstable monarchy, constantly threatened by religious and tribal divisions. The status of the PATHANS in the NORTH-WEST FRONTIER province of Pakistan proved a continuing source of conflict between the two states. In 1973, an army coup overthrew the monarchy and established a republic. In 1978, the military government was deposed in a Marxist coup backed by the Soviet Union. The costly Afghanistan War (1979–89) was fought between government-backed Soviet troops and MUJAHEDDIN guerrillas. In 1988–89, Soviet troops withdrew, but the civil war raged on and the number of refugees continued to mount. In 1992, Mujaheddin forces captured Kabul and set up a moderate Islamic government. Fundamentalists continued to agitate. In 1996, the TALIBAN (Persian, "students"), based in the S city of KANDAHAR, captured Kabul and formed an interim government. An anti-Taliban coalition (United Islamic Front for the Salvation of Afghanistan) failed to prevent further gains, and by 1998 the Taliban controlled 90% of the country. **Economy** Afghanistan is one of the world's poorest countries (1992 GDP per capita, US$819). Agriculture employs *c*.60% of the workforce. Most of the highland farming is semi-nomadic herding. Wheat is the chief crop of the sedentary farming of the valleys. Afghanistan has many mineral deposits, but most are undeveloped. Natural gas is produced, together with some coal, copper, gold, lapis lazuli and salt. Afghanistan has few manufacturing industries. The main exports are karakul skins, cotton, dried and fresh fruit and nuts.

Africa Second-largest continent (after Asia), straddling the equator and lying largely within the tropics. **Land** Africa forms a plateau between the Atlantic and Indian oceans. Its highest features include the ATLAS and Ahaggar mountains in the NW, the Ethiopian Highlands in the E, the Drakensberg Mountains in the S and KILIMANJARO. Lake Assal in the Afar Depression of Djibouti is the lowest point at −153m (−502ft). The huge sunken strip in the E is the African section of the Great RIFT VALLEY. The SAHARA stretches across the N and the KALAHARI and NAMIB are smaller deserts in the S and SW. MADAGASCAR lies off the SE coast. **Structure and**

AFGHANISTAN
AREA: 652,090sq km (251,773sq mi)
POPULATION: 26,511,000
CAPITAL (POPULATION): Kabul (1,565,000)

geology Africa is composed largely of ancient metamorphic rocks overlain with tertiary Mesozoic and Palaeozoic sediments. The mountains of the NW are folded sedimentary material, roughly contemporaneous with the Alps. The Great Rift Valley, formed by the progressive movement of the Arabian Peninsula away from Africa, is mainly igneous in the N and mainly older pre-Cambrian in the S. **Lakes and rivers** The Rift Valley contains the lakes ALBERT, MALAWI and TANGANYIKA. Lake VICTORIA to the E is Africa's largest; Lake CHAD lies in the S Sahara. Rivers include the NILE, NIGER, CONGO and ZAMBEZI. **Climate and vegetation** Much of the continent is hot and (outside the desert areas) humid. The belt along the Equator receives more than 250cm (100in) of precipitation a year and is covered by tropical rain forest. The forest gives way both in the N and S to areas of acacia and brush and then through savanna grassland to desert. The N strip of the continent and the area around the Cape have a Mediterranean climate. **Peoples** Africa is home to over 13% of the world's population divided into more than 700 culturally distinct tribes and groups. North of the Sahara, Arabs and Berbers predominate, while to the S, some of the many black tribes include the Akan, FULANI, GALLA, HAUSA, HOTTENTOTS, IBO, MASAI, MOSSI, SAN, YORUBA and ZULU. Indians and Europeans also form significant minorities. Africa is relatively thinly populated and *c*.75% of the population is rural. **Economy** Agriculture is restricted in central Africa by the large expanse of tropical rain forest, though cash crops such as cocoa, rubber and peanuts are grown on plantations. Along the N coast, crops such as citrus fruits, olives and cereals are grown. The Sahara is largely unproductive, supporting only a nomadic herding community. E and S Africa are the richest agricultural areas, containing large mixed farms and cattle ranching. Apart from South Africa, the continent is industrially underdeveloped. Mining is important. Zambia contains the largest deposits of copper ore in the world, bauxite is extracted in W Africa, and oil is produced in Libya, Algeria and Nigeria. South Africa is extremely rich in minerals, with gold, diamonds and coal being the most important. **Recent History** Before the 1880s Europeans were, except in South Africa, largely confined to the coastal regions. By the end of the 19th century the whole continent, except for Liberia and Ethiopia, was under foreign domination either by European powers or (in the N) by the Ottoman Empire. Beginning in the 1950s, the former colonies secured their independence within the space of 40 years, but the process of rapid decolonization brought unrest and instability to many parts of the continent. A major factor in this unrest was, and continues to be, the artificial boundaries created by colonialism. Area: *c*.30 million sq km (11.7 million sq mi) *Highest mountain* Kilimanjaro (Tanzania) 5,895m (19,340ft) *Longest river* Nile 6,670km (4,140mi) *Population* (1990 est.) 647,518,000 *Largest cities* CAIRO (6,663,000); KINSHASA (3,804,000); ALEXANDRIA (3,170,000); CAPE TOWN (2,350,000) *See also* articles on individual countries

African art Naturalistic rock paintings and engravings, from before 4000 BC are found in the Sahara Desert. They are similar to European PALAEOLITHIC ART. Later African tribal art is inseparable from the ritual life of the community. Examples include: body painting and dance; music and musical instruments (especially the drum); ceremonial masks and small sculptures used in ANCESTOR WORSHIP; and weapons and everyday utensils (such as bowls and stools). Wood is the most commonly used material. Artists were usually professionals and received great respect and cultural status. Except for EGYPTIAN ART, the most fertile artistic region is sub-Saharan Africa. The Nok terracotta heads from Nigeria are the earliest examples of African sculpture yet discovered (*c*.500 BC). The naturalistic bronze heads produced by the YORUBA at Ife, SW Nigeria, reveal an early (12th–15th century) mastery of the CIRE PERDUE process. This skill passed to the ASHANTI of Ghana, who produced highly exaggerated figurative sculpture. The Dogon of Mali are renowned for their wooden sculpture, especially stylized wooden masks featuring recessed rectangles. The stonework of GREAT ZIMBABWE reveals a highly advanced grasp of architectural design. Traditional African art influenced early modern European art, especially PICASSO's development of CUBISM and MODIGLIANI's figurative paintings. *See also* ISLAMIC ART AND ARCHITECTURE

African literatures Oral and written literatures of Africa. **Oral** literature often features musical rhythms and audience participation. Narration is regarded both as performance art and as transmission of historical information. A major theme of Africa's **written** literatures is the conflict between traditional cultures and modernization. African literature written in **indigenous languages** antedates African literature in European languages, but the latter is more widespread. The earliest known indigenous works are religious texts, informed by Christian and Islamic literature. In **North Africa** a tradition of Latin writing dates back to the 5th-century Christian theologian Saint AUGUSTINE. The tradition of North African writing in Arabic has continued into the 20th century, chiefly through the work of Egyptian novelist Naguib MAHFOUZ. In **East Africa** early Swahili poetry was influenced by Islamic verse and written in Arabic, but Latin script later became more common. In **West Africa** the Hausa began to produce literature during the 19th century, while the first **Yoruba** novel, *The Forest of a Thousand Demons* by Daniel Olorunfemi Fagunwa, was not published until 1938. African literatures in **European languages** were mainly born out of colonialism. The Senegalese poet and statesman Léopold SENGHOR, writing in **French**, developed the notion of *négritude*, which asserted the values of traditional African culture. The first known work of **English** literature by an African is *The Interesting Narrative of the Life and Adventures of Olaudah Equiano or Gustavus Vassa, the African* (1789) by Olaudah Equiano. Prominent writers in **Nigeria** include Ben OKRI, Amos TUTUOLA, Wole SOYINKA and Chinua ACHEBE. Major works from **Ghana** include the novel *The Beautyful Ones Are Not Yet Born* (1968) by Ayi Kwei Armah. One of the best-known works of African literature in English is the epic poem *Song of Lawino* (1966) by Ugandan writer Okot p'Bitek. In the late 1970s Kenyan writer Ngugi wa Thiong'o abandoned the language of the colonizer for his native tongue, Gikuyu, signalling a growing trend for indigenous writing.

African mythology North Africans are predominantly Islamic, but the many peoples in sub-Saharan Africa have a rich collection of traditional beliefs. Almost all recognize a supreme being who created the universe. There are also innumerable other gods, whose cults flourish in W Africa. Many Africans believe in the power of the spirit world. Belief in reincarnation is also widespread, and ANCESTOR WORSHIP is an important social ritual. The dead are feared because they possess greater powers than the living. Many Africans believe that people are reborn in living animals or in inanimate objects. MAGIC plays an important part in people's everyday lives. Medicine men make amulets, necklaces and other kinds of charms which are believed to ward off evil. Other objects are used to protect crops and houses or to bring rain. Belief in magic has proved more enduring than the traditional mythologies, which have declined with the advance of CHRISTIANITY and ISLAM.

African National Congress (ANC) South African political party. It was formed in 1912 with the aim of securing racial equality and full political rights for non-whites. By the 1950s, it had become the principal opposition to the APARTHEID regime. A military wing, *Umkhonte We Sizwe* (Spear of the Nation), was set up in the aftermath of the SHARPEVILLE Massacre. It engaged in economic and industrial sabotage. In 1961, the ANC was banned and many of its leaders were arrested or forced into exile. In 1964, the leaders of the ANC, Nelson MANDELA and Walter SISULU, began long sentences as political prisoners. In 1990, the ANC was legalized, Mandela was released from Robben Island, and many of the legislative pillars of apartheid were dismantled. In 1994, in South Africa's first multiracial elections, the ANC gained more than 60% of the popular vote. Nelson Mandela became the first post-apartheid president of South Africa. In 1997, he was succeeded as leader of the ANC by Thabo MBEKI, who became president of South Africa in 1999.

African violet Tropical flowering house plant, with velvety, rounded leaves growing in spreading rosettes around purple, white or pink blossoms with yellow stamens. Height: 10–15cm (4–6in). Family Gesneriaceae; genus *Saintpaulia*.

Afrikaans One of 11 official languages of the Republic of South Africa. It is derived from the language spoken by the original Dutch settlers of the 17th century, but quickly evolved its own forms to become a distinct language. Afrikaans is regarded as a cultural focal point by South Africans of Dutch origin. It is the everyday means of communication for some three million speakers of European, African and mixed descent.

Afrika Korps German armoured force in World War 2 that operated in the N African desert. Under its commander General Erwin ROMMEL it had spectacular but transient success against the British in 1941–42.

Afrikaner (*Boer*, farmer) Descendant of the predominantly Dutch settlers in SOUTH AFRICA. Afrikaners first settled around the Cape region in the 17th century. To avoid British control, the Afrikaners spread N and E from the Cape in the GREAT TREK and founded the independent South African Republic (TRANSVAAL) and Orange Free State. Defeat in the SOUTH AFRICAN WARS (1899–1902) led to the republics merging in the Union of South Africa (1910). *See also* CAPE PROVINCE

Afro-Asiatic languages (Hamito-Semitic) Only family of languages common to both Asia and Africa. They are spoken by *c*.130 million people in N Africa, the Sahara, parts of E, W and central Africa and W Asia. On the African continent, it includes such languages as Berber and the now extinct Coptic and ancient Egyptian. It also includes the SEMITIC LANGUAGES, notably Arabic and Hebrew, that originated in Syria, Mesopotamia, Arabia and Palestine. With a few exceptions, the family uses a script that is read from right to left.

afterbirth PLACENTA, UMBILICAL CORD and fetal membranes expelled from the uterus after birth. The expulsion is brought about naturally by contraction of the uterus.

Agadir Atlantic seaport, SW Morocco. In 1960, Agadir suffered a disastrous earthquake, but it was rebuilt as a tourist centre and is now a popular European tourist destination. Fishing is the other main economic activity. Pop. (1994) 365,965.

Aga Khan Since 1818, title of the leader of the ISHMAILI sect of SHIITE Muslims. Aga Khan III (1877–1957) was the best known. He headed the All-India Muslim League in support of British rule in 1906. He moved to Europe and was known for his enormous wealth and love of horse racing. His grandson, Karim, became Aga Khan IV in 1957 and has continued the family traditions.

Agamemnon In Greek mythology, king of Mycenae, and brother of Menelaus. According to Homer's *Iliad*, he led the Greeks at the siege of TROY. When Troy fell, Agamemnon returned home but was murdered by his wife CLYTEMNESTRA and her lover Aegisthus.

agar Complex substance extracted from seaweed; its powder forms a "solid" gel in solution. It is used as a thickening agent in foods; as an adhesive; as a medium for growing bacteria, MOULD, YEAST and other microorganisms; as a medium for TISSUE CULTURE; and as a gel for ELECTROPHORESIS.

agaric Order of FUNGI that includes edible mushrooms, ink caps and the poisonous AMANITA. Their spores are born on the surface of gills or pores on the undersurface of the cap.

Agassiz, Alexander (1835–1910) US marine zoologist, b. Switzerland. Agassiz was influential in the development of modern systematic zoology and made important studies of the SEAFLOOR. In 1874, he succeeded his father, Louis, as curator of the Harvard Museum of Natural History.

agate Microcrystalline form of quartz with parallel bands of colour. It is regarded as a semi-precious stone and is used for making jewellry. Hardness *c*.6.5; r.d. *c*.2.6.

agave Succulent, flowering plant found in tropical, subtropical and temperate regions. Agaves have narrow, lance-shaped leaves clustered at the base of the plant, and many have large flower clusters. The flower of the well-known century plant (*Agave americana*) of SW North America grows up to 7.6m (25ft) in one season. Other species are SISAL (*A. sisalana*) and mescal (*Lophophora williamsii*), whose fermented sap forms the basis of the liqueur tequila. Family Agavaceae.

Agee, James (1909–55) US writer. A novelist, poet, influential film critic and screenwriter for films such as *The African Queen* (1951, co-scripted with John HUSTON) and *The Night of the Hunter* (1955), Agee is perhaps best known for his study of rural poverty, *Let Us Now Praise Famous Men* (1941). His novel *A Death in the Family* (1957) won a Pulitzer Prize.

agglutination Clumping of BACTERIA or red blood cells by ANTIBODIES that react with ANTIGENS on the cell surface.

agglutinative language Language in which words show a strong tendency to be composed of a series of elements "stuck" together, each one representing only one grammatical category. Japanese or Finnish are examples. In such languages, which are also called agglutinating languages, the elements consist of affixes attached to a core that carries the basic meaning. The affixes specify grammatical features such as plurality of nouns or tense of verbs, or the relationship of the core to other words or phrases within the sentence.

aggression State of mind that is expressed in ways ranging from verbal attack to physical violence. Aggression in animals is generally regarded as instinctive. Psychologists do not agree, however, about the origin of human aggression. Some regard it as instinctive, others as entirely learned, and still others as a mixture of the two. Some theorists believe that children acquire aggressive behaviour as a result of imitating others, including characters seen in films or television.

Agincourt Village in Pas de Calais, NE France. It was the site of the English King HENRY V's victory over the French in 1415 during the HUNDRED YEARS' WAR. Despite being outnumbered, England won due to poor French tactics and the superiority of the English longbow over the French crossbow. The French lost more than 6,000 troops and Henry was able to conquer Normandy.

Agnew, Spiro Theodore (1918–96) US statesman, vice president (1969–73) to Richard NIXON. In 1967, he became governor of his native Maryland. Agnew was a staunch advocate of US involvement in the VIETNAM WAR. During his second term as vice president, Agnew was forced to resign after the discovery of political bribery and corruption in Maryland. He did not contest further charges of tax evasion and was given a three-year probationary sentence and fined US$10,000.

Agnon, Shmuel Yosef (1888–1970) Hebrew writer, b. Poland as Samuel Josef Czaczkes. A key figure in modern Hebrew literature, he shared the 1966 Nobel Prize for literature with Nelly SACHS. Agnon's works include an epic trilogy of novels on the plight of East European Jewry: *The Bridal Canopy* (1919), *A Guest for the Night* (1938) and *The Day Before Yesterday* (1945).

agnosticism Philosophical viewpoint according to which it is impossible either to demonstrate or refute the existence of a supreme being or ultimate cause on the basis of available evidence. It was particularly associated with the RATIONALISM of Thomas HUXLEY and is used as a basis for the rejection of both Christianity and ATHEISM.

agora Civic centre or market-place of ancient Greek towns and cities. Situated in the centre of the town or near the harbour, the agora was a special place for male citizens to conduct their religious, commercial, judicial and social activities. It was usually surrounded by public buildings, temples and colonnades of shops and was ornamented with statues and fountains.

Agostini, Giacomo (1942–) Italian motorcyclist. Racing in both the 350cc and 500cc classes, Agostini won a record 15 world titles and 122 grands prix between 1966 and 1975. Thirteen of his 15 titles were gained on an MV Augusta. He retired from racing in 1975 and became manager of the Yamaha team.

Agra City in Uttar Pradesh, and site of the TAJ MAHAL, N central India. It was founded (1566) by AKBAR I. Agra's importance declined after 1658 when the Mogul capital moved to DELHI. It was annexed to the British Empire in 1803 and later became the capital of North-West Province (1835–62). Agra's fine Mogul architecture make it a major tourist destination. It is an important rail junction and commercial and administrative centre. Industries: glass, shoes, textiles. Pop. (1991) 956,000.

Agricultural Revolution Series of changes in farming practice in the 18th and early 19th centuries. The main changes comprised crop rotation, new machinery, increased capital investment, scientific breeding, land reclamation and ENCLOSURE of common lands. Originating in Britain, these advances led to greatly increased agricultural productivity in Europe.

agriculture Practice of cultivating crops and raising livestock. Modern archaeological dating techniques suggest that the production of CEREALS and the domestication of animals were widespread throughout E Mediterranean countries by *c*.7000 BC. The Egyptians and Mesopotamians (*c*.3000 BC) were the earliest peoples to organize agriculture on a large scale, using irrigation techniques and manure as fertilizer. Farming formed the foundations of later societies in China, India, Europe, Mexico and Peru. By Roman times (200 BC–AD 400), crop farming and the domestication of animals were commonplace in W Europe. In 17th- and 18th-century Europe, selective breeding improved milk and meat yields. The use of the four-field system of crop rotation meant that fields could be used continuously for production with no deterioration in yield or quality of the crops. The greatest changes in agriculture came with the INDUSTRIAL REVOLUTION. Many items of farm machinery were introduced in the 19th century. In Western Europe and North America, mechanization has advanced greatly and a large proportion of agricultural production is now carried out by FACTORY FARMING methods. In much of the underdeveloped world, agriculture is still labour intensive. Three-quarters of the world's workforce is engaged in farming.

Agrigento City in S Sicily, Italy, capital of Agrigento province. One of the great centres of classical times, Agrigento was founded (*c*.580 BC) by Greek colonists from Gela. Agrigento prospered (its population reaching *c*.200,000) until conquered by the Carthaginians in 406 BC. Captured by Romans in 210 BC, its commerce flourished once more. Tourists visit its Greek sites, such as the temples of Hera and Zeus. Pop. (1990) 56,660.

Agrippa, Marcus Vipsanius (b.63 BC) Roman general, adviser to Octavian (later AUGUSTUS). He helped Octavian to power by winning naval battles against Sextus Pompeius in 36 BC and MARK ANTONY at the Battle of ACTIUM in 31 BC.

agronomy Science of soil management and improvement in the interests of agriculture. It includes the studies of particular plants and soils and their interrelationships. Agronomy involves disease-resistant plants, selective breeding and the development of chemical fertilizers.

Agulhas, Cape Southernmost point of Africa, in South Africa, 190km (120mi) ESE of Cape Town.

Ahab (d. *c*.853 BC) King of Israel (*c*.874–853 BC), son and successor of Omri. He secured Israel's borders though wars against Syria and Assyria and through marriage to JEZEBEL, a princess from Tyre. The union saw the introduction of the Phoenician cult of BAAL and Ahab was denounced by the prophet ELIJAH.

Ahern, Bertie (1951–) Irish statesman, taoiseach (1997–). He was first elected to the Dáil Éireann in 1977. Ahern served as vice president (1983–94) of FIANNA FÁIL, before becoming leader. He succeeded John BRUTON as taoiseach.

ahimsa Non-violence or non-injury to both people and animals. It is a central concept of JAINISM and BUDDHISM, and is also important in HINDUISM. This belief inspired the passive resistance of "Mahatma" GANDHI. *See also* KARMA

Ahmadabad (Ahmedabad) City on the River Sabarmati, W India. Founded in 1411 by Ahmad Shah, the Muslim ruler of Gujarat, it is the cultural, commercial and transportation centre of the state, with many magnificent mosques, temple and tombs. It is the headquarters of the INDIAN NATIONAL CONGRESS movement. Main industry: cotton. Pop. (1991) 3,298,000.

Ahmad Shah Durrani (1722–73) Emir of Afghanistan (1747–73) and founder of the Durrani dynasty. He united the Afghan tribes and is sometimes known as the founder of modern Afghanistan.

Ahriman (Angra Mainyu) Supreme evil spirit in ZOROASTRIANISM. Ahriman is the equivalent of Satan in Christian theology, and is permanently at war with AHURA MAZDAH. He heads an army of demons who embody envy and other evil qualities.

Ahura Mazdah (Ormazd or Ormuzd) In ZOROASTRIANISM, the supreme deity and the god of light and wisdom. The Achaemenids elevated Ahura

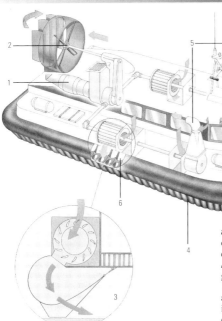

◀ **air-cushion vehicle**
Air-cushion vehicles, or hovercraft, float on a bed of air allowing them to operate on both land and water. A turbine (1) powers a propeller (2) for forward motion. Two main fans (3) provide lift by pulling air into the skirt (4) beneath the vehicle. Two smaller fans (5) blow air through directable nozzles on top of the craft providing manoeuvrability. The skirt is divided into cells (6) that seal the air cushion and act as a giant shock absorber.

aileron Hinged control surface on the outer trailing edge of an AIRCRAFT wing. By moving down or up in opposite directions, ailerons cause the airplane to roll or bank.

Ailey, Alvin (1931–89) US modern dancer and choreographer. He studied dance with Martha GRAHAM. In 1958 Ailey formed the American Dance Theater and acted as its artistic director (1958–89). The company introduced many leading African-American and Asian dancers to worldwide audiences. His work, such as *Roots of the Blues* (1961), incorporates elements of jazz with African and MODERN DANCE.

Ainu Aboriginal people of Hokkaidō (N Japan), Sakhalin and the Kuril islands. Traditionally hunters, fishermen and trappers, they practise ANIMISM and are famed for their bear cult.

air Gases above the Earth's surface. *See* ATMOSPHERE

air conditioning Process of controlling the temperature, humidity, flow and sometimes odour and dust content of air in any enclosed space. Air is cooled by refrigeration or heated by steam or hot water. Odours and dust are removed by filters and the moisture content is adjusted by humidifiers before the air is circulated by fans.

aircraft Any vehicle capable of travelling in the Earth's atmosphere. By far the most common aircraft is the aeroplane, or plane. An **aeroplane** is a heavier-than-air flying machine that depends upon fixed wings for LIFT in the air, as it moves under the THRUST of its engines. This thrust may be provided by an airscrew (propeller) turned by a piston or turbine engine, or by the exhaust gases of a JET engine or rocket motor. **Gliders** differ from planes only in their dependence upon air currents to keep them airborne. The main body of a plane is the fuselage, to which are attached the wings and tail assembly. Engines may be incorporated into or slung below the wings, but are sometimes mounted on the fuselage toward the tail or, as in some fighter aircraft, built into the fuselage near the wings. The landing gear or undercarriage, with its heavy wheels and stout shock absorbers, is usually completely retractable into the wings or fuselage. Wing design varies with the type of plane, high-speed fighters having slim, often swept-back or adjustable wings that create minimal air resistance (drag) at high speeds. At the other extreme, heavy air freighters need broader wings in order to achieve the necessary lift at take-off. A plane is steered by the pilot moving flaps and AILERONS on the wings and rudder and elevators on the tail assembly. This deflects the pressure of air on the AEROFOIL surfaces, causing the plane to rise or descend, to bank (tilt) or swing and turn in

Mazdah into the supreme deity, who created the universe and the twin spirits of good and evil. He became identified with the good spirit, who was in constant conflict with AHRIMAN.

aid, development Funds, goods, equipment and expertise donated or loaned by the world's richer countries to poorer countries and used to promote development. The largest amount of development aid is paid out by the WORLD BANK, specifically through its International Development Association (IDA). All industrialized member states of the UNITED NATIONS (UN) allocate a specific proportion of their own GROSS NATIONAL PRODUCT (GNP) to foreign aid.

Aidan, Saint (d.651) Irish monk from Iona who brought Christianity to NE England. He became the first Bishop of Lindisfarne, where he established a monastery and sent out missionaries all over N England. His feast day is 31 August, the date on which he died.

AIDS *See* ACQUIRED IMMUNE DEFICIENCY SYNDROME

Aiken, Conrad Potter (1889–1973) US poet, novelist and critic. His *Selected Poems* (1929) won him a Pulitzer Prize. Aiken's interest in psychoanalysis and musical form are evident in *Collected Poems* (1953). He also wrote five novels and an autobiography, *Ushant* (1952).

Aiken, Howard (1900–73) US mathematician who was a pioneer in the development of COMPUTERS. In 1939, while working for IBM, Aiken designed an electromechanical automatic calculating machine. In 1944 he helped build the Mark 1 Automatic Sequence Controlled Calculator, one of the first programmable computers.

aikido Martial art based on an ancient Japanese system of self-defence. Unlike some other martial art forms, in which force is met with counter-force, aikido employs the technique of avoiding action by making use of an opponent's forward impetus, causing the attacker to suffer a temporary loss of balance. Some forms of aikido, such as tomiki, are also sports.

the air. RADAR systems aid navigation, an AUTOMATIC PILOT keeps the aircraft steady on a fixed course and pressurized cabins allow passenger planes to fly at heights exceeding 10,000m (33,000ft). *See also* AERODYNAMICS; AEROFOIL; AIRSHIP; BALLOON; GLIDING; HELICOPTER

aircraft carrier Military vessel with a wide open deck that serves as a runway for the launching and landing of aircraft. A modern nuclear-powered carrier may have a flight deck *c*.300m (1,000ft) long, a displacement of *c*.75,000 metric tons, a 4,000-man crew and 90 aircraft.

air-cushion vehicle (ACV) Vehicle that is lifted from the ground by air forced out from under the craft. The best-known example is a HOVERCRAFT. *See artwork* p.15

air force Military air power, first used in World War 1. In 1918 the British government formed the Royal AIR FORCE (RAF), the world's first separate air force. The United States AIR FORCE (USAF) was created in 1947.

Air Force, Royal (RAF) Youngest of the British armed services, formed in 1918 by the amalgamation of the Royal Naval Air Service and the Royal Flying Corps. It was controlled by the Air Ministry from 1919 to 1964, when it was merged into the Ministry of Defence. Total personnel (1996): 68,000.

Air Force, United States (USAF) One of the three major US armed services, established under the Department of Defense in the National Security Act of 1947. It began as the Aeronautical Division of the Army in 1907. The USAF is the world's largest air force. Total personnel (1994): 426,000

air pollution *See* POLLUTION

airship (dirigible) Powered lighter-than-air craft able to control its direction of motion. A gas that is less dense than air, nowadays helium, provides LIFT. A rigid airship, or **Zeppelin**, maintains its form with a framework of girders covered by fabric or aluminium alloy. Non-rigid airships, or **blimps**, have no internal structure. They rely on the pressure of the contained gas to maintain the shape.

air-traffic control System of guidance to allow the safe and orderly movement of aircraft. Air-traffic controllers organize ground and local control for airport vehicles and emergency services. Other operators in radar rooms control aircraft arrivals and departures and monitor the "stacking" and timing of aircraft traffic. A system of route control allows operators to hand over a flight to the next control station on the route.

Aix-en-Provence City in SE France, 27km (17mi) N of Marseilles. Founded in 123 BC by the Romans, it is a cultural centre with a university (1409), an 11th–13th-century cathedral and several art galleries. Industries: wine-making equipment, electrical apparatus, olives, almonds. Pop. (1990) 123,842.

Aix-la-Chapelle, Treaty of (1748) Diplomatic agreement, principally between France and Britain, that ended the War of the AUSTRIAN SUCCESSION (1740–48). The treaty provided for the restitution of conquests made during the war, contributed to the rise of Prussian power, and confirmed British control of the slave trade to Spanish America. An earlier treaty signed at Aix-la-Chapelle ended the War of Devolution (1668).

Ajaccio Seaport capital of CORSICA, France, on the Gulf of Ajaccio; birthplace of Napoleon I. Ajaccio was founded (1492) by the Genoese and was sold to France in 1768. Industries: fishing, shipbuilding. Pop. (1990) 59,320.

Ajax In Greek mythology, name given to two heroes who fought for Greece against TROY. The Greater Ajax is depicted in Homer's *Iliad* as a warrior who led the troops of Salamis against Troy. The Lesser Ajax was shipwrecked by ATHENA for raping CASSANDRA.

Ajmer Town on the banks of the man-made lake Ana Sagar, Rajasthan, NW India. Founded in the 12th century, Ajmer was capital (until 1956) of Ajmer state. Today, it is an administrative centre for the cotton and marble industries. The Durgah Tomb, burial place of the Sufi saint, is a major place of Muslim pilgrimage. Pop. (1991) 402,000.

Akbar I (the Great) (1542–1605) Emperor of India (1556–1605). Generally regarded as the greatest ruler of the MOGUL EMPIRE, he assumed personal control in 1560 and set out to establish Mogul control of the whole of India, extending his authority as far S as Ahmadnagar. Akbar built a new capital at Fatehpur Sikri and endeavoured to unify his empire by conciliation with Hindus. He also tolerated Christian missionaries.

Akhmatova, Anna (1889–1966) Russian poet. Her simple, intense lyrics and personal themes are best represented in the volumes *The Rosary* (1914) and *The Willow Tree* (1940). Her longest work, *Poem Without a Hero* (trans. 1971), is her masterpiece. Although officially ostracized for "bourgeois decadence," she remained popular in the Soviet Union.

Akhnaten (d. *c*.1362 BC) (Akhenaten) Ancient Egyptian king of the 18th dynasty (r. *c*.1379–1362 BC). He succeeded his father, AMENHOTEP III, as Amenhotep IV. In an attempt to counter the influence of the priests of the temple of AMON at LUXOR, he renounced the old gods and introduced an almost monotheistic worship of the sun god, Aten. He adopted the name Akhnaten and established a new capital at Akhetaten (modern Tell el-Amarna). After his death TUTANKHAMEN reinstated Amon as the national god, and the capital reverted to Luxor.

Akiba Ben Joseph (AD 50–135) Jewish rabbi and martyr in Palestine. He developed a new method of interpreting the Halakah, Hebrew oral laws, and supported a revolt (132) against the Roman emperor, Hadrian. He was imprisoned by the Romans and tortured to death.

Akihito (1933–) Emperor of Japan (1989–). In 1959, Akihito married a commoner, Michiko Shoda, the first such marriage in the history of the imperial dynasty. Akihito succeeded his father, HIROHITO.

Akkadia (Agade) Ancient region of MESOPOTAMIA, named after the city-state of Akkad. From the mid-4th millennium BC, the region's cities fought each other, until SARGON I united them in *c*.2340 BC, forming the first empire of BABYLONIA.

Akron City on the Cuyahoga River, NE Ohio. The Ohio and Erie Canal (1827) promoted the city's growth. Once the "rubber capital of the world", the first tyre factory opened here in 1871. Products include plastics and chemicals. Pop. (1996) 217,000.

Aksum (Axum) Town in Tigré province, N Ethiopia. It was capital of a powerful kingdom (1st–6th centuries AD). Aksum was Christianized in the 4th century and remains a major centre of Ethiopian Christianity. According to tradition, its kings were descended from Menelik (legendary son of Solomon). A rich trading centre, Aksum was known for its ivory. Pop. (1984 est.) 18,000.

Alabama Southeastern US state, in the chief cotton-growing region; the state capital is MONTGOMERY. BIRMINGHAM is the largest city and a leading iron and steel centre. Settled by the French in 1702, the region was acquired by Britain in 1763. Most of it was ceded to the US in 1783, and Alabama was admitted as the 22nd state of the Union in 1819. It seceded in 1861 as one of the original six states of the Confederacy, and was readmitted to the Union in 1868. In the 1960s, it was a centre of the Civil Rights movement. The N of the state lies in the Appalachian highlands, which have coal, iron ore and other mineral deposits, and the rest consists of the Gulf coastal plain, crossed by a wide strip of rich soil valuable for agriculture. The Mobile River and its tributaries form the chief river system. The principal crops are peanuts, soya beans and maize, with cotton decreasingly important. Industries: chemicals, textiles, electronics, metal and paper products. Area: 133,915sq km (51,705sq mi). Pop. (2000) 4,447,100.

Alabama claims (1872) Award of US$155 million compensation to the US against the UK for damage inflicted by Confederate ships, especially the cruiser *Alabama*, built in England during the American CIVIL WAR (1861–65). An international tribunal ruled that the British government violated its neutrality by allowing the ships to be built on its territory.

alabaster Fine-grained, massive variety of GYPSUM (calcium sulphate), snow-white and translucent in its natural form. It can be dyed or made opaque by heating and is used for making statues and other ornaments.

Alain-Fournier, Henri (1886–1914) French writer. His reputation was secured by his only completed novel, *Le Grand Meaulnes* (1913), a lyrical and semi-autobiographical account of the experiences of a schoolboy. Alain-Fournier was killed in action at the Battle of the Marne.

Alamo Mission in San Antonio, Texas, scene of a battle between Mexico and the Republic of Texas (1836). About 180 Texans, led by William Travis, Davy CROCK-ETT and James BOWIE, were overwhelmed by a vastly superior Mexican force following a siege of 11 days.

Alaric I (370–410) King of the VISIGOTHS (395–410). His forces ravaged Thrace, Macedonia and Greece and occupied Epirus (395–96). In 401 Alaric invaded Italy. Defeated by the Roman general Stilicho, he formed a pact with him. Emperor Honorius executed Stilicho for treason and Alaric besieged (408) and captured Rome (410). He planned an invasion of Sicily and Africa, but his fleet was destroyed in a storm.

Alaska State in NW North America, separated from the rest of continental US by the province of British Columbia, Canada and from Russia by the Bering Strait. The capital is JUNEAU. The largest city is ANCHORAGE on the S coast. The US purchased the area from Russia in 1867 for $7.2 million. Fishing drew settlers and, after the gold rush of the 1890s, the population doubled in ten years. It became the 49th state of the Union in 1959. About 25% lies inside the Arctic Circle. The main Alaska Range includes Mount McKINLEY (Denali), the highest peak in North America. The chief river is the YUKON. The Alaskan economy is based on fish, natural gas, timber, quartz and, primarily, oil. Tourism to the national parks is also becoming important. Because of its strategic position and oil reserves, Alaska has been developed as a military area and is linked to the rest of the US by the 2,450km (1,523mi) Alaska Highway. Although by far the largest US state, it has the second smallest population (after Wyoming). Of the total state population, 85,698 were registered as Native Americans in the 1990 census (the majority of them Inuit-Aleut Eskimos). Area: 591,004sq mi (1,530,700sq km). Pop. (2000) 626,932.

Alaskan Boundary Dispute (1902–03) Dispute between the US and Britain, representing Canada, over

possession of the inlets between Alaska and Canada after the KLONDIKE GOLD RUSH. It was settled by a six-man panel in favour of the US.

Alban, Saint (active 3rd century AD) First British martyr, from the Roman town of Verulamium (now St Albans). He was killed for hiding a Christian priest from the Romans. In 797, King Offa founded an abbey on the site of Alban's execution. His feast day is 22 June.

Albania Balkan republic; the capital is TIRANA. **Land and climate** About 70% of Albania is mountainous, rising to Mount Korab at 2,764m (9,068ft) on the Macedonian border. Most Albanians live in the farming regions of the W coastal lowlands. Albania is subject to severe earthquakes. The coastal regions have a typical Mediterranean climate, with fairly dry, sunny summers and cool, moist winters. The highlands have heavy winter snowfalls. Maquis covers much of the lowlands. **History** In ancient times, Albania was part of ILLYRIA and in 167 BC became part of the ROMAN EMPIRE. Between 1469 and 1912, Albania formed part of the OTTOMAN EMPIRE. Italy invaded Albania in 1939, and German forces occupied it in 1943. In 1944, Albanian communists, led by Enver HOXHA, took power. In the early 1960s, Albania broke with the Soviet Union after Soviet criticism of the Chinese COMMUNIST PARTY to which it was allied until the late 1970s. In the early 1990s, the Albanian government abandoned communism and allowed the formation of opposition parties. In 1996, the Democratic Party, headed by Sali Berisha, won a sweeping victory. In 1997, the collapse of nation-wide pyramid finance schemes sparked a large-scale rebellion in S Albania and a state of emergency was proclaimed. Berisha formed a government of national reconciliation and agreed to new elections. The Socialist Party of Albania was elected and Rexhep Medjani became president. In 1999, internal unrest was compounded by the crisis in the Serbian province of KOSOVO. **Economy** Albania is Europe's poorest country (1992 GDP per capita, US$3,500), and 56% of the workforce are engaged in agriculture. Under communism, the land was divided into large state and collective farms, but private ownership has been encouraged since 1991. Crops include fruits, maize, olives, potatoes, sugar beet, vegetables and wheat. Livestock farming is also important. Albania has some mineral reserves. Chromite, copper and nickel are exported. Other resources include oil, brown coal and hydroelectricity. Heavy industry has caused severe pollution in some areas.

Albany Capital of New York state, USA, on the Hudson River. Settled by the Dutch in 1614 and British from 1664, it replaced New York City as state capital in 1797. It grew from the 1820s with the building of the Erie Canal, linking it to the Great Lakes, and it is still an important river port. Industries: paper, brewing, machine tools, metal products, textiles. Pop. (1996) 104,000.

Albany Congress (1754) North American colonial conference to discuss Native American relations. Representatives from seven northern and middle colonies met Iroquois leaders and negotiated an alliance against the French. At this meeting Benjamin FRANKLIN proposed a plan for union of the colonies, which was rejected by the colonial governments.

Albany Regency (1820–48) Organization of Democratic Party leaders in New York state. It successfully controlled conventions and appointments until the defeat of Martin VAN BUREN's presidential bid (1848).

albatross Large, migratory oceanic bird found mostly in the South Pacific and famed for its effortless gliding flight. All of the 13 species eat on the wing, landing only to breed. The wandering albatross has a long, hooked

---

ALBANIA

AREA: 28,750sq km (11,100sq mi)

POPULATION: 3,795,000

CAPITAL (POPULATION): Tirana (270,000)

bill, short tail, webbed toes and the greatest wingspan of any living bird – 3.5m (11.5ft) or more. Length: 0.7–1.4m (2.3–4.4ft). Family Diomedeidae.

albedo Fraction of light or other radiation that is reflected from a surface. An ideal reflector has an albedo of 1; those of real reflectors are less; that of the Earth, viewed from satellites, is 0.35.

Albee, Edward Franklin (1928–) US dramatist. Albee's debut play *The Zoo Story* (1959) is a classic text of the Theatre of the ABSURD. His best-known play *Who's Afraid of Virginia Woolf?* (1962) is an intense portrait of a destructive marriage. *A Delicate Balance* (1966), *Seascape* (1975) and *Three Tall Women* (1991) won Pulitzer Prizes.

Albéniz, Isaac (1860–1909) Spanish Romantic composer and pianist. Most of his compositions are for piano. He often used Spanish folk elements in his compositions, notably in the piano suite *Iberia* (1906–09).

Albert, Prince (1819–61) Consort of Queen VICTORIA. First cousin of the queen and prince of Saxe-Coburg-Gotha, he married Victoria in 1840. Albert was her chief adviser and was the principal organizer of the Great Exhibition of 1851. He took an active role in diplomatic affairs and called for moderation in the TRENT AFFAIR (1861). Victoria was devastated by his early death from typhoid.

Albert, Lake Lake in the Rift Valley of E central Africa on the border between the Democratic Republic of Congo and Uganda. It is fed by the River Semliki and the Victoria Nile and drained by the Albert Nile (Bahr el Jebel). Ugandans call it Lake Nyanza and the Zaireans named it Lake Mobuto Sese Seko. Some 160km (100mi) long, it has an average width of 35km (22mi) and its maximum depth is 51m (168ft). Area: 5,350sq km (2,065sq mi).

Alberta Province of W Canada bounded on the W mainly by the Rocky Mountains and in the S by the US; the capital is EDMONTON. Other major cities include CALGARY. Most of Alberta is prairie land. The principal rivers are the Athabasca, Peace and North and South Saskatchewan. Lesser Slave Lake is the largest of many lakes. The area was part of a large territory granted (1670) by Charles II to the HUDSON'S BAY COMPANY, and in 1870 the government of Canada bought the region. In 1882, Northwest Territories was divided into four districts and Alberta was created (named after Queen Victoria's fourth daughter). In 1905, Alberta was admitted to the confederation as a province. The fertile plains support wheat farming and livestock. Major resources are coal, minerals and timber from the forests in the N. Oil and natural gas fields in central Alberta have been a major stimulus to the post-1945 economy. Industries: petroleum, metals, chemicals. Area: 661,188sq km (255,285sq mi). Pop. (1996) 2,696,826.

Alberti, Leon Battista (1404–72) Italian architect, humanist and writer. The first major art theorist of the RENAISSANCE, Alberti's treatise *On Painting* (1435) was highly influential. His buildings include the Rucellai Palace, Florence; Tempio Malatestiano, Rimini; and the Church of San Andrea, Mantua.

Albertus Magnus, Saint (c.1200–80) German philosopher and Doctor of the Church, known as "Doctor Universalis". In 1223, he joined the Dominician order. As a teacher of theology in Paris (1242–48), his pupils included Thomas AQUINAS. He was largely responsible for the rehabilitation of ARISTOTLE in European philosophy. He devoted much of his energies to reconciling Aristotelianism with Christian theology. He was canonized in 1931. His feast day is 15 November.

Albigenses (Cathars) Members of a heretical religious sect that existed in southern France from the 11th to the early 14th centuries and took its name from the French city of Albi. Pope Innocent III ordered a crusade against them in 1200, led mainly by Simon de MONTFORT, which caused much damage in Languedoc and Provence.

albino Person or animal with a rare hereditary absence of the pigment MELANIN from the skin, hair and eyes. The hair is white and the skin and eyes are pink because the blood vessels are visible. The eyes are abnormally sensitive to light and vision is often poor.

Albinoni, Tomaso (1671–1750) Italian violinist and composer. He worked in Venice, where he was a friend of VIVALDI. He was one of the first composers of CONCERTOS for a solo instrument; he also wrote nearly 50 operas.

Albright, Madeleine Korbel (1937–) US stateswoman, secretary of state (1997–2000), b. Czechoslovakia. Following Bill CLINTON's re-election (1996), Albright became the first woman to hold the office of secretary of state. She was a hawkish advocate of US involvement in the GULF WAR and Bosnia. The politics of the Middle East have consumed much of her time.

albumin (albumen) Type of water-soluble PROTEIN occurring in animal tissues and fluids. The principal forms are egg albumin (egg white), milk albumin and blood albumin. In a healthy human, it constitutes about 5% of the body's total weight. It is composed of PLASMA, suspended in which are ERYTHROCYTES (red blood cells), LEUCOCYTES (white blood cells) and PLATELETS.

Albuquerque, Afonso d' (1453–1515) Portuguese military commander, founder of the Portuguese empire in the East Indies. After serving as a soldier in North Africa, Albuquerque became governor-general of the Portuguese settlements in W India. He established control over the spice trade by capturing Goa (1510), Malacca (1511), Calicut (1512) and the Malabar Coast.

Albuquerque City in W central New Mexico, USA, on the Upper Rio Grande River. Traditionally a centre for transport and the livestock trade, it now has a high-tech profile in electronics and solar and nuclear research. A popular health resort and New Mexico's largest city, its population increased by nearly 20% between 1980 and 1992. Pop. (1996) 420,000.

Alcaeus (c.620–580 BC) Greek lyric poet. Credited with inventing the Alcaic verse form, he wrote political odes, hymns and love songs. He was imitated by the poet HORACE. Only fragments of his poems have survived.

Alcatraz (Sp. *álcatraces*, pelican) Island in San Francisco Bay, USA, famous as an escape-proof prison surrounded by shark-infested waters. Discovered by the Spanish in 1769, the island served as a fort and then US federal prison (1933–63). In 1972 it became part of the Golden Gate National Recreational Area.

alcázar (Arabic *Al-qasr*, castle) Moorish fortified palace in Spain. In the 14th and 15th centuries Muslims built several of these massive, rectangular structures with their large corner towers. When the Spanish ousted the Moors, they took these palaces over. The most famous surviving alcázars are in Seville (1364) and Toledo.

alchemy Primitive form of chemistry practised in Western Europe from early Christian times until the 17th century, popularly supposed to involve a search for the philosopher's stone – capable of transmuting base metals into gold – and the elixir of life. It actually involved a combination of practical chemistry, astrology, philosophy and mysticism. Similar movements existed in China and India. *See also* BACON, ROGER

Alcibiades (450–404 BC) Athenian general and statesman. In the PELOPONNESIAN WARS, Alcibiades inspired a disastrous campaign in Sicily (415 BC) and temporarily sided with Sparta. Regaining his position in Athens, he was exiled following the Athenian defeat at Notium and later murdered by Spartan agents.

Alcock, Sir John William (1892–1919) British aviator who, with Arthur Whitten-Brown, was the first to fly non-stop across the Atlantic Ocean. Their transatlantic flight began in St John's, Newfoundland on 14 June, 1919, and landed 16.5 hours later near Clifden, Ireland.

alcohol Organic compound having a hydroxyl (-OH) group bound to a carbon atom. ETHANOL, the alcohol found in alcoholic drinks, has the formula C_2H_5OH. Alcohols are used to make dyes and perfumes and as SOLVENTS in lacquers and varnishes. *See also* METHANOL

Alcott, (Amos) Bronson (1799–1888) US philosopher, teacher and reformer, father of Louisa May ALCOTT. A leading figure in TRANSCENDENTALISM, Alcott helped found a utopian community in Fruitlands, Massachusetts.

Alcott, Louisa May (1832–88) US writer, daughter of Bronson ALCOTT. Her first book, *Flower Fables* (1854), helped ease the family's financial troubles. *Hospital Sketches* (1863) is an account of Alcott's experiences as a nurse in the Civil War. *Little Women* (1868) is one of the most successful children's books ever written. It was originally published in two parts: *Good Wives* appeared in 1869. They form the first of a semi-autobiographical quartet of novels about the New England upbringing of the four March sisters, which includes *An Old-Fashioned Girl* (1870), *Little Men* (1871) and *Jo's Boys* (1886).

Aldrin, "Buzz" (Edwin Eugene) (1930–) US astronaut. He piloted the Gemini XII orbital-rendezvous space flight (November 1966) and the lunar module for the first Moon landing (20 July, 1969). Aldrin followed Neil ARMSTRONG to become the second man on the Moon.

aleatoric Music in which the sequence of notes is determined partly by chance, either at the time of composition or at the discretion of the artists. *See also* CAGE, JOHN

Aleichem, Sholem (1859–1916) Yiddish novelist, dramatist and short-story writer, b. Sholem Yakov Rabinowitz. He portrayed the oppression of Russian Jews with humour and compassion. Aleichem's numerous works include *Tevye the Dairyman* (*c.*1949), which was later adapted as the musical *Fiddler on the Roof* (1964).

Alembert, Jean le Rond d' (1717–83) French mathematician and philosopher. He was a leading figure in the ENLIGHTENMENT. D'Alembert was DIDEROT's co-editor on the first edition of the *Encyclopédie* (1751) and contributed the "Preliminary Discourse". His systematic *Treatise on Dynamics* (1743) provided a solution (d'Alembert's principle) that enables Newton's third law of motion to be applied to moving objects.

Aleppo (Halab) City in NW Syria; Syria's second largest city. Like the capital DAMASCUS, it claims to be the oldest continually inhabited city in the world. It has been part of Syria since 1924. Industries: cotton products, silk weaving, dried nuts and fruit. Pop. (1993) 1,494,000.

Aleut Branch of the ESKIMO people who occupy the ALEUTIAN ISLANDS and Alaska Peninsula. They are divided into two major language groups, the Unalaska and Atka. About 4,000 Aleuts live in scattered villages throughout SW Alaska.

Aleutian Islands Volcanic island chain separating the Bering Sea from the Pacific Ocean. They were purchased with Alaska by the US in 1867 and have several US military bases and wildlife reserves. Industries: fishing, furs. Area: 17,666sq km (6,821sq mi). Pop. (1990) 11,942.

Alexander III (*c.*1105–81) Pope (1159–81). His election to the papacy was opposed by Holy Roman emperor FREDERICK I, who had an antipope, Victor IV, elected. The

schism ended 17 years later with the victory of the LOMBARD LEAGUE over Frederick at the Battle of Legnano.

Alexander I (1777–1825) Russian tsar (1801–25). After repulsing Napoleon's attempt to conquer Russia (1812), he led his troops across Europe and into Paris (1814). Under the influence of various mystical groups, he helped form the Holy Alliance with other European powers. He was named constitutional monarch of Poland in 1815 and also annexed Finland, Georgia and Bessarabia to Russia.

Alexander II (1818–81) Russian tsar (1855–81). He was known as the "Tsar Liberator" for his emancipation of the serfs in 1861. Alexander warred with Turkey (1877–78) and gained much influence in the Balkans. He sold Alaska (1867), but expanded the eastern part of the empire. He brutally put down a revolt in Poland (1863). Alexander was assassinated by revolutionaries.

Alexander III (1845–94) Russian tsar (1881–94). He introduced reactionary measures limiting local government; censorship of the press was enforced and arbitrary arrest and exile became common. Ethnic minorities were persecuted. Toward the end of his reign, Alexander formed an alliance with France.

Alexander III (1241–86) King of Scotland (1249–86). He defeated Haakon IV of Norway at the Battle of Largs (1263) and acquired the Hebrides. Alexander married a daughter of Henry III of England, but resisted English claims to Scotland.

Alexander I (1888–1934) King of the Serbs, Croats and Slovenes (1921–29) and of Yugoslavia (1929–34). In his efforts to forge a united country from the rival national groups and ethnically divided political parties, he created an autocratic police state. Alexander was assassinated by a Croatian terrorist.

Alexander, Harold Rupert Leofric George, 1st Earl Alexander of Tunis (1891–1969) British field marshal and statesman, minister of defence (1952–54). In 1940 he directed the evacuation of DUNKIRK. As commander-in-chief (1942–43) in the Middle East, Alexander supervised the successful North Africa campaign. In 1944, he was made field marshal and Allied commander-in-chief in the Mediterranean. After the war, Alexander served as governor-general of Canada (1946–52) before joining Sir Winston Churchill's Conservative cabinet.

Alexander Nevski, Saint (1220–63) Russian ruler, Grand Duke of Novgorod and Grand Duke of Vladimir. He pragmatically submitted to Mongol rule following their invasion of Russia, and the Great Khan appointed him Grand Duke of Kiev. He defeated the Swedes on the River Neva in 1240 (hence the name "Nevski") and the Teutonic Knights on Lake Peipus in 1242. He was canonized by the Russian Orthodox Church in 1547.

Alexander the Great (356–323 BC) King of Macedonia (336–323 BC), considered the greatest conqueror of classical times. Son of PHILIP II of Macedonia, he became king at the age of 20. Destroying rivals, Alexander rapidly consolidated Macedonian power in Greece. In 334 BC, he began his destruction of the vast ACHAEMENID Persian empire, conquering W Asia Minor and storming Tyre in 332 BC. Alexander subdued Egypt and occupied Babylon, conquering central Asia in 328 BC. In 327 BC, he invaded India but was prevented from advancing beyond the Punjab by the threat of mutiny. Alexander died in Babylon, planning new conquests in Arabia. Although his empire did not outlive him, for he left no heir, he was chiefly responsible for the spread of Greek civilization in the Mediterranean and W Asia.

Alexandria Chief port and second largest city of Egypt, situated on the W extremity of the Nile delta. Founded by

ALEXANDER THE GREAT in 332 BC, it became a great centre of Greek (and Jewish) culture. An offshore island housed the 3rd-century BC Pharos lighthouse, one of the SEVEN WONDERS OF THE WORLD, and the city contained a great library (founded by Ptolemy I and said to contain 700,000 volumes). Today, Alexandria is a deep-water port handling over 75% of the country's trade. The city is the Middle East headquarters for the WORLD HEALTH ORGANIZATION (WHO). Industries: oil refining, cotton textiles, plastics, paper. Pop. (1992 est.) 3,380,000.

alexandrine In prosody, a verse line of 12 syllables. Adopted by Ronsard, it formed the basis of French poetry until challenged by Victor Hugo. In English, it often refers to an iambic hexameter such as Alexander Pope's, "A needless alexandrine ends the song/That like a wounded snake drags its slow length along."

Alexius I (1048–1118) (Alexius Comnenus) Byzantine emperor (1081–1118), founder of the Comnenian dynasty. He held off the Normans who threatened Constantinople and turned the Western armies of the First CRUSADE to his own advantage by using them to reconquer parts of Anatolia.

alfalfa (lucerne) Leguminous perennial plant with spiral pods and purple, clover-like flowers. Like other LEGUMES, it has the ability to enrich the soil with nitrogen and is often grown by farmers and then plowed under. It is a valuable fodder plant. Height: 0.5–1.2m (1.5–4ft). Species *Medicago sativa*. Family Leguminosae.

Alfonso Name of a number of rulers of Spanish kingdoms. **Alfonso V** (994–1028) became king of León and Asturias after his supporters took the city of León in 999. He was killed in battle against the MOORS. **Alfonso VIII** (1155–1214) was king of Castile (1158–1214). He took personal control of the kingdom in 1166 and at first opposed both Moors and fellow Christian kings. In 1212, he forged a coalition with the Christian rulers and won a major victory over the ALMOHADS at Las Navas de Tolosa. **Alfonso X** (1221–84), king of Castile and León (1252–84), was the son and successor of Ferdinand III. He continued his father's wars against the Moors but his ambition was to become Holy Roman emperor. A distinguished scholar, he codified the law and wrote histories of Spain and the world. **Alfonso V** (1396–1458) was king of Aragón (1416–58). He pursued military means to protect his Eastern trade and to curb Turkish power. **Alfonso XIII** (1886–1941) was born after the death of his father, Alfonso XII, and his mother acted as regent until 1902. Although popular, he could not satisfy the conflicting demands of nationalists, socialists, republicans and others. In 1923, he supported the establishment of a military dictatorship under General Miguel PRIMO DE RIVERA. The dictatorship fell in 1930 and a republic was proclaimed.

Alfred the Great (849–99) King of WESSEX (871–99). A warrior and scholar, Alfred saved Wessex from the Danes and laid the foundations of a united English kingdom. After the Danish invasion of 878, he escaped to Athelney in Somerset, returning to defeat the Danes at Edington and recover the kingdom. His pact with the Danish leader, Guthrum (who accepted Christian baptism), roughly divided England in two; the DANELAW occupied the NE. Although he controlled only Wessex and part of

Mercia, Alfred's leadership was widely recognized throughout England after his capture of London (886).

algae Large group of essentially aquatic photosynthetic organisms found in salt and freshwater throughout the world. Algae are a primary source of food for molluscs, fish and other aquatic animals. Algae are directly important to humans as food (especially in Japan) and as FERTILIZERS. They range in size from unicellular microscopic organisms such as those that form green pond scum to huge brown SEAWEEDS more than 45m (150ft) long. Algae belong to the kingdom Protista. *See also* GREEN ALGAE; RED ALGAE; PHOTOSYNTHESIS

Algarve Southernmost province of Portugal, and the most popular of the country's tourist areas. The capital is Faro. Irrigated orchards produce almonds, oranges, figs and olives. The main fish catches are tuna and sardines. Area: 4,986sq km (1,925sq mi). Pop. (1994 est.) 344,300.

algebra (Arabic, *al-jabr* "to find the unknown") Branch of MATHEMATICS dealing with the study of equations that are written using numbers and alphabetic symbols, which themselves represent quantities to be determined. An algebraic equation may be thought of as a constraint on the possible values of the alphabetic symbols. For example, $y + x = 8$ is an algebraic equation involving the variables x and y. Given any value of x the value of y may be determined, and vice-versa. *See also* BOOLE, GEORGE; FUNCTION; SET

Alger, Horatio (1832–99) US author and minister who wrote more than 130 books for young boys on the theme of self-help. The Horatio Alger hero became one who, through hard work, rose from rags to riches. His works include *Ragged Dick* (1867) and *Luck and Pluck* (1869).

Algeria Republic in NW Africa. Algeria is the second largest country in Africa. Most of the people live in the N, either on the fertile coastal plains and hill country bordering the Mediterranean Sea, or in the capital ALGIERS or the second-largest city, ORAN. South of this region are the high plateaux and ranges of the ATLAS Mountains. Over 80% of Algeria is part of the empty wastes of the SAHARA. Some TUAREG nomads roam the desert with their herds. **Climate** Algiers has a Mediterranean climate: summers are warm and dry and winters are mild and moist. The highlands in the N tend to have colder winters and warmer summers. The annual rainfall is less than 200mm (8in). In the summer, the SIROCCO blows from the Sahara. **Vegetation** The N has areas of scrub and farmland, with forests on mountain slopes. The Sahara contains regions of erg (sand dunes), but most of the desert is gravel-strewn plain and bare rock. Date palms and crops flourish around every oasis. **History and Politics** By 2000 BC, BERBERS had established village communities. In the 9th century BC, coastal Algeria (Numidia) formed part of CARTHAGE's trading empire. By the end of the 2nd century BC, Rome had gained control of the coast and parts of the immediate interior. St AUGUSTINE OF HIPPO (now Annaba) was a casualty of the 5th-century invasion of the VANDALS. In the late 7th century, Arabs conquered Algeria and converted the local population to Islam. Arabic became the main language. In the early 10th century, the FATIMIDS rapidly built an empire from their base in NE Algeria. In the late 15th century, as part of the reconquest of S Spain, the Spanish gained control of coastal Algeria. The Spanish were ousted by the Ottomans, and Algeria's coast became a haven for pirates and slave traders. In 1830, France invaded Algeria and rapidly began the process of colonization. ABD AL-KADIR led Algerian resistance until 1847. The European domination of the economy exacerbated

ALGERIA
AREA: 2,381,700sq km (919,590sq mi)
POPULATION: 32,904,000
CAPITAL (POPULATION): Algiers (1,722,000)

discontent among the Muslim population. During World War 2, Algiers served as Allied headquarters in North Africa. At the end of the war, nationalist demands intensified. In 1954, the National Liberation Front (FLN) launched a nationwide revolt against French rule. By 1957 the 500,000-strong French military force had quashed the revolt but not demands for independence. Despite the opposition of the one million French colonists (*colons*) and a section of the French army (the OAS), Charles DE GAULLE persisted with an accord to grant Algeria independence. Following the endorsement of De Gaulle's policy in a 1962 French referendum, the OAS launched a short-lived terrorist campaign against Muslims. The colonists rapidly left Algeria. On 3 July 1962, France declared Algeria independent. The war had claimed *c.*250,000 lives. Ahmed BEN BELLA became prime minister, then president of the newly-reformed republic. In 1965, Ben Bella was overthrown in a military coup, led by the defence minister Colonel Houari Boumédienne, who established a revolutionary council and stepped up the pace of reform. In 1971, he nationalized the French-owned oil and gas industries. Boumédienne died in 1978 and was succeeded by Colonel Chadli Benjedid. In 1989, anti-government demonstrations and riots led to the legalization of opposition parties. The first round of elections in December 1991 saw a decisive victory for the opposition Islamic Salvation Front (FIS), and Benjedid resigned as president. The second round of voting was cancelled and a military government assumed power. In 1992, the FIS was banned and Benjedid's successor, Muhammad Boudiaf, was assassinated. A terrorist campaign was launched by Muslim fundamentalists. In 1995 elections General Liamine Zeroual won a second term as president. Between 1992 and 1997, it is estimated that the civil war claimed 100,000 civilian lives. Algeria continues to suffer from political violence. **Economy** Algeria is a developing country (1995 GDP per capita, US$3,800). Its chief resources are oil and natural gas, which were first discovered under the Sahara in 1956. Its natural gas reserves are the fifth-largest in the world, oil the 14th-largest. Gas and oil account for more than 90% of Algeria's exports. Manufactures include cement, iron and steel, textiles and vehicles. While most larger industries are owned by the government, much of light industry is under private control. Farming employs *c.*14% of the workforce. Barley, citrus fruits, dates, grapes, olives, potatoes and wheat are the major crops.

Algiers Capital and largest city of Algeria, on the Bay of Algiers, N Africa's chief port on the Mediterranean. Founded by the Phoenicians, it has been colonized by Romans, Berber Arabs, Turks (Barbarossa) and Muslim Barbary pirates. In 1830, the French invaded and made Algiers the capital of the French colony of Algeria. In World War 2 it was the headquarters of the Allies and seat of the French provisional government. During the 1950s and 1960s, it was a focus for the violent struggle for independence. The 11th-century Sidi Abderrahman Mosque is a major destination for Muslim pilgrims. Industries: oil refining, phosphates, wine, metallurgy, cement, tobacco. Pop. (1995) 2,168,000.

Algol (Beta Persei) Prototype of a class of eclipsing binaries known as Algol-type variables. The variability in its appearance was first noted in 1669. Algol lies about 100 light years away. *See also* BINARY STAR

Algonquian (Algonkin) Group of Canadian Native American tribes that gave their name to the Algonquian languages of North America. The Algonquian people occupied the Ottawa River area *c.*AD 1600. Driven from

their home by the IROQUOIS in the 17th century, they were eventually absorbed into other related tribes in Canada.

algorithm In arithmetic and computing, a mechanical procedure for determining the value of a FUNCTION from a specified DOMAIN. A finite set of instructions are executed in a stepwise manner to obtain the desired result. Algorithms form the basis of computer PROGRAMS.

Algren, Nelson (1909–81) US novelist. His debut novel was *Somebody in Boots* (1935). Algren's novel about drug addiction, *The Man with the Golden Arm* (1949), won the National Book Award. His work is often set in the slums of Chicago. Other novels include *A Walk on the Wild Side* (1956) and *The Devil's Stocking* (1983).

Alhambra Spanish citadel of the sultans of Granada, a world heritage site and a major tourist attraction. Standing on a plateau overlooking Granada, S Spain, it is one of the most beautiful and well-preserved examples of medieval ISLAMIC ART AND ARCHITECTURE. Most of the complex dates from the period of the Nasrid dynasty (1238–1358).

Ali (*c.*600–61) Fourth Muslim CALIPH (656–61), cousin and son-in-law of the Prophet MUHAMMAD. Ali was married to FATIMA. He is regarded by the SHIITES as the first Imam and rightful heir of Muhammad. Ali succeeded OTHMAN as caliph, despite opposition from Aishah and Muawiya. He was assassinated and his first son, Hasan, abdicated in favour of Muawiya, who founded the UMAYYAD dynasty. His second son, Husayn, led the insurrection against the Umayyads, but was defeated and killed at the Battle of Karbala (680).

Ali, Muhammad (1942–) US boxer, b. Cassius Marcellus Clay. As Cassius Clay, he defeated Sonny Liston to gain the world heavyweight championship (1964). Clay converted to Islam and joined the BLACK MUSLIMS. Ali successfully defended the title nine times. In 1967 he refused to fight in the Vietnam War and the World Boxing Association (WBA) took away his title. In 1971, the US Supreme Court upheld Ali's appeal against the ban, but he was defeated by reigning champion Joe FRAZIER. He regained the title from George Foreman in the 1974 "rumble in the jungle" fight. In 1978, Ali was defeated by Leon Spinks, but won the rematch, becoming the first heavyweight to win the title three times.

Alicante Seaport capital of Alicante province, SE Spain. Founded by the Greeks (325 BC), Alicante was a Roman naval base before falling to the Moors. It was recaptured from the Moors *c.*1265. The centre of a fertile agricultural province, it exports wine, fruit, esparto, cereals and olive oil. Industries: metal products, textiles, tobacco. Pop. (1995) 277,000.

Alice Springs Town on the River Todd, Northern Territory, central Australia. Founded in 1860, Alice Springs is a crucial railhead, livestock shipping centre and supply source for a vast area that includes AYERS ROCK. It is the state's largest town after Darwin. Pop. (1994) 24,852.

Alien and Sedition Acts (1798) Four US acts designed to curb criticism of the government at a time when war with France seemed imminent. The acts imposed stringent rules on residency before naturalization, and gave the president unprecedented powers to deport or imprison undesirable foreigners in time of war.

alienation In psychology, a feeling of estrangement and separation from other people. In existential psychology this meaning is extended to include the perception that one is alienated or estranged from one's "real self" because of being forced to conform to society's expectations. The sociological definition of alienation derives from the work of Hegel and Marx. In *The Economic and Philosophical Manuscripts of 1844* (1930),

Marx outlined four types of alienation caused by industrial capitalism: the commodification of labour; dissociation from the products of one's labour; social detachment; and estrangement from one's own human essence. Emile DURKHEIM developed these ideas in the notion of *anomie*.

alimentary canal Digestive tract of an animal that begins with the MOUTH, continues through the OESOPHAGUS to the STOMACH and INTESTINES, and ends at the anus. It is about 9m (30ft) long in humans. *See also* DIGESTIVE SYSTEM

aliphatic compound Any organic chemical compound whose carbon atoms are linked in straight chains, not closed rings. They include the ALKANES (paraffins), ALKENES (olefins) and ALKYNES (acetylenes).

alkali Soluble BASE that reacts with an ACID to form a SALT and water. A solution of an alkali has a pH greater than 7. Alkali solutions are used as cleaning materials. Strong alkalis include the hydroxides of the ALKALI METALS and ammonium hydroxide. The carbonates of these metals are weak alkalis.

alkali metals Univalent metals forming Group I of the periodic table: LITHIUM, SODIUM, POTASSIUM, RUBIDIUM, CAESIUM and FRANCIUM. They are soft, silvery-white metals that tarnish rapidly in air and react violently with water to form hydroxides.

alkaline-earth metals Bivalent metals forming Group II of the periodic table: BERYLLIUM, MAGNESIUM, CALCIUM, STRONTIUM, BARIUM and RADIUM. They are all light, soft and highly reactive. All, except beryllium and magnesium, react with cold water to form hydroxides (though magnesium reacts with hot water). Radium is important for its radioactivity.

alkaloid Member of a class of complex nitrogen-containing organic compounds found in certain plants. They are sometimes bitter and highly poisonous substances, used as DRUGS. Examples include codeine, morphine, nicotine and quinine.

alkane (C_nH_{2n+2}) HYDROCARBON compound. Alkanes have a single carbon-carbon bond and form an homologous series whose first members are METHANE, ETHANE, PROPANE and BUTANE. Because alkanes are SATURATED COMPOUNDS they are relatively unreactive. Alkanes are used as fuels. *See also* PARAFFIN

alkene (olefin, C_nH_{2n}) Unsaturated HYDROCARBON compound. Alkenes have a carbon-carbon double bond and form an homologous series whose first members are ETHENE and PROPENE. They are reactive, particularly in ADDITION reactions. Alkenes are made by the dehydration of alcohols.

alkyne (acetylene, C_nH_{2n-2}) Unsaturated HYDROCARBON compound. Alkynes have a carbon-carbon triple bond and form an homologous series whose first members are ETHYNE and propyne.

Allah (Arabic *al-Illāh*, "the God") One and only God of ISLAM. Allah is the omnipresent and merciful rewarder, the creator and judge. Unreserved surrender to Allah, as preached in the KORAN, is the heart of the Islamic faith.

Allahabad City at the confluence of the Ganges and Yamuna rivers, Uttar Pradesh state, N central India. Allahabad is a pilgrimage centre for Hindus because of the belief that the goddess Saraswati joined the two rivers at this point. The Kumbh Mela fair, a religious celebration, takes place here every 12 years. It is also an agricultural trade centre. Pop. (1991) 806,000.

allegory Literary work in either prose or verse in which more than one level of meaning is expressed simultaneously. The fables of AESOP and LA FONTAINE are examples of simple allegory. *Pilgrim's Progress* (1684) by John BUNYAN is a sophisticated religious allegory.

Allegri, Gregorio (1582–1652) Italian composer. He composed many works for the papal choir. Allegri's most famous work is the beautiful *Miserere*, which is still widely performed today. He also composed five masses and several other books of church music.

allele One of two or more alternative forms of a particular GENE. Different alleles may give rise to different forms of the characteristic for which the gene codes. Different flower colour in peas is due to the presence of different alleles of a single gene. *See also* MENDEL, GREGOR

Allen, Ethan (1738–89) US frontiersman and soldier. In *c.*1770, he became commander of the GREEN MOUNTAIN BOYS, a volunteer militia. In the American Revolution, Allen and his troops captured Fort Ticonderoga (10 May, 1775) and Crown Point (11 May, 1775). During the invasion of Canada, he was captured (25 September, 1775) and imprisoned in England until 1778, when he returned to Vermont.

Allen, Woody (1935–) US film director, writer and actor, b. Allen Stewart Konigsberg. He made his film debut as an actor and screenwriter in *What's New Pussycat?* (1965). Allen won Academy Awards for best picture, best screenplay and best director for *Annie Hall* (1977). He gained an Oscar nomination for his first serious drama, the BERGMAN-like *Interiors* (1978). His next film, *Manhattan* (1979), marked a return to the semi-autobiographical format. *Hannah and Her Sisters* (1986) won Allen an Oscar for best screenplay. Other films include *Zelig* (1983), *The Purple Rose of Cairo* (1985), *Crimes and Misdemeanors* (1989) and *Mighty Aphrodite* (1996). His separation (1992) from Mia Farrow, his long-standing partner and co-star, was acrimonious and litigious.

Allende Gossens, Salvador (1908–73) Chilean statesman, president (1970–73). He was one of the founders of the Chilean Socialist Party (1933) and served as minister of health (1939–42) and head of the senate (1965–69). Allende's narrow election victory led to the introduction of democratic socialist reforms, which antagonized the Chilean establishment. The nationalization of the US-owned copper industry resulted in a US trade embargo. The CIA began a covert campaign of destabilization, aided by a deteriorating economy. Allende was overthrown and died in a military coup led by General PINOCHET.

allergy Disorder in which the body mounts a hypersensitive reaction to one or more substances (allergens) not normally considered harmful. Typical allergic reactions are sneezing (HAY FEVER), "wheezing" and difficulty in breathing (ASTHMA), and skin eruptions and itching (ECZEMA). A tendency to allergic reactions is often hereditary.

Allies Term used in WORLD WAR 1 and WORLD WAR 2 for the forces that fought the CENTRAL POWERS and AXIS POWERS respectively. In World War 1 they numbered 23 and included Belgium, Britain and its Commonwealth, France, Italy, Japan, Russia and the US. In World War 2 the 49 Allies included Belgium, Britain and the Commonwealth, France, the Netherlands, the Soviet Union and the US.

alligator Broad-snouted, crocodilian REPTILE found only in the US and China. The American alligator, *Alligator mississippiensis*, is found in the SE US; it grows up to 5.8m (19ft) long. The almost extinct smaller Chinese alligator, *A. sinensis*, is restricted to the Yangtze-Kiang river basin. Length: up to 1.5m (5ft). Family Alligatoridea. *See also* CAYMAN; CROCODILE

alliteration Close repetition of consonant sounds within a line of verse or prose. Predominant in Old English poetry, then revived in the 14th century, alliteration is also found in some modern poetry: for example, in this line from W.H. Auden: "By the waters of waking I wept for the weeds."

allium *See* ONION

allopathy Treatment of diseases by methods and remedies that produce effects contrasting with those caused by the disease. The term is usually applied to conventional medicine, as opposed to HOMEOPATHY.

allotropy Property of some chemical elements that enables them to exist in two or more distinct physical forms. Each form (called an allotrope) can have different chemical properties but can be changed into another allotrope – given suitable conditions. Examples of allotropes are molecular oxygen and ozone; white and yellow phosphorus; and graphite and diamond (carbon).

alloy Combination of two or more metals. An alloy's properties are different from those of its constituent elements. Alloys are generally harder and stronger, and have lower melting points. Combinations with the lowest melting points are called eutectic mixtures. Most alloys are prepared by mixing when molten. Some mixtures composed of a metal and a non-metal, such as STEEL, are also referred to as alloys. BRONZE and BRASS have been smelted for the last 5,000 years. The production of ALUMINIUM (c.1890) saw the introduction of new alloys.

All Saints' Day In the Christian liturgical calendar, the day on which all the saints are commemorated. The feast is observed on 1 November in the West and on the first Sunday after Pentecost in the East. The eve of the day is celebrated in some western countries as Halloween.

All Souls' Day Day of remembrance and prayer for all the departed souls. Observed by Roman Catholics and High Church Anglicans on 2 November, or on 3 November if the former falls on a Sunday.

allspice (pimento) Aromatic tree native to the West Indies and Central America. The fruits are used as a spice, in perfume and in medicine. Height: up to 12m (40ft). Family Myrtaceae; species *Pimenta officinalis*

Allston, Washington (1779–1843) US romantic painter. A pupil of Benjamin WEST at London's Royal Academy, Allston was the pioneer of romantic LANDSCAPE PAINTING in the US and a precursor of the HUDSON RIVER SCHOOL. His work in England includes a portrait of Coleridge (1814). In 1818, he returned to the US. Allston's most famous work is the lyrical *Moonlit Landscape* (1819). He spent 20 years working on the disappointing *Belshazzar's Feast*. It remained unfinished.

alluvial fan Generally fan-shaped area of ALLUVIUM (water-borne sediment) deposited by a river when the stream reaches a plain on lower ground and the water velocity is abruptly reduced. Organic matter is also transported, making the soil highly fertile. Valuable minerals are often found in alluvial fans.

alluvium General term that describes the sediments of sand, silt and mud deposited by flowing water along the banks, delta or floodplain of a river or stream. Fine-textured sediments that contain organic matter form soil.

Almaty (formerly Alma-Ata) Largest city and, until 2000, capital of Kazakhstan, near the SE border with Kyrgyzstan. In 1991, it hosted the meeting of 11 former Soviet republics that led to the Alma-Ata Declaration, which created the COMMONWEALTH OF INDEPENDENT STATES (CIS). In 1995, the government decided to move the capital to ASTANA. Industries: foodstuffs, tobacco, timber, printing, film-making, leather, machinery. Pop. (1995) 1,151,000.

Almodóvar, Pedro (1951–) Spanish film director and screenwriter. His debut film was *Dos Putas* (1974). A master of kitsch, black comedies, he achieved international fame with *Women on the Verge of a Nervous Breakdown* (1988) and *Tie Me Up! Tie Me Down!* (1990). Other films include *Kika* (1993) and *All About My Mother* (1999).

Almohad BERBER Muslim dynasty (1145–1269) in North Africa and Spain, the followers of a reform movement within ISLAM. It was founded by Muhammad ibn Tumart, who set out from the Atlas Mountains to purify Islam and oust the ALMORAVIDS from Morocco and Spain. In 1212, Alfonso VIII of Castile routed the Almohads, and in 1269 their capital, MARRAKESH, fell to the Marinids.

almond Small tree native to the E Mediterranean region and SW Asia; also the seed of its nut-like fruit. Family Rosaceae; species *Prunus dulcis*.

Almoravid BERBER Muslim dynasty (1054–1145) in Morocco and Spain. They rose to power under Abdullah ibn Yasin who converted Saharan tribes in a religious revival. ABU BAKR founded MARRAKESH as their capital in 1070; his brother Yusuf ibn Tashufin defeated Alfonso VI of Castile in 1086. Almoravid rule was ended by the rise of the ALMOHADS.

aloe Genus of plants native to S Africa, with spiny-edged, fleshy leaves. They grow in dense rosettes and have drooping red, orange or yellow flower clusters. Family Liliaceae.

alpaca *See* LLAMA

alphabet System of letters representing the sounds of speech. The word alphabet is derived from the first two letters of the Greek alphabet, *alpha* and *beta*. The most important alphabets in use today are Roman, CYRILLIC, GREEK, ARABIC, HEBREW and Devanagari. The Latin alphabet, which grew out of the Greek by way of the Etruscans, was perfected around AD 100 and is the foundation on which Western alphabets are based. In some alphabets, such as the Devanagari of India, each character represents a syllable. BRAILLE and MORSE are coded forms of alphabets invented to meet special needs.

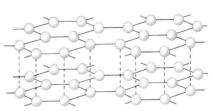

▲ **allotropy** Carbon can exist in two forms, diamond and graphite, known as allotropes of carbon. The top diagram shows the structure of diamond, revealing its sharp, angular structure. The bottom diagram depicts graphite, showing its layered structure. The carbon atoms bond strongly in sheets, but the forces between layers are weak, enabling us to utilize graphite as a lubricant.

Alpha Centauri Brightest star in the constellation Centaurus, and the third-brightest star in the sky. It is a visual BINARY.

alpha particle (alpha ray) Stable, positively charged particle emitted spontaneously from the nuclei of certain radioactive ISOTOPES when undergoing RADIOACTIVE DECAY called **alpha decay**. Alpha particles were discovered (1906) by Ernest Rutherford and later identified as the nuclei of HELIUM atoms consisting of two PROTONS and two NEUTRONS. Their penetrating power is low compared with that of BETA PARTICLES (electrons) but they cause intense ionization along their track. This ionization is used to detect them.

alphorn (alpine horn) Primitive musical instrument, consisting of a long wooden tube, one end of which rests on the ground. ROSSINI used a typical melody played on it by the Alpine herdsmen of Switzerland in the overture to his opera *William Tell* (1829).

alpine plant Small plant found above the tree line in mountain meadows and on rocky slopes, generally at altitudes above 2,300m (7,550ft).

Alps Mountain system in s central Europe, extending *c*.1,200km (750mi) in a broad arc from near the Gulf of Genoa on the Mediterranean Sea through France, Italy, Switzerland, Liechtenstein, Austria, Germany and Slovenia. The system was formed by the collision of the European and African tectonic plates. Glaciers (the longest being the Aletsch Glacier) form the headwaters of many major European rivers, including the Rhine, Rhône and Po. The main ranges are often divided into three groups from w to E: **Western Alps** (Maritime, Cottian, Dauphine and Graian); **Middle Alps** (Pennine, Berner, Lepontine, Glarner, Retiche, Lechtaler Ötztaler and Dolomites); and **Eastern Alps** (Zillertaler, Hohe Tauern, Karnischer, Julian and Karawanken). The highest Alpine peak is MONT BLANC at 4,807m (15,771ft) in the Pennine Alps. Other peaks include the MATTERHORN. Notable passes include the St BERNARD, Mont Cenis and Brenner.

Alsace Region in E France, comprising the departments of Bas-Rhin and Haut-Rhin. STRASBOURG is the leading city, Mulhouse and Colmar are the main industrial centres. Separated from Germany by the River RHINE, the Alsace-LORRAINE region has often caused friction between France and Germany. The art and culture reflect both national influences. There are rich deposits of iron ore and potash. Most of the region is fertile and productive, with German-style, riesling wines the major agricultural product. Industries: steel, textiles, chemicals. Area: 8,280sq km (3,197sq mi). Pop. (1990) 1,624,400.

Altai (Altajsk) Complex mountain system in central Asia stretching from Kazakstan into N China and w Mongolia, and from s Siberia to the Gobi Desert. A densely forested area, it is the source of the Irtyš and Ob rivers. The average height is 2,000–3,000m (6,500–10,000ft), and the highest peak is Mount Belukha at 4,506m (14,783ft).

Altaic languages Family of languages spoken by *c*.80 million people in Turkey, Iran, parts of the former Soviet Union, Mongolia and parts of China. It consists of three branches: the Turkic, Mongolian and Tungusic languages.

Altair Star Alpha Aquilae, whose luminosity is ten times that of the Sun. Characteristics: apparent mag. 0.77; spectral type A7; distance 16 light-years.

Altamira World heritage site of Palaeolithic cave paintings and engravings (*c*.14000–9500 BC) near Santander, N Spain. The roof of the lateral chamber is covered with paintings of animals, including boars, deer, horses and bison, boldly executed in vivid black, red and violet. There are also eight engraved anthropomorphic figures.

Altdorfer, Albrecht (*c*.1480–1538) German painter and engraver, one of the most original German painters of his day. Altdorfer concentrated mainly on religious and historic themes but was also one of the first European artists to take a real interest in landscape. His patrons included the Emperor Maximilian, who commissioned him along with Albrecht DÜRER and others to illuminate his prayer book (*c*.1515), and Duke William of Bavaria for whom Altdorfer painted a series of Classical and Christian histories, including *The Battle of Alexander at Issus* (1529).

alternating current (AC) *See* ELECTRIC CURRENT

alternation of generations Two-generation cycle by which plants and some algae reproduce. The asexual diploid SPOROPHYTE form produces haploid SPORES that, in turn, grow into the sexual GAMETOPHYTE form. The gametophyte produces the egg cell that is fertilized by a male gamete to produce a diploid zygote that grows into another sporophyte.

alternative energy *See* RENEWABLE ENERGY

alternator Electrical GENERATOR that produces an alternating ELECTRIC CURRENT.

Althusser, Louis (1918–90) French philosopher, b. Algeria. He reassessed MARXISM in the light of STRUCTURALISM. Althusser criticized the humanist interpretations of the works of Karl MARX, calling for a more scientific analysis of the modes of social existence. His works include *For Marx* (1965) and *Reading Capital* (1970). In 1980, he was found guilty of murdering his wife and confined to an asylum.

altimeter Instrument for measuring altitude. The simplest type is a form of aneroid BAROMETER. As height increases, air pressure decreases, so the barometer scale can be calibrated to show altitude. Some aircraft have a radar altimeter, which measures the time taken to bounce a radar signal off the ground.

Altiplano High plain in the South American Andes of Peru and Bolivia, at an elevation of *c*.3,650m (12,000ft).

altitude In astronomy, the angular distance of a celestial body above the observer's horizon. It is measured in degrees from 0 (on the horizon) to 90 (at the zenith) along the GREAT CIRCLE passing through the body and the zenith. If the object is below the horizon, the altitude is negative.

altitude sickness Metabolic problems occurring at high altitudes, notably deficiency of oxygen in the blood and tissues. Symptoms include dizziness, palpitations, headache, nosebleed and nausea.

Altman, Robert (1925–) US independent film director. He gained his first Academy Award nomination for *M*A*S*H* (1970). A second Oscar nomination followed for *Nashville* (1975). Following a series of theatre adaptations, Altman returned to exposing the reality behind the myth in *The Player* (1992). *Short Cuts* (1993) was a successful adaptation of Raymond Carver's short stories.

alto In singing, the highest male voice, also called COUNTERTENOR; or the lowest female voice, also called CONTRALTO. It is also used to describe that member of a family of instruments with a range that corresponds to the alto voice; for example, an alto FLUTE is a fourth lower than a standard one.

altruism (It. *altrui* others) Principle of acting for the welfare or interests of someone else. The term was coined by the philosopher Auguste COMTE. It is used in biology to describe the behaviour of an animal that acts in a way that enhances the prospects of survival or reproduction of another individual at the expense of its own interests. Most cases of altruism among animals involve close relatives or young, with whom the animal shares many GENES. So it is, in effect, perpetuating its own genes in the process. *See also* DAWKINS, RICHARD

alum Double sulphate of ALUMINIUM (or another trivalent metal) and another, univalent metal. The most important is potash alum (potassium aluminium sulphate, $KAl(SO_4)_2.12H_2O$); it is used as a mordant in dyeing.

alumina (aluminum oxide, Al_2O_3) Mineral used as an abrasive, electrical insulator and furnace lining. Other forms of alumina include corundum, two impure varieties of which are the gemstones SAPPHIRE and RUBY.

aluminium (symbol Al) Metallic, silvery white element of group III of the periodic table, first obtained in pure form in 1827. It is the most common metal in the Earth's crust; the chief ore is BAUXITE. Bauxite undergoes two processes to yield aluminium. It is first refined to obtain pure alumina (Al_2O_3), which is then smelted to produce aluminium. The **Bayer process**, involving digestion, clarification, precipitation and calcination, is the most common refining process. Smelting involves dissolving alumina in melted cryolite and passing a current through the mixture (ELECTROLYSIS) to yield pure aluminum and carbon dioxide (the **Hall-Heroult process**). Alloyed with other metals, it is used in machined and moulded articles, particularly where lightness is important. It is protected from oxidation (corrosion) by a thin, natural layer of oxide. Properties: at.no. 13; r.a.m. 26.98; r.d. 2.69; m.p. 660.2°C (1,220.38°F); b.p. 1,800°C (3,272°F); most common isotope Al^{27}. *See also* ANODIZING

Alvarez, Luis Walter (1911–88) US physicist who won the 1968 Nobel Prize for physics for developing the liquid-hydrogen BUBBLE CHAMBER. He used it to identify many "resonances" (very short-lived particles). Alvarez also helped construct (1947) the first proton linear ACCELERATOR. He worked on the MANHATTAN PROJECT to develop the atom bomb and invented the radar guidance system for aircraft landings.

alveolus One of a cluster of microscopic air sacs that open out from the alveolar ducts at the far end of each bronchiole in the LUNGS. The alveolus is the site for the exchange of gases between the air and the bloodstream, and is covered in a network of CAPILLARY blood vessels. *See also* GAS EXCHANGE; RESPIRATORY SYSTEM

Alzheimer's disease Degenerative condition characterized by memory loss and progressive mental impairment; it is the most common cause of DEMENTIA. Sometimes seen in the middle years, Alzheimer's becomes increasingly common with advancing age. Many factors have been implicated, but the precise cause is unknown.

AM Abbreviation of AMPLITUDE MODULATION

Amado, Jorge (1912–) Brazilian novelist. His early novels, such as *Sweat* (1934) and *The Violent Land* (1942), are powerful realist novels on poverty in Brazil. Amado's later works, such as *Dona Flor and Her Two Husbands* (1966), are more lyrical, using folklore and humour to examine contemporary Brazilian society.

Amal (Arabic *Afwaj al-Muqawama al-Lubnaniyya*, "masses of the Lebanese resistance"; the acronym means hope) Lebanese SHIITE political movement. Amal was established in 1974 by Musa Sadr to press for greater Shiite political representation in Lebanon. Backed variously by Syria and the Palestinian Liberation Organization (PLO), its members have perpetrated a number of terrorist acts, such as the kidnappings in Lebanon during the 1980s. In 1991, the National Assembly decreed the dissolution of all militias and Amal moderated their stance.

Amalfi Resort town on the Gulf of Sorrento, Campania, s Italy. In the 9th century, Amalfi was an important maritime republic, rivalling Venice and Genoa in terms of wealth and power. In the 1130s, it was sacked by Normans and Pisans and much of the town was destroyed by a storm in 1343. Sites include an 11th century Sicilian-Arab cathedral. Pop. (1990) 5,900.

amalgam Solid or liquid alloy of MERCURY with other metals. Dentists once filled teeth with amalgams usually containing copper and zinc. Most metals dissolve in mercury, although iron and platinum are exceptions.

amanita Large, widely distributed genus of FUNGI. Amanitas usually have distinct stalks and the prominent remains of a veil in a fleshy ring under the cap and at the bulbous base. They include some of the most poisonous fungi known, such as the DEATH CAP. *See also* FLY AGARIC

amaryllis Genus consisting of a single species of bulbous plant, *Amaryllis belladonna*, the belladonna lily, which has several trumpet-shaped pink or white flowers. Amaryllis is also the common name for *Hippeastrum*, a bulbous houseplant.

Amaterasu Sun goddess of the SHINTO pantheon, considered to be the ancestor of the Japanese imperial clan.

Amati Family of Italian violin-makers in Cremona in the 16th and 17th centuries. They included Andrea (*c.*1520–78), the founder of the Cremona school of violin-making. The Amati family are credited with establishing the design of the violin as it is today.

Amazon World's second-longest river (after the NILE), draining the vast Amazon RAINFOREST basin of N South America. It carries by far the greatest volume of water of any river in the world: the average rate of discharge is *c.*95,000m^3 (3,355,000ft^3) every second, nearly three times as much as its nearest rival, the CONGO. The flow is so great that its silt discolours the water up to 200km (125mi) into the Atlantic. At *c.*7 million sq km (2.7 million sq mi), the Amazon river basin comprises nearly 40% of the continent of South America. The European discovery was made by Vincente Pinzón in 1500. In 1541, Francisco de Orellana travelled up the river, and his accounts of a tribe of female warriors gave the river its name. Its tributaries include the XINGU. Length: *c.*6,430km (3,990mi).

Amazon In Greek mythology, a race of female warriors who lived in a totally matriarchal society. As allies of the Trojans, they took part in the defence of TROY, where their queen Penthesilea was slain by ACHILLES after she had killed many Greek warriors.

amber Hard, yellow or brown, translucent fossil resin, mainly from pine trees. Amber is most often found in alluvial soils, in lignite beds or around sea-shores, especially the Baltic Sea. The resin sometimes occurs with embedded fossil insects or plants. Amber can be polished to a high degree and is used to make necklaces and other items of jewellery.

ambergris Musky, waxy solid formed in the intestine of sperm whales. It is used in perfume as a fixative for scent.

Ambrose, Saint (*c.*339–97) Bishop of Milan (374–97) and Doctor of the Church. He was the chief critic of ARIANISM and persuaded Emperor Gratian to outlaw (379) all heresy in the Roman Empire. In 390, Ambrose excommunicated THEODOSIUS I. His preaching and teachings were largely responsible for the conversion of Saint AUGUSTINE. Ambrose's writings, such as *On the Duties of the Clergy*, greatly influenced the thought of the Western church. In 386 he introduced a form of antiphonal PLAINSONG into church services. His feast day is 7 December.

Amenhotep III (*c.*1417–*c.*1379 BC) King of ancient EGYPT. Amenhotep succeeded his father, Thutmose IV. The 18th dynasty was at its height during his reign. His wife, Queen Tiy, played an important role in state affairs. He was succeeded by his son, who took the name AKHNATEN.

America Western Hemisphere, consisting of the continents of NORTH AMERICA and SOUTH AMERICA, joined by the isthmus of CENTRAL AMERICA. It extends from N of the Arctic Circle to 56° s, separating the Atlantic Ocean from the Pacific. NATIVE AMERICANS settled the entire continent by 8000 BC. Norsemen were probably the first Europeans to explore America in the 8th century, but Christopher COLUMBUS is popularly credited with the first European discovery in 1492. The name "America" was first applied in 1507 and derives from Amerigo Vespucci, a Florentine navigator who was falsely believed to be the first European to set foot on the mainland.

American art During the colonial era, American art reflected the taste of European settlers. In Spanish territories, the main demand was for religious art, while in Dutch and English areas, there was a greater emphasis on portraiture. In the 18th century, America produced its first artists of international standing, John Singleton COPLEY and Benjamin WEST. Both spent much of their career in England, where they became leading exponents of history painting. After independence, there was a gradual movement away from European traditions. This was most evident in the field of landscape painting, where artists from the HUDSON RIVER SCHOOL and the Rocky Mountain School recorded the beauty of the wilderness. Thomas EAKINS and Winslow HOMER also celebrated the American way of life, although in a more realistic vein. Realism is the cornerstone of the ASHCAN SCHOOL. In the 20th century, the key event was the ARMORY SHOW of 1913, which encouraged the spread of modern art. Alfred STIEGLITZ was a seminal figure in the development of modern art in the US. Georgia O'KEEFFE and Edward HOPPER were arguably its two greatest stylists. With the development of ABSTRACT EXPRESSIONISM in the 1940s, US artists became the standard-bearers of the avant-garde, a role they have never relinquished. *See also* LUMINISM; NATIVE NORTH AMERICAN ART

American Civil War *See* CIVIL WAR, AMERICAN

American Colonization Society Group founded in 1817 by Robert Finley to return free African Americans to Africa for settlement. More than 11,000 African Americans were transported to Sierra Leone and, after 1821, MONROVIA. Leading members of the society included James MONROE, James MADISON and John MARSHALL.

American Federation of Labor and Congress of Industrial Organizations (AFL-CIO) Largest labour organization in North America. It is a federation of individual trade unions from the US, Canada, Mexico, Panama and some US dependencies. Established in 1955, it merged the American Federation of Labor (AFL) and Congress of Industrial Organizations (CIO). Although each union within the federation is autonomous, the governing body of the AFL-CIO is an executive council made up of president, vice presidents and secretary-treasurer. In recent years, the reduction of union membership (*c*.15% of US workers in 1995) has seen the AFL-CIO concentrate on organizing public sector workers.

American Fur Company First US business monopoly, owned by John Jacob ASTOR. John JAY's Treaty of 1794 permitted US fur trading in the Pacific Northwest. In 1805 Fort Astoria was set up in Oregon. During the WAR OF 1812, the US was unable to defend Astoria, and Astor was forced to sell. As the fur trade declined in the 1840s, Fort Astoria reverted to US control.

American Indians *See* NATIVE AMERICANS

American Legion Association of US military veterans. Founded (1919) in Paris, its US headquarters are in Indianapolis, Indiana. Qualifications for membership are honourable service or honourable discharge. It sponsors many social causes, notably education and sport for young people, and the care of sick and disabled veterans.

American literature English explorers and early colonists produced literary accounts of North America. The first English language work published in New England was the *Bay Psalm Book* (1640). Early colonial literature was often an expression of Puritan piety. Many of the leading figures in the AMERICAN REVOLUTION, such as Thomas PAINE and Benjamin FRANKLIN, produced important literary works. Early 19th-century writers, such as Washington IRVING and James Fenimore COOPER, were influenced by European romanticism. The preeminent US romantic poet was Henry Wadsworth LONGFELLOW. TRANSCENDENTALISM was the first truly distinctive national literary movement. Leading writers included the essayists Henry David THOREAU, Ralph Waldo EMERSON, Oliver Wendell HOLMES and Louisa May ALCOTT. Walt WHITMAN's free-verse epic *Leaves of Grass* (1855–92) is perhaps the most fully realized poetic expression of transcendentalism. The 1840s and 1850s produced many American fiction classics, such as Herman MELVILLE's *Moby Dick* (1851) and Nathaniel HAWTHORNE's *The Scarlet Letter* (1850). Harriet Beecher STOWE's antislavery story *Uncle Tom's Cabin* (1852) was the best-selling novel of the century. Literature of the immediate post-Civil War period is characterized by parochialism. The two great exceptions to the trend were Henry JAMES and Mark TWAIN. While James emigrated to Europe and embraced psychological realism in novels, such as *Portrait of a Lady* (1881), Twain used national dialects in humorous classics, such as *Huckleberry Finn* (1885). Realism fed into NATURALISM, producing writers who either focused on the development of cities (Theodore DRIESER and Edith WHARTON) or those who concentrated on a hostile wilderness (Jack LONDON). Stephen CRANE's *Red Badge of Courage* (1895) was ground-breaking in its naturalistic treatment of the Civil War. In the early 20th century, many US writers went into exile. In Paris, Gertrude STEIN held court over the "Lost Generation", a large group of emigrés that included Ernest HEMINGWAY and Henry MILLER. T.S. ELIOT and Ezra POUND led the search for experimental poetic forms. Eliot's bleak and fragmentary poem *The Wasteland* (1922) is often viewed as the archetype of high MODERNISM. Wallace STEVENS and William Carlos WILLIAMS developed the new poetry. The HARLEM RENAISSANCE witnessed the emergence of African-American writers, such as Langston HUGHES. The style and decadence of the "jazz age" in 1920s New York was captured by F. Scott FITZGERALD in *The Great Gatsby* (1925). The 1920s also witnessed the debut of the first great American dramatist, Eugene O'NEILL. In the 1930s writers such as John STEINBECK, Carson McCULLERS and Eudora WELTY emerged. Post-World War 2 literature and drama can be characterized by a sense of despair when confronted by the violence of the 20th century. In the 1950s, major dramatists such as Arthur MILLER, Edward ALBEE and Sam SHEPARD developed the American theatre. African-American writers, such as Richard WRIGHT, Ralph ELLISON and James BALDWIN, dealt with racial inequality and violence in contemporary US society. Maya ANGELOU and Toni MORRISON focused on the 20th-century history of African-American women. During the 1960s, novelists such as Saul BELLOW, Philip ROTH and Joseph HELLER examined the Jewish urban intellectual approach to American society, often adopting a deeply ironic tone. Humour was also a major outlet for writers such as John UPDIKE, Kurt VONNEGUT and Thomas PYNCHON. Norman MAILER used a more muscular, Hemingway-like approach. The BEAT MOVEMENT (including Jack KEROUAC and Allen GINSBERG) urged the rejection of the established order. A major trend in American poetry was the "confessional" style of personal revelation by poets such as Robert LOWELL and Sylvia PLATH. POST-MODERNISM has informed the work of authors such as Kathy Acker and Bret Easton Ellis.

American Medical Association (AMA) US federation of 54 state and territorial medical associations, founded in 1847. The AMA develops programmes to provide scientific information for the profession and health-education materials for the public. By the mid-1990s there were *c*.300,000 members.

American Revolution (1775–83) (American War of Independence) Successful revolt by the THIRTEEN COLONIES in North America against British rule. A number of issues provoked the conflict, including restrictions on trade and manufacturing imposed by the NAVIGATION ACTS, restrictions on land settlement in the West, and attempts to raise revenue in America by such means as the STAMP ACT (1765) and the Tea Act (1773) that led to the BOSTON TEA PARTY. "No taxation without representation" became the colonial radicals' rallying cry. The intellectual battle for independence was led by Thomas PAINE, Thomas JEFFERSON and Benjamin FRANKLIN. A CONTINENTAL CONGRESS was summoned in 1774, and the first shots were fired at LEXINGTON AND CONCORD, Massachusetts, in April 1775. In May the second Continental Congress met at Philadelphia, established an army under George WASHINGTON, and assumed the role of a revolutionary government. On 4 July, 1776, the DECLARATION OF INDEPENDENCE made the break with Britain decisive. Initially the colonials suffered a series of military defeats, and Washington retreated from New York to Pennsylvania. Crossing the Delaware River, he surprised and captured the British at TRENTON (26 December, 1776). On 3 January, 1777, he defeated the British at PRINCETON, further strengthening American morale. The British attempted a three-pronged attack, focusing on New York State. The strategy failed with the first decisive colonial victory at SARATOGA (17 October, 1777) and brought France into the war against Britain. During the winter of 1777, Washington's forces reorganized in Pennsylvania. In 1778, the British forces focused on the South, taking SAVANNAH in December 1778. Following the defeat at King's Mountain in 1780, the British, under General Charles Cornwallis, were forced to withdraw N to YORKTOWN, Virginia. In 1781, surrounded by American forces and the French navy, Cornwallis surrendered. Fighting ceased and the Treaty of Paris (1783) recognized US independence.

American Samoa US-administered group of five volcanic islands and two coral atolls of the SAMOA island chain in the S Pacific, *c*.1,050km (650mi) NE of Fiji. The principal islands are Tutuila, the Manua group (Ta'u, Ofu and Olosega) and Aun'u. Rose Island (uninhabited) and Swain's Island are coral atolls. In 1899, a treaty between the US, Germany and the UK granted the US rights to the islands E of 171° longitude, and Germany the rights to the W sector. American Samoa remained under the jurisdiction of the US Navy until 1951, when the US naval base at the capital Pago Pago closed down and administration was transferred to the Department of the Interior. In 1978, the first gubernatorial elections took place. The population is largely Polynesian and considered US nationals.

The US government and the tuna fish canning industry are the main sources of employment. Pop. (2000) 39,000.

America's Cup International competition for racing yachts. A trophy was established in 1857 by the New York Yacht Club. Several countries compete in a series of elimination races, before challenging the previous winner. The US has won the best-of-seven series on almost every occasion and traditionally hosted the contest off Newport, Rhode Island.

americium (symbol Am) Radioactive, metallic element of the ACTINIDE SERIES, first made in 1944 by neutron bombardment of PLUTONIUM. It is used in home smoke detectors, and Am^{241} is a source of gamma rays. Properties: at.no. 95; r.a.m.. 243.13; r.d.. 13.67; m.p. 995°C (1,821°F); b.p. unknown; most stable isotope Am^{243} (half-life 7,650 yr).

amethyst Transparent, violet variety of crystallized QUARTZ, containing more iron oxide than other varieties. It is found mainly in Brazil, Uruguay, Canada and North Carolina. Amethyst is a semiprecious gem.

Amharic Official language of Ethiopia since *c*.1300. It is a Semitic language belonging to the SE Semitic subgroup of Afro-Asiatic languages and has many words in common with the ancient form of Ethiopic, the language of religious ritual in the Christian Church in Ethiopia.

Amiens City on the River Somme, PICARDY, N France; capital of Somme department. Amiens has been an important market town and textile centre since the 16th century. It is renowned for its velvet. It was conquered by HENRY IV of France in 1597 and was badly damaged in both world wars. The 13th century Cathedral of Notre Dame is the largest gothic cathedral in France and a world heritage site. Industries: textiles, chemicals. Pop. (1990) 136,230.

Amin, Idi (1925–) President of Uganda (1971–79). He gained power by a military coup in 1971, overthrowing Milton OBOTE. Amin established a dictatorship marked by atrocities and expelled *c*.80,000 Asian Ugandans in 1972. When Tanzanian forces joined rebel Ugandans in a march on Kampala, Amin fled to Libya.

amine Any of a group of organic compounds derived from AMMONIA by replacing hydrogen atoms with alkyl groups. Methylamine (CH_3NH_2) has one hydrogen replaced. Replacement of two hydrogens gives a secondary amine and of three hydrogens, a tertiary amine. Amines are produced in the putrefaction of organic matter and are weakly basic. ANILINE is an aromatic amine compound used in dyeing. *See also* ALKALOID

amino acid Organic acid containing at least one carboxyl group (COOH) and at least one amino group (NH_2). Amino acids are of great biological importance because they combine to form PROTEIN. Amino acids form PEPTIDES by the reaction of adjacent amino and carboxyl groups. Proteins are polypeptide chains consisting of hundreds of amino acids. About 20 amino acids occur in proteins; not all organisms are able to synthesize all of them. **Essential** amino acids are those that an organism has to obtain from its environment. There are ten such essential amino acids for humans: arginine, histidine, isoleucine, leucine, lysine, methionine, phenylalanine, threonine, tryptophan and valine.

Amis, Kingsley (1922–95) English novelist, father of Martin AMIS. Amis' debut novel *Lucky Jim* (1954) is a classic of post-1945 British fiction. A satire on academia, it established Amis as one of the ANGRY YOUNG MEN. Other novels include *That Uncertain Feeling* (1955), *Take a Girl Like You* (1960), *Girl, 20* (1971) and *Stanley and the Women* (1984). His tragicomedy *The Old Devils* (1986) won the Booker Prize.

Amis, Martin (1949–) English novelist and journalist, son of Kingsley AMIS. His debut novel, *The Rachel Papers* (1974), won the Somerset Maugham Award. Amis' humour is more bawdy and dark than his father's. *Money* (1984) is a stylish critique of the dehumanizing tendencies of late capitalism. *Einstein's Monsters* (1987) is a collection of five short stories on nuclear war. *Time's Arrow* (1991) is a complex work on the Holocaust. Other novels include *Success* (1978) and *Night Train* (1997).

Amish Highly conservative, Protestant sect of North America, whose members form an offshoot of the ANABAPTIST MENNONITE Church. The strict Old Order Amish Mennonite Church, to which most sect members belong, was founded in Switzerland in 1693 by Jakob Ammann (c.1645–c.1730). The Amish began migrating to North America in 1720 and eventually died out in Europe. In the US and Canada they established small closed agricultural communities. After 1850, tensions between traditionalist "old order" Amish and more liberal "new order" communities split the sect. Today, a few groups of traditionalist Amish still work the land, practice non-cooperation with the state, wear plain, homemade clothes and shun modern conveniences.

Amman Capital and largest city of Jordan, 80km (50mi) ENE of Jerusalem. Known as Rabbath-Ammon, it was the chief city of the Ammonites in biblical times. A new city was built on seven hills from 1875, and it became the capital of Trans-Jordan in 1921. From 1948 it grew rapidly, partly due to the influx of Palestinian refugees. Industries: cement, textiles, tobacco. Pop. (1994 est.) 1,300,042.

ammeter Instrument for measuring ELECTRIC CURRENT in AMPERES. An ammeter is connected in series in a circuit. In the moving-coil type for DIRECT CURRENT (DC), the current to be measured passes through a coil suspended in a magnetic field and deflects a needle attached to the coil. In the moving-iron type for both direct and ALTERNATING CURRENT (AC), current through a fixed coil magnetizes two pieces of soft iron that repel each other and deflect the needle. Digital ammeters are now common.

ammonia (NH₃) Colourless, nonflammable, pungent gas manufactured by the HABER PROCESS. It is used to make nitrogenous fertilizers. Ammonia solutions are used in cleaning and bleaching. The gas is extremely soluble in water, forming an alkaline solution of ammonium hydroxide (NH₄OH), which gives rise to ammonium salts containing the ion NH₄⁺. Properties: r.d. 0.59; m.p. −77.7°C (−107.9°F); b.p. −33.4°C (−28.1°F).

ammonite Any of an extinct group of shelled cephalopod MOLLUSCS. Most ammonites had a spiral shell, and they are believed to be related to the nautiloids, whose only surviving form is the pearly NAUTILUS. They are common as FOSSILS in marine rocks.

amnesia Loss or impairment of memory. It can be caused by disease or physical injury, especially to the brain, or by psychological disturbance. Selective amnesia, in which only certain unpleasant memories are eliminated, is generally due to emotional disorder.

Amnesty International HUMAN-RIGHTS organization, founded (1961) by Peter Berenson. It campaigns on behalf of prisoners of conscience. Based in the UK and funded entirely by private donations, it champions the rights of individuals detained for political or religious reasons. By the mid-1990s, Amnesty had more than one million members and offices in more than 40 countries. It was awarded the Nobel Peace Prize in 1977.

amnion Membrane or sac that encloses the EMBRYO of a reptile, bird or mammal. The embryo floats in the amniotic fluid within the sac. *See also* UTERUS

amoeba Microscopic, almost transparent, single-celled PROTOZOA of the phylum Rhizopoda. Amoebas have a constantly changing, irregular shape. Found in ponds, damp soil and animal intestines, they consist of a thin outer cell membrane, a large nucleus, food and contractile VACUOLES and fat globules. It reproduces by binary FISSION. Length: up to 3mm (0.1in). Class Sarcodina; species include the common *Ameba proteus* and *Entameba histolytica*, which causes amoebic DYSENTERY.

Amon (Amun) Ancient Egyptian deity of reproduction or the animating force. The "invisible one", Amon is commonly represented as a human being wearing ram's horns and a twin-feathered crown. He gradually assimilated other Egyptian gods, becoming **Amon-Re** (the supreme creator). His cult temple was at Weset (LUXOR).

Amos (active c.750 BC) Old Testament prophet. He was named as the author of the Book of Amos, the third of the 12 books of the Minor Prophets.

Ampère, André Marie (1775–1836) French physicist and mathematician. Ampère founded electrodynamics (now called ELECTROMAGNETISM) and performed numerous experiments to investigate the magnetic effects of electric currents. He devised techniques for detecting and measuring currents, and constructed an early type of galvanometer. Ampère's law – proposed by him – is a mathematical description of the magnetic force between two electric currents. His name is also commemorated in the fundamental unit of ELECTRIC CURRENT, the AMPERE (A).

ampere (symbol A) SI unit of ELECTRIC CURRENT. It is defined as the current in a pair of straight, parallel conductors of infinite length and 1m (39in) apart in a vacuum that produces a force of 2×10⁻⁷ newton per metre (N/m) in their length. This force may be measured on a current balance instrument, the standard against which current meters, such as an AMMETER, are calibrated.

amphetamine (Dexedrine) Drug that stimulates the CENTRAL NERVOUS SYSTEM. The use of amphetamines (known as "pep pills" or "speed") can lead to drug abuse and dependence. They can induce a temporary sense of well-being, often followed by fatigue and depression.

amphibian Class of egg-laying VERTEBRATES, whose larval stages (tadpoles) are usually spent in water but

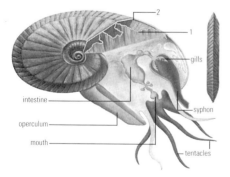

▲ **ammonite** Like the modern nautilus, which lives in the open end of its shell, ammonites had a soft anatomy. As the animal grew, it secreted more shell and moved forward into the new part, walling off the old section with a septum (1).

The walled-off chambers were used for buoyancy, being supplied with air from a siphuncle (2) connecting them all. The septa met the shell wall in suture lines that had patterns for each species and became more complex as the group advanced.

whose adult life is normally spent on land. Amphibians have smooth, moist skin and are cold-blooded. They undergo complete METAMORPHOSIS. Larvae breathe through gills; adults usually have lungs. All adults are carnivorous but larvae are frequently herbivorous. There are three living orders: Urodela (NEWTS and SALAMANDERS), Anura (FROGS and TOADS) and Apoda (CAECILIANS).

amphibole Any of a large group of complex rock-forming minerals characterized by a double-chain silicate structure (Si_4O_{11}). They all contain water as OH^- ions and usually calcium, magnesium and iron. Found in IGNEOUS and METAMORPHIC rocks, they form wedge-shaped fragments on cleavage. Crystals are orthorhombic or monoclinic.

amphitheatre In ancient Rome and the Roman Empire, a large circular or oval building with the performance space surrounded by tiered seating. It was used as a theatre for gladiatorial contests, wild-animal shows and similar events. Many ruined amphitheatres remain; the best-known is the COLOSSEUM in Rome. The term is now used generically to refer to any open, banked arena.

amplifier Device for increasing the magnitude of a signal, such as voltage or current, but not the way it varies. Amplifiers are used in radio and television transmitters and receivers and in audio equipment. For instance, they magnify signals from MICROPHONES or TRANSDUCERS to boost output via LOUDSPEAKERS. The first amplifiers used thermionic valves heated by heat, such as the triode invented (1906) by Lee DE FOREST. These valve amplifiers have largely been replaced by amplifiers with TRANSISTORS. *See also* THERMIONICS

amplitude *See* WAVE AMPLITUDE

amplitude modulation (AM) Form of RADIO transmission. Broadcasts on the short-, medium- and long-wave bands are transmitted by amplitude modulation. The sound signals to be transmitted are superimposed on a constant-amplitude radio signal called the carrier. The resulting modulated radio signal varies in amplitude according to the strength of the sound signal. *See also* FREQUENCY MODULATION (FM)

Amritsar City in Punjab state, NW India. It was founded (1577) by Ram Das, fourth guru of the Sikh religion. Amrtisar is the religious centre of SIKHISM and site of its holiest shrine, the Golden Temple. It was the scene of the Amritsar Massacre in 1919 when hundreds of Indian nationalists were killed by British troops. In 1984, Indian troops stormed the Golden Temple, killing more than 400 people. Amritsar is noted for handicrafts. Industries: textiles, silk weaving, food processing. Pop. (1991) 709,000.

Amsterdam Capital and largest city in the Netherlands, on the River Amstel and linked to the North Sea by the North Sea Canal. Amsterdam was chartered in *c*.1300 and joined the Hanseatic League in 1369. The Dutch East India Company (1602) brought great prosperity to the city. It became a notable centre of learning and book printing during the 17th century. Its commerce and importance declined when captured by the French in 1795 and blockaded by the British during the Napoleonic Wars. A major European port and one of its leading financial and cultural centres, it has an important stock exchange and diamond-cutting industry. Major sights include the Rijksmuseum, the Van Gogh museum and the houses of Anne Frank and Rembrandt. Industries: iron and steel, oil refining, rolling stock, chemicals, glass, shipbuilding. Pop. (1996) 718,000.

Amudarya (ancient **Oxus**) River formed by the confluence of the Vakhsh and Pandj rivers in the Pamir Mountains, central Asia. It forms most of the border between Turkmenistan and Afghanistan and drains into the ARAL SEA. The KARA-KUM Canal carries water from the Amudarya to ASHGABAT.

Amundsen, Roald (1872–1928) Norwegian explorer and the first person to reach the SOUTH POLE. In 1903–06, Amundsen became the first to sail through the NORTHWEST PASSAGE and determined the exact position of the magnetic NORTH POLE. He was beaten by Robert PEARY in the race to the North Pole and turned to ANTARCTICA. Amundsen reached the South Pole on 14 December 1911 (35 days before SCOTT). In 1926, Amundsen and Umberto Nobile made the first flight across the North Pole.

amylase Digestive ENZYME secreted by the SALIVARY GLANDS (salivary amylase) and the PANCREAS (pancreatic amylase). It aids digestion by breaking down starch into MALTOSE (a disaccharide) and then GLUCOSE (a monosaccharide).

Anabaptists Radical Protestant sects in the REFORMATION who shared the belief that infant baptism is not authorized by Scripture, and that it was necessary to be baptized as an adult. The first such baptisms were conducted by the Swiss Brethren sect in Zürich (1525). The sect was the first to completely separate church from state, when they rejected Ulrich ZWINGLI's Reformed Church. Aided by social upheavals (such as the PEASANTS' WAR) and the theological arguments of Martin LUTHER and Thomas Münzer, Anabaptism spread rapidly to Germany and the Netherlands. It stressed the community of believers. The communal theocracy established by John of Leiden at Münster was brutally suppressed (1535).

anabolic steroid Any of a group of hormones that stimulate the growth of tissue. Synthetic versions are used in medicine to treat OSTEOPOROSIS and some types of ANAEMIA; they may also be prescribed to aid weight gain in severely ill or elderly patients. These drugs are associated with a number of side-effects, including acne, fluid retention, liver damage and masculinization in women. Some athletes have been known to abuse anabolic steroids in order to increase muscle bulk.

anabolism *See* METABOLISM

anaconda Large, constricting BOA of South America, the longest (up to 9m/30ft) and heaviest (up to 500kg/1100lb) snake in the world. Anacondas are found chiefly in swamps. They are mainly aquatic, and feed on birds and small mammals. Females give birth to up to 75 live young. Species *Eunectes murinus*. *See also* PYTHON

anaemia Condition in which there is a shortage of HAEMOGLOBIN, the oxygen-carrying pigment contained in ERYTHROCYTES (red blood cells). Symptoms include weakness, pallor, breathlessness, faintness, palpitations and increased chance of infection. It may be due to a decrease in the production of haemoglobin or erythrocytes, excessive destruction of erythrocytes or blood loss. Iron deficiency is the most common cause of anaemia.

anaerobic Connected with the absence of oxygen or air, or not dependent on oxygen or air for survival. An anaerobic organism (anaerobe) is a microorganism that can survive by releasing energy from GLUCOSE and other foods in the absence of oxygen. The process by which it does so is called anaerobic RESPIRATION. Most anaerobes can survive in oxygen but do not need it for respiration. *See also* AEROBIC

anaesthesia State of insensibility or loss of sensation produced by disease or by various anaesthetic drugs used during surgical procedures. During general, or total, anaesthesia the entire body becomes insensible and the individual sleeps; in local anaesthesia only a specific part of the body is rendered insensible and the patient remains conscious. A **general** anaesthetic may be either an injected drug, such as the barbiturate thiopentone, used to induce unconsciousness, or an inhalation agent such as halothane, which is used to maintain anaesthesia for surgery. **Local** anaesthetics, such as lignocaine, numb the relevant part of the body by blocking the transmission of impulses through the sensory nerves which supply it.

Anaheim City in Orange County, part of the greater LOS ANGELES conurbation, s California, USA. Anaheim was founded in 1857. It is home to the Disneyland amusement park (founded 1955). Industries: electronics, aerospace, tourism. Pop. (1992) 274,162.

analgesic DRUG that relieves or prevents pain without causing loss of consciousness. It does not cure the cause of the pain, but helps to deaden the sensation. Some analgesics are also NARCOTICS and many have anti-inflammatory properties. Common analgesics include aspirin, codeine and morphine. *See also* ANAESTHESIA

analogue computer Machine that processes continuously variable information. Information is usually first converted into proportional electrical quantities. These are manipulated by amplifiers and other circuits that perform various mathematical operations. In other words, the COMPUTER solves problems by dealing with quantities (voltages) that are analogous to the quantities in the problem. Analogue computers are time-consuming to set up and operate. Most work once done on analogue computers is now carried out on digital computers.

analogue signal In telecommunications and electronics, transmission of information by means of variation in a continuous waveform. An analogue signal varies (usually in AMPLITUDE or FREQUENCY) in direct proportion to the information content of the signal.

analysis In chemistry, any method of determining the composition of a substance. There are two main types of chemical analysis. **Qualitative** analysis is concerned with finding out what elements or compounds are present in a sample. It makes use of various specific chemical tests. **Quantitative** analysis is used to determine how much of a known substance is present in a sample. There are various quantitative techniques, including volumetric analysis (measuring volumes of reactants), gravimetric analysis (weighing), SPECTROSCOPY and spectrometry (analysis of spectra) and CHROMATOGRAPHY.

analytic geometry (coordinate GEOMETRY) Branch of geometry in which a position is represented by numbers in some coordinate system, lines, curves and surfaces can be represented by algebraic equations. The geometric properties can then be studied by the methods of ALGEBRA. It was first introduced by René DESCARTES in the 17th century. *See also* CARTESIAN COORDINATE SYSTEM

analytic philosophy Dominant movement in 20th-century Anglo-American academic philosophy. It was, in part, a reaction to continental European IDEALISM. In place of essentialism, Bertrand RUSSELL argued for contextual definitions based on the procedures of LOGIC. In *Tractatus Logico-Philosophicus* (1922), Ludwig WITTGENSTEIN posited the notion that significant discourse can be analysed into elementary propositions, such as "not", "and" and "if". The logical content of complex propositions is obscured by ordinary language and can only be analyzed through the reductive method of "logical atomism". Those statements that cannot be broken down into elementary propositions are considered metaphysical. These ideas were taken up by LOGICAL POSITIVISM. Wittgenstein's later work marks a departure from

this view and is often referred to as LINGUISTIC PHILOSOPHY. *See also* AYER, A.J.; QUINE, W.V.

anarchism (Gk. "no government") Political theory that regards the abolition of the state as a prerequisite for equality and social justice. In place of government, anarchy is a social form based upon voluntary cooperation between individuals. The STOICS leader, ZENO OF CITIUM is regarded as the father of anarchism. Millenarian movements of the Reformation, such as the ANABAPTISTS, espoused a form of anarchism. As a modern political philosophy, anarchism dates from the mid-19th century, and writers include P.J. PROUDHON. Often in conflict with emerging COMMUNISM, Mikhail BAKUNIN's brand of violent, revolutionary anarchism led to his expulsion from the First International (1872). Anarchism has been a popular political force only in conjunction with SYNDICALISM. Its support of civil disobedience and sometimes political violence has led to its marginalization.

Anastasia (1901–18) Grand Duchess of Russia, youngest daughter of the last tsar, NICHOLAS II. After the Russian Revolution, Anastasia was presumably murdered, together with other members of the royal family, in July 1918. Since 1920, several women have claimed to be Anastasia, the legal heir to the ROMANOV fortune held in Swiss banks. None of the claimants has been able to prove her identity.

Anatolia *See* ASIA MINOR

anatomy Branch of biological science that studies the structure of an organism. The study of anatomy can be divided in several ways. On the basis of size, there is **gross** anatomy, which is studying structures with the naked eye; **microscopic** anatomy, studying finer detail with a light MICROSCOPE; **submicroscopic** anatomy, studying even finer structural detail with an ELECTRON MICROSCOPE; and **molecular** anatomy, studying with sophisticated instruments the molecular make-up of an organism. Microscopic and submicroscopic anatomy involve two closely related sciences: HISTOLOGY and CYTOLOGY. Anatomy can also be classified according to the type of organism studied: plant, invertebrate, vertebrate or human anatomy. *See also* PHYSIOLOGY

Anaximander (611–547 BC) Greek philosopher, student of THALES. Anaximander's lasting reputation is based on his notion of *apeiron* (Gr. infinite), a non-perceivable substance which he regarded as the primary source material of the natural world. His ideas are considered the precursor of a modern conception of the indestructibility of matter. Anaximander also anticipated the theory of evolution and is said to have made the first map of the Earth, which he conceived of as a self-supporting immobile cylindrical object at the centre of the universe.

ancestor worship Any of various religious beliefs and practices found in societies where KINSHIP is strong. The spirits of dead ancestors or tribal members, believed capable of good or harm, are propitiated by prayers and sacrifices.

Anchorage City in s central Alaska, USA. By far the state's largest city, Anchorage was founded as a railroad town in 1914 and became the supply centre for the gold- and coal-mining regions to the N. Industries: tourism, oil and natural gas. Pop. (1996) 251,000.

anchovy Commercially valuable food fish found worldwide in large shoals in temperate and tropical seas. There are more than 100 species. Length: 10–25cm (4–10in). Family Engraulidae.

ancien régime Term used to describe the political, legal and social system in France before the FRENCH REVOLUTION of 1789. It was characterized by a rigid social order, a fiscal system weighted in favour of the rich and an absolutist monarchy. *See also* STATES GENERAL.

Andalusia (Andalucía) Largest, most populous and southernmost region of Spain, crossed by the River Guadalquivir, and comprising eight provinces. The capital is SEVILLE; other major cities include MÁLAGA, GRANADA and CÓRDOBA. In the N are the Sierra Morena mountains, which are rich in minerals. In the S are the Sierra Nevada, rising to Mulhacén (Spain's highest point), at 3,378m (11,411ft). Farms in the low-lying SW raise horses and cattle (including fighting bulls) and grow most of Spain's cereals; other major crops are citrus fruits, olives, sugar and grapes. Sherry is made from grapes grown in Jerez de la Frontera, near Cádiz. Area: 33,707sq mi (87,268sq km). Pop. (1991) 6,940,522.

andalusite One of many crystalline forms of aluminium silicate, occurring in contact METAMORPHIC ROCK and in other deposits. It is mined commercially in the US, Kazakstan and South Africa to make temperature-resistant and insulating porcelains.

Andaman and Nicobar Islands Territory of India comprising two chains of islands in the Bay of Bengal. The capital is Port Blair (on South Andaman). The main exports are timber, coffee, coconuts and copra. The population of the islands (one of India's seven union territories) almost doubled in the decade to 1991. Total area: 8,300sq km (3,200sq mi). Pop. (1991) 280,661.

Andean Indians *See* NATIVE AMERICANS

Andersen, Hans Christian (1805–75) Danish writer of some of the world's best-loved fairy tales. He gained a reputation as a poet and novelist before his talent found its true expression. Anderson's humorous, delicate, but frequently also melancholy stories, were first published in 1835. They include *The Ugly Duckling*, *The Little Mermaid*, *The Little Match Girl* and *The Emperor's New Clothes*.

Anderson, Carl David (1905–91) US physicist who shared the 1936 Nobel Prize for physics with Victor HESS. In 1932 Anderson discovered the first known particle of antimatter, the POSITRON or anti-electron. He later helped discover the muon, an elementary particle.

Anderson, Elizabeth Garrett (1836–1917) English physician and pioneer of women's rights. She had to overcome intense prejudice against women doctors to become one of the first English women to practise. Later, she became England's first woman mayor.

Anderson, Marian (1902–93) US contralto. She secured her reputation in recital tours of America and Europe (1925–35). In 1955, Anderson made her debut with the METROPOLITAN OPERA COMPANY as Ulrica in Verdi's *Un Ballo in Maschera*; this was the first appearance of a black singer in a leading role at the Metropolitan Opera.

Anderson, Sherwood (1876–1941) US short-story writer and novelist. His best known work is *Winesburg, Ohio* (1919), a series of interrelated stories of life in a small Midwestern town. His novel, *Poor White* (1920), expanded on the theme of conflict between industrial technology and the individual. Other short-story collections include *The Triumph of the Egg* (1921) and *Death in the Woods* (1933). His flat, spare style was a formative influence on Ernest HEMINGWAY and William FAULKNER.

Andes Chain of mountains in South America, extending along the whole length of the W coast. The longest mountain range in the world, it stretches for 8,900km (5,500mi). At their widest it is *c*.800km (500mi) across. There are more than 50 peaks over 6,700m (21,980ft) high. It contains many active volcanoes, including COTOPAXI in Ecuador. Earthquakes are common, and

cities such as LIMA, CALLAO and VALPARAÍSO have been severely damaged. The highest peak is ACONCAGUA, rising to 6,960m (22,834ft) in Argentina. Lake TITICACA (the highest lake in the world) lies in the Andes at 3,810m (12,500ft) above sea-level on the Peru-Bolivia border.

andesite Fine-grained, volcanic rock, second in abundance only to BASALT, found in mountain folds, sills, dykes and lava streams. It is composed of finely crystalline FELDSPARS, with occasional larger crystals (phenocrysts).

Andhra Pradesh State in SE India on the Bay of Bengal; the capital is HYDERABAD. It was created in 1953 from part of MADRAS, and in 1956 incorporated the princely state of Hyderabad. Though mountainous to the NE, most of the region is flat coastal plain. Products include rice and peanuts; coal, chrome and manganese are mined. The principal language is Teluga. Area: 106,878sq mi (276,814sq km). Pop. (1991) 66,508,008.

Andorra Small, independent state situated high in the E Pyrenees between France and Spain. Andorra consists mainly of six valleys that drain to the River Valira. These deep, glaciated valleys lie at altitudes of 1,000 to 2,900m (3,300–9,500ft). In the N, a lofty watershed forms the frontier with France, and to the S the land descends to the Segre Valley in Spain. It is a rare example of a medieval principality. In 1993, a new democratic constitution was adopted that reduced the roles of the president of France and the Spanish bishop of Urgel to purely constitutional figureheads. The main sources of income include agriculture; the sale of water and hydroelectricity to Catalonia; tourism, particularly skiing; and the sale of duty-free goods. Area: 453sq km (175sq mi). Pop. (2000) 49,000.

Andrea del Sarto (1486–1531) (Andrea d'Agnolo di Francesco) Florentine artist. A contemporary of MICHELANGELO and RAPHAEL, he was one of the outstanding painters and draughtsmen of the High RENAISSANCE. He was an excellent portraitist, a master of composition, and he produced many frescos and altarpieces. His frescos include the cycles in the cloister of SS Annunziata (1514–24) and the terra verde grisailles in the Chiostro dello Scalzo (1511–26), Florence.

Andrew, Saint In the New Testament, brother of Simon Peter and one of the original 12 disciples of Jesus. According to tradition, he was crucified on an x-shaped cross. He is patron saint of Scotland and Russia; his feast day is 30 November.

Andric̀, Ivo (1892–1975) Yugoslav novelist. His best known work is an epic trilogy (1945) on Bosnia: *The Bridge on the Drina*, *Bosnian Story* and *Young Miss*. His major theme is man's isolation in a hostile universe. Andric̀ was awarded the 1961 Nobel Prize for literature.

Androcles In Roman legend, a slave who ran away from his master. Androcles removed a thorn from the paw of a suffering lion. When he later faced the same lion in the Roman Arena, the lion refused to harm him.

androgen General name for male sex HORMONES, such as TESTOSTERONE.

Andromache In Greek mythology, the daughter of Eëtion, king of Thebes, and wife of Hector. Her only son, Astyanax, was killed when Troy was taken by the Greeks. She became the captive of Achilles' son, Neoptolemus, and bore him three sons.

Andromeda In Greek mythology, daughter of Cepheus and Cassiopeia, king and queen of Ethiopia. When her country was under threat from a sea dragon, Andromeda was offered as a sacrifice and chained to a rock by the sea. She was saved by PERSEUS.

Andromeda Large constellation of the Northern Hemisphere, adjoining the Square of Pegasus. The main stars lie in a line leading away from Pegasus. The most famous object in the constellation is the ANDROMEDA GALAXY

Andromeda Galaxy Spiral GALAXY in the constellation ANDROMEDA, 2.2 million light years away, the most distant object visible to the naked eye. The Andromeda Galaxy has a mass of more than 300,000 million Suns. Its diameter is *c*.150,000 light-years, somewhat larger than our own Galaxy.

Andronicus I (*c*.1110–85) (Andronicus Comnenus) Byzantine emperor (1183–85). Andronicus succeeded to the throne after murdering his nephew, Alexius II Comnenus, and marrying the boy's 13-year-old widow Agnes-Anna, daughter of the French King Louis VII. His reduction of the power of the nobility and anti-corruption drive were brutally enforced.

Andropov, Yuri Vladimirovich (1914–84) Soviet statesman, president of the Soviet Union (1983–84), general secretary of the Communist Party (1982–84). He played a major role in the suppression of the Hungarian Uprising (1956). As head of the KGB (1967–82), Andropov took a hard line against political dissidence, supporting Soviet intervention in Czechoslovakia (1968) and Poland (1981). In 1973, he joined the Politburo. Andropov succeeded Leonid BREZHNEV as leader. His tenure was the shortest in Soviet history. Perhaps his most significant decision was the promotion of Mikhail GORBACHEV. He was succeeded by Konstantin CHERNENKO.

anemometer Instrument using pressure tubes or rotating cups, vanes or propellers to measure the speed or force of the wind.

anechoic chamber (dead room) Room designed to be echo-free so that it can be used in ACOUSTIC laboratories to measure sound reflection and transmission, and to test audio equipment. The walls, floor and ceiling must be insulated and all surfaces covered with an absorbent material such as rubber, often over inward-pointing pyramid shapes to reduce reflection. The room is usually asymmetrical to reduce stationary waves.

anemone (windflower) Perennial plant found worldwide. Anemones have sepals resembling petals, and many stamens and pistils covering a central knob; two or three deeply toothed leaves appear in a whorl midway up the stem. Many are wild flowers, such as the wood anemone (*Anemone nemorosa*). There are 120 species. Family Ranunculaceae. *See also* BUTTERCUP; SEA ANEMONE

aneurysm Bulging of an artery at a weak point in its wall. Aneurysms can occur almost anywhere in the body. There is always the risk of it rupturing, causing serious, often fatal blood loss. Some aneurysms can be repaired surgically.

Angara River in SE Siberia, Russia, flowing from the SW end of Lake Baikal, N past Irkutsk and Bratsk, then W into the River Yenisei. A source of hydroelectric power, Angara's large drainage basin has iron, coal and gold deposits. Length: *c*.1,850km (1,150mi).

angel (Gk. messenger) Spiritual being superior to man but inferior to God. In the Bible, angels appear on Earth as messengers and servants of God. Angels also form an integral part of Judaism and Islam. *See also* ARCHANGEL

Angel Falls World's highest uninterrupted waterfall, in La Gran Sabrana, E Venezuela. Part of the River Caroni, it was discovered in 1935 and named after Jimmy Angel, a US aviator who died in a crash near the Falls. Total drop: 980m (3,212ft).

angelfish Tropical fish found in the Atlantic and Indo-Pacific oceans, popular as an aquarium fish because of its graceful, trailing fins and beautiful markings. Length: 2–10cm (0.75–4in). Family Cichlidae.

angelica Plant of the CARROT family that grows in northern temperate regions and in New Zealand. Garden angelicas (*Angelica archangelica*) grow to 1.5m (5ft) and have greenish flowers. The stems, usually crystallized, and oil from the roots and seeds, have culinary uses. Family Apiaceae/Umbelliferae

Angelico, Fra (1400–55) (Guido di Pietro) Florentine painter and Dominican friar. Angelico and his assistants painted a cycle of some 50 devotional frescos in the friary of San Marco, Florence (*c*.1438–45). These pictures show great technical skill and are the key to Angelico's reputation as an artist of extraordinary sweetness and serenity. International Gothic influenced his early work, but he found great inspiration in representations of architectural perspective by MASACCIO. His style showed a marked change toward narrative detail in frescos carried out for Pope Nicholas V's Vatican chapel (1447–50).

Angelou, Maya (1928–) US writer and editor. She is best known for five volumes of autobiography, starting with *I Know Why the Caged Bird Sings* (1970), which evokes her childhood in 1930s Arkansas. The fourth volume, *The Heart of a Woman*, deals with her involvement in the 1960s CIVIL RIGHTS movement as the Northern Coordinator for Martin Luther KING. She read her poem "On the Pulse of Morning" at the inauguration of President CLINTON in 1993.

Angevins English royal dynasty named after King HENRY II, son of the Count of Anjou (and grandson of Henry I), who ascended the throne in 1154. The Angevins, who later became the PLANTAGENET royal line, retained the crown until 1485.

angina Pain in the chest due to insufficient blood supply to the heart, usually associated with diseased coronary arteries. Generally induced by exertion or stress, it is treated with drugs, such as glyceryl trinitrate, or surgery.

angiography X-RAY examination of major blood vessels. It is most commonly used to investigate CORONARY ARTERY DISEASE or any disruption of the blood supply to the brain. The technique requires the injection of a radiopaque dye into the bloodstream so that the diseased vessel appears in clear silhouette on the X-ray screen.

angioplasty Surgical repair of diseased or damaged blood vessels. It is a MINIMAL ACCESS SURGERY (keyhole) procedure, in which a balloon-tipped catheter is passed into a main ARTERY, often in the groin, and advanced until it comes to rest in the narrowed vessel; the balloon is then inflated to widen the artery. One of the best-known interventions of this kind, used to treat coronary heart disease, is percutaneous transluminal coronary angioplasty (PTCA), a method of improving blood flow in either of the two arteries supplying the heart.

angiosperm Any of about 250,000 species of plant of the phylum Angiospermophyta, which produce FLOWERS, FRUITS and SEEDS. Angiosperms include most herbs, shrubs, many trees, fruits, vegetables and cereals. Their seeds are protected by an outer covering. There are two main groups: MONOCOTYLEDONS (one seed-leaf), and DICOTYLEDONS (two seed-leaves). *See also* GYMNOSPERM

Angkor Ancient KHMER capital and temple complex, NW Cambodia. The site contains the ruins of several stone temples erected by Khmer rulers, many of which lie within the walled enclosure of Angkor Thom, the capital built (1181–95) by Jayavarman VII (*c*.1120–1215).

Angkor Wat, the greatest structure in terms of its size and the quality of its carving, lies outside the main complex. Thai invaders destroyed the Angkor complex in 1431, and it remained neglected until French travellers rediscovered it in 1858. After restoration, Angkor Wat suffered again when the followers of POL POT ravaged Cambodia in the civil war (1970–75).

angle Measure of the inclination of two straight lines or planes to each other. One revolution is divided into 360 degrees or 2π radians. One degree may be subdivided into 60 minutes, and one minute into 60 seconds.

Angles Germanic tribe from a district of Schleswig-Holstein now called Angeln. In the 5th century they invaded England with neighbouring tribes, including JUTES and SAXONS. They settled mainly in Northumbria and East Anglia. The name England (Angle-land) derives from them.

Anglican Communion Fellowship of 37 independent national or provincial worldwide churches, many of which are in Commonwealth nations. It originated from missionary work by the CHURCH OF ENGLAND. An exception is the EPISCOPAL CHURCH in the US, founded by the Scottish Episcopal Church. There is no single governing authority, but all recognize the leadership of the Archbishop of CANTERBURY. Worship is liturgical, based on the Book of COMMON PRAYER. In 1997, there were c.70 million Anglicans organized into c.30,000 parishes.

angling *See* FISHING

Anglo-Irish Agreement (Hillsborough Agreement) Treaty on the status of Northern IRELAND, signed (1985) by Margaret THATCHER and Garret FITZGERALD. It gave the Republic of Ireland the right of consultation, asserted that any future changes to the status of Northern Ireland would have to be ratified by a majority of its peoples, and set up the Anglo-Irish Intergovernmental Conference (AIIC) to promote closer cooperation. The agreement was denounced by the Ulster Unionists. *See also* DOWNING STREET DECLARATION

Anglo-Maori Wars *See* MAORI WARS

Anglo-Saxon art and architecture Style of art and architecture in Britain following the ANGLO-SAXON invasions from the 5th to the 11th centuries. The most famous archaeological find is the pagan ship-burial at SUTTON HOO. Anglo-Saxon art is predominantly Christian, consisting of stone crosses, ivory carvings and illuminated manuscripts (the most important being the LINDISFARNE GOSPELS). Anglo-Saxon churches are characterized by square apses, aisles or side chambers (*porticus*), pilaster strips and distinctive timber work.

Anglo-Saxon Chronicle Monastic chronicles written in England between the 9th century and 1155. The four surviving versions of the Chronicle are the chief documentary source for ANGLO-SAXON English history.

Anglo-Saxons People of Germanic origin comprising ANGLES, SAXONS and other tribes who began to invade England from the mid-5th century, when Roman power was in decline. By 600, they were well established in most of England. They were converted to Christianity in the 7th century. Early tribal groups were led by warrior lords whose thegns (noblemen) provided military service in exchange for rewards and protection. The tribal groups eventually developed into larger kingdoms, such as Northumbria and WESSEX. The term Anglo-Saxon was first used in the late 8th century to distinguish the Saxon settlers in England from the "Old Saxons" of N

Germany and became synonymous with "English". The Anglo-Saxon period of English history ended with the NORMAN CONQUEST (1066).

Angola Republic in SW Africa. Angola is more than twice the size of France. Most of the country, besides a narrow coastal plain in the W, is part of a huge plateau which makes up the interior of S Africa. In the NE, several rivers flow N into the River CONGO. In the S some rivers, including the Cubango (or Okavango) and the Cuanda, flow SE into the interior of Africa. **Climate** Angola has a tropical climate with temperatures of over 20°C (68°F) throughout the year, though the higher areas are cooler. Rainfall is minimal along the coast S of LUANDA, but increases to the N and E. The rainy season is between November and April. **Vegetation** Grassland covers much of Angola. The coastal plain has little vegetation, and the S coast is a desert region that merges into the bleak NAMIB DESERT. Some rainforest grows in N Angola. **History and Politics** Bantu-speaking people from the N settled in Angola c.2,000 years ago. In the later part of the 15th century, Portuguese navigators, seeking a route to Asia around Africa, explored the coast and, in the early 1600s, the Portuguese set up supply bases. Angola became important as a source of slaves for the Portuguese colony of Brazil. After the decline of the slave trade, Portuguese settlers began to develop the land, and the Portuguese population increased dramatically in the early 20th century. In the 1950s, nationalists began to demand independence. In 1956, the Popular Movement for the Liberation of Angola (MPLA) was founded, drawing support from the Mbundu tribe and *mestizos* (people of mixed African and European descent). The MPLA led a revolt in Luanda in 1961, but it was put down by Portuguese troops. Other opposition movements developed among different ethnic groups. In the N, the Kongo set up the FNLA (Front for the Liberation of Angola), and in 1966 southern peoples, including many of the Ovimbundu, formed the National Union for the Total Independence of Angola (UNITA). Portugal granted independence in 1975, but a power struggle developed among rival nationalist forces. The MPLA formed a government, but UNITA troops (supported by South Africa) launched a civil war. After 16 crippling years a peace treaty was signed (1991) and multiparty elections were held in 1992. The MPLA, which had renounced its Marxist ideology, won a resounding victory, but civil strife resumed as UNITA refused to accept the result. In 1994, a new peace accord was signed in Lusaka, which provided for the formation of a government of national unity, composed of both UNITA and MPLA leaders. In April 1997, the new government was inaugurated. DOS SANTOS remained president, but UNITA leader Jonas SAVIMBI rejected the vice presidency. UNITA retained military control of c.50% of Angola. Fighting continued between government and UNITA forces in rebel-held territory. In September 1997 the UN imposed sanctions on UNITA for failing to comply with the 1994 Lusaka Protocol. As attempts to restart the peace process failed, civil war resumed and in 1999 the UN withdrew its peace-keeping force. **Economy** Angola is a poor developing country (US$1,310) with huge economic potential. More than 70% of the workforce is engaged in subsistence agriculture. The main food crops are cassava and maize and coffee is exported. Angola has large oil reserves, near Luanda and in the Cabinda enclave (separated from Angola by a strip of land belonging to Zaïre). Oil is by far the leading export. Angola is a major diamond producer and has reserves of copper, manganese and phosphates. A growing manufacturing sector is based largely on hydroelectric power.

ANGOLA

AREA: 1,246,700sq km (481,351sq mi)
POPULATION: 13,295,000
CAPITAL (POPULATION): Luanda (2,250,000)

Angora *See* ANKARA

Angry Young Men Loose literary and dramatic term, applied to an anti-establishment group of British writers in the 1950s. Taken from Leslie Allen Paul's autobiography *Angry Young Man* (1951), it was popularized through John OSBORNE's play *Look Back in Anger* (1956). The group included Kingsley AMIS, Arnold WESKER and Alan SILLITOE.

angstrom (symbol Å) Obsolete unit of length, equal to 10^{-10}m or 0.1nm (nanometer). It was used to express the wavelength of light and ultraviolet radiation, and to measure interatomic and intermolecular distances.

Anguilla Island in the West Indies, most northerly of the Leeward Islands. Settled in the 17th century by English colonists, it eventually became part of the St. Kitts-Nevis-Anguilla group. Declared independent in 1967, it re-adopted British colonial status in 1980, and is now a self-governing dependency. The economy of the flat, coral island is based on fishing and tourism. Area: 91sq km (35sq mi). Pop. (2000) 8,000.

anhydride Chemical compound derived from another compound by removing water. Thus, sulphur trioxide (SO_3) is the anhydride of sulphuric acid (H_2SO_4)

aniline (phenylamine, $C_6H_5NH_2$) Highly poisonous, colourless liquid made by the reduction of nitrobenzene. It is an important material in organic compounds such as drugs, explosives and dyes. Properties: r.d. 1.02; m.p. $-6.2°C$ (20.8°F); b.p. 184.1°C (363.4°F). *See also* AMINE

animal Living organism of the animal kingdom, usually distinguishable from members of the PLANT kingdom by its power of locomotion (at least during some stage of its existence), a well-defined body shape, limited growth, its feeding exclusively on organic matter, the production of two different kinds of sex cells and the formation of an embryo or larva during the developmental stage. Higher animals, such as the VERTEBRATES, are easily distinguishable from plants, but the distinction becomes blurred with the lower forms. Some one-celled organisms could easily be assigned to either category. Scientists have classified about a million different kinds of animals in more than twenty phyla. The simplest (least highly evolved) animals include the PROTOZOA, SPONGES, JELLYFISH and WORMS. Other invertebrate phyla include ARTHROPODS (arachnids, crustaceans and insects), MOLLUSCS (shellfish, octopus and squid) and ECHINODERMS (sea urchins and starfish). Vertebrates belong to the CHORDATA phylum, which includes fish, amphibians, reptiles, birds and mammals.

animal classification Systematic grouping of animals into categories based on shared characteristics. The first major classification was drawn up by Aristotle. The current method was devised by Carl LINNAEUS. Each animal is given a two-part Latin name (*see* BINOMIAL NOMENCLATURE), the first part indicating its GENUS, the second its SPECIES. The FAMILY takes in all related genera, and an ORDER is made up of all related families. Similar orders are grouped in a CLASS, and related classes make up a PHYLUM. More than twenty phyla comprise the animal kingdom. For example, the dog is classified: phylum Chordata; class Mammalia; order Carnivora; family Canidae; genus *Canis* and species *familiaris*. *See* TAXONOMY

animal rights Freedom of creatures from subjection to pain and distress, especially applied to those animals used in scientific experimentation for human purposes. Experiments using animals decreased considerably during the 1980s but continue particularly in determining the effects of new medicinal preparations and of the long-term use of consumer products. Animal-rights campaigners wish to extend animal rights to include all farm animals kept, transported or slaughtered in conditions perceived to be inhumane. *See also* HUMAN RIGHTS; VIVISECTION

animation Illusion of motion created by projecting successive images of still drawings or objects. Drawn cartoons are the most common form. Each of a series of drawings is photographed singly. The illusion of motion is created when the photographs are displayed in rapid succession. Computer animation programs have advanced to a point where the drawings themselves are no longer a necessity.

animatism Belief that all inanimate objects and natural phenomena (such as stones, trees, water, fire, stars or thunderstorms) possess a life and consciousness but not a spirit (soul). *See also* ANIMISM

animism Belief that within every animal, plant or inanimate object dwells an individual spirit capable of governing its existence and influencing human affairs. Natural objects and phenomena are regarded as possessing life, consciousness and a spirit. In animism, the spirits of dead animals live on and (if the animals have been killed improperly) can inflict harm. These beliefs are widespread among tribal peoples. *See also* ANIMATISM

anion Negative ION attracted to the ANODE during electrolysis.

anise Annual herb native to Egypt and widely cultivated for its small, ridged, licorice-flavoured seeds. It has small white flowers. Height: up to 76cm (2.5ft). Family Apiaceae/Umbelliferae; species *Pimpinella anisum*.

Anjou Region and former province in W France straddling the lower Loire valley. It was ruled by HENRY II of England after his marriage to Eleanor of Aquitaine, and Louis XI annexed it to the French crown in 1480. Known for its wine, it ceased to be a province in 1790.

Ankara Capital of Turkey, at the confluence of the Cubuk and Ankara rivers. In ancient times it was known as Ancyra, and was an important commercial centre as early as the 8th century BC. It was a Roman provincial capital and flourished particularly under AUGUSTUS. TAMERLANE seized the city in 1402. In the late 19th century, it declined in importance until Kemal ATATÜRK set up a provisional government here in 1920. It replaced Istanbul as the capital in 1923. It is noted for its angora wool and mohair products. Pop. (1995) 2,838,000.

Anna Ivanovna (1693–1740) Empress of Russia (1730–40), daughter of Ivan V and niece of PETER I (THE GREAT). Anna was elected to the throne by the supreme privy council. She restored royal authority with the help of the secret police. Anna restricted the power of the Russian nobility to the advantage of German advisers such as her lover, Ernst Biron. Her expansive foreign policy saw the beginnings of Russia's Asian empire. Anna supported AUGUSTUS III in the War of the Polish Succession. She was succeeded by Ivan VI.

Annam Former kingdom on the E coast of INDOCHINA, now in Vietnam; the capital was Hué. The ancient empire fell to China in 214 BC. It regained self-government but was again ruled by China from 939 to 1428. The French obtained missionary and trade agreements in 1787, and a protectorate was established (1883–84). During World War 2 it was occupied by the Japanese; in 1949 it was incorporated into the Republic of Vietnam.

Annan, Kofi (1938–) Ghanaian diplomat, seventh secretary-general of the UN (1997–). He became the first black African secretary-general. In 1993, Annan was elected under secretary-general for peacekeeping, handling the removal of UN troops from Bosnia. His diplomacy helped secure a peaceful resolution (1998) to the weapons-inspection crisis in Iraq.

Annapolis Seaport capital of Maryland, on the S bank of the Severn River on Chesapeake Bay, USA. It was founded by Puritans in 1649. The site of the signing of the peace treaty ending the American Revolution, it has many buildings dating from colonial times. It is also the seat of the US Naval Academy (founded 1845). Industries: boatyards, seafood packing. Pop. (1992) 34,070.

Annapurna Mountain massif in the HIMALAYAS, in N central Nepal, notoriously dangerous to climbers. It has two of the world's highest peaks: Annapurna I in the N rises to 8,078m (26,504ft); Annapurna II in the E rises to 7,937m (26,041ft). It was first climbed in 1950.

Anne (1665–1714) Queen of Great Britain and Ireland (1702–14), second daughter of JAMES II. Anne succeeded WILLIAM III as the last STUART sovereign and, after the Act of UNION (1707), the first monarch of the United Kingdom of England and Scotland. Brought up a Protestant, she married Prince George of Denmark (1683). Despite 18 pregnancies, no child survived her. The War of the SPANISH SUCCESSION (1701–14) dominated her reign and is often called Queen Anne's War. Anne was the last English monarch to exercise the royal veto over legislation (1707), but the rise of parliamentary government was inexorable. The JACOBITE cause was crushed when Anne was succeeded by GEORGE I. The most lasting aspect of her reign was the strength of contemporary arts and culture.

annealing Slow heating and cooling of a metal, alloy or glass to relieve internal stresses and make up dislocations or vacancies introduced during mechanical shaping, such as rolling or extruding (ejection). Annealing increases the material's workability and durability. *See also* TEMPERING

Anne Boleyn *See* BOLEYN, ANNE

annelid Member of the Annelida phylum of segmented WORMS. It has encircling grooves usually corresponding to internal partitions of the body. A digestive tube, nerves and blood vessels run through the entire body, but each segment has a set of internal organs. Annelids form an important part of the diets of many animals. The three main classes are: **Oligochaeta**, freshwater or terrestrial worms; **Polychaeta**, marine worms; and **Hirudinea**, LEECHES.

Anne of Austria (1601–66) Daughter of Philip III of Spain, wife of LOUIS XIII of France and mother of LOUIS XIV. Her husband died in 1643, and she ruled France as regent in close alliance with Cardinal MAZARIN until her death.

Anne of Cleves (1515–57) Fourth wife of HENRY VIII of England. Her marriage (1540) was a political alliance joining Henry with the German Protestants, but it was never consummated, being declared null after only six months. Anne received a pension, and remained in England until her death. *See also* CROMWELL, THOMAS

Anne, Princess (1950–) Daughter of ELIZABETH II. She was married (1973–92) to Captain Mark Phillips (1948–) with whom she had two children, Peter Mark Andrew (1977–) and Zara Anne Elizabeth (1981–). In 1992 Anne married commander Timothy Laurence (1955–). Anne was a skilled horsewoman and represented Britian at the 1976 Montréal Olympics. In 1987, she was created Princess Royal. Anne has campaigned for many charities, most notably the Save the Children Fund.

annual Plant that completes its life cycle in one growing season, such as the sweet pea or sunflower. Annual plants overwinter as seeds. *See also* BIENNIAL; PERENNIAL

annual ring (growth ring) Concentric circles visible in cross-sections of woody stems or trunks. Each year the CAMBIUM layer produces a layer of XYLEM, the vessels of which are large and thin-walled in the spring and

smaller and thick-walled in the summer, creating the contrast between the rings. Used to determine the age of trees, the thickness of these rings also reveals environmental conditions during a tree's lifetime.

Annunciation Announcement made to the Virgin Mary by the Angel GABRIEL that she was to be the mother of Christ (Luke 1). In many Christian churches the Feast of the Annunciation is kept on 25 March, a date often called "Lady Day". The Annunciation was a common subject for painters during medieval and Renaissance times.

anode Positive electrode of an electrolytic cell that attracts ANIONS during electrolysis. *See also* ELECTROLYSIS

anodizing Electrolytic process to coat ALUMINIUM or MAGNESIUM with a thin layer of oxide to help prevent CORROSION. The process makes the metal the ANODE in an acid solution. The protective coating, steamed to seal the pores, is insoluble and a good insulator. It can also be dyed bright colours.

anorexia nervosa Abnormal loss of the desire to eat. The condition is seen mainly in young women. Anorexia nervosa can result in severe emaciation and in rare cases can be life-threatening. *See also* BULIMIA NERVOSA

Anouilh, Jean (1910–87) French dramatist and screenwriter. A major dramatist of the mid-20th century, Anouilh was influenced by neoclassicism and often reinterpreted Greek myth as a means of exploring oppression. *Antigone* (1944) is perhaps his most celebrated play. His major theme is the contrast between innocence and bitter experience. Other works include *Becket* (1959).

anoxia Deficiency of oxygen in the tissues. It can occur at high altitudes or as a result of underlying disease (such as lung or heart malfunction) or toxic agents. Symptoms include troubled breathing, rapid pulse and cyanosis.

Anschluss Unification of Austria and Germany in 1938. Prohibited by treaty at the end of World War 1, to limit the strength of Germany, Anschluss was nevertheless favoured by many Germans and Austrians. Unification took place through a show of force under Adolf HITLER. It was dissolved by the Allies in 1945.

Anselm of Canterbury, Saint (1033–1109) English theologian, b. Italy. Anselm was an early scholastic philosopher and became Archbishop of Canterbury in 1093. His belief in the rational character of Christian belief led him to propose an ontological argument for the existence of God. His feast day is 21 April. *See also* ONTOLOGY; SCHOLASTICISM

ant Social insect belonging to a family that also includes the BEE and WASP. A typical ant colony consists of one or more queens (fertile females), workers (sterile females) and winged males. Some species also have a caste of soldier ants which guard the colony. Females develop from fertilized eggs, males from unfertilized eggs. Nutrition determines whether a female becomes a queen or worker. First generation larvae are fed entirely by the queen's saliva. Most ants are wingless except at times of dispersal. Mating takes place in flight, after which the male dies. The queen proceeds to lay eggs for the remainder of her life (up to 15 years). Ants range in length from 2–25mm (0.08–1.0in) and are found worldwide except Antarctica. They typically feed on plants, nectar and other insects. Family Formicidae.

antabuse Proprietary name for disulphide, a drug sometimes used in the treatment of alcoholism. It produces unpleasant effects, in particular vomiting, when taken in conjunction with alcohol.

Antakya (formerly Antioch, now also Hatay) City in S Turkey on the River Orontes and capital of Hatay province. Founded in *c*.300 BC by SELEUCUS I, it earned the title "queen of the east". It was taken by POMPEY (64 BC). The modern city occupies only a small part of the ancient Roman site. Products: olives, tobacco, cotton, cereals. Pop. (1990) 118,433.

Antananarivo (Tananarive) Capital and largest city of Madagascar. Founded *c*.1625, Antananarivo became the residence for Imerina rulers in 1794 and the capital of Madagascar. The city was captured by the French in 1895 and became part of a French protectorate. A trade centre for a rice-producing region, it has textile, tobacco and leather industries. Pop. (1990) 802,000.

Antarctica Fifth-largest continent (larger than Europe or Australasia), covering almost 10% of the world's total land area. Surrounding the SOUTH POLE, it is bordered by the Antarctic Ocean and the S sections of the Atlantic, Pacific and Indian oceans. Almost entirely within the ANTARCTIC CIRCLE, it is of great strategic and scientific interest. No people live here permanently, although scientists frequently stay for short periods to conduct research and exploration. Seven nations lay claim to sectors of it. Covered by an ice sheet with an average thickness of *c*.5,900ft (1,800m), it contains *c*.90% of the world's ice and more than 70% of its fresh water. **Land** Resembling an open fan, with the Antarctic Peninsula as a handle, the continent is a snowy desert covering *c*.14.2 million sq km (5.5 million sq mi). Over 95% of Antarctica remains covered in ice throughout the year. The land is a high plateau, having an average elevation of 1,800m (6,000ft) and rising to 5,140m (16,863ft) in the Vinson Massif. Mountain ranges occur near the coasts. The interior, or South Polar Plateau, lies beneath *c*.2,000m (6,500ft) of snow, accumulated over tens of thousands of years. Mineral deposits exist in the mountains, but their recovery has not become practicable. Coal may be plentiful, but the value of known deposits of copper, nickel, gold and iron will not repay the expenses of extracting and exporting them. **Seas and glaciers** Ross Sea and Wendell Sea form the two major coastlines. Antarctic rivers are frozen, inching towards the sea, and instead of lakes there are large bodies of ice along the coasts. The great Beardmore Glacier creeps down from the South Polar Plateau, and eventually becomes part of the Ross Ice Shelf. **Climate and vegetation** Antarctica remains cold all year, with only a few coastal areas being free from snow or ice in summer (December to February). The interior is the coldest place on Earth, with temperatures as low as −90°C (−130°F). Precipitation generally amounts to 17.5–38cm (7–15in) of snow a year, but melting is less than that, allowing a build-up over the centuries. The severity of the climate makes it inhospitable for most life forms, except nematode worms, and

some mosses and plants along the outer rim of the continent. The krill-rich waters of the Antarctic Ocean attract whales, seals and penguins. **History** Antarctic islands were first sighted first in the 18th century and Captain COOK was the first to cross the Antarctic Circle (1772–75). In 1820, Nathaniel Palmer reached the Antarctic Peninsula. Between 1838 and 1840, Charles WILKES discovered enough of the coast to prove that a continent existed, and the English explorer James Clark Ross made coastal maps. In the early 19th century, humans were attracted by the commerical value of seal fur. In the 1890s, Antarctica became the centre of the whaling industry and the focus of many scientific studies. Toward the end of the 19th century, exploration reached inland developing into a race for the South Pole. Roald AMUNDSEN reached the Pole on 14 December, 1911, a month before Robert Falcon SCOTT. The aeroplane brought a new era of exploration, and Richard E. BYRD became the best known of the airborne polar explorers. The Antarctic Treaty (1959), which pledged international scientific cooperation, was renewed and extended in 1991, banning commercial exploitation of the continent.

Antarctic Circle Southernmost of the Earth's parallels, 66.5° s of the equator. At this latitude the sun neither sets on the day of summer SOLSTICE (22 December) nor rises on the winter solstice (21 June). *See also* ARCTIC CIRCLE

Antares (Alpha Scorpii) Bright, supergiant BINARY STAR. Its luminosity and distance are not well determined.

anteater Toothless, mainly nocturnal, insect-eating mammal that lives in swamps and savannahs of tropical America. It has a long, sticky tongue and powerful claws. Length: up to 152cm (60in). Family Myrmecophagidae. *See also* EDENTATE

antelope Hollow-horned, speedy RUMINANT found throughout the Old World, except in Madagascar, Malaya and Australasia; most antelopes are found in Africa. They range in size from that of a rabbit to that of an ox. In some species both sexes bear horns of varied shapes and sizes; in others, only the males are horned. Family Bovidae.

antenna In biology, a long sensory organ (usually of touch and smell) on the heads of insects and most other arthropods. Insects have a single pair of antennae, crustaceans generally two pairs. *See also* ARTHROPOD

anthem Choral composition in Anglican and other English-language church services analogous to the Roman Catholic MOTET in Latin. Developed in the 16th century as a verse anthem with soloists, the anthem was later performed with orchestral accompaniment and by a choir without soloists. Composers of anthems include Henry PURCELL and Ralph VAUGHAN WILLIAMS.

anther In botany, the fertile part of a male sex organ in a flower. The anther produces and distributes pollen and, together with its connecting filament, forms a STAMEN.

Anthony, Saint (*c*.250–*c*.355) Egyptian saint and first Christian monk. He withdrew into complete solitude at the age of 20 to practise ascetic devotion. By the time of St Anthony's death, Christian MONASTICISM was well established. His feast day is 17 January.

Anthony, Susan Brownell (1820–1906) US reformer and woman suffragist. She organized the first woman's TEMPERANCE association and, with Elizabeth Cady STANTON, co-founded the National Woman Suffrage Association (1869). It later became (1890) the National American Woman Suffrage Association, and she acted as president (1892–1900). *See also* SUFFRAGETTE MOVEMENT

anthracite Form of COAL consisting of more than 90% CARBON, relatively hard, black and with a metallic lustre. It burns with the hot, pale-blue flame of complete

▲ **anteater** The giant anteater (*Myrmecophaga tridactyla*) is found in South America, particularly in the swampy regions of the Chaco in Argentina. It uses its powerful claws to rip open termite mounds before scooping up the termites with its long sticky tongue.

combustion. It is the final form in the series of fuels: PEAT, lignite, bituminous COAL and black coal.

anthrax Contagious disease, chiefly of livestock, caused by the microbe *Bacillus anthracis*. Human beings can catch anthrax from contact with infected animals or hides.

Anthropoidea Suborder of PRIMATES including monkeys, apes and human beings. Anthropoids have flatter, more human-like faces, larger brains and are larger in size than prosimian primates.

anthropology Scientific study of human development and how different societies are interrelated. It is concerned with the chronological and geographical range of human societies. Modern anthropology stems from the first half of the 19th century. Public interest in cultural EVOLUTION followed the publication of *On the Origin of Species* by Charles DARWIN (1859). **Physical** anthropologists are concerned with the history of human evolution in its biological sense. **Social** anthropologists study living societies in order to learn about cultural and social evolution. **Applied** anthropology is the specific study of a particular community and its collective and individual relationships. *See also* ETHNOGRAPHY; ETHNOLOGY

antibiotic Substance that is capable of stopping the growth of (or destroying) BACTERIA and other microorganisms. Many antibiotics are themselves produced by microorganisms. Antibiotics are GERMICIDES that are safe enough to be eaten or injected into the body. The post-1945 introduction of antibiotics has revolutionized medical science, making possible the virtual elimination of once widespread and often fatal diseases, including TYPHOID FEVER, PLAGUE and CHOLERA. Some antibiotics are **selective**; that is, effective against specific microorganisms; those effective against a large number of microorganisms are known as **broad-spectrum** antibiotics. Some important antibiotics are PENICILLIN, the first widely used antibiotic, streptomycin and the tetracyclines. Some bacteria have developed ANTIBIOTIC RESISTANCE. *See also* ANTISEPTIC

antibiotic resistance Resistance to antibiotic drugs acquired by many BACTERIA and other PATHOGENS. Because they survive while non-resistant strains are killed, they pass their resistance to their progeny, and resistance increases in the population. Some bacteria have the ability to pass the genes for antibiotic resistance to other organisms of different species on plasmids (small lengths of DNA). Spread of resistance is accelerated by routine prescription of antibiotics to humans and unregulated application to farm animals for the purpose of disease prevention rather than cure. An inadequate dose or failure to complete a course of antibiotics increases the chances of resistant microorganisms surviving to breed. This may lead to the return of epidemics of untreatable infectious diseases.

antibody PROTEIN synthesized in the BLOOD in response to the entry of "foreign" substances or organisms into the body. Each episode of bacterial or viral infection prompts the production of a specific antibody to fight the disease in question. After the infection has cleared, the antibody remains in the blood to fight off any future invasion.

Antichrist Term loosely referring to the supreme enemy of Christ. Martin LUTHER and other REFORMATION leaders applied it to the PAPACY.

anticline Arch-shaped fold in rock strata. Unless the formation has been overturned, the oldest rocks are found in the centre with younger rocks symmetrically on each side.

anticoagulant Substance that prevents or counteracts coagulation, or clotting. Anticoagulants are used to treat diseases caused by blood clots, such as THROMBOSIS. Heparin is a common blood anticoagulant.

Anti-Corn Law League Organization formed (1839) in Manchester, England, to agitate for the removal of import duties on grain. It was led by the Radical members of Parliament, Richard COBDEN and John BRIGHT. By holding mass meetings, distributing pamphlets and contesting elections, it helped bring about the repeal of the CORN LAWS in 1846.

anticyclone Area of high atmospheric pressure around which air circulates. The circulation is clockwise in the Northern Hemisphere and anti-clockwise in the Southern Hemisphere. Anticyclones are often associated with settled weather conditions. In middle latitudes, they bring periods of hot, dry weather in summer and cold, often foggy, weather in winter.

antidepressant *See* DRUG

Antietam, Battle of (17 September, 1862) American CIVIL WAR battle fought around Sharpsburg, Maryland. General George MCCLELLAN's Army of the Potomac made a series of assaults on the Confederates of General Robert E. LEE. Casualties were very heavy. McClellan's losses, *c.*12,000, were slightly greater, but Lee was forced to retreat to Virginia.

antifreeze Substance dissolved in a liquid to lower its freezing point. Ethylene glycol (HOC_2H_4OH) is commonly used in car radiators.

antigen Any substance or organism that induces the production of an ANTIBODY, part of the body's defence mechanism against disease. The antibody reacts specifically with the antigen.

Antigone In Greek mythology, daughter of OEDIPUS and Jocasta, she accompanied her father through his exile until his death. She failed to prevent her brothers Polynices and Eteocles from killing each other in battle. In defiance of King Creon, Antigone buried Polynices and hanged herself rather than face the punishment of being buried alive. The tragedy *Antigone* (*c.*441 BC) by SOPHOCLES is based on the legend.

Antigonus I (382–301 BC) General of ALEXANDER THE GREAT. Antigonus became governor of Phrygia in 333 BC and, in the struggles over the regency, he defeated challengers to gain control of Mesopotamia, Syria and Asia Minor. At Salamis in 306 BC he defeated his former ally, Ptolemy I, but was himself killed at Ipsus.

Antigua and Barbuda Caribbean islands in the LEEWARD ISLANDS group, part of the Lesser ANTILLES. The capital is St John's (on Antigua). **Antigua** is atypical of the Leeward Islands in that it has no rivers or forests; **Barbuda**, by contrast, is a well-wooded, coral atoll. Only 1,400 people live on the game reserve island of Barbuda, where lobster fishing is the main occupation, and none on the rocky island of Redondo. Antigua and Barbuda were linked by Britain after 1860, and gained internal self-government in 1967 and independence in 1981. Both islands rely heavily on tourism, though some attempts at diversification (notably Sea Island cotton) have been successful. Other industries: livestock rearing, market gardening, fishing. Area: 440sq km (170sq mi). Pop. (2000) 79,000.

antihistamine Any one of certain drugs that counteracts or otherwise prevents the effects of HISTAMINE, a natural substance released by the body in response to injury or more often as part of an allergic reaction. Antihistamines are also used to prevent motion sickness. Drowsiness is a common side-effect, and anti-histamines are also prescribed as sedatives. *See also* HAY FEVER

Antilles Collective name for two major island groups in the West Indies archipelago, between the Atlantic Ocean and the Caribbean Sea, stretching in an arc from Puerto Rico to the N coast of Venezuela. The **Greater Antilles** (larger of the two groups) includes CUBA, HISPANIOLA, JAMAICA, PUERTO RICO and the CAYMAN ISLANDS. The **Lesser Antilles** comprises the British VIRGIN ISLANDS, the US VIRGIN ISLANDS, the LEEWARD ISLANDS and WINDWARD ISLANDS, plus small islands off Venezuela.

antimatter MATTER made up of antiparticles, identical to ordinary particles in every way except the charge, SPIN and magnetic moment are reversed. When an antiparticle, such as a POSITRON (anti-electron), antiproton or antineutron meets its respective particle, both are annihilated. Since a PHOTON is its own antiparticle, the possibility exists that there are stars or galaxies composed entirely of antimatter. *See also* ELEMENTARY PARTICLES; SUBATOMIC PARTICLES

antimony (symbol Sb) Toxic, semimetallic element of Group V of the periodic table. Stibnite (a sulphide) is its commonest ore. It is used in some alloys, particularly in hardening lead for batteries and type metal, and in semiconductors. The element has two allotropes: a silvery white metallic and an amorphous grey form. Properties: at.no. 51; r.a.m. 121.75; r.d. 6.68; m.p. 630.5°C (1,166.9°F); b.p. 1,750°C (3,182°F); most common isotope Sb^{121} (57.25%).

antiknock *See* KNOCK, ENGINE

Antioch *See* ANTAKYA

Antiochus III (242–187 BC) King of Syria (223–187 BC), son of SELEUCUS II. After his defeat at Rafa (217 BC) by Ptolemy IV, he invaded Egypt (212–202 BC), seizing land from Ptolemy V with the help of Philip V of Macedon. He recaptured Palestine, Asia Minor and the Thracian Cheronese. The Romans overwhelmed him at Thermopylae (191 BC) and at Magnesia (190 BC). The rebuilt Seleucid empire shrank when he gave up all possessions W of the Taurus. Seleucus IV succeeded him.

antioxidant Chemical additive designed to reduce OXIDATION. Antioxidants are used to prevent fatty foods becoming rancid, deterioration of rubber, formation of gums in petrol, etc. Most are organic AMINES and PHENOLS, functioning by terminating the free-radical chain reaction causing oxidation. Sulphur dioxide and ascorbic acid are often used as antioxidants for foodstuffs.

antiparticle *See* ANTIMATTER

antiphon Alternate short verses or phrases (usually of a PSALM or canticle) sung by two spatially separated halves of a choir (designated *decani* and *cantoris*). More generally, antiphon refers to a short piece of PLAINSONG. The text of the antiphon usually serves to reinforce a psalm's meaning or Christian significance.

antipope Name given to rivals of legitimately elected popes, generally "appointed" by unauthorized religious factions. The first was HIPPOLYTUS (AD 217–35), a Trinitarian heretic and rival of Calixtus I. The most famous were the AVIGNON popes, who rivalled those of ROME during the GREAT SCHISM (1378–1417). *See also* PAPACY

anti-Semitism Discrimination against or persecution of JEWS. Although anti-Semitism predates Christianity, the most organized and persistent persecution of Jews has been by European Christians. The destruction of Jerusalem (AD 70) led to the DIASPORA, and Jews settled throughout Europe and the Roman Empire. In the 4th century Christianity became the official religion of the Empire, and many Jews were forced to convert. In the late Middle Ages, religious pretexts formed the basis of social and economic discrimination. Legislation prevented Jews from owning land, and they were restricted to occupations forbidden by the Christian church, such

as usury (moneylending). The INQUISITION was an organized form of persecution supported by the papacy. The Enlightenment period saw the extension of rights to European Jews. However, the growth of nationalism and the racist ideas of social Darwinism in the 19th century led to the explicit persecution of Jews as a race rather than as followers of JUDAISM. ZIONISM was born as a reaction to this persecution. In the 1880s, POGROMS in Russia and Poland led to the emigration of millions of Jews to other parts of Europe, the USA and Palestine. The DREYFUS AFFAIR (1894) was the most public example of French anti-Semitism. FASCISM encouraged these racist ideas, which found their most virulent expression in NATIONAL SOCIALISM. Anti-Semitism was a central part of the racist ideology of Nazi Germany – about six million Jews died in the HOLOCAUST (1933–45). After World War 2, anti-Semitism persisted, especially in Stalin's Soviet Union. The growth of right-wing nationalism has seen the re-emergence of anti-Semitism in Western Europe.

antiseptic Chemicals that destroy or stop the growth of many microorganisms. Antiseptics are weak germicides that can be used on the skin. The English surgeon Joseph LISTER pioneered the use of antiseptics in 1867. One commonly used is ALCOHOL. *See also* ANTIBIOTIC

antitoxin ANTIBODY produced by the body in response to a TOXIN. It is specific in action and neutralizes the toxin. Antitoxin sera are used to treat and prevent bacterial diseases such as TETANUS and DIPHTHERIA.

antler Bony outgrowth on the skulls of male DEER (and female REINDEER). In temperate-zone species, antlers begin to grow in early summer. They are soft, well supplied with blood and covered with thin, velvety skin. Later, the blood recedes and the dried skin is rubbed off. Antlers then serve as sexual ornaments and weapons until they are shed the following spring.

ant lion LARVA of the neuropteran family Myrmeleontidea, found in most parts of the world. Carnivorous, with large, sickle-shaped jaws, it digs a pit in dry sand where it lies waiting for ants and other insects to fall in. *See also* LACEWING

Antofagasta Seaport and rail centre on the coast of N Chile and the capital of Antofagasta province. Built in 1870 to provide port facilities for the nitrate and copper deposits in the ATACAMA DESERT, it has both ore refining and concentrating plants. The Chuquicamata open-cast copper mine, 135mi (220km) to the NE, is the world's largest. Pop. (1992) 226,749.

Antonello da Messina (1430–79) Sicilian artist. A pioneer of oil painting in Italy, Antonello spent much of his working life in Milan, Naples, Venice and Rome. He probably learned the oil technique in Naples, a centre for Dutch artists. His work married Netherlandish taste for detail with Italian clarity. Apart from religious paintings, such as *Salvator Mundi* (1465) and *Ecce Homo* (1470), he produced some remarkable male portraits. His knowledge of oil glazes had a great influence on Venetian painters, notably Giovanni BELLINI.

Antonescu, Ion (1882–1946) Romanian general and fascist dictator. In 1938 he was imprisoned by King CAROL II for leading an unsuccessful fascist coup. In September 1940, in the face of German aggression, Carol appointed Antonescu premier. Carol was forced to abdicate in favour of his son Michael, and Antonescu assumed dictatorial powers. Romania joined the Axis Powers and helped in the fated invasion of the Soviet Union. At home, Antonescu unleashed pogroms against Romanian Jews. The Red Army invasion of Romania led to his arrest. Antonescu was executed for war crimes.

Antonine Wall Defensive fortification built (c.AD 142) between the firths of Forth and Clyde, the narrowest part (59km/37mi-wide) of central Scotland. The wall was constructed by the Roman emperor Antoninus Pius to mark the N end of the Roman province of Britain. *See also* HADRIAN'S WALL

Antonioni, Michelangelo (1912–) Italian film director. He was a founder of Italian NEO-REALISM. Antonioni's debut was *Cronaca di un amore* (1950). *L'Avventura* (1959) brought international recognition. Antonioni's principal theme is alienation and voyeuristic eroticism. Plot is often subordinate to visual imagery and character development. Other films include *The Red Desert* (1964), *Blow-Up* (1966) and *The Passenger* (1975).

Antony, Mark (82–30 BC) (Marcus Antonius) Roman general and statesman. He fought with distinction in Julius CAESAR's campaign (54–50 BC) in Gaul. In 49 BC Antony became tribune. Civil war broke out between POMPEY and Caesar, and after the decisive Battle of Pharsalus, Antony was made consul. After Caesar's assassination (44 BC), he inspired the mob to drive the conspirators, BRUTUS and CASSIUS, from Rome. Octavian (later AUGUSTUS) emerged as Antony's main rival. Octavian and Brutus joined forces and Antony retreated to Transalpine Gaul. He sued for peace. Antony, Octavian and Lepidus formed the Second Triumverate, which divided up the ROMAN EMPIRE: Antony received Asia. He and CLEOPATRA, queen of Egypt, became lovers. In 40 BC Antony married Octavian's sister Octavia but continued to live with Cleopatra in Alexandria and became isolated from Rome. In 32 BC, the senate deprived Antony of his posts. He was defeated at the Battle of ACTIUM (31 BC). Antony and Cleopatra committed suicide.

Antrim County in Northern Ireland, bounded N by the Atlantic Ocean and NE and E by the North Channel. The capital is BELFAST; other notable centres are Ballymena, Antrim (on the N shore of Lough Neagh) and Larne. Mainly a low basalt plateau, it is noted for the GIANT'S CAUSEWAY. It is chiefly an agricultural region. Industries: linen and shipbuilding, concentrated in Belfast. Area: 3,043sq km (1,175sq mi). Pop. (1991) 665,013.

Antwerp (Flemish *Antwerpen* Fr. *Anvers*) Port city on the River Scheldt, capital of Antwerp province and Belgium's second-largest city. Antwerp rose to prominence in the 15th century and became a centre for English mercantile interests. It was the site of Europe's first stock exchange (1460). Although heavily bombed during World War 2, it retains many attractive old, narrow streets and fine buildings. Industries: oil refining, food processing, tobacco, diamond cutting. Pop. (1996 est.) 456,000.

Anubis In Egyptian mythology, a jackal-headed god. Son of Nephthys and OSIRIS, he conducted the souls of the dead to the underworld and presided over mummification and funerals. Anubis accompanied Osiris on his world conquest and buried him after his murder.

anus Opening at the end of the alimentary canal through which waste material and undigested food are passed from the body in the form of faeces. *See also* DIGESTIVE SYSTEM

anxiety In clinical psychology and psychiatry, state of EMOTION similar to fear and involving apprehension and dread, but not associated with any specific event or stimulus. Chronic anxiety is considered to be one of the primary symptoms of NEUROSIS.

ANZAC (acronym for Australian and New Zealand Army Corps) Volunteer force of 30,000 men that spearheaded the disastrous GALLIPOLI CAMPAIGN in World War 1. Troops landed at GALLIPOLI on 25 April, 1915. Anzac Day (25 April) is a public holiday in Australia and New Zealand. About 8,500 Anzac troops were killed during World War 1.

ANZUS Pact (Australia-New Zealand-United States Treaty Organization) Military alliance organized by the US in 1951. ANZUS was set up in response to waning British power, the Korean War, and alarm at increasing Soviet influence in the Pacific. The treaty stated that an attack on any one of the three countries would be considered as an attack on them all. It was replaced in 1954 by the SOUTHEAST ASIA TREATY ORGANIZATION (SEATO).

aorta Principal ARTERY in the body. Carrying freshly oxygenated blood, the aorta leaves the left ventricle of the heart and descends the length of the trunk, finally dividing to form the two main arteries that serve the legs. *See also* CIRCULATORY SYSTEM; HEART

Apache ATHABASCAN-speaking tribe of Native North Americans that live in Arizona, New Mexico and Colorado. Divided culturally into Eastern Apache (including Mescalero and Kiowa) and Western Apache (including Coyotero and Tonto), they migrated from the NW with the NAVAJO in c.AD 1000 but separated to form a distinct tribal group. They retained their earlier nomadic raiding customs, which brought them into conflict with Mexico and the US during the 19th century. Today, they number c.11,000. *See also* COCHISE; GERONIMO

apartheid Policy of racial segregation practised by the South African government from 1948 to 1990. Racial inequality and restricted rights for non-whites was institutionalized when the AFRIKANER-dominated National Party came to power in 1948. Officially a framework for "separate development" of races, in practice apartheid confirmed white-minority rule. It was based on segregation in all aspects of life, including residence, land ownership and education. Non-whites, around 80% of the population, were also given separate political structures, quasi-autonomous homelands or bantustans. The system was underpinned by extensive repression and measures, such as pass laws, which severely restricted the movements of non-whites. Increasingly isolated internationally and beset by economic difficulties and domestic unrest, the government pledged to dismantle the system in 1990. The transition to nonracial democracy was completed with the elections in April 1994. *See also* AFRICAN NATIONAL CONGRESS (ANC)

apatite Phosphate mineral, usually found as calcium phosphate associated with hydroxyl, chloride or fluoride ions. It occurs in IGNEOUS ROCK and sedimentary deposits as prismatic or tabular hexagonal crystals, as granular aggregates, or in massive crusts. It is usually too soft for cutting and polishing, but there are two gem varieties. Hardness: 5; r.d. 3.1–3.4.

ape Term usually applied to the anthropoid apes (PRIMATES) that are the closest relatives of humans. There are three great apes – CHIMPANZEE, GORILLA and ORANGUTAN – and one lesser, the GIBBON. An ape differs from a MONKEY in being larger, having no visible tail and in possessing a more complex brain. Two MONKEYS are also called "apes" – the BARBARY APE of N Africa and Gibraltar and the black ape of Celebes.

Apennines (Appennino) Mountain range extending the length of Italy, a continuation of the Pennine ALPS. The Apennines form the "backbone" of Italy, stretching c.1,350km (840mi) from the Genoese Riviera to the tip of the country's "toe". Unselective deforestation over the years has caused deep erosion and landslides. Sheep and goats are grazed on its slopes. The highest point is Mount Corno, at 2,914m (9,560ft). *See also* VESUVIUS

aperture In PHOTOGRAPHY, a hole that allows light to pass through the lens onto the film. Modern CAMERAS usually have a diaphragm aperture which works like the iris of a human eye. The photographer can widen or narrow the diaphragm according to a series of points on the lens dial called "f-numbers" or "f-stops". The individual f-numbers represent the focal length of the lens divided by the diameter of the aperture. As the aperture narrows, it gives a greater depth of field.

aphasia Group of disorders of language arising from disease of, or damage to, the brain. In aphasia, a person has problems formulating or comprehending speech and difficulty in reading and writing. *See also* BRAIN DISORDER

aphid (plant LOUSE) Winged or wingless, soft-bodied insect found worldwide. It transmits viral diseases of plants when sucking plant juices. Females reproduce with or without mating, producing one to several generations annually. Common species are also known as blackfly and greenfly. Length: to 5mm (0.2in). Family Aphididae.

Aphrodite Greek goddess of love, beauty and fruitfulness, identified by the Romans as VENUS. She was the daughter of ZEUS and Dione. Her husband was HEPHAESTUS (in Roman mythology, VULCAN). Among her many lovers were ARES, ADONIS and Anchises, the father of AENEAS. Statues of her include the Venus de Milo (Paris) and Aphrodite of Cnidus (Rome).

Apia Capital and chief port of WESTERN SAMOA, on Upolu Island in the SW central Pacific Ocean. Robert Louis Stevenson spent his last years here. Products: coconuts, cacao, bananas, coffee. Pop. (1986) 32,200.

Apis Greek name for the ancient Egyptian sacred bull *Hap*, worshiped at ancient MEMPHIS. The bull was sacred to OSIRIS, believed to be his incarnation, and was mummified upon its death.

Apocrypha Certain books included in the Bible as an appendix to the OLD TESTAMENT in the SEPTUAGINT and in St Jerome's VULGATE translation but not forming part of the Hebrew canon. Nine books are accepted as canonical by the Roman Catholic Church. They are: Tobit, Judith, Wisdom, Ecclesiasticus, Baruch (including the Letter to Jeremiah), 1 and 2 Maccabees and parts of Esther and Daniel. Other books are found in Eastern Orthodox Bibles and in the appendix to the Roman Catholic Old Testament.

Apollinaire, Guillaume (1880–1918) (Wilhelm Apollinaris de Kostrowitzky) French experimental poet, essayist and dramatist. One of the most extraordinary artists of early 20th-century Paris, Apollinaire's *Peintres Cubistes* (1913) was the first attempt to define CUBISM. He also experimented with typography in his poetry collection *Calligrams* (1918). His masterpiece was the wholly unpunctuated *Alcools* (1913), in which he relived the wild romances of his youth.

Apollo In Greek mythology, god of the Sun, archery and prophecy; patron of musicians, poets and physicians; founder of cities; and giver of laws. He was the son of ZEUS and Leto, twin to ARTEMIS. In the TROJAN WAR he sided with Troy, sending a plague against the Greeks.

Apollonius of Perga (*c*.262–190 BC) Greek mathematician and astronomer. He built on the foundations laid by EUCLID. In *Conics*, he showed that an ELLIPSE, a PARABOLA and a HYPERBOLA can be obtained by taking plane sections at different angles through a cone. In astronomy, he described the motion of the planets in terms of epicycles which remained the basis of the system used until the time of COPERNICUS.

Apollo program US SPACE EXPLORATION project to land men on the Moon. Initiated in May 1961 by President John Kennedy, it achieved its objective on 20 July, 1969, when Neil ARMSTRONG set foot on the Moon. The programme terminated with the successful **Apollo-Soyuz** linkup in space during July 1975. It placed more than 30 astronauts in space and 12 on the Moon.

Apostle Missionary sent out and empowered by divine authority to preach the gospel and heal the sick. Jesus commissioned his 12 original DISCIPLES to carry out the purpose of God for man's salvation (Mark 3, Matthew 10, Luke 6). The first qualification for being an Apostle was to have "seen the Lord". The 12 disciples thus became the first and original Apostles. The term is also applied in the New Testament to St PAUL. In modern usage, it is sometimes given to the leader of the first Christian mission to a country. For example, St PATRICK is described as the "Apostle of Ireland".

Apostles' Creed Statement of Christian faith. The last section affirms the tradition of the "holy Catholic Church; the communion of saints; the forgiveness of sins; the resurrection of the body; and the life everlasting". The text evolved gradually, and its present form was fixed by the early 7th century. It is used widely in private and public worship in all the major churches in the West. *See also* NICENE CREED

Appalachians Mountain system stretching 2,570km (1,600mi) from E Canada to Alabama. Comprising a series of parallel ridges divided by wide valleys, the mountains restricted early European settlers to the E coast. It includes the White Mountains, Green Mountains, Catskills, Alleghenies, Great Smoky, Blue Ridge and Cumberland mountains; the highest point is Mount Mitchell, North Carolina, at 2,037m (6,684ft). Rich in timber and coal, they are home to many national parks.

appeasement Policy in which one government grants unilateral concessions to another to forestall a political, economic or military threat. The 1938 MUNICH AGREEMENT is considered a classic example of appeasement.

Appel, Karel (1921–) Dutch painter, sculptor and muralist. In the 1940s, Appel was one of several painters who reacted against the strict formalism of De STIJL and invented a wildly expressionist language of his own, similar to ABSTRACT EXPRESSIONISM. His most powerful work, often portraying fantastic, aggressive and tragic figures, anticipated *Art Informel*.

appendicitis Inflammation of the APPENDIX caused by obstruction and infection. Symptoms include severe pain in the central abdomen, nausea and vomiting. Acute appendicitis is generally treated by surgery. A ruptured appendix can cause peritonitis and even death.

appendix In some mammals, finger-shaped organ, *c*.10cm (4in) long, located near the junction of the small and large intestines, usually in the lower right part of the abdomen. It has no known function in humans but can become inflamed or infected (APPENDICITIS).

Appert, Nicolas (1752–1841) French inventor of the food preservation method of CANNING. In 1810, Appert, a hotel chef, won a prize from the French government

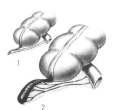

◀ **appendicitis** In appendicitis, the tissues lining the appendix become infected and inflamed, which causes the organ to swell (1) and its vascularization to increase (2). Surgical removal is carried out to prevent the appendix bursting.

for his discovery of the preservation of cooked foods in airtight jars. He also invented the bouillon (stock cube).

Appia, Adolphe (1862–1928) Swiss theorist of modern stage and theatre lighting design. Appia worked on very few productions, but revolutionized stage effects through his writing. He emphasized the need for less elaborate scenery and advocated the use of shadow and light to create atmosphere. Appia's most influential work was *Die Musik und die Inszenierung* (1899).

Appian Way (Lat. *Via Appia*) First road leading southward from Rome to Capua (*c*.210km/130mi), constructed (*c*.312 BC) by the censor Appius Claudius Caecus. It was later extended and formed the first stage of routes to Greece and the East; portions of it remain today.

apple Common name for the most widely cultivated fruit tree of temperate climates. Developed from a tree native to Europe and SW Asia, apple trees are propagated by budding or grafting. From the flowers, which require cross-pollination to produce a desirable fruit, the fleshy fruit grows in a variety of sizes, shapes and acidities; it is generally roundish, 5–10cm (2–4in) in diameter, and a shade of yellow, green or red. A mature tree may yield up to 1cu m (30 bushels) of fruit in a single growing season. Europe produces 50–60% of the world's annual crop, and the US 16–20%. Family Rosaceae; genus *Malus*.

Appleton, Sir Edward Victor (1892–1965) English physicist. He was awarded the 1947 Nobel Prize for physics for his discovery (1925) of the upper (Appleton) layer of the IONOSPHERE. This layer reflects radio waves, and its discovery spurred the development of RADAR.

apricot Tree cultivated throughout temperate regions, after originating in China. The large, spreading tree with dark green leaves and white blossoms bears yellow or yellowish-orange edible fruit, with a large stone. Family Rosaceae; species *Prunus armeniaca*.

apsis (pl. apsides) Either of two points in an object's orbit. The closest point to the primary body is known as the **periapsis**, and the farthest the **apapsis**. The apsides of the Earth's orbit are its perihelion and aphelion; in the Moon's orbit they are its perigee and apogee.

Apuleius, Lucius (125–170) Latin writer, b. North Africa. His narrative romance *Metamorphoses* (or *The Golden Ass*) is the only Latin novel to have survived in its entirety. A satire on contemporary vices, it relates (in 11 parts) the misadventures of a man accidentally turned into an ass and his restoration to human form by the goddess Isis. Some of the tales, such as Cupid and Psyche, have entered into popular mythology. *The Golden Ass* was extremely influential in the development of the NOVEL. Apuleius' *Apologia* is a defence against the charge that he won his wife by magic.

Aqaba (Al 'Aqabah) Only seaport of Jordan, at the head of the Gulf of AQABA on the NE end of the Red Sea. It was an important part of medieval Palestine. In 1917 it was captured from the Turks by T.E. LAWRENCE and finally ceded to Jordan in 1925. It is crucial to Jordan's phosphate exports and is expanding as a port and diving resort. Pop. (1992 est.) 58,000.

Aqaba, Gulf of Northeast arm of the Red Sea between the Sinai Peninsula and Saudi Arabia. AQABA and ELAT lie at the N end of the Gulf. The gulf has played an important role in ARAB-ISRAELI WARS. It was blockaded by the Arabs from 1949 to 1956, and again in 1967, when Israel held strategic points along the Strait of Tiran to guarantee open passage for ships. The Gulf has excellent coral beds and rich marine life.

aqualung *See* SCUBA DIVING

aquamarine *See* BERYL

Aquarius (water bearer) Eleventh constellation of the zodiac, represented by a figure pouring water from a jar.

aquatint Method of engraving on metal plates. Aquatint was invented in the mid-18th century to imitate the effect of brush drawing or watercolour. It involves sprinkling a plate with fine grains of acid-resistant resin, fusing the resin to the metal (modern enamel sprays allow you to avoid this step), and letting acid bite around and through some of the grains. Printmakers can achieve extremely varied effects depending on the thickness of the resin and the immersion time. Aquatint can be used for line engraving or drawing on top of the resin with an acid-resistant varnish. GOYA and PICASSO were masters of the process.

aqueduct Artificial channel for conducting water from its source to its distribution point. While the ancient Romans were not the first to build these conduits, their aqueducts are the most famous because of their graceful architectural structures. One of their most extensive water systems, which served Rome itself, consisted of 11 aqueducts and took 500 years to complete. California has the world's largest conduit system: it carries water over a distance of more than 800km (500mi).

aquifer Rock, often sandstone or limestone, which is capable of both storing and transmitting water owing to its porosity and permeability. Much of the world's human population depends on aquifers for its water supply. They may be directly exploited by sinking WELLS.

Aquinas, Saint Thomas (1225–74) Italian theologian and philosopher, Doctor of the Church. St Thomas is the greatest figure of SCHOLASTICISM. His *Summa Theologiae* (Theological Digest, 1267–73) was declared (1879) by Pope LEO XIII to be the basis of official Catholic philosophy. Aquinas argued that faith and reason are two complementary realms; both are gifts of God, but reason is autonomous. His four hymns for the feast of Corpus Christi are among the greatest devotional pieces. Thomas was canonized in 1323. Thomist METAPHYSICS, a moderate form of REALISM, was the dominant world view until the mid-17th century. Other writings include *Commentary in the Sentences* (1254–56) and *Summa Contra Gentiles* (Against the Errors of the Infidels, 1259–64). His feast day is 7 March. *See also* THOMISM

Aquino, (Maria) Cory (Corazon) (1933–) Philippine stateswoman, president (1986–92), b. Maria Corazon. In 1954 she married Benigno Aquino (1932–83), an outspoken opponent of the MARCOS regime. While he was in prison (1973–81), Cory campaigned tirelessly for his release. Benigno was assassinated by Marcos' agents. Cory claimed victory over Marcos in the 1986 presidential election and accused the government of vote-rigging. A bloodless "people's revolution" forced Marcos into exile. Aquino's government was beset by economic obstacles, and she survived a coup attempt only with US help (1989). She declined to run for re-election in 1992, but supported the campaign of her successor, Fidel Ramos.

Aquitaine Historic region in SW France, named after a Celtic tribe, the Aquitani. Named Aquitania by the Romans, it became (56 BC) an integral part of their empire and included all the land between the Pyrenees and the River Garonne. Aquitaine later formed part of the Carolingian empire. Independent for a time during the early Middle Ages, it became part of France and then, following the marriage (1137) of ELEANOR OF AQUITAINE to HENRY II, part of England. In the early 13th century all but the southern part (Gascony) was returned to France, the rest being restored in 1453 at the end of the HUNDRED YEARS' WAR. The modern region, comprising the departments of Dordogne, Gironde, Landes, Lot-et-Garonne and Pyrénées-Atlantiques, is an important wine-producing region centred on BORDEAUX. Area: 41,308sq km (15,950sq mi). Pop. (1990) 2,795,800.

Arab Peoples of many nationalities, found predominantly in the Middle East and North Africa, who share a common heritage in the religion of ISLAM and their language (ARABIC). The patriarchal family is the basic social unit in a strongly traditional culture that has been little affected by external influences. Wealth from oil has brought rapid modernization in some Arab countries, but a great deal of economic inequality exists. *See also* SEMITES

Arabia Peninsular region of SW Asia bordered by the Persian Gulf (E), the Arabian Sea (S), the Syrian Desert (N) and the Red Sea (W). The original homeland of the ARABS, it is the world's largest peninsula, consisting largely of a plateau of crystalline rock. It is mostly desert, including the vast, barren Rub al-Khali ("Empty Quarter") in the S and the An Nafud in the N. The area was unified by the Muslims in the 7th century and dominated by Ottoman Turks after 1517. HUSSEIN IBN ALI led a successful revolt against the Turks and founded an independent state in the Hejaz region in 1916, but was subsequently defeated by the SAUD family, who founded SAUDI ARABIA in 1925. After World War 2, independent Arab states emerged, many of them exploiting the peninsula's vast reserves of oil. Area: *c.*2.6 million sq km (1 million sq mi).

Arabic Language originating in the Arabian Peninsula and now spoken in a variety of dialects throughout North Africa and the Middle East. It is a Semitic language, belonging to a major subfamily of AFRO-ASIATIC languages. Classical Arabic is the language of the KORAN. It began to spread during the Islamic expansion of the 7th and 8th centuries. It is estimated that 188 million people are native speakers. Arabic uses a script written from right to left. The script has been borrowed for rendering other languages such as URDU.

Arab-Israeli Wars (1948–49, 1956, 1967, 1973–74) Conflicts between ISRAEL and the Arab states. After Israeli independence (14 May, 1948), troops from Egypt, Iraq, Lebanon, Syria and Transjordan (modern Jordan) invaded the country. Initial Arab gains were halted and armistices arranged at Rhodes (January–July 1949). UN security forces upheld the truce until October 1956, when Israeli forces under Moshe DAYAN attacked the SINAI PENINSULA with support from France and Britain, alarmed at Egypt's nationalization of the SUEZ CANAL. International opinion forced a cease-fire in November. In 1967 guerrilla raids led to Israeli mobilization, and in the ensuing SIX-DAY WAR, Israel captured Sinai, the GOLAN HEIGHTS on the Syrian border, and the Old City of JERUSALEM. In the October War of 1973 (after intermittent hostilities), Egypt and Syria invaded on the Jewish holiday of YOM KIPPUR (6 October), and Israel pushed back their advance after severe losses. Fighting lasted 18 days. Subsequent disengagement agreements were supervised by the UN. In 1979, Israel signed a peace treaty with Egypt, but relations with other Arab states remained hostile. In 1982, Israeli forces invaded Lebanon in an effort to destroy bases of the PALESTINE LIBERATION ORGANIZATION (PLO). They were withdrawn (1984) after widespread international criticism. After 1988, the PLO renounced terrorism and gained concessions, including limited autonomy in parts of the occupied territories. *See also* ISRAELI-PALESTINIAN ACCORD

Arab League Organization formed in 1945 to give a collective political voice to the Arab nations. Its members include Syria, Lebanon, Iraq, Jordan, Sudan,

Algeria, Kuwait, Saudi Arabia, Libya, Morocco, Tunisia, Yemen, Qatar and the United Arab Emirates. It has often been divided, notably by the Egyptian peace treaty with Israel (1979) and over the GULF WAR (1991) and has been politically less effective than its founders hoped.

arachnid ARTHROPOD of the class Arachnida, which includes the SPIDER, TICK, MITE, SCORPION and HARVESTMAN. Arachnids have four pairs of jointed legs, two distinct body segments (cephalothorax and abdomen) and chelicerate jaws (consisting of clawed pincers). They lack antennae and wings.

Arafat, Yasir (1929–) Palestinian statesman, first president of Palestine (1996–), leader of the PALESTINE LIBERATION ORGANIZATION (PLO). From a base in Lebanon, Arafat led the anti-ISRAEL guerrilla organization, Fatah. He sought the abolition of Israel and the creation of a secular Palestinian state. The INTIFADA in Israel's occupied territories (GAZA and the WEST BANK) prompted secret talks between Israel and the PLO. In 1993, Arafat and Yitzhak RABIN signed an agreement in which Arafat renounced terrorism and recognized the state of Israel. In return, Rabin recognized the PLO as the legitimate representative of Palestinians and agreed to a withdrawal of Israeli troops from parts of the occupied territories. In 1994, the Palestinian National Authority, headed by Arafat, assumed limited self-rule in the territories relinquished by the Israeli army. In 1996 elections Arafat became president. In 2000, after the failure of peace talks between Arafat and Ehud BARAK, the Intifada in Palestine recommenced.

Aragon, Louis (1897–1982) French writer. Aragon was an early proponent of "automatic writing". His hallucinatory novel *Paris Peasant* (1926) is a seminal work in the literature of SURREALISM. Following a visit to the Soviet Union in 1930, Aragon became a communist and wrote a quartet of socialist realist novels, *The Real World* (1933–44). Other work includes *Holy Week* (1958) and a two-volume novel on Henri Matisse (1971).

Aragón Region in NE Spain. In 1479 the kingdom of Aragón became part of Spain, but retained its own government, currency and military forces until the early 18th century. It is now an autonomous region, comprising the provinces of Huesca, Teruel and Zaragoza. It produces grapes, wheat and sugar-beet. Industries: textiles, chemicals, iron ore, marble, limestone. Area: 47,670sq km (18,500sq mi). Pop. (1991) 1,188,817.

Aral Sea (Aralskoye More) Inland sea in central Asia, SW Kazakstan and NW Uzbekistan. Once the world's fourth largest inland body of water, it has no outlet, contains many small islands, and is fed by the rivers Syrdarya in the NE and Amudarya (OXUS) in the S. It is generally shallow and only slightly saline. The diversion of the rivers for irrigation by the Soviet government led to a disastrous drop in the water level, and the area of the lake shrunk by more than a third between 1960 and 1995. Many fishing communities were left literally stranded. Area: 31,220sq km (12,050sq mi).

Aramaic Ancient Semitic language used as a means of everyday communication in Palestine and other parts of the Middle East at the time of Christ. Originally the language of nomadic groups who established small states in MESOPOTAMIA during the late 2nd millennium BC, it became the common spoken and written language of the Middle East under the Persian Empire until replaced by ARABIC. Parts of the Old Testament were originally written in Aramaic. Minor dialects persist today in small Christian communities of the Near and Middle East.

Aran Islands (Gaelic *Oileain Arann*) Group of three small islands at the entrance to Galway Bay, W Ireland.

They are Inishmore, Inishmaan and Inisheer. The major town is Kilronan. There are pre-Christian ruins of archaeological interest. The islands were vividly described by J.M. Synge. Area: 47sq km (18sq mi). Pop. (1981) 1,381.

Arapaho ALGONQUIAN-speaking tribe of Native North Americans. Their original home was in the Red River Valley; they moved across the Missouri River and split into two groups. After the Treaty of Medicine Lodge (1847), one group joined the Southern Cheyennes in Oklahoma, while the northern band went onto Wind River Reservation with the SHOSHONE. Today, they number *c*.3,000.

Ararat, Mount (Ağri Daği) Two extinct volcanic peaks in the E extremity of Turkey. The highest peaks in Turkey, they are just N of where Noah's Ark is said to have come to rest (Genesis 8). There are two peaks: Great Ararat, at 5,165m (16,945ft), (last eruption 1840), and Little Ararat, at 3,925m (12,877ft).

Araucanian Independent language family of Native South American who live in Chile and Argentina. A loose confederation of Araucanian-speaking sub-tribes (including the Picunche, Mapuche and Huilliche) offered strong resistance to the Spanish invasion under Diego de Almagro in 1536. They drove the Spaniards back to the River Bio-Bio in 1598, and retained parts of Chile to the present day. Their descendants prefer the name *Mapuche* (Land People). The population has declined from *c*.1 million in the 16th century to *c*.300,000 today.

Arawak Largest and most widely spread Native South American language family, at one time spoken from the Caribbean to the GRAN CHACO. Some 40 Arawak tribes remain in Brazil today.

arbitration Resolution of a dispute by an unbiased referee (arbiter) chosen by the parties in conflict. While arbitration may be utilized by individuals in conflict, the procedure is most commonly applied in commercial and industrial disputes and overseen by independent bodies such as the ADVISORY, CONCILIATION AND ARBITRATION SERVICE (ACAS). International cases are often brought before the United Nations International Court of Justice, based at The Hague, Netherlands.

Arbuthnot, John (1667–1735) Scottish writer and court physician (1705–14) to Queen Anne. Arbuthnot is chiefly remembered for his *History of John Bull* (1712), a series of satirical pamphlets on Whig foreign policy.

arbor vitae Common name for five species of trees or shrubs of the genus *Thuja*, resinous, evergreen conifers of the cypress family native to North America and E Asia. They have thin outer bark, fibrous inner bark and flattened branches. Family Cupressaceae.

arc Portion of a curve. For a circle, the length (s) of an arc is found either by $2r\pi \times \theta/360$ or the product of the radius (r) and the angle (θ), measured in RADIANS, that it subtends at the centre: that is, $s = r\,\theta$.

Arc de Triomphe TRIUMPHAL ARCH in the Place Charles de Gaulle, Paris, France. The Arc de Triomphe de l'Etoile is a generalized copy of the triumphal arches erected in ancient Rome to commemorate the victories of individual emperors. Napoleon I commissioned J.F. Chalgrin to design this version, completed in 1836. It is one of the city's most celebrated landmarks.

arch Upward-pointing or curving arrangement of masonry blocks or other load-bearing materials; also used in architectural decoration. The ancient Romans invented traditional masonry arches but later cultures extended their repertoire to include many different and sometimes quite elaborate shapes. The basic structure of a masonry arch consists of wedge-shaped blocks (*voussoirs*) placed on top of each other and a central keystone which holds them together at the top. Modern materials, such as steel and reinforced concrete, are strong and flexible enough to stand on their own and they can also stretch across much wider areas. *See also* VAULT

Archaean Subdivision of pre-Cambrian geological time. It ended *c*.2.5 billion years ago.

Archaebacteria Sub-kingdom of the PROKARYOTAE that, on the basis of both RNA and DNA composition and biochemistry, differ significantly from other BACTERIA. They are thought to resemble ancient bacteria that first arose in extreme environments such as sulphur-rich deep-sea vents. Archaebacteria have unique protein-like cell walls and cell membrane chemistry, and distinctive RIBOSOMES. They include methane-producing bacteria, which use simple organic compounds such as methanol and acetate as food, combining them with carbon dioxide and hydrogen gas from the air, and releasing methane as a by-product. The bacteria of hot springs and saline areas have a variety of ways of obtaining food and energy, including the use of minerals instead of organic compounds. They include both AEROBIC and ANAEROBIC bacteria. Some taxonomists consider Archaebacteria to be so different from other living organisms that they constitute a higher grouping called a DOMAIN.

archaeology Scientific study of former human life and activities through material remains such as artifacts and buildings. An archaeologist excavates and retrieves remains from the ground or sea-bed, recording and interpreting the circumstances in which objects were found, such as their level in the soil and association with other objects. This information can then be used to build a picture of the culture that produced the objects.

archaeopteryx First known bird. About the size of a crow and fully feathered, it has a fossilized skeleton more like that of a reptile than a modern bird, and its beak had pronounced jaws with teeth. It was probably capable only of weak flight.

▲ **archaeopteryx** The earliest known recognizable bird, archaeopteryx dates from the upper Jurassic period. The presence of wings and feathers define it as a bird, but the skeleton is quite reptilian. The wings, instead of being the specialized flying limbs of modern birds, were really elongated forelimbs, complete with claws. The tail resembles a lizard's, and the skull had teeth. The small breastbone shows it was a poor flyer.

Archangel (Archangel'sk) City and major port on the North Dvina delta, NW Russia. Archangel was opened (c.1600) to European trade and was Russia's major port until the founding (1703) of St Petersburg. The monastery of Archangel Michael was built here (1685–99). In the winter, icebreakers keep the large harbour clear, but the port remains ice-free for about six months, essential for commerce in N European Russia. Industries: paper, fishing, shipbuilding. Pop. (1994) 407,000.

archangel One of the rulers or princes of angels in the hierarchy of ANGELS. The archangels MICHAEL, RAPHAEL, GABRIEL and Uriel stand on each of the four sides of God's throne. According to medieval theology, the archangels have the task of ministering to humanity.

archbishop Chief or highest-ranking bishop who is head of an ecclesiastical province or archdiocese. The main function of an archbishop is to supervise and guide the work of subordinate BISHOPS.

archerfish Fish found in brackish waters of SE Asia and Australia. It is yellowish-green to brown with dark markings, and catches insect prey by spitting water "bullets". Length: up to 20cm (8in). Family Toxotidae.

archery Target sport that makes use of a bow and arrow or a crossbow and bolt. Commonly, archers use a longbow to shoot arrows at a target that consists of concentric scoring rings of five colours. The three other divisions of archery are field, flight and crossbow. The world governing body is the *Fédération Internationale de Tir à l'Arc (FITA)*, based in Milan, Italy. Archery returned to the Olympic Games in 1972.

Archimedes (c.287–212 BC) Greek mathematician and engineer. He developed a method for expressing large numbers and made outstanding discoveries about the determination of areas and volumes, which led to a new accurate method of measuring π (pi). In his work *On Floating Bodies*, he stated ARCHIMEDES' PRINCIPLE. He also invented the ARCHIMEDES' SCREW.

Archimedes' principle Observation by ARCHIMEDES that a body immersed in a FLUID is pushed up by a force equal to the weight of the displaced fluid. He supposedly formulated this principle after stepping into a bath and watching it overflow.

Archimedes' screw Machine used for raising water, thought to have been invented by Archimedes in the 3rd century BC. The most common form of the machine is a cylindrical pipe enclosing a helix, inclined at a 45° angle to the horizontal with its lower end in the water. When the machine rotates, water rises through the pipe.

Archipenko, Alexander (1887–1964) Russian-US modernist sculptor, one of the most radical innovators of his day. Largely self-taught, Archipenko helped to introduce the idea of making space an integral element of sculpture, as in the cubist *Walking Woman* (1912). He also developed a form of sculpture using light. Archipenko took part in the ARMORY SHOW (1913) and opened a sculpture school in New York in the late 1930s. His work influenced GABO and Henry MOORE.

architecture Art and science of designing permanent buildings for human use. Architecture can express aesthetic ideas from the most restrained UTILITARIANISM to extravagantly ornate decoration. The difference between "architecture" and "building" is a subject that has exercised theorists since the discipline was invented. In reality, architecture is usually a compromise between aesthetic creation and the demands of practicality. There are many different areas of architecture and apart from the stylistic and historical periods (*see* individual articles), it comes under such broad categories as civic, commercial, religious, recreational and domestic. In the 20th century, traditional barriers between separate artistic disciplines have gradually dissolved, so that it is possible to see architecture as a type of sculpture. Key figures in the development of Western architectural theory include VITRUVIUS, who believed that architecture was merely a form of applied mathematics, and ALBERTI whose pioneering treatise *De re Aedificatoria* (1485) introduced the idea that architecture was an art form in its own right. After the 18th century, European architects tended to regard "building" as a cheap substitute for their profession and something that engineers carried out. Architects began to swing back in the other direction with the arrival of the ARTS AND CRAFTS MOVEMENT, and the introduction of efficient, mass-produced materials. The 20th-century modernists, such as Walter GROPIUS, believed that the form of a building should follow its function. The relationship between the two extremes is continually shifting.

Arctic Vast region of icy seas and cold lands around the NORTH POLE, often defined as extending from the Pole to the ARCTIC CIRCLE. In areas N of latitude 66° 30'N, the Sun neither sets during the height of summer nor rises during the depths of winter. The more southerly areas are frequently referred to as the subarctic. At the centre of the Arctic is the ARCTIC OCEAN, with its many seas and inlets. In the region around the North Pole, the waters of the Arctic are permanently covered with sheet ice or a floating mass of ice debris called the ice pack, but some parts of the ocean are frozen only in winter. When the ice starts to melt in the spring, it disintegrates into floes and drifting pack ice. Icebergs have their origins in freshwater glaciers flowing into the ocean from the surrounding lands. **Lands and climate** Bordering the Arctic Ocean are the most northerly lands of Asia, Europe and North America. By far the greater part of the huge frozen island of GREENLAND lies N of the Arctic Circle. Arctic lands generally have a summer free from ice and snow. Most of the Arctic tundra is flat and marshy in summer but the subsoil is PERMAFROST. For most of the year temperatures are below freezing point. In spring the Sun appears, and some Arctic lands have sunshine every day from March or April to September. **People** Despite the severity of the climate and the restricted food resources, many peoples live in the Arctic. The most scattered are the c.60,000 ESKIMOS spread across polar North America, Greenland and NE Siberia. Several culturally separate groups of people live in N Siberia. In the European part of Russia there are the numerous Zyryans, and in LAPLAND the LAPPS. Most of these peoples follow ancient, traditional patterns of life, but the discovery of great mineral wealth, especially in Alaska and Russia, has brought huge change to their homelands. **History** The Arctic was first explored by Norsemen in the 9th century. The search for the NORTHWEST PASSAGE gave impetus to further explorations in the 16th and 17th centuries, though a route was not found until the early 1900s. The North Pole was first reached in 1909 by Robert PEARY, and the first crossing of the Arctic Ocean under the polar ice-cap was completed in 1959.

Arctic Circle Northernmost of the Earth's parallels, 66.5° N of the equator. At this latitude the Sun neither sets on the day of summer SOLSTICE (21 June) nor rises on the day of winter solstice (22 December).

Arctic fox (white fox or polar fox) Fox found on tundra or mountains of the Arctic. Its fur changes colour in winter either from grey-brown to white or grey to greyblue. Length: 50–60cm (20–24in).

Arctic Ocean Ocean N of the Arctic Circle, between North America and Eurasia. Almost totally landlocked and the Earth's smallest ocean, it is bordered by Greenland, Canada, Alaska, Russia and Norway. Connected to the Pacific Ocean by the Bering Strait and to the Atlantic Ocean by the Davis Strait and Greenland Sea, it includes the Barents, Beaufort, Chukchi, Greenland and Norwegian seas. There is animal life (plankton) in all Arctic water and polar bears, seals and gulls up to about 88° N. Area: 14 million sq km (5.4 million sq mi).

Arctic tern Sea bird whose migrations are the longest of any bird, from summer breeding areas in the far N to wintering areas in Antarctica, a round trip of c.35,500km (22,000mi). It has grey, black and white feathers and a reddish bill and feet. It nests in colonies and lays one to four eggs in a sandy scrape nest. Length: 38cm (15in). Species *Sterna paradisaea*.

Arcturus (Alpha Boötis) Red giant star, the fourth-brightest in the sky, in the constellation of Boötes. Its luminosity is 100 times that of the Sun.

Ardennes (Forest of Ardennes) Sparsely populated wooded plateau in SE Belgium, N Luxembourg, and the Ardennes department of N France. The capital is Charleville-Mézières. It was the scene of heavy fighting in both world wars, notably in the Battle of the BULGE (1944). In the well-preserved forest regions, wild game is abundant, and cleared areas support farming.

area Two-dimensional measurement of a plane figure or body given in square units, such as cm^2 or m^2. The area of a rectangle of sides a and b is ab; the areas of triangles and other polygons can be determined using TRIGONOMETRY. Areas of curved figures and surfaces can be determined by integral CALCULUS.

Arendt, Hannah (1906–75) US philosopher and political scientist, b. Germany. In *The Origins of Totalitarianism* (1951), she examined the common roots of National Socialism and Stalinism in the anti-Semitism, imperialism and nationalism of the 19th-century. *The Human Condition* (1958) incorporated strands of PHENOMENOLOGY into political theory. In 1959 Arendt became the first woman to be appointed to a full professorship at Princeton University. Other works include *Eichmann in Jerusalem* (1963).

Arequipa Second-largest city of Peru and capital of Arequipa department. It was established in 1540 by Francisco PIZARRO on the site of an INCA settlement. Located at the foot of the extinct volcano El Misti (5,822m/19,100ft), it is known as the "White City" because many of its buildings are made of white volcanic stone. Industries: wool processing, textiles, leather. Pop. (1993) 619,156.

Ares In Greek mythology, the god of war, identified with the Roman god MARS. He was the son of Zeus and HERA and lover of APHRODITE. In the Trojan War he sided with the Trojans.

Argentina Republic in S South America. Argentina is the second largest country in South America and the eighth largest in the world. The high Andes Mountains in the w contain ACONCAGUA, the highest peak outside Asia. In s Argentina the Andes overlook PATAGONIA, a plateau region. In E central Argentina lies a fertile plain called the Pampas, which includes the capital BUENOS AIRES. GRAN

ARGENTINA
AREA: 2,766,890sq km (1,068,296sq mi)
POPULATION: 36,238,000
CAPITAL (POPULATION): Buenos Aires (10,990,000)

CHACO lies w of the River PARANÁ, while Mesopotamia is a fertile plain between the Paraná and URUGUAY rivers. **Climate** Argentina's climate ranges from subtropical in the N to temperate in the S, with extremely harsh conditions in the high Andes. Rainfall is abundant in the NE. **Vegetation** Gran Chaco is a forested region, known for its quebracho trees. Mesopotamia and the Pampas are grassy regions with large farms. Patagonia is too dry for crops. **History and Politics** Spanish explorers reached the coast in 1516 and settlers followed in search of silver and gold. Spanish rule continued until revolutionaries, led by General Belgrano, overthrew the viceroy in 1810. By 1816, liberation was complete and Argentina declared independence. A long civil war ensued between centralizers and federalists. Argentina adopted a federal constitution in 1853. For much of World War 2 Argentina was a pro-Axis "neutral" power. In 1944, Ramón Castillo was overthrown in a military coup led by Juan PERÓN, and Argentina switched to the Allies. With the aid of his wife, Eva PERÓN, Perón established a popular dictatorship. In 1955, Perón was overthrown by a military coup and Perónism was suppressed. Political instability dominated the 1960s, with the military seeking to dampen Perónist support. In 1973, an ailing Perón returned from exile to head a civilian government. He was succeeded (1974) by his third wife, Isabel Martinez Perón, who was in turn deposed by a military coup (1976). Military rule (1976–83) was characterized by the so-called "Dirty War". Torture, "disappearances" and wrongful imprisonment were commonplace. In 1982, Argentina invaded the FALKLAND ISLANDS, precipitating the FALKLANDS WAR. Britain quickly recaptured the islands and in 1983 the junta was forced to hold elections. Civilian government was restored. In 1989, the Perónist Carlos MENEM was elected president. The Perónists were defeated by Fernando De la Rúa in 1999 elections. **Economy** Argentina is an upper-middle-income developing country (1995 GDP per capita, US$8,310). The economy is dominated by agriculture. Its main exports are beef, maize and wheat. Other major crops include citrus fruits, cotton, grapes for wine, sorghum, soya beans and sugar cane. Almost 90% of the population live in urban areas. Industries: cars, electrical equipment, textiles.

argon (symbol Ar) Monatomic (single-atom), colourless and odourless gaseous element that is the most abundant NOBLE GAS (inert gas). Argon was discovered (1894) in air by the chemists Lord RAYLEIGH and Sir William RAMSAY. It makes up 0.93% of the atmosphere by volume. Obtained commercially by the fractionation of liquid air, it is used in electric light bulbs, fluorescent tubes, argon lasers, arc welding and semiconductor production. The element has no known true compounds. Properties: at.no. 18; r.a.m. 39.948; r.d. 0.0017837g cm^{-3}; m.p. -189.4°C (-308.9°F); b.p. -185.9°C (-302.6°F).

argonaut (paper NAUTILUS) Ocean-dwelling cephalopod MOLLUSC found in many parts of the world. Related to the OCTOPUS, it has eight arms with suckers. Two of the female's arms are modified to secrete a coiled, paper-thin, ridged shell that is an egg-case. Length: to 16in (40cm). Family Argonautidae.

Argonauts In Greek legend, 50 heroes, including HERACLES, ORPHEUS and CASTOR AND POLLUX, who sailed the ship *Argo* to Colchis, a kingdom at the E end of the Black Sea, in search of the GOLDEN FLEECE. Their leader was JASON, husband of MEDEA.

Argus Name of three figures in Greek legend. One was a giant with 100 eyes, half of which remained open at all times. Another was the shipbuilder who built the ship Argo for JASON and became a member of the crew.

Argus was also the name of the dog who recognized ODYSSEUS on his return to Ithaca.

aria Solo song with instrumental accompaniment, or a lyrical instrumental piece. An important element of operas, cantatas and oratorios, the aria form originated in the 17th century.

Ariadne In Greek mythology, Cretan princess (daughter of MINOS) who fell in love with THESEUS but was abandoned after saving him from the Minotaur. Ariadne was consoled by the god DIONYSUS, whom she later married.

Arianism Theological school based on the teachings of Arius (c.AD 250–336), considered heretical by orthodox Christianity. Arius taught that Christ was a created being, and that the Son, though divine, was neither equal nor co-eternal with the Father. Arianism was condemned by the first Council of NICAEA (325).

Aries (Ram) Constellation in the N sky; it is situated between Pisces and Taurus. Its brightest stars are Hamal (Alpha), magnitude 2.0, and Beta, magnitude 2.6.

Ariosto, Ludovico (1474–1533) Italian Renaissance poet. In 1503 he became a servant of Cardinal d'Este and from 1517 until his death served the Duke of Ferrara. Ariosto's masterpiece, *Orlando Furioso* (published 1532), was intended to glorify the Este family. *Orlando Furioso* follows several love stories from the era of Charlemagne, when Christian knights and Saracens fought for control of Christendom.

Aristarchus of Samos (c.310–230 BC) Greek mathematician and astronomer. Aristarchus tried to calculate the distances of the Sun and Moon from Earth, as well as their sizes. Although his method was sound, the results were inaccurate. He was the first to propose that the Sun is the centre of the Universe (**heliocentric theory**); the idea was not taken up because it did not seem to make the calculation of planetary positions any easier.

aristocracy (lit. "rule by the best") Social system based on privilege. Usually the term has been applied in Western Europe to describe the rule of a hereditary landed nobility, but could also be used to include a "meritocracy" in which leaders are chosen for their ability.

Aristophanes (448–380 BC) Greek comic playwright. Of his more than 40 plays, only 11 survive, the only extant comedies from the period. All follow the same basic plan: caricatures of contemporary Athenians who become involved in absurd situations. Graceful, choral lyrics frame caustic personal attacks. A conservative, Aristophanes parodied EURIPIDES' innovations in drama and satirized the philosophical radicalism of SOCRATES and Athens' expansionist policies. The importance of the chorus in the early works is reflected in the titles, such as *The Wasps* (422 BC), *The Birds* (414 BC) and *The Frogs* (405 BC). Other notable plays include *The Clouds* (423 BC) and *Lysistrata* (411 BC).

Aristotle (384–322 BC) Greek philosopher, founder of the science of LOGIC, and one of the greatest figures in Western philosophy, b. Macedonia. Aristotle studied (367–347 BC) under PLATO at the ACADEMY in Athens. After Plato's death he tutored the young ALEXANDER THE GREAT before founding (335 BC) the Lyceum. In direct opposition to Plato's IDEALISM, Aristotle's METAPHYSICS is based on the principle that all knowledge proceeds directly from observation of the particular. Aristotle argued that a particular object can only be explained through an understanding of causality. He outlined four causes: the **material** cause (an object's substance); **formal** cause (design); **efficient** cause (maker); and the **final** cause (function). For Aristotle this final cause was the primary one. Form was inherent in matter. His ethical philosophy

stressed the exercise of rationality in political and intellectual life. Aristotle's writings cover nearly every branch of human knowledge, from statecraft to astronomy. His principal works are the *Organon* (six treatises on logic and SYLLOGISM), *Politics* (the conduct of the state), *Poetics* (analysis of poetry and TRAGEDY) and *Rhetoric*.

arithmetic Branch of MATHEMATICS using NUMBERS and such operations as addition, subtraction, multiplication and division. The study of arithmetic traditionally involved learning procedures for operations such as long division and extraction of square roots. The procedures of arithmetic were put on a formal, axiomatic basis by Giuseppe Peano in the late 19th century. Using certain postulates, including that there is a unique natural number, 1, it is possible to give formal definition of the set of natural numbers and the arithmetical operations. Thus, addition is interpretable in terms of combining sets: in 2 + 7 = 9, 9 is the cardinal number of a set produced by combining sets of 2 and 7. Multiplication can be thought of as repeated additions, while subtraction and division are the inverse operations of addition and multiplication.

arithmetic progression Sequence of numbers in which each term is produced by adding a constant term (the common difference d) to the preceding one. It has the form $a, a + d, a + 2d$, and so on. An example is the sequence 1, 3, 5, ... The sum of such a progression, $a + (a + d) + (a + 2d) + ...$ is an arithmetic series. For n terms, it has a value $\frac{1}{2}n\,[2a + 0.5(n-1)d]$.

Arizona Southwestern US state, bordering on Mexico. The capital is PHOENIX; other cities include Tucson and Mesa. After the end of the MEXICAN WAR (1848), Mexico ceded most of the present state to the US, and it became the 48th state of the Union in 1912. The Colorado Plateau occupies the N part of the state and is cut by many steep canyons, notably the GRAND CANYON, through which the COLORADO RIVER flows. Arizona's mineral resources, grazing and farmland have long been mainstays of the economy. Mining and agriculture are still important, but since the 1950s manufacturing has been the most profitable sector. The state has many scenic attractions (including the Petrified Forest, Fort Apache and the reconstructed London Bridge at Lake Havasu). Tourism is now a major source of income. It also has the largest Native American population of any US state (203,527 in 1990), with Indian reservations comprising 28% of the land area. Between 1950 and 1970, Arizona's population more than doubled; in the 1970s its annual growth rate was more than 35%. Area: 113,909sq mi (295,025sq km). Pop. (2000) 5,130,632.

ark According to Genesis 6, the floating house Noah was ordered to build and live in with his family and one pair of each living creature during the flood. As the flood waters receded, it came to rest on a mountain top, believed to be Mount ARARAT.

Arkansas South-central US state, bounded on the E by the Mississippi River. The capital (and only large city) is LITTLE ROCK. Arkansas was acquired by the LOUISIANA PURCHASE (1803) and was admitted to the Union as the 25th state in 1836. It was one of the 11 Confederate states during the US Civil War. In the E and S the land is low, providing excellent farmland for cotton, rice and soya beans. The principal waterway is the ARKANSAS River, which (like all the state's rivers) drains into the Mississippi. The NW of the state, including part of the Ozarks, is higher land. Forests are extensive and economically important. Bauxite processing, timber and chemicals are the main industries. Noted for its resistance to the civil rights movement in the 1960s, Arkansas is home to former president Bill Clinton. Area: 53,104sq mi (137,539sq km). Pop. (2000) 2,673,400.

Arkansas River with its source high up in the Rockies of central Colorado, and flowing 2,335km (1,450mi) to the Mississippi River in SE Arkansas. Fourth-longest river in the US, it flows E through Kansas and SE across the NE corner of Oklahoma, and SE to Arkansas.

Ark of the Covenant In Jewish tradition, a gold-covered chest of acacia that contained the stone tablets on which the TEN COMMANDMENTS were inscribed. It rested in the Holy of Holies within the TABERNACLE. Only the high priest could look upon the Ark, and no one could touch it. In Palestine, the Israelites set up a resting place for the Ark in Shiloh. In the 10th century BC, the Ark was moved to the temple built by SOLOMON in Jerusalem. After the destruction of the JERUSALEM TEMPLE in 586 BC, there is no further record of the Ark's location. In today's synagogues, the Ark of the Covenant is a closet or recess in which the sacred scrolls of the congregation are kept.

Arkwright, Sir Richard (1732–92) English inventor and industrialist. Arkwright introduced powered machinery to the textile industry with his water-driven frame for spinning; he started work on the machine in 1764 and patented his invention in 1769.

Arlen, Harold (1905–86) US jazz and popular composer. Many of his songs, such as "Stormy Weather", became jazz standards. In 1939, Arlen won an Academy Award for the song "Over the Rainbow", from the film *The Wizard of Oz*. Other film scores include *A Star is Born* (1954).

Arles Market town at the head of the Camargue delta on the River Rhône, S France. The Romans called their capital of southern Gaul Arelate and linked it by canal to the Mediterranean Sea in 103 BC. The counts of Savoy and kings of France gradually acquired the kingdom of Arles during the 14th century. Vincent van Gogh spent his last and most productive years (1888–90) in Arles, and his reputation boosts the tourist trade. Other industries: boatbuilding, metalworking, sulphur refining. Pop. (1990) 52,590.

Arlington County in N Virginia, USA, across the Potomac River from Washington, D.C. Since 1943 it has been the location of the PENTAGON as well as Arlington National Cemetery (1864). The 200-ha (500-acre) cemetery, built on the former estate of Robert E. LEE, contains the Tomb of the Unknowns, a memorial amphitheatre and the graves of many servicemen and prominent Americans. Originally a part of the District of Columbia, it was made a county of Virginia in 1847. Pop. (1996) 175,000.

Armada, Spanish (1588) Fleet launched by the Catholic PHILIP II of Spain against England to overthrow the Protestant ELIZABETH I. English support for the rebels in the Spanish Netherlands as well as pirate attacks on Spanish possessions convinced Philip that England must be conquered. The 130 ships of the Armada were supposed to collect troops from the Netherlands but, hampered by English attacks and poor planning, this proved impossible. After an indecisive engagement with the English off Gravelines, the Spanish ships ran out of ammunition. They withdrew around N Scotland. Though a blow to Spanish prestige, the defeat had little effect on the balance of naval power.

armadillo Nocturnal, burrowing mammal found from Texas to Argentina, noted for the armour of bony plates that protect its back and sides. When attacked, some species roll into a ball. It eats insects, carrion and plants. Length: 30–150cm (5–60in). Family Dasypodidae.

Armageddon (Hebrew *har megiddo*, "hill of MEGIDDO") Place referred to in Revelation 16, where the final battle between the demonic kings of the Earth and the forces of God will be fought at the end of the world.

Armagh County and town in SE Northern Ireland, near the border with the Republic of Ireland. The town became an ecclesiastical centre in the 5th century and is now the seat of Roman Catholic and Protestant archbishops. It was settled by Protestants in the 16th century. The county is low-lying in the N and hilly in the S. Much of the land is used for farming, and the town is a market centre for agricultural produce. Lurgan and Portadown are centres for textiles and light industries. Area: 676sq km (261sq mi). Pop. (county, 1991) 67,128; (town, 1991) 14,625.

Armani, Giorgio (1935–) Italian fashion designer. He designed (1961–74) for Nino Cerruti, before launching his own menswear label in 1975. Armani's understated style emphasized comfort in a simple cut and elegant lines. He pioneered the "unstructured" suit and his shops and own brand of jeans helped him create a multi-million-dollar international empire.

Armenia Republic in the S Caucasus; the capital is YEREVAN. **Land and climate** Armenia is a rugged mountainous republic. The highest peak is Mount Aragats, 4,090m (13,420ft). Armenia has severe winters and cool summers, but the total yearly rainfall is generally low, between 200 and 800mm (8–30in). The lowest land is in the NE and NW, where Yerevan is situated. Armenia has many fast-flowing rivers that have cut deep gorges in the plateau. The major river is the Araks. The largest lake is Lake Sevan, containing 90% of all Armenia's standing water. Vegetation ranges from tundra to grassy steppe. Oak forests are found in the SE, beech in the NE. **History and politics** Armenia was an advanced ancient kingdom, considered to be one of the original sites of iron and bronze smelting. A nation was established in the 6th century BC, and Alexander the Great expelled the Persians in 330 BC. In 69 BC, Armenia was incorporated into the Roman empire. In AD 303, Armenia became the first country to adopt Christianity as its state religion. From 886 to 1046 Armenia was an independent kingdom. From the 11th–15th centuries the Mongols were the greatest power in the region. By the 16th century, Armenia was controlled by the Ottoman empire. Despite religious discrimination, the Armenians generally prospered under Turkish rule. In 1828, Russia acquired Persian Armenia, and (with promises of religious toleration) many Armenians moved into the Russian-controlled area. In Turkish Armenia, nationalist movements were encouraged by British promises of protection. The Turkish response was uncompromising, and it is estimated that 200,000 Armenians were killed in 1896 alone. In the Russian sector, a process of Russification was enforced. During World War 1, Armenia was the battleground for the Turkish and Russian armies. Armenians were accused of aiding the Russians, and Turkish atrocities intensified. Over 600,000 Armenians were killed by Turkish troops, and 1.75 million were deported to Syria and Palestine. In 1918, Russian Armenia became the Armenian Autonomous Republic; the W part remained part of Turkey, and the NW part of Iran. In 1922, Armenia, Azerbaijan and Georgia were federated to form the Transcaucasian Soviet Socialist Republic (one of the four original republics in the Soviet Union).

ARMENIA
AREA: 29,800sq km (11,506sq mi)
POPULATION: 3,968,000
CAPITAL (POPULATION): Yerevan (1,226,000)

In 1936, Armenia became a separate republic. Earthquakes in 1984 and 1988 destroyed many cities and killed more than 80,000 people. In 1988, war broke out between Armenia and Azerbaijan over NAGORNO-KARABAKH (an Armenian enclave in Azerbaijan). In 1990, the Armenian parliament voted to break from the Soviet Union, and in 1991 joined the newly-established COMMONWEALTH OF INDEPENDENT STATES (CIS). In 1992, Armenia invaded Azerbaijan and occupied Nagorno-Karabakh. In 1994, an uneasy cease-fire left Armenia in control of about 20% of Azerbaijan. In 1998, Robert Kocharyan, a former leader of Nagorno-Karabakh, was elected president of Armenia. In 1999, Prime Minister Vazgen Sarkisyan was shot dead in parliament. **Economy** Armenia is a lower-middle-income nation (1995 GDP per capita, US$2,260). The economy, badly hit by war with Azerbaijan, is in a state of transition. Under communist rule, most economic activity was controlled by the state. Since 1991, the government has encouraged free enterprise, selling farmland and state-owned businesses. Armenia is highly industrialized, and production is dominated by mining and chemicals. Copper is the chief metal; gold, lead and zinc are also mined. Agriculture (centred around the River Araks) is the second-largest sector, with cotton, tobacco, fruit and rice the main products. Despite significant increases in production, Armenia is still dependent on food imports.

Armenian Church (Gregorian Church) Monophysite Christian Church, founded in Armenia (c.AD 300) by St Gregory the Illuminator. In the 4th century, Armenia became the first state to adopt Christianity as the national religion. The Armenian Chuch's endorsement of monophysitism at the Council of CHALCEDON (451) led to its isolation from orthodox Christianity. It is headed by the catholicates of Echmiadzin (Armenia) and Sis (Cilicia) and the patriarchates of Jerusalem and Istanbul. The Armenian Church has c.2 million members, mainly in Armenia and the United States.

Arminius, Jacobus (1560–1609) Dutch theologian whose system of beliefs, especially concerning salvation, became widespread and was later known as Arminianism. Arminius rejected the notion of PREDESTINATION developed by John CALVIN, in favour of a more liberal concept of conditional election and universal redemption. He believed that God will elect to everlasting life those who are prepared to respond in faith to the offer of divine salvation. Arminianism finally achieved official recognition in the Netherlands in 1795. It was a major influence on METHODISM.

armour Protection against weaponry. Soldiers' body armour (usually made of metal or thick leather) has been employed since antiquity to prevent injury. Except for helmets (and occasionally bulletproof VESTS) body armour ceased to be used in European battle in the 17th century. Warships were first armoured in the mid-19th century, using metal plating to deflect small-arms fire. Vehicles acquired armour-plating during World War 1. Armoured vehicles include TANKS, armored personnel carriers and mechanized ARTILLERY.

Armory Show Landmark exhibition of contemporary American and European art held in New York in 1913. The European section caused the greatest excitement. It looked back to IMPRESSIONISM, tracing the history of MODERNISM through NEO-IMPRESSIONISM and POST-IMPRESSIONISM, but came right up to date with examples of CUBISM, ORPHISM and DADA. Marcel Duchamps' painting *Nude Descending a Staircase* caused the most controversy. The exhibition travelled successfully to Chicago and Boston, attracting an estimated half a million visitors. It put avant-garde European art on the American map and revolutionized the country's attitudes, provoking an interest in contemporary art.

arms control Activity undertaken by powerful nations to prevent mutual destruction in warfare, especially with nuclear weapons. The nations attempt to maintain a balance of power by regulating each other's stockpile of weapons. *See also* DISARMAMENT; STRATEGIC ARMS LIMITATION TALKS (SALT)

arms race Rivalry between states or blocs to achieve supremacy in military strength. The first modern instance was the race between Germany and Britain to build up their navies before World War 1. The term refers principally to the race in nuclear weapons between the Soviet Union and the US after World War 2, during the COLD WAR. Examples of arms races at regional level are those of Israel and the Arab states in the Middle East, which started in the 1950s, and of Iran and Iraq in the 1980s.

Armstrong, Henry (1912–88) US boxer, b. Henry Jackson. "Hurricane Hank" is the only boxer to hold world titles at three weights simultaneously: featherweight (1937–38), lightweight (1938–39) and welterweight (1938–40). In 1940, Armstrong narrowly failed to gain a fourth title when he fought a draw with Cerefino Garcia for the middleweight crown. He retired in 1945, with a record of 144 wins. Armstrong died in poverty.

Armstrong, (Daniel) Louis (1900–71) US jazz trumpeter, singer and bandleader, nicknamed "Satchmo" (satchel mouth). Armstrong was one of the most distinctive sounds in 20th-century music. His career spanned over half a century. Armstrong learned to play in New Orleans and in 1922 joined the King Oliver band. The Hot Fives and Hot Sevens recordings (1925–29) are some of the most influential in the history of jazz. In the 1930s he became a successful bandleader. Armstrong also appeared in films such as *Pennies from Heaven* (1936), *New Orleans* (1947) and *High Society* (1956).

Armstrong, Neil Alden (1930–) US astronaut. Armstrong was chosen as a NASA astronaut in 1962 and was the command pilot for the Gemini 8 orbital flight in 1966. On 20 July 1969, he became the first man to walk on the Moon, remarking that it was "one small step for man, one giant leap for mankind".

army Organized group of soldiers trained to fight on land, usually rigidly hierarchical in structure. The first evidence of an army comes from Sumer in the third millennium BC. The Hittites used cavalry and the Assyrians added archers and developed siege machines. In the Middle Ages, armies used improved armour and weapons. The short-term feudal levy by which these armies were raised proved inflexible, and this led to the use of mercenaries. Heavy cavalry was replaced by a combination of infantry and archery. The end of the HUNDRED YEARS' WAR saw the inception of royal standing armies and an end to the chaos caused by mercenary armies. Muskets and bayonets replaced combinations of longbow, pike and infantry, and ARTILLERY was much improved. In the FRENCH REVOLUTIONARY WARS, a citizen army was raised by CONSCRIPTION and contained various specialist groups. Other European armies followed suit, and the age of the mass national army began. The invention of the MACHINE GUN brought about the deadlock of the trench warfare of WORLD WAR 1, which was broken by the TANK, and WORLD WAR 2 saw highly mechanized and mobile armies whose logistics of supply and support demanded an integration of the land, sea and air forces. Since World War 2 nuclear weapons have been deployed both tactically and strategically, and the nature of weaponry has determined an army's structure.

Army, British Ground service of the UK armed forces. In 1998 Regular Army personnel numbered *c*.114,000, including *c*.6,000 women and *c*.10,000 personnel overseas. In addition to the Regular Army, there is a reserve force of *c*.270,000; *c*.57,700 are in the Territorial Army (TA) and the remainder in the Regular Army Reserve. Since 1945 the British Army has formed part of NORTH ATLANTIC TREATY ORGANIZATION (NATO) forces and maintained overseas garrisons in such areas as Falklands, Cyprus and Gibraltar. There are three main sections of the British Army: **staff**, who organize operations; **fighting troops**, which include the Household Cavalry, Royal Armoured Corps, Royal Regiment of Artillery, Corps of Royal Engineers, Royal Corp of Signals and Infantry and Army Air Corp; and **administrative troops**, who provide services such as medical attention and technical support. These include Royal Army Medical Corps, Royal Military Police and Royal Electrical and Mechanical Engineers. The monarch is the official head of the British Army. Control of the army is exercised by the Ministry of DEFENCE, headed by the secretary of state for defence. General supervision is conducted by the chief of the general staff, who heads an army council. The end of the Cold War and financial pressures have seen major cutbacks in conventional forces.

Army, US Ground service of the US armed forces. In 1996 active army personnel numbered *c*.495,000, 32% stationed overseas. Personnel are under the general supervision of the secretary of the army and the army chief of staff, who is the army's highest ranking officer and a member of the Joint Chiefs of Staff. The president is commander-in-chief of the armed forces. The Department of the Army is charged with the organization, training and equipping of these forces, but not their military deployment. The army also provides assistance in disaster relief, conducts weapons research, carries on training at civilian colleges and administers the US Military Academy at West Point. The army has active divisions and helps to maintain National Guard and reserve divisions; major overseas commands are the Seventh Army in Europe and the Eighth Army in Korea. The Continental Army existed from 1775, but the first regular standing army was authorized by Congress in 1785. In 1947, the Department of War became the Department of the Army, and in 1949 it became a part of the Department of DEFENSE. The US Army has taken part in all major wars between the War of 1812 and the Vietnam War. Conscription was occasionally employed and was used in peacetime after World War 2. In 1973, Congress established an all-volunteer Army. In 1980, it resumed registration for conscription of 18-year-old men, and women were, for the first time, among the graduates at West Point.

army worm Moth caterpillar that travels in hordes, destroying crops as they go. The best known army worm is the orange-, brown- and yellow-striped *Pseudaletia unipuncta*. Length: 1.5in (38mm). Outbreaks of this caterpillar occur annually east of the Rocky Mountains in the US. Family Noctuidae.

Arnhem City in E central Netherlands. An important trading centre since medieval times, Arnhem was almost destroyed by an abortive Allied airborne attack in 1944. Industries: metallurgy, textiles, electrical equipment, chemicals. Pop. (1996 est.) 135,000.

Arnhem Land Peninsula in Northern Territory, N Australia. The chief town is Nhulunbuy. The first European discovery was made by Jan Carstensz in 1623. In 1976, the vast majority of Arnhem Land was declared a Native Australian reserve. Tourists are drawn to the aboriginal rock art in Kakudu National Park. Area: *c*.80,808sq km (31,200sq mi).

arnica Large genus of perennials of the DAISY family, native to the Northern Hemisphere. *Arnica montana* was formerly used for treating sprains. Family Compositae.

Arnold, Benedict (1741–1801) American colonial soldier. During the American Revolution, he was wounded at the Battle of SARATOGA (1777) and commanded Philadelphia (1778). In 1780 Arnold became commander of West Point, a fort he planned to betray to the British for money. After the plot was discovered, he fled to the British. His name has become proverbial in modern US usage for treachery.

Arnold, Sir Malcolm (1921–) English composer. Arnold started his career as principal trumpet with the London Philharmonic Orchestra but won immediate acclaim for his compositions. His style is easily accessible and his output includes symphonies, concertos, overtures (*Beckus the Dandipratt*, 1943), ballets (*Homage to the Queen*, 1953) and movie scores (*The Bridge on the River Kwai*, 1957).

Arnold, Matthew (1822–88) English poet and critic, son of Thomas ARNOLD. His writings include literary criticism, such as *Essays in Criticism* (series 1, 1865; series 2, 1888), and social commentary, such as *Culture and Anarchy* (1869), as well as such classic Victorian poems as "Dover Beach" and "The Scholar Gypsy". Arnold's theories on the social and moral benefits of culture were largely responsible for the establishment of ENGLISH LITERATURE as a "core" subject in schools and universities.

Arnold, Thomas (1795–1842) English teacher and scholar, father of Matthew ARNOLD. As headmaster (1827–42) of Rugby School, he introduced educational reforms that were widely influential. In 1841 Arnold was appointed regius professor of modern history at Oxford University. His stewardship of Rugby is recounted in Thomas HUGHES' *Tom Brown's Schooldays* (1857).

Arnulf (850–99) King of the East FRANKS (887–99), last CAROLINGIAN Holy Roman emperor (896–99). Arnulf defeated his uncle CHARLES III (THE FAT) and was proclaimed king. He successfully resisted the Norse invasion (891). At the request of the pope, Arnulf invaded Italy (894), captured Rome (895), and was crowned emperor (896).

aromatic compound Organic chemical compound that contains atoms of carbon (often six) joined to form a stable ring-shaped molecule, as seen in BENZENE. Some of these compounds have rings also containing nitrogen, oxygen or sulphur. *See also* ALIPHATIC COMPOUND

Aroostook War (1838–39) Dispute over the Maine-New Brunswick boundary. The Aroostook Valley was claimed by both Canada and the US, and a conflict arose over Canadian lumber operations. In 1839 a contingent of 50 Maine militia men also moved into the valley. War loomed, but US general Winfield Scott negotiated a truce. It was settled by the Webster-Ashburton Treaty (1842).

Arp, Jean (Hans) (1887–1966) Alsatian sculptor, painter and poet. He founded the Zurich DADA movement with the Romanian artists Tristan Tzara, Marcel Janco and others during World War 1. Arp worked briefly with the BLAUE REITER group and in the 1920s joined the SURREALISM movement. His sculpture spans the divide between Dada humour and the purity of non-iconic ABSTRACT ART. *Navel Shirt and Head* (1926) and *Human Concretion* (1935) are typical.

Arran Island in the Firth of Clyde, W Scotland. The main town is Brodick. A tourist resort, major attractions

▶ **art deco** Examples of art deco-style goods produced in Europe in the 1920s and 1930s. Art deco style is characterized by the nonfunctional use of streamlined, industrial designs for household or consumer objects, such as lamps, radios and teapots. The machine age is reflected also in the deliberate use of man-made materials, such as ceramics, plastics and chrome. Flat, bright colours are often employed in the geometric decoration of materials.

the concept of the Theatre of CRUELTY. Influenced by the psychoanalytical theories of Carl JUNG, Artaud proposed a physical theatre based on unconscious myth and symbol, rather than narrative and psychological realism. His most important work was the volume of essays *The Theatre and its Double* (1938).

art deco Fashionable style of design and interior decoration in the 1920s and 1930s. It took its name from the *Exposition Internationale des Arts Décoratifs et Industriels Modernes* held in Paris (1925). The art deco style is characterized by sleek forms, simplified lines and geometric patterns. *See also* CLIFF, CLARICE

Artemis In Greek mythology, the goddess of hunting and light, identified as DIANA by the Romans. She was the daughter of ZEUS and Leto, and twin sister of APOLLO. Associated with the Moon, she was a virgin who assisted in childbirth and protected infants and animals.

arteriosclerosis Blanket term for degenerative diseases of the arteries, in particular ATHEROSCLEROSIS (hardening of the arteries). It is caused by deposits of fatty materials and scar tissue on the ARTERY walls, which narrow the channel and restrict blood flow, causing an increased risk of heart disease, stroke or gangrene. Evidence suggests that predisposition to the disease is hereditary. Risk factors include cigarette smoking, inactivity, obesity and a diet rich in animal fats and refined sugar. Treatment is by drugs and, in some cases, surgery.

artery One of the BLOOD VESSELS that carry BLOOD away from the HEART. The **pulmonary** artery carries deoxygenated blood from the heart to the lungs, but all other arteries carry oxygenated blood to the body's tissues. An artery's walls are thick, elastic and muscular and pulsate as they carry the blood. A severed artery causes major HAEMORRHAGE.

artesian well Well from which water is forced out naturally under pressure. Artesian wells are bored where water in a layer of porous rock is sandwiched between two layers of impervious rock. The water-filled layer is called an AQUIFER. Water flows up to the surface because distant parts of the aquifer are higher than the wellhead.

arthritis Inflammation of the joints, with pain and restricted mobility. The most common forms are osteoarthritis and rheumatoid arthritis. **Osteoarthritis**, common among the elderly, occurs with erosion of joint cartilage and degenerative changes in the underlying bone. It is treated with analgesics and anti-inflammatories and, in some cases (especially a diseased hip), by joint-replacement surgery. **Rheumatoid arthritis**, more common in women, is generally more disabling. It is an autoimmune disease which may disappear of its own accord but is usually slowly progressive. Treatment includes analgesics to relieve pain. The most severe cases may need to be treated with CORTISONE injections, drugs to suppress immune activity. *See also* RHEUMATISM

arthropod Member of the largest animal phylum, Arthropoda. Living forms include CRUSTACEA, ARACHNID, CENTIPEDE, MILLIPEDE and INSECT. The species (numbering well over one million) are thought to have evolved from ANNELIDS. All have a hard outer skin of CHITIN that is attached to the muscular system on the inside. The body is divided into segments, modified among different groups, with each segment originally carrying a pair of jointed legs. In some animals some of the legs have evolvedaa into jaws, sucking organs or weapons. Arthropods have well-developed digestive, circulatory and nervous systems.

Arthur Legendary British king who was said to rule the Knights of the Round Table. Two medieval chroniclers,

include Brodick Castle, Machrie Moor stone circle and Goat Fell (874m, 2,867ft). Area: *c*.430sq km (166sq mi).

Arras Capital of Pas-de-Calais department on the River Scarpe, NE France. Settled by the Romans, it became a wealthy commercial town in the Middle Ages and was renowned for its tapestry. In the 15th century it was virtually destroyed in the wars between Burgundy and France. In 1492 it was occupied by Spain. By the Treaty of the Pyrenees (1659) it became part of French crown lands. Badly damaged in both world wars, it nonetheless retains much impressive Spanish-Flemish architecture. Industries: food, brewing. Pop. (1990) 42,715.

arrhythmia Irregularity in the rhythm of the heartbeat. Various abnormalities include atrial tachycardia (fast heartbeat), atrial flutter and atrial fibrillation, in which there is erratic and ineffective atrial contraction. In the course of normal activity, however, the HEART rate of a healthy person will have some variety.

arrowroot Tropical and subtropical perennial plant found in wet habitats of America, and some islands of the West Indies. Its leaves are lance-shaped and the flowers are usually white. The ground roots are used in cooking. Family Marantaceae; species *Maranta undinaceae*.

arsenic (symbol As) Toxic, semimetallic element of group V of the periodic table, probably obtained (1250) by Albertus Magnus. Compounds containing arsenic are used as a poison, and to harden lead and make semiconductors. Three allotropes are known: white arsenic, black arsenic and a yellow, nonmetallic form. Properties: at.no. 33; r.a.m. 74.9216; r.d. 5.7; sublimes 613°C (1,135°F); most common isotope As^{75}.

art *See* ARCHITECTURE; DRAWING; PAINTING; SCULPTURE

Artaud, Antonin (1896–1948) French drama theorist and director. In 1927, he co-founded the Théâtre Alfred Jarry, which produced surreal, symbolist plays. His most significant contribution to 20th-century drama was

Gildas and Nennius, tell of Arthur's fighting against the invading West Saxons and his final defeat of them at Mount Badon (possibly Badbury Hill, Dorset) in the early 6th century. However, some consider these sources unreliable, and a modern view is that Arthur was a professional soldier in service to the British kings after the Roman occupation. Geoffrey of Monmouth's 12th century *Historia Regum Brittaniae*, based on Nennius and Welsh folklore, gave the legend – with the Round Table, Camelot, Lancelot, Guinevere and the Holy Grail – the form in which it was transmitted through the Middle Ages.

Arthur, Chester Alan (1830–86) 21st US president (1881–85). In 1880, he was nominated by the Republican Party as vice president in the (justified) hope that he could deliver New York. Arthur became president after the assassination of James GARFIELD and tried to reform the SPOILS SYSTEM, in which incoming presidents replaced government staff with their own appointees. A Civil Service Commission with a merit system was created, but his modest reforms were often frustrated by Congress. Gentlemanly but uninspiring, and suffering from incurable illness, he was not renominated (1884). Arthur was succeeded by Grover CLEVELAND.

Arthurian romance In literature, the numerous medieval stories based on the largely apocryphal life of King ARTHUR of Britain and his knights. The 9th century *Historia Brittonum* by Nennius contains the first references to Arthur as a Christian warrior. Geoffrey of Monmouth's *Historia Regum Brittaniae* (c.1135) embellishes the tale with details of Excalibur (his sword), Merlin the prophet, the CHIVALRY of Arthur's knights, Mordred's treachery, and Arthur's voyage to Avalon. Wace's *Roman de Brut* (1155) translated the tale into French. CHRÉTIEN DE TROYES added the story of the quest for the Holy Grail, which in turn inspired von Eschenbach's *Parzival* (1200–12). Sir Thomas Malory's *Morte d'Arthur* (1485) synthesized all the previous Arthurian material into a coherent cycle. More recent interpretations of the legend include Tennyson's *Idylls of the King* (1859–88).

artichoke (globe artichoke) Tall, thistle-like perennial plant with large, edible, immature flower heads, native to the Mediterranean. It has spiny leaves and blue flowers. Height: 0.9–1.5m (3–5ft). Family Asteraceae/Compositae; species *Cynara scolymus*. A different plant, the Jerusalem artichoke, is grown for its edible tubers. Family Asteraceae/Compositae; species *Helianthus tuberosus*.

Articles of Confederation (1781) First Federal constitution of the US, drafted by the Continental Congress in 1777. Distrust of central authority and state rivalries produced a weak central government, with Congress dependent on the states and unable to enforce its own legislation. The weakness of the Articles was analyzed by Alexander Hamilton and James MADISON in *The Federalist*, and the CONSTITUTIONAL CONVENTION met in 1787 to draft the CONSTITUTION OF THE UNITED STATES.

artificial insemination Method of inducing PREGNANCY without sexual intercourse by injecting SPERM into the female genital tract. Used extensively in livestock farming, artificial insemination allows proven sires to breed with many females at low cost.

artificial intelligence (AI) Science concerned with developing COMPUTERS and computer PROGRAMS that model human intelligence. The most common form of AI involves a computer being programmed to answer questions on a specialized subject. Such "expert systems" are said to display the human ability to perform expert analytical tasks. A closely related science, sometimes known as "artificial life," is concerned with more low-level intelligence. For example, a ROBOT may be programmed to find its way around a maze, displaying the basic ability to interact physically with its surroundings.

artificial selection Breeding of plants, animals or other organisms in which the parents are individually selected in order to perpetuate certain desired traits and eliminate others from the captive population. By this means, most of our domestic crops, livestock and pets have arisen. Artificial selection can be accelerated by techniques such as plant TISSUE CULTURE and the ARTIFICIAL INSEMINATION of livestock. *See also* CLONE; GENETIC ENGINEERING

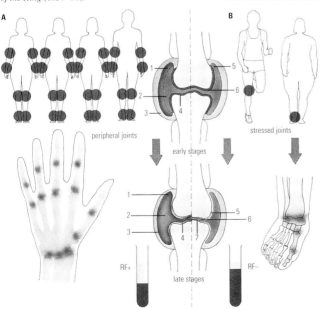

A

B

◄ **arthritis** Meaning inflammation of the joints, arthritis has two main types. In rheumatoid arthritis (A) the synovial membrane (1) becomes inflamed and thickened and produces increased synovial fluid within the joint (2). The capsule and surrounding tissues (3) become inflamed, while joint cartilage is damaged (4). Peripheral joints, as in feet and hands, are involved. Blood tests show rheumatoid factor. Osteoarthritis (B), a degenerative disease, involves thinning of cartilage (5), loss of joint space (6) and bone damage (7). Heavily used or weight-bearing joints are affected. Blood tests are normal.

peripheral joints

stressed joints

early stages

late stages

RF+

RF–

► **art nouveau** Examples of art nouveau style, popular in Europe from the 1880s to the start of World War 1. The movement was known as *Jugendstijl* in Germany, *Sezession* in Austria, and *Modernismo* in Spain. It was most influential in the decorative arts, such as ceramics, jewellery and book illustration. The style of art nouveau was richly ornamental and asymmetrical, characterized by naturalistic plant and animal motifs, and whirling patterns of sinuous lines. Designs are often romantic and exotic in content. The glassware of Tiffany and Lalique is typical. Liberty's department store, London, became famous for its championing of art nouveau.

artillery Projectile-firing weapons with a carriage or mount. An artillery piece is generally one of four types: gun, howitzer, mortar or missile launcher. Modern artillery is classified according to calibre; ranging from under 105mm for light artillery to more than 155mm for heavy. Advances in the 19th century such as smokeless powder, elongated shells, rifling and rapid-fire breach loading, made artillery indispensable in battle. *See also* CANNON

art nouveau Ornamental style which flourished in most of central and w Europe and the US from *c.*1890 to World War 1. The idea originated in England with the ARTS AND CRAFTS MOVEMENT. Focusing mainly on the decorative arts, its most characteristic forms come from sinuous distortions of plant forms and asymmetrical lines. Outstanding art nouveau graphic artists included BEARDSLEY, TIFFANY and Mucha. Charles Rennie MACKINTOSH, Antonio GAUDÍ and Victor Horta were among its most gifted architects.

Arts and Crafts Movement Late 19th- and early 20th-century British movement led by artists who wanted to revitalize the decorative arts by returning to the ideals of medieval craftsmanship. Inspired by William MORRIS, the movement contributed to European ART NOUVEAU, but was eventually transformed by the acceptance of modern industrial methods. *See also* RUSKIN, JOHN

Aruba Dutch island in the Caribbean, off the coast of NW Venezuela; the capital is Oranjestad. An autonomous part of the Netherlands. Industries: oil refining, phosphates, tourism. Area: 193sq km (75sq mi). Pop. (2000) 58,000.

Arunachal Pradesh State of the eastern Himalayas in the far NE of India. The capital is Itanagar. Once a district of ASSAM, it was invaded by the Chinese (1962), but returned to India in 1963. It became a union territory in 1972 and the 24th state of India in 1986.

Most of the state is mountainous forest and jungle. Its main products are coffee, rubber, fruit, spices and rice. It is India's least densely populated state. Area: 81,426sq km (31,438sq mi). Pop. (1991) 864,558.

Aryan Language of an ancient people in the region between the Caspian Sea and Hindu Kush mountains. About 1500 BC one branch entered India, introducing the SANSKRIT language; another branch migrated to Europe. In their 1930s racist propaganda, the Nazis traced German descent from Aryans.

asbestos Group of fibrous, naturally occurring, silicate minerals used in insulating, fireproofing, brake lining and in astronaut suits. Several types exist, the most common being white asbestos. Many countries have banned the use of asbestos, as it can cause lung cancer and asbestosis, a lung disease.

Ascension Island in the S Atlantic Ocean; a UK dependency administered from the colony of St. HELENA. Discovered by the Portuguese (1501), it was occupied by Britain in the early 19th century. It now serves as an Anglo-American telecommunications centre, and was an important base for British forces during the Falklands War. Area: 88sq km (34sq mi). Pop. (1993) 1,117.

Ascension Day Christian feast day that commemorates Christ's ascension into heaven 40 days after his resurrection. It falls on a Thursday, the 40th day after EASTER. It used to be called Holy Thursday.

ascorbic acid *See* VITAMIN

asexual reproduction Type of reproduction in organisms that does not involve the union of male and female reproductive cells. It occurs in three forms: FISSION, BUDDING and VEGETATIVE REPRODUCTION. *See also* CLONE; SEXUAL REPRODUCTION

Asgard In ancient TEUTONIC MYTHOLOGY, the domain of the gods, who resided there in a variety of splendid palaces. The most famous of these was VALHALLA, to which heroes slain in battle were carried in triumph.

ash Group of mainly deciduous trees of the genus *Fraxinus* growing in temperate regions, usually having leaves made up of many small leaflets and winged fruits. The wood is elastic, strong and shock-resistant, and is widely used for furniture. Species include manna ash, *F. ornus*, the flowering ash of S Europe and Asia Minor; the European ash, *F. excelsior*, which grows to 45m (148ft) tall; and *F. floribunda*, a native of the Himalayas. Family Oleaceae. The mountain ash of Europe and Asia (*Sorbus aucuparia*) comes from a different family.

Ascham, Roger (1515–68) English writer and classical scholar. His treatises *Toxophilus* (1545) and *The Scholemaster* (1570) outline the ideal elements of a humanist education. Ascham believed that British scholars should write in English, but recommended a "pure" prose style based on Latin. He was tutor to ELIZABETH I both before and after her accession.

Ashanti Administrative region and ethnic group of central Ghana, W Africa. The capital is KUMASI. The Ashanti people (a matrilineal society) established a powerful empire based on the slave trade with the British and Dutch. In the 18th century, their influence extended into Togo and the Ivory Coast. Conflicts with the British throughout the 19th century were finally resolved in 1902, when the Ashanti territories (a British protectorate since 1896) were declared a crown colony. The region is the main area of Ghana's vital cocoa production. The Ashanti are renowned for their crafts, including high-quality goldwork and weaving. Today, Ashanti is the most populous of Ghana's ten regions. Area: 24,390sq km (9,414sq mi). Pop. (1984) 2,090,100.

Ashcan school Nickname given for group of late 19th- and early 20th-century US artists, including George BEL-LOWS, Robert HENRI and Edward HOPPER, who rejected academic and traditional artistic subjects for the seamier aspects of city life (especially in New York). The inspiration for the group's interest in everyday life came from four core members, William Glackens, John Sloan, George Luks and Everett Shinn, all of whom previously worked as artist-reporters in Philadelphia.

Ashcroft, Dame Peggy (1907–91) English actress. She made her stage debut in 1926. Ashcroft's greatest performances include her Desdemona to Paul ROBE-SON's Othello (1930), Juliet in the John GIELGUD production of *Romeo and Juliet* (1935), and the title role in *Hedda Gabler* (1954). She was made a dame in 1956 and won an Oscar as Best Supporting Actress in *A Passage to India* (1984).

Ashdown, Paddy (Jeremy John Durham) (1941–) British politician, first leader of the Social and LIBERAL DEMOCRATS (1988–99), b. India. He entered Parliament in 1983 and quickly became a leading spokesman for the LIBERAL PARTY. He succeeded David STEEL, who stood down as Liberal leader when the merger with the SOCIAL DEMOCRATIC PARTY (SDP) was formalized. He was succeeded as party leader by Charles KENNEDY.

Ashe, Arthur Robert (1943–93) US tennis player. Ashe won the US (1968), Australian (1970) and Wimbledon (1975) championships. Heart surgery (1979) ended his tournament career, but in 1980 he became the non-playing captain of the US Davis Cup team. He died of AIDS contracted from a blood transfusion.

Ashes, The Cricket trophy, consisting of an urn containing the ashes of stumps and bails, nominally held by the winner of the test series between England and Australia. The urn was presented to the English captain in 1883 after Australia's victory in the 1882 Oval test had prompted a mock obituary to English cricket in the *Sporting Times*.

Ashgabat (formerly Ashkhabad) Capital of the central Asian republic of Turkmenistan, located 40km (25mi) from the Iranian border. Founded in 1881 as a Russian fortress between the Kara-Kum Desert and the Kopet Dagh Mountains, it was largely rebuilt after a severe earthquake in 1948. Its present name was adopted after the republic attained independence from the former Soviet Union in 1992. Industries: textiles, carpets, silk, metalware, glass, light machinery. Pop. (1995) 536,000.

Ashikaga City in central Japan, 80km (50mi) N of Tokyo. An ancient silk-weaving centre, it was the home of the Ashikaga shogunate (1338–1573). Sites include a sacred 12th century temple and an important library of Chinese classics. Pop. (1990) 167,687

Ashkenazim Jews who originally settled in NW Europe, as distinguished from the SEPHARDIM, who settled in Spain and Portugal.

Ashkenazy, Vladimir (1937–) Icelandic pianist and conductor, b. Russia. His interpretations of Russian piano music (especially Rachmaninov) earned international praise, and he shared first prize in the Tchaikovsky Piano Competition (1962). Ashkenazy was principal conductor of the Philharmonia Orchestra (1981–86) and musical director of the Royal Philharmonic Orchestra (1987–94).

Ashoka (*c.*271–238 BC) Indian emperor (r.264–238 BC). The greatest emperor of the MAURYA EMPIRE, at first he fought to expand his empire. Ashoka was disgusted by the bloodshed of war and, renouncing conquest by force, embraced BUDDHISM. He became one of its most fervent supporters and spread its ideas through missionaries to neighbouring countries and through edicts engraved on pillars. His empire encompassed most of India and large areas of Afghanistan.

Ashton, Sir Frederick (1904–88) British choreographer and ballet director, b. Ecuador. In 1935 Ashton joined the Sadler's Wells Ballet (now the Royal Ballet) in London and was its chief choreographer until 1963, then its director (1963–70). His work for dancers such as Margot FONTEYN and Ninette de VALOIS earned him a reputation as Britain's greatest choreographer. His major pieces include *Cinderella* (1948), *Ondine* (1958) and *Marguèrite and Armand* (1963).

Ashurbanipal (d. *c.*627 BC) (Assurbanipal) Last great king of ASSYRIA (668–*c.*627 BC). The Assyrian empire was at its height in his reign, reaching into Upper Egypt, before a rapid decline. Excavations at NINEVEH after 1850 revealed an advanced civilization.

Ash Wednesday First day of LENT

Asia World's largest continent. Entirely in the Eastern Hemisphere, it extends from N of the Arctic Circle in Russia to S of the Equator in Indonesia. **Land** On the W, Asia's boundary with Europe follows a line through the Ural Mountains, W of the CASPIAN SEA and along the Caucasus. Geographically, Europe and Asia are one enormous continent (Eurasia), but historically they have always been regarded as separate continents. Asia has six regions, each defined largely by mountain ranges. Northern Asia includes the massive, inhospitable region of SIBERIA. A large part lies within the Arctic Circle, forming a vast cold, treeless plain (tundra). Southern Siberia includes great coniferous forests (taiga) and the Russian steppes. Its S boundary runs through the TIEN SHAN and Yablonovy Mountains and Lake BAIKAL, the world's deepest lake. The high plateau area of Central Asia extends S to the Himalayas and includes the W Chinese provinces of TIBET and SINKIANG, as well as MONGOLIA. Much of the area is desert, the largest being the GOBI and TAKLA MAKAN. The Tibetan Plateau is mostly barren. Eastern Asia lies between the plateaux of Central Asia and the Pacific. It is a region of highlands and plains, watered by broad rivers. Off the E coast there are many islands, the most important being the Japanese islands of HOKKAIDO, HONSHU and KYUSHU and the Chinese island of TAIWAN. Southeast Asia includes the INDOCHINA peninsula, part of which forms the MALAY PENINSULA, BURMA and a large number of islands, among which the PHILIPPINES and INDONESIA are the most important. The N of this region is mountainous and the S mainly low-lying. Southern Asia consists of the Indian subcontinent and the island of SRI LANKA. In the N it is bounded by the HINDU KUSH, Pamir, KARAKO-RAM and the Himalayan Mountains. In the HIMALAYAS is Mount EVEREST, the world's highest mountain. To the S of the mountains lie wide plains, crossed by rivers flowing from the Himalayas. Farther S is the DECCAN Plateau that rises on its E and W edges, culminating in the E and W GHATS. Southwest Asia includes most of the region known as the MIDDLE EAST. It is made up largely of two peninsulas, Anatolia (ASIA MINOR) and the vast Arabian Peninsula. It is also a region of large inland seas: the Aral, Caspian, Dead and Black seas. **Structure and geology** The most striking feature of the continent is the massive range of Himalayan fold mountains that were formed when the Indo-Australian and Eurasian tectonic plates collided in the Mesozoic era. Most of China and S central Asia is composed of folded Paleozoic and Mesozoic sediments, and large expanses of central Siberia consist of flat-lying sediments of the same age, some completely exposed. The Indian subcontinent is largely pre-Cambrian except for the Deccan Plateau, which is a complex series of lava flows. **Lakes and rivers** Most of the major Asian lakes are found in the centre of the continent and include the Caspian Sea (the largest landlocked body of water in the world), the ARAL SEA and Lake BALKHASH. The River YANGTZE in China, is Asia's longest. The River HUANG HE (Yellow) is China's other major river. Like these rivers, the three principal waterways of SE Asia (IRRAWADDY, SALWEEN, MEKONG) rise on the Tibetan Plateau but flow S instead of E. The INDUS, BRAHMAPUTRA and GANGES are the largest rivers of the Indian subcontinent, and the OB, YENISEI and LENA are the continent's major N-flowing rivers, emptying into the Arctic Ocean. **Climate and vegetation** Except for the climate found on W temperate seaboards, all the world's major climatic divisions (with local variations) are represented in the continent. The monsoon climates of India and W Southeast Asia are peculiar to these regions. Large expanses are covered by desert and semi-arid grassland, with belts of coniferous forest to the N and tropical forest to the S. **Peoples** Asians constitute more than half the world's population. The main language groups are Indo-Aryan, Sino-Tibetan, Ural-Altaic, Malayan and Semitic. Mandarin Chinese has more speakers than any other single language. HINDUISM is the religion with the most adherents, although it is confined to India and SE Asia. ISLAM, CONFUCIANISM, BUDDHISM, SHINTO, CHRISTIANITY, TAOISM and JUDAISM are also important, with the Islamic influence stretching from Turkey to Indonesia. **Recent history** Since World War 2, the history of Asia has been dominated by three main themes: the legacy of COLONIALISM, the growth of COMMUNISM and the rise of Islamic FUNDAMENTALISM. The Indian subcontinent gained its independence from Britain in 1947, when India and Pakistan became separate nations. Indonesia achieved formal independence from the Netherlands in 1949. During the 1950s, Indochina and Malaysia won independence from France and Britain respectively after military confrontations. The spread of communism began with the victory of MAO ZEDONG in China in 1949. North Korea failed, in its war with South Korea (1950–53), to establish a united communist state, and communism was also repulsed with Western help in Indonesia. Communism did finally gain control of Vietnam and Cambodia, following the VIETNAM WAR. The breakup of the Soviet Union led to the creation of eight "new" countries in central Asia, few of which were politically stable or economically strong. In the Middle East, Israel remained on uneasy terms with its Arab neighbours, and Iraq was involved in prolonged war with fundamentalist Iran (1980–88) and later with an international coalition, headed by the US, following Iraq's invasion of Kuwait. **Economy** Agriculture is important, although less than 10% of the continent is cultivated. Asia produces more than 90% of the world's rice, rubber, cotton and tobacco. Rice is the major crop in the E and S; wheat and barley are grown in the W and N. China, Japan and Russia are the most highly industrialized countries in terms of traditional heavy materials. Oil is the most important export of many Middle East countries. Since the 1960s there has been dramatic commercial growth in several countries of SE and E Asia based on a combination of household and high-tech products. Following Japan's example, South Korea, Taiwan, Hong Kong, Singapore, Malaysia and Thailand form the "tiger" economies. In 1997 these economies plunged into recession and are only slowly returning to prosperity. Total area: 17,139,445sq mi (44,391,206sq km) *Highest mountain* Mount Everest (Nepal) 29,029ft (8,848m) *Longest river* Yangtze (China) 3,716mi (5,980km) *Population* 3,193 million *Largest*

cities Shanghai (8,760,000); Tokyo (7,927,000); Beijing (6,560,000) *See also* articles on individual countries

Asia Minor (Anatolia) Great peninsula of W Asia making up most of modern Turkey. The Bosporus, the Sea of Marmara and the Dardanelles divide both Turkey and Europe from Asia. Apart from a very narrow coastal plain, the area is a high, arid plateau. In the SE the Taurus Range rises to more than 3,750m (12,000ft). The area has been inhabited since the Bronze Age, with civilizations such as Troy. The HITTITES established a kingdom here in c.1800 BC. From the 8th century BC, the Greeks established colonies in the area; the Persians invaded in the 6th century BC and the PERSIAN WARS followed. ALEXANDER THE GREAT's empire included this region, although it split into several states after his death. The Romans unified the area in the 2nd century AD. By the 6th century, it had become part of the Byzantine empire. In the 13th–15th centuries, it was conquered by the Ottoman Turks and remained part of the Ottoman Empire until the establishment of the Republic of Turkey in 1923.

Asimov, Isaac (1920–92) US writer and scientist, b. Russia. Although he published several serious scientific works, Asimov is best known for his science fiction novels and short stories. His prolific output contains some of the finest works in the genre, including *I, Robot* (1950) and *The Foundation Trilogy* (1951–53).

Asmara (Asmera) Capital of Eritrea, NE Africa. Occupied by Italy in 1889, it was their colonial capital and the main base for the invasion of Ethiopia (1935–36). Asmara was captured by the British in 1941 and, in the 1950s, the US built Africa's biggest military communications centre here. The city was absorbed by Ethiopia in 1952, and was the main garrison in the fight against Eritrean rebels seeking independence. In 1993, Asmara became the capital of independent ERITREA. Though ravaged by drought, famine and war, it began a strong recovery based on numerous light industries. Pop. (1991) 367,300.

asp Popular name for two species of VIPER, the asp viper of S Europe (*Vipera aspis*), and the Egyptian asp, a horned, side-winding viper of N Africa (*Cerastes cerastes*). They are weakly venomous. Family Viperidae.

asparagus Perennial plants native to Asia and Africa. They have tuberous or fleshy roots, scale-like leaves and small greenish flowers. *Asparagus officinalis* is grown widely for its edible tender shoots. Family Liliaceae.

aspen One of three species of trees of the genus *Populus*, with toothed, rounded leaves. Native to temperate Eurasia, North Africa and North America, they grow up to 30m (100ft). Family Salicaceae.

asphalt *See* BITUMEN

asphyxiation Death resulting from lack of oxygen in air breathed, causing a build up of carbon dioxide in the body tissues. Common causes of asphyxiation are drowning and smoke inhalation.

aspidistra (cast-iron plant) Genus of durable house plants native to Asia, with long, broad, arching leaves. Height: to 91cm (3ft). Family Liliaceae.

aspirin (acetylsalicylic acid) Drug widely used to reduce fever and as an ANALGESIC to relieve minor pain. Recent evidence indicates aspirin can inhibit the formation of blood clots and in low doses can reduce the danger of heart attack and stroke. Aspirin can irritate the stomach and in overdose is toxic and can cause death.

Asplund, (Erik) Gunnar (1885–1940) Swedish architect. He was a pioneer of modernist architecture in Sweden and a major exponent of FUNCTIONALISM. Asplund's graceful and restrained designs include the Woodland Crematorium, Stockholm (1935–40).

Asquith, Herbert Henry, 1st Earl of Oxford and Asquith (1852–1928) British statesman, last Liberal prime minister (1908–16). He entered Parliament in 1886 and served as GLADSTONE's home secretary (1892–95). Asquith was chancellor of the exchequer under Sir Henry CAMPBELL-BANNERMAN, and succeeded him as prime minister. His administration was notable for its social welfare legislation, such as the introduction of old-age pensions (1908) and unemployment insurance (1911). Asquith also passed the Parliament Act (1911) that ended the Lords' power of veto over Commons legislation. His attempts to establish Home Rule for Ireland were rejected by Conservatives and Unionists. Asquith took Britain into WORLD WAR 1 but was an ineffective wartime leader. In 1915, he formed a coalition government with the Conservative Party. He was replaced as prime minister in a cabinet coup led by LLOYD GEORGE. Asquith stayed on as LIBERAL PARTY leader until 1926.

ass Wild, speedy, long-eared member of the HORSE family found in African and Asian desert and mountain areas. Smaller than the horse, it has a short mane and tail, small hoofs and dorsal stripes. The three African races (species *Equus asinus*) are the Nubian, North African and the rare Somali. Height: 90–150cm (3–5ft) at shoulder. Asian races are the kiang and the ONAGER. Family Equidae.

Assad, Hafez al- (1928–2000) Syrian statesman, president (1970–2000). He served as minister of defence (1965–70), before seizing power in a military coup. Assad was elected president in 1971. He took a hardline stance against Israel, and Syrian troops participated in the 1973 ARAB-ISRAELI WAR. Assad was accused of harbouring terrorists. In 1976, Syrian troops were deployed in the Lebanese civil war. In 1987 the Syrian army moved into Beirut to restore order. In the mid-1990s, his stance toward Israel softened and he played an vital role in the Israeli-Palestinian peace negotiations. Syria supported the coalition forces arrayed against Iraq in the Gulf War. He was succeeded as president by his son, Bashar al-Assad.

Assam State in NE India, almost separated from the rest of the country by Bangladesh. The capital is Dispur, and the largest city is Guwahati. It became a state in 1950, but its people have forcibly resisted immigration from West Bengal and Bangladesh. The Bodo minority continue to push for a separate state N of the River BRAHMAPUTRA. Its main products are tea, jute, timber and oil. Area: 78,438sq km (30,277sq mi). Pop. (1991) 22,414,322.

assassin (Arabic, users of hashish) Name given to a Muslim sect of ISMAILIS, founded *c*.1090 by Hasan ibn al-Sabbah. They fought against orthodox Muslims and Christian Crusaders, and committed many political murders until their defeat in the 13th century.

assay Test to determine the amount of a metal present in a sample of material such as ores and alloys. The term is normally applied to tests for gold, silver or platinum.

assembly language COMPUTER LANGUAGE for writing computer PROGRAMS in a form that is closely related to the form that computers can understand directly. Assembly language is a low-level language. Each instruction to be carried out by the computer is represented by a simple code. Programs using these codes are translated by an "assembler" into a form the computer can understand.

asset Anything owned by a person or a company that has a money value. **Current** assets can be easily liquidated to produce their cash value. **Fixed** assets include buildings, machinery and land. Goodwill and PATENTS are described as **intangible** assets because they have potential, rather than actual, money value. Asset stripping is the practice of taking over a business and selling off its assets.

assimilation Process by which an organism uses substances taken in from its surroundings to make new living protoplasm or to provide energy for metabolic processes. It includes the incorporation of the products of food digestion into living tissues in animals and the synthesis of new organic material by a plant during photosynthesis.

Assiniboine Nomadic Native North American tribe. Their language is Siouan, and they are related to the Dakotas. Their culture is that of the Plains Indians. They were peaceful trading partners of the HUDSON'S BAY COMPANY, and their trade helped to destroy the French monopoly among tribes of the region. Today, they number *c*.5,000.

Association of Southeast Asian Nations (ASEAN) Regional alliance formed in 1967 to promote economic cooperation. Its members are Indonesia, Malaysia, Philippines, Singapore, Thailand, Brunei, Vietnam, Laos and Burma. Based in Jakarta, Indonesia, it took over the nonmilitary aspects of the SOUTHEAST ASIA TREATY ORGANIZATION (SEATO) in 1975.

associative law Rule of combination in mathematics in which the result of two or more operations on terms does not depend on the way in which they are grouped. Thus, normal addition and multiplication of numbers follows the associative law, since $a + (b + c) = (a + b) + c$, and $a \times (b \times c) = (a \times b) \times c$.

assonance Imperfect rhyme, where the stressed vowels in the words agree, but the consonants do not. Examples are: "hulks, exults"; "penitent, reticence"; "neck, met." Commonly found in medieval ballads, assonance has also been used as a literary device by such poets as John MILTON and Alfred TENNYSON.

Assumption In the Roman Catholic Church, principal feast of the Blessed Virgin Mary. It is celebrated on 15 August, and marks the occasion when she was taken up into heaven at the end of her life on Earth.

Assyria Ancient empire of the Middle East. It took its name from the city of Ashur (Assur) on the River Tigris near modern Mosul, Iraq. The Assyrian empire was established in the 3rd millennium BC and reached its zenith between the 9th and 7th centuries BC, when it extended

◄ **Assyria** The alabaster relief, originally painted, shows King Ashurbanipal's lion hunt. This is part of a series of narrative wall reliefs (*c*.650) found in the Northern Palace, Nineveh, and represents the highest achievement of Assyrian art.

from the Nile to the Persian Gulf and N into Anatolia. Thereafter it was absorbed by the Persian empire. Under ASHURBANIPAL, art and learning reached their peak. The luxuriance of Ashurbanipal's court at NINEVEH was legendary and, combined with the cost of maintaining his armies, weakened the empire. The capture of Nineveh in 612 BC marked the terminal decline of Assyria.

Assyro-Babylonian mythology Early mythology of the Middle East (Mesopotamia) that described a cosmic order of heaven, Earth and an underworld. Some 4,000 deities and demons directed the physical and spiritual activities of the world.

Astaire, Fred (1899–1987) US dancer, actor and choreographer. His sparkling, improvised solo dances redefined the musical. In 1933, cinema's greatest partnership was formed, when he starred opposite Ginger ROGERS in *Flying Down to Rio*. Fred and Ginger made ten films together. Their first major MGM musical was *The Gay Divorcee* (1934). Classics include *Top Hat* (1935) and *Swing Time* (1936). *The Barkleys of Broadway* (1949) was their last film together. Other dance partners included: Audrey HEPBURN, Rita HAYWORTH and Judy GARLAND.

Astarna (formerly Akmola) Capital-designate of Kazakstan. Astarna lies on the River Ishim in the steppes of N central Kazakstan. Under Soviet rule, it functioned as capital of the Virgin Lands. From 1961 to 1993, it was known as Tselinograd. Pop. (1990) 281,400.

Astarte (Ashtar or Ashtoreth) Phoenician goddess of fertility and love, the equivalent of ISHTAR of the Assyro-Babylonians and APHRODITE of the Greeks. She is represented by a crescent, perhaps symbolic of the Moon or the horns of a cow.

astatine (symbol At) Semimetallic radioactive element that is one of the HALOGENS (group VII of the periodic table). It is rare in nature and is found in radioactive decay. Astatine-211 will collect in the thyroid gland and is used in medicine as a radioactive tracer. Properties: at.no. 85; r.a.m. 211; m.p. 302°C (575.6°F); b.p. 377°C (710.6°F); most stable isotope At^{210} (half-life 8.3hr).

aster Genus of mostly perennial, leafy, stemmed plants native to the Americas and Eurasia. Asters are popular garden plants and most bear daisy-like flowers. Family Asteraceae/Compositae.

asteroid Small body in an independent orbit around the Sun. The majority move between the orbits of Mars and Jupiter, in the main asteroid belt. The largest asteroid (and the first to be discovered) was CERES, with a diameter of 913km (567mi). There are thought to be a million asteroids with a diameter greater than 1km (0.6mi); below this, they decrease in size to dust particles. Some very small objects find their way to Earth as METEORITES. So far nearly 6,000 asteroids have been catalogued and have had their orbits calculated. This figure is increasing by several hundred a year. At least 10,000 more have been observed, but not often enough for an orbit to be calculated. Asteroids almost certainly originate from the time of the formation of the SOLAR SYSTEM.

asthma Disorder of the respiratory system in which the bronchi (air passages) of the lungs go into spasm, making breathing difficult. It can be triggered by infection, air pollution, allergy, certain drugs, exertion or emotional stress. Allergic asthma may be treated by injections aimed at lessening sensitivity to specific allergens. Otherwise treatment is with bronchodilators to relax the bronchial muscles and ease breathing.

astigmatism Defect of vision in which the curvature of the lens differs from one perpendicular plane to another. It can be compensated for by use of corrective lenses.

Aston, Francis William (1877–1945) English physicist. He was awarded the 1922 Nobel Prize for chemistry for his work on ISOTOPES. Aston developed the MASS SPECTROGRAPH, which he used to identify 212 naturally occurring isotopes.

Astor, John Jacob (1763–1848) US financier, b. Germany. In 1808 he founded the AMERICAN FUR COMPANY. After 1812 Astor acquired a virtual monopoly of the US fur trade. In the 1830s he concentrated on land investment and became the wealthiest man in the US. His great-great-grandson William Waldorf Astor (Viscount Astor) (1879–1952) was married to Vicountess Nancy ASTOR.

Astor, Nancy Witcher (Langhorne), Viscountess (1879–1964) British politician, b. USA, the first woman elected to the House of Commons (1919–45). A Conservative, Lady Astor advocated temperance, educational reform and women's and children's welfare. In the 1930s, she and her husband William Waldorf Astor (Viscount Astor) were at the centre of a group of influential proponents of appeasement toward Nazi Germany.

Astrakhan (Astrachan) City-port on the Caspian Sea, S Russia. It was developed by the Mongols in the 13th century. In the Russian civil war (1917–20) the city remained in "White" Russian hands, becoming a base for the Caspian Sea conquest of 1920. Industries: fishing, shipbuilding, engineering, oil-refining. Pop. (1992) 512,000.

astrobiology *See* EXOBIOLOGY

astrolabe Early astronomical instrument for showing the appearance of the celestial sphere at a given moment and for determining the altitude of celestial bodies. The basic form consisted of two concentric disks, one with a star map and one with a scale of angles around its rim, joined and pivoted at their centres (rather like a modern planisphere), with a sighting device attached. Astrolabes were used from the time of the ancient Greeks until the 17th century for navigation, time measurement and terrestrial measurement of height and angles.

astrology Study of the influence supposedly exerted by stars and planets on the natures and lives of human beings. Western astrology draws specifically on the movements of the Sun, Moon, and major planets of the Solar System in relation to the stars that make up the 12 constellations known as the ZODIAC. Astrology originated in ancient Babylon and Persia *c*.3,900 years ago, and rapidly spread through Europe, the Middle East and Asia. In Europe the growing influence of Christianity saw the demise of astrologers. Popular HOROSCOPES still appear in some daily newspapers.

astronaut (Rus. *cosmonaut*) Person who navigates or rides in a space vehicle. The first man to orbit the Earth was the Russian Yuri GAGARIN in 1961. The first man to walk on the Moon was the American Neil ARMSTRONG in 1969. The first woman in space was the Russian Valentina Tereshkova in 1963.

astronomical unit (AU) Mean distance between the Earth and the Sun, used as a fundamental unit of distance, particularly for distances in the Solar System. It is equal to 149,598,000km (92,956,000mi).

astronomy Branch of science concerned with the universe and its components in terms of the relative motions of celestial bodies, their positions on the celestial sphere, physical and chemical structure, evolution and the phenomena occurring on them. It includes celestial mechanics, ASTROPHYSICS, COSMOLOGY and astrometry. **History** Astronomy was first practically used to develop a CALENDAR, the units of which were determined by observing the heavens. The Chinese had a calendar in the 14th century BC. The Greeks developed astronomy significantly between 600 BC and AD 200. THALES introduced geometrical ideas, and PYTHAGORAS saw the universe as a series of concentric spheres. ARISTOTLE believed the Earth to be stationary, but he explained lunar eclipses correctly. ARISTARCHUS put forward a heliocentric theory. HIPPARCHUS used trigonometry to determine astronomical distances. The system devised by PTOLEMY was a geometrical representation of the SOLAR SYSTEM that predicted the motions of the planets with great accuracy. From then on, astronomy remained dormant until the scientific revolution of the 16th and 17th centuries, when COPERNICUS stated his theory that the Earth rotates on its axis and, with all the other planets, revolves round the Sun. KEPLER and his laws of planetary motion refined the theory of heliocentric motion, and his contemporary, GALILEO, made use of the TELESCOPE and discovered the moons of JUPITER. Isaac NEWTON combined the sciences of astronomy and PHYSICS. His laws of motion and universal theory of GRAVITATION provided a physical basis for Kepler's laws and the work of many astronomers from then on, such as the prediction of HALLEY'S COMET and the discovery of the planets URANUS, NEPTUNE and PLUTO. By the early 19th century, the science of celestial mechanics (the study of the motions of bodies in space as they move under the influence of their mutual gravitation) had become highly advanced and new mathematical techniques permitted the solution of the remaining problems of classical gravitation theory as applied to the Solar System. In the second half of the 19th century, astronomy was revolutionized by the introduction of techniques based on photography and SPECTROSCOPY. These encouraged investigation into the physical composition of stars, rather than their position. By this time, larger telescopes were being constructed, which extended the limits of the universe known to man. Harlow SHAPLEY determined the shape and size of our galaxy, and E.P. HUBBLE's study of distant galaxies led to his theory of an expanding universe. BIG BANG and STEADY STATE THEORY of the origins of the universe were formulated. In recent years, space exploration and observation in different parts of the electromagnetic spectrum have contributed to the discovery and postulation of such phenomena as the QUASAR, PULSAR and BLACK HOLE. There are various branches of modern astronomy: **Optical** astronomy is the oldest branch and studies sources of light in space. Light rays can penetrate the atmosphere but, because of disturbances, many observations are now made from above the atmosphere. **Gamma-ray**, INFRARED, **ultraviolet** and **X-ray** astronomy are branches that study the emission of radiation (at all wavelengths) from astronomical objects. Higher wavelengths can be studied from the ground, while lower wavelengths require the use of satellites and balloons. Other branches within astronomy include RADAR ASTRONOMY and RADIO ASTRONOMY.

astrophysics Branch of ASTRONOMY that studies the physical and chemical nature of celestial bodies and their evolution. Many branches of PHYSICS, including NUCLEAR PHYSICS, PLASMA physics, relativity and SPECTROSCOPY, are used to predict properties of stars, planets and other celestial bodies. Astrophysicists also interpret the information obtained from astronomical studies of the electromagnetic spectrum, including light and radio waves.

Asturias, Miguel Ángel (1899–1974) Guatemalan novelist, poet and diplomat. Asturias is best known for his debut novel, *The President* (1946), about the fall and trial of a hated Latin American dictator. A major theme of his novels is the impact of colonialism and industrialization on traditional modes of existence in Latin America. Asturias won the 1967 Nobel Prize for literature.

Asturias Region in NW Spain, bordering the Bay of Biscay and traversed by the Cantabrian Mountains. The capital is Oviedo. The region was named by the Iberians in the 2nd century BC and is famous for its cider and coal mines, the richest in Spain. Industries: coal, manganese, mining, steel and nonferrous metal production, fishing, fruit. Pop. (1991) 1,093,937.

Asunción Capital, chief port and largest city of Paraguay, located on the E bank of the River Paraguay near its junction with the River Pilcomayo. Founded by the Spanish *c.*1536 as a trading post, it was the scene of the Communeros rebellion against Spanish rule in 1721 and was later occupied by Brazil (1868–76). It is an administrative, industrial and cultural centre. Industries: vegetable oil, textiles. Pop. (1992) 637,737.

Aswan City SE Egypt, on the E bank of the River Nile just above Lake Nasser. Aswan was of strategic importance to the Egyptians and Greeks because it controlled all shipping and communications above the first cataract of the NILE. The modern city is a commercial and winter

▲ **astronaut** Astronauts on NASA's shuttle use spacesuits (1) that allow the crew to work in space for up to seven hours. The suit is multi-layered with eight materials combined. The outside is treated nylon to stop damage from tiny meteorites. Four layers of aluminium material then provide a heat shield from solar radiation backed by a fire- and tear-resistant layer. The astronaut is protected from the vacuum of space by a pressure suit of nylon coated with polyeurathane and is kept comfortable in extremes of heat and cold by water pumped through a network of tubes in a nylon chiffon undergarment. (2) The manned manouevring unit (MMU) allows an astronaut to move away from the shuttle. Power comes from 24 thrusters arranged at the corners of the MMU. By releasing pressurized nitrogen from two tanks (3) through nozzles, the astronaut can propel himself/herself through the vacuum. The hand controllers regulate rotation (4) and speed (5). A video camera (6) sends pictures to the shuttle and records the work carried out.

resort centre and has benefited greatly from the construction of the Aswan High Dam. The dam, built with Soviet aid between 1960 and 1970, has a generating capacity of 10 billion kilowatt-hours and supersedes the first Aswan Dam completed in 1902 to establish flood control on the Nile. Many Nubians displaced by the dam's construction have moved to the city. The rock terrain surrounding the lake abounds in Egyptian and Greek temples and although some sites were submerged, the temples of ABU SIMBEL were saved. Industries: copper, steel, textiles. Pop. (1992) 220,000.

Atacama Desert Desert of N Chile, stretching *c*.1,000km (620mi) S from the Peru border. Despite its proximity to the Pacific Ocean it is considered to be the most arid desert in the world; some areas had no recorded rainfall in 400 years. Except where it is artificially irrigated, it is devoid of vegetation. Until the advent of synthetic fertilizers, the desert was mined for sodium nitrate. Large deposits of copper and other minerals remain; nitrates and iodine are extracted from the salt basins.

Atahualpa (1502–33) (Atabalipa) Last Inca ruler of Peru. The son of Huayna Capac, upon his father's death he inherited Quito, while his half-brother Huáscar controlled the rest of the Inca kingdom. In 1532, Atahualpa defeated Huáscar, but his period of complete dominance was to be short-lived. In November 1532, Francisco PIZARRO captured Atahualpa, and he was later executed.

Atalanta In Greek mythology, a swift-footed huntress who was suckled by a she-bear. She offered to marry any man who could outrun her, but to kill those who failed. APHRODITE gave three of the golden apples of the Hesperides to a challenger, Hippomenes. During the race, he dropped them one by one, distracting and delaying Atalanta. They married, but to punish them for consummating their union within the precincts of a temple, ZEUS turned them into lions.

Atatürk, (Mustafa) Kemal (1881–1938) Turkish general and statesman, first president (1923–38) of the Turkish republic. As a young soldier he joined the YOUNG TURKS and was chief of staff to ENVER PASHA in the successful revolution (1908). He fought against the Italians in Tripoli (1911) and defended Gallipoli in the BALKAN WARS. During World War I he led resistance to the Allies' GALLIPOLI CAMPAIGN. The defeat of the OTTOMAN EMPIRE and the capitulation of the sultan persuaded Mustafa Kemal to organize the Turkish Nationalist Party (1919) and set up a rival government in ANKARA. The Treaty of SÈVRES (1920) forced him on the offensive. His expulsion of the Greeks from ASIA MINOR (1921–22) led the sultan to flee Istanbul. The Treaty of Lausanne (1923) saw the creation of a independent republic. His dictatorship undertook sweeping reforms that transformed Turkey into a secular, industrial nation. In 1934, he adopted the title Atatürk (Turkish, father of the Turks). He was succeeded by Ismet INÖNÜ.

atavism Reversion by an organism to a characteristic of its ancestors after an interval of at least one generation in which the trait was absent. The term is no longer in scientific use since the reappearance of ancestral traits is now understood to be the expression of RECESSIVE genes.

ataxia In medicine, a condition where muscles are uncoordinated. It results in clumsiness, irregular and uncontrolled movements, and difficulties with speech. It may be caused by physical injury to the brain or nervous system by a STROKE or by disease.

Aten Ancient Egyptian god. Originally referring to the disc of the Sun, Aten entered into the Egyptian pantheon as the sun god. AKHNATEN elevated his status and virtually established the first monotheistic religion. After Akhnaten's death, the worship of AMON was restored.

Atget, Eugène (1857–1927) French photographer. At the age of 42 he began his photographic record of Paris as reference material for painters. Atget's powerful, serene images of street scenes, people, parks and buildings were "rediscovered" by Berenice Abbott. They form a unique historical document of a vanished era.

Athabasca Lake in W central Canada, on the border between NE Alberta and NW Saskatchewan. Covering *c*.8,080sq km (3,120sq mi) and the fourth largest lake in Canada, it is fed by the Athabasca River from the S and drained by the Slave River to the N. Fort Chipewyan (1788) is preserved at the W end of the lake. There are gold and uranium deposits nearby.

Athabascan (Athapascan or Slave Indians) Tribe and language group of Native North Americans inhabiting NW Canada. They were forced N to the Great Slave Lake and Fort Nelson by the Cree. The term Slave Indian derives from the domination and forced labour exacted by the Cree. The Athabascan tribe has always been closely linked to the Chipewyan, and some authorities regard them as one group. The Athabascan language is a subgroup of the Na-Dene linguistic phylum; there are over 30 languages. Athabascan languages cover the largest geographical area of all Native North American language groups, including Alaska, Yukon, N and W Canada, Oregon, California, New Mexico and W Arizona. Today, the number of Athabascan speakers is believed to exceed 160,000, including the APACHE and NAVAJO.

Athanasian Creed Christian profession of faith, probably written in the 6th century, that explains the teachings of the Church on the Trinity and the incarnation. The Roman Catholic and some Protestant churches accept its authority.

Athanasius, Saint (d.373) Early Christian leader. As patriarch of Alexandria he confuted ARIANISM and, in various writings, defended the teaching that the Son and the Holy Spirit were of equal divinity with God the Father, and so shared a threefold being. He is no longer considered the author of the ATHANASIAN CREED, but he did write the *Life of St Anthony*. His feast day is 2 May.

atheism Philosophical denial of the existence of God or any supernatural or spiritual being. The first Christians were called atheists because they denied Roman religions, but the term is now used to indicate the denial of Christian theism. During the 18th-century ENLIGHTENMENT, David HUME, Immanuel KANT and the Encyclopedists laid the foundations for atheism. In the 19th century, Karl MARX, Friedrich NIETZSCHE and Sigmund FREUD all accommodated some form of atheism into their respective philosophical creeds. In the 20th century, many individuals and groups advocate atheism. *See also* AGNOSTICISM

Athena In Greek mythology, the goddess of wisdom and patroness of the arts and industry, identified with MINERVA. Athena emerged from the head of Zeus fully grown and armed; thereafter, she was her father's most reliable supporter and the sponsor of heroes, such as Heracles, Perseus and Odysseus. In the Trojan War she sided with the Greeks. She helped Argus build the ship *Argo* for JASON and the ARGONAUTS. She received special worship at Athens, where her main temples were the PARTHENON and the Erechtheum.

Athens (Athínai) Capital and largest city of Greece, situated on the Saronic Gulf. The ancient city was built around the ACROPOLIS, a fortified citadel, and was the greatest artistic and cultural centre in ancient Greece, gaining importance after the PERSIAN WARS (500–449 BC). During the 5th century BC, the city prospered under Cimon and PERICLES, who provided a climate in which philosophy and drama were created. The most noted artistic treasures are the PARTHENON (438 BC); the Erechtheum (406 BC); and the Theater of Dionysus (c.500 BC, the oldest of the Greek theatres). Modern Athens and its port of PIRAEUS form a major Mediterranean transport and economic centre. Overcrowding and severe air pollution are damaging the ancient sites. Industries: shipbuilding, tourism, paper, steel machinery, textiles, pottery, brewing, chemicals, glass. Pop. (1991) 3,072,922.

atherosclerosis Most common form of arterial disease. An early stage of ARTERIOSCLEROSIS, it is a thickening of artery walls.

athlete's foot Contagious, fungus-caused infection usually appearing first between the last two toes. Itching, macerated skin and blisters are usual symptoms.

Athelstan (c.895–939) (Aethleston) King of WESSEX (924–39), son and successor of EDWARD THE ELDER. He extended the power of the kingdom built up by his grandfather, ALFRED THE GREAT, by conquest, legislation and marriage alliances. Athelston's victory at the Battle of Brunanburh (937) established him as king of all England.

athletics (track and field) Composite sport that includes running and hurdling events on the track, jumping and throwing field events, cross-country and long-distance road-running and -walking. The first ancient Greek OLYMPIC GAMES (held in 775 BC) featured many athletics events. The first modern Olympic Games were held at Athens in 1896. The world's governing body, the International Amateur Athletic Federation (IAAF), was established in 1912 and the sport maintained its amateur status. During the 1980s and 1990s commercial sponsorship and media coverage has ended top flight amateurism and introduced professional grand prix events.

Athos Holy mountain, 2,032m (6,667ft) high, at the E end of the Acte Peninsula, NE Greece. It is located inside the autonomous Mount Athos community of 20 Byzantine monasteries of the Eastern Orthodox Church established in 962. No women or "beardless boys", or even female animals, are allowed to set foot on the peninsula, and only ten foreigners can visit a day. It forms a special department of Greece in the Macedonia Central region. Area: 336sq km (130sq mi). Pop. (1991) 1,536 (all male).

Atlanta Capital of Georgia, USA, in the NW centre of the state. The land was ceded to Georgia in 1821 by the CREEK and was settled in 1833. The city was founded in 1837 at the E end of the Western and Atlantic Railroad. Originally called Terminus, it became Atlanta in 1845. It served as a Confederate supply depot during the US Civil War. In 1864 Atlanta fell to General SHERMAN, whose army razed the city. It was rapidly rebuilt and soon recovered its importance as a transport and cotton manufacturing center It became the state capital in 1887. It is the headquarters for the Coca-Cola company. Atlanta hosted the 1996 Olympic Games. Industries: textiles, chemicals, iron and steel, electronics. Pop. (1996) 402,000.

Atlantic, Battle of the (1939–43) Campaign for control of the Atlantic sea routes waged by air and naval forces during WORLD WAR 2. The Germans hoped to starve Britain into submission by U-boat attacks on merchant shipping and later to prevent US reinforcements reaching the Mediterranean and Europe. More than 14 million metric tons of shipping were destroyed.

Atlantic Charter Joint declaration of peace aims issued in August 1941 by US President Franklin D. ROOSEVELT and British Prime Minister Winston CHURCHILL. It affirmed the right of all nations to choose their own form of government, promised to restore sovereignty to all nations that had lost it, and advocated the disarmament of aggressor nations.

Atlantic City Resort city in SE New Jersey, USA, built on a 16km (10mi) sandbar in the Atlantic Ocean and settled as a fishing village in 1790. Famous for its 6km (4mi) boardwalk (1896) and its annual Miss America pageant (started in 1921), it became a centre for political and business conventions. In 1976, gambling was legalized and, after the first casinos were opened in 1978, Atlantic City has become a popular tourist centre and stage for sporting events (notably boxing). Pop. (1990) 37,986.

Atlantic Ocean World's second largest ocean stretching from the Arctic Circle in the N to the Antarctic Ocean in the S. Its name derives from the ATLAS Mountains that, for the ancient Greeks, marked the western boundary between the known and the unknown world. Its most striking feature is the MID-ATLANTIC RIDGE that runs N–S for its entire length. At the crest, the ridge is cleft by a deep rift valley, which is frequently offset by E–W transform faults. The age of the crust steadily increases with distance from the central rift, and so there is little doubt that the rift has evolved by SEAFLOOR SPREADING and is associated with the movement of the Americas away from Europe and Africa at a rate of 2–4cm (0.8–1.6in) a year. The average depth of the Atlantic is 3,700m (12,100ft). The greatest known depth is the Milwaukee Deep in the Puerto Rico Trench, which has a depth of 8,650m (28,370ft). The N clockwise gyre is dominated by the fast-flowing GULF STREAM, travelling at speeds of up to 130km (80mi) a day, and forming the W boundary current of the gyre. The S anti-clockwise gyre is atypical in having a weak western boundary current, the Brazil Current. Apart from oil (found mainly in the Gulf of Guinea), sand and gravel are the most important minerals from the Atlantic. The largest single offshore mining operation in the world is located at Ocean Cay on the Grand Bahamas bank, where calcium carbonate is extracted in the form of aragonite. The North Atlantic contains the most valuable fishing grounds in the world, namely the cod fisheries around Iceland, S Greenland and the Grand Banks of Newfoundland. The relatively unexploited fisheries of the South Atlantic are probably less stable than those of the N. Area: 82 million sq km (32 million sq mi).

Atlantis Mythical island in the Atlantic Ocean from which, according to PLATO, a great empire tried to subdue the Mediterranean countries. It has been identified by some with the Greek island of Thera, destroyed by an earthquake c.1450 BC.

Atlas Mountain system in NW Africa, comprising several folded and roughly parallel chains extending c.2,500km (1,500mi) from the coast of SW Morocco to the coast of N Tunisia. North Africa's highest peak, Djebel Toubkal, 4,170m (13,671ft), is found in the High Atlas range in W Morocco.

Atlas In Greek mythology, one of the TITANS, brother of PROMETHEUS. Having fought against Zeus, he was condemned to hold up the heavens.

atman Human soul or self in HINDUISM. *See* BRAHMAN

atmosphere Envelope of gases surrounding the Earth that shields the planet from the harsh environment of space. The gases it contains are vital to life. About 95% by weight of the Earth's atmosphere lies below the 25km (15mi) altitude; the mixture of gases in the lower atmosphere is commonly called air. The atmosphere's composition by weight is: nitrogen 78.09%, oxygen

20.9%, argon 0.93%, 0.03% carbon dioxide, plus 0.05% of hydrogen, the inert gases and varying amounts of water vapor. The atmosphere can be conceived as concentric shells; the innermost is the **troposphere**, in which dust and water vapor create the clouds and weather. The **stratosphere** extends from 10 to 55km (8–36mi) and is cooler and clearer and contains ozone. Above, to a height of 70km (43mi), is the **mesosphere** in which chemical reactions occur, powered by sunlight. The temperature climbs steadily in the **thermosphere**, which gives way to the **exosphere** at c.400km (250mi), where helium and hydrogen may be lost into space. The **ionosphere** ranges from c.50km (30mi) out into the VAN ALLEN RADIATION BELTS.

atmospheric pressure Pressure exerted by the atmosphere because of its gravitational attraction to the Earth (or other body), measured by barometers and usually expressed in units of mercury. Standard atmospheric pressure at sea level is 760mm (29.92in) of mercury. The column of air above each cm^2 of Earth's surface weighs c.1kg (2.2 lb); the column above each in^2 weighs c.6.7kg (14.7lb).

atoll Ring-shaped REEF of CORAL enclosing a shallow LAGOON. An atoll begins as a reef surrounding a slowly subsiding island, usually volcanic. As the island sinks, the coral continues to grow upward until eventually the island is below sea level and only a ring of coral is left at the surface.

atom Smallest particle of MATTER that can take part in a chemical reaction. Every element has its own characteristic atoms. The atom, once thought indivisible, consists of a central, positively charged NUCLEUS orbited by negatively charged ELECTRONS. The nucleus (identified in 1911 by Ernest RUTHERFORD) is composed of tightly packed PROTONS and NEUTRONS. It occupies a small fraction of the atomic space but accounts for almost all of the mass of the atom. In 1913, Niels BOHR suggested that electrons moved in fixed orbits. The study of QUANTUM MECHANICS has since modified the concept of orbits: the Heisenberg UNCERTAINTY PRINCIPLE says it is impossible to know the exact position and MOMENTUM of a SUBATOMIC PARTICLE. The number of electrons in an atom and their configuration determine its chemical properties. Adding or removing one or more electrons produces an ION.

atomic bomb *See* NUCLEAR WEAPON

atomic clock Most accurate of terrestrial CLOCKS. It is an electric clock regulated by such natural periodic phenomena as emitted radiation or atomic vibration; the atoms of CAESIUM are most commonly used. Clocks that run on radiation from hydrogen atoms lose one second in 1.7 million years.

atomic energy *See* NUCLEAR ENERGY

atomic mass number (nucleon number, symbol A) Number of nucleons (PROTONS and NEUTRONS) in the NUCLEUS of an ATOM. In nuclear notation, such as ^7_3Li, the mass number is the upper number and the ATOMIC NUMBER (the number of protons) is the lower one. ISOTOPES of an element have different mass numbers but identical atomic numbers.

atomic mass unit (amu) (symbol u) Unit of MASS used to compare RELATIVE ATOMIC MASS (R.A.M.), defined since 1961 as 1/12th the mass of the most abundant isotope of carbon, carbon–12 (6 electrons, 6 protons and 6 neutrons). One amu is equal to 1.66033×10^{-27} kg.

atomic number (at.no.) (proton number, symbol Z) Number of PROTONS in the NUCLEUS of an ATOM of an element, which is equal to the number of ELECTRONS moving around that nucleus. The atomic number determines the chemical properties of an element and its position in the PERIODIC TABLE. ISOTOPES of an element all have the same atomic number but a different ATOMIC MASS NUMBER.

atomic weight *See* RELATIVE ATOMIC MASS (R.A.M.)

atomism (Gk. *atmos*, "uncuttable") Philosophical theory originated in Greece by Leucippus and elaborated by DEMOCRITUS during the 5th and 4th centuries BC. It held that everything is made of immutable and indivisible particles called atoms. It was an attempt to reconcile the single immutable substance theory of being espoused by Parmenides and other Eleatic philosophers with HERACLITUS' view that all things are subject to change.

atonality Style of music composed using the 12 tones of the chromatic scale without reference to traditional KEYS and HARMONY. Examples include *Pierrot Lunaire* (1912) by Arnold SCHOENBERG. *See also* SERIALISM

atonement In religion, the process by which a sinner seeks forgiveness from, and reconciliation with, God, through an act of expiation such as prayer, fasting or good works.

ATP Abbreviation of ADENOSINE TRIPHOSPHATE

atrium Inner courtyard of a building. It was a common element of Etruscan and ancient Roman dwellings and was also a type of entrance court in early Christian

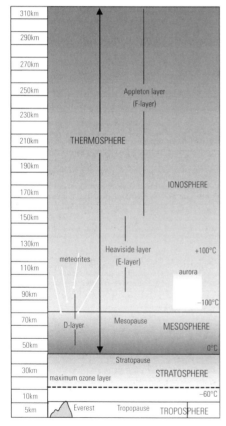

▲ **atmosphere** The Earth's atmosphere is formed of layers. It is believed that the atmosphere has changed three times during the Earth's history. The present atmosphere consists mainly of nitrogen and oxygen.

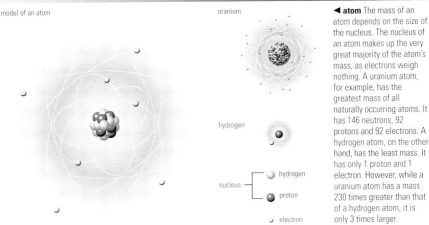

model of an atom

uranium

hydrogen

nucleus — hydrogen

proton

electron

◄ **atom** The mass of an atom depends on the size of the nucleus. The nucleus of an atom makes up the very great majority of the atom's mass, as electrons weigh nothing. A uranium atom, for example, has the greatest mass of all naturally occurring atoms. It has 146 neutrons, 92 protons and 92 electrons. A hydrogen atom, on the other hand, has the least mass. It has only 1 proton and 1 electron. However, while a uranium atom has a mass 230 times greater than that of a hydrogen atom, it is only 3 times larger.

churches. It is also the medical term for one of the upper two chambers of the HEART (also called auricles).

atrophy In medicine, shrinking or wastage of tissues or organs. It may be associated with disease, malnutrition or, in the case of muscle atrophy, with disuse.

atropine Poisonous ALKALOID drug ($C_{17}H_{23}NO_3N$) obtained from certain plants such as *Atropa belladonna* (DEADLY NIGHTSHADE). Atropine is used medicinally to regularize the heartbeat during anaesthesia, to dilate the pupil of the eye and to treat motion sickness.

attar of roses (otto) Essential oil obtained from rose petals, and used as a perfume and perfumery agent. Attar is any fragrant oil derived from plants, though attar of roses (produced by crushing and distilling petals from the damask rose cultivated in the Balkans) is the best known.

Attenborough, Sir David Frederick (1926–) English naturalist and broadcaster, brother of Sir Richard ATTENBOROUGH. He was controller of BBC2 television (1965–68). Since 1954, Attenborough has travelled on zoological and ethnographical filming expeditions, which have formed the basis of such landmark natural history series as *Life on Earth* (1979), *The Living Planet* (1984), *The Trials of Life* (1990) and *The Private Life of Plants* (1995). He was knighted in 1985.

Attenborough, Sir Richard (1923–) English film actor and director. His career has spanned more than 50 years beginning with *In Which We Serve* (1942). Attenborough delivered a menacing performance in *Brighton Rock* (1947). His directorial debut was the World War 1 satire *Oh! What a Lovely War* (1971). Attenborough's acting and directorial style appear to suit biographical films: *Gandhi* (1982) won him Academy Awards for best film and best director. *Shadowlands* (1993), his biopic of C.S. Lewis, brought further critical praise.

Attila (406–53) King of the HUNS (c.439–53), co-ruler with his elder brother until 445. Attila defeated the Eastern Roman emperor THEODOSIUS II, extorting land and tribute, and invaded Gaul in 451. Although his army suffered heavy losses, he invaded Italy in 452, but disease forced his withdrawal. Attila has a reputation as a fierce warrior but was fair to his subjects and encouraged learning. On his death the empire fell apart.

Attlee, Clement Richard, 1st Earl (1883–1967) British statesman, prime minister (1945–51). He entered Parliament in 1922. In 1935, Attlee became leader of the LABOUR PARTY. During World War 2, he served in Winston CHURCHILL's wartime cabinet. Attlee won a

landslide victory in the 1945 general election. His administration was notable for the introduction of important social reforms, such as the NATIONAL HEALTH SERVICE (NHS) and the nationalization of the power industries, the railways and the BANK OF ENGLAND. He also granted independence to India (1947) and Burma (1948). Attlee was re-elected in 1950, but was defeated by Winston Churchill in the 1951 general election. He continued to serve as leader of the opposition until he retired and accepted an earldom in 1955.

attorney general Principal law officer. In the US, the attorney general is the highest law officer of the government and head of the Department of Justice and advises the president and heads of the executive department. In the UK, the attorney general is the chief law officer of the crown and head of the English bar and also legal adviser to the House of Commons and the government.

Atwood, Margaret Eleanor (1939–) Canadian novelist, poet and critic. Best known outside Canada for her novels, she has also published numerous volumes of poetry. Atwood's debut novel, *The Edible Woman* (1969), received immediate acclaim for its stylish and articulate treatment of complex gender relationships. Other novels include *Surfacing* (1972), *The Handmaid's Tale* (1985), *Cat's Eye* (1989) and *Alias Grace* (1996). In 2000, Atwood was awarded the Booker Prize for the novel *The Blind Assassin*.

Auber, Daniel-François-Esprit (1782–1871) French composer. He studied under Cherubini and is regarded as the founder of French grand opera. Auber often collaborated with the librettist Scribe. His 40 operas include *La Muette de Portici* (1828), *Fra Diavolo* (1830) and *La Sirène* (1844).

aubergine (eggplant) Tropical member of the potato (and nightshade) family. The fruit may be eaten as a vegetable. A bushy perennial with violet flowers native to the New World, it is now cultivated in temperate regions. Family Solanaceae; species *Solanum melongena*.

Aubrey, John (1626–97) English biographer and antiquarian. He published only one book in his lifetime, *Miscellanies* (1696). His best-known work was *Lives of Eminent Men* (published 1813). Aubrey's pioneering biographical sketches, which make up in colour what they lack in accuracy, were collected as *Brief Lives* (1898).

Auckland Largest city and chief port of New Zealand, lying on an isthmus on NW North Island. The port, built on land purchased from the Maoris in 1840, handles c.60%

of New Zealand's trade. The first immigrants arrived from Scotland in 1842, and in 1854 the first New Zealand parliament opened here. It was the capital until 1865. Industries: vehicle assembly, boatbuilding, footwear, canning. Auckland has the largest Polynesian population (c.65,000) of any city in the world. Pop. (1994) 929,300.

Auden, W.H. (Wystan Hugh) (1907–73) Anglo-American poet, b. England, one of the major poets of the 20th century. His debut volume, *Poems* (1930), established him as the leading voice in a group of left-wing writers, which included Stephen SPENDER, Louis MAC-NEICE, Cecil DAY-LEWIS and Christopher ISHERWOOD. Auden and Isherwood collaborated on a series of plays, such as *The Ascent of F6* (1936). Auden joined the Republican cause in the Spanish Civil War and wrote *Spain* (1937). In 1939, he emigrated to New York and became a US citizen in 1946. His volume *The Age of Anxiety* (1947) won a Pulitzer Prize. From 1956 to 1961 he was professor of poetry at Oxford University. Auden's poetry adopts many tones, often utilizing colloquial and everyday language. His later poetry is more serious and epistolary, reflecting his conversion to Anglicanism.

audiometry Technique to evaluate hearing ability. An audiometer is an instrument that measures the sensitivity of the ear to sounds.

audit Investigation of private or public business accounting procedures to ensure that the financial statements issued by the organization are in accordance with the actual expenditure, income and valuation of stock, as recorded in any one financial year (or shorter period).

auditory canal Tube leading from the outer EAR to the eardrum. It is c.2.5cm (1in) long.

Audubon, John James (1785–1851) US ornithologist and artist. His remarkable series of some 400 watercolours of birds, often in action, were published in *Birds of America* (1827–38).

Augsburg Historic city on the River Lech, Bavaria. Founded by the Romans (c.15 BC) and named after the Emperor Augustus, it became a free imperial city in 1276 and was a prosperous banking and commercial centre in the 15th and 16th centuries. The AUGSBURG CONFESSION was presented and the Peace of Augsburg (1555) signed here. The cathedral (started 994) claims the oldest stained-glass windows in Europe (11th century). Industries: textiles, engineering, motor vehicles. Pop. (1995) 262,000.

Augsburg, League of (1686) Alliance of the enemies of the French King LOUIS XIV. Composed of Spain, Sweden, the Holy Roman Empire and lesser states, its formation under the Emperor Leopold I was a reaction to French encroachment on the land bordering the Holy Roman Empire. Following the French attack on the PALATINATE in 1688, a new coalition against the French, the Grand Alliance, was formed (1689).

Augsburg, Peace of (1555) Agreement reached by the Diet of the Holy Roman Empire in Augsburg ending the conflict between Roman Catholics and Lutherans in Germany. It established the right of each prince to decide on the nature of religious practice in his lands. Dissenters were allowed to sell their lands and move. Free cities and imperial cities were open to both Catholics and Lutherans. The exclusion of other Protestant sects proved to be a source of future conflict.

Augsburg Confession (1530) Summation of the Lutheran faith, presented to Emperor CHARLES V at the Diet of Augsburg. Its 28 articles were formulated from earlier Lutheran statements principally by Philip MELANCHTHON. It was denounced by the Roman Catholic Church but became a model for later Protestant creeds.

augur In ancient Rome, an interpreter of signs from the gods. Augurs belonged to a priestly college whose job was to "take the auspices" – to perform certain rituals and to study omens, such as the flight of birds. State officials consulted the augurs on the timing of important meetings, battles or other actions.

Augusta State capital of Maine, on the Kennebec River, 72km (45mi) from the Atlantic Ocean. Founded by settlers from Plymouth as a trading post in 1628, it was incorporated in 1797. A dam built across the Kennebec River in 1837 led to Augusta's industry changing from shipping to manufacturing textiles, paper and steel. The city also benefits from tourism. Pop. (1990) 21,325.

Augusta Town on the Savannah River, E Georgia; seat of Richmond county. A trading post was established in 1717 and was named (1735) after the mother of George III. In the American Revolution it was captured (1781) by Continental troops. It served as the capital (1785–95) of Georgia and the US Constitution was ratified here. Augusta expanded rapidly due its tobacco and cotton plantations. Today, it acts as the trade centre for the Central Savannah River Area. Pop. (1990) 47,532.

Augustan Age In literary history, the neoclassical literature of the English RESTORATION. It refers back to the flourishing of literature in the reign (27 BC–AD 14) of Emperor AUGUSTUS, including poets of the ilk of OVID, VIRGIL and HORACE. In late 17th- and early 18th-century England, writers such as DRYDEN, POPE, SWIFT, SHERIDAN, GOLDSMITH, Samuel JOHNSON and Samuel BUTLER extolled the classical values of proportion and elegance. In French literature, the Augustan Age refers to the literature in the reign of Louis XIV (1643–1715), including writers such as RACINE, MOLIÈRE and CORNEILLE.

Augustine, Saint (354–430) Christian theologian and philosopher. His *Confessions* provide an intimate psychological self-portrait of a spirit in search of ultimate purpose. This he believed he found in his conversion to Christianity in 386. As Bishop of Hippo (396–430), North Africa, Augustine defended Christian orthodoxy against MANICHAEISM, DONATISM and Pelagianism. *The City of God* (426) is a model of Christian apologetic literature. Of the Four Fathers of the Latin Church (others being AMBROSE, JEROME and GREGORY I), Augustine is considered the greatest. His feast day is 28 August.

Augustine of Canterbury, Saint (d.604) First Archbishop of CANTERBURY. He was sent from Rome in 596 by Pope GREGORY I, at the head of a 40-strong mission. Arriving in Kent in 597, Augustine converted King ETHELBERT and introduced Roman ecclesiastical practices into England. This led to conflict with the Celtic monks of Britain and Ireland whose traditions had developed in isolation from the continent. The Synod of WHITBY (663) settled disputes in favour of Roman custom. St Augustine's feast day is 28 May (26 May in England and Wales).

Augustinian Name of two distinct and long-established Christian orders. The order of Augustinian Canons was founded in the 11th century. Based on the recommendations of St AUGUSTINE, its discipline was milder than those of full monastic orders. The mendicant order of Augustinian Hermits or Friars was founded in the 13th century and modelled on the DOMINICANS.

Augustus (63 BC–AD 14) (Gaius Julius Caesar Octavianus) First Roman emperor (29 BC–AD 14), also called **Octavian**. Nephew and adopted heir of Julius CAESAR, he formed the Second Triumvirate with Mark ANTONY and Lepidus after Caesar's assassination. They defeated BRUTUS and CASSIUS at Philippi in 42 BC and divided the empire between them. Rivalry between Octavian and

Antony was resolved by the defeat of Antony at ACTIUM in 31 BC. While preserving the form of the republic, Octavian held supreme power. He introduced peace and prosperity after years of civil war. He built up the power and prestige of Rome, encouraging patriotic literature and rebuilding much of the city in marble. He extended the frontiers and fostered colonization, took general censuses, and tried to make taxation more equitable. He tried to arrange the succession to avoid future conflicts, though had to acknowledge an unloved stepson, TIBERIUS, as his successor.

Augustus II (the Strong) (1670–1733) King of Poland (1697–1704, 1709–33) and, as Frederick Augustus I, elector of Saxony (1694–1733). He was elected by the Polish nobles in order to secure an alliance with Saxony, but the result was to draw Poland into the Great NORTHERN WAR on the side of Russia. In 1704 Augustus was forced to give up the crown to Stanislas I Leszcyński. Civil war (1704–09) and invasion by CHARLES XII of Sweden weakened the Polish state. Augustus was restored to the throne after PETER THE GREAT defeated Sweden at the Battle of Poltava in 1709, but at the cost of growing Russian dominance in Polish affairs.

Augustus III (1696–1763) King of Poland (1734–63) and, as Frederick Augustus II, elector of Saxony (1734–63), son and successor of AUGUSTUS II. With the support of the Russian empress ANNA IVANOVA, he gained the throne during the War of the Polish Succession. Augustus opposed MARIA THERESA in the War of the AUSTRIAN SUCCESSION, but later switched allegiances. He was forced into exile during the SEVEN YEARS' WAR (1756–63). Augustus was succeeded by Stanislaus II.

auk Squat-bodied sea bird of colder Northern Hemisphere coastlines. The flightless great auk (*Pinguinus impennis*), or the Atlantic penguin, became extinct in the 1840s; height: 76cm (30in). The razorbill auk (*Alca torda*) is the largest of living species. Family Alcidae.

Aung San (1914–47) Burmese politician who opposed British rule, father of AUNG SAN SUU KYI. Initially collaborating with the Japanese (1942), he later helped expel the invaders. Aung San was assassinated shortly after his appointment as deputy chairman of the executive council.

Aung San Suu Kyi (1945–) Burmese civil rights activist, daughter of AUNG SAN. In 1989 she was placed under house arrest for leadership of the National League for Democracy (NLD), a coalition opposed to Myanmar's oppressive military junta. In 1991 she was awarded the Nobel Peace Prize and the European Parliament's Sakharov Prize (for human rights). The military regime continues to restrict Suu Kyi's movement and communication with NLD supporters. In August 2000, she was detained in her car for ten days while attempting to travel outside Rangoon.

Aurangzeb (1619–1707) Emperor of India (1659–1707). The last of the great Mogul emperors, he seized the throne from his enfeebled father, SHAH JEHAN. Aurangzeb reigned over an even greater area and spent most of his reign defending it. He was a devout Muslim, whose intolerance of Hindus provoked long wars with the MARATHA. The empire was breaking up before his death.

Aurelian (*c*.215–75) Roman emperor. Having risen through the army ranks, Aurelian succeeded CLAUDIUS in 270. His victories against the Goths, reconquest of Palmyra and recovery of Gaul and Britain earned him the title "Restorer of the World". He built the Aurelian Wall to protect Rome and was assassinated in a military plot.

Aurelius, Marcus *See* MARCUS AURELIUS

Auric, Georges (1899–1983) French composer. Auric was artistic director (1962–67) of the Paris Opéra. His many compositions include ballets, songs and film scores, such as those for *Caesar and Cleopatra* (1946) and *Moulin Rouge* (1952). He was a member of Les SIX.

Auriga Large northern constellation, containing the first-magnitude star Capella. Mythologically, it represents Erichthonius, a king of Athens, who invented the four-horse chariot.

aurochs (urus) Extinct European wild ox, the longhorned ancestor of modern domesticated cattle. Once found throughout the forests of Europe and central and SE Asia, it became extinct in 1627. A dark, shaggy animal, it stood up to 2m (7ft) tall at the shoulder. Family Bovidae; species *Bos primigenius. See also* BISON

Aurora In Roman mythology, the goddess of dawn, equivalent to the Greek goddess EOS.

aurora Sporadic, radiant display of coloured light in the night sky, caused by charged particles from the Sun interacting with air molecules in the Earth's magnetic field. Auroras occur in polar regions and are known as **aurora borealis** in the N, and **aurora australis** in the S.

Auschwitz (Oświęcim) Town in Poland. It was the site of a German concentration camp during World War 2. A group of three main camps, with 39 smaller camps nearby, Auschwitz was Hitler's most "efficient" extermination centre. Between June 1940 and January 1945 more than 4 million people were executed here, mostly Jews. The buildings have been preserved as the National Museum of Martyrology. Together with the world's largest burial ground at Brzezinka (Birkenau), one of the other two main camps, Auschwitz is now a place of pilgrimage. Pop. (1989) 45,400.

Austen, Jane (1775–1817) English novelist. Austen completed six novels of great art, insight and wit, casting an ironic but ultimately sympathetic light on the society of upper-middle-class England. In order of composition they are: *Northanger Abbey* (1818), a parody on the contemporary Gothic novel; *Sense and Sensibility* (1811); *Pride and Prejudice* (1813); *Mansfield Park* (1814); *Emma* (1816); and *Persuasion* (1818). Not particularly successful in their time, they have since established their place among the most popular and well-crafted works in English literature. Her work has recently undergone an enthusiastic revival in the public imagination, following several film adaptations, most notably *Sense and Sensibility* (1995).

Austerlitz, Battle of (2 December, 1805) Conflict in Bohemia between the French under NAPOLEON I and the Russians led by Mikhail Kutuzov. One of Napoleon's greatest victories, it was also called the Battle of the Three Emperors.

Austin Capital of Texas, on the Colorado River. Originally called Waterloo, it was first settled in 1835 and renamed after Stephen Austin (the "father of Texas") in 1839. The market centre for a farming and ranching area, Austin hosts national conventions. Industries: high-tech electronics, furniture, machinery, building materials, food processing. Pop. (1996) 541,000.

Australasia Region that includes Australia, New Zealand and Papua New Guinea. The term Australasia is not exact. It is sometimes used to include various Asian countries (principally Indonesia and Malaysia) or extended to include Pacific island groups and the Australian and New Zealand territories in Antarctica – all the lands coming within the same sphere of influence.

Australia Earth's smallest continent, between the Pacific and Indian Oceans. Combined with the island of TASMANIA, it forms the independent Commonwealth nation of Australia, the world's sixth largest country. The huge Western Plateau makes up 66% of its land area and is

AUSTRALIA
AREA: 7,686,850sq km (2,967,893sq mi)
POPULATION: 18,855,000
CAPITAL (POPULATION): Canberra (325,000)

mainly flat and dry. Off the coast of NE Queensland lies the GREAT BARRIER REEF. The GREAT DIVIDING RANGE extends down the entire E coast and into VICTORIA. The mountains of TASMANIA are a southerly extension of the range. The highlands separate the E coastal plains from the Central Lowlands and include Australia's highest peak, Mount KOSCIUSKO, in NEW SOUTH WALES. The capital, CANBERRA, lies in the foothills. The SE lowlands are drained by the MURRAY and Darling, Australia's two longest rivers. Lake EYRE is the continent's largest lake. It lies on the edge of the Simpson Desert and is a dry salt flat for most of the year. ALICE SPRINGS lies in the heart of the continent, close to AYERS ROCK. **Climate** Only 10% of Australia has an average annual rainfall greater than 1,000mm (40in). These areas include some of the tropical N, where DARWIN is situated, the NE coast and the SE. The coasts are usually warm, and many parts of the S and SW, including PERTH, enjoy a Mediterranean climate of dry summers and moist winters. The interior is dry, and many rivers are only seasonal. **Vegetation** Much of the Western Plateau is desert, although areas of grass and low shrubs are found on its margins. The grasslands of the Central Lowlands are used to raise livestock. The N has areas of savanna and rainforest. In dry areas, acacias are common. Eucalyptus grows in wetter regions. **History and Politics** NATIVE AUSTRALIANS (Aborigines) entered the continent from Southeast Asia more than 50,000 years ago. They settled throughout the country and remained isolated from the rest of the world until the first European explorers, the Dutch, arrived in the 17th century. The Dutch did not settle. In 1770, the English explorer Captain James COOK reached BOTANY BAY and claimed the E coast for Great Britain. In 1788 the first British settlement was established (for convicts) on the site of present-day SYDNEY. The first free settlers arrived three years later. In the 19th century, the economy developed rapidly, based on mining and and sheep-rearing. The continent was divided into colonies, which later became states. In 1901, the states of QUEENSLAND, Victoria, Tasmania, New South Wales, SOUTH AUSTRALIA and WESTERN AUSTRALIA, federated to create the Commonwealth of Australia. NORTHERN TERRITORY joined the federation in 1911. A range of progressive social welfare policies were adopted, such as old-age pensions (1909). The federal capital was established (1927) at Canberra, in AUSTRALIAN CAPITAL TERRITORY. Australia fought as a member of the Allies in both world wars. The Battle of the Coral Sea (1942) prevented a full-scale attack on the continent. Post-1945 Australia steadily realigned itself with its Asian neighbours. Robert MENZIES, Australia's longest-serving prime minister, oversaw many economic and social reforms and dispatched Australian troops to the Vietnam War. In 1977, prime minister Gough WHITLAM was removed from office by the British governor-general. He was succeeded by Malcolm FRASER. In 1983 elections Fraser's Liberal Party were defeated by the Labor Party, and Bob HAWKE became prime minister. His shrewd handling of industrial disputes and economic recession helped him win a record four terms in office. In 1991, Hawke was forced to resign as leader and was succeeded by Paul KEATING. Backed by a series of opinion polls, KEATING proposed that Australia

should become a republic by the year 2001. Keating won the 1993 general election and persevered with his free-market reforms. In 1996 elections, Keating was defeated by a coalition led by John HOWARD. In 1998, Howard narrowly secured a second term in office. The historic maltreatment of Native Australians remains a contentious political issue. In 1993, the government passed the Native Title Act which restored to Native Australians land rights over their traditional hunting and sacred areas. **Economy** Australia is a prosperous country (1995 GDP per capita, US$18,940). Its economy was originally based on agriculture, although crops can be grown on only 6% of the land. The country remains a major producer and exporter of farm products, particularly cattle, wheat and wool. Grapes grown for winemaking are also important. Australia is rich in natural resources and is a major producer of minerals, such as bauxite, coal, copper, diamonds, gold, iron ore, manganese, nickel, silver, tin, tungsten and zinc. Australia also produces oil and natural gas. The majority of its imports are manufactured products. They include machinery and other capital goods required by factories. Australia has a highly developed manufacturing sector; the major products include consumer goods, notably foodstuffs and household goods. Tourism is a vital industry (1992 receipts, US$4,000 million).

Australian art Term applied to art produced by Native Australians and also that introduced by European settlers, which has developed its own distinctive style. The art of Native Australians dates back to prehistoric times. They painted on a variety of surfaces, including rock, bark and shells. The most remarkable examples are the so-called X-ray paintings in Arnhem Land, in which hunters depicted the internal anatomy of the beasts they killed, and the *wondjina* figures that were found near water holes in the NW. European influence on the continent dates from 1788, when the first penal colony was established. The Australian landscape attracted a significant number of foreign painters, such as John Glover (1767–1849) and Conrad Martens (1801–78); however, Australian artists still felt the need to train in Europe. The late 19th-century Heidelberg School, based in Heidelberg, Victoria, represented the first truly national movement in Australian art. It was led by Tom Roberts, and their impressionist-inspired landscapes influenced Australian art for many decades. In the 20th century, the Melbourne journal *Angry Penguins* (1940–46) proved a seminal influence, fostering the talents of many avant-garde painters. Among these were the two most celebrated names in Australian art, Sir Sidney NOLAN and Arthur Boyd.

Australian Capital Territory (ACT) (Commonwealth Territory) District within NEW SOUTH WALES but administratively independent of it. It contains the Australian capital, CANBERRA. The area was first settled in 1824 and was set aside as the capital territory in 1908. In 1915, an additional 72sq km (28sq mi) were added, making a total of 2,432sq km (939sq mi). Pop. (1993 est.) 299,400.

Australopithecus *See* HUMAN EVOLUTION

Austria Republic in central Europe. Austria lies at the crossroads of Europe. Mountains constitute about 75% of total land area. The River DANUBE flows through the Vienna Basin, Austria's main farming region and the

AUSTRIA
AREA: 83,850sq km (32,347sq mi)
POPULATION: 7,613,000
CAPITAL (POPULATION): Vienna (1,560,000)

location of its capital, VIENNA. Southern Austria contains ranges of the E ALPS, rising to 3,979m (12,457ft) at Gross Glockner. GRAZ is the major southern city. SALZBURG lies close to the German border. **Climate and Vegetation** Austria's climate is influenced by westerly and easterly winds. Westerlies bring rain and snow and help moderate temperatures. Easterlies bring cold weather in winter and hot weather in summer. Crops are grown on 18% of the land, and another 24% is pasture. Austria has the highest proportion of forest (39%) in Europe. **History and Politics** Austria was part of the HOLY ROMAN EMPIRE, and in 1526 it was united with Bohemia and Hungary. Under HABSBURG rule it became the most important state in the empire. The succession of MARIA THERESA (1740) prompted the War of the AUSTRIAN SUCCESSION. JOSEPH II's reforms encountered fierce resistance. The FRENCH REVOLUTIONARY WARS and the NAPOLEONIC WARS, culminating in defeat at AUSTERLITZ, led to the dissolution of the Holy Roman Empire (1806). Through the auspices of Prince METTERNICH, however, Austria continued to dominate European politics. The REVOLUTIONS OF 1848 forced the succession of FRANZ JOSEPH. Austrian power was further reduced in the AUSTRO-PRUSSIAN WAR (1866). In 1867 Austria and Hungary set up the AUSTRO-HUNGARIAN EMPIRE, whose disregard for individual nationalities precipitated WORLD WAR I. The defeat of the Central Powers led to the establishment of an Austrian republic. ANSCHLUSS with Germany was forbidden. Engelbert DOLLFUSS established a totalitarian state but was unable to stem the rise of Nazi Germany. In 1938, Germany annexed Austria, and they jointly fought in WORLD WAR 2. In 1945, the Allies partitioned and occupied Austria. In 1955 Allied forces withdrew and Austria became a neutral federal republic. A succession of coalition governments was halted by the election of a People's Party government (1970) led by Bruno Kreisky, who remained chancellor until 1983. In 1995, Austria joined the European Union, but was temporarily isolated when the far-right Freedom Party joined a coalition in 2000. **Economy** Austria is a wealthy nation (1995 GDP per capita, US$21,250) which, despite plenty of hydroelectric power, is dependent on the import of fossil fuels. Its leading economic activity is metal manufacture. Dairy and livestock farming are the principal agricultural activities. Austria's 20 million annual visitors (1995) are drawn by its historic cities and the winter sports facilities, especially in the TIROL.

Austrian Succession, War of the (1740–48) Conflict between Austria and Prussia for control of the German states, prompted by the succession (1740) of MARIA THERESA to the Habsburg lands of her father, CHARLES VI. Maria Theresa was faced with counterclaims to her succession from PHILIP V of Spain, AUGUSTUS III of Poland and Charles Albert, elector of Bavaria. The war began with FREDERICK II of Prussia's occupation of the Habsburg province of SILESIA. In 1741, with French aid, Charles Albert captured Prague and was elected as emperor Charles VII. In 1742, with British and Hungarian support, Maria Theresa launched a counter-offensive that overran Bavaria. This first phase (First Silesian War) was concluded by the Treaty of Berlin (1742) in which Prussia gained most of Silesia. The French army was forced to retreat from Prague and was defeated at Dettingen (1743) by GEORGE III of Britain. In 1744, Frederick II launched a second invasion of Silesia, but was repulsed. In 1745, the French won a major victory over the British at Fontenoy. George III and Frederick II signed the Convention of Hanover in which Britain recognized Prussia's claims to

Silesia in return for Frederick's support of the candidacy of the husband of Maria Theresa as Emperor FRANCIS I. War was formally ended by the Treaty of Aix-La-Chapelle (1748). *See also* FRENCH AND INDIAN WARS

Austro-Hungarian Empire (1867–1918) Organization of the old Austrian Empire into the kingdom of Hungary and the empire of Austria, also known as the "Dual Empire." The emperor of Austria and the king of Hungary were the same person, but each nation had its own parliament and controlled its internal affairs. This arrangement ignored other nationalist minorities and pleased neither the Hungarians, who wanted greater autonomy, nor the Austrians, many of whom wanted a realignment with other German states. After World War 1, Hungary and Czechoslovakia declared their independence, the Emperor Charles abdicated, and Austria became a republic.

Austronesian languages (Malayo-Polynesian) Family that includes Malay, Indonesian, Tagalog, Malagasy and numerous other languages spoken in Indonesia, the Philippines and the islands of the Pacific Ocean. There are four branches: Indonesian, Melanesian (which includes Fijian), Micronesian (which includes Chamorro, spoken on Guam) and the Polynesian languages, which include Maori, Tongan, Tahitian and Samoan. There are *c.*175 million speakers.

Austro-Prussian War (1866) Conflict between Prussia and Austria, also known as the Seven Weeks' War. Otto von BISMARCK engineered the war to further Prussia's supremacy in Germany and reduce Austrian influence. Defeat at Sadowa forced Austria out of the German Confederation (a federation of 39 German principalities set up by the Congress of Vienna to replace the HOLY ROMAN EMPIRE).

auteur In film theory, the notion that the director is the prime creator, or "author" of a film. Developed by François TRUFFAUT in 1954, the theory focuses on directorial style and use of recurring motifs to develop a canon of auteurs. Its popularity has waned because it minimizes the collaborative nature of film-making.

authoritarianism System of government that concentrates power in the hands of one person or small group of people not responsible to the population as a whole. Freedom of the press and of political organization are suppressed. Many authoritarian regimes arise from military takeovers.

autism Disorder, usually first appearing in early childhood, characterized by a withdrawal from social behaviour, communication difficulties and ritualistic behaviour. The causes of autism may originate in genetics, brain damage or psychology.

autobiography Narrative account of a person's life, written by the subject. The first important example of the genre was the 4th-century *Confessions* of Saint AUGUSTINE. The modern, introspective autobiography, dealing frankly with all aspects of life, is usually dated from the remarkable *Confessions* of ROUSSEAU (written 1765–72; pub. 1782). *See also* BIOGRAPHY

autochrome Method developed by the LUMIÈRE brothers for colour photography, first marketed in 1907. The screen plate consisted of glass on one side coated with round particles of starch grains dyed red, blue and green and mixed at random and compressed. Carbon black was laid between the dots and the whole plate covered with a varnish. An emulsion was applied to the reverse side. In widespread use for over 30 years, this method was an improvement over the earlier three-colour screen method.

autocracy System of government in which a single person or small group of people wields absolute power.

It is imposed and generally aimed at furthering the interests of an individual or group. Now rarely used, the term is applied to those regimes which came before the development of modern technology and state institutions which made TOTALITARIANISM possible.

autoimmune disease Any one of a group of disorders caused by the body's production of antibodies which attack the body's own tissues. One example of such an autoimmune disease is systemic LUPUS ERYTHEMATOSUS.

Autolycus In Greek mythology, son of Hermes and the mortal Chione. He received from his father the gift of

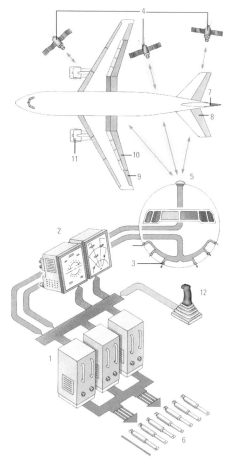

making whatever he touched invisible. In this way he was able to commit numerous thefts until one day he was caught by SISYPHUS, whose oxen he had stolen.

automatic pilot (autopilot) Electronic and mechanical control system that ensures an aircraft follows a pre-programmed flight plan. It monitors the course and speed of the aircraft and corrects any deviations from the flight plan. Systems range from simple wing-levellers in light aircraft to computer-operated units consisting of a GYROSCOPE, an electric SERVOMECHANISM unit and an accelerometer, which measures the aircraft's acceleration.

automation Use of self-governing machines to carry out manufacturing, distribution and other processes automatically. By using FEEDBACK, sensors check a system's operations and send signals to a computer that automatically regulates the process. *See also* MASS PRODUCTION; ROBOT

automobile Road vehicle that first appeared in the 19th century. The first cars were propelled by steam, but were not a success. The age of the automobile really dates from the introduction (1885–86) of the petrol-driven carriages of Gottlieb DAIMLER and Karl BENZ. The INTERNAL COMBUSTION ENGINE for these cars had been developed earlier by several engineers (most notably Nikolaus Otto in 1876). The main components of an automobile remain unchanged: body (**chassis**) to which are attached all other parts, including an **engine** or power plant; a **transmission** system for transferring the drive to the wheels; and steering, braking and suspension for guiding, stopping and supporting the car. Early cars were assembled by a few experts, but modern mass-production began in the early 1900s with Henry FORD and R.E. Olds in the US. In most modern motor factories, component parts are put together on assembly lines. Each worker has a specific task (such as fitting doors or crankshafts). Bodies and engines are made on separate assembly lines that converge when the engine is installed. Overhead rail conveyors move heavy components along the assembly lines, lowering them into position. The assembled car is tested before sale. Recent technology has seen the introduction of robots (properly, robotic arms secured to the workshop floor) on the assembly line. They are usually used for welding and painting. Increasing concern over the environmental impact of the car (such as congestion, pollution and energy consumption) has encouraged governments to examine alternative forms of mass transport, oil companies to produce cleaner fuels, and car manufacturers to look at alternative power plants (such as electric- or gas-powered motors).

autonomic nervous system Part of the body's nervous system that regulates the body's involuntary functions. It helps to regulate the body's internal environment by controlling the rate of heartbeat, PERISTALSIS and sweating. *See also* HOMEOSTASIS; INVOLUNTARY MUSCLE

Auvergne Region and former province of S France, comprising the departments of Allier, Puy-de-Dôme, Cantal and Haute-Loire. The capital is Clermont-Ferrand. Running N–S are the Auvergne Mountains, a scenic chain of extinct volcanoes, with the highest peak at Puy de Sancy, 1,886m (6,188ft). Area: 26,013sq km (10,047sq mi). Pop. (1990) 1,321,200.

auxin Plant hormone produced mainly in the growing tips of plant stems. Auxins accelerate plant growth by stimulating cell division and enlargement and by interacting with other hormones. Actions include the elongation of cells (by increasing the elasticity of cell walls, allowing the cells to take up more water) in geotropism and PHOTOTROPISM, fruit drop and leaf fall. *See also* GIBBERELLIN

▲ **automatic pilot** The diagram shows how an automatic pilot system works. A preprogrammed flight plan is loaded into the aircraft's computers (1). Two visual display units (2) show the aircraft's position, its intended route and its altitude. The change in movement of small vanes (3) on the outside of the aircraft alert the computers to any change in the aircraft's orientation. The aircraft uses the Global Positioning System (4) to determine its position. The receiver is located on top of the aircraft (5). The computers track the aircraft's route and automatically make any adjustments via servos (6) which control the rudder (7), elevators (8), ailerons (9), flaps (10), and throttle settings on the engines (11). The pilots can override the system at any time and revert to manual controls (12).

Avalokitesvara In Buddhism, one of the most distinguished of the BODHISATTVAS. He is noted for his compassion and mercy, and has remained on Earth in order to bring help to the suffering and knowledge to those who have not yet been converted. DALAI LAMAS are considered reincarnations of Avalokitesvara.

Avalon Mythical island where King ARTHUR is supposed to have died, following his battle against Mordred. Avalon was ruled by Morgan Le Fey, and many identify it with Glastonbury, SW England.

avatar In HINDUISM, an incarnation of a god (especially VISHNU) in human or animal form that appears on Earth to combat evil and restore virtue. In Hindu tradition there have been nine incarnations of VISHNU and a tenth is yet to come: these include BUDDHA, KRISHNA and RAMA.

average In statistics, the one score that most typifies an entire set of scores. It is the arithmetic MEAN of the scores. Other calculations that are also used to express what is typical in a set of scores are the MODE (the one score that occurs most often) and the MEDIAN (the middle score in a range which thus divides the set of scores into upper and lower halves).

Averröes (Abu-al-Walid Ibn-Rushd) (1126–98) Leading Islamic philosopher in Spain. In 1182, Averröes

became physician to the Caliph of Marrakesh, but in 1195 was banished to Seville, Spain, for advocating reason over religion. His major work, *Incoherence of the Incoherence*, defends NEOPLATONISM and ARISTOTLE. He exercised a powerful influence on Christian thought that persisted into the Renaissance. *See also* AQUINAS, SAINT THOMAS; SCHOLASTICISM

Avesta (Zend-Avesta) Sacred book of ZOROASTRIANISM. Most of the original was apparently lost when ALEXANDER THE GREAT burned Persepolis, the capital of ancient Persia, in 331 BC. The Gathas, forming the oldest part, originated with Zoroaster. The other remaining parts are the Yashts, Yasna and Vendidad and prayers. The writings were systematized under the Sassanid kings of Persia between the 3rd and 7th centuries AD.

Avicenna (979–1037) (Abu Ali al-Husayn ibn abd Allah ibn Sina) Persian physician and philosopher whose work influenced the science of medicine for many centuries. Avicenna was the greatest philosopher and scientist of the golden age of Islamic learning. His *Canon Medicinae* became a standard work. He also made enduring contributions in the field of Aristotelian philosophy.

Avignon City at the confluence of the rivers Rhône and Durance, Vaucluse department, Provence, SE France. A

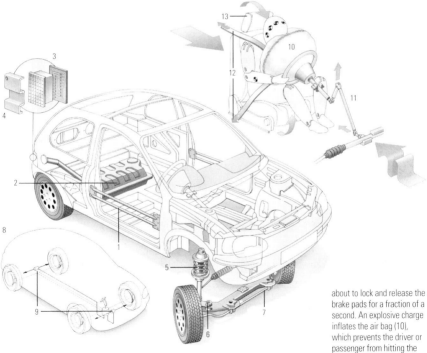

▲ **automobile** A modern car is designed with crumple zones at the front and rear to absorb the energy of a crash and protect the part of the car in which people sit. Side-impact protection bars (1) give strength to the side of the vehicle and spread energy to either side of the passenger cell. Fuel tanks (2)
are situated in front of the rear axle to protect the tank if the car is hit from behind. Some manufacturers have replaced the traditional rear brake lights with LEDs (3) which light more quickly. The cover is stepped (4) to prevent the light being obscured by dirt. The suspension, a MacPherson
strut system, allows vertical movement through the spring (5) while the wishbone (6) and antiroll bar (7) keep the wheels in position and stop excessive roll respectively. Antilock braking systems (ABS) (8) prevent the wheels locking under heavy braking or in poor weather. Sensors (9) detect when a wheel is
about to lock and release the brake pads for a fraction of a second. An explosive charge inflates the air bag (10), which prevents the driver or passenger from hitting the steering wheel or dashboard. The steering column (11) is designed to collapse so the driver is not impaled. Seat belt tensioners use the impact to pull the belt tight (12), holding the passenger in place. The headrest (13) helps stop whiplash injuries when heads snap back in the aftermath of the impact.

thriving city under Roman rule, Avignon was the seat of the popes during their exile from Rome in the 14th century. There is a Papal Palace (1316) and a Romanesque cathedral. The papacy held Avignon until 1791, when it was annexed to France by the Revolutionary authorities. Industries: tourism, soap, wine. Pop. (1990) 83,939.

Avignon popes During the BABYLONIAN CAPTIVITY (1309–77), popes who resided in Avignon instead of Rome. The papal court was established in Avignon by the French pope Clement V. In 1348 the city was bought by CLEMENT VI. The GREAT SCHISM occurred shortly after the court returned to Rome. *See also* PAPACY

avocado Evergreen, broad-leafed tree native to the tropical New World. The name is extended to its green, pear-shaped fruit. Avocados have a high oil content and a nutty flavour. Weight: 200g (7oz) but exceptionally up to 2kg (4.4lb). Family Lauraceae; species *Persea americana*.

Avogadro, Amedeo, Conte di Quaregna (1776–1856) Italian physicist and chemist. His hypothesis, **Avogadro's law** (1811), states that equal volumes of gases at the same pressure and temperature contain an equal number of molecules. This led later physicists to determine that the number of molecules in one gram molecule (the relative molecular mass expressed in grams) is constant for all gases. This number, called **Avogadro's constant**, equals 6.02257×10^{23}. It is both the ratio of the universal gas constant to BOLTZMANN's constant and of FARADAY's constant to the charge of the electron.

Avon Former county in SW England, created in 1974 from areas of GLOUCESTERSHIRE and SOMERSET. It was replaced in 1996 by the unitary authorities of BATH and North-East Somerset, BRISTOL, North-West SOMERSET and South GLOUCESTERSHIRE.

Avon Name of four British rivers. The **Bristol** (Lower) Avon rises in the Cotswold Hills in Gloucestershire and flows S and then W through Bristol, entering the Severn estuary at Avonmouth. Length: 121km (75mi). The **Warwickshire** (Upper) Avon rises in Northamptonshire, and flows SW through Stratford-on-Avon to join the River Severn at Tewkesbury. Length: 155km (96mi). The **Wiltshire** (East) Avon rises near Devizes and flows S into the English Channel. Length: 77km (48mi). The **Scottish** Avon flows E into the Firth of Forth. Length: 29km (18mi).

axiom Assumption used as a basis for deductive reasoning. The axiomatic method is fundamental to the philosophy of modern mathematics: it was used by the Greeks and formalized early in the 20th century by David HILBERT. In an axiomatic system, certain undefined entities (**terms**) are taken and described by a set of axioms. Other, often unsuspected, relationships (**theorems**) are then deduced by logical reasoning. For example, the points, lines and angles of Euclidean geometry are connected by postulates; theorems, such as Pythagoras' theorem, can be deduced. *See also* GÖDEL, KURT

axis Imaginary straight line about which a body rotates. In mechanics, an axis runs longitudinally through the centre of an axle or rotating shaft. In geography and astronomy, it is a line through the centre of a planet or star, about which the planet or star rotates. The Earth's axis between the North and South poles is 12,700km (7,900mi) long and is inclined at an angle of 66.5° to the plane in which the Earth orbits the Sun. A mathematical axis is a fixed line, such as the x, y or z axis, chosen for reference.

Axis Powers Term applied to Germany and Italy after they signed the Rome-Berlin Axis in October 1936. It included Japan after it joined them in the Tripartite Pact

(September 1940). Other states that joined the Axis were Hungary and Romania (1940) and Bulgaria (1941).

axolotl Larval form of certain species of SALAMANDER native to W US and Mexico. Axolotls are aquatic amphibians that normally mature and reproduce without developing into adult salamanders. Length: *c*.25cm (10in). Family Ambystomidae.

Axum *See* AKSUM

ayatollah (Arabic, reflection of God) Honorific title bestowed upon a Muslim leader who has attained significant distinction and, often, political influence. *See also* KHOMEINI, RUHOLLAH

Ayckbourn, Alan (1939–) English dramatist. His first successful play was *Relatively Speaking* (1967). Ayckbourn is acclaimed for his acerbic farces on middle-class values and neuroses, such as *Absurd Person Singular* (1972), the trilogy *The Norman Conquests* (1974) and *A Chorus of Disapproval* (1985). In 2000, Ayckbourn wrote and directed *House* and *Garden*, which were performed simultaneously in the National Theatre using one cast.

aye-aye (aare) Primitive, squirrel-like LEMUR of Madagascar. Nocturnal and tree-dwelling, it has dark shaggy fur and an elongated third finger with which it scrapes insects and pulp from bamboo. Length: 40cm (16in) excluding tail. Species *Daubentonia madagascariensis*.

Ayer, Sir A.J. (Alfred Jules) (1910–89) English philosopher. Building on the ideas of ANALYTICAL PHILOSOPHY from the Vienna Circle of positivists and of George BERKELEY, David HUME, Bertrand RUSSELL and Ludwig WITTGENSTEIN, Ayer introduced LOGICAL POSITIVISM into US and British philosophy. His works include *Language, Truth and Logic* (1936) and *Philosophy and Language* (1960).

Ayers Rock Outcrop of rock, 448km (280mi) SW of Alice Springs, Northern Territory, Australia. Named after the prominent South Australian politician Sir Henry Ayers (1821–97), it remained undiscovered by Europeans until 1872. It stands 348m (1,142ft) high, and is the largest single rock in the world – the distance around its base is *c*.10km (6mi). The rock, caves of which are decorated with ancient paintings, is of great religious significance to Native Australians. It is known to Native Australians as Uluru.

Aymara Major tribe of Native South Americans who live in the highlands of Bolivia and Peru. By 1500 they had been brought into the INCA empire, which was subsequently conquered by the Spanish. Today, the Aymara number *c*.1,360,000. Their struggle to survive in a harsh, semi-desert region accounts for their lack of an artistic heritage. The Ayamara language is spoken by about a million people in Bolivia and 3 million people in Peru.

Ayub Khan, Muhammad (1907–74) Pakistani general and statesman, president (1958–69). After the partition of British India, he assumed control of the army in East Pakistan (now Bangladesh). In 1951, Ayub Khan became commander-in-chief of the army and served as defence minister (1954–56). In 1958, he led the military coup that overthrew Iskander Mirza. Ayub Khan was confirmed as president in a 1960 referendum. His administration was notable for its economic modernization and reforms to the political system. The failure of his regime to deal with poverty and social inequality forced him to resign.

Ayurveda System of medicine practiced by the ancient Hindus and derived from the VEDAS. It is still practised in India.

azalea Name given to certain shrubs and small trees of the genus *Rhododendron* from temperate regions of Asia and North America. Mostly deciduous, they have

AZERBAIJAN
AREA: 86,600sq km (33,436sq mi)
POPULATION: 8,324,000
CAPITAL (POPULATION): Baku (1,740,000)

leathery leaves and funnel-shaped red, pink, magenta, orange, yellow or white flowers. Family Ericaceae.

Azerbaijan Republic in SW Asia. Azerbaijan lies in E Transcaucasia, bordering the CASPIAN SEA to the E. The CAUCASUS Mountains are in the N and include Azerbaijan's highest peak, Mount Bazar-Dyuzi, at 4,480m (14,700ft). Another highland region, including the Little Caucasus Mountains and part of the rugged Armenian plateau, lies in the SW. Between these regions lies a broad plain drained by the River Kura; its eastern part (S of the capital, BAKU) lies below sea level. Azerbaijan also includes the autonomous republic of NAKHICHEVAN on the Iran frontier, totally cut off from the rest of the state by ARMENIA. **Climate and Vegetation** Azerbaijan has hot summers and cool winters. The rainfall is low on the plains, ranging from c.130–380mm (5–15in) a year, but is much higher in the highlands and on the subtropical SE coast. Forests of beech, oak and pine grow on the mountain slopes, while the dry lowlands comprise grassy steppe or semi-desert. **History and Politics** In ancient times the area now called Azerbaijan was often invaded. Arab armies introduced Islam in 642, but most modern Azerbaijanis are descendants of Persians and Turkic peoples who migrated to the area from the E by the 9th century. Azerbaijan was ruled by the MONGOLS between the 13th and 15th centuries and then by the Persian SAFAVID dynasty. By the early 19th century, it was under Russian control. After the Russian Revolution of 1917, attempts were made to form a Transcaucasian Federation made up of Armenia, Azerbaijan and GEORGIA. When these attempts failed, Azerbaijanis set up an independent state, but Soviet forces occupied the area in 1920. Finally, in 1922 Azerbaijan became part of the Soviet Republic of TRANSCAUCASIA, but in 1936 it gained the status of a separate socialist republic within the SOVIET UNION. By 1991, the Soviet Union was defunct and, like its neighbours, Azerbaijan became an independent nation. In 1993, Gaidar Aliev was elected president and Azerbaijan joined the Commonwealth of Independent States (CIS). Since independence, economic progress has been slow, largely because of civil unrest in NAGORNO-KARABAKH, a large enclave within Azerbaijan where the majority of the population are Christian Armenians. In 1992, Armenia occupied the area between its E border and Nagorno-Karabakh, while ethnic Armenians took over Nagorno-Karabakh itself. The ensuing war killed thousands of people and resulted in large migrations of both Armenians and Azerbaijanis. A cease-fire was agreed in 1994, with c.20% of Azerbaijan territory remaining under Armenian control. There was little sign of a long-term solution to the problem, however, and sporadic fighting continued into 1998. **Economy** With its economy in disarray since the dissolution of the Soviet Union, Azerbaijan now ranks the world's lower-middle-income countries (1995 GDP per capita, US$1,460). Its chief resource is oil – Azerbaijan is one of the world's oldest centres of production – with the main oilfields in the Baku region, both on the shore of the Caspian Sea and in the sea itself. In 1994, Azerbaijan invited Western companies to develop and exploit the offshore oil deposits. Manufacturing, including oil refining and the production of chemicals, machinery and textiles, is the most valuable activity. Large areas of land are irrigated, and crops include cotton, fruit, grains, tea, tobacco and vegetables. Fishing is still important, although the Caspian Sea is becoming increasingly polluted.

azimuth Angle between the vertical plane through a celestial body and the N–S direction. Astronomers measure the angle eastward from the N point of the observer's horizon. Navigators and surveyors measure it westward from the S point. Altitude and azimuth form an astronomical coordinate system for defining position.

Aznar, José María (1953–) Spanish statesman, prime minister (1996–). Aznar became president of the Popular Party in 1990. His victory in the 1995 elections over incumbent prime minister Felipe González Márquez ended 13 years of socialist rule in Spain. His minority administration tried to tackle government corruption and enacted reforms that reduced unemployment and brought economic prosperity to Spain. Aznar took Spain into the European single currency (1999) and won a landslide victory in the 2000 elections.

Azores Portuguese island group in the N Atlantic Ocean, 1,290km (800mi) W of Portugal. The capital and chief port is Ponta Delgada (on San Miguel). Although the Azores were known to early explorers such as the Phoenicians and the Norsemen, they were first settled by the Portuguese in the 15th century. In both world wars they were used as military bases. Volcanic in origin, they consist of nine main islands, divided into three groups. A variety of fruits, vegetables and fish are exported. The islands' economy, dependent on small-scale farming and fishing, has improved with the development of tourism. Since 1976, the islands have formed an autonomous region of Portugal. Pico Alto at 2,351m (7,713ft) is Portugal's highest mountain. Area: 2,247sq km (868sq mi). Pop. (1994 est.) 239,900.

Azov, Sea of (Azovskoye More) Northern arm of the Black Sea. A shallow sea with only slight salinity, it has fishing ports on its E and S coasts. The marshes and lagoons at the W (Crimean peninsula) end were so noxious that the sea was known as *Sivash* (putrid lake). Area: 14,520sq mi (37,607sq km).

Aztec (Tenochca) Native-American civilization that rose to a position of dominance in the central valley of Mexico in c.AD 1450. A warlike group, the Aztecs settled near Lake Texcoco in c.1325, where they founded their capital Tenochtitlán (now Mexico City). They established an empire that included most of modern Mexico and extended S as far as Guatemala. The state was theocratic, with a number of deities whose worship included human sacrifice. The Aztecs built temples, pyramids and palaces and adorned them with stone images and symbolic carvings. At the time of the Spanish conquest, Aztec society was based on the exploitation of labour. As a result Hernán CORTÉS used disaffected tribesmen to help him defeat the Aztecs in 1521. *See also* CENTRAL AND SOUTH AMERICAN MYTHOLOGY

B/b, second letter of the Roman alphabet, is probably derived from an Egyptian hieroglyph for a house, which entered the Semitic alphabet 1,500 years later as the letter beth. It then emerged in Greece as beta.

Baade, Walter (1893–1960) US astronomer, b. Germany. From Mount Wilson Observatory, in the 1943 wartime blackout, he was able to observe individual stars in the ANDROMEDA GALAXY and distinguish the younger, bluer Population I stars from the older, redder Population II stars. He went on to show that the Universe was older and larger than previously thought.

Baal Chief god of the Semitic pantheon, akin to the Greek ZEUS. In the ancient Middle East he was linked with fertility as lord of the Earth, the rain and the dew. The Canaanites looked upon him as the foe of Mot, god of death and barrenness.

Baalbek Town in E Lebanon. An early Phoenician settlement, it was occupied by the Greeks in 323 BC and renamed Heliopolis. It was colonized by the Romans in the 1st century BC. It is noted for its Greek and Roman remains, especially the Temple of Jupiter.

Ba'ath Party Arab political party, founded in 1943. Its major objectives are socialism and Arab unity. It is strongest in Iraq and Syria, and militaristic elements of the Ba'ath Party seized power in those countries in 1968 and 1970, respectively. *See also* HUSSEIN, SADDAM

Babbage, Charles (1791–1871) English mathematician. He compiled the first actuarial tables and planned a mechanical calculating machine, the forerunner of the modern COMPUTER. The Royal Society's recommendation that the British government provide financial support was rejected and Babbage failed to complete the machine.

Babbitt, Milton (1916–) US composer, musicologist and teacher. Babbitt's mathematical background influenced his musical style. He systematized the analysis of TWELVE-TONE MUSIC. His compositions include vocal, piano and chamber music. Works include *Ensembles for Synthesizer* (1962–64).

Babel, Isaac Emmanuelovich (1894–1941) Russian short-story writer. His works, many of which are informed by his military service and experience of persecution, include *Tales of Odessa* (1924) and *Red Cavalry* (1926). He died a victim of Stalinist purges in a Siberian concentration camp.

Babel, Tower of Tower begun on the plain of Shinar, in Babylonia, by the descendants of NOAH as a means of reaching heaven (Genesis 11). God prevented its completion by confusing the speech of the people and scattering them throughout the world. The Genesis story was probably inspired by a ZIGGURAT in Babylon, seven stories high and with a shrine to the god Marduk on its top.

Babi faith (Babism) Muslim religious sect founded in 1844 in Persia (Iran) by Sayyid Ali Muhammad, the self-proclaimed prophet Bab (Arabic "gate"). Babists believed in the imminent coming of the Promised One. In 1848 they declared secession from ISLAM, but their rebellion against the new shah was crushed and their founder was executed in 1850. *See also* BAHA'I

Babington Plot (1586) Conspiracy against ELIZABETH I of England, led by Anthony Babington (1561–86), which aimed to restore Roman Catholicism by replacing Elizabeth by MARY, QUEEN OF SCOTS. Sir Francis WALSINGHAM intercepted Babington's correspondence with Mary and the plot was foiled. Babington was executed.

Babi Yar Ravine near Kiev, Ukraine, in which *c.*34,000 Jews were massacred by Nazi German soldiers in 1941. The massacre is commemorated in an eponymous poem (1961) by Yevgeny YEVTUSHENKO and in a novel by Anatoly KUZNETSOV.

baboon Large African MONKEY with a dog-like face, which walks on all fours. Its buttocks have callus-like pads surrounded by brilliantly coloured skin. Baboons are ground dwellers, travelling in families and larger troops led by old males, usually in open, rocky country. Their diet consists of plants, insects and small animals. The males have large canine teeth up to 5cm (2in) long. Weight: 14–41kg (30–90lb). Genus *Chaeropithecus* (or *Papio*).

Babur (1483–1530) First Mogul emperor of India (1526–30) b. Zahir ud-Din Muhammad; Babur (Turk. tiger) became ruler of FERGANA in 1495 and engaged in a long conflict for control of SAMARKAND but ultimately lost both territories. Raising an army, he captured Kabul and carved out a new kingdom for himself in Afghanistan. From here he invaded India, gaining Delhi (1526) and Agra (his future capital, 1527) and conquering N India as far as Bengal.

Babylon Ancient city on the River Euphrates in MESOPOTAMIA, capital of the empire BABYLONIA. It was rebuilt after being destroyed by ASSYRIA *c.*689 BC, and its new buildings included the HANGING GARDENS, one of the SEVEN WONDERS OF THE WORLD. This was the period, under NEBUCHADNEZZAR, of the BABYLONIAN CAPTIVITY of the Jews. After 275 BC, Babylon declined as Seleucia gained ascendancy.

Babylonia Ancient region and empire of MESOPOTAMIA, based on the city of BABYLON. The Babylonian empire was first established in the early 18th century BC by HAMMURABI the Great but declined under the impact of HITTITES and Kassites in *c.*1595 BC. The empire eventually fell to ASSYRIA in the 8th century BC. Babylon's greatness was restored and, in *c.*625 BC, its independence was won by Nabopolassar, who captured the Assyrian capital of NINEVEH. This New Babylonian (Chaldaean) empire defeated Egypt and took the Jews to captivity in Babylon in 586 BC. In 538 BC it fell to the Persians.

Babylonian Captivity Deportation of the JEWS to BABYLON between the capture of Jerusalem in 586 BC by NEBUCHADNEZZAR and the reformation of a Palestinian Jewish state (*c.*538 BC) by CYRUS THE GREAT. Many Jewish religious institutions, such as SYNAGOGUES, were founded in the period of exile, and parts of the Hebrew Bible also date from this time. The term was later applied to the exile of the popes at AVIGNON (1309–77). *See also* DIASPORA; GREAT SCHISM

Bacall, Lauren (1924–) US film actress. Following Bacall's screen debut opposite Humphrey BOGART in *To Have and Have Not* (1944), the two married in 1945. They starred together in a further three films, including the classics *The Big Sleep* (1946) and *Key Largo* (1948).

Bacchus In Roman mythology, the god of wine and fertility, identified with the Greek god DIONYSUS.

Bach, C.P.E. (Carl Philipp Emanuel) (1714–88) German composer, second surviving son of J.S. BACH. The most prolific and famous of Bach's sons, he wrote over 150 keyboard sonatas, 20 symphonies, *c.*50 harpsichord concertos, numerous chamber works, much sacred music and *c.*300 songs. He was widely esteemed as a keyboard player and became a leading theorist with his *Essay on the True Art of Keyboard Playing* (1753–62).

Bach, J.C. (Johann Christian) (1735–82) German composer, youngest son of J.S. BACH. He was organist at Milan Cathedral and composed operas that were staged in Turin and Naples, but he soon moved to London where his operas were better received. In 1763, he was made music-master to Queen Charlotte. Besides 11 operas, he wrote many instrumental and vocal works.

Bach, Johann Sebastian (1685–1750) Prolific German BAROQUE composer. He held a series of court positions as organist and music director and had 20 children, four of whom were also composers. Bach brought contrapuntal forms to their highest expression and is unrivalled in his ability to interweave melodies within the exacting rules of baroque harmony and counterpoint. At the court in Weimar (1708–17), he wrote many of his great organ works (preludes, fugues, toccatas), such as the Fugue in C minor. At Köthen (1717–23), he wrote Book I of the *The Well-Tempered Clavier* and the six *Brandenburg Concertos*. As musical director of St Thomas, Leipzig (1723–50), Bach wrote his celebrated church music, including *St Matthew Passion* (1729) and Mass in B Minor. Other works included the *Goldberg Variations* (1742).

bacillus Genus of rod-like BACTERIA present in the air and soil. One example of a species that is pathogenic in man is *Bacillus anthracis*, which causes ANTHRAX.

background radiation Radiation that is normally present in an environment. Such radiation must be taken into account when measuring radiation from a particular source. On Earth, background radiation is caused by the decay of naturally occurring radioactive substances in surface rocks. In space, the so-called "microwave background" is attributed to the BIG BANG.

Bacon, Francis (1561–1626) English philosopher, statesman and early advocate of the scientific method. Bacon was also an important essayist. He held important government offices but was forced to resign in 1621. None of this interrupted his efforts to break the hold of Aristotelian LOGIC and establish an inductive EMPIRICISM. Bacon entertained the idea of cataloguing all useful knowledge in his *Advancement of Learning* (1605) and *Novum Organum* (1620).

Bacon, Francis (1909–92) British painter, one of the most controversial artists of his generation, b. Ireland. In 1945, Bacon changed the face of English painting when he exhibited his triptych, *Three Studies for Figures at the Base of a Crucifixion*. The shock of the distorted representations of grieving people in his work stems from his violent handling of paint as much as from the subjects themselves. The religious focus of his work continued in a savage series of portraits of Roman Catholic popes.

Bacon, Roger (1220–92) English philosopher and scientist. Strongly influenced by St AUGUSTINE and medieval SCHOLASTICISM, Bacon stressed the importance of studying non-traditional subjects, such as Arabic and mathematics. In 1247, he became a Franciscan. Bacon's three best-known works, *Opus majus*, *Opus minor* and *Opus tertium*, were written (1267–68) for Pope Clement IV. His interest in alchemy and magic earned him the moniker "Doctor Mirabilis".

bacteria Simple, unicellular microscopic organisms. They lack a clearly defined nucleus, and most are without CHLOROPHYLL. Many are motile, swimming around by flagella. Most multiply by FISSION. In adverse conditions many remain dormant inside highly resistant SPORES with thick protective coverings. Bacteria may be AEROBIC or ANAEROBIC. Although **pathogenic** bacteria are a major cause of human disease, many bacteria are harmless or even beneficial to humans by providing an important link

in food chains, as in decomposing plant and animal tissue, and in converting free nitrogen and sulphur into AMINO ACIDS and other compounds that plants and animals can use. Some contain a form of chlorophyll and carry out PHOTOSYNTHESIS. Bacteria belong to the kingdom PROKARYOTAE. *See also* ARCHAEBACTERIA; EUBACTERIA

bacteriology Scientific study of BACTERIA. They were first observed in the 17th century by Anton van LEEUWENHOEK, but it was not until the mid-19th century researches of Louis PASTEUR and Robert KOCH that bacteriology was established as a scientific discipline.

bacteriophage VIRUS that lives on, and infects, BACTERIA. It has a protein head containing a core of DNA and a protein tail. Discovered in 1915, it is important in the study of GENETICS.

Baden-Powell of Gilwell, Robert Stephenson Smyth, 1st Baron (1857–1941) English soldier and founder of the BOY SCOUT movement. He held Mafeking against the Boers (1899–1900). His sister **Agnes** (1858–1945) founded the Girl Guides (1910). His wife, Lady Olave (1889–1977), also did much to promote these movements worldwide.

Baden-Württemberg Federal state in SW Germany, formed in 1952 by the merger of Baden, Württemberg-Baden and Württemberg-Hohenzollern; the capital is STUTTGART. It is a forested and fertile region drained by the Rhine and Danube rivers. Agriculture and livestock rearing are important, but industry is the main economic activity. Chief manufactures include electrical goods, machinery and vehicle-assembly at Stuttgart, MANNHEIM and Karlsruhe. There are famous universities at HEIDELBERG and Freiburg im Breisgau. Visitors are drawn to the spa at Baden-Baden and by the natural beauty of the Neckar Valley and the Black Forest. Area: 35,750sq km (13,803sq mi). Pop. (1993) 10,234,000.

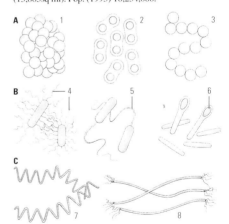

▲ **bacteria** Bacteria occur in three shapes (magnification x 5,000): spherical forms called cocci (A), rod-like bacilli (B), and spiral spirilla (C). **Cocci** can occur in clumps known as staphylococci (1), groups of two called diplococci (2), or chains called streptococci (3). Unlike cocci, which do not move, **bacilli** are freely mobile; some are termed peritrichous and use many flagellae (4) to swim about, while other monotrichous forms use a single flagellum (5). Bacilli can also form spores (6) to survive unfavourable conditions.

Spirilla may be either corkscrew-shaped spirochaetes, like Leptospira (7), or less coiled and flagellated, such as Spirillum (8).

▲ **badger** Eurasian badgers (*Meles meles*) of S China live in large family groups in large burrows known as setts. Setts have a complex network of tunnels and chambers, each serving a particular function.

badger Burrowing, nocturnal mammal that lives in Eurasia, North America and Africa. It has a stocky body with short legs and tail. Eurasian badgers (*Meles meles*) have grey bodies with black-and-white striped heads. American badgers (*Taxidea taxus*) are smaller and have grey-brown to red fur with a white head stripe. Length: 41–71cm (16–28in); weight: 10–20kg (22–44lb). Family Mustelidae.

badlands Eroded, barren plateau in an arid or semi-arid area characterized by steep gullies and ravines. Because of a lack of adequate vegetation (due to climate or human intervention), rainwater runs off very quickly and erodes soft and exposed rock. The best-known examples are the badlands of SW South Dakota and NW Nebraska, USA.

badminton Court game for two or four players, popular in England from the 1870s. The rules were drawn up in Pune, India, and codified with the formation of the Badminton Association (1893). The object is to use light rackets to volley a shuttlecock over a net until missed or hit out of bounds by an opponent. Only the player serving can score a point; games are played to 15 points.

Badoglio, Pietro (1871–1956) Italian soldier and politician. Chief of the general staff in 1919, Badoglio led the Italians at the World War 1 armistice talks. He was chief of staff again from 1925 to 1940. He headed the government that came to power after MUSSOLINI was overthrown in 1943 and arranged an armistice.

Baedeker, Karl (1801–59) German publisher, best known for a series of guidebooks on European cities. Baedeker's first guide (to Koblenz) was published in 1829; the first English editions appeared in 1861. The company's files were destroyed during World War 2, but a great-grandson of Baedeker later revived the business.

Baekeland, Leo Hendrik (1863–1944) US chemist, b. Belgium. Baekeland invented a type of photographic paper, Velox, which could developed under artificial light. He also invented the first thermosetting plastic, BAKELITE, which led to the development of the plastics industry.

Baffin, William (1584–1622) English navigator and explorer. Baffin took part in several expeditions (1612–16) in search of the NORTHWEST PASSAGE. He discovered the Canadian Arctic seaways, the island now named after him, and Lancaster Sound. An outstanding navigator, he published a method of determining longitude by the stars, using nautical tables.

Baffin Island Largest and most easterly island of the Canadian Arctic Archipelago, separated from QUÉBEC province by the Hudson Strait. It is the fifth-largest island in the world, with largely mountainous terrain and an almost entirely Inuit population. Area: 507,451sq km (195,928sq mi).

Bagehot, Walter (1826–77) English economist and writer. Editor of *The Economist* (1860–77), Bagehot is chiefly remembered for his influential treatise *The English Constitution* (1867).

Baghdad Capital of Iraq, on the River Tigris. Established in 762 as capital of the ABBASID caliphate, it became a centre of Islamic civilization and focus of caravan routes between Asia and Europe. In 1921, Baghdad became the capital of newly independent Iraq. In 1991, it was badly damaged during the Persian Gulf War. Notable sights include the 13th-century Abbasid Palace. Industries: building materials, textiles, tanning, bookbinding. Pop. (1987 est.) 3,850,000.

bagpipes Musical instrument with reed pipes connected to a windbag held under the arm and filled by mouth or bellows. The chanter pipe has finger holes for melody, while drone pipes produce monotone accompaniment.

Baha'i Religion founded in the 1860s by BAHAULLAH, an outgrowth of the BABI FAITH. Its headquarters are in Haifa, Israel. Seeking world peace through the unification of all religions, it stresses a simple life dedicated to serving others. It recognizes Bahaullah as the latest prophet of God.

Bahamas Small independent state in the West Indies, in the W Atlantic, SE of Florida. It consists of *c.*700 islands, 2,000 cays and numerous coral reefs. The largest island is Grand Bahama; the capital is NASSAU (on New Providence). The islands consist mainly of limestone and coral, and the rocky terrain provides little chance for agricultural development. Most of the islands are low, flat and riverless with mangrove swamps. The climate is subtropical, with temperatures averaging between 21–32°C (70–90°F). The population is 90% African or African-European; the majority live on New Providence. Anglicanism is the predominant religion and English the official language. San Salvador island is believed to have been the first stop of Christopher Columbus in his quest for the New World (1492). Charles II granted the islands to six lord proprietors of Carolina in 1670, but development was hindered by pirates. Britain assumed direct control by 1729, expelling militants and restoring civil order. Held briefly by Spain (1782) during the American Revolution, the islands were given back to England by the Treaty of Versailles (1783) in exchange for E Florida. In 1834, slavery was abolished. In 1963, a new constitution was drawn up providing for a parliamentary form of government. In 1973, the Bahamas became an independent nation. The main industry is tourism; commercial fishing, salt, rum and handicrafts are also important. Area: 13,860sq km (5,350sq mi). Pop. (2000) 295,000.

Bahaullah (1817–92) Name adopted by Mirza Husayn Ali Nuri, Persian religious leader and founder of the BAHA'I faith. He embraced the BABI FAITH in 1850 but broke away in 1867, proclaiming himself Bahaullah ("The Glory of Allah"), the Promised One foretold by Bab. His work, the *Katabi ikan* (*The Book of Certitude*) is the Baha'i holy book.

Bahia Coastal state in E Brazil; the capital is SALVADOR. Portuguese explorers reached the area in 1501. Declared a province in 1823, it achieved statehood in 1889. Products: cacao, tobacco, hardwood, natural gas, lead, titanium, asbestos, hydroelectricity. Area: 561,026sq km (216,612sq mi). Pop. (1991) 11,801,810.

Bahrain Emirate archipelago in the Persian (Arabian) Gulf, SW Asia; the capital is MANAMA. It comprises 34 small islands and the largest island of Bahrain. Oil was discovered in 1932, and the sheikhdom led the regional development of oil production. It is a hot, desert kingdom linked by a causeway to the Saudi Arabian mainland. From 1861 to 1971, the country was a British protectorate. Since the late 18th century, Bahrain has been governed by the Khalifa family. The 1970s drop in oil production led to economic diversification. Bahrain's aluminium-smelting plant is the Gulf's largest non-oil industrial complex. Other economic sectors have grown, but oil still accounts for 80% of Bahrain's exports and 20% of its GDP. Bahrain is a predominantly Muslim nation. Tensions exist between the SUNNI and majority SHIITE population. During the Iran-Iraq War (1980–88), Bahrain supported Iraq. Area: 678sq km (262sq mi). Pop. (2000) 683,000.

Baikal, Lake (Baykal) World's deepest lake in S Siberia, Russia; the largest freshwater feature in Asia. Fed by numerous small rivers, its outlet is the River ANGARA. It has rich fish stocks and includes the only freshwater seal species. Its ecology has been threatened by industrial pollutants from lakeside factories, and government schemes have been introduced to protect the environment. The city of Irkutsk lies on its N shore. Area: 31,494sq km (12,160sq mi). Max. depth: 1,743m (5,714ft).

Baird, John Logie (1888–1946) Scottish electrical engineer, inventor of TELEVISION. In 1926, Baird demonstrated the first working television to members of the Royal Institution, London. In 1928, he transmitted to a ship at sea, and in 1929 was granted experimental broadcasting facilities by the BRITISH BROADCASTING CORPORATION (BBC). His 240-line, part-mechanical television system was used for the world's first public television service by the BBC in 1936. In 1937, it was superseded by MARCONI's fully electronic scanning.

Baja California (Lower California) Peninsula of NW Mexico, extending SSE for 1,220km (760mi) between the Gulf of California and the Pacific Ocean. The peninsula consists of two states, Baja California Norte (capital Mexicali) and Baja California Sur (capital La Paz). The chief product of the region is long-staple cotton and the main industry is tourism. Area: 143,790sq km (55,517sq mi). Pop. (1990) 1,978,619.

Bakelite Trade name (coined by Leo BAEKELAND) for a thermosetting PLASTIC used for insulating purposes and in making paint. It was the first plastic (1909) made by the process of condensation, in which many molecules of two chemicals (in this case PHENOL and METHANAL) are joined together to form large polymer molecules.

Baker, James Addison (1930–) US Republican Party politician. After serving under Ronald REAGAN as White House chief of staff (1981–85) and secretary of the treasury (1985–88), Baker managed the successful 1988 presidential election campaign of George BUSH. As Bush's secretary of state (1989–92), much of his focus was on the Middle East, particularly Iraq's invasion of Kuwait (1990) and the subsequent GULF WAR (1991). In 1992 Baker became Bush's chief of staff and supervised his unsuccessful bid for re-election.

Baker, Dame Janet Abbott (1933–) English mezzo-soprano. She was renowned as a singer of *Lieder*, oratorio and opera. Well known at the ROYAL OPERA HOUSE (Covent Garden), Sadler's Wells and GLYNDEBOURNE, Baker is particularly admired for her interpretations of Mahler's song cycles.

Baker, Josephine (1906–75) US dancer and singer. After a sensational 1925 Paris debut in *La Revue Nègre*, she became internationally famous for her jazz singing and dancing. She took French citizenship in 1937 and became a member of the French Legion of Honour for her work in the resistance.

baking powder Mixture used in cooking as a substitute for yeast. It contains SODIUM BICARBONATE (sodium hydrogencarbonate) mixed with an acid component, such as tartaric acid or cream of tartar. During cooking, the acid reacts with the sodium bicarbonate to generate carbon dioxide gas, causing the food to rise without the fermentation effects of YEAST.

Baku Capital of Azerbaijan, a port on the W coast of the Caspian Sea. A medieval trade centre, Baku prospered under the Shirvan shahs in the 15th century. Commercial oil production began in the 1870s. At the start of the 20th century, Baku lay at the centre of the world's largest oilfield. The port handles a vast quantity of oil and petroleum products. Industries: oil processing, shipbuilding, electrical machinery, chemicals. Pop. (1993) 1,100,000.

Bakunin, Mikhail Alexandrovich (1814–76) Russian political philosopher. Bakunin became a believer in violent revolution while in Paris in 1848 and was active in the first Communist International until expelled by Karl MARX in 1872. His approach, known as revolutionary ANARCHY, repudiates all forms of governmental authority as fundamentally at variance with human freedom and dignity. In *God and the State* (1882) Bakunin argued that only natural law is consistent with liberty.

Balaclava (Balaklava) Town in the Crimea, site of an inconclusive battle (1854) during the CRIMEAN WAR. The British, French and Turks held off a Russian attack on the supply port of Balaclava. The battle is famous for a disastrous charge by Lord Cardigan's Light Brigade to capture Russian guns, as recorded in a poem by Alfred TENNYSON.

Balakirev, Mili Alexeyevich (1837–1910) Russian composer. Balakirev was one of the RUSSIAN FIVE dedicated to promoting Russian nationalism in 19th-century music. To this end he incorporated Russian folk idioms into his compositional style. Balakirev's best-known compositions are two symphonies, *Islamey* (1869) and incidental music to *King Lear* (1858–61). He founded the St Petersburg Free School of Music in 1862.

balalaika Triangular musical instrument popular in Russia. Strings (usually three) are fingered on a fretted neck and are picked or plucked with the fingers. It sounds similar to the MANDOLIN.

balance Piece of apparatus for making accurate weighings. In a **beam** balance, two pans are suspended at the ends of a beam pivoted at its centre. The mass of the

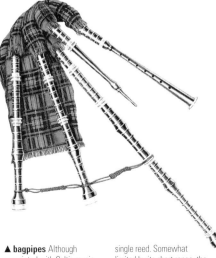

▲ **bagpipes** Although associated with Celtic music, the bagpipes originated in Asia. The drone usually has a single reed. Somewhat limited by its short range, the bagpipes are associated with folk and military music.

object to be weighed, located in one pan, is counterbalanced by known weights added to the other pan. In a **substitution** balance, there is only one pan suspended from the end of an arm with a fixed counterweight at the other end. An **electronic** balance uses an electromagnetic force to restore the balance of a lever arm.

balance of payments Overall surplus or deficit that occurs as a result of the exchange of goods and services between one nation and the rest of the world. A nation with a balance of payments deficit must finance it by borrowing from other nations or the INTERNATIONAL MONETARY FUND (IMF), or by using foreign currency reserves. Such deficits, if frequent, can pose a serious problem as they cause a reduction in the reserves. This in turn leads to economic pressure for DEVALUATION to correct the imbalance.

balance of power System in international affairs by which states seek to keep peace and order by maintaining an approximate balance of forces among rivals.

balance of trade Surplus or deficit incurred by a country in its trading. It is the difference between the sum of imports and exports. *See also* BALANCE OF PAYMENTS

Balanchine, George (1904–83) US choreographer and ballet dancer. One of the greatest artists in 20th-century ballet, Balanchine defected (1924) from Russia to work as principal dancer and choreographer for DIAGHILEV and the BALLETS RUSSES. He moved to the USA in 1933, established the School of American Ballet, and was director (1934–37) of the Metropolitan Opera ballet. He became the first artistic director and choreographer of the New York City Ballet (1948). Credited with creating US neoclassical ballet, he also undertook film choreography for the Ziegfeld and Goldwyn Follies. Ballet pieces include *The Nutcracker* (1954) and *Don Quixote* (1965).

Balaton Largest lake in central Europe, SW of Budapest, central Hungary. Rich in fish, it has many holiday resorts and vineyards on its shores. Area: 600sq km (232sq mi).

Balboa, Vasco Núñez de (1475–1519) Spanish conquistador, the first European to see the Pacific Ocean. Balboa went to Hispaniola in 1500 and to Darién (Panama) ten years later. In September 1513, accompanied by a group of locals, he crossed the isthmus and saw the Pacific, which he called the South Sea. He was later executed on a false charge.

bald cypress (swamp cypress) Deciduous tree growing in shallow water in the SE USA. They have woody growth on the roots that grow above water, and they lose their feathery, light green needles in autumn. Height: to 4.6m (15ft). Family Taxodiaceae; species *Taxodium distichum*.

baldness (alopecia) Loss of HAIR from the scalp. In some cases hair will grow back normally, but in others loss is permanent. Premature baldness is due to the effect of male hormones plus some hereditary component. Hair loss in women occurs later in life and is less pronounced. Baldness may also occur in either sex as a result of dietary deficiency, disease or treatments for cancer.

bald eagle Large bird of prey that lives in North America, where it feeds on fish and small mammals. It is brown with a white head and tail and a yellow bill. Its tail feathers were used in the head-dresses of some Native Americans, and it is the national emblem of the USA. Although now protected by law, it is still an endangered species. Species *Haliaeetus leucocephalus*.

Baldwin I (1171–1205) Count of Flanders and Hainaut, first Latin emperor of Constantinople (1204–05). The capture of Constantinople from the Byzantine Christians by the Western armies of the Fourth Crusade led to the partition of the BYZANTINE EMPIRE, and Baldwin was elected ruler of the newly formed Latin state.

Baldwin, James (1924–87) US novelist and essayist. Baldwin's first novel, *Go Tell It on the Mountain* (1953), was semi-autobiographical and has become an American classic. His prose is inflected with blues and gospel rhythms. His most celebrated novel is *Another Country* (1962). Essay collections include *Notes of a Native Son* (1955) and *The Fire Next Time* (1963). Baldwin was prominent in the US CIVIL RIGHTS movement.

Baldwin, Robert (1804–58) Canadian statesman. Baldwin shared the first premiership of united Canada with Louis la Fontaine, who represented the French of Lower Canada (1841–43, 1847–51). He advocated cooperation between French and British Canadians, organized an effective system of municipal government for Ontario and reorganized the courts.

Baldwin, Stanley, 1st Earl of Bewdley (1867–1947) British statesman, prime minister (1923–24, 1924–29, 1935–37), cousin of Rudyard Kipling. Baldwin was chancellor of the exchequer (1922–23) before succeeding Bonar LAW as Conservative prime minister. Baldwin responded to the General Strike (1926) by passing the Trades Disputes Acts (1927) which made any subsequent general strikes illegal. Baldwin opposed EDWARD VIII's marriage to Wallis Simpson and secured her abdication (1936). His APPEASEMENT of European fascism is often cited as a cause of Britain's lack of preparedness at the start of World War 2.

Balearic Islands Group of Spanish islands in the W Mediterranean off the E coast of Spain; the capital is PALMA. The islands were successively occupied by all the great Mediterranean civilizations of antiquity. In the 11th century, a Moorish kingdom used them as a base for piracy. The chief islands are MAJORCA, Minorca and IBIZA. Industries: tourism, silverworking, olive oil, wine, fruit. Area: 5,014sq km (1,936sq mi). Pop. (1991) 709,138.

Balfour, Arthur James Balfour, 1st Earl of (1848–1930) British statesman, prime minister (1902–05), b. Scotland. Balfour succeeded his uncle, the Marquess of SALISBURY, as prime minister. His government introduced educational reforms (1902), but the CONSERVATIVE PARTY fractured over the tariff reform proposed by Joseph CHAMBERLAIN. Balfour resigned and the Conservatives lost the ensuing general election. He returned to the cabinet in the coalition governments of Herbert ASQUITH and David LLOYD GEORGE. As foreign secretary, he issued the BALFOUR DECLARATION (1917).

Balfour Declaration (1917) Letter written by British foreign minister Arthur BALFOUR to the British Zionist Federation pledging cooperation for the settlement of Jews in PALESTINE. Jews were admitted to the area when it became a British mandate under the League of Nations after World War 1. *See also* ZIONISM

Bali Island province of Indonesia, off the E tip of Java, between the Bali Sea and the Indian Ocean. The main town is Denpasar. Under Javanese control from the 10th century, Bali was a Dutch possession from 1908 to 1949, apart from Japanese occupation during World War 2. It is the centre of Majapahit Hinduism. Its scenic beauty and native culture make it a popular tourist resort. Industries: rice, sweet potatoes, cassava, copra, meat processing. Area: 5,561sq km (2,147sq mi). Pop. (1990) 2,777,811.

Balkan Mountains Major mountain range of the Balkan Peninsula extending from E Serbia through central Bulgaria to the Black Sea; a continuation of the CARPATHIAN MOUNTAINS. It is rich in minerals and forms a climatic barrier for the inland regions. The highest peak is Botev, at 2,375m (7,793ft).

Balkan states Group of countries in the Balkan Peninsula, in SE Europe, consisting of ALBANIA, BOSNIA-HERZEGOVINA, BULGARIA, CROATIA, GREECE, MACEDONIA, ROMANIA, SERBIA and European TURKEY. From the 3rd century AD, the region was ruled by Byzantium. It was later invaded by Slav peoples, and then for 500 years formed part of the Ottoman Empire. The individual countries regained independence in the 19th century.

Balkan Wars (1912–13) Two wars involving the BALKAN STATES and the OTTOMAN EMPIRE. In the first, the Balkan League (Serbia, Bulgaria, Greece and Montenegro) conquered most of the European territory of the Ottoman Empire. The second war (mainly between Serbia and Bulgaria) arose out of dissatisfaction with the distribution of these lands. Serbia's victory added to regional tension before WORLD WAR 1.

Balkhash (Balchaš) Lake in SE Kazakstan extending from the Kazak Hills (NE) to the desert steppes (SW). It has no outlet. The chief inlet is the freshwater River Ili, therefore the W half of the lake is freshwater. Area: 18,428sq km (7,115sq mi). Max. depth: 26m (85ft).

Balla, Giacomo (1871–1958) Italian artist. Influenced by the poet MARINETTI, founder of FUTURISM, Balla adopted the movement's philosophical outlook and urged artists to use art as a means to change Italy's culture through the acceptance of science and technology. His works include *The Street Light – Study of Light* (1909) and *Dynamism of Dog on a Leash* (1912).

ballad (Lat. *ballare*, to dance) Form of popular poetry which is regularly sung, narrative in style with simple metre, rhyme and often a refrain. The first surviving examples date from medieval times and typically consist of four-line stanzas. The ballad was a vital means of perpetuating community myth, the traditions of storytelling and the celebration of rites. Notable later examples include *Lyrical Ballads* (1798), written by WORDSWORTH in collaboration with COLERIDGE. The late-18th century revival of the ballad was central to the rise of ROMANTICISM. It was espoused by SWINBURNE, LONGFELLOW, Sir Walter SCOTT and Rudyard KIPLING.

ballade Non-narrative poem of three (typically eight-line) rhymed stanzas and a final (typically four-line) rhymed stanza (envoy) in which the poet's conclusion or moral is drawn. A widely used form, especially in France where its greatest exponent was François Villon, it flourished in the Middle Ages and was often sung.

Balladur, Edouard (1929–) French statesman, Gaullist premier (1993–95). Balladur was elected to parliament in 1986 and became (1988) minister of economy and finance. In 1995, his lacklustre campaign for the presidency was tainted by charges of corruption, and he lost to Jacques CHIRAC.

Ballard, J.G. (James Graham) (1930–) British novelist and short-story writer, b. China. Ballard is best known for his highly stylized science fiction. Novels such as *The Wind from Nowhere* (1962), *The Drought* (1965), *The Crystal World* (1966) and *Crash* (1973), explore psychological reactions to catastrophic situations. *Empire of the Sun* (1984) dealt with his childhood experiences of a World War 2 Japanese prisoner-of-war camp. Its sequel was *The Kindness of Women* (1991). Other novels include *Cocaine Nights* (1996) and *Super-Cannes* (2000).

ball bearing Type of bearing for rotating machinery. It consists of two concentric rings of steel, which form a "race" for the steel balls positioned between them. The inner ring is fixed to a shaft and the outer one to a support.

Ballesteros, Severiano (1957–) Spanish golfer. Ballesteros was the 20th-century's youngest winner of

the British Open (1979). A brilliant stroke-maker, he won the British Open twice more (1984, 1988) and the US Masters in 1980 and 1983. Ballesteros was an inspiring member of the European Ryder Cup teams from 1985, and captained them to victory in 1997.

ballet Theatrical dance form set to music. The first formal ballet, *Ballet comique de la Reine*, was performed (1581) at the court of Catherine de' Medici. Louis XIV founded the Royal Academy of Dance in 1661. *The Triumph of Love* (1681) was the first ballet to use trained female dancers. The first public performance of a ballet was in 1708. Choreographic notation was developed, and Pierre Beauchamp (1631–1719) established the five classical positions. Jean-Georges NOVERRE (1727–1810), the most influential choreographer of the 18th century, argued for a greater naturalism. The 1832 performance of *Les Sylphides* set the choreographic model for 19th-century romantic ballets, stressing the role of the prima ballerina. Dancing on the toes (*sur les pointes*) was introduced. At the end of the 19th century, Russian ballet emphasized technique and virtuosity. Subsequently, Sergei DIAGHILEV and his BALLETS RUSSES revolutionized ballet with dynamic choreography and dancing. Today, the pre-eminence of Russian ballet is maintained by the KIROV and BOLSHOI companies. In 1930, Dame Marie RAMBERT founded the first English ballet school, and in 1931 Dame Ninette de VALOIS established the Sadler's Wells Ballet (now the Royal Ballet). Rudolf NUREYEV's work for the Royal Ballet enlarged the role and dramatic range of the male dancer. In 1934, the first major US ballet school was instituted under the direction of George BALANCHINE. In 1948, the New York City Ballet was established. It is now one of the world's principal ballet companies. American ballet introduced a more abstract style and an eclectic fusion of classical ballet, jazz and popular and MODERN DANCE. *See also* FOKINE, MICHEL; MACMILLAN, SIR KENNETH; MASSINE, LÉONIDE; MASQUE; NIJINSKY, VASLAV

Ballets Russes Dance company founded (1909) in Paris by Sergei DIAGHILEV, with Michel FOKINE as chief choreographer. It revitalized and reshaped ballet by bringing together great dancers (PAVLOVA and NIJINSKY) and choreographers (MASSINE, NIJINSKY and BALANCHINE). Leading composers, such as STRAVINSKY, DEBUSSY and Richard STRAUSS, composed music for the company, and top artists, such as PICASSO, CHAGALL and MATISSE, designed sets and costumes. It disbanded soon after Diaghilev's death in 1929.

Balliol, John (*c.*1249–1315) King of Scotland (1292–96). His claim to the Scottish throne over ROBERT Bruce was upheld by EDWARD I of England. In return, Edward claimed feudal overlordship of Scotland and Balliol grudgingly acquiesced. In 1295, Balliol formed an alliance with France, which resulted in Edward's invasion (1296) of Scotland. Balliol was defeated and imprisoned (1296–99) in England. He died in exile in Normandy.

ballistics Science of projectiles, including bullets, shells, bombs, rockets and guided MISSILES. **Interior** ballistics deal with the propulsion and motion of the projectile within the firing device. **Exterior** ballistics investigate the trajectory of the projectile in flight. **Terminal** ballistics are concerned with the impact and effect of the projectile at the target.

balloon Unsteerable, lighter-than-air craft, usually made of nylon. Balloons are used for recreation, scientific and military purposes. A gas that is lighter than air lifts the balloon from the ground. The first balloons to fly were of the open-necked hot-air type. This type of balloon uses propane gas to inflate the balloon. Controlled descent is achieved through regulated deflation. Unmanned military, meteorological or other scientific balloons are usually filled with hydrogen. Manned balloons are generally filled with safer helium gas or hot air.

ballooning Travelling in a basket suspended beneath a balloon inflated with a gas lighter than air. Now largely a leisure activity, ballooning was the first means of human "flight". Generally credited with the achievement are the French brothers Jacques and Joseph MONTGOLFIER, who devised a hot-air balloon in which Jean François Pilâtre de Rozier and the Marquis d'Arlandes made the first ascent (21 November 1783). Although hydrogen ballooning is considered by many to be the purest form of the sport, because it is completely silent, it has been largely superseded by the cheaper hot-air method. In this, burning propane gas is used to heat the air through an opening in the bottom of the balloon, which is usually made of nylon fabric. In recent years, there have been many attempts to fly non-stop around the world.

ballot Object used to cast a vote, or process of voting in an election. The word derives from the Italian *ballotta* (little ball) and since 5th-century BC Athens, balls have been used to cast votes. Today, the ballot is often a sheet (or sheets) of paper, although voting machines are frequently used to register votes.

balm Resin from a BALSAM plant and the name of various aromatic plants, particularly those of the genera *Melissa* and *Melittis*, both family Lamiaceae/Labiatae. Also, an old name for any soothing ointment.

Balmoral Private residence of the British monarch in the Scottish Highlands, 85km (53mi) w of Aberdeen. Built in the reign of Queen Victoria, it was left to her by Prince Albert on his death in 1861.

▲ **ballooning** Man's first balloon flight took place on 21 November, 1783, when the Montgolfier brothers' travelled *c.*8km (5mi) across Paris. Made of paper-lined linen and coated with alum to reduce the risk of fire, the balloon (shown here) was 15m (50ft) high, and weighed 785kg (1,730lb). The air was heated by a large mass of burning straw on a wire grid in the centre of the gallery.

balsa Lightweight wood obtained from a South American tree, used for modelling and for building rafts. Family Bombacaceae; species *Ochroma lagopus*.

balsam Aromatic RESIN obtained from plants; healing preparations, especially those with benzoic and cinnamic acid added to the resin; or balsam-yielding trees, such as the balsam fir and balsam poplar. The name is also given to many species of Balsaminaceae that are plants of moist areas, with pendent flowers. *See also* IMPATIENS

balsam fir Evergreen tree native to NE North America. It has flat needles and 6.3cm (2.5in) cones. It is often grown for pulpwood and Christmas trees. Height: to 21.3m (70ft). Family Pinaceae; species *Abies balsamea*.

Baltic languages Branch of the family of INDO-EUROPEAN LANGUAGES, closely related to SLAVIC. The two surviving languages, Latvian (or Lettish) and Lithuanian, are spoken by *c.*5 million peoples in Eastern Europe. A third form, Old Prussian, was submerged into German in the 17th century.

Baltic Sea Part of the Atlantic extending past Denmark, along the N coasts of Germany and Poland and the E coasts of the BALTIC STATES, separating Sweden from Russia and Finland. The sea extends N–S with an arm reaching out to the E. The N part is the Gulf of Bothnia, the E part the Gulf of Finland. The Baltic is the largest body of brackish water in the world. Its low salinity accounts for the ease with which the Gulf of Bothnia freezes in the winter. The tidal range is low and currents are weak. Area: 414,400sq km (160,000sq mi).

Baltic states Countries of ESTONIA, LATVIA and LITHUANIA, on the E coast of the Baltic Sea. The region was settled by various tribes in the 7th century AD, but until the 20th century remained mostly under Danish, Russian or Polish rule. Following the Russian Revolution in 1918, each state became independent, but came under the control of the Soviet Union in 1940. They regained their independence following the breakup of the Soviet Union in 1991.

Baltimore City and port in N Maryland USA, at the mouth of the Patapsco River, on Chesapeake Bay. It was founded (1729) by the Irish baronial family of Baltimore as a tobacco port. In the 19th century, it became an important shipbuilding centre. It is a notable centre of commerce and education, with John Hopkins University and two others, and a major port. Industries: steel, oil refining, shipbuilding, aerospace equipment. Pop. (1990) 736,014.

Baluchistan Region and province in central and SW Pakistan, bordered by Iran (W), Afghanistan (N) and the Arabian Sea (S). Quetta is the capital. The boundaries with Iran and Afghanistan were settled in 1885–96. In 1947, the region became part of Pakistan. The terrain is mostly hilly desert and is inhabited by nomadic tribes such as the Baluchi. Much of the population is employed in sheep raising. Some cotton is grown, and fishing is the chief occupation on the coast. Natural gas is extracted and exported, along with salt and fish. Area: 347,190sq km (134,102sq mi). Pop. (1985 est.) 4,908,000.

Balzac, Honoré de (1799–1850) French novelist. One of the greatest novelists of the 19th century, Balzac's first success was *Les Chouans* (1829). More than 90 novels and short stories followed during a lifetime of extraordinary creative effort. Balzac organized these works into a grand fictional scheme, intended as a detailed, realistic study of contemporary French society, which he called *La Comédie Humaine*. Among his best-known novels are *Eugénie Grandet* (1833) and *Le Pére Goriot* (1835).

Bamako Capital of Mali, on the River Niger, 145km (90mi) NE of the border with Guinea, W Africa. Once a centre of Muslim learning (11th–15th centuries), it was occupied by the French in 1883 and became capital of the French Sudan (1908). Industries: shipping, peanuts, meat, metal products. Pop. (1995 est.) 800,000.

bamboo Tall, tree-like GRASS native to tropical and subtropical regions. The hollow, woody stems grow in branching clusters from a thick rhizome, and the leaves are stalked blades. It is used in house construction and for household implements. Some bamboo shoots are eaten. The pulp and fibre may form a basis for paper production. Height: to 40m (131ft). There are 1,000 species. Family Poaceae/Gramineae; genus *Bambusa*.

banana Long, curved, yellow or reddish fruit of the tree of the same name. It has soft, creamy flesh. A spike of yellow, clustered flowers grows from the centre of the crown of the tree and bends downwards and develops into bunches of 50–150 fruits in "hands" of 10–20. More than 100 varieties are cultivated. Height: 3–9m (10-30ft). Family Musaceae; genus *Musa*.

Bancroft, George (1800–91) US diplomat and historian. Bancroft was appointed secretary of the navy in 1845 and established the US Naval Academy at Annapolis, Maryland. He served as ambassador to Britain (1846–49) and to Germany (1867–74). Bancroft's *History of the United States* (10 vols, 1834–74) is a classic account.

band Instrumental ensemble, usually consisting of wind and percussion instruments. A **big** band performs swing music with about 16 musicians in four sections: trumpets, trombones, saxophones and a rhythm section. A **brass** band contains only brass and percussion instruments. A **dance** band has a rhythm section to provide the strict beat and melody instruments, such as saxophone and violin, to play the tunes. A *jazz* band varies according to the style of JAZZ: a typical jazz quartet consists of piano, bass, drums and saxophone or trumpet. A **military** (marching) band contains brass and woodwind with percussion. A ROCK band has a core of electric guitar, bass guitar and drums.

Banda, Hastings Kamuzu (1902–97) Malawian politician, the country's first president (1966–94). Banda guided Nyasaland to independence as MALAWI (1964), establishing an autocratic regime. He was named president-for-life in 1971. Banda was the only African leader to maintain friendly relations with the South African apartheid regime. In 1994, he was forced to accede to multiparty elections, which he lost.

Bandaranaike, Sirimavo Ratwatte Dias (1916–2000) Sri Lankan stateswoman, prime minister (1960–65, 1970–77, 1994–2000). Following the assassination (1959) of her husband, Solomon BANDARANAIKE, she assumed control of the Sri Lanka Freedom Party and became the world's first woman prime minister. Her daughter, Chandrika Kumaratunga (1945–), became president in 1994, and Sirimavo returned as prime minister.

Bandaranaike, Solomon West Ridgeway Dias (1899–1959) Ceylonese statesman, prime minister (1956–59). He made Sinhalese the official language and founded the Sri Lanka Freedom Party to unite nationalists and socialists. He was assassinated and his wife, Sirimavo BANDARANAIKE, succeeded him.

Bandar Seri Begawan (formerly Brunei Town) Capital of BRUNEI, Borneo, SE Asia. The town port was superseded in 1972 by a new deepwater harbour at Maura. The capital includes the Sultan Omar Ali Saifuddin Masjid, SE Asia's largest mosque. Pop. (1991) 45,867.

bandicoot Australian MARSUPIAL about the size of a rabbit and with similarly long ears, hopping gait and burrowing habits. It eats insects rather than vegetation, and its long pointed snout is probably an adaptation for its insectivorous diet. Genus *Perameles*.

Bandung Capital of West Java province, Indonesia. Founded in 1810, it was the administrative centre of the Dutch East Indies and is now the third largest city in Indonesia. A centre for Sundanese culture, its educational institutions include the Bandung Institute of Technology and two universities. Industries: canning, chemicals, quinine, textiles. Pop. (1990) 2,026,893.

Bandung Conference (1955) International meeting in BANDUNG, Indonesia. Representatives of 29 non-aligned countries of Asia and Africa, including China, met to express their united opposition to COLONIALISM and to gain recognition for the Third World.

bandwidth Range of frequencies spanned by a radio signal of a particular frequency. If a transmitted radio signal is modulated, the bandwidth is the range of frequencies employed on either side of the CARRIER WAVE signal. It is therefore also the range of frequencies used for RADIO BROADCASTING within a particular waveband. The term is also used to describe the frequency range over which a device, such as an amplifier or radio receiver, should not significantly differ from its maximum value. In communications and computing, bandwidth describes that rate at which data is transmitted (for example, by a modem), usually measured in bits per second.

Bangalore (Bangalur) Capital of Karnataka state, S central India. Established in 1537 by the Mysore dynasty, Bangalore was retained by Britain as a military headquarters until 1947. It is the sixth largest city in India and an important industrial and communications centre. Industries: aircraft, machine tools. Pop. (1991) 3,302,296.

Bangkok Capital and chief port of Thailand, on the E bank of the River Menam (Chao Phraya). Bangkok became the capital in 1782 when King Rama I built a royal palace here. It quickly became Thailand's largest city. The Grand Palace (including the sacred Emerald Buddha) and more than 400 Buddhist temples (*wats*) are notable examples of Thai culture and help make the capital a popular tourist destination. It has a large Chinese minority. During World War 2, it was occupied by the Japanese. Today, Bangkok is a busy market centre, much of the commerce taking place on the numerous canals. Industries: building materials, rice processing, textiles, jewellery. Pop. (1993) 5,572,712

Bangladesh Republic in S Asia. Bangladesh is the world's most densely populated country: (1990) 803 people per sq km (2,080 per sq mi). Most of Bangladesh is flat and covered by fertile alluvium spread by the rivers GANGES, BRAHMAPUTRA and Meghna. The capital, DHAKA, is situated on the Ganges delta. The rivers overflow when swollen by the annual monsoon. Floods also occur with the cyclones that periodically strike along its coast. The death toll from the 1991 delta cyclone was 132,000 and more than 5 million people were made homeless. In 1998, the monsoon led to the most prolonged floods on record, killing some 1,500 people and leaving 23 million people homeless. **Climate** Bangladesh has a tropical monsoon climate. In winter, dry winds blow from the N. In spring, moist winds from the S bring heavy rain. It remains hot throughout the monsoon season (June–August). **Vegetation** Though most of Bangladesh is low and cultivated, forests cover *c.*16% of the land. The mangrove swamps of the Sundarbans region are the last sanctuary of the Bengal tiger. On the jungle border with Burma, there are large areas of mahogany forests and rubber plantations. **History and Politics** The early history of Bangladesh is synonymous with that of BENGAL. Islam was introduced in the 13th century. In 1576, Bengal became part of the vast MOGUL EMPIRE under AKBAR I

BANGLADESH
AREA: 144,000sq km (55,598sq mi)
POPULATION: 150,589,000
CAPITAL (POPULATION): Dhaka (Dacca, 3,397,187)

(THE GREAT). In the late-18th century, Bengal fell under the control of the British EAST INDIA COMPANY. In 1905, the British divided Bengal into East and West portions. East Bengal (roughly equivalent to modern Bangladesh) was mainly Muslim. In 1947, British India was partitioned between the mainly Hindu India and Muslim PAKISTAN. Pakistan consisted of two provinces, one to the W of India, and the other to the E, known initially as East Bengal, then East Pakistan. The two provinces were separated by c.1,500km (1,000mi) of India. The majority population of East Pakistan complained of ethnic and economic discrimination by West Pakistan. Complaints turned into riots. In 1970 elections, the Awami League, led by Sheikh Mujibur RAHMAN, won a landslide victory. In March 1971, the League unilaterally declared independence and civil war ensued. During nine months of fighting, over one million East Bengalis were killed and millions more forced into exile, mainly to India. With Indian military assistance, Pakistan was defeated and Bangladesh gained independence. Sheikh Rahman became prime minister. The new state was beset by famine and economic crises. In 1975, Sheikh Rahman assumed the presidency. In 1976, he was assassinated in a military coup and martial law declared. In 1991, Bangladesh held its first free elections since independence. The Bangladesh National Party (BNP) gained a parliamentary majority. In 1996 elections the Awami League, led by Sheikh Hasina, returned to power. In 1998, Begum Zia, the former prime minister, was charged with corruption. **Economy** Bangladesh is one of the world's poorest countries (1995 GDP per capita, US$1,380); agriculture employs more than 50% of the workforce. Rice is the chief crop. Jute processing is the largest manufacturing industry and export.

Bangui Capital of the Central African Republic, on the River Ubangi near the border of the Democratic Republic of Congo. Founded in 1889 by the French, it is the nation's chief port for international trade. Industries: textiles, food processing, beer, soap. Pop. (1995) 553,000.

Bangweulu (Bangweolo) Lake and swamp area in NE Zambia, central Africa. The swamps are formed by the flooding of the lower River Chambezi, which enters the lake from the E. The lake supports commercial fishing. The area was visited by David Livingstone in 1868. Area: c.9,850sq km (3,800sq mi).

banjo Musical instrument with four to nine strings, a body of stretched parchment on a metal hoop, and a long, fretted neck. It is played with a plectrum or the fingers. Probably of African origin, it was taken to the US by slaves. It is often used in Dixieland jazz and folk music.

Banjul (Bathurst) Capital of Gambia, W Africa, on St Mary's Island where the River Gambia enters the Atlantic Ocean. Founded as a trading post by the British in 1816, it is the country's chief port and commercial centre. The main industry is peanut processing, although tourism is rapidly expanding. Pop. (1993) 42,000.

banking Commercial process providing a wide range of financial services, such as holding and transferring money, providing loans and giving stability to the financial sector of the economy. **Clearing** banks in the UK and **commercial** banks in the US deal with the general public, as well as with small- and medium-sized

businesses and corporations; MERCHANT BANKS or investment banks provide services to business and industry, such as investment loans or share flotations. In many countries there are other providers of banking services, such as insurance companies and credit-card issuers, as well as SAVINGS AND LOAN ASSOCIATIONS. A country's CENTRAL BANK, sometimes under government control, can be used as an economic regulator.

Bank of England Britain's central banking institution, founded in 1694 by a group of London merchants. Nationalized in 1946, it regulates foreign exchange, issues bank notes, advises the government on monetary matters and acts as the government's financial agent. It is situated in Threadneedle Street, City of London. The governor of the Bank of England is appointed by the national government. In 1997 the Bank of England was given operational responsibility for setting interest rates.

Bank of the United States Two US national banks. The first was established in 1791. Although it was soundly operated, autonomous state banking interests defeated its rechartering in 1811. Following the War of 1812, a second national bank was chartered by Congress in 1816. There was much opposition to its power to establish local branches. President Andrew JACKSON supported the bank's opponents and vetoed its rechartering. The bank became obsolete in 1836.

bankruptcy Legally determined status of a person or company, usually when debts greatly exceed income and assets. A person or company may ask to be declared bankrupt by the court, or else the creditors may do so. A court-appointed receiver takes charge of the bankrupt's property with the aim of meeting, as far as possible, the bankrupt's financial obligations to his or her creditors.

Banks, Sir Joseph (1743–1820) English botanist. Banks was the senior scientist of the group who sailed to Tahiti with Captain James COOK aboard HMS *Endeavour* in 1768. At Botany Bay, Australia (1770), he collected examples of plants hitherto unknown in Europe, including the shrub BANKSIA named in his honour. Upon his return, Banks helped set up the Royal Botanic Gardens at Kew, W London. In 1778 he became president of the Royal Society.

banksia Any of about 70 species of flowering shrubs and small trees found in Australia and New Guinea that belong to the genus *Banksia*. Their evergreen leaves are long and leathery, and they bear tube-shaped heads of yellowish or reddish flowers. The genus was discovered by Sir Joseph BANKS. Family Proteaceae.

Bann Principal river in Northern Ireland. The Bann rises in the Mourne Mountains and flows N through Lough Neagh and Lough Beg before entering the Atlantic Ocean near Coleraine Length: c.100km (60mi).

Bannister, Sir Roger Gilbert (1929–) English track athlete. On 6 May 1954, Bannister became the first man to run a mile in less than four minutes (3min 59.4sec). He was knighted in 1975.

Bannockburn, Battle of (1314) Major battle fought between EDWARD II of England and ROBERT I (THE BRUCE) at Bannockburn, central Scotland. The c.20,000-strong English army, advancing on Stirling, was intercepted by the Scots and massacred in the river and surrounding marshes. Edward was fortunate to escape with his life. Robert the Bruce became a national hero.

Banting, Sir Frederick Grant (1891–1941) Canadian physician. Banting shared, with J.J.R. Macleod, the 1923 Nobel Prize for physiology or medicine for his work in extracting the hormone INSULIN from the PANCREAS. This made possible the effective treatment of DIABETES.

Bantu Group of African languages generally considered as forming part of the Benue-Congo branch of the Niger-Congo family. Among the most widely-spoken of the several hundred tongues used from the Congo Basin to South Africa are SWAHILI, XHOSA and ZULU. There are more than 70 million speakers of Bantu languages.

banyan Evergreen tree of E India. The branches send down aerial shoots that take root, forming new trunks. Such trunks from a single tree may form a circle up to 100m (330ft) across. Height: to 30m (100ft). Family Moraceae; species *Ficus benghalensis*.

baobab Tropical tree native to Africa. It has a stout trunk containing water storage tissue, and short, stubby branches with sparse foliage. Fibre from its bark is used for rope. Its gourd-like fruit has edible pulp. Height: to 18m (60ft); trunk diameter: to 12m (40ft). Family Bombacaceae; species *Adansonia digitata*.

Bao Dai (1913–97) Emperor of Annam (1932–45), chief of state of Vietnam (1949–55), b. Nguyen Vinh Thuy. Bao Dai cooperated with the Vichy French and Japanese during World War 2. He was forced to resign in 1945 when the Viet Minh led by HO CHI MINH captured Indochina. In 1949, the French regained control and he became head of the new state of Vietnam. French defeat (1954) led to partition and Bao Dai agreed to the appointment of Ngo Dinh DIEM as prime minister. Diem established a republic, and Bao Dai was forced into exile.

baptism Pouring of water on a person's forehead or the immersion of the body in water, used as a rite of initiation into the Christian church. Baptism is one of the SACRAMENTS of the Christian church. Total immersion is practised by the BAPTISTS. In churches which practise infant baptism, the rite is often referred to as christening and is the occasion when a child is given its names.

Baptist Member of various Protestant and Evangelical sects who practise BAPTISM of believers and regard immersion as the only legitimate form sanctioned by the New Testament. Like the ANABAPTISTS, to whom they have an affinity but no formal links, they generally reject the practise of infant baptism, insisting that initiates must have freedom of thought and expression and must already be believers. Baptists originated among English dissenters of the 17th century but have spread worldwide. Baptists cherish the principle of religious liberty. There is no official creed, no hierarchy and individual churches are autonomous. In the mid-1990s, the number of Baptists worldwide was estimated at more than 31 million.

bar Unit of pressure, the pressure created by a column of mercury 75.007cm high. It is equal to 10^5 pascals. Standard atmospheric pressure (at sea level) is 1.01325 bars, or 1,013.25 millibars.

Bar, the *See* INNS OF COURT

Barabbas In the New Testament, convicted criminal or terrorist who was in prison at the time of Jesus Christ's trial before PONTIUS PILATE. In accordance with a PASSOVER custom, Pilate offered to release a prisoner. The Jerusalem mob nominated Barabbas and called for Christ to be crucified (Matthew 27, Mark 15, Luke 23, John 18).

Barak, Ehud (1942–) Israeli statesman, prime minister (1999–). He was chief of staff (1991–94) of the Israeli Defence Forces before joining the cabinet of Yitzhak RABIN. Barak succeeded Shimon PERES as leader of the Labour Party. Despite the optimism that greeted Barak's landslide victory over Binyamin NETANYAHU in the 1999 elections, there was still little immediate progress in the peace process with the Palestinians. In May 2000, Barak presided over the removal of Israeli troops from S Lebanon.

◄ **banjo** Originating in the 18th century, the banjo is popularly supposed to have been brought by slaves from Africa to the US. By the middle of the 19th century, it had become a traditional instrument of African Americans. It has four or more strings, which are plucked, and a resonating body consisting of parchment stretched over a metal hoop.

Barbados Island state in the Windward Islands, West Indies; the capital is BRIDGEPORT. Barbados' warm climate has encouraged the growth of its two largest industries, sugar cane and tourism. Barbados was settled by the British in 1627 and dominated by British plantation owners (using African slave labour until the abolition of slavery) for the next three hundred years. It was not until 1966 that it gained its independence. Area: 430sq km (166sq mi). Pop. (2000) 265,000.

barbarians Term given to all uncivilized tribes by the ancient Greeks and Romans. It is more specifically used to apply to the Germanic and Slavonic tribes that invaded the Roman Empire after about 50 BC.

Barbarossa (1466–1546) (Redbeard) Name given by Christians to two Muslim privateers in the Mediterranean, **Aruj** (d.1518) and Khizr, or **Khayr ad-Din** (d.1546). Aruj was killed in battle against the Spanish, but Khayr seized Algiers from Spain (1533), took Tunis (1534), raided Christian coasts and shipping and gained control of the Barbary States. He acknowledged the Ottoman sultan as his overlord, and from 1533 to 1544 Khayr was the commander of the fleet of SULEIMAN the Magnificent. His forces were finally defeated by Spain and Italy in the famous naval battle of Lepanto.

Barbary ape Tailless, yellowish-brown ape-like MONKEY native to Algeria and Morocco, and introduced into Gibraltar. It is the size of a small dog. The Gibraltar Barbary apes are the only wild monkeys in Europe. Species *Macaca sylvana. See also* MACAQUE; PRIMATE

barbastelle BAT found in Europe and Asia. Up to 6cm (2.5in) long with greyish fur, it catches insects and roosts in buildings or caves. Genus *Barbastella*.

barbel (barb) CARP-like freshwater fish of W Asia and S central Europe. A game and food fish, it has an elongated body, flattened underside and two pairs of fleshy mouth whiskers (barbels). It is a strong swimmer well adapted to fast-flowing rivers. Length: 50–90cm (20–35in); weight: 16kg (35lb). Family Cyprinidae; species *Barbus barbus*.

Barber, Samuel (1910–81) US composer. Barber composed chamber music, notably *Dover Beach* (1931), for voice and string quartet, two symphonies, a piano concerto (1962) and three operas, including *Vanessa* (1958). His style, initially quite romantic, became more dissonant. Barber won two Pulitzer Prizes.

barberry *See* BERBERIS

barbet Brightly coloured, poor-flying tropical bird, known for its monotonous call. It is stout-bodied with a large head, heavy bill, beard-like bristles and short legs. The female lays 2–5 white eggs. Length: 9–30cm (3.5–12in). Family Capitonidae. Genus *Megalaima*.

Barbie, Klaus (1913–91) Nazi chief of the German Gestapo in France during World War 2. Barbie was known as the "Butcher of Lyon" for his persecution and murder of French Resistance fighters and Jews. He sent thousands of people to AUSCHWITZ. After the war, he worked for US counter-intelligence before escaping to Bolivia in 1951. Barbie was captured in 1987, brought back to Lyon and sentenced to life imprisonment.

Barbirolli, Sir John (1899–1970) English conductor. Barbirolli succeeded TOSCANINI as conductor (1937–42) of the New York Philharmonic. He returned to England to lead (1943–68) the Hallé Orchestra, Manchester.

barbiturate DRUG used as a sedative or to induce sleep. Highly addictive and dangerous in high doses or in combination with other drugs, most barbiturates are no longer prescribed. Short-acting barbiturates are used in surgery to induce general anaesthesia; long-acting formulations are prescribed for epilepsy.

Barbizon School French school of landscape painting in the 19th century. Led by Théodore ROUSSEAU in the late 1840s, the group worked in the forest of Fontainebleau near Barbizon, N France. Artists included Charles Daubigny, Diaz de la Peña, Jules Dupré and Constant Troyon. They embraced a longing for the freedom of nature, escaping the restraints of Parisian art. In working directly from nature, they were forerunners of IMPRESSIONISM.

Barbuda Coral island in the West Indies, a dependency of ANTIGUA, with which, along with Redonda, it forms an independent state of the Lesser Antilles. The chief industry is cotton. Area: 161sq km (101sq mi) Pop. (1994) 1,450.

Barcelona City and Mediterranean port in NE Spain, capital of CATALONIA and Spain's second-largest city. Reputedly founded by the Carthaginian Barca family, it was ruled by Romans, Visigoths and Moors, and by the

late Middle Ages had become a major trading centre. It is the focus of radical political and Catalan separatist movements. The autonomous Catalan government based here (1932–39) was swept away by the Spanish CIVIL WAR. Modern Barcelona is the cosmopolitan, cultural capital of Spain. In 1992, the Summer Olympics were held here. Historic buildings include the gothic Cathedral of Santa Eulalia (13th–15th century), the Church of the Sagrada Familia designed by Antonio GAUDÍ (begun 1882) and a Monument to Christopher Columbus. There are two universities, a Museum of Modern Art and the Picasso Museum. Industries: vehicles, textiles, machinery, petrochemicals, electrical goods. Pop. (1995) 1,615,000.

bar code (Universal Product Code) Coded information consisting of thick and thin lines, and designed for computer recognition. A laser beam scans the bar code and a light-sensitive detector picks up the reflected signal, which consists of a pattern of pulses. Bar codes are used on many products for sale in stores and supermarkets. The store's computer translates the bar code into information, including the product's name, weight or size.

bard In Celtic society, poet and singer charged with celebrating the exploits and virtues of the king or chieftain in whose court he lived. The medieval bardic EISTEDDFOD in Wales was revived as an annual event in the 19th century, at which the winner of a national poetry competition is "chaired" as a bard. In popular usage, the term describes any distinguished poet, particularly SHAKESPEARE.

Bardeen, John (1908–91) US physicist known for his research into SEMICONDUCTORS. Bardeen worked for the Bell Telephone Laboratories (1945–51) and was professor of physics (1951–75) at the University of Illinois. He was the first person to win the Nobel Prize twice in the same field, physics: in 1956 he shared with William SHOCKLEY and Walter BRATTAIN for their joint invention of the TRANSISTOR, and in 1972 with Leon Cooper and John Schrieffer for their theory of SUPERCONDUCTIVITY.

Bardot, Brigitte (1934–) French film actress and 1950s sex symbol. Bardot became famous for her roles in *And God Created Woman* (1956) and *Heaven Fell that Night* (1957), directed by her then husband, Roger Vadim. Despite Bardot's long retirement from filmmaking, she has maintained a high public profile, largely due to her animal-rights campaigns.

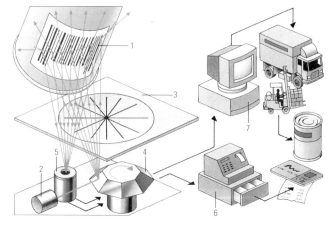

► **bar code** Bar codes represent information concerning a product and its manufacturer in a series of thick and thin black and white lines (1). Two longer, thinner bars mark the beginning and end of the manufacturer and product codes. A laser (2) is reflected through a glass screen (3) onto the bar code by a rotating multi-faceted mirror (4). The laser light is scattered by the white lines and absorbed by the black lines. A sensor (5) detects the reflected laser light and compares the relative width of the lines. Because the relative widths are compared, the bar code does not have to be on a flat surface. The sensor passes the information to the till (6) for billing the customer, and a central computer (7) monitors stock levels and orders supplies of new freight.

Barebone's Parliament (Parliament of the Saints, July–December 1653) Last Parliament of the English COMMONWEALTH. Successor to the RUMP PARLIAMENT, it was named after a prominent member, Praise-God Bare-bone, and representatives were hand-picked by Oliver CROMWELL and the Puritan army chiefs. Religious disputes ruined its effectiveness. It voted its own dissolution and handed over power to Cromwell as Lord Protector.

Barenboim, Daniel (1942–) Israeli pianist and conductor, b. Argentina. He made his recording debut in 1954 (aged 12). As music director (1975–89) of the Orchestre de Paris, Barenboim championed contemporary music. In 1991, he succeeded Sir Georg SOLTI as music director of the Chicago Symphony Orchestra. He was married (1967–74) to the cellist Jacqueline DU PRÉ.

Barents, Willem (d.1597) Dutch navigator and explorer. Barents made three expeditions in search of the NORTHEAST PASSAGE (1594–97). On his third voyage he discovered SVALBARD, and crossing the sea now named after him, reached NOVAYA ZEMLYA. The ship was trapped by ice, and the Dutch sailors built a shelter; most survived until the following year, when they escaped, but Barents died before they reached safety.

Barents Sea Part of the ARCTIC OCEAN lying between Svalbard and NOVAYA ZEMLYA, it was named after Willem BARENTS. The sea-bed consists of an uneven surface distribution of Quaternary sediments. Deeper, older sediments bear evidence of long periods above sea level. The fishing grounds are particularly rich in cod and herring. Area: 1,370,360sq km (529,096sq mi).

Barère de Vieuzac, Bertrand (1755–1841) French revolutionary. During the FRENCH REVOLUTION, Barère supported the execution of King Louis XVI. Despite denouncing his old ally ROBESPIERRE, Barère was imprisoned for his role in the REIGN OF TERROR (1793–94). He escaped and became an agent for Napoleon I but was banished after the Bourbon restoration (1815).

Bari Seaport on the Adriatic, in the Apulia region of SE Italy; capital of Bari province. A Roman colony, it was later ruled by Byzantines, Saracens, Normans and Venetians. The Romanesque cathedral of St Nicholas of Bari is a place of Christian pilgrimage. Bari's traditional industries of shipbuilding and textiles are supplemented by oil refining and nuclear power. Pop. (1996) 337,000.

Baring British family of merchant bankers. Sir Francis Baring (1740–1810) founded the company in 1806. Baring Brothers was a major financier for the Napoleonic Wars. Alexander Baring (1774–1848) was an early investor in United States' trade and helped negotiate the WEBSTER-ASHBURTON Treaty (1842). In 1890, the Bank of England rescued Barings Bank from bankruptcy after Argentina defaulted on debt repayment. In 1995, Barings Bank collapsed as a result of the unsupervised activities of a Singapore-based derivatives trader, Nick Leeson (1967–).

barite Translucent, white or yellow mineral, barium sulphate (BaSO₄), found in sedimentary rocks and ore veins in limestone. It occurs as a gangue mineral with ores of lead, copper and zinc, and as a replacement for limestone. Used as a weighting agent in oil-rig drilling, and in the chemical industry for paper-making, rubber manufacture, high-quality paints and in X-rays. Hardness: 3–3.5; r.d. 4.5.

baritone Name for the register of the human voice which falls between that of TENOR and BASS. It has been much used in operas since the 18th century; Mozart, Verdi and Wagner, among others, have written major roles for the baritone voice.

barium (symbol Ba) Silver-white element of the ALKA-LINE-EARTH METALS, discovered in 1808 by Sir Humphry DAVY. It is a soft metal whose chief sources are heavy spar (barium sulphate) and witherite (barium carbonate). Barium compounds are used as rodent poison, pigments for paints and as drying agents. Barium sulphate (BaSO₄) is taken to allow X-ray examination of the stomach and intestines, because barium atoms are opaque to X-rays; this is called a "barium meal." Properties: at.no. 56; r.a.m. 137.34; r.d. 3.51; m.p. 725°C (1,337°F); b.p. 1,640°C (2,984°F); most common isotope Ba¹³⁸ (71.66%).

bark Outer protective covering of a woody plant stem. It is made up of several layers. The CORK layer, waxy and waterproof, is the thickest and hardens into the tough, fissured outer covering. Lenticels (pores) in the bark allow GAS EXCHANGE between the stem and the atmosphere. *See also* CAMBIUM

Barker, George Granville (1913–91) English poet. His early verse invited comparisons with the New Apocalypse movement. *The Confession of George Barker* (1950) marked the emergence of his mature voice. Other works include *Collected Poems* (1987). Elizabeth Smart's novella *By Grand Central Station I Sat Down and Wept* (1945) was inspired by her relationship with Barker.

Barker, Pat (1943–) English novelist. Barker's novels focus on the plight of women, usually in the N of England. Her debut novel was *Union Street* (1982). *Regeneration* (1991) and *The Eye in the Door* (1993) were the first volumes of a World War 1 trilogy. The final part, *The Ghost Road*, won the 1995 Booker Prize.

Barlach, Ernst (1870–1938) German sculptor, graphic artist, writer and dramatist. Barlach was a major pioneer of the German EXPRESSIONISM movement. His distinctive style was influenced by medieval German wood carving and ART NOUVEAU. Barlach's sculptures, such as the bronze angel in Güstrow Cathedral, Germany, have a raw, emotional quality and vigour.

barley Cereal GRASS native to Asia and Ethiopia, cultivated perhaps since 5000 BC. Three cultivated species are: *Hordeum distichum*, commonly grown in Europe; *H. vulgare*, favoured in the US; and *H. irregulare*, grown in Ethiopia. Barley is eaten by humans and many other animals, and is used to make malt beverages. Family Poaceae/Gramineae.

bar mitzvah Jewish ceremony in which a young male is initiated into the religious community. At the ceremony, which traditionally takes place when he is aged 13 years and 1 day, he reads a portion of the TORAH in a synagogue. The rite is followed by a social celebration. Girls may participate in a similar ceremony (**bas mitzvah**).

barn (symbol *b*) Scientific unit of area used in nuclear physics to measure the cross sections in interactions of particles. A barn equals 10⁻²⁴ cm² per nucleus. This area is a measure of the probability that fission will occur when a neutron moves toward a heavy nucleus.

Barnabas, Saint Early Christian apostle, originally named Joseph He was a companion of St PAUL and travelled with him on two proselytizing missions to Cyprus and the European mainland. His feast day is 11 June.

barnacle Crustacean that lives mostly on rocks and floating timber. Some barnacles live on whales, turtles and fish without being parasitic, although there are also parasitic species. The larvae swim freely until ready to become adults, when they settle permanently on their heads; their bodies become covered with calcareous plates. Two main types are those with stalks (**goose** barnacles) and those without (**acorn** barnacles). Subclass Cirripedia.

Barnard, Christiaan (1922–) South African surgeon. Barnard was the first to perform a human heart transplant

(3 December, 1967). In 1974 he was the first to implant a second heart into a patient and to link the circulations of the hearts so that they worked together as one.

Barnardo, Thomas John (1845–1905) British philanthropist who founded the Dr Barnardo homes for destitute children, b. Ireland. In 1867 Barnardo founded the East End Mission for orphan children, the first of his famous homes. The Barnardo's charity no longer runs homes, but works within communities to help children and families.

Barnes, Julian (1946–). English novelist. His debut novel was *Metroland* (1981). *Flaubert's Parrot* (1984) was an inventive mix of biographical detail and ironic humour. Barnes' *History of the World in 10½ Chapters* (1989) was a popular success. Other works include *Staring at the Sun* (1986) and *England, England* (1999).

barn owl Generally nocturnal bird of prey that lives mainly in the Eastern Hemisphere. The widely distributed common barn OWL (*Tyto alba*) has a heart-shaped face and long legs. It sometimes lives in buildings, and acute hearing enables it to locate rodents and other prey in almost total darkness. Family Tytonidae.

Barnum, P.T. (Phineas Taylor) (1810–91) US showman. Barnum established the American Museum in New York City (1842), where he presented the "dwarf" Tom Thumb, the Fijian mermaid and other "freaks". In 1847, he introduced the Swedish soprano Jenny LIND to US audiences. In 1871, he opened his circus, billed as "The Greatest Show on Earth". He merged with rival James Bailey in 1881 to form Barnum and Bailey's Circus.

barometer Instrument for measuring atmospheric pressure. Barometers are of two basic types. A **mercury** barometer has a vertical column of mercury that changes length with changes in atmospheric pressure. An **aneroid** barometer has a chamber containing a partial vacuum, and the chamber changes shape with changes in pressure. Barometers are used in WEATHER FORECASTING to predict local weather changes: a rising barometer (increasing pressure) indicates dry weather; a falling barometer indicates wet weather. A barometer can also be used in an ALTIMETER to measure altitude by indicating changes in atmospheric pressure. *See also* BAR

Barons' War (1263–67) In English history, conflict between HENRY III and his barons, led by Simon de MONTFORT. In 1261 Henry renounced the provisions of Oxford (1258) and Westminster (1259) that had proposed he rule through a council of barons rather than rely on favourites. The barons decided to force the king to submit and defeated Henry's army in the battle of Lewes (1264). Henry's son, the future EDWARD I, formed an army which defeated the barons, and Montfort was killed at the battle of Evesham (1265).

baroque Term (perhaps derived from the Portuguese *barroca*, a misshapen pearl) applied to the style of art and architecture prevalent in Europe in the 17th and early 18th centuries. Baroque was at its height in the Rome (*c*.1630–80) of BERNINI, BORROMINI and Pietro de Cortona, and in S Germany (*c*.1700–50) with Balthazar Neumann and Fischer von Erlach. High baroque at its best was a blend of light, colour and movement calculated to overwhelm the spectator by a direct emotional appeal. Paintings contained visual illusions; sculpture exploited the effect of light on surface and contour. Buildings were heavily decorated with stucco ornament and free-standing sculpture. Baroque became increasingly florid before merging with the lighter style of ROCOCO. The term is often used to describe the period as well as the style. In music, the period is notable for several stylistic developments. Musical textures became increasingly contrapuntal (polyphonic), culminating in the masterpieces of J.S. BACH and HANDEL. Many purely instrumental forms of increasing virtuosity, such as the fugue, sonata, concerto, suite, toccata, passacaglia and chaconne, emerged and became popular.

barracuda Marine fish found in tropical Atlantic and Pacific waters. Known to attack people, it has a large mouth with many large, razor-sharp teeth. It is long, slender and olive green. Length: usually 1.2–1.8m (4–6ft); weight: 1.4–22.7kg (3–50lb). The great barracuda of the Florida coast grows to 2.5m (8ft). Family Sphyraenidae; there are 20 species.

Barranquilla City and major port on the River Magdalena, N Colombia. It became a river port in the mid-19th century, and the river was deepened to take seagoing ships in 1935. Located in an agricultural region, its industries include textiles, food processing, chemicals, shipbuilding and glass. Pop. (1997) 1,158,000.

barrel organ Mechanical musical instrument in which pins on a rotating drum open valves that let air from a wind-chest enter organ pipes to produce the sound. MOZART and HANDEL wrote compositions for it. It has been used in village churches and by street musicians. The name is sometimes incorrectly applied to a mechanical PIANO or to a hurdy-gurdy.

Barrie, Sir James Matthew (1860–1937) Scottish dramatist and novelist. Barrie is chiefly remembered as the writer of *Peter Pan* (1904), an ever-popular play about a boy who refuses to grow up. Although criticized for his sentimentality, his best works are clever, romantic fantasies. Other plays include *The Admirable Crichton* (1902) and *What Every Woman Knows* (1908).

barrier reef Long, narrow CORAL REEF some distance from, and roughly parallel, to the shore, and separated from it by a lagoon. Australia's GREAT BARRIER REEF is the most famous.

barrow In archaeology, a prehistoric burial mound. In North America, barrows were built by Native Americans known as MOUND BUILDERS. In Europe, barrows are usually either long or round. **Long** barrows were built in the NEOLITHIC period and consist of a vault built of stones, roofed with stone slabs and covered with soil; many were used for multiple burials. **Round** barrows primarily date to the early BRONZE AGE, but some in England were built as late as Roman and Saxon times. Usually containing a single body, they vary in diameter from 1.5m to 50m (4.5–160ft).

Barry, Sir Charles (1795–1860) English architect. Barry redesigned the HOUSES OF PARLIAMENT (1840–67) at Westminster, London, in a Gothic style after the original building burned down. Barry's preference for Italian Renaissance architecture shows in the classical ground plan for the parliament building.

Barrymore US family of actors. **Maurice** (1847–1905) made his stage debut in London in 1872. In 1875, he emigrated to the US, where he married the actress Georgiana Drew. They had three children. **Lionel** (1878–1954), a fine character actor, made many films, including *Dinner at Eight* (1933) and *A Free Soul* (1931), for which he won an Oscar for best actor. **Ethel** (1879–1959) was best known for her stage performances in plays, such as *A Doll's House* (1905) and *The Corn is Green* (1942). She won an Oscar for her part in the film *None But the Lonely Heart* (1944). **John** (1882–1942) was a matinee idol. His many films include *Beau Brummel* (1924), *Don Juan* (1926) and *Grand Hotel* (1932). **Drew** Barrymore (1975–) became a child star in *E.T., The Extra-Terrestrial* (1982).

Barth, Heinrich (1821–65) German explorer and geographer. In 1845 Barth set out on a two-year expedition through N Africa, Asia Minor and Greece. Barth was a member of a British-sponsored exploration (1851–56) of the Sahara. His *Travels and Discoveries in North and Central Africa* (1857–58) is considered a standard text.

Barth, John Simmons (1930–) US writer and founder of post-modern literary pastiche. Among Barth's best-known works are the novels *The Sot-Weed Factor* (1960) and *Giles Goat-Boy* (1966). In 1973 he won the US National Book Award for his three novellas, collectively entitled *Chimera* (1972). Later works include *Sabbatical* (1982), *The Tidewater Tales* (1987) and *The Last Voyage of Somebody the Sailor* (1991).

Barth, Karl (1886–1968) Swiss theologian. Barth was a leading thinker of 20th-century PROTESTANTISM. He tried to lead theology back to the principles of the REFORMATION and emphasized the revelation of God through Jesus Christ. Barth's school has been called dialectical theology or theology of the word. In 1935, he was suspended from his position at the University of Bonn for his anti-Nazi stance, and he returned to Switzerland.

Barthes, Roland (1915–80) French academic, writer and cultural critic. A leading proponent of STRUCTURALISM and SEMIOTICS, his idea of the literary text as a "system of signs" was informed by the linguistics of Ferdinand de SAUSSURE. Perhaps his best-known contribution to literary theory was the notion of the "death of the author," in which the meaning of a text is generated by the reader. His diverse works include *Mythologies* (1957), *S/Z* (1970) and *Camera Lucida* (1980).

Bartholdi, Frédéric Auguste (1834–1904) French sculptor. His most famous piece is *Liberty Enlightening the World* (Statue of Liberty) in New York City harbour, which was dedicated in 1886.

Bartók, Béla (1881–1945) Hungarian composer and pianist. With Zoltán KODÁLY, Bartók amassed a definitive collection of Hungarian folk music. His orchestral works include *Music for Strings, Percussion, and Celesta* (1936), two violin concertos (1908 and 1938) and the Concerto for Orchestra (1943). He wrote one opera, *Bluebeard's Castle* (1911). His compositions combine folk-music idioms with dissonance and great rhythmic energy.

Bartolommeo, Fra (1457–1517) (Bartolommeo della Porta) Florentine painter, draughtsman and Dominican friar. In parallel with RAPHAEL, he contributed to the development of a new type of Madonna with Saints, specific to the High RENAISSANCE, in which the Madonna acts as a central point for the whole composition. Bartolommeo's characteristic style is one of restraint combined with monumentality, exemplified by *The Mystical Marriage of St Catherine* (1511).

Barton, Clara (Clarissa Harlowe) (1821–1912) US humanitarian and founder (1882) of the American National RED CROSS. Barton cared for wounded soldiers during the US Civil War, and was active in the International Red Cross during the Franco-Prussian War (1870–71). She was responsible for the "American amendment" at the 1884 Geneva Convention which enabled the Red Cross to be active in peace-time emergencies.

Baruch, Book of Biblical book in the APOCRYPHA. It consists of an introduction believed to have been written by Baruch (active 600 BC), the disciple of JEREMIAH; a liturgical confession; a sermon; and a set of canticles.

baryon Any ELEMENTARY PARTICLE affected by the strong interaction of nuclear force. The baryon consists of three QUARKS. Baryons are subclasses of HADRONS. The only stable baryons are the proton and (provided it is inside a nucleus) the neutron. Heavier baryons are called hyperons. *See also* LEPTON; MESON

Baryshnikov, Mikhail (1948–) US ballet dancer, b. Russia. A leading member (1969–74) of the KIROV BALLET, Baryshnikov's defection to the West received much publicity. He was with the American Ballet Theatre as principal dancer (1974–78) and artistic director (1980–89). He starred in several films and set up the White Oak Dance Project.

basal metabolic rate (BMR) Minimum amount of energy required by the body to sustain basic life processes, including breathing, circulation and tissue repair. It is calculated by measuring oxygen consumption. Metabolic rate increases well above basal metabolic rate (BMR) during vigorous physical activity or fever or under the influence of some DRUGS (including CAFFEINE). It falls below BMR during sleep, general ANAESTHESIA or starvation. BMR is higher in children.

basalt Hard, fine-grained, basic IGNEOUS ROCK; intrusive or extrusive. Its colour can be dark green, brown, dark grey or black. It can have a glassy appearance. There are many types of basalt with different proportions of elements. It may be compact or vesicular (porous). If the vesicles are subsequently filled with secondary minerals, such as quartz or calcite, it is called **amygdaloidal** basalt. Basalts are the main rocks of ocean floors and form the world's major lava flows, such as the Deccan Trap, India.

base In chemistry, a compound that accepts protons. A base will neutralize an ACID to form a SALT and water. Most are oxides or hydroxides of metals; others, such as ammonia, are compounds that yield hydroxide IONS in water. Soluble bases are called ALKALIS. Strong bases are fully dissociated into ions; weak bases are partially dissociated in solution. *See also* NEUTRALIZATION

base In mathematics, the number of units in a number system that is equivalent to one unit in the next higher counting place. Thus 10 is the base of the decimal system: only the ten digits 0–9 can be used in the units, tens, hundreds and so on. Each number system has a number of symbols equal to its base. In the BINARY SYSTEM (base 2) there are two symbols, 0 and 1.

baseball National summer sport of the US and Canada, also popular in Japan, Korea, Taiwan, Latin America, Australia and parts of Europe. Baseball evolved during the 19th century from various ball games, particularly the English "rounders". The field comprises an inner diamond 27m (90ft) on each side, and an outfield. The diamond has a central pitcher's mound and bases at three corners. The batter stands at the fourth, home plate. Each team has nine players. A run is scored when a batter reaches first base and eventually home plate. To get back to home base with a single hit is a **home run**. A game has nine innings (during which each team bats once). A team's innings ends when a third batter or runner is put out, such as by missing three consecutive valid pitches ("**strikes**"); by a field catch; or if a runner does not reach the next base before the ball is thrown there. Games tied after nine innings are played until there is a winner. Every autumn the top teams of the two North American major leagues (American and National) compete in a World Series.

Basel (Bâle or Basle) City and river port on the Rhine River; capital of Basel-Stadt canton, NW Switzerland. It joined the Swiss Confederation in 1501. It is an economic, financial and historically important cultural centre. There is a cathedral (where ERASMUS is buried), a 15th-century university and a 16th-century town hall. It is the centre of the Swiss chemical and pharmaceutical industries. Pop. (1996) 174,000.

Basel, Council of Ecumenical council convoked at Basel in 1431. It instituted church reforms and conciliated the Hussites in Bohemia. Conflict with Pope Eugene IV led the pope to denounce the council in 1437. In 1439, the council declared Eugene deposed and chose an anti-pope, Amadeus of Savoy, as Pope Felix V. Felix resigned in 1449 and the council was dissolved.

Basho, Matsuo (1644–94) Japanese poet. A student of ZEN Buddhism, he is considered the master of HAIKU verse. Other works include the episodic travelogue *Narrow Road to the Deep North* (1694).

BASIC (Beginners' All-purpose Symbolic Instruction Code) Computer programming language that is relatively easy to learn and uses many everyday words. It is commonly used by both amateur and professional programmers. BASIC computer PROGRAMS usually require a separate program called an **interpreter**, which converts BASIC into the machine code required by the processor.

Basie, Count (William) (1904–84) US jazz band leader, pianist and composer. Basie formed his own band in Kansas City in 1935, centred around a rhythm section of himself, Freddie Green, Walter Page and Jo Jones. The Count Basie Orchestra recordings for Decca (1937–39) are among the most powerful works of the swing era. In 1952, Basie formed a new orchestra, which made the explosive *The Atomic Mr. Basie* (1957).

Basil I (c.813–86) Byzantine emperor (r.867–86) and founder of the Macedonian dynasty. Emperor Michael III assisted Basil in his rise to power. After Michael designated him co-emperor, Basil had his former patron murdered. His most effective policies concerned the conversion of the Bulgars to Orthodox Christianity, military campaigns against the Paulician religious sect in Asia Minor and a revision of Roman legal codes.

Basil II (c.958–1025) Byzantine emperor (976–1025), surnamed Bulgaroctonus ("Bulgar-slayer"). One of Byzantium's ablest rulers, Basil reigned during the heyday of the empire. He is best known for his military victory over the Bulgarian tsar Samuel in 1014, which brought the entire Balkan peninsula under Byzantine control.

basil Common name for a tropical plant of the MINT family, whose dried leaves are used for flavouring. It has white or purple flowers. Family Lamiaceae/Labiatae; species *Ocimum basilicum*.

basilica Roman colonnaded hall used for public business; also an early Christian church based on this design. The main characteristics of a basilica church, established by the 4th century AD, were a rectangular plan with a longitudinal axis, a wooden roof and an E end which was either rectangular or contained a semicircular apse. The body of the church usually had a central nave and two flanking aisles, lower and narrower than the nave.

basilisk Semi-aquatic LIZARD found in trees near streams of tropical America. It has a compressed greenish body, whip-like tail, a crest along its back and an inflatable pouch on its head. It can run over water for short distances on its hind legs, and eats plants and insects. Length: up to 61cm (2ft). Family Iguanidae; genus *Basiliscus*. The basilisk is also a legendary serpent with the body of a cockerel.

Basil the Great, Saint (329–79) Doctor of the Church and one of the four Fathers of the Greek Church. He founded a monastic community and was ordained (370) bishop of Caesarea, Cappadocia. Basil established the dominance of the NICENE CREED and fiercely opposed ARIANISM. He is thought to have composed the *Liturgy of St Basil*, still used in the Eastern Orthodox Church. His feast day is 2 January in the West; 1 January in the East.

Baskerville, John (1706–75) English typographer and pioneer of the English tradition of fine printing. Baskerville set up his own printing house in 1757 and became (1758) printer to Cambridge University. He produced a folio edition of the Bible (1763) and editions of John Milton's poetry. Baskerville's clear typefaces remain in common use.

basketball Game that originated in the USA, and is now played worldwide. Devised in 1891 by Dr James Naismith, it has been an Olympic sport since 1936. It is played by two teams of five (plus substitutes), usually indoors. The court is up to 27.8m (91ft) long and 15m (49ft) wide. At each end is a backboard on which a bottomless netting basket hangs from a hoop 3m (10ft) above the floor. The object is to put the ball down through the opposing team's basket, scoring points. In normal play, 2 points are scored when the ball is thrown from within a zone close to the basket, and 3 points from farther away; a free throw (for a foul) counts 1 point. Players may move with the ball when dribbling it one-handed. With growing commercialization and the worldwide transmission of National Basketball Association (NBA) games, basketball is one of the most popular spectator sports.

Basle *See* BASEL

Basov, Nikolai Gennadiyevich (1922–) Russian physicist who developed the MASER that amplifies microwaves, and the LASER that amplifies light. For these contributions, Basov and his co-worker Alexander PROKHOROV shared the 1964 Nobel Prize for physics with Charles TOWNES.

Basque Country Region of the W Pyrenees in both Spain and France, consisting of the provinces of Alava, Guipúzcoa, part of Navarra, and Vizcaya in Spain and Basse-Navarre, Labord and Soule in France. The main towns are BILBAO and San Sebastian. The region is populated by the BASQUES. It lost its autonomy in the late 18th and early 19th centuries. Separatist movements were formed in response.

Basques Indigenous people of the western Pyrenees in N Spain and SW France, numbering c.3.9 million. Their language is not related to any other European tongue. Throughout history they have tenaciously maintained their cultural identity. The kingdom of NAVARRE, which existed for 350 years, was the home to most of the Basques. After its dissolution in 1512, most of the Spanish Basques enjoyed a degree of political autonomy. This autonomy was removed in 1873, and Basque unrest followed. Basque separatists known as ETA continued to agitate for an independent state. In 1998, ETA announced a cease-fire and opened negotiations with the Spanish government. The cease-fire was called off in November 1999.

Basra (Al-Basrah) City and chief port on the Shatt al-Arab channel, S Iraq; capital of Basra province. An ancient centre of Arabic learning, it was captured by the Turks in 1668. In the early 20th century, large oil fields were discovered nearby. It suffered serious damage during the Iran-Iraq and Gulf wars. Industries: oil refining, flour milling, wool. Pop. (1992 est.) 746,000.

bass Any of several bony fish, both freshwater and marine, and not all closely related. Together they make up a valuable commercial and sport fish. They include the white, black, striped, rock and calico basses. The two main bass families are Serranidae and Centrarchidae.

bass Low or deep pitch. It is used of the lowest-pitched part of a composition or the lowest-pitched member of a family of instruments. It applies to the deepest male singing voice. The bass line in a composition is the bottom note of a chord or the lowest line in polyphony.

basset Short-legged hunting hound, originally bred in France to flush out game. After the BLOODHOUND, it has the most highly developed sense of smell among dogs. Bassets have long bodies and long floppy ears. The short coat is generally tan and white. Standard size: 30–38cm (12–15in) at the shoulder.

Basseterre Capital and chief port of the federated state of ST KITTS-NEVIS, on the SW coast of St Kitts, in the Leeward Islands group, E Caribbean. Founded in 1627, it is an important commercial centre. Industries: sugar refining. Pop. (1994) 13,000.

Basse-Terre Capital of GUADELOUPE in the French West Indies. Founded by the French in 1643, it is an important trade centre. Pop. (1990) 14,000.

bassoon Bass WOODWIND instrument with a range of three octaves, corresponding to that of the CELLO. It has a double-reed mouthpiece and a conical bore, the tube bending back on itself to reduce the basoon's length. They are used in symphonic and chamber music. The double bassoon or contrabassoon is the lowest-pitched wood-wind instrument, sounding an octave below the bassoon.

Bass Strait Channel between Tasmania and Victoria, SE Australia. In 1798, Matthew Flinders and George Bass discovered the Strait, proving that Tasmania was not part of the Australian continent. It has natural gas and oil deposits and rich fishing grounds. Width: 130–240km (80–150mi).

Bastille Fortress and prison in Paris, built in the late 14th century and destroyed during the FRENCH REVOLUTION. Political prisoners were incarcerated here, and it became a symbol of royal oppression. On 14 July 1789, now a national holiday in France, a revolutionary mob stormed it and released its seven prisoners. The Bastille was pulled down soon afterwards.

bat Only MAMMAL that has true flight (although a few others can glide). Bats are nocturnal and found in all tropical and temperate regions. Most are brown, grey or black. A bat's wing is formed by a sheet of skin. Bats are able to navigate in complete darkness by means of a kind of SONAR. Many bats live largely on insects, some are carnivorous, some drink blood, some live on nectar and pollen, and one group – flying foxes – subsist on fruit. Most are small, although they range in wingspan from 25cm–147cm (10–58in). The 178 genera of bats make up the order Chiroptera.

Bates, H.E. (Herbert Ernest) (1905–74) English novelist, playwright and short-story writer. Bates' novels include *Fair Stood the Wind for France* (1944), *The Jacaranda Tree* (1949) and a popular series featuring the Larkin family, including *The Darling Buds of May* (1958) and *A Little of What You Fancy* (1970).

Bates, Henry Walter (1825–92) English naturalist. His work on NATURAL SELECTION in animal MIMICRY lent support to Charles DARWIN's theory of EVOLUTION. On field studies (1848–59) in the Amazon, Bates collected over 8,000 previously unrecorded species of insects.

Bateson, William (1861–1926) English biologist. He discovered and named the science of GENETICS. Bateson translated much of Gregor MENDEL's pioneering work on inheritance in plants, so bringing it recognition. By his own experiments he also extended Mendel's theories to animals, which provided a foundation for the modern understanding of HEREDITY.

Bath Spa city on the River Avon, SW England. The centre of the new unitary authority of Bath and North-East Somerset, Bath has been designated a world heritage site. Its hot springs were discovered in the 1st century AD by the Romans, who named the city *Aquae Solis* (waters of the

◄ **bat** The large mouse-eared bat (*Myotis myotis*) is the largest of all European bats. It has a wingspan of up to 38cm (15in) and migrates up to 200km (125mi) from its summer habitat in S Europe to the Middle East where it spends the winter months. Though it prefers open farmland and woodland, the large mouse-eared bat is sometimes known to live in cellars or the attics of houses. A nocturnal animal, it lives on insects, particularly moths.

sun). The bathing complex and temple are the finest Roman remains in Britain. Bath flourished as a centre for the cloth and wool industries. In the 18th century (under the direction of Beau Nash), the city became a fashionable resort. John Wood transformed the city into a showcase for Georgian architecture. The Royal Crescent, Queen Square and the Circus are among his notable achievements. The city hosts an annual arts festival. The University of Bath was established in 1966. Industries: tourism, printing, bookbinding. Pop. (1991) 79,900.

batholith Huge mass of igneous rock at the Earth's surface. It has an exposed surface of more than 100sq km (40sq mi) and may have originated as an intrusive igneous structure that was eroded into surface material. Most batholiths consist of granite rock types and are associated with the mountain-building phases of PLATE TECTONICS.

batik Method of decorating textiles, practised for centuries in Indonesia and introduced into Europe by Dutch traders. Molten wax is applied to the parts of a fabric that are to remain undyed, before the fabric is dipped into cool vegetable dye. The fabric is then dipped in hot water to remove the wax from the undyed areas.

Batista y Zaldivar, Fulgencio (1901–73) Cuban politician. In 1933, he led a successful military coup, and in 1940 was elected president. In 1944, Batista retired and moved to Florida, but in 1952 a coup returned him to power. In 1959, he was overthrown by Fidel CASTRO.

Baton Rouge Capital city of Louisiana, on the Mississippi River. Founded in 1719 by French colonists, it was ceded to Britain by France in 1763 and to the US with the Louisiana Purchase (1803). It became the state capital in 1849. The city contains both Louisiana State University and Southern University and is the site of a large petrochemical complex. Pop. (1990) 219,531.

Battambang (Batdambung) Second-largest town in Cambodia and capital of Battambang province, W Cambodia. It was ceded to Thailand in 1809, became part of French INDOCHINA in 1907, and was returned to Cambodia in 1946. It is a market centre in a major rice-producing area. Pop. (1981 est.) 551,860.

Batten, Jean Gardner (1909–82) New Zealand aviator who in 1935 became the first woman to make a solo flight from Australia to Britain. Batten also flew solo across the S Atlantic Ocean to South America.

Battenberg, Louis Alexander (1854–1921) British admiral. b. Austria. In 1884, he married Princess Alice, granddaughter of Queen Victoria. In 1917, Battenberg renounced his German titles, anglicised his name as Mountbatten and was created 1st Marquess of Milford

Haven. His youngest son was Louis Mountbatten and his grandson is Prince PHILIP, Duke of Edinburgh.

battery Collection of voltaic cells that convert chemical energy into direct current (DC) electricity. The term is also commonly used for a single cell, particularly a dry cell as used in portable electronic equipment. Most primary cell batteries are not rechargeable; some types of primary cell – such as nickelcadmium (Nicad) batteries – and all accumulators (storage batteries) can be recharged.

battleship Powerful type of naval warship in use during the late 19th and early 20th centuries. The largest battleships, the *Musachi* and the *Yamato*, displaced over 72,000 tonnes and were built by the Japanese. Both were sunk during World War 2. Modern battleships carry a variety of missile systems. *See also* AIRCRAFT CARRIER; CRUISER

baud Unit for measuring the speed of at which a digital communications device carries information. One baud is equal to one BIT per second. Although the term baud rate is still widely used, the speed of modern equipment is often expressed in kilobits per second.

Baudelaire, Charles Pierre (1821–67) French poet and critic. Baudelaire's collection of poems, *Les Fleurs du Mal* (1857), represents one of the highest achievements of 19th-century French poetry. The poems were condemned by the censor and six were subsequently suppressed. Baudelaire was influenced by Edgar Allan POE.

Bauhaus German school for architecture and the applied arts which was instrumental in developing links between design and industry. Founded by Walter GROPIUS in 1919, it aimed to combine great craftsmanship with an ideal of an all-embracing modern art. Although the Bauhaus specialized in architecture and design, several progressive painters, including KANDINSKY and KLEE, taught there. The studios focused on designing products for manufacturing industry, especially furniture, textiles and electric light fittings. In 1928, Hannes Meyer succeeded Gropius

as director. MIES VAN DER ROHE took Meyer's place in 1930, but in 1933, after it moved to Berlin, the Nazis closed the school. Many students and staff emigrated. The school's teaching had an enormous influence on Western design. MOHOLY-NAGY, a Hungarian designer who taught at the Bauhaus in the 1920s, founded the New Bauhaus in Chicago in 1937. This later became the Institute of Design.

bauxite Rock from which most aluminium is extracted. Bauxite is a mixture of minerals, such as diaspore, gibbsite, boehmite and iron. It is formed by weathering and leaching of rocks containing aluminium silicates.

Bavaria (Bayern) Largest state in Germany; the capital is MUNICH. Part of the Roman Empire until the 6th century, it was taken by CHARLEMAGNE in 788, forming part of the Holy Roman Empire until the 10th century. Incorporated into Germany in 1871, it became a state within the German Federal Republic in 1946. Industries: glass, porcelain, brewing. Area: 70,553sq km (27,256sq mi). Pop. (1993) 11,863,313.

Bax, Sir Arnold Edward Trevor (1883–1953) English composer. The influence of Celtic mythology is apparent in his symphonic poems, such as *Tintagel* (1917). His best-known works include seven symphonies (1921–39) and the Second Piano Sonata (1919). Bax became Master of the King's Music in 1942.

bay Tree or shrub of the LAUREL family. The leaves of some varieties are used to flavour food. In classical tradition, head wreaths of bay leaves were awarded as tokens to conquerors. Family Lauraceae; species *Laurus nobilis*.

Bayeux Tapestry (*c*.1080) Strip of linen embroidered in wool, measuring 70m×48cm (231ft×19in), and depicting (in more than 70 scenes) the life of HAROLD I of England and the NORMAN CONQUEST. An unfounded tradition attributes its design to Matilda, wife of WILLIAM I (THE CONQUEROR), but it was probably commissioned by William's half-brother Odo, Bishop of Bayeux. It is now in a museum in Bayeux, N France.

Bayle, Pierre (1647–1706) French philosopher. His major work was the *Historical and Critical Dictionary* (1697), a collection of biographies that examined philosophical and theological doctrines. A champion of religious toleration, Bayle was persecuted for his sceptical assertion that morality was independent of religion. He was a major influence on the ENLIGHTENMENT.

Baylis, Lilian Mary (1874–1937) English theatre manager. In 1912, she became manager of the Old Vic, transforming it into the world's premier house for Shakespearian productions. In 1931, Baylis acquired Sadler's Wells Theatre and turned it into the home of the Royal Ballet and the English National Opera (ENO).

Bay of Pigs (17 April 1961) Unsuccessful effort by Cuban exiles (aided by the US) to overthrow Fidel CASTRO by invading Cuba near the Bay of Pigs. About 1,500 Cubans trained, equipped and transported by the US government, were involved. The invasion was badly planned, and the Cuban army defeated the exiles within three days. President John F. KENNEDY initially denied US involvement and was later subject to much criticism for its failure. *See also* CUBAN MISSILE CRISIS

Bayreuth City in Bavaria, S Germany, where an annual festival is held, staging exclusively the work of composer Richard WAGNER. The festivals are held in the *Festspielhaus*, built to Wagner's specifications. The first festival was held in 1876.

BBC *See* BRITISH BROADCASTING COMPANY (BBC)

BCG (Bacille Calmette Guérin) Vaccine against TUBERCULOSIS. It was named after its discoverers, the French bacteriologists Albert Calmette and Camille Guérin.

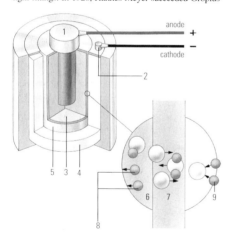

anode **+**
cathode **−**

▲ **battery** Sodium sulphur batteries are the newest type of battery and are lighter than nickel cadmium types. They have a carbon anode (1) and a metal cathode (2). The reactants are arranged in rings around the anode. An inner core of sodium (3) is separated from an outer ring of sulphur (4) by a layer of aluminium (5). The sodium (6) reacts with the aluminium (7), giving up electrons (8) which stream to the anode. The cathode gives electrons to the sulphur atoms (9) that bond with sodium ions to form sodium sulphide. The process creates a voltage.

beach Sloping zone of the shore, covered by sediment, sand or pebbles, that extends from the low-water line to the limit of the highest storm waves. The sediment is derived from coastal erosion or river ALLUVIUM.

Beadle, George Wells (1903–89) US geneticist. During his study of MUTATIONS in bread mould (*Neurospora crassa*), Beadle and Edward Tatum found that GENES are responsible for the synthesis of ENZYMES that control each step of all biochemical reactions occurring in an organism. For this discovery they shared, with J. Lederberg, the 1958 Nobel Prize for physiology or medicine.

beagle Hunting dog used to chase and follow small game. Of ancient origin, the modern breed was developed in England in the mid-1800s. It has a long, slightly domed head with a square-cut muzzle; long, hanging ears; and widely set, large eyes. Average size: (two varieties) not exceeding 38cm (15in) at the shoulder.

Beagle, HMS British survey ship that carried Charles DARWIN as ship's naturalist. The *Beagle* left England in December 1831 and for five years explored parts of South America and the Pacific islands. Darwin's observations formed the basis for his theory of EVOLUTION by NATURAL SELECTION.

Beaker culture Distinctive Neolithic culture that spread throughout Europe in the late 3rd millennium BC. Beaker culture is characterized by single-grave burials in round BARROWS, and a common type of decorated, beaker-shaped pot accompanying the burial. It is likely that the diffusion of this culture represented a gradual spread of new ideas to existing groups, rather than the migration of large numbers of people.

bean Plant grown for its edible seeds and seed pods. The broad bean (*Vicia faba*) is native to N Africa. The string bean (*Phaseolus vulgaris*) is native to tropical South America and is common in the US; several varieties are cultivated. Its long pods or kidney-shaped seeds are eaten as vegetables. The runner (*Phaseolus coccineus*) has scarlet, rather than white or lilac, flowers and shorter, broader seeds. *See also* SOYA BEAN

bear Large, omnivorous mammal with a stocky body, thick coarse fur and a short tail. Bears are native to the Americas and Eurasia. The sun bear is the smallest species, the Kodiak brown bear the largest. Bears have poor sight and only fair hearing, but an excellent sense of smell. They kill prey with a blow from their powerful forepaws. In cold regions most bears become dormant or hibernate in winter. Length: 1.3–3m (4–10ft); weight: 45–725kg (100–1,600lb). Order Carnivora; family Ursidae; there are approximately nine species.

Beardsley, Aubrey (1872–98) English illustrator. His highly wrought, stylized black-and-white drawings epitomize the English ART NOUVEAU style. Associated with the Decadent writers of the 1890s and the AESTHETIC MOVEMENT, Beardsley illustrated the first four volumes of the *Yellow Book* (1894–95) and Oscar Wilde's play *Salome*. His other work, such as *Isolde* (1895), enabled him to produce more outrageous, erotic "Japonesque" illustrations.

beat Style of popular music originating in N England during the early 1960s, also known as the Mersey beat or Liverpool sound. The most famous beat bands were THE BEATLES and The Hollies. Beat groups tended to be all-male, playing guitar-dominated music with catchy vocal lines and harmonies. *See also* BEAT MOVEMENT

beatitudes Blessings spoken by Jesus at the opening of his SERMON ON THE MOUNT upon those worthy of admission to the Kingdom of God. (Luke 6, Matthew 5).

Beatles, The British rock group. Perhaps the most influential band in the history of 20th-century popular music. Formed in Liverpool in 1960, The Beatles initially consisted of John LENNON (1940–80), Paul McCARTNEY (1942–), George Harrison (1943–) and Pete Best (1941–). In 1962 Best was replaced by Ringo Starr (Richard Starkey, 1940–). The Beatles' early style was US-derivative rhythm and blues blended with Lennon and McCartney's songwriting talent and attractive harmonies. From 1964 to 1970, they dominated pop music with 18 albums, including *Revolver* (1966) and *Sgt. Pepper's Lonely Hearts Club Band* (1967). After 1966, they never publicly performed live. The group made four feature films: *A Hard Day's Night* (1964), *Help!* (1965), *Magical Mystery Tour* (1968) and *Let It Be* (1970) and supplied the soundtrack for the cartoon *Yellow Submarine* (1968). The group disbanded in 1970 to pursue individual careers.

beat movement Term derived from John Clellon Holmes' novel *Go* (1952) and applied to a group of US writers in the 1950s, who rejected middle-class values and commercialism. They also experimented with states of perception through drugs and meditation. They included the poets Allen GINSBERG and Lawrence FERLINGHETTI and novelists Jack KEROUAC and William BURROUGHS.

Beaton, David (1494–1546) Scottish churchman, Roman Catholic prelate. Created cardinal in 1538, he succeeded his uncle as archbishop of St Andrews in 1539. In 1542, Beaton arranged the marriage of James V and Mary of Guise. In 1543, he crowned MARY, QUEEN OF SCOTS. Beaton's ruthless persecution of Scottish Protestants culminated in the execution of George Wishart (1546). Beaton was murdered in revenge.

Beaton, Sir Cecil Walter Hardy (1904–80) English photographer, costume and stage designer and writer. Beaton began his career as a fashion photographer in the 1920s and took up stage design in the 1930s. His film and stage designs include *Gigi* (film, 1951), *My Fair Lady* (stage, 1956; film, 1964) and *Coco* (1969).

Beatty, Warren (1937–) US film actor, producer and director, brother of Shirley Maclaine. Beatty made his film debut in *Splendor in the Grass* (1961). He attracted wider recognition for his performance in *Bonnie and Clyde* (1967). Beatty won an Academy Award as best director for *Reds* (1981). After the disastrous *Ishtar* (1987), he returned to form with *Dick Tracy* (1990). Other films include *Bulworth* (1998).

Beaufort, Henry (1374–1447) English statesman and prelate, illegitimate son of John of Gaunt. As chancellor to Henry IV and Henry V, Beaufort considerably influenced English domestic and foreign policy. Guardian of Henry VI (1422), he controlled England in the 1430s.

Beaufort wind scale Range of numbers from 0 to 17 representing the force of winds, together with descriptions of the corresponding land or sea effects. The Beaufort number 0 means calm wind less than 1km/h (0.6mph), with smoke rising vertically. Beaufort 3 means light breeze, 12–19km/h (8–12mph), with leaves in constant motion. Beaufort 11 is a storm, 103–116km/h (64–72mph) and Beaufort 12–17 is a hurricane, 117.5–219+km/h (73–136+mph), with devastation. The scale is named after its inventor, Admiral Sir Francis Beaufort (1774–1857).

Beaumarchais, Pierre Augustin Caron de (1732–99) French dramatist. His principal plays were the related court satires *The Barber of Seville* (1775) and *The Marriage of Figaro*, which were transformed into operas by ROSSINI and MOZART, respectively. Beaumarchais was also employed as a secret agent by the French to supply arms to the Americans during the American Revolution.

Beaumont, Sir Francis (1584–1616) English dramatist closely associated with the dramatist John FLETCHER. Between 1607–13, they produced at least ten outstanding plays, including *Philaster, The Maid's Tragedy* and *A King and No King*. Beaumont is usually credited with sole authorship of two plays, *The Woman Hater* (1607) and *The Knight of the Burning Pestle* (*c*.1607).

Beaumont, William (1785–1853) US army surgeon. He gained gained valuable knowledge of the functioning of the human stomach through a series of experiments he performed on Alexis St. Martin, who, as the result of a gunshot wound, had a small opening into his stomach which refused to close.

Beauregard, Pierre Gustave Toutant (1818–93) Confederate general in the American Civil War. Beauregard served in the Mexican War and was superintendent of West Point until just before the CIVIL WAR broke out (1861). On 13 April 1861, he forced the Union surrender of Fort Sumter in the first action of the war.

Beauvais Town in France, 68km (42mi) NW of Paris. Founded by the Romans, the famed Beauvais tapestry factory was established in the 17th century by Jean Baptiste COLBERT. In 1940, the factory was destroyed and the industry moved to Paris. Landmarks include the unfinished Gothic cathedral of St Pierre (begun 1227), which has the world's highest choir vault at 47m (154ft). Industries: ceramics, textiles, machinery. Pop. (1990) 56,280.

Beauvoir, Simone de (1908–86) French novelist, essayist and critic. De Beauvoir's novels *She Came to Stay* (1943) and *The Mandarins* (1954) are portraits of the existentialist intellectual circle of which she and her lifelong companion, Jean-Paul SARTRE, were members. Her best-known work is the feminist treatise, *The Second Sex* (1949). Other significant works include *The Prime of Life* (1960) and *Old Age* (1970). *See also* EXISTENTIALISM

beaver Large RODENT with fine brown fur, webbed hind feet and a broad scaly tail; it lives in streams and lakes of Europe, North America and Asia. Beavers build "lodges" of trees and branches above water level and dam streams and rivers with stones, sticks and mud. In many places they are hunted for fur. Length: to 1.2m (4ft); weight: up to 32kg (70lb). Family Castoridae; species *Castor fiber*.

Beaverbrook, William Maxwell Aitken, 1st Baron (1879–1964) British newspaper proprietor and politician, b. Canada. Beaverbrook entered Parliament in 1910 and was made a peer in 1917. He was a member of Winston CHURCHILL's war cabinet (1940–45). Beaverbrook bought a majority interest in the *Daily Express* (1916) and later founded the *Sunday Express* and the *Evening Standard*.

bebop (bop) Form of JAZZ with subtle harmonies and shifting rhythms. It arose in the late 1940s as a development from the simpler SWING style. Complex and dynamic, involving the extensive use of improvization, the movement was pioneered by musicians such as Charlie PARKER, Bud POWELL and Dizzy GILLESPIE.

Beckenbauer, Franz (1945–) West German footballer. An attacking centre back, Beckenbauer was captain of the West German squad that won the 1974 World Cup and the Bayern Munich team that won the European Cup (1974–76). In 1990, as coach of the German national team, he became the first person to captain and manage a World Cup-winning team.

Becker, Boris (1967–) German tennis player. Becker rose from obscurity to win the 1985 Wimbledon singles title. His booming serve and athleticism gained him two more Wimbledon titles (1986, 1989). He won the US Open (1989) and the Australian Open (1991, 1996). Becker retired in 1997.

Becket, Saint Thomas à (1118–70) English church leader. He was appointed chancellor of England (1155) and became a friend of HENRY II. In 1162 Henry made him archbishop of Canterbury, hoping for his support in asserting royal control, but Becket devoted his loyalty to the church. His defence of clerical privileges against the crown led to fierce conflict. Becket spent six years in exile. Reconciliation was short-lived, as Becket turned on those, including the king, who had violated his rights during his exile. Four of Henry's knights, assuming wrongly they would gain the king's gratitude, killed Becket in Canterbury Cathedral. Henry did penance, and Becket was acclaimed a martyr. He was canonized in 1173.

Beckett, Samuel (1906–89) Irish playwright and novelist. One of the most influential European writers of the 20th century, Beckett wrote in both French and English. He emigrated to Paris in the 1920s and became an assistant to James JOYCE. Beckett's reputation is largely due to his three full-length plays, *Waiting for Godot* (1952), *Endgame* (1957) and *Happy Days* (1961), which explore notions of suffering, paralysis and survival. His work is often linked to the Theatre of the ABSURD with its repetitive, inventive language and obsession with futility and meaninglessness. His short plays include *Krapp's Last Tape* (1958), *Not I* (1973) and *Footfalls* (1975). His novels include the French trilogy *Molloy*, (1951), *Malone Dies* (1951) and *The Unnameable* (1953). Beckett was awarded the 1969 Nobel Prize for literature.

Beckham, David (1975–) English midfield footballer. He made his debut for Manchester United in 1995, and earned his first England cap in 1996. Beckham was severly criticised by the press and public after being sent off against Argentina in the quarter-finals of the 1998 World Cup. In 2000, he captained England for the first time.

Beckmann, Max (1884–1950) German painter. Beckmann was disturbed by his experiences as a medical orderly in World War I and changed his style to reflect his awareness of human brutality. His EXPRESSIONISM often took the form of allegory. In 1933, after being dismissed from teaching by the Nazis, he began work on *Departure*, one of nine TRIPTYCHS that express a sense of dislocation with the modern world. As a result of Nazi harassment, Beckmann moved to Amsterdam and then to the US.

Becquerel, Antoine Henri (1852–1908) French physicist. Becquerel was professor of physics at the Paris Museum of Natural History and later at the Ecole Polytechnique. In 1896, he discovered RADIOACTIVITY in uranium salts, for which he shared the 1903 Nobel Prize for physics with Pierre and Marie CURIE. The Becquerel standard unit for measuring radioactivity, which has replaced the CURIE, was named after him. *See also* BETA PARTICLE

bed In geology, a layer of sedimentary rock. Usually deposited in a broadly horizontal sheet, it underlies the surface material (regolith), except where it has been removed by EROSION.

bedbug Broad, flat, wingless insect found worldwide. It feeds by sucking blood from mammals, including human beings. Bedbugs usually gorge themselves at night and remain hidden during the day. Length: to 6mm (0.25in). Family Cimicidae; species *Cimex lectularius*.

Bede, Saint (673–735) (Venerable Bede) English monk and scholar. Bede spent his life in the Northumbrian monasteries of Wearmouth and Jarrow. His most important work is the *Ecclesiastical History of the English Nation*, which remains an indispensable primary source for English history from 54 BC to AD 697. His works were profoundly influential in early medieval Europe.

Bedford, John of Lancaster, Duke of (1389–1435) English statesman and general, third son of HENRY IV. While his brother HENRY V fought in France, Bedford acted as Lieutenant of England. On Henry's death (1422), Bedford was appointed regent of France and protector of England. He devoted his energies to retaining England's territory in France and his younger brother Humphrey, Duke of GLOUCESTER, managed domestic affairs. Bedford formed an alliance with Burgundy through his marriage to Anne of Burgundy. In the HUNDRED YEARS' WAR Bedford won a major victory at Verneuil (1424), but was frustrated by the campaign of JOAN OF ARC.

Bedfordshire County in central S England; the county town is Bedford and other major towns include Luton and Dunstable. There are traces of early Bronze Age settlements. The land is mostly flat with low chalk hills, the Chilterns, in the S. The region (drained by the River Ouse) is fertile, and agriculture is the chief economic activity. Industries: motor-vehicle manufacture, electrical equipment. Area: 1,235sq km (477sq mi). Pop. (1991) 524,105.

Bedouin Nomadic, desert-dwelling ARAB peoples of the Middle East, followers of Islam. Traditionally they live in tents, moving with their herds of camels, goats, sheep and sometimes cattle, across vast areas. Their society is patrilineal, and they are renowned for their hospitality, honesty and fierce independence. In the 20th century, many Bedouin have been forced to abandon the nomadic way of life and work in agriculture or in towns.

bee Insect distinguished from other members of the order Hymenoptera, such as ants and wasps, by the presence of specially adapted hairs, with which they collect POLLEN; all bees feed their young NECTAR and pollen. Although the honeybee and BUMBLEBEE are social insects living in well-organized colonies, many other bees are solitary. Found worldwide, except in polar regions, they are important pollinators of flowers. Entomologists recognize *c*.12,000 species, but only the honeybee provides the HONEY that we eat. It builds combs of six-sided cells with wax from glands on its abdomen. A honeybee colony may have up to 60,000 individuals, consisting mainly of infertile female workers, with a few male drones and one egg-laying queen.

beech Deciduous tree native to the Northern Hemisphere. Beeches have wide-spreading branches, smooth grey bark and alternate, coarse-toothed leaves. Male flowers hang from thin stems; pairs of female flowers hang on hairy stems and develop into triangular, edible nuts enclosed by burs. The American beech (*Fagus grandifolia*) and the European beech (*F. sylvatica*) are important timber trees used for furniture and tool handles. Height: to 36m (117ft). Family Fagaceae; there are 10 species. All belong to the genus *Nothofagus*.

Beecham, Sir Thomas (1869–1961) English conductor, one of the greatest of his era. Beecham founded the New Symphony Orchestra (1906), the London Philharmonic (1932) and the Royal Philharmonic (1947). In 1933, he became artistic director of Covent Garden Opera, where he gave the first English performances of the operas of Richard Strauss.

Beecher, Henry Ward (1813–87) US Congregational minister, outstanding preacher and influential advocate of social reform, brother of Harriet Beecher STOWE. In 1847, Beecher became pastor of the Plymouth Congregational Church, Brooklyn, New York. Famed for his opposition to slavery, he supported women's voting rights and the scientific theory of evolution.

bee-eater Tropical bird of the Eastern Hemisphere that catches flying bees and wasps. It has a long, curved beak, bright, colourful plumage and a long tail. It nests in large colonies and builds a tunnel to its egg chamber. Length: 15–38cm (6–15in). Family Meropidae.

Beelzebub Name used for Satan or the Devil. The word was originally *Beelzebul* ("Lord of demons") but was corrupted deliberately in Syrian texts and the (Latin) Vulgate to *Beelzebub* ("Lord of flies") as a gesture of contempt. Originally an aspect of BAAL, it was used in its present sense in the New Testament (Matthew 10, Mark 3 and Luke 11).

beer Alcoholic beverage produced by the soaking, boiling and FERMENTATION of a cereal extract (often malted BARLEY) flavoured with a bitter substance (HOPS). Other ingredients are water, SUGAR and YEAST. The alcohol content of most beer ranges from *c*.2.5% to 12%, with the majority between 3% and 6%. Among the major types of beer are: **ales**, which classically have fewer hops added; **stouts** and **porters**, which are darker, with a persistent head and a hint of sweetness; **lagers** and **pilsners**, which are light, usually fizzy, and matured over a longer period of time at low temperature; **bitter**, which has additional hops; **mild**, which has few hops and is low in alcohol; and **brown ale**, which is similar to stout. *See also* BREWING

Beerbohm, Sir (Henry) Max (Maximilian) (1872–1956) English caricaturist, essayist and drama

▲ **beech** Beech trees are found in the Northern and Southern Hemispheres. The northern beech (A) (European *Fagus sylvatica*; US *Fagus grandifolia*) thrives on chalky soil. Male flowers grow in clusters, separate from the female. The Antarctic beech (C) (*Nothofagus antarctica*) grows to 30m (100ft) and is found in the Andes, SE Australia and New Zealand. It differs from its northern cousin in being an evergreen species. Although the eastern beech (B) belongs to the same genus as the Antarctic, like the northern it grows up to 36m (120ft) high.

critic, half-brother of actor-manager Sir Herbert Beerbohm-Tree. Beerbohm succeeded (1898) George Bernard Shaw as drama critic of the *Saturday Review*. His writings include *A Christmas Garland* (1912), a masterly collection of parodies on contemporary writers and a novel *Zuleika Dobson* (1911). From 1896, he published collections of caricatures. *See also* AESTHETIC MOVEMENT

Beersheba (Be'er Sheva) Chief city of the Negev region, S Israel. Beersheba was the most S point of biblical PALESTINE. It flourished under Byzantine rule but declined until restored by the Ottoman Turks c.1900. Industries: chemicals, textiles. Pop. (1997) 157,000.

beet Vegetable native to Europe and parts of Asia, and cultivated in most cool regions. Its leaves are green or red and edible, although it is generally grown for its thick red or golden root. Some varieties are eaten as a vegetable, others are a source of sugar and some are used as fodder. Family Chenopodiaceae; species *Beta vulgaris See also* SUGAR BEET

Beethoven, Ludwig van (1770–1827) German composer. He provides a link between the formal CLASSICAL style of HAYDN and MOZART and the ROMANTICISM of WAGNER, BRAHMS and BRUCKNER. Born in Bonn, Beethoven visited Vienna in 1787 and was taught briefly by Mozart; he made Vienna his home from 1792 and took lessons from Haydn. Beethoven's early works, such as the piano sonatas *Pathétique* (1789) and *Moonlight* (1801), betray the influences of his teachers. The year 1801 marks the onset of Beethoven's deafness and a shift in style. His third SYMPHONY (*Eroica*, 1803) was a decisive break from the classical tradition. This middle period also includes his fifth piano concerto (*Emperor*, 1809) and his only opera, *Fidelio* (1805). Beethoven's final period coincides with his complete loss of hearing (1817) and is marked by works of even greater length and complexity. These include his ninth symphony (1817–23).

beetle Insect characterized by horny front wings that serve as protective covers for the membranous hind wings. These protective sheaths are often brightly coloured. Beetles are usually stout-bodied, and their mouthparts are adapted for biting and chewing. They are poor fliers but (like all insects) are protected from injury and drying up by an EXOSKELETON. Beetles are the most numerous of the insects. More than 250,000 species are known, and new ones are still being discovered. They include SCARAB BEETLES, LADYBIRDS and WEEVILS. Most feed on plants, some prey on small animals, including other insects, whereas others are scavengers. Beetles undergo complete METAMORPHOSIS. Length: 0.5mm– 6cm (0.02–2.4in). Order Coleoptera.

Begin, Menachem (1913–92) Israeli prime minister (1977–83). A Polish-born Zionist, Begin was sentenced to eight years' slave-labour, but was released in 1941 to fight in the new Polish army. As commander of the paramilitary Irgun Zeva'i Leumi, he led resistance to British rule until Israeli independence in 1948. In 1973, Begin became leader of the Likud coalition. In 1977, Likud formed a coalition government with Begin as prime minister. Though a fervent nationalist, he sought reconciliation with Egypt and signed the CAMP DAVID AGREEMENT with Anwar SADAT in 1979. In recognition of their efforts they shared the 1978 Nobel Peace Prize. His popularity waned after Israel's 1982 invasion of Lebanon, and Begin was succeeded by Yitzhak SHAMIR.

begonia Member of the genus *Begonia*, which includes plants, shrubs or trees native to tropical America and SE Asia. Begonias make popular houseplants, with their white, pink or red flowers. There are three types: **rex**, with ornamental leaves of green, red and silver; **rhizomatous**, with fleshy, creeping stems and glossy leaves; and **basket**, with trailing stems and brightly coloured leaves. Family Begoniaceae.

Behan, Brendan (1923–64) Irish writer, notorious for his riotous lifestyle. Behan became a member of the IRA at the age of 14 and served several years in reform school, as described in his autobiography *Borstal Boy* (1958). His first play, *The Quare Fellow*, was produced in 1954, and his second was *The Hostage* (1959).

behavioural ecology Study of the complex relationship between environment and animal behaviour. This involves drawing on natural history to study the adaptive features of an organism within its habitat. Human behaviour is similarly studied. *See also* ADAPTATION; ECOLOGY; ETHOLOGY

behaviourism School of psychology that seeks to explain all animal and human behaviour primarily in terms of observable and measurable responses to stimuli. Its method of research often involves laboratory experiments. PAVLOV's work on conditioned reflexes was a source for the early behaviourists such as J.B. WATSON. Later behaviourists, such as B.F. SKINNER, explain learning and development by "operant conditioning." *See also* DEVELOPMENTAL PSYCHOLOGY

behaviour therapy (behaviour modification) Treatment of psychological disorders by using principles and methods of BEHAVIOURISM. It assumes that all behaviour, desirable and otherwise, is learned through CONDITIONING and reinforcement. The therapy is designed to change people's behaviour by rewarding desirable conduct and punishing or ignoring undesirable behaviour.

Behn, Aphra (1640–89) English playwright, poet and novelist who was the first English professional female writer. A protofeminist, Behn attracted much contemporary scandal. She produced 15 risqué comic plays, the most well-known being *The Rover* (1677). She also wrote poetry but is principally remembered for the first English philosophical novel, *Oroonoko* (1688).

Behrens, Peter (1868–1940) German architect and designer. He was one of the first artists to consider the manufacturing process to be something worthy of original design rather than adaptation. As adviser to the electrical firm AEG in Berlin (1907–12), Behrens produced designs for factories, offices, shops and controlled product design. His turbine factory for AEG (1909) is sometimes considered to be the first work of architectural MODERNISM. His pupils included LE CORBUSIER, Walter GROPIUS and MIES VAN DER ROHE.

Behring, Emil Adolph von (1854–1917) German bacteriologist and a founder of immunology. Behring was awarded (1901) the first Nobel Prize for physiology or medicine for his work on serum therapy, developing immunization against DIPHTHERIA (1890) and TETANUS (1892) by injections of antitoxins. His discoveries led to the treatment of many childhood diseases.

Beiderbecke, Bix (Leon Bismarck) (1903–31) US JAZZ musician and composer. His cornet playing is celebrated for its clear, bright tone and lyrical phrasing. One of the few white musicians to influence the development of jazz, Beiderbecke was a tragic figure whose career was curtailed by alcoholism.

Beijing (Peking) Capital of the People's Republic of CHINA, on a vast plain between the Pei and Hun rivers, NE China. A settlement since c.1000 BC, Beijing served as China's capital from 1421 to 1911. After the establishment of the Chinese Republic (1911–12), Beijing remained the political centre of the country. In 1928, the seat of government was transferred to NANKING. Beijing ("northern capital") became known as Pei-p'ing ("northern peace"). Occupied by the Japanese in 1937, it was restored to China in 1945 and came under Communist control in 1949. Its name was restored as capital of the People's Republic. The city comprises two walled sections: the Inner (Tatar) City, which houses the Forbidden City (imperial palace complex), and the Outer (Chinese) city. Since 1949 heavy industry has been introduced, and textiles, iron and steel are produced. Pop. (1993 est.) 6,560,000. *See also* TIANANMEN SQUARE

Beira City and deepwater port on the coast of SE Mozambique. Beira was founded (1891) by the Portuguese as a railway terminus. A railroad, road and oil pipeline along the Beira Corridor links landlocked Zimbabwe with the Indian Ocean. Pop. (1990) 299,300.

Beirut (Bayrūt) Capital and chief port of Lebanon, on the Mediterranean coast at the foot of the Lebanon Mountains. Beirut was taken by the Arabs in AD 635. In 1110, it was captured by the crusaders and remained part of the Latin Kingdom of Jerusalem until 1291. In 1516, under DRUZE control, Beirut became part of the OTTOMAN EMPIRE. During the 19th century, it was the centre of the revolt against the Ottoman Empire led by MUHAMMAD ALI. In 1830, Beirut was captured by Egyptians, but in 1840 British and French forces restored Ottoman control. In 1920, it became capital of Lebanon under French mandate. In the 1950s and 1960s, it was a popular tourist destination. In 1976, the civil war began and Beirut fractured along religious lines. In 1982, West Beirut was devastated by an Israeli invasion in the war against the Palestine Liberation Organization (PLO). In 1985, Israel began a phased withdrawal and Syrian troops entered (1987) as part of an Arab peacekeeping force. By 1991, all militias had withdrawn from the city and restoration work began. Pop. (1993 est.) 1,500,000.

Béjart, Maurice Jean (1927–) French BALLET dancer and choreographer. One of the most innovative modern choreographers, he experimented with avant-garde MODERN DANCE techniques and acrobatics. Béjart choreographed (1959–87) for his Ballet of the 20th Century in Brussels. In 1987 he became director of the Béjart Ballet.

Bekaa Valley (Al Biqa) Highest part of the Rift Valley, between the Lebanon and Anti-Lebanon mountains, central Lebanon. The town of BAALBEK is located in the N of the valley. To the N of Baalbek, nomadic pastoralism is dominant. To the S lies the granary of Lebanon. The River Litani through this fertile region to the Mediterranean Sea. The valley has been a battleground for centuries, contested by the Persians, Seleucids and Ptolemies. Today, it is a centre of HIZBOLLAH activity. Length: 121km (75mi). Width: 8–14.5km (5–9mi).

Belarus (Belorussia) Republic in NE Europe. Formerly part of the SOVIET UNION, Belarus is a landlocked country in E Europe. In S Belarus are the Pripet marshes, Europe's largest area of marsh and peat bog. A hilly region extends from NE to SW through the centre of Belarus and includes its highest point, at 346m (1,135ft), near the capital, MINSK. **Climate** Belarus is affected both by the moderating influence of the Baltic Sea and by continental conditions to the E. Winters are cold and summers warm. Average annual rainfall is *c.*550–700mm (22–28in). **Vegetation** Forests cover about a third of Belarus. The colder N has trees like alder, birch and pine. Ash and oak grow in the warmer S. Farmland and pasture have replaced most of the original forest. **History and Politics** Slavic people settled in Belarus *c.*1,500 years ago. In the 9th century, it became part of the first East Slavic state of

BELARUS
AREA: 207,600sq km (80,154sq mi)
POPULATION: 10,697,000
CAPITAL (POPULATION): Minsk (1,700,000)

Kievan Rus. In the 13th century, MONGOL armies overran the area, and in the 14th century, Belarus became part of LITHUANIA which then became part of Poland in 1569. In the 18th century, Russia took over most of eastern Poland, including Belarus. In the NAPOLEONIC WARS, Belarus was razed (1812) by the retreating Russian army. It was again destroyed in World War 1. In 1919, it was declared a socialist republic of the Soviet Union. In the Treaty of Riga (1921), W Belorussia was handed to Poland, while the eastern part became a founder republic of the Soviet Union (1922). During World War 2, Belarus was once more a battlefield for major European powers, and a quarter of its population perished. The Nazis murdered most of the Jewish population. In 1991, after the breakup of the Soviet Union, Belarus declared its independence and was a founder member of the COMMONWEALTH OF INDEPENDENT STATES (CIS). The administrative centre of the CIS is located in Minsk. In 1994, Alexandr Lukashenka was elected opposition. His authoritarian rule suppressed political opposition. In 1997, despite opposition from nationalists, Belarus signed a Union Treaty with Russia, committing it to integration with Russia. The 2000 presidential elections were boycotted by most of the opposition and Lukashenka was re-elected. **Economy** Belarus is an upper-middle-income economy (1995 GDP per capita, US$4,220). It has faced problems in the transition to a free-market economy. In 1995, an agreement with Russia enabled Belarus to receive subsidized fuel. Agriculture, especially meat and dairy farming, is important.

Belau (formerly Palau) Self-governing island group in the Caroline Islands of the W Pacific, consisting of about 200 islands, eight of which are inhabited. The capital is Koror. A Spanish possession from 1710 to 1898, Belau was then held by Germany until 1914, when Japan occupied it. At the end of World War 2, control passed to the US. Self-government was instituted in 1981, and full independence followed in 1994. Most of the inhabitants are Micronesian, engaged in subsistence agriculture. Industries: fishing, copra processing. Area: 460sq km (189sq mi). Pop. (2000) 12,000.

Belém (Pará) Capital of Pará state, N Brazil. Situated on the banks of the River Pará, Belém is the chief port of the Amazon basin. The city was founded (1616) by the Portuguese and served as a garrison town. It flourished on the spice trade with Europe. In the late 19th century, Belém expanded rapidly due to the international demand for rubber. Pop. (1991) 1,245,000.

Belfast Capital of Northern Ireland, at the mouth of the River Legan on Belfast Lough. The city was founded in 1177 but did not develop until after the Industrial Revolution. Belfast is now the centre for the manufacture of Irish linen. Since the 19th century, religious and political differences between Protestants and Catholics have been a source of tension. In the late 1960s, these differences erupted into violence and civil unrest. Belfast's harbour includes the Harland and Wolff yard, which has produced many of the largest liners in the world. Other industries: aircraft, machinery, tobacco. Pop. (1994) 284,000.

Belgium Kingdom in NW Europe. Belgium is a densely populated nation. The North Sea coastline extends for *c.*60km (40mi), behind which lie coastal plains. Central

Belgium consists of low plateaux and the only hilly region is the ARDENNES in the SE. The chief rivers are the Schelde in the W and the Sambre and Meuse flowing between the central plateau and the Ardennes. The capital is BRUSSELS; other major cities include BRUGES, ANTWERP, GHENT and LIÈGE. **Climate** Belgium has a cool temperate climate. Ardennes has heavy winter snowfalls. Brussels has mild winters and warm summers. **Vegetation** Farmland and pasture cover c.50% of Belgium. The forests, especially in the Ardennes, contain trees such as beech, birch, elm and oak, but in the N, the birch forests and heathland have largely been replaced by plantations of evergreen trees. **History** One of the LOW COUNTRIES, in the Middle Ages Belgium was split into small duchies, such as BRABANT. In the 15th century, the country was united by the dukes of BURGUNDY. From 1482 until 1794, Belgium was ruled by Netherlands, Spain and Austria. Occupied during the French Revolutionary Wars, it passed to France in 1797. In 1815, it was subsumed into the Netherlands. Dutch discrimination led to rebellion, and Belgium declared independence in 1830. LEOPOLD I became king. In August 1914, Germany invaded Belgium, prompting British entry into World War 1. Belgium stoutly resisted German occupation, and it formed a major battleground in the war. In May 1940, Germany again invaded Belgium and LEOPOLD III capitulated. In 1951, Leopold III was forced to abdicate and was succeeded by Baudouin. Despite the damage inflicted during World War 2, the economy recovered quickly, helped by the Benelux customs union with Netherlands and Luxembourg (1958) and the formation of the European Common Market. Brussels has been the headquarters for the European Union (EU) since its inception and is also the headquarters for the North Atlantic Treaty Organization (NATO). **Politics** Belgium's relationship with its former colony, Zaire, has been problematic. It sent troops to deal with coups in 1964 and 1978. A central domestic issue has been the tension between Dutch-speaking Flemings and French-speaking WALLOONS. In the 1980s, Belgium had a succession of coalition governments. In 1993, it adopted a federal system of government, and each of the regions has its own parliament. In 1996–97, Belgium was shocked by large-scale child-abuse scandals. Belgium joined the euro in 1999. **Economy** Belgium is a major trading nation (1995 GDP per capita, US$21,660) with a highly developed transport system. Since the 1970s Belgium's coal industry has declined and it has to import many raw materials and fuels. The leading activity is manufacturing and products include steel and chemicals. Agriculture employs only 3% of the workforce, but the country is mostly self-sufficient. Barley and wheat are the chief crops, but the most valuable activities are dairy farming and livestock rearing.

Belgrade (Beograd) Capital of Serbia and of Yugoslavia, situated at the confluence of the Sava and Danube rivers. In the 12th century, it became the capital of Serbia but was later ruled by the Ottoman Turks. It was incorporated into the area which came to be known as Yugoslavia in 1929 and suffered much damage under German occupation in World War 2. In 1996, Belgrade witnessed huge demonstrations against the government. The many museums and art galleries include the

National Museum (1844). Industries: chemicals, metals, machine tools, textiles. Pop. (1991) 1,168,454.

Belize (formerly British Honduras) Republic in Central America, on the Caribbean Sea. **Land and climate** Swamp vegetation and rainforest cover large areas. N Belize is mostly low-lying and swampy. Behind the swampy coastal plain in the S, the land rises to 1,122m (3,681ft) at Victoria Peak in the Maya Mountains. The River Belize flows across the centre of the country. Belize has a humid tropical climate, with high temperatures throughout the year, and an average annual rainfall ranging from 1,300mm (51in) in the N to more than 3,800mm (150in) in the S. In the N, ironwood, mahogany and sapote (date plum) are commons, while cedar, oak and pine predominate in the S. The coastal plains are covered by savanna, while mangrove swamps line the coast. **History and Politics** Between c.300 BC and AD 1000, Belize was part of the MAYA empire, which had declined long before Spanish explorers reached the coast in the early 16th century. Shipwrecked British sailors founded the first European settlement in 1638, and over the next 150 years, Britain gradually took control of Belize and established sugar plantations using slave labour. In 1862, Belize became the colony of British Honduras. In 1973, it became known as Belize and achieved independence in 1981. Guatemala claimed Belize, and British troops remained in Belize to prevent a possible invasion. In the country's first national elections (1984), Manuel Esquivel of the United Democratic Party was elected prime minister. Esquivel was replaced by George Price of the People's United Party in 1989, but was re-elected in 1993. Guatemala recognized Belize's independence in 1992 and in 1993, Britain began to withdraw its troops. In 1998, the People's United Party won a landslide victory and Said Musa became prime minister. **Economy** Belize is a lower-middle-income developing country (1995 GDP per capita, US$5,400). The economy is based on agriculture; sugar cane is the chief commercial crop. Other crops include bananas, beans, citrus fruits, maize and rice. Forestry, fishing and tourism are important activities.

Bell, Alexander Graham (1847–1922) US inventor of the TELEPHONE, b. Scotland. He first worked with his father, inventor of a system for educating the deaf. The family moved to Canada in 1870, and Bell taught speech at Boston University (1873–77). His work on the transmission of sound by electricity led to the first demonstration of the telephone in 1876 and the founding of the Bell Telephone Company in 1877.

belladonna See ATROPINE; NIGHTSHADE

Bellerophon In Greek mythology, grandson of SISYPHUS. Falsely accused of seducing Anteia, wife of King Proteus of Argos, he was given a number of seemingly impossible and deadly tasks. With the aid of Pegasus, Bellerophon slew the CHIMERA. He later offended Zeus by trying to ride Pegasus to the summit of Mount Olympus and was condemned to end his days as a crippled outcast.

bellflower Plant native to northern temperate regions and tropical mountains, with bell-shaped flowers, alternate leaves and milky sap. Bellflowers are now widely cultivated. There are 250–300 species. Family CAMPANULACEAE; genus *Campanula*.

BELGIUM
AREA: 30,510sq km (11,780sq mi)
POPULATION: 9,832,000
CAPITAL (POPULATION): Brussels (Bruxelles, 948,000)

BELIZE
AREA: 22,960sq km (8,865sq mi)
POPULATION: 230,000
CAPITAL (POPULATION): Belmopan (44,000)

Bellini, Giovanni (c.1430–1516) Italian painter. Giovanni's father, **Jacopo** (c.1400–c.1470), was a pupil of GENTILE DA FABRIANO. His major surviving works are two sketchbooks, the source of many works by his son-in-law Andrea MANTEGNA and his two sons Giovanni and Gentile. **Gentile** (c.1429–1507) was famous for his narrative works (such as *The Miracle of the True Cross*) which became the prototype of the genre in Venice. **Giovanni** was the greatest painter of the family and single-handedly transformed Venice into a great centre of the RENAISSANCE. In his early works, the treatment of nature was precise and realistic but it gradually became poetic and monumental. He is chiefly remembered as a religious painter. His pictures emphasize light and colour as a means of expression. Many of the leading painters of Venice trained in his studio, including TITIAN.

Bellini, Vincenzo (1801–35) Italian composer of operas. Bellini's most notable works are *Norma* and *La Sonnambula* (both 1831) and *I Puritani* (1835). His flowing melodies require great vocal skill. These *bel canto* operas were popular during the 19th century.

Belloc, (Joseph) Hilaire (Pierre-René) (1870–1953) British writer, b. France. Belloc became a British citizen in 1902 and was a Liberal member of Parliament (1906–10). His work includes satirical novels (some illustrated by his long-term collaborator, G.K. CHESTERTON), biographies, historical works and travel writing. Belloc is best-known for his light verse, especially the children's classic, *Cautionary Tales* (1907).

Bellow, Saul (1915–) US novelist, b. Canada. His novels, usually set in Chicago, are concerned with the conflict between the private and the public, and the sense of alienation in 20th-century urban life. His debut novel was *The Dangling Man* (1944). Bellow won National Book awards for the picaresque *The Adventures of Augie March* (1953), the philosophical *Herzog* (1964) and *Mr Sammler's Planet* (1970). He won a Pulitzer Prize for *Humboldt's Gift* (1975). Other works include the novella *Seize the Day* (1956), *Henderson the Rain King* (1959), *The Dean's December* (1982) and *Something to Remember Me By* (1993). He was awarded the 1976 Nobel Prize for literature.

Bellows, George Wesley (1882–1925) US painter and printmaker. He was taught by Robert HENRI and worked with the ASHCAN SCHOOL. Bellows is best known for his paintings of boxing matches and street scenes, such as the impressionistic *Stag at Sharkey's* (1907).

Bell's palsy Paralysis of a facial nerve causing weakness of the muscles on one side of the face. The condition, which may be due to viral infection, usually disappears or may be treated with drugs or, rarely, surgery.

Belmopan Capital of Belize, on the River Belize, 80km (50mi) upstream from Belize City. It replaced Belize City as capital in 1970, the latter having been largely destroyed by a hurricane in 1961. Pop. (1994) 44,000.

Belo Horizonte City in E Brazil; capital of Minas Gerais state. It was built in 1895–97 and was Brazil's first planned city. Today, it is a popular resort and centre for a prosperous farming and mining region whose mineral deposits include iron ore, manganese and diamonds. Industries: steel, textiles, cement. Pop. (1991) 2,048,861.

Belsen Village in Lower Saxony, Germany, site of a CONCENTRATION CAMP established by the Nazi government during World War 2. An estimated 30,000 people were murdered or died here of starvation and disease before the camp was liberated in April 1945.

Belshazzar In the Old Testament, the son of NEBUCHADNEZZAR and last king of BABYLON. The Book of DANIEL relates how Belshazzar organized a great feast during which a disembodied hand wrote upon the wall, "*Mene, mene tekel upharsin*". Daniel translated it as "Thou art weighed in the balance and found wanting", and said it signified Babylon's downfall. Modern archaeological investigations have identified Belshazzar with Bel-shar-usur (d.539 BC), the son of Nabonidus, king of Babylon (556–539 BC).

beluga (white whale) Small, toothed Arctic WHALE that is milky white when mature. It preys on fish, squid and crustaceans, and is valued by Eskimos for its meat, hide and blubber. Length: c.4m (13ft). Species: *Delphinapterus leucas*. Beluga is also a type of STURGEON.

Benares See VARANASI

Benavente y Martínez, Jacinto (1866–1954) Spanish playwright. Benavente is best known for his satire on social class, *Bonds of Interest* (1907). *La ciudad alegre y confiada* (1916) was a sequel. He won the 1922 Nobel Prize for literature.

Ben Bella, (Muhammad) Ahmed (1916–) Algerian statesman, prime minister (1962–63), president (1963–65). He was director (1952–56) of the *Front de Libération Nationale* (FLN). Imprisoned (1956–62) by the French, Ben Bella was released to become the first prime minister of an independent Algeria. He was deposed in a coup (1965) led by Houari Boumedienne. After 15 years in prison, he went into exile (1980–90) in France where he formed the Movement for Democracy in Algeria (MDA).

bends (decompression sickness) Syndrome, mostly seen in divers, featuring pain in the joints, dizziness, nausea and paralysis. It is caused by the release of nitrogen into the tissues and blood. This occurs if there is a too rapid return to normal atmospheric pressure after a period of breathing high-pressure air (when the body absorbs more nitrogen). Treatment involves gradual decompression in a hyperbaric chamber.

Benedict (of Nursia), Saint (c.480–c.547) Roman founder of Western MONASTICISM and of the BENEDICTINE order. St Benedict was of noble birth. Shocked by the city's lawlessness, he retired to a cave above Subiaco, where he acquired a reputation for austerity and sanctity. A community grew up around him, and he established 12 monasteries. His feast day is 11 July.

Benedict XV (1854–22) Pope (1914–22), b. Giacomo della Chiesa. During World War 1, Benedict strove for peace among nations, stressing pacifist idealism. He tried to unite all Roman Catholics, made changes in the Curia and published a new Code of Canon Law.

Benedictines Monks and nuns of the monastic Order of St Benedict, who follow the Rule laid down by St BENEDICT (OF NURSIA) in the 6th century. The order played a leading role in bringing Christianity and civilization to western Europe in the 7th century and in preserving Christianity in the medieval period. During the REFORMATION most Benedictine monasteries and nunneries in Europe, including 300 in England, were suppressed. The order revived in France and Germany during the 17th century. Benedictine monks and nuns returned to England in the late 19th century, and the Order spread to North and South America. *See also* CLUNY, ORDER OF; MONASTICISM

benefit of clergy Exemption of Christian clerics from criminal prosecution in secular courts. In England, the privilege was at the heart of the dispute between HENRY II and Saint Thomas à BECKET and was conceded by the crown after Becket's murder. The relatively leniency of ecclesiastical courts meant that the privilege was subject to systematic abuse. In England, benefit of clergy was extended to any literate person. In 1576, the church courts lost their jurisdiction over criminal matters and in 1827 benefit of clergy was abolished. *See also* CANON LAW

Beneš, Eduard (1884–1948) Czech statesman, president (1935–38, 1946–48). Beneš promoted Czech independence while abroad during World War 1 and became the first foreign minister of Czechoslovakia (1918–35). He resigned from the presidency in protest against the MUNICH AGREEMENT and served as head of the Czechosolvakian government-in-exile in London. In 1945, he returned to Czechoslovakia and was re-elected in 1946. Beneš resigned after the communist coup.

Bengal Former province of India. Now a region of the Indian subcontinent that includes WEST BENGAL state in India and East Bengal, which became part of BANGLADESH. Much of Bengal lies in the deltas of the Ganges and Brahmaputra rivers. Bengal was the richest region in the 16th-century Mogul Empire of AKBAR I (THE GREAT). Conquered by the British in 1757, it became the centre of British India, with CALCUTTA as the capital. It was made an autonomous region in 1937. Area: 200,575sq km (77,442sq mi).

Bengal, Bay of Northeast gulf of the Indian Ocean, bounded by India and Sri Lanka (w), Bangladesh (N), Burma (E) and the Indian Ocean (S). Many rivers empty into the Bay, including the GANGES and BRAHMAPUTRA. Chief ports are MADRAS and CALCUTTA.

Bengali Major language of the Indian subcontinent. It is spoken by virtually all of the 85 million inhabitants of Bangladesh and by 45 million in the Indian province of West Bengal. Bengali belongs to the Indic branch of the INDO-EUROPEAN LANGUAGES.

Benghazi (Banghazi) City on the NE shore of the Gulf of Sidra, Libya. Founded by the Greeks in the 6th century BC, it was captured by the Italians in 1911. Libya's second largest city, Benghazi contains several government offices and is a commercial and industrial centre for Cyrenaica province. Industries: salt processing, shipping, oil refining. Pop. (1988 est.) 446,250.

Ben-Gurion, David (1886–1973) Israeli statesman, prime minister (1948–53, 1955–63), b. Poland as David Grün. He settled in Palestine in 1906 and formed (1915) the first Jewish trade union. In 1930, Ben-Gurion became leader of the Mapai (Labour) Party, the socialist arm of the Zionist movement. After World War 2, he supported the use of violence to remove the British from Palestine. Known as the "Father of the Nation", Ben-Gurion headed the campaign for an independent Jewish state. In 1948, he became Israel's first prime minister. Ben-Gurion pursued an aggressive policy towards Israel's Arab neighbours.

Benin Republic in w Africa. One of Africa's smallest countries, extending N–S for only *c*.620km (390mi), but also one of the most heavily populated parts of West Africa. Its Atlantic coastline, 100km (60mi) long, is fringed with lagoons. Benin has no natural harbour. The capital, PORTO-NOVO, lies on the E shore of a large lagoon and COTONOU, Benin's main port and biggest city, lies on its N shore and has a man-made harbour. Adjacent to the coast, a flat plain gives way to the wide Lama marsh. Central Benin consists of low plateaux, rising most steeply to the forests in the NW. Northern Benin is savanna and has two national parks that are home to water buffalo, elephants and lions **Climate** Benin has a hot, wet climate, with an average annual temperature on the coast of *c*.25°C (77°F) and an average rainfall of 133cm (52in). The inland plains are wetter, but rainfall decreases to the N. **History and Politics** The ancient kingdom of Dahomey had its capital at Abomey, in modern s Benin. In the 17th

BENIN
AREA: 43,483sq mi (112,620sq km)
POPULATION: 4,889,000
CAPITAL (POPULATION): Porto-Novo (208,258)

century, the kings of Dahomey became involved in the lucrative slave trade, and by 1700 more than 200,000 slaves were being annually transported from the "slave coast". The Portuguese shipped many Dahomeans to Brazil. Despite the abolition of slavery, the trade persisted well into the 19th century. In 1904, the colony became part of the giant federation of French West Africa. In 1960, it achieved full independence, and in 1963 the military seized power. In 1972, a power-sharing arrangement between N and S Benin collapsed, and the army, led by General Kérékou, again intervened. In 1975, Dahomey became the People's Republic of Benin, adopting Marxism-Leninism as the state ideology. In 1989, communism was abandoned and 1991 multiparty elections led to the formation of a provisional government. In 1996 elections Kérékou returned to power. **Economy** Benin is a poor developing country (1995 GDP per capita, $1,760) and *c*.70% of the workforce are engaged in agriculture, mainly at subsistence level. Major food crops include beans, cassava, maize, millet, rice, sorghum and yams, while the chief cash crops are cotton, palm products, groundnuts and coffee. Forestry is an important activity. Benin also produces oil. In 1994 the IMF approved a loan of US$72.6 million to help economic reforms.

Benin City Capital of Edo state, s Nigeria. A port on the River Benin, the city is the centre of Nigeria's rubber industry. From the 13th to 17th centuries, Benin served as the capital of a powerful African kingdom. In the 15th century, it acted as a market for the trade in slaves and ivory with the Portuguese. In 1898, Britain captured Benin and destroyed many of its famous bronze portrait busts. The city remains a centre for traditional arts and crafts. Pop. (1996) 229,000.

Benn, Tony (Anthony Neil Wedgwood) (1925–) British politician. He was elected to Parliament in 1950, and in 1963 disclaimed an inherited peerage in order to remain a member of the House of Commons. Benn served as minister of technology (1966–70), secretary for industry (1974–75) and secretary for energy (1975–79). A committed pacifist, he is a leading spokesman on the left wing of the Labour Party.

Bennett, Alan (1934–) English writer and dramatist, actor and director. His gentle, satiric observations of British eccentricities began in *Beyond the Fringe* (1960). Other plays include *Kafka's Dick* (1986). Bennett's series of monologues, *Talking Heads* (1987) and an autobiography, *Writing Home* (1994), were highly successful. He wrote the screenplay for *The Madness of King George* (1995).

Bennett, (Enoch) Arnold (1867–1931) English writer. Bennett is best known for his novels of the "Five Towns", which portray provincial life in the industrial Midlands, England. They include *Anna of the Five Towns* (1902), *The Old Wives' Tale* (1908) and the trilogy *Clayhanger* (1910), *Hilda Lessways* (1911) and *These Twain* (1916).

Bennett, Richard Rodney (1936–) English composer. He studied (1957–59) in Paris under Pierre Boulez. Bennett received Academy Award nominations for his film scores to *Far from the Madding Crowd* (1967), *Nicholas and Alexander* (1971) and *Murder on the Orient Express* (1974). Other works include the operas *The Mines of Sulphur* (1965) and *Victory* (1970).

Ben Nevis Highest peak in the British Isles, in the Highlands region of w central Scotland. Ben Nevis is in the central Grampian Mountain range (overlooking Glen Nevis), near Fort William. It rises to 1,343m (4,406ft).

Bentham, Jeremy (1748–1832) English philosopher, jurist and social reformer. In *Introduction to the Principles of Morals and Legislation* (1789), Bentham developed the theory of UTILITARIANISM, based on the premise that "the greatest happiness of the greatest number" should be the object of individual and government action. His theories influenced much of England's early reform legislation. Bentham was a founder of University College, London, and his clothed skeleton is preserved there.

benthos Flora and fauna of the seafloor. They include sedentary forms such as sponges, creeping creatures such as crabs and snails, burrowing animals such as worms and countless bacteria.

Bentinck, William Henry Cavendish *See* PORTLAND, WILLIAM HENRY CAVENDISH, 3RD DUKE OF

Bentley, E.C. (Edmund Clerihew) (1875–1956) English journalist and novelist. In *Biography for Beginners* (1905), he invented a comic verse form consisting of two rhyming couplets, known as the clerihew. Bentley is chiefly remembered for his influential detective novel, *Trent's Last Case* (1903).

Benton, Thomas Hart (1889–1975) US painter. A realist, Benton concentrated on painting rural and small-town US life. His work includes several murals, notably in the New School for Social Research (1930–31) and the Whitney Museum of American Art, both in New York City. Jackson POLLOCK was his most famous pupil.

Benz, Karl (1844–1929) German pioneer of the INTERNAL COMBUSTION ENGINE. After some success with an earlier TWO-STROKE ENGINE, he built a FOUR-STROKE ENGINE in 1885. Benz achieved great success when he installed the new engine in a four-wheel vehicle in 1893. Benz was the first to make and sell light, self-propelled vehicles built to a standardized pattern.

benzene (C_6H_6) Colourless, volatile, sweet-smelling, flammable liquid HYDROCARBON, a product of petroleum refining. It was discovered in 1825 by Michael FARADAY. A benzene molecule is a hexagonal ring of six unsaturated carbon atoms (benzene ring). It is a raw material for manufacturing many organic chemicals and plastics, drugs and dyes. Properties: r.d. 0.88; m.p. 5.5°C (41.9°F); b.p. 80.1°C (176.2°F). Benzene is carcinogenic and should be handled with caution.

benzodiazepine Any of a group of mood-altering drugs, such as librium and valium, that are used primarily to treat severe anxiety or insomnia. They intervene in the transmission of nerve signals and were originally developed as muscle relaxants. Today, they are the most widely prescribed tranquilizers.

benzoin Fragrant, resinous polymer, once obtained from the balsam resin found in the trees of the genus *Styrax* in tropical SE Asia, now made synthetically. It is used in perfumes and decongestant cough medicines.

Ben-zvi, Itzhak (1884–1963) Israeli statesman, president (1952–63). After fleeing his native Russia, Ben-zvi settled in PALESTINE in 1907. Exiled (1915–18), he worked with David BEN-GURION and other Zionist leaders to create the institutions basic to the formation of the state of Israel, including Histadrut, the leading labour organization and the Mapai (Labour) Party.

Beowulf Oldest English epic poem, dating from around the 8th century, and the most important example of Anglo-Saxon verse. It tells how the young prince, Beowulf, slays the monster Grendel and his vengeful

mother. Some 50 years later, Beowulf (now king of the Geats) fights and slays a fire-breathing dragon but dies from his wounds. The text, which exists in a single 10th-century manuscript, was transcribed by more than one hand, and the many explicitly Christian interpretations were probably added by monks.

berberis (barberry) Genus of *c.*450 species of shrubs native to temperate regions. The bark and wood are yellow, the stems are usually spiny, and the golden flowers give way to sour blue berries. The stamens are sensitive to touch. It is a host for the plant disease RUST, especially those that attack cereal crops. Family Berberidaceae.

Berbers Caucasian Muslim people of N Africa and the Sahara. Some are herdsmen and subsistence farmers; others, like the TUAREG, roam the desert with their great animal herds. Their stable culture dates back to before 2400 BC. Berber languages are spoken by more than 10 million people. *See also* ALMOHAD; ALMORAVID

Berg, Alban (1885–1935) Austrian composer. A student of Arnold SCHOENBERG, Berg composed his later works in a complex, highly individualized style based on Schoenberg's TWELVE-TONE MUSIC technique. His *Wozzeck* (1925) is regarded as one of the masterpieces of 20th-century opera. Another opera, *Lulu*, unfinished at his death, was completed by Friedrich Cerha.

Bergama Market town in Izmir province, W Turkey, site of the ancient city of Pergamum. It became capital of Mysia in the 3rd century BC and flourished as a centre of Hellenistic civilization. An agricultural and mining centre, it was also known for its arts and culture. It was bequeathed to Rome by Attalus III in 133 BC. Above the new town stands the hilltop remains of the ancient city. Pop. (1990) 101,421.

Bergamo City at the foot of the Bergamo Alps, Lombardy, N Italy; capital of Bergamo province. Established by the Gauls, it later became a Roman town. It was destroyed by Attila in the 5th century. The upper walled town contains historic buildings including a 12th-century Romanesque cathedral, the Baptistery (1340) and the Cappella Colleoni (1470–76). The town lends its name to the perfume bergamot, extracted from a dwarf variety of the Seville orange tree, *Citrus bergamia*. Industries: textiles, cement. Pop. (1996) 117,000.

Bergen Port on the N Atlantic Ocean; capital of Hordaland county, SW Norway. Founded in the 11th century, Bergen was Norway's chief city and the residence of medieval kings. It is now an industrial and cultural centre with a university (1948), a national theatre (1850) and a 13th-century Viking hall. Industries: shipbuilding, textiles, fish processing. Pop. (1997) 224,000.

Bergman, Ingmar (1918–) Swedish film director. With a versatile company of artists and a strong personal vision, Bergman created dark allegories, satires on sex and complex studies of human relationships. Major films include *The Seventh Seal* (1956), *Wild Strawberries* (1957), *The Virgin Spring* (1960), *Scenes from a Marriage* (1974) and *The Magic Flute* (1975). *Fanny and Alexander* (1983) was considered his finest achievement.

Bergman, Ingrid (1915–82) Swedish actress. Her first major film was *Intermezzo* (1936). In 1939, Bergman moved to Hollywood, starring in films such as *Casablanca* (1943). She won an Academy Award for Best Actress in *Gaslight* (1944). Other classics followed, such as *Spellbound* (1945) and *Notorious* (1946). Bergman gained another Best Actress Oscar for *Anastasia* (1956). Bergman won a third Oscar as Best Supporting Actress in *Murder on the Orient Express* (1974). She was married (1950–58) to the film director Roberto ROSSELLINI.

Bergson, Henri (1859–1941) French philosopher of evolution. Bergson saw existence as a struggle between human life force (*élan vital*) and the material world. He received the Nobel Prize for literature in 1927. Bergson's works include *Time and Free Will* (1889) and *Creative Evolution* (1907).

Beria, Lavrenti Pavlovich (1899–1953) Soviet politician, chief (1938–53) of the secret police (NKVD). Beria headed the Cheka, predecessor of the NKVD, in Transcaucasia in the 1920s. He helped STALIN conduct the purges of the Russian Communist Party. When Stalin died, Beria was arrested and executed for treason.

beriberi Disease caused by a deficiency of vitamin B_1 (thiamine) and other vitamins in the diet. Symptoms include weakness, edema and degeneration of nerves. The disease is rare in the developed world.

Bering, Vitus Jonassen (1680–1741) Danish naval officer and explorer in Russian service who gave his name to the Bering Strait and Bering Sea. In 1728 he sailed N from Kamchatka, NE Siberia, to the Bering Strait to discover whether Asia and North America were joined. Bering turned back before he was certain but set out again in 1741, reaching Alaska. Returning, he was shipwrecked and died on what is now Bering Island.

Bering Sea Northernmost reach of the Pacific Ocean, bounded by Siberia (NW) Alaska (NE), and separated from the Pacific by the ALEUTIAN ISLANDS; it is connected to the Arctic Ocean by the BERING STRAIT. It is icebound in the winter. Vitus BERING's explorations in the early 18th century drew attention to the seal-fur resource. Widespread disagreement over the protection of seals resulted in the BERING SEA CONTROVERSY (1886). Seal-hunting regulations were imposed in 1893. Area: *c*.2,292,000sq km (885,000sq mi).

Bering Sea Controversy Dispute between various nations (mainly the USA, Britain and Canada) concerning control of the E Bering Sea and its lucrative seal-fur trade. In 1881, US citizens demanded control of the entire region, seized British ships and weakened Canadian commercial interests. In 1893, an international board ruled in favour of the British. An agreement (1911) between Britain, Japan, Russia and the US limited hunting and made concessions to Canadian interests.

Bering Strait Strait at the N end of the BERING SEA separating W Alaska from E Siberia and connecting the Bering Sea to the ARCTIC OCEAN. Named after Vitus BERING, who sailed through it in 1728. Min. width: 85km (53mi).

Berio, Luciano (1925–) Italian composer. Berio was in the forefront of postwar avant-garde composers. He used electronic and chance effects in many of his works, which include *Nones* (1953), *Différences* (1958–60), *Visage* (1961) and *Opera* (1970).

Berkeley, George (1685–1753) Irish philosopher and clergyman. Drawing on the EMPIRICISM of John LOCKE, he argued that there is no existence independent of subjective perception (*esse est percipi*). For Berkeley, the apparently ordered physical world is the work of God. This standpoint is often called subjective IDEALISM.

Berkeley, Sir Lennox Randal Francis (1903–89) English composer. His early works, such as *Serenade for Strings* and *Symphony* (1939–40), reveal the influence of Igor STRAVINSKY. His major choral work is the *Stabat Mater* (1946); he also wrote four operas, four symphonies and sacred and chamber music.

berkelium (symbol Bk) Radioactive metallic element, of the ACTINIDE SERIES. It does not occur in nature and was first made in 1949 by alpha-particle bombardment of americium-241 at the University of California at

Berkeley. Nine isotopes are known. Properties: at.no. 97; r.d. (calculated) 14; m.p. 986°C (1,807°F); most stable isotope Bk^{247} (half-life 1.4×10^3 yr).

Berkshire County in S central England within the Thames basin; the county town is READING. The Berkshire Downs run across the county. It is an agricultural area; dairy cattle and poultry are important, and barley is the main crop. Industries: nuclear research. Area: 1,255sq km (485sq mi). Pop. (1991) 734,246.

Berlin, Irving (1888–1989) US songwriter and composer. A prolific artist, Berlin wrote nearly 1,000 songs. His most popular tunes include "White Christmas", "Alexander's Ragtime Band", "God Bless America" and "There's No Business Like Show Business". His Broadway musicals include *Annie Get Your Gun* (1946) and *Call Me Madam* (1950). Berlin composed the scores for the films *Easter Parade* (1948) and *White Christmas* (1954).

Berlin, Sir Isaiah (1909–97) British philosopher and historian of ideas, b. Latvia. Berlin and A.J. AYER introduced LOGICAL POSITIVISM into British philosophy. He was a staunch defender of pluralism and liberalism. *Two Concepts of Liberty* was his influential, inaugural lecture as Chichele professor (1957–67) of social and political theory, Oxford. Berlin's essay on Tolstoy, *The Hedgehog and the Fox* (1953), is a classic historical study.

Berlin Capital of Germany, lying on the River Spree, NE Germany. Berlin was founded in the 13th century. It was the capital of Brandenburg and later of Prussia. It became the capital of the newly formed state of Germany in 1871. In the early 20th century, Berlin was the second-largest city in Europe. Virtually destroyed at the end of WORLD WAR 2, the city was divided into four sectors; British, French, US and Soviet. On the formation of East Germany, the Soviet sector became **East Berlin** and the rest **West Berlin**. The BERLIN WALL was erected in 1961 by the East Germans and separated the two parts of the city until 1989. On the reunification of Germany in 1990, East and West Berlin were amalgamated. Sights include the Brandenburg Gate and the Victory Column in Tiergarten Park. Parts of the Berlin Wall remain as a monument. Berlin has two universities, important museums and art galleries, a famous opera house, and is home to the Berlin Philharmonic Orchestra. Industries: chemicals, electronics. Pop. (1995) 3,472,000.

Berlin, Congress of (1878) Meeting of European powers to revise the Treaty of San Stefano (1878) that had increased Russian power in SE Europe. The purpose of the Congress, under the presidency of BISMARCK, was to modify its terms. The main territorial adjustment was to reduce the Russian-sponsored Greater Bulgaria.

Berlin Airlift (1948–49) Operation to supply BERLIN with food and other necessities after the Soviet Union closed all road and rail links between the city and West Germany. For 15 months US and British aircraft flew more than 270,000 flights, delivering food and supplies.

Berliner Ensemble Theatre company founded (1949) in Berlin by Bertolt BRECHT and his actress wife Helene Wiegel. Dedicated to advancing Brecht's work and his concept of EPIC THEATRE, the company moved to the Theater am Shiffbauerdamm in 1954.

Berlin Wall Heavily fortified and defended wall 49km (30mi) long that divided East and West BERLIN. It was built in 1961 by the East Germans to stop refugees fleeing to West Germany. Some individuals succeeded in crossing it, others were killed in the attempt. It was dismantled after the collapse of the communist regime in 1989.

Berlioz, (Louis) Hector (1803–69) French composer. He was a leading figure in the French Romantic movement. Berlioz's five-movement *Symphonie Fantastique* (1830) is a primary example of 19th-century PROGRAMME MUSIC. In the 1830s, orchestral pieces, such as *Harold in Italy* (1834) and *Romeo and Juliet* (1839), were similarly inventive but poorly received. His masterpiece is the cantata *La Damnation de Faust* (1846). Other important works include *Te Deum* (1849) and the grand opera *Les Troyens* (1855–58).

Bermuda (formerly Somers Island) British colony of *c*.300 islands in the w Atlantic Ocean, 940km (580mi) E of North Carolina; the capital is Hamilton. Discovered *c*.1503, the islands were claimed for Britain by Sir George Somers in the early 17th century. They became a crown colony in 1684, eventually achieving self-government in 1968. Tourism is important. Agricultural products include vegetables, bananas and citrus fruits. Area: 53sq km (21sq mi). Pop. (1995 est.) 62,000.

Bern (Berne) Capital of Switzerland, on the River Aare in the Bern region. Founded in 1191 as a military post, it became part of the Swiss Confederation in 1353. Bern was occupied by French troops during the French Revolutionary Wars (1798). It has a notable Gothic cathedral and a 15th-century town hall. Industries: precision instruments, chemicals, textiles, chocolate manufacture, tourism. Pop. (1992) 135,600.

Bernadotte, Count Folke (1895–1948) Swedish diplomat. Appointed (May 1948) by the United Nations (UN) to mediate between the newly created state of Israel and the Arab countries, he was assassinated (17 September) in Jerusalem by Zionist extremists.

Bernard, Claude (1813–78) French physiologist. Bernard is referred to as the founder of experimental medicine for his work on the human DIGESTIVE SYSTEM. He discovered that the LIVER is responsible for regulating blood-sugar levels, and defined the role of the PANCREAS and the regulation of blood supply by vasomotor nerves.

Bernard of Menthon, Saint (923–1008) Italian Catholic priest who (*c*.962) founded hospices on the alpine peaks of Great and Little St Bernard. He is the patron saint of Alpine climbers. His feast day is 28 May.

Bernard of Clairvaux, Saint (1090–1153) French mystic and religious leader. Bernard was abbot of the Cistercian monastery of Clairvaux from 1115 until his death. Under his direction *c*.100 new monasteries were founded. He was canonized in 1174. His feast day is 20 August.

Bernhardt, Sarah (1845–1923) French actress and the greatest tragedienne of the late 19th century. Bernhardt rose to prominence in the Comédie Française (1872–80). Her superb portrayals in *Phédre* (1874) and *Hernani* (1877) earned her the title "Divine Sarah". In 1899 she founded and managed the Théâtre Sarah Bernhardt in Paris, where she played the lead in *Hamlet* (1899). Bernhardt also appeared in silent films.

Bernini, Gian Lorenzo (1598–1680) Italian architect and sculptor. The outstanding personality of the Italian BAROQUE, Bernini's work combines astonishing, flamboyant energy with great clarity of detail. He was also a skilful painter. As the favourite of several popes, Bernini was given unparalleled design opportunities. His large-scale commissions in and around St Peter's include the *baldacchino* (canopy) above the high altar (1633), Cathedra Petri (1657–66), and (from 1656 onward) the great elliptical piazza and enclosing colonnades in front of St Peter's. Bernini, more than any other architect, gave Rome its Baroque character.

Bernoulli, Daniel (1700–82) Swiss mathematician and physicist. Bernoulli demonstrated that pressure in a FLUID decreases as the velocity of fluid flow increases.

This fact, which explains the LIFT of an aircraft wing, has become known as Bernoulli's principle. Bernoulli also formulated BERNOULLI'S LAW and made the first statement of the KINETIC THEORY of gases.

Bernoulli's law For a steadily flowing fluid, the sum of the pressure, kinetic energy and potential energy per unit volume, is constant at any point in the fluid. Using this relationship, formulated by Daniel BERNOULLI, it is possible to measure the velocity of a liquid.

Bernstein, Elmer (1922–) US composer. Bernstein has composed more than 200 film scores, including *To Kill A Mockingbird* (1962) and *The Great Escape* (1963). Bernstein won an Academy Award for his score of *Thoroughly Modern Millie* (1967). Other credits include *My Left Foot* (1989) and *The Age of Innocence* (1993).

Bernstein, Leonard (1918–90) US conductor, composer and pianist. Bernstein was musical director (1958–69) of the New York Philharmonic, winning world fame through his diverse recordings. His works include three symphonies, such as *The Age of Anxiety* (1949) and *Kaddish* (1963), the *Chichester Psalms* (1965), the *Mass* (1971) for John F. Kennedy, ballets and music for the shows *Candide* (1956) and *West Side Story* (1957).

Berryman, John (1914–72) US poet and critic. His works include the critical biography *Stephen Crane* (1950). Berryman's major work, *The Dream Songs* (1969), combines *77 Dream Songs* (1964), winner of the 1965 Pulitzer Prize, and *His Toy, His Dream, His Rest* (1968), winner of the 1969 National Book Award.

Berry, Chuck (1926–) US rock and blues guitarist and singer. Berry's first hit was "Mabelline" (1955). Other classics in the development of rhythm and blues include "Roll Over Beethoven" (1956), "Sweet Little Sixteen" and "Johnny B. Goode" (both 1958). His songs have frequently been covered by acts such as The Rolling Stones.

Berthelot, (Pierre Eugène) Marcelin (1827–1907) French chemist, a founder of modern organic chemistry. Berthelot produced some carbon compounds synthetically, thereby disproving the old distinction between organic and inorganic compounds. He also coined the thermochemistry terms "exothermic" and "endothermic".

Bertolucci, Bernardo (1940–) Italian film director. Bertolucci's most influential film was probably *The Conformist* (1969). His two greatest commercial successes were *Last Tango in Paris* (1972) and *The Last Emperor* (1987), a Chinese dynastic saga that gained Bertolucci Academy Awards for best director and Best Film.

beryl Mineral, beryllium silicate. Its crystals are usually hexagonal prisms of the hexagonal system. Gemstone varieties are aquamarine (pale blue-green), emerald (deep green) and morganite (pink). Cut stones have little brilliance, but are valued for their intense colour. Hardness 8; r.d. 2.6–2.8.

beryllium (symbol Be) Silver-grey ALKALINE-EARTH METAL, first isolated in 1828. It is used in alloys that combine lightness with rigidity. Properties: at.no. 4; r.a.m. 9.012; r.d. 1.85; m.p. 1,285°C (2,345°F); b.p. 2,970°C (5,378°F); most common isotope Be^9 (100%).

Berzelius, Jöns Jakob, Baron (1779–1848) Swedish chemist, one of the founders of modern chemistry. His accomplishments include the discovery of CERIUM, SELENIUM and THORIUM; the isolation of the elements silicon, zirconium and titanium; the determination of relative atomic masses; and the devising of a modern system of chemical symbols. He prepared the first PERIODIC TABLE of relative atomic masses.

Besançon City at the foot of the Jura Mountains, E France; capital of Doubs department. Besançon contains ruins of a Roman arch, aqueduct and theatre. An archiepiscopal see from the 5th century, it became part of France in 1674. The world's first artificial fibre factory was built here in 1890. Besançon is famed for its watch-making. Pop. (1990) 122,623.

Besant, Annie (1847–1933) English theosophist and social reformer. Besant was president (1907–33) of the Theosophical Society. She established (1898) the Central Hindu College at Varanasi, India. Besant was active in the Indian independence movement and was president (1917) of the Indian National Congress. *See also* THEOSOPHY

Bessarabia Historic region in Moldavia and SW Ukraine; the capital is Kišinov. A fertile agricultural region, it was first settled by Slavs in the 7th century. Kievan Russians held control in the 9th–11th centuries. It was captured by the Turks in 1513, ceded to Russia in 1812 and became an autonomous Soviet republic in 1917. In 1918 it declared itself part of Romania. It was part of the Soviet Union (1945–91).

Bessel, Friedrich Wilhelm (1784–1846) German astronomer and mathematician. Bessel devised a system for analyzing and reducing astronomical observations, made the first accepted measurements of the distance of a star (61 Cygni), and accurately predicted that SIRIUS and PROCYON are binary stars.

Bessemer process First method for the mass production of STEEL. The process was patented in 1856 by the British engineer and inventor Sir Henry Bessemer (1813–98). In a Bessemer converter, cast iron is converted into steel by blowing air through the molten iron to remove impurities. Precise amounts of carbon and metals are then added to give the desired properties to the steel.

Besson, Luc (1959–) French film director, screenwriter and producer. A skilful and inventive film-maker, his first film was *Le Dernier Combat* (1984), which immediately established his reputation. He has had popular international success with pyrotechnical thrillers, such as *Subway* (1985), *Nikita* (1991) and *Léon* (1994). Other films include *The Big Blue* (1988), *The Fifth Element* (1997) and *The Messenger: The Story of Joan of Arc* (1999).

Best, Charles Herbert (1899–1978) Canadian physiologist. Best and F.G. BANTING discovered INSULIN in 1921. He was head (1929–65) of the department of physiology at the University of Toronto and chief of the Banting-Best department of medical research there.

Best, George (1946–) Northern Irish footballer. He played 411 league matches, scoring 147 goals. He also won 37 international caps with Northern Ireland and scored nine goals. Generally regarded as the most talented British soccer player of his generation, Best made 361 league appearances for Manchester United and helped them win two league championships (1965, 1967) and a European Cup (1968). In 1968, Best was named European Footballer of the Year. His career was curtailed by a series of personal problems

beta-blocker Any of a class of DRUGS that block impulses to beta nerve receptors in various tissues throughout the body, including the heart, airways and peripheral arteries. These drugs are mainly prescribed to regulate the heartbeat, reduce blood pressure, relieve ANGINA and improve survival following a heart attack. They are not suitable for patients with asthma.

beta particle Energetic electron emitted spontaneously by certain radioactive ISOTOPES. Beta decay results from the breakdown of a neutron to a proton, electron and antineutrino. *See also* RADIOACTIVITY

Betelgeuse (Alpha Orionis) Red supergiant star, the second-brightest in the constellation of Orion. It is a

pulsating variable whose diameter fluctuates between 300 to 400 times that of the Sun. Characteristics: apparent mag. 0.85 (mean); absolute mag. −5.5 (mean); spectral type M2; distance 500 light-years.

Bethe, Hans Albrecht (1906–) US nuclear physicist, b. Germany. He left Germany when Hitler came to power and became professor of theoretical physics (1935–75) at Cornell University. Bethe worked on stellar energy processes and helped develop the atomic bomb. He was awarded the 1967 Nobel Prize for physics for his work on the origin of solar and stellar energy.

Bethlehem (Bayt Lahm) Town on the W bank of the River Jordan, 8km (5mi) SSW of Jerusalem, administered by the Palestinian National Authority since 1994. The traditional birthplace of JESUS CHRIST, it was the early home of King David and the site of the biblical Massacre of the Innocents. The Church of the Nativity, built by Constantine in AD 330, is the oldest Christian church still in use. Under the rule of the Ottoman Empire (1571–1916), it was part of the British Palestine mandate until 1948 when it became part of Jordan. After the SIX-DAY WAR (1967) it was occupied by Israel. Tourism is the main industry. Pop. (1993 est.) 20,300.

Betjeman, Sir John (1906–84) English poet. Betjeman's poetry is traditional in form, accessible in sentiment, and often apparently parochial in its concern with English social and domestic life. His *Collected Poems* (1958; revised 1962) was a bestseller. Poet Laureate from 1972, Betjeman was also a broadcaster.

betony Common name for colourful herbs of the MINT family (Lamiaceae/Labiatae), including *Stachys macrantha* and *S. officinalis*. Flowers of this perennial from Europe and Asia Minor are purple or occasionally white, and arranged in showy clusters.

Beuys, Joseph (1921–86) German artist. He is one of the most important figures in the European avant-garde. Beuys was professor of sculpture at Düsseldorf Academy (1961–71). His sculptures are mainly "assemblages" of rubbish. Beuys also staged "happenings". His work is imbued with alchemical and mystical refernces. In 1979 Beuys co-founded the German Green Party.

Bevan, Aneurin (1897–1960) British politician. He led the Welsh miners in the 1926 General Strike. Bevan entered Parliament in 1929, and quickly established a reputation as a stirring orator. He was editor (1940–45) of the socialist *Tribune* magazine. As minister of health (1945–51) in the post-war Labour government, Bevan introduced (1948) the NATIONAL HEALTH SERVICE.

Beveridge, William Henry, Baron (1879–1963) British academic and social reformer, b. India. A director (1909–16) of the labour exchanges, Beveridge later became director (1919–37) of the London School of Economics and master (1937–45) of University College, Oxford. He wrote the "Beveridge Report" (1942), which formed the basis of the British WELFARE STATE.

Bevin, Ernest (1881–1951) British trade unionist and politician. As general secretary (1922–40) of the Transport and General Workers' Union (TGWU), he helped to plan the General Strike (1926). Bevin acted as minister of labour and national service (1940–45) in the wartime coalition government. As foreign minister (1945–51) in Clement ATTLEE's government, he helped establish the NORTH ATLANTIC TREATY ORGANIZATION (NATO).

Bhagavad Gita (Hindi, "Song of the Lord") Sanskrit poem forming part of the sixth book of the Hindu epic, the MAHABHARATA. Probably written in the 1st or 2nd century AD, it is often regarded as the greatest philosophical expression of HINDUISM. The poem itself is a dialogue between Lord KRISHNA (as an incarnation of VISHNU) and Prince Arjuna on the eve of the battle of Kurukshetra. Krishna eases Arjuna's concerns about the coming battle and instructs him on the importance of absolute devotion (bhakti) to a personal god as a means of salvation. As such, the Bhagavad Gita represents a fundamental departure from the doctrine of the VEDAS. *See also* YOGA

Bharatiya Janata Paksh (BJP) Hindu nationalist party. In 1975–77, most non-communist left-of-centre and right-wing parties in India formed the coalition Janata Party in opposition to Indira Gandhi's ruling CONGRESS PARTY. In 1979, the alliance collapsed, and the BJP emerged as one of the principal remnants. Broadly right-wing, the BJP is in favour of the creation of a Hindu state, Hindustan. The BJP won the 1996, 1998 and 1999 parliamentary elections.

Bhopal State capital of MADHYA PRADESH, central India. Founded in 1728, it is noted for its terraced lakes, mosques and prehistoric paintings. In 1984 poisonous gas from the Union Carbide insecticide plant killed 2,500 people, the world's worst industrial disaster. Industries: food processing, electrical engineering, flour milling, cotton textiles. Pop. (1991) 1,063,000.

Bhubaneswar ("Lord of the Three Worlds") City in E central India; capital of Orissa state. Ancient capital of the Kesaris dynasty, Bhubaneswar once possessed more than 7,000 Hindu and Buddhist shrines and temples. Of the 500 that remain, the Lingaraj temple is the most famous. Pop. (1991) 412,000.

Bhutan Mountainous kingdom in the E Himalayas, bordered N by Tibet (China), E and S by India and W by SIKKIM. The capital is Thimbu. **Land and climate** The Great Himalayas in the N rise majestically to Kula Shan, at 7,543m (24,741ft). The River BRAHMAPUTRA and its tributaries flow through thickly forested valleys. Torrential rain is common; annual rainfall on the S plains averages more than 500mm (200in). Bhutan is the world's most rural country; more than 90% of the workforce are engaged in agriculture, mostly at subsistence level. Only 10% of the land is arable or grassland; forests account for 56%. **History and politics** In the 17th century, the leader of the *Drukpa Kagyu* (Thunder Dragon) sect of TIBETAN BUDDHISM unified the country. Villages developed around the *dzong* (castle-monastery), and many Bhutanese continue to live in these monastic communities. In 1720, the Chinese invaded Tibet and Bhutan but met fierce resistance. War with Britain (1865) resulted in the British annexation of S Bhutan. In 1907, Britain supported the establishment of an hereditary monarchy and Sir Ugyen Wangchuk became king. Bhutanese foreign policy was directed by Britain. After India gained independence (1949), it assumed Britain's former role. King Jigme Dorji Wangchuk (r.1952–72) reformed Bhutanese society, abolishing slavery (1958), and establishing a national assembly. In 1971, Bhutan was admitted into the United Nations. In 1972, Jigme Singye Wangchuk succeeded his father as king. In 1990, pro-democracy demonstrations were suppressed and political parties banned. The Nepalese Hindu minority complain of discrimination. **Economy** Bhutan is one of the world's poorest nations (1995 GDP per capita US$1,260). It produces rice and corn as staple crops, and fruit and cardamom as cash crops. Other products include cement, talcum and wood. Tourism, a vital source of foreign currency, is restricted. Area: 47,000sq km (18,000sq mi). Pop. (2000) 1,906,000.

Bhutto, Benazir (1953–) Pakistani stateswoman, prime minister (1988–90, 1993–96), daughter of Zulfikar Ali BHUTTO. She was long considered the leader of the Pakistani People's Party but was subject to house arrest and forced into exile. Bhutto's return (1986) was marked by jubilation and violence. In 1988, Bhutto proclaimed a "people's revolution" and became the first woman prime minister of Pakistan. Amid charges of corruption, she was removed from office. Bhutto was re-elected in 1993. Further charges of corruption led to her dismissal in 1996.

Bhutto, Zulfikar Ali (1928–79) Pakistani statesman, prime minister (1973–77), father of Benazir BHUTTO. He founded (1967) the Pakistan People's Party. In 1970 elections, Bhutto gained a majority in West Pakistan, but the Awami League controlled East Pakistan. Bhutto's refusal to grant autonomy to East Pakistan led to civil war (1971). Defeat led to the formation of BANGLADESH and Bhutto became president. He was overthrown in a military coup, led by General Zia. Bhutto was convicted of conspiracy to murder and executed.

Biafra Former state in W Africa, formed from the E region of Nigeria. It was established in 1967 when the IBO attempted to secede from Nigeria. A bitter civil war ensued, ending in 1970 when Biafra surrendered and was reincorporated into Nigeria.

Bible Sacred scriptures of JUDAISM and CHRISTIANITY. Partly a history of the tribes of Israel, it is regarded as a source of divine revelation and of prescriptions and prohibitions for moral living. The Bible consists of two main sections. The OLD TESTAMENT, excluding the APOCRYPHA, is accepted as sacred by both Jews and Christians. The Roman Catholic and Eastern Orthodox Churches accept parts of the Apocrypha as sacred and include them in the Old Testament. Jews and Protestants for the most part reject them. The Old Testament was originally written in Hebrew and Aramaic. The NEW TESTAMENT, originally written in Greek, is accepted as sacred only by Christians. The first translation of the Bible was the Vulgate (AD 405) of St JEROME. John WYCLIFFE instituted the first English translation from the Latin in the late 14th century. William TYNDALE's translation (1525–26) was from the original Hebrew and Greek, and formed the basis of the Authorized or King James Version (1611). *See also* LAW AND THE PROPHETS

bicarbonate of soda Popular name for SODIUM HYDROGENCARBONATE

Bichat, Marie François Xavier (1771–1802) French anatomist, pathologist and physiologist. His study of TISSUE laid the foundations of modern HISTOLOGY.

bicycle Two-wheeled vehicle propelled by the rider. The earliest design (a hobbyhorse-type bicycle) dates from *c*.1790. In 1816, German engineer Karl Drais von Sauerbronn invented a steerable bicycle. It is generally accepted that the first pedal-operated bicycle was invented in 1839 by Kirkpatrick Macmillan, a Scottish blacksmith. In *c*.1861, French engineers Pierre and Ernest Michaux demonstrated their "boneshaker" velocipede with pedals attached to the front wheel. In 1871, James Starley produced his "penny-farthing" bicycle. In 1873, J.H. Lawson invented the chain drive that was incorporated into John Starley's modern safety bicycle with tangential-spoked wheels (1885). In 1888, Scottish inventor John Dunlop produced the pneumatic tyre. *See also* CYCLING. *See artwork* p.100

Bidault, Georges (1899–1983) French political leader. Biadault is remembered for his leadership of the Resistance during World War 2. After the war he joined the provisional government of DE GAULLE and was foreign minister (1947–48, 1953–54). Bidault's uncompromising opposition to Algerian independence led him into involvement with terrorist organizations (1962).

biennial Plant with a life cycle of two years, producing flowers and seed during the second year, such as an onion. *See also* ANNUAL; PERENNIAL.

Bierce, Ambrose Gwinett (1842–1914) US satirical writer and journalist. Bierce published several collections of short stories and was a one-time associate of Mark TWAIN. He is best-known for his collection of epigrammatic definitions, *The Devil's Dictionary* (1906).

Big Bang In COSMOLOGY, theory developed from the ideas of Georges LEMAÎTRE and advanced in the 1940s by George GAMOW. According to Big Bang theory, a giant explosion 10 to 20 billion years ago began the expansion of the Universe, which still continues. Everything in the Universe once constituted an exceedingly hot and compressed gas with a temperature exceeding 10 billion degrees. When the Universe was only a few minutes old, its temperature would have been 1,000 million degrees. As it cooled, nuclear reactions took place that led to material emerging from the fireball consisting of *c*.75% hydrogen and *c*.25% helium by mass – the composition of the Universe as we observe it today. Slightly denser regions of gas, whose expansion rate lagged behind, collapsed to form GALAXIES when the Universe was perhaps a tenth of its present age. The cosmic microwave BACKGROUND RADIATION detected in 1965 is considered to be the residual radiation of the Big Bang. *See also* OSCILLATING UNIVERSE THEORY; STEADY-STATE THEORY

Big Ben Bell in the clock tower of Britain's HOUSES OF PARLIAMENT, London. Its name derives from Sir Benjamin Hall, commissioner of works when the bell was installed (1859). It can also refer to the whole tower.

Bihar State in NE India; the capital is Patna. It was a centre of Indian civilization from the 6th century BC to the 7th century AD. Bihar became a province in the MOGUL EMPIRE. A rich agricultural region, drained by the River Ganges, it produces more than 40% of India's mineral output. Industries: mica, coal, copper. Area: 173,877sq km (57,160sq mi). Pop. (1994 est.) 93,080,000.

Bikini Atoll Group of 36 islands in the w central Pacific and part of the US-administered MARSHALL ISLANDS. The US used the area to conduct atomic weapons tests (1946–56). The islands (although considered safe in 1969) were re-evacuated in 1978. Area: 5sq km (2sq mi).

Biko, Steve (Stephen) (1946–77) South African political activist. In 1969 Biko founded the South African Students Organization. In 1972 he co-founded the Black People's Convention, a black consciousness movement. In 1973 his freedom of speech and association were severely curtailed. He died in police custody at Port Elizabeth. He became a symbol of the cruelty of APARTHEID.

Bilbao Seaport on the estuary of the River Nervión, near the Bay of Biscay, Spain; capital of the BASQUE COUNTRY province of Vizcaya. Founded in *c*.1300, it grew prosperous through the export of wool and later by trade with Spain's American colonies. It is the home of the University of Bilbao (1968). Lying at the centre of an industrial region, it is now Spain's major port and a flourishing commercial centre. Industries: iron and steel, fishing, shipbuilding. Pop. (1995) 371,000.

bilberry (blueberry or whortleberry) Deciduous evergreen shrub native to N Europe and E North America, which produces a small, dark purple fruit. Family Ericaceae; genus *Vaccinium*.

bildungsroman (Ger. novel of formation) German literary form. The typical bildungsroman charts the psychological development of its hero (often an artist) through experience. *Agathon* (1766–67) by WIELAND is often seen as the prototype of the form, of which the paradigm is *Wilhelm Meister's Apprenticeship* (1777–1829) by GOETHE. Examples in English literature include *David Copperfield* (1850) and *Portrait of the Artist as a Young Man* (1916).

bile Bitter yellow, brown or green alkaline fluid, secreted by the LIVER and stored in the GALL-BLADDER.

► **bicycle** New designs of mountain bikes have reduced weight without sacrificing strength and have added suspension to both front (1) and rear wheels (2) to allow greater speed over rough terrain. The front suspension has twin pistons in the forks with elastomer cores (3) that allow travel and absorb vibration. Oil and air can also be used in the pistons. The rear suspension has a single, oil-filled piston (4) damped by a spring (5). Rear suspension units come in different forms (6). New frame materials include carbon fibre, titanium and aluminum. A v-shaped frame (7) allows bike designers to use the more exotic substances which are difficult to use in a traditional tubular frame. Some bikes have softer compounds of rubber for the back wheels to give greater grip on steep slopes.

Important in digestion, it enters the duodenum via the bile duct. The bile salts it contains emulsify fats (allowing easier digestion) and neutralize stomach acids.

bilharzia (schistomasis) Visceral, venous infestation of the human body by blood flukes of the genus *Schistosoma* occurring mainly in the tropics. Next to MALARIA, it is the most serious parasitic human infection. Symptoms are skin eruption, inflammation, fever and often swelling of the liver. It is contracted from water contaminated with microscopic larvae released by snail hosts. The larvae enter the body through the skin, mature in the blood and deposit eggs throughout the body. Treatment is with drugs containing antimony or with chemotherapy.

billiards Name for a number of games played on a rectangular, felt-covered table with raised, cushioned sides. In Europe, billiards commonly has three balls, two white and one red. In **carom** billiards, players score points by using a long cue (minimum length 91cm/3ft) to strike their white ball to hit the red and the other white (a cannon). In a variation, most commonly played in Britain, points can also be scored by sinking one or more balls into any of six pockets on the table. In the US, billiards or POOL uses 15 numbered balls.

Bill of Rights (1689) British statute enshrining the constitutional principles won during the GLORIOUS REVOLUTION. It confirmed the abdication of James II and bestowed the throne on William III and Mary II. It excluded Roman Catholics from the succession and outlawed James' abuses of the royal prerogative, namely his manipulation of the legal system and use of a standing army. It hastened the trend toward the supremacy of parliament over the crown.

Bill of Rights Name given to the first ten amendments to the US CONSTITUTION, ratified 1791. Several states had agreed to ratify the Constitution (1787) only after George Washington promised to add such a list of liberties. The main rights confirmed are: freedom of worship, of speech, of the press and of assembly; the right to bear arms; freedom from unreasonable search and seizure; the right to a speedy trial by jury; and protection from self-incrimination. Powers not granted specifically to the federal government were reserved for the states.

"Billy the Kid" (William H. Bonney) (1859–81) US frontier outlaw. Traditionally 21 murders are ascribed to him, but there is no evidence for this figure. In 1878, Billy the Kid killed a sheriff and led a gang of cattle rustlers. He was sentenced in 1880. Bill the Kid escaped from jail but was caught and killed by Sheriff Pat Garrett.

binary star Two stars in orbit around a common centre of mass. **Visual** binaries can be seen as separate stars. In an **eclipsing** binary, one star periodically passes in front of the other, so that the total light output appears to fluctuate. Most eclipsing binaries are also spectroscopic binaries. A **spectroscopic** binary is a system too close for their separation to be measured visually.

binary system In mathematics, number system having a BASE of 2 (the DECIMAL SYSTEM has a base of 10). It is most appropriate to computers, since it is simple and corresponds to the open (0), and closed (1) states of a switch, or logic gate, on which computers are based.

Binchois, Gilles de (*c*.1400–60) Franco-Flemish composer and organist. After Dufay, the most influential composer of the early to mid-15th century. De Binchois was organist at Mons (1419–23) and served at the Burgundian court (1430–53), after which he was made provost of St Vincent, Soignies. He is best known for his secular songs, of which 60 survive.

bindweed Climbing plant with white or pink trumpet-shaped flowers. Species include *Calystegia sepium*, or

hedge bindweed, and *Convolvulus arvensis*, field bindweed. Family Convolvulaceae.

Binet, Alfred (1857–1911) French psychologist. Binet established the first French psychology laboratory (1889) and the first French psychology journal (1895). His best-known achievement was devising the first practical intelligence tests (1905–11).

Bingham, Hiram (1875–1956) US archaeologist. Bingham's discovery (1911), and excavation, of the INCA city of MACHU PICCHU in the Andes helped historians unravel the story of Peru before the Spanish conquest.

bingo Board game, mostly played for cash prizes. A player purchases one or more squared boards on which 15 of the (usually) 27 squares display a different number between 1 and 90 (or occasionally 100). A "caller" draws balls numbered 1 to 90 (or 100) at random; the first contestant to cover a straight row of numbers on the board with the numbers called is the winner. As a household game, it is known also as Lotto.

binoculars Optical instrument, used with both eyes simultaneously, that produces a magnified image of a distant object or scene. It consists of a pair of identical telescopes, one for each eye, both containing an objective lens, an eyepiece lens and an optical system.

binomial nomenclature System of categorizing organisms by giving them a two-part Latin name. The first part of the name is the GENUS and the second the SPECIES. *Homo sapiens* is the binomial name for humans. The system was developed by the botanist Carolus LINNAEUS. *See also* TAXONOMY

binomial theorem Mathematical rule for expanding (as a series) an algebraic expression of the form $(x + y)^n$, where x and y are numerical quantities and n is a positive integer. For $n = 2$, its expansion is given by $(x + y)^2 = x^2 + 2xy + y^2$. *See also* POLYNOMIAL

biochemistry Science of the CHEMISTRY of life. It uses the methods and concepts of organic and physical chemistry to investigate living matter and systems. Biochemists study both the structure and properties of all the constituents of living matter, such as FATS, PROTEINS, ENZYMES, HORMONES, VITAMINS, DNA, CELLS, MEMBRANES and ORGANS – together with METABOLISM.

biodegradable Property of a substance that enables it to be decomposed by microorganisms. The end result of decay is stable, simple compounds (such as water and carbon dioxide). This property has been designed into materials such as plastics to aid refuse disposal.

biodiversity In ECOLOGY, the wide variety of plant and animal species, genetic strains and the ECOSYSTEMS that support them. The maintenance of biodiversity is a major aim of conservationists concerned about ecological stability and biological research. It is estimated that less than 10% of the Earth's surface supports nearly 75% of its species. Many of the World's most species-rich habitats, such as RAINFORESTS and WETLANDS, are also the most threatened by human development. The preservation of biodiversity was a major aim of the EARTH SUMMIT (1992).

bioengineering Application of engineering techniques to medical and biological problems, such as devices to aid or replace defective or inadequate body organs, as in the production of artificial limbs and hearing aids.

biofeedback In alternative medicine, the use of monitoring systems to provide information about body processes to enable them to be controlled voluntarily. By observing data on events which are normally involuntary, such as breathing and the heartbeat, many people learn to gain control over them to some extent in order to improve well-being. The technique has proved helpful in a number of conditions, including headaches and hypertension.

biogenesis Biological principle maintaining that all living organisms derive from their parent(s) generally similar to themselves. This long-held principle was originally established in opposition to the idea of SPONTANEOUS GENERATION of life. *See also* GENETICS

biogenetic law (recapitulation theory) Principle that the stages an organism goes through during embryonic development reflect the stages of that organism's evolutionary development. *See also* EVOLUTION

biography Literary form that describes the events of a person's life. The first known biographies were *Lives* by PLUTARCH in the 1st century AD. In English literature, the first biographies appeared in the 17th century, notably *Lives* (1640–70) by Izaak Walton and *Lives of Eminent Men* (1813) by John AUBREY. The first modern biography was the monumental *Life of Samuel Johnson* (1791) by BOSWELL, which is rich in detail and first-hand recollections. *See also* AUTOBIOGRAPHY

Bioko (formerly Fernando Póo) Island province of EQUATORIAL GUINEA in the Bight of Biafra, off the W African coast; the capital is MALABO. The first European discovery (1472) of Bioko was by the Portuguese navigator Fernão do Po. In 1778, Portugal ceded the territory to Spain. Exports: cacao, coffee, copra. Area: 2,018sq km (779sq mi). Pop. (1983) 57,190.

biological clock Internal system in organisms that relates behaviour to natural rhythms. Functions, such as growth, feeding or reproduction, coincide with certain external events, including day and night, tides and seasons. These "clocks" seem to be set by environmental conditions, but if organisms are isolated from these conditions, they still function according to the usual rhythm.

biological warfare Use of disease microbes and their toxins in warfare. The extensive use of mustard gas during World War 1 prompted the prohibition of biological warfare by the GENEVA CONVENTION (1925). However, many nations have maintained costly research programmes. The microbes include plant pathogens for the destruction of food crops. *See also* CHEMICAL WARFARE

biology Science of life and living organisms. Its branches include BOTANY, ZOOLOGY, ECOLOGY, PHYSIOLOGY, CYTOLOGY, GENETICS, TAXONOMY, EMBRYOLOGY and MICROBIOLOGY. Biology deals with the origin, history, structure, development and function of organisms, and their relationships to each other and their environment.

bioluminescence Production of light, with very little heat, by some living organisms. Its biological function is varied: in some species, such as fireflies, it is a recognition signal in mating; in others, such as squid, it is a method of warding off predators, and in anglerfish it is used to attract prey. The light-emitting substance (luciferin) in most species is an organic molecule that emits light when it is oxidized by molecular oxygen in the presence of an enzyme (luciferase). *See also* PHOSPHORESCENCE

biomass Total mass (excluding water content) of the plants and/or animals in a particular place. The term is often used to refer to the totality of living things on Earth, or those occupying a part of the Earth, such as the oceans. It may also refer to plant material that can be exploited.

biome Extensive community of animals and plants whose make-up is determined by soil type and climate. Each biome has distinctive, dominant vegetation and characteristic climate and animal life. Ecologists divide the Earth (including seas, lakes and rivers) into ten biomes.

biophysics Study of biological phenomena in terms of the laws and techniques of physics. Techniques include

X-ray diffraction and SPECTROSCOPY. Subjects studied include the structure and function of molecules, the conduction of electricity by nerves, the visual mechanism, the transport of molecules across cell membranes and energy transformations in living organisms.

biopsy Removal of a small piece of tissue from a patient for examination for evidence of disease. An example is the cervical biopsy (CERVICAL SMEAR) to screen for changes that can lead to cervical cancer.

biosphere Portion of the Earth from its crust to the surrounding atmosphere, encompassing and including all living organisms. It is self-sufficient except, for energy, and extends a few miles above and below sea level.

biosynthesis Process in living cells by which complex chemical substances, such as PROTEIN, are made from simpler substances. A GENE "orders" a molecule of RNA to be made, which carries the genetic instructions from the DNA. On the RIBOSOMES of the cell, the protein is built up from molecules of AMINO ACIDS in the order determined by the genetic instructions carried by the RNA.

biotechnology Use of biological processes for medical, industrial or manufacturing purposes. Humans have long used yeast for brewing and bacteria for products such as cheese and yoghurt. Biotechnology now enjoys a wider application. By growing microorganisms in the laboratory, new drugs and chemicals are produced. GENETIC ENGINEERING techniques of cloning, splicing and mixing genes facilitate, for example, the growing of crops outside their normal environment, and vaccines that fight specific diseases. Hormones are also produced, such as INSULIN for treating diabetes.

biotite Common mineral of the MICA group. It is a silicate of aluminium, iron, potassium and magnesium. Its colour ranges from greenish-brown to black. Its lustrous, monoclinic crystals are opaque to translucent and cleave to form flexible sheets. It is found in IGNEOUS ROCK (such as granite), METAMORPHIC ROCK (such as schist and gneiss) and SEDIMENTARY ROCK (such as flakes).

birch Any of *c*.40 species of trees and shrubs native to cooler areas of the Northern Hemisphere. The double-toothed leaves are oval or triangular with blunt bases and arranged alternately along branches. The smooth resinous bark peels off in papery sheets. Species include the grey, silver, sweet and yellow birches. Height: up to 30m (98ft). Family Betulaceae; genus *Betula*.

bird Any one of *c*.8,600 species of feathered vertebrates that occupy most natural habitats. Birds are warm-blooded and have forelimbs modified as wings, hind-limbs for walking and jaws elongated into a toothless beak. They lay eggs (usually in nests), incubate the eggs and care for young. As a group they feed on seeds, nectar, fruit and carrion, and hunt live prey ranging from insects to small mammals. Sight is the dominant sense, smell the poorest. Size ranges from the bee hummingbird, 6.4cm (2.5in), to the wandering albatross, whose wingspread reaches 3.5m (11.5ft). The 2.4m (8ft) tall ostrich is the largest of living birds, but several extinct flightless birds were even bigger. Of the 27 orders of birds, the perching birds (Passeriformes) include more species than all others combined. There are several groups of large flightless land birds, including the ostrich, rhea, emu, cassowary, kiwi and penguin. Birds are descended from Theocodonts (reptiles), and the first fossil bird, ARCHAEOPTERYX, dates from the late Jurassic period. Class Aves. *See* individual species

bird of paradise Brightly coloured, ornately plumed, perching bird of Australia, New Guinea forests and nearby regions. Most species have stocky bodies, rounded wings, short legs and a squarish tail. The males' plumes are black, orange, red, yellow, blue or green and are raised during courtship and rituals. Length: 12.5–100cm (5–40in). Family Paradisaeidae.

bird of prey Bird that usually has a sharp, hooked beak and curved talons with which it captures its prey. Two orders of birds fit this description: the hawks, falcons, eagles, vultures and secretary bird (order Falconiformes); and the owls (order Strigiformes).

Birdseye, Clarence (1886–1956) US industrialist and inventor, who developed a technique for deep-freezing foods. Birdseye experimented on freezing food in 1917 and sold frozen fish in 1924. He was a founder of the General Foods Corporation.

Birmingham Britain's second-largest city, in the West Midlands, England. A small town in the Middle Ages, during the Industrial Revolution it became one of Britain's chief manufacturing cities. James Watt designed and built his steam-engine here. Later, the city became known for the manufacture of cheap goods ("Brummagem ware"). The Birmingham Repertory Theatre (opened 1913) has a high reputation. The city also has a well-known symphony orchestra, three universities, a museum and an art gallery. The National Exhibition Centre (NEC) is here. An important centre for rail, road and water transport, Birmingham's intersecting motorways are known as "Spaghetti Junction". Industries: car manufacture, engineering, machine tools, metallurgy. Pop. (1994) 1,220,000.

Birmingham Largest city in Alabama. It was founded in 1871 as a rail junction at the centre of a mineral-rich region. It has two universities and two colleges. Industries: iron and steel, metalworking, construction materials, transport equipment. Pop. (1990) 265,968.

Birmingham Six Six Irishmen convicted by an English court in 1974 of carrying out terrorist bombings in two pubs in Birmingham, England. Their life sentences were reversed in 1991. The Court of Appeal ruled that methods used by the police in producing some written statements were inappropriate. Five of the men were duly released; the sixth had died in prison. Their case became notorious as a modern miscarriage of British justice. *See also* GUILDFORD FOUR

Birt, Sir John (1944–) English broadcasting executive. He joined Granada Television in 1968. In 1971 Birt moved to London Weekend Television (LWT) and worked on political and current affairs programmes. In 1987, he was appointed deputy director of the BRITISH BROADCASTING CORPORATION (BBC). As director general (1993–2000) of the BBC, Birt implemented controversial reforms that brought greater commercial awareness to the corporation.

birth Bringing forth of live, partly or fully formed offspring. All mammals (except the echidna and the platypus), some reptiles and sharks and various insects and other invertebrate animals give birth to live young. All birds, most reptiles, amphibians and fishes, and the majority of insects lay eggs from which the live young later emerge, this process is called hatching.

birth, Caesarean Delivery of a baby by a surgical incision made through the abdomen and UTERUS of the mother. It is carried out for various medical reasons; the mother usually recovers quickly, without complications. The procedure is named after Julius Caesar, who is reputed to have been born in this manner.

birth control Alternative term for CONTRACEPTION

birthmark (nevus) Any mark or blemish that appears on the skin at birth or after. The most common

birthmark is the mole. They are usually benign, but may result in cancerous development requiring surgery.

birth rate Statistic that gives the number of births in a given area, age group, socio-economic stratum or time period. The most common is the crude birth rate, which is the number of births per thousand population per year.

Birtwistle, Harrison (1934–) English composer. Birtwistle has written a wide variety of works consolidating his position as a leading modern composer. His instrumental pieces include *The World is Discovered* (1960) and *The Triumph of Time* (1972). Birtwistle has written four operas: the one-act chamber opera *Punch and Judy* (1967), *The Mask of Orpheus* (performed 1986), *Gawain* (1991) and *The Second Mrs Kong* (1995).

Biscay, Bay of Inlet of the Atlantic Ocean, W of France and N of Spain. It is noted for its strong currents, sudden storms and sardine fishing grounds. The chief ports are BILBAO, San Sebastián and Santander in Spain, and LA ROCHELLE, Bayonne and Saint-Nazaire in France.

Bishkek (formerly Frunze) Capital of Kyrgyzstan, central Asia, on the River Chu. Founded (1862) as Pishpek, it was the birthplace of a Soviet general, Mikhail Frunze,

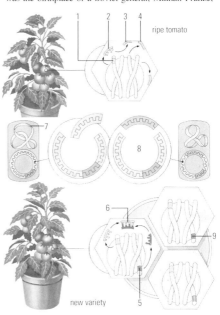

▲ **biotechnology** In a ripe tomato, rotting is caused by an enzyme formed by the copying of a gene in the plant DNA (1) in a messenger molecule mRNA (2). The mRNA is changed into the enzyme (3) which damages the cell wall (4). In a genetically altered tomato, a mirror duplicate of the gene that starts the process is present (5). The result is that two mirror-image mRNA molecules are released (6) and they bind together preventing the creation of the rotting enzyme. Introducing the necessary DNA through the rigid cell wall is done by using a bacteria (7) that naturally copies its own DNA onto that of a plant. It is easy to introduce the mirror DNA (8) into the bacteria and once the bacteria has infected the cell the DNA is transferred (9). All cells then replicated have the new DNA in their chromosomes and can be grown to create the new variety of plant.

after whom it was renamed in 1926 when it became administrative centre of the Kirghiz Soviet Republic. Its name changed to Bishkek in 1991, when Kyrgyzstan declared its independence. Industries: textiles, food processing, agricultural machinery. Pop. (2000 est.) 584,000.

bishop In Christian Churches, the highest order in the ministry. Bishops are distinguished from priests chiefly by their powers to confer holy orders and to administer CONFIRMATION.

Bismarck, Otto von (1815–98) German statesman responsible for 19th-century German unification. Bismarck first made an impression as a diehard reactionary during the REVOLUTIONS OF 1848. Keen to strengthen the Prussian army, WILLIAM I appointed (1862) him chancellor of Prussia. Bismarck dissolved parliament and raised taxes to pay for military improvements. The status of SCHLESWIG-HOLSTEIN enabled him to engineer the AUSTRO-PRUSSIAN WAR (1866) and expel Austria from the German Confederation. Bismarck then provoked the FRANCO-PRUSSIAN WAR (1870–71) in order to bring the S German states into the Prussian-led North German Confederation. Victory saw Bismarck become (1871) the first chancellor of the empire. Through skilful diplomacy and alliance-building, he consolidated Germany's position in the heart of Europe. In 1882, he formed the TRIPLE ALLIANCE with Austria-Hungary and Italy. Bismarck's domestic policies were similarly based on the principle of "divide-and-rule". He passed an antisocialist law (1878) to stem the rise of German SOCIALISM, but was forced to adopt (1883–87) a paternalist programme of social welfare. The rapid process of industrialization encouraged COLONIALISM and the building of a German overseas empire. The accession (1888) of WILLIAM II saw the demise of Bismarck's political influence, and in 1890 the "Iron Chancellor" was forced to resign.

Bismarck State capital of North Dakota, USA, overlooking the Missouri River. It originated in the 1830s, becoming a distribution centre for grain and cattle, and was later an important stop on the Northern Pacific Railroad. Industries: livestock raising, dairying. Pop. (1990) 49,256.

bismuth (symbol Bi) Metallic, silvery-white element of group V of the periodic table, first identified as a separate element in 1753. The chief ores are bismite (Bi_2O_3) and bismuthnite (Bi_2S_3). A poor heat conductor, it is put into low-melting alloys used in automatic sprinkler systems. Bismuth is also used in insoluble compounds to treat gastric ulcers and skin injuries. It expands when it solidifies, a property exploited in several bismuth alloys for castings. Properties: at.no. 83; r.a.m. 208.98; r.d. 9.75; m.p. 271.3°C (520.3°F); b.p. 1,560°C (2,840°F); most common isotope Bi^{209} (100%).

bison Two species of wild oxen formerly ranging over the grasslands and open woodlands of most of North America and Europe. Once numbered in millions, the American bison (often incorrectly called BUFFALO) is now almost extinct in the wild. The wisent (European bison) was reduced to two herds by the 18th century. Both species now survive in protected areas. The American species is not as massive or as shaggy as the European. Length: to 3.5m (138in); height: to 3m (118in); weight: to 1,350kg (2,976lb). Family Bovidae; species American *Bison bison*; wisent *Bison bonasus*.

Bissau Capital of Guinea-Bissau, near the mouth of the River Geba, W Africa. Established in 1687 by the Portuguese as a slave-trading centre, it became a free port in 1869. It replaced Bonama as capital in 1941. Oil processing is the principal industry. Pop. (1992) 145,000.

bit In computing, abbreviation for BINARY system digit, a 1 or 0 used in binary arithmetic. It is the smallest element of storage. Groups of bits form a BYTE, representing letters and other characters. Binary code is used in computing because it is easy to represent each 1 or 0 using electrical components that can be switched between two states (such as "on" and "off"). The code is also easy to store on disk.

bitterling Deep-bodied freshwater fish native to Asia Minor and central Europe. The female deposits her eggs in the mantle cavities of clams and mussels for hatching. Length: to 7.5cm (3in). Family Cyprinidae; species *Rhodeus sericeus*.

bittern Solitary, heron-like wading bird with a characteristic booming call, found in marshes worldwide. A heavy-bodied bird, it is brownish with streaks and spots which help to hide it in swamplands. The female lays 3–6 brownish eggs. Length: 25–90cm (10in–3ft). Family Ardeidae, species *Botaurus stellaris*.

bittersweet *See* NIGHTSHADE

bitumen (asphalt) Material used for roadmaking and for proofing timber against rot. It consists of a mixture of hydrocarbons and organic chemical compounds. Some occurs naturally in pitch lakes, notably in Trinidad, but it can also made by distilling tar from coal or wood.

bivalve Animal that has a shell with two halves or parts hinged together. The term most usually applies to a class of MOLLUSCS – Pelecypoda or Lamellibranchiata – with left and right shells, such as clams, cockles, mussels and oysters. It also refers to animals of the phylum BRACHIOPODA (lampshells) with dorsal and ventral shells. Length: 2mm–1.2m (0.17in–4ft).

Biwa (Biwa-ko) Lake in W central Honshu, Japan, and namesake of the Japanese musical instrument whose shape it resembles. It is the largest lake in Japan and yields freshwater fish. Length: 64km (40mi); width 3–19km (2–12mi); depth 96m (315ft).

Bizerte Seaport in N Tunisia. Strategically placed at the narrowest part of the Mediterranean Sea, it was a naval station under the French, who fortified the outer harbour. A German base in World War 2, it was heavily bombed by the Allies. In 1963, France evacuated its base, which is now an international shipyard. Pop. (1992 est.) 109,000.

Bizet, Georges (1838–75) French romantic composer. Bizet's opera *Carmen* (1875), although a failure at its first performance, has become one of the most popular operas of all time. He also composed other operas, notably *Les pêcheurs de perles* (1863) and orchestral works, including the Symphony in C (1855).

Bjørnson, Bjørnstjerne (1832–1910) Norwegian writer and political figure. His work *Sunny Hill* (1857) was one of the earliest Norwegian novels. Bjørnson played an active role in defending Norwegian independence and one of his poems is Norway's national anthem. His two-part play *Beyond our Power* (1883–95) is an attempt to reconcile Darwinian evolution and religion.

Black, Joseph (1728–99) British chemist and physicist, b. France. Rediscovering "fixed air" (CARBON DIOXIDE), Black found that this gas is produced by RESPIRATION (burning of charcoal and FERMENTATION), that it behaves as an ACID, and that it is found in the atmosphere. He also discovered hydrogen carbonates (bicarbonates) and investigated LATENT HEAT and specific heat.

Black and Tans Nickname for an auxiliary force of the Royal Irish Constabulary, recruited by the British government (1920–21) to suppress Irish nationalists. The 12,000-strong force had no regular uniforms and wore khaki with black hats and belts (hence the name). The strong-arm tactics of the Black and Tans provoked international outrage.

black bear BEAR found in North America and Asia. The American black bear lives in forests from Canada to central Mexico. It eats a variety of plant and animal foods, including carrion. It is timid and avoids humans. Length: 1.5–1.8m (5–6ft); weight: 120–150kg (265–330lb). Species *Euarctos americanus*. The Asiatic black bear lives in bush or forest areas of E and S Asia. Smaller than the American black bear, it has a white crescent marking on the chest. Aggressive, it sometimes kills livestock and humans. Species *Selenarctos thibetanos*.

blackberry (bramble) Fruit-bearing bush, native to northern temperate regions. The prickly stems may be erect or trailing, the leaves oval and toothed, and the blossoms white, pink or red. The edible berries are black or dark red. Family Rosaceae; genus *Rubus*.

blackbird Songbird of the THRUSH family, common in gardens and woodland throughout most of Europe, the Near East, Australia and New Zealand. The male has jet-black plumage and a bright orange bill. The female is brown, with a brown bill. Length: to 25cm (10in). Species *Turdus merula*. In America, the blackbird is a bird of the Icteridae family. The typical red-winged blackbird (*Agelaius phoeniceus*) has a straight bill, long pointed wings and rounded tail. Length: 20–25cm (8–10in).

black body In physics, an ideal body that absorbs all incident radiation and reflects none. Such a body would look "perfectly" black. Wien's law, Stefan's law (*see* Ludwig BOLTZMANN) and PLANCK's law of black-body radiation grew out of the study of black bodies, as did Planck's discoveries in QUANTUM MECHANICS.

blackbuck (Indian antelope) Medium-sized ANTELOPE of the open plains of India. Females and young are fawn-coloured and males are dark. The underparts are white, and there are patches of white on the muzzle. Only males carry long, spiral horns. Length: to 1.2m (47in); height: to 81cm (32in) at the shoulder. Family Bovidae; species *Antilope cervicapra*.

Black Codes (1865–66) Laws passed in former Confederate states restricting the civil and political rights of newly freed blacks. The Black Codes were outlawed by the 14th amendment to the US Constitution (1868).

Black Death (1347–50) Pandemic of PLAGUE, both bubonic and pneumonic, that killed about one-third of the population of Europe. It was first carried to Mediterranean ports from the Crimea and spread throughout Europe, carried by fleas infesting rats. Plague recurred intermittently and less severely until the 18th century.

Blackett, Patrick Maynard Stuart, Baron (1897–1974) English physicist who was awarded the 1948 Nobel Prize for physics for his research on COSMIC RADIATION. Blackett spent 10 years at the Cavendish Laboratory, Cambridge, developing the Wilson cloud chamber into an instrument to study cosmic radiation. He also used it to prove the existence of the POSITRON, the antiparticle of the ELECTRON. *See also* ANTIMATTER

blackfly *See* APHID

Blackfoot Nomadic, warlike Native North American tribes. They are made up of three Algonquian-speaking tribes: the Siksika, or Blackfeet proper; the Kainah; and the Pikuni (Piegan). Living on the N Great Plains E of the Rockies, they depended largely on the bison (buffalo), which was hunted on horseback. Something of their richly ceremonial culture survives among the c.8,000 Blackfeet living today on reservations in Alberta and Montana.

Black Forest (Schwarzwald) Mountainous region between the Rhine and Neckar rivers, Baden-Württemburg, SW Germany. It is heavily forested in the higher areas, particularly around the sources of the Danube and the Neckar rivers. The highest peak is Feldberg, 1,493m (4,898ft). Industries: tourism, timber, mechanical toys, clocks. Area: c.6,000sq km (2,300sq mi).

Black Friday (24 September 1869) Day of financial panic in the US. Jay GOULD and James Fisk attempted to corner the gold market and drove the price of gold up. The price fell after the US government sold part of its gold reserve, and many speculators were ruined.

Black Hawk War (1832) Conflict between the Sac and Fox Native-American tribes and the US army. The Sac chief, Black Hawk (1767–1838), denounced treaties (1804, 1832) that sought to remove the Native Americans from land W of the Mississippi. The shooting of his peace emissary stung Black Hawk into attack. Initial victories against larger white armies were overturned at the Battle of Bad Axe (1832). Black Hawk's surrender was ignored, and most of the tribe were massacred.

black hole Localized region of space from which neither MATTER nor RADIATION can escape – in other words, the escape velocity exceeds the velocity of light. The boundary of this region is called the EVENT HORIZON. Its radius, the **Schwarzschild radius**, depends on the amount of matter that has fallen into the region and it increases linearly as the mass increases. A black hole of stellar mass is thought to form when a massive star undergoes total gravitational collapse. For stars up to about 1.4 solar masses, gravitational collapse can be physically halted to produce a WHITE DWARF. A slightly more massive object will collapse to form a NEUTRON STAR. If, however, the mass exceeds about 3 solar masses, the collapse continues, and (as it contracts below its Schwarzschild radius) the object becomes a black hole and effectively disappears. A star of 3 solar masses has a Schwarzschild radius of c.9km (5.5mi). Inside the event horizon of the black hole, space and time are highly distorted and the stellar matter is increasingly compressed until it forms an infinitely dense singularity. Black holes can have an immense range of sizes. Supermassive black holes with up to a billion solar masses could be the source of energy in quasars and other

▲ **bison** The American bison (*bison bison*) was almost hunted to extinction by European settlers who wanted to free the land for farming and deprive some of the Native Americans of their herds. Strict conservation programs subsequently have ensured the survival of large numbers of this animal in protected areas.

types of active galaxy. Since no light or other radiation can escape from black holes, they are extremely difficult to detect. Any matter encountered by the black hole will most likely go into orbit first rather than being drawn directly into it. A rapidly spinning disk of matter (accretion disk) forms around the object and heats up through friction to such high temperatures that it emits X-rays. Black holes may therefore appear as X-ray sources in BINARY STARS. The most famous candidate is Cygnus X-1. Not all black holes result from stellar collapse. During the BIG BANG, some regions of space might have become so compressed that they formed so-called **primordial black holes**. Such black holes would not be completely black, because radiation could still "tunnel out" of the event horizon at a steady rate, leading to the evaporation of the hole. Primordial black holes could thus be very hot. *See also* STELLAR EVOLUTION; HAWKING, STEPHEN

Black Hole of Calcutta Prison in Calcutta, India, where 64 or more British soldiers were placed by the Nawab Siraj-ad-Dawlah of Bengal in June 1756. The cell was 5.5 × 4.5m (18 × 15ft) and most of the soldiers died of suffocation.

Black Mountain Poets Designation for writers affiliated to Black Mountain College in North Carolina in the 1950s. There the writers came under the influence of Charles Olson. Poets from this school include Robert Creeley, Robert Duncan and Denise Levertov.

Black Muslims African-American nationalist movement in the US. It aims to establish a separatist black Muslim state. Founded (1930) in Detroit by Wallace D. Farad, the movement was led (1934–76) by Elijah MUHAMMAD. The Black Muslims grew rapidly from 1945 to 1960, helped by the rhetorical power of the preacher MALCOLM X. Factions developed within the movement, and in 1963 Malcolm's membership was suspended. In 1976, the movement split into the American Muslim Mission and the Nation of Islam. The former (led by Elijah's son, Wallace D. Muhammad) preach a more integrationist message. The Nation of Islam, led by Louis FARRAKHAN, claims to uphold the true doctrines of Elijah Muhammad and preaches a more racially exclusive message. During the 1980s and 1990s, the Nation of Islam has gained greater popularity in the US. Mass demonstrations, such as the "Million Man March" in Washington, D.C., have generated great media attention. Total membership is *c*.10,000.

Black Panthers Revolutionary party of African Americans in the 1960s and 1970s. It was founded by Huey Newton and Bobby Seale in 1966. The Black Panthers called for the establishment of an autonomous black state and armed resistance to white repression. Armed clashes with police occurred, and several leaders, including Newton, fled abroad to escape prosecution. Leadership conflicts and the decline of black militancy reduced the influence of the Panthers in the 1970s.

Blackpool Town on the Irish Sea, Lancashire, NW England. One of Britain's most popular resorts, it has 11km (7mi) of sandy beaches, a 158m (520ft) tower (built 1895), many indoor and outdoor entertainments and a promenade which is illuminated every autumn. Industries: confectionery, tourism. Pop. (1994) 156,000.

black power Doctrine of radical black movements in the US in the 1960s and later. Principal organizations involved were the Student Nonviolent Coordinating Committee (SNCC), the BLACK MUSLIMS, the Organization of Afro-American Unity and the BLACK PANTHERS. Black Power groups rejected the policy of non-violent civil disobedience associated with Martin Luther KING

and advocated autonomy and self-determination for black communities. *See also* CIVIL RIGHTS

Black Sea (Kara Sea) Inland sea between Europe and Asia, connected to the Aegean Sea by the Bosporus, the Sea of Marmara and the Dardanelles. It receives many rivers (including the Danube) and is a major outlet for Russian shipping. Subject to violent storms in winter, it remains free of ice except in the remote NW. The Black Sea yields large quantities of fish (especially sturgeon). Area: 413,365sq km (159,662sq mi).

Blackshirt Colloquial name for a member of a fascist organization. In 1919 the Squadre d'Azione (SA) was founded in Italy by Benito MUSSOLINI. Organized into paramilitary squads, they violently attacked communists and socialists. In 1922 the Blackshirts' march on Rome helped Mussolini gain power. The name was also applied to the SS in Nazi Germany and Oswald MOSLEY's British Union of Fascists (BUF).

Blackstone, Sir William (1723–80) English jurist and politician. As a Fellow of All Souls' College, Oxford, Blackstone introduced the first English law course into an English university. His *Commentaries on the Laws of England* (1765–69) is a classic study. Blackstone entered Parliament in 1761.

blackthorn Tree or shrub of the rose family that bears white flowers early in the year and has small plum-like fruits (sloes) and long black thorns that give it its name. Family Rosaceae; species *Prunus spinosa*.

black widow Small SPIDER found in many warm regions of the world. It is black and has red, hour-glass-shaped marks on the underside. Its bite is poisonous, though rarely fatal to humans. Length: 25mm (1in); the male is smaller. Family Theridiidae; genus *Latrodectus*.

bladder Large, elastic-walled organ in the lower abdomen in which URINE is stored. Urine passes from each KIDNEY by way of two narrow tubes (ureters) to the bladder, where it is stored until it can be voided. When pressure in the bladder becomes too great, nervous impulses signal the need for emptying. Urine leaves the bladder through a tube called the URETHRA.

bladderwort Mat-like, aquatic INSECTIVOROUS PLANT found in bogs and ponds. It has feathery thread-like leaves with small bladders in which insects and other small creatures are trapped and drowned. Upright stems bear purple or dark pink flowers. Family Lentibulariaceae; genus *Utricularia*.

Blaine, James Gillespie (1830–93) US statesman, secretary of state (1881, 1889–92). An influential Maine Republican, he served as US senator (1876–81). He ran for president in 1884 but lost the election to the Democratic candidate, Grover CLEVELAND, partly because of the defection of reform Republicans (MUGWUMPS).

Blair, Tony (Anthony Charles Lynton) (1953–) British statesman, prime minister (1997–). He entered Parliament in 1983 and joined the shadow cabinet in 1988. Blair was elected leader of the LABOUR PARTY after the death of John SMITH (1994) and rapidly established himself as a modernizer. His reform of the party's structure and constitution ("new Labour") helped him achieve a landslide victory in the 1997 general election. Britain's youngest prime minister of the 20th century, Blair succeeded John MAJOR. Adopting a more presidential approach, his reforms included giving the Bank of England independence in the setting of interest rates and devolution for Scotland and Wales.

Blake, Peter (1932–) English painter. He was a leading figure in British POP ART. Blake created collages of images culled from a variety of media, such as comics and magazine adverts. His most famous piece is the album cover for *Sergeant Pepper's Lonely Hearts Club Band* (1967) by The Beatles.

Blake, Robert (1599–1657) English admiral. A staunch parliamentarian, Blake defended (1643–45) Bristol, Lyme and Taunton against royalist attack in the English Civil War. In 1649, he took command of the parliamentary fleet, and destroyed the royalist navy. In the first (1652–54) of the DUTCH WARS, Blake gained notable victories against a strong Dutch navy. In 1657, he sank the Spanish fleet at Tenerife but died on the voyage home.

Blake, William (1757–1827) English poet, philosopher and artist, one of the most extraordinary personalities of ROMANTICISM. A visionary, he believed that spiritual reality lies hidden behind the visible world of the senses and he attempted to create a visual symbolism to represent his spiritual visions. In the 1780s, Blake worked as a commercial engraver, but from *c*.1787 he began printing his own illustrated poems in colour. The first example was *Songs of Innocence* (1789). Blake's two patrons, Thomas Butts and John Linnell, enabled him to produce the engravings for *Jerusalem* (1804–20). Towards the end of his life, he joined a circle of younger artists who appreciated his remarkable powers, including Samuel PALMER. It was not until the late 19th century that Blake's work achieved general recognition. Among his productions were *Songs of Experience* (1794); prophetic books portraying his private mythologies, such as *The Book of Urizen* (1794) and *The Four Zoas* (1797); and illustrations to *The Book of Job* and to the *Divine Comedy* by Dante.

Blanc, Mont *See* MONT BLANC

blank verse Unrhymed verse, especially iambic pentameter like heroic couplets, widely used in English dramatic and epic poetry. Henry HOWARD introduced blank verse into England in the 16th century. A highly adaptable form, it was transformed by Christopher MARLOWE and William SHAKESPEARE into the characteristic medium of Elizabethan and JACOBEAN drama. John MILTON employed it in *Paradise Lost* (1667) and William WORDSWORTH used it notably in *The Prelude* (1850). It continues to be popular in contemporary poetry.

Blanqui, (Louis) Auguste (1805–81) French socialist leader. A legendary revolutionary campaigner who spent much of his life in prison, Blanqui participated in the revolutions of 1830 and 1848, and in the overthrow of NAPOLEON III in 1870. He became a symbol for European socialists and was president of the PARIS COMMUNE.

Blasco Ibáñez, Vicente (1867–1928) Spanish novelist. Blasco Ibáñez's best works, such as *The Cabin* (1898) and *Reeds and Mud* (1902), deal with rural life in Valencia and express his Republican beliefs. *Blood and Sand* (1908) and *The Four Horsemen of the Apocalypse* (1916) established his international reputation.

blasphemy Speech or action manifesting contempt for God or religion. Severe penalties were prescribed for it in the Old Testament and also by medieval CANON LAW. Jesus Christ was crucified for blasphemy against Judaism. The statutes of many secular countries still include laws against blasphemy. Britain, for example, retains its law, originally designed to ensure social conformity to ANGLICANISM.

blast furnace Cylindrical smelting FURNACE. It is used in the extraction of metals, mainly iron and copper, from their ores. The ore is mixed with coke and a FLUX (limestone in the case of iron ore). A blast of hot compressed air is piped in at the bottom of the furnace to force up temperatures to where the reduction of the oxide ore to impure metal occurs. The molten metal sinks to the bottom and is tapped off. Waste "slag" floats to the top of the metal and is piped off. *See also* OXIDATION-REDUCTION

blastula Stage in the development of the EMBRYO in animals. The blastula consists of a hollow cavity (blastocoel) surrounded by one or more spherical layers of cells. It occurs at or near the end of cleavage.

Blaue Reiter, der Loosely organized group of German expressionist painters. Formed in 1911, it took its name from a picture by Wassily KANDINSKY, one of the group's leading members. Other members included Paul KLEE, August MACKE, Alexei von Jawlensky and Franz Marc. Influenced by CUBISM, the group was the most important manifestation of German modern art before World War I. *See also* EXPRESSIONISM

Blavatsky, Helena Petrovna (1831–91) Russian spiritualist. In 1875, she co-founded the Theosophical Society in New York. In 1878, Blavatsky established the society's headquarters near Madras, India. Her books include *Isis Unveiled* (1877). *See also* THEOSOPHY

Blenheim, Battle of (1704) Decisive battle for the English in the War of the SPANISH SUCCESSION. The Duke of MARLBOROUGH and Prince EUGÈNE OF SAVOY defeated the French at Blenheim in Bavaria. Marlborough was granted a royal manor near Oxford where he built Blenheim Palace, birthplace of his descendant Winston Churchill.

blenny Marine fish in shallow and offshore waters of all tropical and temperate seas. Often scaleless, with a long dorsal fin, it is olive green with varicoloured markings. Length: to 30.5cm (12in). Family Blenniidae.

Blériot, Louis (1872–1936) French aircraft designer and aviator. In 1909, Blériot became the first man to fly an aircraft across the English Channel. The flight from Calais to Dover took 37 minutes. As a designer, he was responsible for a system by which the pilot could operate AILERONS by remote control.

blesbok Small, South African antelope that has a large white mark on its face. Both sexes have horns that grow up to 50cm (20in) long. They are raised successfully as livestock. Family Bovidae, species *Damaliscus dorcas*.

Bleuler, Paul Eugen (1857–1939) Swiss psychiatrist, pioneer in the diagnosis and treatment of PSYCHOSIS. Bleuler coined the term SCHIZOPHRENIA, and unlike his predecessors, attributed the symptoms to psychological rather than physiological origins.

Bligh, William (1754–1817) English naval officer. Bligh was captain of the *Bounty* in 1789, when his mutinous crew cast him adrift. With a few loyal companions, he sailed nearly 6,500km (4,000mi) to Timor. While governor of New South Wales (1805–08), he was arrested by mutineers led by his deputy and sent back to England. He was exonerated.

blight Yellowing, browning and withering of plant tissues caused by various diseases; alternatively, the diseases themselves. Blights may be caused by microorganisms, such as bacteria and fungi, or by environmental factors such as drought. Common blights induced by microorganisms include fire, bean, late and potato blight. They typically affect leaves the most.

blindness Severe impairment (or absence of) vision. It may be due to heredity, accident, disease or old age. The commonest cause of blindness is TRACHOMA. In developed countries, it is most often due to severe DIABETES, GLAUCOMA, CATARACT or degenerative changes associated with ageing. *See also* BRAILLE; COLOUR BLINDNESS; EYE

blind spot Small area on the retina of the EYE where no visual image can be formed because of the absence of light-sensitive cells. It is the area where the optic nerve leaves the eye.

Bliss, Sir Arthur (1891–1975) English composer. Bliss was a pupil of Charles Villiers Stanford, Ralph Vaughan Williams and Gustav Holst. His works include the *Colour Symphony* (1932), a piano concerto (1938), two operas and a number of choral works. From 1953 he was Master of the Queen's Music.

Blitz Name used by the British to describe the night bombings of British cities by the German *Luftwaffe* (air force) in 1940–41. It is an abbreviation of *Blitzkrieg* (lightning war), the name used by the German army to describe hard-hitting, surprise attacks on enemy forces.

Blixen, Karen *See* DINESEN, ISAK

Bloch, Ernest (1880–1959) US composer, b. Switzerland. He emigrated to the US in 1916. Bloch's music combines romanticism with Hebraic themes, such as *Sacred Service* (1933) and *A Voice in the Wilderness* (1937).

Bloch, Felix (1905–83) US nuclear physicist, b. Switzerland. Bloch shared the 1952 Nobel Prize for physics with the US physicist Edward Mills Purcell for their separate development of nuclear MAGNETIC RESONANCE (NMR), used to study atomic nuclei. He was the first director (1954–55) of *Conseil Européen pour la Recherche Nucléaire* (CERN), the European centre in Geneva for research into high-energy PARTICLE PHYSICS.

Bloemfontein City and judicial capital of South Africa; capital of FREE STATE. Dutch farmers settled here in the early 19th century. It contains the oldest Dutch Reformed church in South Africa. The modern city is an important educational centre. Industries: furniture, glassware. Pop. (1991) 300,150.

Blok, Alexander Alexandrovich (1880–1921) Russian poet, leading figure of Russian SYMBOLISM. His most famous early work is *Verses About the Lady Beautiful* (1904), but his increasing concern for social welfare led him through the urban imagery of *The City* (1901–08) to the pro-Bolshevik impressionism of his last and best known work, the epic poem *The Twelve* (1918).

blood Fluid circulating in the body that transports oxygen and nutrients to all the cells and removes wastes such as carbon dioxide. In a healthy human, it constitutes *c.*5% of body weight; by volume, it comprises *c.*5.5l (5.8qts). It is composed of PLASMA in which are suspended microscopic ERYTHROCYTES, LEUCOCYTES and PLATELETS.

blood clotting Protective mechanism that prevents excessive blood loss after injury. A mesh of tight fibres (of insoluble FIBRIN) coagulates at the site of injury through a complex series of chemical reactions. This mesh traps blood cells to form a clot which dries to form a scab. This prevents further loss of blood and also prevents bacteria getting into the wound. Normal clotting takes place within five minutes. The clotting mechanism is impaired in some diseases such as HAEMOPHILIA.

blood group Type into which blood is classified according to which ANTIGENS are present on the surface of its red cells. There are four major types: A, B, AB and O. Each group in the ABO system may also contain the rhesus factor (Rh), in which case it is Rh-positive; otherwise it is Rh-negative. Such typing is essential before BLOOD TRANSFUSION. *See also* LANDSTEINER, KARL

bloodhound Hunting DOG with long, tapered head, loose hanging jowls and ears and a characteristically wrinkled skin. The body is strong and the legs muscular, and the dog weighs up to 50kg (110lb). The smooth coat may be black, tan or red and tan. Height: (at shoulder) up to 69cm (27in).

blood poisoning (septicemia) Presence in the blood of bacteria or their toxins in sufficient quantity to cause illness. Symptoms include chills and fever, sweating and collapse. It is most often seen in people who are already vulnerable, such as the old, the critically ill, or those whose immune systems have been suppressed.

blood pressure Force exerted by circulating BLOOD on the walls of blood vessels due to the pumping action of the HEART. This is measured by a SPHYGMOMANOMETER. It is greatest when the heart contracts and lowest when it relaxes. **High** blood pressure is associated with an increased risk of HEART ATTACK and stroke; abnormally **low** blood pressure is mostly seen in people in SHOCK or following excessive loss of fluid or blood.

blood test Analysis of a sample of BLOOD as an aid to diagnosis. There are a great many tests available, from blood typing, to counts of red or white cells or elaborate assays to trace minute amounts of hormones. Most are performed to evaluate the blood itself, to detect infection or to probe chemical changes in the body.

blood transfusion Transfer of BLOOD or a component of blood from one body to another to make up for a deficiency. This is possible only if the BLOOD GROUPS of the donor and recipient are compatible. It is often done to counteract life-threatening SHOCK following excessive blood loss. Donated blood is scrutinized for readily transmissible diseases, such as HEPATITIS B and ACQUIRED IMMUNE DEFICIENCY SYNDROME (AIDS).

blood vessel Closed channels that carry BLOOD throughout the body. An ARTERY carries oxygenated blood away from the HEART; these give way to smaller arterioles and finally to tiny capillaries deep in the tissues, where oxygen and nutrients are exchanged for cellular wastes. The deoxygenated blood is returned to the heart by way of the VEINS.

Bloody Assizes (1685) Trials held in the w of England following MONMOUTH's Rebellion against James II. Judge Jeffreys conducted the trials. He sentenced about 200 people to be hanged, 800 to transportation and hundreds more to flogging, imprisonment or fines.

bloom Dense population of microscopic algae or CYANOBACTERIA on the surface of lakes or seas, often colouring the water. They may appear suddenly through migration of the population to the water surface. This occurs when the cells float or swim to the surface under calm conditions. They may arise also in response to large increases in nutrients. This happens when sewage or other mineral-rich water enters a lake or sea. Some blooms produce toxins harmful to marine life.

Bloomer, Amelia Jenks (1818–94) US women's rights campaigner. Bloomer published (1849–54) *Lily*, the first US magazine for women. She subsequently continued as editor and wrote articles on education, marriage laws and female suffrage. She popularized the full trousers for women that became known as "bloomers".

Bloomsbury Group Intellectuals who met in Bloomsbury, London, from about 1907. They included the art critics Roger Fry and Clive Bell; novelists E.M. FORSTER and Virginia WOOLF; her husband Leonard, a publisher; economist John Maynard KEYNES; and biographer Lytton STRACHEY.

Blücher, Gebhard Leberrecht von (1744–1819) Prussian field-marshal. He distinguished himself during the NAPOLEONIC WARS, fighting against France (1793–94), and in the campaign of 1805–06. Blücher led the Prussian troops at the Battle of Lützen and helped to defeat NAPOLEON I at Leipzig (1813). In 1815, he was defeated at Ligny but arrived at WATERLOO in time to secure British victory over Napoleon.

Bluebeard Folk villain, murderer of a succession of wives. Bluebeard appears in numerous folk tales from around the world. The best known version is in the collection of fairy tales by Charles PERRAULT, *Tales of Mother Goose* (1697), where Bluebeard is a rich nobleman. Perrault's story forms the basis of a one-act opera, *Bluebeard's Castle* (1911), by Béla BARTÓK.

bluebell Spring-flowering blue flower native to Europe. It grows from a bulb, especially in woodlands, and bears a drooping head of bell-shaped flowers. Height: 20–50cm (8–20in). Family Liliaceae; species *Hyacinthoides non-scripta*.

blueberry *See* BILBERRY

bluebird North American songbird with blue plumage, a member of the thrush subfamily. There are three species. Typically, a bluebird lays its eggs (usually 4–6) in a grass-and-weed-lined nest in a hole in a tree or fence post. Length: 17.8cm (7in). Genus *Sialia*.

bluebottle (blow fly) Black or metallic blue-green FLY, slightly larger than, but similar in habits to, the housefly. The larvae (maggots) usually feed on carrion and refuse containing meat. Family Calliphoridae. Genus *Calliphora*. Length: 6–11mm (0.23–0.43in).

bluefish Predatory marine fish found in most tropical and temperate seas. Fished widely for food and sport, it has an elongated blue/green body and a large mouth with sharp teeth. Length: 1.2m (4ft). Family Pomatomidae; species *Pomatomus saltatrix*.

bluegrass Type of grass that grows in temperate and Arctic regions, and is used extensively for food by grazing animals. Family Poaceae/Gramineae; genus *Poa*.

blue-green algae *See* CYANOBACTERIA

Blue Rider *See* BLAUE REITER, DER

Blue Ridge Mountains East and SE range of the APPALACHIAN Mountains, USA, extending from S Pennsylvania into Georgia. A narrow ridge, 16km (10mi) wide in the N, widens to 113km (70mi) in North Carolina. Heavily forested with few lakes, it includes the Great Smoky Mountains National Park, North Carolina and the Shenandoah National Park, Virginia. The Appalachian Trail takes hikers across the top of the range. Industries: timbering, apple growing, tourism. The highest peak is Mount Mitchell, North Carolina, at 2,039m (6,684ft).

blues Form of African-American music, originating in the late 19th-century, primarily in the South. It evolved from gospel and work songs. The first published blues piece was *The Memphis Blues* by W.C. HANDY (1912). "Jelly Roll" MORTON incorporated a jazzier style in *Jelly Roll Blues*. Great blues vocalists such as Bessie SMITH ("Empress of the Blues"), Robert JOHNSON, Huddie LEDBETTER and "Ma" Rainey, popularized the form. The 1930s northerly migration of African-Americans saw the emergence of a more assertive, urban blues tradition based around Chicago, Illinois. After World War 2, the electric guitar became the dominant voice, with artists such as Muddy Waters and John Lee Hooker. In the 1950s, new forms like RHYTHM AND BLUES and ROCK and roll drew on the blues. During the 1960s, rock and pop bands, such as the Rolling Stones and Grateful Dead, were also directly influenced by the tradition.

blue shift In astronomy, an effect in which the lines in the SPECTRUM of a celestial object are displaced toward the blue end of the spectrum. It results from the DOPPLER EFFECT, because the object and the observer are moving toward each other. The closing speed can be calculated from the extent of the shift. *See also* RED SHIFT

bluestocking Pejorative term applied to a woman with literary pretensions. Dating from the 18th century, it derived from Benjamin Stillingfleet, who wore blue

worsted stockings rather than the black silk of evening dress when attending a London women's literary circle.

bluetooth Specification that defines the software and hardware requirements for short-range, low-power, wireless data networking, enabling electronic devices of all sorts to communicate with each other. Devices that meet the bluetooth standard can send data, up to a rate of 1 megabit per second and within a maximum range of 10m (33ft), in an unlicensed part of the radio spectrum, the 2.4 GHz band. Data security is achieved by encryption and authentication. *See also* WIRELESS APPLICATION PROTOCOL (WAP)

blue whale Endangered baleen WHALE, related to the rorquals. The blue whale is the largest animal that has ever lived, reaching up to 30m (100ft) in length and weighing up to 120 tonnes. In summer it lives in polar seas, feeding on millions of krill each day. Mating occurs at the end of winter and the whales migrate to warmer latitudes to give birth. A single calf is born every two or three years, after a 10–11 month gestation period. They live up to 50 years. Overhunting has led to threat of extinction. Species *Balaenoptera musculus*.

Blum, Léon (1872–1950) French statesman, prime minister (1936–37). He served in the chamber of deputies (1919–40) as a leader of the Socialist Party. Blum formed the Popular Front which became a coalition government. His administration rapidly embarked on a programme of nationalization. Opposed by Conservatives, Blum was forced to resign and became deputy prime minister. He opposed the MUNICH AGREEMENT (1938). Interned by the VICHY GOVERNMENT (1940–45), he briefly (1946–47) led a provisional government.

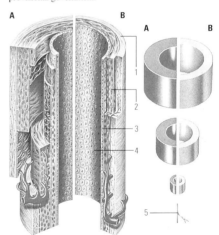

▲ **blood vessels** Arteries (A) and veins (B) conduct blood around the body. They have a common structure consisting of four layers: a protective fibrous coat (1); a layer of smooth muscle and elastic tissue (2), which is thickest in the largest arteries; a thin layer of connective tissue (3); and a smooth layer of cells – endothelium (4). Arteries have thicker walls and a smaller diameter. In veins, inner coat layers are often hard to distinguish. A comparison of the two vessels is shown in half sections of arteries and veins found in the body. Arteries divide into smaller ones, and finally into arterioles (5), where the blood flow can be controlled by autonomic nerves supplying the smooth muscle.

Blunt, Anthony (1907–83) English art historian. He was director (1947–74) of the Courtauld Institute of Art, London, and surveyor of the king's (later queen's) pictures (1945–72). Blunt was a formidable scholar, earning praise for his work on Nicolas POUSSIN. In 1979 his reputation was destroyed when it was disclosed that he had been a Soviet spy during World War 2.

Blyton, Enid Mary (1897–1968) English writer of children's fiction. She wrote more than 400 books and is the third most translated British writer (after Shakespeare and Agatha Christie). Blyton wrote a series of adventure stories based around two groups of child detectives, the "Famous Five" and "Secret Seven". Later characters included Noddy and Big Ears.

boa Large, constricting SNAKE. The boa constrictor (*Constrictor constrictor*) of the American tropics can grow to 3.7m (12ft) in length. The iridescent rainbow boa, the emerald tree boa and the rosy boa are smaller species. Most boas are tree-dwellers, but the rubber boa of the W US is a burrowing species. Family Boidae. *See also* ANACONDA; PYTHON

Boadicea (Boudicca) (d. AD 62) Queen of the ICENI in East Britain. She was the wife of King Prasutagus who, on his death, left his daughters and the Roman emperor as co-heirs. The Romans seized his domain, and Boadicea led a revolt against them. After initial successes, during which her army is thought to have killed as many as 70,000 Roman soldiers, she was defeated and poisoned herself. *See also* ROMAN BRITAIN

boar Male domestic PIG (particularly one that has not been castrated) or, more specifically, the wild pig of Europe, Africa and Asia. It is hunted either for food or sport. The European wild boar is species *Sus scrofa*.

Boas, Franz (1858–1942) US anthropologist, b. Germany. He was the first professor of anthropology at Columbia University (1899–1936). Boas was the leading theorist of cultural relativism, arguing for the study of specific societies in terms of human evolution, archaeology, language and culture. He criticized social studies based on notions of racial difference. In *Kwakiutl Ethnography* (1966), Boas attempted to salvage the culture of a Native American group from colonial domination. Other works include *The Mind of Primitive Man* (1911), *Anthropology and Modern Life* (1928) and *Race, Language and Culture* (1940).

boat Vehicle for passenger and freight transport by water. Today, it usually refers to craft that can be removed from the water; a larger vessel is called a SHIP. The first boats, made in prehistoric times, included rafts, hollowed-out logs and vessels made from plaited reeds. Among the first maritime peoples were the Phoenicians.

▲ **boa** The boa constrictor (*Constrictor constrictor*) is found in many areas of South America. It feeds on birds and small mammals, such as rats and agoutis, which it kills by restricting their ability to breathe. A large snake, it grows to *c*.3.7m (12ft) in length.

They built fleets of galleys, propelled by sails and oars. The later Viking long-boats, also square-sailed, were slimmer and speedier. Lateen (triangular) sails were probably introduced to the West by the empire-building Arabs. Modern boats include SAILING vessels and motor boats, used mainly for pleasure and launches.

boat people Refugees that flee their country by sea to avoid political persecution, or to find greater economic opportunities. The term is closely associated with South Vietnamese refugees, of whom, since 1975, some 150,000 have sailed to Hong Kong and to Southeast Asian countries. Other boat people include Cubans and Haitians attempting to reach the US, usually Florida.

Boat Race In England, annual rowing contest between Oxford and Cambridge University eights, first held in 1829. It is rowed on a 6.8km (4.25mi) course on the River Thames in London, from Putney to Mortlake. Staged on the present course since 1845, the race takes place in March or April.

bobcat (wild cat or red lynx) Vicious, short-tailed cat found throughout swamp, forest and grassland regions of the US, S Canada and Central America. Its reddish-brown coat has black spots with white underparts. The bobcat feeds on rodents and gives birth to 2–4 young following a gestation period of 50–60 days. Length: body 64–76cm (25–30in). Family Felidae; species *Lynx rufus*.

Boccaccio, Giovanni (1313–75) Italian poet, prose writer and scholar, considered to be one of the founders of the Italian RENAISSANCE. His early work, the *Filocolo* (*c*.1336), is considered by many to be the first European novel. Boccaccio is best known for his masterpiece, the *Decameron* (1348–58), ten prose stories with different narrators dealing with contemporary mores, which exercised a tremendous influence on the development of Renaissance literature. His poetry includes *Il Filostrato* (*c*.1338) and *Il Ninfale Fiesolano* (*c*.1344–45). Boccaccio was a friend of PETRACH and biographer of DANTE. *See also* ITALIAN LITERATURE

Boccherini, Luigi (1743–1805) Italian composer and cellist. He was the main exponent of Latin instrumental music during the Viennese classical period. Boccherini was a prolific composer of chamber music, writing over 120 string quintets and nearly 100 string quartets. His orchestral work includes over 20 symphonies.

Bode's law In astronomy, empirical numerical relationship for the mean distances of the planets from the Sun, named after the German astronomer Johann Bode (1747–1826). If the number 4 is added to the sequence 0, 3, 6, 12, 24, 48, 96 and 192, and each sum is divided by 10, the result corresponds reasonably with the mean planetary distances. This aided the discovery of Uranus (1781), but does not work for Neptune and Pluto.

Bodhidharma (active 6th century AD) Indian monk who travelled to China and founded ZEN Buddhism.

bodhisattva (bodhista) In THERAVADA Buddhism, an individual who is about to reach NIRVANA. In MAHAYANA Buddhism, the term is used to denote an individual on the verge of enlightenment who delays his salvation in order to help mankind.

Bodin, Jean (1530–96) French lawyer and political philosopher. In *Six Books of the Republic* (1576), Bodin treated ANARCHY as the supreme political evil and order as the supreme human need.

Bodleian Library Library of OXFORD UNIVERSITY, England. The original library was founded in the 14th century, but destroyed in the reign of Edward VI. It was refounded in 1602 chiefly through the efforts of Sir Thomas Bodley (1545–1613).

Boeotia Department in central Greece, on the N shore of the Gulf of Corinth; the capital is Levádhia. Formed in the 7th century BC, the Boeotian League of Greek cities was dominated by THEBES. It was disbanded after 479 BC. Area: 3,211sq km (1,240sq mi). Pop. (1991) 134,300.

Boer (Afrikaans, farmer) Alternative name for an AFRIKANER

Boer Wars *See* SOUTH AFRICAN WARS

Boethius (*c*.480–524) (Anicius Manlius Severinus) Roman statesman and philosopher under Emperor Theodoric. He attempted to eliminate governmental corruption but was imprisoned on a charge of conspiracy. In prison at Pavia, where he was subsequently tortured and executed, Boethius wrote *On the Consolation of Philosophy* (523). Next to the Bible, this was medieval Europe's most influential book.

bog Spongy, wet soil of decayed vegetable matter; often called a peat bog. It develops in a depression with little or no drainage where the water is cold and acidic and almost devoid of oxygen and nitrogen. A bog nearly has standing water like a MARSH, but plants such as cranberry and the SUNDEW readily grow there.

Bogarde, Sir Dirk (1921–99) English film actor. His first leading role was in Joseph Losey's *The Sleeping Tiger* (1954). Bogarde starred in other Losey films, such as *The Servant* (1963), *King and Country* (1964) and *Accident* (1967). In the 1970s, he appeared in European productions, notably *Death in Venice* (1971). During the 1980s, Bogarde concentrated on writing his memoirs and popular novels. He made a much-praised comeback in *These Foolish Things* (1990). Bogarde was knighted in 1992.

Bogart, Humphrey DeForest (1899–1957) US film actor, often cast as a cynical, wisecracking anti-hero. His association with FILM NOIR and John HUSTON began with roles in *High Sierra* and *The Maltese Falcon* (both 1941). Bogart starred in *Casablanca* (1942). In 1945, he married Lauren BACALL; their sexual magnetism was evident in the *film noir* classic *The Big Sleep* (1946). In 1948, Bogart starred in two Huston classics, *The Treasure of the Sierra Madre* and *Key Largo*. He won a best actor Oscar for *The African Queen* (1951).

Bogotá Capital of Colombia, on a fertile plateau in central Columbia. Bogotá was founded (1538) by the Spanish on the site of a CHIBCHA Indian settlement. In 1819 it was made the capital of Greater Colombia, part of which later became Colombia. Today, it is a centre for culture, education and finance. It has some fine examples of Spanish colonial architecture. Industries: tobacco, sugar, flour, textiles. Pop. (1997) 6,005,000.

Bohemia Historic region which (with MORAVIA) now comprises the CZECH REPUBLIC. Its borders with Germany are formed (NW) by the Erzegebirge (Ore Mountains) and (SW) by the Bohemian Forest. The plateau region is chiefly drained by the rivers ELBE and Vltava. The major cities are PRAGUE and PLZEŇ. Bohemia was established as an independent principality at the end of the 9th century. In the 920s, St WENCESLAS successfully resisted Germanic invasion, but by the end of the 10th century Bohemia formed part of the Holy Roman Empire. In 1198, Ottocar I formed an independent kingdom. At the height of its power during the reign (1253–78) of Ottocar II, Bohemia stretched from the Oder to the Adriatic. Bohemia's golden age was in the reign (1347–78) of Emperor CHARLES IV, who made Prague his capital. In the reigns of WENCESLAS and SIGISMUND, Bohemia was at the centre of nationalist and religious revolts against imperial domination, including the rebellion of Jan HUS. In 1526, Bohemia was inherited by

the HABSBURG dynasty. In 1618, the Defenestration of Prague sparked the THIRTY YEARS' WAR. The process of Germanization was continued by MARIA THERESA and JOSEPH II. LEOPOLD II was the last king of Bohemia. The formation of the AUSTRO-HUNGARIAN EMPIRE failed to satisfy Czech demands for autonomy and independence was finally achieved at the end of World War 1 under Tomás MASARYK. In the MUNICH AGREEMENT (1938) CZECHOSLOVAKIA was forced to cede the SUDETENLAND to Germany. In 1993, the dissolution of Czechoslovakia saw Bohemia and Moravia join to form the Czech Republic.

Böhm, Karl (1894–1981) Austrian conductor famous for his interpretations of Mozart and Richard Strauss. In 1921, Bruno Walter engaged Böhm for the Munich State Opera. He was principal conductor of the Vienna Philharmonic Orchestra from 1933. As director (1934–42) of the Dresden Opera, Böhm conducted several premieres of Strauss' operas. He was director of the Vienna Opera (1943–45, 1954–56).

Bohr, Aage Niels (1922–) Danish physicist, son of Niels BOHR. Bohr shared the 1975 Nobel Prize for physics with Benjamin Mottelson and James Rainwater for devising a "collective model" of the atomic NUCLEUS that assumes the collective vibration of all nucleons.

Bohr, Niels Henrik David (1885–1962) Danish physicist, major contributor to QUANTUM THEORY and the first person to apply it successfully to atomic structure. Bohr worked with J.J. THOMSON and Ernest RUTHERFORD in Britain before teaching theoretical physics at the University of Copenhagen. He escaped from German-occupied Denmark during World War 2 and worked briefly on developing the atom bomb in the US. He later returned to Copenhagen and worked for international cooperation. In the 1920s, Bohr helped to develop the "standard model" of quantum theory, known as the Copenhagen Interpretation. He was awarded the 1922 Nobel Prize for physics for his work on atomic structure and in 1957 received the first Atoms for Peace Award.

boil (furuncle) Small, pus-filled swelling on the skin, often occurring around a hair follicle or SEBACEOUS GLAND. Most boils are caused by infection by a bacterium called a STAPHYLOCOCCUS.

boiler Vessel for heating and converting water to steam. The boiler is an essential part of steam-engines and turbines. It consists of a furnace for burning fuel and a container where water is evaporated into steam. The term is also applied to devices used to provide hot, though not boiling, water in central-heating systems.

boiling point Temperature at which a substance changes phase (state) from a liquid to a vapour or gas. The boiling point increases as the external pressure increases and falls as pressure decreases. It is usually measured at standard pressure of one atmosphere (760mm of mercury). The boiling point of pure water at standard pressure is 100°C (212°F).

Boise Capital and largest city of Idaho, USA, in the valley of the Boise River. Founded in 1863 as a supply post for gold miners, Boise is now a trade centre for the agricultural region of SW Idaho and E Oregon. Crops: sugar beets, potatoes, alfalfa, onions. Industries: steel, sheet metal, furniture. Pop. (1990) 125,738.

Bokassa, Jean Bédel (1921–96) Emperor of the Central African Empire (1977–79). Bokassa came to power in 1966 in a military coup. After serving as president (1966–77) of the Central African Republic, he crowned himself emperor. His regime was brutal. A 1979 coup (with French military aid) removed Bokassa, who went into exile in France.

Boleyn, Anne (1507–36) Second wife of HENRY VIII of England, mother of ELIZABETH I. Henry and Anne were married in 1533, when his first marriage, to CATHERINE OF ARAGON, had been annulled. Henry was desperate for an heir, and following the birth of a still-born boy (1536), Anne was accused of adultery and executed for treason. It is thought that her Protestant sympathies pushed the king toward the break with Rome that unleashed the English REFORMATION.

Bolingbroke *See* HENRY IV (of England)

Bolingbroke, Henry St. John, Viscount (1678–1751) English political leader. A prominent Tory minister under ANNE, he fled to France in 1714 and joined the JACOBITES. Bolingbroke was allowed to return to England in 1723 and continued to oppose the Whig regime under Robert WALPOLE.

Bolívar, Simón (1783–1830) Latin American revolutionary leader, known as "the Liberator". Bolívar achieved no real success until 1819, when his victory at Boyacá led to the liberation of New Granada (later Colombia) in 1821. The liberation of Venezuela (1821), Ecuador (1822), Peru (1824) and Upper Peru (1825) followed, the latter renaming itself Bolivia in his honour. Despite the removal of Spanish hegemony from the continent, his hopes of uniting South America into one confederation were dashed by rivalry between the new states.

Bolivia Republic in W central South America. Bolivia can be divided into two regions. The W is dominated by two parallel ranges of the ANDES Mountains. The W cordillera forms Bolivia's border with Chile. The E range runs through the heart of Bolivia. Between the two, lies the Altiplano. The most densely populated region of Bolivia and site of famous ruins, it includes the seat of government, LA PAZ, close to Lake TITICACA. SUCRE, the legal capital, lies in the Andean foothills. The E is a relatively unexplored region of lush, tropical rainforest, inhabited mainly by Native South Americans. In the SE lies the GRAN CHACO. **Climate and Vegetation** Bolivia's climate varies greatly accrding to altitude. The highest Andean peaks are permanently covered in snow, while the E plains have a humid climate. The main rainy season is between December and February. The windswept altiplano is a grassland region. The semi-arid Gran Chaco is a vast lowland plain, drained by the River Madeira, a tributary of the AMAZON. **History and Politics** The ruins of Tiahuanaco indicate that the Altiplano was the site of one of the great pre-Columbian civilizations. At the time of the Spanish conquest (1532), the AYMARÁ had already been subsumed into the Inca empire by the QUECHUA. The Spanish exploited the Andean silver mines with native forced labour. In 1824, the Spanish were finally expelled with the victory of Antonio José de SUCRE, Simón BOLÍVAR's general. For the next century, the new nation of Bolivia was plagued by corruption and instability. War (1932–35) with Paraguay led to the loss of most of Gran Chaco. In 1941, Victor Paz Estenssoro founded the pro-miner National Revolutionary Movement (MNR) that seized power in 1943 and 1952. Paz nationalized the mines and instituted land reforms for the Native Americans. In 1964, the MNR government was overthrown in a military coup. Guerrilla leader Che GUEVARA was killed in 1967. From 1964 to 1982, Bolivia was ruled by a succession of repressive military regimes, most prominently that of Colonel Hugo Bánzer Suárez (1971–78). In 1982 civilian rule was restored. In 1997, Banzer became president, promising to maintain, with US support, the war against the growing of coca. **Economy** Bolivia is the poorest nation in South America (1995 GDP per capita,

BOLIVIA
AREA: 1,098,580sq km (424,162sq mi)
POPULATION: 9,724,000
CAPITAL (POPULATION): La Paz (1,126,000), Sucre (145,000)

US$2,540). It is the world's sixth-largest producer of tin. The collapse in world tin prices led many into coca production, which experts believe may be its largest (unofficial) export. Agriculture employs 47% of the workforce.

Böll, Heinrich Theodor (1917–85) German novelist and short-story writer. Böll's narratives often contain strident criticisms of German society and Catholic morality, such as the popular novel *The Clown* (1963). Strongly affected by his experiences as a German soldier in World War 2, novels such as *Billiards at Half Past Nine* (1961) attempt to come to terms with the Holocaust. Other novels include *Group Portrait with Lady* (1971) and *The Lost Honour of Katharina Blum* (1974). He was awarded the 1972 Nobel Prize for literature.

Bollywood Term used to describe the film industry in Bombay, India. The centre of Hindi film-making for over 60 years, Bollywood is often used generically to describe Indian cinema as a whole. The largest film industry in the world, India produces more than 900 films annually.

Bologna City in N central Italy, at the foot of Apennines; capital of Bologna and Emilia-Romagna province. Originally an Etruscan town, Felsina, it was colonized by Rome in the 2nd century BC. It has an 11th-century university and the incomplete Church of San Petronio (1390). Industries: mechanical and electrical engineering, publishing. Pop. (1996) 386,000.

Bolsheviks (Rus. majority) Marxist revolutionaries led by LENIN who seized power in the RUSSIAN REVOLUTION of 1917. They narrowly defeated the MENSHEVIKS at the Second Congress of the All-Russian Soviet Democratic Workers' Party in London (1903). The split centred on the means of achieving revolution. The Bolsheviks believed it could be obtained only by professional revolutionaries leading the PROLETARIAT. The Bolsheviks were able to defeat KERENSKY's provisional government with the support of the SOVIETS in Moscow and Petrograd. *See also* MARXISM

Bolshoi Ballet One of the world's leading ballet companies. It adopted its present name in 1825 but was founded as the Petrovsky Theatre in 1776. Based at the Bolshoi Theatre, its choreographers have included Yuri Grigorovich and Alexander Gorsky, and its leading dancers have included Galina ULANOVA and Mikhail Lavrovsky.

Bolshoi Opera Leading Russian opera company, founded in 1780 in Moscow. It performs mostly Russian works and a few foreign operas translated into Russian.

Bolt, Robert Oxton (1924–95) English screenwriter and dramatist. He is best-known for his historical screenplays. Bolt won two Academy Awards for best screenplay for *Dr. Zhivago* (1965) and *A Man for All Seasons* (1960). Other screenplays include *Lawrence of Arabia* (1962), *Ryan's Daughter* (1970) and *The Mission* (1986).

Bolton Town in Greater Manchester, NW England. Since the late 18th century it has been a cotton and wool manufacturing centre (Crompton's spinning mule was invented here in 1779), but these industries are now in decline. Other industries: engineering, chemicals, textile machinery. Pop. (1994) 210,000.

Boltzmann, Ludwig (1844–1906) Austrian physicist, acclaimed for his contribution to statistical mechanics and to the kinetic theory of gases. His research extended the theories of James MAXWELL. Boltzmann's general law asserts that a system will approach a state of thermodynamic equilibrium. He introduced the "Boltzmann equation" (1877) relating the kinetic energy of a gas atom or molecule to temperature. Symbol K in the formula, the gas constant per molecule, is called the "Boltzmann constant". In 1884, he derived a law, often termed the "Stefan-Boltzmann law", for BLACK BODY radiation discovered by his Austrian teacher, Josef Stefan (1835–93). Attacked for his belief in the atomic theory of MATTER, Boltzmann committed suicide. *See also* THERMODYNAMICS

bomb Projectile filled with an explosive charge exploded by a fuse or by impact, and used as a weapon to cause destruction and death. The many specialized types include atomic bombs, high-explosive bombs, smoke bombs to provide a smoke-screen, gas bombs to spread poison gas and fire bombs.

Bombay *See* MUMBAI

Bonaparte, Joseph (1768–1844) King of Spain, b. Corsica. He was the eldest brother of NAPOLEON I. He served as diplomat for the First Republic of France. Napoleon made him king of Naples (1806), and he was king of Spain from 1808 to 1813. After Napoleon's defeat at Waterloo, he resided in the USA (1815–32).

Bonaparte, Napoleon *See* NAPOLEON I

Bonar Law, Andrew *See* LAW, ANDREW BONAR

Bond, Edward (1935–) English dramatist. His early works, such as *Saved* (1965), were controversial in their use of violent imagery to express the cruelty of modern society. *Early Morning* (1968) was the last play to be banned in the UK. Other major plays include *Lear* (1971) and *War Plays* (1985). Bond has written several film scripts, including *Blow Up* (1966).

Bond, William Cranch (1789–1859) US astronomer who discovered Hyperion, Saturn's eighth satellite, and the Crêpe Ring, the faint innermost ring around the planet. Both discoveries were made with his son, George Phillips (1825–65). Bond founded (1839) and was the first director of the Harvard College Observatory. He also produced a daguerreotype of the Moon in 1850.

bond Promissory note guaranteeing the repayment of a specific amount of money on a particular date at a particular fixed rate of interest. Bonds may be issued by corporations, states, cities or the federal government. The US federal government normally pays a lower rate of interest than cities, because US bonds are relatively risk-free. Bonds pay out fixed amounts of interest on a regular basis and appeal to investors seeking a regular income.

Bondfield, Margaret Grace (1873–1953) British Labour politician and trade unionist. In 1923 she became chairman of the TRADES UNION CONGRESS (TUC). As minister of Labour (1923–31), Bondfield was the first woman member of a British cabinet.

bone CONNECTIVE TISSUE that forms the skeleton of the body, protects its internal organs, serves as a lever during locomotion and when lifting objects, and stores calcium and phosphorus. Bone is composed of a strong, compact layer of COLLAGEN and calcium phosphate, and a lighter, porous inner spongy layer containing MARROW in which ERYTHROCYTES and some LEUCOCYTES are produced.

bone china Hard-paste PORCELAIN consisting of kaolin, china stone and bone ash. Josiah SPODE perfected the manufacture of bone china in the 19th century.

bongo Large African antelope of humid forests. Both sexes are red-brown with white vertical stripes and have horns. Height: up to 1.3m (4.2ft) Family Bovidae; species *Taurotragus eurycerus*.

Bonhoeffer, Dietrich (1906–45) German theologian. A Lutheran pastor, he opposed the rise of National Socialism. Arrested by the Nazis in 1943, Bonhoeffer was executed for treason after being linked with a failed conspiracy to assassinate Hitler in 1944. Among his works are *Letters from Prison* (1953) and *Christology* (1966). Bonhoeffer espoused a kind of "secular" Christianity.

Boniface, Saint (675–754) English missionary. He left England in 716 to convert the pagan Germans. For his success he was rewarded with the Archbishopric of Mainz in 751. Boniface was martyred by pagans in Friesland. He is buried in Fulda, Bavaria, and is venerated as the Apostle of Germany. His feast day is 5 June.

Boniface VIII (1235–1303) Pope (1294–1303), b. Benedetto Gaetani. To bring order to Rome and prevent schism, he imprisoned his predecessor, Celestine V. He offered the first plenary indulgence (1300) for all who made a pilgrimage to Rome.

bonito Speedy, streamlined tuna-like fish found in all warm and temperate waters, usually in schools. Bonitos are blue, black and silver, and highly valued as food and game fish. The ocean bonito (*Katsuwonus pelamis*) is also called skipjack tuna or bluefin. Family Scombridae.

Bonn City and capital of former West Germany on the River Rhine, in North Rhine-Westphalia, w Germany. Founded in the 1st century AD as a Roman military establishment, it later became the seat of the electors of Cologne (1238–1797) and was awarded to Prussia by the Congress of Vienna (1815). Bonn was capital of West Germany from 1949 until German reunification in 1990. Sights include a Romanesque cathedral and the Poppelsdorf Palace. Beethoven was born here. Industries: engineering, laboratory equipment. Pop. (1995) 293,000.

Bonnard, Pierre (1867–1947) French painter and graphic artist. Together with his lifelong friend, Jean-Edouard Vuillard, he adapted the traditions of IMPRESSIONISM to create a repertoire of sensuous domestic

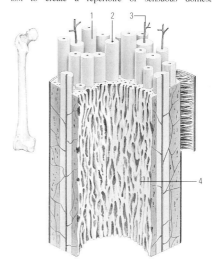

▲ **bone** A magnified cross-section of bone shows that it is composed of rod-like units (1) which have a central channel (2) containing blood vessels (3). These are surrounded by concentric layers or lamellae of collagen fibres, each arranged in a different direction from those in adjacent layers. Calcium salt crystals and bone cells (4) are embedded between the fibres.

interiors. Known as *intimiste*, his paintings are drenched in gorgeous colours. Examples include *The Terrasse Family*, *Luncheon* (1922) and *Martha in a Red Blouse* (1928).

Bonnie and Clyde American couple, Bonnie Parker (1910–34) and Clyde Barrow (1909–34), who robbed banks and shops during the era of the Depression. In 1967 their story was made into a popular film by Arthur Penn.

Bonnie Prince Charlie *See* STUART, CHARLES EDWARD

bonsai Japanese art of dwarfing woody plants and shrubs by pruning and restraining root growth; they are primarily outdoor plants and occur naturally in cliff areas. Bonsai can be 5–60cm (2–24in) tall, depending on the plant used.

booby *See* GANNET

boogie-woogie Type of JAZZ popular in the 1930s. It has a rapid, driving beat, uses BLUES themes and is generally played on the piano. The melody is played over a consistently repeated bass motif played by the left hand.

book Primarily a bound volume of printed pages, it may also be a division within a book (as in the BIBLE) or a statement of accounts. The earliest books were Egyptian writings on papyrus, of which the BOOK OF THE DEAD is often considered the first. Roman books were mostly in the form of rolls, although the Roman period also saw the emergence of the **codex**, the forerunner of the paged book. In the Middle Ages, **vellum**, a fine parchment made from animal skins, became the standard material for books, but by the 15th century they were often written on paper. Modern printed books in Europe date from the invention of movable metal type in 1454 by Johann GUTENBERG (developed earlier in China and Korea), and the first printed book was a German Latin Bible of 1455. *See also* PRINTING; PUBLISHING

bookbinding Craft and commerce of sewing and/or gluing the pages of a BOOK and fixing them between protective covers. The craft began when rolls and scrolls were replaced by the **codex**; the earliest elaborate, decorative examples were used in churches. With the invention of PRINTING, the technique remained relatively unchanged, but the demand increased greatly and other materials were needed. During the 19th century, machine-binding (casing) was introduced, and cloth was used as a binding from 1822. In the 20th century, plastics were introduced to cover books.

Booker Prize British literary prize. The Booker is the most prestigious award for new English-language novels by UK, Commonwealth or Irish writers. Recipients of the prize, first presented in 1969, have included Iris MURDOCH and V.S. NAIPAUL. In 1993, Salman RUSHDIE's *Midnight's Children* (1981) won the "Booker of Bookers".

booklouse Transparent to white, usually wingless insect found worldwide. Booklice feed on moulds in hot, humid, dusty places, such as shelves and books. Length: to 5mm (0.2in). Order Psocoptera; genus *Liposcelis*.

Book of Changes (I-Ching) Ancient Chinese book of wisdom. Although the oldest parts of the text are thought to pre-date CONFUCIUS, he is credited with the commentaries that form a part of the collection. *See also* CHINESE LITERATURE; YIN AND YANG

Book of Common Prayer *See* COMMON PRAYER, BOOK OF

book of hours Book containing the prescribed order of prayers, rites for the canonical hours and readings from the Bible. Such books, developed in the 1300s, were often lavishly decorated by miniaturists and served as status symbols. The most famous extant book of hours is the *Très Riches Heures du Duc de Berry*, illustrated in part by the LIMBOURG brothers.

Book of Kells Illuminated manuscript of the four GOSPELS in Latin. Probably begun in the late 8th century at the Irish monastery of Iona, which later migrated to Kells, County Meath, Ireland, its intricate ILLUMINATION and superb penmanship have earned it the title of "the most beautiful book in the world". After its collation in 1621 by James Usher, it was presented to Trinity College, Dublin, where it has remained.

Book of the Dead Collection of Old Egyptian texts probably dating from the 16th century BC. The papyrus texts, which incorporate mortuary texts from as early as 2350 BC, were placed in the tombs of the dead in order to help them combat the dangers of the afterlife.

Boole, George (1815–64) English mathematician. Largely self-taught, Boole was appointed (1849) professor of mathematics of Cork University. He is remembered for his invention of Boolean ALGEBRA, commonly used in COMPUTERS.

boomslang Venomous snake of the savannas of Africa. It is green or brown with a slender body and a small head. Commonly found in trees or bushes, it eats lizards, frogs and small birds. Length: to 1.5m (4.9ft). Species *Dispholidus typus*.

Boone, Daniel (1734–1820) US frontier pioneer. In 1775 he blazed the famous Wilderness Road from Virginia to Kentucky and founded the settlement of Boonesborough. During the American Revolution, Boone was captured by the Shawnee, but escaped and reached Boonesborough in time to prevent it from falling to the British and their Native-American allies.

Boötes (herdsman) Prominent constellation of the N sky; it contains the bright orange star Arcturus.

Booth, Charles (1840–1916) English social reformer who pioneered the method of social survey in his *Life and Labour of the People in London* (1891–1903). He was instrumental in gaining the passage of the Old Age Pensions Act in 1908.

Booth, John Wilkes (1838–65) US actor and assassin of Abraham LINCOLN. Booth was a Confederate sympathizer. On 14 April 1865, during a performance at Ford's Theater in Washington, D.C., he shot Lincoln, who died the next day. Booth escaped but was either shot or killed himself two weeks later.

Booth, William (1829–1912) English religious leader, founder and first general of the SALVATION ARMY. A Methodist, Booth started his own revivalist movement, which undertook evangelistic and social work among the poor. It became known as the Salvation Army in 1878 and spread to many countries. On his death he was succeeded by his son, William Bramwell Booth.

Boothroyd, Betty (1929–) Speaker of the House of Commons (1992–2000) and Labour MP (1973–2000). After a brief career as a professional dancer, Boothroyd entered politics in 1950. As the first woman speaker, she sought to modernise the British parliamentary system. She was succeeded as speaker by Michael Martin (1948–).

bootlegging Illegal supply and sale of goods that are subject to government prohibition or taxation. Bootleg also refers to unlicensed copies or cheap imitations of goods that are packaged to deceive the buyer. The name is said to derive from the practice of American frontiersmen who carried bottles of illicit liquor in the tops of their boots, for sale to Native Americans. Bootlegging blossomed during the PROHIBITION era (1920–33) in the US.

borage Hairy, annual plant native to s Europe. It has rough, oblong leaves and drooping clusters of pale blue flowers and is cultivated as a food and flavouring.

Height: up to 60cm (2ft). Family Boraginaceae; species *Borago officinalis*.

borax (hydrated sodium borate, $Na_2B_4O_7.10H_2O$) Most common borate mineral. It is found in large deposits in dried-up alkaline lakes as crusts or masses of crystals. Borax may be colourless or white, transparent or opaque. It is used to make heat-resistant glass, pottery glaze, fertilizers and pharmaceuticals.

Bordeaux City and port on the River Garonne; capital of Gironde department, sw France. There is an 11th-century Gothic cathedral, a university (1441) and many fine 18th-century buildings from a period when the slave trade brought prosperity. Bordeaux is a good deep-water inland port and serves an area famous for its fine wines and brandies. Industries: shipbuilding, oil refining, pharmaceuticals. Pop. (1990) 210,336.

Borden, Sir Robert Laird (1854–1937) Canadian statesman, prime minister (1911–20). He was elected to Parliament in 1896, and in 1901 became leader of the Conservative Party. Borden succeeded Sir Wilfrid LAURIER as prime minister. From 1917 to 1920 he headed a coalition government. Borden steered Canada through World War 1 and helped to shape the future constitutional status of the Dominion.

Border, Alan Robert (1955–) Australian cricketer. A tenacious left-handed batsman, he made his test debut in 1978. As Australia's captain (1984–94), Border led his side to three Ashes victories and won the 1987 World Cup. He retired in 1994, after playing a record number of test matches (156). Border holds records for the highest number of runs in test cricket (11,174 runs, including 27 centuries) and the most fielding catches (156).

Borders Region of se Scotland; its s boundary forms the border between Scotland and England. The administrative centre is Newtown St Boswells. The Tweed and Teviot rivers flow e through the region and meet near Kelso. The Cheviot Hills form most of its s border and the Southern Uplands its e border. Livestock farming and forestry are the major economic activities. It was the scene of many battles between the English and Scots. Area: 4,714sq km (1,820sq mi). Pop. (1991) 103,881.

boreal forest Wooded zone of northern latitudes with a cold, dry climate and a poor sandy soil. It consists primarily of conifers and stretches like a broad ribbon across the Northern Hemisphere. Its northern edge is bordered by frozen TUNDRA.

Borg, Björn (1956–) Swedish tennis player. He won five consecutive men's singles titles at Wimbledon (1976–80). In 1981 he lost in a thrilling final to John MCENROE. Borg also won six French Open titles (1974–75, 1978–81) and helped Sweden win the 1975 Davis Cup. He retired in 1983.

Borges, Jorge Luis (1899–1986) Argentinian short-story writer, poet and critic. Borges is best known for his short-story collections, *Dreamtigers* (1960), *The Book of Imaginary Beings* (1967) and *Dr. Brodie's Report* (1970). Dreamlike and poetic, they often use intellectual puzzles, and they established Borges as one of the most significant literary talents of the 20th century.

Borghese Italian princely family, originally of Siena, later Rome. Camillo Borghese (1552–1621) became pope as PAUL V in 1605. Another Camillo (1775–1832) married Marie Pauline Bonaparte, the sister of NAPOLEON I, and was made governor of Piedmont.

Borgia, Cesare (1475–1507) Italian general and political figure, brother of Lucrezia BORGIA. He was made a cardinal (1493) by his father, Pope Alexander VI, but forsook the church to embark on a military campaign

(1498–1503) to establish his dominion in central Italy. Borgia's ruthless campaigns lend credence to the theory that he was the model for Machiavelli's *The Prince*. Imprisoned by Pope Julius II, Borgia escaped to Spain, where he was killed in battle.

Borgia, Lucrezia (1480–1519) Daughter of Pope Alexander VI and sister of Cesare BORGIA. Her marriage to Giovanni Sforza (1493) was annulled by Alexander in 1497 when it failed to produce anticipated political advantages. Lucrezia's marriage to Alfonso, nephew of Alfonso II of Naples, ended with Alfonso's murder (1500) by Cesare's henchman. After the collapse of Borgia aspirations in 1503, she forsook the political intrigue for which she was notorious and lived quietly, a patron of art, at Ferrara with her third husband.

Borglum, John Gutzon (1867–1941) US sculptor. He fashioned a head of Abraham LINCOLN, which now stands in the Capitol rotunda in Washington, D.C. His last and most exacting project was to carve the heads of WASHINGTON, JEFFERSON, LINCOLN and Theodore ROOSEVELT in a rock face at Mount RUSHMORE, South Dakota. The final details were completed by his son.

boric acid (boracic acid, H_3BO_3) Soft, white crystalline solid that occurs naturally in certain volcanic hot springs. It is used as a metallurgical flux, preservative, antiseptic and an insecticide for ants and cockroaches.

Boris Godunov *See* GODUNOV, BORIS

Born, Max (1882–1970) German physicist. He was professor of physics at Göttingen University (1921–33) until the rise of Nazism forced him into exile. Born taught at the universities of Cambridge (1933–36) and Edinburgh (1936–53). In 1954, he returned to Germany. Born was a pioneer in QUANTUM MECHANICS, introducing the notion of an ORBITAL region around an atomic nucleus in which ELECTRONS can move. He shared the 1954 Nobel Prize for physics with Walther BOTHE.

Borneo Island in the Malay Archipelago, 650km (400mi) e of Singapore, se Asia. Mostly undeveloped, Borneo is the world's third largest island, and is divided into four political regions: SARAWAK (w) and SABAH (N) are states of Malaysia; BRUNEI (NW) is a former British protectorate; and KALIMANTAN (E, central and s) covers 70% of the island and forms part of Indonesia. Industries: timber, fishing. Area: 743,330sq km (287,000sq mi).

Bornu Province and former kingdom in NE Nigeria, sw of Lake Chad. From the 14th to the 19th centuries, it was the centre of a powerful Muslim empire that exported slaves and fabrics to N Africa.

Borobudur Ruins of a Buddhist monument in Central Java, built under the Sailendra dynasty *c*.800. It comprises a stupa (relic mound), mandalas (ritual diagrams) and the temple mountain, all forms of Indian GUPTA DYNASTY religious art. *See artwork* p.116

Borodin, Alexander Porfirevich (1833–87) Russian composer and chemist, one of the RUSSIAN FIVE group of composers. Borodin's works include the tone poem *In the Steppes of Central Asia* (1880) and the *Polovtsian Dances* from his opera *Prince Igor* (completed after his death by GLAZUNOV and RIMSKY-KORSAKOV).

boron (symbol B) Nonmetallic element of group III of the periodic table, isolated (1808) by Sir Humphry DAVY. It occurs in several minerals, notably kernite (its chief ore) and BORAX. It has two allotropes: **amorphous** boron is an impure brown powder; **metallic** boron is a black to silver-grey, hard crystalline material. Boron is used in semiconductors and the stable isotope B^{10} is a good neutron absorber, used in nuclear reactors and particle counters. Properties: at.no. 5; r.a.m. 10.81; r.d. 2.34 (cryst.).

2.37 (amorph.); m.p. 2,079°C (3,774°F); sublimes 2,550°C (4,622°F); most common isotope B[11] (80.22%).

Borromini, Francesco (1599–1667) Italian Baroque architect. He was the most inventive of the three masters (BERNINI and Pietro da Cortona) of Roman baroque. Borromini's hallmark was a dynamic, hexagonal design, such as the spectacular Sant' Ivo della Sapienza, Rome (1642). His masterpieces include San Carlo alle Quattro Fontane (1638–41) and Sant' Agnese (1653–55), Rome.

Borrow, George Henry (1803–81) English writer. He worked (1833–40) for the Bible Society in Russia, Spain and Portugal. Borrow's travels formed the basis for *The Zincali* (1841) and *The Bible in Spain* (1843). His literary reputation rests on three semi-autobiographical works: *Lavengro* (1851), *The Romany Rye* (1857) and *Wild Wales* (1857).

borough Originally, in medieval England, a town which had a charter granting privileges and autonomy; now it refers to an urban area granted a charter of incorporation and administered internally. Large metropolitan areas, such as New York City and London, may be divided into separate boroughs. *See also* LOCAL GOVERNMENT

borstal British system of rehabilitation for juvenile offenders between the ages of 16 and 21. The idea originated in 1895 with the Gladstone Committee, and the first institution was established at Borstal Prison, Kent, in 1902. Borstals are residential, providing education, vocational training, regular work and group counselling.

borzoi (Russian wolfhound) Sharp-sighted, speedy hunting DOG with a long narrow head. The body is deep and streamlined, with long legs and curved tail. The coat is long and silky and is usually white with darker markings. Height: (at shoulder) up to 79cm (31in).

Bosch, Hieronymus (*c*.1450–1516) Flemish painter, b. Jerome van Aken, in 's Hertogenbosch. His paintings of grotesque and fantastic visions based on religious themes led to accusations of heresy and greatly influenced 20th-century SURREALISM. His paintings explore the distressing consequences of human sin and innocent figures besieged by horrifying physical torments. About 40 examples of his work survive, including *The Temptation of St Anthony*, *The Garden of Earthly Delights* (often considered his masterpiece) and *Adoration of the Magi*.

Bose, Satyendranath (1894–1974) Indian physicist and mathematician who contributed to the theory of QUANTUM MECHANICS and STATISTICAL MECHANICS. Bose made the initial advances to describe the statistical

properties of certain ELEMENTARY PARTICLES (now called BOSONS). These particles, which include all those that mediate force (like the PHOTON which carries the ELECTRO-MAGNETIC FORCE), all have the property that any number of them can occupy the same quantum state: that is they do not obey Enrico FERMI's EXCLUSION PRINCIPLE. Bose's work was developed by EINSTEIN and the statistics which such particles obey are called **Bose-Einstein statistics**.

Bosnia-Herzegovina Balkan republic in SE Europe. Bosnia-Herzegovina is one of the five republics that emerged from the break-up of the former Federal People's Republic of YUGOSLAVIA. It consists of two main regions – Bosnia in the N, with SARAJEVO as the capital; and Herzegovina in the S, with Mostar the main city. The E half of the nation is dominated by the DINARIC ALPS which slope down gradually to the W. The River Sava, a tributary of the Danube, forms most of its N border with CROATIA. Bosnia-Herzegovina has a narrow, 20km (13mi), outlet to the Adriatic Sea at Neum. **Climate and Vegetation** Coastal areas experience dry, sunny summers and mild, moist winters. Inland, the climate is more extreme, with hot, dry summers and bitterly cold winters. Forests of beech, oak and pine grow in the N. The SW is an arid limestone plateau, interspersed with farmland. **History and Politics** SLAVS settled in the region *c*.1,400 years ago. Bosnia was settled by Serbs in the 7th century and conquered by Ottoman Turks in 1463. The persistence of serfdom led to a peasant revolt (1875). The Congress of Berlin (1878) handed Bosnia-Herzegovina to the AUSTRO-HUNGARIAN EMPIRE, and it was annexed in 1908. Serbian nationalism intensified, and in 1914 Archduke FRANZ FERDINAND was assassinated in Sarajevo, precipitating World War 1. In 1918, Bosnia-Herzegovina was annexed to SERBIA and incorporated into Yugoslavia in 1929. In World War 2, the region became part of the German puppet state of Croatia. In 1946, Bosnia-Herzegovina became a constituent member of TITO's socialist federal republic. In 1991, the republic disintegrated with the secession of Croatia, SLOVENIA and MACEDONIA. Fearing the creation of a Greater Serbia, Croats and Muslims pushed for independence. In March 1992, a referendum, boycotted by Serbian parties, voted for independence. Alija IZETBEGOVIĆ became president of the new state. War broke out between Bosnian government forces and the Serb-dominated Federal Yugoslav Army (JNA). The JNA overran the republic and besieged the government in Saravejo. International pressure forced the JNA to withdraw. The JNA handed its weapons to Bosnian Serbs, who established a separate Serb republic led by Radovan KARADŽIĆ (August 1992). Muslims were forced from their villages in a deliberate act of "ethnic cleansing". In late 1992, the UN deployed peacekeeping forces to distribute humanitarian aid to the starved capital of Sarajevo. In 1993, the UN declared a number of "safe areas" – government-held enclaves where Muslims would not be shelled or persecuted. In February 1994, Bosnian Serbs attacked the enclaves of Sarajevo and Gorazde, prompting UN air-strikes. The governments of Bosnia and Bosnian Croats announced a cease-fire and the formation of a Muslim-Croat Federation. The Dayton Peace Treaty (December 1995) agreed to preserve Bosnia-Herzegovina as a single state but partitioned it between the Muslim-Croat Federation (51%) and Bosnian Serbs (Republika Srpska, 49%). The agreement deployed 60,000 NATO troops as part of a Peace Implementation Force (IFOR). KARADŽIĆ and the Bosnian Serb army leader Ratko MLADIĆ were indicted for war crimes and forced to resign. In 1996 elections Izetbegović was re-elected as

▲ **Borobudur** One of the world's greatest Buddhist shrines, Borobudur was built in the early 9th century to a unique plan involving colossal resources; 570,000cu m (2 million cu ft) of stone were moved from a river bed, dressed, positioned and carved with countless spouts, urns and other embellishments. The walls are covered with reliefs relating to Buddhist doctrine and there are altogether 504 shrines with seated Buddhas.

BOSNIA-HERZEGOVINA
AREA: 51,129sq km (19,745 sq mi)
POPULATION: 4,601,000
CAPITAL (POPULATION): Sarajevo (526,000)

---

head of a tripartite presidency, including a Serb and a Croat representative. NATO troops remained as a "dissuasion" force (DFOR). In 1998, the Serbian nationalist Nikola Poplasen was elected president of Republika Srpska but was dismissed (1999) by the international community's High Representative, Carlos Westendorp, after attempting to oust prime minister Milorad Dorik.
Economy Excluding Macedonia, Bosnia was the least developed of the former republics of Yugoslavia. Its economy has been shattered by the war.

boson ELEMENTARY PARTICLE that transmits FUNDAMENTAL FORCES, such as PHOTONS and gluons (the particles that hold QUARKS together). Bosons have an integer SPIN and are not covered by the EXCLUSION PRINCIPLE. This means that the number of bosons occupying the same quantum state is not restricted. They are named after the physicist Satyendranath BOSE. *See also* FERMION

Bosporus (Karadeniz Bogazi) Narrow strait joining the Sea of Marmara with the Black Sea and separating European and Asiatic Turkey. It is an important strategic and commercial waterway, controlled by the Turks since 1452. Length: 30km (19mi).

Boston State capital and seaport of Massachusetts, at the mouth of the Charles River on Massachusetts Bay. Founded in 1630, it became a Puritan stronghold and the scene of several incidents leading to the outbreak of the American Revolution. A religious and cultural centre, Boston is the home of many important educational establishments, including Boston University and Harvard Medical School. HARVARD UNIVERSITY and the Massachusetts Institute of Technology (MIT) are across the river in Cambridge. Industries: publishing, banking and insurance, shipbuilding. Pop. (1990) 574,283.

Boston Tea Party (1773) Protest by a group of Massachusetts colonists, disguised as Mohawks and led by Samuel ADAMS, against the Tea Act and, more generally, against "taxation without representation". The Tea Act, passed by the British Parliament in 1773, withdrew duty on tea exported to the colonies. It enabled the EAST INDIA COMPANY to sell tea directly to the colonies without first going to Britain and resulted in colonial merchants being undersold. The protesters boarded three British ships and threw their cargo of tea into Boston harbour. The British retaliated by closing the harbour.

Boswell, James (1740–95) Scottish biographer and travel writer. As a young man, he travelled widely in Europe, meeting VOLTAIRE and Jean-Jacques ROUSSEAU. An inveterate hero-worshipper, Boswell found his vocation as the friend and biographer of Samuel JOHNSON. His monumental *Life of Samuel Johnson* (1791) is regarded as one of the greatest biographies in English. Boswell's other works include *An Account of Corsica* (1768) and *The Journal of a Tour to the Hebrides* (1785), an account of his travels with Johnson. His often disconcertingly frank journals paint a colourful picture of contemporary life.

Bosworth Field, Battle of (1485) Final conflict in the English Wars of the ROSES, fought near Bosworth, Leicestershire. RICHARD III was defeated by Henry Tudor. Henry, who claimed to represent the Lancastrian royal house, invaded England from France. Richard was killed,and Henry claimed the throne from HENRY VII.

botanical garden Large garden preserve for display, research and teaching purposes. The first botanical gardens were established during the Middle Ages. In the 16th century, gardens existed in Pisa, Bologna, Padua and Leiden. Aromatic and medicinal herbs still exist in the Botanical Garden of Padua. The first US botanical garden was established by John Bartram in Philadelphia in 1728. Famous botanical gardens include the Royal Botanical Gardens in Kew, near London (1759); Botanical Gardens of Berlin-Dahlem (1646); and Botanical Gardens in Schönbrunn, Vienna (1753).

botany Study of PLANTS and ALGAE, including their classification, structure, physiology, reproduction and evolution. The discipline used to be studied in two parts: lower (non-flowering) plants, which included the algae, mosses and ferns; and higher (seed-bearing) plants, including most flowers, trees and shrubs. Botany also studies the importance of plants to humans.

Botany Bay Large, shallow inlet immediately s of Port Jackson, Sydney Harbour, New South Wales, Australia. It was visited in 1700 by Captain James COOK, who named it because of its flora. It is fed by the Georges and Woronora rivers, and is *c*.1.6km (1mi) wide at its mouth.

botfly Any of several families of stout, hairy, black-and-white to grey fly. Its larvae are parasites of livestock, small animals and even humans. The botfly that attacks deer is possibly the swiftest insect, flying at 80km/h (50mph). Order Diptera; family Oestridae.

Botha, Louis (1862–1919) South African statesman and military leader. In the SOUTH AFRICAN WAR (1899–1902) he was an outstanding commander. Amoderate, Botha advocated reconciliation with the British and became (1910) first prime minister of the Union of SOUTH AFRICA.

Botha, P.W. (Pieter Willem) (1916–) South African statesman. The longest-serving member of the APARTHEID regime, Botha entered parliament in 1948. As defence minister (1966–78), he expanded South Africa's armed forces and was responsible for the military involvement in Angola. Botha became prime minister (1978) and undertook limited reform of apartheid. In 1980, he established the Southwest Africa Territorial Force, as part of a destabilization policy of South Africa's neighbours. Botha became (1980) South Africa's first president and was re-elected in 1987. In 1989, he suffered a stroke and, amid increasing National Party factionalism, resigned and was replaced by F.W. DE KLERK.

Botham, Ian Terence (1955–) English cricketer. In 1974, he made his county debut for Somerset. He had an auspicious test debut against Australia (1977). Botham was one of test cricket's greatest all-rounders, scoring 5,200 runs (including 14 centuries) and taking 373 wickets. In 1979, he became the first player to score a century and take 10 wickets in a test. In 1981, he was largely responsible for England regaining The ASHES. In 1996, he was appointed England coach.

Bothe, Walther Wilhelm Georg Franz (1891–1957) German physicist. During World War 2, he worked on Germany's nuclear energy project and built its first cyclotron. Bothe shared the 1954 Nobel Prize for physics with Max BORN for his development of the coincidence method, which can detect two particles emitted simultaneously from the same nucleus during radioactive decay.

Bothwell, James Hepburn, 4th Earl of (1536–78) Scottish nobleman, third husband of MARY, QUEEN OF SCOTS. Bothwell subdued a rebellion (1565), and after Mary's second husband, Lord Darnley, was implicated in the murder of her secretary, David Rizzio, he became the queen's sole adviser. He was responsible for the murder

(1567) of Darnley, and subsequently married Mary. Faced by a rebellion of Scottish nobles, Bothwell fled abroad and died insane in a Danish prison.

Botswana Landlocked republic in the heart of S Africa; the capital is GABORONE. **Land and climate** Most of the land is flat or gently rolling, with an average height of c.1,000m (3,300ft) and more hilly country in the E. The KALAHARI covers much of Botswana. Most of the S has no permanent streams, but large depressions form inland drainage basins in the N, such as the swamps of the Okavango River delta. Gaborone lies in the wetter and more populous E. Temperatures are high in the summer months (October–April), but winter months are much cooler. The average annual rainfall varies from more than 400mm (16in) in E Botswana to less than 200mm (18in) in the SW. **History** The earliest inhabitants of the region were the nomadic SAN. The Tswana now form the majority population. They settled in E Botswana more than 1,000 years ago. Their arrival led the San to move into the Kalahari. Today, the San form a tiny minority of the population, and many live in permanent settlements. Britain ruled the area as the Bechuanaland Protectorate between 1885 and 1966, after which Botswana gained independence and Seretse Khama became president. He was succeeded (1980) by Ketumile Masire. Masire retired in 1998 and was succeeded by Festus Mogae. **Economy** At independence, Botswana was one of Africa's poorest countries. Many people migrated to work in the mines of South Africa. Today, Botswana is one of Africa's wealthiest nations (1995 GDP per capita $US5,580) and the world's third-largest producer. Its economy was boosted by the discovery of diamonds which account for 70% of its exports. Coal, copper and nickel are valuable resources. Agriculture employs over 40% of the workforce.

Botticelli, Sandro (1444–1510) (Alessandro di Mariano Filipepi) Florentine RENAISSANCE painter. Loved by the PRE-RAPHAELITE BROTHERHOOD and an important influence on ART NOUVEAU, Botticelli was part of a late 15th-century movement which admired the ornamental, linear qualities of GOTHIC ART. He is best known for his mythological allegories, *Primavera* (c.1478), *The Birth of Venus* and *Pallas and the Centaur*. Botticelli was one of the few privileged to decorate the Sistine Chapel in Rome (1481) and was the most popular painter in Florence. He made a series of delicate pen drawings for a copy of Dante's *Divine Comedy*.

botulism Rare but potentially lethal form of food poisoning caused by a toxin produced by the bacterium *Clostridium botulinum*. The toxin attacks the nervous system, causing paralysis and cessation of breathing. The most likely source of botulism is imperfectly canned meat. Botulinum toxin is used medicinally as a treatment for some neuromuscular disorders.

Boucher, François (1703–70) French painter, decorator and engraver. His style was the epitome of ROCOCO frivolity and was distinctly risqué in tone. Boucher was immensely successful and widely imitated. He produced over 11,000 historical, mythological, genre and landscape paintings. Boucher was first painter to Louis XV.

Boucicault, Dion (Dionysius Lardner) (c.1822–90) Anglo-Irish playwright and actor-manager. He was

responsible for the growth of the touring company. A prolific dramatist, Boucicault wrote and adapted nearly 300 plays. The most successful were his comedies and romantic melodramas, such as *London Assurance* (1841) and *The Octoroon* (1859). He was one of the greatest figures of Victorian theatre.

Bougainville, Louis Antoine de (1729–1811) French navigator. A veteran of the French and Indian Wars in Canada, he commanded the first French naval force to circumnavigate the globe (1766–69). Important botanical and astronomical studies were made during the voyage, and Bougainville claimed many of the Pacific islands for France, rediscovering the Solomon Islands. He fought in the American Revolution but was disgraced by a French defeat (1782) in the Caribbean.

Bougainville Volcanic island in the SW Pacific Ocean, E of New Guinea; a territory of Papua New Guinea. It was discovered in 1768 by Louis de BOUGAINVILLE. The island was under German control from 1884 and then under Australian administration after 1914 and again in 1945. It has been the scene of guerrilla warfare since the late 1980s. Kieta is the chief port. Industries: copper mining, copra, cocoa, timber. Area: 10,049sq km (3,880sq mi). Pop. (1990 est.) 128,000.

bougainvillea Tropical, woody vine native to S America, often grown as a garden plant. Its flowers have purple or red bracts. It was named after Louis de BOUGAINVILLE. Family Nyctaginaceae; genus *Bougainvillea*.

Boulanger, Nadia (1887–1979) French music teacher. She was one of the foremost teachers of composition in the 20th century; her pupils included Aaron Copland and Jean Françaix. In the 1930s, Boulanger became the first woman to conduct the Boston Symphony Orchestra and the New York Philharmonic. Her sister, Lili Boulanger (1893–1918), was a composer.

Boulez, Pierre (1925–) French conductor and composer. Boulez aimed to extend serialism into all aspects of a composition, including rhythm and dynamics. His works for voice and orchestra have received much attention, especially *Le Marteau sans maître* (1954) and *Pli selon pli* (1960). Boulez was conductor of the BBC Symphony Orchestra (1971–74) and the New York Philharmonic (1971–78). As director (1975–) of the French Institute for Acoustic and Musical Research (IRCAM), he explored the use of computers in musical composition.

Boulle, André Charles (1642–1732) (André Buhl) French cabinetmaker maintained in the Louvre Palace by Louis XIV as design for the court. Boulle created a distinctive marquetry of tortoiseshell and gilded brass to which he gave his name. There are examples of his work at Versailles and in the Louvre.

Boult, Sir Adrian (1889–1983) English conductor, widely known for his interpretation of early 20th-century English composers. Boult was musical director and principal conductor (1930–50) of the BBC Symphony Orchestra and principal conductor of the London Philharmonic Orchestra (1950–57).

Bounty, Mutiny on the (28 April 1789) British mutiny that took place near Tonga in the South Pacific Ocean. Fletcher Christian led a successful rebellion against Captain William BLIGH, and Bligh and 18 loyal crew members were set adrift. Christian and some of the mutineers founded a colony on Pitcairn Island.

Bourbons European dynastic family, descendants of the CAPETIANS. The ducal title was created in 1327 and continued until 1527. A cadet branch, the Bourbon-Vendôme line, won the kingdom of Navarre. The Bourbons ruled France from 1589 (when Henry of Navarre

---

BOTSWANA
AREA: 581,730sq km (224,606sq mi)
POPULATION: 1,822,000
CAPITAL (POPULATION): Gaborone (182,000)

became HENRY IV) until the FRENCH REVOLUTION (1789). Two members of the family, LOUIS XVIII and CHARLES X, reigned (1814–30) after the restoration of the monarchy. In 1700, the Bourbons became the ruling family of Spain when PHILIP V, grandson of LOUIS XIV of France, assumed the throne. His descendants mostly continued to rule Spain until 1931, when the Second Republic was declared. JUAN CARLOS I, a Bourbon, was restored to the Spanish throne in 1975.

bourgeoisie (middle class) Term originally applied to artisans and craftsmen who lived in medieval French towns. Up to the late 18th century, it was a propertied but relatively unprivileged class, often of urban merchants and tradesmen, who helped speed the decline of the FEUDAL SYSTEM. The 19th century advent of CAPITALISM led to the expansion of the bourgeoise and its division into the **high** (industrialists and financiers) and **petty** (tradesmen and clerical workers) bourgeoisie.

Bourguiba, Habib (1903–2000) First president of Tunisia (1957–87). In 1954, he began negotiations that culminated in Tunisian independence (1956). He became prime minister and, after the abolition of the monarchy, was elected president. In 1975, he was proclaimed president-for-life. Bourguiba maintained a pro-French, autocratic rule until, old and ill, he was overthrown in a coup led by Ben Ali.

Bourke-White, Margaret (1906–71) US photo-journalist. Bourke-White produced dramatic photo-essays for *Time*, *Life* and *Fortune* magazines on a variety of subjects, including the rural South of the 1930s, World War 2, concentration camp victims, the Korean War, South Africa, India and world political leaders.

Boutros-Ghali, Boutros (1922–) Egyptian politician, sixth secretary-general of the UN (1992–96). As Egypt's foreign affairs minister (1977–91), he was involved in much of the Middle East peace negotiations. Boutros-Ghali briefly served as Egypt's prime minister (1991–92) before becoming the first African secretary general of the UN. Early in his term, he faced civil-war crises in the Balkans, Somalia and Rwanda. An independent secretary general, Boutros-Ghali managed to alienate US opinion.

bovine spongiform encephalopathy (BSE) In cattle, degeneration of the brain caused by infectious particles or PRIONS; it may be transmitted by feeding on infected meat. It is also known as "mad cow disease". *See also* CREUTZFELD-JAKOB DISEASE (CJD)

Bowen, Elizabeth Dorothea Cole (1899–1973) Anglo-Irish novelist and short-story writer. Her childhood in Dublin is remembered in *Seven Winters* and *Bowen's Court* (both 1942). Bowen's subtle prose manages to capture the nuances of character and evoke the landscape and weather of the British Isles. Her best known novels are *The Death of the Heart* (1938), *The Heat of the Day* (1949) and *Eva Trout* (1969).

bowerbird Forest bird of New Guinea and Australia. The male builds a simple but brightly ornamented bower to attract the female. After mating, the female lays 1–3 eggs. Adults, mainly terrestrial, have short wings and legs and variously coloured plumage. Length: 25-38cm (10–15in). Family Ptilonorhynchidae.

Bowie, David (1947–) English pop singer, b. David Jones. Fusing a bizarre theatricality to progressive pop, he graduated to international stardom with his album *Ziggy Stardust* (1972). Other albums include *Hunky Dory* (1972) and *Heroes* (1977). Bowie made his film debut in *The Man Who Fell to Earth* (1976).

Bowie, Jim (James) (1796–1836) US frontiersman. He moved to Texas from Louisiana in 1828 and married

the daughter of the Mexican vice-governor. By 1832 he had joined the US colonists who opposed the Mexican government. Bowie was appointed a colonel in the Texas army (1835) and killed at the ALAMO (1836).

Bowles, Paul (1910–99) US writer and composer. He spent his early life composing for opera, ballet and film. From 1952, Bowles resided in Tangier, Morocco. His characteristic theme is the sense of dislocation and spiritual emptiness the Westerner feels when confronted by the "otherness" of the Orient. His works include the novels *The Sheltering Sky* (1949) and *The Spider's House* (1955) and the short-story collection *Pages from Cold Point* (1968). He translated several Moroccan writers.

bowling Indoor sport in which a ball is bowled at pins. It originated in Germany and was brought to the US by Dutch immigrants in the 17th century. Known as ninepins, it soon became a popular gambling game and, when it was banned, a tenth pin was added to circumvent the law. **Ten-pin** bowling is now an highly popular sport. Two players or teams bowl at pins set on a triangular base. Points are scored according to the number of pins knocked over.

bowls Game popular in Britain and Commonwealth countries, in which a series of bowls (woods) are delivered underarm to stop as close as possible to a small white target ball (jack). A point is scored for each bowl closer to the jack than the best opposition bowl.

box Evergreen tree or shrub found in tropical and temperate regions in Europe, North American and W Asia. The shrub is popular for TOPIARY, and boxwood is used for musical instruments. The 100 species include English, or common *Buxus sempervirens*, and larger *Buxus balearica* that grows to 24m (80ft). Family Buxaceae.

boxer Smooth-haired, working DOG bred originally in Germany. It has a broad head with a deep, short, square muzzle and its deep-chested body is set on strong, medium-length legs. The tail is commonly docked, and its coat is generally red or brown, with black and white markings. Height: to 61cm (24in) at the shoulder.

Boxer Rebellion (1898–1900) Anti-western uprising in China. The OPIUM WARS resulted in greater European involvement in China and defeat in the first of the Sino-Japanese Wars further weakened the Qing dynasty. In a bid to restore Manchu authority, the empress dowager CIXI supported the attempts of the Society of Righteous and Harmonious Fists (hence the "Boxers") to forcibly remove Western influence from China. Nationwide attacks on foreigners and Chinese Christians left more than 200 dead. In June 1900, the Boxers began a two-month long siege of Beijing. An international expeditionary force relieved the foreign legations and suppressed the rising. China agreed to pay an indemnity.

boxing Sport of fist-fighting between two people wearing padded gloves within a roped-off ring. Boxers are classified in eight divisions according to weight: minimum weight (under 48kg/105lb), fly, bantam, feather, light, welter, middle and heavyweight (over 88kg/195lb). Professional bouts are scheduled for four to 15 rounds of three minutes' duration. A fight is controlled by a referee in the ring and ends when there is a knockout (a boxer is unable to get to his feet by the count of ten) or a technical knockout (one fighter is seriously injured). If both boxers finish the scheduled number of rounds, the winner is determined by a ringside referee or three judges. Boxing emerged from bareknuckle fighting when the Marquis of QUEENSBURY's rules introduced timed rounds and padded gloves in 1866. The international sport is now controlled by three major rival organizations: the World Boxing

Association (WBA), the World Boxing Council (WBC) and the International Boxing Federation (IBF).

Boycott, Geoffrey (1940–) English cricketer. He was captain of Yorkshire (1971–79). In 1971, Boycott became the first batsman to average more than 100 runs in an English first-class season. He played in 108 test matches for England and his total of 8,114 test runs is surpassed only by Graham GOOCH and David GOWER. In 1982, Boycott was banned from test cricket for touring South Africa. He is now a television sports commentator.

boycott Refusal to deal with a person, organization or country, either in terms of trade or other activities, such as sport. The term originated in 1880 when Irish tenant farmers refused to work for, supply or speak with Charles Boycott, an agent of their landlord. *See also* EMBARGO

Boyd Orr, John, 1st Baron (1880–1971) Scottish nutritionist. He was the first director (1945–48) of the United Nations Food and Agriculture Oragnization. In 1949, Boyd Orr was awarded the Nobel Peace Prize for his efforts to prevent famine.

Boyle, Robert (1627–91) British chemist, b. Ireland. He is often regarded as the father of modern chemistry. At his laboratories in Oxford and London, he conducted research into air, vacuum, metals, combustion and sound. Boyle's *Sceptical Chymist* (1661) proposed an early atomic theory of MATTER. He made an efficient vacuum pump, which he used to establish (1662) BOYLE'S LAW. Boyle formulated the first chemical definitions of an element and a reaction.

Boyle's law Volume of a GAS at constant temperature is inversely proportional to the pressure. This means as pressure increases, the volume of a gas at constant temperature decreases. First stated (1662) by Robert BOYLE, it is a special case of the ideal gas law (involving a hypothetical gas that perfectly obeys the gas laws).

Boyne, Battle of the (1 July 1690) Engagement near Drogheda, Ireland, which confirmed the Protestant succession to the English throne. The forces of the Protestant WILLIAM III of England defeated those of the Catholic JAMES II.

Boy Scouts Worldwide social organization for boys that stresses outdoor knowledge and good citizenship. It was founded (1908) in Britain by Lord BADEN-POWELL with the motto, "Be prepared". A companion organization for girls (Girl Guides, UK; Girl Scouts, US) was founded in 1910. By the 1990s the scouting movement had c.14 million members (including the Cub Scouts and Brownies) in more than 100 countries.

Brabant Province of central Belgium; the capital is BRUSSELS. Mainly Flemish-speaking, it is a densely populated and fertile agricultural region. Industries: chemicals, metallurgy, food processing. Area: 3,372sq km (1,302sq mi). Pop. (1970 est.) 2,178,000.

Brachiopoda (lamp shells) Phylum of c.260 species of small, bottom-dwelling, marine invertebrates. They are similar in outward appearance to bivalve MOLLUSCS. They live attached to rocks by a pedicle (stalk) or buried in mud or sand. There are 75 genera including *Lingula*, the oldest known animal genus. Most modern brachiopods are less than 5cm (2in) across. More than 30,000 fossil species have been found and described.

bracken Persistent, weedy FERN found worldwide. It has an underground stem that can travel 1.8m (6ft) and sends up fronds that may reach 4.6m (15ft) in some climates. The *typica* variety is widespread in Britain. Family Dennstaedtiaceae; species *Pteridium aquilinum*.

bracket fungus (shelf fungus) Any of a large family (Polyporaceae) of common arboreal fungi that have spore-bearing tubes under the cap. Bracket fungi are usually hard and leathery or wood-like and have no stems. They often cover old logs, and their parasitic activity may kill living trees. Some are edible when young.

bract Modified leaf found on a flower's stalk or base. Bracts are usually small and scale-like. In some species they are large and brightly coloured, such as POINSETTIA.

Bradbury, Ray Douglas (1920–) US novelist and short-story writer. Best known for his imaginative science fiction, Bradbury's work includes *The Martian Chronicles* (1950), *Fahrenheit 451* (1953) and *Something Wicked This Way Comes* (1962). He has also written plays, poetry, children's stories, screenplays and volumes of essays, such as *Journey to Far Metaphor* (1994).

Braddock, Edward (1695–1755) British general in the FRENCH AND INDIAN WARS. As commander-in-chief of the British forces in North America, he led the attack on the French stronghold of Fort Dequesne (1755). Progress was slow and, on the advice of George WASHINGTON, Braddock led an advance party. Ambushed by Native Americans, the party was routed and Braddock killed.

Bradford, William (1590–1657) American colonial governor and signatory of the Mayflower Compact. He emigrated to America as one of the PILGRIMS on the *Mayflower* (1620). Bradford was elected governor of Plymouth Colony in 1621 and re-elected for 30 years. He helped draw up a body of laws for the colony in 1636 and wrote a *History of Plymouth Plantation, 1620–46*.

Bradford City in the Aire Valley, West Yorkshire, N England. Since the 14th century, it has been a centre for woollen and worsted manufacturing, but industry has diversified. The city is home to one of England's largest Asian communities. It has a university (established 1966). Industries: textiles, electrical engineering, microelectronics. Pop. (1994) 357,000.

Bradley, Omar Nelson (1893–1981) US general. In World War 2, he commanded the 2nd Corps in N Africa

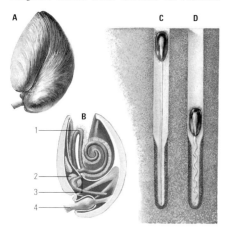

▲ **Brachiopoda** The marine animal known as a brachiopod, or lamp shell, lives in holes in mud flats. It comprises (A) a hinged shell and a stalk with which it grips the rocks. The cross-section (B) shows; lophophore (1) which bears tentacles for feeding; digestive gland (2); mouth (3); and stalks (4). When feeding, *Lingula* (C), rests at the surface of its burrow using feathery cilia to filter water for food particles. When disturbed, its stalk contracts, drawing the animal into the burrow (D), out of sight and reach of its potential predator.

and the invasion of Sicily (1943), and led the 1st Army in the Normandy invasion (1944). Bradley served (1948–49) as chief of staff of the US army and first chairman of the joint chiefs of staff (1949–53).

Bradman, Sir Don (Donald George) (1908–) Australian cricketer and sports administrator, probably the greatest batsmen the game has ever seen. Bradman made his test debut for Australia in 1928 and acted as captain from 1936 until his retirement in 1948. His test record was 6,996 runs in 52 games (an average of 99.94), including 29 centuries and a highest score of 334 (against England at Leeds in 1930). During his first-class career Bradman made a total of 28,067 runs (averaging 95.14), including 117 centuries. He was knighted in 1949.

Braganza Ruling dynasty of Portugal (1640–1910). The dynasty was founded by the Duke of Braganza, who ruled (1640–56) as JOHN IV. During the NAPOLEONIC WARS, the royal family fled to Brazil, then a Portuguese colony. A branch of the house ruled as emperors of Brazil (1822–89).

Bragg, Sir (William) Lawrence (1890–1971) English physicist, b. Australia. He was director (1938–53) of the Cavendish Laboratory at Cambridge. With his father, Sir William Henry Bragg (1862–1942), he determined the mathematics involved in X-ray DIFFRACTION, showed how to compute X-ray wavelengths, and studied CRYSTAL structure by X-ray diffraction. For these advances, they were jointly awarded the 1915 Nobel Prize for physics.

Brahe, Tycho (1546–1601) Danish astronomer. He became the most skilled observer of the pre-telescope era, expert in making accurate naked-eye measurements of the stars and planets. He built an observatory on the island of Hven (1576) and calculated the orbit of the comet seen in 1577. This, together with his study of the supernova, showed that ARISTOTLE was wrong in picturing an unchanging heaven. Brahe could not, however, accept the world system put forward by COPERNICUS. In his own planetary theory (the Tychonian system), the planets move around the Sun, and the Sun itself, like the Moon, moves round the stationary Earth. In 1597, he settled in Prague, where Johann KEPLER became his assistant.

Brahma Creator god in HINDUISM, later identified as one of the three gods in the Trimurti. Brahma is usually thought equal to the gods VISHNU and SHIVA, but later myths tell of him being born from Vishnu's navel. There is only one major temple to Brahma, located at Pushkar, Rajasthan, NW India.

Brahman (Atman) In HINDUISM, the supreme soul of the universe. The omnipresent Brahman sustains the Earth. According to the UPANISHADS, the individual soul is identified with Brahman. Brahman is not God, but rather is *neti neti* (not this, not that) or indescribable.

Brahman cattle (zebu) Many domestic varieties of a species of OX native to India. Tan, grey or black with a hump over the shoulders, brahmans have drooping ears and a large dewlap. Family Bovidae; species *Bos indicus*.

Brahmanism Term denoting an early phase of HINDUISM. It was characterized by acceptance of the VEDAS as divine revelation. The Brahmanas, the major text of Brahmanism, are the ritualistic books comprising the greater portion of Vedic literature. They were complemented by the UPANISHADS. In the course of time deities of post-Vedic origin began to be worshiped and the influence of Brahmanist priests declined.

Brahmaputra River in S Asia. Rising in SW Tibet, it flows E into China, then S into India and WSW across India into Bangladesh (where it becomes the River YAMUNA). Before emptying into the Bay of BENGAL, it

forms (with the GANGES and Meghna rivers) a vast delta. Length: *c.*2,900km (1,800mi).

Brahmin (Brahman) Priestly CASTE that was the highest-ranking of the four *varnas* (social classes) in India during the late Vedic period, the era of BRAHMANISM. The term also denotes a member of that caste. Brahmin were believed to be ritually purer than other castes, and they alone could perform certain spiritual and ritual duties. The recitation of the VEDAS was their preserve, and for hundreds of years, they were the only caste to receive an education and so controlled Indian scholarship. With the later development of HINDUISM as a popular religion, their priestly influence declined, but their secular influence grew, and their social supremacy and privileged status have changed little over the centuries.

Brahmo Samaj (Hindi, Society of God) Indian religious movement, founded (1828) by Ram Mohan Roy in Calcutta. Roy argued for a monotheistic HINDUISM that embraced social reforms. In 1842, Brahmo Samaj was revived by Debendranath Tagore (1817–1905). In 1850 Tagore rejected the Vedic scriptures and a split emerged between the social reformers and the religious reformers.

Brahms, Johannes (1833–97) German composer. Encouraged by his friends Robert and Clara SCHUMANN, Brahms began to earn a living as a composer at the age of 30. He used classical forms rather than the less-strict programmatic style that was becoming popular, and he was a master of contrapuntal HARMONY. Brahms composed in all major musical genres except opera. Among his major works are the *German Requiem* (1868), the *Variations on the St Antony Chorale* (1863), the Violin Concerto in D (1878), four symphonies (1876–1885), two piano concertos (1858, 1881) and *Hungarian Dances* (1873).

Braille System of reading and writing for the blind. It was invented by Louis Braille (1809–52), who lost his sight at the age of three. Braille was a scholar, and later a teacher, at the National Institute of Blind Youth, Paris. He developed a system of embossed dots to enable blind people to read by touch. This was first published in 1829, and a more complete form appeared in 1837.

brain Mass of nerve tissue which regulates all physical and mental activity; it is continuous with the spinal cord. Weighing *c.*1.5kg (3.3lb) in the adult (*c.*2% of body weight), the human brain has three parts: the **hindbrain**, where basic physiological processes, such as breathing and the heartbeat are coordinated; the **midbrain** links the hindbrain and the **forebrain**, which is the seat of all higher functions and attributes (personality, intellect, memory, emotion), as well as being involved in sensation and initiating voluntary movement. *See also* CENTRAL NERVOUS SYSTEM; CEREBRUM; MIND *See artwork* p.122

brain damage Result of any harm done to brain tissue causing the death of nerve cells. It may arise from a number of causes, such as oxygen deprivation, brain or other disease, or head injury. The nature and extent of damage varies. Sudden failure of the oxygen supply to the brain may result in widespread (global) damage, whereas a blow to the head may affect only one part of the brain (local damage). Common effects of brain damage include weakness of one or more limbs, impaired balance, memory loss and personality change; epilepsy may develop.

brain disorder Disturbance of physical or mental function due to abnormality or disease of the brain. Brain disorders should be distinguished from psychological (psychogenic) mental disturbances in which the functioning of the brain itself is not impaired. Brain disorders are associated with impairment of memory, orientation, comprehension and judgment, and also by shallowness of emotional expression. Secondary personality changes may occur, depending upon such factors as the strength and type of personality and the amount of psychological and social stress present. **Acute** disorders are temporary and are generally due to disruption of brain function rather than destruction of brain tissue. They may be caused by such things as infection, drug intoxication and brain trauma. **Chronic** brain disorders are irreversible and include such things as CONGENITAL DISORDER, hereditary disease, senility and BRAIN DAMAGE.

brain stem Stalk-like portion of the BRAIN in vertebrates that includes everything except the CEREBELLUM and the CEREBRAL HEMISPHERES. It provides a channel for all signals passing between the spinal cord and the higher parts of the brain. It also controls automatic functions, such as breathing and heartbeat.

brake Device for slowing the speed of a vehicle or machine. Braking can be accomplished by a mechanical, hydraulic (liquid) or pneumatic (air) system that presses a non-rotating part into contact with a rotating

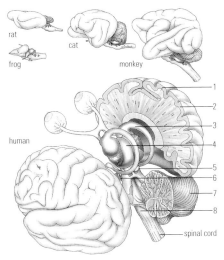

rat
cat
frog
monkey

human

1
2
3
4
5
6
7
8

spinal cord

▲ **brain** The vertebrate brain has three major structural and functional regions – the forebrain, the midbrain, and the hindbrain. In primitive animals, such as amphibians, the forebrain is concerned with smell, the midbrain with vision, and the hindbrain with balance and hearing. In higher animals, such as rats, cats, monkeys, and humans, parts of the brain have adapted to meet the needs of the organism. Most notably, part of the **forebrain**, the cerebrum (1), developed into a complex, deeply fissured structure. It comprises large regions concerned with association, reasoning and judgment. Its outer layer, the cortex (2), contains areas that coordinate movement and sensory information. The limbic system (3) controls emotional responses, such as fear. The thalamus (4) coordinates sensory and motor signals, and relays them to the cerebrum: the hypothalamus (5), along with the pituitary glands, control the body's hormonal system. Visual, tactile and auditory inputs are coordinated by the tectum (6), part of the **midbrain**. In the **hindbrain**, the cerebellum (7) controls the muscle activity needed for refined limb movements and maintaining posture. The medulla (8) contains reflex centres involved in respiration, heartbeat and gastric function.

part, so that friction stops the motion. Some vehicles use electromagnetic effects to oppose the motion and cause braking. A "power" brake utilizes a vacuum system.

Bramante, Donato (1444–1514) Italian architect and painter. Bramante was the greatest exponent of High RENAISSANCE architecture. In 1506, he started rebuilding St Peter's, Rome. His influence was enormous, and many Milanese painters took up his interest in perspective and *trompe l'oeil. See also* ITALIAN ART AND ARCHITECTURE

Branagh, Kenneth Charles (1960–) Northern Irish actor and director. He worked with the Royal Shakespeare Company (RSC) before leaving to form the Renaissance Theatre Company. Branagh moved into directing with the film *Henry V* (1989), receiving Academy Award nominations for best actor and best director. His success in popularizing Shakespeare continued with *Much Ado About Nothing* (1993), *Othello* (1996) and *Hamlet* (1997).

Branch Davidians Late 20th-century religious cult. A breakaway branch of the SEVENTH-DAY ADVENTISTS, the cult had its headquarters near WACO, Texas, and was led by David Koresh. On 28 February 1993, following the shooting of federal officers, the cult was besieged by FBI agents. On 19 April 1993, a fire suddenly broke out and the corpses of more than 80 cult members, including Koresh, were found.

Brancusi, Constantin (1876–1957) French sculptor. Brancusi's primitive style is revealed in a series of wooden sculptures, including *Chimera* (1918). In 1919, his *Bird in Space* was not permitted into the US as a work of art but was taxed on its value as raw metal. This decision was reversed in a suit filed by Brancusi, and the sculpture is now housed in the Museum of Modern Art, New York City. Other works include *The Kiss* (1908), *Prometheus* (1911) and *Flying Turtle* (1943).

Brandenburg State in NE Germany; the capital is POTS-DAM. The region formed the nucleus for the kingdom of Prussia. The March of Brandenburg was founded in 1134 by Albert I (the Bear). It came under the rule of the Hohenzollerns in 1411, and in 1417 Frederick I became the first elector of Brandenburg. Frederick II became the first king of Prussia in 1701. Pop. (1993 est.) 2,543,000

Brando, Marlon (1924–) US actor. In 1951, a reprise of his Broadway role in the film *A Streetcar Named Desire* earned him the first of four consecutive Academy Award nominations. Brando finally won his first best actor Oscar for *On the Waterfront* (1954). He gained a second best actor award for *The Godfather* (1971), but refused to accept the award in protest against the persecution of Native Americans. He received another Oscar nomination for his role in *Last Tango in Paris* (1972). Other credits include *Apocalypse Now* (1979) and an Oscar-nominated performance in *A Dry White Season* (1989).

Brandt, Bill (1904–83) British photographer. He assisted Man RAY in Paris (1929–30) before returning to London where he developed a reputation as a social commentator, as shown in his collection *The English at Home* (1936). During the war he documented life during the Blitz. Brandt is perhaps better known for his nudes.

Brandt, Willy (1913–92) German statesman, chancellor of West Germany (1969–74), b. Karl Herbert Frahm. An active Social Democrat, he fled to Norway and then Sweden during the Nazi era. Brandt returned to Germany after World War 2 and was elected mayor of West Berlin in 1957. In national politics, he was foreign minister (1966–68). As chancellor, he initiated a program of cooperation with the Communist bloc states, for which he was awarded the Nobel Peace Prize in 1971. Brandt resigned after a close aide was exposed as an East German spy.

brandy Alcoholic spirit made by distilling the fermented juice of a fruit, especially grapes in the form of wine. Armagnac and cognac are famous French wine brandies, with an alcohol content of 42%–44%. Marc is a French brandy distilled from grape mush or pomace. Applejack and calvados are brandies distilled from fermented apple juice. Other well known fruit brandies are kirsch (cherries), slivovitz (plums) and peach, apricot, cherry and blackberry brandies.

Brant, Joseph (1742–1807) Mohawk chief. Brant served in the FRENCH AND INDIAN WARS (1754–63) and in PONTIAC'S REBELLION (1763–66). He attended an Anglican school and became an interpreter for missionaries. In return for securing an alliance between the Iroquois and the British, he gained a commission in the British army in 1775. He fought with outstanding courage for the British during the American Revolution.

Braque, Georges (1882–1963) French painter who created CUBISM with PICASSO. Having tried FAUVISM without success, Braque's interest in analytical painting was awakened by CÉZANNE's 1907 memorial show. *Head of a Woman* (1909), *Violin and Palette* (1909–10) and *The Portuguese* (1911) show his transition through the early, analytical phases of cubism. Braque was badly wounded in World War 1, and afterwards evolved a gentler style of painting which earned him enormous prestige. He concentrated on still-life subjects but also produced book illustrations, stage sets and decorative ceramics.

Brasília Capital of Brazil, in W central Brazil. Although the city was originally planned in 1891, building did not start until 1956. The city was laid out in the shape of an aircraft, and Oscar NIEMEYER designed the modernist public buildings. It was inaugurated as the capital in 1960. Pop. (1991) 1,596,274.

Braşov City at the foot of the Transylvanian Alps, E central Romania. Founded in the 13th century by Teutonic knights, Braşov has many inhabitants who are of German descent. It was held by Hungary until 1918, when it was ceded to Romania. During the 1950s, the city was known as Orasul Stalin. Today, Braşov is Romania's second-largest city and a major industrial centre and winter sports resort. Pop. (1994) 324,000.

brass Alloy of mainly copper (55%–95%) and zinc (5%–45%). Brass is yellowish or reddish, malleable and ductile, and can be hammered, machined or cast. Its properties can be altered by varying the amounts of copper and zinc or by adding other metals, such as tin, lead and nickel. Brass is widely used for pipe and electrical fittings, ornamental metalwork and musical instruments.

brass Family of musical wind instruments made of metal and played by means of a cupped or funnel-shaped mouthpiece. Simple brass instruments, such as the BUGLE, produce a limited range of harmonics corresponding to the length of the tube. In most other brass instruments, the length of the air column can be altered by valves or slides to produce the full range of notes. The chief brass instruments of a symphony orchestra are the TRUMPET, FRENCH HORN, TROMBONE and TUBA.

Brassaï (1899–1984) French photographer and painter, b. Hungary as Guyla Halasz. Arriving in Paris in 1923, he worked as a journalist and painter, associating with Picasso and Dali. Brassaï turned to photography in 1930, concentrating on pictures of Paris nightlife and portraits.

brassica Genus of plants with edible roots or leaves. It includes cabbages, cauliflowers, Brussels sprouts (all subspecies of *Brassica oleracea*), turnip (*B.rapa*) and swede (*B. napobrassica*). Some, such as broccoli, have edible flowerheads. Family Brassicaceae/Cruciferae.

Bratislava Capital of Slovakia, on the River Danube, W Slovakia. It became part of Hungary after the 13th century, and was the Hungarian capital from 1526 to 1784. Incorporated into Czechoslovakia in 1918, it become the capital of Slovakia in 1992. Industries: oil refining, textiles. Pop. (1996) 452,000.

Brattain, Walter Houser (1902–87) US physicist. He shared the 1956 Nobel Prize for physics with John BARDEEN and William SHOCKLEY for their development of the TRANSISTOR and research into semiconductivity.

Braun, Eva (1912–45) Mistress of Adolf HITLER. She met Hitler in the early 1930s and they lived together for the rest of their lives. They married in Berlin the day before committing suicide.

Braun, Wernher von (1912–77) US ROCKET engineer, b. Germany. He perfected the V-2 rocket missiles in the early 1940s. In 1945, he went to the USA, becoming a citizen in 1955. In 1958, von Braun was largely responsible for launching the first US satellite, *Explorer 1*. He later worked on the development of the *Saturn* rocket (for the Apollo program) and was deputy associate administrator (1970–72) of the NATIONAL AERONAUTICS AND SPACE ADMINISTRATION (NASA).

Brazil Republic in E South America. Brazil is the world's fifth-largest country, accounting for c.50% of the total area of South America. In the N and W, the AMAZON basin covers more than half of Brazil and is drained by a river system that carries a fifth of the world's running water. The Amazon, the world's second-longest river, has a far greater volume than any other river. The only major city in this region is MANAUS. The NE coast, from the mouth of the Amazon to N Bahia, was the heart of colonial Brazil's sugar plantations. Its major cities are RECIFE and SALVADOR. A narrow coastal strip is bordered by an escarpment, above which lies the vast Brazilian plateau. The capital, BRASÍLIA, was moved here in 1960. The SE is the most developed and heavily populated part of Brazil. It includes the port of RIO DE JANEIRO and the industrial sprawl of SÃO PAULO. BELO HORIZONTE is the centre of the mining region. The S is dominated by the River PARANÁ, which flows into Argentina. **Climate** Brazil lies almost entirely within the tropics, and average monthly temperatures are over 20°C (68°F), with little seasonal variation. Most areas have moderate rainfall with a dry season between May and September. **Vegetation** The Amazon basin contains the world's largest rainforests (*selvas*). The forests are home to countless plants and animals, but many species are threatened by deforestation. The rapid destruction of the forests is also ruining the lives of the last surviving Native Amazonians. The *sertão* is a region of thorny scrub. The SE contains fertile farmland and large ranches. Swamps are found along Brazil's borders with Bolivia and Paraguay, S of the MATO GROSSO. **History and Politics** Portuguese explorer Pedro Alvarez CABRAL claimed Brazil for Portugal in 1500, and colonial development began in the 1530s. Native American and c.4 million African slaves worked on the sugar plantations and in the mines. The growth of mining saw the capital move from Salvador to Rio de Janeiro in 1763. Napoleon's defeat of Portugal led the Portuguese king JOHN VI to flee to Brazil. In 1822, he returned to Portugal and his son, PEDRO I,

BRAZIL
AREA: 8,511,970sq km (3,286,472sq mi)
POPULATION: 156,275,000
CAPITAL (POPULATION): Brasília (179,487,000)

declared Brazil an independent empire. In 1831, Pedro I was forced to abdicate in favour of his son, PEDRO II. During his long reign (1831–89), Brazil's infrastructure developed. In 1888, slavery was finally abolished. In a bloodless revolution, Brazil became a republic (1889) and Marshal Manuel Deodoro da Fonseca became the first president. In 1930, Getúlio VARGAS seized power. His autocratic rule saw the beginnings of industrial development, diversification of agriculture and an emerging national consciousness. In 1945, Vargas was forced to resign, but rampant inflation led to his return to power (1950–54). As part of the development of the interior, the capital was transferred to Brasília (1960). In 1964, the military seized power and maintained control through the use of torture and death squads. Civilian government was finally restored in 1985, and a new constitution (1988) brought liberal reforms and the transfer of powers to Congress. Fernando Collor de Mello was elected president in 1990. In 1992, he was impeached for corruption. In 1995, Fernando Henrique Cardoso was elected president. In 1998, Cardoso was re-elected on a platform of austerity measures to cope with Brazil's economic crisis. **Economy** Brazil is a rapidly industrializing country (1995 GDP per capita, US$5,400). By the mid-1970s, it had also become the world's largest debtor. High rates of inflation (1995, 33%) and unemployment caused widespread poverty and political instability. Its volume of production is one of the largest in the world, but most of the population are excluded from economic benefits. By 1993, industry had become the most valuable activity (37% of GNP), employing 25% of the workforce. Brazil is the world's second-largest producer of iron ore. Other vital resources include tin, manganese, aluminium and diamonds. Brazil is now the world's third-largest producer of commercial vehicles. It remains a major agricultural nation. It is the world's leading producer of oranges, coffee, sugar cane, cassava and sisal. Brazil is the world's second-largest producer of cattle and horses. Forestry is a major industry. Despite international pressure and government promises, deforestation continues at the rate of 1.5% to 4% annually.

Brazil nut Seed of an evergreen tree, which has leathery leaves and grows to 41m (135ft) tall. Its flowers produce a thick-walled fruit 10–30.5cm (4–12in) in diameter which contain 25–40 large seeds. Family Lecythidaceae; species *Bertholletia excelsa*.

brazing Process in which metallic parts are joined by the fusion of alloys that have lower melting points than the parts themselves. The bonding alloy is either preplaced or fed into the joint as the parts are heated. Brazed joints are used extensively in the aerospace industry.

Brazzaville Capital and largest city of the Congo, W Africa, on the River Congo. Founded in 1880, it was capital (1910–58) of French Equatorial Africa. It has a university (1972) and a cathedral. It is a major port, connected by rail to the Atlantic port of Pointe Noire. Industries: foundries, chemicals, shipyards. Pop. (1992) 937,579.

bread Staple food made by mixing flour (containing a little yeast, salt and sugar) with water to make a dough, allowing the yeast to ferment carbohydrates in the mixture (thus providing carbon-dioxide gas which leavens the bread), and finally baking in an oven. Bicarbonate of soda ($NaHCO_3$) may be used instead of yeast. Unleavened bread is flat in shape and heavy.

breadfruit Starchy fruit of a tree of the MULBERRY family (Moraceae) native to SE Asia. The pulp is eaten fresh or cooked, or ground up and baked to make bread. Genus *Atocarpus*.

Breakspear, Nicholas *See* ADRIAN IV

Bream, Julian Alexander (1933–) English guitarist and lutenist. He studied (1945–48) at the Royal College of Music. An outstanding classical guitarist, Bream has had pieces composed for him by, among others, Benjamin BRITTEN and William WALTON.

bream Freshwater fish of E and N Europe. Its stocky body is green-brown and silver, and anglers prize it for its tasty flesh. Length: 30–50cm (12–20in); weight: 4–6kg (9–13lb). Family Cyprinidae; species *Abramis brama*.

breast (mammary gland) Organ of a female mammal that secretes milk to nourish newborn young. In males the glands are rudimentary and nonfunctional. The human female breast, which develops during puberty, is made up of about 15–20 irregularly shaped lobes separated by connective and fat tissues. Lactiferous ducts lead from each lobe to the nipple.

breathing *See* RESPIRATION

breccia Rock formed by the cementation of sharp-angled fragments in a finer matrix of the same or different material. It is formed either inside the Earth by movements of the crust, from scree slopes or from volcanic material. *See also* CONGLOMERATE

Brecht, Bertolt (1898–1956) German playwright, poet and drama theorist. One of the most influential dramatists of the 20th century, his early plays, such as *Baal* (1918), won praise for their radicalism. In the 1920s, Brecht developed his distinctive, politicized theory of EPIC THEATRE. It encouraged audiences to see theatre as staged illusion via a range of "alienation" techniques. His major works were written in collaboration with composers: Kurt WEILL, *The Threepenny Opera* (1928); Hanns Eisler, *The Mother* (1931); and Paul Dessau, *The Caucasian Chalk Circle* (1948). With the rise of Hitler in 1933, Brecht's Marxist views forced him into exile. While in the US, he wrote *Mother Courage and Her Children* (1941) and *The Good Woman of Setzuan* (1943). In 1949, Brecht returned to East Germany to direct the BERLINER ENSEMBLE.

Breckinridge, John Cabell (1821–75) American vice president (1857–61) and Confederate general in the CIVIL WAR. He was a major in the MEXICAN WAR and a congressman (1851) before becoming vice president under James BUCHANAN. Defeated as a pro-slavery presidential candidate in 1860 by Abraham LINCOLN, he became secretary of war (1865) in Jefferson DAVIS' cabinet.

Breda City in Noord-Brabant province, S Netherlands. It is noted for the 1566 Compromise of Breda (a Dutch alliance against Spanish rule) and Charles II of England's Declaration of Breda (1660) before the Restoration. Industries: engineering, textiles. Pop. (1996) 130,000.

Breda, Treaty of (1667) Peace agreement that ended the second of the DUTCH WARS with England. England gave up its claim to the Dutch East Indies but gained control of New York and New Jersey.

breeding Process of producing offspring, specifically the science of changing or promoting certain genetic characteristics in animals and plants. Breeding may involve CROSSBREEDING or INBREEDING to produce the desired characteristics. Scientific breeding has resulted in disease-resistant strains of crops and in animals that give improved food yields. *See also* GENETIC ENGINEERING

Bremen City on the River Weser; capital of Bremen state, N Germany. Bremen suffered severe damage during World War 2, but many of its original buildings (including the Gothic city hall) survived. Industries: shipbuilding, electrical equipment, textiles. Pop. (1995) 549,000.

bremsstrahlung (Ger. braking radiation) ELECTROMAGNETIC RADIATION in the form of X-RAYS emitted when charged particles slow down or change course rapidly.

This happens when high-speed ELECTRONS enter the electric field of an atomic NUCLEUS. Such radiation covers a continuous range of wavelengths within the electromagnetic spectrum.

Brendel, Alfred (1931–) Austrian pianist. One of the world's most critically acclaimed and widely travelled concert artists, Brendel is especially noted for his interpretations of Beethoven and Schubert.

Brentano, Clemens (1778–1842) German poet. Brentano co-founded (with his brother-in-law, Achim von Arnim) the Heidelberg school of ROMANTICISM, devoted to the study of German folklore. He and von Armin collaborated on *Des Knaben Wunderhorn* (1805–08), a collection of German folksongs.

Brescia City in LOMBARDY region, N Italy; capital of Brescia province. An important Roman town, Brescia was sacked by Attila in AD 452. In the 12th century, it became an independent commune. Brescia resisted Austrian occupation and was incorporated into Italy in 1860. The city has many fine examples of Roman, Romanesque, Renaissance and Baroque architecture. Industries: iron and steel, weapons. Pop. (1992) 192,883.

Bresson, Robert (1907–99) French film director. His first feature film was *Angels of the Streets* (1943). Bresson was the epitome of the director as AUTEUR. His films were meticulously crafted, often using a juxtaposition of images to convey a poetic truth. Bresson achieved worldwide recognition for *The Diary of a Country Priest* (1951). Other films include *The Trial of Joan of Arc* (1962), *The Devil, Probably* (1977) and *Money* (1983).

Brest (formerly Brest-Litovsk) City and port at the confluence of the Bug and Muchavec rivers, near the Polish border, W Belarus. It was the site of the signing of the Treaty of BREST-LITOVSK. Industries: food processing, sawmilling, textiles. Pop. (1996) 190,000.

Brest City and port on the Atlantic coast of Brittany, W France. An important naval base, the town was severely damaged in World War 2, when used as a German submarine base. Industries: shipbuilding and repair, chemical manufacture. Pop. (1990) 147,956.

Brest-Litovsk, Treaty of (March 1918) Peace treaty between Russia and the CENTRAL POWERS, confirming Russian withdrawal from World War 1. The Ukraine and Georgia became independent, and Russian territory was surrendered to Germany and Austria-Hungary.

Breton, André (1896–1966) French poet and theorist. A founder and poet of the SURREALISM movement, Breton wrote *Manifeste du surréalisme* (1924) and *Le Surréalisme et la Peinture* (1928). His fictional works include the semiautobiographical novel *Nadja* (1928). *See also* DADA

Breton Celtic language spoken in Brittany, on the NW coast of France. It is a descendant of British, an old Celtic language, and is closely related to Welsh. Breton speakers usually also speak French, which is rapidly replacing it.

Bretton Woods Conference (officially United Nations Monetary and Financial Conference) It met at Bretton Woods, New Hampshire, in July 1944. It was summoned on the initiative of President Franklin ROOSEVELT to establish a system of international monetary cooperation and prevent severe financial crises, such as that of 1929, which had precipitated the GREAT DEPRESSION. Representatives of 44 countries agreed to establish the INTERNATIONAL MONETARY FUND (IMF) and the International Bank for Reconstruction and Development, or WORLD BANK, to provide credit to states requiring financial investment in major economic projects.

Breuer, Marcel Lajos (1902–81) US architect and designer, b. Hungary. One of the great innovators of modern furniture design, Breuer studied and taught (1920–28) at the BAUHAUS, where he created his famous tubular steel chair. In 1937, he settled in the US and subsequently worked with Walter GROPIUS as a partner in architectural projects. He designed the Whitney Museum of American Art, New York (1966).

breviary Roman Catholic liturgical book containing prayers, psalms, hymns and scriptural lessons to be recited by priests as part of the divine office. The book prescribes the texts to be used at specified times of day.

brewing Preparation of BEER and stout by using YEAST as a catalyst in the alcoholic fermentation of liquors containing malt and hops. In beer brewing, a malt liquor (wort) is made from crushed germinated barley grains. Hops are added to the boiling wort both to impart a bitter flavour, and also to help to clarify the beer and keep it free from spoilage by microbes. The clear, filtered wort is cooled and inoculated with brewer's yeast.

Brezhnev, Leonid Ilyich (1906–82) Soviet statesman, effective ruler from the mid-1960s until his death. He rose through the Communist Party of the Soviet Union (CPSU) to become (1957) a member of the presidium (later politburo). In 1964, Brezhnev helped plan the downfall of Nikita KHRUSHCHEV and became party general secretary, at first sharing power with Aleksei KOSYGIN. In 1977, he became president of the Soviet Union. Brezhnev pursued a hard line against reforms at home and in Eastern Europe, but also sought to reduce tensions with the West. After the Soviet invasion of CZECHOSLOVAKIA (1968), he promulgated the "Brezhnev Doctrine" confirming Soviet domination of satellite states, as seen in the 1979 invasion of Afghanistan.

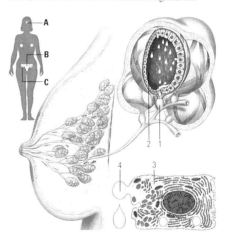

▲ **breast** In humans, there is one pair of mammary glands, which are composed of a mass of epithelial ducts (1, shown magnified) surrounded by fibrous tissue. In women, these ducts enlarge and spread, differentiating into milk-producing tissue. This process occurs under complex hormonal control from the anterior and posterior pituitary glands (A), the placenta during pregnancy (B), and from the ovaries (C). Full development of the glands involves extensive growth of mammary ducts from which specialized lobules proliferate (2). Each lobule, lined by milk-producing cells (3), opens into the ducts leading to the gland nipple. Three to four days after childbirth, the hormone prolactin enables milk containing fat droplets (4) and protein to become available to the child.

Brian Boru (940?–1014) King of Ireland (1002–14). From a power base in Munster, he gained control of the whole of s Ireland. Brian was killed in the aftermath of his victory over the Norsemen at the Battle of Clontarf.

Briand, Aristide (1862–1932) French statesman. A moderate, he was premier of 11 governments between 1909 and 1929. Briand advocated international cooperation and was one of the instigators of the LOCARNO PACT (1925), for which he shared the Nobel Peace Prize with Gustav STRESEMANN in 1926. He was also one of the authors of the KELLOGG-BRIAND PACT of 1928.

brick Hardened block of clay used for building and paving. Usually rectangular, bricks are made in standard sizes by machines that either mould or cut off extruded sections of stiff clay. The first (sun-dried) bricks were used in the Tigris-Euphrates basin *c*.5,000 years ago.

bridge Structure providing a continuous passage over a body of water, roadway or valley. Bridges are prehistoric in origin, the first probably being merely logs. Modern bridges take various forms, including beams, arches, cantilevers, suspension and cable-stayed bridges. They can also be movable or floating pontoons. Construction materials include brick or stone (for arches), steel or concrete.

bridge Card game for four players. **Contract** bridge is the most international of card games, with Olympiads and world championships. It evolved from **auction** bridge, invented by the British in India. Opposite players are partners, and after the cards are dealt, each pair bids for the contract; a bid is a claim of how many "tricks" (rounds of play) will be won. The winner of the bidding must then attempt to win the number of tricks bid.

Bridges, Robert Seymour (1844–1930) English poet. He wrote many lyrics and narrative poems, such as *Eros and Psyche* (1885). After the publication of his *Collected Poems* (1912), Bridges was appointed poet laureate (1913). His most popular work was *The Testament of Beauty* (1929), a philosophical poem on the nature of art and the human soul.

Bridget, Saint (453–523) (St Brigid or St Bride) Patron saint of Leinster, Ireland. She was the founder of a monastic community in Kildare, which may have been Ireland's first nunnery. A legendary figure, Bridget assumed many of the attributes of the Irish goddess Brigit, daughter of the Dagda. Feast day: 1 February.

Bridgetown Capital and port of Barbados, in the West Indies. Founded in 1628, it is the seat of Parliament. Industries: rum distilling, sugar processing, tourism. Pop. (1992) 8,000.

Bridgewater Canal *See* BRINDLEY, JAMES

Bright, John (1811–89) British parliamentary reformer. A Quaker, he and his fellow radical, Richard COBDEN, were leaders of the ANTI-CORN LAW LEAGUE (founded 1839). First elected to Parliament in 1843, Bright subsequently represented Manchester, the home of FREE-TRADE. He lost his seat in 1857 after opposing the Crimean War but was re-elected for Birmingham.

Brighton Resort town on the English Channel, East Sussex, s England. Originally a fishing village, it was popularized as a resort by the Prince Regent (George IV), who had the Royal Pavilion rebuilt here in oriental style by John NASH. It is the seat of the University of Sussex (1961) and the University of Brighton (1992). Industries: food processing, furniture, tourism. Pop. (1991) 143,582.

brill FLATFISH similar and related to the TURBOT. It is fished for food, but unlike the turbot, lacks tentacles. Species *Scophthalmus rhombus*.

Brindley, James (1716–72) English canal-builder who constructed the Bridgewater Canal, the first major

canal in England. It linked Worsley, Lancashire, to Manchester and was commissioned by Francis Egerton, 3rd Duke of Bridgewater (1736–1803). The design included a unique aqueduct over the River Irwell. Brindley was responsible for *c*.565km (350mi) of canals that hastened the INDUSTRIAL REVOLUTION.

Brisbane City and seaport on the River Brisbane; capital of Queensland, E Australia. First settled in 1824 as a penal colony, it became state capital in 1859. It is the location of Parliament House (1869) and the University of Queensland (1909) and is a major shipping and rail centre. Industries: oil refining, shipbuilding, car assembly. Pop. (1993 est.) 1,421,600.

bristle tail *See* SILVERFISH

Bristol City and unitary authority at the confluence of the Avon and Frome rivers, SW England. An important seaport and trade centre since achieving city status in 1155, it was a major centre for the wool and cloth industry. From the 15th to 18th century, it was England's second city and the base for many New World explorations. The 19th century witnessed a gradual decline in the city's economy. Bristol suffered intensive bombing during World War 2. Clifton Suspension Bridge (designed by BRUNEL) was completed in 1864. Other sites include a 12th-century cathedral and the 14th-century church of St Mary Redcliffe. Bristol has two universities: the University of Bristol (1909) and the University of the West of England (1992). Industries: aircraft engineering, chemicals. Pop. (1994) 402,000.

Britain (Great Britain) Island kingdom in NW Europe, officially the UNITED KINGDOM of Great Britain and NORTHERN IRELAND. It is made up of ENGLAND, SCOTLAND, WALES, the CHANNEL ISLANDS and the Isle of MAN.

Britain, ancient British history from PREHISTORY to ROMAN BRITAIN. During the NEOLITHIC age, hunter-gatherers gradually turned to sedentary farming. Old STONE AGE remains have been found at Cheddar Gorge, Somerset, s England. There are numerous examples of New Stone Age burial mounds. During the BRONZE AGE (*c*.2300 BC), the Beaker folk built an advanced civilization, producing the stone circles at STONEHENGE and Avebury, s England. The IRON AGE was dominated by the CELTS. Julius Caesar invaded Britain in 54 BC, and the Roman conquest began in earnest from 43 BC.

Britain, Battle of (1940) Series of air battles fought over Britain. Early in World War 2 (as a prelude to invasion), the Germans hoped to destroy Britain's industrial and military infrastructure and civilian morale by a sustained series of bombing raids. British defences included the first use of RADAR in warfare. Failing to eliminate the spitfires and hurricanes of the Royal Air Force (RAF), the Germans began (7 September) the night bombing (the BLITZ) of London and other cities. In October the Luftwaffe losses (*c*.2,300 aircraft) forced Hitler to abandon his plans for an invasion. The RAF lost some 900 aircraft.

British Antarctic Territory British colony in Antarctica comprising the mainland and islands within a triangular area bounded by latitude 60°s and longitudes 20° and 80°w. It includes the South Shetland Islands, South Orkney Islands and Graham Land. Formerly part of the FALKLAND ISLANDS, the territory became a British Crown colony in 1962, although today Argentina and Chile claim parts of it. There are no permanent settlements, but scientists occupy establishments of the British Antarctic Survey. Area: 1,725,000sq km (666,000sq mi).

British Broadcasting Corporation (BBC) UK state-financed radio and television network. Its directors are appointed by the government but, in terms of policy and content, the BBC is largely independent. It receives its finances from a licence fee. The BBC was set up in 1927 to replace the British Broadcasting Company that had been in operation since 1922. Its first director-general (1927–38) was Lord Reith, whose philosophy of the BBC as an instrument of education and civilization greatly shaped the corporation's policies. *See also* BIRT, SIR JOHN

British Columbia Province of W Canada, on the Pacific coast, bounded N by Alaska, S by Washington state. The Rocky Mountains run N to S through the province. The capital is Victoria, and other major cities include VANCOUVER. The region was first sighted by Sir Francis DRAKE in 1578. Captain COOK landed here in 1778, and George Vancouver took possession of the island that bears his name for Britain in 1794. In 1846, the border with the US was finally settled. Completion of the Canadian Pacific Railway in 1885 spurred the development of the province. The many rivers (principal of which is the Fraser) provide abundant hydroelectric power. Three-fourths of the land is forested, making timber an important industry. Mineral deposits include copper, silver, gold, lead, zinc and asbestos. Dairying and fruit-growing are the chief farming activities. Industries: fishing, paper, tourism, chemicals. Area: 948,600sq km (366,255sq mi). Pop. (1991) 3,282,061.

British Empire Overseas territories ruled by Britain from the 16th to the 20th century. Historians distinguish two empires. The first, based mainly on commercial ventures (such as sugar and tobacco plantations), missionary activities and slave trading, resulted in the creation of British colonies in the Caribbean and North America in the 17th century. This "First Empire" was curtailed by the loss of the 13 US colonies, at the end of the AMERICAN REVOLUTION (1775–81). The "Second Empire" was created in the 19th century, with Queen VICTORIA its empress. The EAST INDIA COMPANY acquired a larger trading empire as a result of the NAPOLEONIC WARS and COLONIALISM increased dramatically from the 1820s. British expansion was predominantly in the Far East, Australia (initially with the penal colonies), Africa and India. As a result of the INDIAN MUTINY (1857), the British government assumed direct responsibility for the administration of India. In 1877, Queen Victoria was proclaimed Empress of India. In the "scramble" for Africa, imperialists such as Cecil RHODES were thwarted in their desire to create a continent-wide empire by the BOER WARS. By 1914, the empire comprised *c.*25% of the Earth's land surface and population. Virtually all the constituent members gained independence in the period after World War 2. Most subsequently became members of the COMMONWEALTH.

British Empire, Order of the (OBE) British military and civil order or knighthood bestowed as a reward for public service to the Commonwealth of Nations. Created in 1917, it has five different classes for men and women: Knights (or Dames) Grand Cross, Knights (or Dames) Commander, Commanders, Officers and Members.

British Honduras *See* BELIZE

British Indian Ocean Territory British colony in the Indian Ocean comprising the islands of the Chagos Archipelago, 1,900km (1,200mi) NE of Mauritius. In 1814, France ceded the territory to Britain, and it was administered by Mauritius. In 1965, Britain bought it from Mauritius in order to build a joint US/UK naval base on Diego Garcia island. In 1976, the islands of Aldabra, Farquhar and Desroches reverted to SEYCHELLES administration. Industries: coconuts, fishing. Area: 80sq km (31sq mi).

British Isles Group of islands off the NW coast of Europe, made up of the UNITED KINGDOM of Great Britain and Northern IRELAND and the Republic of IRELAND. It also includes the Isle of MAN in the Irish Sea (a self-governing island but part of the United Kingdom); and the CHANNEL ISLANDS in the English Channel (also self-governing, but a British crown dependency).

British Legion Organization of ex-service men and women for helping disabled and unemployed war veterans, their widows and families. Each year, during the week preceding Remembrance Day (the Sunday nearest to 11 November), millions of artificial red poppies are sold to commemorate the dead of two World Wars and raise funds for the Legion.

British Library National library of the UK. The British Library was established in 1973 with the amalgamation of the BRITISH MUSEUM Library, the National Central Library and the National Lending Library for Science and Technology. It receives a copy of every book published in the UK. Its collection includes more than 18 million volumes. In 1998, the reference and reading rooms moved from the British Museum to purpose-built accommodation at St Pancras, London. The lending division is located in Boston Spa, West Yorkshire.

British Museum One of the world's greatest public collections of art, ethnography and archaeology (established 1753). Its first displays came from a private collection purchased from the naturalist, Sir Hans Sloane. Later additions included the ROSETTA STONE and the ELGIN MARBLES. The present building by Sir Robert SMIRKE was completed in 1847. The museum's separate departments include the Museum of Mankind and the Department of Prints and Drawings which houses works by Rembrandt, Rubens and Michelangelo.

British North America Act (1867) Act of the British Parliament that created the Dominion of CANADA. It provided a constitution similar to that of Britain. British powers were surrendered in the Canada Act of 1982, when the original act was renamed the Constitution Act.

Brittany (Bretagne) Former duchy and province in NW France, forming the peninsula between the Bay of Biscay and the English Channel. Under Roman rule from 56 BC to the 5th century AD, it was later inhabited by CELTS who gave it its name, language (BRETON) and distinctive culture. England and France disputed its possession, but the duchy retained its independence until it was formally incorporated within France in 1532. In more recent times, the French government has improved the region's infrastructure, and there has been a revival of interest in Breton culture and heritage. Pop. (1990) 2,795,600.

Britten, (Edward) Benjamin (1913–76) English composer. Britten is best known for his operas, among the greatest of the 20th century. He also wrote numerous songs, many especially for Peter PEARS. Britten's operas include *Peter Grimes* (1945), *Billy Budd* (1951), *The Turn of the Screw* (1954), *A Midsummer Night's Dream* (1960) and *Death in Venice* (1973). Other major works include the popular *Young Person's Guide to the Orchestra* (1945) and *War Requiem* (1962). In 1948, he established the music festival held annually at his home-town of Aldeburgh, E England. He was made a peer in 1976.

brittle star (serpent star) Marine ECHINODERM with a small central disc body and up to twenty (though typically five) long, sinuous arms; these break off easily and are replaced by regeneration. Class Ophiuroidea; genera include the phosphorescent *Amphiopholis* and *Ophiactis*.

Brittonic (Brythonic) Group of languages belonging to the Celtic branch of the Italo-Celtic subfamily of Indo-European languages. Its two existing members are WELSH and BRETON. A third Brittonic language, CORNISH, died out in the 18th century, although there are speakers in Cornwall who have revived it in the 20th century. The languages emerged from the CELTIC LANGUAGE spoken in Britain in the 6th century after the Germanic invasions.

Brno (Brünn) Capital city of central Jihomoravský (MORAVIA) region, SE Czech Republic. Founded in the 10th century, it has a 15th-century cathedral. The Bren Gun was designed here. Industries: armaments, engineering, textiles, chemicals. Pop. (1996) 389,000.

broadbill Tropical Eurasian and African bird, named for its broad bill. It weaves a root-and-grass nest suspended over water and lays 2–4 eggs. Length: 12–28cm (5–11in). Family: Eurylaimidae.

broadcasting Transmission of sound or images by radio waves or through electrical or fibre-optic cables to a widely dispersed audience through RADIO or TELEVISION receivers. In the UK, the British Broadcasting Company began radio transmission in 1922 and, as the British Broadcasting Corporation (BBC), was incorporated as a public body in 1927. Until 1973, it enjoyed a monopoly in radio broadcasting. Today, there are five national BBC radio stations. UK public television broadcasting began in 1936 from Alexandra Palace, London. The BBC transmitted on one channel, using 405 lines to build up an image. A second channel, ITV, run by the Independent Broadcasting Authority (IBA) was set up in 1955. BBC2 started broadcasting in 1964; Channel 4 commenced transmission in 1982 and Channel 5 in 1997. BBC1 and BBC2 do not carry commercial advertising, and receive their funding from a licence fee. All five terrestrial channels may be received on television sets with 625 lines. In 1962, Telstar delivered the first transatlantic, SATELLITE television broadcast. Rupert MURDOCH's Sky Television satellite service began broadcasting in 1989, since when CABLE TELEVISION as well as satellite services have grown rapidly in popularity. The launch of digital television in the UK in 1998 greatly increased the number of channels.

Broads, Norfolk Region of shallow lakes and waterways in E England, connected by the rivers Waveney, Yare and Bure, between Norwich and the coast. It is a wildlife sanctuary and a popular sailing area, with 320km 200mi) of waterways.

Broadway Major thoroughfare of New York City that began as the principal N-S axis of the old town. It runs from the S tip of Manhattan to the northern city limit in the Bronx. Famous sites along the route include the Woolworth Building, the Lincoln Center for the Performing Arts, and Columbia University. In the vicinity of Times Square, its theatres and cinemas have made it known worldwide as the "show centre" of the USA.

broccoli (It. sprouts) Variety of CABBAGE cultivated for its edible immature flowers. It is the same variety (*Brassica oleracea botrytis*) as the CAULIFLOWER. **Winter** broccoli has large white heads. **Sprouting** broccoli (calabrese) has tiny green or purple flower buds which gather in compact heads. Family Brassicaceae/Cruciferae.

Broch, Hermann (1886–1951) Austrian novelist. In 1938, he was imprisoned by the Gestapo but escaped into exile in the USA. Broch's novels combine philosophical ideas with modernist form. They include the trilogy *The Sleepwalkers* (1931–32) and *The Death of Virgil* (1945).

Brod, Max (1884–1968) Czech novelist, critic and philosopher. Although chiefly remembered for bringing to public attention the work of Franz KAFKA, of whom he also wrote a biography, Brod was also a novelist. He was a Zionist and settled in Palestine in 1939, where he later became director of the Habina Theatre.

Brodsky, Joseph (1940–96) US poet, b. Russia. Brodsky won the 1987 Nobel Prize for literature and was US poet laureate (1991–92). Before his exile in 1972, he was sent to a Soviet labour camp. His works include *Less Than One*, which won the 1986 US National Book Critics award and *History of the Twentieth Century*.

Broglie, Prince Louis Victor de (1892–1987) French physicist who theorized that all ELEMENTARY PARTICLES have an associated wave. He devised the formula that predicts this wavelength, and its existence was proven in 1927. Broglie developed this form of QUANTUM MECHANICS, called WAVE MECHANICS, for which he was awarded the 1929 Nobel Prize for physics.

bromeliad Any of 1,700 species of the PINEAPPLE family (Bromeliaceae). Most are native to the tropics and subtropics and, besides the pineapple, include many of the larger EPIPHYTES of trees of the rainforests.

bromide Salt of hydrobromic acid or certain organic compounds containing bromine. The bromides of ammonium, sodium, potassium and certain other metals were once extensively used medically as sedatives. Silver bromide is light-sensitive and is used in photography.

bromine (symbol Br) Volatile, liquid element of the HALOGEN group in group VII of the periodic table, first isolated (1826) by the French chemist A.J. Balard. Bromine is the only liquid form of a nonmetallic element. It is extracted by treating seawater or natural brines with chlorine. A reddish-brown fuming liquid having an unpleasant odour, it is used to manufacture photographic film and additives for gasoline. Chemically it resembles CHLORINE, but is less reactive. Properties: at.no. 35; r.a.m. 79.904; r.d. 3.12; m.p. −7.2°C (19.04°F); b.p. 58.8°C (137.8°F); the most common isotope is Br^{79} (50.54%).

bronchitis Inflammation of the bronchial tubes most often caused by a viral infection, such as the common cold or influenza, but exacerbated by environmental pollutants. Symptoms include coughing and the production of large quantities of mucus. It can be acute or chronic, especially in those who smoke.

bronchus (pl. bronchi) One of two branches into which the TRACHEA or windpipe divides, with one branch leading to each of the LUNGS. The bronchus divides into smaller and smaller branches, called bronchioles, which extend throughout the lung, opening into the air sacs, or ALVEOLI.

Brontë, Anne (1820–49) English novelist and poet. The youngest of the Brontë sisters, she became a governess, an experience reflected in *Agnes Grey* (1847). All of her work

▲ **bromeliad** Many bromeliads, such as *Aechmea fasciata*, are epiphytes (air plants), plants that use other plants for support but are not parasitic. Its leaves catch water as it drips through the forest canopy. Bromeliads are members of the pineapple family (Bromeliaceae).

was published under the male pseudonym Acton Bell. Her best-known novel is *The Tenant of Wildfell Hall* (1848).

Brontë, Charlotte (1816–55) English novelist and poet. Brontë suffered from poor health, and her mother, four sisters and dissolute brother Branwell died early. She died in childbirth within a year of her marriage. Her four novels, *The Professor* (1846), *Jane Eyre* (1847), *Shirley* (1849) and *Villette* (1853), are works of remarkable passion and imagination. Her writings initially appeared under the male pseudonym Currer Bell.

Brontë, Emily (1818–48) English novelist and poet. Like her sisters she wrote under a male pseudonym, Ellis Bell. Her love for her native Yorkshire moors and insight into human passion are manifested in her poetry and her only novel, *Wuthering Heights* (1847).

brontosaurus (now known as **apatosaurus**) DINOSAUR of the Jurassic and early Cretaceous periods. It had a long neck and tail and a small head with the eyes and nostrils on the top so that it could remain completely immersed in water. Length: 21m (70ft); weight: to 30 tonnes.

bronze Traditionally an ALLOY of COPPER and no more than 33% tin. It is hard and resistant to corrosion but easy to work. It has long been used in sculpture and bell-casting. Other metals are often added for specific properties and uses, such as aluminium in aircraft parts and tubing, silicon in marine hardware and chemical equipment and phosphorus in springs and electrical parts.

Bronze Age Period between the NEOLITHIC period and the discovery of iron-working techniques (the IRON AGE). In Mesopotamia, BRONZE tools were used from *c*.3200 BC, and the Bronze Age lasted until *c*.1100 BC. In Britain, bronze was used after 2000 BC.

Brook, Peter Stephen Paul (1925–) English director of theatre, opera and film. He joined the ROYAL SHAKESPEARE COMPANY (RSC) as co-director in 1962. His most notable productions were *King Lear* (1962, filmed 1969), *Marat/Sade* (1964) and *Midsummer Night's Dream* (1970). In 1970, Brook established the International Centre for Theatre Research in Paris and in 1985 directed the epic cycle *The Mahabharata* (filmed 1989). Brook also directed the film *Lord of the Flies* (1963).

Brooke, Rupert Chawner (1887–1915) English poet. Brooke wrote some of the most anthologized poems in the English language, including "The Soldier" and "The Old Vicarage, Grantchester", but the romantic image created by his early death during World War 1 has tended to distort his status. His collections include *Poems* (1911) and *1914 and Other Poems* (1915).

Brooklyn Borough of NEW YORK CITY, coextensive with Kings County in SW Long Island; it is connected to Manhattan and Staten Island by bridges (including the famous Brooklyn Bridge), subway trains and ferries. First settled in 1645, it became a borough in 1898. It is the home of Coney Island. Area: 184sq km (71sq mi). Pop. (1990) 2,291,664.

Brookner, Anita (1928–) English novelist. She was the first woman to be Slade professor of art history at Cambridge. After only four years of writing fiction, Brookner won the Booker Prize for her novel *Hôtel du Lac* (1984). Other novels include *A Friend from England* (1987).

Brooks, Louise (1906–85) US film actress. Brooks achieved most of her success in Germany under the direction of G.W. Pabst in his *Diary of a Lost Girl* (1929) and as Lulu in *Pandora's Box* (1929). She never recaptured this early brilliance and retired in 1938.

broom Any of various deciduous shrubs of the PEA family (Fabaceae/Leguminosae). They have yellow, purple or white flowers, usually in clusters. Many belong to the genus *Genista*, which gave its name to the Plantagenate kings of England (Lat. *Planta genista*), who used the broom as their emblem.

Brown, "Capability" (Lancelot) (1715–83) English landscape gardener who revolutionized garden and parkland layout in the 1700s. Brown designed or remodeled nearly 150 estates, including gardens at Blenheim and Kew. He worked to achieve casual effects. He earned his nickname from a habit of saying that a place had "capabilities of improvement".

Brown, Ford Madox (1821–93) English painter closely associated with (although not a member of) the PRE-RAPHAELITE BROTHERHOOD, and grandfather of Ford Madox FORD. The Pre-Raphaelite influence can be seen in *The Last of England* (1855) and *Work* (1852–63).

Brown, Gordon (1951–) British statesman, chancellor of the exchequer (1997–), b. Scotland. Brown entered Parliament in 1983. His first act as chancellor was to give the BANK OF ENGLAND independence in interest-rate policy. *See also* BLAIR, TONY

Brown, James (1933–) US singer and songwriter. An energetic performer, renowned for his dance routines, Brown is hailed as the "Godfather of Soul" and a pioneer of FUNK. His album *Live at the Apollo* (1962) is one of the best-selling pop albums of all time. Brown's hit singles include "Please, Please, Please" (1956), "Papa's Got a Brand New Bag" (1965) and "Say it Loud, I'm Black and I'm Proud" (1968).

Brown, John (1800–59) US anti-slavery crusader. Hoping to start a slave revolt, he led 21 men who captured the US arsenal at Harper's Ferry, Virginia, in 1859. They were driven out the next day by troops under Robert E. LEE. Brown was captured, charged with treason, and hanged. The trial aggravated North-South tensions.

Brown, Robert (1773–1858) Scottish botanist. As the naturalist on Flinder's voyage to Australia (1801–05), he returned with thousands of new species. Brown's studies enabled him to outline the difference between GYMNOSPERMS and ANGIOSPERMS. In *A Brief Account of Microscopical Observations* (1828) he described the movement later known as Brownian motion.

brown bear *See* BEAR

Browne, Robert (*c*.1550–1633) English clergyman, founder of the "Brownists", a separatist religious sect. In *Reformation without Tarrying for Any* (1582), he presented the first argument for CONGREGATIONALISM. In 1584, he was imprisoned and late excommunicated. By 1591, Brown had been reconciled to the CHURCH OF ENGLAND.

Browne, Sir Thomas (1605–82) English scientific and religious writer. Browne's first tract, *Religio Medici* (1642), was an attempt to reconcile science and religion. *Pseudodoxia Epidemica* (or *Vulgar Errors*, 1646) investigated the nature of heresy and superstition. *The Garden of Cyrus* was published jointly (1658) with *Hydriotaphia* (or *Urn-burial*), a treatise on approaches to mortality.

Brownian movement Random, zigzag movement of particles suspended in a fluid (liquid or gas). It is caused by the unequal bombardment of the larger particles from different sides by the smaller molecules of the fluid. The movement is named after Robert BROWN.

Browning, Elizabeth Barrett (1806–61) English poet. In 1846 she secretly married Robert BROWNING and, from 1847, the couple lived in Florence, Italy. *The Seraphim and Other Poems* (1838) and *Poems* (1844) established her popularity, later confirmed by a collection of 1850, which included *Sonnets from the Portuguese* and *Aurora Leigh* (1857). She was regarded as the pre-eminent English woman poet of her generation.

Browning, Robert (1812–89) English poet. "My Last Duchess" and "Soliloquy of the Spanish Cloister", both published in *Bells and Pomegranates* (1846), display his characteristic use of dramatic monologue. In 1846, he and Elizabeth Barrett (BROWNING) secretly married and moved to Florence, Italy, in 1847. Browning published the volumes *Christmas Eve and Easter Day* (1850) and *Men and Women* (1855) before returning to London after Elizabeth's death in 1861. His popularity increased with *Dramatis Personae* (1864) and *The Ring and the Book* (1868–69), often considered to be his masterpiece. One of the foremost poets of the 19th century, Browning is also at times one of the most obscure.

Brownshirts (officially *Sturmabteilung*, or *SA*) German Nazi stormtroopers founded in 1920. By 1933 the Brownshirts, led by Ernst Röhm, numbered *c.*500,000. After the Nazis seized power, the Brownshirts' ideology and challenge to the autonomy of the German army was perceived as a threat by Adolf HITLER. The SA leaders were shot on the "Night of the Long Knives" (29 June 1934), and the SS emerged as their successors.

brucellosis (undulant fever) Infectious disease that can be passed from farm stock to man, usually in unpasteurized milk. It is found mostly in developing nations.

Bruce, Robert *See* ROBERT I (THE BRUCE)

Brücke, Die (1905–13) (The Bridge) First group of German expressionist painters. Founded in Dresden by E.L. KIRCHNER, the group chose their name because they wanted their work to form a bridge with the art of the future. Members of the group included Emil NOLDE, Karl Schmidt-Rottluff, Max Pechstein and Erich Heckel. Their work was characterized by jagged edges, harshly distorted figures and a simplification of colour and form. *See also* EXPRESSIONISM

Bruckner, Anton (1824–96) Austrian composer. He wrote a great deal of church music – cantatas, masses and a *Te Deum* (1881–84) – and nine symphonies. Bruckner's compositions are noted for their massive scale: the symphonies are lengthy, monumental creations greatly influenced by ROMANTICISM. His work is characterized by the use of complex musical form.

Bruegel, Pieter the Elder (1525–69) Netherlandish landscape painter and draftsman. The greatest 16th-century Dutch artist, Bruegel travelled extensively in France and Italy. His return journey through the Alps influenced him profoundly, and he produced a series of sensitive drawings of the region. In 1563, he moved to Brussels and for the rest of his life concentrated on painting. The characteristic rural scenes crowded with tiny peasant figures of his early years gave way during his last six years to paintings with larger figures which illustrated proverbs. His son, **Pieter the Younger** (1564–1637), sometimes copied his father's work. Another son, **Jan** (1568–1625), specialized in highly detailed flower paintings.

Bruges (Brugge) Capital of West Flanders province, NW Belgium. Built on a network of canals, it was a great trading centre in the 15th century. Its importance declined after 1500, but trade revived when the Zeebrugge ship canal was opened in 1907. It has many medieval buildings. Industries: engineering, brewing, lace, textiles, tourism. Pop. (1993 est.) 116,724.

Bruhn, Erik (1928–86) Danish dancer and ballet director. He joined the Royal Danish Ballet Company in 1947. Bruhn combined precision and artistic expression. He was director (1967–73) of the Swedish Opera Ballet and the National Ballet of Canada (1983–86).

Brummell, "Beau" (George Bryan) (1778–1840) Leader of fashion in gentlemen's dress in Regency England between 1798 and 1812. His sense of perfection in dress, accompanied by a sharp wit and a friendship with the Prince Regent (later George IV), gave him enormous social success. The demise of royal patronage and his huge gambling debts forced Brummell into exile (1816) in France, where he lived the rest of his life in poverty.

Brundtland, Gro Harlem (1939–) Norwegian statesman, first woman prime minister of Norway (1981, 1986–89, 1990–96). In her second term, she chaired the World Commission on Environment and Development, which produced the report *Our Common Future* (1987). Brundtland led a succession of minority Labour governments. Most of her third term was overshadowed by the dispute over Norway's entry into the EU. Brundtland served as director general of WHO (1998–).

Brunei Sultanate in N BORNEO, SE Asia; the capital is BANDAR SERI BEGAWAN. **Land and climate** Bounded in the NW by the South China Sea, Brunei consists of humid plains with forested mountains running along its S border with Malaysia. Brunei has a moist, tropical climate. **History and politics** During the 16th century, Brunei ruled over the whole of Borneo and parts of the Philippines, but gradually lost its influence. It became a British protectorate in 1888. Brunei achieved independence from Britain in 1983. **Economy** Oil and gas are the main source of income, accounting for 70% of GDP. Area: 5,765sq km (2,225sq mi). Pop. (2000 est.) 333,000.

Brunel, Isambard Kingdom (1806–59) English marine and railroad engineer who revolutionized British engineering. In 1829 he designed the Clifton Suspension Bridge (completed 1864). Brunel is also noted for his ships; *Great Western* (designed 1837), the first trans-Atlantic wooden steamship, *Great Britain* (1843), the first iron-hulled, screw-driven steamship; and *Great Eastern* (1858), the largest steamship of its era.

Brunel, Sir Marc Isambard (1769–1849) Architect and engineer. A refugee from the FRENCH REVOLUTION, he went to the USA in 1793 and was chief engineer of New York. In 1799, Brunel moved to England, where he was responsible for the construction of the first tunnel (1825–43) under the River Thames, London.

Brunelleschi, Filippo (1377–1446) Florentine architect, first of the great RENAISSANCE architects and a pioneer of PERSPECTIVE. Brunelleschi influenced many later architects, including MICHELANGELO. In 1420, he began to design the dome of Florence Cathedral, the largest since the HAGIA SOPHIA. Other works include the Ospedale degl'Innocenti (1419–26) and the Basilica of San Lorenzo (begun 1421), both in Florence.

Brunhild (Brynhild, Brünnehilde) In Germanic mythology, a female warrior. In the *Volsungsaga*, Brynhild is the chief of the Valkyries, who Odin banishes from Valhalla and places in an enchanted sleep. She is awoken by Sigurd (Siegfried) and they fall in love. Gudrun tricks Sigurd into marrying her and Brynhild is forced to marry Gunnar (Gunther). Brynhild brings about Sigurd's death and kills herself on his funeral pyre.

Bruno, Giordano (1548–1600) Italian philosopher. A fierce opponent of dogmatism and a supporter of the relativity of perception, his pantheistic belief in a deity manifest in the cosmos and his support of COPERNICUS led to his censure for unorthodoxy and his death at the stake.

Brussels (Bruxelles) Capital of Belgium and of Brabant province, central Belgium. During the Middle Ages, it achieved prosperity through the wool trade and became capital of the Spanish Netherlands. In 1830, it became capital of newly independent Belgium. It has many fine buildings, including a 13th-century cathedral, the town hall, art-nouveau-period buildings and academies of fine arts. The main commercial, financial, cultural and administrative centre of Belgium, it is also the headquarters of the EUROPEAN COMMUNITY (EC) and of the NORTH ATLANTIC TREATY ORGANIZATION (NATO). Industries: textiles, chemicals. Pop. (1996) 948,000.

Brussels, Treaty of (1948) Agreement signed by Britain, France and the Low Countries for cooperation in defence, politics, economics and cultural affairs for 50 years. The defence agreement was merged into the NORTH ATLANTIC TREATY ORGANIZATION (NATO) in 1950. In 1954 Italy and West Germany joined, and the name was changed to the Western European Union. It was a forerunner of the EUROPEAN COMMUNITY (EC).

brutalism Architectural movement of the 1950s and early 1960s. It took its inspiration from LE CORBUSIER'S pilgrimage chapel at Ronchamp and his High Court building at CHANDIGARH, India. Other architects, such as James STIRLING, tried to extend Le Corbusier's experiments into aggressive and chunky designs of their own. It should not be confused with the 1950s movement of **new brutalism**, in which Alison and Peter Smithson adopted the uncompromising simplicity of MIES VAN DER ROHE.

Bruton, John Gerard (1947–) Irish statesman, taoiseach (1995–97). He was elected to the Dáil in 1969. A member of FINE GAEL, Bruton rose steadily through the ministerial ranks, earning a reputation as a right-winger. He became leader of Fine Gael in 1990 and succeeded Albert REYNOLDS as taoiseach. Bruton was succeeded by Bertie AHERN.

Brutus (85–42 BC) (Marcus Junius Brutus) Roman republican leader, one of the principal assassins of Julius CAESAR. He sided first with POMPEY against Caesar, but Caesar made him governor of Cisalpine Gaul in 46 BC and city praetor in 44 BC. After taking part in Caesar's assassination, he raised an army in Greece but was defeated at Philippi by MARK ANTONY and Octavian (later AUGUSTUS). Brutus committed suicide.

Bryan, William Jennings (1860–1925) US lawyer and secretary of state (1913–15). A leading advocate of the free coinage of silver, his "Cross of Gold" speech at the 1896 Democratic convention earned him the presidential nomination. Bryan lost the ensuing election to William McKINLEY. Nominated again in 1900, he was again defeated by McKinley. He was defeated a third time (1908) by William Howard TAFT. In return for helping Woodrow WILSON win the 1912 election, he became secretary of state. An opponent of the teaching of evolution, he acted as prosecuting attorney in the SCOPES TRIAL (1925), opposing Clarence DARROW. Bryan won the case but died five days later.

bryony Either of two unrelated plants, both of which are climbers in hedgerows in Europe and elsewhere. **White** bryony, *Bryonia alba*, is a member of the GOURD family (Cucurbitaceae) with large hand-shaped leaves. **Black** bryony, *Tamus communis*, is a member of the YAM family (Dioscoreaceae) and has heart-shaped leaves.

bryophyte Any member of the phylum Bryophyta – small, green, rootless non-VASCULAR PLANTS, including MOSS and LIVERWORT. Bryophytes grow on damp surfaces exposed to light, including rocks and tree bark, almost worldwide from the Arctic to the Antarctic. There are c.24,000 species. *See also* ALTERNATION OF GENERATIONS

BSE *See* BOVINE SPONGIFORM ENCEPHALOPATHY

bubble chamber Device for detecting and identifying ELEMENTARY PARTICLES. It consists of a sealed chamber filled with a liquefied gas, usually liquid hydrogen, kept just below its boiling point by high pressure in the chamber. When the pressure is released, the boiling

point is lowered and a charged particle passing through the superheated liquid leaves a trail of tiny gas bubbles. If a magnetic field is applied to the chamber, the tracks are curved according to the charge, mass and velocity of the particles. Donald GLASER received the 1960 Nobel Prize for physics for inventing the bubble chamber, and it was developed by Luis ALVAREZ.

Buber, Martin (1878–1965) Jewish philosopher, b. Vienna. An ardent early advocate of ZIONISM, he edited *Der Jude* (1916–24), the leading journal of German-speaking Jewish intellectuals. Buber defiantly opposed the Nazis in Germany until forced to move to Palestine in 1938. His most important published work is *I and Thou* (1922) on the directness of the relationship between man and God within the traditions of HASIDISM.

bubonic plague *See* PLAGUE

Buchan, John, 1st Baron Tweedsmuir (1875–1940) British writer and statesman, b. Scotland. Buchan is best-known for his adventure novels, such as *The Thirty-Nine Steps* (1915). He also wrote a four-volume history of World War 1 (1915–19) and biographies. He was governor general of Canada (1935–40).

Buchanan, James (1791–1868) 15th US president (1857–1861). Buchanan entered Congress in 1821 and was Senator (1834–45). President POLK appointed him secretary of state (1845–49). Under President PIERCE, Buchanan served as minister to Great Britain (1853–56). His administration was unpopular, and his attempt to compromise between pro- and anti-SLAVERY factions floundered. His efforts to purchase Cuba and acceptance of a pro-slavery constitution in Kansas contributed to his electoral defeat by Abraham LINCOLN. The Southern states seceded and, shortly after Buchanan left office, the American CIVIL WAR began.

Bucharest (Bucureşti) Capital and largest city of Romania, on the River Dimbovita, s Romania. Founded in the 14th century on an important trade route, it became capital in 1862 and was occupied by Germany in both World Wars. It is an industrial, commercial and cultural centre. The seat of the patriarch of the Romanian Orthodox Church, it has churches, museums and galleries. There are two universities. Industries: oil refining, chemicals. Pop. (1994) 2,061,000.

Buchenwald Site of a Nazi concentration camp, near Weimar in Germany. Established in 1937, it became notorious especially for the medical experiments conducted on its inmates, of whom c.50,000 died. The camp was liberated by US forces in 1945.

Büchner, Georg (1813–37) German dramatist. He died young of typhoid fever, leaving only two completed plays: *Danton's Death* (1835) and *Leonce and Lena* (1850). Büchner is best known, however, for the fragmentary tragedy *Woyzeck* (1837) that formed the basis for Alban Berg's opera *Wozzeck* (1925).

Buck, Pearl S. (Sydenstricker) (1892–1973) US novelist. Buck was brought up in China, which she used as the setting for many of her novels, including *The Good Earth* (1931), which won the 1932 Pulitzer Prize. Her other works include *Sons* (1932), *The Mother* (1934) and *Dragon Seed* (1942). Buck also wrote plays, screenplays, verse and children's fiction, and was awarded the 1938 Nobel Prize for literature.

Buckingham, George Villiers, 1st Duke of (1592–1628) English statesman and court favourite of JAMES I and CHARLES I. He joined the court of James I in 1614 and rapidly acquired a series of titles. His personal extravagance led to Parliamentary investigation. In 1623, Buckingham was largely responsible for the breakdown in the negotiations of marriage between Prince Charles and the Spanish Infanta Maria. In 1624, he arranged Charles' marriage to Henrietta Maria. Buckingham's failure to provide adequate supplies for an English expedition to the Palatinate led to charges of political incompetence. The disastrous expedition to capture Cadiz (1625) led to his impeachment, but Charles I rapidly dissolved parliament. In 1627, Buckingham led another unsuccessful campaign to relieve the HUGUENOTS at La Rochelle. He was murdered by a discontented naval officer.

Buckingham, George Villiers, 2nd Duke of (1628–87) English courtier, son of the 1st duke of BUCKINGHAM. He was educated with CHARLES I's sons and supported the Royalists in the CIVIL WAR (1642–48). A dashing, rakish courtier in Restoration England, Buckingham was a member of the group of ministers known as the CABAL but later joined the opposition to CHARLES II. He wrote several comedies, notably *The Rehearsal* (1671).

Buckingham Palace London residence of British sovereigns since 1837. Formerly owned by the dukes of Buckingham, it was purchased by George III in 1761 and remodeled into a 600-room palace by John NASH in 1825. Sir Aston Webb redesigned the E front in 1913. The changing of the guard takes place here daily.

Buckinghamshire County in SE central England; the county town is Aylesbury. In the Vale of Aylesbury to the N, cereal crops and beans are grown; livestock and poultry are raised in the S. Industries: furniture, printing. Area: 1,877sq km (725sq mi). Pop. (1991) 632,487.

Buckminsterfullerene (buckyball) Allotrope of CARBON that consists of many carbon atoms bonded together in the shape of a hollow sphere. The simplest Buckminsterfullerene has 60 carbon atoms arranged as 12 regular pentagons and 20 hexagons (like the panels on a modern football). It can be made by exposing graphite to a laser beam or electric arc in an inert atmosphere. It is a yellow crystalline solid that dissolves in benzene. It gets its name from the US architect Richard Buckminster FULLER, who invented the GEODESIC DOME structure that the molecules resemble. *See also* ALLOTROPY

bud In plants, a small swelling or projection consisting of a short stem with overlapping, immature leaves covered by scales. Leaf buds develop into leafy twigs, and flower buds develop into blossoms. A bud at the tip of a twig is a terminal bud and contains the growing point; lateral buds develop in leaf axils along a twig.

Budapest Capital of Hungary, on the River Danube. It was created in 1873 by uniting the towns of Buda (capital of Hungary since the 14th century) and Pest on the opposite bank. It became one of the two capitals of the AUSTRO-HUNGARIAN EMPIRE. In 1918 it was declared capital of an independent Hungary. Budapest was the scene of a popular uprising against the Soviet Union in 1956. The old town contains a remarkable collection of buildings, including Buda Castle, the 13th-century Matthias Church, the Parliament Building, the National Museum and Roman remains. Industries: iron and steel, chemicals. Pop. (1997) 1,885,000.

Buddha (Enlightened One) Title adopted by Gautama Siddhartha (*c*.563–*c*.483 BC), the founder of BUDDHISM. Born in Lumbini, Nepal, Siddhartha was son of the ruler of the Sakya tribe, and his early years were spent in luxury. At the age of 29, he realized that human life is little more than suffering. He gave up his wealth and comfort, deserted his wife and small son, and took to the road as a wandering ascetic. He sought truth in a six-year regime of austerity and self-mortification. After abandoning asceticism as futile, he sought his own middle way towards enlightenment. The moment of truth came (*c*.528 BC) as he sat beneath a banyan tree in the village of Buddha Gaya, Bihar, India. After this, he taught others about his way to truth. The title "buddha" applies to those who have achieved perfect enlightenment. Buddhists believe that there have been several buddhas before Siddhartha, and there will be many to come. The term also serves to describe a variety of Buddha images.

Buddhism Religion and philosophy founded (*c*.528 BC) in India by Gautama Siddhartha, the BUDDHA. Buddhism is based on Four Noble Truths: existence is suffering, the cause of suffering is desire, the end of suffering comes with the achievement of NIRVANA and Nirvana is attained through the Eightfold Path of right views, right resolve, right speech, right action, right livelihood, right effort, right mindfulness and right concentration. There are no gods. KARMA, one of Buddhism's most important concepts, says good actions are rewarded and evil ones are punished, either in this life or throughout a long series of lives resulting in **samsara**, the cycle of death and rebirth by REINCARNATION. The achievement of Nirvana breaks the cycle. Buddhism is a worldwide religion. Its main divisions are: THERAVADA, or *Hinayana*, in SE Asia; MAHAYANA in N Asia; Lamaism or TIBETAN BUDDHISM in Tibet; and ZEN in Japan. Today, the total number of Buddhists is estimated at *c*.300 million.

budding Method of asexual reproduction that produces a new organism from an outgrowth of the parent. Hydras, for example, often bud in spring and summer. A small bulge appears on the parent and grows until it breaks away as a new individual.

buddleia Flowering shrub, often conspicuous because of the butterflies attracted to its purple or yellow flowers. Buddleias used to be classified as members of the logania family, native to the tropics, but are now considered to be a separate family, the Buddlejaceae. Genus *Buddleia*.

Budge, (John) Don (Donald) (1915–2000) US tennis player. In 1937, he won the Wimbledon and US Open singles titles. In 1938, Budge became the first man to complete the sport's grand slam of the four major singles titles (Wimbledon, US, Australia, France). In 1937–38, he also won both the mixed and men's doubles titles at Wimbledon and the US Open.

budgerigar (parakeet) Small, brightly coloured seed-eating PARROT native to Australia, and a popular pet. It can be taught to mimic speech. The sexes look alike, but the coloration of the cere (a waxy membrane at the base of the beak) may vary seasonally. Size: 19cm (7.5in) long. Species *Melopsittacus undulatus*.

Buenos Aires Capital of Argentina, on the estuary of the Río de la Plata, 240km (150mi) from the Atlantic Ocean. Originally founded by Spain in 1536, it was rebuilt in 1580 after being destroyed by the indigenous population. It became a separate federal district and capital of the country in 1880. Buenos Aires later developed as a commercial centre for beef, grain and dairy products. It is the seat of the National University (1821). Industries: meat processing, flour milling, textiles, metal works. Pop. (1992 est.) 11,662,050.

Buffalo Industrial city and port on the E shore of Lake Erie, NW New York State, USA. It was first settled in 1803. Its rapid growth was encouraged by its position at the W terminus of the Erie Canal (opened 1825). President MCKINLEY was assassinated at the Pan-American Exposition held here in 1901. It is home to the Albright-Knox art gallery and has two universities. Industries: flour milling, motor vehicles, chemicals. Pop. (1996) 1,175,000.

buffalo Any of several horned mammals, and a misnomer for the North American BISON. The massive ox-like Indian, or water, buffalo (*Bubalus bubalis*) is often domesticated for milk and hides. Height: 1.5m (5ft). Family Bovidae.

"Buffalo Bill" (William Frederick Cody) (1846–1917) US frontiersman, scout and showman. A Pony Express rider at 14, he then served as Union scout during the Civil War. Cody gained his nickname by supplying buffalo meat to railway workers. He became famous through Ned Buntline's dime novels. In 1883 "Buffalo Bill" organized a "Wild West" exhibition, co-starring Annie Oakley and Chief Sitting Bull.

buffer solution Solution to which a moderate quantity of a strong acid or a strong base can be added without making a significant change to its pH value (acidity or alkalinity).

Buffet, Bernard (1928–1999) French painter. Buffet first achieved recognition in the early 1950s for his still-lifes, urban scenes and portraits. The melancholic and monochromatic style of his paintings perfectly captured the mood of French EXISTENTIALISM. He committed suicide in 1999.

Buffon, Georges Louis Leclerc, Comte de (1707–88) French naturalist. From 1739, as keeper of the Jardin du Roi (now Jardin des Plantes) in Paris, Buffon began to collect data for *Histoire naturelle* (44 vols., 1749–1804), a popular compendium of natural history.

bug Any member of the INSECT order Hemiptera, although in the US any insect is commonly called a bug. True bugs are flattened insects that undergo gradual or incomplete metamorphosis, have two pairs of wings and use piercing and sucking mouthparts. Most feed on plant juices, such as the greenfly, although a number attack animals and are carriers of disease.

bugaku Highly stylized formal dances often performed in masks in the Japanese imperial court and characterized by movements in ritualized patterns. The dances were imported from India and China during the 7th century and influenced the development of JAPANESE THEATRE, such as NO DRAMA.

bugle Brass wind instrument resembling a small TRUMPET without valves, capable of playing notes of only one harmonic series. Because its penetrating tones carry great distances, it was often used for military signalling.

bugloss Wild flowering plant, *Anchusa arvensis*, a member of the BORAGE family (Boraginaceae), with bright purplish-blue flowers. The genus *Echium* includes viper's bugloss, a common meadow plant.

Buhl, André Charles *See* BOULLE, ANDRÉ CHARLES

Bujumbura (formerly Usumbura) Capital and chief port of Burundi, E central Africa, at the NE end of Lake TANGANYIKA. Founded in 1899 as part of German East Africa, it was the capital of the Belgian trust territory of Ruanda-Urundi after World War 1 and remained capital of Burundi when the country achieved independence in 1962. It is an administrative and commercial centre. Industries: textiles, cotton. Pop. (1994 est.) 300,000.

Bukhara (Buchara) Ancient city in W Uzbekistan, capital of the Bukhara region. Founded *c*.1st century AD, it was ruled by Arabs (7th–9th century), by Turks and Mongols (12th–15th century), and annexed to Russia in 1868; it was included in Uzbekistan (1924). It is an important Asian trade and cultural centre. Monuments include the 10th-century mausoleum of Ismail Samani. Industries: silk processing, rugs. Pop. (1993) 236,000.

Bukharin, Nikolai Ivanovich (1888–1938) Russian political theorist. After the Russian Revolution (1917), he

became a leading member of the COMMUNIST INTERNATIONAL (Comintern) and editor of *Pravda*. In 1924, Bukharin joined the politburo. He opposed agricultural collectivization and was executed for treason by STALIN.

Bulawayo City in SW Zimbabwe, SE Africa; capital of Matabeleland North province. It was founded by the British in 1893 and was the site of the Matabele revolt in 1896. It is the second largest city in the country. Industries: textiles, motor vehicles. Pop. (1992) 620,936.

bulb In botany, a storage organ consisting of a short stem and swollen scale leaves. Food is stored in the scales, which are either layered in a series of rings, as in the onion, or loosely attached to the stem, as in some lilies. Small buds between the scale leaves give rise to new shoots each year. New bulbs are produced in the axils of the outer scale leaves. *See also* ASEXUAL REPRODUCTION

bulbul Any of numerous species of songbird of Africa and S Asia, where they are kept as cage birds. They are short-necked dull-coloured birds, ranging in size from 15–30cm (6–12in). They feed on berries and other fruits and build a grass nest for 3–5 eggs. Family Pycnonotidae; there are *c*.120 species.

Bulfinch, Charles (1763–1844) US architect. He is particularly noted for his public buildings, including the State House, Boston and University Hall at Harvard University, Cambridge, Massachusetts. From 1818 to 1830, he completed the building of the Capitol in Washington, D.C.

Bulgakov, Mikhail Afanasievich (1891–1940) Russian novelist and dramatist. Bulgakov reworked his novel on the Russian Civil War, *The White Guard* (1925), into a play (*The Day of the Turbines*) which was performed (1926–29) at the Moscow Arts Theatre. The play was banned by Stalin, and his later work also was censored. Bulgakov's masterpiece is the satirical novel *The Master and Margarita* (1928–40).

Bulganin, Nikolai (1895–1975) Soviet statesman and military leader, prime minister (1955–58) and defence minister (1947–49, 1953–55). He served in the army during World War 2. Bulganin became prime minister after the fall of MALENKOV. He was dismissed after disagreements with KHRUSHCHEV.

Bulgaria Balkan republic in SE Europe. Northern Bulgaria consists of a plateau falling to the valley of the River DANUBE, which forms most of Bulgaria's N border with Romania. The heart of Bulgaria is mountainous, and the main ranges include the BALKAN MOUNTAINS (Stara Planina) in the centre and the Rhodope Mountains in the S. The capital, SOFIA, lies close to Bulgaria's highest point, Mount Musala, at 2,925m (9,600ft). Between these ranges lies the valley of the River Maritsa. **Climate** Bulgaria has hot summers and cold winters. Rainfall is moderate. The E has drier and warmer summers than the W, and the Black Sea coast is a popular resort area. **Vegetation** More than half of Bulgaria is given over to crops or pasture, while forests cover *c*.35% of the land. In the Balkan Mountains are the rosefields of Kazanluk, from which attar of roses is exported. **History and Politics** In the late 7th century, BULGAR tribes crossed the Danube and subjugated the SLAVS. The first Bulgarian empire (681–1018) quickly became a major Balkan power. The empire was at its height in the early 10th century, but in 1018 it was annexed to the BYZANTINE EMPIRE by BASIL II. The second Bulgarian empire (1186–1396) conquered the whole of the Balkan peninsula, before it was subsumed into the OTTOMAN EMPIRE. The brutal crushing of a native rebellion (1876) brought Russian assistance, and Bulgaria gained autonomy in 1879. Prince FERDINAND

BULGARIA
AREA: 110,910sq km (42,822sq mi)
POPULATION: 9,071,000
CAPITAL (POPULATION): Sofia (1,117,000)

declared full independence in 1908. Bulgaria was victorious in the first of the BALKAN WARS (1912–13), but fell out with its allies in the second. Defeat in World War 1 led to the abdication of Ferdinand (1918). His successor, Boris III, established a dictatorship in 1935 and allied with Germany in World War 2. In 1944, Soviet troops invaded. Todor Zhivkov led a coup against the monarchy and declared war on Germany. In 1946, Bulgaria became a one-party republic. Industry was nationalized and agriculture collectivized. Bulgaria was a founder member (1955) of the WARSAW PACT. In the early 1950s, the Stalinist regime launched a series of purges of the Communist Party and deported large numbers of Turks. With the collapse of Soviet communism, Zhivkov's presidency (1971–89) came to an abrupt end. The Bulgarian Communist Party was renamed the Bulgarian Socialist Party (BSP). In 1990, the first non-communist president for 40 years, Zhelyu Zhelev, was elected. A new constitution (1991) saw the adoption of free-market reforms. The BSP won the 1994 general election, but virtual economic collapse and anti-government demonstrations prompted the government to resign (1996). Fresh elections (1997) were won by a centre-right coalition. **Economy** Bulgaria is a lower-middle-income developing country (1995 GDP per capita, US$4,480), faced with a difficult transition to a market economy. Since 1989, Bulgaria's major trading partner has been the European Union (EU). Inflation (1994, 96%), unemployment (1993, 16%) and public debt are major economic and social obstacles. Manufacturing is the leading economic activity but has outdated technology. The main products are chemicals, metals, machinery and textiles. Mineral reserves include molybdenum. Wheat and maize are the main crops. The warm valleys of the Maritsa are ideal for growing grapes for winemaking, plums and tobacco. Tourism is increasing rapidly (1995, 2 million visitors).
Bulgars Ancient Turkic people originating in the region N and E of the Black Sea. In c.AD 650, they split into two groups. The western group moved to Bulgaria, where they became assimilated into the Slavic population and adopted Christianity. The other group moved to the VOLGA region and set up a Bulgar state, eventually converting to Islam. The Volga Bulgars were conquered by the Kievan Rus in the 10th century.
Bulge, Battle of the Final German offensive of WORLD WAR 2. The Germans drove a wedge through the Allied lines in the ARDENNES on the French–Belgian frontier in December 1944. Allied forces converged to extinguish the "bulge" in their lines in January 1945, and the advance into Germany was renewed.
bulimia nervosa EATING DISORDER that takes the form of compulsive eating, then purging by induced vomiting or the use of a LAXATIVE or DIURETIC. Confined predominantly to girls and women, the disorder most often results from an underlying psychological problem.
bulldog English bull baiting breed of DOG with a distinctive large head, short upturned muzzle and a projecting lower jaw. The body is large, with muscular shoulders, a broad chest and short stout legs; the tail is short. The smooth coat may be white, tan or brindle. Height: (at shoulder) up to 38cm (15in).

bullfighting National sport of Spain and also popular in Latin America and S France. Classically there are six bulls and three matadors, who are assigned two bulls each. Each matador has five assistants – two *picadors* (mounted on armoured horses) and three *peones* or *banderilleros*. A bullfight starts when the picadors stab the bull to weaken it. The *peones* then plant *banderillas* (barbed sticks) on the withers of the bull. The matador makes several passes with his red cape (*muleta*) before attempting to kill the bull by thrusting a sword between its shoulder blades. In Spain, bullfighting is regarded as an art, to many others worldwide it is a cruel spectacle.
bullfinch Northern European and Asian finch, with a stout, rounded beak. Males have a crimson and grey body and a black head; females have duller colours. It grows to 14cm (5.5in) long; species *Pyrrhula pyrrhula*.
bullfrog FROG found in streams and ponds in the US; it is green or brown and breeds in the spring. The largest North American frog, it can jump long distances; it gets its name from its loud bass voice. Family Ranidae, genus *Rana*. Length: up to 20cm (8in).
bullhead Freshwater catfish, originally found throughout the E US. Now farmed as food, it has been introduced in Europe and Hawaii. It has four pairs of fleshy mouth whiskers and a square tail. Length: to 61cm (24in); weight: to 3.6kg (8lb). Family Ictaluridae; species include yellow *Ictalurus natalis* and brown *Ictalurus nebulosus*.
Bull Run, First Battle of (21 July 1861) American CIVIL WAR engagement fought near Manassas, Virginia. Under-trained Union troops commanded by General Irvin McDowell, at first successful, were eventually routed by Confederate troops under General P.G.T. BEAUREGARD, reinforced by General Thomas J. JACKSON, who earned his nickname "Stonewall" at the battle.
Bull Run, Second Battle of (28 August 1862) American CIVIL WAR battle. On the old battleground of 1861, 48,000 Confederates under General Robert E. LEE beat 75,000 Union soldiers under General John Pope. Union losses were 16,000 to the Confederates' 9,000. Pope was dismissed as commander of the Union army, and General George McCLELLAN reassumed control.
bull terrier Strongly built sporting DOG, originating from England and once used for bear-baiting; it has a large oval head with small erect ears. The broad-chested body is set on strong legs and the tail is short. Height (at shoulder): up to 56cm (22in).
Bülow, Bernhard, Prince von (1849–1929) Chancellor of the German empire (1900–09). His aggressive foreign policy left Germany isolated against the TRIPLE ENTENTE and heightened the tensions in Europe that preceded the outbreak of World War 1. In 1908, Bülow lost the favour of Emperor William II and was forced to resign.
bumblebee (humble bee) Robust, hairy black BEE with broad yellow or orange stripes. The genus *Bombus* live in organized groups in ground or tree nests, where the fertile queen lays her first eggs after the winter hibernation. These become worker bees. Later, the queen lays eggs to produce drones (males) and new queens which develop before the colony dies. The cycle is then repeated. The genus *Psithyrus*, or cuckoo bee, lays its eggs in the nests of *Bombus*, which rear them. Length: up to 2.5cm (1in). Order Hymenoptera; family Apidae.
Bunche, Ralph Johnson (1904–71) US diplomat. He joined the UN in 1947 and helped negotiate a cease-fire (1949) in the Arab-Israeli conflict. In 1950, Bunche became the first African-American to be awarded the Nobel Peace Prize. He directed UN peacekeeping forces

in Suez (1956), the Congo (1960) and Cyprus (1964). Bunche served as UN under-secretary-general (1967–71).

Bunin, Ivan Alekseyevich (1870–1953) Russian writer. Bunin was opposed to the 1917 Revolution and emigrated to France. His works lament the passing of the old Russian order. They include the novel *The Village* (1910) and the short story *The Gentleman from San Francisco* (1916). Bunin was the first Russian to be awarded the Nobel Prize for literature (1933).

bunion Inflammation of the joint at the base of the big toe, causing it to become displaced towards the adjoining toes. A form of BURSITIS, it is caused by ill-fitting shoes. It can be treated by surgery.

Bunker Hill, Battle of (June 1775) Battle in the AMERICAN REVOLUTION fought on Boston's Charlestown peninsula. The first large-scale battle of the war, it was actually fought S of Bunker Hill on Breed's Hill. Although the Americans were driven from their position, the British lost nearly half of their troops (2,400).

Bunsen, Robert Wilhelm (1811–99) German chemist, professor (1852–99) at Heidelberg University. He did important work with organo-ARSENIC compounds and discovered an arsenic poisoning antidote. Bunsen later evolved a method of gas analysis. With his assistant, Gustav KIRCHHOFF, he used SPECTROSCOPY to discover two new elements (CAESIUM and RUBIDIUM). Bunsen invented various kinds of laboratory equipment, such as a carbon-zinc electric cell (Bunsen cell), that was used in arc lamps. He also improved a gas burner that was later named after him. *See* BUNSEN BURNER

Bunsen burner Gas burner widely used in science laboratories. It is named after the German chemist Robert W. BUNSEN. The burner is a 13-cm (5-in) upright tube, usually of brass, attached to a gas source. It has a variable air inlet at its base to control the intensity of its flame.

bunting FINCH found throughout most of the world. Males of the genus *Passerina* are brightly coloured, whereas the females are smaller and duller. Members of the genus *Emberiza* are larger and dull coloured, although the snow bunting is almost white. Family Fringillidae.

Buñuel, Luis (1900–83) Spanish film director. Buñuel and Salvador Dali collaborated on the surrealist masterpiece *Un Chien Andalou* (1928). *L'Age d'Or* (1930) was ferociously critical of the church and social hypocrisy. Other films include *Viridiana* (1961), *Belle de Jour* (1966) and *The Discreet Charms of the Bourgeoise* (1974).

Bunyan, John (1628–88) English preacher and author. During the English CIVIL WAR (1642–52) he fought as a Parliamentarian. In 1653, Bunyan began preaching at a Baptist Church in Bedford. In 1660 he was arrested for unlicensed preaching. Bunyan spent the next 12 years in prison, where he wrote the spiritual autobiography *Grace Abounding* (1666). In 1672, he was reimprisoned and started work on his masterpiece, the Christian ALLEGORY *The Pilgrim's Progress* (1684).

buoyancy Upward pressure exerted on an object by the fluid in which it is immersed. The object is subjected to pressure from all sides. The result of all these pressures is a force acting upward that is equal to the weight of the fluid displaced. *See also* ARCHIMEDES' PRINCIPLE

burbot Bottom-dwelling, freshwater COD found in colder waters of Asia, N America and Europe. It is a slender, brown fish that spawns in winter. Length: to 110cm (38in); weight: to 16kg (36lb). Order Gadiformes; family Gadidae; species *Lota lota*.

burdock Oil-yielding weed found throughout Europe, North Africa and North America. It has large basal leaves and thistle-like purple flower heads covered by stiff, hooked bracts. Common burdock, *Arctium pubens*, is biennial and grows to 0.9m (3ft). Family Asteraceae/Compositae.

bureaucracy Administrative structure of any large organization. Bureaucracies are hierarchically organized. They are set up to apply rules impersonally but are criticized for inflexibility. *See also* WEBER, MAX

Burgas Industrial port on the Black Sea coast, SE Bulgaria; capital of Burgas province. Burgas lies on the site of ancient Thracian and Roman settlements. The construction (1903–04) of a harbour spurred development. In recent years it has become a resort. Industries: food processing. Pop. (1996) 199,000.

Burgess, Anthony (1917–93) English novelist. Burgess' early works are set in Malaya, where he lived and served (1954–60) as part of the Colonial Service. His best-known work is *A Clockwork Orange* (1962), a vision of a modern dystopia in which he deploys a macabre, invented language. Later novels include *Earthly Powers* (1980) and *The Kingdom of the Wicked* (1985).

Burghley, William Cecil, 1st Baron (1520–98) English statesman and chief minister of ELIZABETH I of England. He was secretary of state (1550–53) under EDWARD VI but failed to win MARY I's favour on her accession to the throne. On Mary's death, Elizabeth I made him secretary of state (1558–72) and then lord high treasurer (1572–98). In 1587, Burghley was responsible for ordering the execution of MARY, QUEEN OF SCOTS.

Burgos Capital city of Burgos province, N Spain. Founded in the 9th century, it was the capital of the former kingdom of Castile. During the Spanish Civil War it was General Franco's headquarters. Sites include the burial place of El Cid. It is an important trade and tourist centre. Pop. (1995) 167,000.

Burgundy Historical region and former duchy of E central France that now includes the departments of Yonne, Côte-d'Or, Saône et Loire, Ain and Nièvre. Dijon is the historical capital. Burgundy's golden age began in 1364 when John II of France made his son, Philip the Bold, duke of Burgundy. The succeeding dukes created a state that extended across the Rhine and included the Low Countries. The last duke, Charles the Bold (r.1467–77), failed to have himself crowned king by the Holy Roman emperor, and Burgundy was divided up after his death, France annexing the largest part. The region is a rich agricultural region renowned for its wine. Pop. (1990) 1,609,400.

Burke, Edmund (1729–97) British statesman and writer, b. Ireland. He played a major part in the reduction of royal influence in the House of Commons and sought better treatment for Catholics and American colonists. Burke deplored the excesses of the FRENCH REVOLUTION in his most famous work, *Reflections on the Revolution in France* (1790).

Burke, Robert O'Hara (1820–61) Irish explorer. In 1860, he led the first expedition to cross Australia from S to N. At the River Barcoo, Burke left most of the party and continued with three companions. They reached N Australia in 1861. Only one of the group (King) survived the return journey.

Burkina Faso Landlocked republic in W Africa. Burkina Faso consists of a plateau, *c.*200–700m (650–2,300ft) above sea level, which is cut by several rivers, most of which flow S into Ghana or E into the River Niger. During droughts, some of the rivers dry up and their valleys become marshes. The capital, OUAGADOUGOU, lies in the centre of the country. **Climate** Burkina Faso is hot throughout the year, with most rain occurring between

BURKINA FASO \
AREA: 274,200sq km (105,869 sq mi)
POPULATION: 12,092,000
CAPITAL (POPULATION): Ouagadougou (690,000)

May and September when it is often humid. Rainfall is
erratic and droughts are common. **Vegetation** The sw, is
covered by savanna, while the rest of Burkina Faso is the
semi-desert region of the SAHEL, which merges into the
Sahara. Overgrazing, deforestation and soil erosion are
common problems in the Sahel, causing desertification in
many areas of the country. Large areas of woodland border the rivers. **History and Politics** The people of Burkina Faso are divided into two main groups. The Voltaic
group includes the Mossi (the largest single group) and
the Bobo. The other main group is the Mande. Some
FULANI herders and HAUSA traders also live in Burkina
Faso. From *c*.1100 the Mossi invaded the region and
established small, highly complex states. The powerful
Ouagadougou kingdom was ruled by an absolute
monarch, the Moro Naba. These semi-autonomous states
fiercely resisted domination by the larger Mali and Songhai empires. In the 1890s, France gained control of the
region. In 1919, it became the French protectorate of
Upper Volta. In 1958, Upper Volta became an
autonomous republic within the French Community. In
1960, it achieved full independence. A strong, presidential
form of government was adopted. Persistent drought and
austerity measures led to a military coup in 1966. In 1970,
civilian rule was partially restored, but the military, led by
Sangoulé Lamizana, regained power in 1974. Lamizana
became president in 1978 elections but was overthrown in
1980. In 1983, Thomas Sankara seized power in a bloody
coup. In 1984, Sankara changed the country's name to
Burkina Faso ("land of the incorruptible"). Sankara was
assassinated in 1987, and Captain Blaise Compaoré
seized power. In 1991, Compaoré was elected president,
after opposition parties boycotted the poll. He was re-
elected in 1997. **Economy** Burkina Faso is one of the
world's poorest countries (1995 GDP per capita,
$US780). Nearly 90% of the workforce is engaged in
agriculture, but less than 10% of the land is cultivable
without irrigation, and Burkina Faso remains reliant on
food imports. The chief exports are livestock, groundnuts,
cotton, corn, millet and sorghum. There are some deposits
of gold, manganese, zinc, lead and nickel in the N, but they
remain largely unexploited. Its manufactures are limited
to basic consumer items, such as footwear and bicycles.
Much of the male labour force is forced to migrate to the
Ivory Coast and Ghana to find work.
Burlington, Richard Boyle, 3rd Earl of (1694–1753)
English architect. He was an exponent of PALLADIANISM
in England. Burlington promoted the style through his
own buildings, such as his villa at Chiswick, London.
Burma Republic in SE Asia, officially the Union of Myanmar. The most densely populated part of the country is the
valley of the River IRRAWADDY. MANDALAY, Burma's sec-
ond largest city, lies on the banks of the river. The capital,
RANGOON, lies on the shores of the ANDAMAN SEA.
Burma's land borders are formed by a chain of Himalayan
mountains that rise in the N to 5,881m (19,294ft). In the E,
lies the Shan Plateau, home to the Shan tribe. Burma is federated into tribal areas. Sittwe is the main port of the
Arakan region, on the Bay of BENGAL. In the SE lies the
Tenassserim region, which includes the port of Moulmein.
Climate and Vegetation Burma has a tropical monsoon

climate. The humid rainy season lasts from late May to
mid-October. Mandalay is relatively dry, with an annual
rainfall of 50–100cm (20–50in). The Irrawaddy delta is
one of the world's largest rice-growing areas. About 50%
of Burma is covered by forest. **History and Politics**
Burma's early history was dominated by conflict between
the Burmans and Mons. In 1044 the Burman king
Anawratha unified the Irrawaddy delta region. In 1287
KUBLAI KHAN conquered the Burman capital, Pagan.
Burma was divided: the Shan controlled N Burma, while
the resurgent Mons held the s. In the 16th century, the Burmans subjugated the Shan. In 1758, Alaungapaya reunified
Burma by defeating the Mons kingdom based around
Mandalay and established the Konbaung dynasty. The
19th century was marked by wars between the dynasty and
British India. In the third war (1885), Burma was annexed
to British India. In 1937, Burma gained limited self-government. Helped by the Burmese Independent Army, led
by AUNG SAN, Japan conquered the country in 1942. The
installation of a puppet regime led Aung San to form a
resistance movement. In 1947, Aung San was murdered.
In 1948, Burma achieved independence. The socialist government, led by U NU, was faced with secessionist revolts
by communists and Karen tribesmen. In 1958, U Nu invited General NE WIN to re-establish order. Civilian government was restored in 1960, but in 1962 Ne Win mounted a
successful coup. In 1974, Ne Win became president. Massive demonstrations forced Ne Win to resign (1988), but
the military remained in control in the guise of the State
Law and Order Restoration Council (SLORC). In 1989,
the country's name was changed to Myanmar. Elections in
1990 were won by the National League for Democracy
(NLD), led by AUNG SAN SUU KYI, but SLORC annulled
the result and placed Aung San Suu Kyi under house
arrest. In 1997, SLORC was renamed the State Peace and
Development Council (SPDC). In 1998, NLD calls for the
reconvening of Parliament led to mass detention of political opponents by the SPDC. **Economy** Burma is one of the
world's poorest nations (1992 GDP per capita, $US751).
Agriculture is the main activity, employing 64% of the
workforce, mainly at subsistence level. Teak and rice constitute about two-thirds of exports. Burma is famous for its
precious stones, especially rubies.
Burmese Official language of Burma, spoken by 75%
of the population. It belongs to the Tibeto-Burman
branch of the Sino-Tibetan family of languages.
burn Injury caused by exposure to flames, scalding liquids, caustic chemicals, acids, electric current or ionizing radiation. Its severity depends on the extent of SKIN
loss and the depth of tissue damage. A **superficial** burn,
involving only the EPIDERMIS, causes redness, swelling
and pain; it heals within a few days. A **partial-thickness**
burn (epidermis and DERMIS) causes intense pain, with
mottling and blistering of the skin; it takes a couple of
weeks to heal. In a **full-thickness** burn, involving both
the skin and the underlying flesh, there is charring, and
the damaged flesh looks dry and leathery; there is no
pain because the nerve endings have been destroyed.
Such a burn, serious in itself, is associated with life-
threatening complications, including dehydration and
infection. Treatment includes fluid replacement and
antibiotics; skin grafting may be necessary.
Burne-Jones, Sir Edward Coley (1833–98) English painter and designer. He was associated with the
PRE-RAPHAELITE BROTHERHOOD'S romanticism and
escapism. Burne-Jones often depicted scenes from
Arthurian and similar legends, and was considered an
outstanding designer of stained glass.

BURMA
AREA: 261,228 sq mi (676,577 sq km)
POPULATION: 51,129,000
CAPITAL (POPULATION): Rangoon (Yangon, 2,458,712)

burnet Perennial plant native to N temperate regions, whose leaves are used to give a cucumber-like flavour to salads. Long-stamened, pink flowers are borne on tall stalks. Family Rosaceae; genus *Sanguisorba*.

Burnett, Frances (1849–1924) US writer, b. England. Burnett is chiefly remembered as the author of the children's classics *Little Lord Fauntleroy* (1886), *The Little Princess* (1905) and *The Secret Garden* (1911).

Burney, Fanny (1752–1840) English novelist, dramatist and diarist. The daughter of the musicologist Dr. Charles Burney, she came to fame with her first novel, *Evelina* (1778), a semi-satirical, semi-sentimental look at polite society through the eyes of a young innocent. This was followed by similar works, such as *Cecilia* (1782), *Camilla* (1796) and *The Wanderer* (1814).

Burnham, Forbes (1923–85) Guayanan statesman, prime minister (1964–80) and president (1980–85). Burnham and Cheddi Jegan were the leaders of the independence movement in British Guiana. As prime minister, he oversaw the transition to independence (1966) and the formation of a republic (1970).

Burns, Robert (1759–96) Scottish poet. The success of *Poems, Chiefly in the Scottish Dialect* (1786), which includes "The Holy Fair" and "To a Mouse", enabled him to move to Edinburgh. Although popular, he could not support himself on the revenue from his poetry and so became an excise officer. Scotland's unofficial national poet, his works include "Tam o'Shanter" (1790) and the song "Auld Lang Syne". An annual Burns night is held on his birthday, 25 January.

Burr, Aaron (1756–1836) US statesman, vice president (1801–05), senator for New York (1791–97). His contribution to the formation of a Republican legislature in New York (1800) ensured the election of a Republican president. Burr was supposed to become vice president, but confusion in the ELECTORAL COLLEGE resulted in a tie for president between Burr and Thomas JEFFERSON. Jefferson was elected with the support of Alexander HAMILTON. This mix-up led to the adoption of the 12th amendment to the US Constitution. Burr was an able vice president and was nominated for governor of New York. Hamilton led public attacks on Burr's suitability, which resulted in a duel (1804). Burr killed Hamilton, thus ending his own political career. Embittered, he embarked on an apparent conspiracy to establish an independent republic in SW USA. He was tried for treason but was acquitted (1807).

Burra, Edward John (1905–76) English artist. Fascinated with Harlem, New York and the Marseilles docks, he produced some of his most famous paintings, the Harlem scenes (1933–34). In the mid-1930s Burra turned to fantastic imagery, akin to SURREALISM. His later work, such as *Soldiers* and *War in the Sun*, were provoked by the tragedies of the Spanish Civil War and World War 2.

Burroughs, Edgar Rice (1875–1950) US author of adventure novels. A prolific writer, he is best known as the creator of Tarzan the apeman, who featured in a series of books, beginning with *Tarzan of the Apes* (1912).

Burroughs, William S. (Seward) (1914–97) US novelist, regarded as one of the founders of the BEAT MOVEMENT. Burroughs' best-known work, *Naked Lunch* (1959), deals in part with his heroin addiction. Other

works, experimental in style, include *The Ticket That Exploded* (1962) and *The Western Lands* (1987).

Bursa (Brusa) City in NW Turkey; capital of Bursa province. Bursa is Turkey's sixth-largest city. Founded in the 3rd century BC, it was the first capital (1327–1413) of the Ottoman Empire. In 1402, the city was sacked by Tamerlane. The city has several fine mosques and is famous for its silk manufacturing. Pop. (1995) 1,017,000.

bursitis Inflammation of the fluid-filled sac (bursa) surrounding a joint. It is characterized by pain, swelling and restricted movement. Treatment generally includes rest, heat and gentle exercise. "Housemaid's knee", "tennis elbow" and bunions are common forms of bursitis.

Burton, Richard (1925–84) Welsh stage and film actor, remembered for his deep, passionate and fiery voice. By the 1950s he had a reputation as a leading Shakespearean actor. Burton appeared in such films as *The Robe* (1953), *Look Back in Anger* (1959) and *Becket* (1964). He made a number of films with Elizabeth Taylor, notably *Who's Afraid of Virginia Woolf?* (1966). The couple had a tempestuous relationship and married each other twice.

Burton, Sir Richard Francis (1821–90) English explorer and scholar. In 1853, he travelled in disguise to Medina and Mecca, one of the first Europeans to visit the holy cities. On his second trip to E Africa, with John SPEKE in 1857, Burton discovered Lake Tanganyika. The author of many books, he was best known for his translation of the *Arabian Nights* (1885–88).

Burundi Republic in E central Africa. Burundi is the fifth smallest country on the mainland of Africa and the second most densely populated (after its neighbour RWANDA). West Burundi is part of the Great RIFT VALLEY, which includes Lake TANGANYIKA. The capital, BUJUMBURA, lies on its shores. East of the Rift Valley are high mountains reaching 2,760m (8,760ft). In central and E Burundi, the land descends in a series of step-like grassy plateaux, home to the majority of Burundi's population. **Climate and Vegetation** Bujumbura has a warm climate. A dry season lasts from July to September. The mountains and plateaux are cooler and wetter. The land used to be mainly forest, but farmers have cleared most of the trees. **History and Politics** The Twa pygmies were the first known inhabitants of Burundi. About 1,000 years ago, Bantu-speaking Hutus gradually began to settle in the area, displacing the Twa. From the 15th century, the Tutsi, a tall, cattle-owning people, gradually gained control of Burundi. The Hutu majority were forced into serfdom. The area, called Ruanda-Urundi, was occupied by Belgium in 1916 and became a trust territory. In 1962, Burundi became an independent monarchy, ruled by a Tutsi king. In 1966, the monarchy was overthrown and a republic was established. An attempted Hutu coup led to the establishment of an authoritarian, one-party state (1969). In the early 1970s, further Hutu rebellions were ruthlessly crushed. In 1988, another Hutu coup led to massacres by the Tutsi-dominated army. A new constitution (1991) resulted in multiparty politics and the election (1993) of a Hutu president, Melchior Ndadaye. In 1993, Ndadaye was assassinated in a military coup. Two months of civil war left more than 50,000 dead and created 500,000, mainly Hutu, refugees. Ndadaye was succeeded by another Hutu, Cyprien Ntaryamira. In April 1994, Ntaryamira and Rwanda's president Habyarimana were killed in a rocket attack. A coalition government was unable to contain the genocide, which continued throughout 1995. In 1996, the Tutsi army, led by Pierre Buyoya, seized power. The international community imposed sanctions, but the instability and "ethnic cleansing" that has dominated the region in

BURUNDI
AREA: 27,830 sq km (10,745 sq mi)
POPULATION: 7,358,000
CAPITAL (POPULATION): Bujumbura (300,000)

the 1990s continued. **Economy** Burundi is one of the world's ten poorest countries (1995 GDP per capita, $US630). More than 90% of the workforce is engaged in agriculture, mostly at subsistence level. The main food crops are beans, cassava, maize and sweet potatoes. Coffee accounts for 80–90% of its export earnings.

Bush, George Herbert Walker (1924–) 41st US president (1989–93). Bush served as a fighter pilot during World War 2. In 1966, he entered Congress as a representative for Texas. Under President Richard NIXON, he held several political offices, including ambassador to the United Nations (1971–73). Under President Gerald FORD, Bush was head (1976–77) of the Central Intelligence Agency (CIA). In 1980, after failing to secure the presidential nomination, he became vice president (1981–88) to Ronald REAGAN. In the 1988 presidential election, Bush easily defeated Michael Dukakis. Iraq's invasion (1990) of Kuwait provided the first test of Bush's "new world order" and a threat to America's oil supplies. The Allied forces, led by General SCHWARZKOPF, won the GULF WAR (1991) but failed to remove Saddam HUSSEIN. At home, Bush was faced with a stagnant economy, high unemployment and a massive budget deficit. He was forced (1990) to break his election pledge and raise taxes. This factor, combined with a split in the conservative vote, led to a comfortable victory for his Democratic successor Bill CLINTON.

Bush, George Walker (1946–) 43rd US president (2000–), son of former president George Herbert Walker BUSH. As republican governor of Texas (1995–2000), Bush gained popularity through a policy of "compassionate conservatism", but his wholehearted support for the death penalty provoked widespread criticism. In December 2000, Bush defeated the Democrat candidate Al GORE by the narrowest of margins after the US Supreme Court voted against a recount of votes in the state of Florida.

bushbaby (galago) Primitive, squirrel-like PRIMATE of African forests and bushlands. It is usually grey or brown with a white stripe between its large eyes. It is a gregarious nocturnal tree-dweller which can be domesticated. Length: (excluding tail) to 38cm (15in). Family Lorisidae; genus *Galago*.

Bushehr (Bushire) City in sw Iran, near the head of the Persian (Arabian) Gulf and 185km (115mi) sw of Shiraz. Founded in 1736, it was the chief Iranian port until the rise of Abadan. Industries: carpet-making, cotton. Pop. (1994) 141,000.

bushido (way of the samurai) Moral discipline important in Japan between 1603 and 1868. Requiring loyalty, courage, honour, politeness and benevolence, bushido paralleled European CHIVALRY. Although not a religion, bushido involved family worship and SHINTO rites.

bushmaster Largest pit VIPER, found in central America and N South America. It has long fangs and large venom glands, and is pinkish and brown with a diamond pattern. Length: up to 3.7m (12ft). Family Viperidae; subfamily Crotalidae.

bushrangers Name given to bandits who terrorized the Australian outback in the late 18th and 19th centuries. Some, notably Ned Kelly (executed 1880), cultivated a romantic image.

Busoni, Ferruccio Benvenuto (1866–1924) German-Italian composer and pianist. A virtuoso concert pianist. The influence of Franz LISZT is apparent in his Piano Concerto (1904). Most of Busoni's early output was piano and chamber music, but his mature operas, such as *Turandot* (1917), attempted to synthesize the classical tradition with the radical experimentation of contemporary music.

bustard Large bird found in arid areas of the Eastern Hemisphere. Its plumage is grey, black, brown and white, and its neck and legs are long; in appearance it is quite ostrich-like. A swift runner and a strong, though reluctant flier, it feeds on small animals and lays up to five eggs. Family Otidae. Height: 1.3m (4.3ft).

butane (C_4H_{10}) Colourless flammable gas, the fourth member of the ALKANE series of HYDROCARBONS. It has TWO ISOMERS: n-butane is obtained from natural gas; isobutane is a by-product of PETROLEUM refining. Butane can be liquefied under pressure at normal temperatures and is used in the manufacture of fuel gas and synthetic rubber. Properties: b.p. (n-butane) $-0.3°C$ (31.5°F) and (isobutane) $-10.3°C$ (13.46°F).

Buthelezi, Mangosuthu Gatsha (1928–) ZULU chief and politician. Buthelezi was installed as chief of the Buthelezi tribe in 1953 and became chief minister of KwaZulu, a black homeland within APARTHEID South Africa in 1970. In 1975, he founded the Inkatha "freedom" party. Buthelezi acted as minister for home affairs (1994–99) in Nelson MANDELA's government and, subsequently, in Thabo MBEKI's administration (1999–).

Butler, Richard Austen, Baron (1902–82) British statesman. He entered Parliament in 1929 as a Conservative and was minister of education (1941–45). During this time Butler was responsible for the Education Act (1944) that provided free primary and secondary education for all. He held several major cabinet posts, including chancellor of the exchequer (1951–55), home secretary (1957–62) and deputy prime minister (1962). Butler was narrowly defeated in the contest for the leadership of the Conservative Party by Harold MACMILLAN (1957) and Sir Alec DOUGLAS-HOME (1963).

Butler, Samuel (1612–80) English poet and satirist. Butler is best known for the mock-heroic poem *Hudibras* (1663–78), a three-part satire against Puritanism and the Commonwealth.

Butler, Samuel (1835–1902) English satirical writer. Butler's famous novel *Erewhon* (1872) is a classic utopian criticism of contemporary social and economic injustice. He produced a sequel to his early masterpiece, *Erewhon Revisited* (1901) and the autobiographical *The Way of All Flesh* (1903), a biting attack on Victorian life.

butter Edible fat made from milk. A churning process changes the milk from a water-in-oil emulsion to an oil-in-water emulsion. The fat (oil) globules of the milk collide and coalesce, losing their protective shield of protein and turning into butter, thus separating out from the more watery whey. Commercial butter contains about 80% fat, 1–3% added salt, 1% milk solids and 16% water.

buttercup Herbaceous flowering plant found worldwide; the many species vary considerably but usually have yellow or white flowers and deeply cut leaves. Family Ranunculaceae; genus *Ranunculus*.

butterfly Day-flying INSECT of the order Lepidoptera. The adult has two pairs of scale-covered wings that are often brightly coloured. The female lays eggs on a selected food source and the (CATERPILLAR) larvae emerge within days or hours. The larvae have chewing mouthparts and often do great damage to crops until they reach the "resting phase" of the life cycle, the pupa (chrysalis). Within the pupa, the adult (imago) is formed with wings, wing muscles, antennae, a slender body and sucking mouthparts. *See also* METAMORPHOSIS

butterwort Large group of carnivorous bog plants that trap and digest insects in a sticky secretion on their leaves. They bear single white, purple or yellow flowers on a leafless stalk. The sides of the leaves roll over to enclose the insect while it is digested. Family Lentibulariaceae; species *Pinguicula*. *See also* INSECTIVOROUS PLANT

buttress Mass of masonry built against a wall to add support. Used since ancient times, buttresses became increasingly complex and decorative in medieval architecture. GOTHIC ARCHITECTURE often featured dramatically daring flying buttresses.

Buxtehude, Dietrich (1637–1707) Danish organist and composer of organ and church music. He was organist at Lübeck and became well-known for his evening concerts, *Abendmusik*, for which he composed many works. J.S. BACH was greatly influenced by him.

buzzard Slow-flying bird with broad, rounded wings, fan-shaped tail and sharp hooked beak. The name is used in reference to many BIRDS OF PREY, as in North America for hawks and vultures. Family Accipitridae; genus *Buteo*.

Byatt, A.S. (Antonia Susan) (1936–) English novelist and critic, sister of Margaret DRABBLE. Byatt was best known as a literary scholar until she published her third novel, *The Virgin in the Garden* (1978). *Possession*, a mystery story and romance set in the 19th and 20th centuries, became an unlikely bestseller and won the Booker Prize (1990). Her recent work includes the novellas *Angels and Insects* (1993) and *The Djinn in the Nightingale's Eye* (1994). She was awarded the CBE in 1990.

Byblos Ancient city of the Phoenicians, in Lebanon, 27km (17mi) N of BEIRUT. Byblos was a centre of Phoenician trade with Egypt from the 2nd millennium BC and was particularly famous as a source of PAPYRUS. The Greek word for "book" derived from its name. The city was abandoned after its capture by the Crusaders in 1103.

Byrd, Richard Evelyn (1888–1957) US polar explorer. A naval officer and aviator, Byrd led five major expeditions to the Antarctic (1928–57), surveying more than 2,200,000sq km (845,000sq mi) of the continent. Among other feats, he claimed to be the first man to fly over both the North Pole (1926) and the South Pole (1929).

Byrd, William (1543–1623) English composer. Byrd was appointed by Elizabeth I to be joint organist of the Chapel Royal with Thomas Tallis, whom he succeeded in 1585. With Tallis, he was granted England's first monopoly to print music. Byrd was especially celebrated for his madrigals and church music.

Byron, George Gordon Noel Byron, 6th Baron (1788–1824) English poet. After a childhood scarred by the handicap of a clubfoot and maltreatment from his mother, Byron went to Trinity College, Cambridge (1805). It was with the publication of the first two cantos of *Childe Harold's Pilgrimage* (1812) that he became famous. Byron's romantic image and reputation for dissolute living and numerous sexual affairs vied with his poetic reputation. By 1816, he was a social outcast and went into permanent exile. Abroad, Byron wrote Cantos III and IV of *Childe Harold* (1816, 1818) and *Don Juan* (1819–24), an epic satire often regarded as his masterpiece. In 1823, he travelled to Greece to fight for Greek independence against the Turks and died of fever at Missolonghi.

byte Binary number used to represent letters, numbers and other characters in a computer system. Each byte consists of the same number of BITS. Byte is a contraction of the words "by eight", and originally meant an eight-bit

byte, such as 01101010 (representing j on most systems). Many computers now use 16-, 32-, or 64-bit bytes.

Byzantine art and architecture Art produced in the Roman Empire E of the Balkans. Its greatest achievements fall within three periods. The **first Golden Age** coincided with the reign of Justinian (527–65) and saw the construction of the HAGIA SOPHIA. The **second** Golden Age refers to the artistic revival, which occurred during the time of the Macedonian emperors (867–1057). Finally, the last years of the empire, under the rule of the Palaeologs (1261–1453), are often referred to as the **Byzantine Renaissance**. Most Byzantine art was religious in subject matter and combined Christian imagery with an oriental expressive style. The MOSAIC and ICON were the most common forms. Byzantine church architecture is typically central rather than longitudinal, and the central dome is supported by means of pendentives. Construction is of brick arranged in decorative patterns and mortar. Interiors are faced with marble slabs, coloured glass mosaics, gold leaf and fresco decoration.

Byzantine Empire Christian, Greek-speaking, Eastern ROMAN EMPIRE that outlasted the Roman Empire in the West by nearly 1,000 years. Constantinople (Byzantium or ISTANBUL) was established by the Roman emperor CONSTANTINE I in AD 330. The area of the Byzantine Empire varied greatly, and its history from *c*.600 was marked by continual military crisis and heroic recovery. At its height, under JUSTINIAN I, in the 6th century, it controlled, besides Asia Minor and the Balkans, much of the Near East and the Mediterranean coastal regions of Europe and North Africa. From 1204 to 1261, it was controlled by usurping Crusaders from W Europe and, although Constantinople was recovered, Byzantine territory shrank under pressure from the West and from the Ottoman Turks, who finally captured Constantinople in 1453, extinguishing the Byzantine Empire.

▲ **butterfly** The life cycle of the European swallowtail (*Papilio machaon*) is typical of most species of butterfly. The female adult (1) lays her eggs (2) on the underside of leaves in batches of 100 or more. The eggs then hatch into the first stage larva or caterpillar (3). The caterpillar molts several times before it is fully grown (4). After the final molt, the caterpillar's skin hardens (4, 5) to form the case of the pupa or chrysalis (6). Within the case the tissues of the caterpillar reorganize before the adult butterfly emerges (1).

C/c, third letter of the Roman alphabet, comes from the same root as the letter G/g. It is derived from the Semitic gimel, *meaning throwing stick. It was possibly adapted from the Egyptian* hieroglyph *for a boomerang.*

cabal Advisers to CHARLES II of England in 1667–74. The five members of this group, which is sometimes considered the first CABINET, were CLIFFORD, ARLINGTON, BUCKINGHAM, Ashley (later Earl of SHAFTESBURY) and LAUDERDALE; the first letters of their names spelled "cabal". When it became known that two of them plotted with the king to tolerate Catholicism, the Cabal split up.

Caballé, Montserrat (1933–) Spanish soprano. Caballé made her debut as Mimì in Puccini's *La Bohème* (1957) and performed at the METROPOLITAN OPERA (1965). She specializes in Verdi and Donizetti.

cabbage Low, stout vegetable of the genus *Brassica*. Members include Brussels sprouts, cauliflowers, broccoli, kohlrabi and turnips. They are all biennials that produce "heads" one year and flowers the next. The common cabbage (*Brassica oleracea capitata*) has an edible head and large, fleshy leaves. They grow in temperate regions. Family Brassicaceae/Cruciferae.

cabbage white butterfly BUTTERFLY, the green caterpillar of which is a common pest on cabbage plants. The female adult is almost completely white except for black spots on its wings; the male has no forewing spots. Species *Pieris brassicae*.

cabbala (kabbala) Form of Jewish MYSTICISM. It holds that every word, letter, number, even accent of the Bible contains mysteries to be interpreted, often in the form of codes for YAHWEH. The earliest extant cabbalist work is the 3rd-century *Sefir Yezirah* (Book of Creation). Cabbalism spread throughout Europe in the 13th century and is still practised by some Hasidic Jews.

Cabeza de Vaca, Álvar Núñez (1490–1557) Spanish explorer. In 1528 he was shipwrecked off the Texas coast. Cabeza and three fellow survivors became the first Europeans to explore the American Southwest, eventually settling in Mexico (1536). His published account (1542) and exaggerations encouraged dreams of treasure in the region. His *Comentarios* (1555) recount hardships endured in South America, where he served as governor (1542–45) of the province of Río de la Plata before being disgraced and impoverished through political intrigue.

Cabinda Province of Angola, SW Africa, N of the River Congo, bounded W by the Atlantic Ocean. Separated from the rest of Angola by the Democratic Republic of the Congo; the chief town and port is Cabinda. The Simulambuco Treaty (1885) politically unified Cabinda with Angola. Cabinda refuses to recognize the treaty and claims independence from Angola. There are important offshore oil fields. Industries: oil refining, palm, timber, cacao. Area: 7,270sq km (2,808sq mi). Pop. (1992 est.) 152,100.

cabinet Body of people collectively advising the chief executive in a presidential system or responsible to the legislature for government in a parliamentary system. Most cabinet members have individual responsibility for the management of a department of state. In the UK, cabinet ministers are chosen by the prime minister but officially appointed by the crown. In the US, cabinet members are heads of major executive departments.

cable Wire for mechanical support, for conducting electricity or carrying signals. In civil and mechanical engineering, a cable is made of twisted strands of steel wire. They range in size from small bowden cables to massive supporting cables on the decks of suspension bridges. In electrical engineering, a cable is a conductor consisting of one or more insulated wires. They range greatly in size, from cables used for domestic wiring to the large, armoured underwater cables. These are used for telephone, radio, television and data signals. In a **coaxial** cable, one conductor is cylindrical and surrounds the other. FIBRE-OPTIC cables carry signals in the form of coded pulses of light.

cable television Generally refers to community antenna television (CATV). CATV does not broadcast but picks up signals at a central antenna and delivers them to individual subscribers via coaxial CABLES. Originally designed for areas with poor reception and no local station, cable television, run by private franchise, now serves to increase the variety of local viewing by transmitting channels brought by microwave relay. Cable News Network (CNN) was founded by US entrepreneur Ted Turner (1938–) in 1980. It provides a global 24-hour news service.

Cabot, John (c.1450–c.1498) Italian navigator who made the first recorded European journey to the coast of North America since the Vikings. Supported by the English king Henry VII, Cabot sailed in search of a western route to India and reached Newfoundland (1497). He followed the coast to Cape Breton Island before returning to England. He did not return from a second voyage, but his discovery served as the basis for English claims in North America.

Cabot, Sebastian (1476–1557) Italian navigator, explorer and cartographer, son of John CABOT. Cabot sailed (1508) across the Atlantic in search of a northern passage to China (possibly reaching Hudson Bay) and sailed down the coast of North America. He joined the Spanish navy (1512) and led an expedition (1526) to find a route to the Pacific from the Atlantic, reaching the coast of Brazil. In 1547, Cabot returned to England, where he helped to found the Company of Merchant Adventurers for the Discovery of Cathay. As governor of the company, he organized a series of expeditions (1553–56) in search of a NORTHEAST PASSAGE to China.

Cabral, Pedro Alvares (1467–1520) Portuguese navigator who was the first European to discover Brazil. Supported by the Portuguese king Manuel I, Cabral led an expedition (1500) to the East Indies. To avoid the Gulf of Guinea, he sailed westward and reached Brazil, which he claimed for Portugal.

Cabrini, Saint Frances Xavier (1850–1917) US foundress of orphanages, hospitals, schools and convents, b. Italy. Cabrini was the first US citizen to be canonized (1946). She became a nun in 1877, founded (1880) the Institute of Missionary Sisters of the Sacred Heart, and moved to the US (1889). Her feast day is 22 December.

cacao *See* COCOA

Caccini, Giulio (1550–1618) Italian composer, one of the Florentine *camerata* group which pioneered OPERA. *Euridice* was the first opera to be printed (c.1601) and his *Le Nuove Musiche* (1602) was one of the most influential collections of vocal music in the new monodic style.

cactus Any of more than 2,000 species of succulent plants, found particularly in hot desert regions of the Western Hemisphere. A cactus has long roots, adapted to absorb moisture from desert terrains. Stems are usually spiny, cylindrical and branched. Cactus flowers are usually borne singly in a wide range of colours. Height: 2.5cm (1in) to more than 15m (50ft). *See also* XEROPHYTE

Cadbury, George (1839–1922) English manufacturer and social reformer. In 1861, he and his brother Richard (1835–99) took control of their father's cocoa and chocolate factory. In 1879, Cadbury established a model housing estate for the factory workers at Bourneville.

caddis fly Any of several moth-like insects of the order Trichoptera. Adults have long, many-jointed antennae, hold their wings tent-like over the body and usually grow to *c.*2.5cm (1in) long.

Cade, Jack (d.1450) Irish rebel. He assumed the name of Mortimer and the title of Captain of Kent. In May–June 1450, Cade launched a rebellion against HENRY VI. His march through Kent and Sussex gathered some 40,000 followers. The insurgents held London for two days and were dispersed only on the promise of a pardon. Cade was killed while resisting arrest.

cadence In music, ending of a melodic phrase and/or its accompanying CHORD progression. In Western classical theory, the main kinds of chordal cadence are **perfect** (dominant to tonic chords), **imperfect** (tonic or other chord to dominant), **plagal** (subdominant to tonic) and **interrupted** (dominant to chord other than tonic, often submediant).

Cádiz Port on the Gulf of Cádiz, sw Spain; capital of Cádiz province (founded 1100 BC). It became an important port for shipping routes to the Americas, and in 1587 a Spanish fleet was burned here by Sir Francis Drake. Sights include a 13th-century cathedral. Industries: shipbuilding, sherry, olives, salt, fishing. Pop. (1995) 155,000.

cadmium (symbol Cd) Silvery-white, metallic element in Group II of the periodic table, first isolated (1817) by the German chemist Friedrich Stromeyer. Cadmium is found in greenockite (a sulphide) but is mainly obtained as a by-product in the extraction of zinc and lead. Malleable and ductile, its main uses are as a protective electroplated coating, an absorber of neutrons in nuclear reactors and in nickel-cadmium batteries. Chemically it resembles zinc. Properties: at.no. 48; r.a.m. 112.4; r.d. 8.65; m.p. 320.9°C (609.6°F); b.p. 765°C (1,409°F); most common isotope Cd^{114} (28.86%).

Cadmus In Greek mythology, a prince of Phoenicia. Cadmus and his brothers were sent to find their sister EUROPA, who had been carried off by Zeus. After a fruitless search, he founded the city of Thebes after killing the dragon that guarded the spring there. Cadmus married Harmonia, daughter of ARES and APHRODITE.

caecilian Underground, burrowing amphibian found in Central and South America, s Asia and Africa. Its wormlike body varies from *c.*18 to 135cm (7–53in) in length and its colour from black to pink. There are sensory tentacles between the eyes, which are tiny and often useless.

caecum Dilated pouch at the junction of the small and large intestines, terminating in the APPENDIX. It has no known function in humans. In rabbits and horses, the caecum contains microorganisms which help to break down the cellulose cell walls of the plants they eat.

Caedmon Earliest known English poet, dating from around the 7th century. According to BEDE, he was an illiterate herdsman of Whitby Abbey, Yorkshire, who commanded in a vision to turn the scriptures into poetry. His only surviving work is the fragmentary *Hymn on the Creation.*

Caen Industrial city and port on the River Orne, N France; capital of Calvados department. Once a treasure-house of NORMAN ARCHITECTURE, many of Caen's buildings were destroyed by the Normandy Campaign

of World War 2. The 11th-century abbey church of St Etienne (burial place of William the Conqueror) has survived. Industries: iron-ore mining, textiles, automobiles, electronics. Pop. (1990) 112,846.

Caernarvon Town in Britain, on the Menai Strait, NW Wales. It has a 13th-century castle built by Edward I, whose son, Edward II, was crowned the first Prince of Wales (1301). The princes of Wales are now invested here. Industry: tourism. Pop. (1992 est.) 9,600.

Caesar Name of a powerful family of ancient Rome. The most illustrious representative was Julius CAESAR. The name became the title for the Roman emperor in 27 BC on the accession of Octavian (later AUGUSTUS). *Tsar* and *kaiser* are derived from it.

Caesar, (Gaius) Julius (100–44 BC) Roman general and statesman. After the death of SULLA, Caesar became military tribune. In 63 BC, as *pontifex maximus*, he directed reforms that resulted in the Julian CALENDAR. In 60 BC, Caesar formed the First Triumvirate with POMPEY and CRASSUS, instituted agrarian reforms, and created a PATRICIAN-PLEBEIAN alliance. He conquered Gaul for Rome (58–49 BC) and invaded Britain (54 BC). Refusing Senate demands to disband his army, he provoked civil war with Pompey. Caesar defeated Pompey at Pharsalus (48 BC) and pursued him to Egypt, where he made CLEOPATRA queen. After further victories, he returned to Rome in 45 BC, and was received with unprecedented honours, culminating in the title of dictator for life. Caesar introduced popular reforms, but his growing power aroused resentment. He was assassinated in the Senate on 15 March by a conspiracy led by CASSIUS and BRUTUS. His grandnephew, Octavian (later AUGUSTUS), together with Mark ANTONY, avenged his murder.

Caesarean section *See* BIRTH, CAESAREAN

caesium (symbol Cs) Rare silvery-white metallic element in Group I of the periodic table; the most alkaline and electropositive element. Discovered in 1860 by Robert BUNSEN and Gustav KIRCHHOFF, caesium is ductile and used commercially in photoelectric cells. The isotope Cs^{137} is used in cancer treatments. The decay rate of its most common isotope Cs^{133} is the standard for measuring time. Properties: at.no. 55; r.a.m. 132.9055; r.d. 1.87; m.p. 28.4°C (83.1°F); b.p. 678°C (1,252.4°F). *See also* ALKALI METALS; ATOMIC CLOCK

caffeine ($C_8H_{10}N_4O_2$) White, bitter substance that occurs in coffee, tea and other substances, such as COCOA and ilex plants. It acts as a mild, harmless stimulant and DIURETIC, although an excessive dose can cause insomnia and delirium.

Cage, John (1912–92) US avant-garde composer. He believed that all sounds, including noise and silence, are valid compositional materials. Cage invented the "prepared piano", modified by fixing objects to the strings. *Imaginary Landscape* (1951) is written for 12 randomly tuned radios, *Reunion* (1968) consists of electronic sounds created by chess moves on an electric board, and *4'33"* (1952) has no sound, except for the environment in which it is performed.

Cagliari Seaport capital of Sardinia, Italy. Cagliari lies on the Gulf of Cagliari, s Sardinia, surrounded by beaches and lagoons. Its strategic location in the heart of the w Mediterranean saw it ruled by the Carthaginians, Romans and Arabs. Heavily bombed during World War 2, its surviving monuments include a 5th-century church and the Cathedral of St Cecilia (1257–1312). Industries: salt, ceramics, petrochemicals. Pop. (1996) 175,000.

Cagney, James (1899–1986) US actor. He is best-known as the ruthless gangster in such films as *Public*

Enemy (1930) and *Angels With Dirty Faces* (1936). He won a best actor Academy Award for his performance as US showman George M. Cohan in *Yankee Doodle Dandy* (1942). Cagney made a comeback in *Ragtime* (1981).

Caiaphas Jewish high priest who presided over the *sanhedrin* (religious court) that tried Jesus Christ (Matthew 2, Luke 3, John 18). Caiaphas was one of the priests at the Jerusalem TEMPLE.

Cain First-born son of ADAM and EVE, brother of ABEL. His story is recounted in Genesis 4. God accepted Abel's offering in preference to Cain's, and Cain murdered Abel in anger. Marked by God to preserve him from being murdered, Cain was driven out from the Garden of EDEN and lived in exile in the land of Nod.

Caine, Sir Michael (1933–) English film actor, b. Maurice Micklewhite. His first major role was in *Zulu* (1963). Caine was nominated for an Academy Award as best actor for his performance as the cockney Lothario in *Alfie* (1966). Other films include *The Italian Job* (1969), *Get Carter* (1971), *Sleuth* (1972) and *Educating Rita* (1983). He won Oscars as best supporting actor for *Hannah and Her Sisters* (1986) and *The Cider House Rules* (2000).

Cairngorms Range of mountains in NE central Scotland, in the Grampian region. A major British winter sports area, the highest peak, Ben Macdhui, 1,309m (4,296ft), is the second highest point in the British Isles.

Cairo (Al-Qahirah) Capital of Egypt and port on the River Nile. The largest city in Africa, Cairo was founded (AD 969) by the Fatimid dynasty and subsequently fortified by SALADIN. Medieval Cairo became capital of the MAMELUKE empire, but declined under Turkish rule. Nearby are the SPHINX and the PYRAMIDS of GIZA. Museums include the Museum of Egyptian Antiquities and the Museum of Islamic Art. Old Cairo is a world heritage site containing more than 400 mosques and other fine examples of ISLAMIC ART AND ARCHITECTURE. Its five universities include the world's oldest, the centre of SHIITE Koranic study, housed in the mosque of Al Azhar (972). Industries: tourism, textiles, leather. Pop. (1992 est.) 6,663,000. *See also* EGYPTIAN ARCHITECTURE

Cajun French-speaking settlers in Louisiana, USA. They were driven from Nova Scotia (Acadia) by the British in the 18th century. Cajun music and cooking are popular.

calabash gourd (bottle gourd) Tropical vine with oval leaves and white flowers. It grows to 9–12m (30–40ft). Its smooth, hard fruit is bottle-shaped and grows to 180cm (6ft). Family Cucurbitaceae; species *Lagenaria vulgaris.*

calabrese *See* BROCCOLI

Calabria Region in S Italy, including the provinces of Catanzaro, Cosenza and Reggio di Calabria; the capital is Reggio di Calabria. The local economy is almost exclusively agricultural. Area: 15,080sq km (5,822sq mi). Pop. (1992) 2,074,763.

Calais City and seaport in Pas-de-Calais department, NW France. Calais has been an important port and commercial centre since the Middle Ages. In 1347 it was captured by the English king Edward III and was saved from destruction only by the surrender of the town's burghers (commemorated in Rodin's sculpture). It suffered much damage during World War 2. Calais lies *c.*34km (21mi) across the English Channel from DOVER. Industries: lace making, chemicals, paper. Pop. (1990) 75,309.

calamine Pinkish, odourless powder of zinc oxide and some ferric oxide, dissolved in mineral oils and used in skin ointments to alleviate such disorders as chicken pox, poison ivy and skin rashes.

Calamity Jane (*c.*1852–1903) US frontier heroine, b. Martha Jane Canary. She worked in mining and railroad camps in the West and with the US cavalry as a guide and scout. A fine horsewoman and expert shot, Calamity Jane appeared in various Wild West shows during the 1890s.

calcite (calcium carbonate, $CaCO_3$). Mineral, a major constituent of calcareous sedimentary rock, especially LIMESTONE. The crystals are in the hexagonal system and are tabular (rare), prismatic or needle-like in form. Calcite is usually glassy white but may be red, pink or yellow. It reacts with dilute hydrochloric acid. Hardness 3; r.d. 2.7.

calcium (symbol Ca) Common, silvery-white metallic element of the ALKALINE-EARTH METALS; first isolated (1808) by Sir Humphry DAVY. It occurs in many rocks and minerals, notably LIMESTONE and GYPSUM, and in bones. Calcium helps regulate the heartbeat and is essential for strong bones and teeth. The metal, which is soft and malleable, has few commercial applications but its compounds are widely used. It is a reactive element, combining readily with oxygen, nitrogen and other nonmetals. Properties: at.no. 20; r.a.m. 40.08; r.d. 1.55; m.p. 839°C (1,542°F); b.p. 1,484°C (2,703°F); most common isotope Ca^{40} (96.95%).

calcium bicarbonate Former name of CALCIUM HYDROGENCARBONATE

calcium carbide (calcium acetylide, CaC_2) Chemical made commercially by heating coke and calcium oxide (CaO) in an ELECTRIC FURNACE. It reacts with water to yield ETHYNE. Calcium carbide is also used to manufacture ETHANOIC ACID and ETHANAL.

calcium carbonate ($CaCO_3$) White compound, insoluble in water, that occurs naturally as MARBLE, CHALK, LIMESTONE and CALCITE. Calcium carbonate also forms the shells of mollusks. Crystals are in the hexagonal system and vary in form. Calcium carbonate is used in the manufacture of cement, iron, steel and lime and as a constituent of antacids. Properties: r.d. 2.7 (calcite).

calcium hydrogencarbonate ($Ca(HCO_3)_2$) Salt that is responsible for temporary HARDNESS OF WATER. The hardness is removed when the water is heated and insoluble calcium carbonate is precipitated from the water, forming a "fur" inside pipes and kettles. This also happens when water drips inside caves and forms STALAGMITES and STALACTITES.

calcium oxide (quicklime, CaO) White solid made by heating CALCIUM CARBONATE ($CaCO_3$) at high temperatures. It is used industrially to treat acidic soil and make porcelain, glass, caustic soda, mortar and cement and in the recovery of AMMONIA. Calcium oxide reacts with water to form calcium hydroxide ($Ca(OH)_2$), which dissolves in water to give lime water.

calcium sulphate ($CaSO_4$) Chemical compound that occurs naturally as the mineral anhydrite. The hydrated form ($CaSO_4.2H_2O$) is the mineral GYPSUM, which loses water when heated to form plaster of Paris (calcium sulphate, ($2CaSO_4.H_2O$).

calculus Branch in mathematics involving the techniques of differentiation and integration. DIFFERENTIAL CALCULUS is used to find slopes of curves. INTEGRAL CALCULUS is used to determine the areas or volumes enclosed by a given boundary. The fundamental theorem of calculus is: $\int_a^b f(x)dx = g(b) - g(a)$, where g is any FUNCTION whose DERIVATIVE is the function f. For more than 200 years it was believed that this theorem was discovered (independently) by Gottfried LEIBNIZ and Isaac NEWTON. In 1934 a note written by Newton was discovered in which he acknowledged that his formulation of calculus was based on the work of Pierre de FERMAT.

Calcutta City on the River Hooghly, E India; capital of West Bengal state. Founded *c.*1690 by the EAST INDIA

COMPANY, it was the capital of India under British rule (1772–1912). It has a university (1857) and several important temples. The major port and industrial centre of E India, Calcutta has one of the world's largest jute-milling industries. Other industries: electrical equipment, chemicals, paper, cotton. Pop. (1991) 4,309,819.

Calder, Alexander (1898–1976) US sculptor. Calder created the mobile, a type of colourful, kinetic sculpture with parts that move either by motors or air currents. He also developed non-moving sculptures called "stabiles".

caldera Large, shallow crater formed when a volcano collapses and the MAGMA migrates under the Earth's crust. The caldera of an extinct volcano, if fed by flood-water, rain or springs, can become a crater lake.

Calderón de la Barca, Pedro (1600–81) Spanish dramatist and priest. In 1635 Calderón became court playwright to Philip IV and wrote for the church and public theatre. His *autos sacramentales* are among his finest works. His best-known plays include *Life is a Dream* (*c.*1638) and *The Mayor of Zalamea* (*c.*1640).

calendar Way of reckoning time for regulating religious, commercial and civil life, and for dating events in the past and future. Ancient Egyptians had a system based on the movement of the star SIRIUS and on the seasons. Calendars are based on natural and astronomical regularities: tides and seasons, movements of the Sun and Earth and phases of the Moon. The basic units are day, month and year. The main difficulty in compiling a calendar is that the month is not an exact number of days and the year not an exact number of months. For convenience, extra days (intercalations) are added at intervals to compensate. In the modern **Gregorian**, or New Style, calendar, an extra day (29 February) is added every four years (leap year). The Gregorian calendar was based on the **Julian**, or Old Style, solar calendar. This was introduced by Julius Caesar in the 1st century BC and was developed from an earlier Moon-based calendar. The **Jewish calendar** is semilunar, made up of 12 common years and 7 leap years. The leap years have an additional month (Adar II). The Jewish New Year is celebrated with the festival of ROSH HASHANAH, on the first day of month of Tishri. The Jewish calendar is reckoned from the date of creation (taken to be 7 October 3761 BC). The **Muslim calendar** is wholly lunar, the year always consisting of 12 months without intercalations. The months have alternately 30 and 29 days, except for the twelfth month (Dul-hajj) which has one intercalary day in 11 years out of a cycle of 30 calendar years. The era is counted from the date of Muhammad's flight from Mecca (16 July 622).

Calgary City at the confluence of the Bow and Elbow rivers, S Alberta, Canada. It was founded in 1875 as a post of the Royal Canadian Mounted Police. It is an industrial and commercial centre, and has a university (1945). Industries: flour milling, timber, brick, cement, oil refining. Pop. (1996) 822,000.

Calhoun, John Caldwell (1782–1850) US statesman, vice president (1825–32). After serving in the House of Representatives (1811–17), he was secretary of war (1817–25). Calhoun was vice president under John Quincy ADAMS and Andrew JACKSON, resigning over the NULLIFICATION issue. He was elected to the Senate and was secretary of state (1844–45). A staunch advocate of SLAVERY and states' rights, Calhoun strongly influenced the South in the course that led to the American CIVIL WAR.

Cali City on the River Cali, W Colombia. Founded in 1536, Cali was damaged by an earthquake in 1885. Since the establishment (1954) of the Cauca Valley Authority, the city has grown to become the third largest

in Colombia. It has acquired an unenviable reputation as the centre of a powerful drugs cartel, supplying cocaine to North America. Industries: tourism, tobacco, coffee, sugar. Pop. (1997) 1,986,000.

Calicut (Kozhikode) Seaport on the Malabar coast, Kerala, SW India; Calicut was Vasco de Gama's first port of call in India (1498) and the city developed as a European trading centre. A post of the British EAST INDIA COMPANY was established here in 1664. Calico cloth was first exported to England in the 17th century. Industries: coconuts, coffee, tea, spices. Pop. (1991 est.) 420,000.

California State on the US Pacific coast; the largest state by population and the third largest in area. The capital is SACRAMENTO. Other major cities include LOS ANGELES, SAN FRANCISCO, SAN DIEGO and OAKLAND. The Spanish explored the coast in 1542, but the first European settlement was in 1769, when Spaniards founded a Franciscan mission at San Diego. The area became part of Mexico. Settlers came from the US and, during the MEXICAN WAR, US forces occupied California (1846); it was ceded to the US at the war's end. After gold was discovered in 1848, the GOLD RUSH swelled the population from 15,000 to 250,000 in four years. In 1850, California joined the Union. In the 20th century, the discovery of oil and development of service industries attracted further settlers. Silicon Valley around Sunnyvale is a centre for many electronics and computing industries. In the W, the Coast Ranges run N to S, paralleled by the Sierra Nevada Mountains in the E; between them lies the fertile Central Valley, drained by the Sacramento and San Joaquin rivers. In the SE, is a broad desert area. With a perennial growing season and vast irrigation projects, California is the leading producer of many crops, including a wide variety of fruit and vegetables. Forests cover *c.*40% of the land and support an important timber industry. Mineral deposits include oil, natural gas and a variety of ores valuable in manufacturing (the largest economic sector). Industries: tourism, aircraft, aerospace equipment, electronic components, missiles, wine. Area: 403,971sq km (155,973sq mi). Pop. (2000) 33,871,648.

California redwood (*Sequoia sempervirens*) Conifer that grows to more than 100m (330ft) and is one of the tallest trees. Its close relative from California is the less common big tree or wellingtonia (*Sequoiadendron giganteum*), the heaviest tree in the Western world. Sequoias live to be more than 4,000 years old. Family Taxodiaceae.

californium (symbol Cf) Radioactive, metallic element of the ACTINIDE SERIES, first made (1950) at the University of California, Berkeley, by alpha-particle bombardment of the CURIUM isotope Cm^{242}. Californium presents biological dangers because one microgram releases 170 million neutrons a minute. Properties: at.no. 98; most stable isotope Cf^{251} (half-life 800yr).

Caligula (AD 12–41) (Gaius Caesar) Roman emperor (37–41). Son of Germanicus Caesar, he became emperor after the death of TIBERIUS. Caligula was highly autocratic, made his horse a consul to mock the Senate, and was said to be insane. He was murdered by the Praetorian Guard and succeeded by his uncle, CLAUDIUS I.

caliph Leader of the Muslim community. After the death of MUHAMMAD, ABU BAKR was chosen to be his caliph (successor). The role was originally elective but later became hereditary. The title remained with the Ottoman sultans (1517–1924), after which it was abolished. SUNNI Muslims recognize the first four caliphs: Abu Bakr (632–34), OMAR (634–44), OTHMAN (644–56) and ALI. Shiites accept authority as passing directly from Muhammad to Ali.

Callaghan, (Leonard) James, Baron (1912–) British statesman, prime minister (1976–79). He entered Parliament in 1945 and succeeded (1976) Harold WILSON as prime minister and leader of the Labour Party. Callaghan is the only prime minister in British history to have held all three major offices of state: chancellor of the exchequer (1964–67), home secretary (1967–70) and foreign secretary (1974–76). He also has the distinction of being only the second post-war prime minister never to have won a general election. Callaghan's minority government was marked by delicate negotiations with the Liberal Party (the Lib-Lab Pact) and by strife with the trade unions that culminated in the "winter of discontent". He was defeated by Margaret THATCHER in the 1979 general election. Callaghan was made a life peer in 1987.

Callao Peru's major seaport, on the Pacific coast w of LIMA. Founded (1537) by Francisco Pizarro, Callao was subject to frequent naval attack from Spain's imperial rivals. The city was destroyed by a tidal wave in 1746 and devastated by an earthquake in 1940. Today, it handles 75% of Peru's exports. Industries: oil, sugar refining. Pop. (1993) 369,768.

Callas, Maria (1923–77) Greek soprano. She made her debut in 1941 and attracted international recognition for her performance as Gioconda in Verona (1947). Callas was best-known for her *bel canto* roles, singing Norma at her London (1952) and New York (1956) debuts. She combined dramatic ability with a rich, versatile voice. Callas retired in 1965.

Calles, Plutarco Elías (1877–1945) Mexican statesman, president (1924–28). He joined forces with Venustiano CARRANZA to defeat the regime of Victoriano HUERTA. Calles succeeded Álvaro Obregón as president. His administration attempted to introduce radical changes. Calles' anticlerical policy fomented the Cristero Revolt (1926–27), which was suppressed. He made his National Revolutionary Party (PNR) the dominant force in Mexican politics. Calles brutally suppressed the unions and the church. In 1935, he was toppled by Lázaro CÁRDENAS.

calligraphy Art of fine writing. Calligraphy is freehand, with components in proportion to each other. In Europe there was a marked difference between **uncial** hands used for literary works, which are rounded, easily inscribed letters, and **cursive** hands, used for documents and letters, which are more regularized. Fragments on papyrus from the 3rd century BC show a variety of cursive hands. During the 8th century, the **minuscule** superseded the uncial for ordinary, commercial purposes. The 20th century has seen a revival of calligraphy.

Callisto Second-largest and outermost of Jupiter's GALILEAN SATELLITES, with a diameter of 4,800km (3,000mi). It is the most heavily cratered object known. As well as the dark dense craters, there are large, multiringed impact features, the largest of which is Valhalla, with a diameter of 4,000km (2,500mi).

callus In botany, a protective mass of undifferentiated plant cells formed at the site of a wound in a woody plant. Callus tissue is also formed at the base of cuttings as they start to take root. Callus tissue is important as the starting point for TISSUE CULTURE of plants.

callus Hard, thickened area of skin usually at a place on hands or feet where pressure is continual. A callus may be removed by chemicals or friction.

calotype Photographic process developed and patented in 1841 by Fox TALBOT. The positive-negative process produced a print made from a paper negative that was brushed with silver iodide and other chemicals and exposed in the CAMERA. *See also* PHOTOGRAPHY

calorie Unit of heat. A calorie is the amount of heat required to raise 1 gram of water one degree CELSIUS between 14.5 and 15.5°C (58.1 and 59.9°F). The SI system of units uses the JOULE (1 calorie = 4.184 joules) instead of the calorie. A dietitian's "calorie" is the kilocalorie, 1,000 times larger than a calorie.

calorimeter Apparatus used for experiments involving heat measurements. It is usually a conducting container, such as a copper vessel, that is thermally insulated. There are many types designed for special purposes, such as measuring calories in a food, specific heat capacities, specific latent heats, heats of reaction and heats of formation. A **bomb** calorimeter ignites sealed oxygen to measure heats of combustion, like calories in food.

Calvin, John (1509–64) French theologian of the REFORMATION. He prepared for a career in the Roman Catholic Church but turned to the study of classics. In *c.*1533 Calvin became a Protestant and began work on his *Institutes of the Christian Religion*. In this work he presented the basics of what came to be known as CALVINISM. To avoid persecution, he went to live in Geneva, Switzerland (1536), where he advanced the Reformation.

Calvin, Melvin (1911–97) US chemist. Calvin used radioactive carbon-14 as a trace to label carbon dioxide and track the process by which plants turned it into glucose by PHOTOSYNTHESIS. The series of reactions that take place during photosynthesis is known as the Calvin cycle. Calvin received the Nobel Prize for chemistry in 1961.

Calvinism Set of doctrines and attitudes derived from the Protestant theologian John CALVIN. The Reformed and Presbyterian churches were established in this tradition. Rejecting papal authority and relying on the Bible, Calvinism stresses the sovereignty of God and PREDESTINATION. It usually subordinates state to church and cultivates austere morality, family piety, business enterprise, education and science. These doctrines, particularly predestination, and the rejection of consubstantiation in its eucharistic teaching, caused a split in PROTESTANTISM between LUTHERANISM and PRESBYTERIANISM. Calvinist leaders include John KNOX and Jonathan EDWARDS.

Calvino, Italo (1923–85) Italian novelist and short-story writer, b. Cuba. His early work, such as the novel *Path to the Nest of Spiders* (1947), is in the tradition of Italian neo-realism. Calvino's later style incorporates elements of fantasy, folk tales and formal experimentation. Works include *Invisible Cities* (1972), *If On a Winter's Night a Traveller* (1979) and *Mr Palomar* (1983).

Calypso In Greek mythology, the daughter of Atlas and Tethys. Calypso lived on the mythical island of Ogygia. When ODYSSEUS landed on the island during a storm, she imprisoned him for seven years. Finally, Hermes was sent by Zeus to have Odysseus released.

cambium In botany, layer of cells, parallel to the surface of stems and roots of plants, that divides to produce new cells to allow for growth in diameter of the stem and roots. There are two main types of cambium. **Vascular** cambium produces new PHLOEM on the outside and XYLEM on the inside. **Cork** cambium forms a cylinder just below the epidermis and produces cork cells to replace the epidermis, which ruptures as the stem and root expand, forming the bark and corky outer layer of the older root. *See also* MERISTEM

Cambodia Republic in SE Asia. Cambodia is surrounded by low mountains, except in the SE. The heart of the country is a vast alluvial plain, drained by the River MEKONG. The capital, PHNOM PENH, lies on its banks. In the monsoon, the Mekong floods more than 160,000ha (400,000 acres) of the plain, greatly aiding rice

---

CAMBODIA
AREA: 181,040sq km (69,900sq mi)
POPULATION: 10,046,000
CAPITAL (POPULATION): Phnom Penh (920,000)

---

cultivation. **Climate and Vegetation** Cambodia has a tropical monsoon climate with constant high humidity and temperatures. Coastal regions have the highest rainfall. The dry season lasts from November to April. Forests cover *c*.75% of Cambodia. In the N mountains, on the border with Thailand, are dense tropical rainforests, while mangrove forests line the coast. **History and Politics** In the 6th century the KHMER established an empire roughly corresponding to modern-day Cambodia and Laos. In 889, the empire was reunited, with its capital at ANGKOR. The Angkor period (889–1434) was the golden age of Khmer civilization, culminating in the 12th-century construction of Angkor Wat. In 1434, the Thai captured Angkor and the capital was transferred to Phnom Penh. In the 17th and 18th centuries, Cambodia was a battleground for the empires of Siam and Annam. In 1863 Cambodia became a French protectorate, and was subsumed into the Union of INDOCHINA in 1887. During World War 2, it was occupied by Japan. In 1953, Cambodia achieved full independence from France. Prince NORODOM SIHANOUK became king. In 1955, he abdicated to become prime minister. The VIETNAM WAR (1954–75) dominated Cambodian politics. Initially, Cambodia received US aid, but in 1963 Sihanouk denounced US interference. The build-up of North Vietnamese troops persuaded Sihanouk to seek US help, and in 1969, the US conducted secret bombing raids on communist bases in Cambodia. In March 1970, Sihanouk was overthrown by Lon Nol, and US and South Vietnamese troops entered Cambodia to destroy North Vietnamese camps. Many innocent civilians were killed, and public support rallied to the Cambodian communists (KHMER ROUGE). In October 1970, the Khmer Republic was declared, but the communists already controlled most of rural Cambodia. Civil War broke out. Despite US military aid, the government continued to lose ground. In 1973, the US Congress halted air attacks. In 1975, the Khmer Rouge (led by POL POT) seized Phnom Penh. Cambodia was renamed **Kampuchea**. A brutal form of peasant politics ensued, and a series of purges left 1–4 million people dead. In 1979, Vietnamese and Cambodian troops overthrew Pol Pot, but fighting continued. In 1989, Vietnamese troops withdrew, and in 1992 UN forces began to disarm the various factions. In 1993, elections were held (without the Khmer Rouge) and a coalition government was formed. Sihanouk was restored as king. In 1994, the Khmer Rouge was banned. In 1997, Hun Sen ousted his co-premier, Prince Norodom Ranariddh. Hun Sen claimed victory in 1998 elections, but the opposition parties claimed widespread fraud and voter intimidation. **Economy** Cambodia is a poor nation, wrecked by war. Until the 1970s it was agriculturally self-sufficient but now depends on food imports and economic aid. Farming employs 80% of the work force. Rice, rubber and maize are the major products. Corruption and instability persist.

Cambrian Earliest period of the PALAEOZOIC era, lasting from *c*.590 million to 505 million years ago. Cambrian rocks are the earliest to preserve the hard parts of animals as FOSSILS. The animals lived in the sea, the commonest forms were TRILOBITES, BRACHIOPODS, sponges and snails. Plant life consisted mainly of seaweeds.

Cambridge City on the River Cam, county town of Cambridgeshire, E England. It has one of the world's leading universities. Industries: precision engineering, electronics, printing, publishing. Pop. (1991) 91,933.

Cambridge, University of Founded in 1209 (with claims for an earlier origin), it is one of the oldest scholarly establishments in England. It has a collegiate system, the oldest college being Peterhouse (1284). A centre of Renaissance learning and theological debate in the Reformation, it now offers almost every discipline. In the 20th century, it excelled in scientific research. Its many buildings include Kings College Chapel.

Cambridgeshire County in E central England; the county town is CAMBRIDGE. The area is marshy with chalk hills to the S and is drained by the Ouse and Nene rivers. Ely and Peterborough both have cathedrals. Agriculture is the most important economic activity; crops include wheat, barley and oats. Area: 3,400sq km (1,312sq mi). Pop. (1990) 645,125.

camel Large, hump-backed, UNGULATE mammal of the family Camelidae. There are two species – the two-humped **Bactrian** of central Asia and the single-humped Arabian **dromedary**. Its broad, padded feet and ability to travel several days without water make the camel a perfect desert animal. Camels can carry up to 270kg (600lb) and cover *c*.50km (30mi) a day. Genus *Camelus*.

camellia Genus of evergreen trees or shrubs of the family Theaceae, native to E Asia. It has oval, dark green leaves and waxy, rose-like flowers (pink, red, white or variegated). *Camellia japonica* is the most common species.

Camelot In English mythology, the seat chosen by King ARTHUR for his court. Its site is not known, although many believe it was Cadbury Castle, Somerset, SW England.

cameo Relief carving, usually on striated gemstones, semiprecious stones, or shell. The decoration, often a portrait head, is generally cut on the light-coloured vein, the dark vein being left as a background. Cameos originated from carved stone seals used by Ancient Egyptians, Greeks and Etruscans.

camera Apparatus for taking photographs, consisting essentially of a light-proof box containing photographic film. When a shutter is opened, usually briefly, light from the scene is focused by a lens system onto the film. The amount of light falling on the film is controlled by the shutter speed and by the diameter of the lens APERTURE. Many cameras also have a rangefinder, enabling a focused image to be produced for a given object distance, and a built-in exposure meter to determine the correct combination of shutter speed and aperture for the prevailing light conditions. *See also* PHOTOGRAPHY

Cameroon Republic in W Africa. Cameroon gets its name from the early Portuguese explorers who fished for *camarões* (prawns) along its coast. Behind narrow coastal plains on the Gulf of Guinea, the land rises in a series of plateaux, home of the capital, YAOUNDÉ. In the N, the land slopes down towards the Lake CHAD basin. The mountainous SW region rises to the active volcano, Mount Cameroon at 4,070m (13,354ft). **Climate** Cameroon has one of the wettest climates on Earth. Rainfall is heaviest in the hot and humid SW between July and September. The inland plateaux are cooler. The far N has a hot, dry climate.

CAMEROON
AREA: 475,440sq km (183,567sq mi)
POPULATION: 16,701,000
CAPITAL (POPULATION): Yaoundé (800,000)

Vegetation Rainforests flourish in the S. Inland, the forests give way to savanna. Here national parks (such as the Waza, N of Maroua) contain protected animal species. The far N is semi-desert. **History and Politics** Cameroon is a diverse nation, with more than 160 ethnic groups. Bantu speakers predominate in coastal areas, such as DOUALA. Islam is the dominant force in the N, where major tribal groupings include the FULANI. In 1472, Portuguese explorers (seeking a sea route to Asia) reached the Cameroon coast. From the 17th century, S Cameroon was a centre of the slave trade. In the early 19th-century, SLAVERY was abolished and replaced by the ivory trade, led by Britain. In 1884, Cameroon became a German protectorate. In 1916, the country was captured by Allied troops. After World War 1, Cameroon was divided into two zones, ruled by Britain and France. In 1960, French Cameroon became an independent republic. In 1961, N British Cameroon voted to join the Cameroon Republic (forming the Federal Republic of Cameroon), while S British Cameroon joined Nigeria. In 1966, a one-party state was created, and in 1972, the federation became a unitary state. From 1960 to 1982, Ahmadou Ahidjo was the country's president. His successor, Paul Biya, purged the party of Ahidjo's supporters. In 1984, a failed coup led to many executions, and Biya made Cameroon a republic. Biya was re-elected in 1992, amid charges of electoral malpractice. His autocratic rule was regularly accused of torture and the creation of a police state. In 1995, it became the 52nd member of the COMMONWEALTH OF NATIONS. **Economy** Cameroon is one of West Africa's most successful economies (1995 GDP per capita, \$US2,110). Its wealth, however, is extremely unevenly distributed. Northern Cameroon is impoverished and heavily dependent on cattle-raising. Agriculture dominates the economy, employing 79% of the workforce. Cameroon is self-sufficient in foodstuffs. Major crops include cassava, maize, millet and yams. It is the world's 7th largest producer of cocoa. Other commercial plantations grow coffee, bananas, groundnuts and tobacco. Despite shrinking production, oil accounts for nearly 50% of Cameroon's exports. Other mineral resources include gold and bauxite.

Camões, Luís vaz de (1524–80) Portuguese poet and soldier. In 1572 he published *The Lusiads*, which was adopted as Portugal's national epic and established Camões as the country's greatest national poet.

camouflage Technique used to conceal an object or organism from observation. In the military, a variety of disguises are used to ensure soldiers or weapons blend in with their natural environment, such as nets to break up angular silhouettes or desert tanks painted the colour of sand. Many animals and insects have natural camouflage: the CHAMELEON is the most versatile example.

Campaign for Nuclear Disarmament (CND) Movement in Britain, founded (1958) by Bertrand RUSSELL and Canon John Collins. Advocating unilateral nuclear disarmament, during the 1960s, it organized an annual march. The end of the COLD WAR and disarmament treaties between the US and the former Soviet Union, lessened CND's political prominence.

Campania Region of SW Italy on the Tyrrhenian Sea, including the provinces of Avellino, Benevento, Caserta, Napoli and Salerno; the capital is NAPLES. It is a mountainous area with fertile plains yielding wheat, potatoes, fruit, tobacco, flowers and wine. Area: 13,595sq km (5,249sq mi). Pop. (1992) 5,668,895.

Campanulaceae Bellflower family of herbaceous flowering plants. There are *c*.300 species, including HAREBELL, Canterbury bell, Coventry bell, peach bell-

flower and clustered bellflower. They are cultivated for their delicate blossoms, often a pale or purplish blue.

Campbell, Donald Malcolm (1921–67) English speed record holder, son of Sir Malcolm CAMPBELL. He set seven new world records on water. In 1964 Campbell broke the world water and speed records in Australia. On Lake Dumbleyung he achieved 444.7km/h (276.28mph), while on the salt flats of Lake Eyre he reached 648.72km/h (403mph). Campbell died trying to set a new record. In 1984 his daughter, Gina, set a new women's water speed record.

Campbell, Sir Malcolm (1885–1948) English world speed record holder. In 1935 Campbell became the first man to reach a land speed of 300mph (483km/h), accomplished in *Bluebird* at Utah's Bonneville Salt Flats, USA. He later set a water record of 227km/h (141mph).

Campbell, (Ignatius) Roy Dunnachie (1901–57) South African poet. Campbell's first work was *The Flaming Terrapin* (1924). *The Georgiad* (1931) was a stinging attack on the Bloomsbury Group. *Flowering Rifle* (1939) expressed support for General Franco. He wrote a swaggering autobiography, *Light on a Dark Horse* (1951).

Campbell-Bannerman, Sir Henry (1836–1908) British statesman, prime minister (1905–08). He entered Parliament in 1868, and held minor posts until he became secretary of state for war (1886, 1892–95). In 1899 Campbell-Bannerman became leader of the Liberal Party. As prime minister, he granted self-government to the defeated Boer republics of Transvaal (1906) and Orange River Colony (1907) and enabled the passage of the Trade Disputes Act (1906).

Camp David Agreement (September 1978) Significant step towards Arab-Israeli reconciliation. The agreement resulted from a meeting between Anwar SADAT of Egypt and Menachem BEGIN of Israel, mediated by President Jimmy CARTER at his official country home. Condemned by other Arab leaders, the agreement formed the basis for a 1979 treaty between Egypt and Israel. Sadat and Begin shared the 1978 Nobel Peace Prize.

Campese, David Ian (1962–) Australian rugby union player. A flamboyant winger who played regularly in Italy as well as Australia, he holds the world record for the number of tries scored in international rugby (63). Campese helped Australia win the 1991 World Cup. He retired from international rugby in 1996, after making more than 100 test appearances.

camphor ($C_{10}H_{16}O$) Organic chemical compound. It has a strong odour, which also occurs in the wood and leaves of the camphor tree, *Cinammonum camphora*, native to Taiwan. Camphor is used in medicine for liniments, in the manufacture of celluloid, lacquers and explosives and as an ingredient of mothballs.

Campion, Saint Edmund (1540–81) English Jesuit priest and martyr. He was ordained deacon in the Church of England (1569) but became a Roman Catholic (1571) and later a Jesuit missionary. In 1581 Campion published the pamphlet *Decem Rationes*, defending Roman Catholicism. He was charged with treason and executed. His feast day is 1 December.

Campion, Jane (1955–) New Zealand film director and screenwriter. A sensitive and poetic film-maker, her first feature was *Sweetie* (1989). Campion won a best screenplay Academy Award for *The Piano* (1993). Other films include *Portrait of a Lady* (1997).

Campion, Thomas (1567–1620) English physician, poet and composer. Campion's four *Books of Ayres* (1601–17) for the lute, including "There is a Garden in Her Face", rival the songs of John DOWLAND. *Pomata*

(1595) is a collection of Latin epigrams and elegies. *Observations in the Art of English Poesie* (1602) argues for classical forms rather than rhyme.

Camus, Albert (1913–60) French novelist, playwright and essayist. An active figure in the French Resistance, Camus achieved recognition with his first novel, *The Stranger* (1942), a work permeated with the sense of individual alienation. His later works include the novels *The Plague* (1947) and *The Fall* (1956) and the essay *The Rebel* (1951). Camus was associated with EXISTENTIALISM and the Theatre of the ABSURD. He was awarded the 1957 Nobel Prize for literature.

Canaan Historical region occupying the land between the Mediterranean and the Dead Sea. The Canaanites were a Semitic people, identified with the Phoenicians from *c.*1200 BC. Canaan was the Promised Land of the Israelites, who settled here on their return from Egypt.

Canada Federation in N North America. Canada, the world's second largest country (after Russia), is thinly populated. Much of the land is too cold or mountainous for human settlement, and most Canadians live within 300km (200mi) of the s border with the USA. Western Canada has the most rugged terrain, including the Pacific ranges and the mighty ROCKY MOUNTAINS. Mount LOGAN is Canada's highest peak, at 6,050m (19,850ft). East of the Rockies are the fertile interior plains of Canada's Prairie Provinces (S ALBERTA, MANITOBA and SASKATCHEWAN). This vast farming region is the N extension of the prairies of the United States. In the N are the bleak Arctic islands. The Canadian Shield, in E central Canada, is a vast region of ancient rocks which covers almost half the country, enclosing the HUDSON BAY lowlands. South of the Canadian Shield lie Canada's most populous regions: the lowlands N of Lakes ERIE and ONTARIO and the ST LAWRENCE RIVER valley, including the capital, OTTAWA and TORONTO. The northernmost part of the APPALACHIAN MOUNTAINS are in the far SE. **Climate** Canada has a cold climate, with winter temperatures below freezing throughout most of the country. But VANCOUVER on the w coast has a mild climate, and average temperatures remain above freezing in winter. Western Canada has plenty of rainfall but the prairies are dry with 250–500mm (10–20in) of rain annually. Southeast Canada has a moist climate, and MONTRÉAL has an annual average of *c.*1,040mm (41in) of rain. **Vegetation** Forests of cedar and hemlock grow on the western mountains, with firs and spruces higher up. The interior plains are used mainly for farming and ranching. The far N is tundra. The SE lowlands contain forests of deciduous trees. The Appalachians include beautiful mixed coniferous and deciduous forests. **History and Politics** Canada's first people, ancestors of present-day Native Americans, arrived from Asia *c.*40,000 years ago. Later arrivals were the INUIT, also from Asia. John CABOT was the first European to reach the Canadian coast in 1497. A race began between France and Britain for the riches in this new land. France gained an initial advantage when Jacques CARTIER discovered the St Lawrence River in 1534 and claimed Canada for France. The French established the first European settlement in 1605 and founded QUÉBEC in 1608. The empire was extended by explorers such as LA SALLE. The FRENCH AND INDIAN WARS

(1689–1763) were a protracted battle for colonial domination of Canada. In 1713 the province of NOVA SCOTIA was ceded to Britain in the Treaty of Utrecht. In 1759, Québec was captured by Britain, and France surrendered all of its Canadian lands in the Treaty of Paris (1763). In 1774, the French-Canadian population of Québec gained territory to the Ohio River, and the CONTINENTAL CONGRESS responded by invading Canada. During the American Revolution, Canada remained loyal to the English crown, and American attempts to capture it failed. In 1784, the province of NEW BRUNSWICK was created out of Nova Scotia. The Constitutional Act (1791) divided Canada along linguistic and religious lines: Upper Canada (now Ontario) was English and Protestant; Lower Canada (now Québec) was French and Catholic. Explorers such as Alexander MACKENZIE, James COOK and George Vancouver enabled Britain to form the crown colony of BRITISH COLUMBIA in 1858. Border disputes with the US (*see* AROOSTOOK WAR; WAR OF 1812) continued into the 19th century. Large-scale immigration from Ireland and Scotland increased tension and conflict between the English-speaking majority and the French-speaking minority. In an attempt to reduce conflict, the British passed the British North America Act (1867). This constitutional act established the federation or Dominion of Canada, consisting of Québec, Ontario, Nova Scotia and New Brunswick. In 1869, it acquired the lands of the HUDSON'S BAY COMPANY and other provinces were added: Manitoba (1870), British Columbia (1871), PRINCE EDWARD ISLAND (1873), Alberta and Saskatchewan (1905) and NEWFOUNDLAND (1949). The Dominion's first prime minister, Sir John A. MACDONALD, established the Canadian Pacific Railway, which proved disastrous to his career but provided the means for 3 million Europeans to emigrate to Canada between 1894 and 1914. Canadians fought as part of Allied forces in both World Wars, and in 1949, Canada was a founding member of NATO. Under the leadership of W.L. Mackenzie KING, national unity was strengthened and industry developed. In 1963, Lester PEARSON became prime minister and, as a sign of Canada's growing national confidence, adopted a new national flag. Pierre TRUDEAU's first administration (1968–79) was faced with violent separatist demands for Québec's independence, and martial law was imposed in 1970. In Trudeau's second administration (1980–84), Québec voted (1980) to remain part of the federation. The Canada Act (1981) amended the constitution, and Canada became a fully sovereign state with a Charter of Rights and Freedoms. It was approved by all the provinces except Québec, which claimed power of constitutional veto. In 1985 Brian MULRONEY and provincial leaders signed the Meech Lake Accord, which provided for Québec to be brought into the constitutional settlement as a "distinct society". Manitoba and Newfoundland failed to endorse the Accord, and Canada was plunged into constitutional crisis. Jean CHRÉTIEN was elected in 1993, and re-elected in 1997 and 2000. A 1995 referendum on sovereignty for Québec was narrowly defeated by 50.6% to 49.4%. Canada's new constitution has also enabled Native Americans to press for land claims. In 1999, NORTHWEST TERRITORIES became the Inuit territory of Nunavut. **Economy** Canada is a highly developed and prosperous nation (1995 GDP per capita, US$21,130). Although farmland covers only 8% of the land, farms are highly mechanized and productive. Canada is the world's leading producer of linseed and the second largest producer of oats and rapeseed. It also has huge wood pulp and paper industries. Fishing is important in both Atlantic and Pacific waters. Canada is rich in mineral resources, and is the world's leading pro-

CANADA
AREA: 9,976,140sq km (3,851,788sq mi)
POPULATION: 28,488,000
CAPITAL (POPULATION): Ottawa (313,987)

ducer of uranium, potash and zinc ore. It is also a major producer of petroleum. Manufacturing is highly developed, especially in the cities where 77% of the population live. Canada is a major manufacturer of commercial vehicles. Other products include chemicals, electronic goods, machinery and telecommunications equipment. Canada has long been influenced, both culturally and economically, by the US, and the two countries have the largest bilateral trade flow in the world. Since 1994, Canada, Mexico and the US have been linked through the NORTH AMERICAN FREE TRADE AGREEMENT (NAFTA).

Canada goose North American wild goose found in wide-ranging habitats, which feeds on grasses or vegetation in streams and ponds. It has white cheek pouches and a long black neck. Nesting on stream banks or tundra, it lays white eggs (4–10). Length: 58–100cm (23–40in); weight: 1.3–6kg (3–14lb). Species *Branta canadensis*.

Canadian art and architecture Following Canada's colonization by the French in the 17th century, the Catholic Church provided the main source of patronage. Most art from the colonial period was documentary in nature, such as Paul Kane's portraits of Native Americans. The Royal Canadian Academy of Art, Montréal, and the National Gallery of Canada, Ottawa, were founded in 1880. Landscape painting was the predominant art form in the late 19th and early 20th centuries. Artists, such as J.W. Morrice, used the palette and approach of IMPRESSIONISM to depict the grandeur of the Canadian scenery. In the 1920s, the Group of Seven (Frank Carmichael, Lawren Harris, A.Y. Jackson, Franz H. Johnston, Arthur Lismer, J.E.H. MacDonald and F.H. Varley) rebelled against the prevailing naturalism and produced more expressionist works. Since 1945, Montréal has emerged as a vital artistic centre in Canadian national culture, producing a diverse range of modern and postmodern art from surrealism to op art. Canadian civic architecture has often applied prevailing European and American trends. The Parliament building in Ottawa (*c*.1859) by Thomas Fuller is a notable example of GOTHIC REVIVAL. Devotional and domestic architecture is more distinctive.

Canadian literature Literary work can be divided into two distinct (yet interrelated) traditions, reflecting Canada's dual French and English linguistic and cultural history. In the 1860s, a Québec group emerged, characterized by nationalist romanticism. In the early 20th century, Québec was again the focus for a parochial pastoralism. In Montréal a more innovative poetic SYMBOLISM developed. The first North American novel, *The History of Emily Montague* (1769), was an account of Québec by Frances Moore Brooke. The Confederation of 1867 produced the first national literary movement, the Confederation School of poets. At the turn of the 19th century, prose tended to pastoral romanticism, such as L.M. Montgomery's classic *Anne of Green Gables*. Literature of the 1920s was more critical of Canadian society; post-1945 literature reflected and nurtured a burgeoning national consciousness. Major poets of the period include Earle Birney, Dorothy Livesay and Jay Macpherson. Recent novelists include Margaret ATWOOD, Robertson DAVIES and Mordecai RICHLER.

canal Artificial waterway for irrigation, drainage and navigation or in conjunction with hydroelectric dams. Canals were built 4,000 years ago in ancient Mesopotamia. Today, the longest canal able to accommodate large ships connects the Baltic and White seas in N Europe. It is 227km (141mi) long. The heyday of canal building in the US was in the early 19th century, spurred by the success of the Erie Canal.

Canaletto (1697–1768) (Giovanni Antonio Canal) Italian painter of the VENETIAN SCHOOL, famous for his perspectival views of Venice. Canaletto's early work is more dramatic and free-flowing than his smoother, accurate mature style. In 1746, he travelled to England, where he painted views of London and country houses. Canaletto used a camera obscura to make his paintings more precise, sometimes making the finished work seem stiff and mannered. He managed to infuse his best work with energy, light and colour. Canaletto had an enormous influence on European art.

canary Popular cage-bird that lives wild in the Azores, Canary and Madeira islands. These yellowish FINCHES feed on fruit, seeds and insects and lay spotted greenish-blue eggs. The pure yellow varieties have been domesticated since the 16th century. Family Fringillidae; species *Serinus canarius*.

Canary Islands Archipelago in the N Atlantic Ocean, *c*.110km (70mi) off the NW coast of Africa; the islands constitute two provinces of Spain, LAS PALMAS and SANTA CRUZ DE TENERIFE. Under Spanish rule since the 16th century, the Canaries are mountainous and the climate warm, with little rainfall. Industries: agriculture, fishing, tourism. Area: 7,273sq km (2,808sq mi). Pop. (1991) 1,493,784.

Canberra Capital of Australia on the River Molonglo, Australian Capital Territory, SE Australia. Settled in the early 1820s, it was chosen in 1908 as the new site for Australia's capital (succeeding MELBOURNE). The transfer of all governmental agencies was not completed until after World War 2. Canberra has the Australian National University (1946), Royal Australian Mint (1965), Royal Military College and Stromlo Observatory. The new Parliament House was opened in 1988. Other sites include the National Library, National Museum and National Gallery. Pop. (1993 est.) 324,600.

Cancer Northern constellation between Gemini and Leo. It contains two open clusters: M44, the Praesepe or Beehive Nebula (NGC 2632) and M67 (NGC 2692). The brightest star is Beta Cancri.

cancer Group of diseases featuring the uncontrolled proliferation of cells (tumour formation). Malignant (cancerous) cells spread (metastasize) from their original site to other parts of the body. Known causative agents (**carcinogens**) include smoking, certain industrial chemicals, asbestos dust and radioactivity. Viruses are implicated in some cancers. Some people have a genetic tendency towards particular types of cancer. Treatments include surgery, chemotherapy with cell-destroying drugs and radiotherapy (or sometimes a combination of all three). Early diagnosis can lead to successful treatment.

Cancer, Tropic of Line of latitude, *c*.23.5° N of the equator, which marks the N boundary of the tropics. It indicates the farthest N position at which the Sun appears directly overhead at noon. The Sun is vertical over the Tropic of Cancer on about 21 June, the summer SOLSTICE in the Northern Hemisphere.

candela (symbol cd) SI unit of luminous intensity. It is defined as 1/60 of the luminous intensity of a BLACK BODY at atmospheric pressure and the temperature of solidification of platinum, 1,772°C (3,222°F).

candle Column of wax or tallow with a fibrous wick and used as a light source. Candles were known to the ancient Egyptians, who used tallow wax. Later, the more pleasant-smelling beeswax and spermaceti were used. Modern candles are generally made from a mixture of paraffin wax and stearic acid with a little added beeswax.

cane Term applied to the stems of stalks of a wide variety of plants. Certain species of BAMBOO and reed are referred to commonly as "canes", while rattan and malacca canes are from species of *Calamus* (family Arecacae/Palmae).

Canetti, Elias (1905–94) British writer, b. Bulgaria. His experience of violent anti-semitism in 1930s Europe inspired his masterpiece, *Crowds and Power* (1960). Canetti's fear of the destructive power of mass psychology also informed his only novel, *Auto da Fé* (1935). He was awarded the 1981 Nobel Prize for literature.

canine Any one of four sharp "stabbing" TEETH in the frontal dentition of most mammals. In humans, they are also called eye teeth.

Canis Major (Great Dog) Southern constellation situated s of Monoceros. It contains the bright open cluster M41 (NGC 2287). The brightest star is Alpha Canis Majoris, or Sirius (Dog Star), the brightest star in the sky.

cannabis Common name for the Indian hemp plant, *Cannabis sativa* (family Cannabidaceae), and for the dried plant or extracted resin when used as a psychotropic drug. The drug produces NARCOTIC effect sometimes allied with a feeling of well-being. It is highly carcinogenic and can induce mild psychosis. It has been shown to relieve the symptoms of some illnesses, such as multiple sclerosis.

Cannes Resort on the French Riviera, SE France. During the 19th century Cannes became fashionable with visiting British aristocracy. An international film festival is held here each spring. Industries: tourism, flowers, textiles. Pop. (1990) 68,676.

cannibalism Practice of eating human flesh as food or for ritual purposes. Cannibalism was once widespread but is now almost extinct, although the practice may still exist in remote parts of Papua New Guinea. People were eaten to satisfy vengeance or as a supposed means of acquiring their strength and powers.

Canning, Charles John, Earl (1812–62) British imperial administrator, son of George CANNING. He was governor general of India (1856–58). Canning repressed the INDIAN MUTINY and followed a policy of conciliation that earned him the nickname "Clemency Canning". With the transfer of the government of India to the British Crown, he became the first viceroy of India (1858–62).

Canning, George (1770–1827) British statesman, prime minister (1827). He was Tory foreign minister (1807–10, 1822–24), favouring vigorous measures against NAPOLEON I. He became prime minister, in coalition with the Whigs, but died four months later.

canning Method of food PRESERVATION by sealing it in cans. The method was first applied (1810) by Nicolas Appert (*c.*1750–1841) to foods sealed in bottles and heated. Today, cans are made from tin-plated steel sheet or from aluminium. Any bacteria present in the food are killed, either by dry heat or by steam heat. Once a can is sealed, it must remain airtight to prevent infection by bacteria, particularly those that cause FOOD POISONING.

cannon ARTILLERY piece consisting of a metal tube used to aim and fire missiles propelled by the explosion of gunpowder in the closed end. Cannon, first used in the 14th century, were originally made of bronze or iron.

canoe Light, shallow-draft boat propelled by one or more paddles. Primitive types are dug out of logs or made of skin or bark stretched over wooden frames. Modern types are made of wood, metal or fibreglass.

canoeing Leisure and competitive use of a CANOE. Competitive events includes those for one, two or more canoeists, either seated in a kayak (which has a keel) or kneeling in a Canadian canoe (without a keel). Canoeing became an Olympic sport in 1936.

canon In music, form of COUNTERPOINT using strict imitation. All the voices or parts have the same melody, but each voice starts at a different time.

canon Term used in Christian religion with several meanings. The basic meaning is a rule or standard, such as the official list of SAINTS or the list of books accepted as genuine parts of the BIBLE. This is the meaning embraced by the term CANON LAW. Initially a canon was also a priest in a cathedral or collegiate church, whose life was regulated by the precepts of canon law. They were distinct from secular canons, who lived outside the cathedral and performed a largely administrative role.

canonization Official action by which a member of a Christian church is created a cult figure or SAINT and

▶ **cancer** Cancer can spread in two ways. First, by direct growth into adjacent tissues, called "direct extension" (A), when cancer cells penetrate into bone, soft connective tissue, and the walls of veins and lymphatic vessels. Alternatively, a cancer cell separates from its tumour and is transported to another part of the body. This spread of cancer is called "metastasis" (B). In metastasis, after the tumour has grown to some size, cancer cells or small groups of cells enter a blood or lymph vessel through the vessel wall (1). They travel through the vessel until they are stopped by a barrier, such as a lymph node, where additional tumours may develop, before releasing more cells which

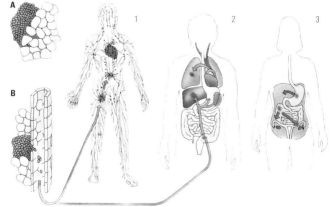

may develop on other lymph nodes. Such cancers, usually carcinomas, may also invade the blood stream and establish more distant secondary growths. Another type of cancer,

sarcomas, tends to spread via venous blood vessels, frequently establishing tumours in the lungs, gastrointestinal tract, or the genito-urinary tract (2). In abdominal cancers

(or transcoelomis-spread cancers), metastasis may also arise as a result of travel across certain body cavities, such as the peritoneal, oral, or pleural cavities (3).

added to the CANON. In the Orthodox Church, a person's sainthood may be proclaimed by a bishop after examining the candidate's case. In the Anglican Church, a commission determines this. In the Roman Catholic Church, officials analyze the evidence of a candidate's reputation for sanctity or virtue and seek out evidence for any miracles done. The results are submitted to the Congregation for the Causes of Saints, and after their findings are ratified by the pope, the candidate is beatified. Further proof is required before full canonization.

canon law In the Roman Catholic, Anglican and Orthodox churches, a body of ecclesiastical laws relating to faith, morals and discipline. It is based on custom and rules laid down by church councils, popes or bishops.

Canopus (Alpha Carinae) Second-brightest star in the sky. Its luminosity and distance are not accurately known, but one estimate classifies it as a bright giant 800 times as luminous as the Sun and 74 light years away.

Canova, Antonio (1757–1822) Italian sculptor. His work expresses the elegance and allusions to antique art which characterize NEOCLASSICISM, but it retains a high degree of individuality. Two important pieces of the 1780s, *Theseus and the Minotaur* and Pope Clement XIV's tomb, catapulted Canova into the limelight. He worked for many distinguished European patrons, notably the papal court.

cantata Musical work consisting of vocal solos and choruses, often alternating with passages of recitative and accompanied by an orchestra. It was a popular form in the 17th and 18th centuries, when Alessandro Scarlatti and J.S. Bach wrote numerous cantatas, both secular and religious.

Canterbury City on the River Great Stour in Kent, SE England. It is the seat of the archbishop and primate of the Anglican Church. The present cathedral (built in the 11th–15th centuries) replaced the original Abbey of St Augustine. Thomas à BECKET was murdered in the cathedral in 1170; after his canonization, Canterbury became a major pilgrimage centre. It contains the University of Kent (1965). Industries: tourism. Pop. (1991) 123,947.

Canterbury, archbishop of Primate of All England and spiritual leader of the worldwide ANGLICAN COMMUNION. The archbishopric was established in 597 when Pope GREGORY I sent a mission to England to convert the Anglo-Saxons. St AUGUSTINE, leader of the mission, became the first archbishop of Canterbury. During the REFORMATION, Archbishop Thomas CRANMER accepted the decision of the English Crown to end papal jurisdiction in England (1534). The archbishop of Canterbury traditionally crowns British monarchs and officiates at other religious ceremonies of national importance. He presides over the Lambeth Conference of worldwide Anglicanism but exercises no jurisdiction outside his own ecclesiastical province.

cantilever bridge BRIDGE in which each half of the main span is rigidly supported at one end only. The other ends are joined in the middle of the bridge.

Canton *See* GUANGZHOU

Cantona, Eric (1966–) French football player. He began his career with Auxerre (1980–88). In 1992 Cantona transferred to Leeds United and, after helping them win the league, moved to Manchester United (1993). Two further championship medals followed. During the 1994–95 season he was banned for kicking an abusive fan. In 1996 Cantona became captain and his self-discipline helped Manchester United win their second consecutive premiership title. Cantona retired in 1997.

Cantonese One of the major languages of China. Within the CHINESE People's Republic, it is spoken by

*c.*50 million people, mainly in the extreme southern provinces of GUANGDONG and GUANGXI. It is also the language spoken by most Chinese in Southeast Asia and the USA.

Cantor, Georg (1845–1918) German mathematician, b. Russia. He was professor of mathematics (1869–1913) at the University of Halle, Germany. His work on INFINITY challenged the existing deductive process of mathematics. Cantor developed the SET THEORY and provided a new definition of IRRATIONAL NUMBERS.

Canute (*c.*994–1035) King of Denmark (1014–28), England (1017–35) and Norway (1028–29). He accompanied his father, Sweyn, on the Danish invasion of England (1013). After his father's death (1014), Canute was accepted as joint king of Denmark with his brother and later became sole king. He invaded England again (1015) and divided it (1016) with the English king Edmund Ironside. Canute became king after Edmund's death. His rule was a just and peaceful one. Canute restored the church and codified English law. His reign in Scandinavia was more turbulent. Canute conquered Norway (1028) made one son king of Denmark (1028) and another king of Norway (1029).

canyon Deep, narrow depression in the Earth's crust. Land canyons are the result of erosion by rivers flowing through arid terrain. Marine canyons may be formed when a river bed and the surrounding terrain is submerged, or by turbulence produced by deep-water currents. *See also* GRAND CANYON

Capa, Robert (1913–54) US photojournalist, b. Hungary. He is remembered for his haunting photos of the brutality of war, especially the image of an execution of a Loyalist prisoner in the Spanish Civil War. Capa covered World War 2 for *Life* magazine and was a founder (1946) of the Magnum photographic agency. He was killed by a landmine in Vietnam.

capacitance (symbol *C*) Property of an electrical circuit or component that describes its ability to store charge in its CAPACITOR. Capacitance is measured in farads: 1 farad is a capacitance needing a charge of one coulomb to raise its potential by 1 volt. Most capacitances are small enough to be measured in microfarads (one millionth of a farad).

capacitor (condenser) Electrical circuit component that stores charge. It has at least two metal plates and is used principally in alternating current (AC) circuits. The various types include parallel-plate condensers and electrolytic capacitors. *See also* ELECTRIC CURRENT

Cape Breton Rocky island in NE Nova Scotia, Canada, separated from the mainland by the Strait of Canso. Industries: timber, fishing, coal mining. Area: 10,311sq km (3,981sq mi). Pop. (1986) 166,116.

Cape Canaveral Low, sandy promontory in E Florida, USA, extending E into the Atlantic Ocean. It is the site of the John F. Kennedy Space Center which, since 1950, has been NASA's main US launch site for space flights and long-range missiles.

Cape Cod Hook-shaped, sandy peninsula in SE Massachusetts, USA. The Pilgrim Fathers landed here in 1620. It extends into the Atlantic Ocean, forming Cape Cod Bay. It was originally a centre for fishing, whaling and salt extraction; tourism is now the major industry.

Cape Horn Southernmost point of South America in S Chile. It was sighted by Francis Drake in 1578 and first rounded in 1616 by Cornelis van Schouten.

Čapek, Karel (1890–1938) Czech dramatist, novelist and essayist. Čapek's dystopic drama *R.U.R.* (Rossum's Universal Robots) (1920) introduced the word "robot" into the English language. He collaborated with his brother Josef (1887–1945) on *The Insect Play* (1921), a satire on totalitarianism. *See also* EXPRESSIONISM

Capella (Alpha Aurigae) Star in the constellation of Auriga, magnitude 0.08 (sixth-brightest in the sky). A spectroscopic binary (comprised of two yellow giants), it is 41 light years from Earth.

caper Flower bud, generally pickled in vinegar, of a shrub native to Sicily and other Mediterranean countries, used as a condiment and to make sauces. Family Capparidaceae; species *Capparis spinosa.*

Cape of Good Hope Peninsula, 48km (30mi) s of Cape Town, South Africa. The first European to sail around it was Bartholomeu Diaz in 1488. The Cape sea route between India and Europe was established by Vasco da Gama in 1497–99.

Cape Province Formerly the largest province in South Africa. In 1994, it was divided into the separate provinces of EASTERN CAPE, WESTERN CAPE and NORTHERN CAPE. The first colony was established (1652) by the Dutch EAST INDIA COMPANY, and slaves were imported to work the land. The BOER settlers' expansion led to territorial wars with indigenous tribes, such as the XHOSA (1779). In 1806, Britain established control and renamed the region, Cape of Good Hope Colony. The new British settlers clashed with the Boers, precipitating the GREAT TREK (1835). In 1867, diamonds were discovered near KIMBERLEY. The British attempt to incorporate TRANSVAAL and Orange FREE STATE into a single state with NATAL and Cape Colony, resulted in the SOUTH AFRICAN WARS (1899–1902). In 1910, the colony became a province of the Union of South Africa. During the 1960s, the apartheid government created the separate tribal areas (bantustans) of Transkei and Ciskei. In 1994, these were integrated into the new Eastern Cape Province.

Capetians French royal family forming the third dynasty that provided France with 15 kings. It began (987) with Hugh Capet, who succeeded Louis V, the last of the CAROLINGIANS. Capetians dominated the feudal forces, extending the king's rule across the whole of France. The last Capetian king, Charles IV, was succeeded (1328) by Philip VI of the House of Valois.

Cape Town City and seaport at the foot of Table Mountain, South Africa. It is South Africa's legislative capital and the capital of WESTERN CAPE province. Founded in 1652 by the Dutch EAST INDIA COMPANY, it came under British rule in 1795. Places of interest include the Union Parliament, a 17th-century castle, the National Historic Museum and the University of Cape Town (founded 1829). It is an important industrial and commercial centre. Industries: clothing, engineering equipment, motor vehicles, wine. Pop. (1991) 2,350,157.

Cape Verde Republic in the E Atlantic Ocean, the most westerly point of Africa. It is made up of 15 islands divided into two groups (Windward and Leeward). The capital is Praia on São Tiago. Cape Verde was colonized by the Portuguese in 1462 and served as a base for the slave trade. The islands gained full independence in 1975. The economy is based on agriculture, fishing and salt. Area: 4,033sq km (1,557sq mi). Pop. (2000 est.) 515,000.

capillarity Movement of a liquid in a narrow opening caused by the surface tension between the liquid and the surrounding material. This is most often seen in a vertical, narrow glass capillary tube, but capillarity also occurs in various directions – as when a sponge or blotting paper soaks up water.

capillary Smallest of BLOOD VESSELS, connecting arteries and veins. Capillary walls consist of only a single layer of cells, so that water containing dissolved oxygen and other nutrients (as well as carbon dioxide and other wastes) can pass easily between the blood and surrounding tissues.

capital In architecture, the block of masonry at the top of a column, often elaborately carved. The design of the capital is characteristic of the ORDERS OF ARCHITECTURE.

capital In ECONOMICS, different forms of wealth. **Fixed** capital includes buildings, tools and equipment; **working** capital (variable or circulating capital) includes raw materials, stock and cash. In accounting, capital is the obligation of a business enterprise has to its owners. Capital includes not only the owner's contribution but also the profits retained within the business for future use.

capitalism Economic system in which property and the means of PRODUCTION are privately owned. Capitalism is based on profit motive, individual enterprise, efficiency through competition and a notion of freedom of choice. It was first articulated by Adam SMITH in his treatise *The Wealth of Nations* (1776). Its development dates from the INDUSTRIAL REVOLUTION and the rise of the BOURGEOISIE. In practice, capitalist governments participate in economic regulation although to a lesser extent than a government within COMMUNISM or SOCIALISM. The collapse of Soviet communism removed capitalism's traditional opponent and created economic uncertainty. *See also* DIVISION OF LABOUR; FREE-TRADE; FRIEDMAN, MILTON; GALBRAITH, J.K.; KEYNES, JOHN MAYNARD; LAISSEZ-FAIRE; MARXISM; MERCANTILISM; MONETARISM

capital punishment Punishing a criminal offence by death. Usual methods of execution include hanging, electrocution, lethal injection, lethal gas or firing squad. The death penalty has been abolished in many Western countries. In the US, capital punishment was effectively in abeyance during the 1970s after several rulings by the Supreme Court, but today 38 states have the death penalty. The use of capital punishment is the subject of much debate: supporters claim that such punishment can be deserved and has a deterrent effect, while opponents state that it is inhuman, does not deter, and that miscarriages of justice cannot be rectified.

Capitol Building in WASHINGTON, D.C., in which the US CONGRESS convenes. The original architect was William Thornton, and the cornerstone was laid by George Washington in 1793. It was burned to the ground by the British in 1814. Benjamin LATROBE and Charles BULFINCH worked on the restoration, which was completed in 1830. The dome reaches a height of 88m (288ft).

Capone, Al (Alphonse) (1899–1947) US gangster of the PROHIBITION era, b. Italy. He inherited a vast crime empire from Johnny Torio. Capone was suspected of many brutal crimes but, ironically, was only ever convicted and imprisoned for income tax evasion (1931).

Capote, Truman (1924–84) US writer. His works, typified by keen social observation and characters on the fringes of society, include the novella *Breakfast at Tiffany's* (1958), the novel *The Grass Harp* (1951) and volumes of shorter pieces such as *Music for Chameleons* (1980). Capote claimed that *In Cold Blood* (1966) was the first non-fiction (faction) novel.

Cappadocia Ancient region of ASIA MINOR, now in E central Turkey, between Lake Tuz and the Euphrates. The principal town is KAYSERI. Cappadocia was an important centre of early Christianity, its pointed, eroded rocks providing cave-havens for hermits.

Capra, Frank (1897–1991) US film director, b. Italy. During the 1930s Depression, Capra made a string of successful screwball comedies. His central theme was the unlikely triumph of idealism and the common man over materialism and bureaucracy. Capra won three

► **carbon cycle**
Elemental carbon is in constant flux. Gaseous carbon dioxide (CO_2) is first incorporated into simple sugars by photosynthesis in green plants. These may be broken down (respired) to provide energy, a process that releases CO_2 back into the atmosphere. Alternatively, animals that eat the plants also metabolize the sugars and release CO_2 in the process. Geological processes also affect the Earth's carbon balance, with carbon being removed from the cycle when it is accumulated within fossil fuels, such as coal, oil, and gas. Conversely, large amounts of carbon dioxide are released into the atmosphere when such fuels are burned.

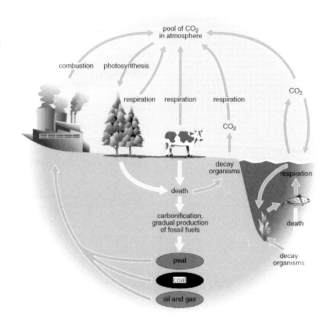

Academy Awards as best director for *It Happened One Night* (1934), *Mr. Deeds Goes to Town* (1936) and *You Can't Take It With You* (1938). Capra's best film, *It's a Wonderful Life* (1947), was a commercial failure.

Capricorn, Tropic of Line of latitude, *c*.23.54° s of the Equator that marks the s boundary of the tropics. It indicates the farthest s position at which the Sun appears directly overhead at noon. The Sun is vertical over the Tropic of Capricorn on about 22 December, which is the summer SOLSTICE in the Southern Hemisphere.

Capricornus (Sea Goat) Southern constellation situated on the ecliptic between Sagittarius and Aquarius; the tenth sign of the zodiac, identified with the Greek god PAN. Usually referred to as Capricorn only for astrological purposes, this constellation contains the faint globular cluster M30 (NGC 7099).

capsicum *See* PEPPER

capuchin Small, diurnal, tree-dwelling monkey found in South and Central America. Black or brown. Omnivorous, but preferring fruit, it grows to 55cm (22in) with a furry, prehensile tail of similar length. Family Cebidae.

Capuchins (officially Friars Minor of St Francis Capuchin, O.F.M.Cap.) Roman Catholic religious order, founded in 1525 as an offshoot of the FRANCISCANS. Capuchins are so-called because of the pointed cowl (*capuche*) which forms part of their habit. They re-emphasized Franciscan ideals of poverty and austerity, and played an important role in the COUNTER-REFORMATION through their missionary activities.

capybara Largest living RODENT, native to Central and South America; it is semi-aquatic with webbed feet, a large, nearly hairless, body, short legs and a tiny tail. Length: 1.2m (4ft). Species *Hydrochoerus hydrochoeris*.

car *See* AUTOMOBILE

Caracalla (188–217) (Marcus Aurelius Antoninus) Roman emperor (211–17). Caracalla murdered his

brother, Geta (212). Excessive expenditure on war caused economic crisis. During his reign, Roman citizenship was extended to all free men in the empire. Caracalla was assassinated by his successor, Macrinus.

Caracas Capital of Venezuela, on the River Guaire. The city was under Spanish rule until 1821. It was the birthplace of Simón BOLÍVAR. Caracas grew after 1930, with the exploitation of oil. It has the Central University of Venezuela (1725) and a cathedral (1614). Industries: motor vehicles, oil, brewing. Pop. (1990) 1,824,892.

Caractacus (d. *c*.AD 54) (Caratacus) British chieftain, son of CYMBELINE. He led the Catuvellauni against the Roman conquest (43–50). Caractacus was captured on the Welsh borders and paraded in Rome by Emperor CLAUDIUS. His life was spared in tribute to his bravery.

Caravaggio, Michelangelo Merisi da (1571–1610) Italian painter, the most influential and original painter of the 17th century. His work brought a new, formidable sense of reality at a time when a feeble MANNERISM prevailed. The majestic *Supper at Emmaus* (*c*.1598–1600), with its beautifully modelled images of Christ and his disciples, shows him gaining confidence. His mature phase (1599–1606) began with two large-scale religious paintings of St Matthew. The use of dramatic shadows (CHIAROSCURO) and a living model, show Caravaggio's revolutionary approach to religious themes. *The Crucifixion of St Peter* and *The Conversion of St Paul* (both 1600–01) are masterpieces of psychological realism.

caraway Biennial herb native to Eurasia and cultivated for its small, brown seed-like fruits that are used for flavouring foods. It has feathery leaves and white flowers. Family Apiaceae/Umbelliferae; species *Carum carvi*.

carbide Inorganic compound of carbon with metals or other more electropositive elements. Many transition metals form carbides, in which carbon atoms occupy spaces between adjacent atoms in the metal lattice.

Some electropositive metals form ionic carbon compounds; the best known is CALCIUM CARBIDE. Carbides are commonly used as abrasives.

carbohydrate Organic compound of carbon, hydrogen and oxygen that is a constituent of many foodstuffs. The simplest carbohydrates are SUGARS. GLUCOSE and FRUCTOSE are monosaccharides, naturally occurring sugars; they have the same formula ($C_6H_{12}O_6$) but different structures. One molecule of each combines with the loss of water to make SUCROSE ($C_{12}H_{22}O_{11}$), a disaccharide. Starch and cellulose are polysaccharides, carbohydrates consisting of hundreds of glucose molecules linked together. *See also* SACCHARIDE

carbon (symbol C) Common nonmetallic element of group IV of the periodic table. Carbon forms a vast number of compounds, which (with hydrogen–hydocarbons and other non-metals) forms the basis of organic CHEMISTRY. Until recently, it was believed there were two crystalline ALLOTROPES: GRAPHITE and DIAMOND. In 1996, a third type, Buckminsterfullerenes (named after Richard Buckminster FULLER), which are shaped like geodesic domes, was discovered. Various amorphous (noncrystalline) forms of carbon also exist, such as coal, coke and charcoal. A synthetic form of carbon is CARBON FIBRE. The isotope C^{14} is used for CARBON DATING of archaeological specimens. Properties: at.no. 6; r.a.m. 12.011; r.d. 1.9–2.3 (graphite), 3.15–3.53 (diamond); m.p. c.3,550°C (6,422°F); sublimes at 3,367°C (6,093°F); b.p. c.4,200°C (7,592°F); most common isotope C^{12} (98,89%).

Carbonari (It. charcoal burners) Members of an early 19th-century Italian secret society advocating liberal, nationalist reforms. The Carbonari were opposed to conservative regimes imposed on Italy after the Congress of Vienna (1815) and were a model for the RISORGIMENTO movement and, in particular, Giuseppe MAZZINI.

carbonate Salt of carbonic acid, formed when carbon dioxide (CO_2) dissolves in water. Carbonic acid is an extremely weak acid, and both it and many of its salts are unstable, decomposing readily to release CO_2. Nevertheless, large parts of the Earth's crust are made up of carbonates, such as CALCIUM CARBONATE and DOLOMITE.

carbon cycle Circulation of CARBON in the biosphere. It is a complex chain of events. The most important elements are the taking up of carbon dioxide (CO_2) by green plants during PHOTOSYNTHESIS and the return of CO_2 to the atmosphere by the respiration and eventual decomposition of animals which eat the plants. The burning of fossil fuels has also, over the years, released CO_2 back into the atmosphere.

carbon dating (radiocarbon dating) Method of determining the age of organic materials by measuring the RADIOACTIVE DECAY of an ISOTOPE of carbon, carbon-14 (^{14}C). This radio-isotope decays to form nitrogen, with a half-life of 5,730 years. When an organism dies, it ceases to take carbon dioxide into its body, so that the amount of ^{14}C it contains is fixed relative to its total weight. Over the centuries, this quantity steadily diminishes.

carbon dioxide (CO_2) Colourless, odourless gas that occurs in the atmosphere (0.03%) and as a product of the combustion of fossil fuels and respiration in plants and animals. In its solid form (dry ice) it is used in refrigeration; as a gas it is used in carbonated beverages and fire extinguishers. Research indicates that its increase in the atmosphere leads to the GREENHOUSE EFFECT and GLOBAL WARMING. Properties: m.p. −56.6°C (−69.9°F); sublimes −78.5°C (−109.3°F). *See also* CARBON CYCLE

carbon fibre Form of carbon made by heating textile fibres to high temperatures. The result is fibres (typically 0.001cm in diameter) which are, weight-for-weight, some of the strongest of all fibres. They are too short to be woven into a super-strong yarn. Instead they are incorporated into plastics, ceramics and glass.

Carboniferous Fifth geologic division of the PALAEOZOIC era, lasting from 360 to 286 million years ago. It is often called the "Age of Coal" because of its extensive swampy forests that turned into most of today's COAL deposits. Amphibians flourished, marine life abounded in warm inland seas, and the first reptiles appeared.

carbon monoxide (CO) Colourless, odourless poisonous gas formed during the incomplete combustion of fossil fuels, occurring, for example, in coal gas and the exhaust fumes of cars. Carbon monoxide poisons by combining with the HAEMOGLOBIN in red blood cells and thus preventing them from carrying oxygen around the body. It is used as a reducing agent in metallurgy. Properties: density 0.968 (air = 1); m.p. −205°C (−337°F); b.p. −191.5°C (−312.7°F).

carboxylic acid Member of a class of organic chemical compounds containing the group COOH. The commonest example is ETHANOIC ACID (acetic acid, CH_3COOH), which is present in vinegar. These acids are weakly acidic, forming salts with bases and esters with alcohols. Esters of high-molecular weight, carboxylic acids, such as stearic, lauric and oleic acids, are present in animal and vegetable fats; for this reason carboxylic acids are often called FATTY ACIDS.

carburettor Component of some petrol-powered INTERNAL COMBUSTION ENGINES, used to vaporize and mix fuel with air in the correct proportion for proper combustion. Generally steady speed requires a ratio of 15:1 air to fuel. Richer ratios of 10:1 air to fuel are necessary for starting cold engines. Efficient carburation is essential for smooth running and efficient engine performance. No carburettor is needed in engines that use fuel injection.

Carcassonne Town on the River Aude, s France; capital of Aude department, Languedoc-Roussillon. Originally fortified by the Romans in the 1st century BC, the old town consists of a hilltop medieval fortress, including the extant 6th-century Visigoth towers. A centre of the ALBIGENSES sect, the fortress was captured (1209) by Simon de Montfort. The new town across the Aude is a farm trading centre. Pop. (1990) 44,990.

carcinogen External substance or agent that causes CANCER, including chemicals, such as the tar present in cigarette smoke, large doses of radiation, and some viruses, such as polyoma.

carcinoma Form of CANCER arising from the epithelial cells present in skin and the membranes lining the internal organs. It is a malignant growth which tends to give rise to metastases (secondary cancers). *See also* SARCOMA

cardamom Pungent spice made from seeds of a plant of the GINGER family (Zingiberaceae). Species *Elettaria cardamomum*.

Cárdenas, Lázaro (1895–1970) Mexican statesman, president (1934–40). In the final phase of the MEXICAN REVOLUTION, Cárdenas accelerated the distribution of communal lands, nationalized oil companies (1938) and encouraged the confederation of labour.

cardiac muscle *See* MUSCLE

Cardiff (Caerdydd) Capital of Wales and port on the River Severn estuary at the mouth of the rivers Taff, Rhymney and Ely, s Glamorgan. The construction of docks (1839) led to the rapid growth of the city, and until the early 20th century, it was a major coal exporting centre. It is the seat of the Welsh National Assembly and the University College of South Wales and

Monmouthshire (1893), and has an 11th-century castle. The Millennium Stadium hosted the 1999 rugby World Cup. Industries: steel manufacturing, engineering, chemicals, food processing. Pop. (1994) 290,000.

Cardin, Pierre (1922–) French fashion designer. Cardin opened his fashion house in 1949 and quickly built a reputation with his oriental styles and sleek coats with huge collars. He was the first couturier to launch menswear (1960) and ready-to-wear (1963) collections. Cardin's "Space Age" collection introduced catsuits and jumpsuits (1964) and shift dresses (1966).

cardinal Priest of the highest rank in the hierarchy of the Roman Catholic Church after the pope. Some cardinals are heads of departments of the CURIA ROMANA, whereas others are PRIMATES of national churches. They are nominated by the pope, whom they advise. On the death of a pope, they meet in secret CONCLAVE to elect his successor.

cardinal (redbird) North American songbird with a clear, whistle-like song. The male has bright red plumage and crest and a thick orange-red bill. They feed on seeds, fruits and insects. A cup-shaped nest holds pale blue, heavily spotted eggs (four) incubated by the female. Length: to 23cm (9in). Family Fringillidae; species *Richmondena cardinalis*.

cardiology Branch of medicine that deals with the diagnosis and treatment of the diseases and disorders of the HEART and vascular system.

Carew, Thomas (1595–1639) English poet. His poetry was largely influenced by that of his friend Ben JONSON and of John DONNE, to whom he wrote an elegy. His work includes *A Rapture* and the masque *Coelum Britannicum*.

Carey, George Leonard (1935–) English cleric, archbishop of Canterbury, and primate of all England (1991–). He was bishop of Bath and Wells (1988–91). He belongs to the evangelical wing of the CHURCH OF ENGLAND. Carey supported the ordination of women priests and environmental conservation efforts. *See also* EVANGELICALISM

Carey, Peter (1943–) Australian novelist and short-story writer. His first book, *The Fat Man in History* (1974), was a collection of short stories. Carey is best-known for his imaginative novels, such as *Bliss* (1981) and *Illywacker* (1985). He won the Booker Prize for *Oscar and Lucinda* (1988). Other works include *The Tax Inspector* (1991) and *Jack Maggs* (1997).

cargo cult Mainly Melanesian religious and political movement in which believers expected their ancestors to return in planes or ships laden with modern goods ("cargo") and bring them prosperity and freedom. Movements of this kind first appeared in the 19th century, when local people were confronted by colonialism. Cults expanded during World War 2.

Carib Major language group and Native American tribe. They entered the Caribbean region from NE South America. About 500 Caribs still live on the island of Dominica; 5,000 migrated to Central America, notably around Honduras, where their descendants still live.

Caribbean Community and Common Market (CARICOM) Caribbean economic union. CARICOM was formed (1973) by the Treaty of Chaguaramas to coordinate economic and foreign policy in the WEST INDIES. Most members rely on the export of sugar and tropical fruits and are heavily dependent on imports. The headquarters is in Georgetown, Guyana.

Caribbean Sea Extension of the N Atlantic Ocean linked to the Gulf of Mexico by the Yucatán Channel and to the Pacific Ocean by the Panama Canal. The first European to discover the Caribbean was Columbus in 1492, who named it after the CARIB. It soon lay on the route of many Spanish expeditions and became notorious for piracy. With the opening of the Panama Canal (1914), its strategic importance increased. Area: *c.*2,640,000sq km (1,020,000sq mi).

caribou *See* REINDEER

caricature (It. *caricare*, load or surcharge) Painting or drawing in which a person is presented in a comic, often ridiculous, light by the distortion of their features. Caricature may be used to interpret the character of a person, event or age. The genre first appeared in the late 16th century. HOGARTH attempted to distinguish between depicting character and comic likeness, but the two traditions merged. In the 20th century, many popular graphic artists have combined caricature with social and political satire, as in political CARTOONS. *See also* CARRACCI, ANNIBALE

caries Decay of teeth or BONE substance. Caries are caused by acids produced when bacteria present in the mouth break down sugars in food. Regular brushing, a reduced sugar intake and fluoride prevent decay.

Carina Part of the dismembered constellation Argo Navis, the ship Argo. It is the brightest and richest part of Argo, representing the ship's keel, and contains CANOPUS.

Carissimi, Giacomo (1605–74) Italian composer. Carissimi is mainly important as an early writer of ORATORIOS, such as *Jephtha*, which give prominence to the role of the chorus. He also wrote chamber CANTATAS

Carl XVI Gustaf *See* CHARLES XVI GUSTAVUS

Carlists Reactionary Spanish political faction in the 19th century. They favoured the royal claims of Don CARLOS and his successors, and figured in several rebellions. The remnants of the Carlists eventually merged with the fascist FALANGE in 1937.

Carlos (1788–1855) Spanish prince and pretender to the throne. His elder brother, Ferdinand VII, changed Spanish law so that his daughter ISABELLA II succeeded him (1833). Carlos was proclaimed king by the CARLISTS, and civil war ensued. Isabella won (1840), and Carlos went into exile. In 1845, he resigned his claim in favour of his son, Don Carlos II.

Carlson, Chester (1906–68) US physicist, inventor of XEROGRAPHY (1938). He patented it in 1940, and in 1947 signed an agreement with the Haloid Company (now Xerox). Carlson's royalties made him a multi-millionaire.

Carlyle, Thomas (1795–1881) Scottish philosopher, critic and historian. His most successful work, *Sartor Resartus* (1836), combined philosophy and autobiography. His histories include *The French Revolution* (1837). Influenced by ROMANTICISM and Goethe in particular, Carlyle was a powerful advocate of the significance of great leaders in history.

Carmelites (officially Order of Our Lady of Mount Carmel) Order founded by St Berthold in Palestine *c.*1154. An order of Carmelite sisters was founded in 1452. The Carmelites devote themselves to contemplation and missionary work.

carnation Slender-stemmed, herbaceous plant native to Europe. It has narrow leaves, swollen stem joints and produces several dense blooms with serrated petals which range from white to yellow, pink and red. Family Caryophyllaceae; species *Dianthus caryophyllus*.

Carné, Marcel (1906–96) French film director. He began his career as an assistant to René CLAIR. Carné collaborated with screenwriter Jacques Prévert on films such as *Quai des Brumes* (1938) and *Le Jour se Lève* (1939). Their partnership culminated in the cinematic masterpiece *Les Enfants du Paradis* (1943). His films went out of fashion with the arrival of the NOUVELLE VAGUE.

Carnegie, Andrew (1835–1919) US industrialist and philanthropist, b. Scotland. He foresaw the demand for iron and steel and founded the Keystone Bridge Company. From 1873, Carnegie concentrated on steel, pioneering mass production techniques. By 1901, the Carnegie Steel Company was producing 25% of US steel. He endowed 2,800 libraries and donated more than $350 million.

Carniola Historic region of SE Europe roughly coextensive with modern SLOVENIA. Once part of the Roman province of Pannonia, Carniola was occupied during the 6th century by the Slovenes. In the 13th century, it was part of the Holy Roman Empire and passed to the Habsburgs in 1335. In 1918 most of the region was awarded to Yugoslavia, until Slovenia gained independence in 1990.

carnival Strictly speaking, a Christian celebration (with parades, masques and pageants) that takes place on Shrove Tuesday (*see* MARDI GRAS). Examples include the street carnivals in Rio de Janeiro, New Orleans, Venice and Rome. Such celebrations have their origins in pagan spring festivals and, during the Roman Empire, reached a peak of debauchery and civil disorder. Unable to suppress these pagan revels, the Catholic Church attempted to adopt them as church ritual. The medieval Feast of Fools parodied Church practice by staging elaborate mock Masses. Eventually the Church managed to relate the festival to the advent of LENT, though carnival retains many of its pre-Christian features, such as sexual licence and social levelling.

carnivore Any member of the order of flesh-eating MAMMALS. Mustelids (WEASELS, MARTENS, MINKS and WOLVERINES) make up the largest family. CATS are the most specialized killers among the carnivores; DOGS, BEARS and RACCOONS are much less exclusively meat eaters; and CIVETS, MONGOOSES and their relatives also have a mixed diet. Related to the civets, but in a separate family, are the HYENAS, large dog-like scavengers. More distantly related to living land carnivores are the SEALS, SEA LIONS and WALRUSES; they evolved from ancient land carnivores who gave rise to early weasel- or civet-like forms. Other extinct carnivores include the sabre-tooth cats, which died out during the Pliocene epoch, 2 million years ago.

carnivorous plant *See* INSECTIVOROUS PLANT

Carnot, Lazare Nicolas Marguerite (1753–1823) French general. He was the outstanding commander of the FRENCH REVOLUTIONARY WARS, his strategy being largely responsible for French victories. Ousted in 1797, Carnot was recalled by Napoleon (1800), who made him minister of war.

Carnot, (Nicolas Léonard) Sadi (1796–1832) French engineer and physicist whose work laid the foundation for the science of THERMODYNAMICS. His major work, *Réflexions sur la puissance motrice du feu* (1824), provided the first theoretical background for the steam engine and introduced the concept of the second law of thermodynamics (involving ENTROPY), which was formulated later by Rudolf CLAUSIUS. Carnot's work was recognized in 1848 by William KELVIN.

Carnot cycle In THERMODYNAMICS, a cycle of events that demonstrates the impossibility of total efficiency in heat engines. Named after Sadi CARNOT, it shows how an engine can never convert all the heat energy supplied to it into mechanical energy. Some heat energy always remains unused in a "cold sink". In an internal combustion engine, this can be thought of as the engine itself.

Caro, Sir Anthony (1924–) English sculptor. He worked as an assistant to Henry MOORE, before making his own sculptures. Caro's distinctive "structures", for example *Ledge Piece* (1978), are made from prefabricated metal, welded and bolted together. He often places his work on the floor to create a greater intimacy.

carob Plant of the E Mediterranean. It belongs to the pea family (Fabaceae/Leguminosae) and bears leguminous fruits that are a foodstuff. Its seeds are used as a substitute for coffee beans. Species *Ceratonia siliqua*.

carol Traditional song usually of religious joy and associated with Christmas. Earliest examples date to the 14th century.

Carol I (1839–1914) Prince of Romania (1866–81); first king (1881–1914). He aided Russia in the first Russo-Turkish War (1877–78). Romanian independence and Carol's sovereignty were recognized by the Congress of Berlin (1878). By 1913 Romania had become the strongest Balkan power. He preserved the neutrality of Romania at the start of World War 1.

Carol II (1893–1953) King of Romania (1930–40), grandnephew of CAROL I. In 1925, he renounced the throne. Carol returned in 1930 and supplanted his son, Michael, as king. He supported the growing fascist movement and hoped to become dictator. German pressure forced him to abdicate in favour of Michael, leaving power in the hands of the fascist leader, Ion ANTONESCU.

Caroline Islands Archipelago of *c.*600 volcanic islands, coral islets and reefs in the W Pacific Ocean, N of the Equator; part of the US Trust Territory of the Pacific Islands. Politically, the islands exist as two entities. In 1979 all the islands, except the BELAU group, became the Federated States of MICRONESIA. Area: 1,130sq km (450sq mi).

Carolingian renaissance Cultural revival in France and Italy under the encouragement of CHARLEMAGNE. The illiterate monarch gathered notable educators and artists from all over the world to his court at Aachen. He promoted Catholicism, art and learning by founding abbeys and encouraging church building. As the first Roman emperor in the West for more than 300 years, Charlemagne imposed a new culture in Europe, combining Christian, Roman and Frankish elements. The outstanding building of the period is the Palatine Chapel, Aachen (805).

Carolingians Second Frankish dynasty of early medieval Europe. Founded in the 7th century by Pepin of Landen, it rose to power under the weak kingship of the MEROVINGIANS. In 732, CHARLES MARTEL defeated the Muslims at Poitiers; in 751 his son, PEPIN III (THE SHORT), deposed the last Merovingian and became king of the Franks. The dynasty peaked under Pepin's son, CHARLEMAGNE (after whom the dynasty is called), who united the Frankish dominions and much of W and central Europe, and was crowned Holy Roman emperor by the pope in 800. His empire was later broken up by civil wars. Carolingian rule finally ended in 987.

Carothers, Wallace Hume (1896–1937) US chemist who discovered the synthetic fibre now called NYLON.

carp Freshwater fish native to temperate waters of Asia. Introduced to the US and Europe, it is an important food fish. It is brown or golden and has four fleshy mouth whiskers called barbels. Length: to 1m (3.2ft). Family Cyprinidae; species *Cyprinus carpio*. *See artwork* p.156

Carpaccio, Vittore (1460–1525) Venetian painter. His narrative paintings relate incidents against a background of an idealized Venice. His cycle of scenes, *The Legend of St Ursula* (1490–98) and *SS George and Jerome* (1502–07), have an exceptional vitality. Carpaccio's range of subjects varied from religious paintings to the enchanting *Two Venetian Ladies*.

Carpathian Mountains Mountain range in central and E Europe, extending NE from the central Czech

Republic to the Polish-Czech border and into Romania and the Ukraine. The N Carpathians (Beskids and Tatra) run E along the border and SE through W Ukraine; the S Carpathians (Transylvanian Alps) extend SW to the River Danube. The highest peak is Gerlachovka, 2,655m (8,711ft). Length: 1,530km (950mi).

carpel Female reproductive part of a flowering plant. A carpel consists of a STIGMA, a STYLE and an OVARY. A group of carpels make up the **gynoecium**, the complete female reproductive structure within a flower.

carpet Floor-covering of soft and durable fabric. Carpets are made from a variety of materials, including wool, cotton and synthetic fibres, synthetics being used in more than 80% of the carpets manufactured today. Most carpets are produced by weaving, tufting, knitting or electrostatic flocking. Pile carpets, in which the cut ends of threads form the upper surface (pile), are woven on power looms. In tufting, pile yarn is stitched to a previously made backing, often of jute; the carpet can then be printed or dyed. In electrostatic flocking, chopped fibres are glued to a backing fabric.

Carracci, Annibale (1560–1609) Italian painter. With his brother Agostino (1557–1602) and cousin Ludovico (1555–1619), he established an influential academy at Bologna. Carracci's major work is the gallery of the Farnese Palace, Rome. It ranks as one of the masterpieces of the early BAROQUE. He also invented CARICATURE.

Carranza, Venustiano (1859–1920) Mexican statesman, president (1914). Carranza supported Francisco MADERO's revolution against Porfirio DÍAZ. When Madero was overthrown by Victoriano HUERTA, Carranza joined Álvaro OBREGÓN, "Pancho" VILLA and Emiliano ZAPATA to defeat Huerta. Villa and Zapata's refusal to recognize Carranza's authority prolonged the civil war. Carranza supported John PERSHING's expedition against Villa. His attempts to prevent the accession of Obregón led to a revolt. Carranza fled and was murdered. *See also* MEXICAN REVOLUTION

Carrel, Alexis (1873–1944) US surgeon and experimental biologist, b. France. Carrel was a member (1912–39) of the Rockefeller Institute. He was awarded the 1912 Nobel Prize for physiology or medicine for his development of anastomosis, a surgical technique for stitching together blood vessels end-to-end. Carrel and Charles A. LINDBERGH invented an artificial heart.

Carreras, José Maria (1946–) Spanish tenor. He made his debut in Barcelona (1970), going on to sing in opera houses worldwide. At the height of his career,

Carreras developed leukaemia. After treatment, he successfully returned to the stage in 1988, becoming a household name as one of the Three Tenors, with Placido DOMINGO and Luciano PAVAROTTI.

Carroll, Lewis (1832–98) English mathematician, photographer and writer, b. Charles Lutwidge Dodgson. An Oxford don, much of whose output consisted of mathematical textbooks, Carroll is remembered for *Alice's Adventures in Wonderland* (1865) and its sequel, *Through the Looking Glass* (1872), along with his nonsense poem *The Hunting of the Snark* (1876).

carrot Herbaceous, generally biennial, root vegetable, cultivated widely as a food crop. The edible, orange taproot is the plant's store of food for the following year. The plant is topped by delicate fern-like leaves and white or pink flower clusters. Family UMBELLIFERAE; Species *Daucus carota*.

Carson, Edward Henry (1854–1935) Northern Irish political leader. A famous barrister, he was the leader of resistance to Irish Home Rule. Organizing the paramilitary Ulster Volunteers (1912), Carson persuaded the British government to exclude the Protestant provinces from the Home Rule Agreement of 1914.

Carson, Kit (Christopher) (1809–68) US guide and soldier. He achieved fame for his work as a guide on FRÉMONT's expeditions (1842–46). In 1854 Carson became an Indian agent in New Mexico and in 1861 became a colonel in the US army, fighting against Confederate forces. In 1868 he became superintendent of Indian affairs for the Colorado Territory.

Carson, Rachel Louise (1907–64) US writer and marine biologist. Carson is best known for her popular books on marine ecology. *The Sea Around Us* (1951) won a National Book Award. *Silent Spring* (1962) directed public attention to the dangers of agricultural pesticides and was a pioneering work in the development of the environmental movement.

Carson City State capital of Nevada, 50km (30mi) S of Reno. The city grew rapidly after silver was discovered in the Comstock Lode in 1859. It was named after Kit CARSON. Gambling is the main industry. Pop. (1990) 40,443.

Cartagena City and port in NW Colombia, on the Bay of Cartagena in the Caribbean Sea; capital of the department of Bolívar. It is the principal oil port of Colombia. There is a university (founded 1824). Industries: oil refining, sugar, tobacco, textiles, tourism. Pop. (1992) 688,306.

Cartagena Major seaport in SE Spain, on the Mediterranean Sea. Founded in *c*.255 BC by the Carthaginians, the settlement later fell to the Romans. Moors captured it in the 8th century, but it was retaken by Spaniards in the 13th century. In 1585, it was destroyed by Francis Drake. It is the site of the medieval Castillo de la Concepción and a modern naval base. Industries: shipbuilding, lead, zinc, iron. Pop. (1991) 166,736.

Carte, Richard D'Oyly (1844–1901) English impresario and producer of the operas of GILBERT and SULLIVAN. He founded the Savoy Theatre, London (1881).

cartel Formal agreement among the producers of a product to fix the price and divide the market among themselves. It usually results in higher prices for consumers and extra profits for the producers. Cartels are illegal.

Carter, Angela (1940–92) English novelist and short-story writer. She is closely associated with MAGIC REALISM. Carter's writing draws on legend and myth, and mixes past and present, a technique used in *Nights at the Circus* (1984). Other works include the novels *The Magic Toyshop* (1967) and *The Passion of New Eve* (1977) and the short-story collection *The Bloody Chamber* (1979).

▲ **carp** Bony fish belonging to the order Cypriniformes, carps have large bodies usually covered evenly with scales, but these may be missing in cultivated types such as the mirror carp.

Carter, Elliott Cook, Jr (1908–) US composer. Carter is widely regarded as the leading modern American composer. His works are notable for elaborate COUNTERPOINT and complex structures. Compositions include a piano (1946) and a cello (1948) sonata, *Variations* (1953–55) and *Concerto* (1970) for orchestra, and four string quartets (1951, 1959, 1971, 1986). Carter received the 1960 Pulitzer Prize for his second string quartet.

Carter, Howard (1874–1939) English Egyptologist. He discovered the tombs of Hatshepsut and Thutmose IV in the Valley of the Kings near LUXOR, Egypt, and supervised excavations for Lord Carnarvon. In 1922 Carter found the tomb of TUTANKHAMUN.

Carter, Jimmy (James Earl), Jr. (1924–) 39th US president (1977–81). He was a Democrat senator (1962–66) and governor (1971–74) for the state of Georgia. In 1976 Carter defeated the incumbent President Gerald FORD. He had a number of foreign policy successes, such as the negotiation of the CAMP DAVID AGREEMENT (1979). These were overshadowed, however, by the disastrous attempt to free US hostages in Iran (April 1980). Following the Soviet invasion of Afghanistan, Carter backed a US boycott of the 1980 Moscow Olympics. An oil price rise contributed to spiralling inflation, which was dampened only by a large increase in interest rates. In the 1980 presidential election, Carter was easily defeated by Ronald REAGAN. Since then, he has sought to promote human rights and acted as a international peace broker.

Cartesian coordinates System in which the position of a point is specified by its distances from intersecting lines (axes). In the simplest type – rectangular coordinates in two dimensions – two axes are used at right angles: y and x. The position of a point is then given by a pair of numbers (x, y). The abscissa, x, is the point's distance from the y axis, measured in the direction of the x axis, and the ordinate, y, is the distance from the x axis. Three axes represent three dimensions.

Carthage Ancient port on the Bay of Tunis, N Africa. It was founded in the 9th century BC by Phoenician colonists. Carthage became a great commercial city and imperial power controlling an empire in North Africa, S Spain and islands of the W Mediterranean. The rise of Rome in the 3rd century resulted in the PUNIC WARS and ended with the destruction of Carthage (146 BC) in the Third Punic War. It was resettled as a Roman colony and in the 5th century AD became the capital of the VANDALS.

Carthusian Monastic order founded by St Bruno in 1084. It is based at the Grande Chartreuse monastery near Grenoble, France. It is a mainly contemplative order in which monks and nuns solemnly vow to live in silence and solitude.

Cartier, Jacques (1491–1557) French navigator and explorer who discovered (1535) the St Lawrence River. Cartier was sent (1534) to North America by Francis I. During this first voyage, he discovered the Magdalen Islands and explored the Gulf of St Lawrence. In 1535–36 he sailed up the St Lawrence River to the site of modern Québec and continued on foot to Hochelaga (present-day Montréal). His third voyage was part of an unsuccessful colonization scheme. Cartier's discoveries laid the basis for French settlements in Canada.

Cartier-Bresson, Henri (1908–) French photographer. In the 1930s, Cartier-Bresson worked as an assistant to Jean RENOIR. He was a co-founder of the photographic agency, Magnum Photos. Cartier-Bresson's photos, exclusively in black-and-white, often capture a unique, fleeting image. His images of post-war Europe are important works of photo-journalism. Cartier-Bresson's books include *The Decisive Moment* (1952), *The World of Henri Cartier-Bresson* (1968) and *About Russia* (1974).

cartilage Flexible, supporting tissue made up of the tough protein COLLAGEN. In the vertebrate EMBRYO, the greater part of the SKELETON is cartilage that is replaced by BONE during development. In humans, cartilage is also present in the larynx, nose and external ear.

cartography Science of map-making. Maps are usually printed on a flat surface using various kinds of projections. A cartographer uses information from land surveys, aerial photographs and other sources. A map may be formed by drawing on paper, engraving lines into plastic or creating an image on a computer screen.

cartoon Originally a preparatory drawing. Italian Renaissance painters made thorough cartoons, such as RAPHAEL, for the Sistine Chapel. Its modern usage as a humorous drawing or satirical picture is derived from a 19th-century competition for fresco designs for Parliament parodied in *Punch* magazine. *See also* CARICATURE

Cartwright, Edmund (1743–1823) English inventor of the power loom. It was patented in 1785, but not used commercially until the early 19th century.

Caruso, Enrico (1873–1921) Italian tenor, one of the most widely acclaimed opera singers of all time. He made his debut in Naples (1894). Caruso was a regular performer (1903–20) at the Metropolitan Opera, and his recordings won him worldwide recognition. The beauty of his voice is best heard in grand opera, especially Verdi.

Carver, George Washington (1864–1943) US agricultural chemist. Carver is best known for his scientific research on the peanut, from which he derived more than 300 products. Born into an African-American slave family, his chief motive was to benefit the impoverished farmers of the South.

Carver, Raymond (1938–88) US short-story writer and poet. Carver's fiction depicts, with uncompromising realism, the lives of US citizens. His short stories are collected in *Will You Please Be Quiet, Please?* (1976), *What We Talk About When We Talk About Love* (1981) and *Cathedral* (1983). He also wrote five books of poetry.

Cary, (Arthur) Joyce (Lunel) (1888–1957) British novelist. His colonial service in Nigeria (1914–20) is reflected in novels, such as *Mister Johnson* (1939). His best-known work is *The Horse's Mouth* (1944).

Casablanca (Dar el-Beida) City in W Morocco, on Africa's Atlantic coast. In 1515, it was resettled by the Portuguese after their destruction of the old town. An earthquake damaged the city (1755). Today, Casablanca is Morocco's largest city and a busy commercial centre, exporting phosphates and importing petroleum products. Industries: tourism, textiles. Pop. (1993) 2,943,000.

Casals, Pablo (Pau) (1876–1973) Spanish (Catalan) cellist and composer. He formed (1919) his own orchestra in Barcelona and organized the annual Casals Festival in Puerto Rico from 1957. Casal's immaculate tone and intellectual rigor are best heard on Bach's cello suites.

Casanova de Seingalt, Giovanni Giacomo (1725–98) Italian libertine and adventurer. From 1750, he travelled through Europe leading a dissolute existence. Casanova amassed a fortune and mixed with high society. His exploits are recounted in his *Memoirs*, not published in unexpurgated form until 1960. His name is synonymous with the amorous adventurer.

Cascade Range Mountain range in W North America, extending from NE California across Oregon and Washington into Canada. The Cascade Tunnel, at 13km (8mi) the longest rail tunnel in the US, passes through them. Crater Lake National Park is in the Cascades. The highest peak is Mount RAINIER, 4,395m (14,410ft). The range also includes Mount ST HELENS, 2,549m (8,363ft).

case One of the forms taken by nouns and pronouns according to their use in a sentence. In Standard English, the pronoun is in the **nominative** case when used as the subject (e.g. *he*, *she*) and in the **accusative** (objective) case when used as the direct object of a verb or governed by a preposition (e.g. *him*, *her*); the noun is in the **possessive** case when it indicates ownership or relation (e.g. *Sarah's*) and otherwise in a single "other" case (e.g. *Sarah*).

casein Principal protein in milk, containing about 15 amino acids. Obtained by the addition of either acid or the enzyme rennet, casein is used to make plastics, cosmetics, adhesives, paints, cheeses and animal feed.

Casement, Sir Roger David (1864–1916) Irish humanitarian and revolutionary. While a British consul (1895–1912), he exposed the exploitation of rubber-gatherers in the Belgian Congo. During World War 1, Casement sought aid for an Irish nationalist uprising and was executed for treason after the British secret service tried to destroy his reputation by publishing the Casement diaries.

cash crop Agricultural crop cultivated for its commercial value, as opposed to a **staple crop** (grown for subsistence). The term is often encountered in development economics. Cash crops, such as coffee, sugar or cotton, were introduced into Africa, Asia and the Americas as part of the colonialist project and intensively farmed via plantation systems.

cashew Evergreen shrub or tree grown in the tropics, important for its nuts. The wood is used for boxes and boats and produces a gum similar to gum arabic. Height: to 12m (39ft). Family Anacardiaceae; species *Anacardium occidentale*.

cashmere Woolly hair of a goat native to Kashmir, India. The warm, lightweight wool is woven for clothing.

Caspian Sea Shallow salt lake, the world's largest inland body of water. The Caspian Sea is enclosed on three sides by Russia, Kazakstan, Turkmenistan and Azerbaijan. The S shore forms the N border of Iran. It has been an important trade route for centuries. It is fed mainly by the River Volga; there is no outlet. The chief ports are BAKU and ASTRAKHAN. It still has important fisheries and a seal trade. Area: *c.*371,000sq km (143,000sq mi).

Cassandra In Greek mythology, the daughter of PRIAM, skilled in the art of prophecy but condemned by Apollo never to be taken seriously. Her warning that the Greeks would capture Troy went unheeded. She was raped by the Greek Ajax the lesser and then carried off as a concubine by AGAMEMNON; they were both murdered by Agamemnon's wife CLYTEMNESTRA and her lover Aegisthus.

Cassatt, Mary (1845–1926) US painter and printmaker. She was influenced by DEGAS and IMPRESSIONISM. Cassatt's finest paintings include *The Bath* (1892). She also did many DRYPOINT and AQUATINT studies of domestic life.

cassava (manioc) Tapioca plant native to Brazil. It is a tall woody shrub with small clustered flowers. A valuable cereal substitute is made from the tuberous roots. Height: up to 2.7m (9ft). Family Euphorbiaceae; species *Manihot esculenta*.

Cassini, Giovanni Domenico (1625–1712) French astronomer, who ran the Paris Observatory. Cassini was the first to accurately measure the dimensions of the SOLAR SYSTEM, and discovered the division in the rings of SATURN that now bear his name, and also four satellites. He also measured Jupiter's rotation period.

Cassiopeia Distinctive northern constellation, representing in mythology the mother of ANDROMEDA. The five leading stars make up a "W" or "M" pattern.

cassiterite (tin oxide, SnO_2) Translucent black or brown mineral; the major ore of tin. It occurs in placer deposits, chiefly in the Malay peninsula, and in pegmatites and other intrusive igneous rock. It takes the form of short, tetragonal prismatic crystals or masses and radiating fibres. Hardness 6–7; r.d. 7.

Cassius, Caius Longinus (d.42 BC) Roman general who led the plot to assassinate Julius CAESAR. Cassius sided with POMPEY against Caesar, but was pardoned after Caesar defeated Pompey at the battle of Pharsalus (48 BC). After the assassination of Caesar in 44 BC, he left for Sicily. Believing he had lost the battle against MARK ANTONY and Octavian (AUGUSTUS) at Philippi, Cassius committed suicide.

Casson, Sir Hugh Maxwell (1910–99) English architect. Director of architecture (1948–51) for the Festival of Britain, Casson was knighted in 1952 and served as professor of interior design (1953–75) at the Royal College of Art and president (1976–82) of the Royal Academy.

cassowary Flightless bird of rainforests in Australia and Malaysia. It has coarse black plumage, a horny crest on its brightly coloured head, large feet, and sharp claws. The male incubates the eggs in a nest on the forest floor. Height: to 1.6m (65in). Family Casuariidae; species *Casuarius casuarius*.

Castagno, Andrea del (1423–57) Florentine painter of the early Renaissance. His use of PERSPECTIVE betrays the influence of MASACCIO. Castagno's realistic and vigorous figure drawing, in turn, greatly influenced LEONARDO DA VINCI and MICHELANGELO. His masterpiece (*c.*1445) is the fresco cycle of the Passion of Christ for the church of Sant' Apollonia, Florence. Best known of these scenes is the *Last Supper*.

caste Formal system of social stratification based on factors such as race, gender or religion, and sanctioned by tradition. An individual is born into a position and cannot change it. It is most prevalent in Hindu society. The four main divisions (*varnas*) are BRAHMINS (priests and professionals), Kshatriyas (nobles and warriors), Vaishyas (farmers and merchants) and Sudras (servants). A fifth group, the "Untouchables" (*harijan* or *dalit*), lie outside the caste system. They perform the most polluting tasks, such as handling animal wastes.

Castiglione, Baldassare (1478–1529) Italian diplomat and writer. Castiglione served in the court of the Duke of Milan and for the Duke of Urbino. While serving as a papal envoy, he wrote *Libro del Cortegiano* (1528), a classic treatise on the role of the Renaissance courtier.

Castile Region and former kingdom in central Spain, traditionally comprising Old Castile (N) and New Castile (S). Old Castile was part of the kingdom of LEÓN until 1230. Castilians captured New Castile from the Moors. Queen ISABELLA I established the union with ARAGÓN in 1479, and in the 16th century Castile became the most influential power in Spain and the core of the Spanish monarchy.

Castile-La Mancha Region in central Spain; includes the provinces of Albacete, Ciudad Real, Cuenca, Guadalajara and Toledo; the capital is TOLEDO. It was captured from the Moors in 1212. Products: olive oil, grapes. Area: 79,226sq km (30,590sq mi). Pop. (1991) 1,658,446.

Castile-León Region in N Spain; includes the provinces of Ávila, Burgos, León, Palencia, Salamanca, Segovia, Soria, Valladolid and Zamora; the capital is Valladolid. Formerly part of the kingdom of LEÓN, Castile and Aragón were united in 1479. Extreme climate and poor soil allow limited grain growing and sheep raising. Area: 94,147sq km (36,350sq mi). Pop. (1991) 2,545,926.

casting Forming objects by pouring molten metal into moulds and allowing it to cool and solidify. Specialized processes, such as plastic moulding, composite moulding, CIRE PERDUE casting and die casting, give greater dimensional accuracy, smoother surfaces and finer detail.

castle Fortified house or fortress, usually the medieval residences of European kings or nobles. Castles evolved from a need for strategic fortresses that could accommodate large households and offer shelter. Built of wood or stone, castles were located often on a hill and surrounded by a water-filled moat. Walls were thick and high enough to withstand attack, with parapets to enable defenders to manoeuvre between the turrets. WINDSOR CASTLE in England is a modified but recognizably medieval castle.

Castlereagh, Robert Stewart, 2nd Viscount (1769–1822) British statesman, b. Ireland. As chief secretary of Ireland (1799–1801), Castlereagh helped secure the passage of the Act of Union with Britain (1800). He resigned over George III's opposition to CATHOLIC EMANCIPATION. As secretary of war (1805–06, 1807–09), Castlereagh reorganized and expanded the army. He resigned after a duel with George CANNING. As foreign secretary (1812–22), Castlereagh formed the QUADRUPLE ALLIANCE that defeated NAPOLEON I and dominated the peace terms at the Congress of VIENNA.

Castor and Pollux (Dioscuri) In Greek mythology, the twin sons of LEDA. They were invoked by sailors seeking favourable winds. Zeus, father of Pollux, transformed them into the Gemini constellation after Castor died and Pollux refused to be parted from him.

castration Removal of the sexual glands (testes or ovaries) from an animal or human. In human beings, removal of the testes has been used as punishment, to sexually incapacitate slaves to produce EUNUCHS, to artificially create soprano voices (CASTRATO) and to stop the spread of cancer. It can also make animals tamer.

castrato Male voice in the soprano or mezzo-soprano register, produced in adult males by CASTRATION during boyhood. Castratos were much used in operas in the 17th and 18th centuries, and in music for the Roman Catholic Church. The most famous castrato was Farinelli. *See also* COUNTERTENOR

Castro, Fidel (1926–) Cuban revolutionary leader and politician, premier (1959–). In 1953, he was sentenced to 15 years' imprisonment after an unsuccessful coup against the BATISTA regime. Two years later, Castro was granted an amnesty and exiled to Mexico. In January 1959, his guerrilla forces overthrew the regime. Castro quickly instituted radical reforms, such as collectivizing agriculture and dispossessing foreign companies. In 1961, the US organized the abortive BAY OF PIGS invasion. Castro responded by allying more closely with the Soviet Union and developing nations. In 1962 the CUBAN MISSILE CRISIS saw the US and Soviet Union on the brink of nuclear war. Castro's attempt to export revolution to the rest of Latin America was largely foiled by the capture (1967) of his ally "Che" GUEVARA. In 1980, he lifted the ban on emigration, and 125,000 people left for Florida. Cuba's economy was heavily dependent on Soviet economic aid. The collapse of Soviet communism and the continuing US trade embargo dramatically worsened the economic climate, forcing Castro to introduce economic reforms.

cat Carnivorous, often solitary and nocturnal mammal of the family Felidae, ranging in size from the rare Siberian tiger to the domestic cat. It has specialized teeth and claws for hunting, a keen sense of smell, acute hearing, sensitive vision and balances well with its long tail (only the Manx cat is tailless). Cats all have fully

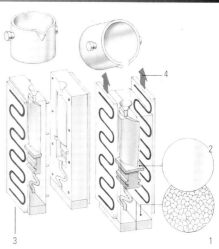

▲ **casting** Metal alloys used to make turbine blades must withstand the huge temperatures and forces inside jet engines. The random crystalline structure formed when the alloy cools normally (as seen in the overflow ,1) can be a source of weakness. The strongest structure is achieved by making a blade from a single crystal (2). This can be done by using heating elements (3). After the molten alloy is poured, the elements move up the sides of the mould (4) ensuring the alloy cools from the bottom and forms a single crystal.

retractile claws, except for the CHEETAH. One of the first animals to be domesticated, cats have appeared frequently in myth and religion. Order Carnivora.

catabolism *See* METABOLISM

catacomb Early Christian, or sometimes Jewish, subterranean cemeteries, often used as refuges from persecution, and as shrines. The extensive catacombs of Rome, a complex of galleries as deep as 8m (25ft), are the best known, but others have been found elsewhere in Europe, N Africa and Syria, dating from the 1st–5th centuries.

Catalan Romance language spoken mainly in NE Spain, but also in the Balearic Islands, Andorra and southern France. There are c.6 million speakers.

Catalonia (Cataluña) Region in NE Spain, extending from the French border to the Mediterranean Sea; the capital is BARCELONA. Catalonia includes the provinces of Barcelona, Gerona, Lérida and Tarragona. United with Aragón in 1137, it retained its own laws and language. During the Spanish Civil War it was a Loyalist stronghold, and recently it has been a focus of separatist movements. The COSTA BRAVA is an important tourist area. Products: grain, fruit, olive oil, wool, wine. Area: 31,932sq km (12,329sq mi). Pop. (1990) 6,059,454.

catalpa Ornamental tree in North America and the West Indies. It has heart-shaped leaves, white or purple flowers and bean-like fruit pods containing many seeds. Common catalpa (*Catalpa bignonioides*) is also called the Indian bean. Height: up to 18m (60ft). Family Bignoniaceae.

catalyst Substance that speeds up the rate of a chemical reaction without itself being consumed. Many industrial processes rely on catalysts such as the HABER PROCESS for manufacturing AMMONIA. Metals or their compounds catalyze by adsorbing gases to their surface, forming intermediates that then readily react to form the desired product while regenerating the original catalytic surface. The METABOLISM of all living organisms depends on biological catalysts called ENZYMES.

catalytic converter Anti-pollution device used in INTERNAL COMBUSTION ENGINES. It consists of a bed of catalytic agents through which flow the gaseous exhaust of fuel combustion. Converters located in mufflers reduce harmful unburned hydrocarbons and carbon monoxide. These converters are adversely affected by tetraethyl lead found in some gasolines.

catalytic cracking *See* CRACKING

catamaran Swift, twin-hulled boat, powered by sails or engine. Originally it was a raft used in Indian and Indonesian waters for cargo carrying and for long voyages by Melanesians and Polynesians. The design has great stability and was adopted in the 1870s by western boatbuilders. Catamarans are now popular for racing.

Catania Port near Mount Etna, E Sicily, Italy; capital of Catania province. Catania was founded by the Greeks in 729 BC. It was devastated by a volcanic eruption in 1669 and an earthquake in 1693. It has Greek and Roman ruins, a Norman cathedral (1091) and a university (1444). Industries: chemicals, cement. Pop. (1996) 342,000.

cataplexy Rare condition where there is sudden loss of power in part or all of the body. Sometimes provoked by strong emotion, it is often associated with NARCOLEPSY.

cataract Opacity in the lens of an eye, causing blurring of vision. Most cases are due to degenerative changes in old age but it can also be congenital, the result of damage to the lens, or some metabolic disorder such as diabetes. Treatment is by removal of the cataract and implanting an artificial lens.

catastrophe theory Mathematical technique published in 1972 by the French mathematician René Thom. It is useful for describing situations in which gradually changing motivations or inputs cause a sudden discontinuous leap in a system's behaviour or output.

catechism Manual of instruction in Christian church teachings for the young or any candidate preparing for membership of a church. In some sects, it provides a medium of instruction for baptized members. A catechism often takes the form of question and answer.

caterpillar Worm-like larva of a BUTTERFLY or MOTH; it has a segmented body, short antennae, simple eyes, three pairs of true legs and chewing mouthparts. Nearly all feed voraciously on plants and are serious crop pests.

catfish Any member of a large family of scaleless fish found in tropical and subtropical waters; it has fleshy barbels on the upper jaw, sometimes with venomous spines. Most species live in freshwater and can be farmed. Length: up to 3.3m (10ft). Order Siluriformes.

cathedral (Gk. *kathedra*, throne or seat) Main church of a bishop's province, containing his throne. In the ROMANESQUE period, cathedrals started to become very large, and many Gothic cathedrals are gigantic structures. The prototype of the true Gothic cathedral is the Abbey Church of St-Denis near Paris. Suger, the abbot, added a chapel and pointed groin VAULT. Bigger windows and slender arches gave it a sense of lightness very different from the static solidity of the Romanesque. Among the great cathedrals of western Europe are Notre-Dame, Paris (begun 1163), and CHARTRES (begun 1194) in France, COLOGNE cathedral in Germany, and MILAN cathedral (begun 1386) in Italy. Some of the finest English examples, such as CANTERBURY and YORK, combine Romanesque and Gothic features. St Mark's, VENICE, is a magnificent Byzantine example. Central and Eastern European cathedrals often amalgamate Byzantine and western features, while many Spanish cathedrals combine Romanesque, French, German and Moorish features. In Latin America, cathedrals are often of Portuguese or Spanish RENAISSANCE and BAROQUE origin. The Episcopal Cathedral of St John the Divine in New York is the world's largest Gothic

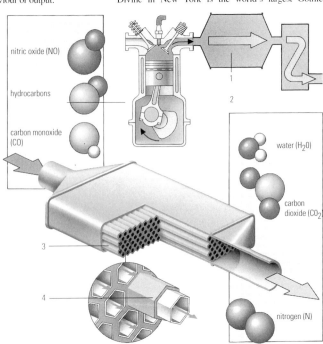

► **catalytic converter**
A catalytic converter is placed in the exhaust system (1) to reduce the pollution produced by combustion engines (2). It comprises a ceramic honeycomb structure (3), which maximizes the surface area of the converter, covered in catalysts – normally platinum and rhodium (4). As exhaust gases, primarily carbon monoxide, nitric oxide, and hydrocarbons from the cylinder, pass through the converter, they react under the influence of the catalysts. The platinum and rhodium accelerate oxidation and reduction in the hot gases. The pollutants are oxidized into water, carbon dioxide and nitrogen.

nitric oxide (NO)

hydrocarbons

carbon monoxide (CO)

water (H_2O)

carbon dioxide (CO_2)

nitrogen (N)

cathedral. *See also* BYZANTINE ART AND ARCHITECTURE; GOTHIC ART AND ARCHITECTURE

Cather, Willa (1876–1947) US novelist and short-story writer. She grew up among immigrant Nebraskan farmers who became the subject of her work. Cather's fiction explores the pioneer spirit: love of the land, loyalty to family and the struggle with nature. Her novels include *O Pioneers* (1913), *A Lost Lady* (1923) and *Death Comes for the Archbishop* (1927).

Catherine I (1684–1727) Empress of Russia (1725–27), b. Martha Skavronskaya. Of peasant origin, Catherine was captured (1702) by Russian soldiers and became the mistress of Alexander Menshikov and later of PETER I (THE GREAT), whom she married in 1712. Catherine was crowned in 1724 and after Peter's death (1725) was proclaimed empress, ruling through a council led by Menshikov. She was succeeded by PETER II.

Catherine II (the Great) (1729–96) Empress of Russia (1762–96), b. Germany. ELIZABETH chose her (1745) as the wife of the future tsar Peter III. Peter succeeded to the throne in 1761. With the help of her lover, Grigori Orlov, Catherine overthrew her husband and shortly afterward he was murdered. Catherine began her reign as an "enlightened despot", with ambitious plans for reform, but after the peasants' revolt (1773–74), led by Pugachev, she became increasingly conservative. In 1785, Catherine extended the powers of the nobility at the expense of the serfs. Catherine's foreign policy, guided by POTEMKIN, vastly extended Russian territory (chiefly at the expense of the Ottoman Empire). In 1764, she secured the accession of her former lover to the Polish throne as Stanislaus II. Russia emerged from the first Russo-Turkish War (1768–74) as the dominant power in the Middle East. Crimea was annexed in 1783, and Alaska was colonized. Her dialogue with leading Enlightenment figures did much to promote her contemporary image in Europe.

Catherine de' Medici (1519–89) Queen of France, wife of HENRY II, and daughter of Lorenzo de' MEDICI. She exerted considerable political influence after her husband's and first son's deaths in 1559. In 1560, Catherine became regent for her second son, CHARLES IX, and remained principal adviser until his death (1574). Her initial tolerance of the HUGUENOTS turned to enmity at the beginning of the French Wars of RELIGION. Catherine's concern for preserving the power of the monarchy led to a dependence on the Catholic House of GUISE, whose growing power she failed to control. Fearing the decline of her own importance at court, she planned the SAINT BARTHOLOMEW'S DAY MASSACRE (1572). When her third son, HENRY III, acceded to the throne in 1574, her effectiveness in policy-making had been compromised.

Catherine of Aragon (1485–1536) Daughter of FERDINAND and ISABELLA, she was the first queen of England's HENRY VIII (1509). Catherine's only surviving child was a daughter (MARY I). The need to produce a male heir, combined with Henry's desire for Anne BOLEYN, induced him to seek an annulment (1527). The pope's procrastination led to the break with Rome and to the English REFORMATION. The annulment was granted by Thomas CRANMER in 1533.

Catherine of Siena, Saint (1347–80) Italian nun. Catherine joined the Third Order of St DOMINIC at the age of 16 and for three years devoted herself to contemplation, the service of the sick and the conversion of sinners. In 1376, she went to Avignon to persuade Pope Gregory XI to return to Rome. She was canonized in 1461 and declared a Doctor of the Church in 1970. Her feast day is 29 April.

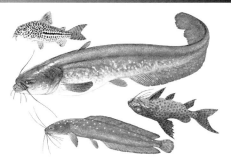

▲ **catfish** A very large family of freshwater fish of the order Siluriformes, catfish tend to be sluggish in their movements and have barbels (whiskers) growing from their mouths. They are scavengers.

catheter Fine tube introduced into the body to deliver or remove fluids. The most common is the urinary catheter, fed into the bladder by way of the URETHRA.

cathode In chemistry, the negative electrode of an electrolytic cell or electron tube. It attracts positive ions (cations) during ELECTROLYSIS.

cathode rays Radiation emitted by the cathode of a thermionic electron valve containing a gas at low pressure. The rays were identified in 1897 by J.J. THOMSON as streams of charged, elementary particles having extremely low mass, later called ELECTRONS. Most electrons are emitted because of collisions between the cathode and positive ions formed in the valve.

cathode-ray tube Evacuated ELECTRON tube used for TELEVISION picture tubes, oscilloscopes and display screens in radar sets and computers. An electron gun shoots a beam of electrons, focused by a grid. The electrons strike a fluorescent screen and produce a spot of light. In a television tube, an electrostatic or magnetic field deflects the beam so that it scans a number of lines on the screen, controlled by the incoming picture signals. *See artwork* p.162

Catholic Church Term used in Christianity with one of several connotations: (1) It is the Universal church, as distinct from local churches. (2) It means the church holding "orthodox" doctrines. (3) It is the undivided church before the schism of East and West in 1054. Following this, the Western church called itself "Catholic", the Eastern church "ORTHODOX". (4) Since the REFORMATION, the term has usually been used to denote the ROMAN CATHOLIC CHURCH, although the ANGLICAN COMMUNION and the OLD CATHOLICS use it to cover themselves as well.

Catholic Emancipation, Act of (1829) Measure by which the statutes (dating back to the REFORMATION) barring Roman Catholics in Britain from holding civil office or sitting in Parliament, were repealed. Emancipation was achieved through a series of acts. In 1778, restrictions against land purchase and inheritance were lifted. In 1791, further restrictions were removed, and by 1793, Catholics were allowed in the services, universities, and the judiciary. The final concession, allowing Catholics to sit in Parliament, was wrung from the Duke of WELLINGTON's government by Daniel O'CONNELL.

Catiline (108–62 BC) (Lucius Sergius Catilina) Roman politician and conspirator. Catiline was made praetor in 68 BC and governor of Africa in 67 BC. False accusations of misconduct led to his defeat by CICERO in elections for consul. Catiline attempted to take the consulship by force (63 BC), but Cicero learned of the conspiracy and denounced him. Catiline fled, and the conspirators were sentenced to death. Julius CAESAR's appeal for mercy merely aroused the wrath of CATO THE YOUNGER. Catiline died in battle at Pistoia, Tuscany.

cation Positive ION that is attracted to the CATHODE during ELECTROLYSIS.

catkin Drooping, scaly spike of unisexual flowers without petals, such as the pussy willow or poplar. This deciduous flower cluster is typical of birches and some beeches.

Cato the Elder (234–149 BC) (Marcus Porcius) Roman leader. As censor, from 184 BC, Cato worked to restore the old ideals of Rome – courage, honesty and simple living. His constant urging in the Senate that CARTHAGE should be destroyed precipitated the Third PUNIC WAR.

Cato the Younger (95–46 BC) (Marcus Porcius Cato Uticensis) Roman politician, great-grandson of CATO THE ELDER. He opposed Julius CAESAR and forced the creation of the First Triumvirate. Cato favoured POMPEY in the civil war against Caesar (49 BC) and, when Caesar emerged victorious, committed suicide.

CAT scan *See* COMPUTERIZED AXIAL TOMOGRAPHY

Catskill Mountains Plateau of the Appalachian system on the w bank of the Hudson River, SE New York, USA. The highest peak is Slide Mountain, 1,282m (4,204ft). Site of the Rip Van Winkle legend, its numerous forests, streams and lakes attracted the painters of the Hudson River School. Today, it is a popular resort.

cattle Large, ruminant mammals of the family Bovidae, including all the varieties of modern domestic cattle (*Bos taurus*), the brahman (*Bos indicus*) and hybrids of these two. The family also includes the YAK, the wild GAUR, the wild banteng and the kouprey. The male is born as a bull calf and becomes a bull if left intact; if castrated, it becomes a steer, bullock or ox if used as a draught animal. The female is a heifer calf, growing to become a heifer and, after calving, a cow. Horns are permanent, hollow and unbranched. Domestic cattle are

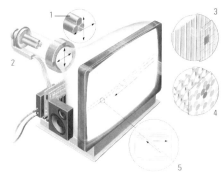

▲ cathode-ray tube Television receivers are a type of cathode-ray tube. Three electron guns (1) receive colour signals from a colour decoder that splits the colour signal into red, green, and blue. The guns fire three beams of electrons through vertical and horizontal deflection coils (2) onto the screen of a "shadow mask tube" (3). This is made up of about a million dots (4), a third of which glow red when bombarded, a third blue, and the remaining third, green. The dots compose the colour picture received by the television. The beam of electrons scans hundreds of lines on the screen (525 in the US, 625 in Europe) making up the moving pictures. The beam scans from left to right, starting top left and finishing bottom right (5).

raised for meat, milk and other dairy products. Leather, glue, gelatin and fertilizers are made from the carcasses.

Catullus, Gaius Valerius (84–54 BC) Roman poet. He is best known for short love lyrics, the most famous of which refer to Lesbia, depicting the woman, Clodia, with whom Catullus was in love. His longer works are the poems *Attis* and *The Marriage of Peleus and Thetis*.

Caucasus (Bol'šoj Kavkaz) Mountain region in SE Europe, Russia, Georgia, Armenia and Azerbaijan, extending SE from the mouth of the River Kuban on the Black Sea to the Apscheron Peninsula on the Caspian Sea. The system includes two major regions: N Caucasia (steppes) and TRANSCAUCASIA. It forms a natural barrier between Asia and Europe. There are deposits of oil, iron and manganese. The highest peak is Mount ELBRUS, at 5,637m (18,493ft). Length: 1,210km (750mi).

Cauchy, Augustin Louis, Baron (1789–1857) French mathematician who formalized many of the ideas of CALCULUS. Following the work of EULER, Cauchy defined the notion of a limit and of a continuous function, and formalized the existing definitions of derivative and integral.

cauliflower Form of CABBAGE with a short thick stem, large lobed leaves and edible white or purplish flower clusters that form tightly compressed heads. Family Brassicaceae; species *Brassica oleracea botrytis*.

caustic soda (sodium hydroxide, NaOH) Strong ALKALI that is prepared industrially by the ELECTROLYSIS of salt (sodium chloride, NaCl). It is a white solid that burns the skin, with a slippery feel because it absorbs moisture from the air. It also absorbs atmospheric carbon dioxide, so forming a crust of sodium carbonate (Na_2CO_3). Caustic soda is used in many industries, such as soap-making and to manufacture ALUMINIUM.

Cavalier (Fr. *chevalier*) Name adopted by the Royalists during the English CIVIL WAR in opposition to the ROUNDHEADS (Parliamentarians). The court party retained the name after the RESTORATION until superseded by the name TORY.

Cavalli, (Pietro) Francesco (1602–76) Italian composer. Successively chorister, organist and choirmaster at St Mark's, Venice, his operas mark an important development of the form in the wake of MONTEVERDI. The verve and brilliance of *Egisto* (1643) and *Calisto* (1651–52) established Venice as the home of Italian opera.

cavalry Mounted troops. Cavalry were first employed by the ancient Egyptians; the first use of cavalry in Europe dates from the invasions of the Huns, Magyars and Mongols. The last prominent use of cavalry occurred in the American CIVIL WAR.

cave Natural underground cavity. There are several kinds, including coastal caves formed by wave erosion, ice caves formed in glaciers and lava caves. The largest are formed in carbonate rocks such as limestone. The largest known cave in the world is in Jean Bernard, France. It is 1,494m (4,900ft) deep.

Cavell, Edith Louisa (1865–1915) English nurse. During World War 1, she was matron of the Berkendael Institute, Brussels. Cavell helped many Allied soldiers to escape from Belgium. She was executed by the Germans.

Cavendish, Henry (1731–1810) English chemist and physicist. He discovered hydrogen and the compositions of water and air, and estimated the Earth's mass and density by a method now known as the "Cavendish experiment". Cavendish also discovered nitric acid (HNO_3) and the gravitational constant, and measured the specific gravity of carbon dioxide (CO_2) and hydrogen. The Cavendish Laboratory at Cambridge University, England, is named after him.

cave painting Drawing made on the wall of a cave by humans of the upper PALAEOLITHIC period. The most famous cave paintings are those at LASCAUX in SW France and at ALTAMIRA in N Spain, all of which were made between 10,000 and 30,000 years ago. Because most cave paintings depict animals that were hunted for food, such as bison, archaeologists believe they were designed to bring good fortune in hunting.

caviar Roe (eggs) of a STURGEON and three less common fish (also occasionally a salmon) which, salted and seasoned, is a gastronomic delicacy, especially in Russia. The roe is extracted from the fish before it can spawn.

Cavour, Camillo Benso, Conte di (1810–61) Piedmontese politician, instrumental in uniting Italy under Savoy rule. From 1852, he was prime minister under Victor EMMANUEL II. Cavour engineered Italian liberation from Austria with French aid, expelled the French with the help of Giuseppe GARIBALDI, and finally neutralized Garibaldi's influence. This led to the formation of the kingdom of Italy (1861). *See also* RISORGIMENTO

cavy (wild guinea pig) Herbivorous South American rodent from which domestic GUINEA PIGS are descended. Small, with dark fur, cavies live in burrows and often form large colonies for protection. Family Caviidae; species *Cavia aperea*.

Caxton, William (1422–91) First English printer. Following a period in Germany (1470–72), where he learned printing, he set up his own press in 1476 at Westminster. Caxton published more than 100 items, many of them his own translations. Among his publications were editions of CHAUCER, GOWER and MALORY.

Cayenne Capital of French Guiana, on an island at the mouth of the River Cayenne. Cayenne was founded (1643) by the French. Cayenne acted (1851–1946) as a French penal settlement. The Pasteur Institute (1940) specializes in the study of tropical diseases. Timber, rum and gold are exported. Pop. (1995) 45,600.

cayenne pepper Hot condiment made from the dried fruits of the sweet pepper plant, a variety of *Capsicum annuum*, native to Mexico and Central America. Family Solanaceae.

Cayley, Sir George (1773–1857) English inventor who founded the science of AERODYNAMICS. Cayley built the first GLIDER to carry a man successfully, developed the basic form of the early aeroplane, and invented a caterpillar tractor.

Cayman Islands British dependency in the West Indies, comprising Grand Cayman, Little Cayman and Cayman Brac, *c.*325km (200mi) NW of Jamaica, in the Caribbean Sea. The capital is Georgetown. The islands were discovered by Columbus in 1503 and ceded to Britain in the 17th century. Industries: tourism, international finance, turtle and shark fishing, timber, coconuts. Area: 259sq km (100sq mi). Pop. (1989) 25,355.

CD-ROM (compact disc read-only memory) Optical storage device for COMPUTER data and programs. It resembles a COMPACT DISC (CD) used in hi-fi systems. A CD-ROM can store much more data than a comparably priced portable MAGNETIC DISK. Computer games, encyclopedias and other software are now available in this form. To use a CD-ROM, the disc is placed in a specialized player connected to, or built in, a computer.

Ceaușescu, Nicolae (1918–89) Romanian statesman, the country's effective ruler from 1965 to 1989. He became general secretary of the Romanian Communist Party in 1965 and head of state in 1967. Ceaușescu promoted Romanian nationalism and pursued an independent foreign policy but instituted repressive domestic policies. He was deposed and executed in the December 1989 revolution.

Cebu Island in the Visayan archipelago, central Philippines; the capital is Cebu. The first European discovery was by Ferdinand MAGELLAN who landed (and died) here in 1521. Founded in 1565, the city of Cebu was the first Spanish settlement in the Philippines. Its good harbour acted as a major Japanese base in World War 2, and the city was destroyed by US bombs. Pop. (1990) 2,617,836 (island); 610,000 (city).

Cecil, Robert, 1st Earl of Salisbury (1563–1612) English statesman, son of Lord BURGHLEY. He became secretary of state to ELIZABETH I on his father's retirement in 1596. Cecil was responsible for negotiating the accession of James I (1603).

cedar Evergreen tree native to the Mediterranean and Asia but found in warm temperate regions worldwide; it has clustered needle-like leaves, long cones and fragrant, durable wood. It is a popular ornamental tree. Height: 30–55m (100–180ft). Family Pinaceae; genus *Cedrus*.

celandine Greater celandine is common to Europe; it has serrated leaves, yellow flowers and narrow seed pods. Its yellow sap was used to cure warts. Family Papaveraceae; species *Chelidonium majus*. The lesser celandine, *Ranunculus ficaria* (family Ranunculaceae), is a low-growing plant with bright yellow flowers in spring, common in the US, Britain, Europe and W Asia.

Celebes Former name of SULAWESI, Indonesia

celeriac (knob celery) Variety of CELERY with an underground stem that is cooked and eaten. Family Apiaceae/Umbelliferae; species *Apium graveolens*.

celery Biennial plant native to the Mediterranean and widely cultivated for its long stalks used as a vegetable. Its fruits are used as food flavouring and in medicine. Family Apiaceae/Umbelliferae; species *Apium graveolens*.

celesta (céleste) Percussion instrument with a range of four octaves. It consists of steel bars that are struck, producing a tinkling tone. Invented by Auguste Mustel in Paris (1886), it features on the "Dance of the Sugar Plum Fairy" in Tchaikovsky's *Nutcracker* ballet (1892).

celestial mechanics Branch of ASTRONOMY concerned with the relative motions of stars and planets that are associated in systems (such as the Solar System or a binary star system) by gravitational fields. Introduced by Isaac NEWTON in the 17th century, celestial mechanics, rather than general RELATIVITY, is usually sufficient to calculate the factors determining the motion of stars and planets around a centre of gravitational attraction.

celestial sphere Imaginary sphere of infinite radius used to define the positions of celestial bodies as seen from Earth, the centre of the sphere. The sphere rotates, once in 24 hours, about a line that is an extension of the Earth's axis. The position of a celestial body is the point at which a radial line through it meets the surface of the sphere. The position is defined in terms of coordinates, such as declination and right ascension or altitude and azimuth, which refer to great circles on the sphere, such as the celestial EQUATOR or the ecliptic.

celestine ($SrSO_4$, STRONTIUM sulphate) Mineral, with distinctive pale blue or white, glassy, orthorhombic crystals, sometimes occurring in fibrous masses. It is found chiefly in sedimentary rock. There are deposits in the US, Britain and Sicily. It is an important source of strontium.

celibacy Commitment to a lifelong abstention from sexual relations. The status of celibacy as a religious obligation is found in Christianity and Buddhism. From the 4th century, it gradually became compulsory for Roman Catholic priests, monks and nuns.

cell In biology, basic unit of which all plant and animal tissues are composed. The cell is the smallest unit of life that can exist independently, with its own self-regulating chemical system. Most cells consist of a MEMBRANE surrounding jelly-like CYTOPLASM with a central NUCLEUS. The nucleus is the main structure in which DNA is stored in CHROMOSOMES. Animal cells vary widely in shape. A red blood cell, for instance, is a biconcave disc, while a nerve cell has a long fibre. The cells of plants and algae are enclosed in a cell wall, which gives them a more rigid shape. Bacterial cells also have a cell wall but do not have nuclei or chromosomes; instead, they have a loop of DNA floating in the cytoplasm. More advanced cells (those that have nuclei) often have other membrane-bounded structures inside the cell, such as MITOCHONDRIA and CHLOROPLASTS. *See also* EUKARYOTE; PROKARYOTE

cell In physics, device from which electricity is obtained due to a chemical reaction. A cell consists of two electrodes (a positive ANODE and a negative CATHODE) immersed in a solution (ELECTROLYTE). A chemical reaction takes place between the electrolyte and one of

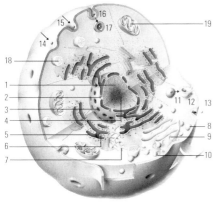

the electrodes. In a **primary** cell, current is produced from an irreversible chemical reaction, and the chemicals must be renewed at intervals. In a **secondary** cell (BATTERY), the chemical reaction is reversible, and the cell can be charged by passing a current through it.

cell division Process by which living CELLS reproduce and enable an organism to grow. In EUKARYOTE cells, a single cell splits in two, first by division of the NUCLEUS (occurring by MITOSIS or MEIOSIS), then by fission of the CYTOPLASM. For growth and asexual reproduction, where the daughter cells are required to be genetically identical to their parents, **mitosis** is used. **Meiosis** results in daughter cells having half the number of chromosomes (HAPLOID). This type of division results in the production of GAMETES (sex cells) that allow genetic information from two parents to be combined at FERTILIZATION. *See also* ALTERNATION OF GENERATIONS; DIPLOID

Cellini, Benvenuto (1500–71) Italian sculptor, goldsmith and writer. Cellini's autobiography (1558–62) is an important primary historical source on Renaissance Italy. Written like a picaresque novel, it relates his Florentine upbringing and his banishment for duelling. Cellini went to Rome, where he entered (1519) the service of Pope Clement VII. He became the most skilled goldsmith of his generation. The best example of his work is the bronze statue *Perseus with the Head of Medusa*.

cello (violoncello) Musical instrument, member of the violin family. It has a soft, mellow tone, one octave below the viola; its strings are tuned to C-G-D-A. It is played with a bow and supported by the knees of a seated player. It was developed in the 16th-century by the AMATI family. Among the most important players of the 20th century are Pablo CASALS and Jacqueline DU PRÉ.

cellophane Flexible, transparent film made of regenerated CELLULOSE and used mostly as a wrapping material. It is made by dissolving wood pulp or other plant material in an ALKALI, to which carbon disulphide is added to form viscose. This is forced through a narrow slit into a dilute acid where it precipitates as a film of cellulose.

cellular telephone *See* MOBILE TELEPHONE

celluloid Hard plastic invented (1869) in the US by John Hyatt. Hyatt made the plastic by mixing cellulose nitrate with pigments and fillers in a solution of camphor and alcohol. When heated it can be moulded into a variety of shapes. It was the first major plastic and used for early motion pictures. It is highly flammable.

cellulose $[(C_6H_{10}O_5)_n]$ POLYSACCHARIDE, CARBOHYDRATE that is the structural constituent of the cell walls of plants and algae. Consisting of parallel unbranched chains of GLUCOSE units cross-linked together, it forms the basic material of the paper and textile industries.

Celsius Temperature scale, devised (1742) by the Swedish astronomer Anders Celsius. The difference between the temperatures of the freezing and boiling points of water is divided into 100 degrees. The freezing point is 0°C and the boiling point is 100°C. The name Celsius officially replaced centigrade in 1948. Degrees Celsius are converted to degrees FAHRENHEIT by multiplying by 1.8 and adding 32. *See also* THERMOMETER

Celt A speaker of a CELTIC LANGUAGE, or descendant from a Celtic language area. After 2000 BC, early Celts spread from E France and W Germany over much of W Europe, including Britain. They developed a village-based, hierarchical society headed by nobles and DRUIDS. Conquered by the Romans, the Celts were pushed into Ireland, Wales, Cornwall and Brittany by Germanic peoples. Their culture remained vigorous, and Celtic churches were important in the early spread of Christianity in N Europe.

▲ **cell** Animal cells are made up of many different components called organelles. The most prominent is the nucleus (1), which contains all the information of the cell in the form of chromosomes. It is surrounded by the nuclear membrane (2), which contains many pores (3) that allow the nucleus to communicate with the rest of the cell. The centre of the nucleus, the nucleolus (4), generates ribosomes (5), which provide the cell with protein. They are found on the rough endoplasmic reticulum (6), a system of flattened sacs and tubes connected to the nuclear membrane. It brings the messenger-RNA molecules, which control the creation of protein, to the ribosomes. The smooth endoplasmic reticulum (7) produces small spheres called vesicles (8) that provide the Golgi apparatus (9) with protein. The Golgi apparatus modifies, sorts and packs large molecules into other vesicles that bud off (10). They are sent to other organelles or secreted from the cell. The fusion of such vesicles with the cell membrane allows particles to be transported out of the cell (exocytosis, 11–13) or brought in (endocytosis, 14–17). Lysosomes (18) break down the molecules entering the cell into enzymes. The mitochondria (19) power the cell, using oxygen and food to generate energy in the form of adenosine triphosphate (ATP). ATP is used in many metabolic processes that are essential for the cell to function.

Celtic art Artworks produced by Celtic peoples in Europe during the prehistoric La Tène period. Its chief characteristic was swirling, abstract design, which found its fullest expression in metalwork and jewellery. The term is sometimes also applied to the La Tène-influenced, early Christian art of western Europe, such as the BOOK OF KELLS.

Celtic languages Group of languages spoken in parts of Britain, Ireland and France, forming a division within the Italo-Celtic subfamily of Indo-European languages. There are two branches of Celtic languages: Brittonic, which includes WELSH, BRETON and Cornish; and Goidelic, including Irish and Scots GAELIC and MANX. The Brittonic or Celtic languages were dominant in the British Isles until the 5th century AD.

Celtic mythology Legends of local deities of the Celtic tribes scattered throughout Europe and the British Isles. Each tribe had an omnipotent god, similar to DAGDA. The gods' world was seen as a reflection of the world of men, while female divinities were more closely identified with nature.

cement Any material in a liquid or plastic form that hardens and bonds other solids together. As a smaller scale adhesive it is also known as GLUE. In building it usually refers to Portland cement, made by heating a mixture of limestone and clay, grinding it and adding GYPSUM.

Cenozoic Most recent era of geological time, beginning c.65 million years ago and extending up to the present. It is subdivided into the TERTIARY and Quaternary periods. It is the period during which present geographical features and plants and animals developed.

censor Public official of ancient Rome, from 443 to 22 BC. Two censors were elected for 18-month terms. Besides taking the census, they supervised public works, finance and morals and filled senatorial vacancies.

censorship Official ban or restriction of any expression deemed to threaten the political, social or moral order. It is usually imposed by the state or church. Rigorous censorship is a feature of authoritarian or totalitarian regimes. In democracies, it is used principally in matters relating to national security. The medieval INQUISITION was a form of censorship. The Reformation and Counter-Reformation used censorship as a means of religious persecution. Until 1948, the Roman Catholic Church published the Index – a list of banned books. Literature has often been subject to censorship, mostly on political or moral grounds. Strict censorship in the Soviet Union was imposed on literary works that contradicted state ideology. In the US and Britain, literary works have occasionally been banned on the grounds of obscenity. Although the Bill of Rights in the US Constitution guarantees freedom of the press, until the 1930s many classic works of art and literature deemed as obscene were prevented from being imported. From 1934 to 1966, the US film industry applied a restrictive, self-regulatory code of morals (the Hays Code). More recently, there have been calls for the censorship of PORNOGRAPHY and racist material. Advanced communications technology (such as the Internet) has made policing more problematic.

census Survey conducted by a government to collect facts about the society it governs. In addition to population counts, most censuses seek information on marital status, age and sex, numbers of children, occupation, education, housing and annual income. Such information helps a government to formulate policy.

centaur In Greek mythology, a creature half-human, half-horse. One of a warlike and lustful race who roamed Mount Pelion in Thessaly, their debauched behaviour was exacerbated by wine. *See also* CHIRON

Centaurus (Centaur) Brilliant southern constellation representing a centaur. The brightest star in Centaurus is ALPHA CENTAURI.

centaury Any plant of the genus *Centaurium* of the GENTIAN family (Gentianaceae). Garden varieties are small plants with flat clusters of reddish flowers.

centigrade *See* CELSIUS

centipede (lit. hundred-legged) Common name for many arthropods of the class Chilopoda. Found in warm and temperate regions, they have flattened, segmented bodies. Most centipedes have c.70 legs (one pair per segment). Many temperate species are 15–30cm (6–12in) long; temperate ones are c.2.5cm (1in). Fast-moving predators, they eat small insects and other invertebrates.

Central Administrative region of central Scotland; the capital is STIRLING. Major towns include Falkirk, Alloa, Grangemouth and Dunblane. In the N, lie the foothills of the Highlands, including the Trossachs. The s is drained chiefly by the River Forth, and is the region's industrial base. The Firth of Forth cuts into the E of the region. Historic sites include BANNOCKBURN battleground and Stirling Castle. Industries: brewing, distilling. Area: 2,635sq km (913sq mi) Pop: 267,492.

Central African Republic Landlocked nation in central Africa; the capital is BANGUI. **Land and climate** It lies on a plateau, mostly between 600–800m (1,970 –2,620ft) above sea level, forming a watershed between the headwaters of two river systems. In the s, the rivers flow into the navigable River Ubangi (a tributary of the River CONGO). The Ubangi and the Bomu form much of the republic's border. In the N, most rivers are headwaters of the River Chari, which flows into Lake CHAD to the N. Bangui has a warm climate with a high average annual rainfall of 1,574mm (62in). The N is drier, with rainfall of c.800mm (31in).Wooded savanna covers much of the country, with open grasslands in the N and rainforests in the SW. The republic has many forest and savanna animals. About 6% of the land is protected in national parks and reserves. **History** Between the 16th and 19th centuries, the population was greatly reduced by slavery and the country is still thinly populated. Most inhabitants migrated into the area during the past 200 years to escape the slave trade. France first occupied the area in 1887, and in 1894 established the colony of Ubangi-Shari at Bangui. In 1906, the colony was united with CHAD, and in 1910 was subsumed into French Equatorial Africa. Forced-labour rebellions occurred in 1928, 1935 and 1946. During World War 2, Ubangi-Shari supported the Free French. In 1958, the colony voted to become a self-governing republic within the French community, and became the Central African Republic. In 1960, it declared independence, but the next six years saw a deterioration in the economy and increasing government corruption and inefficiency under President David Dacko. In 1966, Colonel Jean Bedel BOKASSA assumed power in a bloodless coup. In 1976, Bokassa transformed the republic into an empire and proclaimed himself Emperor Bokassa I. His rule became increasingly brutal, and in 1979 he was deposed in a French-backed coup led by Dacko. In 1981, Dacko, faced with continuing

---

CENTRAL AFRICAN REPUBLIC
AREA: 622,980sq km (240,533sq mi)
POPULATION: 4,074,000
CAPITAL (POPULATION): Bangui (553,000)

unrest, was replaced by André Kolingba. The army quickly banned all political parties. In 1991, the country adopted a new, multiparty constitution. In 1996, an army rebellion was suppressed with the help of French troops. In 1998 a UN peacekeeping force was sent to oversee fresh elections. **Economy** Central African Republic is a low-income developing country (1995 GDP per capita, $US1,070), c.10% of the land is cultivated, and more than 80% of the workforce are engaged in subsistence agriculture. The main food crops are bananas, corn, manioc, millet and yams. Coffee, cotton, timber and tobacco are the main cash crops. Diamonds – the only major mineral resource – are the most valuable single export. Development has been impeded by its remote position, poor transport system, untrained workforce and heavy dependence on foreign aid (especially from France).

Central America Geographical term for the narrow strip of land that connects NORTH AMERICA to SOUTH AMERICA and divides the Caribbean Sea from the Pacific Ocean; it consists of GUATEMALA, EL SALVADOR, HONDURAS, NICARAGUA, COSTA RICA, BELIZE and PANAMA. Highly developed by the Mayas, the region (excluding Panama) was conquered and ruled by the Spanish from the 16th century until 1821. In 1823 the Central American Federation was formed but broke up in 1838. The terrain is mostly mountainous, the climate tropical. It enjoys an economic, ethnic and geological unity. Spanish is the main language. Area: 715,876sq km (276,400sq mi).

Central and South American mythology Traditional beliefs of the native peoples of Central and South America and Mexico. The AZTECS had a rich and complex mythology, much of it taken from the earlier cultures of the TOLTECS and MAYAS. The **Aztecs** believed that there had been four eras (suns) before the one in which they were living, and that each sun had ended in universal destruction. They expected that their own era would end with an earthquake. The Aztec pantheon was headed by HUITZILOPOCHTLI. Other important deities included QUETZALCÓATL. Human sacrifice was a central feature of Aztec culture. They believed that the Sun would cease to rise unless constantly supplied with human blood. The **Mayas** of the Yucatán peninsula in Central America had a god of creation, Hunab Ku, remote from human affairs. In Guatemala, there were creator divinities and also the ancient god Huracán who gave the Mayas fire. In South America, the vast INCA empire of Peru worshiped Inti, the sun god and ancestor of the ruling dynasty. Another important deity was Viracocha, the creator god. ANCESTOR WORSHIP played a central role in **Inca** religious observances. The dead were venerated and the mummies of previous emperors accorded special honours. In tribal groups the shaman still enjoys considerable authority.

Central Asian Republics Economic alliance among the republics of KAZAKSTAN, KYRGYZSTAN and UZBEKISTAN. The alliance was formed in 1994 after the break-up of the Soviet Union.

central bank Institution that regulates and sets policy for a nation's banking system. The UK central bank is the BANK OF ENGLAND, and in the US it is the FEDERAL RESERVE SYSTEM.

Central Intelligence Agency (CIA) US government agency established to coordinate the intelligence activities of government departments and agencies responsible for US national security. Founded in 1947, it played a major role during the COLD WAR, supporting anti-communist movements. At times the CIA has come under attack for overstepping its mandate and interfering in the internal affairs of foreign countries. It was severely criticized for its role in the WATERGATE AFFAIR. It advises, and is directed by, the NATIONAL SECURITY COUNCIL (NSC), and should report any action it proposes to take to Congress and gain presidential authorization.

central nervous system (CNS) Term embracing the brain and spinal cord, as distinct from the PERIPHERAL NERVOUS SYSTEM. The CNS coordinates all nervous activity. *See also* NERVOUS SYSTEM

Central Powers Alliance of Germany and Austria-Hungary (with Bulgaria and Turkey) during World War 1. The name distinguished them from their opponents in the w (Britain, France, Belgium, US) and E (Russia and others).

central processing unit (CPU) Part of a digital COMPUTER circuit that controls all operations. In most computers, the CPU consists of one complex INTEGRATED CIRCUIT (IC), a chip called a MICROPROCESSOR. A CPU contains temporary storage circuits that hold data and instructions; an arithmetic and logic unit (ALU) that performs calculations; and a control unit that organizes operations.

centre of gravity Point at which the weight of a body is considered to be concentrated, and around which its weight is evenly balanced. An object in free flight spins around its centre of gravity (that is moving in a straight line). In a uniform gravitational field, the centre of gravity is the same as the CENTRE OF MASS.

centre of mass Point at which the whole mass of an object or group of objects is considered to be concentrated. Isaac NEWTON first proved his inverse-square law of gravitation by assuming the respective masses of the Earth and Moon were located at their centres.

centrifugal force *See* CENTRIPETAL FORCE

centrifuge Rotating device used for separating substances. In laboratories, centrifuges separate particles from suspensions, and red blood cells from plasma. In the food industry, centrifuges separate cream from milk and sugar from syrup. In each case, the denser substance is forced to the outside of a rotating container.

centripetal force In circular or curved motion, the force acting on an object that keeps it moving in a circular path. For example, if an object attached to a rope is swung in a circular motion above a person's head, the centripetal force acting on the object is the tension in the rope. Similarly, the centripetal force acting on the Earth as it orbits the Sun is gravity. In accordance with NEWTON's laws, the reaction to this, the (theoretical) centrifugal force, is equal in magnitude and opposite in direction.

centurion Military officer of ancient Rome. He commanded 100 men, forming one sixth of a cohort, with ten cohorts making a legion. Centurions were usually soldiers who had risen through the ranks.

Cephalopoda Advanced class of predatory marine molluscs, including SQUID, NAUTILUS, OCTOPUS and CUTTLEFISH. Each has eight or more arms surrounding the mouth, which has a parrot-like beak. The nervous system is well developed, permitting great speed and alertness; the large eyes have an image-forming ability equal to that of vertebrates. Most squirt an inky fluid to alarm attackers. Cephalopods move by squirting water from their mantle edge. Their heavily yolked eggs develop into larval young. Members of this class vary dramatically in size from 4cm (1.5in) to the giant squid, which may reach 20m (65ft). There are more than 600 species.

cephalosporin Class of ANTIBIOTIC drugs derived from fungi of the genus *Cephalosporium*. Similar to PENICILLIN, they are effective against a wide spectrum of BACTERIA, including some resistant to penicillin.

Cepheid variable One of an important class of VARIABLE STARS that pulsate in a regular manner, accompanied by changes in luminosity. Cepheids can expand and contract up to 30% in each cycle. The average luminosity is 10,000 times that of the Sun. Cepheids became important in cosmology (1912) when US astronomer Henrietta Leavitt discovered a relationship between the period of light variation and the absolute magnitude of a cepheid. This law enables the distances of stars to be ascertained.

ceramic In art and technology, article made from inorganic compounds formed in a plastic condition and hardened by heating in a furnace. **Earthenware** is a porous ceramic made from kaolin, ball clay and crushed flint. **Porcelain** is made from kaolin and feldspar, and heated to a higher temperature. It is nonporous and translucent. Special ceramics are made from pure aluminium oxide, silicon carbide, titranates and other compounds. Ceramic ware is ornamented by inlays, relief modelling or by incised, stamped or impressed designs. A creamy mixture of clay and water (slip) can be used to coat the ware. After drying, ceramic ware is baked in a kiln until it has hardened. **Glaze**, a silicate preparation applied to the clay surface and fused to it during firing, is used to make the pottery nonporous and to give it a smooth, colourful, decorative surface. Chinese porcelain dates from the T'ang dynasty, and Chinese stoneware goes back to *c*.3000 BC. The ancient Egyptians developed a faience with a glaze. Mesopotamia and Persia used large architectural tiles with colourful glazes. In the 6th and 5th centuries BC, the Greeks developed red, black and white glazed pottery with figures and scenes, while the Romans used relief decoration. In Spain, lustreware, the first sophisticated ceramic of the modern era, was produced by 9th-century Moors. Later refinements include Italian majolica, Dutch DELFT, German Meissen and English WEDGEWOOD. *See also* POTTERY

cereal Any grain of the grass family (Gramineae) grown as a food crop. Wheat, corn, rye, oats and barley are grown in temperate regions. Rice, millet and sorghum require more tropical climates. Cereal cultivation was the basis of early civilizations, and with the development of high-yielding strains, remains the world's most important food source.

cerebellum Part of the brain located at the base of the CEREBRUM. It is involved in maintaining muscle tone, balance and finely coordinated movement.

cerebral cortex Deeply fissured outer layer of the CEREBRUM. The cortex (grey matter) is the most sophisticated part of the brain, responsible for sensation, initiating voluntary movement, emotions and intellect.

cerebral haemorrhage Form of stroke in which there is bleeding from a blood vessel in the BRAIN into the surrounding tissue. It is usually caused by ARTERIOSCLEROSIS and high blood pressure. Symptoms vary from temporary numbness and weakness on one side of the body to deep coma. A major haemorrhage may be fatal.

cerebral hemispheres Lateral halves of the CEREBRUM, the largest parts of the BRAIN and the sites of higher thought. Because of the crossing of nerve fibres from one hemisphere to the other, the right side controls most of the movements and sensation on the left side of the body, and vice-versa.

cerebral palsy Disorder mainly of movement and coordination caused by BRAIN damage during or soon after birth. It may feature muscular spasm and weakness, lack of coordination, and impaired movement or paralysis and deformities of the limbs. Intelligence is not necessarily affected. The condition may result from a number of causes, such as faulty development, oxygen deprivation, birth injury or infection.

cerebrospinal fluid Clear fluid that cushions the brain and spinal cord, giving some protection against shock. It is found between the two innermost meninges (membranes) in the four ventricles of the BRAIN and in the central canal of the spinal cord. A small quantity of the fluid can be withdrawn by lumbar puncture to aid diagnosis of some brain diseases.

cerebrum Largest and most highly developed part of the BRAIN, consisting of the CEREBRAL HEMISPHERES separated by a central fissure. It is covered by the CEREBRAL CORTEX. It coordinates all higher functions and voluntary activity.

Cerenkov, Pavel Alekseevich (1904–90) Russian physicist. Working at the Institute of Physics of the Soviet Academy of Science, he discovered (1934) that light (CERENKOV RADIATION) is emitted by charged particles travelling at very high speeds. Cerenkov was awarded the 1958 Nobel Prize for physics with his co-workers, I.M. Frank and I.Y. Tamm.

Cerenkov radiation Light emitted when energetic particles travel through a transparent medium, such as water, faster than the velocity of light in that medium. This action is called the **Cerenkov effect**. A cone of light is emitted, trailing the path of the particle. It is named after Pavel CERENKOV. The radiation is used in a Cerenkov counter, a detector of energetic particles.

Ceres In Roman mythology, goddess of food plants, the equivalent of the Greek goddess DEMETER.

Ceres Largest ASTEROID and the first to be discovered (1 January 1801, by Guiseppe Piazzi). Ceres' diameter measures 913km (567mi). It orbits in the main asteroid belt at an average distance from the Sun of 414 million km (257 million mi), the distance of the "missing" planet predicted by BODE'S LAW.

cerium (symbol Ce) Soft, ductile, iron-grey metallic element, the most abundant of the LANTHANIDE SERIES group, first isolated in 1803. The chief ore is monazite. It is used in alloys, catalysts, nuclear fuels, glass and as the core of carbon electrodes in arc lamps. Properties: at.no. 58; r.a.m. 140.12; r.d. 6.77; m.p. 798°C (1,468°F); b.p. 3,257°C (5,895°F). The most common isotope is Ce ^{140} (88.48%).

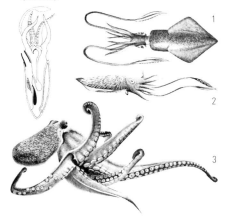

▲ **Cephalopoda** The squid (1), cuttlefish (2) and octopus (3) are all swimming molluscs of the Cephalopoda group. They have advanced, powerful eyes, and tentacles lined with sucker pads which are used to catch fish and small crustaceans. The horny jawed mouth is powerful enough to break up their prey before it is digested in the gut.

cermet One of a group of hard, brittle and heat-resistant materials. Cermet is a combination of ceramic material and metal. Applications include the manufacture of drilling tools, heat shields and turbine blades.

CERN (European Laboratory for Particle Physics) Nuclear research centre located on the Franco-Swiss border, W of Geneva. It was founded in 1954 as an intergovernmental organization, when it was called *Conseil Européen pour la Recherche Nucléaire*. It is the principal European centre for research into PARTICLE PHYSICS.

Cervantes, Miguel de (1547–1616) Spanish novelist, poet and dramatist. Cervantes published two volumes of his masterpiece *Don Quixote de la Mancha* (1605; 1615). Don Quixote is a great archetype of Western fiction, the picaresque hero who misapplies the logic of high Romance to the mundane situations of modern life. It established Cervantes as a towering figure in Spanish letters. Other works include two surviving plays and a collection of short stories, *Novelas Ejemplares* (1613).

cervical smear (pap test) Test for CANCER of the CERVIX, established by George Papanicolaou. A small sample of tissue is removed from the cervix and examined under a microscope for the presence of abnormal, pre-cancerous cells. Treatment in the early stages of cervical cancer can prevent the disease from developing.

cervix Neck of the WOMB (uterus), projecting downwards into the VAGINA. It dilates (expands) widely to allow the passage of the baby during childbirth.

Césaire, Aimé (1913–) West Indian poet, b. Martinique. In his book *Return to My Native Land* (1939), Césaire argued for the cultivation of a collective African identity. This concept of *négritude* was developed by Léopold SENGHOR.

Cetshwayo (d.1884) (Cetewayo) King of the Zulus (1873–79). Nephew of SHAKA, he sought British aid against the BOERS, but British demands for him to disarm led to the ZULU WAR (1879). Eventually defeated, he was deposed, restored briefly in 1883, but died in exile.

Ceylon *See* SRI LANKA

Cézanne, Paul (1839–1906) French painter. He exhibited at the first impressionist show in 1874. *House of the Hanged Man* (1873–74) is characteristic of this period. Cézanne later moved away from IMPRESSIONISM in favour of a more analytical approach using colour to model and express form. Figure paintings, such as *The Card Players* (1890–92), *Madame Cézanne* (*c*.1885) and *The Bathers* (1895–1905) and landscapes, such as *Mont Sainte Victoire* (1904–06), were painted on this principle. Cézanne ranks as one of the great influences on modern art, especially CUBISM. *See also* POSTIMPRESSIONISM

Chabrier, (Alexis) Emmanuel (1841–94) French composer. Chabrier is best known for his orchestral rhapsody, *España* (1883). His lyrical piano music, such as *Impromptu* (1873) and *Bourrée fantasque* (1891), greatly influenced subsequent composers, especially Ravel. Other works include the opera *Le Roi malgré lui* (1887).

Chabrol, Claude (1930–) French film director, a leading member of the NOUVELLE VAGUE. Often making use of the crime genre to explore his favourite themes (food and the indiscreet crimes of the French bourgeoisie), Chabrol was greatly influenced by Alfred Hitchcock. Major films include *Les Biches* (1968), *Le Boucher* (1969), *Ten Days Wonder* (1971) and *Cop au vin* (1984).

Chaco War (1932–35) *See* GRAN CHACO

Chad Republic in N central Africa. Chad is Africa's fifth largest country. Southern Chad is crossed by rivers that flow into Lake CHAD, on the W border with Nigeria. The capital, NDJAMENA, lies on the banks of the River Chari.

CHAD
AREA: 1,284,000sq km (495,752sq mi)
POPULATION: 7,337,000
CAPITAL (POPULATION): Ndjamena (529,555)

Beyond a large depression (NE of Lake Chad) are the Tibesti Mountains, which rise steeply from the sands of the SAHARA Desert. The mountains contain Chad's highest peak, Emi Koussi, at 3,415m (11,204ft). **Climate** Central Chad has a hot tropical climate with a marked dry season between November and April. The S is wetter, with an average yearly rainfall of *c*.1000mm (39in). The hot N desert has an average annual rainfall of less than 130mm (5in). **Vegetation** The far S contains forests, while central Chad is a region of savanna, merging into the dry grasslands of the SAHEL. Plants are rare in the N desert. Droughts are common in N central Chad. A major problem is the increasing rate of desertification. **History and Politics** Chad straddles two, often conflicting worlds: the N, populated by nomadic or semi-nomadic Muslim peoples, such as Arabs and Tuaregs; and the dominant S, where a sedentary population practise Christianity, or traditional religions such as animism. In *c*.AD 700, North African nomads founded the Kanem empire. The Islamic state of Bornu was established in the 13th century. In the late 19th century, the region fell to Sudan. The French defeated the Sudanese in 1900 and, in 1908, Chad became the largest province of French Equatorial Africa. In 1920, it became a separate colony, and in 1960 it achieved full independence. In 1965, President François Tombalbaye declared a one party state and the N Muslims, led by the Chad National Liberation Front (Frolinat), rebelled. By 1973, the revolt had been quashed with the aid of French troops. Libya (supporters of Frolinat) occupied N Chad. In 1981, two leaders of Frolinat, Hissène Habré and Goukouni Oueddi, came to power. In 1983, Libya's bombing of Chad led to the deployment of 3,000 French troops. Libyan troops retreated, retaining only the uranium-rich Aozou Strip. A cease-fire took effect in 1987. In 1990, Habré was removed in a coup led by Idriss Déby. In 1994, the Aozou Strip was awarded to Chad. In 1996, a new democratic constitution was adopted and multiparty elections confirmed Déby as president. **Economy** Hit by drought and civil war, Chad is one of the world's poorest countries (1995 GDP per capita, $US700). Agriculture dominates the economy, more than 80% of the workforce are engaged in farming, mainly at subsistence level. Groundnuts, millet, rice and sorghum are major crops in the wetter S. The most valuable crop is cotton, accounting for *c*.50% of Chad's exports.

Chad, Lake (Tchad) Lake in N central Africa, mainly in the Republic of Chad but partly in Nigeria, Cameroon and Niger. The chief tributary is the River Chari; the lake has no outlet. Depending on the season, the area varies from *c*.10,000–26,000sq km (3,850–10,000sq mi). Max. depth: 7.6m (25ft).

Chadwick, Sir James (1891–1974) English physicist who discovered and named the NEUTRON. He worked on radioactivity with Ernest RUTHERFORD at the Cavendish Laboratory, Cambridge, UK. In 1920, Rutherford had predicted a particle without electric charge in the NUCLEUS of an ATOM, and in 1932 Chadwick proved the neutron's existence and calculated its mass. For this, he received the 1935 Nobel Prize for physics. During World War 2, Chadwick moved to the US to head British research for the MANHATTAN PROJECT to develop the atomic bomb.

chaffinch Small songbird common throughout Europe. It generally perches on low trees, bushes and fences, feeding on plants and insects. The blue and buff colours and pink breast belong to the male only. In winter, flocks consisting solely of males can be seen. Family Fringillidae; species *Fringilla coelebs.*

Chagall, Marc (1887–1985) Russian-French painter. His paintings, with their dream-like imagery, considerably influenced SURREALISM. *I and the Village* (1911) is characteristic of his early style. Chagall worked using ceramics, mosaics and tapestry and in theatre design. He designed stained-glass windows for the Hadassah-Hebrew Medical Centre, Jerusalem (1962), murals for the Metropolitan Opera House, New York (1966), and mosaics and tapestries for the Knesset, Jerusalem (1969).

Chain, Sir Ernst Boris (1906–79) British biochemist, b. Germany. Chain shared the 1945 Nobel Prize for physiology or medicine with Howard FLOREY and Alexander FLEMING for the isolation and development of PENICILLIN as an antibiotic.

chain reaction Self-sustaining nuclear reaction in which one reaction is the cause of a second, the second of a third, and so on. The initial conditions are critical, in that the quantity of fissionable material must exceed the CRITICAL MASS. The explosion of a NUCLEAR WEAPON is an uncontrolled chain reaction. *See* NUCLEAR REACTOR

Chalcedon, Council of (451) Meeting of all the bishops of the Christian church, in the city of Chalcedon, Asia Minor. Convoked by the Emperor Marcian, it reaffirmed the doctrine of two natures (divine and human) in Christ and condemned NESTORIANISM.

chalcedony Micro-crystalline form of QUARTZ. When cut and polished, it is used by gem engravers. It is waxy, lustrous, and there are white, grey, blue and brown varieties. Often coloured by artificial methods, some varieties contain impurities giving a distinctive appearance, such as AGATE (coloured bands), ONYX (striped) and bloodstone (dark green with red flecks).

chalcopyrite (COPPER pyrites, copper iron sulphide CuFeS₂) Most important copper ore. Opaque and brass-coloured, it is found in sulphide veins and in igneous and contact metamorphic rocks. The crystals are tetragonal but often occur in masses. Hardness 3.5–4; r.d. 4.2.

Chaliapin, Fyodor Ivanovich (1873–1938) Russian operatic bass. After singing with the Bolshoi, Chaliapin embarked on international tours, performing at La Scala, Milan (1901); the Metropolitan Opera, New York (1907–08); and with Diaghilev in Paris. He left Russia in 1921 and joined the Metropolitan. Chaliapin was noted for the title role in Mussorgsky's *Boris Godunov.*

chalk Mineral, mainly calcium carbonate (CaCO₃), formed from the shells of minute marine organisms. It varies in properties and appearance; pure forms, such as calcite, contain up to 99% calcium carbonate. It is used in making putty, plaster and cement. Blackboard chalk is now made from calcium sulphate (CaSO₄) or chemically produced calcium carbonate.

Challenger disaster *See* SPACE SHUTTLE

Challenger expedition (1872–76) British expedition in oceanographic research. The *Challenger* ship comprised a staff of six naturalists headed by Charles Wyville Thompson. She sailed *c.*128,000km (69,000 nautical mi) making studies of the life, water and seabed in the three main oceans.

Chamberlain, Sir (Joseph) Austen (1863–1937) British statesman, son of Joseph CHAMBERLAIN. He entered Parliament in 1892. Chamberlain served as chancellor of the exchequer (1903–05, 1919–21) in the governments of Arthur BALFOUR and David LLOYD GEORGE. In 1921, he succeeded Bonar Law as Conservative Party leader. Chamberlain acted as foreign minister (1924–29) in Stanley BALDWIN's administration. For his work on the LOCARNO PACT, he shared the 1925 Nobel Prize for Peace.

Chamberlain, Joseph (1836–1914) British political leader, father of Neville CHAMBERLAIN. He entered Parliament as a Liberal in 1876. In 1880, Chamberlain became president of the board of trade. In 1886, he resigned over GLADSTONE's Home Rule Bill and was leader of the Liberal Unionists from 1889. In 1895, Chamberlain returned to government as colonial secretary, where his aggressive, imperialist stance helped provoke the SOUTH AFRICAN WAR (1899).

Chamberlain, (Arthur) Neville (1869–1940) British statesman, prime minister (1937–40). Son of Joseph CHAMBERLAIN, he entered Parliament in 1918. During the 1920s, Chamberlain served as chancellor of the exchequer (1923–24, 1931–37) and minister of health (1924–29). He succeeded Stanley BALDWIN as prime minister and leader of the Conservative Party. Chamberlain approached Hitler with a policy of APPEASEMENT and signed the MUNICH AGREEMENT (1938). After Hitler's invasion of Poland, he declared war in September 1939. After the loss of Norway, Chamberlain was replaced by Winston CHURCHILL in May 1940.

chamberlain, lord Head of the British sovereign's household. The first lord chamberlain was appointed in 1360. During the reign (1727–60) of George II, the lord chamberlain took over the licensing of all plays presented in Britain. Confirmed by an act of 1844, this function was abolished in 1968.

chamber music Music intended for performance in intimate surroundings. It is usually written for two to eight instruments (or voices). The string quartet (two violins, viola and cello) is the most common arrangement. The term dates from the 17th century and was applied to music played privately in the homes of wealthy patrons. The form has been revived in the late 20th century.

chameleon Arboreal LIZARD, found chiefly in Madagascar, Africa and Asia, notable for its ability to change colour. The compressed body has a curled, prehensile tail and bulging eyes that move independently. Length: 17–60cm (7–24in). Family Chamaeleontidae; genus *Chamaeleo*; there are 80 species.

chamois Nimble, goat-like RUMINANT that lives in mountain ranges of Europe and w Asia. It has coarse, reddish-brown fur with a black tail and horns. Its skin is made into chamois leather. Length: up to 1.3m (50in); weight: 25–50kg (55–110lb). Family Bovidae; species *Rupicapra rupicapra.*

chamomile (camomile) Low-growing, yellow- or white-flowered herb. Several species are cultivated as ground cover. Flowers of the European chamomile (*Chamaemelum nobile*) are used to make herbal tea. Family Asteraceae; genus *Chamaemelum.*

Chamorro, Violeta Barrios de (1939–) Nicaraguan stateswoman, president (1990–96). Chamorro entered politics in 1978 when her husband, Pedro Joáin Chamorro, was assassinated. In 1989, supported by the US, she became leader of the right-wing coalition, the National Opposition Union (UNO). Chamorro became president after defeating the SANDINISTA government in 1990. Her presidency was marked by skirmishes between CONTRA rebels and the Sandinistas, and many of her policies were blocked by reactionary elements in the UNO and by members of the Sandinista Liberation Front.

Champagne District in NE France, made up of the Aube, Marne, Haute-Marne and Ardennes departments. The major city is REIMS. It was a centre for European trade in the 11th–13th centuries. During World War 2, there was heavy fighting along the River Marne. It is an arid region, renowned for its champagne, a sparkling white wine that can only be produced in the district. Area: 25,606sq km (9,886sq mi). Pop. (1990) 1,347,800.

Champaigne, Philippe de (1602–74) French painter, b. Flanders. He was the greatest French portraitist of the 17th century, and a remarkable religious painter. In 1628 Champaigne became artist to Queen Marie de' Medici and Cardinal Richelieu. His beliefs in JANSENISM produced religious paintings characterized by a serene realism. Champaigne's best-known works include portraits and frescos at Vincennes and in the Tuileries.

Champlain, Samuel de (1567–1635) French explorer, founder of New France (Canada). In 1603, following the discoveries of Jacques CARTIER, Champlain travelled up the St Lawrence River as far as Lachine. He returned to New France in 1604, and established a fur-trading colony at Port Royal (now Annapolis Royal, Nova Scotia). Champlain explored the Atlantic coast from Cape Breton to Cape Cod, making the first detailed maps of the area, and in 1608 he founded Québec. With the help of the HURON, he continued to explore the region for the next six years, discovering the lake that bears his name in 1609. In 1615 he travelled up the Ottawa River as far as Lake Huron. The last 20 years of his life were spent as a colonial administrator and patron of further explorations.

Champlain, Lake Lake that lies on the border of New York State and Vermont, USA, and extends into Québec, Canada. It serves as a link in the Hudson-St. Lawrence waterway. Explored (1609) by Samuel de CHAMPLAIN, it was the scene of many battles in the French and Indian Wars, the American Revolution, and the defeat of the British in the War of 1812. Today, the lake is a popular resort area. Area: 1,101sq km (435sq mi).

Champollion, Jean François (1790–1832) French scholar, one of the founders of Egyptology. In 1822, he revealed his decipherment of Egyptian HIEROGLYPHICS through study of the ROSETTA STONE. Champollion was subsequently curator at the Louvre in Paris and first professor of Egyptology at the Collège de France.

chancellor of the exchequer British minister responsible for national finances. The office evolved from the 13th-century clerk of the court of exchequer, assistant to the chancellor. Since the 1850s, it has become probably the second most high-profile cabinet office (after the prime minister).

Chancery In England, court developed in the 15th century for the lord chancellor to deal with petitions from aggrieved persons for redress when no remedy was available in the COMMON LAW courts. By the mid-17th century, Chancery had become a second system of law (equity) rather than a reforming agency. By the Supreme Court of Judicature Act (1925), the court of Chancery was merged into the HIGH COURT OF JUSTICE, of which it is now known as the Chancery Division.

Chandigarh City in NW India at the foot of the Siwalik Hills. The joint capital of Punjab and Haryana states, it is a planned city, designed by LE CORBUSIER and built in the 1950s. Pop. (1991) 511,000.

Chandler, Raymond Thornton (1888–1959) US novelist. His DETECTIVE FICTION features the tough private eye Philip Marlowe in such novels as *The Big Sleep* (1939), *Farewell, My Lovely* (1940) and *The Long Goodbye* (1953). Many have been made into successful films. Chandler's crackling dialogue and seedy plots are distinctive and much copied.

Chandragupta Founder of the Maurya empire in India (ruled c.321–297 BC) and grandfather of ASHOKA. He seized the throne of Magadha and defeated SELEUCUS, gaining dominion over most of N India and part of Afghanistan. His reign was characterized by religious tolerance. He established a vast bureaucracy at Patna. He abdicated and, it is thought, became a Jain monk.

Chandrasekhar, Subrahmanyan (1910–95) US astrophysicist, b. India. He formulated theories about the creation, life and death of stars, and calculated the maximum mass (Chandrasekhar limit) of a white dwarf star before it becomes a neutron star. Chandrasekhar shared the 1983 Nobel Prize for physics with William Fowler.

Chanel, "Coco" (Gabrielle) (1883–1971) French fashion designer. Chanel revolutionized women's fashion, borrowing elements from men's clothing. She is associated with the Chanel suit, jersey dresses, bell-bottom trousers, trench coats and Chanel No.5 perfume.

Chaney, Lon, Sr. (1883–1930) US silent-film actor. The son of deaf-mutes, Chaney was a brilliant mime, noted for his complex disguises in horror films. His major films include *The Hunchback of Notre Dame* (1923) and *The Phantom of the Opera* (1925). His son, Lon Chaney, Jr. (1906–73), was also a film actor.

Changchun (Ch'ang-ch'un) Capital of Jilin province, NE China. As Hsinking, it was the capital (1932–45) of the former state of Manchukuo. Industries: chemicals, textiles, motor vehicles. Pop. (1994) 1,810,000.

Chang Jiang *See* YANGTZE

Channel Islands Group of islands at the SW end of the English Channel, c.16km (10mi) off the W coast of France. The main islands are Jersey, Guernsey, Alderney and Sark; the chief towns are St Helier on Jersey and St Peter Port on Guernsey. A dependency of the British crown since the Norman Conquest, they were under German occupation during World War 2. Guernsey and Jersey each have its own parliament. The islands have a warm climate and fertile soil. Industries: tourism, agriculture. Area: 194sq km (75sq mi). Pop. (1991) 142,949.

Channel Tunnel (Chunnel) Railroad tunnel under the English Channel, 49km (30.6mi) long. The first Channel Tunnel was proposed in 1802 by a French engineer. A start was made in 1882, but was soon abandoned for defence reasons. Another false start was made in the 1970s. In 1985, Eurotunnel, a joint French-English private company, was granted a 55-year concession to finance and operate the tunnel. The French and English sections were linked in 1990, and the tunnel became operational in 1994. It consists of two railroad tunnels and one service tunnel, and links Folkestone, S England, with Calais, N France.

chansons de geste (Fr. songs of deeds) Epic poems written in Old French between the 11th and 14th centuries, generally dealing with the campaigns of CHARLEMAGNE. These anonymous narratives, of which some 80 survive, describe semi-imaginary events.

Chanson de Roland, La French epic, written in Old French by an unnamed author of the late 11th century. It recounts the defeat of CHARLEMAGNE's rearguard at Roncesvalles Pass in the Pyrenees on 15 August 778. A typical CHANSON DE GESTE, the poem alters historical fact.

chant Unaccompanied liturgical singing, especially of PSALMS. Anglican chant developed from Gregorian tones, which were melody formulas defining pitch relationships only. Later, harmonies were added to the melodies and note values designated to English texts of the psalms.

chanterelle Medium-sized, edible, fleshy, terrestrial MUSHROOM. It occurs in beech and oakwoods in autumn. It has a bright yellow, funnel-shaped cap with prominent gills continuing down the stem. Family Cantharellaceae; species *Cantharellus cibarius*.

chaos theory Theory that attempts to describe and explain the highly complex behaviour of apparently chaotic or unpredictable systems which show an underlying order. The behaviour of some physical systems is impossible to describe using the standard laws of physics, the mathematics needed to describe these systems being too difficult for even the largest supercomputers. Such systems are sometimes known as "nonlinear" or "chaotic" systems, and they include complex machines, electrical circuits and natural phenomena such as the weather. Non-chaotic systems can become chaotic, such as when smoothly flowing water hits a rock. Chaos theory provides mathematical methods needed to describe chaotic systems and even allows some general prediction of a system's behaviour. Because it is impossible to know the precise starting conditions of a system, accurate prediction is also impossible.

Chaplin, Charlie (Sir Charles Spencer) (1889–1977) English actor and director, often considered the greatest silent film comedian. In his short films, such as *The Immigrant* (1917) and *A Dog's Life* (1918), he developed his famous character; a jaunty, wistful figure of pathos in baggy trousers and bowler hat, with a cane and a moustache. Chaplin's major films include *The Kid* (1920), *The Gold Rush* (1924), *City Lights* (1931), *Modern Times* (1936), *The Great Dictator* (1940) and *Limelight* (1952). He was attacked for his left-wing politics, and in 1952 left the US to live in Switzerland. In 1972, he returned to Hollywood to accept an honorary Academy Award.

Chapman, George (1560–1634) English poet, dramatist and translator. He completed Christopher MARLOWE's unfinished poem *Hero and Leander* (1598), and worked with Ben JONSON and John Marston. His own works include the plays *The Blind Beggar of Alexandria* (1598) and *Bussy D'Ambois* (1604) and translations of Homer's *Iliad* (1611) and *Odyssey* (1614–15).

Chapultepec National park in central Mexico, SW of Mexico City. A rocky hill region, it is the site of an 18th-century castle, captured by US forces (1847) during the MEXICAN WAR. It was also the scene of a wartime inter-American conference (1945) to ensure assistance and solidarity in the Western Hemisphere.

charcoal Porous form of CARBON, made traditionally by heating wood in the absence of air, and used in W Europe, until late medieval times, for smelting iron ore. Today, charcoal is chiefly used for its absorptive properties, to decolourize food liquids, such as syrups, and to separate chemicals. Artists use charcoal sticks for sketching.

Charcot, Jean Martin (1825–93) French physician and founder of neurology. He made classical studies of HYPNOSIS and HYSTERIA, and taught Sigmund FREUD. Charcot's work centred on discovering how behavioural symptoms of patients relate to neurological disorders.

Chardin, Jean-Baptiste-Siméon (1699–1779) French painter, one of the greatest artists of the 18th century. Chardin's *Rayfish, cat and kitchen utensils* (1728) gained him entry into the Academy. His unsentimentalized scenes of domestic interiors and still-lifes contrasted strongly with the contemporary dominance of historical painting. Chardin painted with brilliant clarity and delicacy, capturing textures with the use of grainy, scumbled paints. His work was often overshadowed by the fashionable ROCOCO style of BOUCHER and

FRAGONARD. Yet, Chardin's abstract style influenced many 19th-century painters, especially MANET.

charge-coupled device (CCD) Type of silicon CHIP designed to capture images. The CCD is divided into a number of microscopic areas (pixels) arranged in rows. When a PHOTON hits a pixel, it knocks off an electron from a silicon atom, which becomes charged. An opposite charge in a layer on the base of the CCD confines this charged silicon atom, and a charge builds up in each pixel relative to the number of photons hitting it. The contents of each pixel are read off 50 times a second, a row at a time, forming an electrical signal used to create television pictures. CCDs are found in video cameras, fax machines and digital cameras.

Charge of the Light Brigade (25 October 1854) British cavalry charge in the CRIMEAN WAR, one of the most notorious mistakes in British military history. It stemmed from Lord Lucan's misreading of an ambiguous order by the British commander, Lord Raglan. As a result, Lord Cardigan led the unsupported Light Brigade straight at a battery of Russian guns. More than 600 men took part, nearly half of whom were casualties. The incident is commemorated in a famous poem by Alfred TENNYSON.

chariot Light two- or four-wheeled vehicle drawn by horses. Chariots were built in Mesopotamia in the 3rd millennium BC. Used for war and hunting in ancient civilizations, they usually carried two men, a driver and an archer. In Roman times, chariot racing was popular.

charismatic movement Movement within the Christian church. It emphasizes the presence of the Holy Spirit in the life of an individual and in the work of the church. It is particularly associated with PENTECOSTAL CHURCHES.

Charlemagne (742–814) (lit. Charles the Great) King of the Franks (768–814) and Holy Roman emperor (800–14). The eldest son of PEPIN III (THE SHORT), Charlemagne inherited half the Frankish kingdom (768), annexed the remainder on his brother Carloman's death (771), and built a large empire. He invaded Italy twice and took the Lombard throne (773). Charlemagne undertook a long and brutal conquest of Saxony (772–804), annexed Bavaria (788), and defeated the Avars of the middle Danube (791–96, 804). He undertook campaigns against the Moors in Spain. In 800, Charlemagne was consecrated as emperor by Pope Leo II, thus reviving the concept of the Roman Empire and confirming the separation of the West from the Eastern, BYZANTINE EMPIRE. He encouraged the intellectual awakening of the CAROLINGIAN RENAISSANCE, set up a strong central authority, and maintained provincial control through court officials. His central aim was Christian reform, both of church and laity.

Charles II (the Bald) (823–77) King of the West Franks (843–77) and Holy Roman emperor (875–77). Younger son of Emperor Louis I, he was involved in the ambitious disputes of his elder brothers. The Treaty of VERDUN (843) made him king of the West Franks, in effect the first king of France. After the death of Louis II, Charles was recognized as Holy Roman emperor.

Charles III (the Fat) (839–88) Holy Roman emperor (881–87) and king of France (884–87) as Charles II. Through the death or incapacity of relatives, he inherited the kingdoms of the East and West Franks. Charles almost reunited the territories of Charlemagne in the 880s but was deposed by his nephew, Arnulf.

Charles IV (1316–78) Holy Roman emperor (1355–78) and king of Bohemia (1347–78). Supported by Pope Clement VI, Charles was a rival of the Wittelsbach Emperor Louis IV, and when Louis died, was elected king of the Germans (emperor-elect). A skilful diplomat, he blocked or appeased his Wittelsbach and Habsburg rivals, and improved relations with the papacy. In 1356, Charles introduced a stable system of imperial government. He ruled from PRAGUE, his birthplace, where he founded Charles University (1348) and built the Charles Bridge. Czech culture reached a peak under his patronage. Charles was succeeded by his son, WENCESLAUS.

Charles V (1500–58) Holy Roman emperor (1519–56) and king of Spain, as Charles I (1516–56). He ruled the Spanish kingdoms, s Italy, the Netherlands and the Austrian Habsburg lands by inheritance and, when he succeeded his grandfather, MAXIMILIAN I, headed the largest European empire since CHARLEMAGNE. In addition, the Spanish conquistadores made him master of a New World empire. Charles' efforts to unify his possessions were unsuccessful, largely due to the hostility of FRANCIS I of France, the Ottoman Turks in central Europe, and the advance of LUTHERANISM in Germany. The struggle with France was centred in Italy: Spanish control was largely confirmed by 1535, but French hostility was never overcome. The Turks were held in check but not defeated, and Charles' attempt to capture Algiers failed (1541). In Germany, Charles, who saw himself as the defender of the Catholic Church, nevertheless recognized the need for reform, but other commitments prevented him following a consistent policy, and LUTHERANISM expanded. Charles increasingly delegated power in Germany to his brother and successor, FERDINAND I, and in 1554–56 surrendered his other titles to his son, Philip II of Spain.

Charles VI (1685–1740) Holy Roman emperor (1711–40) and king of Hungary. His claim to the Spanish throne against the grandson of Louis XIV, PHILIP V, caused the War of the SPANISH SUCCESSION. After his election as emperor, Charles gave up his Spanish claim. His reign was marked by the attempt to secure the succession of his daughter, MARIA THERESA, to the Austrian throne.

Charles I (1887–1922) Austrian emperor (1916–18) and king (as Charles IV) of Hungary (1916–18). When Hungary and Czechoslovakia declared their independence and Austria became a republic in 1918, Charles, the last Habsburg emperor, was forced into exile in Switzerland.

Charles I (1600–49) King of England, Scotland and Ireland (1625–49). Son of JAMES I, he was criticized by Parliament for his reliance on the Duke of BUCKINGHAM and for his Catholic marriage to Henrietta Maria. Although he accepted the PETITION OF RIGHT, Charles' insistence on the "divine right of kings" provoked further conflict with Parliament, and led him to rule without it for 11 years (1629–40). With the support of the archbishop of Canterbury, William LAUD, Charles enforced harsh penalties on nonconformists. When attempts to impose Anglican liturgy on Scotland led to the Bishops' War, Charles was obliged to recall Parliament to raise revenue. The LONG PARLIAMENT insisted on imposing conditions, and impeached Charles' adviser, the Earl of STRAFFORD. In 1641 it presented the GRAND REMONSTRANCE. Relations steadily worsened, and Charles' attempt to arrest five leading opponents (including John PYM and John HAMPDEN) in the Commons precipitated the English CIVIL WAR. After the defeat of the Royalists, attempts by Oliver CROMWELL and other parliamentary and army leaders to reach a compromise with the king failed, and he was tried and executed. *See also* PRIDE'S PURGE; VANE, SIR HENRY

Charles II (1630–85) King of England, Scotland and Ireland (1660–85). After the execution of his father, CHARLES I, he fled to France but in 1650 was invited to Scotland by the COVENANTERS and crowned king in 1651.

Charles' attempted invasion of England was repulsed by Oliver CROMWELL, and he was forced back into exile. In 1660, Charles issued the Declaration of Breda, in which he promised religious toleration and an amnesty for his enemies. Parliament agreed to the Declaration, and Charles was crowned king in May 1660, ushering in the RESTORATION. He attempted to preserve royal power, accepting secret subsidies from the French king LOUIS XIV in exchange for promoting Roman Catholicism. Charles' support of Louis led to a renewal of the DUTCH WARS (1672–74). He clashed with Parliament over both the war and his support of the Catholics. Conflict was further fuelled by strong anti-Catholic feeling, manifest in the "Popish Plot" rumour spread by Titus OATES and the Exclusion Crisis (1679–81), when attempts were made to exclude Charles' brother, the Catholic Duke of York (later JAMES II), from the succession. Unable to resolve his differences with Parliament, Charles dissolved it and ruled with financial support from Louis XIV. Known as the Merry Monarch, Charles had many mistresses (including Nell Gwyn) but left no legitimate heir.

Charles V (the Wise) (1337–80) King of France (1364–80). He regained most of the territory lost to the English in the HUNDRED YEARS' WAR. Charles strengthened royal authority by introducing a regular taxation system, standing army and powerful navy. He established a royal library, encouraged literature and art, and built the BASTILLE. He was succeeded by his son, CHARLES VI.

Charles VI (the Mad) (1368–1422) King of France (1380–1422). Until 1388 he was controlled by his uncle, Philip the Bold of Burgundy. After ruling for four years, Charles suffered recurrent bouts of insanity. Philip and Louis d'Orléans, the king's brother, fought for control of the kingdom. Louis was murdered in 1407, and Philip allied himself with Henry V of England. English victories at Agincourt (1415) and elsewhere forced Charles to sign the Treaty of Troyes (1420), acknowledging Henry as his successor.

Charles VII (1403–61) King of France (1422–61). The son of CHARLES VI, he was excluded from the throne by the Treaty of Troyes (1420). When his father died, Charles controlled lands s of the River Loire, while the N remained in English hands. With the support of JOAN OF ARC, he checked the English at Orléans and was crowned king at Reims (1429). The Treaty of Arras (1435) ended the hostility of Burgundy and, by 1453, the English were driven out of most of France.

Charles VIII (1470–98) King of France (1483–98). He succeeded his father, Louis XI, and until 1491 was controlled by his sister Anne de Beaujeu and her husband. Charles invaded Italy in 1494, beginning the ITALIAN WARS, and in 1495 he entered Naples. A league of Italian states, the papacy and Spain forced him to retreat. One positive result was the introduction of Italian Renaissance culture into France. He was succeeded by his cousin, LOUIS XII.

Charles IX (1550–74) King of France (1560–74). At ten years of age, Charles succeeded his brother FRANCIS II, and his mother CATHERINE DE' MEDICI acted as regent. Her authority waned when, in 1571, the young king fell under the influence of Gaspard de COLIGNY, leader of the HUGUENOTS. Coligny and thousands of his followers were slain in the SAINT BARTHOLOMEW'S DAY MASSACRE (1572), ordered by Charles at the instigation of his mother. He was succeeded by his brother, HENRY III.

Charles X (1757–1836) King of France (1824–30), brother of LOUIS XVI and LOUIS XVIII. He fled France at the outbreak of the FRENCH REVOLUTION (1789) and remained in England until the BOURBON restoration (1814). Charles opposed the moderate policies of LOUIS XVIII. After the assassination of his son in 1820, his reactionary forces triumphed. In 1825, he signed a law indemnifying émigrés for land confiscated during the Revolution. In 1830, Charles issued the July Ordinance, which restricted suffrage and press freedom, and dissolved the newly elected chamber of deputies. The people rebelled, and Charles was forced to abdicate.

Charles III (1716–88) King of Spain (1759–88) and of Naples and Sicily (1735–59), son of Philip V and Elizabeth Farnese. Charles conquered Naples and Sicily in 1734, and inherited the Spanish crown in 1759 from his half-brother Ferdinand VI. He handed Naples and Sicily to his son, Ferdinand. Charles was a highly competent ruler. He encouraged commercial and agrarian reform, and brought the Spanish Catholic Church under state control, expelling the Jesuits in 1767. Allied with France in the SEVEN YEARS' WAR, he received Louisiana in 1763. He was succeeded by his son, CHARLES IV.

Charles IV (1748–1819) King of Spain (1788–1808), son and successor of CHARLES III. Unable to cope with the upheavals of NAPOLEON I, Charles virtually turned over government to his wife, Maria Luisa, and her lover, Manuel de Godoy. Spain was occupied by French troops in the PENINSULAR WAR. He was forced to abdicate in favour of his son, Ferdinand VII, who in turn was forced from the throne by Napoleon.

Charles IX (1550–1611) King of Sweden (1604–11), youngest son of Gustav I. He opposed his brother, John III's, Catholicism. At John's death, Charles became regent (1599–1604) and established Lutheranism. John's son, SIGISMUND III, king of Poland, claimed the throne but was deposed by Charles. Sigismund launched an abortive invasion (1598). In 1600, Charles invaded Livonia, starting the 60-year conflict with Poland. He also embarked on the disastrous Kalmar War (1611–13) with Denmark.

Charles X (1622–60) King of Sweden (1654–60). Charles ascended the throne when his cousin, Queen Christina, abdicated. His efforts to dominate the Baltic resulted in a reign of continuous military activity. Charles invaded Poland unsuccessfully and twice invaded Denmark. He established the natural frontiers in Scandinavia, recovering the s provinces of Sweden from Denmark. He was succeeded by his son, CHARLES XI.

Charles XI (1655–97) King of Sweden (1660–97), son and successor of CHARLES X. A council of regency ruled until he reached his majority (1672). As part of his restriction of the nobility, Charles restored lands to the crown. He led Sweden in the third of the DUTCH WARS. Charles lost (1675) Swedish Pomerania to FREDERICK WILLIAM of Brandenburg. Scandinavia was unified by the Peace of Lund (1679) and Charles' marriage to Princess Ulrika of Denmark. His son succeeded him as CHARLES XII.

Charles XII (1682–1718) King of Sweden (1697–1718), son and successor of CHARLES XI. He was one of the greatest military leaders in European history. Charles defeated Denmark, Poland, Saxony and Russia in a series of brilliant campaigns. Leading the battle, he destroyed the army of PETER I (THE GREAT) at Narva (1700). In 1708 Charles renewed his assault on Russia, but his army, depleted by the severe winter, was decisively defeated at Poltava (1709). He fled to the Ottomans and persuaded the sultan to attack Russia (1711). The sultan turned against him and, in disguise, Charles escaped back to Sweden and devoted his energies to the domestic economy. He was killed while fighting in Norway and was succeeded by his sister, Ulrika Eleanora.

Charles XIV (1763–1844) (Jean Baptiste Bernadotte) King of Sweden and Norway (1818–44), b. France. He fought in the French Revolution and in the Battle of AUSTERLITZ. In effective control of Sweden from 1810, he joined the Allies against Napoleon at the Battle of Leipzig (1814) and forced Denmark to cede Norway to Sweden in the Treaty of Kiel (1814). Charles' subsequent reign brought peace and prosperity to Sweden, and he founded the present Swedish dynasty.

Charles (Prince of Wales) (1948–) Eldest son of ELIZABETH II and heir to the British throne. In 1969, he was invested as the Prince of Wales at Caernarvon. In 1981, Charles married Lady DIANA Spencer. The fairytale marriage rapidly and publicly disintegrated. Their eldest son, Prince William (1982–), is second in line to the throne. Charles is well-known for his work with charities, such as the Prince's Trust, and his advocacy of COMMUNITY ARCHITECTURE.

Charles Edward Stuart *See* STUART, CHARLES EDWARD

Charles, Jacques Alexandre César (1746–1823) French physicist, inventor and mathematician who was the first to use a hydrogen balloon. He discovered the law relating the expansion of a gas to its temperature rise. Joseph GAY-LUSSAC published this work some 15 years after Charles' discovery, and it is alternately known as CHARLES' LAW or Gay-Lussac's law. Charles is credited with inventing a thermometric hydrometer.

Charles, Ray (1930–) US singer and pianist. Blind since the age of six, Charles' fusion of gospel harmonies, jazz instrumentation, and blues lyrics have proved successful since his first hit, "I Got A Woman," (1955). Other standards include "Georgia on My Mind" (1960).

Charles' law Volume of a gas at constant pressure is directly proportional to its absolute temperature. As temperature increases, the volume of a gas also increases at a constant pressure. The relationship was discovered by a French scientist Jacques Charles in 1787. The law is a special case of the IDEAL GAS LAW. It is sometimes called Gay-Lussac's law, because Joseph GAY-LUSSAC established it more accurately in 1802.

Charles Martel (688–741) Frankish ruler, grandfather of CHARLEMAGNE. Charles seized power in a palace coup in Austrasia and reconquered Aquitaine, Neustria, Burgundy and Provence, and established the FRANKS as the rulers of Gaul. He defeated the Moors at the battle of Tours (732–33). His son, PEPIN III (THE SHORT), succeeded him.

Charleston Capital of West Virginia, W central West Virginia, USA, at the confluence of the Elk and Kanawha rivers; seat of Kanawha county. Founded in 1788, the city grew around Fort Lee, home of Daniel BOONE, and was incorporated in 1794. Industries: chemicals, glass, metal, timber, oil, coal. Pop. (1990) 57,287.

Charleston City and port in SE South Carolina, USA. Founded in the 1670s by William Sayle, it became the major SE seaport. The South Carolina Ordinance of Secession was signed here (1860), and the firing on Fort SUMTER was the first engagement of the American Civil War. It has many colonial buildings and the Fort Sumter National Monument. It is the site of a major naval base. Industries: paper, textiles, chemicals. Pop. (1990) 80,414.

Charlton, Sir Bobby (Robert) (1937–) English footballer. He played for Manchester United and was voted European Footballer of the Year (1966). Charlton was a member of England's World Cup winning team. He won 106 international caps, scoring an English record of 49 goals. On retiring, Bobby pursued a career in football administration, and became a director of Manchester

United. His elder brother, **Jack** (1935–), also a member of England's World Cup winning squad, went into club management and led the Republic of Ireland national team to remarkable success before retiring in 1996.

Charon In Greek mythology, boatman of the Lower World who ferried the souls of the dead across the STYX to HADES.

Charpentier, Gustave (1860–1956) French composer, taught by MASSENET. His best-known compositions are the operas *Louise* (1900) and *Julien* (1913) and the orchestral *Impressions d'Italie*.

Chartism (1838–48) British working-class movement for political reform. Combining the discontent of industrial workers with the demands of radical artisans, the movement adhered to the People's Charter (1838), which demanded electoral reform including universal male suffrage. As well as local riots and strikes, the Chartists organized mass petitions (1839, 1842, 1848). The movement faded away after a major demonstration in 1848.

Chartres Town on the River Eure, NW France; capital of Eure-et-Loire department. The stained glass and sculptures in the 12th–13th century gothic Cathedral of Notre Dame make it one of Europe's finest cathedrals. It is a world heritage site. Industries: brewing, leather, agricultural equipment. Pop. (1990) 41,850.

Charybdis In Greek mythology, a female monster of the Straits of Messina. Daughter of Poseidon and Gaia, Zeus hurled her into the sea for stealing Heracles' cattle. A whirlpool formed where she lay.

Chase, Salmon Portland (1808–73) Chief justice of the US Supreme Court (1864–73). Known as the defender of fugitive slaves, he was appointed chief justice by President LINCOLN. Chase presided (1868) over the Senate impeachment proceedings against President Andrew JOHNSON. His dissenting opinion in the Slaughterhouse Cases (1873) became a standard court judgement on the restrictive clause of the 14th Amendment.

chat Any of several birds of the WARBLER group. Chats include the North American yellow-breasted chat (*Icteria virens*) and the red-breasted chat (*Granatellus venustus*) of Central America. It also refers to some European thrushes and Australian wrens.

château (Fr. CASTLE) Term used in France since the 15th century to designate a large country house. Lightly fortified, luxurious country houses, such as the châteaux of Amboise, Blois, Chambord and Chenonceaux, mark the transition between medieval fortress and mansion.

Chateaubriand, François René, Vicomte de (1768–1848) French writer and diplomat whose works contributed to French ROMANTICISM. *The Genius of Christianity* (1802) was a reaction to ENLIGHTENMENT attacks on Catholicism and established his literary reputation. *Atala* (1801) and *René* (1805) are tragic love stories set in the American wilderness. After 1803, Chateaubriand held important diplomatic posts for both Napoleon and the Bourbons and was minister of foreign affairs (1823–24).

Chattanooga City on the Tennessee River, SE Tennessee, USA. Founded as a trading post in the early 19th century, it was an important strategic center in the Civil War. Since 1935 it has been the headquarters of the Tennessee Valley Authority (TVA). Industries: iron and steel, synthetic fibres, tourism. Pop. (1996) 150,000.

Chatterton, Thomas (1752–70) English poet and forger of antiquities. He achieved posthumous fame for poems such as "Bristowe Tragedie" and "Mynstrelles Songe", supposedly composed by Thomas Rowley, an imaginary 15th-century monk. Chatterton's early suicide established him as a hero of the Romantic movement.

Chatterji, Bankim Chandra (1838–94) Indian novelist. His Bengali prose style and theme of India as a divine motherland became the model for nationalist literature. Chatterji's popular novel *Anandamath* (1882) includes the Indian national anthem, "Bandemataram".

Chatwin, Bruce (1940–89) English travel writer and novelist. Chatwin's first book, *In Patagonia* (1977), redefined the art of travel writing with its blend of autobiography, anthropology, history and fiction. Chatwin's best-known work, *Songlines* (1987), outlines his theories on nomadism, and investigates the psychic mapping traditions of the Native Australians. Other books include *The Viceroy of Ouidah* (1980) and *On the Black Hill* (1983).

Chaucer, Geoffrey (1346–1400) English medieval poet. His writings are remarkable for their range, narrative sense, power of characterization and humour. They include *The Book of the Duchess* (1369), *The Parliament of Fowls* and *Troilus and Criseyde* (both *c.*1385). Chaucer's most famous and popular work is *The Canterbury Tales* (*c.*1387–1400), an extraordinarily varied collection of narrative poems, each told by one of a group of pilgrims while travelling to the shrine of Thomas á BECKET. Ranging from the courtly "Knight's Tale" to the bawdy "Miller's Tale", they provide a panoramic view of 14th-century English society and are a landmark in medieval fiction. Chaucer's writings exercised a powerful influence on the future direction of ENGLISH LITERATURE.

Chausson, Ernest Amédée (1855–99) French composer. Chausson studied with Massenet at the Paris Conservatoire. The development of his style can be traced from the symphonic poem *Viviane* (1882) to the elaborate opera *Le roi Arthus* (1886–95). Chausson is best known for his Symphony in B♭ (*c.*1890) and the melancholic *Poème* (1896) for violin and orchestra.

Chávez, Cesar Estrada (1927–93) US labour leader. Born of Mexican-American parents, he migrated to California as a field worker. In 1962, Chávez founded the National Farm Workers Association (NFWA), which in 1966 merged with the Agricultural Workers Organizing Committee of the AFL-CIO, to become the United Farm Workers Organizing Committee. In 1968–70, he led a successful national boycott of California grapes.

Chechenia (formerly Checheno-Ingush Republic) Republic of the Russian Federation, in the N Caucasus; the capital is GROZNY. The region's chief rivers are the Terek and Sunzha, whose valleys are the main source of agricultural products. Chechens, who are Sunni Muslims, constitute 50% of the population, and 40% live in urban areas. Grozny oil field is a major source of Russian oil. The Chechens fiercely resisted tsarist Russia's conquest of the Caucasus, even after absorption in 1859. In the 1920s separate autonomous regions were created by the Soviet Union for the Chechen and Ingush peoples. In 1934 the two were united to form a single region which, in 1936, became the Checheno-Ingush Autonomous Republic. The republic was dissolved in 1943–44 because of alleged collaboration with the German occupying forces in World War 2. The region was reconstituted in 1957. In 1991, the Checheno-Ingush Republic split in two, and General Dudayev was elected president of Chechenya. In 1994, following a period of bloody internal strife, Russia invaded but met fierce resistance. In 1995, Russian troops completed the capture of Grozny at the cost of *c.*25,000 civilian lives. This lead to a protracted guerrilla war. In 1999, Russians launched a second attack on Chechenia, attempting to crush the resistance of Chechen rebels. Industries: oil refining, chemicals. Area: 19,301sq km (7,452sq mi). Pop. (1992) 1,308,000.

cheese Food made by curdling MILK and then processing the curd. The commonest source is cows' milk. Blue cheeses are pierced in order to channel air to a reactive fungus previously introduced. The simplest product is cottage cheese, formed when skimmed milk coagulates.

cheetah Spotted, large CAT found in hot, arid areas of Africa, the Middle East and India. A long-legged animal with blunt, non-retractable claws, it has a tawny brown coat with round black spots. Capable of running at more than 95km/h (60mph), it hunts gazelles and antelopes by sight. Length: body: 140–150cm (55–60in); tail: 75–80cm (30–32in); weight: 60kg (132lb). Family Felidae; subfamily Acinonchinae; species *Acinonyx jubatus*.

Cheever, John (1912–82) US short-story writer and novelist. His works satirize the morals of American suburban life. Cheever's novel *The Wapshot Chronicle* (1957) won a National Book award. Its sequel was *The Wapshot Scandal* (1964). His short-story collection *The Stories of John Cheever* (1978) won a Pulitzer Prize.

Cheka First secret police force in the Soviet Union. Formed shortly after the Russian Revolution (1917). A ferocious reign of terror alienated many Bolshevik organizations and it was disbanded in 1922, replaced first by the GPU and then by the KGB.

Chekhov, Anton Pavlovich (1860–1904) Russian dramatist, who worked closely with Konstantin STANISLAVSKY at the MOSCOW ART THEATRE. His major plays, *The Seagull* (1896), *Uncle Vanya* (1897), *The Three Sisters* (1901) and *The Cherry Orchard* (1904), reveal a deep awareness of human nature and a fine blend of comedy and tragedy. They are detailed portraits of provincial life. Characters often reveal as much by what they leave unsaid as the subtleties of the dialogue itself.

chemical bond Mechanism that holds together atoms to form molecules. There are several types which arise either from the attraction of unlike charges or from the formation of stable configurations through electron-sharing. The number of bonds an atom can form depends upon its valency. The main types are IONIC, COVALENT, metallic and hydrogen bonds. *See also* VALENCE

chemical engineering Application of engineering principles to the making of chemical products on an industrial scale. Unit processes of chemical engineering include OXIDATION-REDUCTION, hydrogenation, nitration and sulphonation, ELECTROLYSIS, polymerization, ion exchange and FERMENTATION.

chemical equation Set of symbols used to represent a CHEMICAL REACTION. Equations show how atoms are rearranged by a reaction, with reactants on the left-hand side and products on the right-hand side. For example, the formation of magnesium oxide when magnesium burns in oxygen is represented by $2Mg + O_2 \rightarrow 2MgO$. The number of atoms of an element on the left-hand side of an equation must equal the number on the right.

chemical equilibrium Balance in a REVERSIBLE REACTION, when two opposing reactions proceed at constant equal rates with no net change in the system. The initial rate of the reactions falls off as the concentrations of reactants decrease and the build-up of products causes the rate of the reverse reaction to increase.

chemical reaction Change or process in which chemical substances convert into other substances. This involves the breaking and formation of CHEMICAL BONDS. Reaction mechanisms include ENDOTHERMIC, EXOTHERMIC, ADDITION, CONDENSATION, combination (formation of a COMPOUND), DECOMPOSITION and OXIDATION-REDUCTION reaction.

chemical warfare Use of chemical weapons such as poison and nerve gases, defoliants and HERBICIDES. Poison gas and mustard gas was used in World War 1. Chemical weapons were not used in World War 2, but the Germans developed a nerve gas. A defoliant, Agent Orange, was employed by the US in the Vietnam War. Although the use of chemical and biological weapons is prohibited by the Geneva Convention (1925), their production, possession and exchange are not. In 1990, the US and Soviet Union agreed to reduce their stockpiles of chemical weapons by 80%. In the 1980s, Iraq used chemical weapons in both the Iran-Iraq War and against the Kurds in N Iraq. Although Allied troops were heavily protected against the threat of chemical weapons during the Gulf War, Saddam Hussein did not resort to chemical warfare. *See also* BIOLOGICAL WARFARE

chemistry Branch of science concerned with the properties, structure and composition of substances and their reactions with one another. Today, chemistry forms a vast body of knowledge with a number of subdivisions; the major division is between organic and inorganic. **Inorganic** chemistry studies the preparation, properties and reactions of all chemical elements and their COMPOUNDS, except most of CARBON. The historic separation from organic chemistry is a false one, since many "inorganic" compounds are found in living organisms, such as common salt (NaCl) in human blood. In education and industry, however, the distinction is frequently still made. **Organic** chemistry studies the reactions of carbon compounds. Organic compounds are *c*.100 times more numerous than nonorganic ones. Organic chemistry also

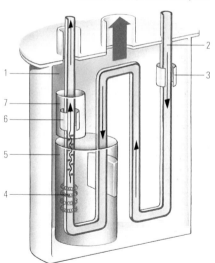

▲ **chemical reaction** Calorimeters measure the amount of heat absorbed or released during a chemical reaction. In a high-pressure flow calorimeter, the apparatus is contained in a vacuum (1) for insulation. A constant flow of liquid or gas enters the calorimeter (2). A platinum resistance thermometer (3) measures the temperature of the substance on entry. A heater (4) puts a known amount of energy into the liquid or gas inside a radiation shield (5) that further lessens any dispersion of energy. The change in temperature is measured by a second thermometer (6) again shielded (7).

studies an immense variety of molecules, including those of industrial compounds such as plastics, rubbers, dyes, drugs and solvents. **Analytical** chemistry deals with the composition of substances. PHYSICAL CHEMISTRY deals with the physical properties of substances, such as their boiling and melting points. Its subdivisions include ELECTROCHEMISTRY, thermochemistry and chemical KINETICS.

Chemnitz (formerly Karl-Marx-Stadt) City on the River Chemnitz, Saxony, SE Germany. Chartered in 1143, Chemnitz's linen trade was devastated by the Thirty Years' War. Recovery followed the opening of cotton mills in the late 17th century. Chemnitz is one of the most heavily polluted cities in Europe. Industries: machine tools, chemicals, textiles, electronics. Pop. (1995) 274,000.

chemoreceptor Tiny region on the outer membrane of some biological cells that is sensitive to chemical stimuli. The chemoreceptor transforms a stimulus from an external molecule into a sensation, such as smell or taste.

chemotherapy Treatment of a disease (usually CANCER) by a combination of chemical substances, or drugs, that kill or impair disease-producing cells or organisms in the body. Specific drug treatment was first introduced in the early 1900s by Paul EHRLICH.

Chénier, André Marie de (1762–94) French poet, b. Turkey. Chénier was secretary (1787–90) to the French ambassador in London but returned to Paris during the French Revolution. Outspoken against Jacobin excesses, he was guillotined. Chénier's poetry, such as *La Jeune Captive* (1795), is both moving and classically precise.

Chennai (formerly Madras) City in SE India, on the Bay of Bengal; capital of Tamil Nadu state. India's second-largest port and fourth-largest city, Chennai was founded in 1639 as a British trading post. As Fort St. George, it became the seat of the EAST INDIA COMPANY and rapidly developed as a commercial centre. It was occupied by the French in 1746, but returned to Britain in 1748. The harbour was constructed in the second half of the 19th century. Industries: textiles, Tamil films, railroad stock, transport equipment. Pop. (1991) 3,841,396.

Chernenko, Konstantin Ustinovich (1911–85) Soviet statesman, president (1984–85). A close ally of Leonid BREZHNEV, he joined the Politburo in 1978. Chernenko succeeded Yuri ANDROPOV as president and general secretary of the Communist Party of the Soviet Union (CPSU). He died after only 13 months in office and was succeeded by Mikhail GORBACHEV.

Chernobyl (Ukrainian, Chornobyl) City on the River Pripyat, N central Ukraine. It is 20km (12mi) from the Chernobyl power plant. On 26 April 1986 an explosion in one of the plant's reactors released 8 tons of radioactive material into the atmosphere. Within the first few hours 31 people died. Fallout spread across E and N Europe, contaminating much agricultural produce.

Containment efforts began with the evacuation of more than 100,000 people from the vicinity of the plant. The reactor was encased in cement and boron. About 25,000 local inhabitants have died prematurely. Two of the three remaining reactors were reworking by the end of 1986. In 1991, Ukraine pledged to shut down the plant, but energy needs dictated its continued output. In 1994, the West pledged economic aid to ensure the plant's closure and it was eventually shut down in 2000.

Chernomyrdin, Viktor (1938–) Russian statesman, prime minister (1992–98). A member (1986–90) of the Central Committee of the Communist Party of the Soviet Union (CPSU), he became prime minister despite the objections of Boris YELTSIN. He broadly supported economic reform but was critical of the pace of privatization. Yeltsin's illness meant that Chernomyrdin acted as caretaker-president throughout much of 1996–97.

Cherokee Largest tribe of Native Americans in the US, member of the Iroquoian language family. The Cherokee migrated S into the Appalachian region of Tennessee, Georgia and the Carolinas. They sided with the British during the American Revolution. When gold was discovered on their land in Georgia in the 1830s, they were forced to move W. This tragic "Trail of Tears" (1838) reduced the population by 25%. One of the Five Civilized Tribes, *c.*47,000 Cherokee descendants now live in Oklahoma and *c.*3,000 in North Carolina.

cherry Widely grown fruit tree of temperate regions, probably native to W Asia and E Europe. Various types are grown for their fruit – round yellow, red or almost black with a round stone. The wood is used in furniture. Height: to 30m (100ft). Family Rosaceae; genus *Prunus*; there are about 50 species.

Cherubini, Luigi Carlo Zenobio Salvatore Maria (1760–1842) Italian composer. He lived in Paris from 1786, and his operas *Lodoïska* (1791) and *Médée* (1797) were rapturously received. In 1822 Cherubini became director of the Paris Conservatoire. His church music includes the C Minor Requiem (1816), and *Cours de contrepoint et de fugue* (1835) is a standard textbook.

chervil Annual herb of the PARSLEY family, native to Eurasia; it is cultivated for its aromatic leaves, used for food flavouring. Height: to 61cm (24in). Family Apiaceae/Umbelliferae; species *Anthriscus cerefolium*.

Chesapeake Bay Inlet of the Atlantic Ocean between Virginia (S) and Maryland (N), USA, at the mouth of the Susquehanna River. Linked to the Delaware River by the Chesapeake and Delaware Canal, it has the world's longest bridge-tunnel system, the Chesapeake Bay Bridge-Tunnel, 29km- (18mi-) long. The first permanent English settlement in North America was on Chesapeake Bay, at Jamestown, Virginia (1607). Length: *c.*320km (200mi). Width: 5–50km (3–30mi).

Cheshire County in NW England, bounded W by Wales and N by Greater Manchester and Merseyside. The county town is CHESTER. Cheshire is drained by the Mersey, Weaver and Dee rivers. It is an important industrial and dairy farming region, noted for its cheese. Industries: salt mining, chemicals, textiles, motor vehicles, oil refining. Area: 2,331sq km (900sq mi). Pop. (1991) 956,616.

chess Game of strategic attack and defence, played on a 64-square checkered board. Two players start with 16 pieces each, white or black, set out along the outer two ranks (rows) of the board. With a black square in the left corner, white's pieces are set out: rook (castle), knight, bishop, queen, king, bishop, knight, rook. Black's pieces align directly opposite. Pawns stand on the second rank. White takes first move, and players move alternately on

▲ **chestnut** Sweet chestnuts may be roasted, boiled, or ground into flour. The best-quality chestnuts grow in Italy. The wood is extremely durable. The American chestnut (*Castanea dentata*) is extinct.

either rank (horizontal), file (vertical), or diagonal, until the king is captured (checkmate). Chess originated in ancient India. Extant references date the game back to the 6th century AD. Modern chess is a high-profile, international game. Since 1948, all male world champion grandmasters (except Bobby Fisher from the USA) have come from Russia or the former Soviet Union.

Chester City and county district on the River Dee, NW England, Cheshire. A Roman garrison town, Chester was a major port until the Dee became silted and Liverpool's port facilities were expanded. Notable buildings include the city wall, a Roman amphitheatre and a medieval cathedral. Industries: tourism, engineering. Area: 448sq km (173sq mi). Pop. (1991) 115,971.

Chesterton, G.K. (Gilbert Keith) (1874–1936) English essayist, novelist, biographer and poet. Best-known for his *Father Brown* stories, which began in 1911, Chesterton also wrote literary criticism and essays. His novels include *The Napoleon of Notting Hill* (1904) and *The Man who was Thursday* (1908). In 1922, he converted to Catholicism, and went on to write the lives of *St Francis of Assisi* (1923) and *St Thomas Aquinas* (1933).

chestnut Deciduous tree native to temperate areas of the Northern Hemisphere. It has lance-shaped leaves and furrowed bark. Male flowers hang in long catkins; females are solitary or clustered at the base of catkins. The prickly husked fruits open to reveal two or three edible nuts. Family Fagaceae; genus *Castanea*; there are four species. *See also* HORSE CHESTNUT

Chevalier, Maurice (1888–1972) French singer and actor. Chevalier danced (1909–13) with the Folies Bergères before making his London debut in *Hullo, America* (1919). His trademark appearance as the debonair *bon viveur* with a straw hat and cane wooed music hall audiences for more than 30 years. Early Hollywood films include *The Merry Widow* (1934). During the 1950s, he made a comeback, appearing in films such as *Love in the Afternoon* (1957) and *Gigi* (1958).

Cheviot Hills Range of hills running 56km (35mi) along the England-Scotland border. Sheep farming is the chief occupation. Since 1945 much of it has been reforested and it is now a National Park area. The highest point is The Cheviot in Northumberland, at 816m (2,676ft).

chewing gum Confection originally made from chicle, a gummy latex exuded from the Central American sapodilla tree. Chewed but never swallowed, it is now usually made from synthetic substances. It was first patented (1869) in the US.

Cheyenne Native North-American tribe. Tribal competition forced them to migrate w from Minnesota along the Cheyenne River. The tribe split (*c*.1830), with the Northern Cheyenne remaining near the Platte River and the Southern Cheyenne settling near the Arkansas River. Following the Colorado Gold Rush (1858), they were restricted to a reservation. War broke out following a US army massacre at Cheyenne (1864). Colonel George CUSTER crushed the Southern Cheyenne, but the Northern Cheyenne helped in his eventual defeat at LITTLE BIGHORN. In 1877, the Cheyenne surrendered and were forced to move to Montana, where *c*.2,000 remain.

Cheyenne State capital of Wyoming and county seat of Laramie County. Founded (1867) as a centre for transporting goods and livestock by railway, it became famous for its connections with figures such as BUFFALO BILL, CALAMITY JANE and Wild Bill Hickok. Industries: packing plants, oil refineries. Pop. (1990) 50,008.

Chiang Ching-kuo (1909–88) Taiwanese statesman, president (1978–88). The eldest son of CHIANG KAI-

SHEK, Chiang rose rapidly through the ranks of the KUOMINTANG. He was minister of defence (1965–72) and premier (1972–78) before becoming president. Chiang began the process of democratization in Taiwan

Chiang Kai-shek (1887–1975) (Jiang Jieshi) Chinese nationalist leader. After taking part in resistance against the QING dynasty, he joined the KUOMINTANG, succeeding SUN YAT-SEN as leader (1925). From 1927, he purged the party of communists and headed a nationalist government in Nanking. During World War 2, with US support, Chiang led the fight against Japan. Civil war resumed in 1945. Chiang was elected president of China (1948), but in 1949 the communists led by MAO ZEDONG drove his government into exile in TAIWAN. Here, Chiang established a dictatorship and maintained that the Kuomintang were the legitimate Chinese government. He remained president of Taiwan until his death.

Chiangmai City in NW Thailand. Founded in the 13th century, it is the commercial, cultural and religious centre of N Thailand. It has air, rail and road links with BANGKOK and is an export point for local produce. Industries: handicrafts, silk. Pop. (1993) 170,000.

chiaroscuro Term for the opposition of light and dark in painting and drawing. CARAVAGGIO and REMBRANDT were masters of the dramatic use of chiaroscuro.

Chiba City and port on Tokyo Bay, central Honshu, Japan; capital of Chiba prefecture. It has an 8th-century Buddhist temple. Industries: textiles, paper. Pop. (1995) 857,000.

Chibcha (Muisca) Late prehistoric culture in South America. Bogotá and Tunja were the main centres. Chibcha culture flourished between 1000 and 1541, and rivalled the INCA. The population (*c*.750,000) developed city-states and excelled in craftwork. The people were conquered by the Spanish (1536–41). Today, Chibcha refers to a Native American language family, whose speakers inhabit S Panama and N Colombia.

Chicago City on the SW shore of Lake Michigan, NE Illinois, USA. In the late 18th century, it was a trading post and became Fort Dearborn military post (1803). With the construction of the Erie Canal and railroads, and the opening up of the prairies, Chicago attracted settlers and industry. Large areas of the city were destroyed by fire in 1871. It became a noted cultural centre in the late 19th century, including the establishment of the Chicago Symphony Orchestra (1891) and several literary magazines. Chicago is the major industrial, commercial, cultural and shipping centre of the Midwest. It has many colleges and universities, the largest rail terminal in the world, and the world's busiest airport, O'Hare. Chicago is renowned for its architecture. The world's first SKYSCRAPER was built here in 1885 and, until 1996, the Sears Tower was the world's tallest building, at 443m (1,454ft). Industries: steel, chemicals, machinery, food processing, metal working. Pop. (1992 est.) 2,833,000.

Chichén Itzá Chief city and shrine of MAYA and TOLTEC peoples between the 9th and 13th centuries AD, in YUCATÁN, Mexico. The earlier Maya city was abandoned *c*.900. The new Toltec city was built *c*.1.5km (1mi) away. Remains include temple-pyramids, a court for ball games and a sacrificial well. In *c*.1200, Chichén Itzá lost its pre-eminence to nearby Mayapan.

Chichester, Sir Francis Charles (1901–72) English yachtsman and aviator. He made a solo flight between England and Australia in a Gypsy Moth biplane (1929). He began ocean sailing in the 1950s and won his first solo transatlantic race in 1960. In *Gypsy Moth IV*, Chichester circumnavigated the globe single-handed (1966–67).

Chichester County town of West Sussex, s England. It is a market centre for the surrounding agricultural region and has a sheltered harbour. There are Roman remains, a Norman cathedral and a modern theatre. An annual drama festival is held here. Pop. (1991) 26,572.

chicken *See* POULTRY

chickenpox (varicella) Infectious disease of childhood caused by a virus of the HERPES group. After an incubation period of two to three weeks, a fever develops and red spots (which later develop into blisters) appear. Recovery is usually within a week, although the possibility of contagion remains until the last scab has been shed.

chick-pea (dwarf pea, garbanzo, chich or gram) Bushy annual plant cultivated since antiquity in s Europe and Asia for its pea-like seeds. It is now also grown widely in the Western Hemisphere. Family Fabaceae/Leguminosae; species *Cicer arietinum*.

chicory Perennial weedy plant whose leaves are cooked and eaten or served raw in salads. The fleshy roots are dried and ground for mixing with (or a substitute for) COFFEE. Chicory has bright blue, daisy-like flowers. Height: 1.5m (5ft). Family Asteraceae/Compositae; species *Chichorium intybus*.

chiffchaff Greenish-brown warbler, named after its distinctive two-note call. It hunts insects in trees, and nests near the ground. Length: 11cm (4.5in). Family Sylviidae; species *Phylloscopus collybita*.

Chifley, Joseph Benedict (1885–1951) Australian statesman, prime minister (1945–49). In 1928 he entered parliament as a Labor member. He served as defence minister (1929–31) and federal treasurer (1941–45), before succeeding John Curtin as prime minister. He continued a policy of nationalization and expanded social services.

chigger (harvest mite or red bug) Tiny red larva of some kinds of MITES. Adults lay eggs on plants, and hatched larvae find an animal host. On humans, chigger bites cause a severe rash and itching. Length: 0.1–16mm (0.004–0.6in). Order Acarina; family Trombiculidae.

Chihuahua Largest state in Mexico, on the N Mexican plateau. The climate and terrain vary from cool mountains (W) to arid desert (E). The state capital, Chihuahua, has a Spanish colonial cathedral. Industries: mining, forestry, tourism, cotton. Area: 247,086sq km (95,400sq mi). Pop. (state, 1990) 2,441,873; (city, 1990) 530,783.

chihuahua Tiny dog (toy group), probably first bred in Central America. It has large, wide-set eyes and large, erect ears. The long, stickle-shaped tail is held in a loop over the back. There are two types of coat – short- and long-haired – which may be any colour. Average size: 12.7cm (5in) at the shoulder; weight: up to 2.7kg (6lb).

chilblain Painful inflammation of the skin caused by exposure to cold; usual areas are toes, fingers and ears. Violent itching develops in areas that are red and swollen; in severe cases, blisters or ulceration may develop.

child abuse Emotional and/or physical (often sexual) maltreatment of a child. Neglect is considered a form of abuse. Physical abuse may be apparent in bruising and lacerations, burns or scars. Sexual abuse is often concealed by the abused out of fear or guilt. Mental effects may result in remoteness or crudely violent outbursts.

childbirth *See* LABOUR

child psychology *See* DEVELOPMENTAL PSYCHOLOGY

Children's Crusade Name given to two 13th-century CRUSADES by children. French children were offered free transport from Marseilles to the Holy Land but were sold as slaves in North Africa. A group of German children bound for the Holy Land travelled to Italy, where the crusade floundered, many dying of starvation and disease.

Chile Republic in SW South America. Chile stretches *c*.4,260km (2,650mi) from N to S, while the maximum E–W distance is only *c*.430km (270mi). The high ANDES mountains form the country's E borders with Argentina and Bolivia. They include Ojos del Salado at 6,863m (22,516ft), the second-highest peak in South America. To the W are basins and valleys, with coastal uplands overlooking the shore. EASTER ISLAND lies 3,500km (2,200mi) off Chile's W coast. Western Chile contains three main land regions. In the N, is the sparsely populated ATACAMA DESERT, stretching *c*.1,600km (1,000mi) S from the Peruvian border. The Central Valley, which contains the capital, SANTIAGO, and the cities of VALPARAÍSO and Concepción, is by far the most densely populated region. In the S, the land has been heavily glaciated; the coastal uplands have been worn into islands, while the inland valleys are arms of the sea. In the far S, the Strait of MAGELLAN separates the Chilean mainland from the TIERRA DEL FUEGO. Punta Arenas is the world's southernmost city. **Climate** Chile's great N–S extent, ranging from the tropics in the N to 55°50′ S at Cape HORN, gives it a variety of climates. Santiago has a Mediterranean climate. Northern Chile has a desert climate, with many places entirely without rain. Southern Chile, by contrast, has a cool temperate climate with frequent storms. **Vegetation** The Atacama Desert is barren, except for some varieties of cactus and shrubs. Central Chile has mixed forests of beech and laurel, while the wet S is a region of thick forests, glaciers, scenic lakes and windswept, rocky slopes. Industrial growth has led to widespread deforestation. **History and Politics** ARAUCANICIANS reached the S tip of South America more than 8,000 years ago. In 1520, Ferdinand MAGELLAN became the first European to sight Chile. In 1541, Pedro de Valdivia founded Santiago. Chile became a Spanish colony. The Native Americans acted as bonded labour on colonial ranches. In 1817, an army, led by José de SAN MARTÍN, surprised the Spanish by crossing the Andes. In 1818, Bernardo O'HIGGINS proclaimed Chile's independence. His dictatorship was followed by democratic reforms. In the War of the Pacific (1879–84), Chile gained mineralrich areas from Peru and Bolivia. In the late 19th century, Chile's economy rapidly industrialized, but a succession of autocratic regimes and its dependence on nitrate exports hampered growth. In 1964, Eduardo FREI Montalvo of the Christian Democratic Party was elected. Frei embarked on a process of reform, such as assuming a majority share in the US-owned copper mines. In 1970, Salvador ALLENDE was elected president. He introduced many socialist policies, such as land reform and the nationalization of industries. In 1973, soaring inflation and public disturbances led to a military coup, with covert US backing. Allende and many of his supporters were executed. General Augusto PINOCHET assumed control and instigated a series of sweeping market reforms and pro-Western foreign-policy initiatives. In 1977, Pinochet banned all political parties. His regime was characterized by repression and human-rights violations. Many political opponents simply "disappeared". In 1981, a new constitution was introduced, and free elections were held in 1989. Patricio Aylwyn was elected president, but Pinochet remained important as commander of the armed

---

CHILE
AREA: 756,950sq km (292,258sq mi)
POPULATION: 15,272,000
CAPITAL (POPULATION): Santiago (5,077,000)

forces. In 1993, Eduardo Frei Ruiz-Tagle was elected president. During the 1990s, Chile's economy has improved and a process of social liberalization continues. Pinochet remained commander-in-chief until 1997, and tension between the government and the army continues. Pinochet is now facing charges of "crimes of genocide and terrorism" in Chile. In 2000, Ricardo Lagos became the first socialist president of Chile since Allende. **Economy** Chile is a lower-middle-income developing nation (1995 GDP per capita, $US9,520). It is the world's largest producer of copper ore, accounting for 22% of total world production in 1993. The most valuable activity is manufacturing, and the main products include iron, steel and wood products. Agriculture employs 18% of the workforce; the chief crop is wheat. Climate and landscape combine to make Chile dependent on imports for more than 50% of its food consumption. Yet, Chile's wine industry is expanding rapidly, and its fishing industry is the world's fifth largest. Chile's economy has become one of the strongest in Latin America.

chilli (chili) Hot, red PEPPER. It is an annual with oval leaves and white or greenish-white flowers that produce red or green seedpods. When dried, the pods are ground. Cayenne comes from the same plant. Height: 2–2.5m (6–8ft). Family Solanaceae; species *Capsicum annuum*.

chimaera (ratfish or ghost shark) One of *c*.28 species of cartilaginous, deep-sea fish with a long poisonous dorsal spine and a slender tail. Some species have an elongated snout. An oil derived from its liver is used as a lubricant in precision equipment. Length: 60cm–2m (23–80in). Families Chimaeridae, Collorhinchidae and Rhinochimaeridae. The term is also used in biology for an animal formed from several different embryos.

Chimera In Greek mythology, a female monster with a lion's head, goat's body and dragon's tail. She was the sister of Cerberus, HYDRA and the SPHINX, and was slain by Bellerophon.

chimpanzee Intelligent great APE of tropical Africa. Chimpanzees are mostly black and powerfully built. A smaller chimpanzee of the Congo is sometimes classified as a separate species. Chimpanzees often nest in trees but spend the day on the ground searching for fruit and nuts. The closest relative to man, they are communicative and highly social. Height: *c*.1.3m (4.5ft); weight: *c*.68kg (150lb). Family Pongidae. Species *Pan troglodytes* (Congo *Pan paniscus*). *See also* PRIMATE

Chimú Large, pre-Columbian state in N Peru. Its centre and capital was the great city of Chan Chan near modern Trujillo, with a population of more than 100,000 inhabitants. From AD 1200 to 1465, when it was conquered by the INCA, Chimú was the most important kingdom in South America. It is noted for its excellent craftwork.

Ch'in Alternative transliteration for the QIN dynasty

China Republic in E Asia. The People's Republic of China is the world's third largest country (after Russia and Canada). Most people live on the E coastal plains in the highlands or the fertile valleys of the rivers HUANG HE and YANGTZE, Asia's longest river, at 6,380km (3,960mi). Western China includes the bleak Tibetan plateau bounded by the HIMALAYAS (the world's highest mountain range). EVEREST, the world's highest peak, lies on the Nepal-TIBET border. Other ranges include the TIAN SHAN. China also has deserts, such as the GOBI on the Mongolian border. **Climate** The capital, BEIJING, in NE China, has cold winters and warm summers, with moderate rainfall. SHANGHAI, in the E central region, has milder winters and more rain. The SE region has a wet, subtropical climate. In the W, the climate is more cold and severe. **Vegetation**

Large areas in the W are covered by sparse grass or desert. The most luxuriant forests are in the SE, such as the bamboo forest habitat of the rare giant panda. **History and Politics** The first documented dynasty was the SHANG (*c*.1523–*c*.1030 BC), when bronze casting was perfected. The ZHOU dynasty (*c*.1030–221 BC) was the age of Chinese classical literature, in particular CONFUCIOUS and LAO TZU. China was unified by QIN SHIHUANGDI, whose tomb near XIAN contains the famous terracotta army. The QIN dynasty (221–206 BC) also built the majority of the GREAT WALL. The HAN dynasty (202 BC–AD 220) developed the empire, a bureaucracy based on CONFUCIANISM, and introduced BUDDHISM. China then split into three kingdoms (Wei, Shu and Wu) and the influence of Buddhism and TAOISM grew. The T'ANG dynasty (618–907) was a golden era of artistic achievement, especially in poetry and fine art. GENGHIS KHAN conquered most of China in the 1210s and established the MONGOL empire. KUBLAI KHAN founded the YÜAN dynasty (1271–1368), a period of dialogue with Europe. The MING dynasty (1368–1644) re-established Chinese rule. It is famed for its fine porcelain. The Manchu QING dynasty (1644–1912) began by vastly extending the empire, but the 19th century was marked by foreign interventions, such as the OPIUM WAR (1839–42) when Britain occupied HONG KONG. Popular disaffection culminated in the BOXER REBELLION (1900). The last emperor (Henry PU YI) was overthrown in a revolution led by SUN YAT-SEN, and a republic established. China rapidly fragmented between a Beijing government supported by warlords, and Sun Yat-sen's KUOMINTANG government in GUANGZHOU. The COMMUNIST PARTY OF CHINA initially allied with the nationalists. In 1926, CHIANG KAI-SHEK's nationalists emerged victorious and turned on their communist allies. In 1930, a rival communist government was established, but was uprooted by Kuomintang troops and began the LONG MARCH (1934). Japan, taking advantage of the turmoil, established the puppet state of MANCHUKUO (1932) under Henry PU YI. Chiang was forced to ally with the communists. Japan launched a full-scale invasion in 1937 and conquered much of N and E China. At the end of World War 2, civil war resumed, with nationalists supported by the US and communists by Russia. The communists triumphed, and the Kuomintang fled to TAIWAN. MAO ZEDONG established the People's Republic of China on 1 October 1949. In 1950, China seized Tibet. In 1958, the GREAT LEAP FORWARD planned to revolutionize industrial production. The CULTURAL REVOLUTION (1966–76) mobilized Chinese youth against bourgeois culture. By 1971, China had a seat on the UN security council and its own nuclear capability. Following Mao's death (1976), a power struggle developed between the GANG OF FOUR and moderates led by DENG XIAOPING; the latter emerged victorious. Deng began a process of modernization, forging closer links with the West. Despite China's economic reforms, political and cultural expression were often suppressed by the party. In 1989, a pro-democracy demonstration was crushed in TIANANMEN SQUARE. In 1997, JIANG ZEMIN succeeded Deng as paramount leader. **Economy** In 1979, special economic zones were created to encourage inward investment. China enjoys most-favoured nation status with the US. In the mid-1980s, agreements were reached

---

CHINA
AREA: 9,596,960 sq km (3,705,386 sq mi)
POPULATION: 1,299,180,000
CAPITAL (POPULATION): Beijing (6,560,000)

on the return of HONG KONG (1997) and MACAU (1999). China has one of the world's largest economies (1995 GDP per capita, $US2,920), and agriculture employs *c.*70% of the workforce. It has vast mineral resources and a huge steel industry.

China Sea Western part of the Pacific Ocean, divided by Taiwan into the SOUTH CHINA SEA and the EAST CHINA SEA.

chinchilla Genus of small, furry RODENTS native to South America. Chinchillas were hunted almost to extinction. They are now bred for their soft fur, the most expensive of all animal furs. Length: 23–38cm (9–15in); weight; 450–900g (1–2lb). Family Chinchilidae.

Chinese Group of languages spoken by *c.*95% of the population of China and by millions more in Taiwan, Hong Kong, Southeast Asia and other countries. There are six major languages that are not mutually intelligible; the most numerous is MANDARIN, spoken by *c.*66% of the Chinese population. All Chinese languages are written in a single, common, non-alphabetic script whose characters number in the thousands and, in some cases, date back several thousand years. This single writing system leads to the classification of all Chinese languages as dialects of one language. Chinese has twice as many users as any other language in the world. *See also* CANTONESE

Chinese architecture Style that as early as the Neolithic period, used columns to support roofs, faced houses south and used bright colours. The characteristic Chinese roof with wide overhang and upturned eaves was probably developed in the ZHOU period (*c.*1030–221 BC). A walled complex with a central axis for temples and palaces was established in the HAN dynasty (202 BC–AD 220), and building residential units around a central courtyard with elaborately planned garden became standard. The pagoda derives from Buddhist influences, notably the Indian stupa, and dates from the 6th century.

Chinese art Longest pedigree of any school in world art, its earliest artifacts (painted pottery) date back to the late Neolithic period. By the time of the SHANG dynasty (*c.*1523–1030 BC), native craftsmen were proficient at casting bronze and making jade carvings, many of which have survived as grave freight. The most elaborate of these belonged to the first emperor of the QIN dynasty, QIN SHIHUANGDI (d.210 BC). It contains a fabulous Terracotta Army of *c.*7,500 life-sized figures and horses. Painting and sculpture were established during the HAN dynasty, though little survives. The T'ANG dynasty (AD 618–907) marked China's artistic zenith. Sculpture reached a peak of refinement, and there were early attempts at landscape painting. The SUNG dynasty saw the first true porcelain. Important technical advances, such as coloured enamels, took place during the MING period (1368–1644). Chinese porcelain became highly valuable in European markets in the QING period. The advent of communism created a rift in this long tradition, as artists adopted Soviet-inspired SOCIALIST REALISM.

Chinese literature Earliest literary texts date from the ZHOU dynasty (*c.*1030–221 BC). This period produced the canonical writings of CONFUCIANISM: the Five Classics, including the first poetry anthology *Shih ching* "Classic of Odes"; and the Four Books, containing doctrinal writings. Traditionally attributed to CONFUCIUS, the *Shih ching* is probably earlier still. In this era, LAO TZU is credited with founding TAOISM. During the HAN dynasty (202 BC–AD 220), elaborate *fu* prose poems, in praise of the dynasty, flourished. The T'ANG dynasty (618–907) marked the golden age of Chinese literature; LI PO, TU FU and Wang Wei were the outstanding poets of the

period. In the SUNG dynasty (960–1279), the novel (often historical) and drama came into being. From the late-17th to early 19th century, much emphasis was placed on formal technique. Ts'ao Chan produced the most memorable work of the period, the novel *Dream of the Red Chamber*. The lyric poem has been the dominant form in Chinese literature. It is normally philosophical, with a quietness of tone and an emphasis on simple, routine experiences. In the first half of the 20th century, Chinese literature became modernized, with the new Chinese republic striving to formulate a new, politicized literary language. During the CULTURAL REVOLUTION, strict censorship was imposed. Recent years have seen a slight liberalization.

Chinese mythology During the SHANG dynasty, divination by means of animal bones was used to consult the spirits of royal ancestors. These ancestors were divine and provided a means of communication with the spirit world. A supreme god, Shang Ti, ruled in heaven as Chinese sovereigns did on earth. During the ZHOU dynasty, Shang Ti was replaced by T'ien ("Heaven") as the supreme being. The emperor, the "Son of Heaven", was responsible for maintaining harmony on earth and assumed the role of both priest and monarch. Chinese creation myths are essentially the reduction of chaos to order. Later, there existed a formal Chinese pantheon ruled by a father-god, the August Personage of Jade. His heavenly court was an almost exact replica of the imperial court at BEIJING. The Sun and the Moon were the objects of an official cult, and the Festival of the Moon was a major annual celebration.

Chinese theatre In its purest form, the traditions of Chinese theatre date back to the SUNG dynasty (960–1279). Traditional theatre is highly stylized, and the symbolism of the various dramatic parts, the actors' costumes, make-up and gestures are considered of far greater importance than the dialogue. Although much recent Chinese theatre has become Westernized, the old dramatic tradition remains enormously popular.

Ch'ing Alternative transliteration for the QING dynasty

chinoiserie European style of furniture and decorative art that became popular in the late 18th century and reflected fanciful and poetic notions of China, based on imports of Chinese ceramics, textiles and travellers' tales.

chinook Warm, dry föhn wind experienced on the E side of the Rocky Mountains in Canada and the USA, and in the European Alps.

Chinook Native American tribe living along the Pacific coast from the Columbia River to The Dalles, Oregon. Although fewer than 1,000, the Chinook travelled widely and the Chinook language was used by others, native and European, during the settlement of the West.

chip *See* SILICON CHIP

chipmunk Small, ground-dwelling SQUIRREL native to North America and Asia. It carries nuts, berries and seeds in cheek pouches, to store underground. Active tree-climbers in summer, they hibernate in winter. Most chipmunks are brown with one or more black-bordered, light stripes. Length: 13–15cm (5–6in) excluding the tail. Family Sciuridae; genera *Eutamias* and *Tamias*.

Chippendale, Thomas (1718–79) English furniture designer. One of the great craftsmen, much of his fame rested upon his *The Gentleman and Cabinet Maker's Directory* (1754–62), a trade catalogue illustrating the designs of his factory. Many of Chippendale's finest pieces were marquetry and inlaid items of neo-classicism.

Chirac, Jacques René (1932–) French statesman, president (1995–). He was first elected to the National Assembly in 1967. In 1974, Chirac was appointed prime minister by President GISCARD D'ESTAING. In 1976, he resigned and formed a new Gaullist party, the Rally for the Republic (RPR). In 1977, Chirac became mayor of Paris. He was again prime minister (1986–88), this time under President François MITTERRAND. In 1995, Chirac succeeded Mitterrand as president. Confronted by the lead-up to European economic and monetary union, Chirac called a surprise prime ministerial election (1997). Victory for the socialists, led by Lionel JOSPIN, was a personal setback for Chirac. In 2000, Chirac was implicated in allegations of covert funding of the RPR in the 1980s.

Chirico, Giorgio de (1888–1978) Italian painter, b. Greece. He was founder of the quasi-surrealist "metaphysical painting" movement. Chirico painted still lifes and empty, dream-like landscapes in exaggerated perspective. In the 1930s he repudiated modern art in favour of the style of the Old Masters. *See also* SURREALISM

Chiron In Greek mythology, wisest and most famous CENTAUR. He taught many of the lesser gods and heroes, including ACHILLES, and was accidently killed by Hercules with a poisoned arrow.

chiropody Diagnosis and treatment of minor disorders of the foot. Typical conditions treated by a chiropodist include ingrowing toenails, verrucas and corns.

chiropractic Non-orthodox medical practice based on the theory that the nervous system integrates all of the body's functions, including defence against disease. Chiropractors aim to remove nerve interference by manipulations of the affected musculo-skeletal parts.

Chisinau (Kishnev) Capital of Moldova, on the River Byk. Founded in the early 15th century, it came under Turkish and then Russian rule. Romania held the city from 1918 to 1940, when it was annexed by the Soviet Union. In 1991 it became capital of independent Moldova. It has a 19th-century cathedral and a university (1945). Industries: plastics, rubber. Pop. (1994) 700,000.

chitin Hard, tough substance that occurs widely in nature, particularly in the hard shells (exoskeletons) of arthropods, such as crabs, insects and spiders. The walls of hyphae (microscopic tubes of fungi) are composed of slightly different chitin. Chemically, chitin is a polysaccharide derived from glucose.

Chittagong Seaport on the River Karnaphuli, near the Bay of Bengal, SE Bangladesh. Under Mogul rule in the 17th century, it was ceded to the British East India Company in 1760. It is Bangladesh's chief port. Industries: jute, tea, oil, engineering. Pop. (1991) 1,363,998.

chivalry (Fr. *chevalerie*, knighthood) Code of ethics and behaviour of the knightly class that developed from FEUDALISM. A combination of Christian ethics and military codes of conduct, the main chivalric virtues were piety, honour, valour, chastity and loyalty. A KNIGHT swore loyalty to God, king and his love. Love was strictly platonic. The Crusades saw the emergence of monastic knighthoods, such as the KNIGHTS HOSPITALLERS and KNIGHTS TEMPLAR. Chivalry was always prone to corruption, and the traditions died out in the 15th century. Chivalric ideals permeate much of medieval literature.

chive Perennial herb whose long, hollow leaves have an onion-like flavour used for seasoning. The flowers grow in rose-purple clusters. Family Liliaceae; species *Allium schoenoprasum*.

chlamydia Small, virus-like BACTERIA that live as PARASITES in animals and cause disease. One strain, *C. trachomatis*, is responsible for TRACHOMA and is also a major cause of pelvic inflammatory disease (PID) in women. *C. psittaci* causes PSITTACOSIS. Chlamydial infection is the most common SEXUALLY TRANSMITTED DISEASE in many developed countries.

chloride Salt of HYDROCHLORIC ACID or some organic compounds containing CHLORINE, especially those with the negative ion Cl‾. The best-known example is common salt, SODIUM CHLORIDE (NaCl). Most chlorides are soluble in water, except mercurous and silver chlorides.

chlorine (symbol Cl) Common nonmetallic element that is one of the HALOGENS, first discovered (1774) by the Swedish chemist Karl SCHEELE. It occurs in common salt (NaCl). It is a greenish-yellow poisonous gas extracted by the electrolysis of brine (salt water) and is widely used to disinfect drinking water and swimming pools, to bleach wood pulp and in the manufacture of plastics, chloroform and pesticide. Chemically, it is a reactive element, and combines with most metals. Properties: at.no. 17; r.a.m. 35.453; m.p. 101°C (149.8°F); b.p. 34.6°C (30.28°F). The most common isotope is Cl^{35} (75.53%).

chlorofluorocarbon (CFC) Chemical compound in which hydrogen atoms of a hydrocarbon, such as an alkane, are replaced by atoms of fluorine, chlorine, carbon and sometimes bromine. CFCs are inert, stable at high temperatures, and are odourless, colourless, nontoxic, noncorrosive and nonflammable. Under the tradename of Freons, CFCs were widely used in aerosols, fire-extinguishers, refrigerators and in the manufacture of foam plastics. When CFCs are used, they slowly drift into the stratosphere and are broken down by the Sun's ultraviolet radiation into chlorine atoms that destroy the OZONE LAYER. It often takes more than 100 years for CFCs to disappear from the atmosphere. Environmental concern led to an international agreement (1990) by governments to reduce and eventually phase out the use of CFCs and other chemicals harming the ozonosphere.

chloroform ($CHCl_3$, trichloromethane) Colourless, volatile, sweet-smelling liquid, prepared by the chlorination of methane. Formerly a major anaesthetic, it is used in the manufacture of fluorocarbons, in cough medicines, for insect bites and as a solvent. Properties: r.d. 1.48; m.p. 63.5°C (82.3°F); b.p. 61.2°C (142.2°F).

chlorophyll Group of green pigments in the CHLOROPLASTS of plants and ALGAE that absorb light for PHOTOSYNTHESIS. There are five types: chlorophyll *a* is present in all photosynthetic organisms except bacteria; chlorophyll *b*, in plants and GREEN ALGAE; and chlorophylls *c*, *d* and *e*, in some algae. It is similar in structure to HAEMOGLOBIN, with a magnesium atom replacing an iron atom.

chloroplast Microscopic green structure within a plant cell in which PHOTOSYNTHESIS takes place. The chloroplast is enclosed in an "envelope" and contains internal membranes to increase the surface area for reactions. Molecules of the light-absorbing pigment CHLOROPHYLL are embedded in these internal membranes. *See artwork* p.182

chocolate Like COCOA, chocolate was originally a drink (introduced to Europe in the 1500s) produced from the seeds of the tropical tree *Theobroma cacao*. The seeds are beans contained in an elliptical pod and do not have the flavour or colour of chocolate until they have been fermented and roasted. The beans are then ground up to make chocolate powder. The first chocolate bar was produced in the late 1700s.

Choctaw One of the largest tribes of Muskogean-speaking Native North Americans, located in SE Mississippi and part of Alabama. As large slave-owners, they supported the South during the American Civil War. A majority of the Choctaw moved to Oklahoma in 1830, where some 40,000 of their descendants still reside.

choir Group of singers who perform together as a musical unit. The earliest choirs were ecclesiastical and sang PLAINSONG in church services. From the 10th century onwards, polyphonic composition gradually replaced unharmonized PLAINSONG in liturgical use. The beginnings of OPERA marked the development of the secular choir or CHORUS. Most modern choirs are mixed sex.

Choiseul, Etienne François, Duc de (1719–85) French statesman, chief minister (1758–1770) of LOUIS XV. As ambassador to Vienna (1757–58), he negotiated the marriage of Marie Antoinette and the future Louis XVI. As minister of foreign affairs he negotiated the Family Compact (1761), allying the BOURBON rulers of France and Spain, and the Treaty of Paris (1763), in which France surrendered French Canada and India to Britain. Choiseul approved the suppression of the Jesuits (1764).

Chola Dynasty of S India. From 985 to 1024, they established an empire that included Sri Lanka, Bengal, parts of Sumatra and Malaya. A great era of Hindu culture finally ended in 1279.

cholera Infectious disease caused by the bacterium *Vibrio cholerae*, transmitted in contaminated water. Cholera, prevalent in many tropical regions, produces almost continuous, watery diarrhoea often accompanied by vomiting and muscle cramps, and leads to severe dehydration. Untreated it can be fatal, but proper treatment, including fluid replacement and antibiotics, results in a high recovery rate. There is a vaccine.

cholesterol White, fatty STEROID, occurring in large concentrations in the brain, spinal cord and liver. It is synthesized in the liver, intestines and skin and is an intermediate in the synthesis of vitamin D and many hormones. GALLSTONES are composed mainly of cholesterol. Meat-rich diets may produce high cholesterol in blood vessels and can lead to ARTERIOSCLEROSIS.

Chomsky, (Avram) Noam (1928–) US professor of linguistics. In *Syntactic Structures* (1957), he developed the concept of a transformational generative grammar, embodying his theories about the relationship between language and the human mind and an underlying universal structure of language. Opposed to BEHAVIOURISM, Chomsky argues that the human capacity for language is partially innate. He has been a consistent critic of US imperialist tendencies and was an outspoken opponent of the Vietnam War. Polemical works include *American Power and the New Mandarins* (1969).

Chongjin City on the Sea of Japan, NE North Korea. From 1910 to 1945 it was controlled by the Japanese, who developed the Musan iron mines. Chongjin was severely damaged during the Korean War (1950–54). Industries: iron, steel, shipbuilding. Pop. (1984 est.) 754,128.

Chongqing *See* CHUNGKING

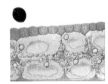

▲ **chloroplast** Found mostly in the cells of plant leaves, chloroplasts absorb sunlight and use it to manufacture special types of sugar. They are able to move about in order to receive the maximum amount of light possible. A section through a leaf reveals that during the day (left), chloroplasts have moved to the outer and inner walls in the direct line of light. During the night (right), they move to the inner and side walls only. Chloroplasts are responsible for the green colour of most plants.

Chopin, Frédéric François (1810–49) Composer for the piano, b. Poland. He gave his first public piano recital in Warsaw at the age of eight. Political repression forced him to move (1831) to Paris, where Chopin rapidly endeared himself in the *salons*. His restrained and delicate style contrasted strongly with contemporary trends. In 1836, Liszt introduced Chopin to the novelist George SAND. In 1838, the couple moved to Majorca, and he composed 24 préludes. Chopin composed almost exclusively for the piano and established it as a solo instrument. His improvisational method produced radical new ideas of HARMONY. Chopin's major works include two piano concertos and three piano sonatas. He died of tuberculosis.

choral music Music written for several voices. Choral compositions were originally religious, CANTATA and ORATORIO being the most usual forms. The foremost composer of cantatas was J.C. BACH and of oratorios HANDEL. Choral music varies from the small-scale madrigals of the 16th century to the large-scale works of the 19th and 20th centuries, such as Verdi's *Requiem* (1874) and Elgar's *Dream of Gerontius* (1900).

chord In music, the simultaneous occurrence of three or more musical tones of different pitch. Chords are categorized as anomalous, characteristic, common, inverted or transient. *See also* HARMONY

chordate Any member of the Chordata, a large phylum of VERTEBRATES and some marine invertebrates, which, at some stage in their lives, have rod-like, cartilaginous supporting structures (notochords). Invertebrate chordates are divided into three subphyla: tunicates (seasquirts), Cephalochordata (amphioxus) and Hemichordata (acorn worms).

chorea Condition characterized by involuntary jerking movements of the face muscles, head and limbs, seen in some neurological diseases. **Sydenham's** chorea, at one time known as St. Vitus' Dance, is a transient disorder of childhood and adolescence, sometimes associated with rheumatic fever. It usually subsides in a few weeks. *See also* HUNTINGTON'S DISEASE

choreography In general, the composition of dance steps and sequences for BALLET and DANCE performance. In the 18th century, choreography was limited to the writing of DANCE NOTATION. *See also* individual choreographers and dancers

chorus In Greek tragedy, the *choros* danced and chanted commentary. Today, a chorus refers to a group of voices. Major works with chorus parts include CANTATAS, OPERAS and ORATORIOS. *See also* CHOIR

Chou Alternative transliteration for the ZHOU dynasty

Chouteau, (Jean) Pierre (1758–1849) US fur trader and political figure. With his half-brother, **René Auguste** Chouteau (1749–1829), he controlled the important trade with the Osage Native Americans. Chouteau established (1796) the first permanent white settlement in Oklahoma. In 1809, he founded the St Louis Missouri Fur Company. His two sons, **Auguste Pierre** (1786–1838) and **Pierre** (1789–1865), developed the family firm so that by the 1850s it controlled most of the fur trade from the Mississippi to the Rockies.

Chrétien, (Joseph-Jacques) Jean (1934–) 20th prime minister of Canada (1993–). He became a member of Parliament in 1963, and held cabinet offices in Pierre TRUDEAU's government. In 1990, Chrétien became leader of the Liberal Party. His populist campaign secured a landslide election victory. Chrétien's main challenge has been to reduce unemployment. He was re-elected, with a much reduced majority, in 1997.

Chrétien de Troyes (active 1160–85) Romance writer of N France, noted for his tales of King ARTHUR. He influenced Geoffrey CHAUCER and Thomas MALORY.

Christ (Gk. *christos*, anointed one) Epithet for the MESSIAH in Old Testament prophecies. Later applied to JESUS, in recognition that he was the expected Messiah.

Christchurch City on South Island, New Zealand; main town of Canterbury. It was founded as a Church of England settlement (1850). The University of Canterbury (1873) is here. Industries: fertilizers, rubber, woollen goods, electrical goods, furniture. Pop. (1996) 314,000.

christening *See* BAPTISM

Christian I (1426–81) King of Denmark (1448–81), Norway (1450–81) and Sweden (1457–64), founder of the Oldenburg dynasty. He was deposed in Sweden and his efforts to regain the throne ended in defeat (1471). His succession (1460) to SCHLESWIG-HOLSTEIN formed the basis of future conflict between Denmark and Germany.

Christian II (1481–1559) King of Denmark and Norway (1513–23) and Sweden (1520–21). Christian won the Swedish crown by conquest, but the subsequent slaughter of Swedish nobles led to the crowning of a rival king, GUSTAVUS I (VASA), and the end of the Kalmar Union. In Denmark, the nobles resented Christian's reforms favouring the middle classes and drove him out. He invaded Norway (1531), but was captured (1532) and imprisoned for the rest of his life.

Christian IV (1577–1648) King of Denmark and Norway (1588–1648), son of Frederick II. Despite a costly war with Sweden (1611–13), and his disastrous participation (1625–29) in the THIRTY YEARS' WAR, he was a popular monarch. Christian's reign brought culture and economic prosperity, and he founded OSLO, Norway.

Christian IX (1818–1906) King of Denmark (1863–1906), successor of Frederick VII. Christian lost SCHLESWIG-HOLSTEIN in a war (1864) with Prussia and Austria. His reign brought reforms to the constitution and the gradual democratization of Danish society.

Christian X (1870–1947) King of Denmark (1912–47) and Iceland (1919–44), succeeding Frederick VIII. In his reign, universal suffrage was established (1915) and social welfare policies were consolidated. Christian defied the Germans during occupation (1940–45).

Christian Follower of JESUS CHRIST. The major Christian Churches regard belief in the divinity of Christ and the Holy TRINITY as the minimum requirement for a Christian.

Christian Democrats Political group combining Christian conservative principles with progressive social responsibility. Christian Democrats have achieved power in many European countries, notably Germany and Italy. Its political principles include individual responsibility allied with collective action, social equality within a welfare state and progress through evolutionary change. Christian Democrats are also represented outside Europe.

Christianity Religion based on faith in JESUS CHRIST as the Son of God. The orthodox Christian faith, summarized in the APOSTLES' and NICENE CREEDS, affirms belief in the TRINITY and Christ's incarnation, atoning death on the cross, resurrection and ascension. The moral teachings of Jesus are contained in the NEW TESTAMENT. The history of Christianity has been turbulent and often sectarian. The first major SCHISM took place in 1054 when the eastern and western churches separated. The next occurred in the 16th-century REFORMATION, with the split of PROTESTANTISM and the ROMAN CATHOLIC CHURCH. In recent times, the ECUMENICAL MOVEMENT, which aims at the reunion of all Christians,

has gained strength. The number of Christians in the world was estimated (1995) at more than one billion.

Christian Science (officially Church of Christ Scientist) Religious sect founded (1879) by Mary Baker EDDY and based on her book *Science and Health with Key to the Scriptures* (1875). Its followers believe that physical illness and moral problems can only be cured by spiritual and mental activity. They refuse medical treatment. "Divine Mind" is used as a synonym for God. Each human being is regarded as a complete and flawless manifestation of the Divine Mind.

Christie, Dame Agatha Mary Clarissa (1891–1976) English writer. She was a prolific and popular writer of detective stories, and *The Mysterious Affair at Styles* (1920) introduced her most famous character, the Belgian detective Hercule Poirot. *Murder at the Vicarage* (1930) featured the aged sleuth Miss Marple. Other novels include *The Murder of Roger Ackroyd* (1926), *Murder on the Orient Express* (1934) and *And Then There Were None* (1939). *Curtain* (1975) killed Poirot off. Christie's plays include *The Mousetrap* (1952), the longest-running play in London.

Christie, Linford (1960–) British athlete, b. Jamaica. In the 1992 Olympics, he captained the British men's team and won the 100m gold medal. Christie won another gold in the 1993 World Championship. He won a hat-trick of gold medals in the European Championships (1986, 1990, 1994). In 1998, he retired to take up coaching athletes.

Christina (1626–89) Queen of Sweden (1632–54). An intellectual of great energy, she brought foreign scholars, such as DESCARTES, to her court. Ruling a Lutheran country, Christina abdicated to become a Roman Catholic. She tried unsuccessfully to obtain the Polish crown (1667).

Christmas Feast in celebration of the birth of JESUS CHRIST, common in Christendom since the 4th century. Although the exact date of Christ's birth is unknown, the feast takes place on 25 December. Christmas is also a secular holiday, marked by the exchange of presents.

Christmas Island *See* KIRITIMATI

Christmas Island Island in the E Indian Ocean, 320km (200mi) S of JAVA. Once under British domination, it was annexed to Australia in 1958. It has important lime phosphate deposits. Area: 135sq km (52sq mi). Pop. (1994 est.) 2,500.

Christoff, Boris (1919–93) Bulgarian bass. Christoff made his opera debut in 1946 (Rome). His powerful voice lent itself to the interpretation of Russian songs and roles such as Boris Godunov and Ivan the Terrible.

Christophe, Henri (1767–1820) Haitian revolutionary leader, president (1806–11) and king (1811–20). Born a free man on the island of Grenada, he participated in the armed struggle against the French in Haiti. Christophe ordered the construction of the citadel of La Ferrière, a fort overlooking Cap-Haitien, the building of which cost many Haitian lives.

Christopher, Saint Patron saint of ferrymen and travellers. His feast day, 25 July, is not officially recognized.

Christopher, Warren (1925–) US secretary of state (1993–97). He served under President Bill CLINTON. Christopher launched an economic assistance programme for Russia, and reopened the Middle East peace negotiations. He was succeeded by Madeleine ALBRIGHT.

chromatic Musical term used in melodic and harmonic analysis for notes not in the scale of the KEY of a passage. Such notes are marked with accidentals; the chords in which they occur are termed chromatic. A chromatic scale is one containing all 12 notes of an octave rather than the seven notes of a DIATONIC scale.

chromatid Either of the two duplicate strands into which each CHROMOSOME in a biological CELL nucleus divides in the first phase of MITOSIS or MEIOSIS (cell division). The pairs of identical chromatids are separated by a long fibrous structure made of proteins, called a mitotic spindle. The separated chromatids become identical daughter chromosomes of the same kind as those of the parent cell on opposite sides of the nucleus.

chromatography Techniques of chemical analysis by which substances are separated from one another, identified and measured. All involve a **mobile** phase consisting of a liquid or gaseous mixture of the substances to be separated, and a **stationary** phase consisting of a material that differentially absorbs the substances in the mixture. The two major types are gas chromatography and paper chromatography. *See also* ELECTROPHORESIS

chromite ($FeOCr_2O_3$) Black mineral, ferrous chromic oxide, separated from magma in the formation of igneous rock. It is weakly magnetic and opaque. Hardness 5.5; r.d. 4.6.

chromium (symbol Cr) Dull grey metal, one of the TRANSITION ELEMENTS, first isolated in 1797. Its chief ore is CHROMITE. Chromium is extensively used as an electroplated coating. Chromium compounds are used in tanning and dyeing. Properties: at.no. 24; r.a.m. 51.996; r.d. 7.19; m.p. 1,890°C (3,434°F); b.p. 2,672°C (4,842°F); most common isotope Cr^{52} (83.76%).

chromosome Structure carrying the genetic information of an organism, found only in the CELL nucleus of EUKARYOTES. Thread-like and composed of DNA, chromosomes carry a specific set of GENES. Each species usually has a characteristic number of chromosomes; these occur in pairs, members of which carry identical genes, so that most cells have a DIPLOID number of chromosomes. GAMETES carry a HAPLOID number. *See also* HEREDITY

chromosphere Layer of the SUN's atmosphere between the PHOTOSPHERE and the CORONA. The chromosphere is *c*.10,000km (6,000mi) thick and is normally invisible because of the glare of the photosphere. It is briefly visible near the beginning and end of a total solar eclipse as a spiky red rim around the Moon's disc, and at other times can be studied by SPECTROSCOPY. At its base, the temperature of the chromosphere is *c*.4,000K, rising to 100,000K at the top. Powerful magnetic fields are believed to cause this rise in temperature.

Chronicles Two historical books of the OLD TESTAMENT. They trace the history of Israel and Judah from the Creation to the end of the BABYLONIAN CAPTIVITY (538 BC).

chronometer Instrument for accurately measuring time. The chronometer was an important navigational aid for ships before radio time signals. Knowing the precise time at which a star reached a certain position enabled a navigator to work out a ship's longitude.

chrysalis Intermediate or pupal stage in the life cycle of all insects that undergo complete METAMORPHOSIS. The chrysalis is usually covered with a hard case, but some pupae, such as the silk moth, spin a silk cocoon. Within the chrysalis, the final stages of the development take place. *See also* LEPIDOPTERA

chrysanthemum Large genus of annual and perennial plants that are native to temperate Eurasia and now widely cultivated. Centuries of selective breeding have modified the original plain daisy-like flowers, and most species have large white, yellow, bronze, pink or red flower-heads. Family Asteraceae/COMPOSITAE.

Chrysostom, St John (*c*.347–407) Doctor of the Church, patriarch of Constantinople. In 386 he was ordained in Antioch, Syria, and his powerful sermons quickly earned him the epithet *Chrysostom* (Gk. golden-mouthed). In 398 he was made archbishop of Constantinople. The zeal with which he approached reform of church and state offended Empress Eudoxia, and led to his banishment (403). His *Homilies* are an invaluable record of religious thought. His feast day is 27 January.

chub Freshwater CARP found in flowing waters. It has a large head, wide mouth and is grey-brown. Length

▶ **chromatography**
Gas-liquid chromatographs can separate the components of tiny amounts of an unknown mixture. A sample of the mixture (1) is injected (2) into a stream of helium (3), or another inert gas. Heating ensures the vaporized gas mixes fully with the helium. After impurities are removed (4) the gas mixture passes into a tube (5) packed with coated granules of silicon (6). A liquid with a very high boiling point (7) covers the 4mm (0.15in) granules. The components of the vaporized mixture have different solubilities (8) and so pass through the liquid around the silicon, and the whole tube, at different speeds. The whole tube is kept at a high temperature to prevent the vaporized gas condensing. As the now-separated parts of the mixture exit the tube (9) they enter a detector (10). Hydrogen (11) and oxygen (12) are added and the gas stream is then burned (13). During burning each compound produces ions that pass a charge between an anode (14) and a cathode (15). This charge is measured and can be compared to known results to determine the make-up of the initial mixture.

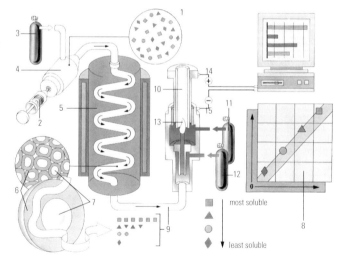

most soluble

least soluble

10–60cm (4–25in). Family Cyprinidae. Chub is also the name of a marine fish of warm seas – oval-shaped with a small mouth and bright colours. Family Kyphosidae.

Chulalongkorn (1853–1910) King Rama V of Siam (1868–1910). He was less insular than his predecessors and embraced Westernization in Siam (Thailand). Chulalongkorn abolished slavery, modernized the legal system, built railways and advanced education and technology. His reforms ensured Siam's independence.

Chungking (Chongqing, Ch'ung-ch'ing) City on the River Yangtze, s China. From the 14th century AD, it was part of a unified China. It became a treaty port in 1891 and was the wartime capital of China (1937–45). It is a transport and shipping centre. Industries: chemicals, steel, iron, silk, cotton. Pop. (1993 est.) 3,780,000.

church Community of believers. Although adopted by non-Christian movements, such as SCIENTOLOGY, it is usually refers to CHRISTIANITY. The characteristics of the Christian Church as the whole body of Christ's followers are described in the NICENE CREED. Church also describes the building used for worship by Christians.

Churchill, Lord Randolph Henry Spencer (1849–95) British statesman, secretary of state for India (1885–86), chancellor of the exchequer (1886). A gifted speaker and loyal member of the Tory Party, he nevertheless attempted widespread Party reform. Churchill's first budget as chancellor proposed deep cuts in military expenditure and was defeated. He was forced to resign. In 1874 he married Jennie Jerome, a US citizen. Their son, Winston, achieved the success denied his father.

Churchill, Sir Winston Leonard Spencer (1874–1965) British statesman, son of Lord Randolph CHURCHILL. He was a reporter in the SOUTH AFRICAN WARS. Elected to Parliament in 1900 as a Conservative, Churchill joined the Liberals in 1904. As first lord of the admiralty under Herbert ASQUITH, he expanded Britain's navy in preparation for World War 1. In LLOYD GEORGE's cabinet, Churchill served as secretary of state for war (1918–21) and, as colonial secretary (1921–22), he oversaw the creation of the Irish Free State. Churchill returned to power as chancellor of the exchequer (1924–29) in Stanley BALDWIN's Conservative government. On the outbreak of WORLD WAR 2, he once more became first lord of the admiralty. In 1940, Churchill replaced Neville CHAMBERLAIN as prime minister. He proved an inspiring war leader, resolute in his opposition to fascism. Cultivating close relations with President Franklin ROOSEVELT, Churchill was the principal architect of the grand alliance of Britain, the US and the Soviet Union (*see* YALTA; POTSDAM). In the 1945 elections, he was defeated by Clement ATTLEE, but Churchill was re-elected in 1950 and reversed some of Labour's nationalizations. He remained an MP until 1964. His extensive writings include a history of World War 2 and the *History of the English-Speaking Peoples* (1956–58). Churchill was awarded the Nobel Prize for literature in 1953.

Church of England Christian Church in England, established by law in the 16th century. During the reign of King HENRY VIII, a process of separation from the Roman Catholic Church began. The initial impetus for this was the pope's refusal to grant Henry a divorce from CATHERINE OF ARAGON. By the Act of Supremacy (1534), the English monarch became head of the church. As the REFORMATION extended to England, the Church of England finally emerged independent of papal jurisdiction and adopted the Elizabethan Settlement. This agreement, while espousing PROTESTANTISM, aimed at preserving religious unity by shaping a national church

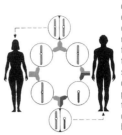

◀ **chromosome** The 46 chromosomes in somatic (non-reproductive) cells contain a single sex-determining pair that consist of an X and Y chromosome in males, or an XX pair in females. Ova contain only the X chromosome, while spermatozoa contain X or Y chromosomes in equal proportions. At fertilization therefore there is a 50% chance of an XX or XY pair being formed.

acceptable to all persons of moderate theological views. This middle course found expression in the doctrinal THIRTY-NINE ARTICLES (1571). The liturgy of the Church of England is contained in the Book of COMMON PRAYER (1662), but since the 1960s alternative forms of worship have come into use. The sovereign bears the title Supreme Governor of the Church of England and formally nominates the bishops. The church is episcopally governed, but priests and laity share in all major decisions by virtue of their representation in the General Synod. Territorially, the church is divided into two provinces, Canterbury and York. The archbishop of CANTERBURY is Primate of All England. The overseas expansion of the Church of England during the period of growth of the British empire resulted in the gradual development of the worldwide ANGLICAN COMMUNION. The Church of England is the only part of the Anglican Communion still established by law as an official state church. In 1992, the General Synod voted in favour of the ordination of women as priests. The first women priests were ordained in 1994.

Church of Ireland Anglican Church in Ireland. It claims to be heir to the ancient Church of the island of Ireland. At the time of the REFORMATION, it ended papal jurisdiction and introduced doctrinal and disciplinary reforms similar to the CHURCH OF ENGLAND. It is territorially divided into two provinces, Armagh and Dublin. The archbishop of Armagh is Primate of All Ireland. It was the legally established Church until 1869.

Church of Scotland National, non-episcopal form of CHRISTIANITY in Scotland, adopting PRESBYTERIANISM by constitutional act in 1689. The church arose as a separate entity during the REFORMATION. Under the leadership of John KNOX, it abolished papal authority and accepted many of the teachings of John CALVIN. The doctrinal position of the Church is based on the Scottish Confession (1560) and the Westminster Confession of 1643. The highest authority resides in the General Assembly, presided over by an annually elected moderator. The Disruption of 1843 led to about one-third of its ministers and members leaving to form the FREE CHURCH OF SCOTLAND. The Church has *c.*850,000 members.

Churriguera Spanish family of architects consisting of three brothers, **José** (1665–1725), **Joaquin** (1674–1724) and **Alberto** (1676–1750). Their most notable works are in Salamanca, Spain. The "Churrigueresque" style of Spanish BAROQUE is characterized by twisted columns and ornate stucco decoration. The most extravagant ornamentation is to be found on Spanish colonial buildings in America. *See also* ROCOCO

chyme Stomach contents, a mixture of partly digested food, gastric acid and digestive enzymes. It passes from the stomach into the small intestine in semi-liquid form. *See also* DIGESTION; DIGESTIVE SYSTEM

chymotrypsin Substance produced in the body that aids in the digestion of food. Chymotrypsin is an ENZYME that breaks down proteins. It is made in the SMALL INTESTINE, by complex chemical reactions, from chymotrypsinogen. This, together with other digestive substances, is secreted by the PANCREAS through the pancreatic duct into the DUO-DENUM that lies between the stomach and the small intestine. Secretion is controlled partly by the AUTONOMIC NER-VOUS SYSTEM and partly by HORMONES. *See also* TRYPSIN

CIA Abbreviation of CENTRAL INTELLIGENCE AGENCY

Ciano, Galeazzo (1903–44) Italian politician. He married (1930) Benito MUSSOLINI's daughter and became foreign minister (1936–43). Ciano was partly responsible for the attack (1940) on Greece that precipitated Italy's entry into World War 2 in 1940. Axis defeats led to his dismissal. Ciano voted for the removal of Mussolini and, when Mussolini was restored to power, he was executed for treason.

Cibber, Colley (1671–1757) English dramatist and actor-manager. His first play, *Love's Last Shift* (1696), began the fashion for sentimental comedy. His appointment as poet laureate in 1730 was ridiculed by Alexander POPE in *The Dunciad* (1742). Cibber's autobiography, *An Apology for the Life of Mr Colley Cibber, Comedian* (1740), is a historic account of the English theatre.

cicada GRASSHOPPER-like insect found in most parts of the world. Males make a loud sound by the vibration of a pair of plates in their abdomen. Females lay eggs in tree branches. The dog-day cicada appears annually in summer. The larvae of the 17-year LOCUST spends up to 17 years in the ground feeding on roots and lives only a week as a winged adult. Length: up to 5cm (2in).

Cicero, Marcus Tullius (106–43 BC) Roman politician, philosopher and orator. A leader of the Senate, he exposed CATILINE's conspiracy (63 BC). Cicero criticized Mark ANTONY, and when Octavian (later AUGUSTUS) came to power, Antony persuaded him to have Cicero executed. His fame rests largely on his political philosophy and oratory. Among Cicero's greatest speeches were *Orations Against Catiline* and the *Phillipics*. His rhetorical and philosophical works include *De Amicitia*.

cichlid Any of a family of freshwater fish related to the PERCH, found in tropical regions, especially the Great Lakes of Africa. Some cichlids, such as the *Tilapia*, breed their young in the mouth. They are popular aquarium fish because of their brilliant colours. Family Cichlidae.

Cid, El (1043–99) (Rodrigo Díaz de Vivar) Spanish national hero. He was a knight in the service of the king of Castile, who spent his whole life fighting, often against the Moors. His greatest achievement was the conquest of Valencia (1094), which he ruled until his death. His exploits have been romanticized in Spanish legend.

cider Drink made from apple juice. In the manufacture of alcoholic cider, the fruit is crushed to a pomace which is squeezed to express the juice and then is fermented in wooden vats or casks. For **sweet** ciders, FERMENTATION is stopped after about three weeks; for **dry** ciders, it is allowed to go to completion. For **still** ciders, carbon dioxide made by the yeast is allowed to escape.

cigar Tight roll of dried and cured TOBACCO leaves prepared for smoking. The practice originated in the Americas and was brought to Europe by sailors. Cigars became established in Spain as a luxury product by *c.*1600.

cigarette Roll of shredded TOBACCO wrapped in thin paper for inhalation by smoking. Because of tar, NICO-TINE (the addictive substance) and other chemicals in the smoke, cigarettes are highly carcinogenic. However,

cigarettes continue to represent a huge industry and source of taxation for governments despite increasing controls, including clear warnings on packets, bans on smoking in public places and restrictions on advertising.

cilia Small, hair-like filaments on cell walls whose wafting motion is used for propulsion or moving matter along a surface. Cilia are present in great quantities on some lining cells of the body, such as those along the respiratory tract. *See also* CILIATE

ciliate Member of the phylum Ciliophora, characterized by CILIA. Ciliates are the largest (*c.*8,000 species) and most complex of the PROTOZOA. They are found in aquatic and terrestrial habitats and many are carnivorous. Ciliates have two nuclei and a variety of organelles, such as a cystome (mouth). Subclasses include Holotrichs (*Paramecium*), Spirotrichs (*Stentor*) and Peritrichs (*Vorticella*).

Cilicia Ancient coastal region of SE Asia Minor, now forming part of Turkey. The major city was Tarsus. The Cilician Gates in the Taurus Mountains was a strategic pass on the trade route between Europe and Asia. It was conquered by Rome in 67 BC. An Armenian state was set up here in 1080 and the region fell to the Turks in 1375.

Cimabue, Giovanni (*c.*1240–*c.*1302) Florentine painter, an important transitional link between the rigid Byzantine style of painting and the greater realism of the 14th-century School of Florence. His best-known work is *Madonna and Child Enthroned*.

Cimarosa, Domenico (1749–1801) Italian composer. He wrote more than 60 operas, the best-known of which is the opera buffa *The Secret Marriage* (1792). Cimarosa also wrote seven cantatas and six oratorios.

cinchona Genus of evergreen trees native to the Andes and grown in South America, Indonesia and Zaire. The dried bark of the trees is a source of QUININE and other medicinal products. Family Rubiaceae.

Cincinnati City on the Ohio River, SW Ohio. Originally named Losantiville, it grew around Fort Washington (established 1789). The completion (1832) of the Miami and Erie Canal made the city a shipping centre for farm produce, and the railway arrived in 1880. Cincinnati has a university (1819). Industries: machine tools, soap products, brewing, meat packing. Pop. (1990) 364,040.

Cincinnatus, Lucius Quinctius (519–438 BC) Legendary Roman patriot. Consul in 460, he was named dictator by the Senate in 458. According to legend, Cincinnatus left his farm to save the Roman army from defeat by the Aequi and promptly resigned as dictator to return to his land. In 439, he was recalled to the dictatorship to defeat the PLEBIANS.

cine camera Apparatus that takes a number of consecutive still photographs, or frames, on film. The illusion of motion is created when the developed film is projected on to a screen. Big-screen cine CAMERAS use 70mm cine film, most professional cameras 35mm, and some smaller cameras 16 or 8mm. *See also* CINEMA; CINEMATOGRAPHY; PHOTOGRAPHY; VIDEO RECORDING

cinema Motion pictures as an industry and artistic pursuit. For much of its history, cinema has been commercially dominated by HOLLYWOOD. Public showings of silent moving pictures, with live musical accompaniment, began in the 1890s, but speech was not heard in a feature film until *The Jazz Singer* (1927). By then cinema was big business with mass appeal. D.W. GRIFFITH's *The Birth of a Nation* (1915) used innovative close-ups and editing techniques. In Russia, Sergei EISENSTEIN used MONTAGE to enhance his political message. In Germany, the EXPRES-SIONISM of Fritz LANG further revealed the creative possibilities of the medium. Technicolour was introduced in

1933, but black-and-white remained the dominant medium until the 1950s. During the 1950s, the growth of television in the US profoundly altered film economics; the decline of Hollywood led to the rise of the independent producer and director. Fewer but more spectacular films were produced. British cinema flourished with institutions such as EALING STUDIOS. Experiments in framing, such as CINEMASCOPE and CINERAMA, attempted to draw audiences back to the cinema. FILM NOIR in the US and NEO-REALISM in Europe explored the social and psychological effects of World War 2. In the 1960s, NOUVELLE VAGUE used faster film stocks and more mobile cameras to develop the notions of the AUTEUR and CINEMA VÉRITÉ. In the 1970s and 1980s, the box-office success of Steven SPIEL-BERG and the development of VIDEO revolutionized the motion picture industry. In the 1990s, the development of computer-generated images brought a new dimension to film. *See also* ANIMATION; CINEMA; CINE CAMERA; CINE-MATOGRAPHY; DOCUMENTARY; PHOTOGRAPHY

Cinemascope Widescreen cinema projection system using an anamorphic lens, originally developed (1928) by Henri Chrétien. Cinemascope was copyrighted (1952) by 20th Century-Fox. The first Cinemascope film, *The Robe* (1953), prompted other studios to develop rival systems.

cinematography Technique of taking and projecting cine film, the basis of the CINEMA industry. Based on the inventions pioneered during the 1880s and 1890s by Thomas EDISON in the US and the LUMIÈRE brothers in France, cinematography was applied professionally soon after the turn of the century.

cinéma vérité Style of film-making, popular during the 1960s, but first practised by Dziga Vertov in the 1920s. It attempted to record truthful action, employing a documentary-like style, often using 16mm cameras. The style was also used in dramas, particularly by François TRUF-FAUT and Jean-Luc GODARD. *See also* NOUVELLE VAGUE

Cinerama Widescreen cinema projection system developed (1952) by Fred Waller. Cinerama used three cameras and projectors to shoot and then project the film onto a large, curved screen. *How the West was Won* (1962) was the first feature film to be shown in Cinerama. *2001: A Space Odyssey* (1968) stretched the creative possibilities of the format. Technical flaws and high production expenses led to its demise in 1973.

cinnabar (HgS) Deep red mineral, mercuric sulphide, the major ore of MERCURY. It occurs as rhombohedral crystals, often twinned, and as granular masses. It is found in hydrothermal veins and volcanic deposits. The ore is reduced to mercury by roasting. It is used in the mineral pigment vermilion. Hardness 2–2.5; r.d. 8.1.

cinnamon Light-brown SPICE made from the dried inner bark of the cinnamon tree. Its delicate aroma and sweet flavour make it a common ingredient in food. It was also used for religious rites and witchcraft. The tree is a bushy evergreen native to India and Burma and cultivated in the West Indies and South America. Family Lauraceae; species *Cinnamomum zeylanicum*.

Cinque Ports Association of certain ports (originally five) in SE England that were granted special privileges in return for defending England's S coast. The grouping of Dover, Hastings, Hythe, Romney (now New Romney) and Sandwich, began under the Anglo-Saxons. The association, which Winchelsea and Rye joined in the 12th century, reached its height during the Hundred Years' War.

cipher *See* CRYPTOGRAPHY

circadian rhythm Internal "clock" mechanism found in most organisms that normally corresponds roughly with the 24-hour day. It relates most obviously to the cycle of waking and sleeping but is also involved in other cyclic variations, such as body temperature.

Circe In Greek mythology, seductive but baleful enchantress whose spells could change men into animals. Mistress of the island of Aeaea, she kept ODYSSEUS with her for a year, changing his men into pigs.

circle Plane geometric figure that is the locus of points equidistant from a fixed point (the centre). This distance is the radius (r). The area of a circle is πr^2, and its perimeter (circumference) is $2\pi r$.

circuit System of electric conductors, appliances or electronic components connected so they form a continuously conducting path. Modern circuits are often printed in copper on a plastic card (printed circuit). *See also* CAPACITOR; CHIP; INTEGRATED CIRCUIT (IC); TRANSISTOR

circuit breaker Automatic switch that disconnects the electricity supply if dangerous conditions occur. A common type of CIRCUIT breaker switches off the current if it exceeds a certain value for more than a specified time. A circuit breaker performs a similar function to a FUSE but is not destroyed in operation.

circulation, atmospheric In climatology, the movement of air in the TROPOSPHERE of Earth's ATMOSPHERE. The poleward circulation, due to CONVECTION, gives rise to large-scale eddies, such as CYCLONES and ANTICY-CLONES, low-pressure troughs and high-pressure ridges. The eddies are also caused by the Earth's rotation maintaining easterly winds towards the Equator and westerly winds towards the poles. *See also* CORIOLIS EFFECT; JET STREAM; OCEANIC CURRENT; TRADE WINDS; WIND

circulatory system Means by which oxygen and nutrients are carried to the body's tissues, and carbon dioxide and other waste products are removed. It consists of BLOOD VESSELS that carry the BLOOD, propelled by the pumping action of the HEART. In humans and other mammals, blood travels to the lungs, where it picks up OXYGEN and loses CARBON DIOXIDE. It then flows to the heart, from where it is pumped out into the AORTA, which branches into smaller arteries, arterioles and CAPILLAR-IES. Oxygen and other nutrients diffuse out of the blood, and carbon dioxide and other tissue wastes pass into the capillaries, which join to form veins leading back to the heart. Blood then returns to the lungs, and the entire cycle is repeated. In fish and many other animals, there is

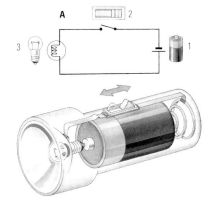

▲ **circuit** This simple electric circuit (A) represents a torch. The power source is a battery (1). The switch (2) breaks the circuit when it is in the off position. When closed, in the on position, power flows to the resistor (3), the bulb, which emits light.

a single circulatory system, with blood passing through the GILLS and on to the rest of the body without an extra boost from the heart. Insects and many other invertebrates have an open circulatory system, where the blood flows freely within the body cavity, but passes through a series of open blood vessels and heart(s).

circumcision Operation of removing part or the whole of the foreskin of the penis or of removing the clitoris. Male circumcision is ritual in some groups, notably Jews and Muslims, and is believed to have sanitary benefits. Female circumcision (genital mutilation) is intended to reduce sexual pleasure and has no medical benefit.

circumference Distance around the boundary of a plane geometric figure, nearly always applied to a circle, for which it has the value $2\pi r$, where r is the radius.

circumnavigation Voyage around the world. It was first accomplished in 1519–22 by the *Victoria* from the expedition commanded by Ferdinand MAGELLAN.

circus (Lat. ring) Circuses originated as round or oval structures for entertainment in the Roman period. Circus Maximus was built (*c*.600 BC) to stage vast chariot races and gladiatorial contests. The modern circus dates from 1768 when Philip Astley built an arena to display his equestrian skills. The modern circus is a travelling show, often held in a tent, featuring trained animals, acrobats and clowns. The main tent, the "big top", is often surrounded by smaller sideshows. The three-ring circus was invented by James A. Bailey, who merged with P.T. BARNUM to provide "The Greatest Show on Earth". In 1907 Barnum and Bailey's was purchased by the Ringling Brothers, and this large circus continues to tour the US.

cire perdue (Fr. lost wax) Method of casting metal objects (usually bronzes) used since classical antiquity. First the object is covered in wax then covered in a heat-proof mould. When heated, the wax melts away and the metal is poured into the space it occupied.

cirque (corrie, cwm) Bowl-shaped, steep-sided hollow in a mountainous region formed by glaciation. A hollow is scoured out of the rock by ice and freeze-thaw activity. When the ice melts, a lake may form in the base of the cirque. Such lakes are often fed by the retreating GLACIER.

cirrhosis Degenerative disease with excessive growth of fibrous tissue in an organ, most often the LIVER, causing inflammation and scarring. Cirrhosis of the liver may be caused by viral hepatitis, prolonged obstruction of the common bile duct, chronic abuse of alcohol or other drugs, blood disorder, heart failure or malnutrition.

cirrocumulus *See* CLOUD

Cistercian Religious order of monks founded (1098) in Citeaux, France, by BENEDICTINE monks led by St Robert of Molesme. St BERNARD OF CLAIRVAUX was largely responsible for the rapid growth of the order in the 12th century. In the 17th century, the order split into two communities: Common Observance and Strict Observance, the latter popularly known as TRAPPISTS.

citizenship Relationship in which a person is a member of a state and owes allegiance to it. Citizenship carries rights and responsibilities. It is acquired at birth either by virtue of having parents who are citizens or being born within the country's territory. It may also be acquired later by a process of naturalization.

citric acid ($C_6H_8O_7$) Colourless, crystalline solid with a sour taste. It is found in a free form in citrus fruits such as lemons and oranges, and is used for flavouring, in effervescent salts and as a mordant (colour-fixer) in dyeing. Properties: r.d. 1.54; m.p. 153°C (307.4°F).

citron Evergreen shrub or small tree of the rue family, native to Asia. It has short spines and oval leaves. It

bears large, oblong, lemon-yellow fruit. Height: up to 3.5m (11.5ft). Family Rutaceae; species *Citrus medica*.

citrus Group of trees and shrubs of the genus *Citrus* in the rue family, native to subtropical regions. They include GRAPEFRUIT, LEMON, LIME, MANDARIN and ORANGE. The stems are usually thorny, the leaves bright green, shiny and pointed. The flowers are usually white, waxy and fragrant. The fruit (hesperidium) is usually ovoid with a thick, aromatic rind. The inside of the fruit is pulpy and juicy, and is divided into segments that contain the seeds. Most citrus fruits contain significant amounts of vitamin C. Family Rutaceae.

cittern (cithern) Musical instrument popular in W Europe in the 16th to 18th centuries. A shallow, flat-backed, guitar-like instrument, its four pairs of wire strings were normally plucked with the fingers.

city Any urban complex larger or more important than a town. Cities have been central to economic, social, cultural and political development since earliest times. In Britain, the term is applied to all towns that have cathedrals; the title of city has also been granted to other large towns by royal charter. In the US, the term is applied to any incorporated municipality.

Ciudad Juárez City on the Rio Bravo del Norte (Río Grande), Chihuahua state, N Mexico. Lying on the US border, it is connected by bridges to El Paso, Texas. It has processing industries for the surrounding cotton-growing region. Pop. (1990) 798,499.

civet (civet cat) Small nocturnal, carnivorous mammal related to the GENET and MONGOOSE, found in Africa, Asia and S Europe. It has a narrow body set on long legs, and its coat is grey-yellow with black markings. There are some 20 species. Length: (overall) 53–150cm (21–59in). Family Viverridae.

civil defence Organized protection of a civilian population to limit the damage caused by enemy attack. In the UK, the Ministry of Home Security was formed (1939) to coordinate protection against air raids and possible invasion during World War 2. By 1968, the UK had largely disbanded its civil defence operations. The US has a Civil Defense Corps to deal with natural emergencies and maintains a network of fallout shelters.

civil disobedience Passive resistance to law or authority practised either as a matter of individual conscience or by a large number of people as a form of non-violent protest. The term originated with Henry THOREAU's essay *Resistance to Civil Government* (1849), in which he argued that disobeying a law is preferable to disobeying one's own conscience. It was practised in India by the supporters of "Mahatma" GANDHI and in the US by the followers of Martin Luther KING, Jr.

civil engineering Field of engineering dealing with large structures and systems. Civil engineers provide facilities for living, industry and transportation, such as roads, bridges, airports, dams, harbours and tunnels. The British Institution of Civil Engineers, founded in London in 1818, is the world's oldest engineering institution.

civil law Legal system derived from ROMAN LAW. It is different from COMMON LAW, the system generally adhered to in England and other English-speaking countries. Civil law is based on a system of codes, the most famous of which is the CODE NAPOLÉON (1804), and decisions are precisely worked out from general basic principles *a priori*. Thus, a civil law judge follows the evidence and is bound by the conditions of the written law and not by previous judicial interpretation. Civil law influences common law in jurisprudence and in admiralty, testamentary and domestic relations; it is also the basis for the system of EQUITY. It is prevalent in Louisiana, Québec (Canada), Latin America and continental Europe.

civil liberties Basic rights that every citizen possesses in a democracy. In some countries, the courts ensure freedom from government control or restraint, except as the public good require. In the US, civil liberties are guaranteed by a BILL OF RIGHTS. In 1998, the European Convention on Human Rights was incorporated into UK law in the form of the Human Rights Act. *See also* CIVIL RIGHTS

civil rights Rights conferred legally upon the individual by the state. There is no universal conception of civil rights. The modern use of the phrase is most common in the US, where it refers to relations between individuals as well as between individuals and the state. It is especially associated with the movement to achieve equal rights for African-Americans. The modern civil rights movement may be said to have begun with the foundation (1910) of the NATIONAL ASSOCIATION FOR THE ADVANCEMENT OF COLORED PEOPLE (NAACP). It gathered pace after the 1954 Supreme Court decision against segregation in schools and, after the foundation of organizations such as the CONGRESS OF RACIAL EQUALITY (CORE), the Southern Christian Leadership Conference led by Martin Luther KING, J., and the Student Nonviolent Coordinating Committee (SNCC). Subsequently, a series of CIVIL RIGHTS ACTS protected individuals from discrimination.

Civil Rights Acts (1866, 1870, 1875, 1957, 1960, 1964, 1968) US legislation. The **Civil Rights Act** (1866) gave African Americans citizenship and extended civil rights to all persons born in the US (except Native Americans). The **1870 Act** was passed to re-enact the previous measure, which was considered to be of dubious constitutionality. The 1870 Act was declared unconstitutional by the US Supreme Court in 1883. The **1875 Act** was passed to outlaw discrimination in public places because of race or previous servitude. The Act was declared unconstitutional by the Supreme Court (1883–85), which stated that the 14th Amendment protected individual rights against infringement by states, not by other individuals. The **1957 Act** established the Civil Rights Commission to investigate violations of the 15th Amendment. The **1960 Act** enabled court-appointed federal officials to protect African-American voting rights. An act of violence to obstruct a court order became a federal offence. The **1964 Act** established as law equal rights for all citizens in voting, education, public accommodations, and in federally assisted programs. The **1968 Act** guaranteed equal treatment in housing and real estate to all citizens.

civil service Administrative establishment for carrying on the work of government. In the UK, the modern service was developed between 1780 and 1870, as the weight of parliamentary business became too heavy for ministers to attend to both policy-making and departmental administration. The Treasury got its first permanent secretary in 1805, the Colonial Office a permanent official in 1825. The two main divisions of the civil service are the Home and Diplomatic services. Since 1968, the civil service has been controlled by the prime minister (as minister of the civil service), but day-to-day management is undertaken by the Lord Privy Seal. In 1981, the secretary to the cabinet was made head of the Home Civil Service. In 1996 the Senior Civil Service was created. The UK civil service has grown away from its centre in Whitehall, London, and now has many regional offices. In 1998, there were *c*.468,180 permanent civil servants in the UK. In the US, the civil service evolved from the ineffective "SPOILS SYSTEM" (1828) established during Andrew JACKSON's presidency, whereby posts were given as rewards for political

support. This system remained in place until the Pendleton Act (1883) created the Civil Service Commission. The commission implemented a merit system, and following the Hatch Acts (1939, 1940), federal employees were no longer allowed to take an active role in party politics.

Civil War, American (1861–65) War fought between the northern states (the Union) and the forces of the 11 southern states which seceded from the Union to form the CONFEDERATE STATES OF AMERICA (the Confederacy). Its immediate cause was the determination of the southern states to withdraw from a Union that the northern states regarded as indivisible. The more general cause was the question of SLAVERY, a well-established institution in the South but one that the northern ABOLITIONISTS opposed. By the 1850s, slavery, abolition and STATES' RIGHTS had created insurmountable differences between North and South. The abolitionists formed the new REPUBLICAN PARTY, and those campaigning for the rights of southern states remained in the DEMOCRATIC PARTY. The 1860 election of a Republican, Abraham LINCOLN, virtually assured southern withdrawal from the Union. The North had superior numbers, greater economic power, and command of the seas. The Confederates had passionate conviction, were fighting for their homeland, and at least early in the war, had superior generals, such as Robert E. LEE and "Stonewall" JACKSON. The war began on 12 April 1861, when Confederate forces attacked FORT SUMTER, South Carolina. The Union's first objective was to take the Confederate capital at Richmond, Virginia, in the First Battle of BULL RUN (July 1861). This campaign was unsuccessful, and the Confederates continued to be victorious, with Lee winning the Peninsular Campaign (April–June 1862) and Jackson victorious in the Shenandoah Valley (March–June 1862). The Confederates were also successful in the Seven Days' Battles (June–July 1862) and the Second Battle of BULL RUN (August 1862). However, Lee's army was checked by the strengthening Union troops (led by General George McCLELLAN) in the Battle of ANTIETAM (September 1862). The Union was defeated at the Battle of FREDERICKSBURG (December 1862) under Ambrose Burnside and at Chancellorsville (May 1863) under Joseph HOOKER. The Union victory in the Battle of GETTYSBURG (June–July 1863) was a turning point. The Union Navy had blocked southern ports, thereby denying the Confederacy essential trade with Europe. The Union strategy was to divide the South by taking control of the Mississippi, Tennessee and Cumberland rivers. The first big Union victory was at Fort Donelson on the Tennessee River (February 1862) under the command of Ulysses S. GRANT. Grant won a victory in the siege of VICKSBURG (November 1862–July 1863) which, with the fall of Memphis (June 1862), gave Union troops control of the Mississippi. In 1864 Grant became supreme commander. He confronted Lee's army in the WILDERNESS CAMPAIGN (May–June 1864) and began the long siege of Petersburg, Virginia – the defence of which was vital to the survival of RICHMOND. Meanwhile, the Union's General William T. SHERMAN cut a devastating swathe across Georgia in 1864, burning ATLANTA on the way. The Union victory at the Battle of Five Forks (1865) blocked the retreat route for Confederate troops in Richmond. Petersburg fell two days later, and Richmond was indefensible. The war ended with Lee's surrender to Grant at Appomattox Court House in April 1865. The Civil War claimed *c*.620,000 lives, more than the combined American dead from all other wars between 1775 and 1975. The Union lost *c*.360,000 soldiers, and the Confederacy *c*.260,000. The South was economically ruined by the war, and RECONSTRUCTION policies poisoned relations between North and South for a century.

Civil Wars, English (1642–45, 1648, 1651) Conflicts in Britain between Crown and Parliament. Following years of dispute between the king and state over the power of the crown, war began when King CHARLES I raised his standard at Nottingham. Royalist forces were at first successful at Edgehill (1642), but there were no decisive engagements and Parliament's position was stronger, as it controlled the SE, London and the navy, and formed an alliance with Scotland. Parliament's victory at Marston Moor (1644) was a turning point, and in 1645 FAIRFAX and Oliver CROMWELL won a decisive victory at Naseby with their NEW MODEL ARMY. In 1646, Charles I surrendered. While negotiating with Parliament, he secretly secured an agreement with the Scots that led to what is usually called the second civil war (1648). A few local Royalist risings came to nothing, and the Scots, invading England, were swiftly defeated. The execution of Charles I (1649) provoked further conflict in 1650, in which Scots and Irish Royalists supported the future CHARLES II. Cromwell suppressed the Irish and the Scots, the final battle being fought at Worcester (1651).

Civil War, Spanish (1936–39) Conflict developing from a military rising against the republican government in Spain. The revolt began in Spanish Morocco, led by General FRANCO. It was supported by conservatives and reactionaries of many kinds, collectively known as the Nationalists and including the fascist FALANGE. The leftist POPULAR FRONT government was supported by republicans, socialists and a variety of ill-coordinated leftist groups, collectively known as Loyalists or Republicans. The Nationalists swiftly gained control of most of rural W Spain. The war represented the first major clash between the forces of the extreme right and the extreme left in Europe. Franco received extensive military support, especially aircraft, from the fascist dictators MUSSOLINI AND HITLER. The Soviet Union provided more limited aid for the Republicans. Liberal and socialist sympathizers from countries such as Britain and France fought as volunteers for the Republicans, but their governments remained neutral. In 1937, the Nationalists extended their control, while the Republicans were weakened by internal quarrels. In 1938, the Nationalists reached the Mediterranean, splitting Republican forces. The fall of Madrid to the Nationalists, after a long siege, in March 1939 ended the war. More than one million Spaniards had been killed.

Cixi (1835–1908) (Tz'u Hsi or Zi Xi) Empress Dowager of China. As mistress of the Emperor Xian Feng and mother of his only son, she became co-regent in 1861 and remained in power until her death by arranging for the succession of her infant nephew in 1875 and displacing him in a palace coup in 1898. Ruthless and reactionary, she abandoned the modernization programme of the "Hundred Days of Reform" and supported the BOXER REBELLION (1900).

CJD *See* CREUTZFELD-JAKOB DISEASE

cladistics System of classifying organisms on the measurable similarities between their respective organs, parts or biological structures. Organisms that share several characteristics are put into taxonomic groups known as **clades**. A **cladogram** is a diagram, resembling a sideways family tree, that shows how pairs or groups of clades diverged from common ancestors. There is considerable disagreement about the validity of cladistics.

Clair, René (1898–1981) French film director. His early work, such as *Entr'acte* (1924) and the silent satire *The Italian Straw Hat* (1927), shows the influence of

SURREALISM. Clair's stylish "talkies", such as *Le Million*, (1931), are masterpieces of early cinema.

clam Bivalve mollusc found mainly in marine waters. It is usually partly buried in sand or mud. With a large foot for burrowing, its soft, flat body lies between two muscles for opening and closing the shells. A fleshy part called the mantle, lies next to the shells. Clams feed on PLANKTON. Class Pelecypoda.

clan Unilineal descent group in which KINSHIP is recognized either through the male line (patrilineal) or through the female line (matrilineal). A notable example is the Highland clans of Scotland, which stress mutual obligations and duties. *See also* MATRIARCHY; PATRIARCHY

Clapham Sect (*c.*1790–*c.*1830) Group of British evangelical reformers. Many of them, including William WILBERFORCE, lived in Clapham, S London, and several were members of Parliament. Originally known as the "Saints", they were especially influential in the abolition of SLAVERY and in prison reform.

Clapton, Eric (1945–) English blues and rock guitarist and songwriter. Clapton was a member of The Yardbirds before forming Cream (1966–68) and Derek and the Dominos (1970–72). His long, blues-based guitar solos led to comparisons with Jimi HENDRIX. *Layla and Other Assorted Love Songs* (1970) is considered a landmark in rock music history. Clapton's solo records include the Grammy award-winning *Unplugged* (1992).

Clare, Saint (1194–1253) Italian nun, founder (1215) with St FRANCIS OF ASSISI of the FRANCISCAN nuns (Poor Clares). A strict order which placed special emphasis on the vow of poverty, it spread throughout Europe in the 13th and 14th centuries. She was canonized in 1255. Her feast day is 12 August.

Clare, John (1793–1864) English poet. The son of an agricultural labourer, his verse contains vivid descriptions of the countryside from the viewpoint of a class which seldom found a poetic voice. His works include *Poems Descriptive of Rural Life and Scenery* (1820), *The Village Minstrel* (1821) and *The Rural Muse* (1835). Briefly lionized as a "peasant" poet, he was declared insane in 1837 and spent most of the rest of his life in asylums.

Clare County between Galway Bay and the Shannon River estuary, Munster province, w Republic of Ireland; the county town is Ennis. The area is hilly and infertile. The chief crops are oats and potatoes. Sheep, cattle, pigs and poultry are raised, and fishing is important. Area: 3,188sq km (1,231sq mi). Pop. (1991) 90,918.

Clarendon, Edward Hyde, 1st Earl of (1609–74) British statesman and historian. A leading adviser to Charles I, he joined CHARLES II in exile, and negotiated the RESTORATION (1660). As chief minister to Charles II, he initiated (but disapproved of) four statutes collectively known as the **Clarendon Code**. The statutes restricted gatherings of PURITANS and Nonconformists, and the movement of their ministers. In addition, all ministers were forced to use the Anglican Book of COMMON PRAYER. Following disagreements with Charles II, he was impeached and forced into exile in 1667, where he completed his *History of the Rebellion* and wrote an autobiography. *See also* NONCONFORMISM

Clarendon, Constitutions of (1164) Sixteen articles issued by HENRY II of England to limit the powers of the church. The most controversial article required clergy who had been convicted in church courts to be punished by royal courts. They played a significant role in the dispute between Henry and Thomas à BECKET.

clarinet Single-reed WOODWIND instrument. It is commonly pitched in B♭ and has a range of over 3 octaves. Other members of the family include the alto clarinet in E♭, the bass in B♭ and the high sopranino in E♭.

Clark, Kenneth McKenzie, Baron (1903–83) English art historian. He was director (1934–45) of the National Gallery, London. *The Nude* (1955) and his monographs on Leonardo da Vinci (1939) and Piero della Francesca (1951) are regarded as standard texts. Clark's television series *Civilisation* (1969) remains a classic work of art history. He was made a life peer in 1969.

Clarke, Arthur C. (Charles) (1917–) English science-fiction writer. He is noted for the realism of his works, such as *Childhood's End* (1953) and *Voices from the Sky* (1965). Stanley Kubrick's film *2001: A Space Odyssey* (1969) was based on his short story *The Sentinel* (1951). Clarke has written three sequels, *2010: Odyssey Two* (1982), *2061: Odyssey Three* (1987) and *3001: The Final Odyssey* (1997).

Clarke, Kenneth Harry (1940–) British statesman, chancellor of the exchequer (1993–97). He became a Conservative MP in 1970. Clarke served in Margaret THATCHER's cabinet as secretary of state for health (1988–90) and education (1991). When John MAJOR became prime minister, he became home secretary (1992). His first budget as chancellor saw an increase in taxation, but the 1996 budget reduced the basic rate by a penny. An outspoken Europhile, after the Conservatives' landslide defeat in the 1997 general election, he was beaten by William HAGUE in the contest for the leadership of the Conservative Party.

class In biology, part of the CLASSIFICATION of living organisms, ranking above ORDER and below PHYLUM.

class In social science, a section of society sharing similar socio-economic status. A person's class is usually determined by the income and wealth of their parents. A class society is a system based on the unequal distribution of wealth. In Marxism, class is defined in relation to the means of PRODUCTION (land, capital). The BOURGEOISIE own the means of production and the PROLETARIAT provide the labour. In the *Communist Manifesto* (1848), Karl MARX and Friedrich ENGELS asserted that "the history of all society up to now is the history of class struggle."

classical Term used in many different and apparently conflicting ways. Literally, it refers to the period between the Archaic and the HELLENISTIC AGE phases of ancient Greek culture. It is used more generally, however, to mean the opposite of romantic or to refer to the artistic styles whose origins can be traced in ancient Greece or Rome. As the antithesis of ROMANTICISM, it is an art which follows recognized aesthetic formulas rather than a style which focuses on individual expression. The RENAISSANCE architect, ALBERTI, took his inspiration from ancient Greek and Roman buildings, and CLASSICISM often suggests descent from antique sources. A classical style of Greek and Roman architecture dominated Europe from 1500 to 1900.

classical economics Term applied to the work of British economists from the late-18th to the mid-19th century. Classical economists range from Adam SMITH to John Stuart MILL. They maintained that markets, if left to their own devices without the interference of government, would find a natural equilibrium. *See also* CAPITALISM; LAISSEZ-FAIRE; MALTHUS, THOMAS

classical music Music composed between *c*.1750 and *c*.1820, whose style is characterized by emotional restraint, the dominance of homophonic melodies (melodies with accompaniment) and clear structures and forms underlying the music. The classical period saw the development of forms such as CONCERTO, SONATA,

SYMPHONY and string quartet, and the piano replace the harpsichord. The greatest composers of this period were HAYDN, MOZART, BEETHOVEN AND SCHUBERT.

classical revival Art and architecture in the style of the ancient Greeks and Romans. The style reflects simplicity, harmony and balance. The Italian RENAISSANCE and the neo-classical style of the early 19th century are examples of classical revivals. *See also* CLASSICISM; NEO-CLASSICISM

classicism Art history term used for an aesthetic attitude and an artistic tradition. The artistic tradition refers to the classical antiquity of Greece and Rome, its art, literature and criticism, and the subsequent periods that looked back to it for their prototypes, such as the CAROLINGIAN RENAISSANCE, the RENAISSANCE and NEO-CLASSICISM. Its aesthetic use suggests the classical characteristics of clarity, order, balance, unity, symmetry and dignity.

classification Organization of organisms into categories based on appearance, structure, genetic sequence or evolution. The categories, from the most inclusive to the most exclusive are KINGDOM, PHYLUM, CLASS, ORDER, FAMILY, GENUS, SPECIES and sometimes variety. For example, the domestic dog is classified as kingdom Animalia, phylum Chordata, class Mammalia, order Carnivora, family Canidae, genus *Canis*, species *Canis familiaris*.

Claude Lorrain (*c*.1604–82) (Claude Gellée) French LANDSCAPE painter, the most influential ideal landscapist. After settling in Rome (1627), he developed a style that combined poetic idealism and his own observations. His mature style evolved between 1640 and 1660, when he explored the natural play of light on different textures. J.M.W. TURNER was among those to absorb his ideas, and he inspired the style known as picturesque.

Claudel, Paul Louis Charles Marie (1868–1955) French dramatist, poet and essayist. Claudel converted to Roman Catholicism in 1886, and many of his works contain religious symbolism. His plays include *The Annunciation to Mary* (1912) and *The Satin Slipper* (1929). The lyrical *Five Great Odes* (1910) contains his finest poetry.

Claudius I (10 BC–AD 54) (Tiberius Claudius Nero Germanicus) Roman emperor (AD 41–54), nephew of TIBERIUS. As successor to CALIGULA, Claudius was the first emperor chosen by the army. He had military successes in Germany, conquered Britain in AD 43, and built both the harbour of Ostia and the Claudian aqueduct. Agrippina the Younger (his fourth wife) supposedly poisoned him and made her son, NERO, emperor.

Clausewitz, Carl von (1780–1831) Prussian soldier and military theorist. He served in the Napoleonic Wars against France. In his theory of large-scale warfare, *On War* (1832), Clausewitz argued that war is simply an extension of politics by other means.

Clausius, Rudolf Julius Emanuel (1822–88) German physicist, regarded as the founder of THERMODYNAMICS. Clausius was the first to formulate the second law of thermodynamics that heat cannot pass from a colder to a hotter object. He also introduced the term ENTROPY.

clavichord Earliest stringed instrument with mechanical action controlled by a keyboard. Possibly originating in the 13th century, it was used extensively from the 16th–18th centuries. The clavichord has a delicate tone; it was superseded by the HARPSICHORD.

clavicle (collar bone) Thin, slightly curved bone attached by ligaments to the top of the STERNUM (breastbone). The clavicle and shoulder-blade make up the SHOULDER girdle, linking the arms to the axis of the body.

Clay, Cassius Former name of Muhammad ALI

Clay, Henry (1777–1852) US statesman. He served in both the House of Representatives (1811–14, 1815–21,

1823–25) and in the Senate (1831–42, 1849–52). Clay was one of the "war hawks" who favoured the WAR OF 1812. He ran for president (1824), and when the election went to the House of Representatives, he supported John Quincy ADAMS. When Adams named Clay secretary of state (1825–29), charges of political corruption were made. One of the founders of the WHIG PARTY, he ran against Andrew JACKSON in 1832. He ran for president again (1844) but was defeated by James POLK. Clay's last years in the Senate were spent trying to work out a compromise between the slave-owning states of the South and the free northern states. The Compromise of 1850 was one result of those efforts.

clay Group of hydrous silicates of aluminium and magnesium, including kaolinite and halloysite, usually mixed with some quartz, calcite or gypsum. It is formed by the WEATHERING of surface GRANITE or the chemical decomposition of FELDSPAR. Soft when wet, it hardens on firing and is used to make CERAMICS, pipes and bricks or to clad the walls of simple buildings.

clearing house Institution established by businesses engaged in similar activities to facilitate transactions among them. Bank clearing houses, for example, aid in the exchange of cheques and drafts without the actual transfer of cash. *See also* BANKING

cleavage In embryology, progressive series of cell divisions that transform a fertilized egg into the earliest embryonic stage (BLASTULA). The egg is divided into blastomeres (smaller cells), each containing a DIPLOID number of chromosomes.

cleavage, rock Formation of definite planes through a rock. It is caused by compression associated with folding and metamorphism, and results in the rock splitting easily parallel to the cleavage.

Cleese, John Marwood (1939–) English actor and screenwriter. He was co-originator of the anarchic television series *Monty Python's Flying Circus* (1969–74). Cleese played a major role in the comedy films spawned by the series, such as *Monty Python's Life of Brian* (1979). He also starred in the television series *Fawlty Towers* (1975–79). Cleese gained an Oscar nomination for best screenplay for *A Fish Called Wanda* (1988).

cleft palate Congenital deformity in which there is an opening in the roof of the mouth, causing direct communication between the nasal and mouth cavities. It is often associated with HARELIP and makes normal speech difficult. Usual treatment includes surgery, special dental care and speech therapy if necessary.

clematis Genus of perennial, mostly climbing shrubs found worldwide. Many have attractive deep blue, violet, white, pink or red flowers, or flower clusters. The leaves are usually compound. Family Ranunculaceae.

Clemenceau, Georges (1841–1929) French statesman, premier (1906–09, 1917–20). A moderate republican, he served in the Chamber of Deputies (1876–1893), favoured compromise in the revolt of the PARIS COMMUNE (1871), and strongly supported Alfred Dreyfus. Clemenceau returned to the Senate in 1902. Concerned with the growing power of Germany, his first term as premier saw the strengthening of relations with Britain. He was succeeded by Aristide BRIAND. After World War I, Clemenceau returned to power and led the French delegation at the VERSAILLES peace conference. *See also* DREYFUS AFFAIR

Clement I, Saint (active late 1st century AD) (Clement of Rome) Pope (*c.*88–*c.*97). His epistle to the church at Corinth (*c.*96) stated the need for unity within the church. He was probably martyred. His feast day is 23 November.

Clement V (*c.*1264–1314) Pope (1305–14), b. Bertrand de Got. He was made archbishop of Bordeaux by BONIFACE VIII. In 1309, Clement moved the papal court to AVIGNON, France. He supported PHILIP IV's suppression of the KNIGHTS TEMPLAR.

Clement VI (1291–1352) Pope (1342–52), b. Pierre Roger. He purchased Avignon and established an extravagant court. Clement offered sanctuary to Jews accused of causing the BLACK DEATH (1348–50) and declared all churches and offices were subject to papal control.

Clement VII (1478–1534) Pope (1523–34), b. Giulio de' Medici. He sided with FRANCIS I in the League of Cognac, thus opposing the Holy Roman Emperor CHARLES V. The imperial troops attacked Rome, and a compromise was drawn up. Clement was unable to deal with the rise of Protestantism, and his indecisiveness over the divorce of Catherine of Aragon and HENRY VIII is thought to have hastened the REFORMATION in England.

Clement of Alexandria (150–215) (Titus Flavius Clemens) Greek theologian and one of the Fathers of the Church. Origen was one of his pupils. In his works, such as *Exhortation to the Greeks*, Clement sought to reconcile Platonic and Christian thought. Though he was regarded as a saint until the 9th century, Clement was condemned by Photius for heresy, andayd he was struck off the list of Roman martyrs. His feast is 5 December.

Clementi, Muzio (1752–1832) British composer and keyboard player, b. Italy. Clementi was an accomplished piano virtuoso and toured (1780–85) throughout Europe. He made a fortune as a piano manufacturer and music publisher. Clementi's best-known compositions are his *c.*70 keyboard sonatas.

Cleopatra (69–30 BC) Queen of Egypt (51–48 BC, 47–30 BC). In 47 BC, she overthrew her husband, brother and co-ruler Ptolemy XIII with the aid of Julius CAESAR, who became her lover. Cleopatra went to Rome with Caesar, but after his assassination in 44 BC, she returned to Alexandria, once again as queen. MARK ANTONY, who had become her lover following Caesar's death, followed her to Egypt, and they married (37 BC). The marriage infuriated Octavian (later AUGUSTUS), brother of Mark Antony's former wife. In 31 BC, Rome declared war on Egypt and defeated Antony and Cleopatra's forces at the Battle of ACTIUM. Mark Antony committed suicide. Cleopatra surrendered to Octavian but then killed herself.

Cleopatra's needles Popular name for two Egyptian obelisks of red granite that were acquired separately in the 1870s. Erected by King Thutmose III in Egypt in the 15th century BC, they are nearly 21m (70ft) tall and weigh *c.*180 tonnes. One stands in New York's Central Park, the other on the Thames Embankment in London.

clergy Collective organization of ordained or consecrated priests and ministers, especially of the Christian church. In the Roman Catholic, Orthodox and Anglican churches, the clergy comprise the orders of bishop, priest and deacon, and may also include members of religious orders. In these churches, bishops exercise authority over priests and deacons. In non-episcopal Protestant churches, the clergy consist of pastors and ministers. Functions of the clergy include administration of the sacrament, preaching and the exercise of spiritual guidance. *See also* ORDINATION OF WOMEN

Clermont-Ferrand City in S central France, capital of Puy-de-Dôme department. Clermont was founded by the Romans and became an episcopal see in the 3rd century. Pope Urban II preached the First Crusade here in 1095. In 1731, Clermont was merged with Montferrand.

Today, it is the industrial centre of the Massif Central and is home to Michelin tyres. Sites include the gothic Cathedral of Notre-Dame (begun 1248). Industries: rubber goods, textiles. Pop. (1990) 136,181.

Cleveland, (Stephen) Grover (1837–1908) 22nd and 24th US president (1885–89, 1893–97). He rose to prominence as governor of New York (1883–84). With the help of Republican MUGWUMPS, he defeated James G. BLAINE to become the first Democratic president since the American Civil War. Cleveland's attempt to reduce the tariff contributed to Benjamin HARRISON's electoral victory in 1888. In his second term, he was faced with a monetary crisis (1893) and secured repeal of the Sherman Silver Purchase Act. In 1895, Cleveland broadened the scope of the MONROE DOCTRINE in response to Britain's boundary dispute with Venezuela. His attempt to maintain the gold standard angered radical Democrats, and Cleveland was not renominated in 1896.

Cleveland City and port at the mouth of the Cuyahoga River, on Lake Erie, NE Ohio, USA. Founded (1796) by Moses Cleaveland, it grew rapidly with the opening of the Ohio and Erie Canal and the arrival of the railway in 1851. In 1870, John D. ROCKEFELLER founded Standard Oil Company here. Cleveland has a symphony orchestra, three universities and an art institute. It is a major Great Lakes port and an iron and steel centre. NASA maintains a research centre here. Industries: chemicals, oil refining, engineering, electronics. Pop. (1990) 505,616.

click beetle (skipjack) Any of a group of beetles that turn over by snapping their bodies and throwing themselves into the air. They make an audible click in the process. Their long, cylindrical larvae are called WIREWORMS.

click language Any of several southern African languages belonging chiefly to the KHOISAN group, and characterized by the use of suction speech sounds called clicks. Clicks are also found in some BANTU languages.

client-server Type of relationship between COMPUTERS in a COMPUTER NETWORK. A client computer makes requests of a designated server computer. The server performs the requested functions and delivers the results.

Cliff, Clarice (1899–1972) English ART DECO pottery designer. Cliff created geometrically shaped ceramics, decorated with bold, brightly coloured abstract designs. Extremely popular in the 1930s, her innovative work was sold under the title "Bizarre".

climate Weather conditions of a place or region prevailing over a long time. The major factors influencing climate are temperature, air movement, incoming and outgoing radiation and moisture movements.

climate change *See* GLOBAL WARMING

climate modelling Use of a COMPUTER to simulate the Earth's climate. Physical data, such as temperature, pressure and wind direction, are manipulated mathematically by a powerful computer to give a model of the Earth's whole climatic system. Researchers can vary various parameters to see what changes occur. In this way they can study the effects of the GREENHOUSE EFFECT and possible GLOBAL WARMING. *See also* CHAOS THEORY

climatology Scientific study of the Earth's climates. **Physical** climatology investigates relationships between temperature, pressure, winds, precipitation and other weather phenomena. **Regional** climatology considers latitude and other geographical factors, such as the influence of large land masses.

climax community In ECOLOGY, stable community that exists at the end of ecological SUCCESSION. During succession, a range of plants and their associated animal life gradually colonize an area, with newcomers usually displacing many of the existing species. At the climax of this process, colonization ceases. *See also* ECOSYSTEM

clinical psychology Field of psychology concerned with diagnosis and treatment of behavioural disorders. Clinical psychologists are engaged in treatment including behaviour therapy and other forms of psychotherapy. Clinical psychologists may work with psychiatrists but do not usually have medical training themselves.

Clinton, Bill (William Jefferson) (1946–) 42nd US president (1993–2000). Clinton became the youngest-ever US governor when he was elected to represent Arkansas (1978–80, 1983–92). Economic recession and Clinton's reformist agenda led to an easy electoral victory (1992) over the incumbent president, George BUSH. As president, Clinton made health-care an immediate priority, appointing his wife, Hillary CLINTON, to head a commission on reform. She was soon removed from the post, and many of the reforms were not realized. Clinton was a chief advocate of the NORTH AMERICAN FREE TRADE AGREEMENT (NAFTA), which won congressional approval in 1993. His first term was dogged by the Whitewater investigation and the blocking of reforms and appointments by a Republican-dominated Congress. Despite allegations of financial and personal impropriety, a buoyant domestic economy and Bob DOLE's lacklustre campaign enabled Clinton to become the first Democratic president since Franklin D. ROOSEVELT to serve successive terms in office. The priorities for his second term were education and welfare reforms, and the expansion of NATO. Economic growth enabled Clinton to announce a balanced budget for 1998. His second term was dogged by sexual scandal. Following the investigations of special prosecutor Kenneth Starr, Clinton was forced to admit that he had an improper relationship with Monica Lewinsky, a White House intern. In 1998, facing charges of perjury over the affair, he became only the second US president (after Andrew JOHNSON) to be impeached. Clinton refused to resign and launched Operation Desert Fox (December 1998), a concerted bombing campaign against Iraq for failing to comply with UN resolutions. He was succeeded by George W. BUSH.

Clinton, George (1739–1812) US statesman, vice president (1805–12). He led the anti-British faction in the New York assembly and was a delegate to the Second Continental Congress. Clinton served as a brigadier general in the Revolution before becoming the first elected governor of New York (1777–95, 1800–04). Clinton became vice president in Thomas JEFFERSON's second term. He stood for president in 1808, but had to accept the vice presidency under James MADISON.

Clinton, Hillary Rodham (1947–) US attorney and first lady. The wife of Bill CLINTON, Hillary drafted (1993) a plan to provide health insurance for all Americans, but it was not implemented. Along with her husband, she was implicated in the Whitewater land and banking scandal. She firmly supported Bill Clinton through a series of allegations of extra-marital liaisons. In 2000, she was elected as senator from New York.

clipper Commercial sailing vessel used throughout the second half of the 19th century. Built primarily for speed, clippers had a long thin hull, usually three masts and many square-rigged sails. One example, the *Cutty Sark*, is preserved in a dry-dock at Greenwich, London.

clitoris *See* VULVA

Clive, Robert, Baron Clive of Plassey (1725–74) British soldier and administrator. In 1743, he travelled to Madras, India, as an official of the British EAST INDIA COMPANY. Clive first attracted attention for his masterly use of guerrilla warfare, such as the capture of Arcot (1751), which prevented the French gaining control of s India. In 1757, he recaptured Calcutta from the nawab of Bengal. As first governor of Bengal (1757–60), Clive established British supremacy in India but his administration was tarnished by corruption. In 1760, he returned to Britain to gain a peerage. Clive returned to Bengal to serve a second term as governor (1765–67). He reformed the civil service and extended the East India Company's control to Bihar. In 1767, he left for England. Clive faced charges of embezzling state funds, but was finally acquitted in 1773. He committed suicide.

cloaca Cavity into which intestinal, urinary and genital tracts open in fish, reptiles, birds and some primitive mammals.

clock Instrument for measuring time. The earliest timekeeping instruments were designed to measure the movements of the Sun, Moon and stars. Examples include neolithic stone columns, ancient Egyptian sundials and water clocks. Candle clocks and sandglasses were later types of non-mechanical clocks. The central feature of all mechanical clocks is an **escapement** mechanism, which enables a clock to tick off time at discrete intervals. This movement is transmitted through a series of gears to the hands which are pushed forward a small distance with every escapement movement. Motive power for mechanical clocks has been provided variously by falling weights, pendulums and coiled springs. In some modern wristwatches, the coiled spring is rewound continually by natural wrist movements. Other modern clocks include those using an electrically oscillated quartz crystal. The latter are accurate, but even more accurate are ATOMIC CLOCKS, which rely upon the natural oscillations of atoms and which measure time to an accuracy of thousandths of a second per year.

cloisonné Enamelling technique in which the design is constructed of wires soldered to a plate, and the cells (cloisons) formed are filled with coloured ENAMEL paste and fired. It was developed in Mycenaean Greece.

clone Set of organisms obtained from a single original parent through some form of ASEXUAL REPRODUCTION or by ARTIFICIAL SELECTION. Clones are genetically identical and may arise naturally from PARTHENOGENESIS in animals. Cloning is often used in plant propagation (including TISSUE CULTURE) to produce new plants from parents with desirable qualities such as high yield. It is now possible to produce animal clones from tissue culture. In 1997, scientists in Scotland announced that they had cloned a sheep. Using nuclear-transfer technology (transfer of a cell NUCLEUS), they produced an embryo from a single udder cell of an adult sheep. The embryo was then implanted into a surrogate mother. In February 1997, Dolly (an identical twin of the sheep that donated the cell) was born. In 1998, Dolly herself gave birth, allaying fears that she would be infertile. In 2000, the same technique was used to implant a gaur embryo in a cow's womb; the first time one species had given birth to another. *See also* GENETIC ENGINEERING

closed-circuit television (CCTV) Television system in which the television camera, receiver and associated controls are most often directly linked by cables. Applications include surveillance and remote monitoring of hazardous environments. CABLE TELEVISION is an extended form of closed-circuit television.

clothes moth Three species of small MOTH whose larvae (caterpillars) attack woollen fabrics and furs. The most destructive is the case-making *Tinea pellionella*, which builds and lives in a small portable case. Wingspan: 1.2cm (0.5in). Family Tinidae.

cloud Masses of water particles or ice crystals suspended in the lower atmosphere. Clouds are formed when water from the Earth's surface becomes vapour through EVAPORATION. As the water vapour rises, it cools and condenses around microscopic salt and dust particles, forming droplets. Where the atmosphere is below the freezing temperature of water, the droplets turn to ice. There are ten different classifications of clouds: **cirrus** are high (above 6,000m/20,000ft), white and threadlike. **Cirrocumulus** are also high clouds, but are often thin sheets. **Cirrostratus** are white, almost transparent, sheets. **Altocumulus** are greyish-white globular clouds found between 2,400m (8,000ft) and 6,000m (20,000ft). **Altostratus** are grey/blue and streaky, and often cover the whole sky. They often produce drizzle. **Nimbostratus** are low, thick and dark and usually shed rain or snow. **Stratocumulus** are masses of white, grey or dark cloud. **Stratus** are low-lying and grey. **Cumulus** are white and fluffy-looking. **Cumulonimbus** are towering, dark clouds which generally produce thunderstorms. Their bases almost touch the ground and extend upward to 23,000m (75,000ft). By day, clouds reflect the rays of the Sun back into the atmosphere, keeping the ground cool. At night, clouds trap and re-radiate heat rising from the Earth, keeping surface temperatures warm. *See also* FOG; HYDROLOGICAL CYCLE

cloud chamber Instrument used to detect and identify charged particles, invented in the 1880s by C.T.R. WILSON to study atomic radiation. The principle is the same as the later BUBBLE CHAMBER, except liquefied gas is replaced by air supersaturated with water or alcohol vapour, and the tracks left are droplets which form around the ionizing particle. The tracks are deflected by a magnetic field and photographed for analysis.

Clouet, François (*c.*1510–72) French portrait painter, son of Jean CLOUET. François succeeded his father as

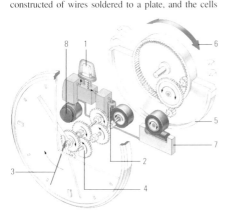

▲ **clock** Many modern clocks and watches use a quartz crystal (1) to tell the time accurately. When electricity is passed through the quartz, it oscillates exactly 32,768 times each second. The oscillations are counted and, on every 32,768th, a pulse of electricity is sent to a motor (2) that moves the hands (3) via gears (4). The need for a battery to power the motor can be removed if a swinging weight (5) is used to generate a current. As the watch moves, the weight rotates (6), turning a generator (7). The current produced by the generator is stored in a capacitor (8) and is smoothed before reaching the quartz crystal.

court painter in 1541. There has been confusion over their respective careers, largely because both used the nickname Janet. Best known of his certain works are the portraits *Pierre Quthe* (1562) and *Lady in her Bath* (*c*.1570).

Clouet, Jean (*c*.1485–1540) French painter in the court of Francis I, father of François Clouet. No authenticated works by him survive, but a few portraits, including *Dauphin François* and *Man holding the Works of Petrarch*, are attributed to him. These follow a Flemish naturalist model, but his drawings show more individuality.

Clough, Arthur Hugh (1819–61) English poet. Only two volumes appeared during his lifetime, *The Bothie of Tober-na-Vuolich* (1848) and *Ambarvalia* (1849). Clough has been posthumously reappraised for his description of Victorian spiritual doubt in works such as *Amours de Voyage* (1858) and the unfinished *Dipsychus* (1865).

clove Tall aromatic, evergreen tree native to the Molucca Islands. The small purple flowers appear in clusters; the dried flower buds are widely used in cookery. Oil of cloves is distilled from the stems. Height: to 12m (40ft). Family Myrtaceae; species *Syzygium aromaticum*.

clover Low-growing annual, biennial and perennial plants native to temperate regions of Europe but now found throughout warmer regions of the Northern Hemisphere. The leaves have three leaflets, rarely four (considered good luck), and the dense flower clusters are white, red, purple, pink or yellow. Some species are grown as food for cattle. Most species are good nitrogen-fixers, due to the bacteria in their ROOT NODULES, which help to enrich soil. Family Fabaceae/Leguminosae; genus *Trifolium*. *See also* NITROGEN CYCLE; NITROGEN FIXATION

Clovis I (465–511) Frankish king of the Merovingian dynasty. He overthrew the Romanized kingdom of Soissons and conquered the Alemanni near Cologne. Clovis and his army later converted to Christianity in fulfilment of a promise made before the battle. In 507, he defeated the Visigoths under Alaric II near Poitiers. Clovis established Merovingian power throughout most of Gaul.

clubmoss Any of *c*.200 species of small evergreen spore-bearing plants which, unlike true MOSSES, have specialized tissues for transporting water, food and minerals. They are related to FERNS and HORSETAILS. The small leaves are arranged in tight whorls around the aerial stems. Millions of years ago, their ancestors formed the large trees of CARBONIFEROUS coal forests. Phylum Lycopodophyta, Family Lycopodiaceae.

Cluj-Napoca City on the River Somesul, at the foot of the w Carpathians, Transylvania, NW central Romania. Built on the Dacian town of Napoca (2nd century BC), Cluj was founded (as Klausenberg) by German colonists in the 12th century. The city was an important cultural centre in the Middle Ages. Stephen Bathory founded (1581) a Jesuit academy, and Cluj became the capital of Transylvania. Part of Austria-Hungary until 1920, it is now Romania's second-largest city. Industries: engineering, chemicals. Pop. (1994) 326,000.

Cluny, Order of Religious order founded (910) by William the Pious, Duke of Aquitaine, at the Monastery of Cluny, France. It was known for its high standards, reflected in strict observance of the BENEDICTINE rule and emphasis on dignified worship, a personal spiritual life and sound economics. Its influence spread throughout s France and Italy, reaching its climax in the 12th century. The monastery at Cluny survived until 1790.

cluster, stellar *See* GLOBULAR CLUSTER; OPEN CLUSTER

clutch Any device placed between the rotating parts of an engine or motor and the drive-shaft to facilitate their quick connection or disconnection. In a car, temporary disengagement of the engine is essential during gearchanges. The clutch usually consists of a pair of friction plates, although there are fluid clutches as well.

clutch, electromagnetic Device that uses magnetic attraction to connect two rotating shafts. Forms include disc clutches with energized coils and magnetic clutch plates. **Eddy current** clutches induce rotational movement in the shaft to be engaged and rotated. **Hysteresis** clutches also transmit rotation without slip. Other electromagnetic clutches employ magnetic metal particles.

Clwyd County in N Wales, bordered by the Irish Sea, Cheshire, Shropshire, Powys and Gwynedd. The county town is Mold. The Vale of Clwyd is a rich agricultural region. Industries: iron and steel, tourism. Area: 2,426sq km (937sq mi). Pop. (1991) 408,090.

Clyde River in SW Scotland. It rises in the Southern Uplands, flows N, then NW, passing over the Falls of Clyde and widening into the Firth of Clyde at Dumbarton. Clydebank, below Glasgow, was Scotland's main shipbuilding region. Length: 170km (106mi).

Clytemnestra In Greek legend, the unfaithful wife of Agamemnon, King of Mycenae, and mother of his son Orestes. On Agamemnon's return from Troy he was murdered by Clytemnestra and her lover Aegisthus.

CND *See* Campaign for Nuclear Disarmament

cnidarian (coelenterate) Any one of the 9,000 species of marine invertebrates of the phylum Cnidaria, which includes JELLYFISH, SEA ANEMONE and CORAL. Charaterized by a digestive cavity that forms the main body, they may have been the first animal group to reach the tissue level of organization. Cnidarians are radially symmetrical, jelly-like with a nerve net and one body opening. Reproduction is sexual and asexual; REGENERATION also occurs.

coal Blackish, solid fuel formed from the remains of fossil plants. In the carboniferous and tertiary periods, swamp vegetation subsided to form PEAT bogs. Sedimentary deposits buried the bogs, and the resultant increase in pressure and heat produced lignite (brown coal), then bituminous coal and finally ANTHRACITE if temperature increased sufficiently. This is termed the coal rank series; each rank of coal represents an increase in carbon content and a reduction in the proportion of natural gas and moisture. Lignite is a poorer fuel than anthracite. *See artwork* p.196

coal tar By-product from the manufacture of COKE. Coal tar comes from bituminous COAL used in the distillation process. It is a volatile substance, important for its organic chemical constituents (coal-tar crudes), which are extracted by further distillation. These are the basic ingredients for the synthesis of many products, such as explosives, drugs, dyes and perfumes.

Coast Mountains Mountain range on the Pacific coast of North America, extending N for *c*.1,600km (1,000mi) through British Columbia, Canada, and into Alaska. An extension of the CASCADE Range, the highest peak is Mount Waddington at 4,042m (13,260ft).

coati (coatimundi) Three species of raccoon-like rodents of SW US and South America. Most have long, slender reddish-brown to black bodies with tapering snouts and long ringed tails. Length: 67cm (26in); weight: 11.3kg (25lb). Family Procyonidae; genus *Nasua*.

coaxial cable Communications CABLE consisting of a central conductor with surrounding insulator and tubular shield. They are used to transmit high-frequency signals. Most domestic television aerials use coaxial cables.

cobalt (symbol Co) Grey TRANSITION ELEMENT first discovered in 1737. Cobalt is found in cobaltite and smaltite, but mostly obtained as a by-product during the processing of other ores. It is a constituent of vitamin B_{12}. Cobalt is used in high-temperature steel, artists' colours (cobalt blue), jet engine manufacture, cutting tools and magnets. Cobalt-60 (half-life 5.26yr) is an artificial isotope used as a source of gamma rays in radiotherapy and tracer studies. Properties: at.no. 27; r.a.m 58.9332; r.d. 8.9; m.p. 1,495°C (2,723°F); b.p. 2,870°C (5,198°F); most common isotope Co^{59} (100%).

Cobbett, William (1763–1835) English journalist and political reformer. He fought for the British in the American Revolution, and (as Peter Porcupine) his criticism of the fledgling democracy in the United States forced his return to England. In 1802, Cobbett founded his weekly *Political Register*. He was an outspoken critic of abuses of political power and a champion of the poor. Cobbett was imprisoned (1810–12) for his attack on flogging in the army and was forced into exile (1817–19) in the US. On his return, Cobbett toured England in the campaign for parliamentary reform. His resultant masterpiece, *Rural Rides* (1830), describes the living conditions of rural workers. He was elected to Parliament in 1832.

Cobden, Richard (1804–65) British Radical politician. With John BRIGHT, he led the campaign for the repeal of the CORN LAWS, and was the chief spokesman in Parliament (1841–57, 1859–65) for the "Manchester School" of free-trade. Cobden negotiated a major trading agreement with France (1860).

Coblenz *See* KOBLENZ

COBOL (Common Business-Oriented Language) Widely used COMPUTER LANGUAGE developed in 1959 for processing business data.

cobra Any of several highly poisonous snakes in the family Elapidae, including the MAMBA, CORAL SNAKE,

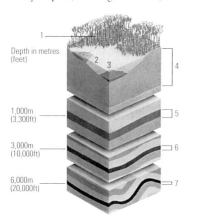

▲ **coal** The process of making coal begins with plant debris (1). Dead vegetation lies in a swampy environment and forms peat (4), the first stage of coal formation. Underwater bacteria remove some oxygen, nitrogen and hydrogen from the organic material. Debris carried elsewhere and deposited by water forms a product called cannel coal (2). Algal material collected underwater forms boghead coal (3). If the dead organic material is buried by sediment, the weight on top of the peat and the higher temperature will turn the peat into lignite (5). With more heat and pressure at increasing depths, lignite becomes bituminous coal (6) and then anthracite (7).

kraits and true cobras. It can expand its neck ribs to form a hood. Found primarily in Africa and Asia, cobras feed on rats, toads and small birds. It is the only snake to make a nest for its young. The king cobra (*Ophiophagus hannah*) reaches 5.5m (18ft) in length, and is the largest venomous snake in the world. The Indian cobra (*Naja naja*) has spectacle-like markings on its hood. Some African species can spit venom into a victim's eyes from more than 2m (7ft), causing temporary or permanent blindness.

coca Shrub native to Colombia and Peru which contains the ALKALOID drug COCAINE. Native Americans chew the leaves. The plant has yellow-white flowers growing in clusters and red berries. Height: *c.*2.4m (8ft). Family Erythroxylaceae; species *Erythroxylon coca*.

cocaine White, crystalline ALKALOID extracted from the leaves of the COCA plant. Once used as a local anaesthetic, it is now primarily an illegal narcotic, with stimulant and hallucinatory effects. It is psychologically habit-forming, but increasing doses are not needed, as the body does not develop tolerance. Habitual use results in physical and nervous deterioration, and withdrawal results in severe depression. *See also* CRACK

coccolith Any microscopic, single-celled flagellate of the Coccolithophorida, a class of ALGAE of the phylum Chrysophyta. The cell is covered with round, chalky platelets, only one or two thousandths of a millimetre in diameter. Many limestone and chalk cliffs are made up entirely of the remains of such platelets.

coccus Small spherical or spheroid bacterium. Average diameter, 0.5–1.25 micrometres. Some, such as *Streptococcus* and *Staphylococcus*, are causes of infection.

cochineal Crimson dye produced from the pulverized dried bodies of certain female scale insects, found in Central America. The dye is still used in cosmetics and foodstuffs, although now often replaced by aniline dyes.

Cochise (1815–1874) Chief of the Chiricahua APACHE. In 1861, the US army falsely imprisoned him, killing five of his relatives. Cochise escaped to lead his tribe in an 11-year war against the army in Arizona. He concluded a treaty that created a reservation. Cochise lived peacefully here until his death, after which the treaty was broken and his people forcibly moved.

cochlea Fluid-filled structure in the inner EAR which is essential to hearing. It has a shape like a coiled shell and is lined with hair cells which move in response to incoming sound waves, stimulating nerve cells to transmit impulses to the BRAIN.

Cochrane, Thomas, 10th Earl of Dundonald (1775–1860) British admiral. He became a hero in the NAPOLEONIC WARS after crippling a French fleet in the Bay of Biscay (1809). In 1814, Cochrane was dismissed from the navy after being found guilty of fraud. In the 1820s he helped in the liberation of Chile, Peru and Brazil. In 1832, Cochrane was reinstated.

cockatiel Small Australian PARROT, with a yellow, crested head and a long tail. Family Psittacidae; species *Nymphicus hollandicus*.

cockatoo Large PARROT with a long, erectile crest. Cockatoos live mainly in Australia and SW Asia. Most are predominantly white, tinged with pink or yellow. They feed on fruit and seeds. Females lay 1–4 white eggs. Length: 38cm (15in). Family Psittacidae.

cockchafer (maybug, June beetle) Any of various large, SCARAB BEETLES whose white grubs feed on the roots of trees and crops, causing severe destruction. They emerge as adults in the spring. Family Scarabaeidae.

Cockcroft, Sir John Douglas (1897–1967) English physicist who, with Ernest WALTON, was the first person to split the ATOM. He and Walton constructed a particle ACCELERATOR with which they created the first artificial nuclear reaction by bombarding lithium atoms with protons (1932). They shared the 1951 Nobel Prize for physics.

Cockerell, Sir Christopher Sydney (1910–99) English engineer who invented the HOVERCRAFT. In the early 1950s, he began research into the development of AIR-CUSHION VEHICLES (ACVs). Cockerell filed the first patent for his hovercraft in 1955.

cockle Marine bivalve mollusc. Its varicoloured, heart-shaped shell has between 20 and 24 strong, radiating ribs. There are *c*.200 recognized species, many edible. Average length: 4–8cm (1.5–3in). Class Bivalvia; family Cardiidae; species include *Cardium aculeatum*.

cock-of-the-rock Fruit-eating, brightly coloured, parrot-like bird of tropical South America. It has a large, erect crest. The birds build their mud nests among rocks or in caves. The males perform communal and ritualistic courtship dances and, after mating, the females lay two eggs. Genus *Rupicola*. Length: 30cm (12in).

cockroach (roach) Member of a group of insects with long antennae and a flat, soft body found worldwide, but mostly in the tropics. Its head is hidden under a shield (pronotum) and it may be winged or wingless. Eggs are laid in special egg cases. Some species are household pests. Length: 13–50mm (0.5–2in). Family Blattidae.

cocoa Drink obtained from the seeds of the tropical American evergreen tree *Theobroma cacao*. The seeds are crushed and some fatty substances are removed to produce cocoa powder. Cocoa is the basic ingredient of CHOCOLATE. The Ivory Coast is one of the world's largest producers. Family Sterculiaceae.

coconut palm (copra plant) Tall palm tree native to the shores of the Indo-Pacific region and the Pacific coast of South America; commercially the most important of all palms. Growing to 30.5m (100ft) tall, it has a leaning trunk and a crown of feather-shaped leaves. Copra, the dried kernel of the coconut fruit, is a valuable source of oil used in the manufacture of margarine and soap. The fibrous husk is used for matting. Family Arecaceae/Palmae; species *Cocos nucifera*.

cocoon Case or wrapping produced by larval forms of animals (such as some MOTHS, BUTTERFLIES and WASPS) for the resting or pupal stage in their life cycle. Most cocoons are made of SILK, and those of the domestic silkworm provide most of the world's commercial silk. *See also* CHRYSALIS; PUPA

Cocos Islands (Keeling Islands) Archipelago in the Indian Ocean, an external territory of Australia, 1,200km (750mi) sw of Java. The 28 small coral islands were discovered (1609) by William Keeling. They came under British control in 1857, but since 1955 have been administered by Australia. The main product is copra. Area: 13sq km (5sq mi). Pop. (1992) 586.

Cocteau, Jean (1889–1963) French writer and filmmaker, an experimental leader of the French avant-garde. He was associated with many leading artistic figures of the 1920s, such as Apollinaire, Picasso, Diaghilev and Stravinsky. His works of surrealist fantasy include the novel, *Les Enfants terribles* (1929; filmed, 1950); the play, *Orphée* (1926; filmed 1950); and the films, *Le Sang d'un poète* (1930) and *La Belle et la bête* (1946).

cod Bottom-dwelling, marine fish found in cold to temperate waters of the Northern Hemisphere. It is grey, green, brown or red with darker speckled markings. Adults feed mainly on crustaceans. Cod is one of the chief food fishes. Length: up to 1.8m (6ft). Family Gadidae.

▲ **cod** The characteristic configuration of the fins – three dorsal fins, two anal fins – reveal this to be a species of cod (*Gadus morhua*). A carnivorous fish, cod can grow to 1.5m (5ft). Hake and haddock are cods.

code *See* CRYPTOGRAPHY

codeine White, crystalline ALKALOID extracted from OPIUM by the methylation of MORPHINE, and with the properties of weak morphine. It is used in medicine as an analgesic to treat mild to moderate pain, as a cough suppresser and to treat diarrhoea.

Code Napoléon French CIVIL LAW, first introduced (1804) by Napoleon I. Based on ROMAN LAW, the Code was intended to end the disunity of French law and was applied to all French territories. It banned social inequality, permitted freedom of person and contract, and upheld the right to own private property. It was revised in 1904 and remains the basis of French civil law.

Cody, William Frederick *See* "BUFFALO BILL"

Coe, Sebastian Newbold (1956–) English athlete. In the 1980 and 1984 Olympic Games, he won gold medals in the 1,500m and silver medals in the 800m. His 800m world record stood for 16 years. He retired in 1990 and became a Conservative MP (1992). Coe lost his seat in the 1997 general election.

coefficient Term multiplying a specified unknown quantity in an algebraic expression. In the expression $1 + 5x + 2x^2$, 5 and 2 are the coefficients of x and x^2, respectively. In physics, it is a ratio that yields a pure number or a quantity with dimensions. *See also* ALGEBRA

coelacanth Bony fish of the genus *Latimeria*. Thought to have become extinct 60 million years ago, it was found in deep waters off the African coast in 1938. It is grey-brown and has lobed fins with fleshy bases. The scales and bony plates are unlike those of modern fish. Length: 1.5m (5ft). Order Crossopterygii; species *Latimeria chalumnae*.

coelenterate Common name for CNIDARIAN

coeliac disease Disorder in which the small intestine fails to absorb food properly. It is caused by intolerance to gluten, a protein in wheat and rye products. Symptoms include depression, diarrhoea and malnutrition.

Coetzee, J.M. (John Michael) (1940–) South African novelist and critic. His novels deal with life under forms of imperialism, including the South African apartheid system in *In the Heart of the Country* (1977) and *Age of Iron* (1990). Coetzee is the only writer ever to have been twice awarded the Booker Prize – for *Life and Times of Michael K* (1983) and *Disgrace* (1999).

coffee Plant and the popular CAFFEINE beverage produced from its seeds (coffee beans). The plants of the genus *Coffea* are evergreen with white fragrant flowers. Native to Ethiopia, they are now cultivated in the tropics, especially Brazil (the world's biggest producer), Colombia and the Ivory Coast. Family Rubiaceae. *See artwork* p.198

cognitive psychology Broad area of human psychology concerned with language, perception, thought and memory. It investigates such matters as the way in which people perceive by sight or hearing; how they organize information; and the use they make of language. In contrast to BEHAVIOURISM, cognitive psychology focuses on internal mental processes and cognitive development. Many practitioners use the computer and the techniques of ARTIFICIAL INTELLIGENCE (AI) to compose a model of the workings of the human brain

cognitive therapy Form of PSYCHOTHERAPY that aims to treat psychological problems through changing patients' attitudes and beliefs. It is used in the treatment of various behavioural problems, phobias and sometimes for children with learning problems.

Cohen, William (1940–) US statesman, secretary of defence (1997–2000). A former Republican senator from Maine, Cohen was appointed by Bill CLINTON partly as an attempt to ensure closer support for foreign policy initiatives from a Republican-dominated Senate.

coherence Property of ELECTROMAGNETIC RADIATION that has a constant phase relationship between two or more sets of waves. A pair of coherent waves produce INTERFERENCE. Light from a LASER is coherent.

cohesion Mutual attraction between the component atoms, ions or molecules of a substance. Weak cohesive forces permit the fluidity of liquids; those of solids are much stronger. Liquids form droplets because of surface tension caused by cohesion.

Cohn, Ferdinand Julius (1828–98) German botanist, one of the founders of BACTERIOLOGY as a separate discipline. Cohn began to study bacteria in 1868 and conducted research into the bacterial causes of infectious disease.

coin Stamped metal discs of standard sizes used as tokens of money in commercial transactions. The earliest coins are of Lydian origin, from the 7th century BC. Early coinage also appeared in China and India. Ancient coins usually contained a specific quantity of precious metal, often gold or silver, and were stamped with the symbol of the issuing authority. With the introduction of banknotes in the late 17th century and the gradual decline of the quantity of precious metal in each coin, they became used for smaller money transactions.

Coke, Sir Edward (1552–1634) English jurist. As chief justice of the King's Bench (1613), he championed the COMMON LAW and, after 1620, developed it in Parliament to oppose the king's assumption of "divine right". He helped to draft the PETITION OF RIGHT (1628), and wrote the influential *Institutes of the Laws of England* (1628).

Coke, Thomas William, Earl of Leicester (1752–1842) English agriculturalist who introduced revolutionary methods of arable farming and cattle breeding. Coke's estate at Holkham, Norfolk, was a model for experimental farms worldwide.

▲ **coffee** The Arabian coffee plant (*Coffea arabica*) is the most common kind of coffee plant. It is a small, evergreen tree that can grow to a height of 7.5m (25ft), but is pruned to 3m (10ft) on plantations. Its leaves are *c*.7.5–15cm (3–6in) long. The white blossoms are followed by tiny green berries, each holding two tough-skinned, greenish beans. The berries ripen to a deep red after six or seven months and are then ready for picking. Instant coffee often uses another genus, *Coffea Robusta*.

coke Stiff, porous, grey mass of carbon mixed with small amounts of minerals, sulphur and residual volatiles. It is left behind as a residue in coking ovens after COAL has been heated without air to drive off most of the volatile matter. It is used mainly in steelmaking for fuelling BLAST FURNACES. Its high calorific value is due to the high carbon content – more than 90%.

Colbert, Claudette (1905–96) (Claudette Chauchoin) US actress, b. France. Her screwball performance in *It Happened One Night* (1934) earned her an Academy Award for best actress. Other credits include *Private Worlds* (1934) and *Since You Went Away* (1936).

Colbert, Jean Baptiste (1619–83) French statesman, the principal exponent of MERCANTILISM. He came to prominence as an adviser to Cardinal MAZARIN. From 1661, when LOUIS XIV began his personal rule, Colbert controlled most aspects of government: reforming taxation and manufacturing, reducing tariffs, establishing commercial companies such as the French EAST INDIA COMPANY, and strengthening the navy.

Colchester City on the River Colne, Essex, SE England. The first Roman colony in Britain was settled here in AD 43 and attacked by Boadicea in AD 61. It has a Roman wall and a fine Norman castle. It is a market centre for the surrounding area. Pop. (1991) 142,515.

colchicine ALKALOID used to treat rheumatism and gout. Its ability to inhibit MITOSIS make it a valuable IMMUNOSUPPRESSIVE DRUG and aid to cancer research. Colchine is extracted from the CORM of colchicum, a genus of *c*.30 species of flowering plants including *C. fallale*. Species grow throughout Eurasia, and have pink, white or purple crocus-like flowers. Family Liliaceae.

cold, common Minor disease of the upper respiratory tract caused by viral infection. Symptoms include inflammation of the nose, headache, sore throat and a cough. A cold usually disappears within a few days. Fever-reducing and pain-relieving drugs, as well as decongestants, may relieve symptoms; rest is recommended for heavy colds. Antibiotics may be prescribed where a bacterial infection is also present. *See also* INFLUENZA

cold-blooded *See* POIKILOTHERMAL

Cold War Political, ideological and economic confrontation between the US and the Soviet Union and their allies from the end of World War 2 until the late 1980s. Despite incidents such as the BERLIN AIRLIFT (1948–49) and the CUBAN MISSILE CRISIS (1962), open warfare never occurred between the NORTH ATLANTIC TREATY ORGANIZATION (NATO) and the WARSAW PACT. Indirect confrontation occurred in the KOREAN WAR and the VIETNAM WAR. DÉTENTE ushered in an era of ARMS-CONTROL negotiations, including the STRATEGIC ARMS LIMITATION TALKS (SALT). The Cold War officially ended with the collapse of Soviet COMMUNISM in the late 1980s and the dissolution of the Warsaw Pact in 1990.

Cole, Nat King (Nathaniel Adams) (1917–65) US singer and pianist, father of Natalie Cole. He was a jazz pianist in the King Cole Trio from 1939 but achieved popularity as a singer with his velvety soft and rich voice. Cole's many hit songs include "Unforgettable", "When I Fall in Love", "Mona Lisa" and "Nature Boy".

Cole, Thomas (1801–48) US landscape painter, b. England. A founder of the HUDSON RIVER SCHOOL, his romantic landscapes depict the grandeur of the Hudson River Valley and Catskill Mountains.

Coleridge, Samuel Taylor (1772–1834) English poet, critic and philosopher. In 1795, he married Sara Fricker, sister-in-law of Robert SOUTHEY. In 1798, Coleridge and William WORDSWORTH published *Lyrical Ballads*, a fundamental work of English ROMANTICISM that opened with Coleridge's ballad "The Rime of the Ancient Mariner". *Christabel and Other Poems* (1816) included the ballad "Christabel" and the fragment "Kubla Khan". In 1800, Coleridge moved to the Lake District, where he fell in love with Wordsworth's sister-in-law Sara Hutchinson. Battling with opium-addiction, Coleridge produced little poetry in his later life, concentrating instead on his lectures. *Biographia Literaria* (1817) is both a meditation on German philosophy and a work of literary criticism.

Colette (1873–1954) French novelist, b. Sidonie Gabrielle Claudine. Her early works, including the first four *Claudine* novels (1900–03), were published under her first husband's pseudonym, Willy. Among her best-known works are *Chéri* (1920), *The Last of Chéri* (1926) and *Gigi* (1944).

colic Severe pain in the abdomen, usually subsiding and then recurring. Intestinal colic may be associated with obstruction of the intestine or constipation.

Coligny, Gaspard II de, Seigneur de Châtillon (1519–72) French Protestant leader. In 1552, he was made Admiral of France. While imprisoned (1557–59) by the Spanish, Coligny converted to CALVINISM. He and Louis I de CONDÉ led the HUGUENOT forces in the first and second of the French Wars of RELIGION. On Condé's death (1569), he was elected commander-in-chief and helped to establish favourable terms at the Treaty of St Germain (1570). Coligny became leading adviser to CHARLES IX. CATHERINE DE' MEDICI's assassination of Coligny led to the SAINT BARTHOLOMEW'S DAY MASSACRE.

colitis Inflammation of the lining of the colon, or large intestine, that produces bowel changes, usually diarrhoea and cramp-like pains. In severe chronic ulcerative colitis, the colon lining ulcerates and bleeds.

collage Composition of various materials (such as cardboard, string and fabric), pasted on to a canvas or other background. Cubist artists, such as PICASSO, BRAQUE and GRIS, developed it into a serious art form.

collagen Protein substance that is the main constituent of bones, tendons, cartilage, connective tissue and skin. It is made up of inelastic fibres.

collective unconscious According to JUNG's psychological theory, the inherited aspect of the UNCONSCIOUS that is common to all members of the human race. The collective unconscious has evolved over many centuries and contains images (archetypes), which are found in dreams and numerous religious and mystical symbols.

collectivism Political and economic theory, opposed to individualism. It emphasizes the need to replace competition with cooperation. SOCIALISM and COMMUNISM are both expressions of the collectivist idea.

collectivization Agricultural policy enforced in the SOVIET UNION under Josef STALIN in 1929 and adopted by China after the communist takeover in 1949. With the object of modernizing agriculture and making it more efficient, small peasant holdings were combined and agriculture brought under state control.

collie Smooth-coated or long-haired working dog. It has a lean, wedge-shaped head with small triangular ears. Its body is set on strong straight legs and the tail is long and curved. The coat, usually black-and-white or tan, may be rough or smooth. Height: to 66cm (26in) at the shoulder.

Collins, Michael (1890–1922) Irish revolutionary. Collins was imprisoned for a year for his role in the EASTER RISING (1916). A leading member of SINN FÉIN, he helped establish (1918) the Dáil Eireann (Irish assembly). Collins was the leader of the IRISH REPUBLICAN ARMY (IRA) campaign against British troops. He

and Arthur GRIFFITH negotiated the treaty (1921) that created the Irish Free State and the partition of Ireland. Collins was assassinated by extremist republicans.

Collins, (William) Wilkie (1824–89) English novelist. Collins made important contributions to the development of DETECTIVE FICTION, especially in his two enduringly popular novels, *The Woman in White* (1860) and *The Moonstone* (1868). He collaborated with Charles DICKENS in writing plays and stories.

Collodi, Carlo (1826–90) Italian writer and journalist. Collodi is best known for his children's tale *Pinocchio* (1881), the story of a puppet transformed into a boy. It was made into an animated film (1940) by Walt Disney.

colloid Substance composed of fine particles which can be readily dispersed throughout a second substance. A sol is a solid dispersed in a liquid, an AEROSOL is a solid or liquid in a gas, an **emulsion** is a liquid in a liquid, and a **foam** is a gas in either a liquid or solid.

Cologne (Köln) City on the River Rhine, Nordrhein Westfalen, w Germany. In AD 50, the Romans built a fortress here. In 785, Cologne was made an archbishopric by Charlemagne and it enjoyed great influence during the Middle Ages. It was heavily bombed during World War 2. Notable buildings include a cathedral (started 1248, completed 1880) and the Gürzenich (a Renaissance patrician's house). Its university was founded in 1388. Cologne is a commercial, industrial and transport centre. Industries: oil refining, petrochemicals, chemicals, engineering, textiles. Pop. (1995) 964,600.

Colombia Republic in NW South America. Colombia is the only South American country to have coastlines on both the Pacific Ocean and the Caribbean Sea. CARTAGENA is the main Caribbean port. Colombia is dominated by three ranges of the Andean Mountains. On the edge of the w Cordillera lies the city of CALI. The Central Cordillera is a chain of lofty volcanoes that divides the valleys of the rivers Magdalena and Cauca. It includes the city of MEDELLÍN. The E Cordillera contains the capital, BOGOTÁ, at *c.*2,800m (9,200ft). East of the ANDES lie plains drained by headwaters of the AMAZON and ORINOCO rivers. This region accounts for two-thirds of the land, but only 2% of the population. **Climate and Vegetation** The Pacific lowlands have a tropical, rainy climate, but Bogotá has mild annual temperatures. The Caribbean lowlands and the Magdalena valley have dry seasons. Colombia's vegetation varies from dense rainforest in the SE to the tundra of the snow-capped Andean peaks. Coffee plantations line the w slopes of the E Cordillera. Mangrove swamps lie along the Pacific coast. The NE plains are covered by savanna (*llanos*). **History** The advanced, pre-Colombian CHIBCHA civilization lived undisturbed in the E cordillera for many thousands of years. In 1525, the Spanish established the first European settlement at Santa Marta. By 1538, the conquistador Gonzalo Jiménez de Quesada had conquered the Chibcha and established Bogotá. Colombia became part of the New Kingdom of Granada, whose territory also included Ecuador, Panama and Venezuela. Bogotá became the colonial capital. In 1819, Simón BOLÍVAR defeated the Spanish at Boyacá and established Greater Colombia. Bolívar became president. In 1830, Ecuador and Venezuela gained independence. In 1885, the

COLOMBIA
AREA: 1,138,910sq km (439,733sq mi)
POPULATION: 39,397,000
CAPITAL (POPULATION): Bogotá (6,005,000)

Republic of Colombia was formed. Differences between republican and federalist factions proved irreconcilable, and the first civil war (1899–1902), claimed *c*.100,000 lives. In 1903, aided by the US, Panama achieved independence. The second civil war, *La Violencia* (1949–57), was even more bloody. Political corruption, violence and repression became endemic. In 1957, Liberal and Conservative parties formed a National Front Coalition, which remained in power until 1974. Throughout the 1970s, Colombia's illegal trade in cocaine grew steadily, creating wealthy drug barons. In the 1980s, armed cartels (such as the Cali) became a destabilizing force and political and media assassinations were frequent. A new constitution (1991) protected human rights. In 1994, the Liberal leader Ernesto Samper was elected president. The 1998 presidential elections were won by the Social Conservative Party (PSC) candidate Andrés Pastrana Arango. In an effort to end the guerrilla war that has lasted for 30 years, Pastrana entered into negotiations with the Revolutionary Armed Forces of Colombia (FARC) and the National Liberation Army (ELN). In October 1998, the ELN attacked an oil pipeline in Antioquia, NW Colombia, killing more than 66 people. **Economy** Colombia is a lower-middle-income developing country (1995 GDP per capita, $US1,105). It is the world's second-largest coffee producer. Other crops include bananas, cocoa and maize. Colombia also exports coal, oil emeralds and gold. In 1997, the collapse of the world coffee and banana market led to a massive budget deficit and added to the high unemployment rate. In September 1998, as part of new austerity measures, Colombia devalued the peso. It triggered the longest (20 days) strike in Colombia's history.

Colombo Capital and chief seaport of Sri Lanka, on the SW coast. Settled in the 6th century BC, it was taken by Portugal in the 16th century and later by the Dutch. In 1796, Colombo was captured by the British. It gained independence in 1948. Colombo has one of the world's largest artificial harbours. Apart from shipping, the city has light industries. Pop. (1992 est.) 684,000.

Colombo Plan International organization with headquarters in COLOMBO, Sri Lanka, which seeks to promote the economic and social development in S and SE Asia. Initiated (1951) by the Commonwealth of Nations, it now includes 26 states including the US, Canada, Japan and the UK.

Colón Port at the Caribbean end of the Panama Canal, central Panama. Colón was founded (1850) as Aspinwall by Americans working on a trans-Panama railway. It became a free-trade zone in 1953 and is now the world's second-largest duty-free port. Pop. (1990) 140,908.

colon Part of the large INTESTINE in mammals that extends from the small intestine to the RECTUM. The colon absorbs water from digested food and allows bacterial action for the formation of faeces. *See also* DIGESTIVE SYSTEM

colonialism Control by one country over a dependent area or people. Although associated with modern political history, the practice is ancient. In European colonial history, economic, political and strategic factors were involved in the world empires of countries, such as Britain and France, subjugating mainly African and Asian states and often creating artificial boundaries. After World War 2, colonialist exploitation was widely recognized, and colonial powers conceded, willingly or not, independence to their colonies. *See also* IMPERIALISM

Colorado State in W central USA; the state capital is DENVER. Other major cities include Colorado Springs and Pueblo. It is the highest state in the nation, with an average elevation of 2,073m (6,800ft). In the W half are

the ranges of the ROCKY MOUNTAINS, and in the E the GREAT PLAINS. Major rivers are the Colorado, Rio Grande, Arkansas and South Platte. The US acquired the E of the state from France in the LOUISIANA PURCHASE (1803). The remainder was ceded by Mexico after the MEXICAN WAR (1848). The discovery of gold and silver encouraged immigration, and Colorado was made a territory in 1861. It achieved statehood in 1876. The most important agricultural activity is the raising of sheep and cattle. Sugar beet, maize and hay are grown. Industries: tourism, transport, electrical equipment. Area: 268,658sq km (103,729sq mi). Pop. (2000) 4,301,261.

Colorado Major river in SW USA, which rises in the Rocky Mountains of N Colorado and flows SW into the Gulf of California, passing through the GRAND CANYON. There are many national parks and hydroelectric power projects on the river. Length: 2,333km (1,450mi).

Colosseum Amphitheatre in Rome built (AD 72–81) by Emperor Vespasian. It measures 189 × 156m (620 × 513ft) by 45.7m (150ft) high, and seated *c*.50,000 people. Citizens of Rome came here to watch gladiatorial contests and, according to tradition, the martyrdom of Christians.

Colossians, Epistle to the Book of the New Testament taking the form of a letter written by either St PAUL or a disciple to the Church at Colossae, a city in SW Phrygia (now central Turkey). The letter, written from prison in Rome (*c*.AD 61), is a warning to the Colossians not to adopt ideas from other faiths.

Colossus of Rhodes One of the SEVEN WONDERS OF THE WORLD, a bronze statue of the Sun god overlooking the harbour at Rhodes. It stood more than 30.5m (100ft) high. It was built, at least in part, by Chares of Lindos between *c*.292 BC and *c*.280 BC and destroyed by an earthquake *c*.224 BC.

colostomy Operation to bring the COLON out through the wall of the abdomen in order to bypass the lower section of the bowel. An artificial opening is created so that faecal matter is passed into a bag, worn outside the body. *See also* DIGESTION

colour Sensation experienced when light of sufficient brightness and of a particular wavelength strikes the RETINA of the EYE. Normal daylight (white light) is made up of a spectrum of colours, each a different wavelength. These colours can be placed in seven bands – red, orange, yellow, green, blue, indigo and violet – of decreasing wavelength. A pure spectral colour is called a **hue**. If the colour is not pure but contains some white, it is "desaturated" (**tint**). A colour may also have luminosity (**brightness**) which determines its shade. Any colour is perceived as a mixture of three primary colours: red, green and blue in light; of red, yellow and blue in paint.

colour blindness General term for various disorders of colour vision. The most common involves red-green vision, a hereditary defect almost exclusively affecting males, in which the person cannot tell red from green. Total colour blindness, an inherited disorder in which the person sees only black, white and grey, is rare.

Colt, Samuel (1814–62) US inventor. Colt patented (1835–36) the revolver, a single-barrelled pistol with an automatic revolving set of chambers, brought into successive alignment. He also invented a submarine battery and a submarine telegraph cable. His Colt's Patent Firearms Manufacturing Company at Hartford, Connecticut, was the first assembly-line in manufacturing.

Coltrane, John William (1926–67) US JAZZ saxophonist. Coltrane first attracted attention as a member (1955–61) of the Miles DAVIS quintet, on albums such as *Kind as Blue* (1959). In 1957, he worked with

Theolonious MONK and became a bandleader. *Giant Steps* (1959) was a landmark album in the development of modern jazz. In 1961, he formed a quartet. After making the masterpiece *A Love Supreme* (1964), the quartet disbanded. Other albums include *Africa/Brass Vols. 1&2* (1961), *Impressions* (1963) and *Ascension* (1965).

Colum, Padraic (1881–1972) Irish writer. A key figure in the Irish literary renaissance, Colum helped found the ABBEY THEATRE and wrote a memoir of James JOYCE. From 1914 he lived mainly in the US. His verse is collected in *Collected Poems* (1953).

Columba, Saint (521–97) Irish Christian missionary in Ireland and Scotland. He founded several monasteries in Ireland before leaving in 563 to found an important monastery on the island of Iona. His feast day is 9 June.

Columban, Saint (543–615) (Columbanus) Irish Christian missionary to the continent of Europe. Accompanied by 12 fellow monks, Columban left (*c*.590) Ireland for Gaul where he founded two monasteries. Columban's adherence to Celtic practices led to his expulsion from here in 610. In 612 he founded an abbey at Bobbio, Italy, where he died. His feast day is 23 November.

Columbia Capital of South Carolina, USA, in the centre of the state on the Congaree River. Founded as state capital in 1786, it was nearly destroyed in the Civil War. It is home to the University of South Carolina (1801), Columbia College (1854), Allen University (1870) and the Woodrow Wilson Museum. Industries: textiles, printing. Pop. (1990) 98,052.

Columbia River in SW Canada and NW USA. It flows from Columbia Lake in British Columbia, Canada, through Washington and Oregon, and enters the Pacific Ocean N of Portland. It has one of the largest drainage basins on the continent, *c*.668,220sq km (258,000sq mi). Length: 1,953km (1,214mi).

Columbia, District of *See* WASHINGTON, D.C.

columbine Any of *c*.100 species of perennial herbaceous plant native to cool climates of the Northern Hemisphere. They have five-petalled, spurred flowers and notched leaflets. Height: to 90cm (3ft). Family Ranunculaceae; genus *Aquilegia*.

columbium *See* NIOBIUM

Columbus, Christopher (1451–1506) Italian explorer credited with the discovery of America. Columbus believed he could establish a route to China and the East Indies by sailing across the Atlantic since, along with many learned contemporaries, he believed the circumference of the Earth to be much smaller than it is. He secured Spanish patronage from FERDINAND V and ISABELLA I. In 1492 Columbus set out with three ships (*Niña*, *Pinta* and *Santa Maria*) and made landfall in the Bahamas, the first European to reach the Americas since the Vikings. Believing he had reached the East, he called the inhabitants "Indians". On a second, larger expedition (1493), a permanent colony was established in Hispaniola. Columbus made two more voyages (1498 and 1502), exploring the Caribbean region. He never surrendered his belief that he had reached Asia. His discoveries laid the basis for the Spanish empire in the Americas.

Columbus Capital of Ohio, USA on the Scioto River. Founded in 1812, it grew rapidly with the arrival of the railway in 1850. It is a major transport, industrial and trading centre. Columbus has numerous universities and colleges. The Battelle Memorial Institute (1929) conducts scientific, technological and economic research. Industries: machinery, aircraft. Pop. (1990) 632,910.

column In architecture, a vertical post, supporting part of a building. A column may be free-standing, with a capital, base and shaft, or it may be partly attached to a wall. Triumphal columns such as Trajan's Column in Rome, had narrative reliefs to depict battle victories. *See also* ORDERS OF ARCHITECTURE

coma Unconsciousness caused by a head injury, brain disease, drugs or lack of blood supply to the BRAIN.

Comanche Shoshonean-speaking Native American nation. They separated from the parent SHOSHONE in the distant past and migrated from E Wyoming into Kansas. Numbering *c*.15,000, they introduced the horse to the Northern Plains tribes. Conflict with US forces resulted in their near extinction by 1874. Today, *c*.4,500 Comanche live on reservations in SW Oklahoma.

Comaneci, Nadia (1962–) Romanian gymnast. She was the star of the 1976 Olympic Games, winning five medals – three golds, a silver and a bronze. Comaneci was the first gymnast to be awarded a perfect score of 10 (uneven bars and beam). In the 1980 Olympics, she won two gold and two silver medals. She retired in 1984 to manage the Romanian gymnastics team. In 1989, Comaneci defected to the US.

Combination Acts British acts of Parliament of 1799 and 1800 making combinations (or TRADE UNIONS) of workers illegal. The government feared they were potentially subversive. Trade unions nevertheless multiplied after 1815, and in 1824 the acts were repealed. A later Combination Act (1825) restricted the right to strike and, as the TOLPUDDLE MARTYRS (1834) demonstrated, trade-union organizers could still be prosecuted.

combustion Burning, usually in oxygen. The combustion of fuels is used to produce heat and light. An example is a fire. Industrial techniques harness the energy produced using combustion chambers and furnaces.

COMECON Acronym for the COUNCIL FOR MUTUAL ECONOMIC ASSISTANCE

Comédie-Française French national theatre, founded (1680) by Louis XIV and revised in 1803 by Napoleon I. There are two kinds of members: *pensionnaires*, chosen by audition, and *sociétaires*, to which position the *pensionnaire* can be elevated only upon the death, retirement or resignation of a *sociétaire*.

comedy One of the two main types of DRAMA. It differs from TRAGEDY in its lightness of style and theme, and its tendency to resolve happily. It originated in early Greek fertility rites and, in modern usage, refers not only to a humorous play or film, but also to the growing tradition of "stand-up" routines. As theatre has developed, the once clear division between the two dramatic forms has been blurred. *See also* ARISTOPHANES; GREEK DRAMA

Comenius, John Amos (1592–1670) Czech religious leader and educational reformer, who influenced modern education. Comenius believed in equal education for all children. His best-known book was *Orbis Sensualum Pictus* (*The Visible World in Pictures*, 1658).

comet Small, icy solar system body in an independent orbit around the Sun. F.L. Whipple's (1906–) "dirty snowball" theory of comets is largely accepted. The solid nucleus of a comet is small, that of HALLEY'S COMET measures just 16 × 8km (10 × 5mi), and comprises rock and dust particles embedded in ice. As the comet approaches the Sun and gets warmer, evaporation begins and jets of gas and dust form the luminous, spherical coma. Later, radiation pressure from the Sun and the SOLAR WIND may send dust and gas streaming away as a tail, as much as 150 million kilometres in length. They are three main types of comet: **short-period** comets often have their aphelia at approximately the distance of Jupiter's orbit. **Long-period** comets (such as Halley's) have aphelia near or beyond Neptune's orbit. Comets with very long periods have such great orbital eccentricities that their paths are almost parabolic. It is now thought that comets originated with the rest of the solar system. *See also* METEOR

comfrey Any plant of the genus *Symphytum* of the BORAGE family (Boraginaceae), native to Eurasia. Comfreys have small yellow or purple flowers and hairy leaves. Boiled concoctions of *S. officinale* were once used to treat wounds.

comic Magazine consisting of stories told by strip cartoons with "balloons" containing the characters' speech. Comics evolved from the comic strip in the 1930s. A tradition of adult, politicized, subversive and often erotic comics, along with explicit graphic novels, has established itself during the latter part of the 20th century.

comic opera Musico-dramatic work with some spoken dialogue and a light or amusing plot. The term is used indiscriminately and includes musical comedy and OPERETTA. In operatic works, it approximates most closely to early 18th-century Italian OPERA BUFFA, but bears little relation to the French OPÉRA COMIQUE.

Cominform (acronym for Communist Information Bureau) Agency established in 1947 to coordinate and provide information to the Communist Party of the Soviet Union and other European communist parties. It replaced the COMMUNIST INTERNATIONAL, abolished in 1943. Cominform was dissolved in 1956.

Comintern *See* COMMUNIST INTERNATIONAL

commedia dell' arte Style of Italian comedy, popular from the mid-16th to late-18th century, which spread throughout Europe. Professional players performed on street stages or at court functions. Plays were comic, often coarse and crudely improvised on briefly outlined scenarios. Commedia produced several (now standard) masked characters: Harlequin (clown), Capitano (braggart soldier), Pantalone (deceived father or cuckolded husband), Colombina (maid) and Inamorato (lover).

commensalism Situation in nature in which two species live in close association but only one benefits. One of the species (the commensal) may gain from increased food supply or by procuring shelter, support or means of locomotion, but the other (the host) neither gains nor loses. *See also* MUTUALISM; SYMBIOSIS

commodity market Market in which goods or services are bought and sold. Commodities are raw materials such as tea, rubber, tin or copper. The actual commodities are seldom present, and what is traded is their ownership. The largest commodity exchange in the world is in Chicago, Illinois, USA.

Commodus, Lucius Aelius Aurelius (161–192) Roman emperor (180–192), son and successor of MARCUS AURELIUS. Commodus' profligate, perhaps insane, rule was mainly spent organizing gladiatorial contests. He was assassinated by a wrestler.

Common Agricultural Policy (CAP) System of support for agriculture within the EUROPEAN UNION (EU). The CAP was incorporated in the Treaty of ROME (1957). It was designed to increase food production within the EU, and to ensure a reasonable income for farmers. The EU sets target prices for commodities. If prices fall below target to a level known as intervention prices, the EU buys up the surplus, creating the so-called "beef mountains" and "wine lakes". In 1988, to prevent overproduction, the EU introduced a policy of paying farmers to set aside part of their land as fallow. By 1994, the CAP was absorbing 51% of the total EU budget, having soared to 75% in the 1970s. It is one of the most contentious issues in the Union, and demands for reform are frequent.

common law Legal system developed in England and adopted in most English-speaking countries. Distinguished from CIVIL LAW, its chief characteristics are judicial precedents, trial by jury and the doctrine of the supremacy of law. Based originally on the king's court, "common to the whole realm", rather than local or manorial courts, it dates back to the constitutions of CLARENDON (1164). It is the customary and traditional element in the law accumulating from court decisions. A proliferation of statutes have come to supersede common law. *See also* ROMAN LAW

Common Market *See* EUROPEAN UNION (EU)

Common Prayer, Book of Official liturgy of the ANGLICAN COMMUNION. It was prepared originally (1549) as a reformed version of the old Roman Catholic liturgy for England's Henry VIII by Thomas CRANMER. In 1552 it was revised under the Protestant government of Edward VI. The THIRTY-NINE ARTICLES were added (1562) by Matthew PARKER. The Prayer Book was further revised in 1662 after the RESTORATION of Charles II.

Commons, House of *See* HOUSE OF COMMONS

Commonwealth (1649–60) Official name of the republic established in England after the execution of CHARLES I. The PROTECTORATE was set up in 1653, in which Oliver CROMWELL was given almost regal powers. The Commonwealth ended with the RESTORATION of CHARLES II. *See also* RUMP PARLIAMENT

Commonwealth Games Sports competition originating as the British Empire Games (1930). Competitors are members of the COMMONWEALTH OF NATIONS. Based on the OLYMPIC GAMES, they are held every four years.

Commonwealth of Independent States (CIS) Alliance of 12 of the former republics of the SOVIET UNION. The CIS was formed in (1991) by ARMENIA, AZERBAIJAN, BELARUS, GEORGIA, KAZAKSTAN, KYRGYZSTAN, MOLDOVA, RUSSIA, TAJIKISTAN, TURKMENISTAN, UKRAINE and UZBEKISTAN. The BALTIC STATES (ESTONIA, LATVIA and LITHUANIA) did not join. All members, except Ukraine, signed a treaty of economic union in 1993, creating a free-trade zone. Russia is the dominant power, with overall responsibility for defence and peacekeeping.

Commonwealth of Nations Voluntary association of 53 states, largely consisting of English-speaking countries that were formerly part of the BRITISH EMPIRE. It was established by the Statute of Westminster (1931). Headed by the British sovereign, it exists largely as a forum for discussion of issues of common concern. A Commonwealth secretariat is located in London. Several countries have withdrawn from the Commonwealth, notably Burma (1947), the Republic of Ireland (1949) and Fiji (1989). Pakistan left in 1972, but rejoined in 1989.

commune Usually a community of people who choose to live together for a shared purpose. In the 19th century, many communes tried to apply utopian socialist ideals. In the 1960s, communes were formed intending to be cooperative, self-supporting and free of the values of mainstream society. In China, farming communes exist, similar to the state farms of the former Soviet Union.

communications Processes for sharing information and ideas. Facial expressions, hand signals, writing and speech are examples. The 15th-century invention of the PRINTING press revolutionized communications. The 20th century has witnessed a further revolution, primarily in terms of increased access. TELECOMMUNICATIONS inventions, such as the TELEPHONE, RADIO, TELEVISION and COMPUTER NETWORK, have facilitated rapid, global mass communication. The INTERNET is the latest in a long line of technological innovations.

Communications Satellite (COMSAT) Private company that provides worldwide SATELLITE communications systems. COMSAT, established by the US Congress, began with the launch of the *Early Bird* satellite in 1965. Other nations now participate in projects.

communism Political outlook based on the principle of communal ownership of property. The theory is derived from the interpretation placed by Karl MARX and Friedrich ENGELS on the course of human history. As outlined in the *Communist Manifesto* (1848), *Capital* (vol. 1, 1867) and other writings, Marx asserted that social and political relations depend ultimately upon relations of economic production. All value (and so wealth) is produced by labour, yet in a capitalist system, workers' salaries do not represent the full value of their labour. Thus, the working CLASS (PROLETARIAT) and the class that is in control of CAPITAL and production (BOURGEOISIE) have conflicting interests. CAPITALISM, it is asserted, is merely one stage in the progress of human institutions. As the forces of production (technology and capital stock) increase, the relations of production must change in order to accommodate them. Marx postulated that the bourgeoisie (by the nature of its operations) brought into being the urban proletariat. Conflicting interests within capitalism would inevitably lead to the overthrow of the bourgeoisie by the proletariat and so the collapse of the system itself. This would be replaced, first by SOCIALISM and eventually by a communist society in which production and distribution would be democratically controlled, summarized in the slogan "From each according to their ability, to each according to their need". A socialist experiment was attempted by LENIN in Russia following the RUSSIAN REVOLUTION (1917). STALIN turned communism into an ideology to justify the use of dictatorial state power to drive rapid economic development. This process was used as a model for other communist countries, such as China and Cuba.

Communist International (Comintern, Third International) Communist organization founded (1919) by LENIN. He feared that the reformist Second International might re-emerge and wished to secure control of the world socialist movement. The Comintern was made up mainly of Russians, and failed to organize a successful revolution in Europe in the 1920s and 1930s. The Soviet Union abolished the Comintern in 1943.

Communist Party, Chinese Political organization established (July 1921) by Li Dazhao and Chen Duxiu. The Party was strengthened by its alliance (1924) with CHIANG KAI-SHEK's nationalist KUOMINTANG, but virtually shattered when the communists were expelled from Chiang's group in 1927. MAO ZEDONG was the guiding force in revitalizing the Party in the early 1930s. Under his leadership, solidified during the LONG MARCH (1934–35), the Party revised the Soviet proletariat-based model to fit the peasant-oriented economy of China and, after another four years of civil war from 1945, the People's Republic was proclaimed in TIANANMEN SQUARE (October 1949). The Party had achieved complete political and military power. Its structure and hierarchy was nearly destroyed during the CULTURAL REVOLUTION, but was rebuilt after Mao's death (1976) by DENG XIAOPING. Following the pro-democracy demonstrations (May 1989) the Party swung away from political reform. Yet, its flexible approach to economic reform enabled it to survive the collapse of Soviet COMMUNISM. In 1993, Jiang ZEMIN became president. The National People's Congress is the supreme legislative body and nominally elects the highest officers of state. The Party has more than 40 million members (1995).

Communist Party of the Soviet Union (CPSU) Former ruling party of the SOVIET UNION. It wielded all effective political power in the country and, via the COMMUNIST INTERNATIONAL, had considerable influence over Communist parties in other countries. At its height the CPSU had *c*.15 million members organized into *c*.400,000 local units (cells) throughout the Soviet Union. Party organization paralleled the hierarchy of local government administration, thus enabling party control of every level of government. There were Party cells in almost all areas of Soviet life, such as the school system, armed forces, factories, collective farms and the media. After the break-up of the Soviet Union in 1991, the Party was dissolved following a number of decrees by Boris YELTSIN. There remains a strong, traditional conservative power base of ex-Party members who are politically active in Russia. *See also* COMMUNISM; LENIN; individual party leaders

community In ECOLOGY, naturally occurring group of plants or animals living within a particular HABITAT. A community in a particular ECOSYSTEM is interdependent in many ways, such as the FOOD CHAIN. During ecological SUCCESSION, the structure of a community is constantly shifting until a stable, climax community is established.

community architecture Programmes, mainly for housing, that involve a study of the prevailing social conditions, and consultation with the people who are going to use them. In Britain, the idea developed during the 1970s as a reaction to mass housing developments. Its most prominent supporter is Prince Charles.

commutative law Property of an operation and a set of elements in mathematics. Two elements are said to be commute under the operation * if a*b = b*a: that is, if the result of the operation is the same regardless of the order of the elements. Addition and multiplication of numbers is commutative, since $a + b = b + a$ and $ab = ba$. Matrix multiplication and vector cross-products do not obey the commutative law.

Como City on the SW shore of Lake Como, Lombardy, N Italy; capital of Como province. Originally a Roman colony, it was liberated from Austrian rule by Garibaldi in 1859. Sites include a 14th-century marble cathedral. The province is a popular resort area. Lake Como is the deepest lake in N Italy. Depth: 412m (1,353ft). Length: 50km (31mi) Industries: silk, tourism. Pop. (1990) 89,602.

Comoros (Comores) Independent republic in the Indian Ocean off the E coast of Africa between Mozambique and Madagascar. The three major volcanic islands are Grande Comore (home of the capital, Moroni), Anjouan and Mohéli. The islands are mountainous, the climate tropical and the soil fertile. Farming is the chief occupation. Coconuts, copra, vanilla, cocoa and sisal are the main crops. France owned the islands between 1841 and 1909. Independence was granted in 1975. In 1978, European mercenaries overthrew the government and democracy was restored only in 1984. The 1996 presidential election was won by Muhammad Taki. In 1997, a referendum on Anjouan voted for independence. Area: 1,862sq km (719sq mi). Pop. (2000) 670,000.

compact disc (CD) Disc used for high-quality digital sound reproduction. The disc has a shiny metal layer and a transparent, protective plastic coating. The sound signal consists of millions of tiny pits, pressed into one side of the metal. When it is played, a narrow laser beam is reflected from the rotating disc's surface. A sensor detects changes in the beam, and forms an electrical signal of pulses. This is processed and decoded to form a sound signal that can be amplified for reproduction on loudspeakers. *See also* CD-ROM *See artwork* p.204

company Group of people who agree to work together as a firm or business. The legal responsibility of running a company rests with its board of directors which, if the business has raised finance by selling shares in the company, has to account to its shareholders. In a **private** company, the directors sell shares to whomever they please. The shares of a **public** company can be bought and sold freely through a STOCK EXCHANGE. In a **public limited company (plc)**, the legal liability of its shareholders is limited to the value of their shares. *See also* CORPORATION

compass Direction-finding instrument also used to show direction of a MAGNETIC FIELD. It is a horizontal magnetic needle on a vertical pivot whose north-seeking end can turn to point towards magnetic N. Adjustments can be made to give true N. The compass has been used in Europe since the 12th century when the "needle" was a piece of lodestone. Today, NAVIGATION often uses the motor-driven GYROCOMPASS.

compiler Computer PROGRAM that translates the symbols of a programming language into instructions readable directly by a COMPUTER. Most programs are written in high-level languages, such as "C", Pascal or BASIC, which are made up of words and symbols easily comprehended by humans. A compiler takes these programs and renders them into a form readable by the computer.

complex In psychology, collection of repressed memories and desires. When this charge remains in the unconscious, it can exert a dominating influence on behaviour. The term was introduced by Carl JUNG, who deduced that certain associations were repressed because of their immoral or disagreeable content. Such associations can give rise to various NEUROSES.

complex number Number of the form $a + bi$, where $i = \sqrt{-1}$, and a and b are REAL NUMBERS. To obtain a solution to the equation $x^2 + 1 = 0$, we need to introduce a new number i, such that $i^2 = -1$. The solutions to similar equations then give rise to a set of numbers of the general form $a + bi$. These are known as the complex numbers. Since b can be equal to zero, the set of complex numbers includes the real numbers.

Compositae Family of *c*.20,000 species of plants in which the "flower" is actually a composite flower-head consisting of a cluster of many, usually tiny, individual flowers (florets). In a typical composite, such as the DAISY, the flower-head has a central yellow disc, consisting of a cluster of tiny bisexual florets lacking visible petals. The outer ring of female ray florets has large white petals. In composites such as the DANDELION and CHICORY, the flower-head consists entirely of ray florets. Others, such as THISTLES, consist entirely of disc florets. Composites make up by far the largest family of plants. The Compositae are often known as the Asteraceae.

composite Material such as CONCRETE, FIBREGLASS or plywood, made by combining two or more other materials. A composite usually has qualities superior to those of the materials from which it is made.

compound Substance formed by chemical combination of two or more elements that cannot be separated by physical means. Compounds are produced by the rearrangement of VALENCE (outer ELECTRONS of an atom) seeking to attain more stable configurations. They usually have properties quite different from those of their constituent elements. IONIC COMPOUNDS have ionic bonds – they are collections of oppositely charged ions. The ions are packed together in a regular arrangement called a CRYSTAL lattice. Ionic compounds, such as sodium chloride, are solids at room temperature and have high melting and boiling points. COVALENT bonding occurs where non-metal atoms share electrons. Such compounds can be classified as simple molecular structures (such as carbon dioxide) with low melting and boiling points; or giant molecular structures (such as graphite and diamond). Their properties depend on the arrangement of the atoms in the macromolecule. *See also* MOLECULE

comprehensive school System of secondary education based on the notion of inclusivity rather than selectivity. In principle, comprehensive schools admit any child regardless of ability or aptitude. In practice, a degree of selection or "streaming" according to ability often occurs. In the US, Sweden and Russia the majority have schools have been comprehensive in the 20th century. In the UK, the widespread introduction of comprehensive schools was started in 1965 by the Labour government, and by 1997 more than 87% of the secondary-school pupils attended comprehensive schools.

compressor Machine that delivers air or gas at pressure. It is used for furnace blast systems, ventilation and refrigeration systems, pneumatic drills and for inflating vehicle tyres. Reciprocating and rotary compressors are the two basic types.

Compton, Arthur Holly (1892–1962) US physicist. He discovered that wavelengths of X-RAYS increase when the rays collide with ELECTRONS (the Compton effect). This helped prove that X-rays could act as particles. Compton shared the 1927 Nobel Prize for physics with C.T.R. WILSON. As head of the early phase of the MANHATTAN PROJECT to develop the atom bomb, he helped create the first sustained nuclear CHAIN REACTION.

Compton-Burnett, Dame Ivy (1892–1969) English novelist. Compton-Burnett's novels are set in the sombre, domestic interiors of the Edwardian gentry, uncovering a world of cruelty and hypocrisy. They include *A House and its Head* (1935), *Elders and Betters* (1944) and *Mother and Son* (1955). She was made a dame in 1967.

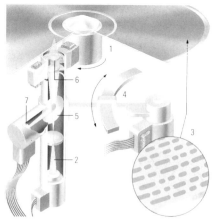

▲ **compact disc** A compact disc player reads digital information from a compact disc (1) using a focused laser (2). Music or other information is written on the underside of the disc in a spiral track of pits (3) representing a digital code of zeros and ones. The disc spins and the laser, mounted on a swing arm (4), moves as the disc plays. The laser passes through a semi-silvered mirror (5) and is focused on the disc (6). When the laser hits a flat area, it is reflected back via the mirror to a sensor (7), and the information sent to a chip. When the laser hits a pit, it is scattered.

computer Device that processes data (information) by following a set of instructions called a PROGRAM. All digital computers work by manipulating data represented as numbers. The origins of the computer can be traced back to the ABACUS and mechanized adding machines. Charles BAB-BAGE first conceived of a machine that could be given instructions to perform many different calculating tasks. By the mid-1940s, mechanical machines were replaced by electronic versions. Some of these used groups of electromagnetic switches, called relays, to register binary numbers. At any instant, each switch could be either on or off, corresponding to the digits 1 or 0 in the BINARY SYSTEM. Stages in the long-term development of electronic digital computers are termed **computer generations**. A **first-generation** computer was developed by engineers at the University of Pennsylvania in 1946. The 27-tonne machine called the Electronic Numerical Indicator and Computer (ENIAC) used electronic VALVES instead of relays. Programming ENIAC to do a particular task was a lengthy process that consisted of changing wired connections. John VON NEUMANN helped to develop techniques for storing programs in code to avoid this problem. In 1951, UNIVAC 1 became the first computer offered for general sale. This **second-generation** computer used TRANSISTORS and became smaller and more practical. In the 1960s, a **third generation** of computers appeared with the invention of INTEGRATED CIRCUITS, leading to a further reduction in size. **Fourth-generation** computers, developed in the 1980s, were even smaller, utilizing powerful MICROPROCESSORS. Microprocessors contain a complete CENTRAL PROCESSING UNIT (CPU) that controls operations. The latest microprocessors contain more than a million transistors and other components, all in a package little bigger than a postage stamp. **Fifth-generation** computers using **very large-scale integration (VLSI)** chips will utilize the developments of ARTIFICIAL INTELLIGENCE (AI) and commonly may be controlled by spoken commands. **Read-Only Memory (ROM)** and **Random Access Memory (RAM)** chips respectively act as permanent and temporary electronic memories for storing data. A typical desktop computer system consists of: a main unit containing a central processor, together with memory chips and storage devices (usually MAGNETIC DISKS); a monitor with a CATHODE-RAY TUBE; a keyboard and a mouse; and a printer. Computer programs are usually stored on disks and transferred to the machine's RAM when required. The keyboard and mouse are called **input devices**, since they allow the user to feed information into the computer. The **keyboard** enables the user to enter letters, numbers and other symbols. The **mouse** is a small device moved by hand, which enables the user to control the computer by positioning a pointer on the monitor screen, to select functions from a list. A magnetic disk drive, such as a HARD DISK, can supply programs and data to the computer and store its output. Many computers have CD-ROM drives. Many other **peripherals** are used, such as a scanner which converts images into an electronic signal so that they can be stored and displayed by the computer. The modern computer market is dominated by PCs – the generic term used to refer to machines based on the original IBM personal computer produced in the early 1980s. All these machines use an operating system (such as DOS or Windows) produced by the giant SOFTWARE corporation, Microsoft. Other popular operating systems include Apple Macintosh (MacOS) and UNIX. *See artwork* p.206
computer-aided design (CAD) Use of COMPUTER GRAPHICS to assist the design of, for example, fabrics, electronic circuits, buildings and vehicles. With CAD, designers can make alterations and analyze their effect.

computer-aided manufacture (CAM) Use of computers to control industrial production. Its main applications involve the control of ROBOTS and automated machine tools in factories to achieve rapid and consistent manufacturing without the possibility of human error. Often CAM is linked to COMPUTER-AIDED DESIGN (CAD).
computer graphics Illustrations produced on a COMPUTER. Simple diagrams and shapes may be produced by typing on the keyboard. Complex images require a mouse, painting or drawing SOFTWARE.
computerized axial tomography (CAT) Method of taking X-rays that provides images of "slices" through the body. Inside a CAT scanner is an X-ray source that produces a narrow beam of radiation. This passes through a patient's body and is detected by an electronic sensor. The X-ray source and detector are rotated around the patient's body so that views are taken from all angles. A computer analyzes the output to build up a picture of the slice of the body.
computer language System of words and rules used to PROGRAM a computer. Most COMPUTERS work using a binary-coded language (using 1s and 0s) called **machine code**. A language consisting of words and symbols that relate more directly to normal language can be used to instruct a computer. A COMPILER, assembler or other such program then translates this into machine code. Several kinds of programming language have been designed for different purposes. **Fortran** is for scientific and mathematical use, COBOL (Common Business-Oriented Language) for business programs, ALGOL for mathematical applications, and BASIC and **Pascal** were originally for use by learners. Today, the majority of applications for personal computers are written in a language called "C", or derivatives of it. *See also* ASSEMBLY LANGUAGE
computer network Number of computers linked together for communications purposes. A typical **local area network (LAN)** links computers within the same building, enabling staff to exchange data and share printers. A **wide area network (WAN)** covers longer

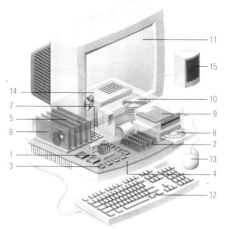

▲ **computer** Components of a computer include (1) the central processing unit (CPU), (2) RAM, (3) BIOS and ROM chips, (4) the mother board, (5) expansion cards, (6) video card, (7) expansion slots, (8) optical disk drive, (9) floppy disk drive, (10) hard disk, (11) monitor, (12) keyboard, (13) mouse, (14) power supply and (15) loudspeaker.

distances and may link LANs. The interconnections are made through public TELEPHONE services via electronic units called MODEMS, or through the INTEGRATED SERVICES DIGITAL NETWORK (ISDN), a dedicated high-speed line that carries digital signals. *See also* INTERNET

computer program *See* PROGRAM

computer virus Sequence of computer PROGRAM code that is able to copy itself from one COMPUTER to another, and is usually designed to disrupt the normal operation of a computer. Some viruses find their way into computers all over the world. A virus may remain undetected for months before springing into action. The worst cause loss or alteration of data held on the computer.

COMSAT *See* COMMUNICATIONS SATELLITE (COMSAT)

Comte, Auguste (1798–1857) French philosopher, founder of POSITIVISM. He proposed a law of three stages (theological, metaphysical and positive) to represent the development of the human race. In the first two stages, the human mind finds religious or abstract causes to explain phenomena, while in the third, explanation of a phenomenon is found in a scientific law. Comte influenced John Stuart MILL and was the founder of SOCIOLOGY. His works include *System of Positive Polity* (1830–42).

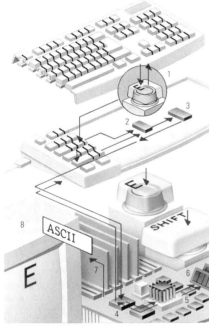

▲ **computer** Pressing a key (1) or pair of keys changes the current flowing through the key's circuit. A microprocessor (2) scans the circuits and detects when they change. A scan code is transmitted to the microprocessor in the memory buffer in the keyboard (3). The scan code then travels through the cable connecting the keyboard to its controller chip (4) in the body of the computer. The controller chip informs the (5) central processing unit (CPU), which finds the keyboard program in read-only memory (ROM) (6) and cancels the scan code in the keyboard's memory buffer. ROM converts the scan code into the PC's language, ASCII (7), and then instructs the monitor (8) to display the character, in this instance an uppercase E.

Conakry Capital city of Guinea, W Africa, on Tombo Island, in the Atlantic Ocean. Founded in 1884, it is a major port and the administrative and commercial centre of Guinea. Conakry exports alumina and bananas. Pop. (1995) 1,508,000.

concentration camp Detention centre for military or political prisoners. The British set up camps for Afrikaner civilians during the SOUTH AFRICAN WARS (1899–1902). The most notorious were those established by the Nazi regime in Germany in the 1930s for people considered racially or socially undesirable and political opponents. Some of these camps provided slave labour while others were the sites of mass execution. In Poland, more than 6 million people, mostly Jews, were murdered in the gas chambers. GULAGS were widely employed during Stalin's purges, and re-education camps were used in the Chinese CULTURAL REVOLUTION and by the KHMER ROUGE. *See also* AUSCHWITZ; BELSEN; BUCHENWALD; DACHAU

Concepción City near the mouth of the River Bío-Bío, S central Chile; capital of Concepción province. Founded in 1550 by Pedro de Valdivia, it was destroyed (1570, 1730, 1751, 1835, 1939) by earthquakes and was severely damaged in 1960. The modern city is the third-largest in Chile. More than 80% of Chile's coal is mined nearby and shipped via its Pacific port, Talcahuano. Other industries: textiles, glass, sugar. Pop. (1995) 350,000.

conceptual art Art giving primacy to idea over craftsmanship. The notion was first asserted by Marcel DUCHAMP, but a movement only began to take shape in the 1960s. Conceptual art questions the nature of art and emphasizes the elimination of art as an object or commodity for reproduction. The "viewer" is often implicated in the production of art as performance or "happening". Artists include Claes OLDENBURG and Joseph BEUYS.

conceptualism Philosophical theory in which the universal is found in the particular, a position between NOMINALISM and REALISM. It asserts that the mind is the individual that universalizes by experiencing particulars.

concerto Musical work for instrumental soloists accompanied by orchestra. Alessandro Stradella (1644–1682) is credited with originating the **concerto grosso**, in which a small section of soloists on various instruments, the *concertino*, is contrasted with the full orchestra, the *ripieno*. J.S. BACH's Brandenburg Concertos are fine examples of this form. VIVALDI composed most of his concertos for one soloist and orchestra and used the three-movement form (fast-slow-fast) which was to become standard in CLASSICAL MUSIC, such as the brilliant concertos of MOZART and BEETHOVEN. In the 19th century, concertos involved increasing virtuosity, as in the works of LISZT and RACHMANINOV.

conclave Originally a place of private or secret assembly, then the assembly itself. More particularly, the assembly of CARDINALS that elects a new pope.

Concord Capital of New Hampshire on the Merrimack River. Founded as a trading post (1660), it was settled in 1727. It was the site of New Hampshire's ratification of the Constitution as the deciding state on 21 June 1788. Industries: electrical equipment. Pop. (1992) 36,364.

Concord *See* LEXINGTON AND CONCORD, BATTLES OF

concordat Agreement between church and state regulating relations between them on matters of common concern. The term is usually applied to treaties between individual states and the VATICAN.

concrete Hard, strong building material made by mixing CEMENT, sand, gravel and water. It is an important building material. It can be reinforced by embedded steel rods. Pre-stressed concrete contains piano wires instead of steel. Its modern use dates from the early 19th century, although the Romans made extensive use of concrete.

concussion Temporary loss of consciousness due to a blow to the head. It may last from a few seconds to a few hours. There may be no structural damage to the brain, but a scan will detect signs of bruising. It is often associated with confusion and AMNESIA. Treatment consists of rest and close observation.

Condé (1530–1830) Junior branch of the French royal house of BOURBON. Notable members of the line included **Louis I**, Prince de Condé (1530–69), a HUGUENOT leader. The third prince was **Henry II** (1588–1646), a Catholic, who was arrested for blackmail and sedition (1616), but was reconciled to the crown under LOUIS XIII. **Louis II**, the Great Condé (1621–86), was a famous general. Victorious against Spain at Rocroi (1643), he was later involved in the civil conflict known as the FRONDES. **Louis Joseph** de Bourbon-Condé (1736–1818) led the émigré nobility during the FRENCH REVOLUTION.

condensation Formation of a liquid from a gas or vapour, caused by cooling or an increase in pressure. It changes water vapour in the air into water droplets, forming mist, cloud, rain or drops on cold surfaces.

condenser *See* CAPACITOR

conditioning In experimental psychology, learning in which human or animal subjects learn to respond in a certain way to a stimulus. Classical conditioning stems from the work of Ivan PAVLOV, while operant conditioning was first described by B.F. SKINNER.

condom *See* CONTRACEPTION

condor Common name for two species of the American VULTURE: the black Andean condor (*Vultur gryphus*) and the rare grey-brown California condor (*Gymnogyps californianus*). They are two of the largest flying birds and feed on partly rotted carrion. Length: up to 127cm (50in). Wingspan: up to 3.5m (10ft).

Condorcet, Marie Jean Antoine Nicolas de Caritat, Marquis de (1743–94) French philosopher, mathematician and politician. His *Essay on the Application of Analysis to the Probability of Majority Decisions* (1785) was a valuable contribution to mathematics. Condorcet was the only leading *philosophe* to play an active part in the French Revolution. A moderate GIRONDIN, he was condemned by the JACOBINS and died in prison. In *Sketch for a Historical Picture of the Progress of the Human Mind* (1795), he suggests the progress of man to ultimate perfection.

conductance (symbol G) Ability of a material to conduct ELECTRICITY. In a direct current (DC) circuit, it is the reciprocal of electrical RESISTANCE. For example, a conductor of resistance R has a conductance of 1/R. In an alternating current (AC) circuit, it is the resistance divided by the square of impedance (the opposition of a circuit to the passage of a current; $G = R/Z^2$. SI units of conductance are siemens (symbol S).

conduction Thermal conduction is the transfer of heat from a hot region of a body to a cold region. If one end of a metal rod is placed in a flame, the heat energy received causes increased vibratory motion of the molecules in that end. These molecules bump into others farther along the rod, and the increased motion is passed along until finally the end not in the flame becomes hot. **Electrical** conduction is the progress of charged particles through a substance resulting in an electric charge. In metals, it is the flow of free ELECTRONS. In gases, it is the flow of IONS. *See also* SEMICONDUCTOR; SUPERCONDUCTIVITY

conductivity Measure of the ease with which a material allows electricity (**electrical** CONDUCTION) or heat

(**thermal** conduction) to pass through it. For a solid substance, the electrical conductivity is the CONDUCTANCE. For an ELECTROLYTE, conductivity is the ratio of the current density to the field strength.

conductor In physics, substance or object that allows easy passage of free ELECTRONS. Conductors have a low electrical RESISTANCE. Metals, the best conductors, have free electrons that become an ELECTRIC CURRENT when made to move. The resistance of a metallic conductor increases with temperature because the lattice vibrations of atoms increase and scatter the free electrons.

conductor In music, a person who coordinates the performance of a band, orchestra or choir, and directs and inspires the interpretation of the music. Before the 19th century, a harpsichordist or first violinist "directed" orchestral playing. As the size of orchestras increased, it became common practice for a musician to stand before the players and conduct with a baton.

cone Solid, geometric figure swept out by a line (**generator**) that joins a point moving in a closed curve in a plane, to a fixed point (**vertex**) outside the plane. In a right circular cone, the vertex lies above the centre of a circle (base), and the cone's generators join the vertex to points on the circle. Such a cone has a volume $\frac{1}{3}\pi r^2 h$ and a curved surface area πrs, where h is the vertical height, s the slant height, and r the radius of the base.

Confederate States of America (1861–65) (Confederacy) Southern states which seceded from the Union following the election of Abraham LINCOLN. South Carolina left in December 1860, and was followed closely by Alabama, Florida, Georgia, Louisiana, Mississippi and Texas. In March 1861, Jefferson DAVIS was elected president and a new constitution protected STATE'S RIGHTS and retained SLAVERY. A capital was established at MONTGOMERY, Alabama. On 12 April, the American CIVIL WAR began, and Arkansas, North Carolina, Tennessee and Virginia joined the Confederacy. The capital was moved to RICHMOND, Virginia. The Confederacy received little external support, and internal problems contributed to its defeat and dissolution in April 1865.

Confederation, Articles of *See* ARTICLES OF CONFEDERATION

Confederation of British Industry (CBI) UK organization founded (1965) to promote the prosperity and interests of industry. Financed by *c*.250,000 companies, which are also its members, the CBI advises the government on policy affecting Britain's industrial interests.

confession Acknowledgment of SINS. In the Jewish and Christian traditions, it may be made by a congregation in the course of worship or by individual penitents.

confirmation Sacrament of the Christian Church by which the relationship between God and an individual, established by BAPTISM, is confirmed or strengthened in faith. Candidates for confirmation take the baptismal vows previously made on their behalf by godparents.

Confucianism Philosophy that dominated China until the early 20th century and still has many followers, mainly in Asia. It is based on the *Analects*, sayings attributed to CONFUCIUS. Strictly an ethical system to ensure a smooth-running society, it gradually acquired quasi-religious characteristics. Confucianism views man as potentially the most perfect form of *li*, the ultimate embodiment of good. It stresses the responsibility of sovereign to subject, of family members to one other, and of friend to friend. Politically, it helped to preserve the existing order, upholding the status of the MANDARINS. When the monarchy was overthrown (1911–12), Confucian institutions were

CONGO
AREA: 342,000sq km (132,046sq mi)
POPULATION: 3,167,000
CAPITAL (POPULATION): Brazzaville (937,579)

ended, but after the Communist Revolution (1949), many Confucian elements were incorporated into Maoism.

Confucius (551–479 BC) (K'ung-fu-tzu) Founder of CONFUCIANISM. Born in Lu, he was an excellent scholar and became an influential teacher of the sons of wealthy families. He is said to have been prime minister of Lu. In his later years, he sought a return to the political morality of the early ZHOU dynasty. *See also* CHINESE LITERATURE

congenital disorder Abnormal condition present from birth caused by faulty development, infection or the mother's exposure to drugs or other toxic substances during pregnancy. SPINA BIFIDA is such a condition.

conglomerate In geology, a sedimentary rock made up of rounded pebbles embedded in a fine matrix of sand or silt, commonly formed along beaches or on river beds.

Congo Equatorial republic in W central Africa; the capital is BRAZZAVILLE. The main port is Pointe Noire on the Gulf of Guinea. **Land and climate** Congo generally has a hot, wet equatorial climate. Its narrow, treeless coastal plain is dry and cool. Inland, the River Niari has carved a fertile valley through the forested highlands. Central Congo consists of luxuriant savanna with valley forests. Tree species include the valuable okoumé and mahogany. The N contains large swamps in the tributary valleys of the Zaire and Ubangi rivers. **History** Between the 15th and 18th centuries, part of Congo probably belonged to the huge Kongo kingdom. The Congo coast became a centre of the European slave trade. European exploration of the interior took place in the late 19th century, and the area came under French protection in 1880. It was later governed as part of a larger region called French Equatorial Africa and remained under French control until 1960. In 1964, Congo adopted Marxism-Leninism as the state ideology. In 1968, the military, led by Marien Ngouabi, seized power. Ngouabi created the Congolese Workers Party (PCT). In 1977, Ngouabi was assassinated, but the PCT retained power under Colonel Sassou-Nguesso. In 1990, the PCT renounced Marxism and Sassou-Nguesso was deposed. In 1992, democratic elections were won by the Pan-African Union for Social Democracy (UPADS), led by Pascal Lissouba. In 1997, Lissouba was deposed and Sassou-Nguesso was reinstalled as president. **Economy** Congo is a lower-middle-income developing country (1995 GDP per capita, US$2,050). More than 60% of the workforce is engaged in subsistence agriculture. Major food crops include bananas, cassava, maize and rice, while cash crops are coffee and cocoa. Congo's main exports are oil (70% of the total) and timber.

Congo, Democratic Republic of (formerly Zaïre) Republic in W central Africa. The second largest nation in Africa, the Democratic Republic of Congo is dominated by the River CONGO. The Congo basin is the world's second largest drainage system. Behind a narrow Atlantic coastline, on the opposite bank of the Congo from Brazzaville, lies the Republic's capital, KINSHASA. North, central Congo consists of a high plateau, 1,000 to 1,400m (3,300–4,600ft) high, and includes the city of KISANGANI. In the E, the plateau rises to 5,109m (16,762ft) in the RUWENZORI Mountains. Lakes ALBERT and Edward form much of Congo's NE border with Uganda. Lake Kivu lies along its border with Rwanda. Lake TANGANYIKA forms

the entire border with Tanzania. All the lakes lie in an arm of the Great RIFT VALLEY. The S highland province of Shaba (Katanga) includes Congo's second largest city, Lubumbashi. **Climate** Much of Congo has an equatorial climate with high temperatures and heavy rainfall throughout the year. The S has a more sub-tropical climate. **Vegetation** Dense, equatorial rainforests grow in N Congo. The S plateau is an area of savanna and swamps. **History and politics** By *c.*1000 AD, Bantu-speakers had largely displaced the native pygmy population. From the 14th century, large Bantu kingdoms began to emerge. In 1482, a Portuguese navigator became the first European to reach the mouth of the Congo. In the 19th century, slave and ivory traders formed powerful states. Henry Morton STANLEY's explorations (1874–77) into the interior established the route of the River Congo. In 1878, King LEOPOLD II of Belgium employed Stanley to found colonies along the Congo. In 1885, Leopold proclaimed the foundation of the Congo Free State. Leopold's personal empire was gradually extended, and concessionaires were granted control of the lucrative rubber trade. Sir Roger CASEMENT's denunciation of the inhuman exploitation of the native population resulted in international criticism. In 1908, Belgium responded by establishing direct control as the colony of Belgian Congo. European companies exploited African labour to develop the copper and diamond mines. Internal opposition to colonial rule was banned. In 1958, the French offered the Congo a free vote on independence. Nationalists in Belgian Congo demanded similar elections. In June 1960, independence was granted as the Republic of the Congo. Patrice LUMUMBA became prime minister. Belgium had not properly secured institutional changes, and the state rapidly fractured. The mineral-rich province of Katanga demanded independence. Belgian troops, sent to protect its citizens and mining interests, were replaced by UN troops. In September 1960, Joseph MOBUTU, commander-in-chief of the Congolese National Army, seized power. Lumumba was imprisoned and later murdered. In 1963, UN and government forces combined to force Katanga to drop its demands for secession. Following the withdrawal of UN troops in 1964, Belgian Congo was again plunged into civil war. Belgian troops once more intervened. In 1965, Mobutu proclaimed himself president. Mobutu began a campaign of "Africanization": Leopoldville became Kinshasa (1966); the country and river renamed Zaïre (1971); Katanga became Shaba (1972); and Mobutu adopted the name Mobutu Sese Seko. Zaire became a one-party state. Unopposed, Mobutu was re-elected in 1974 and 1977. Political repression and endemic corruption led to renewed civil war in Shaba (1977–78). Secessionist forces were again defeated with European aid. An ailing Mobutu, whose personal wealth was estimated at US$5 billion, came under increasing pressure to reform. In 1990, he was forced to allow the formation of opposition parties. National elections were repeatedly deferred and a succession of transitional governments remained under Mobutu's control. In 1995, millions of Hutus fled from RWANDA into E Zaïre to escape possible Tutsi reprisals. In 1996, rebel forces, led by Laurent Kabila, launched a successful offensive against Mobutu's regime. Mobutu was forced into exile. Zaïre was renamed the Democratic Republic of Congo (DRC). Kabila's presidency held out the hope of democratic reforms. In 1998, the DRC was plunged into civil war between government forces and the Tutsi-dominated Congolese Rally for Democracy (RCD). In August 1999, the warring factions signed the Lusaka Peace Agreement that ushered in a fragile ceasefire. In 2000, political dialogue broke down

CONGO, DEMOCRATIC REPUBLIC OF
AREA: 2,344,885 (905,365sq mi)
POPULATION: 49,190,000
CAPITAL (POPULATION): Kinshasa (3,804,000)

and fighting resumed. **Economy** the Democratic Republic of Congo is a low-income developing country (1995 GDP per capita, US$490). It is the world's leading producer of cobalt and the second largest producer of diamonds (after Australia). Copper is the major export. The Republic has enormous potential for hydroelectricity; the Inga Dam, near Kinshasa, is one of the world's largest. A major economic problem is an inadequate infrastructure, especially the poor standard of the roads. Agriculture employs 71% of the workforce, mainly at subsistence level. Palm oil is the most important cash crop. Other cash crops include cocoa, coffee, cotton and tea. Food crops include bananas, cassava, maize and rice. Corruption and hyperinflation are major obstacles to economic growth.

Congo (Zaïre River) River in central and W Africa; the second-longest in the continent. It rises in the S of the Democratic Republic of Congo and flows in a massive curve to the Atlantic Ocean. Its rate of flow and size of drainage basin make it Africa's largest untapped source of hydroelectric power. The chief ocean port is Matadi. The main headstream is the Lualaba, and the Kasai and Ubangi are among its many large tributaries. Length: 4,670km (2,900mi)

Congregationalism Christian church denomination in which local churches are autonomous; members have been called Brownists, Separatists and Independents. It is based on the belief that Christ is the head of the church and all members are priests. Modern Congregationalism began in England in c.1580. In the UK, the Congregational Church in England and Wales merged with others as the United Reformed Church (1972). In the US, the Congregational Christian Churches united with others as the United Church of Christ (1957).

Congress Legislative branch of the US federal government established by the US CONSTITUTION (1789). Congress comprises the SENATE (the upper house) and the HOUSE OF REPRESENTATIVES (the lower house). The main powers of Congress include the right to assess and collect taxes, introduce legislation, regulate commerce, propose constitutional amendments, mint money, raise and maintain armed forces, establish lower courts and declare war. Legislation must be passed by both houses and the president to become law. If the president uses his power of veto, Congress can still pass the bill with a two-thirds majority in each house. The first meeting of Congress took place in 1789 in New York City. The Senate can approve treaties and presidential appointments and tries the president if he is impeached. The House of Representatives initiates all tax bills and has the power to impeach the president. The Constitution requires that Congress meet at least once every year, and the president may call special sessions. The preparation and consideration of legislation is largely accomplished by the 17 standing committees in the Senate and a further 21 in the House of Representatives.

Congress of Industrial Organizations (CIO) See AMERICAN FEDERATION OF LABOR AND CONGRESS OF INDUSTRIAL ORGANIZATIONS (AFL-CIO)

Congress of Racial Equality (CORE) US civil rights organization, founded (1942) in Chicago by James Farmer. CORE first attracted national attention for its sponsorship of the FREEDOM RIDES (1961) to end segregation on public transport. Using the tactics of non-violence espoused by Martin Luther KING, Jr., it organized sit-ins, pickets, and boycotts to combat racial discrimination. CORE co-sponsored the March on Washington (1963).

Congress Party (officially Indian National Congress) Oldest political party in India, whose fortunes were often intertwined with the Nehru dynasty. It was founded in 1885, but was not prominent until after World War 1, when "Mahatma" GANDHI transformed it into a mass independence movement. Jawaharlal NEHRU became president of the Congress in 1929, and at independence (1947) became prime minister. In 1966, Nehru's daughter, Indira GANDHI, became prime minister in 1966, but the party later split, and Indira's Congress (I) suffered a landslide defeat at the elections of 1977. The party regained power in 1979, and in 1984 (after Indira's assassination) her son, Rajiv GANDHI, became leader. Following a further split, Congress was defeated in 1989, and Rajiv was assassinated in 1991. Under new leaders, the party lost the 1996, 1998 and 1999 elections.

congress system Attempt during the early 19th century to conduct diplomacy through regular conferences between the European allies that had defeated Napoleonic France. It originated in the Treaty of PARIS (1815). The four powers (Austria, Britain, Prussia and Russia) met in 1818, 1820 and 1821. Britain withdrew (1822) after opposing proposals to intervene against revolutionary forces in South America and elsewhere. Differences between the three remaining powers at St Petersburg in 1825 caused the abandonment of the system.

Congreve, William (1670–1729) English dramatist. His elegant satire represents the peak of RESTORATION DRAMA. Congreve's comedies include *Love for Love* (1695) and *The Way of the World* (1700). He also wrote a tragedy, *The Mourning Bride* (1697).

conic (conic section) Curve found by the intersection of a plane with a CONE. Circles, ellipses, parabolas or hyperbolas are conic sections. Alternatively, a conic is the locus of a point that moves so that the ratio of its distances from a fixed point (the focus) and a fixed line (the directrix) is constant. This ratio is called the ECCENTRICITY (e): $e = 1$ gives a parabola, $e >1$ a hyperbola, $e<1$ an ellipse and $e = 0$ a circle.

conifer Cone-bearing trees, generally evergreen, such as pines, firs and redwoods. They are some of the Earth's largest plants, reaching heights of up to 99m (325ft). Conifers are a major natural resource of the Northern Hemisphere. *See also* GYMNOSPERM

conjunctivitis Inflammation of the conjunctiva, the fine membrane that lines the eyelid and covers the front of the eye. It can be caused by infection, usually bacterial, by exposure to irritants or by allergy, and it produces watery, burning and itching eyelids.

Connecticut Northeastern US state; its state capital and largest city is HARTFORD. One of the original 13 colonies, Connecticut was first settled by the English in the 1630s. Puritans flocked to the area, and in 1662 the colony received a charter from Charles II. Connecticut was one of the first states to ratify the Constitution and joined the union in 1788. The Connecticut River valley separates the W and E highlands. Hartford is one of the world's leading insurance centres. The state economy is based on manufacturing. Industries: transport equipment, machinery. Dairy produce, eggs and tobacco are the main farm products. Fishing is also important. Area: 12,549sq km (4,845sq mi). Pop. (2000) 3,405,565.

connective tissue Supporting and packing tissue that helps to maintain the body's shape and hold it together.

Bones, ligaments, cartilage and skin are types of connective tissue.

Connery, Sean (1930–) Scottish film actor. He starred in *Dr No* (1962), the first film adaptation of Ian FLEMING's James Bond spy stories. Connery made a further six Bond films, including *Diamonds are Forever* (1971) and *Never Say Never Again* (1983). He became a versatile character actor in films such as *The Name of the Rose* (1986). Connery won an Academy Award as Best Supporting Actor for *The Untouchables* (1987).

Connolly, James (1870–1916) Irish nationalist leader. He went to the US in 1903 and helped establish the INDUSTRIAL WORKERS OF THE WORLD (IWW). Returning to Ireland, he was a leader in the EASTER RISING of 1916, and was executed by the British authorities.

Connors, Jimmy (James Scott) (1952–) US tennis player. He won more Grand Prix singles titles (109) than any other player. In 1974, Connors won the US, Australian and Wimbledon singles titles. He won the US Open four more times (1976, 1978, 1982–83) and Wimbledon in 1982. Connors also won doubles titles with Ilie Nastase.

conquistador (Sp. conqueror) Leader of the Spanish conquest of the New World in the 16th century. Conquistadores were often ex-soldiers unemployed since the Christian reconquest of Spain. The most famous were Hernán CORTÉS and Francisco PIZARRO.

Conrad II (990–1039) Holy Roman emperor (1027–39), first of the Salian dynasty. Conrad became king of Germany (emperor-elect) in 1024. As emperor, he suppressed early revolts in Lotharingia and Italy. In 1034, Conrad annexed Burgundy. His son succeeded him as HENRY III.

Conrad III (1093–1152) First German king (1138–52) of the HOHENSTAUFEN dynasty. In 1128, Conrad was crowned as an anti-king to LOTHAIR II but was forced to submit in 1135. Upon Lothair's death, he was officially crowned king. Anxious to deprive Lothair's son (Henry the Proud) of a power base, Conrad awarded Saxony to Albert the Bear. Henry's son, HENRY THE LION, launched a civil war out of which emerged the rival factions of the GUELPHS and GHIBELLINES. Conrad joined the Second Crusade, but was never crowned by the pope.

Conrad IV (1228–54) German king (1237–54), king of Sicily and Jerusalem (1250–54), son of FREDERICK II. The conflict between Frederick and Pope INNOCENT IV saw the election (1246) of an anti-king, and Germany lurched into civil war. Conrad inherited Sicily and Jerusalem upon Frederick's death but was never crowned emperor. The pope excommunicated him (1254).

Conrad, Joseph (1857–1924) British novelist and short-story writer, b. Poland. His eventful years as a ship's officer in Asian, African and Latin American waters permeated the exotic settings of many of his novels. Conrad was a central figure in the development of literary MODERNISM. His major works include *Lord Jim* (1900), *Heart of Darkness* (1902), *Nostromo* (1904), *The Secret Agent* (1907), *Under Western Eyes* (1911) and *Chance* (1914).

conscription Compulsory enlistment in the armed forces. In Britain, conscription was used in both World Wars and continued in peacetime as National Service until 1962. In the US, conscription was used during the Civil War, but dropped until 1940, when it was re-introduced, finally being abolished in 1973.

conservation Term that has a number of different, if associated, meanings in the preservation of nature and its resources. Conservation requires planning and organization to make the best use of resources or to preserve the natural landscape and wildlife. It is also used to describe the preservation, and sometimes renovation, of ancient and historic man-made structures. *See also* ECOLOGY

conservation, laws of Physical laws stating that some property of a closed system is unaltered by change in the system. The most important are the laws of conservation of MATTER and ENERGY. Mass and energy are interconvertible according to the equation $E = mc^2$; what is conserved is the total mass and its equivalent in energy.

conservatism Political philosophy seeking to preserve the historic continuity of a society's laws, customs, social structure and institutions. Its modern expression derives from the response, first in Germany, to the liberal doctrines of the Enlightenment and the French Revolution. Originally, conservatives supported MERCANTILISM in preference to LAISSEZ-FAIRE economics, but in the 20th century they have adopted the principles of the free-market and MONETARISM. *See also* BURKE, EDMUND; CHRISTIAN DEMOCRATS; CONSERVATIVE PARTY; LIBERALISM; SOCIALISM

Conservative Party (officially Conservative and Unionist Party) Oldest political party in Britain. Its origins lie in the transformation of the early 19th-century TORY PARTY into the Conservative Party under Sir Robert PEEL in the 1830s; it was mainly a party of landed interests. After the Reform Act of 1867, the urban and commercial element in the Party increased. It held power for 31 of the 71 years between 1834 and 1905, and for most of the 1920s and 1930s, either alone or in coalition. In the post-war period, it held office in 1951–64 and 1970–74. In 1979, the Party swung further to the right under the leadership (1975–90) of Margaret THATCHER. With the support of traditional LABOUR PARTY voters, it was able (under Thatcher and John MAJOR) to win four consecutive elections. In 1997, William HAGUE became the youngest leader of the Party since William PITT (the Younger) in 1783.

Constable, John (1776–1837) English painter, a leading Western landscapist. He attended (1795–1802) the Royal Academy and studied the paintings of CLAUDE LORRAIN. Constable studied every effect of clouds and light on water. His first success came when *The Haywain* (1821) and *View on the Stour* (1817) were shown at the Paris Salon in 1824, although recognition in England only came after his death.

Constance (Konstanz) City-port on Lake Constance, Baden-Württemberg, SW Germany. Founded as a Roman fort in the 4th century AD, it became a free imperial city in 1183 and was the site of the Council of CONSTANCE. Constance passed to Austria in 1548 and to Baden in 1805. Notable sites include an 11th-century cathedral and the Kaufhaus (1388). Industries: tourism, textiles, chemicals. Pop. (1990 est.) 75,000.

Constance, Council of (1414–18) Ecumenical council that ended the GREAT SCHISM. It was convoked by the anti-pope John XXIII. MARTIN V was elected pope in 1417. The Council also attempted to combat heresy, notably that of Jan HUS.

Constance, Lake (Bodensee) Lake bounded by Austria, Germany and Switzerland. Fed and drained by the River Rhine, it divides into two arms near the city of Constance. Area: 543sq km (210sq mi).

Constant (de Rebecque), (Henri) Benjamin (1761–1830) French politician and novelist, b. Switzerland. A member of Napoleon's tribunate (1799–1802), he went into exile in 1803. After the BOURBON restoration, Constant led the liberal opposition (1819–22, 1824–30). His chief work was the psychological novel *Adolphe* (1816).

constant In mathematics, a quantity or factor that does not change. It may be universal, such as the ratio of the circumference of a circle to its diameter, or it may be particular, such as a symbol that has a fixed value in an algebraic equation.

Constanţa City in E Romania, on the Black Sea. Founded in the 7th century BC as a Greek colony, it was taken by the Romans in 72 BC, and named in the 4th century AD by Emperor Constantine. It is Romania's chief port and a major trade centre. It has Roman and Byzantine ruins, several mosques and a naval and air base. Industries: shipbuilding, oil refining, textiles. Pop. (1994) 349,000.

Constantine I (the Great) (285–337) Roman emperor (306–37), and founder of the Christian empire. A series of feuds for control of Italy ended when Constantine adopted Christianity and defeated Maxentius (312). Constantine and Licinius signed the Edict of Milan (313) that extended tolerance to Christians throughout the empire. In 324, he defeated Licinius and became sole ruler. Constantine presided over the first council of the Christian church at NICAEA (325), which condemned ARIANISM. He rebuilt (330) Byzantium as his capital and renamed it Constantinople (now ISTANBUL). Constantine centralized imperial power but divided the empire before his death.

Constantine II (1940–) King of Greece (1964–73). In 1967, a military junta seized power in Greece and Constantine launched an abortive coup against the generals. He was forced into exile and was formally deposed in 1973. The junta was overthrown (1974) and Greece became a republic.

Constantinople Former name of ISTANBUL

Constantinople, Latin Empire of (1204–61) Empire established after the sacking of Constantinople (now ISTANBUL) by the leaders of the Fourth CRUSADE. It lay on both sides of the Dardanelles and was divided among the Crusaders. Constantinople was under the control of BALDWIN I. It was constantly under attack from its neighbours, and declined rapidly: Thessalonica fell in 1222, and Asia Minor in 1224. The Latin Empire ended in 1261, when Constantinople was recaptured by the Byzantine emperor Michael VIII.

constellation Grouping of stars, forming an imaginary figure traced on the sky. The groupings have no physical basis as each star is a different distance from Earth. There are 88 constellations that were assigned boundaries on the CELESTIAL SPHERE by the International Astronomical Union in 1930. *See individual constellations*

constipation Incomplete or infrequent evacuation of stools that are hard and difficult to pass. It may arise from a number of causes, ranging from a poor diet to emotional stress; it may also be a symptom of bowel disease. Constipation may be eased by adding roughage to the diet or by laxatives or enemas.

constitution Code of laws, or collection of customary practices, delineating the powers and organization of the various organs of government within a nation, and some of the rights and obligations of its citizens. In states with a written constitution, courts often have specific powers relating to the constitution and likely points of conflict. In the US, where there is a federal system of government, the SUPREME COURT often resolves conflict between the individual states and the central government. In countries without a written constitution, such as Britain, constitutional law is more imprecise and problems are addressed within the political process.

Constitutional Convention (1787) Meeting of delegates, in Philadelphia, from 12 of the 13 US states (Rhode Island abstained), which resulted in the creation of the US CONSTITUTION. The Convention was called to revise the ARTICLES OF CONFEDERATION (1781), and to redress the lack of power wielded by the existing government structure. There was demand for a more stable and centralized federal government that had tighter monetary control. The major disagreement centred on how each state should determine its share of this centralized power. A bicameral system was agreed, whereby the House of Representatives was elected according to population and the Senate was chosen by the states.

Constitution of the United States Fundamental laws and basis of US government. Adopted (September 1787) by the CONSTITUTIONAL CONVENTION in Philadelphia, it was ratified in 1788, and went into effect in 1789. It replaced the ARTICLES OF CONFEDERATION (1781), which had proved inadequate, giving too much power to each state. It was designed to create a system of "checks and balances" to prevent one branch of government gaining dominance over others. Opponents who feared that the federal government would be too powerful and the rights of the individual unprotected, succeeded in having ten amendments, collectively known as the BILL OF RIGHTS, added. Seventeen other amendments have been ratified, the most recent in 1992. The Constitution was designed not as a code of laws, but as a statement of principles to which laws should adhere, thus allowing considerable flexibility in judicial interpretation.

constructivism Russian abstract art movement founded, *c*.1913, by the sculptor Vladimir TATLIN. Other members were the brothers Naum GABO and Antoine PEVSNER. Influenced by CUBISM and FUTURISM, their sculptures attempted to relate to contemporary technology. From 1921, the Soviet regime condemned the movement, and Gabo and Pevsner left Russia. Through them and other exiles, constructivism spread and informed modern European architecture and sculpture.

consul One of the two chief magistrates of ancient Rome. The office was established *c*.510 BC. Consuls were elected yearly to administer civil and military matters. After 367 BC, one consul was a PATRICIAN, the other a PLEBEIAN – each having the power to veto the other's decisions.

consumerism Belief that consumers should influence the policies and practices regulating the standards and methods of manufacturers, advertisers and sellers. Interest in consumerism first arose in the 1960s, with Ralph NADER raising the issue in the US public consciousness.

consumption *See* TUBERCULOSIS

consumption In economics, expenditure on goods and services, excluding expenditure on capital goods such as machinery. Consumption can be divided into public and private sectors. **Public** consumption consists of government spending on services, such as health and education. **Private** consumption is household expenditure on non-durables, such as cars and clothing. It is the largest component of national income. The primary importance of private consumption was first stated by Jeremy BENTHAM. Adam SMITH made it the sole reason for production. John Maynard KEYNES proposed the theory of **consumptive function**, which describes the relationship between consumer income and consumption. Governments seek to control consumption by taxation and interest rates.

contact lens Lens worn on the CORNEA to aid defective vision. They were invented (1887) by Adolf Frick and were initially made of glass. Modern contact lenses, developed (1948) by Kevin Tuohy, are made of plastic. Hard (corneal) lenses cover the pupil and part of the cornea. They are usually gas-permeable (allowing oxygen to reach the cornea). Soft (hydrophilic) lenses cover the whole cornea and are hydrated in saline solution.

continent Large land masses on the Earth's surface. The continents are EUROPE and ASIA (or Eurasia), AFRICA, NORTH AMERICA, SOUTH AMERICA, AUSTRALIA and ANTARCTICA. They cover *c*.30% of the Earth above sea level and extend below sea level, forming continental shelves. All continents have four components, which make up the continental crust. **Shields** are areas of relatively level land, within a few hundred metres height above sea level, consisting of crystalline rocks. **Stable platforms** are areas that have a thin covering of sedimentary rock. **Sedimentary basins** are broad, deep depressions filled with sedimentary rocks formed in shallow seas. **Folded mountain** belts are younger sedimentary rocks in long, linear zones of intensely folded and faulted rocks that have been metamorphosed and intruded by igneous and volcanic activity. The continental crust is composed of rocks moving very slowly over the surface of the Earth by CONTINENTAL DRIFT. Its thickness is mainly between 30 and 40km (20–25mi), except under mountain chains (up to 70km/45mi). *See also* PLATE TECTONICS

continental divide Line of separation running the length of a continent that determines to which side of the continent rivers flow. Such divides exist in the US, Canada, S America and Australia.

Continental Congress (1774–89) Federal legislature of the American colonies during the AMERICAN REVOLUTION and the period of Confederation. Its first meeting, at Philadelphia in September 1774, resulted in unified opposition to British rule and agreed on a boycott of trade with Britain. In May 1775, the Congress

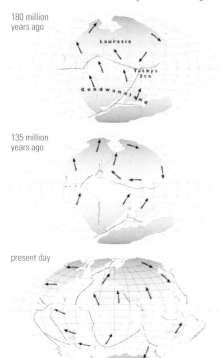

180 million years ago

Laurasia

Tethys Sea

Gondwanaland

135 million years ago

present day

▲ **continental drift** About 200 million years ago, the original Pangaea land mass began to split into two continental groups, which further separated over time to produce the present-day configuration.

reconvened and appointed George WASHINGTON to command the American army. In July 1776, the Second Congress adopted the DECLARATION OF INDEPENDENCE and drafted the ARTICLES OF CONFEDERATION. The adoption of the CONSTITUTION (1787) made the Congress redundant, although it continued to meet until 1789.

continental drift Theory that the continents change position very slowly, moving over the Earth's surface at a rate of only a few centimetres per year, adding up to thousands of kilometres over geological time. Early supporters of continental drift claimed that the jigsaw shapes of the present-day continents could be pieced together to form an ancient land mass which, at sometime in the past, split and drifted apart. Continental drift became accepted with the development of PLATE TECTONICS in the 1960s. In recent years, continental movement has been measured by global positioning satellites. *See also* GONDWANALAND; PANGAEA

continental margin Region of the ocean floor that lies between the shoreline and the abyssal ocean floor. It includes the continental shelf, the continental slope and the continental rise.

Continental System Trade blockade of Britain introduced (1806) by NAPOLEON I to cripple the British economy and force favourable peace terms in the NAPOLEONIC WARS. Extended to Russia by the Treaty of Tilsit (1807) and to Spain and Portugal in 1808, the Continental System also included neutral countries and prompted a retaliatory British blockade against France and its allies. The system was highly unpopular, and the economic war probably caused more deprivation on the continental mainland than in Britain, which maintained command of the sea. The restrictions contributed to the WAR OF 1812.

Contra Right-wing Nicaraguan revolutionary group active between 1979 and 1990. In support of the former dictator General Anastasio SOMOZA, ousted in 1979, the Contra aimed to overthrow the elected, left-wing SANDINISTA government. The Contra received financial and military assistance from the US government from mid-1986. Elections were subsequently held in Nicaragua in 1990, at which the US-funded Union of National Opposition (UNO), effectively the political wing of the Contra, was victorious. The Contra were officially disbanded. *See also* IRAN-CONTRA AFFAIR

contraception (birth control) Use of devices or techniques to prevent pregnancy. The PILL is a hormone preparation that prevents the release of an egg (OVUM) and thickens the cervical mucus. The intra-uterine device (IUD) is a small spring, made from plastic or metal, inserted into the womb. It stops the fertilized egg embedding itself in the uterine lining. Barrier methods include the male and female condom and the diaphragm. The male condom is a latex sheath that covers the penis and collects the ejaculated semen; the female condom lines the inside of the vagina, preventing any sperm entering the womb. The use of condoms is widely advocated because they help protect against some sexually transmitted diseases, including ACQUIRED IMMUNE DEFICIENCY SYNDROME (AIDS). Devices such as diaphrams or caps cover the cervix thus preventing sperm entering the womb. Less effective is the "rhythm method", which involves the avoidance of sex on days when conception is most likely (when the woman is ovulating). It is not a reliable method. Emergency contraception, known as the "morning-after pill", can be taken up to 72 hours after unprotected sexual intercourse; it prevents the fertilized ovum embedding itself in the womb. It is not suitable to be used regularly. *See also* SEXUAL REPRODUCTION

contralto Lowest range (below SOPRANO and MEZZO-SOPRANO) of the female singing voice. A male voice in this range is called a COUNTERTENOR. *See also* ALTO

control system Means by which a process is made to conform to prescribed instructions, either by maintaining the values of certain parameters at a constant level (**regulator**) or by forcing the controlled variable to change with time in a predetermined manner (SERVO-MECHANISM). A central heating thermostat is an example of a regulator. Control systems may be mechanical, electromechanical, electronic or fluidic. All systems depend on **feed-forward** or FEEDBACK. Many complex industrial systems are computer-controlled.

convection Transfer of heat by the flow of currents within fluids (gases or liquids). Warm fluids have a natural tendency to rise (because they are less dense), whereas cooler fluids tend to fall. This movement subsides when all areas of the fluid are at the same temperature. Convection in the form of winds is the main method of heat transfer in the Earth's atmosphere. Liquid convection is used in a car's cooling system.

convection current In geology, heat generated from radioactivity deep within the Earth's MANTLE causing rock to flow towards the CRUST. At the top of the mantle, the rising rock is deflected laterally below the crust before sinking. This mantle convection is thought to be the process driving PLATE TECTONICS.

convergence In mathematics, property of an infinite series (or sequence) having a unique and finite limiting value. Thus, for the series $1 + 1/2 + 1/2^2 + 1/2^3 + ...$, the sum of the first two terms is 1.5, the first three 1.75, and the first four 1.875; as more and more terms are taken, the sum approaches 2, called the limit of the series. Such a series is said to converge. *See also* DIVERGENCE

convolvulus *See* BINDWEED

Conway Cabal (1771) In US history, a failed plot (supposedly led by Thomas Conway) to remove George WASHINGTON as commander of Revolutionary forces and replace him with Horatio GATES. Investigations later revealed that the plot was not instigated by Conway.

Cook, James (1728–79) British naval officer and explorer. He charted the approaches to Québec during the Seven Years' War. In 1768–71, Cook led an expedition to Tahiti to observe an eclipse of the Sun and to investigate the strategic and economic potential of the South Pacific. He conducted a survey of the unknown coasts of New Zealand and charted the E coast of Australia, naming it New South Wales and claiming it for Britain. On a second expedition to the S Pacific (1772–75), Cook charted much of the Southern Hemisphere and circumnavigated Antarctica. On his last voyage (1776–79), he discovered the Sandwich (Hawaiian) Islands, where he was killed in a dispute with the inhabitants. Cook is generally regarded as the greatest European explorer of the Pacific in the 18th century.

Cook, Robin (1946–) British statesman, foreign secretary (1997–). He entered Parliament in 1974. A skilful parliamentary speaker, Cook held various posts (1987–97) in Labour's shadow cabinet. As foreign secretary, he sought to promote a greater ethical dimension to British foreign policy.

Cook, Thomas (1808–92) English founder of worldwide tourist agency, Thomas Cook and Son. As a missionary, he arranged the first group tours for temperance organizations (1841–44). In 1845, Cook founded his own firm. He offered foreign tours in 1855, the grand tour of Europe in 1856, and the first round-the-world tour in 1872.

Cook, Mount Mountain in W central South Island, New Zealand. The highest peak in New Zealand, it lies in Mount Cook National Park and has the Tasman Glacier on its SE slope. Height: 3,764m (12,349ft).

Cook Islands Group of 15 islands in the S Pacific Ocean, NE of New Zealand, consisting of the Northern (Manihiki) Cook Islands and the Southern (Lower) Cook Islands; a self-governing territory in free association with New Zealand. Discovered by James Cook in 1773, the islands became a British protectorate in 1888, and were annexed to New Zealand in 1901. They achieved self-governing status in 1965. Products: copra, citrus fruits. Area: 293sq km (113sq mi). Pop. (1992 est) 17,900.

Cooke, (Alfred) Alistair (1908–) English broadcaster and journalist. He was chief correspondent in America (1948–72) for *The Guardian* newspaper. Cooke wrote the successful television documentary *America: A Personal History of the United States* (1972–73). He is best-known for his weekly *Letter from America*, the longest-running radio feature programme (first broadcast in 1946).

Cookson, Dame Catherine (1906–98) English novelist. Her bestselling romantic novels are set often in her native NE England. Her debut novel was *Kate Hennigan* (1950). Cookson has written more than 70 novels, including the Mallen trilogy and the Mary Ann octet (1954–67). She was made a dame in 1993.

Coolidge, (John) Calvin (1872–1933) 30th US President (1923–29). Stern action in the Boston police strike of 1919 earned him the Republican nomination as vice president in 1920. He became president on the death of Warren HARDING in 1923, and was re-elected in 1924. A conservative with no dramatic political programme, his administration was characterized by a laissez-faire approach to business and commerce, summed up by his phrase, "the business of America is business". Many argue that this attitude was partly responsible for the unsustainable bullishness of the US stock market.

Cooper, Gary (1901–61) US film actor. His laconic style soon became an archetype for the cowboy hero in Westerns such as *The Virginian* (1929). In the 1930s, Cooper's acting diversified in films such as *Mr. Deeds Goes to Town* (1936). He won two Academy Awards as best actor: *Sergeant York* (1941) and *High Noon* (1952).

Cooper, James Fenimore (1789–1851) US novelist. He was one of the earliest American novelists and among the first to gain international recognition. Cooper's most successful works were the romantic "Leatherstocking Tales" about the frontier, of which the best known are *The Pioneers* (1823), *The Last of the Mohicans* (1826) and *The Deerslayer* (1841).

cooperative movement Variety of worldwide organizations, founded to provide mutual assistance in economic enterprises for the benefit of their members. The first such movement was founded (1844) in England by the Rochdale Pioneers, who established a cooperative retail society to eliminate the middleman and share profits among its members. The cooperative movement has been extended to include cooperative agriculture, cooperative manufacturing and cooperative banking and finance. *See also* COOPERATIVE PARTY; COOPERATIVE WHOLESALE SOCIETY; OWEN, ROBERT

Cooperative Party British political party, formed in 1917 as the political wing of the Cooperative Union. It is associated with the LABOUR PARTY, and since 1946 all of its parliamentary candidates have stood for election jointly as Labour cooperative candidates.

Cooperative Wholesale Society Organization formed (1863) in the north of England to provide for consumer cooperation. It was a development of the early cooperative experiments of Robert OWEN and the Rochdale Pioneers, which encouraged consumers to form their own retail societies and share the profits.

coordinate geometry (analytic geometry) Branch of mathematics combining the methods of pure GEOMETRY with those of ALGEBRA. Any geometrical point can be given an algebraic value by relating it to coordinates, marked off from a frame of reference. Thus, if a point is marked on a square grid so that it is x_1 squares along the x axis and y_1 squares along the y axis, it has the coordinates (x_1, y_1). Polar coordinates can also be used. It was first introduced in the 17th century by René DESCARTES. *See* CARTESIAN COORDINATE SYSTEM

coot Aquatic bird of freshwater marshes. Related to the RAILS, it takes flight awkwardly but is a strong swimmer and diver and feeds in or near water. All coots have white bills and foreheads. The female lays 8 to 12 eggs on a floating reed nest. Family Rallidae; genus *Fulica*.

Copenhagen (København) Capital and chief port of Denmark on E Sjaelland and N Amager Island, in the Øresund (The Sand). A trading and fishing centre by the early 12th century, Copenhagen became the capital in 1443. It has a 17th-century stock exchange, the Amalienborg Palace (home of the royal family) and the Christianborgs Palace. Other sights include the Tivoli amusement park and the "Little Mermaid" sculpture. The commercial and cultural centre of Denmark, it has shipbuilding, chemical and brewing industries. Pop. (1994) 620,970.

copepod Marine or freshwater CRUSTACEAN. Copepods are possibly the most numerous animals in the world and are a major component of the marine food chain. Some are parasitic on aquatic animals, especially fish. Their segmented, cylindrical bodies have a single median eye and no carapace. Length: 0.5–2mm (0.02–0.08in); length of parasitic forms may be more than 30.5cm (1ft). There are 7,500 species. Subclass Copepoda.

Copernicus, Nicolas (1473–1543) (Mikolaj Kopernik) Polish astronomer. Through his study of planetary motions, Copernicus developed a heliocentric (Sun-centred) theory of the universe in opposition to the accepted geocentric (Earth-centred) theory conceived by PTOLEMY nearly 1,500 years before. In the **Copernican system** (as it is now called), the planets' motions in the sky were explained by their orbit of the Sun. The motion of the sky was simply a result of the Earth turning on its axis. An account of his work, *De revolutionibus orbium coelestium*, was published in 1543. *See also* ARISTOTLE; GALILEO; KEPLER

Copland, Aaron (1900–90) US composer, especially known for combining folk and jazz elements with 20th-century symphonic techniques. His highly popular ballet music includes *Billy the Kid* (1938), *Rodeo* (1942) and *Appalachian Spring* (1944), for which he was awarded a Pulitzer Prize. Copland wrote symphonies, chamber music and patriotic pieces such as *A Lincoln Portrait* (1942). He was also a conductor and an admired teacher.

Copley, John Singleton (1738–1815) US painter. A gifted draughtsman and colourist, he produced some ground-breaking historical paintings that introduced the notion of portraying subjects just because they were exciting. Copley's paintings include *Colonel Epes Sargent* (*c*.1760) and *The Death of Major Peirson* (1783).

copper (symbol Cu) Red-pink TRANSITION ELEMENT. Reddish copper occurs native (free or uncombined) and in several ores including cuprite (an oxide) and chalcopyrite (a sulphide). Ores are often treated with acids

and the copper recovered by ELECTROLYSIS. It is malleable; a good thermal and electrical conductor, second only to silver; and is extensively used in boilers, pipes, electrical equipment and alloys, such as brass and bronze. Copper tarnishes in air, oxidizes at high temperatures, and is attacked only by oxidizing acids. It forms two series of salts, termed copper(I) (cuprous) and copper(II) (cupric). Properties: at.no. 29; r.a.m. 63.546; r.d. 8.96; m.p. 1,083°C (1,981°F); b.p. 2,567°C (4,653°F); most common isotope Cu^{63} (69.09%).

copperhead Any of various species of snakes, so-called because of the colour of their head. The N American copperhead is a pit viper, rarely more than 1m (3ft) long. The Australian copperhead is a venomous snake of the cobra family, often reaching 1.5m (5ft) in length. The Indian copperhead is a rat snake.

Coppola, Francis Ford (1939–) US film director, producer and screenwriter. In 1969, he established Zoetrope, an independent production company. Coppola won an Academy Award for best picture for *The Godfather* (1972). Its sequel, *Godfather II* (1974), won him Oscars for best picture and best director. Coppola followed this success with *Apocalypse Now* (1975). Other credits include *Peggy Sue Got Married* (1986), *Godfather III* (1990) and *Dracula* (1992).

copra Dried kernel (meat) of the COCONUT and the principal commercial product of that nut. The husk is usually removed and the exposed kernel dried by the sun and later by artificial heat. The oil is pressed out and the residue, copra, sold as animal feed.

Coptic Church Largest Christian church in Egypt. Its members form 5–10% of Egypt's population. The Coptic Church is led by the patriarch of Alexandria. Of ancient origin, the Copts trace the history of the church to St MARK. As a result of its Monophysite creed (denying the humanity of Christ), the Coptic Church was declared heretical by the Council of Chalcedon (451) and became isolated from other Christian churches. In 642, the Arab conquest of Egypt brought mass conversion to Islam.

copyright Legal authority protecting an individual's or company's works of art, literature, music and computer programs from reproduction or publication without the consent of the owner of the copyright. Since the Universal Copyright Convention (1952), works must carry the copyright symbol (©) followed by the owner's name and the first year of publication. This right lasts for the copyright holder's lifetime, and for 70 years after his or her death. In the UK, the Copyright, Designs and Patents Act (1988) introduced the notion of intellectual property. *See also* PATENT

coral Small, coelenterate marine animal of class Anthozoa, often found in colonies. The limestone skeletons secreted by each animal polyp accumulate to form a CORAL REEF. Reef-building corals are found only in waters with temperatures in excess of 20°C (68°F).

coral reef Rock formation found in shallow, tropical seas. Such reefs are formed from the calcium carbonate secreted by living coral organisms as protection against predators and wave action. The way in which the coral, and therefore the reef, grows is strongly influenced by the currents and temperature of the sea water.

Coral Sea Arm of the SW Pacific Ocean between the Great Barrier Reef off the E coast of Australia, Vanuatu (E) and New Guinea (NW). It was the scene of a US naval victory over the Japanese in 1942.

coral snake Poisonous, burrowing snake of the Americas and SE Asia. It is shy and docile, but has fatal venom. Most species are brightly coloured, ringed with red, yellow and black. It feeds on lizards, frogs and other snakes. Family Elapidae.

cor anglais (English horn) Reed instrument of the OBOE family. Longer than the oboe, its range is a fifth lower. Its bell is pear-shaped, and its double reed is inserted in a curved mouthpiece. A modern counterpart for the curved oboe da caccia in the music of J.S. Bach, parts have been scored for it in many 19th-century works, especially those of BERLIOZ and WAGNER.

Corbusier, Le See LE CORBUSIER

Corday, Charlotte (1768–93) French patriot. A noblewoman, she was one of the GIRONDINS who disagreed with the radical policies espoused by the JACOBIN Jean Paul MARAT. On 13 July 1793, Corday stabbed Marat to death in his bath and was guillotined on 17 July.

Córdoba (Cordova) City on the River Guadalquivir, Andalusia, S Spain; capital of Córdoba province. A flourishing centre of learning under Abd ar-Rahman III (first caliph of Córdoba), it was captured by Ferdinand III of Castile in 1236, who imposed Christian culture on the city. The Great Mosque (8–10th century) is a world heritage site. Industries: tourism, coal and lead mining, engineering. Pop. (1995) 323,000.

Córdoba City in central Argentina, capital of Córdoba province. Founded in 1573, it is now Argentina's second largest city. Córdoba flourished during the colonial era, being on a trade route from Buenos Aires to Chile. It is the site of Argentina's oldest university (founded 1613). Córdoba is both a cultural and commercial centre, and exports farm produce from the surrounding region. Industries: leather, textiles, glass. Pop. (1991) 1,179,067.

core Central area of the Earth from a depth of 2,885km (1,790mi). It accounts for 16% of the Earth's volume and 31% of its mass. Measurement of seismic waves indicate that the outer part is liquid, because shear (S) waves will not travel through it, whereas the inner core, from 5,150km (3,200mi) to the centre of the Earth, is interpreted as solid because seismic velocities are lower. The core is thought to be composed of iron-nickel alloy (90% iron, 10% nickel). Temperature estimates for the core vary from 4,000 to 7,000°C (7,200 to 12,600°F). Convection in the iron, liquid outer core is thought to be responsible for producing the Earth's magnetic field.

Corelli, Arcangelo (1653–1713) Italian BAROQUE composer. He achieved early distinction as a violinist. Corelli helped to develop the CONCERTO grosso, composed many sonatas, and did much to consolidate the principles behind modern violin playing.

Corfu (Kérkyra) Island in NW Greece, second largest of the Ionian island group; the major town is Corfu. In 433 BC, the island was allied with Athens against Corinth. The Romans held Corfu from 229 BC, and it was part of the Byzantine Empire until the 11th century. It was occupied by the Venetians (1386–1797), and then fell under British protection (1809–64), before passing to Greece. Products: olives, fruit. Industries: tourism, fishing. Area: 593sq km (229sq mi). Pop. (1991) 107,592.

Cori, Carl Ferdinand (1896–1984) US biochemist, b. Czechoslovakia. Cori shared the 1947 Nobel Prize for physiology or medicine with his wife, Gerty Theresa (1896–1957), and B.A. HOUSSAY for their discovery of how the chemical energy of GLYCOGEN, a carbohydrate, is broken down to be used by the body.

coriander (cilantro) Strong-smelling herb of the CARROT family native to the Mediterranean and Near East. The leaves, the seeds and oil from the seeds are used as an aromatic flavouring in foods, medicines and liqueurs. Family Apiaceae/Umbelliferae; species *Coriandrum sativum*.

Corinth (Kórinthos) Capital of Corinth department, NE Peloponnesos, at the SW tip of the Isthmus of Corinth, Greece. One of the largest and most powerful cities of ancient Greece, it was a rival of Athens and friend of Sparta, with which it was allied in the PELOPONNESIAN WAR (431–404 BC). Destroyed by the Romans in 146 BC, it was rebuilt by Julius Caesar in 44 BC. Ruled by the Venetians (1687–1715), then by the Turks, it became part of Greece in 1822. The modern city is 5km (3mi) NE of ancient Corinth, which was destroyed by an earthquake in 1858. The ruins include a temple of Apollo and amphitheatre. It is a major transport centre. Industries: chemicals, winemaking. Pop. (1991 est.) 29,000.

Corinthian order See ORDERS OF ARCHITECTURE

Corinthians, Epistles to the Two books of the New Testament consisting of two letters by St PAUL addressed to the Christian Church in Corinth, Greece. The letters cover several issues, but centre on the teething troubles of the newly founded Christian community at Corinth.

Coriolanus, Gnaeus Marcius (5th century BC) Roman general. He captured the Volscian town of Corioli. According to legend, he was banished from Rome (491 BC) after opposing the distribution of grain to relieve a famine. Coriolanus joined forces with the Volsci to march on Rome. According to PLUTARCH, he was dissuaded from sacking the city by the entreaties of his wife and mother. The story forms the basis of SHAKESPEARE's history *Coriolanus* (c.1607).

Coriolis effect (Coriolis force) Apparent force on particles or objects due to the rotation of the Earth under them. The motion of particles or objects is deflected towards the right in the Northern Hemisphere and towards the left in the Southern Hemisphere, but their speed is unaffected. The direction of water swirling round in a drain or whirlpool demonstrates this force.

Cork County and county town in S Republic of Ireland, in Munster province. The largest Irish county, it has a rugged terrain with fertile valleys. The chief occupations are farming and fishing along the rocky coastline. In the 9th century, the Danes took Cork, but were driven out in 1172 by Dermot McCarthy, who swore allegiance to the English throne. Oliver Cromwell occupied Cork in 1649. Many public buildings were destroyed in nationalist uprisings in 1920. The city has both Catholic and Protestant cathedrals, the University College of Cork (1845) and a large harbour. The largest export is farm produce, but it is also famous for tweed and linen. Area: 7,462sq km (2,881sq mi). Pop. (1991) 410,369.

cork Outer, dead, waterproof layer of the BARK of woody plants. The bark of the cork oak, native to Mediterranean countries, is the chief source of commercial cork. Family Fagaceae; species *Quercus ruber*.

corm Fleshy underground STEM that produces a plant such as the CROCUS. In most plants, new corms form on top of old ones, which last for one season. See also ASEXUAL REPRODUCTION

cormorant Bird found in coastal and inland waters throughout the world. It has a hooked bill, a black body and webbed feet. It dives well, and in some areas of SE Asia it is trained to catch and retrieve fish. There are 30 species. Length: to 1m (3.3ft). Family Phalacrocoracidae; genus *Phalacrocorax*. See artwork p.215

corn Main CEREAL plant of a country or region. In Britain, corn normally refers to WHEAT, in North America to MAIZE, and in Scandinavia to BARLEY.

corncrake Bird of the RAIL family common in grain fields of N Europe. It has a brown body and a short bill, and its specific name describes its call. Family Rallidae; species *Crex crex*.

cornea Transparent membrane at the front of the EYE. It is curved and acts as a fixed LENS, so that light is to some extent focused before it reaches the lens.

Corneille, Pierre (1606–84) French dramatist. Corneille and RACINE are regarded as the masters of classical French tragedy. Corneille's comedy *Mélite* (1629) attracted the attention of Cardinal Richelieu. His masterpiece is the epic tragedy *Le Cid* (1637). Other tragedies include *Horace* (1640), *Cinna* (1641) and *Polyeucte* (1643). His tragedies assert the human will against fate in classically precise ALEXANDRINE lines.

cornet BRASS musical instrument similar to a TRUMPET. One of the first brass instruments to have valves, and capable of playing a full range of notes. Hector Berlioz was one of the many 19th-century composers to take advantage of this ability. Its range is about the same as a trumpet's, but its tone is mellower. It is used in brass and military bands.

cornflower (bachelor's button) Annual of the composite family common in many parts of Europe. Family Asteraceae/Compositae; species *Centaurea cyanus*.

Cornforth, Sir John Warcup (1917–) Australian chemist. Cornforth shared the 1975 Nobel Prize for chemistry with Vladimir Prelog for his work on the stereochemistry of enzyme-catalyzed reactions, and for his demonstration of how CHOLESTEROL is made in the body.

Corn Laws Series of acts regulating the import and export of grain in Britain. The Act of 1815 prevented the import of wheat until the domestic price exceeded a certain figure. This kept the price of bread high. Opposition led to repeal by the ANTI-CORN LAW LEAGUE (1846).

Cornish One of the languages of the BRITTONIC group of CELTIC LANGUAGES, closely related to BRETON and WELSH. It died out as a medium of natural everyday communication in the late 18th century, although traces remain today in Cornish place names.

Cornwall County in SW England, on a peninsula bounded by the Atlantic Ocean, the English Channel, and Devon; the county town is Bodmin. Major towns include Truro, St Austell and Penzance. A rocky coast with hills and moors inland, it is drained by the Camel, Fowey, Tamar and Fal rivers. It is a popular tourist region. Area: (including Scilly Isles) 3,512sq km (1,356sq mi). Pop. (1991) 468,425.

► **cormorant** The common cormorant (*Phalacrocorax carbo*) is the largest of the cormorant species. It grows to a height of up to 1m (3ft). This particular species is found in or near coastal regions of N Europe, Iceland, W Greenland, Africa, Asia and New Zealand.

Cornwallis, Charles, 1st Marquess (1738–1805) British general and statesman. In 1778, he became second in command of British forces in the AMERICAN REVOLUTION. In 1780, Cornwallis took command of the Carolina Campaign. His surrender at the Siege of YORKTOWN (1781) signalled the end of the war. As governor general of India (1786–93, 1805), he reformed the civil service and defeated TIPU SAHIB of Mysore. Cornwallis resigned as viceroy of Ireland (1798–1801) after GEORGE III refused to accept the Act of CATHOLIC EMANCIPATION.

corona Outermost layer of the SUN's atmosphere, extending for many millions of kilometres into space. It is visible to the naked eye only during a total solar eclipse. The corona emits strongly in the X-ray region and has been studied by X-ray satellites. The corona has a temperature of 1–2 million K.

coronary heart disease ARTERIOSCLEROSIS of the coronary ARTERIES. It is the most common cause of death in the Western world. Atheriosclerosis can lead to the formation of a blood clot in one or other of the coronary arteries supplying the HEART (**coronary thrombosis**). The patient experiences sudden pain in the chest (ANGINA) and the result may be a HEART ATTACK (**myocardial infarction**), when the flow of blood to the heart is suddenly stopped. Smokers are much more likely to die suddenly from atheriosclerosis. Evidence suggests that a high intake of POLYUNSATURATES can protect against coronary heart disease. *See also* ANGIOPLASTY

coronation Ceremony of crowning a monarch. The form of coronation used in Britain was first drafted by St Dunstan, who crowned King Edgar in 973. Since 1066, British sovereigns have been crowned in Westminster Abbey, London. The Merovingian kings of the Franks were probably the first to introduce Christian coronation to Europe (*c*.5th century AD).

coroner Dating from 12th-century England, public official who inquires into deaths that have apparent unnatural causes by means of an inquest and/or postmortem. In both the UK and US, coroners are often assisted by a jury. In the UK, coroners also inquire into cases of "treasure trove". In the US, coroners are usually elected by voters within a county.

Corot, (Jean-Baptiste) Camille (1796–1875) French painter, a leading 19th-century landscapist. After 1827, Corot gained success at the Paris Salon with traditionally romantic paintings in a soft-edged style, unlike the precisely observed scenes of his earlier work. He was a major influence on CÉZANNE and POSTIMPRESSIONISM.

corporal punishment Punishment by caning, flogging or beating. As a judicial practice authorized by a court, it is unlawful in many countries, although it occurs particularly in Islamic states as a penalty under Sharia law. *See also* CAPITAL PUNISHMENT

corporate state Concept of government in which workers and employers from similar industries are organized into CORPORATIONS; these, together with other corporations, select representatives who determine national policy. Fascist Italy adopted features of the corporate state, with Benito Mussolini acting as the final arbitrator.

corporation Business organization that is legally a separate entity, which gives it limited liability, as compared to a proprietorship or partnership. The owners or shareholders are not individually responsible for the legal dealings of the corporation, except in the extent of their holdings. The corporation form is most usual in large organizations, especially in the US. In the UK, the term COMPANY is often used.

Corpus Christi Feast of thanksgiving for the institution of the EUCHARIST, observed by the Roman Catholic Church and many high church Anglicans. It is observed on the Thursday after Trinity Sunday.

Corregidor Small island at the mouth of Manila Bay, Philippines. Corregidor's strategic position led to its fortification by Spain in the 18th century. In 1898, it was acquired by the US, who further strengthened its defences. It was such a formidable stronghold that, in the early stages of World War 2, it protected Manila from Japanese invasion for five months before finally surrendering in May 1942. Corregidor was recaptured by US troops in February 1945. Area: 5sq km (2sq mi).

Correggio (*c*.1490–1534) (Antonio Allegri) Italian painter from Correggio who worked mainly in Parma. His oil paintings and frescos produced daring foreshortening effects. One of the first painters to experiment with the dramatic effects of artificial light, Correggio is the major link between the early illusionism of Andrea MANTEGNA and the great Baroque ceiling painters.

correlation In STATISTICS, a number that summarizes the direction and degree of relationship between two or more dimensions or variables. Correlations range between 0 (no relationship) and 1.00 (a perfect relationship), and may be positive (as one variable increases, so does the other) or negative (as one variable increases, the other decreases).

correspondence Property of two geometric figures in which angles, lines and points in one bear a similar relationship to those in another. Also, two sets *A* and *B* are said to be in one-to-one correspondence if every element of *A* can be mapped to an element of *B* by a single function, with no two elements of *A* mapping to the same element in *B*.

corrie *See* CIRQUE

corrosion Gradual tarnishing of surface, or major structural decomposition, by chemical action on solids, especially metals and alloys. It commonly appears as a greenish deposit on copper and brass, RUST on iron or a grey deposit on aluminium, zinc and magnesium. Some metals, such as aluminium, corrode readily to form an oxide.

Corsica (Corse) Mountainous island in the Mediterranean Sea, *c*.160km (100mi) SE of the French coast. It is a region of France comprising two departments. The capital is Ajaccio. It was a Roman colony, before passing into the hands of a series of Italian rulers. In 1768, France purchased all rights to the island. Napoleon was born here in 1769. Products: grapes, olives, mutton. Area: 8,681sq km (3,352sq mi). Pop. (1990) 250,400.

Cortés, Hernán (1485–1547) Spanish CONQUISTADOR and conqueror of Mexico. In 1518, he sailed from Cuba to Central America with 550 men. Cortés marched inland towards the Aztec capital, Tenochtitlán (now Mexico City), gaining allies among the subject peoples of the Aztec king, Montezuma II. In November 1519, Cortés took Montezuma hostage. The Aztecs subsequently rebelled, forcing the Spanish to retreat. Cortés regained (1521) the city after a three-month siege, gaining the Aztec empire for Spain.

cortex In animal and plant anatomy, outer layer of a gland or tissue. Examples are the cortex of the ADRENAL GLANDS; the cerebral cortex (outer layer) of the brain; the cortical layers of tissue in plant roots and stems, lying between the bark or EPIDERMIS and the hard wood or conducting tissues.

corticosteroid Any HORMONE produced by the cortex (outer layer) of the ADRENAL GLANDS. There are two types of corticosteroids. **Mineralocorticoids**, such as alderosterone, regulate the balance of fluids and salts in

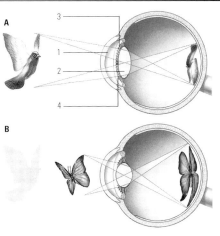

▲ **cornea** Focusing of light rays from distant objects (A) is mainly done by the cornea (1) with a little help from the lens (2). Ciliary muscles (3) encircling the lens relax and stretch ligaments (4), which pull the lens flat. Rays from a near object (B) are bent by a thick lens produced when the ligaments slacken as the ciliary muscles contract. This process, which is called accommodation, is essential for sharp focusing.

the body. **Glucocorticoids**, such as CORTISONE and hydrocortisone, regulate the use of CARBOHYDRATES, FATS and PROTEINS. Some corticosteroids have been synthesized and are used to treat disorders, such as rheumatoid arthritis, asthma and severe allergies. *See also* STEROID

cortisone HORMONE produced by the cortex of the ADRENAL GLANDS and essential for carbohydrate, protein and fat metabolism; kidney function; and disease resistance. Synthetic cortisone is used to treat adrenal insufficiency, rheumatoid arthritis and other inflammatory diseases, and rheumatic fever.

Cortona, Pietro da (1596–1669) Italian painter and architect, with BERNINI and BORROMINI one of the leading exponents of the BAROQUE style in Rome. Cortona's mastery of illusionistic decoration is shown in the huge fresco *Allegory of Divine Providence and Barberini Power* (1633–39) on the ceiling of the Barberini Palace, Rome. Other frescoes are to be found in the Pitti Palace, Florence. His architectural masterpiece is the façade of Santa Maria della Pace, Rome (1656–57).

corundum (aluminium oxide, Al_2O_3) Translucent to transparent mineral in many hues. It is found in igneous, pegmatitic and metamorphic rocks, occurring as pyramidal or prismatic crystals in the rhombohedral class and as granular masses. It is the hardest natural substance after DIAMOND. Gemstone varieties are sapphire and ruby. It is an industrial abrasive. Hardness 9; r.d. 4.

cosecant In TRIGONOMETRY, ratio of the length of the hypotenuse to the length of the side opposite an acute angle in a right-angled triangle. The cosecant of angle *A* is usually written cosec *A*, and is equal to the reciprocal of its SINE.

Cosgrave, William Thomas (1880–1965) Irish statesman, prime minister (1922–32) of the Irish Free State. A member of SINN FÉIN, he took part in the EASTER RISING (1916). Cosgrave served in the provisional government of the Dáil Éireann in 1919. In 1932 elections, he was defeated by Eamon DE VALERA. Cosgrave served (1932–44) as leader of the FINE GAEL opposition. His son, **Liam Cosgrave** (1920–), was leader (1965–77) of Fine Gael and served as taoiseach (1973–77) of the Republic of Ireland.

cosine In TRIGONOMETRY, ratio of the length of the side adjacent to an acute angle to the length of the hypotenuse in a right-angled triangle. The cosine of angle *A* is abbreviated cos *A*.

cosmetics Preparations externally applied to change or enhance the beauty of human skin, hair or nails. Body-marking has been common since prehistoric times. The ancient Egyptians used kohl (a mixture of soot, lead ore, burnt copper, rosewater and sandalwood) to darken their eyes, and dyed their hands with henna. Rouge and chalk were used to colour the face by the ancient Greeks and Romans. The use of cosmetics declined after the French Revolution (1789-99) and was frowned on by the Puritans and Victorians. The 20th century has witnessed the growth of a huge cosmetics industry based on scientific testing. Many Western cosmetics are wax-based. Petroleum jelly, liquid paraffin and pigments are also used. Mascara mixes soot with paraffin and carnauba wax.

cosmic radiation (cosmic rays) Charged particles from space that constantly bombard the Earth at velocities approaching the speed of light. The extraterrestrial nature of cosmic RADIATION was discovered (*c*.1912) by Victor HESS, and has contributed greatly to the development of PARTICLE PHYSICS. **Primary** cosmic radiation consists mainly of PROTONS (hydrogen nuclei) and some ALPHA PARTICLES (helium nuclei). These are the most energetic particles known; as high as 10^{20} electron volts (eV), or nearly one billion times more energetic than the highest energy yet produced in a particle ACCELERATOR. There are two main types of primary radiation, galactic and solar. It is believed that **galactic** rays originate chiefly from SUPERNOVAE. The energy for **solar** rays appears to be obtained from **solar flares**. Some primary nuclei penetrate Earth's magnetic field and enter the upper atmosphere, where they collide with other nuclei to produce **secondary** cosmic radiation of nucleons (protons and NEUTRONS), MESONS, LEPTONS (such as ELECTRONS) and high-energy GAMMA RADIATION. Cosmic radiation contributes to BACKGROUND RADIATION.

cosmology Branch of scientific study that brings together ASTRONOMY, MATHEMATICS and PHYSICS in an effort to understand the make-up and evolution of the Universe. Once considered the province of theologians and philosophers, it is now an all-embracing science. In the 1920s, the discovery by the US astronomer Edwin HUBBLE that galaxies are receding from each other promoted the BIG BANG theory. Associated with this is the OSCILLATING UNIVERSE THEORY. The other main theory of cosmology is the STEADY-STATE THEORY.

Cosmos (Gk. order) Universe considered as an ordered whole. PLATO and ARISTOTLE conceived of the Universe as ordered by an intelligent principle. This concept became the basis of modern natural science.

Cossacks Bands of Russian adventurers who undertook the conquest of Siberia in the 17th century. Of ethnically mixed origins, they were escaped serfs, renegades and vagabonds who formed independent, semi-military groups on the fringe of society. After the Russian Revolution (1917), the Cossacks opposed the BOLSHEVIKS and strongly resisted collectivization.

Costa Brava (Sp. wild coast) Coastal strip on the Mediterranean Sea, Gerona province, Catalonia, NE Spain. Since World War 2, the area has developed a very important tourist industry.

Costa del Sol Andalusian coast between the Strait of Gibraltar (W) and the Capa de Gata (E), S Spain. The Costa del Sol has attractive beaches and large tourist resorts, including Málaga, Torremolinos and Marbella. Although tourism expanded rapidly since the 1970s, the Spanish government has taken measures to control further development and safeguard the area's natural beauty.

Costa Rica Republic in Central America; the capital is SAN JOSÉ. **Land and climate** Central Costa Rica consists of mountain ranges and plateaux with many volcanoes. In the SE, the densely populated Meseta Central and Valle del General have rich volcanic soils. The highlands descend to the Caribbean lowlands and the Pacific coast region. San José stands at *c*.1,170m (3,840ft) above sea-level and has a pleasant climate with an average annual temperature of 20°C (68°F), compared with more than 27°C (81°F) on the coast. The NE trade winds bring heavy rains to the Caribbean coast. Evergreen forests (including mahogany and tropical cedar) cover *c*.50% of Costa Rica. **History** Christopher Columbus reached the Caribbean coast in 1502, and rumours of treasure soon attracted many Spanish settlers. Spain ruled the country until 1821. In 1822, Spain's Central American colonies broke away to join the Mexican Empire. In 1823, the Central American states formed the Central American Federation. This large union gradually disintegrated, and Costa Rica achieved full independence in 1838. The nation held its first free, democratic elections in 1890. In the 20th century, Costa Rica's reputation for stable, parliamentary democracy has been twice threatened. First, General Tinoco formed a military dictatorship (1917–19). Second, a revolt against the president-elect in 1948 led to the abolition of a standing army. The presidency (1953–74) of José Figueres saw the founding of the modern state. In 1986, Oscar Arias Sánchez was elected president. Arias was awarded the 1987 Nobel Prize for Peace for his efforts to secure peace in the civil wars that raged throughout Central America during the 1980s. In 1994, José María Figueres Olsen, son of José Figueres, was elected president. He was succeeded (1998) by Miguel Angel Rodríguez. **Economy** Costa Rica is a lower-middle-income developing nation with one of the most prosperous economies in Central America (1995 GDP per capita, US$5,850). The country has high educational standards and life expectancy (average 73.5 years). Agriculture employs 24% of the workforce. Major crops include coffee, bananas and sugar. Other crops include beans, citrus fruits and cocoa. Cattle ranching is important. Costa Rica has rich timber resources, but lacks minerals. Tourism is a fast-growing industry.

Costner, Kevin (1955–) US film actor and director. Costner's breakthrough film was *The Untouchables* (1987). Other leading roles followed, such as *Bull Durham* (1988). Costner won Academy Awards for best director and best actor in his directorial debut *Dances With Wolves* (1990), an epic Civil War-era Western. Other acting credits include *JFK* (1991), *The Bodyguard* (1992) and *The Postman* (1998).

cost of living Income necessary to purchase a certain level of goods and services. Most countries publish cost-of-living indices that show the ways in which prices are rising over specific time periods.

COSTA RICA
AREA: 51,100sq km (19,730sq mi)
POPULATION: 3,711,000
CAPITAL (POPULATION): San José (303,000)

costume In the theatre, clothing worn by actors during a performance. The history of theatrical costume is rooted in religious ceremony and in the actor's need to assume a disguise. In GREEK DRAMA, costume was stylized and symbolic, with masks used for quick character changes. **Roman theatre** had more exaggerated masks, as well as everyday dress for domestic comedies. The simplicity of medieval costume was later replaced by lavish splendour of dress, especially in the courts of 16th- and 17th-century Europe. In the 18th and 19th centuries, authentic detail in elaborate period costumes reflected the concern for historical accuracy. Today, with more emphasis on interpretation, stage costume is linked with the creative approach of the director.

cotangent Ratio of the length of the side adjacent to an acute angle, to vcm. the length of the side opposite the angle in a right-angled triangle. The cotangent of angle A is usually abbreviated cot A and is equal to the reciprocal of its TANGENT.

cot death (sudden infant death syndrome) Sudden, unexpected death of an infant less than two years old from an unidentifiable cause. In the UK, cot death accounts for $c.20\%$ of infant mortality. It appears that the most important factor is the position in which the infant sleeps: babies who sleep on their fronts have an increased risk. Post-mortem examinations have shown that nearly half of affected infants have had a viral infection in their upper respiratory tract within the 48 hours before death.

Côte d'Ivoire *See* IVORY COAST

Cotman, John Sell (1782–1842) British landscape painter and etcher, co-founder (with John CROME) of the Norwich School. One of Britain's most important 19th-century watercolourists, Cotman's paintings include *Greta Bridge* (c.1805) and *Chirk Aqueduct*.

cotoneaster Genus of c.50 species of deciduous shrubs of the ROSE family (Rosaceae), mostly native to China. With small white flowers and small red or black, berry-like fruit, they are often cultivated as ornamental plants.

Cotonou City in s Benin, w Africa. The former capital and largest city in Benin, it is an important port and distribution centre for the offshore oil industry. Industries: textiles, brewing. Pop. (1994) 537,000.

Cotopaxi Active volcano in the Andes Mountains, N central Ecuador, 65km (40mi) s of Quito. It is the highest continually active volcano in the world. Its frequent eruptions have caused severe damage. Height: 5,896m (19,344ft).

Cotswolds Range of limestone hills in w England, lying mainly in Gloucestershire, and extending 80km (50mi) NE from Bath. The local stone is widely used as a building material. The region is also known for its breed of sheep.

cotton Annual shrub native to subtropical regions. Most cotton is grown to make fabric from the fibres that envelop the seeds. Family Malvaceae; genus *Gossypium*.

cotton gin Machine for separating COTTON lint from seeds, a task previously done by hand. The gin, patented (1794) by Eli WHITNEY, contributed to the prosperity of US cotton plantations and to the industrialization of the textile industry.

cottonmouth *See* WATER MOCCASIN

cotyledon First leaf, or pair of leaves, produced by the embryo of a flowering plant. Its function is to store and digest food for the embryo plant, and if it emerges above ground, to photosynthesize for seedling growth. *See also* DICOTYLEDON; MONOCOTYLEDON

couch grass (quack or twitch grass) Persistent, perennial GRASS that spreads rapidly by rhizomes, or underground stems. It is a common weed in the Northern Hemisphere. Family Poaceae/Gramineae; species *Elymus repens* (formerly *Agropyron repens*).

cougar *See* PUMA

Coulomb, Charles Augustin de (1736–1806) French physicist. He invented the torsion balance that led to the discovery of **Coulomb's law**: the force between two point electric charges is proportional to the product of the charges, and inversely proportional to the square of the distance between them. The SI unit of ELECTRIC CHARGE is the coulomb.

Council for Mutual Economic Assistance (COMECON) International organization (1949–91) aimed at the coordination of economic policy among communist states, especially in Eastern Europe. Led by the Soviet Union, its original members were Bulgaria, Czechoslovakia, East Germany, Hungary, Poland and Romania; later joined by Cuba, Mongolia and Vietnam. Cooperation took the form of bilateral trade agreements.

Council of Europe European organization founded (1949) with the aim of strengthening pluralist democracy and human rights, and promoting European cultural identity. Originally a Western European organization, it admitted former communist countries in the 1990s. It has adopted around 150 conventions, the most important of which is the EUROPEAN CONVENTION ON HUMAN RIGHTS. The organization is based in Strasbourg, France.

counterpoint In music, technique in composition involving independent melodic lines sung or played simultaneously to produce HARMONY. Counterpoint (contrapuntal) writing reached its height in the 16th century in the work of William Byrd, Orlando di Lasso and Giovanni Palestrina, the organ compositions of J.S. Bach in the 18th century, and in the late works of Beethoven.

Counter-Reformation Revival of the Roman Catholic Church in Europe during the 16th and early 17th centuries. It began as a reaction to the Protestant REFORMATION and was intended to strengthen the Church against PROTESTANTISM and the prevailing HUMANISM of the RENAISSANCE. The reforms were essentially conservative, trying to remove many of the abuses that had crept into the late medieval church and win new prestige for the papacy. Girolamo SAVARONAROLA highlighted the secularization, corruption and growing materialism within the church hierarchy, but his prescription for change was too radical. The fifth LATERAN COUNCIL introduced minor changes and Pope CLEMENT VII founded new monastic orders to act as evangelical bulwarks against LUTHERANISM, but the major impetus for reform emerged from the pontificate of PAUL III and the founding of the

◀ **cotton** The cotton plant (*Gossypium* sp.) is a shrub-like annual native to the world's subtropical regions. After rapid flowering, small green seedpods (bolls) develop. The cotton seeds within the bolls sprout a mass of fine fibre hairs. When mature the bolls rupture and soft cloud of cotton erupts. The crop is either harvested by hand or machine and then taken to be ginned (separating the seed from the fibres), cleaned, carded, and spun into yarn.

Society of Jesus (JESUITS). The Council of TRENT (1545–63) was the engine of the Counter-Reformation. It eradicated simony (such as the sale of indulgences), standardized Roman Catholic theology, and undertook institutional reforms. Paul IV brought discipline and morality back to the papal court. PIUS IV oversaw the last session of the Council. The second phase (1563–90) of the Counter-Reformation was administered by PIUS V, GREGORY XIII and SIXTUS V. *See also* CAMPION, ST EDMUND; VINCENT DE PAUL

counter-tenor Male voice of the same register as the female CONTRALTO. It is most common in Britain, where some traditional church choirs prefer male altos.

country and western Popular music originally associated with rural areas of S USA. The music typically features sentimental lyrics and instrumental music played with stringed instruments such as the guitar, banjo or fiddle. Its origins lie in the folk music of British immigrants. NASHVILLE, Tennessee, is the music's spiritual home.

county One of the main administrative divisions of local government in the UK, the US and some Commonwealth countries. Counties are usually responsible for policing, local judicial administration, maintaining public roads and other public facilities, such as a fire service. *See also* LOCAL GOVERNMENT

Couperin, François (1668–1733) French composer. He was organist and harpsichordist at the court of Louis XIV. "Le Grand", as he was known, is now principally remembered for his many harpsichord pieces.

Courbet, Gustave (1819–77) French painter, the leading exponent of REALISM. Largely self-taught, Courbet rejected traditional subject matter and instead painted peasant groups and scenes from life in Paris. His nudes shocked contemporary society. His controversial political activity forced him into exile in Switzerland in 1873. Courbet's rejection of both romantic and classical ideals prepared the way for IMPRESSIONISM.

courgette (zucchini) Variety of MARROW

Court, Margaret (1942–) Australian tennis player. Her singles titles include the US Open (1962, 1965, 1968–70, 1973), Wimbledon (1963, 1965, 1970), the Australian Open (1960–66 1969–71, 1973) and the French Open (1962, 1964, 1969–70, 1973). Court won more Grand Slam titles (64) than any other player in the history of women's tennis.

Courtauld, Samuel (1793–1881) English industrialist. He founded the firm of Courtaulds in 1816. At first it specialized in the production of silks, but from 1904 produced viscose rayon, nylon and other artificial fibres. In 1931, Courtauld's grandson, Samuel (1876–1947), bequeathed his London home (Home House) and his collection of 19th-century French painting to the University of London, in order to form a department for the research and study of art (the Courtauld Institute).

court martial Court of the armed services for trial of service persons accused of breaking military law. Offences range from murder to desertion. Courts martial do not utilize the JURY system. Members of the court martial are serving officers, in certain cases advised by a judge advocate.

courts of law Judicial assemblies to try legal cases and to impose punishment or remedy a damage. The history of the court system lies in the English assumption of COMMON LAW as its legal basis (which Britain introduced to its former colonies, including the US and Canada) as opposed to ROMAN LAW in many other countries around the world. In the US and the UK, courts are hierarchically organized, and try suits of two different

types – CIVIL or CRIMINAL. In the UK, civil law cases are heard by county courts and the HIGH COURT OF JUSTICE, while those of criminal law are heard by CROWN COURTS or MAGISTRATES' court. The Court of Appeal is divided into civil and criminal divisions, and hears appeals from crown courts, county courts and the High Court. Appeals from the High Court are heard by the HOUSE OF LORDS, the Supreme Court of Appeal. In the US, there are two court systems. **Federal** courts administer cases involving the nation, federal laws, interstate disputes and non-US nationals. Federal courts include the SUPREME COURT, courts of appeal, district courts and special courts. **State** courts are divided into superior and inferior courts. **Superior** courts include the state supreme court, and county and municipal courts. **Inferior** courts include magistrates' courts, and tribunals such as traffic courts, juvenile courts and small claims courts.

Cousteau, Jacques Yves (1910–97) French oceanographer. Co-inventor (with Emile Gagnan) of the AQUALUNG, he also invented a process of underwater television and conducted a series of undersea living experiments (1962–65). Many of the expeditions made by his research ship *Calypso* were filmed for television.

covalent bond CHEMICAL BOND in which two atoms share a pair of electrons, one from each atom. Covalent bonds with one shared pair of electrons are called single bonds; double and triple bonds also exist. The molecules tend to have low melting and boiling points and to be soluble in non-polar solvents. Covalent bonding is most common in organic compounds.

Covenanters Scottish Presbyterians pledged by the National Covenant (1638) to uphold their religion. They opposed CHARLES I's efforts to impose an Anglican episcopal system and supported Parliament in the English CIVIL WAR, in exchange for a promise to introduce PRESBYTERIANISM in England and Ireland. The Scots changed sides when this promise was broken, but were soon defeated by Oliver CROMWELL. Covenanter revolts against Charles II were suppressed, but Presbyterianism was restored in Scotland in 1688.

Coventry City and county district in West Midlands, central England. An important weaving centre in the Middle Ages, it later became known for its clothing manufacture. Coventry was badly damaged by bombing during World War 2, and the 14th-century cathedral was destroyed. A new cathedral (designed by Sir Basil Spence) was completed in 1962. It is the home of the University of Warwick (1965) and Coventry University (1992). Industries: motor vehicles, telecommunications, engineering. Pop. (1994) 303,000.

Coverdale, Miles (1488–1569) English cleric who issued the first printed English Bible (1535) and the "Great Bible" (1539). Influenced by the REFORMATION, he helped William TYNDALE on his Bible translation.

cow Of CATTLE, a mature female that has borne at least one calf. It is also applied to other female mammals, such as elephants and seals.

Coward, Sir Noel Pierce (1899–1973) English dramatist, composer and performer. Coward was known for his urbane comedies such as *Hay Fever* (1925), *Bitter Sweet* (1929), *Private Lives* (1930) and *Blithe Spirit* (1941). His plays frequently lampooned drab high-society etiquette. Other works include the films *In Which We Serve* (1942) and *Brief Encounter* (1945). He also composed many songs, such as "Mad Dogs and Englishmen".

cowboy (cowhand) US ranch hand. Traditionally living and working in the West, cowboys increased after the Civil War. They have been romanticized in books and films as a symbol of the rugged independence, colour and vigour of the old "Wild West". *See also* GAUCHO

Cowdrey, Sir (Michael) Colin (1932–2000) English cricketer. He scored 42,719 runs and 107 centuries in first-class cricket for Kent and England. He was captain of Kent from 1957 to 1971. He played in 114 tests (27 as captain) and scored 7,624 runs (22 centuries).

Cowell, Henry Dixon (1887–1965) US composer, influenced by non-Western music. Cowell created "tone clusters" (dissonances produced by striking piano keys with the fist or forearm), such as *Advertisement* (1914). Other piano pieces are played directly on the strings by plucking or striking, for example *Aeolian Harp* (1923).

Cowley, Abraham (1618–67) English poet. A committed Royalist, he served as secretary to Queen Henrietta Maria. Cowley's first collection of METAPHYSICAL POETRY was *The Mistress* (1647). His *Poems* (1656) included the scriptural epic "Davideis" and "Pindaric Odes", the latter introducing this poetic form to English.

Cowper, William (1731–1800) English poet and hymn writer. He contributed several poems to John Newton's *Olney Hymns* (1779), including "God moves in a Mysterious Way". Despite bouts of near insanity, Cowper's poetry is lucid and direct, often drawing engagingly on the countryside or the details of domestic life, as in the long blank-verse poem *The Task* (1785) and the comic ballard *John Gilpin* (1782).

cowrie (cowry) Gastropod MOLLUSC identified by an ovoid, highly polished shell with a long, toothed opening and varied markings. It is found on coral shores. Length: 8.3–152mm (0.33–6in). Family Cypraeidae; more than 160 species, including the map cowry *Cypraea mappa*.

cowslip Most commonly either the English primrose native to Europe (*Primula veris*) or the US marsh marigold (*Caltha palustris*), both yellow-flowered herbs. The term is also sometimes used for the shooting star and the Virginia cowslip.

coyote Wild DOG originally native to w North America. Coyotes have moved into many areas formerly inhabited by wolves in the E United States. Usually greyish-brown, they have pointed muzzles, big ears and bushy tails. Length: 90cm (35in); weight: *c*.12kg (26lb). Species *Canis latrans*.

coypu Large, aquatic RODENT, native to South America. It now also lives in North America and parts of Europe. Coypus have brown outer fur and soft, grey underfur, commercially known as nutria. Overall length: 1m (3.5ft); weight: 8kg (20lb). Species *Myocastor coypus*.

crab Flattened, triangular or oval ten-legged crustacean covered with a hard shell. Primarily marine, some crabs are found in freshwater and a few are terrestrial. Their short abdomen, often called a tail, is bent under. Most have a pair of large foreclaws, a pair of movable eyestalks and a segmented mouth. Crabs usually move sideways. Size: pea-sized to 3m (12ft). Order Decapoda.

crab apple Small, sour fruit produced by certain apple trees. The various species grow in Europe, North America and Asia. The fruit is used in making preserves and jelly. Family Rosaceae; genus *Malus*.

Crabbe, George (1754–1832) English poet. Crabbe's poetry is imbued with the atmosphere of his native Suffolk and is unflinchingly anti-sentimental, as in *The Village* (1783) and *The Borough* (1810), the latter the basis for Benjamin Britten's opera *Peter Grimes* (1945).

Crab nebula NEBULA located *c*.6,500 light years away in Taurus. It is the remnant of a supernova noted by Chinese astronomers in July 1054, when it shone as brightly as Venus, visible even in daylight. The nebula

was discovered in 1731 by the English astronomer John Bevis and, independently, by Charles Messier in 1758.

crack Street drug that is a COCAINE derivative. It is supplied in the form of hard, crystalline lumps, which are heated to produce smoke inhaled for its stimulant effects. It imposes considerable strain on the heart and blood vessels, and may result in heart failure or a stroke. Psychotic episodes may also occur.

cracking Stage in PETROLEUM refining during which the products of the first distillation are treated to break up large HYDROCARBONS into smaller molecules by the controlled use of heat, catalysts and often pressure. The cracking of petroleum yields heavy oils, petrol and gases such as ETHANE, ETHENE and PROPENE, which are used in the manufacture of plastics, textiles, detergents and agricultural chemicals.

Craig, Edward Gordon (1872–1966) English stage designer, son of Ellen TERRY. In *On the Art of the Theatre* (1905), Craig proposed that actors become "super-marionettes" controlled by the director-designer-creator. He advocated non-representational scenery and atmospheric lighting.

Craig, James (1871–1940) Northern Irish statesman and soldier, first prime minister of Northern Ireland (1921–40). With Sir Edward CARSON, Craig helped organize Unionist resistance and was instrumental in keeping Ulster part of the United Kingdom. As prime minister he abolished (1929) proportional representation and, through boundary changes, ensured a Protestant majority.

crake *See* RAIL

Cranach (the Elder), Lucas (1472–1553) German painter and engraver, court artist to the electors of Saxony. A friend and follower of Martin LUTHER, Cranach designed many propaganda woodcuts for the Protestant cause. He also produced some of the first full-length portraits.

cranberry Plant of the HEATH family, distributed widely in N temperate regions. It is a creeping or trailing shrub, and bears red berries with an acid taste used to make sauce and juice. Family Ericaceae; Genus *Vaccinium*.

Crane, (Harold) Hart (1899–1932) US poet. He is acclaimed as one of the most brilliant and creative 20th-century US poets. Crane's major work, *The Bridge* (1930), is a series of related poems in which New York City's Brooklyn Bridge serves as a mystical symbol of the creative power of civilization.

Crane, Stephen (1871–1900) US writer, poet and war correspondent. His best known work is *The Red Badge of Courage* (1895), a grimly realistic story of an American Civil War soldier. Other works include a novel, *Maggie: A Girl of the Streets* (1893) and a collection of short stories, *The Open Boat and Other Tales of Adventure* (1898).

crane Any of several species of tall, wading birds found in most parts of the world except s America. It has brownish, greyish or white plumage with a bright ornamental head and it feeds on almost anything. After courtship dances, the female lays two eggs in a bulky nest. Height: to 150cm (60in). Family Gruidae.

crane Machine for lifting and placing heavy loads. The large, tower cranes seen on building sites have a long jib, or arm, counterbalanced by a weight on a shorter arm. Other heavy cranes, such as those moving on wheels or rails in foundries, form a bridge over the load. Climbing and crawling cranes are used in the construction of high-rise buildings and large bridges. Small cranes, or hoists, are mounted on road vehicles for breakdown work.

cranefly Non-biting, true fly of the order Diptera. It has a slender body, long fragile legs and one pair of wings.

The larvae (leatherjackets) live in the soil where they feed on plant roots and stems, frequently becoming serious agricultural pests. Family Tipulidae; species *Tipula simplex*. Length: to 3cm (1.2in).

cranesbill Common name for certain species of wild GERANIUM. Some are grown for ornamental ground cover.

cranium Dome-shaped part of the SKULL that protects the brain. It is composed of eight bones fused together.

Cranmer, Thomas (1489–1556) English prelate and religious reformer. Cranmer was appointed archbishop of Canterbury by HENRY VIII in 1533. He secured the annulment of Henry's marriage to CATHERINE OF ARAGON despite opposition from the pope. Cranmer, a friend of Thomas CROMWELL, promoted the introduction of PROTESTANTISM into England and compiled the first Book of COMMON PRAYER in 1549. Following the accession of the Roman Catholic MARY I in 1553, Cranmer's reforms were halted. He was burned at the stake.

Crashaw, Richard (1612–49) English poet. Crashaw taught at Cambridge University (1635–43), then fled to Europe and converted to Roman Catholicism. His religious poetry is notable for its ornate and exuberant imagery, such as *Steps to the Temple* (1646).

Crassus, Marcus Licinius (115–53 BC) Roman political and military leader. He commanded an army for Sulla in 83 BC, amassed a vast personal fortune, and raised and led the troops who defeated the slave rebellion of Spartacus in 71 BC. With POMPEY and Julius CAESAR, Crassus formed (60 BC) the First Triumvirate and became governor of Syria in 54 BC.

crater Roughly circular depression usually with steep sides, found in the surface of some planets, notably the Moon. It is formed either by meteoric impact, when shock waves blast out a hole in the ground, or at the vent of a volcano, when lava is expelled explosively.

crater lake Accumulation of water, usually by precipitation of rain or snow but sometimes groundwater, in a volcanic crater (caldera). Should an eruption occur, the resulting mud flow (lahar) is often more destructive than a lava flow. Crater Lake in Crater Lake Park, Oregon, USA, was formed by precipitation, and the waters are maintained solely by rain and snow.

Crawford, Joan (1904–77) US film actor, b. Lucille Fay le Sueur. Determined and versatile, she remained a star for nearly half a century. Crawford started in musicals before graduating to dramatic roles in films, such as *Grand Hotel* (1932) and *The Women* (1939). She won a best actress Academy Award for *Mildred Pierce* (1945). Other films include *Possessed* (1947) and *What Ever Happened to Baby Jane?* (1962).

Craxi, Bettino (1934–) Italian statesman, prime minister (1983–87). As Italy's first socialist prime minister, he cracked down on public expenditure in an effort to control inflation. Between 1994 and 1996 he received several prison sentences after being found guilty of corruption.

crayfish Edible, freshwater, ten-legged crustacean in rivers and streams of temperate regions. Smaller than LOBSTERS, crayfish burrow into the banks of streams and feed on animal and vegetable matter. Some cave-dwelling species are blind. Length: normally 8–10cm (3–4in). Families Astacidae (Northern Hemisphere), Parastacidae (Southern Hemisphere), Austroastacidae (Australia).

Crazy Horse (1842–77) Chief of the Oglala SIOUX. He was a leader of Sioux resistance to the advance of white settlers in the Black Hills, and assisted SITTING BULL in the destruction of Colonel George CUSTER at the BATTLE OF LITTLE BIGHORN in 1876. Persuaded to surrender, he was killed a few months later, allegedly while trying to escape.

creationism Belief that all things owe their origin to God's acts of creation. Some conservative Christians believe in the literal truth of the biblical account of the creation given in the Book of Genesis, which states that God created Heaven and Earth in six days. Such people oppose Charles DARWIN's theory of EVOLUTION. Roman Catholics use the term creationism to denote the doctrine that God creates a soul for every single human being at conception. *See also* ORIGINAL SIN

creation myth In most mythologies and religions, an account of the origin of the world, as well as of the human race and all the other creatures on Earth. There is a remarkable similarity in the creation stories as recounted in the holy books of major religions, and in the myths and legends of ethnic groups.

Crécy, Battle of (1346) First major battle of the HUNDRED YEARS' WAR. The English, led by EDWARD III and his son, EDWARD THE BLACK PRINCE, defeated the French led by PHILIP VI. The English longbow, as well as superior tactics, accounted for their victory.

Cree People belonging to the ALGONQUIAN language family of Native Americans in Canada, who ranged from James Bay to the Saskatchewan River. Like the related Chippewa, Cree served as guides and hunters for French and British fur traders. Many of the Plains Cree intermarried with the French. The current population is *c*.130,000.

creed (Lat. *credo*, I believe) In Christian churches, personal yet formal statement of commitment to doctrinal belief. *See also* APOSTLES' CREED; ATHANASIAN CREED; NICENE CREED

Creek Confederation of NATIVE AMERICANS, part of the Muskogean-language group. One of the largest groups in SE USA, the Creek ranged from Georgia to Alabama. They formed a settled, agricultural society, with land owned communally. Individual settlements had a degree of autonomy. After the Creek Wars (1813–14), they were removed to Oklahoma, where *c*.60,000 remain.

cremation Ritual disposal of a corpse by burning. It was a common custom in parts of the ancient civilized world, and is still the only funeral practice among Hindus and Buddhists. Early Christians rejected cremation because of their belief in the physical resurrection of the body. Its legitimacy is now recognized by all Christian churches.

Cremona City on the River Po, Lombardy, N Italy; capital of Cremona province. Founded (218 BC) by the Romans, Cremona was a centre of learning in the Middle Ages. In the late Renaissance, it was renowned for its school of painting. Since the 17th century, Cremona has been famous for the manufacture of violins: the Amati, Guarneri and Stradivari families were based in the city. Pop. (1990) 75,160.

Creole Person born in the S USA, West Indies or Latin America but of foreign or mixed descent. Generally a Creole's ancestors were either African slaves or French, Spanish or English settlers. In the US, it can also refer to someone of mixed European and African ancestry. Creole language is a PIDGIN, adopted as the native language of a community (English, French, Portuguese).

crescent Symbol of the MOON in its first quarter. The symbol has been associated with ISLAM since the capture of Constantinople by the Ottoman Turks in 1453. It is on the Turkish and other Islamic nation flags.

cress Any of several small, pungent-leaved plants of the mustard family (Brassicaceae/Cruciferae), generally used in salads and as garnishes. The best known is WATERCRESS. Species *Nasturtium officinale*.

Cretaceous Last period of the MESOZOIC era, lasting from 144 to 65 million years ago. DINOSAURS became extinct at the end of this period. The first true placental and MARSUPIAL mammals appeared, and modern flowering plants were common.

Crete (Kreti, Kríti) Largest island of Greece, in the E Mediterranean Sea, SSE of the Greek mainland; the capital is IRÁKLION. MINOAN CIVILIZATION flourished on Crete from 2000 BC, and the palace of KNOSSOS was built in c.1700 BC. Crete was conquered by Rome in 68–67 BC, and later came under Byzantine (395), Arab (826), and Venetian (1210) rule. In 1669, Crete fell to Turkey. Foreign intervention forced Turkey to evacuate Crete (1898), and it was eventually united with Greece (1908). It was occupied by German forces in World War 2. Crete has a mountainous terrain upon which sheep and goats are raised. The mild climate supports the cultivation of cereals, grapes, olives and oranges. Products: wool, hides, cheese, olive oil, wine. Tourism is important. Area: 8,336sq km (3,218sq mi). Pop. (1991) 540,054.

Creutzfeld-Jakob disease (CJD) Rare, degenerative brain disease that causes physical deterioration and dementia, usually progressing to death within a year of onset. Caused by an abnormal protein called a PRION, it is related to SCRAPIE in sheep and BOVINE SPONGIFORM ENCEPHALOPATHY (BSE) – "mad cow disease". Typically it affects older people, but in 1996 a new variant form of CJD (nvCJD) was found in younger victims. In 1997, scientists confirmed that the agent responsible for this variant was identical to that of BSE, confirming the link between CJD and the consumption of infected beef. As yet, there is no known cure.

Crick, Francis Harry Compton (1916–) English biophysicist. In the 1950s, with James WATSON and Maurice Wilkins (1916–), he established the double-helix molecular structure of deoxyribonucleic acid (DNA). The three were jointly awarded the Nobel Prize for physiology or medicine in 1962.

cricket Brown to black insect with long antennae and hind legs adapted for jumping, found worldwide. Males produce a chirping sound by rubbing their wings together. Length: 3–50mm (0.8–2in). Family Gryllidae.

cricket Bat and ball game, popular in Britain and other Commonwealth nations, originating in c.1700. Two teams of 11 players compete on an oval or round field. The game revolves around two wickets, 20.1m (66ft, 22yd) apart. A wicket comprises three wooden stumps 71.1cm (28in) high, connected at the top with two small crosspieces (bails). Leading nations compete against each other in a series of test matches, the most famous of which is probably The ASHES. A test match is held over a maximum of five days and two innings per side. In an innings, all the players of one team bat once, while the other team fields, providing the bowlers and a wicket-keeper. A batsman stands within a marked area (crease) on the pitch (the strip between the wickets), 1.2m (4ft) from the wicket. The bat is traditionally made of willow wood. Fielders are placed at strategic positions around the ground. A bowler is allowed to bowl six consecutive overarm deliveries (an over) at the wicket defended by a batsman; this is followed by another over from the opposite end of the pitch by a different bowler. The ball is made of stitched leather with a seam. A run is usually scored by a batsman making contact with the ball and running between the wickets with his partner before the ball can be returned to either wicket. If the ball reaches the boundary of the field it scores four runs, or six if it does not bounce. A batsman can be given out in a number of ways: by being bowled (when the ball delivered by a bowler hits the wicket); by being caught (the ball struck by the bat or glove is caught before bouncing by a player); by being run out or "stumped" (a player dislodges the bails with the ball when a batsman is outside the crease), by being "leg before wicket", or "lbw" for short (the ball hits a batsman's padded leg and would, in the opinion of the umpire at the bowler's end, have hit the wicket); or by hitting his own wicket. The game is adjudicated by two umpires on the field. If they are uncertain of a run-out or catch, a third umpire (off the field) decides on the basis of television replays. Since the 1960s, one-day or "limited overs" cricket has become increasingly popular. Since 1975, cricketing nations have competed every four years in the World Cup, a competition of one-day matches. The sport's administrative and historical headquarters is at Lord's Cricket Ground, London.

Crimea (Krym) Peninsula in S Ukraine that extends into the Black Sea W of the Azov Sea and joined to the mainland by the Perekop Isthmus. Simferopol is the capital. The Crimea was inhabited from the 10th to 8th century BC by the Cimmerians. During the 5th century, it was colonized by the Greeks and then by Romans, Ostrogoths, Huns, Mongols, Byzantines and Turks, before being annexed to Russia in 1783. In 1921, it became an autonomous republic of Russia, and in 1954 was transferred to the Ukraine as the Krymskaya oblast. In 1991, it was made an autonomous republic of an independent Ukraine. The region has many mineral resources and much intensive agriculture. Area: c.27,000sq km (10,400sq mi). Pop. (1991 est.) 2,549,800.

Crimean War (1853–56) Fought by Britain, France and the Ottoman Turks against Russia. In 1853 Russia occupied Turkish territory, and France and Britain, determined to preserve the OTTOMAN EMPIRE, invaded the Crimea (1854) to attack SEVASTOPOL. The War was marked on both sides by incompetent leadership and organization, the CHARGE OF THE LIGHT BRIGADE is the best-known example. The major battles of the War were at Balaclava and Inkerman (both 1854). Sevastopol was eventually captured (1855). At the Treaty of Paris (1856), ALEXANDER II surrendered Russia's claims on the Ottoman Empire. More than 250,000 soldiers were lost on both sides, many from disease in the appalling military hospitals. *See also* NIGHTINGALE, FLORENCE

Criminal Investigation Department (CID) Non-uniformed branch of the London Metropolitan Police (founded 1878) dealing with the prevention and investigation of crime, and with the preparation of information on criminal trends. There are c.1,600 CID officers, whose headquarters are at New Scotland Yard.

criminal law Body of law that defines crimes, lays down rules of procedure for dealing with them, and establishes penalties for those convicted. Broadly, a crime is distinguished from a TORT by being deemed injurious to the state. In many countries, the criminal law has been codified. Criminal law remains what it was originally, a part of COMMON LAW, although since the 18th century it has been greatly added to by statute law.

Crippen, Hawley Harvey (1862–1910) US murderer. In January 1910, he poisoned his wife at their London home, and attempted to flee with his mistress to Canada aboard the SS *Montrose*. The ship was notified using radio (believed to be the first use of wireless telegraphy for police purposes). Crippen was arrested and returned to London, where he was convicted and executed.

Cripps, Sir (Richard) Stafford (1889–1952) British statesman, chancellor of the exchequer (1947–50). He belonged to the left wing of the LABOUR PARTY and was ambassador to Russia (1940–42), later serving in Winston

CHURCHILL's war cabinet. As chancellor in the reforming government of Clement ATTLEE, Cripps' austerity programme helped to reconstruct the post-war economy.

critical angle Angle at which a significant transition occurs. In optics, it is the angle of incidence with a medium at which total internal REFLECTION occurs. In telecommunications, it is the angle at which radio waves are reflected by the IONOSPHERE.

critical mass Minimum mass of fissionable material required in a FISSION bomb or nuclear reactor to sustain a CHAIN REACTION. The fissionable material of a fission bomb is divided into portions less than the critical mass; when brought together at the moment of detonation, they exceed the critical mass.

Crivelli, Carlo (1430–93) Italian painter. He combined a linear approach with an intensely decorative style of drawing. Crivelli's masterpiece is *The Annunciation* (1486).

Croatia (Hrvatska) Balkan republic in SE Europe. Croatia was one of the six republics that made up the former federated state of YUGOSLAVIA. It achieved independence in 1991. The DALMATIA region borders the Adriatic Sea and is dominated by the limestone mountains of the Dinaric Alps. The major port is SPLIT. Other highlands lie in the NE, but Croatia chiefly consists of the fertile Pannonian plain. The River Drava forms most of its border with Hungary. The capital, ZAGREB, lies on the River Sava. **Climate** The coastal area has hot, dry summers and mild, moist winters. Inland, the climate is more continental. Winters can be bitterly cold, while summer temperatures often soar to 38°C (100°F). **Vegetation** Farmland, including pasture, covers 70% of Croatia, with forest and woodland occupying only 15%. Sparse Mediterranean scrub (maquis) predominates in Dalmatia. **History and Politics** SLAV peoples settled in the area *c*.1,400 years ago. In 803, Croatia became part of the Holy Roman Empire, and the Croats soon adopted Christianity. Croatia was an independent kingdom in the 10th and 11th centuries. In 1102, an 800-year union of the Hungarian and Croatian crowns was formed. In 1526, part of Croatia fell to the Ottoman Empire, while the rest of Croatia came under the Austrian HABSBURGS. In 1699, all of Croatia came under Habsburg rule. Following the defeat of Austria-Hungary in World War 1, Croatia became part of the new Kingdom of the Serbs, Croats and Slovenes, renamed Yugoslavia (1929). Germany occupied Yugoslavia during World War 2, and Croatia was proclaimed independent, though it was really a pro-Nazi puppet state (*Ustashe*). After the War, communists took power, and Josip Broz TITO became leader of Yugoslavia. During the 1980s, economic and ethnic problems (including a deterioration in relations between Croatia and SERBIA) threatened the country's stability. In 1990, the Croatian Democratic Union (HDZ), led by Franjo TUDJMAN, won Croatia's first democratic elections. A 1991 referendum voted overwhelmingly in favour of Croatia becoming an independent republic. The Yugoslav National Army was deployed, and Serb-dominated areas took up arms in favour of remaining in the federation. SERBIA supplied arms to Croatian Serbs, and war broke out between Serbia and Croatia. In 1992, United Nations' peacekeeping troops were deployed to maintain an uneasy cease-fire; Croatia had ceded 30% of its territory. Tudjman was re-elected president. In 1992, war broke out in BOSNIA-HERZEGOVINA, and Bosnian Croats occupied parts of Croatia. In 1993, Croatian Serbs in E Slavonia voted to establish the separate republic of Krajina. In 1994, the Bosnian, Bosnian Croat and Croatian governments formed a federation. In 1995, Croatian government forces seized Krajina, and 150,000 Serbs fled.

CROATIA
AREA: 56,538sq km (21,824sq mi)
POPULATION: 4,960,000
CAPITAL (POPULATION): Zagreb (726,770)

Following the Dayton Peace Accord (1995), Croatia and the rump Yugoslav state formally established diplomatic relations (August 1996). An agreement between the Croatian government and Croatian Serbs provided for the eventual reintegration of Krajina into Croatia (1998). In January 2000, following Tudjman's death, Stipe Mesic of the centrist coalition was elected president. **Economy** The wars have badly disrupted Croatia's relatively prosperous economy (1994 GDP per capita, $US2640). Croatia has a wide range of manufacturing industries, such as steel, chemicals, oil refining and wood products. Agriculture is the principal employer. Crops include maize, soya beans, sugar beet and wheat.

Croce, Benedetto (1866–1952) Italian philosopher and politician. He was a senator (1910–20) and minister of education (1920–21). When Mussolini came to power, Croce retired from politics in protest against fascism. He re-entered politics following the fall of Mussolini in 1943. As leader of the Liberal Party, he played a prominent role in resurrecting Italy's democratic institutions. His works include the idealistic *Philosophy of the Spirit* (1902–17).

Crockett, "Davy" (David) (1786–1836) US frontiersman and politician. He served in the Tennessee legislature (1821–26) and the US Congress (1827–31, 1833–35). A Whig, Crockett opposed the policies of Andrew JACKSON and the Democrats. He died at the ALAMO.

crocodile Carnivorous, lizard-like REPTILE found in warm parts of every continent, except Europe. Most crocodiles have a longer snout than ALLIGATORS. All lay hard-shelled eggs in nests. There are about 12 species including two dwarf species in Africa. The Asian saltwater crocodile (*Crocodylus porosus*) sometimes attacks humans. Family Crocodylidae. Length: up to 7m (23ft).

crocus Hardy, perennial flowering plant. It is low, with a single tubular flower, and grass-like leaves rising from an underground corm. Family Iridaceae; genus *Crocus*.

Croesus (d. *c*.546 BC) King of Lydia in Asia Minor (r. *c*.560–546 BC). Renowned for his wealth, he was overthrown and captured by CYRUS THE GREAT. According to HERODOTUS, Croesus threw himself upon a funeral pyre.

Crohn's disease Chronic inflammatory condition that may affect any part of the human gastrointestinal tract. The cause is unknown, but possibly represents an exaggerated response to an allergen or infective agent. The ileum and colon are most commonly affected.

Cro-Magnon Tall, Upper Palaeolithic race of HUMANS, possibly the earliest form of modern *Homo sapiens*. Cro-Magnon people settled in Europe *c*.35,000 years ago. They made a variety of sophisticated flint tools, as well as bone, shell and ivory jewellery and artifacts. Cro-Magnon artists produced the cave paintings of France and N Spain. Cro-Magnon remains were first found (1868) in Les Eyzies-de-Tayac, Dordogne, France.

Crome, John (1768–1821) English landscape painter, known as "Old Crome". Crome was a founder of the Norwich School. His paintings are almost all scenes of rural Norwich. Crome's beautifully simple style is best appreciated in *Mousehold Heath* (1816) and *Porlingland Oak* (*c*.1818). His son, **John Bernay** Crome (1794–1842), "Young Crome", painted scenes of rivers and coasts.

Crompton, Richmal (1890–1969) English writer. Crompton created one of the most popular characters in British children's fiction, William, a scruffy, prankish schoolboy. The stories were first collected as *Just William* (1922), and more than 30 William novels followed.

Crompton, Samuel (1753–1827) English inventor of a spinning machine. His "spinning mule" of 1779 proved a boon to the textile industry, reducing thread-breakage and producing very fine yarn.

Cromwell, Oliver (1599–1658) Lord Protector of England (1653–58). A committed Puritan, he entered Parliament in 1628 and was an active critic of CHARLES I in the LONG PARLIAMENT (1640). In the first of the English CIVIL WARS, his Ironsides helped defeat the Cavaliers at MARSTON MOOR (1644). In 1645, Cromwell helped to form the NEW MODEL ARMY. After a decisive victory at NASEBY (1645), he emerged as the leading voice of the army faction. Cromwell favoured a compromise with CHARLES I, but Charles' duplicity convinced him of the need to execute the king. In the second civil war, Cromwell defeated the Scottish Royalists at Preston (1648). His influence was strengthened in PRIDE'S PURGE (1648) of Parliament. The RUMP PARLIAMENT pressed for Charles' execution and established the COMMONWEALTH republic (1649). Cromwell ruthlessly suppressed opposition in Ireland, and defeated CHARLES II in the third civil war (1651). The failure of BAREBONE'S PARLIAMENT (1653) led to the "Instrument of Government" that established the PROTECTORATE. Cromwell became a virtual military dictator as "lord protector". The Humble Petition and Advice (1657) offered him the throne, but he refused. Cromwell's expansionist foreign policy was both anti-Stuart and pro-Protestant. The DUTCH WARS (1652–54) and the war (1655–58) with Spain were financially exorbitant. He was succeeded by his son, Richard CROMWELL.

Cromwell, Richard (1626–1712) Lord protector of England (1658–59), son of Oliver CROMWELL. Richard lacked his father's qualities of leadership. He was ousted from power after eight months, and spent 20 years in exile before returning to England in 1680.

Cromwell, Thomas, Earl of Essex (1485–1540) English statesman. Cromwell was secretary to Cardinal Thomas WOLSEY, and succeeded him as HENRY VIII's chief minister in 1531. He was responsible for the acts of the REFORMATION parliament that established the CHURCH OF ENGLAND with the king as supreme head. Cromwell's ruthless management of the DISSOLUTION OF THE MONASTERIES (1536–40) was demonstrated by the PILGRIMAGE OF GRACE (1536). He fell from power after the failure of Henry's marriage to ANNE OF CLEVES and was executed.

Cronin, A.J. (Archibald Joseph) (1896–1981) Scottish novelist. He was a medical inspector of mines and general physician until the success of his first work, *Hatter's Castle* (1931). Many of his novels were filmed, such as *The Stars Look Down* (1935), *The Citadel* (1937), *The Keys of the Kingdom* (1942) and *The Green Years* (1944).

Cronus (Kronos) In Greek mythology, youngest son of URANUS and GAIA. Youngest of the TITANS, he ruled the universe after castrating his father. Cronus devoured all of his children by his sister Rhea, except ZEUS. Zeus was raised secretly in Crete and overthrew his father.

Crookes, Sir William (1832–1919) English chemist and physicist. He invented the radiometer (which measures ELECTROMAGNETIC RADIATION) and the Crookes tube, which led to the discovery of the electron by J.J. THOMSON. Crookes was the first to suggest that CATHODE RAYS consist of negatively charged particles. He also discovered THALLIUM. *See also* X-RAY

crop rotation Practice of successively growing different crops on the same field. Rotated crops generally complement each other, each providing nutrients required by the others.

croquet Lawn game in which wooden balls are hit with wooden mallets through a series of six wire hoops towards a peg. The first to complete 12 hoops (each hoop in both directions) and reach the peg wins. Croquet developed in France in the 17th century.

Crosby, "Bing" (Harry Lillis) (1904–77) US popular singer and actor. He became one of the most successful "crooners" in the US. Crosby worked with Bob HOPE on the acclaimed *Road* series and won a best actor Academy Award for *Going My Way* (1944). His recording of the Irving BERLIN song "White Christmas" (1942) is one of the best-selling records of all time.

cross Ancient symbol with different significance to many cultures. In Christianity, it is associated with Christ's sacrificial death by CRUCIFIXION for the redemption of mankind. An image of a cross is usually placed on, above, or near the altar in churches, and is often carried in religious processions. Other crosses are still used as religious or secular symbols. They include the crosses of St George, St Andrew, the Victoria Cross, the Red Cross and the Maltese Cross. As a religious symbol, the cross existed in ancient Egypt, Babylonia and Assyria.

crossbill Parrot-like, forest FINCH found in the N of the Northern Hemisphere. It has a heavy, curved, scissor-like bill in which the upper and lower mandibles cross, which it uses to pry seeds from cones of evergreens. Length: 15cm (6in). Family Fringillidae; genus *Loxia*.

crossbow *See* ARCHERY

Crossman, Richard Howard Stafford (1907–74) British statesman, secretary of state for health and social services (1968–70). He entered Parliament in 1945. Crossman held several cabinet positions in the Labour administrations of Harold WILSON. He is best-known for his detailed political *Diaries* (1975–77), which were published posthumously, despite attempts to suppress them.

▲ **crocodile** A visual comparison between alligators (1) and crocodiles (2) shows the different shapes of their snouts. Another sign of difference is that the long lower fourth tooth protudes from the closed jaw of a crocodile. In general, crocodiles are more aggressive than alligators. Both are strong enough to kill an animal the size of a cow. The gharial, or gavial, (3) of the Indian subcontinent has a very elongated snout.

croup Respiratory disorder of small children, caused by inflammation of the LARYNX and airways. It is mostly triggered by viral infection. Symptoms are a harsh cough, difficult breathing, restlessness and fever.

Crow Large tribe of Siouan-speaking Native Americans that separated in the early 18th century from the HIDATSA. They migrated into the Rocky Mountains region from the upper Missouri River. Today, *c.*4000 Crow occupy a large reservation in Montana, where they were settled in 1868. They are noted for their fine costumes, artistic culture and complex social system.

crow Large, black bird found in many temperate woodlands and farm areas worldwide. Living in large flocks, crows prey on small animals and eat plants and carrion. They can be crop pests. They are intelligent birds and can sometimes be taught to repeat phrases. The female lays three to six greenish eggs. Family Corvidae. *See also* JAY; MAGPIE; RAVEN; ROOK

crown court In England, court established (1971) to replace the assize court and court of quarter session. They are superior courts with a general jurisdiction, presided over by High Court judges. *See also* COURTS OF LAW

crown jewels Crown, orb and sceptre and other precious objects belonging to the British monarchy and kept on display in the TOWER OF LONDON. They include St Edward's Crown, which weighs more than 2kg (5lb), and the Imperial Crown of State, weighing 1.6kg (3.5lb). The Scottish jewels, called the Honours of Scotland, are kept in Edinburgh Castle.

crucifixion Form of capital punishment commonly used in the Roman Empire, in which a person was nailed or bound to a CROSS by the wrists and feet and left to die. Crucifixion was applicable only to slaves and those without civil rights. It was often preceded by flagellation. JESUS CHRIST (30 BC) and SPARTACUS (71 BC) died on the cross. The punishment was abolished by Constantine.

Cruelty, Theatre of French dramatic movement of the late 1920s. It developed under the influence of Antonin ARTAUD, who advocated a physical theatre expressing stark emotions. Violence was used as a theatrical device to disturb audience perception. Performance was considered more important than a specific text.

Cruikshank, George (1792–1878) English illustrator and cartoonist, well known for his political and theatrical illustrations. Cruikshank illustrated more than 800 books, of which the best known are Dickens' *Sketches by Boz* and *Oliver Twist.*

Cruise, Tom (1962–) US film actor. His career began in teenage-oriented films. His roles in *Top Gun* (1986) and

Rain Man (1988) gained him a wider audience. Cruise earned Academy Award nominations for his performances in *Born on the Fourth of July* (1989), *Jerry Maguire* (1996) and *Magnolia* (1999). He is married to fellow actor Nicole Kidman (1967–).

cruise missile Self-propelled MISSILE that travels, generally at low altitudes, following the contours of the terrain. This allows it to avoid conventional radar defenses. The siting of American cruise missiles on European soil during the 1980s led to large-scale public demonstrations. In 1991 and 1998 the US navy fired Tomahawk cruise missiles against ground targets in Iraq.

cruiser Warship, smaller, lighter and faster than a BATTLESHIP, ranging in size from 7,500 to 21,000 tonnes. After World War 1, arms-limitation treaties restricted its guns to 200mm (8in). Since World War 2, cruisers have replaced battleships as the major warships of a modern navy.

Crusades Series of military expeditions (11th–14th centuries) from Christian Europe to recover the Holy Land (Palestine) from the Muslims. In the 7th century, JERUSALEM was captured by the caliph OMAR. In the early 11th century, persecution of Christians had intensified under the FATIMIDS. In 1071, control of Jerusalem passed to the SELJUK Turks. The Seljuk capture (1085) of Antioch (ANTAKYA) from the BYZANTINE EMPIRE presaged Turkish domination of ASIA MINOR, and Emperor ALEXIUS I appealed to the West for assistance. In Europe, the concept of a holy war against Islam was given credence by greater economic and military confidence, the strength of millenarian movements, and the growth of pilgrimages. Self-advancement of Crusaders and commercial motives were also significant. In 1095, Pope URBAN II convoked the Council of Clermont, assuring potential knights of the spiritual rewards for their endeavours. The **First Crusade** (1095–99) was the most successful. In 1097, the Crusaders captured Antioch and Nicaea. In July 1099, they celebrated the recapture of Jerusalem by slaughtering the entire Muslim and Jewish population. The victorious factions established four Crusader states in the Levant, including the Latin Kingdom of Jerusalem. The **Second Crusade** (1147–49) was led by Emperor CONRAD III and the French king LOUIS VII. It was an unmitigated failure. The **Third Crusade** (1189–92) was called by Pope Gregory VIII in response to SALADIN's capture (1187) of Jerusalem. In 1190, Emperor FREDERICK I (BARBAROSSA) drowned, and leadership of the Crusade passed to RICHARD I of England and PHILIP II of France. In 1191, they captured Acre, but disagreements forced a truce with Saladin. The **Fourth Crusade** (1202–04) was diverted to Constantinople by the Venetians, and saw the establishment of the Latin Empire of CONSTANTINOPLE under BALDWIN I. After the disastrous CHILDREN'S CRUSADE (1212), Pope INNOCENT III made Egypt the target of the **Fifth Crusade** (1218–21). Emperor FREDERICK II embarked on the diplomatic **Sixth Crusade** (1228–29), which saw him crowned king of Jerusalem. In 1244, Jerusalem was retaken for Islam. LOUIS IX of France responded by launching the **Seventh Crusade** (1248–54) against Egypt. In 1268, Jaffa and Antioch were recaptured for Islam. Louis IX launched the **Eighth Crusade** (1270) but died in Tunis. The **Ninth Crusade** (1271–72) was led by Prince Edward (later EDWARD I of England). In 1291, Acre, the last Christian foothold in the Levant, fell to Islam. *See also* KNIGHTS HOSPITALLERS; KNIGHTS TEMPLAR; TEUTONIC KNIGHTS

crust In geology, the thin outermost solid layer of the Earth. The crust represents less than 1% of the Earth's

▲ **crow** The American crow (*Corvus brachyrhynchas*) is found throughout North America. A large crow, its wingspan can reach up to 90cm (3ft). It feeds on some eggs and chicks, as well as insects and rodents. Crows are easily tamed and can mimic some human sounds.

volume, and varies in thickness from c.5km (3mi) beneath the oceans, to c.70km (45mi) beneath mountain chains such as the Himalayas. Oceanic crust is generally thinner, averaging 7km (4.5mi) thick and is basaltic in composition, whereas continental crust is mainly between 30 and 40km (20 and 25mi) thick and of granitic composition. The lower boundary of the crust is defined by a marked increase in seismic velocity, known as the Mohorovičić discontinuity. *See also* MOHO

crustacean Any member of the class Crustacea, consisting of c.30,000 species of ARTHROPODS. The class includes the decapods (CRABS, LOBSTERS, SHRIMP and CRAYFISH), isopods (pill millipedes and WOODLICE) and many varied forms. Most crustaceans are aquatic (marine or freshwater) and breathe through gills or the body surface. They are typically covered by a hard exoskeleton. They range in size from the ocean plankton, as little as 1mm (0.04in) in diameter, to the Japanese spider crab, up to 3m (12ft) across.

cryogenics Branch of physics that studies materials and effects at temperatures approaching ABSOLUTE ZERO. Some materials exhibit highly unusual properties such as SUPERCONDUCTIVITY or SUPERFLUIDITY at such temperatures. The **Joule-Thomson effect** can be used to reduce temperatures to 0.3K. To cool gases even further requires magnetic process such as the **adiabatic process.** Cryogenics has been used to freeze human bodies in the uncertain hope that future technology may be able to revive the subjects.

cryolite (sodium-aluminium fluoride, Na_3AlF_6) Brittle, icy-looking, red, brown or black halide mineral, found in pegmatite dykes and used in aluminium processing. It occurs as crystals in the monoclinic system, occasionally the cubic system, sometimes as granular masses. The crystals are frequently twinned. Greenland has the only large deposit. Cryolite is also a source of aluminium salts and fluorides.

cryptography Form of written message in which the original text (plaintext) is replaced by a series of other signs according to a prearranged system, in order to keep the message confidential. Unlike a **code**, in which each letter of the plaintext is replaced by another sign, a **cipher** cannot be "cracked" without a key. Typically, a key is a complex pattern of letters or symbols forming the basis upon which the plaintext is enciphered. The receiver reverses this process to decipher the message. Ciphers were used by the ancient Greeks and were employed widely during the medieval and Renaissance periods. Mechanical devices for producing complex ciphers were developed between the two World Wars. The best-known cipher machine was the German Enigma device. Today, fast computers are used by intelligence services for constructing and breaking complex ciphers.

crystal SOLID with a regular geometrical form with characteristic angles between its faces, having limited chemical composition. The structure of a crystal, such as common salt, is based upon a regular 3–D arrangement of atoms, ions or molecules (a crystal or ionic **lattice**). Crystals are produced when a substance passes from a gaseous or liquid phase to a solid state, or comes out of solution by evaporation or precipitation. Slow cooling produces large crystals, whereas fast cooling produces small crystals.

crystallography Study of the formation and structure of crystalline substances. It includes the study of CRYSTAL formation, chemical bonding in crystals and the physical properties of solids. In particular, crystallography is concerned with the internal structure of crystals. *See also* X-RAY CRYSTALLOGRAPHY

Crystal Palace First building of its size, 124 × 564m (408 × 1,850ft), to be made of glass and iron. England's Sir Joseph PAXTON designed it for the Great Exhibition held in Hyde Park, London (1851). It was the first building prefabricated in sections and assembled on site. After the exhibition it was dismantled and re-erected on Sydenham Hill, SE London, where it stood until accidentally destroyed by fire in 1936.

Cuba Caribbean island republic, at the entrance to the Gulf of Mexico. Cuba is the largest and most westerly of the WEST INDIES archipelago. It consists of one large island, Cuba, together with the Isla de la Juventud (Isle of Youth) and many small islets. The highest mountain range, the Sierra Maestra in the SE, reaches 2,000m (6,562ft) at Pico Turquino. The rest of the land consists of gently rolling hills or coastal plains. **Climate** Cuba has a semi-tropical climate. May to October is the rainy season. Fierce hurricanes may occur between August and October. **Vegetation** Farmland covers about half of Cuba, and 66% of this is given over to sugar cane. Pine forests still grow, especially in the SE. Mangrove swamps line some coastal areas. **History and Politics** When Christopher Columbus discovered Cuba in 1492, it was inhabited by Native Americans. The first Spanish colony was established in 1511. The indigenous population was quickly killed, replaced by African slave labour. Cuba formed a base for Spanish exploration of the American mainland. In 1868, discontent at Spanish rule erupted into war. Slavery was abolished in 1886. In 1895, a second war of independence was led by José MARTÍ. In 1898, the sinking of the US battleship *Maine* precipitated the SPANISH-AMERICAN WAR. From 1898 to 1902, Cuba was under US military occupation before becoming an independent republic. In order to protect US-owned plantations, the US occupied Cuba (1906–09, 1912). Fulgencio BATISTA ruled Cuba from 1933 to 1959, maintaining good relations with the US. In 1952, he imposed martial law. After an abortive coup attempt in 1953, Fidel CASTRO (supported by Che GUEVARA) launched a revolution in 1956. In 1959, Castro became premier. Castro's brand of revolutionary socialism included the nationalization of many US-owned industries. In 1961, the US broke off diplomatic ties and imposed a trade embargo. Castro turned to the Soviet Union. Cuban exiles, supported by the US government, launched the disastrous BAY OF PIGS invasion. In 1962, the potential siting of Soviet missiles fuelled the CUBAN MISSILE CRISIS. Castro's attempt to export revolution to the rest of Latin America ended in diplomatic alienation. Cuba turned to acting as a leader of developing nations and providing support for revolutionary movements. Between 1965 and 1973, more than 250,000 Cubans went into voluntary exile. Emigration was legalized in 1980, and many disaffected Cubans chose to leave. In 1998, Pope John Paul II became the first pontiff to visit Cuba and the UN called for an end to the US economic embargo. **Economy** Cuba's economy has been devastated (1992 GDP per capita, $US3,412) by the dissolution of the Soviet Union and the US trade embargo. Restrictions on private ownership of industry were relaxed in 1993. Cuba is over-dependent on its sugar industry (75% of exports). It is the world's fourth-

---

CUBA
AREA: 110,860sq km (42,803sq mi)
POPULATION: 11,504,000
CAPITAL (POPULATION): Havana (2,241,000)

largest producer of sugar cane. Nickel ore is the second-largest export. Other exports include cigars, fish and rum.

Cuban Missile Crisis (October 1962) US and Soviet Union confrontation over the installation of Soviet nuclear rockets in Cuba, perhaps the closest the world has yet come to nuclear war. President John KENNEDY warned Premier Nikita KHRUSHCHEV that any missile launched from Cuba would be met by a full-scale nuclear strike on the Soviet Union. On 24 October, Cuba-bound Soviet ships bearing missiles turned back, and Khrushchev ordered the bases to be dismantled.

cube In mathematics, the result of multiplying a given number by itself twice. Thus the cube of a is $a \times a \times a$, written a^3. A cube is also described as the third power of a number. The cube root is the number that must be multiplied by itself twice over to give a specified number. A cube is a regular six-sided solid figure (all its edges are equal in length, and all its faces are squares).

cubism Revolutionary, 20th-century art movement. It originated in c.1907, when PICASSO and BRAQUE began working together to develop a new pictorial language able to represent ideas as well as objective reality. They built up three-dimensional images on the canvas using fragmented solids and volumes. In 1908, Braque held an exhibition of his new paintings that provoked the critic Louis Vauxcelles to describe them as bizarre arrangements of "cubes". The initial experimental, "**analytical**" phase (1907–12), of which Picasso and Braque were the main exponents, was inspired mainly by African sculpture and the later works of CÉZANNE. The "**synthetic**" phase (1912–14) introduced more colour and decoration, and the techniques of COLLAGE and papiers collés were very popular. Cubist painters included LÉGER, Robert DELAUNAY and Sonia DELAUNAY-TERK and art. Frantis˘ek KUPKA. The most important cubist sculptors (apart from Picasso) were ARCHIPENKO, LIPCHITZ and Ossip Zadkine. Cubism revolutionized artistic expression and lent itself easily to adaptation and development. It is probably the most important single influence on 20th-century progressive

Cuchulainn Irish legendary hero. He was king of Ulster during the 1st century BC, and hero of the legend *The Cattle Raid of Cooley*, in which he defended his kingdom against the rest of Ireland. The Cuillin Hills in Skye, NW Scotland, are named after him.

cuckoo Widely distributed forest bird. Related species are the ani, ROAD RUNNER and coucal. True Old World cuckoos are generally brownish, although a few species are brightly coloured and notable for parasitic behaviour. Their chief food is insects. Length: 15–75cm (6–30in). Family Cuculidae; genus *Cuculus*.

cuckoopint (wake robin or lords-and-ladies) Tuberous plant native to Europe. It has arrow-shaped leaves and sends up stout SPATHES, each of which unfurls to reveal a SPADIX that gives off a fetid carrion scent, attractive to insects. Red poisonous berries form as the spathe dies off. Family Araceae; species *Arum maculatum*.

cucumber Trailing, annual vine covered in coarse hairs; it has yellowish flowers and the immature fruit is eaten raw or pickled. Family Cucurbitaceae; species *Cucumis sativus*.

Cugnot, Nicolas Joseph (1725–1804) French engineer who invented (1769) the first self-propelled road vehicle. This three-wheeled, two-cylinder steam tractor was designed to pull guns and travelled at nearly 5km/h (3mph).

Cukor, George (1899–1983) US stage and film director, noted for his stylish comedies and literary dramas. He extracted remarkable performances from his leading actresses, such as Greta Garbo in *Camille* (1936); Joan Crawford in *The Women* (1939); Katherine Hepburn in *A Bill of Divorcement* (1932), *Holiday* (1938) and *The Philadelphia Story* (1940); Judy Holliday in *Born Yesterday* (1950); and Judy Garland *A Star is Born* (1954). Cukor won an Academy Award for *My Fair Lady* (1961).

Culloden, Battle of (1746) Decisive battle of the JACOBITE rising of 1745. The Jacobites, predominantly Highlanders, led by Charles Edward STUART, were defeated near Inverness by government forces under the Duke of Cumberland, son of George II. Culloden ended STUART attempts to regain the throne by force. The battle was followed by ruthless subjugation of the Highland clans.

cult System of religious beliefs, rites and observances connected with a divinity or group of divinities, or the sect devoted to such a system. Within a religion, such as HINDUISM, many gods have their own cults, notably SHIVA. Animals are the focus of some cults, such as the INUIT whale cult. A deified human being may also be the object of worship, as in the emperor cults of ancient Rome. In the 20th century, a cult often denotes a quasi-religious organization that controls its followers by means of psychological manipulation. Leaders of cults are usually forceful, charismatic personalities.

Cultural Revolution (1966–76) The "Great Proletarian Cultural Revolution" was initiated by MAO ZEDONG and his wife, JIANG QING, to purge the Chinese COMMUNIST PARTY of his opponents and to instill current revolutionary attitudes. Senior party officials were removed from their posts, and intellectuals and others suspected of revisionism were victimized and humiliated. A new youth corps, the RED GUARDS, violently attacked reactionary ideas. By 1968 China was near civil war. The Red Guards were disbanded, and the army restored order.

culture In ANTHROPOLOGY, all knowledge that is acquired by human beings by virtue of their membership of a society. A culture incorporates all the shared knowledge, expectations and beliefs of a group. Culture in general distinguishes human beings from animals, since only humans can pass on accumulated knowledge.

Cumans Turkic people originating in N Asiatic Russia. They conquered S Russia in the 11th century AD, set up a state on the coast of the Black Sea, and traded with the Byzantine Empire and Hungary. After defeat by Mongols in c.1240, many Cumans moved to Hungary.

Cumbria County in NW England, bounded by the Solway Firth (N, and the Irish Sea (W); the county town is CARLISLE. The region includes the LAKE DISTRICT and the Cumbrian Mountains. Area: 6,808sq km (2,629sq mi). Pop. (1991) 483,163.

cumin Annual herb native to the Middle East and widely cultivated for its seed-like fruit used as a food flavouring. It has a branching stem and small pink or white flowers. Height: to 15cm (6in). Family Apiaceae/Umbelliferae; species *Cuminum cyminum*.

cummings, E.E. (Edward Estlin) (1894–1962) US poet. His first work was a novel, *The Enormous Room* (1922). Cummings' reputation rests on his poetry, which usually exhibits sentimental emotion and/or cynical realism. It is characterized by unconventional spelling, punctuation and typography. His verse was collected in *Complete Poems 1913–1962* (1972).

cumulus *See* CLOUD

cuneiform System of writing developed (c.3000 BC) in Mesopotamia. The system consists of wedge-shaped strokes, derived from the practice of writing on soft clay with a triangular stylus as a "pen". Cuneiform developed from pictograms that came to serve as an "ALPHABET" of more than 500 characters. Most stood for words, but some stood for syllables or speech-sounds.

Cunningham, Merce (1919–) US dancer and choreographer. He was a soloist (1940–55) with the Martha GRAHAM Company. In 1952 Cunningham formed his own MODERN DANCE company. He is best-known for his work with avant-garde artists and composers, such as Andy Warhol and John Cage. Cunningham incorporated improvisational techniques into dance through his method of "chance composition", in which dances are performed according to the roll of a die. His productions include *How to Pass, Kick, Fall, and Run* (1965).

Cupid In Roman mythology, god of love, equivalent to the Greek god EROS.

cuprite (cuprous oxide, Cu_2O) Reddish-brown, brittle, translucent oxide mineral. Formed by the oxidation of other ores, such as copper sulphide, it is an important source of copper.

Curaçao Largest island of the NETHERLANDS ANTILLES in the West Indies, in the S Caribbean Sea; the capital is Willemstad. Most inhabitants are descended from African slaves imported during the 17th and 18th centuries; the indigenous Arawak are now extinct. Curaçao derives most income from tourism and oil-refining. Products: peanuts, tropical fruits, Curaçao liqueur. Area: 444sq km (171sq mi). Pop. (1993 est.) 146,828.

curare Poisonous, resinous extract obtained from various tropical South American plants of the genera *Chondodendron* and *Strychnos*. Most of its active elements are ALKALOIDS. Causing muscle paralysis, it is used on the poisoned arrows of Native South Americans when hunting. It is also used as a muscle relaxant in abdominal surgery and setting fractures.

Curia Romana Official administrative body of the Roman Catholic Church. It is based in the VATICAN and consists of a court of officials through which the pope governs the Church. It includes three groups – congregations, tribunals and curial offices – and is concerned with all aspects of the life of the Church and its members.

Curie, Marie (1867–1934) Polish scientist who specialized in work on RADIATION. Marie and her husband **Pierre** Curie (1859–1906) (who specialized in the electrical and magnetic properties of crystals) worked together on a series of radiation experiments. In 1898, they discovered RADIUM and POLONIUM. In 1903, they shared the Nobel Prize for physics with A.H. BECQUEREL. In 1911, Marie became the first person to be awarded a second Nobel Prize (this time for chemistry), for her work on radium and its compounds. She died of leukaemia caused by laboratory radiation. Their daughter, **Irène Joliot-Curie** (1897–1956) and her husband, **Frédéric** Joliot-Curie (1900–58), were awarded the 1935 Nobel Prize for chemistry for producing artificial radioactive substances.

curie (symbol Ci) Unit formerly used to measure the activity of a radioactive substance. Named after Marie CURIE, it is defined as that quantity of a radioactive isotope that decays at the rate of 3.7×10^{10} disintegrations per second. The curie has been replaced by an SI unit, the becquerel (symbol Bq).

Curitiba City in SE Brazil; capital of Paraná state. Brazil's eighth-largest city, its development dates from the influx of Europeans in the late 19th century, when it became a distribution centre for the surrounding agricultural region. It has a cathedral and two universities. Industries: textiles, paper, tobacco. Pop. (1991) 1,290,142.

curium (symbol Cm) Synthetic, radioactive metallic element of the ACTINIDE SERIES. It was first made in 1944 by the US nuclear chemist Glenn SEABORG and his colleagues by the alpha particle bombardment of plutonium-239 in a cyclotron. Silvery in colour, curium is chemically reactive, intensely radioactive and is toxic if absorbed by the body. It provides power for orbiting satellites. Properties: at.no. 96; r.d. (calculated) 13.51; m.p. 1,340°C (2,444°F); 14 isotopes, most stable Cm^{247} (half-life 1.6×10^7 yr).

curlew Long-legged, wading bird with a down-curved bill and mottled brown plumage. Often migrating long distances, it feeds on small animals, insects and seeds, and nests on the ground, laying two to four eggs. Length: to 48–62cm (19–25in). Species *Numenius arquata*.

curling Game resembling lawn bowling on ice that is a major winter sport of Scotland, and popular in Canada, N USA and Nordic countries. The game is played by two teams of four players on an ice surface, 42m (138ft) long by 4.3m (14ft) wide. Each player has two smooth circular stones with a handle. At each end of the ice is a circular target with a central area known as the tee. One player sends his stone towards the tee, and teammates use brooms to sweep the surface in front of it to give it a smoother surface over which to glide. Each player delivers two stones. One point is scored for each stone lying nearer the tee than an opponent's stone.

currant Any of several mainly deciduous shrubs and their fruits, rich in vitamin C. Black, red and white currants are included in the genus *Ribes*: they are popular plants, cultivated widely. The fruits are used in pies, preserves and syrups. Family Grossulariaceae.

current, electric *See* ELECTRIC CURRENT

current, ocean *See* OCEANIC CURRENT

Curtin, John Joseph (1885–1945) Australian statesman, prime minister (1941–45). He entered parliament in 1928 and became leader of the Labor Party in 1935. Curtin organized the mobilization of national resources during the Japanese War. He died in office.

Curzon, George Nathaniel, 1st Marquess of Kedleston (1859–1925) British statesman. He entered Parliament as a Conservative in 1886. As viceroy of India (1899–1905), Curzon reformed administration and education and established (1901) the North-West Frontier Province. He resigned after a dispute with Lord KITCHENER. During World War 1 (1914–18), he served in the coalition cabinets of Herbert ASQUITH and LLOYD GEORGE. He continued as foreign secretary (1919–24) in Bonar LAW's government, and helped negotiate the Treaty of Lausanne.

Cushing, Harvey Williams (1869–1939) US surgeon. His pioneering techniques for surgery on the brain and spinal cord helped advance neurosurgery. He first described the syndrome produced by over-secretion of adrenal hormones that is now known as Cushing's syndrome. It is characterized by weight-gain in the face and trunk, high blood pressure, excessive growth of facial and body hair, and diabetes-like effects.

Cushing, Peter (1913–94) English film actor. After his performance as Baron Frankenstein in *Time Without Pity* (1957), he almost exclusively played horror roles for Hammer Films. Cushing's brooding, chiselled features and gaunt physique perfectly suited the genre.

Custer, George Armstrong (1839–76) US military leader. A flamboyant, headstrong character, Custer was the youngest Union general in the American CIVIL WAR. Following the War, he was posted to the frontier, but was court-martialled (1867) for disobeying orders and suspended. In 1868, he returned to service and led campaigns against the Cheyenne. His decision to divide his regiment and attack a superior force of Sioux at the

Battle of LITTLE BIGHORN (1876) resulted in the death of Custer and his entire regiment.

Cuthbert, Saint (635–87) Celtic monk and missionary. In 661 he became prior at Melrose. In 664 Cuthbert moved to Lindisfarne and became its bishop in 685. He lived for long periods as a hermit on the island of Farne. His life is told by St BEDE. His feast day is 20 March.

cuticle Exposed outer layer of an animal. In humans it is the EPIDERMIS, especially the dead skin at the edge of fingers. In botany, it is the waxy layer on the outer surface of epidermal cells of leaves and stems of vascular plants. It helps to prevent excessive water loss.

cuttlefish Cephalopod MOLLUSC related to the SQUID and OCTOPUS. Like squid, cuttlefish swim rapidly by the propulsion of a jet of water forced out through a siphon. They have ten sucker-covered arms on the head, two much longer than the rest. Their flattened bodies contain the familiar chalky cuttlebone. Capable of rapid colour changes, they can also eject blue-black "ink" as a means of protection. Family Sepiidae; species *Sepia officinalis*.

Cuvier, Georges, Baron (1769–1832) French geologist and zoologist, a founder of comparative anatomy and palaeontology. His scheme of classification stressed the form of organs and their correlation within the body. Cuvier applied this system to fossils and came to accept the theory of catastrophic changes.

Cuyp, Albert (1620–91) Dutch painter, son and pupil of **Benjamin Gerritsz** Cuyp (1612–52). His father was a genre painter much influenced by REMBRANDT. Albert is regarded as one of the greatest Dutch landscape painters. His calm, colourful river scenes, and landscapes with cows, use glowing light effects.

Cuzco City in S central Peru; capital of Cuzco department. An ancient capital of the Inca empire from *c*.1200, it fell to the Spaniards in 1533. Cuzco was destroyed by earthquakes in 1650 and then rebuilt. It is a centre of archaeological research. Pop. (1993) 255,568.

cyanide Salt or ester of hydrocyanic acid (prussic acid, HCN). The most important cyanides are sodium cyanide (NaCN) and potassium cyanide (KCN), both of which are deadly poisonous. Cyanides have many industrial uses – in electroplating, for the heat treatment of metals, in the extraction of silver and gold, in photography and in insecticides and pigments.

cyanobacteria (formerly blue-green algae) One of the major BACTERIA phyla, distinguished by the presence of the green pigment CHLOROPHYLL and the blue pigment phycocyanin. They perform PHOTOSYNTHESIS with the production of oxygen. Genetic analysis of CHLOROPLASTS show that they evolved from cyanobacteria by ENDOSYMBIOSIS. Many cyanobacteria perform NITROGEN FIXATION. They are most abundant in lakes, rivers and oceans. Some produce toxic BLOOMS.

cybernetics Study of communication and CONTROL SYSTEMS in animals, organizations and machines. The term was first used in this sense by Norbert Wiener in 1948. Cybernetics makes analogies between processes in the brain and nervous system, and those in COMPUTERS and other electronic systems. Analyzing, for example, the mechanisms of FEEDBACK and data processing.

cyberspace Popular term for the perceived "virtual" space within computer memory or networks. The term is a product of science fiction, where it usually refers to direct INTERFACE between brain and computer. It is often used to refer to the INTERNET and the worldwide web.

cycad Any member of the phylum Cycadophyta, primitive palm-like shrubs and trees that grow in tropical and subtropical regions. Although they are GYMNOSPERMS, they have feathery palm- or fern-like leaves (poisonous in most species) at the top of stout (usually unbranched) stems. In addition to their main roots, they also have special roots containing CYANOBACTERIA that carry out NITROGEN FIXATION. These plants first flourished *c*.225 million years ago. Most of the 100 or so surviving species are less than 6.1m (20ft) tall.

Cyclades (Kikládhes) Large group of Greek islands in the S Aegean Sea, off the SE coast of Greece; the capital is Hermoupolis (on Síros). The name is derived from the Greek *kyklos* (ring), since, in antiquity, it was held that the islands encircled the sacred island of Delos. The islands were annexed to Greece in 1829 from the Ottoman Empire. Mineral deposits include bauxite, lead and sulphur. Products: wheat, grapes, fish, olive oil, tobacco, marble. Area: 2,572sq km (993sq mi). Pop. (1991) 100,100.

cyclamen Genus of 20 species of low-growing perennial herbs, native to central Europe and the Mediterranean region. They have swollen, tuberous corms and heart- or kidney-shaped leaves. The drooping blooms are white, pink, lilac or crimson. Family Primulaceae.

cycle In physics, series of changes through which any system passes which brings it back to its original state. For example, alternating current starts from zero voltage, rises to a maximum, declines through zero to a minimum and rises again to zero. In the INTERNAL COMBUSTION ENGINE, a two-stroke engine completes one cycle each downward plunge and return.

cycling Sport for individuals and teams competing on BICYCLES. Now a regular event at the Olympic Games, cycle racing first became popular following the invention of the pneumatic tire (1888). There is a diversity of formats and events, road racing being the best-known form. The most famous cycle race is the TOUR DE FRANCE (inaugurated 1903).

cyclone System of WINDS, or a storm, that rotates inwards, around a centre of low atmospheric pressure (depression). The winds flow anti-clockwise in the Northern Hemisphere, and clockwise in the Southern

► **cypress** The Lawson cypress (*Chamaecyparis lawsonia*) can grow to a height of 60m (200ft) and live for up to 600 years. Also known as the Oregon cedar, this tree is native to Oregon and California, USA, where it is grown for its timber and natural beauty.

Hemisphere. Cyclones in middle latitudes are associated with cloudiness and high humidity, and the development of a FRONT. A strong tropical cyclone can give rise to a HURRICANE. *See also* CIRCULATION, ATMOSPHERIC; TORNADO

Cyclopes In Greek mythology, three demons, each having one eye in the centre of its forehead, who forged the thunderbolts of ZEUS. They were depicted by Homer as giant herdsmen living on an island. ODYSSEUS escaped from the Cyclops Polyphemus by blinding him.

cyclotron *See* ACCELERATOR, PARTICLE

Cygnus One of the most conspicuous constellations in the N sky, lying in the Milky Way. Its brightest star, Deneb, is the most luminous to the naked eye, 50,000 time the Sun's light. It forms part of the Northern Cross. Cygnus A was the first RADIO GALAXY to be discovered.

cylinder Solid figure or surface formed by rotating a rectangle, using one side as an axis. If the vertical height is h and the radius of the base r, then the volume is $\pi r^2 h$, and the curved surface area $2\pi rh$.

cymbal Saucer-shaped percussion instrument. It is made of brass with a small dome in the centre and is usually without definite pitch. It is played by clashing a pair together with both hands or by striking a suspended cymbal with a beater. It is used in symphony orchestras, brass bands and in most jazz and rock groups.

Cymbeline (Cunobelinus) (d. *c*.AD 42) Ancient British king. An ally of the Romans, he was king of the Catuvellauni tribe. After conquering the Trinovantes, he became the strongest ruler of S Britain. Shakespeare's play *Cymbeline* (*c*.1610) was based on Holinshed.

Cynewulf Anglo-Saxon poet of the early 8th century, presumed to be the author of *Elene*, *The Fates of the Apostles*, *The Ascension* and *Juliana*. The poems suggest that he was a priest in Mercia or Northumbria.

Cynics School of philosophy founded (*c*.440 BC) by Antisthenes, a pupil of SOCRATES. Cynics considered virtue to be the only good. Its teachings were developed by DIOGENES. *See also* STOICS

cypress Tall, evergreen tree native to North America and Eurasia. It has scale-like leaves, roundish cones and a distinctive symmetrical shape. The wood is durable and fragrant, and is of value commercially. Height: 6–24m (20–80ft). Family Cupressaceae; genus *Cupressus*. There are about 20 species.

Cyprian, Saint (200–258) Father of the Church, bishop of Carthage (248–58). Cyprian was a pagan rhetorician who was converted (*c*.246) to Christianity. His theological treatise, *The Unity of the Catholic Church* (251), argued for the restoration of church unity based on episcopal authority. Cyprian's strict views on apostasy and heresy resulted in his eventual martyrdom under VALERIAN. His feast day is 16 September.

Cyprus Island republic in the NE Mediterranean Sea; the capital is NICOSIA. **Land and climate** Cyprus has scenic mountain ranges, the Kyrenia and the Troodos, the latter rising to 1,951m (6,401ft) at Mount Olympus. The island contains fertile lowlands, used extensively for agriculture. It has a Mediterranean climate, with hot, dry summers and mild winters. Pine forests grow on the mountain slopes. **History and People** Greeks settled on Cyprus *c*.3,200 years ago. From AD 330, the island was part of the Byzantine Empire. In the 1570s, it became part of the Ottoman Empire. Turkish rule continued until 1878, when Cyprus was leased to Britain. In 1925, Britain proclaimed it a colony. In the 1950s, Greek Cypriots, who made up 80% of the population, began a campaign for *enosis* (union) with Greece. Their leader was the Greek Orthodox Archbishop MAKARIOS III. A guerrilla force

CYPRUS
AREA: 9,250 sq km (3,571 sq mi)
POPULATION: 762,000
CAPITAL (POPULATION): Nicosia (189,000)

(EOKA) attacked the British, who exiled Makarios. In 1960, Cyprus became an independent country and Makarios was its first president. The constitution provided for power-sharing between the Greek and Turkish Cypriots. It proved unworkable, however, and fighting broke out between the two communities. In 1964, the UN sent in a peacekeeping force. In 1974, Greek-led Cypriot forces overthrew Makarios. This led Turkey to invade N Cyprus, occupying *c*.40% of the island. Many Greek Cypriots fled from the Turkish-occupied area, which in 1979 was proclaimed to be a self-governing region. In 1983, the Turkish Cypriots declared the N to be an independent state, called the Turkish Republic of Northern Cyprus; the only country to recognize it is Turkey. The UN regards Cyprus as a single nation under the Greek Cypriot government in the S. It is estimated that more than 30,000 Turkish troops are deployed in N Cyprus. Despite UN-brokered peace negotiations (1997), there are frequent border clashes between the two communities. In 1998 Cyprus began accession negotiations with the European Union. **Economy** Cyprus got its name from the Greek word *kypros*, meaning copper, but little copper remains; the chief minerals today are asbestos and chromium. Industry employs 37% of the workforce, and manufactures include cement, footwear, tiles and wine. Crops include barley, citrus fruits, grapes, olives, potatoes and wheat. The most valuable activity in Cyprus is tourism. The economy of the Turkish Cypriot North lags behind that of the Greek Cypriot South.

Cyrano de Bergerac, Savinien (1619–55) French writer. His novels and plays combine free thinking, humour and burlesque romance. As an author, he is best known for two posthumously published prose fantasies, *Journey to the Moon* (1656) and *The Comical Tale of the States and Empires of the Sun* (1662). He is perhaps equally famous as the eponymous hero of the popular but historically inaccurate play by Edmond ROSTAND.

Cyrenaics School of Greek philosophy, founded by Aristippus of Cyrene, which flourished in the late 4th and early 3rd century BC. Cyrenaics espoused an early form of HEDONISM, believing that pleasure is the only good and that all pleasures are equal in value. The school declined under the challenge of EPICURUS.

Cyril, Saint (826–69) Greek Christian missionary. With his brother, Methodius, he is one of the two so-called "Apostles to the Slavs" who were sent to convert the Khazars and Moravians to Christianity. Cyril is said to have invented the CYRILLIC alphabet. His feast day is 14 February in the West and 11 May in the East.

Cyrillic ALPHABET based on Greek letter forms that is now used for writing several Slavic languages, most notably Russian and Serbian.

Cyrus II (the Great) (d.529 BC) King of Persia (559–529), founder of the ACHAEMENID Persian empire. He overthrew the Medes, then rulers of Persia, in 549 BC, defeated King CROESUS of Lydia (*c*.546 BC), and captured BABYLON (539 BC) and the Greek cities in Asia Minor. His empire stretched from the Mediterranean to India. He delivered the Jews from their BABYLONIAN CAPTIVITY.

cyst Hollow cavity or sac in the body that contains liquid or semi-solid matter. It may occur in a glandular organ, such as breast or prostate or in the skin. It may be caused by infection or by a blocked duct. A cyst may be removed for medical or cosmetic reasons.

cystic fibrosis Hereditary glandular disease in which the body produces abnormally thick mucus that obstructs the breathing passages, causing chronic lung disease. There is a deficiency of pancreatic enzymes, an abnormally high salt concentration in the sweat and a failure to gain weight. The disease is treated with antibiotics, pancreatic enzymes and a high-protein diet.

cystitis Inflammation of the urinary bladder, usually caused by bacterial infection. It is more common in women. Symptoms include frequent and painful urination, low back pain and slight fever.

cytokinin (kinetin or kinin) Any of a group of plant hormones that stimulate cell division. Cytokinins work in conjunction with AUXINS to promote swelling and division in the plant cells producing lateral buds. They are used commercially to produce seedless grapes, to stimulate germination of barley in brewing and to prolong the life of green, leaf vegetables.

cytology Study of living CELLS and their structure, behaviour and function. Cytology began with Robert HOOKE's microscopic studies of cork in 1665, and the microscope is still the main tool. In the 19th century, a theory was developed which suggested that cells are the basic units of organisms. Recently, cytochemistry has focused on the study of the chemistry of cell components.

cytoplasm Jelly-like matter inside a CELL and surrounding the NUCLEUS. Cytoplasm contains various bodies known as organelles, with specific metabolic functions. The proteins needed for cell growth and repair are produced in the cytoplasm.

Czartoryski, Adam Jerzy (1770–1861) Polish politician. A hostage at the Russian court, he befriended the future tsar, ALEXANDER I, who appointed him foreign minister (1803–06). Czartoryski was responsible for the adoption (1815) of the Polish constitution. He opposed NICHOLAS I's ambitions and, following an insurrection, headed (1830–31) a Polish provisional government. After its failure, he was forced into exile in Paris.

Czech Language spoken in the Czech Republic (Bohemia and Moravia) by *c.*10 million people. A Slavic language, it is closely related to SLOVAK.

Czechoslovakia Former federal state in central Europe. Formed after World War 1 from parts of the old AUSTRO-HUNGARIAN EMPIRE, Czechoslovakia was formally recognized as a new republic by the Treaty of St Germain (1918). A democratic constitution was established in 1920, and the nation was first led by Tomás MASARYK and then by Eduard BENEŠ. Nationalist tensions caused unrest: the SLOVAKS had long wanted autonomy, and the large German population in the N wanted to join with Germany. Hitler's rise to power and annexation of Austria led to the MUNICH AGREEMENT (1938), which ceded land to Germany. Poland and Hungary also acquired territory, and Beneš resigned. In 1939, Hitler occupied Czechoslovakia, and Beneš formed a government-in-exile in London. In 1945, the country was liberated by Soviet and US troops, and Beneš was restored as president. A 1946 election gave the communists a majority in the coalition. By 1948, they had assumed complete control, and Beneš resigned. Czechoslovakia became a Soviet-style state. Unrest during the 1950s led to some liberalization, but it was not until the PRAGUE SPRING (1968) and the reforms of Alexander DUBČEK that any great democratization occurred. Soviet troops crushed the

revolution. When democratic reforms were introduced in the Soviet Union in the late 1980s, CZECHS also demanded reforms. In 1989, anti-government demonstrations and the democratization of Eastern Europe finally led to the resignation of Communist Party leaders. Non-communists came to power, and the "Velvet Revolution" was complete when Vaclav HAVEL became president. Free elections were held in 1990, but differences between the Czechs and Slovaks led to the partitioning of the country on 1 January, 1993. The break was peaceful, and the two new nations, the CZECH REPUBLIC and the SLOVAK REPUBLIC, have retained many ties. *See also* BOHEMIA; MORAVIA

Czech Republic Republic in central Europe. The Czech Republic is made up of two regions: the plateau of BOHEMIA in the W, and the lowland of MORAVIA in the E. The capital, PRAGUE, and PLZEŇ are Bohemia's largest cities. BRNO is the major Moravian city. Mountains form most of the N border. Some rivers, such as the ELBE, ODER and Vltava flow N into Germany, while others in the S flow into the DANUBE basin. **Climate** Moderate Atlantic air streams give Prague warm summers, while easterly winds from Russia bring bitterly cold winters. The average annual rainfall is moderate, with 500mm to 750mm (20in–30in) common in lowland areas. **Vegetation** Many of the republic's forests have been cut down to create farmland, but oak and spruce remain. Acid rain is damaging trees in the N. **History and Politics** CZECHS began to settle in the area *c.*1,500 years ago. In the 10th century Bohemia became important as a kingdom within the Holy Roman Empire. In 1526, the Austrian Habsburgs assumed control, but a Czech rebellion in 1618 led to the THIRTY YEARS' WAR. Although Austria continued to rule Bohemia and Moravia, Czech nationalism continued to grow throughout the 19th century. CZECHOSLOVAKIA was created after World War 1. Germany occupied the country in World War 2. In 1946, the communists emerged as the strongest party, but Eduard BENEŠ became president. By 1948, communist leaders had assumed absolute control. Democratic reforms culminated in the PRAGUE SPRING (1968). Warsaw Pact troops invaded to crush the "Velvet Revolution" and the formation of a noncommunist administration. Free elections were held in 1990, resulting in the re-election of Vaclav HAVEL. In 1992, the government agreed to the secession of the SLOVAK REPUBLIC and, on 1 January 1993, the Czech Republic was created. Havel was re-elected in 1998. In 1999 the Czech Republic joined NATO. **Economy** Under communism, Czechoslovakia became one of the most industrialized parts of Eastern Europe (1995 GDP per capita, US$9,770). The country has deposits of coal, uranium, iron ore, magnesite, tin and zinc. Manufacturing employs 40% of the workforce. Industries include chemicals, beer, iron and steel and machinery. The Czech Republic is mainly self-sufficient in food. Private ownership of land is gradually being restored. Agriculture employs 12% of the workforce. Livestock raising is important. Crops include grains, fruit and hops for brewing. In 1998, talks began on formal accession to the European Union (EU).

CZECH REPUBLIC
AREA: 78,864sq km (30,449sq mi)
POPULATION: 10,500,000
CAPITAL (POPULATION): Prague (1,210,000)

D/d, fourth letter of the Roman alphabet. It is derived from the Semitic daleth, *meaning door, and the Greek delta. It took its current form c.AD 114. In Roman numerals, D stands for 500.*

dab Marine FLATFISH; a valuable food fish. The upper, "sighted" side is brown with darker spots; the underside is almost white. Length: to 25cm (10in). Species *Pleuronectes limanda*.

dace Any of several small freshwater fish of the CARP family, Cyprinidae. The common European dace (*Leuciscus leuciscus*) is silvery and can grow up to 30cm (12in) long. The Moapa dace (*Moapa coriacea*) is an endangered species.

Dachau Town in Bavaria, SW Germany, site of the first Nazi CONCENTRATION CAMP established in March 1933. Up to 70,000 people died or were murdered here before liberation in 1945. The site is preserved as a memorial.

dachshund Small German hunting dog bred to follow badgers to earth. It has a long tapered head and rounded pendulous ears; the long body is set on short legs and the tail is held in line with the back. Its coat may be smooth, wiry or long. There are two types, standard and miniature. Height: (at shoulder) up to 23cm (9in).

Dacia Ancient region of Europe (now in Romania). It was colonized (101–106) by TRAJAN. Dacia was later overrun by Goths, Huns and Avars. The language was retained and is the basis of modern Romanian.

Dada (Dadaism) Movement in literature and the visual arts, started in Zürich (1915). Contributors included Jean ARP, Marcel DUCHAMP, Max ERNST and Man RAY. The group promulgated complete nihilism, espoused satire and ridiculed civilization. Dadaists participated in deliberately irreverent art events designed to shock a complacent public. In the early 1920s, conflicts of interest led to the demise of Dadaism. *See also* SURREALISM

Dadd, Richard (1817–61) English painter. Dadd showed early promise as an artist, but murdered his father in 1843 and spent the rest of his life in asylums. He continued to paint, specializing in highly imaginative fairy and fantasy pictures. His finest work is *The Fairy Feller's Master-stroke* (1855–64), a minutely detailed piece of whimsical invention.

daddy-longlegs European name for the CRANE FLY

Daedalus In Greek mythology, an architect and sculptor. He constructed the LABYRINTH for King MINOS of Crete. Denied permission to leave the island, he made wings of wax and feathers to escape with his son ICARUS.

daffodil Bulbous flowering plant, family Amaryllidaceae. The single flowers are yellow or yellow and white, with a bell-like central cup and oval petals. Height: to 45cm (18in). Genus *Narcissus*.

Dafydd ap Gwilym (*c.*1320–*c.*1380) Welsh poet. Born into nobility, he composed in a bardic tradition akin to the TROUBADOURS. Dafydd wrote entirely in Welsh using the complex *cywydd* metre. His major themes are chivalry and social satire.

Dagda (lit. "good god") Ancient Irish deity, father of BRIGIT. He possessed the powers of fire and magic. With his mighty club, he could both kill and restore life.

Dagestan Republic in the Russian Federation, bounded on the E by the CASPIAN SEA, SE European Russia. The capital is Makhachkala. Islam was introduced in the 7th century, and the majority of the present population is Muslim. Annexed by Russia in the early 19th century, Dagestan's gained autonomy in 1921. In 1991, it claimed full republic status. Dagestan is dominated by the CAUCASUS mountains. Lowlands to the N support wheat, maize and grapes. The rivers Samur and Sulak provide hydroelectric power. Difficulty of access has left mineral resources untapped. Industries: engineering, oil, chemicals. Area: 50,300sq km (19,416sq mi). Pop. (1994) 1,953,000.

Daguerre, Louis Jacques Mandé (1789–1851) French painter and inventor. In 1829 Daguerre and Niepce invented the daguerreotype, an early photographic process in which a unique image is produced on a copper plate without an intervening negative. Their process was announced in 1839. *See also* PHOTOGRAPHY

Dahl, Roald (1913–90) English writer, chiefly of short stories. He is best-known for his witty, imaginative children's fiction. Dahl's books, such as *James and the Giant Peach* (1961) and *Charlie and the Chocolate Factory* (1964), are popular with all ages. He is also noted for his adult stories, such as *Someone Like You* (1953) and *Kiss, Kiss* (1959).

dahlia Genus of perennial plants with tuberous roots and large flowers. The common garden dahlia (*Dahlia pinnata*) has been developed into more than 2,000 varieties. Height: to 1.5m (5ft). Family Asteraceae/Compositae.

Dáil Éireann Lower house of the two-chamber Parliament of the Republic of Ireland (the upper house is the *Seanad Éireann*). It has 166 members elected for five-year terms by a system of proportional representation.

Daimler, Gottlieb (1834–1900) German engineer and automobile manufacturer. In 1883, with Wilhelm Maybach, Daimler developed an INTERNAL COMBUSTION ENGINE. He used this to power his first car (1886). In 1890, he founded the Daimler Motor Company, which made Mercedes cars and became Daimler-BENZ (1926).

dairy farming Production of milk and its products. Through management of dairy cows and cultivation of feed crops, an efficient kind of farming is carried on. Dairy breeds include Jersey, Ayrshire and Fresian.

daisy Any of several members of the family Asteraceae/Compositae, especially the common English garden daisy, *Bellis perennis*. It has long stalks with solitary flower heads, each of which has a large, yellow central disk and small, radiating white petal-like florets.

Dakar Capital and largest city on the Atlantic coast, Senegal, W Africa. Founded in 1857 as a French fort, it later became capital of French West Africa. There is a Roman Catholic cathedral and a Presidential Palace. Dakar has excellent educational and medical facilities, including the Pasteur Institute. Industries: textiles, oil refining, brewing. Pop. (1995) 1,500,000.

Dakota *See* NORTH DAKOTA; SOUTH DAKOTA

Dakota *See* SIOUX

Daladier, Édouard (1884–1970) French statesman, prime minister (1933, 1934, 1938–40). As prime minister and minister of defence, he signed the MUNICH AGREEMENT (1938). In 1940, he was arrested by the new VICHY GOVERNMENT and deported (1942) to Germany. He was released at the end of World War 2 and became a member of the National Assembly (1946–58).

Dalai Lama (Grand Lama) Supreme head of the Yellow Hat Buddhist monastery at LHASA, TIBET. The title was bestowed upon the third Grand Lama by the Mongol ruler Altan Khan (d.1583). In 1950–51, **Tenzin Gyatso** (1935–), 14th Dalai Lama, temporarily fled Tibet after it was annexed by the People's Republic of China.

Following a brutally suppressed Tibetan uprising (1959), he went into exile in India. In TIBETAN BUDDHISM the Dalai Lama is revered as the BODHISATTVA *Avalokitesvara*. When a Dalai Lama dies, his soul is believed to pass into the body of an infant, born 49 days later.

Dalhousie, James Andrew Broun Ramsay, 1st Marquess of (1812–60) British statesman, governor general of India (1847–56). After serving as an MP and president of the Board of Trade (1845), he was appointed governor general of India. Dalhousie initiated many public works, such as developing the railway and sewage systems. In the second of the SIKH WARS, he annexed Punjab (1849) and the further acquisitions of Rangoon (1852) and Oudh (1856) fuelled the INDIAN MUTINY (1857).

Dali, Salvador (1904–89) Spanish artist. His style, a blend of meticulous realism and hallucinatory transformations of form and space, made him an influential exponent of SURREALISM. His dream-like paintings exploit the human fear of distortion, as in *The Persistence of Memory* (1931). Dali collaborated with Luis BUÑUEL on the films *Un Chien andalou* (1928) and *L'Age d'or* (1930).

Dallapiccola, Luigi (1904–75) Italian composer. He was the first Italian composer to use ATONALITY, adopting the TWELVE-TONE system of SCHOENBERG in the 1930s as in the opera *Volo di notte* (1940). Persecuted by Mussolini during World War 2, he wrote pieces concerned with freedom, notably *Canti di Prigonia* (1941).

Dallas City in NE Texas, USA. First settled in the 1840s, Dallas expanded with the 20th-century development of its oil fields. President KENNEDY was assassinated here on 22 November 1963. A commercial and transport centre of the Southwest, it has many educational and cultural institutions. Industries: oil refining, electronic equipment. Pop. (1990) 1,006,877.

Dalmatia Region of Croatia on the E coast of the ADRIATIC SEA; the provincial capital is SPLIT. From the 10th century, it was divided N and S between Croatia and Serbia. By 1420, most of Dalmatia was controlled by Venice. The Treaty of Campo Formio (1797) ceded the region to Austria. After World War 1 it became part of Yugoslavia. The coastline stretches along the Adriatic from Rijeka to the border with Montenegro and from the 1960s has been a popular tourist destination. Most of the inland area is mountainous. In 1991, Dalmatia was the scene of heavy fighting between Croats and Serbs. Other major cities include Zadar (the historic capital) and DUBROVNIK.

dalmatian Dog characterized by its white coat with black or brown spots. It has a long, flat head with long muzzle and high-set ears. Its powerful body is set on strong legs and the tail is long and tapered. Height: to 58cm (23in) at the shoulder.

Dalton, John (1766–1844) English chemist, physicist and meteorologist. He researched TRADE WINDS, the cause of rain and the AURORA borealis. Dalton described COLOUR BLINDNESS based on personal

▶ **dalmatian** Perhaps best known from the Disney animated film *101 Dalmatians* (1961), dalmatians are thought to have been developed as carriage dogs in the Croatian region of Dalmatia.

experience. His study of gases led to Dalton's law of partial pressures: the total pressure of a gas mixture is equal to the sum of the partial pressures of the individual gases, provided no chemical reaction occurs. Dalton's atomic theory states that each element is made up of indestructible, small particles. He also constructed a table of relative atomic masses.

Dam, (Carl Peter) Henrik (1895–1976) Danish biologist. In 1939 he discovered VITAMIN K, the fat-soluble vitamin needed for blood clotting. Dam isolated it from hempseed and the seeds of other plants, and he also discovered it in liver. For this work, he shared the 1943 Nobel Prize for physiology or medicine with E.A. DOISY.

dam Barrier built to confine water (or check its flow) for irrigation, flood control or electricity generation. The first dams were probably constructed by the Egyptians 4,500 years ago. **Gravity** dams are anchored by their own weight. **Single-arch** dams are convex to the water they retain, supported at each end by river banks. Multiple-arch and **buttress** dams are supported by buttresses rooted in the bedrock. The cheapest commercial source of electricity comes from hydroelectric projects made possible by dams, such as the ASWAN High Dam, Egypt.

Damascus Capital of Syria, on the River Barada, SW Syria. Perhaps the oldest continuously occupied city in the world, today it is Syria's administrative and financial centre. In 2000 BC, Damascus formed part of the Egyptian Empire. In 332 BC, ALEXANDER THE GREAT captured the city from Persia, and it was subsumed into the SELEUCID empire. Under Roman rule Damascus became a prosperous commercial city and an early centre of Christianity. THEODOSIUS I built (AD 379) a Christian church that, under UMAYYAD rule (661–750), was converted into the Great Mosque. The city withstood the CRUSADES and was part of the Ottoman Empire for 400 years (1516–1918). In 1918, it was captured by the British and came under French administration. It became capital of independent Syria in 1941. Industries: damask fabric, metalware. Pop. (1993 est.) 1,497,000.

Damocles In Greek history, a courtier of Dionysius I of Syracuse (Sicily). Dionysius suspended a sword by a fragile thread above Damocles' head to make him realize that wealth and power were insecure.

Dampier, William (1651–1715) English navigator and buccaneer. His early career included a raiding expedition (1679–81) against Spanish America and a voyage (1688) across the Pacific Ocean. He explored the coasts of Australia, New Guinea and New Britain, and the Dampier Archipelago and Dampier Strait are named after him. In 1708 he rescued Alexander Selkirk, on whom DEFOE based Robinson Crusoe.

damselfly Delicate insect resembling the DRAGONFLY. Almost all have a slender, elongated blue abdomen and a pair of membranous wings that are held vertically over the body when at rest. Length: to 5cm (2in). Order Odonata.

damson Small tree and its edible fruit. The name is often applied to varieties of PLUM (*Prunus domestica*). The fleshy DRUPE is generally borne in clusters, has a tart flavour and is made into jam. Family Rosaceae. The damson-plum of tropical America is a separate species, *Chrysophyllum oliviforme*, Family Sapotaceae.

Dana, Richard Henry (1815–82) US writer and lawyer. He sailed (1834) as an ordinary seaman around Cape Horn to California. Dana's concern for the injustices suffered by sailors prompted his book, *Two Years Before the Mast* (1840), a classic of maritime literature.

Danby, Thomas Osborne, 1st Earl of (1632–1712) (subsequently Marquis of Carmarthen, Duke of Leeds)

Leading minister of CHARLES II, he was impeached and imprisoned (1679–84) for trying to secure a secret subsidy from LOUIS XIV of France. Danby organized a group, later known as TORIES, who supported the succession of the future JAMES II, but he later changed sides and served WILLIAM III (1690–95) until again impeached for bribery.

dance Ancient art of ordered, stylized body movements, normally performed to music or voices. Primitive dance was probably part of courtship and religious ritual. In China, Japan and India, graceful MIME is the distinctive feature, whereas the dances of Africa have rapid, athletic movements. In 18th-century Europe, BACH and HANDEL, among others, composed music for formal courtly dances, such as the gavotte and minuet. Ballroom dances, such as the waltz, foxtrot, tango and quickstep, became popular in the 19th and early 20th centuries. From the 1940s to the 1960s, many new dances, from the jitterbug to the twist, were introduced. *See also* BALLET; FOLK DANCE; MODERN DANCE

dance of death According to popular belief, probably originating in 13th or 14th-century morality poems and plays, the means by which the dead rose up at night to attract the curious and unsuspecting to their deaths. The superstition was reinforced through recital and performance, with stylized dance pageants, paintings, illustrations and verse in which the dance symbolized death.

dandelion Widespread perennial weed, with leaves growing from the base and yellow composite flowers. It reproduces by means of parachute seeds. The leaves are used in salads, the flowers in wine-making. Family Asteraceae (COMPOSITAE); species *Taraxacum officinale*.

Dandolo, Enrico (*c.*1108–1205) Venetian statesman, founder of the Venetian empire. In 1192, he became Doge of Venice. Dandolo led the Fourth CRUSADE in the capture (1204) of Constantinople and established the Latin Empire of CONSTANTINOPLE. In 1205, he and BALDWIN I were defeated at Adrianople, Dandolo, aged and blind, led the Latin army home.

Danelaw Large region of NE England occupied by Danes in the late 9th century. Its independence was confirmed by Alfred and Guthrum's Pact (886). Alfred's son, Edward the Elder, and grandson, Athelstan, restored it to English control in the early 10th century.

Daniel Legendary Jewish hero and visionary of the 6th century BC, who was at the court of the Babylonian kings NEBUCHADNEZZAR and BELSHAZZAR. The OLD TESTAMENT Book of Daniel, probably written *c.*165 BC, relates events in Daniel's life during the BABYLONIAN CAPTIVITY. The last six of its 12 chapters consist of visions and prophesies.

D'Annunzio, Gabriele (1863–1938) Italian writer and soldier. His erotic novel, *The Flame of Life* (1900), describes his affair with Eleanora DUSE. D'Annunzio's masterpiece is the impressionistic collection of lyrics, *Halcyon* (1903). His rhetoric was instrumental in persuading Italy to join the Allies in World War 1. D'Annunzio fought with spectacular bravery. He established personal rule (1919–21) of Fiume (Rijeka). D'Annunzio supported the rise of Mussolini's fascist movement.

Dante Alighieri (1265–1321) Italian poet. He helped defeat the GHIBELLINES at the battle of Campaldino (1289). *La Vita Nuova* (*The New Life*, *c.*1292) celebrates Dante's idealized love for Beatrice Portinari (1266–90), who remained the inspiration for much of his life's work. Dante's support for the moderate White GUELPHS against the papal faction of Black Guelphs led to his exile (1302). He never returned to Florence, but wrote under the patronage of various nobles until his death in Ravenna. His allegorical masterpiece, *The Divine Comedy*, a three-book

epic in *terza rima*, is one of the great works of Western literature. It depicts the poet's spiritual journey through Hell, Purgatory and Paradise. Other works include *The Banquet* (*c.*1304–07) and *On Monarchy* (*c.*1313).

Danton, Georges Jacques (1759–94) French statesman, a leader of the FRENCH REVOLUTION. He was instrumental in the arrest of LOUIS XVI (10 August 1792). Danton, DESMOULINS, ROBESPIERRE and MARAT formed a revolutionary tribunal. Danton dominated the first Committee of Public Safety (April–July 1793) but was ousted by Robespierre and the JACOBINS. He called for an end to the REIGN OF TERROR and for leniency towards the GIRONDINS. Danton was arrested for conspiracy, tried and guillotined.

Danube (Donau) River in central and SE Europe. Europe's second-longest river, it rises in SW Germany and flows NE then SE across Austria to form the border between Slovakia and Hungary. It then flows S into Serbia, forming part of Romania's borders with Serbia and Bulgaria. It continues N across SE Romania to the Black Sea. Length: *c.*2,859km (1,770mi).

Danzig *See* GDAŃSK

Da Ponte, Lorenzo (1749–1838) Italian poet, b. Emanuele Conegliano. Da Ponte wrote the libretti for Mozart's *The Marriage of Figaro* (1786), *Don Giovanni* (1787) and *Così fan tutte* (1790).

Daphne Nymph in GREEK MYTHOLOGY. APOLLO, struck by a gold-tipped arrow of EROS, fell in love with Daphne. She had been shot with one of Eros' leaden points, and so scorned all men. To protect her from Apollo, the gods transformed her into a laurel tree.

Darby, Abraham (1677–1717) English iron manufacturer. In 1709 Darby developed the first COKE-fired BLAST FURNACE, at Coalbrookdale, Shropshire. The relatively cheap and abundant supplies of coke fuelled the INDUSTRIAL REVOLUTION. His grandson, **Abraham Darby III** (1750–91), built the world's first cast-iron bridge, at Ironbridge Gorge, Shropshire.

Dardanelles (Çanakkale Bogazi) Narrow strait between the Sea of Marmara and the Aegean Sea, separating Çanakkale in Asian Turkey from GALLIPOLI in European Turkey. With the BOSPORUS Strait, the Dardanelles forms a waterway whose strategic and commercial importance has been recognized since ancient times (known then as the Hellespont). In the Byzantine and Ottoman Empires and both World Wars, it was of strategic importance in the defence of Constantinople (ISTANBUL). The strait was the scene of the GALLIPOLI CAMPAIGN in World War 1. Length: 61km (38mi). Width: 1.2–6km (0.75–4mi).

Dar es Salaam Former capital of Tanzania, on the Indian Ocean, E Tanzania. Founded in the 1860s by the sultan of Zanzibar, it was capital of German East Africa (1891–1916) and of Tanganyika (1916–74). It is Tanzania's commercial centre, largest city and port. Industries: textiles, chemicals. Pop. (1988 est.) 1,360,850.

Darío, Rubén (1867–1916) (Félix Rubén García Sarmiento) Nicaraguan poet, father of the *modernismo* movement. His early works, such as *Blue* (1881) and *Profane Hymns* (1896), show the influence of French Parnassians and symbolists Darío's masterpiece, *Songs of Life and Hope* (1905), is more historical and political.

Darius I (the Great) (*c.*558–486 BC) King of Persia (521–486 BC) of the ACHAEMENID dynasty. He extended the Persian empire, chiefly through the conquests of Thrace and Macedonia. Darius divided the empire into provinces (satrapies), made great improvements to transport infrastructure, and was tolerant of religious diversity. He was defeated by the Greeks at Marathon in 490 BC.

Darius III (380–330 BC) King of Persia (336–330 BC). By underestimating the strength of ALEXANDER THE GREAT, he brought about the demise of the ACHAEMENID Persian empire. Defeated at Issus (333 BC) and Gaugamela (331 BC), Darius was forced to flee to Ecbatana and then to Bactria, where he was killed.

Darjeeling City at the foot of the Himalayas, West Bengal, NE India. A former British hill station, it is noted for its teas. Pop. (1981) 57,603.

Dark Ages Period of European history from the fall of the Roman Empire in the 5th century to the 9th or 10th century. The term appears to imply cultural and economic backwardness, but in fact indicates ignorance of the period due to lack of historical evidence.

Darling, Grace (1815–42) English heroine. Daughter of a lighthouse keeper on Farne Islands, Northumberland, in 1838 Darling helped her father rescue five crew from the shipwrecked boat *Forfarshire*.

Darmstadt City in Hesse state, W central Germany. The old town dates from the Middle Ages. The city was severely damaged during World War 2. It is a cultural centre, with a music school. Industries: chemicals, aerospace engineering, steel. Pop. (1995) 139,000.

Darnley, Henry Stuart, Lord (1545–67) Scottish aristocrat, second husband of MARY, QUEEN OF SCOTS, and father of JAMES I of England. In 1565 he married Mary (his cousin). Darnley's debauched lifestyle made him unpopular at court. In 1566 he conspired in the murder of Mary's secretary, David Rizzio (1566), and became estranged from the queen. Darnley was murdered in a plot led by the Earl of BOTHWELL.

Darrow, Clarence Seward (1857–1938) US lawyer. He unsuccessfully defended (1894) Eugene V. DEBS (1894) following the Pullman strike. A staunch opponent of capital punishment, none of the 100 people charged with murder who Darrow defended were ever sentenced to death. In 1906 he secured the acquittal of William HAYWOOD. In the famous SCOPES TRIAL (1925), Darrow unsuccessfully defended the right to teach evolution in school, but his cross-examination of William Jennings BRYAN discredited the Fundamentalist stance.

darts Indoor target game developed in 15th-century England. Three weighted, metal-pointed darts are thrown at a board 2.4m (8ft) away. The standard board is divided into 20 even wedges, with a triple scoring band in the middle and a double scoring band on the outside, fanning out from two small circles in the centre (the bull's-eye, worth 50 points, and around it the "25"). Starting with a certain number of points (usually 501), the object is to reach zero, finishing with a "double".

Darwin, Charles Robert (1809–82) English naturalist, who developed the organic theory of EVOLUTION. In 1831, he joined a five-year, round-the-world expedition on HMS BEAGLE. Observations made of the flora and fauna of South America (especially the Galápagos Islands) formed the basis of his work on animal variation. The development of a similar theory by A.R. WALLACE led Darwin to present his ideas to the Linnean Society in 1858. In 1859, he published *The Origin of Species*, one of the world's most influential science books. Thomas HUXLEY championed Darwin's ideas and engaged in a heated debate with theologians, since Darwin's notion of a common ancestral origin contradicted a literal interpretation of the Book of GENESIS. Drawing on the work of Thomas MALTHUS, Darwin argued that organisms reproduce more than is necessary to replenish their population, creating competition for survival. Opposed to the ideas of LAMARCK, Darwin

argued that each organism was a unique combination of genetic variations. The variations that prove helpful in the struggle to survive are passed down to the offspring of the survivors. He termed this process NATURAL SELECTION. NEO-DARWINISM supplemented his ideas with modern research into HEREDITY, especially MUTATION.

Darwin, Erasmus (1731–1802) English physician, grandfather of CHARLES DARWIN. Many of his ideas on evolution, proposed in *Zoonomia, or the Laws of Organic Life* (1794–96), anticipated later theories. Many of his other scientific works were written in verse. Darwin also cultivated a large botanical garden.

Darwin Port on the Beagle Gulf, N Australia, capital of Northern Territory. Founded in the late 1860s as Palmerston, it became Port Darwin in 1911. Allied headquarters in N Australia during World War 2, it was bombed by the Japanese (1942). In 1974 most of the city was destroyed by a cyclone. Darwin's harbour is the major shipping point for N Australia. Pop. (1993 est.) 77,900.

Darwinism *See* EVOLUTION

dasyurus Genus of mainly nocturnal, carnivorous MARSUPIALS found in Australia, New Guinea and Tasmania. They have large canine teeth, separate digits and long tails. Family Dasyuridae.

data Information, such as lists of words, quantities or measurements or codes representing a picture. A computer PROGRAM works by processing data that may be entered using a keyboard or other input device and then stored as a data file on a MAGNETIC DISK. Data may come from a variety of sources, including the INTERNET.

database Collection of DATA produced and retrieved by a COMPUTER. The data is usually stored on MAGNETIC DISK or tape. A database PROGRAM enables the computer to generate files of data and later search for and retrieve specific items or groups of items.

data processing Systematic sequence of operations performed on DATA, especially by a COMPUTER, in order to calculate or revise information stored on MAGNETIC DISK or tape. The main processing operations performed by a computer are arithmetical and logical operations that involve decision-making based on comparison of data.

data protection Measures taken to guard DATA against unauthorized access. Many governments have passed legislation ensuring that such DATABASES are registered and that the information they contain is protected.

date palm Tree native to the Near East. It has large flower clusters that produce the popular edible fruit. Height: up to 30m (100ft). Family Arecacae/Palmae.

dating, radioactive (radiometric dating) Any of several methods using the laws of RADIOACTIVE DECAY to assess the ages of archaeological remains, fossils, rocks and of the Earth itself. The specimens must contain a very long-lived radioisotope of known HALF-LIFE, which, with a measurement of the ratio of radioisotope to a stable ISOTOPE (usually the decay product), gives the age. In **potassium-argon** dating, the ratio of potassium-40 to its stable decay product argon-40 gives ages over ten million years. In **rubidium-strontium** dating, the ratio of rubidium-87 to its stable product strontium-87 gives ages up to several thousand million years. In CARBON DATING, the proportion of carbon-14 (half-life 5,730 years) to stable carbon-12 absorbed into once-living matter, such as wood or bone, gives ages up to several thousand years.

datura Genus of North American plants with large, trumpet-shaped, sweet-smelling flowers. Some produce useful drugs, others are ornamentals. THORN APPLE (*Datura stramonium*) is the source of a drug used in the treatment of asthma. Family Solanaceae (NIGHTSHADE).

Daudet, Alphonse (1480–97) French writer. Daudet first gained attention for his sketches of life in his native Provence, collected in *Lettres de mon moulin* (1869). *Tartarin de Tarascon* (1872) introduced the comic character of Tartarin.

Daumier, Honoré (1808–79) French painter, sculptor and caricaturist. Daumier produced more than 4,000 lithographs lampooning French middle-class society.

dauphin Title of the heir to the French throne from 1350 to 1830. The name was originally that of the rulers of Viennois, SE France, deriving from lands known as the Dauphiné, which were acquired by the French crown in 1349 and bestowed on the heir to the throne.

Davao Seaport on MINDANAO Island, S Philippines. During the 1960s its industry grew and its population more than doubled. It is the largest city on Mindanao and the commercial centre of a prosperous farming region. Products: hemp, timber. Pop. (1994) 961,000.

Davenant, Sir William (1606–68) English dramatist and poet, rumoured to be the illegitimate son of Shakespeare. His plays include the comedies *Love and Honour* (1634) and *The Wits* (1636). He succeeded Ben JONSON as Poet Laureate in 1638. Davenant was responsible for the revival of English theatre at the end of the Protectorate and the start of the Restoration. In 1656 he staged the first English opera, *The Siege of Rhodes*.

David, Saint (d. *c*.600) Patron saint of Wales. He founded a monastery at what is now St Davids. Little is known of his life, but legends abound. His feast day is 1 March.

David (d. *c*.962 BC) King of ancient Israel (*c*.1010–970 BC), successor of SAUL. His career is related in the OLD TESTAMENT books of SAMUEL. David's military successes against the Philistines, led Saul to plot his demise. As king, he united Judah and Israel. David captured Jerusalem, making it his capital and building his palace on Mount Zion. The later part of his reign was an era of decline, marked by the revolts of his sons ABSALOM and Adonijah. David was succeeded by SOLOMON, his son by Bathsheba. According to the Jewish Prophets, the MESSIAH must be a descendant of David.

David I (c.1084–1153) King of Scotland (1124–53), son of Malcolm III and successor of Alexander I. He strengthened the monarchy by granting land to the aristocracy and developing the burghs. In 1136, David invaded England in support of his niece Matilda's claim to the throne. He was defeated at the Battle of the Standard (1138). In 1141, David gained control of Northumberland.

David, Gerard (1460–1523) Flemish painter. Influenced by van EYCK and van der WEYDEN, David has a distinctive, austere grace. He was commissioned by the town of BRUGES to paint several works: *The Judgement of Cambyses* and *The Flaying of Sisamnes* warned officials of the retribution for injustice.

David, Jacques Louis (1748–1825) French painter, a leader of NEOCLASSICISM. His output reflected his JACOBIN views and support for Napoleon I. His most famous work is *Oath of the Horatii* (1784). Others include *Death of Socrates* (1787) and *Death of Marat* (1793).

Davies, Sir Peter Maxwell (1934–) English composer. He has written four operas, including *Taverner* (1972) and *Resurrection* (1988). Much of his work reflects the landscape and culture of his adopted home, the remote Orkney Islands, N Scotland, notably the opera *The Martyrdom of St Magnus* (1977).

Davies, Robertson (1913–95) Canadian writer. Davies is best known for *The Deptford Trilogy* (1970–75), which exhibits his characteristic mixture of myth, satire and psychological symbolism. Other works

include *The Salterton Trilogy* (1951–58) and a number of plays, including *A Jig for the Gypsy* (1954).

Da Vinci, Leonardo *See* LEONARDO DA VINCI

Davis, Angela (1944–) US political activist. Beginning in the 1960s, Davis was an advocate for both African-Americans' and women's CIVIL RIGHTS. In 1970 a judge was murdered with guns registered in Davis's name. Charged with conspiracy, murder and kidnapping, Davis was acquitted after a sensational trial.

Davis, Bette (1908–89) US film actress. She is remembered for her intense character portrayals in films such as *Of Human Bondage* (1934). Davis won two best actress Academy Awards – *Dangerous* (1935) and *Jezebel* (1938). Other films include *All About Eve* (1950) and *What Ever Happened to Baby Jane* (1962).

Davis, Sir Colin (1927–) English conductor. He was principal conductor of the BBC Symphony Orchestra (1967–71), and musical director at the Royal Opera House (1971–86). In 1983, Davis became chief conductor of the Bavarian Radio Symphony Orchestra.

Davis, Jefferson (1808–89) American statesman, president of the CONFEDERATE STATES during the CIVIL WAR (1861–65). Davis was elected to Congress in 1845 but resigned to fight in the MEXICAN WAR. A strong advocate for the extension of SLAVERY, he acted as senator for Mississippi (1849–51). In 1853, Franklin PIERCE made him secretary of war. In 1857, he rejoined the Senate and acted as leader of the Southern bloc. He resigned when Mississippi seceded from the Union (1861) and was soon elected leader of the Confederacy. Following Lee's surrender, Davis was captured and imprisoned (1865–67).

Davis, John (*c*.1550–1605) English navigator. He made three voyages (1585, 1586, 1587) in search of a NORTHWEST PASSAGE, in the last of which he sailed through Davis Strait into Baffin Bay. In 1592, Davis discovered the Falkland Islands. He invented a double quadrant that was used for more than a century.

Davis, Miles Dewey (1926–91) US jazz trumpeter and composer. During the 1940s he played BEBOP with Charlie PARKER. *The Birth of the Cool* (1949) marked a change of style with greater texture and restraint. In 1955, Davis formed a quintet (including the saxophonist John COLTRANE) that made such landmark recordings as *Relaxin'* (1956). *Kind of Blue* (1959) is widely regarded as the first exercise in "modal" jazz. In the late 1960s Davis pioneered a fusion of jazz and rock music. He retired from playing (1975–80) but returned with a series of pop-jazz records such as *You're Under Arrest* (1985).

Davis, Steve (1957–) English snooker player. Davis dominated snooker in the 1980s, winning the world championship six times (1981, 1983–84, 1987–89).

Davis, Stuart (1894–1964) US painter, leading US exponent of CUBISM. The greatest impact on his style was the ARMORY SHOW (1913). After a visit to Paris (1928–29), he turned toward cubism's synthetic phase, introducing natural forms arranged in flat areas of pattern in bright, contrasting colours. His later abstract style used lettering that resembled advertising slogans, such as *Owh! in San Pao* (1951).

Davitt, Michael (1846–1906) Irish nationalist. In 1870 he was sentenced to 15 years' penal servitude for smuggling arms to the FENIAN MOVEMENT. Davitt and Charles Stewart PARNELL founded (1879) the Irish Land League to organize tenant farmers against evictions and high rents. He was elected to Parliament in 1882, 1892 and 1895.

Davy, Sir Humphry (1778–1829) English chemist, a founder of ELECTROCHEMISTRY. He was invited to join the Royal Institution after discovering the anaesthetic value of nitrous oxide (laughing gas). In 1807, using the process of ELECTROLYSIS, Davy discovered potassium. In 1808, he isolated the elements sodium, barium, strontium, calcium and magnesium. His investigation into the conditions under which firedamp (methane and other gases) and air explode, led to his invention of the miner's safety lamp. He employed Michael Faraday as his assistant.

Dawes, Charles Gates (1865–1951) US statesman, vice president (1925–29). He served (1897–1902) as comptroller of the currency under President William McKINLEY. Dawes was awarded the 1925 Nobel Peace Prize for his work that produced the DAWES PLAN (1924) for stabilizing the German economy.

Dawes Plan (1924) Measure devised by a committee chaired by Charles DAWES to collect and distribute German REPARATIONS after World War 1. It established a schedule of payments and arranged for a loan of 800 million marks by US banks to stabilize the German currency.

Dawkins, Richard (1941–) English zoologist. Dawkins' first popular science book, *The Selfish Gene* (1976), examines animal behaviour in the context of EVOLUTION, proposing that genes govern behaviour in order to survive. *The Blind Watchmaker* (1986) is a good introduction to NEO-DARWINISM.

Day, Doris (1924–) US singer and actress. Her recordings, such as "Secret Love" (1954), sold millions during the 1940s and 1950s. Day's wholesome, energetic performances in films such as *Calamity Jane* (1953) and *Send Me No Flowers* (1964) won her an even greater audience. She received an Oscar nomination for *Pillow Talk* (1959).

Dayaks (Dyaks) Malayo-Polynesian-speaking indigenous peoples of Borneo and Sarawak. Groups include the Ibans (Sea Dayaks) of Sarawak and the Land Dayaks of SW Borneo. They live in wooden long-houses, cultivating rice, fishing and hunting with blowpipes.

Dayan, Moshe (1915–81) Israeli general and statesman. In World War 2, he led a Palestinian Jewish force against the Vichy French. In 1956, he led the invasion of the Sinai Peninsula and, as minister of defence, became a hero of the SIX-DAY WAR (1967). He was foreign minister (1977–79).

▶ **Davy** Perhaps best known for the invention of the miner's safety lamp (Davy lamp), Sir Humphry Davy was a significant chemist who inspired Michael Faraday. The lamp comprised a two-layer, metal-gauze chimney that ensured that any methane gas in the mine would not ignite the flame inside the lamp.

Day-Lewis, Cecil (1904–72) British poet and critic, b. Ireland. He wrote detective novels under the pseudonym Nicholas Blake. Day-Lewis is often compared to W.H. AUDEN. His best political poetry is contained in OVERTURES TO A DEATH (1938). Other work, such as *A Time to Dance* (1935) is more lyrical. He was professor of poetry at Oxford (1951–56) and Poet Laureate from 1968.

Day-Lewis, Daniel Michael (1957–) Irish actor, b. England, son of Cecil DAY-LEWIS. He first achieved recognition in *My Beautiful Laundrette* (1986). Day-Lewis won an Academy Award as best actor for *My Left Foot* (1989). Other films include *The Age of Innocence* (1993) and *In the Name of the Father* (1993).

Dayton City at the confluence of the Great Miami and Stillwater rivers, SW Ohio, USA. Settled in 1796, it is a commercial centre for the surrounding agricultural region. In 1995 the Dayton Peace Accord ended the Bosnian civil war. Pop. (1990) 182,044.

D-day (6 June 1944) Codename for the Allied invasion of Normandy during WORLD WAR 2. Commanded by General EISENHOWER, Allied forces landed on the French coast between Cherbourg and Le Havre. It was the largest amphibious operation in history, involving *c*.5,000 ships. Despite fierce resistance, bridgeheads were established by 9 June. It was the first step in the liberation of Europe.

DDT (**d**ichloro**d**iphenyl**t**richloroethane) Organic compound used as an insecticide. It acts as a contact poison, disorganizing the nervous system. Though effective against most insect pests, it proved to have long-lasting toxic effects and is now banned in many countries.

deacon (Gk. *diakonos*, helper) Ordained minister who serves as a priest's assistant in Christian churches. The institution of the diaconate can be traced to the New Testament, which describes the ordination of seven deacons (Acts 6).

deadly nightshade (belladonna) Poisonous perennial plant native to Europe and W Asia. It has large leaves, purple flowers and black berries. ALKALOIDS, such as ATROPINE, are obtained from its roots and leaves. Family Solanaceae; species *Atropa belladonna*.

Dead Sea (Al-Bahr-al-Mayyit) Salt lake in the Jordan valley, on the Jordan-Israel border. It is fed by the JORDAN River. The surface, 403m (1,320ft) below sea level, is the lowest point on Earth. It is situated in a hot, dry region. One of the world's saltiest waters, it supports no life, and much salt is commercially extracted.

Dead Sea Scrolls Ancient manuscripts discovered from 1947 in caves at Qumran near the DEAD SEA. Written in Hebrew or Aramaic, they date from between the 1st century BC and the 1st century AD. They include versions of much of the OLD TESTAMENT. Some are a thousand years older than any other biblical manuscript.

deafness Partial or total hearing loss. **Conductive** deafness is usually due to infection or inherited abnormalities of the middle ear. **Perceptive** deafness may be hereditary or due to injury or disease of the COCHLEA, auditory nerve or hearing centres in the brain. Treatment ranges from removal of wax to delicate microsurgery. Hearing aids, sign language and lip-reading are techniques that help the deaf to communicate.

Deakin, Alfred (1856–1919) Australian statesman, prime minister (1903–04, 1905–08, 1909–10). As attorney general, he helped to draft Australia's constitution. Deakin introduced the notorious White Australia Policy.

Dean, James (1931–55) US film actor. Dean played the restless son in the film of John Steinbeck's *East of Eden* (1954) and appeared as a misunderstood teenager in *Rebel Without a Cause* (1955). Dean was killed in a car crash before the release of his third and final film *Giant* (1956). He has become a cult hero.

death Cessation of life. In medicine, death has traditionally been pronounced on cessation of the heartbeat. However, modern resuscitation and life-support techniques have led to the revival of patients whose hearts have stopped. In a tiny minority of cases, while breathing and heartbeat can be maintained artificially, the potential for life is extinct. In this context, death may be pronounced when it is clear that the brain no longer controls vital functions. The issue is highly controversial.

death cap (deadly amanita) Highly poisonous FUNGUS that grows in woodland. It has a yellowish-green cap and a white stem with a drooping ring and sheathed base. If eaten, the poison causes great pain and, in most cases, death. Species *Amanita phalloides*.

death penalty *See* CAPITAL PUNISHMENT

Death Valley Desert basin in E California, USA. It has the lowest point in the Western Hemisphere, 86m (282ft) below sea level. Temperatures can reach 57°C (134°F), the highest in the USA. Length: 225km (140mi).

deathwatch beetle Small beetle that tunnels through wood. It makes a faint ticking sound once said to presage death. It is the mating signal of the female as it taps against the wood. Length: to 0.9cm (0.3in). Family Anobiidae; species *Xestobium rufovillosum*.

de Beauvoir, Simone *See* BEAUVOIR, SIMONE DE

Debrecen City in E Hungary. It was a stronghold of Protestantism in the 16th century. Louis Kossuth proclaimed Hungary's independence here in 1849. It is an important commercial and cultural centre. Industries: food processing, furniture. Pop. (1997) 210,000.

Debs, Eugene Victor (1855–1926) US labour organizer. He was a founder and first president (1893–97) of the American Railroad Union (ARU). When federal troops broke up the Pullman strike (1894), Debs was imprisoned. In 1898, he formed the Social Democratic Party and was its presidential candidate (1900, 1904, 1908, 1912). Debs was also a founder (1905) of the INDUSTRIAL WORKERS OF THE WORLD (IWW). He condemned US participation in World War 1 and was convicted (1918) under the Espionage Act. While still in prison, Debs ran for president (1920) and polled nearly one million votes.

Debussy, Claude Achille (1862–1918) French composer, exponent of IMPRESSIONISM. He wrote highly individual music that was delicate and suggestive, and explored new techniques of harmony and orchestral colour. Some critics cite his *Prélude à l'après-midi d'un faune* (1894) as the beginning of 20th-century music. Other orchestral works are *Nocturnes* (1899), *La Mer* (1905) and *Images* (1912). His piano works, such as *Suite Bergamasque* (1890) and *Etudes* (1915), are among his most important works. His one completed opera was *Pelléas and Mélisande* (1902).

Debye, Peter Joseph Wilhelm (1884–1966) US chemist, b. Netherlands. He was best known for his work on molecular structure and ionization. Debye pioneered X-RAY CRYSTALLOGRAPHY and was awarded the 1936 Nobel Prize for chemistry.

decathlon Sports event comprising ten different track and field activities: 100m, long jump, shot put, high jump, 400m, 110m hurdles, discus, pole vault, javelin and 1,500m. It has been an Olympic event since 1912.

Decatur, Stephen (1779–1820) US naval officer. In the TRIPOLITAN WAR (1801–05), Decatur's daring destruction of the captured US frigate, *Philadelphia*, earned him a captaincy. His capture of the British frigate, *Macedonian*, in the WAR OF 1812 saw him rise to commodore. Decatur was killed in a duel with James Barron.

Deccan Plateau in central India, S of the River Narmada. In attempting to conquer it in the 17th century, Aurangzeb fatally weakened the MOGUL dynasty. In the late 18th century, the British defeated the French here. On its E and W edges, the Deccan rises to the GHATS. The plateau is covered with rich volcanic soils. Cotton, cereal, coffee and tea are grown.

decibel (symbol dB) Logarithmic unit, one tenth of a bel, used for comparing two power levels and for expressing the loudness of a sound. The faintest audible sound (2×10^{-5} pascal) is given an arbitrary value of 0dB. The human pain threshold is c.120dB. Ordinary conversations occur at 50 to 60 dB.

deciduous Annual or seasonal loss of all leaves from a tree or shrub; it is the opposite of EVERGREEN.

decimal fraction Number in the DECIMAL SYSTEM (based on 10) written as a digit to the right of a decimal point. The number 52.437 represents an INTEGER (whole number, 52) added to a decimal fraction (0.437). It is composed of 52 + $(4 \times 10^{-1}) + (3 \times 10^{-2}) + (7 \times 10^{-3})$, which may also be written 52 + (4/10 + 3/100 + 7/1000), 52 + 437/1000, or 52,437/1000. Decimal fractions are added, subtracted, multiplied and divided like integers, but the decimal point must be correctly positioned after each operation.

decimal system Commonly used system of writing numbers, using a base ten and the Arabic numerals 0 to 9. It is a positional number system, each position to the left representing an extra power of ten. Thus 6,741 is (6 $\times 10^3) + (7 \times 10^2) + (4 \times 10^1) + (1 \times 10^0)$. Note that $10^0 = 1$. Decimal fractions are represented by negative powers of ten placed to the right of a decimal point.

Declaration of Independence (4 July 1776) Statement of principles in which the THIRTEEN COLONIES of North America justified the AMERICAN REVOLUTION and separation from Britain. Its blend of idealism and practical statements have ensured its place as one of the world's most important political documents. The Declaration was drafted by a committee that included Thomas JEFFERSON, and was based on the theory of NATURAL RIGHTS, propounded by John LOCKE to justify the GLORIOUS REVOLUTION in England. It was approved by the CONTINENTAL CONGRESS on 4 July. The Declaration states the necessity of government having the consent of the governed, of government's responsibility to its people, and contains the famous paragraph: "We hold these truths to be self-evident, that all men are created equal, that they are endowed by their Creator with certain unalienable Rights, that among these are Life, Liberty and the Pursuit of Happiness."

Declaration of Rights *See* BILL OF RIGHTS

Declaration of the Rights of Man and Citizen (1789) Statement of principles of the FRENCH REVOLUTION, adopted by the National Assembly, accepted by Louis XVI and included in the 1791 constitution. Influenced by the American DECLARATION OF INDEPENDENCE and the ideas of Jean Jacques ROUSSEAU, it established the sovereignty of the people and a balance of rights and responsibilities embodied in "liberty, equality and fraternity".

declination (dec. symbol δ) Angular distance of a celestial object north or south of the celestial equator. It is calculated positively from 0 to 90 (from the equator to the north celestial pole), and negatively from 0 to 90 (from the equator to the south celestial pole). *See also* CELESTIAL SPHERE

decoder In telecommunications and electronics, a device that converts the information content of a signal into a more intelligible form. In a satellite-television receiver, it decodes encrypted signals; in a colour television, it separates the red, blue and green components.

decomposition Natural degradation of organic matter into simpler substances, such as carbon dioxide and water. Organisms of decay are usually BACTERIA and FUNGI. Decomposition recycles nutrients by releasing them back into the ECOSYSTEM.

decompression sickness *See* BENDS

deconstruction In architecture, a term used to describe work dating from the early 1980s that explores ways of reconciling traditional oppositions in building design, such as structure–decoration or abstraction–figuration. Deconstruction is also a literary and philosophical term of critical analysis, pioneered by the philosopher Jacques DERRIDA. Patterns of opposition, which form a given text, are broken down and considered.

Decorated style Style of English Gothic architecture that flourished *c.*1250–1350. The most exuberant phase of English Gothic, it featured double-curving ogee arches and intricate, curvilinear window tracery. The windows of Exeter Cathedral are excellent examples of Decorated stone carving. *See also* GOTHIC ART AND ARCHITECTURE

deep scattering layer (DSL) Sound-reflecting layers in the oceans that are distinct enough at times to create a "false bottom". Various layers that can be detected during the day by sonar equipment disappear at night. Shoals of small deep-dwelling fish, crustaceans and squid that feed at the water surface at night seem to be the cause. DSLs are found usually at depths of 400 to 800m (600–1,200ft).

deep-freezing Method of FOOD PRESERVATION, usually at $-5°C$ (23°F) or below. Three methods are widely used for commercial deep freezing: in **blast** freezing, a flow of cold air is passed over the food; in **contact** freezing, the food is placed between refrigerated plates, or in a refrigerated alcohol bath; and in **vapour** freezing, liquid nitrogen or solid carbon dioxide (dry ice) is made to vapourize in the food compartment. *See also* REFRIGERATION

deer Long-legged, hoofed RUMINANT. There are 53 species in 17 genera distributed worldwide. In most species, the male (buck, hart or stag) bears ANTLERS. Only in REINDEER does the female (hind or doe) bear antlers. Deer often gather in herds. They are generally brown, with spotted young (fawns). They eat bark, shoots, twigs and grass. Humans exploit them for their meat (venison), hides and antlers (for hunting trophies). The deer family Cervidae has existed since the Oligocene epoch. The Chinese water deer is the smallest, measuring only 55cm (22in) tall at the shoulder; the ELK, at 2m (6.5ft), is the largest.

Defence, Ministry of British department of state. First formed in 1940, in 1964 it was reorganized to combine the old War Office, Admiralty and Air Ministry. It is presided over by a secretary of state and two ministers of state.

defence mechanism UNCONSCIOUS or involuntary reaction adopted by people to protect themselves from threatening and anxiety-producing mental or physical events. The term was first used by Sigmund FREUD and includes REPRESSION, PROJECTION and SUBLIMATION.

Defender of the Faith (Lat. *Fidei Defensor*) Title adopted by the monarchs of England since 1521. The title was first given to Henry VIII by Pope Leo X after the publication of a tract by Henry attacking the Protestant MARTIN LUTHER.

deflation Falling prices, accompanied by falls in output and employment. The opposite of INFLATION, it normally occurs during a RECESSION or DEPRESSION and can be measured by the price index. Excess production capacity leads to an excess of supply that usually causes deflation.

Defoe, Daniel (1660–1731) English journalist and novelist. Defoe championed William III in his first notable poem, *The True-born Englishman* (1701). A

politically controversial journalist, he was twice imprisoned, once for *The Shortest Way with the Dissenters* (1702). Defoe's enduringly popular novels include *Robinson Crusoe* (1719), *Moll Flanders* (1722), *Colonel Jack* (1722) and *Roxana* (1724). He is among the most prolific writers in the English language.

De Forest, Lee (1873–1961) US inventor. He was a pioneer in the development of RADIO communication. In 1906 he invented the audion triode valve (ELECTRON TUBE). The triode could amplify signals and became essential in radio, television, radar and computer systems. In 1947 valves were replaced by the TRANSISTOR. *See also* THERMIONICS

deforestation Clearing away of forests and their ECOSYSTEMS, usually on a large scale, by humans. There is an immediate danger that the vital topsoil will be eroded by wind (such as the DUST BOWL) or, in hilly areas, by rain. Proposals to clear whole regions of the Amazonian rainforests, which play a key role in maintaining the oxygen balance of the Earth, could, if fully implemented, cause an environmental catastrophe.

Degas, (Hilaire Germain) Edgar (1834–1917) French painter and sculptor. He studied (1854–59) Renaissance art in Italy and exhibited in the Salon (1865–70). After meeting Édouard MANET, Degas took part in exhibitions of IMPRESSIONISM. While sharing an interest in depicting scenes of everyday life, he differed from his colleagues in the stress he placed on composition, draftsmanship and the use of the studio. His favourite themes, ballet and horse racing, reveal his preoccupation with the depiction of movement. Inspired by photography and Japanese prints, Degas' paintings, such as *Foyer of the Dance* (1874), are characterized by informal poses and unusual viewpoints. For the last 20 years of his life he was almost blind and produced much freer work in glowing pastels or sculpting in wax.

De Gasperi, Alcide (1881–1954) Italian statesman, prime minister (1945–53). He was born in Trentino, then under Austrian rule. De Gasperi struggled successfully for its reunification with Italy. A staunch anti-fascist, he was imprisoned twice in the 1920s. During World War 2 he founded the Italian Christian Democratic Party. De Gasperi is regarded as the chief architect of Italy's post-war recovery.

De Gaulle, Charles André Joseph Marie (1890–1970) French general and statesman, first president (1959–69) of the Fifth Republic. In 1940 he became undersecretary of war but fled to London after the German invasion. De Gaulle organized French resistance (Free French) forces and in June 1944 was proclaimed president of the provisional French government. Following liberation he resigned, disenchanted with the political settlement. In 1958, De Gaulle emerged from retirement to deal with the war in Algeria. In 1962, he was forced to cede Algerian independence. France gained an independent nuclear capability, but alienated the UK and US by its temporary withdrawal from NATO and by blocking British entry into the EEC. In 1965, De Gaulle was re-elected, but resigned after defeat in a 1969 referendum.

degree In mathematics, unit of angular measure equal to 1/360 of a complete revolution. One degree is written 1° and can be divided into 60 parts called minutes (e.g. 20'), which may in turn be divided into 60 parts called seconds (e.g. 25"). In physics and engineering, a degree is one unit on any of various scales, such as the CELSIUS temperature scale.

De Havilland, Sir Geoffrey (1882–1965) English aircraft designer. During both World Wars his aircraft firm designed and manufactured many military aircraft, including the Tiger Moth and the Mosquito.

dehydration Removal or loss of water from a substance or tissue. Water molecules can be removed by heat, catalysts or a dehydrating agent such as concentrated sulphuric acid. Dehydration is used to preserve food. In medicine, excessive water loss is often a symptom or result of disease or injury.

Deighton, Len (Leonard Cyril) (1929–) English novelist. His spy thrillers *The Ipcress File* (1962) and *Funeral in Berlin* (1964) were made into films starring Michael Caine. Bernard Samson is the central character of the *Game, Set and Match* trilogy: *Berlin Game* (1983), *Mexico Set* (1984) and *London Match* (1986).

deism System of natural religion, first developed in England in the late 17th century. It affirmed belief in one God but held that He detached himself from the universe after its creation and made no revelation. Reason was man's only guide. Deist writings include John Toland's *Christianity not Mysterious* (1696) and Matthew Tindal's *Christianity as Old as the Creation* (1730). Deism was a great influence on the ENLIGHTENMENT. VOLTAIRE, ROUSSEAU and DIDEROT were its chief exponents.

Dekker, Thomas (*c*.1570–1632) English dramatist and pamphleteer. He collaborated with Thomas MIDDLETON (*The Honest Whore*, 1604) and John Webster (*Westward Ho*, 1604). Dekker's best-known play is the comedy *The Shoemaker's Holiday* (1599). His pamphlets include *The Seven Deadly Sins of London* (1606).

de Klerk, F.W. (Frederik Willem) (1936–) South African statesman, president (1989–94). He entered Parliament in 1972 and joined the cabinet in 1978. In 1989, De Klerk led a "palace coup" against P.W. BOTHA and became president and National Party leader. Following a narrow electoral victory, he began the process of dismantling APARTHEID. In 1990 the ban on the AFRICAN NATIONAL CONGRESS (ANC) was lifted and Nelson MANDELA was released. In 1991, the main apartheid laws were repealed and victory in a 1992 whites-only referendum marked an end to white minority rule. In 1993, de Klerk shared the Nobel Peace Prize with Nelson Mandela. Following the 1994 elections, de Klerk became deputy president in Mandela's government of national unity. In 1996, he resigned and led the Nationalists out of the coalition. In 1997, he retired as leader of the National Party.

de Kooning, Willem (1904–97) US painter, b. Netherlands. In the 1930s, he explored several different styles and in 1948 became one of the leaders of ABSTRACT EXPRESSIONISM. Unlike POLLOCK, he kept a figurative element in his work and shocked the public with violently distorted images, such as the *Women* series (1953). His emphasis on technique is known as ACTION PAINTING.

Delacroix, (Ferdinand Victor) Eugène (1798–1863) French painter, the greatest French artist of ROMANTICISM. He was heralded as the leader of the romantic movement following the exhibition of his first major painting, *The Barque of Dante* (1822). Opposed to the prevailing NEOCLASSICISM, he was inspired by history, politics, mythology and literature (especially Shakespeare and Byron). *Massacre at Chios* (1824) and *Greece Expiring on the Ruins of Missolonghi* (1827) were inspired by the Greek War of Independence. A visit to Morocco (1832) inspired sketches that developed into paintings, such as *Women of Algiers* (1834). In the 1830s, Delacroix's work underwent a major change as he began to exploit divisionism. From 1833, he worked on decorations for civic buildings, such as the Louvre. His portraits of contemporaries include *Paganini* (1832) and *Chopin and George Sand* (1838).

de la Mare, Walter (1873–1956) English poet, writer and anthologist. His technically accomplished collections of poems include *Songs of Childhood* (1902), *Winged Chariot* (1951) and the anthology *Come Hither* (1923). His prose includes the novel, *Memoirs of a Midget* (1921).

Delaunay, Robert (1885–1941) French painter, cofounder (with his wife Sonia DELAUNAY-TERK) of ORPHISM. Delaunay was an influence on the BLAUE REITER group. Many of his works are abstract cityscapes. The Eiffel Tower series is his most famous.

Delaunay-Terk, Sonia (1885–1979) French painter, b. Russia. Co-founder (with her husband Robert DELAUNAY) of ORPHISM. Among her most notable works are the lyrical *Simultaneous Contrasts* (1912) and delightful abstract illustrations for the *Prose du Trans-Sibérien*.

Delaware Confederation of Algonquian-speaking NATIVE AMERICANS. They occupied land from Long Island, New York, to Pennsylvania and Delaware. Pressured by settlers and the IROQUOIS CONFEDERACY, the Delaware migrated to Ohio in the 18th century. They lost these lands by a treaty of 1795 and became scattered.

Delaware State in E USA, on the Atlantic coast, occupying a peninsula between Chesapeake and Delaware bays. The capital is DOVER, the largest city is WILMINGTON. Discovered by Henry Hudson in 1609, it was named after the British governor of Virginia, Baron de la Warr. Delaware was settled by Swedes in 1638. The Dutch, under Peter Stuyvesant, conquered the territory by 1655. It was under English control from 1664 to 1776. One of the original THIRTEEN COLONIES, it was the first to ratify the Articles of Confederation (1789). Despite being a slave state, it remained in the Union during the American Civil War. It is the second-smallest state (after Rhode Island), and most of its land is coastal plain. The Delaware River, an important shipping route, forms part of the E boundary. Industries: chemicals, rubber, plastics. Agriculture: cereal crops, soya, dairy produce. Area: 5,328sq km (2,057sq mi). Pop. (2000) 783,600.

Delaware River in NE USA. The Delaware rises in the Catskill Mountains, SE New York and flows along the New York–Pennsylvania and Pennsylvania–New Jersey borders. The Delaware becomes navigable at Trenton, New Jersey. It is second only to the Mississippi River in annual freight tonnage carried. Length: 450km (280mi).

Delft City in South Holland province, SW Netherlands. Founded in the 11th century, it was an important commercial centre until the 17th century. Industries: Delftware pottery, ceramics, china. Pop. (1994) 91,941.

Delhi Union territory and city on the River Yamuna, N central India. Strategically placed midway between the Ganges and Indus valleys, the city has been of strategic importance for more than 2,000 years. The union territory consists of NEW DELHI, the capital of India since 1912, and Old Delhi, whose walls were built (1638) by SHAH JAHAN. With the construction of the Red Fort imperial palace, Delhi became capital of the MOGUL EMPIRE. Shah Jahan also built the Jami Masjid. Other sites include Rajghat (a shrine where Gandhi was cremated). Industries: cotton textiles, handicrafts. Pop. (1991) 7,206,704.

Delhi Sultanate (1206–1526) Succession of ruling Muslim dynasties in India. In 1192 Muhammad of Ghor captured DELHI from the Hindus led by Prithvi Raj. In 1206, Qutb ud-Din proclaimed himself sultan of Delhi and established the so-called Slave dynasty. His successor, Iltutmish, made Delhi his permanent capital. In 1290, the Khaji dynasty came to power. By 1320, in the reign of Ala ud-Din Khaji, the sultanate's power extended as far as S India. In 1398, the empire fell to TAMERLANE.

Delian League Confederation of Greek city-states formed (478 BC) under Athenian leadership after the losses of the PERSIAN WARS. The treasury was initially held on the island of Delos, but was moved to Athens by PERICLES. It was disbanded after the PELOPONNESIAN WARS.

Delibes, (Clément Philibert) Léo (1836–91) French composer. He was famous for his ballet music, especially *Coppélia* (1870), and also wrote several operas, such as *Lakmé* (1883), and sacred and secular choral works.

Delilah Philistine woman in the Old Testament (Judges 16). The mistress of SAMSON, she betrayed him to the Philistines by cutting his hair, the source of his strength, while he slept.

delirium State of confusion in which a person becomes agitated, incoherent and loses touch with reality; often associated with DELUSIONS or HALLUCINATIONS. It may be seen in various disorders, brain disease, fever and drug or alcohol intoxication.

Delius, Frederick (1862–1934) English composer. He combined ROMANTICISM with IMPRESSIONISM, most notably in orchestral pieces, such as *Brigg Fair* (1907) and *On Hearing the First Cuckoo in Spring* (1912). His love of nature is evident in the operas, *A Village Romeo and Juliet* (1901) and *Fennimore and Gerda* (1910).

DeLillo, Don (1936–) US novelist. A leading figure in POST-MODERNISM, his complex works examine the state of contemporary American society. Novels include *White Noise* (1986), *Libra* (1988) and *Underworld* (1997).

De Long, George Washington (1844–81) US naval officer and Arctic explorer. He set sail in 1879, but his ship was caught in polar ice and drifted until 1881 when it was crushed. De Long was one of 14 survivors to reach Siberia, only to die of cold and starvation.

Delphi Ancient city state in Greece, near Mount Parnassus. The presence of the ORACLE of APOLLO made it a sacred city. The Pythian Games were held at Delphi every four years. The Temple of Apollo was sacked in Roman times, and the oracle closed (AD 390) with the spread of Christianity.

delphinium (larkspur) Any of *c*.250 species of herbaceous plants native to temperate areas, with spirally arranged leaves and loose clusters of flowers. Petals form a tubular spur. Garden delphiniums are varieties of *Delphinium elatum*. Family Ranunculaceae.

delta Fan-shaped body of ALLUVIUM deposited at the mouth of a river. It is formed when a river deposits sediment as its speed decreases while it enters the sea. Most deltas are fertile areas but subject to frequent flooding.

delusion False or irrational belief based upon a misinterpretation of reality. Mild delusions are quite common, but fixed delusions can be a symptom of PARANOIA.

Delvaux, Paul (1897–1994) Belgian painter, one of the most distinctive surrealists. His characteristic themes were skeletons and an idealized type of female figure, portrayed nude or half-clothed in unlikely settings. Delvaux's paintings are dream-like and convey a strong sense of eroticism. *See also* SURREALISM

dementia Deterioration of personality and intellect that can result from disease of, or damage to, the BRAIN. It is characterized by memory loss, impaired mental processes, personality change, confusion, lack of inhibition and poor personal hygiene. Dementia is more common in the elderly. *See also* ALZHEIMER'S DISEASE

Demeter In GREEK MYTHOLOGY, the goddess of nature, sister of ZEUS and mother of PERSEPHONE.

De Mille, Agnes (1906–93) US dancer and choreographer. Her choreography for the Broadway musical *Oklahoma* (1943) rendered dance integral to the plot

and turned it into a serious art form. Other musicals include *Carousel* (1945), *Brigadoon* (1947), *Gentlemen Prefer Blondes* (1949), *Paint Your Wagon* (1951) and *Come Summer* (1969). De Mille also created ballets, such as *Rodeo* (1942) and *Fall River Legend* (1948).

De Mille, Cecil B. (Blount) (1881–1959) US film producer and director. His debut film, *The Squaw Man* (1913), established Hollywood as the world's film production capital. Many of his films deal with biblical themes, such as *The Ten Commandments* (1923, 1956) and *King of Kings* (1927). Other films include *Union Pacific* (1939) and *The Greatest Show on Earth* (1952).

Demirel, Süleyman (1924–) Turkish statesman, prime minister (1965–71, 1975–77, 1979–80, 1991–93) and president (1993–2000). In 1964 he became leader of the Justice Party. Demirel was ousted by military coups in 1971 and 1980. He led the Truth Path Party (1987–93). In 2000 presidential elections, Demirel was succeeded by Ahmet Necdet Sezer.

democracy (Gk. *demos kratia*, people authority) Rule of the people, as opposed to rule by one (autocracy) or a few (oligarchy). Ancient GREECE is regarded as the birthplace of democracy, in particular ATHENS (5th century BC). Small Greek city-states enabled direct political participation but only among its citizens (a small political elite). As societies grew, more refined systems were needed. In a FEUDAL SYSTEM, the king selected tenants-in-chief to provide counsel. In late 13th-century England, a PARLIAMENT evolved but remained answerable to the monarchy. The Roundheads' victory in the English CIVIL WAR was a victory for parliamentary sovereignty. A fundamental shift in emphasis was the transition from natural law to NATURAL RIGHTS, as expounded by John LOCKE: in addition to responsibility (to crown or church), people possessed inalienable rights. ROUSSEAU developed these notions into the SOCIAL CONTRACT, which influenced the FRENCH and AMERICAN REVOLUTIONS: government was limited by law from impinging on individual freedoms. During the 19th century the FRANCHISE was extended. In the 20th century democratic representation has been a matter of debate and sometimes bloody dispute. Common to modern liberal democracy is the principle of free multi-party elections with universal adult suffrage.

Democratic Party US political party, descendant of the Anti-Federalist Party and Thomas JEFFERSON's Democratic-Republican Party. It became the Democratic Party during the presidency (1829–37) of Andrew JACKSON, and remained the dominant force in US politics until Abraham LINCOLN's victory over James BUCHANAN in 1861. The party was split by the American CIVIL WAR (1861–65), with support mainly restricted to the South and West. Despite the presidencies of Grover CLEVELAND and Woodrow WILSON, it was not until the advent of Franklin D. ROOSEVELT's "New Deal" that it was once more regarded as a progressive force. Roosevelt was succeeded by Harry S. TRUMAN. Democratic presidents were in office from 1961 to 1969 (John F. KENNEDY, Lyndon B. JOHNSON), a period marked by progressive economic and social policy, such as the passing of CIVIL RIGHTS legislation. In the 1970s and 1980s, only Jimmy CARTER (1977–81) held the presidency. The REPUBLICAN PARTY dominated until Bill CLINTON (1992–2000) recaptured the centre ground but, returned to power in 2000 with the election of George W. BUSH.

Democritus (460–370 BC) Greek philosopher and scientist. Democritus contributed to the theory of ATOMISM, propounded by his teacher Leucippus, by suggesting that all matter consisted of tiny, indivisible particles.

demography Term introduced (1855) by Achille Guillard for the scientific study of human populations and their changes, movements, size, distribution and structure. The primary sources of data are the census and vital statistics. Demographic methods are used for gauging and anticipating public needs.

De Morgan, Augustus (1806–71) British mathematician and logician, b. India. In 1828 he became the first professor of mathematics at University College, London. De Morgan contributed to the development of SET THEORY and worked with George BOOLE on the creation of symbolic LOGIC. *See also* ALGEBRA

Demosthenes (383–322 BC) Athenian orator and statesman. In 351 BC he delivered the first of his famous *Philippics*, urging the Greeks to unite and resist PHILIP II of Macedon. The Greeks were defeated at the Battle of Chaeronea (338 BC) and Demosthenes was put on trial. His defence, "On the Crown", is a masterpiece of political oratory. Demosthenes committed suicide after the failure of the Athenian revolt against Macedon.

Dempsey, Jack (1895–1983) US heavyweight boxer. Nicknamed the "Manassa Mauler", Dempsey was the first boxer to generate a $1 million gate. He became world champion after knocking out Jess Willard (1919). Dempsey lost the title to Gene Tunney (1926) on points. In the "Battle of the Long Count" rematch (1927), Dempsey floored Tunney but failed to return to a neutral corner, thus delaying the referee's count. Tunney went on to win.

Dench, Dame Judi (Judith) Olivia (1934–) English actress. Dench began her career with the Old Vic (1957–61) before joining the Royal Shakespeare Company (RSC). Her films include *84 Charing Cross Road* (1986), *A Handful of Dust* (1987) and *Mrs Brown* (1997).

dendrochronology Means of estimating time by the growth rings in trees. Chronology based on the bristlecone pine extends back more than 7,000 years.

Deneb (Alpha Cygni) White supergiant star in the constellation of Cygnus. It is 60,000 times more luminous than the Sun and located *c.*1,500 light-years away.

Deneuve, Catherine (1943–) French actress. Her beauty and nonchalant elegance were established in Roman POLANSKI's psychological horror film *Repulsion* (1965) and Luis BUÑUEL's *Belle de Jour* (1967). Deneuve received an Oscar nomination for *Indochine* (1992).

dengue Infectious virus disease transmitted by the *Aedes aegypti* MOSQUITO. Occurring in the tropics and some temperate areas, it produces fever, headache and fatigue, followed by severe joint pains, aching muscles, swollen glands and a reddish rash. Recovery usually follows, but relapses are common.

Deng Xiaoping (1904–97) Chinese statesman. He took part in the LONG MARCH, served in the Red Army. In 1945, he became a member of the central committee of the Chinese COMMUNIST PARTY. After the establishment of the People's Republic (1949), he held several important posts, becoming general secretary of the party in 1956. During the CULTURAL REVOLUTION, he was denounced for capitalist tendencies and dismissed. Deng returned to government in 1973, was purged by the GANG OF FOUR in 1976, but reinstated in 1977. Within three years he had become the paramount leader of party and government. Deng introduced rapid economic modernization, encouraging foreign investment, but without social and political liberalization. He officially retired in 1987 but was still in control at the time of the TIANANMEN SQUARE massacre (1989).

De Niro, Robert (1943–) US film actor. A powerful presence, he first gained critical acclaim in Martin SCORSESE's *Mean Streets* (1973). De Niro won an Academy Award as best supporting actor for *The Godfather, Part II* (1974). After a powerful performance in *Taxi Driver* (1976), he was nominated for an Oscar in *The Deer Hunter* (1978). De Niro won a best actor Academy Award for *Raging Bull* (1981). His first film as director was *A Bronx Tale* (1993).

Denmark Kingdom in W Europe. Denmark is the smallest country in Scandinavia. It consists of a peninsula, Jutland, and more than 400 islands, 89 of which are inhabited. The capital, COPENHAGEN, lies on Sjaelland (the largest island). It faces Sweden across The Sound, a narrow strait that leads from the Baltic Sea to the Kattegat and the North Sea. ODENSE lies on the island of Fyn. To the NW of Denmark lie the self-governing Danish dependencies of GREENLAND and the FARÖE ISLANDS. The granite island of Bornholm, off the S tip of Sweden, is a separate administrative region. Denmark is flat: the highest point is only 171m (561ft) above sea level. **Climate and vegetation** Denmark has a cool but pleasant climate due to North Atlantic Drift. In cold winter spells, The Sound may freeze over. Summers are warm and rainfall occurs throughout the year. The wettest seasons are summer and autumn. Much of Denmark is a patchwork of green fields, lakes and sandy beaches. **History and Politics** By *c.*2000 BC, the Danes had developed an advanced Bronze Age culture. Between the 9th and 11th centuries VIKINGS terrorized much of W Europe. In the 11th century, King CANUTE ruled over Denmark, Norway and England. In 1397, Queen Margaret unified the crowns of Denmark, Sweden and Norway. Sweden broke away in 1523, while Norway was lost to Sweden in 1814. Denmark adopted LUTHERANISM as the national religion in the 1530s, and Danish culture flourished in the 16th and early 17th centuries. CHRISTIAN IV led Denmark into costly wars with Sweden, and the THIRTY YEARS' WAR (1618–48) weakened the Danish aristocracy. Serfdom was abolished in 1788. In 1866, SCHLESWIG-HOLSTEIN was lost to Prussia. The Social Democratic Party dominated 20th-century Danish politics. Denmark remained neutral in World War 1. In 1918, ICELAND became self-governing. During the 1920s, Denmark adopted progressive social welfare policies. In 1940, Germany occupied Denmark. Many Jews escaped to Sweden. In 1943, CHRISTIAN X was arrested and martial law declared. In 1945, Denmark was liberated by British forces. Denmark played an important part in European reconstruction. In 1949, it relinquished its neutrality and joined the North Atlantic Treaty Organization (NATO). In 1973, Denmark became the first Scandinavian member of the European Economic Community (EEC). In 1992, Denmark rejected the MAASTRICHT TREATY, but reversed the decision in a second referendum (1993). In 1998, the Amsterdam Treaty was ratified by a further referendum. **Economy** Danes enjoy a high standard of living (1995 GDP per capita, US$21,230). In the 1980s and 1990s, the Danish economy suffered from high unemployment and foreign debt. Other problems include pollution and the high cost of welfare provision. Despite being self-sufficient in oil and natural gas, Denmark has few natural resources. Manufacturing employs 27% of the workforce. Products include furniture, electrical goods and textiles. Services, including tourism, form the largest

DENMARK
AREA: 43,070sq km (16,629sq mi)
POPULATION: 5,153,000
CAPITAL (POPULATION): Copenhagen (620,970)

sector, accounting for 63% of GDP. Farms cover c.75% of the land. Farming employs only 4% of the workforce but is highly productive. Fishing is also important.

density Ratio of mass to volume for a given substance, usually expressed in SI units as kg/m³. It is an indication of the concentration of particles within a material. The density of a solid or liquid changes little over a wide range of temperatures and pressures. **Relative density** (r.d.), or specific gravity (s.g.), is the ratio of the density of one substance to that of a reference substance (usually water) at the same temperature and pressure. The density of a gas depends on both pressure and temperature.

dentistry Profession concerned with the care and treatment of the mouth, particularly the TEETH and their supporting tissues. Dentistry includes specialities such as **oral surgery** (repair of injury to the jaw and tooth extraction), **orthodontics** (correction of malpositioned teeth) and **periodontics** (care of the gums and tissues supporting teeth). The most common disorder is gum disease, promoted by the build-up of PLAQUE. Dentistry was studied in China from 620 and toothbrushes have been found from the 10th century. The first dental school was established in Philadelphia, USA, in 1840. The Royal Dental Hospital, London, was founded in 1858.

dentition Type, number and arrangement of TEETH. An adult human has 32 teeth. In each jaw are four **incisors**, two **canines**, four **premolars**, four **molars** and, in most adults, up to four **wisdom** teeth. Children lack the premolars and four molars. The incisors are used for cutting; the canines for gripping and tearing; and the molars and premolars for crushing and grinding food. The dental formula is written: $\frac{2}{2}\frac{1}{1}\frac{2}{2}\frac{3}{3}$. A herbivore has relatively unspecialized teeth that grow throughout life to compensate for wear. A carnivore has a range of specialized teeth related to killing, gripping and crushing bones. In carnivores, unspecialized unspecialized milk teeth are replaced by specialized adult teeth, which have to last a lifetime.

denudation In geology, wearing away of land by WEATHERING and EROSION, and the transportation of material. Together with DEPOSITION, denudation is the major process which creates the Earth's landscape.

Denver Capital and largest city of Colorado, USA, at the foot of the Rocky Mountains. At an altitude of 1,608m (5,280ft), it is nicknamed the "Mile High City". Founded in 1860, it became state capital in 1867. Its prosperity was boosted with the discovery of gold and silver. After World War 2, Denver's dramatic growth and high altitude led to serious pollution problems. During the 1970s, exploitation of oil deposits created further growth. Denver is the site of many government agencies, including a US mint. Sites include the Denver Art Museum, the Boettcher Botanical Gardens and a university (1864). It has the world's largest airport in area, Denver International, and its proximity to the Rockies and the ski resort of Aspen make it a major tourist centre. Denver has many aerospace and electronics industries. Pop. (1990) 467,610.

deoxyribonucleic acid See DNA

Depardieu, Gérard (1948–) French film actor. Burly and charismatic, he was France's leading actor in the 1980s. He is equally adroit playing an historical figure, such as *Danton* (1982), or a hunchback tax-collector in *Jean de Florette* (1986). *Green Card* (1990) was his first major English-speaking role. His performance as *Cyrano de Bergerac* (1990) was definitive. He made his directorial debut with *Tartuffe* (1984). Other films include *Trop Belle pour Toi* (1989) and *Germinal* (1993).

Depp, Johnny (1964–) US film actor. After bit parts in major films such as *Nightmare on Elm Street* (1984),

his big break was the title role in *Edward Scissorhands* (1990). A reputation for quirky comedy performances was enhanced by *Benny and Joon* (1993), *What's Eating Gilbert Grape* (1993) and *Ed Wood* (1994). Other films include *Sleepy Hollow* (1999).

deposition In geology, laying down of material which has been removed by DENUDATION. Most of the material will be sediment and therefore a possible source of SEDIMENTARY ROCKS when consolidated. Much of the material will eventually be dumped on the seabed by rivers. However, there will be some deposition on land – for example, SILT on flood plains, TILL deposited by ice and LOESS deposited by wind. Together with denudation, deposition is the major process which creates the Earth's landscape.

depreciation Decline in the value of an ASSET over the asset's economic life. It includes the decrease in value or usefulness because of wear and tear, obsolescence or fall in market prices, but does not cover unexpected losses due to accident or natural disaster.

depression In economics, a period of economic hardship, more severe than a RECESSION. It is usually measured by a fall in output and a rise in unemployment. The most severe and widespread was the GREAT DEPRESSION of the 1930s.

depression In meteorology, a region of low atmospheric pressure with the lowest pressure at the centre. It usually brings unsettled or stormy weather. *See also* CYCLONE

depression In psychiatry, disorder characterized by feelings of guilt, failure or worthlessness. Often stress-related, depression leads to low self-esteem, self-recrimination and obsessive thoughts. Insomnia, loss of appetite and lethargy can be present; in severe cases there is a risk of suicide. *See also* MANIC DEPRESSION.

De Quincey, Thomas (1785–1859) English essayist and critic. He was an associate of WORDSWORTH and COLERIDGE, whom he memorialized in *Recollections of the Lakes and the Lake Poets* (1834–39). De Quincey is best known for his *Confessions of an English Opium Eater* (1822).

Derain, André (1880–1954) French painter, sculptor and printmaker. He was an early exponent of FAUVISM, such as his portrait of MATISSE (1905). Derain's use of bold brush-strokes and bright colours is epitomised in Mountains at Collioure (1905). After 1906 he turned towards CUBISM and more architectural forms. From c.1920 he concentrated on pastiches of the Old Masters.

Derby, Edward George Geoffrey Smith Stanley, 14th Earl of (1799–1869) British statesman, prime minister (1852, 1858–59, 1866–68). He entered Parliament as a WHIG in 1827 and acted as chief secretary for Ireland (1830–33). He resigned shortly after becoming colonial secretary (1833) and joined the CONSERVATIVE PARTY. He was colonial secretary (1841–45) under Robert PEEL but resigned over the repeal of the CORN LAWS. From 1846 to 1868 Derby led the Tory protectionists, briefly heading two administrations. In 1866 he became prime minister for the last time and introduced the REFORM ACT (1867). Derby was succeeded by Benjamin DISRAELI.

Derby City and county district on the River Derwent, Derbyshire, central England. Industries: railroad and aerospace engineering, textiles and ceramics (Derby ware china). Pop. (1994) 232,000.

Derbyshire County in N central England; the county town is DERBY, other major towns are Chesterfield and Alfreton. Low-lying in the S, it rises to the PEAK DISTRICT in the N, and is drained by the River Trent and its tributaries, the Dove, Derwent and Wye. Agriculture is important, such as dairy farming, wheat and oats. There are coal deposits in the E. Industries: steel, textiles. Area: 2,631sq km (1,016sq mi). Pop. 887,600.

derivative Rate of change of the value of a mathematical FUNCTION with respect to a change in the independent VARIABLE. The derivative is an expression of the instantaneous rate of change of the function's value: in general it is itself a function of the variable. An example is obtaining the velocity and acceleration of an object that moves distance x in time t according to the equation $x = at^n$. The velocity increases with time. The expression dx/dt, called the first derivative of distance with respect to time, is equal to the velocity of the object; in this example it equals nat$^{(n-1)}$. The result is obtained by DIFFERENTIAL CALCULUS. In this example, the second derivative, written d^{2}x/dt^2, is equal to the acceleration.

dermatitis Inflammation of the skin. In acute form it produces itching and blisters. In chronic form it causes thickening, scaling and darkening of the skin. *See also* ECZEMA

dermis Thick inner layer of the SKIN, which lies beneath the EPIDERMIS. It consists mainly of loose CONNECTIVE TISSUE, richly supplied with BLOOD and lymph vessels, nerve endings, sensory organs and sweat glands.

Derrida, Jacques (1930–) French philosopher, b. Algeria. Drawing on the work of STRUCTURALISM, Derrida proposed a philosophy of DECONSTRUCTION. He argued that Western philosophy is based on a series of metaphysical binary oppositions, such as speech/text, which privilege one term over another, in this instance speech. Derrida revealed the limits or margins of these oppositions and sought to **defer** assimilation (*différance*) through an appeal to intertextuality, multiple meanings and the free play of language. His work proved most influential in the field of literary theory. Writings include *Writing and Difference* (1967) and *Margins of Philosophy* (1972).

Derry City and administrative district on the River Foyle near Lough Foyle, NW Northern Ireland. In AD 546, St Columba founded a monastery here. In 1600, English forces seized the city, and in 1613, James I granted Derry to the citizens of London. It was renamed **Londonderry**, a new city was laid out and Protestant colonization began. In 1688–89 James II unsuccessfully besieged the city. In recent years the city has been plagued by sectarian violence. In 1984 its name reverted to Derry. Industries: clothing manufacture. Area: 347sq km (149sq mi). Pop. (1991) 95,371.

dervish Member of a Muslim fraternity. Communities arose within SUFISM and by the 12th century had established themselves in the Middle East. The chief devotion of dervishes is *dhikr* (remembering of God). Its encouragement of emotional display and hypnotic trances has earned dervishes the epithet "whirling".

Desai, Morarji Ranchhodji (1896–1995) Indian statesman, prime minister (1977–79). He was an early supporter of "Mahatma" GANDHI. Desai was defeated by Indira GANDHI in the contest for leadership of the CONGRESS PARTY. He was detained (1975–77) during the state of emergency. In 1977, Desai became leader of the newly formed opposition party, Janata Dal. As prime minister, he restored democratic government to India.

desalination Extraction of pure water from water containing dissolved salts, usually seawater. The commonest and oldest method is DISTILLATION. Another method is to freeze the salt solution; salt is excluded from the ice crystals which can then be melted.

Descartes, René (1596–1650) French philosopher and mathematician. Descartes is often regarded as the father of modern philosophy. His philosophical principles are outlined in *Discourse on Method* (1637), *Meditations on the First Philosophy* (1641) and *Principles of Philosophy* (1644). His methods of deduction and intuition inform modern metaphysics. He reached one indubitable proposition: "I am thinking", and from this he concluded that he existed: *cogito ergo sum* (I think, therefore I am). Descartes also founded analytic geometry, introduced the CARTESIAN COORDINATE SYSTEM, and helped establish the science of optics.

desert Arid region of the Earth, at any latitude, characterized by scant, intermittent rainfall of less than 25cm (10in) per year, and little or no vegetation. Regions with 25 to 50cm (10–20in) of rainfall are semi-deserts. Cold deserts, areas almost permanently covered with snow or ice, extend over one-sixth of the Earth's surface, and hot deserts over one-fifth. Most desert regions lie in the horse latitudes between 20° and 30° N and S of the Equator. These include the Australian, KALAHARI and SAHARA (the world's largest desert). Deserts, such as the ATACAMA and NAMIB, occur in W coastal regions where offshore currents make the land exceptionally dry. There are also deserts in the middle of the largest continents where no onshore winds can reach to bring rain, such as the GOBI and MOJAVE deserts and DEATH VALLEY. *See also* TUNDRA

desertification Process by which a DESERT gradually spreads into neighbouring areas of semi-desert. It may result from a natural event, such as fire or climatic change, but occurs most frequently as a result of overgrazing, overpopulation and deforestation. *See also* SAHEL

De Sica, Vittorio (1901–74) Italian film director and actor. He is noted for his use of amateur actors in realistic dramas. Working with Cesare Zavattini, he made a significant contribution to Italian NEO-REALISM with films such as *Shoeshine* (1946) and *Bicycle Thieves* (1948). Other films include *Umberto D* (1952), *Two Women* (1961) and *A Brief Vacation* (1975).

desktop publishing (DTP) Use of a COMPUTER to prepare text and pictures for publication. The technique uses computer PROGRAMS, such as QuarkXpress, that display documents on the computer screen. The operator can control the type font, size, line length and column organization of text, and incorporate scanned images if necessary. The result can be output in forms ready for conventional PRINTING and PUBLISHING.

Des Moines Capital and largest city of Iowa, USA, near the confluence of the Des Moines and Raccoon rivers. Founded in 1843, it is an industrial and transport centre for the Corn Belt. Flooded in 1954, the city is protected by dams and reservoirs. Industries: mechanical and aerospace engineering. Pop. (1990) 193,187.

Desmoulins, Camille (1760–94) French revolutionary. His pamphlets, such as *Révolutions de France et de Brabant* (1789), were widely read, and he was responsible for inciting the mob to attack the BASTILLE on 12 July 1789, precipitating the FRENCH REVOLUTION. Initially Desmoulins attacked the Girondins, but later (with DANTON) urged moderation. He was arrested and guillotined.

De Soto, Hernando (1500–42) Spanish explorer. After taking part in the conquest of the Inca under Francisco PIZARRO, he was appointed governor of Cuba (1537) with permission to conquer the North American mainland. His expedition landed in Florida (1539) and advanced as far north as the Carolinas and as west as the Mississippi. The ruthless search for non-existent treasure and extreme brutality toward the native inhabitants led to a costly battle at Maubilia (1540). De Soto died after returning to Mississippi; the survivors eventually reached Mexico (1543).

Des Prés, Josquin *See* JOSQUIN DESPREZ

Dessalines, Jean Jacques (1758–1806) Haitian ruler. In 1802, he succeeded TOUSSAINT L'OUVERTURE as leader of the revolution. Having driven out the French, he declared independence in 1804, changing the country's name from St Domingue to Haiti. As Emperor Jacques, he ruled despotically and was assassinated.

destroyer Warship, smaller than a CRUISER, usually equipped with guns, torpedoes, depth charges and missiles. It evolved from torpedo boats in the British Royal Navy in the 1890s and played a major role in both world wars convoying Allied merchant ships. The first nuclear-powered destroyer was built by the US in 1962.

detective fiction Literary form in which a crime is solved by a detective (usually amateur). The greatest exponents of the genre include Edgar Allan POE, Wilkie COLLINS, Arthur Conan DOYLE, G.K. CHESTERTON, Agatha CHRISTIE, Raymond CHANDLER and Dorothy L. SAYERS.

détente Term in international relations for the reduction of tension between states. It chiefly refers to the efforts of the USA, the Soviet Union and their respective allies to end the COLD WAR and to establish closer links of mutual understanding. Détente was marked by a series of ARMS-CONTROL agreements and confidence-building measures, such as the STRATEGIC ARMS LIMITATION TREATY (SALT) signed in 1974. *See also* DISARMAMENT

detergent Synthetic chemical cleansing substance. The most common type is alkyl sulphonate. Detergents have molecules that possess a long hydrocarbon chain attached to an ionized group. This chain attaches to grease, while the ionized group has an affinity for water (so the grease is washed away with the water).

determinism Philosophical thesis that every event is the result of its causes. Nothing is accidental. It usually involves the denial of FREE WILL, though Thomas HOBBES and David HUME struggled to reconcile the two ideas. CALVIN's PREDESTINATION is a form of determinism.

Detroit City on the Detroit River, SE Michigan, USA. Founded (1710) as a French trading post, it was captured by the British in 1760, who used it as a base during the American Revolution. Britain took it again in the WAR OF 1812, but US forces regained it in 1813. The largest city in Michigan, Detroit is a GREAT LAKES centre and headquarters of General Motors, Chrysler and Ford. Industries: motor vehicles, steel. Pop. (1990) 1,027,974.

deuterium ISOTOPE (D or H^2) of hydrogen whose nuclei contain a neutron in addition to a proton. Deuterium occurs in water as D_2O (heavy water), from which it is obtained by ELECTROLYSIS. Heavy water is used as a moderator in some FISSION reactors. At. no. 2; r.a.m. 2.0144.

Deuteronomy Biblical book, fifth and last of the PENTATEUCH or TORAH. It contains three discourses ascribed to MOSES, which frame a code of civil and religious laws. The book was probably written long after Moses.

De Valera, Eamon (1882–1975) Irish statesman, prime minister (1932–48, 1951–54, 1957–59). He was active in the Irish independence movement and after the Easter Rising (1916) was elected president of SINN FÉIN while imprisoned in England. In 1924, De Valera founded FIANNA FÁIL. He defeated Cosgrave in 1932. In 1959, De Valera became president of the republic. He retired in 1973.

devaluation Lowering the value of one nation's currency with respect to that of another or to gold. The decision to devalue is made by a central government usually when the nation is having BALANCE OF PAYMENTS problems. Devaluation stimulates the economy by reducing the foreign currency price of exports.

developing countries *See* LESS DEVELOPED COUNTRIES (LDCs)

developmental psychology Study of behaviour through all life stages, from foetus to old age. Psychologists study normal growth, change and self-actualization.

devil Evil spirit considered in many religions to be the arch-enemy of the Supreme Being. In Christianity, the Devil is the chief of the fallen angels cast out of heaven for their sins. The devil was named as SATAN, BEELZEBUB or the Prince of Darkness. The biblical account of Christ's temptation in the desert leads to the perception of the Devil as the tempter of men's souls. In Islam, Iblis is the name of the devil figure, the supreme tempter.

Devil's Island (Île du Diable) Smallest and southernmost of the Îles du Salut in the Caribbean Sea, off the coast of French Guiana. It was a French penal colony from 1852 to 1938.

Devine, George (1910–65) English theatre manager, director and actor. He founded the London Theatre Studio. Devine taught (1947–52) at the Old Vic and was director (1952–56) of the Young Vic. As artistic director (1956–65) of the English Stage Company at the Royal Court Theatre, London, he promoted many new writers.

devolution Delegation of authority and political power from a central legislature to a regional government. Central government retains overall constitutional control. In the UK, central government has devolved power to Scotland, Wales and Northern Ireland with the establishment of separate parliaments. The Scottish parliament has tax-varying powers.

Devolution, War of (1667–68) Conflict over the Spanish Netherlands. LOUIS XIV of France claimed that the disputed territories had devolved on him through his wife Maria Theresa, daughter of PHILIP IV of Spain. the French army overran Flanders, prompting the United Provinces, England and Sweden to form the TRIPLE ALLIANCE (1668). Peace was made at Aix-la-Chapelle.

Devon County in SW England, bounded by the English Channel (S) and the Bristol Channel (N); the county town is EXETER. During the Middle Ages, tin mining was a major industry. Devon is a hilly region that includes Dartmoor and Exmoor. Industries: tourism, fishing, dairy products, textiles. Area: 6,711sq km (2,591sq mi). Pop. (1991) 1,009,950.

Devonian Fourth-oldest period of the PALAEOZOIC era, lasting from 408 to 360 million years ago. Many marine and freshwater remains include jawless fishes and forerunners of today's bony and cartilaginous fishes. The first known land vertebrate, the amphibian *Ichthyostega*, appeared at this time. Land animals included scorpions, mites, spiders and the first insects. Land plants included CLUB MOSS and FERNS.

De Vries, Hugo (1848–1935) Dutch botanist. His experimental methods led to the rediscovery (1900) of MENDEL's laws of HEREDITY and the development of a theory of MUTATION. De Vries argued that GENETIC mutation was the chief engine of EVOLUTION.

dew Water droplets formed, usually at night, by condensation on vegetation and other surfaces near the ground.

Dewar, Donald (1937–2000) Scottish statesman, first minister of the Scottish Parliament (1999–2000). A committed socialist, Dewar was Labour MP for South Aberdeen (1966–70) and Glasgow (1978–97, 1997–2000), before being appointed secretary of state for Scotland (1997–2000). He drafted the Scotland Bill that laid the foundations for the new Scottish Parliament, thus realising his dream of self-rule for Scotland. As first minister, he presided over the turbulent inception of the new Parliament. He was succeeded by Harry McLeish.

Dewar, Sir James (1842–1923) Scottish chemist and physicist. He is chiefly remembered for his work on CRYOGENICS. In 1872, Dewar invented the vacuum flask, commercially known as the Thermos flask. In 1898, he liquified hydrogen. Dewar and **Sir Frederick Abel** (1826–1902) invented the propellant cordite.

Dewey, John (1859–1952) US educator and philosopher. He was professor of philosophy (1904–30) at Columbia University. Influenced by PRAGMATISM and UTILITARIANISM, Dewey proposed a philosophy of **instrumentalism**. He regarded intelligence as an instrument to overcome practical problems. In *Democracy and Education* (1916) Dewey emphasized the importance of experimentation and practical application in education. A leading figure in the development of PROGRESSIVE EDUCATION, he urged that learning should be vocational, equipping students with the skills to integrate into society.

Dewey decimal system Means of classifying books, devised (1873) by US librarian Melvil Dewey (1851–1931). Books are divided by subject into ten main classes, each class containing 100 numbers. The main disciplines within each subject are subdivided into groups of ten, and decimal numbers are used for even more precise definitions. For example, class 600–699 is technology and applied sciences; 630–639 is agriculture; useful insects is 638; and beekeeping is 638.1.

dew point Temperature at which a vapour begins to condense, for example when water vapour in the air condenses into cloud as the air becomes saturated with vapour.

Dhaka (Dacca) Capital of Bangladesh, a port on the Ganges delta, E Bangladesh. In the 17th century, it was the Mogul capital of Bengal. In 1765, Dhaka came under British control. At independence (1947) it became capital of the province of East Pakistan. Severely damaged during the war of independence from Pakistan, in 1971 Dhaka became capital of independent Bangladesh. Sites include the Dakeshwari temple. It is in the centre of the world's largest jute-producing area. Industries: engineering, textiles, printing. Pop. (1991) 3,397,187.

dharma Religious concept relating to what is true or right, found in the principal religions of India. In HINDUISM, it is the moral law or code governing an individual's conduct in life. In BUDDHISM, dharma is the doctrine of universal truth proclaimed by the BUDDHA. In JAINISM, dharma is moral virtue. *See also* KARMA

dhole Rare, reddish-brown wild dog native to S and SE Asia. It hunts large mammals in packs, running its prey to exhaustion. Length: (without tail) to 1m (3.3ft). Family Canidae. species *Cuon alpinus*.

diabetes Disease characterized by lack of INSULIN needed for sugar METABOLISM. This leads to HYPERGLYCAEMIA and an excess of SUGAR in the blood. Symptoms include abnormal thirst, over-production of urine and weight loss; degenerative changes occur in blood vessels. Untreated, it progresses to diabetic coma and death. **Type 1** usually begins in childhood and is an autoimmune disease. Those affected owe their survival to insulin injections. Milder **type 2** mostly begins in middle-age. There is some insulin output and the disease is managed with dietary restrictions and oral insulin. Susceptibility to *diabetes mellitus* is inherited and more common in males.

diagenesis Physical and chemical processes whereby sediments are transformed into solid rock, usually at low pressure and temperature.

Diaghilev, Sergei Pavlovich (1872–1929) Russian ballet impresario. He was active in the Russian avantgarde before moving to Paris, where he formed (1911) the BALLETS RUSSES and acted as its director until his death. Diaghilev was responsible for revolutionizing the world of BALLET, integrating music and scene design with innovative choreography. Dancers such as NIJINSKY, PAVLOVA and MARKOVA performed pieces choreographed by the likes of Michel FOKINE and George BALANCHINE. STRAVINSKY, DEBUSSY, RAVEL and Richard STRAUSS composed for the company, while artists such as Pablo PICASSO designed the sets and costumes.

dialect Regional variety of a language, distinguished by features of pronunciation, grammar and vocabulary. Dialectal differences may be relatively slight (as in the dialects of American English), or so great (Italian) that mutual comprehension becomes difficult or impossible.

dialectic Method of argument through conversation and dialogue, based on the philosophy of SOCRATES, in particular the *Dialogues*. HEGEL went on to argue that ordinary logic is static and lifeless. In the *Science of Logic* (1812–16) he claimed to satisfy the need for a dynamic method. LOGIC was to be dialectical, or a process of resolution by means of conflict of categories. *See also* DIALECTICAL MATERIALISM

dialectical materialism Scientific theory and philosophical basis of MARXISM. It asserts that everything is material and that change results from the struggle of opposites according to definite laws. Its main application was in the analysis of human history. Karl MARX agreed with HEGEL that history is logically dialectical, so that true social change can only occur when two opposing views are resolved through a new synthesis, rather than one establishing itself as true. According to Marx's theory of historical materialism, history was derived from economic or social realities.

dialysis Process for separating particles from a solution by differing rates of diffusion through a semi-permeable membrane, discovered by Thomas Graham (1805–69). In the artificial KIDNEY machine, invented in 1943 by Willem Kolff (1911–), molecules of waste products are separated out to purify the blood. **Electrodialysis** uses a direct electric current to accelerate the process, especially useful for isolating proteins.

diamond Crystalline form of carbon (C). The hardest natural substance known, it is found in kimberlite pipes and alluvial deposits. Appearance varies according to its impurities. Bort, inferior in crystal and colour, carborondo, an opaque grey to black variety, and other non-gem varieties are used in industry. Industrial diamonds are used as abrasives, bearings in precision instruments such as watches, and in the cutting heads of drills for mining. Synthetic diamonds, made by subjecting GRAPHITE, with a catalyst, to high pressure and temperatures of c.3,000°C (5,400°F) are fit only for industry. Diamonds are weighed in carats (0.2gm) and points (1/100 carat). The largest producer is Australia. Hardness 10; s.g. 3.5.

Diana In Roman religion, the virgin huntress and patroness of domestic animals. She was identified with ARTEMIS. A fertility deity, she was invoked to aid conception and childbirth.

Diana, Princess of Wales (1961–97) Former wife of the heir to the British throne. The daughter of Earl Spencer, Diana married CHARLES, Prince of Wales in 1981, and they had two sons, William (1982–) and Harry (1984–). A popular, glamorous figure, she worked for many public-health and children's charities. Their marriage fell apart acrimoniously and publicly, and they divorced in 1996. Diana continued to campaign for humanitarian causes until her tragic death in a car crash.

diaphragm Sheet of muscle that separates the abdomen from the THORAX. During exhalation it relaxes and allows the chest to subside; on inhalation it contracts and flattens, causing the chest cavity to enlarge.

diarrhoea Frequent elimination of loose, watery stools, accompanied by cramps and stomach pains. It arises from infection, intestinal irritants or food allergy. Mild attacks can be treated by replacement fluids.

diary (Lat. day) Record of events and observations kept by an individual at the time of their occurrence. The earliest diary of literary worth is the account of the Gallic Wars by CAESAR. Diaries may be of either historical or literary interest, and the most notable diarists, such as Samuel PEPYS, combine both qualities. Significant modern diarists include Anne FRANK (1929–45), who documented her two years of hiding in an Amsterdam room to escape Nazi persecution. The late 20th-century diary may take the form of a video or cinematic, as well as literary, record.

Diaspora (Gr. dispersion) Jewish communities outside Palestine. Although there were communities of Jews outside Palestine from the time of the BABYLONIAN CAPTIVITY (6th century BC), the Diaspora essentially dates from the destruction of Jerusalem by the Romans (AD 70). The majority of Jews remain in the Diaspora. *See also* JUDAISM; ZIONISM

diathermy Medical treatment that uses heat generated by high-frequency (short-wave) alternating electric current. The heat stimulates local blood circulation and tissue repair. It is used to treat back pain, to aid muscle and tendon repair, and in neurosurgery.

diatom Any of a group of microscopic single-celled ALGAE (phylum Bacillariophyta) characterized by a shell-like cell wall made of silica. Diatoms live in salt and fresh water, and even soil and tree bark.

diatonic Pertaining to the musical scale that uses seven of the 12 notes of the OCTAVE, the notes moving in the tonic sol-fa system. A diatonic scale can be major or minor. Diatonicism has been the basic scale of Western polyphonic music since the 16th century. *See also* CHROMATIC; MUSICAL NOTATION

Diaz, Bartholomeu (c.1450–1500) Portuguese navigator, the first European to round the CAPE OF GOOD HOPE. In 1487 Diaz sailed three ships around the Cape, opening the long-sought route to India. He took part in the expedition of CABRAL that discovered Brazil, but was drowned when his ship foundered.

Díaz, Porfirio (1830–1915) Mexican statesman, president (1876–80, 1884–1911). He supported Benito JUÁREZ in the war (1861–67) against Emperor MAXIMILIAN. Díaz refused to accept defeat in the 1871 and 1876 presidential elections and began a revolt that overthrew President Sebastián Lerdo. His 35-year dictatorship was brutally effective. His fraudulent re-election (1910) sparked a popular uprising led by Francisco MADERO, and Díaz was forced into exile.

Dickens, Charles John Huffam (1812–70) English novelist. After a difficult early life, he began his writing career as a parliamentary reporter for the *Morning Chronicle*. Dickens' first success was a series of satirical pieces collected as *Sketches by Boz* (1836). *The Pickwick Papers* (1836–37) launched his literary career. All of Dickens' novels first appeared in serial form. His early work includes *Oliver Twist* (1838), *Nicholas Nickleby* (1839), *The Old Curiosity Shop* (1841) and *Barnaby Rudge* (1841). In 1842 Dickens travelled to the USA, recording his thoughts in *American Notes*. In 1843 he finished *Martin Chuzzlewit* and wrote *A Christmas Carol*. His mature novels included *David Copperfield* (1850), *Bleak House* (1853), *Hard Times* (1854), *Little Dorrit* (1857) and *A Tale of Two Cities* (1859). Dickens'

last novels, *Great Expectations* (1861), *Our Mutual Friend* (1865) and the incomplete *The Mystery of Edwin Drood*, are bleak depictions of the destructive powers of money and ambition. His prolific output provided some of the most memorable characters in ENGLISH LITERATURE and captured the mood of Victorian London.

Dickinson, Emily Elizabeth (1830–86) US poet. From the age of 30 she lived in almost total seclusion in Amherst, Massachusetts. Dickinson wrote 1,775 short lyrics, only seven of which were published in her lifetime. *Poems by Emily Dickinson* appeared in 1890, and her collected works were not published until 1955. They rank among the greatest works in AMERICAN LITERATURE. Her rich verse explores the world of emotion and the beauty of simple things.

dicotyledon Larger of the two subgroups of flowering plants, or ANGIOSPERMS, characterized by two seed leaves (COTYLEDONS) in the seed embryo. Dicotyledons have broad leaves with branching veins; flower parts in whorls of fours or fives; vascular bundles in a ring in the stem and root; and a taproot. There are c.250 families of dicotyledons, such as the ROSE and DAISY.

dictatorship Absolute rule without consent of the governed. In many modern dictatorships, all power resides in the dictator. Personal freedom is severely limited, censorship is generally enforced, education is tightly controlled, and legal restraints on governmental authority are abolished. *See also* AUTHORITARIANISM

dictionary Book that lists words and their definitions in alphabetical order. A dictionary may be general or subject oriented. In the former category, Samuel JOHNSON's *A Dictionary of the English Language* (1755) is the pioneering work in English. The first great US lexicographer was Noah WEBSTER, who published *An American Dictionary of the English Language* in 1828. The *Oxford English Dictionary* (*OED*) was first published in 1884.

Diderot, Denis (1713–84) French philosopher and writer. He was chief editor of the *Encyclopédie* (1751–72), an influential publication of the ENLIGHTENMENT. A friend of ROUSSEAU, he was imprisoned briefly (1749) for irreligious writings. He broadened the scope of the *Encyclopédie* and, with d'ALEMBERT, recruited contributors, including VOLTAIRE. As a philosopher, Diderot progressed gradually from Christianity through DEISM to ATHEISM. *On the Interpretation of Nature* (1754) and *d'Alembert's Dream* (1769) reveal his scientific MATERIALISM. *Jacques the Fatalist* (1796) illustrates his DETERMINISM. He also wrote plays, and art and literary criticism.

Dido In Greek and Roman legend, Phoenician princess and founder of CARTHAGE. Dido's hand was sought by the king of Libya. To escape him she stabbed herself. VIRGIL made Dido a lover of AENEAS and attributes her suicide to his decision to abandon her.

Diefenbaker, John George (1895–1979) Canadian statesman, prime minister (1957–63). He was Canada's first Conservative prime minister since Richard B. Bennett (1930–35). In 1958, Diefenbaker gained the largest parliamentary majority in Canada's history. As prime minister, he secured the adoption of a Bill of Rights (1960). Economic crisis forced him to devalue the Canadian dollar and adopt austerity measures.

Diem, Ngo Dinh (1901–63) Vietnamese statesman, prime minister of South Vietnam (1954–63). In 1955, he formed a republic, forcing Bao Dai into exile. At first, Diem received strong US support but corruption and setbacks in the VIETNAM WAR led to growing discontent. With covert US help, army officers staged a coup in which he was murdered.

Dien Bien Phu Fortified village in N Vietnam. In a 1954 battle the French stronghold was captured by the Vietnamese Viet Minh after a siege lasting 55 days. French casualties were c.15,000. The resultant cease-fire ended eight years of war.

diesel engine (compression-ignition engine) INTERNAL COMBUSTION ENGINE invented (1897) by German engineer Rudolf Diesel (1858–1913). Heat for igniting the lower grade diesel oil is produced by compressing air.

diet Range of food and drink consumed by an animal. The human diet falls into five main groups of necessary nutrients: PROTEIN, CARBOHYDRATE, FAT, VITAMIN and MINERAL. An adult's daily requirement is about one gram of protein for each kilogram of body weight. Beans, fish, eggs, milk and meat are important protein sources. Carbohydrates (stored as GLYCOGEN) and fat are the chief sources of energy and are found in cereals, root vegetables and sugars. Carbohydrates make up the bulk of most diets. Fats are a concentrated source of energy and aid the absorption of fat-soluble vitamins (vitamins A, D, E and K). Water and minerals, such as iron, calcium, potassium and sodium, are also essential.

Diet Legislative assembly or administrative council, principally important in German history. CHARLES IV established the diet of the Holy Roman Empire by his Golden Bull of 1356. It comprised three estates – the seven electors (of the Holy Roman emperor), other lay and church nobility, and representatives of the imperial cities – each of which met separately. Approval by each estate and the consent of the emperor were required on all matters. After the Treaty of Westphalia (1648), the diet lost much of its legislative power and importance.

Dietrich, Marlene (1904–92) German actress and cabaret singer. Her glamourous, sultry image evolved in films directed by Josef von Sternberg, such as *The Blue Angel* (1930) and *Blonde Venus* (1932). Later films include *Destry Rides Again* (1939), *Rancho Notorious* (1956) and *Judgement at Nuremberg* (1961).

differential In mathematics, small change in the value of a mathematical expression due to a change in a VARIABLE. If $f(x)$ is a function of x, the differential of the function, written df, is given by $f'(x)\,dx$, where $f'(x)$ is the DERIVATIVE of $f(x)$.

differential In mechanics, a set of circular gears that transmits power from an engine to the wheels. When a car is turning a corner, the differential allows the outside drive wheel to rotate faster than the inner one.

differential calculus (differentiation) Form of CALCULUS used to calculate the rate of change (DERIVATIVE) of one quantity with respect to another of which it is the FUNCTION.

differential equation Equation containing DERIVATIVES. For example, $dN/dt = AN$, where N is the number of people in a population, t time, A constant, and dN/dt the derivative of population with respect to time; this differential is a simplified equation for population growth. *See also* CALCULUS

diffraction Spreading of a wave, such as a LIGHT beam, on passing through a narrow opening or hitting the edge of an obstacle, such as sound being heard around corners. It is evidence for the wave nature of light. All waves are diffracted by obstacles.

diffusion Movement of a substance in a mixture from regions of high concentration to regions of low concentration, due to the random motion of atoms or molecules. Diffusion ceases when there is no longer a concentration gradient. Its rate increases with temperature.

digestion Process of the DIGESTIVE SYSTEM in which food is broken down into smaller molecules that can be

readily absorbed. Digestion occurs mainly by means of chemical agents called ENZYMES.

digestive system (alimentary system) Group of organs of the body concerned with the DIGESTION of foodstuffs. In humans, it begins with the mouth, and continues into the OESOPHAGUS, which carries food into the STOMACH. The stomach leads to the small INTESTINE, which opens into the COLON. After food is swallowed, it is pushed through the digestive tract by PERISTALSIS. On its journey, food is transformed into small molecules that can be absorbed into the bloodstream and carried to the tissues. CARBOHYDRATE is broken down to sugars, PROTEIN to AMINO ACIDS, and FAT to FATTY ACIDS and GLYCEROL. Indigestible matter, mainly CELLULOSE, passes into the RECTUM and is eventually eliminated from the body (as faeces) through the ANUS.

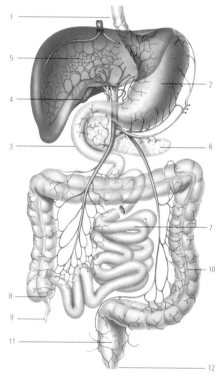

▲ **digestive system** The digestion and absorption of food takes place within the digestive tract, a coiled tube some 10m (33ft) long which links mouth to anus. Food is passed down the oesophagus (1) to the stomach (2), where it is partially digested. Chyme is released into the duodenum (3), the first part of 7m (23ft) of small intestine. The duodenum receives bile secreted by the gall bladder (4) in the liver (5), and enzymes secreted by the pancreas (6). Most absorption takes place in the jejunum and ileum, the remaining parts of the small intestine (7). Any residue passes into the caecum (8), the pouch at the start of the large intestine. At one end of the caecum is the 10cm (4in) long vermiform appendix (9), which serves no useful purpose in humans. Water is re-absorbed in the colon (10). Faeces form and collect in the rectum (11) before being expelled as waste matter through the anus (12).

▶ **digital audio tape** A digital audio tape (DAT) recorder records sound, an analogue signal, in digital form. The analogue signal enters via a microphone (1) and passes through a converter (2), which transcribes the sound wave into a series of zeros and ones. Two magnetic heads, tiny electromagnets (3) in a rotating drum (4), receive the digital signal as electrical pulses that polarize diagonal strips of magnetic tape (5) (moving right to left, 6) as it is scanned diagonally (7). The heads align the magnetic elements of the tape representing a zero or a one. Each head records one half of a stereo recording. One head records parallel to the tape (8), one perpendicular (9) to avoid interference. The units of an blank tape are jumbled (10). When a tape (11) is played, the head reads the polarization of the tape.

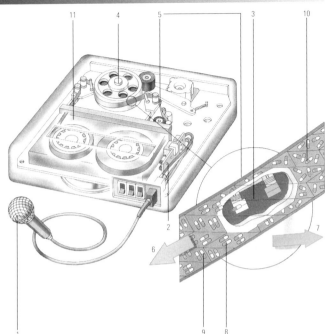

Diggers (1649–50) English millenarian social and religious sect, an extreme group of the LEVELLERS. Their egalitarian agrarian community was destroyed by local farmers. The main Digger theorist, Gerrard Winstanley, proposed communalization of property to establish social equality in *Law of Freedom* (1652).

digital DATA expressed in terms of a few discrete quantities, often associated with a digital COMPUTER. Data is represented as a series of zeros and ones in a BINARY SYSTEM. Digital can also refer to displaying information in numbers, as opposed to continuously varying analogue.

digital audio tape (DAT) Technology for recording data in DIGITAL form on magnetic TAPE. DATs are smaller and longer than analogue cassettes. They are used primarily for computer back-ups and studio-recording.

digitalis Drug obtained from the leaves of the FOX-GLOVE (*Digitalis purpurea*), used to treat HEART disease. It increases heart contractions and slows the heartbeat.

digital signal Group of electrical or other pulses in a COMPUTER or COMMUNICATIONS system. They may represent DATA, sounds or pictures. Pulses are represented by zeros and ones in the BINARY SYSTEM.

Dijon City in E France; capital of Côte-d'Or department. In the 11th century the dukes of BURGUNDY made it their capital. It was annexed to France (1477). Sites include Dijon University (1722) and the Church of Notre Dame. Exports: wine, mustard. Pop. (1990) 146,703.

dill Aromatic annual herb native to Europe. Its small oval seeds and feathery leaves are used in cooking. Family Apiaceae/Umbelliferae; species *Anethum graveolens*.

Dillinger, John Herbert (1903–34) US gangster. He was imprisoned (1923–33) for attempted armed robbery. Upon his release, Dillinger and his gang terrorized the Midwest, killing 16 people. He escaped from jail twice and was declared "public enemy number one", before being betrayed by his mistress (the "lady in red") and shot dead outside a Chicago cinema.

DiMaggio, Joe (Joseph Paul) (1914–99) US baseball player. He played for the New York Yankees (1936–42, 1946–51) and held the record for hitting safely in 56 consecutive games. He married (1954) Marilyn MONROE and was elected to the Baseball Hall of Fame (1955).

Dimbleby, Richard (1913–65) English broadcaster. He was the BBC's first war correspondent and covered the fall of Berlin and the tragedy of Belsen. For many years Dimbleby anchored the current affairs programme *Panorama*. He brought dignity and authority to television coverage of state occasions. His sons **David** (1938–) and **Jonathan** (1944–) are also broadcasters.

dimension In mathematics, the spatial dimension is the number specifying the extent of an object in different directions. A figure with length only is one-dimensional; a figure having area but not volume, two-dimensional; and a figure having volume, three-dimensional.

diminishing returns, law of (law of increasing costs) In economics, if more of a variable input, such as labour, is added to the production process, while all other factors are held constant, the addition to total output per unit input begins to decline at some point.

Dinaric Alps (Dinara Planina) Mountain range parallel to the E coast of the Adriatic Sea. Forming part of the E ALPS, it extends from the Istrian peninsula (Croatia) to NW Albania. Length: 640km (400mi).

D'Indy, Vincent (1851–1931) French composer and teacher. He co-founded the *Schola Cantorum* for the study of church music (1894). D'Indy taught composition here until his death. His pupils included SATIE. He composed operas, orchestral, choral, chamber and piano music.

Dinesen, Isak (1885–1962) (Karen Blixen) Danish writer. She described her life on a Kenyan coffee plantation in *Out of Africa* (1937). Her collections of short stories include *Shadows on the Grass* (1960).

dingo Yellowish-brown wild DOG found in Australia; it is probably a descendant of early domestic dogs introduced by Native Australians. It feeds mainly on rabbits and other small mammals. Height (at shoulder): *c*.61cm (24in). Family Canidae; species *Canis dingo*.

Dinka Nilotic people of the southern Sudan. The Dinka are transhumant cattle herders. The *c*.2 million population are organized into many independent tribes.

dinosaur (Gr. terrible lizard) Any of a large number of REPTILES that lived during the MESOZOIC era, between 225 and 65 million years ago. They appeared during the Triassic period, survived the JURASSIC, and became extinct at the end of the Cretaceous. Dinosaurs were mostly egg-laying animals, ranging in size from 91cm (30in) to the 27-m (90-ft) DIPLODOCUS. There were two orders: **Saurischia** ("lizard hips"), included the bipedal carnivores and the giant herbivores; the **Ornithiscia** ("bird hips") were smaller herbivores. There is evidence that some birds are the living descendants of ornithischians. Many theories are advanced to account for their extinction. One theory is that they died because of the devastating atmospheric effects from the impact of a large meteor. *See also* BRONTOSAURUS; PTERODACTYL; TRICERATOPS; TYRANNOSAURUS

Diocletian (245–313) Roman emperor (284–305). Of low birth, he was made emperor by the army. Diocletian reorganized the empire to resist the Barbarians, sharing power with Maximilian, Constantius I and Galerius. He ordered the last great persecution of the Christians (303).

diode Electronic component with two electrodes, used as a RECTIFIER to convert alternating current (AC) to direct current (DC). SEMICONDUCTOR diodes have largely replaced ELECTRON-TUBES, and allow ELECTRIC CURRENT to flow freely in only one direction. A Zener diode blocks current until a critical voltage is reached.

Diogenes (active 4th century BC) Greek philosopher. He founded the CYNIC school of philosophy. He believed that by reducing personal needs to a minimum, one can have mastery over one's soul.

Dionysius the Areopagite, Saint (1st century AD) First bishop of Athens, converted by St Paul. His name was used by a Palestinian writer of *c*.500, now known as Pseudo-Dionysius, whose mystical works of NEOPLATONISM had a great influence on SCHOLASTICISM.

Dionysius the Elder (430–367 BC) Tyrant of Syracuse (405–367 BC). His ambitions were to spread Hellenism beyond the city. He tried to form an empire in Lower Italy by seizing Rhegium (387), Caulonia and Croton (379). He then mixed the various populations. An erstwhile playwright, he once sold Plato as a slave.

Dionysus Greek god of wine and fertility, identified with the Roman god BACCHUS. Son of ZEUS and Semele, he was reared by nymphs and taught men the secrets of cultivating grapes and making wine.

Dior, Christian (1905–57) French fashion designer. In 1947 he launched the "New Look" whose wide shoulders and long, shapely skirts signalled an end to war austerity. Dior created the A-line dress in 1956.

diorite Deep-seated, coarse-grained IGNEOUS ROCK, similar to GRANITE in texture but made up mainly of plagioclase feldspar and hornblende, with BIOTITE or augite. It is usually dark grey.

dioxin Any of various poisonous chemicals. The compound most commonly known as dioxin is 2,3,7,8-tetrachlorodibenzo-p-dioxin (TCDD), a by-product and impurity in the manufacture of disinfectants and HERBICIDES. Dioxin causes skin disfigurement and is linked with birth defects, cancer and miscarriages. Accidental releases of dioxin from chemical plants have caused major disasters. TCDD was a constituent of Agent Orange.

dip, magnetic Angle between the direction of the Earth's magnetic field and the horizontal. A freely suspended magnetic needle in London dips, with its north pole pointing down, at an angle of 71.5° to the horizontal.

diphtheria Acute infectious disease characterized by the formation of a membrane in the throat which can cause asphyxiation; there is also release of a toxin which can damage the nerves and heart. Caused by a bacterium, *Corynebacterium diphtheriae*, it is treated with antibiotics.

Diplodocus DINOSAUR that lived in N USA during the JURASSIC period. The longest land animal that has ever lived, it had a long slender neck and tail and was a swamp-dwelling herbivore. Length: up to 27m (90ft).

diploid CELL that has its CHROMOSOMES in pairs. Diploids are found in almost all animal cells, except GAMETES, which are HAPLOID. Cells of flowering plants and gymnosperms are also diploid. In diploids, the chromosomes of each pair carry the same GENES. *See also* ALTERNATION OF GENERATIONS

diplomatic service Body of public servants who are responsible for intergovernment negotiations. The Congress of Vienna (1815) established a hierarchy of diplomatic ranks: ambassador or papal legate; minister penipotentiary and envoy; minister; and chargé d'affairs. Diplomats enjoy diplomatic immunity. They are allowed communications and transport without interference. *See also* EXTRATERRITORIALITY

dipole Separation of ELECTRIC CHARGE in a molecule. In a COVALENT BOND, the electron pair is not equally shared. In hydrogen chloride (HCl), ELECTRONS are attracted toward the more electronegative chlorine atom, giving it a partial negative charge and leaving an equal positive charge on the hydrogen atom. Dipoles contribute to the chemical properties of molecules.

dipper Bird found near mountain streams. It feeds on small fish and aquatic invertebrates. It has a thin, straight bill, short wings and greyish-brown plumage. Length: to 19cm (7.5in). Family Cinclidae; genus *Cinclus*.

Dirac, Paul Adrien Maurice (1902–84) English physicist. He made valuable contributions to the development of QUANTUM THEORY. In 1928 Dirac introduced a notation for quantum equations that combined SCHRÖDINGER's use of DIFFERENTIAL EQUATIONS with HEISENBERG's use of matrices. In 1930 he applied EINSTEIN's theory of RELATIVITY to quantum mechanics in order to describe the SPIN of an ELECTRON. The resultant equation predicted the existence of ANTIMATTER. Dirac shared the 1933 Nobel Prize for physics with Schrödinger.

direct current (DC) *See* ELECTRIC CURRENT

director In the theatre, the person who has the primary responsibility for making a play. The director approves the script, decides the cast and production team, and controls the actors' performances. In late 19th-century theatre, the ensemble approach of the MEININGEN PLAYERS was developed further by Konstantin STANISLAVSKY. Stanislavsky's technique encouraged greater theatrical REALISM. Adolphe APPIA promoted the expressive use of lighting. Max REINHARDT emphasized the power of theatre as spectacle. Ervin PISCATOR and Bertolt BRECHT developed a politicized EPIC THEATRE. In the USA, the STANISLAVSKY-inspired work of the ACTORS' STUDIO, led by Lee STRASBERG, was influential. The experimentation of the theatre of the ABSURD and the Theatre of CRUELTY informed the work of Peter BROOK, Peter HALL and Jonathan MILLER. *See* also CINEMA

Directory (1795–99) Government of the First Republic of France, consisting of five directors elected by the Council of Five Hundred and the Council of Ancients. It was established as part of the Thermidorian reaction to the REIGN OF TERROR. Success in the FRENCH REVOLUTIONARY WARS inspired greater independence among the generals, and the coup of 18 Brumaire (9 November), 1799, led to the accession of NAPOLEON I. *See also* CARNOT, LAZARE; FRENCH REVOLUTION

disaccharide Type of sugar (including common sugar) formed by the condensation of two monosaccharides with the removal of water. Cane sugar, SUCROSE, is a disaccharide, which, on hydrolysis with dilute acid, yields both GLUCOSE and FRUCTOSE (monosaccharides). LACTOSE (the sugar in milk) and MALTOSE are other important disaccharides.

disarmament Refers principally to attempts post-1918 (and especially post-1945) to reach international agreements to reduce armaments. The United Nations established the Atomic Energy Commission (1946) and the Commission for Conventional Armaments (1947). In 1952, these were combined into the Disarmament Commission. It produced no results, and the Soviet Union withdrew in 1957. The USA and the Soviet Union signed the Nuclear Test Ban Treaty (1963) and the Nuclear Non-Proliferation Treaty (1968), which provided for an international inspectorate. This was followed by a series of STRATEGIC ARMS LIMITATION TALKS (SALT). In 1986, SALT was superseded by START (strategic arms reduction talks), resulting in the Intermediate Nuclear Forces (INF) Treaty (1987) that reduced the superpowers' arsenal of short-range, intermediate missiles by *c.*2,000 (4% of the total stockpile) and provided for on-site inspection. Conventional Forces in Europe Treaty (1990) set limits on equipment and troop levels. Attempts to sign a comprehensive Test Ban Treaty have been thwarted by China, France, India and Pakistan. Following the break-up of the Soviet Union, the four republics with nuclear weapons (Russia, Ukraine, Belarus, Kazakstan) agreed in 1991 to implement the START treaties.

disciple One of the followers of Jesus Christ during his life on Earth, especially one of his 12 close personal associates. These 12 men were his first APOSTLES.

discontinuity *See* MOHO

discus Field event in which a wooden and metal disc is thrown. The thrower rotates in a circle (diameter 2.5m/8.2ft) several times before releasing the discus. Originally an ancient Greek sport, it was revived for the first modern Olympic Games held in Athens (1896).

disease Any departure from health, with impaired functioning of the body. Disease may be **acute**, with severe symptoms for a short time; **chronic**, lasting a long time; or **recurrent**, returning periodically. There are many types and causes of disease: infectious, caused by harmful BACTERIA or VIRUSES; hereditary and metabolic; growth and development; IMMUNE SYSTEM diseases; neoplastic (TUMOUR-producing); nutritional; deficiency; ENDOCRINE SYSTEM diseases; or diseases due to environmental agents. Treatment may be **symptomatic** (relieving symptoms) or **specific** (attempting to cure an underlying cause). Disease prevention includes eradication of harmful organisms, VACCINES, public health measures and medical checks.

disinfectant (germicide) Agent that kills or inhibits the growth of bacteria and other microorganisms on inanimate objects. ANTISEPTIC is used on contaminated living tissue. Joseph LISTER introduced carbolic acid (PHENOL) as a medical disinfectant in the 1870s. Today, chlorinated phenols are used in pharmaceutical products. CHLORINE and chlorine compounds are commonly used to kill bacteria, especially in water. IODINE is used in food preparation. ALCOHOL is an effective disinfectant. AMMONIUM is the most common agent in household cleaners. It also acts as a DETERGENT.

disk Form of computer DATA storage. Disks come in many different forms, some using magnetic methods to store data, such as the HARD DISK, while others use optical systems like the COMPACT DISC (CD) and CD-ROM.

disk operating system (DOS) COMPUTER operating system developed in the early 1980s by Bill GATES and Microsoft for early International Business Machines (IBM) personal computers. DOS is the SOFTWARE that governs a computer's data storage and PROGRAM execution. It is rapidly being replaced by Windows-based operating systems (also developed by Microsoft).

Disney, Walt (Walter Elias) (1901–66) US film animator, producer and executive. Disney has become synonymous with family entertainment and a menagerie of cartoon characters, such as Mickey Mouse, Donald Duck and Pluto. Disney's first success, *Steamboat Willie* (1928), was the first cartoon to use sound and featured his own voice as Mickey Mouse. Disney's first feature was *Snow White and the Seven Dwarfs* (1937). A series of popular classics followed: *Pinocchio* (1940), *Fantasia* (1940), *Dumbo* (1941) and *Bambi* (1942). In 1950, Disney diversified into live action features with *Treasure Island* (1950). In 1955, the first amusement park, Disneyland, opened in Anaheim, California. Disney collected a total of 29 Academy Awards. The Walt Disney Company (founded 1923) is one of the world's most powerful media corporations.

Disraeli, Benjamin, 1st Earl of Beaconsfield (1804–81) British statesman and novelist, prime minister (1868, 1874–80). Disraeli was elected to Parliament in 1837. His brand of Toryism is expressed in the trilogy of novels, *Coningsby* (1844), *Sybil* (1846) and *Tancred* (1847). Following the split in the TORY PARTY over the repeal of the CORN LAWS (1846), Disraeli became leader of the land-owning faction. His opposition to Robert PEEL was rewarded when he became chancellor of the exchequer (1852, 1858–59, 1866–68) under Lord DERBY. Disraeli succeeded Derby as prime minister but soon was ousted by William GLADSTONE. His second term coincided with the greatest expansion of the second BRITISH EMPIRE. Disraeli led Britain into the Zulu War (1879), and the second Afghan War (1878–79), and sought to diminish the strength of Russia. In 1875, Britain purchased the Suez Canal from Egypt. In 1880, Disraeli was defeated for a second time by Gladstone.

Dissolution of the Monasteries (1536–40) Abolition of English MONASTICISM in the reign of HENRY VIII. The operation, led by Thomas CROMWELL, was a result of the break with Rome but also provided additional revenue, since the monasteries owned *c.*25% of the land in England, all of which passed to the crown.

distemper Contagious, often fatal, disease of young dogs, wild canines and weasels. Symptoms include fever, shivering, muscular spasms and loss of appetite. Death is caused by inflammation of the brain.

distillation Extraction of a liquid by boiling a solution and cooling the vapour so that it condenses and can be collected. Distillation is used to separate liquids in solution, or liquid solvents from dissolved solids, to yield drinking water from sea water or to produce alcoholic spirit. Fractional distillation, which uses a vertical column for condensation, is used in OIL refining.

distilling Production of liquor by DISTILLATION, especially of ethyl ALCOHOL. In wine, yeast FERMENTATION produces a maximum alcohol content of *c.*15%. Distillation concentrates alcohol to a much higher degree to produce spirit. Most spirits are *c.*40% proof.

distributive law Rule of combination in mathematics, in which an operation applied to a combination of terms is equal to the combination of the operation applied to each individual term. Thus, in arithmetic $3\times(2+1) = (3\times2)+(3\times1)$ and, in algebra $a(x + y) = ax + ay$.

District of Columbia Federal district, coextensive with WASHINGTON, DC, the US capital. It is governed under federal law. It was created in 1790–91 from land taken from the states of Maryland and Virginia. The Virginia portion was returned in 1846. Area: 179sq km (69sq mi).

diuretic Drug used to increase the output of URINE. It is used to treat raised blood pressure and OEDEMA.

diver *See* LOON

diverticulitis Inflammation of diverticula, pockets of herniation on the wall of the large intestine, usually caused by infection. Symptoms include abdominal pain and either diarrhoea or constipation. It usually responds to antibiotics and a bland diet.

dividend Net earnings of a public company that is paid to its stockholders. The dividend is a percentage of the par value of the stock or is calculated on a per share basis. It is a share of the profits.

divination Foretelling the future by interpreting various signs. Divination is a form of magic with worldwide distribution. OMENS are often thought to be found in the entrails of sacrificed animals, cards and palms.

diving Water sport in which acrobatic manoeuvres are performed off a springboard or platform. Points are awarded for level of difficulty, technique and grace of flight, and cleanness of entry into the water. Techniques include tuck, pike, twist and somersault.

diving, deep-sea Underwater activity for commercial or leisure purposes. Deep-sea diving developed with the introduction of the diving bell and diving suit. It refers to descents to depths of more than $c.11\mathrm{m}$ (36ft). Divers need to ascend slowly from such depths to avoid the BENDS. *See also* SCUBA DIVING

division of labour In economics, the specialization of the functions and roles involved in production. The term was introduced by Adam SMITH in his *Wealth of Nations* (1776). Modern MASS PRODUCTION is based on **occupational** division of labour, where each worker is allocated to a specific task.

divorce Legal dissolution of marriage. The ease with which a divorce may be obtained, if at all, varies greatly. In most Western countries, adultery was for many years the only ground for divorce. Desertion, insanity and mental cruelty were added over the years. More recently, irretrievable breakdown, which apportions blame on neither partner, is cited. In many contemporary Western societies, more than one in three marriages ends in divorce.

Diwali Festival of lights in HINDUISM. Homes are lit with numerous tiny clay lamps in commemoration of the defeat of Ravana by RAMA. The story is symbolic of the return of light after the monsoon.

Dix, Otto (1891–1969) German painter and engraver. He was a pitiless satirist of inhumanity, notably in a series of 50 etchings called *The War* (1924). Dix attacked the corruption of post-World War 1 Germany. The Nazis banned him from teaching (1933), and he was jailed for an alleged plot to kill Hitler (1939). After World War 2, he concentrated on religious themes.

Dixieland Style of JAZZ music originating in NEW ORLEANS in the 1900s. It consists of a steady beat with interweaving melodic lines played by a small group (typically, clarinet, trumpet, trombone and rhythm section). King Oliver and Louis ARMSTRONG were two of its most famous exponents.

Djibouti (Jibouti) Republic on the NE coast of Africa; the capital is DJIBOUTI. **Land and Climate** Djibouti occupies a strategic position around the Gulf of Tadjoura where the RED SEA meets the Gulf of Aden. Behind the coastal plain lie the Mabla Mountains, rising to Moussa Ali at 2,020m (6,627ft). Djibouti contains the lowest point on the African continent, Lake Assal, at 155m (509ft) below sea-level. Djibouti has one of the world's hottest and driest climates; summer temperatures regularly exceed 42°C (100°F) and average annual rainfall is 130mm (5in). Nearly 90% of the land is semi-desert, and shortage of pasture and water make farming difficult. **History and politics** Islam was introduced in the 9th century. The subsequent conversion of the Afars led to conflict with Christian Ethiopians. In 1888, France set up French Somaliland. Full independence as the Republic of Djibouti was achieved in 1977, and Hassan Gouled Aptidon of the Popular Rally for Progress (RPP) was elected president. In 1981, he declared a one-party state. Continuing protests against the Issas-dominated regime forced the introduction of a multi-party constitution in 1992. The Front for the Restoration of Unity and Democracy (FUUD), supported primarily by Afars, boycotted 1993 elections, and Aptidon was re-elected for a fourth six-year term. FUUD rebels continued an armed campaign for political representation. In 1994, government and FUUD forces signed a peace accord, and in 1996 FUUD was recognized as a political party. **Economy** Djibouti is a poor country, heavily reliant on food imports. A free-trade zone, it has no major resources, and manufacturing is on a very small scale. The only important activity is livestock raising, and 50% of the population are pastoral nomads.

Djibouti (Jibouti) Capital of DJIBOUTI, on the S shore of the Gulf of Tadjoura, NE Africa. Founded in 1888, it became capital in 1892 and a free port in 1949. Ethiopian emperor Menelik II built a railroad from ADDIS ABABA, and Djibouti became the chief port for Ethiopian trade. When ERITREA was federated with ETHIOPIA (1952–93), it lost this status. Pop. (1995) 383,000.

Djilas, Milovan (1911–95) Yugoslav politician and writer. Djilas was an architect of Yugoslavia's independence from the Soviet Union. In 1954, he was dismissed suddenly from office by TITO. Djilas' support for the Hungarian revolution (1956) and criticism of the authoritarian regime in *New Class* (1957) led to a prison term (1956–61). His next work, *Conversations with Stalin* (1962) brought a second prison sentence (1962–66).

DNA (deoxyribonucleic acid) NUCLEIC ACID that is the major constituent of the CHROMOSOMES of EUKARYOTE cells and some viruses. DNA is often referred to as the "building block" of life since it stores the GENETIC CODE that functions as the basis of HEREDITY. The molecular structure of DNA was first proposed by J.D. WATSON and F.H. CRICK in 1953. It consists of a double helix of two long strands of alternating SUGAR molecules and PHOSPHATE groups linked by nitrogenous bases. The whole molecule is shaped like a twisted rope ladder with the nitrogenous bases forming the rungs. The sugar is deoxyribose, and the four bases are adenine (A), cytosine (C), guanine (G) and thymine (T). The bases are always paired in the same way: adenine always binds with

---

DJIBOUTI

AREA: 23,200sq km (8,958sq mi)
POPULATION: 552,000
CAPITAL (POPULATION): Djibouti (383,000)

thymine, guanine with cytosine. This regularity ensures accurate self-replication. During replication the two DNA strands separate, each providing a template for the synthesis of a new strand of RNA (messenger RNA). This process of transcription, mediated by ENZYMES, results in an identical copy of the original helix. In the process of replication the amount of DNA doubles as the chromosomes replicate themselves before MITOSIS; in the ovum and sperm the amount is half that of the body cells (*see* MEIOSIS). A base and its associated sugar and phosphate are known as a **nucleotide**; the whole strand is a polynucleotide chain. The genetic code is stored in terms of the sequence of nucleotides: three nucleotides code for one specific AMINO ACID; a series of them constitutes a GENE. *See also* BIOTECHNOLOGY; GENETIC ENGINEERING; RECOMBINANT DNA RESEARCH

Dnepropetrovsk City in Ukraine, on the River Dnieper; capital of Dnepropetrovsk region. Founded in 1787 as Ekaterinoslav by Grigori Potemkin for Catherine II, it was renamed in 1926. Industries: iron and steel, chemicals, cement. Pop. (1996) 1,147,000.

Dnieper (Dnepr) River in E Europe. Rising in the Valdai Hills, w of Moscow, it flows s through Belarus and Ukraine to the Black Sea. It is the third longest river in Europe. The Dneproges dam (completed 1932) made the river entirely navigable. It has several hydroelectric power stations. Length: 2,286km (1,420mi).

Dobell, Sir William (1899–1970) Australian painter. He was a controversial winner of the Archibald Prize for portraiture of *Joshua Smith* (1943). Dobell used impressionistic brushwork in a style reminiscent of Hogarth.

doberman Strong guard dog, bred in late 19th-century Germany. It has a long head; its ears are often clipped to a short, erect shape. The smooth coat may be black, red or fawn. Height: to 71cm (28in) at the shoulder.

Dobzhansky, Theodosius (1900–75) US geneticist, b. Russia. He was influential in the development of population GENETICS as a separate study. His writings include *Genetics and the Origin of Species* (1937) and *Genetics of the Evolutionary Process* (1970).

dock Any of more than 200 species of flowering plants native to N US and Europe. Curled dock (*Rumex crispus*) has scaly brown flowers. Dock leaves are a country remedy for nettle stings. Family Polygonaceae.

Doctorow, E.L. (Edgar Lawrence) (1931–) US author. Doctorow's novels have a strong political edge and concern for history. *Ragtime* (1975), his best known novel, deals with late 19th-century racism in the US. Other works include *The Book of Daniel* (1971), *Billy Bathgate* (1988) and *The Waterworks* (1994).

documentary Factual film. The term was first applied to Robert Flaherty's *Nanook of the North* (1921), a first-hand account of life among the Inuit. Documentaries soon rivalled newspapers and became a major means of television news, current affairs and science presentation. Other ground-breaking documentaries include Donn Alan Pennebaker's *Don't Look Back* (1967) and Marcel OPHÜLS' *A Sense of Loss*. *See also* CINÉMA VÉRITÉ

dodder Leafless, parasitic, twining plant with a thread-like stem and clusters of small yellow flowers. It feeds using haustoria, modified roots that enter the host plant. Family Convolvulaceae; species *Cuscuta europaea*.

Dodecanese (Dhodhekánisos) Group of 20 islands in the SE Aegean Sea, between Turkey and Crete; a department of Greece. The capital and largest island is RHODES. The islands were under Ottoman control (1500–1912) before passing to Greece (1947). The main occupation is agriculture, such as fruit growing, livestock raising and diving for sponges. Area: 2174sq km (839sq mi). Pop. (1991) 163,476.

Dodge City City on the Arkansas River, SW Kansas, USA. The city was founded with the arrival of the Sante Fe Railway in 1872 and rapidly became the world's largest cattle market. A frontier town, Dodge City became notorious for its gunfights, and Wyatt EARP was called upon to keep the peace. Boot Hill, the old burial ground for cowboys, has been preserved. Today, it is the commercial centre of an agricultural region. Pop. (1990) 21,129

Dodgson, Charles Lutwidge *See* CARROLL, LEWIS

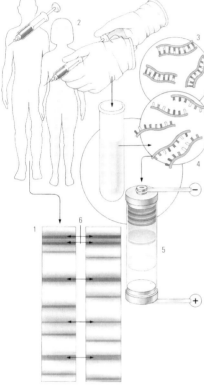

▲ **DNA** Using a technique known as DNA fingerprinting, a person can be accurately identified. The process allows a person's DNA to be represented in visual form (1). Each DNA pattern is unique (like a fingerprint) – with the exception of identical twins. In a case of disputed paternity, DNA fingerprinting allows the relationship to be settled beyond doubt. DNA is present in all cells, so a sample can be taken from blood (2), skin or even sweat. DNA is separated out (3), and an enzyme that divides DNA is added. The enzyme attacks the mini-satellite region between the genes (4). The genes are then sorted by size by an electric field (5). Gel electrophoresis exploits the fact that small sections of DNA carry a charge to force them through a gel. The size of the sections controls how far they travel, giving a pattern unique to each individual. A child combines DNA from both parents, so will have a partially similar pattern. Paternity is confirmed by the matching marks (6).

dodo Extinct flightless bird that lived on the Mascarene Islands in the Indian Ocean. The last dodo died in c.1790. The true dodo (*Raphus cucullatus*) of Mauritius was a heavy-bodied bird with a large head and large hooked bill. Weight: to 23kg (50lb).

Dodoma Capital of Tanzania, central Tanzania. In 1974 Dodoma replaced DAR ES SALAAM as capital. It is in an agricultural region, and crops include grain, seeds and nuts. Pop. (1988) 203,833.

dog Domesticated, carnivorous mammal closely related to the jackal, wolf and fox. Typically it has a slender, muscular body; long head with slender snout; small paws, five toes on the forefeet, four on the hind; non-retractile claws; and well-developed teeth. Smell is the dog's keenest sense; its hearing is also acute. The gestation period is 49 to 70 days; one or more puppies are born. Dogs developed from the tree-dwelling *miacis*, which lived c.40 million years ago. The dog was domesticated c.10–14,000 years ago. There are c.400 breeds classified in various ways, such as TERRIER, sporting, hound, working and toy. Length: 34–135cm (13.4–53.2in); tail 11–54cm (4.3–21.3in); weight: 0.1kg–70kg (2–150lb). Family Canidae; species *Canis familiaris*. *See also* individual breeds

Doge's Palace Residence of the *doge* (chief magistrate of Venice, 697–1797), in ST MARK'S Square, VENICE, Italy. It was begun in the 9th century and rebuilt several times, and the present version (by Giovanni and Bartolomeo Buon) is in Venetian Gothic style.

dogfish SHARK found in marine waters worldwide. Generally greyish with white spots, it lacks a lower tail lobe. Eggs are laid in cases (mermaids' purses). Dogfish are divided into two groups: spiny and spineless. A food fish, they are sold as rock salmon. Length: spiny, 0.6–1.2m (2–4ft); spineless, 7.3m (24ft). Suborder Squalidae.

dogwood Any of several small trees and shrubs in the genus *Cornus* of the family Cornaceae. Wild flowering dogwoods are in deciduous forests. They have small flowers in four large petal-like, white bracts.

Doha Capital of QATAR, on the E coast of the Qatar peninsula in the Persian (Arabian) Gulf. Doha was a small fishing village until oil production began in 1949. It is now a modern city and trade centre. Industries: oil refining, shipping, engineering. Pop. (1993) 339,000.

Dohnányi, Ernst (Ernö) von (1877–1960) Hungarian composer, conductor and pianist. Hungarian folk influences are evident, in pieces such as the piano suite *Ruralia Hungarica* (1926). He also composed operas, concertos and orchestral pieces.

Doisy, Edward Adelbert (1893–1986) US biochemist. He researched blood buffers, vitamins and metabolism. Doisy also isolated the female sex hormones, oestrone (1929) and oestradiol (1935). He shared the 1943 Nobel Prize for physiology or medicine with Henrik DAM for their analysis of vitamin K.

Dolby system Electronic circuit for reducing the background hiss created in SOUND RECORDING on magnetic TAPE. It was invented (1966) by Ray Dolby (1933–). The hiss is caused by the granular nature of the tape coating. It is reduced by artificially boosting the higher frequencies before recording and restoring them to their original levels on playback.

doldrums Region of the ocean near the EQUATOR, characterized by calms and light winds. It corresponds approximately to low pressure around the Equator.

dolerite (diabase) Medium-grained, dark green, basic igneous rock. It consists of plagioclase feldspar and pyroxene crysatls It is found worldwide in dykes and sills.

Dole, Bob (Robert Joseph) (1923–) US politician. Dole served as a Republican representative from Kansas (1960–69), before joining the Senate. He was President Gerald FORD's running mate in the unsuccessful Republican campaign (1976). Dole served as majority leader of the Senate (1984–86, 1994–96). In 1996 he finally gained the Republican presidential nomination but ran a lacklustre campaign and lost the election to Bill CLINTON.

Dolin, Sir Anton (1904–83) English ballet dancer and choreographer, b. Patrick Kay. He joined Diaghilev's BALLETS RUSSES in 1921, becoming principal dancer in 1924. Dolin is best-known for his partnership with Alicia MARKOVA, and the couple formed the Markova-Dolin Ballet (1935) and the London Festival Ballet (1949). He was knighted in 1981.

dollar ($) Standard monetary unit of the USA since 1792. It was derived from the Spanish *dolar*, the most widely used coin in the American colonies. Divided into a hundred cents, the value was based on the gold price until 1934. Many other countries have adopted the dollar.

Dollfuss, Engelbert (1892–1934) Austrian chancellor (1932–34). Determined to preserve Austrian independence, he dissolved the National Socialist (Nazi) Party, which had demanded union with Germany (1933), and assumed authoritarian powers. He was assassinated by Austrian Nazis in an unsuccessful coup.

dolmen Megalithic monument of a stone lintel supported by upright stones. Dolmens were used as burial chambers and covered by a BARROW. They are most common in Cornwall, SW England, and Brittany, NW France.

dolomite ($CaMg(CO_3)_2$, calcium-magnesium carbonate) Carbonate mineral found in altered limestones. It is usually colourless or white. A rhombohedral class prismatic crystal, it is often found as a gangue mineral in hydrothermal veins. It is also a sedimentary rock, probably formed by the alteration of limestone by sea water.

Dolomites (Dolomiti or Dolomiten) Alpine range in NE Italy. The Dolomites are composed of dolomitic limestone, eroded to form a striking landscape popular with mountaineers and tourists. The highest peak is Marmolada, 3,342m (10,964ft) high.

dolphin Aquatic mammal, any of the small toothed WHALES of the family Delphinidae. There are c.50 species, both salt and fresh water. The best-known are the dark-blue-backed common dolphin (*Delphinus delphis*), the blue-grey bottle-nosed (*Tursiops truncatus*) and the KILLER WHALE. Larger than a PORPOISE, a dolphin has a distinct beak, slender body, a tail fin for propulsion and a dorsal fin for steering. It breathes through a single blow-hole and can remain underwater for 15 minutes. Dolphins are the fastest and most agile of the whales, achieving speeds up to 39km/h (24mph) and leaps of 9m (30ft). They swim in large, hierarchically-organized schools, feeding on fish and crustacea. Dolphins have a gestation period of 12 months. Their intelligence and playful behaviour have contributed to a wealth of maritime literature and mythology. Dolphins communicate through a complex language and map their environment by ECHOLOCATION. Length: to 4m (13ft).

Domagk, Gerhard (1895–1964) German chemist. He is known for his discovery (1932) of the antibacterial properties of the dye, prontosil. Domagk was awarded the 1939 Nobel Prize for physiology or medicine, but was prevented by Nazi decree from accepting it until 1947.

domain In mathematics, a set of values that can be assigned to the independent VARIABLE in a function or relation; the set of values of the dependent variable is called the range. For example, let the function be $y = x^2$, with x restricted to 0, 1, 2, 3 and −3. Then y takes the values 0, 1, 4, 9 and 9, respectively. The domain is {0, 1, 2, 3, −3} and the range is {0, 1, 4, 9}.

domain In TAXONOMY, the domain is sometimes seen as a higher category than KINGDOM. In this scheme, the two subkingdoms of PROKARYOTAE (ARCHAEBACTERIA and EUBACTERIA) constitute two domains, called Archaea and Bacteria. All other living organisms are included in a third domain, EUKARYOTES. *See also* PHYLOGENETICS; PLANT CLASSIFICATION

dome In architecture, a hemispherical roof. One of the earliest monumental domes is the PANTHEON, Rome. The dome was an important element in ISLAMIC ART AND ARCHITECTURE, especially MOSQUES. It was a significant element in Renaissance and Baroque styles.

Domenichino (1581–1641) Leading painter of the Italian BAROQUE. In 1602, he worked with Annibale Carracci on the FARNESE Palace. His masterpiece is *The Last Communion of St Jerome* (1614) altarpiece in the Vatican.

Dome of the Rock (Qubbat al-Sakhrah) MOSQUE and shrine built (685–692) by Abd al-Malik on a Jewish temple site in JERUSALEM. The Dome covers the summit of Mount Moriah, where the prophet MUHAMMAD is believed to have ascended to Heaven. According to the Old Testament, the Rock is also where ABRAHAM was to have sacrificed ISAAC. *See also* TEMPLE, JERUSALEM

Domesday Book (1085–86) Census of the English kingdom commissioned by WILLIAM I (THE CONQUEROR) to ascertain potential crown revenue. The most complete survey in medieval Europe, it is an important primary historical source. It lists property and resources by manors.

Domingo, Placido (1941–) Spanish tenor, one of the leading opera singers of his generation. In 1961 he made his debut at Monterrey, Mexico. Domingo is an outstanding interpreter of the Italian romantic repertoire. In

the 1990s, he achieved popularity as one of the Three Tenors. *See also* CARRERAS, JOSÉ; PAVAROTTI, LUCIANO

Dominic, Saint (1170–1221) (Domingo de Guzmán) Spanish priest, founder of the DOMINICANS. In 1203, Pope INNOCENT III sent him to preach to the ALBIGENSES. Dominic founded a monastery at Prouille, S France. He developed an order based on scholastic and democratic principles, and rules derived from St AUGUSTINE. His feast day is 4 August.

Dominica Independent island nation in the E Caribbean Sea, West Indies; the capital and chief port is ROSEAU. The largest of the WINDWARD ISLANDS, it was named after *dies dominica* (Sunday), the day it was discovered by Christopher COLUMBUS (1493). The original inhabitants were CARIB, but the present population are mainly the descendants of African slaves. Dominica is mountainous and heavily forested, and the climate is tropical. Possession of Dominica was disputed between Britain and France, until it was awarded to Britain in 1783. It became a British crown colony in 1805 and was a member of the Federation of the West Indies (1958–62). It achieved complete independence as a republic within the Commonwealth of Nations in 1978. Dominica is one of the poorest Caribbean countries. Agriculture is the dominant economic sector. Exports: copra, bananas, citrus fruit. Area: 750sq km (290sq mi). Pop. (2000) 87,000.

Dominican Republic Independent nation occupying the E two-thirds of the island of Hispaniola in the West Indies; the capital is SANTO DOMINGO. Dominican Republic is mountainous: the Cordillera Central range includes the highest point in the Caribbean, Duarte Peak, at 3,175m (10,417ft). The most fertile agricultural region is the Cibao Valley. Hispaniola was visited by Christopher COLUMBUS in 1492, and a Spanish settlement was established at Santo Domingo. In 1697, the W third of the island (now HAITI) was ceded to France. In 1795, the whole island came under French rule, but the E part was returned to Spain in 1809. In 1821, the colony declared itself the independent Dominican Republic but was annexed by Haiti. It won independence a second time in 1844. Its subsequent history was punctuated by dictatorships and US military interventions. The most notorious dictator was Rafael Trujillo, who ruled from 1930 to 1961. In 1965, a left-wing revolt was suppressed with the help of US troops. In 1966, Joaquín Balaguer was elected president and a new constitution was adopted. Antonio Guzmán Fernández was president, 1978–1986, after which Balaguer returned to power. In 1996, he was succeeded by Leonel Fernández Reyna. In 2000, Hipóliti Mejía was elected president. Mineral deposits are an increasingly important export, though agriculture is still the economic mainstay. Tourism is encouraged. Chief crops: sugar cane, coffee. Area: 48,442sq km (18,703sq mi). Pop. (2000) 8,621,000.

Dominicans (officially *Ordo Praedicatorum*, Order of Preachers, O.P.) Roman Catholic religious order, founded (1215) by St DOMINIC. They are also known as Black Friars or Jacobins. Dominicans are one of the four great mendicant orders of Roman Catholicism. Devoted to preaching and study, the order operates worldwide and includes a contemplative order of nuns. Noted scholars include St Thomas AQUINAS and Saint ALBERTUS MAGNUS.

Domino, "Fats" (Antoine) (1928–) US pianist and singer. Domino's blend of BOOGIE-WOOGIE piano and rhythm-and-blues sold 23 million records between 1949 and 1960. His hits included "Ain't that a Shame" (1955) and "Blueberry Hill" (1956).

dominoes Game played with rectangular tiles. The standard game, played by 2 to 6 players, uses a set of 28 wood-

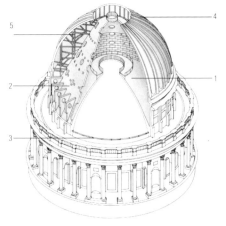

▲ **dome** The dome of St Paul's Cathedral, London, was designed (1675–1711) by Sir Christopher Wren. To make it as airy and as light as possible, it has a triple construction: a brick inner dome (1), its "eye" rising 65m (213ft) above the floor; an intermediate, brick cone (2) reinforced with iron chains (3) and an outer dome (4), resting on the intermediate cone and built out with timber framing (5) and lead covering to obtain the desired silhouette.

en or plastic tiles. The top of every domino is divided into two equal squares, each of which contains a number from 0 (blank) to 6 in dice format. The dominoes are played one at a time with identical numbers placed adjacent to each other. The first to dispose of all their dominoes wins.

domino theory Political doctrine that affected US foreign policy during the COLD WAR. It held that if one country became communist, its neighbours would inevitably follow. The doctrine was widely used in support of US military involvement in VIETNAM.

Domitian (AD 51–96) Roman emperor (81–96). A son of VESPASIAN, he succeeded his brother TITUS. His rule was at first orderly but became increasingly tyrannical. After several attempts, he was assassinated. Domitian was partly responsible for building the COLOSSEUM.

Don River of SW Russia. Rising SE of Tula, it flows S, then SW to the Sea of Azov. Rostov is the major port. Annual floods are controlled by the Tsimlyansk Reservoir. The Don is navigable for 1,370km (850mi) and is an important shipping route for grain, timber and coal. It is linked to the River VOLGA. Length: 1,930km (1,200mi).

Donatello (c.1386–1466) Italian artist, greatest European sculptor of the 15th century, joint creator of RENAISSANCE ART in Florence. His work marks a turning point in European sculpture, moving from a formulaic GOTHIC style to a more vital means of expression, inspired by humanism. His initial innovations included standing figures of saints in Orsanmichele, Florence. Donatello invented the technique of *stiacciato* ("like drawing in marble"). After a visit to Rome (1430–32), his work, such as the bronze *David*, adopted a more CLASSICAL feel. His late work, such as *Judith and Holofernes* and a wood carving of *Mary Magdalene* (1455), shows even greater emotional intensity. Donatello greatly influenced MICHELANGELO.

Donatism Schismatic Christian movement founded in 4th-century N Africa. The movement was led by Donatus. In the tradition of Montanism followers claimed that only those without sin belonged to the Church, and they supported re-baptism. Despite condemnation by the Synod of Arles (314), by the mid-5th century Donatism had become the dominant form of Christianity in Africa. Only with the teachings of St AUGUSTINE did Donatism decline.

Doncaster City and county district on the River Don, South Yorkshire, NE England. Founded as a Roman fort, it was an important staging post on route from Lincoln to York. The racecourse hosts the St Leger, Britain's oldest horse-race. Other sites include Mansion House. Industries: railway engineering, mechanical engineering. Pop. (1991) 288,854.

Donegal County in NW Republic of Ireland, bounded by Northern Ireland (E) and the Atlantic Ocean (N and W). The county town is Lifford. There is a rocky, indented coastline and much of the county is hilly. The chief rivers are the Finn, Foyle and Erne. Agriculture is the main activity. Tourism and fishing are also important. Area: 4,830sq km (1,865sq mi). Pop. (1991) 128,117.

Donets Basin (Donbas or Donec) Industrial region in E Ukraine and S Russia; the capital is Donetsk. It is a major coal and steel producer. Development of one of the world's most concentrated industrial areas began c.1870. By 1989, it was producing more than 200 million tonnes of coal a year. In the 1990s, there was a slump in production due to exhausted deposits and antiquated technology. Area: c.25,900sq km (10,000sq mi).

Dönitz, Karl (1891–1980) German admiral. He was commander-in-chief (1943–45) of the German navy during WORLD WAR 2. On the death of HITLER, Dönitz

became chancellor and negotiated the German surrender. He was imprisoned (1946–56) for war crimes.

Donizetti, Gaetano (1797–1848) Italian composer. He wrote 75 comic and serious operas. Initially influenced by ROSSINI, he formed his own melodic style. Operas include *L'Elisir d'Amore* (1832), *Lucia di Lammermoor* (1835), *Roberto Devereux* (1837) and *Don Pasquale* (1843).

Don Juan Legendary Spanish philanderer of a medieval folk tale, the earliest printed version being *The Rake of Seville* (1630) by Tirso de Molina. Notable versions of his amorous adventures are Mozart's opera *Don Giovanni* (1787) and Lord Byron's poem *Don Juan* (1819–24).

donkey Domesticated ASS used by humans since well before 3000 BC. Crossed with a horse it produces a MULE.

Donleavy, J.P. (James Patrick) (1926–) Irish author, b. USA. Donleavy's first novel, *The Ginger Man* (1955), was not published in uncensored form in Britain and the USA until 1963. Other novels include *A Singular Man* (1963), *The Onion Eaters* (1971) and *That Darcy, That Dancer, That Gentleman* (1991).

Donne, John (1572–1631) English poet and cleric. Donne's METAPHYSICAL POETRY is among the greatest work in ENGLISH LITERATURE. His early poetry, from the 1590s, consists mainly of love poems, elegies and satires. The love poetry is intense, erotic and rhetorical; the elegies, colloquial and racy; the satires, witty and cynical. Donne's marriage (1601) to a minor, Anne More, ruined his court career. His poetry, such as *An Anatomy of the World* (1611) and *Of the Progress of the Soul* (1612), became more philosophical. Donne's rejection of Catholicism and conversion to Anglicanism is evident in the prose-work *Pseudo-Martyr* (1610). He was ordained in 1615 and became dean (1621) of St Paul's Cathedral, London (1621). Donne's late poetry is devotional in tone, such as the powerful *Holy Sonnets*. Donne's *Collected Poems* were published in 1633.

Doolittle, Hilda (1886–1961) (H.D.) US poet, associated with Ezra POUND and IMAGISM. Her published verse includes the collections *Sea Garden* (1916) and *The Flowering of the Rod* (1946). She also wrote prose, such as *Palimpsest* (1926) and *Hermione* (1981).

Doors, The US psychedelic rock group formed in 1965 by Jim Morrison (1943–71) and Ray Manzarek (1935–). The other two members were John Densmore and Robby Krieger. Their first album, *The Doors* (1967), contains probably their most famous tune "Light My Fire". The band achieved notoriety through Morrison's poetic lyrics and flamboyant stage performances.

dopamine Chemical normally found in the corpus striatum region of the brain. Insufficient levels are linked with PARKINSON'S DISEASE. Dopamine is a NEUROTRANSMITTER. *See also* ADRENALINE; NORADRENALINE

Doppler, Christian Johann (1803–53) Austrian physicist and mathematician. Doppler is famous for his prediction (1842) of the DOPPLER EFFECT.

Doppler effect Change in frequency of a wave when there is relative motion between the wave source and the observer. The amount of change depends on the velocities of the wave, source and observer. With a sound wave, the effect is the drop in pitch of a vehicle's siren as it passes an observer. With light, the velocity must be large for an appreciable effect, such as the RED SHIFT of a rapidly receding galaxy. *See also* NAVIGATION

Dorchester County and market town of Dorset, on the River Frome, S England. It was the setting for Judge JEFFREYS' "Bloody Assizes" (1685). The Iron-Age earthworks of Maiden Castle lie on the outskirts of the town. Dorchester was the model for Casterbridge in the novels of Thomas HARDY. Pop. (1991) 15,037.

Dordogne River in SW France. Rising in the AUVERGNE hills, it is formed by the convergence of the rivers Dor and Dogne. It flows SW then W to meet the River Garonne and forms the Gironde estuary. It has famous vineyards along its 471km (293mi) course.

Doré, Gustave (1832–83) French illustrator, painter and sculptor. He is best known for his engraved book illustrations, such as *Inferno* (1861), *Don Quixote* (1862) and the Bible (1866).

Dorian Greek-speaking people who settled in N Greece *c.*1200 BC. They displaced the culturally superior MYCENAEAN CIVILIZATION because they mastered the use of iron. Their arrival marks the start of a 400-year "dark age" of ancient Greece.

Doric order One of the five ORDERS OF ARCHITECTURE

dormancy Temporary state of inaction or reduced METABOLISM in plants and animals. Animals may become dormant (HIBERNATION) during winter months when food resources are scarce; dormant plant seeds cease to grow or develop for a time. An organism can return to a fully active state when conditions, such as temperature, moisture or day length, change.

dormouse Squirrel-like RODENT of Eurasia and Africa in temperate climates. Most dormice are active at night. They eat nuts, fruit, seeds, insects and other tiny animals. They were once bred for human food. Length: 10–20cm (4–8in), excluding tail. Family Gliridae.

Dorset County on the English Channel, SW England; the county town is DORCHESTER. Dorset's most famous prehistoric monument is the Iron Age hill fort, Maiden Castle. It is traversed W to E by the North Dorset and South Dorset Downs. Cereal crop cultivation and livestock raising are important. Industries: tourism, marble quarrying. Area: 2,654sq km (1,025sq mi). Pop. (1991) 361,919.

Dortmund City and port on the Dortmund-Ems Canal, Nodrhein-Westfalen state, NW Germany. In the 13th century Dortmund flourished as a member of the HANSEATIC LEAGUE. It declined in the late 17th century but grew as an industrial centre from the mid-19th century. Industries: iron and steel. Pop. (1995) 474,000.

dory (John Dory) Marine fish found worldwide. It is deep-bodied with a large mouth. The species *Zeus faber* of the Mediterranean Sea and Atlantic Ocean is a valuable food fish. Length: to 1m (3.3ft). Family Zeidae.

DOS Acronym for DISK OPERATING SYSTEM

Dos Passos, John Roderigo (1896–1970) US novelist. His characteristic style was first evident in *Manhattan Transfer* (1925). Dos Passos' masterpiece, the trilogy *United States*, consisting of *The 42nd Parallel* (1930), *1919* (1932) and *The Big Money* (1936), develops his ambitious idea of a "collective" portrait of early 20th-century USA using multiple narrative forms, including STREAM OF CONSCIOUSNESS.

Dos Santos, José Eduardo (1942–) Angolan statesman, president (1979–). Dos Santos' succession to the presidency was marked by violence between the Cuban-backed People's Movement for the Liberation of Angola (MPLA) government and the South African-backed National Union for the Total Independence of Angola (UNITA), led by Jonas SAVIMBI. The Lusaka Protocol (1994) paved the way for a government of national unity, headed by Dos Santos.

Dostoevsky, Fyodor Mikhailovich (1821–81) Russian novelist, one of the greatest 19th-century writers. After completing *Poor Folk* and *The Double* (both 1846), he joined a revolutionary group, was arrested and sentenced to death (1849). He was reprieved at the eleventh hour, and his sentence was commuted to four years' hard labour.

Dostoevsky returned to St Petersburg in 1859, where he wrote *Notes from the Underground* (1864). After *Crime and Punishment* was published (1866), he left Russia, partly to escape creditors. His last major work was his masterpiece, *The Brothers Karamazov* (1879–80).

dotterel Wading bird of the plover family. The Eurasian dotterel (*Eudromias morinellus*) has a stocky body, short tail and mottled-brown plumage with a rust-coloured breast. Length: 22cm (8.5.in). Family Charadriidae.

Douai Bible English translation (from the Latin Vulgate) of the BIBLE, authorized by the Roman Catholic Church for use after the REFORMATION. Gregory Martin, living in exile at Douai, France, was the main translator. The NEW TESTAMENT was published at Reims (1582), the OLD TESTAMENT at Douai (1609–10). It was revised by Richard Challoner (1749–50).

Douala Chief port of Cameroon, on the Bight of Biafra, W Africa. As Kamerunstadt, it was capital of the German Kamerun Protectorate (1885–1901), then became Douala (1907) and was capital of French Cameroon (1940–46). Industries: ship repairing, textiles, palm oil. Pop. (1992) 1,200,000.

double bass Largest stringed instrument. It has four strings tuned in fourths (E-A-D-G) and sounds one OCTAVE below the musical notation. It resembles a large violin but has sloping shoulders. The double bass is held vertically. A bow is generally used for classical music, but the strings are usually plucked in jazz.

double star Two stars that appear close together. There are two types of double star: BINARY STARS and **optical doubles** (two stars quite distant from each other, but appearing close as a result of chance alignment).

Douglas, Gavin (1475–1522) Scottish medieval poet, important in the emergence of Scots as a distinct language. Douglas' rhymed-couplet version of Virgil's *Aeneid* in Scots (1513) was the first translation of a classic into an English-based language.

Douglas, Kirk (1916–) US actor and producer, b. Issur Danielovitch, father of Michael DOUGLAS. His first major role was in the boxing film *Champion* (1949). Douglas earned Academy Award nominations for *The Bad and the Beautiful* (1952) and as Vincent Van Gogh in *Lust for Life* (1956). Other films include *Gunfight at the OK Corral* (1957) and *Spartacus* (1960).

Douglas, Michael (1944–) US actor and producer, son of Kirk DOUGLAS. His acting career soared in the adventure-comedies *Romancing the Stone* (1984) and *Jewel of the Nile* (1985). Douglas won a best actor Oscar for *Wall Street* (1987). Other films include *Fatal Attraction* (1986), *Basic Instinct* (1992) and *Wonder Boys* (2000).

Douglas, Stephen Arnold (1813–61) US politician. Known as the "Little Giant", he was a senator (1847–61). His doctrine of "popular sovereignty" proposed that each territory be given the right to chose whether it wanted SLAVERY or not. Douglas sponsored the KANSAS-NEBRASKA ACT (1854). His debates with Abraham LINCOLN in the 1858 senate campaign on the issue of slavery attracted great attention. Douglas was returned to the Senate but had alienated many Southern Democrats. In 1860, his nomination as presidential candidate for the Democrats split the party. Lincoln won the election, and Douglas supported him when the American CIVIL WAR broke out.

Douglas fir Conifer tree native to W North America. The Douglas fir is, in fact, a pine tree. Named after a Scottish botanist, David Douglas (1798–1834), it grows 60 to 90m (200–300ft) tall and has long, flat needles and hanging cones. It is the most valuable provider of timber in North America. Family Pinaceae.

Douglas-Home, Sir Alec (1903–95) British statesman, prime minister (1963–64). He entered Parliament in 1931, and served as parliamentary private secretary (1937–39) to Neville CHAMBERLAIN. He joined (1951) the House of Lords as Lord Home of the Hirsel and had a succession of cabinet posts, including foreign secretary (1960–63). Douglas-Home renounced his peerage to succeed Harold MACMILLAN as Conservative prime minister. He was also foreign secretary under Edward HEATH (1970–74).

Douglass, Frederick (1817–95) African-American abolitionist and social reformer. An escaped slave, he became (1841) a lecturer for the Massachusetts Anti-Slavery Society. Douglass wrote *Narrative of the Life of Frederick Douglass* (1845) and, fearing capture, went into exile in England. In 1847 he bought his freedom and returned to the USA to found the abolitionist newspaper, *North Star*. A lifelong supporter of equal rights, he served as minister to Haiti (1889–91).

Doukhobors (Dukhobors, Rus. spirit wrestlers) Russian nonconformist Christian sect founded in the 18th century. Doukhobors rejected ecclesiastical and state authority in favour of a pacifist, communal society. Under the leadership of Peter Verigin and with the help of Leo Tolstoy and English QUAKERS, 7,000 Doukhobors emigrated (1899) to w Canada where they established successful agricultural communities. Internal divisions emerged, and the sect split (1945) into the Union of the Doukhobors and the more radical Sons of Freedom.

Douro (Duero) River in Spain and Portugal. Rising in N central Spain, it flows w to form part of the Spanish-Portuguese border. It then turns w through N Portugal to empty into the Atlantic Ocean near OPORTO. Length: 895km (556mi).

dove Cooing, plump-bodied bird found almost worldwide. Doves are related to PIGEONS and have small heads, short legs and dense, varied plumage. They feed mostly on vegetable matter. Length: 15–83cm (6–33in). Family Columbidae.

Dover Seaport on the Strait of Dover, Kent, SE England. One of the cinque ports, Dover is a resort and cross-Channel ferry port. The nearest point to France on mainland Britain, it was fortified by the Romans. In World War 1 it was an important naval base, and it suffered intensive bombing during World War 2. Its medieval castle contains the remains of a Roman lighthouse and a Saxon stronghold. Pop. (1991) 34,322.

Dover State capital of Delaware, USA, on the St Jones River. Founded in 1683, it has been state capital since 1777. It is a shipping and canning centre for the surrounding agricultural region. Industries: gelatin food products, synthetic polymers. Pop. (1990) 27,630.

Dowding, Hugh Caswell Tremenheere, Baron (1882–1970) British air chief marshal, b. Scotland. As commander-in-chief (1936–40) of Fighter Command, he organized the air defence that defeated the Luftwaffe in the Battle of Britain (1940). Dowding retired in 1942.

Dowell, Sir Anthony (1943–) English ballet dancer, director of the Royal Ballet (1986–2001). He joined the Royal Ballet in 1961 and was principal dancer (1966–86). Dowell's most famous partnership was with Antoinette Sibley. In 1978–79, he danced with the American Ballet Theatre. Dowell was knighted in 1973.

Dowland, John (1563–1626) English composer of songs and lute music. His songs, written for voice and lute, are widely considered to be the finest of his generation, due to their great emotional range. He also composed much instrumental music, such as the famous set of variations, *Lachrimae* (1605).

Down District on the Irish Sea coast, SE Northern Ireland; the administrative centre is Downpatrick. The Mountains of Mourne lie in the S. Anglo-Normans invaded (12th century), and from the 16th century English and Scottish settlers made their home here. Agriculture dominates the economy. Industries: agricultural machinery, textiles. Area: 650sq km (250sq mi). Pop. (1991) 58,008.

Downing Street Street in London, off Whitehall, named after the diplomat Sir George Downing (1623–84). It includes the official residence of the British prime minister at No. 10, chancellor of the exchequer at No. 11 and chief whip at No. 12.

Downing Street Declaration (15 December 1993) Joint declaration issued by the UK prime minster John MAJOR and the Irish leader Albert REYNOLDS. Continuing the momentum of the ANGLO-IRISH AGREEMENT, it set a framework for peace talks in NORTHERN IRELAND. It stated that all political parties (including SINN FÉIN) could be involved in an all-Ireland forum if they committed themselves to permanently ending paramilitary violence. The UK and Irish governments also agreed that the status of Northern Ireland could only change with majority consent of its people, and Ireland's future would be determined only by the peoples of the island of Ireland.

Down's syndrome Human condition caused by the presence of an extra copy of CHROMOSOME 21. It gives rise to varying degrees of mental retardation, decreased life expectancy and perhaps physical problems, such as heart and respiratory disorders. The syndrome was first described by British physician J.L.H. Down (1828–96). There is evidence that the risk of having a Down's child increases with maternal age. It was originally called "Mongolism" by Down, but this term is now obsolete.

Doyle, Sir Arthur Conan (1859–1930) English physician and novelist. The novel, *A Study in Scarlet* (1887), introduced his famous characters Sherlock Holmes and Dr. Watson. A succession of highly popular Sherlock Holmes stories followed, including *The Adventures of Sherlock Holmes* (1892), *The Memoirs of Sherlock Holmes* (1894) and *The Hound of the Baskervilles* (1902). Other works include *The Lost World* (1912).

Doyle, Roddy (1958–) Irish novelist, dramatist and screenwriter. Doyle established his reputation with *The Commitments* (1987), which formed a trilogy with *The Snapper* (1990) and *The Van* (1991). The film version of *The Commitments* (1991), directed by Alan PARKER, received widespread acclaim. In 1993, Doyle was awarded the Booker Prize for *Paddy Clarke Ha Ha Ha*. Other novels include *The Woman Who Walked into Doors* (1996) and *A Star called Henry* (1999).

D'Oyly Carte, Richard *See* CARTE, RICHARD D'OYLY

Drabble, Margaret (1939–) English novelist, sister of A.S. BYATT. *The Millstone* (1965) was filmed as *A Touch of Love*. Later work includes the trilogy, *The Radiant Way* (1987), *A Natural Curiosity* (1989) and *The Gates of Ivory* (1991).

Draco (active 7th century BC) Athenian political leader and lawmaker. He drew up the first written code of laws in Athens. They were famous for their severity, and the death penalty was prescribed even for minor offenses.

Draco (Dragon) Long, winding N constellation, representing the dragon slain by Hercules. It extends between URSA MAJOR and URSA MINOR, with the dragon's head near the star VEGA.

drag (air resistance) Force opposing the motion of a body through a gas or liquid. Aircraft experience drag as the friction of air over external surfaces. To combat drag, aircraft and cars have streamlined designs.

dragon Mythical scaly lizard, snake or fire-breathing monster. Often depicted with wings, talons and a lashing tail, in some traditions it has many heads or changes shape at will. Sometimes, such as the tale of St GEORGE and the dragon, it is used symbolically as the incarnation of evil. In China and Japan, the dragon is identified with a beneficent force of nature. The term can also refer to certain lizards, such as the KOMODO DRAGON.

dragonfly Swift-flying insect of the order Odonata. It has a long, slender, often brightly coloured abdomen, and two pairs of large membranous wings. Like the DAMSELFLY, it mates while flying. The carnivorous nymphs are aquatic. Wing span: to 17cm (7in).

Drake, Sir Francis (*c*.1540–96) English mariner. In 1577–80, he circumnavigated the world in the *Golden Hind*, looting Spanish ships and settlements and claiming California for England. Drake was knighted by Elizabeth I on his return. His raid on CADIZ in 1587 postponed the Spanish ARMADA, which he helped to defeat in 1588. Drake died in a raid on the Spanish colonies.

Drakensberg Mountains (Kwathlamba) Major mountain range in S Africa, extending through Lesotho, KwaZulu-Natal, Free State and Transvaal. The highest peak is Thabana Ntlenyana in Lesotho, at 3,485m (11,425ft). Length: *c*.1,130km (700mi).

drama Art form, probably derived from primitive religious rituals. In the West, drama developed into a sophisticated art form in 5th-century BC Greece with the plays of AESCHYLUS, SOPHOCLES, EURIPIDES and ARISTOPHANES. GREEK DRAMA followed the unity of action, defined by ARISTOTLE in his *Poetics*. Classical Roman drama relied heavily on Greek models, and these in turn strongly influenced ELIZABETHAN and JACOBEAN drama, such as the plays of William KYD, Francis BEAUMONT, John FLETCHER, Christopher MARLOWE, Ben JONSON and William SHAKESPEARE. In Spain, Lope de VEGA established the *comedia*, written in verse with three acts. NEOCLASSICISM flourished in the reign of LOUIS XIV with the tragedies of CORNEILLE and RACINE. The comedies of MOLIÈRE reflected the influence of the COMMEDIA DELL'ARTE. Twentieth-century drama received its impetus from the NATURALISM of CHEKHOV, IBSEN and STRINDBERG. The

verse dramas of T.S. ELIOT marked the beginnings of MODERNISM. These experiments were extended by EPIC THEATRE, theatre of CRUELTY and theatre of the ABSURD. SURREALISM influenced the work of PIRANDELLO and Samuel BECKETT. *See also* CHINESE THEATRE; COMEDY; INDIAN THEATRE; JAPANESE THEATRE; TRAGEDY

draughts (checkers) Board game played between two people on a chessboard. Each player starts with a set of 12 counters, arranged on the dark squares of the first three rows. The players take it in turn to move pieces one square diagonally forwards. If a square is occupied by an opponent's piece, it may be taken or "jumped" and the opponent's piece is removed from the board. A counter reaching the opponent's back line can be "crowned" as a king, which is able to move diagonally backwards as well as forwards. The object of the game is to capture all the opponent's pieces.

Dravidian Family of languages spoken in S India by *c*.10 million people. The four major Dravidian languages are Telugu, Tamil, Kannada and Malayalam. Tamil is also spoken in Sri Lanka. Brahui is spoken in Pakistan.

dream Mental activity associated with rapid-eye-movement (REM) sleep. It is usually a train of thoughts, scenes, and desires expressed in visual images and symbols. On average, a person dreams for a total of 1.5–2 hours in eight hours of sleep. For centuries, dreams have been regarded as a source of prophecy or visionary insight. In PSYCHOANALYSIS, patients' dreams are often examined to reveal a latent content.

Dreiser, Theodore Herman Albert (1871–1945) US writer. His first novel, *Sister Carrie* (1900), was considered immoral by its publisher, and Dreiser distributed it himself. *Jennie Gerhardt* (1911) was attacked for its uncompromising NATURALISM. Dreiser's masterpiece, *An American Tragedy* (1925), is based on a real murder case.

Dresden City on the River Elbe, capital of Saxony, SE Germany. First settled by Germans in the early 13th century, it suffered almost total destruction from Allied bombing in World War 2. Industries: optical and precision instruments. Pop. (1995) 474,000.

Dreyer, Carl Theodor (1889–1968) Danish film director. His silent masterpiece, *The Passion of Joan of Arc* (1928), used prolonged close-ups and elaborate sets. His best-known film, *Day of Wrath* (1943), is a slow-burning allegory on the Nazi occupation of Denmark.

Dreyfus Affair French political crisis arising from the conviction of Captain Alfred Dreyfus (1859–1935) for treason in 1894. Dreyfus was a Jewish army officer convicted on false evidence. In 1898, publication of *J'accuse*, an open letter by Emile ZOLA in defence of Dreyfus, provoked a bitter national controversy. Dreyfus, initially imprisoned, later received a presidential pardon.

dromedary Large domesticated CAMEL, a pack and riding animal. It has a long neck and legs, wide feet suited to walking on sand and snow, and a single fatty hump on its back. Height: to 2m (7ft) at the shoulder.

drongo Noisy, pugnacious, insect-eating bird of South Africa, SE Asia and Australia. It has a thick, hooked bill, bristled nostrils, long forked tail, iridescent blackish plumage and, in some species, ornamental feathers and crests. Length: 18–38cm (7–15in). Family Dicruridae.

Drosophila *See* FRUIT FLY

drought Condition that occurs when EVAPORATION and TRANSPIRATION exceed PRECIPITATION for long periods. Four kinds are recognized: **permanent**, typical of desert and semi-arid regions; **seasonal**, in climates with well-defined dry and rainy seasons; **unpredictable**, an abnormal failure of expected rainfall; and **invisible**, when even

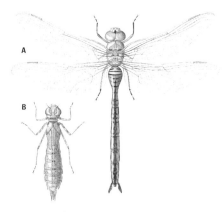

▲ dragonfly An incomplete metamorphosis, such as occurs in dragonflies, may be an adaptation to take advantage of different habitats. The adult form (A) of *Anax imperator* is a fast-flying predator of other insects, while the nymph (B) is aquatic, preying on a variety of life in ponds.

frequent showers do not restore sufficient moisture. In the In sub-Saharan Africa a series of droughts in the late 1960s and 1980s caused major famine. In Britain, an absolute drought is defined as a period of at least 15 consecutive days on none of which more than 0.25mm of rain falls.

drug In medicine, a substance used to diagnose, prevent or treat disease, or aid recovery from injury. Although many drugs are still obtained from natural sources, scientists are continually developing synthetic drugs. Such drugs include ANTIBIOTICS. Some drugs interfere in physiological processes, such as anti-coagulants which render the blood less prone to clotting. Drugs also may be given to make good some deficiency, such as hormone preparations for an underactive gland.

drug addiction Psychological or physical dependence on a DRUG. **Physical** addiction is often manifested by symptoms of withdrawal (such as vomiting and convulsions) if the drug dose is decreased or stopped. Long-term drug use often produces tolerance and increased doses are required to reproduce the psychological effect. Physical dependence on drugs has only been medically proven for NARCOTICS (such as HEROIN), depressants (such as BARBITURATES or ALCOHOL) and some STIMULANTS (such as NICOTINE). Other drugs, such as hallucinogens or hashish, are not thought to be physically addictive, but can produce PSYCHOSIS or PARANOIA. Two of the most common addictions are alcohol and nicotine, since these are legal and easily available. In comparison, addiction to "hard" (addictive) drugs (such as HEROIN or CRACK cocaine) is not common, yet drug-related crime makes up a significant percentage of crime statistics in many countries.

Druids Pre-Christian Celtic religious leaders of ancient Britain, Ireland and Gaul. Little is known of them but they appear to have been judges and teachers as well as priests. In Britain and Gaul, druidism was suppressed by the Romans, but it survived in Ireland until the 5th century.

drum Percussion instrument, generally a hollow cylinder or vessel with a skin stretched across the openings. It is struck with hands or a variety of sticks. Drums were among the earliest musical instruments; examples have been found dating from 6000 BC. Drums first appeared in European CLASSICAL MUSIC in the 18th century. In the 20th century, the role of drums in popular music has greatly expanded. Since the 1980s, electronic drum machines have shaped the sound of much contemporary dance music. *See also* PERCUSSION; TIMPANI

drumlin Smooth, oval-shaped mound of glacial TILL, one end of which is blunt, the other tapered. Drumlins usually occur in groups called a "drumlin field" or "drumlin swarm". They are believed to be formed beneath the other zone of an advancing ice sheet, which deposits and streamlines material. The long axis of a drumlin lies parallel to the movement of the GLACIER.

Drummond of Hawthornden, William (1585–1649) Scottish poet. He was the first Scottish poet to write in a non-Scottish English. Drummond's works include *Poems* (1616) and *Flowers of Sion* (1623). He also wrote many Royalist pamphlets.

drupe (stone fruit) Any FRUIT with a thin skin, fleshy pulp, and hard stone or pit enclosing a single seed.

Druse (Druze) Middle Eastern religious sect. A breakaway group of the ISMAILIS, the Druse originated in the reign of al-Hakim (996–1021), sixth Fatimid CALIPH of Egypt. They are named after al-Darazi, the first to proclaim the cult. Stressing pure MONOTHEISM, they emphasize the possibility of direct communication with divinity as a living presence. There are *c*.500,000 Druses living in Syria, LEBANON and Israel.

dryads In Greek mythology, nymphs of the woodlands and guardian spirits of trees.

dry cleaning Method of cleaning fabrics using special solvent fluids and soaps without water. It was discovered by accident in 1849 by a French tailor, Jolly-Belin, when he noticed the cleaning effect of some spilt turpentine. Introduced into Britain in 1866, it now uses non-flammable solvents in special machines (washing by hand was originally used). Clothes are washed with solvent and dried in a warm-air tumbler.

Dryden, John (1631–1700) English poet and playwright. He first attracted attention for his *Heroic Stanzas* (1659) on the death of Oliver CROMWELL. Dryden also celebrated the RESTORATION with *Astraea Redux* (1660). His account of the events of 1666, *Annus Mirabilis* (1667), saw him become the first official poet laureate (1668–88). For the next decade, Dryden concentrated on dramatic writing, such as *Tyrannic Love* (1669) and the comedy *Marriage à la mode* (1673). *All for Love* (1678) was his first play in blank verse. *MacFlecknoe* (1684) lampooned Thomas Shadwell, his eventual successor as poet laureate. Dryden converted to Catholicism, and *The Hind and the Panther* (1687) is a religious ALLEGORY.

dry ice Popular name for frozen CARBON DIOXIDE

drypoint Quick ENGRAVING technique, probably originating in the 15th century, using a sharply pointed tool to draw lines in a metal plate. Qualities of line are determined by the amount of pressure.

dualism Doctrine in philosophy and metaphysics that recognizes two basic and mutually independent principles, such as mind and matter, body and soul, or good and evil. Dualism contrasts with MONISM. Both PLATO and DESCARTES were dualists, but modern philosophers have tended toward monism.

Dubai One of the seven federated states of the UNITED ARAB EMIRATES (UAE), on the Persian (Arabian) Gulf, SE Arabia; the capital is Dubai. First settled in the late 18th century, it was a dependency of ABU DHABI until 1833. At the end of the 19th century, it became a British protectorate. Dubai was at war with Abu Dhabi from 1945 to 1948. In 1971, it became a founder member of the UAE. Oil was discovered in the early 1960s and is the largest sector of Dubai's prosperous, export-driven economy. Area: *c*.3,890sq km (1,500sq mi). Pop. (1985) 419,104.

Du Barry, Marie Jeanne Bécu, comtesse (1743–93) French courtesan and noblewoman. She was mistress of Jean du Barry, who engineered her acceptance as last mistress of Louis XV in 1769. A great patron of the arts, she was arrested and executed for treason by the Revolutionary Tribunal.

Dubček, Alexander (1921–92) Czechoslovak statesman, Communist Party secretary (1968–69). Dubček was elected party leader at the start of the PRAGUE SPRING. His liberal reforms led to a Soviet invasion in August 1968, and Dubček was forced to resign and was expelled from the party. Following the collapse of Czech communism, he was publicly rehabilitated and served as speaker (1989–92) of the federal parliament.

Dublin (Baile Átha Cliath) Capital of the Republic of Ireland, at the mouth of the River Liffey on Dublin Bay. In 1014, Brian Boru recaptured it from the Danish. In 1170, it was taken by the English and became the seat of colonial government. Dublin suffered much bloodshed in nationalist attempts to free Ireland from English rule. From 1913, a series of strikes culminated in the EASTER RISING (1916). Dublin was the centre of the late-19th-century Irish literary renaissance. George Bernard SHAW, James JOYCE and Oscar WILDE were born here. It is now the commercial and cultural centre of the Republic. Notable sites include Christ Church Cathedral (1053), St Patrick's Cathedral (1190), Trinity College (1591) and the ABBEY THEATRE (1904). Industries: brewing, textiles, clothing. Pop. (1996) 1,024,000.

Dublin County in E Republic of Ireland, in Leinster province, on the Irish Sea; the county town is DUBLIN. Low lying in the N, the land rises to the Wicklow Mountains in the S and is drained chiefly by the River Liffey. Cattle are raised; crops include wheat, barley and potatoes. Area: 356sq mi (922sq km). Pop. (1991) 1,025,304.

dubnium (symbol Db) Synthetic, radioactive, metallic element, first of the transactinide elements, atomic number 104. The longest-lived of its ten ISOTOPES has a half-life of 70 seconds (the longest yet identified). Previously named "unnilquodium", "dubnium" was adopted in 1995 as a compromise between the proposed US name of "rutherfordium" and the Russian proposal of "kurchatovium".

Du Bois, W.E.B. (William Edward Burghardt) (1868–1963) US civil rights leader, writer and educator. In 1905, he co-founded the Niagara movement that evolved into the NATIONAL ASSOCIATION FOR THE ADVANCEMENT OF COLORED PEOPLE (NAACP). Du Bois helped organize the first Pan-African Congress (1919). Works include *The Souls of Black Folk* (1903). *See also* PAN-AFRICANISM

Dubrovnik Adriatic seaport, DALMATIA, Croatia. As a free city, it was an important trading post between the Ottoman Empire and Europe, and a traditional place of asylum for persecuted peoples. It was devastated by an earthquake (1979) and a 1991 Serbian siege. Sites include a 14th-century mint. It is an important tourist centre. Products: grapes, cheese, olives. Pop. (1991) 49,730.

Dubuffet, Jean (1901–85) French painter and sculptor. Among his best-known works are assemblages of materials (such as glass, sand, rope) arranged into crude shapes, called *pâtes*. He collected the work of untrained artists, coining the phrase *art brut*.

Duccio di Buoninsegna (c.1265–c.1319) Italian painter, first great artist of the Sienese School. He infused the rigid Byzantine style of figure painting with humanity and lyricism. Surviving works include *Rucellai Madonna* (1285) and the Maestà altarpiece (1308–11).

Duchamp, Marcel (1887–1968) French painter and theorist, one of the most radical art theorists of the 20th century. His *Nude Descending a Staircase* outraged visitors to the 1913 ARMORY SHOW. Duchamp produced relatively few paintings, concentrating on abolishing the concept of aesthetic beauty. He was a leading member of New York DADA, inventing the "ready-made". His main work, *The Bride Stripped Bare by Her Bachelors, Even* (1915–23), is a "definitively unfinished" painting of metal COLLAGE elements on glass.

duck Worldwide waterfowl, related to the SWAN and GOOSE. Most nest in cool areas and migrate to warm areas in winter. All have large bills, short legs and webbed feet. Their colour is varied, and dense plumage is underlaid by down and waterproof feathers. There are two groups: **dabbling** ducks, which feed from the surface; and **diving** ducks. All eat seeds, insects, crustacea and molluscs. Most lay a large clutch of eggs. There are seven tribes: EIDERS, shelducks, dabbling ducks, perching ducks, pochards, sea ducks and stiff-tailed ducks. There are c.200 species. Length: 30–60cm (1–2ft); weight: to 7.2kg (16lb). Family Anatidae.

duck-billed platypus *See* PLATYPUS

duckweed Family (Lemnaceae) of four genera, including 25 species of tiny, floating, aquatic flowering plants. The disc-like leaflets have one 15cm (6in) trailing root.

ductility Ability of metals and some other materials to be stretched without being weakened. Copper is said to be a ductile metal, as it is easily drawn out to form wire, and silver and gold are even more ductile than copper.

due process of law Formal legal procedure to ensure that no one is deprived of life, freedom or property before proper legal authority has been obtained. It is enshrined in England's MAGNA CARTA. A major element of the process is a TRIAL.

Dufay, Guillaume (1400–74) Burgundian composer. His MOTETS were grand, complex compositions written for specific events. Dufay also wrote masses.

Dufy, Raoul (1877–1953) French painter. Dufy was associated with IMPRESSIONISM and FAUVISM, and is famous for his decorative racing and boating scenes. The bright, luminous colours and linear simplicity of *Riders in the Wood* (1931) is typical of his work.

dugong (sea cow) Large, plant-eating aquatic mammal found in shallow coastal waters of Africa, Asia and Australia. Grey and hairless, the dugong has no hind legs, and its forelegs are weak flippers. Length: 2.5–4m (8–13ft); weight: 270kg (600lb). Family Dugongidae.

duiker (duikerbok) Small, sub-Saharan African ANTELOPE. The female is larger than the male and occasionally carries stunted horns; the horns of the male are short and spiky. Duikers are grey to reddish-yellow. Height: up to 66cm (26in) at the shoulder; weight: up to 17kg (37lb). Family Bovidae; species *Sylvicapra grimmia*.

Duisburg City at the confluence of the rivers Rhine and Ruhr, Nordrhein-Westfalen state, NW Germany. Chartered in 1129, it remained a free imperial city until the late 13th century. During World War 2, Dusiburg was the centre of the German armaments industry and suffered extensive bombing damage. It is Europe's largest inland port. Industries: iron, steel, textiles. Pop. (1995) 536,000.

Dukas, Paul (1865–1935) French composer. His best-known work, the orchestral scherzo *The Sorcerer's Apprentice* (1897), shows his skilful orchestration and individual style.

dulcimer Medieval stringed instrument, originally Persian, with a flat, triangular sounding board and ten or more strings struck with hand-held hammers.

Dulles, John Foster (1888–1959) US statesman, secretary of state (1953–59). He served (1945–49) as a US delegate to the United Nations. In 1951 Dulles drew up the peace treaty with Japan. As secretary of state to Dwight D. EISENHOWER, he advocated the proliferation of nuclear weapons to counter the perceived threat of communism.

Duma National parliament in Russia, principally the Imperial Duma established after the RUSSIAN REVOLUTION OF 1905. Count Witte established an upper house and a duma (lower house elected by suffrage) with limited powers. The first two dumas (1906, 1907) were dissolved rapidly by Tsar NICHOLAS II. The third duma (1907–12) passed limited reforms. The fourth duma (1912–17) was in perpetual conflict with the tsar. Nicholas II dissolved the duma, but it refused to disband. The RUSSIAN REVOLUTION led to its abolition.

Dumas, Alexandre (1802–70) (*père*) French novelist and dramatist. He achieved success with romantic historical plays, such as *La Tour de Nesle* (1832). Dumas wrote popular swashbuckling novels, such as *The Count of Monte Cristo*, *The Three Musketeers* (1844–45) and *The Black Tulip* (1850).

Dumas, Alexandre (1824–95) (*fils*) French dramatist and novelist, illegitimate son of Alexandre DUMAS (*père*). His first great success was *La Dame aux Camélias* (1852), the basis of Verdi's opera *La Traviata*.

His didactic later plays, such as *Les idées de Madame Aubray* (1867), helped to provoke French social reform.

Du Maurier, Dame Daphne (1907–89) English novelist. Du Maurier's romantic novels include *Jamaica Inn* (1936), *Rebecca* (1938), *Frenchman's Creek* (1941) and *My Cousin Rachel* (1951). She also wrote plays, and short stories (including "The Birds").

Dumfries and Galloway Region in SW Scotland, bounded SE by England, S by the Solway Firth; the capital is Dumfries. Major towns include Castle Douglas, Lockerbie and Stranraer. An agricultural region, sites include the Galloway Hills and the runic Ruthwell Cross. Area: 6,396sq km (2,470sq mi). Pop. (1991) 147,805.

dump In computing, information copied from COMPUTER memory to an output or storage device. It may be the entire contents of a file copied to another DISK, or a print-out of the screen (screen dump).

Dunant, Jean Henri (1828–1910) Swiss philanthropist and founder of the International RED CROSS. His account of the Battle of Solferino, *Recollections of Solferino* (1862), inspired the adoption (1864) of the Geneva Convention for the treatment of wounded and prisoners-of-war. Dunant shared the first Nobel Peace Prize (1901) with Frédéric Passy.

Dunbar, Paul Laurence (1872–1906) US writer. His poetry, written in African-American dialect, is a bittersweet mixture of sadness and humour. Dunbar's *Lyrics of Lowly Life* (1896) concerns Southern black life before the Civil War. His novels include *The Love of Landry* (1900).

Duncan, Isadora (1877–1927) US dancer, pioneer of MODERN DANCE. She achieved fame in Europe for her emotional, expressive style. Duncan died tragically when her scarf caught in the wheel of her car and strangled her.

Dundee, John Graham of Claverhouse, 1st Viscount (c.1649–89) Scottish soldier. He defeated the COVENANTERS at Bothwell Brig (1679) and was made a viscount (1688). After the GLORIOUS REVOLUTION (1688–89), "Bonnie Dundee" led a JACOBITE rebellion in support of JAMES II of England. He was mortally wounded in the victorious Battle of Killiecrankie.

Dundee City on the N shore of the Firth of Tay, Tayside, E Scotland. A centre of the REFORMATION in Scotland, Dundee is an important port and has a university (founded 1881). Industries: textiles, confectionery, engineering. Pop. (1994) 160,000.

dune Ridge of wind-blown particles, most often sand. They occur in deserts in many shapes: **barchans** (crescent-shaped) are formed by a constant wind; **seifs** are narrow ridges.

Dunedin (Gaelic, Edinburgh) City on SE South Island, New Zealand. Founded in 1848 by Scottish Free Church settlers, Dunedin grew after the discovery of gold in the 1860s. It has the University of Otago (1871). Industries: agricultural machinery. Pop. (1996) 121,000.

Dunfermline Industrial city in Fife, E Scotland, near the Firth of Forth. Robert I (the Bruce) and Queen Margaret are buried in the 11th-century Benedictine abbey. The birthplace of Andrew CARNEGIE, Dunfermline is the headquarters for the Carnegie trusts. The Rosyth Royal Naval dockyards are nearby. Industries: textiles, coalmining, electronics. Pop. (1991) 55,000.

dung beetle Small to medium-sized SCARAB BEETLE. Some species form balls of dung as food for their larvae and may roll the balls some distance before burying them. Family Scarabaeidae; species *Geotrupes stercorarius*.

Dunkirk (Dunkerque) Port at the entrance to the Straits of Dover, Nord department, NW France. It came under French rule in 1662. In World War 2, more than 300,000 Allied troops were evacuated from its beaches between 29 May and 3 June 1940, when the German army broke through to the English Channel. It is France's third-largest port and a major iron and steel producer in W Europe. Industries: oil refining, shipbuilding. Pop. (1990) 70,331.

Dunlop, John Boyd (1840–1921) Scottish inventor. In 1888, Dunlop invented the first successful pneumatic bicycle TYRE. In 1889, he formed a company (Dunlop Rubber Company) for the commercial production of the tyre.

Duns Scotus, John (1265–1308) Scottish Franciscan theologian and philosopher. He founded a school of SCHOLASTICISM called Scotism. Duns Scotus challenged the ideas of St Thomas AQUINAS that faith and reason are complementary, arguing that faith was a matter of will.

Dunstable, John (c.1390–1453) English composer. Little is known about him, but masses, motets and a few secular works have survived. Dunstable gained recognition for his experiments in counterpoint and influenced Guillaume DUFAY and Gilles de BINCHOIS.

Dunstan, Saint (c.910–88) English monk, archbishop of Canterbury (960–88). He negotiated a peace treaty with the Danes that helped to unify England. Dunstan revived English monasticism and acted as adviser to several kings of Wessex. His feast day is 19 May.

duodenum First section of the small INTESTINE, shaped like a horseshoe. The pyloric sphincter, a circular muscle, separates it from the STOMACH. Alkaline BILE and pancreatic juices are released into the duodenum to aid the DIGESTION of food.

Du Pont de Nemours, Eleuthère Irénée (1771–1834) US industrialist, b. France. Founder of a huge chemical company and family empire that continues as E.I. Du Pont de Nemours and Co. In 1799, he came to the US with his father, **Pierre Samuel** Du Pont de Nemours (1739–1817). They started a business producing high-quality gunpowder and prospered from the War of 1812. The Du Pont company pioneered the production of NYLON and other synthetic fibres.

Du Pré, Jacqueline (1945–87) English cellist, wife of Daniel BARENBOIM. Soon after her London debut (1961), Du Pré became widely acknowledged as a remarkable talent. Her interpretation of Elgar, Beethoven and Brahms drew special acclaim. In 1973, her career was cut short by multiple sclerosis, but she continued to teach.

Durango State in NW Mexico. In W Durango, the SIERRA MADRE Occidental contains mineral deposits such as silver, gold and lead. The capital, Victoria de Durango, has been the major mining town since its foundation in 1563. To the E, the arid plains provide excellent pastures, and many crops are cultivated in the fertile River Nazas valley. Industries: timber, tanning, textiles, tourism. Area: 119,648sq km (46,196sq mi). Pop. (1990) 1,349,378.

Duras, Marguérite (1914–96) French novelist and dramatist, b. Indochina. Her novels include *The Sea Wall* (1950), *Destroy, She Said* (1969), *The Lover* (1984) and *Summer Rain* (1990). Duras also wrote the screenplay for the film *Hiroshima mon amour* (1959).

Durban Seaport on the N shore of Durban Bay, South Africa. Founded in 1835, the national convention initiating the Union of South Africa was held here. It has the University of Natal (1949) and Natal University College (1960). Industries: shipbuilding, oil refining, chemicals. Pop. (1991) 1,137,378.

Dürer, Albrecht (1471–1528) German painter, engraver and designer of woodcuts; the greatest artist of the northern RENAISSANCE. During his visits to Italy, Dürer was influenced by artists such as LEONARDO DA VINCI. Dürer's synthesis of N and S European traditions shaped European art. His album of woodcuts, *The Apocalypse* (1498), has remarkable paint-like tones. His paintings include *The Feast of the Rose Garlands* (1506) and *Four Apostles* (1526), which reveal his preoccupation with Lutheranism. Dürer is often credited as the founder of etching.

Durga In the Hindu pantheon, one of the names of the wife of SHIVA. Depicted as a 10-armed goddess, she is both destructive and beneficent but is worshiped today as a warrior against evil. Her festival, the Durga-puja, which occurs around September, is a time for family reunions.

Durham, John George Lambton, 1st Earl of (1792–1840) British statesman. One of the drafters of the Great REFORM ACT of 1832, he led the radical wing of the Whig Party. Governor-general of Canada (1838), he formulated the basis of British colonial policy.

Durham City and administrative district on the River Wear, NE England; the county town of Co. Durham. Founded by monks in the 10th century, it became a defensive outpost against the Scots and the seat of prince-bishops. Its cathedral (1093) contains the tomb of the Venerable BEDE, and an 11th-century castle is now part of the university (founded 1832). Industries: textiles, carpet-weaving, engineering. Pop. (1991) 85,800.

Durham City in the Piedmont region, central North Carolina, USA. Settled *c.*1750, Durham was the site of Confederate General Joseph E. Johnston's surrender (1865) to the Union General William T. SHERMAN to end the American CIVIL WAR. After the war, it became a centre of the tobacco industry. Today, it is a research and education centre that includes Duke University. Industries: textiles, hosiery, cigarettes. Pop. (1990) 136,611.

Durkheim, Emile (1858–1917) French sociologist. Influenced by the POSITIVISM of Auguste COMTE, Durkheim used the methods of natural science to study human society and is considered (with Max WEBER) a founder of SOCIOLOGY. In *The Division of Labour in Society* (1893) and the *Elementary Forms of Religious Life* (1912), Durkheim argued that religion and labour were basic organizing principles of society. *Suicide* (1897) outlines his theory of alienation.

Durrell, Gerald Malcolm (1925–95) British naturalist and author, brother of Lawrence DURRELL, b. India. His humorous and stylish novels include *My Family and Other Animals* (1956) and *A Zoo in My Luggage* (1960).

Durrell, Lawrence George (1912–90) British novelist and poet, brother of Gerald DURRELL, b. India. His life in Greece and Egypt provided inspiration for most of his writing. His major work is the inventive tetralogy, *The Alexandria Quartet*: *Justine* (1957), *Balthazar* (1958), *Mountolive* (1958) and *Clea* (1960).

Dürrenmatt, Friedrich (1921–90) Swiss dramatist, novelist and essayist. Influential in the post-1945 revival of German theatre, his works are ironic and display a nihilistic, black humour. *Woyzeck* (1972) is his most frequently performed play.

Durrësi (Durrës) City on the Adriatic coast of W Albania; capital of Durrësi province. It was founded in 625 BC as a colony of Corinth. Ceded to Venice in 1392, it was captured by the Turks in 1501. Durrësi was capital of independent Albania from 1913 to 1921. It was occupied by Austria and Italy in World War 1 and by Italy in World War 2. Today, it is Albania's largest port exporting grain, olive oil and tobacco. Industries: textiles, leather. Pop. (1991) 86,900.

Duse, Eleanora (1859–1924) Italian actress. She was regarded as the greatest actress of her generation. Duse is best-known for her roles in plays by her lover, Gabriele D'ANNUNZIO, and Henrik IBSEN.

Dushanbe (Dušanbe) Capital of Tajikistan, at the foot of the Gissar Mountains, Central Asia. Founded in the 1920s, it was known as Stalinabad from 1929 to 1961. An industrial, trade and transport centre, it has Tadzhik University and Academy of Sciences. Industries: cotton, engineering. Pop. (1994) 524,000.

Düsseldorf Capital of North Rhine-Westphalia, at the confluence of the rivers Rhine and Düssel, NW Germany. Founded in the 13th century, it was the residence of the dukes of Berg in the 14th–16th centuries. It became part of Prussia in 1815 and was under French occupation from 1921 to 1925. It is a cultural centre. Industries: chemicals, textiles. Pop. (1995) 573,000.

dust bowl Area of *c.*40 million ha (100 million acres) of the GREAT PLAINS, that suffered from wind erosion. Due to drought, over-planting and mismanagement, much of the topsoil was blown away in the 1930s. Soil conservation programmes have helped restore productivity.

Dutch Official language of the Netherlands, spoken by almost all of the country's 13 million inhabitants and also in Netherlands Antilles and Surinam. Dutch is a Germanic language, belonging to the Indo-European family.

Dutch art Before the 16th century, most Netherlandish art was commissioned by the church. Artists such as LUCAS VAN LEYDEN produced elaborate altarpieces. After independence from Spain, the chief patrons were the merchant class. The 17th century was a golden age, producing artists of the calibre of REMBRANDT, Jan VERMEER, Frans HALS and Jacob van RUISDAEL. The 19th-century Hague School rekindled the Dutch landscape tradition. Vincent VAN GOGH, though Dutch-born, had closer links with 19th-century FRENCH ART. In the 20th century, the main artistic contributions have come from Piet MONDRIAN and the De STIJL group.

Dutch East India Company *See* EAST INDIA COMPANY

Dutch East Indies Until 1949 the part of Southeast Asia that is now INDONESIA. An overseas territory of the Netherlands, it comprised the Malay Archipelago, including SUMATRA, JAVA, BORNEO (except North Borneo), SULAWESI, MOLUCCAS and the Lesser Sunda Islands (except Portuguese TIMOR). The islands were first colonized by the Dutch in the early 17th century.

Dutch elm disease Highly infective fungus infection that attacks the bark of ELM trees and spreads inward until it kills the tree. It is spread by beetles whose grubs make a series of linked tunnels in the wood below the bark.

Dutch Wars Three 17th-century naval conflicts between Holland and England arising from commercial rivalry. The **first war** (1652–54) ended with England holding the advantage. The **second war** (1665–67) followed England's seizure of New Amsterdam (New York). The Dutch inflicted heavy losses and destroyed Chatham naval base, England; England modified its trade laws. The **third war** (1672–74) arose from English support of a French invasion of the Netherlands. The Dutch naval victory forced England to make peace.

Duvalier, "Baby Doc" (Jean-Claude) (1951–) President of Haiti (1971–86). He succeeded his father, "Papa Doc" DUVALIER, as president-for-life. Although he introduced several important reforms and disbanded the Tonton Macoutes, he retained his father's brutal methods. Civil unrest forced his exile to France in 1986.

Duvalier, "Papa Doc" (François) (1907–71) President of Haiti (1957–71). He declared himself president-for-life and relied on the feared Tonton Macoutes, a vigilante group, to consolidate his rule. Under Duvalier's ruthless regime, the longest in Haiti's history, the country's economy severely declined.

Duve, Christian René de (1917–78) Belgian biochemist, b. England. He was a pioneer in the field of CELL biology. Duve's analysis of biochemical activity in the cell led him to discover the lysosome, an organelle that contains the ENZYMES. He shared the 1974 Nobel Prize for physiology or medicine.

dvd (digital video disc) *See* VIDEO DISC

Dvořák, Antonín (1841–1904) Czech composer. He adapted Czech FOLK MUSIC to a classical style. Best known for his orchestral works, which include nine symphonies, two sets of *Slavonic Dances* and several symphonic poems, Dvořák's Cello Concerto (1895) is one of the supreme achievements of the form. His stay in the USA (1892–95) inspired his most popular work, the Symphony in E minor ("From the New World").

dwarfism Condition of abnormally short stature. The commonest cause is malnutrition. It is also associated with several inherited disorders, of which **achondroplasia** is the most common. In this condition the head and trunk are of normal size but the limbs are very short. In **pituitary** dwarfism, caused by a deficiency of growth hormone, the body is of normal proportions.

dye Substance, natural or synthetic, used to impart colour to various substances. Natural dyes have mostly been replaced by synthetic dyes, many derived from coal tar. Dyes are classified according to their application: **direct** dyes, such as sulphur and vat dyes, can be applied directly to fabric because they bind to the fibres. **Indirect** dyes, such as ingrain and mordant dyes, require a secondary process to fix the dye.

Dyfed County in SW Wales; the administrative centre is Carmarthen. The Cambrian Mountains extend to the coast. Agriculture is based on livestock rearing and crops. Industries: fishing, timber, textiles, tourism. Area: 5,765sq km (2,226sq mi). Pop. (1990) 343,543.

Dyke, Sir Anthony van *See* VAN DYCK, SIR ANTHONY

dyke (dike) In engineering, a barrier or embankment designed to confine or regulate the flow of water. Dykes are used in reclaiming land from the sea by sedimentation (as practised in The Netherlands) and also as controls against river flooding. In geology, a dyke is an intrusion of igneous rock whose surface is different from that of the adjoining material.

Dylan, Bob (1941–) US popular singer and composer, b. Robert Allen Zimmerman. Dylan successfully combined social protest poetry and FOLK MUSIC on records such as *The Times They Are A-Changin'* (1963) and *Highway 61 Revisited* (1965). His switch to ROCK music and electric instrumentation initially alienated many fans. Classic albums from this period include *Blood on the Tracks* (1975).

dynamics Branch of MECHANICS that studies objects in motion. Its two main branches are **kinematics**, which studies motion without regard to cause and KINETICS, which takes into account forces that cause motion. *See also* INERTIA; MOMENTUM; NEWTON'S LAWS

dynamite Solid, blasting EXPLOSIVE. Invented (1866) by Alfred NOBEL. It contains NITROGLYCERINE incorporated in an absorbent base, such as charcoal or wood pulp. Dynamite is used in mining, quarrying and engineering.

dynamo (GENERATOR) Device that converts mechanical energy into electrical energy by the principle of ELECTROMAGNETIC INDUCTION. In a simple dynamo, a CONDUCTOR, usually an open coil of wire (armature), is placed between the poles of a permanent magnet. This armature is rotated within the magnetic field, inducing an ELECTRIC CURRENT. *See also* ALTERNATOR

dysentery Infectious disease characterized by DIARRHOEA, bleeding and abdominal cramps. It is spread in contaminated food and water, especially in the tropics. There are two types: **bacillary** dysentery, caused by BACTERIA of the genus *Shigella*; and **amoebic** dysentery, caused by a type of PROTOZOA. Both are treated with antibacterials and fluid replacement.

dyslexia Impairment in reading ability. Dyslexia is usually diagnosed when difficulty in learning to read is clearly not due to inadequate intelligence, brain damage or emotional problems. Symptoms may include difficulty with writing, especially in spelling correctly.

dyspepsia (indigestion) Pain or discomfort in the stomach or abdomen arising from digestive upset.

dysprosium (symbol Dy) Silvery-white, metallic rare-earth element of the LANTHANIDE SERIES, first identified (1886) by Lecoq de Boisbaudran. Its chief ores are monazite and bastnaesite. Its capacity to absorb neutrons makes it important in nuclear technology. Its compounds are also used in lasers. Properties: at.no. 66; r.a.m. 162.5; r.d. 8.54; m.p. 1,409°C (2,568°F); b.p. 2,335°C (4,235°F); most common isotope Dy[164] (28.18%).

dystrophy, muscular Any of a group of inherited disorders featuring weakness or wasting of muscles. The commonest form, **Duchenne** muscular dystrophy, is almost entirely confined to boys, developing usually before the age of four. There is no cure and death is usual before the age of 20.

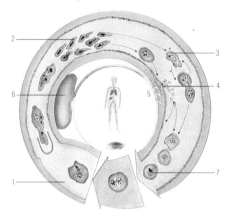

▲ **dysentery** Amoebic dysentery is caused by a microscopic organism (*Entamoeba histolytica*), found in contaminated water or food. *Entamoeba* is a natural inhabitant of the gut; however, under certain conditions, invasion of the gut wall occurs. Ingested *Entamoeba* cysts undergo division and multiplication in the large intestine (1). After division, eight trophozoites (feeding protozoa) are produced (2); non-infective trophozoites remain in the intestine (3) feeding on bacteria and food particles. Infective trophozoites invade the gut wall (4), multiply, and dissolve tissues by protein-digesting enzymes. If organisms enter the blood stream (5) they can be carried to the lungs (6), liver and brain where abscesses develop. Those released from gut abscesses re-invade tissues or form cysts (7) and are passed in the faeces. The disease is transmitted if flies carry cysts from faeces to food or, more commonly, if contaminated water is drunk (8).

E/e, fifth letter of the Roman alphabet. Derived from an Egyptian hieroglyph of a man rejoicing, it entered the Semitic alphabet as the letter he. It was adopted by the Greeks as the letter epsilon before taking its present form.

EARTH DATA

DIAMETER (EQUATORIAL): 12,756km (7,926mi)
MASS: 5,378 billion billion tons
VOLUME: 1,083 billion cubic km (260 billion cubic mi)
DENSITY (WATER = 1): 5.52
ORBITAL PERIOD: 365.3 days
ROTATION PERIOD: 23hr 56min 04sec
SURFACE TEMPERATURE: 290K

eagle Strong, carnivorous diurnal BIRD OF PREY. Sea and fishing eagles, such as the BALD EAGLE, are large birds found by sea coasts and lakes, where they feed on fish, small animals and carrion. **Serpent** eagles are stocky, reptile-eating birds. Large, **harpy** eagles inhabit tropical forests. True (booted) eagles (*Aquila*) have long hooked bills, broad wings, powerful toes with long curved talons and feathered legs. They nest high on sea coasts or island mountains, building huge stick nests (eyries). One or two light-brown or spotted eggs are laid. Length: 40–100cm (16–40in) Family Accipitridae. *See also* FALCON

Eakins, Thomas (1844–1916) US painter and photographer, regarded as one of the greatest artists of the 19th century. Eakin's painstaking search for anatomical accuracy aroused much controversy. His use of CHIAROSCURO and psychological insight attract comparison with Rembrandt. Eakin's most celebrated paintings are *Gross Clinic* (1875), *The Chess Players* (1876), *The Swimming Hole* (1883) and *Agnew Clinic* (1889). He had a profound impact on the ASHCAN SCHOOL. *See also* LUMINISM

Ealing Studios British film studios founded in 1929. Ealing produced a series of classic British comedies, such as *Passport to Pimlico* (1949), *The Lavender Hill Mob* (1951) and *The Ladykillers* (1955). Original screenplays and a nucleus of actors led by Alec GUINNESS, assured their success. The studios were sold in 1952, and bought by the BBC in 1994.

ear Organ of hearing and balance. It converts sound waves to nerve impulses which are carried to the BRAIN. In most mammals, it consists of the outer, middle and inner ear. The **outer** ear carries sound to the eardrum. The **middle** ear is air-filled, and has three tiny bones (ossicles) that pass on and amplify sound vibrations to the fluid-filled inner ear. The **inner** ear contains the COCHLEA. Vibrations stimulate tiny hairs which cause

impulses to be sent via the auditory nerve to the brain. The inner ear also contains semicircular canals that maintain orientation and balance.

Earhart, Amelia (1898–?1937) US aviator, first woman to fly solo across the Atlantic (1932). In 1937, she attempted to fly around the world but disappeared in the Pacific Ocean.

Early, Jubal Anderson (1816–94) Confederate general in the American CIVIL WAR. He was brigadier general at the first battle of BULL RUN (1861) and fought in the Battle of Chancellorsville, the GETTYSBURG CAMPAIGN (1863) and the WILDERNESS CAMPAIGN (1864). Early was routed by General CUSTER at Waynesboro (March 1865), and General LEE relieved him of command.

Early English First phase of English GOTHIC ARCHITECTURE (13th century). It followed NORMAN ARCHITECTURE. In *c.*1250, French-inspired English stonemasons developed a native Gothic idiom: CANTERBURY Cathedral is a very early example. Later works emphasized appearance rather than structure: builders ornamented and enhanced visible walls, or made prominent use of VAULT ribbing. *See also* DECORATED STYLE; PERPENDICULAR STYLE

Early English (Anglo-Saxon, Old English) ENGLISH language from *c.*AD 450 to 1100. It is the earliest form of English, directly descended from the Germanic languages of the early ANGLO-SAXONS. It had a vocabulary of *c.*50,000 words. It comprised four main dialects: Northumbrian, Mercian, Kentish and West Saxon. The best of Early English literature, such as BEOWULF, was written in Northumbrian. West Saxon became the chief dialect as a result of ALFRED THE GREAT's unification of England.

Earp, Wyatt Berry Stapp (1848–1929) US law officer. In 1879 he became deputy sheriff of Tombstone, Arizona. In 1881 the Earp brothers and Doc Holliday fought the Clanton gang in the gunfight at the O.K. Corral.

▶ **ear** The ear is divided into three parts – the outer, middle and inner ear. The outer consists of the pinna and the auditory canal. The pinna funnels sound waves via the canal to the ear drum, tympanic membrane, of the middle ear. The sound waves are amplified and transmitted by tiny bones, the ossicles, which cause the oval window to vibrate. This sets the fluids of the inner ear in motion. Hair cells in structures of the inner ear, the cochlea and semicircular canals, are stimulated and generate impulses interpreted by the brain as sound.

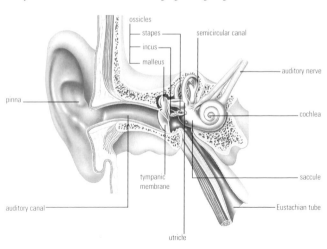

Earth Third major planet from the Sun, and the largest of the four inner, or terrestrial planets. Some 70% of the surface is covered by water. This fact and the Earth's average surface temperature of 13°C (55°F), make it suitable for life. Continental land masses make up the other 30%. Our planet has one natural satellite, the MOON. Like all the terrestrial planets, there is a dense CORE rich in iron and nickel, surrounded by a MANTLE of silicate rocks. The thin, outermost layer of lighter rock is the CRUST, which can vary in depth from between 40km (25mi) – the thickest **continental** crust – to 5km (3mi) – the thinnest **oceanic** crust. The boundary between the crust and the mantle is called the MOHO. The solid, inner core rotates at a different rate from the molten, outer layers, and this, together with currents in the outer core, gives rise to the Earth's MAGNETIC FIELD. The crust and the uppermost mantle together form the **lithosphere**, which consists of tightly fitting slabs called **plates**. The plates, which float on a semi-molten layer of mantle called the **asthenosphere**, move in interactions known collectively as PLATE TECTONICS. *See also* ATMOSPHERE; GEOLOGICAL TIME

earthquake Tremor below the surface of the Earth which causes shaking to occur in the crust. Shaking lasts only for a few seconds, but widespread devastation can result. According to PLATE TECTONICS, earthquakes are caused by the movement of crustal plates, which produces FAULT lines. The main earthquake regions are found along plate margins, especially on the edges of the Pacific, such as the SAN ANDREAS FAULT. A large earthquake is usually followed by smaller "aftershocks". An earthquake beneath the sea can result in a TSUNAMI. Earthquake prediction is a branch of SEISMOLOGY. The world's largest recorded earthquake (1976) at Tangshan, China, killed more than 250,000 people and measured 8.2 on the RICHTER SCALE.

Earth sciences General term used to describe all the sciences concerned with the EARTH. It includes the basic subject of GEOLOGY, with its subclassifications of GEOCHEMISTRY, GEOMORPHOLOGY, GEOPHYSICS; MINERALOGY and PETROLOGY; SEISMOLOGY and VOLCANISM; OCEANOGRAPHY; METEOROLOGY; PALAEONTOLOGY

Earth Summit (June 1992) United Nations' Conference on Environment and Development, held in Rio de Janeiro, Brazil. It was the first serious global acknowledgment of the problems created by the impact of industrial society on the environment. The Rio Declaration imposed limits on the emission of gases, responsible for the GREENHOUSE EFFECT and GLOBAL WARMING. A second Earth Summit (June 1997) called for progress in the reduction of CARBON-DIOXIDE emissions. *See also* ECOLOGY

earthworm Annelid with a cylindrical, segmented body and tiny bristles. Most worms live in moist soil. Their burrowing aerates the soil, helping to make it fertile. Length: 5cm–33m (2in–11ft). There are several hundred species. Class Oligochaeta; genus *Lumbricus*.

earwig Slender, flattened, brownish-black insect found in crevices and under tree bark. There are some 900 species worldwide. All have a pair of forceps at the hind end. Order Dermaptera; genus *Forficula*.

East Anglia Region of E England, made up of the counties of NORFOLK and SUFFOLK, and parts of CAMBRIDGESHIRE and ESSEX. The protection afforded by the fenlands made it one of the most powerful Anglo-Saxon kingdoms of the late 6th century. A fertile agricultural region, farming includes grain and vegetable growing and livestock raising. Industries: farming, tourism, fishing.

East China Sea Northern branch of the China Sea, bordered by Korea and Japan (N), China (W), Taiwan

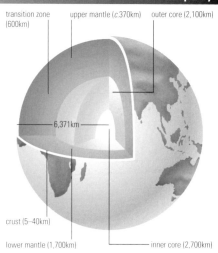

▲ **Earth** Formed *c.*4,600 million years ago, the first humans (*Homo habilis*) appeared only 2 million years ago. The Earth consists of concentric rings, from the uppermost crust to a solid inner core of nickel and iron.

(S) and the Ryukyu Islands (E). Area: *c.*1,249,160sq km (482,300sq mi).

Easter Feast in celebration of the resurrection of JESUS CHRIST on the third day after his crucifixion. It is the oldest and primary Christian feast, celebrated on the Sunday following the first full moon between 21 March and 25 April. The exchange of Easter eggs is a pre-Christian rite.

Easter Island (Isla de Pascua) Volcanic island in the SE Pacific; the chief town is Hanga Roa. The most isolated island in Polynesia, it was discovered by a Dutch navigator on Easter Day, 1722, and has been under Chilean administration since 1888. It is famous for the curious hieroglyphs (*rongorongo*) and statues carved in stone, standing up to 12m (40ft) high. Industries: farming, tourism. Area: 163sq km (63sq mi). Pop. (1982) 1,867.

Eastern Cape Province in SE South Africa; the capital is East London. Created (1994) from the E part of the former CAPE PROVINCE, it incorporates the former, apartheid-created homelands of Transkei and Ciskei. Area: 169,600sq km (65,466sq mi). Pop. (1994 est.) 6,436,790

Eastern Orthodox Church *See* ORTHODOX CHURCH, EASTERN

Easter Rising (24 April 1916) Rebellion by Irish nationalists against British rule, led by Patrick PEARSE of the Irish Republican Brotherhood (IRB) and James CONNOLLY of SINN FÉIN. An arms shipment from Germany was intercepted by the British navy and Roger CASEMENT (the IRB's contact with Germany) was arrested, but the insurrection went ahead as planned. On Easter Monday, *c.*1,500 volunteers seized buildings in Dublin, including the General Post Office, and proclaimed Ireland a republic. By 29 April, the British had crushed the rising. Sixteen of the ringleaders were executed and 2,000 people imprisoned. In 1917, Eamon DE VALERA was granted an amnesty and nationalist sentiment produced an electoral victory for Sinn Féin.

East India Company Name of several organizations set up by European countries in the 17th century to trade E of Africa. The French company was founded (1664) by Louis XIV and set up colonies on several islands in the Indian

▶ **echidna** An example of
a primitive mammal, the
echidna (spiny anteater) is
classified as a monotreme.
Instead of giving birth to live
young like other mammals,
it is an egg-layer. The tiny
egg (1) is soft-shelled and
resembles a reptile's egg.
Once the egg is laid, the
echidna uses its hind limbs
to roll it to a special
incubation groove (2). The
minute hatchling is c.1.25cm
(0.5in) long.

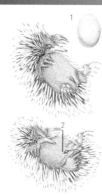

Ocean. It was abolished in 1789. The Dutch company was
founded (1602), with headquarters in Jakarta from 1619. It
was dissolved in 1799. The British company was set up in
1600 to compete for the East Indian spice trade, but competition with the Dutch led it to concentrate on India. In the
18th century, Robert CLIVE defeated the challenge of the
French company and captured BENGAL (1757). Corruption
and financial mismanagement led William PITT (THE
YOUNGER) to make the company responsible to Parliament. Increasingly it became an administrative arm of
colonial government in India and the company lost its
commercial monopolies in 1813. The INDIAN MUTINY
(1857) led to its powers being transferred to the British
Crown and the company was dissolved in 1873.

Eastman, George (1854–1932) US inventor, industrialist and philanthropist who popularized the art of
PHOTOGRAPHY. Eastman invented (1879) a dry-plate
process and began to mass produce photographic plates.
In 1884 he designed a roll film. The first Kodak camera
was produced in 1888. The Eastman Kodak Company
was founded in 1892.

East Sussex County of SE England. The county town is
Lewes; other major towns include BRIGHTON and East-
bourne. Its S border is the English Channel. The chalky
South Downs run parallel to the coast. In the N, the Weald
plains are drained by the River Ouse. Most of the region
was included in the kingdom of WESSEX. In 1066, William
the Conqueror defeated the forces of Harold II in the Battle of HASTINGS. Industries: agriculture, services, tourism.
Area: 1,795sq km (693sq mi). Pop. (1991) 670,600.

East Timor *See* TIMOR

Eastwood, Clint (1930–) US film actor and director.
He began his career in the television series *Rawhide*
(1959–65). Eastwood played the no-nonsense drifter in
a trilogy of "spaghetti WESTERNS" by Sergio LEONE, *A
Fistful of Dollars* (1964), *For a Few Dollars More*
(1965) and *The Good, the Bad and the Ugly* (1967).
Dirty Harry (1971) and its four sequels were also tough
and uncompromising films. As a director, he earned
praise for *The Outlaw Josey Wales* (1976) and *Bird*
(1988). Eastwood won Academy Awards for best picture and best director for *Unforgiven* (1992).

eating disorders Range of disorders involving eating
habits and appetites. The most common are ANOREXIA
NERVOSA and bulimia nervosa.

Ebla Influential city-state in the third millennium BC,
located in modern N Syria. In 1975, archaeologists discovered more than 15,000 clay tablets (c.2300 BC)
recording the city's development. The tablets contain
the earliest known reference to Jerusalem.

Ebola Virus that causes haemorrhagic fever. Thought to
have been long present in animals, the Ebola virus was
first identified in humans during an outbreak in Zaïre (now
Congo) in 1976. It is acquired through contact with contaminated body fluids. The death rate can be as high as 90%.

ebony Hard, fine-grained dark heartwood of various
Asian and African trees of the genus *Diospyros* in the
ebony family (Ebenaceae). Its major commercial tree is
the macassar ebony (*D. ebenum*) of S India and Malaysia.

Ebro River in N Spain. Rising at Fontibre in the
Catabrian Mountains, it flows ESE and then SE through
Logrono and ZARAGOZA, and into the Mediterranean
below Tortosa. It is the longest river whose entire course
is in Spain. Length: 910km (565mi).

eccentricity (symbol *e*) One of the elements of an
ORBIT. It indicates how much an elliptical orbit departs
from a circle. A circle has an eccentricity of 0, a parabola an eccentricity of 1.

Eccles, Sir John Carew (1903–97) Australian
physiologist. He showed that nerve impulses are conducted by the release of a chemical neurotransmitter
across the synapses. Eccles shared the 1963 Nobel
Prize for physiology or medicine. *See also* NEURONS

Ecclesiastes Old Testament book of aphorisms, compiled under the pseudonym "the Preacher, the son of
David". An example of WISDOM LITERATURE, the book is
traditionally ascribed to SOLOMON but clearly dates from
after the BABYLONIAN CAPTIVITY. Its theme is the vanity
and emptiness of life, relieved only by faith in God.

Ecclesiasticus Book of the APOCRYPHA, an example
of Jewish WISDOM LITERATURE. The work of a Jewish
scribe, Jesus ben Sirach, written in c.180 BC. A hand-
book of practical and moral advice, the central theme is
the relationship between wisdom and God.

echidna (spiny anteater) MONOTREME related to the
PLATYPUS, found in Australia, Tasmania and New
Guinea. It is a primitive egg-laying mammal with a
CLOACA, spines on the upper body, and an elongated
snout. Length: 30–77cm (12–30in).

echinoderm Any member of the phylum Echinoder-
mata, a group of spiny-skinned, marine invertebrate animals. Radially symmetrical with five axes, they have a
skeleton of calcareous plates in their skin. Their body
cavity includes a complex, internal fluid-pumping system and tube feet. They reproduce sexually and produce
a bilaterally symmetrical larva. Species include SEA
URCHIN, SEA CUCUMBER and STARFISH.

Echo In Greek mythology, a mountain nymph condemned to speak only in echoes, because her chattering
distracted the goddess HERA from the infidelity of ZEUS.

echo Reflected portion of a wave, such as SOUND or
RADAR, from a surface so that it returns to the source and
is heard after a short interval. High notes provide a better
echo than low notes. Echoes are useful in NAVIGATION.

echolocation In animals, system of navigation used
principally by WHALES and BATS. The animal emits a
series of short, high-frequency sounds, and from the
returning ECHO, it gauges its environment. Bats also use
the system for hunting. *See also* SONAR

echo sounder Device that sends ultrasonic sound
pulses through water and detects their reflection – from
the sea bottom, schools of fish, or any submerged
object. Continuous chart recordings can provide a profile of the sea bottom. *See also* SONAR

Eck, Johann Maier von (1486–1543) German
Roman Catholic theologian. He held a public debate
(1519) with Martin LUTHER in Leipzig. Eck forced Luther
to deny the authority of the Council of CONSTANCE and

engineered his excommunication for heresy (1521). He helped produce the AUGSBURG CONFESSION (1530).

Eckhart, Johannes (*c*.1260–*c*.1327) (Meister Eckhart) German Dominican theologian and mystic. An evangelical preacher, his sermons stressed the path to salvation through personal spiritual development. In 1526, he was accused of heresy but died before his condemnation by Pope JOHN XXII.

eclampsia Occurrence of convulsions not associated with any other disease in a pregnant woman with pre-eclampsia. The condition, which threatens the lives of mother and baby, must be treated immediately or coma and death will follow. Delivery may be hastened or Caesarean section performed. The cause is unknown.

eclipse In astronomy, partial or total obscuration of the light from one celestial body as it passes through the shadow cast by another body. Eclipses are transitory; the most familiar are lunar and solar eclipses. Within any given year, a maximum of seven eclipses can occur, either four solar and three lunar or five solar and two lunar. A **solar** eclipse occurs when the MOON passes between the EARTH and the SUN, blocking the Sun's light from the part of the Earth on which the Moon's shadow falls. It can only happen at new Moon. The maximum duration of a **total** solar eclipse is 7min 8sec. A **lunar** eclipse occurs when the Earth intervenes between the Sun and the Moon, blocking the Sun's light from the Moon. It can only happen at full Moon. The longest duration of a total lunar eclipse is 1hr 42min. Because the Earth and Moon shine only by the reflected light of the Sun, each casts a shadow into space in the direction away from the Sun. The shadow consists of a region of total darkness (**umbra**) and partial darkness (**penumbra**). The solar eclipse in 1919 was particularly valuable in checking Einstein's theory of RELATIVITY.

Eco, Umberto (1932–) Italian writer and academic. Eco's best-known work is the erudite philosophical thriller *The Name of the Rose* (1981). Other novels include *Foucault's Pendulum* (1989) and *The Island Before Time* (1994). He is a professor of SEMIOTICS.

ecology Biological study of relationships of organisms to their ENVIRONMENT and to one another. The term was coined (1866) by Ernst Haeckel. Ecologists study **populations** (groups of individual organisms), **communities** (different organisms sharing the same environment), or ECOSYSTEMS (a community and its physical environment).

The maximum population that can be sustained by a particular environment's resources is called its **carrying capacity**. The role of a species within its community is termed its **ecological niche**. Within the BIOSPHERE, natural cycles (CARBON CYCLE, HYDROLOGICAL CYCLE, NITROGEN CYCLE and oxygen cycle) are assisted when the biological diversity of species fill these various ecological niches. This diversity produces CLIMAX COMMUNITIES, and an extensive climax COMMUNITY is called a BIOME. **Applied ecology** is the practical management and preservation of natural resources and environments.

econometrics Application of mathematical methods and statistical tests to ECONOMICS. It is widely used in forecasting trends and testing economic theories.

economics Social science studying the allocation of scarce RESOURCES in the PRODUCTION of commodities, and the distribution of these commodities for CONSUMPTION in society. Adam Smith's *The Wealth of Nations* (1776) is often cited as the first economic treatise. Smith's arguments in favour of FREE-TRADE form the basis of CLASSICAL ECONOMICS. Thomas MALTHUS argued that population would outstrip food supply and lead to famine. David RICARDO's theory of labour value was adopted by Karl MARX. Marx provided a detailed critique of CAPITALISM and a prescription for change. Refinements to classical economics included the theory of marginal utility, which argued that value was determined by need. John Maynard KEYNES produced more fundamental modifications. His *General Theory of Employment, Interest and Money* (1936) was an attempt to deal with economic DEPRESSION and mass UNEMPLOYMENT. The pressures of INFLATION led to the development of MONETARISM and the re-emergence of high UNEMPLOYMENT. In recent years, economics has developed into two broad areas: **microeconomics** studies the economics of firms and individuals, and the workings of individual market mechanisms; while **macroeconomics** studies whole economic systems. *See also* CONSERVATISM; DIVISION OF LABOUR; FEUDAL SYSTEM; LAISSEZ-FAIRE; MERCANTILISM; SOCIALISM; SUPPLY AND DEMAND, LAW OF

economies of scale Theory that as a business expands and produces more, its profitability increases due to lower unit costs, higher productivity, better use of plant and machinery, and greater bargaining power. It is often used to support mergers and acquisitions, but there

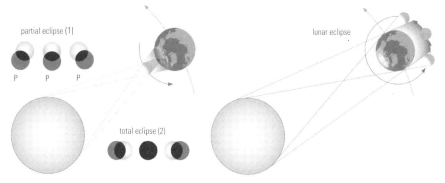

▲ **eclipse** When the Moon passes between the Sun and the Earth it causes a partial eclipse of the Sun (1) if the Earth passes through the Moon's outer shadow (P), or a total eclipse (2) if the inner cone shadow crosses the Earth's surface. In a lunar eclipse, the Earth's shadow crosses the Moon and, again, provides either a partial or total eclipse. Eclipses of the Sun and the Moon do not occur every month because of the 5° difference between the plane of the Moon's orbit and the plane in which the Earth moves.

can be diseconomies of scale, such as greater difficulty in monitoring and control, and increased bureaucracy.

ecosystem Basic unit in ECOLOGY, consisting of a COMMUNITY of organisms in a physical ENVIRONMENT. Study of these systems is based often on energy flow. The chemicals necessary for life are recycled by the FOOD CHAIN, CARBON CYCLE, HYDROLOGICAL CYCLE, NITROGEN CYCLE and oxygen cycle. Interference with these natural processes, such as POLLUTION, climate change, or the loss of a species, can disrupt the entire ecosystem.

ecstasy (MDMA) (3,4–methylnedioxymethylamphetamine) AMPHETAMINE-based drug, which raises body temperature and blood pressure by inducing the release of epinephrine and targeting the neurotransmitter, SEROTONIN. Users experience short-term feelings of euphoria, rushes of energy and increased tactility. Withdrawal can involve bouts of depression and insomnia. Some deaths have resulted from using the drug.

ectopic Occurrence of a pregnancy outside the UTERUS, such as in the FALLOPIAN TUBE. The EMBRYO cannot develop normally and spontaneous ABORTION often occurs. If not, urgent surgery is necessary to save the mother from serious haemorrhage.

Ecuador Republic in NW South America. Ecuador straddles the Equator. Three ranges of the high ANDES mountains form its backbone. The snowcapped Andean peaks include Mount Chimborazo and the world's highest active volcano, Cotopaxi, at 5,896m (19,344ft). Earthquakes are frequent and often devastating. Ecuador's capital, QUITO, lies in the high Andean plateaux, which are home to nearly half of the nation's population. West of the Andes lie flat coastal lowlands, which include Ecuador's largest city and port, GUAYAQUIL. The E lowlands (Oriente) are drained by headwaters of the River AMAZON. The GALÁPAGOS ISLANDS, a province of Ecuador in the Pacific Ocean, lie c.1,050km (650mi) off the W coast. **Climate** Although the coast is cooled by the Peruvian current, temperatures remain between 23° and 25°C (73°F–77°F) throughout the year. Quito, at 2,500m (8,200ft), experiences temperatures of 14°C to 15°C (57°F–59°F). **Vegetation** Vegetation in the Andes varies from high snowfields to grassy meadows in the foothills. Beans, maize and wheat are grown in the highlands; citrus fruits, rice and sugar cane on the coastal lowlands. These lowlands also include deciduous woodland and large tropical forests in N coastal areas. The S border with Peru is desert. A dense rainforest covers the Oriente. **History and Politics** The INCA conquered the kingdom of Quito in the late 15th century, and their language, QUECHUA, remains widely spoken. In 1532, Spanish forces, under Francisco PIZARRO, defeated the Incas at Cajamarca and established the Spanish viceroyalty of Quito. A revolutionary war culminated in Antonio José de SUCRE's defeat of the Spanish at the battle of Mount Pichincha (1822). Simón BOLÍVAR negotiated the admittance of Quito to the federation of Gran Colombia, along with Colombia and Venezuela. In 1830, Ecuador seceded. The 19th century was characterized by internal instability. For the first half of the 20th century, the army dominated politics. In the Treaty of Rio (1942), Ecuador was forced to cede more than 50% of its Amazonian territory to Peru.

Post-1945 politics was dominated by José María Velasco Ibarro. During the 1950s, his authoritarian regime improved Ecuador's infrastructure. In 1970, faced with student riots and economic recession, Velasco established a dictatorship. In 1972, he was deposed by an army coup. Ecuador returned to democracy in 1979. Durán Ballen's presidency (1992–96) saw the start of privatization. Austerity measures provoked civil unrest. A border war with Peru (1995) led to the establishment of a demilitarized zone. In 1996, Ballen was defeated by Abdala Bucaram. In 1997, Bucaram was declared mentally incompetent and removed from office. The 1998 election was won by Jamil Mahaud. **Economy** Ecuador is a lower-middle-income developing nation (1995 GDP per capita, US$4,220). Agriculture employs 33% of the workforce. Ecuador is the world's third largest producer of bananas. Cocoa and coffee are also vital crops. Fishing is important, forestry is a vital industry and mining is increasingly important. The economy was transformed by the discovery (1972) of oil in the Oriente.

ecumenical council (general council) Ecclesiastical convention of worldwide church representatives. Pronouncements are considered binding on all church members. All Christians recognize the first seven councils, the last of which was held in NICAEA in 787. Since then, the Roman Catholic Church has recognized 21 councils convened by popes. Since the REFORMATION, the councils have been restricted to Roman Catholics. The most recent was the Second VATICAN COUNCIL (1962–65). *See also* BASEL, COUNCIL OF; CHALCEDON, COUNCIL OF; CONSTANCE, COUNCIL OF; LATERAN COUNCILS; TRENT, COUNCIL OF

ecumenical movement Movement to restore the lost unity of Christendom. In its modern sense, the movement began with the Edinburgh Missionary Conference of 1910, and led to the foundation of the WORLD COUNCIL OF CHURCHES in 1948.

eczema Inflammatory condition of the skin, a form of DERMATITIS characterized by dryness, itching, rashes and blister formation. It can be caused by contact with a substance, such as a detergent, or a general ALLERGY. Treatment is usually with a corticosteroid ointment.

Edda One of two collections of Old Icelandic literature. The *Poetic Edda*, or *Elder Edda*, is a collection of 34 mythological and heroic poems written between AD 800 and 1200. It is the most valuable collection of Norse literature. The *Prose Edda*, or *Younger Edda* (c.1220), by Snorri Sturluson is a guide to early Icelandic poetry, the first half of which deals with TEUTONIC MYTHOLOGY.

Eddington, Sir Arthur Stanley (1882–1944) English astronomer and physicist. Eddington pioneered the use of atomic theory to study the internal constitution of stars. Among his discoveries were the mass-luminosity relationship and the degeneration of matter by WHITE DWARFS. Eddington helped popularize Einstein's theory of RELATIVITY and, in 1919, obtained experimental proof of the general theory that gravity bends light by measuring stars close to the Sun during a solar ECLIPSE.

Eddy, Mary Baker (1821–1910) US founder of CHRISTIAN SCIENCE (1879). Her doctrine of healing based on the Bible was expounded in *Science and Health With Key to the Scriptures* (1875). In 1879, Eddy organized the Chuch of Christ, Scientist, and actively directed the movement until her death.

edelweiss Small, perennial plant native to the Alps and other high Eurasian mountains. It has white, downy leaves and small, yellow flower heads enclosed in whitish-yellow bracts. Family Asteraceae (COMPOSITAE); species *Leontopodium alpinum*.

ECUADOR

AREA: 283,560sq km (109,483sq mi)
POPULATION: 13,319,000
CAPITAL (POPULATION): Quito (1,488,000)

Eden, Sir (Robert) Anthony, 1st Earl of Avon
(1897–1977) British statesman, prime minister
(1955–57). He was Britain's youngest foreign secretary (1935). Eden resigned (1938) in protest at the
APPEASEMENT policy of Neville CHAMBERLAIN. He
served again as foreign secretary (1940–45, 1951–55)
and succeeded Winston CHURCHILL as Conservative
prime minister. Ill health and his mishandling of the
SUEZ CANAL Crisis forced Eden to resign. He was succeeded by Harold MACMILLAN.

Eden, Garden of In GENESIS 2, garden created by God
as the home of ADAM and EVE. Adam and Eve lived in
the garden and enjoyed its fruits without toil, until they
were banished for eating the forbidden fruit from the tree
of knowledge. The garden of Eden is also mentioned in
the KORAN and is popularly equated with paradise.

Ederle, Gertrude Caroline (1906–) US swimmer.
At the 1924 Olympics she won a gold medal as a member of the US women's relay team and two individual
bronze medals. In 1926 Ederle became the first woman
to swim the English Channel.

edentate (Lat. with all the teeth removed) Any of a
small order of North and South American mammals
found from Kansas to Patagonia. There are c.30 species
of edentates, including ARMADILLO, SLOTH and
ANTEATER. Only anteaters are truly toothless.

Edgar (943–75) King of England (959–75), younger
son of EDMUND I. In 957, he succeeded his brother
Edwy as king of Mercia and Northumberland. In 958,
Edgar recalled Saint DUNSTAN from exile and assisted in
the revival of monasticism. His CORONATION (973) at
Bath was the first of its kind. He was succeeded by his
son, EDWARD THE MARTYR. *See also* DANELAW

Edgar the Aetheling (c.1050–1125) English prince,
grandson of EDMUND II. He was heir to EDWARD THE
CONFESSOR, but was overlooked in favour of HAROLD II.
On Harold's death at the Battle of HASTINGS (1066),
Edgar led resistance to WILLIAM I (THE CONQUEROR) and
formed an alliance with King MALCOLM III of Scotland.
In 1074, he made peace with William. Edgar fought for
Robert II, Duke of Normandy, against Henry I and was
captured at the Battle of Tinchebrai (1106).

Edgehill, Battle of (23 October 1642) First encounter
of Parliamentarians and Royalists in the English CIVIL
WARS, near Banbury, Oxfordshire. The Royalists were
outnumbered (11,000 men to the Parliamentarians'
13,000), but the result was to their advantage.

Edgeworth, Maria (1767–1849) Irish novelist, b. England. Her first work, *Letters to Literary Ladies* (1795),
argued for the education of women. Edgeworth is best
remembered for her novels of Irish provincial life, including *Castle Rackrent* (1800) and *The Absentee* (1812).

Edinburgh, Duke of *See* PHILIP, PRINCE, DUKE OF
EDINBURGH

Edinburgh Capital of Scotland, in Lothian region. The
city grew steadily when Malcolm III made Edinburgh
Castle his residence (11th century), and it became the
capital of Scotland in the early 15th century. It flourished
as a cultural centre in the 18th and 19th centuries around
figures such as David HUME, Adam SMITH, Robert BURNS
and Sir Walter SCOTT. Sites include: Palace of Holyroodhouse (official residence of the monarch in Scotland);
Chapel of St Margaret (part of Edinburgh Castle and the
city's oldest building); the Royal Mile (linking the Castle
with Holyroodhouse); the 15th-century St Giles Cathedral; the home of the Protestant reformer John KNOX; and
Princes Street. The University of Edinburgh was founded
in 1583. It has two other universities, Heriot-Watt (1966)

and Napier (1992). Museums and art galleries include the
National Gallery of Scotland and the Royal Museum of
Scotland. The new devolved Scottish assembly is based
in Edinburgh. Edinburgh has held an international arts
festival since 1947. Industries: brewing, tourism, chemicals, printing and publishing. Pop. (1994) 445,000.

Edirne (Adrianople) Fortified city at the confluence of
the rivers Meric and Tundzha. Rebuilt by the Roman
Emperor Hadrian (c.AD 125) as Adrianopolis, it was the
scene of a Roman defeat (378) by the Visigoths. Edirne
was capital of Ottoman Turkey from 1361 to 1453. Captured by the Russians (1829, 1879) and the Bulgarians
(1913), Edirne was ceded to Greece in 1920. It was
returned to Turkey in 1923. It is an agricultural trading
centre. Industries: textiles, tanning. Pop. (1990) 102,300.

Edison, Thomas Alva (1847–1931) US inventor.
With little formal education, he became the most prolific inventor of his generation. In 1876, Edison opened a
laboratory in Menlo Park, New Jersey. Here, he invented the carbon transmitter for TELEPHONES (1876), and
the phonograph or RECORD PLAYER (1877). Using a carbon filament, Edison invented of the first commercially
viable ELECTRIC LIGHT (October 21, 1879) that ensured
his fame. In New York City, he built (1881–82) the
world's first permanent electric power plant for distributing electric light. In 1892, most of his companies were
merged into the General Electric Company (GEC). In
1914, Edison developed an experimental talking motion
picture. By the time of his death, he had patented more
than 1,300 inventions.

Edmonton Capital of ALBERTA, on the North
Saskatchewan River, Canada. The "Gateway to the
North", Edmonton is the northernmost city in North
America. Founded as a fur-trading post by the Hudson's
Bay Company in 1795, it developed with the arrival of
the railway in 1891 and the Klondike gold-rush (1898). It
became the capital of Alberta in 1905. The discovery of
oil (1947) made Edmonton a major metropolitan area.
The city is home to the University of Alberta (1906).
Industries: coal mining, natural gas. Pop. (1991) 616,741.

Edmund, Saint (c.1175–1240) English cleric and
scholar, b. Edmund Rich. He was archbishop of Canterbury (1234–40). Edmund taught at Oxford University
and preached (1227) in favour of the Sixth CRUSADE. His
outspoken opposition to HENRY III led to the neutralization of his episcopacy. His feast day is 16 November.

Edmund I (921–46) King of Wessex (939–46), half-
brother and successor of ATHLESTAN. On his accession,
Edmund was faced with a Viking invasion led by Olaf
Guthrithson. He was forced to relinquish Northumbria
and much of the E Midlands. Between 942 and 944, he
regained most of the territory and reunited the kingdom.

Edmund II (c.980–1016) (Edmund Ironside) King of the
English (1016), son and successor of ETHELRED II (THE
UNREADY). In 1015, he became ruler of the Danelaw.
Edmund led resistance to the Danish king CANUTE II, but
was defeated at the Battle of Ashingdon (1016). He was
forced to divide the kingdom, retaining only Wessex.
Edmund died shortly after, leaving Canute as sole ruler.

Edo *See* TOKYO

education Process, either formal or informal, of acquiring knowledge and skills, leading to the development of
understanding, attitudes and values. **Formal** education is
organized instruction undertaken by society. In c.3000 BC,
the first SCHOOLS for reading and writing were founded by
the Egyptians and Sumerians. Western education is based
largely on the ancient Greek model. In c.387 BC, Plato
founded a school of philosophy, known as the ACADEMY.

SOCRATES' and CICERO's works proved highly influential in the development of teaching and LEARNING techniques. In medieval Europe, education was usually undertaken by the church. The establishment of the first modern universities, especially in Paris and Oxford, contributed to the growth of SCHOLASTICISM. The humanist ideals of the Renaissance and the invention of printing saw an expansion in formal education. The ENLIGHTENMENT brought new disciplines and teaching methods. The early 19th century saw the beginnings of state education. In 1841, Friedrich FROEBEL opened the first kindergarten. Elementary education became free and compulsory throughout most of Europe by the early 20th century. In the UK, the Education Act (1944) established a system of COMPREHENSIVE SCHOOLS. Maria MONTESSORI's theories on the importance of creative learning proved highly influential. John DEWEY emphasized the role of VOCATIONAL EDUCATION. DEVELOPMENTAL PSYCHOLOGY, especially the work of Jean PIAGET, has informed new educational models.

Education, UK Department of (DES) British government department responsible for the promotion of EDUCATION and the fostering of civil science in England. Headed by the secretary of state for education, its specific function is the broad allocation of capital resources for education, provision and training of teachers, and the setting of basic educational standards. The department works in cooperation with local education authorities (LEAs), which administer the day-to-day running of schools, and with the University Grants Committee which administers the universities. The departmernt derives from the Board of Education and was set up as the Ministry of Education by the Education Act (1944).

Edward I (1239–1307) King of England (1272–1307), son and successor of HENRY III. His suppression of the BARONS' WAR (1263–65), led by Simon de MONTFORT, made him king in all but name. Edward joined the Ninth CRUSADE (1270) and was crowned on his return (1274). He conquered Wales and incorporated it into England (1272–84). In 1296, Edward captured the Scottish coronation stone from Scone, but William WALLACE and ROBERT I (THE BRUCE) led Scottish resistance. His reforms are central to Britain's legal and constitutional history. The Statutes of WESTMINSTER codified common law. Edward's foreign ambitions led to the formation of the MODEL PARLIAMENT (1295). His son, EDWARD II, inherited high taxation and the enmity of Scotland.

Edward II (1284–1327) King of England (1307–27), son and successor of EDWARD I. Edward's reliance on his friend and adviser Piers Gaveston alienated his barons. The barons drafted the Ordinances of 1311, which restricted royal power and banished Gaveston. In 1312, they killed Gaveston. Renewing his father's campaign against the Scots, Edward was routed at BANNOCKBURN (1314). In 1321, Thomas, Earl of Lancaster, led an unsuccessful revolt against the king and his new favourite, Hugh le Despenser. In 1325, Edward's

estranged queen, Isabella, went as envoy to France. In 1326, she formed an army with her lover, Roger Mortimer, which invaded England and forced Edward to abdicate in favour of his son, EDWARD III. Edward II was murdered in Berkeley Castle, Gloucestershire, England.

Edward III (1312–77) King of England (1327–77), son and successor of EDWARD II. For the first three years of his reign, his mother, Isabella, and Roger Mortimer wielded all political power. In 1330, Edward mounted a successful coup. His reign was dominated by the outbreak of the HUNDRED YEARS' WAR (1337). Edward led several campaigns to France, won a famous victory at CRÉCY (1346), and claimed the title king of France, although only conquering Calais. The BLACK DEATH accelerated the abolition of serfdom. PARLIAMENT was divided into two houses and permanently sited at Westminster. In old age, his sons, EDWARD THE BLACK PRINCE and JOHN OF GAUNT, took over government. He was succeeded by his grandson, RICHARD II.

Edward IV (1442–83) King of England (1461–70, 1471–83). On the death (1460) of his father, Richard, Duke of York, in the Wars of the ROSES, Edward became the Yorkist candidate for the throne. He was crowned after the defeat of the Lancastrians at Towton. When the powerful Earl of WARWICK changed sides, Edward was forced into exile but returned to defeat Warwick at Barnet (1471). He encouraged trade, restored order and enforced royal absolutism. Edward died leaving two young sons, "the Princes in the Tower", but the throne was usurped by his brother, RICHARD III.

Edward V (1470–83) King of England for 77 days in 1483. He succeeded his father, EDWARD IV (1483). His uncle, the Duke of Gloucester, placed Edward and his younger brother, Richard, in the Tower of London, taking the throne for himself as RICHARD III. The disappearance of "the Princes in the Tower" was attributed to Richard although some suspect HENRY VII.

Edward VI (1537–53) King of England (1547–53), only legitimate son of HENRY VIII. He reigned under two regents, the dukes of SOMERSET (1547–49) and NORTHUMBERLAND (1549–53). Clever but frail, Edward died after willing the crown to Northumberland's daughter-in-law, Lady Jane GREY, to exclude his Catholic sister, MARY I.

Edward VII (1841–1910) King of Great Britain and Ireland (1901–10), son of Queen VICTORIA. As Prince of Wales, his views and lifestyle led to his exclusion from government by his mother. As king, he restored court pageantry and contributed to the ENTENTE CORDIALE with France. He was succeeded by his son, GEORGE V.

Edward VIII (1894–1972) King of Great Britain and Ireland (1936), subsequently Duke of Windsor. Edward's proposed marriage to an American divorcee, Wallis Simpson, was opposed by Stanley BALDWIN's government. Edward refused to back down and was forced to abdicate after a 325-day reign.

Edwards, Jonathan (1703–58) US revivalist minister and theologian. A powerful preacher in Massachusetts (1729–50), he gained a wide following. With his Calvinist themes of PREDESTINATION and man's dependence on God, Edwards brought about the GREAT AWAKENING.

Edward the Black Prince (1330–76) Prince of Wales (1343–76), eldest son of EDWARD III of England. In the HUNDRED YEARS' WAR, he distinguished himself at the Battle of CRÉCY (1346), and captured JOHN II (THE GOOD) of France at Poitiers (1356). As ruler (1362–71) of Aquitaine, Edward was responsible for the massacre at Limoges (1371). He ensured the accession of his son as RICHARD II.

▲ **eel** Moray eels (*Gymnothorax undulatus* – right – and *G. favagineus*) are found in all tropical seas. They can inflict severe bites if disturbed.

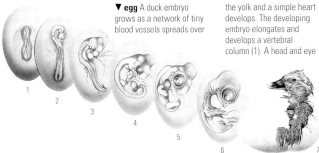

▼ **egg** A duck embryo grows as a network of tiny blood vessels spreads over the yolk and a simple heart develops. The developing embryo elongates and develops a vertebral column (1). A head and eye start to form, and the heart folds into its final position (2). The gut forms, the brain enlarges, and the embryo starts to curl (3–4). The limbs appear, and the tail and mouth form (5). By 13 days (6), it is possible to identify the bird from its bill. Some species of bird hatch shortly after this stage; others, such as the mallard duck (7), continue to develop in the egg.

Edward the Confessor, Saint (1002–66) King of England (1042–66), son of ETHELRED II (THE UNREADY). Before succeeding HARDECANUTE, Edward was resident in Normandy. His perceived favouritism towards Normans resulted in a rebellion, led by his father-in-law, Godwin. Edward's reign is noted for the rebuilding of WESTMINSTER ABBEY. His name resulted from his piety and, having taken a vow of chastity, he produced no heir. Though said to have promised the throne to William I (the Conqueror), Edward acknowledged HAROLD II, son of Godwin, as his rightful heir. He was canonized in 1161. His feast day is 13 October.

Edward the Elder (d.925) King of Wessex (899–925), son of and successor to ALFRED THE GREAT. Edward completed the reconquest of the S DANELAW (918), and by 920 was considered overlord by the rulers of Northumbria and Wales. He was succeeded by his son, ATHELSTAN.

Edward the Martyr (d.978) King of England (975–78). He was murdered, perhaps by his stepmother, and succeeded by his step-brother ETHELRED II (THE UNREADY). Miracles were reported at his grave, and he was popularly regarded as a saint.

eel Marine and freshwater fish found worldwide in shallow temperate and tropical waters. Eels have snake-like bodies, dorsal and anal fins, and an air bladder at the throat. Length: up to 3m (10ft). Types include freshwater, moray and conger. Order Anguilliformes.

eelworm Tiny, thread-like nematode found worldwide in soil, fresh and saltwater. Most species are parasitic, and can cause extensive damage to crops. They have been used to control other pests. *See* ROUNDWORM

efficiency Work a MACHINE does (output) divided by the work put in (input). It is usually expressed as a percentage. A perfect machine would have an efficiency of 100%, but in mechanical systems there are always ENERGY losses such as those caused by FRICTION. Electrical generators have an efficiency of more than 99%, while internal combustion engines have an efficiency of *c*.25%. For very simple machines, efficiency can be defined as the mechanical advantage (force ratio) divided by the distance ratio (velocity ratio).

EFTA *See* EUROPEAN FREE TRADE ASSOCIATION

Egbert (d.839) King of Wessex (802–39). In 825, he defeated the Mercians at Ellendun, Wiltshire, and went on to gain Essex, Kent, Surrey and Sussex. Egbert's conquest of Mercia was short-lived, but in 838 he gained control of Cornwall. Egbert laid the foundations for the supremacy of Wessex.

egg (OVUM) Reproductive cell of female organisms. Its nucleus supplies half the chromosome complement of a future ZYGOTE and almost all the CYTOPLASM, upon union with the male gamete (SPERM). Once fertilized, an animal egg is surrounded by ALBUMIN, shell, egg case, or MEMBRANE, depending on the species. The egg provides a reserve of food for the EMBRYO in the form of yolk.

ego Self or "I" which the individual consciously experiences. According to Sigmund FREUD, it is the conscious level of personality that deals with the external world and also mediates the internal demands made by the impulses of the ID and the prohibitions of the SUPEREGO.

egret White HERON of temperate and tropical marshy regions. It is known for its plumes. Egrets are long-legged, long-necked, slender-bodied wading birds with dagger-like bills. They feed on small animals and nest in colonies. Height: 50–100cm (20–40in). Family Ardeidae; genus *Egretta*.

Egypt Country in NE Africa. Egypt is Africa's second most populous country (after Nigeria), and its capital, CAIRO, is Africa's largest city. ALEXANDRIA is Egypt's largest port. Most of Egypt is desert, and almost all the people live either in the NILE valley and its fertile delta or along the SUEZ CANAL. The region N of Cairo is often called **Lower** Egypt; S of Cairo, **Upper** Egypt. On the Sudanese border, S of the ASWAN High Dam, lies Lake Nasser. Egypt has three other largely uninhabited regions: the Western (Libyan) and Eastern (Arabian) deserts (parts of the SAHARA), and the SINAI PENINSULA, with Egypt's highest peak, Gebel Katherina, at 2,637m (8,650ft). **Climate** Egypt is a dry country, and sparse rainfall occurs in winter. It has mild winters and hot summers. **Vegetation** The Nile valley forms a long, green ribbon of fertile farmland. Dry landscape covers 90% of Egypt. **History and Politics** The Egyptian state was formed in *c*.3100 BC. The Old Kingdom saw the building of the PYRAMIDS at GIZA. The ruins of the Middle Kingdom's capital at LUXOR bear testament to Egypt's imperial power (*see* EGYPT, ANCIENT). In 332 BC, Egypt was conquered by Alexander the Great and the capital moved to ALEXANDRIA. After CLEOPATRA, the Roman Empire was dominant. In AD 642, Egypt was conquered by the UMAYYAD dynasty, who were supplanted by the ABBASIDS. ARABIC became the official language and ISLAM the dominant religion. Under the FATIMIDS, Cairo became a centre of SHIITE culture. SALADIN's rule (1169–93) was notable for the defeat of the CRUSADES. His dynasty was overthrown (1250) by MAMELUKE soldier slaves. In 1517, Egypt was conquered by the OTTOMANS, who ruled for nearly three centuries. Egypt was occupied (1798–1801) by Napoleon I. France was expelled by MUHAMMAD ALI, who established the modern Egyptian state. The construction (1867) of the Suez Canal encouraged British imperial ambitions. In 1882, Britain subdued Cairo, and the British army remained even after Egypt became an independent monarchy (1922) under FUAD I. Fuad

EGYPT
AREA: 1,001,450sq km (386,660 sq mi)
POPULATION: 64,210,000
CAPITAL (POPULATION): Cairo (9,656,000)

was succeeded by FAROUK (r.1936–52). The creation (1948) of Israel saw the involvement of Egypt in the first of the ARAB-ISRAELI WARS. In 1953, the monarchy fell, and Gamal Abdal NASSER led (1954–70) the new republic. Nasser's nationalization of the Suez Canal (1956) was briefly contested by Israel, Britain and France. In 1958, Egypt, Syria and Yemen formed the short-lived United Arab Republic. Egypt was defeated by Israel in the SIX- DAY WAR (1967). Nasser was succeeded by Anwar SADAT. After defeat in the Yom Kippur War (1973), Sadat signed the CAMP DAVID AGREEMENT (1979) with Israel, which withdrew from Sinai (1982). Egypt was expelled from the Arab League, and Sadat was assassinated by Islamic extremists. Hosni MUBARAK became president (1981–). A state of emergency has existed since 1981. Mubarak led Egypt back into the Arab League (1989) and improved relations with the West. In 1992, Muslim fundamentalists restarted their armed campaign. In 1997, 58 tourists were murdered in Luxor, damaging the vital tourist industry. Mubarak was re-elected in 1999. **Economy** Egypt is Africa's second most industrialized country (after South Africa), but it remains a poor developing country (1995 GDP per capita, US$3,820). Farming employs 34% of the workforce. Egypt is the world's second-largest producer of dates. Textiles are the second most valuable export (after oil).

Egypt, ancient Civilization that flourished along the Nile River in NW Africa from c.3400 BC–30 BC. The dynasties are numbered from 1 to 30, and the kingdoms of Upper and Lower Egypt were united c.3100 BC by the legendary MENES. Ancient Egyptian history is separated into a number of periods. The highlight of the **Old Kingdom** was the building of the PYRAMIDS of GIZA during the 4th dynasty. After the death of Pepy II in the 6th dynasty, central government disintegrated. This was the **First Intermediate Period**. Central authority was restored in the 11th dynasty, and the capital was moved to Thebes (now LUXOR). The **Middle Kingdom** (c.2040–1640 BC) saw Egypt develop into a great power. Amenemhet I, founder of the 12th dynasty (c.1991 BC), secured Egypt's borders and created a new capital. Literature, art and architecture flourished. At the end of this Kingdom, Egypt again fell into disarray **(Second Intermediate Period)** and control was seized by the HYKSOS. The **New Kingdom** began c.1550 BC and brought great wealth. Massive temples and tombs, such as TUTANKHAMUN'S, were built. Wars with the HITTITES under RAMSES II weakened Egypt, and subsequent ineffectual rulers led to the decline of the New Kingdom. The 21st to 25th dynasties (**Third Intermediate Period**) culminated in Assyrian domination. The Persians ruled from 525 until 404 BC, when the last native dynasties appeared. In 332 BC, Egypt fell to the armies of ALEXANDER THE GREAT, who moved the capital to ALEXANDRIA. After Alexander's death, his general became ruler of Egypt, as PTOLEMY I. The Ptolemies maintained a powerful empire for three centuries, and Alexandria became a centre of learning. Roman power was on the ascendancy, and when Ptolemy XII asked POMPEY for aid in 58 BC, it marked the end of Egyptian

independence. CLEOPATRA tried to assert independence through associations with Julius CAESAR and Mark ANTONY, but she was defeated at ACTIUM. Her son, Ptolemy XV (whose father was probably Julius Caesar), was the last Ptolemy; he was killed by Octavian (AUGUSTUS), and Egypt became a province of Rome.

Egyptian architecture, ancient Architecture developed since 3000 BC and characterized by post and lintel construction, massive walls covered with hieroglyphic and pictorial carving, flat roofs, and structures such as the mastaba, obelisk, pylon and PYRAMID. Perhaps the great architect of the ancient period was Imhotep.

Egyptian art, ancient (2686–2181 BC) Works were chiefly relief sculpture and painting, characterized by front and side views of the human figure, flat colour tones, symmetry in sculpture and static figures. Relief-decorated private tombs and temples portrayed daily life.

Egyptian mythology Ancient Egyptians worshipped many deities that represented every aspect of nature and human activity. Early tribal deities took the form of totemic animals that gradually acquired human characteristics. The sun-god RA emerged out of primeval chaos to create the air and father the sky-goddess, Nut, and the Earth-god, Geb. Ra was the chief deity. His symbol, the PYRAMID, became the design for the tombs of ancient Egypt's rulers. The pharaohs administered the will of the gods and built huge temples in their honour at LUXOR. Nut and Geb gave birth to OSIRIS. Osiris was both protector of nature and judge of the dead. He was murdered by his brother, SETH, but restored to life by his sister and wife, the mother goddess ISIS. Their son, HORUS, represented the triumph of good over evil. By the XIX dynasty, Ra had become united with the god AMON. AKHNATEN asserted the supremacy of the god ATEN. The ancient Egyptians believed in REINCARNATION, and the BOOK OF THE DEAD outlines the precautions needed to ensure immortality *See also* HATHOR; MUMMY; THOTH

Egyptology Study of ancient EGYPT, its people and its antiquities. Important landmarks in Egyptology include the discovery of the ROSETTA STONE, the temple of AMON and the tomb of TUTANKHAMEN at LUXOR, and the moving of the temples at ABU SIMBEL.

Ehrlich, Paul (1854–1915) German bacteriologist. He shared (with Ilya Metchnikoff) the 1908 Nobel Prize for physiology or medicine for his work on immunization. Ehrlich's search for a "magic bullet" against disease and his discovery of salvarsan, a chemical effective against syphilis microorganisms, introduced CHEMOTHERAPY.

Eichmann, (Karl) Adolf (1906–62) German Nazi, head of the notorious subsection IV-B-4 of the Reich Central Security Office in WORLD WAR 2. Eichmann supervised the fulfilment of the Nazi policies of deportation, slave labour and mass murder in the CONCENTRATION CAMPS that led to the death of c.6 million Jews. In 1945, he escaped to Argentina but was abducted (1960) by the Israel secret police, and tried and executed in Israel.

eider Large sea DUCK found in N Europe and North America. Its down is used to fill pillows and comforters. When breeding, the male grows striking black and white plumage. Family Anatidae; genus *Somateria*.

Eiffel Tower Landmark built for the Paris *Exposition* of 1889. Designed by Alexandre Gustave Eiffel, the iron-framed tower rises 300m (984ft). Lifts and stairs lead to observation platforms.

Eijkman, Christiaan (1858–1930) Dutch physician. In 1929 he shared (with Frederick Hopkins) the Nobel Prize for physiology or medicine for his discovery of the antineuritic vitamin. Eijkman was the first to recognize a dietary deficiency disease, demonstrating that beriberi was produced by a lack of a certain dietary substance, later identified as VITAMIN B_1.

Eindhoven City on the River Dommel, *c*.90km (55mi) SE of ROTTERDAM in North Brabant province, s Netherlands. Eindhoven has been an industrial centre since the Philips electrical company was founded here in 1891. Industries: radio, electrical and electronic equipment, engineering, motor vehicles, textiles. Pop. (1996) 197,000.

Einstein, Albert (1879–1955) US physicist, b. Germany, best known for his theories of RELATIVITY. In 1905 Einstein published four papers that revolutionized physical science. "The Electrodynamics of Moving Bodies" announced his special theory of relativity. Drawing on the work of H.A. LORENTZ, Einstein's **special theory** of relativity discarded the notion of absolute motion in favour of the hypothesis that the speed of light is constant for all observers in uniform (unaccelerated) motion. Measurements in one uniformly moving system can be correlated with measurements in another uniform system, if their **relative** velocity is known. It asserted that the speed of light was the maximum velocity attainable in the Universe. A corollary of this special theory – the equivalence of MASS and ENERGY ($E = mc^2$) – was put forward in a second paper. A third paper, on BROWNIAN MOVEMENT, confimed the atomic theory of MATTER. Lastly, Einstein explained the PHOTOELECTRIC EFFECT in terms of quanta or photons of light. For this insight, which forms the basis of modern QUANTUM THEORY, Einstein received the 1921 Nobel Prize for physics. In 1911 he asserted the equivalence of GRAVITATION and INERTIA. Einstein extended his special theory into a **general theory** of relativity (1916) that incorporated systems in non-uniform (accelerated) motion. He asserted that matter in space causes curvature in the space-time continuum, resulting in gravitational fields. This explained the peculiar motion of the planet Mercury and was confirmed (1919) by Arthur EDDINGTON's study of starlight. Fearful of the rise of Nazism, Einstein accepted a post (1933–55) at the Institute of Advanced Study, Princeton, New Jersey, USA. In 1940 he became a US citizen. Einstein devoted the rest of his career to a UNIFIED FIELD THEORY, combining ELECTROMAGNETISM and GRAVITATION.

einsteinium Radioactive, synthetic metallic element (symbol Es) of the ACTINIDE SERIES. The isotope, Es^{253}, was first identified in 1952 at the University of California at Berkeley. Eleven isotopes have been identified. Properties: at.no. 99; most stable isotope Es^{254} (half-life 276 days). *See also* TRANSURANIC ELEMENTS

Eire *See* IRELAND, REPUBLIC OF

Eisenhower, Dwight David ("Ike") (1890–1969) 34th US president (1953–61). As supreme commander of the Allied Expeditionary Force from 1943, Eisenhower was largely responsible for the integration of Allied forces in the liberation of Europe. In 1950, he became Supreme Allied Commander (Europe) and helped establish the NORTH ATLANTIC TREATY ORGANIZATION (NATO). In 1952, Eisenhower gained the Republican nomination and secured an easy victory over Adlai STEVENSON in the presidential election. He enforced a prompt end to the KOREAN WAR and, with John Foster DULLES, established a staunchly anti-communist foreign policy. In 1956, Eisenhower was resoundingly re-elected. In 1957, he ordered Federal troops into Little Rock, Arkansas, to end segregation in schools. His second term was dominated by the COLD WAR. He was succeeded by John F. KENNEDY.

Eisenstein, Sergei (1898–1948) Soviet film director. Although he completed just six films in 25 years, he is one of the most influential artists in the history of CINEMA. Eisenstein developed the use of creative editing for narrative and expressive effect. His films include *The Battleship Potemkin* (1925) and *October/Ten Days That Shook the World* (1928). *See also* MONTAGE

El Alamein Village in N Egypt. In October 1942, the British 8th Army (under General MONTGOMERY) successfully attacked Axis forces here and eventually drove them back to Tunisia. The battle was a turning point in the North Africa campaign of WORLD WAR 2.

Elam Ancient country of MESOPOTAMIA; the capital was Susa. Elamite civilization became dominant *c*.2000 BC with the capture of BABYLON. It flourished until the Muslim conquest in the 7th century. Susa was an important centre under the ACHAEMENID kings of Persia and contained a palace of DARIUS I; archaeological finds include the stele of HAMMURABI, inscribed with his code of law.

eland Largest living ANTELOPE, native to central and s Africa. Gregarious and slow-moving, elands have heavy, spiral horns. Height: up to 1.8m (5.8ft) at the shoulder; weight: up to 900kg (2,000lb). Family Bovidae.

elasticity Capability of a material to recover its size and shape after deformation by STRESS and strain. When an external force is applied, a material develops stress, which results in strain (a change in dimensions). *See also* HOOKE'S LAW

Elat (Eilat) Seaport in s Israel on the Gulf of AQABA. A holiday resort, it is also the site of an oil pipeline terminal. Its location close to the SINAI PENINSULA and its harbour make it a vital gateway for Israel's trade with Africa. Industries: fishing, tourism. Pop. (1990 est.) 26,000.

Elba Italian island in the Tyrrhenian Sea, largest of the Tuscan Archipelago; the chief port and town is Portoferraio. Napoleon I was exiled here (1814–15). Industries: fisheries, wine, tourism. Area: 223sq km (86sq mi). Pop. (1984 est.) 28,907.

Elbe River in central Europe. It rises as the Labe on the s slopes of the Riesengebirge in the Czech Republic, flows N and NW through Germany, and enters the North Sea at Cuxhaven. Length: 1,167km (725mi).

Elbert, Mount Mountain in the Sawatch Range of the ROCKY MOUNTAINS, central Colorado, USA. It is the highest peak in the Rockies, at 4,402m (14,433ft).

Elbrus, Mount (Gora El'Brus) Two peaks in s European Russia, in the CAUCASUS range on the border with Georgia. Extinct volcanoes; the W peak, rising to 5,633m (18,481ft), is the highest in Europe. The E peak is 5,595m (18,356ft) high.

elder Shrub or small tree found in temperate and subtropical areas. It has divided leaves and clusters of small white flowers. Its small, shiny black berries are used for making wine and jelly and in medicine. There are 40 species. Family Caprifoliaceae, genus *Sambucus*.

El Cid *See* CID, EL

El Dorado (Sp. The Golden One) Mythical city of fabulous wealth, supposedly in South America, the focus of many Spanish expeditions in the 16th century.

Eleanor of Aquitaine (1122–1204) Queen consort of France and later of England. She married LOUIS VII of France and accompanied him on the Second Crusade (1147–49). Divorced in 1152, she married the future HENRY II of England but later supported their sons, the future RICHARD I and JOHN, in revolt against Henry.

Eleanor of Castile (1246–90) Queen consort (1272–90) of EDWARD I of England, daughter of Ferdinand III of Castile. According to legend, she saved Edward's life by sucking the poison from a wound he gained while they were on a Crusade (1270–73).

Eleanor died at Hadby, Nottinghamshire, and memorial "Eleanor crosses" were erected at the 12 places her funeral cortège stopped on route to London. The last stop was at Charing Cross, where a replica now stands.

election Process of choosing candidates for office. In the modern world, elections have been inseparable from the rise of DEMOCRACY. In most countries, age and residency qualifications govern a person's eligibility to vote; candidates must also meet certain requirements. The first elections to PARLIAMENT in England were held in the 13th century. In the 19th century, various reform acts widened the FRANCHISE and a secret BALLOT was introduced in 1872. In the US, congressional elections are held every two years and presidential elections every four years. *See also* ELECTORAL COLLEGE; PRIMARY; PROPORTIONAL REPRESENTATION

electoral college US body, elected by voters in the states, which casts the votes to elect the president and vice president. The number of electors from each state equals the number of its representatives in both houses of CONGRESS. State committees or conventions of each political party select candidates for electors. In an ELECTION, the candidate who wins a plurality of a state's popular vote usually receives all the state's electoral vote. Thus, a candidate may be elected to the presidency without a majority of the popular vote.

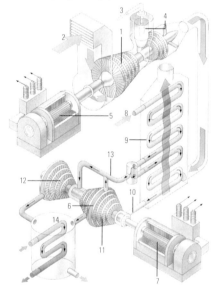

▲ **electricity sources** A combined cycle power station burns gas to generate electricity. It is more efficient than traditional fossil fuel power plants. The first turbine (1) sucks in air (2), compressing it before mixing it with the fuel (3) and burning the mixture (4). Exhaust gases spin a second turbine, connected to the first turbine and a generator (5). The energy of the gases is harnessed to power a second multiple turbine (6) connected to another generator (7). Gases are used to superheat water (8), looping through a special vessel (9). To maximize power generation, superheated steam (10) turns a high-pressure turbine (11) before passing into a lower-pressure turbine (12). Steam is fed into the turbine from the heating loops (13) and is cooled (14) before returning to the circuit.

Electra Daughter of AGAMEMNON, leader of the Greeks in the Trojan War. She helped her brother Orestes avenge their father's murder by plotting to kill their mother CLYTEMNESTRA and stepfather Aegisthus.

Electra complex *See* OEDIPUS COMPLEX

electric car AUTOMOBILE powered by a rechargeable BATTERY. The electrical energy stored in the BATTERY is converted to mechanical power by an ELECTRIC MOTOR. Electric cars do not produce exhaust pollutants, do not consume scarce petroleum resources, and they are quieter. The major disadvantage of electric cars is their range – they can only travel *c*.160km (100mi) before the battery needs recharging. The maximum speed of an electric car is usually less than 100km/h (62mph). The first electric cars were produced in Europe in the late 1800s.

electric charge Quantity of ELECTRICITY. Electric charges (measured in coulombs) are either positive or negative. They can be stored on insulated metal spheres (VAN DE GRAAFF GENERATOR), insulated plates (CAPACITOR) or in chemical solutions (electric BATTERY).

electric current Movement of ELECTRIC CHARGES, usually the flow of ELECTRONS along a CONDUCTOR or the movement of ions through an ELECTROLYTE. Current (symbol I) flows from a positive to a negative terminal, although electrons actually flow along a wire in the opposite direction. It is measured in AMPERES. Direct current (DC) flows continuously in one direction, whereas alternating current (AC) regularly reverses direction. The frequency of AC current is measured in HERTZ (Hz). *See also* ELECTRICITY; PARTICLE PHYSICS

electric field (electrostatic field) Region around an ELECTRIC CHARGE in which any charged particle experiences a force. The strength of the field (E) upon unit charge at a distance r from a charge Q is equal to $Q/4\pi r^2 E$, where E is the permittivity (degree to which molecules polarize). *See also* ELECTROMAGNETISM

electric furnace FURNACE heated to a very high temperature by an ELECTRIC CURRENT. Electric furnaces are used in industry for melting metals and other materials.

electricity Form of energy associated with static or moving ELECTRIC CHARGES. Charge has two forms – positive and negative. Like charges repel, and unlike attract, as described by Charles COULOMB in Coulomb's law. ELECTRIC CHARGES are acted upon by forces when they move in a MAGNETIC FIELD; this movement generates an opposing magnetic field (FARADAY'S LAWS). Electricity and MAGNETISM are different aspects of ELECTROMAGNETISM. The flow of charges constitutes a current, which in a CONDUCTOR consists of negatively charged ELECTRONS. For an ELECTRIC CURRENT to exist in a conductor, there must be an ELECTROMOTIVE FORCE (EMF) or POTENTIAL DIFFERENCE between the ends of the conductor. If the source of potential difference is a BATTERY, the current flows in one direction as a direct current (DC). If the source is the power supply, the current reverses direction twice every cycle as alternating current (AC). The AMPERE is the unit of current, the coulomb is the unit of charge, the OHM the unit of RESISTANCE, and the VOLT is the unit of ELECTROMOTIVE FORCE. OHM'S LAW and the laws of KIRCHHOFF are the basic means of calculating circuit values.

electricity sources Devices that convert other forms of energy into ELECTRICITY. Most of the world's electricity is produced in power stations from the chemical energy of fossil fuels (COAL, OIL or NATURAL GAS). The heat from burning fossil fuels turns water into steam. The steam drives a TURBINE, linked to an electricity GENERATOR. In a nuclear power station, heat comes from the FISSION of nuclei in a NUCLEAR REACTOR. A BATTERY and fuel cell converts chemical energy directly into electricity. SOLAR CELLS convert SOLAR ENERGY into electricity. Wind generators and water turbines produce electricity from the energy of movement in wind and water. *See also* ENERGY SOURCES; HYDROELECTRICITY; RENEWABLE ENERGY

electric motor Machine that converts electrical ENERGY into mechanical energy. In a simple form of electric MOTOR, an ELECTRIC CURRENT powers a set of ELECTROMAGNETS on a rotor in the MAGNETIC FIELD of a permanent MAGNET. Magnetic forces set up between the permanent magnet and the electromagnet cause the rotor to turn. Electric motors may use alternating current (AC) or direct current (DC).

electrocardiogram (ECG) Recording of the electrical activity of the HEART traced on a moving strip of paper by an electrocardiograph. It is used to diagnose heart disease.

electrochemistry Branch of chemistry concerned with the relationship between ELECTRICITY and chemical changes. It includes the properties of IONS in solution, the CONDUCTIVITY of ELECTROLYTES, and the study of the processes in electrochemical cells and in ELECTROLYSIS.

electroconvulsive therapy (ECT) Controversial treatment of MENTAL DISORDER by an electric current passed via ELECTRODES to one or both sides of the brain to induce convulsions. Given under anaesthesia, it is mainly prescribed for severe depression that has failed to respond to other treatments. It can produce unpleasant side effects, such as confusion, memory loss and headache.

electrocution Death caused by the passage of an ELECTRIC CURRENT through the body. The current may come from a low- or (more often) a high-voltage source or from lightning. A major shock either causes chaotic disruption of the heartbeat (fibrillation) or stops the heart completely. Severe burns may be visible where the current has entered the body and also at its point of exit.

electrode CONDUCTOR, usually a wire or rod, through which an ELECTRIC CURRENT flows into or leaves a medium. In ELECTROLYSIS, two electrodes – a positive (ANODE) and a negative (CATHODE) – are immersed in an ELECTROLYTE.

electroencephalogram (EEG) Recording of electrical activity of the BRAIN. ELECTRODES are attached to the scalp to pick up the tiny oscillating currents produced by brain activity. Electroencephalography is used mainly in the diagnosis and monitoring of EPILEPSY.

electrolysis CHEMICAL REACTION caused by passing a direct current (DC) through an ELECTROLYTE. This results in positive IONS migrating to the negative ELECTRODE (CATHODE) and negative ions migrating to the positive electrode (ANODE). Electrolysis is an important method of obtaining chemicals. *See* ELECTROPLATING

electrolyte Solution or molten salt that can conduct ELECTRICITY, as in ELECTROLYSIS. In electrolytes, current is carried by IONS, rather than by ELECTRONS.

electromagnet MAGNET constructed from a soft iron core around which is wound a coil of wire. A MAGNETIC FIELD is set up when an ELECTRIC CURRENT is passed through the wire.

electromagnetic force One of the four FUNDAMENTAL FORCES in nature. Within an ATOM, the electromagnetic force binds the negatively charged ELECTRONS to the positively charged NUCLEUS. *See also* GRAND UNIFIED THEORY (GUT); UNIFIED FIELD THEORY

electromagnetic induction Use of MAGNETISM to produce an ELECTROMOTIVE FORCE (EMF). If a bar magnet is pushed through a wire coil, an ELECTRIC CURRENT is induced in the coil when the magnet is moving. An

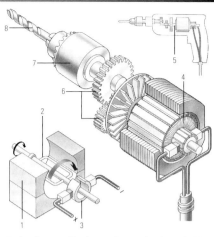

▲ **electric motor** Electric motors work using the interaction of a magnet (1) and a wire with a current passing through it (2). With the current flowing, the magnetic field produced by the loop interacts with the field of the magnet. A downward force acts on the right side, an upward force on the left side. When the loop reaches the vertical the split ring (through which the current reaches the loop) (3) reverses the current and so the magnetic field. Electric motors use multiple coils (4) to ensure constant power. In an electric drill, the turning shaft (5) emerges from the magnetic coils and is then geared (6) through a chuck (7) to the drill bit (8).

electric current is also induced in the coil if it is rotated around the magnet, as in a DYNAMO, ELECTRIC MOTOR or transformer. *See also* INDUCTANCE; INDUCTION

electromagnetic radiation ENERGY in the form of transverse waves. It travels through free space at close to the speed of light, c.300,000km (186,000mi) per second. In general, electromagnetic waves are set up by electrical and magnetic vibrations that occur universally in ATOMS. The WAVELENGTH of electromagnetic radiation varies inversely with the WAVE FREQUENCY. These waves make up the **electromagnetic spectrum**, which includes (in ascending order of frequency): RADIO waves (including MICROWAVES), INFRARED WAVES, LIGHT, ULTRAVIOLET RADIATION, X-RAYS and GAMMA RADIATION. They can undergo REFLECTION, REFRACTION, INTERFERENCE, DIFFRACTION and polarization. In some instances, such as the PHOTOELECTRIC EFFECT, electromagnetic radiation behaves in a manner that can only be explained by assuming the radiation to be composed of quanta of energy (photons). *See also* QUANTUM THEORY

electromagnetic series (electrochemical series) List of METALS and the gas hydrogen, whose order indicates their relative tendency to be oxidized, or to lose ELECTRONS in chemical reactions (*see* OXIDATION-REDUCTION). The series starts with the metal that tends to lose the most electrons in reaction. Those that lose electrons more readily than hydrogen are termed **electropositive**; those that lose electrons less readily are called **electronegative**. The order of some common metals is: potassium, aluminium, zinc, iron, cobalt, nickel, tin, lead, hydrogen, copper, mercury, silver and gold.

electromagnetism Branch of physics dealing with the laws and phenomena that involve the interaction or interdependence of ELECTRICITY and MAGNETISM. The

▶ **electron microscope**
In an electron microscope, a beam of electrons (1) streams from the heated tungsten cathode (2) of an electron gun (3) and is focused by upper (4) and lower (5) electromagnetic lenses. It then passes through an aperture ring (6) and a scan coil (7) before being focused by a projector lens (8) onto the sample (9). The process takes place in a vacuum with air evacuated (10) by a pump. A computer controls the scan coil, which directs the beam across the sample. The sample is placed in an airlock (11) and manipulated into position (12). An image of the sample is created by detecting electrons dislodged (13) from the sample. These electrons correlate to the topography of the sample and are measured by a flash detector (14) when they hit a fluorescent target (15). The image is displayed on a computer monitor (16): here *Lactobacillus bulgaricus* magnified 1,000 times (17).

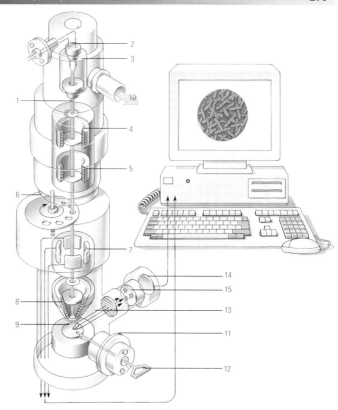

region in which the effect of an electromagnetic system can be detected is known as an **electromagnetic field**. When a magnetic field changes, an electric field can always be detected. When an electric field varies, a magnetic field can always be detected.

electromotive force (emf) Potential difference between the terminals in a source of ELECTRIC CURRENT, measured in volts. It is equal to the energy liberated when this voltage drives the current round an electric circuit. *See also* ELECTRICITY

electron (symbol e) Stable ELEMENTARY PARTICLE with a negative charge (-1.602×10^{-19}C), a rest mass of 9.1×10^{-31} kg and a SPIN of $\frac{1}{2}$ fermion. Electrons were first identified (1879) by J.J. THOMSON. In 1913, Robert MILLIKAN determined their charge. Electrons are one of the three primary constituents of ATOMS. They form ORBITALS that surround the positively charged NUCLEUS. In a free atom, the electrons' total negative charge balances the positive charge of the PROTONS in the nucleus. Removal or addition of an atomic electron produces a charged ION. **Free electrons** (not bound to an atom) are responsible for electrical conduction. Beams of electrons are used in electronic devices, such as CATHODE-RAY TUBES, OSCILLOSCOPES and ELECTRON MICROSCOPES. An electron is classified as a LEPTON. Its anti-particle is the POSITRON. *See also* BROGLIE, PRINCE LOUIS VICTOR DE; CHEMICAL BOND; MATTER; NEUTRONS; PARTICLE PHYSICS; PHOTOELECTRIC EFFECT; VALENCE

electronic mail (e-mail) Correspondence sent via a COMPUTER NETWORK. Messages produced using word-processing programs are transmitted over a network and

stored in a computer called a **mail server** until people transfer them to their own computer. *See also* INTERNET

electronic music Music in which electronic methods are used to generate or modulate sounds. The first pieces produced on tape recorders were composed in the 1920s. In Paris, Pierre Schaeffer and Pierre Henry manipulated recorded sounds, producing one of the first major works, *Symphonie pour un homme seul* (1950). The invention of the SYNTHESIZER inspired many composers, particularly Karlheinz STOCKHAUSEN. In the 1960s, it became possible to use computers for complex electronic sounds; Yannis XENAKIS and Pierre BOULEZ are two of the many composers to have used computers.

electronics Study and use of CIRCUITS based on the conduction of ELECTRICITY through valves and SEMICONDUCTORS. The DIODE valve, invented by John FLEMING, and the triode valve, invented by Lee DE FOREST, provided the basic components for all the electronics of RADIO, TELEVISION and RADAR until the end of World War 2. In 1948, a team led by William SHOCKLEY produced the first semiconducting TRANSISTOR. Semiconductor devices do not require the high operating voltages of valves and can be miniaturized as an INTEGRATED CIRCUIT (IC). This has led to the production of COMPUTERS and automatic control devices. *See also* CATHODE-RAY TUBE; ELECTRON; MICRO-ELECTRONICS; PRINTED CIRCUIT; THERMIONICS

electron microscope MICROSCOPE used for producing an image of a minute object. It "illuminates" the object with a stream of ELECTRONS, and the "lenses" consist of magnets that focus the electron beam. The image is obtained by converting the pattern (made by electrons passing through the object) into a video display, which may be photographed. These microscopes can magnify from 2,000 to a million times.

electron volt (symbol eV) Unit of energy equal to the energy acquired by an ELECTRON in falling freely through a POTENTIAL DIFFERENCE of one VOLT. It is equal to 1.602×10^{-19} joules.

electrophoresis Movement of electrically charged colloidal particles through a fluid from one ELECTRODE to another when a voltage is applied across the electrodes. It is used in the analysis and separation of colloidal suspensions, especially colloidal proteins. *See also* CHROMATOGRAPHY; COLLOID

electroplating Deposition of a coating of metal on another by making the object to be coated the CATHODE in ELECTROLYSIS. Positive ions in the ELECTROLYTE are discharged at the cathode and deposited as metal. Electroplating is used in silver-plated utensils and chromium-plated automobile parts.

electroscope Instrument to detect the presence of an ELECTRIC CHARGE or radiation. The commonest type is the gold-leaf electroscope, in which two gold leaves hang from a conducting rod held in an insulated container. A charge applied to the rod causes the leaves to separate, and the amount of separation indicates the amount of charge.

electrostatics *See* STATIC ELECTRICITY

element Substance that cannot be split into simpler substances by chemical means. All atoms of a given element have the same ATOMIC NUMBER (at.no.) and thus the same number of PROTONS and ELECTRONS. The atoms can have different ATOMIC MASS NUMBERS, and a natural sample of an element is generally a mixture of ISOTOPES. The known elements range from hydrogen (at.no. 1) to element 112. Elements of the first 95 atomic numbers exist in nature; the higher numbers have been synthesized. *See also* PERIODIC TABLE

element 104 *See* DUBNIUM

element 105 *See* HAHNIUM

element 106 *See* RUTHERFORDIUM

elementary particle In physics, a SUBATOMIC PARTICLE that cannot be subdivided. Such particles are the basic constituents of MATTER. There are three groups of elementary particles: QUARKS, LEPTONS (light particles) and gauge BOSONS (messenger particles). All elementary particles have an associated anti-particle.

elephant Largest land animal, the only surviving member of the mammal order *Proboscidea*, which included the MAMMOTH and the MASTODON. It is native to Africa (*Loxodonta africana*) and India (*Elephas maximus*). The tusks, the source of ivory, are elongated upper incisors that it uses for digging up roots. The Indian cow (female) elephant has no tusks. The trunk is an elongated nose and upper lip that it uses for drinking and picking up food. The African elephant is taller and heavier than its Indian counterpart. A bull (male) elephant may weigh as much as 7,000kg (eight tonnes), and can charge at speeds up to 40km/h (25mph). It also has much larger ears, up to 100cm (40in) in diameter. Elephants are herbivores and browse in herds led by a bull. The cow (female) gives birth to its calf after 18 to 22 months gestation. Elephants live for 60 to 70 years. Indian elephants are used as beasts of burden but do not breed in captivity. The hunting of elephants for their tusks saw the population reduce from 1.3 million in 1979 to 600,000 in 1989. A ban on hunting has led to a resurgence.

elephantiasis Condition in which there is gross swelling of the tissues due to blockage of lymph vessels. It is usually caused by parasitic worms, as in FILARIASIS.

Eleusinian Mysteries Religious rites in ancient Greece at Eleusis, Attica, to honour DEMETER and PERSEPHONE. The rites probably began as a fertility festival.

Elgar, Sir Edward (1857–1934) English composer. His individual style is first evident in his set of 14 orchestral variations, the *Enigma Variations* (1899). Elgar's oratario, *The Dream of Gerontius* (1900), established him as a leading European composer. Other works include a violin concerto (1910), a cello concerto (1919) and two symphonies. His third symphony was completed (1998) by Anthony Payne. Elgar is perhaps best-known for the patriotic piece "Land of Hope and Glory", one of the five *Pomp and Circumstance* marches (1901–30).

Elgin Marbles Group of sculptures from the Acropolis of Athens, including sculptures of the PARTHENON. They were transported (1803–12) by the 7th Earl of Elgin (1766–1841), sold to the British Government in 1816, and are now on display in the British Museum, London. The Greek government has campaigned for their return.

El Greco *See* GRECO, EL

Elijah (active 9th century BC) Old Testament prophet. He rebuked King AHAB for his attitude to the Phoenician cult of BAAL introduced by Ahab's wife, JEZEBEL (1 Kings 17, 2 Kings 2). Elijah, aided by his disciple ELISHA, contested that there was no God but YAHWEH.

Eliot, George (1819–80) English novelist, b. Mary Ann Evans. Her unconventional relationship with G.H. LEWES began in 1853. Eliot's first work of fiction was the collection, *Scenes of Clerical Life* (1858). Three novels of provincial life followed: *Adam Bede* (1859), *The Mill on the Floss* (1860) and *Silas Marner* (1861). *Romola* (1862–63) was her only historical romance. *Middlemarch* (1871–72) is regarded as Eliot's masterpiece. Her last novel was *Daniel Deronda* (1874–76).

Eliot, T.S. (Thomas Stearns) (1888–1965) British poet, playwright and critic, b. USA. His first volume, *Prufock and Other Observations* (1917), includes "The Love Song of J. Alfred Prufock". Eliot's poem *The Waste Land* (1922) is a keystone of literary MODERNISM. Later poems, notably *Ash Wednesday* (1930) and the *Four Quartets* (1935–43), concerned religious faith. Eliot also wrote verse plays, including *Murder in the Cathedral* (1935) and *The Cocktail Party* (1950). His children's poems, *Old Possum's Book of Practical Cats* (1939), formed the basis for the musical *Cats*. Eliot was awarded the 1948 Nobel Prize for literature.

Elisha Old Testament prophet of Israel, disciple and successor of ELIJAH (2 Kings 2–13). He appeared in the 9th century BC and destroyed the Phoenician cult of BAAL. Elisha is portrayed as a miracle-worker, healer, and fulfiller of God's commissions to his master Elijah.

Elizabeth, Saint In the New Testament, wife of Zacharias and mother of JOHN THE BAPTIST. She was related to MARY, mother of Jesus. Her feast day is 5 November.

Elizabeth (1709–62) Empress of Russia (1741–62), daughter of PETER I (THE Great). She came to the throne after overthrowing her nephew, Ivan VI. Elizabeth waged war (1741–43) against Sweden and annexed (1743) the southern portion of Finland. A great patron of the arts, she was succeeded by her nephew, PETER III.

Elizabeth I (1533–1603) Queen of England (1558–1603), daughter of HENRY VIII and Anne BOLEYN. During the reigns of her half-brother and half-sister, EDWARD VI and MARY I, she avoided political disputes. Once crowned, she re-established Protestantism. The Elizabethan Settlement, conducted by Matthew PARKER, saw the CHURCH OF ENGLAND adopt the THIRTY-NINE ARTICLES (1571). Various plots to murder Elizabeth and place the Catholic MARY, QUEEN OF SCOTS, on the throne resulted in Mary's imprisonment and execution (1587), and increasing discrimination against Catholics. Elizabeth relied on a small group of advisers, such as Lord BURGHLEY and Sir Francis WALSINGHAM. For most of her reign, England was at peace, and commerce and industry prospered. ELIZABETHAN DRAMA reflected this "golden age". The expansion of the navy saw the development of the first BRITISH EMPIRE and the defeat of the Spanish ARMADA (1588). Despite pressure to marry, Elizabeth remained single. Her favourites included Robert Dudley, Earl of LEICESTER, and Robert Devereux, 2nd Earl of ESSEX. She was the last of the TUDORS, and the throne passed to the JAMES I, a STUART.

Elizabeth II (1926–) Queen of Great Britain and Northern Ireland and head of the Commonwealth of Nations (1952–), daughter of GEORGE VI. In 1947 she married PHILIP Mountbatten, Duke of Edinburgh, with whom she had four children, CHARLES, ANNE, Andrew and Edward. Popular and dutiful, Elizabeth has had to contend with criticism of royal wealth and scandals associated with the marriage failures in the royal family, particularly that of Charles and DIANA, PRINCESS OF WALES.

Elizabeth (1900–) (Queen Mother) British queen consort of GEORGE VI. Born Lady Bowes-Lyon, she married George in 1923. They had two children, Elizabeth (later ELIZABETH II) and MARGARET. In 1936, she became queen when George's brother, EDWARD VIII, abdicated. A popular figure, her 100th birthday was celebrated nationwide.

Elizabethan drama Drama staged in England during the reign (1558–1603) of ELIZABETH I. Drawing on classical and medieval thought, as well as folk drama, Elizabethan drama is characterized by a spiritual vitality and creativity. Dramatists of the period include William SHAKESPEARE, Christopher MARLOWE and Ben JONSON.

elk Name of two different species of deer: the European elk (*Alces alces*), known in North America as the MOOSE, and the American elk or WAPITI. The elk, found in N Eurasia, is the largest of all deer. Height at the shoulder: to 1.9m (6ft); weight 816kg (1,800lb). Family Cervidae.

Ellesmere Island Mountainous island in the Arctic Ocean, NW of Greenland, forming part of the Northwest Territories of Canada. It is the second largest and northernmost island of the Arctic Archipelago. Area: 196,236sq km (75,767sq mi).

Ellice Islands Former name (until 1976) of TUVALU

Ellington, "Duke" (Edward Kennedy) (1899–1974) US jazz composer, pianist and bandleader. Ellington's early pieces, performed (1927–32) at the Cotton Club, Harlem, New York, include "Black and Tan Fantasy" (1927) and "Mood Indigo" (1930). The "jungle" style gave way to the elegance of standards such as "Take the A Train" (1941). His orchestral suite *Black, Brown and Beige* (1943) was written for a concert at Carnegie Hall.

ellipse CONIC section formed by cutting a right circular cone with a plane inclined at such an angle that the plane does not intersect the base of the cone. When the intersecting plane is parallel to the base, the conic section is a circle. Most planetary orbits are ellipses.

Ellis, (Henry) Havelock (1859–1939) English psychologist and author. His seven-volume *Studies in the Psychology of Sex* (1897–1928) promoted the scientific study of sex and helped change public attitudes.

Ellis Island Island in Upper New York Bay, near MANHATTAN, SE New York. It acted as the main US immigration centre from 1892 to 1943. The Ellis Island Immigration Museum opened in 1990. Area: 11ha (27 acres).

Ellsworth, Lincoln (1880–1951) US polar explorer. In 1926 he and Roald AMUNDSEN became the first humans to fly over the North Pole. In 1935 Ellsworth became the first person to fly over Antarctica.

elm Hardy, tall, deciduous tree of N temperate zones. Elms have fan-shaped crowns, which make them ideal shade trees. Species include the American (*Ulmus americana*) and the Wych elm (*U. procera*). Both species are attacked by the fungus known as Dutch elm disease. Height: more than 30m (100ft). Family Ulmaceae.

El Niño (Sp. (Christ) child) Periodic easing or reversing of the TRADE WINDS over the S Pacific Ocean, causing the warm surface waters that have "piled-up" in the W Pacific to flow back and raise the coastal waters of South America by 2 to 3°C. It occurs around Christmas time. El Niño has a dramatic effect on climate patterns in Australia and Southeast Asia and may be implicated in changed rainfall patterns as far away as Africa. In normal years, trade winds blow E to W along the Equator, dragging sun-warmed surface waters into a pool off N Australia and monsoon rains to Indonesia. In the W Pacific, the Humboldt Current pushes the surface waters away from the coast of Peru, bringing cold, nutrient-rich water to the surface. This upwelled, nutrient-rich water stimulates the production of phytoplankton and swells the population of anchovies, which themselves are prey to seabirds (such as boobies and brown pelicans) and the Peruvian fishing industry. In an El Niño year, the upwelling ceases and the biological productivity of the area collapses. In 1982–83, for instance, the catch of anchovies was reduced by 600%. In addition, mean se-level along the coast of Latin America may increase by as much as 50cm (20in), causing widespread flooding. Some scientists believe that the frequency and effects of El Niño may be increasing.

El Paso City and port of entry in W Texas, USA, across the Rio Grande from Juárez, Mexico; seat of El Paso county. The area was visited by Spanish missionaries in the 16th century, but no settlement was made until 1827. The coming of the railway (1881) spurred development. In 1963, the border with Mexico was finally resolved. Industries: cotton clothing, oil refining. Pop. (1996) 600,000.

El Salvador Republic in Central America. El Salvador is the smallest and most densely populated country in Central America. It has a narrow coastal plain along the Pacific Ocean. The majority of the interior is mountainous with many extinct volcanic peaks, overlooking a heavily populated central plateau. In 1854 an earthquake destroyed the capital, SAN SALVADOR, and another in October 1986 killed 400 people. **Climate** The coast has a hot tropical climate. Inland, the climate is moderated by altitude. There is a wet season between May and October. **Vegetation** Grassland and some virgin forests are found in the highlands. The central plateau and valleys have areas of grass and deciduous woodland, while coastal regions are covered by tropical savanna or forest. **History and Politics** In 1524–26 the Spanish explorer Pedro de Alvarado conquered Native American tribes such as the Pipil, and the region became part of the Spanish viceroyalty of Guatemala. Independence was achieved in 1821, and El Salvador joined (1823) the Central American Federation. The federation was dissolved in 1839.

EL SALVADOR
AREA: 21,040sq km (8,124sq mi)
POPULATION: 6,739,000
CAPITAL (POPULATION): San Salvador (1,522,000)

Maximiliano Hernández Martínez seized power in a palace coup (1931). His brutal dictatorship was overthrown by a general strike (1944). A period of progressive government was followed by a military junta headed first by Julio Adalberto Rivera (1962–67) then Fidel Sánchez Hernández (1967–72). The "Soccer War" (1969) broke out with Honduras following an ill-tempered World Cup qualifying match between the two countries. Within four days, El Salvador had captured much of Honduras. A cease-fire was announced and the troops withdrew. In the 1970s El Salvador's socio-economic problems were compounded by the repressive National Republican Alliance (ARENA) regime. In 1979 civil war broke out between US-backed government forces and the Farabundo Marti National Liberation Front (FMLN). The 12-year war claimed 75,000 lives. A cease-fire came into effect in 1992, and the FMLN became a recognized political party. In 1993 a UN Truth Commission led to the removal of senior army officers for human-rights abuses, and FMLN arms were decommissioned. In 1994 Armando Calderón Sol of the ruling ARENA party was elected president. In 1999, he was succeeded by Francisco Flores. **Economy** El Salvador is a lower-middle-income developing country (1995 GDP per capita, US$2,610). Farmland and pasture account for *c*.60% of land use. El Salvador is the world's 10th largest producer of coffee. Sugar and cotton are grown on the coastal lowlands. Fishing is important. The civil war devastated the economy.

Éluard, Paul (1895–1952) French poet, b. Eugène Grindel. Along with André BRETON and Louis ARAGON, he was one of the founders of SURREALISM in literature. His debut collection was *Capital of Grief* (1926). In 1942 he joined the Communist Party and later works, such as *Poetry and Truth* (1942), are more political.

Elysium In Greek mythology, the Elysian fields. The abode of blessed mortals after their removal from the Earth, it is the realm to which heroes departed.

Emancipation Proclamation (1 January 1863) Declaration issued by Abraham LINCOLN abolishing SLAVERY in the CONFEDERATE STATES OF AMERICA. It was designed to enhance the Union's support from abroad, especially Britain, and to reduce the South's fighting force. Slavery was finally abolished by the 13th Amendment to the US CONSTITUTION (December 1865).

embalming Artificial preservation of dead bodies. The custom was highly advanced in ancient Egypt as early as 4000 BC. The body was soaked in a soda solution and the cavities filled with spices, oils and resins. Viscera were sometimes embalmed separately and placed in canopic jars. The science of anatomy revived the process, commonly by injecting formaldehyde into the vascular system and draining the blood.

embargo Order prohibiting exchange of goods. It usually refers to the restriction by government on the departure of merchant ships from its ports. Embargoes may form part of a package of SANCTIONS.

Embargo Act (1807) Act passed by Thomas JEFFERSON to force England and France to remove restrictions on US trade, following attacks on US merchant shipping. It prohibited all ships from entering or leaving US ports. The act hurt the US economy, and merchants resorted to smuggling. Resistance led to the Non-Intercourse Act (1809) that ended the 14-month embargo.

embolism Blocking of a blood vessel by an obstruction called an embolus, usually a blood clot, air bubble or particle of fat. The effects depend on where the embolus lodges; a cerebral embolism causes a STROKE. Treatment is with anticoagulants or surgery. *See also* ARTERIOSCLEROSIS

embroidery Decorative needlework (specifically stitching) on cloth. It has sometimes served as a means to depict historic events, such as the BAYEUX TAPESTRY. During the Renaissance, it was an important art of many courts. There was also a tradition of rural and folk embroidery, particularly in E Europe and in the quilting of the early English settlers in N America.

embryo Early developing stage of an animal or plant. In animals, the embryo stage starts at FERTILIZATION, and ends when the organism emerges from the egg or from its mother's UTERUS. In mammals, an embryo is sustained through blood supplied by the mother via the PLACENTA. In humans, the embryo is called a FETUS after the first eight weeks of pregnancy. In invertebrate animals the embryo is usually called a LARVA. In plants, the embryo is found in the seed, and the embryo stage ends on GERMINATION. An embryo results when the nuclei of an EGG and a SPERM or male sex cell fuse to form a single cell, called a ZYGOTE. The zygote then divides into a ball of cells called a BLASTULA. The blastula and then the embryo undergoes rapid changes in which the cells differentiate themselves to form features, such as limbs and organs. **Embryology** is the biological study of the origin, development and activities of embryos. Concern in the UK over the experimental use of human embryos formed by in vitro fertilization led to the establishment (1990) of the Human Fertilization and Embryology Authority, which acts as a licensing authority for the use of embryos. *See also* MEIOSIS; MITOSIS

emerald Variety of BERYL, highly valued as a gemstone. The colour varies from light to dark green according to the amount of chromium. The finest emeralds are found in Colombia.

Emerson, Ralph Waldo (1803–82) US essayist, philosopher and poet. He was a minister in the Unitarian

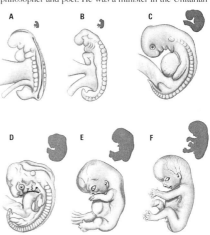

▲ **embryo** After 3 weeks a human embryo bears a primitive heart and head (A). By the 4th week, the heart is pumping blood around the body and into the placenta, and 25 pairs of tissue blocks (somites) appear, which later give rise to bone and muscle tissue (B). After 5 weeks, limb buds and rudimentary eyes are visible (C). The limbs become well developed, and the tail region recedes by the 6th week (D). The head grows rapidly; eyes, ears, and teeth buds appear by the 7th week (E). The tail portion vanishes and almost all the organs and tissues have developed by the 8th week (F). It is now known as a fetus.

Church but became disillusioned and left (1832). Emerson settled in New England, where he formed a circle that included Nathaniel HAWTHORNE, Henry David THOREAU and Bronson ALCOTT. His essay *Nature* (1836) set out the principles of TRANSCENDENTALISM. In 1840 Emerson co-founded *The Dial* magazine. Emerson's lectures formed the basis of *Essays* (1841, 1844). His poetry was collected in *Poems* (1847) and *May-Day* (1867). Other collections of lectures include *Representative Men* (1850), *The Conduct of Life* (1860) and *Society and Solitude* (1870).

émigré In French history, a refugee who fled France after the storming of the Bastille (14 July 1789). Émigrés were mainly royalist nobles who feared for their lives in the FRENCH REVOLUTION. In exile, they formed a counter-revolutionary force under Prince Louis Joseph de CONDÉ. In 1802 Napoleon I pardoned the émigrés and many returned to France. With the restoration of the BOURBONS, the émigrés received compensation.

Emilia-Romagna Region in N central Italy, bordering the Adriatic Sea; the capital is BOLOGNA. It was incorporated in the kingdom of Italy in 1860. The N part forms a vast plain. In the S lies the central part of the APENNINES. Industries: tourism, motor vehicles. Area: 22,124sq km (8,542sq mi). Pop. (1991) 3,909,512.

emotion Human feelings and behavioural tendencies involving complex mental and physiological reactions. The subtlety and complexity of emotions mean that intuitive understanding or the systematic study of subjective experience is often the best way of comprehending their nature. Emotions, however, are associated with predictable physiological changes, such as increased heart and breathing rates, sweating and trembling.

Empedocles (c.495–c.435 BC) Greek scientist and philosopher. Empedocles taught the doctrine of the four elements (earth, water, air and fire) and, anticipating modern physics, he explained change as being alterations in the proportions of these four elements.

emphysema Accumulation of air in tissues, most often in the lungs (pulmonary emphysema). **Pulmonary** emphysema, characterized by breathlessness, is the result of damage to and enlargement of the ALVEOLUS. It is associated with chronic bronchitis and smoking.

Empire State Building Skyscraper in New York, USA. Completed in 1931, it was the highest building in the world until 1972. It is 381m (1,250ft) tall, or 449m (1,472ft) to the top of its television mast. Its name derives from the nickname of New York state.

Empire style Neo-classical style in interior decoration, associated with the reign (1804–14) of NAPOLEON I. It made affected use of Egyptian decorative motifs. *See also* NEO-CLASSICISM; REGENCY STYLE

empiricism Philosophical doctrine that all knowledge is derived from experience. It was developed mainly by LOCKE, BERKELEY and HUME, in reaction to the RATIONALISM of DESCARTES, SPINOZA and LEIBNIZ, who claimed the existence of *a priori* knowledge (innate ideas). *See also* EPISTEMOLOGY; LOGICAL POSITIVISM

Empson, William (1906–84) English poet and critic. He expanded the ideas of I.A. RICHARDS in *Seven Types of Ambiguity* (1930). Empson wrote detailed analyses of specific texts, a technique that became known as the New Criticism. His other critical works include *The Structure of Complex Words* (1951) and *Milton's God* (1961).

emu Large, dark-plumed, flightless Australian bird. It is a strong runner with powerful legs. Large, greenish eggs (8–10) are hatched by the male in a ground nest. Height: 1.5m (5ft); weight: to 54kg (120lb). Species *Dromaius novaehollandiae*.

emulator COMPUTER configured in such a way that it acts like another type of computer. Emulators are often used in the development of new microprocessors.

emulsion SUSPENSION of one liquid in another. For example, when a water-based paint is diluted, the paint forms an emulsion with the water. It does not dissolve in the water, but is dispersed into very fine droplets or particles which take an extremely long time to settle out. Fats can form emulsions with water. During DIGESTION, salts from the bile pass into the gut and act on the fats there, reducing their surface tension so that they can form smaller droplets.

enamel Decorative or protective glazed coating produced on metal surfaces, or a type of paint. Ceramic enamels are made from powdered glass and calx, with metal oxides to add colour. Enamel paints consist of zinc oxide, lithopone and high-grade varnish. The finish is hard, glossy and durable. *See also* CLOISONNÉ

encephalitis Inflammation of the brain, usually associated with a viral infection; often there is an associated MENINGITIS. Symptoms include fever, headache, lassitude and intolerance of light; in severe cases there may be sensory and behavioural disturbances, paralysis, convulsions and coma.

enclosure In European history, the fencing-in by landlords of common land. Complaints against this practice date from the 13th century. Enclosure usually led to increased agricultural productivity at the cost of depriving people of free grazing and firewood. It was a cause of popular rebellions, especially in the 16th century. The AGRICULTURAL REVOLUTION of the 18th century produced another phase of enclosure.

encyclical Letter addressed by the Pope to all members of the Roman Catholic Church. Recent encyclicals have condemned contraception (Paul VI, 1968) and ecumenism (John Paul II, 1995).

encyclopedia Compendium of knowledge, containing information in all fields (general) or in a particular field (specialist). Some of the first encyclopedic works were compiled by ARISTOTLE and PLINY, but the first modern work was probably John Harris' *Lexicon Technicum* (1704) that contained sophisticated bibliographies and cross-referencing. Perhaps the most influential work was the *Encyclopédie* (1772) compiled by DIDEROT. The *Encyclopædia Britannica* was first published in 1771.

endangered species Animals or plants threatened with extinction as a result of such activities as habitat destruction and overhunting. In 1948 the International Union for the Conservation of Nature and Natural Resources (IUCN) was founded to protect endangered species. The IUCN publishes the *Red Data Book*, which currently lists more than 1,000 animals and 20,000 plants considered endangered. The Convention on Trade in Endangered Species of Wild Flora and Fauna (CITES) was signed in 1973. It seeks to prevent international trade in c.30,000 species. In the UK, the Wildlife and Countryside Act (1981) gives legal protection to a wide range of wild animals and plants. *See also* BIODIVERSITY; CONSERVATION; ECOLOGY; HABITAT; WETLAND

Enders, John Franklin (1897–1985) US microbiologist. He shared the 1954 Nobel Prize for physiology or medicine with Frederick C. Robbins and Thomas H. Weller for the discovery that POLIOMYELITIS viruses can be grown in cultures of various types of tissues. This work was fundamental to the development of the polio vaccine.

endive Leafy annual or biennial plant widely cultivated for its sharp-flavoured leaves. There are two main types: curly CHICORY (escarole) with slender, wavy-edged leaves, and a variety with broad, flat leaves. Family Asteraceae/Compositae; species *Cichorium endivia*.

endocrine system Body system made up of all the endocrine (ductless) glands that secrete HORMONES directly into the bloodstream to control body functions. The chief endocrine glands are the PITUITARY GLAND, THYROID GLAND, ADRENAL GLAND and sex gland or GONAD (TESTIS in males and OVARY in females).

endocytosis In biology, process by which a CELL takes in substances. When a cell's MEMBRANE comes into contact with food, a portion of the cytoplasm surrounds the substance and a depression forms within the cell wall. There are two types of endocytosis: **pinocytosis** is the incorporation and digestion of dissolved substances, and **phagocytosis** is the engulfing and digestion of microscopic particles. In higher animals, PHAGOCYTE cells are an important part of the IMMUNE SYSTEM.

endometriosis Common gynaecological disorder in which tissue similar to the ENDOMETRIUM is found in other parts of the pelvic cavity. It is treated with analgesics, hormone preparations or surgery.

endometrium Mucous membrane, well supplied with blood vessels, that lines the UTERUS. It is shed each month during menstruation.

endoplasmic reticulum Network of membranes and channels in the CYTOPLASM of EUKARYOTE cells. It helps to transport material inside the CELL.

endorphin (endogenous MORPHINE) Naturally occurring PEPTIDE neurotransmitter found in the pituitary gland that has similar pain-relieving effects as morphine and other derivatives of OPIUM. Endorphins block the sensation of pain by binding to pain receptor sites. Two endorphins (**enkephalins**) occur in the brain, spinal cord and gut. ACUPUNCTURE is thought to provide pain relief by inducing the release of endorphins. *See also* ANALGESIC; NEURON; NEUROTRANSMITTER

endoscope Instrument used to examine the interior of the body. Early types of endoscope, such as the opthalmoscope, were developed in the 19th century. FIBRE OPTICS has revolutionized the design of endoscopes. The modern endoscope is a flexible glass fibre instrument that can be swallowed by a patient or introduced through a tiny incision in the body. Most endoscopy is for diagnostic purposes, but modern instruments are used in biopsy and MINIMAL ACCESS SURGERY.

endosperm Tissue that surrounds the developing EMBRYO of a seed and provides food for growth. It is triploid (each cell has three sets of CHROMOSOMES), being derived from the fusion of one of the male GAMETES from the germinated pollen grain and two of the haploid nuclei in the embryo sac.

endosymbiosis Mutually beneficial relationship in which one organism lives inside another. For example, bacteria were engulfed by EUKARYOTE cells and formed symbiotic relationships with them, eventually becoming so interdependent that the cells behaved as a single organism; the bacteria became MITOCHONDRIA and CHLOROPLASTS. *See also* SYMBIOSIS

endothermic reaction CHEMICAL REACTION in which heat is absorbed from the surroundings, causing a fall in temperature – as in the manufacture of water-gas from coal and steam. *See also* EXOTHERMIC REACTION

energy In physics, capacity for doing WORK. It is measured in JOULES (J). POWER, the rate at which energy is produced or consumed, is measured in WATTS (W). POTENTIAL ENERGY is an object's ability to do work because of a change in the object's position or shape. KINETIC ENERGY is the energy an object has because it is

moving. The many forms of energy include electrical, NUCLEAR, thermal, LIGHT and chemical. Energy can be transferred from one body to another through work processes, heating, ELECTROMAGNETIC RADIATION or ELECTRICITY. Energy can also be converted from one form to another. The law of CONSERVATION of energy states that energy cannot be created or destroyed. The concept of energy began with GALILEO and Sir Isaac NEWTON. The idea that MASS is a form of energy was established by Albert EINSTEIN, who recognized that energy (E) and mass (m) could be transformed into each other according to the relation $E = mc^2$, where c is the velocity of light.

energy sources Naturally occurring substances, processes and phenomena from which we obtain ENERGY. Most energy is derived originally from the Sun. FOSSIL FUELS are the remains of life that was dependent on the Sun's energy. HYDROELECTRICITY derives from the solar energy that maintains the HYDROLOGICAL CYCLE, while wind is generated by uneven heating of the atmosphere and its energy harnessed by wind farms. The movements of the oceans – waves and tides – are caused by wind and the pull of the Moon and have been used to generate energy. Increasingly, SOLAR ENERGY is being used to heat some domestic water supplies directly and to provide electricity from PHOTOELECTRIC CELLS. GEOTHERMAL ENERGY is obtained from underground hot rocks. Other major energy sources are radioactive metals, such as URANIUM and PLUTONIUM, which provide NUCLEAR ENERGY. *See also* TIDAL POWER; WIND POWER

Engels, Friedrich (1820–95) German political philosopher. Engels and MARX formulated the theory of DIALECTICAL MATERIALISM and co-wrote the *Communist Manifesto* (1848). His materialist reworking of the dialectics of HEGEL is most evident in *Anti-Dühring* (1878) and *Socialism, Utopian and Scientific* (1882). From 1870 until Marx's death in 1883, Engels helped financially with Marx's research and continued to help him with his writings, particularly *Das Kapital*. His own works include *Condition of the Working Class in England* in 1844 (1845) and *The Origin of the Family, Private Property and the State* (1884).

engine Machine that produces useful energy of motion from some other form of energy. The term is usually restricted to combustion engines, which burn fuel. These machines include the STEAM ENGINE, DIESEL ENGINE, JET ENGINE and ROCKET engine. Such engines are distinct from ELECTRIC MOTORS. An external combustion engine burns its fuel outside the chamber in which motion is produced. An INTERNAL COMBUSTION ENGINE burns its fuel and develops motion in the same place. *See artwork* p.284

engineering Application of scientific principles for practical purposes, such as construction and developing power sources. There are many different fields in engineering including MECHANICAL, CIVIL, CHEMICAL, electrical and nuclear. *See also* ELECTRONICS

England Largest nation within the United Kingdom, bounded by the North Sea (E), the English Channel (S), Wales and the Irish Sea (W), and Scotland (N); the capital is LONDON. **Land and economy** In general, the N and W are higher and geologically older than the S and E. The chief rivers are the SEVERN, THAMES, TRENT, Great OUSE, HUMBER and MERSEY. The principal lakes include WINDERMERE and Derwentwater in the LAKE DISTRICT. The S of the country has low hills and downs, while much of E England is flat fenland. The N is predominantly upland and includes the PENNINES, CHEVIOT HILLS and Cumbrian Mountains. **History** There are traces of PALAEOLITHIC settlements in England. Occupied by the CELTS from *c.*400

BC, England was later conquered by the Romans, whose rule lasted until the 5th century. Germanic tribes began arriving in the 3rd century AD and gradually established independent kingdoms. Christianity was introduced into the country in the 6th century. In the 9th century, ALFRED THE GREAT led a united England against the Danes. The NORMAN CONQUEST (1066) brought strong central government and inaugurated the FEUDAL SYSTEM. IRELAND was conquered in the late 12th century, and WALES became a principality of England in 1284. The 13th century saw the foundations of PARLIAMENT and the development of statute law. During the Middle Ages, English kings laid claim to French territory. The Wars of the ROSES curbed the power of the nobility. Under the TUDORS, Wales was united politically with England and became a strong Protestant monarchy. The reign of ELIZABETH I was one of colonial expansion and growing naval power. In 1603, JAMES I merged the English and Scottish crowns. For subsequent history of England, *see* UNITED KINGDOM. Area: 130,362sq km (50,333sq mi). Pop. (1991) 47,055,204.

English Language belonging to the Germanic branch of the INDO-EUROPEAN family. It may be said to have come into existence with the arrival of the ANGLO-SAXONS in England in the 5th century AD. During more than 1,500 years of development, it has been transformed from an inflected language with grammatical gender to one with very few inflections and employing a sex-correlated gender system (he, she and it). Its vocabulary has been massively expanded by the inclusion of numerous foreign, technical and slang words. It is the mother tongue of *c*.300 million people, and a second language for hundreds of millions more worldwide.

English architecture Between the 6th and the 17th centuries, there were at least five distinctive styles of English architecture, including SAXON, NORMAN and GOTHIC, and RENAISSANCE and BAROQUE. England was influenced by European trends in architecture towards the end of their development. For example, Inigo JONES brought his revolutionary Renaissance ideas relatively late to the 17th-century STUART court, and Christopher WREN

introduced Baroque forms to England at the end of his career. The GEORGIAN period (1702–1830) is subdivided into English Baroque, PALLADIANISM and NEO-CLASSICISM. In the 19th century, the Victorian age was marked by earnestness and solidity, while the Great Exhibition (1851) paved the way for MODERNISM. William MORRIS and the ARTS AND CRAFTS MOVEMENT encouraged purity of design in the late 19th century and, a trend that continued into the early 20th century with the work of LUTYENS and VOYSEY. In the late 20th century, notable English modernist and post-modernist architects include Basil SPENCE, Richard ROGERS and Norman FOSTER.

English art England's earliest artistic traditions were shaped by invading forces. The ANGLO-SAXONS had an enduring influence. Their most notable achievement came with the BAYEUX TAPESTRY. The Church remained the dominant patron of the arts until the arrival of Hans HOLBEIN at the court of Henry VIII. In the 17th century, the Flemish painters RUBENS and VAN DYCK worked in the courts of James I and Charles I. A native tradition eventually emerged in the 18th century, with William HOGARTH and Thomas GAINSBOROUGH. The ROYAL ACADEMY OF ARTS (RA) was founded in 1768, and Joshua REYNOLDS was the first president. In the 19th century, England's two most influential artists were J.M.W. TURNER and John CONSTABLE. The work of the PRE-RAPHAELITE BROTHERHOOD bridged ROMANTICISM and SYMBOLISM, while William MORRIS was a seminal influence on the ARTS AND CRAFTS MOVEMENT. The major 20th-century figures were Stanley SPENCER and Francis BACON. Modern English sculptors, including Jacob EPSTEIN, Henry MOORE and Barbara HEPWORTH, have exerted a widespread influence.

English Channel (Fr. *La Manche*) Arm of the Atlantic Ocean between France and Britain, joining the North Sea at the Strait of Dover. A cross-channel train-ferry service was started in 1936, and the CHANNEL TUNNEL was completed in 1994. Width: 30–160km (20–100mi); length: 564km (350mi).

English horn *See* COR ANGLAIS

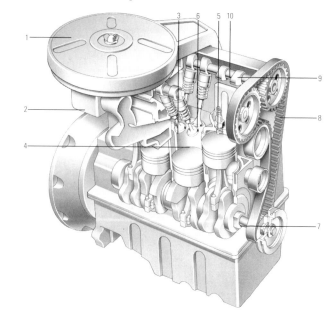

► **engine** In an in-line, four-cylinder petrol engine, air is sucked into the engine (1) through the carburettor (2). The air mixes with petrol which enters through the dual inlet valves (3) on each cylinder (4). The spark plug (5) then ignites the mixture, forcing the cylinder down rapidly. The burnt gases are expelled through the outlet valves (6). The reciprocal motion of the cylinders is converted into rotation by the crankshaft (7). The crankshaft also turns the timing belt (8), which controls the opening of the valves and the firing of the spark plug through the cams (9) located on the camshaft (10).

English literature Earliest surviving works are from the EARLY ENGLISH period (475–1100). Mainly poems in the heroic mould, epics such as Beowulf belong to an oral tradition but were written down in the 7th century. King Alfred began a tradition of English prose by translating a number of Latin works into the vernacular and initiating the *Anglo Saxon Chronicle*. Norman French replaced Old English as the language of the ruling classes after 1066, and the influence of FRENCH LITERATURE was reflected in the numerous CHANSONS DE GESTE and the ARTHURIAN ROMANCES. The native tradition of alliterative poetry re-emerged in the 14th century in the works of William LANGLAND, Thomas MALORY and Geoffrey CHAUCER. William SHAKESPEARE and Christopher MARLOWE were the leading figures in ELIZABETHAN DRAMA. Shakespeare's late works formed a bridge with the JACOBEAN era. Edmund SPENSER and Philip SIDNEY ensured the period was also a golden age for poetry. John DONNE and the METAPHYSICAL poets continued this tradition, but the poetry of MILTON was unsurpassed in the 17th century. English prose flourished with the production of the Authorized Version of the Bible in 1611. After the RESTORATION, drama revived in the comedies of CONGREVE; the classical ideals of the AUGUSTAN AGE (*c.*1690–1740) are typified in the satiric prose of SWIFT, the poetry of POPE, and the criticism of Samuel JOHNSON. The NOVEL emerged in the early 18th century, with works by DEFOE, RICHARDSON, FIELDING, STERNE and SMOLLETT, and was developed in the 19th century by Jane AUSTEN, Walter SCOTT, THACKERAY, the BRONTËS, George ELIOT and DICKENS. The romantic movement, heralded in BLAKE's poetry, gained full flight with WORDSWORTH and COLERIDGE, and was developed by KEATS, BYRON and SHELLEY. The major Victorian poets were TENNYSON and Robert and Elizabeth BROWNING. The wit of SHAW and WILDE, and the bleak novels of HARDY, gave way to the cynicism of war poets such as Siegfried SASSOON. The formal experiments of MODERNISM were realized best in the novels of James JOYCE, Virginia WOOLF and D.H. LAWRENCE, and the verse dramas of T.S. ELIOT. W.B. YEATS looked back to the visions of Blake. The novel diversified with the writings of Aldous HUXLEY, Evelyn WAUGH and Graham GREENE. In the 1930s, W.H. AUDEN produced explicitly political poems and Noel COWARD lampooned the British class system. The 1950s saw the emergence of the "ANGRY YOUNG MEN", including John OSBORNE and Kingsley AMIS, and the absurdist plays of Samuel BECKETT. Post-war novelists include Anthony BURGESS, William GOLDING, Iris MURDOCH, Angela CARTER and Salman RUSHDIE; dramatists include Harold PINTER, Tom STOPPARD, Joe ORTON and David HARE; poets include Dylan THOMAS, Philip LARKIN, Ted HUGHES and Seamus HEANEY.

English National Opera (ENO) English opera company with a policy of performing all operas in English. The ENO moved from Sadler's Wells to its present location at the London Coliseum in 1968. It has given the first British performance of numerous operas, such as GLASS' *Akhnaten*, and many premières, such as BIRTWISTLE's *The Mask of Orpheus*. Its musical directors have included Sir Charles MACKERRAS (1970–78) and Paul Daniel (1997–).

engraving INTAGLIO printing process; it describes various methods of making prints by cutting lines into metal or wood. Variations include ETCHING and AQUATINT. *See also* WOODCUT

Enlightenment (Age of Reason) Philosophical movement of 18th-century Europe and America. It was inspired by the scientific and philosophical revolutions of the late 17th century. The spirit of rational inquiry of the Scientific Revolution, embodied by the work of Isaac NEWTON, the RATIONALISM of DESCARTES, the religious ideas of SPINOZA and PASCAL and the EMPIRICISM of Francis BACON and John LOCKE, filtered into the fabric of 18th-century society. The *Encyclopédie* was the central text of the Enlightenment. In France, the Philosophes (VOLTAIRE, de MONTESQUIEU, Jean-Jacques ROUSSEAU and DIDEROT) championed a scientific approach to socio-political and economic affairs. They attacked established religion (*see* DEISM) and viewed the state as the instrument for social change. Rational human behaviour was at the centre of the economic theories of Adam SMITH, Jeremy BENTHAM and Baron TURGOT. The importance of the individual was underlined in the philosophies of Immanuel KANT and David HUME. The work of Thomas PAINE, Thomas JEFFERSON and Benjamin FRANKLIN epitomized the political spirit of the age.

Ennius, Quintus (239–169 BC) Roman poet, sometimes known as the father of Latin poetry. He is best known for his epic history of Rome, *Annales*.

Enoch Name of several Old Testament figures. One was the father of METHUSELAH and writer of PSEUDEPIGRAPHA, such as the Books of Enoch. Another was the eldest son of CAIN.

Ensor, James (1860–1949) Belgian painter and etcher, a forerunner of EXPRESSIONISM and SURREALISM. In Brussels he was a founder of the avant-garde group Les Vingt. His most celebrated work, *Entry of Christ into Brussels* (1888), was rejected as scandalous.

Entebbe City on the NW shore of Lake Victoria, S central Uganda, E Africa. Founded in 1893, it was capital of the British protectorate of Uganda (1894–1962). Pop. (1991) 41,638.

Entente Cordiale (1904) Friendly understanding between Britain and France. Its outward aim was the mutual recognition of each other's colonial interests, especially Britain's in Egypt and France's in Morocco. It also sought to counteract the growing power of Germany. In 1907 the Entente was extended into the TRIPLE ENTENTE.

enteritis Inflammation of the lining of the intestine, usually causing diarrhoea. It can arise from infection or exposure to some irritant or radioactive source. Treatment includes a bland diet. *See also* GASTROENTERITIS

enthalpy (symbol H) In THERMODYNAMICS, amount of HEAT energy possessed by a substance. The enthalpy of a system equals the sum of its internal energy and the product of the pressure and volume. In an ENDOTHERMIC REACTION, there is an increase in enthalpy. The reverse occurs in an ENDOTHERMIC REACTION.

entomology (Gk. *entomon*, insect) Term for the scientific study of INSECTS, coined by ARISTOTLE. The ancient Greeks were the first serious entomologists.

entropy Quantity that specifies the disorder of a physical system; the greater the disorder, the greater the entropy. In THERMODYNAMICS, it expresses the degree to which thermal energy is available for work – the less available it is, the greater the entropy.

Enver Pasha (1881–1922) Turkish general and politician. Involved in the Young Turk revolution (1908), he became virtual dictator after a coup (1913). Enver Pasha was instrumental in bringing Turkey into World War 1 as an ally of Germany. He was killed leading an anti-Soviet expedition in Bukhara.

environment In ECOLOGY, the physical and biological surroundings of an organism. The environment covers both non-living (abiotic) factors, such as temperature, soil, atmosphere and radiation, and also living (biotic) organisms, such as plants, microorganisms and animals.

enzyme (Gk. *zymosis*, fermentation) PROTEIN that functions as a CATALYST in biochemical reactions. The FERMENTATION properties of yeast cells have long been utilized in the brewing trade. In 1926 the US biochemist James B. Sumner became the first person to isolate an enzyme, urase, in pure crystal form and proved that enzymes are protein molecules. In the next decade, PEPSIN, TRYPSIN and CHYMOTRYPSIN were crystallized. Today, more than 1,500 catalysts have been identified. In 1969 scientists first synthesized an enzyme, ribonuclease. Chemical reactions can occur several thousand or million times faster with enzymes than without them. They operate within a narrow temperature range (usually 30°C to 40°C) and have optimal pH ranges. Many enzymes have to be bound to non-protein molecules in order to function effectively. These molecules include **trace elements** (such as metals) and **coenzymes** (such as vitamins). The lack or malfunction of enzymes can cause a variety of metabolic diseases. Enzymes are widely used in the manufacture of detergents and food.

Eocene Second of the five epochs of the TERTIARY period, *c.*55–38 million years ago. The fossil record shows members of modern plant genera, including beeches, walnuts and elms, and indicates the apparent dominance of mammals, including the ancestors of camels, horses, rodents, bats and monkeys.

Eos In Greek mythology, the goddess of dawn, identified with the Roman goddess, Aurora. Daughter of HYPERION, and sister of HELIOS and SELENE, she drove through the sky in a horse-drawn chariot.

ephedrine Drug, chemically similar to ADRENALINE. It stimulates the autonomic nervous system and is used to treat some allergies, to treat bronchial asthma by dilating bronchioles, to dilate pupils of the eyes, as a nasal decongestant and to treat low blood pressure.

ephemeris (pl. ephemerides) Table giving the predicted positions of a celestial object, such as a planet or comet, at given intervals.

Ephesians NEW TESTAMENT epistle dictated, according to tradition, by St PAUL during his captivity in Rome (*c.*AD 60) and addressed to the Christian Church at Ephesus. The letter describes the supreme power and authority invested by God in Christ and stresses the unity of love and faith in the Christian church.

Ephesus (Efes) Ancient Ionian city of W Asia Minor (modern Turkey). A prosperous port under the Greeks and Romans, it was a centre of the cult of Artemis (Diana). The Temple of Artemis was the largest Greek temple ever built and one of the SEVEN WONDERS OF THE WORLD. Ephesus was captured by Croesus (*c.*550 BC), Cyrus the Great (*c.*546 BC) and Alexander the Great (334 BC), falling under Roman control (133 BC). Today, it is one of the world's principal archaeological sites.

epic Long, narrative poem in grandiose style. The earliest known form of GREEK LITERATURE, epics were originally used to transmit history orally. Using highly formalized language, epics tend to involve gods, men and legendary battles. HOMER is the author of two of the most famous epics, the *Iliad* and the *Odyssey*. Later examples include the *Aeneid* by VIRGIL, *Paradise Lost* (1667) by John MILTON and *The Faerie Queene* (1589–96) by Edmund SPENSER.

epic theatre Theory of dramatic presentation formulated in the late 1920s by BRECHT and PISCATOR. Its attempts to undermine theatrical illusion by distancing effects in the use of costume, sets, songs, argument and self-conscious soliloquies are intended to lead the audience to view events objectively and critically.

Epicureanism School of Greek philosophy founded by EPICURUS. He proposed that the sensations of pleasure and pain were the ultimate measures of good and evil, and that pleasure should be actively pursued. *See also* HEDONISM

Epicurus (341–270 BC) Greek philosopher, founder of EPICUREANISM. Born on the island of Samos, he began teaching philosophy at the age of 32. He embraced a theory of physics derived from the ATOMISM of DEMOCRITUS.

epidemic Outbreak of an infectious or communicable disease rapidly spreading to many people. The study of epidemics is known as EPIDEMIOLOGY. An epidemic sweeping across many countries, such as the BLACK DEATH, is termed a pandemic.

epidemiology Study of the incidence and patterns of disease, with a view to finding means of prevention or control. Modern epidemiology is concerned with environmental and lifestyle factors in disease causation.

epidermis In animals, outer layer of cells that contains no blood vessels. In many invertebrates it is only one cell thick; in vertebrates it may comprise several layers and forms part of the SKIN. In plants, it is the outermost layer of a leaf or of an unthickened stem or root.

epiglottis Small flap of CARTILAGE projecting upward behind the root of the tongue. It closes off the LARYNX during swallowing to prevent food entering the windpipe.

epigram (Gk. inscription) In classical literature, a brief Greek or Latin poem expressing, in a pointed, witty manner, a single thought. The epigrams of the 1st century Latin poet Martial served as the model for epigrammatists, such as Ben JONSON and Oscar WILDE.

epilepsy Disorder characterized by abnormal electrical discharges in the brain that provoke seizures. Attacks are often presaged by warning symptoms, the "aura". Seizure types vary from the momentary loss of awareness seen in *petit mal* attacks ("absences") to the major convulsions of *grand mal* epilepsy. They may be triggered by a number of factors, including sleep deprivation, flashing lights or excessive noise. Epilepsy is controlled with anti-convulsant drugs.

Epiphany Christian feast celebrated on 6 January. It originated in the Eastern Church as an observance of the baptism of JESUS CHRIST. In the West it became associated with the manifestation of Christ to the Gentiles and the coming of the Magi (Three Wise Men).

epiphyte (air plant) Plant that grows on another plant but is not a PARASITE. Epiphytes usually have aerial roots and produce their own food by PHOTOSYNTHESIS. They are common in tropical forests. Examples are some FERNS, orchids, Spanish moss and many BROMELIADS.

Episcopal Church Anglican church of the US. CHURCH OF ENGLAND services were held in the first American colonies. With the American Revolution, the Church of England was disestablished and a national church organized in its place. Known as the Protestant Episcopal Church, its constitution and its own version of the Book of COMMON PRAYER were established in 1789. In 1989 it appointed the first woman bishop in the ANGLICAN COMMUNION. The church has more than 2.5 million members.

epistemology Branch of PHILOSOPHY that critically examines the nature, limits and validity of knowledge and the difference between knowledge and belief. In RATIONALISM, the existence of innate ideas are maintained along with ideas derived from experience. EMPIRICISM rejected the existence of innate ideas. Immanuel KANT attempted to combine both positions. A.N. WHITEHEAD proposed a causal theory of knowledge. PRAGMATISM focused on the practical data derived from the senses. Sir Karl POPPER rejected the certainty of scientific knowledge, since it depends on unpredictable insight.

epistles Collection of 20 letters forming most of the middle section of the NEW TESTAMENT. More than half are attributed to the apostle St PAUL – the so-called Pauline Epistles – while the rest are by various writers: two by PETER, three by JOHN, one by JAMES and one by JUDE. The author of the Epistle to the Hebrews is unknown.

epithelium Layer of cells closely packed to form a surface for a body tube or cavity. Epithelium covers the SKIN and various internal organs and surfaces, such as the intestines, nasal passages and mouth. Epithelial cells may also produce protective modifications, such as hair and nails, or secrete substances, such as ENZYMES.

epoxy resin Group of thermosetting POLYMERS with outstandingly good mechanical and electrical properties, stability, heat and chemical resistance, and adhesion. Epoxy RESINS are used as adhesives, in casting and in protective coatings.

Epstein, Sir Jacob (1880–1959) British sculptor, b. USA. His series of 18 nude figures (1907–08) caused a public outcry. Epstein scandalized Paris with the angel for Oscar Wilde's tomb (1912). His most revolutionary sculpture was *The Rock Drill* (1913–14), an ape that has mutated into a robot. Epstein also produced religious works, including the bronze *Visitation* (1926).

Epstein-Barr virus Organism responsible for GLANDULAR FEVER. Symptoms include fatigue, headache, muscular ache, sore throat and enlarged lymph nodes. Epstein-Barr virus is also implicated in the causation of a number of other diseases. The virus is spread by droplet infection.

equation Mathematical statement of VARIABLES, equal to some subset of all possible variables. The equation $x^2 = 8 - 2x$ is true only for certain values (solutions) of x ($x = 2$ and $x = -4$). This type of equation is contrasted with an identity, such as $(x + 2)^2 = x^2 + 4x + 4$, which is true for all values of x. Equations are said to be linear, QUADRATIC, cubic, quartic, etc., according to whether their degree (the highest power of the variable) is 1, 2, 3, 4, etc. *See also* SIMULTANEOUS EQUATIONS

equator Name given to two imaginary circles. The **terrestrial** Equator lies midway between the North Pole and South Pole and is the zero line from which latitude is measured. It divides the Earth into the Southern and Northern hemispheres. The **celestial** equator lies directly above the Earth's Equator and is used as a reference to determine the position of a star.

Equatorial Guinea (formerly Spanish Guinea) Republic in W central Africa, consisting of a mainland territory between Cameroon and Gabon, Mbini (Río Muni), and five islands in the Gulf of Guinea, the largest of which is Bioko (Fernando Póo). The capital is MALABO (on Bioko). **Land and climate** Bioko is a volcanic island with fertile soils. It is also mountainous, rising to 3,008m (9,869ft), and has heavy rainfall. There is a marked dry season from December to February. Mainland Mbini (90% of Equatorial Guinea's land area) consists mainly of hills and plateaux behind the coastal plains. Its main river, the Lolo, rises in Gabon. Mbini has a similar climate to Bioko. Dense rainforest covers most of Mbini. **History**

and Politics Portuguese navigators reached the area in 1471. In 1778, Portugal ceded the islands and commercial mainland rights to Spain. In 1827, Spain leased bases on Bioko to Britain, and the British settled some freed slaves. Descendants of these former slaves (*Fernandinos*) remain on the island. Spain returned to the area in the mid-19th century. Bioko and Mbini were made provinces of overseas Spain (1959). They achieved independence in 1968. In 1979, the nation's first president, Francisco Macias Nguema, was deposed by a supreme military council, led by Colonel Mbasogo. A 1991 referendum voted to set up a multi-party democracy, consisting of the ruling Equatorial Guinea Democratic Party (PDGE) and ten opposition parties. Elections (1993) were boycotted by the main parties and most of the electorate. The PDGE formed a government. In 1996 elections, President Mbasogo claimed 99% of the vote. In 1997, the main opposition, the Progress Party, was banned. Mbasogo's regime has been accused of routine arrests and torture of opponents. **Economy** Agriculture employs 66% of the workforce. The main food crops are bananas, cassava and sweet potatoes. The most valuable crop is cocoa. Timber and coffee are also exported. GDP per capita (1999) \$US2000.

equestrian sports Three Olympic equestrian disciplines of dressage, show-jumping and trials (or eventing) that test a horse's training, development and ability to execute defined movements. **Show-jumping** tests a horse's speed and jumping ability over obstacles set in a confined area. **Trials**, held over 1–3 days, test its ability at dressage, over obstacles, across country and in show-jumping.

equilibrium In physics, a stable state in which any variety of forces acting on a particle or object negate each other, resulting in no net force. An object with constant velocity is also said to be in equilibrium. The term can also be ascribed to a body with a constant temperature; this is known as **thermic** equilibrium. *See also* GRAVITY; LEVER; THERMODYNAMICS

equinox Either of the two days each year when day and night are of equal duration. They occur on the two occasions, (one spring, one autumn) when the Sun crosses the celestial EQUATOR. In the Northern Hemisphere, the **vernal** (spring) equinox occurs around 21 March and the **autumnal** equinox around 23 September.

equity In law, a field of jurisdiction that enables the judiciary to apply principles or morals. In medieval England it became clear that the strict application of COMMON LAW produced cases of injustice. In such cases, the chancellor reviewed petitions made to the king and made remedies where appropriate. Eventually, the chancellor became head of a court of equity known as the CHANCERY. Equity was based on ROMAN LAW and CANON LAW but soon established its own set of precedents. In 1873, law and equity were merged in a High Court of Justice.

Erasmus, Desiderius (1466–1536) (Gerhard Gerhards) Dutch scholar and teacher, considered the greatest of the RENAISSANCE humanists. His Latin translation of the Greek New Testament revealed flaws in the VULGATE text. Among his original works, the *Manual of the Christian Knight* (1503) called for reform of the church. Erasmus had an early influence on Martin LUTHER and other Protestant reformers but sought change from within the Catholic Church and disagreed with the course of the REFORMATION. In *On Free Will* (1524) he openly clashed with Luther. *See also* HUMANISM

Erastianism Complete control of church affairs by the state. It is named after Thomas Erastus (1524–85), a Swiss theologian and physician. In contrast to CALVINISM, he denied that the church alone had disciplinary powers.

EQUATORIAL GUINEA
AREA: 28,050sq km (10,830 sq mi)
POPULATION: 455,000
CAPITAL (POPULATION): Malabo (35,000)

Hence, Erastianism is a distortion of his position, which assumed cooperation between church and state.

Eratosthenes (*c*.276–*c*.194 BC) Greek scholar who first measured the Earth's circumference by geometry. Eratosthenes administered the library of ALEXANDRIA.

erbium (symbol Er) Metallic element of the LANTHANIDE SERIES. There are six isotopes naturally occurring, and the chief ores are monazite and bastnaesite. Nine radioactive isotopes have been identified. Soft and malleable, erbium is used in some alloys. Erbium oxide is used as a pink colourant for glass. Properties: at.no. 68; r.a.m. 167.26; m.p. 1,522°C (2,772°F); b.p. 2,863°C (5,185°F); r.d. 9.045; most common isotope Er^{166} (33.41%).

Erfurt City on the River Gera, Thuringia, central Germany. One of Germany's oldest cities, it was first mentioned by St Boniface in the 8th century and was an important centre in the Carolingian empire. Napoleon I and Alexander I met at the Congress of Erfurt (1808). Pop. (1995) 213,100.

ergonomics (human-factors engineering) Study of the relationship between human beings and their work environment. In particular, it examines the physical and psychological interaction of man and machine. The science of ergonomics dates from the beginnings of MASS PRODUCTION. In recent years, it has focused on human-computer interaction (HCI). Applications include the design of aircraft and automobile interiors.

ergot Fungus disease of rye plants and other small grasses. Part of the fungal body contains alkaloids that are generally poisonous but, when purified and in appropriate doses, can be used medicinally. Genus *Claviceps.*

Erhard, Ludwig (1897–1977) German statesman and economist, chancellor (1963–66). As economics minister of West Germany (1949–63), he was largely responsible for West German economic recovery after World War 2. Erhard succeeded Konrad ADENAUER as chancellor.

Eric XIV (1533–77) King of Sweden (1560–68), son of GUSTAVUS I (VASA). Eric expanded the power of the monarchy, but aggressive foreign policy led to war (1563–70) with Denmark.

Eric the Red (active late 10th century) Norse chieftain who settled on Greenland. He settled in Iceland, from which he was banished after a murder. Eric the Red set off to the west and discovered the land he named Greenland in *c*.981.

Erie, Lake Great Lake in North America, bordered by Ontario (W), New York (E), Ohio and Pennsylvania (S) and Michigan (SW); part of the GREAT LAKES ST LAWRENCE SEAWAY. Site of a British defeat in the WAR OF 1812, Lake Erie is the shallowest and second smallest of the lakes (after Lake ONTARIO). It has been polluted by the cities (Buffalo, Erie, Cleveland and Toledo) that line its shores. Government incentives are aiding recovery. Area: 25,667sq km (9,910sq mi). Max. depth: 64m (210ft).

Erie Canal Artificial waterway in New York, connecting Buffalo on LAKE ERIE to ALBANY on the Hudson River. The first major waterway to be built (1817–25) in the USA, it aided the commercial growth of New York City by joining the Great Lakes to the Atlantic Ocean. Although largely superseded by the railways, it was revitalized and lengthened to 843km (524mi) in 1918.

Eritrea Independent state in NE Africa, on the Red Sea; the capital is ASMARA. The chief ports are Aseb and Massawa. **Land** Much of Eritrea is a continuation of the high Ethiopian plateau, sloping down to plains in the E and W. Unreliable rainfall is a frequent cause of drought. **History** Eritrea was a dependency of ETHIOPIA until the 16th century, when it was annexed to the Ottoman Empire. During the 19th century, control of the region was disputed between Ethiopia, Egypt and Italy. In 1890, it became an Italian colony. From 1941 to 1952, it was under British military administration. In 1952, it was federated with Ethiopia, becoming a province in 1962. Eritrean separatists began a 30-year campaign of guerrilla warfare, and 700,000 refugees fled to Somalia. In 1991, the Eritrean People's Liberation Front (EPLF) helped topple Mengistu's Ethiopian government and won a referendum on independence. In 1993, Eritrea formally gained independence. The new EPLF government, led by Isaias Afwerki, began the process of reconstructing a country impoverished by war and famine. Eritrea faced border conflicts with Sudan and Djibouti. In 1998, a border dispute with Ethiopia flared into a war that had claimed *c*.50,000 lives by mid-1999. **Economy** The war-devastated economy is mainly agricultural. Industries: textiles, leather goods, salt. Area: 117,599sq km (45,405sq mi). Pop. (2000 est.) 4,523,000.

ermine Known as a STOAT in Eurasia or a short-tailed WEASEL in North America.

Ernst, Max (1891–1976) German painter and sculptor, founder of Cologne DADA (1919), later influential in SURREALISM. Ernst developed ways of adapting COLLAGE, photomontage and other radical pictorial techniques. His most important works include *L'Eléphant Célèbes* (1921) and *Two Children Threatened by a Nightingale* (1924). He lived in New York (1941–48). *See also* MONTAGE

Eros Elongated asteroid with an irregular-shaped orbit. In 1931 and 1975 it approached to within 24 million km (15 million mi) of Earth. Longer diameter: 27km (17mi). Mean distance from the Sun: 232 million km (144 million mi). Mean sidereal period: 1.76yr.

Eros In Greek mythology, god of love, equivalent to the Roman god Cupid. Depicted as a winged boy carrying a bow and arrows, and often blindfold, he was the youngest and most mischievous of the gods. He married PSYCHE.

erosion Alteration of landforms by the wearing away of rock and soil, and the removal of any debris (as opposed to WEATHERING). Erosion is carried out by the agents of wind, water, GLACIERS and living organisms. In **chemical** erosion, minerals in the rock react to other substances, such as weak acids found in rain water, and are broken down. In **physical** erosion, powerful forces such as rivers and glaciers physically wear rock down and transport it. *See also* GEOMORPHOLOGY

erratic In geology, a rock that has been transported some distance from its source by glacial action and is therefore of a different type to the surrounding rocks.

erysipelas Contagious skin infection caused by a STREPTOCOCCUS bacterium. Symptoms include pain and heat in the affected part and coarse skin rashes that become red, shiny and swollen.

erythrocyte Red BLOOD cell, usually disc-shaped and without a nucleus. It contains HAEMOGLOBIN that combines with oxygen and gives blood its red colour. Normal human blood contains an average of five million such cells per cu mm of blood.

Esaki, Leo (1925–) Japanese physicist, who developed the tunnel DIODE, a SEMICONDUCTOR that allows electrons to cross normally impassable electronic barriers. US physicist Ivar Giaever extended Esaki's research to the field of SUPERCONDUCTIVITY. For this work, they shared the 1973 Nobel Prize for physics with Brian JOSEPHSON.

Esau (Heb. hairy) Old Testament figure, son of ISAAC and REBECCA. Esau sold his inheritance for a bowl of stew to his scheming brother, JACOB.

escape velocity Minimum velocity required to free a body from the gravitational field of a celestial body or stellar system. Escape velocities are, for the Earth 11.2km/sec (7mi/s) and Moon 2.4km/sec (1.5mi/s).

eschatology In systematic theology, the formalized doctrine concerning the end of the world or the end of time. It comprises the study of teaching and theory about the coming of the kingdom of God. *See also* MESSIAH; MILLENARIANISM

Escher, Maurits Cornelis (1898–1972) Dutch graphic artist. He is best known for his prints based on mathematical ideas. These contain metamorphoses, illusions and paradoxes, as in *Ascending and Descending* (1960).

Escoffier, (Georges) Auguste (1846–1935) French chef. He gained a reputation as the "king of cooks" while managing the kitchens at the Savoy (1890–99) and Carlton (1899–1919) hotels in London. Escoffier's culinary creations include the peach Melba.

Escorial Spanish monastery and palace near Madrid. Built (1563–84) for PHILIP II, it comprises a massive group of buildings and houses a notable art collection.

Esfahan *See* ISFAHAN

Eshkol, Levi (1895–1969) Israeli statesman, prime minister (1963–69), b. Ukraine. Eshkol established one of the first *kibbutzim* (cooperative farms), became minister of finance (1952–53), and created the Israel Labour Party.

Eskimo (Algonquian, eaters of raw flesh) Aboriginal inhabitants (*c*.60,000) of Arctic and sub-Arctic regions of North America (the INUIT), Greenland and Siberia. Sharing the common language family of Eskimo-ALEUT, Eskimos have adapted to harsh climates and are proficient hunters of sea mammals. In some areas, a nomadic existence has been replaced by village settlements and work in the oil and mining industries. The eating of raw meat preserves scarce resources and provides essential nutrients. In winter, igloos (snow huts) provide temporary shelter. In summer, tents are made from animal skins. Eskimos are skilled artisans, producing kayaks and finely crafted tools from skin, ivory, bone, copper or stone. Their spiritual life is dominated by invisible forces of nature (*innua*). SHAMANISM plays an important role in everyday life.

esparto (needlegrass, alfa) Coarse perennial grass, native to Spain and n Africa. It is used to make paper, rope and twine. There are *c*.150 species. Heights: to 0.9m (3ft). Family Gramineae; genera *Stipa* and *Lygeum*.

Esperanto Language devised (1887) by Ludwik Zamenhof (1859–1917), as a language of international communication. Its vocabulary is mostly derived from w European languages.

espionage Act of obtaining secret information, especially for one state about the political, military and industrial matters of a rival. The importance of espionage in military affairs was recognized in ancient China, Greece and Egypt. MATA HARI was the most renowned spy in World War 1. The secret police (KGB) in the Soviet Union wielded considerable political power. In the US, the CENTRAL INTELLIGENCE AGENCY (CIA) was established in 1947. The COLD WAR witnessed a dramatic increase in espionage activity. *See also* INTELLIGENCE SERVICE

essay (Fr. *essai*, attempt) Usually short, non-fictional prose composition, written expressing a personal point of view. It originated with the 16th-century French writer MONTAIGNE. Noted British essayists include Francis BACON, Henry FIELDING, Dr Samuel JOHNSON, Oliver GOLDSMITH, Matthew ARNOLD and Charles LAMB.

Essen City on the River Ruhr, Nordrhein-Westfalen state, NW Germany. With a major coalfield, Essen underwent a huge industrial expansion during the 19th century. The city was heavily bombed in World War 2. Industries: mining, iron and steel. Pop. (1995) 618,000.

Essenes Jewish religious sect that existed in Palestine from the 2nd century BC to the end of the 2nd century AD. A secrecy developed about the sect, and they shunned public life and temple worship. The DEAD SEA SCROLLS are said to contain their sacred books.

essential oil Oil found in flowers, fruits or plants. It is the source of their odour and is widely used in aromatherapy, potpourri and perfumed toiletries.

Essex, Robert Devereux, 2nd Earl of (1566–1601) English courtier and soldier. A favourite of ELIZABETH I, he attacked Cadiz in 1596. Following a quarrel with Elizabeth, Essex was reluctantly made lord lieutenant of a rebellious Ireland. He returned in disgrace six months later, attempted a coup d'état, and was executed for treason.

Essex, Robert Devereux, 3rd Earl of (1591–1646) Parliamentary commander in the English CIVIL WARS from July 1642. A poor strategist, he was effectively superseded by Oliver CROMWELL when the NEW MODEL ARMY was formed in 1645. His failures may have helped to prolong the war.

Essex County in SE England; the county town is Chelmsford. Colonized by the Romans at COLCHESTER, it was invaded by the Anglo-Saxons in the 5th century and later came under Danish control. Low-lying on the E coast, the land rises to the NW providing pasture for dairy and sheep farming. Wheat, barley and sugar beet are important crops. Industries: machinery, electrical goods. Area: 3,674sq km (1,419sq mi). Pop. (1991) 1,528,577.

estate Organized social CLASS with separate representation in government. The disintegration of the FEUDAL SYSTEM saw the emergence of three estates – nobility, clergy and commons (BOURGEOISIE). The English PARLIAMENT developed out of this classification; the nobility and clergy were represented in the HOUSE OF LORDS, and the bourgeoisie in the HOUSE OF COMMONS. The rise of the bourgeoisie can be clearly traced in the history of the French STATES GENERAL. Sometimes the media are called the FOURTH ESTATE.

ester Any of a class of organic compounds formed by reaction between an ALCOHOL and an ACID.

Esther OLD TESTAMENT book narrating how the legendary Queen Esther persuaded her husband, XERXES I, to prevent the massacre of the Jews in Babylon. The event is celebrated in the Jewish feast of PURIM.

Estonia Republic on the E coast of the Baltic Sea, Estonia is the smallest of the three Baltic states that gained independence from the Soviet Union in 1991. **Land and Climate** Estonia is mostly flat. The area is strewn with moraine. It is dotted with more than 1,500 small lakes. Lake Peipus and the River Narva make up most of Estonia's Russian border. Estonia has more than 800 islands that make up *c*.10% of total area; the largest is Saaremaa. Despite its northerly position, it has a fairly mild climate. Rainfall averages from 480 to 580mm (19–23in). Farmland and pasture account for more than 33% of land use. **History and Politics** The original settlers were related to the Finns. The TEUTONIC KNIGHTS introduced Christianity in the 13th century, and by the 16th century German noblemen owned much of the land. In 1561, Sweden took the N part of the country and Poland the S. In 1625, Swe-

ESTONIA
AREA: 44,700sq km (17,300sq mi)
POPULATION: 1,647,000
CAPITAL (POPULATION): Tallinn (427,000)

den assumed complete control but surrendered the region to Russia in 1721. In 1918, Estonia became independent. In 1940, Soviet forces occupied Estonia, but were driven out by Germany in 1941. Soviet troops returned in 1944, and Estonia became one of the 15 socialist republics of the Soviet Union. Estonians strongly opposed Soviet rule, and many were deported to Siberia. In 1990, Estonia declared independence, and the Soviet Union recognized this in 1991. In 1992, Estonia adopted a new constitution and and Lennart Meri (1929–) was elected president. In 1994, the last Soviet troops withdrew from Estonia. Since independence Estonia has been ruled by a succession of coalition or minority governments. **Economy** Under Soviet rule, Estonia was the most prosperous of the Baltic states (1995 GDP per capita, $4,220). Privatization and free-trade reforms have increased foreign investment and trade with the European Union. Chief natural resources are oil shale and forests. Manufactures include petrochemicals, fertilizers and textiles. Agriculture and fishing are important. Barley, potatoes and oats are major crops.

estuary Coastal region where a river mouth opens into the ocean and fresh water from the land mixes with salt water from the sea. Estuaries often provide good harbours and breeding grounds for many kinds of marine life.

etching Method of INTAGLIO (incised) printing used for black-and-white designs. A metal plate, usually copper, is coated with an acid-proof ground. A design is etched with a needle so that the lines penetrate the ground. The plate is then placed in an acid that eats away the exposed line so that it will hold ink. When the plate is finished, it is rolled with ink and placed in an etching press to be printed.

ethanal (acetaldehyde, CH_3CHO) Colourless volatile, flammable liquid manufactured now by catalytic oxidation of ETHENE or ETHANOL, or catalytic hydration of ETHYLENE. It is used in the breathalyzer test and to silver mirrors. Properties: r.d. 0.788; m.p. $-123.5°C$ ($-190.3°F$); b.p. $20.8°C$ ($69.4°F$).

ethane (CH_3CH_3) Colourless, odourless gas, the second member of the ALKANE series of HYDROCARBONS. It is a minor constituent of natural gas. *See also* SATURATED COMPOUND

ethanoate (acetate) Salt or ester of ethanoic acid. A compound containing the ion CH_3COO^- or the group CH_3COO-. It is used in synthetic fibres, lacquers and acetate film.

ethanoic acid (acetic acid, CH_3COOH) Colourless corrosive liquid made by the oxidation of ETHANOL by catalysis or by the action of bacteria. It is the active ingredient in VINEGAR and has many uses in the organic chemicals industry. Properties: r.d. 1.049; m.p. $16.6°C$ ($61.9°F$); b.p. $117.9°C$ ($244.4°F$).

ethanol (ethyl alcohol, C_2H_5OH)) Colourless, flammable and volatile ALCOHOL, produced by the FERMENTATION of sugars, molasses and grains, or by the catalytic hydration of ETHYLENE. Its many uses include alcoholic beverages, rocket fuels, cosmetics and pharmaceuticals. Properties: r.d. 0.789; b.p. $78.5°C$ ($173.3°F$).

Ethelbert (d.616) King of Kent (560–616). He was the strongest ruler in England s of the River Humber and was the first Christian king in Anglo-Saxon England.

Ethelred I (d. AD 871) King of Wessex and Kent (865–71), son of Ethelwulf and elder brother of ALFRED THE GREAT. His reign was dominated by resistance to the Viking invaders. Ethelred died after victory at Ashdown, and was succeeded by Alfred.

Ethelred II (the Unready) (968–1016) (Old English, evil *rede* or counsel) King of England (978–1013, 1014–16). Following continuous Danish attacks, he paid

off the raiders with money raised by the Danegeld (994). The Danes returned nevertheless in 997 and again in 1002, when they were massacred by Ethelred's forces. The Danish King Sweyn retaliated and conquered England (1013). Ethelred was made king again on Sweyn's death but was succeeded by Sweyn's son, CANUTE II.

ethene (ethylene, C_2H_4) Colourless gas derived from the CRACKING of PROPANE and other compounds. Vast quantities are used in polyethylene production. Ethene is also used for many other chemical syntheses.

ether In physics, hypothetical medium that was supposed to fill all space and offer no resistance to motion. It was disproved (1887) by MICHELSON and MORLEY.

ether (diethyl ether, $C_2H_5OC_2H_5$) Colourless, volatile, inflammable liquid prepared by the action of sulphuric acid on ethanol followed by distillation. It is used as an industrial solvent, fuel additive and decreasingly as an anaesthetic. **Diethyl ether** is a typical member of the ethers with the general formula ROR', where R,R' are hydrocarbon radicals. Properties: m.p. $-116.2°C$ ($-117.2°F$); b.p. $34.5°C$ ($94.1°F$).

ethics (moral philosophy) Study of voluntary human actions, both individual and collective, according to moral precepts. Judaism, Christianity, Islam, Hinduism and Buddhism all incorporate moral teachings. For ARISTOTLE, happiness was achieved through the cultivation of virtue. PLATO's ethical system was based on metaphysical IDEALISM. HEDONISM taught that the pursuit of pleasure was the highest good. STOICS advocated virtue achieved through harmony with nature. RATIONALISM postulated conscience as the basis of moral behaviour. EMPIRICISM argued that conscience was acquired by experience. Immanuel KANT put moral duty above happiness. He argued that an act is only truly moral if it is motivated solely by duty. The ethics of UTILTARIANISM are based on the principle of the greatest good for the greatest number. *See also* AYER, A.J.; DEWEY, JOHN

Ethiopia Landlocked republic in E Africa. Ethiopia is dominated by the Ethiopian Plateau, a block of volcanic mountains. Its average height is 1,800m–2,450m (6,000ft–8,000ft), rising in the N to 4,620m (15,157ft) at Ras Dashen. The plateau is bisected by the Great RIFT VALLEY. The Eastern Highlands include the Somali Plateau and the desert of the Ogaden Plateau. The Western Highlands include the capital, ADDIS ABABA, the Blue NILE (Abbay) and its source, Lake Tana (Ethiopia's largest lake). The Danakil Desert forms Ethiopia's border with ERITREA. **Climate** Ethiopia's climate is greatly affected by altitude. Addis Ababa, at 2,450m (8,000ft), has an average annual temperature of 20°C (68°F). Rainfall is generally more than 1,000mm (39in), with a rainy season from April to September. The NE and SW lowlands are extremely hot and arid with less than 500mm (20in) rainfall. **Vegetation** Grass, farmland and trees cover most of the highlands. Semi-desert and tropical savanna cover parts of the lowlands. A dense rainforest grows in the SW. **History and Politics** According to tradition, the Ethiopian kingdom was founded (*c.*1000 BC) by Solomon's son, Menelik I. The expansion of Islam led to the isolation of AKSUM, and the kingdom fragmented in the 16th century. In 1855, Kasa re-established unity, proclaimed himself Emperor

ETHIOPIA
AREA: 1,128,000sq km (435,521sq mi)
POPULATION: 61,841,000
CAPITAL (POPULATION): Addis Ababa (2,316,000)

Theodore and founded the modern state. The late 19th century was marked by European intervention, and Menelik II became emperor with Italian support. He expanded the empire, made Addis Ababa his capital (1889), and defeated an Italian invasion (1895). In 1930, Menelik II's grandnephew, Ras Tafari Makonnen, was crowned Emperor HAILE SELASSIE I. In 1935, Italian troops invaded Ethiopia (Abyssinia). During World War 2, British and South African forces recaptured Ethiopia, and Haile Selassie was restored as emperor. In 1952, Eritrea was federated with Ethiopia. Following famine in N Ethiopia, Selassie was deposed by a military coup in 1974. The Provisional Military Administrative Council (PMAC) abolished the monarchy. Military rule was repressive, and civil war broke out. In 1977, Somalia seized land in the Ogaden Desert. The PMAC leader, Mengistu Mariam, recaptured territory in Eritrea and the Ogaden with Soviet military assistance. In 1984–85, widespread famine received global news coverage, and 10,000 FALASHAS were airlifted to Israel. In 1987, Mengistu established the People's Democratic Republic of Ethiopia. In 1991, the Tigrean-based Ethiopian People's Revolutionary Democratic Front (EPRDF) and the Eritrean People's Liberation Front (EPLF) brought down Mengistu's regime. In 1993, Eritrea achieved independence. Multiparty elections (1995) were won by the EPRDF and Negasso Gidada was elected president. A border war with Eritrea had claimed *c*.50,000 lives by mid-1999, more than 40,000 of whom were killed in the Battle of Badme (February 1999). **Economy** Ethiopia is the world's poorest country (1995 GDP per capita, US$450), 88% of the workforce are engaged in agriculture, mostly at subsistence level, and 67% of exports are food products. Coffee is the main cash crop. Ethiopia remains heavily dependent on foreign aid.

ethnography Study of the culture of an ethnic group or society. Ethnographers gather anthropological data by direct observation of a group's economic and social life. *See also* ANTHROPOLOGY; ETHNOLOGY

ethnology Comparative study of cultures. Historical ethnology was developed in the late 19th century in an attempt to trace cultural diffusion. *See also* ANTHROPOLOGY

ethology Study of animal behaviour, especially in the natural environment, first outlined in the 1930s by Konrad LORENZ and Niko TINBERGEN. Ethologists study natural processes, such as courtship, mating and self-defence. *See also* EVOLUTION; IMPRINTING; NATURAL SELECTION

ethyl alcohol *See* ETHANOL

ethylene *See* ETHENE

ethyne (acetylene, C_2H_2) Colourless, flammable gas manufactured by cracking of petroleum fractions. The simplest ALKYNE, it is explosive if mixed with air. When burned with oxygen, it produces extremely high temperatures up to 3,480°C (6,300°F) and is used in oxyacetylene torches. It is polymerized to manufacture plastics, synthetic fibres, resins and neoprene (synthetic rubber). It is also used to produce ethanal and ethanoic acid. Properties: r.d. 0.625; m.p. −80.8°C (−113.4°F); b.p. −84°C (−119.2°F).

Etna Volcanic mountain on the E coast of Sicily, Italy. The first known eruption was in 475 BC, others occurring in 1169, 1669 and 1971. It is the highest active volcano in Europe and the highest mountain in Italy S of the Alps. Height: *c*.3,340m (10,958ft).

Eton Town on the River Thames, Berkshire, S England. It is the site of a famous private school, Eton College, founded by Henry VI in 1440. Pop. (1981) 3,559.

Etruscan Inhabitant of ancient Etruria (modern Tuscany and Umbria), central Italy. Etruscan civilization

flourished in the first millennium BC. Their sophisticated society was influenced by Greece and organized into city-states. Etruscan civilization reached its peak in the 6th century BC. Their wealth and power was based primarily on their skill at ironworking and their control of the iron trade. They are famed for their naturalistic bronze busts and black *bucchero* pottery. The Etruscan cult of the dead led them to produce elaborate tombs. From the 5th to the 3rd century BC, they were gradually overrun by neighbouring peoples, particularly the Romans.

etymology Branch of PHILOLOGY dealing with the origin and history of words. The word *telephone*, for example, is a combination of two elements derived from Greek, *tele* (distant) and *phone* (sound or voice).

EU Abbreviation for the EUROPEAN UNION

Eubacteria Sub-kingdom of the kingdom PROKARYOTAE, sometimes considered a separate DOMAIN. Eubacteria include all multicellular BACTERIA, including those that photosynthesize, deriving their carbon from the air. They do not have the unique types of cell walls, RIBOSOMES and RNA of the other subkingdom, ARCHAEBACTERIA. *See also* PHOTOSYNTHESIS

Euboea (Évvoia) Island in the W Aegean Sea, SE central Greece; the capital is Khalkís. Under Athenian domination from 506 to 411 BC, it was taken by Philip II of Macedon in 338, then held successively by the Romans, Byzantines, Venetians and Turks, before being incorporated into Greece in 1830. Industries: livestock, grapes. Area: 3,654sq km (1,411sq mi). Pop. (1991) 208,408.

eucalyptus (gum tree) Genus of evergreen shrubs and slender trees, native to Australia and cultivated in warm and temperate regions. They are valuable sources of hardwood and oils. Leaves are blue/white, and they bear woody fruits and flowers without petals. Height: to 122m (400ft). There are *c*.600 species. Family Myrtaceae.

Eucharist (Gk. thanksgiving) Central act of Christian worship in which the priest and congregation partake in Holy Communion – one of the principal SACRAMENTS. The Eucharist is a commemorative re-enactment of the LAST SUPPER. *See also* TRANSUBSTANTIATION

Euclid (*c*.330–*c*.260 BC) Greek mathematician who taught at Alexandria, Egypt. Euclid is remembered for his classic textbook on GEOMETRY *Elements* (Lat. pub. 1482). His axioms, that parallel lines never meet and the angles of a triangle always add up to 180°, remained the basis for geometry until the development of **non-Euclidean geometry** in the 18th century.

Eudoxus of Cnidus (*c*.408–*c*.355 BC) Greek mathematician and astronomer. His greatest contribution was to give a precise definition of a REAL NUMBER in the framework of a general theory of proportion. In astronomy, he proposed the first system for describing the motions of the heavenly bodies.

Eugène of Savoy (1663–1736) French-born prince and Austrian general. He displayed courage and leadership for Austria against the Ottoman Turks at Vienna (1683) and Zenta (1697). In the War of the SPANISH SUCCESSION (1702–13), Eugène joined the Duke of MARLBOROUGH in victories over the French at BLENHEIM (1704), Oudenarde (1708) and Malplaquet (1709).

eugenics Study of human improvement by selective breeding, founded in the 19th century by Sir Francis GALTON. Eugenics was discredited in the early 20th century owing to its ethical implications and its racist and class-based assumptions. Advances in GENETICS have given rise to the modern field of genetic counselling, through which people known to have defective genes that could cause disorders in offspring are warned of the risks.

Eugénie (1826–1920) Consort of NAPOLEON III and French empress. She became the wife of Napoleon III shortly after he declared the Second Empire in 1852. Regent in her husband's absences at war (1859, 1865, 1870), her influence as a Catholic and conservative was often felt in French affairs. After Napoleon was deposed in 1870, the couple fled to England.

Euglenophyta Phylum of single-celled ALGAE which includes the genus *Euglena*. Members of this group have both animal and plant characteristics. They swim by means of flagella. Many species contain CHLOROPLASTS and employ PHOTOSYNTHESIS, but some are colourless and feed on BACTERIA and DIATOMS. *See also* FLAGELLATE

eukaryote Organism whose CELLS have a membrane-bound NUCLEUS, with DNA contained in CHROMOSOMES. Making up one of the three DOMAINS, eukaryotes include all ANIMALS, PLANTS, FUNGUS and PROTISTA. They have a complex CYTOPLASM with an ENDOPLASMIC RETICULUM, and most of them possess MITOCHONDRIA. *See also* KINGDOM; PROKARYOTAE

Euler, Leonhard (1707–83) Swiss mathematician. He is best known for his geometric theorem, which states that for any polyhedron (many-sided figure), $V - E + F = 2$, where V is the number of vertices, E the number of edges and F the number of faces. Euler conducted much research into the number e, the base of natural LOGARITHMS.

eunuch Castrated man, originally used as keeper of a HAREM. They were employed as servants in royal and wealthy households, especially in the Byzantine and Ottoman Empires. *See also* CASTRATO

euphonium BRASS musical instrument, related to the TUBA. Invented in 1843, it is pitched in C or B♭.

Euphrates (Firat) River of SW Asia. Formed by the confluence of the rivers Murat and Karasu, it flows from E Turkey across Syria into central Iraq, where it joins the River TIGRIS NW of BASRA to form the SHATT AL-ARAB and eventually flows into the PERSIAN GULF. The ancient civilizations of BABYLONIA and ASSYRIA developed along the lower Euphrates. Length: 2,800km (1,740mi).

Eureka Stockade (1854) Armed rebellion of gold diggers at Ballarat, Victoria, Australia. Resentment at exploitative administration of the goldfields culminated in some 150 diggers forming a stockade and firing on a contingent of 280 police and troops. They were quickly overcome and 30 men killed. None of the rebels were subsequently convicted.

eurhythmics System of musical and dance training that has influenced BALLET and acting. Developed in Switzerland and Germany by Emile Jaques-Dalcroze (1865–1950), it evolved from interpretive gymnastic exercises performed to music.

Euripides (c.480–450 BC) Greek playwright; with AESCHYLUS and SOPHOCLES, one of the three great writers of Greek TRAGEDY. Euripides' plays caused contemporary controversy, with their cynical depiction of human motivation. The significance of the CHORUS was reduced in favour of an examination of individual behaviour, especially women in love. His works, such as *Medea, Electra, Hecuba* and the anti-war satire *Trojan Women*, achieved great posthumous popularity.

euro Single currency unit for the EUROPEAN UNION (EU). The MAASTRICHT TREATY (1992) established a timetable for economic and monetary union (EMU). A European Currency Unit (ECU) acted as a theoretical unit until the birth of the euro on 1 January 1999. In this first stage, 11 member states (Austria, Belgium, Finland, France, Germany, Ireland, Italy, Luxembourg, Netherlands, Portugal and Spain) fixed their exchange rates against each other and against the euro. International financial transactions began to be calculated in euros and the European Central Bank took control of a single monetary policy. In its first two years of existence the euro fell in value by more than 30% against the sterling and the dollar. In a "second wave", the euro will enter public circulation on 1 January 2002 and will circulate alongside national currencies for six months, after which national currencies will be abolished. Denmark and the UK have "opted out" of this first wave. *See also* EUROPEAN MONETARY SYSTEM (EMS); EXCHANGE RATE MECHANISM (ERM)

Europa Smallest of Jupiter's GALILEAN SATELLITES, with a diameter of 3,138km (1,950mi). Mainly rock, Europa's smooth water-ice crust is criss-crossed by a network of light and dark linear markings. There are very few craters.

Europa Beautiful Phoenician princess of Greek legend. She was abducted and ravished by ZEUS who carried her across the sea to Crete. She bore three sons, including MINOS, who became king of Crete.

Europe Earth's second smallest continent, comprising the western fifth of the Eurasian landmass. It is separated from Asia by the URALS (E), CASPIAN SEA and the CAUCASUS (SE), BLACK SEA and DARDANELLES (S), and from Africa by the MEDITERRANEAN SEA. **Land** Europe is dominated by the Alpine mountain chain, the principal links of which are the PYRENEES, ALPS, CARPATHIAN MOUNTAINS, BALKAN MOUNTAINS and the Caucasus. Between the Scandinavian peninsula and the Alpine chain is the great European plain, which extends from the Atlantic coast in France to the Urals. Much of the plain is fertile farmland. Major islands include the British Isles, Sicily, Sardinia, Corsica and Iceland. **Structure and geology** Much of N Europe is made up of large sedimentary plains overlying an ancient Precambrian shield, outcrops of which remain in N Scandinavia, Scotland and the Urals. There are also worn-down Palaeozoic highlands. Many upland areas N of the Alps were formed during the Carboniferous period, including Ireland, the moorlands of Devon and Cornwall and the PENNINES, England. Southern Europe is geologically younger. Alpine folding began in the Oligocene period. Europe's longest river is the VOLGA; other major rivers are (from W to E) the TAGUS, LOIRE, RHÔNE, RHINE, ELBE and DANUBE. The Caspian Sea is the world's largest lake. **Climate and vegetation** Europe's climate varies from subtropical to polar. The Mediterranean climate of the S is dry and warm. Much of the land is scrub (maquis), with some hardwood forests. Further N, the climate is mild and quite humid, moderated by prevailing westerly winds and the GULF STREAM. The natural vegetation is mixed forest, but this has been extensively depleted. Mixed forest merges into boreal forests of conifers. In SE European Russia, wooded and grass steppe merge into semidesert to the N of the Caspian Sea. In the far N, lies the tundra. **History** The Mediterranean region was the cradle of the ancient Greek and Roman civilizations. The collapse of the Western Roman Empire and the barbarian invasions brought chaos to much of Europe. During the Middle Ages, Christianity was the unifying force throughout the continent. The post-medieval period witnessed the SCHISM in the Catholic Church and the emergence of the nation state. European powers began to found vast empires in other parts of the globe (*see* COLONIALISM; EXPLORATION; IMPERIALISM), and the FRENCH REVOLUTION ushered in an era of momentous political changes. During the 20th century, a period overshadowed by two World Wars and the rise of COMMUNISM, Europe began to lose some of its pre-eminence in world affairs. After World War 2, the countries of Europe became divided into two ideological blocs: Eastern Europe, dominated by the Soviet Union; and Western Europe, closely aligned with the USA. The rivalry was known as the COLD WAR. The NORTH ATLANTIC TREATY ORGANIZATION (NATO) was established to act as a deterrent to the spread of COMMUNISM; the Warsaw Pact was its E European counterpart. Several economic organizations, in particular the EUROPEAN COMMUNITY (EC), worked towards closer intra-national cooperation. In 1991, the collapse of Soviet communism added to the momentum for a kind of supranational union in the form of a EUROPEAN UNION (EU). **Economy** Almost half of European land is unproductive because of climate, relief, soil or urbanization. A quarter of land is forested; the lumber industry is particularly important in Scandinavia and the mountainous areas of E Europe. Fishing is a major industry in countries with Atlantic or North Sea coastlines. Two-thirds of cultivated land is arable. Cereals are the principal crop: wheat is the most important, replaced by oats in the N and sometimes by maize in the S. Rice is grown with the aid of irrigation. Sheep are grazed on many upland areas, but dairy farming is by far the most important form of animal husbandry. In Mediterranean areas many fruits, early vegetables and grapevines (mainly for wine) are cultivated. Europe produces more than one-third of the world's coal. Germany, Poland, Czech Republic and Russia are the leading producers. Other mineral deposits include bauxite, mercury, lead, zinc and potash. Romania was the largest producer of oil in Europe until North Sea states, especially Britain, began to exploit their resources. Europe is highly industrialized, and manufacturing employs a high proportion of the workforce. The largest industrial areas are in W central Europe, in particular N and NE France, the RUHR, and around the North Sea ports of ANTWERP, AMSTERDAM, ROTTERDAM and HAMBURG. *Area* c.10,360,000sq km (4,000,000sq mi) *Highest mountain* Mount Elbrus (Russia) 5,633m (18,481ft) *Longest river* Volga 3,750km (2,330mi) *Population* (1990 est.) 785,700,000 *Largest cities* MOSCOW (8,881,000); LONDON (6,679,700); ST PETERSBURG (4,952,000); BERLIN (3,419,000) *See also* articles on individual countries

European Atomic Energy Commission (Euratom) Organization formed by the second of the Treaties of ROME (1957). It was founded to coordinate non-military nuclear research and production, and provide capital for investment, specialists and equipment. It is administered by the EUROPEAN COMMISSION.

European Commission Institution responsible for initiating and implementing the policies of the EUROPEAN UNION (EU). The Commission drafts policy proposals which it submits to the EUROPEAN COUNCIL OF MINISTERS and the EUROPEAN PARLIAMENT. It was established (1967) with the creation of the EUROPEAN COMMUNITY (EC). There are 20 commissioners, two from France, Germany, Italy, Spain and the UK, and one each from the remaining member states. Each commissioner has responsibility for a different policy area and pledges loyalty to the EU rather than individual member states. The President of the Commission is elected by the commissioners for a four-year term. The Commission heads a secretariat of c.15,000 civil servants based in Brussels. It is collectively responsible to the European Parliament, which can remove it on a censure motion carried by a two-thirds majority. In 1999, following charges of corruption, the entire Commission resigned.

European Community (EC) Historical organization of Western European countries dedicated to closer economic and political cooperation in Europe. In 1952 the European Coal and Steel Community (ECSC) was established to integrate the coal and steel industries primarily of France and West Germany to create a more unified Europe. The success of the ECSC led to the Treaties of ROME (1957) that established the **European Economic Community** (EEC), or Common Market, and the EUROPEAN ATOMIC ENERGY COMMISSION (EURATOM). The aim was to create a common economic approach to agriculture, employment, trade and social development, and to give Western Europe more influence in world affairs. Original members included France, West Germany, Italy, Belgium, Netherlands and Luxembourg. In 1962, the COMMON AGRICULTURAL POLICY (CAP) came into effect. In 1967, the EEC, ECSC and EURATOM merged to form the European Community (EC). The United Kingdom, Ireland and Denmark joined in 1973; Greece in 1981; Spain and Portugal in 1986; and Austria, Finland and Sweden in 1995. In 1993, the EC was superseded by the EUROPEAN UNION (EU).

European Convention on Human Rights (1950) Agreement to protect the rights and freedoms of the individual, signed by the members of the COUNCIL OF EUROPE. The Convention listed 12 basic rights, including the right to life, to a fair trial, to peaceful assembly and association, and to freedom of expression and from slavery and torture. An additional protocol provides for the abolition of the death penalty. *See also* HUMAN RIGHTS

European Council of Ministers Policy-making body of the EUROPEAN UNION (EU). The Council, which meets in Brussels, consists of ministers from government of each of the member states. It formally comprises the foreign ministers of each state, but in practice the minister depends on the subject under review. Council decisions are made by qualified majority vote, simple majority or unanimity. Unanimity votes are taken on sensitive issue, such as taxation and constitutional matters. Qualified majority voting is weighted according to the relative population sizes of each of the member states. The **European Council**, comprising the heads of government of the member states, meets twice a year to provide overall policy direction.

European Court of Human Rights Created in 1959, the court is presided over by one judge from member states that are signatories of the EUROPEAN CONVENTION ON HUMAN RIGHTS (1950). It decides whether or not an individual's rights have been disregarded by a member state in cases when the two parties have already failed to reach a settlement through the European Commission of Human Rights.

European Court of Justice (officially Court of Justice of the European Communities) Court responsible for the interpretation and implementation of European Union laws. The court will also rule in cases where member states are alleged to have broken EC laws. It was established in the first of the Treaties of ROME (1957) and is based in Luxembourg.

European Economic Area (EEA) Economic union agreed (1992) between the 12 members of the EUROPEAN COMMUNITY (EC) and six of the seven members (Switzerland rejected the notion) of the EUROPEAN FREE TRADE ASSOCIATION (EFTA). The EEA extended the EU's Single Market principles to EFTA. In 1995 Austria, Finland and Sweden joined the EUROPEAN UNION (EU), leaving only Norway, Iceland and Liechtenstein as non-EU members.

European Free Trade Association (EFTA) Organization seeking to promote free trade among its European members. Established in 1960, it originally comprised

Austria, Denmark, Ireland, Norway, Portugal, Sweden, Switzerland and the UK. By 1995 all but Norway and Switzerland had joined the EUROPEAN UNION (EU), while Iceland and Liechtenstein joined EFTA in 1970 and 1991, respectively. *See also* EUROPEAN ECONOMIC AREA (EEA)

European Monetary System (EMS) System set up in 1979 to bring about monetary stability among the then nine members of the EUROPEAN COMMUNITY (EC). The EMS had three main components: the European Currency Unit (ECU), a monetary unit weighted according to the size of each member state's economy and the value of its trade; the EXCHANGE RATE MECHANISM (ERM), where each member state agreed to keep their national currencies within set margins (initially either 2.25% or 6% above or below) of a central rate of exchange against the ECU; and the credit mechanisms. The MAASTRICHT TREATY (1992) set a timetable for achieving economic and monetary union (EMU) and the establishment of a single currency (the EURO). In 1998 11 member states were chosen to participate in the first stage of EMU. On 1 January 1999, the euro was born and a European Central Bank was given control of a single monetary policy.

European Parliament (EP) Representative assembly of the EUROPEAN UNION (EU). It originated (1952) as the Common Assembly of the European Coal and Steel Community (ECSC). The Parliament was expanded by the Treaties of ROME (1957) to serve two new bodies, the European Economic Community (EEC) and the EUROPEAN ATOMIC ENERGY COMMISSION (EURATOM). Direct elections to the EP were first held in 1979. In June 1994 elections the Parliament expanded from 518 to 567 seats. In 1995 it expanded to 626 members with the accession of Austria, Finland and Sweden to the EU. In June 1999 British MEPs will for the first time by elected by a system of PROPORTIONAL REPRESENTATION (PR). The EPs powers were greatly increased by the Single European Act (1986), which introduced the cooperation procedure, the MAASTRICHT TREATY (1991), which extended the cooperation procedure and introduced the co-decision procedure, and the Amsterdam Treaty (1997), which extended the co-decision procedure to all areas except economic and monetary union (EMU). Although it cannot initiate legislation, it can advise and has the power of consultation on all EU issues, including the EU budget. The Parliament meets in Strasbourg and Brussels.

European Space Agency (ESA) Organization formed (1976) by the partial merger of the European Space Research Agency (ESRO) and the European Launcher Development Organization (ELDO). It aims to promote space research and provides for the implementation of a common European space policy. Since 1980 Arianespace has been responsible for the **Ariane** Launcher, the rocket responsible for putting ESA satellites into orbit.

European Union (EU) Organization of fifteen European countries (Austria, Belgium, Denmark, Finland, France, Germany, Greece, Ireland, Italy, Luxembourg, Netherlands, Portugal, Spain, Sweden and the United Kingdom) established (1993) following the ratification of the MAASTRICHT TREATY (1992). The EU assumed control of the existing framework and institutions of the EUROPEAN COMMUNITY (EC), such as the EUROPEAN COMMISSION and EUROPEAN PARLIAMENT (EP), but extended the role and scope of the EC according to the criteria of the Maastricht Treaty. The member states agreed to greater cooperation, particularly in areas such as foreign and security policies (*see* WESTERN EUROPEAN UNION (WEU)), and internal and judicial policies. The UK and Denmark "opted out" of the first stage in the creation of a single European currency (the EURO). Some argue that the Union will lead inevitably to a federal Europe. In addition to reforms of existing policies, such as the COMMON AGRICULTURAL POLICY (CAP), the EU is faced with the challenge of enlargement. In 1998, formal accession negotiations were opened with Hungary, Poland, Estonia, Czech Republic, Slovenia and Cyprus. In addition to the Commission and Parliament, the EU's institutional structure comprises the EUROPEAN COUNCIL OF MINISTERS, the Economic and Social Committee (which advises on draft EU legislation), the European Central Bank and the EUROPEAN COURT OF JUSTICE. *See also* EUROPEAN MONETARY SYSTEM (EMS)

europium (symbol Eu) Silvery-white, metallic rare-earth element of the LANTHANIDE SERIES. Its chief ores are monazite and bastnaesite. The metal is used in the manufacture of colour television screens and lasers, and in control rods in nuclear reactors. Properties: at.no. 63; r.a.m. 151.96; r.d. 5.25; m.p. 822°C (1,512°F); b.p. 1,597°C (2,907°F); most common isotope Eu[153] (52.18%).

Eurydice In Greek mythology, the nymph married to ORPHEUS.

eustachian tube Small channel that connects the middle EAR to the back of the throat. It opens when swallowing, to allow the pressure in the middle ear to remain the same as the pressure of air outside the body.

Euston Road School School of painting and drawing founded (1937) in London by Graham Bell (1910–43), William Coldstream (1908–87), Victor PASMORE (1908–98) and Claude Rogers (1909–79). Inspired by SICKERT and CÉZANNE, they rejected the prevailing trend towards abstraction and surrealism in favour of a more straightforward naturalism.

euthanasia (Gk. good death) Inducing the painless death of a person (usually with a terminal illness), often by a drug. It is illegal in most countries. **Voluntary** euthanasia, the taking of life with the consent of the patient, is accepted in practice in The Netherlands. **Passive** euthanasia, the withholding of life-supporting treatment, is a form of voluntary euthanasia. In the UK groups, such as Exit, campaign for the right to a dignified death.

eutrophication Process by which a stream or lake becomes rich in inorganic nutrients by agricultural run-off or other artificial means. Compounds of nitrogen, phosphorus, iron, sulphur and potassium are vital for plant growth in water; in excess they overstimulate the growth of surface ALGAE or CYANOBACTERIA producing BLOOM that can consume all available dissolved oxygen with devastating effects on marine life.

evangelicalism (Gk. *euangelos*, good news or gospel) Term applied to several, generally Protestant, tendencies within the Christian Church. Evangelicalism denotes the school that stresses personal conversion and witness of salvation by faith in the atoning death of Jesus Christ.

evangelist Person who preaches the gospel, announcing the good news of redemption through Jesus Christ and the hope of everlasting life. The word also applies by extension to the authors of the four gospels of the New Testament: Saints MATTHEW, MARK, LUKE and JOHN. *See also* GREAT AWAKENING; METHODISM

Evans, Sir Arthur John (1851–1941) English archaeologist. He excavated the ruins of KNOSSOS in Crete and found evidence of a Bronze Age (2000–1400 BC) civilization, which he named the MINOAN CIVILIZATION.

Evans, Dame Edith Mary (1888–1976) English stage and screen actress. While with the OLD VIC (1925–26, 1936), she played a variety of roles, including the Nurse in *Romeo and Juliet*. Evans' best-remembered roles include Lady Bracknell in *The Importance of Being Earnest*. She won the New York Film Critic's Award for her performance in *The Whisperers* (1967).

Evans, Walker (1903–75) US photographer. He is famed for his portrait images of the poverty-stricken South of the 1930s, many published in *Let Us Now Praise Famous Men* (1941).

Evans-Pritchard, Sir Edward Evan (1902–73) English anthropologist. He was chair of social anthropology (1946–70) at the University of Oxford. Evans-Pritchard's fieldwork in East Africa resulted in the classic studies of tribal societies, *Witchcraft, Oracles and Magic Among the Azande* (1937) and *The Nuer* (1940).

evaporation Process by which a liquid or solid becomes a vapour. The reverse process is CONDENSATION. Solids and liquids cool when they evaporate because they give up energy (LATENT HEAT) to the escaping molecules.

Eve In the Bible (GENESIS 2), the first woman, created by God from ADAM's rib to be his companion and wife in the Garden of EDEN. She succumbed to temptation and disobeyed God by eating the fruit of the tree of the knowledge of good and evil and sharing it with Adam. For this act the couple became mortal and were banished from the garden. She was the mother of CAIN, ABEL and Seth.

Evelyn, John (1620–1706) English diarist. He was a founder member of the Royal Society. Evelyn is best-known for his *Diary* (published posthumously in 1818), a vivid account of life in 17th-century England.

evening primrose Any of various plants of the genus *Oenothera*, many of which are native to W North America. They have yellow, pink or white flowers that open in the evening. Height: 1.8m (5.3ft). Family Onagraceae.

event horizon Boundary of a BLACK HOLE, from which nothing can escape. Observers outside the event horizon can therefore obtain no information about the black hole's interior. The radius of the event horizon is called the **Schwarzschild radius**. At the event horizon, the ESCAPE VELOCITY equals the velocity of light with the consequence that all ELECTROMAGNETIC RADIATION is trapped. Its presence can only be detected by its powerful gravitational force.

Everest, Mount (Nepalese *Sagarmatha*; Tibetan *Chomo-Langma*, Mother Goddess of the World) Highest mountain in the world, in the central Himalayas on the borders of Tibet and Nepal. It is named after George Everest, first surveyor-general of India. Everest was conquered on 29 May 1953 by Sir Edmund HILLARY and Tenzing Norgay. Height: 8,848m (29,029ft).

Everglades Large tract of marshland in S Florida, extending from Lake Okeechobee to Florida Bay. The region is made up of mangrove forests, sawgrass and hummocks (island masses of vegetation). In the late 19th and early 20th century, large areas were drained for agricultural use. Water shortages and fires damaged the fragile ecosystem, and the Everglades National Park was established in 1947. It supports abundant animal life, including alligators, snakes, turtles, egrets and bald eagles. Total area: *c*.10,000sq km (4,000sq mi).

evergreen Plant that retains its green foliage, unlike DECIDUOUS plants. There are two groups: narrow-leaved, or CONIFERS, and broad-leaved. Conifers include fir, spruce, pine and juniper. Among the broad-leaved evergreens are holly and rhododendron.

Evert, Chris (Christine Marie) (1954–) US tennis player. She won a total of 18 Grand Slam titles. Evert won seven French Open titles (1974–75, 1979–80, 1983, 1985–86), six US Opens (1975–78, 1980, 1982), three Wimbledon titles (1974, 1976, 1981), and two Australian

Opens (1982, 1984). She was the first woman to win US\$1 million in prize money. Evert retired in 1989.

evolution Theory that a SPECIES undergoes gradual changes to survive and reproduce in a competitive, and often changing, environment, and that a new species is the result of change from the ancestral forms. Early work on evolutionary theory was initiated by Jean LAMARCK, but it was not until Charles DARWIN published *The Origin of Species* (1959) that the theory was considered worthy of argument. Present-day evolutionary theory is largely derived from the work of Darwin and Gregor MENDEL and maintains that in any population or gene pool, there is VARIATION, including random MUTATION, in genetic forms and characteristics. Most species produce greater quantities of offspring than their environment can support, so only those members best adapted to the environment survive. When new characteristics provide survival advantages, those individuals that possess them pass on these characteristics to their offspring through the process of HEREDITY. *See also* ADAPTATION; ADAPTIVE RADIATION; DAWKINS, RICHARD; GENETICS; GOULD, STEPHEN JAY; HUMAN EVOLUTION; NATURAL SELECTION; NEO-DARWINISM; PUNCTUATED EQUILIBRIUM

Ewing, William Maurice (1906–74) US geophysicist. He was the first (1935) to take seismic measurements of the ocean that greatly aided understanding of marine sediments and ocean basins. Ewing also took (1939) the first deep-sea photographs.

exchange rate In economics, the rate at which one nation's currency can be converted to that of another. It varies according to fluctuations on the world's FOREIGN EXCHANGE markets. *See also* GOLD STANDARD

exchange rate mechanism (ERM) System for keeping the currencies of member states of the EUROPEAN UNION (EU) stable, as part of the EUROPEAN MONETARY SYSTEM (EMS). The ERM worked well for a time, but currency speculation forced two currencies, the UK pound sterling and the Italian lira, to leave it in 1992, because they were unable to keep their value above the minimum limit (6% and 2.25% respectively). The ERM was near collapse, and to save it several currencies were allowed to fluctuate by as much as 15% above or below their central rate. The lira rejoined in 1996. *See also* EURO; FOREIGN EXCHANGE

excited state Condition of an atom, ion or molecule, when its energy level is higher than that of the ground (lowest) state. For example, an ATOM can be in an excited state having absorbed a PHOTON. The increased energy causes one of the ELECTRONS to occupy an ORBITAL of higher energy; the atom may restore its former state by various emissions.

exclusion principle Basic law of QUANTUM MECHANICS proposed by Wolfgang PAULI in 1925, stating that no two ELECTRONS in an atom can possess the same energy and SPIN. More precisely, the set of four QUANTUM NUMBERS characterizing certain ELEMENTARY PARTICLES called FERMIONS must be unique.

excommunication Formal expulsion from the communion of the faithful, from sacraments and from rites of a religious body. Largely abandoned by Protestants, excommunication has been retained by Jewish congregations and by the Roman Catholic Church. In the days when the church held great temporal (as well as spiritual) authority, excommunication was a severe punishment for HERESY or BLASPHEMY.

excretion Elimination of materials from the body that have been involved in METABOLISM. Such waste materials, particularly nitrogenous wastes, would be toxic if allowed to accumulate. In mammals these wastes are excreted mainly as URINE and to some extent also by sweating. Carbon dioxide is excreted through the lungs during breathing.

executor Person responsible for carrying out the provisions of a WILL. Normally the executor is named in the will by the **testator** (person who has made the will). The executor's duties are to arrange the funeral of the deceased, to pay outstanding debts and to distribute the property among the beneficiaries.

Exeter City on the River Exe; county town of Devon, SW England. Ancient buildings include the Norman cathedral (c.1275), the 12th-century Guildhall and the remains of Roman walls. Exeter University was established in 1955. Industries: tourism, textiles, leather. Pop. (1994) 107,000.

existentialism Any of several philosophical systems concerned with the nature of existence or being. Søren KIERKEGAARD is regarded as the founder of the movement. He rejected METAPHYSICS, arguing that an individual is forced to make their own ethical decisions. Martin HEIDEGGER developed these ideas in relation to the PHENOMENOLOGY of Edmund HUSSERL. Karl JASPERS argued that the greatest insights into existence were experienced in extreme situations. For Jean-Paul SARTRE, the central tenet of existentialism was that existence precedes essence. He declared that there was no God and that individuals were "condemned to be free". Sartre's writings influenced Simone de BEAUVOIR and Albert CAMUS.

exobiology (astrobiology) Search for life on other planets. Exobiology is concerned with attempts to detect environmental conditions beyond Earth.

Exodus OLD TESTAMENT book of the Bible, the second book of the PENTATEUCH or TORAH. The first part details the flight of the Israelites from Egypt; the second part contains a catalogue of religious instructions that formed the basis of Mosaic law. *See also* MOSES; PASSOVER; TEN COMMANDMENTS

exorcism Ritual expulsion of evil spirits from a person, place or thing, usually performed by a priest or SHAMAN. Exorcism is a practice common to many religions. In the Christian Church, it is performed by means of the laying-on of hands and incantation.

exoskeleton Protective skeleton or hard supporting structure forming the outside of the soft bodies of certain animals, notably ARTHROPODS and MOLLUSCS. In arthropods, it consists of a thick horny covering attached to the outside of the body and may be jointed and flexible. The exoskeleton does not grow as the animal grows; instead it is shed periodically and the animal generates a new one.

exothermic reaction CHEMICAL REACTION in which heat is evolved. A common example is COMBUSTION. *See also* ENDOTHERMIC REACTION; ENTHALPY

expanding Universe Theory of the origin and direction in time of the UNIVERSE. Physicists have attempted to explain the RED SHIFT phenomena of some stars as resulting from a single, huge explosion which causes these stars to be moving away from our section of the Universe. The RED SHIFT occurs when, due to the DOPPLER EFFECT, the perceived wavelengths of light from some stars are lengthened because of their outwards movement. There is also the opposite effect, a BLUE SHIFT, but this does not occur as often. Today, the balance of opinion is in favour of the theory of the Universe expanding following the BIG BANG. *See also* HUBBLE CONSTANT

expansion (expansivity) In physics, a change in the size of an object with change in TEMPERATURE. Most substances expand on heating, although there are exceptions – water expands when it cools from 4°C (39°F) to its

freezing point at 0°C (32°F). A solid has three coefficients of expansion: **linear**, **superficial** and **volume**, equal to the fractional increase in length, area or volume (respectively) per unit temperature rise. For a gas, the coefficient of expansion is the rate of change of volume with temperature (at constant pressure), or of volume with pressure (at constant temperature). *See also* CHARLES' LAW

exploration Phoenicians, Greeks and Carthaginians undertook vast journeys across the oceans for the purposes of trade and colonization. The conquests of Alexander the Great opened up intercourse between East and West. For almost 1,000 years after the collapse of the Roman Empire (in the 5th century AD), the Chinese and Arabs dominated exploration. European knowledge of Asia was advanced by MARCO POLO. The European "age of discovery" was motivated by financial gain and the missionary zeal of Christianity. In 1487 Bartholomeu DIAZ rounded the Cape of Good Hope in search of a sea route to the spices of India. In 1498, Vasco da GAMA completed the first voyage from Portugal to India. In 1492, Christopher COLUMBUS sailed westward towards Asia, landing in America. Similarly, in 1500, Pedro CABRAL accidentally discovered Brazil en route to India. The search for a trade route to the East spurred Ferdinand MAGELLAN's circumnavigation of the globe (1519–22). The lure of gold in South America prompted the explorations of Hernán CORTÉS and Francisco PIZARRO. In the 17th century, the interior of North America was revealed by Samuel de CHAMPLAIN, Sieur de LA SALLE, Louis JOLIET and Jacques MAQUETTE. The Portuguese and Spanish monopoly of the Atlantic trade routes led to the search for new routes. Francis DRAKE, James COOK and Vitus BERING explored the Pacific and Indian oceans. In the mid-19th century, the interior of Africa was mapped by H.M. STANLEY and David LIVINGSTONE. European exploration and colonization devastated indigenous peoples, either through the spread of new diseases or SLAVERY. In the late 19th century, explorations began to motivated more by science than economics. In 1909, Richard E. PEARY reached the North Pole. In 1911, Roald AMUNDSEN beat Robert SCOTT to the South Pole. Richard BYRD was a pioneer of exploration by airplane. The launch of Sputnik 1 (1957) opened up the era of SPACE EXPLORATION.

Explorer I First of a series of US scientific satellites. It was launched in 1958, and the programme continued into the 1970s. The early Explorers provided information about the VAN ALLEN RADIATION BELTS.

explosive Substance that reacts rapidly and violently, emitting heat, light, sound and shock waves. There are tow broad types of explosive: **deflagrating**, or low explosives, and **detonating**, or high explosives. Low explosives, such as GUNPOWDER , are used as propellants for bullets and shells and in quarrying or mining. Some explosives are highly nitrated **chemical** compounds or mixtures that decompose violently. These include TNT, NITROGLYCERINE and DYNAMITE. Nuclear explosives are radioactive metals, the atoms of which can undergo nuclear FISSION or FUSION, to release radiant energy and devastating shock waves. *See also* NUCLEAR WEAPON

exponent Superscript number placed to the right of a symbol indicating its POWER, for example in $a^4 (= a \times a \times a \times a)$, 4 is the exponent.

exponential In general, a FUNCTION of x of the form a^x, where a is a constant. The exponential function e^x, where e is the base of natural LOGARITHMS, 2.7182818..., can be represented by a power series $1 + x + x^2/2! + x^3/3! + ...$

expressionism Style of art in which conventional methods of NATURALISM are replaced by distorted and exaggerated images to express intense, subjective emotion. The term expressionism is often used in relation to a radical German art movement between the 1880s and *c*.1905 that reached its apogee in the work of the BLAUE REITER. It was inspired by the work of VAN GOGH, GAUGHIN and MUNCH. In the theatre, the plays of STRINDBERG and WEDEKIND are often described as expressionist. In music, the term is often applied to the early works of BERG and SCHOENBERG, while in literature the novels of DOSTOEVSKY and KAFKA are expressionist in conception. *See also* BRÜCKE, DIE

extensor *See* MUSCLE

extinction Dying out of a species or population. Extinction is part of the process of EVOLUTION in which certain species of plants and animals die out, often to be replaced by others. *See also* CONSERVATION; ENDANGERED SPECIES

extrasensory perception (ESP) Perception that takes place outside the known sensory systems. The term covers alleged parapsychological phenomena such as clairvoyance, telepathy and precognition. ESP has been the subject of serious investigation, beginning with the establishment (1882) of the Society for Psychical Research in London.

extraterritoriality State of legal immunity granted to members of the DIPLOMATIC SERVICE, their families, and the premises they occupy. This includes exemption from arrest or prosecution and from search or seizure.

extroversion Personality type characterized by outgoing behaviour; the opposite of INTROVERSION. The term was popularized by Carl JUNG.

extrusion In geology, the breaking out of IGNEOUS ROCK from below the Earth's surface. In industry, extrusion is the forcing of metals or plastics at optimum temperature through a die to make rods or tubes. *See also* VOLCANO

Eyck, Jan van (*c*.1390–1441) Flemish painter. His best-known work is the altarpiece for the Church of St Bavon, Ghent, which includes the *Adoration of the Lamb* (1432) and the *Arnolfini Wedding* (1434). He perfected the manufacture and technique of oil paint. His brother **Hubert** van Eyck (*c*.1370–1426) probably assisted Jan on the St Bavon alterpiece.

eye Organ of vision. It converts light energy to nerve impulses that are transmitted to the visual centre of the brain. Most of the mass of a human eye lies in a bony protective socket, called the orbital cavity, which also contains muscles and other tissues to hold and move the eye. The eyeball is spherical and composed of three layers: the sclera (white of the eye), which contains the transparent CORNEA; the choroid, which connects with the IRIS, PUPIL and LENS, and contains blood vessels to provide nutrients and oxygen; and the RETINA, which contains rods and cones for converting the image into nerve impulses. The aqueous humour (a watery liquid between the cornea and iris) and the vitreous humour (a jelly-like substance behind the lens) both help to maintain the shape of the eye. *See also* SIGHT

eyebright Any of several small annual and perennial plants found in temperate and subarctic regions. They have terminal spikes of white, yellow or purple flowers. Some are hemiparasites, whose roots form attachments to those of other plants. European eyebright (*Euphrasia officinalis*) was formerly used to treat eye diseases. Family Scrophulariaceae.

Eyre, Lake Salt lake in NE South Australia. It is the lowest point on the continent, *c*.15m (50ft) below sea level, and the largest salt lake in Australia. Area: 9,324sq km (3,600sq mi). Max. depth: 1.2m (4ft).

Eysenck, Hans Jürgen (1916–97) British psychologist and pioneer of BEHAVIOUR THERAPY, b. Germany. Much of Eysenck's work focused on developing a biological definition of PERSONALITY. Many of his works, such as *Uses and Abuses of Psychology*, were best-sellers. His research methodology and views on genetic determination courted controversy.

Ezekiel Old Testament prophet who was among the Jews deported during the BABYLONIAN CAPTIVITY. He is traditionally considered the author of the Old Testament Book of Ezekiel. He was the last of the "greater" Old Testament prophets, the successor of ISAIAH and JEREMIAH.

Ezra In the Old Testament, a continuation of Chronicles I and II. It records the priest Ezra's journey from Babylon to Jerusalem to spread the law of MOSES.

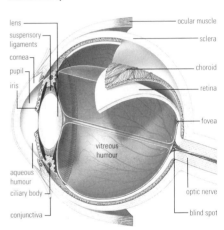

lens · ocular muscle
suspensory ligaments · sclera
cornea · choroid
pupil · retina
iris · fovea
vitreous humour
aqueous humour · optic nerve
ciliary body · blind spot
conjunctiva

▲ **eye** Light entering the human eye passes through a lens, which is controlled by muscles and ligaments. The lens focuses the image of the object onto the retina. The retina comprises light-sensitive nerve cells, called rods and cones, which convert the image into nerve impulses. These impulses are relayed to the brain via the optic nerve.

F/f, sixth letter of the Roman alphabet, is derived from the Semite letter waw, meaning hook. It entered the Greek alphabet as digamma. The Greeks used it to represent the sound w in English. It gained its present form c.AD 114.

Fabergé, Peter Carl (1846–1920) Russian jeweller. He took over his father's business in 1870, making decorative objects in gold and precious stones. Fabergé was famed for his many jewelled Easter eggs for European royalty, the first for Tsar Alexander III in 1884. He left Russia after the Russian Revolution of 1917.

Fabian Society British society of non-Marxists, founded in 1883, who believed that SOCIALISM could be attained through gradual political change. With George Bernard SHAW, Annie BESANT and Sidney and Beatrice WEBB as leaders, the society gained widespread recognition and helped found the Labour Representation Committee (1900) that became the British LABOUR PARTY in 1906. Today, the Fabian Society is affiliated to the Labour Party and publishes a journal and pamphlets.

Fabius Maximus Verrucosus, Quintus (d.203 BC) Roman general and political leader, called Cunctator (Lat. "Delayer"). He is famed for his strategy of avoiding pitched battle against HANNIBAL during the Second PUNIC WAR. When his strategy was rejected, the Romans suffered a disastrous defeat at Cannae in 216 BC. Fabius' strategy was resumed, eventually eroded Hannibal's strength.

fable Literary genre that takes the form of a short allegorical tale intended to convey a moral. The oldest fables are the Greek tales of AESOP and the Indian stories of the *Panchatantra*. Other notable collections of fables were made by Jean de LA FONTAINE and John GAY. More recent fables include James THURBER's *Fables for Our Time* (1940). *See also* ALLEGORY

Fabricius, Hieronymus (1537–1619) (Girolamo Fabrici) Italian anatomist. He was a pupil of Gabriello Fallopius, whom he succeeded (1562) as professor of anatomy at Padua. His book, *On the Formed Foetus* (1600), describes his pioneering research in EMBRYOLOGY. Fabricius also gave the first complete description of the valves in veins, although he misunderstood their function.

facies In geology, all the features of a rock that show the history of its formation. Geologists often distinguish age by facies. It is also applied to gradations of IGNEOUS ROCK.

factor In mathematics, any number that divides exactly into a given number. For example, the factors of 72 are 1, 2, 3, 4, 6, 8, 9, 12, 18, 24 and 36.

factory Place of manufacture characterized by extensive use of machinery and the DIVISION OF LABOUR. The INDUSTRIAL REVOLUTION saw the development of textile factories. Factory production was revolutionized by Eli WHITNEY who introduced (1798) interchangeable parts. Henry FORD pioneered the assembly line method of MASS PRODUCTION. Many modern factories use ROBOTS for the AUTOMATION of various tasks. **Factory farming** is the intensive rearing of livestock in large, densely populated enclosures. Feed is usually automatically dispensed. Some believe that this mass production of food contravenes ANIMAL RIGHTS.

Factory Acts Series of laws in Britain to regulate conditions of employment of FACTORY workers. A response to the atrocious conditions resulting from the INDUSTRIAL REVOLUTION, the first Factory Acts (1802, 1819) limited the hours of work for children and forbade the employment of children under the age of nine respectively. The 1833 Act set up a central body of inspection. The Acts of 1844 and 1847, sponsored by the 7th Earl of SHAFTESBURY, extended protection to the mining industry and reduced the working day to ten hours. The INTERNATIONAL LABOUR ORGANIZATION was founded in 1919. In Britain, workers have been protected by further legislation, including the Factories Act (1961), Health and Safety at Work Act (1974) and the Employment Act (1989). The social chapter of the MAASTRICHT TREATY (1992) sought to harmonize labour laws throughout the European Union (EU).

Faeroe Islands (Faroe Islands) Group of 22 volcanic islands (17 inhabited) in the N Atlantic between Iceland and the Shetland Islands. The largest are Streymoy and Esturoy. Settled in the 7th century, the group was part of Norway from the 11th century until 1380, when it was ceded to Denmark. In 1852 parliament was restored, and since 1948 it has enjoyed a degree of autonomy. Capital and chief port: Tórshavn (Streymoy), pop. (1996) 15,000; Language: Faroese; Industries: fishing, sheep-rearing. Area: 1,339sq km (540sq mi). Total pop. (2000) 49,000.

Fahrenheit, Gabriel Daniel (1686–1736) German physicist and instrument-maker. He invented the alcohol THERMOMETER (1709), the first mercury thermometer (1714) and devised the FAHRENHEIT TEMPERATURE SCALE. Fahrenheit also showed that the boiling points of liquids vary with changes in pressure.

Fahrenheit temperature scale System for measuring temperature based on the freezing point (32°F) and the boiling point (212°F) of water. The interval between them is divided into 180 equal parts. The Fahrenheit scale is still used in the US for non-scientific measurements. Fahrenheit is converted to CELSIUS by subtracting 32 and then dividing by 1.8. *See also* THERMOMETER

fainting (syncope) Loss of consciousness accompanied by general weakness of the muscles. A faint may be preceded by giddiness, nausea and sweating. Its causes include insufficient flow of blood to the brain and shock.

Fairbanks, Douglas (1883–1939) US film actor, b. Julius Ullman. In 1919, he founded United Artists (UA) with Charlie CHAPLIN, D.W. GRIFFITH and his wife Mary Pickford. Fairbanks' swashbuckling acrobatics made him a screen idol in adventures such as *The Mark of Zorro* (1920) and *Robin Hood* (1922). His son, **Douglas Fairbanks, Jr** (1909–2000) appeared in films such as *Catherine the Great* (1934) and *The Prisoner of Zenda* (1937).

Fair Deal *See* TRUMAN, HARRY S.

Fairfax of Cameron, Thomas, 3rd Baron (1612–71) English Parliamentary general in the English CIVIL WARS. He succeeded ESSEX as commander-in-chief (1645) of the NEW MODEL ARMY. In 1650, Fairfax was replaced as commander by Oliver CROMWELL for refusing to march against the Scots. He later headed the commission to the Hague to arrange the RESTORATION of Charles II (1660).

fairy In folklore, a supernatural being who possesses magical powers. Often depicted as tiny humans, fairies are usually mischievous or even malicious. Frequently associated with nature, they are usually invisible. Fairyland is often depicted as an underworld ruled by OBERON and TITANIA. Fairies have been a source for literature, such as *A Midsummer Night's Dream* (1595) by Shakespeare, Grimm's *Fairy Tales* (1812–15), Sir James M. Barrie's *Peter Pan* (1904) and Tolkien's *Lord of the Rings* (1955).

Faisal I (1885–1933) King of Iraq (1921–33). He joined T.E. LAWRENCE in the Arab revolt (1916) against the Turks. Faisal was installed as king by the British nd helped Iraq achieve independence. His grandson uled (1939–58) as **Faisal II**. He was assassinated in a military coup.

Faisal ibn Abdul Aziz *See* SAUD, AL-

Faith healing Use of spiritual force to cure physical or mental illness. In Christianity, it is traced back to the MIRACLES of the Holy Spirit performed through Christ and his apostles, as recorded in the New Testament. In the Catholic churches, healing is connected to the administering of the sacraments and pilgrimmages to shrines such as LOURDES. *See also* CHRISTIAN SCIENCE

fakir (Arabic, poverty) Initiate in SUFISM, who practises self-denial in order to be closer to God. *See also* DERVISH; ISLAM

Falange (Sp. phalanx) Spanish political party founded (1933) by José Antonio PRIMO DE RIVERA. Modelled on other European fascist parties, it was merged with other groups under the FRANCO regime and became the sole legal political party. It was heavily defeated in free elections in 1977. *See also* FASCISM

Falashas Ethnic group of black Jews in Ethiopia, probably descended from early converts to JUDAISM. Their religion relies solely on observance of the OLD TESTAMENT. After suffering much discrimination at home, more than 7,000 were airlifted to Israel in 1984–85.

falcon Widely distributed BIRD OF PREY, sometimes trained by man to hunt game (falconry). Similar to HAWKS, falcons have keen eyesight, short hooked bills, long pointed wings, streamlined bodies, strong legs with hooked claws, and grey or brownish plumage with lighter markings. The females are much larger than the males. Falcons feed on insects, smaller birds and small ground animals. Sweeping down (stoops) at speeds of up to 280km/h (175mph), they can kill on the wing using their talons. They lay two to five brown-spotted white eggs, often in abandoned nests. The best-known species are the KESTREL and PEREGRINE FALCON. Length: 15–64cm (6–25in). Family Falconidae.

Faldo, Nick (Nicholas Alexander) (1957–) English golfer. He has won the British Open (1987, 1990, 1992), and the US Masters (1989, 1990, 1996), the only player apart from Jack NICKLAUS to win in successive years. Faldo was also a member of victorious European Ryder Cup teams (1995, 1997).

Falkland Islands (Islas Malvinas) British crown colony in the S Atlantic Ocean, *c*.520km (320mi) off the E coast of Argentina; the capital is STANLEY (on East Falkland). It includes two large islands (East and West Falkland) and 200 smaller ones. First explored by Europeans in the late 16th century, the Falklands have been under Spanish, French and British control. Argentinian denials of UK sovereignty led to the FALKLANDS WAR (1982). The main activity is sheep farming. Area: *c*.12,200sq km (4,600sq mi). Pop. (2000) 2,000.

Falklands War (April–June 1982) Military conflict fought between the UK and Argentina on the question of sovereignty over the FALKLAND ISLANDS. On 2 April, after the breakdown of negotiations, Argentine forces invaded and occupied the Falklands, South Georgia and South Sandwich Islands, administered by Great Britain since the 19th century. The British blockaded the islands and landed at Port San Carlos. They surrounded the Argentine troops at the capital, Port Stanley, and forced them to surrender (14 June). The war cost 254 British and 750 Argentine lives. The victory helped secure a second term for Margaret THATCHER. Although the British resumed their administration of the islands, the basic issue of sovereignty remains unresolved.

Falla, Manuel de (1876–1946) Spanish composer. He developed a Spanish style by using folk songs combined with rich modern harmonies. Among his works are the opera *La Vida Breve* (1905), *Nights in the Gardens of Spain* (1916) for piano and orchestra, and the music for the ballet *The Three-Cornered Hat* (1919).

Fallopian tube (oviduct) In mammals, either of two narrow ducts leading from the upper part of the UTERUS into the pelvic cavity and ending near each OVARY. After ovulation, the OVUM travels through the Fallopian tube where FERTILIZATION can occur. The fertilized ovum, or EMBRYO, is then implanted into the uterus.

fallout Widely scattered radioactive material produced by an explosion of a NUCLEAR WEAPON or at a NUCLEAR REACTOR. Fallout consists of radioactive ISOTOPES. **Local** fallout, within *c*.500km (300mi) of the blast site, consists of heavier particles, which fall to earth within several hours. **Distant** fallout of lighter particles entering the troposphere usually returns to Earth at about the same latitude as the source within several weeks. If fallout enters the stratosphere, it can be scattered across the globe often years later. RADIOACTIVE DECAY particles include strontium-90, potassium-40, carbon-14 and iodine-131. These elements contaminate food and water, and when accumulated in the human body, can cause RADIATION SICKNESS, leukaemia and bone cancer. *See also* TEST BAN TREATY

fallow deer Medium-sized DEER native to woodlands in Asia Minor and parts of Europe. The summer coat is fawn with white spots. Its winter coat is a uniform greyish-brown. The males have broad antlers. Height: 90cm (3ft) at the shoulder. Species *Dama dama*.

family Taxonomic category ranking above a GENUS and below an ORDER. *See also* TAXONOMY

family Basic unit of social organization. Most families are based on KINSHIP through blood, MARRIAGE or ADOPTION. The family's primary functions are reproductive, economic, social and educational. A **nuclear** family consists only of parents and their children. Polygamy and the cohabitation of several related nuclear families creates an **extended** family. Since the 19th century, economic and social developments have altered the traditional family structure in Western industrialized societies. In particular, the increasing rate of DIVORCE has created many more one-parent families.

family planning Alternative term for CONTRACEPTION

famine Extreme prolonged shortage of food, produced by both natural and man-made causes. If famine persists, it can result in widespread starvation and death. Famine is often associated with DROUGHT or alterations in weather patterns which lead to crop failure and the destruction of livestock. However, warfare and complex political situations are equally likely causes.

Fangio, Juan Manuel (1911–95) Argentine racing driver. One of the best drivers of all time, he was Formula One world champion five times (1951, 1954–57), and on his retirement (1958) had won a total of 24 grands prix.

Fanon, Frantz Omar (1925–61) Martinique psychiatrist and theorist of Third World revolution. Educated in France, he left to practise psychiatry in Algeria. Fanon wrote *Black Skin, White Masks* (1952) and *The Wretched of the Earth* (1961). In the latter, he called for a peasant revolution against Western colonialism.

fantail Small bird with a long, fan-shaped tail, native to the forests of SE Asia and Australasia. They are often classified with FLYCATCHERS in the family Muscicapidae; others put them in a separate family, Rhipiduridae. There are *c*.40 species in the genus *Rhipidura*. Length: 15–20cm (6–8in). A fantail is also a variety of domestic PIGEON.

FAO *See* FOOD AND AGRICULTURE ORGANIZATION

Farabi, Abu Nasr al- (d.950) Islamic philosopher. Influenced by NEOPLATONISM, he argued that prophets should fulfil the legislative role accorded to poets by Plato. Al-Farabi attempted to reconcile ARISTOTLE and Islam. *See also* AVICENNA

farad (symbol F) Unit of CAPACITANCE. It is equal to the capacitance of a CAPACITOR that acquires a charge of 1 coulomb when a POTENTIAL DIFFERENCE of 1 VOLT is applied across the plates. It is a very large unit, and the microfarad (symbol μF), or one millionth of a farad, and the picofarad (symbol pF), or one million-millionth of a farad are commonly used.

Faraday, Michael (1791–1867) English experimental physicist and chemist. A student of Sir Humphry DAVY, in 1825 he became director of the laboratories at the Royal Institution, London. Faraday's early work was on the liquefaction of gases, and in 1825 he discovered BENZENE. After discovering (1832) the process of ELECTROLYSIS, he went on to formulate the laws that control it (FARADAY'S LAWS). Faraday also discovered the relationship between ELECTRICITY and MAGNETISM, providing proof of ELECTROMAGNETIC INDUCTION. In 1831, he built the first electrical GENERATOR and the first TRANSFORMER. The unit of CAPACITANCE (the farad) is named after him. Faraday's work was developed by James Clerk MAXWELL into a single mathematical theory of ELECTROMAGNETISM. He inaugurated the annual Christmas lectures at the Royal Institution.

Faraday's laws Two laws of ELECTROLYSIS and three of ELECTROMAGNETIC INDUCTION formulated by Michael FARADAY. The **electrolysis** laws state that (1) the amount of chemical change during electrolysis is proportional to the charge passed, and (2) the amount of chemical change produced in a substance by a certain amount of ELECTRICITY is proportional to the electrochemical equivalent of that substance. Faraday's laws of **induction** state that (1) an electromagnetic force is induced in a CONDUCTOR if the MAGNETIC FIELD surrounding it changes, (2) the electromagnetic force is proportional to the rate of change of the field, and (3) the direction of the induced electromagnetic force depends on the field's orientation.

farce (lat. *farcire*, to stuff) Comic drama typified by stereotypical characterizations, improbable plot lines and emphasis on physical humour. One of the earliest examples is Shakespeare's *Comedy of Errors* (c.1593). The "bedroom farce" was developed in France by Georges FEYDEAU. Oscar Wilde's *The Importance of Being Earnest* (1895) opened up new dramatic possibilities.

Far East Countries of E and SE Asia. They include China, Japan, North and South Korea, Mongolia, E Siberia in Russia, Vietnam, Laos, Cambodia, Thailand, Malaysia, Burma (Myanmar), Indonesia and the Philippines.

Fargo, William George (1818–81) US businessman. In 1844 he organized, with Henry Wells, a carrier service between Buffalo and the West. Wells, Fargo and Company then set up an express service between New York and San Francisco to cater for the gold rush. In 1850, the company merged with two others to form the American Express Company.

farming *See* AGRICULTURE

Farnese Italian family who ruled (1545–1731) the duchy of Parma and Piacenza. In 1534, **Alessandro** Farnese (1468–1549) became pope as PAUL III. He created the duchy for his family and commissioned Antonio da Sangallo to build the Farnese Palace, Rome. Paul III's grandson, **Alessandro** Farnese (1545–92), was a general in the service of PHILIP II of Spain. He distinguished himself against the Turks at the Battle of LEPANTO (1571). In 1578,

Alessandro was appointed governor-general of the Spanish Netherlands. He captured Antwerp (1585) and secured possession of the S Netherlands. In 1590, Alessandro forced HENRY IV of France to raise the siege of Paris.

Farouk (1920–65) King of Egypt (1936–52), son of King FUAD I. He alienated many Egyptians by his personal extravagance and corruption. His ambitious foreign policy ended in defeat in the first ARAB-ISRAELI WAR (1948), and he was overthrown in a military coup led by Gamal Abdel NASSER.

Farquhar, George (1678–1707) Irish playwright. His RESTORATION DRAMAS were distinguished by their humour and depth of character. Among his plays are *The Constant Couple* (1699), *The Recruiting Officer* (1706) and *The Beaux' Stratagem* (1707).

Farragut, David Glasgow (1801–70) US admiral. He served under David Porter in the WAR OF 1812. In 1862 Farragut was given command of the Western Gulf Blockading Squadron in the American CIVIL WAR and sailed up the Mississippi River to defeat the Confederate flotilla protecting the New Orleans forts. Farragut's most famous victory was at the Battle of Mobile Bay (1864), where he ignored torpedoes to capture the Confederate forts. He became (1866) the first US admiral.

Farrakhan, Louis (1933–) US leader of the Nation of Islam, a black separatist organization. He was recruited into the BLACK MUSLIMS in the 1950s by MALCOLM X. Farrakhan is a charismatic advocate of its racial exclusivity, and in 1976 formed the Nation of Islam, claiming greater adherence to the teachings of Elijah MUHAMMAD. He has been accused of inciting anger against other US minorities, particularly Jews. In 1995, Farrakhan organized a large political demonstration, assembling 400,000 men in a "Million Man March" on Washington.

Farrell, J.T. (James Thomas) (1904–79) US writer. He is best known for his trilogy about Studs Lonigan (1932–35). Set in a poor Irish community in Chicago, it is typical of his harshly realistic treatment of modern city life. Later fiction includes 10 novels of a projected 25-volume series called *A Universe of Time*.

Farrell, Terry (1938–) English post-modern architect known for his witty imagery and anthropomorphism. Farrell's projects include the redevelopment (1991) of Charing Cross Station, London. His strategies include breaking down the verticality of buildings by introducing variations in colour and banding. *See also* POST-MODERNISM

fascism Political movement founded in Italy by Benito MUSSOLINI (1919), characterized by NATIONALISM, TOTALITARIANISM and anti-communism. The term also applied to the regimes of Adolf HITLER in Germany (1933) and Francisco FRANCO in Spain (1936). A reaction to the RUSSIAN REVOLUTION (1917) and the spread of COMMUNISM, the movement based its appeal on the fear of financial instability among the middle-classes and on a wider social discontent. Basic to fascist ideas were: glorification of the state and total subordination to its authority, suppression of all political opposition, stern enforcement of law and order, the supremacy of the leader as the embodiment of high ideals and an aggressive militarism aimed at achieving national greatness. It also typically encouraged racist and xenophobic attitudes and policies. Fascism was discredited by defeat in World War 2, but in the 1990s, far-right nationalist groups have re-emerged in many countries. *See also* NATIONAL SOCIALISM

Fashoda Incident (1898) Confrontation between British and French forces on the Upper Nile, Sudan. Britain's aim to establish a link between the Cape and the Nile conflicted with French ambition to expand from the

Atlantic to the Red Sea. A British force under Lord KITCH-ENER met a French column under Jean Baptiste Marchand. Conflict was avoided when the French withdrew.

Fassbinder, Rainer Werner (1946–82) German film director. A leading figure in modern German cinema, he was known for his radical, hypnotic, low-budget productions. Fiercely political, Fassbinder's films include *The Bitter Tears of Petra von Kant* (1972), *The Marriage of Eva Braun* (1979) and *Veronika Voss* (1982).

fast breeder reactor *See* NUCLEAR REACTOR

fat Mixture of LIPIDS that is solid at normal body temperatures. They are insoluble in water, but dissolve in organic solvents such as ether, carbon tetrachloride, chloroform and benzene. Most common biological fats are triglycerides: ESTERS in which one molecule of GLYCEROL is bound to three molecules of FATTY ACIDS, each having 12 to 18 carbon atoms. Animal fats are esters of **saturated** fatty acids; vegetable OILS are esters of **unsaturated** fatty acids. Animal fats are used in food, SOAP and CANDLES. Vegetable fats and oils are used in soap, MARGARINE, PAINT and LUBRICANTS. Fats are the major storage energy for plants and animals, having twice the calorific value of CARBOHYDRATES. In animals, fat is deposited in the subcutaneous layer beneath the skin and deep within the body as a specialized ADIPOSE TISSUE. It serves as an insulator and protects internal organs. **Brown** fat is found particularly in newborn and hibernating mammals. It is more richly supplied with blood vessels and is more readily converted into heat. OBESITY (excess of body fat) occurs when diet exceeds physical exercise. Research indicates that the consumption of high levels of saturated animal fats can increase the risk of heart disease.

Fatah, al- *See* PALESTINE LIBERATION ORGANIZATION

Fates In Greek mythology, the three goddesses of human destiny. Called the *Moirae* by the Greeks, they correspond to the Roman *Parcae* and the Germanic NORNS. Clotho spun the thread of life; Lachesis, the element of chance, measured it; and Atropos, the inevitable, cut it.

Fathers of the Church Early Christian writers whose works are held as orthodox. They include the Apostolic Fathers and the eight **Doctors of the Church**. The four Doctors of the Latin Church are St AMBROSE, St JEROME, St AUGUSTINE and St GREGORY I. The four Doctors of the

Greek church are St BASIL THE GREAT, St John CHRYSOS-TOM, St ATHANASIUS and St Gregory Nazianzen.

fatigue In general, mental or physical tiredness after activity; in physiology, an inability to function at normal levels of physical and mental activity. Muscle fatigue results from the accumulation of LACTIC ACID in the muscle tissue and the depletion of GLYCOGEN.

Fatima (606–32) Daughter of the prophet MUHAMMAD, and wife of ALI. Fatima is revered by the SHI'A sect of ISLAM.

Fatimid SHI'A dynasty who claimed the caliphate on the basis of their descent from FATIMA. The dynasty was founded by Said ibn Husayn at the end of the 9th century. The Fatimids quickly overthrew the SUNNI rulers in most of NW Africa. By ibn Husayn's death (934), the Fatimid empire had expanded into s Europe, and in 969 they captured Egypt and established the Mosque and University of Al-Azhar, Cairo. By the end of the 11th century, Egypt was all that remained of the empire.

fatty acid Organic compound consisting of a CAR-BOXYLIC ACID group (–COOH) bound to a long hydrocarbon chain. Examples of **saturated** fatty acids (those with only single bonds in their hydrocarbon chain) are acetic acid and palmitic acid; **unsaturated** fatty acids (one double bond) include oleic acid, and **polyunsaturated** fatty acids (two or more double bonds) include linoleic acid. FATS normally contain saturated fatty acids; OILS contain unsaturated fatty acids. **Essential** fatty acids (EFAs) are polyunsaturated. They are essential to the human DIET because they cannot be manufactured by the body. They act as precursors of PROSTAGLANDIN. Diets in which EFAs form a high proportion of total fat intake result in lower levels of CHOLESTEROL. An adult human requires 2–10g of linoleic acid or its equivalent per day.

Faulkner, William Cuthbert (1897–1962) US novelist. *Sartoris* (1929) was the first in a series of novels set in the fictional Mississippi county of Yoknapatawpha. *The Sound and the Fury* (1929) and *As I Lay Dying* (1930) utilize a STREAM OF CONSCIOUSNESS narrative. *Light in August* (1932) and *Absalom, Absalom!* (1936) examine the effects of racism in the Deep South. Faulkner was awarded the 1949 Nobel Prize for literature. He won Pulitzer Prizes for *A Fable* (1951) and his final novel, *The*

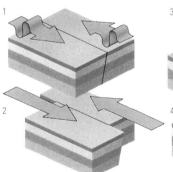
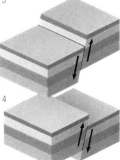
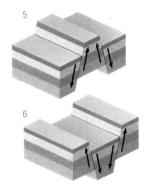

▲**fault** The Earth's crust is subjected to enormous forces, and the stress creates faults. In a tear fault (1) the stresses cause horizontal movement. The forces build up until they are released in a sudden movement (2), often causing earthquakes. In a normal fault (3) the rocks are pulled apart, causing one side to slip down along the plane of the fault. In a reverse fault (4) the rocks on either side of the fault are forced together. One side rises above the other along the fault plane. In a horst fault (5) the central section is left protruding due to compression from both sides or the sinking of the bracketing rock. A rift valley (6) has a sunken central section, formed either by compression or the outward movement of the two valley sides.

▶ **fax** A fax machine converts text or images fed into the machine (1) into a digital code (2). The code is created by shining light on tiny strips of the document in turn (3). Sensors (4) detect the amount of light that bounces back. Where ink is present, little light is reflected, creating an electrical pulse of low voltage. A high voltage results when light is reflected from white paper. The digital code is converted by a modem in the fax into an analogue signal (5) and transmitted to the receiving fax machine (6) via the telephone network. A modem in the second machine converts the analogue code back into a digital code (7), then a printer (8) interprets the digital code and produces the hard facsimile copy (9). Each machine has its own number which is dialled in via a keyboard (10) on the sending machine.

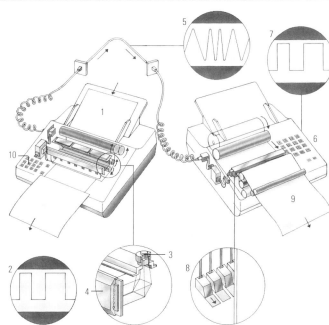

Reivers (1962). Faulkner wrote the screenplays for *To Have and Have Not* (1945) and *The Big Sleep* (1946).

fault In geology, a fracture in the Earth's crust along which movement has occurred. The result of PLATE TEC-TONICS, faults are classified by the type of movement. Vertical movements in the crust cause **normal** and **reverse** faults, while horizontal movements result in **tear** faults. Faults can occur in groups creating **horsts** (block mountains) or **grabens** (rift valleys). *See artwork*, p.301

Fauré, Gabriel Urbain (1845–1924) French Romantic composer renowned for his intimate, restrained compositions. They include many songs, such as *Clair de lune* (1889); chamber music, such as *Elégie* (1883); and the *Requiem* (1887). Fauré was director (1905–22) of the Paris Conservatoire.

Faust Semi-legendary German doctor and magician of the early 16th century. According to legend, he sold his soul to the DEVIL (Mephistopheles). The story inspired Christopher Marlowe's play *Dr Faustus* (1604). In his two-part poetic drama *Faust* (1808, 1832), GOETHE transformed the doctor into a romantic symbol.

fauvism Expressionist art style based on vivid, non-naturalistic colours. MATISSE was the leading figure and, with SIGNAC and DERAIN, exhibited at the Salon d'Automne (1905). A critic described their work as something produced by wild animals (*fauves*). Other members of the group included DUFY, VLAMINCK and BRAQUE. Although fauvism was short-lived, its influence on EXPRESSIONISM was profound.

Fawcett, Dame Millicent Garrett (1847–1929) English feminist, sister of Elizabeth Garrett ANDERSON. As president of the National Union of Women's Suffrage Societies (1897–1919), she was a leading figure in the SUFFRAGETTE MOVEMENT. Fawcett was a vigorous campaigner in the struggle to extend the FRANCHISE to women. She also founded Newnham College, Cambridge, one of the first women's colleges of higher education in Britain.

Fawkes, Guy (1570–1606) English conspirator in the GUNPOWDER PLOT (1605). He was enlisted by Roman Catholic conspirators in a plot against JAMES I and Parliament. The plot was betrayed, and Fawkes was arrested, surrounded by barrels of gunpowder, and later executed. Traditionally, an effigy called a "guy" is burned on 5 November, the anniversary of the intended explosion.

fax (facsimile transmission) Equipment by which text, photographs and drawings can be transmitted and received through a TELEPHONE system. The image, on paper, is scanned to translate it into a series of electrical pulses. Inside the fax machine, a MODEM converts the pulses into a form that can be transmitted through the telephone system. At the receiving end, the fax machine's modem converts the signals back into pulses, and prints these as dots to build up a copy of the original document.

FBI *See* FEDERAL BUREAU OF INVESTIGATION

feather One of the skin appendages that make up the plumage of birds. Feathers are composed of the fibrous protein KERATIN and they provide insulation and enable flight. They also serve camouflage and display functions. Most birds moult at least twice a year. *See also* MOULTING

February Revolution (1848) French insurrection that overthrew the government of LOUIS PHILIPPE. The Revolution began in Paris following the economic crisis of 1847–48 and agitation for parliamentary reform. Led by bourgeois radicals and working-class revolutionaries, it created the short-lived Second Republic in France, and set off popular uprisings and unrest throughout Europe. *See also* REVOLUTIONS OF 1848

Fechner, Gustav Theodor (1801–87) German physician and psychologist who helped found experimental psychology by using objective methods to study psychophysics – the relationships of physical stimuli to sensation and PERCEPTION. **Fechner's law** states (incorrectly) that the relationship between the strength of a stimulus and the perceived intensity of a sensation is logarithmic.

Federal Bureau of Investigation (FBI) US federal government agency that investigates violations of federal law. Its findings are reported to the attorney general and various nationwide attorneys for decisions on prosecution. Established in 1908, its autonomy was strengthened under the directorship of J. Edgar HOOVER (1924–72). The agency was criticized for its role in the WATERGATE SCANDAL (1972–74). Its headquarters are in Washington, D.C., and its director is appointed by the president, subject to Senate approval.

federalism Political system that allows states united under a central government to maintain a measure of independence. Examples include the USA, Australia, Canada, Germany, India and Switzerland. Central government has supreme authority, but the component states have a considerable amount of autonomy in such matters as education and health. *See also* DEVOLUTION

Federalist Party Early US political party that favoured FEDERALISM. *The Federalist* (1788) was a series of 85 political essays mainly written by Alexander HAMILTON, assisted by James MADISON and JOHN JAY. Following the ratification of the Constitution, George WASHINGTON formed a new government. A major split soon emerged within the cabinet, between a Federalist group led by Alexander Hamilton and an Anti-Federalist Party led by Thomas JEFFERSON. The Anti-Federalists later formed the DEMOCRATIC PARTY. The Federalists were conservatives; favouring business and land-owning interests, and pursuing a pro-British foreign policy. The election of a second Federalist president, John ADAMS, led to the ALIEN AND SEDITION ACTS (1798). The Federalists increasingly became the party of New England, and they disintegrated after the election of 1816.

Federal Reserve System CENTRAL BANK of the United States, established (1913) to maintain sound monetary and credit conditions. Twelve regional banks are supervised by a Federal Reserve Board of governors appointed by the president. All national banks are members, as are many state and commercial banks. The Federal Reserve System regulates money flow and credit by varying its discount rate on loans to member banks and by varying the percentage of total deposits member banks must keep in reserve.

feedback In technology, process by which an electronic or mechanical CONTROL SYSTEM monitors and regulates itself. Feedback works by returning part of the "output" signal of a system to its "input" device. **Negative** feedback tends to reduce the input and is used in AMPLIFIERS to reduce noise distortion. **Positive** feedback tends to reinforce the input signal and can cause the output to oscillate, producing the high-pitched screech heard on public-address systems when the MICROPHONE picks up feedback from the LOUDSPEAKERS. *See also* BIOFEEDBACK

Feininger, Lyonel (1871–1956) US painter. In 1887, he left the US for Europe and became involved with CUBISM. Feininger evolved a distinctive style, portraying figurative scenes in patterns of interconnecting planes coloured to resemble prisms. He exhibited with the BLAUE REITER (1913) and taught at the BAUHAUS (1919–33). In 1937, Feininger returned to the US and produced some of his best work, such as *Dawn* (1938).

Feldman, Morton (1926–87) US composer. In the 1950s, he worked with John CAGE. Some of his works explore chance, with decisions left for the performers to make. Works include *Rothko Chapel* (1971) and *The Viola in my Life* (1970–71).

feldspar (felspar) Most important group of rock-forming minerals and the constituents of IGNEOUS ROCK. Feldspars all contain aluminium, silicon and oxygen, but with varying proportions of potassium, sodium and calcium. The two major types are ORTHOCLASE and PLAGIOCLASE. Hardness 6–6.5; r.d. 2.5–2.8.

Fellini, Federico (1920–93) Italian film director. His second film, *I Vitelloni* (1953), established his characteristic blend of satire, autobiography and humanism. *La Strada* (1954) won an Academy Award for best foreign film. Fellini won a second Oscar for *Le notti di Cabiria* (1957). *La Dolce Vita* (1960) was a controversial success. Fellini won two more Oscars for best foreign film: $8\frac{1}{2}$ (1963) and *Amarcord* (1974).

feminism Movement that promotes equal rights for women. One of the first feminist texts was Mary Wollstonecraft's *Vindication of the Rights of Women* (1792). In the US, Elizabeth Cady STANTON organized (1848) the Seneca Falls Convention on WOMEN'S RIGHTS. In late 19th-century Britain, the SUFFRAGETTE MOVEMENT was formed, leaders included Emmeline PANKHURST and Millicent Garrett FAWCETT. The women's movement gained further impetus during the two World Wars, as women took on employment previously confined to men. The growing economic independence of women was championed by Virginia WOOLF in *A Room of One's Own* (1929). The **women's liberation** movement grew out of texts such as *The Second Sex* (1949) by Simone de BEAUVOIR, *The Golden Notebook* (1962) by Doris LESSING, *The Feminine Mystique* (1963) by Betty FRIEDAN and *The Female Eunuch* (1970) by Germaine GREER. "Women's lib" argued that issues of sexual politics were relevant in both professional and personal relationships. It also challenged gender stereotypes. Practical demands were focused on attaining social and economic equality. In the US, the Equal Employment Opportunity Commission was created (1964) and Betty Friedan organized (1966) the National Organization for Women (NOW). The contraceptive PILL, introduced in the 1960s, appeared to give women greater control over their own SEXUAL REPRODUCTION. In the UK, the Abortion Act (1967) ushered in the notion of a women's right to choose whether to bear a child. The Equal Pay Act (1970), the Sex Discrimination Acts (1975, 1976) and the creation (1975) of the Equal Opportunities Commission gave legal force to many feminist demands.

femur Thigh bone extending from the hip to the knee. It is the longest and strongest bone of the human SKELETON.

fencing Sport of swordsmanship using blunt weapons: the foil, épée and sabre. Fencers wear protective jackets and breeches, gloves and wire-mesh masks. In competitions, electronic sensors register hits, which score one point each. It has been an Olympic sport since 1896.

feng shui (Chin. under the canopy of heaven) Study of harmony with nature, based on the Chinese philosophy of TAOISM. The BOOK OF CHANGES outlines the principles of YIN AND YANG, whose balance provides harmony. Feng shui extends these ideas to architecture and interior design.

Fenian movement Secret Irish-American revolutionary society, named after the Fianna, an ancient Irish military force. The Great Potato Famine (1845–49) spurred the Young Ireland uprising (1848), whose failure prompted many revolutionaries to emigrate. In the United States, John O'Mahoney founded (1848) the Fenian Brotherhood. In Ireland, James Stephens formed (1858) the **Irish Republican Brotherhood (IRB)**. The growing strength of the transatlantic movement led the British government to arrest the leaders of the IRB. In 1867, James Kelly led the abortive Fenian Rising. The Fenians split into several factions: the HOME RULE and Land League movements led by Charles Stewart PARNELL and Michael DAVITT, and SINN FÉIN led by Arthur

GRIFFITH. Patrick PEARSE led the IRB in the abortive EASTER RISING (1916). In 1919, Michael COLLINS formed the IRISH REPUBLICAN ARMY (IRA).

fennec fox (desert FOX) Nocturnal fox native to the deserts of N Africa and Kuwait; smallest member of the DOG family. It has a sandy-coloured coat and huge, pointed ears. The fennec fox feeds on rodents, lizards, birds and insects. Length excluding tail: 40cm (16in).

fennel Tall, perennial herb of the PARSLEY family, native to S Europe. The seeds and extracted oil are used to add a liquorice flavour to medicines, liqueurs and foods. It grows to 1m (3.2ft). Family Apiaceae/Umbelliferae; genus *Foeniculum vulgare*.

Fens Lowland region of E England, W and S of the WASH, including parts of Lincolnshire, Cambridgeshire, Suffolk and Norfolk. In the 17th century, a major reclamation of this marshy area created the Bedford Level. The Fens are extremely fertile and intensive cultivation yields cereals, fruits and vegetables. Length: *c*.117km (73mi). Width: 55km (35mi).

Fenton, Roger (1819–69) English photographer whose carefully composed portraits and landscape studies earned him enduring acclaim. Fenton's plates of the Crimean War are among the first photographs of combat.

fenugreek Annual herb native to the Mediterranean. Its brownish seeds are used in curries and the leaves in salads.

Ferber, Edna (1887–1968) US writer. She won a Pulitzer Prize for her first novel, *So Big* (1924). Many of her later novels were made into films, such as *Show Boat* (1926), *Cimarron* (1930), *Giant* (1952) and *Ice Palace* (1958). Ferber also wrote several plays with George S. KAUFMAN, including *Dinner at Eight* (1932).

Ferdinand I (1503–64) Holy Roman emperor (1558–64), king of Bohemia and of Hungary (1526–64). His rule in Hungary was contested by JOHN I, then by JOHN II, both of whom were aided by the Turkish sultan. In Bohemia, Ferdinand secured the absolute rule of his HABSBURG dynasty. In Germany, he helped defeat the Protestant Schmalkaldic League (1546–47). Although a devout Catholic, Ferdinand negotiated the Peace of AUGSBURG (1555) and worked for reconciliation between the two churches. He was succeeded by Maximilian II.

Ferdinand II (1578–1637) Holy Roman emperor (1619–37), king of Bohemia (1617–37) and Hungary (1618–37), grandson of FERDINAND I. Educated by the Jesuits, he championed the COUNTER REFORMATION. In 1619 the mainly Protestant diet of Bohemia chose FREDERICK V as their ruler, precipitating the THIRTY YEARS' WAR. Ferdinand regained Bohemia (1620) and Hungary (1621). GUSTAVUS II of Sweden's entry into the war turned the tide against Ferdinand. He was succeeded by his son, FERDINAND III.

Ferdinand III (1608–57) Holy Roman emperor (1637–57), king of Bohemia and Hungary (1625–57), son of FERDINAND II. In 1634, he succeeded WALLENSTEIN as commander of the imperial army in the THIRTY YEARS' WAR. After Ferdinand's accession, the HABSBURG empire suffered a devastating series of defeats, and he was forced to conclude the Peace of WESTPHALIA (1648).

Ferdinand (1861–1948) Prince (1887–1908) and tsar (1908–18) of Bulgaria. In 1908, he declared Bulgaria independent of the Ottoman Empire. Ferdinand allied Bulgaria with Serbia, Greece and Montenegro in the first of the BALKAN WARS (1912), but Bulgaria's territorial gains were largely lost in the second war (1913) to its former allies. In a bid to regain territory, Ferdinand entered World War 1 on the side of the CENTRAL POWERS. Further defeats saw him abdicate in favour of his son, Boris III.

Ferdinand V (1452–1516) (Ferdinand the Catholic) King of Castile and León (1474–1504), of Aragon (as Ferdinand II) (1479–1516), of Sicily (1468–1516), and of Naples (as Ferdinand III) (1504–16). Ferdinand became joint king of Castile and León after marrying ISABELLA I in 1469, and inherited Aragon from his father, John II, in 1479. After he and Isabella conquered the Moorish kingdom of Granada (1492), they ruled over a united Spain. They sponsored the voyage of Christopher COLUMBUS to the New World (1492), expelled the Jews from Spain, and initiated the Spanish INQUISITION. After Isabella's death (1504), Ferdinand acted as regent in Castile for their insane daughter, Joanna, and then for her son, Charles I (later Holy Roman emperor CHARLES V).

Ferdinand I (1345–83) King of Portugal (1367–83). He fought three wars for control of Castile. The first war (1369–71) was settled by Ferdinand's promise of marriage to Leonor, daughter of Henry II of Castile. He reneged on the agreement and launched a second war (1372) with JOHN OF GAUNT that resulted in the Castilian siege of Lisbon (1373). A third war (1381–82) also ended in humiliation for Ferdinand.

Ferdinand VI (*c*.1712–1759) King of Spain (1746–59), son and successor of PHILIP V. He dismissed his father's chief minister, Ensenada, and reduced the influence of his stepmother Elizabeth Farnese. The death of his wife (1758) plunged Ferdinand into a deep grief from which he never recovered.

Ferdinand VII (1784–1833) King of Spain (1808–33), son of CHARLES IV. As prince, he felt excluded from government by Godoy and his mother, and sought the support of NAPOLEON I. In 1807, Ferdinand was arrested for treason by his father. In 1808, a rising resulted in his father's abdication, but Napoleon began the PENINSULAR WAR that toppled Ferdinand and installed Joseph Bonaparte. During the war, Ferdinand was imprisoned in France. In 1812, Spain proclaimed a liberal constitution. Upon his restoration (1814), Ferdinand abolished the new constitution. Liberal opposition organized secret societies, such as the Carbonari, that forced him to reinstate the constitution (1820). In 1823, with the help of French troops, Ferdinand crushed the liberals and revoked the constitution. During his reign, Spain lost all of its North American colonies. He abandoned the Salic law so that his daughter, ISABELLA II, could succeed him. Conservatives (CARLISTS) supported the claim of Ferdinand's brother, Don Carlos, and civil war ensued.

Ferdinand I (1751–1825) King of the Two Sicilies (1816–25), son of the future CHARLES III of Spain. He inherited the kingdoms of Naples and of Sicily on his father's accession (1759). In 1816, they were combined as the Kingdom of the Two Sicilies. Ferdinand's marriage (1768) to Marie Caroline, sister of MARIE ANTOINETTE, encouraged him to pursue reactionary and pro-Austrian policies. He was driven from his throne by the French during the FRENCH REVOLUTIONARY WARS and NAPOLEONIC WARS but was restored in 1815. In 1820, a rising forced him to concede constitutional monarchy, but with Austrian aid, absolutism was restored in 1821.

Fergana Region in the Uzbekistan mountains, W central Asia on the SILK ROUTE. It is one of the world's oldest continuously farmed areas. The chief town of the valley is now also called Fergana pop. (1990) 183,000.

Ferguson, Alex (Alexander) Chapman (1941–) Scottish football manager. In Scotland, he managed St Mirren (1974–78) and Aberdeen (1978–86). In 1983, he won the European Cup Winner's Cup. As manager (1986–) of Manchester United, Ferguson led them to victory in the European Cup (1999), six Premier League championships (1993, 1994, 1996, 1997, 1999, 2000) and three FA Cup victories (1990, 1994, 1996).

Ferlinghetti, Lawrence (1919–) US poet. A leader of the BEAT MOVEMENT, he opened (1953) the City Lights bookstore in San Francisco and began publishing beat authors such as Allen GINSBERG. His colloquial poetry includes *A Coney Island of the Mind* (1958).

Fermanagh District in SW Northern Ireland; the county town is Enniskillen. The district is hilly in the NE and SW. Cattle raising is important. Area: 1,876sq km (724sq mi). Pop. (1991) 54,033.

Fermat, Pierre de (1601–65) French mathematician . With Blaise PASCAL, he helped to formulate the theory of PROBABILITY and, by showing that light travels along the shortest optical path (**Fermat's principle**), he laid the foundation for geometric optics. In mathematics, Fermat is best known for his development of modern NUMBER THEORY. It was recently discovered that DIFFERENTIAL CALCULUS, though, to be invented by Sir Isaac NEWTON, was communicated to him in a series of letters by Fermat. *See also* FERMAT'S LAST THEOREM

Fermat's last theorem Hypothesis, first stated by Pierre de Fermat, that for all integers $n > 2$, there are no natural NUMBERS x, y and z that satisfy the equation $x^n + y^n = z^n$. Fermat wrote that he had found a proof, but died without revealing it. Attempts at a valid proof enriched the area of algebraic number theory. In 1993, Andrew Wiles of Princeton University announced a proof, but it was found to contain a gap. Further work repaired this, and the proof was widely accepted in 1995.

fermentation Energy-yielding metabolic process by which sugar and starch molecules are broken down to carbon dioxide and ALCOHOL in the absence of air (ANAEROBIC respiration). Catalyzed by ENZYMES, it is used for WINE- and BREAD-making, beer-BREWING and CHEESE maturation. The intoxicating effect of fermented fruits has been known since 4000 BC.

Fermi, Enrico (1901–54) US physicist, b. Italy. His early career in Italy was spent developing (independently of Paul DIRAC) a form of quantum statistics, now known as **Fermi-Dirac statistics**. Unlike the method developed by Satyendranath BOSE and Albert EINSTEIN, Fermi-Dirac statistics assumes that the SUBATOMIC PARTICLES known as FERMIONS behave according to the EXCLUSION PRINCIPLE outlined by Wolfgang PAULI. Fermi was awarded the 1938 Nobel Prize for physics for his work on the bombardment of URANIUM by NEUTRONS. In 1940, in the USA, Fermi produced the first synthetic transuranic element, NEPTUNIUM. In 1942, he produced the first controlled nuclear CHAIN REACTION. At Los Alamos, Fermi worked on the MANHATTAN PROJECT to develop the atomic bomb. He opposed Edward TELLER on the development of the HYDROGEN BOMB. The element FERMIUM was named after him. *See also* NUCLEAR WEAPON; QUANTUM THEORY

fermion Any SUBATOMIC PARTICLE that obeys the EXCLUSION PRINCIPLE and has a half-odd integer SPIN (such as 0.5, 1.5, or 2.5). Examples are PROTONS, ELECTRONS and QUARKS. *See also* BOSON

fermium (symbol Fm) Radioactive metallic TRANSURANIC ELEMENT of the ACTINIDE SERIES. First identified (1952) as a decay product of U^{255} from the first HYDROGEN BOMB explosion. Ten isotopes have been identified. Properties: at.no. 100; most stable isotope Fm^{257} (half-life 80 days).

fern Non-flowering plant. Ferns grow in warm, moist areas; there are $c.$10,000 species. The best-known genus *Pteridium* (BRACKEN) grows on moors and in open woodland. Ferns are characterized by two generations: the conspicuous SPOROPHYTE, which possesses leafy fronds, stems, RHIZOMES and roots, and reproduces by SPORES usually on the leaves; and the GAMETOPHYTE, which resembles moss and produces sperm and ova. Fronds unroll from curled "fiddleheads". Phylum Filicinophyta.

Ferrara Medieval walled city in N Italy, capital of Ferrara province. It contains the cathedral of St Giórgio (1135) and Este Castle (1385–1570). An independent commune in the 10th century, it was ruled by the House of Este from 1240, who made it a centre of the RENAISSANCE. Under papal rule from 1598, its prosperity declined. In 1797, it was ceded to France but restored to papal control in 1815. Industries: agriculture, chemicals. Pop. (1996) 135,000.

Ferrari, Enzo (1898–1988) Italian racing and sports car designer and manufacturer. He began driving in 1920 with Alfa Romeo. In 1939, Ferrari founded his own company that produced the first Ferrari racing car in 1947. The company also manufactures production sports cars.

ferret European POLECAT. WEASEL-like animals, they have long necks, slender bodies, long tails, short legs and white fur. They are agile killers used to hunt rats and rabbits. Body length: 36cm (14in); weight: 700g (1.5lb). Family Mustelidae; species *Mustela putorius*.

ferry Passenger, vehicle or freight-carrying BOAT. Some high-speed passenger ferries are HYDROFOILS. Recently there has been concern over the safety of **roll-on, roll-off** (ro-ro) ferries, following disasters such as the sinking of the *Estonia* in the Baltic Sea (September 1994) that resulted in more than 900 fatalities.

Fertile Crescent Rich strip of land extending from the head of the Persian Gulf through the basins of the rivers Tigris and Euphrates and then along the Mediterranean coasts of Syria, Lebanon and Israel to the lower Nile valley. The term was coined by US archaeologist James H. Bearsted (1865–1935) to refer to the cradle of early civilizations such as those of BABYLON, ASSYRIA, ancient EGYPT, PHOENICIA and MESOPOTAMIA.

fertility drug Drug taken to increase a woman's chances of conception and pregnancy. One of the major causes of female sterility results from insufficient secretion of pituitary HORMONES, and this can be treated with either human chorionic GONADOTROPIN or clomiphene citrate, although use of the latter has resulted in multiple births. In cases where FERTILIZATION occurs but the uterine lining is unable to support the developing fetus, the hormone progesterone may be used. *See also* ENDOMETRIOSIS

fertilization Key process in SEXUAL REPRODUCTION during which the nuclei of female and male GAMETES (sex cells) fuse to form a ZYGOTE. The zygote contains the genetic material (CHROMOSOMES) from both parents (*see* HEREDITY). In animals, the female sex cell is called the OVUM and the male cell SPERM. After fertilization, the zygote begins to divide to form an EMBRYO. Fertilization of the female OVUM by the male SPERM can be external (as in most fish, amphibians and aquatic invetebrates) or internal (as in reptiles, birds, mammals and insects). In PLANTS, the male gamete is found in POLLEN, and for most higher plants, POLLINATION occurs before fertilization. *See also* DIPLOID; HAPLOID

fertilizer Organic or inorganic substance containing nutrients – mainly nitrogen, phosphorus and potassium– that is added to soil to aid plant growth. **Organic** fertilizers include manure and compost, fish and bone meal, and guano. **Nitrogen** fertilizers are the most widely used inorganic fertilizers. Phosphorus fertilizers (**phosphates**) are made from the mineral apatite. **Potassium** fertilizers are extracted from deposits of potassium chloride. Nitrogen fertilizer in surface water promotes the growth of algae that degrades water quality and can cause EUTROPHICATION. Inorganic fertilizers suppress nitrogen-fixing bacteria, making agriculture increasingly dependent on artificial fertilizer.

Fessenden, Reginald Aubrey (1866–1932) US physicist and RADIO engineer, b. Canada. He is thought to have broadcast the first radio programme (using speech signals, not Morse code) in 1906, from a transmitter he constructed at Brant Rock, Massachusetts. Fessenden developed a new type of wireless system using continuous waves. His c.500 patents included AMPLITUDE MODULATION (AM) and the high-frequency ALTERNATOR.

fetish Inanimate object (charm) believed to possess magical power. The fetish may be a natural object, such as a stone, or a man-made object, such as a carved statue. Fetishism is a form of ANIMISM. They are believed to bring good luck or ward off evil. In psychiatry, fetishism is an abnormal sexual attachment to an inanimate object, such as a shoe or type of clothing. See also TABOO

fetus (foetus) Stage of EMBRYO development in a mammal after the main adult features are recognizable. In humans it dates from about eight weeks after conception.

feudal system Social system in most of Europe from the 9th century to the late Middle Ages, based on the tenure of land. The system originated from the need to provide a permanent group of knights to assist the king in his wars. All land was theoretically owned by the monarch, and leased to his tenants-in-chief for their attendance at court and military assistance; they in turn let out fiefs to knights in return for military service and other obligations. The lowest rank, serfs, worked their lord's land in return for the right to grow their own produce. The system ended in the 16th century in England, but lasted until the 18th century in parts of Europe and Russia. See also CAPITALISM

Feuerbach, Ludwig Andreas (1804–72) German philosopher. He studied under G.W.F. Hegel but came to reject Hegel's IDEALISM for a naturalistic form of MATERIALISM. Feuerbach's major work, The Essence of Christianity (1841), argued that religion was "the dream of the human mind", and that the proper subject of study for philosophy was man's physical nature. Feuerbach was a major influence on Karl MARX.

fever Elevation of body temperature above normal, that is 37°C (98.6°F). It is mainly caused by bacterial or viral infection and can accompany most infectious diseases.

Feydeau, Georges (1862–1921) French playwright. He wrote many popular plays, with absurd plots and sparkling dialogue, in which he pioneered 19th-century French FARCE. These include Hotel Paradiso (1894), The Lady from Maxim's (1899) and A Flea in Her Ear (1907).

Feynman, Richard Phillips (1918–88) US theoretical physicist. He worked on the MANHATTAN PROJECT to develop the atomic bomb. An inspiring teacher and orator, Feynman was professor of theoretical physics (1950–88) at the California Institute of Technology. In 1949, he introduced a graphic technique (**Feynman diagrams**) for illustrating the electromagnetic interactions between ELEMENTARY PARTICLES. In 1957, Feynman and Murray GELL-MANN proposed the theory of WEAK NUCLEAR FORCE. He shared the 1965 Nobel Prize for physics for his part in the development of QUANTUM ELECTRODYNAMICS (QED). In 1986, he was a key member of the committee that investigated the Challenger space shuttle disaster.

Fez (Fès) City in N central Morocco. Founded c.790, it is a former capital of Morocco and a sacred city of Islam containing many mosques. Industries: leather, pottery, traditional crafts, metalworking. Pop. (1993) 564,000.

Fianna Fáil ("Soldiers of Destiny") Irish political party. It was formed (1926) by those opposed to the partition of Ireland. In 1932, the party achieved power under Eamon DE VALERA, and has formed the government alone or in coalition for most years since then. It seeks the reunification of Ireland by peaceful means. See also FINE GAEL

Fibonacci, Leonardo (c.1170–c.1240) Italian mathematician. He wrote Liber abaci (c.1200), the first Western work to adopt the Arabic numerical system. Fibonacci produced the mathematical sequence named after him, in which each term is formed by the addition of the two terms preceding it. The sequence begins 0, 1, 1, 2, 3, 5, 8, 13, 21.... and so on. Many natural forms, such as leaf systems, are delimited by the **Fibonacci series**.

fibre Any of various materials consisting of thread-like strands. Natural fibres can be made into yarn, textiles and other products, including carpets and rope. The fibres consist of long narrow cells. **Animal** fibres are based on protein molecules and include WOOL, SILK, mohair, angora and horsehair. **Vegetable** fibres are based mainly on CELLULOSE and include COTTON, LINEN, FLAX, JUTE, SISAL and KAPOK. The mineral ASBESTOS is a natural, inorganic fibre. Regenerated fibres are manufactured from natural products, modified chemically. For example, RAYON is made from cellulose fibre obtained from cotton or wood. **Synthetic** fibres are made from a molten or dissolved plastic resin by forcing it through fine nozzles (spinnerets). The result is a group of filaments that are wound onto bobbins. These fibres can be used as single-strand yarn or spun to form multi-strand yarn and woven into textiles. Some synthetic fibres are made into rope, carpets and other products. Synthetic fibres include NYLON and other polyamides, POLYESTERS and ACRYLICS. Other synthetic fibres, such as carbon or metals, can be used to reinforce resins to produce extremely strong materials.

fibreglass Spun glass used as a continuous filament in textiles and electrical insulation, and in a fibrous form to reinforce plastics or for sound or heat insulation. Molten glass is drawn through spinnerets or spun through holes in a revolving dish. Combined with layers of resin, fibreglass is used for car bodies, boats and aircraft parts.

fibre optics Fine strands of glass or plastic, less than 1mm (0.04in) thick, able to transmit digital information in the form of pulses of light. Such transmission is possible because light entering an optical fibre is conducted by reflection from one end of the fibre to the other with very little loss of intensity. Fibre-optic cables can carry more information than traditional copper cables and are immune to electromagnetic interference. **Single-mode** fibres have extremely small cores and accept light only along the axis of the fibres. They are used mainly in long-distance communication. **Multi-mode** fibres are larger and accept light from a variety of angles. Optical fibres have various applications, such as the ENDOSCOPE. See also OPTICS

fibrin Insoluble, fibrous protein that is essential to BLOOD CLOTTING. Developed in the blood from a soluble protein, fibrinogen, fibrin is laid down at the site of a wound in the form of a mesh which then dries and hardens so that the bleeding stops.

fibula Long, thin outer bone of the lower leg of four- and two-legged VERTEBRATES, including humans. It articulates with the other lower leg bone (TIBIA) just below the knee.

Fichte, Johann Gottlieb (1762–1814) German philosopher. Fichte was strongly influenced by the IDEALISM of Immanuel KANT, but his Critique of All Revelation (1792) rejected Kant's doctrine of "things-in-themselves", holding that reason and man's ego structured all experience. In The Science of Knowledge (1794), Fichte argued that the absolute ego (God) is the source of all morality and knowledge, and creates both the external world and the individual ego. His patriotic lectures, *Addresses to the German Nation* (1807–08), tried to awaken German nationalism against Napoleon I.

fiddler crab Small, burrowing CRAB of the genus *Uca*. They are found worldwide on sandy beaches and salt marshes. The male has one huge claw, held in front of the body. This pincer is used in courtship displays and fights with other males. They are poor swimmers and remain in burrows during high tide. Order Decapoda.

field In physics, region in which an object is affected by a FORCE as a result of the presence nearby of another object or objects. There are various kinds of field, including ELECTRIC FIELDS and MAGNETIC FIELDS. *See also* FARADAY, MICHAEL; GRAVITATION; RELATIVITY

Fielding, Henry (1707–54) English novelist and dramatist. In the 1730s, Fielding wrote a number of satirical plays, such as *Pasquin* (1736). His first work of fiction, *An Apology for the Life of Mrs Shamela Andrews* (1741), was a parody of Samuel RICHARDSON's *Pamela* (1740). *Joseph Andrews* (1742) was his first NOVEL. Other works include *The Life of Mr Jonathan Wild the Great* (1743). Fielding strengthened the NOVEL genre through his depiction of character and narrative sophistication. His masterpiece is the picaresque novel, *Tom Jones* (1749). Fielding also founded Britain's first organized police force, the Bow Street Runners.

Field of the Cloth of Gold (1520) Meeting near Calais, N France, between HENRY VIII of England and FRANCIS I of France. Despite ostentatious displays of wealth and swaggering festivities, Francis failed to win English support for the Valois cause and Henry later formed an alliance with the Habsburg Emperor CHARLES V.

Fields, Dame Gracie (1898–1979) English singer and comedienne, b. Grace Stansfield. Her success as a music-hall entertainer led to a series of film comedies, notably *Sally in Our Alley* (1931) and *Sing As We Go* (1934). Fields' sentimental tunes, such as "Sally", entertained the troops in World War 2. She was created a dame in 1978.

Fields, W.C. (William Claud) (1880–1946) US vaudeville, film and radio comedian. Field was famous for his portrayal of hard-drinking, misanthropic braggarts in such films as *My Little Chickadee* (1940) and *Never Give a Sucker an Even Break* (1941).

Fife Region in E central Scotland between the firths of Tay and Forth; the capital is Glenrothes. Central Fife is mostly low-lying farmland. Coalfields lie in the W and E. Along the North Sea coast there are many fishing villages. St Andrews is the seat of Scotland's oldest university (1410) and the home of the Royal and Ancient Golf Club. Area: 1,305sq km (504sq mi). Pop. (1991) 341,199.

Fifteen Rebellion (1715) *See* JACOBITES

fifth column Saboteurs, spies and other non-uniformed paramilitary elements active behind the battle line, working to undermine the enemy's cause. The term dates from the Spanish CIVIL WAR (1936–39) and described Republican sympathizers in Madrid.

fig Tree, shrub or climber of the MULBERRY family, growing in warm regions, especially from the E Mediterranean to India and Malaysia. The common fig (*Ficus carica*) has tiny flowers without petals that grow inside fleshy flask-like receptacles; these become the thick outer covering holding the seeds, the true, edible fruit of the fig tree. Height: to 11.8m (39ft). Family Moraceae, genus *Ficus*.

figwort Common name for *c.*3,000 plant species of the genus *Scrophularia*. They are perennial herbaceous plants distributed worldwide. Most species have a

strong smell and bear small, greenish-yellow or purple flowers. Family Scrophulariaceae.

Fiji Independent nation in the S Pacific Ocean, consisting of more than 800 mostly volcanic islands and islets; the capital is Suva on Viti Levu island. The two largest islands, Viti Levu and Vanua Levu, rise sharply from the fertile, heavily populated coastal region to a mountainous and rugged interior. Settlement of the region dates back to the second millennium BC. Discovered by Abel TASMAN in 1643, the islands were visited by British explorers in the 18th century and became a British crown colony in 1874. Indians were subsequently imported to work on the sugar plantations and by the 1950s outnumbered the native Fijian population. In 1970, Fiji achieved independence within the Commonwealth of Nations. The election of an Indian-majority government (1987) led to a military coup by native Fijians, led by Colonel Stiveni Rabuka, and the proclamation of a republic. In 1992, Rabuka became prime minister. In 1997, Fiji was readmitted to the Commonwealth. Mahendra Chaudhry defeated Rabuka in the 1999 elections, but was ousted from parliament following a coup (May 2000), led by George Speight. Speight held Chaudhry and his cabinet hostage for 56 days, until his demands for Fiji's multiracial constitution to be abolished were met. Agriculture is the most important sector of the economy; the main products are copra, sugar and rice. Gold and silver are mined and tourism is important. Area: 18,272sq km (7,055sq mi). Pop. (2000 est.) 833,000.

filariasis Group of tropical diseases caused by infection with a nematode worm, *filaria*. The parasites, which are transmitted by insects, infiltrate the lymph glands, causing swelling and impaired drainage. Drug treatment reduces the symptoms. *See also* ELEPHANTIASIS

file In computing, a block of stored data. A file may contain information (such as a group of addresses), a document or a complete PROGRAM. It is usually stored on a HARD DISK or floppy MAGNETIC DISK. With random-access files, any item of data can be accessed immediately. With serial files, the data must be read through from the beginning until the required item is reached. *See also* DATABASE

filibuster Method of delaying a vote of a legislative assembly by making long speeches. It has particular reference in the US Senate, which did not have any method for voting to end debate until 1917. Since then a two-thirds majority has been required to close a debate.

Fillmore, Millard (1800–74) 13th US president (1850–53). He served (1833–43) in the House of Representatives, and in 1834 joined the newly formed WHIG PARTY. In 1848, Fillmore was elected vice president to Zachary TAYLOR and succeeded as president when Taylor died. In order to mediate between pro- and anti-slavery factions, he agreed to the Compromise of 1850. Fillmore's attempt to enforce the Fugitive Slave Law embittered ABOLITIONISTS and split the party. He failed to win renomination in 1852, and was succeeded by Franklin PIERCE. In the 1856 elections, Fillmore stood for the KNOW-NOTHING MOVEMENT, but was defeated by Abraham LINCOLN.

film In PHOTOGRAPHY, sensitized strips of CELLULOSE acetate or other plastic, coated on one side with a light-sensitive EMULSION, used to record photographic images. The emulsion of a black-and-white film consists of a suspension of finely divided grains of silver bromide in gelatin. After exposure, the film is kept in darkness until the latent image is made visible by developing and fixing. Film is rated according to its "speed" or sensitivity to light. This is a measure of the size of the silver bromide grains contained in the emulsion. A "fast" black-and-white film (high ASA or DIN number) gives rise to a grainy, high-contrast image, whereas "slower" film captures a greater range of tones. *See* CINEMA; SILVER NITRATE

film noir Genre of cynical, bleak films, originating in Hollywood in the 1940s. Bathed in gloomy shadows, the ominous mood of the films depicts an uneasy world, lacking ideals or moral absolutes. John HUSTON's *The Maltese Falcon* (1941) was the blueprint for other genre classics, such as *The Big Sleep* (1946) and *Touch of Evil* (1958).

filter Device for separating SOLID particles from a LIQUID or GAS, in a process known as filtration. Cars have several filters that operate by trapping solid particles in porous materials, such as paper or meshes, or by circulating the material to be filtered through a maze, such as an air filter.

fin External organ used in swimming by aquatic animals, and most highly evolved in FISHES. Fins are named according to their position. **Median** fins include the tail (caudal), typically used for propulsion and the **dorsal** and **anal** fins, used for balancing. The paired **pectoral** fins and **pelvic** fins are used for steering.

finch Any of a family (Fringillidae) of small or medium-sized birds. Finches account for more than half of the world's known bird species and are found on all continents, except Australasia and Antarctica. Most have a cone-shaped bill and feed on seeds. They are classified into three groups: those with small, triangular bills, such as the BUNTING, CANARY and SPARROW, and those specifically called finches, such as the BULLFINCH, CHAFFINCH and GOLDFINCH; those with thick, rounded bills, such as the CARDINAL and GROSBEAK; and the crossbills. Most finches build cup-shaped nests for their three to six speckled eggs.

Fine Gael Irish political party. It was founded in 1933 as a successor to the party under William COSGRAVE that had held power since the inception of the Irish Free State. Overshadowed by FIANNA FÁIL, Fine Gael has held office only four times, always in coalition with the Labour Party (1948–51, 1954–57, 1973–77, 1994–97).

Fingal's Cave Cave on Staffa Island, Inner Hebrides, Scotland. Spectacularly composed of clustered balsaltic columns, it inspired Mendelssohn's overture (1829).

Finger Lakes Series of 11 long, narrow, glacial lakes in central New York state, USA. Cayuga and Seneca are the longest, both more than *c*.60km (35mi) long. New York's wine industry is based here. Hammondsport, at the end of Keuka Lake, is the area's commercial centre. Cornell University is situated on Cayuga Lake. Finger Lakes is a popular tourist destination.

fingerprint Pattern of ridges in the dermis or deeper skin on the end of the fingers a nd thumbs. Fingerprints are specific to an individual and remain unchanged in pattern throughout life. In 1901, the British police force introduced fingerprinting as a means of identifying criminals. Today, Scotland Yard maintains a library of more than two million prints. *See also* DNA; FORENSIC SCIENCE

Finland (Suomi) Republic in N Europe. Finland has four geographical regions. In the s and w, on the gulfs of Bothnia and Finland, is a low, narrow coastal strip where most Finns live. The capital and largest city, HELSINKI, is here. The ÅLAND ISLANDS lie in the entrance to the Gulf of Bothnia. Most of the interior is a beautiful wooded plateau, with more than 60,000 lakes. The Saimaa area is Europe's largest inland water system. A third of Finland lies within

the Arctic Circle; this "land of the midnight sun" is called *Lappi* (LAPLAND). **Climate** Finland has short, warm summers; Helsinki's July average is 17°C (63°F). In Lapland, the temperatures are lower, and in June the sun never sets. Winters are long and cold; Helsinki's January average is –6°C (21°F). The North Atlantic Drift keeps the Arctic coasts free of ice. **Vegetation** Forests (birch, pine and spruce) cover 60% of Finland. The vegetation becomes more and more sparse to the N, until it merges into Arctic tundra. **History** In the 8th century, the LAPPS were forced N by Finnish-speaking settlers. In the 13th century, Sweden conquered the country. Lutheranism was established in the 16th century. Finland was devastated by wars between Sweden and Russia. Following the NORTHERN WAR (1700–21), Russia gained much Finnish land. In the NAPOLEONIC WARS, Russia conquered Finland, and it became a grand duchy (1809). Despite considerable autonomy, Finnish nationalism gained strength, fuelled by important Finnish language works. Tsar NICHOLAS II's programme of Russification (1899–1905) met fierce resistance. Following the Russian Revolution (1917), Finland declared independence. Civil war (January–May 1918) broke out between the Russian-backed Red Guard and the German-backed White Guard, led by Carl MANNERHEIM. The White Guard triumphed, and a republic was established (1919). At the outbreak of World War 2 (1939–45), Finland declared its neutrality. The Russo-Finnish War was prompted by a Soviet invasion (November 1939) and, in March 1940, Finland ceded part of KARELIA and Lake LADOGA. In 1941, Finland allied itself with Germany, and in 1944 Soviet troops invaded and forced Finland to agree armistice terms based on the 1940 resolution. Much of N Finland was destroyed in the ensuing war with Germany. The Paris Treaty (1947) confirmed the 1944 armistice agreement. In 1955, Finland joined the UN and the Nordic Council and maintained a policy of neutrality during the Cold War. Urho Kaleva Kekkonen led (1956–81) Finland through the process of reconstruction. In 1986, Finland became a full member of EFTA, and in 1995 it joined the European Union (EU). In 2000, Tarja Halonen became Finland's first female president. **Economy** In 1999, Finland was one of the 11 countries to participate in the "first wave" of the European single currency. Forests are Finland's most valuable resource. Forestry accounts for *c*.35% of exports. The chief manufactures are wood and paper products. Post-1945, the economy has diversified. Engineering, shipbuilding and textile industries have grown. Farming employs only 9% of the workforce. Livestock and dairy farming are the chief activities. The economy is slowly recovering from the recession and unemployment caused by the collapse of the Soviet bloc.

Finnish One of the two official languages of Finland and a member of the FINNO-UGRIC group of languages. It is spoken by more than 4.5 million people in Finland and by nearly a million people in Sweden, Russia and the US. SWEDISH is the other official language of Finland, spoken by *c*.300,000 inhabitants.

Finn MacCumhail (Finn MacCool or Fingal) (active 2nd or 3rd century AD) Semi-mythical Irish leader of a group of soldiers known as the Fianna. Their exploits were recorded in many ballads and poems, including those in the 12th-century *Book of Leinster* and others said to have been written by his son, OSSIAN.

Finno-Ugric Group of related languages spoken by more than 22 million people in Finland and N Norway, in Estonia and Karelia, at the N end of the River Volga and each side of the Urals, and in Hungary. The languages are unrelated to the INDO-EUROPEAN family. The

FINLAND
AREA: 338,130sq km (130,552sq mi)
POPULATION: 5,077,000
CAPITAL (POPULATION): Helsinki (532,000)

Finnic branch includes FINNISH, Estonian, Lappish, Mordvinian, Mari, Komi, Votyak, Cheremiss and Zyrian; the Ugric branch comprises HUNGARIAN, Ostyak and Mansi (Vogul). Together with the Samoyed languages, Finno-Ugric makes up the Uralic family.

Finzi, Gerald (1901–56) Influenced by Ralph VAUGHAN WILLIAMS and Edward ELGAR, Finzi mainly composed vocal works. His compositions include *Dies Natalis* (1939), a setting of passages from Thomas Traherne, and *Intimations of Immortality* (1950), a setting for tenor, chorus and orchestra of the WORDSWORTH ode. His clarinet concerto (1949) is also much admired.

fir Any of a number of evergreen trees of the PINE family, native to alpine regions of the Northern Hemisphere. The pyramid-shaped trees are prized for their beauty and fragrance. They have flat needles and cylindrical cones that shed their scales when mature. The North American BALSAM FIR is the source of Canadian BALSAM. Height: 15–90m (50–300ft). Family Pinaceae; genus *Abies*. The DOUGLAS FIR is not a true fir.

Firdausi (935–1020) Persian poet. He wrote the *Shah Nama* (*Book of Kings*), an epic poem about the history of Persia. The first major work in Persian literature, it was presented to Mahmud of Ghazni in 1010.

fire COMBUSTION of fuel to produce heat and light, often accompanied by flames and smoke. Fuels are of three types: solids, liquids and gases. The fuel must be heated to an **ignition temperature** in the presence of oxygen for fire to begin. Carbon monoxide forms when there is insufficient oxygen to burn the fuel completely. In ancient Greece and Rome, fire was considered one of the four elements. In ZOROASTRIANISM, fire is sacred. *See also* VESTA

firearm Term used usually to describe a small arm – a weapon carried and fired by one person or a small group of people. Firearms were used in Europe in the 14th century. They were, however, ineffective in close combat until *c.*1425, when a primitive trigger to bring a lighted match into contact with the gunpowder charge was invented. These **matchlocks** were heavy and cumbersome and needed a constantly lit match. The lighter flintlock (which used the spark produced by flint striking steel to ignite the powder) superseded the matchlock in the mid-17th century. In 1805, the explosive properties of mercury fulminate were discovered and, with the invention of the percussion cap (1815), it provided a surer, more efficient means of detonation. It permitted the development by 1865 of both the **centre-fire cartridge** (which has basically been the type of ammunition used in firearms ever since) and breech-loading. Another major 19th-century advance was **rifling**, which was the cutting of spiral grooves along the inside of a barrel in order to make the bullet spin in flight. In the 1830s, Samuel COLT perfected the revolver, a PISTOL which could fire several shots without the need to reload. By the 1880s, magazine RIFLES were also in use and were made more effective when a bolt action was incorporated after 1889. Development of a weapon that could fire a continuous stream of bullets began with the manually operated GATLING GUN, but the first modern MACHINE GUN was the Maxim gun, invented in the 1880s. Guns of this type dominated the trench warfare of World War 1, and by World War 2 more portable automatic weapons, light machine guns such as the Bren gun and sub-machine gun, were in use. Newer developments include gas-operated rifles, firearms with several rotating barrels and extremely high rates of fire, and small firearms that use explosive bullets.

fireball (bolide) Very bright METEOR. Fireballs have been loosely defined as meteors brighter than the planets.

firedamp In COAL mining, flammable and explosive gas

◀ **fir** Although not strictly a true fir, the largest Douglas firs, named for the botanical explorer David Douglas, grow to *c.*90m (300ft) and can live for more than 400 years. In damp conditions, a Douglas fir will grow 1m (3ft) a year for the first 30 years of its life.

emitted by coal seams. It is composed mostly of METHANE (natural gas, CH_4) but also contains some hydrogen, oxygen and carbon dioxide, and occasionally a little ethane. Firedamp has caused many disastrous pit explosions; it is detectable with a Davy lamp (after Sir Humphry DAVY), the flame of which elongates when the gas is present.

fire extinguisher Canister of chemicals for extinguishing FIRES. Some fire extinguishers contain liquid carbon dioxide under high pressure. When the extinguisher is operated, the pressure is released and the liquid changes to carbon dioxide gas. This is denser than air and extinguishes flames by smothering them and excluding oxygen. Carbon tetrachloride vapour is more effective, as it is much denser than carbon dioxide. Another kind of chemical extinguisher sprays powdered sodium bicarbonate. When heated by the flames, this powder releases carbon dioxide gas. Others spray water or foam onto the fire.

fire-fighting Extinguishing, prevention and detection of FIRE. Fire prevention measures include regulations to use FIRE RETARDANT materials in the manufacture of goods. Fire protection involves the provision of fire drills, overhead heat- and smoke-sensitive detectors, alarms, fire-fighting personnel, sprinkler system and other FIRE EXTINGUISHERS. Fire-fighting methods are dependent on the fuel that ignited the fire. In the case of fires ignited by **solids** (such as wood or coal), water is most commonly used. In fires caused by **liquids** (such as oil or gasoline), foam is most often used. For **electrical** fires, the most effective agents are halogen compounds and carbon dioxide.

firefly Light-emitting beetle in moist places of temperate and tropical regions. Organs underneath the abdomen usually give off rhythmic flashes of light. The luminous larvae and wingless females of some species are called GLOW-WORMS. Length: to 25mm (1in). There are *c.*1,000 species. Family Lampyridae.

Fire of London (2–6 September 1666) Accidental fire that destroyed most of the City of London, England. It started in a baker's shop in Pudding Lane, now marked by the Monument, and it spread rapidly through the closely packed wooden houses. The fire provided an opportunity for rebuilding London on a more spacious plan, but, for the most part, only the famous churches of Sir Christopher WREN (including ST PAUL'S Cathedral) were built.

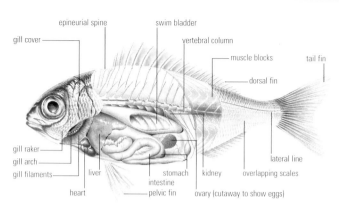

gill cover
epineurial spine
swim bladder
vertebral column
muscle blocks
dorsal fin
tail fin
gill raker
gill arch
gill filaments
liver
heart
intestine
stomach
pelvic fin
kidney
lateral line
overlapping scales
ovary (cutaway to show eggs)

◀ **fish** There are more than 22,000 species of bony fish. Although they vary in shape and the way they swim, they share many common features. All have a tail with equal upper and lower lobe sizes, which provides neither up nor down thrust. Such fish achieve natural buoyancy by adjusting their density using the swim bladder. The fish can expand or contract the swim bladder by secreting gas into or absorbing gas out of it, so adjusting the volume and external pressure, and counteracting the tendency to sink or float to the surface.

fire retardant Chemical solution consisting mainly of boric acid and borax impregnated into flammable materials to slow down the process of COMBUSTION. In construction, fire-resistive buildings are made of reinforced concrete or protected steel. ASBESTOS is no longer considered to be a safe building material.

fireweed (willow herb) Any of several species of perennial plants, especially *Epilobium angustifolium*. It has a long, unbranched stem with narrow, willow-like leaves and purple-red flowers. Height: to 1m (3ft). Family Onagraceae; genus *Epilobium*.

firework Combustible device, normally used for display purposes, which when ignited by a fuse produces coloured flames, sparks, smoke and noise. Fireworks were being produced in China by AD 600. The basic EXPLOSIVE, usually GUNPOWDER, is combined with metallic salts to produce colours: strontium salts for red; sodium for yellow; barium for green; copper for blue. Metal filings provide sparks. The manufacture and sale of fireworks is strictly controlled. *See also* FAWKES, GUY

first aid Immediate treatment of a victim of an accident, sudden illness, or other medical emergency. If the victim appears to have a broken bone or internal injuries, they should not be moved. If the victim is unconscious, their head should be turned to one side to prevent choking. Check that the victim has an open airway – if not, they may have respiratory failure (asphyxia). **Asphyxia** may be caused by the obstruction of air passages, in which case the Heimlich manoeuvre is recommended. For asphyxia caused by fumes or gas, such as carbon monoxide, the victim should be moved to a clear atmosphere before administering artificial respiration. The best method of **artificial respiration** is mouth-to-mouth resuscitation. Place the victim on their back, put one hand under the victim's chin and the other on the forehead. Tilt the victim's head back by lifting with the hand under the chin and pressing down on the forehead. If the victim is an adult, pinch the nostrils shut, take a deep breath, cover the mouth tightly and breathe hard into their mouth. If the victim is a child, both mouth and nose can be covered. Repeat this procedure every five seconds. If the victim has swallowed a poisonous substance, identify the **poison** and then call the emergency services. They may recommend inducing vomiting with syrup of ipecac. In an animal **bite or sting**, the wound should be cleaned with soap and water before applying antiseptic and a bandage. For poisonous SNAKEBITE, the wound should be cooled with ice to slow

down the absorption of poison. A few snakebites require anti-venoms. In order to stop the victim **bleeding** severely, apply direct pressure, preferably with a sterile dressing. If bleeding continues, apply pressure to the artery that supplies blood to the area. To treat **shock**, place the victim on their back with their legs raised slightly and place a blanket over the body. In the case of first- and second-degree **burns**, cold water should be applied before dressing with sterile bandages.

Fischer, Bobby (Robert James) (1943–) US chess player, world champion (1972–75). In 1959, aged 15, he became the youngest ever grandmaster. In 1972, Fischer defeated Boris Spassky to become the first American to hold the world title. From then until 1992, he never played a single game of chess in public. Fischer forfeited his world title to Anatoly KARPOV.

Fischer, Emil Hermann (1852–1919) German chemist. He is remembered for his research on the structure and synthesis of SUGARS and PURINES. Fischer is regarded as the founder of STEREOCHEMISTRY for his discovery that the optical activity of sugars is dependent on the three-dimensional structure of their molecules. He synthesized several polypeptides, including glucose and fructose. Fischer was awarded the 1902 Nobel Prize for chemistry. *See also* ENZYME; ISOMER

Fischer, Hans (1881–1945) German biochemist who received the 1930 Nobel Prize for chemistry for his structural studies of CHLOROPHYLL and of the red BLOOD pigment haemin. Fischer was able to synthesize haemin and almost completely synthesized one of the chlorophylls.

Fischer-Dieskau, Dietrich (1925–) German baritone. He made his concert debut in 1947. Fischer-Dieskau is best known for his brilliant recordings of *lieder*. His recordings of the songs and song-cycles of Schubert, Brahms, Schumann and Wolf are definitive.

fish Cold-blooded, aquatic vertebrate animal characterized by fins, gills for breathing, a streamlined body almost always covered by scales or bony plates onto which a layer of mucus is secreted, and a two-chambered heart. Fish are the most ancient form of vertebrate life, dating back more than 450 million years. They reproduce sexually, and fertilization may be external or internal. The eggs develop in water or inside the female, according to species. Fish have lateral line organs, which are fluid-filled pits and channels that run under the skin of the body. Sensitive fibres link these channels to the central nervous system and detect changes of pressure in the water and changes of strength and direction in currents.

About 75% of all fish live in the sea. A few fish, such as SALMON and EEL, divide their lives between salt and fresh-water habitats. Fish are usually divided into three classes: Agnatha, which are jawless fish, including the HAGFISH and LAMPREY; Chondrichthyes (**cartilaginous** fish), which includes SHARK, SKATE, RAY and CHIMERA; and the numerous Osteichthyes (**bony** fish), including subclasses of soft-rayed fish (LUNGFISH) and the successful teleost fish, such as salmon and COD. There are c.22,000 species of bony fish, and they represent c.40% of all living vertebrates. They are divided into 34 orders and 48 families.

Fisher, Saint John (1469–1535) English Roman Catholic prelate. Fisher opposed Henry VIII's proposed divorce from Catherine of Aragon in 1529. He was tried and executed for denying that Henry was supreme head of the church under the Act of Supremacy. He was canonized in 1935. His feast day is 9 July.

Fisher, Sir R.A. (Ronald Aylmer) (1890–1962) English geneticist and statistician. His book, *The Genetical Theory of Natural Selection* (1929), is a fundamental work on population GENETICS. Fisher was knighted in 1952.

fishing and **fisheries** Harvesting fish for commercial uses. Commercial fishing boats and fleets employ several methods for catching fish, including pole and line, purse seine, gill netting, trawling and stunning. About 70% of the commercial fish catch is taken in the Northern Hemisphere, with the greatest catches taken between the Philippines and Japan. Other fishing areas include the North Atlantic, North Pacific and North Sea. The most significant Southern Hemisphere areas are the Pacific coast of Peru and the South African coast. Herrings, sardines and anchovies make up the largest percentage of the total catch. Other species caught in large commercial quantities include cod, haddock, hake, redfish, sea bream, mackerel, tuna and salmon. The major fishing nations (by catch) are China, Japan, Peru, Chile, Russia and the United States. By the late 1970s, fish stocks were severely depleted. While attempts have been made to allow stocks to return to previous levels, such as the 1983 United Nations "Law of the Sea" resolution that allowed countries to enforce an exclusive 320km (200mi) limit around their coastlines, stocks are still low.

fission In biology, form of ASEXUAL REPRODUCTION in unicellular organisms. The parent cell divides into two or more identical daughter cells. Binary fission produces two daughter cells (as in bacteria). Multiple fission produces 4, 8, or, in the case of some protozoa, more than 1,000 daughter cells, each developing into a new organism.

fission, nuclear In physics, form of nuclear reaction in which a heavy atomic NUCLEUS splits into two, with the release of two or three NEUTRONS and large amounts of heat and nuclear RADIATION. Fission may occur spontaneously, or may be made to occur by bombarding certain nuclei with low-energy (slow) neutrons or PROTONS. The only naturally occurring fissionable material is URANIUM-235. Natural uranium is not capable of sustaining a CHAIN REACTION because its major isotope, U^{238}, tends to absorb neutrons before they can split another atom. Currently, there are two main methods of creating a sustained chain reaction in uranium fuel. In the first, the neutrons released by fission of U^{235} are slowed down by a **moderator** composed of light atoms, such as DEUTERIUM, which does not absorb neutrons. This method is used in most NUCLEAR REACTORS. Alternatively, the uranium may be **enriched** (increasing the amount of the fissionable material). This is the method employed in fast breeder reactors. Nuclear fission and nuclear FUSION are used in NUCLEAR WEAPONS.

Fitzgerald, Edward (1809–83) English poet and translator. He is remembered for his classic free-verse translation, *The Rubáiyát of Omar Khayyám* (1859). Fitzgerald's paraphrase of the text by OMAR KHAYYÁM was lauded by Dante Gabriel ROSSETTI.

Fitzgerald, Ella (1917–96) US jazz singer. The "First Lady of Song" was discovered by Chick Webb at Harlem's Apollo Theater (1934). Her first hit was "A-Tisket A-Tasket" (1938). Her "Songbook" series of renditions of popular "standards" by George Gershwin, Jerome Kern and Cole Porter have become definitive.

Fitzgerald, F. Scott (Francis Scott Key) (1896–1940) US writer. He began his debut novel, *This Side of Paradise* (1920), while in the US army. Along with *The Beautiful and Damned* (1922), this established Fitzgerald as a chronicler of what he christened the "Jazz Age". He spent much of the 1920s in Europe, mingling with wealthy and sophisticated expatriates. Fitzgerald's masterpiece is *The Great Gatsby* (1925). His final novels were *Tender is the Night* (1934) and the unfinished *The Last Tycoon* (1941).

Fitzgerald, George Francis (1851–1901) Irish physicist who researched into ELECTROLYSIS and ELECTROMAGNETISM, and who is noted for his theory of ELEC-

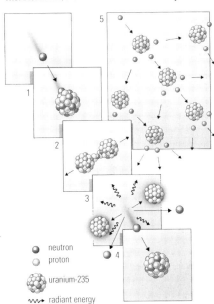

▲ **fission** Most nuclear power stations use uranium-235 as fuel. When a uranium-235 nucleus is struck by a slow-moving neutron (1), it absorbs the neutron to form uranium-236. This is unstable and splits violently (2) forming two smaller nuclei, generating radiant energy (some in the form of heat) and releasing several neutrons (3). These neutrons can then start the process again (4), splitting further nuclei, which in turn release yet more neutrons (5). Such a process is known as a chain reaction and can spread at lightning speed. In a nuclear reactor, many of the neutrons are absorbed to prevent the chain reaction from running out of control and causing an excessive release of energy. Atom bombs are designed to encourage the chain reaction to spread extremely rapidly.

neutron
proton
uranium-235
radiant energy

TROMAGNETIC RADIATION. As an explanation of the Michelson-Morley experiment to determine the Earth's movement through the ETHER, Fitzgerald suggested the theory that objects change length (the **Lorentz-Fitzgerald contraction**) due to this type of movement. This theory was incorporated into Albert EINSTEIN's special theory of RELATIVITY. *See also* LORENTZ, HENDRIK ANTOON; MICHELSON, ALBERT ABRAHAM

Five Civilized Tribes Term adopted by early writers to include those NATIVE-AMERICAN tribes regarded as more advanced, due to agricultural, political and social successes. They were the CHEROKEE, Chickasaw, CHOCTAW, CREEK and SEMINOLE tribes.

Five-Year Plan Series of economic goals, especially those set by the former SOVIET UNION. In 1928, Joseph STALIN launched the first Five-Year Plan; it was designed to speed up the industrialization of the USSR and the COLLECTIVIZATION of agriculture. It focused on the development of heavy industry. The third plan (1938–42) was interrupted by World War 2. The seventh plan (1959–65) failed to meet its agricultural production targets. The ninth plan (1971–75) concentrated on light industry. The twelfth and final plan (1986–90) saw the Soviet economy slide into recession.

fives Game in which players alternately hit a small cork-and-rubber ball against a wall with a gloved hand. There are three major variants: Eton (the original, dating from 1825), Rugby and Winchester, named after the British public schools where they were devised. Eton fives is played by two pairs in a three-walled court incorporating a buttress and step. Only the serving side can score; first to score 12 wins, usually in five games. Rugby and Winchester fives are played as singles or doubles in a four-walled court.

fjord (fiord) Narrow, steep-sided inlet on a sea coast. They were formed by GLACIERS moving toward the sea, and were flooded when the ice melted and sea levels rose.

flagellant Religious zealot who uses flagellation, or flogging, for disciplinary or devotional purposes. Now almost obsolete, the practice of flagellation has been part of many religions, including those of ancient Greece and Rome, some Native-American cultures and Christianity. In most cases, flagellants have used self-inflicted beatings as a means of doing penance for sins or for purification.

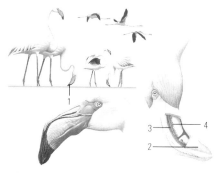

▲ **flamingos** feed by lowering their heads into the water so that their bills are upside down (1). Its crooked shape allows the front half of the bill to lie horizontally in the water (2). Tiny hook-like lamellae (3) strain food as the water is pumped through them by a backward and forward motion of the tongue. Protuberances on the tongue (4) scrape the particles of food off the lamellae for ingestion as the tongue moves back and forth.

flagellate Any member of the class Mastigophora. Flagellates are PROTOZOA that possesses, at some stage of their development, one or several whip-like structures (FLAGELLUM) for locomotion and sensation. There are two major groups: **phytoflagellates** resemble plants (in that they obtain their energy through PHOTOSYNTHESIS), the **zooflagellates** resemble animals (in that they obtain energy through feeding). Most have a single NUCLEUS. Reproduction may be asexual (FISSION) or sexual.

flagellum (pl. flagella) Long, whip-like extension of a cell. There may be a single flagellum or a group of them. Many cells, such as SPERM cells and some BACTERIA, PROTOZOA and single-celled algae, beat their flagella as a means of locomotion – they "swim" through fluids in this way. In sperm and protozoa, the structure and movement of the flagella resembles that of CILIA. *See also* FLAGELLATE

Flagstad, Kirsten (1895–1962) Norwegian soprano. In 1935, she made her debut with the Metropolitan Opera Company, New York. Flagstad was acclaimed for her Wagner roles, especially Isolde (*Tristan and Isolde*) and Brünnhilde (the *Ring* cycle). She was the first director (1958–60) of the Royal Norwegian Opera.

Flaherty, Robert Joseph (1884–1951) US film director. He made the first feature-length DOCUMENTARY film, *Nanook of the North* (1922). Other films include *Moana* (1926), *Man of Aran* (1934) and *Louisiana Story* (1948).

flamboyant style Final phase of French GOTHIC ARCHITECTURE (14th–16th century). The name comes from the flame-like forms of the elaborate tracery used in cathedrals, as on the west façade of Rouen Cathedral (1370). The English DECORATED STYLE is a close equivalent.

flamenco Traditional song, dance and instrumental music, thought to have developed from an amalgam of Romany, Jewish and Arab cultures in Andalusia, s Spain. There are three types of song, of which the most demanding is the *cante hondo*. The dances epitomize pride, poise and sensuality. Songs and dances are accompanied by hand-claps, finger-snapping and rhythmic rolls on the guitar.

flamingo Long-necked, long-legged wading bird of tropical and subtropical lagoons and lakes. They have webbed feet, and a plumage that varies in colour from pale to deep pink. Their bills have fine, hair-like filters which strain food from the muddy water. Height: to 1.5m (5ft). Family Phoenicopteridae.

Flamsteed, John (1646–1719) English astronomer, the first Astronomer Royal (1675). His book *British Catalogue of Stars* contained a record of his observations and listed nearly 3,000 stars; it was the most accurate of its time and served as the standard work for many years.

Flanders Historic region now divided between Belgium and France. In Belgian Flanders, FLEMISH is the major language. From the 10th century, Flanders grew prosperous on the cloth industry, and the old nobility gradually lost authority to the cities, such as BRUGES, ANTWERP and GHENT. By 1400, it was part of Burgundy, passing to the Habsburgs in 1482 before becoming part of the Spanish Netherlands. It was frequently fought over by France, Spain and later Austria, and was the scene of devastating trench warfare in World War 1.

flare, solar *See* SOLAR FLARE

flatfish Any of more than 500 species of bottom-dwelling, mainly marine fish found worldwide. Flatfish have a laterally flattened body, with one anal and one dorsal fin. Both eyes are on the same side. The fish lie on their "blind" side, which is generally white. The upper surface is coloured to blend with their surroundings, and some species are able to alter their pigmentation.

Examples include HALIBUT, PLAICE, TURBOT, SOLE, DAB and FLOUNDER. Order Pleuronectiformes.

flatworm Simple, carnivorous, ribbon-like creature which, having no circulatory system and sometimes no mouth or gut, feeds by absorption through its body wall. Almost all are hermaphrodites. The FLUKE and TAPEWORM are parasites of animals. Order Platyhelminthes.

Flaubert, Gustave (1821–80) French novelist of the 19th-century realist school. An extremely craftsman-like and elegant writer, Flaubert remains one of the most highly respected of European novelists. *Madame Bovary* (1857), his masterpiece, represents the transition from ROMANTICISM to REALISM in the development of the NOVEL. Other fiction includes *The Temptation of St Anthony* (1847), *Salammbô* (1862), *A Sentimental Education* (1869) and the short stories *Three Tales* (1877).

flax Slender, erect, flowering plant cultivated for its fibres and seeds. The fibres are spun into yarn to make LINEN. The seeds yield linseed oil. Family Linaceae; species *Linum usitatissimum*.

Flaxman, John (1755–1826) English sculptor and illustrator. His early career was spent as a pottery designer for Josiah WEDGWOOD. While studying (1789–94) in Rome, Flaxman gained a reputation as a neoclassical artist with his illustrations for the *Iliad* and *Odyssey* (both 1793). His best-known works are the memorial sculptures of Sir Joshua Reynolds and Lord Nelson in St Paul's Cathedral, London. *See also* NEOCLASSICISM

flea Any of 1,000 species of wingless, leaping insects found worldwide. They are external parasites on warm-blooded animals. In moving from one host to another, they can carry disease. Length: to 1cm (0.4in). Order Siphonaptera.

fleabane Any of *c*.250 species of plants of the genus *Erigeron* that grow in temperate climates. Most have lance-shaped leaves and daisy-like flowers with yellow central discs and white, yellow, pink or purple florets. Canada fleabane is dried and used in the treatment of diarrhoea. Height: to 1m (3.3ft). Family Compositae.

Flecker, James Elroy (1884–1915) English poet. His best-known works are the verse collection *The Golden Journey to Samarkand* (1913) and the play *Hassan* (1922).

Fleming, Sir Alexander (1881–1955) Scottish bacteriologist, discoverer of PENICILLIN. In 1922, he discovered lysozyme, a natural antibacterial substance found in saliva and tears. In 1928, while conducting research on staphylococci, Fleming noticed that a mould, identified as *Penicillium notatum*, liberated a substance that inhibited the growth of some BACTERIA. He named it penicillin; it was the first ANTIBIOTIC. Howard FLOREY and Ernst CHAIN refined the drug's production, and in 1941 it was produced commercially. In 1945, Fleming, Florey and Chain shared the Nobel Prize for physiology or medicine.

Fleming, Ian Lancaster (1908–64) English novelist. He wrote 13 escapist spy thrillers about the secret agent James Bond, "007", which won great popularity for their realistic detail, and sexual and violent fantasy. They include *Casino Royale* (1952) (in which Bond makes his first appearance), *From Russia with Love* (1957) and *Goldfinger* (1959). The subsequent films based on his novels have become a movie institution.

Fleming, Sir John Ambrose (1849–1945) English electrical engineer, inventor of the THERMIONIC valve. Fleming's valve was a RECTIFIER, or DIODE, consisting of two electrodes in an evacuated glass envelope. The diode permitted current to flow in one direction only. It could detect RADIO signals. *See also* FLEMING'S RULES

Fleming's rules In physics, ways of remembering the relationships between the directions of the current, field, and mechanical rotation in electric MOTORS and GENERATORS. In the **left-hand** rule (for motors), the forefinger represents field, the second finger current, and the thumb, motion; when the digits are extended at right-angles to each other, the appropriate directions are indicated. The **right-hand** rule applies the principles to generators. The rules were devised by John Ambrose FLEMING.

Flemish One of the two official languages of Belgium (the other being FRENCH). It is spoken mainly in the N half of the country, by *c*.50% of the population. Flemish is virtually the same language as DUTCH, but for historical and cultural reasons, it is called Flemish in Belgium and Dutch in The Netherlands.

Flemish art (Netherlandish art) Loose art history term used to describe artists working in what roughly corresponds to modern-day Netherlands, Belgium and Luxembourg. In the 14th and early 15th centuries, Flemish artists were masters of the International Gothic style, brilliantly characterized by the illuminated manuscripts of the LIMBOURG brothers. Naturalism became a hallmark of Flemish art, as in the portraits and altarpieces of van EYCK and van der WEYDEN and the LANDSCAPE PAINTINGS of BRUEGEL. The greatest figures of the next generation were Anthony VAN DYCK, who spent much of his career in England, and Peter Paul RUBENS, the chief exponent of BAROQUE art in N Europe. After 1650, Flemish art went into decline. In the 19th century, James ENSOR was a precursor of EXPRESSIONISM. In the 20th century, MAGRITTE and Paul Delvaux both made significant contributions to the SURREALISM movement. *See also* DUTCH ART

Fletcher, John (1579–1625) English dramatist and poet. From *c*.1607 to 1616, he collaborated with Francis BEAUMONT on romantic tragicomedies such as *Philaster*, *The Maid's Tragedy* and *A King and No King*. Fletcher may have worked with Shakespeare on *Henry VIII* and *The Two Noble Kinsmen*. His own work includes *The Faithful Shepherdess* (1608) and *The Chancer* (1623).

flight *See* AERODYNAMICS; AERONAUTICS; AIRCRAFT

flight recorder (black box) Device for automatically recording data during the operation of an AIRCRAFT. Investigators analyze the data after a crash or malfunction. A small aircraft may have a simple cockpit voice recorder (CVR) that records all cockpit sounds and radio contact with air traffic control. Larger aircraft carry a separate flight data recorder (FDR). Control settings, instrument readings and other data are recorded on magnetic wire.

Flinders, Matthew (1774–1814) English navigator and explorer. In 1798, he and George Bass sailed around Tasmania. Flinders circumnavigated (1801–03) Australia. His charts and surveys of the region were highly valuable.

Flint City in S Michigan, USA. Founded in 1819 as a fur-trading post, Flint became a centre for vehicle production. General Motors was founded here in 1908, and Flint is second only to DETROIT as the leading producer of automobiles in the United States. Pop. (1996) 135,000.

flint (SiO_2) Granular variety of QUARTZ of a fine crystalline structure. It is usually brown or dark grey, although the variety known as chert is paler. It occurs in rounded nodules and is found in chalk or other sedimentary rocks containing calcium carbonate. Of great importance to early humans during the STONE AGE, when struck a glancing blow, flint is flaked, leaving sharp edges appropriate for tools and weapons; two flints struck together produce a spark which can be used to make fire.

flood Innundation of land that is normally dry through the overflowing of a body of water, usually a river. The commonest cause of flooding is when heavy rainfall or melting snow or ice exceeds the carrying capacity of the river system. In many regions, such as the NILE valley, annual floods follow the rains of spring. Very heavy rains followed by rapid runoff can cause **flash floods**. They are most common in areas with little or no vegetation. **Flood control** measures include slowing down the rate of runoff in the headwaters by planting vegetation or constructing DAMS, and building levees on the lower flood plains. Major flood control projects in the UK include the Thames Barrier, London.

Flood, the Primeval deluge sent by God to devastate the Earth as a punishment for wickedness. As related in the Old Testament (Genesis 6–9), God sent rain upon the Earth for 40 days and nights, destroying everything he had created. Only NOAH, his family, and a pair of every living creature, contained in the Ark that he had built, were spared to start creation afresh. The Genesis account bears some resemblance to part of the epic of GILGAMESH.

floppy disk *See* MAGNETIC DISK

Flora In Roman mythology, personification and goddess of springtime and of budding fruits, flowers and crops. Flora was honoured as a fertility goddess.

Florence (Firenze) Capital of Tuscany and Firenze province, on the River Arno, Italy. Initially an Etruscan town, it was a Roman colony from the 1st century BC to 5th century AD. In the 12th century, it became an independent commune and major trading centre. The site of many factional power struggles, especially the 13th-century war between the GUELPHS and GHIBELLINES, it nevertheless became the cultural and intellectual centre of Italy. Florence's period of dominance coincided with the rule of the MEDICI family. It became a city-state and one of the leading centres of the RENAISSANCE. Artists who contributed to the flourishing city included MICHELANGELO, LEONARDO DA VINCI, RAPHAEL and DONATELLO. In 1569, Florence became the capital of the Grand Duchy of Tuscany. From 1865 to 1871, Florence was the capital of the kingdom of Italy. Its many notable churches include: the Duomo gothic cathedral (1296); San Lorenzo, Florence's first cathedral rebuilt in 1425 by BRUNELLESCHI, including the New Sacristy built by Michelangelo; and the monastery San Marco which holds FRA ANGELICO masterpieces. Major art collections include the UFFIZI Museum and the Bargello Palace. Industries: tourism, craft, fashion. Pop. (1996) 384,000.

Florence, school of Painters and sculptors who flourished in Florence during the RENAISSANCE. Major figures include GIOTTO, Fra ANGELICO, LEONARDO, MICHELANGELO, BOTTICELLI and RAPHAEL.

Florey (of Adelaide), Sir Howard Walter, Baron (1898–1968) British pathologist, b. Australia. He shared,

with Alexander FLEMING and Ernst CHAIN, the 1945 Nobel Prize for physiology or medicine for his part in the development of PENICILLIN. Florey isolated the antibacterial agent from the mold, thus making possible the large-scale preparation of penicillin. *See also* ANTIBIOTIC

Florida State in the extreme SE USA, occupying a peninsula between the Atlantic Ocean and the Gulf of Mexico; the capital is TALLAHASSEE. Florida forms a long peninsula with thousands of lakes, many rivers and vast areas of swampland. At the S tip there is a chain of small islands, the FLORIDA KEYS, stretching W. The biggest attractions are the EVERGLADES, Florida Keys and DISNEY World in ORLANDO. Discovered in 1513, the first permanent settlement in Florida was at St Augustine. Originally Spanish, the land passed to the English (1763), then returned to the Spanish in 1783. America purchased Florida in 1819 and, although the state seceded from the Union in 1861, it was little affected by the Civil War. It developed rapidly after 1880 when forest-clearing and drainage schemes were begun. Florida's historic ties with Cuba are particularly evident in MIAMI, Florida's second largest city after JACKSONVILLE. Industries focus on the John F. Kennedy Space Center at CAPE CANAVERAL. Chief agricultural products: citrus fruits, sugar cane, vegetables. Area: 151,670sq km (58,560sq mi). Pop. (2000) 15,982,378.

Florida Keys Chain of small US coral and limestone islands, extending in a curve, *c.*240km (150mi) long, from Biscayne Bay, Miami, to Key West. Most of the islands are connected by the overseas Highway 1; the best-known are Key West and Key Largo. The Florida Keys area is a major tourist area. Other industries: fishing.

flounder Marine FLATFISH found in the Arctic, Atlantic and Pacific oceans. It is grey, brown or green on the upper, sighted, side; the blind underside is nearly white. It is an important food fish. Length: to 90cm (35in). Order Pleuronectiformes; species *Platichthys flesus*.

flour Fine or coarse powder prepared by sifting and grinding GRAIN. Most flour is made from WHEAT and is used to bake BREAD. MILLET is used in India, the former Soviet Union and China. The main protein in wheat is GLUTEN. Bread flour contains *c.*11% protein, cake flour less than 9%. Self-raising flour contains a leavening agent, SODIUM HYDROCARBONATE. Flour dough is often bleached and enriched with vitamins and minerals.

flower Reproductive structure of all ANGIOSPERMS (flowering plants). It has four sets of organs set in whorls on a short apex (RECEPTACLE). The leaf-like SEPALS protect the bud and form the calyx. The brightly coloured PETALS form the corolla; the STAMENS are stalks (filaments) tipped by ANTHERS (pollen sacs); the CARPELS form the PISTIL with an OVARY, STYLE and STIGMA. Flowers are bisexual if they contain stamens and carpels, and unisexual if only one of these is present. Reproduction occurs following POLLINATION, when POLLEN is transferred from the anthers of one flower to the stigma of another flower of another plant (**cross-pollination**), or to the same flower or flower of the same plant (**self-pollination**). A pollen tube grows down into the ovary where FERTILIZATION occurs and a SEED is produced. The ovary bearing the seed ripens into a FRUIT containing the seed, and the rest of the flower wilts.

flu Abbreviation of INFLUENZA

fluid Any substance that is able to flow. Of the three common states of MATTER, GAS and LIQUID are considered fluid, while a SOLID is not.

fluidics Technology of devices operated by a FLUID for CONTROL SYSTEMS and instruments. Fluidic systems simulate electronic circuits. They were developed in the US in the 1960s for ROCKET and AIRCRAFT guidance.

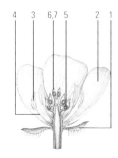

► **flower** A typical flower has four main parts: sepals, petals, stamens and carpels. The sepals (1) protect the developing bud and lie outside the showy petals (2). Each male stamen is made up of an anther (3), which contains the pollen grains, borne on a filament (4). The female carpels are found at the centre of the flower, each containing ovaries (5) and a style (6) which supports the stigma (7).

fluid mechanics Study of the behaviour of liquids and gases. **Fluid statics** is the study of FLUIDS at rest and includes the study of pressure, density and the principles of PASCAL and ARCHIMEDES. **Fluid dynamics** is the study of moving fluids and includes the study of streamline flow, BERNOULLI'S LAW and the propagation of waves. Engineers use fluid mechanics in the design of bridges, dams and ships. AERODYNAMICS is a branch of fluid mechanics.

fluke FLATWORM, an external or internal PARASITE of animals. Flukes have suckers for attachment to the host. Human infection can result from eating uncooked food containing encysted larvae or from penetration of the skin by larvae in infected waters. The worms enter various body organs, such as the liver, lungs and intestines, causing oedema (swelling) and decreased function. Phylum Platyhelminthes, class *Trematoda*.

fluorescence Emission of radiation, usually light, from a substance when its atoms have acquired excess energy from a bombarding source of radiation, usually ultraviolet light or electrons. Unlike PHOSPHORESCENCE, fluorescence ceases when the source of energy is removed. Television tubes use fluorescent screens. *See also* FLUORESCENT LAMP

fluorescent lamp Lamp that generates light by FLUO-RESCENCE. It consists of a glass tube coated on the inside with a chemical phosphor and containing, at low pressure, small quantities of mercury. When an electric current is passed through the tube, the atoms of mercury emit ULTRAVIOLET RADIATION, which impinges on the phosphor coating, causing it to glow brightly.

fluoridation Addition of inorganic FLUORIDES to the water supply to reduce dental CARIES. The additive is usually sodium fluoride, at a concentration of about one part per million. Since its inception in the 1930s fluoridation has been adopted in many countries.

fluoride Any salt of hydrogen fluoride (HF); more particularly, fluoride compounds added to drinking water or toothpaste to build up resistance to tooth decay.

fluorine (symbol F) Gaseous toxic element of the HALOGEN group, isolated (1886) by Henri Moissan. Chief sources are fluorspar and cryolite. The pale yellow element, obtained by ELECTROLYSIS, is the most electronegative element and the most reactive non-metallic element. It is in FLUORIDE in drinking water and is used in making FLUOROCARBONS and in extracting URANIUM. Properties: at.no. 9; r.a.m. 19; m.p. −219.6°C (−363.3°F); b.p. −188.1°C (−306.6°F); single isotope F^{19}.

fluorite (fluorspar) Mineral, calcium fluoride (CaF_2). It has cubic system crystals with granular and fibrous masses. Brittle and glassy, it can be yellow, purple or green. It is used as a flux in steel production, and in ceramics and chemical industries. Hardness 4; r.d. 3.1.

fluorocarbon (technically chlorofluoromethane) Organic compound that is produced by replacing the hydrogen atoms of hydrocarbons with FLUORINE atoms. Their inertness, low toxicity and ability to withstand high temperature, make them ideal for use in plastics, such as PTFE (POLYTETRAFLUOROETHYLENE) or Teflon. Many of these chemicals also contain CHLORINE and are called CHLOROFLUOROCARBONS (CFCs).

flute WOODWIND musical instrument. Air is blown across a mouth-hole near one end of a horizontally held tube. It has a range of three octaves, with a mellow tone in the lower register and a brighter tone in the higher.

flux In CERAMICS, any substance that promotes vitrification when mixed with CLAY. When the ware is fired, the flux melts, filling the porous clay form. As the piece cools, it hardens, becoming glossy and non-porous.

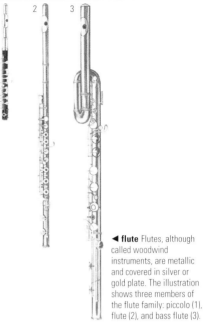

◀ **flute** Flutes, although called woodwind instruments, are metallic and covered in silver or gold plate. The illustration shows three members of the flute family: piccolo (1), flute (2), and bass flute (3).

Fluxes include FELDSPAR rock, SILICA and BORAX. In METALLURGY, a flux is added to the charge of a smelting FURNACE to purge impurities from the ore and to lower the melting point of the slag.

flux In physics, rate of flow of energy or matter past a surface at right angles to the surface. *See also* MAGNETIC FLUX

fly Any of a large order (Diptera) of two-winged insects. They range in size from midges 1.6mm (0.06in) long to robber flies more than 76mm (3in) in length. The 60,000–100,000 species are found worldwide. All flies undergo METAMORPHOSIS. A female lays between one and 250 eggs at a time. The larva (MAGGOT) typically lives on rotting flesh or plants. Adult flies have compound eyes and sucking mouthparts. Many are pests and vectors, especially HORSEFLIES, MOSQUITOES and TSETSE FLIES. The common housefly is species *Musca domestica*.

flycatcher Common name for two families (Old World Muscicapidae, New World Tyrannidae) of birds that catch insects in midflight. The Tyrannidae (tyrant flycatchers) includes the KINGBIRD.

flying bomb Popular name for the V1, V2 ROCKETS used by the Germans in World War 2.

Flying Dutchman Ghost ship of ill potent, haunting the seas around the Cape of Good Hope. In legend, its captain swore to round the Cape or be forever damned. The story inspired Wagner's opera *The Flying Dutchman* (1843).

flying fish Tropical marine fish found worldwide. It is dark blue and silver, and uses its enlarged pectoral and pelvic fins to glide above the water surface for several yards. Length: to 45.7cm (18in). Family Exocoetidae; species *Cypselurus opisthopus*.

flying fox Popular name for a species of FRUIT BAT

flying squirrel Small, nocturnal SQUIRREL that lives in forests. They can glide more than 50m (150ft) by means of furry flaps of skin that stretch out flat and taut on both sides of the body when the limbs are extended. Flying squirrels nest high up in hollows of trees. There are 33 species of the genus *Pteromys* in Asia (one reaches SE

Europe) and two species of the genus *Glaucomys* in North America. The giant flying squirrel of s Asia grows up to 120cm (4ft) long.

Flynn, Errol (1909–59) US film actor, b. Tasmania. He made his name with *Captain Blood* (1935), and won worldwide fame playing romantic, swashbuckling heroes, as in *The Adventures of Robin Hood* (1938). He had a scandalous off-screen reputation, and published an autobiography, *My Wicked, Wicked Ways* (1959).

FM Abbreviation of FREQUENCY MODULATION (FM)

Fo, Dario (1926–) Italian playwright and director. Fo's drama incorporates elements of farce and the carnivalesque. His most famous works are *Accidental Death of an Anarchist* (1970) and *Can't Pay? Won't Pay!* (1975). In 1997, Fo was awarded the Nobel Prize for literature.

focal length Distance from the midpoint of a curved mirror or the centre of a thin LENS to the focal point of the system. For converging systems, it is given a positive value; for diverging systems, a negative value.

Foch, Ferdinand (1851–1929) French general. In WORLD WAR 1, he helped repel the German advance at MARNE (1914), but the disastrous offensives at YPRES (1915) and the SOMME (1916) led to his dismissal. In 1917, Foch returned as chief of the French general staff. In April 1918, he became commander in chief of all Allied forces in France and led the counter-offensive that ended in German surrender.

fog Mass of water droplets immediately above the Earth's surface that reduces visibility to less than 1km (0.6mi). A light fog is called **mist** or haze. Fog is caused by water vapour condensing as the air becomes cooler. This condensation takes place around particles of dust. **Advection** fog develops from air flowing over a surface of a different temperature, such as steam fog that results from cold air passing over warm water; **frontal** fog forms when warm rain falls through cold air near the ground; **radiation** fog occurs when the ground cools on a still, clear night and is most common in valleys; **upslope** fog develops when air cools as it ascends a slope. *See also* DEW POINT

Fokine, Michel (1880–1942) Russian-American choreographer. He revolutionized BALLET through his efforts at unity of music, drama, dance and décor. From 1909, Fokine was chief choreographer for DIAGHILEV and his BALLETS RUSSES in Paris. In 1932, he became a naturalized American. His best-known works include *Les Sylphides* (1909), *Firebird* (1910) and *Petrushka* (1916).

Fokker, Anthony Herman Gerard (1890–1939) US aircraft manufacturer, b. Java. In 1912, he opened an aircraft factory in Germany that supplied triplanes and biplanes to the German airforce in World War 1. Fokker also developed a method of firing a machine gun through the propeller of an aircraft. In 1922, he went to the US.

fold In geology, a bend in a layer of rock. An upfold is an ANTICLINE; a downfold, a SYNCLINE. A monocline (flexure) slopes in one direction only and usually passes into a FAULT. Folds occur as part of the process of PLATE TECTONICS, where rock strata buckle and bend under pressure. If the compression is fairly gentle and even, the resulting fold is **symmetrical**. If the pressure is uneven, then **asymmetrical** folds will form. In many cases, the folds are pushed right over to form **recumbent** features. Eventually the rock strata may break under the pressure, to form an overthrust or a **nappe**.

folic acid Yellow, crystalline derivative of glutamic acid, it forms part of the VITAMIN B complex.

folk art Term used to describe the art of folk cultures, especially those of rural and ethnic minority communities. It is usually practised by people who have not had

formal training and who use local craft processes. The decoration of everyday objects features strongly in folk art, often with motifs that have been handed down from generation to generation. *See also* PRIMITIVISM

folklore Traditions, customs and beliefs of the people. The most prevalent form of folklore is the **folk tale**. In contrast to literature, which is transmitted through written texts, the folk tale has an oral basis and is transmitted primarily through memory and tradition. Often the tales take the form of myths, fables and fairy tales. The best-known work on folklore is Sir James Frazer's anthropological study, *The Golden Bough* (1890).

folk music Music deriving from, and expressive of, a particular national, ethnic or regional culture; it is nearly always vocal. Its main theme tends to be the history of a people, so that folk songs are usually narrative. The musical structure is the simple repetition of a tune (with or without chorus), sometimes with a freedom of rhythm which adheres more to the natural metre of the word than to the more formal requirements of composition. Some modern writers of popular music, such as Bob DYLAN, have applied the folk idiom to their compositions.

Folsom Prehistoric inhabitants of North America whose existence was proved first by the discovery (1926) of fluted stone spearheads near Folsom, New Mexico. The tools were found with the bones of extinct mammals, such as the mastodon, and appear to date from *c*.9000 BC.

Fonda, Henry (1905–82) US actor. Cast as the model of American decency and homespun wisdom, he appeared in a series of John FORD films, such as *Young Mr Lincoln* (1939), *The Grapes of Wrath* (1940) and *Twelve Angry Men* (1957). Fonda won a best actor Academy Award for his performance opposite his daughter, Jane FONDA, in *On Golden Pond* (1981). Other films include *The Lady Eve* (1941), *My Darling Clementine* (1946) and *Mister Roberts* (1955).

Fonda, Jane (1937–) US film actress, daughter of Henry FONDA. Following a lauded performance in *They Shoot Horses, Don't They?* (1969), Fonda won a Best Actress Academy Award for *Klute* (1971). A second award followed for *Coming Home* (1978). She starred opposite her father in *On Golden Pond* (1981). Her personal fitness program, *Jane Fonda's Workout Book* (1981), was a worldwide bestseller.

Fontainebleau Town in the Forest of Fontainebleau, N France, famed for its royal palace. The 16th-century palace was commissioned by Francis I. Built on the site of a previous royal residence, it is a world heritage site and a masterpiece of French Renaissance architecture. Napoleon's imperial headquarters, it was also the location for the signing of his first abdication (1814). It is now a museum and the presidential summer residence. The town was headquarters of the military branch of NATO from 1945 to 1965. Pop. (1982) 18,750.

Fontainebleau school Style of painting associated with a group of artists working at the French court in the 16th century. In a bid to match the magnificence of the Italian courts, FRANCIS I gathered an international team of artists to decorate his palace at FONTAINEBLEAU. Led by the Florentine artists Fiorentino Rosso and Francesco Primaticcio, the group evolved a unique style of MANNERISM, blending sensuality and elegance.

Fonteyn, Dame Margot (1919–91) English ballerina. She was a member of the Royal Ballet (1934–59) and a guest artist with every major US and European ballet company. Fonteyn made her debut (1935) in Sir Frederick ASHTON's production of *The Fairy's Kiss*. She was acclaimed as one of the most exquisite classical dancers of the 20th century. Fonteyn continued to dazzle audiences late in her career, especially in partnership with Rudolf NUREYEV.

food Material taken into an organism to maintain life and growth. Important substances in food include: PROTEINS, FATS, CARBOHYDRATES, MINERALS and VITAMINS. *See also* FOOD CHAIN

food additive Substance introduced into food to enhance flavour, to act as a preservative, to effect a better external coloration or more appetizing appearance, or to restore or increase nutritional value. Other additives include thickeners, stabilizers and anti-caking agents. The use of food additives is strictly regulated by law and requires prominent labelling. The 208 food additives approved for use in the EU carry an **E number**.

Food and Agriculture Organization (FAO) Specialized agency of the UNITED NATIONS (UN) established in 1946. It aims to eliminate hunger and improve world nutrition. Its headquarters are in Rome.

food chain Transfer of energy through a series of organisms. The Sun provides the energy that **primary producers**, such as green plants, convert into food by PHOTOSYNTHESIS. Plants also need **abiotic** substances from the water and soil to grow. **Primary consumers** (HERBIVORES) eat the plants and in turn serve as food for **secondary consumers** (CARNIVORES). Decomposers complete the food chain by breaking down dead organic matter into simple nutrients. *See also* DECOMPOSITION; ECOSYSTEM

food poisoning Acute illness caused by consumption of food which is itself poisonous or which has become contaminated with BACTERIA. Frequently implicated are SALMONELLA bacteria, found in cattle, pigs, poultry and eggs, and listeria, sometimes found in cheese. Symptoms include abdominal pain, DIARRHOEA, nausea and vomiting. Treatment includes rest and fluids to prevent dehydration. *See also* BOTULISM; GASTROENTERITIS

food preservation Treatment of foodstuffs to prolong the time for which they can be kept before spoiling. Salting, pickling and FERMENTATION preserve food chemically. Chemical preservatives, such as sodium benzoate, can be added to foods. Cold storage at 5°C (41°F) prolongs the life of foods temporarily, while deep-freezing at $-5°C$ ($-3°F$) or below greatly extends the acceptable storage period. In **freeze-drying**, frozen foods are placed in a vacuum chamber and the water in them is removed as vapour; the foods can be fully reconstituted at a later date. Since 1990, **irradiation** (the preservation of food by subjecting it to low-level radiation in order to kill microorganisms) has been increasingly used. *See also* CANNING; DEEP-FREEZING

food technology Application of scientific techniques to the generation, mass production, packaging and preservation of all types of food. Generating new and better forms of food often involves GENETIC ENGINEERING. The genetic material in edible plants is improved in order to achieve greater yield and resistance to disease. Improving genetic strains is also important in the mass production of all forms of meat farming. The scientific provision of an idealized environment can increase the size and quality of vegetables and animals. Animals can be further scientifically bioengineered through the careful introduction of hormones. *See also* BIOTECHNOLOGY; FOOD PRESERVATION

Foot, Michael (1913–) British politician, writer and leader of the Labour Party (1980–83). Foot was editor of the *Evening Standard* (1942–44) and *Tribune* (1955–60) and a leading member of the Campaign for Nuclear Disarmament (CND). First elected to parliament in 1945, he joined (1974) Harold WILSON's cabinet as secretary of state for employment, later becoming leader of the House of Commons. In 1980, Foot succeeded James CALLAGHAN as leader of the party, but resigned after Labour's disastrous defeat in the 1983 general election.

foot In poetry, unit of verse metre. Each foot is composed of a group of two or more syllables, some of which are stressed. Most commonly used feet are anapest, dactyl, iamb and trochee.

football, American Contact sport played in the USA, where it is second in popularity only to baseball. It is played by two teams of 11 people on a field 91.5 × 49m (100 × 53yd). The field is marked off by latitudinal stripes every 4.6m (5yd) and is flanked on each end by an end zone, 9.1m (10yd) long. At each end of the end zone are H-shaped goalposts. An inflated leather, spheroid ball is used, with the object of moving the ball – by ground or air – across the opponent's goal line. Most football teams have defensive and offensive units that alternate on the field according to possession of the ball. The field leader is the quarterback. Before each play, the two teams face each other along the line of scrimmage. A game consists of two halves, each having two 15-minute quarters. Each half starts with a kickoff, and after the receiving team has run back the ball, it must advance 10 yards in 4 attempts (downs) or turn the ball over to the opponents. The defending team must stop the ball carrier by pushing him out of bounds or tackling him. The ball is usually turned over by punting (kicking) on the last down. If a player fumbles, has a pass intercepted, or loses possession of the ball during the series of downs, the opposing team takes over the ball. Scoring can occur in five ways: a **touchdown** (crossing the opponent's goal line) scores six points ; an "**extra point**" (kicking the ball through the goal post after a touchdown) scores one point; a **conversion** (running or completing a pass into the opponent's end zone after a touchdown) scores two; a **field goal** (kicking the ball between the uprights) scores three; and a **safety** (downing the ball carrier behind his own goal line) scores two. Substitutions are freely allowed. The game dates from 1874. In 1920, the American Professional Football Association was formed, and in 1922 it was renamed the National Football League (NFL). In 1959, a separate league, the American Football League (AFL), was formed. In January 1967, the first Super Bowl was held between the winners of the AFL and the NFL. In 1970, the two leagues merged to form the present NFL, consisting of two conferences of 15 teams each.

football, association (soccer) Arguably the most popular worldwide sport. It involves two teams of 11 players who attempt to force a round ball into their opponents' goal. It is played on a rectangular pitch of maximum size 120 × 90m (390 × 300ft), minimum 90 × 45m (300 × 150ft). The goals, two uprights surmounted by a crossbar, are 7.32m × 2.44m (8ft × 24ft) wide. Only the goalkeeper may handle the ball, and then only in the penalty area of the goal he is defending. The other players may play the ball in any direction with any other part of the body, essentially it is kicked or headed. A game is played over two 45-minute periods and controlled by a referee. Modern football rules were formulated in 19th-century England, and the Football Association (FA) was founded in 1863. The FA Cup, established in 1872, is the world's oldest knockout football competition. The introduction of professionalism in 1885 led to the foundation (1888) of the Football League Championship. Football soon spread beyond Britain and, in 1904, *Fédération internationale de football association* (FIFA) was formed to control the sport at world level. Football has been played at the Olympic

Games since 1908. The first of the four-yearly World Cup competitions was held in 1930. In Europe, the winners of each national league annually compete for the European Champions Cup (established 1955) Recent years have seen a significant increase in commercial sponsorship and television coverage. In 1992, the English FA changed the "four-division" structure of the Football League, primarily to raise the commercial profile of leading clubs. The new structure consisted of a "Premier" league of the top 20 clubs as a separate entity within the FA, and the First, Second and Third Divisions of the Football League.

football, Australian rules Type of football popular in Australia and Papua New Guinea. It is played over four 25-minute quarters between two teams of 18 players using an oval-shaped ball on an oval pitch 135–185m (440–600ft) long and 110–155m (345–504ft) wide. The ball may be kicked or punched, and although players can run with the ball, they must bounce it on the ground every 10m (33ft). The object of the game is to score points by kicking the ball between goalposts 6.4m (21ft) apart (6 points). There are two other posts farther apart, one 6.4m (21ft) each side of the goalposts; a ball passing between one of these and a goal post scores a "behind" (1 point).

football, Canadian Game similar to American FOOTBALL. The Grey Cup is the highlight of the professional season. The principal differences are that teams have 12 players, are allowed only three downs, and play on a larger field, 100 × 59.4m (110 × 65yd).

football, Gaelic Sport popular in Ireland and dating from the 16th century. Each side has 15 men who may kick, punch or pass the ball, but not throw it. Players may not pick the ball up from the ground with the hands; it may be carried for four paces and has to be bounced, kicked or punched away. The field is 128–146m (140–160yd) long and 77–91m (80–100yd) wide with goalposts at each end. One point is scored for putting the ball over the bar and three for driving it under the bar. The game generally lasts 60 minutes with two halves.

foraminiferan Amoeboid PROTOZOAN animal that lives among plankton in the sea. They have multi-chambered chalky shells (tests) and vary in size from microscopic to 5cm (2in) across. Many remain as fossils and are useful in geological dating. When they die, their shells sink to the ocean floor to form large deposits, the source of chalk and limestone. Order Foraminifera.

force (symbol F) Push, pull or turn. A force acting on an object may (1) balance an equal but opposite force or a combination of forces so that it does not move, (2) change the state of motion of the object (in magnitude or direction), or (3) change the shape or state of the object. There are four FUNDAMENTAL FORCES in nature.

Ford, Ford Madox (1873–1939) English novelist, poet and critic, b. Ford Madox Hueffer. He provided influential support to such writers as Ezra POUND, while editing the *Transatlantic Review* in Paris, and Joseph CONRAD and D.H. LAWRENCE during his editorship of the *English Review*. His novels include *The Good Soldier* (1915) and the tetralogy *Parade's End* (1924–28).

Ford, Gerald Rudolph (1913–) 38th US president (1974–77). Elected to the House of Representatives in 1948, he gained a reputation as an honest and hard-working Republican. He was nominated by President NIXON to replace the disgraced Spiro AGNEW as vice president (1973). When Nixon resigned, Ford became president – the only person to hold the office without winning a presidential or vice-presidential election. One of his first acts was to pardon Nixon. His attempts to counter economic recession with cuts in social welfare and taxes were

hindered by a Democrat-dominated Congress. Renominated in 1976, he narrowly lost the election to Jimmy CARTER.

Ford, Harrison (1942–) US film actor. His breakthrough film was *Star Wars* (1977). Ford's reputation as the all-action adventure hero was strengthened by *Indiana Jones* (1981) and its sequels, and the classic science-fiction film *Blade Runner* (1982). He was nominated for a best actor Academy Award for *Witness* (1985). Other films include *Sabrina* (1995).

Ford, Henry (1863–1947) US industrialist. He developed a gas-engined car in 1892 and founded Ford Motors in 1903. In 1908 Ford designed the Model T. His introduction of an assembly line (1913) revolutionized industrial MASS PRODUCTION, and over 15 million Model T's were sold before it was discontinued in 1928. In 1914, Ford raised the minimum wage to $5 a day and reduced the workday to eight hours. He refused, however, to allow union organization in his factories until 1941. In 1945, with the company losing *c*.$9 million a month, he handed control of the company to his grandson, **Henry Ford II** (1917–87). Henry Ford II transformed the business, introducing new models, such as the Thunderbird and Mustang, and bringing the company back into profit.

Ford, John (1586–1639) English playwright who, with Cyril Tourneur, pioneered post-JACOBEAN drama. His major plays include *The Broken Heart* (*c*.1630), *Love's Sacrifice* (*c*.1630), *'Tis Pity She's a Whore* (*c*.1633) and *Perkin Warbeck* (1634). Incest and thwarted passion are common themes, and plays emphasize the difference between public and private morality.

Ford, John (1895–1973) US film director. Ford won four Academy Awards for best director: *The Informer* (1935), *The Grapes of Wrath* (1940), *How Green Was My Valley* (1941) and *The Quiet Man* (1952). His WESTERN classics include *Stagecoach* (1939), *My Darling Clementine* (1946), *The Horse Soldiers* (1959) and *The Searchers* (1956).

foreign exchange Buying and selling national currencies. All currencies have an underlying value relative to the value of gold, registered with the INTERNATIONAL MONETARY FUND (IMF). This value may deviate, and governments can control the amount of deviation by trading on foreign-exchange markets. Speculators may trade in the hope of profiting from short-term fluctuations in the value, an activity known as **arbitrage**. International commercial companies and financial institutions also buy and sell foreign currencies. *See also* EURO

Foreign Legion Professional military group of mixed national origin, created (1831) by LOUIS PHILIPPE to serve in French colonies. In 1962, after fighting in the two World Wars and later French colonial struggles, the Legion moved its headquarters from Algeria to Aubagne, s France. It is renowned for its harsh discipline.

forensic science (medical jurisprudence) Application of medical, scientific or technological knowledge to the investigation of crimes. Forensic medicine involves examination of living victims and suspects, as well as the pathology of the dead. The cause of death, if there is doubt, is established at an autopsy. Modern developments include testing bodily specimens (blood, semen, and so on) linked to the crime to provide a DNA "fingerprint" to be compared with the defendant's. *See also* FINGERPRINT

forest Large area of land covered with a dense growth of trees and plants. Earth's first forests developed *c*.365 million years ago. In the early 1800s forests covered 60% of the Earth, today they account for *c*.30%. DEFORESTATION is a major environmental concern, since forests make such a vital contribution to Earth's atmosphere and also act as a

WATERSHED. Forests have been an important source of timber, food and other resources since prehistoric times. The forest ECOSYSTEM has five basic strata; canopy, understory, shrub layer, herb layer and forest floor. **Tropical hardwood** forests, including RAINFORESTS, are predominantly EVERGREEN. They account for *c*.7% of Earth's landmass, but *c*.50% of Earth's species. **Temperate hardwood** forests are mostly DECIDUOUS. BOREAL FORESTS, consisting mainly of CONIFERS, lie in the far N. *See also* FORESTRY

Forester, C.S. (Cecil Scott) (1899–1966) British novelist, b. Egypt. Forester is most famous for his 12-novel saga about Horatio Hornblower, a naval officer during the Napoleonic Wars; the series began with *The Happy Return* (1937). Other works include *The African Queen* (1935) and *The Gun* (1933).

forestry (silviculture) Management of forest resources for human benefit, in particular the production of timber through reforestation. It also includes the conservation of soil, water and wildlife. Forests account for 10% of total land use in the UK. There are two million hectares of productive woodland in Britain, nearly half of which is owned by the Forestry Commission and managed by its executive agency, Forest Enterprise. The Forestry Commission is the government department responsible for forestry policy in Great Britain. The National Forest is being planted in 52,000ha (128,000acres) of Derbyshire, Leicestershire and Staffordshire. *See also* DEFORESTATION

forget-me-not Any of *c*.50 species of hardy perennial and annual herbs of the genus *Myosotis* found in temperate regions. Its five-petalled flowers are sky blue but may change colour with age. Family Boraganacea (BORAGE).

forging Shaping of metal by hammering or by applying pressure against a shaped die. Blacksmiths forge horseshoes and other iron items by hammering the red-hot metal on an anvil. In mass-manufacturing processes, pressure from a hydraulic forging press shapes metal parts by forcing them against a hard-metal die.

formaldehyde *See* METHANAL

Forman, Miloš (1932–) Czech film director. After making several films in Czechoslovakia, including *Fireman's Ball* (1967), he moved to the US (1968). *One Flew Over the Cuckoo's Nest* (1975) is one of only three films to gain Academy Awards for best film, best director, best actor and best actress. Forman won a further Oscar as best director for *Amadeus* (1984).

formic acid *See* METHANOIC ACID

Formosa Former name of TAIWAN

Forster, E.M. (Edward Morgan) (1879–1970) English novelist. Forster wrote six novels before giving up fiction at the age of 45: *Where Angels Fear to Tread* (1905), *The Longest Journey* (1907), *A Room with a View* (1908), *Howards End* (1910), *A Passage to India* (1924) – widely seen as his masterpiece – and the posthumously published homosexual love story, *Maurice* (1971). He made a significant contribution to the development of the realist NOVEL, and *Aspects of the Novel* (1927) is a collection of literary criticism. Other works include the essay collections *Abinger Harvest* (1936) and *Two Cheers for Democracy* (1951).

Forsyth, Frederick (1938–) English writer. Forsyth's political thrillers lend themselves to film adaptation, such as *The Day of the Jackal* (1970), *The Odessa File* (1972), *The Dogs of War* (1974) and *The Fourth Protocol* (1984).

forsythia Genus of hardy deciduous shrubs of the OLIVE family Oleaceae, named after the Scottish botanist William Forsyth (1737–1804). They are commonly cultivated in temperate regions. The small yellow flowers look like golden bells. Height: to 3m (10ft).

Fort-de-France Capital of the French overseas department of Martinique, on Fort-de-France Bay. First settled in the 17th century, it remained undeveloped until the beginning of the 20th century, when a volcanic eruption destroyed St Pierre. It is now a popular tourist resort. Exports: sugar cane, rum, cacao. Pop. (1990) 101,540.

Forth River in SE Scotland, formed at Aberfoyle by the confluence of Duchray Water and the Avondhu from Ben Lomond. It meanders E before widening into the **Firth of Forth** estuary and emptying into the North Sea. Total length: 186km (116mi).

Fort Lauderdale City on the Atlantic coast of SE Florida, USA; seat of Broward county. It was established (1838) as a military post by Major William Lauderdale. There are more than 435km (270mi) of waterways. Port Everglades is one of the world's largest passenger ports. Industries: tourism, computing. Pop. (1990) 149,377.

Fort Sumter Fort in South Carolina, USA, scene of the first hostilities of the CIVIL WAR. In 1860 South Carolina seceded from the Union and demanded all Federal property to be handed to the state. President James BUCHANAN refused, and South Carolina prepared to seize the fort held by federal forces under Major Robert

▲ **fossil** Animal fossils are not only made from their bones or shells, often their tracks can also be fossilized. Typically, a footprint (1) is left behind in soft mud, which partially hardens to form a cast. If the mud becomes flooded (2), sediment is laid over the mud especially quickly (3) helping to preserve the shape of the footprint. Over the course of time, the mud and sediment become compressed and turn to rock (4). The original mud-based rock forms a mold of the footprint (5) and the sediment-based rock forms a cast (6).

Anderson. The Confederate General BEAUREGARD called on Anderson to surrender, but he refused. On 12 April the Confederates began to bombard the fort. On 13 April it surrendered. The Confederates held Fort Sumter until 1865. It became a national monument in 1948.

Fort Wayne City in NE Indiana, USA, at the confluence of the St Joseph and St Mary rivers. The French built a trading post here *c*.1680. It was captured by the British during the French and Indian War (1755–63) and held by Native Americans (1763) during PONTIAC'S REBELLION. Development was spurred by the opening of the Wabash and Erie canals. Industries: heavy vehicles, copper wire, stainless steel, mining machinery. Pop. (1996) 185,000.

Fort Worth City in N central Texas, USA, *c*.50km (30mi) W of DALLAS. It was settled in 1843 and the US army established a post here in 1847. In the 1870s, the city was a supply centre on the cattle route from Texas to Kansas. It is famous for its oil and cattle. Industries: aerospace, electronic equipment. Pop. (1996) 480,000.

Forty-Five Rebellion *See* JACOBITES

fossil Direct evidence of the existence of an organism more than 10,000 years old. Fossils document evolutionary change and enable geologic dating. Some are original structures, such as bones, shells or wood (often altered through mineralization or preserved as moulds and casts), or imprints, such as tracks and footprints. Leaves can be preserved as a carbonized film outlining their form. Occasionally organisms are totally preserved in frozen soil (such as mammoths), peat bogs and asphalt lakes, or trapped in hardened resin (such as insects in amber). Fossil excrement (coprolite) frequently contains undigested and recognizable hard parts. *See artwork* p.319

fossil fuels COAL, OIL and NATURAL GAS – FUELS that were formed millions of years ago from fossilized remains. They are a non-renewable energy source.

Foster, Jodie (1962–) US film actress and director. In 1976, aged 13, she received an Academy nomination for her role in *Taxi Driver*. Foster has won two Best Actress Oscars, one for a controversial performance as a rape victim in *The Accused* (1988) and another for *The Silence of the Lambs* (1991). Her first film as a director was *Little Man Tate* (1991). Other films include *Sommersby* (1993).

Foster, Sir Norman (1935–) English architect. He formed Team 4 with Sue and Richard ROGERS and his wife, Wendy. Foster is noted for his use of advanced engineering technology. His huge glass and steel exoskeletons seem to exemplify modernist ideals of efficiency. Foster's works include the HSBC building, Hong Kong (1986), Stansted airport terminal, Essex (1991), the German Reichstag, Berlin (1999), the Millennium Bridge, London (2000) and the new London Assembly (2001).

Foster, Stephen Collins (1826–64) US songwriter. Influenced by Negro spirituals, his popular songs include "Oh! Susannah" (1848), "Camptown Races" (1850), "Swanee River" (1851), "My Old Kentucky Home" (1853) and "Jeanie with the Light Brown Hair" (1854).

Foucault, Jean Bernard Léon (1819–68) French physicist. He used a PENDULUM (Foucault's pendulum) to prove that the Earth spins on its axis. Foucault invented (1852) the GYROSCOPE and devised a method to measure the absolute velocity of light (1850), showing it to be slower in water than in air. With Armand Fizeau, he took the first clear photograph of the Sun. He also discovered eddy currents (Foucault currents).

Foucault, Michel (1926–84) French philosopher and historian. He was professor of the history of systems of thought (1970–84) at the *Collège de France*. Foucault examined the social and historical contexts of ideas and institutions, such as school, prison, police force and asylum. His main theme was how systems of knowledge (such as psychiatry) have changed humans into subjects. Foucault's works include *Madness and Civilization* (1961), *Discipline and Punish* (1975), *The Order of Things* (1966) and *The History of Sexuality* (1976).

Fouché, Joseph, Duc d'Otrante (1763–1820) French revolutionary, minister of police (1799–1802, 1804–10, 1815). At the start of the FRENCH REVOLUTION he joined the GIRONDINS, but switched to the JACOBINS and supported the REIGN OF TERROR. Fouché was instrumental in the overthrow of ROBESPIERRE and helped NAPOLEON I to power in the coup of 18 Brumaire. As minister of police, he formed an espionage system that saw France become a virtual police state.

Fountains Abbey Ruined CISTERCIAN monastery near Ripon, North Yorkshire, England. A world heritage site, it was founded in 1132 and became the wealthiest Cistercian community in England.

Fouquet, Jean (1420–80) French court painter. His work is monumental and sculptural. Notable works include a portrait of Charles VII (*c*.1447), Books of Hours (1450–60) and the *Pietá* at Nouans.

Fouquet, Nicolas (1615–80) French minister of finance (1653–61). Fouquet plundered the treasury for personal gain. Jean-Baptiste COLBERT alerted King LOUIS XIV, who ordered his arrest (1661). A three-year trial led to a sentence of exile, later commuted to life imprisonment.

Fourier, (François Marie) Charles (1772–1837) French socialist. He supported cooperativism and made detailed plans for the organization of communities (phalanxes). Fourier suggested that capital for the enterprise come from the capitalist, and he provided for payment to capital in his division of output. *See also* UTOPIANISM

Fourier, Jean Baptiste Joseph (1768–1830) French mathematician and physicist, scientific adviser (1798–1801) to Napoleon in Egypt. Fourier's application of mathematics to the study of HEAT led him to discover a technique (**Fourier analysis**) of expressing complex periodic functions in terms of sums of SINE and cosine WAVES. His belief that many periodic phenomena could be described by the **Fourier series** of sine and cosine functions has been largely vindicated.

four-stroke engine Engine in which the operation of each piston is in four stages, each stage corresponding to one movement of a piston along a cylinder. The stages are: induction (the fuel-air mixture enters the cylinder), compression, expansion (the exploding mixture forces the piston along the cylinder), and exhaust. This system, used by many INTERNAL COMBUSTION ENGINES, is called the four-stroke cycle, or Otto cycle, after its inventor, Nickolaus Otto (1832–91).

Fourteen Points (January 1918) Programme presented by President Woodrow WILSON for a just peace settlement of World War 1. In general, the programme called for greater liberalism in international affairs and supported national self-determination. It made useful propaganda for the Allies and was the basis on which Germany sued for peace in 1918. Some points found expression in the Treaty of VERSAILLES. The 14th Point laid the basis for the LEAGUE OF NATIONS.

fourth estate Name sometimes given to the press. The phrase was coined by Thomas Babington MACAULAY when he wrote (1828) of the House of Commons that: "The gallery in which the reporters sit has become a fourth estate of the realm". This was an expansion of the concept of the three ESTATES – the lords spiritual, lords temporal and commons.

Fourth of July US national holiday. It celebrates the approval by the CONTINENTAL CONGRESS of the DECLARATION OF INDEPENDENCE (4 July 1776). It has been a national holiday since then.

fowl Domestic birds, such as chicken or turkey, and game such as pheasant and duck. *See also* POULTRY

Fowler, H. W. (Henry Watson) (1858–1933) English lexicographer and grammarian. With his brother F.G. Fowler (1870–1918) he compiled the first *Concise Oxford Dictionary* (1911). Fowler is best known for his *Dictionary of Modern English Usage* (1926). He also wrote *The King's English* (1906).

Fowler, William Alfred (1911–95) US astrophysicist. He and Fred HOYLE were members of a research group that applied the insights of nuclear physics to astronomy. Fowler is most famous for his theory of STELLAR EVOLUTION in which chemical elements are formed in nuclear reactions within stars. He shared the 1983 Nobel Prize for physics with Subrahmanyan CHANDRASEKHAR.

Fowles, John Robert (1926–) English novelist. His first novel, *The Collector* (1963), about an obsessive who kidnaps a young woman, was made into a successful film (1965). *The Magus* (1966) and *The French Lieutenant's Woman* (1969) were also filmed. Later novels include *Mantissa* (1983) and *A Maggot* (1985).

Fox, Charles James (1749–1806) British statesman and orator, the main parliamentary proponent of liberal reform in the late 18th century. Fox entered parliament in 1768 and served as lord of the Admiralty (1770–72), and lord of the Treasury (1773–74) under Lord NORTH. He was dismissed by GEORGE III for his opposition to government policy on North America. Fox became foreign secretary (1782) in Rockingham's government and formed a short-lived coalition government (1783) with Lord North. Thereafter, he led WHIG opposition to the government of William PITT, urging the abolition of slavery and the extension of the franchise. On Pitt's death (1806), Fox briefly returned as foreign secretary.

Fox, George (1624–91) English religious leader, founder of the QUAKERS. In 1646 Fox embarked upon his evangelical calling in response to an "inner light". Imprisoned eight times between 1649 and 1673, he travelled to the Caribbean and America to visit Quaker colonists (1671–72). His *Journal* (1694) is a valuable record of the early Quaker movement.

fox Any of several carnivores of the DOG family. The red fox (*Vulpes vulpes*) is typical. Distinguished by its sharp features, rather large ears and long bushy tail, it feeds on insects, fruit, carrion, small birds and mammals and carrion. Foxes usually stalk their prey. They are solitary animals, living in dens only for the mating season. The female fox (vixen) bears four or five cubs. Foxes are hunted by larger carnivores and humans. Height: 38cm (15in) at the shoulder; weight: c.9kg (20lb). Family Canidae. *See also* ARCTIC FOX; FENNEC FOX; FOXHUNTING

Foxe, John (1516–87) English Anglican clergyman and historian whose writings promoted Protestantism and influenced English people's perception of Roman Catholicism. Foxe returned from exile in France in Elizabeth I's reign and wrote *Actes and Monuments of these latter and perillous Dayes*, better known as *Foxe's Book of Martyrs* (1563).

foxglove Hardy, Eurasian plants of the genus *Digitalis*. They have long, spiky clusters of drooping tubular flowers. The common biennial foxglove (*D. purpurea*), source of DIGITALIS, is grown for its showy purple or white flowers. Family Scrophulariaceae.

foxhound Medium-sized dog (sporting group) used in FOXHUNTING. The coat is short and smooth, the ears droop and the tail is carried erect. They are black, tan and white, and are noted for their speed and stamina. The American foxhound, a separate breed, is slighter than the English variety. Height: 53–63cm (21–25in) at the shoulder.

fox-hunting Blood sport, in which a fox is pursued across country by horse riders with FOXHOUNDS. The hunting season lasts from November to April. In the UK, calls for the abolition of foxhunting have widespread public support.

fractal Geometrical figure in which an identical motif is repeated on a reducing scale; the figure is "self-similar". The term was coined by Benoit MANDELBROT, and fractal geometry is closely associated with CHAOS THEORY. Fractal objects include shells, cauliflowers, mountains and clouds. They are also produced mathematically in computer graphics.

fraction Quotient written in the form of one number divided by another. A fraction is a/b, where a is the **numerator** and b the **denominator**. If a and b are whole numbers, the quotient is a **simple** fraction. If a is smaller than b, it is a **proper** fraction; if b is smaller than a, it is an **improper** fraction. In an **algebraic** fraction, the denominator, or the numerator and denominator, are algebraic expressions, for example $x/(x^2 + 2)$. In a **composite** fraction, both the numerator and denominator are themselves fractions.

fracture Break in a BONE usually as a result of injury, but occasionally as a result of disease (pathological fractures). In a **simple** fracture the ends of the broken bone are not displaced; in a **compound** fracture the bone pierces the skin. A **stress** fracture is a crack in a bone arising from repeated pressure. Simple breaks can be realigned with a splint.

Fragonard, Jean-Honoré (1732–1806) French painter. Fragonard is best known for the light-hearted spontaneity of his erotic scenes, such as *The Swing* (c.1766) and *The Progress of Love* (1771).

Frame, Janet (1924–) New Zealand short-story writer and novelist. Her works draw on her first-hand experience of the treatment of mental health patients. Frame's autobiographical work *An Angel at My Table* (1984) was filmed by Jane CAMPION.

franc Monetary unit of France, Belgium, Switzerland and Luxembourg, as well as of the African Financial Community (CFA) and the French Pacific Community. It is divided into 100 centimes.

France, Anatole (1844–1924) (Jacques Anatole François Thibault) French author. He achieved recognition with the novels, *The Crime of Sylvester Bonnard* (1881) and *Thaïs* (1890). France supported Emile ZOLA during the DREYFUS AFFAIR, and his writing grew more political, as in the four-volume novel series, *Contemporary History* (1897–1901), and *Penguin Island* (1908). He was awarded the 1921 Nobel Prize for literature.

France Republic in W Europe. France is Europe's second-largest country (after Ukraine). Almost half of its 5,500km (3,440mi) of frontier is sea. The PYRENEES form its SW border with Spain. The JURA MOUNTAINS and the ALPS form the E and SE borders with Switzerland and Italy. MONT BLANC is W Europe's highest peak, 4,807m (15,771ft). The RHINE forms part of the border with Germany. The MASSIF CENTRAL, between the RHÔNE-Saône valley and the Aquitaine basin, covers 15% of France. LYON and MARSEILLES are connected to the Rhône. The ÎLE-DE-FRANCE province, W of the River LOIRE, includes the capital, PARIS. *See* individual gazetteer articles. **Climate** The climate in w France is mild, moderated by the effects of the Atlantic Ocean. The e experiences greater seasonal variation. The Mediterranean Sea coast has hot, dry summers and mild, moist winters. The Alps, Jura and Pyrenees have good snowfall and are popular for winter sports. **Vegetation** A patchwork of fields and meadows cover *c.*60% of the land. Forests occupy *c.*27%. **History** Julius Caesar completed the Roman conquest of Gaul in 51 BC. The Roman Empire began to decline in the 3rd century AD. In 486 the Franks, led by CLOVIS I, established the MEROVINGIAN dynasty. Following his death, the kingdom fragmented. In 687, the CAROLINGIANS reunited Gaul and PEPIN III (THE SHORT) overthrew the Merovingians (757). His son, CHARLEMAGNE, was crowned (800) emperor of the West. He expanded the Empire and provided sound administration. Charlemagne's empire soon disintegrated and in 843, his grandson, CHARLES II (THE BALD), became ruler of the area of present-day France. Hugh Capet is often seen as the first king of France (987), and the CAPETIANS gradually subdued the nobility. The NORMAN CONQUEST (1066) marked the start of a long history of Anglo-French rivalry. PHILIP II regained land lost through dowry to the English. In 1328, the first Valois king, PHILIP VI, acceded to the throne. The HUNDRED YEARS' WAR (1337–1453) was a series of battles for the French succession. By 1422, England controlled most of France. JOAN OF ARC helped to crush the siege of Orléans (1428), and by 1453 England had been expelled from France. LOUIS XI restored royal authority and crushed the ANGEVINS. FRANCIS I's reign marked the beginning of the RENAISSANCE in France and the struggle with the HABSBURGS. The rise of the HUGUENOTS led to the Wars of RELIGION (1562–98). The GUISE faction lost, and HENRY IV became the first BOURBON king (1589). Cardinals RICHELIEU and MAZARIN led France to victory in the THIRTY YEARS' WAR (1618–48). LOUIS XIV's court at VERSAILLES was the richest in Europe. Yet, the *ancien régime* of LOUIS XV and LOUIS XVI was bankrupted by war and incapable of reform. The FRENCH REVOLUTION (1789–99) saw the execution of the king, and ROBESPIERRE's brutal REIGN OF TERROR. The DIRECTORY ended when NAPOLEON I proclaimed himself emperor (1799). The success of the NAPOLEONIC WARS was wiped out at WATERLOO (1815). Napoleon was forced into exile, and the Bourbons restored to the throne. The FEBRUARY REVOLUTION (1848) established a Second Republic. Napoleon I's nephew seized power as NAPOLEON III (1852). His defeat in the FRANCO-PRUSSIAN WAR (1870–71) led to the formation of the Third Republic (1870–1940). The PARIS COMMUNE (1871) was violently suppressed. The DREYFUS Affair polarized France. France was the battleground for much of WORLD WAR 1. CLEMENCEAU and BRIAND led France to peace. Léon BLUM and Édouard DALADIER failed to tackle Germany's increasing power. In June 1940, German troops completed the conquest of France and established the VICHY GOVERNMENT. Charles DE GAULLE became head of a government-in-exile. In August 1944 Paris was liberated, and a Fourth Republic was founded (1946). Political instability and colonial war, especially in ALGERIA, slowed the postwar recovery. In 1958, de Gaulle was elected president and established a Fifth Republic. Gaullist foreign policy

alienated the US and UK. In 1969 De Gaulle resigned, replaced first by Georges POMPIDOU, then Valéry GISCARD D'ESTAING. François MITTERRAND's presidency was marked by nationalization, civic rebuilding, decentralization and advocacy of the EUROPEAN UNION (EU). Following Mitterrand's death (1995), his rival Jacques CHIRAC was elected president. His welfare reforms and attempts to meet the criteria for Economic and Monetary Union (EMU) brought strikes and unemployment and led to the election (1997) of a socialist prime minister, Lionel JOSPIN. **Economy** France is a leading industrialized nation (1995 GDP per capita, US\$21,030). It is the world's fourth-largest manufacturer of cars. Industries include chemicals and steel. It is the leading producer of farm products in w Europe. Livestock and dairy farming are vital sectors. It is the world's second-largest producer of cheese and wine. Wheat is the principal crop. Tourism is a major industry (1992 receipts, US\$25 million).

Francesca, Piero della *See* PIERO DELLA FRANCESCA

Franche-Comté Historic region of e France; its capital was Dôle until 1674 and BESANÇON thereafter. Founded in the 12th century as the "free county" of the Burgundians, it was disputed between the Holy Roman Empire, France, Burgundy, Spain and Switzerland throughout the Middle Ages. After LOUIS XIV's conquest of 1674, it was finally recognized as part of France in 1678. Area: 16,202sq km (6,254sq mi). Pop. (1991) 1,097,300.

franchise Right or privilege of an individual to vote in public political ELECTIONS, granted by government. Franchise is conferred according to a set of criteria, which may include age, sex, race and class. In contemporary democracies, the intention is that anyone over a specific age has the right to vote. In Britain, the modern basis of the franchise dates from the 1832 Reform Act and subsequent acts which, by 1918, ensured all men over the age of 21 and women over 30 were entitled to vote (the first country to give women the vote was New Zealand). By 1928 women aged over 21 were enfranchised, and in 1969 the voting age was lowered to 18. In the US, the franchise is granted by each state, and this is overseen by the CONSTITUTION. The 14th and 15th Amendments (1868 and 1870 respectively) forbid any state to deny voting rights to resident adult men aged over 21 on the grounds of race, colour or previous servitude. The 19th Amendment (1920) gave women the vote. In US political practice, voting rights for African Americans, especially in the South, were restricted until the 1960s through such practices as state-constitution clauses, literacy tests and poll taxes. The 24th Amendment (1964) banned poll taxes. The Voting Rights Act outlawed literacy tests and installed poll observers to prevent voter intimidation. The 26th Amendment (1971) lowered the voting age to 18. *See also* BALLOT; DEMOCRACY; SUFFRAGETTE MOVEMENT

Francis I (1708–65) Holy Roman emperor (1745–65), Duke of Lorraine (1729–35) and Tuscany (1737–65). In 1736 he married the Habsburg heiress, MARIA THERESA. Her accession (1740) precipitated the War of the AUSTRIAN SUCCESSION against FREDERICK II. Francis succeeded Charles VIII as emperor, but the real ruler was his wife.

Francis II (1768–1835) Last Holy Roman emperor (1792–1806), first emperor of Austria, as Francis I (1804–35), and king of Bohemia and of Hungary (1792–1835). Francis was repeatedly defeated by the armies of NAPOLEON I in the FRENCH REVOLUTIONARY WARS, and his territory steadily diminished, culminating in the rout at the Battle of AUSTERLITZ (1805) and the abolition of the HOLY ROMAN EMPIRE. In 1810, Prince METTERNICH secured the marriage of Francis' daughter,

FRANCE
AREA: 551,500sq km (212,934sq mi)
POPULATION: 58,145,000
CAPITAL (POPULATION): Paris (9,469,000)

Marie Louise, to Napoleon. Austria was preserved by this alliance, and in 1813 Francis joined the coalition that defeated Napoleon. He then formed the HOLY ALLIANCE.

Francis I (1494–1547) King of France (1515–47), cousin and son-in-law and successor of LOUIS XII. A leader of the RENAISSANCE, he is best remembered for his patronage of the arts and his palace at FONTAINEBLEAU. Persecution of the WALDENSES, centralization of monarchial power, and foolish financial policies made Francis unpopular at home. A costly struggle with the Emperor CHARLES V over the imperial crown led to defeat at Pavia (1525). Francis was imprisoned and in the Treaty of Madrid (1526) forced to give up Burgundy and renounce his claims to Italy. Two more wars (1527–29, 1536–38) ended ingloriously. In 1542 Francis concluded a treaty with SULEIMAN I and attacked Italy for a fourth time. Charles, in alliance with Henry VIII, responded by invading France, and Francis lost further territory. He was succeeded by his son, HENRY II.

Francis II (1544–60) King of France (1559–60), eldest son of HENRY II and CATHERINE DE' MEDICI. Married to Mary Queen of Scots at the age of 14, he was a sickly youth and his kingdom was controlled by the GUISE family. *See also* RELIGION, WARS OF

Franciscans Friars belonging to an itinerant religious order founded by St FRANCIS OF ASSISI. The first order, known as the Friars Minor, now comprises three subdivisions: the Observants; the CAPUCHIN; and the Conventual, who are allowed to own property corporately. The second order, the Poor Clares, an order of nuns founded by St Francis and St CLARE, came into being in 1212.

Francis Joseph *See* FRANZ JOSEPH

Francis of Assisi, Saint (1182–1226) Italian founder of the FRANCISCANS, b. Giovanni di Bernardone. The son of a wealthy merchant in Assisi, in 1205 he renounced his worldly life for one of poverty and prayer. In 1209 Francis received permission from Pope INNOCENT III to begin a monastic order. The Franciscans were vowed to humility, poverty and devotion to the task of helping people. In 1212, with St CLARE, he established an order for women, popularly called the Poor Clares. In 1224, while Francis prayed on Monte della Verna, near Florence, the stigmata wounds of the Crucifixion appeared on his body. He was canonized in 1228. His feast day is 4 October.

Francis of Sales, Saint (1567–1622) French Roman Catholic bishop and devotional writer. He was a leader of the COUNTER REFORMATION in Savoy. Francis converted many of the population of Chablais from CALVINISM. In 1602 he was appointed Bishop of Geneva, where he founded the Visitation Nuns. His writings include *Introduction to the Devout Life* (1609).

Francis Xavier, Saint (1506–52) Early JESUIT missionary, often called the **Apostle of the Indies**. Francis was an associate of St IGNATIUS OF LOYOLA, with whom he took the vow founding the Society of Jesus (JESUITS). From 1541 he travelled through India, Japan and the East Indies, making many converts. Francis died while on a journey to China. His feast day is 3 December.

francium (symbol Fr) Radioactive metallic element, discovered (1839) by Marguerite Perey. It occurs naturally in uranium ores and is a decay product of actinium. Properties: at.no. 87; most stable isotope Fr^{223} (half life 22 minutes).

Franck, César Auguste (1822–90) French Romantic composer, b. Belgium. Franck wrote major works for the organ and is best remembered for the *Symphonic Variations* for piano and orchestra (1885), the popular *Symphony in D Minor* (1888), and significant chamber works.

Franck, James (1882–1964) US physicist, b. Germany. With Gustav Hertz, he experimented with ELECTRON bombardment of gases, providing support for the theory of atomic structure proposed by Niels BOHR and information for the QUANTUM THEORY of Max PLANCK. Franck and Hertz shared the 1925 Nobel Prize for physics. He worked on the MANHATTAN PROJECT to develop the atom bomb and presented the "Franck petition" which opposed the use of the bomb against Japanese civilians.

Franco, Francisco (1892–1975) Spanish general and dictator of Spain (1939–75). He joined the 1936 military uprising that led to the Spanish CIVIL WAR and assumed leadership of the fascist FALANGE. By 1939, with the aid of Nazi Germany and Fascist Italy, Franco had won the war and become Spain's dictator. He kept Spain neutral in World War 2, after which he presided over its accelerating economic development, while maintaining rigid control over political expression. In 1947 Franco declared Spain a monarchy with himself as regent, and in 1969 he designated JUAN CARLOS as heir to the throne.

Franco-Prussian War (1870–71) Prussian victory in the AUSTRO-PRUSSIAN WAR (1866) alarmed NAPOLEON III. The Prussian chancellor, BISMARCK, used the prospect of French invasion to frighten the s German states into joining the North German Confederation dominated by Prussia. The nominal cause of the war was a dispute over the Spanish succession. Prussia was fully prepared for the French declaration of war (14 July 1870), and General von Moltke launched a devastating offensive into Alsace. In September the emperor and 100,000 French troops were captured at Sedan. Napoleon III abdicated, and Paris was surrounded and starved into submission. An armistice was agreed in January 1871, and Alsace and Lorraine were ceded to the new German empire under WILLIAM I. Paris refused to surrender its weapons, and the PARIS COMMUNE was formed.

frangipani (pagoda tree) Shrub or small tree (*Plumeria rubra*) native to tropical America. It is widely cultivated in the Old World tropics for its fragrant white, yellow, pink or red flowers, which are used as offerings in Buddhist temples. A perfume is prepared from the flowers. Frangipani has a poisonous milky sap. Family Apocynaceae; genus *Plumeria*.

Frank, Anne (1929–45) German Jew who became a symbol of suffering under the Nazis. Born in Frankfurt am Main, she fled with her family to the Netherlands in 1933. The Franks were living in Amsterdam at the time of the German invasion in 1940 and went into hiding from 1942 until they were betrayed in August 1944. Anne died in Bergen-Belsen concentration camp. The diary she kept during her years in hiding was published in 1947 and attracted worldwide readership.

Frankenthaler, Helen (1928–) US painter, sculptor and graphic artist who provides the link between ABSTRACT EXPRESSIONISM and colour field painting. Her seminal work is *Mountains and Sea* (1952). She was married (1958–71) to Robert MOTHERWELL.

Frankfort Capital of Kentucky, USA, on the Kentucky River, N central Kentucky. First settled in 1779, it was made the state capital in 1792. Notable buildings include "Liberty Hall" (1796), reportedly designed by Thomas Jefferson, and the Old Capitol (1827–30). Industries: tobacco, whisky distilling, textiles. Pop. (1990) 25,535.

Frankfurt City and port, on the River Main, Hesse state, W Germany. It was one of the royal residences of Charlemagne; the Holy Roman emperors were elected here, and the first German National Assembly met here in 1848. Notable buildings include a Gothic cathedral, an art museum and a university. Frankfurt is Germany's banking centre and a venue for international fairs. Industries: chemicals, electrical equipment, telecommunications, publishing. Pop. (1995) 652,000.

Frankfurter, Felix (1882–1965) US jurist and educator, associate justice of the US Supreme Court (1939–62). He helped found the American Civil Liberties Union (1920). An adviser to Franklin D. ROOSEVELT, Frankfurter was a liberal Supreme Court justice. He advocated judicial restraint and government self-regulation in civil liberties.

Frankfurt School Influential German philosophical and sociological movement associated with the Institute for Social Research founded (1923) within the University of Frankfurt. Its members included Theodor ADORNO, Herbert MARCUSE, Erich FROMM, Max Horkheimer and Jürgen HABERMAS. In 1934, the Institute closed and many members fled to New York, USA. It returned to Frankfurt in the 1950s. The Frankfurt School developed **critical theory**, a social philosophy based on the writings of Karl MARX and Sigmund FREUD. It argued that thought is a product of social processes and that science and POSITIVISM are not objective but subject to social values.

frankincense (olibanum) Gum resin extracted from the bark of trees of the genus *Boswellia*, found in Africa and parts of the Middle East. Used in religious ceremonies and one of the gifts of the MAGI, it is burned as incense, and the fine spicy oil extracted from the resin is used as a fixative in perfumes.

Franklin, Aretha (1942–) US gospel and soul singer. Known as the "Queen of Soul", Aretha has had more million-selling singles than any other female artist. Her classic songs include "I Never Loved a Man (The Way I Love You)", "Respect" (1967) and "I Say a Little Prayer" (1967).

Franklin, Benjamin (1706–90) American statesman, scientist and inventor. A successful printer in Philadelphia, where he published *Poor Richard's Almanac* (1732–57), he gave the business up to devote his life to scientific research. His experiments in electricity, which he identified in lightning, were influential. Franklin was deputy paymaster general (1753–74) of the colonies. At the ALBANY CONGRESS (1754), he proposed a union of the colonies. Franklin pressed for moderate opposition to the STAMP ACT (1768). A leading delegate to the CONTINENTAL CONGRESS, he became an architect of the new republic. When war broke out, Franklin went to Paris and negotiated a treaty of alliance (1778). His peace proposals formed the basis of the final Treaty of Paris (1783) with Great Britain. Franklin was president of Pennsylvania's executive council (1785–88) and, as a member of the CONSTITUTIONAL CONVENTION (1787), helped form the US CONSTITUTION.

Franklin, Sir John (1786–1847) English Arctic explorer. He served as a naval officer in the Battle of Trafalgar (1805). Franklin's first overland exploration of N Canada (1819–22) crossed from Great Slave Lake to the Arctic coast. His second expedition (1825-27) descended the Mackenzie River. Franklin served as governor of Tasmania (1836–43). In 1845, he embarked on a fated search for the NORTHWEST PASSAGE. The first of 40 search parties was launched in 1848. These expeditions greatly advanced knowledge of the Arctic and eventually established (1859) that Franklin had died with his entire 129-man crew after they became caught in ice in the Victoria Strait.

Franklin, Rosalind Elsie (1920–58) English molecular biologist. Using X-RAY CRYSTALLOGRAPHY, Franklin obtained excellent diffraction photographs of the structure of DNA. Her work enabled James WATSON, Francis CRICK and Maurice WILKINS to determine the full molecular structure of DNA.

Franks Germanic people who settled in the region of the Rhine River in the 3rd century. Under CLOVIS I in the late 5th century, they overthrew the remnant of Roman rule in Gaul and established the MEROVINGIAN empire. This was divided into the kingdoms of Austrasia, Neustria and Burgundy, but was reunited by the CAROLINGIANS, notably by CHARLEMAGNE. The partition of his empire into the East and West Frankish kingdoms is the origin of Germany and France.

Franz Ferdinand (1863–1914) Archduke of Austria, nephew of FRANZ JOSEPH. He became heir apparent in 1889. On an official visit to Bosnia-Herzegovina, Franz Ferdinand and his wife were assassinated by a Serb nationalist, Gavrilo Princip, in Sarajevo (28 June 1914). The incident led directly to the outbreak of WORLD WAR 1.

Franz Josef Land (Zemlya Franca-iosifa) Russian archipelago in the Arctic Ocean, forming part of Archangel'sk oblast. A group of c.85 islands, it includes Alexandra Land, George Land and Graham Bell Island. The most northerly lands in the Eastern Hemisphere, its average mean temperature is −14.2°C (6.5°F). Franz Josef Land was discovered (1873) by an Austrian expedition and was incorporated in the Soviet Union in 1926. Area: c.20,700sq km (8,000sq mi).

Franz Joseph (1830–1916) Emperor of Austria (1848–1916) and king of Hungary (1867–1916). He succeeded his uncle Ferdinand, who abdicated during the REVOLUTIONS OF 1848, and quickly brought the revolutions under control, defeating the Hungarians under Louis KOSSUTH in 1849. With the formation (1867) of the AUSTRO-HUNGARIAN EMPIRE, Franz Joseph was forced to grant Hungary co-equal status. He died in the midst of World War 1, two years before the final collapse of the HABSBURG empire.

Frasch process *See* SULPHUR

Fraser, (John) Malcolm (1930–) Australian statesman, prime minister (1975–83). In 1955, he entered parliament as the youngest-ever Liberal MP. Fraser served in the cabinet (1966–71) before becoming Liberal Party leader (1975) and forming a coalition government. An uncompromising politician, he was defeated in 1983 elections by Bob HAWKE and resigned.

Fraser Chief river of British Columbia, NW Canada. It rises at Yellowhead Pass in the Rocky Mountains and flows NW to Prince George, then S around the Cariboo Mountains and into the Strait of Georgia at Vancouver. It was discovered in 1793 by Sir Alexander Mackenzie and named after Simon Fraser, who followed (1808) the river to its mouth. It is the major spawning ground in North America for the Pacific salmon. The Fraser River canyon has spectacular scenery. Length: c.1,370km (850 mi).

Fraunhofer, Joseph von (1787–1826) German physicist and optician, founder of astronomical spectroscopy. By studying the DIFFRACTION of light through narrow slits, he developed the earliest form of diffraction grating. He observed and began to map the dark lines in the Sun's spectrum (1814), now called **Fraunhofer lines**.

Frazier, Joe (1944–) US heavyweight boxer. In 1968, he won a version of the world's heavyweight title when he beat Buster Mathis and became undisputed champion after he defeated Jimmy Ellis (1970). In 1973, Frazier lost the title to George Foreman. His bouts with Muhammad ALI, whom he defeated in 1971, were his most notable. After losing again to Foreman and twice to Ali, he retired in 1976.

Frederick I (Barbarossa) (1123–90) Holy Roman emperor (1155–90) and king of Germany (1152–90); nephew and successor to Emperor CONRAD III. He hoped to end the division between the houses of HOHENSTAUFEN and GUELPH. He was crowned emperor by ADRIAN IV. In 1156, Frederick restored Bavaria to HENRY THE LION. In 1158, he captured Milan and declared himself king of the Lombards. Frederick set up an antipope to ALEXANDER III, who excommunicated him and formed the LOMBARD LEAGUE. In 1176, Frederick was defeated at Legnano by the League and was forced to recognize Alexander as pope and make peace (1183) with the Lombards. In 1180, he defeated Henry the Lion and partitioned Bavaria. Frederick was drowned on the Third Crusade. His son succeeded as HENRY VI.

Frederick II (1194–1250) Holy Roman emperor (1215–50) and German king (1212–20), king of Sicily (1198–1250), and king of Jerusalem (1229–50); son of Emperor HENRY VI. After his father's death, Germany was plunged into factional strife between the HOHENSTAUFENS, led by his uncle Philip of Swabia, and the GUELPHS led by OTTO IV. Otto prevailed, but his invasion of Italy prompted Pope INNOCENT III to promote Frederick. He devoted himself to Italy and Sicily, and although he promised to make his son, Henry, king of Sicily, Frederick secured his election as king of Germany (1220) instead. His claims on Lombardy and postponement of a crusade angered Pope Honorius III, who excommunicated him and revived the LOMBARD LEAGUE. He finally embarked on a crusade in 1228 and proclaimed himself *stupor mundi* (wonder of the world). In Sicily, Frederick set up a centralized royal administration, while in Germany he devolved authority to the princes. The latter policy led Henry to rebel against his father. In 1235, Frederick imprisoned Henry, gave the German throne to CONRAD IV, and issued a land peace. In 1239 he captured most of the papal states. In 1245 Pope Innocent IV deposed him.

Frederick III (1415–93) Holy Roman emperor (1452–93) and German king (1440–93). He attempted to win the thrones of Bohemia and Hungary after the death of his ward, Ladislas V (1458). Instead, he lost Austria, Carinthia, Carniola and Styria to Matthias Corvinus of Hungary, only recovering them on Matthias' death (1490). By marrying his son Maximilian to Mary, heiress of Burgundy, in 1477, he acquired an enormous inheritance for the HABSBURGS.

Frederick III (1831–88) Emperor of Germany (1888). Son of William I, he married (1858) Victoria, eldest daughter of the British Queen VICTORIA. Liberal and popular, he died 90 days after his accession and was succeeded by his son, William II.

Frederick II (the Great) (1712–86) King of Prussia (1740–86). Succeeding his father, FREDERICK WILLIAM I, he made PRUSSIA a major European force. In the War of the AUSTRIAN SUCCESSION (1740–48) against MARIA THERESA, Frederick gained the province of Silesia from Austria. During the SEVEN YEARS' WAR (1756–63), his brilliant generalship preserved the kingdom from a superior hostile alliance. In 1760, Austro-Russian forces occupied Berlin (1760), but Russia's subsequent withdrawal from the war enabled Frederick to emerge triumphant at the peace. He directed Prussia's remarkable recovery from the devastation of war. Gaining further territory in the first partition of Poland (1772), he renewed the contest against Austria in the War of the Bavarian Succession (1778–79). Artistic and intellectual, he was a friend and patron of Voltaire. He wrote extensively in French, built the palace of Sans Souci and was a gifted musician.

Frederick V (1596–1623) (Winter King) King of Bohemia (1619–20), elector palatine (1610–20). A Calvinist prince of the Wittelsbach family, he married the daughter of James I of England (1613). In 1619 he was chosen as king by the Protestant rebels of Bohemia in preference to the Holy Roman emperor FERDINAND II, provoking the outbreak of the THIRTY YEARS' WAR. Defeat at the Battle of the White Mountain (1620) resulted in the loss of both Frederick's titles.

Fredericksburg City on the Rappahannock River, N Virginia, USA. Planned in 1727, it has many historic landmarks that make it a major tourist attraction. It is particularly associated with the American Revolution and Civil War. From 1760, the Rising Sun Tavern was a meeting place for American patriots. Many sites are connected to George WASHINGTON, including the site of the signing of a 1775 resolution of American Independence. The Civil War battle of Fredericksburg (1862) was a one-sided victory for the Confederate army of Northern Virginia, led by General Robert E. LEE, over the Union Army of the Potomac, led by Major General Ambrose BURNSIDE. Nearly 13,000 Union troops were killed or wounded. In comparison, the Confederate troops of Stonewall JACKSON and James Longstreet lost *c*.5,300. Industries: tourism, clothing, shoes. Pop. (1990) 19,030.

Frederick William I (1688–1740) King of Prussia (1713–40), son and successor of Frederick I. He strengthened the army and economy and centralized the government, laying the basis for the rise of Prussia as a great power. Frederick William treated his gifted son, the future FREDERICK II (THE GREAT), with brutality but bequeathed him a full treasury and the finest army in Europe.

Frederick William II (1744–97) King of Prussia (1786–97), nephew and successor of FREDERICK II (THE GREAT). He joined (1792) the alliance against France but made peace in 1795 in order to consolidate his acquisitions in the E as a result of the second (1793) and third (1795) partitions of Poland. He kept an extravagant court and left Prussia virtually bankrupt.

Frederick William III (1770–1840) King of Prussia (1797–1840), son and successor of FREDERICK WILLIAM II. He declared war on France (1806), suffered a disastrous defeat at Jena, and was forced to sign the Treaty of Tilsit (1807). In Prussia, some progressive reforms were made, but a constitution, though promised, was never produced, and the king later became increasingly reactionary. The reorganized Prussian army re-entered the NAPOLEONIC WARS in 1813 and played a major part in NAPOLEON I's eventual defeat.

Frederick William IV (1795–1861) King of Prussia (1840–61), son and successor of FREDERICK WILLIAM III. He granted a constitution in response to the REVOLUTIONS OF 1848, but later amended it to eliminate popular influence. He refused the crown of Germany (1849) because it was offered by the Frankfurt Parliament, a democratic assembly. From 1858, the future Emperor WILLIAM I ruled as regent.

Frederick William (1620–88) (Great Elector) Elector of Brandenburg (1640–88). He inherited a collection of small and impoverished territories ravaged by the THIRTY YEARS' WAR. By the end of his reign, his organizational powers had created a unified state with a centralized tax system and a formidable standing army. The powers of the provincial estates (assemblies) were reduced. The Elector encouraged commerce and industry. He acquired Eastern Pomerania at the Peace of WESTPHALIA and, by his interventions in the war between Poland and Sweden (1655–60), gained sovereignty over Prussia.

Fredericton City in E Canada, at the head of the Saint John River; capital of the province of New Brunswick. Settled in the early 18th century by the French, it was made provincial capital in 1785. It is an important trade and rail centre. Industries: timber. Pop. (1991) 45,364.

Free Church Any of a number of Protestant churches which are independent of the established church of a country. In England CONGREGATIONALISM, METHODISM, PRESBYTERIANISM and the BAPTIST movements formed a National Council of Evangelical Free Churches.

Free Church of Scotland Grouping of Scottish Presbyterians formed as a result of the secession of nearly one-third of the membership of the established CHURCH OF SCOTLAND in the Disruption of 1843. In 1900, all but a small minority of this Free Church joined the United Presbyterian Church to become the United Free Church of Scotland. In 1929, following the acceptance of the Church of Scotland's spiritual independence, the United Free Church of Scotland reunited with it. The tiny Presbyterian minority who had opposed the initial union retained their independence and kept the name United Free Church.

Freedmen's Bureau US government agency established in 1865 at the end of the CIVIL WAR to aid newly freed African-Americans. Administered by the War Department, with General Oliver O. HOWARD as its commissioner, the agency was one of the most powerful instruments of RECONSTRUCTION. The bureau also acted as a political machine, recruiting voters for the REPUBLICAN PARTY. President Andrew JOHNSON viewed the bureau's work as an unconstitutional interference in the Southern states. It was disbanded in 1872.

Freedom of Information Act (1967) US law giving greater public access to government records. It permits government agencies full discretion about disclosure of information only in such areas as national defence, confidential financial information and law enforcement. The act was weakened by agency reclassification of information under permitted exemptions. A Freedom of Information Act is being prepared for the UK.

Freedom Rides Civil rights trips to the US South in 1961 sponsored by the CONGRESS OF RACIAL EQUALITY (CORE). They led to the desegregation of interstate terminals and subsequently to the Interstate Commerce Commission's ruling providing "nonracial" seating in buses.

Free French Group formed by Charles DE GAULLE on the creation of the VICHY GOVERNMENT in 1940. Its purpose was to continue French opposition to Germany. Operating outside France, the group was soon aligned with internal Resistance groups. The Free French aided the Allies throughout the war, forming a provisional government after the D-DAY invasion.

freemasonry Customs and teachings of the secret fraternal order of Free and Accepted Masons, an all-male secret society with national organizations worldwide. Freemasonry is most popular in the UK and countries once in the British empire. It evolved from the medieval guilds of stonemasons and cathedral builders. Its ceremonies, which use many symbolic gestures and allegories, demand a belief in God as the architect of the Universe. The first Grand Lodge (meeting place) was founded in England (1717). The first US lodge was founded (1730) in Philadelphia. Many of the leaders of the American Revolution were masons, and 13 US presidents have been lodge members. Historically associated with liberalism, freemasonry teaches morality, charity and law-abiding behaviour. In recent times, they have incurred criticism because of their strict secrecy, male exclusivity and alleged use of influence within organizations, such as the police or local government, to benefit members. It is estimated that there are c.6 million Masons worldwide.

free port Area in which goods may be landed and reshipped without customs intervention. Free ports aid in quicker movement of ships and goods. When the goods are moved to the consumer, they then become subject to customs duties. Free ports include New York City, Copenhagen, Singapore and Stockholm.

free radical Short-lived molecule (less than 1ms) that has an unpaired ELECTRON and, therefore, rapidly binds with other molecules. Occurring as by-products of normal CELL chemistry, free radicals are highly reactive and can cause extensive damage in the body, even though cells have some protective enzymes. They are thought to play a role in ageing and a number of disease processes.

freesia Genus of perennial herbs of the IRIS family, native to South Africa. Species of freesia are widely cultivated for their fragrant yellow, white or pink flowers. They are grown in greenhouses for winter blooming.

Free State (formerly Orange Free State) Province in E central South Africa; the capital is BLOEMFONTEIN. The region consists principally of fertile high plains, with the DRAKENSBERG MOUNTAINS as part of its E border with Lesotho. The River ORANGE forms its S border with Northern Cape. Boers began to settle in large numbers after the GREAT TREK (1836). It was annexed (1848) by the British, achieved independence (1854), and after its involvement in the SOUTH AFRICAN WARS (1899–1902) was again annexed by Britain. Regaining independence in 1907, the Orange Free State joined the Union of South Africa in 1910. The economy is dominated by agriculture and gold. Pop. (1995 est.) 2,782,500.

freethinkers People whose opinions and ideas, especially on matters of religion, are not influenced by CANON law or dogma. The original freethinkers were part of a post-Reformation movement that sought to assert reason over religious authority. DEISM emerged as the chief expression of freethought during the 17th and 18th centuries. *See also* ATHEISM; HUMANISM

Freetown Capital and chief port of Sierra Leone, W Africa. Freetown was founded (1787) by the British as a settlement for freed slaves from England, Nova Scotia and Jamaica. It was the capital of British West Africa (1808–74). In 1961 Freetown was made capital of independent Sierra Leone. Industries: platinum, gold, diamonds, oil refining, palm oil. Pop. (1992) 505,080.

free trade Commerce conducted between nations without restrictions on imports and exports. In the 19th century, the repeal of England's CORN LAWS (1846) and the Anglo-French free-trade treaty (1860) were hallmarks of free trade. Twentieth-century agreements include the EUROPEAN FREE TRADE AGREEMENT (EFTA) (1959) and the NORTH AMERICAN FREE TRADE AGREEMENT (NAFTA) (1994). Protectionists oppose free trade, advocating import duties and restrictive quotas to safeguard domestic industry from foreign competition. *See also* MERCANTILISM

free verse Verse with no regular metre and no apparent form, relying primarily on cadence. The rhythm is close to prose. Walt WHITMAN and Arthur RIMBAUD were early users of free verse, which is now a common form.

free will In philosophy, doctrine that individuals are able to choose some of their own actions. It is often compared with DETERMINISM. PLATO argued that choices are determined by the good course. ARISTOTLE contested this, arguing that people often desire something they know is bad for them. In Christian theology, free will is contested by PREDESTINATION. In the 5th century St AUGUSTINE held that man could only be saved by divine grace, while PELAGIUS believed man can choose salvation or damnation. *See also* EXISTENTIALISM; NIETZSCHE, FRIEDRICH WILHELM

freezing *See* DEEP-FREEZING; FOOD PRESERVATION

freezing point Temperature at which a substance changes from LIQUID to SOLID. For most substances, it increases with pressure. Melting point is the change from solid to liquid and is the same as freezing point.

Frege, Gottlob (1848–1925) German philosopher. He was a professor of mathematics at Jena (1879–1918). With George BOOLE, Frege was one of the founders of modern symbolic LOGIC. In his *Foundations of Arithmetic* (1884), Frege attempted to derive all mathematics from logical axioms.

Frei (Montalva), Eduardo (1911–82) Chilean statesman, president (1964–70). In 1964, he defeated Salvador ALLENDE to become the first Christian Democrat leader of Chile. Frei's ambitious package of reforms, including the nationalization of Chile's copper industry and the redistribution of land and wealth, floundered amid economic recession. In 1970 Frei was defeated by Allende. His son, Eduardo **Frei Ruiz-Tagle** (1942–), also served as president (1993–2000).

Fremantle Major port in w Australia, at the mouth of the River Swan and part of PERTH metropolitan area. In 1829, Captain Charles Fremantle founded the city as a penal colony. It overtook Albany as Western Australia's main port at the end of the 19th century. Pop. (1991) 23,834.

Frémont, John Charles (1813–90) US explorer and general. Following his exploration and mapping of the Oregon Trail (1842), Frémont crossed the Sierra Nevada in the winter of 1843–44. A second expedition (1845) led to the Bear Flag Revolt by American settlers, and he became civil governor. In 1848, he resigned his commission in 1848 and made a fortune in the gold rush. Frémont was the first REPUBLICAN PARTY presidential candidate, losing to James BUCHANAN. He became governor of Arizona (1878–83).

French, John Denton Pinkstone, 1st Earl of Ypres (1852–1925) British field marshal. He distinguished himself in the second of the SOUTH AFRICAN WARS and was made chief of the Imperial General Staff (1912–14). At the outbreak of WORLD WAR 1, France was given command of the British Expeditionary Force. Criticized for indecisiveness, he resigned (December 1915) in favour of Sir Douglas HAIG. French also served a controversial term as lord lieutenant of Ireland (1918–21).

French Major language, spoken in France and parts of Belgium, Switzerland, Canada, Haiti, Africa and other areas. There are some 80–100 million French speakers worldwide. Descended from Latin, it is a Romance language of the INDO-EUROPEAN family. It is one of the six official languages of the United Nations (UN).

French Academy *See* ACADÉMIE FRANÇAISE

French and Indian Wars (1689–1763) Collective name for four colonial wars in North America, fought between Great Britain and France with Native American nations fighting on both sides. The aim of the wars in North America was for control of the eastern part of the continent, with ports and forts that controlled trade to the Old World. **King William's War** (1689–97) was a development of the War of the GRAND ALLIANCE and ended inconclusively. **Queen Anne's War** (1702–13) corresponds to the War of the SPANISH SUCCESSION. Britain gained Newfoundland, Acadia and Hudson Bay. **King George's War** (1744–48) grew out of the War of the Austrian Succession. It ended inconclusively. The **French and Indian War** (1754–63) was the most significant conflict, forming part of the SEVEN YEARS' WAR. British

efforts (1754–55) to capture French forts in w America were unsuccessful. After 1756, British resources improved, and forts at Louisburg and Duquesne (1758) were captured. Ticonderoga fell in 1759. In the battle for Québec on the Plains of Abraham (1759), both the French and English generals, Louis Joseph de MONTCALM and James WOLFE, were killed, but Britain emerged victorious. In 1760, the British captured Montréal. The Treaty of Paris (1763) established British control of Canada.

French architecture From the 8th to early 19th centuries, French architects were dependent on royal patronage, although the 10th-century Benedictine abbey at Cluny had an influence on cathedral architecture. During the 11th and 12th centuries, CATHEDRALS in the ROMANESQUE style were constructed. In the 13th century, Gothic cathedrals, such as CHARTRES and NOTRE-DAME, were built. In 1494 the influence of Italian RENAISSANCE ARCHITECTURE grew and inspired kings, such as Francis I and Henry IV, to commission magnificent palaces, including FONTAINEBLEAU, the LOUVRE and Chambord. Royal influence climaxed in the 17th century with Louis XIV's palace at VERSAILLES. After 1685, a lighter note prevailed, but in the mid-18th century, official architecture turned to NEOCLASSICISM, introducing designs based on the DORIC order. In the 19th century, patronage shifted from the court to the bourgeoisie. Baron Haussman designed the wide boulevards of Paris, and between 1850 and 1870, mansard roofs and pavilions marked a Renaissance revival. The EIFFEL TOWER (1889) heralded MODERNISM, and ART NOUVEAU faded quickly. In the 1920s and 1930s, BAUHAUS had a large influence, and the Domino frame buildings of LE CORBUSIER spearheaded the INTERNATIONAL STYLE.

French art Studies of French art usually begin with the 12th century. There were several important centres of manuscript illumination in Cistercian abbeys. During the Renaissance, the art of the Court was heavily influenced by Italian trends, as is evident with Jean FOUQUET and the FONTAINEBLEAU SCHOOL. It was not until the 17th century that artists of international stature emerged such as CLAUDE LORRAIN and Nicolas POUSSIN, who were masterful exponents of classical landscape painting. Poussin was particularly important, and his rigorous draftsmanship was used as a benchmark for academic standards well into the 19th century. The twilight-years of the *ancien régime* were celebrated in the light-hearted ROCOCO fantasies of François BOUCHER and Jean-Honoré FRAGONARD. As the Revolution drew near, however, these gave way to the stern moralizing of neoclassical painters such as Jacques Louis DAVID. He remained influential into the romantic period, when the leading French artist was Eugène DELACROIX. In the late 19th century, there were a succession of movements which increased artistic freedom. These began with the REALISM of Gustave COURBET and culminated in IMPRESSIONISM, POST-IMPRESSIONISM and SYMBOLISM. This creativity continued into the 20th century, when the School of Paris fostered many new developments. France remained the leading force in avant-garde art until after World War 2, when its mantle passed to the US.

French Guiana Overseas department of France, in South America. **Land and Climate** The coastal plain includes cultivated areas, particularly near the capital,

FRENCH GUIANA
AREA: 90,000sq km (37,749sq mi)
POPULATION: 130,000
CAPITAL (POPULATION): Cayenne (45,000)

CAYENNE. The River Maroni forms the border with SURINAM, and the River Oyapock its E border with Brazil. The climate is hot and equatorial, with high annual temperatures. Rainfall is heavy, although August to October is dry. Rainforest covers *c*.90% of the land. Mangrove swamps line parts of the coast, while other areas are covered by tropical savanna. **History** Europeans first explored the coast in 1500. The French were the first settlers (1604), and Cayenne was founded in 1637 by French merchants. It became a French colony in the late 17th century. The colony, whose plantation economy depended on African slaves, remained French except for a brief period in the early 19th century. From the time of the French Revolution, France used the colony as a penal settlement for political and other prisoners. In 1848 slavery was abolished, and Asian labourers were introduced. **Politics** In 1946 French Guiana became an overseas department of France and, in 1974, also an administrative region. **Economy** Despite rich forest and mineral resources, it is a developing country with high unemployment. It depends on France to finance services. Since 1968, Kourou has been the EUROPEAN SPACE AGENCY's rocket-launching site. Industries: fishing, forestry, gold mining, agriculture. Crops include bananas, cassava, rice and sugar cane. Exports include shrimp, timber and rum.

French horn BRASS musical instrument. It has a flared bell, long coiled conical tube, three or four valves and a funnel-shaped mouthpiece.

French literature Although the earliest surviving works of French literature, written in the *langue d'oïl*, date from the 10th century, major works date from the 12th century when the CHANSONS DE GESTE celebrated the military exploits of the nobility. Allegorical romances by Chrétien de TROYES and others gave way to more intimate poetry in the 15th century by writers such as Francois VILLON. The poems of the 16th century poet Pierre de Ronsard (leader of La PLÉIADE) rivalled that of Renaissance Italy, and in prose, the comic genius of RABELAIS contrasted with the pithy originality of the essayist MONTAIGNE. The great dramatists CORNEILLE, RACINE and MOLIÈRE, and the writings of philosophers DESCARTES and PASCAL ensured that the 17th century was a golden age of French literature. They were succeeded in the 18th century by the writers of the ENLIGHTENMENT, the rationalists ROUSSEAU, DIDEROT and VOLTAIRE; and BEAUMARCHAIS, who wrote social farces. The Romantic movement of the early 19th century produced novels and poems by the prolific Victor HUGO, and LAMARTINE and DUMAS (*père* and *fils*). Writers such as STENDHAL, BALZAC, FLAUBERT, MAUPASSANT and ZOLA reacted against ROMANTICISM, producing works of NATURALISM and REALISM. Poets BAUDELAIRE and RIMBAUD paved the way for SYMBOLISM and modern poetry, typified by the works of VERLAINE and VALÉRY and APOLLINAIRE in the 20th century. PROUST and GIDE dominated French fiction until 1940, backed up by MAURIAC and Duhamel, with SARTRE, de BEAUVOIR, CAMUS, MAUROIS, MALRAUX and SAINT-EXUPÉRY producing the finest post-war work. The most original dramatists of the post-war period are Jean GENET, IONESCO and BECKETT.

French Polynesia French overseas territory in the S central Pacific Ocean, consisting of more than 130 islands, divided into five scattered archipelagos: SOCIETY ISLANDS, MARQUESAS ISLANDS, Tuamotu Archipelago, Gambier Islands and Tubuai Islands; the capital is Papeete on TAHITI (Society Islands). The larger islands are volcanic with fertile soil and dense vegetation. The more numerous coral islands are low-lying. The climate is tropical, and humidity is high. Missionaries arrived in Tahiti at the end of the 18th century, and in the 1840s France began establishing protectorates. In 1880–82, the islands were annexed by France and became part of the colony of Oceania. In 1958 they were granted the status of an overseas territory. In the 1960s the French government began nuclear testing on Mururoa atoll, leading to worldwide protests. In recent years there have been increasing demands for autonomy in Tahiti, the largest and most populous island. In 1995 the French government put forward proposals to grant Polynesia the status of an autonomous overseas territory. Copra and vanilla are the leading agricultural products, and cultured pearls are exported. Tourism has grown rapidly in recent years. Area: 3,265sq km (1,260sq mi). Pop. (1994 est.) 216,600.

French Revolution (1789–99) Series of events that removed the French monarchy, transformed government and society, and established the First Republic. Suggested causes include economic pressures, antiquated social structure, weakness of the – theoretically absolute – royal government, and the influence of the ENLIGHTENMENT. Beginning in June 1789, when the STATES GENERAL met at Versailles during a political crisis caused by attempts to tax the nobility, representatives of the BOURGEOISIE demanded reform and proclaimed themselves a National Assembly. Popular resistance, epitomized by the storming of the BASTILLE, forced the government to accede to demands which included the abolition of the aristocracy, reform of the clergy, and the DECLARATION OF THE RIGHTS OF MAN AND CITIZEN (1789). The Legislative Assembly was installed (October 1791) and, faced with growing internal and external pressure, declared war on Austria (April 1792). It was soon in conflict with most other European states whose governments viewed events in France with fear. The war hastened political change: LOUIS XVI was deposed (August 1792), and the National Convention met to proclaim a republic (September 1792). After a period of rivalry between JACOBINS and GIRONDINS (November 1792–June 1793), strong central government, marked by fanaticism and violence, was imposed during the REIGN OF TERROR, and Louis was executed. Social anarchy and runaway inflation characterized the Thermidorean Reaction (July 1794–October 1795), which followed the fall of ROBESPIERRE. Another new constitution imposed the DIRECTORY (1795–99). The Consulate (1799–1804), dominated by NAPOLEON I, put an end to the decade of revolution.

French Revolutionary Wars (1792–1802) Series of campaigns in which the armies of revolutionary France fought combinations of European foes. Fear and hatred of the FRENCH REVOLUTION fuelled the hostility of Austria in particular. The French declared war on Austria and Prussia in April 1792. The success of the French generals Dumouriez and Kellermann at Valmy and Jemappes provoked other states, including Britain, Netherlands and Spain, to form the First Coalition (1793). By 1794 France was once more on the offensive. After concluding peace treaties with Netherlands and Prussia (1795), France concentrated on war with Austria. Peace with Austria was concluded at Campo-Formio (1797). Napoleon Bonaparte (*see* NAPOLEON I) conducted a brilliant campaign in Italy. Britain, having established naval superiority, remained at war. Horatio NELSON defeated Napoleon's fleet at Aboukir, Egypt. A Second Coalition was formed in 1799, consisting of Russia, Austria, Britain, Turkey, Portugal and Naples. France defeated Naples (1799), and Russia's withdrawal weakened the alliance. In the coup of 18 Brumaire, Napoleon became first consul. The events of 1800 proved decisive. Napoleon defeated the Austrians at Marengo, and

Moreau crushed the Allies at Hohenlinden. Britain captured Malta and Egypt (1801) but lacked the will to fight alone and made peace at Amiens. *See* NAPOLEONIC WARS

frequency Rate of occurrence. In statistics, the number of times a numerical value, event, or special property occurs in a population in a given time. In physics, the number of oscillations occurring in a given time (measured in HERTZ), such as sound, light and radio WAVES, or a swinging PENDULUM or vibrating springs. Frequency is the reciprocal of period. *See also* WAVE FREQUENCY

frequency modulation (FM) Form of RADIO transmission. It is the variation of the FREQUENCY of a transmitted radio carrier wave by the signal being broadcast. It makes radio reception fairly free from static interference and, although restricted in range to receivers in line-of-sight of the transmitter, has become the most favoured transmission method. *See also* AMPLITUDE MODULATION (AM)

fresco (It. fresh) Method of painting on freshly spread plaster that is still damp. In true fresco (*buon fresco*) paint combines with moist plaster so that, when dry, the painted surface does not peel. Dry fresco (*fresco secco*) is the application of paint in a water and glue medium to a dry plaster wall. It does not last as well as true fresco. The palace at Knossos, Crete (*c*.1700 BC), was decorated with frescos. GIOTTO and MICHELANGELO created great frescos.

Fresnel, Augustin Jean (1788–1827) French physicist and engineer. His pioneering work in OPTICS was instrumental in establishing the wave theory of LIGHT. Fresnel researched the conditions governing interference phenomena in POLARIZED LIGHT, studied double refraction, and devised a way of producing circularly polarized light. He also invented a convex lens (**Fresnel lens**) consisting of a series of stepped concentric rings.

Fresno City in s central California, USA; seat of Fresno County. The city was settled with the arrival of the railway in 1872 and Fresno was incorporated in 1885. In the centre of the fertile San Joaquin valley, Fresno produces nearly 80% of the nation's raisins. Industries: agriculture, wines. Pop (1990) 354,091.

Freud, Anna (1895–1982) British psychotherapist, youngest daughter of Sigmund FREUD, b. Austria. She applied PSYCHOANALYSIS to child development and was an early advocate of play therapy. Her books include *Normality and Pathology in Childhood* (1968).

Freud, Lucian (1922–) British painter, b. Germany, grandson of Sigmund FREUD. One of the strongest modern figure painters, Freud's most characteristic subjects are portraits, such as *Francis Bacon* (1952), and nudes.

Freud, Sigmund (1856–1939) Austrian physician and founder of PSYCHOANALYSIS. With Josef Breuer he developed methods of treating mental disorders by free association and the interpretation of dreams. These methods derived from his theories of ID, EGO and SUPEREGO, and emphasized the unconscious and subconscious as agents of human behaviour. Freud developed theories of neuroses involving childhood relationships to one's parents and stressed the importance of sexuality in behaviour. He believed that each personality had a tripartite structure: the **id**, the unconscious emotions, desires and fears which may surface in dreams or madness; the **ego**, the conscious rationalizing section of the mind; and the **superego**, which may be compared to the conscience. The ego comes to mediate the selfish needs of the id and the idealistic demands of the superego. The adoption of a satisfactory superego is dependent on the resolution of the OEDIPUS COMPLEX. His works include *The Interpretation of Dreams* (1900), *The Psychopathology of Everyday Life* (1904) and *The Ego and the Id* (1923).

friar Member of certain religious orders. The four main orders – the DOMINICANS, FRANCISCANS, CARMELITES and AUGUSTINIANS – were founded in the 13th century. Friars differ from cloistered monks in that they are involved in widespread outside activity.

friction Resistance encountered when surfaces in contact slide or roll against each other, or when a fluid flows along a surface. Friction is directly proportional to the force pressing the surfaces together and the surface roughness. When the movement begins, it is opposed by a static friction up to a maximum "limiting friction" and then slipping occurs. Aircraft reduce air (fluid) friction by having a streamlined design. *See also* AERODYNAMICS

Friedan, Betty Naomi (1921–) US feminist. Her book, *The Feminine Mystique* (1963), challenged the notion of woman as housewife and mother, rather than wage-earner. Friedan was founder and first president (1966–70) of the National Organization for Women (NOW).

Friedman, Milton (1912–) US economist. An influential member of the Chicago School of Economics, he supported MONETARISM as the best means of controlling the economy. His works include: *A Monetary History of the United States 1867–1960* (1963), written with Anna Schwartz, and a key book in monetary economics; *A Theory of the Consumption Function* (1957); and *Capitalism and Freedom* (1962). Friedman was awarded the 1976 Nobel Prize for economics.

Friedrich, Caspar David (1774–1840) German painter. One of the greatest romantic artists, he created eerie, symbolic landscapes, such as *Shipwreck on the Ice* (1822) and *Man and Woman Gazing at the Moon* (1824).

Friel, Brian (1929–) Irish dramatist. He achieved international recognition with *Philadelphia, Here I Come!* (1964). Friel's plays, such as *Translations* (1980) and *Dancing at Lughnasa* (1990), focus on the modern history of Ireland.

Friends, The Religious Society of *See* QUAKERS

Friese-Greene, William (1855–1921) English photographer. In 1889, he developed the first motion-picture CAMERA using a ribbon of paper "film". Friese was also the first to show a celluloid film (1890).

Frisch, Karl von (1886–1982) Austrian zoologist. He shared the 1973 Nobel Prize for physiology or medicine with K. LORENZ and N. TINBERGEN for his pioneering work in ETHOLOGY. He deciphered the "language of bees" by studying their dance patterns (waggle dance) in which one bee tells others in the hive the direction and distance of a food source. In his earlier work, he showed that fish and bees see colours, fish can hear and that bees can distinguish various flower scents.

Frisch, Max (1911–91) Swiss novelist and dramatist. His early plays, greatly influenced by BRECHT, are experimental in form and often satirical. They include: *The Chinese Wall* (1946), *The Fire Raisers* (1953) and *Andorra* (1961). His later plays, including *Triptych* (1979), and the novels *Stiller* (1954) and *A Wilderness of Mirrors* (1964), involve man's quest for identity.

fritillary Common name for several genera of butterflies including large fritillaries (silverspots) of the genus *Speyeria* and small fritillaries of the genus *Boloria*. The larvae (caterpillars) are largely nocturnal. Family Nymphalidae

Frobisher, Sir Martin (*c*.1535–94) English navigator. In 1756 he made his first voyage in search of the Northwest Passage and discovered what was to become Frobisher Bay, Canada. He was knighted for his part in the defeat of the Spanish Armada (1588).

Froebel, Friedrich Wilhelm August (1782–1852) German educator and influential educational theorist.

His main interest was in preschool-age children, and in 1841 he opened the first kindergarten. He stressed the importance of environment, self-directed activity, physical training and play in the development of the child.

frog Tailless AMPHIBIAN, found worldwide. Frogs have long hind limbs, webbed feet and external eardrums behind the eyes. Most begin life as TADPOLES after hatching from eggs, usually laid in water. Some frogs remain aquatic, some terrestrial, living in trees or underground. Most have teeth in the upper jaw and all have long sticky tongues attached at the front of the mouth to capture live food, usually insects. Length: 2.5–30cm (1–12in). Subclass Salientia (or Anura), divided into 17 families; the most typical genus is *Rana. See also* TOAD

froghopper Any of various small, hopping insects whose eggs and young are covered with a protective frothy mass called cuckoo spit. Adults are triangular and grey, greenish or brown. They feed on plants. Length: to 1.5cm (0.6in). Order Homoptera; family Cercopidae.

Froissart, Jean (c.1337–c.1410) Flemish poet and historian. His four *Chronicles* of European history between 1325 and 1400 are a valuable (if partial) primary source of information on events such as the HUNDRED YEARS' WAR.

Fromm, Erich (1900–80) US psychoanalyst, b. Germany. Fromm applied PSYCHOANALYSIS to the study of peoples and cultures, stressing the importance of interpersonal relationships in an impersonal, industrialized society. His books include *Escape from Freedom* (1941) and *The Art of Loving* (1956). *See also* FRANKFURT SCHOOL

Fronde (1648–53) Series of rebellions against oppressive government in France. The **Fronde of the Parlement** (1648–49) began when ANNE OF AUSTRIA tried to reduce the salaries of court officials. It gained some concessions from the regent, LOUIS XIV. The **Fronde of the Princes** (1650–53) was a rebellion of the aristocratic followers of CONDÉ and forced Cardinal MAZARIN into temporary exile. Condé briefly held Paris, but the rebellion soon collapsed, and promised reforms were withdrawn.

front In meteorology, the boundary between two air masses of different temperatures or densities. **Cold** fronts occur as a relatively cold and dense air mass moves under warmer air. With a **warm** front, warmer air is pushing over colder air and replacing it. An **occluded** front is composed of two fronts: a cold front overtakes a warm or stationary front. In a **stationary** front, air masses remain in the same areas and the weather is mostly unchanged.

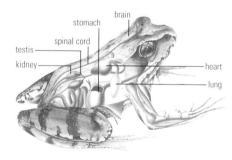

▲ **frog** The common frog (*Rana temporaria*) is just one of the 2,500 or so species of frog or toad. Although most live in wetland habitats, some species are adapted to live in tropical forests, grassland, and even deserts. A common feature of all frogs and toads is that they undergo a complete change of form (metamorphosis) during their life cycle.

Frontenac, Louis de Baude, Comte de Palluau et de (1620–98) French governor of New France, (1672–82, 1689–98). The architect of French expansion in Canada, he promoted the fur trade and encouraged the explorations of LA SALLE, JOLLIET and others. His independent policies led to his recall to France. Frontenac's second term was dominated by the start of the FRENCH AND INDIAN WARS. His defence of Québec and attacks on British forts enabled France to maintain its empire in New France.

frontier In US history, the westernmost region of white settlement. In the 17th century the frontier began in the foothills of the APPALACHIAN Mountains and gradually moved westward until the late 19th century, when no new land remained for pioneer homesteaders. In the US, the frontier notions of rugged individualism and free enterprise were promoted by Frederick Jackson Turner in *The Significance of the Frontier in American History* (1893). The existence of a frontier region, where a dominant group was able to expand (usually at the expense of native inhabitants), has been an important factor in the history of other countries, such as South Africa.

Frost, Robert Lee (1874–1963) US poet. His work is shaped by the landscape of his native New England. Frost's first two volumes of lyric poems, *A Boy's Will* (1913) and *North of Boston* (1914), established his reputation. His best known poems include: "Stopping by Woods on a Snowy Evening", "The Road Not Taken", and "Mending Wall". Frost received the Pulitzer Prize for poetry (1924, 1931, 1937, 1943).

frost In meteorology, atmospheric temperatures at Earth's surface below 0°C (32°F). The visible result of a frost is usually a deposit of minute ice crystals formed on exposed surfaces from DEW and water vapour. In freezing weather the "degree of frost" indicates the number of degrees below freezing point. When white **hoar-frost** is formed, water vapour passes directly from its gaseous state to a solid, without becoming a liquid.

frostbite Freezing of living body tissue in sub-zero temperatures. Frostbite is an effect of the body's defensive response to shut down blood vessels at the extremities in order to preserve warmth at the core of the body. It mostly occurs in the face, ears, hands and feet. In superficial frostbite, the affected part turns white and cold; it can be treated by gentle thawing. If freezing continues, ice crystals form in the tissues; the flesh hardens, and there is no sensation. Deep frostbite, which causes tissue death, requires urgent medical treatment.

fructose (fruit sugar, $C_6H_{12}O_6$) Simple, white monosaccharide, found in honey, sweet fruits and flower nectar. Sweeter than SUCROSE, it is made commercially by the HYDROLYSIS of beet or cane sugar and is used in foods as a sweetener. Its derivatives are a vital source of energy.

fruit SEED-containing mature OVARY of an ANGIOSPERM, in which the seeds are enclosed by the PERICARP. Fruits serve to disperse plants and are an important food source (they provide vitamins, acids, salts, calcium, iron and phosphates). **Simple** fruits, dry or fleshy, are produced by one ripened ovary of a single PISTIL (unit comprising a stigma, style and ovary) and include LEGUMES (peas and beans) and NUTS. **Aggregate** fruits develop from several simple pistils; examples are RASPBERRY and BLACKBERRY. **Multiple** fruits develop from a flower cluster; examples are PINEAPPLES and FIGS. Although considered fruits in culinary terms, APPLES and PEARS are regarded botanically as "false" fruits, as the edible parts are created by the RECEPTACLE and not the carpel walls. *See also* DRUPE; BERRY

fruit bat Any of c.160 species of nocturnal, fruit-eating BATS found in tropical regions of the Old World. They have an independent, clawed second digit and rely on sight, rather than ECHOLOCATION for orientation. They are capable of powerful, sustained flight. The Pteropodidae, or **flying foxes**, live in SE Asia. The largest of all bats, they have a foxlike head and can cause substantial damage to fruit crops. Length: to 40cm (16in); Wingspan: to 1.5m (5ft). Genus *Pteropus.*

fruit fly (drosophilia) Common name for any of the flies of the families Tephritidae or Drosophilidae. The Tephritidae (**peacock flies**) contains *c*.1,200 species that lay their eggs directly in the pulp of fruit. Larvae tunnel their way through fruit, and they are a serious pest of fruit. The Drosophilidae (**pomace flies**) feed mainly on the yeasts of rotting fruit. *Drosophila melangogaster* is used extensively in GENETIC studies. Order Diptera.

Frunze Former name of BISHKEK

Fry, Christopher (1907–) English dramatist, b. Christopher Harris. His witty blank-verse plays are often set in ancient or medieval times. They include *A Phoenix Too Frequent* (1946), *The Lady's Not for Burning* (1948) and *Venus Observed* (1950).

Fry, Elizabeth (1780–1845) English prison reformer and philanthropist. She was a committed Quaker. Horrified by conditions in Newgate Prison, London, Fry agitated for more humane treatment of women prisoners.

Fry, Roger (1866–1934) English art critic and painter. He was Slade professor of fine art (1933–34) at Cambridge. Fry is chiefly remembered for introducing the works of Cézanne and the French postimpressionists to English audiences. As a critic, he espoused a formal theory of aesthetics. His books include *Cézanne* (1927).

Fuad I (1868–1936) King of Egypt. Son of ISMAIL PASHA, he was sultan (1917–22) and first king of modern Egypt (1922–36). Fuad reigned under British influence and in conflict with the nationalist Wafd Party. His grandson reigned briefly as **Fuad II** (1952–53).

Fuchs, Klaus (1912–88) British physicist and Communist spy, b. Germany. Fuchs worked on the atom bomb in the United States (1943) and returned to Britain (1946) to head the theoretical physics division of the atomic research centre at Harwell. Imprisoned (1950) for passing secrets to the Soviet Union, his British citizenship was revoked. After release (1959), he went to East Germany to work at the nuclear research centre.

Fuchs, Sir Vivian Ernest (1909–99) English antarctic explorer and geologist. He led the British Commonwealth Trans-Antarctic Expedition (1957–58) that completed the first overland crossing of Antarctica. Fuchs crossed from Shackleton Base via the South Pole (where they met Sir Edmund HILLARY's New Zealand expedition) to Scott Base (3,500km/2,200mi). He served as director (1958–73) of the British Antarctic Survey.

fuchsia Genus of shrubby plants found in tropical and subtropical South and Central America and parts of New Zealand. They are widely cultivated. Named after the German herbalist Leonard Fuchs (1501–66), they have oval leaves and pink, red or purple trumpet-shaped, waxy flowers. The 100 or so species include the crimson-purple *Fuchsia procumbens* and *F. speciosa.* Family Onagraceae. *See* EVENING PRIMROSE

fuel Substance that is burned or otherwise modified to produce energy, usually in the form of heat. Apart from FOSSIL FUELS, firewood and charcoal, the term also applies to radioactive materials used in nuclear power stations. *See also* ENERGY SOURCES; NATURAL GAS; OIL

fuel cell Electrochemical CELL for direct conversion of the energy of oxidation of a fuel to electrical energy. Specialized electrodes are immersed in an ELECTROLYTE, and

◄ **fruit bat** The grey-headed fruit bat (*Pteropus poliocephalus*) of Australia grows to 40cm (16in) and has a wingspan of more than 1m (3.5ft). They feed in groups on various wild and cultivated fruits

the fuel (such as hydrogen) is supplied to one and the oxidizer (such as oxygen) to the other. Electrode reactions occur leading to oxidation of the fuel, with production of electric current. Fuel cells are used in space vehicles.

Fuentes, Carlos (1928–) Mexican novelist and short-story writer. His first two novels, *Where the Air is Clean* (1958) and *The Death of Artemio Cruz* (1962), share a critical view of Mexican society and earned him an international reputation. Other fiction includes *The Hydra Head* (1978) and *Distant Relations* (1980). Among his recent work are the novel *The Campaign* (1991) and the essays *Geography of the Novel* (1993).

Fugard, Athol (1932–) South African dramatist, director and actor. Fugard achieved international acclaim for his plays *The Blood Knot* (1961), *Sizwe Bandi is Dead* (1972) and *My Children! My Africa* (1990). His work often explores the effects of apartheid on South Africa's black population.

fugitive slave laws US federal acts of 1793 and 1850 that provided for the return of escaped slaves to their owners. When SLAVERY was abolished in Northern states, the UNDERGROUND RAILROAD helped Southern slaves obtain freedom. Northern states also passed laws that prevented escaped slaves from being returned to slave states. The **Compromise of 1850** had a tougher fugitive slave law than the 1793 statute, with heavy penalties for aiding fugitive slaves. According to the 1850 laws, fugitive slaves were denied legal rights. The law was so harsh that it helped the ABOLITIONISTS' cause, and many citizens openly flouted the new regulations

fugue (It. flight) In music, a composition of several parts or voices where the same melodic line or theme is stated and developed in each voice. Generally the theme begins in one part and others are added in sequence. Popular in the BAROQUE period, fugue writing reached its peak with J.S. BACH. *See also* COUNTERPOINT

Fujiyama (Mount Fuji) Highest mountain in Japan, in the Fuji-Hakone National Park. An extinct volcano, it is seen as the most sacred mountain in Japan. It is a summer and winter sports area. Height: 3,776m (12,389ft).

Fukuoka City on the SE shore of Hakata Bay, N Kyushu, S Japan. In medieval times, Hakata was one of Japan's major ports. There is a rich agricultural region to the N. Industries: textiles, machinery, chemicals, fishing. Pop. (1995) 1,285,000.

Fulani (Fulah or Fulbe) People of W Africa, numbering *c*.6 million. Their language belongs to the W Atlantic group of the NIGER-CONGO. Originally a pastoral people, they helped the spread of Islam throughout W Africa from the 16th century, establishing an empire lasting until British colonialism in the 19th century.

Fulbright, James William (1905–95) US Senator from Arkansas (1945–74). He sponsored the Fulbright Act (1946) that provided funds for educational exchanges (**Fulbright scholarships**) between the US and other countries. As chairman of the Senate committee on foreign relations (1959–74), Fulbright was critical of US military involvement abroad, especially in Vietnam.

Fuller, (Richard) Buckminster (1895–1983) US architect and engineer. Believing that only technology can solve modern world problems, he invented several revolutionary designs. The most widely used is the GEO-DESIC DOME. His books include *Operating Manual for Spaceship Earth* (1969) and *Earth Inc.* (1973).

Fuller, Margaret (1810–50) US writer and editor. A leader of TRANSCENDENTALISM, she served as editor-in-chief of *The Dial* (1840–42). In 1845, Fuller became the first literary critic of the New York *Tribune*. Her feminist treatise, *Woman in the Nineteenth Century* (1846), explored the discrimination of women.

Fuller, Melville Weston (1833–1910) US lawyer, chief justice of the Supreme Court (1888–1910). He was a strict constructionist. Important cases include: *Plessy* v. *Ferguson* (1896), which upheld "separate but equal" laws of segregation; and *Lochner* v. *New York* (1905), a "due process" clause interpreted so the state could not set a 10-hour day for bakers. Fuller helped settle a boundary dispute between Venezuela and Great Britain (1899), and was a member of the Hague Tribunal (1900–10).

Fuller, Roy Broadbent (1912–91) English poet and novelist. The progress of his verse, from Audenesque works to a more individual voice, can be traced in *Collected Poems 1936–61* (1962) and *New and Collected Poems* (1985). Novels include: *Image of a Society* (1956), *My Child, My Sister* (1965) and *Stares* (1990). Fuller also wrote an autobiography, *Spanner and Pen* (1991).

fuller's earth Clay-like substance containing more than 50% SILICA. Once used for fulling (removing oil and grease from wool), it is now used to bleach petroleum and refine vegetable oils.

Fulton, Robert (1765–1815) US inventor and engineer. Designing torpedoes and other naval weapons, his main interest was in navigation. Fulton pioneered (1807) the use of steamboats for carrying passengers and freight, travelling from New York City to Albany on his craft *Clermont*.

Funchal Capital and chief port of MADEIRA. Founded in 1421, it was ruled by Spain from 1580 to 1640 and was briefly under British administration in the early 19th century. It is now an industrial and resort centre for all the islands in the Madeira archipelago. Industries: sugar-milling, distilling, wine, handicrafts. Pop. (1981) 44,111.

function In mathematics, rule that assigns a unique value to each element of a given SET. The given set is the **domain** of the function, and the set of values is the **range**. Two or more elements of the DOMAIN may be assigned the same value, but a function must assign only one value to each element of the domain. A function *f* maps each element *x* of the domain to a corresponding element (or value) *y* in the range. Here *x* and *y* are variables, with *y* dependent on *x* through the functional relationship *f*. The dependent variable *y* is said to be a function of the independent variable *x*. For example, the square-root of a function, its domain and range being the non-negative real numbers. *See also* TRIGONOMETRIC FUNCTION

functionalism In art and architecture, an early 20th-century style based on UTILITARIANISM. Functionalism rejected ornamentation and stressed the basic structure of the work and of the materials used. Major proponents included GROPIUS, BAUHAUS and LE CORBUSIER.

functionalism Sociological and anthropological theory outlined by Emile DURKHEIM. The theory attempts to understand the function of each part of society (customs, institutions, objects, roles, religion) in relation to each other and to the whole society. It attempts to explain how each separate cultural phenomenon corresponds to the "needs" of the whole of society.

fundamental forces Four basic forces that exist in physics. The most familiar, and the weakest, is GRAVITATION. Much stronger is the ELECTROMAGNETIC FORCE, which "binds" particles together. The two other forces operate only on the subatomic level. The WEAK NUCLEAR FORCE, associated with the decay of particles, is intermediate in strength between the gravitational and electromagnetic force, whereas the STRONG NUCLEAR FORCE, associated with the "glue" that holds nuclei together, is the strongest natural force.

fundamentalism Movement within some Protestant denominations, particularly in the US, which originated in the late 19th and early 20th centuries as a reaction against biblical criticism and theories of evolution. The name is derived from *The Fundamentals*, a series of 12 tracts published between 1909 and 1915 by eminent US evangelical leaders. The doctrines most emphasized are the inspiration and infallible truth of the BIBLE, the divinity of Christ, the VIRGIN BIRTH, ATONEMENT by Christ bringing expiation and salvation for all, the physical RESURRECTION and the SECOND COMING. Fundamentalism has been loosely used to refer to any extreme orthodox element within a religion, such as Islamic fundamentalists.

fungicide Chemical that kills fungi. For example, creosote is used to prevent dry rot in wood.

fungus Any of a wide variety of organisms of the KINGDOM Fungi, which are unable to photosynthesize and which reproduce by means of spores and never produce cells with flagella. They include MUSHROOMS, MOULDS and YEASTS. There are *c*.100,000 species. Fungi have relatively simple structures, with no roots, stems or leaves. Their cell walls contain the polysaccharide CHITIN. The main body of a typical multicellular fungus consists of an inconspicuous network (mycelium) of fine filaments (hyphae), which contain many nuclei and which may or may not be divided into segments by cross-walls. The hypha nuclei are HAPLOID. The mycelia may develop spore-producing, often conspicuous, fruiting bodies, mushrooms and TOADSTOOLS. Fungal PARASITES depend on living animals or plants: SAPROPHYTES utilize the materials of dead plants and animals, and symbionts obtain food in a mutually beneficial relationship with plants. Fungi feed by secreting digestive ENZYMES onto their food, then absorbing the soluble products of digestion. Many cause diseases in crops, livestock and humans (athlete's foot). Moulds and yeasts are used in the production of BEER and CHEESE; some fungi, such as *Penicillium*, are sources of ANTIBIOTICS.

funk Style or energy of popular music. It was originally employed in the 1950s to summarize a form of modern JAZZ which, although influenced by BEBOP harmonies, emphasized modern melodies. Funk was developed by such artists as James BROWN and George Clinton.

fur Soft, dense hair covering the skin of certain mammals, such as mink, fox, ermine, musquash, wolf, bear, squirrel and rabbit. Most are hunted and killed for their pelts which, when manufactured into clothing, may command high prices. Some fur-bearing animals are now protected by law because overhunting has threatened extinction.

Furies (Erthyes and Eumenides) In Greek mythology, three hideous goddesses of vengeance whose main task was to torment those guilty of social crimes.

furnace Enclosed space raised to a high temperature by the combustion of fuels or by electric heating. Most furnaces are used in the extraction of metals or the making of alloys. An **arc** furnace relies on the heat generated by an electric arc (spark), often between two large carbon electrodes, which are slowly consumed. A **resistance** furnace is heated by passing an electric current through a heating element or directly through metallic material. An **induction** furnace uses ELECTROMAGNETIC INDUCTION to cause a current to flow in a metallic charge. The resulting heat is sufficient to melt the metal.

fur trade Vital commercial factor in the development of the North American wilderness. The fur trade began in the 1500s as a form of exchange between Native Americans and Europeans. By the late 1500s, fur had become a valuable commodity in Europe, encouraging Europeans to explore further into the interior. In 1608, Samuel de CHAMPLAIN established a fur-trading post at Québec. In 1670, the HUDSON'S BAY COMPANY was established. Control of the fur trade was a major factor in the FRENCH AND INDIAN WARS. In the 1770s, the rival North West Company was formed, which merged with the Hudson's Bay Company in 1821. The LEWIS AND CLARK EXPEDITION (1804–06) led to the development of the trade in the West. John Jacob ASTOR formed the AMERICAN FUR COMPANY. Mountain men, such as Kit CARSON, explored the Rocky Mountains. In the 19th century, the fur trade declined dramatically due to changes in fashion and the clearance of land for settlements.

Furtwängler, Wilhelm (1886–1954) German conductor. He became conductor of the Berlin Philharmonic Orchestra in 1922 (life appointment in 1952) and of the Vienna Philharmonic Orchestra in 1930. Furtwängler appeared frequently at the Bayreuth and Salzburg festivals and was a specialist in the works of Beethoven and Wagner. His ambiguous relationship with the Nazi government aroused controversy.

furze *See* GORSE

fuse In electrical engineering, a safety device to protect against overloading. Fuses are commonly strips of easily melted metal placed in series in an electrical circuit such that when overloaded, the fuse melts, breaking the circuit and preventing systemic damage.

fusion, nuclear Form of **thermonuclear reaction** in which nuclei of light atoms (such as hydrogen) combine to form one or more heavier nuclei with the release of large amounts of energy. The process takes place in the Sun and other stars, and has been reproduced (1952) on Earth in the HYDROGEN BOMB. Since then efforts have been largely concentrated on producing a thermonuclear reactor. Two main methods have been employed. In the first, a PLASMA of tritium and deuterium is raised to a temperature above 100 million°C in a **tokamak** (ring-shaped) reactor. The second method is laser fusion, in which a pellet of tritium and deuterium is imploded by laser. At present, both methods have failed to produce more energy from fusion than the input into the system. *See also* FISSION, NUCLEAR; NUCLEAR ENERGY

futures In economics, commodities, currencies or securities bought or sold for a fixed price on delivery at a specified date in the future. As opposed to OPTIONS, a futures contract guarantees a purchase or sale. It provides an opportunity for regular buyers or suppliers to protect themselves against price fluctuations.

futurism Art movement that originated in Italy with the publication (1909) of the futurist manifesto by Filippo MARINETTI. It aimed to glorify machines and to depict speed and motion by means of an adapted version of CUBISM. Its ideas were absorbed by DADA and SURREALISM. Russian futurism, led by Vladimir MAYAKOVSKY, was mainly a literary movement that embraced formal experimentation.

Fuzhou (Fuzhou or Fu-chou) City and port on the River Min Chiang, capital of Fukien province, SE China. Fuzhou was founded in the T'ang dynasty (618–907). It was one of the first treaty ports to be opened to foreign trade (1842) and flourished as China's largest tea-exporting centre. It declined in the early 20th century. In 1949, after the Communist takeover, Fuzhou was blockaded by the Nationalists. Industries: engineering, chemicals, textiles. Pop. (1993 est.) 1,290,000.

fuzzy logic System of LOGIC able to represent statements that are true or false depending on context. For example, the statement "this is warm", applied to the inside of a freezer that is not working, is true only in the context that the freezer is not literally "freezing". Computer-controlled devices programmed on the principles of fuzzy logic are able to put into context information they receive and respond flexibly to the environment.

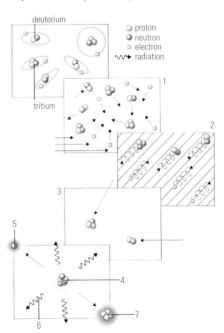

▲ **fusion** In experiments to generate power by nuclear fusion, the aim is usually to produce energy by fusing tritium and deuterium. These are isotopes of hydrogen, and the process can only occur at a temperature above 100 million°C and enormous pressure. Deuterium has one proton, one neutron and one electron, while tritium has one proton, two neutrons and an electron. In a fusion reactor the mixture of the two isotopes is heated by intense radio emissions, ion bombardment and electrical pulses (1). The plasma which results is suspended in a magnetic field (2). The tritium and deuterium nuclei fuse (3), creating a helium nucleus (4), a loose neutron (5), radiation (6), and energy when the products hit the edge of the plasma (7).

G/g, seventh letter of the Roman alphabet. Like the letter c, it probably derived from the Egyptian hieroglyph for a boomerang. The Greeks made it the third letter of their alphabet, gamma. The letter g is the symbol for gravity and gram.

g Symbol for the universal constant of GRAVITATION. g is also the symbol for acceleration of free fall due to Earth's gravity. One g is $c.9.8m/s^2$ ($32ft/s^2$).

G8 Abbreviation of GROUP OF EIGHT

gabbro Coarse-grained IGNEOUS ROCK composed of sodium and calcium FELDSPAR, with OLIVINE and PYROXENE.

Gable, Clark (1901–60) US film actor. His magnetism made him "king" of 1930s Hollywood. Gable won an Academy Award for best actor in *It Happened One Night* (1934). His performance as Rhett Butler in *Gone With the Wind* (1939) is one of cinema's most enduring. Other films include the posthumously released *The Misfits* (1961).

Gabo, Naum (1890–1977) US sculptor and architect, b. Russia as Naum Pevsner. A founder of CONSTRUCTIVISM, Gabo published the *Realist Manifesto* (1920) with his brother Antoine Pevsner.

Gabon The Gabonese Republic lies on the Equator in w central Africa; the capital is LIBREVILLE. **Land and Climate** Behind the coastline is a narrow plain. The land then rises to hills, plateaux and mountains divided by deep valleys carved by the River Ogooué and its tributaries. Gabon has high temperatures and humidity most of the year. Dense rainforest covers $c.75\%$ of Gabon, with tropical savanna in the E and S. **History** Portuguese explorers reached the Gabon coast in the 1470s, and the area later became a source of slaves. France established a settlement in 1839, later named Libreville. In the 1880s, Gabon became a French colony. In 1960, it achieved full independence. In 1968, after the death of Gabon's first president, Leon Mba, it became a one-party state. Free elections took place in 1990. The Gabonese Democratic Party (PDG), formerly the only party, won a majority in the National Assembly. President Bongo, of the PDG, won the presidential elections in 1993, although accusations of fraud and corruption led to riots in Libreville. Bongo was condemned by the international community for his harsh suppression of popular demonstrations. In 1998, Bongo was re-elected. **Economy** Gabon's abundant natural resources, including forests, oil, manganese and uranium, make it one of Africa's richer states (1992 GDP per capita, US$3,913). However, agriculture still employs $c.75\%$ of the workforce. Crops include bananas, cassava, maize and sugar cane, while cocoa and coffee are grown for export.

Gabor, Dennis (1900–79) British physicist b. Hungary. He was awarded the 1971 Nobel Prize for physics for his invention (1947) of HOLOGRAPHY. He developed the basic technique of creating a three-dimensional image, but it was not until the invention (1960) of the LASER by Charles H. TOWNES that holography was commercially feasible.

> **GABON**
> AREA: 267,670sq km (103,347sq mi)
> POPULATION: 1,612,000
> CAPITAL (POPULATION): Libreville (418,000)

Gaborone Capital of Botswana, s Africa. First settled in the 1890s, it served as the administrative centre of the former Bechuanaland Protectorate. In 1966, it became capital of an independent Botswana. Pop. (1995) 182,000.

Gabriel Archangel mentioned in the Old and New Testaments and in the Koran. In the Old Testament, Gabriel helps DANIEL to interpret his visions. In the New Testament he foretells the birth of St JOHN THE BAPTIST to his father, ZACHARIAS, and that of JESUS CHRIST to his mother, MARY. In the Koran, he is the angel who appears to MUHAMMAD. The Christian Church celebrates Gabriel's feast day on 24 March.

Gabrieli Two Italian composers, uncle and nephew. **Andrea** Gabrieli ($c.1533–86$) was organist at St. Mark's, Venice. He wrote vocal and organ music, his nephew **Giovanni** Gabrieli ($c.1553–1612$), succeeded him as organist at St. Mark's. He developed the new CONCERTO style and was a major influence on the early BAROQUE.

Gaddafi, Muammar al *See* QADDAFI, MUAMMAR AL

Gaddi, Taddeo ($c.1300–c.1366$) Leading member in a family of Florentine artists. Taddeo's father, **Gaddo di Zanobi** ($c.1259–c.1330$), was a noted painter and mosaicist. **Taddeo** served as an apprentice to GIOTTO His best-known work is the fresco series *Life of the Virgin* (completed in 1338). Taddeo's son, **Agnolo** (d.1396), also painted frescoes; the most famous is the *Legend of the True Cross* ($c.1380$).

gadolinium (symbol Gd) Silvery-white metallic element of the LANTHANIDE SERIES. Chief ores are gadolinite, monazite and bastnaesite. Its uses include neutron absorption and the manufacture of certain alloys. Properties: at.no. 64; r.a.m. 157.25; r.d. 7.898; m.p. $1,311°C$ ($2,392°F$); b.p. $3,233°C$ ($5,851°F$); most common isotope Gd^{158} (24.87%).

Gaelic Language spoken in parts of Ireland and Scotland. The two branches diverged in the 15th century and are mutually unintelligible. The Irish variety is one of the official languages of the Republic of Ireland. In Scotland, Gaelic has no official status and is dying out.

Gagarin, Yuri Alekseyevich (1934–68) Russian cosmonaut, the first man to orbit the Earth. On 12 April 1961 he made a single orbit in 1 hour 29 minutes.

Gage, Thomas (1721–87) British general and administrator. He became governor of Montréal in 1760 and was made head of the British forces in North America in 1763 and governor of Massachusetts in 1774. His soldiers provoked the patriots at Concord (April 1775), leading to the Battles of LEXINGTON AND CONCORD that began the AMERICAN REVOLUTION.

Gaia (Gaea) In Greek mythology, mother goddess of the Earth. Wife (and in some legends, mother) of URANUS, she bore the TITANS, the CYCLOPES and the Hecatoncheires ("those of a hundred hands").

Gaia hypothesis Scientific theory that interrelates the Earth's many and varied processes – chemical, physical and biological. Popular in the 1970s, when it was proposed by James Lovelock, it conceives of Earth as a single living organism. *See also* ECOLOGY

Gainsborough, Thomas (1727–88) English portrait and landscape painter. Influenced by the Dutch landscape painters, he developed a style that is remarkable for its characterization and use of colour. Among his best landscapes is *The Watering Place* (1777). Gainsborough's portraits, such as *Viscount Kilmorey* (1768) and *Blue Boy* ($c.1770$), rivalled those of Sir Joshua REYNOLDS.

Gaitskell, Hugh Todd Naylor (1906–63) British statesman, leader of the Labour Party (1955–63) and chancellor of the exchequer (1950–51). He entered Parliament in

1945. Gaitskell served in Clement ATTLEE's cabinet as minister of fuel and power (1947–50) and minister of state for economic affairs (1950) before becoming chancellor. He defeated Aneurin BEVAN in the 1950 leadership elections A period of consensus between the two main parties, known as "Butskellism" (*see* BUTLER, R.A.), ensued in British politics. On the right-wing of the Labour Party, Gaitskell refused to accept the 1960 conference's decision to adopt a policy of unilateral disarmament and defeated a leadership challenge from his eventual successor Harold WILSON.

Galápagos Islands (Sp. *Archipiélago de Colón*) Pacific archipelago on the Equator; a province of Ecuador, *c*.1,050km (650mi) W of mainland South America. The capital is Baquerizo Moreno, on San Cristóbal. Other main islands include Santa Cruz, San Salvador and Isabela. The islands are volcanic with sparse vegetation, except for dense forests on the high lava craters, which rise to 1,707m (5,633ft) at Volcán Wolf (Isabela). Mangrove swamps and lagoons teem with wildlife. Many animal species are unique to the islands, such as the giant land tortoises. The Galápagos National Park is a world heritage site. In 1832, Ecuador annexed the archipelago and established a settlement. In 1835, Charles DARWIN spent six weeks studying the Galápagos fauna. Area: 7,845sq km (3,029sq mi) Pop. (1990) 9,785.

galaxy Huge assembly of STARS, dust and gas, held together by gravitational interactions. There are three main types of galaxy, as originally classified (1925) by Edwin HUBBLE. The most common are **elliptical** galaxies (E). These are round or elliptical systems, showing a gradual decrease in brightness from the centre outwards. Consisting of old stars and predominantly free of dust and gas, elliptical galaxies are graded E0 to E7 according to increasing ellipticity. **Spiral** galaxies (S), such as our own GALAXY, are flattened, disc-shaped systems in which young stars, dust and gas are concentrated in spiral arms coiling out from a central bulge, the nucleus. **Barred spiral** galaxies (SB) are distinguished by a bright central bar from which the spiral arms emerge. In addition to these three main classes are **lenticular** galaxies, systems with a disc and nucleus but with no apparent spiral arms. **Irregular** galaxies, such as the MAGELLANIC CLOUDS, are systems with no symmetry. Galaxies can exist singly or in clusters. About one galaxy in a million is a RADIO GALAXY, emitting strong ELECTROMAGNETIC RADIATION. A SEYFERT GALAXY has a bright, compact nucleus and is a strong emitter of INFRARED WAVES. A **Markarian** galaxy emits strong ULTRAVIOLET RADIATION. **N-type** galaxies have a star-like nucleus with a very faint haze surrounding it. They are usually strong radio sources, and it has been hypothesized that they evolve into QUASARS. Current theories suggest that all galaxies were formed from immense clouds of gas soon after the BIG BANG, *c*.10,000 million years ago.

Galaxy (G) Star system that contains the SOLAR SYSTEM. The Galaxy is spiral and is *c*.100,000 light-years in diameter. Our SUN and Solar System are located at the edge of one of the spiral arms, *c*.30,000 light-years from the centre. The spiral arms form a **disk-shaped** system, with a bulging core (**nucleus**) in the direction of SAGITTARIUS. Old Population II stars are found in the nucleus; younger, hotter Population I stars make up the spiral arms. The stars of the spiral arms form the MILKY WAY. Surrounding it all is the spheroidal **galactic halo**, which contains very old Population II stars including GLOBULAR CLUSTERS. The whole Galaxy is rotating but the rate of rotation decreases with distance from the centre. Our Sun circles the centre at *c*.250km/s, taking 220 million years per orbit. The Galaxy

forms part of the **Local Group**, which includes the ANDROMEDA GALAXY and the MAGELLANIC CLOUDS.

Galbraith, J.K. (John Kenneth) (1908–) US economist, b. Canada. Three of his most famous works are *American Capitalism: The Concept of Countervailing Power* (1952); *The Affluent Society* (1958); and *The New Industrial State* (1967). Galbraith takes the position that many accepted theories about the functioning of capitalist economies are outmoded. He advocates higher public spending on education and other services. He was an adviser to former US president John F. Kennedy.

Galen (*c*.129–*c*.199) Greek physician, whose work and writings provided much of the foundation for the development of medical practice. He made anatomical and physiological discoveries, including ones concerning heart valves, secretions of the kidney, respiration and nervous function. He was among the first to study physiology by means of detailed animal dissection.

galena (lead sulphide, PbS) Grey metallic mineral, the major ore of LEAD. It is widely found in hydrothermal veins and as a replacement in limestone and dolomite rocks. Hardness 2.5–2.7; r.d. 7.5.

Galicia Region of SE Poland (Western Galicia) and W Ukraine (Eastern Galicia), on the slopes of the Carpathian Mountains (N) and bordering the Czech Republic (S). The major cities are KRAKÓW (Poland) and LVOV (Ukraine). After passing to Austria in 1772, Galicia became the centre of HASIDISM. After World War I, Poland seized Western Galicia and was awarded Eastern Galicia at the 1919 Paris Peace Conference. The 1939 partition of Poland between Nazi Germany and the Soviet Union gave most of Eastern Galicia to the Ukraine, a position ratified by the 1945 Polish-Soviet Treaty. The region is mainly agricultural, although there are oil fields. Products: grain, flax, potatoes and tobacco. Area: 78,500sq km (30,309sq mi).

Galicia Autonomous region in NW Spain, comprising the provinces of La Coruña, Lugo, Orense and Pontevedra; the capital is Santiago de Compostela. It was a centre of resistance to the Moorish invasions in the 8th century and passed to Castile in the 13th century. It was the focus of a literary and cultural revival in the 19th century. Galicia has a mountainous interior. Its economy is based on livestock; fishing and mining are also important. Area: 29,434sq km (11,361sq mi). Pop. (1991) 2,731,669.

Galilean satellites Four chief SATELLITES of JUPITER: GANYMEDE, CALLISTO, Io and EUROPA, named after GALILEO, who first observed them in 1610.

Galilee, Sea of (Lake Tiberius or Yam Kinneret) Freshwater lake in N Israel fed by the River Jordan. Israel's major reservoir, it is an important fishing ground and the source of water for irrigation of the Negev Desert. The surface is *c*.215m (705ft) below sea level. Area: 166sq km (64sq mi).

Galileo (1564–1642) (Galileo Galilei) Italian physicist and astronomer whose experimental methods laid the foundations of modern science. He was a lecturer at Pisa, later moving to Florence and then to Padua. According to legend, Galileo observed that a hanging lamp in Pisa Cathedral took the same time to complete one oscillation however long the swing, and he suggested the PENDULUM could be used for timekeeping. He later studied falling bodies and disproved ARISTOTLE's view that they fall at different rates according to weight. Galileo is reputed to have demonstrated this law of uniform acceleration by dropping weights from the Leaning Tower of Pisa. He also discovered the parabolic flight path of projectiles. In 1609, Galileo used one of the first astronomical TELESCOPES to discover sunspots, lunar craters, Jupiter's major satellites and the phases of Venus. In *Sidereus Nuncius* (1610) he supported COPERNICUS' heliocentric system that the Earth moves around the Sun. Galileo was forbidden by the Roman Catholic Church to teach that this system represented physical reality, but in *Dialogue on the Two Great World Systems* (1632) he defied the pope by making his criticism of PTOLEMY's system even more explicit. As a result, Galileo was brought before the INQUISITION and forced to publicly recant. He is reported to have murmured "*eppur si muove*" (still it moves – referring to the Earth, which the Church insisted was stationary at the centre of the universe. Galileo remained under house arrest until his death. In 1992, the Vatican absolved him of heresy.

Galileo Space probe to JUPITER, launched in October 1989. The probe passed the asteroids Gaspra and Ida in October 1991 and August 1993, respectively. Galileo went into orbit around Jupiter in 1995.

gall Abnormal swelling of plant tissue stimulated by an invasion of any of a wide variety of parasitic or symbiotic organisms, including bacteria, fungi and insects. Most gall organisms only stunt the affected plants.

Galla Hamitic people who make up 40% of the population of Ethiopia, living mainly in the s. They are predominantly nomadic pastoralists and practise Christianity, Islam and animism.

gall bladder Muscular sac, found in most vertebrates, which stores BILE. In humans it lies beneath the right lobe of the LIVER and releases bile into the DUODENUM by way of the bile duct.

Galliano, John (1960–) British fashion designer, b. Gibraltar. A graduate of St Martin's School of Art, London, he quickly became associated with flamboyant and daring designs. In 1995, Galliano was appointed creative head of Givenchy, Paris.

Gallic Wars (58–51 BC) Campaigns in which the Romans, led by CAESAR, conquered GAUL. By 57 BC, Caesar had subdued sw and n Gaul. In 56 BC, he conquered the Veneti, leaders of an anti-Roman confederation, and in 55–54 BC invaded Germany and Britain. Caesar defeated a united Gallic revolt in 52 BC.

Gallipoli (Gelibolu) Peninsula and port in w Turkey, on the European side of the DARDANELLES. Colonized by the ancient Greeks, it has been of strategic importance in the defence of Istanbul (Constantinople). It was the first European city to be conquered (1354) by the Ottoman Turks. In 1915–16, it was the scene of the GALLIPOLI CAMPAIGN. Pop. (1985) 16,715.

Gallipoli Campaign (1915–16) Allied operation against the Turks during WORLD WAR 1. Some 45,000 British and French and 30,000 ANZAC troops were involved. After eight months of inconclusive fighting and more than 145,000 casualties, the Allies withdrew.

gallium (symbol Ga) Grey metallic element of group III of the periodic table. It was discovered in 1875. Chief sources are bauxite and some zinc ores. The metal, liquid at room temperature, is used in lasers, semiconductors and high-temperature thermometers. Properties: at.no. 31; r.a.m. 69.72; r.d. 5.9; m.p. 29.78°C (85.60°F); b.p. 2,403°C (4,357°F); most common isotope Ga^{69} (60.4%).

Gallo, Robert Charles (1937–) US scientist who identified (1984) the virus that causes ACQUIRED IMMUNE DEFICIENCY SYNDROME (AIDS). Now called the HUMAN IMMUNODEFICIENCY VIRUS (HIV), the organism was identified by Gallo a year after its independent discovery by the French virologist Luc Montagnier.

Galloway *See* DUMFRIES AND GALLOWAY

gallstone (cholelithiasis) Hard mass, usually composed of cholesterol and calcium salts, which forms in the GALL

BLADDER. Gallstones may cause severe pain (biliary colic) or become lodged in the common bile duct, causing obstructive JAUNDICE or cholecystitis. Treatment is by removal of the stones themselves or of the gall bladder.

Gallup, George Horace (1901–84) US pollster. His sampling of public opinion on social, political and business matters became a feature of political life after he correctly forecasted the outcome of 1936 US presidential election.

Galois, Évariste (1811–32) French mathematician who laid the foundation of GROUP THEORY. His work was dismissed by the mathematical establishment as incomprehensible, and he turned to political activism, being arrested twice. Galois died after a duel.

Galsworthy, John (1867–1933) English novelist and dramatist. He wrote more than 31 plays, including *Strife* (1909). Galsworthy is best known for a quartet of novels, collectively known as the *The Forsyte Saga* (1906–21), that trace three generations of a fictional English upper-middle-class family. Other chronicles include *A Modern Comedy* (1924–28) and *End of the Chapter* (1931–33). He was awarded the 1932 Nobel Prize for literature.

Galton, Sir Francis (1822–1911) English scientist, cousin of Charles DARWIN. He helped in the development of the modern weather chart and pioneered the use of fingerprints for identification. Galton is remembered as the founder of EUGENICS. In *Hereditary Genius* (1869) he argued that intelligence was inherited. *See also* HEREDITY

Galvani, Luigi (1737–98) Italian physiologist. His experiments with frogs' legs indicated a connection between muscular contraction and electricity. He believed "animal electricity" was created in the muscle and nerve His findings were disputed by Alessandro VOLTA.

galvanizing Coating of iron or steel articles with zinc in order to protect from CORROSION. The coating can be applied directly in a bath of molten zinc, electroplated from cold zinc sulphate solutions, or dusted on and baked.

galvanometer Instrument for detecting, comparing or measuring ELECTRIC CURRENTS. It is based on the principle that a current through a CONDUCTOR (usually a coil) creates a MAGNETIC FIELD which reacts with a magnet giving a deflection. The main types are the **moving-coil** galvanometer and the **moving-magnet instrument**.

Galway County in Connaught province, w Republic of Ireland; the county town is Galway. Bounded by the Atlantic (w), it is mountainous in the w, low-lying in the E, and drained by the River SHANNON. It is an agricultural region. Industries: tourism, agriculture, cotton-spinning, sugar-refining, handicrafts. Area: 5,939sq km (2,293sq mi). Pop. (1991) 129,511.

Gama, Vasco da (1469–1524) Portuguese navigator. He was charged with continuing Bartholomeu DIAZ's search for a sea route to India. Da Gama's successful expedition (1497–99) rounded the Cape of Good Hope and sailed across the Indian Ocean to Calicut. In 1502–03, he led a heavily armed expedition of 20 ships to Calicut and brutally avenged the killing of Portuguese settlers left there by CABRAL. Da Gama thereby secured Portuguese supremacy in the Eastern spice trade. In 1524, he returned to India as viceroy, dying there shortly afterwards.

Gambetta, Léon Michel (1838–82) French statesman, premier (1881–82). A political opponent of NAPOLEON III, he organized French resistance in the FRANCO-PRUSSIAN WAR (1870–71). He helped form the Third Republic.

Gambia, The The smallest country in mainland Africa; the capital is BANJUL. **Land and Climate** The Gambia consists of a narrow strip of land bordering the River Gambia, and is enclosed by Senegal, except for a short Atlantic coastline. The middle part of the River Gambia is bordered

---

GAMBIA
AREA: 4,363sq mi (11,300sq km)
POPULATION: 1,119,000
CAPITAL (POPULATION): Banjul (42,000)

---

by terraces (*banto faros*), which are flooded after heavy rains. The upper river flows through a sandstone plateau. Gambia has hot, humid summers. In winter, temperatures drop to *c*.16°C (61°F). Mangrove swamps line the river banks. Much land has been cleared for farming. Gambia is rich in wildlife. **History and politics** Portuguese mariners reached Gambia's coast in 1455 when the area was part of the Mali empire. In the 16th century, Portuguese and English slave traders operated in the area. In 1664, the British established a settlement and later founded a colony, Senegambia (1765), which included parts of present-day Gambia and Senegal. In 1783, this was handed over to France. In 1816, Britain founded Bathurst (now Banjul) as a base for its anti-slavery operations. In 1888, The Gambia became a British colony and remained under British rule until it achieved full independence in 1965. In 1970, The Gambia became a republic. In 1981, an attempted coup was defeated with the help of Senegalese troops. In 1982, The Gambia and Senegal formed a defence alliance, the Confederation of Senegambia, but this ended in 1989. In 1992, Sir Dawda Jawara was re-elected as president for a fifth term. In July 1994, he was overthrown in a military coup, led by Yahya Jammeh. In 1996, Jammeh was elected president. **Economy** The Gambia is a poor, developing country (1995 GDP per capita, US$930). Agriculture employs more than 80% of the workforce. The main food crops are cassava, millet and sorghum; groundnuts are the leading export. Tourism is becoming important.

gamelan Traditional Indonesian orchestra using xylophones, marimbas, gongs and drums. Used to accompany ceremonies, the rhythmically complex music has inspired composers such as Claude DEBUSSY and Philip GLASS.

gamete Reproductive sex cell that joins with another sex cell to form a new organism. Female gametes (ova) are usually motionless; male gametes (SPERM) often have a tail (flagellum) enabling them to swim to ova. All gametes are HAPLOID. *See also* OVUM; SEXUAL REPRODUCTION

game theory In mathematics, the analysis of problems involving conflict. Initially it was based on the assumption that participants in conflict adopt strategies that maximize personal gain and minimize loss. Later, more complex motivations, such as morality, were included. Distinctions are made between games involving one, two, or more players, as in solitaire, chess and poker respectively. Game theory is applied in business management, sociology, economics, ecology and warfare. The theory was first introduced by Émile Borel and developed (1928) by John VON NEUMANN.

gametophyte Generation of plants and algae that bears the female and male GAMETES. In flowering plants these are the germinated pollen grains (male) and the embryo sac (female) inside the ovule. *See also* ALTERNATION OF GENERATIONS; FERN

gamma globulin One of the protein components of the serum of mammalian BLOOD. It contains approximately 85% of the circulating ANTIBODIES of the blood. It gives temporary IMMUNITY in patients who have been exposed to certain diseases, such as measles.

gamma radiation Form of very short wavelength ELECTROMAGNETIC RADIATION emitted from the nuclei of some radioactive atoms. High-energy gamma rays have even greater powers of penetration than X-RAYS. They are used in medicine to attack cancer cells and in the food industry to kill microorganisms. *See also* RADIOACTIVITY

Gamow, George (1904–68) US nuclear physicist, b. Russia. In cosmology, he developed the BIG BANG theory and explained (with Ralph Alpher and Hans BETHE) the abundances of chemical elements in the universe. In molecular biology, Gamow deduced the triplet code (codon) of bases in DNA. With Edward TELLER, he established the Gamow-Teller theory of beta decay.

Gance, Abel (1889–1991) French film director. An influential film-maker and a technical innovator, he employed revolutionary techniques, such as mobile cameras, tracking shots, close-ups and montage. His major works include the World War 1 pacifist statement *J'accuse* (1919), *La Roue* (1923) and *Napoléon* (1927).

Gandhi, Indira (1917–84) Indian stateswoman, prime minister (1966–77, 1980–84), daughter of Jawaharlal NEHRU. She served as president of the Indian National CONGRESS PARTY (1959–60) before succeeding Lal Shastri as prime minister. In 1975, amid growing social unrest, Gandhi was found guilty of breaking electoral rules in the 1971 elections. She refused to resign, invoked emergency powers, and imprisoned many opponents. In 1977 elections, the Congress Party suffered a heavy defeat at the hands of Morarji DESAI, and the party split. In 1980, leading a faction of the Congress Party, Gandhi returned to power. In 1984, after authorizing the use of force against Sikh dissidents in the Golden Temple at AMRITSAR, she was killed by a Sikh bodyguard. She was succeeded by her eldest son Rajiv GANDHI.

Gandhi, Mohandas Karamchand (1869–1948) Indian nationalist leader. In 1888, "Mahatma" (Sanskrit, Great Soul) Gandhi went to England to study law. In 1893 he moved to South Africa to practise law, and championed the rights of the minority Indian community. While in South Africa Gandhi launched (1907) his first non-cooperation (*satyagraha*) campaign, involving non-violent (AHIMSA) civil disobedience. In 1914, he returned to India. Following the massacre at AMRITSAR (1919), Gandhi organized several campaigns of *satyagraha* and was imprisoned (1922–24) for conspiracy. Resistance methods included strikes, refusal to pay taxes and non-respect of colonial law. After his release, Gandhi served as president (1925–34) of the Indian National CONGRESS. He campaigned for a free, united India; the revival of craft industries, especially the spinning of cloth; and the abolition of untouchability (*see* CASTE). In 1930, he made his famous 400km (250mi) protest march against a salt tax. In 1934, Jawaharlal NEHRU succeeded Gandhi as leader of the Congress. In 1942, after the British rejected his offer of cooperation in World War 2 if Britain granted immediate independence, Gandhi launched the Quit India movement. He was then interned until 1944. Gandhi played a major role in the post-war talks with Nehru, Lord MOUNTBATTEN and Muhammad Ali JINNAH that led to India's independence (1947). Gandhi opposed partition and the creation of a separate Muslim state (Pakistan). When violence flared between Hindus and Muslims, Gandhi resorted to fasts for peace. A figure of huge international and moral stature, he was assassinated by a Hindu fanatic in New Delhi.

Gandhi, Rajiv (1944–91) Indian statesman, prime minister (1984–89), eldest son of Indira GANDHI. He was a pilot before reluctantly entering politics. Rajiv became prime minister after his mother's assassination. He worked to placate India's Sikh extremists, but his reputation was tarnished by a bribery scandal. Defeated in the 1989 election, Rajiv was assassinated while campaigning for re-election.

Ganesh Elephant-headed Hindu god, son of SHIVA and PARVATI. He is the patron of learning and is said to have written down the MAHABHARATA. *See also* HINDUISM

Ganges (Ganga) River of N India. It rises in the Himalayas, then flows SE and empties into the Bay of Bengal through the BRAHMAPUTRA–Ganges delta. The plains of the Ganges are extremely fertile and support the densely populated cities of DELHI, AGRA, VARANASI and LUCKNOW. In HINDUISM, it is the earthly form of the Goddess Ganga, and pilgrims purify themselves in its waters. Length: 2,512km (1,560mi).

ganglion Cluster of nervous tissue containing cell bodies and SYNAPSES, usually enclosed in a fibrous sheath. In a VERTEBRATE, most ganglia occur outside the CENTRAL NERVOUS SYSTEM.

Gang of Four Radical faction that tried to seize power in China after the death of MAO ZEDONG. In 1976 both Chairman MAO and prime minister ZHOU ENLAI died, leaving a power vacuum. The Gang of Four, Zhang Chunjao, Wang Hungwen, Yao Wenyuan and their leader JIANG QING (Mao's widow), tried to launch a military coup but were arrested for treason by premier HUA GUOFENG. They were sentenced to life imprisonment.

gangrene Death of body tissues associated with loss of blood supply, possibly with bacterial contamination.

gannet Diving seabird related to the tropical booby. Gannets are heavy-bodied with tapering bills, long pointed wings and webbed feet. Their plumage is white with black wing tips. They nest in huge colonies on rocky islands. Length: 63–100cm (25–40in). Family Sulidae.

Gansu (Kansu) Province in NW central China, bordered E by Inner Mongolia; the capital is Lanzhou. The region became Chinese territory in the 3rd century BC. Wheat, cotton, rice, maize and tobacco are grown under irrigation. Mineral deposits include iron ore, oil and coal. Area: 366,625sq km (141,550sq mi). Pop. (1990) 22,930,000.

Ganymede Largest of Jupiter's GALILEAN SATELLITES, with a diameter of 5,262km (3,270mi). Its cratered terrain is covered with grooves suggesting geological activity.

gar Primitive, freshwater bony fish found in shallow waters of North America. Its cylindrical body is covered with diamond-shaped plates. Length: to 300cm (10ft); Weight: to 135kg (300lb). Family Lepisosteidae.

Garbo, Greta (1905–90) Swedish film actress. Her aura of mystery and enigmatic beauty made her an adored screen idol. Her first major role was in *Torrent* (1926). Her first "talkie" was *Anna Christie* (1930). Garbo played the leads in the classics *Grand Hotel* (1932), *Anna Karenina* (1935), *Camille* (1937) and the comedy *Ninotchka* (1939). She retired in 1941.

García Lorca, Federico *See* LORCA, FEDERICO GARCÍA

García Márquez, Gabriel (1928–) Colombian novelist. His popular novel, *One Hundred Years of Solitude* (1967) achieves a unique combination of realism, lyricism and mythical fantasy, making it a central text of MAGIC REALISM. Later works include *The Autumn of the Patriarch* (1975), *Love in the Time of Cholera* (1985) and *The General in His Labyrinth* (1989). He was awarded the 1982 Nobel Prize for literature.

Garda, Lake Largest lake in Italy, forming the border between Lombardy and Venetia. It has many tourist resorts along its shoreline. Area: 370sq km (143sq mi).

gardenia Genus of more than 60 species of evergreen shrubs and small trees native to tropical and subtropical Asia and Africa. They have white or yellow fragrant, waxy flowers. Height: to 5.5m (18ft). Family Rubiaceae.

Gardiner, Stephen (1483–1555) English prelate and politician. In 1533, he became secretary to HENRY VIII,

helping to annul Henry's marriage to CATHERINE OF ARAGON. However, Gardiner opposed the REFORMATION and was imprisoned (1548) by EDWARD VI. In 1553, he was appointed lord chancellor by MARY I, supporting her persecution of Protestants and advocacy of Catholicism.

Gardner, Erle Stanley (1889–1970) US writer, creator of the detective lawyer Perry Mason. He wrote 80 novels featuring Perry Mason, the first of which was *The Case of the Velvet Claws* (1933).

Garfield, James Abram (1831–81) 20th US President (1881). He served in the American Civil War until 1863, when he was elected to the House of Representatives. In 1876 Garfield became the Republican leader of the house. The 1880 Republican convention was deadlocked and, on the 36th ballot, he became the compromise presidential candidate. Garfield's four-month administration was characterized by party squabbles over federal jobs and political patronage. He was assassinated on 2 July 1881 and was succeeded by vice president Chester A. ARTHUR.

Garibaldi, Giuseppe (1807–82) Italian patriot and soldier, who helped to achieve Italian unification. Influenced by MAZZINI, he participated in a republican rising (1834), and was forced into exile in South America. Garibaldi returned to fight against the Austrians in the REVOLUTIONS OF 1848 and in the unsuccessful defence of Rome against the French, but was again forced to flee. In 1860, he led his 1,000-strong band of "Red Shirts" against the Kingdom of the Two Sicilies, a dramatic episode in the RISORGIMENTO. Garibaldi handed his conquests over to King VICTOR EMMANUEL II, and they were incorporated into the new kingdom of Italy. *See also* CAVOUR, CONTE DI

Garland, Judy (1922–69) US singer and film actress, b. Frances Gumm. Garland's performance as Dorothy in *The Wizard of Oz* (1939) made her a worldwide star. Other films include *Meet Me in St Louis* (1944), *Easter Parade* (1948) and *A Star is Born* (1954). Her daughter is the actress and singer *Liza Minelli* (1946–).

garlic Bulbous herb native to S Europe and central Asia. It has onion-like foliage and a bulb made up of cloves, used for flavouring. It is also claimed to have medicinal properties. Family Liliaceae; species *Allium sativum*.

garnet Two series of orthosilicate minerals found in metamorphic rocks and pegmatites. Some varieties are important as gemstones. Hardness 6.5–7.5; r.d. 4.

Garonne River in SW France. Rising on the slopes of the Pyrenees in Spain, it flows NW through Toulouse to join the River DORDOGNE N of Bordeaux and form the Gironde estuary, which empties into the Atlantic Ocean. Length: 575km (357mi).

Garrick, David (1717–79) English actor, theatre manager and dramatist. A pupil of Samuel JOHNSON, he is credited with replacing the formal declamatory style of acting with easy, natural speech. Garrick made his acting debut (1741) in *Richard III*. He was manager (1747–76) of Drury Lane Theatre, London.

Garrison, William Lloyd (1805–79) US abolitionist. In 1831, he started the *Liberator* in Boston, an influential journal in the anti-slavery movement. After the American Civil War (1861–65), he concentrated on other reforms, including temperance and women's suffrage.

Garter, Order of the Premier order of knighthood in Britain, founded (1348) by Edward III. The monarch is the Grand Master, and the number of companion knights is limited to 24. Its motto is *"Honi soit qui mal y pense"* ("Shame on him who thinks badly of it").

Garvey, Marcus (1887–1940) US black nationalist leader, b. Jamaica. In 1914 he founded the Universal Negro Improvement Association (UNIA) designed to "promote the spirit of race pride". Garvey believed that black people could not achieve equality within white-dominated Western countries, so he created a "back-to-Africa" movement. He established the Black Star Line shipping company as a means of transporting black people back to Africa. By the 1920s, Garvey was the most influential black leader in the USA, via his *Negro World* newspaper. In 1922, the Black Star Line and the UNIA collapsed. Garvey was convicted of fraud, jailed (1925), pardoned (1927) by President Coolidge and deported to Jamaica (1927). RASTAFARIANISM is influenced by his philosophy.

gas Phase of MATTER in which molecules are free to move in any direction; a gas spreads by DIFFUSION to fill a container of any size. Because of their low densities, most gases are poor conductors of heat and electricity. When cooled, gases become LIQUIDS. Some, such as carbon dioxide, can be liquefied by pressure alone. All gases follow certain laws, such as AVOGADRO'S law, BOYLE'S LAW, CHARLES' LAW, GRAHAM'S law and IDEAL GAS LAWS. *See also* PLASMA; SOLID

Gascoigne, Paul John (1967–) English footballer. "Gazza" has played club football for Newcastle United (1985–88), Tottenham Hotspur (1988–91), Lazio (1992–95), Glasgow Rangers (1995–98), Middlesbrough (1998–2000) and Everton (2000–). He cried after his booking in the 1990 World Cup semi-final against Germany meant that he would be prevented from playing in the final. He sustained a serious knee injury in a reckless tackle in the 1991 FA Cup final. A gifted goal-scoring midfielder, his off-field behaviour has been widely criticised.

Gascony Former province in SW France, bounded by the PYRENEES (S) and the Bay of BISCAY (W). Part of Roman Gaul, it was later overrun by the Visigoths and the Franks. In the 6th century Gascony was conquered by the Vascones. It passed to AQUITAINE in the 11th century. In 1154, Gascony fell to the English. It was a major battleground in the Hundred Years' War and was finally restored to France in 1453.

gas exchange In biology, the uptake and output of gases, especially oxygen and carbon dioxide, by living organisms. In animals and other organisms that obtain their energy by AEROBIC respiration, gas exchange involves the uptake of oxygen and the output of carbon dioxide. In plants, algae and bacteria that carry out PHOTOSYNTHESIS, the opposite may occur, with a carbon dioxide uptake and oxygen output. At the cellular level, gas exchange takes place by DIFFUSION across cell MEMBRANES in solution. *See also* BREATHING; CIRCULATORY SYSTEM; RESPIRATION; RESPIRATORY SYSTEM; VENTILATION

Gaskell, Elizabeth Cleghorn (1810–65) English novelist. Gaskell explored the problems of the industrial poor in her novels *Mary Barton* (1848) and *North and South* (1855). Other works include *Cranford* (1853), *Wives and Daughters* (1866) and a biography of Charlotte Brontë.

gasoline *See* PETROLEUM

Gasperi, Alcide de (1881–1954) Italian statesman, prime minister (1945–53). A founder member of the Italian People's Party, he entered the Italian parliament in 1921. A strong opponent of FASCISM, Gasperi was imprisoned during MUSSOLINI'S regime. During World War 2, he was active in the resistance and helped to create the Christian Democratic Party. Gasperi contributed greatly to the post-war reconstruction in Italy.

Gassendi, Pierre (1592–1655) French philosopher and physicist. He espoused a form of ATOMISM based on the work of EPICURUS. His criticisms of Descartes and Aristotle had a strong influence on Robert BOYLE and Isaac NEWTON. *See also* SCEPTICISM

gastric juice Fluid comprising a mixture of substances, including PEPSIN and hydrochloric acid, secreted by GLANDS of the stomach. Its principal function is to break down proteins into polypeptides during DIGESTION.

gastroenteritis Inflammation of the STOMACH and INTESTINES causing abdominal pain, diarrhoea and vomiting. Severe cases can cause dehydration.

gastropod Member of the Gastropoda class of MOLLUSCS that includes the SNAIL, SLUG, WHELK, LIMPET, ABALONE and SEA SLUG. Many possess a single spiral shell that has been produced by chemical precipitation from the mantle. Many types of gastropods live immersed in seawater, breathing through gills. Some freshwater snails, however, breathe through lungs and need to surface periodically for air. Sea slugs are entirely without shells.

gas turbine Type of INTERNAL-COMBUSTION ENGINE that is driven by a continuous stream of hot gas passing over the the blades of a TURBINE. In most cases, air is fed under pressure into a COMPRESSOR before passing into combustion chambers, where it is mixed with a fuel, such as oil, and burned. *See also* JET ENGINE

Gates, Bill (William Henry) (1955–) US businessman, reputedly the world's wealthiest person. In 1975, Gates co-founded Microsoft Corporation which rapidly became the dominant computer SOFTWARE producer. He is noted for his innovative thinking and aggressive marketing and business tactics. In 2000, he fought to prevent the break-up of the Microsoft Corporation after the US government ruled that the company had broken US anti-monopoly laws.

Gates, Horatio (1727–1806) American general, b. England. He served in the British army under General Edward BRADDOCK in the FRENCH AND INDIAN WARS before emigrating (1772) to Virginia and joining the colonists' cause in the AMERICAN REVOLUTION. In 1776, Gates became commander of the army in the N and defeated the British at the Battle of SARATOGA (1777). He lost his command after his defeat at Camden, South Carolina (1780).

Gatling gun Early MACHINE GUN invented (1862) by Richard Gatling (1818–1903). Adopted by the US Army in 1866, it had several barrels mounted in a cylinder that was rotated by a crank so that each barrel fired in turn.

GATT Acronym for the GENERAL AGREEMENT ON TARIFFS AND TRADE

gaucho COWBOY of the Argentine, Paraguayan and Uruguayan pampas. Originally nomadic, the gauchos became farmhands and superb horse soldiers. They were an important political force in the 18th and 19th centuries.

Gaudí (y Cornet), Antonio (1852–1926) Spanish architect. An idiosyncratic exponent of ART NOUVEAU, Gaudí employed sculptural, organic forms and ceramic ornamentation on buildings such as the Palau Güell (1885–89), Caso Battló (1905–07) and the unfinished church of the Sagrada Familia, all in Barcelona.

Gaudier-Brzeska, Henri (1891–1915) French sculptor who lived in England from 1911. A friend of Ezra POUND, he was part of the VORTICISM movement. Two of his best-known works are *Red Stone Dancer* (1913) and *Crouching Figure* (*c*.1914). He was killed in World War 1.

Gauguin, (Eugène Henri) Paul (1848–1903) French painter who, with VAN GOGH and CÉZANNE, ranks as the greatest artist of POST-IMPRESSIONISM. In his early career, Gauguin exhibited (1881–86) with the impressionists in Paris. In 1886, he moved to Brittany. *The Vision After the Sermon* (1888) is a key work in Gauguin's break with the naturalism of IMPRESSIONISM. His belief that form and pattern should represent mental images influenced SYMBOLISM. Gauguin developed his own "synthetist" style of EXPRESSIONISM characterized by bold contours and large areas of unmodulated colour. Inspired by "primitive" art, he left France for Tahiti in 1891. The late works, often of South Sea islanders, convey a sense of mystery and myth. They include *Where do we come from? What are we? Where are we going?* (1897) and *Faa Iheihe* (1898).

Gaul Ancient Roman name for the land N of the Pyrenees, S and W of the Rhine and W of the Alps. In 900 BC, Celtic tribes began to migrate across the Rhine and spread southwards. In 222 BC, the Romans conquered the region S of the Alps, calling it **Cisalpine** Gaul. By 121 BC, the Romans had captured the area N of the Alps, known as **Transalpine** Gaul. In the GALLIC WARS (58–51 BC) Caesar completed the conquest of Gaul, dividing it into three ethnic regions: AQUITANIA, Celtic Gaul (modern central France) and Belgica (roughly modern Belgium). *See also* CELT

Gaultier, Jean-Paul (1952–) French fashion designer. At the age of 18, he joined Pierre CARDIN. In 1977 Gaultier launched his first collection. His designs for women and men convey an anarchic sense of humour, mixing textures and cuts with unconventional features.

gaur (seladang) Species of wild cattle found in forested hilly country in India and Malaysia. Gaurs are dark brown in colour with a white "sock" on each leg. Length: up to 3.8m (12.4ft) long. Family Bovidae; species *Bos gaurus*.

Gauss, Karl Friedrich (1777–1855) German mathematician. His *Disquisitiones Arithmeticae* (1798) was the first modern text on NUMBER THEORY. Gauss made many discoveries that were not credited to him, such as non-Euclidean geometry and quaternions. In 1801, he calculated the orbit of the asteroid Ceres. Gauss served as director (1807–55) of the astronomical observatory at the University of Göttingen. From 1821 he was involved in the first worldwide survey of the Earth's magnetic field, for which he invented a heliograph. In 1833, Gauss invented the electric telegraph. The unit of magnetic flux density is named after him. *See also* LOBACHEVSKY, NIKOLAI

Gauteng Province in N central South Africa; the capital is JOHANNESBURG. Formed in 1994 from the TRANSVAAL as PWV (PRETORIA-WITWATERSRAND-Vereeniging), the province was renamed Gauteng in 1995. It is South Africa's smallest but most populous province. Area: 18,810sq km (7,260sq mi). Pop. (1995 est.) 7,048,300.

Gautier, Théophile (1811–72) French poet, novelist and critic. His poems, such as *Albertus* (1833), *España* (1845) and *Enamels and Cameos* (1852), exhibit the formalist aesthetic theory of art that influenced SYMBOLISM.

Gavaskar, Sunil Manohar (1949–) Indian cricketer. Gavaskar scored a record 10,122 runs in 125 test matches (including 106 consecutive tests) for India (1971–87). In 1993, his record was surpassed by Allan BORDER.

gavial Reptile native to N India. It has a long, narrow snout, an olive or brownish back and a lighter belly.

▲ **gecko** The banded gecko (*Coleonyx variegatus*) is one of a great many species of gecko inhabiting desert regions. It is nocturnal, hiding under rocks during the day and foraging for insects at night.

Length: to 5m (15.4ft). Family Gavialidae; species *Gavialis gangeticus*. *See also* CROCODILE

gavotte Originally a 15th-century folk dance. It became fashionable in court society in the 18th century.

Gay, John (1685–1732) English dramatist and poet. His verse includes *The Shepherd's Week* (1714) and *Trivia* (1716). Gay collaborated with Alexander POPE and John ARBUTHNOT on the play *Three Hours After Marriage* (1717). His best-known work is the ballad-opera *The Beggar's Opera* (1728), a political satire and burlesque of Italian opera. Its sequel was *Polly* (1729).

Gaya City on the River Phalgu, Bihar state, NE India. It is a pilgrimage centre sacred to both Hindus and Buddhists. Buddha received enlightenment nearby. It is the seat of Magadha University (1962). Pop. (1991) 292,000.

Gaye, Marvin (1939–84) US singer-songwriter. In 1961, he joined Motown Records. His hit singles included "I Heard It Through The Grapevine" (1968) and "Too Busy Thinking 'Bout My Baby" (1968). In the 1970s, Gaye released a string of classic soul albums, including *What's Going On* (1971) and *Let's Get It On* (1973). His album *Midnight Love* (1982) included the single "Sexual Healing". Gaye was shot dead by his father.

Gay-Lussac, Joseph Louis (1778–1850) French chemist and physicist. He discovered (1808) the law that gases combine in a simple ratio by volume (Gay-Lussac's law). Gay-Lussac also discovered the law of gas expansion, often attributed to J.A.C. CHARLES. He prepared (1808) the elements boron and potassium.

Gaza Strip Strip of territory in SW Israel, bordering on the SE Mediterranean Sea. Following the ARAB-ISRAELI WAR (1948–49) it became an Egyptian possession and served as a centre for Palestinian refugees. Occupied by Israel from 1967, it was the scene of the INTIFADA against Israel in 1988. In 1994, its administration was taken over by the Palestinian National Authority. Area: 363sq km (140sq mi). Pop. (1994) 724,500.

gazelle Any of several species of graceful, small to medium antelopes native to Africa and Asia, often inhabiting plains. Most are light brown with a white rump and horns. Family Bovidae; genus *Gazella*.

GCSE *See* GENERAL CERTIFICATE OF SECONDARY EDUCATION

Gdańsk (Danzig) City and seaport on the Gulf of Gdańsk, N Poland; capital of Gdańsk province. Settled by Slavs in the 10th century, it was a member of the HANSEATIC LEAGUE. It was taken by Poland in the 15th century but passed to Prussia in 1793. The Treaty of Versailles (1919) established Gdańsk as a free city, and annexation (1939) by Germany precipitated World War 2. In the 1980s, its shipyards became a focus of opposition to Poland's communist regime. Industries: metallurgy, chemicals, machinery, timber. Pop. (1996) 463,000.

GDP Abbreviation of GROSS DOMESTIC PRODUCT (GDP)

gear Wheel, usually toothed, attached to a rotating shaft. The teeth of one gear engage those of another in order to transmit and modify speed of rotation and TORQUE.

gecko Any of *c*.650 species of LIZARDS, native to warm regions of the world. They owe their remarkable climbing ability to minute hooks on their feet. Length: 3–15cm (1–6in). Family Gekkonidae.

Geddes, Sir Patrick (1854–1932) Scottish sociologist, biologist and town planner. Geddes pioneered the use of social surveys in town planning. His ideas, published in *City Developments* (1904), were far ahead of his time, although they left their mark on some of his pupils, notably Lewis MUMFORD.

Geelong Port in S Victoria, SE Australia. Located on Corio Bay, Geelong is the largest city in the state of

Victoria. It was settled in the 1830s. Exports: wool, wheat, meat and hides. Pop. (1993 est.) 151,900.

Geiger, Hans (Johannes Wilhelm) (1882–1945) German physicist who, with Ernest RUTHERFORD, devised (1908) the GEIGER COUNTER. In 1909 Geiger and Ernest Marsden studied the deflection of alpha particles by thin metal foil, providing the basis for Rutherford's discovery of the atomic NUCLEUS. *See also* RADIATION, NUCLEAR

Geiger counter (Geiger-Müller counter) Instrument used to detect and measure the strength of nuclear RADIATION by counting the number of ionized particles produced. Low-pressure argon gas is held in an aluminium cylinder that acts as one electrode and a wire containing low-pressure argon gas and a wire along the central axis of the cylinder that acts as a second electrode. A potential difference of *c*.400 V is applied, just less than that required to produce a discharge in the gas. The gas becomes ionized when the counter is brought close to radioactive substances and makes a circuit. The current is amplified to produce an audible click.

gel Homogeneous mass consisting of minute particles dispersed in a LIQUID to form a fine network throughout the mass. A gel's appearance can be elastic or jelly-like, as in GELATIN, or quite rigid and solid, as in silica gel.

gelatin Colourless or yellowish protein obtained from COLLAGEN in animal cartilages and bones. It is used in film emulsions, capsules for medicines, as a culture medium for bacteria, and in foodstuffs such as jellies.

Geldof, Sir Bob (Robert Frederick Xenon) (1954–) Irish rock musician. He was the lead singer (1975–86) with the Boomtown Rats. In 1984 Geldof organized the pop charity "Band Aid", which raised £8 million for famine-relief in Africa, especially Ethiopia. The 1985 "Live Aid" concerts in London and Philadelphia were screened worldwide and raised more than £48 million. Geldof received an honorary knighthood in 1986.

Gell-Mann, Murray (1929–) US theoretical physicist. In 1954 he introduced the concept of "strangeness" to account for the relative longevity of HADRONS. In 1962 Gell-Mann predicted the existence of a new particle (**omega-minus**). In 1964 he coined the term "QUARK" to describe the basic constituent of the BARYON and MESON. Gell-Mann was awarded the 1969 Nobel Prize for physics for his work on ELEMENTARY PARTICLES. *See also* PARTICLE PHYSICS

gem Any of about 100 minerals valued for their beauty, rarity and durability. Transparent stones, such as DIAMOND, RUBY and EMERALD are the most highly valued. PEARL, AMBER and CORAL are gems of organic origin.

Gemayel, Pierre (1905–84) Lebanese politician. A MARONITE Christian, he founded (1935) the right-wing Phalange Party. Gemayel served (1960–84) in the Lebanese parliament. He led the Phalange militia forces in the Lebanese civil war. His youngest son, **Bashir** (1947–82) was assassinated while president-elect. His eldest son, **Amin** (1942–) served as president (1982–88).

Gemini (the Twins) Northern constellation, situated on the ecliptic between Taurus and Cancer. Its brightest stars are Castor (Alpha Geminorum) and Pollux (Beta Geminorum).

gender In linguistics, any of several categories into which nouns and pronouns are divided for grammatical purposes. In some languages, adjectives or verbs may take different forms to agree with the different genders. A three-gender system, with categories labelled masculine, feminine and neuter, exists in such languages as German and Russian, while a two-gender system, with masculine and feminine, operates in such languages as French and Welsh.

gene Unit by which hereditary characteristics are passed on from one generation to another in plants and animals. A gene is a length of DNA that codes (*see* GENETIC CODE) for a particular protein or peptide. Genes are usually found along the CHROMOSOMES. In most cell nuclei, genes occur in pairs, one located on each of a chromosome pair. Where different forms of a gene (ALLELES) are present in a population, some forms may be RECESSIVE to others (DOMINANT genes) and will not be expressed unless present on both members of a chromosome pair. *See also* GENETICS; GENETIC ENGINEERING; HEREDITY

gene bank Genetic material kept for possible future use. Material stored includes bacteria and moulds; seeds, spores and tubers; frozen sperm, eggs and embryos; and even live animals and plants. The material can be used in plant and animal BREEDING, GENETIC ENGINEERING and in medicine. Live species are used for restocking natural habitats in which species are in danger of EXTINCTION.

General Agreement on Tariffs and Trade (GATT) United Nations agency of international trade, subsumed into the new WORLD TRADE ORGANIZATION (WTO) in 1995. Founded in 1948, GATT was designed to prevent "tariff wars" (the retaliatory escalation of tariffs) and to work towards the reduction of tariff levels. Most non-communist states were party to GATT.

General Certificate of Secondary Education (GCSE) Secondary education qualification gained through public examination in the UK, except Scotland. It replaced GCE Ordinary level and the Certificate of Secondary Education in 1988. Advanced level (A-level) examinations are taken by many students at 18 and are used for higher-education entrance.

General Strike (4–12 May 1926) Nationwide strike in Britain involving *c*.3 million members of the Trades Union Congress (TUC). It was called in support of the National Union of Mineworkers (NUM), whose members had been locked out of the mines after refusing to accept a reduction in pay and an increase in working hours. Stanley BALDWIN's government responded by employing special constables and volunteers to run essential service and issuing an anti-strike propaganda journal, *The British Gazette*. The TUC called off the strike and the Trade Union Act (1927) restricted trade union rights.

generator Device for producing electrical energy. The most common is a machine that converts the mechanical energy of a TURBINE or INTERNAL COMBUSTION ENGINE into ELECTRICITY by employing ELECTROMAGNETIC INDUCTION. There are two main types of generators: alternating current (AC) and direct current (DC), often called an ALTERNATOR and a DYNAMO. Each has an armature (or ring) that rotates within a magnetic field creating an induced ELECTRIC CURRENT. *See also* ACCELERATOR, PARTICLE; BATTERY; ELECTRICITY SOURCES; FUEL CELL; SOLAR CELL; VAN DE GRAAFF GENERATOR

Genesis First book of the OLD TESTAMENT and of the PENTATEUCH or TORAH. It relates the creation of the universe and progresses from ADAM and EVE to ABRAHAM, JOSEPH and the descent into Egypt.

Genet, Jean (1910–86) French dramatist and novelist. His experiences as a homosexual in reform schools, brothels and prisons are recounted in *Our Lady of the Flowers* (1944), *Miracle of the Rose* (1946) and *The Robber's Journal* (1949). A leading exponent of the Theatre of the ABSURD, He used violent eroticism and bizarre illusion in plays such as *The Maids* (1947) and *The Balcony* (1957).

genet Cat-like carnivore of the CIVET family, native to W Europe and S and E Africa. Solitary and nocturnal, genets have slender bodies, grey to brown spotted fur, and banded

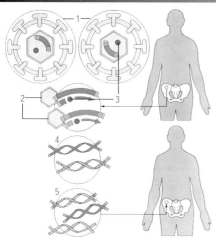

▲ gene therapy GRT is used to treat severe combined immunodeficiency (SCID), where the gene responsible for production of the enzyme adenosine deaminase (ADA) is missing. As ADA is essential for white blood cell production, this renders the body open to infection. Two retroviruses (1) are introduced into the bone marrow. These have the ability to produce RNA from their DNA (2) using a reverse transcriptase enzyme (3). This DNA is then incorporated into the human chromosomes (4). When these chromosomes multiply, new viral RNA and viral proteins, as well as ADA are produced (5). The first two produce more new viruses, while the ADA is used by the body to produce vital white blood cells. The process then repeats and spreads throughout the bone marrow.

tails. Length: body to 58cm (22in); tail to 53cm (21in); weight: to 2kg (4.4lb). Family Viverridae; genus *Genetta*.

gene therapy (gene replacement therapy, GRT) Medical treatment involving the replacement or alteration of faulty GENES by means of GENETIC ENGINEERING. Although first used on humans in 1990, it remains a largely experimental procedure. A healthy gene is packaged into some kind of vector (usually a suitably doctored virus) so that it can be targeted at the affected cells. Initially, gene therapy was restricted to the treatment of hereditary disorders such as CYSTIC FIBROSIS and SICKLE-CELL DISEASE. Research is being conducted into its suitability as a method for the treatment of certain cancers.

genetic code Arrangement of information stored in GENES. It is the ultimate basis of HEREDITY and forms a blueprint for the entire organism. The genetic code is based on the genes that are present, which in molecular terms depends on the arrangement of nucleotides in the long molecules of DNA in the cell CHROMOSOMES. Each group of three nucleotides specifies, or codes, for an AMINO ACID or for an action such as "start" or "stop". By specifying which PROTEINS to make and in what quantities, the genetic code not only **directly** controls production of structural materials, but also, by coding for ENZYMES, **indirectly** codes for the production of other cell materials.

genetic engineering Construction of a DNA molecule containing a desired GENE. The gene is then introduced into a bacterial, fungal, plant or mammalian cell, so that the cell produces the desired protein. It has been used to produce human growth hormone, insulin and enzymes for biological washing powder. *See also* BIOTECHNOLOGY; CLONE

genetic fingerprinting Forensic technique that uses genetic material, specifically the DNA within sample body cells, to identify individuals. It is used in paternity suits to detect the true father of a child and sometimes in rape cases. It was first used in the UK courts in 1987.

genetics Study of HEREDITY. Geneticists study how the characteristics of an individual organism depend on its GENES, how the characteristics are passed down to the next generation, and how changes may occur through MUTATION. A person's behaviour, learning ability and physiology may be explained partly by genetics, although the person's environment also has a considerable influence. In 1865, Gregor MENDEL established the basic laws of inheritance by cross-breeding strains of pea plants. The molecular structure of heredity was revealed by Francis CRICK, James WATSON and Maurice WILKINS' discovery (1953) of DNA. *See also* BIOTECHNOLOGY; GENETIC ENGINEERING

Geneva City at the S end of Lake Geneva, SW Switzerland. A Roman town, it was taken by the Franks in the 6th century and passed to the HOLY ROMAN EMPIRE in the 12th century. During the REFORMATION, it became the centre of PROTESTANTISM under John CALVIN. It joined the Swiss Confederation in 1814. It was the seat of the LEAGUE OF NATIONS (1919–46) and is the headquarters of the Red Cross and the World Health Organization (WHO). Industries: banking, watch-making and jewellery, precision instruments, tourism. Pop. (1996) 174,000.

Geneva, Lake (Fr. Lac Léman, Ger. Genfersee) Lake in SW Switzerland and E France. Crescent-shaped, it lies between the ALPS and the JURA MOUNTAINS. Its S shore forms part of the French–Swiss border. It is drained to the W by the River Rhône. Length: 72km (45mi). Width: up to 14km (9mi). Area: 580sq km (224sq mi).

Geneva conventions Series of international agreement on the conduct of warfare, chiefly the treatment of wounded soldiers, prisoners-of-war and noncombatants, and the neutrality of the medical services. Inspired by Henri DUNANT's founding of the RED CROSS, the first convention was held in Geneva in 1864. Subsequent conventions (1906, 1929, 1949, 1977) extended its terms, including the prohibition of attacks on unarmed civilians.

Genghis Khan (c.1162–1227) Conqueror and founder of the MONGOL empire, b. Temüjin. In 1206, according to the *Secret History of the Mongol Nation* (c.1240), he united Mongolia and was proclaimed Genghis Khan (Universal Ruler). Organizing his cavalry into a highly mobile and disciplined squadron (*ordus*, hence "hordes"), Genghis Khan demonstrated his military genius by capturing Beijing (1215) and subjugating most of N China. He went on to create one of the largest empires ever known, by annexing Afghanistan, Iran, Uzbekistan and invading Russia as far as Moscow. On his death, the empire was divided among his sons.

Genoa (Genova) Seaport on the Gulf of Genoa, NW Italy; capital of Liguria region. An influential trading power during the Middle Ages, its fortunes declined in the 15th century, and it came under foreign control. Genoa has a university (1471) and an Academy of Fine Arts (1751). Industries: oil refining, motor vehicles, textiles, chemicals, paper, shipbuilding. Pop. (1996) 659,000.

genocide Systematic and deliberate destruction of a racial, religious or ethnic group in times of war or peace. After the HOLOCAUST (1933–45) in Nazi Europe, the United Nations (UN) signed the Convention on the Prevention and Punishment of the Crime of Punishment (1948).

genome Entire complement of genetic material carried within the CHROMOSOMES of a single cell. In effect, a genome carries all the genetic information about an individual; it is coded in sequence by the DNA that makes up the chromosomes. The term has also been applied to the whole range of GENES in a particular species. *See also* HUMAN GENOME PROJECT

genotype Genetic constitution of an individual organism. The particular set of GENES present in each cell of an organism is distinct from the PHENOTYPE, the observable characteristics of the organism.

genre painting Art term used to define paintings that portray scenes of everyday life. It was first used in the late 18th century to define the small paintings of household interiors popularized by 17th-century DUTCH ART.

gentian Perennial herb native to temperate regions, although many species are alpines. It has heart-shaped leaves and usually blue tubular flowers. Among 500 species are the dark blue *Gentiana clusii*, the Chinese *G. sino-ornata* and yellow *G. lutea*, whose bitter root is used as a tonic. Family Gentianaceae; genus *Gentiana*.

Gentile da Fabriano (*c.*1370–1427) Italian painter. A leader of the INTERNATIONAL GOTHIC style, he greatly influenced Florentine art with frescoes and the *Adoration of the Magi* (1423) for the Church of Santa Trinita, Florence.

genus (pl. genera) Part of the TAXONOMY of living organisms, ranking below FAMILY and above SPECIES. The genus name is usually a Latin or Greek noun.

geochemistry Study of the chemical composition of the EARTH. It is concerned with the abundance, distribution and migration of the elements and their isotopes in Earth's atmosphere, mantle, crust and core.

geochronology Dating of rocks or of Earth processes. Absolute dating techniques (radiometric DATING) involve the measurement of RADIOACTIVE DECAY to determine the actual date in years for a given rock. Relative dating involves the use of fossils, sediments or relationships between structures to place rock sequences and geological events in order. *See also* CARBON DATING; DENDROCHRONOLOGY

geodesic dome Architectural structure of plastic and metal, based upon triangular or polygonal facets. It was invented (1947) by R. Buckminster FULLER. *See also* BUCKMINSTERFULLERENE

geodesic surveying Method of surveying that covers areas large enough to involve consideration of the Earth's curvature. Geodesic surveying is used to establish features such as national boundaries and for mapping whole states or countries.

Geoffrey of Monmouth (*c.*1100–54) Welsh priest and chronicler, best known for his *History of the Kings of Britain* (*c.*1136). Though accepted as reliable until the 17th century, Geoffrey essentially told folk tales. His book was the chief source for the legend of King ARTHUR, and it was Shakespeare's source for *King Lear* and *Cymbeline*.

geography Study of the physical nature of the Earth (**physical** geography) and people's relationship to it (**human** geography). As a modern discipline, geography was founded in the 19th century by Baron von HUMBOLDT.

geological timescale Scale of the history of the Earth. Until recently, only methods of relative dating were possible by studying the correlation of rock formations and fossils. The largest divisions of geological time are eras (PALAEOZOIC, MESOZOIC and CENOZOIC); these are broken down into periods and the TERTIARY and QUATERNARY periods are further subdivided into epochs. Epochs consists of several **ages**, and ages can be divided into **chrons**. Eras are grouped together as **eons**.

geology Study of the materials of the Earth, their origin, arrangement, classification, change and history. Geology is divided into several categories, the major ones being MINERALOGY (arrangement of minerals), PETROLOGY (rocks and their combination of minerals), STRATIGRAPHY (succession of rocks in layers), PALAEONTOLOGY (study of fossilized remains), GEOMORPHOLOGY (study of landforms), structural geology (classification of rocks and the forces that produced them) and environmental geology (study of use of the environment).

geomagnetism Branch of GEOPHYSICS that studies the Earth's MAGNETIC FIELD. Geomagnetism is thought to be caused by the metallic composition of the Earth's CORE. The gradual movements of magnetic North result from currents within the MANTLE. *See also* MAGNETISM *See artwork,* p.344

geometric mean Geometric mean of *n* numbers is the *n*th root of their product. For example, the geometric mean of 8 and 2 is $\sqrt{(8 \times 2)} = 4$.

geometry Branch of mathematics concerned with shapes and space. **Euclidean** geometry deals with simple plane and solid figures. **Analytic** geometry (CARTESIAN COORDINATE SYSTEM) introduced (1637) by René DESCARTES, applies ALGEBRA to geometry and allows the study of more complex curves. **Projective** geometry, introduced (1822) by Jean-Victor Poncelet, is concerned with projection of shapes and with properties that are independent of such changes. More abstraction occurred in the early 19th century with formulations of **non-Euclidean** geometry by Janos Bolyai and N.I. LOBACHEVSKY, and **differential** geometry, based on the application of CALCULUS. *See also* EUCLID; GAUSS, KARL FRIEDRICH; TOPOLOGY

geomorphology Scientific study of features of the Earth's surface and the processes that have formed them.

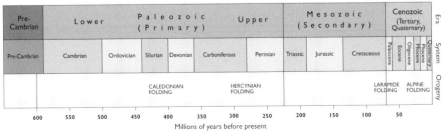

Pre-Cambrian	Lower		Paleozoic (Primary)			Upper		Mesozoic (Secondary)			Cenozoic (Tertiary, Quaternary)	
Pre-Cambrian	Cambrian	Ordovician	Silurian	Devonian	Carboniferous	Permian	Triassic	Jurassic	Cretaceous			
			CALEDONIAN FOLDING		HERCYNIAN FOLDING				LARAMIDE FOLDING	ALPINE FOLDING		
600	550	500	450	400	350	300	250	200	150	100	50	

Millions of years before present

▲ **geological timescale**
The 4.6 billion years since the formation of the Earth are divided into four great eras, which are further split into periods and, in the case of the most recent era, epochs. The present era is the Cenozoic ("new life"), extending backward through "middle life" and "ancient life" to the Precambrian. Although traces of ancient life have since been found, it was largely the proliferation of fossils from the beginning of the Palaeozoic era onward some 570 million years ago, which first allowed precise sub-divisions to be made.

geophysics Study of the characteristic physical properties of the Earth as a whole system. It uses CHEMISTRY, GEOLOGY, ASTRONOMY, SEISMOLOGY, METEOROLOGY and many other disciplines. From the study of seismic waves, geophysicists have deduced the Earth's interior structure.

George, Saint (active 3rd–4th century) Early Christian martyr who became patron saint of England in the late Middle Ages. Many stories grew up about him, including the 12th-century tale of his killing a dragon to save a maiden. His feast day is 23 April.

George I (1660–1727) King of Great Britain and Ireland (1714–27) and Elector of Hanover (1698–1727). A Protestant, he succeeded Queen ANNE as the first monarch of the House of HANOVER. George favoured the WHIGS over the Tories, suspecting the latter of JACOBITE sympathies. As king of England, he preferred his native Hanover and spoke little English. As a result, power passed to Parliament and ministers such as Sir Robert WALPOLE.

George II (1683–1760) King of Great Britain and Ireland and Elector of Hanover (1727–1760), son of GEORGE I. Like his father, he was more German than English. Sir Robert WALPOLE dominated politics early in the reign. George survived a JACOBITE revolt (1745) and was the last British king to lead his army in battle, at Dettingen (1746). British prosperity was growing fast, and George witnessed victories overseas in the SEVEN YEARS' WAR.

George III (1738–1820) King of Great Britain and Ireland (1760–1820) and King of Hanover (1760–1820), grandson of GEORGE II. He was the first thoroughly English monarch of his line. George shared the blame with Lord NORTH for the loss of the American colonies in the AMERICAN REVOLUTION (1775–83), but was quick to appreciate the talents of William PITT THE YOUNGER. His reign witnessed the beginnings of the INDUSTRIAL REVOLUTION and the birth of METHODISM. In 1765, he suffered his first attack of apparent insanity, now known to be symptoms of porphyria. They grew worse, and in 1811 his son, the future GEORGE IV, was made prince regent.

George IV (1762–1830) King of Great Britain and Ireland (1820–30), son of GEORGE III. He served as regent for his father from 1811, ascending the throne in 1820. Self-indulgent and extravagant, George was bored by government but was a strong patron of the arts. His marriage (1795) to Caroline of Brunswick became a source of scandal, and he contracted (1785) a legally invalid marriage with Mrs Fitzherbert. *See also* REGENCY STYLE

George V (1865–1936) King of Great Britain and Northern Ireland and Emperor of India (1936–47),

second son and successor of EDWARD VII. In 1893 he married Princess Mary of Teck. In 1917, during WORLD WAR 1, George changed the name of the royal house from the German SAXE-COBURG-GOTHA to Windsor. He was a conscientious monarch, helping in the formation of the National Government under Ramsay MACDONALD.

George VI (1895–1952) King of Great Britain and Northern Ireland (1936–52) and Emperor of India (1936–47), son of GEORGE V. He became king when his brother, EDWARD VIII, abdicated. In 1923, George married Lady ELIZABETH Bowes-Lyon. In an inspiring display of solidarity, he decided to remain with his family in London during the BLITZ. In 1949 he became head of the newly formed COMMONWEALTH.

George I (1845–1913) King of the Hellenes (1863–1913). Made king by Great Britain, France and Russia with approval of a Greek national assembly, he backed the constitution of 1864 giving power to an elected parliament. George gained territory for Greece in the BALKAN WARS. He was assassinated in 1913 and was succeeded by his son as Constantine I.

George, Stefan (1868–1933) German poet. George was influenced by NIETZSCHE and by French SYMBOLISM. The Nazis misinterpreted his visions of noble youth and a new German culture in *The Seventh Ring* (1907) and *The New Reich* (1928), and he went into exile rather than accept their patronage.

Georgetown Capital and largest city of Guyana, at the mouth of the River Demerara. Founded (1781) by the British, it was the capital of the united colonies of Essequibo and Demerara and was known as Stabroek during the brief Dutch occupation from 1784. Renamed George Town by the British in 1812, it is Guyana's major port. Industries: shipbuilding, food processing, brewing and rum distilling. Pop. (1995) 254,000.

Georgetown *See* PENANG

Georgia State in SE USA on the Atlantic Ocean, N of Florida; the capital is ATLANTA. Other major cities are Columbus, Macon and SAVANNAH. In the S and E of the state is a broad coastal plain and the Okefenokee Swamp. The central area consists of the Piedmont plateau. In the N are the BLUE RIDGE MOUNTAINS and the Appalachian plateau. The area is drained by the Savannah, Ogeechee and Altamaha rivers. The Spanish were the first Europeans to arrive in the area. In 1732, it was settled by British colonists. By the end of the 18th century, cotton had become the major crop. Georgia was one of the original six states of the Confederacy in the American CIVIL WAR. Ravaged by the armies of General SHERMAN in 1864, it was readmitted to the Union in 1870. Cotton, once the chief crop, has declined in favour of tobacco, peanuts, livestock and poultry. Textiles are a major industry, but chemicals, paper and timber, and the manufacture of ships and aircraft are increasingly significant. Area: 152,488sq km (58,876sq mi). Pop. (2000) 8,186,453.

Georgia Republic in SE Europe. The Transcaucasian republic of Georgia contains two autonomous republics of ABKHAZIA and Ajaria, and the province of Tskhinvali (South OSSETIA). It has four geographical areas: the CAUCASUS Mountains form its N border with Russia and include its highest peak, Mount Kazbek, at 5,042m (16,541ft); the fertile Black Sea coastal plain in the W; the E end of the Pontine Mountains forms its S borders with Turkey and Armenia; and a low plateau in the E extends into Azerbaijan. Between the mountains lie the Kura valley and the capital, TBILISI. **Climate** The Black Sea lowlands are subtropica, while the alpine Caucasus are permanently snow-covered. Tbilisi has moderate rainfall, hot

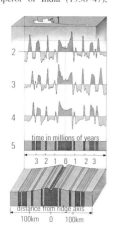

▶ **geomagnetism** A magnetic survey from a ship (1) sailing back and forth over a mid-oceanic ridge gives readings (2, 3, 4) that indicate that the magnetism of the rocks of the seafloor points alternately N and S in a series of bands parallel to the ridge (6). The pattern is identical at each side of the axis and corresponds to the pattern of reversals in the Earth's magnetic field for the last few million years (5). The rocks moving away from the axis carry a record of the Earth's magnetic field.

time in millions of years

3 2 1 0 1 2 3

distance from ridge axis
100km 0 100km

GEORGIA

AREA: 69,700sq km (26,910sq mi)
POPULATION: 5,777,000
CAPITAL (POPULATION): Tbilisi (1,253,000)

summers and cold winters. **Vegetation** Forest and shrub cover c.50% of Georgia. The coastal plain has apple orchards and orange groves. **History and politics** The land of the legendary Golden Fleece, Georgia has a strong national culture and a long literary tradition based on its own language and alphabet. Georgia was an independent kingdom from c.4th century BC, and the Georgians formed the two Black Sea states of Colchis and Iberia in c.1000 BC. The Persian SASSANIDS ruled during the 3rd and 4th centuries AD. Christianity was introduced in AD 330, and the established church is independent Eastern Orthodox. In the 11th century, independence was gained from the Turkish SELJUK empire. The 12th century witnessed Georgia's greatest period of cultural, economic and military expansion. In 1555, Georgia was divided between Persia (W) and Turkey (E). In the early 19th century, Georgia was absorbed into the Russian empire. Despite a brief period of independence after the Russian Revolution (1917), Georgia became a constituent republic of the SOVIET UNION in 1921. Russia combined Georgia, Armenia and Azerbaijan into a single republic of TRANSCAUCASIA. This federation was broken up in 1936, and Georgia became a separate Soviet republic. After violent demonstrations in 1989, Georgia declared independence in May 1991. By the close of 1991, President Gamsakhurdia's authoritarian regime had brought civil war to the streets of Tbilisi. In 1992, Eduard SHEVARDNADZE was elected president. Faced by conflict from Gamsakhurdia's supporters and secessionist movements in Abkhazia and South Ossetia, Shevardnadze called in Russian troops to defeat the rebellion. In return for Russian support, Georgia joined the COMMONWEALTH OF INDEPENDENT STATES (CIS) and allowed Russia ultimate economic power. Minority demands for secession continued, and in 1995, South Ossetia was renamed Tskhinvali, and Abkhazia was granted autonomous status. Shevardnadze was re-elected in 1995 and again in 2000. Conflict continues in the region and CIS peacekeeping forces are deployed in Abkhazia. **Economy** Georgia is a developing country (1995 GDP per capita, US$1,470), its economy devastated by civil war and the break-up of the Soviet Union. Agriculture engages 58% of the workforce, although the rugged terrain makes farming difficult. The E region is famous for its grapes, used to make wine. The coastal lowlands produce tea and tropical fruit and are a tourist destination. Georgia is rich in minerals, such as barite, coal and copper. Georgia has huge potential for generating hydroelectric power, but is desperately short of energy and dependent on Ukraine, Azerbaijan and Russia for oil.
Georgian Language of GEORGIA. The most important member of the South Caucasian (Kartvelian) language family, it is used by nearly 4 million people.
Georgian architecture Building styles in Britain and its colonies (1714–1830). The name derives from the Hanoverian kings who reigned during this period (George I to George IV). The various Georgian styles include PALLADIANISM, ROCOCO, NEO-CLASSICISM, GOTHIC REVIVAL and REGENCY STYLE. BATH in SW England has many fine Georgian buildings.
geostationary orbit Location of an artificial SATELLITE so that it remains above the same point on a planet's

surface because it completes one ORBIT in the same time it takes the planet to rotate once on its axis. Communications and remote-sensing satellites are often placed in geostationary orbits.
geothermal energy Heat contained in the Earth's crust. It is produced by RADIOACTIVITY within the Earth's core and by PLATE TECTONIC movement. It is released by hot springs, GEYSERS and VOLCANOES, and can be used as a source for generating ELECTRICITY. The world's first geothermal power-station was built (1913) at Larderello, Italy.
geranium Any of 400 hardy, herbaceous perennial plants of the genus *Pelargonium*. They bear pink, purple or white flowers over a long season. Family Geraniaceae.
gerbil Nocturnal RODENT native to arid areas of Asia and Africa, and a popular pet. It has long hind legs and tail. Its fur may be fawn, grey, brown or red. It is a subterranean herbivore and often hoards food. Family Cricetidae.
Géricault, (Jean Louis André) Théodore (1791–1824) French painter. A forerunner of the romantic movement, he began by painting battles. His most famous work, the *Raft of the Medusa* (1817), depicts the survivors of a shipwreck.
germ Popular term for any infectious agent. Germs can be bacteria, fungi or viruses. In biology, it denotes a rudimentary stage in plant growth.
German *See* GERMANIC LANGUAGES
German architecture Architecture of Germany including, in its early days, that of Austria. The earliest surviving buildings date from CHARLEMAGNE. They are in the ROMANESQUE style, at its best in Worms Cathedral (c.1180). Romanesque was superseded by GOTHIC, seen in ecclesiastical architecture and provincial buildings, such as the *Rathaus* (town hall) typical of NE German towns. There is little RENAISSANCE architecture in Germany, an exception being the rebuilt façade of the *Rathaus* in Bremen. The BAROQUE period extended into the ROCOCO, examples including the elaborate Church of the *Vierzehnheiligen* (1772) by Balthasar Neuman and masterpieces by Fischer von Erlach and Matthaeus Pöppelmann. In the late 1700s, NEO-CLASSICISM inspired buildings in Berlin and Munich by Friedrich Schinkel, Leo von Klenze and others. New materials such as cast iron were exploited, as in Vienna's *Dianabad* by Karl Etzel (1843). Walter GROPIUS and the BAUHAUS dominated the beginning of the 20th century. In the 1930s, MIES VAN DER ROHE exemplified the INTERNATIONAL STYLE, which was replaced by the re-adoption of neo-classicism under HITLER, with "official" Nazi architect Albert SPEER. After World War 2, most new buildings adopted principles of EXPRESSIONISM or MODERNISM.
German art National tradition dating back to the illuminated manuscripts of the 9th and 10th centuries. By the end of the Middle Ages, a flourishing tradition in woodcarving had grown up in the S with the work of Veit Stoss and Tilman Riemenschneider. In the 16th century, Germany was at the forefront of the Northern RENAISSANCE, led by Albrecht DÜRER and Hans HOLBEIN THE YOUNGER. This was a golden age for German painting and, although Caspar FRIEDRICH made an important contribution to ROMANTICISM, it was only in the 20th century that EXPRESSIONISM and BAUHAUS achieved comparable status.
Germanic languages Group of languages, a subdivision of the INDO-EUROPEAN family. One branch (**West** Germanic) includes English, German, Yiddish, Dutch, Flemish and Afrikaans; another (**North** Germanic) includes Swedish, Danish, Icelandic and Faroese. **German** is spoken by c.120 million people in Germany, Austria and Switzerland. **High** German (*Hochdeutsch*), of S Germany and Austria, is now the standard dialect.

Low German (*Plattdeutsch*) was spoken widely in the N but is now declining.

Germanicus Caesar (15 BC–AD 19) Roman general, nephew and adopted son of TIBERIUS. He commanded the Gallic and German provinces. After defeating the German leader Arminius (AD 16), Tiberius also gave him command of the E provinces. Germanicus' children included Agrippina the Elder, mother of NERO and CALIGULA.

germanium (symbol Ge) Grey-white metalloid element in group IV of the periodic table, discovered in 1886. A by-product of zinc ores or the combustion of certain coals, it is important in SEMICONDUCTOR devices. Properties: at.no. 32; r.a.m. 72.59; r.d. 5.35; m.p. 937°C (1,719°F); b.p. 2,830°C (5,126°F); most common isotope Ge^{74} (36.54%).

German literature German literature has a long and fine tradition, dating back to the Middle High German period and the 13th-century courtly poems of Hartmann von Aue, Wolfram von Eschenbach and Gottfried von Strassburg, as well as the *Minnesang* of Walther von der Vogelweide and the heroic epic, the *Nibelungenlied*. During the next few centuries, German literature was dominated by the classical conventions of FRENCH LITERATURE. In the late 18th century a truly national literary movement, STURM UND DRANG, emerged. Two of Germany's greatest writers, the Weimar classicists, GOETHE and SCHILLER were early proponents of the movement. CLASSICISM found its major literary expression in the BILDUNGSROMAN. Germany's great classicist poet was Friedrich HÖLDERLIN. ROMANTICISM flourished in the late 18th and early 19th centuries, when writers such as SCHLEGEL, NOVALIS, BRENTANO, E.T.A. HOFFMANN, KLEIST and the GRIMM BROTHERS encouraged a romanticization of German history and folklore, often through fairy tales. HEINE's work marks the beginnings of German REALISM. At the start of the 20th century, Stefan GEORGE and RILKE's lyrical poetry was in part a reaction against the prevailing realist tone. Among anti-naturalist novelists were major figures like Thomas MANN, Erich REMARQUE, Hermann HESSE and Robert MUSIL. German EXPRESSIONISM was a combination of formal experimentation and political content. Major figures in the movement included Franza KAFKA and Bertolt BRECHT. During the Third Reich, many writers were branded as "undesirable" because of their race or politics. Many "forbidden" texts were burned. Post-war German writers, such as Günther GRASS, Max FRISCH and Heinrich BÖLL, examined aspects of German complicity during the Nazi period.

German measles (rubella) Viral disease usually contracted in childhood. Symptoms include a sore throat, slight fever and pinkish rash. Women developing rubella during the first three months of pregnancy risk damage to the fetus. Immunization is recommended for all children.

German shepherd (Alsatian) Working dog bred in Germany by c.1900. It has woolly underhair and is black, grey, or black and tan. Height: c.64cm (25in) at the shoulder; weight: 27–38kg (60–85lb).

Germany Federal republic in central Europe. Germany lies in the heart of Europe. It is the fifth-largest country in Europe (after Ukraine, France, Spain and Sweden), and the world's 12th most populous country. **Land and climate** Germany can be divided into three geographical

GERMANY
AREA: 356,910sq km (137,803sq mi)
POPULATION: 76,962,000
CAPITAL (POPULATION): Berlin (3,472,000)

regions: the N German plain; central highlands; and the S Central Alps. The fertile N **plain** is drained by the rivers ELBE, ODER and Weser. It includes the industrial centres of HAMBURG, BREMEN, HANOVER and KIEL. In the E lies the capital, BERLIN, and the former East German cities of LEIPZIG, DRESDEN and MAGDEBURG. Northwest Germany (especially the RHINE, RUHR and Saar valleys) is Germany's industrial heartland. It includes the cities of COLOGNE, ESSEN, DORTMUND, DÜSSELDORF and DUISBURG. The **central highlands** include the HARZ MOUNTAINS and the cities of MUNICH, FRANKFURT, STUTTGART, NUREMBERG and AUGSBURG. **Southern** Germany rises to the Bavarian ALPS on the border with Switzerland, which include Germany's highest peak, Zugspitze, at 2,963m (9,721ft). The BLACK FOREST, overlooking the Rhine valley, is a major tourist attraction. The region is drained by the DANUBE (Europe's second-largest river). Germany has a temperate climate. The NW is warmed by the North Sea. The Baltic lowlands in the NE are cooler. In the S, the climate becomes more continental. (*See* individual *länder*) **Vegetation** The N German plain contains large areas of heath. The forests of central and S Germany include pine, beech and oak. **History** In c.200 BC, German tribes began to displace the Celts. In the 5th century AD, they conquered much of the western Roman Empire. In 486, the MEROVINGIAN king CLOVIS I conquered S and W Germany and THURINGIA. His son CHARLEMAGNE expanded the territory to the Elbe and was crowned emperor (800). His empire rapidly fragmented, and the FEUDAL SYSTEM created powerful local duchies. In 918, HENRY I (THE FOWLER) began a century of SAXON rule, and his son OTTO I (THE GREAT) established the HOLY ROMAN EMPIRE (first *Reich*) (962). In 1152, FREDERICK I founded the HOHENSTAUFEN dynasty. FREDERICK I's conflict with the papacy created civil war. In 1273, RUDOLF I founded the HABSBURG dynasty. City states formed alliances, such as the HANSEATIC LEAGUE. CHARLES V's reign (1519–58) brought religious and civil unrest, such as the REFORMATION and the PEASANTS' WAR. Catholic and Protestant conflict culminated in the devastating THIRTY YEARS' WAR (1618–48). The reign (1740–86) of FREDERICK II (THE GREAT) saw the emergence of the state of PRUSSIA. The NAPOLEONIC WARS (1803–15) ended in humiliating defeat and the Congress of VIENNA (1815) created the German Confederation. The 19th century brought growing nationalism, fuelled by German ROMANTICISM. The REVOLUTIONS OF 1848 led to the election of BISMARCK as chancellor (1862–90). Prussian victories in the AUSTRO-PRUSSIAN WAR (1866) and the FRANCO-PRUSSIAN WAR (1870–71) created the second German *Reich* under the HOHENZOLLERN king, WILLIAM I. Prince von BÜLOW's imperial ambitions were a cause of WORLD WAR 1 (1914–18). The Treaty of VERSAILLES (1919) placed a heavy price on German defeat. WILLIAM II was forced to abdicate, and the WEIMAR REPUBLIC (1919–33) was created. Mass unemployment, crippling inflation, war reparations and world depression created the conditions for FASCISM. The leader of the National Socialist (Nazi) Party, Adolf HITLER, was elected (1933) to build a THIRD REICH. NATIONAL SOCIALISM pervaded all areas of society, dissent was crushed by the GESTAPO, opposition parties and elections banned. Hitler, as *Führer*, became the father of the nation through GOEBBELS' propagandizing. CONCENTRATION CAMPS were set up and armaments stockpiled. Hitler remilitarized the RHINELAND (1936), aided Franco in the Spanish CIVIL WAR (1936–39) and annexed Austria (1938). The MUNICH AGREEMENT (1938) marked the failure of appeasement; Germany invaded Czechoslovakia

(March 1939) and Poland (September 1939), precipitating WORLD WAR 2. Initial success was halted by failure in the Battle of BRITAIN and Hitler's disastrous Soviet offensive (June 1941). The blanket bombing of German cities devastated German industry and morale. Faced with defeat, Hitler committed suicide (30 April 1945). Germany surrendered (8 May 1945), and leading Nazis faced the NUREMBERG TRIALS. Germany was divided into four military zones. COLD WAR tension increased. Following the BERLIN AIRLIFT (1949), American, British and French zones were joined to make the Federal Republic of Germany (West Germany); the Soviet zone formed the German Democratic Republic (East Germany). Berlin was also divided: East Berlin became capital of East Germany, BONN de facto capital of West Germany. Walter ULBRICHT became leader (1950–71) of **East Germany**. Economic deprivation led to a revolt in 1953, which Soviet troops subdued. In 1955 East Germany joined the Warsaw Pact. Between 1945 and 1961, four million people crossed to the west. The BERLIN WALL was built to halt the exodus. Ulbricht was replaced (1971) by Erich HONECKER. Relations with West Germany thawed, and travel was permitted between the two. Honecker's refusal to adopt reforms led to civil unrest. In November 1989, a rally of 500,000 people demanded reunification, the Wall was opened and the regime collapsed. Christian Democrats won the first free elections (March 1990). In July 1990, East and West Germany were formally unified. Konrad ADENAUER was elected as the first chancellor (1949–63) of **West Germany**. He was committed to German reunification. In 1955 West Germany became a member of NATO. The economy continued to grow dramatically under Kurt KIESINGER (1963–69). Willy BRANDT's chancellorship (1969–74) was noted for his *Ostpolitik* (establishing better relations with the Soviet bloc). His successor was Helmut SCHMIDT (1974–82). Helmut KOHL's chancellorship (1982–98) was more conservative. In December 1990, Kohl was elected in the first all-German elections since 1933. In 1998, Kohl was defeated by Gerhard Schröder of the Social Democratic Party (SPD). Schröder formed a coalition government with The Greens. **Politics** Reunification has meant massive investment to restructure the former East German economy, which has strained federal resources and entailed tax increases. High unemployment, unequal distribution of wealth, crime and the rise of neo-Nazi groups are all serious social and political problems. Germany is a major supporter of the EUROPEAN UNION (EU), and Helmut Köhl was the drving force behind the creation of the EURO. **Economy** Germany is one of the world's greatest economic powers (1995 GDP per capita, US\$20,070). Services form the largest economic sector. Machinery and transport equipment account for 50% of exports. It is the world's third-largest car producer. Other major products: ships, iron, steel, petroleum, tyres. It has the world's second-largest lignite mining industry. Other minerals: copper, potash, lead, salt, zinc, aluminium. Germany has a large agricultural sector. It is the world's second-largest producer of hops and beer, and fifth-largest wine-producer. Other products: cheese and milk, barley, rye, pork.

germination Growth of the EMBRYO in the SEED of a new plant. To germinate, a seed or spore needs favourable conditions of temperature, light, moisture and oxygen. *See also* DICOTYLEDON

Geronimo (1829–1908) Chief of the Chiricahua APACHE. Escaping from a reservation into which he and his tribe were forced, he led a band of followers in raids against white settlers in Arizona for more than ten years.

After surrendering in 1886, he was imprisoned in Florida, Alabama and finally confined in Fort Sill, Oklahoma. He became a farmer and national celebrity.

gerrymander Practice of redrawing electoral boundaries to favour a particular party. It is named after Elbridge Gerry, governor of Massachusetts (1810–12). One of his redefined districts was said to resemble a salamander.

Gershwin, George (1898–1937) US composer and songwriter, b. Jacob Gershovitz. His brother, **Ira** Gershwin (1896–1983), mostly wrote the lyrics. Gershwin composed hit musicals, such as *Lady Be Good* (1924), a jazz opera *Porgy and Bess* (1935), and some orchestral works, such as *Rhapsody in Blue* (1924) and *An American in Paris* (1928).

gestalt psychology School of psychology characterized by the expression "the whole (*Gestalt*) is greater than the sum of its parts". It opposed the dominant theories of BEHAVIOURISM. The school was founded in Germany (*c*.1912) by Max WERTHEIMER, Wilhelm WUNDT, Wolfgang KÖHLER and Kurt KOFFKA. They were mainly concerned with providing an adequate description of PERCEPTION. They argued that subjective mental processes are an organizing force. For instance, when a succession of different still photographs are rapidly passed by the human eye, they are perceived as "motion pictures".

Gestapo (*Geheime Staatspolizei*) State secret police of Nazi Germany. Founded (1933) by GOERING, it became a powerful national organization under HIMMLER from 1934, as an arm of the SS. With up to 50,000 members by 1945, the Gestapo and SS ran the CONCENTRATION CAMPS.

gestation (PREGNANCY) Period during which a developing EMBRYO is carried in the UTERUS.

Gesualdo, Carlo (*c*.1560–1613) Italian composer. He is best known for his harmonically daring MADRIGALS, which in their complexity and modernity set him apart from his contemporaries. He published six books of madrigals and also wrote motets and religious songs.

Gethsemane In the New Testament, a garden, probably an olive grove at the foot of the W slope of the Mount of Olives, E of Jerusalem, where JESUS CHRIST was betrayed by JUDAS ISCARIOT.

Getty, Jean Paul (1892–1976) US businessman and art collector. In 1930, he became president of his father's oil company. He lived in England from 1959. Getty personal fortune was estimated at more than \$1,000 million. He founded the J. Paul Getty Museum in Malibu, California.

Gettysburg, Battle of (1–3 July 1863) Decisive campaign of the American CIVIL WAR, fought near Gettysburg, Pennsylvania. The Union army of George Gordon Meade checked the invasion of Pennsylvania by the Confederate forces of Robert E. Lee. The battle was a turning point. The heavy casualties (*c*.20,000 each side) prompted Abraham LINCOLN's GETTYSBURG ADDRESS.

Gettysburg Address (19 November 1863) Speech by President Abraham LINCOLN at the dedication of the national cemetery on the battlefield of GETTYSBURG. It ended by describing democracy as "government of the people, by the people, and for the people". One of the most famous political addresses, the text of the speech is carved onto the Lincoln Memorial in Washington, D.C.

Getz, Stan (1927–91) US jazz saxophonist, b. Stanley Gayetsky. He played in Woody Herman's big band, before forming his own group. Getz's lyrical, mottled tone bridged the gap between BEBOP and the birth of "cool" jazz. He is best-known for the bossa nova tune "The Girl From Ipanema" (1963) with Astrid Gilberto.

geyser Hot spring that erupts, throwing up jets of superheated water and steam to a height of *c*.60m (200ft) and

followed by a shaft of steam with a thunderous roar. Geysers occur in the United States, Iceland and New Zealand.
Ghana Republic in W Africa. Ghana (formerly Gold Coast) faces the Gulf of Guinea in West Africa. The densely populated s coastal plains are lined by lagoons and include the capital, ACCRA. In the SW plateau lies the ASHANTI region and its capital, KUMASI. Ghana's major river is the VOLTA. The Aksombo Dam, built 1964, created one of the world's largest artificial lakes, Lake Volta. The dam is used to generate hydroelectricity. **Climate** Accra has a tropical climate yet is cooler than many equatorial areas. Rain falls throughout the year, especially heavily in the SW. The N is warmer than the S. The winter months (November– March) have a low average rainfall. **Vegetation** Tropical savanna dominates the coastal region and the far N. Rainforest covers most of the central region. **History and politics** Various African kingdoms existed in the region before the arrival of Portuguese explorers in 1471, who named it the Gold Coast after its precious mineral resource. In 1642, the Dutch gained control, and the Gold Coast was a centre of the 17th-century slave trade. Following the abolition of slavery (1860s), the European powers withdrew under the advance of the Ashanti. In 1874, Britain colonized the region, excluding Ashanti. In 1901, Ashanti was also subdued. The British developed cacao plantations. After World War 2, nationalist demands intensified, and in 1951 elections were held. Kwame NKRUMAH became prime minister. In 1957, Ghana became the first African colony to gain full independence. British Togoland was incorporated into the new state. The country was renamed Ghana after a powerful, medieval West African kingdom. In 1960, Ghana became a republic with Nkrumah as president. In 1964, Ghana became a one-party state. The economy slumped, burdened by debt, corruption

GHANA
AREA: 238,540sq km (92,100sq mi)
POPULATION: 16,944,000
CAPITAL (POPULATION): Accra (949,013)

and the falling cacao price. Nkrumah was deposed in a military coup (1966). Ghana briefly returned to civilian rule (1969–72). The National Redemptive Council (NRC), led by Colonel Acheampong (1972–78), continued to nationalize industry. In 1979, Flight-Lieutenant Jerry Rawlings overthrew the government and executed opposition leaders. A civilian government was formed. In 1981, this was toppled by Rawlings. In 1992, a new constitution paved the way for multiparty elections. Opposition parties and voters boycotted the elections, and The National Democratic Council (NDC), led by Rawlings, secured a victory. In 1996, Rawlings was re-elected. **Economy** Ghana is a developing country (1995 GDP per capita, US$1,990). Agriculture employs 59% of the workforce and accounts for more than 66% of exports. Ghana is the world's fifth largest producer of cocoa beans. Other cash crops: coffee, coconuts, palm kernels. Minerals are the second largest export; timber is also important. Ghana is the world's tenth largest producer of manganese. The Ashanti Goldfields Corporation is one of the world's largest producers.

gharial *See* GAVIAL
Ghats Two mountain systems in India, running parallel to the coast on both sides of the Deccan Plateau. The **Western** Ghats extend from the River Tapti to Cape Comorin. The **Eastern** Ghats extend from the River Mahanadi to the Nilgiri Hills. Length: (Western) 1,600km (1,000mi); (Eastern) 1,400km (875mi).
Ghazali, al- (1058–1111) Islamic philosopher. In 1095, he abandoned his post as professor of philosophy at Baghdad to become a mendicant mystic. Ghazali's greatest work *The Revival of the Religious Sciences* made SUFISM an acceptable part of orthodox ISLAM. His critique of ARISTOTLE was rebutted by AVERROËS.
Ghent (Gent, Gand) City in NW central Belgium. A major cloth centre in the 13th century, it came under Austrian control from 1714 and was captured by the French in 1792, becoming part of independent Belgium in 1830. Industries: plastics, chemicals, steel, electrical engineering, motor vehicles. Pop. (1996) 226,000.
Ghent, Treaty of (1814) Agreement ending the WAR OF 1812 between Britain and the USA. It restored territorial allocations to their pre-war position and appointed a commission to settle the dispute over the US–Canada border.
ghetto (It. foundry) Section of a city inhabited by a minority group. The term originated in 16th-century Venice, designating a area of the city to which Jews were restricted. In the 20th century, the concept of a Jewish ghetto was revived by the Nazis in WARSAW.
Ghibelline Political faction in 13th-century Italy that supported the HOHENSTAUFEN dynasty of the HOLY ROMAN EMPIRE and opposed the pro-papal GUELPHS. During the struggles between FREDERICK II and the popes in the mid-13th century, Ghibellines came to designate those on the imperial side. They were defeated by the Guelphs in 1268, and the family went into decline.
Ghiberti, Lorenzo (1378–1455) Italian sculptor, goldsmith, architect, painter and writer; he was a major transitional figure between the late GOTHIC and RENAISSANCE worlds. Ghiberti made two pairs of bronze doors for the Baptistery in Florence. One pair, the "Doors of Paradise" (1425–52), is considered his masterpiece.

A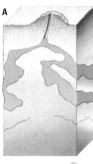
C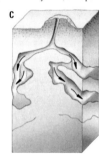

B

▲ **geyser** A plume of hot water and steam, a geyser is the result of the boiling of water at depth in a series of interconnecting chambers by volcanic heat (A). The expansion of steam produced drives the water and steam above it out at the surface (B), and this is followed by a period of refilling and heating, making it a periodic phenomenon (C).

Ghirlandaio, Domenico (1449–94) Florentine painter, best known for his religious frescoes, b. Domenico di Tommaso Bigordi. He worked on the Sistine Chapel with BOTTICELLI and others, producing *Christ Calling the First Apostles* (1482). Ghirlandaio's (It. garland-maker) major work was the fresco cycle *Life of St John the Baptist* (1486–90) in S. Maria Novella, Florence.

Ghose, Aurobindo (1872–1950) (Sri Aurobindo) Indian mystic philosopher and nationalist leader. In 1908 he was imprisoned for agitating against British rule in Bengal. After his release, Ghose devoted himself to Hindu philosophy. He founded an *ashram* (retreat) at Pondicherry, SE India. In works such as *The Synthesis of Yoga* (1948) Ghose formulated his system of integral YOGA based on a two-way path to union with BRAHMAN.

Giacometti, Alberto (1901–66) Swiss sculptor and painter. His early works, such as *The Palace at 4am* (1923), show the influence of SURREALISM. Giacometti's most characteristic works are emaciated, elongated figures built of plaster on a wire base, such as *Pointing Man* (1947). His paintings have the same agitated quality.

Giant's Causeway Promontory on the N coast of County Antrim, Northern Ireland. It extends 5km (3mi) along the coast and consists of thousands of basalt columns of varying heights.

gibberellin Any of a group of plant HORMONES that stimulate cell division, stem elongation, and response to light and temperature. They increase crop yields.

Gibbon, Edward (1737–94) English historian. He conceived the idea of his great work, *The Decline and Fall of the Roman Empire* (1776–88), while among the ruins of ancient Rome. The six-volume text is still widely used.

gibbon Smallest of the APES, native to forests in SE Asia. It has a shaggy brown, black or silvery coat and is very agile. It has long, powerful arms. Height: 41–66cm (16–26in). Family Pongidae; genus *Hyloblates*.

Gibbons, Grinling (1648–1721) British woodcarver, b. Holland. He became Master Carver to the Crown after being introduced to Charles II by John Evelyn. His decorative carvings of fruit, flowers and cherub's heads adorn the choir stalls of St Paul's Cathedral, London.

Gibbons, Orlando (1583–1625) English composer. He wrote sacred music, viol fantasies and madrigals, such as *The Silver Swan* (1612). He was a master of POLYPHONY.

Gibbs, James (1682–1754) Scottish architect. He was inspired by Sir Christopher WREN. Gibbs was an individualist, fitting into neither the BAROQUE style, which preceded him, nor the later Palladian. His best-known work is the church of St Martin in the Fields, London (1722–26).

Gibbs, Josiah Willard (1839–1903) US mathematical physicist and chemist. His application of thermodynamics to physical processes led to statistical mechanics. He devised the phase rule and developed vector analysis.

Gibraltar British crown colony, a rocky peninsula on the S coast of Spain. The MUSLIM conquest of Spain began in AD 711, and Gibraltar remained under Moorish control until 1462. In 1704, it was captured by an Anglo-Dutch fleet and ceded to Britain in the Peace of UTRECHT (1713). In 1964, it was granted self-government, and a 1967 referendum showed Gibraltarians' wish to remain British. Industries: tourism, re-exportation of petroleum and petroleum products. Area: 6.5sq km (2.5sq mi). Pop. (1993 est.) 28,051.

Gibson, Mel (1956–) Australian film actor and director, b. US. International recognition followed his starring roles in *Mad Max* (1979) and *Gallipoli* (1981). He showed his versatility in the ZEFFIRELLI production of *Hamlet* (1990). Gibson won Academy Awards for best director and best picture for *Braveheart* (1995).

Gide, André Paul Guillaume (1869–1951) French novelist, dramatist and critic. His *Journals* (1885–1950) show a constant struggle between puritan and pagan elements. His novellas *The Immoralist* (1902) and *Strait is the Gate* (1909) were inspired by his marriage to his cousin. Gide's mature works, such as *The Counterfeiters* (1926), dramatize a search for spiritual truth. He was awarded the 1947 Nobel Prize for literature.

Gideon (Jerubbaal) In the Old Testament, a Judge of Israel, an Israelite hero, and father of Abimelech (Judges 6–8). Gideon belonged to one of the clans making up the tribe of Manasseh. Called by an angel of Yahweh, he destroyed the Canaanite altar of BAAL. After a victorious attack on the Midianite camp with only 300 soldiers (chosen by God), he refused to be made king.

Gielgud, Sir Arthur John (1904–2000) English actor and director. He made his stage debut in 1921. Gielgud established his reputation in *Hamlet* (1929). He played almost every major Shakespearian role and was acclaimed in *The Importance of Being Earnest* (1930, 1939) and *The Cherry Orchard* (1961). Gielgud won an Oscar for Best Supporting Actor in *Arthur* (1981). Other films include *Gandhi* (1982) and *Prospero's Books* (1991). He was knighted in 1953.

Giffard, Henri (1823–1882) French engineer. His AIRSHIP (1852) had the first STEAM ENGINE that was light and powerful enough to be used to power a balloon. The engine drove a 3.5m (11ft) propeller at the rate of 110rpm to power the 44m (144ft) craft at *c*.9km/h (5.6mph).

Gifu City on the River Kiso, S Honshu, Japan. A former medieval castle town, it was a centre of civic strife in the 17th century. Industries: tourism, chemicals, motor vehicles, textiles, paper, sake. Pop. (1995) 407,000.

Gila monster Poisonous nocturnal LIZARD that lives in deserts of SW USA and N Mexico. It has a stout body, massive head, flat tail and scales of orange, yellow and black. It eats mammals and eggs. Length: 50cm (20in). Family Helodermatidae; species *Heloderma suspectum*.

Gilbert, Sir Humphrey (1539–83) English explorer and colonizer. A scholar and soldier, he proposed the existence of the NORTHWEST PASSAGE in his *Discourse* (1576) and unsuccessfully sailed in search of it in 1578 and 1583. On his second trip, Gilbert established a colony at St. John's, Newfoundland. On the voyage home, Gilbert's ship foundered and he was drowned off Nova Scotia.

Gilbert, Walter (1932–) US molecular biologist. Gilbert shared the 1980 Nobel Prize for chemistry for his work on the composition of nucleic acids and their role in the formation of genes.

Gilbert, William (1544–1603) English physicist and physician to Elizabeth I. In *De Magnete* (1600) he was the first to recognize terrestrial MAGNETISM and coined the terms magnetic pole, electric attraction and electric force.

Gilbert, Sir W.S. (William Schwenck) (1836–1911) English librettist and playwright. He collaborated with Sir Arthur SULLIVAN on an immensely successful series of 14 comic operettas, nearly all first performed by the D'Oyly CARTE company. Their works include *HMS Pinafore* (1878), *The Pirates of Penzance* (1879), *The Mikado* (1885) and *The Gondoliers* (1889).

Gilbert and Ellice Islands Two groups of coral islands in the W Pacific Ocean, 4,000km (2,500mi) NE of Australia. In 1915 the islands became a British colony. Separated from the Ellice Islands in 1975, the Gilbert Islands are now part of KIRIBATI. The Ellice Islands are now called TUVALU.

Gilbert and George English artists. **Gilbert** Proesch (1943–) and **George** Passmore (1942–). They first attracted attention as "singing sculptures" in an eight-hour rendition of *Underneath the Arches* (1969). Since the 1970s they have produced photopieces.

Gilgamesh Hero of the great Assyro-Babylonian myth, the Epic of Gilgamesh. He went in search of the secret of immortality. Having overcome monsters and gods, Gilgamesh found the flower of immortality, only to have it snatched from him by a serpent.

Gill, (Arthur) Eric (Rowton) (1882–1940) English engraver and sculptor. He designed many typefaces, including Perpetua (1925) and Gill Sans Serif (1927). Gill's major sculptures include the *Stations of the Cross* (1914–18) in Westminster Cathedral, London, and *Ariel and Prospero* (1931) on Broadcasting House, London.

gill Organ through which most fish, some larval amphibians and many aquatic invertebrates obtain oxygen from water. When a fish breathes it opens its mouth, draws in water, and shuts its mouth again. Water is forced through the gill slits, over the gills, and out into the surrounding water. Oxygen is absorbed into small capillary blood vessels, and at the same time, waste carbon dioxide carried by the blood diffuses into the water.

Gillespie, "Dizzy" (John Birks) (1917–93) US jazz trumpeter and bandleader. He played in the SWING bands of Cab Calloway and Billy Eckstine before forming his own orchestra. With Charlie PARKER and Bud POWELL, "Dizzy" was a pioneer of BEBOP. His dazzling tone and harmonic invention is evident on *Shaw 'Nuff* (1946).

Gillray, James (1757–1815) English caricaturist. His political and social satire was wider in scope than that of HOGARTH. Gillray lampooned George III as "Farmer George". William Pitt and Napoleon I appear in "The Plum Pudding in Danger".

gin Distilled alcohol containing flavouring substances from the berry of the JUNIPER tree, *Juniperus communis*. English and American gins are alcohol distilled from fermented grain diluted to the required strength – between 80° and 94° proof spirit – and flavoured with juniper and small amounts of orris, cassia and other aromatic substances. Dutch gin is distilled from barley malt and has a lower alcoholic content.

ginger Herbaceous PERENNIAL plant native to tropical E Asia and Indonesia and grown commercially in Jamaica and elsewhere. It has fat tuberous roots and yellow-green flowers. The kitchen spice is made from the tubers of *Zingiber officinale*. Family Zingiberaceae.

Gingrich, Newt (Newton Leroy) (1943–) US Republican politician. He entered Congress in 1979. In 1994 Congressional elections, Gingrich persuaded Republicans to subscribe to his "Contract with America", a commitment to cut wasteful government spending. As Speaker of the House of Representatives (1995–98), he led the Republican-dominated Congress into conflict with President CLINTON. In 1997, financial scandals reduced his power, but he remained an outspoken foe of Clinton.

ginkgo (maidenhair tree) Oldest living species of GYMNOSPERM, native to temperate regions of China, occurring only rarely in the wild. It dates from the late Permian period. It has fan-shaped leaves, small, foul-smelling fruits and pitlike seeds. Height: to 30m (100ft). Phylum Ginkgophyta; species *Ginkgo biloba*.

Ginsberg, Allen (1926–97) US poet. His work was influenced by Zen Buddhism, meditation and the use of hallucinogens. His first collection of verse, *Howl and Other Poems* (1956), was a searing indictment of American society and established him as the leading poet of the BEAT MOVEMENT. Other work includes *Kaddish and Other Poems* (1961), a lament for his mother.

ginseng Either of two perennial plants found in the USA (*Panax quinquefolius*) and E Asia (*P. ginseng*). It has yellow-green flowers and compound leaves. The dried tuberous roots are used in Chinese traditional medicine. Height: to 51cm (20in). Family Araliaceae.

Giolitti, Giovanni (1842–1928) Italian statesman, five times prime minister between 1892 and 1921. He introduced measures of social welfare and broadened the franchise. Although Giolitti instigated the Italo-Turkish War of 1911, he opposed Italy's entry into World War 1. He initially backed MUSSOLINI, withdrawing support in 1924.

Giordano, Luca (1632–1705) Neapolitan painter. His prolific output earned him the epithet *Luca fa presto* ("Luca works quickly"). At first influenced by José de RIBERA, Giordano's style became more decorative after visits to Venice. In 1682 he completed the ceiling fresco in Palazzo Medici-Riccardi, Florence.

Giorgione (*c*.1478–1510) Italian painter, b. Giorgio da Castlefranco. A pupil of BELLINI, he became one of the major painters of the Venetian High RENAISSANCE. He had an enigmatic romantic style, as in *Tempest* (*c*.1505). His *Sleeping Venus* was probably completed (*c*.1510) by TITIAN.

Giotto (di Bondone) (*c*.1266–1337) Florentine painter. A pupil of CIMABUE, he is a central figure of the early RENAISSANCE. Giotto rejected the stylized form of Italo-Byzantine art in favour of a more realistic style, best represented by the frescoes (*c*.1305–08) in the Arena Chapel, Padua. In 1334 he became architect of Florence and designed the campanile of the Duomo. Controversy rages over the attribution of the frecoes in S. Francesco, Assisi.

giraffe Any of nine subspecies of herbivorous, hoofed mammals, native to Africa. The tallest land animal, giraffes have very long necks, short, tufted manes and two to four skin-covered horns. The coat is pale brown with red-brown blotches. Giraffes can gallop at speeds up to 50km/h (30mph). Height: to 5.5m (18ft). Family Giraffidae; species *Giraffa camelopardalis*.

Giraudoux, Jean (1882–1944) French dramatist and novelist. His early poetic novels include *Suzanne and the Pacific* (1921). Giraudoux is best-known for his stylized plays based on Greek myths, including *Amphitryon 38* (1929), *Intermezzo* (1933) and *Tiger at the Gates* (1935). Other plays include *The Madwoman of Chaillot* (1946).

Girl Guides Organization for girls founded (1910) in England by Agnes Baden-Powell, sister of Lord BADEN-POWELL, founder of the BOY SCOUTS. Today, there are *c*.7 million guides worldwide, including *c*.870,000 guides in Britain. They are divided into three groups, Brownie Guides, Guides and Ranger Guides, according to age.

Girondins Political group in the FRENCH REVOLUTION named after deputies from Gironde, SW France. From 1792 the moderate and middle-class Girondins tried to prevent the execution of LOUIS XVI and reduce the power of Paris. In 1793 they were expelled from the National Congress by the JACOBINS and their leaders executed.

Giscard d'Estaing, Valéry (1926–) French statesman, president (1974–81). He was elected to the National Assembly in 1956. Giscard d'Estaing served as finance minister (1962–66) under Charles de GAULLE. After his dismissal, he formed the Independent Republican Party. Giscard d'Estaing returned as finance minister under Georges POMPIDOU. He defeated François MITTERRAND to become president, but narrowly lost to him in 1981. He has been leader of the centre-right Union for French Democracy (UDF) since 1988.

Gish, Lillian (1896–1993) US actress. She was noted as a virtuous heroine in the silent classics by D.W. GRIFFITH, including *The Birth of a Nation* (1915) and *Intolerance* (1916). Gish was later acclaimed as a character actress in such films as *The Night of the Hunter* (1935).

Gissing, George Robert (1857–1903) English novelist. His debut novel, *Workers in the Dawn* (1880), established his naturalistic style. Gissing's best-known work is *New Grub Street* (1891), a bleak portrayal of poverty and literary ambition. Other novels include *The Odd Women* (1893) and *The Private Papers of Henry Ryecroft* (1903).

Giulini, Carlo Maria (1914–) Italian conductor. A pupil of TOSCANINI, his first major appointment was principal conductor (1951–56) of La Scala, Milan. Giulini worked with the New Philharmonia Orchestra and at the Royal Opera House, London. He was conductor (1978–84) of the Los Angeles Philharmonic.

Giulio Romano (*c*.1499–1546) Italian painter and architect, b. Giulio Pippi. One of the founders of MANNERISM, his early career was spent as chief assistant to RAPHAEL. In 1524 Giulio left Rome for Padua and began (1526) the design for the anti-classical Palazzo del Tè. The palace includes the splendid Hall of Giants (1532–34).

Giza (Al-Jizah) City in N Egypt. It is the site of the Great SPHINX, the PYRAMID of Khufu (Cheops), the University of Cairo (relocated in 1924) and Egypt's film industry. A suburb of Cairo, it is a resort and agricultural centre. Industries: cotton textiles, footwear, cigarette-manufacturing. Pop. (1992) 2,144,000.

glacier Large land mass of ice and firn (granular snow), which moves slowly downhill or outward in all directions due to the stress of its own weight. The flow terminates where the rate of melting is equal to the advance of the glacier. There are three main types: the mountain or **valley** glacier, originating above the snow line; the **piedmont**, which develops when valley glaciers spread out over lowland; and the **ice-sheet** and ICE-CAP. **Glaciation** is the action of glacier ice on the Earth's surface. **Upland** glaciation mainly causes EROSION. It leaves jagged peaks and arêtes, CIRQUES, U-shaped and hanging valleys, finger lakes and tarns and crevasses. **Lowland** glaciation is mainly characterized by DEPOSITION, producing features such as MORAINES, drumlins, eskers, glacial lakes and roche moutonnées. *See also* ICE AGES

gladiator In ancient Rome, prisoner of war, slave or condemned convict trained to fight one another or wild animals in public arenas. Their fate, life or death, was often decided by the spectators. In AD 325, gladiatorial contests were officially abolished by Constantine the Great, but they persisted into the 5th century.

gladiolus Genus of 250 species of perennial plants native to Europe and Africa but cultivated widely. Gladioli pass the dry season as CORMS, which sprout in spring to produce a spike of funnel-shaped flowers and tall, lance-shaped leaves. Height: to 1m (3ft). Family Iridaceae.

Gladstone, William Ewart (1809–98) British statesman, prime minister (1868–74, 1880–85, 1886, 1892–94). He was elected to Parliament as a Tory in 1832 and served (1843–45) as president of the Board of Trade under Robert PEEL. Gladstone sided with the Peelites over the repeal of the CORN LAWS and served as chancellor of the exchequer (1852–55) in George ABERDEEN's coalition and again (1857–66) under Viscount PALMERSTON. In 1867, Gladstone succeeded Palmerston as leader of the LIBERAL PARTY. In his first term, he disestablished (1869) the Irish Church and introduced (1870) a system of national education and the first Irish Land Act. In 1874, Gladstone was defeated by Benjamin DISRAELI and briefly resigned as Liberal leader. His stinging criticism of Disraeli's imperialist tendencies won him the 1879

elections. In his second term, Gladstone passed a second Irish Land Act (1881) and several REFORM ACTS (1884, 1885) that extended the FRANCHISE. The government's failure to help General GORDON in Khartoum forced him to resign. Gladstone's last ministries were dominated by his advocacy of HOME RULE for Ireland.

gland Cell or tissue that manufactures and secretes special substances. There are two basic types: **exocrine** glands make such substances as hydrochloric acid, sweat, sebaceous fluids and ENZYMES and secrete these usually through ducts to an external or internal body surface. **Endocrine** glands contain cells that secrete HORMONES directly into the bloodstream. *See also* ENDOCRINE SYSTEM

glandular fever (infectious mononucleosis) Acute disease, usually of young people, caused by the EPSTEIN-BARR VIRUS. There are an increased number of white cells (monocytes) in the blood, and symptoms include fatigue, sore throat, headache, fever and painful enlargement of the LYMPH nodes.

Glaser, Donald Arthur (1926–) US physicist who invented the BUBBLE CHAMBER, using it to study ELEMENTARY PARTICLES. Glaser was awarded the 1960 Nobel Prize for physics.

Glasgow Largest city and port in Scotland on the River CLYDE, Strathclyde region. Founded in the 6th century, it developed with the American tobacco trade in the 18th century and the cotton trade in the 19th century. Nearby coalfields and the Clyde estuary promoted the growth of heavy industry, chiefly iron and steel and shipbuilding (now in decline). A cultural centre, Glasgow has three universities, the Glasgow School of Art and the Kelvingrove Art Gallery and Museum. Industries: shipbuilding, heavy engineering, flour milling, brewing, textiles, tobacco, chemicals, printing. Pop (1994) 720,000.

Glashow, Sheldon Lee (1932–) US physicist and educator. He shared the 1979 Nobel Prize for physics with Steven WEINBERG and Abdus SALAM for their independent formulation of a QUANTUM THEORY that unified ELECTROMAGNETIC FORCE and WEAK NUCLEAR FORCE. In this gauge theory "electroweak" interaction is mediated by PHOTONS and BOSONS.

glasnost (Rus. openness) Term adopted (1986) by Mikhail GORBACHEV to refer to the adoption of a more liberal social policy. One result was popular criticism of the Soviet system and the COMMUNIST PARTY, leading to the breakup of the SOVIET UNION and the fall of Gorbachev. *See also* PERESTROIKA

Glass, Philip (1937–) US composer. Glass studied with Nadia BOULANGER in Paris, where he met Ravi SHANKAR and became interested in non-Western music. A pioneer in the development of MINIMALISM, his characteristic style is the hypnotic repetition of short motifs

◄ **giraffe** The world's tallest mammal, the giraffe (*Giraffa camelopardalis*) reaches a height of 5.5m (18ft). The giraffe's long neck makes up about half its height and enables it to browse from the higher branches of trees of the African savanna.

within a simple harmonic idiom. Glass attracted attention with his first opera, *Einstein on the Beach* (1976). Other operas include *Satyagraha* (1980), *Akhnaten* (1984) and *The Voyage* (1992). *See also* REICH, STEVE

glass Brittle, transparent material. It behaves like a solid but is actually a liquid that is cooled to prevent particles organizing themselves into a regular pattern. It is made by melting together SILICA (sand), sodium carbonate (SODA) and CALCIUM CARBONATE (limestone). It can only be worked when hot and pliable. There are many types of glass. **Soda-lime** glass is used in the manufacture of bottles and drinking vessels. **Flint** glass refracts light well and is used in lenses and prisms. **Toughened** glass (laminated with plastic) is used in car windscreens. Glass was probably invented in Egypt in the 3rd millennium BC. GLASS-BLOWING was not practised until *c*.100 BC (in Syria). The Romans were highly skilled in glass-making. The art of crystal glass was perfected in Venice in the 15th century. *See also* FIBREGLASS; FIBRE OPTICS

glass-blowing Art of shaping molten GLASS by inflating it through a hollow tube, or blowpipe. Glass blowing was probably invented (*c*.100 BC) by Syrian craftsmen. Molten glass is picked up on the end of the blowpipe, then formed by blowing, swinging and rolling on a smooth stone or iron surface. The mass production of hollow items, such as bottles, is achieved by machines blowing glass into rotating moulds.

glass snake (glass lizard) Legless LIZARD found in North America, Eurasia and Africa. The cylindrical body has a groove along each side and is brown or green, although some species are striped. Length: 60–120cm (24–48in). Family Anguidae; genus *Ophisaurus*.

Glastonbury Ancient and historic market town in Somerset, SW England. According to legend, it was the site of the first Christian church in England founded by Joseph of Arimathea. Glastonbury is also the legendary burial place of King ARTHUR and Queen GUINEVERE and as such has been identified with Avalon. Pop. (1991) 7,747.

Glauber, Johann Rudolf (1604–68) German chemist and physician. Glauber made valuable contributions to chemistry, mainly concerning the preparation of salts. He prepared hydrochloric acid, hydrated sodium sulphate (known as **Glauber's salt**) and tartar emetic.

glaucoma Condition in which the pressure within the eye is increased due to an excess of aqueous humour, the fluid within the chamber. It occurs when the normal drainage of fluid is interrupted, posing a threat to vision. Most frequently found in the over 40s, the disease cannot be cured but is managed with drugs and surgery.

Glazunov, Alexander Konstantinovich (1865–1936) Russian composer, in the romantic tradition of TCHAIKOVSKY. His works include eight symphonies, chamber music, two violin concertos and the ballets *Raymonda* (1897) and *The Seasons* (1898).

Glendower, Owen *See* GLYN DŴR, OWAIN

Glenn, John Herschel, Jr (1921–) US astronaut. On 20 February 1962, aboard the spacecraft *Friendship 7*, he became the first person to orbit the Earth. Glenn became a US senator (Democrat) from Ohio and failed to win the 1984 Democratic presidential nomination. In 1998, at the age of 77, Glenn flew his second space mission on the space shuttle *Discovery*, becoming the oldest person in space. *See also* SPACE EXPLORATION

gliding Leisure activity involving flight in a glider. The unpowered glider is launched by a sling mechanism or towed by a small aircraft and then released. Once airborne, gliders descend relative to the surrounding air. If this air is a rising updraft, a glider may gain altitude, thus prolonging its flight. The first manned glider flight was made (1891) by Otto LILIENTHAL. *See also* HANG GLIDING

Glinka, Mikhail (1804–57) Russian composer, the first to receive international acclaim. His two operas, *A Life for the Czar* (1836) and *Russlan and Ludmila* (1841), inspired the RUSSIAN FIVE. Later in his life, Glinka lived in Italy and Spain, writing songs and orchestral music.

global warming Trend towards higher average temperatures on Earth's surface. During the last few million years, there have been several periods when surface temperatures have been significantly higher or lower than at present. During cold periods (ICE AGES) much of the land area has been covered by GLACIERS. The Earth is currently in the middle of a warm period (interglacial), which began *c*.10,000 years ago. Since the 1960s, some scientists have called attention to signs that the Earth is becoming unnaturally warmer as the result of an increased GREENHOUSE EFFECT caused by human activity.

Globe Theatre Elizabethan theatre associated with William SHAKESPEARE. Built (1599) on Bankside, London, it had polygonal walls with a roof over the stage and galleries. Destroyed by fire in 1613 and rebuilt in 1614, it was closed down by the Puritans in 1642 and demolished in 1644. The Globe was rebuilt and reopened in 1995.

globular cluster Near-spherical cluster of very old stars in the halo of our GALAXY and others. Globular clusters contain anything from 100,000 to several million stars, concentrated so tightly near the centre that they cannot be separately distinguished by ground-based telescopes.

glockenspiel (Ger. bell play) Percussion instrument with a bell-like sound. Its tuned metal bars are struck with a hammer, either freehand or from a miniature keyboard.

glomerulus Mass of capillary blood vessels within a Bowman's capsule, the funnel-shaped end of a NEPHRON in the KIDNEY. Fluid passes from the blood in the capillaries into the capsule and then down the tubule of the nephron. It passes out of the kidney along the ureter as urine.

Glorious Revolution (1688–89) Abdication of JAMES II of England and his replacement with WILLIAM III (OF ORANGE) and MARY II. After James had antagonized powerful subjects by his favour towards Roman Catholics, political leaders invited William to take the throne. William landed in November 1688, and James fled to France. It was called "glorious" because it occurred virtually without violence. In 1689, William and Mary ratified the BILL OF RIGHTS. In 1690, James was defeated at the Battle of the BOYNE.

Gloucester, Humphrey, Duke of (1391–1447) Protector of England (1422–29), youngest son of HENRY IV and brother of John, Duke of BEDFORD. He served as protector during his brother's absences in France. Gloucester proved an inept ruler and argued with Henry BEAUFORT. In 1447 he was arrested for treason and died in prison.

Gloucester County town of GLOUCESTERSHIRE on the River SEVERN, W England. A market town, it was the Roman city of Glevum and capital of Mercia in Saxon times. There is an 11th-century cathedral where Edward II is buried. Industries: aerospace, agricultural machinery, railway equipment and fishing. Pop. (1994) 102,000.

Gloucestershire County in SW England; the county town is GLOUCESTER. The COTSWOLDS, to the E, sustain dairy and arable farming. The fertile Severn valley is also devoted to dairying. Industries: engineering, scientific instruments, plastics. Area: 2,642sq km (1,020sq mi). Pop. (1991) 528,370.

glow-worm Any of a number of wingless female BEETLES or beetle larvae of the genus *Lampyris* that possess organs that emit a glow of light, especially the European beetle *Lampyris noctiluca*. A winged male is known as a FIREFLY. Family Lampyridae.

Gluck, Christoph Willibald von (1714–87) German operatic composer. His early operas were composed in the Italian tradition. In *Orfeo ed Euridice* (1762), Gluck attempted to reform opera by unifying musical and dramatic components. He turned to the French tradition in *Iphigénie en Tauride* (1779). Gluck influenced Mozart.

glucose (dextrose) Colourless crystalline SUGAR ($C_6H_{12}O_6$) occurring in fruit and honey. It requires no digestion before absorption. INSULIN lowers the blood-glucose level by causing the liver to convert glucose into GLYCOGEN. A monosaccharide CARBOHYDRATE, it is prepared commercially by the hydrolysis of starch using hydrochloric acid and is used in food and pharmaceuticals.

glue Adhesive traditionally made by boiling animal skin, bones, horns and hooves. It consists of a jelly of hydrolyzed collagen (fibrous protein) and other substances. It forms a tough skin when dry. **Vegetable** glues are made from starch (flour and water), rubber, soya beans and other sources. **Synthetic** adhesives include EPOXY RESINS, a group of POLYMERS that have additional properties of heat and chemical resistance.

gluten Main protein substance in WHEAT flour. Not present in barley, oats or maize, gluten contributes the elasticity to dough. It is used to make gluten bread for diabetics and as an additive to chocolate. *See also* COELIAC DISEASE

glycerol (glycerine) Thick, syrupy, sweet alcohol (1,2,3–trihydroxypropane, $CH_2OHCH(OH)CH_2OH$) obtained as a by-product of SOAP, and synthesized industrially from PROPENE. It is used in the manufacture of various products, including paints, cosmetics and EXPLOSIVES.

glycogen CARBOHYDRATE stored in the body, principally by the LIVER and muscles. Glycogen is a polymer of GLUCOSE. When the body needs energy, glycogen is broken down to glucose. *See also* RESPIRATION

glycolysis First stage in the biochemical process of RESPIRATION in which GLUCOSE is converted to pyruvic acid ($C_3H_4O_3$). The process results in a net gain of two molecules of ADENOSINE TRIPHOSPHATE (ATP) per glucose molecule. In AEROBIC respiration, pyruvate enters the KREBS CYCLE, with the ultimate yield of 12 more molecules of ATP. In ANAEROBIC respiration, pyruvic acid is converted to LACTIC ACID. In FERMENTATION, the hydrogen atoms taken from glucose are transferred to pyruvic acid via coenzymes. *See also* ENZYME

Glyndebourne Estate in East Sussex, England, site of an annual opera festival. John Christie built an opera theatre here in 1931. A larger theatre was opened in 1994.

Glyn Dŵr, Owain (Owen Glendower) (*c*.1359–1416) Welsh chief. A member of the house of Powys, he led a rebellion (1401) against HENRY IV. Proclaimed Prince of Wales, Glyn Dŵr allied himself with Henry's English enemies, Sir Henry PERCY and the Mortimer family. By 1404, he had captured Harlech and Aberystwyth castles. By 1409, Glyn Dŵr had lost both castles and retreated to the hills to maintain guerrilla warfare against the English.

GMT Abbreviation of GREENWICH MEAN TIME

gnat Common name for several small flies, mainly of the family Culicidae, the female of which bites human beings. *See also* MOSQUITO.

gneiss METAMORPHIC ROCK with a distinctive layering or banding. The darker minerals are likely to be hornblende, augite, mica or dark feldspar. Before metamorphism, gneiss was an IGNEOUS ROCK, possibly a granite.

Gnosticism Religious movement, embracing numerous sects, based on belief in *gnosis* (Gk. knowledge). This was occult knowledge that released the spiritual part of human beings from the evil bondage of the material world. Gnosticism was widespread by the 2nd century AD.

gnu (wildebeest) Large, ox-like African ANTELOPE. The **white-tailed** gnu (*Connochaetes gnou*) is almost extinct. The **brindled** gnu (*Connochaetes taurinus*) lives in E and S Africa, where large herds migrate annually. It has a massive, buffalo-like head and a slender body. Both sexes are horned. Length: up to 2.4m (7.8ft); height: 1.3m (4ft); weight: up to 275kg (600lb). Family Bovidae.

Goa State in SW India on the Arabian Sea; the capital is Panaji. It was ruled by Hindu dynasties until it fell under Muslim domination in the 15th century. Captured by the Portuguese in 1510, it became a flourishing trade centre and the hub of Portugal's Asian empire. In 1962, it was annexed by India and made a Union territory of India. In 1987, Goa became a separate state. Products: rice, cashews, spices, pharmaceuticals, footwear, pesticides. Area: 3,702sq km (1,429sq mi). Pop. (1991) 1,169,793

goat Horned RUMINANT raised for milk, meat, leather and hair. Closely related to sheep, they are brown or grey in colour. The male is a ram or billy, the female a doe or nanny, and the young a kid. Wild species are nomadic, living in rugged mountain areas. The five species include

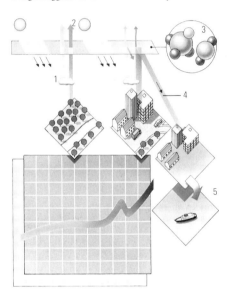

▲ **global warming**
Shortwave solar radiation enters the Earth's atmosphere warming the planet (1). Cloud cover and the surface of the Earth reflect energy at a longer wavelength. Most of the energy then radiates out into space (2). When, however, the products of the burning of fossil fuels have polluted the atmosphere (3), the radiation is trapped and bounces back to the surface a second time (4), increasing the energy input into the Earth. This is known as the greenhouse effect, because the same principle warms the interior of greenhouses. The incoming shortwave rays can enter the greenhouse through the glass panels but the reflected longwave rays are blocked by the same glass trapping the energy. On a global scale, scientists believe the greenhouse effect could raise the temperature of the Earth, resulting in the melting of the polar icecaps and subsequent sea-level rise and flooding of low-lying areas (5).

the IBEX (*Capra ibex*), markhor (*Capra falconeri*) and the pasang (*Capra aegagrus*). Length: to 0.85m (2.8ft); height: to 1.4m (4.5ft). Family Bovidae; genus *Capra*.

goatsucker *See* NIGHTJAR

Gobbi, Tito (1915–84) Italian baritone. In 1938, he made his debut in Verdi's *La traviata* in Rome. Gobbi sang in most of the great opera houses. He was highly acclaimed for his powerful acting ability.

Gobelins, Manufacture nationale des State-controlled TAPESTRY factory in Paris, founded (*c*.1440) by Jean Gobelin. The factory converted (1601) from a dye-works to making tapestry. In 1662 Louis XIV bought the premises to create a royal tapestry and furniture works. It was directed (1663–90) by Charles LE BRUN.

Gobi (Sha-moh) DESERT area in central Asia, extending over much of S Mongolia and N China. One of the world's largest deserts, it is on a plateau, 900–1,500m (3,000–5,000ft) high. The fringes are grassy and inhabited by nomadic Mongolian tribes who rear sheep and goats. The Gobi has cold winters, hot summers and fierce winds and sandstorms. Area: *c*.1,300,000sq km (500,000sq mi).

Gobind Singh (1666–1708) Tenth and last Sikh guru, who laid the foundations of Sikh militarism. In 1699 he created the *Khalsa*, a military fraternity of devout Sikhs, which became the basis of the Sikh army he led against the MOGUL empire. The turban and the common attachment of Singh ("lion") to Sikh names date from his reign.

Gobineau, Joseph Arthur, comte de (1816–82) French writer and anthropologist. First known as a novelist, he evolved racist theories, pervaded by anti-Semitism, in such works as *Essay on the Inequality of the Human Races* (1854). His claim for the intellectual and moral superiority of Aryans influenced Adolf HITLER.

God One of the supernatural, divine and usually immortal beings worshiped by followers of a polytheistic religion, such as those of ancient Greece and Rome; also a single supreme being, creator of the universe, as worshiped by the followers of monotheistic religions, such as JUDAISM or ISLAM. ALLAH is God of Islam, and YAHWEH is God of Judaism. CHRISTIANITY, a monotheistic religion, conceives of one God with three elements – Father, Son and Holy Spirit. In HINDUISM, BRAHMA is considered the soul of the world, but there are lesser gods. *See also* AGNOSTICISM; ATHEISM; BUDDHISM; DEISM; POLYTHEISM; MONOTHEISM; ZEUS

Godard, Jean-Luc (1930–) French film director. His contributions to *Cahiers du Cinéma* established him as a spokesman of the NOUVELLE VAGUE. Godard's debut feature *A Bout de Souffle* (1960) revolutionized film-making with its jump cuts and shaky hand-held shots. His next film on the Algerian war, *Le Petit Soldat* (1963), was banned for three years. After making *Alphaville* (1965), *La Chinoise* (1967) and *Weekend* (1965), Godard collaborated on propaganda films such as *Tout va bien* (1972).

Goddard, Robert Hutchings (1882–1945) US physicist. A pioneer in ROCKET development, he developed and launched (1926) the first liquid-fuelled rocket.

Gödel, Kurt (1906–78) US logician, b. Moravia. He is best known for his "undecidability" or "incompleteness" theorem, first published in 1931. **Godel's theorem** states that any AXIOM-based mathematical system contains statements that can neither be proved nor disproved within the system. In 1940, he emigrated to the USA, joining Albert EINSTEIN at the Institute of Advanced Study at Princeton. *See also* NUMBER THEORY

Godfrey of Bouillon (*c*.1060–1100) French crusader, Duke of Lower Lorraine (1089–95). He led the First CRUSADE (1096). Godfrey played a major role in the siege and

capture (1099) of Jerusalem. He was elected king, but preferred the title Defender of the Holy Sepulchre.

Godiva, Lady (d.*c*.1080) English benefactress, wife of Leofric, Earl of Mercia. According to tradition, she rode naked through the streets of Coventry in 1040 to persuade her husband to reduce the burden of excessive taxation.

Godoy, Manuel de (1767–1851) Spanish statesman, chief minister (1792–97, 1801–08) of CHARLES IV. His rapid promotion at court was due to his affair with Queen María Luisa. Godoy joined the First Coalition in the FRENCH REVOLUTIONARY WARS, but made peace and signed the Treaty of San Ildefonso (1796) against England. His alliance with France in the NAPOLEONIC WARS resulted in defeat at the Battle of Trafalgar (1805). Godoy's corrupt administration became more unpopular at the start of the PENINSULAR WAR and he was overthrown with Charles by FERDINAND VII.

Godthåb Danish name for NUUK, capital of Greenland

Godunov, Boris (1551–1605) Tsar of Russia (1598–1605). Chief minister and brother-in-law of IVAN IV (THE TERRIBLE), he became regent to Ivan's imbecile son Fyodor; he was popularly supposed to have murdered Fyodor's brother and heir, Dmitri, in 1591. On Fyodor's death in 1598, Boris was elected tsar. Godunov gained recognition for the Russian Orthodox Church as an independent patriarchate, but his suppression of the boyars led to the "Time of Troubles" (1604–12).

Godwin, William (1756–1836) English political philosopher and novelist, husband (1794–97) of Mary WOLLSTONECRAFT. In *An Enquiry Concerning Political Justice* (1793), he advocated anarchy as the fullest expression of Enlightenment RATIONALISM. Godwin expanded on his philosophy in the gothic novel *Caleb Williams* (1794). In 1797, Wollstonecraft died giving birth to their daughter, Mary SHELLEY. His work was a major influence on ROMANTICISM. *See also* ANARCHISM

Goebbels, (Paul) Joseph (1897–1945) German Nazi leader. He joined the Nazi Party in 1924, and founded the newspaper *Der Angriff* in 1926. When the Nazis came to power in 1933, Goebbels became minister of propaganda. He took total control of the media, which he manipulated to support Nazi aims. Goebbels committed suicide with his entire family in April 1945.

Goering, Hermann Wilhelm (1893–1946) German Nazi leader. As commander of the *Luftwaffe* (air force) from 1933 and overall director of economic affairs from 1936, he was second in command to Adolf HITLER. His reputation declined with the failure of the Luftwaffe to subdue the British or the Russians during World War 2. Captured in 1945, he was sentenced to death at the NUREMBERG TRIALS but committed suicide.

Goes, Hugo van der (*c*.1440–82) Flemish painter, one of the greatest artists of the 15th century. In 1474, he was elected dean of the painter's guild in Ghent and in the following year entered a monastery. His triptych (1745) known as the *Portinari Altarpiece* (the only work definitely ascribed to him) is a masterpiece of emotional intensity.

Goethe, Johann Wolfgang von (1749–1832) German poet, dramatist, novelist and statesman. While studying law at Strasbourg, HERDER inspired him to appreciate Shakespeare. Goethe's first play, *Götz von Berlichingen* (1773), was in the tradition of STURM AND DRANG. His epistolary novel *The Sorrows of Young Werther* (1774) won him international fame. In 1775, Goethe moved to Weimar, where he served as chief minister (1775–85). His visits to Italy (1786–88, 1790) fired his enthusiasm for classicism, evidenced in the historical drama *Egmont* (1788) and the poetical drama *Iphigenie* *auf Tauris* (1789). Goethe's novel *Wilhelm Meister's Apprenticeship* (1796) became the model for the German BILDUNGSROMAN. His lyrical poems *Westöstlicher Diwan* (1819) were inspired by the Persian poet HAFIZ. Goethe's most enduring work, the dramatic poem *Faust*, was published in two parts (1808, 1832). He is buried at Weimar, next to his friend and fellow giant of ROMANTICISM Friedrich von SCHILLER. *See also* GERMAN LITERATURE.

Gog and Magog In Ezekiel, Gog from the land of Magog attacks Israel. In Revelation, Gog and Magog are attenders of SATAN. In British folklore Gog and Magog are survivors of s race of giants destroyed by Brutus, founder of London. A pair of statues depicting them has stood in London's Guildhall since the reign of Henry V.

Gogol, Nikolai Vasilievich (1809–52) Russian novelist and dramatist. His work marks the transition from ROMANTICISM to early realism. Gogol made his reputation with stories, such as *The Nose* (1835), and the drama *The Government Inspector* (1836). He turned to religion and lived mostly in Rome from 1836 to 1848. Here he wrote the first part of his picaresque novel *Dead Souls* (1842) and the story *The Overcoat* (1842).

Goh Chok Tong (1941–) Singaporean statesman, prime minister (1990–). He entered Parliament in 1976. Goh Chok Tong rose steadily through the ministerial ranks and succeeded Lee Kuan Yew as prime minister and leader of the People's Action Party (PAP).

goitre Swelling in the front of the neck due to enlargement of the THYROID GLAND. Causes range from a lack of iodine in the diet to a thyroid cancer. *See also* HYPERTHYROIDISM; HYPOTHYROIDISM; MYXOEDEMA

Golan Heights (Ramat Ha Golan) Range of hills in SW Syria on the border with Israel. During the Arab-Israeli War of 1967, Israel occupied the area and later annexed it. Of great strategic importance to Israel, it has remained a source of conflict between Syria and Israel. Area: 1,150sq km (444sq mi). Pop. (1983 est.) 19,700.

gold (symbol Au) Naturally occurring metallic element. It is also obtained as a by-product in the refining of copper. Gold is used in jewellery, in connectors for electronic equipment and as a form of money. Gold in the form of a COLLOID is sometimes used in colouring glass. The isotope Au^{198} (half-life 2.7 days) is used in radiotherapy. The metal is unreactive but dissolves in aqua regia, a mixture of nitric and hydrochloric acids. The gold content of alloys is measured in carats, with 24 carats corresponding to pure gold. Properties: at.no. 97; r.a.m. 196.9665; r.d. 19.30; m.p. 1,063°C (1,945°F); b.p. 2,796°C (5,072°F); most common isotope Au^{197} (100%).

goldcrest Smallest British bird. Its head is capped with bright orange and a black stripe. Its body is green and its wings are black with a white stripe. Length: *c*.8.4cm (3.3in). Family Muscicapidae; species *Regulus regulus*.

Golden Fleece In Greek mythology, fleece of the ram that saved Helle and Phrixus from their stepmother Ino. On arrival in Colchis, Phrixus sacrificed the ram and hung the fleece in a wood guarded by a dragon. The fleece was seized by JASON and the ARGONAUTS.

Golden Gate Strait on the coast of California, USA, linking the Pacific Ocean with San Francisco Bay. The first landing was made (1769) by Francisco de Ortega. It is spanned by the Golden Gate Bridge, completed in 1937.

Golden Horde Name given to the Mongol state established in s Russia in the early 13th century. The state derived from the conquests of GENGHIS KHAN and was extended by his successors, who took over the whole of the Russian state centred on Kiev. It was conquered by TAMERLANE in the late 14th century and split up.

golden mean (golden section, golden ratio) Classical ratio created when a line is divided into two parts in such a way that the ratio of the shorter to the longer is as the longer to the whole, that is. $a/b = b/(a + b)$, where $a + b$ is the line's length. The ratio is approximately 3:5, or exactly $1:(\sqrt{5} + 1)/2$ (*see* FIBONACCI SEQUENCE). The golden mean was cited by VITRUVIUS as the basis of proportion in classical GREEK ARCHITECTURE.

goldfinch Any of various small, seed-eating birds of the genus *Carduelis*. The red-faced European goldfinch (*C. carduelis*) has a brown body with yellow and black wings. The males of the American goldfinches, such as *C. tristis*, have yellow plumage in the summer. Family Fringillidae.

goldfish Freshwater CARP originally found in China. The most popular aquarium fish, it was domesticated in China *c*.1,000 years ago. The wild form is plain and brownish, but selective breeding has produced a variety of colours. Family Cyprinidae; species *Carassius auratus*.

Golding, Sir William Gerald (1911–93) English novelist. His debut novel was the allegorical *Lord of the Flies* (1954). Golding's fascination with maritime history is revealed in the trilogy *The Ends of the Earth* (1991), which includes the Booker Prize-winning *Rites of Passage* (1980), *Close Quarters* (1987) and *Fire Down Below* (1989). Other novels include *Pincher Martin* (1956). He was awarded the 1983 Nobel Prize for literature.

Goldman, Emma (1869–1940) US anarchist and feminist, b. Lithuania. In New York, she co-edited (1906–17) the anarchist monthly *Mother Earth*. Goldman was imprisoned (1916, 1917) for advocating birth control and opposing conscription during World War 1. In 1919, she was deported to Russia. Goldman was active in the Spanish Civil War. *See also* ANARCHISM

Goldmark, Peter Carl (1906–77) US inventor and engineer, b. Hungary. In 1940, he made the first colour TELEVISION broadcast. Goldmark also developed (1948) the 33$^1/_3$ r.p.m. long-playing record. He invented the first VIDEO recorder and a scanning system that enabled the Lunar Orbiter to send photos of the Moon back to Earth.

gold rush Rapid influx of population in response to reports of the discovery of gold. The largest gold rush brought some 100,000 prospectors to California, USA, (1849–50). Some of the miners, known as Forty-Niners, went on to Australia (1851–53). There were also gold rushes to South Africa (1886), to the Klondike in the Yukon, Canada (1896), and to Alaska (1898).

Goldsmith, Oliver (1730–74) Anglo-Irish dramatist, novelist, essayist and poet. After a colourful but penurious early life, he became known as a lively comic writer. Goldsmith first attracted attention with the collection of essays *The Citizen of the World* (1762). His poems *The Traveller* (1764) and *The Deserted Village* (1770) were similarly well-received. Goldsmith wrote one novel, *The Vicar of Wakefield* (1766). His plays include *The Good-Natured Man* (1768) and *She Stoops to Conquer* (1773).

gold standard Monetary system in which the gold value of currency is set at a fixed rate and currency is convertible into gold on demand. It was adopted by Britain in 1821, by the USA, France and Germany in the 1870s, and by most of the rest of the world by the 1890s. It produced nearly fixed EXCHANGE RATES and was intended to foster monetary stability. The GREAT DEPRESSION forced many countries to depreciate their exchange rates in an attempt to foster trade. By the mid-1930s, the gold standard had been abandoned.

Goldwyn, Samuel (1882–1974) US film producer, b. Poland as Schmuel Gelbfisz. He was noted for his commercially successful films, including *Wuthering Heights* (1939), *The Best Years of Our Lives* (1946), *Guys and*

Dolls (1955) and *Porgy and Bess* (1959). He formed Goldwyn Pictures in 1917 and later merged with Louis B. Mayer to form (1924) Metro-Goldwyn-Mayer.

golf Game in which a small, hard ball is struck by a club. There are three basic types of club: woods, irons and putters. A play may use a maximum of 14 clubs. The object of the game is to hit the ball into a sequence of holes (usually 18), in the least possible number of shots. The length of each hole varies from c.90m to 450m (100–500yd). Each hole consists of a **tee**, from where the player hits the first shot; a **fairway** of mown grass bordered by trees and longer grass, known as the **rough**; and a **green**, a putting area of smooth, short grass and the site of the hole. A player may have to circumvent hazards, such as lakes or bunkers. Each hole is given a par, the number of shots it should take to complete the hole. Competition is usually over 18, 36 or 72 holes; the winner is decided by the lowest total of strokes (stroke play) or the most holes won (match play). The major tournaments are the US Open, British Open, US Professional Golfer's Association (PGA) and the US Masters. In 1754, the Royal and Ancient Golf Club, ST ANDREWS, Scotland, was formed and the basic rules of golf were codified.

Golgi body Collection of microscopic vesicles, or sacs, observed near the nucleus of many living CELLS. It is a part of a cell's ENDOPLASMIC RETICULUM, specialized for the purpose of packaging and dispatching proteins made by the cell. It was discovered (1873) by Italian histologist Camillo Golgi (1844–1926)

Goliath In the Old Testament, the PHILISTINE giant slain by the shepherd boy DAVID (1 Samuel 17). David killed Goliath with a stone from his catapult.

Gómez, Juan Vicente (1857–1935) Venezuelan statesman. Vice president under Cipriano Castro, he seized power during Castro's absence abroad and ruled Venezuela, either as elected president (1908–15, 1922–29, 1931–35) or through puppets, until his death. Gómez's dictatorial rule was brutally effective. While he amassed a personal fortune, he did improve Venezuela's infrastructure and enable it to pay off its foreign debt.

Gomulka, Wladyslaw (1905–82) Polish statesman, president (1956–70). During World War 2, he was secretary general of the outlawed Polish Communist Party. Gomulka served as vice president (1945–48) in the first post-war government, but was dismissed and imprisoned (1951–54) for his criticism of Stalinism. In 1956, popular uprisings led to Gomulka heading a more liberal regime. As the economy declined, however, his rule became more oppressive. He resigned after sharp rises in food prices.

gonad Primary reproductive organ of male and female animals, in which develop the GAMETES or sex cells. Thus, the gonad in the male is a TESTIS and in the female an OVARY. Hermaphrodite animals possess both types. *See also* SEXUAL REPRODUCTION

gonadotrophin One of several HORMONES that stimulate the development and function of the gonads (OVARY and TESTIS). The PITUITARY GLAND produces three gonadtrophins: **luteinizing hormone (LH)**, which stimulates the production of OESTROGEN and PROGESTERONE; **follicle-stimulating hormone (FSH)**, which promotes ovulation in females by stimulating the Graafian follicles in the ovary, encourages the production of SPERM in males, and is used in many FERTILITY DRUGS; and **prolactin**, which triggers LACTATION. The PLACENTA produces **human chorionic gonadotrophin (hCG)**. Pregnancy tests work by measuring the levels of hCG in urine.

Goncharov, Ivan Alexandrovich (1812–91) Russian novelist. A civil servant from 1834 to 1867, he spent many years in the ministry of censorship. His best-known work is the satirical *Oblomov* (1859); other works include *A Common Story* (1847) and *The Precipice* (1869).

Goncourt, Edmond de (1822–96) French novelist and social historian. Edmond collaborated with his brother **Jules** (1830–70) on *The Journal of the Goncourts* (1836–40), a personal account of Parisian society, and the naturalistic novels *Germinie Lacerteux* (1864) and *Madame Gervaisais* (1869). In his will, Edmond provided for the Prix Goncourt, France's top literary award.

Gondwanaland Southern supercontinent. It began to break away from the single land mass, PANGAEA, c.200 million years ago. It became South America, Africa, India, Australia and Antarctica. The northern supercontinent, which eventually became North America and Eurasia without India, was Laurasia.

Góngora y Argote, Luis de (1561–1627) Spanish poet and chaplain to the king (1616–26). Influential in its time and subsequently much imitated, his poetry includes *Galatea* and *Las Soledades* (1613). Góngora's works became increasingly complex, allusive and BAROQUE, giving rise to the term gongorism.

gonorrhoea SEXUALLY TRANSMITTED DISEASE (STD) caused by the bacterium *Neisseria gonorrhoeae*, giving rise to inflammation of the genital tract. Symptoms include pain on urination and the passing of pus. Gonorrhoea is treated with antibiotics. If not treated, it may spread, causing sterility and threatening other organs.

Gooch, Graham Alan (1953–) English cricketer. In 1973, he made his county debut for Essex. In 1975, Gooch played in the first of his 118 test matches for England. In 1982, he captained the "rebel" side that toured South Africa and was banned from test cricket for three years. Gooch was captain of England (1988–93). In 1993, he surpassed David GOWER as England's leading run-scorer. Gooch scored a career total of 8,900 test runs.

Good Friday Friday before EASTER Day. It is observed by all Christians as marking the day of the crucifixion of Jesus. For many, it is a day of fasting and abstinence.

Good Friday Agreement (10 April 1998) Northern IRELAND peace accord signed by British Prime Minister Tony BLAIR and Irish Taoiseach Bertie AHERN and representatives from eight political parties in Northern Ireland. The Agreement provided for a new, 108-seat Northern Ireland Assembly with legislative powers devolved from the British Parliament. It created a North-South Ministerial Council to coordinate policies between the Republic of IRELAND and Northern Ireland, and a "council of the isles", which replaced the intergovernmental conference established by the ANGLO-IRISH AGREEMENT (1985). Other major points included: the Republic of Ireland dropping its constitutional claim to Northern Ireland; the decommissioning of terrorist weapons; the release of paramilitary prisoners; a reduction in the British security presence in Northern Ireland. The Assembly met for the first time in July, but the peace process stalled when First Minister David TRIMBLE refused to appoint two SINN FÉIN members to the executive committee until the IRISH REPUBLICAN ARMY (IRA) had started decommissioning. US Senator George MITCHELL conducted a review of the Agreement and secured concessions that, in December 1999, produced home rule in Northern Ireland for the first time since 1974. In February 2000, the Assembly was suspended after deadlock on the issue of decommissioning. It was reconvened in June, after the IRA agreed to partial weapons inspection and the British government announced a new deadline for decommissioning (June 2001). *See also* ADAMS, GERRY; HUME, JOHN; PAISLEY, IAN

Goodman, Benny (Benjamin David) (1909–86) US jazz clarinetist and bandleader. In 1934, he formed his famous big band. Goodman was the first big band-leader to employ black and white musicians together. With theme songs such as "Stompin' at the Savoy" and "One O'Clock Jump", he was labelled the "King of Swing". Goodman also played classical music; Bartók and Copland composed pieces for him. *See also* SWING

Good Neighbor Policy US policy of non-intervention in the affairs of Latin America, initiated by President Franklin D. ROOSEVELT. THE ORGANIZATION OF AMERICAN STATES (OAS), founded (1945) to foster hemispheric solidarity, was an extension of this policy.

Goodyear, Charles (1800–60) US inventor. In 1839, Goodyear discovered the process of VULCANIZATION, which increases the durability of RUBBER. In 1844, he patented the process (1844). Goodyear died in poverty.

goose Widely distributed waterfowl, related to the DUCK and SWAN. Geese have blunt bills, long thick necks, short-ish legs, webbed feet and, in the wild, a combination of grey, brown, black and white dense plumage underlaid by down. They live near fresh or brackish water and spend time on land, grazing on meadow grasses. Wild geese breed in colonies in northern latitudes, mate for life and build grass-and-twig, down-lined nests for 3 to 12 eggs. They migrate in summer, flying in skeins in V-formation. There are 14 species, including the CANADA GOOSE. Weight: 1.4–5.9kg (3–13lb). Family Anatidae.

gooseberry Hardy, deciduous, spiny shrub and its edible fruit. It is generally green and hairy and fairly acidic. Family Grossulariaceae; species *Ribes grossularia*.

Goossens, Sir (Aynsley) Eugene (1893–1962) British conductor and composer of Belgian descent. He was director (1931–46) of the Cincinnati Orchestra and conductor (1948–56) of the Sydney Symphony Orchestra. He composed an oboe concerto for his brother **Leon** (1897–1988). Goosens was knighted in 1955.

gopher Small, stout burrowing rodent of North and Central America. It has fur-lined external cheek pouches and long incisor teeth outside the lips. It lives underground for shelter and food storage, digging tunnels to find roots and tubers. Length: 13–46cm (5–18in). Family Geomyidae.

Gorbachev, Mikhail Sergeyevich (1931–) Soviet statesman, president of the SOVIET UNION (1988–91) and general secretary of the Communist Party of the Soviet Union (1985–91). After succeeding Konstantin CHERNENKO as leader, Gorbachev embarked on a programme of reform based on two principles: PERESTROIKA (restructuring) and GLASNOST (openness). He played a major role in the nuclear DISARMAMENT process, withdrew Soviet troops from Afghanistan and acquiesced to the demise of communist regimes in Eastern Europe (1989–90), effectively ending the COLD WAR. In Russia, the benefits of radical socioeconomic change were slow to take effect, and Gorbachev's popularity fell as prices rose. In August 1991, Communist hardliners mounted an unsuccessful coup. In December 1991, the Communist Party was abolished. Gorbachev was forced to dissolve the Soviet Union and hand power to his rival, Boris YELTSIN. Gorbachev was awarded the Nobel Peace Prize in 1990.

Gordian knot Complicated binding, tying the yoke to the pole of a wagon belonging to Gordius, legendary King of Phrygia. An oracle foretold that whoever could release the knot would conquer all Asia. In 333 BC ALEXANDER THE GREAT was said to have slashed the binding before going on to fulfil the prophecy.

Gordimer, Nadine (1923–) South African writer. Her works, critical of apartheid, are concerned with contemporary politics and social morality. Among Gordimer's collections of short stories are *Face to Face* (1949) and *Jump* (1991). Her early novels include *The Lying Days* (1953). Gordimer won the Booker Prize for *The Conservationist* (1974). Other novels include *July's People* (1981) and *My Son's Story* (1990). She was awarded the 1991 Nobel Prize for literature.

Gordon, Charles George (1833–85) British soldier and administrator. He fought in the CRIMEAN WAR and OPIUM WAR and was employed by the Chinese government to put down the TAIPING REBELLION. He was governor-general of the Sudan (1877–80) and returned to Khartoum in 1884 to evacuate Egyptian forces threatened by the MAHDI. He was killed two days before the arrival of a relief force.

Gordon Riots (1780) Violent demonstrations against Roman Catholics in London, England. Protestant extremists led by Lord George Gordon (1751–93) marched on Parliament to protest against the Catholic Relief Act (1778), which lifted some restrictions on Catholics. The march degenerated into a week-long riot; *c*.450 people were killed or injured.

Gore, Al (Albert Arnold) (1948–) US statesman, vice president (1993–2000). He was a Democratic congressman (1977–85) and senator (1985–93) for Tennessee. As vice-president to Bill CLINTON, he championed environmental issues. In 2000, Gore narrowly lost the presidential elections to George W. BUSH in a highly contentious election.

Górecki, Henryk (1933–) Polish composer. He studied under Oliver MESSIAEN in Paris. Górecki's early works were influenced by WEBERN and SERIAL MUSIC, but his later output, such as the Third Symphony (1976) is inspired more by medieval Polish chants, Renaissance polyphony and the richness of the Wagnerian orchestra.

Gorgons In Greek mythology, three monsters named Stheno, Euryale and MEDUSA. With golden wings and snakes for hair, they turned anyone who looked directly at them to stone. PERSEUS killed Medusa by using his shield as a mirror, holding it so that she saw her own reflection.

gorilla Powerfully built great APE native to the forests of equatorial Africa. The largest primate, it is brown or black, with long arms and short legs. It walks on all fours and is herbivorous. Height: to 175cm (70in); weight: 140–180kg (308–396lb). Family Pongidae; species *Gorilla gorilla*.

Gorky, Arshile (1905–48) US painter, b. Armenia. His work bridged SURREALISM and ABSTRACT EXPRESSIONISM. In 1920, he emigrated to the USA, where he joined a group of European surrealists in New York in the 1940s. He became fascinated by the work of MIRÓ, who inspired some of his paintings, such as the different versions of *Garden in Sochi* (1940) and *Mojave* (1941–42).

Gorky, Maxim (1868–1936) Russian writer. He championed the worker in *Sketches and Stories* (1898), the play *The Lower Depths* (1902), and the novel *Mother* (1907). Gorky was imprisoned for his role in the Russian Revolution of 1905 and lived much of his life in exile in Italy. He is best-known for an autobiographical trilogy (1913–23). In 1931, Gorky returned to the Soviet Union. As first president of the Soviet Writers Union, he championed SOCIALIST REALISM.

Gormley, Anthony (1950–) English sculptor. Much of Gormley's work has focused on the human figure. In 1994, he was awarded the Turner Prize for *Field for the British Isles*. His *Angel of the North* (1998), an enormous statue overlooking the A1 road, near Gateshead, brought both admiration and criticism.

gorse (furze) Any of several dense thorny shrubs (genus *Ulex*) found mainly in Europe; The common European species, *U. europaeus*, bears yellow flowers and thrives in open hilly regions. Family Fabaceae/Leguminosae.

gospel Central content of the Christian faith, the good news (*god spell* in Old English) that human sins are forgiven. The first four books of the NEW TESTAMENT, ascribed to the Evangelists Matthew, Mark, Luke and John, are known as the four Gospels.

gospel music African-American vocal church music. It first arose in the depression years of the 1930s from the fusion of Protestant hymn harmony with African rhythmic and melodic features. Gospel music emphasizes the "good news" aspect of revivalist Christianity. Powerfully expressive, it often uses a call-and-response form, with a choir answering a soloist/preacher.

Gothenburg (Göteborg) City in sw Sweden, at the confluence of the Göta and Kattegat rivers; chief seaport and second largest city in Sweden. Founded (1619) by Gustavus II, it soon flourished as a commercial centre. Industries: shipbuilding, vehicles, food-processing, chemicals, textiles. Pop. (1997) 454,000.

Gothic art and architecture Architecture of medieval Europe from the 12th to 16th centuries. Gothic architecture was the successor to the ROMANESQUE. It is characterized by the pointed ARCH and ribbed VAULT.

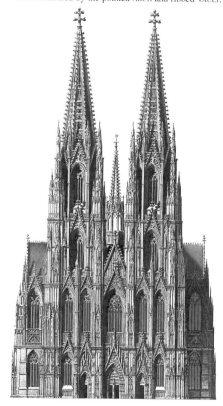

▲ **Gothic art and architecture** Cologne Cathedral, Germany, was begun in 1248, but the present building was completed between 1842 and 1880. The largest Gothic church in N Europe, the illustration shows the w façade. The cathedral's grandeur lies predominantly in its highly decorated, spiny twin towers, which rise to 152m (502ft).

The style is religious in inspiration and ecclesiastical in nature. Its greatest and most characteristic expression is the CATHEDRAL. The introduction of flying BUTTRESSES was a technical advance that made the large windows possible. An early prototype is the Abbey Church of St Denis, France (1140–44). Ever higher and lighter structures followed, with increasingly intricate vaulting and tracery. In architectural convention English Gothic is divided into three phases: EARLY ENGLISH (Lincoln Cathedral), DECORATED (Exeter Cathedral) and PERPENDICULAR (Chapel of King's College, Cambridge). Gothic sculpture was elegant and more realistic than the Romanesque, emphasizing line and silhouette. In painting, the Gothic style manifested itself most successfully in manuscript ILLUMINATION. *See also* GOTHIC NOVEL; GOTHIC REVIVAL; INTERNATIONAL GOTHIC

Gothic novel Genre of English fiction popular in the late 18th and early 19th centuries. Gothic novels often rely on eerie medieval externals, such as old castles, monasteries and hidden trapdoors, for their symbolism. Horace WALPOLE wrote an important prototype, *The Castle of Otranto* (1764). Later examples include *The Mysteries of Udolpho* (1794) by Ann Radcliffe, *The Monk* (1796) by M.G. Lewis and *Frankenstein* (1818) by Mary SHELLEY. The genre was parodied by Jane AUSTEN in *Northanger Abbey* (1818).

Gothic revival (neo-Gothic) Architecture based on the GOTHIC ART AND ARCHITECTURE of the Middle Ages. Beginning in the late 18th century, it peaked in 19th-century Britain and the USA, also appearing in many European countries. British exponents, notably John RUSKIN, A.W.N. PUGIN and Sir George Gilbert SCOTT, insisted on the need for authentic, structural re-creation of medieval styles. Notable examples are the Houses of Parliament, London, by Pugin and Sir Charles BARRY, and Trinity Church, New York City, by Richard Upjohn.

Goths Ancient Germanic people, groups of whom settled near the Black Sea in the 2nd and 3rd centuries AD. The **Visigoths** were driven westward into Roman territory by the HUNS in 376, culminating in their sacking Rome under ALARIC in 410. They settled in sw France, then, driven out by the Franks in the early 6th century, in Spain. Some groups united to create the **Ostrogoths**, who conquered Italy under THEODORIC THE GREAT (489). They held Italy until conquered by the Byzantines under Belisarius and Narses (536–53).

Gotland Island and county of Sweden, off the E coast in the Baltic Sea; the capital is Visby. The island had ancient trading links with both Rome and Byzantium and later with Russia. In the 12th century it was colonized by Germans. Nominally under Swedish rule, it was conquered by Denmark in the 14th century and eventually returned to Sweden in 1645. Industries: tourism, sugarbeet processing, cereals, cement manufacture. Area: 3,140sq km (1,212sq mi). Pop. (1994 est.) 58,237.

gouache WATERCOLOUR paint made opaque by the addition of white. It lightens in colour when dry and cracks if used thickly. Popular among manuscript illuminators in the Middle Ages, gouache has been used by 20th-century painters and commercial artists.

Gould, Glenn (1932–82) Canadian pianist and composer. He became a soloist with the Toronto Symphony Orchestra at the age of 14. Gould is famous for his interpretations of J.S. Bach and Ludwig Beethoven. His first string quartet was premiered in 1956. In later years he concentrated on recording.

Gould, Stephen Jay (1941–) US palaeontologist. He proposed that EVOLUTION could occur in sudden spurts rather than gradually. Gould's theory of PUNCTUATED EQUILIBRIUM suggested that sudden accelerations in the evolutionary process could produce rapid changes in species over the comparatively short time of a few hundred thousand years. He has written many popular science books, including *Hen's Teeth and Horses' Toes* (1983) and *Bully for Brontosaurus* (1992). *See also* MUTATION

Gounod, Charles François (1818–93) French composer and organist. Gounod is best known for his operas, which include *Faust* (1859), *Mireille* (1863) and *Roméo et Juliette* (1864).

gourd Annual VINE and its ornamental, hard-shelled fruit. These range from almost spherical, as in *Cucurbita pepo*, to irregular or bottle-shaped, as in *Lagenaria siceraria*. The rind may be smooth or warty. Family Cucurbitaceae. *See also* PUMPKIN

gout Form of ARTHRITIS, featuring an excess of uric acid crystals in the tissues. More common in men, it causes attacks of pain and inflammation in the joints. It is treated with anti-inflammatories.

Gower, David Ivon (1957–) English cricketer. A left-handed batsman. He made his county debut for Leicestershire in 1975, and his England debut in 1978. Gower captained England (1984–86, 1989) and helped regain (1985) The Ashes from Australia. He scored 8,231 runs in 117 test matches. In 1993, he retired to pursue a media career. *See also* GOOCH, GRAHAM

Gower, John (1330–1408) English poet. Ranked in his time with Lydgate and CHAUCER, his work includes *Vox Clamantis* (1379–82), an attack on social injustice, and his most famous work, *Confessio Amantis* (1386–93), a collection of allegorical tales on the subject of Christian and courtly love.

Goya (y Lucientes), Francisco José de (1746–1828) Spanish painter and engraver. A severe illness (1791) provoked a vein of fantastic works, one of the most vicious and sinister of which is *Los Caprichos*, a series of 82 engravings published in 1799. Goya enjoyed the royal patronage of CHARLES IV, despite mercilessly realistic paintings such as *The Family of Charles IV* (1800). His bloody scenes, *The Second of May, 1808* and *The Third of May, 1808*, portray the Spanish resistance to the French invasion. *The Disasters of War* (1810–14) is a savage suite of 65 etchings. Obsessed with the dark side of the human psyche, his last works are the so-called *Black paintings*, 14 murals in sombre colours in which Goya unleashed yet more horrors from his tortured imagination.

Goyen, Jan Josephszoon van (1596–1656) Dutch painter. A pioneer of Dutch realistic painting, he attempted to capture natural light and space and to depict calm atmospheric effects using a narrow range of colours. Many of his paintings are town views and river scenes.

Gozzoli, Benozzo (1421–97) Italian painter. He is famous for his numerous frescos, such as *The Journey of the Magi* (1459–61) in the Medici Palace, Florence.

Graaf, Regnier de (1641–73) Dutch anatomist and doctor. The **Graafian follicles** – thin-walled cavities in the OVARIES of MAMMALS in which eggs develop – were named after him. De Graaf investigated the functions of the PANCREAS and the nature of the sexual organs. He was the first to use the term "ovary".

Grable, Betty (1916–73) US film actress. She starred in many Hollywood musicals, and her wholesome popularity was inextricably linked to the 1940s boom in musicals. Her fabled legs were insured for US$1 million. Grable's films include *Tin Pan Alley* (1940) and *I Wake Up Screaming* (1941). She was the World War 2 "pin-up" girl for American soldiers.

Gracchus, Gaius Sempronius (153–121 BC) Roman statesman. As tribune (123–121 BC), he continued to implement the social reforms of his brother **Tiberius**, who was killed (133 BC) for attempting to reform agrarian law to benefit the poor. Gaius sought to check the power of the Senate by uniting the PLEBEIANS and the equites. These reforms were short-lived; he was defeated in the election of 121 BC, and killed in the ensuing riots.

Grace, W.G. (William Gilbert) (1848–1915) English cricketer. He played for England, Gloucestershire and London County. He scored a total of 54,896 runs (including 126 centuries), took 2,876 wickets and held 877 catches in first-class matches. He led England in 13 of his 22 Test matches (1880–99).

grace Undeserved favour from God or a gift demonstrating this. In Christian theology, the spontaneous gift of divine favour or goodwill is a necessary part of the salvation of those who have sinned. Grace is also a state of mind brought about by divine influence in an individual for his rebirth and sanctification. Faith, regular worship and the sacraments are all means of receiving grace.

Graces In Greek mythology, three goddesses who represented intellectual pleasures: beauty, grace and charm. Associated especially with poetry, Aglaia, Euphrosyne and Thalia were often linked with the MUSES. They were also described as daughters or granddaughters of ZEUS.

grackle Several species of stout-billed, New World blackbirds within the genera *Quiscalus* and *Cassidix* of the family Icteridae. Sometimes called crow blackbirds, they have blackish, iridescent plumage. The common grackle, *Q. quiscula*, of the USA, may reach 30cm (12in) in length. Species of Asian MINA birds of the genus *Gracula* are also called grackles.

Graf, Steffi (Stephanie) (1969–) German tennis player. In 1987, she succeeded Martina NAVRATILOVA as the world's No 1 woman tennis player. Despite injury problems, her powerful serve and forehand play dominated the women's game. In 1988, Graf completed a Grand Slam. She won the Australian Open (1988–90, 1994), French Open (1987, 1988, 1993, 1995, 1996), Wimbledon (1988, 1989, 1991–93, 1995, 1996) and the US Open (1988, 1989, 1993, 1995, 1996). In 1999, Graf announced her retirement.

grafting In surgery, organ or tissue transplanted to replace a part of the body that is damaged or diseased. The replacement tissue may be taken from elsewhere on a patient's body (**autograft**) or from a donor (**allograft**). The use of an organ from a donor can lead to rejection, when the patient's immune system attacks the grafted tissue. The first skin graft was performed in 1817. *See also* TRANSPLANT

grafting In horticulture, method of plant propagation. A twig of one variety (the **scion**), is established on the roots of a related variety (the **stock**). Most fruit trees are propagated by a similar process called budding, in which the scion is a single bud.

Graham, Billy (William Franklin) (1918–) US evangelist. A charismatic preacher, he led Christian revivalist crusades all over the world, including communist countries. Graham was consulted by several US presidents, especially Richard NIXON. *See also* EVANGELICALISM

Graham, Martha (1894–1991) US choreographer and dancer. She was a leading figure in MODERN DANCE. In the early 1920s, she broke with traditional BALLET, employing highly individual forms based on natural movement. In 1929 she formed her own company. Her works include *Appalachian Spring* (1944).

Graham, Thomas (1805–69) Scottish chemist. He is best remembered for **Graham's law**, which states that the diffusion rate of a GAS is inversely proportional to the square root of its density. This law is used in separating isotopes by the diffusion method and has important industrial applications. Graham also discovered DIALYSIS.

Grahame, Kenneth (1859–1932) Scottish writer of children's fiction. Grahame wrote the children's classic *Wind in the Willows* (1908), which featured the riverbank characters of Mole, Rat, Badger and Toad. It formed the basis for the A.A. MILNE play *Toad of Toad Hall* (1929).

grain Fruits of various CEREAL plants, or the plants themselves. The main kinds of grain are WHEAT, MAIZE and RICE. They are an important food, not only rich in carbohydrates but also containing proteins and vitamins.

Grainger, (George) Percy (Aldridge) (1882–1961) Australian-American composer and pianist. He was a pupil of Ferruccio Busoni and a protégé of Edvard GRIEG, who encouraged him to collect, edit and arrange English and Irish folk-songs. In 1914 Grainger moved to the USA. His arrangements include *Shepherd's Hey* (1911) and *Molly on the Shore* (1921). Grainger also wrote highly experimental music.

grammar Branch of LINGUISTICS that studies the structure of words (**morphology**) and how words combine into phrases, clauses and sentences (SYNTAX). Sometimes it also includes PHONOLOGY and SEMANTICS. **Prescriptive** grammar is a value-based subject that establishes conventions of "correct" usage. **Descriptive** grammar describes actual usage patterns. In 1957 Noam CHOMSKY developed the concept of **generative** grammar, which aims to provide a formal description of the finite set of linguistic rules that generate the infinite number of grammatical sentences in a language. **Transformational** grammar is a form of generative grammar which seeks to explain the structural relationship between words in a sentence and sentences themselves.

grammar school In England, Wales and Northern Ireland, a form of secondary education based on the principle of selection. Pupils are usually chosen on the basis of an examination at the age of 11 (the elevenplus). The oldest grammar schools date from the Middle Ages, and were established to teach Latin in preparation for university or certain professions. Since 1965, the widespread introduction of COMPREHENSIVE SCHOOLS by the Labour government has seen the gradual phasing-out of grammar schools. Today, *c*.4% of pupils inEngland and Wales are educated in grammar schools.

gramophone *See* SOUND RECORDING

Grampian Region in NE Scotland, bordered by the North Sea, the Grampian Highlands and the Cairngorms; the capital is ABERDEEN. The W of the region is mountainous, rising to 1,311m (4,301ft) at Ben Macdhui. The E is drained by the rivers Spey, Dee and Don. Along the banks of the Spey lie many whisky distilleries. Industries: beef farming, fishing, tourism. Area: 8,707sq km (3,361sq mi). Pop. (1991) 503,900.

Grampians Mountain range in N central Scotland. It is the highest mountain system in Britain, running between Glen More and the Scottish Lowlands. Rivers rising in the Grampians include the Spey and Findhorn (flowing N), the Don and Dee (flowing E), and the Tay and Forth (flowing S). Highest peak: BEN NEVIS, 1,343m (4,406ft).

Gramsci, Antonio (1891–1937) Italian political theorist and activist. A founder (1921) of the Italian Communist Party (PCI), he became its leader and was elected (1924) to the Chamber of Deputies. In 1926, MUSSOLINI's Fascist government banned the Communist Party and Gramsci was imprisoned. While in prison, he wrote his *Prison Letters* (1947) which greatly influenced the future shape of Italian communism. Gramsci died shortly after his release.

Granada City in Andalusia, S Spain; capital of Granada province. Founded in the 8th century as a Moorish fortress, it became the capital of the independent Muslim kingdom of Granada in 1238. The last Moorish stronghold in Spain, it surrendered to the Christian armies of Ferdinand and Isabella (1492). The central splendour of Granada is the ALHAMBRA. Industries: tourism and textiles. Pop. (1991) 254,034.

granadilla Edible fruit of the PASSION FLOWER

Granados, Enrique (1867–1916) Spanish composer. He was inspired by the rhythms and melodies of Spanish folk music. Granados used his piano suite *Goyescas* (1911) as the basis for an opera (1916). He was drowned when HMS *Sussex* was torpedoed in the English Channel.

Gran Chaco Lowland plain of central South America, stretching across the borders of Argentina, Bolivia and Paraguay. Arid and largely unpopulated, the region is famous for its quebracho trees, a major source of TANNIN. The discovery of oil in the Chaco Boreal, and Bolivia's subsequent need for a route to the sea, led to the Chaco War (1932–35) between Bolivia and Paraguay. More than 100,000 soldiers died before an agreement gave 75% of Gran Chaco to Paraguay, and allowed Bolivia use of the River Paraguay.

Grand Banks Submerged plateau off the SE coast of Newfoundland, Canada. It is one of the world's richest fishing grounds for cod, as well as halibut, haddock and herring. International fishing is regulated by the Canadian government. Area: *c*.93,000sq km (36,000sq mi).

Grand Canal Main waterway in Venice, Italy. It is crossed by three bridges, the most famous of which is the Rialto. It forms, with smaller canals, the major Venetian transport system. Length: 3km (2mi); width: 30–60m (100–200ft).

Grand Canal Ancient inland waterway in NE China, between Beijing and Hangzhou. The first part, between the rivers Yangtze and Huai Ho, was built in the 6th century BC. It was extended to Hangzhou in the 6th century AD and to Beijing by KUBLAI KHAN in the 13th century. Total length: *c*.1,600km (1,000mi).

Grand Canyon Deep gorge in NW Arizona, carved by the Colorado River. It is 450km (280mi) long and varies from 6km (4mi) to 18km (11mi) in width. In some places it is more than 1.5km (1mi) deep. With its magnificent multicoloured rock formations revealing hundreds of millions of years of geological history, the Grand Canyon is one of the great natural wonders of the world.

Grand Coulee Dam World's largest concrete dam, located in N central Washington, USA, on the Columbia River. Constructed between 1933 and 1942, it is used for irrigation, flood control and navigation. The dam is the largest source of hydroelectricity in the US. Height: 168m (550ft). Length: 1,273m (4,173ft).

Grand National English National Hunt steeplechase, held in March. First run (1836) at Maghull, the horse race moved to its present home at Aintree near Liverpool in 1839. A handicap for six-year-olds and upwards, the gruelling 7.2km (4mi 4 furlong) course includes 31 fences.

Grand Remonstrance (November 1641) Statement of grievances by the LONG PARLIAMENT presented to CHARLES I. It listed numerous objections to the royal government and demanded parliamentary approval of ministers. It was passed in the House of Commons by only 11 votes, and Charles rejected it. It hardened the division between the Crown and Parliament, which culminated in the English CIVIL WARS.

grand unified theory (GUT) Theory that attempts to express WEAK NUCLEAR FORCE, ELECTROMAGNETIC FORCE and STRONG NUCLEAR FORCE in a single gauge theory. In the 1970s Sheldon GLASHOW, Steven WEINBERG and Abdus SALAM formulated a QUANTUM THEORY that unified electromagnetic force and weak nuclear force as the "electroweak force". It has so far improved impossible to prove that this electroweak force is unified with strong nuclear force. If GRAVITATION could be incorporated, then a UNIFIED FIELD THEORY would be produced.

granite Coarse-grained, light-grey, durable IGNEOUS ROCK, composed chiefly of FELDSPAR and QUARTZ, with some mica or hornblende. It is thought to have solidified from magma (molten rock).

Grant, Cary (1904–86) US film actor, b. Britain as Archibald Leach. A dashing and charming actor, he specialized in playing romantic leads. Grant's films include screwball comedies such as *Bringing Up Baby* (1938), *His Girl Friday* (1940) and *The Philadelphia Story* (1941), tearful romances such as *An Affair to Remember* (1957), and stylish thrillers such as *North by Northwest* (1959).

Grant, Duncan James Corrowr (1885–1978) Scottish painter and designer, cousin of Lytton STRACHEY. A member of the BLOOMSBURY GROUP, he participated (1912) in the second exhibition of POST-IMPRESSIONISM. Grant was a co-director (1913–19) of Roger FRY's Omega Workshops. A pioneer of Briitish abstract art, his paintings include *Abstract kinetic collage painting* (1914).

Grant, Ulysses S. (Simpson) (1822–85) US Civil War general and 18th US President (1869–77). He served in the MEXICAN WAR (1846–48) and the US CIVIL WAR. Grant masterminded the Vicksburg Campaign (1862–63). In 1864, Abraham LINCOLN gave him overall command of the Union forces. He co-ordinated the final campaigns and accepted the surrender of Robert E. LEE (1865). As president, Grant achieved foreign policy successes but failed to prevent the growth of domestic corruption. Comfortably re-elected in 1872, he saw members of his own administration implicated in corruption scandals, and he retired at the end of his second term.

Granville-Barker, Harley (1877–1946) English theatre manager, director and actor. After a career in acting, he became co-manager (1904–07) of the Royal Court Theatre, London. Granville-Barker championed the plays of George Bernard SHAW. He also wrote plays, such as *The Voysey Inheritance* (1905), and a series of Prefaces (1927–45) to Shakespeare's plays.

grape Vines that grow in temperate and subtropical climates, producing fruit that is eaten raw, dried or used for making WINE. The classical European vine (*Vitis vinifera*) had its origins in Asia. The climate, soil, topography and methods of cultivation all determine the quality of the crop. Family Vitaceae.

grapefruit Evergreen CITRUS-fruit tree of the family Rutaceae; also its yellow edible fruit, which is a valuable source of vitamin C. The tree, which may reach 6m (20ft), is grown mainly in subtropical climates in the USA, Israel, South Africa and Argentina. Family Rutaceae.

graph Diagram representing a relationship between numbers or quantities. Many graphs use the CARTESIAN COORDINATE SYSTEM. Other forms include bar charts, in which a series of figures is represented by lines of various lengths, and pie charts, in which quantities are represented by sectors of a circle.

graphical user interface (GUI) Computer PROGRAM enabling a user to operate a COMPUTER using simple

symbols. Early personal computers used operating systems that were text-based. Commands were often obscure combinations of letters and numbers, which made using the systems difficult for the uninitiated. A GUI replaces these commands with a screen containing symbols called icons. The user manipulates these using a "mouse".

graphite (plumbago) Dark-grey, soft crystalline form of CARBON. It occurs naturally in deposits of varying purity and is made synthetically by heating petroleum coke. It is used in pencils, lubricants, electrodes, brushes of electrical machines, rocket nozzles and as a moderator that slows down neutrons in nuclear reactors. Graphite is a good conductor of heat and electricity. Hardness 1–2; r.d. 2.1–2.3.

Grass, Günter Wilhelm (1927–) German novelist, poet and playwright. His prose combines evocative description with historical documentation in the mannerist style. He used powerful techniques to grotesque comic effect in *The Tin Drum* (1959) and *Cat and Mouse* (1961), and he satirized the Nazi era in *Dog Years* (1963). Later works include *The Flounder* (1977) and *The Rat* (1986). In 1999, he was awarded the Nobel Prize for literature.

grass Herbaceous plants with fibrous roots that have long, narrow leaves enclosing hollow, jointed stems. The stems may be upright or bent, lie on the ground, or grow underground. The flowers are small, without PETALS and SEPALS. The leaves grow from the base, and so removal of the tips does not inhibit growth, making grass suitable for lawns and pastures. CEREAL grasses, such as rice, millet, maize and wheat, are cultivated for their seeds. Others are grown for fodder, erosion control and ornament. BAMBOO is the only woody species. There are *c*.9,000 species. Family Poaceae/Gramineae. *See also* MONOCOTYLEDON

grasshopper Plant-eating insect. It is a powerful jumper owing to enlarged hind legs. The forewings are leathery, and the hind wings are membranous and fan-shaped; when the insect is at rest, the wings are folded over its back. Length: 8–11cm (0.3–4.3in). Order Orthoptera; families Acrididae and Tettingoniidae. *See also* LOCUST

grass snake (water snake) Non-poisonous snake found in Europe, N Africa and central Asia. It swims readily, but is generally found in long grass and undergrowth. It is greenish-brown with a yellow collar. In Britain it is sometimes mistaken for the ADDER. Length: to 1m (3.3ft). Family Colubridae; species *Natrix natrix*.

Grattan, Henry (1746–1820) Irish statesman. He entered the Irish parliament in 1775. A compelling orator, he became leader of the Patriotic Party. In 1782,

▲ **grasshopper** Because they have problems visually attracting mates in long grass, grasshoppers (order Orthoptera) seek partners using sound signals. By scraping a row of protruding pegs on the inside of each back leg against hardened ridges on their forewings, they make high-frequency mating calls. The calls, known as stridulation, vary from species to species depending on the number of pegs on each leg.

Grattan helped to obtain legislative independence. He strongly opposed the Act of UNION (1801) that merged the Irish and British parliaments. As a member of the Westminster Parliament (1805–20), Grattan fought for CATHOLIC EMANCIPATION.

gravel Mixed pebbles and rock fragments 2mm or more in diameter. Gravel beds are the remains of ancient seashores or river beds. Some are mined for their metal content, such as the California gold-bearing gravels. Gravel is often used as an aggregate in CONCRETE.

Graves, Robert von Ranke (1895–1985) English poet, novelist and critic. His early poetry, such as *Fairies and Fusiliers* (1917), relates his experiences in World War 1. After publishing the autobiographical farce, *Goodbye To All That* (1929), Graves emigrated to Majorca, Spain. He is best-known for the historical novels *I, Claudius* (1934) and *Claudius the God* (1939). Graves' critical work includes *The White Goddess* (1948) on the nature of the poetic Muse. His *Collected Poems* appeared in 1975.

gravitation Force of attraction that is exercised by every particle of MATTER as a result of its MASS. Gravitation dominates astronomical phenomena, but is the weakest of the four FUNDAMENTAL FORCES. This is because it increases as the mass of the interacting objects increase (**nonsaturation**). Gravitation was first described (1687) by Sir Isaac NEWTON, whose **law of gravitation** stated that gravitational force is directly proportional to the masses of the interacting bodies and inversely proportional to the square of the distance between them. Thus, the gravitational force F between two masses m_1 and m_2 a distance d apart was found to be $F = Gm_1m_2/d^2$, where G is a constant of proportionality called the **universal constant** of gravitation ($6.670 \times 10^{-11} \mathrm{Nm^2kg^{-2}}$). Newton's law accurately predicts the movement of the planets around the Sun, but breaks down when the gravitational force is very strong. A more complete treatment of gravitation was developed (1915) by Albert EINSTEIN, who showed in his **general** theory of RELATIVITY that gravitation is a manifestation of the curvature of the SPACE-TIME continuum. **Gravity** is the intensification of gravitation at the surface of a planet or other celestial body. The Earth's gravity produces an acceleration of $c.9.8$ m/s^{-2} ($c.32\mathrm{ft/s^{-2}}$) for any unsupported body.

gravure Style of printing from an INTAGLIO plate. In this kind of printing, the design that is printed is lower than the surface of the plate. Ink at different depths on the plate creates varying tones. In photogravure printing, the plate is made by a photographic process.

Gray, Asa (1810–88) US botanist. Gray's contributions to PLANT CLASSIFICATION include the classic textbook *Manual of Botany for the Northern United States* (1848).

Gray, Thomas (1716–71) English poet. His masterpiece was "Elegy Written in a Country Churchyard" (1751). Other poems include "Ode on the Death of a Favourite Cat" (1748) and "The Descent of Odin" (1768).

gray (symbol Gy) SI unit of absorbed radiation dose. One gray is equivalent to supplying 1 joule of energy per kilogram of irradiated material. It superseded the rad (1 gray = 100 rad).

grayling Freshwater food and sporting fish of the salmon group found in N North America and Eurasia. It is characterized by an unusually long, tall dorsal fin and a small mouth. Length: to 60cm (24in). Family Salmonidae; species include *Thymallus thymallus*.

Graz City at the foot of the Schlossberg mountain, on the River Mur, SE Austria; capital of Styria. Austria's second-largest city, Graz's many historic buildings include a 15th-century Gothic cathedral, the *Uhrturm* clock tower

(1561) and the Renaissance Landhaus. Johannes Kepler taught at the state university (founded 1586) and Frederick II is buried here. Industries: iron and steel, paper, leather, glass, chemicals, textiles. Pop. (1991) 237,810.

Great Australian Bight Wide bay of the Indian Ocean in S Australia, situated between Cape Pasley (W) and Port Lincoln (E). The coast is backed by the steep cliffs of the Nullarbor Plain. During winter months the sea in the area is very stormy. Width: 1,200km (750mi).

Great Awakening Series of 18th-century religious revivals in the American colonies. It was inspired in the 1730s by the preaching of Jonathan EDWARDS and George WHITEFIELD. Baptist revivals occurred in 1760, and METHODISM evolved in the pre-Revolutionary period. The movement led to a great deal of Christian missionary work among the Native American tribes.

Great Barrier Reef World's largest CORAL REEF, in the Coral Sea off the NE coast of Queensland, Australia. It was first explored by James COOK in 1770. It forms a natural breakwater and is up to 800m (2,600ft) wide. The reef is separated from the mainland by a shallow lagoon 11–24km (7–15mi) wide. It is a world heritage site and major tourist destination. Length: 2,000km (1,250mi). Area: c.207,000sq km (80,000sq mi).

Great Basin Desert area in W USA comprising most of Nevada and parts of Utah, Idaho, California, Wyoming and Oregon. This sparsely populated area includes DEATH VALLEY and the MOJAVE DESERT. The few streams drain into saline lakes, the largest being GREAT SALT LAKE. Mineral deposits include gold, magnesite, mercury and beryllium ore. Area: c.492,000sq km (190,000sq mi).

Great Bear Lake Lake in Northwest Territories, NW Canada; the largest lake in Canada and fourth largest in North America. It was first explored (1825) by John FRANKLIN. It is drained in the W by the Great Bear River. The lake remains frozen for eight months of the year. Area: c.31,800sq km (12,300sq mi).

Great Britain Island lying to the West of mainland Europe, and political entity containing ENGLAND, SCOTLAND and WALES. Wales was united with England in 1536. The Act of UNION (1707) united Scotland with England, and the Act of Union (1801) established the UNITED KINGDOM of Great Britain and Ireland.

great circle Circle on a spherical surface, whose centre is coincident with the centre of the sphere. On the celestial sphere, the EQUATOR is a great circle, as are all MERIDIANS. The shortest distance between any two points on a sphere, great circles are used for mapping aircraft routes.

Great Dane (German mastiff) Large hunting dog, originally bred in Germany more than 400 years ago. One of the largest dog breeds, it has a long narrow head and large blunt muzzle. Its deep-chested body is set on long, strong legs. The smooth coat may be various colours. Height: up to 92cm (36in) at the shoulder.

Great Depression Severe economic DEPRESSION that afflicted the USA throughout the 1930s. At the close of the 1920s, economic factors such as overproduction, unrealistic credit levels, stock market speculation, lack of external markets and unequal distribution of wealth all contributed to the prolonged economic crisis. The dramatic collapse of the Wall Street stock market in October 1929 saw $30 billion wiped off stock values in the first week. Bank failures became commonplace. At the depth of the Depression (1932–33), unemployment stood at 16 million, almost 33% of the total workforce. The gross national product (GNP) fell by almost 50%. The Hawley-Smoot Tariff Act increased US tariffs and effectively

spread the depression worldwide. Franklin D. Roosevelt, sensing the national emergency, instituted the
New Deal, which helped to mitigate the worst effects of
the crisis. However, the economy only really started to
pick up with increased defence spending in the 1940s.

Great Dividing Range (Eastern Highlands) Series
of mountain ranges along the E coast of Australia.
They extend S from the Atherton Tableland in Queensland to the Grampian Mountains in Victoria (S). The
highest peak is Mount Kosciusko, at 2,230m (7,316ft).
Length: 3,703km (2,300 mi).

Greater Antilles Largest of three major island groups
in the West Indies, between the Atlantic Ocean and the
Caribbean Sea. The group includes Cuba, Hispaniola,
Jamaica, Puerto Rico and the Cayman Islands.

Great Exhibition (1851) *See* Crystal Palace

Great Lakes World's largest expanse of freshwater; five
lakes in central North America, between Canada and the
USA. They are, from W to E, lakes Superior, Michigan,
Huron, Erie and Ontario. Connected by straits, rivers
and canals, they provide a continuous waterway. They are
drained by the St Lawrence River, the deepening of
which opened up the lakes to world shipping. The growth
in industry and commerce has brought people and pollution to the lakes' shores. Major cities include Chicago,
Toronto, Detroit, Buffalo, Cleveland and Milwaukee. Total surface area: *c.*245,300sq km (94,700sq mi).

Great Leap Forward Five-year economic plan in China
begun (1958) by Mao Zedong. It aimed to double industrial production and boost agricultural output. Tens of millions of workers were mobilized to smelt steel in primitive
furnaces, but much of the steel proved useless. Collective
farms were merged into communes, but progress was
dashed by a succession of poor harvests. After four years
the government was forced to concede failure.

Great Plains High, extensive region of grassland in
central North America. The Great Plains extend from
the Canadian provinces of Alberta, Saskatchewan and
Manitoba through W central USA to Texas. The plateau
slopes down and E from the Rocky Mountains. It is a
sparsely populated region with a semi-arid climate,
prone to high winds. The chinook wind warms an otherwise bitter winter. Most of the land is prairie, and cattle-
ranching and sheep-rearing are the main economic
activities. Wheat is the principal crop. The Great Plains
were roamed by Native Americans until Europeans
destroyed the herds of Bison. The railroads brought settlers in the late 19th century, but by the 1930s drought
and mismanagement had created the Dust Bowl.

Great Red Spot (GRS) Large oval area in the S hemisphere of Jupiter. Since it was first observed (1664) by
Robert Hooke, it has varied in size and colour, from
*c.*11,000 to 14,000km wide by 24,000 to 40,000km long
(7,000–9,000mi by 15,000–25,000mi), and from a deep
red to a light pink, occasionally fading away altogether.
It is an atmospheric phenomenon, a huge anticyclone,
projecting above the surrounding cloud-tops. The red
colour may be produced by phosphorus.

Great Rift Valley *See* Rift Valley

Great Salt Lake Large, shallow saltwater lake in NW
Utah, USA. It is fed by the Bear, Weber and Jordan
rivers, and its depth and area vary with climatic
changes. The heavy brine supports only shrimp and
algae. It is the remnant of the prehistoric Lake Bonneville, which covered much of the Great Basin of
North America. Bonneville Salt Flats, famous for land
speed records, lies in the Great Salt Desert. Area: from
*c.*2,500sq km (960sq mi) to *c.*6,200sq km (2,400sq km).

Great Schism (1378–1417) Split within the Roman
Catholic Church following the election of two rival
popes to succeed Gregory XI. In 1309 Pope Clement V
moved the papacy from Rome to Avignon, France. The
attempt to return the papacy to Rome saw the Italian cardinals elect an Italian pope, Urban VI, and the French
cardinals elect a rival "Antipope", Clement VII. The
schism ended with the Council of Constance
(1414–17), which established Martin V as sole pope.

Great Slave Lake Second largest lake in Canada, W
Northwest Territories; the deepest lake in North America. It is named after the Slave tribe of Native Americans. Europeans discovered the lake in 1771. It is
drained by the Mackenzie River. Area: *c.*28,400sq km
(10,980sq mi). Max. depth: 615m (2,015ft).

Great Smoky Mountains Part of the Appalachians,
on the North Carolina–Tennessee border, USA. One of
the oldest ranges on Earth, it includes the largest virgin
forest of red spruce. The highest point is Clingmans
Dome, 2,026m (6,643ft). Area: 2,090sq km (806sq mi).

Great Trek (1835–40) Migration of *c.*12,000 Boers
from Cape Colony into the South African interior. Their
motives were to escape British control and to acquire
cheap land. The majority settled in what became Orange
Free State, Transvaal and Natal.

Great Wall of China Defensive frontier and world
heritage site, *c.*2,400km (1,500mi) long, extending from
the Huang Hai (Yellow Sea) to the central Asian Desert,
N China. It is an amalgamation of fortifications constructed by various dynasties. Sections of the wall were
first built by the Warring States. In 214 BC, Qin Shihuangdi ordered that they should be joined to form a
unified boundary. The present wall was mostly built 600
years ago by the Ming dynasty. It averages 7.6m (25ft)
high and up to 9m (30ft) thick. A section of the wall outside Beijing is open to tourists.

Great Zimbabwe Ruined city and world heritage site,
SE Zimbabwe. It was the capital of a Bantu-speaking
kingdom (12th–15th century). At the height of its power,
the city's population probably numbered more than
15,000. The city's 9m (30ft) tower is a national symbol.

grebe Brown, grey and black freshwater diving bird
found worldwide. It flies laboriously and has legs set so
far back that it cannot walk. There are six common
species in North America and five in Britain and W
Europe. Length: to 48cm (19in). Family Podicepidae;
genus *Podiceps.*

Greco, El (1541–1614) Cretan painter, b. Domenikos
Theotokopoulos. He studied under Titian in Venice,
Italy. By 1577 El Greco had settled in Toledo, N Spain,
where he remained for the rest of his life. His earliest
work here, *The Assumption of the Virgin* (1579), combines Spanish influences with the Italian. His characteristically elongated and distorted figures disregard normal rules of perspective. El Greco's later paintings, such
as *Burial of Count Orgasz* (1586), *Agony in the Garden*
(1610) and *Assumption* (1613), express his profound
religious conviction. *See also* Mannerism

Greece (Hellas) Republic in SE Europe. The mountainous, maritime Hellenic Republic can be divided into four
geographical regions: **Northern** Greece includes the

GREECE
AREA: 131,990sq km (50,961sq mi)
POPULATION: 10,193,000
CAPITAL (POPULATION): Athens (3,097,000)

historic regions of THRACE and MACEDONIA and its second-largest city, THESSALONÍKI; **Central** Greece, N of the Gulf of Corinth, includes the capital and largest city, ATHENS, and its highest peak, Mount OLYMPUS at 2,917m (9,570ft); **Southern** Greece is the PELOPONNESOS peninsula and includes the city of CORINTH; the fourth region is the **Greek Islands**, which constitute c.20% of Greece. The largest island, CRETE, lies in the Mediterranean Sea. In the Aegean Sea lie the Sporades archipelago (including EUBOEA), the DODECANESE (including RHODES), the Cyclades group, and the NE island of LESBOS. The Ionian islands include CORFU and Cephalonia. **Climate** Low-lying areas have mild, moist winters and hot, dry summers. The E coast has c.50% of the rainfall of the W. The mountains have a much more severe climate. **Vegetation** Much of Greece's original vegetation has been destroyed. Some areas are covered by maquis. **History and Politics** Crete was the centre of MINOAN CIVILIZATION, between c.3000 and 1450 BC. The Minoans were followed by the MYCENAEAN CIVILIZATION, which prospered until the DORIANS settled (c.1200 BC). Powerful city-states emerged, such as SPARTA and Athens. SOLON established DEMOCRACY in Athens (5th century BC). The revolt of the IONIANS started the PERSIAN WARS (499–479 BC). (*See GREECE, CLASSICAL*) Athens was defeated in the PELOPONNESIAN WAR (431–404 BC), and Corinth and THEBES gained control. In 338 BC, MACEDON, led by PHILIP II, became the dominant power. His son, ALEXANDER THE GREAT, ushered in the HELLENISTIC AGE. In 146 BC, Greece became a Roman province. Greece formed part of the BYZANTINE EMPIRE from AD 330 to 1453. In 1456, the Ottomans conquered Greece. The Greek War of Independence (1821–27) was supported by the European powers, and an independent monarchy was established (1832). As king of the Hellenes (1863–1913), GEORGE I recovered much Greek territory. In 1913, Greece gained Crete. In 1917, Greece finally entered World War 1 on the Allied side. In 1923, 1.5 million Greeks from Asia Minor were resettled in Greece. In 1936, Joannis METAXAS became premier. His dictatorial regime remained neutral at the start of World War 2. By May 1941, Germany had occupied Greece. By 1944, resistance groups had recaptured most of the territory, and the Germans withdrew. From 1946 to 1949, a civil war raged between communist and royalist forces. In 1951, Greece was admitted to NATO. In 1955, Kónstantinos KARAMANLIS became prime minister, the economy improved, but tension with Turkey over CYPRUS surfaced. In 1964, a republican, George Papandreou, became prime minister. In 1967, a military dictatorship seized power. The "Greek Colonels" imposed harsh controls on dissent. In 1973, the monarchy was abolished and Greece became a presidential republic. Civil unrest led to the 1974 restoration of civilian government, headed by Karamanlis. In 1981, Greece joined the European Community, and Andreas PAPANDREOU became Greece's first socialist prime minister (1981–89, 1993–96). In 1990, Karamanlis returned as president. He was succeeded (1995–) by Constantine Stephanopoulos. The 1996 election was won by the Panhellenic Socialist Party (PASOK) led by Kostas Simitis. Simitis was re-elected in 2000, pledging to take Greece in to the European single currency (the euro). In 1998, forest fires raged over one million hectares of Attica, killing more than seven people. **Economy** Despite improvements in infrastructure and industry, Greece is one of the poorest members of the European Union (1995 GDP per capita, US$11,710). Manufacturing is important. Products: textiles, cement, chemicals, metallurgy. Minerals: lignite,

bauxite, chromite. Farmland covers c.33% of Greece, grazing land 40%. Major crops: tobacco, fruit (olives, grapes), cotton, wheat. Livestock are raised. Shipping and tourism are also major sectors.
Greece, classical Period beginning with the defeat of the second Persian invasion in 479 BC and ending with the death of ALEXANDER THE GREAT in 323 BC. Warring city-states flourished as centres of trade. ATHENS, the most wealthy and powerful, developed a democratic system under the guidance of PERICLES. Its main rival was the military state of SPARTA. Classical Greece was the birthplace of many ideas in art, literature, philosophy and science – among them those of PLATO and ARISTOTLE. It is traditionally regarded as the birthplace of Western civilization. *See also* HELLENISTIC AGE
Greek INDO-EUROPEAN LANGUAGE spoken in Greece since c.2000 BC. In ancient Greece there were several dialects: Attic, spoken in Athens, is the most common in literary records. Greek was widely spoken in the Middle East during the HELLENISTIC AGE. It was the official language of the Byzantine Empire and began to evolve into its modern form in c.1000 AD. After the fall of Byzantium, it developed two forms: "demotiki", the spoken language also used in most literary forms; and "katharevousa", used in official documents.
Greek art and architecture Greek architecture came into its own in the 6th century BC when stone replaced wood as the building material for civic and temple buildings. Distinct ORDERS OF ARCHITECTURE began to emerge. The earliest remaining DORIC temple is the Temple of Hera at Olympia (late 7th century BC), and the most outstanding example is the PARTHENON. Among IONIC temples, the Erechtheum is considered the most perfect. The Corinthian mausoleum at HALICARNASSUS (350 BC) was one of the SEVEN WONDERS OF THE WORLD. Greek art may be divided into four chronological periods: Geometric (late 11th–late 8th century BC), Archaic (late 8th century–480 BC), Classical (480–323 BC) and Hellenistic (323–27 BC). Only a few small bronze horses survive from the **Geometric** period. During the **Archaic** period, stone sculpture appeared, vase painting proliferated and the human figure became a common subject. Civic wealth and pride was a feature of the **Classical** period, and sculpture reached its peak of serene perfection. The **Hellenistic** period is noted for increasingly dramatic works.
Greek drama First form of DRAMA in Western civilization, which took three forms, TRAGEDY, COMEDY and SATYR plays. Tragedy and comedy were the two main forms. **Tragedy** developed from religious festivals, at which a CHORUS sang responses to a leader. AESCHYLUS introduced a second actor, and SOPHOCLES added a third. The other major tragedian was EURIPIDES. Greek tragedy usually dealt with mythical subjects, but sometimes (as in Aeschylus' *The Persians*) used recent history for its setting. A tradition of Greek **comedy** arose in the 5th century BC. It was often highly topical and lampooned politics and the conventions of tragedy; its best-known exponent was ARISTOPHANES. Comedy flourished in the Hellenistic Age (323–27 BC), especially in the work of MENANDER. **Satyr** plays were bawdy works written to accompany tragedies.
Greek literature One of the longest surviving traditions in world literature. The earliest Greek literature took the form of EPIC poems, as epitomized by the *Iliad* and the *Odyssey* of HOMER and the didactic poetry of Hesiod, such as the *Theogony*. It also saw the development of lyric poetry, exemplified by the choric lyrics and odes of PINDAR. In Classical GREECE (480–323 BC), there was a tradition of

fine literature in poetry and prose writing. During the HEL-
LENISTIC AGE (323–27 BC), epic, epigrammatic and didactic poetry flourished in the works of Apollonius of Rhodes,
Aratus and Callimachus. During the Roman period (*c.*27
BC–*c.*AD 330), important figures included PLUTARCH,
MARCUS AURELIUS and PTOLEMY. Writing in Greek died
out after the Turkish invasions of the 15th century and was
only revived after their overthrow in 1828. Prominent
among the new generation were Dionysios Solomos and
Andreas Kalvos. Modern Greek writers of international
stature include Nikos KAZANTZAKIS.

Greek mythology Collection of stories mainly concerning the adventures of gods and heroes. In the myths,
the gods are not wholly admirable figures: they have
similar weaknesses to humans and are capable of great
vindictiveness, revenge and favouritism. Greek myths
were often explanatory, offering answers to questions of
human nature and the universe, clarifying abstract ideas,
or explaining religious matters in a more rational manner. From the time of HOMER (9th century BC) Greek
polytheism formed a coherent system, with a pantheon
of 12 deities who dwelt on Mount OLYMPUS: ZEUS,
HERA, POSEIDON, ATHENA, APOLLO, ARTEMIS,
APHRODITE, HEPHAESTUS, ARES, DEMETER, HESTIA and
HERMES. Major religious centres included Delphi and
Olympia. *See also* DIONYSUS; HADES; NYMPH

Greeley, Horace (1811–72) US journalist and political leader. In 1841 he founded the *New York Tribune*. In
his editorials, Greeley supported liberal reforms and
vigorously opposed slavery. His advocacy of Western
settlement was encapsulated in his advice, "Go West,
young man, go West". His bid for the presidency (1872)
was defeated by Ulysses S. GRANT.

green algae Large group of marine and freshwater
ALGAE (phylum Chlorophyta). They are distinct from
other algae by virtue of possessing cup-shaped CHLORO-
PLASTS that contain chlorophyll b, and by producing
cells with FLAGELLA at some stage in their lives. Green
algae range in size from microscopic single-cell types to
large, complex SEAWEEDS. *See also* LICHEN

Greenaway, Kate (1846–1901) English artist. She is
best remembered for her illustrations in children's
books, such as *The Birthday Book* (1880) and *Mother
Goose* (1881). An annual medal for the best British children's book illustration is named after her.

Greenaway, Peter (1942–) Welsh film director and
screenwriter. An innovative and painterly director, his
breakthrough film was *The Draughtsman's Contract*
(1983). Other films include *The Cook, The Thief, His
Wife, and Her Lover* (1989), *Prospero's Books* (1991)
and *The Pillow Book* (1996).

green belt Area of open land maintained as a barrier
between adjoining built-up areas. The concept of green
belts was first proposed (1898) in Britain by Ebenezer
Howard (1850–1928) in his plans for garden cities.
Howard used them to distinguish residential from industrial sections. The Town and Country Planning Act
(1947) established a green belt around London. Green
belts provide protection from factories and urban
sprawl, but they add to urban overcrowding.

Green, T.H. (Thomas Hill) (1836–82) English
philosopher. He was professor of moral philosophy at
Oxford University from 1878. A representative of English
IDEALISM, he reacted against EMPIRICISM and stressed self-
determination against free ethical choice. His most
important work is *Prolegomena to Ethics* (1883).

Greene, (Henry) Graham (1904–91) English novelist, journalist, travel writer and dramatist. In 1926,

Greene converted to Catholicism; religion, guilt and the
search for redemption are consistent themes in his novels. His psychological thrillers are among the most popular and critically acclaimed works of 20th-century fiction. Greene's debut novel was *The Man Within* (1929).
Stamboul Train (1932) was the first in a series of "entertainments" that included the screenplay for *The Third
Man* (1950) and *Our Man in Havana* (1958). Novels that
explored religious issues included *Brighton Rock* (1938),
The Power and the Glory (1940), *The Heart of the Matter* (1948) and *The Quiet American* (1955). Other works
include *A Burnt-Out Case* (1961), *The Honorary Consul*
(1973) and *Travels with My Aunt* (1978).

Greene, Nathanael (1743–86) American general. He
was George WASHINGTON'S second-in-command in the
AMERICAN REVOLUTION. In 1776, Greene skillfully led
the left wing of the American forces at the battle of Trenton, Princeton and Brandywine. In 1780, he assumed
command of the Southern army. His reorganization and
strategy ensured the success of the Carolina Campaign
(1780–82) that resulted in numerous British defeats.

greenfinch Greenish bird with yellow wing markings It
is found in parts of Europe and in N Asia. Length: 14.7cm
(5.8in). Family Fringillidae; species *Carduelis chloris*.

greenfly *See* APHID

Greenham Common Site of a former US airbase, near
Newbury, Berkshire, S England. During the 1980s, the
Women's Peace movement established a protest camp
outside the base, to campaign against the deployment of
CRUISE MISSILES. The base was closed in 1991.

greenhouse effect Raised temperature at a planet's
surface as a result of heat energy being trapped by gases
in the ATMOSPHERE. As the Sun's rays pass through Earth's
atmosphere, some heat is absorbed but most of the short-
wave SOLAR ENERGY passes through. This energy is re-
emitted by the Earth as long-wave radiation, which cannot pass easily through the atmosphere. More heat is
retained if there is a CLOUD layer. In the last 100 years,
more heat has been retained due to an increase of more
than 15% in concentrations of carbon dioxide (CO_2)
through the burning of FOSSIL FUELS. Tiny particles of
CO_2 form an extra layer, which acts like the glass in a
greenhouse. The effect is compounded by the damage to
the OZONE LAYER caused by CHLOROFLUOROCARBONS
(CFCs). Scientists of the Intergovenmental Panel on Climate Change (IPCC) have estimated that a doubling of
the present carbon dioxide emissions could led to GLOBAL
WARMING on the scale of an average surface temperature
rise of between 1 to 3.5°C. *See also* EARTH SUMMIT

Greenland World's largest island, in the NW Atlantic
Ocean, lying mostly within the Arctic Circle. It is a self-
governing province of Denmark; the capital is NUUK
(Godthåb). More than 85% of Greenland is covered by
PERMAFROST, with an average depth of 1,500m (5,000ft).
Settlement is confined to the SW coast, which is warmed
by Atlantic currents. Most of Greenland's inhabitants are
INUIT. Its European discovery is credited to ERIC THE
RED, who settled in 982, founding a colony that lasted
more than 500 years. In 1380, Greenland became a Danish possession and was incorporated into the kingdom in
1953. Following a referendum, Greenland achieved
home rule (1979) and self-government (1981). In 1985,
it withdrew from the European Union (EU). Greenland's
economy is heavily dependent on subsidies from Denmark. Fish forms the basis of the economy. Lead and
zinc are mined in the NW, and the S has untapped reserves
of uranium. Tourism is increasing. Area: 2,175,000sq km
(840,000sq mi). Pop. (2000) 60,000.

green movement Campaign to preserve the environment and to minimize pollution or destruction of the Earth's natural habitats. The green movement formed its own active pressure groups GREENPEACE and Friends of the Earth in the early 1970s. It gained political representation shortly afterwards in the form of various European GREEN PARTIES. In affluent Western societies, effects of the movement have included the production of environmentally safe products and a heightened concern with the recycling of waste products, such as paper and plastics.

Green Party Any of a number of European political parties embodying the principles of the GREEN MOVEMENT. Major Green parties were founded in the early 1970s. In the UK, traditional political parties adopted many Green policies in the 1990s and the Green vote declined. In 1998, the Greens in Germany joined a coalition government.

Greenpeace International pressure group. It was founded (1971) in Canada, initially to oppose US nuclear testing in Alaska. Greenpeace promotes environmental awareness and campaigns against environmental abuse. It gains wide media coverage for its active, non-violent demonstrations against whaling and toxic-waste dumping.

green revolution Intensive plan of the 1960s to increase crop yields in developing countries by introducing higher-yielding strains of plant and new FERTILIZERS and PESTICIDES. The scheme began in Mexico in the 1940s and was successfully introduced in parts of India, SE Asia, the Middle East and Latin America.

greenshank Shy, wading bird with a long, slightly upturned bill. It breeds in Scotland and Scandinavia, and has characteristic olive-green legs. Height: 30cm (12in). Family Charadriidae; species *Tringa nebularia*.

green turtle Marine TURTLE found in tropical waters of the Atlantic and Pacific. It has a large head, shell, and powerful forelegs that act as flippers. It is an endangered species. Length: to 1.2m (4ft); weight: to 225kg (500lb). Family Cheloniidae; species *Chelonia mydas*.

Greenwich Borough in SE London, England. In Greenwich Park stands the former Royal Observatory (founded 1675). The prime meridian forms the basis of GREENWICH MEAN TIME (GMT). Greenwich has a rich maritime history. The Royal Naval College was formerly the Greenwich Hospital, partly designed (1696) by Sir Christopher WREN. It stands on the site of a Tudor royal palace, birthplace of Henry VIII, Mary I and Elizabeth I. The *Cutty Sark* tea clipper and *Gypsy Moth IV* yacht are moored at Greenwich Pier. Queen's House was the first Renaissance building in England, designed (1616) by Inigo JONES. The Millennium Dome was built in Greenwich to celebrate the dawning of the third millennium. Pop. (1991) 207,650.

Greenwich Mean Time (GMT) Local time at GREENWICH, London, situated on the prime MERIDIAN (0° LONGITUDE). It has been used as the basis for calculating standard time in various parts of the world since 1884.

Greenwich Village Residential area between Spring and West 14th streets, MANHATTAN, NEW YORK CITY, USA. Once a separate village, in the latter half of the 19th century, Greenwich Village became a cultural centre, popular with writers, artists and musicians. Some 19th-century wooden houses remain, and it is popular with tourists.

Greer, Germaine (1939–) Australian feminist and writer. Her book, *The Female Eunuch* (1970), challenged the misrepresentation of female sexuality by a patriarchal society. Other works include *Sex and Destiny: the Politics of Human Fertility* (1984), *The Change: Women, Aging and the Menopause* (1991) and *The Whole Woman* (1999). *See also* FEMINISM

Gregorian chant PLAINSONG music of the early and medieval Christian Church. It is still sung in some high Anglican and Roman Catholic churches. It is named after Pope GREGORY I (r.590–604) but is now believed to have originated shortly after Gregory's time. Before the Reformation, psalms, canticles and texts of the Roman Catholic LITURGY were sung to Gregorian chants. *See also* MODE

Gregory I (the Great), Saint (c.540–604) Pope (590–604), last of the Latin FATHERS OF THE CHURCH. He devoted himself to alleviating poverty and hunger among the Romans. Gregory was responsible for enforcing the spiritual supremacy of the papacy and establishing the temporal independence of the pope. His reforms included changes in the LITURGY, such as the development of GREGORIAN CHANT. Gregory initiated the conversion of the LOMBARDS and sent Saint AUGUSTINE to England to convert the ANGLO-SAXONS. He encouraged MONASTICISM and his doctrinal writings were influential in the development of SCHOLASTICISM. His feast day is 12 March.

Gregory VII, Saint (c.1020–85) Pope (1073–85), b. Hildebrand. He condemned lay investiture, simony and clerical marriage. Emperor HENRY IV opposed the reforms and deposed Gregory (1076). Gregory responded by excommunicating Henry. In 1077 Henry was forced to do penance at Canossa, Italy. In 1079, Gregory decreed Henry deposed. Henry retorted by appointing an antipope (Clement III). In 1084, Henry captured Rome, forcing Gregory to flee to Salerno. Gregory failed to establish the independence of the papacy, but his example inspired the Concordat of WORMS (1122). His feast day is 25 May.

Gregory XIII (1502–85) Pope (1572–85), b. Ugo Buoncompagni. He supported education, training for the clergy and missionary activity, especially the JESUITS. He promoted church reform and sought to carry out the decrees of the Council of TRENT. He is best known for his reform of the Julian CALENDAR (1582).

Grenada Independent island nation in the SE Caribbean Sea, the most southerly of the WINDWARD ISLANDS, c.160km (100mi) N of Venezuela. It consists of Grenada and the smaller islands of the Southern Grenadines dependency; the capital is ST GEORGE'S. The country is volcanic in origin, with a ridge of mountains running N–S. It has a tropical climate with occasional hurricanes. First sighted (1498) by Christopher COLUMBUS, the islands were then inhabited by the Carib. In the mid-17th century, Grenada was settled by the French. It became a permanent British possession in 1783 and a crown colony in 1877, and was a member of the West Indian Federation (1958–62). In 1974, it became an independent Commonwealth state. In 1979, the New Jewel movement, led by Maurice Bishop, seized power and proclaimed a People's Revolutionary Government. In October 1983, Bishop was killed in a military coup. US forces invaded the island and completed (1985) a phased withdrawal after the re-establishment of democratic government. In 1995, a general election was won by the New National Party (NNP), led by Dr Keith Mitchell. In 1999, the NNP was re-elected. The economy is mainly agricultural, based on cocoa, bananas, sugar, spices and citrus fruits. It is also heavily dependent on tourism. Area: 344sq km (133sq mi). Pop. (2000) 83,000.

Grenadines Group of c.600 small islands in the S Windward Islands, Caribbean Sea, WEST INDIES. The S Grenadines are included in GRENADA. The N Grenadines form part of ST VINCENT AND THE GRENADINES. Industries: cotton, limes, livestock, tourism.

Grenville, Sir Richard (1541–91) English naval commander, cousin of Sir Walter RALEIGH. In 1585, he commanded the fleet that carried Raleigh's colonists to Roanoke, Virginia. In 1591, as commander of the *Revenge*, Grenville bravely fought alone against a Spanish fleet off the Azores. He was mortally wounded in the 15-hour battle.

Gresham, Sir Thomas (1519?–79) English financier. In 1566 he founded the Royal Exchange, London. Gresham acted as chief financial adviser to ELIZABETH I. In 1579, he founded Gresham College, London, which later evolved into the Royal Society. He was erroneously attributed with **Gresham's law**, which states that "bad money drives out good".

Grey, Charles, 2nd Earl (1764–1845) British statesman, Whig prime minister (1830–34). Grey secured the passage of the parliamentary REFORM ACT (1832). He also steered the Act abolishing slavery in the British Empire.

Grey, Sir George (1812–98) British colonial administrator, prime minister of New Zealand (1877–79). As governor of New Zealand (1845–53, 1861–68), Grey attempted to negotiate a peaceful settlement of the MAORI WARS.

Grey, Lady Jane (1537–54) Queen of England for nine days in July 1553, great-granddaughter of Henry VII. She was married to the son of the Duke of NORTHUMBERLAND, regent for the ailing EDWARD VI. On Edward VI's death she was proclaimed queen, but the rightful heir, MARY I, was almost universally preferred. Lady Jane and her husband were executed.

Grey, Zane (1875–1939) US novelist, b. Pearl Grey. His WESTERN stories present brawny heroes loyal to the ethics of the American frontier. Grey's most popular novel was *Riders of the Purple Sage* (1912).

greyhound Coursing dog traditionally used to hunt hares and also used for racing. It has a long, tapered head and muzzle with small ears set at the back. Its broad muscular back and well-arched loins are set on long lean legs. The tail is long and tapered, and the coat is smooth. Greyhounds can reach speeds of up to 70km/h (45mph). Height: 66cm (26in) at the shoulder; weight 29kg (65lb).

Grieg, Edvard Hagerup (1843–1907) Norwegian composer. A pioneer of IMPRESSIONISM in music, he used Norwegian folk themes in many of his compositions. Grieg wrote the incidental music for Henrik IBSEN's play *Peer Gynt* (1876). Other major works include the Piano Concerto (1868) and *Holberg Suite* (1884).

Griffith, Arthur (1872–1922) Irish statesman, president of the Irish Free State (1922). From 1899, he edited the republican newspaper, *United Irishman*. In 1905, Griffith founded SINN FÉIN. He took no part in the EASTER RISING (1916), but was imprisoned by the British (1916–18). In 1919, he became vice president of the unofficial Irish parliament, the Dáil Éireann. Griffith and Michael COLLINS were the chief negotiators of the Anglo-Irish Treaty (1921) that created the Irish Free State and *de facto* acceptance of partition. Eamon DE VALERA rejected the settlement and Griffith became president.

Griffith, D.W. (David Wark) (1875–1948) US film director. His expressive use of the camera, lighting and dramatic editing established film as an independent art form. In 1915 Griffith released the Civil War epic *The Birth of a Nation*, often cited as the most important document in cinematic history but also condemned as racist. *Intolerance* (1916) was his response, examining the persistence of prejudice. In 1919, he co-founded United Artists. *Abraham Lincoln* (1930) was his first "talkie" and *The Struggle* (1931) his final film. In 1935, Griffith won an honorary Oscar.

griffon (griffon vulture) Carrion-eating bird of prey of Eurasia and N Africa, with gold or sandy-brown plumage.

It is gregarious and nests in large flocks. Length: 1m (3.3ft). Family Accipitridae; species *Gyps fulvus*.

Grimaldi, Joseph (1779–1837) English entertainer. From 1800 to 1828, he dominated the PANTOMIME season at Covent Garden, London. Grimaldi's performance as "Joey the Clown" influenced the modern circus act.

Grimm brothers German philologists and folklorists. **Jakob Ludwig Karl** (1785–1863) formulated **Grimm's law**, which detailed the regular shifting of consonants (such as *p* to *f*, as in the Latin word *pater* to the English *father*) in INDO-EUROPEAN LANGUAGES. It was a landmark in the study of language. He and his brother, **Wilhelm Karl** (1786–1859), are popularly known for their enduring collection of folk tales, *Grimm's Fairy Tales* (1812–15). It was a major text of ROMANTICISM.

Grimmelshausen, Hans Jakob Christoffel von (1621–76) German novelist. He served in the Imperial and Swedish armies. Grimmelshausen is known for his picaresque novels, *Simplicissimus* (1669–72), that serve as social commentary on the THIRTY YEARS' WAR (1618–48).

Grimond, Jo (Joseph), Baron (1913–93) British politician, Liberal Party leader (1956–67). He entered Parliament in 1950. Grimond modernized the LIBERAL PARTY and proposed a political realignment, which captured new supporters. He opposed nuclear weapons and favoured Britain's entry into the European Community (EC). After the forced resignation of Jeremy Thorpe (1976), Grimond became caretaker leader of the Party until David STEEL took over.

Gris, Juan (1887–1927) Spanish painter. In 1906, he settled in Paris, where he became acquainted with PICASSO. Gris influenced the development of synthetic CUBISM, as seen in *Homage to Picasso* (1912). Later works include collages, architectonic paintings, stage sets and costumes for DIAGHILEV. *See also* BRAQUE, GEORGES

grizzly bear Large BEAR, generally considered to be a variety of brown bear (*Ursus arctos*) although sometimes classified as a separate species (*Ursus horribilis*). Once widespread in W North America, the grizzly is now rare except in W Canada, Alaska, and some US national parks. Length: to 2.5m (7ft); weight: 410kg (900lb).

Gromyko, Andrei (1909–80) Soviet statesman, foreign minister (1957–85), president (1985–88). As Soviet ambassador to the USA (1943–46), he took part in the Yalta and Potsdam peace conferences (1945). He then acted as the permanent Soviet delegate to the United Nations (1946–48). As foreign minister, Gromyko represented the Soviet Union throughout most of the COLD WAR and helped arrange the summits between BREZHNEV and NIXON. He was given the largely honorary role of president by Mikhail GORBACHEV.

Groningen City at the confluence of the Hoornse Diep and the Winschoter Diep, NE Netherlands; capital of Groningen province. A member of the HANSEATIC LEAGUE from 1284, it controlled most of Friesland. Groningen remained loyal to the Habsburgs but was forced to surrender to the Dutch in 1594. The surrounding fertile agricultural land makes it one of the Netherland's largest markets. Industries: shipbuilding, electrical equipment. Pop. (1996) 170,000.

Gropius, Walter (1883–1969) German-US architect, founder of the BAUHAUS (1919–28). Gropius transformed the Weimar School of Art into the Bauhaus, which was relocated (1926) to his newly designed buildings in Dessau. He fled Nazism (1934) and became professor of architecture (1937–52) at Harvard University. Gropius was a pioneer of FUNCTIONALISM and INTERNATIONAL STYLE in particular. The results of his cooperative, group-work design methods can be seen in the Harvard Graduate Center (1949) and the US Embassy, Athens (1960).

grosbeak Any of several birds of the FINCH family (Fringillidae). They have short, thick, seed-cracking beaks. Found in woodlands of the Americas, Europe and Asia, species include the rose-breasted grosbeak (*Pheucticus ludovicianus*) of North and South America, and the pine grosbeak (*Pinicolor enucleator*) of Canada and N Europe. Length: 18–25cm (7–10in).

gross domestic product (GDP) Total amount of goods and services produced by a country annually. It does not include income from investments or overseas possessions. GDP gives an indication of the wealth of a nation. *See also* GROSS NATIONAL PRODUCT (GNP)

gross national product (GNP) Total market value of all goods and services produced by a country annually, plus net income from abroad. GNP is a universal indicator of economic performance and provides an assessment of different economic sectors. GNP is the sum of four types of spending: private consumption (goods and services bought by the community), government expenditure, balance of trade and business investment. *See also* GROSS DOMESTIC PRODUCT (GDP)

Grossmith, George (1847–1912) English actor and writer. He played the baritone role in many of GILBERT and SULLIVAN's operettas. Grossmith is best remembered for the novel *Diary of a Nobody* (1882), written in collaboration with his brother *Weedon* (1854–1919).

Grosz, George (1893–1959) German illustrator and painter. A founder of the DADA movement in Berlin, Grosz mercilessly satirized capitalist decadence, German militarism and the rise of fascism in drawings and caricatures, such as *Ecce Homo* (1923). In 1932 he fled to the USA. Late works show some affinity with SURREALISM.

Grotius, Hugo (1583–1645) Dutch jurist and diplomat, b. Huig de Groot. Grotius' legal treatise *De Jure Belli et Pacis* (1625) is regarded as the founding text of modern international law.

groundhog *See* WOODCHUCK

groundnut *See* PEANUT

ground squirrel (gopher) Terrestrial SQUIRREL native to Eurasia and North America. Ground squirrels eat plants, seeds, insects, small animals and eggs. Most have greyish-red to brown fur; some are striped or spotted. Length: to 40.5cm (16in); weight: 85–1,000g (0.1–2.2lb). Family Sciuridae; genus *Citellus* (and others).

groundwater Water that lies beneath the surface of the Earth. It comes chiefly from rain, although some is of volcanic or sedimentary origin. It moves through porous rocks and soil and can be collected in WELLS. Groundwater can dissolve minerals and leave deposits, creating structures such as CAVES, STALAGMITES and STALACTITES. *See also* WATER TABLE

grouper Tropical marine fish found from the coast of Florida to South America, and in the Indian and Pacific oceans. It has a large mouth, sharp teeth, a mottled body and the ability to change colour. Length: to 3.7m (12ft); weight: to 450kg (1,000lb). Family Serranidae; species: giant, *Epinephelus itajara*; Australian, *Epinephelus lanceolatus*. *See also* BASS

Group of Eight (G8) (formerly Group of Seven – G7) Eight nations that meet for an annual economic summit meeting. In 1975, the heads of government of what were regarded as the world's seven wealthiest nations – the USA, Japan, Germany, Britain, France, Canada and Italy – met in the first of these meeting. The changing world economy has led other countries to seek membership. In 1997, Russia was formally admitted to the group.

group theory Branch of mathematics applicable to SETS with symmetric properties. A group is a set with elements (together with an operation) that must obey four rules: closure; association; existence of an inverse; and existence of an identity. The theory was developed by Évariste GALOIS. Group theory is particularly useful in quantum mechanics, spectroscopy and particle physics.

group therapy Form of PSYCHOTHERAPY in which several individuals interact on a cognitive and emotional basis. Groups meet regularly with a trained therapist (facilitator) who can be directive or non-directive, allowing the group to set the agenda. The shared experiences and the reproduction of interpersonal relationships may enable individuals to recognize patterns of behaviour and act out new behaviours. Group therapy is often used in cases of CHILD ABUSE, DRUG ADDICTION and marriage counselling. The technique was formalized (1905) by US physician J.H. Pratt (1872–1942). There are various types of group therapy, including BEHAVIOUR THERAPY and GESTALT PSYCHOLOGY.

grouse Plump game bird of N areas of the Northern Hemisphere. Grouse are fowl-like, but have feathered ankles and toes and brightly coloured air sacs on the neck. Family Tetraonidae. *See also* PRAIRIE CHICKEN

Grove, Sir George (1820–1900) English musicologist. Grove was the founder and first editor of the *Dictionary of Music and Musicians* (1878–89). He was director (1882–95) of the Royal College of Music, London.

Groznyy City in the Caucasus Mountains, SW Russia; capital of CHECHENIA. Founded in 1818, it has been an oil-producing centre since 1893 and has a pipeline to the Black Sea and the Donets Basin. Groznyy was severely damaged in fighting (1994–2000) between Russian forces and Chechen rebels, and there were many civilian casualties. Industries: oil, petrochemicals. Pop. (1994) 364,000.

Grünewald, Matthias (1470–1528) German painter, b. Mathis Gothardt. A contemporary of DÜRER, he was court painter at Mainz (1508–14) and Brandenburg (1515–25). Grünewald's masterpiece is the altarpiece at Isenheim, Alsace (*c*.1515). His use of dazzling colour and distorted figures was a major influence on EXPRESSIONISM.

Guadalajara City in W central Mexico; capital of Jalisco state. Situated at an altitude of 1,567m (5,141ft), it is the second-largest city in Mexico. Founded in 1531, Guadalajara has become a major industrial centre. It has some fine Spanish colonial architecture, including a 16th-century cathedral and 18th-century university. Noted for its mountain scenery and mild climate, it is a popular health resort. Industries: engineering, textiles, food processing, pottery, glassware. Pop. (1990) 1,650,205.

Guadalcanal Largest of the Solomon Islands, *c*.970km (600 mi) E of New Guinea, W central Pacific Ocean; the capital is Honiara. Guadalcanal was the scene of heavy fighting between Japanese and US troops in World War 2. The chief products are coconuts, fish, fruit and timber. Area: 5,302sq km (2,047sq mi). Pop. (1991 est.) 60,692.

Guadalupe-Hidalgo, Treaty of (1848) Peace settlement ending the MEXICAN WAR. Mexico ceded the present US states of Texas, New Mexico, Arizona, California, Nevada and Utah, plus parts of Colorado and Wyoming. The USA paid $15 million in compensation.

Guadeloupe French overseas department (since 1946), consisting of the islands of Basse-Terre (W), Grande-Terre (E) and several smaller islands in the Leeward Islands, E WEST INDIES. Discovered in 1493 by Columbus, Guadeloupe was settled by the French (1635), briefly held by Britain and Sweden, and reverted to French rule in 1816. Chief crops are sugar cane and bananas. Industries: distilling, tourism. Area: 1,780sq km (687sq mi). Pop. (1990) 378,178.

Guam Southernmost and largest of the MARIANA ISLANDS in the W Pacific Ocean; the capital is Agaña. An unincorporated US territory, Guam was discovered (1521) by Ferdinand MAGELLAN and ceded to the USA in 1898. It was the first US territory to be occupied by the Japanese during World War 2. Industries: oil refining, palm oil, fish products. Area: 541sq km (209sq mi). Pop. (2000) 128,200.

guanaco Large species of LLAMA (*Lama guanicoe*) native to the Andean foothills and the pampas of South America. A New World relative of the CAMEL, it is used as beast of burden. It has a brown, soft woolly coat and grey head. Height: up to 110cm (3.25ft) at shoulder.

Guangdong (Kwangtung) Province in S China, bordered S by the South China Sea; the capital is GUANGZHOU. Guangdong possesses 20% of China's entire length of coastline. The province, which faces HONG KONG and MACAO, is at the heart of China's economic resurgence, with the special economic zones of Shantou, Shenzen and Zhuhai. The SW seaport of Zhanjiang on the Leizhou peninsula is a major contributor to the economic growth of the province. Nearly 50% of overseas Chinese are from Guangdong. The River Pearl delta regions are the most populous. Industries: fishing, sugar cane, mining. Area: 197,000sq km (76,000 sq mi). Pop. (1990) 63,210,000.

Guangxi (Kwangsi) Autonomous region in S China; the capital is Nanning. It was established in 1958 for the Zhuang, China's largest minority nationality. Cultivation is limited by the mountainous terrain. Minerals include manganese, zinc, tin, tungsten and antimony. Industries: oil refining, fertilizers. Area: 220,495sq km (85,133sq mi). Pop. (1990) 21,000,000.

Guangzhou (Canton) Largest city in S China, on the River Pearl; capital of Guangdong province. It has been an important trading port since 300 BC. The birthplace of SUN YAT-SEN, it was the focal point of the nationalist revolution (1911). A military academy was established in 1924 under CHIANG KAI-SHEK. It is S China's leading industrial and commercial city. Industries: textiles, rubber products, shipbuilding, sugar refining, iron, steel. Pop. (1994) 3,114,000.

guano Dried excrement, mainly of seabirds and bats, that accumulates along coastlines and in caves. A valuable natural fertilizer, containing phosphorus, nitrogen and potassium, it is found mainly on islands off South America and Africa where there is a large population of pelicans, gannets and cormorants. Seal guano is also used.

Guantánamo City in E Cuba, served by the port of Caimanera on Guantánamo Bay, 10mi (16km) to the N. The US maintains a naval base on Guantánamo Bay under the terms of a treaty first signed in 1903. The city is the processing centre for a prosperous coffee and sugar-producing region. Pop. (1990 est.) 200,383.

guarana Climbing, fruit-bearing plant native to the Amazon basin. Locally, the fruit is prized for its single seed, which is roasted, ground and dissolved in water. Guarana's stimulant properties have become well-known in the West, where it is marketed in the form of soft drinks, tablets and chewing gum. Family Sapindaceae.

Guaraní Native South American tribe and language. The tribe's population has decreased greatly, although most Paraguayans are descended from Guaraní. Their language has survived as Paraguay's second national language.

Guardi, Francesco (1712–93) Venetian painter. His vivid, fluid views of Venice were "discovered" by the 19th-century Impressionists. His work is much freer than CANALETTO's.

Guarini, Guarino (1642–83) Italian architect and mathematician, b. Camillo Guarini. Influence by BORROMINI, he developed his own unique blend of BAROQUE and GOTHIC architecture. Guarini was responsible for the spread of the Baroque style beyond Italy. His surviving monuments include the Church of San Lorenzo (1667–82) and the Sindone Chapel (1673–77).

Guarneri Family of violin-makers who worked in Cremona, Italy. **Andrea** (*c*.1626–98) designed and built his instruments in the AMATI style, but the greatest craftsman of the family was his great-nephew (or possibly grandson) **Giuseppi Antonio** (1698–1744). He is known for the original designs of his violins, which can be compared in quality to those of STRADIVARI.

Guatemala Republic in Central America. Guatemala contains a densely populated, fertile mountain region. The capital, GUATEMALA CITY, is situated here. The highlands run in an E – W direction and contain many volcanoes. Guatemala is subject to frequent earthquakes and volcanic eruptions. Tajmulco, an inactive volcano, is the highest peak in Central America, at 4,211m (13,816ft). South of the highlands lie the Pacific coastal lowlands. North of the highlands is the thinly populated Atlantic plain and the vast Petén tropical forest. Guatemala's largest lake, Izabal, drains into the Caribbean Sea. **Climate** Guatemala lies in the tropics, and the lowlands are hot and rainy. The central mountain region is more temperate. Guatemala City, at *c*.1,500m (5,000ft) above sea level, has a pleasant, warm climate, with a marked dry season between November and April. **Vegetation** Hardwoods, such as mahogany, rubber, palm and chicozapote (from which chicle, used in chewing gum, is obtained), grow in the tropical forests in the N and mangrove swamps line the coast. Oak and willow grow in the highlands, with fir and pine at higher levels. Much of the land on the Pacific plains is farmed. **History and Politics** Between AD 300 and 900, the QUICHÉ branch of the MAYA ruled much of Guatemala but inexplicably abandoned their cities on the N plains. The Quiché ruins at Tikal are the tallest temple PYRAMIDS in the Americas. In 1523–24 the Spanish conquistador Pedro de Alvarado defeated the native tribes. In 1821, Guatemala became independent. From 1823 to 1839, it formed part of the Central American Federation. Various dictatorial regimes interfered in the affairs of other Central American states, arousing much resentment and leading to the establishment of the Central American Court of Justice. In 1941, Guatemala nationalized the German-owned coffee plantations. After World War 2, Guatemala embarked on further nationalization of plantations. In 1960, the mainly Quiché Guatemalan Revolutionary National Unity Movement (URNG) began a guerrilla war, which has killed more than 100,000 people. During the 1960s and 1970s, Guatemala was beset by terrorism, human rights abuses and political assassinations. In 1976, Guatemala City was devastated by an earthquake, which killed more than 22,000 people. In 1983, Guatemala reduced its claims to BELIZE. In 1984, civilian rule was restored, after the USA withdrew backing for the Guatemalan military. In 1995, an accord was signed recognizing the rights of the indigenous population. Sup-

---

GUATEMALA
AREA: 108,890sq km (42,042sq mi)
POPULATION: 12,222,000
CAPITAL (POPULATION): Guatemala City (1,167,000)

port for the URNG has dwindled. In 1996, Alvaro Arzú was elected president and a peace agreement with the URNG ended 35 years of civil war. In 1999, Alfonso Portillo was elected president, despite admitting that he had killed two men. **Economy** Guatemala is a lower-middle-income developing nation (1995 GDP per capita, US$3,340). Agriculture employs 50% of the workforce. Coffee, sugar, bananas and beef are leading exports. Other important crops are cardamom and cotton. Maize is the chief food crop, but Guatemala has to import food. Forestry is a major activity. Tourism and manufacturing are growing in importance. Manufactures: processed farm products, textiles, wood products, handicrafts.

Guatemala City (Ciudad Guatemala) Capital of Guatemala, on a plateau in the Sierra Madre; largest city in Central America. Founded in 1776, the city was the capital (1823–39) of the Central American Federation. It was badly damaged by earthquakes in 1917–18 and in 1976. Industries: mining, furniture, textiles, handicrafts. Pop. (1995) 1,167,000.

guava Any of 100 species of fruit-bearing trees or shrubs native to tropical America and the West Indies. The large white flowers produce a berry-like fruit, usually yellow with white, pink, or yellow flesh. Family Myrtaceae.

Guayaquil City on the River Guayas near the Gulf of Guayaquil, W Ecuador; chief port and largest city of Ecuador. Founded by the Spanish in the 1530s, Guayaquil was frequently attacked by buccaneers in the 17th and 18th centuries. Industries: textiles, pharmaceuticals, leather goods, cement, iron products, oil refining, fruit. Pop. (1997) 1,974,000.

gudgeon Freshwater CARP found in rivers from Britain to China. It has an elongated body, variable colour and a small mouth with barbels. Length: 20cm (8in). Species *Gobio gobio*.

guelder rose Plant of the HONEYSUCKLE family (Caprifoliaceae). It has globular clusters of white or pink flowers. Species *Viburnum opulus*.

Guelph Political faction in medieval Italy, opposed to the GHIBELLINE. The two factions were linked to rival families contending for the HOLY ROMAN EMPIRE in the 12th century. In 1198 OTTO IV (a Guelph) became Holy Roman emperor. In the battle for control of Italy, the Guelphs took the side of the papacy, while the Ghibellines backed the emperor FREDERICK II. The Ghibellines were defeated (1268) by the Guelphs at Tagliacozzo, but the feud lived on. *See also* HOHENSTAUFEN

guenon Any of *c*.17 species of long-tailed, slender, medium-sized African MONKEYS found S of the Sahara Desert. Guenons are omnivorous tree-dwellers, living in small troops dominated by an old male. Genus *Cercopithecus*.

Guernica Town in Vizcaya province, N Spain. It is a centre of BASQUE nationalism. The bombing of Guernica by German aircraft during the Spanish CIVIL WAR inspired Picasso's masterpiece, *Guernica* (1937).

Guernsey Second largest island in the CHANNEL ISLANDS; the capital is St Peter Port. It constitutes a bailiwick with several smaller islands, including Alderney and SARK. Its mild, sunny climate is ideal for dairy farming and horticulture. Tourism is also important. Area: 78sq km (30sq mi). Pop. (1991) 58,867.

guerrilla warfare Small-scale ground combat operations frequently designed to harass, rather than destroy, the enemy. The term was coined to describe the Spanish partisans actions against Napoleon I's armies in the PENINSULAR WAR (1807–14). Such tactics are especially suited to difficult terrain and rely on lightning attacks and aid from civilian sympathizers. In the 20th century, guerrilla tactics

have been used by many nationalist and communist movements, such as the Viet Cong in the VIETNAM WAR.

Guevara, "Che" (Ernesto) (1928–67) Argentine revolutionary leader. Guevara became associated with Fidel CASTRO in Mexico and returned with him to Cuba to play a leading role in the Cuban revolution (1956–59) against the BATISTA regime. Guevara became a minister in Castro's government. In 1965, he disappeared from public view. Two years later, he was captured and killed while trying to establish a communist guerrilla base in Bolivia. His remains were returned to Cuba in 1997.

Guggenheim US family of industrialists and philanthropists. **Meyer Guggenheim** (1828–1905), b. Switzerland, immigrated to Philadelphia (1847) and prospered in the lace import business. He bought silver and lead mines in Colorado. He retired, leaving control of his enterprises to his seven living sons. **Daniel** Guggenheim (1856–1930) took the leading role in expanding the family businesses. A prominent philanthropist, he established the Daniel and Florence Guggenheim Foundation. **Solomon R.** Guggenheim (1861–1949) endowed a foundation to foster nonobjective art: the Guggenheim Museum opened in New York City in 1959. **Simon** Guggenheim (1867–1941) was a US senator. In memory of his son, he established the John Simon Guggenheim Memorial Foundation, which offers fellowships to scholars and artists. **Harry Frank** Guggenheim (1890–1971) was US ambassador to Cuba (1929–33). **Peggy** Guggenheim (1898–1979) was a patron and collector of modern art.

guided missile Missile controlled throughout its flight by exterior or interior control systems. There are four types: surface-to-surface, surface-to-air, air-to-air and air-to-surface. The first guided missiles were the V1, V2 ROCKETS launched (1944) by Germany during World War 2. Post-war developments included the huge intercontinental ballistic missiles (ICBMs), with nuclear warheads and ranges of 10,000km (6,000mi). Submarine systems included Polaris and Trident. The multiple independently targeted re-entry vehicles (MIRVs) – ICBMs with many sub-missiles were developed in the late 1960s. The CRUISE MISSILE has wings like an airplane, making it capable of flying at low altitudes. Long-range ballistic missiles and cruise missiles use **inertial** guidance systems in which GYROSCOPES are connected to a computer that automatically adjusts the flight to follow a preset course without reference to the destination. They also possess **active** radar guidance, the missile itself containing a radio receiver and transmitter. Shorter-range missiles may be steered by an operator, via radio signals or trailing wire. "**Fire-and-forget**" missiles carry detectors that lock on to radiation emitted from their target. Those using **infrared** guidance lock on to heat sources, while radar-homing missiles home in on RADAR signals.

guild Association of craftsmen or merchants in medieval Europe. Merchant guilds probably developed from earlier religious associations and sometimes became more or less synonymous with municipal government. Guilds controlled economic conditions in the interest of their members but were eclipsed by the development of capitalism.

Guildford Four Three men and a woman of Irish extraction convicted in an English court of terrorist bombings in Guildford and Woolwich, S England, in 1975. Their life sentences were quashed on appeal in 1989. *See also* BIRMINGHAM SIX

Guillaume de Lorris (1210–37) French romance writer. He wrote the earlier part of the *Roman de la Rose* (*c*.1230), an allegory in which a courtly lover becomes enamoured of a rosebud. Guillaume died before it was finished, and Jean de Meung composed the second part.

guillemot Small, usually black and white seabird of the AUK family (Alcidae). It lives on cold Northern Hemisphere coastlines and dives for food. Length: *c*.43cm (17in). Genera *Cepphus* and *Uria*.

guillotine Mechanized device for execution by beheading adopted during the FRENCH REVOLUTION. First used in 1792, *c*.1,400 died under it during the REIGN OF TERROR. It remained in use in France until the abolition of CAPITAL PUNISHMENT in 1981. The term also describes a British parliamentary procedure, first used in 1887, by which a set time is allotted to various stages of a bill in order to speed its passage into law.

Guimard, Hector (1867–1942) French architect. He designed several entrances to the Paris Métro (1899–1901), using plant-like forms in cast iron. His Castel Béranger, an apartment block in Paris (1898), was one of the first examples of French ART NOUVEAU.

Guinea Republic in West Africa. Guinea lies on the Atlantic coast of West Africa. It can be divided into four regions: an alluvial coastal plain, which includes the capital, CONAKRY; the highland region of the Fouta Djallon, the source of one of Africa's longest rivers, the NIGER; the NE savanna; and the SE Guinea Highlands, which rise to 1,752m (5,748ft) at Mount Nimba. **Climate** Guinea has a tropical climate. Conakry has heavy rains between May and November. During the dry season, hot, harmattan winds blow from the SAHARA. **Vegetation** Mangrove swamps grow along parts of the coast. The Fouta Djallon is largely open grassland. Northeastern Guinea is tropical savanna, with acacia and shea scattered across the grassland. Rainforests of ebony, mahogany and teak grow in the Guinea Highlands. **History and politics** The NE Guinea plains formed part of the medieval empire of Ghana. The Malinke formed the Mali empire, which dominated the region in the 12th century. It was replaced by the SONGHAI empire. In the mid-15th century Portuguese explorers arrived, and the slave trade began soon afterwards. From the 17th century, other European slave traders became active in Guinea. In the early 18th century, the FULANI gained control of the Fouta Djallon. Following a series of wars, France gained control and made Guinea the colony of French Guinea (1891). France exploited Guinea's bauxite deposits, and mining unions developed. In 1958, Guinea voted to become an independent republic. France severed all aid. Guinea's first president, Sékou Touré (1958–84), adopted a Marxist programme of reform and embraced Pan-Africanism. Opposition parties were banned and dissent was brutally suppressed. In 1970, Guinea was invaded by Portuguese Guinea (GUINEA-BISSAU). Conakry acted as the headquarters for independence movements in Guinea-Bissau. A military coup followed Touré's death and Colonel Lansana Conté established (1984) the Military Committee for National Recovery (CMRN). Conté improved relations with the West and introduced free enterprise policies. In 1992, civil unrest forced the introduction of a multiparty system. Conté was elected president amid claims of electoral fraud. In 1996, a military coup was defeated. Conté was re-elected in 1998. **Economy** Guinea is a low-income

developing country (1992 GDP per capita, US$592). It is the world's second-largest producer of bauxite (after Australia), which accounts for 90% of its exports. Guinea has 25% of the world's known reserves of bauxite. Other natural resources include diamonds, gold, iron ore and uranium. Agriculture (mainly at subsistence level) employs 78% of the workforce. Major crops include bananas, cassava, coffee and palm kernels. Cattle and other livestock are raised in highland areas.

Guinea-Bissau Small republic in West Africa; the capital and chief port is BISSAU. **Land and climate** Guinea-Bissau is mostly low-lying, with a broad, swampy coastal plain and broad river estuaries. The land rises to low plateaux in the E. Guinea-Bissau has a tropical climate, with a dry season (December to May) and a rainy season. Mangrove forests line the coasts, and dense rainforest covers much of the coastal plain. Inland, forests merge into tropical savanna, with open grassland on the high ground. **History** It was first visited by Portuguese navigators in 1446. Between the 17th and early 19th centuries, Portugal used the coast as a base for the slave trade. In 1836, Portugal appointed a governor to administer Guinea-Bissau and the CAPE VERDE Islands, but in 1879 the two territories were separated and Guinea-Bissau became the colony of Portuguese Guinea. In 1956, African nationalists founded the African Party for the Independence of Guinea and Cape Verde (PAIGC). Portugal's determination to keep its overseas territories forced the PAIGC to begin a guerrilla war (1963), and by 1968 it held 66% of the country. In 1972, a rebel National Assembly in the PAIGC-controlled area voted to form the independent republic of Guinea-Bissau. In 1974, it formally achieved independence (followed by Cape Verde in 1975). In 1980, an army coup led by Major João Vieira overthrew the government. The new Revolutionary Council resisted unification with Cape Verde, concentrating on national policies and socialist reforms. In 1991, the PAIGC voted to introduce a multiparty system. The PAIGC won the 1994 elections, and Vieira was re-elected president. In 1998, hundreds of people were killed in fighting between government forces backed by Senegalese troops and rebels led by General Ansumane Mane. Kumba Yalá of the Party for Social Renovation defeated the PAIGC in the 2000 elections. **Economy** Guinea-Bissau is a poor country, (1995 GDP per capita, $US790) with agriculture (mostly subsistence) employing more than 80% of its workforce. Coconuts and peanuts constitute 40% of Guinea-Bissau's exports. Fishing is also important.

guinea fowl Pheasant-like gamebird of s Africa. The common domestic guinea hen (*Numida meleagris*) is blue, grey or black with white spots and an ornamental crest. Length: to 50cm (20in). Family Numididae.

guinea pig Type of CAVY found in South America. The domestic *Cavia porcellus* is a popular pet. It has a large head, soft fur, short legs and no tail. It eats grass and other green plants. *Cavia aperea* is a wild species. Family Caviidae.

Guinevere In ARTHURIAN ROMANCE, King ARTHUR's queen who was loved by LANCELOT OF THE LAKE. In Thomas MALORY's *Morte d'Arthur* (*c*.1469) she betrayed the king and was sentenced to die. Guinevere was rescued by Lancelot and later restored to Arthur.

GUINEA
AREA: 245,860sq km (94,927sq mi)
POPULATION: 7,830,000
CAPITAL (POPULATION): Conakry (1,508,000)

GUINEA-BISSAU
AREA: 36,120sq km (13,946sq mi)
POPULATION: 1,197,000
CAPITAL (POPULATION): Bissau (145,000)

Guinness, Sir Alec (1914–2000) English stage and film actor. His acclaimed stage roles included Hamlet (1938) and Macbeth (1966). He is best-known for his film performances in the EALING STUDIOS comedies, such as *The Kind Hearts and Coronets* (1949), *Lavender Hill Mob* (1951) and *The Ladykillers* (1955). Guinness won an Academy Award for best actor in *Bridge on the River Kwai* (1957). Other films include *Lawrence of Arabia* (1962), *Doctor Zhivago* (1965), *Star Wars* (1977), *A Passage to India* (1984) and *Little Dorrit* (1988). He also appeared as George Smiley in the television adaptations of John Le Carré's *Tinker, Tailor, Soldier, Spy* (1979) and *Smiley's People* (1982). He was knighted in 1959.

Guiscard, Robert (1015–85) Norman French nobleman and soldier. He drove the Byzantines out of southern Italy and established Norman power in Sicily. He delivered Pope GREGORY VII from Emperor HENRY IV.

Guise, House of Ducal house of Lorraine, the most powerful family in 16th-century France. **Claude**, Duke of Lorraine (1496–1550), founded the house in 1528. His eldest son, **Francis** (1519–63), supervised the massacre of HUGUENOTS at Vassy in 1562, precipitating the French Wars of RELIGION. His second son, **Charles** (1524–74), cardinal of Guise, played a major role at the Council of TRENT. His daughter, **Mary of Guise**, married JAMES V and was the mother of MARY, QUEEN OF SCOTS. Francis' son, **Henri** (1550–88), helped to organize the SAINT BARTHOLOMEW'S DAY MASSACRE (1572) and led the Holy League, which vehemently opposed Protestantism. Guise power declined when HENRY IV took the throne.

guitar Plucked stringed musical instrument. The guitar is first known with the Moors, who introduced it to Spain perhaps as early as the 12th century. The early guitar had four double strings and was similar to the LUTE. The popularity of the lute in the 17th century extended to the guitar; the most famous guitarist of the time was Robert de Visée (*c*.1650–*c*.1725). The modern guitar dates from the design of Antonio de Torres Jurado (1817–92). Guitar technique was developed by Fernando Sor (1778–1839). The Spanish guitar has a flat back, round sound hole, fretted fingerboard and six strings usually tuned in fourths. In the 20th-century, the virtuoso playing of Andrés SEGOVIA inspired compositions by Manuel de FALLA and Heitor VILLA-LOBOS. In 1946, Les Paul invented the electric guitar, now a standard instrument in blues, pop and rock music. Acoustic and semi-acoustic guitars are also widely used in folk and jazz. The **bass** guitar usually has four strings, tuned one octave below the lowest strings of the standard guitar.

Guiyang (Kuei-yang, or Kweiyang) City in sw China; capital of GUIZHOU province. An administrative centre under the Ming and Qing dynasties, it developed rapidly after World War 2, and is now an important rail junction and industrial base. Industries: iron and steel, cement, paper, textiles, chemicals. Pop. (1994) 1,131,000.

Guizhou (Kweichow) Province in s China; the capital is Guiyang. Guizhou became a Chinese province in the Ming dynasty. During World War 2 it served as a military base for Allied forces. It was taken by Chinese communists in 1950. Industries: coal mining, iron ore, mercury. Area: 174,060sq km (67,204sq mi). Pop. (1990) 32,370,000.

Gujarat State in w India, on the Arabian Sea; the capital is Gandhinagar. Absorbed into the MAURYAN EMPIRE in the 3rd century BC, it was a centre of JAINISM under the Maitraka Dynasty (5th–8th centuries AD). In the early 15th century it was an autonomous Muslim sultanate. Under British rule it became a province (1857).

After independence it was established as a separate state. It is highly industrialized with substantial reserves of oil and gas. Industries: cotton textiles, salt mining, electrical engineering, petrochemicals. Area: 195,984sq km (75,669sq mi). Pop. (1994 est.) 44,235,000.

Gujarati (Gujerati) Modern language of N India, the official language of GUJARAT. Belonging to the Indic branch of INDO-EUROPEAN LANGUAGES, it began to evolve in *c*.AD 1000. Gujarati is spoken by more than 30 million inhabitants of Gujarat and other Asian communities worldwide.

gulag Network of detention centres and forced-labour prisons within the former Soviet Union. The term is an acronym in Russian for Chief Administration of Corrective Labour Camps. Established in 1918, gulags were secret CONCENTRATION CAMPS used to silence political and religious dissenters. The regime was forcefully described by Alexander Solzhenitsyn in *The Gulag Archipelago* (1973).

Gujranwala City in the Punjab, NE Pakistan. It was a major centre of SIKH power in the 18th and 19th centuries. Gujranwala is a market centre for a district producing wheat, rice, sugar and oilseed. Industries: ironware, textiles, handicrafts. Pop. (1995) 1,663,000.

Gulf of Mexico *See* MEXICO, GULF OF

Gulf States Countries around the Persian (Arabian) Gulf, including IRAN, IRAQ, KUWAIT, SAUDI ARABIA, QATAR, the UNITED ARAB EMIRATES and the BAHRAIN islands. Since the 1960s, the political and economic importance of the states has been bolstered by the extensive exploitation of oil reserves. The term also applies to the US states bordering the Gulf of Mexico: Florida, Alabama, Mississippi, Louisiana and Texas.

Gulf Stream Relatively fast-moving current of the N Atlantic Ocean. It flows from the straits of Florida, USA, along the E coast of North America, then E across the Atlantic to the NW European coast. The current warms coastal climates along its course.

Gulf War (16 January 1991–28 February 1991) Military action by a US-led coalition of 32 states to expel Iraqi forces from KUWAIT. Iraqi forces invaded Kuwait (2 August 1990) and claimed it as an Iraqi province. On 7 August 1990, Operation Desert Shield began a mass deployment of coalition forces to protect Saudi oil reserves. Economic sanctions failed to secure Iraqi withdrawal, and the UN Security Council set a deadline of 15 January 1991, for the removal of Iraqi forces. Iraqi president Saddam HUSSEIN ignored the ultimatum, and General Norman SCHWARZKOPF launched Operation Desert Storm. Within a week, extensive coalition air attacks had secured control of the skies. Iraqi ground forces were defenceless against the coalition's technologically advanced weaponry. Iraq launched Scud missile attacks on Saudi Arabia and Israel, in the hope of weakening Arab support for the coalition. On 24 February, the ground war was launched. Iraqi troops burned Kuwaiti oil wells as they fled. Kuwait was liberated two days later, and a cease-fire was declared on 28 February. Saddam Hussein remained in power. The Gulf War claimed the lives of 234 Allied troops and between 85,000 and 150,000 Iraqi soldiers. Some 33,000 Kuwaitis were killed or captured.

gull (seagull) Any of various ground-nesting birds found along coastlines worldwide. They eat carrion, refuse, fish, shellfish, eggs and young birds. The herring gull (*Larus argentatus*) is grey and white with black markings, hooked bill, pointed wings and webbed feet. It grows to 56–66cm (22–26in). The black-headed gull (*L. ridibundus*) is smaller, with black feathers on its head in summer. Family Laridae.

gum Sticky secretions of plants. Gums are chemically complex, consisting mainly of various saccharides bound to organic acids. **Gum arabic** is the most widely used of the water-soluble adhesives. **Gum tragacanth** is used as a binding agent in pill manufacture and as a food emuslifier. *See also* AGAR; EUCALYPTUS; RESIN

gun Tubular weapon firing a projectile, usually by force of explosion. The term is now restricted to ARTILLERY pieces with a relatively high muzzle velocity and a flat trajectory. PISTOLS, RIFLES and MACHINE GUNS are usually described as guns; mortars and howitzers are not.

Gunn, Thom (Thomson William) (1929–) English poet. Shortly after the publication of his debut collection of verse, *Fighting Terms* (1954), Gunn took up permanent residence in the USA. Other volumes include *My Sad Captains* (1961) and *The Passages of Joy* (1982).

Gunnell, Sally Janet Jane (1966–) English athlete. In the 1992 Olympic Games, she captained the British women's team and won a gold medal in the 400m hurdles. Gunnell repeated this success in the 1993 World Championships, breaking the world record. A foot injury prevented her defence of the world title in 1995, and forced her retirement from the 1996 Olympic Games.

gunpowder EXPLOSIVE mixture of saltpetre (potassium nitrate), charcoal and sulphur. Invented by the Chinese, gunpowder was used in European warfare from the 14th century to *c*.1900, when it was replaced by smokeless powders, such as DYNAMITE.

Gunpowder Plot (November 1605) Failed Roman Catholic conspiracy to blow up JAMES I of England and his Parliament. The leader was Robert Catesby, and the chief perpetrator was Guy FAWKES. The plotters were arrested on 5 November, a date now celebrated in Britain as Guy Fawkes Day (Bonfire Night).

guppy Small, freshwater fish native to NE South America and the West Indies. A popular aquarium fish, male guppies have metallic blue-green coloration. The females breed live young at monthly intervals. They feed on mosquito larvae and algae. Length: up to 6cm (2.5in).

Gupta dynasty (*c*.AD 320–*c*.550) Ruling house whose kingdom covered most of N India. It was founded by Chandragupta I. The Gupta dynasty embraced Buddhism and is seen as a golden age. It reached its greatest extent at the end of the 4th century but declined at the end of the 5th century under concerted attack from the HUNS.

Gurdjieff, George Ivanovich (1877–1949) Russian spiritualist. In Paris he founded (1922) the Institute for the Harmonious Development of Man. His students were taught to attain a higher level of consciousness through dance, lectures and labour. His writings include *Meetings with Remarkable Men* (1963).

Gurdwara (Sanskrit, Guru's doorway) Sikh temple housing a copy of the *Adi Granth*, the holy scripture of SIKHISM. There are several historically important *gurdwaras*, such as the Golden Temple of AMRITSAR, Punjab.

Gurkha Hindu ruling caste of Nepal since 1768. They speak a SANSKRIT language. The name also denotes a Nepalese soldier in the British or Indian army.

gurnard Tropical, marine, bottom-dwelling fish. It has a large spiny head and enlarged pectoral fins. Length: to 50cm (20in). Family Triglidae.

guru Personal teacher and spiritual master. In traditional Hindu education, boys lived in the home of a *guru*, who guided their studies of the VEDAS and saw to their physical health and ethical training. In SIKHISM, the title *guru* was assumed by the first ten leaders. Guruship was terminated in 1708.

Gustavus I (Vasa) (1496–1560) King of Sweden (1523–60) and founder of the Vasa dynasty. In 1520, he led a victorious rebellion against the invading Danes. In 1523 Gustavus was elected king. During his reign Sweden gained independence, the Protestant church was established and the Bible was translated into Swedish.

Gustavus II (Adolphus) (1594–1632) King of Sweden (1611–32). His reign was distinguished by constitutional and educational reforms. Gustavus ended war with Denmark (1613) and Russia (1617). Hoping to increase Sweden's control of the Baltic, he entered the THIRTY YEARS' WAR (1618–48). Gustavus' victory over Walllenstein at the Battle of Breitenfeld (1631) earned him the epithet "Lion of the North". He was killed during the Swedish victory at the Battle of Lützen.

Gustavus III (1746–92) King of Sweden (1771–92). During his reign, known as the Gustavian Enlightenment, he instituted financial reforms, religious toleration, a free press and a strong navy. A gifted writer and patron of the arts, he founded the Swedish Academy.

Gutenberg, Johann (1400–68) German goldsmith and printer, credited with inventing PRINTING from movable metallic type. He produced the first printed Bible, known as the *Gutenberg Bible* or *Mazarin Bible* (*c*.1455).

Guthrie, "Woody" (Woodrow Wilson) (1912–67) US folk singer, guitarist and songwriter. His social-protest poetry captured the spirit of the Great Depression and championed workers' rights. Guthrie's most famous song is probably "This Land Is Your Land" (1944). He greatly influenced later artists, such as Bob DYLAN.

Guyana (formerly British Guiana) Republic on the Atlantic Ocean, NE South America; the capital is GEORGETOWN. **Land and climate** More than 80% of Guyana is forested. Its interior includes rainforests, savannas, valleys of the River Essequibo and the Pakaraima Mountains, which rise to 2,772m (9,094ft) at Mount Roraima. The narrow, alluvial coastal plain is largely reclaimed marshland and mangrove swamp. Guyana has a hot and humid climate, but temperatures are lower in the S and W highlands. Rainfall is heavy. There are two dry seasons: February to April, and August to November. **History** The Dutch settled here in 1581, and the Treaty of Breda (1667) awarded them the area. Land reclamation for plantations began in the 18th century, under the control of the Dutch West India Company. Britain gained control in the early 19th century and set up the colony of British Guiana (1831). In 1838, slavery was abolished. After World War 2, progress towards self-government was achieved with a new constitution (1952) and the election of Dr Cheddi Jagan. In 1966, British Guiana became independent, and Forbes Burnham of the socialist People's National Congress (PNC) became the first prime minister. Ethnic conflict between the majority East Indian and African minority marred much of the late 1960s. In 1970, Guyana became a republic. In 1980, Burnham became president, and a new constitution increased his power. After Burnham's death (1985), Desmond Hoyte introduced liberal reforms. In 1992 elections, Hoyte was defeated by Jagan. Jagan's People's Progressive Party (PPP) formed the first non-PNC government since independence. After Jagan's death (1997), his wife, Janet Jagan, was elected president.

GUYANA
AREA: 214,970sq km (83,000sq mi)
POPULATION: 891,000
CAPITAL (POPULATION): Georgetown (254,000)

In 1999, she resigned on grounds of poor health and was replaced by Bharrat Jagdeo. **Economy** Guyana is a poor, developing country (1995 GDP per capita, $US2,420). The economy is dominated by mining and agriculture. Principal exports: sugar, rice, bauxite. Diamond and gold mining are important. Fishing and forestry industries are expanding, as is eco-tourism.

Guy of Lusignan (1140–94) King of the Latin kingdom of Jerusalem (1186–92) and of Cyprus (1192–94). He was defeated and captured by SALADIN at Hattin (1187). Guy later fought in the Third CRUSADE (1189–91), resigned the throne to Conrad of Montferrat (1192) and was granted Cyprus by Richard I of England.

Guzmán Blanco, Antonio (1829–99) Venezuelan statesman, president (1870–88). An autocrat, he enacted extensive social reforms, including free education.

Gwalior City in Madhya Pradesh, central India. Founded in the 6th century, it was the capital of the former princely state of Gwalior (dissolved 1956). The city is overlooked by the Gwalior fort, a stronghold on the Rock of Gwalior, which houses elaborate shrines, temples and the palace of Man Singh. Industries: cotton, flour, oilseed processing, textiles, porcelain, plastics. Pop. (1991) 691,000.

Gwent Former county in SE Wales. It was formed in 1974 from most of Monmouthshire, part of Breconshire, and Newport. It 1996 Gwent was abolished and Monmouthshire was re-constituted with new boundaries and four new county boroughs, including Blaenau Gwent.

Gwyn, Nell (1650–87) English actress. Originally an orange-seller, see took to the boards in John Dryden's *The Indian Emperor* (1665). Nell Gwyn was CHARLES II's mistress, probably bearing him two sons.

Gwynedd County in NW Wales, on the Irish Sea coast; the administrative centre is CAERNARVON. Gwynedd is rugged and mountainous and includes most of the SNOWDONIA National Park. Industries: slate quarrying, hydroelectric power, tourism. Area: 3,866sq km (1,493sq mi). Pop. (1990) 235,452.

gymnastics Multidisciplined sport requiring suppleness, strength and poise in a variety of regulated exercises. Men and women compete separately in individual and team events. Men perform in six events: vault, parallel bars, horizontal bars, pommel horse, rings and floor exercises. Women perform in four events: vault, balance beam, asymmetrical bars and floor exercises. Exercises are rated in terms of difficulty, and marks out of ten are awarded for technical skill and artistry. The World Championships were inaugurated in 1950, and women's gymnastics became an Olympic sport in 1952.

gymnosperm Seed plant with naked seeds borne on scales, usually cones. Most EVERGREENS are gymnosperms. LARCH and some other CONIFERS, however, are DECIDUOUS. All living seed-bearing plants are divided into two main groups: gymnosperms and ANGIOSPERMS. In the Five KINGDOMS classification system, gymnosperms comprise three distinct phyla: Coniferophyta (such as PINE, SPRUCE, and CEDAR); Ginkgophyta (a single species, the GINKGO); and Gnetophyta (strange plants such as *Welwitschia*, *Ephedra* and *Gnetum*).

gynaecology Area of medicine concerned with the female reproductive organs. Its study and practice is often paired with OBSTETRICS.

Györ City and port in NW Hungary, at the confluence of the rivers Rába and Danube. Famous for its 12th-century cathedral, its main industries are steel, textiles, flour milling and distilling. Pop. (1997) 127,000.

gypsum (hydrated calcium sulphate, $CaSO_4.2H_2O$) Most common sulphate mineral. Huge beds of gypsum occur in sedimentary rocks, where it is associated with HALITE. It crystallizes in the monoclinic system. Varieties are ALABASTER, selenite (transparent and foliated), and satin spar (silky and fibrous). It is a source of plaster of Paris. Hardness 2; r.d. 2.3.

gypsy *See* ROMANY

gypsy moth Small tussock MOTH with black zigzag markings; the female is a lighter colour. Length: 5cm (2in). Family Lepidoptera; species *Lymantria dispar*.

gyrfalcon Largest of all FALCONS, *Falco rusticolus*, is native to the mountains and tundra of Scandinavia and Arctic regions. It hunts low to the ground, feeding mainly on ground-dwelling birds. Plumage is a mottled greybrown. Length: to 61cm (24in). Family Falconidae.

gyrocompass Navigational aid incorporating a continuously driven GYROSCOPE. The spinning axis of the gyroscope is horizontal, and its direction indicates true N, irrespective of the course of the craft. Invented *c*.1908, the gyrocompass has replaced the magnetic COMPASS for NAVIGATION in most ships and aircraft.

gyroscope Symmetrical spinning disc that can adapt to any orientation, being mounted in gimbals (a pair of rings with one swinging freely in the other). When a gyroscope is spinning, a change in the orientation of the gimbals does not change the orientation of the spinning wheel. This means that changes in direction of an aircraft or ship can be determined without external references. A gyrostabilizer is used to steady the roll of a craft, and a GYROCOMPASS is a gyroscope modified to act as a COMPASS. When TORQUE is applied to a fast-spinning gyroscope, it produces a phenomenon known as PRECESSION: the gyroscope revolves about a fixed point with the axis of spin describing a cone around the vertical. The gyroscope was invented (1852) by Jean FOUCAULT. *See also* AUTOMATIC PILOT; NAVIGATION

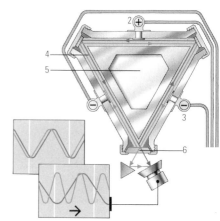

▲ **gyrocompass** A laser gyrocompass measures rotation by comparing the wavelength of lasers (1). A current is passed from a cathode (2) to two anodes (3) creating two lasers in a gas-filled triangular chamber (4) drilled in a solid glass block (5). Part of the lasers are bled out at one end of the gyrocompass (6) and the wavelength measured. If the gyrocompass rotates to the left the path of the laser travelling to the left is reduced fractionally reducing its wavelength. The opposite occurs to the other laser. A sensor (7) compares the two lasers to measure the rotation.

H/h, eighth letter of the Roman alphabet. It is derived from an Egyptian hieroglyph for rope. The Semites modified it to form the letter cheth. *It was taken into the Greek alphabet (c.600 BC) as the letter* eta.

Haakon IV (1204–63) King of Norway (1217–63). He reigned at the start of medieval Norway's "golden age" (1217–1319). Haakon secured the submission of Iceland and Greenland to his rule. A patron of learning and the arts, SNORRI STURLUSON lived at his court. Haakon died in the Orkneys after a campaign against the Scots that saw the loss of the HEBRIDES to Alexander III.

Haakon VII (1872–1957) King of Norway (1905–57). He was elected king when Norway regained its independence from Sweden. In 1940 Haakon was forced into exile by the German invasion and led a government-in-exile (1940–45) in London, England.

Haarlem City on the River Spaarne, W Netherlands; capital of North Holland province. By the 12th century Haarlem was a fortified town. A centre of Dutch painting in the 16th and 17th centuries, it is famous for its tulip bulbs. Industries: electronic equipment, publishing, printing. Pop. (1994) 150,213.

habeas corpus (Lat. you should have the body) Writ in law for the protection of the liberty of the individual. Of the several kinds of *habeas corpus*, the most important is the *habeas corpus ad subjiciendum*, which commands a person who holds another in custody to bring the prisoner before the court and to state the cause of detention.

Haber process Industrial process for converting atmospheric nitrogen into AMMONIA. A mixture of nitrogen and hydrogen is passed over a heated CATALYST at a pressure of c.1,000 atmospheres. The chemical reaction $N_2 + 3H_2 \rightarrow 2NH_3$ occurs. By "fixing" atmospheric nitrogen, it is possible to convert ammonia to NITRIC ACID and thus produce the NITRATES that are used in the manufacture of fertilizers and explosives. It was invented (1908–09) by German chemists Fritz Haber and Carl Bosch. *See also* NITROGEN FIXATION

Habermas, Jürgen (1929–) German social philosopher. A member of the FRANKFURT SCHOOL, he continued Theodor ADORNO's reappraisal of MARXISM. Habermas' early works, such as *Knowledge and Human Interests* (1968), sought to reveal the ideological history behind the development of science. His later works, such as *Theory of Communicative Action* (1982), adopt a more language-based approach while retaining a commitment to truth and rational consensus.

habitat Place in which an organism normally lives. A habitat is defined by characteristic physical conditions and the presence of other organisms. *See also* ECOSYSTEM

Habsburg (Hapsburg) Austrian royal dynasty, a leading ruling house in Europe from the 13th to 19th century. It became a major force when RUDOLF I was elected (1273) king of the Germans. He established the core of the Hapsburg dominions in AUSTRIA, Styria and Carniola. FREDERICK III arranged the marriage (1477) by which his son, Maximilian, gained Burgundy, The Netherlands and Luxembourg. MAXIMILIAN I extended his father's marriage diplomacy to his own son, Philip, who acquired (1496) Castile, Aragón, Granada, Spanish America, Naples, Sicily and Sardinia. When CHARLES V became emperor in 1519, he ruled over the largest European empire since Charlemagne. His brother, FERDINAND I, gained Hungary and Bohemia through marriage. In 1556, Charles abdicated, leaving his Spanish titles to his son, PHILIP II, and his Austrian titles to Ferdinand I. In 1700, the Spanish line ended and in the subsequent War of the SPANISH SUCCESSION (1703–13) power passed to the BOURBONS. In 1740, the male line of the Austrian branch ended, but MARIA THERESA re-established the house as that of Habsburg-Lorraine, although she lost Silesia. At the end of the Napoleonic Wars (1803–15) the habsburgs lost the Austrian Netherlands and the title of Holy Roman Emperor, but continued to control Austria. By 1867, the Habsburg Empire was reduced to the AUSTRO-HUNGARIAN EMPIRE. FRANZ JOSEPH saw the disintegration of his empire in World War 1. It finally broke up in 1918, when CHARLES I was deposed. *See also* HOLY ROMAN EMPIRE

hacker In computing, person who obtains unauthorized access to a computer DATABASE. A hacker, who usually gains access through the public telephone system using a MODEM, may read or alter the information in the database.

Hackman, Gene (1931–) US film actor. He gained an international reputation with character parts in such films as *Bonnie and Clyde* (1967) and *I Never Sang for My Father* (1969). Hackman won an Academy Award for best actor in *The French Connection* (1971) and went on to star in *The Conversation* (1974) and *Mississippi Burning* (1988). His performance in *Unforgiven* (1992) earned him an Oscar for best supporting actor.

haddock Marine fish found in cold and temperate waters, mainly in the Northern Hemisphere. Dark grey and silver, it has a dark blotch near the pectoral fins. Length: to c.90cm (36in); weight: to 11kg (24.5lb). Family Gadidae; species *Melanogrammus aeglefinus*.

Hades In Greek mythology, god of the dead; the name is also applied to the realm over which he ruled. The dead were ferried by CHARON across the river STYX to the realm of Hades. Once there, the virtuous went to ELYSIUM. The wicked were confined to Tartarus, the bottomless pit. Hades' queen was PERSEPHONE. In Roman mythology Hades was known as PLUTO.

Hadlee, Sir Richard John (1951–) New Zealand cricketer. He played English county cricket for Nottinghamshire. A right-arm fast bowler and left-handed batsman, Hadlee took 431 wickets and scored 3,124 runs in 86 test matches between 1973 and 1990. He is the second highest wicket-taker in test match history (after KAPIL DEV). Hadlee was knighted in 1990.

Hadrian, Publius Aelius (AD 76–138) Roman emperor (117–138). Nephew and protégé of Emperor TRAJAN, Hadrian adopted a policy of imperial retrenchment, discouraging new conquests, relinquishing territory hard to defend and ordering the construction of HADRIAN'S WALL in Britain. One of the most cultured of the Roman emperors, he erected many fine buildings, notably the vast Hadrian's Villa at Tivoli, and also rebuilt the PANTHEON. The erection of a shrine to Jupiter on the site of the Temple in Jerusalem provoked a Jewish revolt (132–135), which was ruthlessly suppressed.

Hadrian's Wall Defensive fortification in N England, erected (AD 122–36) on the orders of the Roman Emperor HADRIAN. It extended 118km (74mi) and was c.2.3m (7.5ft) thick and 1.8 to 4.6m (6–15ft) high. Forts were built along its length. Extensive stretches survive.

hadron Group of SUBATOMIC PARTICLES that are influenced by the STRONG NUCLEAR FORCE. The group can be divided into BARYONS, which have a half-integral SPIN, and MESONS, which have zero or integral spin. More than

150 hadrons have been discovered and, with the exception of the proton and antiproton, they are all unstable. LEPTONS are not subject to strong nuclear force and do not have a substructure of QUARKS. *See also* MATTER

haemoglobin Red-coloured PROTEIN present in the ERYTHROCYTES (red-BLOOD cells) of vertebrates. It carries oxygen to all cells in the body by combining with it to form oxyhaemoglobin. Oxygen attaches to the haem part of the protein, which contains iron; the globin part is a globular PROTEIN.

haemophilia Hereditary BLOOD clotting disorder causing prolonged external or internal bleeding, often without apparent cause. **Haemophilia A** is caused by inability to synthesize blood factor VIII, a substance essential to clotting. This can be managed with injections of factor VIII. The rarer **haemophilia B** is caused by a deficiency of blood factor IX. The gene for both types is passed on almost exclusively from mother to son.

haemorrhage Loss of BLOOD from a damaged vessel. It may be external, flowing from a wound, or internal, as from internal injury or a bleeding ulcer. Blood loss from an artery is most serious, causing shock and death if untreated. Chronic bleeding can lead to ANAEMIA. Internal bleeding is signalled by blood in the urine or sputum.

haemorrhoids (piles) Distended blood vessels at the juncture of the rectum and the anal canal. Often caused by prolonged constipation, they are usually treated by injections of a sclerosing agent. If they cause discomfort, bleed and protrude from the anus, surgery may be required.

haemostasis Process by which bleeding stops. BLOOD vessels constrict, platelets aggregate and plasma coagulates to form filaments of FIBRIN.

Hafiz (*c*.1325–*c*.1390) (Shams ud-Din Mohammad) Persian poet. His verse, in rhyming couplets, deals powerfully with sensual pleasures, most famously in the *Divan*. Hafiz was a devout Sufi and DERVISH, and much of his poetry is religious in content. *See also* SUFISM

hafnium (symbol Hf) Silvery metallic element, one of the TRANSITION ELEMENTS, discovered in 1923. Hafnium's chief source is as a by-product in obtaining the element ZIRCONIUM. It is used as a neutron absorber in reactor control rods. Properties: at.no. 72; r.a.m. 178.49; r.d. 13.31; m.p. 2,227°C (4,041°F); b.p. 4,602°C (8,316°F); most common isotope Hf^{180} (35.24%).

Haganah (Heb. defence) Jewish militia in Palestine formed (1920) to protect Jewish settlements from Palestinian attack. Allied with the extreme Irgun group in 1945, it attempted to change British policy on Jewish immigration and received aid from US Zionists. After the creation of the state of ISRAEL in 1948, the Haganah became the official Israeli army. *See also* ZIONISM

hagfish (slime eel) Eel-like, primitive, jawless fish found in temperate to cold marine waters. It has underdeveloped eyes and four to six fleshy whiskers around its sucking mouth. It is a scavenger and feeds on dead or dying fish. It secretes a slimy mucus from pores along its sides. Length: to 80cm (32in). Family Myxinidae.

Haggadah Story of the EXODUS and redemption of the people of Israel by God, read during PASSOVER services. Developed over centuries, it includes excerpts from the Bible, rabbinical writings, psalms, stories and prayers.

Haggai (active 6th century BC) Old Testament prophet, probably not the author of the Book of Haggai, the tenth of the 12 books of the Minor Prophets. The book records four prophesies made by Haggai in 521 BC, in which he urged the Jews to make haste in rebuilding the TEMPLE.

Haggard, Sir (Henry) Rider (1856–1925) English novelist. His colonial service in South Africa provided the background for his hugely successful romantic adventure novels, such as *King Solomon's Mines* (1885), *She* (1887) and *Allan Quatermain* (1887). Other books include *Rural England* (1902). He was knighted in 1912.

Hagia Sophia (Aya Sofia) Byzantine church in Istanbul. It was built (532–37) for Emperor JUSTINIAN I. A masterpiece of BYZANTINE ARCHITECTURE, it was the first building to use pendentives to support a central DOME. A series of domes extends the lofty interior space. The church was converted into a mosque in 1453. The Hagia Sophia now acts as a museum.

Hague, William Jefferson (1961–) British politician, Conservative Party leader (1997–). He entered parliament in 1989. In 1995, Hague joined John MAJOR's cabinet as secretary of state for Wales. After the Conservative's landslide defeat in the 1997 general election, Hague emerged as the youngest Tory leader since William PITT in 1783. His anti-European single currency platform pushed the party towards the Thatcherite right.

Hague, The ('s-Gravenhage or Den Haag) City in the w Netherlands; capital of South Holland province. It is the seat of the Dutch government. Founded in the 15th century, the city has been an intellectual and political centre since the 17th century. The Hague has been the seat of the International Court of Justice since 1945. Much of the economy depends on its diplomatic activities. Industries: textiles, pottery, furniture, chemicals. Pop. (1996) 443,000.

Hahn, Otto (1879–1968) German physical chemist. He worked on RADIOACTIVITY with William RAMSAY and Edward RUTHERFORD. In 1906, Hahn returned to Germany to work with Lise MEITNER. In 1917, they discovered the radioactive element PROTACTINIUM. Assisted by Fritz Strassmann, Hahn and Meitner investigated Enrico FERMI's work on the NEUTRON bombardment of URANIUM. In 1938 Meitner was forced to flee Nazi Germany, shortly before Hahn and Strassmann discovered nuclear FISSION. Hahn was awarded the 1944 Nobel Prize for chemistry.

Hahnemann, (Christian Friedrich) Samuel (1755–1843) German physician. He popularized HOMEOPATHY, a system of medical treatment based on the idea that a disease should be treated with minute doses of agents that produce the symptoms of the disease.

hahnium (symbol Ha) Synthetic, radioactive TRANSACTINIDE ELEMENT. Six isotopes have been synthesized. It was first reported (1967) by a Soviet team at Dubna. They claimed the isotopes of mass numbers 260 and 261, as a result of bombarding AMERICIUM with neon ions. In 1970 a team at the University of California claimed the isotope 260 (half-life 1.6 seconds) obtained by bombarding CALIFORNIUM with nitrogen nuclei. The element is named after Otto HAHN. Properties: at.no. 105

Haifa (Hefa) City on Mount Carmel, Israel. It is the centre of the BAHA'I religion. Haifa is Israel's major port and third-largest city. Industries: textiles, chemicals, shipbuilding, oil-refining. Pop. (1992) 251,000.

Haig, Douglas, 1st Earl (1861–1928) British field marshal. During World War 1, he served as commander-in-chief (1915–18) of British forces in France. Haig's policy of attrition inflicted appalling losses among British troops, particularly in the campaigns of the SOMME and PASSCHENDAELE. Under the supreme command of Marshal FOCH, he led the final assault on the Hindenburg line. In 1921 Haig helped establish the Royal BRITISH LEGION.

haiku In JAPANESE LITERATURE, a poetic form consisting of 17 syllables in five-seven-five pattern. Haikus originally evoked a moment in nature. Matsuo BASHO is considered to be the finest exponent of the form.

hail Precipitation from cumulonimbus clouds in the form of balls of ice. Hailstorms are associated with atmospheric turbulence extending to great heights combined with warm, moist air nearer the ground.

Haile Selassie I (1892–1975) (Ras Tafari Makonnen) Emperor of Ethiopia (1930–74). When Italy invaded Ethiopia in 1935, he was forced into exile (1936). In 1941, Haile Selassie drove out the Italians with British aid. Subsequently he became a leader among independent African nations, helping to found (1963) the Organization of African Unity (OAU). Unrest at corruption and lack of reform led to his overthrow by a military coup in 1974. He died while under arrest. *See also* Rastafarianism

Hainan Island off s China, separated from the mainland by the Hainan Strait; the capital is Haikou. It has been under Chinese authority from the 2nd century BC. In 1988, it was designated a special economic zone. Products: rubber, coffee, rice, timber, tin, copper and steel. Area: 33,991sq km (13,124sq mi). Pop. (1990) 6,420,000.

Haiphong Port on the Red River delta, N Vietnam. Founded in 1874, it became the chief naval base of French Indochina. Haiphong was occupied by the Japanese during World War 2 and bombed by the French in 1946. During the Vietnam War it suffered intensive bombardment by the USA and its harbour was mined. Industries: cement, glass, chemicals, cotton. Pop. (1992) 783,000.

hair Threadlike structure covering the skin of mammals. It has insulating, protective and sensory functions. Hair grows in a follicle, extending down through the epidermis to the dermis. New cells are added to the base of the hair; older hair cells become impregnated with keratin and die. Hair colour depends on the presence of melanin in the hair cells. A small muscle attached to the base of the hair allows it to be erected in response to nerve signals sent to the follicle. Erecting the hairs traps a thicker layer of air close to the skin, which acts as insulation. *See also* fur

hairstreak Any of a group of butterflies of the family Lycaenidae. They are grey and brown, and found in open areas on every continent, especially in the tropics. Hairstreaks have a quick, erratic flight. Genus *Strymon*.

Haiti Independent nation occupying the w third of the Caribbean island of Hispaniola and including the islands of Tortuga and Gonâve; the capital is Port-au-Prince. Much of the country is mountainous, with a humid tropical climate. After being discovered by Christopher Columbus in 1492, it had Spanish settlements established at the e end of the island, and within 100 years most of the native Arawaks had died through disease or ill-treatment. In the 17th century French corsairs set up plantations in the w part of the island; in 1697 the Spanish recognized the area as French territory. Known as Saint Dominque, the region prospered in the 18th century. The sugar and coffee plantations were worked by African slaves, who soon formed the majority of the population. In 1790, Toussaint L'Ouverture led a slave revolt against the colonial rulers. In 1801, as governor general, he abolished slavery, but he was killed by the French two years later. In 1804, the country was declared independent, under the name of Haiti, and Jean Jacques Dessalines became emperor. During the 19th century, Haiti experienced much political instability. From 1915 to 1934, it was virtually governed by the USA. In 1957, the election of François Duvalier as president inaugurated a period of corruption. Attempts to establish a democratic government in the 1980s and 1990s, after the deposition of the Duvalier family, were frustrated by the army. In 1991, the democratically elected president Jean-Bertrand Aristide was removed from office by a military coup, but was restored in 1994 with US backing. In 1995, René Préval was elected president, but divisions within the government were not resolved until 1999 when Préval appointed a new government by decree. In 2000, Aristide was re-elected as president. Haiti is the poorest country in the Western Hemisphere (1995 GDP per capita, US$910) and is reliant on food imports. Coffee accounts for about one-third of total exports.

Haitink, Sir Bernard (1929–) Dutch conductor, principal conductor of the Amsterdam Concertgebouw Orchestra (1961–87) and the London Philharmonic (1967–79). As musical director of the Royal Opera House (1987–), Haitink was noted for outstanding Wagner performances.

Hajj (Arabic, migration) Pilgrimage to Mecca made in the 12th month of the Muslim year. All Muslims are required to undertake the Hajj. It is the last of the Five Pillars of Islam, the religious duties defined by the Koran.

hake Relative of the cod found in temperate waters of the Atlantic and Pacific oceans. It is silver and brown. Length: to 1m (40in); weight: to 14kg (30lb). Family Gadidae or Merluccidae; species Atlantic *Merluccius bilinearis*; Pacific *M. productus*.

Hakluyt, Richard (*c.*1552–1616) English geographer. Hakluyt's detailed history of maritime exploration, *Principal Navigations* (1589), stimulated further voyages of discovery and English colonization.

Halcyon Greek mythological figure. The daughter of Aeolus, she is best known as the wife of Ceyx, king of Thessaly. When Ceyx was drowned, Halcyon ran to the seashore to find his body and drowned herself. The gods changed the couple into kingfishers.

Haldane, J.B.S. (John Burdon Sanderson) (1892–1964) British biologist and geneticist, nephew of Richard Burdon Haldane. His work formed the basis of population genetics. His book *The Causes of Evolution* (1933) examined the theory of natural selection in the light of modern genetic research. Haldane was the first to estimate (1932) the mutation rate of a human gene. His book *Daedalus, or Science and the Future* (1924) was an early attempt to popularize science. In 1956, he became disillusioned with Marxism and emigrated to India.

Haldane, Richard Burdon, 1st Viscount (1856–1928) British statesman, secretary of war (1905–12) and lord chancellor (1912–16). In 1895 he helped found the London School of Economics (LSE). In 1905, Haldane reorganized the British Army along German lines and created the Territorial Army.

Hale, George Ellery (1868–1938) US astronomer who organized a number of observatories, including the Yerkes Observatory (1897), the Mount Wilson Observatory (1917) and the Palomar Observatory (1949). Each observatory featured, in turn, the largest telescope of its day. The last two observatories were renamed the Hale Observatories in 1970 in his honour. Hale also invented the spectroheliograph.

Haley, Bill (William John Clifton) (1925–81) US singer. White idol of the rock and roll era, he had his first real success with "Crazy Man Crazy" (1953). Haley's achieved international fame with "Rock around the Clock" (1954) and "Shake, Rattle and Roll" (1955).

half-life Time taken for one-half of the nuclei in a given amount of radioactive isotope to decay (change into

---

HAITI
AREA: 27,750sq km (10,714sq mi)
POPULATION: 8,003,000
CAPITAL (POPULATION): Port-au-Prince (1,402,000)

another element or isotope). Only the half-life is measured because the decay is never considered to be total. Half-lives remain constant under any temperature or pressure, but there is a great variety among different isotopes. Oxygen-20 has a half-life of 14 seconds and uranium-234 of 250,000 years. A radioactive isotope disintegrates by giving off alpha or beta particles. The term "half-life" also refers to particles that spontaneously decay into new particles, such as a free neutron being transformed into an electron. *See also* DATING, RADIOACTIVE; RADIOACTIVITY

half-tone process Production of zinc or copper plates for PRINTING illustrations. By breaking down the continuous image of the original into separate dots of varying size, it is possible to reproduce the full tone values of a photograph or artwork. The image required is photographed through a glass screen bearing ruled lines crossing each other at right angles; the resultant image is exposed on a sensitized printing plate. Georg Meisenbach is usually credited as the inventor (1882) of the half-tone process, but the Levy brothers of Philadelphia, USA, were the first to use it commercially.

halibut FLATFISH found worldwide in deep, cold to temperate seas. It is brownish on the eye side and white below. Family Pleuronectidae; species, Atlantic *Hippoglossus hippoglossus*, giant Pacific *H. stenolepis*.

Halicarnassus (modern Bodrum, Turkey) Ancient Greek city in sw Asia Minor. Under Persian rule from the 6th century BC, it grew rich because of its trading position. In the 4th century BC it was a semi-independent state under the Persian governor, Mausolus, whose tomb was one of the SEVEN WONDERS OF THE WORLD.

halide Salt of one of the HALOGENS, or a compound containing a halogen and one other element; examples are sodium fluoride and potassium chloride. The alkyl halides (haloalkanes) are organic compounds, such as methyl chloride (chloromethane CH_2Cl).

Halifax, Charles Montagu, 1st Earl of (1661–1715) English Whig statesman. He entered Parliament in 1689. As a lord of the treasury (1692–94), Halifax established the national debt (1692) and founded the BANK OF ENGLAND (1694). As chancellor of the exchequer (1694–95), he introduced new coinage. In 1697, Halifax became first lord of the treasury but resigned when the Tories came to power (1699). On Queen ANNE's death (1714), he was made a member of the council of regency and resumed as lord of treasury under GEORGE I. He was also a patron of writers.

Halifax City and seaport in E Canada, on the Atlantic Ocean; capital of Nova Scotia. Founded in 1749, it developed as an important naval base. In 1912, many of the victims from the *Titanic* were buried here. In 1917, it was the scene of a huge explosion on a munitions ship, which killed more than 2,000 people. Industries: commercial fishing, shipbuilding, oil refining. Pop. (1992) 114,455.

halite (NaCl) Sodium chloride, or common (rock) SALT. It is found in evaporite sedimentary rocks and in salt domes and dried lakes. It is colourless, white or grey. It has a cubic system of interlocking cubic crystals, granules and masses. It is important as table salt and as a source of CHLORINE. Hardness 2.5; r.d. 2.2.

Hall, Sir Peter Reginald Frederick (1930–) English theatre director. He was a founder and director (1961–73) of the ROYAL SHAKESPEARE COMPANY (RSC). Hall directed opera at GLYNDEBOURNE and the ROYAL OPERA HOUSE. His films include *Akenfield* (1974). Hall was director of the National Theatre of Great Britain (1973–88) and formed his own Peter Hall Company in 1987.

Hall, (Marguerite) Radclyffe (1883–1943) English novelist and poet. Hall is best-known for *The Well of*

Loneliness (1928), a sympathetic study of lesbianism, that was banned as obscene in Britain for many years.

Hallé, Sir Charles (1819–95) British conductor and pianist, b. Germany. In 1857, he formed a symphony orchestra in Manchester, which subsequently became the Hallé Orchestra. In 1893, he was a founder of the Royal Manchester College of Music.

Halle City on the River Saale, Saxony-Anhalt state, SE Germany. It was founded in the 9th century as a fortress. There is some lignite, salt and potash mining in the area. Industries: chemicals, sugar refining, electrical goods. Pop. (1995) 290,000.

Haller, Albrecht von (1708–77) Swiss biologist, physician and poet. As a botanist, he was celebrated for his descriptions of alpine flora. In 1736, Haller researched the contractile properties of muscle tissue, and his resulting treatise (1757–66) laid the foundations of modern neurology and physiology.

Halley, Edmond (1656–1742) English astronomer and mathematician. He was Astronomer Royal (1720–42). Halley's most famous discovery (1696) was that COMETS have periodic ORBITS. In 1705, he accurately predicted the return of the comet now known as HALLEY'S COMET in 1758. Halley founded modern geophysics, charting variations in Earth's magnetic field and establishing the magnetic origin of the AURORA borealis. He showed that atmospheric pressure decreases with altitude. Halley financed Isaac NEWTON to write *Principia* (1687).

Halley's comet Bright periodic COMET. It takes 76 years to complete an ORBIT that takes it from within Venus's orbit to outside Neptune's. It was first observed by Edmond HALLEY in 1682; later he deduced that it was the same comet that had been seen in 1531 and 1607, and predicted its return in 1758. There are records of every return since 240 BC. In 1986, the Giotto space probe showed the nucleus to be an irregular object measuring $15 \times 8km$ ($9 \times 5mi$) and consisting of ice.

hallmark Offical stamp used by British government ASSAY offices to mark the standard of gold and silver. The mark has four elements: the standard mark, showing the purity of the metal; the office mark, bearing the assay office's cipher; the date mark; and the maker's mark.

Hallowe'en (contraction of All Hallows Eve) In medieval times, a holy festival observed on 31 October, the eve of All Saints' Day. It was merged with the ancient Celtic festival of Samhain, when fires were lit to frighten away evil spirits and to guide the souls of the dead who were supposed to revisit their homes on this day. Today, Halloween is observed as a festival for masquerading and for children's "trick or treat".

Hallstatt Small town in w central Austria, believed to be the site of the earliest IRON AGE culture in w Europe. Iron was worked here from *c*.700 BC. The site contains a large Celtic cemetery and a deep salt mine. Fine bronze and pottery objects have also been discovered.

hallucination Apparent perception of something that is not present. Although they may occur in any of the five senses, auditory hallucinations and visual hallucinations are the most common. While they are usually symptomatic of MENTAL ILLNESS, especially PSYCHOSIS, hallucinations may result from fatigue or emotional upsets. Hallucinogenic drugs include ECSTASY, LSD and MESCALINE.

halogen Elements (FLUORINE, CHLORINE, BROMINE, IODINE and ASTATINE) belonging to Group VII of the PERIODIC TABLE. They react with most other elements and with organic compounds. The halogens are highly electronegative; they react strongly because they require only one electron to achieve the "stable 8" inert gas configuration. They produce crystalline salts (HALIDES) containing negative ions of the type F⁻ and Cl⁻.

halon Any of several gases used in FIRE EXTINGUISHERS. Chemically halons can be considered as simple HYDRO-CARBONS that have had some or all of their hydrogen atoms replaced by a HALOGEN. Similar to CHLOROFLUO-ROCARBONS (CFCs), they are even more destructive to the OZONE LAYER.

Hals, Frans (*c*.1580–1666) Dutch painter. He is best known for his paintings of robust figures, such as the *Laughing Cavalier* (1624), and his group portraits. His more subdued later works have a dignity and strength approaching those of his contemporary, REMBRANDT.

Hamburg City-state and port on the River Elbe, N Germany. Founded in the 9th century by CHARLE-MAGNE, it became one of the original members of the HANSEATIC LEAGUE. Severely bombed during World War 2, it is now Germany's second largest city and a major cultural centre. Industries: electronic equipment, brewing, publishing, chemicals. Pop. (1995) 1,706,000.

Hamilcar Barca (d.228 BC) Carthaginian commander. Initially successful in the first of the PUNIC WARS, he was defeated in 241 BC. Hamilcar suppressed a revolt of Carthaginian mercenaries in 238 BC and the following year conquered much of Spain. He was the father of HANNIBAL and Hasdrubal Barca.

Hamilton, Alexander (1755–1804) US statesman. During the American Revolution he served as George WASH-INGTON's aide-de-camp and secretary. After the war he became a member of the Continental Congress and a delegate to the Constitutional Convention. Hamilton was the principal contributor to *The Federalist Papers* (1788), advocating the new US CONSTITUTION. As the first secretary of the treasury (1789–95), he established the national currency and the Bank of the United States (1791). In 1800, he alienated many within the FEDERALIST PARTY by supporting Thomas JEFFERSON's bid for presidency. In 1804, he thwarted Aaron BURR's campaign for governor of New York. Burr challenged him to a duel and killed him.

Hamilton, Lady Emma (1765–1815) English mistress of Admiral NELSON. She was married to Sir William Hamilton (1730–1803), British ambassador to Naples, where her relationship with Nelson, tacitly accepted by her husband, began in 1798. They had two daughters.

Hamilton, James Hamilton, 1st Duke of (1606–49) Scottish political and military leader. As CHARLES I's commissioner in Scotland (1638–39), he failed to achieve a compromise with the COVENANTERS and led an army against them in 1639. He fought for Charles in the English CIVIL WARS. In 1648, he led Scottish forces in support of the king. He was defeated by Oliver CROMWELL at Preston, and executed.

Hamilton, Richard (1922–) English artist, a leader of the POP ART movement. He produced collages using images taken from commercial art. His best-known work is *Just what is it that makes today's homes so different, so appealing?* (1956).

Hamilton, William D. (1936–) New Zealand biologist. He developed the theory of **inclusive fitness**, an idea in GENETICS that sought to explain the EVOLUTION of ALTRU-ISM in animals in terms of Darwinian NATURAL SELECTION. Hamilton theorized that if an organism sacrificed itself to save its relatives, it was doing so to ensure that at least some of its own GENE variants were passed on to the following generation. The success with which an individual's alleles are passed on is called inclusive fitness.

Hamilton Capital and chief port of Bermuda, on Great Bermuda, at the head of Great Sound. Founded in 1790, it

became the capital in 1815 and was made a free port in 1956. Tourism is the major industry. Pop. (1994) 1,100.

Hamilton City in Canada, in SE Ontario. Founded in 1813, it is an important communication and manufacturing centre. Industries: iron, steel, vehicles, electrical equipment, textiles. Pop. (1991) 318,499.

Hamito-Semitic languages *See* AFRO-ASIATIC LANGUAGES

Hammarskjöld, Dag (1905–61) Swedish diplomat, second secretary-general (1953–61) of the UNITED NATIONS (UN). He brought great moral authority to the office. In 1956, Hammarsköld played a leading role in resolving the SUEZ CRISIS. He sent a UN peacekeeping force to the Congo. He died in an air crash over Zambia while on a mission to the Congo. Hammarsköld was posthumously awarded the 1961 Nobel Peace Prize.

hammer Men's field event in which a spherical, metallic weight attached to a steel wire is thrown. The "hammer" weighs 7.26kg (16lb). The thrower stands within a circle 2.13m (7ft) in diameter and, by rotating two or three times, builds up momentum before releasing the hammer. It has been an Olympic event since 1900.

hammerhead Aggressive SHARK found in tropical marine waters and warmer temperate zones. It can be recognized by its head, which has extended sideways into two hammer-like lobes, with one eye and one nostril located at the tip of each. Length: to 6.1m (20ft); weight: to 906kg (2,000lb). Family Sphyrnidae.

Hammerstein II, Oscar (1895–1960) US lyricist and librettist. Hammerstein collaborated with Jerome KERN on *Show Boat* (1927) and with Richard RODGERS on *Oklahoma!* (1943), *Carousel* (1945), *South Pacific* (1949), *The King and I* (1951) and *The Sound of Music* (1959).

Hammett, (Samuel) Dashiell (1894–1961) US novelist, the originator of realistic DETECTIVE FICTION. Hammett drew on his own experience as a Pinkerton detective to create the investigators Sam Spade and Nick Charles. His books include *Red Harvest* (1929), *The Maltese Falcon* (1930) and *The Thin Man* (1934).

Hammurabi (d. *c*.1750 BC) King of BABYLONIA (*c*.1792–*c*.1750 BC). By conquering neighbours, such as SUMERIA, he extended his rule in Mesopotamia and reorganized the empire under the Code of HAMMURABI. A good administrator, Hammurabi improved productivity by building canals and granaries.

Hammurabi, Code of Ancient laws compiled under HAMMURABI. A copy of the code is in the Louvre, Paris. It is composed of 282 provisions with harsh penalties for offenders and includes the maxim, "An eye for an eye, a tooth for a tooth". Covering family life, property and trade, it provides information on social and economic conditions in ancient Babylonia.

Hamnett, Katharine (1948–) English fashion designer. In 1979, she founded her own company and attracted attention for her innovative use of Haboti silk, stone-washing techniques and garment dyeing.

Hampshire County in S England, bordering the English Channel; the county town is WINCHESTER. There are traces of Iron Age hill forts. The area was settled in Roman times. Predominantly agricultural, Hampshire contains the port of SOUTHAMPTON and the naval base at PORTSMOUTH. Its coastal resorts and the NEW FOREST woodland are tourist attractions. Industries: agriculture, oil refining, chemicals, brewing, electronics. Area: 3,782sq km (1,460sq mi). Pop. (1991) 1,541,547.

Hampden, John (1594–1643) English parliamentarian, a leader of the opposition to CHARLES I. As a result of his criticism and his part in drawing up the GRAND

REMONSTRANCE, Hampden was one of the five members whom the king tried to arrest in the House of Commons in 1642, an act that precipitated the English CIVIL WARS.

Hampton Seaport on the James River and Hampton Roads, SE Virginia, USA. First settled in 1610, it is reputedly the oldest settlement founded by the English in the USA to be in continuous use. Industries: defence, tourism, seafood packing, fertilizers. Pop. (1990) 133,793.

Hampton Court Palace Palace situated beside the River Thames, 23km (14mi) from Westminster, London, England. Cardinal WOLSEY began construction in 1515, and he gave it to HENRY VIII in 1526, hoping to regain his favour. It is noted for the splendour of its architecture and its garden with maze. Christopher WREN rebuilt and extended parts of the palace between 1696 and 1704.

hamster Small, mainly nocturnal, burrowing RODENT native to Eurasia and Africa. It has internal cheek pouches for carrying food. The golden hamster (*Mesocricetus auratus*) is a domestic pet and all are descended from one female captured in Syria in 1930. Length: up to 18cm (7in). Family Cricetidae; species *Cricetus mesocricetus*.

Hamsun, Knut (1859–1952) Norwegian novelist, pseudonym of Knut Pederson. He first gained attention for *Hunger* (1890). Hamsun's distrust of modern mass culture is reflected in *The Growth of the Soil* (1917). He was awarded the 1920 Nobel Prize for literature.

Han Imperial Chinese dynasty (202 BC–AD 220). It was founded by a rebellious peasant, Liu Pang, who overthrew the QIN dynasty and established the capital at Chang'an. Under the Han, CONFUCIANISM became the state philosophy, and China achieved unprecedented power, prosperity, technological invention and cultural growth, especially under Han Wu Ti in the 2nd century BC. A usurper, WANG MANG, interrupted the dynasty between AD 8 and 25; the dynasty is divided by that period into the Former Han and Later Han.

Han (Han-Jen) Ethnic group that makes up *c*.94% of the population of China. They consist of various groups sharing the same culture, traditions and written language, although within the Han Chinese language are several dialects. Their ancient hierarchical society, based on Taoist, Confucian and Buddhist tenets, has been reorganized under Communism.

Hancock, Tony (Anthony John) (1924–68) English comedian. He became a household name with his lugubrious wit in the radio, and later television, series *Hancock's Half Hour* (1954–61). A tragic figure, plagued by self-doubt, Hancock committed suicide.

handball Name given to two games played mostly in Ireland and the USA. One is played with a hard, small ball by two or four gloved players on courts of one, three or four walls. A variant of this game that uses wooden rackets is called **paddleball**. The other game, sometimes called **team handball**, is played on a court where, between two goals, players catch, pass and throw a ball with the object of hurling it past the opposing goalkeeper. *See also* FIVES

Handel, George Frideric (1685–1759) English composer, b. Germany. In 1712, after some success as an operatic composer in Italy, he moved to England. Handel wrote (*c*.1717) the *Water Music* to serenade GEORGE I's procession down the River Thames. In 1720, he became the first director of the Royal Academy of Music, London. From 1729 to 1734, he wrote a series of operas for the Kings Theatre, London, including *Orlando* (1733). From 1739, Handel concentrated on creating a new form, the ORATORIO, producing such masterpieces as *Saul* (1739), *Israel in Egypt* (1739), *Messiah* (1742) and *Judas*

Maccabaeus (1747). In 1749 he composed *Music for the Royal Fireworks*. In 1751 he began to lose his sight.

Handy, W.C. (William Christopher) (1873–1958) US composer and musician, the "Father of the BLUES". From 1903 he led his own band, writing tunes such as "Memphis Blues" (1911) and "St Louis Blues" (1914).

hang gliding GLIDING using a lightweight craft, usually with a triangular wing that is stabilized by the weight of the pilot's body underneath. Take-off is made by running down a slope, assisted by a steady updraft. The pilot hangs from a harness and, by using a control bar to shift body weight, steers the glider.

Hanging Gardens of Babylon One of the SEVEN WONDERS OF THE WORLD. The gardens are thought to have been spectacular, rising in a series of terraces and ingeniously irrigated by water pumped up from the Euphrates. They were probably built by NEBUCHADNEZ-ZAR. Nothing remains of them.

hanging valley Valley that ends high up the face of a larger valley, possibly with a stream running through it and ending in a waterfall. Most hanging valleys result form glacial deepening of the main valley. *See also* GLACIER

Hanks, Tom (1956–) US film actor and director. Initially typecast in comedy roles, his early films included *Splash* (1984) and *Big* (1988). Hanks' performance as a gay AIDS victim in *Philadelphia* (1993) demonstrated his dramatic versatility and won him an Academy Award for best actor. He won a second Oscar for *Forrest Gump* (1994). In 1996 he made his directorial debut with *That Thing You Do!* He was acclaimed for his dramatic role in Steven SPIELBERG's *Saving Private Ryan* (1998).

Hannibal (247–183 BC) Carthaginian general in the second of the PUNIC WARS, son of HAMILCAR BARCA. One of the greatest generals of ancient times, in 218 BC he invaded N Italy after crossing the Alps with 40,000 troops and a force of elephants. Hannibal won a series of victories but was unable to capture Rome. Recalled to CARTHAGE to confront the invasion of SCIPIO AFRICANUS, he was defeated at Zama (202 BC). After the war, as chief magistrate of Carthage, he alienated the nobility by reducing their power. They sought Roman intervention, and Hannibal fled to the Seleucid kingdom of ANTIOCHUS III. He fought under Antiochus against the Romans, was defeated, and committed suicide.

Hanoi Capital of Vietnam and its second largest city, on the Red River. In the 7th century the Chinese ruled Vietnam from Hanoi; it later became capital of the Vietnamese empire. Taken by the French in 1883, the city became the capital of French Indochina (1887–1945). From 1946 to 1954, it was the scene of fighting between the French and the Viet Minh. It was heavily bombed during the VIETNAM WAR. Industries: engineering, vehicles, textiles, rice-milling. Pop. (1996) 3,056,000.

Hanover (Hannover) City on the River Leine, N Germany; capital of Lower Saxony. Chartered in 1241, the city joined the HANSEATIC LEAGUE in 1386. GEORGE I of Britain was elector of Hanover. Hanover was badly damaged during World War 2, but many old buildings were later reconstructed. Industries: machinery, steel, textiles, rubber, chemicals. Pop. (1995) 526,000.

Hanover (Hannover) Former kingdom and province of Germany. In 1692, Duke Ernest Augustus, one of the dukes of Brunswick-Lüneberg, was created elector of Hanover; his lands were known thereafter as Hanover. In 1714 his son succeeded to the British throne as GEORGE I. Divided during the Napoleonic era, Hanover was reconstituted as a kingdom in 1815. Allied with Austria in the AUSTRO-PRUSSIAN WAR (1866), it was annexed by

Prussia after Austria's defeat. After World War 2 it was incorporated into the state of Lower Saxony.

Hanover, House of German royal family and rulers of Britain, from 1714 to 1901. The electors of Hanover succeeded to the English throne in 1714 under the terms of the Act of Settlement (1701) and the Act of Union (1707). GEORGE I, the first elector also to be king of England, was succeeded in both England and Hanover by GEORGE II, GEORGE III, GEORGE IV and WILLIAM IV. Salic law forbade Queen VICTORIA's accession to Hanover; the Hanoverian title was inherited by her uncle, the Duke of Cumberland, and the crowns of Britain and Germany were separated.

Hansard Colloquial name for the daily record of the proceedings of the British Houses of Parliament. It is named Luke Hansard (1752–1828), printer to the Commons.

Hanseatic League Commercial union formed (1241) by *c*.160 N German cities (Hanse towns), including Bremen, Cologne, Hamburg and Lübeck. The League protected its merchants by controlling the trade routes from the Baltic region to the Atlantic. It began to decline in the late 15th century with the opening up of the New World and aggressive trading by the British and Dutch.

Hanukkah (Chanukah or Feast of Lights) Eight-day festival celebrated in JUDAISM. It commemorates the rededication of the Jerusalem TEMPLE in 165 BC, and the miracle of a one-day supply of oil lasting for eight days. It is celebrated with the lighting of candles on a special eight-branched holder called a menorah.

Hanuman In Hindu mythology, the monkey general who helped RAMA to find and rescue his wife, Sita. His attributes include great strength, agility and wisdom.

haploid Term describing a CELL that has only one member of each CHROMOSOME pair. All human cells except GAMETES are DIPLOID, having 46 chromosomes. Gametes are haploid, having 23 chromosomes. The body cells of many lower organisms, including many algae and single-celled organisms, are haploid. *See also* ALTERNATION OF GENERATIONS; MEIOSIS

happening Spontaneous or improvised multimedia event emphasizing audience participation and an element of surprise. Most popular in the 1960s, happenings draw on elements of DADA, SURREALISM and POP ART.

Hapsburg *See* HABSBURG

Harare (formerly Salisbury) Capital of Zimbabwe, in the NE part of the country. Settled by Europeans in 1890 as Fort Salisbury, it became capital of Southern Rhodesia in 1902. The city served as capital of the Federation of Rhodesia and Nyasaland (1953–63) and of Rhodesia (1965–79). It has a university (1957) and two cathedrals. Industries: gold mining, textiles, steel, tobacco, chemicals, furniture. Pop. (1992) 1,184,169.

Harbin (Haerbin) City on the River Sungari, NE China; capital of Heilungkiang province. It was a place of refuge for White Russians after the Revolution of 1917. Under Japanese rule from 1932 to 1945, it was then briefly occupied by Soviet forces before falling to the Chinese Communists in 1946. Industries: oil, coal, turbines and generators, mining equipment, paper. Pop. (1994) 2,505,000.

hard disk Rigid MAGNETIC DISK for storing computer PROGRAMS and DATA. The built-in hard disk drive in a typical personal COMPUTER consists of a number of hard platters coated with a magnetic material set on a common spindle. They are housed inside a sealed container, with a motor to spin the stack of platters, a head to write (record) and read (replay) each side of each platter, and associated electronic circuits. Hard disk capacity is continually being

increased: most computers are now sold with a disk of at least 500 megabytes (Mb) capacity.

Hardecanute (*c*.1019–42) King of Denmark (1035–42) and last Danish king of England (1040–42). The legitimate son and heir of CANUTE II, he was able to assume the English throne only after the death of HAROLD I, his stepbrother. Because he was childless, the throne reverted to an English holder, EDWARD THE CONFESSOR, on his death.

Hardie, (James) Keir (1856–1915) Scottish socialist politician. In 1888, he founded the Scottish Parliamentary Labour Party. In 1892, Hardie entered Parliament as the first socialist MP. In 1893, he founded the Independent Labour Party. In 1906, Hardie became a co-founder and first leader (1906–08) of the LABOUR PARTY. A committed pacifist, he withdrew from Labour politics in World War 1.

Harding, Warren Gamaliel (1865–1923) 29th US President (1921–23). A senator (1915–20), he was the Republican compromise candidate to run for president in 1920. Harding's campaign for a return to "normalcy" easily defeated the Democratic challenge. While in office, he left government to his cabinet and advisers. This administration, known as the "Ohio Gang", was one of the most corrupt in US history. The Teapot Dome Scandal forced a Congressional investigation. Harding died before the worst excesses became public knowledge, and he was succeeded by the vice president, Calvin COOLIDGE.

hardness Resistance of a material to abrasion, cutting or indentation. The **Mohs scale** is a means of expressing

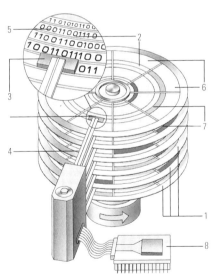

▲ **hard disk** A computer hard disk is made up of multiple rotating platters (1), each one of which has circular magnetic tracks (2) that are read and written on by a magnetic head (3) held by an arm (4). The disks spin at 100 times per second. The magnetic heads, tiny electromagnets, align magnetic particles on the surface of the platters to represent a digital code of zeros and ones (5). The magnetic tracks on the platters are divided into sectors (6), and when information is written on the hard disk, files are split into different sectors on the platters (7). A file allocation table tells the chip (8) controlling the hard disk where information is held on the platters.

the comparative hardness of materials, particularly minerals, by testing them against ten standard materials. These range from (1) talc to (10) diamond (the hardest).

hardness of water Reluctance of water to produce a lather with soap, due to various dissolved salts, mainly those of calcium and magnesium. These salts give rise to an insoluble precipitate, which causes "scale" in boilers, pipes and kettles. Hardness may be temporary (removed by boiling), caused by calcium bicarbonate; or permanent (not affected by boiling), caused by calcium sulphate.

Hardouin-Mansart, Jules (1646–1708) French architect to LOUIS XIV. His bold BAROQUE style can be best seen in the Palace of VERSAILLES, such as the Hall of Mirrors (1678–84), the Orangery (1681–86), and the Grand Trianon (1687–88).

hardware In computing equipment as opposed to the programs, or SOFTWARE, with which a computer functions. The computer, keyboard, printer and electronic circuit boards are examples of hardware.

Hardy, Thomas (1840–1928) English novelist and poet. His birthplace, Dorset, SW England, formed the background for most of his writing. His first major success was *Far from the Madding Crowd* (1874). The often tragic tales that followed remain among the most widely read 19th-century novels and include *The Return of the Native* (1878), *The Mayor of Casterbridge* (1886), *Tess of the d'Urbervilles* (1891) and *Jude the Obscure* (1895). The latter was attacked for its immoral tone, and thereafter Hardy devoted himself to poetry, including *Wessex Poems* (1898) and *The Dynasts* (1903–08).

Hare, David (1947–) English dramatist. He collaborated with Howard Brenton on *Pravda* (1985), a study of media corruption. Hare wrote a "State of the Nation" trilogy on the British establishment: *Racing Demon* (1990) on the Church of England; *Murmuring Judges* (1991) on the legal system; and *The Absence of War* (1993) on politics. His s creenplays include *Plenty* and *Wetherby* (both 1985). Other plays include *The Blue Room* (1999), an adaption of SCHNITZLER's *La Ronde*, and *Via Dolorosa* (1998), a monologue about his experiences in Israel.

hare Large member of the RABBIT family (Leporidae). True hares (genus *Lepus*) have ears that are longer than their heads, and are born with open eyes and a full coat of fur. Length: to 76cm (30in); weight: to 4.5kg (10lb). Hares include the JACK RABBIT and snowshoe rabbit.

harebell Flowering plant of the bellflower family (CAMPANULACEAE), a common wildflower in pastures and also cultivated in gardens. It has drooping, bell-shaped, mid-blue flowers. Species *Campanula rotundifolia*.

Hare Krishna (International Society for KRISHNA Consciousness) Hindu sect, founded (1965) in New York by Swami Prabhupada (A.C. Bhaktivedanta). The movement is based on the philosophy that Krishna is the supreme God and stresses the importance of asceticism. Public perception of the movement has been enhanced by the proselytizing of its shaven-headed, saffron-robed devotees, who practise self-denial, vegetarianism, meditation and chanting of MANTRAS. *See also* HINDUISM

harelip Congenital cleft in the upper lip caused by the failure of the two parts of the palate to unite. It is a congenital condition, often associated with CLEFT PALATE.

harem Women's quarters in a Muslim household. It contained a man's wives, concubines and female servants. The most famous harems were those of the Turkish sultans in ISTANBUL, which often had several hundred women and were guarded by EUNUCHS.

Hargreaves, James (1722–78) English inventor and industrialist. In 1764, near Blackburn, Lancashire, he invented the spinning jenny. This machine greatly speeded the spinning process of COTTON by producing eight threads simultaneously. In 1768, local spinners destroyed the jenny, fearing that it threatened their jobs. Hargreaves moved to Nottingham and, with Thomas James, built a mill and became one of the first great factory owners.

Harlem Residential area of New York City, USA, bounded s by 110th Street and N by 168th Street. The area is a political and cultural focus for African-Americans. The Center for Research in Black Culture is located here, next to the Countee Cullen library, which has been a meeting place for black writers since the 1920s. The Apollo Theater is a noted venue for black performers.

Harlem Renaissance Period of creativity, particularly in literature, among African-Americans in the 1920s. Centred in HARLEM, the Renaissance produced many fine writers, such as Countee Cullen, Zora Neale HURSTON, Langston HUGHES and Claude McKay.

harlequin English name derived from the character Arlecchino of the COMMEDIA DELL'ARTE, who was a quick-witted, unscrupulous serving man. A harlequin today appears in comedy and pantomime as a mute jester, dressed in diamond-patterned, multi-coloured tights.

Harlow, Jean (1911–37) US movie actress, known as the "blonde bombshell", an almost legendary figure in 1930s Hollywood. Her first major role was in *Hell's Angels* (1930). Other films include *The Public Enemy* (1931) and *Platinum Blonde* (1931). Soon after completing *Saratoga* (1937), Harlow died of cerebral oedema.

harmonica (mouth organ) Musical instrument consisting of a small metal case containing metal reeds. The reeds vibrate as the player blows or inhales through slots along one edge of the case.

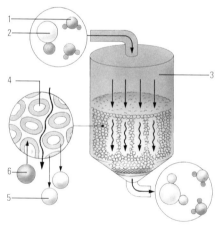

▲ **hardness of water** Scale in kettles and water pipes is caused by the presence in water (1) of dissolved calcium carbonate (2), usually from the chemical weathering of limestone. In hot or boiling water, calcium carbonate precipitates, forming solid limescale deposits on surfaces, such as the inside of kettles. Calcium carbonate also prevents soap from lathering. In an ion exchange tank (3), the tank is filled with grains of sodium-coated material with which the water has to come into contact (4). Sodium ions (5), which are more reactive than calcium, are exchanged for calcium ions (6). Because of the different properties of the sodium ions, the sodium salts formed remain in solution even when boiled.

harmonics (overtones) In acoustics, additional notes whose frequencies are multiples of a basic (fundamental) note. When a violin string is plucked, the sounds correspond to vibrations of the string. The loudest note corresponds to the fundamental mode of vibration. Other weaker notes, corresponding to subsidiary vibrations, sound at the same time. Together these notes make up a harmonic series.

harmony In music, structure of CHORDS and the relationships between them. Before *c*.1600, POLYPHONY was the norm in Western musical composition. The early Baroque era witnessed the establishment of a system of TONALITY based on the DIATONIC scale. The basic element of harmony is the triad: a three-note chord built by a note of the SCALE of the tonality of the composition and the notes a third and a fifth above it (for example, C, E and G in the KEY of C). A **harmonic progression** consists of a particular sequence of chords, especially one modulating into another tonality. The tonic, dominant and subdominant chords are the primary chords of a key (C, G and F chords in the key of C). Chords involving notes from outside the major or minor scale are said to be CHROMATIC. In the last half of the 19th century, composers such as WAGNER became increasingly chromatic. In the early 20th century, SCHOENBERG adopted ATONALITY and then SERIALISM. *See also* COUNTERPOINT; MELODY

Harold I (d.1040) (Harold Harefoot) Danish king and ruler of England (1035–40). An illegitimate son of CANUTE II, he claimed the crown, ruling as regent (1035–37). Elected king at Oxford, he disposed of his rival, Alfred the Aethling, and displaced the heir, his half-brother HARDECANUTE.

Harold II (1022–66) Last Anglo-Saxon king of England (1066). He was elected king following the death of EDWARD THE CONFESSOR, despite having pledged to support William of Normandy's (WILLIAM I) claim to the throne. England was immediately invaded by HAROLD III of Norway, whom he defeated. Three days later he was defeated and killed by William at the Battle of HASTINGS.

Harold III (Hardrada) (1015–66) King of Norway (1045–66). He served as a mercenary for the Byzantine Empire, returning to Norway in 1045. He made vain attempts to conquer Denmark. Harold was killed at Stamford Bridge during his invasion of England.

harp Ancient musical instrument consisting of a frame over which strings are stretched. Variations have been found in the Egyptian, Greek and Celtic civilizations. A modern orchestral harp has a large triangular frame that carries 47 strings. Seven pedals ensure the whole chromatic range is covered by altering the pitch of the strings.

harpsichord Keyboard musical instrument. Its metal strings are mechanically plucked by quill plectrums. Its volume can barely be regulated, although stops may be used to bring extra strings into use. Historic instruments may have had two or, rarely, three keyboards. The harpsichord was the principal keyboard instrument from 1500 to 1750 but was later replaced by the PIANO.

harrier Medium-sized HAWK. Active by day, it flys low over grasslands where it swoops on small animals. It has a small bill and long wings, legs and tail. Length: 38–50cm (15–20in). Family Accipitridae; genus *Circus*.

Harriman, William Averill (1891–1986) US diplomat. He was US ambassador to the Soviet Union (1943–46) and Britain (1946) and secretary of commerce under President TRUMAN (1955–59). Harriman was roving ambassador under President KENNEDY and ambassador at large for President JOHNSON. He was also chief negotiator at the Paris peace talks on the Vietnam War (1968, 1969).

Harris, Sir Arthur Travers (1892–1984) British air marshal. Known as "Bomber Harris", he served in the Royal Flying Corps in World War 1. As commander-in-chief (1942–45) of RAF Bomber Command during World War 2, Harris was responsible for the mass bombing of German industrial cities. He was knighted in 1942.

Harris, Joel Chandler (1848–1908) US writer. From 1879, Harris published his *Uncle Remus* stories, which are retellings of African-American folktales. The character of Br'er Rabbit is perhaps his most memorable.

Harrisburg Capital of Pennsylvania, USA, in the SE of the state on the Susquehanna River. Established as a trading post in *c*.1718, a town was established by 1785, which was the scene of the Harrisburg Convention (1788). It became the state capital in 1812. Industries: textiles, machinery, electronic equipment. Pop. (1992 est.) 53,430.

Harrison, Benjamin (1833–1901) 23rd US President (1889–93), grandson of William Henry HARRISON. After one term in the US Senate, he was selected (1888) as the Republican presidential nominee against President Grover CLEVELAND. Harrison won with a majority of the electoral votes, although Cleveland had the most popular votes. As president, he signed into law the Sherman Antitrust Act and the McKinley Tariff Act (both 1890). He was defeated by Cleveland in 1892.

Harrison, William Henry (1773–1841) Ninth US President (1841). He is remembered chiefly for his military career, especially his victory at Tippecanoe over Native Americans (1811) and later in the WAR OF 1812. He was elected president in 1840, with John Tyler as vice president, under the famous slogan "Tippecanoe and Tyler too". Harrison died after one month in office. He was the grandfather of Benjamin HARRISON.

Hart, Moss (1904–61) US dramatist. He worked with George S. KAUFMAN on many comedies, including *You Can't Take It With You* (1936). His most successful musical was *Lady in the Dark* (1941), written with Kurt WEILL and Ira GERSHWIN. He directed *My Fair Lady* (1956).

hartebeest Large ANTELOPE native to African grasslands S of the Sahara Desert. They have reddish or yellowish-brown coats and short, sharply rising horns united at the base. Length: up to 200cm (80in); height: to 150cm (60in); weight: up to 180kg (400lb). Family Bovidae.

Hartford Capital of Connecticut, USA, on the Connecticut River. More than 25 insurance companies have their headquarters here. Manufactures include precision instruments and electrical equipment. Pop. (1990) 139,739.

Hartford Convention (1814–15) Meeting of leaders from New England states opposed to the WAR OF 1812 because it disrupted trade. Convention resolutions sought to strengthen states' rights over conscription and taxation; some delegates favoured withdrawal from the Union.

Hartley, L.P. (Lesley Poles) (1895–1972) English novelist, short-story writer and critic. He won acclaim with his trilogy of novels *The Shrimp and the Anemone* (1944), *The Sixth Heaven* (1946) and *Eustace and Hilda* (1947). Hartley's best-known novel, *The Go-Between* (1953), is a psychological drama of the loss of childhood innocence.

Hartmann, Nicolai (1882–1950) German realist philosopher. Although influenced by PLATO and Immanuel KANT, he proposed, in *Outlines of a Metaphysics of Knowledge* (1921), that existence is an essential prerequisite for knowledge, a reversal of Kant's idea. He finally rejected Kantian ideas in his book, *New Ways of Ontology* (1942). *See also* REALISM

Harun al-Rashid (764–809) ABBASID caliph of Baghdad (786–809). His reign has gained romantic lustre from the stories of the *Arabian Nights*. He engaged in successful war with the BYZANTINE EMPIRE, but his effort to reconcile competing interests by dividing the empire between his sons led to civil war.

Harvard University Oldest US college, founded in 1636 by John Harvard at Cambridge, Massachusetts. It was originally intended for the instruction of Puritan ministers. Harvard has two undergraduate divisions: Harvard College for men and Radcliffe College for women. All classes are co-educational. It has ten graduate schools.

harvestman (daddy-longlegs) ARACHNID with legs that may be several times its body length. It feeds on insects and plant juices. Body: 2.5–13mm (0.1–0.5in). Family Phalangidae.

harvest-mite *See* CHIGGER

Harvey, William (1578–1657) English physician and anatomist who discovered the circulation of the BLOOD. His findings were published in *De Motu Cordis et Sanguinis* (1628). He also studied EMBRYOLOGY.

Haryana State in N central India; the capital is CHANDIGARH. It was formed in 1966 from part of the state of the Punjab. Industries: machine and farming tools, cement, paper, bicycles. Area: 44,222sq km (17,074sq mi). Pop. (1991) 16,403,648.

Harz Mountains Mountain range in central Germany, extending 96km (60mi) between the rivers Weser and Elbe. The highest peak is the Brocken, 1,142m (3,747ft).

Hasdrubal Barca Name of two Carthaginian generals. The elder (d.221 BC) expanded Carthaginian power and founded Cartagena, Spain. The younger (d.207 BC) was the son of HAMILCAR BARCA and the brother of HANNIBAL. He took command in Spain when Hannibal went to Italy. After defeat there, he fled to Italy, where he died in battle.

Hašek, Jaroslav (1883–1923) Czech novelist and short-story writer. He wrote the best-selling satirical novel *The Good Soldier Schweik* (1920–23).

Hashemite Arab princely family descended from the Prophet MUHAMMAD, including the fourth caliph ALI and King HUSSEIN of Jordan.

hashish Resin obtained from the flowering tops of the hemp plant *Cannabis sativa* and used as a psychotropic drug. When smoked or eaten it generally induces heady sensations and often a feeling of detachment. Possession of the drug is illegal in the UK. *See also* CANNABIS

Hasidism Popular pietist movement within JUDAISM founded by Israel ben Eliezer (c.1699–c.1761), known as the Baal Shem Tov (Master of the Good Name). The movement, centred in E Europe until World War 2, strongly supports Orthodox Judaism. Its main centres are now in Israel and the USA.

Hassan II (1929–99) King of Morocco (1961–99), son of Muhammad V. He dissolved the National Assembly in 1965 and introduced a new constitution, approved by referendum (1971), which left his authority supreme.

Hastings, Warren (1732–1818) British colonial administrator, first British governor general of India (1774–85). Hastings reformed the administration and finances of the British East India Company and consolidated Britain's military control of India. He made many enemies and returned to England (1785) to face charges of corruption. In 1795 he was acquitted, but his career was ruined.

Hastings, Battle of (14 October 1066) Fought near Hastings, SE England, by King HAROLD II of England against an invading army led by WILLIAM, Duke of Normandy. The Norman victory and death of Harold marked the end of the Anglo-Saxon monarchy and produced a social revolution.

hatchetfish Carnivorous hatchet-shaped fish with light-emitting organs on the underside of its muscular abdomen.

There are two groups: **deep-sea** hatchetfish (family Sternoptychidae) related to salamander; and **flying** hatchetfish (family Gasteropelecidae) of South America which "fly" by beating their pectoral fins. Length: to 10cm (4in).

Hathor Ancient Egyptian goddess of love and happiness, music and dance. She was depicted as a cow or with the horns of a cow.

Hatshepsut (d.1482 BC) Queen of Egypt (c.1494–1482 BC). Daughter of THUTMOSE I, she married Thutmose II. After his death (c. 1504 BC), she ruled first as regent for her nephew and then in her own right, the only woman to rule as pharaoh.

Hatta, Muhammad (1902–80) Indonesian statesman. Exiled by the Dutch in 1935 for revolutionary activities, Hatta and SUKARNO collaborated with the Japanese in World War 2. In 1948 he led the fight for Indonesian independence from the Dutch and became vice-president (1950–56) of the new republic. Hatta resigned after a dispute with Sukarno, but returned as an adviser to SUHARTO.

Haughey, Charles (1925–) Irish statesman, taoiseach (1979–81, 1982, 1987–92). He entered parliament in 1957. Haughey succeeded Jack Lynch as taoiseach and president (1979–92) of FIANNA FÁIL. In 1987, he returned to power after defeating Dr Garrett FITZGERALD. Haughey was forced to resign after a phone-tapping scandal.

Hauptmann, Gerhart (1862–1946) German dramatist, poet and novelist. His play, *Before Dawn* (1889), marked the birth of German naturalist drama. Other plays include *The Weavers* (1892). Hauptmann was awarded the 1912 Nobel Prize for literature.

Hausa Mainly Muslim people, inhabiting NW Nigeria and S Niger. Hausa society is feudal and based on patrilineal descent. Its language is the LINGUA FRANCA of N Nigeria and a major trading language of W Africa. Hausa crafts include weaving, leatherwork and silversmithing.

haustorium Invasive, sucker-like or tube-like structure in a parasitic plant or fungus. It penetrates the outer tissues of a host plant in order to absorb nourishment.

Havana (La Habana) Capital of CUBA, on the NW coast; largest city and port in the West Indies. It was founded (15151) by the Spanish explorer Diego Velázquez and moved to its present site in 1519. Havana became Cuba's capital at the end of the 16th century. By the early 19th century it was a wealthy commercial centre. The city's fortunes declined later in the century. Industries: oil refining, textiles, sugar. Pop. (1994) 2,241,000.

Havel, Vaclav (1936–) Czech statesman and dramatist. He wrote a series of plays, such as *The Garden Party* (1963), that were highly critical of Czechoslovakia's communist regime. Havel was the leading spokesman for the dissident group Charter 77 and was imprisoned (1979–83) by the regime. In 1989 he served another brief spell in prison before founding the Civic Forum. Following the "Velvet Revolution" (December 1989) Havel was elected president of Czechoslovakia. He resigned (1992) in protest at the partition of Czechoslovakia, but returned by popular demand as president of the Czech Republic. He was re-elected in 1998.

Hawaii US state in the N Pacific Ocean, c.3,350km (2,100mi) WSW of San Francisco; the capital is HONOLULU. It consists of eight large and 124 small volcanic islands. The highest point is MAUNA KEA, at 4,205m (13,678ft). There is an important US naval base at PEARL HARBOR. Settled by Polynesians in the 9th century AD, the islands were united in the late 18th century by King KAMEHAMEHA. In 1778, they were visited by Captain Cook, who named them the Sandwich Islands. In 1893, the monarchy was overthrown and was annexed by the

US in 1898. In 1900, Hawaii became a US territory and was the last state to be admitted (1959) to the Union. The economy is based on agriculture and tourism. Exports: bananas, pineapples, sugar, nuts, coffee. Area: 16,705sq km (6,450sq mi). Pop. (2000) 1,211,537.

hawfinch Largest European FINCH, nesting in temperate regions. It has mostly chestnut plumage, with black and white patches. Length: 18cm (7in). Species *Coccothraustes coccothraustes*.

hawk BIRD OF PREY of the family Accipitridae, which includes the true hawks, BUZZARDS, EAGLES, HARRIERS, KITES, OSPREYS and VULTURES. They range in size from the tiny SPARROW HAWK to the harpy eagle. Hawks have short, hooked bills for tearing meat and strong claws for killing and carrying prey. Common coloration is red, brown or grey plumage with streaks on the wings. Length: 28–66 cm (11–26in). Order Falconiformes. *See also* FALCON

Hawke, Bob (Robert) (1929–) Australian statesman, prime minister (1983–91). He entered Parliament in 1980 and in 1983 became leader of the Australian Labor Party. Hawke held office for an unprecedented four terms. He was succeeded by Paul KEATING.

Hawke, Edward, 1st Baron (1705–81) British admiral. In 1747 he was knighted for the defeat of the French at Finisterre. During the SEVEN YEARS' WAR Hawke destroyed the French fleet at Quiberon Bay, thus ending France's invasion plans.

Hawking, Stephen William (1942–) English theoretical physicist. He used the general theory of RELATIVITY and QUANTUM MECHANICS to produce theories on BIG BANG and the formation of BLACK HOLES. He found that the powerful gravitational field around super dense black holes can radiate matter. Hawking wrote the popular science bestseller *A Brief History of Time* (1988). Since the 1960s, he has suffered from a progressive motor neurone disease.

Hawkins, Coleman (1904–69) US jazz saxophonist. He began his career in 1923 with the Fletcher Henderson orchestra. From 1934 to 1939, "the Hawk" lived in Europe, where he recorded with Django REINHARDT. Hawkins' definitive recording of "Body and Soul" was one of the first recordings of an extended jazz solo.

Hawkins, Sir John (1532–95) English naval commander. With the support of Elizabeth I, he led two lucrative expeditions to Africa and the West Indies (1562–63, 1564–65), but on his third expedition (1567–69) the Spanish destroyed most of his ships. He played an important role in the defeat of the Spanish ARMADA in 1588.

Hawks, Howard (1896–1977) US film director. In a career spanning six decades, he proved himself adept in every film genre. Hawks made gangster films such as *Scarface* (1931), screwball comedies such as *Bringing Up Baby* (1938), film noir thrillers such as *The Big Sleep* (1946), musicals such as *Gentleman Prefer Blondes* (1953), and westerns such as *Rio Bravo* (1959).

Hawksmoor, Nicholas (1661–1736) English BAROQUE architect. He started his career as an assistant to Sir Christopher WREN on the construction of St Paul's, London, and worked with Sir John VANBRUGH at Castle Howard and Blenheim Palace. Hawksmoor is celebrated for his six London church designs, including St Mary's, Woolnoth (1716–27) and St George's, Bloomsbury (1716–31).

hawthorn Any of more than 200 species of thorny DECIDUOUS shrubs and trees of the genus *Crataegus*, growing in N temperate parts of the world. Their flowers are white or pink, and small berries are borne in clusters. They are widely used in hedgerows. Family Rosaceae.

Hawthorne, Nathaniel (1804–64) US novelist. He helped develop the American short-story. His reputation was made with *The Scarlet Letter* (1850). Other works include *The House of the Seven Gables* (1851), *The Blithedale Romance* (1852) and *The Snow Image and Other Twice-Told Tales* (1851). Much of his work is set in Puritan New England and examines the conflict between emotion and repressive social strictures.

Hay, John Milton (1838–1905) US secretary of state (1898–1905) under Presidents MCKINLEY and Theodore ROOSEVELT. His "open-door policy" was a demand for equal trading status for foreign powers in China, and he negotiated the HAY-PAUNCEFOTE TREATY ensuring US control of the Panama Canal.

Haydn, Franz Joseph (1732–1809) Austrian composer. Haydn brought the SONATA form to masterful fruition in more than 100 symphonies, notably the *Military*, the *Clock* and the *London* (all 1793–95). His most famous choral works are the oratorios *The Creation* (1798) and *The Seasons* (1801). He also wrote many string quartets, chamber works, concertos and masses.

Hayek, Friedrich August von (1899–1992) British economist, b. Austria. In *The Road to Serfdom* (1944) he criticized the creation of the WELFARE STATE and championed free-market economics and MONETARISM. Hayek shared the 1974 Nobel Prize for economics.

Hayes, Helen (1900–93) US actress. In a distinguished stage career, her most notable roles were in *Dear Brutus* (1918), *Victoria Regina* (1935–39) and *The Glass Menagerie* (1948). Hayes' film credits include *The Sin of Madelon Claudet* (1931) for which she won an Academy Award for best actress; *What Every Woman Knows* (1934); *Anastasia* (1956); and *Airport* (1969), which won her an Academy Award for best supporting actress.

Hayes, Rutherford Birchard (1822–93) 19th US President (1877–81). As governor of Ohio, he won the Republican nomination for president in 1876. Some of the electoral votes were disputed, but an electoral commission awarded all of them to Hayes, giving him victory over Samuel J. Tilden. As president, Hayes removed all federal troops from the South and tried to promote civil-service reform. He retired after one term.

hay fever Seasonal ALLERGY induced by grass POLLENS. Symptoms include ASTHMA, itching of the nose and eyes and sneezing. Symptoms are controlled with an ANTIHISTAMINE.

Hay-Pauncefote Treaty (1901) Agreement promising equal rates through the PANAMA CANAL to all nations and all vessels. It also granted the USA the full right to build and manage the canal. It was negotiated by John HAY and Lord Pauncefote, British ambassador to the USA.

Hayworth, Rita (1918–87) US film actress. Her image as the sultry temptress was established in *Blood and Sand* (1941). Hayworth was the dancing partner of Gene KELLY in *Cover Girl* (1944), and Fred ASTAIRE in *You Were Never Lovelier* (1941). Orson WELLES (one of her five husbands) directed her in *The Lady From Shanghai* (1948).

hazel Any of about 15 bushes or small trees of the genus *Corylus*, native to N temperate regions. There are separate male and female flowers. The fruit is a hazelnut, also called cobnut or filbert. Family Betulaceae.

Hazlitt, William (1778–1830) English critic and essayist. A friend to many leading talents of the Romantic movement, his volumes of critical essays include *Lectures on the English Poets* (1818), *Table Talk* (1821–22) and *The Spirit of the Age* (1825).

Health, UK Department of Government department responsible for the administration of the NATIONAL

HEALTH SERVICE and local authority social services. It also provides information on public and environmental health and is responsible for public ambulance services. The head of the Department is the secretary of state for health.

Health and Safety Commission British government body created by the Health and Safety at Work Act (1974) to instigate and monitor measures to protect people in work and the public at large from industrial or commerical hazards. The Health and Safety Executive has an inspectorate to enforce health and safety law in working premises.

Heaney, Seamus (1939–) Irish poet, b. Northern Ireland. His early volumes, such as *Death of a Naturalist* (1966), establish a strong link between soil and language. Later works, such as *North* (1975), *Field Work* (1979) and *Station Island* (1984), examine the political and historical connotations of words. Heaney won the Whitbread Prize for *The Spirit Level* (1996). His essay collections include *The Government of the Tongue* (1988). Heaney was awarded the 1995 Nobel Prize for literature. Other works include a translation of Beowulf (2000), which won the Whitbread Prize.

hearing Process by which sound WAVES are experienced. SOUND waves enter the EAR and vibrate the eardrum. The vibrations are transmitted by three small bones to the COCHLEA, where receptors generate nerve impulses that pass via the auditory nerve to the brain to be interpreted.

hearing aid Electronic sound-reproducing device to increase the sound intensity at the EAR. Modern aids use a small crystal microphone, a battery-powered amplifier and an earpiece. Cochlear implants (electrodes implanted in the cochlea of the ear) are now being used to help profoundly deaf people.

Hearne, Samuel (1745–92) British explorer of Canada. In 1766 he joined HUDSON'S BAY COMPANY and was posted to the Churchill River. In 1770–72 Hearne became the first European to reach the Arctic Ocean overland, via the Coppermine River.

Hearst, William Randolph (1863–1951) US media tycoon. He built a nationwide publishing empire that included newspapers, magazines, news services, radio stations and film studios. With his rival, Joseph PULITZER, Hearst practised sensational journalism and promoted the Spanish-American War. His career inspired Orson Welles' film *Citizen Kane* (1941).

heart Muscular ORGAN that pumps BLOOD throughout the body. In humans, the heart MUSCLE is located behind the breastbone between the lower parts of the lungs. Divided longitudinally by a muscular wall, the right side contains only deoxygenated blood, the left side only oxygenated blood. The pulmonary ARTERY carries deoxygenated blood from the heart to the lungs. Each side is divided into two chambers, an atrium and a ventricle. The average heart beat rate for an adult at rest is 70–80 beats per minute.

heart attack (myocardial infarction) Death of part of the HEART muscle due to the blockage of a coronary ARTERY by a blood clot (thrombosis). It is accompanied by chest pain, sweating and vomiting. Modern drugs treat abnormal heart rhythms and dissolve clots in the coronary arteries. **Heart failure** occurs when the heart is unable to pump blood at the rate necessary to supply body tissues and may be due to high BLOOD PRESSURE or CORONARY HEART DISEASE. Symptoms include shortness of breath, OEDEMA and fatigue. Treatment is with a DIURETIC and heart drugs. *See also* ANGINA; ARTERIOSCLEROSIS

heart-lung machine Apparatus used during some surgery to take over the function of the heart and lungs. It consists of a mechanical pump to circulate blood around the body and a filter to add oxygen to the blood and remove carbon dioxide. It was first used in 1953.

heat (symbol Q) Form of ENERGY that is transferred as a consequence of a difference in TEMPERATURE. The amount of heat gained or lost by a body is equal to the product of its heat capacity and the temperature through which it rises of falls. Heat is transferred in three forms: CONVECTION, CONDUCTION and RADIATION. The total KINETIC and POTENTIAL ENERGY of a body is known as its internal energy (U). If this body changes temperature, there is a corresponding change (ΔU) in its internal energy. According to the first law of THERMODYNAMICS, $\Delta U = Q - W$, where Q is the heat and W is the WORK. The SI unit of heat and energy is the JOULE (J).

heat capacity (thermal capacity) Ratio of the heat supplied to an object to the rise in its TEMPERATURE. It is measured in joules/kelvin. *See also* SPECIFIC HEAT CAPACITY

Heath, Sir Edward Richard George (1916–) British statesman, prime minister (1970–74). He entered Parliament in 1950, becoming lord privy seal (1960–63). In 1965 Heath succeeded Sir Alec DOUGLAS-HOME as leader of the CONSERVATIVE PARTY. He defeated Harold WILSON in the 1970 general election. As prime minister, Heath secured (1973) Britain's membership of the European Community (EC), but poor industrial relations led to a bitter miners' strike and the "three-day week" (1974) to conserve energy. After two general election defeats in 1974, he was replaced (1975) as Conservative leader by Margaret THATCHER. Heath was a staunch critic of "Thatcherism" and an outspoken advocate of European integration during John MAJOR's terms in office.

heath Any of various woody, evergreen shrubs of the genus *Erica*, found in Europe, North America and Africa. They usually have bell-shaped blue or purple

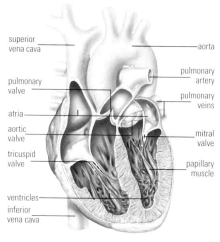

superior vena cava
aorta
pulmonary artery
pulmonary valve
pulmonary veins
atria
aortic valve
mitral valve
tricuspid valve
papillary muscle
ventricles
inferior vena cava

▲ **heart** The human heart contains four chambers – two atria and two ventricles – and four sets of valves. Blood from the body passes into the right atrium, via the vena cavae. Flow of blood into the right ventricle is controlled by the tricuspid valve. Pulmonary arteries carry blood from the right ventricle to the lungs, while the pulmonary veins carry oxygenated blood back from the lungs to the left atrium. In a similar way, the mitral valve controls the flow of blood between the left atrium and the left ventricle. The aorta conducts the oxygenated blood from the left ventricle to all parts of the body.

flowers. Family Ericaceae.

heather (ling) Evergreen shrub native to Europe and Asia Minor. It has bell-shaped flowers of pink, lavender or white. Family Ericaceae; species *Calluna vulgaris*.

heatstroke Condition in which human body temperature rises above 41°C (106°F). It is brought on by exposure to extreme heat. In mild cases there is lassitude and fainting; in severe cases, collapse, coma and death may ensue.

heaven Abode of divine beings or a world of bliss beyond death. In the later Jewish tradition (after the 3rd or 2nd century BC), it was the dwelling place of God and the angels and of those human beings who had died after leading a virtuous life. Christian theology adopted this conception but modified it to be the destination after death of the true followers of Jesus Christ. *See also* HADES; HELL; LIMBO; NIRVANA; PURGATORY

Heaviside-Kennelly layer (E-layer) Charged region within the IONOSPHERE of Earth's ATMOSPHERE responsible for the reflection of RADIO waves back to Earth. itwas independently discovered (1902) by Oliver Heaviside (1850–1925) and Arthur Kennelly (1861–1939).

heavy water *See* DEUTERIUM

Hebrew Language of the SEMITIC branch of the AFROASIATIC family. Spoken in Palestine from ancient times, it is the language of the OLD TESTAMENT. It declined during the BABYLONIAN CAPTIVITY and was overtaken by ARAMAIC. Hebrew persisted as a literary and liturgical language among Jews. It was revived as a spoken language by the 19th century Zionist movement and became the official language of ISRAEL in 1948. *See also* YIDDISH

Hebrews, Epistle to the Part of the NEW TESTAMENT. It contains a letter of encouragement to a group of Jewish converts to Christianity and a review of Israel's history and Jesus' place in it. Its author is unknown.

Hebrides (Western Isles) Group of more than 500 islands in the Atlantic Ocean off the w coast of Scotland. They are divided into the Inner Hebrides (principal islands: Skye, Rhum, Eigg, Islay, Mull) and the Outer Hebrides (principal islands: Lewis with Harris, North and South Uist). First inhabited in the 4th millennium BC, the islands, from the 3rd century AD, were settled by Picts and later by Scots. In the 8th century, they were invaded by Vikings and became a Norwegian dependency. In the 13th century, they were ceded to Scotland by Norway. Less than 100 of the islands are inhabited, and agriculture is limited. Industries: fishing, farming, woollen clothing.

Hebron (El Khalil) City in the Israeli-occupied WEST BANK. An ancient city, it came under Arab control in the 7th century AD and was occupied by the Crusaders (12th–13th centuries) before reverting to Arab rule. It later became part of the Ottoman Empire. In 1948, it was annexed to Jordan but was occupied by Israel during the SIX-DAY WAR (1967). It has witnessed much Israeli–Arab tension, especially during the INTIFADA. The ISRAELI-PALESTINIAN ACCORD granted Palestinian self-rule to 85% of the city. Hebron is sacred to both Jews and Muslims. The Tomb of the Patriarchs (the Cave of Machpelah) is the traditional burial place of Abraham, Sarah, Isaac, Rebecca, Jacob and Leah. Industries: tanning, glass making, food processing. Pop. (1995 est.) 117,000.

Hecate Goddess in Greek mythology. Associated with ARTEMIS, she bestowed wealth and blessings, and presided over witchcraft, graveyards and cross-roads.

Hector In Greek legend, the greatest of the Trojan heroes, eldest son of PRIAM. He was slain by ACHILLES.

hedgehog Small, nocturnal Eurasian and African mammal of the family Erinaceidae. It has short, sharp spines and defends itself by rolling into a ball with the

▲ **hedgehog** The spines of the European hedgehog (*Erinaceus europus*) are actually hairs modified into hollow tubes with reinforcing ridges on the inside walls, making for a strong but light structure. The spines are raised when the animal is threatened.

spines outermost. It feeds on insects and other small animals. Genus *Erinaceus*

hedonism Pursuit of pleasure, or any of several philosophical or ethical doctrines associated with it. Aristippus (*c*.435–*c*.356 BC) taught that pleasure was the highest good. EPICURUS advocated discrimination in the seeking of pleasure. LOCKE believed that the idea of "good" can be defined in terms of pleasure. BENTHAM and J.S. MILL adapted a psychological view of hedonism in formulating UTILITARIANISM.

Hegel, Georg Wilhelm Friedrich (1770–1831) German philosopher, whose method of dialectical reasoning had a strong influence on his successors, notably Karl MARX. In 1818, he succeeded Johann FICHTE as professor of philosophy at Berlin University. He developed a metaphysical system that traced the self-realization of spirit by dialectical movements towards perfection. These progressions took the form of battles between a thesis and an antithesis, eventually resolved in a synthesis at a higher level of truth. Hegel wrote two major books, *Phenomenology of Mind* (1807) and *Science of Logic* (1812–16). *See also* DIALECTICAL MATERIALISM

hegemony Leadership or dominance of one state over others. The term originated in ancient Greece where the cities of Athens, Sparta and Thebes held hegemony over Greece in the 5th and 4th centuries BC. The term was also employed by the Italian Marxian theorist Antonio GRAMSCI to refer to the phenomenon of one social CLASS monopolizing the creation and transmission of values.

Hegira (Arab. exodus) Flight of MUHAMMAD from MECCA to MEDINA in AD 622 to escape persecution. OMAR set this date as the start of the Islamic CALENDAR.

Heidegger, Martin (1889–1976) German philosopher. A founder of EXISTENTIALISM and a major influence on modern philosophy, Heidegger's most important work was *Being and Time* (1927). Influenced by HERMENEUTICS, PHENOMENOLOGY and Christian ONTOLOGY, his central concern was how human self-awareness is dependent on the concepts of time and death. For Heidegger, Western science and philosophy have led to NIHILISM and prevent people from rediscovering their true selves. His later work focused more on the role of language. His support for the Nazi Party has damaged his reputation.

Heidelberg City on the River Neckar, Baden-Württemberg, sw Germany. Founded in the 12th century, it has the oldest university in Germany (1386) and a medieval castle. Industries: printing machinery, precision instruments, publishing, textiles. Pop. (1995 est.) 139,000.

Heifetz, Jascha (1901–87) US violinist, b. Russia. He made his debut at the age of six and first performed in London in 1920, rapidly establishing a reputation for technical virtuosity. he commissioned a number of new violin works, including Walton's Violin Concerto (1939).

Heimlich manoeuvre FIRST AID technique, developed by Dr Henry J. Heimlich for relieving blockage in the windpipe. The rescuer uses his or her arms to encircle the choking person's chest from behind, positioning one fist in the space just beneath the breastbone and covering it with the other hand. The rescuer then thumps their fist into the patient's midriff.

Heine, Heinrich (1797–1856) German poet and prose writer. The *Book of Songs* (1827), a collection of verse, is his best-known work. It was followed by the four-volume satirical *Pictures of Travel* (1826–31). SCHUMANN and SCHUBERT both set his lyrics to music.

Heinkel, Ernst Heinrich (1888–1958) German AIRCRAFT designer. He developed the SEAPLANE and light passenger aircraft. In 1939, Heinkel designed the first jet aircraft (HE-178) and the first plane powered by a liquid-fuel ROCKET motor (HE-176). Heinkel's aircraft were used in World War 2 by the German Luftwaffe.

Heisenberg, Werner Karl (1901–76) German physicist and philosopher, one of the pioneers of QUANTUM MECHANICS. He studied under Max BORN and Niels BOHR. In 1926, Heisenberg developed a form of QUANTUM THEORY based on matrix ALGEBRA, known as matrix mechanics. Paul DIRAC showed that Heisenberg's theory was equivalent to Erwin SCHRÖDINGER's notion of WAVE MECHANICS. In 1927, Heisenberg published his famous UNCERTAINTY PRINCIPLE, which stated that the momentum and position of a SUBATOMIC PARTICLE cannot be accurately measured simultaneously. He was awarded the 1932 Nobel Prize for physics. During World War 2 Heisenberg worked with Otto HAHN on the development of a nuclear reactor.

Hejaz Region in NW Saudi Arabia, on the Red Sea coast. The centre of ISLAM, it contains the Muslim holy cities of MECCA and MEDINA. It has been part of Saudi Arabia since 1932. Area: 388,500sq km (150,000sq mi).

Helen In Greek legend, the beautiful daughter of LEDA and ZEUS. She married Menelaus, King of Sparta, but was carried off by PARIS, Prince of TROY, thus provoking the TROJAN WAR.

Helena Capital of Montana, W central Montana, USA. Settled by prospectors in 1864, by 1868 US$16 million worth of gold had been mined. In 1889, it became state capital. Industries: mineral-smelting. Pop. (1990) 24,569.

helicopter AIRCRAFT that gains lift from power-driven rotors (rotating AEROFOILS). A helicopter is capable of vertical takeoff and landing (VTOL), hovering, and forwards, backwards and lateral flight. Each rotor blade can move independently of the others. At take-off, all blades have a steep pitch in order to acheive maximum LIFT. The circular movement of the blades generates an opposite, reactive force on the helicopter that is overcome by another set of opposite-turning rotors, or by another small rotor in the tail generating THRUST in the opposite direction. The first successful helicopter was built (1939) by Igor SIKORSKY.

heliocentric theory *See* COPERNICUS, NICOLAS

Heliopolis Ancient city in N lower Egypt, in the Nile delta, 10km (6mi) NE of Cairo. It was noted as a centre of Sun worship for the god RA, from *c.*1580 to 1090 BC, and was the site of the obelisks CLEOPATRA'S NEEDLES.

Helios In Greek mythology, god of the Sun, identified with the Roman god APOLLO. Helios appears driving a four-horse chariot through the sky.

helium (symbol He) Nonmetallic element, a NOBLE GAS, discovered in 1868. First obtained in 1895 from the mineral clevite, the chief source today is from natural gas. It is also found in some radioactive minerals and in the Earth's atmosphere (0.0005% by volume). It has the lowest melting and boiling points of any element. It is colourless, odourless and nonflammable and is used in light-air balloons, to make artificial "air" (with oxygen) for deep-sea divers, and in welding, semiconductors and lasers. Liquid helium is used in CRYOGENICS. Properties: at.no. 2; r.a.m. 4.0026; r.d. 0.178; m.p. $-272.2°C$ ($-458°F$); b.p. $-268.9°C$ ($-452.02°F$); single isotope He[4].

helix Curve generated when a point moves over the surface of a cylinder so that it traces a path inclined at a constant angle to the cylinder's axis, as in a coil spring.

hell Abode of evil spirits and the place or state of eternal punishment after death for the wicked. In modern Christian theology, hell is conceived as eternal separation from God. Hell is paralleled in other religions and mythologies, for example, the Hebrew *sheol* or the Greek HADES. *See also* HEAVEN; LIMBO; PURGATORY

hellebore Any of *c.*20 species of poisonous, herbaceous plants of the genus *Helleborus*, native to Eurasia. Best known is the Christmas rose, *H. niger*, which bears white flowers from mid-winter to early spring. Family Ranunculaceae.

Hellenistic age (323–27 BC) Period of Classical Mediterranean history from the death of ALEXANDER THE GREAT to the accession of AUGUSTUS. Alexander's conquests helped to spread Greek civilization over a wide area. The age was distinguished by remarkable scientific and technological advances, especially in ALEXANDRIA, and by more elaborate and naturalistic styles in the visual arts.

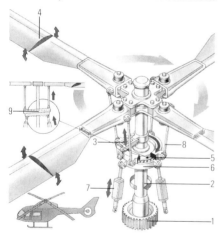

▲ **helicopter** A helicopter rotor head transfers the power of the engines to the rotor blades via gears (1) and the rotor shaft (2). The swish plate controls the tilt of the rotor (3) and also the pitch of the blades (4). The upper (5) and lower (6) swish plates are controlled by hydraulic cylinders (7) attached to the lower plate. The upper plate is connected to the rotor blades by control rods (8). The pitch of the blades controls the amount of lift generated, while the attitude of the whole rotor controls how the helicopter moves horizontally. If the rear of the swish plate is raised (9), the rotor dips toward the nose of the helicopter, causing it to travel forward.

Heller, Joseph (1923–) US novelist. His debut novel, *Catch–22* (1961), is a masterful satire on the stupidity of war. Other works include the play *We Bombed in New Haven* (1968), and the novels *Something Happened* (1974), *God Knows* (1984) and *Closing Time* (1994).

Hellespont *See* DARDANELLES

Hellman, Lillian (1905–84) US dramatist. Her debut play, *The Children's Hour* (1934), was a controversial success. Hellman's drama *The Little Foxes* (1939) was a damning critique of American capitalism. A committed socialist and feminist, Hellman and her partner, Dashiell HAMMETT, were blacklisted during the McCarthy era. Her memoirs started with *An Unfinished Woman* (1969) and concluded with *Maybe* (1980).

Helmholtz, Hermann Ludwig Ferdinand von (1821–94) German physicist and physiologist. He made contributions in ACOUSTICS and OPTICS, expanding Thomas Young's three-colour theory of vision. His experiments on the speed of nerve impulses led him to formulate a principle of conservation of energy vital to THERMODYNAMICS.

Helmont, Jan Baptista van (1580–1644) Flemish chemist and physician. He believed in transmutation (the changing of base substance of the Earth. Helmont carried out was the basic substance of the Earth. Helmont carried out quantitative experiments and coined the word "GAS" (Greek *chaos*). He also discovered CARBON DIOXIDE.

Héloïse *See* ABELARD, PETER

Helsinki (Helsingfors) Capital of Finland, in the S of the country, on the Gulf of Finland. Founded (1550) by GUSTAVUS I (VASA), it became the capital in 1812. It has two universities (1849, 1908), a cathedral (1852), museums and art galleries. The administrative centre of Finland, it is also its largest port. Industries: shipbuilding, engineering, ceramics, textiles. Pop. (1997) 532,000.

Helvétius, Claude Adrien (1715–71) French philosopher and educator. His best-known work, *De L'Esprit* (1758), attacked the religious basis of morality, arousing great opposition. Helvétius claimed that everybody is intellectually equal but some have less desire to learn than others. This led him to claim, in *De l'homme* (1772), that all human problems could be solved by education.

hematite One of the most important iron ores, containing mainly ferric oxide, Fe_2O_3. Containing 70% iron by weight, it occurs in several forms and varies in colour from steel-grey to black, but sometimes red.

Hemingway, Ernest Millar (1899–1961) US writer. After serving as an ambulance driver in World War 1, he became a journalist, first in Paris and later as a war correspondent in the Spanish Civil War and World War 2. The novel, *The Sun Also Rises* (1926), chronicled the LOST GENERATION and established his reputation. Later works include *A Farewell to Arms* (1929), *For Whom the Bell Tolls* (1940) and the novella *The Old Man and the Sea* (1952). He was also an acclaimed short-story writer. Hemingway was awarded the 1954 Nobel Prize for literature. Prone to severe depression, he committed suicide.

hemlock Poisonous herbaceous plant native to Eurasia. It has a long taproot and flat clusters of white flowers. The leaf stalks have purple spots. Family Apiaceae/Umbelliferae; species *Conium maculatum*.

hemp Herb native to Asia and cultivated in Eurasia, North America and parts of South America. It has hollow stems with fibrous inner bark, also called hemp, which is used to make ropes and cloth. Oil from the seeds is used in soap and paint. Some strains of the plant, generally known as CANNABIS, are used to produce MARIJUANA and HASHISH. Height: to 5m (16ft). Family Cannabinaceae; species *Cannabis sativa*.

Hendrix, Jimi (James Marshall) (1942–70) US rock musician. His improvised guitar solos have influenced generations of rock and jazz artists. In 1965, he formed "The Jimi Hendrix Experience" with Mitch Mitchell and Noel Redding. His debut album was *Are You Experienced?* (1965). Hendrix was a headline act at WOODSTOCK (1970). Other albums include *Band of Gypsies* (1970).

Hendry, Stephen Gordon (1969–) Scottish snooker player. In 1987, he became the youngest player to win a major title. In 1988, Hendry became British Open champion. The youngest-ever world champion in 1990, he held the world title six times in the next seven years.

Henley Royal Regatta Oldest rowing regatta in the world, begun in 1839 in Henley-on-Thames, Oxfordshire, England. Held every July, the regatta is as famous as a social event as it is for rowing. Trophies include the Grand Challenge Cup and the Diamond Challenge Sculls.

henna (Egyptian privet) Small shrub native to the Middle East and N Africa. Since ancient times, people have extracted a red-brown dye from the leaves to colour hair and skin. Family Lythraceae; species *Lawsonia inerma*.

Hennepin, Louis (1640–1701) French explorer. A Franciscan missionary, he sailed to Canada in 1675 and became chaplain to LA SALLE. Hennepin accompanied him on the 1679 expedition, writing the first description of Niagara Falls and being held prisoner by the Sioux. His exaggerated account, *Description de la Louisiane* (1683), was very popular.

Henri, Robert (1865–1929) US painter, a founder of the ASHCAN SCHOOL. Henri is best known for his realistic urban scenes such as *West 57th Street, New York* (1902).

Henrietta Maria (1609–69) Queen consort of CHARLES I of England and daughter of HENRY IV of France. Her Roman Catholicism and support for Charles's absolutist tendencies incurred Parliament's hostility and helped precipitate the ENGLISH CIVIL WARS.

Henry I (the Fowler) (*c.*876–936) King of the Germans (918–36). Duke of Saxony, he was elected to succeed CONRAD I as king. He asserted his authority over the German princes and reconquered Lotharingia (Lorraine, 925). In 933, he defeated the Magyar raiders. He was succeeded by his son, OTTO I, first Holy Roman Emperor.

Henry II (973–1024) Holy Roman Emperor (1002–24). Succeeding his cousin, Otto III, he concentrated on cementing his rule in Germany. Henry was crowned in Rome in 1014 and canonized in 1146.

Henry III (1017–56) German king (1039–56) and Holy Roman Emperor (1046–56). He succeeded his father, CONRAD II. Imperial power reached its zenith in Henry's reign as he subdued rebellious vassals in Saxony and Lorraine and compelled the rulers of Poland, Bohemia and Hungary, as well as the S Italian princes, to pay him homage.

Henry IV (1050–1106) German king (1056–1106) and Holy Roman Emperor (1084–1106). Embroiled in the dispute with the papacy over the lay investiture of clerics, he deposed Pope GREGORY VII and was in turn excommunicated by the pope (1076). Rebellion in Germany weakened Henry's position. In 1077, he was forced to do penance at Canossa. In 1084, Henry captured Rome, deposed Gregory and set up an antipope, Clement III. In 1105, he was deposed by his son, HENRY V.

Henry V (1081–1125) German king (1105–25) and Holy Roman Emperor (1111–25). Having deposed his father, HENRY IV, he resumed the quarrel with the papacy over investiture, while antagonizing German princes by the ruthless assertion of his power. Henry was defeated in Germany and compelled to compromise with the papacy. The Concordat of WORMS (1122) ended the investiture conflict.

Henry VI (1165–97) German king (1190–97) and Holy Roman Emperor (1191–97), son of FREDERICK I (BARBAROSSA). In 1186 he married Constance, heiress of the kingdom of Sicily, and much of his reign was devoted to securing that inheritance. After 1194, the empire was at the height of its power. Although he failed to make the empire hereditary in the HOHENSTAUFEN line, his infant son, FREDERICK II, was accepted as his successor.

Henry I (1068–1135) King of England (1100–35), youngest son of WILLIAM I (THE CONQUEROR). He rescinded unpopular taxes and married a Scottish princess of Anglo-Saxon descent. He thus won the support that helped him to defeat his brother ROBERT II, Duke of Normandy, and regain Normandy for the English crown (1106). Henry settled the dispute over the investiture involving Archbishop ANSELM.

Henry II (1133–89) King of England (1154–89), son of Geoffrey of Anjou and Matilda (daughter of HENRY I). He inherited the ANGEVIN lands and obtained AQUITAINE by marrying ELEANOR in 1152. He re-established stable royal government in England, instituting reforms in finance, local government and justice. His efforts to extend royal justice to priests led to his quarrel with Thomas à BECKET. His later reign was troubled by the rebellions of his sons, including two future kings, RICHARD I and JOHN.

Henry III (1207–72) King of England (1216–72). The influence of foreigners on his administration antagonized the nobles. He was forced to accept the Provisions of Westminster (1259), giving more power to his councillors, but renounced them in 1261, provoking the BARONS' WAR. The leader of the barons, Simon de MONTFORT, was defeated at Lewes (1264) by Henry's son, the future EDWARD I, who thereafter ruled on his father's behalf.

Henry IV (1367–1413) King of England (1399–1413), son of JOHN OF GAUNT. Henry Bolingbroke was exiled in 1399 by RICHARD II. He returned and overthrew Richard, claiming the crown for himself. As a usurper Henry had to overcome revolts, notably by Owain GLYN DŴR and Sir Henry PERCY.

Henry V (1387–1422) King of England (1413–22), son of HENRY IV. Henry renewed the English claims against France in the HUNDRED YEARS WAR and won a decisive victory at AGINCOURT in 1415. Further conquests in 1417–19 resulted in the Treaty of Troyes (1420), when CHARLES VI of France recognized him as his heir.

Henry VI (1421–71) King of England (1422–61, 1470–71). He succeeded his father, HENRY V, as a baby and came of age in 1437. In 1445, Henry married MARGARET OF ANJOU, who thereafter dominated government. His reign was characterized by military disasters in France and by the dynastic conflict in England known as the Wars of the ROSES. Deposed by the Yorkists led by EDWARD IV (1461), he was restored in 1470 but was again deposed and murdered.

Henry VII (1457–1509) King of England (1485–1509), founder of the TUDOR dynasty. Having come to the throne by defeating RICHARD III in the final battle of the Wars of the ROSES at BOSWORTH FIELD (1485), Henry united the houses of LANCASTER and YORK by marrying the Yorkist heiress, Elizabeth. His financial acumen restored England's fortunes after the devastation of civil war. He took effective action against pretenders to his throne, securing the succession of his son HENRY VIII.

Henry VIII (1491–1547) King of England (1509–47), second son of HENRY VII. He became heir (1502) on the death of his elder brother, Arthur. His aggressive foreign policy, administered by Cardinal WOLSEY, depleted the royal treasury. Henry, supported by Thomas CROMWELL, presided over the first stages of the English REFORMATION, brought about largely because the pope refused to grant Henry a divorce from his first wife, CATHERINE OF ARAGON. With the legislation in place, Henry divorced Catherine and married Anne BOLEYN (1533), mother of the future ELIZABETH I. In 1535, Anne was executed for adultery. Thomas MORE, Henry's former chancellor, was also executed for refusing to accept Henry as head of the church. Henry then married Jane Seymour, who died shortly after the birth of the future EDWARD VI. His next marriage, to ANNE OF CLEVES, ended in divorce (1540) and with the execution of Cromwell. Shortly after, he married Catherine HOWARD (executed 1542) and finally Catherine Parr (1543) who survived him. Henry's reign will also be remembered for the DISSOLUTION OF THE MONASTERIES (1536–40), which brought temporary relief from financial problems but at the cost of social unrest.

Henry II (1519–59) King of France (1547–59), son and successor of FRANCIS I. In 1533, he married CATHERINE DE' MEDICI. Henry was dominated by his mistress, Diane de Poitiers, and by the rival families of GUISE and Montmorency. After bankrupting the royal government, the war with Emperor CHARLES V was concluded at the Peace of Cateau-Cambrésis (1559). Henry began the persecution of HUGUENOTS, which led to the Wars of RELIGION.

Henry III (1551–89) King of France (1574–89). As Duke of Anjou, he fought against the HUGUENOTS in the Wars of RELIGION. By making peace with the Huguenots (1576), he antagonized extremist Roman Catholics, who formed the Catholic League led by the House of GUISE. After the League provoked a revolt in 1588, Henry had the Guise leaders killed and made an alliance with the Huguenot, Henry of Navarre (later HENRY IV). The king was assassinated by a member of the league.

Henry IV (1553–1610) King of France (1589–1610), first of the BOURBON dynasty. From a Protestant upbringing, he was recognized as leader of the HUGUENOTS. Henry's marriage to Margaret of Valois was marred by the SAINT BARTHOLEMEW'S DAY MASSACRE (1572). Henry survived, but was forced to convert to Roman Catholicism. In 1584, he became legal heir to HENRY III. On Henry III's death, the GUISE family refused to recognize his claim, but were subdued. In 1593, Henry willingly converted to Roman Catholicism, allegedly remarking "Paris is well worth a Mass". He ended the French Wars of RELIGION by the Edict of NANTES (1598), but remained sympathetic to Protestantism, secretly supporting the revolt of the Protestant Netherlands against Spain. A popular king, with a keen sense of social justice, he was assassinated by François Ravaillac.

Henry, Joseph (1797–1878) US physicist, whose work on ELECTROMAGNETISM was essential for the development of the telegraph. His work on INDUCTION led to the production of the TRANSFORMER. The unit of inductance is named after him.

Henry, O. (1862–1910) US short-story writer, b. William Sydney Porter. He supposedly took his name from a contraction of Ohio Penitentiary, where he served a sentence for embezzlement. His short-stories about ordinary New Yorkers include the collection *The Four Million* (1906).

Henry, Patrick (1736–99) American patriot and statesman. As a member of the CONTINENTAL CONGRESS, he called the colonists to arms in March 1775 with the demand, "Give me liberty or give me death". Henry served as governor of Virginia (1776–79, 1784–86). A strong believer in STATES' RIGHTS, he opposed ratification of the US CONSTITUTION in 1787.

Henry the Lion (1129–95) Duke of Saxony (1142–80) and of Bavaria (1156–80). A GUELPH, he recovered the lands lost by his father, Henry the Proud, to the Emperor Conrad III. As Duke of Saxony he promoted German expansion beyond the River Elbe. In 1180, after refusing to support the Italian wars of the Emperor FREDERICK I (Barbarossa), he was deprived of most of his lands.

Henry the Navigator (1394–1460) Portuguese prince, son of JOHN I. Henry sponsored Portuguese voyages to the Atlantic coast of Africa, which later led to the discovery of the route to India via the Cape of Good Hope.

Henze, Hans Werner (1926–) German composer. Influenced by SCHOENBERG, he investigated the possibilities of TWELVE-TONE MUSIC. Henze's politically-inspired pieces include a requiem for Che Guevara, *The Raft of the Medusa* (1968). He is best known for his operas, such as *Elegy for Young Lovers* (1961).

hepatitis Inflammation of the liver, usually due to a generalized infection. Early symptoms include jaundice, fever, nausea, vomiting, abdominal swelling, skin rashes and joint pains. Seven different hepatitis viruses are known: A, B, C, D, E, F and G. The most common single cause is the infectious **hepatitis A** virus (HAV). Hepatitis A is usually a mild feverish disorder, which is transmitted by contaminated water or food. More serious is the serum **hepatitis B** virus (HBV), which can lead to chronic inflammation or complete failure of the liver and, sometimes, to liver cancer. Hepatitis B is transmitted by sexual intercourse, contact with infected blood products, or contaminated needles. Vaccines are available against HAV and HBV. **Hepatatis C** and **G** are transmitted in the same way as hepatis B. **Hepatatis D** (HDV) can only replicate in the presence of HBV. **Hepatits E** may cause epidemics in countries with poor sanitation.

Hepburn, Audrey (1929–93) US actress, b. Belgium. Her ingénue performance in *Roman Holiday* (1953) earned her an Academy Award for best actress. *Sabrina* (1954) and *Funny Face* (1957) won her further popular success. Other mature roles include *Breakfast at Tiffany's* (1961) and *My Fair Lady* (1964).

Hepburn, Katharine (1909–) US stage and film actress. She won her first Academy Award for best actress in *Morning Glory* (1933). Hepburn made nine films with Spencer TRACY, beginning with *Woman of the Year* (1952), and ending with an Oscar-winning performance in *Guess Who's Coming to Dinner* (1967). She won her third Oscar for best actress in *The Lion in Winter* (1968). Her performance in *On Golden Pond* (1981) gained her a fourth award. Other films include *Bringing up Baby* (1938), *The Philadelphia Story* (1940), *The African Queen* (1951), *Suddenly Last Summer* (1959) and *Long Day's Journey into Night* (1962).

Hephaestus Ancient Greek god of fire and crafts. Son of ZEUS and HERA, he is equivalent to the Roman VULCAN. Blacksmith and armourer to the Olympian gods, with a forge under volcanic Mount Etna, he was depicted as crippled and uncouth. His consort was APHRODITE.

Hepplewhite, George (d.1786) English furniture designer and cabinet-maker. His chairs have tapered legs with shield backs, and his neoclassical furniture combines pale woods with mahogany, often in the form of inlay.

heptathlon Track and field discipline for women consisting of seven events contested over two days.

Hepworth, Dame Barbara (1903–76) English sculptor. She shared Henry MOORE's interest in the techniques of carving. Hepworth's early pieces were mainly in wood and stone, using the natural qualities of these materials to produce fluid forms such as *Figure in sycamore* (1931). She was married (1932–51) to the abstract painter Ben NICHOLSON and her works are almost exclusively non-figurative. In the 1950s, Hepworth began to work in bronze. Later works include the memorial to Dag Hammerskojd, *Single form* (1963). She died in a fire at her studio in St Ives, Cornwall.

Hera In Greek mythology, queen of the Olympian gods, sister and wife of ZEUS. She appears as a scold who persecuted her rivals but helped JASON and ACHILLES.

Heracles In Greek mythology, greatest of the Greek heroes (in Roman mythology known as **Hercules**). Condemned to serve King Eurystheus, he performed 12 labours: he killed the Nemean lion and the Hydra; caught the Erymanthian boar and the Ceryneian hind; drove away the Stymphalian birds; cleaned the Augean stables; caught the Cretan bull and Diomedes' horses; stole the girdle of Hippolyte; killed Geryon; captured Cerberus; and stole the golden apples of Hesperides. After his death, he was allowed to ascend as a god to Olympus.

Heraclitus (536–470 BC) Greek philosopher, b. Ephesus, Asia Minor. Heraclitus believed that the outward, unchanging face of the universe masked a dynamic equilibrium in which all things were constantly changing, but with opposites remaining in balance. The elemental substance connecting everything was fire. He is credited with two sayings that sum up his world view: "All things change" and "You cannot step into the same river twice". Only fragments of his one book survive.

Heraclius (575–641) Byzantine Emperor (610–41). An outstanding military leader, he came to power at a time of economic, political and military crisis. Heraclius re-established government and army, defeated the Persians and took the Byzantine Empire to unrivalled power. By the time of his death, however, the Arabs had conquered much of the Empire.

Heraklion *See* IRÁKLION

heraldry Historic system in which personal and inherited symbols are granted for the practice of bearing and displaying ensigns on armour. During the Middle Ages heraldic symbols were displayed on the shield and helm. The herald, frequently a tournament official, became an expert at identifying families by their insignia; his function evolved into one of designing and granting armorial bearings. Its origin dates to 12th-century Germany. In England heraldry is controlled by the College of Arms (formed 1484). The Court of the Lord Lyon (1592) has a similar function in Scotland.

Herat (Harat) City in w Afghanistan, on the River Hari Rud; capital of Herāt province. Originally the ancient city of Aria, Herāt, which lay on an important trade route, served as TAMERLANE's capital in the early 15th century. Industries: textiles. Pop. (1990) 187,000.

herb Seed-bearing plant, usually with a soft stem that withers away after one growing season. Most herbs are ANGIOSPERMS. The term is also applied to any plant used as a flavouring, seasoning or medicine, such as ANGELICA, BASIL, BORAGE, CHAMOMILE, CHERVIL, DILL, FENNEL, MARJORAM, MINT, PARSLEY, ROSEMARY, SAGE and THYME. Herbs are usually grown in temperate climes, whereas SPICES are usually found in the tropics.

Herbert, George (1593–1633) English poet and churchman. His verse, some of the finest METAPHYSICAL POETRY, was published posthumously as *The Temple* (1633). It is noted for its devotional tone and technical complexity.

herbicide PESTICIDE used to kill weeds and other unwanted plants. Selective herbicides kill the weeds growing with crops, leaving the crops unharmed; non-selective herbicides, such as paraquat, kill all the vegetation. There are concerns over their toxicity to humans and their persistence in the environment.

herbivore Animal that feeds solely on plants. The term is most often applied to MAMMALS, especially RUMINANTS. Herbivores are characterized by broad molars and blunt-edged teeth, which they use to pull, cut and grind their food. Their digestive systems are adapted to the assimilation of cellulose. *See also* RODENT

Herculaneum Ancient city on the Bay of Naples, Italy, the site of modern Resina. Devastated in AD 62 by an earthquake, it was buried in AD 79 by the eruption of VESUVIUS. Archaeological excavations unearthed the Villa of the Papyri, which contained a library, well-preserved furniture, and victims who died on the seashore.

Hercules *See* HERACLES

Herder, Johann Gottfried von (1744–1803) German philosopher and poet. He believed human society to be an organic, secular totality that develops as the result of a historical process. Herder was a founder of German ROMANTICISM and a critic of KANT. *Outlines of a Philosophy on the History of Man* (1784–91) is regarded as his masterpiece.

heredity Transmission of characteristics from one generation of plants or animals to another. Characteristics, such as red hair, may be specific to individuals within a group; others, such as the possession of external ears, may be typical of a group as a whole. The combination of characteristics that makes up an organism and makes it different from others is set out in the organism's GENETIC CODE, passed on from its parents. The first studies of heredity were conducted by Gregor MENDEL. *See also* GENETICS

Hereford and Worcester County in W central England, bounded W and SW by Wales; the county town is WORCESTER. It is drained by the Severn, Wye and Teme rivers. The Malvern Hills divide the county into two lowland plains. The Vale of Evesham in the S provides rich soil for market gardening. Agriculture is the main activity. Industries: agricultural machinery, fruit canning and processing. Area: 3,926sq km (1,516sq mi). Pop. (1991) 676,747.

heresy Denial of, or deviation from, orthodox religious belief. The concept is found in most organized religions with a rigid dogmatic system. The early Christian church fought against heresies such as ARIANISM and NESTORIANISM. In the Middle Ages, the Catholic Church set up the INQUISITION to fight heresy. After the REFORMATION, the Catholic Church described Protestants as heretics because of their denial of many papally defined dogmas, while Protestants applied the term to those who denied their interpretation of the major scriptural doctrines.

Hereward the Wake (d. *c*.1080) Anglo-Saxon thegn who led resistance to the Norman Conquest of WILLIAM I (THE CONQUEROR). Hereward held out against William's forces on the Isle of Ely for nearly a year (1070–71).

hermaphrodite Organism that has both male and female sexual organs. Most hermaphrodite animals are invertebrates, such as the EARTHWORM and SNAIL. They reproduce by the mating of two individuals, each of which receives SPERM from the other. Some hermaphrodites are self-fertilizing. *See also* REPRODUCTION

hermeneutics Study of the principles of the interpretation of texts. The term particularly applies to the interpretation of scriptural or literary works.

Hermes In Greek mythology, messenger of the gods and patron of travellers and commerce. Represented with winged hat and sandals and carrying a golden wand, he is identified with the Roman MERCURY.

hermit crab Small CRAB found in shallow waters worldwide. Unlike other crabs it has a soft abdomen, which it protects with sea-snail shells. It changes shells as it grows. Some hermit crabs are terrestrial and do not use shells as adults. Family Paguridae.

hernia (rupture) Protrusion of an organ, or part of an organ, through its enclosing wall. Common hernias include: the protrusion of part of the intestine through the abdominal wall (**inguinal** hernia), which commonly occurs in the groin; protrusion of an intestinal loop through the umbilicus (**umbilical** hernia); or protrusion of part of the stomach or oesophagus into the chest cavity (**hiatus** hernia).

Hero In Greek mythology, a priestess of Aphrodite at Sestos. Each night Leander swam across the Hellespont from Abydos to court Hero. One stormy night Leander was drowned and Hero drowned herself in sorrow.

Herod Agrippa I (AD 10–44) King of Judaea (41–44), grandson of HEROD THE GREAT. He attracted the favour of

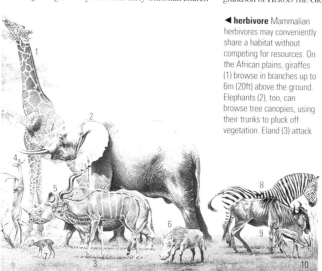

◄ **herbivore** Mammalian herbivores may conveniently share a habitat without competing for resources. On the African plains, giraffes (1) browse in branches up to 6m (20ft) above the ground. Elephants (2), too, can browse tree canopies, using their trunks to pluck off vegetation. Eland (3) attack the middle branches with their horns, twisting twigs to break them off, while gerenuk (4) stand on their hind legs to reach higher branches. The black rhino (5) uses its hook-like upper lip to feed on bark, twigs and leaves (white rhinos have lengthened skulls and broad lips for grazing the short grasses that they favour). The wart hog (6) and dik-dik (7) eat buds and flowers and will also dig up roots and tubers. Such sharing of a single resource also occurs among grazers. Migrating zebra (8) crop the taller, coarse grasses; wildebeest (9) feed on the leafy centre layer, allowing small gazelles (10) to reach the tender new shoots.

CALIGULA, who confirmed him as ruler of most of Palestine. He imprisoned St PETER and executed St JAMES.

Herod Agrippa II (27–93) King of Chalcis (50–93) and of Judaea (53–70), son of HEROD AGRIPPA I. The last of the Herodian dynasty, he presided over the trial of St PAUL. Herod tried to prevent the Jewish revolt (66) and afterwards sided with Rome.

Herodotus (c.485–c.425 BC) Greek historian. His *Histories* are the first great prose work in European literature. His main theme was the struggle of Greece against the Persian empire in the PERSIAN WARS, but he also provides an insight into the contemporary Mediterranean world.

Herod the Great (73–04 BC) King of Judaea (37–04 BC). Supported by MARK ANTONY and AUGUSTUS, he endeavoured to reconcile Jews and Romans, and was responsible for many public works, including the rebuilding of the TEMPLE in Jerusalem. Herod later became cruel and tyrannical. According to the New Testament, he was king of Judaea when JESUS was born.

heroin Drug derived from MORPHINE. It produces effects similar to morphine, but acts more quickly and is effective in smaller doses. It is prescribed to relieve pain in terminal illness and severe injuries. Widely used illegally, it is more addictive than morphine. *See also* DRUG ADDICTION

heron Any of several species of wading bird that live near rivers. Herons have white, grey or brown plumage, long neck and legs and a sharp bill. They feed mainly on fish. Height: to 1.8m (6ft). Family Ardeidae.

Herophilus (c.335–c.280 BC) Greek anatomist. He practised at Alexandria and was one of the first to experiment with post-mortem examinations. Herophilus compared human and animal anatomy and made detailed studies of the human brain and spinal cord.

herpes Infectious disease caused by one of the herpes viruses. **Herpes simplex 1** infects the skin and causes cold sores. **Herpes simplex 2** is a SEXUALLY-TRANSMITTED DISEASE (STD). Symptoms include painful blisters on the genitals. **Herpes zoster** attacks nerve ganglia, causing SHINGLES. The same virus is responsible for CHICKENPOX.

Herrick, Robert (1591–1674) English poet, disciple of Ben JONSON. Ordained in 1623, he was ejected from his post (1647) for royalist sympathies. He regained the position after the RESTORATION. His poems, notably the collection *Hesperides* (1648), have great lyrical freshness.

herring Marine fish found worldwide. It is one of the most important food fish, and various species are canned as PILCHARD or SARDINE or sold fresh, pickled (rollmops) or smoked (as kippers or bloaters). Herrings have a laterally compressed body and a deeply forked tail fin. They feed on plankton. Length: 8–46cm (3–18in). Family Clupeidae; the 190 species include *Clupea harengus*.

Herschel, Sir John Frederick William (1792–1871) English astronomer, son of Sir William HERSCHEL. He extended his father's work on DOUBLE STARS and NEBULAE. In 1834 at the Cape of Good Hope, Herschel undertook a systematic survey of the southern sky, discovering more than 1,200 doubles and 1,700 nebulae and clusters. He combined these and his father's observations into a *General Catalog of Nebulae and Clusters* (1864).

Herschel, Sir William (1738–1822) English astronomer, b. Germany. He discovered URANUS (1781) and later two SATELLITES of Uranus (1787), and two of Saturn (1789). He observed many DOUBLE STARS and more than 2,000 NEBULAE and clusters, and published catalogues of them. Herschel realized that the Milky Way is the plane of a disc-shaped universe, whose form he calculated by counting the numbers of stars visible in different directions. In 1800, he discovered and investigated infrared radiation.

Hertfordshire County in London's "commuter belt", SE England; the county town is Hertford. Other major towns include ST ALBANS, Watford, Hatfield and Letchworth (Britain's first garden city). The terrain is flat apart from an extension of the Chiltern Hills in the NW. The main rivers are the Lea, Stort and Colne. Agriculture is important. Industries: engineering, electrical equipment, printing. Area: 1,636 sq km (631sq mi). Pop. (1994) 1,005,400.

Hertz, Heinrich Rudolf (1857–94) German physicist. In his early career he worked as an assistant to Hermann HELMHOLTZ. In 1888 Hertz discovered, broadcasted and received the RADIO waves predicted by James Clerk MAXWELL. He also demonstrated that heat and light are kinds of ELECTROMAGNETIC RADIATION. The unit of FREQUENCY, the HERTZ (Hz), is named after him.

hertz (symbol Hz) SI unit of FREQUENCY. A periodic phenomenon with a period of one second (such as one oscillation per second) is equivalent to 1Hz.

Hertzog, James Barry Munnik (1866–1942) South African statesman, prime minister (1924–39). He led the Orange Free State forces in the second of the SOUTH AFRICAN WARS (1899–1902). A member (1910–12) of the first Union government under Louis BOTHA, Hertzog founded the opposition National Party in 1914. He led two coalition governments. In 1939, Hertzog resigned from the coalition with Jan SMUTS in protest against South Africa's support for Britain in World War 2.

Hertzsprung-Russell diagram (H-R diagram) Plot of the absolute MAGNITUDE of stars against their spectral type; this is equivalent to plotting their LUMINOSITY against their surface temperature or colour index. Brightness increases from bottom to top, and temperature increases from right to left. The diagram was devised (1913) by Henry Norris Russell, independently of Ejnar Hertzsprung, who had the same idea in 1911. The H-R diagram reveals a pattern in which most stars lie on a diagonal band, the main sequence.

Herzegovina *See* BOSNIA-HERZEGOVINA

Herzl, Theodor (1860–1904) Jewish leader and founder of ZIONISM, b. Budapest. He worked as a lawyer and a journalist. In 1897 Herzl became president of the World Zionist Organization, which worked throughout Europe to establish a Jewish national home in Palestine.

Herzog, Werner (1942–) German film director. A leaders of the revival in German cinema in the 1970s, his recurring themes are obsession and alienation in extreme environments. His films include *Aguirre, Wrath of God* (1973), *The Enigma of Kasper Hauser* (1975), *Nosferatu* (1979), *Fitzcarraldo* (1982) and *Cobra Verde* (1988).

Heseltine, Michael Ray Dibdin (1933–) British statesman, deputy prime minister (1995–97). He entered Parliament in 1966. Under Margaret THATCHER, Heseltine served as secretary of state for the environment (1979–83) and defence secretary (1983–86), resigning over the Westland Affair. He rejoined the cabinet as secretary of state for the environment (1990–92) under John MAJOR's leadership. As secretary of state for trade and industry (1992–95), he announced a drastic programme of pit closures. Despite a heart attack, Heseltine continued as a combative deputy prime minister. Following electoral defeat (1997), he took a less active role in CONSERVATIVE PARTY politics.

Hesiod (active 8th century BC) Greek poet. Little is known of his life; he seems to have been a farmer in Boeotia and lived slightly later than HOMER. Hesiod's two major works are the *Theogony*, which presents a genealogy of the gods, and *Works and Days*, containing information and advice for farmers.

Hess, Rudolf (1894–1987) German Nazi leader. He joined the Nazi Party in 1921 and took part in the abortive MUNICH PUTSCH. Hess was the nominal deputy leader under Hitler from 1933. In 1941, he flew to Scotland in a mysterious one-man effort to make peace with the British. In 1945, Hess was sentenced to life imprisonment at the NUREMBERG TRIALS and spent the rest of his life in Spandau prison, Berlin, for many years its sole inmate.

Hess, Victor Francis (1883–1964) US physicist, b. Austria. As a result of his investigations into the ionization of air, he suggested that radiation similar to X-rays, later named cosmic RADIATION, comes from space. He shared the 1936 Nobel Prize for physics with Carl ANDERSON.

Hesse, Hermann (1877–1962) German novelist and poet. He lived in Switzerland after 1911 and became a Swiss citizen in 1923. Hesse studied Indian mysticism and Jungian psychology, subjects that find expression in novels such as *Demian* (1919), *Siddhartha* (1922) and *Steppenwolf* (1927). Other novels include *Narcissus and Goldmund* (1930) and *The Glass Bead Game* (1943). He was awarded the 1946 Nobel Prize for literature.

Hessen Region of central Germany. It was divided by a strip of Prussian territory until 1945. Industries: chemicals, manufacturing, electrical engineering. Area: 21,114sq km (8,150sq mi). Pop. (1993) 5,967,305.

Hestia In Greek mythology, virgin goddess of the hearth. In Rome, she was worshiped as VESTA.

Heston, Charlton (1923–) US actor. He won an Academy Award for best actor in *Ben Hur* (1959). Heston lent his powerful physical presence to other historical epics such as *The Ten Commandments* (1956), *El Cid* (1961), *Khartoum* (1966) and *Julius Caesar* (1970). Other films include *Planet of the Apes* (1968) and *Soylent Green* (1973).

heterosexuality Attraction of a male or female to members of the opposite SEX. The word is used to distinguish such attraction from HOMOSEXUALITY.

heterozygote Organism possessing two contrasting forms (ALLELES) of a GENE in a CHROMOSOME pair. In cases where one of the forms is dominant and one RECESSIVE, only the dominant form will be expressed in the PHENOTYPE. *See also* HOMOZYGOTE

Hewish, Antony (1924–) English radio astronomer. He shared the 1974 Nobel Prize for physics with Martin Ryle (1918–84) for their work on PULSARS.

hexagon Six-sided plane figure. Its interior angles add up to 720°. In a regular hexagon, whose sides and interior angles are all equal, each interior angle is 120°.

Heyerdahl, Thor (1914–) Norwegian ethnologist. With five crew, he drifted on the balsa raft *Kon Tiki* c.8,000km (5,000mi) across the Pacific Ocean from Peru to Polynesia (1947) in an attempt to prove that the Polynesians came from South America and not from SE Asia. In 1977 he sailed from Iraq to Djibouti in a reed boat, the *Tigris*.

Heywood, Thomas (1574–1641) English dramatist and actor. He was a prolific playwright, writing more than 220 plays. His best-known plays are *A Woman Killed with Kindness* (1603) and *The Fair Maid of the West* (1631).

Hiawatha (active 16th century) Native American leader of the Onondaga. In c.1575, he founded the five-nation IROQUOIS CONFEDERACY to halt intertribal wars. His semi-mythic reputation is partly the result of association with the fictional hero of the LONGFELLOW poem, *The Song of Hiawatha* (1855).

hibernation Dormant (sleep-like) condition adopted by some animals to survive harsh winters. Adaptive mechanisms to avoid starvation and extreme temperatures include reduced body temperature and slower heartbeat, breathing rate and metabolism.

hibiscus Genus of plants, shrubs and small trees native to tropical and temperate regions, and cultivated worldwide. Their large white, pink, yellow, blue or red bell-shaped flowers have darker centres. Family Malvaceae.

Hickok, "Wild Bill" (James Butler) (1837–76) US frontiersman. A renowned marksman, he was a scout with the Union Army during the CIVIL WAR and after the war for George CUSTER. He served as US marshal (1869–71) in Kansas and later toured with the Wild West show of "BUFFALO BILL". He was shot dead while playing poker.

hickory Deciduous tree of the WALNUT family native to E North America. Hickories are grown for ornament, timber and for their nuts. Height: 25m (80ft). Family Juglandaceae; genus *Carya*. *See also* PECAN

Hidalgo y Costilla, Miguel (1753–1811) Mexican priest and revolutionary. Of Creole birth, he was a priest in Dolores, Guanajuato, where he plotted a revolt against Spain. With an untrained army of 80,000, he captured Guanajuato and Valladolid. Defeated at Calderón Bridge, Hidalgo fled but was captured and executed.

hieroglyphics Writing system used in ancient EGYPT and, by extension, those of ancient Crete, Asia Minor, Central America and Mexico. The Egyptian system of hieroglyphics (pictorial characters) arose sometime before 3100 BC. At first they were purely picture symbols. The word "sun" was represented by a circle with a dot inside. In due course, they also came to be used conceptually, with symbols such as that for "sun" also standing for "day". Eventually, many symbols were used phonetically. The "sun" symbol, for instance, stood for a syllable that contained the same combination of consonants but had a different meaning. By the 7th century, hieroglyphics were used for business and literary purposes. As ancient Egyptian was supplanted by Greek, hieroglyphics died out. Most Egyptian texts have been deciphered, thanks to the discovery of the ROSETTA STONE (1799).

High Court of Justice In English law, court established primarily to hear civil cases. It also hears appeals from the magistrates' courts. It consists of three divisions: the Queen's Bench, the CHANCERY and the Family division.

high-definition television (HDTV) Form of TELEVISION on which the picture is made up of 1,250 or 1,125 scanning lines instead of 625 or 525. The increased number of lines makes the TV image sharper. It relies on digital transmission along FIBRE OPTICS rather than the transmission of electronic signals by radio waves.

high-fidelity (hi-fi) SOUND RECORDING and reproduction with the minimum of distortion, usually involving the use of high-quality components and circuits. The original sound source may be a COMPACT DISC (CD), gramophone record, magnetic TAPE, a radio signal or a live performance. An AMPLIFIER is required to "magnify" the signals, and one or more LOUDSPEAKERS are needed to make the source audible. Domestic hi-fi systems have been produced since the 1920s, but did not become common until the advent of long-playing gramophone records (LPs) in the 1950s and 1960s.

high jump Track-and-field event in which a competitor attempts to jump over a bar supported between two uprights. It has been an Olympic sport since 1896. A competitor may have a maximum of three attempts to clear each height to which the bar is raised.

Highland Scottish mountain and moorland region, lying N of a line running roughly SW to NE from Dumbarton to Stonehaven; the administrative centre is Inverness. The area is split geologically into the Northwest Highlands and the GRAMPIAN Highlands (separated by Glen More). Hydroelectric power and forestry schemes have been introduced in an effort to halt the decline in population through emigration. Industries: tourism, forestry, fishing. Area: 25,396sq km (9,804sq mi). Pop. (1991) 204,000

Highland Games Series of athletic competitions featuring traditional Scottish events. The term specifically refers to the Royal Braemar Games held annually in Scotland since 1819. The programme includes highland dancing, bagpipe playing and the tossing of the caber.

high-level language COMPUTER LANGUAGE that is reasonably close to spoken English. A high-level language is converted by a COMPILER into a form the COMPUTER can use. Most computer languages are now high-level.

Hilbert, David (1862–1943) German mathematician, b. Russia. He was professor of mathematics (1895–1943) at the University of Göttingen. Hilbert's *Foundations of Geometry* (1899) had the most profound influence on the study of GEOMETRY since EUCLID, establishing a rigorous axiomatic basis for the subject. His attempt to ground all mathematics on axioms was later discredited by Kurt GÖDEL. Hilbert's On Numbers (1897) systematized all the known results of algebraic NUMBER THEORY. His work on integral equations led to the concept of **Hilbert** space, crucial to the development of QUANTUM MECHANICS. In 1900, Hilbert proposed 23 problems for the mathematicians of the new century to tackle. Most of these have now been solved and have led to profound new understandings in mathematics.

Hill, Geoffrey (1932–) English poet. He usually writes on historical and religious themes. His volumes of poetry include *For the Unfallen* (1959), *King Log* (1968), *Mercian Hymns* (1971), *Tenebrae* (1978) and *The Mystery of the Charity of Charles Péguy* (1983).

Hill, Graham (1929–75) English motor racing driver. His long Formula 1 career included over 176 starts and 14 winning races. In 1962, Hill won his first Grand Prix and the world driver's championship. In 1968, he was again world champion. In 1972, Hill became the first Formula 1 champion to win the Le Mans 24-hour race. His son, **Damon** (1960–), is also a successful Formula 1 driver, becoming world champion in 1996.

Hill, Octavia (1838–1912) English housing reformer and co-founder (1895) of the NATIONAL TRUST. In 1864, with the help of John RUSKIN, she launched her first project to refurbish London slums.

Hill, Sir Rowland (1795–1879) English postal reformer. In 1840 he introduced the nationwide "penny post", adopting the first adhesive pre-paid postage stamp.

Hillary, Sir Edmund Percival (1919–) New Zealand explorer and mountaineer. On 29 May 1953, Hillary and the Sherpa guide, Tenzing Norgay, were the first climbers to reach the summit of Mount EVEREST. He also led (1955–58) the New Zealand group of the Commonwealth Trans-Antarctic Expedition organized by Vivian FUCHS.

Hilliard, Nicholas (1547–1619) English miniaturist and goldsmith. He portrayed many of the leading figures of the time in an exquisitely graceful style.

Himachal Pradesh State in the W Himalayas, NW India; the capital is Simla. It suffered numerous invasions before coming under British rule in the 19th century. It is mountainous and heavily forested, with highly cultivated valleys. Timber provides the main source of income. Area: 55,673sq km (21,495sq mi). Pop. (1991) 5,170,877.

Himalayas System of mountains in S Asia, extending *c.*2,400km (1,500mi) N – S in an arc between Tibet and India-Pakistan. The mountains are divided into three ranges: the Greater Himalayas (N), which include Mount EVEREST and K2; the Lesser Himalayas; and the Outer Himalayas (S).

Himmler, Heinrich (1900–45) German Nazi leader. In 1929 he became head of the SS. After the Nazis came to power in 1933, Himmler assumed control of the German GESTAPO and of the CONCENTRATION CAMPS. In 1945 he was captured by the British and committed suicide.

Hindemith, Paul (1895–1963) German composer, who emigrated to the USA in 1939. Among his works are symphonies, concertos, ballets, chamber music and operas. In the 1930s, with Kurt WEILL, he developed *Gebrauchsmusik* (Ger. utility music) written for amateur performance. His best-known work is the symphony he derived from his opera *Mathis der Maler* (1934).

Hindenburg, Paul Ludwig Hans von Beneckendorf und von (1847–1934) German statesman and general, president (1925–34). Commanding the army on the E front in World War 1, he defeated the Russians in the Battle of Tannenberg. In 1916, Hindenburg became supreme commander and, with his chief-of-staff, Erich LUDENDORFF, directed the German retreat on the Western Front (to the **Hindenburg line**). As second president of the WEIMAR REPUBLIC, he reluctantly appointed Adolf HITLER as chancellor in 1933.

Hindi Most widespread language in India, spoken in the north-central area by 154 million people. Hindi and English are the official languages of India. It derives from SANSKRIT and belongs to the Indo-European family.

Hinduism Traditional religion of India, characterized by a philosophy and a way of life rather than by a dogmatic structure. It was not founded by an individual and has been developing gradually since *c.*3000 BC, absorbing external influences. There are several schools within Hinduism, but all Hindus recognize the VEDAS as sacred texts. DHARMA is the eternal moral law underpinning existence. KARMA is the law of cause of effect that energises REINCARNATION. Liberation from the cycle of suffering and rebirth (*moksha*) and a return to BRAHMAN is the chief aim in life. One of the features of Hindu society is the CASTE system, but modern Hindu scholars maintain that it is not part of the religion. The main Hindu gods are BRAHMA, VISHNU and SHIVA (the Trimurti). Popular deities include KRISHNA, GANESH, PARVATI, LAKSHMI and INDRA. BRAHMANISM, the early phase of Hinduism, culminated in the classic texts of the MAHABHARATA (incorporating the BHAGAVAD GITA) and the RAMAYANA (relating the adventures of RAMA). Today, there are *c.*800 million Hindus worldwide. *See also* ADVAITA; AHIMSA; BRAHMO SAMAJ; HARE KRISHNA; MANTRA; UPANISHADS; VEDANTA

Hindu Kush Mountain range in central Asia, a continuation of the HIMALAYAS extending WSW for 800–960km (500–600 mi) from N Pakistan and NE Afghanistan. The highest peak is Tirich Mir, 7,700m (25,260ft).

Hindustani Member of the Indo-Iranian branch of INDO-EUROPEAN LANGUAGES, closely related to HINDI and URDU. More than 300 million people are thought to speak or understand Hindustani in India and Pakistan.

hip Joint on each side of the lower trunk, into which the head of the femur fits; the hip bones form part of the PELVIS.

hip-hop RAP music and its associated culture, originating in New York in the early 1980s. The music is characterized by a strong drumbeat, percussive "scratching" of vinyl records and rap vocals.

Hipparchus (active 2nd century BC) Greek astronomer. He estimated the distance of the Moon from the Earth and drew the first accurate star map. He developed an organization of the Universe that, although it had the Earth at the centre, provided for accurate prediction of the positions of the planets.

hippies Term used, especially in the 1960s, to refer to people in the West who rejected conventional middle-class values. Most were young people who renounced materialism, the work ethic and war, in particular the Vietnam War, and emphasized brotherhood and love. They adopted irregular life styles and were associated with the use of hallucinogenic drugs.

Hippocrates (*c*.460–*c*.377 BC) Greek physician, often called "the father of medicine". He emphasized clinical observation and provided guidelines for surgery. He is credited with the **Hippocratic oath**, a code of professional conduct still followed by doctors.

Hippolytus In Greek mythology, son of THESEUS and Hippolyta. When he spurned the advances of his stepmother, PHAEDRA, she turned his father against him. Put to death, he came back to life when his innocence was proved.

hippopotamus (Gr. river horse) Two species of bulky, herbivorous mammal, native to Africa. *Hippopotamus amphibius* has a massive grey or brown body with a large head and bulbous snout, short legs and tail. They have the largest mouth of any mammal, which gapes open to reveal long incisor and cannine teeth. Their skin dehydrates easily and they spend the day in water, emerging at night to graze on pastures. Males can weigh up to 3,200kg (7,050lb). **Pygmy** hippopotamuses, *Choeropsis liberiensis*, are much smaller and spend more time on land. They weigh *c*.180kg (400lb). Family Hippopotamidae.

hire purchase (HP) Method of acquiring goods by making a deposit, then paying the rest, with interest, in regular instalments. The vendor usually has an agreement with a financier who pays the full price of the goods. The buyer becomes full owner of the goods only after repaying the financer completely.

Hirohito (1901–89) Emperor of Japan (1926–89). He was the first crown prince to travel abroad (1921). Although he generally exercised little political power during his reign, Hirohito persuaded the Japanese government to surrender to the Allies in 1945. Under the new constitution of 1946, he lost all power and renounced the traditional claim of the Japanese emperors to be divine. He was succeeded by his son AKIHITO.

Hiroshige, Ando (1797–1858) Japanese master of the UKIYO-E (coloured WOODCUT). Together with HOKUSAI and UTAMARO, he was one of the leading Japanese printmakers of his era. Hiroshige is best known for his landscapes, such as *Fifty-Three Stages of the Tokaido Highway* (1833), which influenced IMPRESSIONISM.

Hiroshima City on the delta of the River Ota, SW Honshu, Japan; the river divides the city into six islands connected by 81 bridges. Founded in 1594, it was a military headquarters in the SINO-JAPANESE and RUSSO-JAPANESE wars. In August 1945, it was the target of the first atomic bomb dropped on a populated area. The city centre was obliterated and more than 70,000 people were killed. The event is commemorated in the Peace Memorial Park. Industries: brewing, shipbuilding, motor vehicles, chemicals. Pop. (1995) 1,109,000.

▶ **hippopotamus** The common hippopotamus, *Hippopotamus amphibius*, has the largest mouth of any mammal. Its canine teeth can reach 60cm (2ft) in length. The female produces a single calf. They usually travel in herds of 10 to 15 animals.

Hirst, Damien (1965–) English sculptor. He made his name by exhibiting sculptures of animals preserved in formaldehyde. One of these pieces, *Mother and Child Divided* (1993), which consists of the severed halves of a cow and calf displayed in four tanks, helped to win him the Turner Prize in 1995.

Hispaniola Island in the West Indies, in the N central Caribbean Sea, between Cuba (W) and Puerto Rico (E). It was discovered in 1492 by Christopher COLUMBUS. HAITI occupies the W third of the island, and the DOMINICAN REPUBLIC the remaining portion. It is a mountainous, agricultural region with a sub-tropical climate. Industries: coffee, cacao, tobacco, rice, sugar cane, some mining. Area: 76,480sq km (29,521sq mi).

Hiss, Alger (1904–96) US public official. He worked for the US state department (1936–47). In 1948, a former Soviet agent accused Hiss of passing confidential information documents to the Soviets. He denied the charges before a congressional committee, was tried (1949, 1950) for perjury, found guilty and sentenced to five years' imprisonment. The Hiss trial divided US public opinion. In 1992, papers released from KGB archives appeared to confirm Hiss' innocence.

histamine Substance derived from the amino acid histidine, occurring naturally in many plants and in animal tissues, and released on tissue injury. It is implicated in allergic reactions that can be treated with ANTIHISTAMINES.

histogram Bar chart. The bars represent the frequency (in absolute terms or as a percentage of the total) with which certain values (or ranges of value) occur within a given set of data.

histology Biological, especially microscopic, study of TISSUES and structures in living organisms.

historical novel Novel in which the main characters, plot and setting are based on historical persons, events or places. Examples include Walter SCOTT's *Ivanhoe* (1819) and Charles DICKENS' *A Tale of Two Cities* (1859).

history Written record of the human past; often used to mean the events themselves rather than the record of them. The Western historical tradition began with the Greek historians HERODOTUS and THUCYDIDES. China, and countries influenced by it, had a different, even older historical tradition in which the past was seen as the source of wisdom, and historians strove to distinguish comprehensible patterns in it.

Hitchcock, Sir Alfred (1899–1980) English film director. His full debut was *The Pleasure Garden* (1925). *Blackmail* (1929) was the first British film with synchronous sound. Hitchcock's appearances as an extra, the thrilling chases, sinister mood and sudden shocks, greatly influenced the French NOUVELLE VAGUE. *The Man Who Knew Too Much* (1934) was an international success. After *The 39 Steps* (1935) and *The Lady Vanishes* (1938), Hitchcock left for Hollywood. *Rebecca* (1940) won an Academy Award for best picture. Though less consistent in the 1940s, his credits included *Suspicion* (1941) and *Spellbound* (1945). An extraordinary sequence began with *Strangers on a Train* (1951), followed by the classic thrillers *Rear Window* (1954), *Vertigo* (1958), *North by Northwest* (1959) and *Psycho* (1960).

Hitler, Adolf (1889–1945) German fascist dictator (1933–45), b. Austria. He served in the German army during World War 1 and was decorated for bravery. In 1921 Hitler became leader of the small National Socialist Workers' Party (Nazi Party). While imprisoned for his role in the failed MUNICH PUTSCH, he set out his extreme racist and nationalist views in *Mein Kampf* (1925). Economic distress and dissatisfaction with the WEIMAR

REPUBLIC led to electoral gains for the Nazis and, by forming an alliance with orthodox Nationalists, Hitler became chancellor in January 1933. He made himself dictator of a one-party state in which all opposition was ruthlessly suppressed by the SS and GESTAPO. The racial hatred he incited led to a policy of extermination of Jews and others in the HOLOCAUST. Hitler pursued an aggressive foreign policy aimed at territorial expansion in E Europe. The invasion of Poland finally goaded Britain and France into declaring war on Germany in September 1939. Hitler himself played a large part in determining strategy during WORLD WAR 2. In April 1945, with Germany in ruins, he committed suicide.

Hittites People of Asia Minor who controlled a powerful empire in the 15th–13th centuries BC. They founded a kingdom in Anatolia (Turkey) in the 18th century BC; their capital was Hattusas (Boğazköy). They expanded E and S in the 15th century BC and conquered N Syria before being checked by the Egyptians under RAMSES II. Under attack from ASSYRIA, the Hittite empire disintegrated c.1200 BC.

hives (urticaria or nettle rash) Transient, itchy reddish or pale raised skin patches. Hives may be caused by an ALLERGY, by irritants such as sunlight or by stress.

Hizbullah (Hezbollah) Iranian-backed Islamic-fundamentalist group. It was formed in the early 1980s to encourage the integration of SHIITE religious militants into Middle Eastern politics. Hezbollah has been responsible for terrorist and military activities in the Middle East and elsewhere, including missile attacks on Israel.

Hobart Port and state capital of TASMANIA, SE Australia. Founded as a penal colony in the early 1800s, it became capital in 1812. It has one of the world's best natural harbours. Industries: fruit processing, textiles, zinc. Pop. (1994 est.) 52,900.

Hobbema, Meindert (1638–1709) Dutch painter. Hobbema's serene landscapes, especially the masterpiece *Avenue of Middelharnis* (1689), were highly influential on 18th and early 19th-century English landscape artists.

Hobbes, Thomas (1588–1679) English philosopher. In *De Corpore* (1655), *De Homine* (1658) and *De Cive* (1642), he maintained that matter and its motion comprise the only valid subjects for philosophy. His greatest work, *Leviathan* (1651), argued that man is inherently selfish but obeys a SOCIAL CONTRACT to maintain civilized society.

Hobbs, Sir Jack (John Berry) (1882–1963) English cricketer. His first-class record of 61,237 runs (including 197 centuries) remains unbeaten. He played cricket for Surrey (1904–30) and England (1908–30). Hobbs scored 5,410 runs (3,636 against Australia) in 61 tests. He was knighted in 1953.

hobby Typical FALCON, a day-active BIRD OF PREY found in temperate regions, especially in Europe. A brown-and-white streaked bird, it lives in or near open woodland country. Length: 33cm (13in). Species *Falco subbuteo*.

Hochhuth, Rolf (1931–) German dramatist. His controversial plays include *The Representative* (1963), which attacked the non-intervention of the pope in World War 2, and *Soldiers* (1967), which accused Winston Churchill of complicity in the death of Polish general Sikorski.

Ho Chi Minh (1890–1969) (Nguyen That Thanh) Vietnamese statesman, president of North Vietnam (1954–69). He founded the Vietnamese Communist Party in 1930. Forced into exile, he returned to Vietnam in 1941 to lead the VIET MINH against the Japanese. In 1945, Ho Chi Minh declared Vietnamese independence and led resistance to French colonial forces. After the French defeat at DIEN BIEN PHU (1954), Vietnam was partitioned and he became president of North Vietnam.

Ho Chi Minh organized and supported the VIET CONG against South Vietnam and committed North Vietnamese forces against the USA in the VIETNAM WAR.

Ho Chi Minh City (Saigon) City in S Vietnam, at the mouth of the River Saigon in the MEKONG delta; the largest city in Vietnam. It was an ancient Khmer settlement. In 1859, Saigon was seized by the French and made capital of Cochin China and then French INDOCHINA (1887–1902). In 1954, it became capital of independent South Vietnam. During the VIETNAM WAR it served as the military headquarters for US and South Vietnamese forces. Taken by the North Vietnamese in 1975, it was later renamed Ho Chi Minh City. It is the commercial and industrial centre of Vietnam. Industries: shipbuilding, textiles, pharmaceuticals. Pop. (1992) 4,322,000.

hockey (field hockey) Game played by two teams of 11 players, in which a hooked stick is used to strike a small, solid ball into the opponents' goal. The field of play classically measures 91.47 × 54.9m (300 × 180ft), usually grassed. There are two 35-minute halves. To score, a player must be within the semi-circle marked out in front of the goal. Body contact is forbidden and a ball is prohibited from being hit above shoulder height. The modern game dates from the formation of the English Hockey Association in 1875 and has been an Olympic sport since 1908. Recent developments in the UK include the introduction of a national club league system. *See also* ICE HOCKEY

Hockney, David (1937–) English painter. He made his name with witty POP ART paintings such as *Flight into Italy–Swiss Landscape* (1962). In the late 1960s and the 1970s, Hockney developed a more realistic, classical style, with pictures such as *A Bigger Splash* (1967) and his portraits in spacious interiors. His graphic work, including his series of etchings, *A Rake's Progress* (1961–63), are often regarded as being more innovative than his painting.

Hoddle, Glenn (1957–) English football player and coach. A creative midfield player, he made 377 appearances for Tottenham and earned 53 international caps. After a brief spell at Monaco, Hoddle became player-manager at Swindon Town and then Chelsea. He succeeded Terry VENABLES as England's national coach (1996–99). Hoddle led England in the 1998 World Cup finals, but was forced to resign following controversial remarks about the disabled. He was succeeded by Kevin KEEGAN.

Hodgkin, Sir Alan Lloyd (1914–98) English physiologist. During World War 2 he worked on the development of RADAR. Hodgkin and Andrew Huxley researched the transmission of nerve impulses in the giant squid. They discovered the ionic mechanisms involved in the excitation and inhibition of the membranes of nerve cells (NEURONS). Hodgkin and Huxley shared the 1963 Nobel Prize for physiology or medicine with John Eccles.

Hodgkin's disease Rare type of CANCER causing painless enlargement of the LYMPH GLANDS, lymphatic tissue and spleen, with subsequent spread to other areas. Named after the pathologist Thomas Hodgkin (1798–1866), its treatment consists of RADIOTHERAPY, surgery, drug therapy or a combination of these. It is curable if caught early.

Hoffa, Jimmy (James Riddle) (1913–?75) US trade union leader, president of the International Brotherhood of Teamsters (1957–71). In 1967, Hoffa was imprisoned for jury tampering, mail fraud and mishandling of union funds. In 1971, his sentence was commuted by President NIXON. In 1975, Hoffa disappeared and is presumed dead.

Hoffman, Dustin (1937–) US film actor. His debut in *The Graduate* (1967) earned an Academy Award nomination for best actor. Hoffman won further nominations for his roles as a derelict in *Midnight Cowboy* (1969)

and as a comedian in *Lenny* (1974). He finally won an Oscar for best actor in *Kramer vs. Kramer* (1979). Hoffman won a second Oscar for *Rain Man* (1988).

Hoffmann, E.T.A. (Ernst Theodor Amadeus) (1776–1822) German writer, musician and music critic. He wrote many gothic fantasies, several of which formed the basis for OFFENBACH's opera, *The Tales of Hoffmann* (1881). Tchaikovsky's *Nutcracker Suite* (1892) is also based on one of his stories. *The Devil's Elixir* (1815–16) and *The Educated Cat* (1820–22) are his two novels.

Hofmann, August Wilhelm von (1818–92) German chemist and teacher. He discovered a method, known as the Hofmann reaction, for converting an amide organic compound into an AMINE with one carbon atom fewer. He also discovered METHANAL (formaldehyde).

Hofmannsthal, Hugo von (1874–1929) Austrian dramatist and librettist. He was a co-founder of the Salzburg Festival and his play *Everyman* (1911) opened the 1920 festival. Hofmannsthal wrote the libretti for Richard Strauss' operas *Der Rosenkavalier* (1911) and *Ariadne auf Naxos* (1912).

Hofstadter, Robert (1915–90) US physicist. He proposed that PROTONS and NEUTRONS have a positively charged core surrounded by a cloud of elementary particles (pions). Hofstadter shared the 1961 Nobel Prize for physics with Rudolf Mössbauer.

hog *See* PIG

Hogan, (William) Ben (Benjamin) (1912–97) US golfer. After winning the US PGA (1946, 1948) and the US Open (1948), Hogan was seriously injured in a car accident. He made a remarkable recovery and went on to win three further US Opens (1950, 1951, 1953), two US Masters' (1951, 1953) and the British Open (1953).

Hogarth, William (1697–1764) English painter and engraver. He established his reputation with *A Harlot's Progress* (1731–32), the first in a series of "modern moral subjects". Hogarth painted narrative pictures that satirically exposed the follies and vices of his age. He is best known for *A Rake's Progress* (1733–35) and the masterpiece *Marriage à la Mode* (1743–45). He reached a wider audience by producing engravings of his paintings. Hogarth also excelled at portraiture, such as *Captain Coram* (1740). His *Analysis of Beauty* (1753) is a masterful exposition of ROCOCO aesthetics.

Hogg, James (1770–1835) Scottish poet, known as "the Ettrick shepherd". He had little formal education and worked tending sheep in the Borders. His poetic reputation was established with *The Queen's Wake* (1813). Hogg's masterpiece is the disturbing psychological novel *The Private Memoirs and Confessions of a Justified Sinner* (1824).

Hohenstaufen German dynasty that exercised great power in Germany and the HOLY ROMAN EMPIRE from 1138–1254. It is named after the castle of Staufen, built by Frederick, Count of Swabia, whose son became CONRAD III of Germany and Holy Roman Emperor in 1138. From Conrad III to CONRAD IV, the family occupied the Imperial throne, except between 1209 and 1215 (when OTTO IV, the representative of their great rivals, the GUELPHS, was Emperor). The greatest of the dynasty was FREDERICK II.

Hohenzollern German dynasty that ruled BRANDENBURG, Prussia and Germany. In 1415, the family acquired Brandenburg, and Prussia was added in 1618. FREDERICK WILLIAM (the Great Elector) further expanded their territories, and his son, Frederick I, adopted the title "King in Prussia". FREDERICK WILLIAM I built up the famous Prussian army, and FREDERICK II used it to great effect against the HABSBURGS. Germany was finally united in

1871 under the Hohenzollern emperor, WILLIAM I. His grandson WILLIAM II abdicated at the end of World War I.

Hokkaido (formerly Yezo) Most northerly and second largest of the main islands of JAPAN, bounded W by the Sea of Japan and E by the Pacific Ocean; the capital is SAPPORO. Until the late 19th century, it was the homeland of the Ainu aboriginals. It is mountainous and forested, with some active volcanoes. Linked to HONSHU island by the Seikan Tunnel, it is Japan's chief farming region and coal-producer. Crops: rice, maize, wheat, soya beans, potatoes, sugar beet. Industries: fishing, forestry, coal-mining, natural gas. Area: 83,451sq km (32,212sq mi). Pop. (1992 est.) 5,659,000.

Hokusai, Katsushika (1760–1849) Japanese master of UKIYO-E (coloured WOODCUT), especially famous for his landscapes, who influenced late 19th-century European painters. His most famous series of prints is *Views of Mount Fuji* (1835). *See also* HIROSHIGE, ANDO

Holbein, Hans, the Elder (*c*.1465–1524) German painter, father of HANS HOLBEIN THE YOUNGER. He was best known as a painter of altarpieces, producing some of his finest work for the Dominican convent of St Catherine, Augsburg. Holbein's later pictures reflect the increasing influence of Italian art.

Holbein, Hans, the Younger (1497–1543) German painter. His early work included religious paintings, such as *Dead Christ* (1521) and woodcuts such as *Dance of Death* (*c*.1523–25). Holbein's portraits of his friend ERASMUS earned him the patronage (1526–28) of Sir Thomas MORE. In 1532, he settled permanently in London and became (1536) court painter to HENRY VIII. Holbein's masterpieces include *The Ambassadors* (1533) and superb portraits of *Christina of Denmark, Duchess of Milan* (1538) and *Anne of Cleves* (1540).

Holden, William (1918–81) US film actor. An immediate star in his debut feature *Golden Boy* (1939), his career spanned six decades. Holden's ability was best captured by roles in Billy WILDER films, including the Hollywood satires *Sunset Boulevard* (1950) and *Fedora* (1978). He won an Academy Award for best actor in *Stalag 17* (1953).

Hölderlin, (Johann Christian) Friedrich (1770–1843) German poet. With the help of SCHILLER, he published the two-volume philosophical novel *Hyperion* (1797, 1799). From 1802, Hölderlin was increasingly troubled by mental illness, provoked by the death of his love Susette. In the 20th century, his lyrical poetry was critically reappraised for its synthesis of symbolism and classical Greek forms.

Holguin City in SE Cuba, its port on the Atlantic Ocean. Founded *c*.1720, it was the focus for rebellions against Spanish rule (1868–78, 1895–98). Located on a fertile plateau, it exports tobacco and cattle products. Industries: sugar cane, coffee, timber. Pop. (1994) 242,000.

Holiday, Billie (1915–59) US blues and jazz singer, nicknamed "Lady Day". She became famous in the 1930s with the bands of Count BASIE and Artie Shaw. Holiday's melancholic renditions of "My Man, Mean to Me" (1937) and her own "God Bless the Child" (1941) are legendary in the history of jazz.

Holland Popular name for the NETHERLANDS but properly referring only to a historic region, now divided into two provinces. A fief of the Holy Roman Empire in the 12th century, Holland was united with the county of Hainaut in 1299. It passed to Burgundy in 1433 and to the Habsburgs in 1482. In the 16th century, Holland led the Netherlands in their long struggle for independence.

Hollerith, Herman (1860–1929) US COMPUTER pioneer. In 1890, he invented a mechanical tabulating machine that used punched cards to record and process data. These gave rise to the Hollerith code (later employed by early computers) that uses 12 bits per alphanumeric character. Hollerith's firm, the Tabulating Machine Company, later expanded to become International Business Machines (IBM).

Holly, Buddy (1936–59) US rock and roll singer and songwriter, b. Charles Hardin Holley. In 1957, Buddy Holly and the Crickets had a string of hits including "That'll be the Day", "Oh Boy" and "Peggy Sue". Holly was a pioneer of double-tracking and the standard rock grouping of drums and bass, rhythm and lead guitars. He was killed in an air crash.

holly Any of c.300 species of trees or shrubs of the widely distributed genus *Ilex*. They have alternate, simple leaves. The small male and female flowers usually grow on separate trees. In winter the female flowers develop into red berries. The English holly tree (*I. aquifolium*) has spiny evergreen leaves. It is used for Christmas decoration. Height: to 15m (50ft). Family Aquifoliaceae.

Hollywood District of LOS ANGELES, California, USA. After 1911, it became the primary centre for film-making in the USA, and by the 1930s its studios dominated world CINEMA. Tourist attractions include Hollywood Boulevard.

Holmes, Oliver Wendell (1809–94) US writer and physician. His best literary work takes the form of humorous table talk, such as *The Autocrat of the Breakfast Table* (1857–58), *The Professor at the Breakfast Table* (1860) and *The Poet at the Breakfast Table* (1872). He was also a respected professor of medicine at Harvard University.

holmium (symbol Ho) Metallic element of the LANTHANIDE SERIES, first identified spectroscopically in 1879. Its chief ore is monazite. The element has few commercial uses. Properties: at.no. 67; r.a.m. 164.9304; r.d. 8.795 (25°C); m.p. 1,474°C (2,685°F); b.p. 2,695°C (4,883°F); most common isotope Ho^{165} (100%).

Holocaust, The (1933–45) Extermination of European Jews and others by the Nazi regime in Germany. The Nazi persecution reached its peak in the "Final Solution", a programme of mass extermination adopted in 1942, and carried out with murderous efficiency by Adolf EICHMANN. Jews, as well as others considered racially inferior by the Nazis, were killed in CONCENTRATION CAMPS such as AUSCHWITZ, BELSEN, DACHAU, Majdanek and Treblinka. Total Jewish deaths are estimated at more than 6 million, about three-quarters of the population of European Jews. The Holocaust has raised theological and moral problems about the course of European civilization.

Holocene (Recent epoch) Division of GEOLOGICAL TIME extending from c.10,000 years ago to the present. It includes the emergence of humans as settled members of communities; the first known villages date from c.8,000 years ago.

holography Process of making a hologram. One or more photographs are formed on a single film or plate by INTERFERENCE between two parts of a split LASER beam. The photograph appears as a flat pattern until light hits the plate in the correct position; it then becomes a 3-D image. The theory of holography was proposed (1947) by Denis Gabor, but only became practicable with the invention of the laser.

Holst, Gustav (Gustavus Theodore von) (1874–1934) English composer. His early works were often influenced by Hinduism, as in the opera *Sita* (1906), and English folksong, as in *Somerset Rhapsody* (1907). Among his works are several operas, including *The Perfect Fool* (1922), songs, chamber music and the popular orchestral suite *The Planets* (1914–16).

Holy Alliance (1815) Agreement signed at the Congress of VIENNA by the crowned heads of Russia, Prussia and Austria. Its purpose was to re-establish the principle of hereditary rule and to suppress democratic and nationalist movements, which had sprung up in the wake of the FRENCH REVOLUTION. The agreement, signed later by every European dynasty except the king of England and the Ottoman Sultan, came to be seen as an instrument of reaction and oppression.

Holy Communion *See* EUCHARIST

Holy Grail In medieval legend, cup supposedly used by JESUS CHRIST at the LAST SUPPER and by JOSEPH OF ARIMATHEA at the crucifixion to catch the blood from Jesus' wounds. The quest for the grail, especially by the knights in ARTHURIAN ROMANCE, became a search for mystical union with God.

Holyoake, Sir Keith Jacka (1904–83) New Zealand statesman, prime minister (1957, 1960–72). One of New Zealand's longest-serving statesman, he entered Parliament in 1932. In 1957, Holyoake succeeded Sir Sidney Holland as prime minister and leader of the National Party. He was governor-general (1977–80) of New Zealand.

Holy of Holies Innermost part of the Jewish TABERNACLE (Exodus 25–31) and later of the Jerusalem TEMPLE. Originally it contained the ARK OF THE COVENANT. It could only be entered once a year by the high priest on YOM KIPPUR.

Holy Roman Empire European empire centred on Germany (10th–19th centuries), which echoed the empire of ancient Rome. It was founded (962) when the German king OTTO I (THE GREAT) was crowned in Rome, although some historians date it from the coronation of CHARLEMAGNE in 800. The Emperor, who was elected by the German princes, claimed to be the temporal sovereign of Christendom, ruling in cooperation with the spiritual sovereign, the pope. However, the Empire never encompassed all of western Christendom, and relations with the papacy were often difficult. From 1438, the title was virtually hereditary in the HABSBURG dynasty. After 1648, the Empire became little more than a loose confederation, containing hundreds of virtually independent states. It was finally abolished by NAPOLEON I in 1806.

Holyrood House Royal palace in Edinburgh, Scotland. Begun in 1501, it was burned down in 1650. The existing house was reconstructed in the 1670s.

Holy Sepulchre Tomb in the old city of JERUSALEM traditionally held to be the site of the burial and resurrection of JESUS CHRIST. It was believed to have been discovered by St Helena, mother of Emperor CONSTANTINE I, who built the first "Church of the Holy Sepulchre" there c.336. Several churches have been built, destroyed, and rebuilt on the site over the centuries. Most of the present church dates from 1810.

Holy Spirit (Holy Ghost) Third person of the TRINITY in Christian theology. The Holy Spirit represents the spiritual agent through whom God's grace is given.

Holy Week Seven-day period preceding EASTER. It begins with Palm Sunday, commemorating Christ's entry into Jerusalem; Maundy Thursday marks his institution of the EUCHARIST; Good Friday marks his betrayal and crucifixion.

Home, Sir Alec Douglas- *See* DOUGLAS-HOME, SIR ALEC

Home Counties Counties surrounding London, England, consisting of BERKSHIRE, BUCKINGHAMSHIRE, ESSEX, HERTFORDSHIRE, KENT and SURREY.

Home Office British department of state, dating from 1782. The Home Office deals with all matters of national administration not entrusted to another department. The head of the department, the Home Secretary, is a cabinet position; there are separate secretaries of state for Scotland and Wales. There is a separate Northern Ireland office.

homeopathy Unorthodox medical treatment that involves administering minute doses of a drug or remedy that causes effects similar to those that are being treated. It was popularized by Christian HAHNEMANN.

homeostasis In biology, processes that maintain constant metabolic conditions within a cell or organism in response to either internal or external changes.

Homer (active 8th century BC) Greek poet. Homer is traditionally considered to be the author of the great early epics of GREEK LITERATURE, the *Iliad* and the *Odyssey*. Nothing factual is known about Homer, he is supposed have been blind and lived in Ionia. Literary scholarship has shown that the Homeric poems are a synthesis of oral, bardic stories. The *Iliad* relates the siege of Troy in the TROJAN WAR. The *Odyssey* tells of the post-war wanderings of ODYSSEUS on his way back to Penelope in Ithaca.

Homer, Winslow (1836–1910) US painter and illustrator. He won international acclaim for his coverage of the US Civil War in *Harper's Weekly* and particular recognition as a painter with *Prisoners from the Front* (1866). Homer is best known for haunting oil and watercolour seascapes, such as *Northeaster* (1895).

Home Rule, Irish Movement to gain Irish legislative independence from the British Parliament in the 19th century. The Act of UNION (1800) between Britain and IRELAND was unsuccessfully challenged by Daniel O'CONNELL's Repeal Association in the 1830s and 1840s. In the 1870s, Isaac Butt began the Home Rule League. His successor, Charles PARNELL, won GLADSTONE's support, but the first Home Rule Bill of 1886 split the LIBERAL PARTY and sent Liberal Unionists into the arms of the CONSERVATIVE PARTY. This coalition defeated a second bill in 1893. A third bill, presented by ASQUITH, was passed by Parliament in 1912. Implementation of the bill was postponed by the start of World War 1. The EASTER RISING (1916) and the landslide victory for SINN FÉIN in Irish elections were followed by a guerrilla war led by the IRISH REPUBLICAN ARMY (IRA). In 1919, the Dáil Eireann claimed independence. In 1920, LLOYD GEORGE's government passed a fourth Home Rule Bill establishing separate parliaments in Dublin and Belfast. In 1921, Arthur GRIFFITH and Michael COLLINS signed the Anglo-Irish Treaty that created the Irish Free State and gave *de facto* recognition to Northern IRELAND. The treaty was opposed by Eamon DE VALERA and the Irish Free State plunged into civil war.

Homo Genus to which humans belong. Modern humans are classified *Homo sapiens sapiens*. *See also* CRO-MAGNON; HOMO ERECTUS; HOMO HABILIS; HOMO SAPIENS; HUMAN EVOLUTION; NEANDERTHAL

Homo erectus ("upright man") Species of early human, presumably evolved from HOMO HABILIS, dating from *c*.1.5 million to 0.2 million years ago. **Java Man** was the first early human fossil to be found, late in the 19th century. Both it and **Peking Man**, another early discovery, represent more advanced forms of *Homo erectus* than older fossils found more recently in Africa. Our own species, HOMO SAPIENS, is thought to have evolved from **Heidelberg Man**. *See also* HUMAN EVOLUTION

Homo habilis ("handy man") Species of early human, discovered (1964) by Louis LEAKEY in the OLDUVAI GORGE, East Africa. Its fossil remains are between *c*.1.8 and *c*.1.2 million years old, contemporary with those of *Australopithecus*. The physical development is much more like that of modern human and it is thought they evolved into HOMO ERECTUS. *See also* HUMAN EVOLUTION

homoiothermic (endothermic or warm-blooded) Animal whose body temperature does not fluctuate as the temperature of its surroundings fluctuates. Mammals and birds are homoiothermic. They maintain their body temperature through METABOLISM. *See also* POIKILOTHERMIC

homology Similarity in essential structure of organisms based on a common genetic heritage. It often refers to organs that now have a different superficial appearance and function in different organisms. For example, a human arm and a seal's flipper are homologues, having evolved from a common origin. *See also* EVOLUTION

homophony In music, sounding in unison of voices or instruments. Also, a musical texture with a predominant melody part and an accompaniment, as opposed to monophony (music in a single part) or POLYPHONY.

Homo sapiens ("wise man") Our own species, which is thought to have evolved *c*.500,000 years ago from HOMO ERECTUS. The earliest fossils of *Homo sapiens* have been discovered in Africa. Modern man, *Homo sapiens sapiens*, developed sophisticated tools (*c*.40,000 years ago) that enabled it to colonize all Earth's continents except Antarctica by the PLEISTOCENE epoch (*c*.10,000 years ago).

homosexuality Emotional or sexual attraction to members of one's own sex. Male and female homosexuals are popularly known as gays and lesbians respectively. Historically, homosexuality was seen as a pathological condition and many psychoanalytic and psychiatric theories served to reinforce this impression. Doctors now agree that homosexuality is a normal aspect of sexuality. There is some evidence, from the study of twins, that genetic factors may partly determine homosexuality, but there is also evidence to show the influence of social factors. In the UK homosexual acts between consenting adults in private was legalised in 1967. In 1999, the minimum age of consent for homosexual acts was equalised with the heterosexual age of consent at 16 years of age. In the UK gays and lesbians have long sought to obtain equal rights and opportunities in such areas as housing, employment and the legal status of gay relationships. In Western countries the higher incidence among gay men of ACQUIRED IMMUNE DEFICIENCY SYNDROME (AIDS) has unified much of the gay community into promoting the importance of safe sex and increased funding for AIDS research.

homozygote Organism possessing identical forms of a GENE on a CHROMOSOME pair. It is a purebred organism and always produces the same kind of GAMETE. *See also* HETEROZYGOTE

Homs (Hims) City in W central Syria, on the River Orontes. Known in ancient times as Emesa, it was taken by Muslims in 636 and passed to the Ottomans in 1516. Sites include a Crusader fortress. Industries: oil refining, sugar refining, textiles, fertilizers. Pop. (1994) 644,000.

Honduras Republic in Central America. It has two coastlines: the N Caribbean coast, which extends for *c*.600km (375mi); and a narrow, 80km (50mi) long Pacific outlet to the Gulf of Fonseca. The deep waters off the N coast prompted the Spanish to name the country Honduras (Sp. depths). Along the N coast are vast banana plantations. In the E lies the MOSQUITO COAST. The Cordilleras highlands form 80% of Honduras and include the capital, TEGUCIGALPA. **Climate** Honduras has a tropical climate. The

---

HONDURAS
AREA: 112,090sq km (43,278 sq mi)
POPULATION: 6,846,000
CAPITAL (POPULATION): Tegucigalpa (814,000)

rainy season is from May to October. The N coast can be hit by fierce hurricanes. **Vegetation** Pine forests cover 75% of Honduras. The N coastal plains contain rainforest and tropical savanna. The Mosquito Coast contains mangrove swamps and dense forests. **History and politics** From AD 400 to 900 the MAYA civilization flourished. The magnificent ruins at Copán in W Honduras were discovered by the Spaniards in 1576 but became covered in dense forest and were only rediscovered in 1839. Christopher Columbus sighted the coast in 1502. In 1524, Pedro de Alvarado founded the first Spanish settlements. The native population was gradually subdued, and gold and silver mines were established. In 1821, Honduras gained independence, forming part of the Mexican empire. Between 1823 and 1838, Honduras was a member of the Central American Federation. Throughout the rest of the 19th century, it was subject to continuous political interference, especially from Guatemala. Britain controlled the Mosquito Coast. In the 1890s, US companies developed the banana plantations and exerted great political influence. Honduras became known as a "banana republic". After World War 2, demands grew for greater national autonomy and workers' rights. In 1963, the Liberal government was overthrown by a military coup. Honduras' expulsion of Salvadorean immigrants led to the brief "Soccer War" (1969) with El Salvador, following an ill-tempered World Cup qualifying match between the two countries. In 1982, civilian government was restored. During the 1980s, Honduras acted as a base for the US-backed CONTRA rebels from Nicaragua. Honduras was dependent on US aid. In 1988, popular demonstrations against the Contras led to the declaration of a state of emergency. In 1990, the war in Nicaragua ended. In 1992, Honduras signed a treaty with El Salvador, settling the disputed border. In 1997, the Liberal Party leader Carlos Flores was elected president. In 1998, Hurricane Mitch killed more than 5,500 people and left 14 million homeless. **Economy** Honduras is the least industrialized country in Central America, and the poorest developing nation in the Americas (1995 GDP per capita US$1,900). It has few mineral resources, other than silver, lead and zinc. Agriculture dominates the economy, forming 78% of exports and employing 38% of the workforce. Bananas and coffee are the leading exports, and maize the principal food crop. Cattle-raising, fishing and forestry are also important. Honduras has vast timber resources. Development is hampered by the lack of an adequate transport infrastructure.

Honecker, Erich (1912–94) East German communist leader (1971–89). Imprisoned by the Nazis (1935–45), he rose rapidly in the East German Communist Party after World War 2 and succeeded Walter ULBRICHT as party leader, pursuing policies approved by Moscow. With the reforms under Mikhail GORBACHEV and the collapse of European communism, Honecker resigned.

Honegger, Arthur (1892–1955) French composer. One of a group of Parisian composers known as *Les Six*, he caused a sensation with *Pacific 231* (1923), an orchestral description of a steam locomotive. His other compositions include five symphonies, two operas and the dramatic psalm *King David* (1921).

honey Sweet, viscous liquid manufactured by honeybees from nectar. It consists of the sugars fructose and dextrose, traces of minerals and c.17% water. *See also* BEE

honeyeater (honey sucker) Any of a group of Australian birds that feed on nectar and fruit, pollinating the flowers they feed on. Family Meliphagidae.

honeysuckle Woody twining or shrubby plant that grows in temperate regions worldwide. It has oval leaves and tubular flowers. In Eurasia, *Lonicera periclymenum* climbs to 6m (20ft). Family Caprifoliaceae.

Hong Kong (Xianggang Special Administrative Region) Former British crown colony off the coast of SE China; the capital is Victoria on Hong Kong Island. Hong Kong comprises Hong Kong Island, ceded to Britain by China in 1842; the mainland peninsula of Kowloon, acquired in 1860; the New Territories on the mainland, leased for 99 years in 1898; and some 230 islets in the South China Sea. The climate is sub-tropical, with hot, dry summers. In 1984 the UK and China signed a Joint Declaration in which it was agreed that China would resume sovereignty over Hong Kong in 1997. It also provided that Hong Kong would become a special administrative region, with its existing social and economic structure unchanged for 50 years. It would remain a free port. The last British governor Chris Patten (1992–97) introduced a legislative council. The handover to China was completed on 1 July 1997 and Chief Executive Tung Chee-hwa was sworn in and a provisional legislative council appointed. Hong Kong is a vital international financial centre with a strong manufacturing base. In 1997, the financial crisis in SE Asia caused the Hang Seng index to lose half of its value. In 1998, the administration spent more than US$15.2 billion defending the Hong Kong dollar. Industries: textiles, electronic goods, cameras, toys, plastic goods, printing. Area: 1,071sq km (413sq mi). Pop. (1996) 6,311,000

Honolulu Capital and chief port of Hawaii, USA, on SE Oahu Island. It became the capital of the kingdom of Hawaii in 1845 and remained the capital after the annexation of the islands by the USA in 1898. Landmarks include the Iolani Palace, Waikiki Beach and the Diamond Head Crater. Tourism is of major importance. Industries: sugar refining, pineapple-canning. Pop. (1990) 365,272. *See also* PEARL HARBOR

Honshu Largest of Japan's four main islands, lying between the Sea of Japan (W) and the Pacific Ocean (E). It includes Mount FUJI and Lake Biwa (BIWA-KO). The S of the island is highly industrial with six of Japan's largest cities: TOKYO, YOKOHAMA, OSAKA, NAGOYA, KOBE and KYOTO. Other cities include KAWASAKI and HIROSHIMA. The majority of the population inhabit the coastal lowlands. Industries: shipbuilding, oil-refining, chemicals, textiles, rice, tea, fruit. Area: 230,782sq km (89,105sq mi). Pop. (1990) 82,569,581.

Honthorst, Gerrit van (1590–1656) Dutch painter. He was influenced by CARAVAGGIO and was particularly skilful in depicting dramatic, candle-lit interiors, notably *Samson and Delilah* (c.1620).

Hooch, Pieter de (1629–84) Dutch painter. He is best known for his serene, domestic interiors and courtyards, such as *The Courtyard of a House in Delft* (1658).

Hooke, Robert (1635–1703) English physicist and inventor. Interested in astronomy, he claimed to have stated the laws of planetary motion before Isaac NEWTON. Hooke studied the ELASTICITY of solids, which led to HOOKE'S LAW. Among his inventions were a practical telegraph system and the reflecting MICROSCOPE.

Hooke's law Law applying to the ELASTICITY of a material. The law states that the stress (internal tension) is proportional to the strain (a change in dimensions). It was discovered in 1676 by Robert HOOKE.

hookworm Two species (*Necator americanus* and *Ancyclostoma duodenale*) of ROUNDWORM. A human PARASITE, hookworm larvae usually enter the host through the skin of the feet and legs and attach to the wall of the small intestine. Symptoms can include anaemia and constipation. Phylum Nematoda.

hoopoe Striped, fawn-coloured bird that inhabits open areas in warmer parts of Eurasia. It has a fan-like crest, a curved bill and feeds on small invertebrates. Length: 30cm (12in). Family Upupidae; species *Upupa epops*.

Hoover, Herbert Clark (1874–1964) 31st US President (1929–33). Acclaimed for his work with victims of war, he was secretary of commerce under presidents HARDING and COOLIDGE. After winning the Republican nomination for president in 1928, Hoover easily defeated Alfred E. Smith. During his first year in office, the economy was shattered by the Wall Street Crash and the ensuing GREAT DEPRESSION. With his belief in individual enterprise and distrust of government interference, Hoover failed to provide sufficient government resources to deal with the Depression. In 1932, he was resoundingly defeated by Franklin ROOSEVELT's promise of a NEW DEAL.

Hoover, J. (John) Edgar (1895–1972) US administrator, director (1924–72) of the US FEDERAL BUREAU OF INVESTIGATION (FBI). He reorganized the Bureau, compiling a vast file of fingerprints and building a crime laboratory. During the 1930s, Hoover fought organized crime. After World War 2, he concentrated on what he saw as the threat of communist subversion in the USA.

Hoover Dam One of the world's largest dams, on the Colorado River between Arizona and Nevada, USA. Opened in 1935, its waters irrigate land in S California, Arizona and Mexico. Height: 221m (726ft). Length: 379m (1,244ft).

hop Twining vine native to Eurasia and the Americas. It has heart-shaped leaves and small male and female flowers on separate plants. The female flowers of *Humulus lupulus* are used to flavour BEER. Family Cannabiaceae.

Hope, Bob (1903–) US comedian, b. England. He started his career in vaudeville, and in 1938 the Bob Hope Show began on radio. Hope starred in more than 50 films, including the *Road* series with Bing CROSBY, *The Paleface* (1947) and *The Seven Little Foys* (1955).

Hopi Shoshonean-speaking tribe of Native Americans, famous for having retained the purest form of pre-Columbian life to have survived in the USA today. Today, *c*.6,000 Hopi people inhabit 11 villages in Arizona.

Hopkins, Sir Anthony (1937–) Welsh film and stage actor. His film career experienced several false starts before a dramatic resurgence in the 1990s. Hopkins won an Academy Award for best actor for his hypnotic performance in *The Silence of the Lambs* (1991). Other films include *Shadowlands* (1993) and *Nixon* (1995). *August* (1995) was his directorial debut.

Hopkins, Sir Frederick Gowland (1861–1947) English biochemist. He shared the 1929 Nobel Prize for physiology or medicine with Christiaan EIJKMAN for his work on VITAMINS. Hopkins pointed out that some diseases, such as SCURVY and RICKETS, might be caused by deficiency in the diet of a substance necessary for proper health, the so-called vitamin concept

Hopkins, Gerard Manley (1844–89) English poet and Jesuit priest. Hopkins contributed the principle of "sprung rhythm" to English poetry. His writing is concerned with problems of faith. The sinking of a German ship carrying five nuns inspired "The Wreck of the Deutschland" (1875). All of his poems were published posthumously.

Hopper, Edward (1882–1967) US realist painter. A pupil of Robert HENRI, he was greatly influenced by the ASHCAN SCHOOL. Hopper's paintings of scenes in New England and New York City, such as *Early Sunday Morning* (1930), convey a sense of melancholic romanticism.

Horace (65–08 BC) Roman poet, b. Quintus Horatius Flaccus. His first *Satires* appeared in *c*.35 BC, and were followed by *Epodes* (*c*.30 BC), *Odes* (*c*.23 BC) *Epistles* (*c*.20 BC) and *Ars Poetica* (*c*.19 BC). His simple Latin lyrics provided a vivid picture of the Augustan age.

horizon, celestial GREAT CIRCLE on the CELESTIAL SPHERE. It lies midway between the observer's ZENITH and NADIR.

hormone Chemical substance secreted by living cells. Hormones affect the metabolic activities of cells in other parts of the body. In MAMMALS, hormones are secreted by glands of the ENDOCRINE SYSTEM and are released directly into the bloodstream. They exercise chemical control of physiological functions, regulating growth, development, sexual functioning, METABOLISM and (in part) emotional balance. They maintain a delicate equilibrium that is vital to health. The HYPOTHALAMUS, adjacent to the PITUITARY GLAND at the base of the BRAIN, is responsible for overall coordination of the secretion of hormones. Most hormones are PROTEINS or STEROIDS. Hormones include THYROXINE, ADRENALINE, INSULIN, OESTROGEN, PROGESTERONE and TESTOSTERONE. In PLANTS, hormones control many aspects of metabolism, including cell elongation and division, direction of growth, initiation of flowering, development of fruits, leaf fall and responses to environmental factors. The most important plant hormones include AUXIN, GIBBERELLIN and CYTOKININ. *See also* GONADOTROPHIN; HOMEOSTASIS

hormone replacement therapy (HRT) Use of the female HORMONES progestogen (usually PROGESTERONE) and OESTROGEN in women who are either menopausal or who have had both ovaries removed. HRT relieves symptoms of MENOPAUSE; it also gives some protection against heart disease and OSTEOPOROSIS. The oestrogen causes a thickening of the lining of the uterus, which may increase risk of cancer of the ENDOMETRIUM. The progestogen causes a regular shedding of the lining, similar to menstruation, which may lessen this risk.

horn BRASS musical instrument traditionally used in hunting and ceremonies. Horns appeared in the opera orchestras of 17th-century Europe and in the 19th-century with Wagner and Strauss. The modern instrument (French horn) consists of a coiled tube of conical bore that widens to a flared bell; most have three valves.

hornbeam Any of a number of small, hardy trees of the genus *Carpinus*, found throughout the N Hemisphere.

▲ **hornbill** The great hornbill (*Buceros bicornis*) is just one of the 45 species of hornbill, all of which are found in tropical Asia and Africa. The enormously developed bill of the great hornbill is used for display and nesting purposes rather than for feeding.

They have smooth bark, a short trunk, spreading branches and clusters of green nuts. Family Betulaceae.

hornbill Brownish or black-and-white bird, native to tropical Africa and SE Asia. It has a large, brightly coloured bill. The female lays one to six eggs in a hole high up in a tree trunk and then sometimes erects a barricade, imprisoning herself and her eggs there for 4 to 11 weeks. The male feeds her through a slit in the wall. Length: 38–152cm (15–60in). Family Bucerotidae.

hornblende Black or green mineral found in IGNEOUS and METAMORPHIC ROCKS. It is the commonest form of AMPHIBOLE, and contains iron and silicates of calcium, aluminium and magnesium. Hardness 5.5; r.d. 3.2.

Horne, Marilyn (1934–) US mezzo-soprano. She studied with Lotte LEHMANN and made her debut in *The Bartered Bride*, Los Angeles (1954). Her international career has included a cycle of Rossini and Bellini operas with Joan SUTHERLAND.

hornet Large orange-and-brown WASP native to Europe, or yellow-and-black wasp of the USA. They build egg-shaped paper nests with one queen and many nectar-gathering workers. They have a powerful sting but are less aggressive than the common wasp. Family Vespidae.

Horney, Karen (1885–1952) US psychoanalyst, b. Germany. She challenged orthodox Freudian PSYCHOANALYSIS by emphasizing the role of environmental and cultural factors in the development of women's sexuality. In 1941, Horney formed the Association for the Advancement of Psychoanalysis. *See also* FREUD, SIGMUND

horoscope Map of the stars and planets at the time of a person's birth. It shows the position of the celestial bodies in relation to the 12 signs of the ZODIAC and is the basis of ASTROLOGY.

Horowitz, Vladimir (1904–89) US concert pianist, b. Russia. He was world-famous by the age of 20 for his virtuoso technique and great sensitivity. From 1950, Horowitz appeared only rarely on the concert platform but continued to make recordings.

horse Hoofed mammal. It evolved in North America but became extinct there during the late Pleistocene epoch. Early horse forms crossed the land bridge across the Bering Strait, dispersed throughout Asia, Europe and Africa, and produced the modern horse family. The only surviving true wild horse is Przewalski's horse. The horse was first domesticated *c*.5,000 years ago in central Asia. Horses returned to the New World with the Spanish conquistadores in the 1500s. Horses are characterized by one large functional toe, molars with crowns joined by ridges for grazing, an elongated skull and a simple stomach. Fast runners, they usually live in herds. Family Equideae; species *Equus caballus. See also* MULE

horse chestnut Any of 25 species of deciduous trees that grow in temperate regions, especially the common horse chestnut, *Aesculus hippocastanum*. It has large leaves, long flower spikes and round prickly fruits containing one or two inedible nuts. Family Hippocastanaceae. Height: to 30m (100ft).

horsefly Any of several species of flies in the family Tabanidae, especially *Tabanus lineola*. It is a pest to livestock and human beings. The female inflicts a painful bite and sucks blood. Length: to 3cm (1.2in).

Horse Latitudes Either of two areas of high pressure found near 25°N and 25°S of the Equator. The air rises at or near the Equator because of low pressure and then circles in the atmosphere, but much falls near the tropics of CANCER and CAPRICORN. The falling air gives rise to fairly permanent regions of high pressure. The TRADE WINDS blow from the Horse Latitudes towards the Equator.

horsepower (hp) Unit indicating the rate at which WORK is done, adopted by James WATT in the 18th century. He defined it as the weight, 250kg (550lb), a horse could raise 0.3m (1ft) in one second. The electrical equivalent of 1 hp is 746 watts.

horse racing Sport in which horses guided by jockeys race over a course of predetermined length. Most popular is thoroughbred racing, although harness racing (in which horses draw a light two-wheeled carriage) is also popular. In the UK thoroughbred racing includes **flat racing** organized by the Jockey Club, and hurdle racing and **steeplechasing** organized according to National Hunt rules. Horse racing began in Assyria in *c*.1500 BC. The world's oldest flat race is the English Derby, held annually at Epsom, Surrey, since 1780. It is one of the five English Classics: 1,000 Guineas, 2,000 Guineas, Oaks and St Leger. The GRAND NATIONAL steeplechase dates from 1839. *See also* EQUESTRIAN SPORTS

horseradish Perennial plant native to Eastern Europe. It is cultivated for its pungent, fleshy root, which is a useful seasoning. It has lance-shaped, toothed leaves, and white flower clusters. Height: 1.2m (4ft). Family Brassicaceae/Cruciferae; species *Armoracia rusticana*.

horsetail Any of *c*.30 species of flowerless plants that are related to ferns and grow in all continents except Australasia. The hollow stems have a whorl of tiny leaves at each joint. Spores are produced in a cone-like structure at the top of a stem. Horsetails date from the Carboniferous period. Phylum Sphenophyta, genus *Equisetum*.

Horthy, Miklós Nagybánai (1868–1957) Hungarian statesman and regent (1920–44). He commanded the Austro-Hungarian fleet in World War 1. Horthy took part in the counter-revolution that overthrew Béla KUN, becoming regent and effective head of state. His highly conservative regime suppressed political opposition and resisted the return of CHARLES I. Allied with the Axis Powers in 1941, he tried to arrange a separate peace with the Allies in 1944 but was arrested by the Germans.

horticulture Growing of vegetables, fruits, seeds, herbs, shrubs and flowers on a commercial scale. Techniques employed include propagation by leaf, stem and root cuttings, and by stem and bud GRAFTING. Fruit trees, shrubs and vines are usually propagated by grafting the fruiting stock on to a hardier rootstock. SEED is a major horticultural crop. Close scientific control of POLLINATION is essential for producing crops of specific quality.

Horus In Egyptian mythology, falcon-headed god, son of ISIS and OSIRIS. He came to be closely identified with all the pharaohs, who used his name as the first of their titles and were thought to rule as him on Earth.

Hosea (Osee) (8th century BC) OLD TESTAMENT prophet. The Book of Hosea uses the adultery of his wife as an allegory of the unfaithfulness of Israel to God.

hospital Institution for the care and treatment of the sick, injured, or physically or mentally incapacitated. The earliest hospitals may be traced to ancient Greece, where the sick gathered at the temples of Aesculapius (the god of healing). After the advent of Christianity, hospitals were established throughout Western Europe. In medieval Europe, the monasteries took in the poor and sick and became centres of pharmaceutical and medical knowledge, such as St Bartholomew's (1123) and St Thomas's (1207) London, England. In the early 19th century voluntary hospitals were founded by philanthropists. The NATIONAL HEALTH SERVICE (NHS) was founded in 1946 to provide a comprehensive health service free at the point of delivery.

Hospitaller *See* KNIGHTS HOSPITALLERS

Hottentot (Khoikhoi) KHOISAN-speaking people of s Africa, now almost extinct. Traditionally nomadic, many were displaced or exterminated by Dutch settlers. Descendants have mostly been absorbed into the South African population.

Houdini, Harry (1874–1926) US magician and escape artist, b. Erich Weiss in Hungary. Houdini escaped from packing cases, handcuffs and straitjackets, often while in a tank underwater.

Houphouët-Boigny, Félix (1905–93) Ivory Coast statesman, first president (1960–93). He served in the French colonial government, becoming president on independence. Maintaining close relations with France, the Ivory Coast became one of the more affluent West African countries. In the 1980s, a recession, exacerbated by expenditure on grandiose projects, caused unrest, and he was forced to legalize opposition parties (1990).

house music Form of dance music popular in the USA and Britain from the late 1980s. Using drum machines and sampled sound effects, often put into repetitive loops, house music increased the creative role of the disc jockey (DJ). It has produced a number of other forms of dance music.

House of Commons Lower house of the British PAR-LIAMENT. The upper house is the unelected HOUSE OF LORDS. The House of Commons dates from the 13th century. It is the major forum for discussion and voting on intended legislation and questioning of ministers. Its 659 members are elected by their constituents in a secret ballot, usually in general elections that must be held at least every five years. The PRIME MINISTER is the leader of the majority party in the Commons, and most members of the CABINET are drawn from the Commons, although some may be from the Lords. Debates and proceedings are controlled by the speaker. Select committees scrutinize legislation.

House of Lords Upper house of the British PARLIAMENT. In its legislative capacity, the Lords is completely subordinated to the HOUSE OF COMMONS. The Parliament Acts of 1911 and 1949 checked virtually all its power, except to delay passage of a bill for one year. Members of the House of Lords include the Lords Spiritual (26 archbishops and bishops), Lords Temporal (c.1,000 hereditary and life peers) and the Lords of Appeal (Law Lords). The Law Lords form Britain's highest court of appeal. In 1999, the number of hereditary peers was reduced to 92 as a first step to major reform of the House. The Law Lords continue to form Britain's highest court of appeal.

House of Representatives Lower house of the US legislature, which together with the SENATE forms the CONGRESS. It has 435 members. Each state has at least one representative; the larger the population of a state the more representatives are allowed. They are directly elected and serve two-year terms. The House considers bills and has exclusive authority to originate revenue bills, initiate impeachment proceedings and elect the president if the electoral college is deadlocked.

Houses of Parliament (Palace of Westminster) First large-scale public building of the GOTHIC REVIVAL in Britain. After a fire destroyed the old Palace of Westminster, Charles BARRY, together with PUGIN, a passionate Gothic specialist, created a building that combined a functional plan and modern technology with Gothic detail (1868).

Housman, A.E. (Alfred Edward) (1859–1936) English poet and scholar. He is best known for *A Shropshire Lad* (1896), a series of 63 lyrics on nature and love. Its idealized view of the English countryside proved extremely popular. His *Collected Poems* were published in 1939.

Houssay, Bernado Alberto (1887–1971) Argentinian physiologist who greatly advanced knowledge of the ENDOCRINE SYSTEM. He shared the 1947 Nobel Prize for physiology or medicine for discovering the role played by the hormone of the anterior PITUITARY GLAND lobe in regulating the metabolism of sugar. He demonstrated the complex interlocking action of various HORMONES of the body.

Houston City and port in SE Texas, USA, connected to the Gulf of Mexico by the Houston Ship Canal. Founded in 1836, it was capital of the Republic of Texas (1837–39, 1842–45). Its greatest growth came after the building of the canal (1912–14). The largest city in Texas, it is a major cultural centre with five universities, a symphony orchestra and many art galleries and museums. It is also a leading industrial, commercial and financial centre, with vast oil refineries and a massive petrochemical complex. Industries: space research (the Johnson Space Center is nearby), shipbuilding, meat-packing, electronics, chemicals, brewing, sugar and rice processing, synthetic rubber, printing, publishing. Pop. (1990) 1,630,553.

hovercraft (AIR-CUSHION VEHICLE) Fast, usually amphibious craft. A horizontal fan produces a cushion of air supporting the craft just above the ground or water. Vertical fans propel the craft. Most hovercraft are powered by gas turbine or diesel engines. Hovercraft travel at speeds up to c.160km/h (100mph). The first hovercraft was built by Christopher Cockerell in 1939. They are used as marine ferries and as military vehicles.

Hovhaness, Alan (1911–2000) US composer. His works, some of which reflect his Armenian ancestry, include *Mysterious Mountain* (1955), *Magnificat* (1957) and *And God Created Great Whales* (1970).

Howard, Catherine (1520–42) Fifth queen of HENRY VIII. She was brought to Henry's attention by opponents of Thomas CROMWELL and they married in July 1540. Evidence of premarital indiscretions led to her execution.

Howard, Henry See SURREY, HENRY HOWARD, EARL OF

Howard, John (1726–90) English campaigner for prison reform. Howard toured prisons in England and Wales and in 1774 had two Acts of Parliament passed to ensure minimum standards of sanitation and decency. The Howard League for Penal Reform, founded in 1866, is dedicated to improving prison conditions.

Howard, John Winston (1939–) Australian statesman, prime minister (1996–). Howard was elected to the House of Representatives in 1974. In 1982, he became deputy leader of the Liberal Party and was made leader in 1985. He held many shadow cabinet positions, and in 1995 was appointed leader of the Opposition. In 1996, Howard led the Liberal-National coalition to victory against Paul KEATING's ruling Labor Party government. He was re-elected in 1998.

Howard, Trevor (1916–88) English actor. He made his screen debut as the romantic lead in David LEAN's *Brief Encounter* (1945). Other films include *The Third Man* (1949), *Sons and Lovers* (1960), *Ryan's Daughter* (1970), *Gandhi* (1982) and *White Mischief* (1987).

Howe, Sir Geoffrey (1926–) British politician, chancellor of the exchequer (1979–83), foreign secretary (1983–89), deputy prime minister and leader of the House of Commons (1989–90). A leading figure in the Conservative cabinet of Margaret THATCHER, he made a damning resignation speech after he voiced her hostility to the EURO.

Howe, Sir William (1729–1814) British general during the AMERICAN REVOLUTION. He fought at Bunker Hill and became commander-in-chief of British forces in North America in 1775. He captured New York

(1776) and occupied Philadelphia (September 1777). After defeat at Saratoga (1777), he resigned and returned to England (1778).

Hoxha, Enver (1908–85) Albanian statesman, prime minister (1946–54), first secretary of the Communist Party (1954–85). In 1941, he founded the Albanian Communist Party and led the resistance to Italian occupation during World War 2. In 1946, the Republic of Albania was established and Hoxha became prime minister. His dictatorial control of party, army and state led to accusations of Stalinism. In 1961, Hoxha withdrew from the WARSAW PACT. The later break with Peking led to Albania's isolation and economic impoverishment.

Hoyle, Sir Fred (Frederick) (1915–) English astrophysicist and cosmologist. He developed the STEADY-STATE THEORY which, although it was subsequently displaced by the BIG BANG theory, sparked important research into NUCLEOSYNTHESIS in stars. Hoyle has often attracted controversy with his unorthodox ideas.

Hua Guofeng (1920–) (Hua Kuofeng) Chinese statesman, premier and chairman of the Chinese COMMUNIST PARTY (1976–81). When DENG XIAOPING was ousted as prime minister in 1976, he was replaced by Hua. After the death of MAO ZEDONG, he also became chairman of the party and thus successor to both Mao and ZHOU ENLAI. His pragmatic approach to policy led to his isolation within the party. Hua resigned and was replaced by ZHAO ZIYANG as premier and HU YAOBANG as party chairman. In 1982, he was ousted from the central committee.

Huang Hai (Yellow Sea) Shallow branch of the Pacific Ocean, N of the East China Sea between the Chinese mainland and the Korean peninsula. It is connected to the Chihli and Liaodong gulfs by the Strait of Chihli. The HUANG HE, Liao and Yalu drain into it; the yellow loess (fine-grained silt) from these rivers gives the sea its popular name. Area: *c*.466,000sq km (180,000sq mi).

Huang He (Huang Ho, or Yellow) River in N central China; China's second longest (after the YANGTZE). It rises in the Kunlun mountains and flows E to LANZHOU. It then takes a "great northern bend" around the Ordos Desert. Near Baotau, it turns S through Shanxi province. It then flows E through Henan province and NE through Shandong to enter the Bo Hai Gulf, an arm of the HUANG HAI. The river gets its popular name from the huge amounts of yellow silt it collects in its middle course. The silting of the river bed makes the river prone to serious flooding, but the threat has been greatly reduced by dykes and dams. Length: *c*.5,500km (3,400mi).

Hubbard, L. Ron (Lafayette Ronald) (1911–86) US science-fiction writer and the guiding spirit of the Church of SCIENTOLOGY. His works *Dianetics: The Modern Science of Mental Health* (1950) and *Science and Survival* (1951) formed the basis of Scientology. Hubbard was executive director of the church (1955–66).

Hubble, Edwin Powell (1889–1953) US astronomer. In 1925 he published his classification of GALAXIES and his discovery that spiral NEBULAE were resolvable as independent star systems. Using the telescope at Mount Wilson Observatory, Hubble measured the distance to the ANDROMEDA GALAXY. He attributed the RED SHIFT of the spectral lines of galaxies to the recession of galaxies, and hence to the EXPANDING UNIVERSE. In 1929, he proposed a linear relation between the distance of a galaxy from Earth and their velocity of recession (HUBBLE'S LAW).

Hubble's law Proposed by HUBBLE (1929), it claimed a linear relation between the distance of galaxies from us and their velocity of recession, deduced from the RED SHIFT in their spectra. The **Hubble constant** (symbol

H_0) is the rate at which the velocity of recession of galaxies increases with distance from Earth. The inverse of the Hubble constant is the **Hubble time**, which gives a maximum age for the universe on the assumption that there has been no slowing of the expansion.

Hubble Space Telescope (HST) Optical telescope that was placed in Earth orbit by the SPACE SHUTTLE in 1990. Images transmitted back to Earth revealed that the telescope's main mirror was incorrectly shaped. A shuttle repair team corrected the fault in 1993, and it was again repaired in 1997. The HST now produces accurate images of bodies that cannot be observed clearly by terrestrial telescopes due to atmospheric distortion.

Huddleston, (Ernest Urban) Trevor (1913–98) British Anglican priest and anti-APARTHEID activist. In 1943 he moved to Johannesburg, South Africa. Huddleston's conviction that the principle of universal brotherhood in Christ should be applied everywhere was evident from his book *Nought for your Comfort* (1956). From 1960 to 1968, he was Bishop of Masai, Tanzania. In 1969, he became vice president of the Anti-Apartheid Movement. He was bishop of Mauritius and archbishop of the Indian Ocean (1978–83).

Hudson, Henry (d.1611) English maritime explorer. He made several efforts to find a NORTHEAST PASSAGE. Employed by the Dutch EAST INDIA COMPANY (1609), Hudson was blocked by ice and crossed the Atlantic to search for a NORTHWEST PASSAGE, becoming the first European to sail up the HUDSON River. In 1610, he embarked on another voyage to discover the Northwest Passage and reached HUDSON BAY. Forced by ice to winter in the bay, his crew set him adrift to die in an open boat.

Hudson River in E New York state, USA. It rises in the ADIRONDACK MOUNTAINS and flows S to New York Bay, NEW YORK CITY. First explored (1609) by Henry HUDSON, it has become one of the world's most important waterways. The New York State Barge Canal connects it with Lake Champlain, the Great Lakes and the St Lawrence River. Length: *c*.493km (306mi).

Hudson Bay World's largest inland sea, in E Northwest Territories, Canada, also bounded by Québec (E), Ontario (S) and Manitoba (SW). It is connected to the Atlantic by the Hudson Strait (NE) and to the Arctic Ocean by the Foxe Channel (N). Explored in 1610 by Henry HUDSON, the bay contains Southampton, Mansel and Coats Islands. The Churchill and Nelson rivers drain into the bay, which is ice-free from July to October. Area: *c*.1,243,000sq km (480,000sq mi).

Hudson River School (*c*.1825–75) Group of US landscape painters influenced by European ROMANTICISM. They were so named because of their idealized scenes of the HUDSON River Valley. The group included Thomas COLE and Frederick E. Church.

Hudson's Bay Company English company chartered in 1670 to promote trade in the HUDSON BAY region of North America and to seek a NORTHWEST PASSAGE. The company had a fur-trading monopoly and was virtually a sovereign power in the region. Throughout the 18th century, it fought with France for control of the bay. In 1763, France ceded control of CANADA to England, and the North West Company was formed. Intense rivalry forced the Hudson's Bay Company into a more active role in W exploration, and in 1771 Samuel Hearne proved the lack of a short Northwest Passage out of the Bay. In 1821, the companies merged to control territory stretching from the Atlantic to the Pacific. After the Confederation of Canada (1867), challenges to its monopoly power increased, and in 1869 it was forced to cede all its territory to Canada. As the FUR TRADE declined in the early 20th century, the company diversified and was divided up in 1930.

Huerta, Victoriano (1854–1916) Mexican statesman and general, president (1913–14). Instructed by President Francisco MADERO to suppress the revolt led by Félix Díaz, Huerta instead joined forces with the rebels. Madero was arrested and killed, and Huerta became president. Defeated by the Constitutionalists led by Venustiano CARRANZA, Huerta fled to the USA.

Huggins, Sir William (1824–1910) English astronomer. He pioneered the use of SPECTROSCOPY in astronomy. Huggins discovered the RED SHIFT in the spectral lines of stars. He distinguished between nebulae that are uniformly gaseous and those with stellar clusters.

Hughes, Howard Robard (1905–76) US industrialist, aviator and film producer. Hughes inherited an industrial corporation (1923) and became a billionaire as head of the Hughes Aircraft Company. In 1935 he set the world speed record of 567km/h (352mph) in an aircraft of his own design. He occasionally produced films, including *Hell's Angels* (1930) and *The Outlaw* (1943).

Hughes, Langston (1902–67) US poet. Hughes was a leading figure of the HARLEM RENAISSANCE. A prolific writer, he had a distinctive musical style that combined African-American dialect with the rhythms of jazz and blues. His works include *Shakespeare in Harlem* (1942) and *One-Way Ticket* (1949).

Hughes, Ted (Edward James) (1930–98) English poet. He succeeded Sir John BETJEMAN as poet laureate in 1984. One of the most distinctive voices in contemporary English verse, Hughes focused on the raw, primal forces of nature. Collections include *Hawk in the Rain* (1957), *Lupercal* (1960), *Wodwo* (1967), *Crow* (1970), *Moortown* (1979) and *Wolfwatching* (1989). His creative translation of the Greek poet *Tales from Ovid* (1997) won the Whitbread Prize. Hughes was married (1956–62) to Sylvia PLATH. His last volume, *Birthday Letters* (1998), was a personal reflection on their relationship and posthumously won him a second Whitbread Prize. His books for children include *The Iron Man* (1968).

Hughes, Thomas (1822–96) English novelist. A Christian socialist, Hughes is best known for the novel *Tom Brown's Schooldays* (1857), a semi-fictional account of his education under Thomas ARNOLD at Rugby School.

Hugo, Victor Marie (1802–85) French poet, dramatist and novelist. A major force in 19th-century French literary life, he received a pension from Louis XVIII for his first collection of *Odes* (1822), and presented his manifesto of ROMANTICISM in the preface to his play *Cromwell* (1827). Later works include the plays *Hernani* (1830) and *Ruy Blas* (1838), and the novels *The Hunchback of Notre Dame* (1831) and *Les Misérables* (1862). Some of his most important works were written whilst in exile, such as the satirical poems *The Punishments* (1853). On the fall of the Second Republic he returned to Paris, where he became a senator.

Huguenots French Protestants who arose in Roman Catholic France during the REFORMATION and suffered persecution. In 1559, a national synod of Huguenot congregations adopted an ecclesiastical structure highly influenced by John CALVIN. During the Wars of RELIGION (1562–98), Huguenots continued to face persecution and thousands died. HENRY IV, a Huguenot, came to the throne in 1589 and, despite adopting the Roman Catholic faith in 1593, promulgated the Edict of NANTES (1598), which recognized Catholicism as the official religion but gave Huguenots certain rights. In 1685, it was revoked by LOUIS XIV, and thousands of Huguenots fled France.

In 1789, their civil rights were restored, and the CODE NAPOLÉON (1804) guaranteed religious equality.

Huitzilopochtli Chief deity of the AZTEC, revered as a Sun god and god of war. He is usually shown in armour decorated with hummingbird feathers. His cult required a daily nourishment of human blood. *See also* CENTRAL AND SOUTH AMERICAN MYTHOLOGY

Hull, Clark Leonard (1884–1952) US psychologist, best known for his experimental studies of LEARNING and behaviour. He accepted some of the ideas of PAVLOV and FREUD but attempted to apply rigorous scientific methods. His theory of learning, based on the principle of reward for the appropriate response to a stimulus, was developed in works such as *Principles of Behavior* (1943).

Hull, Cordell (1871–1955) US politician. A member of the House of Representatives (1907–21, 1923–31), author of the first federal income-tax law (1913), and secretary of state (1933–44) under Franklin D. ROOSEVELT. Hull was an important diplomatic figure in World War 2 and played a key role in gaining US acceptance of the United Nations. He was awarded the 1945 Nobel Peace Prize.

Hull (officially Kingston upon Hull) City in NE England, on the N bank of the Humber estuary. Britain's third largest port, it was founded in the late 13th century and grew around its fishing industry. The decline of the fishing industry has been partly offset by the construction of the Humber Bridge (1981), one of the world's longest single-span suspension bridges. Pop. (1994) 274,000.

human Primate MAMMAL of the genus *Homo*, the only living species of which is *Homo sapiens*. When compared with near relatives, the CHIMPANZEE, GORILLA and ORANGUTAN, humans are distinguishable by a number of features. They walk upright, their body is only patchily hairy, their big toes are not opposable to the other toes, their backbone is more S-shaped than straight and their forehead is higher than that of any ape. Microscopically, humans are distinguishable from great APES by the size, number and shape of their chromosomes. Another distinction is the human capacity for language. Socially, humans are similar to lesser PRIMATES, preferring a family or other small group.

human body Physical structure of a HUMAN. It is composed of water, PROTEIN and other organic compounds, and some minerals. The SKELETON consists of more than 200 bones, sheathed in voluntary MUSCLE to enable movement. A SKULL surrounds the large BRAIN. The body is fuelled by nutrients absorbed from the DIGESTIVE SYSTEM and oxygen from the LUNGS, which are pumped around the body by the CIRCULATORY SYSTEM. Metabolic wastes are eliminated mainly by EXCRETION. Continuation of the species is enabled by the reproductive system. Overall control is exerted by the NERVOUS SYSTEM, working closely with the ENDOCRINE SYSTEM. The body surface is covered by a protective layer of SKIN.

human evolution Process by which HUMANS developed from pre-human ancestors. The FOSSIL record of human ancestors is patchy and unclear. Some scientists believe that our ancestry can be traced back to one or more species of Australopithecines that flourished in S and E Africa *c*.4–1 million years ago. Other scientists believe that we are descended from some as yet undiscovered ancestor. The earliest fossils that can be identified as human are those of HOMO HABILIS, which date from 2 million years ago. The next evolutionary stage was HOMO ERECTUS, who first appeared *c*.1.5 million years ago. The earliest fossils of our own species, HOMO SAPIENS, date from *c*.250,000 years ago. An apparent side-branch, the NEANDERTHALS, existed in Europe and W Asia some 130,000–40,000 years ago. Fully modern humans, *Homo sapiens sapiens*, first appeared *c*.50,000 years ago. All human species apart from *Homo sapiens sapiens* are now extinct.

Human Genome Project International scientific programme to map the entire sequence of *c*.100,000 GENES in human DNA. Begun in 1988, the study is expected to take 15 years. Researchers are located in more than 20 centres around the world, and their efforts are coordinated primarily in the USA and France by the Human Genome Organization (HUGO). The study is expected to increase understanding of genetic disorders, such as ALZHEIMER'S DISEASE and MUSCULAR DYSTROPHY. It will also provide insight into HUMAN EVOLUTION and identify genetic similarities between humans and other species.

human immunodeficiency virus (HIV) Organism that causes ACQUIRED IMMUNE DEFICIENCY SYNDROME (AIDS). A RETROVIRUS identified in 1983, HIV attacks the IMMUNE SYSTEM, leaving the person unable to fight infection. There are two distinct viruses: **HIV-1**, which has now spread worldwide; and **HIV-2**, which is concentrated almost entirely in W Africa. Both cause AIDS. There are three main means of transmission: from person to person by sexual contact; from mother to baby during birth; and by contact with contaminated blood or blood products (for example, during transfusions or when drug-users share needles). People can carry the virus for many years before developing symptoms.

humanism Philosophy based on a belief in the supreme importance of human beings and human values. The greatest flowering of humanism came during the RENAISSANCE, spreading from Italy to other parts of Europe. Early adherents included PETRARCH and ERASMUS. Modern humanism developed as an alternative to traditional Christian beliefs. This movement, which has been associated with social reform, was championed by Bertrand RUSSELL. *See also* ATHEISM; EXISTENTIALISM

human rights Entitlements that an individual may arguably possess by virtue of being human and in accordance with what is natural. The concept of the inalienable rights of the human being has traditionally been linked to the idea of natural law, on which commentaries were written by several Greek and Roman writers. John LOCKE helped to shape ideas of fundamental human rights and liberal DEMOCRACY in *Two Treatises on Government* (1690). The concept of human rights has been most notably formulated in a number of historic declarations, such as the US DECLARATION OF INDEPENDENCE (1776) and the CONSTITUTION (1789) and particularly its first amendments in the BILL OF RIGHTS (1791), and the French DECLARATION OF THE RIGHTS OF MAN AND CITIZEN (1789). These documents owed much to the English PETITION OF RIGHT (1628) and BILL OF RIGHTS (1689), which extended the concept of individual freedom proclaimed earlier in the MAGNA CARTA (1215). The responsibility of the international community for the protection of human rights is proclaimed in the Charter of the United Nations (1945) and the Universal Declaration of Human Rights (1948). *See also* CIVIL RIGHTS

Humber Estuary in Humberside, NE England, formed by the confluence of the rivers TRENT and OUSE near Goole. HULL lies on its N shore. It is crossed by the Humber Bridge (opened 1981), the longest single-span suspension bridge in the world with a main span of 1,410m (4,626ft). Length: 64km (40mi).

Humboldt, Friedrich Heinrich Alexander, Baron von (1769–1859) German naturalist and explorer. He explored (1799–1804) South America, studying volcanoes, tropical storms and the increase in magnetic intensity from the Equator towards the poles. His five-volume *Kosmos* (1845–62) describes the physical universe.

Hume, Basil (1923–) English Roman Catholic cardinal and BENEDICTINE monk. He was magister scholarum (1957–63) of the English Benedictine Congregation. In 1976, Hume was created archbishop of Westminster and a cardinal.

Hume, David (1711–76) Scottish philosopher, historian and man of letters. Hume's publications include *A Treatise of Human Nature* (1739–40), *History of England* (1754–63), and various philosophical "enquiries". Widely known for his humanitarianism and philosophical SCEPTICISM, Hume's philosophy was a form of EMPIRICISM that affirmed the contingency of all phenomenal events. He argued that it was impossible to go beyond the subjective experiences of impressions and ideas. *See also* BERKELEY, GEORGE; LOCKE, JOHN

Hume, John (1937–) Northern Irish politician, leader (1983–) of the nationalist SOCIAL DEMOCRATIC LABOUR PARTY (SDLP). He was a founder member and president (1964–68) of the Credit Union League. Hume entered

▲ human evolution
Although the fossil record is not complete, we know that humans evolved from ape-like creatures. Our earliest ancestor, *Australopithecus afarensis*

(A), lived in NE Africa some 5 million years ago. Over the next 3 to 4 million years *A. africanus* (B) evolved. *Homo Habilis* (C), who used primitive stone tools, appeared

c.500,000 years later. *H. erectus* (D) is believed to have spread from Africa to other continents *c*.750,000 years ago. Records indicate that from *H. erectus* evolved two

species: Neanderthal man (E), who died out 40,000 years ago and who could have been made extinct by the other species; and the earliest modern man, *H. sapiens sapiens* (F).

► **hummingbird** The sword-billed hummingbird (*Ensifera ensifera*) is one of the 300 or so species of hummingbird found in the Americas. Hummingbirds live largely on nectar, and their long bills are perfectly suited to extracting the nectar from deep within the flowers.

Parliament in 1983. His commitment to peace in Northern Ireland helped secure an IRA cease-fire. Hume shared the 1998 Nobel Peace Prize with David TRIMBLE, leader of the ULSTER UNIONISTS.

humerus Bone in the human upper arm. A depression on the posterior, roughened lower end of the humerus provides the point of articulation for the ULNA.

humidity (relative humidity) Measure of the amount of water vapour in air. It is the ratio of the actual vapour pressure to the saturation vapour pressure at which water normally condenses and is usually expressed as a percentage. Humidity is measured by a HYGROMETER.

hummingbird Popular name for small, brilliantly coloured birds of the family *Trochilidae*, found in S and N America. They feed in flight on insects and nectar, usually by hovering in front of flowers. Their speed can reach 100km/h (60mph) and their wings, which beat 50–75 times a second, make a humming sound. Length: 6–22cm (2.2–8.6in).

Humperdinck, Engelbert (1854–1921) German teacher and composer. His works include incidental music, songs, and seven operas, the first of which, *Hansel and Gretel* (1893), is his most popular work. He worked with WAGNER in the preparation of *Parsifal* (1880–81).

humus Dark brown organic substance resulting from partial decay of plant and animal matter. It improves soil by retaining moisture, aerating and increasing mineral nutrient content and bacterial activity.

Hunan Province in SE central China, S of Tungting Lake; the capital is Changsha. The region is largely forested, but agriculture is important; rice, tea, rape seed and tobacco are produced. Hunan has valuable mineral resources. Area: 210,570sq km (81,301sq mi). Pop. (1990) 60,600,000.

Hundred Days (20 March–28 June 1815) Period between the escape of NAPOLEON I from Elba and the second restoration of Louis XVIII, following the Allied victory at WATERLOO.

Hundred Years' War (1337–1453) Sporadic conflict between France and England. In 1328, PHILIP VI was crowned. In 1337, he captured AQUITAINE, prompting King EDWARD III of England to invade France. English victories at CRÉCY (1346) and POITIERS (1356) led to the Peace of Brétigny (1360) which ceded large territories to Edward. The accession of HENRY VI to the English throne revived French fortunes. In 1429, the siege of ORLÉANS was broken by JOAN OF ARC. In 1453, the French captured Bordeaux, leaving only Calais in English hands (until 1558).

Hungarian (Magyar) Official language of Hungary, spoken by the country's 10.3 million inhabitants and by about 3 million more in parts of Romania, Slovakia and other countries bordering Hungary. It belongs to the Ugric branch of the FINNO-UGRIC languages.

Hungary Landlocked republic in central Europe. Hungary is mostly low-lying. The DANUBE River forms much of its N border with the Slovak Republic. The capital, BUDAPEST, lies on the banks of the Danube. To the E of the river is the Great Hungarian Plain (*Nagyalföld*) including Hungary's second-largest city, DEBRECEN. To the W lies the Little Plain (*Kisalföld*) and the region of Transdanubia, which includes central Europe's largest lake, Lake BALATON. In the NE, the Mátra Mountains rise to the Kékes peak, at 1,015m (3,330ft). **Climate** Hungary has a continental climate, with hot summers and cold winters. **Vegetation** Much of Hungary's original vegetation has been cleared. Large forests remain in the scenic NE highlands. **History and Politics** MAGYARS first arrived in the 9th century. In the 11th century Hungary's first king, Saint STEPHEN, made Roman Catholicism the official religion. In 1222, the Golden Bull established a parliament. In the 14th century the ANGEVIN dynasty extended the empire. In the Battle of Mohács (1526), Hungary was defeated by the Ottomans. In 1699, LEOPOLD I expelled the Turks and established HABSBURG control. The accession of FRANZ JOSEPH led to war with Austria (1848). Austrian defeat in the AUSTRO-PRUSSIAN WAR (1866) led to the compromise solution of the AUSTRO-HUNGARIAN EMPIRE (1867–1918). As defeat loomed in World War 1, nationalist demands intensified. In 1918, independence was declared. In 1919, communists, led by Béla KUN, briefly held power. In 1920, Miklós HORTHY became regent. World War 1 peace terms saw the loss of all non-Magyar territory (66% of Hungarian land). In 1941, Hungary allied with Nazi Germany, regaining much of its lost territory. Virulent anti-semitism saw the extermination of many Hungarian Jews. Hungary's withdrawal from the war led to German occupation (March 1944). The Soviet expulsion of German troops (October 1944–May 1945) devastated much of Hungary. In 1946, Hungary became a republic, headed by Imre NAGY. In 1948, the Communist Party gained control, forcing Nagy's resignation and declaring Hungary a People's Republic (1949). Hungary became a Stalinist state. Industry was nationalized and agriculture collectivized. Economic crisis forced the brief reinstatement (1953–55) of Nagy. In 1955, Hungary joined the Warsaw Pact. In 1956, the Hungarian Revolution led to Nagy forming a government. János KÁDÁR formed a rival government and called for Soviet military assistance. Soviet troops brutally suppressed the uprising. Nagy was executed and 200,000 people fled. From 1968, Kádár's regime gradually adopted a more liberal stance. In the 1980s, Hungary began to seek Western aid to modernize its economy. In 1989, Kádár was forced to resign and the Communist Party was disbanded. In 1990, multiparty elections were won by the conservative Democratic Forum. The Hungarian Socialist Party (HSP), composed of ex-communists, won the 1994 elections and set up a coalition government with the liberal Alliance of Free Democrats. Gyula Horn of the HSP became prime minister. In 1998 elections, the Federation of Young Democrats-Hungarian Civic Party (Fidesz-MPP) emerged as the largest party and Viktor Orban became prime minister. **Economy** Since the early 1990s, Hungary has adopted

HUNGARY
AREA: 93,030sq km (35,919sq mi)
POPULATION: 10,531,000
CAPITAL (POPULATION): Budapest (1,885,000)

market reforms and privatization programmes. The economy (1995 GDP per capita, US$6,410) has suffered from the collapse in exports to the former Soviet Union and Yugoslavia. Transitional costs have resulted in an increase in national debt, unemployment and inflation. The manufacture of machinery and transport is the most valuable sector. Hungary's resources include bauxite, coal and natural gas. Agriculture accounts for 14% of GDP. Major crops include grapes for wine-making, maize, potatoes, sugar beet and wheat. Tourism is a growing sector.

Huns Nomadic people of Mongol or Turkic origin who expanded from central Asia into E Europe. Under ATTILA, they overran large parts of the Roman Empire in 434–53, exacting tribute, but after his death they disintegrated.

Hunt, (William) Holman (1827–1910) English painter who was one of the founders (1848) of the PRE-RAPHAELITE BROTHERHOOD. His works, such as *The Light of the World* (1854) and *The Scapegoat* (1856), combine meticulous precision with heavy, didactic symbolism.

Hunt, (James Henry) Leigh (1784–1859) English critic, journalist and poet. He was instrumental in introducing the work of SHELLEY and KEATS to the public. He founded the literary periodical *The Examiner*, and also contributed to *The Indicator* and *The Liberal*.

Hunter, Holly (1956–) US film and stage actress. In 1987, her film performances in *Broadcast News* and *Raising Arizona* won awards, and she gained further praise for the repeat of her stage role in *Miss Firecracker* (1989). Hunter's powerful performance in *The Piano* (1993) won her an Academy Award for best actress.

hunting and gathering Practice of small societies in which members subsist by hunting and by collecting plants rather than by agriculture. The groups are always small bands and have sophisticated kinship and ritualistic systems. Today, hunter-gatherer societies are most numerous in lowland South America and parts of Africa.

Huntington's disease (Huntington's chorea) Acute degenerative disorder. It is genetically transmitted and usually occurs in early midlife. It is caused by the presence of abnormally large amounts of glutamate and aspartate. Physical symptoms include loss of motor coordination. Mental deterioration can take various forms.

hurling (hurley) Game that is one of the national sports of Ireland. It is played by two teams of 15 on a field 137 × 82m (450 × 270ft), at each end of which are goalposts. The object is to score points by propelling the ball between the goal uprights, either above (1 point) or below (3 points) the crossbar. Every player carries a hurley, a hooked stick, on which the ball may be balanced as the player runs or with which it may be batted upfield towards a teammate; the ball may be kicked.

Huron Confederation of Iroquoian-speaking tribes of Native Americans who once occupied the St Lawrence Valley E of Lake Huron. In wars for control of the fur trade with the IROQUOIS CONFEDERACY (1648–50), their population was reduced from 15,000 to c.500. After a period of wandering, they settled in Ohio, the Great Lakes area and Kansas. Today, c.1,250 live on reservations in Ohio and Oklahoma, USA, and in Ontario, Canada.

Huron, Lake Second largest of the GREAT LAKES of North America, forming part of the boundary between the US and Canada. It drains Lake SUPERIOR and feeds Lake ERIE as part of the Great Lakes–St Lawrence Seaway system and is navigable by ocean-going vessels. Area: 59,596sq km (23,010sq mi). Max. depth: 230m (750ft).

hurricane Wind of Force 12 or greater on the BEAU-FORT WIND SCALE; intense tropical cyclone with winds ranging from 120–320km/h (75–200mph), also known

as a typhoon in the Pacific. Originating over oceans around the Equator, hurricanes have a calm central hole, or eye, surrounded by inward spiralling winds and cumulonimbus clouds.

Hurston, Zora Neale (1901–60) US writer and folklorist. An anthropologist, she collected the folklore of S African-American communities. Hurston infused her fiction with these folk tales and speech rhythms. Her best-known novel is *Their Eyes Were Watching God* (1937). She was a major figure in the HARLEM RENAISSANCE.

Hurt, William (1950–) US film actor. His first film was *Altered States* (1980), but he achieved wider recognition for *The Big Chill* (1983). Hurt won an Academy Award for best actor in *Kiss of the Spider Woman* (1985). His performances in *Children of a Lesser God* (1986) and *Broadcast News* (1987) earned him further Academy nominations.

Hus, Jan (1369–1415) Bohemian religious reformer. He studied and later taught at Prague, where he was ordained priest. Influenced by the writings of John WYCLIFFE, Hus was excommunicated in 1411. In *De Ecclesia* (1412), he outlined his case for reform of the Church. He was tried by the Council of CONSTANCE (1415) and burned at the stake as a heretic. His followers, known as HUSSITES, launched a civil war against the Holy Roman Empire.

Hussein I (1935–99) HASHEMITE king of Jordan (1953–99). He sought to maintain good relations with the West while supporting the Palestinians' cause in the ARAB-ISRAELI WARS. In 1967 Hussein led Jordan into the SIX-DAY WAR, losing the WEST BANK and East JERUSALEM to Israel. In 1970, he ordered his army to suppress the activities of the PALESTINE LIBERATION ORGANIZATION (PLO) in Jordan. In 1974, Hussein relinquished Jordan's claim to the West Bank to the PLO. In the 1990s, he supported efforts to secure peace in the Middle East, signing a treaty with Israel in 1994 and attending the funeral of Itzhak RABIN in 1995. He was succeeded by his son Abdullah (1962–).

Hussein, Saddam (1937–) Iraqi statesman, president of Iraq (1979–). In 1959, he was forced into exile for his part in an attempt to assassinate the Iraqi prime minister. In 1963, Saddam returned home and was imprisoned in 1964. After his release, he played a prominent role in the 1968 coup led by the BA'ATH PARTY. The civilian government was replaced by a Revolutionary Command Council (RCC). In 1979, Saddam became chairman of the RCC. His invasion of Iran marked the beginning of the IRAN-IRAQ WAR (1980–88). At home, Saddam ruthlessly suppressed all internal opposition. His 1990 invasion of Kuwait provoked worldwide condemnation. In the ensuing GULF WAR (1991), a multinational force expelled the Iraqi forces from Kuwait. Further uprisings by KURDS and Iraqi SHIITES were ruthlessly suppressed, and Saddam survived punitive economic sanctions.

Husserl, Edmund (1859–1938) German philosopher, founder of PHENOMENOLOGY. He studied consciousness as it related to objects and the structure of experience. His works include *Ideas: General Introduction to Pure Phenomenology* (1913) and *Cartesian Meditations* (1931).

Hussites Followers of the religious reformer Jan HUS in Bohemia and Moravia in the 15th century. The execution of Hus in 1415 provoked the Hussite Wars against the Emperor SIGISMUND. Peace was agreed at the Council of Basel (1431), but it was rejected by the radical wing of the Hussites, the Taborites, who were defeated at the Battle of Lipany (1434).

Huston, John (1906–87) US film director, writer and actor. His first feature as a director was *The Maltese Falcon* (1941). Huston won an Academy Award for best director for *The Treasure of the Sierra Madre* (1946).

▶ **hydrofoil** Hydrofoils use the lift of underwater "wings" (1) to push the boat out of the water. They work in water the same way aerofoils work in air. A low-pressure zone is created above the top surface of the hydrofoil, pushing the wing upwards (2).This lessens the drag, allowing the boat to travel faster. The Boeing Jetfoil (shown) scoops up water (3) and uses gas turbines (4) to drive high-pressure pumps (5) that throw the water from the rear, creating thrust. The jetfoil can reach speeds of up to 75km/h (45 mph).

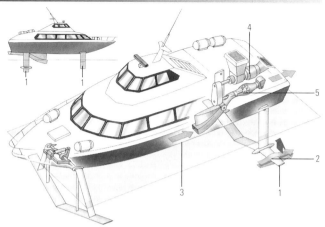

Other classics followed, such as *Key Largo* (1948), *The Asphalt Jungle* (1950) and *The African Queen* (1951). Other credits include *The Man Who Would be King* (1975), *Prizzi's Honor* (1985) and *The Dead* (1987).

Hutton, James (1726–97) Scottish geologist. In *A Theory of the Earth* (1795) he outlined his ideas on the origin of the Earth. Hutton's conclusions on the timescale of geological forces at work led him to believe that the Earth was much older than previously believed. His discoveries formed the basis of modern GEOLOGY.

Hutton, Sir Len (Leonard) (1916–90) English cricketer. An opening batsman for Yorkshire, he was the first professional captain of England (1953). Hutton captained England for 23 of his 79 test matches (1937–55), scoring 6,971 test runs. In 1938, he scored 364 against Australia, a world record until Gary SOBERS' innings (1958).

Huxley, Aldous Leonard (1894–1963) English novelist, grandson of Thomas HUXLEY. He published several volumes of poetry before writing novels such as *Crome Yellow* (1921), *Antic Hay* (1923) and *Point Counter Point* (1928), which satirized the hedonism of the 1920s. His best-known work, *Brave New World* (1932), presents a nightmarish vision of a future society. *Island* (1962) evokes a Utopian community. *Eyeless in Gaza* (1936) and *The Doors of Perception* (1954) explore his interest in mysticism and states of consciousness. Among his finest works are the *Collected Short Stories* (1957).

Huxley, Sir Julian Sorell (1887–1975) English biologist, grandson of Thomas HUXLEY. His books on animal behaviour and evolution include *The Individual in the Animal Kingdom* (1911) and *Evolutionary Ethics* (1943).

Huxley, Thomas Henry (1825–95) English biologist. Huxley championed DARWIN's theory of EVOLUTION. His works include *Zoological Evidences as to Man's Place in Nature* (1863), *Manual of Comparative Anatomy of Vertebrated Animals* (1871) and *Evolution and Ethics* (1893).

Hu Yaobang (1915–89) Chinese statesman, general secretary of the Chinese COMMUNIST PARTY (1980–87). He joined the Communists in 1933 and took part in the LONG MARCH. Hu became associated with DENG XIAOPING in the war against Japan (1937–45), during which he served as a political commissar. In 1952, he became head of the Young Communist League, but lost his post (1966) during the CULTURAL REVOLUTION. Hu was rehabilitated after MAO ZEDONG's death (1976). Accused of sympathizing with student demonstrations for democracy, Hu was dismissed. The TIANANMEN SQUARE protests followed his death.

Huygens, Christiaan (1629–95) Dutch physicist and astronomer. In 1655, he discovered Saturn's rings and its largest satellite, Titan. In 1656, Huygens built the first PENDULUM clock. He also introduced the convergent eyepiece for TELESCOPES. In 1678, Huygens presented his WAVE theory of LIGHT to explain RELECTION and REFRACTION.

hyacinth Bulbous plant native to the Mediterranean region and Africa. It has long, thin leaves and spikes of bell-shaped flowers, which may be white, yellow, red, blue or purple. Family Liliaceae; genus *Hyacinthus*.

hybrid Offspring of two parents of different GENE composition. It often refers to the offspring of different varieties of a species or or of the cross between two separate species. Most inter-species hybrids, such as MULES, are unable to produce fertile offspring.

hybridization Cross-breeding of plants or animals between different species to produce offspring that differ in genetically determined traits. Changes in climate or in the environment of an organism may give rise to natural hybridization, but most hybrids are produced by human intervention to produce plants or animals that may be hardier or more economical than the original forms.

Hyderabad City on the River Musi, S India; capital of Andhra Pradesh. Founded in 1589, Hyderabad has a number of notable buildings, including the Char Minar (1591). It is an educational centre with four universities. Industries: tobacco, textiles, handicrafts. Pop. (1991) 3,145,939.

Hyderabad City on the River INDUS, Sind province, SE Pakistan. Founded in 1768, it was the capital of Sind until captured by the British in 1843. Industries: chemicals, pottery, shoes, furniture. Pop. (1995) 1,107,000.

Hyder Ali (1722–82) Sultan of Mysore (1761–82). An able general, he commanded the army of Mysore from 1749. His expansionist policies led to confrontation with the British, whom he defeated in 1767 and 1780. In 1781, he was himself defeated by Sir Eyre Coote.

Hydra Largest constellation in the sky. It represents the water snake killed by HERACLES in classical mythology.

hydra Popular name for a group of small, freshwater organisms including JELLYFISH, CORAL and SEA ANEMONE.

hydrangea Genus of 80 deciduous woody shrubs, small trees and vines, native to the Western Hemisphere and Asia. They are grown for their showy clusters of flowers, which may be white, pink or blue. Family Hydrangeaceae.

hydraulics Physical science and technology of the behaviour of FLUIDS in both static and dynamic states. In

1795 Joseph Bramah invented the hydraulic press. In the 19th century hydraulic power was used for cranes and swing-bridges. Oil later replaced water as the main working fluid. Most modern cars have hydraulic brakes. *See also* FLUID MECHANICS

hydrocarbon Organic compound containing only CARBON and HYDROGEN. There are many different hydrocarbons, including open-chain compounds such as the ALKANES (paraffins), ALKENES (olefins) and acetylenes. Petroleum, natural gas and coal tar are major sources.

hydrocephalus Excess of cerebrospinal fluid (CSF) in the BRAIN. Hydrocephalus exerts dangerous pressure on brain tissue. It can be due to obstruction or a failure of natural reabsorption. In babies it is congenital; in adults it may arise from injury or disease. It is treated by a shunting system to drain the CSF into the abdominal cavity.

hydrochloric acid Solution of hydrogen chloride (HCl) gas in water. It is obtained by the action of SULPHURIC ACID on common SALT, as a by-product of the chlorination of hydrocarbons, or by combination of HYDROGEN and CHLORINE. Hydrochloric acid is used in industry and is produced by humans cells in the stomach lining to allow the enzyme PEPSIN to digest proteins.

hydroelectricity ELECTRICITY generated from the motion of water. In all installations this ENERGY of movement, or kinetic energy, is first converted into mechanical energy in the spinning blades of a water TURBINE and then into electricity by the spinning rotor of a GENERATOR. Many power stations are driven by water held back by large DAMS to regulate flow, such as the HOOVER DAM. Hydroelectric power (HEP) provides cheap energy for mountainous areas with high rainfall.

hydrofoil Boat or ship whose hull is lifted clear of the water, when moving at speed, by submerged wings. They usually have gas-turbine or diesel engines that power propellers or water jets. Speeds range from 30 to 60 knots.

hydrogen (symbol H) Gaseous, nonmetallic element, first identified as a separate element in 1766 by Henry CAVENDISH. Colourless and odourless, hydrogen is the lightest and most abundant element in the universe (76% by mass), mostly found combined with oxygen in water. It is used to manufacture AMMONIA by the HABER PROCESS and in rocket fuels. Properties: at.no. 1; r.a.m. 1.00797; r.d. 0.0899; m.p. −259.1°C (−434.4°F); b.p. −252.9°C (−423.2°F); most common isotope H[1] (99.985%).

hydrogen bomb (H-bomb) NUCLEAR WEAPON developed by the USA in the 1940s and first exploded in 1952 in the Pacific. The explosion results from nuclear FUSION when hydrogen nuclei are joined to form helium nuclei, releasing great destructive energy and radioactive fallout.

hydrogen peroxide (H_2O_2) Liquid compound of hydrogen and oxygen. It is prepared by electrolytic oxidation of sulphuric acid and also by oxidation-reduction. Hydrogen peroxide is used as a bleach, disinfectant and an oxidizer for rocket fuel and submarine propellant. Properties: r.d. 1.44; m.p. −0.9°C (30.4°F); b.p. 150°C (302°F).

hydrogen sulphide (H_2S) Colourless, poisonous gas with the smell of bad eggs. It is produced by decaying matter, found in crude oil, and prepared by the action of sulphuric acid on metal sulphides. Properties: m.p. −85.5°C (−121.9°F), b.p. −60.7°C (−77.3°F).

hydrological cycle (water cycle) Circulation of water around the Earth. Water is evaporated from the sea; most falls back into the oceans, but some is carried over land. There it falls as precipitation, and by surface run off or infiltration and seepage, it gradually finds its way back to the sea. Less than 1% of the world's water is involved in this cycle.

hydrology Study of the Earth's waters, their sources, circulation, uses and chemical and physical composition. The HYDROLOGICAL CYCLE is the Earth's natural water circulation system. Hydrologists are concerned with the provision of fresh water, building dams and irrigation systems and controlling floods and water pollution.

hydrolysis Chemical reaction in which molecules are split into smaller molecules by reaction with water, often assisted by a CATALYST. For example, in digestion, ENZYMES catalyze the hydrolysis of CARBOHYDRATES, PROTEINS and FATS into smaller, soluble molecules that the body can assimilate.

hydrophyte (aquatic plant) Plant that grows only in water or in damp places. Examples include WATER LILIES, WATER HYACINTH, DUCKWEED and PONDWEED.

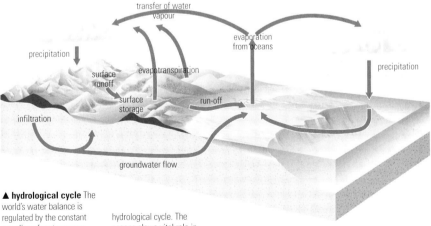

▲ **hydrological cycle** The world's water balance is regulated by the constant recycling of water among the oceans, the atmosphere and the land. The movement of water among these three "reservoirs" is called the hydrological cycle. The oceans play a vital role in this cycle: 74% of the total precipitation falls over the oceans, and 84% of the total evaporation comes from the oceans. Water vapour in the atmosphere circulates around the planet, transporting energy as well as water itself. When the vapour cools, it falls as rain or other precipitation.

hydroponics (soil-less culture or tank farming) Growing of plants with their roots in a mineral solution or a moist inert medium (such as gravel) containing the necessary nutrients, instead of soil.

hydroxide Inorganic chemical compound containing the hydroxyl group –OH, which acts as a BASE. The strong inorganic bases, such as potassium hydroxide (KOH), dissociate in water almost completely to provide many hydroxyl ions.

hydrozoa Class of animals without backbones, all living in water, belonging to the phylum Coelenterata. They vary in shape and size from the large PORTUGUESE MAN-OF-WAR to the simple HYDRA. *See also* COELENTERATE

hyena Predatory and scavenging carnivore native to Africa and S Asia. The spotted or laughing hyena (*Crocuta crocuta*) of the sub-Sahara is the largest. The brown hyena (*Hyaena brunnea*) of S Africa is smaller. Weight: 27–80kg (60–176lb). Family Hyaenidae.

hygrometer Instrument to measure the HUMIDITY of the ATMOSPHERE. One type, the **psychrometer**, compares the wet and dry bulb temperatures of the air; other types measure absorption or condensation of moisture from the air, or chemical or electrical changes caused by that moisture.

Hyksos Invaders, probably from Palestine, of EGYPT in the 17th century BC. They are attributed with the first use of horses and chariots. They ruled Egypt from *c.*1674 to 1567 BC as the 15th and 16th dynasties. They were overthrown by a native revolt.

Hymen In Greek mythology, god of marriage. Son of APOLLO, he is represented as a youth attending APHRODITE.

hymn Song of praise or gratitude to a god or hero. The oldest forms are found in ancient Egyptian and Greek writings and in the Old Testament psalms of rejoicing. In strict Christian church usage, hymns are religious songs sung by the choir and congregation in a church, distinct from a psalm or a canticle.

hyperactivity (attention-deficit disorder) Condition characterized by excessive activity, restlessness, impulsiveness and short attention span. It occurs most commonly in children, particularly boys. Treatment is generally based on BEHAVIOUR THERAPY.

hyperbola Plane curve traced out by a point that moves so that its distance from a fixed point bears a constant ratio, greater than one, to its distance from a fixed straight line. The fixed point is the focus, the ratio is the eccentricity, and the fixed line is the directrix. The curve has two branches and is a CONIC section. Its standard equation in Cartesian coordinates x and y is $x^2/a^2 - y^2/b^2 = 1$.

hyperglycaemia Condition in which blood-sugar level is abnormally high. It can occur in a number of diseases, most notably DIABETES. *See also* HYPOGLYCAEMIA

Hyperion In Greek mythology, sometimes said to be the original Sun god. He was one of the TITANS, the son of URANUS and GAIA, and the father of HELIOS the Sun, SELENE the Moon and EOS the dawn.

hypertension Persistent high BLOOD PRESSURE. It can damage blood vessels and may increase the risk of strokes or heart disease. *See also* HYPOTENSION

hyperthermia Abnormally high body temperature, usually defined as being 41°C (106°F) or more. It is usually due to overheating (as in HEATSTROKE) or FEVER.

hyperthyroidism Excessive production of thyroid HORMONE, with enlargement of the THYROID GLAND. Symptoms include protrusion of the eyeballs, rapid heart rate, high blood pressure, accelerated metabolism and weight loss. *See also* HYPOTHYROIDISM

hyperventilation Rapid breathing that is not brought about by physical exertion. It reduces the carbon dioxide

level in the blood, producing dizziness, tingling and tightness in the chest; it may cause loss of consciousness.

hypnosis Artificially induced, sleep-like state during which suggestions are readily obeyed. It was first described more than two centuries ago. It is physiologically different from sleep and closer to a state of relaxed wakefulness. Its reduction of critical faculties and effects on memory have been used in PSYCHOANALYSIS.

hypochondria (hypochondriasis) Neurotic condition characterized by an exaggerated concern with ill health. Hypochondriacs imagine they have serious diseases and often consult several doctors in the hope of a "cure".

hypoglycaemia Abnormally low blood-sugar level. It may result from fasting, excess INSULIN in the blood, or various metabolic and glandular diseases, notably DIABETES. Symptoms include dizziness, headache, sweating and mental confusion. *See also* HYPERGLYCAEMIA

hypotension Condition in which BLOOD PRESSURE is abnormally low. It is commonly seen after heavy blood loss or excessive fluid loss due to prolonged vomiting or diarrhoea. It also occurs in many kinds of serious illness. Temporary hypotension may cause sweating, dizziness and fainting. *See also* HYPERTENSION

hypotenuse Side opposite the right angle in a right-angled triangle. It is the longest side of the triangle.

hypothalamus Region at the base of the brain containing centres that regulate body temperature, fluid balance, hunger, thirst and sexual activity. It is also effects emotions, sleep and the integration of HORMONE and nervous activity.

hypothermia Fall in body temperature to below 35°C (95°F). Insidious in onset, it can progress to coma and death. Hypothermia is sometimes induced during surgery to lower the body's oxygen demand. It occurs naturally in animals during HIBERNATION.

hypothesis Assumption or proposal made in order to account for or correlate known facts. Consequences inferred from a hypothesis are put to further inquiry, thus enabling the assumption to be tested in a particular situation. A set of hypotheses, logically connected and leading to the prediction of a wide range of naturally occurring events or states, is called a theory.

hypothyroidism Deficient functioning of the THYROID GLAND. Congenital hypothyroidism can lead to cretinism in children. In adults the condition is called **myxedema**. More common in women, it causes physical and mental slowness, weight gain, sensitivity to cold and susceptibility to infection. It can be due to a defect of the gland or a lack of iodine in the diet. It is treated with the hormone thyroxine.

hyrax Small, herbivorous, hoofed mammal of Africa and SW Asia. Rock hyraxes (genus *Procavia*), which live in deserts and hills, are larger than the solitary, nocturnal, tree-dwelling hyraxes (genus *Dendrohyrax*). Length: to 50cm (20in). Family Procaviidae.

hysterectomy Removal of the UTERUS, possibly with surrounding structures. It is performed to treat fibroids or cancer or to put an end to heavy menstrual bleeding.

hysteresis Phenomenon occurring in the magnetic and elastic behaviour of substances in which the strain is greater when the stress is decreasing than when it is increasing because of a lag in the effect. When the stress is removed, a residual strain remains.

hysteria In psychology, a group of disorders characterized by emotional instability, dissociation, hallucinations and the presence of physical symptoms of illness with no physiological cause. Hysteria is no longer used as a diagnostic term. Leading researchers in this field have included Jean Martin CHARCOT, Pierre Janet and Sigmund FREUD.

I/i, ninth letter of the Roman alphabet, is derived from the Semitic letter yod, meaning hand. *It passed to the Greek alphabet, where it was called* iota. *In the Roman alphabet it was pronounced* ee.

Iasi City in NE Romania, 16km (10mi) from the border with Moldova. It was the capital of Moldavia from 1562 to 1861. Notable buildings include the 15th-century Church of St Nicholas. It remains an important commercial and administrative centre. Industries: textiles, machinery, pharmaceuticals, food products. Pop. (1994) 340,000.

Ibadan City in SW Nigeria; capital of Oyo state. The second-largest city in Nigeria, it was established in the 1830s as a YORUBA military base. Ibadan handles the regional cacao and cotton trades. Industries: plastics, cigarettes, brewing, chemicals. Pop. (1992 est.) 1,295,000.

Ibáñez, Vicente Blasco *See* BLASCO IBÁÑEZ, VICENTE

Iberian Peninsula Part of SW Europe occupied by SPAIN and PORTUGAL, separated from Africa by the Strait of Gibraltar and from the rest of Europe by the PYRENEES. The early Iberian inhabitants were colonized by Phoenicians, the Carthaginians and, in the 2nd century BC, the Romans. Visigoth incursions in the 4th century AD were followed by the Moorish invasions from North Africa. With the capture of GRANADA (1492), the Christian reconquest of the peninsula was complete. Area: 596,384sq km (230,264sq mi).

Ibarruri, Dolores (1895–1989) Spanish politician. She was a founder (1920) of the Spanish Communist Party and the Spanish delegate to the Third International (1933, 1935). During the Spanish CIVIL WAR (1936–39), Ibarruri's inspirational oratory for the Republican cause earned her the epithet "*La Pasionaria*". In 1939, she went into exile in the Soviet Union. In 1977, Ibarruri returned to Spain and was re-elected to the National Assembly.

ibex Any of several species of wild Old World GOATS. The long, backward curving horns grow up to 1.5m (5ft) long on the male, and both sexes have long, yellow-brown hair. Ibexes are renowned for their agility. Height: 85cm (3ft) at shoulder. Family Bovidae.

ibis Tropical lagoon and marsh wading bird with long down-curved bill, long neck and lanky legs. Closely related to the SPOONBILL, it may be black, whitish or brightly coloured. It feeds on small animals and nests in colonies. The sacred ibis, *Threskiornis aethiopicus*, was worshipped by the ancient Egyptians as a symbol of the god Thoth. Length: 60–90cm (2–3ft). Subfamily: Threskiornithidae.

Ibiza Island of Spain, 130km (80mi) off the E coast, in the W Mediterranean; part of the Balearic group. The mild climate and beautiful scenery have made Ibiza a popular tourist resort. Other activities include fishing, salt mining and the cultivation of figs and olives. Area: 572sq km (221sq mi). Pop. (1991) 70,000.

Iblis Islamic counterpart of the archangel SATAN. According to the KORAN, Iblis disobeyed God and was cast out of heaven but given the power to tempt mankind into evil.

Ibn Batuta (1304?–68?) Arab traveller and writer. Born in Tangier, Morocco, he began his adventures in *c*.1325 with a pilgrimage to Mecca by way of Egypt and Syria. Travel was to occupy the next 30 years of his life, when he visited parts of Africa, Asia and Europe. In *c*.1350, he returned to Morocco to write an account of his travels.

Ibn Khaldun *See* KHALDUN, IBN

Ibo (Igbo) Kwa-speaking people of E NIGERIA. Their patrilineal society originally consisted of politically and socially separate village units, but during the 20th century a unified political movement developed in reaction to British colonial rule. In 1967, the Ibo attempted to secede from Nigeria as the Republic of BIAFRA.

Ibrahim Pasha (1789–1848) Egyptian general and governor, son of MUHAMMAD ALI. He campaigned (1816–18) against the Wahhabis of Arabia and fought the Greek insurgents with equal success until the Ottoman defeat at NAVARINO (1827). When his father defied Ottoman supremacy, Ibrahim conquered Syria (1832–33) and became its governor until forced to withdraw in 1841.

Ibsen, Henrik Johan (1828–1906) Norwegian dramatist and poet. His first published play was *Catilina* (1850), and he came to international attention for the poetic drama, *Peer Gynt* (1867). The NATURALISM of Ibsen's presentation of social issues in tragedies such as *A Doll's House* (1879), *Ghosts* (1881), *An Enemy of the People* (1882) and *Hedda Gabler* (1890) established his reputation. His later works, such as *The Master Builder* (1892) and *John Gabriel Borkman* (1896), are more symbolic.

Icarus In Greek mythology, the son of DAEDALUS. Daedalus made wings of feathers and wax in order to escape from Crete to the mainland and was successful. But Icarus flew too near the Sun, the heat of which melted his wings, and he fell into the sea and drowned.

ice WATER frozen to 0°C (32°F) or below, when it forms complex six-sided crystals. It is less dense than water and floats. When water vapour condenses below the freezing point, ice crystals are formed. Clusters of crystals form snowflakes. *See also* GLACIER

Ice Ages Periods in the Earth's history when ICE-SHEETS and GLACIERS advance to cover areas previously not affected by ice. There is evidence of at least six ice ages having occurred throughout the Earth's history, the earliest dating back to 2.3 billion years ago. The best known is the most recent Ice Age, which began *c*.2 million years ago and lasted until the retreat of the ice to its present extent *c*.10,000 years ago. The present time may be a warmer period known as an interglacial. The last ice age produced many of the landforms seen in northern continents and affected sea level on a global scale.

iceberg Large drifting piece of ice, broken off from a GLACIER or polar ICECAP. In the Northern Hemisphere the main source of icebergs is the SW coast of Greenland. In the Southern Hemisphere, the glacial flow from Antarctica releases huge tabular icebergs. Icebergs can be dangerous to shipping, since only a small portion is visible above the surface of the water.

ice-cap Small ICE-SHEET, often in the shape of a flattened dome, which spreads over the mountains and valleys of

◀ **ibis** The scarlet ibis (*Eudocimus ruber*) is found in marsh regions of tropical South America. It grows to a height of *c*.60cm (24in). It has distinctive scarlet plumage with black wing tips.

polar islands. The floating ice fields surrounding the North Pole are sometimes incorrectly called an ice-cap.

ice hockey Fast-action sport on an oval ice rink in which two teams of six players wearing ice skates (and protective clothing) use special hockey sticks to try to propel a vulcanized rubber disc (puck) into the opponents' goal. The rink is usually 61m × 26m (200ft × 85ft) and surrounded by walls c.1.2m (4ft) high. It is evenly divided into three zones – attacking, neutral and defending – each 18.3m (60ft) long. The goals are within the playing area, 3 to 4m (10–15ft) from each back line. Games consist of three 20-minute periods of actual timed play. Substitutions are allowed at any time, and the game is controlled by a referee and two linesmen. A penalized player may be banished to the "sin bin" for two or more minutes, and the team meanwhile remains a player short on the ice unless the opponents score. The National Hockey League (NHL) of North America was instituted in 1917. The major trophy is the Stanley Cup. It has been included in the Winter Olympics since 1920.

Iceland Small Scandinavian republic in the North Atlantic Ocean, N Europe; the capital is REYKJAVÍK. **Land and climate** Iceland sits astride the Mid-Atlantic Ridge, which is slowly widening as the ocean is being stretched apart by CONTINENTAL DRIFT. Molten lava wells up to fill the gap in the centre of Iceland. Iceland has c.200 volcanoes, and eruptions are frequent. Geysers and hot springs are also common features. Ice-caps and glaciers cover c.12% of the land; the largest is Vatnajökull in the SE. The only habitable regions are the coastal lowlands. Vegetation is sparse or nonexistent on 75% of the land. Treeless grassland or bogs cover some areas, and Iceland also has some spruce trees in sheltered areas. Deep fjords fringe the coast. **History and politics** In AD 874, Norwegian Vikings colonized Iceland, and in 930 the settlers founded the world's oldest parliament (*Althing*). In 1262, Iceland united with Norway, and when Norway united with Denmark in 1380, Iceland came under Danish rule. During the colonial period Iceland lost much of its population due to migration, disease and natural disaster. In 1918, Iceland became a self-governing kingdom, united with Denmark. During World War 2, Iceland escaped German occupation, largely due to the presence of US forces. In 1944, a referendum decisively voted to sever links with Denmark, and Iceland became a fully independent republic. In 1946, it joined the North Atlantic Treaty Organization (NATO). The USA maintained military bases on Iceland. In 1970 Iceland joined the European Free Trade Association (EFTA). The extension of Iceland's fishing limits in 1958 and 1972 precipitated the "Cod War" with the UK. In 1977, the UK agreed not to fish within Iceland's 370km (200 nautical mi) fishing limits. The continuing US military presence remains a political issue. Vigdis Finnbogadottir served as president from 1980 to 1996. She was succeeded by Olafur Ragnar Grimsson. In 1991, David Oddsson was elected prime minister. In 1995, he was re-elected as the head of a new centre-right coalition. **Economy** Fishing and fish processing are the principal industries, accounting for 80% of Iceland's exports. (1995 GDP per capita, US$20,460.) Overfishing is a major economic problem. Barely 1% of the land is used to grow crops,

---

ICELAND
AREA: 103,000sq km (39,768sq mi)
POPULATION: 274,000
CAPITAL (POPULATION): Reykjavík (105,000)

---

mainly root vegetables and fodder for livestock, and 23% is used for grazing sheep and cattle. Iceland is self-sufficient in meat and dairy products. Vegetables and fruits are grown in greenhouses. Manufacturing is important. Products: aluminium, cement, electrical equipment, fertilizers. Geothermal power is an important energy source and heats Reykjavík. Tourism is increasingly important.

Icelandic Official language of Iceland, spoken by virtually all of the island's 268,000 inhabitants. It belongs to the Germanic family of Indo-European languages and is descended from the Old Norse that was taken to Iceland by Norwegian Vikings in the 9th and 10th centuries AD. By the time of the earliest works of ICELANDIC LITERATURE, many dialectal characteristics had arisen to distinguish it from Norwegian. Icelandic has, however, undergone little linguistic change since the 12th century apart from pronunciation, which has altered greatly. The language has three grammatical genders, a system of noun declensions involving case forms, and complex verb conjugations similar to those of modern German.

Icelandic literature Early Icelandic literature emerged in the 13th century from the oral tradition of Eadic and Skaldic poetry, both of which were based on ancient Icelandic mythology. Other early writings (14th–16th centuries) include the sagas of Norse monarchs, translations of foreign romances and religious works. From the 14th to 19th centuries, the *rímur*, a narrative verse poem, was the dominant form. The 19th century was probably the most important period in the development of Icelandic literature, with the rise of Icelandic realism late in the period. Important 20th-century writers include Gunnar Gunnarsson (1889–1975) and Halldór LAXNESS.

Iceni Ancient British tribe that occupied the area now known as Norfolk and Suffolk. The territory had been ruled by Prasutagus, a client-king, but on his death (AD 60) the Romans attempted to annex it. This led to a widespread revolt led by Prasutagus' queen, BOADICEA. The Iceni sacked Colchester, London and St Albans before they were crushed by the Roman governor, Suetonius Paulinus.

ice-sheet Also described as a continental GLACIER. The term may be used for any vast ICE-CAP covering Greenland and Antarctica. The ice at the edges of an ice-sheet breaks away to form ICEBERGS, often many square miles in area.

ice skating Winter leisure activity and all-year-round indoor competitive sport in which participants use steel skates to glide on ice. The three disciplines of competition ice skating are solo skating, pairs skating and (pairs) ice dancing. **Solo** and **pairs** skating comprise compulsory figure skating, a short programme of compulsory elements and free skating (to the skater's choice of music). The **ice dancing** competition is structured similarly but based on set styles of dancing. **Speed** skating has two disciplines: international-track and short-track.

I Ching *See* BOOK OF CHANGES

ichneumon Parasitoid WASP that consumes other insects and spiders. Found worldwide, they are characterized by an ovipositor (often longer than the body) that is used to inject eggs into hosts. They are usually 1cm (0.4in) long. Family Ichneumonidae.

icon Type of religious painting or sculpture, often of Christ, the Virgin and Child or individual saints. The term is particularly used of Byzantine pictures and later Russian imitations. Icons were already being produced as early as the 5th century; they have been used as an aid to prayer from the 6th century. In the Eastern Christian Church the veneration of icons was banned (726–843).

iconography Study and interpretation of themes and symbols in the figurative arts. In the 18th century, the term referred to the classification of ancient monuments by motifs and subjects, but by the 19th century it was more concerned with symbolism in Christian art. Modern iconographers also study secular art and that of religions other than Christianity.

id In psychoanalytic theory, the deepest level of the personality that includes primitive drives (hunger, anger, sex) demanding instant gratification. Even after the EGO and the SUPEREGO develop and limit these instinctual impulses, the id is a source of motivation and of unconscious conflicts.

Idaho State in NW USA, on the border with Canada; the capital and largest city is BOISE. Idaho remained unexplored until 1805. The discovery of gold in 1860 brought many immigrants, although the Native American population was not subdued until 1877. The state was admitted to the Union in 1890 and by the turn of the century had begun to develop its resources. The terrain is dominated by the Rocky Mountains and is drained chiefly by the Snake River, whose waters are used to generate hydroelectricity and for irrigation. The principal crops are potatoes, hay, wheat and sugar beets and cattle are reared. Silver, lead, antimony and zinc are mined, and industries include food processing and timber. Area: 216,412sq km (83,557sq mi). Pop. (2000) 1,293,953.

ideal gas law Law relating pressure, temperature and volume of an ideal (perfect) gas: $pV = NkT$, where N is the number of molecules of the gas and k is a constant of proportionality. This law implies that at constant temperature (T), the product of pressure and volume (pV) is constant (BOYLE'S LAW); and at constant pressure, the volume is proportional to the temperature (CHARLES' LAW).

idealism Philosophical doctrine that assigns metaphysical priority to the mental over the material. It denies the claim within REALISM that material things exist independently of the MIND. Idealism in the West dates from the teachings of PLATO. The term is also applied to artistic pursuits to denote a rendering of something "as it ought to be" rather than as it actually is.

ideology Collection of beliefs or ideas reflecting the interests and aspirations of a country or its political system. In the 20th century the term has been applied to various political theories, including FASCISM, MARXISM and COMMUNISM. *See also* CLASS

Idris I (1890–1983) King of Libya (1951-69). Head of the Cyrenaican government and leader of the Islamic Sanusi sect, he sided with the British in World War 2, and was ruler of Libya when it became independent in 1950. In 1969 Idris was deposed by a military junta with socialist aims, dominated by Muammar al-QADDAFI.

idyll In classical Greek literature, a brief poem, generally part of a group of poems describing pastoral scenes or events. The form is especially associated with the 3rd-century BC poet THEOCRITUS. More recent examples include *Idylls of the King* (1842–45) by TENNYSON and *Dramatic Idylls* (1879–80) by Robert BROWNING.

Ignatiev, Count Nikolai Pavlovich (1832–1908) Russian diplomat. The border agreement he negotiated with China in 1859 enabled Russia to become a major Pacific power. Ambassador to Turkey in 1864–78, he helped to draw up the Treaty of San Stefano, which ended the Russo-Turkish War (1877–78).

Ignatius of Antioch, Saint (active 1st century AD) Bishop of Antioch and influential theologian of the early Christian Church. On his way to Rome, where he died for his faith, Ignatius wrote his seven *Epistles*, valuable sources for an assessment of the doctrine of the early Church.

Ignatius of Loyola, Saint (1491–1556) Spanish soldier, churchman and founder of the JESUITS. In 1534,

with FRANCIS XAVIER and other young men, he made vows of poverty, chastity and obedience. Ignatius was ordained in 1537 and moved to Rome where, in 1540, Pope PAUL III approved his request to found the Society of Jesus, or Jesuits. He spent the rest of his life in Rome supervising the growth of the order, which was to become the leading force in the COUNTER-REFORMATION. Ignatius wrote the influential *Spiritual Exercises* (1548). He was canonized in 1622. Feast day: 31 July.

igneous rock One of three major classes of rock produced by the cooling and solidifying of molten MAGMA. All igneous rocks are crystalline and most are quite resistant to erosion. **Extrusive** or volcanic igneous rocks, such as BASALT, are formed by the rapid cooling of molten material at the surface. **Intrusive** or hyperbyssal rocks, such as DOLERITE, are formed in SILLS or DYKES at intermediate depth. **Plutonic** rocks, such as GRANITE, are formed in BATHOLITHS at greater depth. The major chemical constituent is SILICA. **Acid** rocks contain high amounts of QUARTZ, FELDSPAR or MICA, and are light in colour. Basic rocks are darker and contain 45% to 55% silica, including minerals such as HORNBLENDE. *See also* GABBRO; METAMORPHIC ROCK; SEDIMENTARY ROCK

Iguaçu Falls (Iguassu) Series of spectacular waterfalls on the River Iguaçu on the border between Brazil and Argentina, South America. A world heritage site, the 275 falls are interspersed among rocky islands along a 3km- (2mi-) long escarpment. Total drop: 2,470m (8,104ft).

iguana Any of numerous species of terrestrial, arboreal (tree-dwelling), burrowing or aquatic LIZARDS that live in tropical America and the Galápagos Islands. The common iguana (*Iguana iguana*) is greenish-brown with a serrated dewlap and a crest along its back. Length: to 2m (6.5ft). Family Iguanidae.

Ijsselmeer Large lake in the NW Netherlands. It was formed in 1932 by the completion of a dyke that divided the Zuider Zee into the saline Wadden Zee and the freshwater Ijsselmeer. Length of dyke: 32km (20mi). Area: 1,200sq km (460sq mi).

ileum Major part of the small INTESTINE, about 4m (13ft) long. Its inner wall is lined with finger-like villi, which increase the area for the absorption of nutrients.

Iliescu, Ion (1930–) Romanian statesman, president (1990–96). In 1971, he became propaganda secretary in Nicolae CEAUȘESCU's regime, but was later banished to Timișoara for his opposition to Ceaușescu's growing cult of the personality. Following the "Christmas Revolution" (1989) and the execution of Ceaușescu, Iliescu was elected president. He was succeeded by Emil Constantinescu. He was re-elected in 2000.

Illinois State in N central USA, on the E bank of the Mississippi River; the capital is SPRINGFIELD. Illinois was explored first by the French in 1673. Ceded to the British in 1763, it was occupied by American troops during the

◀ **iguana** The common iguana (*Iguana iguana*) is one of the world's largest lizards, growing up to 2m (6.5ft) or more in length. It lives near rivers in tropical America. The young feed mainly on insects, whereas adults eat leaves and fruit.

American Revolution. Illinois became a state of the Union in 1818. The state is mostly flat prairie land and is drained by many rivers flowing SW to the Mississippi. The fertile soil supports crops such as hay, oats and barley; livestock farming is also important. Mineral deposits are found in the S. CHICAGO (the largest city) is a transport centre and port on Lake MICHIGAN. Area: 146,075sq km (56,400sq mi). Pop. (2000) 12,419,293.

illiteracy Inability to read and write. The eradication of illiteracy is a major aim of public and compulsory education around the world, and yet the problem remains huge. It is estimated that some one billion adults in the world (about 1 in 5 of the world's population) are unable to read.

illumination Coloured decorations serving to beautify manuscripts of religious books. The practice of illumination began in about the 5th century. The style ranges from decoration of initial letters and borders to miniatures and full-page illustrations. Illumination reached its height during the 14th and 15th centuries with such Flemish and French artists as the LIMBOURG brothers and Jean FOUQUET. *See also* BOOK OF KELLS

Illyria Historic region on the N and E shores of the Adriatic Sea, now mainly in Albania. The tribes of Illyria were conquered by the Romans after 168 BC, and the region was later divided into the provinces of Dalmatia and Pannonia. Several late Roman emperors were of Illyrian origin.

image In optics, representation of an object produced when rays of light from the object are either reflected by a MIRROR or refracted by a LENS. A **real** image can be projected onto a screen and recorded in a photograph; a **virtual** image, such as that produced by a plane mirror, cannot.

imaginary number In mathematics, the SQUARE ROOT ($\sqrt{}$) of a negative quantity. The simplest, $\sqrt{-1}$, is usually represented by i. The NUMBERS are so called because when first discovered they were widely regarded as meaningless. But they are necessary for the solution of many QUADRATIC EQUATIONS, the roots of which can be expressed only as COMPLEX NUMBERS, which are composed of a real part and an imaginary part. They also find applications in alternating current (AC) theory.

imagism Movement in poetry that flourished in the USA and England from 1912 to 1917. The imagists believed that poetry should use the language and flexible rhythms of common speech. Amy LOWELL, the principal exponent, produced three anthologies called *Some Imagist Poets* (1915–17). Among the most distinguished contributors was Ezra POUND.

imago Adult, reproductive stage of an insect that has undergone full METAMORPHOSIS. Imagos are the winged insects, such as butterflies and dragonflies, that emerge from PUPAS or develop from NYMPHS.

Imam Leader of a Muslim community invested with spiritual or temporal authority. Imam is also a title of honour for ISMAILI leaders, such as the AGA KHAN.

IMF Abbreviation of INTERNATIONAL MONETARY FUND

Imhotep (active 27th century BC) Egyptian architect. He is often credited with designing the step PYRAMID at Saqqara for Pharaoh Zoser in the Third Dynasty of the Old Kingdom. He was later deified as the patron of scribes and the son of Ptah, the builder god of Memphis. The Greeks identified him with Asclepius.

Immaculate Conception Roman Catholic belief that the Blessed Virgin MARY was free of all ORIGINAL SIN from the moment that she was conceived. It was defined as a dogma by Pope PIUS IX in 1854.

immigration MIGRATION of people as permanent settlers into a country other than their native land. The majority of immigrants are economic, seeking better economic or employment opportunities and improved standards of health and welfare. Some migrants are REFUGEES fleeing political or religious persecution or natural disasters. Most of the early settlers in North America were from England or France. SLAVERY brought enforced migration for 15 million Africans. Most immigration in the 19th and 20th centuries has been from Europe to the continents of North America, South America and Australasia. From 1820 to 1930 the USA received *c*.60% of the world's immigrants. Before 1890, these were mainly economic migrants from N and W Europe, principally from the UK, Ireland and Germany. After 1890, the largest group of immigrants to the US were Roman Catholics and Jews from E and S Europe. In recent years, the major flow of immigration has been from less developed to more developed economies, in particular Germany, the USA, UK, Australia, Canada and Italy. Most countries place legal restrictions on the numbers of immigrants they will accept, and impose conditions for the right of citizenship. In the UK, immigration is mainly governed by the Immigration Act (1970). British and Commonwealth citizens with the right of abode before 1983 and citizens of the EU or EEA are not subject to immigration control. In 1994, 31% of immigrants to the UK were from the EU. In 1995, only 6% of the more than 55,000 applications for political asylum were accepted.

immune system Mechanism by which an organism resists DISEASE. In humans, acquired IMMUNITY is conferred by LYMPHOCYTES and PHAGOCYTES (white blood cells), INTERFERON and ANTIBODIES in the bloodstream.

immunity In medicine, protection or resistance to DISEASE. **Innate** immunity is influenced by genetic factors and general health. **Acquired** immunity is the body's second line of defence. An infecting agent stimulates the IMMUNE SYSTEM to produce ANTIBODIES (**humoral** immunity) and T-LYMPHOCYTES (**cell-mediated** immunity). Antibodies are PROTEINS produced by B-lymphocytes in response to the presence of ANTIGENS. They attach themselves to the antigen and either destroy it or "mark" it so a PHAGOCYTE can engulf the antigen. Subsequent exposure to the same harmful antigen, such as a VIRUS, causes an accelerated immune response. In **cell-mediated** immunity sensitized cells react directly with the antigen. This form of immunity is suppressed by HUMAN IMMUNODEFICIENCY VIRUS (HIV). Immunity may be induced artificially by IMMUNIZATION. *See also* ACQUIRED IMMUNE DEFICIENCY SYNDROME (AIDS); AUTOIMMUNE DISEASE; MACROPHAGE; PATHOGEN; TOXIN

immunization Practice of conferring IMMUNITY against DISEASE by artificial means. **Passive** immunity may be conferred by the injection of an antiserum containing ANTIBODIES. **Active** immunity involves VACCINATION with dead or attenuated (weakened) organisms to stimulate production of specific antibodies and so provide lasting immunity.

immunoglobulin PROTEIN found in the bloodstream that plays a role in the body's IMMUNE SYSTEM. Immunoglobulins act as ANTIBODIES for specific ANTIGENS. They can be obtained from donor plasma and injected into people at risk of particular diseases.

immunology Study of IMMUNITY and the IMMUNE SYSTEM. It is concerned with preventing disease by VACCINATION – **active** immunity; or by injections of ANTIBODIES – **passive** immunity. Immunologists also study disorders of the immune system, such as ALLERGY, and the possible rejection of TRANSPLANTS.

immunosuppressive drug Any drug that suppresses the body's IMMUNE SYSTEM to infection or "foreign" tissue. Such drugs are used to prevent rejection of TRANSPLANTS and to treat AUTOIMMUNE DISEASES and some CANCERS.

impala (pala) Long-legged, medium-sized African ANTELOPE. Long, lyre-shaped horns are found only on the males, but both sexes have sleek, glossy, brown fur with black markings on the rump. Length: to 1.5m (5ft); height: to 1m (3.3ft) at the shoulder. Family Bovidae; species *Aepyceros melampus.*

impatiens (busy Lizzies) Genus of 450 species of succulent annual plants, mostly native to the tropics of Asia and Africa. They have white, red or yellow flowers and seedpods, which, when ripe, pop and scatter their seeds. Some species are known as touch-me-not. Family Balsaminaceae. *See also* BALSAM

impeachment Prosecution of a public official by the legislature of a state. In Britain, it is conducted by the House of Commons with the House of Lords as judge, and in the USA by the House of Representatives with the Senate as judge.

impedance (symbol Z) Property of a component in an ELECTRIC CIRCUIT that opposes the passage of current. In a **direct current (DC)** circuit, the impedance corresponds to the RESISTANCE (R). In an **alternating current (AC)** circuit with CAPACITANCE or INDUCTANCE, the additional property of reactance (X) has to be allowed for, as expressed in the equation $Z^2 = R^2 + X^2$. All of these quantities are measured in OHMS.

imperialism Domination of one people or state by another. Imperialism can be economic, cultural, political or religious. With the age of EXPLORATION came the setting up, from the 16th century, of trading empires by major European powers such as the British, Spanish, French, Portuguese and Dutch. They penetrated Africa, Asia and North America, their colonies serving as a source of raw materials and providing a market for manufactured goods. With few exceptions, imperialism imposed alien cultures on native societies. In the 20th century, most former colonies have gained independence. *See also* COLONIALISM

imperial system Units of measurement developed in the UK. It is based on the foot, pound and the second. *See also* METRIC SYSTEM.

impetigo Contagious skin condition caused by streptococcal or staphylococcal infection, most common in children. It causes multiple, spreading lesions with yellowish-brown crusts, primarily affecting the face, hands and feet.

impotence In men, the inability to perform SEXUAL INTERCOURSE. It may be temporary or permanent, brought about by illness, injury, the effects of certain drugs, fatigue or psychological factors. *See also* VIAGRA

impressionism Major French anti-academic art movement of the late 19th century, gaining its name from a painting by MONET entitled *Impression, Sunrise* (1874). In the words of Monet, the movement's leading painter, impressionists aimed to create "a spontaneous work rather than a calculated one". In the 1860s, Monet, RENOIR, Alfred SISLEY and Frédéric Bazille formed a close-knit group exploring the possibilities of painting outdoors and the effects of light on nature. The first impressionist exhibition took place in 1874. Although not accepted at first, impressionism became widely influential from the late 1880s and spread throughout Europe. DEGAS and PISSARRO were prominent impressionists, and CÉZANNE exhibited with them twice. MANET was influenced by, and influenced, impressionism. Other impressionists include Mary CASSATT. RODIN has been called an impressionist because of his interest in the effects of light on his sculpture. In music, the term impressionism refers to a period lasting from c.1890 to c.1930 and is usually applied to the work of Claude DEBUSSY, who influenced Maurice RAVEL, Frederick DELIUS and Manuel DE FALLA. *See also* ROMANTICISM

imprinting Form of LEARNING that occurs within a critical period in very young animals. A complex relationship develops between the newborn infant and the first animate object it encounters, which is usually a parent. The future emotional development of the infant depends upon this relationship. Imprinting in birds has been studied by Konrad LORENZ, who believed that it is an irreversible process.

inbreeding Mating of two closely blood-related organisms. It is the opposite of outbreeding. Over successive generations it causes much less variation in GENOTYPE and PHENOTYPE than is normal in a wild population. A form of GENETIC ENGINEERING, it can be used to improve breeds in domestic plants and animals. In humans, it can have harmful results, such as the persistence of HAEMOPHILIA in some European royal families.

Inca South American people who migrated from the Peruvian highlands into the CUZCO area c.AD 1250. The Incas conquered and assimilated the CHIMÚ. They consolidated their empire slowly and steadily until the reigns of Pachacuti (r.1438–71) and his son, Topa (r.1471–93), when Inca dominance extended over most of the continent W of the Andes. Although highly organized on bureaucratic lines, the Inca empire collapsed when the Spanish invasion (1532) led by PIZARRO coincided with a civil war between ATAHUALPA and Huáscar. *See also* CENTRAL AND SOUTH AMERICAN MYTHOLOGY; MACHU PICCHU

incandescence Emission of LIGHT by a substance at a high temperature. An incandescent object is never at a temperature below c.400°C (750°F). An object like a fluorescent lamp can emit bright light without being incandescent. *See also* FLUORESCENCE

incarnation Act of appearing in, or assuming, living or bodily form, especially the assumption of human form by a divine being, as in Hinduism or Christianity. All orthodox Christians believe that the eternal Son of God, the creator and sole deity, took on bodily form and lived on Earth as a mortal, JESUS of Nazareth. The doctrine of the Incarnation was stated in the GOSPEL of St JOHN and St Paul's Epistle to the COLOSSIANS and confirmed by the first Council of NICAEA (325) and the Council of CHALCEDON (451).

incendiary bomb Bomb designed to burn its target, rather than destroy it by explosion. They were first used in World War 1. In World War 2 they had phosphorus or thermite as the charge. They were also used during the Vietnam War in the form of NAPALM.

incest Sexual relations within a FAMILY or KINSHIP group, the TABOO on which is universal but definitions and proscriptions vary between societies. In many countries incest is a crime that carries a prison sentence. It is likely that the rules of many primitive communities prohibited marriage between close relatives long before the possible adverse genetic effects of such relationships were realized.

Inchon City and port on the Yellow Sea, NW South Korea. First opened to foreign trade in the 1880s and was the scene of a Russo-Japanese naval battle (1904). In 1950, US forces landed here at the start of the KOREAN WAR. It is one of South Korea's major commercial centres. Industries: iron and steel, textiles, chemicals. Pop. (1995) 2,308,000.

incisor Any of the chisel-shaped cutting TEETH in the front of the mouth between the canines in the dentition of mammals. There are eight in humans, four in the centre front of each jaw. *See also* DENTITION

inclination Angle made by a free-floating MAGNET with the Earth's magnetic lines of force. At the north magnetic pole the inclination is zero; at the magnetic equator it is 90°. *See also* DECLINATION

income tax Federal or state annual assessment of tax on income, profits and financial gains of any type. It is a

direct tax on money earned or acquired, as distinct from a tax levied on goods or services such as VALUE-ADDED TAX (VAT). Income tax is usually a **progressive** form of TAXATION, in the sense that tax rates increase with levels of taxable income (there is also usually a non-taxable allowance). The wealthy pay more tax in proportion to their income than the lower paid, thereby acting as a limited form of wealth redistribution. Governments can use tax rates as a means of regulating CONSUMPTION: if tax rates rise, consumers have less disposable income and thus less money to buy goods. In Britain, income tax is administered by the Board of Inland Revenue. It was first imposed by William PITT (THE YOUNGER) in 1798.

incubation In biology, process of maintaining stable, warm conditions to ensure that eggs develop and hatch. Incubation is carried out naturally by birds and by some reptiles. It is accomplished by sitting on the eggs, by making use of volcanic or solar heat or the warmth of decaying vegetation, or by covering the eggs with an insulating layer of soil or sand.

incunabula BOOKS published in the infancy of modern PRINTING. It encompasses European books printed before 1500. Georg Wolfgang Panzer produced the first catalogue of such books in five volumes (1793–97).

Independence Day *See* FOURTH OF JULY

Index Librorum Prohibitorum (Lat. Index of Prohibited Books) List of books banned by the Roman Catholic Church as being dangerous to the faith or morals of its members. It was first issued (1559) by Pope Paul IV and revised at intervals until it was finally discontinued by the Second VATICAN COUNCIL in 1966.

India World's seventh-largest country and second-most populous (after China). The Republic of India can be divided into three geographical regions: **Northern** India is dominated by the HIMALAYAS. The rivers BRAHMAPUTRA, INDUS and GANGES rise in the Himalayas and form the fertile, alluvial **central plains**. A densely populated area, the plains include the capital, NEW DELHI. CALCUTTA lies in the Ganges delta. In the w is the THAR DESERT and India's largest state, RAJASTHAN. **Southern** India consists of the large DECCAN plateau, bordered by the Western and Eastern GHATS. India's largest city is MUMBAI. *See individual gazetteer articles* **Climate** India has three main seasons: a cool season from October to February; a hot season between March and June; and the monsoon season from mid-June to September. There are wide regional variations in temperature and rainfall. **Vegetation** The KARAKORAM RANGE in the far N has permanently snow-covered peaks. The E Ganges delta has mangrove swamps. Between the gulfs of Kutch and Cambay are the deciduous forest habitats of the last of India's wild lions. The Ghats are clad in heavy rainforest. **History and politics** One of the world's oldest civilizations flourished in the lower INDUS Valley, *c*.2500 to *c*.1700 BC. In *c*.1500 BC, Aryans conquered India and established an early form of HINDUISM. Between 327 and 325 BC, Alexander the Great conquered large parts of NW India. In *c*.321 BC, CHANDRAGUPTA founded the MAURYA EMPIRE. In the 3rd century BC, his grandson, ASHOKA, unified India and established BUDDHISM. In the 2nd century AD, the CHOLA established a s trading kingdom. In the 4th and 5th centuries AD, N India flourished under the

GUPTA DYNASTY. The 7th century is seen as the classical period of India's history. In 1192, the DELHI SULTANATE became India's first Muslim kingdom and dominated the region. In 1526, BABUR founded the MOGUL EMPIRE (1526–1857). In the 16th century, SIKHISM was founded by NANAK. In the 17th century, India became a centre of ISLAMIC ART AND ARCHITECTURE under SHAH JAHAN (who built the TAJ MAHAL) and AURANGZEB. In the early 18th century, the MARATHA successfully resisted European imperial ambitions in the guise of the EAST INDIA COMPANY. In 1757, Robert CLIVE established the BRITISH EMPIRE (1757–1947). The PUNJAB was annexed to British India after British victory in the SIKH WARS (1845–46, 1848–49). Growing civil unrest culminated in the INDIAN MUTINY (1857–58). Reforms failed to dampen Indian nationalism, and the CONGRESS PARTY was formed in 1885. In 1906, the MUSLIM LEAGUE was founded to protect Muslim minority rights. Following World War 1, "Mahatma" GANDHI began his passive resistance campaigns. The AMRITSAR Massacre (1919) intensified Indian nationalism. In August 1947, British India was partitioned into India and the Muslim state of PAKISTAN. The ensuing mass migration killed more than 500,000 people. India became the world's largest democratic republic. Jawaharlal NEHRU of the Congress Party was India's first prime minister. The first of the INDIA-PAKISTAN WARS (1947–49) was fought over the status of JAMMU AND KASHMIR. In 1965, Nehru's daughter, Indira GANDHI, became prime minister. In 1971, India provided military support to create an independent BANGLADESH. In 1974, India became the world's sixth nuclear power. In 1984, faced with demands for an independent Sikh state in Punjab, troops stormed the Golden Temple in Amritsar. In October 1984, Indira Gandhi was murdered by her Sikh bodyguards and was succeeded by her son, Rajiv GANDHI. In 1984, the world's worst industrial accident occurred at BHOPAL. In 1991, Rajiv Gandhi was assassinated by TAMIL militants. Between 1947 and 1996, India was ruled by the Congress (I) Party for all but four years. In 1996, the United Front formed a coalition government. In 1998, the withdrawal of Congress (I) support led to fresh elections and the formation of a coalition government led by the BHARATIYA JANATA PARTY (BJP) with Atari Bihari Vajpayee as prime minister. In April 1999, the BJP government fell, but was re-elected in October and Vajpayee resumed the post of prime minister. **Economy** India has rapidly industrialized; manufacturing is its largest export sector. Rich in mineral resources, it is the world's third-largest producer of bituminous coal. Agriculture employs 62% of the workforce, and food crops account for 75% of cultivated areas. India is the world's second-greatest producer of rice and third-largest producer of wheat and the largest exporter of tea. In 1991, India abandoned command economics and introduced free market reforms. Poverty and urban overcrowding are major problems (1995 GDP per capita, US$1,400).

Indiana State in N central USA, s of Lake Michigan; the capital is INDIANAPOLIS. Indiana was explored by the French in the early 18th century. In 1763, it was ceded to the British and passed to the USA after the American Revolution. The Native American population was not subdued until 1811. Indiana remained a rural area until late 19th century industrialization. Access to Lake Michigan and the Ohio River in the s ensures efficient distribution of the state's agricultural and manufacturing products. Indiana is one of the country's richest farming regions. The development of heavy industry in the NW has made it one of the leading producers of machinery. Industries: grain, soya beans, livestock, coal, limestone, steel,

---

INDIA
AREA: 3,287,590sq km (1,269,338sq mi)
POPULATION: 1,041,543,000
CAPITAL (POPULATION): New Delhi (301,800)

electrical machinery, motor vehicles, chemicals. Area: 93,993sq km (36,291sq mi). Pop. (2000) 6,080,485.

Indianapolis State capital of INDIANA, USA, at the centre of the state, on the White River. Built on a specially selected site, it became the state capital in 1825. It is home to the Motor Speedway, where the Indianapolis 500 motor race takes place. The city is the major cereal and livestock market in a fertile agricultural area. Industries: electronic equipment, vehicle parts, pharmaceuticals, meat packing. Pop. (1990) 741,952.

Indian art and architecture Earliest examples of Indian art date from the ancient civilization of the Indus Valley (c.2300 to c.1750 BC). Excavations at Harappa (Punjab) and Mohenjo-daro (Sind) show fortified cities with a variety of buildings and sophisticated sanitation. Art in the MAURYAN EMPIRE (320–185 BC) was intensely Buddhist in motivation. It can be seen in the development of the stupa and the *chaitya* (shrines) and *vihara* (monastic halls) hollowed out of solid rock at Ajanta. The GUPTA DYNASTY (AD 320–550) was the golden age of Buddhist art. The Buddhist temple, with a porch and cella (main sanctuary), originated at this time. The temples at Khajuraho show the sophistication of sculpture. From the 6th century AD, a typical Hindu temple plan developed. In the 7th and 8th centuries, a Dravidian style of Hindu temple emerged in S India. ISLAMIC ART AND ARCHITECTURE were introduced after the Muslim conquest (1192). Between the 16th and 18th centuries, during the MOGUL EMPIRE, an Indo-Islamic style evolved, influenced by Persian prototypes. The TAJ MAHAL stands as the most perfect example of Mogul architecture. By the late 16th century, Indian taste was emerging in bright colouring and in detailed backgrounds. The influence of Britain was most keenly felt in public architecture, such as Sir Edwin LUTYENS's designs for New Delhi. Major modern painters include Rabindranath TAGORE, Jamini Roy, Amrita Sher Gil and Francis Souza.

Indian literature SANSKRIT LITERATURE is divided into three periods: the **Vedic** period (c.1500–c.200 BC) includes the VEDAS and the UPANISHADS; the **Epic** period (c.400 BC–c.AD 400) includes the MAHABHARATA, the BHAGAVAD GITA and the RAMAYANA; and the **Classical** period (from c.AD 200), which includes the lyrics of KALIDASA. During the 19th century various regional vernacular literatures emerged. **Bengali literature** was particularly influential in the development of a nationalist literature, including writers such as Rabindranath TAGORE and Bankim Chandra CHATTERJI.

Indian Mutiny (1857–58) Large-scale uprising against British rule. It is known in India as the first war of independence. It began (10 May 1857) at Meerut as a mutiny among 35,000 Indian troops (sepoys) in the Bengal army. The immediate cause was the introduction of cartridges lubricated with the fat of cows and pigs, a practice offensive to both Hindus and Muslims. A more general cause was resentment at modernization and Westernization. The mutineers captured Delhi and, with the support of local maharajahs and many civilians in Uttar Pradesh and Madhya Pradesh, the British garrison at Lucknow was besieged. On 14 September 1857, British forces recaptured Delhi and the revolt petered out. Atrocities were perpetrated on both sides. The revolt resulted in the British government taking over control of India from the EAST INDIA COMPANY in 1858.

Indian National Congress *See* CONGRESS PARTY

Indian Ocean Third largest ocean in the world, bounded by Asia (N), Antarctica (S), Africa (W) and Southeast Asia and Australia (E). Known in ancient times as the Erythraean Sea, the Indian Ocean was the first to be extensively navigated. Branches of the ocean include the ARABIAN SEA, the Bay of BENGAL and the Andaman Sea. Its largest islands are MADAGASCAR and SRI LANKA. The average depth is 4,000m (13,000ft) although there is a Mid-Oceanic Ridge, extending from Asia to Antarctica; several of its peaks emerge as islands. The deepest part is the Java Trench, reaching 7,725m (25,344ft). The climate of the nearby land masses is strongly influenced by the ocean's winds and currents. There are three wind belts: the MONSOONS, which pick up moisture from the ocean, bringing heavy rainfall to W India and Southeast Asia; the TRADE WINDS from the SE; and the prevailing westerly winds, bringing tropical storms. The currents are governed by these winds, the seasonal shift of the monsoon dictating the flow of water N of the Equator. Area: c.73.6 million sq km (28.4 million sq mi).

Indians, American *See* NATIVE AMERICANS

Indian Territory Area set aside for Native Americans by the US government. The Indian Removal Act of 1830 gave the president authority to designate specific western lands for settlement by NATIVE AMERICANS removed from their native lands. In 1834, the Indian Intercourse Act set aside Kansas, Nebraska and Oklahoma N and E of the Red River as the Indian Territory. In 1854, Kansas and Nebraska were redesignated territories open to white settlement. In 1889, Western Oklahoma was opened to white settlement. In 1907, the last of the Indian Territory was dissolved when Oklahoma became a state.

Indian theatre Classical and modern dramatic traditions of the Indian subcontinent, including Sanskrit, Kutiyattam and Kathakali. Sanskrit (Hindu) classical drama, the two great epics of which are the MAHABHARATA and the RAMAYANA, can be traced back as far as the 3rd century BC and survived into the 11th century AD, dying out probably as a result of Muslim disapproval. Sanskrit was followed by a more eclectic tradition that emphasized music, poetry and dance in its performance. This developed in tandem with Indian folk drama. Largely as a result of Western influence, modern drama appeared during the latter half of the 20th century. There is also an enormously strong tradition of puppetry in Indian theatre.

Indian wars In American history, series of conflicts between NATIVE AMERICANS and early European settlers. The **Spanish** were involved in conflicts with Native Americans in the SW. The **French** had generally good relations with Native Americans although they were involved in occasional conflict with the Iroquois Confederacy. The **British** settlers were involved in numerous conflicts along the E coast. Events include PONTIAC'S REBELLION and KING PHILIP'S WAR. Once settlers started moving W, the level of conflict escalated, as the US army fought against tribes refusing to be pushed out of their traditional lands. The SIOUX, the APACHE and the CHEYENNE offered the fiercest resistance. Violent opposition did not abate until the end of the 19th century.

India–Pakistan Wars Three conflicts between INDIA and PAKISTAN after they became separate and independent states in 1947. The **first** (1947–49) arose from a dispute over JAMMU AND KASHMIR. Inconclusive fighting continued until January 1949, when the UN arranged a truce, leaving KASHMIR partitioned. It remained a source of friction and was the chief cause of the **second** war (1965), fought over another territorial dispute. Both sides invaded the other's territory, but military stalemate soon resulted in a cease-fire. The **third** India–Pakistan war (1971) arose out of the civil war between East and West Pakistan. India intervened in support of East Pakistan (BANGLADESH), and (West) Pakistan suffered a decisive defeat.

indicator In chemistry, substance used to indicate acidity or alkalinity. Usually shown by a change of colour. Indicators, such as the dye LITMUS, can detect a change of pH that measures a solution's acidity (litmus turns red) or alkalinity (turns blue). Universal indicator (liquid or paper) undergoes a spectral range of colour changes from pH 1 to 13.

indigestion *See* DYSPEPSIA

indigo Violet-blue DYE traditionally obtained from plants of the genus *Indigofera*. It has been produced synthetically since the 1890s.

indium (symbol In) Silvery-white metallic element of Group III of the periodic table. Its chief source is as a by-product of zinc ores. Malleable and ductile, indium is used in semiconductors and as a mirror surface. Properties: at.no. 49; r.a.m. 114.82; r.d. 7.31; m.p. 156.6°C (313.9°F); b.p. 2,080°C (3,776°F); most common isotope In[115] (95.77%).

Indochina Peninsula of SE Asia, including BURMA, THAILAND, CAMBODIA, VIETNAM, West MALAYSIA and LAOS. The name refers more specifically to the former federation of states of Vietnam, Laos and Cambodia, associated with France within the French Union (1945–54). European penetration of the area began in the 16th century. By the 19th century, France controlled Cochin China, Cambodia, ANNAM and TONKIN, which together formed the Union of Indochina in 1887; Laos was added in 1893. By the end of World War 1, France had announced plans for a federation within the French Union. Cambodia and Laos accepted the federation but fighting broke out between French troops and Annamese nationalists who wanted independence for Annam, Tonkin and Cochin China as Vietnam. The war ended with the French defeat at DIEN BIEN PHU. French control of Indochina was officially ended by the Geneva Conference of 1954.

Indo-European languages Family of languages spoken throughout Europe and SW and S Asia, and used in the areas of European colonial settlement, such as Australia and New Zealand, South Africa, Canada, the USA and Latin America. It consists of the following subgroups: the GERMANIC LANGUAGES, the CELTIC LANGUAGES and the Indo-Iranian languages (including PERSIAN, Avestan and the Indo-Aryan or Indic languages SANSKRIT, PALI and modern HINDI). It also includes are Armenian, Albanian, GREEK, the Italic languages (including LATIN and its descendants, the ROMANCE LANGUAGES), the Baltic group (including Latvian and Lithuanian) and the Slavic group (including Old Church Slavonic, RUSSIAN, POLISH, CZECH, Serbian, Croatian and others). About half the world's population speaks one of these Indo-European languages.

Indonesia Republic in SE Asia. Indonesia is the world's most populous Muslim nation and fourth most populous nation on Earth. It is also the world's largest archipelago, with 13,677 islands (less than 6,000 of which are inhabited). Three-quarters of its area and population is included in five main islands: the Greater Sunda Islands of SUMATRA, JAVA, SULAWESI and KALIMANTAN; and IRIAN JAYA (W New Guinea). More than 50% of the total population live on Java, where the capital, JAKARTA, is situated. The Lesser Sunda Islands include BALI, TIMOR and Lombok. Indonesia is mountainous and prone to earthquakes. It has more active volcanoes (c.100) than any other country. **Climate**

INDONESIA
AREA: 1,904,570sq km (735,354sq mi)
POPULATION: 218,661,000
CAPITAL (POPULATION): Jakarta (7,885,519)

Indonesia lies on the Equator and is hot and humid throughout the year. Rainfall is generally heavy; only the Sunda Islands have a dry season. **Vegetation** Mangrove swamps line the coast. Tropical rainforests remain the major vegetation on less populated islands. Much of the larger islands have been cleared by logging and shifting cultivation. **History and politics** In the 7th and 8th centuries, the Indian GUPTA DYNASTY was the dominant force and was responsible for the introduction of Buddhism and the building of BOROBUDUR, Java. In the 13th century, Buddhism was gradually replaced by Hinduism. By the end of the 16th century Islam had become the principal religion. In 1511, the Portuguese seized MALACCA. By 1610, the Dutch had acquired all of Portugal's holdings, except East Timor. During the 18th century, the Dutch EAST INDIA COMPANY controlled the region. In 1799, Indonesia became a Dutch colony. In 1883, KRAKATOA erupted, claiming c.50,000 lives. In 1927, SUKARNO formed the Indonesian Nationalist Party (PNI). During World War 2, the Japanese expelled the Dutch (1942) and occupied Indonesia. In August 1945, Sukarno proclaimed its independence; the Dutch forcibly resisted. In November 1949, Indonesia became a republic, with Sukarno as its first president and Muhammad HATTA as vice-president. During the 1950s, economic hardship and secessionist demands were met with authoritarian measures. In 1962, Indonesian paratroopers seized Netherlands NEW GUINEA and, in a 1969 referundum, Netherlands New Guinea formally became part of Indonesia as Irian Jaya. In 1966, General SUHARTO deposed Sukarno. The Communist Party was banned and alleged communists executed. In escalating violence up to 750,000 people were killed. In 1968, Suharto was appointed president. In 1975, Indonesian forces seized East Timor and declared it a province of Indonesia. Resistance to Indonesian rule has killed more than 200,000 East Timorese. The UN does not recognize the annexation. In 1997–98, Indonesia suffered from dangerously high levels of smog caused by forest fires exacerbated by deforestation and drought. In 1997, Suharto's government was destabilized by the economic crisis in Southeast Asia. Steep rises in food prices led to student demonstrations in which six protesters were shot dead by security forces in Jakarta. Nationwide riots and looting forced Suharto to resign in May 1997. He was replaced by his deputy, B.J. Habibie. Suharto faced charges of corruption, allegedly amassing a personal fortune of up to US$20 billion. East Timor gained independence in 1999, but the population suffered greatly at the hands of pro-Indonesian militias. Habibie was replaced by Abdurrahman Wahid (Gus Dar). Secessionist forces continue to oppose Indonesian settlement on Irian Jaya and in Aceh, N Sumatra. In 1999–2000, there was increased sectarian conflict in the Malaccas. **Economy** In 1997, the Indonesian economy collapsed (1995 GDP per capita, US$3,800). Despite the IMF agreeing a US$49.2 billion rescue package, the value of the rupiah fell by 300%. In 1998, inflation was running at 100% per annum and the economy was expected to contract by 15%. Agriculture employs 56% of the workforce. Oil is the most valuable resource. Indonesia is the world's second-largest exporter of natural gas and second-largest exporter of rubber. Coffee and rice production are important.

Indore City on the Saraswati and Khan rivers, Madhya Pradesh, W central India. It became important in the 18th century as the capital of the Holkar dynasty. It is now a commercial centre. Industries: iron and steel, textiles, chemicals, furniture. Pop. (1991) 1,092,000.

Indra In Vedic mythology, the ruler of heaven, great god of storms, thunder and lightning, worshiped as rain-maker and bringer of fertility. Indra slew Vritra, dragon of drought, to produce the Sun and water on the Earth.

inductance Property of an electric circuit or component that produces an ELECTROMOTIVE FORCE (EMF) following a change in the current. The SI unit of inductance is the henry (symbol *H*). **Self-inductance** (symbol *L*) occurs when the current flows through the circuit or component, and **mutual inductance** (symbol *M*) when current flows through two circuits or components that are linked magnetically. *See also* ELECTROMAGNETIC INDUCTION

induction In medicine, initiation of LABOUR before it starts of its own accord. It involves perforating the foetal membranes and administering the hormone oxytocin to stimulate contractions of the UTERUS.

induction In physics, process by which magnification or electrification is produced in an object. In ELECTRO-MAGNETIC INDUCTION, an electric current is produced in a CONDUCTOR when placed within a varying MAGNETIC FIELD . The magnitude of the current is proportional to the rate of change of MAGNETIC FLUX. In a TRANSFORMER, the alternating current in the primary coil creates a changing magnetic field that induces a current in the secondary coil. *See also* FARADAY'S LAWS; INDUCTANCE

inductive logic Method of reasoning by which a general proposition is supported through consideration of particular examples. Valid inductive reasoning does not guarantee the truth of its conclusion. This is in contrast with deductive LOGIC, which is a systematic method of reasoning, by which conclusions arrived at cannot be false if they follow necessarily and logically from a true premise. *See also* POPPER, SIR KARL

indulgence In Roman Catholic theology, remission by the Church of temporal punishment for SIN. An indulgence, once granted, obviates the need for the sinner to do PENANCE, although it does not necessarily remove guilt and may itself be only a partial rather than a full (plenary) indulgence. Previously available from bishops, indulgences are today granted only by the pope. Abuses connected with the sale of indulgences in the later Middle Ages were one of the major causes of the REFORMATION.

Indus River of s Asia. It rises in the Kailas mountain range in Tibet and flows WNW through the Jammu and Kashmir region of India, then SW through Pakistan and into the Arabian Sea. Semi-navigable along its shallow lower part, the Indus is used chiefly for irrigation and hydroelectric power. In its lower valley there are traces of an urban civilization that flourished in the 3rd millennium BC. Length: c.3,050km (1,900mi).

industrial relations Relationship between employers and employees, usually represented respectively by management and TRADE UNIONS. The aims of management may be at odds with the objectives of workers. This is often expressed in disputes over rates of pay and working practices. Employers and unions attempt to settle their differences by **collective bargaining**. Industrial disputes can be settled by **arbitration** and **conciliation**, usually via an independent third party such as the ARBITRATION AND CONCILIATION ADVISORY SERVICE (ACAS).

Industrial Revolution Social and economic transformation of agricultural societies into industrial societies. The Industrial Revolution began in Britain in the 18th century. By 1870 France, Germany and the USA were rapidly developing an industrial base. The RUSSIAN REVOLUTION (1917) led to the rapid industrialization of the Soviet Union and industries developed in Japan, India and China. In the UK, the Industrial Revolution was preceded by a rapid increase in population, which was both a cause and result of the AGRICULTURAL REVOLUTION. The

PRODUCTION of textiles was revolutionized by the inventions of Richard ARKWRIGHT, Edmund CARTWRIGHT, Samuel CROMPTON and James HARGREAVES. The new machines necessitated the building of FACTORIES. The STEAM ENGINE, invented (1769) by James WATT, was the main driving force of the Industrial Revolution and led to the siting of factories near coalfields. Industrialization led to the growth of large industrial cities, especially in Scotland, the North, the Midlands and South Wales. MASS PRODUCTION required an expansion of the network of CANALS and roads. The construction of RAILWAYS began in c.1830. Work in the factories was based on the DIVISION OF LABOUR. At first, the economic doctrine of LAISSEZ-FAIRE allowed the growth of industrialization without restrictions on working conditions. The FACTORY ACTS later brought regulations in employment of children and the length of the working day. The Industrial Revolution produced major social changes, in particular the creation of an industrial working CLASS. Relations between CAPITAL and LABOUR became antagonistic, leading to the development of MARXISM. *See also* CAPITALISM

Industrial Workers of the World (IWW) US trade union; also known as the "Wobblies". The IWW was formed (1905) in Chicago by Daniel DeLeon, Eugene V. DEBS and William D. Haywood. It was designed to combine both skilled and unskilled labour in one organization. The group advocated a socialist society and employed militant tactics. It split up after World War 1.

industry In economic terms, all businesses that produce goods or services. The term is also used to define a group of firms producing a similar kind of product, such as the computer industry. Industries are often classified into three groups: **manufacturing** industries process commodities; **agriculture** provides food; and **service** industries provide largely intangible services, such as entertainment.

inequality Mathematical statement that one expression is less, or greater, than another. The symbols >, for "is greater than", and <, for "is less than", are used. The symbols ≥ and ≤ are also used, for "greater than or equal to" or "less than or equal to", respectively.

inert gas *See* NOBLE GAS

inertia Property possessed by all MATTER as a measure of the way an object resists changes to its state of motion. Isaac NEWTON formulated the first law of motion, sometimes called the law of inertia, stating that a body will remain at rest or in a uniform motion unless acted upon by external forces.

inertial guidance In aeronautics, system using components that respond to changes in INERTIA to control GUIDED MISSILES or spacecraft the orbits of which are largely above the Earth's atmosphere. The main components include GYROSCOPES for reference and for detecting changes in orientation, motors or jets for correcting differences between planned and actual flight paths, and ACCELEROMETERS for determining velocity and position. The system can be supplemented by RADAR observations and control to correct gyro drift. Inertial guidance was first developed (1942) by VON BRAUN for the V2 ROCKET. *See also* NAVIGATION

infant mortality Statistic representing the number of deaths per 1,000 live births occurring among infants under one year of age. It includes deaths from congenital conditions and birth complications, as well as those caused by diseases and post-natal accidents. The figure gives an indication of the quality of ante-natal and post-natal care in a country or region. Infant mortality rates are much lower in prosperous, developed countries than they are in emerging countries. For instance, in the 1990s the USA averaged c.8 deaths per 1,000 births, while Afghanistan had c.162.

infantry Foot soldiers carrying portable firearms and equipment. Modern infantry forces are equipped with rifles, machine guns, mortars, grenades and other light-weight weapons, as well as supplies.

infarction Death of part of an organ caused by a sudden obstruction in an artery supplying it. In a myocardial infarction (HEART ATTACK), a section of heart muscle dies.

infection Invasion of the body by harmful microorganisms (PATHOGENS) that multiply and give rise to DISEASE. Bacterial infections include PNEUMONIA, SCARLET FEVER, TUBERCULOSIS and WHOOPING COUGH. Most infections caused by BACTERIA can be cured with ANTIBIOTICS. Some viral infections can be prevented by IMMUNIZATION. VIRUSES cause Acquired Immune Deficiency Syndrome (AIDS), CHICKENPOX, the common COLD, INFLUENZA, MEASLES, POLIO and SMALLPOX (among others).

infertility Inability to reproduce. In a woman it may be due to a failure to ovulate (release an OVUM for FERTILIZATION), obstruction of the FALLOPIAN TUBE or disease of the ENDOMETRIUM; in a man it is due to inadequate SPERM production. In plants, the term refers to inability to reproduce sexually. Infertility occurs in a HYBRID between different species, which are unable to produce viable GAMETES (eggs or male sex cells). *See also* ARTIFICIAL INSEMINATION; IN VITRO FERTILIZATION (IVF)

infinity (symbol ∞) Abstract quantity that represents the magnitude of an object without limit or end. In geometry, the "point at infinity" is where parallel lines can be considered as meeting. In algebra, $1/x$ approaches infinity as x approaches zero. In set theory, the set of all integers is an example of an infinite set.

inflammation Reaction of body tissue to infection or injury, with resulting pain, heat, swelling and redness. It occurs when damaged cells release HISTAMINE, which causes blood vessels at the damaged site to dilate. LEUCOCYTES invade the area to engulf bacteria. MACROPHAGES remove dead tissue, sometimes with the formation of pus.

inflation In economics, continual upward movement of prices. Although often associated with periods of prosperity, inflation may also occur during RECESSIONS. It usually occurs when there is relatively full employment. Under "cost-push" inflation, prices rise because producers' costs increase. Under "demand-pull" inflation, prices increase because of excessive consumer demand for goods. Low inflation is a major economic objective for most governments. Instruments for controlling inflation include changes in INTEREST rates, prices and incomes policy, increased TAXATION and cuts in government spending. *See also* CONSUMPTION; DEFLATION; DEPRESSION; MONETARISM

inflection Variation in the form of a lexical item (word) that serves to distinguish its grammatical relationship to other words in a sentence without altering its part of SPEECH. In a common type of inflection, affixes are added to a stem or root form in order to distinguish tense, person, number, gender, voice or case. In English, this is usually achieved by adding endings to the word stem – singular noun "house" gives plural "houses". Another type uses internal vowel differences within the word stem – the verb "sing" gives simple past tense "sang". Even closely related languages may differ widely in inflection.

inflorescence FLOWER or flower cluster. Inflorescences are classified according to branching characteristics. A **racemose** inflorescence has a main axis and lateral flowering branches with flowers opening from the bottom up or from the outer edge in; types include panicle, raceme, spike and umbel. A **cymose** inflorescence has a composite axis with the main stem ending in a flower and lateral branches bearing additional, later-flowering branches.

influenza (flu) Viral INFECTION affecting the airways, with chesty symptoms, headache, joint pain and fever. It is treated by bed-rest and pain-killers. Vaccines are available to confer IMMUNITY to some strains. Epidemics occur because influenza mutates so quickly, producing new strains that are resistant to the body's immune system and existing vaccines. *c.*20 million people died in a 1918–19 epidemic.

information technology (IT) COMPUTER and TELECOMMUNICATIONS technologies used in processing information of any kind. Word processing, the use of a DATABASE and the sending of ELECTRONIC MAIL (E-MAIL) over a COMPUTER NETWORK all involve the use of information technology. Television stations employ information technology to provide viewers with TELETEXT services. IT has revolutionized retailing and banking through the development of BAR CODES and electronic funds transfer (EFT). In manufacturing IT has enabled the development of COMPUTER-AIDED MANUFACTURE (CAM) using CONTROL SYSTEMS and ROBOTS. *See also* ARTIFICIAL INTELLIGENCE

information theory Mathematical study of communication. It is primarily concerned with the measurement of information, and the methods of coding, transmitting, storing, retrieving and processing this information. The theory was outlined by Claude E. Shannon in *The Mathematical Theory of Communication* (1949). *See also* PROBABILITY

infrared astronomy *See* ASTRONOMY

infrared radiation ELECTROMAGNETIC RADIATION that produces a sensation of heat emitted by hot objects. It was discovered in 1800 by Sir William HERSCHEL. Intermediate in energy between visible light and microwaves, its wavelength range is *c.*750nm to 1mm. It has applications in astronomy, medicine and warfare.

Ingenhousz, Jan (1730–99) Dutch physician and plant physiologist. In 1799 Ingenhousz discovered the process of PHOTOSYNTHESIS in green plants.

Ingres, Jean Auguste Dominique (1780–1867) French painter. A pupil of DAVID, he is one of the great figures of French NEOCLASSICISM. Ingres was an outstanding portraitist, especially of women in high society, such as *Madame d'Haussonville* (1845). He also produced sensual nudes, such as *Bather of Valpinçon* (1808). Ingres was a staunch opponent of ROMANTICISM.

Ingushetia Autonomous Russian republic; the capital is Nazran. Ingushetia lies on the N side of the Caucasus Mountains. The majority population (85%) are Ingush with a Chechen minority. The economy is based on oil and cattle raising. For much of the 20th century, Ingushetia's history was tied to CHECHENIA. In 1991, the Chechen-Ingush Republic declared its independence. The Ingush desire to distance itself from the Chechen-dominated decision led to the deployment of Russian troops and formal separation from Chechenia (1992). In 1993, Ingushetia became a member of the Russian Federation.

injection In medicine, use of a syringe and needle to introduce drugs or other fluids into the body to diagnose, treat or prevent disease. The three major types of injections are **intravenous** (into a vein), **intramuscular** (into a muscle) and **subcutaneous** (under the skin).

ink Coloured liquid used for writing, drawing or printing. Inks were used in China before 1000 BC. Early inks were a mixture of carbon, oil and gum. In the 15th century, varnish was added to PRINTING ink, enabling the development of LITHOGRAPHY and GRAVURE. Printing inks are differentiated by their drying methods. Lithographic ink dries by penetration and gravure by evaporation. Ordinary blue-black permanent writing ink contains ferrous sulphates, mineral acid and other DYES. Indian ink, used for drawing, contains carbon black and SHELLAC. The ink in ballpoint pens consists of a synthetic dye Printing ink is Some inks dry by evaporation of a volatile solvent.

Inkatha Freedom Party South African political organization, founded (1975) by Chief BUTHELEZI to represent South Africa's ZULU population. Its initial aim was to work towards a democratic, non-racial political system, but it was accused of complicity with the APARTHEID regime. In the early 1990s, Inkatha was involved in violent conflict with the AFRICAN NATIONAL CONGRESS (ANC). In terms of representation, it ranks third among political parties. Its strongest base is in KWAZULU-NATAL.

Inner Mongolia (Chin. Nei Mongol) Autonomous region in n China, bordered n by Mongolia and Russia, s by the GREAT WALL of China and w by the GOBI DESERT; the capital is Hohhot. Area: 1,183,000sq km (460,000sq mi). Pop. (1990) 21,456,798.

Innocent III (1161–1216) Pope (1198–1216), b. Lotario di Segni. He extended the temporal and spiritual power of the papacy. Innocent successfully intervened in the dispute over the imperial crown, backing the claim of FREDERICK II over OTTO IV. He regained control of the PAPAL STATES. Innocent excommunicated King JOHN of England for refusing to recognize Stephen LANGTON as Archbishop of Canterbury. He condemned PHILIP II of France and proclaimed the fourth CRUSADE (1204). The fourth LATERAN COUNCIL (1215) defined the doctrine of the EUCHARIST, establishing the concept of TRANSUBSTANTIATION.

Innsbruck City on the River Inn, w Austria; capital of TIROL. Founded in the 12th century, the city grew rapidly because of its strategic position on a historic transalpine route. Innsbruck is a commercial and industrial centre and an important winter sports resort. Industries: manufacturing, metalworking, textiles. Pop. (1991) 118,112.

Inns of Court Four legal societies in London, England: Lincoln's Inn (established 1310), Inner Temple (1340), Middle Temple (1340) and Gray's Inn (1357). They have the exclusive right to admit persons to practise as barristers in English courts. Most London barristers have chambers at the Inns of Court. Each Inn is governed by Masters of the Bench ("benchers"), who are mainly judges or Queen's Counsels (QCs).

Inönü, Ismet (1884–1973) Turkish statesman, prime minister (1923–37, 1961–65) and president (1938–50), b. Mustafa Ismet. As chief-of-staff (1919–22) to Mustafa Kemal (ATATÜRK), he defeated the Greeks at Inönü. In 1923 he became the prime minister of the new Turkish republic, introducing many secular reforms. In 1938 Inönü succeeded Atatürk as president.

inorganic chemistry *See* CHEMISTRY

Inquisition (Holy Office) Ecclesiastical court founded by Pope Gregory IX for the prosecution of heresy. In 1223, Gregory ordered the Dominicans to crush the ALBIGENSIANS. In 1232, he appointed Dominican and Franciscan inquisitors to hunt out other heretics, such as the WALDENSES. The use of torture to extract confessions was authorized (1252) and punishments ranged from penances to banishment and death by fire. In 1479, the Inquisition was revived in Spain. Under the first grand inquisitor, TORQUEMADA, the **Spanish Inquisition** acquired a reputation for its brutal persecution of Jews and Muslims. It was not formally abolished until 1834. In 1542, a Roman Inquisition was set up to check the growth of PROTESTANTISM. In 1557, the Roman Catholic Church published the INDEX LIBRORUM PROHIBITORUM. In 1965, the Holy Office became the Sacred Congregation for the Doctrine of the Faith.

insect Any of more than a million species of small, invertebrate animals, including the BEETLE, BUG, BUTTERFLY, ANT and BEE. There are more species of insects than all other species combined. Adult insects have three pairs of jointed legs, usually two pairs of wings, and a segmented body with a horny outer covering or exoskeleton. The head has three pairs of mouthparts, a pair of compound eyes, three pairs of simple eyes and a pair of antennae. Most insects can detect a wide range of sounds through ultrasensitive hairs on various parts of their bodies. Some can "sing" or make sounds by rubbing together parts of their bodies. Most insects are plant-eaters, many being serious farm and garden pests. Some prey on small animals, especially other insects, and a few are scavengers. There are two main kinds of mouthparts – chewing and sucking. Reproduction is usually sexual. Most insects go through four distinct life stages, in which complete METAMORPHOSIS is said to take place. The four stages are OVUM (egg), LARVA (caterpillar or grub), PUPA (chrysalis) and IMAGO (adult). Young grasshoppers and some other insects, called NYMPHS, resemble wingless miniatures of their parents. The nymphs develop during a series of moults (incomplete metamorphosis). SILVERFISH and a few other primitive, wingless insects do not undergo metamorphosis. Phylum Arthropoda; class Insecta. *See also* ARTHROPOD

insecticide Substance used to destroy or control insect pests. Insecticides may be **stomach** poisons, such as lead

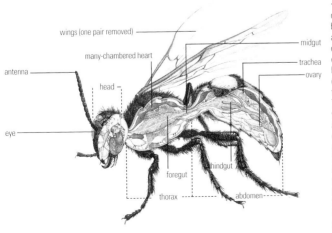

◀ **insect** The internal anatomy of all insects, such as the honey bee shown here, is all contained and protected within the confines of the tough, flexible exoskeleton. The typical insect body contains organs of digestion, respiration, circulation, excretion and reproduction. There are muscles through which movement is effected and a nervous system that coordinates and controls insect actions on the basis of information received by the sense organs, most important of which are the large compound eyes and the feelers and antennae. All insect bodies comprise three parts: the head, thorax and abdomen.

wings (one pair removed)

many-chambered heart

antenna

head

eye

midgut

trachea

ovary

hindgut

foregut

thorax

abdomen

arsenate and sodium fluoride; **contact** poisons, such as DDT and organophosphates; or **systematic** poisons, such as octamethylpyrophosphoramide, which are toxic to insects that eat plants into which they have been absorbed. **Organophosphates** are preferred to chlorinated HYDRO-CARBONS (such as DDT) because they eventually break down into non-toxic substances. They are, however, hazardous to humans and must be handled with care.

insectivore Small order of carnivorous MAMMALS (Insectivora), many of which eat insects. Almost worldwide in distribution, some species live underground, some on the ground and some in streams and ponds. Most insectivores have narrow snouts, long skulls and five-clawed feet. Three families are always placed in the order: Erinaceidae (moon rats, gymures, HEDGEHOGS); Talpidae (MOLES, shrew moles, desmans) and Soricidae (SHREWS). But six other families – including tree shrews and tenrecs and solenodons – are also often included in the order.

insectivorous plant (carnivorous plant) Any of several plants that have poorly developed root systems and are often found in nitrogen-deficient sandy or boggy soils. They obtain the missing nutrients by trapping, "digesting" and absorbing insects. Some, such as the Venus's fly-trap (*Dionaea muscipula*), are active insect trappers. The sundews (*Drosera*) snare insects with a sticky substance and then enclose them in their leaves. Bladderworts (*Utricularia*) suck insects into their underwater bladders. Other plants have vase-shaped leaves, such as the pitcher plant (*Sarracenia flava*).

instinct Behaviour that is inherited, as opposed to behaviour that is learned. In the 19th century instincts were often cited to explain behaviour, but the term fell into disrepute with the advent of BEHAVIOURISM. The term has recently been revived in the work of such ethologists as Konrad LORENZ. Instinct is important in animal behaviours such as reproduction and feeding. *See also* HEREDITY; LEARNING

insulation Technique for reducing or preventing the transfer of heat, electricity, sound or other vibrations. Wool, fibreglass and foam plastic are good **heat** insulating materials because they contain air. This trapped air reduces the transfer of heat by CONDUCTION. Water is also a good heat insulator. A diver's wet suit keeps the wearer warm by trapping a layer of water around the body. **Electrical** insulation materials include rubber, POLYVINYL CHLORIDE (PVC), polythene, glass and porcelain. **Sound** insulating materials absorb sound and change it to heat by FRICTION.

insulator In electricity, substance that provides a high resistance to an ELECTRIC CURRENT. Insulators are used to prevent contact between CONDUCTORS in electrical circuits. The thickness of the insulation necessary depends on the voltage. Common insulators are rubber, POLYVINYL CHLORIDE (PVC), mica, Teflon, glass, asbestos, thermoplastics and porcelain.

insulin HORMONE secreted by the islets of Langerhans in the PANCREAS, which controls blood-glucose levels. Insulin lowers the blood-glucose level by helping the uptake of glucose into cells and by causing the liver to convert glucose to GLYCOGEN. In the absence of insulin, glucose accumulates in the blood and urine, resulting in DIABETES. Insulin was isolated in 1921 by Frederick BANTING and Charles BEST. Its three-dimensional structure was discovered by Frederick SANGER.

insurance Procedure whereby one party (the insured) transfers the financial consequences of risk of loss to another (the insurer) for a consideration (the premium). Each insured contributes to a common fund, and the losses of the unfortunate few are reimbursed from the fund.

Modern practices date back to the 16th and 17th centuries. It covers such areas as life, fire, accident and theft.

intaglio Incised carving on gemstones, hardstones or glass, in which the design is sunk below the surface. In PRINTING, the term is used to describe processes in which ink is applied to incisions and hollows in a printing plate, as in ETCHING. *See also* ENGRAVING; GRAVURE

integer Negative or positive whole number and zero, for example ... −3, −2, −1, 0, 1, 2, 3,..... There is a limitless (infinite) number of integers. The positive integers are the natural NUMBERS. The existence of negative integers and zero allow any integer to be subtracted from any other integer to give an integer result.

integral calculus In mathematics, the branch of CAL-CULUS that deals with integration: the finding of a function, one or more derivatives of which are given. There are many applications of integral calculus. It is used to find the areas and volumes of curved shapes. In engineering calculations, DIFFERENTIAL EQUATIONS are solved by integral calculus. Its principles are also incorporated in many measuring and control instruments.

integrated circuit (IC) Complete miniature electronic CIRCUIT incorporating SEMICONDUCTOR devices such as the TRANSISTOR and RESISTOR. **Monolithic** integrated circuits have all the components manufactured into or on top of a single crystal of silicon (commonly called a silicon CHIP). **Hybrid** integrated circuits have separate components attached to a ceramic base. Components in both types are joined by conducting film. *See also* PRINTED CIRCUIT

Integrated Services Digital Network (ISDN) High-speed TELEPHONE lines designed to carry digital information. There are various grades of ISDN that can carry information more than a thousand times faster than conventional analogue voice lines. ISDN lines connect directly to a COMPUTER and do not need a MODEM.

integration *See* INTEGRAL CALCULUS

intelligence General ability to learn and to deal with problems, new situations and abstract concepts. It can be manifest in many different ways, including skills in adaptability, memory and reasoning. Fierce debate has raged over the roles of hereditary and environmental factors in developing intelligence. Intelligence tests measure abstract reasoning and problem-solving abilities.

intelligence quotient (IQ) Classification of the supposed INTELLIGENCE of a person. It is computed by dividing a person's assessed "mental age" by their real age, then multiplying by 100. "Mental age" is determined by reference to the average performance of people of various ages on a standard intelligence test. *See also* APTITUDE TEST

intelligence service Government organization maintained in most countries to obtain information concerning activities that might endanger the state. Intelligence services are usually secretive in their operations. In the UK, **MI-5** (Military Intelligence-5) is responsible for domestic counter-ESPIONAGE. **MI-6** is responsible for overseas intelligence. *See also* CENTRAL INTELLIGENCE AGENCY (CIA); FEDERAL BUREAU OF INVESTIGATION (FBI); KGB

intensive-care unit (ICU) Specialized HOSPITAL unit treating patients with acute, life-threatening conditions. It is characterized by the use of continuous (electronic) monitoring and life-support technology, together with intensive nursing and the judicious use of drugs. The intention is to offer short-term support to critically ill or injured patients.

interest In economics, price paid to the lender by the borrower for the "use" of money over a specified period of time, usually calculated as a percentage of the principal (sum lent). **Simple** interest is paid regularly and calculated as a percentage of the original principal. In **compound**

interest, the interest calculated for one period (such as a year) is added to the original principal, and the interest for the next period is calculated as a percentage of this total. The **interest rate** is the percentage payable: for instance, an **annual percentage rate (APR)** of 5% on a principal sum of £10,000 gives the lender £50 interest per year.

interface Way that a computer PROGRAM or system interacts with its user. The simplest form of computer interface is the keyboard, through which the user controls the computer by typing in commands. The most common type for personal computers is the GRAPHICAL USER INTERFACE (GUI).

interference In optics, the interaction of two or more WAVE motions, such as those of light and sound, creating a disturbance pattern. **Constructive** interference is the reinforcement of the wave motion because the component motions are in PHASE. **Destructive** interference occurs when two waves are out of phase and cancel each other.

interferometer Instrument in which a WAVE, especially a light wave, is split into component waves that are made to travel unequal distances to recombine as INTERFERENCE patterns. The patterns have such uses as quality control of lenses and prisms, and the measurement of WAVELENGTHS.

interferon PROTEIN produced by body cells when infected with a VIRUS. Interferons can help uninfected cells to resist infection by a virus and also may impede virus replication and protein synthesis. In some circumstances they can inhibit cell growth; human interferon is now produced by GENETIC ENGINEERING for therapeutic use, to treat some CANCERS, HEPATITIS and MULTIPLE SCLEROSIS. Interferon was discovered in 1957 by Alick Isaacs. *See also* IMMUNITY

interlude Short theatrical piece, prominent in the late 15th and early 16th centuries, which provided entertainment during royal and noble banquets. Performed by a small travelling company, it combined moral messages with clowning, and was the immediate precursor of ELIZABETHAN DRAMA.

intermezzo Light theatrical entertainment performed to music between the acts of a drama or OPERA. The earliest intermezzi date from the late 15th century. The 18th-century intermezzi of operas were the basis for OPERA BUFFA. Today, the term commonly refers to an instrumental interlude during an opera.

internal combustion engine Engine in which fuel is burned inside, so that the gases formed can produce motion, widely used in AUTOMOBILES. An internal combustion engine may be a TWO-STROKE ENGINE or a FOUR-STROKE ENGINE. In the most common type of engine, a mixture of PETROLEUM vapour and air is ignited by a spark. The gases produced in the explosion usually drive a piston along a cylinder. A crankshaft changes the reciprocating (to-and-fro) movement of the pistons into rotary motion. In the WANKEL ENGINE, the gases produced in the explosions drive a triangular rotor. Nikolaus OTTO built the first practical internal combustion engine in 1867. Rudolf Diesel designed the first DIESEL ENGINE in 1897. Because combustion is incomplete and reliant on FOSSIL FUELS, internal combustion engines are a major cause of air pollution.

International Atomic Energy Agency (IAEA) Specialized intergovernmental agency of the UNITED NATIONS (UN). It was founded in 1957 to promote peaceful uses of NUCLEAR ENERGY and establish international control of nuclear weapons. The organization's headquarters are in Vienna, Austria.

International Court of Justice Supreme judicial body of the UNITED NATIONS (UN) for hearing disputes between

countries involving treaties and INTERNATIONAL LAW. It replaced the League of Nations' Permanent Court of Justice in 1947. Its 15 judges are chosen by the UN, each coming from a different state and serving for nine years. The president and vice-president serve three-year terms. The court sits at The Hague, Netherlands.

International Brigades Volunteer forces which fought on the Republican side against FRANCO during the Spanish CIVIL WAR (1936–39). Although recruited by the COMMUNIST INTERNATIONAL, they were a rallying point for anti-Fascists of all persuasions. They distinguished themselves at the siege of Madrid (1936), but were too small (never more than 20,000 strong) and badly organized to influence the result of the war. They were disbanded in 1938.

international gothic Style of painting which spread throughout Europe between c.1375 and c.1425. A sophisticated linear style, it originated in French GOTHIC art, particularly ILLUMINATION, and is characterized by naturalistic detail, elegant elongated figures and jewel-like colour. Examples include the *Très Riches Heures* (1413–15) by the LIMBOURG brothers in Burgundy, and the work of PISANELLO and GENTILE DA FABRIANO in Italy. A variant found in German art is known as the **soft style**.

International Labour Organization (ILO) Specialized intergovernmental agency of the UNITED NATIONS (UN). Its aim is to facilitate improved industrial relations and conditions of work. It was formed as an agency of the LEAGUE OF NATIONS by the Treaty of VERSAILLES (1919) and has a membership comprising government, employer and worker representatives. Its headquarters are in Geneva, Switzerland.

international law Body of rules deemed legally binding that have resulted from treaties, agreements and customs between nations. Its sources are also decisions by agencies, conferences or commissions of international organizations

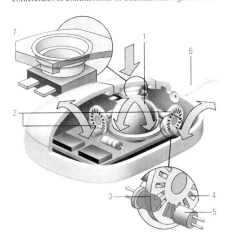

▲ **interface** Computer operators use a variety of means to interact with the computer. A hand-held mouse, for example, moves a cursor on a monitor screen. The central ball (1) rotates as the mouse moves. As the ball moves, spoked wheels (2) turn according to sideways and up-and-down movement.

An LED (3) shines through the spokes (4). The rate of rotation of both wheels is detected by sensors (5), which send information to the computer via a cable (6), moving the cursor appropriately. Buttons at the front of the mouse (7) can be used to click on areas of the screen or call up menus.

such as the United Nations (UN), as well as international tribunals, such as the INTERNATIONAL COURT OF JUSTICE. It remains difficult to enforce. *See also* GROTIUS, HUGO

International Monetary Fund (IMF) Specialized, intergovernmental agency of the UNITED NATIONS (UN), and administrative body of the INTERNATIONAL MONETARY SYSTEM. Established by the BRETTON WOODS CONFERENCE (1944), its main function is to provide assistance to member states troubled by BALANCE OF PAYMENTS problems and other financial difficulties. The IMF does not actually lend money to member states; rather, it exchanges the member state's currency with its own **Special Drawing Rates (SDR)** (a "basket" of other currencies) in the hope that this will alleviate balance of payment difficulties. These exchanges are usually conditional upon the recipient country agreeing to pursue prescribed policy reforms. The organization is based in Washington, D.C.

international monetary system Structure of world monetary relationships. When countries exchange goods and services with other countries, it is not uncommon for exports to exceed imports or imports to exceed exports, thus creating a BALANCE OF PAYMENTS deficit or surplus. When a deficit exists, one country must pay another the difference. This payment may involve the exchange of gold or some mutually acceptable monetary unit (usually a so-called "hard" currency, such as the US dollar). *See also* BRETTON WOODS CONFERENCE; EUROPEAN MONETARY SYSTEM (EMS); INTERNATIONAL MONETARY SYSTEM (IMF)

international style Name for the architectural style developed in Europe in the 1920s and 1930s that stressed FUNCTIONALISM and avoided superfluous decoration in design. It characteristically featured austere white walls, asymmetrical cubic shapes and large expanses of glass. LE CORBUSIER and Walter GROPIUS were early exponents. *See also* ART DECO; BAUHAUS; BRUTALISM; MODERNISM

Internet (Net) Worldwide communications system consisting of hundreds of small COMPUTER NETWORKS, interconnected by TELEPHONE systems. It is a network of networks in which messages and data are sent using short local links from place to place. This enables users to send a message anywhere in the world by ELECTRONIC MAIL (E-MAIL) for the cost of a local phone call. The Internet or **Information Superhighway** was started in 1969 with funds from the US Department of Defense. *See also* WORLD WIDE WEB (WWW)

interplanetary matter Material in the space between the planets. It is made up of atomic particles (mainly PROTONS and ELECTRONS) ejected from the Sun via the SOLAR WIND, and dust particles (mainly from COMETS, but some possibly of cosmic origin) in the plane of the ecliptic.

Interpol (International Criminal Police Organization) Intergovernmental organization. Established in 1923, its main function is to provide member states with information about international criminals and to assist in their arrest. Its headquarters are in Lyon, France.

intersection Point, or LOCUS of points, common to two or more geometrical figures. Two non-parallel lines in the same plane meet in a point; two non-parallel planes meet in a line. *See also* SET

intestine Lower part of the ALIMENTARY CANAL beyond the STOMACH. Food is moved through the intestine by a wave-like action known as PERISTALSIS. It undergoes the final stages of DIGESTION and is absorbed into the bloodstream in the small intestine, which extends from the stomach to the large intestine. In the large intestine (CECUM, COLON and RECTUM) water is absorbed from undigested material, which is then passed out of the body through the anus.

Intifada (Arabic, uprising) Campaign of violent civil disobedience by Palestinians in the Israeli-occupied territories of the WEST BANK of the River JORDAN and the GAZA STRIP. The Intifada began in 1987 and was a sustained attempt to disrupt Israel's heavy-handed policing tactics. It claimed more than 1,400 Palestinian and 230 Jewish lives. The Intifada resulted in the ISRAELI-–PALESTINIAN ACCORD (1993). *See also* PALESTINE LIBERATION ORGANIZATION (PLO)

Intolerable Acts (Coercive Acts, 1774) British legislation designed to punish the American colonists after the BOSTON TEA PARTY. They closed the Boston port and moved the customs house to Salem. Under the Administration of Justice Act, British officials accused of capital offences would be tried in England; another law (the Massachusetts Government Act) annulled the Massachusetts Charter, imposing a military government on Massachusetts. The colonists' opposition resulted in the calling of the First CONTINENTAL CONGRESS.

intoxication Condition arising when the body is poisoned by any toxic (harmful) substance, whether liquid, solid or gas. Symptoms vary according to the ingested substance. The term is most commonly used in connection with excessive alcohol consumption.

intrauterine device (IUD) Plastic or metal loop inserted by a doctor inside a woman's womb as a means of CONTRACEPTION. It is a reliable form of birth-control, but some women suffer serious side-effects, including cramps and heavy bleeding.

intravenous drip Apparatus for delivering drugs, blood and blood products, nutrients and other fluids directly into the bloodstream. A hollow needle is inserted into an appropriate vein and then attached to a length of tubing leading from a bag containing the solution.

introversion Preoccupation with one's own responses and impressions, coupled with a preference for reflection over action and a dislike of social activity. The term was coined by C.G. JUNG as a polar opposite to EXTROVERSION. Extreme introverts can be passive and withdrawn.

intrusion In geology, emplacement of rock material that was either forced or flowed into spaces among other rocks. An igneous intrusion (pluton) consists of MAGMA that never reached the Earth's surface but filled cracks and faults, then cooled and hardened. *See also* IGNEOUS ROCK

Inuit Collective name for the ESKIMO people of Nunavut, Arctic Québec and N Labrador areas of Canada, and Alaska and Greenland. Many Inuit still live by the traditional skills of fishing, trapping, and hunting.

Inverness City at the head of the Moray Firth on the River Ness; capital of Highland region, N Scotland. A tourist centre with a long boatbuilding history, Inverness lies at the NE end of the Caledonian Canal. The castle was destroyed at the Battle of CULLODEN (1746), but rebuilt in Victorian times. Pop. (1991) 41,230.

invertebrate In zoology, the term for an animal without a backbone. There are more than one million species of invertebrates, divided into 30 major groups. One of these is Arthropoda (joint-legged animals), the largest of all animal phyla in terms of numbers of species. Most are INSECTS, but it also includes crustaceans and ARACHNIDS. MOLLUSCS make up the second largest group of invertebrates. *See also* ARTHROPOD; CRUSTACEA; PHYLUM

investment In economics, the acquisition of financial or productive assets. **Financial** assets are bought with the objective of obtaining an income or capital gain. An element of risk accompanies intangible investment. The purchasing of government stocks and bonds is usually more secure but yields limited gains; while buying shares or unit trusts has a higher risk but a greater potential profit. **Fixed** investment is the purchase of capital goods (plant and machinery) used in the manufacture of consumer goods or services. Investment and CONSUMPTION constitute the national income.

in vitro fertilization (IVF) (test-tube baby) Use of artificial techniques that join an OVUM with SPERM outside a woman's body to help infertile couples to have children of their own. The basic technique of IVF involves removing eggs from a woman's ovaries, fertilizing them in the laboratory and then inserting them into her UTERUS. In **zygote intrafallopian transfer (ZIFT)**, a fertilized egg (ZYGOTE) is returned to the FALLOPIAN TUBE, from which it makes its own way to the uterus. The zygote then divides to form an EMBRYO. In **gamete intrafallopian transfer (GIFT)**, the eggs are removed, mixed with sperm, then both eggs and sperm are inserted into a Fallopian tube to be fertilized in the natural setting. *See also* FERTILIZATION; INFERTILITY

involuntary muscle One of three types of MUSCLE in the body, so called because, unlike SKELETAL MUSCLE, it is not under the conscious control of the brain but is stimulated by the AUTONOMIC NERVOUS SYSTEM and by HORMONES in the bloodstream. It is of two kinds. Smooth muscle is the muscle of the alimentary canal, blood vessels and bladder. Cardiac muscle powers the HEART.

Io Innermost satellite of JUPITER. It was discovered by GALILEO in 1610 and is larger than the Moon. Io is the most volcanically active body in the Solar System. It is more than 3,600km (2,200mi) in diameter and is 422,000km (262,000mi) above the surface of the planet.

iodine (symbol I) Nonmetallic element that is the least reactive of the HALOGEN group (elements in Group VII of the periodic table). The black volatile solid gives a violet vapour and has an unpleasant odour that resembles CHLORINE. Iodine was discovered in 1811 by the French chemist Bernard Courtois. Existing in seawater, seaweeds and other plants, it is also extracted from Chile saltpeter and oil-well brine. Iodine is essential for the functioning of the THYROID GLAND. It is used as a medical antiseptic and in photography. Properties: at.no. 53; r.a.m. 126.9; r.d. 4.93; m.p. 113.5°C (236.3°F); b.p. 184.4°C (363.9°F); most stable isotope I^{127} (100%).

ion Atom or group of atoms with an electric (positive or negative) charge resulting from the loss or gain of one or more ELECTRONS. Positive ions are called **cations** and move towards the CATHODE in ELECTROLYSIS; negative ions are called **anions** and move towards the ANODE. The process of forming ions is called ionization. *See also* IONIC BOND; IONIC COMPOUND

Iona Island off the coast of W Scotland in the Inner HEBRIDES. The island has an abbey, founded in AD 563 by St Columba, that became the centre of the Celtic church. It has been restored in the 20th century. Tourism is the main source of income. Area: 13sq km (5sq mi).

Ionesco, Eugène (1912–94) French dramatist, b. Romania. A major figure in the Theatre of the ABSURD, Ionesco had his first success with *The Bald Prima Donna* (1950), a satire on the futility of verbal communication. Other plays include *The Chairs* (1951) and *Rhinoceros* (1960).

Ionia Historic region on the W coast of Asia Minor (Turkey), including neighbouring Aegean islands. The area was settled by people from Mycenae in Greece in the 11th and 10th centuries BC. Miletus and EPHESUS became the most important of the prosperous Ionian cities. Ionia was conquered by the Persians in the 6th century BC, then fell under Athenian domination until the Persians regained control in the 4th century BC. After the conquests of ALEXANDER THE GREAT, Ionia was

ruled by Hellenistic kings and from the 2nd century BC was part of the Roman Empire.

Ionians In ancient Greece, inhabitants of Attica, BOEOTIA and IONIA. They spoke a dialect distinct from that of the DORIANS and Aeolians. There was always potential hostility between Ionians and Dorians, neither regarding the other as fully Greek, which appears in the contest between Athens and Sparta in the PELOPONNESIAN WARS. The term is also applied to the inhabitants of Ionia alone.

ionic bond (electrovalent bond) Type of chemical bond in which ions of opposite charge are held together by electrostatic attraction.

ionic compound Substance formed by ionic bonding, a chemical bond of positively and negatively charged IONS. Salts, bases and some acids are ionic compounds. As crystalline solids, such compounds have high melting points and boiling points. As solids, they are also nonconductors of electricity and are usually soluble in water but insoluble in organic solvents. In the liquid and molten states, ionic compounds are good conductors.

Ionic order One of the Classical ORDERS OF ARCHITECTURE.

ionosphere Wide region of the Earth's ATMOSPHERE in which there are free ELECTRONS and IONS produced by ULTRAVIOLET RADIATION and X-RAYS from the Sun. The ionosphere extends from *c.*80km (50mi) to 1,000km (650mi) at the limits of the atmosphere in the VAN ALLEN RADIATION BELTS. It is divided into layers distinguished by the concentration of electrons. The lowest layer is the **D** or daytime layer. The **E** layer (Heaviside-Kennelly layer) undergoes molecular ionization. The upper **F** layer (Appleton layer) undergoes atomic ionization. These layers reflect RADIO waves of long wavelengths (*c.*30MHz) while shorter wavelengths can pass through undisturbed.

Iowa State in N central USA, lying between the Missouri and Mississippi rivers; the capital is DES MOINES. First explored by Europeans in 1673, the land was claimed for France in 1682. In 1803, the region was sold to the USA in the LOUISIANA PURCHASE. In 1846, Iowa was admitted to the Union. Industrial development was encouraged after World War 2. Originally prairie that was ploughed to create farmland, the region is known for its fertile soil. Maize and other cereals are produced, and Iowa stands second only to Texas in the raising of prime cattle. Industries: food processing, farm machinery. Area: 145,790sq km (56,290sq mi). Pop. (2000) 2,926,324.

Iphigenia In Greek legend, daughter of AGAMEMNON and CLYTEMNESTRA and sister of ELECTRA and ORESTES. She was sacrificed by her father to the goddess ARTEMIS in exchange for favourable winds for his journey to TROY.

Ipoh City in N Malaysia, on the River Kinta; capital of Perak state. It developed in the 1890s, when Chinese were brought in to work in the tin mines. It remains Malaysia's major tin-mining centre. There are also rubber plantations and limestone quarries. Pop. (1991) 383,000.

Ipswich City and port in E England, on the Orwell estuary; the county town of SUFFOLK. The wool trade brought prosperity in the Middle Ages. After a decline, Ipswich's fortunes were revived in the 19th century with the introduction of light industry. Industries: milling, brewing, printing, agricultural machinery. Pop. (1994) 115,000.

IQ Abbreviation of INTELLIGENCE QUOTIENT.

Iqbal, Sir Muhammad (1875–1938) Indian political leader, poet and philosopher. Iqbal was an advocate of an independent Muslim state and became president of the MUSLIM LEAGUE in 1930. His best-known poetic work is *The Secrets of the Self* (1915).

Iquitos City and inland port on the upper River Amazon, NE Peru. It is a centre for commercial shipping and oil exploration in the Amazonian region. Exports: coffee, cotton, timber, rubber. Pop. (1993 est.) 274,759.

IRA *See* IRISH REPUBLICAN ARMY

Iráklion (Heraklion or Candia) Seaport and largest city on the island of Crete, S Greece; capital of Iráklion prefecture. Founded in the 9th century by the Saracens, it was conquered by the Byzantines in 961, the Venetians (1204) and the Ottoman Turks (1669). It became part of Greece in 1913. The ruins of KNOSSOS are nearby. Tourism is important. Exports: wine, olive oil, almonds, raisins. Pop. (1991) 115,124.

Iran Islamic republic in SW Asia. Iran contains a barren central plateau, which covers *c.*50% of the country. It includes the *Dasht-e-Kavir* (Great Salt Desert) and the *Dasht-e-Lut* (Great Sand Desert). The Elburz Mountains, N of the plateau, contain Iran's highest point, Damavand, at 5,604m (18,368ft), and the capital, TEHRAN. To the NE lies Iran's second city, MASHHAD. On the NW edge of the plateau lies the city of QOM. The W of the plateau is bounded by the Zagros Mountains, including the cities of ISFAHAN and SHIRAZ. In the far NW lies its largest lake, Lake Urmia, and the city of TABRIZ. The SHATT AL ARAB forms part of its border with Iraq. Iran is susceptible to earthquakes. **Climate** Iran has hot summers and cold winters. Precipitation is highest in the N, often in the form of winter snow. **Vegetation** Forest covers *c.*10% of Iran, mainly in the Elburz and Zagros mountains. Semi-desert and desert cover most of the country. **History and politics** Until 1935 Iran was known as PERSIA. Aryans settled in Persia *c.*2000 BC. In 550 BC, the Persian king CYRUS THE GREAT founded the ACHAEMENID dynasty. In 331 BC, the Persian Empire fell to Alexander the Great. In AD 224, Persian rule was restored by the SASSANIDS. In AD 641 Arabs conquered Persia and introduced ISLAM. For the next two centuries Persia was a centre of ISLAMIC ART AND ARCHITECTURE. In the 11th century, SELJUK Turks conquered Persia, but in 1220 the land was overrun by the MONGOLS. The SAFAVID dynasty (1501–1722) was founded by Shah ISMAIL, who established the SHIITE theocratic principles of modern Iran. NADIR SHAH expelled Afghan invaders. His despotic rule (1736–47) was noted for imperial ambition. The Qajar dynasty (1794–1925) witnessed the gradual decline of the Persian Empire in the face of European expansion. Britain and Russia competed for influence in the area. The discovery of oil in SW Iran led to the Russian and British division of Iran in 1907. In a 1919 treaty Iran effectively became a British protectorate. In 1921, Reza Khan seized power in a military coup. In 1925, he deposed the Qajar dynasty and proclaimed himself Reza Shah PAHLAVI. He annulled the British treaty and began a process of modernization. In 1941, British and Soviet forces occupied Iran. Reza Shah abdicated in favour of his son, Muhammad Reza Shah PAHLAVI. The 1943, Tehran Declaration guaranteed Iran's independence. In 1951, the oil industry was nationalized. The shah fled Iran, but soon returned with US backing and restored Western oil rights (1953). During the 1960s, the shah undertook large-scale reforms, such as land ownership and extending the franchise to women (1963). Discontent surfaced over increasing westernization and economic inequality. The secret police crushed all dissent. Iranian clerics, led by Ayatollah

KHOMEINI, openly voiced their disapproval of the secularization of society. In 1971 Britain withdrew its troops from the Persian Gulf. Iran increased its defence spending to become the largest military power in the region. Following his expulsion, Khomeini called for the abdication of the shah (1978). In January 1979, the shah fled, and Khomeini established an Islamic republic. The theocracy was profoundly conservative and anti-western. In July 1979, the oil industry was renationalized. In November 1979, militants seized the US embassy in Tehran, taking 52 American hostages. In September 1980, the Iraqi invasion marked the start of the IRAN-IRAQ WAR (1980–88). The war claimed more than 500,000 Iranian lives. In 1986 the USA covertly agreed to supply Iran with arms, in return for influence over the return of hostages (*see* IRAN-CONTRA AFFAIR). In February 1989, Khomeini imposed a fatwa (death penalty) on the Anglo-Indian writer Salman RUSHDIE. In June 1989, Khomeini died and was succeeded by RAFSANJANI. Rafsanjani's regime began to ease relations with the West. Free market reforms were adopted and Iran supported international sanctions against Iraq in 1991. Allegations of support for international terrorism and development of a nuclear capability led the USA to impose trade sanctions in 1995. In 1997, elections Rafsanjani was defeated by the liberal reformer Muhammad Khatami. In July 1999, student protests against the conservatives' blocking of the reforms of Khatami were suppressed by the police and the military. The reformers won the 2000 parliamentary elections. **Economy** Iran's prosperity is based on oil production (1995 GDP per capita, US$5,470). Oil accounts for 95% of its exports, and it is the world's fourth-largest producer of crude oil. The Iran-Iraq War devastated Iran's industrial base. Oil revenue has been used to diversify the economy and develop manufacturing. Industry now employs 26% of the workforce. Attempts have been made to reduce Iran's dependence on food imports. Agriculture employs 30% of the workforce. Iran is the world's largest producer of dates. Other major crops include wheat and barley. Iran is famous for its fine carpets. Tourism has great potential, but the political situation discourages many visitors.

Iran-Contra affair (1987–88) (Irangate) US political scandal. It involved a secret agreement to sell weapons to Iran via Israel, in order to secure the release of US hostages held in the Middle East. The profits were diverted to support the Nicaraguan CONTRAS, who were attempting to overthrow the SANDINISTA government. The affair, negotiated by Colonel Oliver NORTH with the support of national security advisers to the White House, was revealed by a congressional investigative committee in 1987. North and his superiors, plus several other officials, were later convicted of various charges, including obstructing Congress. In 1992, they were controversially pardoned by President George BUSH.

Iranian languages Group of languages forming a subdivision of the Indo-Iranian family of INDO-EUROPEAN LANGUAGES. The major Iranian languages are Persian, Pashto, Kurdish, Mazanderani and Gilaki (of Iran), Baluchi (of Iran and Pakistan), and Tajik and Ossetic, spoken in the republic of Tajikistan and in South Ossetia (a part of Georgia) and North Ossetia (an autonomous region of the Russian Federation).

Iran-Iraq War (1980–88) Contest for supremacy in the Persian Gulf. The war began when Iraq, partly in response to Iranian encouragement of revolt among the Shiites of S Iraq, invaded Iran, which was disorganized after the Islamic fundamentalist revolution of 1979. Iraq's objective was the SHATT AL ARAB waterway, but

---

IRAN

AREA: 1,648,000sq km (636,293sq mi)

POPULATION: 68,759,000

CAPITAL (POPULATION): Tehran (6,750,000)

stiff Iranian resistance checked its advance and forced its withdrawal (1982). The conflict bogged down in stalemate, with sporadic Iranian offensives. US-led intervention in 1987 was seen as tacit support for Iraq. A UN cease-fire resolution (1987) was accepted by Iraq and, after several Iraqi successes, by Iran also. Estimated total casualties were more than 1 million.

Iraq Republic in sw Asia. Iraq has only a narrow outlet, via the SHATT AL ARAB delta, to the PERSIAN GULF. Its main port, BASRA, is located here. Part of the Syrian Desert forms most of w Iraq, and there are mountains in the NE. Central Iraq is dominated by the valleys of the EUPHRATES and TIGRIS rivers, and includes the capital, BAGHDAD. **Climate** Iraq's climate varies from temperate in the N to sub-tropical in the S and E. The central feature is the lack of adequate rainfall, except in the NE. **Vegetation** Forests account for 3% of the land. Dry grassland and low shrubs grow in the N. The desert provides winter grazing land. The S is mainly marshland. Dates are grown in the sandy SE. **History and politics** The ancient region of MESOPOTAMIA roughly corresponds with modern Iraq. SUMERIA was the first great civilization, c.3000 BC. In c.2340 BC SARGON I conquered Sumeria. In the 18th century BC, HAMMURABI established the first empire of BABYLONIA. In the 8th century BC, Babylonia fell to ASSYRIA. In the 1st century BC, the Assyrian kings SARGON II, SENNACHERIB and ASHURBANIPAL added to the splendour of NINEVEH. NEBUCHADNEZZAR extended the New Babylonian Empire and was responsible for the BABYLONIAN CAPTIVITY. In 539 BC Babylon fell to CYRUS THE GREAT, who founded the ACHAEMENID dynasty. Mesopotamia became part of the Persian Empire. In AD 637, ISLAM was introduced via the Arab conquest. Baghdad became capital of the ABBASID caliphate (750–1258). In 1258, Mongols captured Baghdad. From 1534 Mesopotamia was part of the Ottoman Empire. In 1916, Britain invaded Mesopotamia. In 1920, it became a British mandated territory. Britain renamed the country Iraq and set up an Arab monarchy. In 1932, Iraq finally achieved independence, and oil was first exported in 1934. As a member of the Arab League, Iraq participated in the 1948 ARAB-ISRAELI WAR. By the 1950s, oil dominated Iraq's economy and funded national development programmes. In 1958, a proposal to form an Arab Union with Jordan precipitated a military coup. A republic was established and the king executed. In 1962, the KURDS of N Iraq demanded autonomy, beginning a protracted war of secession. In 1968, the BA'ATH PARTY emerged as the dominant power. Iraq participated in the 1973 Arab-Israeli War. In 1979, Saddam HUSSEIN became president and purged the Ba'ath Party. Iraq invaded Iran, starting the IRAN-IRAQ WAR (1980–88). The Kurdish rebellion continued and poison gas was used against villagers. On 2 August 1990, Iraqi troops invaded Kuwait (see GULF WAR). In 1991, following Iraq's forced withdrawal from Kuwait, rebellion broke out in the Kurdish N highlands and SHIITE S marshlands. The revolt was brutally suppressed by Iraqi forces and UN forces formed "no-fly" zones to protect the civilian population. In 1994, an autonomous Kurdish administration collapsed amid bitter in-fighting. In 1995, UN weapons inspectors (UNSCOM) discovered evidence of Iraq's attempts to gain a nuclear

capability. Continued lack of cooperation with UNSCOM led to US and British bombing raids on Iraq in December 1998. Confrontations in the "no-fly" zones continued in 1999. **Economy** Wars, sanctions and financial mismanagement have created economic chaos. Oil traditionally accounts for 98% of revenue and 45% of GNP. Since 1990 a UN embargo has halted oil exports. In 1996 concern about severe hardship suffered by the civilian population led to a UN "oil-for-food" deal. Farmland covers c.20% of Iraq. Products are barley, cotton, dates and fruits, but Iraq is dependent on food imports. Manufacturing is dominated by petroleum products.

Ireland, John Nicholson (1879–1962) English composer, influenced by Brahms, Dvořák and Ravel. His works, firmly grounded in ROMANTICISM and often inspired by landscape, include *The Forgotten Rite* (1913), *Mai-Dun* (1921), *These Things Shall Be* (1937), the overture *Satyricon* (1946) and many songs and piano pieces.

Ireland Second largest island of the BRITISH ISLES. Ireland is w of Great Britain. The Irish Sea and St Georges Channel run between the two islands. At present, Ireland is divided into two separate countries, the Republic of IRELAND and Northern IRELAND. **Land and climate** The central area of Ireland is a lowland with a mild, wet climate. This area is covered with peat bogs (an important source of fuel) and sections of fertile limestone (the location of dairy farming). Most coastal regions are barren highlands. The interior of Ireland has many lakes and wide rivers (loughs). It boasts the longest river in the British Isles, the SHANNON. **History** From c.3rd century BC to the late 8th century, Ireland was divided into five kingdoms inhabited by Celtic and pre-Celtic tribes. In the 8th century AD, the Danes invaded, establishing trading towns, including DUBLIN, and creating new kingdoms. In 1014, BRIAN BORU defeated the Danes, and for the next 150 years Ireland was free from invasion but subject to clan warfare. In 1171, HENRY II of England invaded Ireland and established English control. In the late 13th century, an Irish parliament was formed. In 1315, English dominance was threatened by a Scottish invasion. In the late 15th century HENRY VII restored English hegemony and began the plantation of Ireland by English settlers. Edward Poynings forced the Irish Parliament to pass Poynings Law (1495), stating that future Irish legislation must be sanctioned by the English Privy Council. Under JAMES I the plantation of ULSTER was intensified. An Irish rebellion (1641–49) was eventually thwarted by Oliver CROMWELL. During the GLORIOUS REVOLUTION, Irish Catholics supported JAMES II, while Ulster Protestants supported WILLIAM III. After James' defeat, the English-controlled Irish Parliament passed a series of punitive laws against Catholics. In 1782, Henry GRATTAN forced trade concessions and the repeal of Poynings Law. William PITT's government passed the Act of UNION (1801), which abolished the Irish assembly and created the United Kingdom of Great Britain and Ireland. In 1829, largely due to the efforts of Daniel O'CONNELL, the Act of CATHOLIC EMANCIPATION was passed, which secured Irish representation in the British Parliament. A blight ruined the Irish potato crop and caused the IRISH FAMINE (1845–49). Nationalist demands intensified. Gladstone failed to secure Irish HOME RULE amid mounting pressure from fearful Ulster Protestants. In 1905, Arthur GRIFFITH founded SINN FÉIN. In 1914, Home Rule was agreed, but implementation was suspended during World War 1. In the EASTER RISING (April 1916), Irish nationalists announced the creation of the Republic of Ireland. The British Army's brutal crushing of the rebellion was a propaganda victory for Sinn

IRAQ
AREA: 438,320sq km (169,235sq mi)
POPULATION: 26,339,000
CAPITAL (POPULATION): Baghdad (3,850,000)

Féin and led to a landslide victory in Irish elections (1918). Between 1918 and 1921, the IRISH REPUBLICAN ARMY (IRA), founded by Michael COLLINS, fought a guerrilla war against British forces. In 1920, a new Home Rule bill established separate parliaments for Ulster and Catholic Ireland. The Anglo-Irish Treaty (1921) led to the creation of an Irish Free State in January 1922 and *de facto* acceptance of partition. (For history post-1922, *see* IRELAND, NORTHERN; IRELAND, REPUBLIC OF)

Ireland, Northern Part of the UNITED KINGDOM, 26 districts occupying the NE of IRELAND, traditionally divided into the six counties of ANTRIM, ARMAGH, DERRY, DOWN, FERMANAGH and TYRONE; the capital is BELFAST. Other major towns include DERRY, Coleraine, Ballymena, Lisburn, Newry, Armagh and Enniskillen. (For land and climate, and pre-1922 history, *see* IRELAND.) **History** In 1920, the six counties of Ulster became the self-governing province of Northern Ireland with a separate, Protestant-dominated parliament. The British government affirmed the inclusion of Northern Ireland within the UK under the principle of self-determination. The Irish Free State (now Republic of Ireland) constitution upheld the unity of the island of Ireland. In 1955, the IRISH REPUBLICAN ARMY (IRA) began a campaign of violence for the creation of an independent, unified Ireland. In 1962, the Republic of Ireland condemned the use of terrorism. Northern Catholics felt aggrieved at discrimination in employment, housing and political representation. In 1967, the Civil Rights Association was established to campaign for equal rights. In 1968, civil rights marches resulted in violent clashes, especially in Derry. Catholic fear of the increasing Protestant domination of local security forces was compounded when the Royal Ulster Constabulary (RUC) was supplemented by the sectarian Ulster Defence Regiment (UDR). The British Army was brought in to protect the Catholic populations in Belfast and Derry. The IRA and Protestant LOYALIST paramilitary organizations, such as the Ulster Defence Association (UDA), increased their campaigns of sectarian violence. In 1972, the Northern Ireland parliament (Stormont) was suspended, replaced by direct rule from Westminster. On 30 January 1972 ("Bloody Sunday"), British troops shot and killed 13 civil rights demonstrators. In 1974, the Council of Ireland, formed by the British and Irish governments to promote cooperation between Ulster and the Irish Republic, quickly collapsed under pressure from a Unionist-led general strike. The IRA campaign widened to include terrorist attacks on Great Britain and British military bases in W Europe. In 1981 hunger strikes by IRA prisoners were more successful in gaining worldwide sympathy. In 1985, the ANGLO-IRISH AGREEMENT gave the Republic of Ireland a consultative role in the government of Northern Ireland. In 1986, a Northern Ireland Assembly was re-established, but quickly failed under the Unionists' boycott. In 1993, following secret talks between the British government and SINN FÉIN, the DOWNING STREET DECLARATION offered all-party negotiations following a cessation of violence. In 1994, provisional IRA and loyalist paramilitaries announced a cease-fire, raising hopes of an end to a sectarian conflict that had claimed more than 2,700 lives. In 1996, disputes over the decommissioning of arms stalled the process and the IRA resumed its terrorist campaign on the British mainland. In July 1997, another cease-fire was agreed, and in October Sinn Féin and Unionists took part in joint peace talks for the first time since partition. On 10 April 1998, the Good Friday Agreement was signed. It provided for an elected Northern Ireland assembly; a North-South Ministerial Council and a British-Irish Council. The Republic of Ire-

land agreed to abandon its constitutional claim to Northern Ireland and processes were established for the decommissioning of weapons and releases of paramilitary prisoners. In May 1998, the agreement was overwhelmingly approved in referenda in Northern Ireland and the Republic of Ireland. In June 1998, elections were held for the new Northern Ireland Assembly. David TRIMBLE of the Ulster Unionists became First Minister. In 1999, the timing of the decommissioning of terrorist weapons continued to be the main stumbling block to peace. After further problems on the issue of arms-decommissioning, the Assembly was suspended in February 2000. It was reconvened in June, after the IRA agreed to partial weapons inspection and the British government announced a new deadline for decommissioning (June 2001). **Economy** More than 80% of Northern Ireland is farmed. Chief crops are potatoes and barley. Heavy industry is concentrated around the port of Belfast. Industries: shipbuilding, vehicle manufacture, textiles (especially linen). The majority population is Protestant; Catholics form a significant minority of 38%. Northern Ireland's economic prosperity is not equally shared: the Catholic community has a much higher rate of unemployment. The economy has been devastated by civil war. Area: 14,121sq km (5,452sq mi). Pop. (1991) 1,573,836.

Ireland, Republic of (Éire) Republic occupying more than 80% of the island of Ireland. It is divided into four provinces of 26 counties (*see* individual articles). The capital is DUBLIN. Other major cities include CORK and LIMERICK. (For land, climate and pre-1922 history and politics, *see* IRELAND) **History and politics** In January 1922, the Irish Free State was created as a Dominion within the British empire. Arthur GRIFFITH of SINN FÉIN became taoiseach. Civil war (1922–23) ensued between supporters of the settlement and those who refused to countenance the partition of Ireland and the creation of Northern IRELAND. The anti-settlement party, led by Eamon DE VALERA, were defeated by Irish Free State forces led by Michael COLLINS. Collins was assassinated and William COSGRAVE became prime minister (1922–32). In 1926, De Valera formed a separate party, FIANNA FÁIL, and became taoiseach (1932–48, 1951–54, 1957–59). In 1933, FINE GAEL was founded. In 1937, a new constitution declared the sovereign nation of Éire to be the whole island of Ireland and abolished the oath of loyalty to the English crown. During World War 2, Éire remained neutral. It opposed Allied operations in Northern Ireland, and the IRISH REPUBLICAN ARMY (IRA) pursued a pro-German line. In 1949, Ireland became a republic outside of the Commonwealth. Its claim to the six counties of Northern Ireland was reiterated. In 1955, Ireland was admitted to the UN. In 1959, de Valera became president (1959–73). During the 1950s, the IRA was banned by both Irish governments and, as a secret organization, it conducted bombing campaigns in Northern Ireland and England. Relations with Northern Ireland improved. In 1973, Ireland joined the European Community (EC). During the 1980s, a series of short-lived coalition governments led by Charles HAUGHEY and Dr Garrett FITZGERALD caused political uncertainty. The ANGLO-IRISH AGREEMENT (1985) gave Ireland a consultative role in the affairs of Northern Ireland. In 1990 Mary ROBINSON was elected as Ireland's first

> **IRELAND, REPUBLIC OF**
> AREA: 70,280sq km (27,135sq mi)
> POPULATION: 4,086,000
> CAPITAL (POPULATION): Dublin (1,024,000)

female president. The DOWNING STREET DECLARATION (1993), signed by John Major and Albert REYNOLDS, continued the momentum for a peaceful settlement in Northern Ireland. The Republic agreed to relinquish its claim to Northern Ireland if a majority of the peoples of the North voted to remain in the United Kingdom. In 1995 elections, Reynolds was defeated by John BRUTON, leader of Fine Gael. Following a 1995 referendum, divorce was legalized. Abortion remains a contentious political issue. In 1997 elections, Bertie AHERN became taoiseach and Mary McAleese became president. In the GOOD FRIDAY AGREEMENT (1998), the Irish Republic gave up its constitutional claim to Northern Ireland and a North-South Ministerial Council was established. In 1999, Ireland joined the EURO. **Economy** Ireland has benefited greatly from its membership of the European Union (1995 GDP per capita, US$15,680). Common Agricultural Policy (CAP) grants have enabled the modernization of farming. Agriculture employs 14% of the workforce. Food and live animals account for more than 20% of exports. Major products include cereals, cattle and dairy products, sheep, sugar beet and potatoes. Fishing is also important. Industry has greatly expanded and accounts for 35% of GNP. Traditional sectors, such as brewing, distilling and textiles, have been supplemented by high-tech industries, such as electronics. The service sector employs 57% of the workforce and accounts for more than 50% of GNP. Tourism is the most important component; receipts from tourism amounted to US$1,620 million (1992). Unemployment remains high and economic migration, though decreasing, is common.

Irian Jaya (West Irian or Irian Barat) Province of E INDONESIA, comprising the W half of NEW GUINEA and adjacent islands; the capital is Djajapura. In the central part of the province, a mountain range rising to more than 5,000m (16,500ft) runs c.650km (400mi) from E to W. Much of the region N of the mountain range is covered by tropical rainforest. Irian Jaya is noted for the richness of its flora and fauna. First explored by Europeans in the 16th century, it was formally claimed by the Netherlands in 1828 and became known as Dutch New Guinea. In 1962, Irian Jaya achieved independence in 1962, but was incorporated into Indonesia in 1963. The economy is predominantly agricultural. Major products include copra, peanuts, rice and timber. Copper and crude oil are exported. Area: 422,170sq km (162,900sq mi). Pop. (1990) 1,648,708.

iridium (symbol Ir) Silver-white metallic element discovered (1804) by the English chemist Smithson Tennant. A PLATINUM-type metal, iridium is hard and brittle and the most corrosion-resistant metal. It is used in making surgical tools, scientific instruments, pen tips and electrical contacts. Properties: at.no. 77; r.a.m. 192.22; r.d., 22.42; m.p. 2,410°C (4,370°F); b.p. 4,130°C (7,466°F); most common isotope Ir^{193} (62.6%).

iris Coloured part of the EYE. It controls the amount of light that enters the PUPIL in the centre of the eye by increasing or decreasing the size of the pupil. This is effected by muscles in the iris contracting or relaxing.

Iris In Greek mythology, goddess of the rainbow and messenger of the gods. Depicted as swift-footed and golden-winged, she appears in Euripides' *Herakles*.

iris Genus of c.300 species of monocotyledonous flowering plants widely distributed, mostly in temperate areas. They may have BULBS or RHIZOMES. Height: up to 90cm (3ft). Family Iridaceae. *See also* CROCUS; GLADIOLUS

Irish *See* GAELIC

Irish Famine (1845–51) (Great Potato Famine) Widespread starvation of Irish peasantry. In 1845, a blight affected the potato, destroying the staple crop. Many farmers could not meet their rents and were evicted. The famine was exacerbated by an epidemic of typhus. It is estimated that one million people died of starvation and another million emigrated, mostly to the United States.

Irish literature Oral storytelling traditions were the preserve of the DRUIDS. Earliest written works, mainly heroic sagas, date from the 7th to the 12th centuries and were composed in GAELIC. The **Ulaid cycle** forms the 12th-century *Book of the Dun Cow*. The **Fenian cycle** includes the legendary exploits of FINN MACCUMHAIL and OSSIAN, in the 12th-century *Book of Leinster*. The **Ulster cycle** includes the heroic account of CUCHULAINN in *The Cattle Raid of Cooley*. Between the 13th and 17th centuries, Gaelic was gradually eroded by Norman and English encroachment, preserved only in poetic works commissioned by wealthy patrons. Leading figures in ENGLISH LITERATURE, such as Jonathan SWIFT, Laurence STERNE and Oscar WILDE, were of Irish descent. Inspired by the movement for Irish HOME RULE, the late 19th and early 20th centuries saw an Irish literary renaissance. Although largely writing in English, the movement drew on the traditions of Gaelic culture. The revival was led by W.B. YEATS. The ABBEY THEATRE hosted the resurgence in Irish drama, staging plays by J.M. SYNGE, George Bernard SHAW and Sean O'CASEY. James JOYCE and Samuel BECKETT reflected on Irish culture from self-exile. Leading contemporary Irish writers include Brian FRIEL and Seamus HEANEY. *See also* BEHAN, BRENDAN; COLUM, PADRAIC; O'BRIEN, EDNA; O'BRIEN, FLANN; RUSSELL, GEORGE

Irish Republican Army (IRA) Guerrilla organization, dedicated to the forceful reunification of IRELAND. Formed in 1919 by Michael COLLINS as the militant wing of SINN FÉIN, the IRA waged war against British rule. Some members ("irregulars") rejected the Anglo-Irish Treaty of 1921, fighting a civil war until 1923. During World War 2 it remained pro-German. Outlawed by both Irish governments in the 1950s, the IRA went underground. In 1970 the organization split into an "official" wing (which emphasized political activities) and a "provisional" wing (committed to armed struggle). The **Provisional IRA** perpetrated terrorist acts in Great Britain and Northern Ireland and Europe, including the Birmingham pub bombing (1974), the murder of Lord Mountbatten (1979), the attempted assasination of the British prime minister in Brighton (1984) and Downing Street (1991), and the Remembrance Day bombing in Enniskillen (1987). In 1994, it declared a cease-fire, but resumed its campaign in 1996. In 1997, it announced another cease-fire. The timing of the decommissioning of IRA weapons is a major issue in the peace process. In 2000, the IRA agreed to partial weapons inspection as a move towards decommissioning.

Irish Sea Part of the Atlantic Ocean, lying between Ireland and Britain. It is connected to the Atlantic by the North Channel (N) and by St George's Channel (S). Scotland, Wales, and England are on its E shore and Ireland on the W shore. Area: 103,600sq km (40,000sq mi).

Irkutsk City on the River Angara, E Siberia, Russia; capital of Irkutsk oblast. It grew as a result of trade with China and the completion of the Trans-Siberian railway. Irkutsk is an important industrial and educational centre. Gold from the Lena goldfields is transshipped, and there is also trade in furs. Industries: ship repairing, timber, machine tools, heavy machinery. Pop. (1994) 632,000.

iron (symbol Fe) Common metallic element of the first transition series, known from the earliest times. Its chief ores are HEMATITE (Fe_2O_3), MAGNETITE (Fe_3O_4) and iron

PYRITES (FeS$_2$). **Pig** iron is obtained in a BLAST FURNACE by SMELTING iron oxide with carbon monoxide from COKE, using limestone to form a slag. **Cast** iron is made from pig iron by remelting and cooling. Wrought iron is made from pig iron by heating with ferric oxide. Iron corrodes to form RUST. The pure metal – a reactive soft element – is rarely used; most iron is alloyed with carbon and other elements in the various forms of STEEL. Properties: at.no. 26; r.a.m. 55.847; r.d. 7.86; m.p. 1,535°C (2,795°F); b.p. 2,750°C (4,982°F); most common isotope Fe^{56} (91.66%).

Iron Age Period succeeding the BRONZE AGE, dating from c.1100 BC in the Near East, later in W Europe. During this period people learned to smelt IRON, although the HITTITES had probably developed the first significant iron industry in Armenia soon after 2000 BC. In Africa the Iron Age succeeded the STONE AGE.

ironclad Wooden warship protected by iron armour, the precursor of the modern BATTLESHIP. Naval losses in the CRIMEAN WAR (1854–56) prompted France to build (1859) the first ironclad warship, the frigate *Gloria*. In 1862 the MONITOR AND MERRIMACK contested the first battle between ironclads in the US CIVIL WAR.

Iron Curtain Colloquial term for the barrier between communist East Europe and the capitalist West during the COLD WAR. The term passed into common use after it was used (March 1946) by Winston CHURCHILL in a speech in Fulton, Missouri, USA.

iron lung Popular name for the **Drinker respirator**, a device that provides long-term artificial RESPIRATION. It consists of a metal tank in which the patient's body is enclosed (with the head outside). Breathing is sustained by alternating negative and positive air pressure inside the tank.

irony Use of words to convey, often satirically, the opposite of their literal meaning. It was first developed by PLATO in his Socratic dialogues, in which SOCRATES often feigned ignorance to evoke admissions from other people. Dramatic irony refers to situations in which the audience possesses information that the protagonist does not.

Iroquois Confederacy League of Native Americans occupying the Mohawk Valley and the Lakes area of New York state. They called themselves Oñgwanósioñi (Hodinonhsioni), "people of the long house", after the distinctive shape of their bark dwellings. The original tribes were the MOHAWK, SENECA, Onondaga, Cayuga and Oneida. The Tuscarora joined later. The Iroquois had a highly developed political system and were renowned warriors. Their total number has halved since 1600; in the mid-1990s they numbered c.10,000, living in New York, Wisconsin, Oklahoma and Canada.

Iroquois War (1642–53) Conflict for territorial expansion carried out by the IROQUOIS CONFEDERACY. The Iroquois, or Five Nations, enlarged their New York territory to the N, W, and, S by dispersing the HURONS (1649), the Tabacco, Neutral Nations (1650), the Eries (1656), Conestogas (1675) and Illinois (1684).

irradiation Exposure to nuclear or ELECTROMAGNETIC RADIATION. Materials are often irradiated with high-energy NEUTRONS in NUCLEAR REACTORS, to make them temporarily radioactive. More portable sources of such radiation are radioisotopes such as cobalt-60 and caesium-137, which are used in the irradiation treatment for cancer. Treatment also involves the use of particle ACCELERATORS, including PROTON and neutron beam machines. Radioactive sources are used industrially, such as in FOOD PRESERVATION. **Ionizing** radiation is used to destroy bacteria and microorganisms in some foodstuffs, while in other foods, such as soft fruits, it increases shelf-life. The process of

irradiation in FOOD TECHNOLOGY is still being closely monitored. Some people fear it not only destroys harmful bacteria but also beneficial nutrients. *See also* FOOD PRESERVATION; RADIATION, NUCLEAR

irrational number In mathematics, any number that cannot be expressed as the ratio of two INTEGERS. An example is √2: like other IRRATIONAL NUMBERS, its expression as a decimal is infinite and non-repeating. Irrational numbers, together with the RATIONAL NUMBERS, make up the set of REAL NUMBERS.

Irrawaddy (Irawadi) River in central Burma (Myanmar), formed by the union of the Mali and Nmai rivers. A vast delta extends 290km (180mi) from Henzada to the Andaman Sea. One of Asia's major rivers, it lies at the centre of an important rice-producing region. Length: c.2,100km (1,300mi).

irrigation Artificial watering of land for growing crops. Irrigation enables crops to grow in regions with inadequate precipitation. The first irrigation systems date from before 3000 BC in Egypt, Asia and the Middle East. Today, most WATER for irrigation is surface water (from streams, rivers and lakes) or GROUNDWATER (obtained from wells). In some regions, freshwater for irrigation is obtained by DESALINATION. Canals, ditches, pumps and pipes are used to convey water to fields.

Irving, Sir Henry (1838–1905) English actor-manager, b. John Henry Brodribb. He made his first stage appearance in 1856 and became the leading Shakespearean actor of his generation. From 1878 to 1902 Irving was manager of the Lyceum Theatre, London, and engaged Ellen TERRY as his leading lady. In 1895 he became the first actor to receive a knighthood.

Irving, Washington (1783–1859) US essayist and short-story writer. He wrote the burlesque *History of New York* (1809) under the pseudonym Dietrich Knickerbocker. From 1815 to 1832 he lived mostly in Europe. Under the pseudonym Geoffrey Crayon, Irving wrote *The Sketch Book* (1819–20) that contains the famous stories "Rip Van Winkle" and "The Legend of Sleepy Hollow". In 1832 he returned to the USA, where his continuing literary output included *Astoria* (1836).

Isaac Biblical character of the Old Testament, and one of the Patriarchs. He was the only son of ABRAHAM and Sarah. As a test of faith in God, Abraham was prepared to sacrifice Isaac as commanded, but at the last minute Isaac was told to sacrifice a lamb instead. Isaac took as his wife Rebecca and became the father of JACOB and ESAU.

Isabella I (1451–1504) Queen of Castile (1474–1504), whose marriage to Ferdinand II of Aragon (FERDINAND V of Castile and León) led to the unification of Spain and its emergence as a dominant European power. Daughter of John II, she won a dispute over the succession by 1468 and married Ferdinand (1469). With his support Isabella reformed royal administration in Castile and encouraged humanist scholarship in Spain, although she was also responsible for the Spanish INQUISITION (1487) and the expulsion of the Jews (1492). Her popularity was enhanced by the conquest of Granada (1492). Isabella supported the voyages of COLUMBUS, which led to the establishment of the Spanish empire in the New World.

Isabella II (1830–1904) Queen of Spain (1833–68), daughter of FERDINAND VII. She was challenged by her uncle, Don CARLOS, resulting in the first CARLIST civil war. In 1868 a liberal revolt led by army officers forced her into exile, and in 1870 she abdicated in favour of her son, ALFONSO XII.

Isabella of France (1292–1358) Queen consort of EDWARD II of England (1308–27), daughter of PHILIP IV of

France. In 1325, she returned to France. In 1326, Isabella and her lover Roger de Mortimer launched a successful invasion of England, forced Edward to abdicate and then assasinated him. In 1327, Edward and Isabella's son acceded to the throne as EDWARD III. In 1330, Edward III executed Mortimer and banished his mother to a nunnery.

Isaiah (Isaias) (active c.8th century BC) Old Testament prophet who was active in Jerusalem from the 740s until the end of the century and gave his name to the Old Testament Book of Isaiah. Isaiah's career coincided with the westward expansion of the Assyrian empire. The Book of Isaiah was written in both verse and prose. Only part of it is attributed to Isaiah. The rest has been thought to be the work of one or even two authors from a later period. The book contrasts Judah's perilous present-day state with glimpses into the future, when God shall send a king to rule over his people.

ISDN *See* INTEGRATED SERVICES DIGITAL NETWORK

Isfahan (Esfahan) City on the River Zaindeh, central Iran. The ancient city of Aspadana, it was occupied successively by Arabs, Seljuk Turks and Mongols. In the late 16th century the SAFAVID dynasty made it their capital and transformed it into one of the most beautiful cities of the age. After its capture by the Afghans in 1722, the city declined. The third-largest city in Iran, it has steel and textile industries as well as the traditional crafts of carpets and rugs, metalwork and silverware. Pop. (1994) 1,224,000.

Isherwood, Christopher William Bradshaw (1904–86) English writer. His novels, characteristically dealing with the sensibility of the homosexual artist, include *All the Conspirators* (1928) and *Mr Norris Changes Trains* (1935), set in pre-war Germany. The musical *Cabaret* (1966) was based on a short story from his *Goodbye to Berlin* (1939). Isherwood collaborated on three plays with W.H. AUDEN, including *The Ascent of F6* (1936). In 1939 he emigrated to the USA and became interested in Hinduism.

Ishiguro, Kazuo (1954–) Japanese novelist, resident in the UK since 1960. His first novels, *A Pale View of Hills* (1982) and *An Artist of the Floating World* (1986), are set in Japan. *The Remains of the Day* (1989) won the Booker Prize. *The Unconsoled* (1995) marked a departure from the elegantly crafted economy of his early style. *When We Were Orphans* (2000) was nominated for the Booker Prize.

Ishmael Any of several biblical figures, most notably ABRAHAM's son by Hagar and half-brother to ISAAC. He married an Egyptian and fathered 12 sons and one daughter, who married ESAU, Isaac's son.

Ishtar Principal goddess of Assyro-Babylonian mythology. She is the daughter of both Anu, the sky god, and Sin, the moon god. Through the centuries, Ishtar came to exhibit diverse attributes, those of a compassionate mother goddess and of a lustful goddess of sex and war. She is identified with the Sumerian Inanna, Phoenician ASTARTE, and the biblical Ashtoreth.

Isidore of Seville, Saint (c.560–636) Spanish ecclesiastic and last of the western Fathers of the Church. In c.600 he became Archbishop of Seville. Isidore is famous for his encyclopedia of knowledge, *Etymologies*. He was canonized by Pope Clement VIII in 1589. His feast day is 4 April.

isinglass Clear, almost pure GELATIN that is prepared from the air bladders of sturgeon and other sources. It is used primarily to clarify wines and beers. The name also refers to an abundant silicate material, also called muscovite, used as an insulator.

Isis In Egyptian mythology, wife and sister of OSIRIS, and mother of HORUS. After Osiris was murdered, Isis put together the dismembered parts of Osiris' body and magically revived him. The epitome of fidelity and maternal devotion, she was worshiped throughout the ancient world up through Roman times.

Islam (Arabic, submission to God) Monotheistic religion founded by MUHAMMAD in Arabia in the early 7th century. At the heart of Islam stands the KORAN, considered the divine revelation in Arabic of God to Muhammad. Members of the faith (MUSLIMS) date the beginning of Islam from AD 622, the year of the HEJIRA. Muslims submit to the will of Allah by five basic precepts (pillars). First, the *shahadah*, "there is no God but Allah, and Muhammad is his prophet". Second, *salah*, five daily ritual prayers. At the MOSQUE a Muslim performs ritual ablutions before praying to God in an attitude of submission, kneeling on a prayer mat facing MECCA with head bowed, then rising with hands cupped behind the ears to hear God's message. Third, *zakat* or alms-giving. Fourth, *sawm*, fasting during RAMADAN. Fifth, HAJJ, the pilgrimage to Mecca. The rapid growth in Islam during the 8th century can be attributed to the unification of the temporal and spiritual. The community leader (CALIPH) is both religious and social leader. The Koran was soon supplemented by the informal, scriptural elaborations of the Sunna (Muhammad's sayings and deeds), collated as the Hadith. A Muslim must also abide by the SHARIA or religious law. While Islam stresses the importance of the unity of the *summa* (nation) of Islam, several distinctive branches have developed, such as SUNNI, SHIITE and SUFISM. Today, there are c.935 million Muslims worldwide.

Islamabad Capital of Pakistan, in the N of the country. Construction of a new capital to replace KARACHI began in 1960, and in 1967 Islamabad became the official capital. It lies at the heart of an agricultural region, but administrative and governmental activities predominate. Pop. (1981) 204,000.

Islamic art and architecture Lacking a strong, independent tradition, Islamic art began to develop as a unique synthesis of the diverse cultures of conquered countries from the 7th century. Early Islamic art and craft is perhaps best illustrated in the architecture of the MOSQUE. Two of the most impressive surviving examples of early Islamic architecture are the DOME OF THE ROCK (685–92) in Jerusalem and the UMAYYAD Mosque in Damascus (c.705). Common architectural forms, such as the DOME, MINARET, *sahn* (courtyard), and the often highly-decorated *mihrab* (prayer niche) and *mimbar* (prayer pulpit) developed in the 9th century. Mosques also acquired rich surface decorations of mosaic, carved stone and paint. In Spain, Moorish architecture developed independently after the Umayyads were forced to flee there by the ABBASID dynasty. It is characterized by its use of the horseshoe arch, faience and stone lattice screens, as seen in the ALHAMBRA. Islamic CAIRO is a world heritage site of Muslim architecture, often derived from Persian innovation. The Ibn Tulun Mosque (879) is a fine example of early brick and stucco form. The Al-Azhar mosque displays 10th century developments. The masterwork of Persian mosques, with their distinctive onion-shaped domes and slender pencil minarets, is the ISFAHAN Imperial Mosque (1585–1612). The Persians influenced the Islamic architecture of India and Turkey. Because of a religious stricture on the representation of nature, Islamic art developed stylized figures, geometrical designs and floral-like decorations (arabesques). The KORAN was the focus for much of the development of calligraphy and illumination. Many of the cursive scripts were developed in the 10th century, and the most commonly used script, Nastaliq, was perfected in the 15th century. Muslim secular art included highly ornamented metalwork (often inlaid with red copper), which developed in the 13th century around Mosul in N Mesopotamia. The art of pottery and ceramics was extremely advanced, with excellent glazes and decoration. The Islamic *minai* (enamel) technique reached its zenith in the 16th century in Isfahan, where entire walls were decorated in faience. Perhaps the best-known art of the Islamic world is that of rug-making.

Isle of Man *See* MAN, ISLE OF

Isle of Wight *See* WIGHT, ISLE OF

Ismail (1486–1524) Shah of Persia (1501–24), founder of the SAFAVID dynasty. A national and religious hero in Iran, he re-established Persian independence and established SHIITE Islam as the state religion. He warred successfully against the UZBEKS in 1510 but was defeated by the Ottoman sultan, Selim I, at the Battle of Chaldiran (1514).

Ismailis Smaller of the two SHIITE branches of ISLAM. Comprised of two groups; "Twelvers", who trace the succession to the 12th IMAM, and "Severners", who believe that the succession halted with the 7th Imam, ISMAIL. Their leader is the AGA KHAN.

Ismail Pasha (1830–95) Viceroy of Egypt (1863–79), grandson of MUHAMMAD ALI. In 1867 he received the title of khedive from the Ottoman sultan. Profits from cotton enabled Ismail to build extensively in Alexandria and Cairo, but later financial difficulties forced him to sell Egypt's share in the Suez Canal Company to Britain and forced him to resign in favour of his son, Tewfik Pasha.

isobar Line on a weather map connecting points of equal pressure, either at the Earth's surface or at a constant height above it. The patterns of isobars depict the variation in ATMOSPHERIC PRESSURE, showing areas of high and low pressure on the map.

isolationism Avoidance by a state of foreign commitments and alliances. It is connected in particular with the foreign policy of the USA. US isolationism was not applied to the Americas, considered an exclusively US area of interest under the MONROE DOCTRINE, nor did it prevent US involvement in China and elsewhere in pursuit of commercial gains. With respect to Europe, it was interrupted when the USA entered World War 1 in 1917 and permanently abandoned in 1941, although it continues to have some advocates.

isomers Chemical compounds having the same molecular formula but different properties due to the different arrangement of ATOMS within the MOLECULES. **Structural** isomers have atoms connected in different ways. **Geometric** isomers, also called cis-trans isomers, differ in their symmetry about a double bond. **Optical** isomers are mirror images of each other. *See also* STEREOCHEMISTRY

isotope One of two or more ATOMS with the same ATOMIC NUMBER but a different number of NEUTRONS. Both mass number and mass of the nucleus are different for different isotopes. The RELATIVE ATOMIC MASS (R.A.M.) of an ELEMENT is an average of the isotope masses. The isotopes of an element have similar chemical properties, but physical properties vary slightly. Most elements have two or more naturally occurring isotopes, some of which are radioactive (radioisotopes). **Radioisotopes** are used in medicine, research and industry. Isotopes are also used in radioactive DATING.

Israel Name given in the Old Testament to JACOB and to the nation that the Hebrews founded in CANAAN. Jacob was renamed Israel after he had wrestled with the mysterious "man" who was either an angel or God Himself (Genesis 32:28). As a geographical name,

Israel at first applied to the whole territory of Canaan captured or occupied by the Hebrews after the Exodus from Egypt. This territory was united as a kingdom under DAVID in the early 10th century BC, with its capital at JERUSALEM. Following the death of David's son, SOLOMON, the ten northern tribes seceded, and the name Israel thereafter applied to the kingdom they founded in N Palestine; the remaining two tribes held the southern kingdom of JUDAH.

Israel Small state in SW Asia, on the Mediterranean Sea. Israel can be divided into four geographical regions: a narrow, fertile coastal plain, site of Israel's main industrial cities, HAIFA and TEL AVIV; the Judaeo-Galilean highlands; the NEGEV Desert, which occupies the S half of Israel extending to ELAT on the Gulf of AQABA, and includes the city of BEERSHEBA; in the E lies part of the Great RIFT VALLEY, including the Sea of GALILEE, the River JORDAN and the DEAD SEA, the world's lowest point, at 396m (1,302ft). Israeli-occupied territories are the GAZA STRIP, the WEST BANK (including East JERUSALEM), and the GOLAN HEIGHTS. **Climate** Israel has a Mediterranean climate with hot, dry summers and mild, rainy winters. Temperature and rainfall vary with elevation and proximity to the sea. The Dead Sea region has only 70mm (2.5in) of rainfall a year, and temperatures rise to 49°C (120°F). **Vegetation** Despite reforestation schemes, forests account for only 6% of land use. Farmland covers *c*.20% of the land, with pasture making up another 40%. The arid Negev Desert is partly irrigated with water pumped from the Sea of Galilee. **History and politics** Israel is part of a historic region that makes up most of the Biblical Holy Lands (for history pre-1947, *see* PALESTINE). In the late 19th century ZIONISM began to agitate for a Jewish homeland. In 1947, the United Nations (UN) agreed to partition Palestine into an Arab and a Jewish state, but the plan was rejected by the Arabs. On 14 May 1948, the State of Israel was proclaimed. Hundreds of thousands of Palestinians fled. In the first of the ARAB-ISRAELI WARS, Egypt, Iraq, Jordan, Lebanon and Syria invaded. The HAGANAH successfully defended the state. An Israeli government was formed with Chaim WEIZMANN as president and David BEN-GURION as prime minister. In 1949, Israel was admitted to the UN, and the capital transferred from Tel Aviv to Jerusalem. In 1950, the Law of Return provided free citizenship for all immigrant Jews. Following Egypt's nationalization of the SUEZ CANAL, Israel captured Gaza and the SINAI PENINSULA. In 1957, Israel withdrew. In 1963, Ben-Gurion resigned and Levi ESHKOL became prime minister (1963–69). In 1967, NASSER blockaded Elat. Israel's defence minister Moshe DAYAN launched a pre-emptive attack against Egypt and Syria. Within six days Israel had occupied the Gaza Strip, the Sinai peninsula, the Golan Heights, the West Bank and East Jerusalem. In 1969 Eshkol died, and Golda MEIR became prime minister (1969–74). On 6 October 1973 (YOM KIPPUR), Egypt and Syria attacked Israeli positions in Sinai and the Golan Heights. Recovering from the initial surprise, Israeli troops launched a counter-offensive and retained its 1967 gains. Yitzhak RABIN's government (1974–77) is chiefly remembered for the daring rescue of Israeli hostages at ENTEBBE. Rabin was succeeded by

---

ISRAEL

AREA: 26,650sq km (10,290sq mi)
POPULATION: 5,321,000
CAPITAL (POPULATION): Jerusalem (591,000)

Menachem BEGIN (1977–83). Begin's hard-line government encouraged Jewish settlement on the West Bank and suppressed Palestinian uprisings. Following the CAMP DAVID AGREEMENT, Egypt and Israel signed a peace treaty (1979) in which Egypt recognized the Israeli state and regained Sinai. In 1982, Begin launched a strike against nuclear installations in Iraq and a full-scale invasion of LEBANON (1982–85) to counter the PALESTINE LIBERATION ORGANIZATION (PLO). In 1987, the INTIFADA began in Israeli-occupied territory. From 1989 to 1992, Israel's population expanded by 10%, due to the immigration of FALASHAS and Soviet Jews. Increasing Jewish settlement inflamed the popular uprising. During the GULF WAR (1991) Israel was the target for Iraqi scud missiles, but under US pressure it did not respond. In 1992, Rabin was re-elected and began "peace-for-land" negotiations with the PLO. In 1993, Rabin and Yasir ARAFAT signed the ISRAELI-PALESTINIAN ACCORD. In 1994, the Palestinian National Authority (PNA) assumed limited autonomy over the West Bank town of JERICHO and the Gaza Strip. On 4 November 1995, Rabin was assassinated by a Jewish extremist. His successor, Shimon PERES, continued the peace process. Peres was narrowly defeated in the 1996 general election by the Likud leader NETANYAHU who, while vowing to maintain the peace process, favoured a more hardline policy. Jewish settlement on the West Bank intensified, despite US and UN disapproval. In January 1997, Israeli troops withdrew from HEBRON and the process crept forward. Further Jewish settlement on the West Bank threatened to stall the process. In October 1998, the US-brokered Wye agreement broke the stalemate with Israel agreeing to redeploy troops on the West Bank, and the PLO promising to cancel anti-Israeli provisions in its charter. Opposition to the agreement led to fresh elections in May 1999, which were won by a Labour coalition, One Israel. The new prime minister, Ehud BARAK, attempted to advance the peace process but, in January 2000, talks with Syria broke down. By June 2000, the Israeli government had withdrawn all troops from Lebanon. **Economy** Israel is a prosperous nation (1995 GDP per capita, US$16,490). In 1948, Israel was heavily reliant on food imports and was hit by Arab boycotts during the 1950s. Now it is self-sufficient and a major exporter of fruits and vegetables. Agriculture, which employs 4% of the workforce, is highly scientific. Manufactured goods are the leading export; products include chemicals, electronic and military equipment, jewellery, plastics and scientific instruments. Diamonds account for 23% of exports. About 66% of the workforce is employed in the service sector. Tourism is a major source of foreign currency.

Israeli–Palestinian Accord Agreement that aimed to end hostilities between Palestinians and Israelis, especially in the WEST BANK and GAZA STRIP. Secret talks began in the mid-1980s. On 13 September 1993, a "Declaration of Principles" was signed by Yitzhak RABIN and Yasir ARAFAT. The PLO recognized Israel's right to exist and renounced terrorism. In return, Israel recognized the PLO as the legitimate representative of Palestinians and agreed to a staged withdrawal of troops from parts of the occupied territories. On 18 May 1994, the Israeli army completed its redeployment in the Gaza Strip and withdrew from JERICHO. The Palestinian National Authority (PNA), headed by Arafat, assumed limited autonomy. In September 1995 Rabin agreed to withdraw Israeli troops from a further six towns and 85% of HEBRON. In October 1995, 1,100 Palestinian prisoners were released. The assassination of Rabin and the election of Benjamin

NETANYAHU halted the process, and Jewish settlement on the West Bank accelerated. In 1997, despite the withdrawal of most Israeli troops from Hebron and desperate attempts by the US government to encourage dialogue, Israel's determination to build more Jewish settlements in E Jerusalem stalled the process. The Wye agreement (1998) appeared to break the deadlock, but met concerted opposition within Israel. *See also* INTIFADA

Istanbul City and seaport in NW Turkey, on both sides of the BOSPORUS, partly in Europe and partly in Asia, at the entrance to the Sea of Marmara. The city was founded by Greek colonists in the 7th century BC. It was known as **Byzantium** until AD 330 when CONSTANTINE I chose it as the capital of the Eastern Roman Empire and renamed it **Constantinople**. Captured by the OTTOMAN Turks in 1453, the city was largely destroyed by an earthquake in 1509 and rebuilt. When the new Turkish Republic was established after World War 1, the capital was moved to ANKARA, and Constantinople was renamed Istanbul. Today, it is the commercial and financial centre of Turkey. Industries: shipbuilding, cement, textiles, glass, pottery, leather goods. It also derives a valuable income from tourism. Pop. (1995) 7,774,000.

Italian Language of Italy, where it is spoken by 58 million inhabitants, and of the canton of Ticino, in Switzerland. It is one of the ROMANCE LANGUAGES descended from spoken LATIN and so belongs ultimately to the Italic group of INDO-EUROPEAN LANGUAGES. There are many Italian dialects, and the official language is based on those of central Italy, particularly Tuscan. During the 20th century, broadcasting and the movies standardized the language greatly, but most Italians continue to use a regional dialect for everyday communication.

Italian art and architecture Painting, sculpture and other art produced in Italy following the Roman period. By the 6th century, trade with the Byzantine Empire had brought the influence of BYZANTINE ART AND ARCHITECTURE to Italian art, which lasted through the 11th century. The chief centres of the Italo-Byzantine style were Venice, Tuscany, Rome and the deep south. Mosaics and stylized geometric forms became standard as decorations for GOTHIC cathedrals and churches. Icon panels were the main type of paintings from the 11th to the 13th centuries, with major schools in SIENA, Lucca and PISA. By the time of the RENAISSANCE, the emphasis was on balance and harmony, with such masters as LEONARDO DA VINCI, GHIBERTI, DONATELLO, BOTTICELLI and MICHELANGELO. MANNERISM developed in Florence late in the Renaissance but faded by the end of the 16th century, giving way to the BAROQUE style of the 17th century. This was typified by artists such as the painter CARAVAGGIO and the architect BERNINI. In the 18th and 19th centuries, the NEO-CLASSICAL movement was inspired by Classical Roman art, the subject of PIRANESI's engravings. The 20th century saw the birth of FUTURISM, as well as the more tranquil works of MODIGLIANI and DE CHIRICO.

Italian literature Body of work produced in Italy from the 13th century on. Italian vernacular literature emerged in the 13th century with the work of the Sicilian poets at the court of FREDERICK II; they extensively employed the SONNET. Religious poetry also flourished. Major figures of the 14th century were DANTE, the poet PETRARCH and BOCCACCIO, who influenced the works of CHAUCER. The RENAISSANCE produced outstanding poetry and philosophy, especially in the work of Torquato TASSO, Lodovico ARIOSTO and the politician, MACHIAVELLI. During the 18th-century Age of ENLIGHTENMENT, a new literary language was required to reflect modern experience. The poet Carlo Porta (1775–1821) employed regional dialects, while Giuseppe Parini (1729–99) wrote in a more conventional style. The lyrical works of Giacomo Leopardi (1798–1837) and the novels of Alessandro MANZONI helped to take Italian literature into its Romantic period. The 19th-century RISORGIMENTO movement for Italian unification and independence inspired a literary flowering. The major figure to emerge was Gabriele D'ANNUNZIO. Luigi PIRANDELLO revived the traditions of Italian theatre. Important 20th-century novelists include Alberto MORAVIA, Cesare PAVESE, Eugenio MONTALE, Umberto ECO and Italo CALVINO. The poets Salavatore QUASIMODO and Eugenio MONTALE and the dramatist Dario FO received Nobel prizes for literature.

Italian Wars (1494–1559) Struggle for control of the independent Italian states between the VALOIS kings of France and the HABSBURGS. In 1494, CHARLES VIII of France captured Naples, but was forced to retreat. In 1499, LOUIS XII occupied Milan and Genoa. In 1504 Louis was forced to concede control of Naples to FERDINAND V of Spain. In 1510, Pope JULIUS II formed the Holy League against France. The capture of FRANCIS I by Emperor CHARLES V's forces at the Battle of Pavia (1525) permanently weakened the French position. The final settlement of Câteau-Cambrésis (1559) left Habsburg Spain dominant.

italics Style of handwriting developed by the Florentine humanist Niccolò Niccoli in the 15th century. By the 16th century it had replaced Gothic script in most European countries. The 20th century has seen its revival. It is now used in printed works for special purposes, such as to indicate emphasis or foreign words.

Italy Republic in S Europe. Italy is bordered in the N by the ALPS, which include its highest peak, Gran Paradiso, at 4,061m (13,323ft). In the NE lies Italy's largest lake, Lake GARDA, framed by the DOLOMITES. The Alps drop down to a vast, fertile plain, drained by Italy's longest river, the PO. This is the richest industrial and agricultural region. The APENNINES form central Italy's backbone. Either side of the range are narrow coastal lowlands. On the Tyrrhenian side lies the capital, ROME. SICILY is the largest Mediterranean island and includes Mount ETNA. *See individual gazetteer articles* **Climate** Italy has a Mediterranean climate, except for Sicily, which is subtropical. Alpine winters are long, and the frequent snow is ideal for winter sports. **History and politics** By tradition ROMULUS AND REMUS founded ancient ROME in 753 BC. The ETRUSCANS were overthrown by the Romans, who established a republic (509 BC). In the PUNIC WARS, Rome gained a Mediterranean empire. POMPEY was defeated by Julius CAESAR, whose assassination led to the formation (27 BC) of the ROMAN EMPIRE under AUGUSTUS. DIOCLETIAN divided the empire into Eastern (BYZANTINE EMPIRE) and Western sections. The PAPACY ensured the continuation of Rome's influence. PEPIN III (THE SHORT) expelled the LOMBARDS and enabled the creation of the PAPAL STATES. In AD 800, Pepin's son, CHARLEMAGNE, was crowned emperor of the West. In 962 OTTO I conquered Italy and established the HOLY ROMAN EMPIRE. Central and N Italy were controlled by

powerful city-states, while the S established a FEUDAL SYSTEM under the HOHENSTAUFEN and Angevin dynasties. The 13th-century battle between imperial and papal power divided the cities and nobles into the GUELPH and GHIBELLINE factions. The RENAISSANCE profoundly affected western civilization. ITALIAN ART AND ARCHITECTURE was a formative force across Europe. In the 16th century Spain gained Sicily, Naples and Milan. The FRENCH REVOLUTIONARY WARS failed to bring reunification. Nationalist groups, such as the RISORGIMENTO, emerged. In 1861, MAZZINI's republicans were defeated by monarchists led by GARIBALDI, and the kingdom of Italy was unified under VICTOR EMMANUEL II. The papacy refused to concede the loss of Rome, and VATICAN CITY was set up as a sovereign state (1929). The late 19th century was marked by industrialization and empire-building. VICTOR EMMANUEL III's reign (1900–46) saw Italy enter World War 1 on the Allied side (1915). Italian discontent at the post-war settlement culminated in D'ANNUNZIO's seizure of TRIESTE and the emergence of FASCISM. In 1922, Benito MUSSOLINI assumed dictatorial powers. Aggressive foreign policy included the seizure of ETHIOPIA and Albania. In 1936, Mussolini entered an alliance with HITLER. During World War 2, Italy fought on the Axis side, but after losing its North African empire, Mussolini was dismissed and Italy surrendered (1943). Germany invaded and Italy declared war. In 1944, Rome fell to the Allies. The Christian Democrat Party emerged as the dominant postwar political force, with DE GASPERI as prime minister (1945–53). In 1948, Italy became a republic and was a founding member of NATO (1949) and the European Economic Community (1958). Italy has been riven by political instability (56 governments since 1945), endemic corruption (often linked to the MAFIA), social unrest and the wealth gap between N and S. In 1993, popular discontent with traditional political parties and the political structure led to the adoption of a "first-past-the-post" system and the emergence of the Northern League and anti-corruption parties. Elections in 1996 were won by the left-wing Olive Tree alliance and Romano Prodi became prime minister (1996–98). In 1998, the Communist Refoundation (RC) withdrew its support for Prodi's government and Massimo D'Alema, leader of the Party of the Democratic Left (PDS), became prime minister. In 1999, Italy joined the EURO. In April 2000, after rifts within the coalition government widened, D'Alema resigned and was replaced by Giuliano Amato. **Economy** Italy's main industrial region is the NW triangle of MILAN, TURIN and GENOA (1995 GDP per capita, US$19,870). It is the world's eighth-largest car and steel producer. Machinery and transport equipment account for 37% of exports. Italy has few mineral resources. Agricultural production is important. Italy is the world's largest producer of wine. Tourism is a vital economic sector (1992 receipts $21,577 million).

Ito, Hirobumi (1841–1909) Japanese statesman. The leading figure in the modernization of Japan after the MEIJI RESTORATION (1868), he served in several government posts and took part in the Iwakura Mission (1871–73) to study Western governments. After the RUSSO–JAPANESE WAR (1904-05), Ito headed the Japanese administration in what was then the protectorate of Korea. He was assassinated by a Korean nationalist.

Itúrbide, Agustín de (1783–1824) Mexican general and politician, who helped Mexico achieve independence (1821) and was emperor (1822–23). Dissent crystallized when SANTA ANNA and Guadalupe Victoria

ITALY
AREA: 301,270sq km (116,320sq mi)
POPULATION: 57,195,000
CAPITAL (POPULATION): Rome (2,654,000)

called for the creation of a republic. Iturbide abdicated and was exiled. Early in 1824 he returned to Mexico and was promptly arrested and shot.

Ivan III (the Great) (1440–1505) Grand Duke of Moscow (1462–1505). He laid the foundations of the future empire of Russia. By 1480 Moscow's northern rivals, including Novgorod, were absorbed by conquest or persuasion, domestic rebellion was crushed, and the TATAR threat was ended permanently. Ivan's later years were troubled by conspiracies over succession. He began to use the title *tsar* ("caesar") and employed Italian artists in the buildings of the KREMLIN.

Ivan IV (the Terrible) (1530–84) Grand Duke of Moscow (1533–84) and first tsar of Russia (1547–84). In 1547 he married Anastasia, a ROMANOV. At first, Ivan was an able and progressive ruler, reforming law and government. By annexing the TATAR states of Kazan and Astrakhan, he gained control of the River Volga. Ivan established trade with W European states and began Russian expansion into Siberia. Defeat by the Poles in the Livonian War (1558–82) left Russia financial crippled. After his wife's death in 1560, he became increasingly unbalanced, killing his own son in a rage. Ivan established a personal dominion, the *oprichnina*, inside Russia. He created a military force, the *oprichniki*, which pursued a reign of terror against the boyars.

Ives, Charles (1874–1954) US composer. His use of polytonality and polyrhythms anticipated the work of Schoenberg and Stravinsky. Ives first attracted attention with his second piano sonata *Concord* (1915). His work was often inspired by American folk music, such as *Variations on America* for organ (1891) and Symphony No. 2 (1902). Ives was awarded the 1947 Pulitzer Prize for music for Symphony No. 3 (1904).

IVF Abbreviation of IN VITRO FERTILIZATION

ivory Hard, yellowish-white dentine of some mammals. The most highly prized variety is obtained from elephant tusks. The term also refers to the teeth of hippopotamuses, walruses, sperm whales and several other mammals.

Ivory Coast (officially Côte d'Ivoire) Republic in W Africa; the capital is YAMOUSSOUKRO. The SE coast features lagoons enclosed by sandbars, on one of which the former capital and chief port of ABIDJAN is situated. Rocky cliffs line the SW coast. Coastal lowlands give way to a plateau. The NW highland borders with Liberia and Guinea are an extension of the Guinea Highlands. **Climate** Ivory Coast has a hot and humid tropical climate with high temperatures throughout the year. The S has two distinct rainy seasons, May to July and October to November. Inland, rainfall decreases and the N has a dry season and only one rainy season. **Vegetation** Rainforests once covered the S lowlands, but much of the land has been cleared for farming. Tropical savanna covers the plateau, and forests occupy much of the Guinea Highlands. **History and politics** European contact with the region dates back to the late 15th century, and trade in ivory and slaves soon became important. French trading posts were founded in the late 17th century, and Ivory Coast became a French colony in 1893. From 1895, Ivory Coast was governed as part of French West Africa, a massive union that also included modern-day Benin, Burkina Faso, Guinea, Mali, Mauritania, Niger and Senegal. In 1958, Ivory Coast voted to remain within the French Community, but achieved full independence in 1960. Its first president, Félix HOUPHOUËT-BOIGNY, was the longest-serving African head of state, with an uninterrupted 33-year presidency until his death in 1993. He was a paternalistic, pro-Western leader. His dialogue with South Africa's apartheid

IVORY COAST
AREA: 322,460sq km (124,502sq mi)
POPULATION: 17,600,000
CAPITAL (POPULATION): Yamoussoukro (120,000)

government enraged many fellow African states. In 1983 the National Assembly agreed to move the capital from Abidjan to Yamoussoukro, the president's birthplace, but economic setbacks delayed the completion of the transfer, and government offices remained in Abidjan until 1990. Civil unrest continued throughout the 1980s and led to the adoption of a new constitution (1990) that legalized opposition parties. Houphouët-Boigny was succeeded by Henri Konan Bédié. In 1995, Bédié was re-elected, after an opposition boycott. In 1999, Bédié was overthrown in a military coup led by General Robert Guei. The 2000 presidential elections were boycotted by the main parties, and Laurent Gbagbo of the socialist opposition replaced Guei as president. **Economy** Agriculture employs *c*.66% of the workforce and accounts for *c*.50% of Ivory Coast's exports. Ivory Coast is the world's largest producer of cocoa beans and fourth-largest producer of coffee (1995 GDP per capita, US$1,580). Other exports include cotton, bananas, palm oil, pineapples and hardwoods. Food crops include cassava, rice and yams. Manufactures include fertilizers, refined oil, textiles and timber.

ivy Woody, EVERGREEN vine with leathery leaves, native to Europe and Asia. Its long, climbing stems cling to upright surfaces, such as trees or walls, by aerial roots. The common English ivy (*Hedera helix*) is propagated by cuttings and grows outdoors in moist shady or sunny areas. Family Araliaceae.

Ivy League Group of eight long-established, prestigious US universities and one college. The universities are HARVARD, YALE, PRINCETON, University of Pennsylvania, Brown, Columbia and Cornell. The college is Dartmouth. They are organized as an intercollegiate athletic league.

Iwo Jima (formerly Sulphur Island) Largest of the Volcano Islands in the W Pacific Ocean, Japan. During World War 2, Iwo Jima was captured by the USA at great human cost (1945). The US flag being planted on its highest peak, Mount Suribachi, became a US symbol of the Pacific conflict and the basis for a sculpture near ARLINGTON National Cemetery, Washington, D.C. Iwo Jima was returned to Japan in 1968. Industries: sugar refining, sulphur mining. Area: 21sq km (8sq mi).

Izetbegović, Alija (1925–) Bosnian statesman, president of BOSNIA-HERZEGOVINA (1992–2000). He was imprisoned (1945–48, 1983–88) by the Yugoslavian government for pan-Islamic activities and for his Islamic Declaration of 1970. In 1990, Izetbegović was elected leader of the Party of Democratic Action (PDA), promising to establish a multi-faith republic. He led Bosnia-Herzegovina's coalition government from 1990 until its declaration of independence in 1992. Izetbegović retained his position as president throughout the civil war and signed the Treaty of Paris (1995), which ended the Bosnian War. He was re-elected in 1996. In October 2000, he retired.

Izmir (formerly Smyrna) City and seaport on the Gulf of Izmir, W Turkey. It was settled by Greeks at the beginning of the 1st millennium BC. Izmir was part of the Ottoman Empire from 1424–1919, when it was assigned to Greece. It passed to Turkey under the Treaty of Lausanne (1923). Industries: tourism, tobacco, silk, carpets, cotton and woollen textiles, petrochemicals, foodstuffs, cement. Pop. (1995) 2,018,00.

J/j, tenth letter of the Roman alphabet. It evolved from the letter i and was the last letter to be incorporated into the modern alphabet; its early history is the same as that of the letter i. The j developed from the tail form of the letter i.

jabiru Large STORK of the New World, found in swamps from Mexico to Argentina. Length: 1.5m (5ft); wingspan: 2m (7ft). Family Ciconiidae; species *Jabiru mycteria*.

Jabotinsky, Vladimir (1880–1940) Jewish leader in Palestine, b. Russia. In 1920, he organized HAGANAH, the Jewish self-defence movement. Jabotinsky was a leading supporter of ZIONISM. During the 1930s, he worked for the establishment of a separate Jewish state. The terrorist group, Irgun Zvai Leumi, was founded by his associates.

jaçana (lily trotter) Long-toed water bird of tropical lakes with a slender body, narrow bill, wrist spurs and tapered claws. It is black or reddish-brown. It runs over floating vegetation, feeding on aquatic plants and small animals. Length: to 51cm (20in). Family Jacanidae.

jacaranda Genus of trees native to tropical America. The ornamental *Jacaranda mimosifolia* and *J. cuspidifolia* have showy blue flowers and fern-like leaves. There are 50 species. Family Bignoniaceae.

jackal Wild dog that resembles a COYOTE in habits, size and general appearance. It preys on small animals and eats fruit and seeds. There are several species of jackal, distributed throughout Asia and Africa. Length: to 74cm (29in). Family Canidae; genus *Canis*.

jackdaw Gregarious, black-and-grey, European bird that frequents open country. Smaller than its relative, the CROW, it has a grey head and white-rimmed eyes. It lives in colonies. Family Corvidae; species *Corvus monedula*.

Jacklin, Tony (Anthony) (1944–) English golfer. In 1969, he became the first Briton in 18 years to win the British Open. In 1970, Jacklin became the first British player in 50 years to win the US Open. He captained two victorious European Ryder Cup teams (1985, 1987).

jackrabbit Any of several large, slender, long-eared HARES of W North America. Jackrabbits rely on their speed and agility to escape from predators. Most are grey with white underparts. Family Leporidae; genus *Lepus*.

Jackson, Andrew (1767–1845) Seventh US president (1829–37). He became a national hero in the WAR OF 1812 when he defeated the British at New Orleans (1815). His popular appeal narrowly failed to defeat John Quincy ADAMS in the 1824 presidential election. His supporters built the basis of the new DEMOCRATIC PARTY and, in 1828, he was elected with John C. CALHOUN as his vice president. Jackson faced staunch opposition from the establishment and set up a SPOILS SYSTEM of political appointments. Calhoun resigned over the NULLIFICATION issue, and Jackson faced further conflict over STATES' RIGHTS, the expansion of the FRONTIER and the TARIFF. His second term (1832–37) was marked by his trenchant opposition to the BANK OF THE UNITED STATES. He was succeeded by Martin VAN BUREN.

Jackson, Glenda (1936–) English actress and politician. She reprised her stage role in her film debut *Marat/Sade* (1967). Jackson won two Academy Awards for Best Actress in *Women in Love* (1969) and *A Touch of Class* (1973). Other films include *Sunday Bloody Sunday* (1971) and *Hedda* (1975). She became a labour MP in 1992 and was re-elected in 1997.

Jackson, Jesse Louis (1941–) US political leader and CIVIL RIGHTS activist. Ordained a Baptist minister in 1968, he worked with Martin Luther KING JR in the Southern Christian Leadership Conference. In 1971, he formed Operation PUSH (People United to Save Humanity) to combat racism. An inspiring orator, Jackson campaigned for the Democratic presidential nomination in 1984 and 1988; although he did not achieve the nomination, he inspired many people to register to vote. In 1986, he became president of the National Rainbow Coalition.

Jackson, Mahalia (1911–72) US gospel singer. She began her career in her father's Baptist church. In 1950, Jackson made her Carnegie Hall debut. In 1958, she sang Duke Ellington's *Black, Brown and Beige* suite at the Newport Festival. She was also a CIVIL RIGHTS activist and campaigned with Martin Luther KING, JR.

Jackson, Michael (1958–) US pop singer and songwriter. At the age of five, he was the youngest member of The Jackson Five. Jackson launched his solo career with the albums *Got To Be There* (1971) and *Off the Wall* (1979). His album *Thriller* (1982), backed by spectacularly choreographed videos, sold more than 35 million copies. Later albums included *Bad* (1987) and *Dangerous* (1991). In 1993, he was forced to cancel a worldwide tour after allegations of child abuse. In 1994, Jackson married Lisa Marie Presley (1968–), daughter of Elvis PRESLEY. The couple separated in 1996.

Jackson, "Stonewall" (Thomas Jonathan) (1824–63) Confederate general in the American CIVIL WAR. His stand against overwhelming odds at the first Battle of BULL RUN (1861) gained him the nickname "Stonewall". He fought, again greatly outnumbered, in the Shenandoah Valley (1862) and played an important part in the Confederate victories after the second Battle of Bull Run. Jackson was accidentally shot and killed by his own men at the Battle of Chancellorsville.

Jackson State capital and largest city of Mississippi, USA, on the Pearl River, in the SW part of the state. Originally a trading post established in the 1790s, it was chosen as the site of the state capital in 1821. Industries: natural gas, glass, textiles. Pop. (1990) 196,637.

Jacksonville Seaport and largest city in Florida, USA, in the NE part of the state, on the St John's River. It served as a CONFEDERATE base during the Civil War, developed as a port in the 19th century and was devastated by fire in 1901. It has shipyards and a naval air station. Industries: cigars, canning, wood products. Pop. (1994 est.) 676,718.

Jack the Ripper Unidentified murderer of at least seven prostitutes in Whitechapel, E London, in 1888. The bodies of his victims were mutilated in a manner that suggested a knowledge of anatomy. The case remains unsolved.

Jacob Old Testament figure who was a grandson of ABRAHAM and, by tradition, ancestor of the nation of ISRAEL. He was the second-born son of ISAAC and Rebecca, and younger twin brother of ESAU. Stories about him and his family form the last part of Genesis (25:19–50:13). Jacob had 12 sons and one daughter by his two wives, Rachel and Leah, and their respective maids. The descendants of his 12 sons became the 12 tribes of Israel.

Jacob, François (1920–) French biologist. Jacob and Jacques Monod discovered that messenger RNA (mRNA) carried hereditary information from the cell NUCLEUS to the sites of PROTEIN synthesis, and that operator GENES control the activity of other genes. They shared the 1965 Nobel Prize for physiology or medicine with French biologist André Lwoff. *See also* DNA

Jacobean (Lat. *Jacobus*, James) Term designating the artistic styles of the reign of JAMES I (1603–25). The major literary art form was drama, typical examples of which are the works of WEBSTER and the late plays of SHAKESPEARE. METAPHYSICAL POETRY, such as the work of John DONNE, was also a feature. In architecture the major achievement was the work of Inigo JONES. Jacobean painters were not as distinguished.

Jacobins Political club of the FRENCH REVOLUTION. In 1789, Breton members of the STATES-GENERAL met in a Dominican (Fr. Jacobin) monastery to form the Jacobin Club. By 1791, it had branches throughout France. By 1792, ROBESPIERRE had seized control of the Jacobins and the club adopted more radical policies. In 1793, the Jacobins engineered the expulsion of the GIRONDINS and the club became an instrument of the REIGN OF TERROR. It collapsed soon after Robespierre's downfall in 1794.

Jacobites Supporters of JAMES II of England and his STUART descendants, who attempted to regain the English throne after the GLORIOUS REVOLUTION of 1688. Jacobitism was strong in the Scottish Highlands and parts of Ireland. In 1715 (the "**Fifteen Rebellion**"), a rising at Braemar, led by the Earl of Mar, proclaimed James Edward STUART as king. The movement collapsed with the defeat of the rebels at Preston. In 1745, a second rising (the "**Forty-Five Rebellion**"), led by Bonnie Prince Charlie (Charles Edward STUART), captured Scotland and advanced as far as Derby, central England, before retreating. In 1746, the Highlanders were decisively defeated at the Battle of CULLODEN and the British government embarked upon a policy of suppression of the Highland clans that ended the Jacobite threat.

Jacob's ladder Any of 50 species of wild and cultivated plants of temperate areas. It has clusters of delicate blue, violet or white flowers and alternate compound leaves. Height: up to 90cm (3ft). Family Polemoniaceae.

Jacopone da Todi (1230–1306) Italian poet. After the death of his wife in the 1260s, he became a monk and wrote numerous fervid, personal hymns. The Latin canticle *Stabat mater dolorosa* is attributed to him.

Jacquard, Joseph Marie (1752–1834) French silk weaver. In 1801 he perfected a loom that could weave patterns automatically. By 1812, there were 11,000 Jacquard looms in use in France. The first automated machine, the loom was controlled by punched cards.

jade Semi-precious silicate mineral of two major types: the rarer **jadeite**, which is often translucent; and **nephrite**, which has a waxy quality. Both types are extremely hard and usually green or white in colour. Nephrite was used in China in the 3rd millennium BC. Hardness 5–6; r.d. 3–3.4.

Jade, August Personage of In Chinese mythology, the supreme god of heaven and, according to some traditions, the creator of human beings. He concerned himself exclusively with the affairs of the emperor, leaving his heavenly ministers to deal with lesser mortals.

Jakarta (Djakarta) Capital of Indonesia, on the NW coast of Java. It was founded (as Batavia) by the Dutch

jaeger (skua) Gull-like, predatory, fast-flying seabird that breeds in the Arctic and winters in the sub-tropics. It has a dark, stocky body with pointed wings and long tail feathers. It feeds on small land animals and seabirds. Length: 33–51cm (13–20in). Genus *Stercorarius*.

Jaffa City and port in W Israel, a suburb of TEL AVIV. Mentioned in the Bible, it was captured by ALEXANDER THE GREAT in 332 BC. It was taken back by the Jews during the Hasmonean revolt but was destroyed by the Roman emperor Vespasian in AD 68. It changed hands many times in the Middle Ages. In the 20th century, it became a focus of Palestinian resistance to Jewish settlement. In 1948, the city was settled by Israelis and united with Tel Aviv in 1950. Pop. (1995 est.) 355,000.

Jagiello (Jagello) Medieval Polish dynasty. It began with the marriage (1386) of Grand Duke Jagiello of Lithuania to Queen Jadwiga of Poland, uniting Poland and Lithuania. In the 15th century, the dynasty also controlled Hungary and Bohemia. Defeated by the Turks at the Battle of MOHACS (1526), the Habsburg Ferdinand I assujimed power in Hungary and Bohemia and the Jagiello dynasty ended in 1572.

jaguar Largest New World CAT, found in woodland or grassland from SW USA to Argentina. It has a chunky body and a spotted, yellowish coat with black rosettes. The black rings distinguish it from the LEOPARD. It eats large mammals, turtles and fish. Length: up to 2.5m (8ft), including tail; weight up to 136kg (300lb). Family Felidae; species *Panthera onca*.

jaguarundi Small, ground-dwelling CAT found in Central and South America. It is black, brown, grey or fox red. Length: to 67cm (26in), excluding tail; weight: to 9kg (20lb). Family Felidae; species *Felis yagouaroundi*.

Jahangir (1569–1627) Emperor of India (1605–27), son and successor of AKBAR I (THE GREAT). He continued the expansion of the MOGUL EMPIRE. Jahangir granted trading privileges to the Portuguese and the British and was a patron of poetry and painting.

Jainism Ancient religion of India originating in the 6th century BC as a reaction against conservative BRAHMANISM. It was founded by Mahavira (599–527 BC), venerated as the last of 24 *tirthankaras* (saints). Jains do not accept Hindu scriptures, rituals or priesthood, but they do accept the doctrines of KARMA and REINCARNATION. Jainism lays special stress on AHIMSA – non-injury to living creatures. Today, there are *c*.4 million Jains worldwide.

Jaipur State capital of Rajasthan, W India. The walled city was founded in 1727. The most notable of its distinctive pink sandstone buildings are the Hawa Mahal ("Palace of Winds", 1739) and the Jantar Mantar observatory (1726). Jaipur is famous for its carpets, jewellery, enamels and printed cloth. Pop. (1991) 1,458,000.

◄ **jaguar** The largest cat in the Americas, the jaguar (*Panthera onca*) is now extinct in most of N America. It is a solitary hunter and an excellent swimmer and tree-climber. Unlike most big cats, it does not roar.

*c.*1619 as a fort and trading post, and it became the headquarters of the Dutch EAST INDIA COMPANY. It became the capital after Indonesia gained its independence in 1949. Industries: ironworking, printing, timber. Exports: rubber, tea, quinine. Pop. (1994 est.) 7,885,519.

Jakobson, Roman (1896–1982) US linguist, b. Russia. An important figure in Russian formalism, Jakobson developed the structural linguistics of Ferdinand de SAUSSURE. In 1941, he emigrated to the USA and became a professor (1949–67) at Harvard University. In *Fundamentals of Language* (1956), Jakobson outlined a universal system of phonology. *See also* STRUCTURALISM

Jamaica Independent island nation in the Caribbean, 145km (90mi) S of Cuba; the capital is KINGSTON. The third largest island in the Caribbean, Jamaica's coast is ringed with beautiful, palm-fringed beaches. In E Jamaica the Blue Mountains rise to 2,255m (7,402ft). It has a tropical maritime climate. Jamaica was discovered by Christopher COLUMBUS in 1494 and remained a Spanish possession until captured by the British in 1655. Its sugar plantations brought prosperity, but the economy declined after the abolition of slavery in 1834. In 1865, British rule was threatened by a black rebellion. In 1944, the colony was granted internal self-government within the Commonwealth and in 1958 joined the Federation of the WEST INDIES. In 1962, after the collapse of the Federation, William A. Bustamante of the Jamaican Labour Party (JLP) negotiated full independence for Jamaica. In 1973, Michael Manley of the People's National Party (PNP) took Jamaica into CARICOM. He retired in 1992 and was succeeded by Percival J. Patterson of the PNP. Patterson was re-elected in 1993 and 1997. Chief crops are sugar cane, bananas and other fruits. The economy is based on light engineering, construction and mining. Jamaica is the world's third largest producer of bauxite (aluminium ore). Tourism is also important. Area: 10,962sq km (4,232sq mi). Pop. (2000) 2,735,000.

James the Great, Saint (d. *c.*44 AD) One of the 12 DISCIPLES and first APOSTLES of JESUS CHRIST, son of Zebedee and brother of St JOHN. James was beheaded by HEROD AGRIPPA I. His shrine at Santiago de Compostela, N Spain, is a place of pilgrimage. His feast day is 25 July.

James the Just, Saint (d. *c.*AD 62) According to tradition, the first bishop of the Christian church in Jerusalem; referred to in the Gospels as a "brother" of JESUS CHRIST. In Roman Catholicism, James is identified with St **James the Less**, who witnessed Christ's crucifixion. The Epistle of St JAMES is attributed to him. He was condemned to death by the SANHEDRIN. His feast day is 3 May.

James I (1566–1625) King of England (1603–25) and, as James VI, king of Scotland (1567–1625). Son of MARY, QUEEN OF SCOTS, and Lord DARNLEY, he acceded to the Scottish throne as an infant on his mother's abdication. In 1589, James married Anne of Denmark. In 1603 he inherited the English throne on the death of ELIZABETH I, and thereafter confined his attention to England. James supported the Anglican Church, at the cost of antagonizing the PURITANS, and sponsored the publication (1611) of the Authorized, or King James, Version of the BIBLE. The GUNPOWDER PLOT (1605) was foiled and James cracked down heavily on Catholics. In 1607, the first English colony in America (Jamestown) was founded. James' insistence on the divine right of kings brought conflict with Parliament. In 1611, he dissolved Parliament, and (excluding the 1614 Addled Parliament) ruled without one until 1621. The death (1612) of Robert CECIL saw James' increasingly dependent on corrupt favourites such as Robert Carr and George

Villiers, 1st Duke of BUCKINGHAM. He was succeeded by his son, CHARLES I. *See also* JACOBEAN

James II (1633–1701) King of England (1685–88), second son of CHARLES I. After the second English CIVIL WAR (1648) James escaped to Holland. In 1659, he married Anne Hyde, daughter of the Earl of CLARENDON, and the couple had two daughters (later Queens MARY II and ANNE). At the RESTORATION (1660) of his brother CHARLES II, James was appointed lord high admiral. In 1669, he converted to Roman Catholicism and was forced to resign his offices. On his accession, James was confronted by the Duke of MONMOUTH's Rebellion (1685). His pro-Catholic policies and the birth of a son (James Edward STUART) to his second wife, Mary of Moderna, provoked the GLORIOUS REVOLUTION (1688–89). Mary and her husband, WILLIAM OF ORANGE, assumed the crown and James fled to France. With French aid, he invaded Ireland but was defeated by William at the Battle of the BOYNE (1690). *See also* JACOBITES

James I (1394–1437) King of Scotland (1406–37). His father, Robert III, sent him to France for safety, but he was intercepted by the English (1406). He was not ransomed until 1424. James then restored royal authority by ruthless methods. He carried out reforms of the financial and judicial systems and encouraged trade. His campaign against the nobility made him many enemies, and he was assassinated at Perth.

James II (1430–60) King of Scotland (1437–60). Succeeding his father, JAMES I, at the age of six, his minority was dominated by aristocratic factions, particularly the Douglases. In 1452, he killed the earl of Douglas and seized control. During the English Wars of the ROSES, James supported the Lancastrians against the Yorkists, who were allied with the Douglases, and was killed by an exploding cannon at Roxburgh.

James III (1451–88) King of Scotland (1460–88), son and successor of JAMES II. James was challenged by his brother Albany, whom EDWARD IV of England recognized as king in 1482. Peace was arranged, but a new rebellion resulted in James' defeat and murder.

James IV (1473–1513) King of Scotland (1488–1513), son and successor of JAMES III. He captured and killed the nobles responsible for his father's death. James defended royal authority against the nobility and the church, and endeavoured to promote peace with England, marrying HENRY VIII's sister, Margaret Tudor. Henry's attack on Scotland's old ally, France, drew him into war (1513), and he was killed at Flodden.

James V (1512–42) King of Scotland (1513–42), son and successor of JAMES IV. In 1538, James married Mary of Guise as a safeguard against his aggressive uncle, HENRY VIII. Failure to gain the support of the nobility contributed to the defeat of his forces by the English at Solway Moss (1542). He was succeeded by his daughter, MARY, QUEEN OF SCOTS.

James Edward Stuart *See* STUART, JAMES EDWARD

James, C.L.R. (Cyril Lionel Robert) (1901–89) Trinidadian historian and political theorist. In 1933, he emigrated to England. James wrote a history of TOUSSAINT L'OUVERTURE's Haitian revolution, *The Black Jacobins* (1938). He is best known for *Beyond a Boundary* (1963), a unique combination of cricketing and social history.

James, Henry (1843–1916) US novelist, short-story writer and critic, brother of William JAMES. In 1876, he settled in England and became a British subject in 1915. James' early masterpiece, *The Portrait of a Lady* (1881), features a recurrent theme – the conflict between the values of American and European society. The novels of his middle period, such as *The Bostonians* (1886), deal with American politics. James' last novels, *The Wings of the Dove* (1902), *The Ambassadors* (1903) and *The Golden Bowl* (1904), show his mastery of the psychological novel. His shorter fiction includes *The Turn of the Screw* (1898).

James, Jesse Woodson (1847–82) US outlaw. With his brother, Frank, he fought for the Confederacy during the US Civil War. In 1867, they formed an outlaw band and terrorized the frontier, robbing banks and trains in Missouri and neighbouring states. He was shot dead by Robert Ford, a member of his own gang, for a large reward.

James, P.D. (Phyllis Dorothy), Baroness (1920–) English novelist. She brought greater realism to the genre of DETECTIVE FICTION. The poet-detective Adam Dalgleish features in novels such as *Death of an Expert Witness* (1977) and *A Taste for Death* (1986). Her other leading character is the private detective Cordelia Gray, heroine of *An Unsuitable for a Woman* (1972) and *Skull Beneath the Skin* (1982).

James, William (1842–1910) US philosopher and psychologist, elder brother of Henry JAMES. He held that the feeling of emotion is based on the sensation of a state of the body; the bodily state comes first and the emotion follows. As a philosopher, James influenced PRAGMATISM. His most famous works are *The Principles of Psychology* (1890) and *Varieties of Religious Experience* (1902).

James, Epistle of St Letter of the New Testament, traditionally attributed to St JAMES the Less, "brother" of JESUS CHRIST. It exhorts Christians to live righteous lives, warning that profession of Christian faith should not take the place of good works.

Jameson, Sir Leander Starr (1853–1917) South African statesman, b. Scotland. In 1878 he emigrated to South Africa. In 1895, Jameson, supported by Cecil RHODES, led an abortive raid on the Afrikaner republic of Transvaal and was imprisoned. After his release, he served as prime minister (1904–08) of Cape Colony.

Jamestown First successful English settlement in America. It was established in 1607 on the James River, Virginia. On the verge of collapse from disease and starvation, it was saved by Captain John SMITH (1608) and the timely arrival of new supplies and colonists (1610). From 1614, survival was assured thanks to tobacco planting.

Jammu and Kashmir State in NW India, bounded N by Pakistan-controlled KASHMIR, W by Pakistan and E by China. The region is mountainous and the Himalayas tower above the heavily populated valleys of the rivers Indus and Jhelum. The capitals are Srinagar (summer) and Jammu (winter). Industries: rice, animal husbandry, silk, rice and flour milling, tourism. Area: 100,569sq km (38,845sq mi). Pop. (1994 est.) 8,435,000.

Jamshedpur City at the confluence of the rivers Subarnareka and Karkhaiin, Bihar, NE India. Situated close to iron and coal deposits, it was founded (1907) as a steel town by the industrialist Dorabji Tata. It remains the centre of India's iron and steel industry. Pop. (1991) 461,000.

Janáček, Leoš (1854–1928) Moravian composer. He integrated the inflections and rhythms of the Czech language and Moravian folk music into his compositions. His pieces include orchestral works such as *Taras Bulba* (1918) and *Sinfonietta* (1926), choral works such as the *Glagolitic Mass* (1927), and operas including *Jenufa* (1904), *Kátya Kabanová* (1921), *The Cunning Little Vixen* (1924) and *The Makropoulos Affair* (1926).

Janissaries Elite corps of the Ottoman army, founded in the 14th century. The Janissaries were a highly effective fighting force until the 17th century, when

discipline and military prestige declined. They were abolished by MAHMUD II in 1826.

Jansen, Cornelis Otto (1585–1638) Dutch Roman Catholic theologian and founder of JANSENISM. His four-volume work, *Augustinus* (1640), argued that the teachings of St AUGUSTINE on grace and salvation were contrary to the precepts of the JESUITS. It was condemned by Pope Urban VIII in 1642.

Jansenism Theological school that grew up in the Roman Catholic Church in the 17th and 18th centuries. It was named after Cornelis JANSEN, but the movement was strongest in France. The Jansenists believed that man is incapable of carrying out the commandments of God without divine "grace", which is bestowed only on a favoured few. French Jansenists, such as Blaise PASCAL, incurred the hostility of the JESUITS and of the French crown, and they were condemned by the pope in 1713.

Jansky, Karl (1905–50) US engineer. In 1931, he discovered unidentifiable radio signals from space. Jansky concluded that they were stellar in origin and that the source lay in the direction of Sagittarius. His discovery is considered to be the beginning of RADIO ASTRONOMY. The unit measuring radio emission is named after him.

Janus Roman god of thresholds and beginnings. He was usually depicted with two faces, one looking forwards and the other looking backwards. The month of January is named after him.

Japan Archipelago state in E Asia. Its four largest islands are (in decreasing order of size) HONSHU, HOKKAIDO, KYUSHU and SHIKOKU. These constitute 98% of the total land area and enclose the Inland Sea (Sea of Japan). Japan has thousands of other small islands, including the RYUKYU ISLANDS. OKINAWA forms part of the Ryukyu archipelago. The four main islands are mostly mountainous. The highest peak is the sacred FUJIYAMA, at 3,776m (12,389ft). Japan has more than 150 volcanoes, *c*.60 of which are active. Many of the small islands are the tips of volcanoes. Volcanic eruptions, earthquakes and tsunami occur frequently. Around the coast are small, densely populated, fertile plains covered by alluvium deposited by the short rivers that rise in the mountains. The Kanto plain stretches from the S coast of Honshu to N Kyushu, and is Japan's industrial heartland. The plain includes the capital and world's sixth largest city, TOKYO. If YOKOHAMA is included, this is the world's most densely populated area. Other major cities in the region include NAGOYA, KYOTO, OSAKA, KOBE and FUKUOKA. **Climate** The climate of Japan varies greatly from cool temperate in the N to subtropical in the S. SAPPORO on Hokkaido has cold, snowy winters with temperatures below −20°C (4°F). Summer temperatures sometimes exceed 30°C (86°F). Tokyo has higher rainfall and temperatures. **Vegetation** Forests and woodland cover *c*.66% of the land. The N forests include fir and spruce. Central Japan has mixed forests of beech, maple and oak. Deciduous trees dominate in the S. The cherry tree is found throughout Japan. **History and politics** Most Japanese people are descendants of migrants from mainland Asia. One of the earliest groups are the AINU, *c*.15,000 of whom still live on Hokkaido. According to legend, Japan's first emperor, Jimmu, ascended the throne in 660 BC. The native religion was SHINTO. The

---

JAPAN
AREA: 377,800sq km (145,869sq mi)
POPULATION: 128,470,000
CAPITAL (POPULATION): Tokyo (7,894,000)

Yamato established the Japanese state in the 5th century and made Kyoto the imperial capital. In the 6th century, BUDDHISM was introduced. CONFUCIANISM was part of the profound cultural influence that China has had on JAPANESE ART AND ARCHITECTURE and JAPANESE LITERATURE. In the 12th century, civil war gave way to the power of the SHOGUN, who ruled in the emperor's name. For the next 700 years Japan was ruled by these warrior-kings. European contact began when Portuguese sailors reached Japan in 1543. Following unsuccessful invasions of Korea and China, the TOKUGAWA shogunate (1603–1867) unified Japan and established their capital at Edo (Tokyo). Through the codes of BUSHIDO, the Tokugawa ensured total loyalty. Japan pursued an isolationist path. In 1854 Matthew C. PERRY forced the Tokugawa shogunate to open its ports to Western trade. Western powers plotted the overthrow of the shogunate and the re-establishment of imperial power (MEIJI RESTORATION, 1868). The Emperor MEIJI's reign (1868–1912) was characterized by social and economic modernization, headed by the ZAIBATSU. Japanese nationalism created the desire for empire-building. The first of the SINO-JAPANESE WARS (1894–95) saw Japan acquire Formosa (Taiwan). Japan's decisive victory in the RUSSO-JAPANESE WAR (1904–05) marked its emergence as the dominant power in the region. In 1910, Japan annexed Korea. During the 1920s Japan concentrated on building its economy, interrupted only by an earthquake (1923) that claimed 143,000 lives and devastated Tokyo and Yokohama. Militarists began to dominate Japanese politics. In 1930, Japan invaded MANCHURIA and set up the puppet state of MANCHUKUO. In 1937, Japan invaded China and precipitated the second Sino-Japanese War. At the start of WORLD WAR 2, Japan signed a pact with Germany and Italy. In 1941, Japan launched an attack on the US naval base at PEARL HARBOR. Japan conquered a huge swathe of Pacific territory, but gradually the Allies regained ground. In 1945, the USA dropped atom bombs on the cities of HIROSHIMA and NAGASAKI and forced Japan's unconditional surrender (14 August 1945). The US occupation (1945–52) of Japan under Douglas MACARTHUR undertook the demilitarization of industry and the adoption of a democratic constitution. Emperor HIROHITO declaimed his divinity and became a constitutional monarch. In 1951, Japan concluded a security treaty with the USA that allowed US bases to be stationed on Japan in return for securing its defences. During the 1960s and early 1970s, Japan witnessed popular demonstrations against US interference. In 1972, under the administration of Eisaku SATO, the USA completed the return of the Ryukyu Islands to Japan. In 1989 Hirohito died and was succeeded by his son, AKIHITO. The Liberal Democratic Party (LDP) governed Japan almost continuously from 1948 to 1993. In the early 1990s, Japan was rocked by a series of political corruption scandals. In 1993 the LDP split: the three splinter parties formed a short-lived coalition government. In 1994, a new electoral system was introduced with an element of proportional representation. Tomiichi Murayama became Japan's first socialist prime minister. In 1996, he was replaced by Ryutaro Hashimoto, leader of the LDP. In 1998, the economic crisis in Southeast Asia spread to Japan. The government's slow and inadequate response forced Hashimoto to resign. He was replaced as prime minister by leader of the LDP by Keizo Obuchi. In 2000, Obuchi suffered a stroke and was succeeded by Yoshiro Mori. **Economy** Japan is the world's second largest (1995 GDP per capita, US$22,110) economic power (after the USA). Its success is based on the latest industrial technology, a skilled and committed labour force, vigorous export policies and a comparatively small defence expenditure. But economic success has brought problems: the rapid growth of industrial cities has led to high land prices, housing shortages and pollution. Its ageing workforce also presents problems. In 1997 economic crisis in Southeast Asia badly hit Japan's financial institutions, wiping 25% off the value of the Nikkei Dow. Unemployment rose to its highest level (4.5%) since 1945. The US government agreed a US$2 billion rescue package. Services form the largest sector of Japan's economy. Despite having to import most of its raw materials and fuels, manufacturing is a vital sector of the Japanese economy. Machinery and transport equipment account for more than 70% of exports. Japan is the world's leading automobile, ship and steel producer. It is also the world's second-largest iron and cement producer. Other important manufactures include electrical and electronic equipment, chemicals and textiles. Japan has the second-largest fish catch (after China). Attempts have been made to reduce its whaling. Because Japan is so mountainous, only 15% of land is farmed and it is forced to import 30% of its food. Rice is the chief crop, taking up *c*.50% of total farmland. Other products include fruits, cereals, tea and vegetables. Japan is under increasing pressure to lift its protectionist policies of import restrictions and high tariffs.

Japanese Official language of Japan and the native tongue of more than 120 million people in Japan and the Ryukyu and Bonin islands. Some scholars classify Japanese as a member of the Ural-Altaic family, which also includes Finnish, Hungarian and Turkish. Japanese uses a pitch accent. There are at least four different forms of spoken Japanese, and a modern literary style. Japanese writing uses a combination of some 1850 Chinese characters and tables of syllabic symbols called *kana*.

Japanese art and architecture Earliest surviving examples of **Japanese art** are Jomon pottery figurines (*c*.1000 BC). In the 6th century AD, Chinese influence was strong. LACQUER work, sculpture and ink painting developed during the Nara period (AD 674–794). The later Yamato-e tradition was based on national, rather than Chinese, aesthetic standards. It flowered during the Kamakura military rule (1185–1333). The profound influence of ZEN Buddhism on Japanese art is particularly apparent in the Muromachi period (1333–1573). Many of the best-known

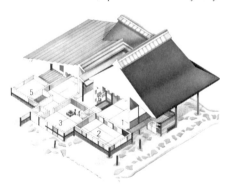

▲ **Japanese architecture**
The Shonkintei garden pavilion at the palace of Katsura in Kyoto (1641) is typical of Japanese architecture. It comprises two large rooms

(1) and (2) divided by *shoji* (translucent screens), a tea room (3), lobby (4) and pantry section (5). The *tokonoma* (6) is an alcove for the display of flowers and objects of art.

examples of Japanese art were produced in the Edo (TOKUGAWA) period (c.1600–1868). The UKIYO-E prints of UTAMARO, HOKUSAI, HIROSHIGE and others date from this period. Modern Japanese artists have made important contributions to 20th-century art and design. **Japanese architecture** derives from Chinese Buddhist structures. The 7th-century Horuji Temple at NARA served as the model for future constructions and includes the world's oldest extant wooden buildings. The Todaji (East Great Temple) also at Nara is the world's largest wooden building. Temples have curved wooden columns, overhanging roofs and thin exterior wood and plaster walls. A gateway, drum tower and PAGODA are also built, usually on a picturesque wooded hillside. Domestic structures are traditionally built with interior wooden posts supporting the roof. The outer walls are movable panels of wood or rice paper that slide in grooves. The interior is flexibly subdivided by screens and decorated with simplicity and delicacy.

Japanese literature One of the world's oldest and richest literary traditions. The earliest extant works are the *Kojiki* (712) and the *Nihongi* (720), which histories written in Chinese characters used phonetically. The earliest recorded Japanese poetry is in the *Manyoshu* (760), which contains poems dating from the 4th century. The **Heian Period** (794–1185) is noted for the *Kokinshu* (905), an anthology of poetry commissioned by the emperor, which provided a pattern for *tanka* (short poems). Classical prose developed during this period, and accounts of court life flourished. The most significant work was Murasaki Shikibu's *Genji Monogatari* (c.1010), the first true novel. During the **Middle Ages** (1185–1603) NO DRAMA was refined. The "war tales" genre appeared in this period, typified by *Heike Monogatari*. In the **Tokugawa Period** (1603–1868), literature, once the preserve of the aristocracy, became the field of the commoners. HAIKU became popular; Matsuo BASHO was the greatest exponent of this poetic form. There were also developments in PUPPET THEATRE and KABUKI THEATRE. In the **Modern Period**, foreign contacts increased and Western literature had a major influence. Poetry flourished, and major figures such as Yosano Akiko (1878–1942), Ishikawa Takuboku (1885–1912) and Hagiwara Sakutaro (1886–1942) found new means of expression. Modern writers such as Yukio MISHIMA and the Nobel prizewinners Yasunari KAWABATA and Kenzoburo Oe have won an international reputation.

Japanese theatre Dramatic forms, including NO DRAMA, PUPPET THEATRE (*bunraku*) and KABUKI THEATRE. Japanese theatre descended from ritual dances, and involves music, song and dance in addition to dialogue. More modern styles of drama, known as *shinpa* and *shingeki* (new theatre), which were influenced by Western theatre, developed out of the desire to portray modern events and ideas in a more realistic style.

Jarman, Derek (1942–94) English film director. A candid and confrontational figure in the vanguard of the "queer film" movement, Jarman developed a style that was politicized, experimental and erotic. His films include *Caravaggio* (1986), *War Requiem* (1989) and *Wittgenstein* (1993). Jarman died of AIDS.

Jarrow March (October 1936) British protest march of unemployed workers from Jarrow, County Durham, to London. Unemployment was especially high in Jarrow, a small, shipbuilding town dependent on one company, which had closed down in 1933. About 200 people took part in the march. *See also* GREAT DEPRESSION

Jarry, Alfred (1873–1907) French playwright, poet and satirist. Jarry is best-known for his avant-garde farce *Ubu Roi* (1896). His work foreshadowed SURREALISM.

Jaruzelski, Wojciech (1923–) Polish general and statesman, prime minister (1981–85), head of state (1985–89) and president (1989–90). In 1981, he imposed martial law and banned the trade union SOLIDARITY, led by Lech WALESA. Jaruzelski was replaced as president by Lech Walesa.

jasmine Any evergreen or deciduous shrub or vine of the genus *Jasminum*, common in the Mediterranean. It has fragrant yellow, pink or white flowers. Its oil is used in perfumes. Height: to 6.5m (20ft). Family Oleaceae.

Jason In Greek mythology, hero and leader of the ARGONAUTS. Sent on a quest for the GOLDEN FLEECE, Jason sailed aboard the *Argo*. After surviving many perils, he found the fleece in Colchis and stole it, with the help of the sorceress MEDEA, whom he married.

Jaspers, Karl (1883–1969) German philosopher and psychopathologist. His major work, *Philosophy* (1932), presents an interpretation of EXISTENTIALISM. Jaspers argued that the deepest insights into human nature are revealed in "limit situations", such as death. Other works include *Truth and Symbol* (1947) and *Philosophical Faith and Revelation* (1962).

Jatakas (birth stories) Buddhist writings that drew moral conclusions from stories of the BUDDHA in a previous existence. The main character usually appears as an animal whose present circumstances are the result of past acts.

jaundice Yellowing of the skin and the whites of the eyes, caused by excess of BILE pigment in the blood. Mild jaundice is common in newborn babies. In adults jaundice may occur when the flow of bile to the intestine is blocked by an obstruction such as a GALLSTONE, or in diseases such as CIRRHOSIS, HEPATITIS or ANAEMIA.

Jaurès, Jean Léon (1859–1914) French socialist leader. He campaigned on behalf of Alfred Dreyfus in the DREYFUS AFFAIR. In 1905, Jaurès formed the United Socialist Party from various socialist groupings in France. In 1914, he founded the journal *L'Humanité*. Jaurès was assassinated by a nationalist fanatic for advocating arbitration rather than war with Germany.

Java (Jawa) Indonesian island, between the Java Sea and the Indian Ocean, SE of Sumatra; the largest city is JAKARTA. In the early centuries AD, the island was ruled by Hindu kingdoms. Islam began to spread in the 16th century. By the 18th century, the island was mainly under Dutch control. It was occupied by the Japanese during World War 2. Java is a mountainous country, with a volcanic belt in the S and an alluvial plain to the N. It is thickly forested and has many rivers. It produces rice, tea, coffee, sugar cane, textiles, tobacco and rubber. Silver, gold and phosphate are mined in the N. Area: 126,501sq km (48,842sq mi). Pop. (1990) 107,581,306.

javelin Lightweight, tapered, tubular spear thrown in a field event: the longest throw wins, provided the javelin lands point-first. The modern javelin is made of a metal alloy, is up to 2.7m (8.9ft) long, and weighs a minimum of 800g (28.2oz) for men and 600g (21oz) for women.

Jay, John (1745–1829) US statesman, first chief justice of the Supreme Court (1789–95). Jay was president of the CONTINENTAL CONGRESS (1778–79) and negotiated the peace treaty with Great Britain. He was secretary of foreign affairs (1784–89) and contributed to *The Federalist* (1787–88). In 1794, he concluded JAY'S TREATY. *See also* FEDERALIST PARTY

jay Any of 37 species of harsh-voiced birds of the CROW family. Jays often have blue wing markings. Many are crested, including the Eurasian jay *Garrulus glandarius*. Length: c.34cm (13in). Family Corvidae.

Jay's Treaty (1794) Agreement between the USA (represented by John JAY) and Britain (represented by Lord Grenville) principally to settle points of dispute outstanding since the American Revolution. Its trade provisions helped establish American commerce. The USA agreed not to aid privateers hostile to Britain, and Britain withdrew from the Northwest Territory.

jazz Style of music that developed in the S states of the USA in the late 19th century. It evolved from Negro spirituals and African slave songs. It is traditionally characterized by a syncopated rhythm drawn from RAGTIME; prominence of melody, often with elements derived from the BLUES; and improvisation. The form was taken up by white musicians as DIXIELAND music. Early practitioners included Buddy Bolden, "Jelly Roll" MORTON, King Oliver and Bix BEIDERBECKE. Louis ARMSTRONG's trumpet-playing developed the role of the soloist. By the end of the 1920s, jazz had spread to other US cities and influenced European classical composers, such as Ravel and Stravinsky. In the late 1920s, SWING developed in in Kansas City and Harlem. The role of improvisation diminished in favour of big-band orchestration. Major jazz composers and bandleaders emerged, such as Duke ELLINGTON, Count BASIE, Benny GOODMAN and Glenn MILLER. The big bands nurtured the talents of Billie HOLIDAY, Coleman HAWKINS and Lester YOUNG. In the 1930s, "Django" REINHARDT fused European folk music with swing. In the 1940s, Charlie PARKER and Dizzy GILLESPIE led the BEBOP revolution in New York City, characterized by the use of the flatted fifth, complex rhythms and harmonic rather than melodic progression. Other leading players included Bud POWELL and Theolonius MONK. In the late 1940s, Miles DAVIS and Stan GETZ pioneered "cool" jazz. In the 1950s, Davis and John COLTRANE introduced MODES as the basis for improvisation. Charles MINGUS returned to the bluesy roots of jazz. In the 1960s, avant-garde or free jazz introduced atonality, polyharmonies and polyrhythms. In the 1970s, Miles Davis led experiments with a fusion of jazz and other popular forms, such as funk. In the 1980s and 1990s, musicians such as Wynton MARSALIS reflected on the historical progression of jazz.

Jeans, Sir James Hopwood (1877–1946) English astrophysicist and astronomer. He investigated stellar dynamics and proposed the tidal theory of planetary origin, in which the matter of the planets was drawn out of the Sun by the attraction of a passing star. Jeans popularized the science of astronomy in works such as *The Universe Around Us* (1929).

Jedda *See* JIDDAH

Jefferies, (John) Richard (1848–87) English novelist. He is celebrated for his detailed, unsentimental descriptions of rural England in autobiographical works such as *Bevis* (1882) and *The Story of My Heart* (1883).

Jefferson, Thomas (1743–1826) Third US president (1801–09), vice president (1797–81). Jefferson was a leading member of the CONTINENTAL CONGRESS and the primary author of the DECLARATION OF INDEPENDENCE (1776). His governorship of Virginia (1779–81) was ended by the AMERICAN REVOLUTION. Jefferson returned to Congress (1783–84) before succeeding Benjamin FRANKLIN as minister to France (1785–89). He was persuaded by George WASHINGTON to serve as his first secretary of state (1789–93). Disagreements with Alexander HAMILTON saw the formation of the precursor of the DEMOCRATIC PARTY. Narrowly defeated by John ADAMS in the 1796 presidential election, Jefferson became vice president. He led opposition to the ALIEN AND SEDITION ACTS (1798). The landmarks of his first administration

(1801–05) were the LOUISIANA PURCHASE (1803) and the LEWIS AND CLARK EXPEDITION (1804–06). His second term (1805–09) overcame the Aaron BURR conspiracy. He managed to avoid war with Britain, instead passing an EMBARGO ACT (1807). He was a slave owner, although in principle opposed to slavery.

Jefferson City State capital of Missouri, USA, on the Missouri River. It was chosen as state capital in 1821. The Capitol building (1911–18) was built in the Italian Renaissance style. Industries: shoes, clothes, electrical appliances, bookbinding. Pop. (1990) 35,480.

Jeffreys, George, 1st Baron (1648–89) English judge. He became lord chief justice in 1683 and lord chancellor in 1685. He presided over the BLOODY ASSIZES for JAMES II. After the GLORIOUS REVOLUTION (1688), he was caught trying to flee the country and was imprisoned in the Tower of London, where he died. *See also* MONMOUTH, JAMES SCOTT, DUKE OF

Jehovah Latinized form of YAHWEH

Jehovah's Witnesses Religious sect founded in the 1870s by Charles Taze Russell (1852–1916) of Pittsburgh, Pennsylvania, USA. In 1884 they published the first edition of the magazine *The Watchtower*. The sect believes in the imminent end of the world for all except its own members. They hold to the theory of a theocratic kingdom (a kingdom ruled by God), membership in which cannot be reconciled with allegiance to any country. They deny most fundamental Christian doctrines and believe the Bible prohibits blood transfusion and military service. Today, the sect has *c*.2 million members worldwide.

Jellicoe, John Rushworth, 1st Earl (1859–1935) British admiral. He was commander-in-chief (1914–16) of the Grand Fleet in World War 1. Jellicoe was criticized for the stalemate at the Battle of JUTLAND (1916). He organized the convoy system of defence against U-boats. He served (1920–24) as governor-general of New Zealand.

jellyfish Marine COELENTERATE found in coastal waters and characterized by tentacles with stinging cells. The adult form is the **medusa**. It has a bell-shaped body with a thick layer of jelly-like substance between two body cell layers, many tentacles and four mouth lobes surrounding the gut opening. Jellyfish propel theselves by contracting muscles and expelling water from the mouth. Diameter: 7.5–30.5cm (3–12in). Class Scyphozoa. *See also* POLYP

Jenkins (of Hillhead), Roy Harris, Baron (1920–) British statesman, home secretary (1965–67) and chancellor of the exchequer (1967–70). He was elected to Parliament in 1958. Jenkins served in Harold WILSON's Labour government. He acted as president (1977–81) of the European Commission. In 1981, Jenkins co-founded and became first leader of the SOCIAL DEMOCRATIC PARTY (SDP). In 1983, he stood down in favour of David OWEN. In 1998, Jenkins headed the commission that recommended the introduction of PROPORTIONAL REPRESENTATION (PR) in British elections. His historical biographies include *Mr Attlee* (1948) and *Gladstone* (1995).

Jenkins' Ear, War of (1738–41) Conflict between Britain and Spain that arose from commercial competition in South America. In 1738, Captain Robert Jenkins claimed his ear had been cut off by Spanish coastguards. Sir Robert WALPOLE reluctantly declared war on Spain. The war merged into the War of the AUSTRIAN SUCCESSION.

Jenner, Edward (1749–1823) English physician who pioneered VACCINATION. In 1796, aware that cowpox (a minor disease) seemed to protect people from SMALLPOX, Jenner inoculated a healthy boy with cowpox from the sores of an infected dairymaid. The boy was later found to be immune to smallpox.

jerboa (desert rat) Nocturnal, herbivorous, burrowing RODENT of Eurasian and African deserts, with long hind legs . It has a satiny, sand-coloured body and a long tail. Length: to 15cm (6in), excluding tail. Family Dipodidae.

Jeremiah (c.650–c.586 BC) Hebrew prophet who gave his name to the Old Testament Book of Jeremiah. He spoke out against social injustices in Jerusalem during the reign of Josiah, prophesising the fall of Judah to Babylon. In 586 BC NEBUCHADNEZZAR captured Judah. Jeremiah remained in the city and was later exiled in Egypt. His revelations were preserved by his secretary BARUCH.

Jerez de la Frontera Picturesque town close to the Portuguese border, Cadiz province, Andalusia, S Spain. Jerez is the centre of the sherry-making industry and lends its name to the wine. Pop. (1995) 191,000.

Jericho Ancient city of Palestine, on the WEST BANK of the River Jordan, N of the Dead Sea. It is one of the earliest known sites of continuous settlement, dating from c.9000 BC. According to the Old Testament, Joshua captured Jericho from the Canaanites (c.300 BC) when the city walls collapsed at the blast of the army's trumpets. HEROD THE GREAT sacked Jericho and built a new city to the s. In 1993, the city was selected as the centre for Palestinian self-rule. It lies in an agricultural area, producing citrus fruit and dates. Pop. (1994 est.) 25,000.

Jeroboam Name of two kings of Israel (N Palestine). **Jeroboam I** (active late 10th century BC) led an unsuccessful revolt against King SOLOMON and was forced to flee to Egypt. After Solomon's death he returned to lead the secessionist kingdom of Israel in Palestine's N hills. **Jeroboam II**'s reign (c.783–c.741 BC) brought peace and economic progress, but corruption was widespread.

Jerome, Saint (c.AD 342–420) Doctor of the Church and author of the VULGATE Bible, b. Dalmatia as Eusebius Hieronymous. He studied in Rome before travelling to Antioch. Jerome lived as a hermit in the desert before returning to Rome. He acted as papal secretary (382–85) to Pope Damasus I (r.366–94). In 386, Jerome settled in Jerusalem, where he founded a monastery and compiled the Latin version of the Bible. Feast Day: 30 September.

Jerome, Jerome K. (Klapka) (1859–1927) English humourist, novelist and dramatist. His most successful works include the play *The Passing of the Third Floor Back* (1907) and the novel *Three Men in a Boat* (1889).

Jersey Largest of the CHANNEL ISLANDS, lying c.16km (10 mi) off the NW coast of Normandy in France. Fruit and dairy farming are important. The capital is St Helier. Area: 117sq km (45sq mi). Pop. (1991) 84,082.

Jerusalem Capital of Israel, a sacred site for Christians, Jews and Muslims. Originally a Jebusite stronghold (2000–1500 BC), the city was captured by King DAVID after 1000 BC. Destroyed by NEBUCHADNEZZAR (c.587 BC), Jerusalem was rebuilt (c.35 BC) by HEROD THE GREAT, but was again destroyed (AD 70) by TITUS. The Roman colony of Aelia Capitolina was established, and Jews were forbidden within city limits until the 5th century. In 614, Christian control was ended by the Persians. In 1071, Jerusalem was conquered by the SELJUKS, whose maltreatment of Christians precipitated the CRUSADES. It was held by the OTTOMAN Turks from 1244 to 1917 before becoming the capital of the British-mandated territory of Palestine. In 1948, it was divided between Jordan (the east) and Israel (the west). In 1967, the Israeli army captured the old city of East Jerusalem. In 1980, the united city was declared the capital of Israel, although this status is not recognized by the UN. Notable monuments within the old city include the DOME OF THE ROCK, the El Aqsa Mosque and the WESTERN WALL. Jerusalem is an administrative and cultural centre, with banking, insurance and public service employment. The main industries are tourism and diamond cutting. Pop. (1997) 591,000.

Jesuits Members of the Society of Jesus, a Roman Catholic religious order for men founded (1540) by St IGNATIUS OF LOYOLA and Francis XAVIER. The Jesuits were the leading force in the COUNTER-REFORMATION. They were active missionaries, but antagonized many European rulers because they gave allegiance only to their general in Rome and to the pope. In 1773, under pressure from the kings of France, Spain and Portugal, Pope Clement XIV abolished the order, but it continued to exist in Russia. The order was re-established in 1814.

Jesus Christ (active 1st century AD) Hebrew preacher who founded the religion of CHRISTIANITY, hailed and worshipped by his followers as the Son of God. Knowledge of Jesus' life is based mostly on the biblical gospels of St MATTHEW, St MARK and St LUKE. The date of Jesus' birth in Bethlehem, Judaea, is conventionally given as c.4 BC, near the end of the reign of HEROD THE GREAT. MARY, believed by Christians to have been made pregnant by God, gave birth to Jesus. The birth was said to have taken place in a stable and been attended by the appearance of a bright star and other unusual events. Jesus grew up in Nazareth and may have followed his father, JOSEPH, in becoming a carpenter. In c.AD 27, Jesus was baptized in the River Jordan by JOHN THE BAPTIST. Thereafter Jesus began his own ministry, preaching to large numbers as he wandered throughout the country. He also taught a special group of 12 of his closest disciples, who were later sent out as his APOSTLES to bring his teachings to the Jews. Jesus' basic teaching, summarized in the SERMON ON THE MOUNT, was to "love God and love one's neighbour". He also taught that salvation depended on doing God's will rather than adhering to the letter and the contemporary interpretation of the TORAH. Such a precept angered the

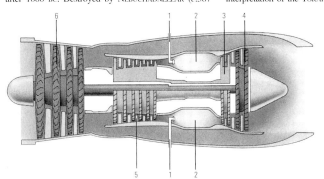

◀ **jet engine** A turbofan engine is used on civil jet aircraft. Fuel entering the engine (1) mixes with compressed air and burns in the combustion chamber (2). The expanding gases rotate high-speed (3) and low-speed (4) turbines. These, in turn, drive a compressor (5), which forces air into the combustion chamber. Fans (6) push air round the chamber and into the tail pipe, providing thrust by means of displacement.

hierarchy of the Jewish religion. In c.AD 30, Jesus and his disciples went to Jerusalem. His reputation as preacher and miracle-worker preceded him, and he was acclaimed as the MESSIAH. A few days later Jesus gathered his disciples to partake in the LAST SUPPER. At this meal, he instituted the EUCHARIST. Before dawn the next day, Jesus was arrested by agents of the Hebrew authorities, accompanied by JUDAS ISCARIOT, and summarily tried by the SANHEDRIN, the Supreme Council of the Jews. He was then handed to the Roman procurator, PONTIUS PILATE, on a charge of sedition. Roman soldiers crucified Jesus at Golgotha (Calvary). After his death, Jesus' body was buried in a sealed rock tomb. Two days later, according to the gospel accounts, he rose from the dead and appeared to his disciples and to others. Forty days after his resurrection, he is said to have ascended into heaven. *See also* TRINITY

jet engine Form of GAS TURBINE engine that derives forward motion by reaction to the rapid discharge of a jet of gas in the opposite direction. In a jet engine, fuel burns in oxygen from the air to produce a fast-moving stream of exhaust gases. These are ejected from the back of the jet engine and produce forward THRUST in accordance with NEWTON'S LAWS of MOTION. The jet engine was patented in 1930 by Frank WHITTLE. In 1939, the He-178, designed by Ernst Heinrich HEINKEL, became the first jet aeroplane to fly. Early commercial aircraft used **turboprop** engines, in which a PROPELLER is driven by the turbine shaft. The **turbojet** engine provides greater efficiency at speeds above 800km/h (500mph). The turbine drives one or more compressors but the remaining energy in the gas provides jet propulsion. The turbofan engine incorporates a large fan that compresses air outside the engine to provide greater acceleration. *See also* ROCKET *See artwork* p445

Jet Propulsion Laboratory (JPL) Space centre in Pasadena, California, USA, for the development and control of unmanned spacecraft. The California Institute of Technology runs JPL for the NATIONAL AERONAUTICS AND SPACE ADMINISTRATION (NASA). JPL scientists sent the Surveyor probes to the Moon in the 1960s. Other notable achievements include the MARINER PROGRAM, the VIKING SPACE MISSION and the VOYAGER PROGRAM.

jet stream Narrow, swiftly moving band of wind between slower currents at altitudes of 10–16km (6–10mi) in the upper troposphere or lower stratosphere, principally in the zone of prevailing westerlies. The jet stream can blow at speeds of up to 370km/h (230mph).

Jews Traditionally, the descendants of JUDAH, fourth son of JACOB, who settled in ancient Palestine towards the end of the 2nd millennium BC; historically, followers of the religion of JUDAISM. In c.1020 BC, SAUL founded the HEBREW state of ISRAEL. DAVID united the kingdoms of Judaea and Israel. His son, Solomon, built the TEMPLE in JERUSALEM. In 587 BC, the Temple was destroyed by NEBUCHADNEZZAR and Jews were deported from Jerusalem, beginning the period of the BABYLONIAN CAPTIVITY. In 538 BC, CYRUS THE GREAT delivered the Jews from Babylon. In the 2nd century BC, the MACCABEE dynasty gained political independence from the Greeks. In AD 70, the Temple was destroyed for a second time by the Romans and the DIASPORA began. The descendants of Jews who emigrated to Spain and Portugal are known as the SEPHARDIM; those who settled in NW Europe are known as the ASHKENAZIM. In Christian Europe Jews were victims of ANTI-SEMITISM. They were forced into GHETTOS and given menial occupations such as USURY. In 1290, Jews were driven out of England. In 1492, they were expelled from Spain. During World War 2 (1939–45), six million Jews were killed in the HOLOCAUST. In 1948, having

struggled against British rule in modern Palestine, the modern state of ISRAEL was proclaimed, despite opposition from Arab and other Islamic states. Today, there are c.17.5 million Jews worldwide, including c.7 million in the USA and c.5 million in Israel. *See also* FALASHAS; SEMITIC LANGUAGES; YIDDISH; ZIONISM

Jezebel (d. c.843 BC) Phoenician princess who became the wife of AHAB, king of Israel. She introduced into Israel the worship of the Phoenician deity BAAL and came into conflict with the priests of YAHWEH. Jezebel clashed most severely with the prophet ELIJAH, who foretold her brutal death. She was crushed under the chariot of the usurper, Jehu.

Jiang Qing (1914–92) Chinese politician, third wife of MAO ZEDONG. A former actress, she became a high-ranking party official and the leader of the CULTURAL REVOLUTION. One of the radical GANG OF FOUR that sought power after Mao's death in 1976, Jiang was arrested the following year, convicted of treason and imprisoned for life.

Jiangsu (Kiangsu) Province in E China; the capital is NANKING. Under the rule of the Ming dynasty from 1368 to 1644, it became a separate province in the 18th century. Taken by Japan in 1937, the province was freed by Chinese nationalists in 1945 and fell to the Chinese communists in 1949. One of China's smallest and most densely populated provinces, it is an extremely fertile region that includes the YANGTZE delta. It is highly industrialized: SHANGHAI, the largest city, is the chief manufacturing centre of China. Products: rice, cotton, wheat, barley, soya beans, peanuts, tea. Industries: silk, oil refining, textiles, food processing, cement. Area: 102,240sq km (39,474sq mi). Pop. (1990) 68,170,000.

Jiangxi (Kiangsi) Province in SE China; the capital is Nan-ch'ang. Originally known as Kan under the Zhou dynasty (770–435 BC), the region was ruled by the dynasties of W QIN, S SUNG and T'ANG, until it came under the QING dynasty (1644–1911). It has a mountainous terrain and fertile areas drained by the River Kan. Products: rice, wheat, beans, citrus fruits, tobacco, sugar cane, cotton. Industries: textiles, paper, fishing, porcelain, farm machinery, fertilizers, petrochemicals, tungsten, coal and tin mining. Area: 164,865sq km (63,654sq mi). Pop. (1990) 38,280,000.

Jiang Zemin (1926–) Chinese statesman, general secretary of the Chinese Communist Party (1989–). A cautious proponent of reform, he was elected to the central committee in 1982 and served as mayor of Shanghai (1985–88). Jiang succeeded ZHAO ZIYANG as general secretary. In 1997, he succeeded DENG XIAOPING as China's paramount leader.

Jiddah (Jedda) Administrative capital and largest port of Saudi Arabia, on the Red Sea, c.75km (50mi) w of Mecca. Under Turkish rule until 1916, it was taken in 1925 by IBN SAUD. It acts as a port of entry for the HAJJ. Oil wealth has also expanded the city and port. Industries: steel rolling, oil refining, cement, pottery. Pop. (1991) 1,500,000.

jihad (jehad) Religious obligation imposed upon Muslims through the KORAN to spread ISLAM and protect its followers by waging war on non-believers. There are four ways in which Muslims may fulfil their jihad duty: by the heart, by the tongue, by the hand and by the sword.

Jim Crow laws Laws enacted in S US states after RECONSTRUCTION, enforcing racial segregation in public places and on public transport. They were overturned by the CIVIL RIGHTS legislation of the 1950s and 1960s.

Jinnah, Muhammad Ali (1876–1948) Indian statesman, founder of PAKISTAN. A British-trained lawyer, he joined the Indian National Congress in 1906 but left it in

1920 when his demand for a separate Muslim electorate was rejected. Jinnah led the MUSLIM LEAGUE in campaigning for political equality for Indian Muslims, while continuing to seek agreement with Hindus. By 1940 he had adopted the aim of a separate Muslim state. This was realized when India was partitioned in 1947.

Joan of Arc, Saint (*c.*1412–31) (Jeanne d'Arc) French saint and national heroine, also known as Joan of Lorraine or the Maid of Orléans. A peasant girl, she claimed to hear heavenly voices urging her to save France during the HUNDRED YEARS WAR. In 1429, Joan of Arc led French troops in breaking the English siege of Orléans. She drove the English from the Loire towns and persuaded the indecisive dauphin to have himself crowned as CHARLES VII of France at Reims. In 1430, Joan of Arc was captured and handed over to the English. Condemned as a heretic, she was burned at the stake. Joan of Arc was canonized in 1920. Feast day: 30 May.

Job Old Testament book describing the crises in the life of Job, a well-to-do man from a town E of Palestine. The main theme is that suffering comes to good and bad people alike. *See also* WISDOM LITERATURE

Jodhpur (Marwar) Walled city on the edge of the Thar Desert, Rajasthan, NW India. Founded in 1459, it was the capital of the former princely state of Jodhpur. It is now an important road and rail junction. Industries: textiles, lacquerware, bicycles. Pop. (1991) 668,000

Jodrell Bank Site of the Nuffield Radio Astronomy Laboratories of the University of Manchester, Cheshire, England. It has one of the world's largest steerable radio telescopes. Diameter: 76m (250ft).

Joffre, Joseph Jacques Césaire (1852–1931) French marshal. He was commander-in-chief (1914–16) of the French armies during World War 1. Determined to take the offensive, Joffre was forced to retreat but recouped his forces, and his reputation, in the first Battle of the MARNE (September 1914). After heavy losses at VERDUN and the SOMME (both 1916), he resigned.

Johannesburg City on the WITWATERSRAND, capital of GAUTENG province, NE South Africa. The largest city in modern South Africa, Johannesburg was founded as a gold-mining town in 1886. In 1900, it was captured by the British in the second of the SOUTH AFRICAN WARS. It developed rapidly as the administrative headquarters for South Africa's gold-mining industry. Today, it is the republic's leading industrial and commercial city. Industries: pharmaceuticals, metal, machinery, textiles, engineering, diamond cutting. Pop. (1991) 1,916,063.

John, Saint (active 1st century AD) (St John the Apostle or St John the Evangelist) In the New Testament, one of the 12 Apostle of JESUS CHRIST, son of Zebedee and brother of St JAMES THE GREATER. He is traditionally held to be the author of the fourth gospel according to Saint JOHN and the three epistles of John. He is also identified with St John the Divine, author of the Book of REVELATION. Together with St James and St PETER, St John belonged to the inner group of disciples. His feast day is 27 December.

John VIII (820–882) Pope (872–882). He served in the Curia for 40 years. As pope, he built fortifications to protect Rome, founded the papal navy and asked Christians to protect Europe against the SARACENS. He crowned Louis II king of France in 878.

John XXII (1245–1334) Pope (1316–34), b. Jacques Duèse. Second of the AVIGNON POPES, in 1323 he condemned the doctrine of absolute poverty, espoused by the FRANCISCANS, as heretical. He remained the final arbiter between Louis of Bavaria and Frederick of Austria in their contest for the HOLY ROMAN EMPIRE.

John XXIII (1370–1419) ANTIPOPE (1410–15), b. Baldassare Cossa. Elected antipope by the Council of Pisa, he convoked the Council of CONSTANCE (1414) to end the GREAT SCHISM. The Council called for his resignation along with the other papal contenders, Gregory XII (Rome) and Benedict XIII (Avignon). He fled but was brought back and forced to resign. He was imprisoned until 1418 when he acknowledged MARTIN V as pope.

John XXIII (1881–1963) Pope (1958–63). b. Angelo Giuseppe Roncalli. He served as a medical chaplain in World War 1 and was subsequently in the papal diplomatic service. Regarded as a compromise choice, John XXIII supported ecumenicalism. He spoke out against social injustice and communism. In 1962, John XXIII convened the Second VATICAN COUNCIL to promote reform and renewal within the Church.

John (1167–1216) King of England (1199–1216), youngest son of HENRY II and ELEANOR OF AQUITAINE. He ruled during RICHARD I's absence on the Third CRUSADE. Disgraced for intriguing against Richard, John nevertheless succeeded him as king. He waged a disastrous war (1204–05) against PHILIP II of France that resulted in the loss of vast territories in France. In 1209, he was excommunicated by Pope INNOCENT III for refusing to accept Stephen Langton as Archbishop of Canterbury. In 1214, his nephew and ally Emperor OTTO IV was defeated by Philip II and John attempted to collect further tax from the nobles to finance war. In 1215, John was compelled by his barons to sign the MAGNA CARTA. His subsequent disregard of the terms led to the first Barons' War (1215–17).

John II (the Good) (1319–64) King of France (1350–64), son of PHILIP VI. In 1356, he was captured by the English at Poitiers in the HUNDRED YEARS WAR and held in captivity in England. John was released on the promise of a large ransom, but when he was unable to provide it, he returned to England, where he died.

John I (1487–1540) (John Zapolya) King of Hungary (1526–40), governor of Transylvania (1511–26). He was crowned king after Louis II was killed by the Ottomans at the Battle of MOHACS (1526). In 1529, with the help of SULEIMAN I (THE MAGNIFICENT), he defeated Emperor Frederick I.

John II (1540–71) (John Sigismund Zapolya) King of Hungary and prince of Transylvania. In 1541, SULEIMAN I (THE MAGNIFICENT) invaded Hungary and placed the government in the hands of George Martinuzzi. Martinuzzi was assassinated by Emperor Ferdinand I.

John II (1609–72) (John Casimir) King of Poland (1648–68), son of SIGISMUND III. His turbulent reign is known in Polish history as the Deluge. In 1651, he defeated the joint forces of the Cossacks, Tatars and Ottomans. In 1654, Russia invaded Poland and John was forced (1667) to cede E UKRAINE. In 1655, CHARLES X of Sweden invaded and gained (1660) N Livonia. In 1657, Frederick William of Brandenburg allied himself with John in return for E Prussia.

John III (1624–96) (John Sobieski) King of Poland (1674–96). In 1673, he won a brilliant victory over the Turks at Khotin. In 1683 he allied himself with Emperor LEOPOLD I and defeated a superior Turkish force to raise the siege of Vienna. John pursued the retreating Ottoman army into Hungary. His failure to gain Moldavia and Wallachia fuelled domestic unrest in Poland.

John I (1357–1433) King of Portugal (1385–1433). After the death of his half-brother, FERDINAND I, he resisted the proposed regency of Ferdinand's daughter, Beatrice of Castile, and was elected king. In 1385, John defeated the Castilians at Ajubarrota. In 1387, he married Philippa, daughter of John of Gaunt. In 1415, John captured Ceuta, Morocco, the first European possession in Africa.

John III (1502–57) King of Portugal (1521–57). John's reign marked the climax of Portuguese expansion, including the colonization of Brazil, but the empire began to decline by its end. In 1536, he introduced the INQUISITION into Portugal and generally favoured clerical, particularly Jesuit, interests.

John IV (1605–56) King of Portugal (1640–56). As duke of Braganza, he was leader of a Portuguese revolt against Spanish rule (1640) and became king. Portuguese independence was confirmed by victory at Montijo (1644).

John VI (1767–1826) King of Portugal (1816–26). Because of the insanity of his mother, Queen Maria, he was effectively sovereign from 1792, officially regent from 1799. In 1807, he fled to Brazil to escape the invading army of NAPOLEON I and did not return to claim the throne until 1822, when he accepted the constitutional government proclaimed in 1820.

John, Augustus Edwin (1878–1961) English painter. He was an opponent of academicism. Although he was influenced by the Old Masters and by POST-IMPRESSIONISM, his high-toned colour and solidity of drawing were unique. His works include *Galway* (1916) and the portraits *Dorelia* and *Bernard Shaw* (c.1914).

John, Sir Elton (1947–) English rock singer and pianist, b. Reginald Kenneth Dwight. John collaborated with lyricist Bernie Taupin (1950–) on albums such as *Goodbye Yellow Brick Road* (1973) and singles "Rocket Man" and "Daniel" (both 1972). In 1997, he sang a revised version of "Candle in the Wind" (1973) at the funeral of Diana, Princess of Wales. He was knighted in 1998.

John, Gospel according to Saint Fourth and last gospel of the New Testament, recounting the life and death of JESUS CHRIST and believed to be the work of the Apostle JOHN. It is more concerned with the spiritual meaning of events than with historical facts or historical sequence.

John, Gwen (1876–1939) English painter. The antithesis of her brother, Augustus JOHN, she created restrained, grey-toned portraits of single figures. Her subtle characterization and tonal relationships are demonstrated in *Self Portrait* (c.1900) and *Portrait of a Nun* (c.1920–30).

John Bull Symbolic representation of the typical Englishman and, by extension, of England itself. The name became popular after the appearance of the *History of John Bull* (1712) by Dr John Arbuthnot.

John Dory *See* DORY

John of Austria, Don (1545–78) Spanish admiral and general, illegitimate son of Emperor CHARLES V. In 1570, he defeated a revolt by the Moors in Grenada. John commanded the Holy League fleet that defeated the Turks at the Battle of LEPANTO (1571). In 1573 he captured Tunis, N Africa. In 1576, John was appointed governor-general of the Netherlands. His lack of diplomacy fuelled conflict.

John of Gaunt (1340–99) English nobleman, Duke of Lancaster (1362–99), fourth son of EDWARD III and father of HENRY IV. In 1359, he acquired the Lancastrian estates through marriage to Blanche. John fought under his brother, EDWARD THE BLACK PRINCE, in the HUNDRED YEARS WAR. His second marriage to Constance, daughter of Peter the Cruel of Castile, gained him a claim to the throne of Castile. He was effective ruler of England during the senility of his father and the minority of RICHARD II. John supported the religious reforms of John WYCLIFFE.

John of the Cross, Saint (1542–91) Spanish mystic and poet, b. Juan de Yepes y Álvarez. With St TERESA OF AVILA he founded the Discalced Carmelites, a branch of the Carmelite order. John's spiritual poems, such as "The

Dark Night of the Soul", are regarded as the pinnacle of Spanish mystical literature. His feast day is 14 December.

John Paul I (1912–78) Pope (1978), b. Albino Luciani. He became the 263rd pope of the Roman Catholic Church. A modest but gregarious man, he was popular despite the brevity of his reign – 34 days.

John Paul II (1920–) Pope (1978–), b. Poland as Karol Wojtyla. He studied literature before being ordained in 1946. He became auxiliary bishop of Kraków (1958), archbishop (1964) and then cardinal (1967). In 1978, he became the first non-Italian pope in 455 years. Theologically conservative, John Paul II upheld papal infallibility and condemned artificial methods of birth control and the ordination of women as priests.

Johns, Jasper (1930–) US painter, sculptor and printmaker. Together with Robert RAUSCHENBERG, he led the movement away from ABSTRACT EXPRESSIONISM towards POP ART and MINIMAL ART. His characteristic style features canvases covered with banal, everyday images, such as *Three Flags* (1958) and *Target With Four Faces* (1955).

Johnson, Amy (1903–41) English pilot, the first woman to fly solo from England to Australia (1930). In 1932 she broke the record held by her husband for a solo flight to the Cape of Good Hope, South Africa. She died in a plane accident while serving as a pilot in the Air Transport Auxiliary during World War 2.

Johnson, Andrew (1808–75) 17th US president (1865–69), vice president (1864–65). He was a Democrat governor (1853–57) and senator (1857–62) for Tennessee. He was the only Southerner to remain in the Senate after the outbreak of the CIVIL WAR. Johnson was elected with the incumbent Republican president Abraham LINCOLN on a National Union ticket and became president when Lincoln was assassinated. His policy of RECONSTRUCTION saw the restoration of civil government to the South. The hostility of the predominantly Republican congress to his support for the southern states led to his impeachment trial in the Senate for "crimes and misdemeanurs". Johnson was acquitted by one vote.

Johnson, Jack (John Arthur) (1878–1946) US boxer. He was the first African-American to win the world heavyweight title, defeating Tommy Burns (1908). In 1915 Johnson lost the title to Jess Willard.

Johnson, Lyndon Baines (1908–73) 36th US president (1963–69), vice president (1960–63). He represented Texas as a Democrat in the House of Representatives (1937–48) and the Senate (1948–60). Johnson served as vice president to John F. KENNEDY and became president after Kennedy's assassination (1963). He showed considerable skill in securing passage of the CIVIL RIGHTS ACT (1964) and was overwhelmingly re-elected in 1964. Johnson carried out an ambitious domestic reform programme, but its success was overshadowed by the escalation of the VIETNAM WAR, which, together with severe race riots between 1965 and 1968, dissuaded him from seeking re-election in 1968. He was succeeded as president by Richard NIXON.

Johnson, "Magic" (Earvin) (1959–) US professional basketball player. He led the Los Angeles Lakers to five National Basketball Association (NBA) championships (1980, 1982, 1985, 1987, 1988) and was voted Most Valuable Player three times (1987, 1989, 1990). In 1991, Johnson retired after announcing he was HIV-positive. He returned to win a gold medal with the US "Dream Team" in the 1992 Olympics.

Johnson, Michael (1967–) US track athlete. In 1991, he became the 200m world champion. In 1995, Johnson became 200m and 400m world champion. At the 1996

Olympics, he became the first man in Olympic history to win 200m and 400m gold medals.

Johnson, Philip Cortelyou (1906–) US architect. He studied under Marcel BREUER at Harvard University and became a proponent of the INTERNATIONAL STYLE. Johnson collaborated with MIES VAN DER ROHE on the Seagram Building, New York City, USA (1958). Other designs include the Lincoln Center, New York City (1964).

Johnson, Samuel (1709–84) English lexicographer, poet and critic. In 1749, he published the long poem *The Vanity of Human Wishes*. His reputation was established by the masterly *Dictionary of the English Language* (1755). Other works include the essay collection *The Idler* (1758–61), the philosophical romance *Rasselas* (1759), an edition (1765) of Shakespeare and the critical *Lives of the Poets* (1779–81). A trenchant conversationalist, Johnson co-founded (1764) "The Club" with Joshua REYNOLDS, later known as "The Literary Club". He toured Scotland in 1773 with his biographer James BOSWELL. Johnson published his notes as *A Journey to the Western Isles of Scotland* (1775).

John the Baptist (active 1st century AD) Prophet who heralded the appearance of JESUS CHRIST and the coming of the kingdom of God. The son of ZECHARIAH and Elizabeth, he was born in Judaea six months before Jesus. John baptized Jesus in the River Jordan, recognizing him as the MESSIAH. He was beheaded by Herod Antipas, after SALOME asked for his head as a reward for her dance.

Johor State in S peninsular Malaysia, separated from Singapore by the Johor Strait. The capital is Johor Baharu. The land is dominated by swamps and forests. It was founded by Sultan Mahmud of MALACCA. In 1512, it was captured by the Portuguese. In 1641, it helped the Dutch acquire Malacca. Industries: rubber, tin, bauxite, palm oil, pineapples. Area: 19,000sq km (7,400sq mi) Pop. (1990) 2,106,500.

joint In anatomy, place where one BONE meets another. In **movable** joints, such as those of the knee, elbow and spine, the bones are separated and cushioned from one another by pads of CARTILAGE. In **fixed** joints, cartilage may be present in infancy but disappears later as the bones fuse together, as in the SKULL. In the movable joints of bony VERTEBRATES, the bones are held together by LIGAMENTS. SYNOVIAL FLUID lubricates the joint.

Joliot-Curie, Irene *See* CURIE, MARIE

Jolliet, Louis (1646–1700) French explorer, b. Québec, Canada. In 1673, Jolliet and Jacques Marquette became the first Europeans to travel the Mississippi River, from its confluence with the Wisconsin River to the mouth of the Arkansas River.

Jolson, Al (1886–1950) US music-hall singer and comedian, b. Russia as Asa Yoelson. He began his career working in minstrel shows. Jolson starred in *The Jazz Singer* (1927), the first feature film with sound, and had his own radio show. He is remembered for his sentimental renditions of "Swanee" and "Mammy".

Jonah Fifth of the 12 minor prophets and central character in the Old Testament Book of Jonah. This book relates how Jonah disobeyed God's command to preach to the Gentiles in Nineveh. He attempted to flee from the Assyrian capital in a ship, but was thrown overboard in a storm and swallowed by a whale. Three days later Jonah was regurgitated alive on shore. He repented and carried out God's commandment.

Jones, Inigo (1573–1652) English architect and painter. He introduced England to a pure CLASSICAL style based on the work of Andrea PALLADIO. His knowledge of Italian architecture gained him enormous prestige. His most noted buildings include the Queen's House, Greenwich (1616–35), and Banqueting House, Whitehall (1619–21).

Jones, John Paul (1747–92) American naval officer in the American Revolution, b. Scotland as John Paul. In 1775, he joined the Continental navy and proved successful at capturing supplies and enemy vessels. With his flagship *Bonhomme Richard* he engaged the British ship *Serapis* in an epic battle off the coast of England (1779). He boarded and captured the *Serapis* while his ship burned and then sank.

Jones, Marion (1975–) US track and field athlete. Jones won five medals at the 2000 Olympics. She won gold medals in the 4x400m relay, and the 100m and 200m events, and bronze in the 4x100m relay and the long jump.

Jongkind, Johan Barthold (1819–91) Dutch painter and etcher. His work had close affinities with IMPRESSIONISM. Many of his oil paintings were based on watercolours and drawings executed outside his studios.

Jonson, Ben (1572–1637) English dramatist, poet and actor. In 1598, he killed a fellow actor in a duel. His first major play, *Every Man in His Humour* (1598), included SHAKESPEARE in its cast. Jonson's next "comedies of humours", *Every Man out of His Humour* (1599) and *Cynthia's Revels* (1600), were less successful. *The Poetaster* (1601) satirized fellow playwrights Thomas DEKKER and John Marston. His Roman tragedies, *Sejanus* (1603) and *Catiline* (1611) were critical failures. Jonson's major works are the four comedies *Volpone* (1606), *Epicoene* (1609), *The Alchemist* (1610) and *Bartholomew Fair* (1614). He collaborated on several MASQUES for the court of James I and became the first poet laureate. His collected verse includes *Epigrams* (1616) and *The Forest* (1616), featuring "Song: To Celia". *See also* ELIZABETHAN DRAMA; JACOBEAN

Joplin, Scott (1868–1917) US composer. He wrote RAGTIME piano music such as "Maple Leaf Rag" (1900) and "The Entertainer" (1902), as well as the opera *Treemonisha* (1911).

Jordaens, Jacob (1593–1678) Flemish painter. He is known for his allegorical and mythological works and for his naturalistic depictions of peasant life.

Jordan, Michael Jeffrey (1963–) US basketball player. He led the Chicago Bulls to six National Basketball Association titles (1991–93, 1996–98) and was named Most Valuable Player five times (1988, 1991, 1992, 1996, 1997). Jordan played in the US teams that won gold medals at the 1984 and 1992 Olympics. In 1993, he switched to baseball, but returned to the Bulls in 1995. Jordan retired in 1999.

Jordan HASHEMITE kingdom in SW Asia. Jordan can be divided into three geographical areas: the Transjordan plateau in the E constitutes 90% of total land area and is the most populous region. It includes the capital, AMMAN. Central Jordan forms part of the Great RIFT VALLEY and contains the River JORDAN and the DEAD SEA. West Jordan (now the WEST BANK) is part of historic PALESTINE and includes the region of SAMARIA; this area is now occupied by ISRAEL. Jordan has a coastline on the Gulf of AQABA. The ancient city of PETRA lies close to Jordan's highest peak, Jabal Ram, at 1,754m (5,755ft). **Climate** The Transjordan plateau is a transition zone between a Mediterranean climate to the W and a desert climate to the E. **Vegetation** Most of Jordan is desert or semi-desert. Parts of the W plateau have scrub vegetation, and there are some areas of dry grassland. **History and politics** The region was conquered by the SELEUCIDS in the 4th century BC. In the 1st century BC, the Nabatean empire developed a capital at Petra. The Romans, led by Pompey, captured the region in the 1st century AD. In AD 636, Arab armies

JORDAN
AREA: 89,210sq km (34,444sq mi)
POPULATION: 5,558,000
CAPITAL (POPULATION): Amman (1,300,042)

conquered the territory and introduced Islam. After the First CRUSADE the region was incorporated into the Latin kingdom of Jerusalem (1099). In 1517, it became part of the OTTOMAN EMPIRE. After the defeat of the Ottomans in World War 1, the area E of the River Jordan was included in the British League of Nations mandated territory of Palestine. In 1921, the E region was administered separately as Transjordan. In 1928, it became a constitutional monarchy ruled by the Hashemite dynasty. In 1946, Transjordan achieved independence. The creation of the state of Israel (1948) led to the first of the ARAB-ISRAELI WARS (1948–49). Hundreds of thousands of Palestinians fled to Jordan. Under the peace terms, Transjordan annexed the remaining Arab parts of Palestine (West Bank and EAST JERUSALEM). This incensed the Palestinians, and King ABDULLAH was assassinated in 1951. In 1953, HUSSEIN I acceded. In 1958, Jordan formed the short-lived Arab Federation with Iraq. The SIX-DAY WAR (1967) ended in the Israeli occupation of East Jerusalem and the West Bank: more than one million Palestinian refugees now lived in E Jordan. In 1970, Jordan became embroiled in a bloody civil war with Palestinian independence movements. By 1971, Jordan had ejected all guerrillas operating from its soil. In 1974, King Hussein recognized the PALESTINIAN LIBERATION ORGANIZATION (PLO) as the legitimate representative of the Palestinians. In 1988, Jordan gave up its claim to the West Bank and approved the creation of an independent Palestine. Jordan sided with Iraq in the IRAN-IRAQ WAR and the GULF WAR. In 1991, opposition parties were legalized, and the first multiparty elections were held in 1993. In October 1994, Jordan and Israel signed a peace treaty that ended the state of war existing since 1948. The border between Elat and Aqaba was opened and King Hussein was granted custodial rights of Islamic sites in Jerusalem. Elections in 1997 were boycotted by opposition parties, including the Islamic Action Front (IAF). In 1999, King Hussein died and was succeeded by his son, Abdullah. **Economy** Jordan is the world's seventh-largest producer of phosphates and potash. Just over half of the land is farm or pasture land. Major crops include barley, citrus fruits, grapes, olives and wheat. Jordan has an oil refinery and produces natural gas. Tourism is developing rapidly and reforms are helping to expand the economy (1995 GDP per capita, US$4,060).

Jordan River in the Middle East, rising in the Anti-Lebanon Mountains at the confluence of the rivers Hasbani, Dan and Baniyas. It flows S through Israel and the Sea of Galilee and empties into the Dead Sea. Since 1967, the S part of the river has formed a section of the Israel-Jordan border. Length: 320km (200mi).

Joseph, Saint In the New Testament, husband of MARY and the legal father of JESUS CHRIST. He was a carpenter from Nazareth, N Palestine. His feast day is 19 March.

Joseph In the Old Testament, 11th son of JACOB and first from his marriage to Rachel. Jacob's gift to Joseph of a richly woven, multicoloured coat, aroused the jealousy of his half-brothers who sold him into slavery. Joseph's powers of prophecy gained him high office in the Pharoah's court. He saved Egypt from famine and was reconciled with his brothers. As Yusuf, Joseph is regarded as a prophet in Islam.

Joseph I (1678–1711) Holy Roman Emperor (1705–11), king of Hungary (1687–1711) and of Bohemia (1705–11). His reign was dominated by revolt in Hungary, and by the War of the SPANISH SUCCESSION. He was succeeded by his brother, CHARLES VI.

Joseph II (1741–90) Holy Roman emperor (1765–90), king of Hungary and Bohemia (1780–90), son of MARIA THERESA and Emperor Francis I. Until 1780, he ruled the Habsburg lands jointly with his mother. As sole ruler, he introduced sweeping liberal and humanitarian reforms, including the abolition (1781) of serfdom. His radical programme required autocratic means and the support of ministers such as KAUNITZ. Despite the visit (1782) of Pope Pius VI he suppressed the monastic orders. The scale and pace of change led to revolts in Hungary and the Austrian Netherlands. He was succeeded by LEOPOLD II.

Joséphine (1763–1814) Consort of NAPOLEON I and empress of the French (1804–09). Her first marriage, to Vicomte Alexandre de‑Beauharnais, ended with his death in 1794 during the REIGN OF TERROR. She married Napoleon in 1796. Her inability to bear him a son caused Napoleon to obtain annulment of their marriage in 1809.

Joseph of Arimathea, Saint In the New Testament, a wealthy member of the SANHEDRIN who secretly supported JESUS CHRIST. He claimed Christ's body from PONTIUS PILATE after the crucifixion and attended to its burial. In legend he brought the HOLY GRAIL to England and founded the first English Christian church at GLASTONBURY. His feast day is 17 March.

Josephson, Brian David (1940–95) Welsh physicist. In 1962, he deduced that an electric current would flow between two superconductors separated by a thin layer of insulator (the "Josephson effect"). Josephson shared the 1973 Nobel Prize for physics with Leo ESAKI and Ivar Giaever. *See also* SUPERCONDUCTIVITY.

Josephus, Flavius (AD 37–100) Jewish leader and historian, b. Joseph ben Mattityahu. As governor of Galilee, he took part in the revolt against Rome (AD 66–70) and was captured. Josephus found favour with VESPASIAN and settled in Rome (70). His writings include *The Jewish War* (75–79 and *Antiquities of the Jews* (93).

Joshua Heroic figure among the Israelites who became their commander after the death of MOSES and led them into CANAAN following the exodus from Egypt. His subsequent exploits are recorded in the Book of Joshua, the sixth book of the Old Testament.

Jospin, Lionel (1937–) French statesman, prime minister (1997–). In 1995, he succeeded François MITTERRAND as leader of the French Socialist Party (PS) but lost the ensuing presidential election to Jacques CHIRAC. In the 1997 prime ministerial elections, Jospin won a surprise victory against the incumbent, Alain Juppé.

Josquin Desprez (1445–1521) (Josquin Des Prés) Flemish composer. He wrote three books of masses, more than 100 motets and many secular songs. The expressiveness and inventiveness of his music mark him as the most prominent composer of Renaissance Europe.

Joule, James Prescott (1818–89) English physicist. In a series of experiments (1843–78) he showed that HEAT is a form of ENERGY (the first law of THERMODYNAMICS) and established the mechanical equivalent of heat (the basis for HELMHOLTZ's law of conservation of energy). In 1841, he measured the heat loss of an electric current due to the resistance of the wire (**Joule's law**) The JOULE is named after him.

joule (symbol J) SI unit of energy. One joule is the work done by a force of one NEWTON acting over a distance of one metre. It was named after James JOULE.

Joyce, James (1882–1941) Irish novelist. In 1904, he renounced Catholicism and left Ireland to live and work in Europe. Joyce's experiments with narrative form and STREAM OF CONSCIOUSNESS place him at the centre of literary MODERNISM. His first work was the short-story collection *Dubliners* (1914). *A Portrait of the Artist as a Young Man* (1916) was a fictionalized autobiography of Stephen Daedalus. His masterpiece, the novel *Ulysses* (1922), presents a day (16 June 1904) in the life of Leopold Bloom. *Finnegan's Wake* (1939) is an allusive mix of Irish history and myth.

Juan Carlos (1938–) King of Spain (1975–), grandson of ALFONSO XIII. He succeeded FRANCO and set about the democratization of Spanish society. In 1962, Juan Carlos married Princess Sophia of Greece. In 1981, he survived an attempted military coup.

Juárez, Benito Pablo (1806–72) Mexican statesman, president (1858–62, 1867–72). Elected governor of his native state of Oaxaca (1847), he was exiled (1853–55) by SANTA ANNA. As president, Juárez won a victory over conservatives in the "War of Reform", and headed resistance to the French invasion (1862) until the fall of MAXIMILIAN (1867).

Judah Fourth son of JACOB and his first wife, Leah, and forefather of the most important of the 12 tribes of ancient ISRAEL. After the exodus and Joshua's conquest of CANAAN, the tribe of Judah received the region south of JERUSALEM. This territory later became known as Judaea. The tribe of Judah eventually became the dominant one. Israel's greatest kings, DAVID and SOLOMON, belonged to it, and prophets foretold that the MESSIAH would arise from among its members.

Judaism Monotheistic religion developed by the ancient HEBREWS in the Near East during the third millennium BC and practised by modern JEWS. Tradition holds that Judaism was founded by ABRAHAM who, in *c.*20th century BC, was chosen by God to receive favourable treatment in return for obedience and worship. Having entered into this covenant with God, Abraham moved to CANAAN, from where centuries later his descendants migrated to Egypt and became enslaved. God accomplished the Hebrews' escape from Egypt and renewed the covenant with their leader MOSES. Through Moses, God gave the Hebrews a set of strict laws. These laws are revealed in the TORAH, the core of Jewish scripture. Apart from the PENTATEUCH, the other holy books are the TALMUD and several commentaries. In the 10th century BC, SOLOMON built the first TEMPLE of Jerusalem as a repository for the ARK OF THE COVENANT. Local worship takes place in a synagogue, a building where the Torah is read in public and preserved in a replica of the Ark of the Covenant. A RABBI undertakes the spiritual leadership and pastoral care of a community. Modern Judaism is split into four large groups: Orthodox, Conservative, Reform and Liberal Judaism. **Orthodox** Judaism, followed by most of the world's 18 million Jews, asserts the supreme authority of the Torah and adheres most closely to traditions, such as the segregation of men and women in the synagogue. **Reform** Judaism denies the Jews' claim to be God's chosen people and is more liberal in its interpretation of certain laws and the Torah. **Conservative** Judaism is a compromise between Orthodox and Reform Judaism, adhering to many Orthodox traditions but seeking to apply modern scholarship in interpreting the Torah. **Liberal** Judaism, also known as Reconstructionism, is a more extreme form of Reform Judaism, seeking to adapt Judaism to the needs of society.

Judas Iscariot (d. *c.*AD 30) Disciple who betrayed JESUS CHRIST to the Jewish hierarchy. He was one of the 12 apostles originally chosen by Jesus. When Jesus and his disciples arrived in Jerusalem, Judas assisted the chief priests in arresting Jesus. In return for 30 pieces of silver, he led the chief priests' agents to the Garden of Gesthemane and pointed Jesus out to them by greeting him with a kiss. Later, in remorse, he committed suicide.

Jude, Epistle of New Testament book of the Bible. It consists of a letter exhorting all Christians to keep the faith and live righteously. The author calls himself the brother of James, probably the one mentioned in Mark 6:3.

Judges Seventh book of the Old Testament. It covers a 200-year period in the history of ancient ISRAEL, from the death of JOSHUA to the establishment of the first Israelite kingdom (*c.*11th century BC).The judges are leaders inspired by God to fight battles on behalf of the fledgling nation against neighbouring enemies. The Book of Judges contains some of the oldest material in the Bible.

judicial review In England and Wales, the re-examination in the HIGH COURT OF JUSTICE (acting as supreme court of appeal) of a previous verdict. The review may decide on various courses of action, such as overturning a verdict, changing the sentence on a conviction or issuing an INJUNCTION.

Judith Heroine of an Old Testament book considered apocryphal by Protestants and Jews. She is described as a beautiful young widow who heroically rescued the Israelite city of Bethulia from siege by the Assyrians.

judo Form of JUJITSU and one of the most popular of the Japanese martial arts. It places emphasis on physical fitness and mental discipline. A system of belt colours displays a practitioner's standard. Manoeuvres include holds, trips and falls. Scoring is according to the finality of a throw or hold.

Juggernaut (Jagganath) Form of the Hindu god KRISHNA, worshipped in Puri, E India. At an annual festival, statues of the god, his brother and his sister are pulled around the town on heavy carts. The term juggernaut has come to mean any large, heavy vehicle.

jugular In anatomy, term that applies to any structure in the neck, and especially to any of several veins. The external jugular veins receive blood from the outside of the cranium, the neck and the deep tissues of the face. Others receive blood from the back of the neck, the larynx, tissues below the lower jaw, the brain and the face.

jujitsu Method of unarmed self-defence used in hand-to-hand combat. It involves such techniques as striking, holding, throwing, choking and joint locking. There are *c.*50 systematized variants (including JUDO, KARATE and AIKIDO) that have been refined over a period of 2,000 years in Japan, China and Tibet. In the early 19th century, when the SAMURAI were forbidden to carry weapons, jujitsu became a form of self-defence.

jujube Either of two species of small thorny trees and their fruit of the genus *Zizyphus*. *Z. jujuba*, native to China, has elliptical leaves and reddish brown, plum-sized fruits, which have a crisp, white, sweet flesh. *Z. mauritanica* of India has smaller fruit. Family Rhamnaceae.

Julian of Norwich (c.1342–c.1413) English mystic. According to legend she lived as a recluse near St Julian's Church, Norwich. She is celebrated for her visionary work *Revelations of Divine Love* (c.1393).

Julian (the Apostate) (331–63) Roman Emperor (361–63). He achieved power on the death of Constantine II. Julian tried to restore paganism without persecuting Christians. He was killed in battle against the Sassanids.

Julius II (1443–1513) Pope (1503–13), b. Guiliano della Rovere. He tried to recover papal lands and, in 1506, established the Swiss Guard to protect the pope and Rome. He built up the treasury through the sale of benefices and began the building of St Peter's Basilica.

Julius Caesar *See* CAESAR, (GAIUS) JULIUS

July Revolution (1830) Insurrection in France. The immediate cause was the July Ordinances, which dissolved the chamber of deputies, reduced the electorate and imposed rigid press censorship. CHARLES X was forced to abdicate and LOUIS PHILIPPE was proclaimed king with a more liberal constitution.

Juneau State capital of Alaska, USA; a seaport on the Gastineau Channel, bordering British Columbia. It grew rapidly after the discovery of gold in 1880 and was made capital of Alaska territory 1900 and state capital 1959. Industries: mining, timber, salmon canning, tourism. Pop. (1990) 26,751.

Jung, Carl Gustav (1875–1961) Swiss psychiatrist. He worked closely (1907–13) with Sigmund FREUD but disagreed that sexuality was the prime cause of NEUROSIS. Jung founded analytical psychology, based on psychic "individuation". He argued that the UNCONSCIOUS had two dimensions – the personal and archetypes of a collective unconscious. Jung believed INTROVERSION and EXTROVERSION to be basic personality types.

Jungfrau Mountain peak in the Swiss Alps. First climbed in 1811, it is the site of an alpine research station. Height: 4,158m (13,642ft).

juniper Any evergreen shrub or tree of the genus *Juniperus*, native to temperate regions of the Northern Hemisphere. Junipers have needle-like or scale-like leaves. The aromatic timber is used for making pencils, and the berry-like cones of common juniper (*J. communis*) for flavouring gin. Family Cupressaceae.

Junkers Landed aristocracy of Prussia. Descendants of the knights who conquered large areas of E Germany in the Middle Ages, they came to dominate the government and army in Russia and, after 1871, the German Empire. Intensely conservative, their hostility to the WEIMAR REPUBLIC contributed to the success of the Nazis.

Juno Asteroid discovered by Karl Harding in 1804. It is the tenth-largest asteroid. Diameter: 244km (152mi).

Juno In Roman mythology, the principal female deity and consort of Jupiter, depicted as a statuesque, matronly figure.

Jupiter Fifth major planet from the Sun, and the largest of the giant planets. It is one of the brightest objects in the sky. Through a telescope, Jupiter's yellowish elliptical disc is seen to be crossed by brownish-red bands, known as belts and zones. The most distinctive feature is the **Great Red Spot (GRS)**, first observed (1664) by Robert HOOKE. Spots, streaks and bands are caused by Jupiter's rapid rotation and turbulent atmosphere. Eddies give rise to the spots, which are cyclones or (like the GRS) anticyclones. Hydrogen accounts for *c.*90% of Jupiter's atmosphere and helium for most of the rest. At 1,000km (600mi) below the cloud tops there is a ocean of liquid hydrogen. At the centre of Jupiter there is probably a massive iron–silicate core surrounded by an ice

mantle. The core temperature is estimated to be 30,000K. The deep, metallic hydrogen "mantle" gives Jupiter a powerful magnetic field. Its magnetosphere is huge, several times the size of the Sun, and is the source of the planet's powerful radio emissions. Jupiter has 16 known SATELLITES, the four major ones being the GALILEAN SATELLITES. Knowledge of the planet owes much to visits by space probes: Pioneers 10 and 11, Voyagers 1 and 2, Ulysses and GALILEO.

Jupiter King of the Roman gods, identified with the Greek god ZEUS. He could take on various forms: the light-bringer (Lucetius), god of lightning and thunderbolts (Fulgur) and god of rain (Jupiter Elicius).

Jura Mountains Mountain range in E France and NW Switzerland. Forming part of the Alpine system, it extends from the River Rhine at Basel to the River Rhône SW of Geneva. It has several hydroelectric schemes.

Jurassic Central period of the MESOZOIC era, from 213 to 144 million years ago. In this period, there were Saurischian and ornithischian DINOSAURS, such as *Allosaurus* and *Stegosaurus*. Plesiosaurs, pterosaurs and ARCHAEOPTERYX date from this period. Primitive mammals had also begun to evolve.

jurisprudence Philosophy and science of the law, which dates back to PLATO and ARISTOTLE. Jurisprudence seeks to discover the source and justification of the law and its scope and function in a particular society.

jury Group of people summoned to pass judgment under oath. The 12-member jury in criminal trials dates from the mid-12th century, but it was only in the 17th century that jury members ceased to give evidence and simply passed judgment on the basis of evidence heard in court.

Justinian I (482–565) Byzantine emperor (527–565), sometimes called "the Great". His troops, commanded by Belisarius, regained much of the old Roman Empire, including Italy, North Africa and part of Spain. Longer-lasting achievements were the **Justinian Code**, a revision of the whole body of ROMAN LAW, and buildings in Constantinople. Heavy taxation, to pay for wars, drained the strength of the Empire.

Justin Martyr, Saint (*c.* AD 100–165) Father of the Church, b. Samaria. In *c.*130 he was converted to Christianity, probably while at Ephesus. Justin defended Christian doctrine in his two *Apologies* (*c.*150–60) and was put to death in Rome. His feast day is 1 June.

jute Natural plant fibre obtained from *Corchorus capsularis* and *C. olitorius*, both native to India. The plants grow up to 4.6m (15ft) tall. The fibre is obtained from the bark by soaking (retting) and beating. Jute is used to make sacking, twine and rope. Family Tileaceae.

Jutes Germanic people who invaded Britain in the 5th century along with Angles, Saxons and others. They settled mainly in Kent and the Isle of Wight.

Jutland, Battle of (1916) World War 1 naval battle between Britain and Germany off the Jutland peninsula, NW Europe. The only full-scale engagement of the war involving the two main fleets, it ended indecisively. Although British losses were greater, the German fleet remained in harbour for the rest of the war.

Juvarra, Filippo (1678–1736) Italian architect, one of the finest exponents of the BAROQUE style. His greatest achievements are the Superga (1717–31), just outside Turin, and the Church of the Carmine (1732), Turin.

Juvenal, Decimus Junius (AD 55–140) Roman poet. His 16 *Satires* (*c.*98–128) denounced the immorality of Roman society under Emperor DOMITIAN. Juvenal contrasted the decadence in imperial Rome with the virtues of the republic.

JUPITER DATA
DIAMETER (EQUATORIAL): 142,800km (88,700mi)
MASS (EARTH = 1): 317.9
VOLUME (EARTH = 1): 1,319
DENSITY (WATER = 1): 1.33
ORBITAL PERIOD: 11.86 years
ROTATION PERIOD: 9h 50m 30s
AVERAGE SURFACE TEMPERATURE: −150°C (−238°F)

TIME ZONES

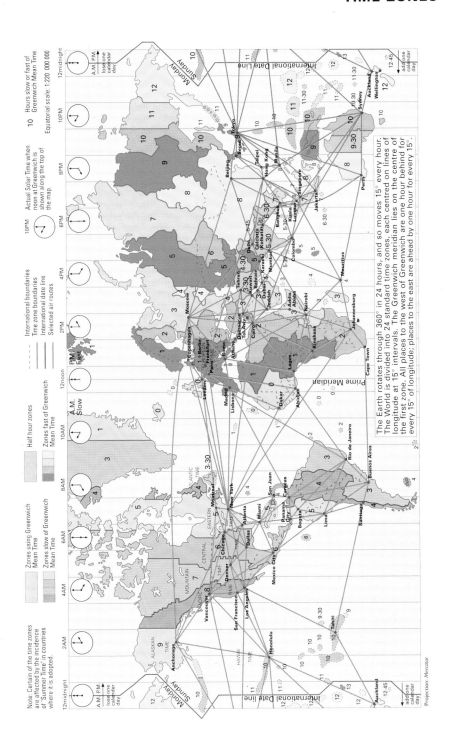

Note: Certain of the time zones are affected by the incidence of 'Summer Time' in countries where it is adopted.

Zones using Greenwich Mean Time

Zones fast of Greenwich Mean Time

Zones slow of Greenwich Mean Time

Half hour zones

International boundaries

Time zone boundaries

International date line

Selected air routes

10 Hours slow or fast of Greenwich Mean Time

Equatorial scale: 1:220 000 000

Actual Solar Time when noon at a Greenwich is shown along the top of the map.

The Earth rotates through 360° in 24 hours, and so moves 15° every hour. The World is divided into 24 standard time zones, each centred on lines of longitude at 15° intervals. The Greenwich meridian lies on the centre of the first zone. All places to the west of Greenwich are one hour behind for every 15° of longitude; places to the east are ahead by one hour for every 15°.

Projection: Mercator

WORLD POLITICAL

Alaska (U.S.A.)

Arctic Circle

GREENLAND (Den.)

ICEL

CANADA

UNIT KING

IRELAND Lon

Chicago

San Francisco

UNITED STATES

New York

NORTH

Los Angeles

Tropic of Cancer

Bermuda (U.K.)

Azores (Port.)

ATLANTIC

PORTUGAL

MOROCCO

Canary Is. (Spain)

WESTERN SAHARA

Hawaiian Is. (U.S.A.)

MEXICO

Mexico

BAHAMAS

CUBA

OCEAN

PACIFIC

JAMAICA HAITI DOM. REP

BELIZE

GUATEMALA HONDURAS

EL SALVADOR NICARAGUA

Puerto Rico (U.S.A.)

ST. KITTS & NEVIS

ANTIGUA & BARBUDA

DOMINICA

ST. LUCIA

ST. VINCENT ◦ BARBADOS

TRINIDAD & TOBAGO

MAURITANIA

CAPE VERDE IS.

SENEGAL

GAMBIA

GUINEA BISSAU

GUINEA

SIERRA LEONE

LIBERIA

IVOR COAS

BU

Kiritimati

Equator

COSTA RICA

PANAMA

Bogota

COLOMBIA

VENEZUELA

GUYANA

SURINAM

FRENCH GUIANA

OCEAN

Galapagos Is. (Ecuador)

ECUADOR

Ascension · (U.K.)

Marquesas Islands (France)

FRENCH POLYNESIA

PERU

Lima

BRAZIL

St. Helena (U.K.)

Society Islands (France)

Cook Islands (N.Z.)

Tahiti (France)

Tuamotu Archipelago (France)

BOLIVIA

Sao Paulo

Rio de Janeiro

SOUTH

Tubuai Islands (France)

Tropic of Capricorn

Pitcairn Island (U.K.)

Easter Island (Chile)

CHILE

Santiago

ARGENTINA

URUGUAY

Buenos Aires

ATLANTI

Tristan da Cunha(U

Chatham Islands (N.Z.)

OCEAN

Falkland Is. (U.K.)

South Georgia (U.K.)

Antarctic Circle

West from Greenw

Projection: Hammer Equal Area

EUROPE

Arctic Circle

ICELAND
Reykjavík

Norwegian
Sea

Tromsø

Faroe Is.
(Den.)

SWEDEN

Shetland
Is.

NORWAY
Trondheim

ATLANTIC

Hebrides

Orkney
Is.

Bergen

Oslo
Örebro
Uppsala

Gävle

Stavanger

Vänern

Jönköping

UNITED
KINGDOM

SCOTLAND
Aberdeen

Dundee

North

Skagerrak

Kattegat

Vättern

Gotla

Glasgow
Edinburgh

N.
IRELAND
Belfast

Ålborg
Gothenburg

DENMARK
Århus

Balti

IRELAND
Dublin

Newcastle-
upon-Tyne

Sea

Copenhagen
Malmö

Cork

Manchester
Leeds
Liverpool
Sheffield

Kiel

Gdańsk

OCEAN

WALES
Birmingham
Cardiff
ENGLAND
Bristol

Amsterdam **NETHER-**
The Hague **LANDS**
Rotterdam

Hamburg
Bremen
Elbe

Szczecin
Bydgoszcz

POL

Plymouth
Southampton

LONDON

BELGIUM
Antwerp

Hannover
Magdeburg

Berlin

Poznań

Łódź
Wrocław

English Channel

Lille
Brussels

Essen
Dortmund
Cologne
Bonn
Wiesbaden

GERMANY
Halle
Leipzig

Oder

Dresden

Katowice

Channel Is.
Le Havre
Rouen

Chemnitz

Ostrava

Brest
Seine
PARIS
Luxembourg
LUX.

Frankfurt
am Main

Prague

CZECH REP.

Nantes
Loire

Strasbourg

Rhine
Stuttgart

Nuremberg

SL
Vienna
Bratislav

FRANCE

Dijon

Munich

Linz

Salzburg

Limoges

St-Étienne

Lyons

Zürich
LIECH.
SWITZERLAND
Bern Vaduz
Geneva
Innsbruck

AUSTRIA
Graz

HUN

Bay of
Biscay

Bordeaux

Garonne

Grenoble

Milan

Venice

Ljubljana

SLOVENIA
Zagreb

La Coruña

Vigo

Toulouse

Rhône

Turin

Genoa

Bologna

Trieste

CROATIA

Porto
Douro

Bilbao

Ebro

Nice
MONACO

Florence

BOSNIA-
HERZ.

Valladolid

ANDORRA
Andorra
la-Vella

Marseilles

Toulon

Corsica

SAN
MARINO

Split

Sarajevo

MON
NEG

PORTUGAL

Lisbon
Tagus

SPAIN
Madrid

Zaragoza

Barcelona

Ajaccio

ITALY
Rome

Adriatic

Sea

Guadiana

Valencia

Tira

Seville
Guadalquivir

Córdoba
Murcia

Alicante

Balearic Is.
Palma

Minorca

Sardinia

Tyrrhenian

Naples
Taranto

Cádiz
Granada

Ibiza
Majorca

Sea

Bari

Str. of Gibraltar
Málaga
Tangier
Gibraltar (U.K.)
Ceuta (Sp.)
Melilla (Sp.)

Algiers

Mediterranean

Cagliari

Sea

Palermo
Messina

Sicily
Catania

Ionia
Sea

MOROCCO

Africa

ALGERIA

Annaba

Constantine **TUNISIA**
Tunis

Pantelleria
(Italy)

MALTA
Valletta

Projection: Bonne   West from Greenwich   0   East from Greenwich   5   10   15

■ **LONDON** Capital Cities

ft   m

15 000   5000

12 000   4000

6000   2000

3000   1000

1200   400

600   200

0

200   600

1000   3000

2000   6000

4000   12 000

m   ft

SCANDINAVIA AND THE BALTIC LANDS

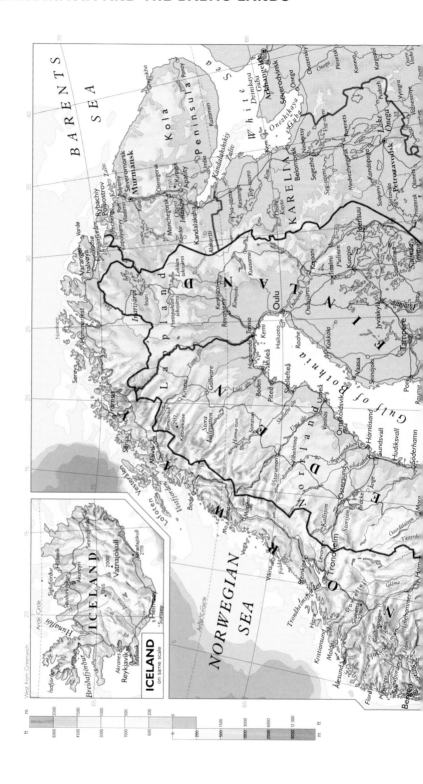

SCANDINAVIA AND THE BALTIC LANDS

BRITISH ISLES

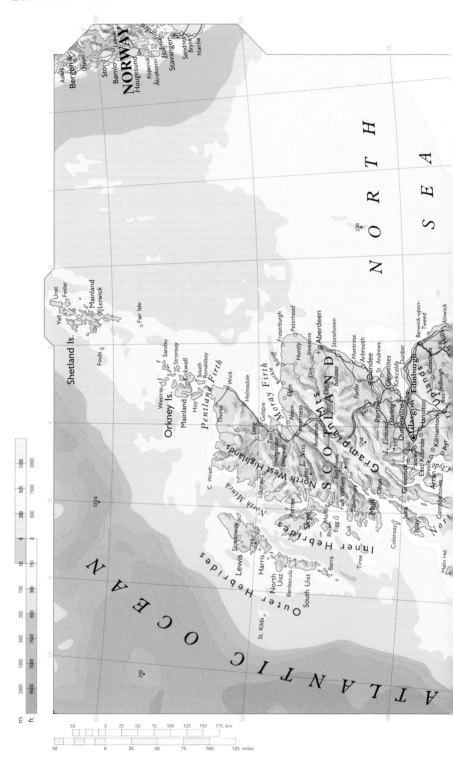

NORWAY

Askøy Oslo Bergen Leirvik Lervik Bolt Strod Bømlo Stavanger Sandnes Bryne Nærbø
Haugesund Kopervik Akrahamn

N O R T H   S E A

Shetland Is.
Yell Unst Fetlar
Foula Mainland Lerwick

Fair Isle

Orkney Is.
Westray Sanday Stronsay
Mainland Kirkwall
Hoy South Ronaldsay

Pentland Firth
Wick
Thurso Helmsdale
C. Wrath Golspie
Tain Loch
Lairg
Invergordon
Dingwall
Ullapool Inverness
L. Ness
Aviemore

Moray Firth
Buckie
Elgin Nairn

Fraserburgh Peterhead
Banff
Huntly Inverurie Aberdeen
Stonehaven

S C O T L A N D
G r a m p i a n   M t s.
North West Highlands

Ben Nevis 1343
Fort William
Fort Augustus
Mallaig
Oban
Mull
Eigg
Rhum
Coll
Tiree

Inner Hebrides

Outer Hebrides
Lewis
Harris
North Uist
Benbecula
South Uist
Barra

St. Kilda

Ballater
Forfar
Perth
Dundee
Montrose
Arbroath
St. Andrews
Glenrothes
Kirkcaldy
Dunbar
Stirling
Dunfermline
Edinburgh
Hamilton
East Kilbride
Kilmarnock
Ayr
Paisley
Glasgow
Greenock
Irvine
Campbeltown
Arran
Jura
Islay
Colonsay

Southern Uplands
Galashiels
Berwick-upon-Tweed
Alnwick

Clyde

Malin Hd.

A T L A N T I C   O C E A N

1224

316

238

50   0   25   50   75   100   125   150   175 km

50   0   25   50   75   100   125 miles

m ft
1000   3000
500   1500
200   600
50   150
0   0
50   150
100   300
500   1500
1000   3000
2000   6000

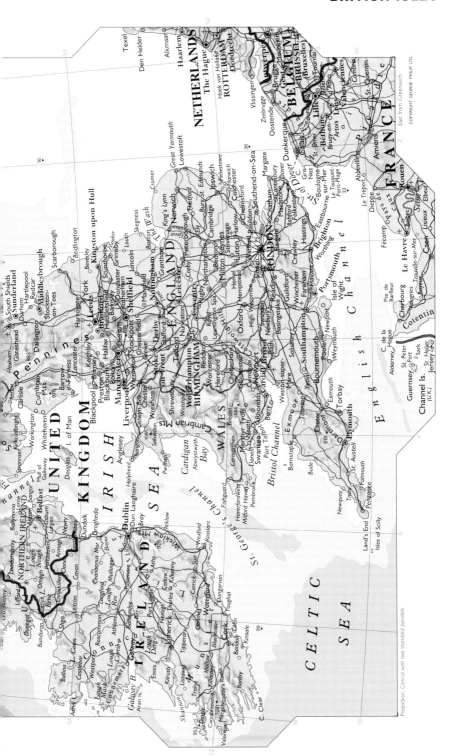

Projection: Conical with two standard parallels

East from Greenwich

COPYRIGHT GEORGE PHILIP LTD.

SOUTHWEST EUROPE

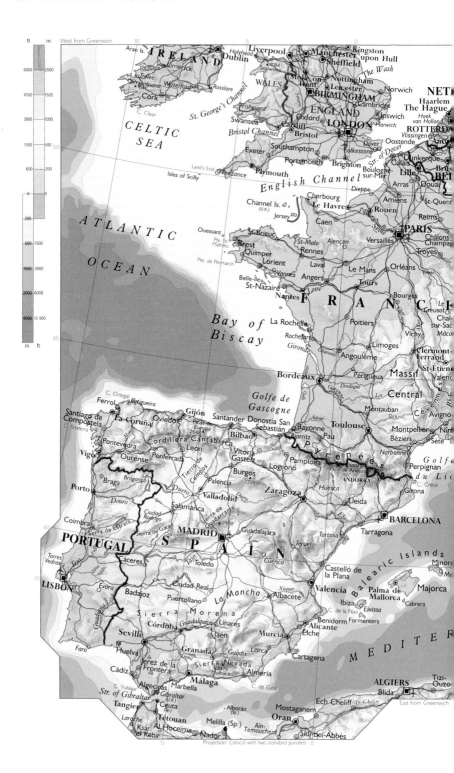

SOUTHWEST EUROPE

SOUTHEAST EUROPE, MIDDLE EAST AND TURKEY

Slovyansk
Kramatorsk
Lysychansk
Stakhanov
Artemovsk
Alchevsk
Krasnyy Luch
Lugansk
avlohrad
Gorlovka
Slavyansk
DONETSK
Makiyivka
Novoshakhtinsk
aporozhye
Mariupol
Taganrog
ROSTOV
Azov
Novocherkassk
Shakhty
Don Kotelnikovo
Volgodonsk
KALMYKIA
Volga
Krasnyy Yar
Astrakhan
Melitopol
Berdyansk
Yeysk
Salsk
Ozero Manych
Gudilo
Veselovsk
Vdkhr.
Ergeni
Vozneshensmost
Elista
E
Sea of Azov
Kerch
Tikhoretsk
RUSSIA
Kropotkin
Stavropol
Blagodarnyy
Budennovsk
Neftekumsk
Kuma
Feodosiya
Krasnodar
Armavir
Nevinnomyssk
Kuban
Maykop
Labinsk
Cherkessk
Georgiyevsk
Kizlyar
Terek
Novorossiysk
Tuapse
KARACHEY-
Kislovodsk
Pyatigorsk
Mozdok
Sochi
CHERKESSIA
Nalchik
KABARDINO-
CHECHENIA
Gagra
Ebrus
5642
NORTH
Grozny
Makhachkala
ABKHAZIA
BALKARIA
OSSETIA
Sokhumi
Vladikavkaz
DAGESTAN
Derbent
Kutaisi
South
Ossetia
Tskhinvali
4131
Xacmaz
S E A
Poti
GEORGIA
Telavi
Quba
Batumi
TBILISI
Rustavi
AJARIA
Mingäçevir
Su Anbari
AZERBAIJAN
Gyumri
Vanadzor
Gänca
Sumqayit
BAKU
Bafra
Samsun
Ordu
Trebolu
Rize
Artvin
Kars
ARMENIA
Naġorno-
Karabakh
Xankändi
Alat
Giresun
Trabzon
Kaçkar
3937
YEREVAN
Gəris
Neftçala
inop
Amasya
Şebinkarahisar
Alucra
Agri
Agri Daği
5165
Naxçivan
Länkäran
Tokat
Pontine Mts.
Erzincan
Karayazi
NAXÇIVAN
Naxçivan
Astara
Erzurum
Firat
Ordubad
Araks
Kelkit
um
Sivas
Murat
Malazgirt
Khvoy
Marand
TABRÍZ
Ardabíl
Kayseri
Gürün
Muş
Van Gölü
1720
Van
Daryácheh-ye
Orúmiyeh
IRAN
Miäneh
Keban
Baraji
Keban
Palu
Tatvan
5297
Orúmiyeh
Qezel Owzan
Kahramanmaraş
Malatya
Elaziğ
KEY
Cilo Daği
4135
Maragheh
Zanjän
Gaziantep
Batman
Atatürk
Baraji
Diyarbakir
Mardin
Cizre
Miändowäb
Saqqez
maniye
Nusaybin
Al Qámishli
NINAWÁ
Arbíl
As Sulaymäniyah
Sanandaj
ADANA
Iskenderun
Al Hasakah
Mosul
ALEPPO
Ar Raqqah
Kirkúk
Antakya
Bahret
Assad
Zab al Saġir
Bäkhtärän
Al Lädhiqiyah
Dayr az Zawr
SYRIA
Khänaqín
Hamäh
Himş
S
Tikrit
Sämarrá
ipli
Tudmur
Mileh Tharthär
BAGHDAD
BANON
Zakah
Hit
Euphrates
Ba'qúbah
BEIRUT
Ar Ramädi
DAMASCUS
IRAQ
Tigris
Al Hillah
MMAN
JORDAN
An Najaf
Al Amärah
Dead Sea
SAUDI
ARABIA
Ma'än
'Aqabah

East from Greenwich

COPYRIGHT GEORGE PHILIP LTD.

ASIA

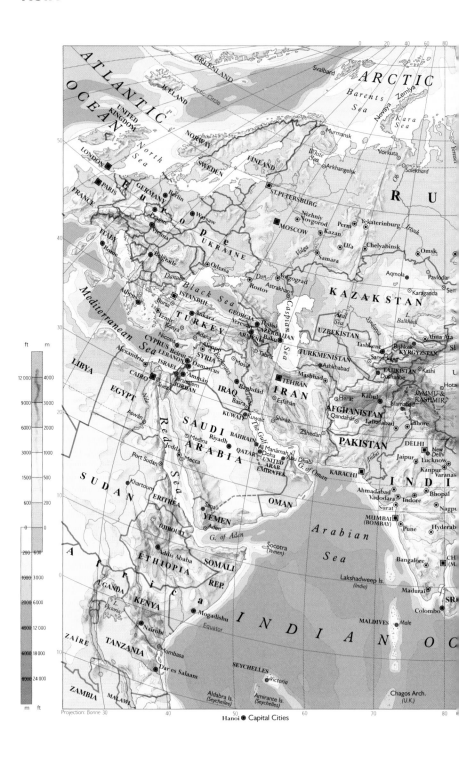

Projection: Bonne 30

Hanoi ● Capital Cities

ASIA

ARCTIC OCEAN

Laptev Sea

New Siberian Is.

Wrangel I.

ALASKA (USA)

Bering Sea

Aleutian Is. (USA)

Khatanga

Verkhoyansk

Gizhiga

Magadan

Kamchatsky

Petropavlovsk-Kamchatsky

A S I A

Lena

Yakutsk

Okhotsk

Sea of Okhotsk

Sakhalin

Kuril Is.

PACIFIC OCEAN

Angara

Krasnoyarsk

Bratsk

Chita

L. Baikal

Amur

Komsomolsk

Khabarovsk

Yuzhno-Sakhalinsk

Hokkaido

Sapporo

Irkutsk

Ulan Ude

Blagoveshchensk

Hailar

Qiqihar

Harbin

Changchun

Jilin

Vladivostok

Honshu

JAPAN

TOKYO

Novokuznetsk

Ulan Bator

MONGOLIA

SHENYANG

Jinzhou

Anshan

NORTH KOREA

P'yongyang

SOUTH KOREA

SEOUL

Pusan

Kyoto

Nagoya

Yokohama

Osaka

Ürümqi

Hami

Baotou

BEIJING

TIANJIN

Taiyuan

Jinan

Dalian

Hiroshima

Kyushu

Kagoshima

Bonin Is. (Japan)

Yumen

Lanzhou

Hwang-ho

Xi'an

Nanjing

SHANGHAI

East China Sea

Volcano Is. (Japan)

Tropic of Cancer

C H I N A

Chengdu

Wuhan

HANGZHOU

Nanchang

Fuzhou

Ryukyu Is.

GUAM (USA)

Mt. Everest 8850

Lhasa

Thimphu

BHUTAN

Brahmaputra

Kunming

Changsha

CHONGQING

Yangtze

Taipei

TAIWAN

Ganges

BANGLADESH

DACCA

CALCUTTA

BURMA

(MYANMAR)

Chittagong

Hanoi

Haiphong

Hainan

Si Kiang

GUANGZHOU

Macau

HONG KONG

Luzon

MANILA

PHILIPPINES

FED. STATES OF MICRONESIA

PALAU

Bay of Bengal

Andaman Is. (India)

Rangoon

LAOS

Vientiane

Mekong

THAILAND

BANGKOK

VIETNAM

Cebu

South China Sea

Sulu Sea

Palawan

Mindanao

Davao

Nicobar Is. (India)

CAMBODIA

Phnom Penh

Ho Chi Minh City

G. of Thailand

Zamboanga

IRIAN JAYA

Medan

Str. of Malacca

PEN. MALAYSIA

Kuala Lumpur

MALAYSIA

SINGAPORE

BRUNEI

Bandar Seri Begawan

SABAH

SARAWAK

Borneo

Celebes Sea

Manado

Celebes

Ceram

Halmahera

Ambon

Ceram

Banda Sea

Arafura Sea

Sumatra

Palembang

Banjarmasin

I N D O N E S I A

Ujung Pandang

EAST TIMOR

JAKARTA

Bandung

Java

Semarang

Surabaya

Java Sea

Flores

Sumba

Timor

Timor Sea

AUSTRALIA

Greenwich

COPYRIGHT GEORGE PHILIP LTD.

CHINA AND SOUTHEAST ASIA

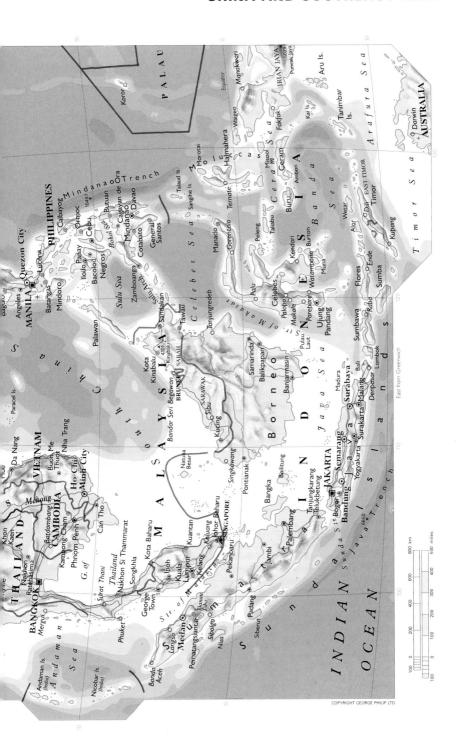

SOUTHERN ASIA

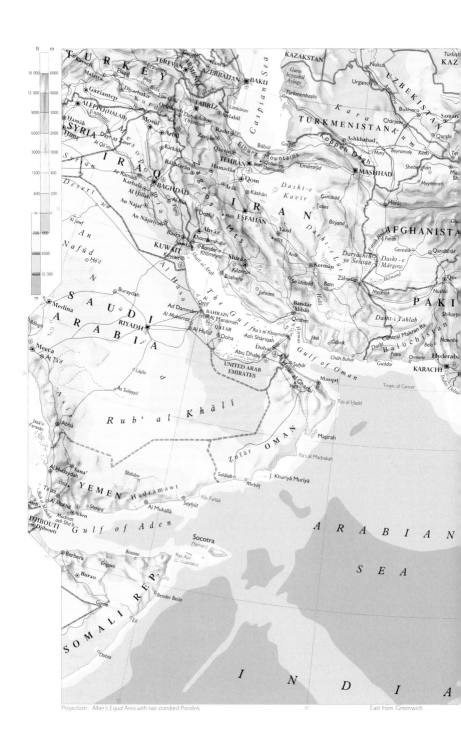

Projection : Alber's Equal Area with two standard Parallels

East from Greenwich

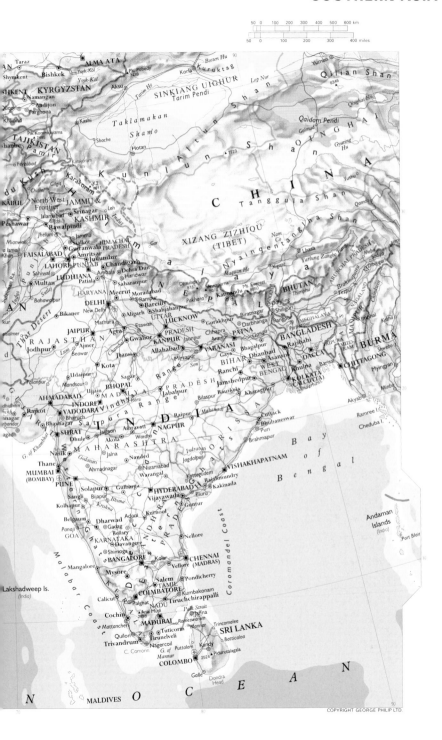

AFRICA

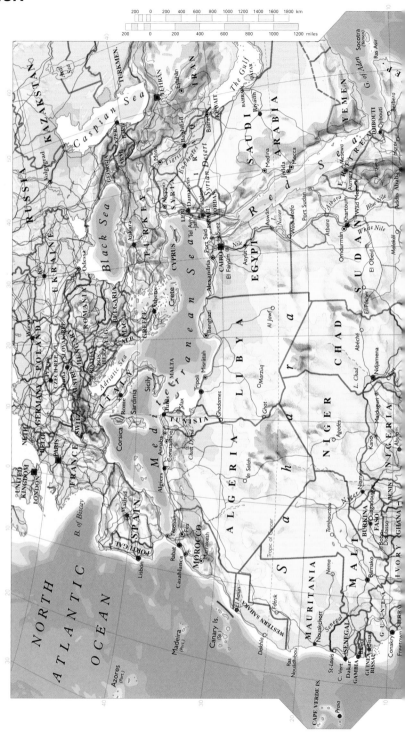

AFRICA

● Dakar Capital Cities

Projection Azimuthal Equidistant

INDIAN OCEAN

SEYCHELLES

MAURITIUS
Réunion (Fr.)

MADAGASCAR
Antananarivo
Toamasina
Antsiranana
Mahajanga
Fianarantsoa

COMOROS
Mayotte

Aldabra Is.
C. Delgado

Mozambique Channel

SOMALIA
Mogadishu
Kismayu

KENYA
Nairobi
Mombasa
Kisumu
L. Turkana
Gulu

UGANDA
Kampala
L. Victoria

TANZANIA
Dodoma
Dar es Salaam
Zanzibar
Kilimanjaro 5895
L. Tanganyika

RWANDA
Kigali

BURUNDI
Bujumbura

CONGO
(DEM. REP. OF THE)
Kisangani
Lubumbashi
Lualaba
L. Mweru
L. Edward
L. Kivu

Juba
L. Albert

CAMEROON
Yaoundé
Douala

EQUATORIAL GUINEA
Malabo
Annobon

GABON
Libreville
C. Lopez

CONGO
Brazzaville
Pointe Noire

Congo (Zaire)
Ubangi
Bangui

NIGERIA
Port Harcourt

Bight of Benin
Gulf of Guinea

Porto Novo
Accra
Sekondi-Takoradi
Abidjan
Monrovia

SÃO TOMÉ & PRINCIPE

ANGOLA
Luanda
Lobito
Benguela
Namibe
Cuando
Cubango
C. Fria

CABINDA (Angola)
Matadi
Kinshasa
Kananga
Kasai

ZAMBIA
Lusaka
Ndola
Kitwe

MALAWI
Lilongwe
Blantyre
L. Malawi

MOZAMBIQUE
Beira
Maputo
Zambezi

ZIMBABWE
Harare
Bulawayo

BOTSWANA
Gaborone
Kalahari

NAMIBIA
Windhoek

SOUTH AFRICA
Pretoria
Johannesburg
Durban
Cape Town
C. of Good Hope
Port Elizabeth
East London
Kimberley
SWAZILAND
LESOTHO
Maseru

St. Helena (U.K.)

Ascension I. (U.K.)

SOUTH ATLANTIC OCEAN

Tristan da Cunha

Tropic of Capricorn

Equator

West from Greenwich   East from Greenwich

m / ft scale bar

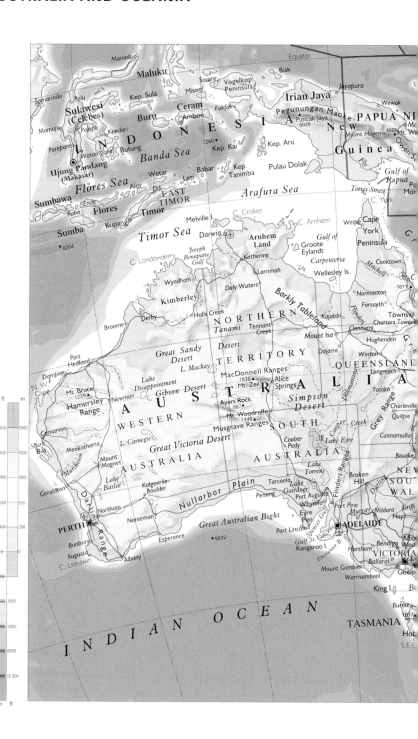

Equator

Manado
Maluku
Sorong
Biak
Jayapura
Vogelkop
Peninsula
Wewak
Samarinda
Palu
Kep. Sula
Misool
Irian Jaya
Pegunungan Maoke PAPUA NE
Sulawesi
(Celebes)
Buru
Ceram
Ambon
Fakfak
Puncak Jaya
5029
New
Mamuju
Mamuju
Palopo
Kendari
Fakfak
Mount Hagen
4508
Mt. Wi

Parepare
Watampone
Butung
Kep. Kai
1260
Kep. Aru
Guinea
Owen S

Ujung Pandang
(Makasar)
Banda Sea
Wetar
Babar
Kep.
Pulau Dolak
Fly
Gulf of
Papua

Sumbawa
Flores Sea
Alor
Dili
Leti
Tanimba
Torres Strait
Mor
Raba
Ende
EAST
TIMOR
Arafura Sea
C. York
Flores
Timor
C. Croker
Weipa
Cape
Sumba
6204
Kupang
Melville I.
Darwin
C. Arnhem
York
Peninsula

Timor Sea
C. Londonderry
Joseph
Bonaparte
Gulf
Arnhem
Land
Katherine
Gulf of
Groote
Eylandt
Carpenteria
Cooktown
Wyndham
Daly Waters
Larrimah
Wellesley Is.
Mitchell
1611

Kimberley
Halls Creek
NORTHERN
Tanami
Tennant
Creek
Kajabbi
Normanton
Forsayth
Townsvil
Charters Towers
Broome
Derby
TERRITORY
Mount Isa
Cloncurry
Hughenden

Great Sandy
Desert
L. Mackay
Dajarra
Winton
Longreach
QUEENSLAND
Port
Hedland
Lake
Disappointment
MacDonnell Ranges
1510
Mt. Zeil
Alice
Springs
Yaraka

Dampier
Mt. Bruce
1235
Newman
Gibson Desert
Ayers Rock
867
Simpson
Desert
Charleville
N.W.
Cape
Hamersley
Range
AUSTRALIA
Mt. Woodroffe
1440
Musgrave Ranges
SOUTH
Cooper Creek
Quilpie
Cunnamulla

Carnarvon
WESTERN
L. Carnegie
Great Victoria Desert
AUSTRALIA
Lake Eyre
Bourke
NEW
Shark
Bay
Meekatharra
Mount
Magnet
Coober
Pedy
Lake
Torrens
Broken
Hill
SOU
WAL
Geraldton
Lake
Barlee
AUSTRALIA
Tarcoola
Lake
Gairdner
Darling
Mildura
Griff
Northam
Kalgoorlie-
Boulder
Nullarbor Plain
Penong
Port Augusta
Whyalla
Murray
Hay
PERTH
Norseman
Eyre
Pen.
Port Pirie
ADELAIDE
Alb
Bunbury
Great Australian Bight
Port Lincoln
Spencer Gulf
Wod
Augusta
Esperance
5632
Gulf St. Vincent
Kangaroo I.
Bendigo
Ballarat
Geelo
C. Leeuwin
Albany
Encounter B.
Horsham
VICTORIA

Mount Gambier
Warrnambool
King I.
Be

INDIAN OCEAN
TASMANIA
Burnie
607
Hob
S.E.C

ft	m
6000	2000
4500	1500
3000	1000
1500	500
600	200
	0
200	
500	1500
1000	3000
2000	6000
4000	12 000
m	ft

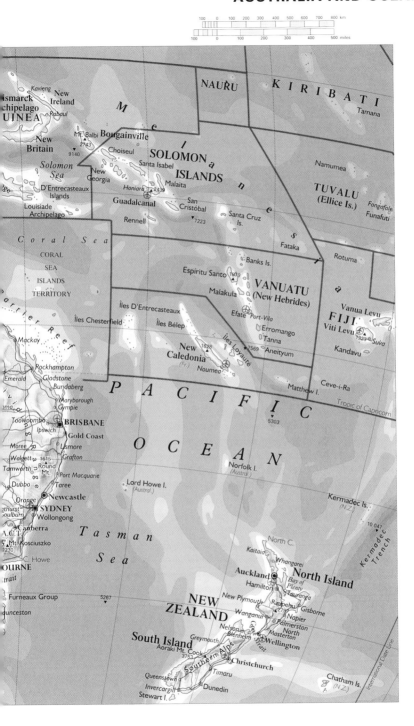

100 0 100 200 300 400 500 600 700 800 km
100 0 100 200 300 400 500 miles

Kavieng
New Ireland
ismarck
chipelago
UINEA Rabaul

NAURU

K I R I B A T I

Tamana

M
e
New
Britain Mt Balbi Bougainville
2743
9140 Choiseul
Solomon New Santa Isabel SOLOMON
Sea Georgia
D'Entrecasteaux Honiara 2439 ISLANDS
Islands Guadalcanal Malaita
Louisiade San
Archipelago Cristóbal
Rennell 7223

Namumea

l
a
n
d
s

TUVALU
(Ellice Is.)

Fongafale
Funafuti

Santa Cruz
Is.

Fataka

Rotuma

C o r a l   S e a

CORAL
SEA
ISLANDS
TERRITORY

Banks Is.
Espíritu Santo 1879
VANUATU
(New Hebrides)
Malakula
Efate Port-Vila
Erromango
Tanna
Aneityum

Vanua Levu
FIJI
Viti Levu 7323 Suva
Kandavu

Ceve-i-Ra

Íles D'Entrecasteaux

Íles Chesterfield

Íles Bélep

New
Caledonia
(Fr.) 1828
Noumea Íles Loyauté 7569

Matthew I.

Tropic of Capricorn

a
r
r
i
e
r   R
e
e
f
Mackay

Rockhampton
Gladstone P A C I F I C
Emerald Bundaberg
oma Maryborough
Gympie 5303
Toowoomba O C E A N
Ipswich BRISBANE
Gold Coast
Moree Lismore
Walgett 1615 Grafton Norfolk I.
Tamworth Round (Austrl.)
Dubbo Mt. Port Macquarie
Taree Lord Howe I. Kermadec Is.
Orange Newcastle (Austrl.) (N.Z.)
sthurst SYDNEY
oulburn Wollongong 10 047
A.C.T. Canberra T a s m a n
Mt. Kosciuszko North C.
2230 C. Howe S e a Kaitaia Whangarei
OURNE Auckland North Island
trait Hamilton Bay of
Plenty Tauranga
Furneaux Group 5267 New Plymouth Ruapehu Gisborne
unceston NEW Wanganui 2797 Napier
ZEALAND Nelson Palmerston
North
South Island Greymouth Blenheim Masterton
Aoraki Mt. Cook Wellington
3753 Christchurch
Queenstown Timaru
Invercargill Dunedin Chatham Is.
Stewart I. (N.Z.)

Kermadec
Trench

International Date Line

NORTH AMERICA

NORTH AMERICA

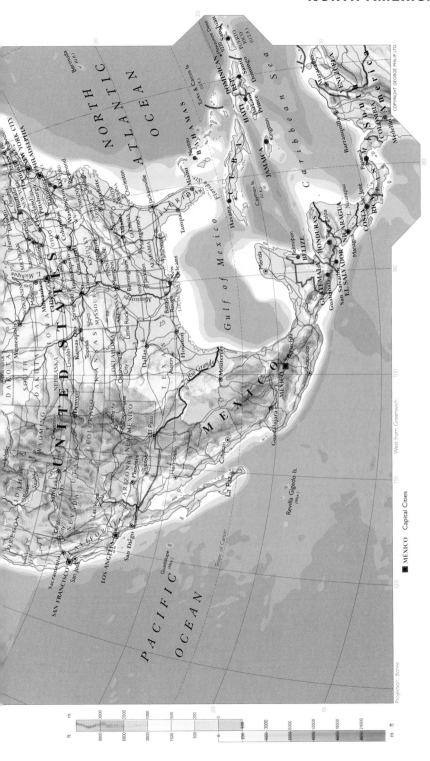

UNITED STATES OF AMERICA

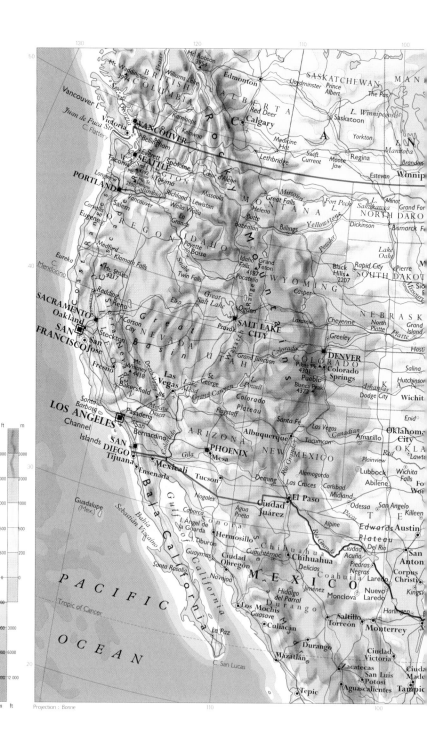

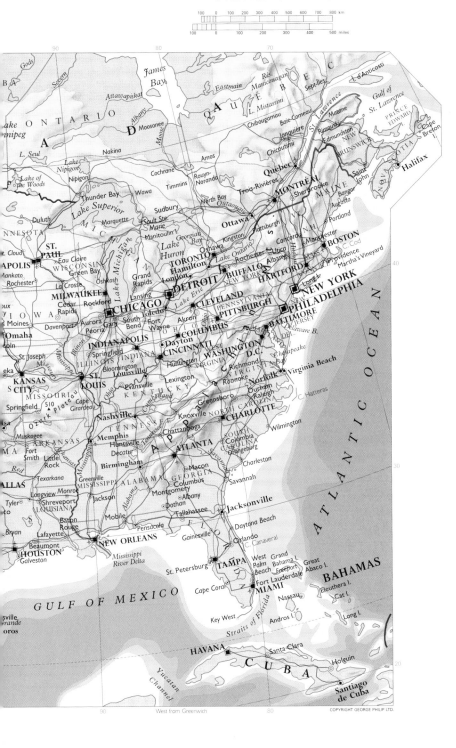

NORTHEASTERN USA

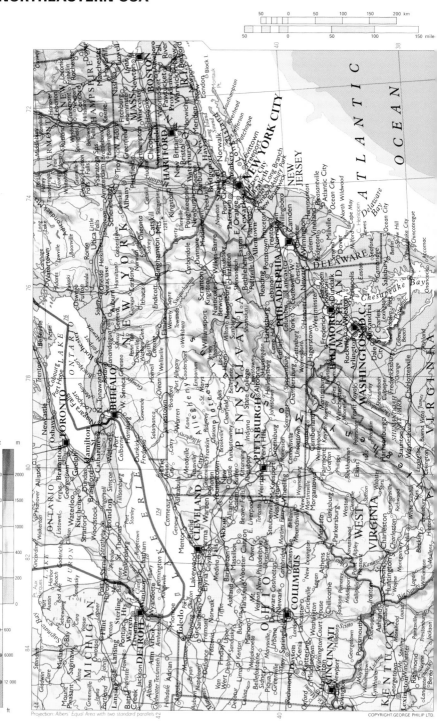

Projection: Albers' Equal Area with two standard parallels

CENTRAL AMERICA AND THE CARIBBEAN

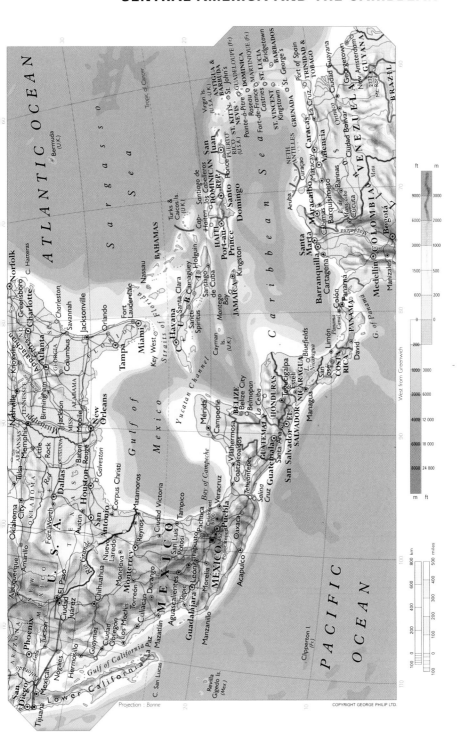

SOUTH AMERICA

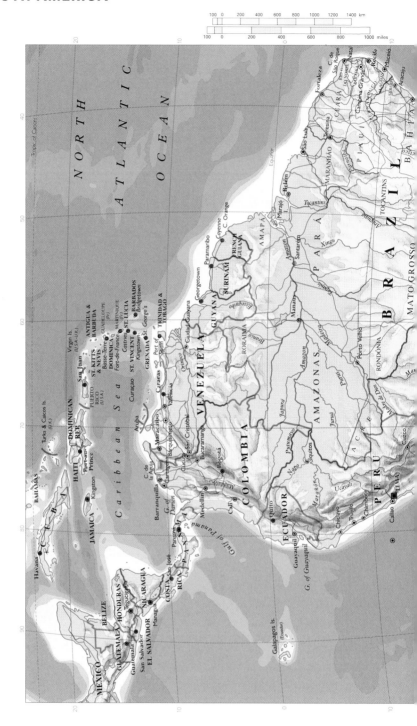

SOUTH

ATLANTIC

OCEAN

South Georgia (U.K.)

FALKLAND IS.
West Falkland
East Falkland
Stanley
60° West from Greenwich 50

C. Horn
Tierra del Fuego
Magellan's Str.
Punta Arenas

PACIFIC

OCEAN

San Félix (Chile)
San Ambrosio (Chile)

Arch. de Juan Fernández (Chile)

Tropic of Capricorn

Projection: Lambert's Azimuthal Equal Area

MINAS GERAIS
ESPÍRITO SANTO
Vitória
Campos
Niterói
RIO DE JANEIRO
SÃO PAULO
PARANÁ
Curitiba
RIO GRANDE DO SUL
Pôrto Alegre
Pelotas
URUGUAY
Montevideo
Río de la Plata
Mar del Plata
Bahía Blanca
PARAGUAY
Asunción
Corrientes
Resistencia
Santa Fe
Rosario
Paraná
BUENOS AIRES
Córdoba
San Juan
Mendoza
A R G E N T I N A
Viedma
Comodoro Rivadavia
Gulf of San Jorge
Gulf of Penas
Valdivia
Puerto Montt
Concepción
SANTIAGO
Valparaíso
Viña del Mar
Mt. Aconcagua
San Miguel de Tucumán
Salta
Cochabamba
Santa Cruz
Sucre
Goiânia
MATO GROSSO DO SUL
Belo Horizonte
Ouro Prêto
Goiâna
Antofagasta
Iquique
Arequipa
C H I L E

■ LIMA   Capital Cities

m
4000
3000
2000
1000
500
200
0
ft
12000
9000
6000
3000
1500
600
0

ft
3000
6000
12000
18000
24000
m

COPYRIGHT GEORGE PHILIP LTD.

ANTARCTICA

Projection: Zenithal Equidistant

K/k, eleventh letter of the Roman alphabet. It is derived from the Semitic letter kaph, *possibly from an earlier Egyptian hieroglyph for hand. In Greek it became* kappa *and in that form passed to the Roman alphabet.*

K2 Mountain in NE Pakistan on the border with China. It is the world's second-highest peak and the highest in the Karakoram range. It was first climbed in 1954 by Ardito Desio. Height: 8,611m (28,251ft).

Kaaba (Ka'abah or Ka'ba) Central shrine of ISLAM, located in the Great Mosque, MECCA, Saudi Arabia. In prayer, Muslims face the meridian that passes through the Kaaba. Each pilgrim who undertakes the HAJJ circles the shrine seven times, touching the Black Stone for forgiveness. The Black Stone is said to have been given to Abraham by the Archangel Gabriel.

Kabardino-Balkaria Republic of the Russian Federation in the N Caucasus Mountains on the border with Georgia; the capital is Nalchik. It was annexed to Russia in 1827, constituted as a republic of the Soviet Union in 1936 and became a federal republic of Russia in 1991. The population consists of Muslim Kabardinos (48%), Russians (32%) and Turkic-speaking Balkars (10%). Industries: ore-mining, timber. Pop. (1989) 235,000.

kabbala Variant spelling of CABBALA

kabuki theatre Stylized mixture of dance and music, mime and vocal performance; a major form of moralizing entertainment in Japan since the mid-17th century. In contrast to NO DRAMA, which originated with the nobility, Kabuki was the theatre of the common people. *See also* JAPANESE THEATRE

Kabul Capital of Afghanistan, on the River Kabul, in the E part of the country. It is strategically located in a high mountain valley in the HINDU KUSH. It was taken by Genghis Khan in the 13th century. Later it became part of the MOGUL EMPIRE (1526–1738). The capital of Afghanistan since 1776, it was occupied by the British during the Afghan Wars in the 19th century. Following the Soviet invasion in 1979, Kabul was the scene of bitter fighting. Unrest continued into the mid-1990s, as rival Muslim groups fought for control. Industries: textiles, leather goods, furniture, glass. Pop. (1993 est.) 700,000.

Kádár, János (1912–89) Hungarian statesman, premier (1956–58, 1961–65) and first secretary of the Hungarian Socialist Workers' Party (1956–88). He fought in the resistance during World War 2, and later served as minister of the interior (1948–50). In 1956, Kádár replaced Imre NAGY as premier after crushing the Hungarian uprising. In 1968, he gave military support to the Soviet invasion of Czechoslovakia. Kádár's policy of "consumer socialism" revitalised the domestic economy.

Kaddish Ancient Jewish prayer used particularly at services of mourning for the dead. It is a formal statement of praise and faith in the coming of God's Kingdom.

Kafka, Franz (1883–1924) German novelist, b. Czechoslovakia. He suffered from intense self-doubt, publishing only essays and short stories, such as *Metamorphosis* (1916), during his lifetime. Kafka requested that his friend Max BROD destroy his works after his death. Brod overrode his wishes and published the trilogy of unfinished novels for which Kafka is best known today: *The Trial* (1925), *The Castle* (1926) and *Amerika*

(1927). They are disturbing studies of the alienation of the individual in a bureaucratic and totalitarian society.

Kahlo, Frida (1907–54) Mexican painter. In 1925, a serious traffic accident left her a permanent semi-invalid and, during her convalescence, she taught herself to paint. In 1929, Kahlo married fellow artist Diego RIVERA. Her subsequent style was influenced by his work but also by Mexican folk art and, to a lesser extent, SURREALISM. Her paintings, such as *The Broken Column* (1944), are largely autobiographical, concentrating on her disability.

Kahn, Louis Isadore (1901–74) US architect, b. Estonia. He followed the example of LE CORBUSIER, GROPIUS and MIES VAN DER ROHE, using bare concrete to create his severely beautiful designs. Kahn broke with the INTERNATIONAL STYLE of MODERNISM, drawing on neoclassicism to create a pure geometrical style that integrated form and function. His designs include the Richards Medical Center, University of Pennsylvania, Philadelphia (1958–60) and the Jonas Salk Institute of Biological Studies, La Jolla, California (1959–65).

Kaieteur Falls Waterfall on the River Potaro in the Guyana Highlands, central Guyana, South America. It was discovered in 1870 by Barrington Brown of the US Geological Survey. The surrounding area became the Kaieteur National Park in 1930. Height: 226m (741ft).

Kaifeng City in Henan province, E central China. It was first settled in the 4th century BC and (as Pienching) served as capital of China during the Five Dynasty period (907–60) and the Northern Sung dynasty (960–1127). It is the site of a Jewish settlement that flourished from 1163 until the 15th century. Industries: electrical goods, agricultural machinery, chemicals, silk, flour. Pop. (1990) 690,000.

kaiser German title derived from the Latin *Caesar*. In 962 OTTO I assumed the title as Holy Roman Emperor. In 1871, WILLIAM I adopted the title with the unification of Germany after the FRANCO-PRUSSIAN WAR. His son, WILLIAM II (r.1888–1918), was the last kaiser.

Kaiser, Georg (1878–1945) German dramatist. His expressionist plays, such as *The Burghers of Calais* (1914), *Gas I* (1918) and *Gas II* (1920), attacked the dehumanizing nature of the machine age. Kaiser's work was banned by the Nazis. *See also* EXPRESSIONISM

kala-azar *See* LEISHMANIASIS

Kalahari Desert plateau in S Africa between the rivers Orange and Zambezi, mainly in SW Botswana but also covering parts of SE Namibia and Northern Cape, South Africa. Thorn scrub and forest grow in some parts of the desert, and it is possible to graze animals during the rainy season. The Kalahari is sparsely populated, mainly by the nomadic SAN. In the S lies the Kalahari Game Reserve. Area: c.260,000sq km (100,000sq mi).

kale Hardy variety of CABBAGE. It is short-stemmed and has large, bluish-green, curly-edged leaves. It may reach a height of 61cm (24in). Family Brassicaceae; (sub)species *Brassica oleracea acephala*.

Kali Hindu goddess of destruction, consort of SHIVA. She is also known as DURGA, PARVATI and Shakti. Kali represents the all-devouring aspect of Devi, the mother-goddess of India, who in other forms is calm and peaceful.

Kalidasa (active 5th century AD?) Indian dramatist and poet. Kalidasa is regarded as the major figure in classical SANSKRIT LITERATURE. He is chiefly remembered for his play *Sakuntala*, the love story of King Dushyanta and the nymph Sakuntala.

Kalimantan Region of Indonesia, forming the S part of the island of BORNEO. In the 16th century, Muslim states were created. In the 17th century, the Dutch gradually established colonial rule over what became part of the Netherlands East Indies. In 1950, Kalimantan came under Indonesian control. Products: rice, copra, pepper, oil, coal, industrial diamonds, timber. Area: 539,460sq km (208,232sq mi). Pop. (1990) 9,099,874.

Kalinin, Mikhail Ivanovich (1875–1946) Soviet statesman, head of state of the Soviet Union (1919–46). He was a founder (1912) of the newspaper *Pravda* and fought in the RUSSIAN REVOLUTION (1917). A supporter of Stalin, Kalinin served in the politburo (1925–46).

Kaliningrad (formerly Königsberg) City and seaport on the Baltic coast, W Russia; capital of Kaliningrad oblast. Founded in 1255, the city was a member of the HANSEATIC LEAGUE. In 1525, Königsberg became the residence of the dukes of Prussia. In 1946, it was incorporated into the Soviet Union. Following the break-up of the Soviet Union, Kaliningrad oblast is now separated from Russia proper and shares a border with Poland and Lithuania. Industries: shipbuilding, fishing, motor vehicle parts. Pop. (1993) 411,000.

Kalmykia Republic of the Russian Federation on the Caspian Sea, SE European Russia; the capital is Elista. In the early 17th century the Kalmyks migrated here from W China. In 1935, the region was constituted as a republic of the Soviet Union. In World War 2 the Kalmyks were deported to Soviet Central Asia for alleged collaboration with the Germans. They returned in 1957 and Kalmykia was re-established (1958) as an autonomous republic. In 1991, it became a republic of the Russian Federation. Industries: fishing, animal farming. Area: *c.*75,900sq km (29,300sq mi). Pop. (1994) 320,600.

Kamakura City at the head of the Miura-hanto peninsula, SE Honshu, Japan. It was capital (1192–1333) of Japan during the Kamakura shogunate. Kamakura is a major centre of Buddhism and its chief landmark is a 13-m-high (52-ft) bronze Buddha (1292). Pop. (1995) 170,000.

Kamchatka Vast peninsula in E Siberia, Russia, separating the Sea of Okhotsk (W) from the Bering Sea and the Pacific Ocean (E). The region has 22 active volcanoes. Mineral resources include oil, coal, gold and peat. Area: *c.*270,000sq km (104,000sq mi).

Kamehameha Five kings of Hawaii. **Kamehameha I** (r. *c.*1758–1819) united all the Hawaiian islands. He instituted harsh laws but abolished human sacrifice. His son, **Kamehameha II** (r.1819–25), admitted the first US missionaries. **Kamehameha III** (r.1825–54) introduced a liberal constitution and land reform. **Kamehameha IV** (r.1854–63) made social and economic reforms and resisted US influence. His brother, **Kamehameha V** (r.1863–72), abandoned the constitution and strengthened royal authority. The dynasty ended with his death.

Kamerlingh-Onnes, Heike (1853–1926) Dutch physicist. In 1908, using a liquid HYDROGEN cooling system, he liquefied HELIUM and achieved a temperature within one degree of ABSOLUTE ZERO. In 1911, Onnes discovered the property of SUPERCONDUCTIVITY in some metals. He was awarded the 1913 Nobel Prize for physics.

kamikaze (Jap. divine wind) Name given to pilots or their explosive-laden aircraft used by the Japanese during World War 2. Their suicidal method of attack was to dive into ships of the enemy fleet. In the Battle of Okinawa (1945) more than 1,400 pilots died in the process of destroying 26 US battleships.

Kampala Capital and largest city in Uganda, on the N shore of Lake Victoria. Founded in the late 19th century on the remains of a royal palace of the kings of Buganda, it replaced Entebbe as capital when Uganda attained independence in 1962. Kampala is the trading centre for the

agricultural goods and livestock produced in Uganda. Industries: textiles, food processing, tea blending, coffee, brewing. Pop. (1995) 954,000.

Kampuchea *See* CAMBODIA

Kanchenjunga (Kinchinjunga or Kanchanjanga) Third-highest mountain in the world, in the E Himalayas on the border between Nepal and Sikkim. It was first climbed in 1955 by a British expedition led by Charles Evans. The highest of its five peaks reaches 8,586m (28,169ft).

Kandahar (Qandahar) City and provincial capital in S Afghanistan. Because of its strategic location on important trade routes, it was occupied by many foreign conquerors before becoming the first capital of an independent Afghanistan (1747–73). It was the scene of fighting after the Soviet invasion of Afghanistan in 1979 and became the headquarters of the TALIBAN in the 1990s. It is a market centre for regional products such as wool, grain and tobacco. Pop. (1992 est.) 293,000.

Kandinsky, Wassily (1866–1944) Russian painter and theorist, a founder of ABSTRACT ART. His early paintings, including the many numbered *Compositions*, express great lyricism. From 1911, Kandinsky was an active member of der BLAUE REITER. His writings, especially *Concerning the Spiritual in Art* (1914), show the influence of Oriental art philosophy. After World War 1, his work became more controlled. *White Line* (1920) and *In the Black Circle* (1921) demonstrate the beginnings of a refinement of geometrical form that developed during his years (1922–33) at the BAUHAUS.

Kandy City in Sri Lanka. Former capital of the ancient kings of Ceylon, it was occupied by the Portuguese and the Dutch before being captured by the British in 1815. Kandy is a market centre for a region producing tea, rice, rubber and cacao. The chief industry is tourism. Pop. (1990) 104,000.

kangaroo Largest MARSUPIAL mammal. Kangaroos have powerful hind legs designed for leaping and fighting. The short front legs are used for grasping. The long, muscular tail acts as a balance while hopping, and as a prop when it stands on its hind legs. The single offspring (joey) is suckled in the female's (flyer) pouch for six months. They feed on roots and fungi and often live in burrows. Red kangaroos (*Macropus rufus*) graze on the Australian plains. Males (boomers) of the species may grow to more than 2m (7ft) tall and weigh up to 90kg (200lb). The grey kangaroo (*M. kanguru*) inhabits open woodland in Australia and Tasmania. The wallaroo or euro (*M. robustus*) lives in rocky hills. Kangaroos can perform single leaps of up to 8m (26ft) and travel up to 48km/h (30mph). Family Macropodidae. *See also* WALLABY

kangaroo rat Tiny, desert-dwelling RODENT of W North America. It has long hind legs and a long tail, and hops. It stores seeds in its cheek pouches. Length: to 41cm (16in), including tail. Family Heteromyidae; genus *Dipodomys*.

Kang Youwei (1858–1927) Chinese political reformer and philosopher. In *One World Philosophy* (1900), he developed a reformist form of CONFUCIANISM. In 1898, Kang persuaded Emperor Guangxu to pass a series of decrees known as the "Hundred Days of Reform". Empress Dowager CIXI imprisoned Guangxu and annulled most of the reforms. Kang fled to Canada.

Kano City in N central Nigeria; capital of Kano state. The city dates from before the 12th century and became a Muslim possession in the 16th century. In the early 19th century Kano was conquered by the FULANI. Today, it is a trading centre for a region producing cotton and nuts. Industries: textiles, leather goods, brewing, chemicals. Pop. (1996) 674,000.

Kanpur (Cawnpore) City on the River Ganges, Uttar Pradesh, N India. In 1801, Kanpur was ceded to the British and became a frontier post. During the INDIAN MUTINY (1857) the entire British garrison in Kanpur was massacred. The city is now a major industrial and commercial centre. Industries: chemicals, leather goods, textiles. Pop. (1991) 1,879,420.

Kansas State in central USA; the capital is TOPEKA. Other major cities are Wichita and KANSAS CITY. First visited by Spanish explorers in the 16th century, the area passed from France to the new United States under the LOUISIANA PURCHASE (1803). It was Native American territory until 1854, when the Territory of Kansas was created and the area opened up for settlement. It was admitted to the Union as a free state in 1861. Part of the Great Plains, the land rises from the prairies of the E to the semi-arid high plains of the W. The area is drained by the Kansas and Arkansas rivers. Kansas is the leading US producer of wheat. Maize, hay and sorghum are also grown, and cattle raising is important. Industries: transport equipment, chemicals, petroleum products, machinery. Area: 213,094sq km (82,276sq mi). Pop. (2000) 2,688,418.

Kansas City City in W Missouri, USA, on the Missouri River, adjacent to KANSAS CITY, Kansas. Established in 1821 as a trading post, it developed in the 1860s with the introduction of the railway and the growth in cattle trade. Industries: aerospace equipment, vehicles, chemicals, petroleum products, livestock, grain. Pop. (1990) 435,146.

Kansas City City in NE Kansas, USA, at the confluence of the Kansas and Missouri rivers, adjacent to KANSAS CITY, Missouri. Part of a Native American reservation, it was acquired by Wyandotte Native Americans in 1843 and sold to the US government in 1855. The modern city was established in 1886. Industries: livestock, motor vehicles, metal products, chemicals. Pop. (1990) 149,767.

Kansas-Nebraska Act (May 30, 1854) US Congressional measure, sponsored by Senator Stephen A. DOUGLAS, which allowed US territories to decide for themselves such domestic matters as whether to allow slavery. The act failed to satisfy pro- and anti-slavery forces alike.

Kant, Immanuel (1724–1804) German metaphysical philosopher. He was a teacher and professor of logic and METAPHYSICS at the University of Königsberg. The order and modesty of Kant's life was undisturbed by the notoriety caused by his publications. Kant's philosophy of IDEALISM, outlined in *Critique of Pure Reason* (1781), sought to discover the nature and boundaries of human knowledge. It was much influenced by Isaac NEWTON and David HUME. Kant's system of ethics, described in the *Critique of Practical Reason* (1790), places moral duty above happiness and asserts the existence of an absolute moral law (the "categorical imperative"). His views on aesthetics are embodied in his *Critique of Judgment* (1790). Kant also produced several essays in support of religious liberalism and the ENLIGHTENMENT.

kaolin (china clay) Fine clay composed chiefly of KAOLINITE, a hydrous silicate of aluminium. It is used in the manufacture of coated paper, ceramics and fine porcelains.

kaolinite Sheet silicate mineral, hydrous aluminium silicate ($Al_2Si_2O_5(OH)_4$). It is a product of the weathering of feldspar and has triclinic system tabular crystals. It is white with a dull lustre. Hardness 2–2.5; r.d. 2.6.

Kapil Dev (1959–) Indian cricketer. One of the game's greatest all-rounders, he captained India to victory in the 1983 World Cup. Kapil Dev played 131 tests (1978–94), taking a record 434 wickets and scoring 5,248 runs.

Kapitza, Peter Leonidovich (1894–1984) Russian physicist. He conducted research on MAGNETISM with Ernest RUTHERFORD at the Cavendish Laboratory (1924–32). In 1934, Kapitza returned to Russia. In 1938, he discovered the SUPERFLUIDITY of liquid helium. Kapitza shared the 1978 Nobel Prize for physics.

kapok Tropical tree with compound leaves and white or pink flowers. Its seed pods burst to release silky fibres, commonly used for stuffing and insulation. Height: to 50m (165ft). Family Bombacaceae; species *Ceiba pentandra*.

Karachai-Cherkassia Republic of the Russian Federation in the N Caucasus Mountains; the capital is Cherkessk. Karachai was a separate autonomous region within the Soviet Union (1926–43) until Stalin deported much of the Muslim population. In 1957, Karachai-Cherkassia was established as an autonomous region. In 1992, it became a republic of the Russian Federation. Area: 14,100sq km (5,442sq mi). Pop. (1995) 436,000.

Karachi City and seaport on the Arabian Sea, SE Pakistan; capital of Sind province. Settled in the early 18th century, in 1843 it passed to the British, who developed it as a major port. Karachi was the first capital of Pakistan (1947–59) and remains the country's largest city. It is an important trade centre for agricultural produce. Industries: steel, engineering, textiles, chemicals, printing and publishing. Pop. (1991 est.) 6,700,000.

Karadžić, Radovan (1945–) Serbian politician. In 1990, he founded the Serbian Democratic Party. In 1992, Bosnia-Herzegovina voted for independence from the Serb-dominated federation of Yugoslavia. Karadžić declared a separate Bosnian Serb state, Republika Srpska, with himself as president. With the support of Serbian president Slobodan MILOŠEVIĆ, he instituted a policy of "ethnic cleansing" of non-Serbs from the republic and waged war against the Bosnian state. In 1995, Milošević withdrew his support and Karadžić was forced to sign the Dayton peace accord with Bosnian President IZETBEGOVIĆ. In 1996, he was indicted by the United Nations (UN) for war crimes but remained at large.

Karajan, Herbert von (1908–89) German conductor. He conducted the Berlin State Opera (1938–45) and was director of the Vienna State Opera (1945–1964). As musical director of the Berlin Philharmonic Orchestra (1955–89) and artistic director of the Salzburg Festival (1956–60, 1964), Karajan dominated the European classical music scene.

Karakalpak Autonomous republic in W Uzbekistan; the capital is Nukus. In 1925, it was made an autonomous region of Kazakstan (1925) and a separate republic of the Soviet Union in 1933. In 1936, it became part of the Uzbek Soviet Republic and retained its autonomous status within independent Uzbekistan. Crops include alfalfa, rice, cotton, maize and jute. Livestock raising is important, and there is some light industry. Area: 165,600sq km (63,940sq mi). Pop. (1990) 1,244,700.

Karakoram Range Mountain range in central Asia, extending SE from E Afghanistan to Jammu and Kashmir in India. It includes some of the world's highest mountains, among them K2. Length: c.480km (300mi).

Kara-Kum Desert in central Asia, extending from the Caspian Sea (W) to the River Amudarya (E), and including most of TURKMENISTAN. The Kara-Kum Canal carries water c.800km (500mi) from the Amudarya to ASHGABAT to irrigate a cotton-producing region. Area: c.350,000sq km (135,000sq mi).

Karamanlis, Konstantinos (1907–98) Greek statesman, prime minister (1955–63, 1974–80), president (1980–85, 1990–95). He entered Parliament in 1935. On becoming prime minister, he formed his own party, the National Radical Union (ERE). In 1963, Karamanlis resigned after an election defeat. He opposed the military junta from self-imposed exile. In 1974, he returned as leader of the new Democratic Party (ND).

karate Martial art popularized in Japan in the 1920s. The technique, which involves a formal method of physical and mental training, includes a variety of blows using the hand, legs, elbows and head. In competition, scoring depends on the finality of the blow. *See also* JUJITSU

Karelia Republic of the Russian Federation in NW European RUSSIA, bounded by the White Sea to the E and FINLAND to the W; the capital is Petrozavodsk. In the Middle Ages the region was an independent Finnish state. Split in the 12th century between Sweden and NOVGOROD, it was unified under Swedish rule in the 17th century. The E was returned to Russia in 1721, while the W was part of Finland until 1940. After the Soviet-Finnish War (1939–40), the E sector absorbed 36,000sq km (14,000sq mi) of Finnish land and became a constituent republic of the Soviet Union. During World War 2 the Finns occupied most of Karelia, but it was returned to the Soviet Union in 1944. In 1992, it became a republic of the Russian Federation. Climate restricts farming to the S, where vegetables and cereal crops are grown and livestock are raised. Fishing and timber are the chief industries. The region has valuable mineral deposits. Area: 172,400sq km (66,564sq mi). Pop. (1994) 794,200.

Karen Thai-Chinese cultural group, mostly farmers, living in the Kayah state of Burma. They form *c*.10% of Burma's population. The hill tribes practise an animistic religion, while the plains-dwellers are Christians and Buddhists. Their tonal languages are of the Sino-Tibetan family. The Karen have fiercely opposed Burmese domination and have a large measure of local autonomy.

Karloff, Boris (1887–1969) US actor, b. England as William Henry Pratt. His portrayal of the monster in *Frankenstein* (1931) led to a series of roles in horror films. Karloff and Bela LUGOSI formed a macabre duo in films such as *The Raven* (1935) and *The Body Snatcher* (1945).

Karlsruhe City on the River Rhine, Baden-Württemberg, SW Germany. Founded in 1715 by the margrave of Baden-Durlach, it was the capital of the state of Baden. Karlsruhe suffered severe damage during World War 2. It has a university and several colleges, and has been a centre of atomic research since 1956. Industries: jewellery, chemicals, pharmaceuticals, oil refining. Pop. (1995) 277,000.

karma (Sanskrit, action) Central moral doctrine in HINDUISM, BUDDHISM and JAINISM. It is a natural, impersonal law of moral cause and effect, unconnected with divine punishment for sins. In Hinduism and Jainism, karma is the sum of a person's actions which are passed on from one life to the next and determine the nature of rebirth. Buddhism rejects this continuity of the "soul" through REINCARNATION. The intention behind an action determines the fate of an individual. Release from rebirth into NIRVANA depends on knowledge of the Real, which in turn enables neutral action. *See also* YOGA

Karnak *See* LUXOR

Karnataka State in SW India; the capital is BANGALORE. It was known as **Mysore** until 1973. A predominantly agricultural state, coffee is the major cash crop. Hill forests provide most of the world's sandalwood. Karnataka formed part of the MAURYA EMPIRE (*c*.321–185 BC). In 1313, it was conquered by the DELHI SULTANATE, but was quickly restored to Hindu control. In 1761 HYDER ALI captured the region. In 1799, his son, TIPPOO SAHIB, was defeated by the British. Pop. (1991) 44,817,400.

Karpov, Anatoly (1951–) Russian chess player. In 1975, he became world champion by default after

Bobby FISCHER failed to play. Karpov successfully defended his title against Victor Korchnoi (1978, 1981). In 1985, he was defeated by Gary KASPAROV. Karpov suffered further defeats against Kasparov (1986, 1987, 1990) before Kasparov formed his own chess federation and forfeited the old title (1993–2000) to him.

karst Limestone plateau characterized by irregular protuberant rocks, sinkholes, caves, disappearing streams and underground drainage. Such topography is named after its most typical site in the Karst region of Slovenia.

Kashmir Region in N India and NE Pakistan; former Indian princely state. When the Indian subcontinent was partitioned in 1947, the maharaja of Kashmir acceded to India, precipitating war between India and Pakistan. A cease-fire agreement left it divided between the Indian-controlled state of JAMMU AND KASHMIR and the Pakistan-controlled areas in the N and W of the region. The N area of Kashmir is ruled directly by the Pakistan government; the W area, **Azad Kashmir**, is partly autonomous. The **Aksai Chin** area of Kashmir, on the border with Tibet, is occupied by China. Indian Jammu and Kashmir has remained in a state of unrest. Kashmir includes parts of the HIMALAYAS and the KARAKORAM RANGE. The Vale of Kashmir, in the valley of the River Jhelum, is the most populated area, and wheat and rice are grown. Total area: 222,236sq km (85,806sq mi).

Kasparov, Gary (1963–) Azerbaijani chess player, b. Gary Weinstein. In 1985, he defeated Anatoly KARPOV to become the youngest-ever chess world champion. Kasparov successfully defended his title against Karpov in 1986, 1987 and 1990. In 1996, he defeated the IBM Deep Blue chess computer, but in 1997 he was defeated by an enhanced version of Deep Blue. In 2000, he lost his world title to Vladimir Kramnik.

Kassel City on the River Fulda, Hesse, central Germany. Founded in the 10th century, it was capital of Hesse-Kassel from the mid-16th century and of Hesse-Nassau from 1866 to 1944. Kassel was almost completely destroyed in World War 2. Industries: vehicles, machinery, textiles, optical instruments. Pop. (1990) 197,900.

Katmandu (Kathmandu) Capital of Nepal, situated *c*.1,370m (4,500ft) above sea level in a valley of the Himalayas. It was founded in AD 723. It was an independent city from the 15th century until 1768, when it was captured by Gurkhas. Katmandu is Nepal's administrative, commercial and religious centre. Industries: tourism. Pop. (1993) 535,000.

Katowice City in S Poland. Founded in the 16th century and chartered in 1865, it was occupied by Germany throughout World War 2. It is one of Poland's foremost industrial centres, producing coal, iron and steel, heavy machinery and chemicals. Pop. (1996) 334,000.

katydid (bush CRICKET) Green to brown leaf-like insect found throughout the world, named after its distinctive call. Its wings are arched over its back, and it has long antennae. Length: to 3.5.cm (1.4in). Family Tettigoniidae.

Katz, Sir Bernard (1911–) British biophysicist, b. Germany. He shared the 1970 Nobel Prize for physiology or medicine with Ulf von Euler and Julius Axelrod for work on the chemistry of nerve transmission. Katz discovered how the NEUROTRANSMITTER acetylcholine is released by neural impulses, causing muscles to contract.

Kauffmann, Angelica (1741–1807) Swiss painter. In 1766, she went to England, where she earned a reputation for her neoclassical portraits. A protégée of Sir Joshua REYNOLDS, Kauffmann was a founder-member (1768) of the Royal Academy (RA). She decorated houses designed by Robert and James ADAM. From 1781, she lived in Italy.

Kaufman, George Simon (1889–1961) US dramatist. He collaborated on more than 40 plays. Kaufman won the Pulitzer Prize for the musical *Of Thee I Sing* (1931). He won a second Pulitzer Prize for *You Can't Take It With You* (1936), written in collaboration with Moss HART. Kaufman and Hart also produced *The Man Who Came To Dinner* (1939). He worked with Edna Ferber on *Stage Door* (1936). Kaufman directed *Guys and Dolls* (1950).

Kaunas City and port in S Lithuania. Founded in the 11th century, it became part of Russia in 1795. It was capital of independent Lithuania (1918–40). Industries: iron and steel, electrical machinery, chemicals, textiles. Pop. (1996) 411,000.

Kaunda, Kenneth David (1924–) Zambian statesman, president (1964–91). In 1959 he was imprisoned for membership of the banned Zambia African National Congress. In 1960, Kaunda became leader of the United National Independence Party (UNIP). Kaunda led Northern Rhodesia to independence as Zambia, becoming its first president. In 1972, he imposed single-party rule. Kaunda was a staunch opponent of APARTHEID and played a leading role in establishing an independent Namibia (1990). In 1991, severe economic problems and political unrest forced him to allow multiparty elections in which he was defeated by Frederick Chiluba. In 1997, following a failed military coup, Kaunda was imprisoned. In 1998, he was released and resigned as leader of UNIP.

Kaunitz, Wenzel Anton, Count von (1711–94) Austrian statesman. In 1748, he negotiated the treaty ending the War of the AUSTRIAN SUCCESSION. As chancellor and foreign minister (1753–92) under MARIA THERESA and JOSEPH II, Kaunitz favoured France over Austria's traditional ally, Prussia. His defensive alliance with France and Russia (1756) precipitated the SEVEN YEARS' WAR (1756–63). In 1772, Kaunitz secured Austria a share in the partition of Poland. The French Revolution (1789) destroyed the French alliance.

kauri pine Broad-leaved CONIFER, *Agathis australis*, native to New Zealand. It has flaky bark, bronze-green leaves and round cones. It was extensively milled by the early settlers of New Zealand. The trees made fine masts and its fossilized gum (copal) is used in the manufacture of lacquers and varnishes. Maoris regard the trees as forest gods. Height: to 45m (150ft). Family Araucariaceae.

Kawabata, Yasunari (1899–1972) Japanese novelist. Kawabata's first major work, *The Izu Dancer* (1925), established him as a leader in Japanese neo-impressionism. Other works, such as *Snow Country* (1935–47) and *The Sound of the Mountain* (1949–54), are compelling, melancholic reflections on love. He was the first Japanese writer to be awarded a Nobel Prize for literature (1968).

Kawasaki Industrial city on Tokyo Bay, SE Honshu, Japan. Kawasaki suffered extensive damage from bombing during World War 2. Industries: iron and steel, motor vehicles, oil, shipbuilding. Pop. (1995) 1,203,000.

Kayseri City in E Turkey, spectacularly situated at the foot of Mount Erciyas in Cappadocia. As Caesarea Cappadociae, it was capital of a Roman province in the 1st century AD. Taken by the Seljuk Turks in the 11th century, it was renamed Kayseri. It was subsequently captured by the Mongols (1243) and the Mamelukes (1419) before becoming part of the Ottoman Empire in 1515. Industries: textiles, sugar, cement, aircraft parts. Pop. (1994) 464,000.

Kazak Turkic-speaking Muslim people who inhabit KAZAKSTAN (*c*.6.5 million) and the adjacent Sinkiang province of China (*c*.800,000). Traditionally nomadic, in the 20th century they settled within the collective farm system of the former Soviet Union.

Kazakstan Republic in Central Asia. A vast flat country, it stretches more than 3,000km (2,000mi) from the VOLGA and CASPIAN SEA lowlands in the W to the ALTAI and TIAN SHAN mountains in the E. The Caspian Sea lowlands extend E through the ARAL SEA region and include the Karagiye depression at 132m (433ft) below sea level. Eastern Kazakstan contains several freshwater lakes, the largest of which is Lake BALKHASH. Kazakstan's rivers have been used extensively for irrigation, causing ecological problems: the ARAL SEA has shrunk from 66,900sq km (25,830sq mi) in 1960 to 33,642sq km (12,989sq mi) in 1993. Whole fishing villages are now barren desert. **Climate** Kazakstan has a continental dry climate. Winters are cold. At ALMATY, snow covers the ground for an average of 100 days each year. **Vegetation** Kazakstan has very little woodland. Grassy steppe covers much of the N, while the S is desert or semi-desert. Large dry areas between the Aral Sea and Lake Balkhash are irrigated farmland. **History** Little is known of the early history of Kazakstan, except that it was the home of nomadic peoples. In 1218, the Mongol Emperor GENGHIS KHAN conquered the region. Following his death the empire was divided into khanates. Feudal trading towns emerged beside the oases. In the late 15th century, the towns formed a Kazak state, which fought for its independence from the neighbouring khanates. In 1731, Kazakstan appealed to Russia for protection and voluntarily acceded to the Russian empire. In the early 19th century, Russia abolished the khanates and encouraged Russian settlement throughout Kazakstan. The conscription of Kazaks during World War 1 aroused much resentment, and after the Russian Revolution (1917), demands for independence grew. In 1920, Kazakstan became an autonomous Soviet republic and in 1936 a full constituent republic. During the 1920s and 1930s, the process of Russification increased. Stalin's forced collectivization of agriculture and rapid industrialization led to great famine. Soviet minorities were transported to Kazakstan. In the 1950s, the "Virgin Lands" project sought to turn vast areas of grassland into cultivated land to feed the Soviet Union. The Soviets placed many of their nuclear missile sites in Kazakstan and also built their first fastbreeder nuclear reactor at Mangyshlak. In 1986, nationalist riots were prompted by the imposition of a Russian to lead the republic. Following the dissolution of the Soviet Union, Kazakstan declared independence (December 1991) and joined the COMMONWEALTH OF INDEPENDENT STATES (CIS). **Politics** A former Communist Party leader, Nursultan Nazarbayev, was Kazakstan's first elected president. He introduced free-market reforms and a new constitution. Multiparty elections were held in 1994. In a 1995, referendum Nazarbayev was confirmed as president until 2000. In 1996, the government announced plans to move the capital to Aqmola by 2000. Aqmola is nearer to the main industrial areas and mineral resources in the N. **Economy** Kazakstan is a developing country (1995 GDP per capita, US$3,010). The break-up of the Soviet Union hit Kazak exports. In 1994, it entered into a single market agreement with other Central Asian states. Free-market reforms have encouraged inward investment. Kazakstan is rich in mineral resources. It is the world's ninth-largest producer of bituminous coal. Its gas, oil and gold reserves

---

KAZAKSTAN
AREA: 2,717,300sq km (1,049,150sq mi)
POPULATION: 19,006,000
CAPITAL (POPULATION): Aqmola (280,000)

are being increasingly exploited. In 1996, construction started on a pipeline to Russia. Agriculture is highly developed. Grain is the principal crop.

Kazan, Elia (1909–99) US film director and novelist, b. Turkey. Kazan was one of the founders of the ACTORS' STUDIO. His work in the cinema includes *A Tree Grows in Brooklyn* (1945), *Gentleman's Agreement* (1947) and *On the Waterfront* (1954). He wrote two best-selling novels, *America, America* (1962) and *The Arrangement* (1967).

Kazan City and port on the River Volga, E European Russia; capital of TATAR REPUBLIC. Founded in the 13th century, Kazan became the capital of the Tatar khanate in 1438. Conquered by Ivan IV, it served as the E outpost of Russian colonization. Industries: electrical equipment, engineering, oil refining, chemicals, fur. Pop. (1994) 1,092,000.

Kazantzakis, Nikos (1885–1957) Greek writer. His epic poem *The Odyssey* (1938) is an ambitious modern sequel to Homer's work. Kazantakis is best-known for religious and philosophical novels, such as *Zorba the Greek* (1946) and *The Last Temptation of Christ* (1951).

Kean, Edmund (c.1787–1833) English actor. In 1814, he made a notable London debut as Shylock at Drury Lane Theatre. Kean became renowned for his interpretations of Shakespearean tragic roles.

Keating, Paul John (1944–) Australian statesman, prime minister (1991–96). He entered Parliament in 1969 and served as treasurer (1983–91) in the government of Bob HAWKE. Keating succeeded Hawke as prime minister. An outspoken advocate of republicanism, he won the 1993 general election. In 1996 elections, Keating was defeated by John HOWARD.

Keaton, Buster (Joseph Francis) (1895–1966) US actor and director. Keaton's acrobatic stunts and deadpan features made him one of the biggest comedy stars of the silent-film era. His ten full-length features include the classics *The Navigator* (1924) and *The General* (1926). The advent of the "talkies" marked a decline in his career.

Keats, John (1795–1821) English poet, one of the major figures of ROMANTICISM. His first volume, *Poems* (1817), included "On First Looking into Chapman's Homer". Keats was savagely criticized for the four-volume romance *Endymion* (1818). *Lamia, Isabella, The Eve of St Agnes and Other Poems* (1820) included the ballad "La Belle Dame sans Merci" and the magnificent lyrics "Ode on a Grecian Urn", "Ode to a Nightingale" and "Ode to Autumn". Keats died of tuberculosis in Rome, leaving unfinished the epic *Hyperion*. Percy SHELLEY mourned his passing in his elegy *Adonais* (1821)

Keble, John (1792–1866) English churchman and poet. His poetic volume *The Christian Year* (1827) led to an appointment as professor of poetry (1831–41) at Oxford University. In 1833 Keble preached a sermon on "National Apostasy" that is widely held to mark the start of the OXFORD MOVEMENT.

Keegan, Kevin (1951–) English footballer and manager. He played as a forward for Liverpool (1971–77), Hamburg (1977–80), Southampton (1980–82) and Newcastle (1982–84). Keegan earned 63 caps for England (1972–82). He was European Footballer of the Year in 1978 and 1979. In 1992, Keegan became manager of Newcastle United, leading them in to the Premier League. In 1997, he moved to Fulham. In 1999, Keegan succeeded Glenn HODDLE as England coach.

Keelung (Chilung) City on the East China Sea, N Taiwan. Occupied by the Spanish in the early 17th century, it was later briefly in Dutch hands. Under Japanese occupation (1895–1945) Keelung developed rapidly. An important commercial centre, it is Taiwan's principal

naval base. Industries: fishing, chemicals, shipbuilding. Pop. (1992) 355,894.

Keillor, Garrison Edward (1942–) US writer and humourist. His bittersweet stories about the fictional community of Lake Wobegon include *Happy To Be Here* (1981), *Leaving Home* (1987) and *We Are Still Married* (1989).

Kekulé von Stradonitz, Friedrich August (1829–96) German chemist. He discovered the ring structure of BENZENE. He worked on the structure of organic molecules and on the concept of valence, particularly with respect to benzene and other aromatic compounds.

Keller, Helen Adams (1880–1968) US social worker, writer and lecturer. With the help of her teacher, Anne Sullivan, Keller overcame the loss of sight, hearing and speech, caused by an early illness, to master several languages and lecture throughout the world. Her books include *The Story of My Life* (1902), *The World I Live In* (1908) and *The Open Door* (1957).

Kellogg-Briand Pact (1928) International peace agreement negotiated by US secretary of state Frank B. Kellogg and French foreign minister Aristide BRIAND. It renounced war as a means of settling international disputes and was subsequently signed by most of the world's governments.

Kelly, Gene (1912–96) US dancer, choreographer, film star and director. His major films, co-directed with Stanley Donen, were *On the Town* (1949), *An American in Paris* (1951) and the hugely popular *Singin' in the Rain* (1951).

Kelly, Grace Patricia (1929–82) US film actress. She appeared in *High Noon* (1952) and *Mogambo* (1953), and won an Academy Award for her role in *The Country Girl* (1954). She retired from the screen after marrying Prince Rainier of Monaco in 1956. Kelly died in a car accident.

kelp Any of several brown SEAWEEDS commonly found on Atlantic and Pacific coasts, a type of brown ALGAE. A source of iodine and potassium compounds, kelps are used in a number of industrial processes. Giant kelp (*Macrocystis*) exceeds 46m (150ft) in length. Phylum Phaeophyta.

Kelvin, William Thomson, 1st Baron (1824–1907) Scottish physicist and mathematician after whom the absolute scale of TEMPERATURE is named. The Kelvin temperature scale has its zero point at ABSOLUTE ZERO and degree intervals the same size as the degree Celsius. The freezing point of water occurs at 273K (0°C or 32°F) and the boiling point at 373K (100°C or 212°F). In THERMODYNAMICS he resolved conflicting interpretations of the first and second laws.

Kemal Atatürk *See* ATATÜRK, KEMAL

Kempis, Thomas à (1380–1471) German Augustinian monk and spiritual writer. Ordained in 1413, he remained in the monastery of the Brethren of the Common Life, near Zwolle, for most of his life. He wrote or edited numerous treatises on the life of the soul. The most famous work attributed to him is *Imitation of Christ* (c.1415–24). Other works include *Soliloquium Animae* and *De Tribus Tabernaculis*.

Kendall, Edward Calvin (1886–1972) US chemist who worked on the biological effects of the HORMONES of the ADRENAL GLANDS, in particular CORTISONE, which he isolated. He shared the 1950 Nobel Prize for physiology or medicine.

Keneally, Thomas Michael (1935–) Australian novelist. His best-known work, *Schindler's Ark* (1982), won the Booker Prize, and formed the basis of Steven SPIELBERG's film *Schindler's List* (1993).

Kennedy, Charles (1959–) British politician, leader of the LIBERAL DEMOCRATS (LD) (1999–). In 1982, Kennedy entered the House of Commons as MP for

Ross, Cromarty and Skye. In 1999, he succeeded Paddy ASHDOWN as Party leader. He has pursued a policy of constructive engagement with the Labour government and argued for Britain's entry into the euro.

Kennedy, Edward Moore (1932–) US senator. In 1962, he was elected as Massachusetts senator to finish the term of his brother John KENNEDY, who had become president. Following the assassination of his brothers, John and Robert, Teddy Kennedy's own presidential chances were shattered by his involvement in a fatal car accident (1969) on Chappaquiddick Island, Massachusetts. An effective critic of the REAGAN administration, he was re-elected to the Senate (1982, 1988, 1994).

Kennedy, John Fitzgerald (1917–63) 35th US President (1961–63). He was elected to Congress as a Democrat from Massachusetts in 1946, serving in the Senate from 1953 to 1960. Kennedy gained the presidential nomination in 1960 and narrowly defeated Richard NIXON. He adopted an ambitious and liberal programme, under the title of the "New Frontier", and embraced the cause of CIVIL RIGHTS, but his planned legislation was frequently blocked by Congress. In foreign policy, Kennedy founded the "Alliance for Progress", the aim of which was to improve the image of the USA abroad. Adopting a strong anti-communist line, he was behind the BAY OF PIGS disaster (1961) and outfaced KHRUSHCHEV in the ensuing CUBAN MISSILE CRISIS, which was followed by a US-Soviet treaty banning nuclear tests. He increased military aid to South Vietnam. Kennedy was assassinated in Dallas, Texas, on 22 November 1963.

Kennedy, Joseph Patrick (1888–1969) US businessman and politician. He was chairman of the Securities and Exchange Commission (1934–35) and ambassador to Great Britain (1937–40). He was involved in many philanthropic endeavours, especially the Joseph P. Kennedy Memorial Foundation, founded for a son killed in World War 2. He was determined that his sons, Joseph P. Kennedy Jr., John F. KENNEDY, Robert KENNEDY and Edward KENNEDY, should enter politics.

Kennedy, Nigel (1956–) English violinist. He has performed with many of the world's leading orchestras and also in jazz concerts with the violinist Stephane Grappelli. His recording of Vivaldi's *Four Seasons* was a bestseller.

Kennedy, Robert Francis (1925–68) US lawyer and politician. He served on the Senate Select Committee on Improper Activities in Labor or Management Field (1957–59) where he clashed with the Teamsters' Union president Jimmy HOFFA. In 1960, he managed the successful presidential campaign of his brother John F. KENNEDY. He became US attorney general (1961–64), vigorously enforcing CIVIL RIGHTS laws and promoting the Civil Rights Act of 1964. After his brother's assassination, he left the cabinet and was elected (1964) senator for New York. While a candidate for the Democratic presidential nomination, he was assassinated (4 June) in Los Angeles.

Kennedy Space Center *See* CAPE CANAVERAL

Kent County in SE England, S of the Thames estuary and NW of the Strait of Dover; the county town is Maidstone. Roman settlement began in AD 43. It later became an Anglo-Saxon kingdom and remained a separate kingdom until the 9th century. Apart from the North Downs, the area is mainly low-lying. It is drained by the rivers Medway and Stour. Cereals, hops, fruit and vegetables are grown, and sheep and cattle are reared. DOVER, FOLKESTONE and Ramsgate are ports. There are Norman cathedrals at CANTERBURY and Rochester. Industries: paper-making, shipbuilding, chemicals, brewing. Area: 3,723sq km (1,441sq mi). Pop. (1991) 1,508,873

Kentucky State in SE central USA; the capital is FRANKFORT. Other major cities include Lexington and Louisville. Ceded to Britain by France in 1763, Kentucky became the 15th state. Its loyalties were divided at the outbreak of the CIVIL WAR, and the state was invaded by both sides. Most of the area consists of rolling plains. In the SE, the Cumberland Mountains dominate a rugged plateau region. The state is drained chiefly by the Ohio and Tennessee rivers. Tobacco is the chief crop, followed by hay, maize and soya beans. The state is noted for breeding thoroughbred racehorses. Industries: electrical equipment, machinery, chemicals, primary metals, coal production. Area: 104,623sq km (40,395sq mi). Pop. (2000) 4,041,769.

Kenya Republic in E Africa. Kenya straddles the Equator. Most of Kenya comprises high plains. MOMBASA lies on the narrow coastal plain. In the NW is an area of high scrubland around Lake Turkana. In the SW are the Kenyan highlands, including Mount KENYA, the country's highest peak at 5,199m (17,057ft), and the capital, NAIROBI. The Great RIFT VALLEY cuts through W Kenya. **Climate** Mombasa is hot and humid. Inland, the climate is moderated by elevation: Nairobi has summer temperatures $c.10°C$ ($18°F$) lower than Mombasa. **Vegetation** The coast is lined with mangrove swamps. The inland plains are bushlands. Much of the N is semi-desert. Forests and grasslands are found in the densely populated SW highlands. **History and politics** Some of the earliest hominid fossils have been found in S Kenya. Kenya's coast has been a trading centre for more than 2,000 years. In the 8th century, the Arabs founded settlements. In the 16th century, Portuguese traders controlled the area. In 1729, Arab dynasties regained control. In 1895, Britain gained rights to the coast. Colonization began in 1903, and land was acquired from the KIKUYU for plantations and farms. The territory was divided into the inland Kenya Colony and the coastal Protectorate of Kenya. European settlement intensified. The employment of Africans as plantation and farm labourers led to social unrest. MAU MAU waged an armed struggle (1952–56) for land rights and independence. Britain declared a state of emergency and imprisoned its leader, Jomo KENYATTA. In 1963, Kenya achieved independence, becoming a republic in 1964. Jomo Kenyatta was the first president. His authoritarian regime tried to establish unity. Drought and territorial disputes with Uganda and Tanzania created civil unrest. In 1978, Kenyatta died and was succeeded by Daniel arap MOI. Moi rejected calls for democracy and cracked down on dissent. In 1982, the Kenya African National Union (KANU) became the sole legal political party. Following nationwide riots in 1988, the government agreed to electoral reform. In 1992 multiparty elections, Moi was re-elected, but independent observers claimed the elections were rigged. Prior to 1997 elections, 14 pro-democracy demonstrators were killed by police. Moi was re-elected amid allegations of electoral malpractice. In 1998, fighting between the Kikuyu and Kalenjin tribes killed more than 100 people. **Economy** Kenya is a developing country (1995 GDP per capita, US$1,380). Agriculture employs $c.80\%$ of the workforce. Kenya is the world's fourth-largest tea producer. Coffee is an important cash crop. The chief food crop is maize. Kenya's wildlife parks and reserves attract many tourists.

KENYA
AREA: 580,370sq km (224,081sq mi)
POPULATION: 35,060,000
CAPITAL (POPULATION): Nairobi (2,000,000)

Kenya, Mount Extinct volcanic mountain in central Kenya. The second-highest mountain in Africa, it was first climbed in 1899. It consists of three peaks, the highest of which is Batian, rising to 5,200m (17,058ft).

Kenyatta, Jomo (1893–1978) Kenyan statesman, president of Kenya (1964–78). A KIKUYU, he led the struggle for Kenyan independence from 1946. Kenyatta was imprisoned (1952–61) by the British colonial authorities for alleged involvement in the MAU MAU uprising. As leader of the Kenya African National Union (KANU), he became the first president of an independent Kenya. Although Kenyatta suppressed domestic opposition, he presided over a prosperous economy and generally followed pro-Western policies. He was succeeded by Daniel arap MOI.

Kepler, Johannes (1571–1630) German mathematician and astronomer. He supported the heliocentric theory put forward by COPERNICUS. Kepler succeeded Tycho BRAHE as imperial mathematician to Emperor Rudolf II. From Brahe's observations, he concluded that Mars moves in an elliptical orbit, and he went on to establish his three laws of planetary motion: **law one** states that the orbit of a planet is an ellipse with the Sun at one of the foci; **law two** (law of areas) states that the line joining the planet to the Sun (radius vector) sweeps out equal areas in equal times; **law three** states that the square of the period of revolution (P) is directly proportional to the cube of the mean distance of the planet from the Sun. The *Rudolphine Tables* (1627), based on Brahe's observations and Kepler's laws, remained the most accurate until the 18th century.

Kerala State on the Arabian Sea, SW India; the capital is Trivandrum. One of India's smallest states, it is the most densely populated. Fishing is important. Products: rubber, tea, coffee, coconuts, cashew nuts, ivory, textiles, teak, chemicals, minerals. Area: 38,864sq km (15,005sq mi). Pop. (1991) 29,098,518.

keratin Fibrous PROTEIN present in large amounts in SKIN cells, where it serves as a protective layer. Hair and fingernails are made up of cells filled with keratin, which is also the basis of claws, horns and feathers.

Kerensky, Alexander Feodorovich (1881–1970) Russian moderate political leader. He became prime minister of the provisional government in July 1917, shortly after the overthrow of the Tsar. Deposed by the BOLSHEVIKS, he fled to France. *See also* RUSSIAN REVOLUTION

Kern, Jerome David (1885–1945) US songwriter of film and show music. His outstanding musical is *Showboat* (staged 1927; filmed 1936, 1959), containing the song "Ol' Man River". He influenced Richard RODGERS and George GERSHWIN.

kerosene (paraffin) Distilled petroleum product that is heavier than petrol but lighter than diesel fuel. Kerosene is used in camping stoves, tractor fuels and fuels for jet and turboprop aircraft.

Kerouac, Jack (1922–69) US poet and novelist. His debut novel was *The Town and the City* (1950). *On the Road* (1957) established Kerouac as the leading novelist of the BEAT MOVEMENT. Later works include *The Dharma Bums* (1958), *Desolation Angels* (1965) and the posthumously published *Visions of Cody* (1972).

Kerry County in Munster province, SW Republic of Ireland; the county town is Tralee. It is a mountainous region with an indented coastline and many lakes. Oats and potatoes are grown, and sheep and cattle raised. Industries: tourism, fishing, footwear, woollen goods. Area: 4,701sq km (1,815sq mi). Pop. (1991) 121,894.

kestrel (windhover) Small FALCON that lives mainly in Europe, and hovers over its prey before attacking. It feeds mainly on rodents, insects and small birds. Length: 30cm (12in). Species *Falco tinnunculus*.

Kesselring, Albert (1885–1960) German general. During World War 2, he commanded the LUFTWAFFE, later becoming commander-in-chief in Italy (1943) and then supreme commander on the Western Front (1945). In 1947 Kesselring was sentenced to death for his part in the massacre of Italian hostages in 1943. The sentence was commuted to life imprisonment and he was freed in 1952.

Kew Gardens (Royal Botanic Gardens) Collection of plants and trees in SW London, UK. Founded in 1760 by George III's mother, they were given to the nation by Queen Victoria in 1840. Much plant research is carried out here. *See also* BANKS, SIR JOSEPH

key In music, term used to indicate TONALITY in a composition, based on one of the major or minor scales. The key of a piece of music is indicated by the key signature at the left hand end of the stave. The key of a passage may, however, change by the addition of accidentals before prescribed notes; a change of key is known as a modulation.

keyboard instrument Large group of musical instruments played by pressing keys on a keyboard. Notes are sounded by hitting or plucking a string (as in the PIANO or HARPSICHORD), forcing air through a pipe or reed (ORGAN or ACCORDION), or electronically (SYNTHESIZER).

Keynes, John Maynard (1883–1946) English economist. In *The General Theory of Employment, Interest and Money* (1936), which was strongly influenced by the GREAT DEPRESSION, Keynes established the foundation of modern MACROECONOMICS. He advocated the active intervention of government in the economy to stimulate employment and prosperity. He was highly influential as an economic adviser in World War 2, and took a leading role in the BRETTON WOODS CONFERENCE of 1944.

KGB (*Komitet Gosudarstvennoye Bezhopaznosti*, Rus. Committee for State Security) Soviet secret police. In the 1980s, it employed *c.*500,000 people and controlled all police, security and intelligence operations in the Soviet Union. It also gathered military and political information on other countries. The KGB opposed liberalization under GORBACHEV, and its chief led an attempted coup against him in 1991. After the collapse of communism and the break-up of the Soviet Union, it underwent extensive reform.

Khachaturian, Aram Ilyich (1903–78) Armenian composer. He wrote a piano concerto (1936) and a violin concerto (1940), but his best-known works are probably the ballets *Gayane* (1942) and *Spartacus* (1953).

Khafre, Great Sphinx of Monumental statue of the SPHINX at GIZA, Egypt. Its name derives from the pharaoh whose pyramid it sits in front of and whose portrait is said to be represented by the sphinx's face. The strange and compelling symbolism of its part human, part animal body continues to baffle archaeologists.

Ibn Khaldun (1332–1406) Arab historian, b. Tunis. He served the sultan of Morocco, but was forced into exile in Spain after being implicated in a rebellion. He worked as an envoy for the Muslim king of Granada, but his political career suffered amidst the endless intrigues that beset the decline of the ALMOHAD empire. He abandoned politics in order to write the *Kitab al'Ibar* (*Universal History*) of Muslim North Africa. In his *Introduction to History* (*Muqaddimah*), Ibn Khaldun posited a cyclical philosophy of history in which civilizations alternate between growth and decay. He also argued for the creation of a "science of culture" to study the political and economic factors responsible for transformations in human society. In 1382, Ibn Khaldun became a teacher at the al-Azhar University, Cairo. He negotiated with TAMERLANE in an attempt to relieve the siege of Damascus in 1401.

Khan, (Niazi) Imran (1952–) Pakistani cricketer and politician. He made his test debut for Pakistan in 1971. He played English county cricket for Worcestershire (1975–77) and Sussex (1978–88). He captained Pakistan for most of the decade 1982–92, leading them to victory in the 1992 World Cup. An outstanding allrounder, he took 325 wickets in test matches and became only the second player to score a century and take ten wickets in a test (1983). In the 1997 Pakistan elections, his political aspirations suffered a setback.

Kharkov (Kharkiv) City in NE Ukraine. It was founded in the 17th century to serve as a stronghold for the Ukrainian Cossacks defending Russia's S border. During the 19th century it developed industrially, stimulated by nearby coalfields. From 1919 to 1934, it was capital of the Ukrainian Soviet Socialist Republic. Industries: mining machinery, ball-bearings, chemicals, electrical goods. Pop. (1995) 1,555,000.

Khartoum Capital of Sudan, at the junction of the Blue NILE and White Nile rivers. Khartoum was founded in the 1820s by MUHAMMAD ALI. In 1885, it was besieged by Mahdists, and General GORDON was killed. In 1898 it became the seat of government of the Anglo-Egyptian Sudan, and from 1956 the capital of independent Sudan. Industries: cement, gum arabic, chemicals, glass, cotton textiles, printing. Pop. (1993) 925,000.

Khatami, Muhammad (1943–) Iranian statesman, president (1997–). A leading opponent of Shah Muhammad Reza PAHLAVI, he was elected to Iran's national assembly after the Islamic Revolution (1979). In 1982, Khatami was appointed minister of culture and Islamic guidance by Ayatollah KHOMEINI. Conservative clerics criticized Khatami's relatively liberal stance on press freedom, and he was forced to resign in 1992. In the 1997 presidential elections, Khatami was supported by the outgoing President Hashemi RAFSANJANI. Khatami's campaign for economic reform and greater social freedom gained him 70% of the vote. His moderate government faced strong opposition from the conservative establishment, and their blocking of reforms produced widespread unrest in 1999. His reforms were overwhelmingly endorsed in the 2000 parliamentary elections.

Khayyám, Omar *See* OMAR KHAYYÁM

Khazars Turkic people who first appeared in the lower Volga region *c*.2nd century AD. Between the 8th and 10th centuries, their empire prospered and extended from N of the Black Sea to the River Volga and from W of the Caspian Sea to the River Dnieper. They conquered the Volga Bulgars and fought the Arabs, Russians and Pechenegs. In the 8th century, their ruling class adopted JUDAISM. In 965, their empire was destroyed by the army of Sviatoslav, Duke of Kiev.

Khmer Language of up to 85% of the inhabitants of Cambodia. It belongs to the Mon-Khmer language group and has given its name to the people who speak it. A Khmer empire was set up between the 9th and 15th centuries AD. In 1970, Cambodia was renamed the Khmer Republic. When the Republic fell to the KHMER ROUGE in 1975, the country was renamed Kampuchea; the name Cambodia was restored in 1989.

Khmer Rouge Cambodian communist guerrilla organization. It gained control of Cambodia in 1975. Led by POL POT and Khieu Samphan, it embarked on a forced communist transformation of Cambodian society, during which an

estimated 2 to 3 million people died. The regime lost power to the Vietnamese after a period of intense conflict in 1977–78. The Kampuchean National United Front for National Salvation, supported by the Vietnamese, founded a People's Republic in 1979. In 1982, the Khmer Rouge joined a coalition with Prince SIHANOUK (the former Cambodian leader) and the Khmer Peoples National Liberation Front. From 1988, attempts were made to settle the political situation by peaceful means. In 1991, each faction signed a cease-fire agreement, which was to be monitored by UNITED NATIONS (UN) troops. After an election in 1993, in which the Khmer Rouge refused to take part, Prince Sihanouk's parliamentary monarchy was re-established. Since being banned in 1994 membership of the Khmer Rouge has declined rapidly. In 1998 Pol Pot died.

Khoisan Group of South African languages. The Khoikhoi and SAN are the two largest groups of native speakers of these languages. The Khoisan languages also include Sandawe and Hadza, spoken by small tribal groups in Tanzania. *See also* CLICK LANGUAGE

Khomeini, Ruhollah (1900–89) Iranian ayatollah (religious leader). An Islamic scholar with great influence over his SHIITE students, he published (1941) a virulent attack on Riza Shah Pahlavi and remained an active opponent of his son, Muhammad Reza Shah PAHLAVI. Exiled in 1964, he returned to Iran in triumph after the fall of the Shah in 1979. His rule was characterized by strict religious orthodoxy, elimination of political opposition and economic turmoil. In 1989, Khomeini issued a *fatwa* (death order) against author Salman RUSHDIE. He was succeeded by Hojatoleslam RAFSANJANI. *See also* IRAN-IRAQ WAR

Khorana, Har Gobind (1922–) US biochemist who shared the 1968 Nobel Prize for physiology or medicine with Robert W. Holley and Marshall W. NIRENBERG for discoveries about the way in which GENES determine cell function. They established that most codons, combinations of three of the four different bases found in DNA and RNA, eventually cause the inclusion of a specific AMINO ACID into the cell proteins.

Khrushchev, Nikita Sergeyevich (1894–1971) Soviet statesman, first secretary of the Communist Party (1953–64) and Soviet prime minister (1958–64). Noted for economic success and ruthless suppression of opposition in the Ukraine, he was elected to the Politburo in 1939. After STALIN died, Khrushchev made a speech denouncing him and expelled his backers from the central committee. Favouring détente with the West, he yielded to the USA in the CUBAN MISSILE CRISIS. Economic setbacks and trouble with China led to his replacement by Leonid BREZHNEV and Aleksei KOSYGIN in 1964.

Khyber Pass Mountain pass in the Safid Kuh range, on the frontier between Afghanistan and Pakistan, linking the Kabul valley in Afghanistan (W) with Peshawar in Pakistan (E). Height: 1,073m (3,520ft). Length: 50km (30mi).

kibbutz Collective settlement in Israel that is owned by its members. The idea developed from the pioneering communities established by the Jewish settlers in a part of ancient Palestine that became Israel in 1948.

Kidd, William (1645–1701) Scottish pirate, commonly known as Captain Kidd. In 1696, after a successful career as a privateer, he turned to piracy on an expedition to East Africa. In 1699, Kidd was arrested in Boston, Massachusetts, USA, and sent to England where he was tried and hanged for piracy.

Kiddush Blessing recited before a meal on the eve of the Jewish Sabbath or of a festival. The head of the household says the prayer over a cup of wine, which is then passed around to each member to sip.

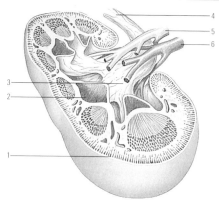

▲ **kidney** The human kidney is enclosed in a fibrous capsule and consists of an outer cortex region (1), a medulla region (2) with pyramidal-shaped areas and an inner pelvis region (3) that leads into the ureter (4). The renal artery (5) conducts blood into the kidney to be filtered, and it is then carried away by the renal vein (6).

kidney In vertebrates, one of a pair of organs responsible for regulating blood composition and EXCRETION of waste products. The kidneys are at the back of the abdomen, one on each side of the backbone. The human kidney consists of an outer cortex and an inner medulla with *c*.1 million tubules (NEPHRONS). Nephrons contain numerous CAPILLARIES, which filter the blood entering from the renal ARTERY. Some substances, including water, are reabsorbed into the blood. URINE remains, which is passed to the URETER and on to the BLADDER. *See also* HOMEOSTASIS

kidney machine (artificial kidney) Equipment designed to remove toxic wastes from the blood in kidney failure. Plastic tubing is used to pipe blood from the body into the machine, where waste products are filtered out by DIALYSIS.

Kiel City and seaport in N Germany, at the head of the Kiel Canal linking the North Sea and the Baltic Sea; capital of SCHLESWIG-HOLSTEIN state. Today, Kiel is a yachting centre. Industries: shipbuilding, textiles, precision instruments, printed matter. Pop. (1995) 247,000.

Kierkegaard, Søren (Aaby) (1813–55) Danish philosopher and theologian, regarded as the founder of modern EXISTENTIALISM. He believed that individuals must exercise FREE WILL and make deliberate decisions about the direction of their lives. Critical of HEGEL's speculative philosophy, he considered that religious faith was, at best, blind obedience to an irrational God. His books include *Either/Or* (1843) and *Philosophical Fragments* (1844).

Kiesinger, Kurt Georg (1904–88) German statesman, chancellor of West Germany (1966–69). He was elected to the Bundestag as a Christian Democrat in 1949. As federal chancellor, Kiesinger maintained the conservative policy of his predecessors, ADENAUER and ERHARD.

Kieslowski, Krzysztof (1941–96) Polish film director. He gained international praise for the ten-part epic *Dekalog* (1988), which drew on the commandments to reflect the pessimism and humanism in modern Poland. He received great critical acclaim for his final work, the *Three Colours* film trilogy: *Blue* (1993), *White* (1993), and *Red* (1994).

Kiev (Kiyev) Capital of Ukraine and a seaport on the River Dnieper. Founded in the 6th or 7th century, Kiev was the capital of Kievan Russia. It later came under Lithuanian then Polish rule before being absorbed into Russia. It became the capital of the Ukrainian Soviet Socialist Republic in 1934 and of independent Ukraine in 1991. Industries: shipbuilding, machine tools, footwear, furniture. Pop. (1993) 2,600,000.

Kigali Capital of Rwanda, central Africa. It was a trade centre during the period of German and Belgian colonial administration, becoming the capital when Rwanda achieved independence in 1962. Industries: tin mining, cotton, tanning, textiles, coffee. Pop. (1993) 234,500.

Kikuyu Bantu-speaking people of the highlands of Kenya, E Africa. British conquest strained their political and agricultural system; the result was an outbreak of terrorism during the 1950s by a group known as MAU MAU. After Kenya gained independence in 1963, they were the country's most important tribe, forming 20% of the population.

Kilauea Volcanic crater in Hawaii, USA, on SE Hawaii Island. It last erupted in 1968 and is the largest active crater in the world. Height: 1,247m (4,090ft). Depth: 152m (500ft).

Kildare County in Leinster province, E Republic of Ireland; the county town is Naas. A low-lying region, its chief rivers are the Liffey, Boyne and Barrow. Primarily agricultural, Kildare is noted for its breeding of racehorses. Area: 1,694sq km (654sq mi). Pop. (1991) 122,656.

Kilimanjaro Mountain in NE Tanzania, near the border with Kenya. The highest mountain in Africa, it is an extinct volcano with twin peaks joined by a broad saddle. Coffee is grown on the intensely cultivated S slopes. Height: Kibo 5,895m (19,340ft); Mawenzi 5,150m (16,896ft).

Kilkenny County in Leinster province, SE Republic of Ireland; the county town is Kilkenny. Part of the central plain of Ireland, it is drained by the rivers Suir, Barrow and Nore. Farmers grow cereal crops and vegetables, and cattle are reared. The chief industries are brewing and coal mining. Area: 2,062sq km (796sq mi). Pop. (1991) 73,635.

killer whale Large, toothed WHALE of the DOLPHIN family that lives mainly in the Pacific and Antarctic oceans. It is black above and white below, with a white patch above each eye. A fierce predator, it hunts in packs. Length: 9m (30ft). Species: *Orcinus orca*.

kiln In ceramics, an oven for firing ware. Early kilns were holes in the ground into which the ware was placed and covered by a large fire. Later, special wood- or coal-fired, oven-type kilns were built. Today, most kilns use gas or electricity.

kilogram (symbol kg) SI unit of mass defined as the mass of the international prototype cylinder of platinum-iridium kept at the International Bureau of Weights and Measures near Paris, France. One kilogram is equal to 1,000g (2.2lb).

Kimberley City in South Africa; capital of Northern Cape province. It was founded in 1871 after the discovery of diamonds nearby. Today, it is one of the world's largest diamond centres. Other industries include the processing of gypsum, iron and manganese. Pop. (1991) 167,060.

Kim Il Sung (1912–94) Korean statesman, first premier of North Korea (1948–72) and president (1972–94). He joined the Korean Communist Party in 1931 and led a Korean unit in the Soviet army during World War 2. In 1950, Kim led a North Korean invasion of South Korea, precipitating the KOREAN WAR (1950–53). Chairman of the Korean Workers' Party from 1948, his government suppressed all opposition and pursued strictly orthodox communist policies. He was succeeded by his son, KIM JONG IL.

Kim Jong Il (1941–) North Korean statesman, president (1994–), son of KIM IL SUNG. In 1980, he was officially named as his father's successor, assuming a more important role in government and being included in the personality cult that surrounded his father.

Kim Young Sam (1927–) South Korean statesman, president (1992–97). He was president of the New Democratic Party (NDP) from 1974. In 1979, he was banned from politics for his opposition to President Park. The ban was lifted in 1985. As leader of the Democratic Liberal Party (DLP), Kim Young Sam became president of South Korea.

kinetic energy (symbol K) Energy that an object possesses when in motion. It is the energy given to an object to set it in motion; it depends on the mass (m) of the object and its velocity (v), according to the equation $K = \frac{1}{2}mv^2$. On impact, it is converted into other forms of energy, such as heat, sound and light. *See also* POTENTIAL ENERGY

kinetics In physics, one of the branches of DYNAMICS. In chemistry, a branch of physical chemistry that deals with the rates of chemical reactions.

kinetic theory Theory in physics dealing with matter in terms of the forces between particles and the energies they possess. There are five principles to the kinetic theory: matter is composed of tiny particles; these are in constant motion; they do not lose energy in collision with each other or the walls of their container; there are no attractive forces between the particles or their container; and at any time the particles in a sample may not all have the same energy.

King, B.B. (Riley B.) (1925–) US blues guitarist and singer-songwriter. His albums include *Blues is King* (1967) and *Lucille Talks Back* (1975).

King, Billie Jean (1943–) US tennis player. She won the US Open women's singles four times (1967, 1971–72, 1974); a record 20 Wimbledon titles, including six singles titles (1966–68, 1972–73, 1975); the Australian Open (1968); and the French Open (1972). King also dominated women's doubles and advocated parity in the prize money for men's and women's competitions.

King, Martin Luther, Jr (1929–68) US Baptist minister and CIVIL RIGHTS leader. In 1956, he led the boycott of segregated public transport in Montgomery, Alabama. As founder (1960) and president of the Southern Christian Leadership Council (SCLC), he became a national figure. King opposed the Vietnam War and demanded measures to relieve poverty, organizing a huge march on Washington (1963) where he made his most famous ("I have a dream...") speech. In 1964, he became the youngest person to be awarded the Nobel Peace Prize. He was assassinated0 (4 April, 1968) in Memphis, Tennessee, where he had gone to support striking workers. His wife, **Coretta Scott King** (1927–), became a civil rights leader after his death. His son, **Martin Luther King III**, became leader of the SCLC in 1998.

King, Stephen (1947–) US novelist and short-story writer. King is a master of the modern horror novel. Many of his books, such as *The Shining* (1977) and *Misery* (1987), have been made into successful films.

King, William Lyon Mackenzie (1874–1950) Canadian statesman, prime minister (1921–30, 1935–48). His career was marked by the drive for national unity, culminating in the Statute of WESTMINSTER (1931). He made concessions to the Progressives, and he was conciliatory toward French-Canadian demands. In foreign policy his basic sympathies were isolationist and anti-British, but he cooperated closely with Britain and the US during World War 2.

kingbird (tyrant flycatcher) New World flycatcher whose habitat is mainly in tropical America. It dives at intruders and snaps up insects. It grows to 17cm (6.8in).

kingdom Topmost level (taxon) of the most widely adopted TAXONOMY for living organisms, the Five Kingdoms system. The Five Kingdoms are Animalia (ANIMAL), Plantae (PLANT), Fungi (FUNGUS), PROKARYOTAE and PROTISTA. Two subkingdoms are often recognized within Prokaryotae, ARCHAEBACTERIA and EUBACTERIA, but the bacteria are so diverse that many taxonomists consider that they comprise more than one kingdom. Some believe that they merit the status of a new, even higher category, DOMAINS. *See also* EUKARYOTE; PLANT CLASSIFICATION

kingfisher Compact, brightly coloured bird with a straight, sharp bill, which dives for fish along rivers, streams and lakes. It nests in a horizontal hole in an earth bank. Length: 13–43cm (5–17in). Family Alcedinidae.

King George's War (1744–48) Inconclusive struggle between France and Britain for control over North America. Both sides enlisted Native American allies in fighting over disputed boundaries in Nova Scotia, New England and the Ohio Valley. By the Peace of Aix-la-Chapelle (1748), conquered territory was restored by mutual agreement.

King Philip's War (1675–76) War between English settlers and Native Americans in New England. The Wampanoags, under their chief Philip (Metacomet), rebelled against increasing white aggression. Colonial forces eventually gained the upper hand and wreaked still greater destruction on native settlements. King Philip was killed in 1676.

Kings I and II Two books in the OLD TESTAMENT, called Third and Fourth Kingdoms in the Greek SEPTUAGINT. These books recount the history of the kingdom of ISRAEL from the end of the reign of DAVID (*c*.970 BC) to the fall of Judah and the destruction of Jerusalem by the Babylonians in 586 BC.

Kingsley, Charles (1819–75) English writer. He was one of the first clergymen to support Charles DARWIN, whose ideas he partly incorporated into *The Water Babies* (1863). His immensely popular historical novels include *Hypatia* (1843) and *Hereward the Wake* (1866).

Kingston Capital and largest city of Jamaica. It was founded in 1693. It rapidly developed into Jamaica's commercial centre, based on the export of raw cane sugar, bananas and rum. In 1872 it became the island's capital. Kingston is the cultural heart of Jamaica. In recent years it has been plagued by urban disturbances and armed drug gangs. Pop. (1993) 644,000.

Kingston-upon-Hull Official name of HULL

Kingstown Capital and chief port of St Vincent and the Grenadines, on the SW coast. Exports: cotton, sugar cane, molasses, cacao, fruit. Pop. (1991) 26,223.

King William's War *See* FRENCH AND INDIAN WARS

▲ **killer whale** The large triangular dorsal fin and the black and white body are the two obvious features of the killer whale (*Orcinus orca*). It is found mostly in polar seas and is generally considered to be the most ferocious of whales. Almost any creature in the sea is considered as food by the 9m (30ft) killers.

kinkajou Nocturnal, foraging mammal of the RACOON family that lives in forests of Central and South America. Primarily a fruit and insect eater, it lives almost entirely in trees. Length: to 57.5cm (22.7in); weight: to 2.7kg (6lb). Family Procyonidae; species *Potos flavus*.

Kinnock, Neil Gordon (1942–) British politician, leader of the Labour Party (1983–92). He was elected to Parliament in 1970. Kinnock succeeded Michael FOOT as leader of the LABOUR PARTY and led opposition to the Conservative government of Margaret THATCHER. Despite reforming the Labour Party, he was unable to overcome Mrs Thatcher's huge majority in the 1987 general election and narrowly lost to John MAJOR in the 1992 general election. Kinnock resigned in favour of John SMITH. In 1994, he became a European Commissioner for transport. In 1999, he was appointed vice-president of the EC.

Kinsey, Alfred Charles (1894–1956) US zoologist, noted for his studies on human sexual behaviour. He was director of the Institute for Sex Research, Indiana University and is best known for *Sexual Behavior in the Human Male* (1948) and *Sexual Behavior in the Human Female* (1953).

Kinshasa (formerly Léopoldville) Capital of the Democratic Republic of Congo. A port on the River Congo, it replaced Boma as the capital of the Belgian Congo in 1923. When Zaire gained independence in 1960, it continued as capital, changing its name in 1966. Industries: tanning, chemicals, brewing. Pop. (1994) 3,804,000.

kinship Relationship by blood or marriage, sometimes extended to cover relations of affinity. It also refers to a complex of rules in society governing descent, succession, inheritance, residence, marriage and sexual relations. *See also* INCEST

Kipling, (Joseph) Rudyard (1865–1936) British writer, b. India. His *Barrack Room Ballads and Other Verses* (1892), which include the poems "If" and "Gunga Din", is a classic text of British colonialist literature. His novels include *The Light That Failed* (1890) and *Kim* (1901). He also wrote many children's stories, including *The Jungle Book* (1894), the *Just So Stories* (1902) and *Puck of Pook's Hill* (1906). Kipling was the first English writer to be awarded the Nobel Prize for literature (1907).

Kirchhoff, Gustav Robert (1824–87) German physicist. With Robert BUNSEN, he developed the spectroscope, with which they discovered CAESIUM and RUBIDIUM in 1860. He is famous for two laws that apply to multiple-loop electric circuits. Kirchhoff's laws state that: (1) at any junction the sum of the currents flowing is zero; and (2) the sum of the ELECTROMOTIVE FORCES (EMF) around any closed path equals the sum of the products of the currents and impedances (resistances).

Kirchner, Ernst Ludwig (1880–1938) German painter and printmaker, a leader of the expressionist artists known as Die BRÜCKE. Kirchner characteristically portrayed urban scenes, such as *The Street* (1913). His art was condemned by the Nazis as degenerate, and he committed suicide. *See also* EXPRESSIONISM

Kiribati (formerly Gilbert Islands) Independent nation in the W Pacific Ocean, comprising *c*.33 islands, including the Gilbert, Phoenix and Line Islands, and straddling the Equator; the capital is Bairiki (on Tarawa). British navigators first visited the islands in the late 18th century. They became a British protectorate in 1892. Full independence within the Commonwealth of Nations was granted in 1979. The mining of phosphates dominated the economy until 1980, when production ended because of diminishing resources. Agriculture is the major economic activity. Land area: 717sq km (277sq mi). Pop. (2000) 72,000

Kiritimati (Christmas Island) Largest atoll in the world, one of the Line Islands, forming part of KIRIBATI. It was the site of nuclear tests by Britain (1956–62) and the USA (1962). Area: 575sq km (222sq mi). Pop. (1990) 2,537.

Kirov, Sergei Mironovich (1888–1934) Soviet politician. An effective speaker, he was elected to the Communist Party Politburo in 1930. His murder, probably on STALIN's orders, served as a pretext for the Stalin purges (1934–38).

Kirov Former name (1934–92) for VYATKA.

Kirov Ballet Ballet company founded in 1735 at St Petersburg. Under the direction of PETIPA (1862–1903), the Kirov Ballet was the world's top company, with principal dancers such as PAVLOVA and NIJINSKY. Later stars include Michel FOKINE, Rudolf NUREYEV and Mikhail BARYSHNIKOV. The **Kirov Opera** has also made a distinguished contribution to Russian culture.

Kisangani (formerly Stanleyville) City and port on the River Congo, N Democratic Republic of Congo (DRC). Kisangani was founded in 1883 by the English explorer Henry M. STANLEY. During the 1950s, it was the headquarters of the Congolese National Movement led by Patrice LUMUMBA. During the 1960s, it was the focus for a series of unsuccessful rebellions. In 1996, it was at the centre of the Hutu refugee crisis in the DRC. Pop. (1994) 373,000.

Kissinger, Henry Alfred (1923–) US statesman and political scientist, secretary of state (1973–77), b. Germany. In 1969 he became President NIXON's assistant for national security and chief adviser on foreign policy, helping to establish the STRATEGIC ARMS LIMITATION TALKS (SALT) with the Soviet Union. As secretary of state, Kissinger shared the Nobel Peace Prize (1973) with Le Duc Tho for his part in negotiating a cease-fire in the VIETNAM WAR. His "shuttle diplomacy" brought a cease-fire agreement between Egypt and Israel in the 1973 Yom Kippur War. After the fall of Nixon, Kissinger continued as secretary of state for President FORD.

Kitaj, R.B. (Ronald Brooks) (1932–) British painter, b. USA. He has loose associations with the POP ART movement. Kitaj paints in flat, soft-edged areas of bright colour, often on very large canvases.

Kitasato, Shibasaburo (1852–1931) Japanese bacteriologist who isolated the bacilli that cause the diseases tetanus, anthrax and dysentery. In 1890, Kitasato prepared a diphtheria antitoxin. He also discovered, independently of Alexandre YERSIN, the infectious organism that causes bubonic plague.

Kitchener, Horatio Herbert, 1st Earl (1850–1916) British field marshal and statesman. He took part in the unsuccessful relief of General GORDON at Khartoum (1883–85), but reconquered Sudan in 1898, and became its governor-general. Kitchener served as chief of staff in the second of the SOUTH AFRICAN WARS (1900–02) and established the first concentration camps. After service in India and Egypt, he was appointed secretary of state for war at the outbreak of World War 1. Kitchener's image appeared on the recruitment posters.

kite Diverse group of HAWKS of the sub-family Milvinae, found in open country worldwide. Kites have hooked bills, long wings and a long forked tail. They are usually scavangers. The red kite, *Milvus milvus*, is common throughout rural Europe. Length: 60cm (24in). Family Accipitridae.

kittiwake Arctic GULL with a greenish-yellow bill, black wing-tips and short dark legs. It flies low over open seas, hunting for fish. The female lays one to three spotted pale eggs in a cup-shaped nest in cliffs. Length: to 41cm (16in); Family Laridae: species *Rissa tridactyla*.

kiwi Any of three species of flightless, fast-running, forest and scrubland birds of New Zealand, especially the common brown kiwi, *Apteryx australis*. Mainly nocturnal, it has a long, flexible bill with which it probes for food in the ground. Family Apterygidae.

Klaus, Václav (1941–) Czech statesman, prime minister (1993–97). Following the "Velvet Revolution" (1989), he became finance minister in Václav HAVEL's administration. In 1991, Klaus founded the Civic Democratic Party (ODS). He became prime minister of the Czech republic following the break-up of Czechoslovakia, but was forced to resign in 1997 amid financial scandal. He was replaced (1998) by Milos Zeman of the social democrats.

Klee, Paul (1879–1940) Swiss painter and graphic artist. In 1912, he joined Kandinsky's der BLAUE REITER group. Klee evolved his own pictorial language based on correspondences between line, colour and plane. Some of his images are entirely ABSTRACT, but some are recognizable figures. He taught at the BAUHAUS (1920–31) and at Düsseldorf Academy (1931–33), but returned to Switzerland in 1933, after the Nazis had condemned his work as degenerate. Characteristic works include *Graduated Shades of Red-Green* (1921) and *Revolutions of the Viaducts* (1937).

Klein, Melanie (1882–1960) Austrian psychoanalyst who developed therapy for young children. In *The Psychoanalysis of Children* (1932) Klein presented her methods and ideas of child analysis; she believed play was a symbolic way of controlling anxiety and analysed it to gain insight into the psychological processes of early life.

Klein, Yves (1928–62) French painter and experimental artist, one of the pioneers of CONCEPTUAL ART. Klein is best known for hand and body prints in his characteristic colour scheme of bright blue ("Klein blue") on white.

Kleist, (Bernd) Heinrich (Wilhelm) von (1777–1811) German dramatist. The central themes of his romantic dramas are the conflict between reason and emotion and the blurred distinction between illusion and reality. Kleist wrote comedies such as *Amphitryon* (1807) and historical tragedies such as *The Prince of Homburg* (1821). He shot himself in a suicide pact.

Klemperer, Otto (1885–1973) German conductor. He was celebrated for his interpretations of Beethoven, Brahms and Mahler. In 1933, with the rise of Nazism in Germany, he went to the USA and became conductor of the Los Angeles Philharmonic. In 1946, he returned to Europe as director of the Budapest Opera (1947–50).

Klimt, Gustav (1862–1918) Austrian painter and designer, a founder of the Vienna SEZESSION and the foremost ART NOUVEAU painter in Vienna. Klimt's works combines stylized nudes with bejewelled clothing or backgrounds reminiscent of Byzantine mosaics. His style considerably influenced the painters Egon SCHIELE and Oskar KOKOSCHKA. His works include *The Kiss* (1908).

Klondike Gold Rush (1896–1904) Mass migration of gold prospectors to the Klondike region, Yukon Territory, NW Canada. The rich gold deposits discovered (1896) in the Klondike River brought more than 30,000 prospectors to the territory. Within a decade more than $100 million worth of gold had been extracted. The easily accessible lodes were exhausted (*c*.1910), but mining continues.

Klopstock, Friedrich Gottlieb (1724–1803) German poet. He anticipated the STURM UND DRANG movement and influenced other poets such as GOETHE, RILKE and HÖLDERLIN. Klopstock's major work is the epic *The Messiah* (1745–73) based on Milton's *Paradise Lost* (1667).

Kneller, Sir Godfrey (1646–1723) British painter, b. Germany. He settled in London in 1674 and became the foremost portrait painter in England. In 1711, Kneller founded the first English academy of painting. His best-known works include 48 portraits of the members of the Kit-Cat Club (*c*.1702–17).

knight In medieval Europe, a mounted warrior of intermediate rank. The knight began as a squire and was knighted with a sword touch on the shoulder after a period of trial. Knights were often landholders, owing military service to their overlord. Honorary orders of knighthood, such as the Knights of the Garter (1349), were founded towards the end of the Middle Ages, a tradition that continued into the modern era.

Knights Hospitallers Military Christian order founded to defend Jerusalem after its capture in the first CRUSADE. After the fall of Jerusalem (1187) to Saladin, they moved to Acre, then Cyprus. In 1310 the Knights Hospitallers captured Rhodes, from where they were expelled by the Ottoman Turks in 1522. In 1530 Emperor Charles V gave them the island of Malta, where they remained until driven out by Napoleon in 1798. The order still exists as an international, humanitarian charity.

Knights Templar Military religious order established in 1118, with headquarters in the supposed Temple of Solomon in Jerusalem. With the KNIGHTS HOSPITALLERS, the Templars protected routes to Jerusalem for Christians during the CRUSADES. The possessions of the Templars in France attracted the envious attention of King PHILIP IV, who urged Pope Clement V to abolish the order in 1312.

knitting Hand-weaving of a textile by using rod-like needles to interlace loops of spun yarn. Knitting was apparently unknown in Europe before the 15th century, when the practice began in Spain and Italy, having arrived there probably from the Arab world. The first knitting machine was invented in England in 1589.

knock, engine (pre-ignition or pinking) Metallic noise produced in an INTERNAL COMBUSTION ENGINE, caused by detonation of part of the compressed fuel-air mixture before a spark from the spark plug ignites the remainder. It lowers the efficiency of the engine but can be overcome by adding an anti-knocking agent to the fuel. The traditional additive is lead(IV) tetraethyl, but because this compound releases lead into the atmosphere and thereby contributes to pollution, its use has declined with the introduction of unleaded petrol.

Knossos Ancient palace complex in N central Crete, 6.4km (4mi) SE of modern Iráklion. In 1900, Sir Arthur Evans began excavations that revealed that the site had been inhabited before 3000 BC. His main discovery was a palace from the MINOAN CIVILIZATION (built *c*.2000 BC and rebuilt *c*.1700 BC). Close to the palace were the houses of Cretan nobles. The complex also contains many frescoes. Knossos dominated Crete *c*.1500 BC, but the palace was occupied *c*.1400 BC by invaders from MYCENAE.

knot Unit of measurement equal to one nautical mile per hour – 1 knot equals 1.852km/h (1.15mph). The speeds of ships and aircraft are generally expressed in knots, as are those of winds and currents.

Knox, John (1514–72) Leader of the Protestant REFORMATION in Scotland. Ordained a Catholic priest, he was later converted to Protestantism and took up the cause of the Reformation. Captured by French soldiers in Scotland, he was imprisoned in France (1547), then lived in exile in England and Switzerland. In 1559, Knox returned to Scotland, where he continued to promote the Protestant cause. In 1560, the Scottish Parliament, under Knox's leadership, made PRESBYTERIANISM the state religion. In 1563, he was tried for treason but acquitted.

koala Small marsupial that lives in eucalyptus trees of Australia, eating their leaves. A single immature young is born, nurtured in its mother's pouch until fully formed, then carried on her back for a further six months. Length: 85cm (33in). Species *Phascolarctos cinereus*.

Kobe City and seaport on the N shore of Osaka Bay, SW Honshu Island, Japan. It is Japan's leading port and a major industrial centre. In January 1995, more than 5,000 people were killed and 27,000 injured in an earthquake. Industries: shipbuilding, iron and steel, electronics, chemicals. Pop. (1995) 1,424,000.

Koblenz (Coblenz) City at the confluence of the Rhine and Mosel rivers, W Germany; capital of Koblenz province. Founded in the 9th century BC as a Roman camp, it was later a residence of Frankish kings; from 10th to late 18th century it was held by archbishops of Trier. During World War 2, most of Koblenz was destroyed. Remaining sites include the Church of St Castor (836) and the 11th-century fortress of Ehrenbreitsen. Koblenz is a major wine-trading centre. Industries: pianos, furniture, textiles. Pop. (1995) 110,000.

Koch, Robert (1843–1910) German bacteriologist. He was awarded the 1905 Nobel Prize for physiology or medicine for his discovery of the bacillus that causes TUBERCULOSIS. This work laid the foundation for methods of determining the causative agent of a disease.

Kodály, Zoltán (1882–1967) Hungarian composer. With BARTÓK he collected and systematized Hungarian folk music, which was the principal influence in his work. His best-known compositions include the *Psalmus Hungaricus* (1923) and the comic opera *Háry János* (1927).

Koestler, Arthur (1905–83) British novelist and philosopher, b. Hungary. *Darkness at Noon* (1940), his best-known novel, is a biting indictment of Stalinist totalitarianism. His other novels also embody political themes. He died in a suicide pact with his wife.

Koffka, Kurt (1886–1941) US psychologist, b. Germany. With Wolfgang KÖHLER and Max Wertheimer, he was a founder of GESTALT PSYCHOLOGY. He wrote *The Growth of the Mind* (1921) and *Principles of Gestalt Psychology* (1935).

Kohl, Helmut (1930–) German statesman, chancellor (1982–98). Between 1976 and 1982, he led the Christian Democratic Union (CDU) Party opposition to Helmut SCHMIDT. Kohl succeeded Schmidt as chancellor. His conservative approach advocated strong support for NATO and a return to the traditional values of the West German state. Kohl strongly supported closer integration in the European Union (EU) and the establishment of the EURO. In 1990, he presided over the reunification of East and West Germany and was elected as the first chancellor of the new unified Germany. Re-elected in 1994 and 1996, Kohl lost the 1998 election to Gerhard SCHRÖDER.

Köhler, Wolfgang (1887–1967) US psychologist, b. Estonia. With Kurt KOFFKA and Max Wertheimer, he was a key figure in GESTALT PSYCHOLOGY. His work on animal learning and problem solving is summarized in *The Mentality of Apes* (1917).

kohlrabi Edible crop vegetable with lobed leaves and a greenish-white or purple, turnip-like stem. It is unusual in that both the stem and leaves may be eaten. Family Brassicaceae/Cruciferae; (sub)species *Brassica oleracea gongylodes*.

Kokoschka, Oskar (1886–1980) Austrian painter. He was influenced by the elegance of KLIMT but soon developed his own type of EXPRESSIONISM. His work is characterized by forceful, energetic draftsmanship and restless brushwork.

kolanut (colanut) Fruit of the evergreen kola tree, native to tropical Africa. The nuts are high in caffeine

and act as a powerful stimulant. Family Sterculiaceae; species *Cola acuminata*.

Kollwitz, Käthe (1867–1945) German graphic artist and sculptor. She was influenced by experiences of the poverty-stricken districts of N Berlin. Her best-known works depict suffering, especially of women and children. She made her name with the expressionist etchings *The Weavers' Revolt* (1897–98) and *Peasants' War* (1902–08).

Kommunizma Pik (Communism Peak) Mountain in the Pamirs region, SE Tajikistan, central Asia. Known as Mount Garmo until 1933 and Stalin Peak until 1962, it was the highest peak in the former Soviet Union. Height: 7,495m (24,590ft).

komodo dragon Giant monitor lizard that lives on four islands to the E of Java, Indonesia; it is the largest lizard in the world. Length: 3m (10ft). Family Varanidae; species *Varanus komodoensis*.

Königsberg *See* KALININGRAD

Konya City in S central Turkey. Known in ancient times as Iconium, it was first settled in the 8th century BC. The capital of the SELJUK sultanate of Rum from 1099, it was annexed by the Ottoman sultan in 1472. It is the religious centre of the whirling DERVISHES. Industries: cotton, leather, carpets. Pop. (1993) 585,000.

kookaburra (laughing jackass) Large KINGFISHER of Australia, known for its call resembling fiendish laughter. Groups often scream in unison at dawn, mid-day and dusk. They feed on animals. Species *Dacelo gigas*.

Koons, Jeff (1955–) US sculptor. In the 1980s, he burst onto the art scene with a series of sexually explicit pieces. Other exhibits, such as his vacuum cleaners in perspex cases, were intended as a comment on modern consumer society and have their roots in the POP ART movement of the 1960s.

Koran (Qur'an) Sacred book of ISLAM. According to Muslim belief, the Koran contains the actual word of God (Allah) as revealed by the angel GABRIEL to the Prophet MUHAMMAD. Muhammad is said to have received these revelations over two decades beginning (*c.*AD 610) on the Night of Power (commemorated at RAMADAN) and ending in 632, the year of his death. The 114 *suras* (chapters) of the Koran are the source of Islamic belief and a guide for the whole life of the community. The central teachings of the Koran are that there is no God but Allah and all must submit to Him, that Muhammad is the last of His many messengers (which have included Abraham, Moses and Jesus), and that there will come a day of judgment. In addition to these teachings, the Koran contains rules that a Muslim must follow in everyday life.

Korbut, Olga (1955–) Soviet gymnast. Korbut won three gold medals (beam, floor exercises, team) and a silver medal at the 1972 Olympic Games. In 1976, she won a team gold and a silver. In 1991, she moved to the USA.

Korda, Sir Alexander (1893–1956) British film director, b. Hungary as Sándor Kellner. His lavish films include *The Scarlet Pimpernel* (1935), *Lady Hamilton* (1941), *Anna Karenina* (1948) and *The Third Man* (1949).

Korea Peninsula in E Asia, separating the Yellow Sea from the Sea of Japan. The rivers Yalu and Tumen form most of its N border with China. **Land and climate** The E seaboard is mountainous, rising in the NE to 2,744m (9,003ft) at Mount Paektu. The mountains descend in the W to coastal lowlands. The traditional capital, SEOUL, lies close to the 38th parallel border between North KOREA and South KOREA. The Korean Archipelago lies off the S coast and includes the province of Cheju-do. North Korea experiences long and severe winters but warm summers. South Korea has a more tropical climate with occasional

KOREA, NORTH
AREA: 120,540sq km (46,540sq mi)
POPULATION: 26,117,000
CAPITAL (POPULATION): Pyongyang (2,639,448)

KOREA, SOUTH
AREA: 99,020sq km (38,232sq mi)
POPULATION: 46,403,000
CAPITAL (POPULATION): Seoul (10,229,000)

typhoons in the rainy months (July–August). **History** Korea's calendar starts in 2333 BC. China was a dominant influence. The first native Korean state was established in the 1st century AD, and Korea was unified under the Silla dynasty in the 7th century. Korea was invaded by Mongols in 1231 and eventually surrendered. The Yi dynasty ruled Korea from 1392 to 1910. Early in the Yi period, Seoul was made the new capital and CONFUCIANISM became the official religion. In the 17th century, Korea was a semi-independent state, dominated by the MANCHU dynasty. A long period of isolationism followed. In the late 19th century, Korea became more active in foreign affairs, due to the growing power of Japan. After the RUSSO-JAPANESE WAR (1904–05), Korea was effectively a Japanese protectorate and was formally annexed in 1910. Japan's enforced industrialization of Korea caused widespread resentment. Following Japan's defeat in World War 2, Korea was divided into two zones of occupation: Soviet forces N of the 38th parallel, and US forces S of the line. Attempts at reunification failed, and in 1948 two separate regimes were established: the Republic of Korea in the S and the Democratic People's Republic in the N. In June 1950, North Korea invaded South Korea. The ensuing KOREAN WAR (1950–53) resulted in millions of deaths and devastated the peninsula. An uneasy truce has prevailed ever since. Attempts at reunification continue.

Korea, North Republic in E Asia, occupying the N part of the Korean peninsula. North Korea is largely mountainous. The capital, PYONGYANG, lies on the W coastal plain. North Korea's border with South Korea is based on the 38th parallel. (For land, climate and pre-1953 history, *see* KOREA and KOREAN WAR) **History and politics** In 1948, North Korea established a communist government led (1948–94) by KIM IL SUNG. His Stalinist regime exploited North Korea's rich mineral resources. Industry was nationalized. Heavy industry and arms production greatly increased. Agriculture was collectivized and mechanized. After the KOREAN WAR several million Koreans fled Kim Il Sung's dictatorial regime. North Korea remained largely closed to outside interests. Alliances were formed with China and the Soviet Union, but the collapse of the latter had adverse effects on North Korea's economy. Its emphasis on the military industry had a destabilizing effect on regional politics and internal economic planning. Since 1991, Korea's economy has slumped. In 1991, North and South Korea signed a non-aggression pact and agreed on a series of meetings on reunification. The process was halted in 1994 with the death of Kim Il Sung. He was succeeded by his son, KIM JONG IL. During the early 1990s, North Korea's nuclear weapons building programme gathered momentum. In 1994 North Korea, briefly withdrew from the Nuclear Non-Proliferation Treaty. It rejoined after agreeing to halt the reprocessing of plutonium, in return for guarantees on energy supplies and the establishment of economic and diplomatic relations with the USA. In 1995, severe flooding caused more than US$15 billion of damage and devastated agricultural production. In 1996, the UN sent emergency food aid to relieve famine. In 1998, North Korea launched a ballistic missile over Japanese airspace. **Economy** North Korea has considerable mineral resources, including coal, copper, iron ore, lead, tin, tungsten and zinc. Despite these resources, it is a net consumer of energy and is reliant on oil imports (1992 GDP per capita, US$3,026). Industries include chemicals, iron and steel, machinery and textiles. Agriculture employs more than 40% of the workforce. Rice is the leading crop.

Korea, South Republic in E Asia, occupying the S part of the Korean peninsula. South Korea is largely mountainous. The capital, SEOUL, lies on the W coastal lowlands. Other major cities include INCHON, TAEGU and the main port of PUSAN, on the SE coast. Cheju-do, the largest island, includes Mount Halla, South Korea's highest peak, at 1,950m (6,398ft). (For land, climate and pre-1953 history, *see* KOREA and KOREAN WAR) **History and politics** South Korea's first government, led (1948–60) by Syngman RHEE, was beset by economic problems. South Korea was a predominantly agricultural economy, heavily dependent on the N for energy and resources. South Korea's infrastructure was devastated by the Korean War. Rhee's corrupt and repressive regime became increasingly unpopular. In 1960, the massacre of student protesters sparked nationwide disturbances, and a military junta, led by General PARK, seized power in 1961. Park's presidency (1963–79) brought rapid economic growth. Helped by US aid, South Korea became a major manufacturer and exporter. In 1972, Park introduced martial law and passed a new constitution that gave him almost unlimited powers. His regime pursued increasingly authoritarian social policies. In 1979, Park was assassinated, but the military continued to dominate the government. In 1987, a new constitution ensured the popular election of the president and reduced the presidential term to five years. In 1988, Seoul hosted the summer Olympic Games. Relations with North Korea continued to improve, and in 1991 the two countries signed a non-aggression pact and established a series of summit meetings on reunification. In 1992, the long-standing opposition leader, KIM YOUNG SAM, became president. His administration was South Korea's first full civilian government in 32 years. The death of North Korean president KIM IL SUNG stalled reunification talks, but the momentum had been established. In 1998, Kim Dae Jung succeeded Kim Young Sam as president. **Economy** South Korea is an upper-middle-income developing country (1992 GDP per capita, US$9,250). During the late 20th century, it was one of the world's fastest growing industrial economies. US aid of more than $6,000 million (1945–78) played a large part in the success story. South Korea's industrial conglomerates (*chaebols*) benefited from a highly educated workforce and import controls. South Korea's protectionist policies are slowly giving way to free market reforms. The largest sector of the economy is services, employing 50% of the workforce. The manufacturing sector is South Korea's greatest asset. Manufactured goods, machinery and transport equipment make up 66% of South Korea's exports. South Korea is the world's fifth-largest car producer and is a major producer of iron and steel, cement, and electrical and electronic products. Major chaebols include Hyundai, Daewoo and Samsung. Agriculture employs 17% of the workforce. South Korea is self-sufficient in grain and is the world's eighth-largest producer of rice. Fishing is another vital sector. In 1997, Hanbo and several other major *chaebols* in South Korea collapsed. The over-lending by South Korea's banks and the crisis in the rest of Southeast Asia devastated the country's finances. The International Monetary Fund (IMF) agreed to a record US$21 billion rescue package. Labour reform laws led to redundancies and rising unemployment.

Korean National language of North and South Korea. Some scholars class it as one of the ALTAIC LANGUAGES. It is spoken by more than 50 million people. The Korean alphabet developed in the 15th century.

Korean War (1950–53) Conflict between North KOREA (supported by China) and South KOREA (supported by UN forces dominated by the USA). In June 1950 South Korea was invaded by forces from the North. The United Nations (UN) Security Council, during a boycott by the Soviet Union, voted to aid South Korea. Major US forces, plus token forces from its allies, landed under the overall command of General Douglas MACARTHUR. The invaders were driven out, but when UN forces advanced into North Korea, China intervened and drove them back, recapturing Seoul. After more heavy fighting, UN forces slowly advanced until virtual stalemate ensued near the 38th Parallel, the border between North and South Korea. Negotiations continued for two years before a truce was agreed in July 1953. Total casualties were estimated at 4 million.

Kornberg, Arthur (1918–) US biochemist. In 1959, he shared (with Severo Ochoa) the Nobel Prize for physiology or medicine for work on the synthesis of RNA and DNA, an important contribution to the study of genetics.

Korngold, Erich Wolfgang (1897–1957) US composer, b. Austria. By the age of 12, he had gained recognition in Europe for chamber and orchestral works. In 1934, Korngold emigrated to the USA. He received two Academy Awards for best film score for the highly chromatic incidental music in *Anthony Adverse* (1936) and *The Adventures of Robin Hood* (1938).

Kornilov, Lavr Georgievich (1870–1918) Russian general. Appointed supreme military commander by the KERENSKY government in August 1917, he launched an unsuccessful rebellion in September 1917. After the RUSSIAN REVOLUTION (November 1917), he led the anti-communist White forces at the start of the Russian Civil War. He was killed in action at Ekaterinodar (now Krasnodar).

Korolyov, Sergei Pavlovich (1906–66) Soviet engineer. He was chief designer at the Scientific Research Institute near Moscow and directed the design and manufacture of the Vostok and Soyuz manned spacecraft, including Vostok I, in which Yuri GAGARIN made the first manned space flight in 1961.

Kosciuszko, Mount Mountain in SE Australia, in the Great Dividing Range in SE New South Wales. The highest mountain in Australia, it lies inside a national park and is a winter sports resort. Height: 2,228m (7,310ft).

Kościuszko, Thaddeus (1746–1817) Polish general and patriot. After the second partition of Poland in 1793, he led a revolutionary movement to regain Polish independence. It was initially successful, but the invading armies of Russia and Prussia proved too strong, and Kościuszko was imprisoned (1794–96) and then exiled.

kosher Ritually correct or acceptable for Jews. A word of Hebrew origin, it is applied by Orthodox Jews to food that conforms to Jewish dietary laws and customs.

Kosovo Autonomous province in s Serbia; the capital is Pristina. Ottoman victory in the Battle of Kosovo Field (1389) broke the power of Serbia. In 1913, it was reclaimed by Serbia and was incorporated into Yugoslavia in 1929. After World War 2 it became an autonomous province of Serbia. In 1974, Kosovo was granted a degree of autonomy. In 1990, the 80% Albanian population demanded greater autonomy. Serbia responded by imposing direct rule. The violent suppression of Albanian demonstrations led to a full-scale war in 1999. Peace talks sought to reinstate its autonomous status. Area: 10,887sq km (4,205sq mi). Pop. (1991) 1,956,200.

Kossuth, Lajos (1802–94) Hungarian statesman. In 1848 Kossuth led the Hungarian Revolution against Habsburg rule and was appointed provisional governor of the independent republic. In 1849, the Russians crushed the uprising, forcing him to flee. He continued to champion Hungarian independence from exile in Europe and the USA but the Compromise of 1867, which created the Dual Monarchy of the AUSTRO-HUNGARIAN EMPIRE, put an end to his hopes.

Koštunica, Vojislav (1944–) Serbian statesman, president of the Federal Republic of YUGOSLAVIA (2000–). In the late 1980s, Koštunica formed the Democratic Party of Serbia. In September 2000, Koštunica defeated Slobodan MILOŠEVIĆ in the presidential elections as leader of an opposition coalition, the Democratic Oppostition of Serbia (DOS). Attempts to sabotage election results by Milošević's supporters led to mass demonstrations in Belgrade, and Milošević was forced to concede defeat.

Kosygin, Aleksei Nikolayevich (1904–80) Soviet statesman, premier (1964–80). He was elected to the Communist Party Central Committee in 1939 and the Politburo in 1948. Kosygin served as an economics expert to Joseph STALIN. He was removed on the accession of Nikolai KHRUSHCHEV, but returned to share power with Leonid BREZHNEV.

Koussevitzky, Sergei Aleksandrovich (1874–1951) US musician, b. Russia. A virtuoso double-bass player, he became even more famous as conductor of the Boston Symphony Orchestra (1924–49).

Kowloon Peninsula on the SE coast of China, part of HONG KONG. One of the most densely populated areas of the world, it was ceded to Britain by China in 1860 and returned to China in 1998. Industries: shipbuilding. Area: 9sq km (3.5sq mi). Pop. (1986) 2,301,691.

Krakatoa Small volcanic island in w Indonesia, in the Sunda Strait between Java and Sumatra. In 1883 one of the world's largest volcanic eruptions destroyed most of the island. The resulting tidal waves caused 50,000 deaths and great destruction.

Kraków (Cracow) City in s Poland. Founded in the 8th century, Kraków was made a residence of the Polish kings in the 12th century and subsequently capital of Poland. In 1795, it was ceded to Austria. After a period of independence (from 1815), it was restored to Austria in 1846. The city became part of Poland after World War 1. Historic buildings include the Wawel Cathedral. The Jagiellonian University (1364) is one of the oldest in Europe. Today, Kraków is a manufacturing centre. Industries: chemicals, metals, machinery, clothing, printing. Pop. (1996) 745,000.

Krasnodar City and port on the E bank of the River Kuban, SW European Russia; capital of Krasnodar Kray. Founded in 1794 by CATHERINE II as a frontier outpost, it was known as Yekaterinodar until 1920. Industries: oil refining, machine tools, textiles, metalworking. Pop. (1994) 638,000.

Krasnoyarsk City and port on the w bank of the upper River Yenisei, w Siberian Russia; capital of Krasnoyarsk Kray. Founded in 1628 by the COSSACKS, it was attacked in the later 17th century by Tatars and other tribes. It developed rapidly after the discovery of gold in the area. Industries: shipbuilding, heavy machinery, electrical goods, cement, timber, flour milling. Pop. (1994) 914,000.

Krebs, Sir Hans Adolf (1900–81) British biochemist, b. Germany. In 1953, he shared (with F.A. Lipmann) the Nobel Prize for physiology or medicine for his discovery of the CITRIC ACID cycle (KREBS' CYCLE) that results in the production of energy in living organisms (RESPIRATION).

Krebs cycle (citric acid or tricarboxylic acid cycle) Biochemical pathway by which most EUKARYOTE organisms obtain much of their energy by oxidizing foodstuffs. Occurring in the MITOCHONDRIA of CELLS, the Krebs cycle comprises a number of complex chemical reactions, many of which release energy, in association with a process called the electron transport system, as ADENOSINE TRIPHOSPHATE (ATP) becomes ADENOSINE DIPHOSPHATE (ADP). ATP provides chemical energy for metabolic reactions. The Krebs cycle is an essential part of the process of cell RESPIRATION and METABOLISM. It is named after Sir Hans KREBS.

Kreisler, Fritz (1875–1962) US violinist and composer, b. Austria. He studied at the Vienna and Paris conservatories and made his debut in the USA in 1889. He was a world-famous violin virtuoso and also composed numerous short violin pieces.

Kremlin (Rus. citadel) Historic centre of Moscow. It is a roughly triangular fortress covering c.36.5ha (90 acres). The Kremlin walls were built of timber in the 12th century and its first stone walls were built in 1367. Within the walls several cathedrals face on to a central square; the Great Kremlin Palace was the tsar's Moscow residence until the revolution. In March 1918, the Supreme Soviet established the Kremlin complex as the location of all government offices. Today, the Kremlin is the home of the Russian presidential offices.

Krenek, Ernst (1900–91) US composer, b. Austria, who emigrated to the USA in 1938. From 1920, he experimented with atonal music in Berlin, and, living in Vienna after 1930, he adopted the TWELVE-TONE MUSIC technique of SCHOENBERG. He created a sensation with the jazz opera *Johnny Strikes Up* (1926).

krill Collective term for the large variety of marine crustaceans found in all oceans. They are strained and used as food by various species of baleen WHALE.

Krishna Most celebrated hero of Hindu mythology. He was the eighth AVATAR (incarnation) of VISHNU and primarily a god of joyfulness and fertility. Many devotional cults grew up around him, as well as legends and poems. Krishna is the hero of the MAHABHARATA and the deliverer of the BHAGAVAD GITA. He is commonly depicted as a youth with a blue face. *See also* HARE KRISHNA

Krishnamurti, Jiddu (1895–1986) Hindu religious leader. He founded the World Order of Star with Annie BESANT, the theosophist leader, dissolving it in 1929, and in 1969 founded the Krishnamurti Foundation in Ojai, California, USA.

Kroeber, Alfred Louis (1876–1960) US anthropologist, one of the most important cultural anthropologists of the early 20th century. He helped to advance the study of Native North American ethnology, linguistics and folklore.

Kronos *See* CRONUS

Kropotkin, Peter Alexeievich (1842–1921) Russian anarchist. He was jailed for seditious propaganda in 1874 but escaped into exile in 1876. Living mostly in Britain, Kropotkin became one of the most important theorists of anarchist socialism, criticizing the centralizing tendencies of Marxism. He argued in *Mutual Aid* (1902) that

cooperation rather than competition is the natural order of things. He returned to Russia in 1917. *See also* ANARCHISM

Kruger, Paul (Stephanus Johannes Paulus) (1825–1904) South African statesman and soldier, president (1883–1902) of the South African Republic. In the 1830s, he took part in the GREAT TREK. In 1877, Britain annexed Transvaal and Kruger led the fight for independence. He fought in the first of the SOUTH AFRICAN WARS and was elected the first president of the South African Republic. Kruger was re-elected in 1888, 1893 and 1898. His refusal to grant equal status to non-BOER settlers precipitated the second South African War. Kruger was forced into exile, where he sought support for the Boer cause. He died in Switzerland.

Kruger National Park Game reserve in Northern Province, South Africa, on the Mozambique border. Founded in 1898 by Paul Kruger as the Sabi Game Reserve, it became a national park in 1926. Area: c.20,720sq km (c.8,000sq mi).

Krupp German munitions firm. The world's largest manufacturers of munitions, the Krupp family monopolized the manufacture of arms in Germany during World War 1. **Alfred** Krupp (1812–87) was the first steelmaker to install the BESSEMER PROCESS and was one of the leaders in the industrial development of the Ruhr valley. His son, **Friedrich** Alfred Krupp (1854–1902), expanded into shipbuilding and the manufacture of chrome and nickel steel alloys and armour plate. One of their best-known products was Big Bertha, a gun that shelled the Paris area from a distance of 132km (82mi). Under Friedrich's son-in-law, Gustav von Bohlen und Halbach, the Krupp works were a mainstay in the Nazi war effort. His son, **Alfred** Krupp (1907–67), was imprisoned for his war activities and was required to sell a portion of his Krupp interests. The business passed from family control and became a corporation in 1967.

krypton (symbol Kr) Gaseous non-metallic element, a NOBLE GAS. Discovered in 1898, krypton makes up c.0.0001% of the Earth's atmosphere by volume and is obtained by the fractional distillation of liquid air. It is used in fluorescent lamps, lasers and electronic heart valves. Properties: at.no. 36; r.a.m. 83.80; r.d. 3.73; m.p. −156.6°C; (−249.9°F); b.p. −152.3°C; (−242.1°F); most common isotope Kr^{84} (56.9%).

Kuala Lumpur Capital of Malaysia, in the S Malay peninsula. Founded in 1857, it was made the capital of the Federated Malay States in 1895, of the Federation of Malaya in 1957 and of Malaysia in 1963. A commercial centre, it has two universities and many striking modern buildings including one of the world's tallest buildings, the twin Petronas Towers, at 452m (1.483ft). Industries: tin, rubber. Pop. (1991) 1,145,000.

Kubelik Name of two Czech musicians. **Jan** (1880–1940) was a violinist and composer, highly regarded for his technical mastery. His son, **Rafael** (1914–96), was an eminent conductor as well as a composer. He was musical director of the Metropolitan Opera Company, New York (1973–74).

Kublai Khan (1215–94) Mongol Emperor (1260–94). Grandson of GENGHIS KHAN, he completed the conquest of China in 1279, establishing the YUAN dynasty, which ruled until 1368. He conquered the Southern SUNG dynasty and extended operations into SE Asia, although his attempt to invade Japan was thwarted by storms. He conducted correspondence with European rulers and apparently employed Marco POLO.

Kubrick, Stanley (1928–99) US film director. An ambitious, fiercely independent AUTEUR, his films include *Dr Strangelove* (1963), *2001: A Space Odyssey* (1968), *A Clockwork Orange* (1971), *The Shining* (1980) and *Full Metal Jacket* (1987). His final film was *Eyes Wide Shut* (1999).

kudu Large African ANTELOPE found S of the Sahara. The body is grey-brown with vertical white stripes, and the male bears long, spiral horns. Genus *Tragelaphus*.

Kuiper, Gerard Peter (1905–73) US astronomer, b. Netherlands. He discovered the satellites Miranda (of Uranus) in 1948 and Nereid (of Neptune) in 1949. He found methane in the atmospheres of Uranus, Neptune and Titan, and carbon dioxide in the atmosphere of Mars.

Ku Klux Klan (KKK) Name of two secret, white, racist groups in the USA. The first Ku Klux Klan was organized in the South in 1866. Opposed to RECONSTRUCTION, it attempted to enforce labour discipline in plantation districts and to maintain white supremacy by preventing blacks from voting. Dressed in white robes and hoods, klansmen terrorized black communities. By 1872, the Klan had been suppressed by Federal authorities. A second Ku Klux Klan was founded in 1915, embracing broader-based racism directed also against Catholics, Jews and communists. By the mid-1920s its membership was estimated at four million. It declined thereafter, but there was a minor resurgence in the 1960s and in some Southern states in the 1990s.

Kumasi City in central Ghana; capital of ASHANTI region. The second-largest city in Ghana, it was the capital of the Ashanti kingdom in the 17th and 18th centuries before being annexed by the British in 1901. It is a commercial centre for a cocoa-growing region. Industries: food processing, handicrafts, timber. Pop. (1988) 385,000.

Kun, Béla (1886–1937) Hungarian political leader. With the support of LENIN, Kun led communist agitation against the new republic of Hungary and led a communist regime for a few months in 1919. His attempt to turn Hungary into a Soviet-style republic was defeated by Romanian troops. He probably died in Stalin's purges.

Küng, Hans (1928–) Swiss Roman Catholic theologian. He became the first important Roman Catholic theologian to question the doctrine of papal infallibility and the dogma of the Virgin Mary, for which he was censured by the Vatican (1979) and forbidden to teach Catholic theology.

kung fu Ancient Chinese martial art based on the idea that the best form of defence against violence utilizes actions that combine attack and defence.

Kuniyoshi, Yasuo (1893?–1953) US painter, b. Japan. His work, which has been described as Asian in spirit but Western in technique, includes *Child* (1923), *Landscape* (1924) and *Upside Down Table and Mask* (1940).

Kuomintang (Guomindang) Nationalist Party in China, which was the major political force during and after the creation of a republic in 1911. It was first led by SUN YAT-SEN. It cooperated with the Chinese COMMUNIST PARTY until 1927 when Sun's successor, CHIANG KAI-SHEK, turned against the communists, initiating a civil war. Between 1937 and 1945, cooperation was renewed in order to repel the Japanese, after which the civil war resumed. With the communists victorious, Chiang set up a rump state on the island of TAIWAN, where the Kuomintang continues to govern.

Kupka, František (1871–1957) Czech painter, etcher and illustrator. In 1911, he joined the ORPHISM movement of Robert DELAUNAY. Kupka was a pioneer of ABSTRACT ART. His works include *Fugue in Red and Blue* (1912).

Kurdistan Extensive mountainous and plateau region in SW Asia, inhabited by the KURDS and including parts of E Turkey, NE Iran, N Iraq, NE Syria, S Armenia and E Azerbaijan. Plans for the creation of a separate Kurdish state were put forward after World War 1 but subsequently abandoned. Area: *c*.192,000sq km (74,000sq mi).

Kurds Predominantly rural, Islamic population, who live in a disputed frontier area of SW Asia that they call KURDISTAN. Traditionally nomadic herdsmen, they are mainly SUNNI Muslims who speak an Iranian dialect. For 3,000 years they have maintained a unique cultural tradition, although internal division and constant external invasion have prevented them from uniting into one nation. In recent times, their main conflicts have been with Turkey and Iraq. After the IRAN-IRAQ WAR (1988), Iraq destroyed many Kurdish villages and their inhabitants. The Iraqi response to a Kurdish revolt after the GULF WAR (1991) caused 1.5 million Kurds to flee to Iran and Turkey. The UN formed "safe havens" for the Kurds. In 1996, Iraqi troops invaded the region and captured the Kurdish city of Irbil. The USA responded by launching cruise missiles at Iraqi military installations. In Turkey, Kurd nationalists have campaigned for an independent homeland since 1925. Today, *c*.8 million Kurds live in E Turkey, 6 million in Iran, 4 million in N Iraq, 500,000 in Syria and 100,000 in Azerbaijan and Armenia.

Kuril Islands (Kurilskiye Ostrova) Chain of 30 large and 26 smaller islands in SAKHALIN region, Russia, extending 1,200km (750mi) from the S Kamchatka Peninsula to NE Hokkaido, Japan, and separating the Sea of Okhotsk from the Pacific Ocean. The N islands were settled by Russians, the S islands by Japanese. In 1875, Russia gave the islands to Japan in exchange for full control of SAKHALIN island. After World War 2 the islands were ceded to the Soviet Union. The chief economic activities are sulphur mining and whaling. Area: 15,600sq km (6,023sq mi).

Kurosawa, Akira (1910–98) Japanese film director. In *Rashomon* (1950), he introduced the world of the SAMURAI warriors to Western audiences. The popularity of this genre was confirmed with *The Seven Samurai* (1954). *Dursu Uzala* (1975) and *Ran* (1985) both won Academy Awards for best foreign language film.

Kursk City in W Russia at the confluence of the rivers Tuskoc and Seim. Founded in 1095, it was destroyed by the TATARS in 1240 and rebuilt as a frontier post in 1586. Industries: iron and steel, chemicals, synthetic fibres, shoes, electrical equipment. Pop. (1994) 439,000.

Kush Kingdom and former state in NUBIA. Lasting from *c*.1000 BC to *c*.AD 350, it conquered Egypt in the 7th–8th centuries BC. It was later defeated by the Assyrians and moved its capital to Meroë in the Sudan. After Roman and Arab attacks in the N, Meroë was captured by the Aksumites *c*.AD 350. The Kushites are thought to have fled west. *See also* AKSUM

Kuti, Fela (Anikulapo) (1938–97) Nigerian singer-songwriter and saxophonist. Known for protesting against oppression and respected for his intricate Afro-beat music, his albums include *Coffin for Head of State* (1978) and *Underground System* (1992).

Kutuzov, Mikhail Illarionovich (1745–1813) Russian general. At the start of the NAPOLEONIC WARS (1803–15), he was defeated by NAPOLEON I at the Battle of AUSTERLITZ (1805). In 1812, Kutuzov was appointed commander-in-chief of the Russian army. Defeated at the Battle of Borodino (1812), he decided to retreat and split his army. This decision led to Napoleon's ruin.

KUWAIT
AREA: 17,820sq km (6,880sq mi)
POPULATION: 2,639,000
CAPITAL (POPULATION): Kuwait City (418,000)

Faced by the freezing Russian winter, the French retreated from Moscow with Kutuzov in relentless pursuit.

Kuwait (Al Kuwayt) Small state in the NE Arabian Peninsula, N of the Persian Gulf. The capital is Kuwait City. Kuwait was founded in the early 18th century. In 1899, it became a British protectorate, becoming fully independent in 1961. In 1990, it was invaded by IRAQ. Many thousands of Kuwaitis were killed, kidnapped or taken hostage. In the GULF WAR (1991) allied coalition forces, led by the USA, liberated Kuwait. Iraqi troops set light to oil wells as they retreated, causing widespread environmental damage. The cost of post-war reconstruction was estimated at $100 billion. In 1992, Kuwait held its first parliamentary elections. The Amir, Shaikh Jabir al-Sabah, holds executive power. Oil was discovered in 1938 and Kuwait's huge oil reserves have made it one of the world's richest countries (1995 GDP per capita, US$23,790). Other industries include shipbuilding, petrochemicals and fertilizers. Despite the desert terrain, agriculture is being developed.

Kuznetsov, Anatoly (1929–79) Ukrainian writer. His writings include the novels *Continuation of a Legend* (1957) and *Babi Yar* (1966). *See also* BABI YAR

Kwakiutl Tribe of Native North Americans. They speak the Wakashan language and are closely related to the Bella Bella. They number *c*.2,000 and occupy N Vancouver Island in British Columbia, Canada.

Kwa languages Group of languages making up a branch of the Niger-Congo family of African languages. Kwa languages include Yoruba and Ibo in S Nigeria; Ewe of Ghana, Togo and Benin; Akan of Ivory Coast and Ghana; Gä of Accra city; and Bini of Benin.

Kwanzaa Holiday celebrated by African-Americans. Developed in 1966, it is based on traditional African harvest festivals. It begins on 26 December, and lasts for seven days, each day commemorating a different virtue. In addition, families gather for communal meals and some exchange gifts.

kwashiorkor Severe protein deficiency in small children. Common in parts of Africa with a high incidence of malnutrition, it is characterized by retarded growth, swollen abdomen, OEDEMA, diarrhoea and apathy.

KwaZulu-Natal Province in E South Africa, bordered by the Indian Ocean and the Drakensberg Mountains; the capital is Pietermaritzburg. It was created in 1994 from the Zulu homeland, KwaZulu and the former province of Natal. Industries: sugar, textiles, tanning, oil refining. Area: 92,180sq km (33,578sq mi). Pop. (1995 est.) 8,713,100.

Kyd, Thomas (1558–94) English dramatist who achieved popular success with *The Spanish Tragedy* (*c*.1589). Kyd was a member of the literary circles of his day, associating with Christopher MARLOWE. In 1593, he was arrested for atheism.

Kyoto City on W central Honshu Island, Japan; capital of Kyoto prefecture. Founded in the 6th century, it was the capital of Japan for more than 1,000 years. Industries: porcelain, lacquerware, textiles, precision tools. Pop. (1995) 1,464,000.

Kyrgyz Turko-Mongolian people who inhabit the Republic of KYRGYZSTAN in central Asia. Of the Muslim faith, they are Turkic-speaking nomadic pastoralists who began to settle in the TIAN SHAN region of KYRGYZSTAN in the 7th century. They were colonized by the Russians during the 19th century. After fighting the BOLSHEVIKS in the Russian Civil War (1917–21), many Kyrgyz perished in the ensuing famine.

Kyrgyzstan (formerly Kirghizia) Landlocked republic between China, Tajikistan, Uzbekistan and Kazakstan, NE Middle Asia. **Land and climate** A mountainous country, the highest mountain, Pik Pobedy, is 7,439m (24,406ft) above sea level. The largest of Kyrgyzstan's many lakes is Ozero (Lake) Issyk-Kul in the NE. The lowlands of Kyrgyzstan have warm summers and cold winters, but in the mountains, January temperatures drop to −28°C (−18°F). Much of Kyrgyzstan has a low annual rainfall. Mountain grassland is the dominant vegetation, with woodland covering only a small area, mainly in the lower valleys. Less than a tenth of the land is used for crops. **History and politics** The area that is now Kyrgyzstan was populated in ancient times by nomadic herders. MONGOL armies conquered the region in the early 13th century. Islam was introduced in the 17th century. China gained control of the area in the mid-18th century, but in 1876 Kyrgyzstan became a province of Russia. In 1916 Russia put down a rebellion and many local people fled to China. In 1922, when the Soviet Union was formed, Kyrgyzstan became an autonomous region. In 1936, it became a Soviet Socialist Republic. Under communism, nomads were forced to live on government-run farms. In August 1991, Kyrgyzstan declared independence. The Communist Party was dissolved. President Askar Akayev began to introduce free-market reforms. In 1994, a new constitution was adopted. In 2000, Akayev was re-elected. There are tensions between the rural nomadic Kirghiz and the urban Russians and Uzbeks. **Economics** In 1997, private ownership was legalized. Agriculture, especially livestock raising, is the chief activity (1995 GDP per capita, US$1,800). Major products include cotton, eggs, fruits, grain, tobacco, vegetables and wool. Industries are concentrated around the capital, BISHKEK, and manufactures include machinery, processed food, metals and textiles. The largest single export is gold. Economic cooperation agreements have been signed with Kazakstan, Uzbekistan and Belarus.

Kyushu Island in S Japan; the southernmost of the four principal Japanese islands. The terrain is mountainous, and the irregular coastline has many natural harbours. It is the most densely populated of the Japanese islands. The chief port is NAGASAKI. Products: rice, tea, tobacco, fruit, soya beans. Industries: mining, fishing, timber, textiles, porcelain, metals, machinery. Area: 42,149sq km (16,274sq mi). Pop. (1992 est.) 13,314,000.

Kyung Wha Chung (1948–) Korean violinist. At the age of nine she played the Mendelssohn concerto in Seoul. Three years later she went to the Juilliard School of Music, New York City, where she won the Leventritt Award jointly with Pinchas Zukerman.

Kyzyl Kum (Kizil Kum) Desert of central Asia, in Uzbekistan and S Kazakstan, between the rivers Amudarya and Syrdarya. Cotton and rice are grown in the irrigated river valleys, and karakul sheep are raised by tribespeople. Area: *c*.230,000sq km (89,000sq mi).

KYRGYZSTAN
AREA: 198,500sq km (76,640sq mi)
POPULATION: 5,403,000
CAPITAL (POPULATION): Bishkek (584,000)

L/l, 12th letter of the alphabet, can be traced to the Semitic letter lamedh, *which passed into Greek as* lambda. *It became slightly modified in the Roman alphabet and in this form has passed into English.*

Laban, Rudolph von (1879–1958) Slovakian choreographer and dancer. Laban organized the dance routines for the 1936 Olympic Games. His system of dance notation (Labanation) proved highly influential in the development of MODERN DANCE.

Labor Party Social democratic party in Australia. Founded in 1891, it is the oldest surviving political party in Australia. It first held federal office in 1904. In 1916, the party split over involvement in World War 1. Prime Minister W.M. Hughes led the majority pro-conscription wing into the breakaway National Party. In 1929, the Labor Party returned to office under J.H. Scullin, but it fractured again over policies to combat the GREAT DEPRESSION. Between 1939 and 1949 the Labor government introduced important social welfare reforms. In 1955, the party split again over attitudes to communism. In 1972, the party returned to power under Gough WHITLAM. Bob HAWKE held office for a record four terms and was succeeded as prime minister by Paul KEATING.

labour In childbirth, stages in the delivery of the FOETUS at the end of pregnancy. In the first stage, contractions of the UTERUS begin and the sac containing the amniotic fluid ruptures. In the second stage, the contractions strengthen and the baby is propelled through the birth canal. The third stage is the expulsion of the PLACENTA and foetal membranes, together known as the afterbirth.

labour In economics, one of the factors of PRODUCTION that makes commodities through the application of human physical and intellectual effort. In the FEUDAL SYSTEM agricultural labour was performed mainly by SERFS. The Middle Ages saw the development of trade GUILDS. The INDUSTRIAL REVOLUTION brought the DIVISION OF LABOUR in FACTORIES. TRADE UNIONS were established to improve wages and conditions of work. *See also* CAPITAL; CLASS

Labour Party Social democratic party in the UK. The first British socialist parties, founded in the 1880s, united in the Independent Labour Party (ILP) in 1893, whose president was Keir HARDIE, the first socialist member of Parliament. In 1900, the ILP created the Labour Representation Committee, which was renamed the Labour Party in 1906. In 1918, it adopted a constitution written by Sidney WEBB. In 1924, Labour formed a brief minority government under Ramsay MACDONALD and again held office from 1929 to 1931. Labour joined the wartime coalition of World War 2 and its leader, Clement ATTLEE, was deputy prime minister (1942–45) in Winston CHURCHILL's government. After a landslide Labour victory in 1945, the Attlee government introduced a series of social reforms that strengthened the WELFARE STATE and SOCIAL SECURITY. In 1946, Aneurin BEVAN founded the NATIONAL HEALTH SERVICE (NHS). It also set about the NATIONALIZATION of British industry. Labour returned to power under Harold WILSON (1964–70). In 1974, Wilson formed a minority government. In 1976, he resigned and was succeeded as prime minister and Labour leader by James CALLAGHAN. In 1979, Callaghan was defeated by Margaret THATCHER. In 1981, the Labour Party split with the "gang of four" (Roy JENKINS, David OWEN, Shirley WILLIAMS and Bill Rogers) forming the SOCIAL DEMOCRATIC PARTY (SDP). The Labour Party, led (1980–83) by Michael FOOT, was heavily defeated in the 1983 elections. Neil KINNOCK's leadership (1983–92) introduced important internal reforms and changes in policy, but the party remained in opposition. John SMITH continued the democratization of the party. In 1994, Tony BLAIR became party leader and stepped up the pace of "modernization" under the slogan of "New Labour". The Labour Party won a landslide victory in the 1997 general election, and Blair became the first Labour prime minister for 18 years.

Labrador Mainland part of NEWFOUNDLAND province, E Canada, bordered W and S by Québec and E by the Atlantic Ocean. It is mountainous with an indented coastline. In 1498, the coast was visited by John CABOT. It passed to Britain under the Treaty of Paris (1736). Between 1809 and 1827 the boundaries between Newfoundland and Québec were under dispute. In 1949, Labrador became part of Canada. Industries: timber, fishing, iron ore mining. Area: 292,220sq km (112,826sq mi).

La Bruyère, Jean de (1645–96) French satirist. He ridiculed French life in his only work, *The Characters of Theophrastus, Translated from the Greek, with the Characters and Mores of This Age* (1688).

laburnum Any of several Eurasian shrubs and small trees of the genus *Laburnum*, especially the common Laburnum, *L. anagyroides*, which has drooping clusters of bright yellow flowers. It bears pods having poisonous seeds. Family Fabaceae/Leguminosae.

labyrinth Intricate structure of chambers and passages, generally constructed to confuse anyone within it. In Greek mythology, MINOS had a labyrinth built by DAEDALUS to confine the MINOTAUR.

lac Name of an insect and the sticky substance it secretes onto twigs; the deposit is harvested in Asia for use in shellac and red lac dye. Species *Laccifer lacca*.

Lacaille, Nicolas Louis de (1713–62) French astronomer. From 1751 to 1753 he surveyed the skies of the Southern Hemisphere, introducing 14 new S constellations. In 1761, Lacaille made an accurate measurement of the Moon's distance; this made possible a more accurate method of determining terrestrial longitude.

lacemaking Manufacture of lace, an openwork ornamental fabric made from fine threads of linen, cotton, silk, wool or artificial fibres. **Needlepoint** lace was made with needle and thread, using embroidery stitches on a linen backing. **Bobbin** lace (pillow lace) was made using bobbins of thread. The threads were crossed, braided, twisted or woven around pins stuck in a pillow. Most lace is now made by machine.

lacewing Any of numerous species of neuropteran insects, especially members of the families Chrysopidae

▲ **lacewing**
The European lacewing (*Eurolean europaeus*), also known as the ant lion, grows to 2cm (0.8in). A member of the Neuroptera order, lacewings are found throughout the world. The larva of the lacewing is an extremely fierce predator of certain small insects, particularly aphids.

and Hemerobiidae, which are found worldwide. Common green lacewings have a slender greenish body, long antennae and two pairs of delicate, lacy, veined wings. Length: to 2cm (0.8in).

lachrymal gland Organ that produces tears. It is located in the orbital cavity and is controlled by autonomic nerves. It produces slightly germicidal tears that flow through ducts to the surface of the eye to lubricate it.

Laclos, Pierre (Ambroise François) Choderlos de (1741–1803) French general and novelist. His epistolary novel, *Les Liaisons Dangereuses* (1782), caused a sensation and was only belatedly recognized as a great work.

lacrosse Ball game that originated among the Iroquois Native Americans of Canada and the USA. It is played by teams of 10 male or 12 female players. They carry sticks that have a thonged meshwork head like a flexible scoop. The ball may be conveyed, passed, kicked or hit with the stick, but only the goalkeepers are allowed to handle it. Lacrosse became Canada's national game in 1867.

lactation Secretion of MILK to feed the young. In pregnant women, HORMONES induce the breasts to enlarge, and prolactin (a pituitary hormone) stimulates breast cells to begin secreting milk. The milk appears in the breast immediately after the birth of the baby. Its flow is stimulated by suckling.

lactic acid Colourless organic acid (2-hydroxypropanoic acid, $CH_3CHOHCOOH$) formed from LACTOSE by the action of bacteria. It is also produced in muscles, when ANAEROBIC respiration occurs due to insufficient oxygen and causes muscle fatigue. Lactic acid is used in foods and beverages, in tanning, dyeing and adhesive manufacture. Properties: r.d. 1.206; m.p. 18°C (64.4°F); b.p. 122°C (251.6°F).

lactose (milk sugar) Disaccharide present in MILK, made up of a molecule of GLUCOSE linked to a molecule of galactose. It is important in cheesemaking, when lactic bacteria turn it into LACTIC ACID. This sours the milk and results in the production of cheese curd.

Ladoga (Rus. *Ladozhskoye Ozero*, Finnish, *Laatokka*) Europe's largest lake, in NW Russia (near the Finnish border). It is drained by the River Neva. Formerly divided between Finland and the Soviet Union, it has been entirely within the Russian border since the Russian invasion of Finland in 1940. Area: 17,678sq km (6,826sq mi).

ladybird (ladybug) Any of a large number of small, brightly coloured beetles; most common species are red with conspicuous black spots and a black and white head. Ladybirds and their larvae are regarded as useful by farmers because their diet consists primarily of APHIDS. Family Coccinellidae.

Lady Day *See* ANNUNCIATION

lady's smock (cuckooflower) North American and Eurasian perennial flowering plant, common in moist meadows. It has a stout stem, fine leaves and clusters of pink or purplish flowers. Family Brassicaceae/Cruciferae; species *Cardamine pratensis*.

Lafayette, Marie Joseph Gilbert de Motier, marquis de (1757–1834) French general and statesman. He fought for the colonists in the AMERICAN REVOLUTION, distinguishing himself in the Yorktown campaign (1781). Returning to France, Lafayette presented the DECLARATION OF THE RIGHTS OF MAN to the States General (1789). After the storming of the Bastille, he commanded (1789–91) the National Guard in the first phase of the FRENCH REVOLUTION. In 1791, Lafayette lost popular support by ordering his troops to fire on a riotous crowd. In 1792, hounded by the JACOBINS, he deserted to the Austrians. In 1799, Lafayette was

◀ **ladybird** The seven-spot ladybird or ladybug (*Coccinealla septempuctata*) is found throughout Europe. It is the largest of the European ladybirds, growing to 8mm (0.4in). Both the adults and larvae feed on aphids, making them popular with gardeners. During the winter, large numbers hibernate together.

rehabilitated by Napoleon and returned to France. He played a major role in the JULY REVOLUTION (1830) that installed LOUIS PHILIPPE as king of France.

La Fontaine, Jean de (1621–95) French poet. He is chiefly remembered for his *Fables* (1668–94), verse interpretations of 240 FABLES from writers such as AESOP. He also wrote *Contes* (1664–74), a bawdy collection of poetic treatments of stories by authors such as BOCCACCIO. *See also* FRENCH LITERATURE

Lagerkvist, Pär Fabian (1891–1974) Swedish writer. Lagerkvist's verse collection *Anguish* (1916) established him as one of Sweden's greatest lyric poets. He is chiefly remembered for his novels *The Hangman* (1933), *The Dwarf* (1944) and *Barabbas* (1950). His central theme is the brutality of man and the search for transcendental meaning. He was awarded the Nobel Prize for literature in 1951.

Lagerlöf, Selma Ottiliana Lovisa (1858–1940) Swedish novelist. Her native Värmland is the rural setting for many of her works. Her novels include *The Saga of Gösta Berlings* (1891) and *Jerusalem* (1901). Her short-story collection *The Wonderful Adventures of Nils* (1906) is a classic work of children's literature. In 1909, she became the first woman to be awarded the Nobel Prize for literature.

lagoon Shallow stretch of seawater protected from waves and tides by a strip of land or coral.

Lagos Largest city and chief port of Nigeria, in the S of the country, on the Gulf of Guinea. From the 17th century Lagos developed as a YORUBA settlement, coming under British control in 1861 after years of Portuguese exploitation through the slave trade. In 1960, it became the capital of independent Nigeria but was replaced by ABUJA in 1982. Industries: brewing, ship repairing, textiles, crafts. Pop. (1992) 1,347,000.

Lagrange, Joseph Louis (1736–1813) French mathematician and astronomer, b. Italy. His early researches at the University of Turin included work on the calculus of variations and the harmonics of sound. In 1766, Lagrange succeeded Leonhard EULER as head of the Berlin Academy of Sciences. His major work is *Analytical Mechanics* (1788), developing a new approach to mechanics based entirely on ALGEBRA and CALCULUS. *See also* CELESTIAL MECHANICS; LAGRANGIAN POINTS

Lagrangian points One of the five points at which a celestial body can remain in equilibrium with respect to two much more massive bodies orbiting each other.

Lahore City on the River Ravi, NE Pakistan; capital of Punjab province and Pakistan's second-largest city. It was used as a royal residence under the MOGUL EMPIRE. It was part of the Sikh kingdom from 1767 and passed to the British in 1849. From 1955 to 1970, it was capital of West Pakistan. It is an important commercial and industrial centre. Industries: iron, steel, textiles. Pop. (1995). 5,085,000.

Laibach, Congress of (1821) Conference of European powers at Laibach (now Ljubljana, Slovenia). It confirmed Austria's right to suppress revolution in Naples but caused a split between Britain and France and the HOLY ALLIANCE (Austria, Prussia and Russia).

Laing, R.D. (Ronald David) (1927–89) Scottish psychiatrist. He was an exponent of existential psychology and produced radical work on the nature of SCHIZOPHRENIA. Laing believed that the mentally ill are not necessarily maladapted: a psychotic disorder may be a reasonable reaction to the stresses of the world. His major work is *The Divided Self* (1960).

laissez-faire In economics, the doctrine that an economic system functions best when self-interest and the profit motive are allowed free reign without the interference of government. The concept was developed in reaction to MERCANTILISM by the French physiocrats in the 18th century. Adam SMITH adopted the doctrine, arguing that FREE-TRADE and competition were the basis of a healthy economy. John Stuart MILL and Jeremy BENTHAM developed Smith's ideas into the philosophy of UTILITARIANISM. In the 1840s, Richard COBDEN and John BRIGHT formed the "Manchester school" that secured the repeal of the CORN LAWS. In the 20th century the development of monopoly CAPITALISM led to state intervention to protect competition. In the 1930s, John Maynard KEYNES promoted the intervention of government to fight against unemployment and guard against recession.

laity Members of a Christian Church who are not part of the clergy. The distinction has greater significance in the Anglican, Roman Catholic and Orthodox Churches.

lake Inland body of water, generally of considerable size and too deep to have rooted vegetation completely covering the surface. The expanded part of a river and a reservoir behind a dam are also termed lakes. *See also* OXBOW

Lake District Region of Cumbria, NW England, containing the principal English lakes. Its spectacular mountain and lakeland scenery and its literary associations make it a major tourist attraction. Among its 15 lakes are Derwent Water, Grasmere, Buttermere and WINDERMERE. The highest point is SCAFELL PIKE at 978m (3,210ft). The Lake District National Park was established in 1951. Area: 2,243sq km (866sq mi).

Lake poets Name for three poets who lived (*c*.1800) in the LAKE DISTRICT, NW England: William WORDSWORTH, Samuel Taylor COLERIDGE and Robert SOUTHEY.

Lakshmi (Padma or Sita) In Hindu mythology, the lotus goddess, wife of VISHNU, who existed at the beginning of creation, rising from the ocean borne by a lotus. Lakshmi was the goddess of beauty and youth, and was also worshipped as goddess of wealth and good fortune.

Lalande, Joseph Jérôme LeFrançais de (1732–1807) French astronomer whose main achievement was a catalogue of more than 47,000 stars. In 1762, Lalande became professor of astronomy at the Collège de France, a post he held for 46 years. In 1768, he was made director of the Paris Observatory.

Lalique, René (1860–1945) French jewellery designer whose work significantly contributed to the ART NOUVEAU movement. In 1920, he began to produce Lalique glass, a product whose popularity has endured.

Lamaism *See* TIBETAN BUDDHISM

Lamarck, Jean-Baptiste Pierre Antoine de Monet, chevalier de (1744–1829) French biologist. His theories of EVOLUTION (Lamarckism), according to which ACQUIRED CHARACTERISTICS are inheritable, influenced evolutionary thought throughout most of the 19th century, but were disproved by Charles DARWIN.

Lamartine, Alphonse-Marie Louis de (1790–1869) French romantic poet and statesman. His *Méditations Poétiques* (1820), a nostalgic eulogy to his serenely happy childhood, won him immediate fame, while his later poems, collected in *Recueillements Poétiques* (1839), echoed his liberal political convictions. Lamartine briefly served in the provisional government after the FEBRUARY REVOLUTION (1848).

Lamb, Charles (1775–1834) English writer. He is best known for his essays, most famously collected as *The Essays of Elia* (1823, 1833). Lamb is also remembered for his children's books, which include the perennially popular *Tales from Shakespeare* (1807), on which he collaborated with his sister, **Mary** (1764–1847).

Lamb, Willis Eugene, Jr (1913–) US physicist who applied new techniques to measure the lines of the hydrogen SPECTRUM. He found that the WAVELENGTHS varied from those predicted by Paul DIRAC. For this research, he shared the 1955 Nobel Prize for physics.

Lambert, (Leonard) Constant (1905–51) English composer, conductor and critic. He was commissioned by DIAGHILEV to write the ballet *Romeo and Juliet* (1926). Lambert was musical director (1905–51) of the Sadler's Wells Ballet. His best-known composition is the jazz-inflected choral work *Rio Grande* (1927). He wrote *Music Ho!* (1934), an influential critical work.

Lambert, John (1619–84) English parliamentary general in the English CIVIL WARS. He commanded the cavalry in several victorious battles, including MARSTON MOOR (1644) and Preston (1648). Lambert headed the group that overthrew Richard CROMWELL and ruled the country as head of the "Committee of Safety" until the RESTORATION. He was convicted of treason and sentenced to life imprisonment.

Lamentations Old Testament book bewailing the destruction (*c*.587 BC) of JERUSALEM and its TEMPLE; it is often attributed to the author of the Book of JEREMIAH.

Lammas Christian festival of thanksgiving for the harvest, celebrated on 1 August in medieval England. It was originally one of the QUARTER DAYS.

Lamming, George (1927–) Caribbean novelist and poet. His native Barbados forms the background to his debut novel, *In the Castle of My Skin* (1953). *The Emigrants* (1954) describes the problems facing West Indians in England, where he settled in the 1950s. Later novels include *Natives of My Person* (1972).

lamp Form of artificial lighting. Early lamps burned fuels, such as animal fat, wax and oil. Coal gas was used from the early 1800s. The electric light became popular in the early 1900s. Most modern lamps are electrically powered and are of three main types: incandescent, discharge and FLUORESCENT LAMPS. *See also* INCANDESCENCE

Lampedusa, Giuseppe Tomasi di (1896–1957) Sicilian prince whose posthumously published novel, *The Leopard* (1958), portrayed the microcosmic and isolated life of Sicily with memorable force.

lamprey Eel-like, jawless vertebrate found in marine and freshwater on both sides of the Atlantic and in the Great Lakes. It feeds by attaching its mouth to fish and sucking their blood. Length: to 91cm (3ft). Family Petromyzondiae.

Lancashire County in NW England, bordered by Cumbria (N), North and West Yorkshire (E), Greater Manchester and Merseyside (S), and the Irish Sea (W); the county town is Preston. Other major towns include Lancaster (the administrative centre), Blackpool and Blackburn. It was occupied in Roman times and later formed part of an Anglo-Saxon kingdom. From the 16th century, textile manufacturing became increasingly important, and by the early 19th century cotton goods were vital to Lancashire's economy. In the 20th century, cotton and its other traditional industry, coal, sharply declined. It is drained by the rivers Lune and Ribble, and its lowland regions are predominantly agricultural. Area: 3,064sq km (1,183sq mi). Pop. (1994) 1,424,000.

Lancaster, Burt (1913–94) US film actor and producer. A former circus acrobat, he made his film debut in *The Killers* (1946). He won an Academy Award for best actor in *Elmer Gantry* (1960). Other films include *Bird Man of Alcatraz* (1962), *The Leopard* (1963) and *Atlantic City* (1980).

Lancaster, Duchy of English estate first given by HENRY III to his son Edmund in 1265. The revenues from the duchy passed permanently to the crown in 1399, with the accession of the Lancastrian king HENRY IV.

Lancaster, House of English royal dynasty. The first Earl of Lancaster was Edmund "Crouchback" (1245–96), son of HENRY III. In 1361 the title and lands passed to JOHN OF GAUNT via his wife. Their son became HENRY IV in 1399. During the Wars of the ROSES in the 15th century, the royal houses of Lancaster and York, both PLANTAGENETS, contended for the crown.

Lancelot of the Lake In ARTHURIAN ROMANCE, the father of Galahad and one of the most famous knights; he is portrayed as the lover of GUINEVERE, wife of King ARTHUR.

Lanchow *See* LANZHOU

Land, Edwin Herbert (1909–91) US physicist, inventor of the "instant" camera. By 1936, he had developed "Polaroid", a light-polarizing material later used in sunglasses. In 1947, he developed a camera that produced a finished print within one minute.

Landau, Lev Davidovich (1908–68) Soviet physicist. His many contributions included the basic theories describing ferromagnetism and liquid HELIUM. In 1927, Landau proposed a concept for energy called the density matrix, which was later used in QUANTUM MECHANICS. He received the 1962 Nobel Prize for physics for his research into the SUPERFLUIDITY of helium.

Land League Irish association formed (1879) to campaign for land reform and tenants' rights in Ireland. It was organized by Michael DAVITT and Charles PARNELL. Its aims were mainly realized in the Irish Land Act (1881). *See also* FENIAN MOVEMENT; HOME RULE

Landor, Walter Savage (1775–1864) English writer. His lyrics include *Gebir: a Poem in Seven Books* (1798). Landor is chiefly remembered for his prose dialogues, *Imaginary Conversations of Literary Men and Statesmen* (1824–29).

Landowska, Wanda Louise (1877–1959) Polish harpsichordist and pianist who lived in Paris from 1919 and in the USA from 1941. An authority on early music, she founded (1925) the Ecole de Musique Ancienne, Paris.

landscape gardening Arranging gardens to produce certain effects. Two main traditions are the Sino-English, with its retention of the informality of nature, and the Franco-Italian, with its geometric patterns. The second tradition arose in Italy during the RENAISSANCE. It is best exemplified in the *parterres* of VERSAILLES, designed by André LE NÔTRE. In England, the naturalist style developed in the 18th century with William Kent and "Capability" BROWN.

landscape painting Art of portraying natural scenery. While landscape painting was central to the art of the East, especially China, the West did not recognize it as a separate genre until the 16th century. Landscape painting came into full flower in 17th-century Holland; Jacob van RUISDAEL is regarded as the greatest Dutch landscape painter.

In Italy, Annibale CARRACCI invented the "ideal landscape". CLAUDE LORRAIN and Nicholas POUSSIN arranged natural elements into artificial compositions. In the 19th century, mystical and romantic landscapes were created by painters such as Caspar FRIEDRICH in Germany and J.M.W. TURNER in Britain, as well as a number of North American artists. Jean-Baptiste COROT and John CONSTABLE introduced a more naturalistic approach, which led to the enormous popularity that landscape achieved through IMPRESSIONISM. In the 20th century, abstract and surrealist painters once more reinvented the genre.

Landseer, Sir Edwin Henry (1802–73) English painter and sculptor. He achieved immense popularity with his sentimental paintings of animals, such as the stag in *Monarch of the Glen* (1851). His best-known sculptures are the lions in Trafalgar Square, London (1867).

landslide Relatively rapid displacement of rock or soil slipping over a definite surface. Landslides are frequently caused by water lubricating the slip surface.

Landsteiner, Karl (1868–1943) US pathologist, b. Austria. He discovered the four different BLOOD GROUPS (A, B, AB and O) and demonstrated that certain blood groups are incompatible with others. He was awarded the 1930 Nobel Prize for physiology or medicine. In 1940, with A.S. Wiener, he identified the rhesus (Rh) factor.

Lanfranc (*c*.1010–89) Italian theologian. He was a BENEDICTINE monk whose priory at Bec in Normandy became a centre for European scholars in the 1040s. As a counsellor of WILLIAM I (THE CONQUEROR), he became Archbishop of Canterbury (1070–89).

Lanfranco, Giovanni (1582–1647) Italian painter, one of the pioneers of the high BAROQUE style in Rome. He was born in Parma and trained under Agostino Carracci in Bologna. In 1602, he moved to Rome to assist Annibale CARRACCI on the decorations in the Farnese Palace. After 1612, Lanfranco executed a series of important frescos in the city, including *The Assumption of the Virgin* (1625–27) at Santa Andrea della Valle.

Lang, Andrew (1844–1912) Scottish anthropologist and historian. His anthropological works include *Custom and Myth* (1884) and *Myth, Ritual and Religion* (1887–99). As a historian, he is best known for his *History of Scotland* (1900–07).

Lang, Fritz (1890–1976) Austrian film director. His debut feature was *Halbblut* (1919). Lang's first major success was the two-part crime thriller *Dr Mabuse* (1922). His best-known film, *Metropolis* (1927), has become a science-fiction classic. Perhaps his greatest film was his first sound feature, the expressionistic, psychological thriller *M* (1931). Fleeing Nazism, Lang moved to the USA. His first Hollywood film was *Fury* (1936). Later films include *The Big Heat* (1953), *While the City Sleeps* (1956) and *The 1000 Eyes of Dr Mabuse* (1960).

Lange, Dorothea (1895–1965) US photographer. Her portraits of urban poor and migrant labourers in California during the GREAT DEPRESSION, and her images of rural America taken for the Farm Security Administration (1935–42), are classics of documentary photography.

Langevin, Paul (1872–1946) French physicist. In 1905, he was the first to interpret paramagnetism (weak MAGNETISM) and diamagnetism (opposition to a magnetic force) in terms of the behaviour of electrons in atoms. During World War 1, he built the first submarine detector based on ultrasonic waves. *See also* SONAR

Langland, William (1331–99) English poet. His poem *Piers Plowman* (*c*.1367–70), a late flowering of the alliterative tradition in English verse, is considered one of the most important works of medieval literature.

Langley, Samuel Pierpont (1834–1906) US astronomer. In 1880 he invented the bolometer for measuring the Sun's infrared radiation. In 1896 Langley built the first successful unmanned heavier-than-air aircraft.

Langmuir, Irving (1881–1957) US physical chemist. His inventions include a gas-filled tungsten lamp and the atomic-hydrogen welding process. In 1932, Langmuir was awarded the 1932 Nobel Prize for chemistry for his work in surface chemistry.

Langton, Stephen (c.1150–1228) English cardinal and scholar who was one of England's most controversial archbishops of Canterbury. His appointment (1207) by Pope INNOCENT III was bitterly opposed by King JOHN, and he was prevented from entering England and occupying his post until 1213. Langton supported the barons concerning the MAGNA CARTA (1215).

Langtry, Lillie Emilie Charlotte (1853–1929) British actress, b. Jersey as Emilie Charlotte le Breton. Noted for her beauty, she was one of the first English women aristocrats to appear on the stage. In 1881, Langtry made her acting debut at the Haymarket Theatre, London. Oscar WILDE wrote *Lady Windermere's Fan* (1892) for her. She became the mistress of the Prince of wales, later EDWARD VII.

language System of human communication. Although there are more than 4,000 different languages (*see individual entries*), they have many characteristics in common. Almost every human language uses a fundamentally similar grammatical structure, or SYNTAX, even though they may not be linked in vocabulary or origin. **Families** of languages have been constructed (AFRO-ASIATIC, AUSTRONESIAN, DRAVIDIAN, INDO-EUROPEAN, NIGER-CONGO, SINO-TIBETAN) but their composition and origins are the subject of continuing debate. Historical studies of language are undertaken by the disciplines of ETYMOLOGY and PHILOLOGY. LINGUISTICS usually involves contemporary language. *See also* AGGLUTINATIVE LANGUAGE; CHOMSKY, NOAM; DIALECT; GRAMMAR; HUMBOLDT, WILHELM VON; INFLECTION; SAUSSURE, FERDINAND DE; SIGN LANGUAGE

Languedoc-Roussillon Region of s France, extending from the Rhône valley to the foothills of the Pyrenees; the capital is MONTPELLIER. Languedoc was originally settled by the Romans. It later became part of the CAROLINGIAN empire before passing to the French crown in 1271. Languedoc-Roussillon is one of the world's major wine-producing regions. The industry is based on the fertile soils along the River Garonne and the alluvial Mediterranean coastal plain. Area: 27,736sq km (10,706sq mi). Pop. (1990) 1,926,514.

langur Any of c.15 species of medium to large MONKEYS of SE Asia and the East Indies. They are slender, with long hands and tails. Tree dwellers, they are found from sea-level to snowy Himalayan slopes up to an elevation of 4,000m (13,000ft). Length: 43–78cm (17–31in). Family Cercopithecidae; genus *Presbytis*.

lanolin Purified, fat-like substance derived from sheep's wool and used with water as a base for ointments and cosmetics.

Lansing Capital city of Michigan, USA, on the Grand River, s Michigan. First settled in the 1840s, it was made the state capital in 1847. Industries: motor vehicles, metal goods, machinery. Pop. (1991) 127,321.

lantern fish Any of numerous species of marine fish in Atlantic and Mediterranean waters, especially *Diaphus rafinesquiei*. It is identified by light organs along its sides. Length: 7.5cm (3in). Family Myctophidae.

lanthanides (rare-earth elements) Series of 15 rare metallic elements with atomic numbers from 57 to 71. They are, in order of increasing atomic numbers: LAN-THANUM (sometimes not considered a member), CERIUM, PRASEODYMIUM, NEODYMIUM, PROMETHIUM, SAMARIUM, EUROPIUM, GADOLINIUM, TERBIUM, DYSPROSIUM, HOLMIUM, ERBIUM, THULIUM, YTTERBIUM and LUTETIUM. Their properties are similar. They occur in monazite and other rare minerals, and are placed in Group III of the periodic table.

lanthanum (symbol La) Silvery-white, metallic element, first identified in 1839. One of the LANTHANIDES, its chief ores are monazite and bastnasite. Soft, malleable and ductile, lanthanum is used as a catalyst in cracking crude oil, in alloys and to manufacture optical glasses. Properties: at.no. 57; r.a.m. 138.9055; r.d. 6.17; m.p. 920°C (1,688°F); b.p. 3,454°C (6,249°F); most common isotope La^{139} (99.91%).

Lanzhou (Lanchow) City on the River Huang He, w China; capital of Gansu province. An old walled city dating from the 6th century BC, it is now a major transport centre. The principal industry is oil refining. Since 1960 it has been the base for the Chinese nuclear industry. Pop. (1994) 1,296,000.

Laocoon Priest of APOLLO during the TROJAN WAR. In Virgil's *Aeneid*, he exhorts the Trojans to fear the Greeks even when they are bearing gifts. He and his sons were strangled by two sea-serpents sent by Apollo.

Laos Landlocked republic in SE Asia; the capital is VIENTIANE. **Land and climate** Mountains and high plateaus cover most of Laos. The highest point is Mount Bia, at 2,817m (9,242ft), in central Laos. Most people live on the plains bordering the River MEKONG and its tributaries. The Mekong is one of Asia's longest rivers and forms much of Laos's NW and SW borders. The Annam Cordillera mountains form the E border with Vietnam. Laos has a tropical monsoon climate, with dry, sunny winters. Temperatures rise until April, when moist SW winds herald the monsoon season. Forests cover c.60% of the land. **History and politics** In 1353, Fa Ngoun founded the kingdom of *Lan Xang* (Land of a Million Elephants). Theravada BUDDHISM was adopted as the official religion. In 1707, the kingdom divided into the N kingdom of Luang Prabang and the S kingdom of Vientiane. In the early 19th century, the kingdoms were controlled by Siam. In 1893, Siam deferred to French power, and Laos was ruled as part of French INDOCHINA. In 1945, Laos was occupied by Japan. In 1947, in the aftermath of World War 2, Laos became a semi-autonomous constitutional monarchy. In 1953, Laos achieved independence, but was plunged into civil war. The communist Patriotic Front (Pathet Lao) controlled most of N Laos, and royalist forces controlled Vientiane. For most of the next 22 years, Laos was riven by sectarian conflict. The North Vietnamese use of the Ho Chi Minh Trail through Laos as a military supply line saw US bombardment of E Laos, and US military and financial support to the Laotian government against the Pathet Lao. By 1974, the Pathet Lao had secured most of Laos. The victory of the Viet Cong in the VIETNAM WAR (1957–75) enabled the final victory of Pathet Lao. The king abdicated and a democratic republic was proclaimed. Vietnam remained a powerful influence on Laos. In 1997, Laos joined the ASSOCIATION OF SOUTHEAST ASIAN NATIONS (ASEAN). The 1991 constitution confirmed the Lao People's Revolutionary Party (LPRP) as the only legal political party. In 1998, Khamtay

---

LAOS

AREA: 236,800sq km (91,428sq mi)
POPULATION: 5,463,000
CAPITAL (POPULATION): Vientiane (332,000)

Siphandon was elected president. **Economy** Laos is one of the world's poorest countries (1992 GDP per capita, US$1,760). Agriculture employs c.76% of the workforce and accounts for 60% of GDP. Rice is the main crop; timber and coffee are also exported. Hydroelectricity is produced at power stations along the Mekong. The "Golden Triangle", on the border with Cambodia and Burma, is the centre for the illegal production of opium. Laos is thought to be the world's third-largest producer of opium. In 1986, Laos began to introduce free-market reforms.

Lao Tzu (Laozi) (active 6th century BC) Chinese philosopher, credited as the founder of TAOISM. According to tradition he was a contemporary of CONFUCIUS and developed Taoism as a mystical reaction to CONFUCIANISM. He is said to have written *Tao Te Ching*, the sacred book of Taoism. In parables and verse it advocates harmony with the *Tao* (path). *See also* YIN AND YANG

La Paz Administrative capital and largest city of Bolivia, in the W of the country. Founded by the Spanish in 1548 on the site of an Inca village, it was one of the centres of revolt in the War of Independence (1809–24). Located at 3,600m (12,000ft) in the Andes, it is the world's highest capital city. Industries: chemicals, tanning, flour milling. Pop. (1993) 1,126,000.

Laplace, Pierre Simon, Marquis de (1749–1827) French astronomer and mathematician. Laplace made significant advances in PROBABILITY theory. His study and application of NEWTON's theory of GRAVITATION to the Solar System was summarized in his book *Celestial Mechanics* (1798–1827). Laplace proposed that the Solar System had condensed out of a vast, rotating gaseous NEBULA (the **nebular hypothesis**). He also did fundamental work in the study of heat, magnetism and electricity.

Lapland Region in N Europe, lying almost entirely within the Arctic Circle and including N Norway, the northernmost parts of Sweden and Finland and the W part of the Kola Peninsula of Russia. Mountains are in Norway and Sweden, while TUNDRA predominates in the NE. The S regions are forested. The harsh climate has restricted settlement. Industries: hydroelectricity, fishing, mining for iron ore, copper and nickel. Tourism is important. Area: c.388,500sq km (150,000sq mi).

La Plata City in E Argentina, 56km (35 mi) SE of Buenos Aires. Founded in 1882, the city was called Eva PERÓN from 1946 to 1955. La Plata is Argentina's largest oil-refining centre. Its port, Ensenada, is a major exporter of oil, cereals and frozen meat. Pop. (1991) 640,000.

La Plata, Río de *See* PLATA, RÍO DE LA

Lapps People inhabiting LAPLAND, N Europe. The mountain Lapps are nomadic herders of reindeer, while those of the forest and coast are semi-nomadic and live by hunting, trapping and fishing. Their racial origins are uncertain. They speak Lapp, a FINNO-UGRIC LANGUAGE. Lapps have largely abandoned shamanism for Lutheran Christianity. Today, they number c.30,000.

lapwing (peewit) Eurasian PLOVER, *Vanellus vanellus*. A wading bird with a conspicuous crest. It commonly nests in open agricultural land and defends its young by luring predators away, feigning a broken wing. Length: 30cm (12in). Family Charadriidae.

Lara, Brian Charles (1969–) West Indian cricketer, b. Trinidad. A left-handed batsman, he made his debut for West Indies in 1990. In 1994, Lara scored 375 against England in Antigua, beating Gary SOBERS (1957) of the most runs in a single test innings. Also in 1994, playing English county cricket for Warwickshire, Lara scored a first-class record of 501 not out against Durham. His captaincy (1997–99) of West Indies was less consistent.

larch Any CONIFER tree of the genus *Larix*, native to cool and temperate regions of the Northern Hemisphere. Larches bear cones and needle-like leaves that, unusually for a conifer, are shed annually. Family Pinaceae.

lares Roman gods of cultivated land, worshipped at crossroads where field boundaries met, and also gods of the household. The worship of the lares (which were stylized as figurines) moved into the houses to join that of the PENATES, the gods of the threshold.

lark Any of several small birds, known for their melodious songs. Most common in Europe are the woodlark (*Lullula arborea*), skylark (*Alauda arvensis*) and shorelark (*Eremophila alpestris*). All are mottled brown. They feed on insects, larvae, crustaceans or berries. Length: to 18cm (7in). Family Alaudidae.

Larkin, Philip Arthur (1922–85) English poet. His first verse collection was *The North Ship* (1945), but he established his colloquial style in *The Less Deceived* (1955). Other works include *The Whitsun Weddings* (1964) and *High Windows* (1974). Larkin edited the *Oxford Book of Twentieth Century Verse* (1973). His *Collected Poems* appeared in 1988, and his controversial letters in 1992.

larkspur *See* DELPHINIUM

La Rochefoucauld, François, Duc de (1613–80) French writer of maxims and epigrams. In 1635, he was involved in an intrigue against Cardinal RICHELIEU and took part in the FRONDES revolts (1648–53). He wrote *Réflexions ou Sentences et Maximes Morales* (1665).

La Rochelle Seaport on the Bay of Biscay, W France; capital of Charente-Maritime department. An English possession during the 12th and 13th centuries, it changed hands several times during the HUNDRED YEARS WAR (1337–1453). In the 16th century, it became a HUGUENOT stronghold but capitulated to the forces of Cardinal RICHELIEU in 1628. Industries: shipbuilding, oil refining, sawmilling. Pop. (1990) 71,094.

Larousse, Pierre (1817–75) French lexicographer. In 1852, he co-founded the publishing house of Larousse. Larousse edited the 15-volume *Great Universal Dictionary of the 19th Century* (1866–76), the first in a series of dictionaries and encyclopedias.

larva Developmental stage in the METAMORPHOSIS of many invertebrates and some other animals. A common life cycle, typified by the BUTTERFLY, is egg, larva, PUPA and IMAGO (adult). The larva pupates to become an adult. Names for the larva of different organisms include MAGGOT, CATERPILLAR and TADPOLE.

Larwood, Harold (1904–95) English cricketer. He was a fast bowler for Nottinghamshire and England. Larwood took 78 wickets in 21 test matches (1926–33). He spearheaded the English attack in the infamous "bodyline" series (1932–33) against Australia.

laryngitis Inflammation of the LARYNX and vocal cords. Symptoms include sore throat, coughing and breathing difficulties. It is usually due to a respiratory tract infection.

larynx (voice box) Triangular cavity between the TRACHEA (windpipe) and the root of the tongue. It contains the vocal cords. These are thin bands of elastic tissue that vibrate when outgoing air passes over them, setting up resonant waves that are changed into sound by the action of throat muscles and the shape of the mouth. *See artwork* p.478

La Salle, (René) Robert Cavelier, Sieur de (1643–87) French explorer of North America. In 1668, he sailed for Canada to make his fortune in the fur trade. He explored the GREAT LAKES area and was governor of Fort Frontenac on Lake Ontario (1675). On his greatest journey, he followed the Mississippi to its mouth (1682), naming the land Louisiana and claiming it for France.

La Scala (*Teatro alla Scala*) One of the world's greatest opera houses, in Milan, Italy. Designed by Giuseppe Piermarini, it opened in 1776, and has been the scene of many famous premieres, among them Bellini's *Norma*, Verdi's *Otello* and Puccini's *Madame Butterfly*.

Las Casas, Bartolomé de (1474–1566) Spanish missionary, known as the Apostle of the Indies. He went to Hispaniola in 1502 and spent his life trying to help the Native Americans; his *History of the Indies* documents their persecution by Spanish colonists.

Lascaux Complex of caves in the French Pyrenees, discovered in 1940. They contain examples of 13 different styles of PALAEOLITHIC wall paintings, depicting horses, ibex, stags and a reindeer. The caves were closed in 1963 in order to halt the deterioration of the CAVE PAINTINGS.

laser (acronym for light amplification by stimulated emission of radiation) Optical MASER, a source of a narrow beam of intense coherent light or ultraviolet or infrared radiation. The laser was invented in 1960 by US physicist Theodore H. Maiman. The source can be a solid, liquid or gas. A large number of its atoms are excited to a higher energy state. One PHOTON of radiation emitted from an excited atom then stimulates the emission of another photon, of the same frequency and direction of travel, which in turn stimulates the emission of more photons. The photon number multiplies rapidly to produce a laser beam of very high energy content. It has applications in medicine, research, engineering, telecommunications, holography and other fields.

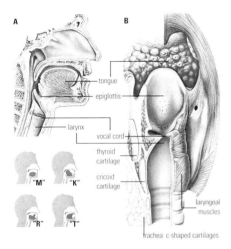

▲ **larynx** The larynx, together with the epiglottis, tongue, and mouth and lips is a principal organ of speech. A side view (A) and back view (B) of these organs are shown. Air pushed out from the lungs through the larynx causes the vocal cords to vibrate, producing a continuous singing tone, the "voice". This tone can be altered in "pitch" by varying the arrangement of the cartilages of the larynx

(thyroid and cricoid) by action of the associated muscles. As air passes through the mouth, the voice is modulated and broken up by changing the position and shape of the other organs to produce speech. The different vowels are produced by altering the shape of the mouth. Consonants (four shown) are formed when the stream of air is suddenly emitted or cut off.

Labels on figure: tongue, epiglottis, larynx, vocal cord, thyroid cartilage, cricoid cartilage, laryngeal muscles, trachea: c-shaped cartilages. "M" "K" "R" "T"

laser printer Computer printer with a LASER diode to control image formation. The laser beam scans lines across an electrically charged drum. The beam flashes on and off according to whether each point is to be light or dark. Exposed areas become discharged. The charged areas attract toner powder, thus forming an image. Charged plain paper picks up the powder image from the drum. A heated roller fuses the powder onto the paper to make the image permanent.

laser surgery Surgical treatment carried out using a LASER beam. The high energy in an extremely narrow laser beam can burn through body tissues to make a fine "cut". The heat also seals blood vessels, so there is much less bleeding than when a knife is used. Some forms of skin cancer are treated in this way.

Laski, Harold Joseph (1893–1950) English political scientist and teacher. A prominent figure in the FABIAN SOCIETY, he served as chairman (1945–46) of the Labour Party. As professor of political science (1926–50) at the London School of Economics (LSE), he influenced a number of the first wave of post-colonial leaders. His writings include *Faith, Reason, Civilization* (1944).

Las Palmas (Las Palmas de Gran Canaria) Spanish city in NE Grand Canary Island; capital of Las Palmas province. Founded in 1478, the city expanded considerably after the building of the port in 1883. It is now a tourist resort. Its port, Puerto de la Luz, is the chief port in the Canary Islands, exporting bananas, sugar, tomatoes and almonds. Pop. (1995) 374,000.

Lassa fever Acute viral disease, classified as a haemorrhagic fever. The virus, first detected in 1969, is spread by a species of rat found only in W Africa. It causes internal bleeding, fever, headache and muscle pain.

Lasso, Orlando di (1532–94) Flemish composer. Employed by Albert V of Bavaria after 1556, he became famous throughout Europe and is ranked as one of the greatest composers of the late 16th century. He was known for his madrigals, masses and motets.

Last Supper (Lord's Supper) Final meal shared by JESUS CHRIST and his disciples in Jerusalem during or just before the Passover, in the course of which Jesus instituted the Christian EUCHARIST.

Las Vegas Largest city in Nevada, USA, in the S of the state. It is a world-famous gambling and entertainment centre. With more than 13 million visitors per year, Las Vegas is one of the USA's major tourist destinations. The Mormons established a colony on the site in 1855–57. In 1931 Nevada legalized gambling, and the city grew rapidly. Its first big gambling casino opened in 1946. Las Vegas is also the commercial centre for a mining and ranching area. Pop. (1990) 258,295.

La Tène Archaeological site in Switzerland, discovered in the 19th century. It gives its name to the second phase of CELTIC culture (*c*.500–*c*.50 BC). The origin of the culture, which replaced the HALLSTATT, was contact with Greek and Etruscan influences. It was a highly war-like culture, hierarchically organized with kings, a priestly class (the DRUIDS), warriors, farmers and slaves. La Tène weaponry was late IRON AGE. The La Tène conquered central Europe in the 4th and 3rd centuries, but, by 50 BC, they had submitted to German invaders from the N and Romans from the S.

latent heat (symbol L) Heat absorbed or given out by a substance as it changes its phase at constant temperature. When ice melts, its temperature remains the same until it has been completely melted into water; the heat necessary to do this is called the latent heat of fusion.

Lateran Councils Five ECUMENICAL COUNCILS of the Western Church, held in the Lateran Palace, Rome. The

first (1123) confirmed the Concordat of WORMS of 1122. The **second** (1139) condemned simony and the marriage of the clergy. The **third** (1179) decreed that the pope was to be elected by a two-thirds majority of the College of Cardinals. The **fourth** (1215) defined the doctrine of the EUCHARIST, officially using the term "TRANSUBSTANTIATION". The **fifth** (1512–17) introduced minor reforms in the wake of the REFORMATION.

Lateran Treaty (1929) Agreement between Italy and the VATICAN. The Italian government recognized the Vatican as an independent sovereign state with the pope as its temporal head, and the Vatican surrendered the PAPAL STATES and Rome. Roman Catholicism was affirmed as Italy's state religion.

laterite Reddish, hard-baked soil found in the tropics. It results when hot, wet conditions wash away most of the nutrient content of the soil, leaving behind hydrated oxides of iron and aluminium. Some laterites contain sufficient iron to be of commercial value.

latex Milky fluid produced by certain plants, the most important being the RUBBER TREE. Rubber latex is GUM resin and fat in a watery medium. It is used in paints, special papers and adhesives, and to make sponge RUBBERS. Synthetic rubber latexes are also produced.

Latimer, Hugh (c.1485–1555) English clergyman and Protestant martyr. He defended King HENRY VIII's divorce from Catherine of Aragon. In 1535 Latimer was made bishop of Worcester but resigned his see in 1539 as a protest against the temporary reaction in favour of Catholicism. With the accession (1547) of EDWARD VI, he resumed preaching. When the Roman Catholic MARY I came to the throne (1553), he was charged with heresy and, refusing to recant, was burned at the stake.

Latin Language of ancient ROME, the ROMAN EMPIRE, and of educated medieval European society. It belongs to the family of INDO-EUROPEAN LANGUAGES. Its earliest written records are inscriptions and legal formulas of the late 6th century BC. As Rome extended its rule throughout Italy, Latin gained supremacy. The richest phase of LATIN LITERATURE was the AUGUSTAN AGE (43 BC– AD 14). Spoken Latin was used throughout the Roman Empire. It eventually broke up into numerous dialects, which formed the basis of the ROMANCE LANGUAGES. Latin remained the language of the church, science, medicine, law, education, and most written transactions in Europe throughout the Middle Ages. It was still used in some scholarly and diplomatic circles in the 19th century, and the Roman Catholic mass in Latin until the 1960s.

Latin America Those parts of the Western Hemisphere (excluding French-speaking Canada) where the official or chief language is a ROMANCE LANGUAGE. Commonly it refers to the 18 Spanish-speaking republics and Brazil (Portuguese) and Haiti (French). Occasionally it includes some islands of the WEST INDIES.

Latin literature Literature of the ROMAN EMPIRE, ancient ROME and medieval Europe. The earliest works date from the 3rd century BC and were imitations of GREEK DRAMA and GREEK LITERATURE by Livius Andronicus and Naevius. In the 2nd century BC, the influence of Greek drama was adapted to Roman themes by PLAUTUS and TERENCE. ENNIUS introduced the hexameter into LATIN in his *Annals*. The "Golden Age" of Latin literature (c.70 BC–c.AD 14) was heralded in the prose works of CICERO and the poetry of CATULLUS and LUCRETIUS. The AUGUSTAN AGE (43 BC–AD 14) was marked by the *Metamorphoses* of OVID, the *Aeneid* of VIRGIL, the lyrics of HORACE and the prose histories of LIVY. The despotic reign of NERO saw the suicide of PETRONIUS. The reign of

TRAJAN was noted for the writings of PLINY THE ELDER. The so-called "Silver Age" (AD 98–138) saw the tragedies of SENECA, the satires of JUVENAL and the sceptical histories of TACITUS. With the exception of APULEIUS, Latin literature declined until its revival in the 5th century as the lingua franca of Christian discourse by Saint AUGUSTINE. The trend was continued by BOETHIUS and BEDE. Latin prose writers of the Middle Ages included Pierre ABELARD, Thomas AQUINAS and Thomas à KEMPIS. In the 16th century age of HUMANISM, Latin was again revived by ERASMUS and Sir Thomas MORE.

latitude Distance N or S of the EQUATOR, measured at an angle from the Earth's centre. All lines of latitude are parallel to the Equator, which is the zero line of latitude.

La Tour, Georges de (1593–1652) French painter of religious and genre scenes. He is famous for his nocturnal scenes lit by a single candle. Many art historians consider him to be one of the most important representatives of 17th-century French CLASSICISM. His work includes *Christ and St Joseph in the Carpenter's Shop* (c.1645) and the *Lamentation over St Sebastian* (1645).

Latrobe, Benjamin Henry (1766–1820) US architect, b. England. His monumental public buildings include some of the earliest examples of Greek revival and Gothic revival in the USA, including the Bank of Pennsylvania, Philadelphia (1789). He also worked on the rebuilding of the Capitol, Washington, D.C. (1815–17).

Latter Day Saints, Church of *See* MORMONS

Latvia Baltic republic in NE Europe; the capital is RIGA. **Land and climate** Latvia consists mainly of flat plains separated by low hills. Small lakes and peat bogs are common, and its highest point is only 311m (1,020ft) above sea level. Latvia's main river is the Daugava (Western Dvina). Riga has warm summers, but the winter months (December to March) are sub-zero and the sea often freezes. Moderate rainfall occurs throughout the year, with light snow in winter. Forests cover c.40% of Latvia and c.27% of the land is farmed. **History and politics** The ancestors of most modern Latvians settled in the area c.2,000 years ago. Between the 9th and 11th centuries, the region was attacked by Vikings from the W and Russians from the E. In the 13th century, German invaders took over. From 1561, the area was partitioned between various groups, including Poles, Lithuanians and Swedes. In 1710, PETER I (THE GREAT) took Riga, and, by the end of the 18th century, Latvia was under Russian rule. In 1918, Latvia declared independence and this was confirmed at the Treaty of Versailles (1919). In the secret Molotov-Ribbentrop Pact (1939), Germany and the Soviet Union agreed to divide up parts of E Europe. In 1940, Soviet troops invaded Latvia, which became part of the Soviet Union. In 1941, German forces seized Latvia, but Soviet troops returned in 1944. Under Soviet rule, many Russian immigrants settled in Latvia. In the late 1980s, when reforms were being introduced in the Soviet Union, Latvia's government relaxed communist laws, allowed press and religious freedom, and made Latvian the official language. In 1990, Latvia declared independence an act that was finally recognized by the Soviet Union in September 1991. In 1993, Latvia held its first multiparty elections. In 1994, it adopted a law restricting the

---

LATVIA
AREA: 64,589sq km (24,938sq mi)
POPULATION: 2,768,000
CAPITAL (POPULATION): Riga (826,000)

naturalization of non-Latvians, including many Russian settlers. In 1995, Latvia joined the Council of Europe and formally applied to join the European Union (EU). In 1997, Prime Minister Andris Skele of the People's Party resigned following charges of government corruption. In 1998 elections the People's Party emerged as the largest single party, but a coalition government was formed by Vilis Kristopans of Latvia's Way. In 1999, Viara Vike-Freiberg became the first woman head of state in post-communist Eastern Europe. **Economy** Latvia is a lower-middle-income country (1995 GDP per capita, US$3,370). It faces many problems in transforming from a command economy to a mixed economy. The country lacks natural resources and has to import many of the materials needed for manufacturing. Latvia produces only *c*.10% of the electricity it needs, and the rest has to be imported from Belarus, Russia and Ukraine. Manufactures include electronic goods, farm machinery and fertil-Farm exports include beef and dairy products and pork.

Laud, William (1573–1645) English cleric, archbishop of Canterbury (1633–45) and religious adviser to CHARLES I. Working closely with Charles I, he imposed press censorship, enforced a policy regulating wages and prices and sought to remove PURITANS from important positions in the church. His attempt to impose the English Prayer Book upon the Scots was one of the causes of the English CIVIL WARS. Laud was impeached (1640) by the LONG PARLIAMENT.

Lauda, Niki (Nikolas) (1949–) Austrian motor racing driver. He won the world drivers' championship in 1975, 1977 (both Ferrari) and 1984 (McLaren). In 1976, he suffered near-fatal injuries at the Nurburgring, Germany.

Lauder, Sir Harry (1870–1950) Scottish music-hall comedian and singer. Lauder entertained the troops in World War 1 with songs such as "Roamin' in the Gloamin'" and "I Love a Lassie".

Laue, Max Theodor Felix von (1879–1960) German physicist. He was director of the Institute for Theoretical Physics in Berlin. Using IONS in a crystal as a grating, he produced X-RAY interference patterns, showing that X-rays are waves. For the discovery of X-ray diffraction in crystals, Laue received the 1914 Nobel Prize for physics.

lauraceae Large family of flowering plants, mostly evergreen shrubs and trees, including LAUREL, CINNAMON and SASSAFRAS; it is found in warm and temperate regions worldwide. The flowers are generally green and are followed by berries.

Laurasia Ancient N continent, containing North America and Eurasia, which formed when a rift split PANGAEA (the Earth's single original land mass) from E to W along a line slightly N of the Equator. CONTINENTAL DRIFT and PLATE TECTONICS caused Laurasia to split up into the separate continents that exist today.

laurel Evergreen shrubs and trees native to S Europe and cultivated in the USA. Included is the noble, or bay, laurel (*Laurus nobilis*) with leathery, oval leaves, tiny yellowish flowers and purple berries. Height: 18–21m (60–70ft). Family LAURACEAE

Laurel and Hardy US comedy team who starred in more than 100 films. **Stan Laurel** (1890–1965), b. England, played the thin, bumbling oaf. His US partner, **Oliver Hardy** (1892–1957), played the fat, irascible would-be leader. The naïve duo always wore derby hats. Their films include *Leave 'em Laughing* (1928), *Another Fine Mess* (1930), *The Music Box* (1932) and *Way Out West* (1937).

Laurier, Sir Wilfrid (1841–1919) Canadian statesman, prime minister (1896–1911). Laurier was the first French-Canadian to lead (1887–1919) a federal party (the Liberals). He created a separate Canadian navy in 1909 and signed a reciprocal tariff agreement with the USA in 1911.

Lausanne City on the N shore of Lake Geneva, SW Switzerland; capital of Vaud canton. Originally a Celtic settlement, it became an episcopal see in the 6th century. In 1536, it was conquered by BERN and accepted the Reformation. Industries: leather, brewing, chemicals. Pop. (1991) 265,000.

Lautrec, Henri Toulouse See TOULOUSE-LAUTREC, HENRI MARIE RAYMOND DE

lava Molten rock or MAGMA that reaches the Earth's surface and flows out through a volcanic vent in streams or sheets. There are three main types of lava: vesicular, such as pumice; glassy, such as obsidian; and even-grained. Chemically, lavas range from acidic to ultrabasic.

Laval, Pierre (1883–1945) French statesman, prime minister (1931–32, 1935–36). His government fell as a result of the unpopularity of the Hoare-Laval Pact, which approved Italy's conquest of Ethiopia. In 1940, Laval joined the VICHY GOVERNMENT, becoming its head under Marshal PÉTAIN. This was seen as treason by the FREE FRENCH, and he was executed after the war.

Laver, Rod (Rodney George) (1938–) Australian tennis player. He won the US (1962, 1969), British (1961, 1962, 1968, 1969), Australian (1960, 1962, 1969) and French (1962, 1969) singles championships, becoming the first man to win the "Grand Slam" twice (1962, 1969).

Lavoisier, Antoine Laurent (1743–94) French chemist who founded modern chemistry. He demolished the PHLOGISTON theory (which said that phlogiston was lost during combustion) by demonstrating the function of oxygen in COMBUSTION. Lavoisier named oxygen and hydrogen and showed how they combined to form water. In collaboration with Claude Berthollet, he published *Methods of Chemical Nomenclature* (1787), which laid down the modern method of naming substances.

Law, (Andrew) Bonar (1858–1923) British statesman, prime minister (1922–23), b. Canada. He entered Parliament in 1900. In 1911, Bonar Law became the first leader of the Conservative Party to come from a manufacturing background. He was chancellor of the exchequer (1916–19) before becoming prime minister.

law System of rules governing society, enforced by punishments specified by society. The major systems are COMMON LAW, ROMAN LAW and EQUITY.

Law and the Prophets Two major divisions of the OLD TESTAMENT. The Law, or the Law of Moses, is the first five books of the Old Testament, known as the TORAH in Hebrew and the PENTATEUCH in Greek. The Prophets consists of several books grouped differently according to Jewish or Christian tradition. The groupings include: (a) Joshua, Judges, I and II Samuel, and I and II Kings; (b) Isaiah, Jeremiah and Ezekiel; and (c) Hosea, Joel, Amos, Obadiah, Jonah, Micah, Nahum, Habakkuk, Zephaniah, Haggai, Zechariah and Malachi.

Lawrence, D.H. (David Herbert) (1885–1930) English novelist, short-story writer and poet. A miner's son, his first poems were published (1909) by Ford Madox FORD in the English Review. His debut novel was *The White Peacock* (1911). In 1912, Lawrence published his second novel, *The Trespasser*, and eloped to Germany with Frieda Weekley (*née* von Richthofen). His first major novel was the semi-autobiographical *Sons and Lovers* (1913). *The Rainbow* (1915), perhaps his greatest novel, was banned as obscene. *Women in Love* (1921) appeared in censored form. After completing *Aaron's Rod* (1922), Lawrence and Frieda went into self-imposed exile. *Kangaroo* (1923) was inspired by his travels in

Australia and *The Plumed Serpent* (1926) was set in Mexico. His last novel, *Lady Chatterley's Lover*, was privately published (1928) in Florence, but until 1960 remained available only in expurgated form in England.

Lawrence, Ernest Orlando (1901–58) US physicist. In 1930, as professor at the University of California at Berkeley, he built the first cyclotron, a subatomic particle ACCELERATOR. He received the 1939 Nobel Prize for physics. LAWRENCIUM was named after him.

Lawrence, T.E. (Thomas Edward) (1888–1935) (Lawrence of Arabia) British soldier. He joined the army in World War 1, and in 1916 led the Arab revolt against the Turks. He was a successful guerrilla commander, leading (October 1918) Arab forces into Damascus, Syria. In 1926, he privately published his remarkable account of the Arab revolt, *The Seven Pillars of Wisdom*.

Lawrence, Sir Thomas (1769–1830) English painter. He was considered one of the most brilliant British portrait painters of his age. His portrait of *Queen Charlotte* (1789) won immediate acclaim. He became Painter in Ordinary to the King and was sent to Europe to paint the allied leaders involved in the defeat of Napoleon.

lawrencium (symbol Lr) Radioactive metallic element, one of the ACTINIDE SERIES. It was first made in 1961 at the University of California at Berkeley by bombarding CALIFORNIUM with boron nuclei. Properties: at.no. 103; r.a.m. 262; most stable isotope Lr^{256} (half-life 27 seconds).

Law Society Either of two inclusive organizations of solicitors in Britain – the Law Society in England and Wales, and the Law Society of Scotland – as incorporated in 1831 by Act of Parliament. Each Law Society regulates and enforces the standards by which solicitors operate. It administers LEGAL AID to those entitled to it and retains a fund from which compensation may be made in the case of a solicitor's fraud or negligence.

laxative Any agent used to counteract constipation. They include bulk-forming drugs, stimulant laxatives, faecal softeners and saline purgatives.

Laxness, Halldór Kiljan (1902–98) Icelandic novelist. He was awarded the 1955 Nobel Prize for literature for his novels about the fishing villages and farms of Iceland. His fiction includes *Independent People* (1934–35), *The Atom Station* (1948), *Paradise Reclaimed* (1960). The trilogy *Iceland's Bell* (1943–46) was influenced by the SAGAS of NORSE LITERATURE.

Lazarus Either of two men mentioned in the New Testament. In John 11 Lazarus was the brother of Mary and Martha of Bethany. Four days after his death, Jesus miraculously restored him to life. In Luke 16 Lazarus is the poor man in Christ's parable about a beggar and a rich man.

L-dopa (levodopa) Naturally occurring amino acid used to relieve some symptoms of PARKINSON'S DISEASE. It sometimes suppresses the trembling, unsteadiness and slowness of movement that characterize the condition.

leaching In geology, process by which chemicals and nutrients are removed from a soil. Rainwater, especially in warm climatic regions, will dissolve anything soluble and wash it away. Once removed, these solubles can only be replaced slowly. As a result, leached soils become coarse and infertile. Saline soils can, however, be reclaimed for agriculture by leaching out salts.

Leacock, Stephen Butler (1869–1944) Canadian humourist, b. Britain. His *Literary Lapses* (1910) proved popular for their gentle satire and love of the absurd. Leacock also wrote *Sunshine Sketches of a Little Town* (1912).

lead (symbol Pb) Metallic element of Group IV of the periodic table. Its chief ore is GALENA (lead sulphide),

from which lead is obtained by roasting. Exposure to lead from paints, pipes, petrol and other sources can lead to lead poisoning. Soft and malleable, it is used as a shield for X-rays and nuclear radiation, and in batteries, cable sheaths and alloys such as pewter and solder. Chemically, lead is unreactive and a poor conductor of electricity. Properties: at.no. 82; r.a.m. 207.19; r.d. 11.35; m.p. 327.5°C (621.5°F); b.p. 1,740°C (3,164°F); most common isotope Pb^{208} (52.3%).

Leadbelly *See* LEDBETTER, HUDDIE

leaf Part of a plant, an organ that contains the green pigment CHLOROPHYLL and is involved in PHOTOSYNTHESIS and TRANSPIRATION. It usually consists of a blade and a stalk (petiole) that attaches it to a stem or twig. Most leaves are simple (undivided), but some are compound.

leafhopper Any of numerous species of small, slender insects of the family Cicadellidae. Leaf hoppers feed by sucking the sap of plants and may, in large numbers, do a great deal of damage. Many species are brightly coloured.

leaf insect Any of several species of flat, green insects that resemble leaves and are found throughout tropical Asia. The female has large leathery fore-wings with markings like leaf veins. Order Phasmida; family Phylliidae. *See also* STICK INSECT

League of Nations International organization, forerunner of the UNITED NATIONS (UN). Created by the Treaty of VERSAILLES (1919) ending World War 1, it was impaired by the refusal of the USA to join. The threats to peace from Germany, Italy and Japan caused the League to collapse in 1939. It was dissolved in 1946.

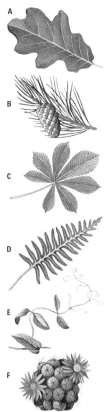

◀ **leaf** Leaves exhibit a wide variety of shapes. The pendunculate oak (*Quercus rober*) (A) and the Scots pine (*Pinus sylvestris*) (B) have simple leaves, with a single leaf blade, while the horse chestnut (*Aesculus hippocastrum*) (C) and ferns, such as Polypodium (D) have compound leaves. The leaflets of compound leaves either radiate from one point (**palmate**) as in the case of the horse chestnut, or are arranged in opposite pairs down the main stalk (**pinnate**) as is the case with ferns. The primary function of leaves is photosynthesis, but in addition leaflets may be modified into climbing tendrils (E), or protective spines, as in the cactus *Mammillaria zeilmannia* (F).

Leakey, Louis Seymour Bazett (1903–72) English archaeologist and anthropologist. He discovered fossils in East Africa that proved humans to be older than had been thought. In 1931, he began to research OLDUVAI GORGE in Tanzania with his wife, **Mary** (1913–96). After his death, she continued working in East Africa, often with their son Richard LEAKEY.

Leakey, Richard Erskine Frere (1944–) Kenyan palaeoanthropologist and archaeologist, son of Mary and Louis LEAKEY. At Lake Turkana, Kenya, Leakey discovered (1972) a *c*.1.9 million year-old skull of *Homo habilis*. Other discoveries include a *Homo erectus* skeleton *c*.1.6 million years old. Leakey became director (1988–94) of the Kenyan Wildlife Service. His campaign against the ivory trade brought him into the political arena. In 1995, he co-founded the Safina Party. *See also* HUMAN EVOLUTION

Lean, Sir David (1908–91) English film director. His early films, such as *In Which We Serve* (1942) and *Brief Encounter* (1945), were collaborative projects with Noel COWARD. These were followed by the Dickens' adaptations *Great Expectations* (1946) and *Oliver Twist* (1948). Lean is remembered for his meticulously crafted spectaculars, such as *The Bridge on the River Kwai* (1957) and *Lawrence of Arabia* (1962), both of which gained him Academy Awards for best director. Other films include *Doctor Zhivago* (1965) and *Ryan's Daughter* (1970). His last film was *A Passage to India* (1984). He was knighted in 1984.

Lear, Edward (1812–88) English poet, painter and draftsman. He is famous for his tragicomic nonsense verse for children. Lear invented such characters as the Owl and the Pussycat. His works include *A Book of Nonsense* (1846) and *Laughable Lyrics* (1877).

learning Acquisition of skills and concepts by a variety of processes. The oldest theories held learning to be an associative process by which ideas, images and events become linked in the mind. Behaviourists believed that learning was related to conditioning. GESTALT PSYCHOLOGY dealt with such learning potentials as problem solving; modern COGNITIVE PSYCHOLOGY concentrates on mental processes, such as concept formation.

learning disability Disorder that prevents students from learning as well as would be expected from their ability, as measured on an intelligence test. It covers a wide range of learning problems, including difficulties with learning reading, writing, mathematics or communication skills. In the UK the term is sometimes used with "learning difficulties" to mean MENTAL HANDICAP.

leather Animal hide, treated to make it hard-wearing and resistant to decay. Most leather is made from cattle hide, but many other kinds of skin are used too. The skin is first cured via a drying process or the application of salt. It is then washed and prepared for tanning, a process that usually consists of treating the skin with a solution of chromium salts or plant extract (TANNIN).

Leavis, F.R. (Frank Raymond) (1895–1978) English literary critic. His works of criticism include *The Great Tradition* (1948), *The Common Pursuit* (1952) and *D.H. Lawrence, Novelist* (1955). Leavis' views on society and education are expounded in *Mass Civilization and Minority Culture* (1933).

Lebanon Republic on the E shores of the Mediterranean Sea, SW Asia. A narrow coastal plain contains the capital, BEIRUT, the second-largest city of TRIPOLI, and the historic city of TYRE. Behind the plain are the rugged Lebanese Mountains, which rise to 3,088m (10,131ft). The Anti-Lebanon Mountains form the E border with Syria. Between the two ranges is the BEKAA VALLEY, a

---

LEBANON
AREA: 10,400sq km (4,015sq mi)
POPULATION: 3,327,000
CAPITAL (POPULATION): Beirut (1,500,000)

---

fertile farming area and site of the ancient city of BAAL-BEK. **Climate** Coastal regions have a typical Mediterranean climate, with hot, dry summers and mild, wet winters. Onshore winds bring heavy winter rain to the W slopes of the mountains. **Vegetation** Lebanon was famous in ancient times for its cedar forests, but these have largely disappeared. Forests now cover only 8% of the land. **History and politics** In *c*.3000 BC, Canaanites founded Tyre and BYBLOS, establishing what became known as PHOENICIA. In 332, ALEXANDER THE GREAT conquered the territory. In 64 BC, the region fell to the Romans. Christianity was introduced in AD 325. Arab conquest in the 7th century saw the introduction of Islam, but Christian MARONITES predominated. Lebanon was one of the principal battlefields of the CRUSADES (1100–1300). In 1516, Lebanon became part of the Ottoman Empire, and Turkish rule continued until World War 1. After the war Lebanon and Syria were mandated to France. In 1945, Lebanon became fully independent. During the 1950s Lebanon's economy grew rapidly and it pursued a pro-Western foreign policy. This infuriated the Arab population, and US troops were called in to crush a 1958 rebellion. In the late 1960s, Lebanon came under increasing military pressure from Israel to act against Palestinian guerrillas operating in S Lebanon. In 1975, civil war broke out between Maronite, SUNNI, SHI'ITE and DRUSE militias. About 50,000 Lebanese died and the economy was devastated. In 1976, Syrian troops imposed a fragile cease-fire. In 1978, Israel invaded S Lebanon to destroy Palestinian bases. UN peacekeeping forces were called in to separate the factions. In 1982, Israel launched a full-scale attack on Lebanon. The 1983 deployment of US and European troops in Beirut was met by a terrorist bombing campaign. In 1984, multinational forces left, and Israeli troops withdrew to a buffer zone in S Lebanon. In 1987, Syrian troops moved into Beirut to quell disturbances. In 1990, an uneasy truce was called. Syria maintained troops in West Beirut and the Bekaa Valley. The Syrian- and Iranian-backed HIZBULLAH and the Israeli-backed South Lebanon Army (SLA) continued to operate in S Lebanon. The presidency of Elias Hrawi (1989–98), began the difficult task of economic reconstruction and social reconciliation. In 1998, General Emile Lahoud was appointed president. In 1996 and 2000, Israel launched major bombing raids on Lebanon, but finally agreed to withdraw troops by July 2000. **Economy** The civil war devastated Lebanon's valuable tourism, trade and financial sectors (1992 GDP per capita, $2,500). Manufacturing was also badly damaged. Manufactures include chemicals, electrical goods and textiles. Farm products include fruits, vegetables and sugar beet.

Lebed, Aleksander Ivanovich (1950–) Russian general and politician. As commander of the Tula Airborne Troops Division, he stood guard at the Supreme Soviet building during the attempted coup of August 1991. Running against YELTSIN in the 1996 presidential elections, Lebed's support was such that Yeltsin offered him a government position to win his votes. He was appointed national security adviser but dismissed later in 1996.

Leblanc, Nicolas (1742–1806) French chemist. In 1790 he devised a process for producing soda ash (sodium carbonate, Na_2CO_3) from salt (sodium chloride, NaCl) by treating it with sulphuric acid.

Le Brun, Charles (1619–90) French painter. As chief painter to LOUIS XIV, he created the Galerie d'Apollon at the Louvre (1661) and much of the interior of VERSAILLES, including the Hall of Mirrors (1679–84). In 1663 he became director of the ACADÉMIE FRANÇAISE.

Le Carré, John (1931–) English novelist, b. David John Moore Cornwell. His debut novel, *Call for the Dead* (1961), introduced his best-known character, George Smiley. Le Carré's espionage thrillers are carefully plotted studies of history and character. Other novels include *The Spy Who Came in from the Cold* (1963), *Tinker, Tailor, Soldier, Spy* (1974), *Smiley's People* (1980), *The Little Drummer Girl* (1983), *A Perfect Spy* (1986) and *The Russia House* (1989).

Le Châtelier's principle Rule announced (1888) by the French chemist Henry Louis Le Châtelier (1850–1936). It states that if a system in a state of equilibrium is disturbed, it tends to restore the equilibrium.

Leclanché cell Electric CELL (*c.*1865) invented by French chemist Georges Leclanché (1839–82). Its ANODE was a zinc rod, and its CATHODE a carbon plate surrounded by packed manganese dioxide. These electrodes were dipped into a solution of ammonium and zinc chlorides. It is the basis of the dry cell or BATTERY.

Leconte de Lisle, Charles Marie René (1818–94) French poet. He was the leader of the anti-romantic Parnassian school. His collected works, including *Poèmes antiques* (1852) and *Poèmes barbares* (1862), are disciplined and pessimistic. In 1866, he was elected to the Académie Française.

Le Corbusier (1887–1963) French architect, b. Switzerland as Charles Édouard Jeanneret. His early work exploited the qualities of reinforced concrete in cube-like forms. His Unité d'Habitation, Marseilles (1946–52), was a modular design widely adopted for modern mass housing. Later, Le Corbusier evolved a more poetic style, of which the highly sculptural chapel of Notre-Dame-du-Haut at Ronchamp (1955) is the finest example. In the 1950s he laid out the town of Chandigarh, India, and built its majestic supreme courts. His last major work was the Visual Arts Center at Harvard University, Cambridge, Massachusetts (1963). His book *Towards a New Architecture* (1923) was a key text of the INTERNATIONAL STYLE.

Leda In Greek mythology, Queen of Sparta, wife of Tyndareus and mother of CLYTEMNESTRA. She was also the mother of CASTOR AND POLLUX and HELEN by ZEUS. The myth reveals that Zeus came to her in the form of a swan.

Ledbetter, Huddie (1888–1949) US composer and blues singer, better known as Leadbelly. Folklorist John A. Lomax discovered him in prison and used his songs in the book *Negro Folk Songs as Sung by Lead Belly* (1936). He composed many classic blues songs, including "Goodnight, Irene" and "Rock Island Line".

Lee, Ann (1736–84) British mystic, member of the United Society of Believers in Christ's Second Appearing, popularly called the SHAKERS. The Shaker sect was persecuted in Britain, and in 1774 Lee and eight others fled to the American colonies. In 1776 she founded a colony near Albany, New York.

Lee, Jennie, Baroness (1904–88) British politician. In 1929, she became the youngest-ever woman MP. In 1934 Lee married Aneurin BEVAN. As minister for the arts (1967–70), she was responsible for establishing the Open University (OU). In 1970, she was made a life peer.

Lee, Laurie (1914–97) English writer. His collections of poetry include *The Sun My Monument* (1944) and *My*

Many-Coated Man (1955). He is best known for his autobiography, *Cider with Rosie* (USA: *The Edge of Day*) (1959), and his accounts of travels in Spain during the Spanish Civil War, *As I Walked Out One Midsummer Morning* (1969) and *A Moment of War* (1991). He also wrote short stories.

Lee, Robert Edward (1807–70) Commander of the Confederate forces in the American CIVIL WAR. In 1862, he was appointed commander of the main Confederate force, the Army of Virginia. Lee won the second Battle of BULL RUN (1862) and defeated the Union forces at FREDERICKSBURG (1862) and Chancellorsville (1863). In July 1863, his invasion of the North ended in decisive defeat at GETTYSBURG. In April 1865, Lee was finally trapped and forced to surrender by Ulysses S. GRANT.

Lee, Spike (Shelton Jackson) (1957–) US film director. His debut feature, the stylish black-and-white comedy *She's Gotta Have It* (1986), was a commercial success. *Do the Right Thing* (1989) was a bleak meditation on racism in the USA. Lee made the controversial *Jungle Fever* (1991), a pessimistic view of racial integration. Other films include *Malcolm X* (1992), *Crooklyn* (1994) and *Bamboozled* (2000).

Lee, Tsung-Dao (1926–) US physicist, b. China. He and his colleague, Chen Ning YANG, showed that among the weak interactions of SUBATOMIC PARTICLES, the law of conservation of parity (that nature, in effect, makes no distinction between right- and left-handedness) does not always hold. For this, Lee and Yang were awarded the 1957 Nobel Prize for physics.

leech Any of numerous species of freshwater, marine or terrestrial annelids found in tropical and temperate regions. Its tapered, ringed body has a sucking disc at each end. Many species live on the blood of animals. Length: 13–51mm (0.5–2in). Class Hirudinea.

Leeds City and county district on the River Aire, West Yorkshire, N England. Founded in Roman times, it forms part of one of England's major industrial regions. Its woollen industry dates from the 14th century, but it was in the 18th and 19th centuries that Leeds became famous for its cloth manufacture. It remains the centre of England's wholesale clothing trade. Leeds has two universities (1904, 1992) and is host to an international piano competition. Other industries: aircraft components, textile machinery, engineering, chemicals. Pop. (1994) 529,000.

leek Biennial plant related to the onion; it originated in the Mediterranean region and is cultivated widely for culinary purposes. Family Liliaceae, species *Allium porrum*.

Lee Teng-hui (1923–) Chinese politician, president of Taiwan (1988–). A member of the ruling Nationalist Party (KUOMINTANG), he became vice president of the party (and of Taiwan) in 1984. On the death of CHIANG CHING-KUO, Lee Teng-hui became president and was subsequently elected (1996). He was largely responsible for the rapid liberalization of Taiwan.

Leeuwenhoek, Anton van (1632–1723) Dutch scientist. He built simple microscopes with a single lens that were so accurate they had better magnifying powers than the compound microscopes of his day. He investigated and described many microorganisms.

Leeward Islands Group of islands in the West Indies, comprising the N section of the Lesser Antilles; it includes the US and British VIRGIN ISLANDS, GUADELOUPE, ANGUILLA, ANTIGUA AND BARBUDA, MONTSERRAT, ST KITTS-NEVIS and St Martin. Colonization began in the early 17th century. For the next 200 years control of the islands fluctuated between Britain and France. The economy is based on agriculture and tourism. Major crops include fruits and sugar.

legal aid British system by which those below a certain income can receive free or subsidized legal representation or advice. In criminal cases, it is paid for mainly from public funds. In civil cases, costs will usually be met from the costs awarded by the court. It was introduced in Britain in 1949 and is now covered in Scotland by the Legal Aid (Scotland) Act (1986), and in England and Wales by the Legal Aid Act (1988). The high cost of legal advice is placing strain on the scheme.

Léger, Fernand (1881–1955) French painter. An influential member of the School of Paris, he evolved a form of CUBISM jokingly called "tubism" because of its emphasis on cylindrical, mechanical forms. Examples include the series *Contrast of Forms* (1913). Léger directed the first non-narrative film *Ballet méchanique* (1924).

Leghorn *See* LIVORNO

legion Basic organizational unit of the Roman army until the fall of the empire in the West in the 5th century AD. During the great period of Rome's expansion, a legion was *c.*6,000 men strong, consisting mainly of heavy infantrymen (legionnaries), with some light troops and cavalry in support. The legion was subdivided into cohorts (420 men each), maniples (120 men each) and centuries (100 men each).

legionnaire's disease Pneumonia-like lung disease caused by the bacterium *Legionella pneumophila*. It takes its name from the serious US outbreak (1976) that occurred during a convention of the American Legion held in Philadelphia, Pennsylvania.

Legion of Honour (Légion d'Honneur) French award, created (1802) by NAPOLEON I to reward civil and military service. The highest class of award is the great cross (*grand-croix*). The usual award is Knight of the Legion (*Chevalier de la Légion*), marked by a red ribbon.

legislation *See* LAW

legislature Representative assembly whose primary function is the enactment of laws. Legislatures can be either unicameral or bicameral (composed of one or two chambers). In most democracies, including Britain, the "lower" or more directly elected chamber is more powerful than the "upper" chamber filled by government appointees or hereditary members. In the USA, the SENATE is constitutionally more powerful than the HOUSE OF REPRESENTATIVES, and both houses are elected. *See also* HOUSE OF COMMONS; HOUSE OF LORDS; PARLIAMENT

legume Member of the PEA family of flowering plants, including many trees, shrubs, vines and herbs whose roots bear nodules that contain nitrogen-fixing bacteria. The fruit is typically a pod (legume) containing a row of

seeds. Food species include the pea, runner BEAN, SOYA BEAN, LENTIL, broad bean and kidney bean. *See also* NITROGEN FIXATION; NITROGEN CYCLE; ROOT NODULE

Lehár, Franz (1870–1948) Austrian composer, b. Hungary. From 1890, he travelled as a bandmaster in Austria. He composed more than 30 operettas, of which *The Merry Widow* (1905) is the most popular today.

Le Havre City and seaport at the mouth of the River Seine, N France, on La Manche (the English Channel). Founded in the 16th century on the site of a fishing village, it was enlarged and fortified and is now France's second-largest port. It is the principal export point for Paris and a transatlantic and cross-Channel passenger port. Industries: chemicals, fertilizers, timber, food processing, oil-refining. Pop. (1990) 195,854.

Lehmann, Lotte (1888–1976) US soprano, b. Germany. She was the most illustrious singer of operatic roles and Lieder of her time. She sang with the Vienna State Opera (1914–38) and the Metropolitan Opera Company, New York, from 1934 until her retirement in 1961.

Leibniz, Gottfried Wilhelm (1646–1716) German philosopher and mathematician. He made many practical inventions, including a calculating machine (1671). In 1684, Leibniz published his discovery of differential and integral CALCULUS, made independently of Sir Isaac NEWTON. His philosophy that the universe comprises a hierarchy of constituents (monads) with God at the top asserting a divine plan was satirized in VOLTAIRE's *Candide* (1759). His major works include *New Essays Concerning Human Understanding* (1704).

Leicester, Robert Dudley, Earl of (1532–88) English courtier. He was a favourite of Queen ELIZABETH I, who ennobled him. Marriage to Elizabeth seemed possible, but instead, Elizabeth proposed his marriage to MARY, QUEEN OF SCOTS, who rejected him.

Leicester City in central England; county town of Leicestershire. It was founded in the 1st century AD as a Roman town (*Ratae Coritanorum*) and was conquered by the Danes in the 9th century. In 1589 Queen Elizabeth I granted a charter to the city. Leicester became famous for its hosiery and footwear. Pop. (1994) 297,000.

Leicestershire County in E central England; the county town is LEICESTER. The area is drained chiefly by the Soar and Wreak rivers. The uplands of the E are devoted to farming, and the W has more industry. Wheat, barley, sheep and dairy cattle are important, and the region is famous for its hosiery and Stilton cheese. Area: 2,553sq km (986sq mi). Pop. (1994) 916,900.

Leiden (Leyden) City on the River Oude Rijn, W Netherlands, 9mi (15km) NE of The Hague. Leiden received its city charter in the 13th century and developed a textile industry. The Pilgrim Fathers lived here before setting out for America in 1620. Industries: textiles, printing, publishing. Pop. (1996) 116,000.

Leif Ericsson (*c.*970–1020) Norse adventurer and explorer, son of ERIC THE RED. In 1003 he sailed from Greenland to investigate land in the west. Among the places he visited were Helluland (probably Baffin Island), Markland (Labrador) and VINLAND.

Leigh, Mike (1943–) English film director, playwright and screenwriter. His debut feature, *Bleak Moments* (1971), established his reputation for innovative social realism. After a long break, Leigh made the acclaimed *High Hopes* (1988), and the similarly satirical *Life is Sweet* (1990). *Naked* (1993) and *Secrets and Lies* (1995) gained him international recognition.

Leigh, Vivien (1913–67) British film and stage actress, b. India. She received Academy Awards for her

▲ **lemur** The ring-tailed lemur (*Lemur catta*), like the 16 or so other species of lemur, is found only in Madagascar and small neighbouring islands. The various species range in size, the smallest being no larger than a rat, while the largest reaches a similar size to a cat. All species are arboreal and omnivorous, feeding on fruit, insects, and small mammals.

performances as Scarlett O'Hara in *Gone With The Wind* (1939) and for her moving portrayal of Blanche du Bois in *A Streetcar Named Desire* (1951). She was married (1937–60) to the actor Laurence OLIVIER.

Leighton, Frederic, Baron (1830–96) English painter and sculptor. His first exhibited painting, *Cimabue's Madonna Carried in Procession* (1855), was bought by Queen Victoria. Leighton was president (1878–96) of the Royal Academy. His refined classical style contrasted with the romantic PRE-RAPHAELITE BROTHERHOOD (PRB).

Leinster Province in E Republic of Ireland, comprising the counties of Carlow, Dublin, Kildare, Kilkenny, Laois, Longford, Louth, Meath, Offaly, Westmeath, Wexford and Wicklow. It is the most populous of Ireland's four provinces and includes the most fertile farmland in the republic. The province's major city is DUBLIN. Area: 19,635sq km (7,581sq mi). Pop. (1991) 1,860,949.

Leipzig City in E central Germany, at the confluence of the rivers Pleisse, White Elster and Parthe. Founded as a Slavic settlement in the 10th century, it became a commercial centre. It was the scene of the Battle of the Nations (1813). Leipzig was the second-largest city (after Berlin) in the former East Germany. The birthplace of Richard Wagner, it was also home to J.S. Bach for 27 years. The printing industry (founded in 1480) is important. Industries: textiles, machinery. Pop. (1995) 481,000.

leishmaniasis (kala-azar) Insect-borne disease carrying a high mortality and caused by infection with the parasite *Leishmania donovani*, transmitted by sandflies. The spleen is particularly affected and becomes enlarged. Symptoms include fever, anaemia, and wasting. The disease occurs primarily in Mediterranean Europe, Africa, Asia and Central and South America.

leitmotiv German word for a guiding theme in musical compositions. It is a theme that recurs throughout a work, usually an OPERA or a piece of PROGRAMME MUSIC.

Leitrim County in Connacht province, N Republic of Ireland, narrowly bounded on the NW by Donegal Bay; the capital is Carrick-on-Shannon. Hilly in the N, undulating in the S, it is drained by the River Shannon and its tributaries. Farming is the main occupation. Area 1,525sq km (589sq mi). Pop. (1991) 25,301.

Lely, Sir Peter van der Faes (1618–80) Dutch portrait painter, active in England. Principal painter to CHARLES II, he is associated with the Restoration court. He established the tradition of the society portrait. His best-known paintings include two series, *The Windsor Beauties* (1660s) and the famous *Admirals* (1666–67).

Lemaître, Abbé Georges Édouard (1894–1966) Belgian astrophysicist who formulated the BIG BANG theory for the origin of the Universe. He saw the Universe as originally analogous to a radioactive ATOM, with all the energy and matter concentrated into a kernel that he called the "primeval atom". Lemaître argued that an EXPANDING UNIVERSE would have originated in the explosion of that primeval atom.

Le Mans City in NW France; capital of Sarthe department. It is world-famous as the venue of the Le Mans 24-hour race for sports cars. Pop. (1990) 145,502.

lemming Any of several species of RODENTS, native to Arctic regions. They have brown fur, small ears and a short tail. They occasionally migrate in large numbers, and some species in Norway have suffered great losses by drowning while doing so. Family Cricetidae.

lemon Evergreen tree and its sour, yellow citrus fruit. Grown primarily in the USA and sub-tropical regions, it is mostly used in cooking and in drinks. Height of tree: to 6m (20ft). Family Rutaceae; species *Citrus limon*.

Lemmon, Jack (1925–) US film actor. He won an Academy Award as best supporting actor in *Mister Roberts* (1955). Lemmon won the best actor Oscar for his performance in *Save the Tiger* (1973). A versatile player, he has starred in Billy WILDER comedies such as *Some Like It Hot* (1959), *The Apartment* (1960) and *The Front Page* (1975), as well as in serious dramas such as *The China Syndrome* (1979) and *Missing* (1982).

lemur Any of several small primitive, mainly arboreal (tree-dwelling) and nocturnal, herbivorous PRIMATES that live in Madagascar. It resembles a squirrel, but has grasping monkey-like hands. Lemurs are the only surviving members of the ancient group of prosimian primates. Family Lemuridae. *See also* AYE-AYE

Lena River in E central Russia. It rises in the Baikal Mountains, flows generally N through the central Siberian uplands and empties through a wide delta into the Laptev Sea (part of the Arctic Ocean). Although navigable for 3,437km (2,135mi) of its 4,400km (2,730mi) route, it is frozen from early autumn to late spring.

Lenard, Philipp Eduard Anton (1862–1947) German physicist, b. Hungary. He was awarded the 1905 Nobel Prize for physics for his studies of CATHODE RAYS. His work was important in the development of ELECTRONICS and NUCLEAR PHYSICS.

Lendl, Ivan (1960–) Czech tennis player. Lendl led the world rankings for a record 270 weeks, winning seven Grand Slam singles titles, but never Wimbledon.

lend-lease US programme of assistance during World War 2. The Lend-Lease Act was passed in March 1941, before the USA became a combatant. It empowered President Franklin ROOSEVELT to transfer military equipment to other countries in the US national interest. The first beneficiaries were Britain and China. The programme was later extended to other allies, notably the Soviet Union.

L'Enfant, Pierre Charles (1754–1825) US architect and engineer, b. France. He went to America (1777) and served in the Continental army. At George Washington's invitation, he planned the national capital (1791), but the high cost of construction caused his dismissal. More than a century later, the development of Washington, D.C., was pursued according to his plans.

Lenin, Vladimir Ilyich (1870–1924) Russian revolutionary and statesman, b. Vladimir Ilyich Ulyanov. He evolved a revolutionary form of SOCIALISM (MARXISM-Leninism) that emphasized the need for a vanguard party to lead the revolution. In 1900, Lenin went into exile, founding (1903) what became the BOLSHEVIKS. After the first part of the RUSSIAN REVOLUTION of 1917, he returned to Russia. Lenin denounced the liberal government of KERENSKY and demanded armed revolt. After the Bolshevik revolution (November 1917), he became the head of state. Lenin withdrew Russia from World War 1. With the help of Leon TROTSKY, Lenin's government survived famine and the Russian Civil War (1918–22) by instituting a centralized command economy. In 1919, he founded the third COMMUNIST INTERNATIONAL. In 1921, the New Economic Policy (NEP) marked a return to a mixed economy. In 1922, Lenin became head of the newly formed SOVIET UNION. In 1923, a new constitution established the supremacy of the COMMUNIST PARTY OF THE SOVIET UNION (CPSU). Lenin's authority was unchallenged until he was crippled by a stroke in 1922. After his death, a power struggle ensued between Trotsky and Joseph STALIN.

Leningrad Former name for ST PETERSBURG

Lennon, John (1940–80) English singer and songwriter, a member of the BEATLES. Lennon co-wrote the vast majority of the Beatles' songs with Paul MCCARTNEY

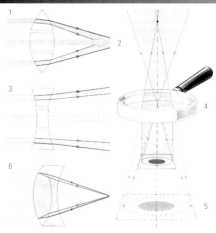

▲ **lens** A convex lens (1) focuses light on a single point (2) by diffracting the beams of light towards each other. A concave lens (3) diffracts parallel rays of light, making them diverge. A magnifying glass (4) is a convex lens. The glass makes the rays of light diverge, making it appear that they come from a larger image (5) than is the actual case. Cameras use a combination of convex and concave lenses (6) to focus light on the film without separation of the colours of the spectrum.

and appeared in the band's films and in *How I Won the War* (1967). He published *In His Own Write* (1964) and *A Spaniard in the Works* (1965). A major figure in the peace movement, he married Yoko Ono in 1969. Lennon was shot dead by Mark Chapman in New York City.

Le Nôtre, André (1613–1700) French landscape gardener. His grandiose, geometric style established the French garden as the leading style in contemporary Europe. In 1637, Le Nôtre became gardener to LOUIS XIV and created such famous gardens as VERSAILLES, Chantilly, and the Tuileries in Paris.

lens Piece of transparent glass, plastic, quartz or organic matter, bounded by two surfaces, usually both spherical, that changes the direction of a light beam by REFRACTION. A convex lens bends light rays towards the lens axis. A concave lens bends rays away from the axis. The optical IMAGE may be right side-up or inverted, real or virtual, and magnified or reduced in size.

Lent Period in the Christian year that precedes EASTER. In the Western Churches it begins on Ash Wednesday and is 40 days long (Sundays are not included); in the Eastern Church it lasts 80 days (neither Saturdays nor Sundays are counted). Lent is a time of fasting, abstinence and penitence to prepare for the remembrance of the crucifixion and resurrection of JESUS CHRIST.

lentil Annual plant of the PEA family that grows in the Mediterranean region, SW Asia and N Africa. It is cultivated for its nutritious seeds. Height: to 51cm (20in). Family Fabaceae/Leguminosae; species *Lens culinaris*.

Lenya, Lotte (*c.*1898–1981) Austrian singer and actress. Lenya became famous in two notable BRECHT plays with musical scores by her husband, Kurt WEILL, *The Threepenny Opera* (1928) and *The Rise and Fall of the City of Mahagonny* (1930). In 1935, she emigrated to the USA.

Leo I, Saint (d.AD 461) (Leo the Great) Pope (440–61). He established important points of doctrine, including the dual nature of Christ, which he propounded at the Council of CHALCEDON (449). By personal intervention, he saved Rome from ATTILA (452) and the Vandal Gaiseric (455).

Leo III, Saint (*c.*750–816) Pope (795–816). With the help of CHARLEMAGNE, Leo imposed his rule on Rome and crowned Charlemagne emperor on Christmas Day, 800. This strengthened papal authority in Rome and led to recognition of the pope and emperor as religious and secular leaders of Western Christendom.

Leo IX, Saint (1002–54) Pope (1048–54), b. Bruno of Egisheim. Leo's wide-ranging programme of reform was against abuses such as SIMONY. Efforts to strengthen papal authority in s Italy provoked war with the Normans, who held him prisoner in 1053. The excommunication of the Patriarch of Constantinople by Leo's legate (1054) led to the permanent SCHISM between Eastern (Greek) and Western (Latin) Churches.

Leo X (1475–1521) Pope (1513–21), b. Giovanni de' Medici, son of Lorenzo de' MEDICI. He presided over the Fifth of the LATERAN COUNCILS, which failed to enact church reforms. In 1517, Martin LUTHER published his theses at Wittenberg and was excommunicated by Leo in 1521. He gave HENRY VIII the title Defender of the Faith.

Leo XIII (1810–1903) Pope (1878–1903), b. Vincenzo Gioacchino Pecci. He reconciled Roman Catholic attitudes to the scientific and political theories of the time. He was a devoted scholar, opening the Vatican secret archives to the public. He sponsored several universities and advanced the philosophy of THOMISM.

León City in w Nicaragua, the country's second-largest city. It was founded (1524) near Lake Managua. In 1610, a severe earthquake forced the city's reconstruction on its present site. For 300 years it served as the nation's capital. In 1821, when Nicaragua gained independence from Spain, a bitter rivalry between León and Granada led to civil war. In 1858, MANAGUA was proclaimed the new capital. León was the scene of bitter fighting between SANDINISTA guerrillas and government forces in the late 1970s. Industries: food processing, leather goods, cigars, cotton. Pop. (1994 est.) 158,577.

León City in NW Spain; capital of León province. A military camp in Roman times, it was occupied by the Moors in the 8th century. Recaptured (882) by Alfonso III of Asturias, it was capital of the medieval kingdom of Asturias and León until 1230. Industries: leather, cotton, textiles, iron, glass, pottery, tourism. Pop. (1995) 124,000.

Leonardo da Vinci (1452–1519) Florentine painter, sculptor, architect, engineer and scientist. Leonardo was the founder of the High RENAISSANCE style. By the 1470s, he had developed his characteristic style of painting figures who seem rapt in sweet melancholy. In *c.*1482, Leonardo moved to Milan where he worked mainly for Ludovico SFORZA. While in Milan, he worked on an altarpiece, *The Virgin of the Rocks* (1483–85). Leonardo painted the *Last Supper* (*c.*1498) on the walls of Santa Maria delle Grazie, Milan, using a new MURAL technique that proved unstable. When the French invaded Milan in 1499, he left for Florence. From 1500 to 1506, Leonardo created his finest easel paintings, including the enigmatic *Mona Lisa* (*c.*1504–05). His 19 notebooks contain detailed scientific drawings, including plans for a helicopter-like flying machine, a tank and a submarine.

Leoncavallo, Ruggiero (1858–1919) Italian composer. He travelled all over Europe working as an accompanist and composer of music-hall songs. Of his operas, *I Pagliacci* (1892) alone has withstood the test of time.

Leone, Sergio (1921–89) Italian film director, creator of the "spaghetti western". The "Man With No Name" trilogy of *A Fistful of Dollars* (1964), *For a Few Dollars*

More (1965) and *The Good, The Bad and The Ugly* (1966) revived Clint EASTWOOD's career. The epics *Once Upon a Time in the West* (1968) and *Once Upon a Time in America* (1984) were commercially unsuccessful but later reappraised as his masterworks.

leopard (panther) Solitary big CAT found throughout Africa and S Asia. It has a round head with a short nose and a long, thin tail. The coat may be yellow and white with dark spots, or almost completely black. It feeds on birds, monkeys, antelopes and cattle. Length: to 2.1m (7ft) including tail; weight: to 91kg (200lb). Family Felidae; species *Panthera pardus*.

Leopold I (1640–1705) Holy Roman Emperor (1658–1705). He helped revive HABSBURG power in Europe. In 1683, with the help of JOHN III of Poland, Leopold defeated the Ottoman siege of Vienna. In 1699, he regained Hungary from the Turks. Leopold joined the European defensive alliances (1686, 1689, 1701) that inflicted heavy defeats in Germany on LOUIS XIV of France. *See also* SPANISH SUCCESSION, WAR OF

Leopold II (1747–92) Holy Roman Emperor (1790–92), grand duke of Tuscany as Leopold I (1765–90), third son of MARIA THERESA. He succeeded his father, FRANCIS I, as ruler in Tuscany and his brother JOSEPH II as Holy Roman Emperor. By reversing many of Joseph's reforms, Leopold pacified much of the Empire. He was involved in the Declaration of Pillnitz, which aimed to restore Louis XVI. It was one of the main causes of the FRENCH REVOLUTIONARY WARS.

Leopold I (1790–1865) First king of independent Belgium (1831–65). Son of the duke of Saxe-Coburg-Saalfield, he became a British subject after marrying the daughter of the future King GEORGE IV (1816). He was an important influence on Queen VICTORIA, his niece, and was largely responsible for her marriage to Prince ALBERT.

Leopold II (1835–1909) King of Belgium (1865–1909). He initiated colonial expansion and sponsored the expedition of Henry STANLEY to the Congo (1879–84). In 1885, Leopold established the Congo Free State (Zaire) under his own personal rule. In 1908, he was forced to cede the Congo to the Belgian state.

Leopold III (1901–83) King of Belgium (1934–51). When the Germans invaded Belgium (1940) during World War 2, he declined to accompany the government into exile and surrendered. He remained in Belgium during the war, until removed to Germany in 1944. On his return, he encountered such fierce opposition that he abdicated in favour of his son, Baudouin.

Lepanto, Battle of (1571) Naval engagement in the Gulf of Patras, off Lepanto, Greece. The last great battle

between fleets of war galleys, it was the first major victory of the Christians over the Ottoman Turks.

lepidoptera Order of insects that includes MOTHS and BUTTERFLIES; they are found worldwide except Antarctica.

leprosy (Hansen's disease) Chronic, progressive condition affecting the skin and nerves, caused by infection with the microorganism *Mycobacterium leprae*. **Lepromatous** leprosy is a contagious form in which raised nodules appear on the skin and there is thickening of the skin and peripheral nerves. In **tuberculoid** leprosy there is loss of sensation in parts of the skin, sometimes with loss of pigmentation and hair. Now confined almost entirely to the tropics, leprosy is treated with a combination of drugs, but the nerve damage is irreversible.

lepton One of a class of ELEMENTARY PARTICLES. There are 12 types, including the ELECTRON and electron-NEUTRINO, muon and muon-neutrino, tau and tau-neutrino, together with their antiparticles (anti-leptons). Leptons are governed by the WEAK NUCLEAR FORCE. They have no QUARK substructure.

Lermontov, Mikhail Yurevich (1814–41) Russian poet and novelist. He was exiled to the Caucasus for his revolutionary poem to Tsar Nicholas I on the death of PUSHKIN. Lermontov is chiefly remembered for his semi-autobiographical novel *A Hero of Our Time* (1840) and the long narrative poem *The Demon* (1841).

Le Sage, Alain René (1668–1747) French novelist and dramatist. The best of his *c*.100 comic plays is *Turcaret* (1709). His PICARESQUE work, *Gil Blas* (1715–35), was translated by Tobias SMOLLETT and influenced the development of the realist NOVEL.

lesbianism Term that describes female HOMOSEXUALITY.

Lesbos (Lesvos or Mylini) Third-largest Greek island, 10km (6mi) off the NW coast of Turkey in the Aegean Sea; the capital is Mitilíni. It was settled by the Aeolians *c*.1000 BC. In the 7th and 6th centuries BC, it was a cultural centre. It was held by Persia, Greek city-states, Macedonia, Rome and Byzantium. The Ottomans occupied the island from 1462 to 1913, when it passed to Greece. Products: olives, wheat, grapes, citrus fruits. Industries: fishing, tourism. Area: *c*.1,630sq km (630sq mi). Pop. (1991) 103,700.

lesion Any abnormality in a body tissue due to injury or disease. Examples are ulcers and tumours.

Lesotho (formerly Basutoland) Enclave kingdom within the Republic of South Africa; the capital is MASERU. **Land and climate** The scenic Drakensberg Range forms Lesotho's NE border with KWAZULU-NATAL, and includes its highest peak, Thabana Ntlenyana, at 3,482m (11,424ft). Most people live in the W lowlands, site of Maseru, or in the S valley of the River Orange, which rises in NE Lesotho

◀ **leopard** The leopard (*Panthera pardus*) and the "black panther", a member of the same species but with different coloration, are found in tropical rainforests of Africa and Asia. Powerful, agile hunters, they feed on any animal they can overpower. If they are unable to consume their prey at one sitting, leopards will drag the carcass into a tree out of the reach of scavengers.

LESOTHO

AREA: 30,350sq km (11,718sq mi)
POPULATION: 1,836,000
CAPITAL (POPULATION): Maseru (367,000)

---

and flows through South Africa to the Atlantic Ocean. All land in Lesotho is held by the king in trust for the SOTHO nation. Lesotho's climate is greatly affected by altitude; 66% of the land lies above 1,500m (4,921 ft). Maseru has warm summers and cold winters. Rainfall averages c.700mm (28in). Grassland covers much of Lesotho. **History and politics** The early 19th-century, tribal wars dispersed the Sotho. In the 1820s, a Sotho kingdom was formed by Moshoeshoe I in present-day Lesotho. Moshoeshoe I was forced to yield to the British, and in 1868 the area became a protectorate. In 1871, it became part of the British Cape Colony, but after British failure to disarm the Sotho, the area fell under direct rule. In 1966, Sotho opposition to incorporation into the Union of South Africa saw the creation of the independent kingdom of Lesotho. Moshoeshoe II, great-grandson of Moshoeshoe I, became king. In 1970, Leabua Jonathan suspended the constitution and banned opposition parties. The next 16 years were characterized by civil conflict between the government and Basuto Congress Party (BCP) forces. In 1986, a military coup led to the reinstatement of Moshoeshoe II. In 1990, he was deposed and replaced by his son, Letsie III. The BCP won the 1992 multiparty elections, and the military council was dissolved. In 1994, Letsie III attempted to overthrow the government. In January 1995, Moshoeshoe II was restored to the throne. His death (1996) saw the restoration of Letsie III. In 1997, a majority of BCP politicians formed a new governing party, the Lesotho Congress for Democracy (LCD). Accusations of fraud in May 1998 elections led to violent protests and an army mutiny. In September 1998, South African forces restored order and fresh elections were called in 2000. **Economy** Lesotho is a low-income, less-developed country (1995 GDP per capita, US$1,780). It lacks natural resources, except diamonds. Agriculture, mainly at subsistence level, is the main activity. Major crops include maize and sorghum. Tourism is developing. Large numbers of the population work in South Africa.

less developed countries (LDCs) Those countries, primarily of Africa, Asia and Latin America, that have little or no industrial base. Characteristically, they have high rates of population growth, high infant mortality, short life expectancy, low levels of literacy and poor distribution of wealth.

Lesseps, Ferdinand Marie, Vicomte de (1805–94) French diplomat and engineer. He conceived the idea of a canal through the isthmus of Suez, linking the Red Sea with the Mediterranean. He formed the Suez Canal Company, securing finance from the French government. Digging began in 1859, and the canal was opened in November 1869. In 1879, he launched a scheme to construct the PANAMA CANAL but it was abandoned in 1886 when his company failed.

Lesser Antilles See ANTILLES

Lessing, Doris May (1919–) British novelist, b. Persia, who was brought up in Rhodesia. Her first novel, *The Grass Is Singing* (1950), is a story of racial hatred. Her *Children of Violence* quintet (1952–69) explores the social position of women; *The Golden Notebook* (1962) is a key feminist text. Lessing also wrote the science-fiction quintet *Canopus in Argos* (1979–83), which

includes *The Making of the Representative for Planet 8* (1982). Other works include *The Good Terrorist* (1985).

Lessing, Gotthold Ephraim (1729–81) German philosopher, dramatist and critic. His commitment to the German enlightenment is evident in the verse play, *Nathan der Weise* (1779). Other works include the tragedy *Emilia Galotti* (1772) and the critical work *Laocoon* (1766).

Lethe In Greek mythology, the river of forgetfulness in HADES. All who drank from it lost their memories.

lettuce Annual plant widely cultivated in salads. Most varieties of *Lactuca sativa* are cool-weather crops. The leaves form a compact head or loose rosette.

leucite Grey or white feldspar mineral, a potassium aluminium silicate, $KAl(SiO_3)_2$. Unstable at high pressures, it can be found in potassium-rich lava flows and volcanic plugs. Hardness 5.5–6; r.d. 2.5.

leucocyte (white BLOOD cell) Colourless structure containing a NUCLEUS and CYTOPLASM. There are two types of leucocytes – LYMPHOCYTES and PHAGOCYTES. Normal blood contains 5,000–10,000 leucocytes per cu mm. Excessive numbers of leucocytes are seen in such diseases as LEUKAEMIA. *See also* ANTIBODIES; IMMUNE SYSTEM

leucotomy (prefrontal lobotomy) Surgical operation on the BRAIN. It was first performed in the 1930s to treat psychiatric disorders by severing tracts of nerve fibres leading to the frontal lobes. It may cause irreversible deterioration of personality. Drugs have made the operation redundant.

leukaemia Any of a group of cancers in which the bone marrow and other blood-forming tissues produce abnormal numbers of immature or defective LEUCOCYTES. This over-production suppresses output of normal blood cells and PLATELETS, leaving the person vulnerable to infection, anaemia and bleeding. **Acute lymphoblastic leukaemia** (ALL) is predominantly a disease of childhood; **acute myelogenous leukaemia** (AML) is mainly seen in older adults. Both forms are potentially curable.

Le Vau, Louis (1612–70) French architect. Inspired by contemporary Italian BAROQUE buildings, he evolved a classic 17th-century French style, seen in his designs for the Palace of VERSAILLES (1669–85).

levee Natural embankment formed alongside a river by the deposition of silt when the river is in flood. Levees can help to prevent flooding and are sometimes built up and strengthened artificially. Some are totally artificial.

Levellers (1645–49) Members of a radical movement in England in the COMMONWEALTH period. They campaigned for the abolition of the monarchy and House of Lords, the extension of the franchise, religious toleration and a more egalitarian society. In 1647, their leaders, including John LILBURNE, presented a constitution to Oliver CROMWELL. When their demands were not met, several mutinies broke out in the NEW MODEL ARMY, resulting in their suppression. *See also* DIGGERS

lever Simple machine used to multiply the force applied to an object, usually to raise a heavy load. A lever consists of a rod and a point (fulcrum) about which the rod pivots. An example is the crowbar.

Leverhulme, William Hesketh Lever, 1st Viscount (1851–1925) English industrialist and philanthropist. He began the manufacture of soap from vegetable oil under the tradename Sunlight. In 1884, Lever Brothers founded Port Sunlight, a model industrial village. The company forms the core of the modern multinational Unilever.

Leverrier, Urbain Jean Joseph (1811–77) French astronomer. In 1846 he successfully predicted that an unknown planet (Neptune) was responsible for discrepancies between the calculated and observed orbital motion of Uranus.

Levi, Primo (1919–87) Italian writer. A Jew, he joined a guerrilla movement in World War 2. He was captured and sent to Auschwitz. Levi survived but was haunted by the HOLOCAUST. His books, such as *If This is a Man* (1947), *The Truce* (1963) and *The Periodic Table* (1984), attempt to come to terms with the experience.

Leviathan In the Old Testament, an immense serpent living in the depths of the ocean. It embodied everything evil.

Levine, James (1943–) US pianist and conductor. In 1964, he became assistant conductor of the Cleveland Orchestra. He was later principal conductor (1973) and then musical director (1975) of the New York METROPOLITAN OPERA. In 1982, he made his debut at Bayreuth. He is acknowledged as a leading interpreter of Wagner.

Lévi-Strauss, Claude (1908–90) French anthropologist. In *The Elementary Structures of Kinship* (1949) and *Structural Anthropology* (1958), Lévi-Strauss outlined the science of STRUCTURALISM. In 1959, he became professor of anthropology at the College of France. In 1973, he was elected to the Académie Française.

Levites Clan of religious officials in ancient Israel. It is possible that they once were one of the 12 tribes of Israel mentioned in the Old Testament, descended from Levi, the third son of JACOB. By the time of JESUS CHRIST, the Levites ran the entire TEMPLE organization with the exception of the priesthood.

Leviticus Third book of the PENTATEUCH or TORAH. It is primarily a manual for the instruction of priests.

Lewes, George Henry (1817–76) English journalist and critic. He wrote dramatic criticism as well as philosophical works, including *A Biographical History of Philosophy* (1845) and the hugely successful *The Life and Works of Goethe* (1855). Separated from his wife, he lived with George ELIOT, whose work he encouraged.

Lewis, (Frederick) Carl (Carlton) (1961–) US track and field athlete. In the 1984 Olympics, Lewis won four gold medals (100m, 200m, 4×100m relay, long jump), equalling Jesse OWEN's feat. In 1988, he won two Olympic gold medals (100m, long jump). At the 1992 Olympics, Lewis again won two gold medals (long jump, 4×100m relay). At the 1996 Olympics in Atalanta, he won his ninth gold medal (long jump).

Lewis, C.S. (Clive Staples) (1898–1963) English scholar, critic and writer. He is best known for his religious and moral books written after his conversion to Christianity, particularly *The Screwtape Letters* (1942) and his autobiography *Surprised by Joy* (1955). Lewis wrote a number of highly acclaimed children's books, including *The Lion, the Witch and the Wardrobe* (1950).

Lewis, (Harry) Sinclair (1885–1951) US writer. His first novel, *Main Street* (1920), set out his central theme – the hypocrisy and parochialism of small-town Midwestern society. *Babbitt* (1922), often cited as his masterpiece, is the story of a businessman who refuses to conform. Lewis rejected the Pulitzer Prize for *Arrowsmith* (1925). In 1930, he became the first US writer to be awarded the Nobel Prize for literature.

Lewis, (Percy) Wyndham (1884–1957) British painter, critic and novelist, b. Canada. He was the central figure of the VORTICISM movement. His work was greatly influenced by FUTURISM and NIETZSCHE. After World War 1, he produced a series of novels and essays.

Lewis and Clark Expedition (1804–06) US expedition to seek a route by water from the Mississippi to the Pacific Ocean. Instigated by President JEFFERSON, it was led by army officers Meriwether Lewis and William Clark, with the assistance of a Shoshone woman, Sacajawea. It reached the Pacific at the mouth of the

Columbia River and produced valuable information about the country and peoples of the Northwest.

Lexington City in the bluegrass region of NE central Kentucky, USA. Lexington is a famous breeding ground for thoroughbred horses. It also has the world's largest tobacco market. Other industries: automobile parts, electrical machinery, distilling. Pop. (1992) 232,252.

Lexington and Concord, battles of (April 1775) First battles of the AMERICAN REVOLUTION. British troops marching from Boston to Concord, Massachusetts, were intercepted by militiamen at Lexington Green. Several minutemen were killed, and the British advanced to Concord and destroyed military supplies. Returning to Boston the British were involved in several skirmishes and suffered nearly 300 casualties.

Leyden jar Earliest and simplest device for storing static electricity, developed (*c.*1745) in Leyden, Holland. The original electrical condenser (capacitor), it consists of a foil-lined glass jar partly filled with water and closed with a cork through which protrudes a brass rod wired to the foil. To charge the jar, friction is applied to the tip of the rod.

Leyte Gulf, Battle of (October 1944) Air and naval engagement between Japanese and US forces in the Philippines. In the largest naval battle in history, the Japanese lost 40 ships and 405 aircraft.

Lhasa Capital of Tibet (Xizang Zizhiqu) Autonomous Region in SW China, on a tributary of the Brahmaputra, at 3,600m (11,800ft) in the N Himalayas. An ancient religious centre, it was occupied by the Chinese in 1951. After the Tibetan revolt against the occupation (1959–60), many of Lhasa's temples and monasteries were closed. The 17th-century Potala Palace was the home of the DALAI LAMA. Today, Lhasa is an important trading centre, also manufacturing chemicals and processing gold and copper. Pop. (1994) 118,000.

liana Any ground-rooting, woody vine that twines and creeps extensively over other plants for support; it is common in tropical forests. Some species may reach a diameter of 60cm (24in) and a length of 100m (330ft).

Liaoning Coastal province in NE China, bordering North Korea; the capital is Shenyang. Japan conquered the Liaotung peninsula during the RUSSO-JAPANESE WAR (1904–05) and developed the province's industries and railroads. It later formed part of the Japanese puppet state MANCHUKUO (1932–45). After World War 2, it fell under the joint control of Russia and China. Since 1955, it has been a Chinese province. Liaoning is the chief site of China's heavy industry. The province has rich coal and iron ore reserves and supplies 20% of China's electrical power. It includes the cities of Anshan, Fushun and Dalian (China's major port). The principal river is the Liao. Area: 151,000sq km (58,300sq mi). Pop. (1990) 39,980,000.

Libby, Willard Frank (1908–80) US chemist. From 1941 to 1945, he worked on the separation of isotopes for the atomic bomb. In 1960, Libby was awarded the Nobel Prize for chemistry for his development of CARBON DATING.

Liberal Democrats (LD) (officially Social and Liberal Democrats) British political party, formed in March 1988 by the merger of the LIBERAL PARTY and the SOCIAL DEMOCRATIC PARTY (SDP). Its first leader (1988–99) was Paddy ASHDOWN. He was succeeded (1999) by Charles KENNEDY. In the 1988 election, it returned 20 MPs. The smallest of the three main political parties, it has vigorously campaigned for PROPORTIONAL REPRESENTATION (PR). In the 1997 general election, the Liberal Democrats returned 46 MPs. It faces a dilemma over the nature and extent of its participation with the LABOUR PARTY.

liberalism Political and intellectual belief that advocates the right of the individual to make decisions, usually political or religious, according to the dictates of conscience. Its modern origins lie in the 18th-century ENLIGHTENMENT. In politics it opposes arbitrary power and discrimination against minorities (see CIVIL RIGHTS). In the late 18th century, it became associated with the doctrines of FREE-TRADE and LAISSEZ-FAIRE. By the end of the 19th century, it was committed to the WELFARE STATE and a mixed economy. See also HAYEK, FRIEDRICH AUGUST von; RAWLS, JOHN

Liberal Party British political party. It grew out of the early 19th-century WHIGS. The first official use of the name was the National Liberal Federation founded (1877) by Joseph CHAMBERLAIN, although the administration (1855–58) of Lord Palmerston is often regarded as Liberal. Its predominant interests were FREE-TRADE, religious and individual liberty, financial retrenchment and constitutional reform. Its greatest leader was William GLADSTONE, who led four governments (1868–74, 1880–85, 1885–86, 1892–94). The government of (1905–08) Henry CAMPBELL-BANNERMAN legalized TRADE UNIONS, reformed the House of Lords and introduced progressive SOCIAL SECURITY measures. In 1908, Herbert ASQUITH became leader and prime minister. In 1916, LLOYD GEORGE formed a coalition government with the CONSERVATIVE PARTY. Since Lloyd George, it has never formed a government. After the formation (1980) of the SOCIAL DEMOCRATIC PARTY (SDP), the Liberal Party entered into an alliance and then merged with it in 1987. In 1988, the Liberal members and most of the SDP formed the LIBERAL DEMOCRATS. A small Liberal Party still exists.

Liberal Party Canadian political party. Holding principles similar to the British LIBERAL PARTY, it was formed in 1854. Its first administration (1873–78), under Alexander Mackenzie, was anti-railroad and advocated FREE-TRADE. Under the leadership (1896–1911) of Wilfrid LAURIER, the Liberals supported ethnic conciliation, independence and immigration. It later held power under Lester PEARSON (1963–68), Pierre TRUDEAU (1968–79, 1980–84), John Turner (1984) and Jean CHRÉTIEN (1993–).

Liberal Party Australian political party. It was formed (1913) in opposition to the LABOR PARTY. In 1944, Robert MENZIES created a new Liberal Party from the collapse of the United Australia Party. In 1949, Menzies became prime minister of a Liberal-Country coalition government. In 1966, Menzies was succeeded as prime minister and Liberal Party leader by Harold Holt. The Liberals returned to office under John Gorton (1968–71) and William McMahon (1971–72). In 1975, Malcolm FRASER defeated Gough WHITLAM to become prime minister (1975–83). In 1996, after five successive Labor governments, the Liberal Party regained power under John HOWARD.

Liberia Republic on the Atlantic coast of W Africa. **Land and climate** Liberia's coastline stretches more than 500km (300mi), and is the site of the capital and chief port, MONROVIA. A narrow coastal plain rises to a plateau region, with the highest land on the border with Guinea. The most important rivers are the Cavally, which forms the border with Ivory Coast, and the St Paul. Liberia has a tropical climate with high annual temperatures and

humidity. There are two rainy seasons. Mangrove swamps and lagoons line the coast, while inland, forests cover nearly 40% of the land. Liberia also has areas of tropical savanna. Only 5% of the land is cultivated. **History and politics** In 1821 Liberia was founded by the AMERICAN COLONIZATION SOCIETY. In 1822, the Society landed African-American former slaves at a coastal settlement that they named Monrovia. In 1847, Liberia became a fully independent republic. For many years Americo-Liberians controlled Liberia's government, and the US Firestone Company's rubber plantations covered more than 400,000ha (1 million acres). Under the leadership (1944–71) of William Tubman, Liberia's economy grew and social reforms were adopted. In 1980, Tubman's successor, William R. Tolbert, was assassinated in a military coup and Master-Sergeant Samuel Doe led a new military government. In 1985, Doe's brutal and corrupt regime won a fraudulent election. In 1989, civil war broke out, and the Economic Community of West African States (ECOWAS) sent a five-nation peacekeeping force. Doe was assassinated, and an interim government, led by Amos Sawyer, was formed. Civil war raged on, and by mid-1993, an estimated 150,000 people had died and hundreds of thousands were homeless. In 1995, a ceasefire was agreed and a council of state, composed of formerly warring leaders, was established. Conflict resumed when one faction's leader, Roosevelt Johnson, was dismissed from the council. In July 1996, a further cease-fire was agreed. In 1997 elections, former warlord Charles Taylor and his National Patriotic Council secured a resounding victory. In September 1998, Roosevelt Johnson was arrested in clashes that killed 47 people. **Economy** Civil war has devastated Liberia's economy (1992 GDP per capita, US$1,045). Until the 1950s, Liberia was a plantation economy. Agriculture still employs 75% of the workforce, mainly at subsistence level. Chief food crops include cassava, rice and sugar cane. Rubber, cocoa and coffee are grown for export. Timber is also exported. Crude materials, principally iron ore, account for more than 90% of Liberia's exports.

Liberty, Statue of See STATUE OF LIBERTY

libido In PSYCHOANALYSIS, term used by Sigmund FREUD to describe instinctive sexual energy. Freud later enlarged its meaning to include all mental energy (or life energy) that accompanies strong desires.

Library of Congress US national library in Washington, D.C. It is supported mainly by congressional appropriations. The library was originally established (1800) to serve as a research facility for members of Congress. Its collection includes more than 60 million items. The librarian is appointed by the president. See also BRITISH LIBRARY

libretto Text of an opera or operetta. From 1597 libretti were printed to commemorate performances; by the mid-18th century, public audiences used them to follow the opera's story. A number of composers have written their own libretti, notably Wagner.

Libreville Capital and largest city of Gabon, W central Africa, at the mouth of the River Gabon on the Gulf of Guinea. Founded by the French in 1843 and named Libreville (Fr. Freetown) in 1849, it was initially a refuge for escaped slaves. The city has expanded with the development of Gabon's mineral industry. Other industries: timber (hardwoods), palm oil, rubber. Pop. (1993) 418,000.

Libya Republic in N Africa. Libya consists of three geographical areas. The NW and NE Mediterranean coastal plains are home to the majority of Libya's population; the NE plain includes Libya's capital, TRIPOLI; the NW plain its second-largest city, BENGHAZI. The SAHARA occupies 95%

LIBERIA
AREA: 111,370sq km (43,000sq mi)
POPULATION: 3,575,000
CAPITAL (POPULATION): Monrovia (962,000)

LIBYA
AREA: 1,759,540sq km (679,358sq mi)
POPULATION: 6,500,000
CAPITAL (POPULATION): Tripoli (990,697)

of Libya, and is inhabited only at scattered oases. The desert rises to 2,286m (7,500ft) at Bette Peak, on the s border with Chad. **Climate** The coastal plains have a Mediterranean climate, with hot, dry summers and mild, moist winters. Inland, the average annual rainfall drops to 100mm (4in) or less. **Vegetation** Shrubs and grasses grow on the N coasts, with some trees in wetter areas. At the desert oases, date palms provide shade from the sun. **History and politics** The earliest known inhabitants of Libya were the BERBERS. Between the 7th century BC and the 5th century AD, the region came under the rule of Greeks, Carthaginians, Romans and Vandals. Magnificent Roman ruins survive. In AD 642, Arabs invaded Libya and Islam remains the dominant religion. From 1551, Libya was part of the Turkish Ottoman Empire; power resided with local rulers or JANISSARIES. During the 17th century, Barbary pirates attacked shipping from bases on the Libyan coast. In the 19th century, US, British and French forces attempted to stop the piracy. In 1911, Italy invaded Libya, and by 1914 had conquered the whole territory. Attempts at colonization were made in the 1930s, and in 1939 Libya was formally incorporated into Italy. During World War 2, the country was a battleground for many of the North Africa campaigns. Following the Allied victory Libya was placed under UN mandate until 1951, when it became an independent monarchy. In 1953, Libya joined the Arab League, and in 1955 became a member of the United Nations (UN). In 1969, the king was overthrown in a military coup led by Colonel Muammar al-QADDAFI. A Revolutionary Command Council set about the nationalization of industry, the establishment of an Islamic state and the reduction of foreign interference. In 1971, Libya entered a federation with Egypt and Syria. Libya maintained an anti-Israel foreign policy, and Qaddafi aided the Palestine Liberation Organization (PLO). During the 1980s, Libyan and US relations deteriorated further. Following an attack on US forces, the USA placed an oil embargo on Libya. In 1986, following evidence of Libyan support of international terrorism, the USA bombed Tripoli and Benghazi. In 1992, Libya was accused of sheltering the terrorists responsible for the bombing (1988) of Pan-Am flight 103 over Lockerbie, Scotland, and refused to extradite them to the USA or the UK. Libya has a long-standing territorial dispute with Chad, and sent troops to intervene in the civil war. In 1994, the International Court of Justice dismissed Libya's claim to the Aozou Strip in N Chad. Qaddafi has attracted worldwide criticism for his support of revolutionary movements. In 1995, all Palestinians were deported from Libya in protest against the PLO-Israeli peace agreement. In 1999, Libya agreed to extradite the two suspects in the Lockerbie case and UN sanctions were suspended. **Economy** The discovery of oil in 1958 transformed Libya's economy. Formerly one of the world's poorest countries, it has become Africa's richest (1992 GDP per capita, US$9,782). Oil accounts for more than 95% of exports, but Libya remains a developing country. Agriculture is important, but it is dependent on food imports. Economic sanctions have badly hit the economy.

lice *See* LOUSE

lichen Plant consisting of a FUNGUS in which microscopic (usually single-celled) ALGAE are embedded. The fungus and its algae form a symbiotic association in which the fungus contributes support, water and minerals, while the algae contribute food produced by PHOTOSYNTHESIS. *See also* SYMBIOSIS

Lichtenstein, Roy (1923–97) US painter, sculptor and graphic artist. He is regarded as a leading exponent of POP ART. Among his best-known paintings are *Whaam!* (1963) and *Good Morning, Darling* (1964).

licorice *See* LIQUORICE

Lie, Trygve Halvdan (1896–1968) Norwegian statesman, first secretary-general of the UNITED NATIONS (UN) (1946–52). He blamed both sides for the COLD WAR but antagonized the Soviet Union by his support for UN intervention (1950) in the KOREAN WAR.

Liebig, Baron Justus von (1803–73) German chemist. He was the first to realize that animals use oxygen to get energy from food. Liebig also showed that plants derive their minerals from the soil, and he introduced synthetic fertilizers into agriculture.

Liebknecht, Karl (1871–1919) German revolutionary, son of Wilhelm LIEBKNECHT. With Rosa LUXEMBURG, he was a leader of the communist group known as the SPARTACISTS. After the failure of the Spartacist uprising in Berlin (1919), they were murdered in police custody.

Liebknecht, Wilhelm (1826–1900) German revolutionary, father of Karl LIEBKNECHT. After taking part in the REVOLUTION OF 1848, he was exiled to England where he became an associate of Karl MARX. In 1869, Liebknecht and August BEBEL founded the Social Democratic Party (SPD). They were imprisoned (1872–74) by Otto von BISMARCK for their opposition to the FRANCO-PRUSSIAN WAR (1870–71). In 1874, he entered the Reichstag.

Liechtenstein Independent principality in W central Europe at the E end of the Alps, between Austria (E) and Switzerland (W); the capital is Vaduz. The principality was formed in 1719 through the merging of Vaduz and Schellenberg. It remained part of the Holy Roman Empire until 1806. A member of the German Confederation from 1815, it gained independent status in 1866. In 1921, Liechtenstein entered into a currency union with Switzerland and, in 1923, a customs union. Until 1990 Switzerland also handled its foreign policy. In 1990, the principality joined the UN. Liechtenstein has a constitutional and hereditary monarchy; the ruling family is the Austrian house of Liechtenstein. Women finally received the vote in 1984. Liechtenstein is the fourth-smallest country in the world and one of the richest (1995 GDP per capita, $34,000). Since 1945, it has rapidly developed a specialized manufacturing base. The major part of state revenue is derived from international companies attracted by the low taxation rates. Tourism is increasingly important. It is world-famous for its postage stamps. Area: 157sq km (61sq mi). Pop. (2000) 28,000.

lied (Ger. song) It has a more specific connotation in current usage as the art song of German Romantic composers – especially Franz SCHUBERT, Hugo WOLF, Johannes BRAHMS and Robert SCHUMANN.

lie detector (polygraph) Electronic device that may be capable of detecting lies. The lie detector monitors such factors as heart rate, breathing rate and perspiration, all of which may be affected when a person tells an untruth.

Liège (Flemish, Luik) City and river port in E Belgium, at the confluence of the rivers Meuse and Ourthe; capital of Liège province. Settled in Roman times, it became part of Belgium in 1830. During the 19th century, it was one of the first steel-making and coal-mining centres. Liège was occupied by the Germans in both world wars and severely damaged in the Battle of the Bulge

(1944–45). After World War 2 the city's steel industry drastically declined. Liège is a commercial centre. Industries: chemicals, electronics. Pop. (1991) 195,201.

life Feature of organisms that sets them apart from inorganic matter. Life can be regarded as the ability to obtain energy from the Sun or from food and to use this for growth and reproduction. The current theory on life's origin is that giant molecules, similar to proteins and nucleic acids, reacted together in the watery surface environment of the young Earth that is now commonly called the primordial soup.

life expectancy Potential length of individual human life based on the average for any given group. It is affected by such factors as the economy, modernization, standards of health and hygiene and INFANT MORTALITY rates.

lift In AERODYNAMICS, force that acts upwards on the undersurface of an AEROFOIL, or wing. The lift force is a result of the upwards pressure underneath the aerofoil being greater than the downwards pressure on the top.

lift (elevator) Machine for raising and lowering passengers and freight from one level to another inside or outside buildings. Early lifts were driven by steam or hydraulic power. The first lift was installed (1856) in a New York City store by Elisha Otis, who invented a safety system that incorporated ratchets along the lift shaft to ensure that the body of the lift could not drop accidentally. In 1889, the first electric lift was installed, also in New York City.

ligament Bands of tough fibrous CONNECTIVE TISSUE that join bone to bone at the joints.

Ligeti, György (1923–) Hungarian composer whose avant-garde works involve shifting patterns of tone colours. After 1956, Ligeti's work on electronic sound influenced his compositions, especially *Atmosphères* (1961) and *Lux Aeterna* (1966).

light ELECTROMAGNETIC RADIATION to which the human eye is sensitive. Visible light is in the wavelength range from $c.400$nm (violet) to 770nm (red). The speed (symbol c) at which electromagnetic radiation (including light) travels in a vacuum is 299, 792,458ms^{-1}. Light exhibits typical phenomena of WAVE motion, such as REFLECTION, REFRACTION, DIFFRACTION, light polarization and INTERFERENCE. The properties of light were investigated in the 17th century by Sir Isaac NEWTON, who was the first to split white light light into its component colours (SPECTRUM) with a PRISM. Newton believed in a corpuscular (particle) theory of light, but the wave theory was well established by the second decade of the 19th century after the work of Thomas YOUNG and Augustin Jean FRESNEL. At the beginning of the 20th century, experiments on the PHOTOELECTRIC EFFECT and the work of Max PLANCK revived the idea that light can behave like a stream of particles. This dilemma was resolved by the QUANTUM THEORY, according to which light consists of elementary particles called PHOTONS. When light interacts with matter, as in the photoelectric effect, energy is exchanged in the form of photons and so light seems to be particles. Otherwise, it behaves as a wave. *See also* ETHER; HOLOGRAPHY; LASER; RELATIVITY

lighthouse Building, often in the form of a tower, with a light at the top to guide vessels at night. Lighthouses are built on land and at sea. Some mark ports and harbours, while others warn of shallow waters or dangerous rocks. Originally, a lighthouse keeper was always in attendance, but modern lighthouses are often unmanned and operated by remote control. The light system may produce a steady beam, a rotating beam or a pattern of flashes. Today, lighthouses are becoming less important as many vessels are equipped with satellite-aided NAVIGATION equipment called global positioning system (GPS).

lightning Visible flash of light accompanying an electrical discharge between clouds or between clouds and the surface, most commonly produced in a THUNDERSTORM. The potential difference causing the discharge can be as much as 1,000 million volts.

light-year Unit of astronomical distance equal to the distance travelled in free space or a vacuum by light in one tropical year. One light-year is equal to 9.4607×10^{12} km $(5.88 \times 10^{12}$ mi).

lignin Complex noncarbohydrate substance in woody tissues (especially XYLEM of plants), often in combination with cellulose. It is lignin that gives wood its strength. To obtain pure CELLULOSE for the paper and rayon industries, the lignin has to be removed.

lilac Any of 20 species of evergreen ornamental shrubs and small trees of the genus *Syringa*, which bear pointed clusters of tiny fragrant white to purple flowers. Height: to 6m (20ft). Family Oleaceae.

Lilburne, John (1614–57) English republican, leader of the LEVELLERS. Imprisoned (1638–40) under CHARLES I, he fought for Parliament during the CIVIL WARS (1642–45). Captured, he escaped execution when Parliament arranged an exchange of prisoners. Demanding greater equality and religious freedom, he led protests against the COMMONWEALTH of CROMWELL. Often imprisoned, he spent his last years among Quakers.

Lilienthal, Otto (1849–96) German engineer and pioneer of GLIDER design. In 1891 Lilienthal became the first person to control a glider in flight. He made $c.2,500$ more flights before his death in a biplane crash.

Lille (Flemish, Lisle) City in NW France, near the Belgian border; capital of Nord department. A fortified town in the 11th century, it changed hands several times. It flourished in the 16th century under the dukes of Burgundy. In the late 17th century, Lille became capital of French Flanders, and the building of its stock exchange established its commercial reputation. Lille is a major industrial and commercial city. Industries: textiles, engineering. Pop. (1990) 172,142.

Lilongwe Capital of Malawi, SE Africa, in the centre of the country, $c.80$km (50mi) W of Lake Malawi. Lilongwe was originally an agricultural trade centre. It replaced Zomba as the capital in 1975 and has rapidly become Malawi's second-largest city. Pop. (1994) 395,000.

lily Any of species of perennial, BULB-producing plants of the genus *Lilium*, from temperate and sub-tropical regions. They have erect stems and various leaf arrangements. The showy flowers may be almost any colour.

lily of the valley Perennial woodland plant native to Europe, Asia and E USA. It has broad, elongated leaves and bears stalks of tiny, white, bell-shaped fragrant flowers. Family Liliaceae; species *Convallaria majalis*.

Lima Capital and largest city of Peru, on the River Rímac at the foot of the Cerro San Cristóbal. Lima was founded in 1535 by Francisco PIZARRO. It functioned as the capital of the Spanish New World colonies until the 19th century. During the War of the Pacific, Lima was occupied (1881–83) by Chilean forces. It is the commercial and cultural centre of Peru. With the oil-refining port of Callao, the Lima metropolitan area is the third-largest city of South America, and it handles more than 75% of Peru's manufacturing. Pop. (1993) 6,386,308.

limbic system Collection of structures in the middle of the brain. Looped around the HYPOTHALAMUS, the limbic system is thought to be involved in emotional responses, such as fear and aggression, the production of mood changes and the laying down of memories.

limbo In Roman Catholic theology, the abode of souls excluded from HEAVEN but not condemned to any other punishment. This concept, which never became doctrine, said unbaptized infants go to limbo after death.

Limbourg, Pol de (active 1380–1416) Franco-Flemish manuscript illustrator. Pol and his brothers, Jan and Hermann, became court painters to Jean, duc de Berry in 1411. Their masterpiece is a BOOK OF HOURS known as *Les Très Riches Heures du Duc de Berry* (1413–15). *See also* ILLUMINATION

lime Name for any of the deciduous linden trees that grow in the N temperate zone. It has serrated, heart-shaped leaves with small, fragrant, yellowish flowers. The common British linden, *Tilia vulgaris*, is one of the three British species. The American lime, *T. americana*, is also called basswood. Family Tiliaceae.

lime Small tropical tree (*Citrus aurantifolia*) of the rue family (Rutaceae). The trees grow to 2.4–4.6m (8–15ft) and yield small, green, acid fruits. Lime juice was used on long voyages by English sailors in the 18th and 19th centuries; the vitamin C helped to ward off SCURVY.

lime *See* CALCIUM OXIDE

Limerick City on the Shannon estuary, SW Republic of Ireland; capital of Limerick county, Munster province. In the 9th century it was sacked by Norse invaders. At the beginning of the 11th century, Brian Boru made Limerick the capital of Munster. In the 12th century, the city was occupied by English forces who built a castle. During the 17th century, the city was besieged by the armies of both Oliver Cromwell and William III. Industries: lacemaking, salmon fishing. Pop. (1993 est.) 75,436.

limestone SEDIMENTARY ROCK composed primarily of carbonates. Generally formed from deposits of the skeletons of marine invertebrates, it is used to make cement and lime and as a building material.

Limoges City on the River Vienne, W central France; capital of the department of Haute-Vienne. A Roman settlement, it was later a tribal capital of the Gauls. Its enamel industry culminated in the 16th-century craftsmanship of Léonard Limousin but was devastated during the THIRTY YEARS' WAR. In the late 18th century, the city flourished once more with the establishment of manufacturing porcelain. Since 1945, economic expansion has been led by the exploitation of uranium mines near Ambazac. Pop. (1990) 133,464.

limpet Primitive gastropod MOLLUSC commonly found fixed to rocks along marine shores. It has a cap-like shell and a large muscular foot. Length: to 13cm (5in). Families: Patellacea, Acmaeidae and Fissurellidae.

Limpopo (Crocodile) River in S Africa. It rises in NE South Africa in the former Transvaal province. It forms part of the border between South Africa and Botswana, then the border of South Africa and Zimbabwe before crossing Mozambique to enter the Indian Ocean NE of Maputo. Length: *c*.1,770km (1,100mi).

Lin Biao (1907–71) Chinese communist statesman and general. His defeat of CHIANG KAI-SHEK in Manchuria, helped to secure the victory of the Red Army in 1949. In 1959, Lin became defence minister. He served as vice-chairman (1966–69) to Mao Zedong during the CULTURAL REVOLUTION (1966–69) and compiled Mao's *Little Red Book*. Mao's likely successor, Lin was killed in a mysterious air crash after launching a failed coup.

Lincoln, Abraham (1809–65) 16th US President (1861–65). Elected to the Illinois legislature for the WHIG PARTY in 1834, he studied to become a lawyer. He served (1847–49) in the House of Representatives and unsuccessfully ran for the Senate for the new REPUBLICAN PARTY against Stephen A. DOUGLAS in 1858. He was Republican candidate for president in 1860.

Lincoln's victory made the secession of the Southern, slave-owning states inevitable, and his determination to defend FORT SUMTER began the CIVIL WAR. A strong commander-in-chief, he played a leading role in military planning. In September 1862, he issued the EMANCIPATION PROCLAMATION and, in November 1863, delivered his famous GETTYSBURG ADDRESS. In 1864, Lincoln was re-elected and saw the war to a successful conclusion. On 14 April 1865, five days after the surrender of Robert E. LEE, Lincoln was shot by John Wilkes BOOTH, a Southern sympathizer. He died the next day.

Lincoln City in E England; the county town of LINCOLNSHIRE. It was founded by the Romans as *Lindum Colonia*. As one of the five boroughs of the DANELAW, Lincoln thrived on its wool trade until the 14th century. In the 19th century, the draining of surrounding fenland revived the local economy. The castle was begun (1068) in the reign of William I, and houses one of the original copies of the Magna Carta. Lincoln Cathedral (begun *c*.1073) has a central tower 83m (271ft) high. Industries: farm machinery. Pop. (1991) 81,900.

Lincoln State capital and second-largest city of Nebraska, USA. Founded in 1856 as Lancaster, its name was changed in honour of Abraham LINCOLN. The city was made state capital when Nebraska was admitted to the Union in 1867. Lincoln is a centre for livestock and grain, and more recently for insurance. Industries: rubber products, pharmaceuticals. Pop. (1990) 191,972.

Lincolnshire County in E England, bordering the North Sea; the county town is LINCOLN. The area was settled by the Romans, and an Anglo-Saxon kingdom was later established in Lindsey. In the Middle Ages it was a prosperous farming region. In 1974, part of N Lincolnshire was incorporated into the new authority of Humberside. Apart from the undulating Wolds, the region is flat, drained by the rivers Trent, Welland and Witham. Agriculture, the mainstay of the economy, includes cereals, sugar beets and sheep. Area: 5,886sq km (2,273sq mi). Pop. (1994) 605,800.

Lind, Jenny (1820–87) Swedish operatic soprano, b. Johanna Lind Goldschmidt. The "Swedish nightingale" made her debut in 1838. Lind achieved worldwide success in coloratura roles. In *c*.1852, she settled in London and founded several musical scholarships.

Lindbergh, Charles Augustus (1902–74) US aviator. He became an international hero when, in *The Spirit of St Louis*, he made the first non-stop transatlantic solo flight, from New York to Paris (1927) in 33 hours 30 minutes. In 1932, his baby son was kidnapped and murdered.

Lindisfarne Gospels Manuscript illuminated in the Hiberno-Saxon style in the late 7th or 8th century. It may have been executed for Eadfrith, Bishop of Lindisfarne (698–721). *See also* ILLUMINATION

Lindsday, (Nicholas) Vachel (1879–1931) US writer who styled himself the "vagabond poet". He travelled throughout the USA holding poetic revival meetings to stimulate a popular taste for poetry. *The Congo and Other Poems* (1914) and *General William Booth Enters into Heaven* (1913) contain much of his best work.

linear accelerator Type of particle ACCELERATOR in which charged particles travel in straight lines through a vacuum chamber. Early linear accelerators were electrostatic accelerators. In more modern types, a high-frequency, alternating electric field is used to accelerate the particles. Final energies depend on the length of the chamber, and can reach several GeV (million ELECTRON VOLTS). The linear accelerator at Stanford University is 3.2km (2mi) long and produces electrons with energies of 20GeV.

linear script Early form of writing, found on clay tablets in Crete and Greece. **Linear A** was in extensive use during the middle period of the MINOAN CIVILIZATION (c.2100–c.1450 BC). **Linear B** was an adaptation of Linear A, used by the MYCENAEAN CIVILIZATION of mainland Greece to write their early form of Greek. Linear B was used from c.1450 BC to the end of the Mycenaean period, c.1150 BC. In 1952, Michael Ventris deciphered Linear B; Linear A still defies analysis.

Lineker, Gary Winston (1960–) English footballer. A goal-poaching striker, he played for Leicester City (1976–85) and Everton (1985–86), before becoming the leading scorer in the 1986 World Cup finals in Mexico. He moved to Barcelona (1986–89), before following manager Terry VENABLES to Tottenham Hotspur (1989–92). Lineker scored 48 goals in 80 internationals, one goal short of Bobby CHARLTON's scoring record for England. In 1995, he retired from football and took up sports journalism.

linen Yarn and fabric made of fibres from the FLAX plant. The fibres are released from the substance that binds them by retting (soaking) the long stems in water. The fibres are spun to form yarn that is then woven.

ling Food fish related to the COD, found in the Atlantic Ocean. It is brown and silver and has long dorsal and ventral fins. Length: to 2m (7ft); weight: 3.6kg (8lb). Family Gadidae; species *Molva molva*.

lingua franca Language that serves as a medium of communication between people who otherwise lack a common tongue. A lingua franca may be a simplified form of the language of the dominant power, such as PIDGIN English, or it may be a hybrid, such as SWAHILI, which consists of words of both Arabic and Bantu origin.

linguistic philosophy Part of the tradition of ANALYTIC PHILOSOPHY, whose central principle is that the traditional problems of philosophy are merely confusions generated by the misuse of or misunderstandings about language. Ludwig WITTGENSTEIN's later work suggested that meaning in language lies in the rules for its use in ordinary life. These ideas were developed by J.L. Austin and Gilbert Ryle.

linguistics Systematic study of LANGUAGE, its nature, structure, constituent elements and changes. As a discipline, linguistics embraces PHONETICS, phonology (the study of sound systems within languages), GRAMMAR (including SYNTAX), SEMANTICS and pragmatics (the study of language use). *See also* CHOMSKY, NOAM; SAUSSURE, FERDINAND DE; STRUCTURALISM

Linnaeus, Carolus (1707–78) (Carl von Linné) Swedish botanist and taxonomist. His *Systema Naturae* (1735) laid the foundation of the modern science of TAXONOMY by including all known organisms in a single classification system. He devised the system of BINOMIAL NOMENCLATURE, which gave standardized Latin names to every organism. *See also* GENUS; SPECIES

linnet Small songbird of the family Carduelidae. *Carduelis cannabina* of Europe inhabits hedgerows and thickets, moving to open country in colder seasons. Both sexes are brown and grey, but the male has a red breast and crown in the summer. Length: to 13cm (5in).

linseed *See* FLAX

linseed oil Oil pressed from seeds of cultivated FLAX *(Linum usitatissimum)*. Because of its drying qualities, it is an important ingredient of oil paints and printing inks and is used to make VARNISH and linoleum.

Linz City and major port on the River Danube, NW Austria; capital of Upper Austria. Founded in Roman times as *Lentia*, it became a provincial capital of the Holy Roman Empire in the late 15th century. Austria's third-largest city, Linz is a commercial and industrial centre. Industries: iron and steel, chemicals, fertilizers. Pop. (1991) 203,044.

lion Large CAT that lives on African savannas south of the Sahara and on reserves in SW Asia. It is golden yellow with light spots under the eyes. The male has a deep neck mane. The smaller female does most of the hunting and preys on antelopes, zebras and bush pigs. Lions live in prides of four to 30 individuals. They travel and hunt mainly at twilight and can cover 48km (30mi) in a single night. Lionesses can reach speeds of 48km/h (30mph). Length of male: to 2.5m (8.5ft) including tail. Family Felidae; species *Panthera leo*.

Lipchitz, Jacques (1891–1973) French sculptor, b. Lithuania. He created one of the first cubist sculptures, *Man with Guitar* (1914). After moving to the USA in 1941, his work became more spiritual and more solid in structure. His works include *Sailor with a Guitar* (1914) and *Prayer* (1943). *See also* CUBISM

Li Peng (1928–) Chinese statesman, premier (1987–). He was adopted by ZHOU ENLAI after his father was executed by the KUOMINTANG. In 1983, he became deputy premier. In 1985, he joined the politburo. In 1989, Li Peng declared martial law during the pro-democracy demonstrations in TIANANMEN SQUARE, Beijing.

lipid One of a large group of fatty organic compounds in living organisms. They include animal fats, vegetable oils and natural waxes. Lipids form an important food store and energy source in plant and animal cells.

Lipmann, Fritz Albert (1899–1986) US biochemist, b. Germany. He isolated and partially explained the molecular structure of COENZYME A, derived from the B vitamin, pantothenic acid. For this and other work on metabolism, he shared the 1953 Nobel Prize for physiology or medicine with the biochemist Hans KREBS.

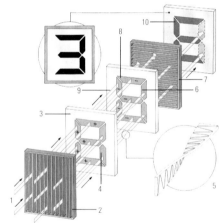

▲ **liquid crystal** Liquid-crystal displays use the property of liquid crystals to twist the polarization of light to produce numbers or symbols. Incoming light (1) is first regimented in one plane by a polarizer (2) before it passes through the first of two plates of glass (3) on which are fixed electrodes (4). Seven electrodes are needed to represent Arabic numerals. The liquid crystal lies between the two plates of glass (5) and twists light (5) passing through uncharged electrodes (6). This light can pass through the second polarizer (7) and can be seen. The light passing through the charged electrodes (8) is not twisted (9), is blocked by the polarizer, and cannot be seen forming the components of the number (10).

Li Po (AD 701–62) Chinese poet of the T'ANG dynasty. He was a Taoist, and the influence of TAOISM can be seen in the sensual and spiritual aspects of his work. He is said to have drowned while drunk.

Lippi, Filippino (1457–1504) Florentine painter, son of Fra Filippo LIPPI. He studied with BOTTICELLI. In 1484, Lippi completed the frescos of MASACCIO in Santa Maria del Carmine. His fresco cycles are in the Caraffa Chapel, Santa Maria sopra Minerva, Rome (1488–93), and the Strozzi Chapel, Santa Maria Novella, Florence. He also painted altarpieces.

Lippi, Fra Filippo (1406–69) Florentine painter. His early work shows the influence of MASACCIO, but from *c.*1440 he developed his own style. His most characteristic subject was the Virgin and Child. His finest fresco cycle (1452–64) depicts the lives of St Stephen and St John in Prato Cathedral. Lippi was a major influence on the 19th-century PRE-RAPHAELITE BROTHERHOOD.

Lippmann, Gabriel (1845–1921) French physicist. The first person to produce a colour photograph of the visible spectrum, he also invented the direct colour process of PHOTOGRAPHY. His work was important in the development of holograms. In 1908, he was awarded the Nobel Prize for physics. *See also* HOLOGRAPHY

liquid PHASE of MATTER intermediate between a GAS and a SOLID. A liquid substance has a relatively fixed volume but flows to take the shape of its container. A liquid at room temperature, such as water, can be changed into a vapour (its gaseous state, steam) by heating or into a solid (ice) by cooling.

liquid crystal Substance that can exist halfway between the liquid and solid states with its molecules partly ordered. By applying a carefully controlled electric current, liquid crystals turn dark. They are used in liquid crystal displays (LCDs) in pocket calculators.

liquorice (licorice) Perennial plant of the PEA family, native to the Mediterranean region and cultivated in temperate and sub-tropical areas. It bears spikes of blue flowers. The dried roots are used to flavour confectionery, tobacco and medicines. Height: to 90cm (3ft). Family Fabaceae/Leguminosae; species *Glycyrrhiza glabra*.

Lisbon (Lisboa) Capital, largest city and chief port of Portugal, at the mouth of the River TAGUS, on the Atlantic Ocean. An ancient Phoenician settlement, the city was conquered by the Romans in 205 BC and, after waves of Teutonic invasions in the 5th century AD, fell to the Moors in 716. In 1147, the Portuguese reclaimed Lisbon, and in 1260 it became the nation's capital. It declined under Spanish occupation (1580–1640). In 1755, the city was devastated by an earthquake. Lisbon is an international port and tourist centre. Sights include the 16th-century Tower of Belém and the 15th-century Jerónimos Monastery, built to commemorate Vasco da Gama's voyage to India. Industries: steel, shipbuilding, chemicals. Pop. (1991) 2,561,000.

Lissitzky, El (Eliezor) Markovich (1890–1941) Russian painter and designer. In the 1920s, MALEVICH inspired him to create a series of paintings (*Prouns*) that simulated 3-D architectonic constructs. He designed many books, including Mayakovsky's *For the Voice*. *See also* CONSTRUCTIVISM; SUPREMATISM

Lister, Joseph, 1st Baron (1827–1912) English surgeon who introduced the principle of antisepsis. Using carbolic acid (phenol) as the ANTISEPTIC agent, in conjunction with heat sterilization of instruments, he brought about a dramatic decrease in post-operative fatalities.

Liszt, Franz (1811–86) Hungarian composer and pianist, father-in law of Richard WAGNER. He was the greatest pianist of his generation. Liszt's challenging compositions for piano include *Transcendental Studies* (1851). He invented the SYMPHONIC POEM. Although his output was predominantly piano pieces, Liszt also wrote orchestral works, such as the *Faust Symphony* (1857), Hungarian rhapsodies and choral music. He was patron to Frédéric CHOPIN and Edvard GRIEG.

litany Prayer taking the form of a series of petitions and responses. A member of the clergy intones or speaks the petitions, to each of which the congregation replies with the same response, such as "pray for us". In the Anglican Church, a general supplication entitled "the Litany" is included in the BOOK OF COMMON PRAYER.

literary criticism Discipline concerned with literary theory and the evaluation of literary works. It effectively began with PLATO's comments on the role of poets in his *Republic*; ARISTOTLE's response to this, the *Poetics*, represents the first systematic attempt to establish principles of literary procedure. Notable later contributions to the debate include Sir Philip SIDNEY's *The Defence of Poesie* (1595); DRYDEN's *Of Dramatick Poesie* (1668); WORDSWORTH's preface to *Lyrical Ballads* (1798); SHELLEY's *A Defence of Poetry* (1820); and the critical works of Matthew ARNOLD, in particular, *Culture and Anarchy* (1869). The 20th century has seen an explosion of literary critical effort, such as the writings of T.S ELIOT, I.A. Richards, William EMPSON, and F.R. LEAVIS; also important are the writings of STRUCTURALISM and post-structuralism, notably Roland BARTHES, Michel FOUCAULT and Jacques DERRIDA. The late 20th century saw new critical approaches such as DECONSTRUCTION and FEMINISM.

literature Collections of writings, usually grouped according to language, period and country of origin (*see individual articles*). Within such groupings, literature may be subdivided into forms, such as POETRY and PROSE, and within these again into categories, such as verse DRAMA, NOVELS, EPIC poems, TRAGEDIES, COMEDIES, SATIRES and so on. *See also* LITERARY CRITICISM

lithium (symbol Li) Common silvery metallic element, one of the ALKALI METALS, first isolated in 1817. Ores include lepidolite and spodumene. Chemically it is similar to sodium. The element, which is the lightest of all metals, is used in alloys and in glasses and glazes; its salts are used in medicine. Properties at.no. 3; r.a.m. 6.941; r.d. 0.534; m.p. 180.5°C (356.9°F); b.p. 1,347°C (2,456.6°F); most stable isotope Li^7 (92.58%).

lithography In art, method of PRINTING from a flat inked surface. In traditional lithography, invented in the 1790s, the design is made on a prepared plate or stone with a greasy pencil, crayon or liquid. Water applied to the surface is absorbed where there is no design. Oil-based printing ink, rolled over the surface, sticks to the design but not to the moist areas. Pressing paper onto the surface produces a print.

lithosphere The upper layer of the solid EARTH; it includes the CRUST and the uppermost MANTLE. Its thickness varies but is *c.*60km (40mi); it extends to a depth of *c.*200km (125mi). It is made up of tectonic plates that move independently, giving rise to PLATE TECTONICS.

Lithuania Baltic republic in NW Europe; the capital is VILNIUS. **Land and climate** Lithuania is a mostly lowland country with SE highlands. Ice Age moraine covers most of Lithuania and includes more than 2,800 lakes. The longest river is the Neman, which rises in Belarus and flows through Lithuania to the Baltic Sea. Winters are cold: average January temperature, –5°C (23°F). Summers are warm: average July temperature 17°C (63°F). Average rainfall is *c.*630mm (25in). Farmland covers

---

LITHUANIA
AREA: 65,200sq km (25,200sq mi)
POPULATION: 3,935,000
CAPITAL (POPULATION): Vilnius (573,000)

---

*c.*75% of Lithuania, and forests only 16%. **History and politics** The first independent, unified Lithuanian state emerged in 1251 and by the 14th century had expanded E as far as Moscow. In 1386, Lithuania entered into a dynastic union with Poland. In 1569, the two countries were unified as a Commonwealth. The final partition of Poland saw Lithuania become part of the Russian empire (1795). In February 1918, Lithuania declared its independence. In 1920, it signed a peace treaty with the Soviet Union, and Poland captured Vilnius. In 1926, a military coup established a dictatorial government. In 1940 the Soviet Union annexed Lithuania as a Soviet republic. In 1941, German troops occupied Lithuania and many Lithuanian Jews were murdered. In 1944, Soviet troops recaptured the territory. In 1989, nationalist demands forced the Lithuanian Communist Party to agree to multiparty elections. The 1990 elections were won by the nationalists and Lithuania proclaimed its independence. In January 1991, Soviet troops and nationalist forces fought on the streets of Vilnius. A referendum voted overwhelmingly in favour of independence, and the Soviet Union recognized Lithuania as an independent republic in September 1991. The former Communist Party, the Democratic Labour Party, won 1992 elections. In 1993, Soviet troops completed their withdrawal. In 1996, Lithuania signed a treaty of association with the European Union (EU). Following 1996 elections, the Homeland Union and the Christian Democratic party formed a coalition government. In 1998, an independent candidate, Valdas Adamkus, was elected president. **Economy** Lithuania is a developing country (1995 GDP per capita, US$4,120). As a Russian republic, it rapidly industrialized. Since independence it has experienced many problems of transition from a command economy into a mixed economy. It lacks natural resources and is dependent on Russian raw materials. Manufacturing is the most valuable export sector: major products include chemicals, electronic goods and machine tools. Dairy and meat farming and fishing are also important activities.

litmus Dye that is purple in neutral aqueous solutions; it is used to indicate acidity (turning red) or alkalinity (turning blue). It is most familiar in the form of litmus paper used as an acid-base indicator. *See also* PH

litre (symbol l or L) Metric unit equal to a cubic decimetre, one thousandth of a cubic metre. Another definition, used from 1901–68, was that 1 litre equalled the volume of 1kg of pure water at 4°C (39°F). A litre is equivalent to 0.22 imperial gallons or 0.264 US gallons.

Little Bighorn, Battle of (25 June 1876) Victory of SIOUX and CHEYENNE Native Americans against the US cavalry led by Colonel George CUSTER. Sometimes known as "Custer's Last Stand", it was the last major victory of Native Americans against the US army. The cavalry regiment of 225 men was annihilated by the Sioux, led by SITTING BULL and CRAZY HORSE, near the Little Bighorn River in Montana.

Little Entente (1920–38) Alliance between Romania, Yugoslavia and Czechoslovakia after World War 1 to maintain post-war boundaries. It helped to prevent ANSCHLUSS (uniting of Germany and Austria) until 1938.

Little Richard (1935–) US singer-songwriter and pianist, b. Richard Penniman. He achieved fame in the late 1950s with songs such as "Tutti Frutti" (1956) and "Good Golly Miss Molly" (1958). After a near-fatal plane accident, he was ordained a minister in the Church of the Seventh Day Adventists and has oscillated between music and ministry ever since.

Little Rock Capital and largest city of Arkansas, USA, on the Arkansas River. Founded in 1814, it became the state capital in 1821. In 1957, federal troops enforced a US Supreme Court ruling against racial segregation in schools. Industries: electronics, textiles. Pop. (1992) 176,870.

Litvinov, Maxim Maximovich (1876–1951) Russian revolutionary and diplomat. In 1903, he joined the Bolsheviks and participated in the RUSSIAN REVOLUTION OF 1905. As foreign minister (1930–39) for the Soviet Union, Litvinov pursued a policy of collective security and cooperation with the West and gained American recognition (1933) of the new state. His anti-Nazi stance led to his replacement as foreign minister by MOLOTOV. He served (1941–43) as ambassdor to the United States.

liturgy Established order of the rituals of public ceremonies and worship of an organized religion. In Christianity, the term also refers to the Divine Office or to the rites proper to specific days, such as GOOD FRIDAY, or to particular sacraments, such as BAPTISM. In the Eastern Orthodox Church, the Divine Liturgy refers specifically to the celebration of the Eucharist.

Liu Shaoqi (1898–1974) (Liu Shao-ch'i) Chinese staesman, chairman (1959–68) of the People's Republic of China. A leader of the trades union movement, he was the chief theorist of the early Chinese COMMUNIST PARTY. In 1949, he was appointed chief vice-chairman of the party. In 1959, Liu became second-in-command to MAO ZEDONG. He was purged during the CULTURAL REVOLUTION and died in prison.

Lively, Penelope (1933–) British novelist, b. Egypt. Lively has written many children's books, including *The Ghost of Thomas Kempe* (1973) and *A Stitch in Time* (1976). Her first work for adults was *The Road to Lichfield* (1977). *Moon Tiger* (1987) won the Booker Prize. Other novels include *According to Mark* (1984), *City of the Mind* (1991) and *Cleopatra's Sister* (1993).

liver Large organ located in the upper right abdomen of VERTEBRATES. Weighing up to 2kg (4.5lbs) in an adult human, it is divided into four lobes and has many functions. It is extremely important in the control of the body's internal environment (HOMEOSTASIS). It receives nutrients from the INTESTINE and is a site of METABOLISM of proteins, carbohydrates and fats. It synthesizes BILE and some vitamins, regulates the BLOOD-glucose level, produces blood-clotting factors, breaks down worn-out ERYTHROCYTES and removes toxins from the blood. Its many metabolic reactions are the body's main source of heat, distributed by the blood. *See also* INSULIN

Liverpool, Robert Banks Jenkinson, 2nd Earl of (1770–1828) British statesman, prime minister (1812–27). He entered Parliament in 1790. Liverpool served as home secretary (1804–06, 1807–09) and secretary for war and the colonies (1809–12) before becoming Tory prime minister. His government oversaw the end of the NAPOLEONIC WARS and the WAR OF 1812 with the USA. Liverpool resisted political reform and the CATHOLIC EMANCIAPTION. He suspended HABEAS CORPUS after the PETERLOO MASSACRE (1819).

Liverpool City and seaport on the N side of the River Mersey estuary, Merseyside, NW England. Liverpool was founded in the 10th century and became a free borough in 1207. The first wet dock was completed in 1715, and the city expanded rapidly to become Britain's largest

Llywelyn ap Iorwerth

port. In the early 20th century, it was the major embarkation port for emigration to the New World. Liverpool suffered severe bomb damage during World War 2. The construction (1972) of a container terminal and the completion of a rail tunnel link with Birkenhead improved the city's trade and transport links. In the 1980s, inner-city regeneration schemes included the Albert Dock refurbishment. Liverpool Free Port (Britain's largest) was opened in 1984. The sixth-largest city in England and the principal Atlantic port, Liverpool has more than 800ha (2,000 acres) of dockland. Pop. (1994) 664,000.

liverwort Any of *c*.9,000 species of tiny non-flowering green plants that, like the related mosses, lack specialized tissues to transport water, food and minerals. Liverworts belong to the plant phylum Bryophyta.

Livingstone, David (1813–73) Scottish explorer of Africa. In 1841 he went to South Africa as a missionary and became famous through his account of a journey (1853–56) across Africa from Angola to Mozambique. In 1866 he set off to find the source of the Nile. Livingstone disappeared and was found in 1871 by Henry Morton STANLEY on Lake Tanganyika.

Livy (59 BC–AD 17) (Titus Livius). One of the greatest Roman historians. He began his *History of Rome c.*28 BC. Of the original 142 books, 35 have survived in full.

lizard REPTILE found on every continent; there are 20 families, *c*.3,000 species. Most have a scaly cylindrical body with four legs, a long tail and moveable eyelids. Some species such as GLASS SNAKES, SLOW WORMS and some SKINKS, have reduced or absent limbs. Most lizards are terrestrial, and many live in deserts. There are also semi-aquatic and arboreal forms. Many lizards have an autotomic defence mechanism – they shed their tail when attacked. Most lay eggs rather than bear live young. They feed mainly on insects and vegetation. They range in size from the *c*.5cm (2in) GECKO to the 3m (10ft) KOMODO DRAGON. Order Squamata; sub-order Sauria. *See also* CHAMELEON; GECKO; IGUANA; MONITOR

Ljubljana (Laibach) Capital and largest city of Slovenia, at the confluence of the rivers Sava and Ljubljanica. Ljubljana was founded, as Emona, by the Roman Emperor Augustus in 34 BC. From 1244, it was the capital of Carniola, an Austrian province of the Habsburg Empire. During the 19th century, it was the centre of the Slovene nationalist movement. The city remained under Austrian rule until 1918, when it became part of the kingdom of Serbs, Croats and Slovenes (later Yugoslavia). When Slovenia achieved independence (1991), Ljubljana became the capital. Industries: textiles, paper and printing. Pop. (1996) 270,000.

llama Domesticated South American even-toed, ruminant mammal. It has been used as a beast of burden by Native Americans for more than 1,000 years. It has a long woolly coat and slender limbs and neck. The smaller alpaca is bred for its wool. Family Camelidae; genus *Lama*.

Lloyd, Harold (1893–1971) US film actor. In 1914, he was hired by Hal ROACH to star in short comedies. Lloyd modelled himself on Charlie CHAPLIN, but added death-defying stunts, such as hanging from a clockface in *Safety Last* (1923). His success waned with the arrival of "talkies", and his final film was *Mad Wednesday* (1947).

Lloyd George, David (1863–1945) British statesman, prime minister (1916–22). A Welsh Liberal, he entered Parliament in 1890. As chancellor of the exchequer (1908–15), Lloyd George increased taxation to pay for social measures such as old-age pensions. His "People's Budget" (1909) provoked a constitutional crisis that led to a reduction of the powers of the House of Lords. He was an effective minister of munitions (1915) during World

War 1. In 1916, he led a cabinet rebellion to dislodge the prime minister, Herbert ASQUITH. Lloyd George led a coalition government with the Conservatives for the rest of the war. In 1918, he won an easy electoral victory and was a leading figure at the peace conference at VERSAILLES. In 1921, he negotiated with SINN FÉIN to create the Irish Free State and the Conservatives withdrew their support. He was succeeded as prime minister by BONAR LAW.

Lloyd's Insurance market in London dealing especially in marine insurance. Lloyd's began in the 17th century as a coffee house, where businessmen willing to insure shipping gathered. Lloyd's as an institution does not insure anything; it is merely the market where individual underwriters (known as "names" and grouped in syndicates) can meet. Between 1988 and 1993, some syndicates sustained substantial losses, leading to a change in the regulation of names, allowing some to have limited liability.

Lloyd Webber, Andrew (1948–) British composer. He composed *Joseph and the Amazing Technicolor Dreamcoat* (1967) while still a student. The lyricist, Tim Rice, was also his collaborator on the rock opera *Jesus Christ Superstar* (1971) and the musical *Evita* (1978). *Cats* (1981) was a long-running hit, as were *The Phantom of the Opera* (1986) and *Sunset Boulevard* (1993). His brother **Julian** (1951–), is a highly respected cellist.

Llywelyn ap Gruffydd (d.1282) (Llywelyn the Last) Prince of Wales, grandson of LLYWELYN AP IORWERTH. Allied with the rebellious English barons, he gained control of much territory and was recognized as Prince of Wales by the Treaty of Montgomery (1267). The accession of EDWARD III brought his ruin. In 1282, he renewed his rebellion and was killed in battle.

Llywelyn ap Iorwerth (1173–1240) (Llywelyn the Great) Welsh prince of Gwynedd. He captured Mold from the English (1199) and established his suzerainty in Gwynedd, then gained control of Powys. He allied himself with the English barons against John and was recognized as suzerain by all the Welsh princes.

▲ **llama** Domesticated for more than a thousand years, llama (*Lama peruana*, shown) are used primarily as pack animals in s and w South America, from sea level to elevations of 5,000m (16,500ft). They thrive in a semi-desert habitat feeding on mountain grass. They grow to 1.2m (4ft) long and to a height at the shoulder of 1.2m (4ft).

Loach, Ken (1936–) English film and television director. His first television drama, *Cathy Come Home* (1966), received both acclaim and criticism for its realistic portrayal of homelessness. Many of his films, such as *Kes* (1971), *Riff Raff* (1991), *Raining Stones* (1993) and *My Name is Joe* (1998), focus on working-class Britain and reflect Loach's socialist perspective. Other films include *Hidden Agenda* (1990), about Northern Ireland, and *Land and Freedom* (1995), about the Spanish Civil War.

loach Small freshwater fish in mountain streams of Asia and Europe; there are more than 200 species. British loaches are the stone loach (*Nemachilus barbatula*) and the spined loach (*Cobitis taenia*).

Lobachevsky, Nikolai Ivanovich (1793–1856) Russian mathematician. In 1826, he announced the creation of one of the first comprehensive systems of non-Euclidean GEOMETRY. *See also* EUCLID; RELATIVITY

lobelia Genus of 365 species of flowering plants found worldwide, mainly used for bedding plants. The flowers may be blue, red or white and irregularly shaped, and the leaves are simple. Family Lobeliaceae.

lobotomy *See* LEUCOTOMY

lobster Large, long-tailed, marine decapod CRUSTACEAN. True lobsters (Homaridae) possess enlarged bulbous chelae (claws) and a segmented body. Some species are prized edible shellfish. They live in rocky crevices at the bottom of the ocean, feeding at night on seaweed and animals. Weight: up to 23kg (50lbs).

local government System of regional administration differing in each country. The systems that developed in France, the former Soviet Union and England have served as models for much of the rest of the world. Local government in England developed from the Municipal Reform Act (1835), which first established elected councils in cities; the Local Government Act (1888) set up county

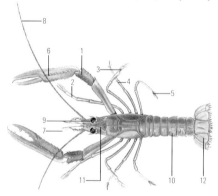

▲ **lobster** The Norway lobster (*Nephrops norvegicus*), a small burrowing form up to 20cm (8in) long found off NE Atlantic coasts, is a typical crustacean. With the crabs, crayfish, prawns, and shrimps, it is classified in a sub-group of the order Decapoda ("10 legs") called the Reptantia ("walking", although they are able to swim short distances). The

legs are borne in pairs (1–5), the first of which is enlarged to form nipping claws (chelae) (6). Of the two pairs of antennae (7, 8), the second may be far longer than the body. With the eyes (9), the antennae are the principal sense organs. The body segments are visible only on the abdomen (10) for the thorax is covered by a shell (carapace) (11). The tail (12) is a fan shape.

councils elsewhere. In 1974, a two-tier system was established in England, Scotland and Wales, with counties subdivided into districts, each with an elected council. Some metropolitan counties were abolished in 1986 and replaced by a single tier of smaller local borough councils.

Local Group Small group of about 30 galaxies that includes our GALAXY, the two MAGELLANIC CLOUDS, the ANDROMEDA GALAXY and the Triangulum spiral. They are distributed over a roughly ellipsoidal space *c*.5 million light-years across. The members are gravitationally bound, so that, unlike more distant galaxies, they are not receding from us or from each other.

Locarno Pact (1925) Group of international agreements that attempted to solve problems of European security outstanding since the Treaty of VERSAILLES of 1919. The pact established Germany's W borders and enabled Germany to enter the LEAGUE OF NATIONS. The general peace established at Locarno was soon disturbed by HITLER.

loch (Scot. lake) *See individual gazetteer articles*

Lochner, Stefan (1410–51) German painter. His most important surviving work is *The Adoration of the Magi* (*c*.1448), which is now in Cologne Cathedral, Germany. DÜRER gazed "with wonder and astonishment" at the delicate naturalism of his style.

lock Structure built into a stretch of inland waterway to raise or lower water levels. Each lock consists of two sets of lock gates. A vessel enters the lock, the gates are closed and sluices are opened to admit or release enough water to bring the vessel to the same level as the water beyond the second pair of gates.

Locke, John (1632–1704) English philosopher. His friendship with the Earl of SHAFTESBURY, accused of conspiracy against CHARLES II, made him a target of suspicion and he went into exile in the Netherlands (1683–89). Locke returned to England only after the GLORIOUS REVOLUTION. His *Essay Concerning Human Understanding* (1690) is regarded as the founding text of EMPIRICISM. Locke rejected the concept of "innate ideas" and held that all knowledge is gained from sense-experience. He is chiefly remembered for his political theory of LIBERALISM expounded in *Two Treatises on Civil Government* (1690). Locke argued that all men had equal rights to "life, health, liberty, or possessions". He rejected the divine right of kings, advocating that the state, guided by NATURAL LAW, be formed by SOCIAL CONTRACT.

lockjaw *See* TETANUS

Lockyer, Sir (Joseph) Norman (1836–1920) English astronomer. In 1868, 40 years before its discovery on Earth, he detected HELIUM in the Sun's atmosphere. In 1869, Lockyer founded the scientific journal *Nature*.

locomotive Engine that draws a train, usually on a RAILWAY. In 1804, English engineer Richard TREVITHICK built the first STEAM ENGINE locomotive for transporting heavy loads at an ironworks. The first steam locomotive providing a railway service for passengers was George Stephenson's *Locomotion*, built in 1825. Electric-powered locomotives arrived in the late 19th century. Diesel, diesel-electric and gas-turbine locomotives were introduced in the 20th century.

locus In geometry, the path of a specified point when it moves to satisfy certain conditions. A circle is the locus of a point in a plane moving in such a way that its distance from a fixed point (the centre) is constant.

locust Insect (a type of GRASSHOPPER) that migrates in huge swarms. They may contain up to 40 billion insects, and cover an area of *c*.1,000sq km (385sq mi). Length: 12.5–100mm (0.5–4in). Order Orthoptera; species *Schistocerca gregaria*.

Łódź Second-largest city in Poland, *c.*120km (75mi) SW of Warsaw. A small market town until the 19th century, Łódź grew under Russian occupation after 1820 to become the centre of the Polish textile industry. Taken by the Russians in 1815, the town was returned to Poland in 1918. Industries; textiles, machinery. Pop. (1996) 826,000.

loess Fine-grained clay, a sedimentary material made up of rock fragments. It is earthy, porous and crumbly, usually yellowish or brown in colour. Loess consists of mainly quartz and calcite from glaciated areas, blown by the wind and often built up into thick layers. The largest expanse is in the Huang He valley, N China.

Logan, Mount Peak in the St Elias Mountains, SW Yukon, Canada. At 6,050m (19,849ft), it is the highest in Canada and second-highest in North America.

loganberry Biennial, hybrid, red-berried bramble. A cross between the BLACKBERRY and RASPBERRY, it is disease-prone and is grown only in sheltered areas. Family Rosaceae; species *Rubus ursinus loganobaccus*.

logarithm Aid to calculation devised by John NAPIER in 1614 and developed by the English mathematician Henry Briggs. A number's logarithm is the power to which a base must be raised to equal the number, i.e. if $b^x = n$, then $\log_b n = x$, where n is the number, b the base, and x the logarithm. Common logarithms have base 10, and so-called natural logarithms have base e (2.71828...). Logarithms to the base 2 are used in computer science and information theory.

logic Branch of philosophy that deals with the processes of valid reasoning and argument. Logic defines the way in which one thing may be said to follow from, or be consequent upon, another. This is known as **deductive** logic. **Inductive** logic, in which a general conclusion is drawn from a particular fact or facts, is the preserve of science. Although logical systems were devised in China and India, the history of logic in the West began in the 4th century BC with the Greek philosopher ARISTOTLE. In the Middle Ages, Pierre ABELARD used logic in the synthesis of ideas, the goal of SCHOLASTICISM. Various post-Renaissance scholars, including LEIBNIZ, developed the foundations of modern logic. **Symbolic**, or mathematical, logic was outlined in the 19th century by George BOOLE and developed by Gottlob FREGE. Modern formal logic or symbolic logic utilizes symbols to represent precisely defined classes of proposition connected to each other by such operators as "and", "or", "if... then."

logical positivism Early 20th-century school of philosophy whose adherents consider that only empirically verifiable scientific propositions are meaningful. Its roots were in the LOGIC of Gottlob FREGE and Bertrand RUSSELL, the POSITIVISM of Ernst Mach and, above all, the claim of Ludwig WITTGENSTEIN that philosophy was the clarification of thought.

logos In philosophy, intellect or reason; in a larger sense the rational principle that orders the universe. As used in the New Testament Gospel of St John, the Greek word *logos* was in the Authorized Version translated as "the Word". The Word can be either the intention of God (His rational principle) or the outward expression of that intention – both describing JESUS CHRIST.

Loire Longest river in France. The Loire rises in the Cévennes range, on the SE edge of the MASSIF CENTRAL, and flows N and NW to Orléans. It then turns SW into a wide, fertile basin. The cities of TOURS and Angers lie on its banks. It then flows through the Pays de la Loire to NANTES, emptying into the Bay of BISCAY at St-Nazaire. It is connected by a series of canals to the RHÔNE and SEINE rivers. Length: 1,020km (635mi).

Lollards Followers of the 14th-century English religious reformer John WYCLIFFE. They helped to pave the way for the REFORMATION and challenged many doctrines and practices of the medieval church, including TRANSUBSTANTIATION, clerical celibacy and the authority of the PAPACY. They went among the people as "poor preachers", teaching that the Bible was the sole authority in religion. After 1401, many Lollards were burned as heretics, and in 1414 they had an unsuccessful uprising in London and then went underground.

Lombard League Defensive alliance of the cities of Lombardy in N Italy (1167). Its purpose was to resist the re-establishment of imperial authority by FREDERICK I. Led by Pope ALEXANDER III, the league defeated the emperor at Legnano (1176). By the Peace of Constance in 1183, the cities retained independence. The league was active again in 1226 against FREDERICK II.

Lombards Germanic peoples who inhabited the area E of the lower River Elbe until driven W by the Romans in AD 9. In 568 they invaded N Italy under Alboin and conquered much of the country, adopting Catholicism and Latin customs. The Lombard kingdom reached its peak under Liutprand (d.744). It went into decline after defeat by the Franks under CHARLEMAGNE (775).

Lombardy (Lombardia) Region in N Italy, bordering Switzerland in the N; the capital is MILAN. Lombardy is Italy's most populous and industrial region. It is divided into the provinces of Bergamo, Brescia, Como, Cremona, Mantova, Milano, Pavia, Sondrio and Varese. North Lombardy is an Alpine region with many lakes. South Lombardy is dominated by the fertile plain of the River Po. The plains have been a major European battleground. Area: 23,834sq km (9,202sq mi). Pop. (1991) 8,856,074.

Lomé Capital and largest city of the Republic of Togo, W Africa, on the Gulf of Guinea. Made capital of German Togoland in 1897, it later became an important commercial centre. It was the site of conferences in 1975 and 1979 that produced a trade agreement (known as the Lomé Convention) between the European Community and 46 African, Caribbean and Pacific states. Its main exports are coffee and cocoa. Pop. (1992) 590,000.

Lomond, Loch Long, narrow lake in Strathclyde and Central regions, W central Scotland. It is drained by the River Leven into the Firth of Clyde. The largest Scottish loch, it is 37km (21mi) long and 190m (625ft) deep at its deepest part. It is dominated at the N end by Ben Lomond (height: 973m/3,192ft). Area: 70sq km (27.5sq mi).

London, Jack (1876–1916) US novelist and short-story writer, b. John Griffith Chaney. He is best known for his Alaskan novels, such as *Call of the Wild* (1903) and *White Fang* (1906).

London Capital of the United Kingdom and (after Moscow) the second-largest city in Europe, located on both banks of the River THAMES, 65km (40mi) from its mouth in the North Sea, SE England. Since 1965 it has been officially called Greater London: comprising the square mile of the City of London and 13 inner and 19 outer boroughs, covering a total of 1,580sq km (610sq mi). Little is known of London before the Romans set up camp in the 1st century AD. Called *Londinium*, it was their most important town in Britain, developing as a port and commercial centre. By the 3rd century, the population numbered *c.*40,000. After the Romans left Britain, London declined until the 9th century, when ALFRED THE GREAT made it the seat of government. Edward the Confessor built WESTMINSTER ABBEY and made WESTMINSTER his capital in 1042. The prosperity of England during the Tudor period firmly established London's wealth and importance. In the reign of Elizabeth I, the population increased from fewer than 100,000 to *c*.250,000. During the 17th century, the area between Westminster and the City was built up. The plague of 1665 killed 75,000 Londoners. In 1666, the FIRE OF LONDON destroyed many buildings. Sir Christopher WREN played an important role in the reconstruction of the city, designing many churches, including ST PAUL'S. During the 19th century, the population reached 4 million. By the end of the century, London was the world's biggest city. Much of E London was rebuilt after bomb damage during World War 2, and in the late 1980s the largely derelict docklands were rapidly developed. London remains one of the world's most important administrative, financial, commercial and industrial cities. Industries: tourism, entertainment, engineering, chemicals, paper, printing and publishing, clothing, brewing. Pop. (1994) 6,966,800. *See also* DOWNING STREET; GREENWICH; HAMPTON COURT PALACE; HOUSES OF PARLIAMENT; INNS OF COURT; LLOYD'S; NATIONAL THEATRE; ROYAL OPERA HOUSE; TUSSARD, MADAME

London, University of University in London, England, founded in 1836, originally comprising King's College and University College. The university now comprises 14 colleges, 6 medical schools and 11 postgraduate medical institutions, as well as various other academic institutes.

Londonderry *See* DERRY

Longfellow, Henry Wadsworth (1807–82) US poet. He is chiefly remembered for his narrative poems, such as *Evangeline* (1847), *The Song of Hiawatha* (1855), *The Courtship of Miles Standish* (1858) and *Tales of a Wayside Inn* (1863), which includes "Paul Revere's Ride". Influenced by European romanticism, Longfellow combined archaic rhythms to enliven American mythology. *Ballads and Other Poems* (1842) contains two of his most popular shorter poems, "The Wreck of the Hesperus" and "The Village Blacksmith".

Longhi, Pietro (1702–85) Italian painter. He devoted himself chiefly to small-scale genre pictures, especially scenes of the domestic manners of the Venetian middle classes, such as *The Exhibition of a Rhinoceros at Venice*.

longhorn Almost extinct breed of beef cattle, originally from Mexico, descended from European cattle introduced by Spanish conquistadors. They are now used only as rodeo and show animals.

Long Island Island in SE New York State, USA, bounded on the S by the Atlantic Ocean and separated from Manhattan by the East River and from Connecticut by Long Island Sound. Originally inhabited by the Delaware Native Americans, it was settled by the Dutch West India Company and the Massachusetts Bay Colony in the 17th century. About 190km (120mi) long, it has commuter towns, light industry, fishing and holiday resorts. Area: 4,463sq km (1,723sq mi). Pop. (1990) 6,861,454.

longitude Angular measurement around the Earth, usually in degrees E or W of an imaginary N–S line through the prime MERIDIAN at Greenwich, London. All N–S lines either meridians or lines of longitude. *See also* LATITUDE

long jump Field event in which competitors run up to a take-off board and try to leap the farthest. The length of the jump is measured from the forward edge of the board to the nearest imprint the jumper leaves in the sandpit.

Long March (1934–35) Enforced march of the Chinese RED ARMY during the war against the Nationalist (KUOMINTANG) forces. Led by Zhu De and MAO ZEDONG, 90,000 communist troops, accompanied by *c*.15,000 civilians, broke through a Nationalist encirclement of their headquarters and marched some 10,000km (6,000mi) from Jiangxi province, SE China,

to Shanxi province in the NW. Under frequent attack, they suffered 45,000 casualties. The march prevented the extermination of the Chinese COMMUNIST PARTY.

Long Parliament English Parliament initially summoned by CHARLES I in November 1640. It followed the SHORT PARLIAMENT, which lasted only weeks. Antagonism between Charles and Parliament resulted in the outbreak of the English CIVIL WARS. The Long Parliament sat, with intervals, for 20 years. Oliver CROMWELL expelled hostile members in PRIDE'S PURGE (1648), and thereafter it was known as the RUMP PARLIAMENT.

long-sightedness (hypermetropia) Defect of vision that causes distant objects to be seen more clearly than nearby ones. In a long-sighted person, the focusing distance of the eyeball is too short and, as a result, light rays entering the eye strike the retina before they can be properly focused. Long-sightedness is corrected by convex lenses. *See also* MYOPIA

loom Frame or set of frames on which threads are woven into cloth. The loom enables a set of threads, called the weft, to be passed over and under a set of lengthwise threads, called the warp. The simplest kind of loom is a single frame on which WEAVING is done by hand. Such looms have been used for more than 7,000 years. In 1785, Edmund CARTWRIGHT invented a loom powered by a steam engine to speed cloth production. Today, most advanced commercial looms are computer-controlled and have mechanisms that thread the weft through the warp at speeds of *c*.100km/h (60mph).

loon (diver) Diving bird of the Northern Hemisphere, known for its harsh call. It has black, white and grey plumage. An excellent swimmer, it often stays submerged while fishing. Length: 88cm (35in). Family Gaviidae.

Loos, Adolf (1870–1933) Czech architect, a pioneer of MODERNISM. His rationalist designs were informed by Louis SULLIVAN and the Chicago School. His austere style, stripped of ornamentation, is evident in Steiner House and Michaelerplatz, Vienna (both 1910). Loos influenced the development of FUNCTIONALISM and the INTERNATIONAL STYLE.

Loran (**Lo**ng **ra**nge **n**avigation) RADIO system of NAVIGATION for ships and aircraft. Pairs of transmitters emit signal pulses that are picked up by a receiver. By measuring the difference in time between the signals reaching the receiver, the vessel's position can be plotted.

Lorca, Federico García (1898–1936) Spanish poet and dramatist. His poetry, ranging from *Gypsy Ballads* (1928) to *The Poet in New York* (1940), was internationally acclaimed. In the theatre, his early farces gave way to tragedies such as the trilogy *Blood Wedding* (1933), *Yerma* (1935) and *The House of Bernarda Alba* (1936). He was killed by nationalists in the Spanish CIVIL WAR.

lord chancellor Head of the British legal system, an office of cabinet rank. His duties include acting as head of the judiciary and as speaker of the House of Lords.

Lord's CRICKET ground in London, England. Founded by Thomas Lord in 1787, it has been at its present location in St John's Wood since 1814. It is the home of Marylebone Cricket Club (MCC) and Middlesex County Cricket Club. Since 1884, every test series in England has included a match at Lord's.

Lord's Prayer Prayer JESUS CHRIST taught his disciples. Found in Matthew 6:9–13 and, slightly differently, in Luke 11:2–4. It is also called *Pater Noster* (Lat. Our Father).

Lorelei Large rock in the River Rhine near Sankt, Goarshausen, W Germany. According to legend, a beautiful maiden called Lorelei drowned herself in despair over her faithless lover, only to rise as a siren to lure fishermen to their doom on the rock.

Loren, Sophia (1934–) Italian film actress. Her sensuous performance in *The Black Orchid* (1959) set Hollywood alight. Loren won an Academy Award for best actress in *Two Women* (1960). Other films include *Marriage Italian Style* (1964).

Lorentz, Hendrik Antoon (1853–1928) Dutch physicist. His early work was concerned with the theory of ELECTROMAGNETIC RADIATION devised by James Clerk MAXWELL. This led him to the **Lorentz transformation** (connecting the space and time co-ordinates of an event as observed from two frames of reference) and the prediction of the **Lorentz-Fitzgerald contraction** (objects change length due to their movement relative to the observer), both of which helped Albert EINSTEIN to develop his special theory of RELATIVITY. Lorentz also worked on the ZEEMAN EFFECT, for which he and Pieter Zeeman were awarded the 1902 Nobel Prize for physics. *See also* FITZGERALD, GEORGE FRANCIS

Lorenz, Konrad Zacharias (1903–89) Austrian zoologist, a founder of ETHOLOGY. He observed that INSTINCT played a major role in animal behaviour, as for example in IMPRINTING. In 1973, he shared, with N. TINBERGEN and K. von FRISCH, the Nobel Prize for physiology or medicine.

loris Any of several species of primitive, tailless, tree-dwelling, nocturnal PRIMATES of S Asia and the East Indies. They have soft, thick fur and large eyes, and feed mainly on insects. Length: 18–38cm (7–15in). Family Lorisidae; genera *Loris* and *Nycticebus*.

Lorrain, Claude *See* CLAUDE LORRAIN

Lorraine (Ger. Lothringen) Region of NE France, bounded N by Belgium, Germany and Luxembourg, E by ALSACE, S by FRANCHE-COMTÉ and E by CHAMPAGNE. The capital is Mietz. Lorraine is divided into four departments. In the 10th century it was divided into two duchies, Upper and Lower Lorraine. In 1766, it became a French province. In 1871, E Lorraine was joined to form the German territory of Alsace-Lorraine, which was returned to France in 1919. The area was again disputed during World War 2. Industries: brewing, winemaking. It also has rich iron ore deposits. Area: 23,547sq km (9,089sq mi). Pop. (1990) 2,305,700. *See also* LOTHARINGIA

Los Alamos Town in New Mexico, USA, site of a large scientific laboratory. During World War 2 the laboratory was one of the centres for the MANHATTAN PROJECT, which produced the first NUCLEAR WEAPON. After the war, the laboratory developed the HYDROGEN BOMB.

Los Angeles, Victoria de (1923–) Spanish soprano. In 1949 she made her debut at the Paris Opéra and La Scala, Milan. In 1950 she made her American debut at Carnegie Hall and joined the Metropolitan Opera Company.

Los Angeles (City of Angels) City on the Pacific coast, SW California, USA; the second-largest US city (after New York City) and the nation's leading manufacturing base. The city was founded in 1781 by Mexican settlers. At the conclusion of the MEXICAN WAR (1848), the USA acquired Los Angeles. The city grew with the completion of the Southern Pacific (1876) and Santa Fe (1885) railways. The discovery of oil (1894) and the development of the HOLLYWOOD film and television industry encouraged further growth. During World War 2 the city's industry boomed with the need for aircraft and munitions, and many African Americans migrated to the city to work in the factories. In 1965, five days of riots in the Watts district left 34 dead and US$200 million damages. In 1992, the acquittal of four policemen on a charge of beating an African American suspect sparked off further race riots, which left 58 dead and US$1 billion damages. A 1994 earthquake killed 57 people and caused US$15–30 billion of damage. Air pollution is also a major problem. Greater Los Angeles sprawls over 1,200sq km (465sq mi) joined by a freeway network. More than 600,000 Mexican-Americans live here, more than in any other US city, the majority in the overcrowded barrio of E Los Angeles. More than 500,000 African Americans also live in the city, concentrated especially in the S central district of Watts. Central Los Angeles consists mainly of Hollywood. Beverley Hills is known for its opulent homes. Greater Los Angeles includes ANAHEIM (home of Disneyland) and Santa Monica. Industries: tourism, aerospace, film and television, oil refining, electronic equipment. Pop. (1990) 3,489,779.

Lost Generation Designation for disillusioned expatriate American intellectuals, writers and artists after World War 1. The term is attributed to a remark ("You are all of a lost generation") made by Gertrude STEIN to Ernest HEMINGWAY. Other Lost Generation writers include F. Scott FITZGERALD, Ezra POUND and John DOS PASSOS.

Lot Biblical character who was living in SODOM at the time when God decided to destroy it (Genesis 11:31–14:16. 19). Lot survived, but his wife looked back at the city and was turned into a pillar of salt.

Lothair I (795–855) Frankish emperor (840–55), eldest son of LOUIS I. He was co-emperor with his father from 817. War broke out on the death of Louis (840) between Lothair and his two brothers. Lothair was defeated at Fontenoy (841), and the Frankish empire was divided in three by the Treaty of Verdun (843). Lothair retained the title of emperor and ruled the Middle Kingdom, consisting of the Low Countries, N France, Switzerland and N Italy.

Lothair II (826–869) King of Lotharingia (855–869), son of LOTHAIR I. He inherited LOTHARINGIA (Lorraine) from his father, and the kingdom of Provence from his brother (863).

Lotharingia Part of CHARLEMAGNE's empire inherited by his descendant LOTHAIR II, after whom it is named. Roughly, Lotharingia included modern LORRAINE (whose name is itself a corruption of Lotharingia), Alsace, NW Germany, Luxembourg, Belgium and the Netherlands.

Lothian Region in E central Scotland, bounded N by the Firth of Forth, E by the North Sea and S by the Lammermuir, Moorfoot and Pentland Hills; the capital is EDINBURGH. Industries: coal-mining, engineering, whisky distilling. Area: 1,755sq km (677sq mi). Pop. (1991) 726,000.

lottery Form of gambling whereby participants pay to enter and winners are picked by a method based on chance. This method often involves participants choosing numbers. They win if their numbers correspond to numbers picked randomly by the lottery organizer during a subsequent draw.

Lotto, Lorenzo (1480–1556) Italian painter. Lotto's painting was very inconsistent, but the best examples, such as *The Crucifixion* (*c*.1528) at Monte San Giusto, Bergamo, show great freshness of observation and psychological insight.

lotus Common name for WATER LILIES of the genus *Nelumbo* and several tropical species of the genus *Nymphaea*. The circular leaves and flowers of some species may be 60cm (2ft) across. Family Nymphaeaceae. The genus *Lotus* is made up of the trefoils of the unrelated Fabaceae/Leguminosae family.

loudspeaker Device for converting changing electric currents into sound. The most common type has a moving coil attached to a stiff paper cone suspended in a strong MAGNETIC FIELD. By ELECTROMAGNETIC INDUCTION, the changing currents in the coil cause the cone to vibrate, thus creating sound waves. Many modern loudspeakers give faithful sound reproduction between 80 and 20,000 hertz. *See also* MICROPHONE; SOUND RECORDING

Louis I (the Pious) (778–840) Emperor of the Franks (814–840), only surviving son of CHARLEMAGNE. He struggled to maintain his father's empire. Louis' attempts to provide an inheritance for his four sons provoked civil war.

Louis II (the German) (*c*.804–876) King of the East Franks (843–876), son of LOUIS I (THE PIOUS). His brother, LOTHAIR I, became emperor in 840, but Louis and another brother, Charles, forced him to divide the empire in three by the Treaty of Verdun (843). Louis received the lands extending from the Rhine to the E frontier of the empire, essentially those that later formed Germany. He has been regarded as the founder of the German kingdom.

Louis IV (the Bavarian) (*c*.1287–1347) Duke of Bavaria (1294–1347), king of Germany and Holy Roman Emperor (1314–47; crowned 1328). Denied confirmation of his kingship by the papacy, Louis was excommunicated, but elector princes made him Emperor nonetheless. In 1346, he was deposed by Pope CLEMENT VI but fought against his successor, Charles.

Louis IV (921–54) King of France (936–54). He was raised in England, hence his nickname d'Outremer ("from overseas"). His attempt to re-establish his father's claim to Lorraine (938) was blocked by his CAPETIAN rival, Hugh the Great, count of Paris, whom he finally defeated in 950.

Louis VI (1081–1137) King of France (1108–37). He was the effective ruler for several years before he succeeded his father, Philip I. He re-established control of the royal domain, increasing the authority of the royal courts and enjoying the strong support of the church. In 1137, he secured the marriage of his heir, LOUIS VII, to ELEANOR OF AQUITAINE.

Louis VII (*c*.1120–80) King of France (1137–80). His marriage to ELEANOR OF AQUITAINE extended the French crown's lands to the Pyrenees. As king, he consolidated royal power. Returning from the Second CRUSADE, he divorced Eleanor for alleged infidelity. She married HENRY II of England, whose French territories then became greater than those of Louis. Louis retaliated by supporting the rebellions of Henry's sons.

Louis VIII (1187–1226) King of France (1223–26). In 1216, he invaded England at the invitation of barons opposing King JOHN, but was defeated at Lincoln (1217) and returned to France. He successfully concluded the crusade against the heretical ALBIGENSES in S France.

Louis IX (1214–70) King of France (1226–70), later known as St Louis. His mother, Blanche of Castile, was regent from 1226 to 1236 and during his absence from France (1248–54). In 1242, Louis defeated the English at Taillebourg. He was captured on the Sixth CRUSADE.

Louis XI (1423–83) King of France (1461–83), son of CHARLES VII. He rebelled against his father and was driven out of his province of the Dauphiné in 1456 and sought refuge at the court of Burgundy. As king, he suppressed rebellious nobles. His greatest rival was Charles the Bold of Burgundy, but after Charles' death (1477), Louis gained Burgundy and also, after another convenient death, Anjou. He strengthened the French monarchy.

Louis XII (1462–1515) King of France (1498–1515). On becoming king, he had his first marriage annulled to wed Anne of Britanny, resulting in the incorporation of Britanny in France. He succeeded his cousin, CHARLES VIII, and was involved throughout his reign in the dynastic wars arising from Charles' invasion of Italy in 1494. Louis continued this policy, invading Italy in

1499. He was defeated by the HOLY LEAGUE and forced to surrender all his Italian acquisitions (1513).

Louis XIII (1601–43) King of France (1601–43), son of Henry IV and MARIE DE MÉDICIS. In 1617 he finally ended his mother's regency and exiled her. He increasingly relied on Cardinal RICHELIEU, who exercised total authority from 1624. Louis approved the domestic crushing of the HUGUENOTS at home while making alliances with Protestant powers abroad, in opposition to the Habsburgs, during the THIRTY YEARS WAR.

Louis XIV (1638–1715) King of France (1643–1715). The first part of his reign was dominated by Cardinal MAZARIN. From 1661, Louis ruled personally as the epitome of absolute monarchy and became known as the "Sun King" for the luxury of his court. As ministers, he chose men of low rank or the junior nobility, such as the able COLBERT. Louis' wars of aggrandisement in the Low Countries and elsewhere drained the treasury. His revocation of the Edict of NANTES drove Huguenots abroad, weakening the economy. In the War of the SPANISH SUCCESSION, the French armies were decisively defeated.

Louis XV (1710–74) King of France (1715–74), great-grandson and successor of LOUIS XIV. He failed to arrest France's slow decline. Disastrous wars, especially the War of the AUSTRIAN SUCCESSION and the SEVEN YEARS' WAR, resulted in financial crisis and the loss of most of the French empire. The monarchy became deeply unpopular.

Louis XVI (1754–93) King of France (1774–92), grandson and successor of LOUIS XV. In 1770, he married the Austrian archduchess MARIE ANTOINETTE. Louis' lack of leadership qualities allowed the *parlements* (supreme courts) and aristocracy to defeat the efforts of government ministers, such as Jacques NECKER, to carry out vital economic reforms. The massive public debt forced Louis to convoke the STATES GENERAL to raise taxation. His indecisiveness on the composition of the States General led the third (popular) estate to proclaim itself a National Assembly, signalling the start of the FRENCH REVOLUTION. The dismissal of Necker and rumours that Louis intended to forcibly suppress the assembly led to the storming of the BASTILLE (14 July 1789). In October 1789, the royal family was confined to the Tuileries palace. Early French defeats in the war against Austria and Prussia led to the declaration of a republic. Louis was tried for treason by the Convention and found guilty. He was guillotined on 21 January 1793.

Louis XVII (1785–95) Son of LOUIS XVI, proclaimed king of France by royalists in 1793. He was placed in the care of a shoemaker by the Republican government after the execution of his father and probably died of neglect.

Louis XVIII (1755–1824) King of France (1814–24), brother of LOUIS XVI. He fled from the FRENCH REVOLUTION to England. Louis was restored to the throne in 1814 but was forced to flee again during the HUNDRED DAYS until NAPOLEON I's final defeat at Waterloo (1815). He agreed to a constitution providing for parliamentary government and a relatively free society.

Louis I (the Great) (1326–82) King of Hungary (1342–82) and Poland (1370–82). The son of Charles I, Louis was appointed king of Poland by Casimir III. Though the union of the two countries was not a success (Louis ruled Poland through regents), Louis had control of one of the largest realms in Europe. Hungarian might was acknowledged throughout the Balkans. He encouraged commerce, industry and science.

Louis, Joe (1914–81) US boxer, b. Joseph Louis Barrow. He was nicknamed the "Brown Bomber". In 1937, Louis won the world heavyweight title from James J.

Braddock. He retired undefeated in 1949. Louis fought 25 successful defences and scored 21 knockouts, including the historic 1938 defeat of Max Schmeling. He returned to the ring, lost on points to Ezzard Charles (1950), and was knocked out by Rocky Marciano (1951). Louis held the title longer than any other heavyweight.

Louisiana State on the Gulf of Mexico, s central USA; the capital is BATON ROUGE. Louisiana consists of the MISSISSIPPI alluvial plain and the Gulf coastal plain. The Mississippi Delta in the SE of the state was formed by silt. It covers c.33,700sq km (13,000sq mi), c.25% of the state's total area. The tidal shoreline is 12,426km (7,721mi) long. Nearly 15% of the state is marshland. North of the marshes, rolling prairies stretch to the Texas border. Almost half the state is forested. It has a mainly sub-tropical climate. Low-lying land and heavy rainfall make it prone to flooding. In 1699 the French colony of Louisiana was founded. It was later ceded to Spain but regained by France in 1800. In the LOUISIANA PURCHASE (1803) Napoleon sold it to the USA. In 1861, it joined the Confederacy, being readmitted to the Union in 1868. The discovery of oil and natural gas in the early 20th century provided a great boost to the economy. Racial discrimination left the African American community (30% of the population) politically powerless until the 1960s. It is a leading producer of soya beans, sweet potatoes, rice and sugar cane. Fishing is a major industry, particularly shrimp and crayfish. Louisiana is second only to Texas in US mineral production. Petroleum and coal account for more than 95% of mining income. Area: 125,674sq km (48,523sq mi). Pop. (2000) 4,468,976.

Louisiana Purchase (1803) Transaction between the USA and France, in which the USA bought, for 60 million francs ($15 million), 2,144,500sq km (828,000sq mi) of land between the Mississippi River and the Rocky Mountains. President Thomas JEFFERSON sent James MONROE to France to negotiate the purchase from Napoleon I, who had lost interest in a colonial empire in the New World. The Louisiana Purchase doubled the area of the USA, and 13 states were admitted from the territory.

Louis Philippe (1773–1850) King of France (1830–48). In 1814 he returned to France from exile. In 1830 Louis gained the throne after the JULY REVOLUTION. Although known as the "Citizen King", he retained much personal power. The FEBRUARY REVOLUTION (1848) forced him to abdicate and the Second Republic was declared. He died in exile in England.

Louisville City in NW Kentucky, USA, a port on the Ohio River; largest city in Kentucky. Established as a military base in 1778 by George Rogers Clark, it was named after LOUIS XVI of France. It developed into a coal-shipping centre by the mid-19th century. Host to the famous Kentucky Derby, the city has many stud stables. Industries: bourbon whiskey, tobacco. Pop. (1990) 269,063.

Lourdes Town in Hautes-Pyrénées department, sw France,; a centre of religious pilgrimage. In 1858, a 14-year-old peasant girl called Bernadette Soubirous claimed to have had visions of the Virgin Mary in the nearby grotto of Massabielle, where there is an underground spring. In 1862, the Roman Catholic Church declared the visions to be authentic. The waters of the spring, believed to have healing powers, are the focus of pilgrimages by up to 5 million visitors a year. Pop. (1990) 16,580.

louse Common name for various small, wingless insects, parasitic on birds and mammals. There are two main groups in different sub-orders of Phthiraptera. The chewing lice (Mallophaga) feed mainly on the feathers of birds. The biting or sucking lice (Anoplura)

feed only on the blood of mammals. Both are small, pale and flattened, with leathery or hairy skins.

Louth County in the NE Republic of Ireland, in Leinster province, bordering Northern Ireland (N) and the Irish Sea (E); the capital is Dundalk. It is a low-lying region, except in the hilly NW and the mountainous N, drained by the rivers Fane, Dee and Castletown. Industries: textiles, footwear, Area: 821sq km (317sq mi). Pop. (1991) 90,724.

Louvre France's national museum and art gallery in Paris. It holds a collection of more than 100,000 works, including paintings, drawings, prints and sculpture. Originally a royal palace, the Louvre became a museum in the 18th century and opened as the first national public gallery in the Revolution in 1793. In 1989, a glass pyramid, designed by I.M. Pei, was built in the forecourt.

lovebird Any of nine species of small parrots that live mainly in Africa and Madagascar. Both sexes are brightly coloured and are often kept as cage birds. The largest species is the rosy-faced lovebird (*Agapornis roseicollis*) of South Africa.

Lovelace, Richard (1618–58) English CAVALIER poet. A flamboyant and ardent royalist, he was imprisoned in 1642 and 1648, during which time he wrote *To Althea, from Prison* and *To Lucasta, Going to the Wars*.

Lovell, Sir Alfred Charles Bernard (1913–) English astronomer. He was director (1951–81) of the JODRELL BANK experimental station for radio astronomy near Manchester, England, and oversaw the construction of the world's first large steerable radio telescope.

Low, Sir David Alexander Cecil (1891–1963) British cartoonist, b. New Zealand. In 1919, he moved to England. Low worked (1927–50) for the *Evening Standard*, creating the character of Colonel Blimp.

Low Countries Region of NW Europe now occupied by the NETHERLANDS, BELGIUM and LUXEMBOURG. It was the most advanced and prosperous region of N Europe during the Middle Ages and Renaissance, under the dukes of BURGUNDY from 1384 and the HABSBURGS from 1477. The Dutch gained independence as the United Provinces in 1609. The southern Netherlands (Belgium) became an independent kingdom in 1830. Luxembourg was ruled by the Dutch house of Orange until 1890, when it passed to another branch.

Lowell, Amy (1874–1925) US poet and critic, sister of Percival LOWELL. Her first volume was the sensuous *A Dome of Many-colored Glass* (1912). Following the exit of Ezra Pound, Lowell became the leader of the IMAGISM movement. Sword Blades and Poppy Seed (1914) was an experiment with "polyphonic prose".

Lowell, James Russell (1819–91) US poet, editor and ABOLITIONIST. His satirical series *The Biglow Papers* (1848) influenced the anti-slavery movement. In He founded and edited the *Atlantic Monthly* (1857–61).

Lowell, Percival (1855–1916) US astronomer, brother of Amy LOWELL. In 1894, he built an observatory at Flagstaff, Arizona. He observed Mars, producing intricate maps of the so-called canals, which he ascribed to the activities of intelligent beings. He studied the orbits of URANUS and NEPTUNE, and calculated that their orbital irregularities were caused by an undiscovered Planet X. This led to the discovery of the planet PLUTO in 1930.

Lowell, Robert (1917–77) US poet. Lowell was perhaps the most important voice in American poetry to emerge after World War 2. His early work, such as the Pulitzer Prize-winning *Lord Weary's Castle* (1946), is rich in Catholic symbolism. He is best known for his later, more intimate "confessional" style, best represented by the autobiographical *Life Studies* (1959). Lowell and other confessional poets, such as Sylvia Plath, reappraised the gap between the public and the private. He won a second Pulitzer Prize for *The Dolphin* (1973).

Lower Saxony Region of N Germany, formed in 1946 by the merging of Hanover, Brunswick, Oldenberg and Schaumberg–Lippe. Agriculture focuses on cereal crops. Industries: machinery, electrical engineering. Area: 47,606sq km (18,376sq mi), Pop. (1993 est.) 7,648,004.

Lowry, L.S. (Lawrence Stephen) (1887–1976) English painter. He is best known for the highly personal way cityscapes of his native Salford, Greater Manchester, NW England. In works such as *The Pond* (1950) Lowry painted matchstick figures set against a bleak industrial landscape of brick and iron.

Loyalist In Northern Ireland, a person who wishes the province to remain part of the United Kingdom. In contrast, a Republican is one who wishes Northern Ireland to unite with the Republic of Ireland. In US history, loyalists were those North American colonists who refused to renounce their loyalty to the British crown after the DECLARATION OF INDEPENDENCE (July 1776).

LSD (lysergic acid diethylamide) Hallucinogenic drug, causing changes in mental state, sensory confusion and behavioural changes, resulting from the drug blocking the action of serotonin in the brain. First synthesized in the 1940s, LSD was made illegal in the UK in the mid-1960s.

Luanda Capital, chief port, and largest city of Angola, on the Atlantic coast of SW Africa. First settled by the Portuguese in 1575, its economy was based on the shipment of more than 3 million slaves to Brazil until the abolition of slavery in the 19th century. Today, it exports crops from the province of Luanda. Industries: oil refining, metalworking. Pop. (1995) 2,250,000.

Lübeck Baltic port at the mouth of the River Trave, Schleswig-Holstein, NE Germany. A Slavonic city in the 11th century, it was destroyed by fire in 1138. In 1143, it was refounded as part of Holstein. In 1226, it was made a free imperial city and later rose to a pre-eminent position in the HANSEATIC LEAGUE. During the 16th century the city began to decline. In 1937, it was incorporated into Schleswig-Holstein. The city was badly damaged by Allied bombing during World War 2. The port is the principal employer. Industries: shipbuilding, aeronautical equipment. Pop. (1995) 217,000.

Lublin City in SE Poland. Founded in the late 9th century as a fortified settlement, Lublin developed as a trade centre, acquiring municipal rights in 1317. The city has twice produced national governments: Poland's first Council of Workers' Delegates (a temporary authority) was formed in 1918; and in 1944, following the retreat of the German army, the provisional government was convened in Lublin. Today, it is the focus for a farming region and a transport and industrial centre, producing heavy machinery, textiles and electrical goods. Pop. (1996) 353,000.

lubricant Oil, grease or other substances placed between moving parts to reduce friction and dissipate heat. Most lubricants are now derived from petroleum.

Lucas, George (1944–) US film director and producer. He began his career as an assistant to Francis Ford COPPOLA. His breakthrough film was *American Graffiti* (1973). Lucas is best known for the science-fiction classic *Star Wars* (1977), which used groundbreaking special effects and was one of the most successful films of all time. Lucas was executive producer of the *Star Wars* sequels *The Empire Strikes Back* (1980) and *Return of the Jedi* (1983). He also worked with Steven SPIELBERG on the "Indiana Jones" trilogy.

Lucas van Leyden (1494–1533) Dutch painter and engraver. His engravings (which are regarded as second only to those of DÜRER) include *Ecco Homo* and *Dance of the Magdalene* (1519). Among his paintings are *Chess Players* (c.1508) and *Last Judgment* (1526).

Lucerne (Luzern) City on Lake Lucerne, central Switzerland. It joined the Swiss Confederation in 1332. In 1803, Lucerne became the capital of the French-inspired Helvetic Republic but rejoined the Confederation in 1848. It is an important summer resort and plays host to a music festival. It is the centre of the cereal-growing canton of Lucerne. Industries: engineering, metal goods, chemicals, textiles. Pop. (1994 est.) 61,656.

Lucifer Name given in ancient Roman times to the planet VENUS. In classical mythology, Lucifer's Greek counterpart was Phosphorus. In Christian mythology, Lucifer is an epithet of SATAN and a symbol of overbearing pride.

Lucknow City on the River Gomati, N India; capital and largest city of Uttar Pradesh. The first Mogul Emperor of India conquered the city in 1528. It was the capital of the kingdom of Oudh (1775–1856), then of Oudh province (1856–77) and of the United Provinces (1887). Lucknow was the centre of the MUSLIM LEAGUE in its campaign (1942–47) for an independent Pakistan. Industries: papermaking, distilling, chemicals, printing, handicrafts. Pop. (1991) 1,642,000.

Lucretia In Roman legend, the beautiful and pure wife of Lucius Tarquinius Collatinus. After being raped by Sextus Tarquinius, son of the Etruscan king of Rome, she demanded that her father and husband should avenge her and then stabbed herself to death. Lucius Junius Brutus then led the populace in a rebellion, and the Roman Republic was established.

Lucretius (c.95–c.55 BC) (Titus Lucretius Carus) Latin poet and philosopher. His six-volume poem *On the Nature of Things* is based on the philosophy of EPICURUS.

Luddites Unemployed workers in early 19th-century England who vandalized the machines that had put them out of work. They were chiefly hand-loom weavers who had been replaced by mechanical looms. The riots started in the Nottingham area in 1811 and spread to Lancashire and Yorkshire before dying out after 1815.

Ludendorff, Erich (1865–1937) German general. He played a major part in revising the SCHLIEFFEN PLAN before World War 1. In 1914, Ludendorff masterminded the victory over the Russians at Tannenberg. In 1916, he and HINDENBURG were given supreme control of Germany's war effort. He served (1924–28) in the Reichstag as a member of the Nazi Party.

Luftwaffe German air force. In English-speaking countries, the term refers specifically to the air force of Nazi Germany. Built up rapidly in the 1930s, it was designed primarily as part of German *Blitzkrieg* tactics and was highly effective in the early stages of WORLD WAR 2 and during the invasion of the Soviet Union (1941). It was less successful as a high-explosive bombing force in the Battle of BRITAIN (1940). *See also* BLITZ

Lugosi, Bela (1884–1956) US film actor, b. Hungary. In 1927 he achieved fame on Broadway in the play *Dracula*. Lugosi reprised his role in the classic horror film *Dracula* (1931). He appeared with Boris KARLOFF in films such as *The Black Cat* (1934) and *The Raven* (1935).

lugworm Marine WORM that lives in the sand of the seabed. With the aid of bristles, it burrows a u-shaped tunnel in sand or mud from which it rarely emerges. Length: up to 30cm (12in). Genus *Arenicola*.

Lukacs, György (1885–1971) Hungarian literary critic and philosopher. Lukacs was a key figure in the 1956

Hungarian rising. His writings include *History and Class Consciousness* (1923) and *The Historical Novel* (1955).

Luke, Saint Author, according to Christian tradition, of the gospel that bears his name and of the ACTS OF THE APOSTLES in the New Testament. He is said to have been a physician, to have been able to speak and write Greek, and may have been a non-Jew born in Antioch, Syria. Luke is the patron saint of painters. His feast day is 18 October.

Luke, Gospel according to Saint Third book of the New Testament and one of the three SYNOPTIC GOSPELS. It is traditionally attributed to St LUKE. One of its sources is the Gospel according to St MARK.

Lully, Jean-Baptiste (1632–87) French composer, b. Italy. In 1652 he joined the court musicians to Louis XIV. After collaborating with Molière on comedies such as, *Le Bourgeois Gentilhomme* (1670), Lully turned to opera. His *Cadmus and Hermione* (1673) has been called the first French lyrical tragedy. Other operas include *Alceste* (1674) and *Proserpine* (1680).

lumbago Pain in the lower region of the back. It is due to strain or poor posture. When associated with SCIATICA, it may be due to a slipped disc. *See also* RHEUMATISM

lumen (symbol lm) SI unit measuring the amount of light in a certain area for one second. The light is emitted in a unit solid angle (one steradian) from a source of unit intensity (one CANDELA).

Lumière Two French brothers, **Louis Jean** (1864–1948) and **Auguste** (1862–1954), who were pioneers of CINEMATOGRAPHY. They invented an early combination of motion-picture camera and projector called the "Cinématographe". Their film, *Lunch Break at the Lumière Factory* (1895), is considered to be the first motion picture. By 1895, the brothers had made improvements in colour photography. *See also* CINEMA

luminescence *See* FLUORESCENCE; PHOSPHORESCENCE

luminism Art style followed by a group of 19th-century US painters. The Luminists were concerned with the depiction of light and atmospheric effects. They used careful gradations of tone to achieve these effects, so that no brushwork was apparent. The leading figures were George Caleb Bingham, Asher Durand and members of the HUDSON RIVER SCHOOL.

luminosity Absolute brightness of a star, given by the amount of energy radiated from its entire surface per second. It is expressed in watts (joules per second) or in terms of the Sun's luminosity. Bolometric luminosity is a measure of the star's total energy output at all wavelengths. Absolute magnitude is an indication of luminosity at visual wavelengths. *See also* HERTZSPRUNG-RUSSELL DIAGRAM

lumpfish (lumpsucker) Marine fish of the North Atlantic coasts, the pectoral fins of which join to form a sucker with which it attaches itself to rocks. Length: up to 61cm (2ft); weight 6kg (13lb). Family Cyclopteridae.

Lumumba, Patrice Emergy (1925–61) Congolese statesman, prime minister (1960–61) of Congo. He was leader of the Congolese nationalist movement against the Belgians and became first premier of the independent Republic of the Congo. The country was plunged into civil war when the mineral-rich province of Katanga tried to secede. Lumumba appealed to the United Nations for assistance and a peacekeeping force was sent. Lumumba was dismissed and imprisoned by MOBUTU. He escaped, but was recaptured and killed.

lunar eclipse *See* ECLIPSE

lungfish Elongated fish from which the first AMPHIBIANS developed, found in shallow freshwater and swamps in Africa, South America and Australia. It has primitive lungs, and during a dry season the various species can breath air or survive total dehydration by burrowing into the mud. Order Dipnoi.

lungs Organs of the RESPIRATORY SYSTEM of vertebrates, in which the exchange of gases between air and blood takes place. They are located in the pleural cavity within the ribcage. This cavity is lined by two sheets of

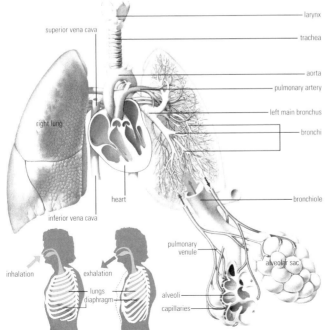

◄ **lungs** Breathing introduces air into the lungs for the exchange of oxygen and carbon dioxide. Air is funnelled into the trachea, the flexible windpipe ringed with cartilage. The trachea forks into the left and right bronchi. Each bronchus branches into several small segments, or bronchi, terminating in 250,000 respiratory bronchioles, each about 0.5mm (0.02in) in diameter. Beyond lie the alveolar ducts leading into hollow alveoli. Here in the alveoli, networked with capillaries only one cell in width, diffusion occurs across a fine membrane. Stale blood is reoxygenated and makes its way back to the heart to be pumped to each living cell in the body. Carbon dioxide is eliminated from the lungs in expired air. The inset diagram shows the position of the diaphragm during breathing.

larynx
superior vena cava
trachea
aorta
pulmonary artery
left main bronchus
right lung
bronchi
heart
bronchiole
inferior vena cava
pulmonary venule
inhalation　exhalation
alveolar sac
lungs
diaphragm
alveoli
capillaries

► **lute** Capable of great expressiveness, the lute requires a high degree of skill on the part of the player, or lutenist. The instrument was once played throughout w Europe and Middle Eastern countries, from where, it is assumed, the lute originated.

TISSUE (the pleura), one coating the lungs and the other lining the walls of the thorax. Between the pleura is a fluid that cushions the lungs and prevents friction. Light and spongy, lung tissue is composed of tiny air sacs, called ALVEOLI that are served by networks of fine CAPILLARIES. *See also* GAS EXCHANGE; VENTILATION

Luoyang (formerly Honan) Industrial city on the River Luo, Honan province, N central China. It was the capital of the Eastern Chou dynasty (770–256 BC) and the T'ang dynasty (AD 618–907). Nearby are the Longmen caves, containing *c.*100,000 carvings of Buddha. Pop. (1994) 863,000.

lupin Any annual or perennial plants of the genus *Lupinus*, in the pea family. They have star-shaped compound leaves and tall showy spikes of flowers. Height: to 2.4m (8ft). Family Fabaceae/Leguminosae.

lupus Autoimmune disease affecting the skin and connective tissue. The most common form, **lupus vulgaris**, is a tuberculous infection of the skin. **Lupus erythematosus (LE)** is an inflammation of tissues caused by the body's immune system. Discoid LE causes red patches covered with scales, often on the cheeks and nose. Nine times more common in women than in men, the disease is treated mainly with corticosteroids.

Lusaka Capital and largest city of Zambia, in the s central part of the country, at an altitude of 1,280m (4,200ft). Founded (1905) by Europeans to service the local lead mining, it replaced Livingstone as the capital of Northern Rhodesia (later Zambia) in 1935. Lusaka is the centre of a fertile agricultural region and is a major financial and commercial city. Industries: textiles, shoe manufacture. Pop. (1990) 982,000.

Lusitania British passenger liner sunk (7 May 1915) off the Irish coast by a German U-boat. Of the 1,195 lives lost, 128 were Americans and the incident aroused anti-German feeling that ultimately led Woodrow Wilson to abandon his policy of neutrality and America to enter the war.

lute Plucked stringed instrument popular in 16th- and 17th-century Europe. It has an almond-shaped body and fretted neck and originally had 11 gut strings. It was played to accompany songs and stylized dances and has been revived in recent years as a concert instrument.

lutetium (symbol Lu) Metallic element of the lanthanide group, first isolated in 1907 from the element ytterbium. Chief ore is monazite (phosphate). Lutetium

has no commercial uses. Properties: at.no. 71; r.a.m. 174.97; r.d. 9.835; m.p. 1,656°C (3,013°F); b.p. 3,315°C (5,999°F); most common isotope Lu^{175} (97.41%).

Luther, Martin (1483–1546) German Christian reformer, a founder of PROTESTANTISM and leader of the German REFORMATION. In 1517 he affixed his 95 Theses to the door of the Schlosskirche in Wittenberg. This was a document that attacked, among other things, the sale of INDULGENCES. This action led to a quarrel between Luther and church leaders, including the pope. Luther decided that the Bible was the true source of authority and renounced obedience to Rome. In 1521, Luther was excommunicated at the Diet of WORMS. His view that salvation could not be attained by good works but was a free gift of God's grace led to a rift with ERASMUS. In 1529, Luther defended consubstantiation against ZWINGLI. Although Luther initially merely sought to reform the Catholic Church his approval of MELANCHTHON's AUGSBURG Confession (1530) established LUTHERANISM. Luther's translation (1522–34) of the Bible into High German helped the development of German literature.

Lutheranism Doctrines and Church structure that grew out of the teaching of Martin LUTHER. The principal Lutheran doctrine is that of justification by faith alone (*sola fide*). Luther held that grace cannot be conferred by the Church but is the free gift of God's love. He objected to the Catholic doctrine of TRANSUBSTANTIATION. Instead, Luther believed in the real presence of Christ "in, with and under" the bread and wine (consubstantiation). These and other essentials of Lutheran doctrine were set down by Philip MELANCHTHON in the AUGSBURG CONFESSION (1530), which has been the basic document of the Lutherans ever since. In 1947 the Lutheran World Federation was formed. Today, the Lutheran Church has *c.*25 million members worldwide.

Luthuli, Albert John Mvumbi (1898–1967) South African civil-rights leader. Elected chief of a Zulu community, he became president of the AFRICAN NATIONAL CONGRESS (ANC) in 1952 during a period of increasing militancy that led to the banning of the ANC in 1960. In 1960 he became the first African to be awarded the Nobel Peace Prize. Thereafter his movements were closely restricted by the APARTHEID government, and in 1962 his publications were banned.

Lutoslawski, Witold (1913–94) Polish composer. He gained international recognition with his Concerto for Orchestra (1954). He later experimented with SERIALISM, notably in *Funeral Music* (1958), and aleatory techniques, as in *Venetian Games* (1961).

Lutyens, Sir Edwin Landseer (1869–1944) English architect. He built a reputation on original designs for houses. Lutyens developed a talent for more majestic commissions in his World War 1 memorials, notably The Cenotaph (1922) in Whitehall, London. His most ambitious project was his plan for the imperial capital of New Delhi (1913–30), India.

Lutyens, (Agnes) Elizabeth (1906–83) English composer, daughter of Sir Edwin LUTYENS. She worked mainly within the TWELVE-TONE MUSIC system. Her works include various symphonies as well as *Quincunx for Orchestra* (1959–60) and the operas *The Numbered* and *Isis and Osiris* (both 1973)

lux (symbol lx) SI unit of illumination, equal to one LUMEN per square metre.

Luxembourg Independent grand duchy in w Europe, bordered by Belgium, France and Germany; the capital is LUXEMBOURG. **Land and climate** Luxembourg is divided geographically into the forested ARDENNES plateau and

LUXEMBOURG
AREA: 2,590sq km (1,000sq mi)
POPULATION: 377,000
CAPITAL (POPULATION): Luxembourg (78,000)

the fertile Bon Pays in the s. In the E, the Moselle and Sauer river valleys provide fertile farmland. Luxembourg has a temperate climate. Forests cover c.20% of Luxembourg, farms 25% and pasture another 20%. **History and politics** In the 11th century the county of Luxembourg formed one of the largest fiefs of the Holy Roman Empire. In 1354, Luxembourg became a duchy. In 1482, it passed to the HABSBURG dynasty, and in the 16th century it was incorporated in the Spanish Netherlands. In 1714, it passed to Austria. It was occupied by France during the NAPOLEONIC WARS and was made a Grand Duchy at the CONGRESS OF VIENNA (1815). In 1839, Belgium acquired a large part of the duchy. In 1867, Luxembourg was recognized as an independent state, and its neutrality was guaranteed by the European powers. Luxembourg was occupied by Germany in World War 1 and in 1940 Germany invaded again. In 1948, it joined NATO. In 1960, Belgium, the Netherlands and Luxembourg formed the economic union of Benelux. Luxembourg was one of the six founders of the European Community (EC). In 1964, Prince Jean became Grand Duke. Following 1994 elections, the Christian Social People's Party (CD) and the Luxembourg Socialist Workers' Party (SOC) formed a coalition government. Jean-Claude Juncker (CD) became prime minister. In 1998, Grand Duke Jean conferred many constitutional powers upon his son and heir, Prince Henri. In 1999, Luxembourg adopted the European single currency (the euro). **Economy** There are rich deposits of iron ore, and Luxembourg is a major producer of iron and steel (1995 GDP per capita, US$37,930). Other industries include chemicals, textiles, tourism, banking and electronics. Farmers raise cattle and pigs. Major crops include cereals, fruits and grapes for winemaking. The city of Luxembourg is a major centre of European administration and finance.

Luxembourg Capital of the Grand Duchy of Luxembourg, at the confluence of the Alzette and Pétrusse rivers. Luxembourg was a stronghold in Roman times. The walled town developed around a 10th-century fortress. The Treaty of London (1867) dismantled the fortress. It is the seat of the European Court of Justice, the Secretariat of the European Parliament, the European Monetary Fund, the European Investment Bank and the European Coal and Steel Union. Industries: iron and steel, chemicals, textiles, tourism. Pop. (1997) 78,000.

Luxemburg, Rosa (1871–1919) German revolutionary, b. Poland. In 1893, she founded the Polish Communist Party. In 1898, she gained German citizenship. In 1915, Luxemburg was imprisoned for her opposition to World War 1. While in prison, she and Karl LIEBKNECHT founded (1916) the socialist and pacifist Spartacist League (the SPARTACISTS). In 1918, after her release, she formed the German Communist Party. In 1919, she and Liebknecht were murdered while under arrest after an abortive uprising in Berlin.

Luxor (El Uqsur) City in E central Egypt, on the E bank of the River Nile; known to the ancient Egyptians as Weset and to the ancient Greeks as **Thebes**. After the PYRAMIDS, Luxor's temples and tombs constitute Egypt's greatest pharaonic monuments. There are remains of many temples and tombs, dating back nearly 4,000 years.

Luxor Temple lies on the banks of the Nile in the heart of the city where, until the 19th century, it remained half buried. It was linked to the **Karnak** temple, 2.5km (1mi) N of Luxor, by an avenue of sphinxes. Karnak's temple complex covers 40ha (100 acres) and was built over 1,300 years. The site has three separate temples, the greatest of which is the Temple of AMON. The Valley of the Kings, on the Nile's W bank, contains the tombs of many pharaohs. The 1922 discovery of Tutankhamen's tomb revealed the lavish treasure buried with kings. In 1997, Muslim fundamentalists killed 58 tourists outside HATSHEPSUT's Temple. Pop. (1992) 146,000.

Luzon Largest island of the PHILIPPINES, occupying the N part of the group; the main cities are QUEZON CITY and the nation's capital, MANILA. Luzon accounts for about one-third of the land mass of the Philippines and more than 50% of its population. The coastal areas are generally mountainous, the highest peak being Mount Pulog at 2,928m (9,606ft). The fertile central plain is a major rice-producing region. The indigenous Igorots also farm rice on the steep mountain terraces. The Bicol peninsula in the SE has many coconut plantations. Luzon also has gold, chromite and copper. Manila Bay is one of the world's finest natural harbours. Luzon led revolts first against Spanish rule in 1896 and then against US rule in 1899. In 1941, the island was invaded by the Japanese. US forces staged a last desperate stand on BATAAN peninsula in 1942. In 1945, the Japanese were finally expelled. Several US bases have remained on the island since World War 2. Area: 104,688sq km (40,420sq mi). Pop. (1992 est.) 30,500,000.

Lvov, Prince Georgi Yevgenevich (1861–1925) Russian political leader. A constitutional democrat, he was elected by the Duma to form a provisional government after the first RUSSIAN REVOLUTION (March 1917) had forced the abdication of Tsar NICHOLAS II. His government was feeble and brought in a number of socialists whose first loyalty was to the SOVIETS. In July 1917, Lvov resigned in favour of KERENSKY. He was imprisoned by the BOLSHEVIKS after the November revolution but escaped to France.

Lvov (Lemberg) City on a tributary of the River Bug, close to the Polish border, in W Ukraine. Founded in 1256 by a Ukrainian prince, it was captured by Poland in 1340. Lvov became part of Austria in 1772, and in 1918 was briefly the capital of the independent Ukrainian Republic before reverting to Poland. It was annexed by the Soviet Union (1945–91). Industries: heavy machinery, chemicals, oil refining. Pop. (1996) 802,000.

Lyceum School in Classical Athens where ARISTOTLE taught. In later times the name was adopted by many educational institutions, such as French secondary schools (lycées), and a US group devoted to adult education, founded in 1826, in which Ralph Waldo EMERSON and Henry THOREAU took part.

Lycopodophyta (Phylum) of c.1,000 species of VASCULAR PLANTS related to ferns, which includes the CLUB MOSSES, selaginellas and quillworts. They have branching underground stems (RHIZOMES) and upright shoots supported by roots. Some species are EPIPHYTES.

Lycurgus (active 7th century BC?) Semi-mythical lawgiver of ancient SPARTA. He has been cited as the author of the political and social system in Sparta. Many scholars now doubt that one individual was responsible for the Spartan social system.

Lydia Ancient kingdom of W Asia Minor. Under the Mermnad dynasty (c.700–547 BC), it was a powerful and prosperous state, the first to issue a coinage, with its capital at Sardis. Its last king was CROESUS, famous for his wealth, who was defeated by the Persians under CYRUS THE GREAT in 547 BC.

Lyell, Sir Charles (1797–1875) Scottish geologist. His popular three-volume *Principles of Geology* (1830–33) discredited the catastrophic view of geology in favour of a long, slow gradual change. It influenced Charles DARWIN's formulation of a theory of EVOLUTION. Other works include *Elements of Geology* (1838) and *The Geological Evidence of the Antiquity of Man* (1863).

Lyly, John (1553–1606) English poet, dramatist and writer of prose romances. His prose comedies and pastoral romances include *Sappho and Phao* (1584), *Endymion: the Man in the Moon* (1591) and *Midas* (1592). Lyly is best known for the elaborate prose style that he evolved in *Euphues* (1578).

lyme disease Condition caused by a spirochete transmitted by the bite of a TICK that lives on deer. It usually begins with a red rash, often accompanied by fever, headache and pain in the muscles and joints. Untreated, the disease can lead to chronic arthritis, and there may also be involvement of the nervous system, heart, liver or kidneys. It is treated with ANTIBIOTICS.

lymph Clear, slightly yellowish fluid derived from the BLOOD and similar in composition to plasma. Circulating in the LYMPHATIC SYSTEM, it conveys LEUCOCYTES (white blood cells) and some nutrients to the tissues.

lymphatic system System of connecting vessels and organs in vertebrates that transport LYMPH through the body. Lymph flows into lymph capillaries and from them into lymph vessels, or lymphatics. These extend throughout the body, leading to lymph glands that collect lymph, storing some of the LEUCOCYTES (white blood cells). Lymph nodes empty into large vessels,

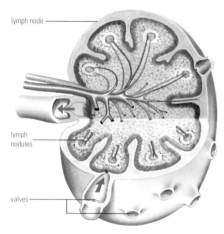

lymph node

lymph nodules

valves

▲ **lymph** The lymph system is a network of lymphatic vessels that collects tissue fluid (the lymph) and conducts it back to the bloodstream. In the process it transports nutrients from blood to cells and cell wastes back into capillaries. Lymph drains through the system but the lymphatics possess valves to prevent backflow.

Lymph nodes are scattered along the lymph vessels but particularly in the neck, armpits and groin. In the tissue around the nodes, microorganisms are destroyed by macrophage cells, while antibody-synthesizing white blood cells, the lymphocytes, are produced by the lymph nodules.

linking up into lymph ducts that empty back into the CIRCULATORY SYSTEM. The lymphatic system plays a major role in the body's defence against disease.

lymph gland (lymph node) Mass of tissue occurring along the major vessels of the LYMPHATIC SYSTEM. Lymph glands are filters and reservoirs that collect harmful material, notably bacteria and other disease organisms, and they often become swollen when the body is infected.

lymphocyte Type of LEUCOCYTE (white blood cell) found in vertebrates. Produced in the bone marrow, they are mostly found in the LYMPH and blood and around infected sites. In human beings lymphocytes form *c*.25% of white blood cells and play an important role in combating disease. **B-lymphocytes** produce ANTIBODIES and **T-lymphocytes** maintain IMMUNITY.

Lynch, David (1946–) US film director. His penchant for the grotesque and surreal was evident in *Eraserhead* (1977). Lynch gained widespread recognition for *The Elephant Man* (1980). Other films include *Blue Velvet* (1986), *Wild at Heart* (1990) and *Highway* (1998). He also made the television series *Twin Peaks* (1990).

Lynn, Dame Vera (1917–) English singer, b. Vera Margaret Lewis. She was the British "Forces Sweetheart" during World War 2. Lynn is remembered for her renditions of "We'll Meet Again" and "White Cliffs of Dover".

lynx Any of several small CATS in forests of central and N Europe, along the French-Spanish border and in the USA. It may be yellow-grey or reddish-brown. It has long legs, tufted ears and characteristic beard-like hair on its cheeks. Length: to 116cm (46in). Family Felidae.

Lyon (Eng. Lyons) City and river port at the confluence of the Rhône and Saône rivers, SE France; capital of Rhône department. Lyon was founded by the Romans as *Lugdunum* in 43 BC and became the capital of Roman GAUL. Its historic association with silk began in the 15th century. It was also one of the first printing centres. In 1793, Lyon was devastated by French Revolutionary troops. During World War 2 it was a stronghold of the French resistance movement. Lyon is the third-largest city in France and Europe's biggest producer of silk and rayon fabrics. Pop. (1990) 415,487.

lyre Ancient stringed musical instrument. Used originally by the Sumerians, it was introduced into Egypt and Assyria in the second millennium BC. In classical Greek times it usually had seven strings supported by a wooden frame and attached to a sound box at the base; the strings were plucked using a bulky plectrum. In Europe since the Middle Ages, lyres have been commonly been played with a bow.

lyrebird Either of two shy Australian songbirds: the superb lyrebird (*Menura superba*) and Albert's lyrebird (*M. alberti*). These large, perching birds have lyre-shaped tails displayed during courtship performances.

Lysander (d.395 BC) Spartan general. He was responsible for the victory over Athens during the PELOPONNESIAN WAR (429–404 BC), defeating the Athenian fleet in 406 and 405 and obtaining Persian support for Sparta. He lost influence in Sparta after the accession of King Agesilaus II in 399 BC.

Lysenko, Trofim Denisovich (1898–1976) Russian agronomist and geneticist. He expanded the theory of LAMARCK with his own ideas of plant genetics (Lysenkoism). Lysenko promised the Soviet government vast increases in crop yields through the application of his theories. He enjoyed official sanction under Stalin.

Lytton, Edward George Earle Bulwer-Lytton, 1st baron (1803–73) English novelist. He wrote historical novels such as *The Last Days of Pompeii* (1834).

M/m, the 13th letter of the alphabet, is derived from the Semitic letter mem *(meaning water). The corresponding Greek letter was* mu, *which went via the Etruscan alphabet to Latin as* m.

Maastricht City on the River Maas (Meuse), SE Netherlands; capital of Limburg province. The city's strategic location, close to the Belgian and German borders, has meant frequent occupation by foreign armies. In 1992, the MAASTRICHT TREATY was signed here. The city is the commercial, industrial and transport centre for a wide region. Industries: dairy products, paper, leather goods, glass. Pop. (1996) 119,000.

Maastricht Treaty (7 February 1992) Agreement on EUROPEAN UNION (EU) signed by the leaders of 12 European nations at MAASTRICHT, SE Netherlands. The treaty included a timetable for the introduction of a single currency (the EURO); a Common Foreign and Security Policy (CFSP), with the WESTERN EUROPEAN UNION (WEU) as a possible defence arm of the EU; a common European citizenship for nationals of all member states and the extension of European cooperation in justice and home affairs. The treaty introduced the principle of subsidiarity whereby decisions are taken at the most appropriate level: local, regional or national. It extended qualified majority voting in the EUROPEAN COUNCIL OF MINISTERS and increased the powers of the EUROPEAN PARLIAMENT (EP) over the budget and the EUROPEAN COMMISSION. A separate protocol on social policy (the social chapter) was adopted by 11 states with the UK opting-out. The UK signed up to the social chapter by the Amsterdam Treaty (1997).

Maazel, Lorin (1930–) US conductor, b. France. He made his debut in 1953. Maazel was director of Deutsche Oper (1965–71) and Vienna State Opera (1982–84). A methodical, lively performer, he was music director of the Cleveland Orchestra (1971–82) and the Pittsburgh Symphony Orchestra (1986–).

Mabuse (*c*.1478–1536) (Jan Gossaert) Netherlandish painter. He began his career in the tradition of Gerard DAVID and Hugo van der GOES but changed his style dramatically after a visit to Italy as an assistant to Philip of Burgundy in 1508–09. Italianate features appeared within his Netherlandish style, as seen in his *Neptune and Amphitrite* (1516).

McAdam, John Loudon (1756–1836) Scottish engineer who invented the macadam road surface. He proposed that roads should be raised above the surrounding ground with a base of large stones covered with smaller stones and bound together with fine gravel.

macadamia Genus of Australian trees of the family Proteaceae. Most species have stiff, oblong, lance-like leaves. The edible seeds are round, hard-shelled nuts, covered with thick husks that split when ripe. Height: to 18m (60ft).

Macao (Macau) Former Portuguese overseas province in SE China, 64km (40mi) W of Hong Kong, on the River Pearl estuary; it consists of the 6sq km (2sq mi) Macao Peninsula and the nearby islands of Taipa and Colôane. The city of Santa Nome de Deus de Macao (coexistence with the peninsula) is connected by a narrow isthmus to the Chinese province of GUANGZHOU. The first European discovery was by Vasco da GAMA in 1497. In 1557, the Portuguese colonized the island. In 1849, Portugal declared it a free port. In 1887, the Chinese government recognized Portugal's right of "perpetual occupation". Competition from Hong Kong and the increased silting of Macao's harbour led to the port's decline toward the end of the 19th century. In 1974, Macao became a Chinese province under Portuguese administration. It was returned to China in December 1999. Macao's economy is based on gambling and tourism. Other industries: textiles, electronics, plastics. Pop. (2000) 656,000.

macaque Diverse group of omnivorous, medium-sized to large Old World MONKEYS found from NW Africa to Japan and Korea. Most are yellowish brown and are forest dwellers and good swimmers. Weight: to 13kg (29lb). Genus *Macaca. See also* BARBARY APE; RHESUS

MacArthur, Douglas (1880–1964) US general. A division commander in World War 1, he became army chief of staff in 1930 and military adviser to the Philippines in 1935, retiring from the US army in 1937. He was recalled in 1941 and conducted the defence of the Philippines until ordered out to Australia. As supreme Allied commander in the SW Pacific (1942–45), he directed the campaigns that led to Japanese defeat and administered the subsequent US occupation (1945–50) of Japan. In 1950, he was appointed commander of UN forces in the KOREAN WAR. Autocratic and controversial, he was relieved of his command by President TRUMAN in 1951.

Macaulay, Thomas Babington (1800–59) English historian and statesman. He upheld liberal causes in Parliament (1830–38) and served on the British governor's council in India (1834–38), where he introduced a Western education system. He re-entered Parliament (1839–47, 1852–56) but spent most of his later years writing his five-volume *History of England* (1849–61).

macaw Any of several species of tropical American harsh-voiced PARROTS. All have sword-shaped tails and large powerful bills. Most species are brightly coloured, such as the scarlet macaw (*Ara macao*), which has a red tail and yellow wings with bright blue on its back and wings. Order Psittacidae.

Macbeth (d.1057) King of Scotland (1040–57). In 1040, he killed Duncan I, his cousin, in battle and seized the throne. English intervention on behalf of Duncan's son (later Malcolm III Canmore) resulted in his defeat by Siward, Earl of Northumbria, at Dunsinane Hill, near Scone (1054). Macbeth fled north and was eventually killed by Malcolm at Lumphanan. Shakespeare based his *Macbeth* (1605) on Holinshed's inaccurate *Chronicle*.

Maccabees, Books of Four historical books, the first two (I and II) of which are included in the Roman Catholic Deuterocanonical books of the Bible and the Protestant APOCRYPHA. **Maccabees I and II** are modelled on the OLD TESTAMENT books of CHRONICLES and are a valuable historical source. They record the Jewish dynasty of the Maccabees. In 165 BC, **Judas Maccabee** led a revolt against the SELEUCID occupation of JERUSALEM. His reconsecration of the TEMPLE (165 BC) is celebrated by the Jewish feast of HANUKKAH. Judas and his two brothers, Jonathan and Simon, were murdered (161? BC, 143 BC, 135 BC respectively) in JUDAEA's resistance to Syrian domination. Maccabees III and IV are PSEUDEPIGRAPHA.

McCarthy, Joseph Raymond (1908–57) US Republican senator, leader of the crusade against alleged communists in the US government. Taking advantage of anti-communist sentiment in the COLD WAR, he widened his attack to other sectors of public life including the film industry. During the period of

"McCarthyism", many of those accused of communism were blacklisted. McCarthy polarised US society; many regarded his hearings as show trials or witch-hunts, while others considered him a hero. In 1954, his House Un-American Activities Committee (HUAC) turned its attention to the army. The hearings were televised, and McCarthy's accusations were shown to be baseless.

McCarthy, Mary (1912–89) US writer and drama critic. She wrote several novels, including *A Charmed Life* (1955) and *The Group* (1963). Among her non-fiction works are *Venice Observed* (1956) and *Memories of a Catholic Girlhood* (1957).

McCartney, Sir Paul (1942–) English singer-songwriter. He was the bass player in The BEATLES and co-wrote most of the band's hit songs with John LENNON. The release of his solo album, *McCartney* (1970), marked the break-up of The Beatles. McCartney formed his own group, Wings (1971–81), with his wife Linda (1942–98). In 1977, "Mull of Kintyre" became the UK's bestselling single. In 1995, he was involved in a brief reformation of The Beatles. During the 1990s, McCartney turned to more classically inspired work, such as *Liverpool Oratorio* (1991) and *Standing Stone* (1997). He was knighted in 1997.

McCormick, Cyrus Hall (1809–84) US inventor. In 1931 he invented the reaper. A large-scale manufacturing operation and widespread advertising, together with his inventions of the twine binder and side-rake, revolutionized harvesting and brought him financial success.

McCullers, Carson (1917–67) US writer. McCullers' remarkable debut novel, *The Heart is a Lonely Hunter* (1940), showed her to be a sensitive exponent of the "southern gothic" style epitomized by Tennessee WILLIAMS and William FAULKNER. Other works include *Reflections in a Golden Eye* (1941) and the novella *The Ballad of the Sad Cafe* (1951), dramatized by Edward ALBEE in 1963.

MacDiarmid, Hugh (1892–1978) Scottish poet and critic, b. Christopher Murray Grieve. A nationalist and communist, he was a founder member of the SCOTTISH NATIONALIST PARTY (SNP). MacDiarmid was the dominant voice in Scottish poetry from the early 1920s. His revival of Scots as a poetic language was influential in the 20th-century Scottish renaissance. MacDiarmid's masterpiece is *A Drunk Man Looks at the Thistle* (1926).

Macdonald, Flora (1722–90) Scottish JACOBITE heroine. After the Battle of CULLODEN (1746), she smuggled the Young Pretender, Charles Edward STUART, to Skye, disguised as her maid. From there, he sailed safely to Europe.

Macdonald, Sir John Alexander (1815–91) Canadian statesman, first prime minister of the Dominion of Canada (1867–73, 1878–91). He strengthened the Dominion by introducing protective tariffs, encouragement of western settlement, and the acquisition of HUDSON'S BAY COMPANY lands (1869). His efforts to organize a transcontinental railway led to the Pacific Scandal and electoral defeat (1873).

MacDonald, (James) Ramsay (1866–1937) British statesman, prime minister (1924, 1929–31, 1931–35), b. Scotland. He entered Parliament in 1906, and became leader of the LABOUR PARTY in 1911. His opposition to Britain's participation in World War 1 lost him the leadership in 1914, and his seat in 1918. Re-elected in 1922, he regained the party leadership and became Britain's first Labour prime minister. His minority government fell within months when the Liberals withdrew their support. In 1929, he became prime minister again, but the Great Depression led to the collapse of the Labour

government (1931). MacDonald remained as prime minister at the head of a Conservative-dominated national government. In 1935, he resigned and was succeeded as prime minister by Stanley Baldwin.

Macedon Ancient country in SE Europe, roughly corresponding to present-day MACEDONIA, Greek Macedonia and Bulgarian Macedonia. The Macedonian king Alexander I (d.420 BC) initiated a process of Hellenization. In 348 BC PHILIP II founded the city of Thessaloníki and he was acknowledged as king of Greece in 338 BC. His son, ALEXANDER THE GREAT, built a world empire, but this rapidly fragmented after his death (323 BC). Macedon was eventually defeated by the Romans in the Macedonian Wars, and the empire was restricted to Macedonia proper. In 146 BC Thessaloníki became capital of the first Roman province. In AD 395, Macedonia became part of the Eastern Roman (Byzantine) empire. Slavs settled in the 6th century, and from the 9th to the 14th century, control of the area was contested mainly by Bulgaria and the Byzantine empire. A brief period of Serbian hegemony was followed by Ottoman rule from the 14th to 19th century. In the late 19th century, Macedonia was claimed by Greece, Serbia and Bulgaria. In the first of the BALKAN WARS (1912–13), Bulgaria gained much of historic Macedonia, but it was decisively defeated in the Second Balkan War and the present-day boundaries were established.

Macedonia Greek region, bordering the Former Yugoslav Republic of MACEDONIA; the capital is THESSALONÍKI. A mountainous region, it includes many ancient sites, such as the former capital, Pella.

Macedonia Balkan republic in SE Europe. The landlocked Former Yugoslav Republic of Macedonia is a largely mountainous country. The land rises to Mount Korab, at 2,764m (9,068ft), on the border with Albania. Most of Macedonia is drained by the River Vardar, and the capital, SKOPJE, lies on its banks. In the SW, Macedonia shares the large lakes of Ohrid and Prespa with Albania and Greece. **Climate** Macedonia's climate is mainly continental, with hot summers, cold winters and often heavy snowfall. Rainfall is slightly heavier in early summer and autumn. **Vegetation** Mountain forests of beech and oak are common, but farmland covers *c*.30% of Macedonia. **History and Politics** (*for history pre-1913, see* MACEDON) The BALKAN WARS (1912–13) ended with the flight of thousands of Macedonians into Bulgaria and the division of Macedonia into Greek Macedonia, Bulgarian Macedonia and Serbian Macedonia (the largest portion, in the N and centre). At the end of World War 1, Serbian Macedonia became part of the Kingdom of the Serbs, Croats and Slovenes (later YUGOSLAVIA). Macedonian nationalists waged an armed struggle against Serbian domination. Between 1941 and 1944, Bulgaria occupied all Macedonia, but a peace treaty restored the 1913 settlement. In 1946, President TITO created a federal Yugoslavia, and Macedonia became one of its constituent republics. Regional tension between Greece, Bulgaria and Yugoslavia remained strong. In 1990, multiparty elections produced the first post-1945, non-communist regional government, with Kiro Gligorov as president. In September 1991, the break-up of the Yugoslav Federation led to Macedonia's declaration of independence. It

---

MACEDONIA
AREA: 24,900sq km (9,600sq mi)
POPULATION: 2,157,000
CAPITAL (POPULATION): Skopje (541,000)

renounced all territorial claims to Greek and Bulgarian Macedonia, but (under pressure from Greece) the EC refused to recognize its sovereignty on the grounds that its name, flag and currency were signs of its territorial intentions. A compromise was reached, and the country temporarily became known as the Former Yugoslav Republic of Macedonia (FYRM). In 1993, the UN accepted the new republic as a member and all the EC members, except Greece, established diplomatic relations with the FYRM. In 1994, Greece banned Macedonian trade through Greece. The ban was lifted in 1995, when Macedonia agreed to redesign its flag and remove any claims to Greek Macedonia from its constitution. Internal tensions exist between Macedonians and the Albanian minority. In 1998, elections a right-wing coalition formed a new government. The war in the Serbian province of KOSOVO led to the influx of c.245,000 ethnic Albanian refugees. In 1999, Gligorov was replaced as president by Boris Trajkovski. **Economy** Macedonia is a developing country (1995 GDP per capita, US$1,550). The poorest of the six former republics of Yugoslavia, its economy was devastated by UN trade sanctions against the rump Yugoslav federation and by the Greek embargo. In 1995 unemployment was running at 36% and inflation at 57%. The extent of national debt is also a major obstacle. Manufactures, especially metals, dominate exports. Macedonia mines coal, but imports oil and natural gas. Agriculture employs nearly 17% of the workforce, and Macedonia is nearly self-sufficient in food. Major crops include cotton, fruits, maize, tobacco and wheat.

McEnroe, John Patrick, Jr (1959–) US tennis player, b. Germany. He was an exquisite stroke-maker whose fiery temperament often led to conflict with officials. McEnroe won the US Open singles four times (1979–81, 1984) and Wimbledon three times (1981, 1983–84). He and Peter Fleming also captured 10 Grand Slam doubles titles.

McEwan, Ian (1948–) English novelist. McEwan's early collections of short stories, *First Love, Last Rites* (1975) and *In Between the Sheets* (1977), and his novella *The Cement Garden* (1978), portrayed themes of sexual perversion and psychological disturbance. These themes continued to dominate his novels, which include *The Child in Time* (1987), *The Innocent* (1990) *Black Dogs* (1992) and *Enduring Love* (1997) McEwan's short novel *Amsterdam* (1998) was awarded the Booker Prize.

Machaut, Guillaume de (c.1300–77) French poet, musician and diplomat. His best-known poetry, which influenced CHAUCER and anticipated the ballade and the rondeau, is to be found in *Le livre de Voir-dit* (1361–65). A leading figure of the *ars nova*, he was among the first to compose polyphonic settings of poetry and the Mass.

Machiavelli, Niccolò (1469–1527) Florentine statesman and political theorist. He served from 1498 to 1512 as an official in the republican government of Florence but lost his post when the Medici family returned to power. His most famous work, *The Prince* (1513), offered advice on how the ruler of a small state might best preserve his power, including judicious use of force. The term "Machiavellian", to describe immoral and deceitful political behaviour, arose from a simplification of Machiavelli's ideas.

machine Device that modifies or transmits a FORCE in order to do useful WORK. In a basic, or simple, machine, a force (**effort**) overcomes a larger force (**load**). The ratio of the load (output force) to the effort (input force) is the machine's **force ratio** (formerly MECHANICAL ADVANTAGE). The ratio of the distance moved by the

load to the distance moved by the effort is the distance ratio (formerly velocity ratio). The ratio of the work done by the machine to that put in it is the EFFICIENCY, usually expressed as a percentage. The three primary machines are the inclined plane (which includes the screw and the wedge), the LEVER and the wheel (which includes the PULLEY and the WHEEL AND AXLE).

machine code In computing, instructions that the CENTRAL PROCESSING UNIT (CPU) of a COMPUTER can execute directly, without the need for translation. Machine-code statements are written in a binary-coded (low-level) COMPUTER LANGUAGE. Programmers usually write computer PROGRAMS in a high-level language (such as FORTRAN or C), which a COMPILER program then translates into machine code for execution. *See also* BINARY SYSTEM

machine gun Weapon that loads and fires automatically and is capable of sustained rapid fire. The firing mechanism is operated by recoil (backwards thrust) or by gas from fired ammunition. The gun may be water- or air-cooled. The first widely used machine gun, the Maxim gun, was invented (1883) by Hiram MAXIM. *See also* GATLING GUN

machine tools Power-driven machines for cutting and shaping metal and other materials. Shaping may be accomplished in several ways, including shearing, pressing, rolling and cutting away excess material using lathes, shapers, planers, drills, milling machines, grinders and saws. Other techniques include the use of machines that use electrical or chemical processes to shape the material. Advanced machine-tool processes include cutting by means of LASER beams, high-pressure water jets, streams of PLASMA (ionized gas) and ULTRASONICS. Today, computers control many cutting and shaping processes carried out by machine tools and ROBOTS.

Mach number Ratio of the speed of a body or fluid to the local speed of SOUND. Mach 1 therefore refers to the local speed of sound. An aircraft flying at below Mach 1 is said to be subsonic. SUPERSONIC FLIGHT means flying at speeds above Mach 1. Mach numbers are named after the Austrian physicist Ernst Mach (1838–1916).

Machu Picchu Ancient fortified town, 80km (50mi) NW of Cuzco, Peru. The best-preserved of the INCA settlements, it is situated on an Andean mountain saddle, 2,057m (6,750ft) above sea level. A complex of terraces extends over 13sq km (5sq mi), linked by more than 3,000 steps. Machu Picchu was discovered in 1911 by the American explorer Hiram BINGHAM, who dubbed it the "lost city of the Incas".

Macintosh, Charles (1766–1843) Scottish chemist and inventor after whom the mackintosh coat is named. In 1823, he invented a method of making waterproof cloth by joining two pieces of fabric using a solution of rubber in coal-tar naphtha. However, it was not until 1839, with the advent of vulcanized rubber that withstood temperature changes, that the mackintosh became a practical garment.

Macke, August (1887–1914) German painter. He was a prominent member of der BLAUE REITER and specialized in sensitive watercolours, such as *The Zoo* (1912). During visits to Paris (1907–12), he was influenced by Robert DELAUNAY and by experimental groups, notably FAUVISM and ORPHISM.

McKellen, Sir Ian (1939–) English film and stage actor. In 1965, he joined the National Theatre. McKellen gained his reputation with the Royal Shakespeare Company (1974–78). His films include *Scandal* (1989), *Six Degrees of Separation* (1993), *Richard III* (1995) and *Restoration* (1995). He was nominated for an Academy

Award for his performance in *Gods and Monsters* (1998). He is a leading figure in the gay rights movement Stonewall. McKellen was knighted in 1991.

Mackenzie, Sir Alexander (1764–1820) Canadian fur trader and explorer, b. Scotland. He moved to Montréal in 1778, and in 1787 became a partner in the fur-trading North West Company. In 1793, Mackenzie's journey to the Pacific via the Peace and Fraser rivers proved the impossibility of a sea passage to the west, although it was the first crossing of the continent N of Mexico. He wrote *Voyages...to the Frozen and Pacific Oceans* (1801).

Mackenzie, Sir (Edward Montague) Compton (1883–1972) British novelist. He wrote the popular novels *Sinister Street* (1913–14) and *Whisky Galore* (1947).

Mackenzie River in NW Canada. The longest river in Canada, it flows *c*.1,800km (1,120mi) NW from the Great Slave Lake to the Arctic Ocean. Between the Great Slave and Athabasca lakes, the Mackenzie is called the Slave River. Minerals are the principal economic resource of the basin.

mackerel Fast-swimming, agile marine food fish related to the TUNA and found in shoals in the N Atlantic, N Pacific and Indian oceans. The mackerel has a streamlined body and powerful tail. The body colour is silvery blue with dark side bars. It has a voracious appetite and lives on smaller fish and plankton. Length: 61cm (2ft). Family Scombridae.

Mackerras, Sir (Alan) Charles (1925–) Australian conductor, b. USA. He was musical director (1970–79) of English National Opera (ENO). In 1986, he became music director of Welsh National Opera. His most distinctive contribution has been as an interpreter of Czech music, notably Leós JANÁCEK.

McKinley, William (1843–1901) 25th US president (1897–1901). He served as a Republican representative (1876–90) and was elected governor of Ohio in 1891. In 1896 McKinley defeated William Jennings BRYAN in the presidential election. A strong and effective president, he was largely preoccupied by foreign affairs. McKinley gained the support of Congress for the SPANISH-AMERICAN WAR (1898) and sanctioned US participation in suppression of the BOXER REBELLION in China (1900). McKinley declared that ISOLATIONISM was "no longer possible or desirable". Re-elected in 1900, he was shot dead by an anarchist on 6 September 1901. McKinley was succeeded by Theodore ROOSEVELT.

McKinley, Mount Peak in S central Alaska in the Alaska Range, and the highest peak in North America. Permanent snowfields cover more than half the mountain. Wildlife is abundant on the lower slopes, in particular caribou and white Alaskan mountain sheep. It is included in Mount McKinley National Park (since 1980 known by the Aleutian name of Denali). Height: 6,194m (20,321ft).

Mackintosh, Charles Rennie (1868–1928) Scottish architect, artist and designer. He was one of the most successful and gifted exponents of ART NOUVEAU. His buildings, such as the Glasgow School of Art (1898–1909), were notable for their simplicity of line and skillful use of materials. Mackintosh's ideas had an enormous influence on early 20th-century European architecture, especially in Germany and Austria.

MacLeish, Archibald (1892–1982) US poet and playwright. One of the US expatriates in Paris during the 1920s, he was strongly influenced by Ezra POUND and T.S. ELIOT. His works include the epic poem *Conquistador* (1932) and *Collected Poems* (1952), both of which won Pulitzer Prizes, as did his verse play, *J.B.* (1958). Other successful plays include *Nobodaddy* (1926) and *The Trojan Horse* (1952).

McLuhan, (Herbert) Marshall (1911–80) Canadian academic and expert on communications. His view that the forms in which people receive information (such as television, radio and computers) are more important than the messages themselves was presented in his books *The Mechanical Bride: Folklore of Industrial Man* (1951), *Understanding Media* (1964) and *The Medium is the Message* (1967).

McMillan, Edwin Mattison (1907–91) US physicist. In 1951, he shared the Nobel Prize for chemistry with Glenn SEABORG for their discovery of NEPTUNIUM and other TRANSURANIC ELEMENTS. McMillan worked on the atomic bomb at Los Alamos, New Mexico, then on the cyclotron with Ernest LAWRENCE at the University of California at Berkeley. He developed the synchrocyclotron that led to modern nuclear ACCELERATORS, for which he shared the 1973 Atoms for Peace Prize.

Macmillan, (Maurice) Harold (1894–1986) British statesman, prime minister (1957–63). He entered Parliament in 1924. Macmillan held a succession of Conservative cabinet posts, including minister of defence (1954–55) and chancellor of the exchequer (1955–57), before succeeding Anthony EDEN as prime minister.

► **Mackintosh** Glasgow School of Art (1909). Scottish architect Charles Rennie Mackintosh based his work upon the tradition of Scottish baronial architecture, arriving at a simplified style stripped of all formal ornamentation. The clarity of line of the Glasgow School of Art is a hallmark of his austere style of art nouveau.

Macmillan improved Anglo-American relations and sought a *rapprochement* between Moscow and Washington. His attempt to lead Britain into the European Economic Community (EEC) faltered in the face of French Premier Charles De Gaulle's opposition. Macmillan's campaign on the theme of domestic prosperity ("you've never had it so good") won him a landslide victory in the 1959 general election. His second term was beset by recession and the Profumo scandal. Macmillan resigned on grounds of ill health and was succeeded by Alec Douglas-Home. In 1984, he became Earl of Stockton.

Macmillan, Sir Kenneth (1929–92) Scottish choreographer and dancer. He was director (1970–77) of the Royal Ballet. Macmillan's modern ballets include *Romeo and Juliet* (1965), *Manon* (1974) and *Mayerling* (1978). He was knighted in 1983.

MacNeice, Louis (1907–63) Northern Irish poet. MacNeice was a leading member of a left-wing group of writers of the 1930s, later dubbed the "Auden circle". MacNeice and W.H. Auden collaborated on *Letters from Iceland* (1937). Other volumes include *Autumn Journal* (1939) and *Solstices* (1961). Other works include the verse play *The Dark Tower* (1947).

McQueen, Steve (1930–80) US film actor. He had a tough, raw screen talent, trading on his maverick personality. McQueen is chiefly remembered for roles in action films of the 1960s and 1970s, such as *The Magnificent Seven* (1960) and *The Great Escape* (1962). Often performing the stunts himself, McQueen made the chase scene a trademark in later films, including *Bullitt* (1968) and *The Getaway* (1972).

Macready, William Charles (1793–1873) English actor and theatrical manager. Macready was hailed as the greatest Shakespearean actor of his generation in the roles of Macbeth, Lear and Hamlet. His productions were noted for their meticulous attention to detail.

macroeconomics Study of the economic system as a whole, rather than the study of individual markets (*see* microeconomics). It involves the determination of items such as gross national product (GNP) and the analysis of unemployment, inflation, growth and the balance of payments. *See also* economics; Keynes, John Maynard

macromolecule Molecule up to 1,000 times greater in diameter than the molecules of most substances. Many proteins, nucleic acids, plastics, resins, rubbers and natural and synthetic fibres are made up of such giant units.

macrophage Large white blood cell (leucocyte) found mainly in the liver, spleen and lymph nodes. It engulfs foreign particles and microorganisms by phagocytosis. Working together with other lymphocytes, it forms part of the body's immune system. *See also* phagocyte

Madagascar Island republic in the Indian Ocean, 390km (240mi) off the e coast of Mozambique, se Africa. Madagascar is the world's fourth-largest island. In the w, a wide coastal plain gives way to the central highlands, mostly between 600m and 1,220m (2,000ft–4,000ft). This is Madagascar's most densely populated region and home of the capital, Antananarivo. The land rises in the n to the volcanic peak of Tsaratanana, at 2,876m (9,436ft). The land slopes off in the e to a narrow coastal strip. **Climate** Antananarivo lies in the tropics, but temperatures are

moderated by altitude. Winters (April to September) are dry, but heavy rain falls in summer. The e coastlands are warm and humid, while the w is drier. **Vegetation** Grass and scrub grow in the s. Forest and tropical savanna once covered much of the country, but large areas have been cleared for farming, destroying natural habitats and seriously threatening Madagascar's unique and diverse wildlife. **History and politics** Africans and Indonesians arrived more than 1,400 years ago, and Muslims arrived in the 9th century. In the early 17th century Portuguese missionaries vainly sought to convert the native population. The 17th century saw the creation of small kingdoms. In the early 19th century, the Merina began to subdue smaller tribes, and by the 1880s they controlled nearly all the island. In 1896, the French defeated the Merina, the monarchy was abolished and Malagasy (as the island was then known) became a French colony. In 1942, Vichy colonial rule was overthrown by the British, and the Free French reasserted control. In 1946–48, a rebellion against French power was brutally dispatched, and as many as 80,000 islanders died. In 1958, republican status was adopted. In 1960, full independence was achieved. President Tsiranana's autocratic government adopted many unpopular policies, such as the advocacy of economic relationships with South Africa's apartheid regime. In 1972, the military took control of government. In 1975, Malagasy was renamed Madagascar, and Lieutenant Commander Didier Ratsiraka proclaimed martial law and banned opposition parties. During the 1980s, Madagascar was beset by civil strife and numerous failed coups. In 1991, the opposition formed a rival government, led by Albert Zafy. In 1993, multiparty elections Zafy became president. In 1995, he was granted the right of prime ministerial appointment. In 1996, Zafy was impeached. In the 1997 elections, Ratsiraka regained the presidency. Madagascar was devastated by floods and tropical storms in 2000. **Economy** Madagascar is one of the world's poorest countries (1995 GDP per capita, US$640). The land has been badly eroded by deforestation and overgrazing. Farming, fishing and forestry employ *c*.80% of the workforce. Food and live animals form 66% of all exports. The major cash crop is coffee. Madagascar produces *c*.66% of the world's natural vanilla. Other exports include cloves, sisal and sugar. Madagascar's food crops include bananas, cassava, rice and sweet potatoes. It is hoped that interest in Madagascar's 150,000 unique species of plants and animals will encourage eco-tourism.

mad cow disease Popular name for bovine spongiform encephalopathy (BSE)

Madeira Islands Archipelago and autonomous Portuguese region, off the nw African coast, *c*.420km (260mi) n of the Canary Islands, in the Atlantic Ocean; capital and chief port is Funchal (on Madeira). Madeira, the largest, and Porto Santo are the only inhabited islands. The region's warm and stable climate makes it a popular European tourist destination. Industries: production of Madeira (a fortified wine), sugar cane, fruit and embroidery. Area: 794sq km (307sq mi). Pop. (1991) 253,400.

Maderna, Bruno (1920–73) Italian composer, conductor, and leader of the Italian avant-garde. In 1955, he and Luciano Berio co-founded the electronic music studio of Italian Radio. His use of electronic media was often combined with live performance.

Madero, Francisco Indalecio (1873–1913) Mexican statesman, president (1911–13). In 1910, Madero was imprisoned for his opposition to the dictatorship of Porfirio Díaz and was forced to flee to Texas, where he called for a Mexican Revolution. With the aid of

MADAGASCAR

AREA: 587,040sq km (226,656sq mi)
POPULATION: 16,627,000
CAPITAL (POPULATION): Antananarivo (1,053,000)

"Pancho" VILLA and Emiliano ZAPATA, Madero overthrew Díaz. Madero was a weak president, and the revolutionary movement rapidly and violently fragmented. He was murdered during a military coup led by his former general Victoriano HUERTA.

Madhya Pradesh State in central India; the capital is BHOPAL. Other major cities include GWALIOR and INDORE. Lying between the DECCAN and Gangetic plains, it is the largest state in India. During the 16th–17th centuries, the region was ruled by the indigenous Gonds. In the 18th century, the MARATHAS assumed control. In 1820, it was occupied by the British, and from 1903 to 1950 it was known as the Central Provinces and Berar. In 1956, Madhya Bharat, Vindhya Pradesh and Bhopal were incorporated into the new state of Madhya Pradesh. The economy is dominated by agriculture. Major crops include wheat, rice and cotton. Madhya Pradesh is also rich in mineral resources, such as bauxite, iron ore and manganese. Bhopal has chemical and electrical industries. Area: 443,446sq km (171,261sq mi). Pop. (1991) 66,181,170.

Madison, James (1751–1836) Fourth US President (1809–17). Madison was a close adviser to George WASHINGTON until, dismayed by the growing power of the executive, he broke with the FEDERALIST PARTY, his former allies. Madison became associated with Thomas JEFFERSON. Jefferson, as president, made him secretary of state in 1801, and he succeeded Jefferson in the presidency, winning the election easily. As president Madison was unable to avoid the WAR OF 1812 with Britain, which provoked threats of secession in New England. The successful conclusion of the war restored national prosperity, and Madison, the "Father of the Constitution", retired to his Virginia plantation as an admired elder statesman.

Madison State capital and second-largest city of Wisconsin, on an isthmus between lakes Mendota and Monona. Founded as the state capital in 1836, it was incorporated as a city in 1856. It is an educational and manufacturing centre in a dairy-farming region. Industries: agricultural machinery, meat and dairy products, medical equipment. Pop. (1990) 191,262.

Madonna (1958–) US popular singer and actress, b. Madonna Louise Veronica Ciccone. Her first hit was "Like A Virgin" (1984). After a promising acting debut in *Desperately Seeking Susan* (1985), Madonna's film career was less consistent and she turned to other media. The documentary *Madonna: Truth or Dare* (1991) was followed by the book *Sex* (1992). Albums include *Like A Prayer* (1989), *Erotica* (1992) and *Ray of Light* (1998). Other films include *Evita* (1996).

Madonna Representation in painting or sculpture of the Virgin MARY, usually with the infant Jesus. The early Christians painted the Madonna in their catacombs, and she was a feature of many outstanding Byzantine ICONS. The advent of the Renaissance brought less stylized representations, and portraits of her during that period were produced by almost every great painter and sculptor.

Madras Former name of CHENNAI

Madrid Capital and largest city of Spain, lying on a high plain in the centre of the country on the River Manzanares. It is Europe's highest capital city, at an altitude of 655m (2,149ft). Madrid was founded in the 10th century as a Moorish fortress. In 1083 it was captured by Alfonso VI of Castile. In 1561 Philip II moved the capital from Valladolid to Madrid. The French occupied the city during the PENINSULAR WAR (1808–14). The city expanded considerably in the 19th century. During the Spanish CIVIL WAR Madrid remained loyal to the Republican

cause and was under siege for almost three years. Its capitulation in March 1939 brought the war to an end. Modern Madrid is a thriving cosmopolitan centre of commerce and industry. Major economic activities include tourism, banking and publishing. Pop. (1995) 3,030,000.

madrigal Form of unaccompanied vocal music originating in Italy in the 14th century. Early madrigals feature two or three parts and a highly ornamented upper part. During the 16th and early 17th centuries, the number of voices was increased and the style became more contrapuntal. The middle period of madrigal composition (c.1540–80) was dominated by Italian masters, such as Andrea GABRIELI and PALESTRINA, and Flemish composers such as Orlando di LASSO. The late period (c.1580–1620) was dominated by Italians such as Carlo GESUALDO and MONTEVERDI and English composers such as William BYRD, Orlando GIBBONS and Thomas Weelkes.

Madurai City on the River Vaigai, in Tamil Nadu state, S India. It served as the capital of the Pandya dynasty (5th century BC–11th century AD) and the Nayaka kingdom (c.1550–1736) before passing to the British in 1801. Industries: weaving, brassware, woodcarving, coffee, tea, tourism. Pop. (1991) 1,094,000.

Maecenas, Gaius (70–08 BC) Roman statesman and literary patron. He was a close supporter of Octavian (later Emperor AUGUSTUS). Hugely wealthy, Maecenas is remembered best for his patronage of poets such as HORACE and VIRGIL. His name has become a synonym for a wealthy benefactor of the arts.

maenad Female follower of DIONYSUS. Maenads are depicted carrying staffs entwined with ivy and surmounted by a pine cone while dancing in orgiastic revels.

Maeterlinck, Maurice (1862–1949) Belgian dramatist. His plays include *The Princess Maleine* (1889), *Pelléas and Mélisande* (1892) and *The Blue Bird* (1908), first produced in Moscow by STANISLAVSKY. Maeterlinck was awarded the 1911 Nobel Prize for literature.

Mafeking, Siege of (1899–1900) Siege during the second of the SOUTH AFRICAN WARS. British troops, led by BADEN-POWELL, were held in Mafeking, N South Africa, by Boer forces for 217 days. The lifting of the siege was a cause for national celebration in England.

Mafia (It. boldness) Name given to organized groups of Sicilian bandits. Originating in feudal times, the Mafia spread to the USA in the early 20th century and became involved in organized crime during the PROHIBITION era.

Magdalene, Mary See MARY MAGDALENE, SAINT

Magdeburg City on the River Elbe, central Germany; capital of Saxony-Anhalt state. In the 13th century the city was granted a charter, and Magdeburg prospered as a leading member of the HANSEATIC LEAGUE. During the 16th century it was one of the centres of the Protestant REFORMATION. In 1631, during the THIRTY YEARS WAR, Magdeburg was sacked and destroyed by fire. The city also suffered heavy bomb damage in World War 2. A major inland port, it is linked to the Rhine and the Ruhr by the Mittelland Canal. Industries: iron and steel, scientific instruments, chemicals. Pop. (1995) 265,000.

Magellan, Ferdinand (1480–1521) Portuguese explorer, leader of the first expedition to circumnavigate the globe. He sailed to the East Indies and may have visited the Spice Islands (Moluccas) in 1511. Subsequently he took service with Spain, promising to find a route to the Moluccas via the New World and the Pacific. In 1519, Magellan set out with five ships and nearly 300 men. He found the waterway near the S tip of South America that is now named Magellan's Strait. After severe hardships, the expedition reached the Philippines, where Magellan was killed in a local conflict. Only one ship, the *Victoria*, completed the round-the-world voyage.

Magellanic Clouds Two small satellite GALAXIES of the MILKY WAY galaxy, visible in skies around the South Pole as misty stellar concentrations. The Small Cloud (**Nubecula Minor**), located in the constellation of Tucana, is irregular; the Large Cloud (**Nubecula Major**), mostly in the constellation of Dorado, is vaguely spiral. Their distance is *c*.150,000 light-years away.

maggot Name commonly given to the legless LARVA of a FLY. It is primarily used to describe those larvae that infest food and waste material; others are generally called grubs or CATERPILLARS. *See also* METAMORPHOSIS

Maghreb Arabic term for NW Africa, generally applied to MOROCCO, ALGERIA, TUNISIA and sometimes LIBYA.

Magi (sing. Magus) Members of a hereditary priestly class of ancient Persia (Iran), responsible for certain religious ceremonies and cultic observances. By the time of Christ, the term Magi applied to astrologers, soothsayers and practitioners of the occult. The coming of the Magi to JESUS is marked in the Western Church by the feast of EPIPHANY. In the East it is celebrated at Christmas.

magic Use or apparent use of natural or spirit forces to produce results that seem logically impossible. Belief in magic is associated mainly with primitive societies, although traces can still be found (such as superstitions) in developed countries. There are two main types of magic: **black** magic (which makes use of evil spirits and delights in evil for evil's sake) and **white** magic (used to good purpose and to counteract the evil effects of black magic). *See also* WITCHCRAFT

magic realism Twentieth-century school of fiction. Particularly associated with post-1945 Latin American novelists, magic realism is characterized by the interweaving of realistic and fantastical or supernatural elements. Gabriel GARCÍA MÁRQUEZ's novel *One Hundred Years of Solitude* (1967) is perhaps the greatest example of the genre.

magistrate In England, anyone invested by the state with authority to administer the law. A magistrate is a judicial officer, inferior to a judge, who presides over a magistrate's court. There are two kinds, the unpaid justice of the peace (JP) and, in larger towns, the stipendiary (paid) magistrate.

Maginot Line French fortifications on the border with Germany. Designed to prevent a German invasion, it was built between the world wars and named after André Maginot, French minister of war (1929–32). It contained its own underground railway, hospitals and barracks and was considered impregnable. When the Germans invaded France in 1940 they advanced through Belgium, outflanking the Maginot Line. *See also* WORLD WAR 2

magma Molten material that is the source of all IGNEOUS ROCKS. The term refers to this material while it is still under the Earth's crust. In addition to its complex silicate composition, magma contains gases and water vapour.

Magna Carta (June 1215) "Great Charter" issued by King JOHN of England. He was forced to sign the charter by his rebellious barons at Runnymede, an island in the River Thames. The 63 clauses of the Magna Carta were mainly concerned with defining, and therefore limiting, the feudal rights of the king and protecting the privileges of the church. While it failed to prevent the first BARONS' WAR (1215), it has endured as a key text of the English constitution.

magnesia Magnesium oxide (MgO), a white, neutral, stable powder formed when magnesium is burned in oxygen. It is used industrially in firebrick and medicinally in antacid remedies. Magnesium carbonate, found as magnesite and also used as an antacid, is often called magnesia.

magnesium (symbol Mg) Silvery-white metallic element, one of the ALKALINE-EARTH METALS. Its chief sources are magnesite and DOLOMITE. Magnesium burns in air with an intense white flame and is used in flashbulbs, fireworks, flares and incendiaries. Its alloys are light and used in aircraft fuselages, jet engines, missiles and rockets. Chemically, magnesium is similar to CALCIUM. Hydrated magnesium sulphate is called Epsom salts. Properties: at.no. 12; r.a.m. 24.312; r.d. 1.738; m.p. 648.8°C (1,200°F); b.p. 1,090°C (1,994°F); most common isotope Mg^{24} (78.7%).

magnet Object that produces a MAGNETIC FIELD, an area around the magnet in which other magnetizable objects experience a force. Lodestones, which are naturally magnetic, were used as early magnets, and strong magnetic materials were later recognized as containing either iron, cobalt, nickel or their mixtures. A typical **permanent** magnet is a straight or horseshoe-shaped magnetized iron bar. The Earth is a giant magnet, its magnetic lines of force being detectable at all latitudes. An ELECTROMAGNET is much stronger than a permanent one and is used for raising heavy steel weights and scrap. A **superconducting** magnet, the strongest of all, has special alloys cooled to very low temperatures. *See also* ELECTRICITY; MAGNETISM

magnetic disk Plastic disk coated with magnetic material and used for storing computer PROGRAMS and DATA (information) as a series of magnetic spots. Most COMPUTERS contain a HARD DISK unit for general storage. Hard magnetic disks can store larger amounts of data and come in cartridges that slot into a special drive unit. Computers also usually have a disk drive for inserting portable, lower-capacity **floppy disks**. Data is stored magnetically on both sides of a floppy disk, and is read by magnetic heads in the computer as the disk rotates at *c*.300rpm. *See also* CD-ROM

magnetic field Region surrounding a MAGNET, or a CONDUCTOR through which a current is flowing, in

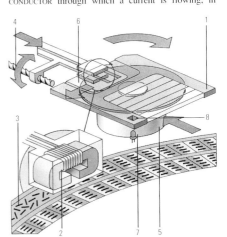

▲ **magnetic disk** A magnetic floppy disk (1) uses a magnetic head, a tiny electromagnet (2), to polarize magnetic particles in the surface of the disk (3). The polarization represents zeros and ones. A screw (4) moves the head across the disc, which is spun by a motor (5).

When the disk is inserted, a lever moves aside the protective window over the disk (6). An LED (7) checks whether the disk is write-protected. If the light can pass through a window on the disk (8) it is protected, and no new data can be stored on the disk or old data removed.

▶ **magpie** Found in temperate regions of Europe, Asia, North Africa, and NW North America, magpies are members of the crow family. The common magpie (*Pica pica*) of Europe and North America, which grows to 46cm (18in), has gained an unfavourable reputation. This is primarily due to its aggressive behaviour towards other birds and its tendency to kill distressed lambs or sickly calves.

which magnetic effects, such as the deflection of a compass needle, can be detected. A magnetic field can be represented by a set of lines of force (flux lines) spreading out from the poles of a magnet or running around a current-carrying conductor. The direction of a magnetic field is the direction a tiny magnet takes when placed in the field. **Magnetic poles** are the field regions in which MAGNETISM appears to be concentrated. If a bar magnet is suspended to swing freely in the horizontal plane, one pole will point north; this is called the north-seeking or **north pole**. The other pole, the south-seeking or **south pole**, will point south. Unlike poles attract each other; like poles repel each other. The Earth's magnetic poles are the ends of the huge "magnet" that is Earth.

magnetic flux (symbol Φ) Measure in webers (Wb) of the strength and extent of a MAGNETIC FIELD. The flux through an area A at right angles to a uniform magnetic field is $\Phi = \mu H A$, where μ is the magnetic permeability of the medium and H is the magnetic field intensity. Magnetic flux density is the flux per unit area (symbol B), which equals μH. Change of magnetic flux through an electric circuit induces an ELECTROMOTIVE FORCE.

magnetic recording Formation of a record of electrical signals on a wire or tape by means of a pattern of magnetization. In an audio tape recorder, plastic tape coated with iron oxide is fed past an electromagnet that is energized by the amplified currents produced by a MICROPHONE. By ELECTROMAGNETIC INDUCTION, variations in magnetization (from the oscillating current produced by the sound) are induced in the particles of iron oxide on the tape. When played back, the tape is fed past a similar electromagnet that converts the patterns into sound, which is in turn fed to an AMPLIFIER and LOUD-SPEAKER. *See also* SOUND RECORDING

magnetic resonance Absorption or emission of ELECTROMAGNETIC RADIATION by atoms placed in a MAGNETIC FIELD. Spectrometers for nuclear magnetic resonance (NMR) use radio frequencies for chemical analysis and research in nuclear physics, and medically to analyze body tissues. MAGNETIC RESONANCE IMAGING (MRI) is a medical scanning system for the brain, spinal cord and other soft tissues of the body.

magnetic resonance imaging (MRI) Diagnostic scanning system, based on the use of powerful MAGNETS, which produces images of soft tissues in the body. Magnetic resonance imaging (MRI) is invaluable for producing images of the brain and spinal cord in particular. The scanner's magnet causes the nuclei within the atoms of the patient's body to line themselves up in one direction. A brief radio pulse is then beamed at the nuclei, causing them to spin. As they realign themselves

to the magnet, they give off weak radio signals that can be recorded and converted electronically into images.

magnetism Properties of MATTER and of electric currents associated with a field of force (MAGNETIC FIELD) and with a north–south polarity (magnetic poles). All substances possess these properties to some degree because orbiting ELECTRONS in their ATOMS produce a magnetic field; similarly, an external magnetic field will affect the electron orbits. All substances possess weak magnetic (**diamagnetic**) properties and will tend to align themselves with the field, but in some cases this diamagnetism is masked by the stronger forms of magnetism: paramagnetism and ferromagnetism. **Paramagnetism** is caused by electron SPIN and occurs in substances having unpaired electrons in their atoms or molecules. The most important form of magnetism, **ferromagnetism**, is shown by substances such as iron and nickel, which can be magnetized by even a weak field due to the formation of tiny regions, called domains, that behave like miniature magnets and align themselves with an external field. In 1864, James Clerk MAXWELL produced a unified mathematical theory of ELECTRICITY and magnetism (ELECTROMAGNETISM).

magnetite Iron oxide mineral (Fe_3O_4). It is a valuable iron ore, found in igneous and metamorphic rocks. It is black, metallic and brittle. Permanently magnetized deposits are called lodestone. Hardness 6; r.d. 5.2.

magnetosphere Region of space surrounding a planet in which the planet's MAGNETIC FIELD predominates over the SOLAR WIND, and controls the behaviour of PLASMA (charged particles) trapped within it. The boundary of the magnetosphere is called the **magnetopause**, outside which is a turbulent magnetic region called the **magnetosheath**. Downwind from the planet, the solar wind draws the magnetosphere out into a long, tapering **magnetotail**. Mercury, Earth, and the giant planets have magnetospheres. The Earth's contains the VAN ALLEN RADIATION BELTS of charged particles.

magnification Measure of the enlarging power of a MICROSCOPE or TELESCOPE. It is the size of an object's image produced by the instrument compared with the size of the object viewed with the unaided eye. In an astronomical telescope, magnification is equal to the ratio of the FOCAL LENGTH of the objective (the lens or lenses nearest the object) to the focal length of the eyepiece.

magnitude In astronomy, numerical value expressing the brightness of a celestial object on a logarithmic scale. **Apparent** magnitude is the magnitude as seen from Earth, determined either by eye, photographically or photometrically. It ranges from positive through zero to negative values, the brightness increasing rapidly as the magnitude decreases. **Absolute** magnitude indicates intrinsic LUMINOSITY and is defined as the apparent magnitude of an object at a distance of 10 parsecs (32.6 light-years) from the object.

magnolia Any of *c*.40 species of trees and shrubs of the genus *Magnolia*, native to North and Central America and E Asia. They are valued for their white, yellow, purple or pink flowers. Height: to 30m (100ft). Family Magnoliaceae.

magpie Bird of the CROW family, closely related to the JAY, found mostly in the Northern Hemisphere. The common magpie (*Pica pica*) has a chattering cry, a long greenish-black tail and short wings. It has a clearly defined white underside with black above. They are attracted to shiny objects. Length: 46cm (18in). Family Corvidae.

Magritte, René (1898–1967) Belgian painter. Influenced by DADA, his *The Menaced Assassin* (1926) is a landmark in the development of SURREALISM. Magritte concentrated on the analysis of pictorial language, placing familiar objects in incongruous surroundings and disturbing the link between word and image. Other works that explore paradox and ambiguity include *The Key of Dreams* (1930).

Magyars People who founded the kingdom of HUNGARY in the late 9th century. From their homeland in NE Europe, they moved gradually south over the centuries and occupied the Carpathian basin in 895. Excellent horsemen, they raided the German lands to the west until checked by OTTO I in 955. They adopted Christianity and established a powerful state that included much of the N Balkans, but lost territory to the Ottoman Turks after the Battle of MOHÁCS (1526). The remainder of the kingdom subsequently fell to the HABSBURG Empire.

Mahabharata (Sanskrit, Great Epic of the Bharata dynasty) Poem of *c.*100,000 couplets, written between *c.*400 BC–C.AD 200. It is considered one of India's two major Sanskrit epics, the other being the RAMAYANA. The verse is important both as literature and as Hindu religious instruction and incorporates the BHAGAVAD GITA (Song of the Lord). Its central theme is the dynastic feud between the Kauravas and the Pandavas.

Maharashtra State in W India, bordering on the Arabian Sea; the capital is MUMBAI. From the 14th to 17th centuries, the area was under Muslim rule. In the 17th centur, it came under the control of the local Maratha tribe. Britain incorporated Maharashtra into its Indian empire in the early 19th century. India's third-largest state in both area and population, it was formed in 1960 and is composed of five sub-regions: Konkan, Deccan, Khandesh, Marathwada and Vidarbha. Most of the land lies on the dry W DECCAN plateau where farming is poor. Rice is grown along the coast. The area has rich mineral deposits, including manganese and coal. Industries, such as textiles and chemicals, are concentrated in the major cities, especially Mumbai. Area: 307,762sq km (118,827sq mi). Pop. (1991) 78,707,000.

Mahatma (Sanskrit, Great Soul) Person of special holiness. The term is used by Hindus but has no specific place in organized Hindu religion. The most famous Mahatma of modern times was Mohandas K. GANDHI.

Mahayana (Sanskrit, greater vehicle) One of the two main schools of BUDDHISM, the other being the THERAVADA, also known as *Hinayana* (smaller vehicle). Mahayana Buddhism was dominant in India from the 1st to the 12th century and is now prevalent in Tibet, China, Korea and Japan. Unlike the *Hinayana* school, it conceives of the BUDDHA as divine, the embodiment of the absolute and eternal truth.

Mahdi Messianic Islamic leader. The title usually refers to Muhammad Ahmad (1844–85) of Sudan, who declared himself to be the Mahdi (the Rightly Guided One) in 1881 and led the attack on KHARTOUM (1885). He set up a great Islamic empire with its capital at Omdurman. His reign lasted less than six months as he died in June 1885. His followers were defeated at Omdurman (1898).

Mahfouz, Naguib (1911–) Egyptian novelist and short-story writer. He is celebrated mainly for the "Cairo Trilogy" (1956–57) of realist novels (*Palace Walk*, *Palace of Desire*, *Sugar Street*), which examines the fate of one middle-class family in Cairo between 1917 and the birth of the republic in 1952. His religious allegory *Children of Gebelawi* (1959) was banned in much of the Arab world. In 1988, Mahfouz became the first writer in Arabic to be awarded the Nobel Prize for literature.

mahjong Game for four players that involves collecting winning combinations of rectangular tiles. It is

believed to have originated as a card game in China in the 1st millennium BC, but in its current form it dates only from *c.*1920. There are 144 tiles: 108 suit tiles (three suits of 36); 28 honour tiles; and eight flower or season tiles. Drawn from a "wall" or common pool, they are exchanged or strategically discharged.

Mahler, Gustav (1860–1911) Austrian composer and conductor. He conducted the Vienna State Opera (1897–1907) and Metropolitan Opera (1908–10). Mahler completed nine symphonies (the unfinished tenth was left as a full-length sketch) that incorporated folk elements and expanded the size of the orchestra. His second, fourth and eighth symphonies feature choral parts. Other works include the song cycles *Das Lied von der Erde* (1908) and *Kindertotenlieder* (1902).

Mahmud II (1785–1839) Sultan of the OTTOMAN EMPIRE (1808–39). His reign saw conflict with Greece, Russia and Egypt. He was initially successful against Greece in the Greek War of Independence, but Russian and British intervention forced him to capitulate (1829) and started the Russo-Turkish war (1828–29). Mahmud then lost the support of the viceroy of Egypt, Muhammad ALI, which led to the invasion of Turkey, precipitating Egyptian independence.

mahogany Any of numerous species of tropical American deciduous trees and their hard, reddish wood, valued for furniture making. Mahogany has composite leaves, large clusters of flowers and winged seeds. Height: to 18m (60ft). Family Meliaceae.

maidenhair fern Dainty FERN found in limestone areas in Europe and N America. The wedge-shaped leaves are borne on slender, shiny, black stalks. Leaves of most species are pink as they unfold, then turn pea-green. Height: 25–50cm (19–20in). Family Adiantaceae; genus *Adiantum*, especially *Adiantum capillus-veneris*.

Mailer, Norman (1923–) US novelist. Mailer's debut novel, *The Naked and the Dead* (1948), was one of the major works on World War 2. His combative political journalism, such as *Why are we in Vietnam?* (1967) and *The Prisoner of Sex* (1971), have courted controversy. *Armies of the Night* (1968) and *The Executioner's Song* (1979) both won Pulitzer Prizes. Mailer has experimented with a variety of genres, from thrillers, such as *Tough Guy's Don't Dance* (1984), to historical novels, such as *Ancient Evenings* (1983). *The Gospel According to the Son* (1997) was a political reworking of the life of Jesus.

Maillol, Aristide (1861–1944) French sculptor. Initially a painter and tapestry designer, he concentrated on sculpture after 1900, and his work was almost exclusively of the female nude. He turned away from the fluid forms and emotive romanticism of RODIN towards the ideals of classical Greek sculpture.

Maimonides, Moses (1135–1204) Jewish philosopher, Hebrew scholar and physician, b. Spain. As a youth he was attracted to Aristotelian philosophy, which influenced his well-known *Guide of the Perplexed*, a plea for a more rational philosophy of Judaism. In 1159, he emigrated to Egypt after a tyrannical Muslim sect took over his native Córdoba. In Cairo he became court physician to SALADIN and was the recognized leader of Egyptian Jewry. His *Mishneh Torah* is a systematic compilation of Jewish oral law. Other works on Jewish law and philosophy and on medicine confirmed him as one of the most influential thinkers of the Middle Ages.

Maine State in NEW ENGLAND, extreme NE USA; the capital is AUGUSTA. The largest city is PORTLAND. The land is generally rolling country with mountains in the W and more than 2,000 lakes. The chief rivers are the St

John, Penobscot, Kennebec and St Croix. Inhabited by the Abenaki Native Americans, Maine was explored by John Cabot in 1498. The first British settlement, Fort St George, was established in 1607 but quickly abandoned. Firm colonization began in the 1620s. In 1652, it fell under the administration of the MASSACHUSETTS BAY COMPANY and then of MASSACHUSETTS proper in 1691. In 1820, Maine achieved statehood and became the 23rd state of the Union. Economic development was rapid, based on the trading ports and Maine's timber resources for shipbuilding. Three-quarters of Maine is forested. The major economic sector is the manufacture of paper and wood products. Economic development has been hampered by poor soil, a short growing season, geographic remoteness and a lack of coal and steel. Broiler chickens and blueberries are the major agricultural products. Lobsters are the economic mainstay of the modern fishing industry. Tourism is an increasingly important sector. Sites of interest include the Acadia National Park and the start of the Appalachian Trail. Area: 86,026sq km (33,215sq mi). Pop. (2000) 1,174,923.

Mainz City in W Germany, at the confluence of the Rhine and Main rivers; capital of Rhineland-Palatinate. It was founded (1 BC) as a Roman camp. In AD 1118, it was made a free city. In the 15th century, Mainz flourished as a major European centre of learning. Today, it is an important transport and commercial centre. Pop. (1995) 185,000.

maize (corn or sweet corn) CEREAL plant of the grass family. Originally from Central America, it is the key cereal in subtropical zones. Edible seeds grow in rows upon a cob, protected by a leafy sheath. height: to 5m (16ft). Species *Zea mays*.

Major, John (1943–) British statesman, prime minister (1990–97). He entered parliament in 1979. In 1989, Margaret THATCHER unexpectedly made him foreign secretary then chancellor of the exchequer. Following Mrs Thatcher's resignation, Major emerged as her compromise successor. He moderated the excesses of Thatcherism, such as scrapping the unpopular POLL TAX. Major lent full military support to the USA in the GULF WAR (1991). He led the CONSERVATIVE PARTY to a surprise victory in the 1992 general election. The catastrophic events of "Black Wednesday" (16 September 1992) forced Britain to withdraw from the EUROPEAN MONETARY SYSTEM (EMS) and devalue the pound. The issue of Europe haunted the rest of his term and fractured the Conservative Party. Political scandals and sleaze contributed to Tony BLAIR's landslide victory at the 1997 general election. Major resigned as party leader and was succeeded by William HAGUE.

Majorca (Mallorca) Largest of the BALEARIC ISLANDS, in the W Mediterranean, *c.*233km (145mi) off the Spanish coast; the capital is PALMA. The island is administered by Spain as part of the Baleares autonomous region. In 1229, James I of Aragon captured the island from the Moors and founded the kingdom of Majorca. During the Spanish Civil War it served as a base for Italian forces supporting General Franco. Excluding the mountainous NW, the island is chiefly fertile, with rolling hills and a mild climate. Agricultural products include olives, figs and citrus fruits. Tourism is the island's economic mainstay. Area: 3,639sq km (1,405sq mi). Pop. (1987 est.) 605,512.

Makarios III (1913–77) Greek-Cypriot leader. In 1950 Makarios was appointed Greek Orthodox archbishop of CYPRUS and led the movement for *enosis* (union with Greece). In 1956, he was deported by the British. In 1959, Makarios became the first president of an independent Cyprus. In 1974, he was briefly overthrown by Greek Cypriots still demanding *enosis*. The coup provoked unrest among Turkish Cypriots and led to a Turkish invasion. Makarios was unable to prevent the subsequent partition of Cyprus into Greek and Turkish sections.

Malabo Seaport capital of Equatorial Guinea, on BIOKO island, in the Gulf of Guinea, W central Africa. Founded in 1827 as a British base to suppress the slave trade, it was known as Santa Isabel until 1973. The city stands on the edge of a volcanic crater that was breached by the Atlantic to create a natural harbour. Industries: fish processing, hardwoods, cocoa, coffee. Pop. (1992) 35,000.

Malacca (Melaka) State in Malaysia, in SW Malay Peninsula, on the Strait of Malacca; the capital is Malacca. The city was founded in 1403 and prospered as the leading trade centre for E Asia. The Muslim sultanate of Malacca became the region's most powerful empire and the centre for the spread of Islam throughout Malaya. In 1511, Malacca was conquered by the Portuguese. In 1641, it passed to the Dutch and in 1824 it was ceded to Britain. In 1957, it became a state of independent Malaya and, in 1963, of Malaysia. Area: 1,658sq km (640sq mi). Pop. (1993 est.) 583,400.

Malachi Last of the books of the 12 minor prophets and last book of all of the OLD TESTAMENT in the Authorized Version. Probably written *c.*460 BC, it addresses the Jews who had returned to Judaea after the Babylonian Captivity but were disillusioned by the continuing harshness of their existence.

Málaga City and seaport on the coast of Andalusia at the mouth of the River Guadalmedina, S Spain; capital of

▲ **malaria** The life cycle of the malaria parasite *Plasmodium* requires two hosts, the *Anopheles* mosquito and a human host, with adverse effects of infection only appearing in the human host. An infected mosquito injects thousands of *Plasmodium* organisms into the bloodstream when it bites a human (1). These penetrate liver cells, multiply, and cause cell rupture (2). Released organisms may reinfect liver cells (3) but usually progress to infect erythrocytes (red blood cells) (4, 5). Male and female parasites shortly appear in the erythrocytes (6). At this stage another mosquito bites the human and takes infected blood from them (7). Fertilization occurs within the mosquito, the "embryo" penetrating the stomach wall (8). Within the cyst formed (9), thousands or organisms develop. The cyst ruptures, organisms released travel to the salivary glands, and from here they are injected into a second human host (10).

Málaga province. It was founded in the 12th century BC by the Phoenicians. Modern tourism has swollen the city's population and spilled over into the nearby resorts of Torremolinos, Marbella and Fuengirola. Industries: wine, beer, textiles, food processing. Pop. (1995) 532,000.

Malagasy *See* MADAGASCAR

Malamud, Bernard (1914–86) US novelist and short-story writer. The son of Russian Jewish immigrants, his common theme is the nature of a Jewish identity. His novels include *The Assistant* (1957) and *A New Life* (1961). Malamud won a Pulitzer Prize for his novel *The Fixer* (1966). His short-story collections include *Rembrandt's Hat* (1973).

malaria Parasitic disease resulting from infection with one of four species of *Plasmodium* PROTOZOA. Transmitted by the *Anopheles* MOSQUITO, it is characterized by fever and enlargement of the spleen. Attacks of fever, chills and sweating typify the disease and recur as new generations of parasites develop in the blood. The original antimalarial drug, QUININE, has given way to synthetics, such as chloroquine. With 270 million people infected, malaria is one of the most widespread diseases, claiming two million lives a year.

Malawi Republic in E central Africa. Malawi is dominated by Lake MALAWI, which constitutes 50% of the nation's area. The lake forms most of its E border with Tanzania and Mozambique, and is drained in the S by the River Shire (a tributary of the ZAMBEZI). The capital, LILONGWE, lies in a valley of the central plateau. Mountains fringe the W edge of Lake Malawi, rising in the S to 3,000m (9,843ft) at Mlange. **Climate** The lowlands are hot and humid throughout the year, but the uplands have a pleasant climate. Lilongwe has a warm, sunny climate, with occasional frosts in July and August. **Vegetation** Grassland and tropical savanna cover much of Malawi. Woodland grows in wetter regions. **History and politics** The SAN were gradually displaced by Bantu-speakers, who formed the Maravi kingdom (15th–18th century). In the early 19th century, the area was a centre of the slave trade. In 1891, it became a British protectorate: slavery was abolished and coffee plantations established. In 1907, it became known as Nyasaland. In 1915, a rebellion against British domination was suppressed. In 1953, Nyasaland became part of the Federation of Rhodesia (modern Zimbabwe) and Nyasaland (the Federation also included present-day Zambia). The Congress Party, led by Dr Hastings BANDA, strongly opposed the Federation. In 1959, a state of emergency was declared. In 1963, the Federation was dissolved and in 1964 Nyasaland achieved independence as Malawi. Banda was the first post-colonial prime minister, and when Malawi became a republic (1966), he was made president. Malawi became a one-party state, and in 1967 Banda's autocratic government established diplomatic relations with South Africa's apartheid government. In 1971, as the newly appointed president-for-life, Banda became the first post-colonial, black African head of state to visit South Africa. Malawi became a shelter for rebels and refugees from the civil war in Mozambique – more than 600,000 were accommodated in the late 1980s. Banda's repression of opposition became more brutal. In 1992, international famine-relief aid was tied to improvements in human rights and the establishment of multiparty democracy. In 1994 elections Banda and his Malawi Congress Party were defeated and Bakili Muluzi of the United Democratic Front became president. In 1995, Banda and his close associates were acquitted of murder charges. Muluzi was re-elected in 1999. **Economy** Malawi is one of the world's poorest

> **MALAWI**
> AREA: 118,480sq km (45,745sq mi)
> POPULATION: 12,458,000
> CAPITAL (POPULATION): Lilongwe (395,000)

countries (1995 GDP per capita, US$750). Agriculture employs more than 80% of the workforce, mostly at subsistence level. Food crops include cassava, maize and rice. Chief export crops include tobacco, tea, sugar and cotton. Malawi lacks mineral resources and has few manufacturing industries. Lake fishing is an important activity.

Malawi, Lake (formerly Lake Nyasa) Lake in E central Africa in the Great RIFT VALLEY, bordered by Tanzania (N), Mozambique (E) and Malawi (S and W). First sighted by the explorer Caspar Boccaro in 1616, the lake was visited by David LIVINGSTONE in 1859. The third-largest lake in Africa, it is fed chiefly by the River Ruhuhu and drained by the Shire. Area: 28,500sq km (11,000sq mi). Length: 580km (360mi). Width: 24–80km (15–52mi).

Malayalam Language spoken on the W coast of extreme S India, principally in the state of Kerala. It belongs to the Dravidian family of languages and there are c.20 million speakers. It is one of the 15 constitutional languages of India.

Malayo-Polynesian Languages Alternative name for the AUSTRONESIAN LANGUAGES

Malay Peninsula Promontory of SE Asia, stretching for c.1,100km (700mi) between the Strait of MALACCA and the South China Sea. The N part of the peninsula is now S Thailand, and the S part forms Malaya (W MALAYSIA). SINGAPORE lies off its S tip. A mountain range is the backbone of the peninsula, rising to 2,190m (7,186ft) at Mount Gunong Tahang. Most of the vegetation is dense tropical rainforest. The peninsula is one of the world's largest producers of tin and rubber. Today, the peninsula is populated equally by Malays and Chinese. The region was controlled almost continuously from the 8th to the 13th centuries by the Buddhist Sailendra dynasty from SUMATRA. In the 15th century, the Malaccan empire held sway. For the next three centuries the region came under the control of the various European imperial powers. In 1909, Britain assumed control of a majority of the states and reached a border agreement with Siam (Thailand). Area: c.180,000sq km (70,000sq mi).

Malaysia Federation of SE Asian states. It consists of two main parts: **West Malaysia** is on the MALAY PENINSULA between the Strait of Malacca and the SOUTH CHINA SEA. It is home to c.80% of the population and includes the capital, KUALA LUMPUR. **East Malaysia** consists of the states of SABAH and SARAWAK, in N BORNEO. Within Sarawak is the independent nation of BRUNEI. East and West Malaysia consist of coastal lowlands with mountainous interiors. The highest peak is Kinabalu (in Sabah), at 4,101m (13,455ft). **Climate** Malaysia has a hot and rainy climate. There are monsoon seasons in the SW and NW. Kuala Lumpur averages 200 days of rain per year. **Vegetation** Dense rainforest covers c.60% of Malaysia; only 13% of the land is farmed. **History and politics** (*for early history, See* MALAY PENINSULA, SABAH and SARAWAK) In 1641, the Dutch captured MALACCA and controlled much of the trade through the narrow strait. In 1795, Britain conquered Malacca. In 1819, Britain founded SINGAPORE and in 1826 formed the Straits Settlement, consisting of Penang, Malacca and Singapore. In 1867, the Straits Settlement became a British colony. In 1888, Sabah and Sarawak became a British protectorate. In 1896 the states

MALAYSIA
AREA: 329,750sq km (127,316sq mi)
POPULATION: 21,983,000
CAPITAL (POPULATION): Kuala Lumpur (1,231,500)

of Perak, Selangor, Pahang and Negeri Semblian were federated. In 1909, the states of Johor, Kedah, Kelantan, Perlis and Terengganu formed the Unfederated Malay States. Japan occupied Malaysia throughout World War 2. After Japan's defeat, the British expanded the Federation of Malaya (1948) to include the unfederated states and Malacca and Penang. Communists (largely from the Chinese population) began a protracted guerrilla war, and many Chinese were forcibly resettled. In 1957, the Federation of Malaya became an independent state within the Commonwealth of Nations. In 1963, Singapore, Sabah and Sarawak joined the Federation, which became known as Malaysia. In 1965, tension over Chinese representation led to the secession of Singapore. The New Economic Policy (1970–90) was largely successful in reducing ethnic tension caused by economic inequality. The United Malays National Organization (UMNO) has held power, either alone or in coalition, since independence. In 1997, choking pollution from smog and the economic crisis in SE Asia led to criticism of Dr Mahathir Muhammad's premiership (1979–). In January 1998, the government announced the deportation of all non-Indonesian foreign workers. In September 1998, after publicly calling for Mahathir's resignation, Deputy Prime Minister Anwar Ibrahim was arrested on charges of corruption and sodomy. The closing ceremony of the 1998 Commonwealth Games was marred by running battles between police and demonstrators on the streets of Kuala Lumpur. Mahathir was re-elected in 1999. **Economy** Malaysia is an upper-middle-income developing country (1995 GDP per capita, US$9,020). The National Development Policy (1990–2000) was the second stage in its rapid industrialization. In the early 1990s, economic growth averaged 8% per annum. In 1997, Thailand's devaluation of its currency triggered a regional economic crisis. Malaysia's stock market lost 60% of its value, and its currency (the ringgit) lost one-third of its value against the US dollar. In 1998, the ringgit was withdrawn from international foreign exchange markets. Manufactured goods account for 78% of exports. Malaysia is the world's largest producer of palm oil, second-largest producer of tin and third-largest producer of natural rubber. Agriculture is an important activity. Rice is the chief food crop.

Malcolm III (Canmore) (c.1031–93) King of Scotland (1058–93), son of Duncan I. He gained the throne after killing MACBETH. His second marriage was to an English princess, later Saint Margaret (d.1083). Malcolm launched five invasions of Norman England. In 1072, he was forced to swear allegiance to WILLIAM I of England. He was killed at Alnwick, N England.

Malcolm X (1925–65) US African-American nationalist leader, b. Malcolm Little. He joined the BLACK MUSLIMS while in prison and, after his release (1953), became their leading spokesman. Following an ideological split with the founder of the movement, Elijah MUHAMMAD, he made a pilgrimage to MECCA, became an orthodox Muslim and formed a rival group. His assassination may have been authorized by the Black Muslims.

Maldives Republic in the Indian Ocean, c.640km (400mi) SW of Sri Lanka, consisting of c.1,200 low-lying coral islands grouped into 26 atolls; the largest island and capital is MALE. The islands (of which 200 are inhabited) are prone to flooding. The climate is tropical, and the monsoon season lasts from April to October. Coconuts and copra are the primary crop. Fishing is traditionally the major industry, and the leading export-earner is the bonito (Maldives tuna). Since 1972, tourism has been encouraged to boost foreign reserves. The chief religion is Sunni Muslim. From the 14th century, the country was ruled by the ad-Din dynasty. In 1518, the islands were claimed by the Portuguese. From 1665 to 1886, they were a dependency of Ceylon (Sri Lanka). In 1887, they became a British protectorate. In 1965, they achieved independence as a sultanate. In 1968, the sultan was deposed and a republic was declared. In 1982, Maldives joined the Commonwealth. An attempted coup in 1988 was suppressed with the aid of Indian troops. Area: 298sq km (115sq mi). Pop. (2000) 283,000.

Male Largest of the Maldive Islands, in the Indian Ocean. The island atoll forms the only urban area in the group, trading in bonito (Maldives tuna), breadfruit, copra and other coconut products. The building of a modern international airport has boosted tourism. Pop. (1995) 63,000.

Malenkov, Georgi Maksimilianovich (1902–88) Soviet statesman, prime minister (1953–55). He succeeded Joseph Stalin as prime minister and leader of the COMMUNIST PARTY OF THE SOVIET UNION (CPSU). Malenkov was soon superseded by Nikita KHRUSHCHEV as party leader and in 1955 lost the premiership to Nikolai BULGANIN. In 1957, he was implicated in an unsuccessful coup against Khrushchev and dispatched to manage a power station in Siberia. In 1961, he was expelled from the party.

Malevich, Kasimir (1878–1935) Russian painter, a pioneer of geometric ABSTRACT ART. Malevich absorbed ideas from CUBISM (LÉGER in particular) and FUTURISM and experimented with the fragmentation and multiplication of images, as in *The Knife Grinder* (1912). In 1913, he founded the SUPREMATISM movement and later concentrated on developing CONSTRUCTIVISM. His suprematist work culminated in the *White on White* (c.1918) series.

Mali Landlocked republic and largest country in W Africa. It is generally flat. Northern Mali forms part of the Sahara, which rises to the border with Algeria. This region contains many wadis (dry river valleys). The old trading city of TIMBUKTU lies on the edge of the desert. The main rivers, the Sénégal and the Niger, are both in S Mali. The capital, BAMAKO, lies on the banks of the Niger. **Climate** Northern Mali has a hot, arid climate. The S has enough rain for cultivation. Dry and dusty harmattan winds blow from the Sahara. **Vegetation** More than 70% of Mali is desert or semi-desert with sparse vegetation. Central and SE Mali is a dry grassland region known as the SAHEL. In prolonged droughts, the N Sahel dries up and becomes part of the Sahara. Southern Mali, the most densely populated region, is covered by fertile farmland and tropical savanna. **History and politics** Mali has lain at the heart of many of Africa's historic empires. From the 4th to the 11th centuries, the region was part of the ancient GHANA empire. The medieval empire of Mali was one of the world's most powerful and prosperous powers; its gold riches were legendary. The 14th-century reign of Emperor MANSA MUSA saw the introduction of Islam and the development of Timbuktu as a great centre of learning and the trans-Saharan trade. The SONGHAI empire dominated the region during the 15th century. In the 19th century, France gradually gained control. In 1893, the region became known as French Sudan and in 1898 was incorporated into the Federation of West Africa. Nationalist

MALI
AREA: 1,240,190sq km (478,837sq mi)
POPULATION: 12,685,000
CAPITAL (POPULATION): Bamako (800,000)

movements grew more vocal in their opposition to colonialism. In 1958, French Sudan voted to join the French Community as an autonomous republic. In 1959, it joined with Senegal to form the Federation of Mali. Shortly after gaining independence, Senegal seceded and in 1960 Mali became a one-party republic. Its first president, Modibo Keita, was committed to nationalization and pan-Africanism. In 1962, Mali adopted its own currency. In 1963, Mali joined the Organization of African States (OAS). Economic crisis forced Keita to revert to the franc zone and permit France greater economic influence. In 1968, Keita was overthrown in a military coup. The army group formed a National Liberation Committee and appointed Moussa Traoré as prime minister. During the 1970s, the Sahel suffered a series of droughts that contributed to a devastating famine that claimed thousands of lives. In 1979, a new constitution was adopted, and Traoré was elected president. In 1991, Traoré was overthrown in another military coup. In 1992, a new constitution established a multiparty democracy and Alpha Oumar Konaré, leader of the Alliance for Democracy in Mali (ADEMA), won the ensuing presidential election. A political settlement provided a special administration for TUAREGS in N Mali. In 1997, Konaré was re-elected and Traoré was sentenced to life imprisonment. **Economy** Mali is one of the world's poorest countries (1995 GDP per capita, US$550). Agriculture, including nomadic pastoralism, employs 85% of the workforce. Farming is hampered by water shortages, and only 2% of the land is cultivated. Another 25% is used for grazing animals. Food crops include millet, rice and sorghum. The chief cash crops are cotton, groundnuts and sugar cane. Fishing is an important economic activity. Mali has vital mineral deposits of gold and salt. In 1984, Mali rejoined the franc zone. In 1998, the IMF provided Mali with debt relief of US$250 million.

Malinowski, Bronislaw (1884–1942) English anthropologist, b. Poland, considered by many to be one of the pioneers of social ANTHROPOLOGY. His work with primitive peoples led him to believe that every aspect or norm of a society is a function vital to its existence.

mallard Common freshwater duck. The male is black, white, brown and grey with a green head, whereas the female is mottled brown with blue wing markings. It dabbles or feeds from the surface. Length: 63cm (28in). Species *Anas platyrhynchos*.

Mallarmé, Stephane (1842–98) French poet, leading exponent of SYMBOLISM and precursor of MODERNISM. His allusive poetic style defies definitive statement in favour of sound associations. Mallarmé's best known poems are *Hérodiade* (1869) and *L'Après-Midi d'un faune* (1876). His work was a defining influence on Paul VALÉRY.

Malle, Louis (1932–95) French film director. His debut feature, *Ascenseur pour l'Echaufaud* (1957) was a landmark in the French NOUVELLE VAGUE. Other films from this period include *Les Amants* (1958) and *Le Feu Follet* (1963). Malle's first English language film was *Pretty Baby* (1978). Other US films include *Atlantic City* (1981) and *My Dinner with Andre* (1981). His best-known film was *Au Revoir Les Enfants* (1987). Malle's final film was *Vanya on 42nd Street* (1995).

malleability Property of metals (or other substances) that can be permanently shaped by hammering or rolling without breaking. In some cases it is increased by raising temperature.

mallow Annual, biennial or perennial plants occurring in tropical and temperate regions. The flowers are pink and white. The mallow family includes more than 900 species of plants, of which COTTON, OKRA and HIBISCUS are among the best known. Family Malvaceae; especially genus *Malva*.

Malmö Fortified port and city on the Øresund opposite Copenhagen, SW Sweden. Founded in the 12th century, Malmö is Sweden's third-largest city. It is a major industrial centre. Industries: shipbuilding, textiles. Pop. (1997) 248,000.

malnutrition Condition resulting from a DIET that is deficient in necessary components such as PROTEINS, FATS or CARBOHYDRATES. It can lead to deficiency diseases, increased vulnerability to infection and death.

Malory, Sir Thomas (d.1471) English writer. His major work, *Le Morte d'Arthur*, is a seminal text of ARTHURIAN ROMANCE. It was printed by Caxton in 1485.

Malpighi, Marcello (1628–94) Italian physiologist. He was a founder of microscopic anatomy, demonstrating how blood reaches the tissues through tiny vessels (capillaries), as William HARVEY had conjectured. Malpighi explained the network of capillaries on the surface of the lung. The Malpighian tubules of the kidney are among the structures named after him.

Malraux, André (1901–76) French novelist and politician. He witnessed (1925–27) the Communist uprising in China, and fought for the Republicans in the Spanish Civil War and the French resistance in World War 2. Malraux was a loyal supporter of Charles DE GAULLE and served (1959–69) as minister of cultural affairs. He is celebrated chiefly for his novels *La Condition humaine* (1933) and *L'Espoir* (1937).

malt Germinated grain, usually BARLEY, used in beverages, beer and foods. The grain is softened in water and allowed to germinate. This activates ENZYMES, which convert the starch to malt sugar (maltose). The grain is then kiln-dried.

Malta Archipelago republic in the Mediterranean Sea, c.100km (60mi) S of Sicily; the capital is VALLETTA (on Malta). Malta consists of: two main islands, Malta (area: 246sq km/95sq mi) and Gozo (67sq km/26sq mi); the small island of Comino, located between the two large islands; and two tiny islets. The islands are low-lying. Malta island is composed mostly of limestone. Gozo is largely covered by clay, and as a result its landscapes are less arid. The climate is typically Mediterranean, with hot, dry summers and mild, wet winters. In spring, the sirocco may raise temperatures and damage crops. Malta has no forests, and 38% of the land is arable. **History and politics** Malta has evidence of Stone Age settlement dating back c.4,000 years. In c.850 BC, the Phoenicians colonized Malta. They were followed by the Carthaginians, Greeks and Romans. In AD 395, Malta became part of the E Roman (Byzantine) Empire. In 870, Islam was introduced via Arab invasion, but Christian rule was restored (1091) by Roger I, Norman king of Sicily. A succession

MALTA
AREA: 316sq km (122sq mi)
POPULATION: 366,000
CAPITAL (POPULATION): Valletta (102,571)

of feudal lords ruled Malta until the early 16th century. In 1530, the Holy Roman emperor gave Malta to the KNIGHTS HOSPITALLERS. In 1565, the Knights, who had fought in the CRUSADES, held Malta against a Turkish siege. In 1798, the French captured Malta but, with help from Britain, they were driven out in 1800. In 1814, Malta became a British colony and a strategic military base. In World War 2, Italian and German aircraft bombed the islands. In 1942, in recognition of the bravery of the Maltese resistance, the British king George VI awarded the George Cross to Malta. In 1953, Malta became a NATO base. In 1964, Malta became independent, and in 1974 it became a republic. In 1979, Britain's military agreement with Malta expired, and all British forces withdrew. In the 1980s, Malta declared itself a neutral country. In 1990, Malta applied to join the European Community. In 1997, the newly-elected Malta Labour Party pledged to rescind the application. The Nationalist Party, led by the pro-European Edward Adami, regained power in 1998 elections. **Economy** Malta is an upper-middle-income developing country (1992 GDP per capita, US$8,281), although it lacks natural resources. Machinery and transport equipment account for more than 50% of exports. Malta's historic naval dockyards are now used for commercial shipbuilding and repair. The state-owned Malta Drydocks is Malta's leading industry. Manufactures include chemicals, electronic equipment and textiles. The largest sector is services, especially tourism. The rocky soil makes farming difficult, and Malta produces only 20% of its food. The main crops are barley, fruits, vegetables and wheat. Malta has a small fishing industry.

Malthus, Thomas Robert (1766–1834) English economist and clergyman. In his famous *Essay on Population* (1798), Malthus argued that population

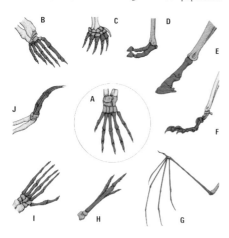

▲ **mammal** The feet of mammals have evolved in many different ways from the basic mammalian foot (A), possessed by the earliest shrewlike mammal. Seals (B) have developed evenly graduated toes for a webbed paddle. Moles (C) have truncated toes for leverage when digging. The camel's two toes (D) are padded for walking on sand. Horses have a hoof (E) instead of claws, and elongated feet for speed, as has the cheetah (F). Bats (G) have enormously elongated digits to support wings. Kangaroos' toes (H) are for hopping. Lemurs (I) and sloths (J) have forelimbs for grasping trees.

increases geometrically but food supply can increase only arithmetically, so that population must eventually overtake it, with famine, war and disease as consequences. He prescribed controls on the birth rate.

maltose (malt sugar) Disaccharide ($C_{12}H_{22}O_{11}$) that contains two molecules of the simple sugar GLUCOSE. It is produced by the hydrolysis of STARCH by the enzyme AMYLASE and by the breakdown of starches and GLYCOGEN during digestion.

mamba Any of several large, poisonous African tree snakes of the COBRA family, Elapidae. The **black mamba** (*Dendroaspis polylepsis*) is the largest species. It is grey, greenish-brown or black and is notoriously aggressive; its bite is almost always fatal. Length: to 4.3m (14ft).

Mameluke (Arabic, slave) Military elite in Egypt and other Arab countries. In 1250, the Mamelukes of Egypt overthrew the Ayyubid dynasty. They halted the MONGOLS, defeated the Crusaders and crushed the ASSASSINS. In 1517, Egypt was conquered by the Ottoman Turks, but the Mamelukes continued to control Egypt until suppressed by MUHAMMAD ALI in 1811.

Mamet, David (1947–) US dramatist and film director. He is noted for his sharp, perceptive dialogue. Mamet won a Pulitzer Prize for *Glengarry Glen Ross* (1983). Other plays include *American Buffalo* (1975) and *Oleanna* (1992). Screenplays include *The Postman Always Rings Twice* (1981) and *The Untouchables* (1987). He made his directorial debut with *House of Games* (1987).

mammal Class (Mammalia) of VERTEBRATE animals characterized by mammary glands in the female and full, partial, or vestigial hair covering. Mammals are warm-blooded. They have a four-chambered heart with circulation to the lungs separate from the rest of the body. As a group, mammals are active, alert and intelligent. They usually bear fewer young than other animals and give them longer parental care. Before birth, most mammals grow inside the mother's body and are nourished from her by means of a PLACENTA. When born, they continue to feed on milk from the mother's mammary glands. There is a wide range of features, shapes and sizes among mammals. Mammals include 17 orders of placentals, one MARSUPIAL order – all live-bearing – and an order of egg-laying MONOTREMES. They probably evolved *c.*180 million years ago from a group of warm-blooded reptiles. Today, mammals range in size from shrews weighing a few grams to the blue whale, which can weigh up to 150 tonnes.

mammary gland *See* BREAST

mammoth Extinct PLEISTOCENE ancestor of the ELEPHANT. Many were covered with long red or brown hair. The prominent tusks were long and curved, sometimes crossing in adult males. In summer months the permafrost of Siberia has been known to yield whole specimens that have been frozen for as long as 30,000 years. Genus *Mammuthus*.

man Zoological term for a HUMAN BEING

Man, Isle of Island off the NW coast of England, in the Irish Sea; the capital is Douglas. In the Middle Ages, it was a Norwegian dependency, subsequently coming under Scottish, then English rule. It has been a British crown possession since 1828, and has its own government (the Tynwald). The basis of the economy is tourism. Agricultural products include oats, fruit and vegetables. Area: 572sq km (221sq mi). Pop. (1991) 69,788.

Managua Capital of Nicaragua, in the W central part on the S shore of Lake Managua. In 1855, it became the national capital. Managua suffered damage from earthquakes in 1931 and 1962. It is the economic, industrial and commercial hub of Nicaragua. Industries: textiles, tobacco, cement. Pop. (1995) 864,000.

Manama (Al-Manamah) Capital of Bahrain, on the N coast of Bahrain Island in the Persian Gulf. It was made a free port in 1958, and a deepwater harbour was built in 1962. Manam is Bahrain's principal port and commercial centre. Industries: oil refining, banking, boatbuilding. Pop. (1995) 148,000.

manatee Any of three species of large, plant-eating, sub-ungulate, aquatic mammals found primarily in shallow coastal waters of the Atlantic Ocean. It has a tapered body ending in a large rounded flipper; there are no hindlimbs. Length: to 4.5m (14.7ft); weight: 680kg (1,500lb). Family Trichechidae; genus *Trichechus. See also* DUGONG

Manaus City and river port in NW Brazil, on the Rio Negro 16km (10mi) from its confluence with the Amazon; capital of Amazonas state. Founded in 1669, the city remained undeveloped until the late 19th-century Although more than 1,600km (1,000mi) from the Atlantic, the port can accommodate ocean-going vessels. Oil from Peru is refined here. Exports: jute, timber, nuts, rubber. Pop. (1991) 1,010,558.

Manchester City on the River Irwell, NW England. In AD 79 the Celtic town was occupied by the Romans, who named it *Mancunium.* The textile industry (now in decline) dates back to the 14th century. In 1830, the world's first passenger railway was constructed between LIVERPOOL and Manchester. In 1838, Manchester was incorporated as a borough. It was the headquarters of the 19th-century Anti-Corn Law League. In 1894, the Manchester Ship Canal opened, providing the city with its own access to the sea. The University of Manchester Institute of Science and Technology (UMIST) was founded in 1824 and the University of Manchester in 1880. Manchester is home to the Hallé Orchestra. It plays host to the 2002 Commonwealth Games. Sites include the Town Hall, designed (1877) by Alfred Waterhouse, and the Royal Exchange (1869). Industries: banking, chemicals, pharmaceuticals, printing and publishing. Pop. (1991) 404,861.

Manchu Nomadic peoples of MANCHURIA. They established the QING dynasty.

Manchukuo Japanese puppet state in MANCHURIA (1932–45). It was under the nominal rule of the pretender to the QING throne, Henry PU YI. The state of Manchukuo was not recognized by most foreign governments, and after the defeat of Japan in 1945, Manchuria was returned to China.

Manchuria Region of NE China, now included in the provinces of Heilongjiang, Jilin and Liaoning. Manchuria is rich in mineral deposits and has become one of China's leading sites for heavy industry. It is a major agricultural area, whose chief product is soya beans. Dalian is the principal port. The Manchus conquered China in the 17th century, and at the end of the 19th century the Chinese constructed the railways and the Russians developed the naval facilities at Port Arthur. In the RUSSO–JAPANESE WAR (1904–05) Japan seized control of S Manchuria and Port Arthur. In 1931, Japan occupied the whole of Manchuria and established the puppet state of MANCHUKUO. During World War 2 the region's industry aided the Japanese war effort. In 1945, Manchuria was occupied by Soviet forces, who destroyed many factories. In 1948, the Chinese communists defeated the Manchurian nationalists, and reconstruction began. From 1960 to 1990, the region was at the forefront of Sino-Soviet hostilities. Area: c.1.5 million sq km (600,000sq mi).

Manchurian Incident (1931) Japanese seizure of Manchuria. The Japanese seized Mukden in September

and rapidly overran the province, setting up the puppet state of MANCHUKUO. The ensuing SINO-JAPANESE WAR later merged into World War 2. After the defeat of Japan (1945), Manchuria was returned to China.

Mandalay City in central Burma (Myanmar), on the River Irrawaddy; capital of Mandalay division. Founded in 1857, Mandalay was the last capital (1860–85) of the Burmese kingdom before it was annexed to Britain. The city was occupied by the Japanese during World War 2 and suffered severe damage. Pop. (1983) 532,985.

mandarin (mandarine) Type of ORANGE popular because of its sweet flavour. The **tangerine** is a flattish, loose-skinned species of mandarin orange. Family Rutaceae; species *Citrus reticulata.*

Mandarin Major dialect of CHINESE, the spoken language of c.70% of the population of China. It was originally the language of the imperial court. Mandarin is the basis of modern standard Chinese.

Mandela, Nelson Rolihlahla (1918–) South African statesman, president (1994–99). He joined the AFRICAN NATIONAL CONGRESS (ANC) in 1944, and for the next 20 years led the campaign of civil disobedience against South Africa's APARTHEID government. Following the SHARPEVILLE Massacre (1960), Mandela formed *Umkhonte We Sizwe* (Spear of the Nation), a paramilitary wing of the ANC. In 1961, the ANC was banned. In 1962, Mandela was acquitted on charges of treason, but in 1964 he was sentenced to life imprisonment for political offences. He spent the next 27 years in prison on Robben Island, becoming a symbol of resistance to apartheid. International sanctions forced F.W. DE KLERK to begin the dismantling of apartheid. In February 1990, Mandela was released and resumed his leadership of the newly legalized ANC. In 1993, Mandela and de Klerk shared the Nobel Peace Prize. In 1994, Mandela gained two-thirds of the popular vote in South Africa's first multi-racial democratic elections. A strong advocate of the need for reconciliation, he made de Klerk deputy president (1994–96) in his government of national unity. In 1996, he divorced his wife, **Winnie** (1934–), who was convicted of kidnapping and of being an accessory to assault. In 1997, Mandela was replaced as leader of the ANC by Thabo MBEKI, who also succeeded him as president.

Mandelbrot, Benoit B. (1942–) US mathematician, b. Poland. He has made major contributions to CHAOS THEORY and is best known for coining the term FRACTAL. His book, *The Fractal Geometry of Nature* (1982), contains many examples of natural fractals. The Mandelbrot set, a fractal object, is named after him.

Mandelstam, Osip (1891–1938) Russian poet. One of the Acmeist group of poets (with Anna AKHMATOVA), he reacted against the mysticism of Russian SYMBOLISM. Mandelstam's poetry, such as *Stone* (1913) and *Tristiya* (1922), exhibits a desperate longing for a peaceful and harmonious society. His work ran counter to Stalinist ideology and he was arrested in 1934. Mandelstam is believed to have died in a labour camp in Vladivostok.

Mandelson, Peter (1953–) British politician, son of Herbert MORRISON. Mandelson was director of communications for the Labour Party (1985–92), before being elected (1992) as Labour MP for Hartlepool. In 1997, he was appointed minister for trade and industry, but resigned (1998) over allegations that he had accepted a personal loan from a colleague but failed to register it with the House of Commons. In 1999, he returned to the cabinet as secretary of state for Northern Ireland.

mandolin Stringed musical instrument related to the LUTE and associated with 18th-century Italy. It has four or six paired wire strings that are played with a plectrum. Today, the mandolin is most often as an accompaniment to folk songs and dances.

mandrake Plant of the potato family, native to the Mediterranean region and used since ancient times as a medicine. It contains the ALKALOIDS hyoscyamine, scopolamin and mandragorine. Leaves are borne at the base of the stem, and the large greenish-yellow or purple flowers produce a many-seeded berry. Height: 40cm (16in); family Solanaceae; species *Mandragora officinarum*.

mandrill Large BABOON that lives in dense rainforests of central W Africa. Mandrills roam in small troops and forage for their food on the forest floor. The male has a red-tipped, pale blue nose, yellow-bearded cheeks and a reddish rump. Height: 75cm (30in) at the shoulder; weight: to 54kg (119lb). Species *Mandrillus sphinx*.

Manet, Édouard (1832–83) French painter. Although Manet's name is usually linked with the IMPRESSIONISM movement, he did not consider himself an impressionist. The famed *Le Déjeuner sur l'Herbe* (1863) was violently attacked by critics for its realistic depiction of the female nude. *Olympia* (1865), a portrait of a well-known courtesan, was similarly scorned. Manet finally achieved recognition with later works, such as *Le Bar aux Folies-Bergère* (1881).

manganese (symbol Mn) Grey-white metallic element that resembles iron and was first isolated in 1774. Its chief ores are pyrolusite, manganite and hausmannite. The metal is used in alloy steels, ferromagnetic alloys, fertilizers and paints, and as a petrol additive. Properties: at.no. 25; r.a.m. 54.938; r.d. 7.20; m.p. 1,244°C (2,271°F); b.p. 1,962°C (3,564°F); most common isotope Mn^{55} (100%). *See also* TRANSITION ELEMENTS

mango Evergreen tree native to SE Asia and grown widely in the tropics for its fruit. It has lanceolate leaves, pinkish-white clustered flowers and yellow-red fruit that is eaten ripe or preserved when green. Height: to 18m (60ft). Family Anacardiaceae; species *Mangifera indica*.

mangosteen Small tropical fruit tree, Garcinia mangostana, native to SE Asia. The roundish fruit has a thick, hard purple rind surrounding its white edible flesh.

▲ **mandrill** A species of baboon, the mandrill (*Mandrillus sphinx*) is found in Equatorial West Africa. The extraordinary colours of the mandrill's face intensify if the animal becomes agitated. Zoologists believe that this display has replaced the baring of teeth to express anger common to other baboons.

mangrove Common name for any of *c*.120 species of tropical trees or shrubs found in marine swampy areas. Its stilt-like aerial roots, which arise from the branches and hang down into the water, produce a thick undergrowth, useful in the reclaiming of land along tropical coasts. Some species also have roots that rise up out of the water. Height: to 20m (70ft). Chief family: Rhizophoraceae.

Manhattan Borough of NEW YORK CITY, SE New York state, USA; lying mainly on Manhattan Island and bounded w by the HUDSON River. In 1625, the Manhattan Indians sold the island to the Dutch West India Company, and the town of New Amsterdam was built. In 1664, the British captured the Dutch colony and renamed it New York. In 1898, Manhattan became one of five boroughs established by the Greater New York Charter. Industries: electrical goods, chemicals, fabricated metals, finance, tourism, entertainment, broadcasting, publishing. Pop. (1990) 1,487,536.

Manhattan Project Code name given to the development of the US atomic bomb during WORLD WAR 2. Work on the bomb was carried out in great secrecy by a team including Enrico FERMI and J. Robert OPPENHEIMER. The first test took place on 16 July 1945, near Alamogordo, New Mexico, and in August the first atomic bombs were dropped on NAGASAKI and HIROSHIMA, Japan. *See also* NUCLEAR WEAPON

Mani (216–276) Persian prophet, founder of MANICHAEISM. As a youth he saw a vision of an angel, which was himself, and several years later, when the vision returned, he believed that he was the prophet of a new religion. Although he was martyred, his ideas spread throughout Europe, Africa and Chinese Turkistan.

mania Mental illness marked by feelings of intense elation and excitement. Speech is rapid and physical activity frenetic. In extreme cases mania is accompanied by violent behaviour.

manic depression (bipolar disorder) Mental illness featuring recurrent bouts of DEPRESSION, possibly alternating with periods of MANIA. Depressive and manic symptoms may alternate in a cyclical pattern, be mixed, or be separated by periods of remission and disturbances of thought and judgment.

Manichaeism Religious teaching of the prophet MANI based on a supposed primeval conflict between light and darkness. The Manichaean sect, which was influenced by ZOROASTRIANISM and CHRISTIANITY, spread rapidly to Egypt and Rome, where it was considered a Christian heresy, and eastward to Chinese Turkistan, where it survived probably until the 13th century.

Manila Capital of the Philippines, on Manila Bay, SW Luzon island. Manila is the industrial, commercial and administrative heart of the Philippines. The River Pasig bisects the city. On the S bank stands the old walled city (**Intramuros**), built by the Spanish in the 16th century on the site of a Muslim settlement. It became a trading centre for the Pacific area. On the N bank lies **Ermita**, the administrative and tourist centre. In 1942, it was occupied by the Japanese. In 1945, a fierce battle between Japanese and Allied forces destroyed the old city. Pop. (1990) 1,587,000.

Manipur State in NE India, on the Burmese border; the capital is Imphal. Manipur was governed by the state of ASSAM until 1949 when it was made a Union Territory. It was established as a state in 1972. Crops include rice, pulses, mustard and sugar cane. Industries: cotton and silk weaving, carpentry. Area: 22,356sq km (8,632sq mi). Pop. (1991) 1,837,149.

Manitoba Province in S central Canada, the easternmost of the prairie provinces, bordered by Hudson Bay

(NE) and the USA (S); the capital and largest city is WIN-NIPEG. The terrain varies from the prairie country and lake district of the S to the rugged upland of the Canadian Shield of the NE and the tundra of the far N. In 1670 Charles II granted the land to the HUDSON'S BAY COMPANY. In 1869, the company sold it to the newly created confederation of Canada. In 1870, Manitoba gained provincial status. Manitoba is famous for its wheat fields. Dairy farming and the rearing of poultry are also important. Mineral deposits include nickel, copper and zinc. There are large oil fields in the SW of the province and extensive timber reserves. Industries: food products, clothing, electrical products, machinery, metals, transport equipment. Area: 649,947sq km (250,946sq mi). Pop. (1994 est.) 1,131,100.

Manley, Michael Norman (1923–97) Jamaican statesman, prime minister (1972–80, 1989–92). In 1969, he became leader of the People's National Party. As prime minister, Manley introduced socialist policies such as the establishment of a system of free education and nationalization of industry.

Mann, Thomas (1875–1955) German novelist and essayist. An outstanding figure of 20th-century GERMAN LITERATURE, Mann linked individual psychological problems to the decline in European culture. His debut novel, *Buddenbrooks* (1901), a family saga, was an immediate success. Shorter works include the novella *Death in Venice* (1912) and the autobiographical essay *Reflections of a Non-political man* (1918). *The Magic Mountain* (1924) is widely acclaimed as his masterpiece. *Mario and the Magician* (1930) was an allegorical critique of fascism. In 1933, Mann left Germany, moving to Switzerland then the United States. Other works include the tetralogy *Joseph and His Brothers* (1933–43), *Dr Faustus* (1947) and the picaresque *Felix Krull* (1953). He was awarded the 1929 Nobel Prize for literature.

manna (flowering ash) Tree of the OLIVE family that grows in S Europe and Asia Minor. The pinnate leaves have rust-coloured hairs underneath. The flowers are white and showy with large petals. A sugary substance, mannite, is collected from cuts made in the bark and used medicinally. Height: to 18m (60ft); family Oleaceae: species *Fraxinus ornus*. The name manna is also given to similar substances of various origins, especially sweet substances exuded by attacking insects such as APHIDS.

Mannerheim, Carl Gustav Emil, Baron von (1867–1951) Finnish field marshal and statesman, president (1944–46). He served in the Russian army and was a general in World War 1. In 1918, Mannerheim led the anti-Bolshevik forces to victory in the Finnish Civil War and became regent of an independent Finland. In 1919, he retired after defeat in presidential elections. In 1931, as head of the defence council, he planned the Mannerheim Line across Karelia. Mannerheim commanded Finnish forces in the Finnish-Russian War (1939–40, 1941–44) and led the first post-war Finnish administration.

mannerism In art history, loose term generally applied to the art and architecture of Italy between the High RENAISSANCE and the BAROQUE (c.1520–1600). A self-conscious style, it aimed to exceed the Renaissance in terms of emotional impact. In architecture, mannerism is best represented by GIULIO ROMANO's Palazzo del Tè, Mantua (1526). Mannerist painting is characterized by elongated figures in distorted poses, often using a lurid palette of colours. Leading painters included VASARI, PARMIGIANO, PONTORMO and Giovanni LANFRANCO. Theorists are still debating the scope of mannerism: it has been extended to include MICHELANGELO, RAPHAEL, El

GRECO, the FONTAINEBLEAU SCHOOL and the Romanist painters of the Netherlands. *See also* CELLINI, BENVENUTO

Mannheim City and river port on the E bank of the River Rhine, at the mouth of the River Neckar, Baden-Württemberg, central Germany. Originally a fishing village, it was fortified in 1606 and destroyed by the French in 1689. It was rebuilt in 1697, became the seat of the Rhine Palatinate (1719–77), and passed to Baden in 1803. Industries: chemicals, oil refining, engineering, paper, textiles. Pop. (1995) 316,000.

Manning, Olivia (1912–80) English novelist. Her debut novel was *The Wind Changes* (1937). Manning's attention to characterization and historical detail is best represented by the popular Balkan trilogy: *The Great Fortune* (1960), *The Spoilt City* (1962) and *Friends and Heroes* (1965). Its sequel was the Levant trilogy: *Danger Tree* (1977), *The Battle Lost and Won* (1978) and *The Sum of Things* (1980). The two trilogies together tform the *Fortunes of War*.

manor Type of unit, or estate, characteristic of medieval Europe. Typically, a manor was divided into the lord's demesne (on which the peasants were bound to labour), an area assigned to the peasants for their own use and an area of common land. The lord, or his steward, occupied the manor house.

Mansa Musa (d.1337) Muslim emperor of MALI (1312–37). His reign marked Mali's greatest period of economic and cultural dominance. His impressive displays of the golden wealth of the imperial treasury, such as his pilgrimage to Mecca (1324–25) and his lavish gifts to Egypt, gained Mali wide international recognition.

Mansell, Nigel (1953–) English motor-racing driver. In 1980, he made his Formula 1 debut for Lotus (1980). In 1985, he joined Williams and won his first race, the European Grand Prix. In 1992, Mansell won the world driver's championship. He then left Formula 1 to compete in the US IndyCar championships, becoming World Series champion (1993).

Mansfield, Katherine (1888–1923) British short-story writer, b. New Zealand. Her debut volume, *In a German Pension* (1911), shows the influence of CHEKHOV. Mansfield's delicate humour and deceptively simple style are best represented by *The Garden Party* (1922) and *The Dove's Nest* (1923). She led a troubled life and died of tuberculosis.

Manson, Charles (1934–) US cult leader. In 1967, he established a commune based on free love and complete subservience to him. In 1969, members of the cult committed a series of brutal murders, including that of Roman POLANSKI's wife, Sharon Tate (1943–69). Manson and his accomplices were sentenced to death, later commuted to life imprisonment.

Mantegna, Andrea (1431–1506) Italian painter and engraver. In 1460, he became court painter to the Gonzaga family in Mantua and decorated the bridal chamber in the Gonzago Palace. The murals on the ceiling of the room are the first example of illusionist architecture to have been created since antiquity. Mantegna's other great work was his series of nine oil paintings, *The Triumph of Caesar* (c.1480–95).

mantis (praying mantis) Any of several species of mantids, insects found throughout the world. They have powerful front legs used to catch and hold their insect prey. Colours range from brown and green to bright pinks. Length: 25–150mm (1–6in). Family Mantidae.

mantissa Decimal part of a LOGARITHM.

mantle Layer of the EARTH between the CRUST and the CORE, which extends to a depth of 2,890km (1,795mi).

The mantle forms the greatest bulk of the Earth: 82% of its volume and 68% of its mass. The uppermost part is rigid, solid and brittle, and together with the Earth's crust, forms the **lithosphere**. From a depth of *c*.60km (40mi) down to 200km (125mi), the mantle has a soft zone called the **asthenosphere**. Temperature and pressure are in balance so that much of the mantle material is near melting point or partly melted and capable of flowing. The remainder of the mantle is thought to be more solid but still capable of creeping flow. In the lower mantle several changes in seismic velocity can be detected. The chemical constitution of the mantle is uncertain, but it is thought to be made up of iron-magnesian silicates.

mantra Sacred word, verse or formula recited during prayers or meditation in HINDUISM and BUDDHISM. Mantras include such chantings as the symbolic sound Om (Aum). *See also* TANTRISM

Manu In Hindu mythology, the hero of the deluge. Manu caught a fish that offered to save him in exchange for its life. The fish had Manu build a ship, which it towed to the Himalayas when the FLOODS came. There it was tied to a tree until the waters receded. Manu is the generic name for each of the 14 consecutive rulers of the Earth. The present ruler is the seventh, the son of the Vedic Sun god, Vivasvan. *See also* NOAH

Manx Language formerly spoken in the Isle of Man. Closely related to Scottish GAELIC, it was spoken by most of the native inhabitants until *c*.1700, when English was introduced. By 1900 there were only a few thousand speakers left.

Manzoni, Alessandro (1785–1873) Italian novelist and poet. His poetry expressed his religious faith, but his masterpiece is a historical novel, *The Betrothed* (1827), one of the outstanding works of Italian literature.

Maori Polynesian population, the original inhabitants of New Zealand. Traditionally, Maoris lived by agriculture, hunting and fishing. They retain strong attachments to their language, culture and customs. In Maori society, tattooing, carving and weaving were developed arts, and their war chants (*haka*) are still kept alive. Since the 1970s, the Maoris have been increasingly politically active, and some of their land has been returned to them. *See also* MAORI WARS

Maori Wars (1843–48, 1860–72) Series of conflicts in which the indigenous MAORIS resisted the British colonization of New Zealand. Both Maori Wars were really a succession of rebellions and were confined mainly to the North Island. They arose when the settlers broke the terms of the Treaty of Waitangi (1840) that guaranteed the Maoris possession of their lands. The rebellions of the 1840s were led by the Maori chiefs Hone Heke and Te Rauparaha. Sir George GREY was appointed governor in an effort to quell revolts. The second phase (the Taranaki Wars) was led by the Kingitanga unity movement. An 1861 truce was short-lived as Britain invaded Waikato (July 1863). In 1865 a native land court was established. In 1867, a Maori school system was formed and the Maoris allowed to have four elected members in the New Zealand legislature. British troops withdrew in 1870.

Mao Zedong (1893–1976) Chinese statesman, founder and chairman (1949–76) of the People's Republic of China. In 1921, Mao helped found the Chinese COMMUNIST PARTY. After the nationalist KUOMINTANG, led by CHIANG KAI-SHEK, dissolved the alliance with the communists in 1927, Mao helped established rural soviets. In 1931, he was elected chairman of the Soviet Republic of China, based in JIANGSU. The advance of nationalist forces forced Mao to lead the Red Army on the LONG MARCH (1934–35) NW to Shanxi. In 1937, the civil war was suspended as communists and nationalists combined to fight the second SINO–JAPANESE WAR. The communists' brand of guerrilla warfare gained hold of much of rural China. Civil war restarted in 1945, and by 1949 the nationalists had been driven out of mainland China. Mao became chairman of the People's Republic and was re-elected in 1954. ZHOU ENLAI acted as prime minister. In 1958, Mao attempted to distinguish Chinese COMMUNISM from its Soviet counterpart by launching the GREAT LEAP FORWARD. The programme ended in mass starvation, and the withdrawal of Soviet aid. Mao's leadership was challenged. The CULTURAL REVOLUTION was an attempt by Mao and his wife, JIANG QING, to reassert Maoist ideology. The cult of the personality was encouraged, political rivals were dismissed, and Mao became supreme commander of the nation and army (1970). Mao and Zhou Enlai's death created a power vacuum. A struggle developed between the GANG OF FOUR, HUA GUOFENG, and DENG XIAOPING. *Quotations from Chairman Mao Zedong* (popularly known as "The Little Red Book", 1967) is a worldwide bestseller.

map Graphic representation of part or all of the Earth's surface. Maps are usually printed on a flat surface using various kinds of projections based on land surveys, aerial photographs and other sources. *See also* MAP PROJECTION

maple Genus of deciduous trees native to temperate and cool regions of Europe, Asia and North America. They have yellowish or greenish flowers and winged seeds. They are grown for ornament, shade or timber, depending on the species; the sugar maple is also tapped for maple syrup. Height: 4.6–36m (15–120ft). Family Aceraceae; genus *Acer*.

Mapplethorpe, Robert (1946–89) US photographer. Much of his work, because of his explorations of racial imagery and homoeroticism, has caused controversy. His techniques, such as the use of platinum prints, endow his work with a fragile elegance. He died of AIDS.

map projection Any systematic method of drawing the Earth's meridians and parallels on a flat surface. Only on a globe can areas and shapes be represented with any fidelity. Projections are either geometrical derivations (cylindrical, conical or azimuthal) or networks and grids derived mathematically in transposition from globe to flat surface. **Mercator's projection** is a modified cylindrical projection.

Maputo (formerly Lourenço Marques) Capital and chief port of Mozambique, on Maputo Bay in the S of the country. It was visited by the Portuguese in 1502 and was made the capital of Portuguese East Africa in 1907, being known as Lourenço Marques until 1976. It is linked by rail to South Africa, Swaziland and Zimbabwe, and is a popular resort area. Industries: footwear, textiles, rubber. Pop. (1993 est.) 2,000,000.

marabou *See* ADJUTANT STORK

Maracaibo City and port between Lake Maracaibo and the Gulf of Venezuela, NW Venezuela. Founded in 1529, it was sacked in 1669. It expanded after the discovery of oil in 1917 and is now Venezuela's second-largest city. Industries: oil processing, coffee, cacao, sugar. Pop. (1990) 1,207,513.

Maradonna, Diego (1960–) Argentine footballer. A gifted striker, in 1984 he transferred to Napoli for £6.9 million, helping the Italian team win two Serie A titles (1987, 1990), the Italian Cup (1990) and the UEFA Cup (1989). Maradonna was captain of Argentina's World Cup-winning team of 1986, infamously scoring a goal with his hand in the quarter-final against England. He won more than 80 caps for Argentina, leading them to two more World Cups (1990, 1994). He was banned from playing in the 1994 World Cup after failing a drugs test.

Marat, Jean Paul (1743–93) French revolutionary, b. Switzerland. A physician, he founded *L'Ami du Peuple* (Friend of the People), a vitriolic journal that supported the JACOBINS. His murder by Charlotte Corday, a member of the GIRONDINS, was exploited for propaganda by the Jacobins and contributed to the ensuing REIGN OF TERROR.

Maratha (Mahratta) Hindu warrior people of W central India, who rose to power in the 17th century. They extended their rule throughout W India by defeating the MOGUL EMPIRE and successfully resisting British supremacy in India during the 18th century. They were finally defeated in 1818.

marathon Long-distance race. The standard marathon is 42.2km (26.2mi), which was the distance run by the Greek soldier who brought news of the victory over the Persians at Marathon to Athens in 490 BC.

Marathon, Battle of (490 BC) Victory of the Greeks, mainly Athenians, during the PERSIAN WARS. The defeat of a much larger Persian army on the Marathon plain NE of Athens secured Attica from the invasion of CYRUS THE GREAT.

marble Metamorphic rock composed largely of recrystallized limestones and dolomites. The colour is normally white, but when tinted by serpentine, iron oxide or carbon can vary to shades of yellow, green, red, brown or black. It has long been a favourite building and sculpting material.

Marceau, Marcel (1923–) French mime artist. His best known creation is Bip, a sad, white-faced clown with a tall, battered hat. Marceau made several films, including *Un jardin public* (1955), and made a memorable appearance in *Silent Movie* (1976).

Marche Region in E central Italy between the Apennines and the Adriatic Sea; the capital is Ancona. Except for a narrow coastal plain, Marche is mountainous. Farming is the principal economic activity; major crops include cereals, olives and grapes. Area: 9,692sq km (3,743sq mi). Pop. (1990) 1,435,570.

Marciano, Rocky (1923–69) US boxer, b. Rocco Francis Marchegiano. In 1951, he became only the second boxer to knock out Joe LOUIS. In 1952, Marciano won the world heavyweight title by knocking out Joe Walcott. In 1956, Marciano retired undefeated.

Marconi, Guglielmo (1874–1937) Italian physicist who developed RADIO. By 1897, Marconi was able to demonstrate radio telegraphy over a distance of 19km (12mi) and established radio communication between France and England in 1899. By 1901, radio transmissions were being received across the Atlantic Ocean. In 1909, Marconi was awarded the Nobel Prize for physics.

Marco Polo *See* POLO, MARCO

Marcos, Ferdinand Edralin (1917–89) Philippine statesman, president (1965–86). He was elected to the Philippine Congress in 1949. As president, Marcos received support from the US for his military campaigns (1969) against communist guerrillas on Panay and Moro secessionists on MINDANAO. Continued civil unrest led to the imposition of martial law in 1972. A new constitution (1973) gave Marcos authoritarian powers. His regime acquired a reputation for corruption and repression, symbolized by the extravagance of his wife, **Imelda** (1930–). In 1983, his main rival, Benigno Aquino, was assassinated and political opposition coalesced behind Benigno's widow, Cory AQUINO. Marcos appeared to win the 1986 general election, but allegations of vote-rigging forced

him into exile. In 1988, US authorities indicted both him and Imelda for fraud. Ferdinand was too ill to stand trial and died in Hawaii. Imelda was subsequently acquitted, but on her return (1991) to Manila she was indicted for embezzlement. In 1992, Imelda unsuccessfully ran for president. In 1993, she was sentenced to 18 years imprisonment, but appealed the judgement.

Marcus, Rudolph (1923–) US physical chemist, b. Canada, who developed what is now known as the "Marcus theory" for electron transfer (OXIDATION-REDUCTION) reactions of solvent molecules. His formula calculates the size of the energy barrier the electrons must surmount to move from one molecule to another. The theory is applicable to such processes as photosynthesis and the electrical conductivity of polymers. He received the Nobel Prize for Chemistry in 1992.

Marcus Aurelius Antoninus (AD 121–180) Roman emperor (161–180) and philosopher of the STOIC school. Between 161 and 169, he ruled as co-emperor with his adoptive younger brother Lucius Aurelius Verus (d.169). His only surviving work, the much-admired *Meditations*, is a collection of philosophical thoughts and ideas that occurred to him during his campaigns. He died in battle on the Danube frontier.

Marcuse, Herbert (1898–1979) US radical political philosopher, b. Germany. He is noted for his critical reinterpretations of MARXISM and for his Freudian analysis of 20th-century industrial society. In the 1920s, Marcuse was a founder member of the FRANKFURT SCHOOL. Fleeing Nazi Germany in 1933, he settled in the USA and worked for the US government (1941–50). Marcuse's advocacy of civil resistance found favour with left-wing students of the 1960s. His works include *Eros and Civilization* (1955) and *One-Dimensional Man* (1964). *See also* ALIENATION

Mardi Gras Community festival or CARNIVAL held on Shrove Tuesday, the day before the beginning of Lent, in many Roman Catholic countries, particularly France. In the USA, most notably New Orleans, it includes street parades, concerts and dances.

Margaret I (1353–1412) Queen of Denmark, Norway and Sweden, daughter of WALDEMAR IV. In 1363 she married King Haakon VI of Norway. Her son, Olaf, succeeded Waldemar in Denmark (1375) and Haakon in Norway (1380). In 1387, Olaf died and Margaret ruled as queen. In 1389, she defeated the Swedish king Albert of Mecklenburg. In 1397, Margaret established he Kalmar Union of the three crowns.

Margaret II (1940–) Queen of Denmark, daughter of Frederick IX. In 1972, she became the first queen regent since MARGARET I and the first democratically appointed sovereign in Denmark's history. In 1967, Margaret married the French count Henri Laborde Monpezat.

Margaret (Rose), Princess (1930–) Youngest daughter of King GEORGE VI, sister of ELIZABETH II. Margaret was married (1960–78) to Anthony Armstrong-Jones (later Lord Snowdon). The couple had two children David, Viscount Linley (1961–) and Lady Sarah Chatto (1964–).

Margaret of Anjou (1430–82) Queen consort of HENRY VI of England from 1445. During the Wars of the ROSES she led the Lancastrian cause, raising troops in France. After her only son, Edward, was killed at Tewkesbury (1471), Margaret was taken prisoner. Ransomed by LOUIS XI of France in 1476, she left England for good.

margarine Butter-like substance made from vegetable fats blended with aqueous milk products, salt, flavouring, food colouring, emulsifier and vitamins A and D. It is used for cooking and as a spread.

marguerite Perennial herb of the daisy family native to the Canary Islands. It has white-rayed, yellow-centred flower heads. Height: to 91cm (3ft). Family Asteraceae/COMPOSITAE; species *Argyranthemum frutescens*.

Mariana Islands Volcanic island chain in the w Pacific Ocean, stretching over 800km (500mi) of the Marianas Trench, *c*.2,400km (1,500mi) E of the Philippines. The group comprises GUAM and the islands of the Northern Marianas: Saipan, Tinian, Rota, Pagan and 11 smaller islands. Discovered by Ferdinand MAGELLAN in 1521 and named Islands of Thieves, the islands were renamed the Marianas in 1668. The Northern Marianas came under German control in 1898, subsequently passing to Japan. In 1944, they were taken by US forces and in 1947 became part of the US Trust Territory of the Pacific Islands. In 1978, the Commonwealth of the Northern Mariana Islands was formed in association with the USA, and in 1986 the islanders acquired US citizenship. Trusteeship status was ended in 1990. Exports include sugar cane, coconuts and coffee. Tourism is important. Area (excluding Guam): 464sq km (179sq mi). Pop. (1990) 43,345.

Mariana Trench Deep trench in the w Pacific Ocean. It is the site of the Challenger Deep, at 11,033m (36,198ft) the greatest known depth in the Pacific. Challenger Deep is deeper than Mount Everest is high.

Maria Theresa (1717–80) Archduchess of Austria, ruler of the Austrian HABSBURG Empire (1740–80). She succeeded her father, the Emperor CHARLES VI, but was challenged by neighbouring powers in the War of the AUSTRIAN SUCCESSION (1741–48), losing Silesia to Prussia but securing the imperial title for her husband, FRANCIS I. Count von KAUNITZ negotiated an alliance with France, but failed to regain Silesia in the SEVEN YEARS' WAR (1756–63). From 1765, she jointly ruled with her son, Emperor JOSEPH II.

Marie Antoinette (1755–93) Queen of France, daughter of Emperor FRANCIS I and MARIA THERESA of Austria, she married the future LOUIS XVI in 1770. Her life of pleasure and extravagance contributed to the outbreak of the FRENCH REVOLUTION in 1789. She initiated the royal family's attempt to escape in 1791, was held prisoner and was finally guillotined.

Marie de Médicis (1573–1642) Queen of France. A member of the Medici family, daughter of the Grand Duke of Tuscany, she married HENRY IV of France (1600). He was assassinated, possibly with her connivance, the day after she was crowned queen in 1610. As regent for her son, LOUIS XIII, she relied on Italian advisers and reversed Henry's anti-Habsburg policy. She was constantly at odds with Louis after 1614 and antagonized Cardinal RICHELIEU. Failing to have him dismissed in 1630, she was forced to leave France, settling in Brussels (1631).

Marie Louise (1791–1847) French Empress, daughter of Emperor FRANCIS II. In 1810 she married NAPOLEON I. In 1811 she gave birth to the future NAPOLEON II. Marie Louise acted briefly as regent during Napoleon's absences on campaign. Alienated from him by 1814, she was made duchess of Parma.

marigold Any of several mostly golden-flowered plants, mainly of the genera *Chrysanthemum, Tagetes*, and *Calendula*, all of the daisy family (Asteraceae/COMPOSITAE). Those most commonly cultivated are the French marigold (*Tagetes patula*) and the African marigold (*T. erecta*).

marijuana Narcotic drug prepared from the dried leaves of the Indian hemp plant (*Cannabis sativa*); it is different from HASHISH, which is prepared from resin obtained from the flowering tops of the plant. Possession of the drug is illegal in many countries. *See also* CANNABIS

marimba PERCUSSION instrument with tuned wooden bars, ranging five to six octaves, that are set in a frame over resonators and struck with mallets. The modern marimba was developed in South America, although it probably originated in Africa.

Marine Corps, US Branch of the US armed forces that is a service within the department of the Navy. It consists of *c*.196,000 personnel and conducts the land operations connected with naval operations.

Mariner program Series of US space probes to the planets. **Mariner 2** flew past Venus in 1962, and **Mariner 4** flew past Mars in July 1965, photographing craters on its surface. **Mariner 5** passed Venus in October 1967, making measurements of the planet's atmosphere. **Mariners 6 and 7** obtained further photographs of Mars in 1969. **Mariner 9** went into orbit around Mars in November 1971. It made a year-long photographic reconnaissance of the planet's surface and obtained close views of the two moons, Phobos and Deimos. **Mariner 10**, the last of the series, was the first two-planet mission, passing Venus in February 1974 and then encountering Mercury three times, in March and September 1974 and March 1975.

Marinetti, Filippo Tommaso (1876–1944) Italian poet, novelist, dramatist and founder of FUTURISM. In such works as *Futurismo e Fascismo* (1924), Marinetti embraced FASCISM and advocated the glorification of machinery, speed and war.

Marius, Gaius (157–86 BC) Roman general and politician. His policy of recruiting poor men without property contributed to the bond between Roman troops and their commanders. He also revised army training and equipment. His rivalry with SULLA forced him out of Rome, but he raised an army and recaptured the city (87 BC).

marjoram Perennial herb of the MINT family (Lamiaceae/Labiatae) *c*.60cm (24in) tall with purplish flowers. It is native to the Mediterranean region and w Asia and is cultivated as an annual in northern climates. Species *Origanum vulgare*.

Mark, Saint (active 1st century AD) Apostle and possibly one of the four evangelists of the New Testament. He is identified with John Mark (Acts 12:12, 15:37), the cousin of the apostle St BARNABAS. He accompanied both Barnabas and St PAUL on several missionary journeys until a disagreement with Paul caused him to detach himself. Christian tradition says that he went off to become secretary to St PETER and to write the first gospel. His feast day is 25 April.

Mark, Gospel according to Saint Second GOSPEL in the NEW TESTAMENT, but the earliest in composition. It was written *c*.AD 55–65 and is believed to be one of two reference works (the other being "Q") used by St MATTHEW and St LUKE in compiling their gospels. It is traditionally attributed to St MARK and is one of the three SYNOPTIC GOSPELS – those presenting a common view of Jesus Christ's life.

Mark Antony *See* ANTONY, MARK

market economy Economy in which resources are controlled by the operation of free-markets (in which the forces of supply and demand operate without interference). The opposite is a controlled economy, in which market forces are under governmental control; in a mixed economy, there is partial governmental control.

market research Study of consumer preferences and demand, for the purpose of increasing the sales of commercial products. It involves the collection, recording and analysis of data derived from testing a product on a representative sample of likely consumers. Interviewing to ascertain popular preferences for products is another method.

Markievicz, Constance, Countess (1868–1927) Irish nationalist. She fought in the Easter Rising (1916) and was imprisoned. In 1918, standing for Sinn Féin, Markievicz became the first woman to be elected to the British Parliament. She did not take her seat.

Markova, Dame Alicia (1910–) English ballerina, b. Lilian Alicia Marks. In 1931, she joined the Vic-Wells Ballet and was its first prima ballerina. Classical ballets in which she excelled include *Giselle*, *Les Sylphides* and *Swan Lake*. In 1935, she founded the Markova-Dolin Ballet with Anton DOLIN.

Marlborough, John Churchill, 1st Duke of (1650–1722) English general. In 1685, he helped JAMES II defeat MONMOUTH, but switched allegiance in support of the Protestant GLORIOUS REVOLUTION (1688). Partly due partly to his wife's friendship with Queen ANNE, Marlborough was appointed Captain-General of the Allied armies in the War of the SPANISH SUCCESSION. His strategic skill gained great victories at BLENHEIM (1704), Ramillies (1706), Oudenaarde (1708) and Malplaquet (1709). Churchill was rewarded with a dukedom and Blenheim Palace. When his wife lost the Queen's favour and the Tories regained power, Marlborough was dismissed (1711) and went into exile.

Marley, Bob (Robert Nesta) (1945–81) Jamaican singer-songwriter. Marley and his band, The Wailers, transformed REGGAE into an internationally popular music form with hit singles such as "Get Up, Stand Up" (1973) and "No Woman No Cry" (1974). He combined faith in RASTAFARIANISM with political statement. Marley's albums include *Natty Dread* (1975), *Exodus* (1977) and *Uprising* (1980).

marlin Any of several species of large marine fish found in warm waters of the Atlantic and Pacific oceans, especially the blue marlin (*Makaira mitsukurii*); it is often fished for sport. The marlin is blue with a coppery tint and violet side markings. The fins and long snout are sharply pointed. Length: to 8m (26ft); weight: 635kg (1,400lb). Family Istiophoridae.

Marlowe, Christopher (1564–93) English dramatist and poet. He helped make BLANK VERSE the vehicle of ELIZABETHAN DRAMA. Much of Marlowe's success derives from his ability to humanize his overreaching heroes, as in *Tamburlaine the Great* (1590), *The Tragical History of Doctor Faustus* (1604) and *The Jew of Malta* (1633). His masterpiece is *Edward II* (1592). Marlowe's greatest poems are *Hero and Leander* (1598) and *The Passionate Shepherd* (1599). He served as a spy in Francis WALSINGHAM's intelligence service and was killed in a tavern brawl.

marmoset Small diurnal, arboreal PRIMATE of South America. Among the smallest of the MONKEYS, marmosets are the size of small squirrels. They have soft, dense fur and pointed, sickle-shaped nails. Family Callitrichidae; typical genus *Callithrix*.

marmot (groundhog) Stocky GROUND SQUIRREL, native to North America, Europe and Asia. Most marmots have brown to grey fur, short, powerful legs and furry tails. Length: 30–60cm (12–24in) excluding tail; weight: 3–8kg (6.5–16.5lb). Family Sciuridae. *See also* WOODCHUCK

Marne, Battles of Two WORLD WAR 1 battles fought beside the River Marne, N France. The first (September 1914) was a counterattack directed by General JOFFRE, which checked the German drive on Paris. The second (July 1918) was another Allied counter-stroke, which stopped the last German advance and preceded the final Allied offensive.

Maronite Member of a Christian community of Arabs in Lebanon and Syria, who have spread by emigration to Egypt, Cyprus, s Europe and North and South America. The Maronite Church claims origins both from St Maron (d.407), a Syrian hermit, and St John Maro, patriarch of Antioch (685–707). In 680, the Maronites were condemned as Monotheletic heretics by the Third Council of Constantinople. In 1182, they returned to communion with the pope. They have the status of a uniate Church – that is, an Eastern Church in union with Rome but retaining its own rite and canon law. The 19th-century massacre of Maronites by the DRUSE led to French intervention in Lebanon and Syria. Today, Maronites number more than 1 million. Some 400,000 of which live in Lebanon.

Marquesas Islands Volcanic island group in the Pacific Ocean, s of the Equator. The islands, part of French Polynesia, include Fatu Hiva, Hiva Oa and Nuku Hiva; the capital is Taiohae (on Nuku Hiva). The islands were first discovered by a Spanish navigator in 1595. The French took possession in 1842. During the 19th century, diseases brought by Europeans killed many native Polynesians. The islands are mountainous, with fertile valleys and several good harbours. Exports include tobacco, vanilla and copra. Area: 1,049sq km (405sq mi). Pop. (1988) 7,538.

Marquette, Father Jacques (1637–75) French Jesuit missionary and explorer in North America. In 1666, Marquette arrived in Québec as a missionary priest. In 1673, Marquette and Louis JOLLIET led the first European expedition along the upper Mississippi River, exploring as far as the mouth of the Arkansas River.

Márquez, Gabriel García *See* GARCÍA MÁRQUEZ, GABRIEL

Marrakech (Marrakesh) City at the NW foot of the Atlas Mountains, W central Morocco. Founded in 1062 by the ALMORAVIDS, it was the country's capital until 1147 and subsequently served as the sultan's residence. The second-largest city in Morocco, sights include the 12th century Koutoubia mosque and the Medina. Industries: tourism, leather goods. Pop. (1993) 602,000.

marram grass (beach grass) Important grass of sand dunes. Its long RHIZOMES and roots help to bind the sand together and so prevent dune movement. *Ammophila arenaria* has long leaves that are curled into cylindrical spikes to resist water loss.

marriage In the modern Western sense, legal status of a man and a woman joined by ceremony as husband and wife. This is known as MONOGAMY, but some societies practise polyandry and POLYGAMY. The modern stress on the importance of individual choice of partner is historically and culturally very unusual. Arranged marriages, for instance, are the norm in Hindu and Muslim communities. *See also* FAMILY; KINSHIP

marrow In anatomy, soft tissue containing blood vessels, found in the hollow cavities of BONE. The marrow found in many adult bones is somewhat yellowish and functions as a store of fat. The marrow in the flattish bones is reddish and contains cells that give rise eventually to ERYTHROCYTES (red blood cells) as well as to most of the LEUCOCYTES (white blood cells), but not LYMPHOCYTES and platelets. *See artwork* p.530

marrow In botany, climbing or trailing annual vine (*Cucurbita pepo*), probably native to tropical America but now grown worldwide. Marrows produce elongated fruits (SQUASHES) that are popular vegetables. Varieties

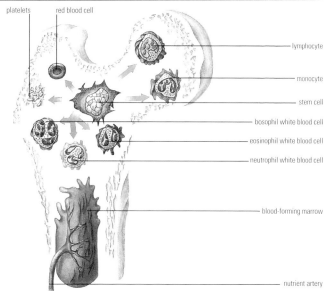

► **marrow** Most bones have hollow cavities that are filled with spongy bone marrow. Some of this (not, however, in the long bones) forms new red and white blood cells. Little more than 250g (0.5lb) of bone marrow is sufficient to provide the 5 billion red cells a day needed to replace old cells that have worn out after their 120-day lifetime in the body. Some white cells are also formed in the lymph nodes.

platelets — red blood cell — lymphocyte — monocyte — stem cell — bosophil white blood cell — eosinophil white blood cell — neutrophil white blood cell — blood-forming marrow — nutrient artery

include the courgette. Family Cucurbitaceae. *See also* GOURD; PUMPKIN

Mars Fourth major planet from the Sun. Mars appears red to the naked eye because of the high iron content of its surface crust, and is also known as the Red Planet. The atmosphere consists mainly of 95% carbon dioxide, 2.5% nitrogen and 1.5% argon, with smaller quantities of oxygen, carbon monoxide and water vapour. Its axial tilt is similar to the Earth's, so it passes through a similar cycle of SEASONS. The surface temperature on Mars varies between extremes of 130K and 290K. Its surface reveals a long and complex history of geological activity. The major difference in terrain is between the largely smooth, lowland volcanic plains of the northern hemisphere and the heavily cratered uplands of the south. The biggest volcanic structure on Mars is Olympus Mons, which is hundreds of kilometres across and 27km (17mi) high. Other geographical features, such as some giant canyons, are channels in which rivers once flowed. The variable polar ice caps appear to be composed of solid carbon dioxide with underlying caps of water ice. Mars has two tiny SATELLITES in very close orbits, Phobos and Deimos. In 1996, scientists investigating a meteorite, thought to have originated on Mars, found fossilised microorganisms that some believe indicate the presence of primitive life on the planet.

Mars Ancient Roman god of war, often depicted as an armed warrior; one of the three protector-deities of the city of Rome itself (with JUPITER and Quirinus). He was originally associated with agriculture but later took on his dominant military aspects; the wolf and woodpecker were sacred to him.

Marsala Fishing port in W Sicily, S Italy. It was founded (397 BC) by the Cathaginians. It lends its name to a dessert wine that was originally made here. Pop (1990) 80,760.

Marsalis, Wynton (1961–) US jazz musician. Before forming his own group, he was a member (1980–82) of Art Blakey's Jazz Messengers. Marsalis is one of the few jazz players to successfully cross over into classical music. His albums include *Black Codes (From the Underground)* (1984) and the Grammy Award-winning *Blood on the Fields* (1996).

Marseilles (Marseille) City and seaport on the Gulf of Lyon and connected to the River Rhône by an underground canal, SE France; capital of Bouches-du-Rhône department. The oldest city in France, it was founded in 600 BC by Greeks. During the Crusades, Marseilles was a commercial centre and shipping port for the Holy Land. The 19th-century French conquest of Algeria and the opening of the Suez Canal (1869) brought great prosperity. Today, Marseilles is the second-largest city in France. Industries: flour milling, soap, vegetable oil, cement, sugar refining, chemicals, engineering. Pop. (1990) 800,550.

Marsh, Dame Ngaio (1899–1982) New Zealand novelist. She moved to England in 1928. Her theatrical detective novels, mostly featuring Superintendant Roderick Alleyn, include *Opening Night* (1951) and *Final Curtain* (1957).

marsh Flat WETLAND area, devoid of peat, saturated by moisture during one or more seasons. Typical vegetation includes grasses, sedges, reeds and rushes. Marshes are valuable wetlands and maintain water tables in adjacent ecosystems. Unlike BOGS, they have alkaline, not acidic, soil. *See also* SWAMP

Marshall, George Catlett (1880–1959) US general and statesman, secretary of state (1947–49) and defense secretary (1950–51). He served as US chief of staff (1939–45) during World War 2. He initiated the MARSHALL PLAN of economic assistance for post-war Europe. In 1953 Marshall was awarded the Nobel Peace Prize.

Marshall, John (1755–1835) Chief justice of the US Supreme Court (1801–35). At the Virginia constitutional

MARS DATA
DIAMETER (EQUATORIAL): 6,787km (4,217mi)
MASS (EARTH = 1): 0.11
VOLUME (EARTH = 1): 0.15
DENSITY (WATER = 1): 3.94
ORBITAL PERIOD: 687.0 days
ROTATION PERIOD: 24h 37m 23s
SURFACE TEMPERATURE: −23°C (−9°F)

ratification convention (1788), Marshall argued successfully for the CONSTITUTION against Patrick HENRY. Marshall raised the Supreme Court to great prestige and established basic precepts for constitutional interpretation. Important cases include Marbury v. Madison (1803).

Marshall, Thurgood (1908–93) US lawyer and Supreme Court justice. As counsel (1938–62) for the National Association for the Advancement of Colored People (NAACP), he played a key role in obtaining US Supreme Court judgments against racial segregation in schools. Marshall was the first African-American associate justice of the US Supreme Court (1967–91).

Marshall Islands Republic in the w Pacific Ocean, E of the Caroline Islands, consisting of a group of atolls and coral reefs; the capital is Dalap-Uliga-Darrit (on Majuro Atoll). They consist of two great chains, the Ralik (w) and the Ratak (E), which cover an ocean area of 11,650sq km (4,500sq mi).The islands were first explored by Spain in the early 16th century. Annexed to Germany in 1885, the group was occupied by Japan in 1914 and by US forces in World War 2. In 1947, the islands became part of the US-administered Trust Territory of the Pacific Islands. In 1990, the Trusteeship ended, and in 1991 the islands joined the UN as a full member state. Products: copra, coconuts, tropical fruits, vegetables, fish. Land area: c.180sq km (70sq mi). Pop. (2000) 70,000.

Marshall Plan US programme of economic aid to European countries after World War 2. Promoted by the secretary of state, General MARSHALL, its purpose was to repair war damage and promote trade within Europe, while securing political stability. The Soviet Union and E European countries declined to participate. Between 1948 and 1951, 16 countries received a total of $12 billion.

Marston Moor (2 July 1664) Site of the largest battle in the English CIVIL WARS, 11km (7mi) w of York. Royalist forces under Prince RUPERT were defeated by the Parliamentarians under Thomas FAIRFAX, with Scots allies.

marsupial MAMMAL of which the female usually has a pouch (marsupium) within which the young are suckled and protected. The young are born in a very undeveloped state. Most marsupials are Australasian and include such varied types as the KANGAROO, KOALA, WOMBAT, TASMANIAN DEVIL, PHALANGER, BANDICOOT and marsupial mole. The only marsupials to live outside Australasia are the OPOSSUMS in the Americas. See also MONOTREME

marten Any of several species of carnivorous mammals of the WEASEL family that live in forested areas of Europe, Asia and North and South America. Martens have a long body and short legs and are hunted for their fur. The dark brown skins of the SABLE (*Martes zibellina*) are the most valuable. Family Mustelidae.

Martí, José (1853–95) Cuban poet and essayist. His verse reflected his belief that poetry and politics were inseparable. He was forced into exile and lived in New York before returning to Cuba, where he died fighting the Spanish. Many Latin American writers were strongly influenced by his works. *Ismaelillo* (1882) and *Versos sencillos* (1891) contain his best poems.

Martial, Marcus Valerius (c.AD 40–104) Latin epigrammatist, b. Spain. He wrote c.1,500 satirical short poems on contemporary Roman society.

martial arts See AIKIDO; JUDO; JUJITSU; KARATE; KUNG FU; SUMO WRESTLING; TAE KWON DO; TAI CHI

martial law Maintenance of civic order by using military personnel. Martial law may be declared on a local short-term basis by a government in an emergency, as when sending in the army to deal with pockets of civil

unrest. It may also be declared on a nationwide, long-term basis following a military coup.

Martin, Saint (c.315–c.397) Patron saint of France, bishop of Tours (371–97). As a Roman soldier, he is reputed to have torn his cloak to share it with a beggar. In c.360, Martin founded the first monastery in Gaul, at Poitiers. He was an evangelical bishop. His feast day (11 November) is known as Martinmas.

Martin V (1368–1431) Pope (1417–31), b. Oddone Colonna. After 39 years of schism, he tried to restore papal prestige and church unity through political means. Martin reorganized the Curia and sought to reopen diplomatic links with the Eastern Orthodox Church in Constantinople, but failed.

Martin, Frank (1890–1974) Swiss composer. His distinctly personal style shows a mastery of counterpoint, harmony and emotional continuity; in later works he used a modified 12-note system. His best-known work is the *Petite Symphonie Concertante* (1945). Other works include a piano quintet (1920), a string trio (1936) and a concerto for harpsichord and orchestra (1952).

martin Fast-flying bird closely related to the SWALLOW and native to Europe and North America. It has long, pointed wings and short legs. Species include the house martin (*Delichon urbica*), purple martin (*Progne subis*) and sand martin (*Riparia riparia*). Family Hirundinidae.

Martin du Gard, Roger (1881–1958) French novelist. His major works are *Jean Barois* (1913) and an eight-novel series, *Les Thibault* (1922–40), on family life in early 20th century France. He was awarded the 1937 Nobel Prize for literature.

Martineau, Harriet (1802–76) English writer. Deaf from birth, her works include the nine-volume *Illustrations of Political Economy* (1832–34). In 1834 she visited the USA and her anti-slavery views are contained in *Society in America* (1837).

Martini, Simone (c.1284–1344) Italian painter. His imposing fresco, the *Maestà* (1315) combines elements of BYZANTINE ART and GOTHIC ART and presages the RENAISSANCE. The *Annunciation* (1333) is often considered to be his most accomplished work.

Martinique Caribbean island in the Windward group of the Lesser Antilles, forming an overseas department of France; the capital is Fort-de-France. Discovered in 1502 by Christopher COLUMBUS, Martinique was inhabited by Carib Indians until they were displaced by French settlers after 1635. Attacked in the 17th century by the Dutch and the British, the island became a permanent French possession after the Napoleonic Wars. Of volcanic origin, it is the largest of the Lesser Antilles. The original capital, St Pierre, was completely destroyed by a volcanic eruption in 1902. Industries: tourism, sugar, rum, fruits, cocoa, tobacco, vanilla, vegetables. Area: 1,079sq km (417sq mi). Pop. (2000) 362,000.

Martins, Peter (1946–) Danish dancer, choreographer and ballet director. His partnership with Suzanne Farrell was one of the greatest in the history of ballet. Martins was principal dancer (1969–83) with the New York City Ballet, before becoming its joint ballet master (with Jerome ROBBINS), then director (1990–). His choreographed works include *Les Gentilhommes* (1987) and *A Musical Offering* (1991).

Martinů, Bohuslav (1890–1959) Czech composer. Much of his music is based on Bohemian folk rhythms and Czech dances. Martinů's works include the opera *Julietta* (1938) and Symphony No. 6 (1955).

martyr Person who dies willingly rather than renounce his or her religious faith. The term, which is taken from the Greek word for "witness", is particularly applied to Christians who suffered death for their beliefs. The first Christian martyr was St STEPHEN. In Judaism, the six million Jews murdered by the Nazis are regarded as martyrs. *See also* SAINT

Marvell, Andrew (1621–78) English metaphysical poet and satirist. In his lifetime he was known for his withering satires on corruption and mismangement in the court of Charles II. Today, Marvell is chiefly remembered for his lyric poetry, first collected in 1681 in a volume that included "The Garden", "Bermudas" and his best-known poem, "To His Coy Mistress".

Marx, Karl Heinrich (1818–83) German social philosopher, political theorist and founder (with Friedrich ENGELS) of international COMMUNISM. He produced his own philosophical approach of DIALECTICAL MATERIALISM. Marx proclaimed that religion was "the opium of the people" and in *The German Ideology* (1845–46), written with Engels, described the inevitable laws of history. In Brussels he joined the Communist League and wrote with Engels the epoch-making *Communist Manifesto* (1848). Marx took part in the revolutionary movements in France and Germany, then went to London (1849) where he lived until his death. His work at the British Museum produced a stream of writings, including *Das Kapital* (3 vols., 1867, 1885, 1894, the last two edited by Engels), which became the "Bible of the working class". In 1864, the International Workingmen's Association (the First International) was formed, and Marx became its leading spirit. His expulsion of BAKUNIN from the Association in 1872 led to its collapse. Marx was one of the most important political theorists of modern times. *See also* MARXISM

Marx Brothers US team of vaudeville and film comedians. The Marx Brothers consisted of **Chico** (Leonard, 1891–1961), **Harpo** (Arthur, 1893–1964), **Groucho** (Julius, 1895–1977), Gummo (Milto, 1894–1977) and Zeppo (Herbert, 1901–79), the latter two both withdrew from the group by 1935. Their riotous, wise-cracking comedies include *Animal Crackers* (1930), *Duck Soup* (1933) and *A Night at the Opera* (1935).

Marxism School of SOCIALISM that arose in 19th-century Europe as a response to the growth of industrial CAPITALISM. It is named after Karl MARX. According to Marxism, a communist society was historically inevitable. Capitalism, because of its emphasis on profits, would eventually so reduce the condition of workers that they would rebel, overthrow the capitalists and establish a classless society in which the means of production were collectively owned. *The Communist Manifesto* (1848) and *Das Kapital* (1867, 1885, 1894) both contain ideas central to Marxism, which forms the basis of COMMUNISM and strongly influenced the related ideology, socialism. *See also* CLASS; DIALECTICAL MATERIALISM; LENIN, VLADIMIR ILYICH; MAO ZEDONG

Mary I (1516–58) (Mary Tudor) Queen of England (1553–58), daughter of HENRY VIII and CATHERINE OF ARAGON. During the reign of her half-brother, EDWARD VI, she remained a devout Catholic. On Edward's death, the Duke of NORTHUMBERLAND arranged the brief usurpation of Lady Jane GREY but Mary acceded with popular support. In 1554, a Spanish alliance was secured by her marriage to the future King PHILIP II of Spain. The marriage provoked a rebellion, led by Sir Thomas WYATT, and hostility intensified after England lost Calais to France in 1558. Mary's determination to re-establish papal authority saw the restoration of heresy laws. The resultant execution of *c.*300 Protestants, including

CRANMER, LATIMER and RIDLEY, earned her the epithet "Bloody Mary". She was succeeded by ELIZABETH I.

Mary (Blessed Virgin Mary) (active 1st century AD) Mother of JESUS CHRIST. She figures prominently in the first two chapters of the Gospels according to St MATTHEW and St LUKE, which record Christ's birth. Mary has always been held in high regard in Christendom. In the early church, the principal Marian feast was called the Commemoration of St Mary, from which developed the later feast of the ASSUMPTION (15 August). Other Marian feasts are the Nativity (8 September), the ANNUNCIATION or Lady Day (25 March), the Purification or Candlemas (2 February), the Visitation (2 July) and (for Roman Catholics) the IMMACULATE CONCEPTION (8 December).

Mary II (1662–94) Queen of England, Scotland and Ireland, eldest daughter of JAMES II. Despite her father's conversion to Catholicism, Mary was brought up a Protestant. In 1677 she married her cousin, William of Orange, and moved to Holland. The GLORIOUS REVOLUTION (1688–89) resulted in the exile of James II, and she and her husband were invited to assume the English throne as Mary II and WILLIAM III (OF ORANGE).

Mary, Queen of Scots (1542–87) Daughter of JAMES V, she succeeded him as queen when one week old. She was sent to France aged six, and married the future FRANCIS II of France in 1558. On his death in 1560, she returned to Scotland, where, as a Catholic, she came into conflict with Protestant reformers. Her marriage to Lord DARNLEY was also resented and soon broke down. After Darnley's murder (1567), she married James BOTHWELL, possibly her husband's murderer, which alienated her few remaining supporters. Following a rebellion of Scottish nobles, she was forced to abdicate in favour of her infant son, James VI (later JAMES I of England). Although she raised an army, it was defeated at Langside (1568), and Mary fled to England. Kept in captivity, she became involved in plots against ELIZABETH I and was eventually executed.

Maryland State in E USA, on the Atlantic Ocean; capital is ANNAPOLIS. The largest city is BALTIMORE. The W half of the state forms part of the Piedmont plateau region. Maryland is dominated by Chesapeake Bay and its coastal marshlands. The first settlements were founded in 1634. Maryland (which was one of the 13 original states) was active in the struggle for American independence. In 1791, the state ceded an area of land on the Potomac River to create the District of Columbia, the site of the national capital WASHINGTON, D.C. During the CIVIL WAR, Maryland was one of the border states that did not secede from the Union, but its citizens served in both armies. The rearing of cattle and chickens is the most important farming activity. Maize, hay, tobacco and soya beans are the chief crops. Industries: iron and steel, shipbuilding, metals, transport equipment, chemicals, electrical machinery, fishing. Area: 25,316sq km (9,775sq mi). Pop. (2000) 5,296,486.

Mary Magdalene, Saint (active 1st century AD) Early follower of JESUS CHRIST, from the village of Magdala on the W shore of the Sea of Galilee. According to the gospels, Christ freed her of seven demons. She accompanied Christ on his preaching tours in Galilee, witnessed his crucifixion and burial, and was the first person to see him after his resurrection. She is often identified as a repentant prostitute. Her feast day is 22 July.

Masaccio (1401–28?) Florentine painter of the early RENAISSANCE, b. Tommaso Giovanni di Mone. His three most important surviving works are: a polyptych (1426) for the Carmelite Church, Pisa (now in London, Berlin and Naples); a fresco cycle that he created with Masolino portraying the life of St Peter, in the Brancacci Chapel, Santa Maria del Carmine, Florence (*c*.1425–28); and the *Trinity* fresco in Santa Maria Novella, Florence (*c*.1428).

Masada Fortified hill near the Dead Sea, SE Israel. It was the scene of the final defence of the Jewish ZEALOTS against the Romans during the Jewish revolt that began in AD 66. The defenders, *c*.1,000 in number, committed mass suicide rather than surrender (AD 73).

Masai African people of Kenya and Tanzania, consisting of several subgroups who speak a Nilotic language. They are characteristically tall and slender. Their patrilineal, egalitarian society is based on nomadic pastoralism, cattle being equated with wealth. The traditional Masai *kraal* is a group of mud houses surrounded by a thorn fence.

Masaryk, Tomáš (1850–1937) Czech statesman and philosopher, first president of CZECHOSLOVAKIA (1918–35). In 1900, he founded the Czech Peoples Party to represent Czech interests in the AUSTRO-HUNGARIAN EMPIRE. Masaryk fled at the outbreak of World War 1 and (with Eduard BENEŠ) formed the Czechoslovak national council. In 1918, he returned as president. Revered as the "father" of the nation, Masaryk enacted land reforms and pursued a liberal path on minority rights. He was succeeded by Beneš.

Mascagni, Pietro (1863–1945) Italian composer and conductor. His reputation rests mainly on the one-act opera *Cavalleria Rusticana* (1890).

Masefield, John Edward (1878–1967) English poet and novelist. He early seafaring experiences inform much of his work. Masefield's debut volume *Salt-Water Ballads* (1902) includes "Sea Fever". He was poet laureate from 1930. Masefield is best-known for his long narrative poems such as *The Everlasting Mercy* (1911) and *Reynard the Fox* (1919).

maser (acronym for **m**icrowave **a**mplification by **s**timulated **e**mission of **r**adiation) Device using atoms artificially kept in states of higher energy than normal to provide amplification of high-frequency radio signals. They are used to measure signals from outer space. In 1953, the first maser was built by Charles TOWNES, for which he shared the 1964 Nobel Prize for physics with Nikolai BASOV and Alexander PROKHOROV. It used electrostatic plates to separate high-energy ammonia atoms from low-energy ones. Radiation of a certain frequency would then stimulate the high-energy ammonium atoms to emit similar radiation and strengthen the signal. *See also* LASER

Maseru Capital of Lesotho, on the River Caledon, near the W border with South Africa. It was capital of British Basutoland protectorate (1869–71, 1884–1966)and remained the capital when the kingdom of Lesotho achieved independence in 1966. It is a commercial, transport and administrative centre. Pop. (1995) 297,000.

Mashhad (Arabic, shrine of martyrdom) City in NE Iran, close to the border with Turkmenistan; capital of Khorasan province. It is an Islamic holy city and a place of pilgrimage for SHIITE Muslims. In 809 the Abbasid Caliph HARUN AL-RASHID was buried here, and in 818 the Imam Ali Riza died while visiting Harun's grave. An ornate shrine was built over both their tombs. In the 18th-century, Mashhad became the capital of Persia. Today, Mashhad is Iran's second-largest city and a major trade centre. It is famous for its carpet and textile manufacture. Pop. (1994) 1,964,000.

Mason-Dixon Line Border of Pennsylvania with Maryland and West Virginia, USA. It is named after the men who surveyed it in the 1760s. It was regarded as the dividing line between slave and free states at the time of the MISSOURI COMPROMISE (1820–21) and became the

popular name for the boundary between North and South in the USA.

masque Dramatic presentation that originated in Italy but became popular in the English court and the great houses of the nobility during the late 16th and early 17th centuries. The masque consisted of verse, comedy, and, as an essential feature, a dance for a group of masked revellers. The earliest masque text is *Proteus and the Adamantine Rock* (1594).

mass Celebration of the EUCHARIST in the Roman Catholic Church and among some High Church Anglicans. The Catholic rite comprises the Liturgy of the Word and the Liturgy of the Eucharist, which includes the Offertory, the sacrifice of Christ's body and blood under the guise of bread and wine. In the late 20th century, the mass underwent a number of changes following the Second VATICAN COUNCIL (1962–65). *See also* TRANSUBSTANTIATION

mass In music, a setting of the Roman Catholic religious service in Latin. Composers from all eras have written masses. One of the most famous is J.S. BACH's Mass in B minor. In the 19th century, mass settings increased in scale until they were more likely to be performed in concert halls than in church services.

mass (symbol *m*) In physics, measure of the quantity of MATTER in an object. Scientists recognize two types of mass. The **gravitational** mass of a body is determined by its mutual attraction to another, reference body, such as the Earth, as expressed in NEWTON'S LAW OF GRAVITATION. Spring balances and platform balances proved a measure of gravitational mass. The **inertial** mass of a body is determined by its resistance to a change in state of motion, as expressed in the second law of motion. INERTIA balances provide a measure of inertial mass. According to EINSTEIN's principle of equivalence, upon which his general theory of RELATIVITY is based, the inertial mass and the gravitational mass of a given body are equivalent. *See also* WEIGHT

Massachusetts State on the Atlantic coast of NEW ENGLAND, NE USA; the capital and largest city is BOSTON. Other major cities are Worcester, Springfield, Cambridge and New Bedford. The first settlement was made (1620) at PLYMOUTH on Massachusetts Bay by the PILGRIMS. In 1630, Boston was founded by English Puritans, and it became the centre of the MASSACHUSETTS BAY COLONY. The state played a leading role in events leading up to the American Revolution and was the scene of the first battle. After achieving statehood in 1788, Massachusetts prospered. In the E of the state is a low-lying coastal plain. The uplands of the interior are divided by the Connecticut River valley and the Berkshire valley. The principal rivers are the Housatonic, Merrimack and Connecticut. A highly industrialized region, Massachusetts is one of the most densely populated states in the nation. Agricultural produce includes cranberries, tobacco, hay, vegetables and market garden and dairy products. Industries: electronic equipment, plastics, footwear, paper, machinery, metal and rubber goods, printing and publishing, fishing. Area: 20,300sq km (7,838sq mi). Pop. (2000) 6,349,097.

Massachusetts Bay Company English company chartered in 1629. Its purpose was trade and colonization of the land between the Charles and Merrimack rivers in North America. A group of Puritans, led by John WINTHROP, gained control of the company and founded the Massachusetts Bay Colony in 1630. They took the company's charter with them to MASSACHUSETTS and enjoyed considerable autonomy. Within 10 years, *c*.20,000 people, mainly English Puritans, had settled in the colony.

Massachusetts Institute of Technology (MIT)
University in Cambridge, Massachusetts, USA. It is recognized as a leading technical college, with facilities
that include a large nuclear reactor, a high-energy particle accelerator and a nuclear science laboratory. There
are more than 70 special laboratories either directly
associated with or affiliated with MIT.

Massenet, Jules Émile-Frédéric (1842–1912)
French composer. He dominated 19th-century French
lyric opera. Massenet composed many operas, including
Le Cid (1885), *Werther* (1892) and *Thérèse* (1909). His
two masterpieces are considered to be *Manon* (1884)
and *Thaïs* (1894). *See also* ROMANTICISM

Massif Central Extensive mountainous plateau in SE
central France. The volcanic AUVERGNE Mountains
form the core of the region, which also includes the
Cévennes (SE) and the Causses (SW). Sheep and goats
are grazed on the slopes. Hydroelectric power is generated there, and coal and kaolin are mined. The highest
peak is Puy de Sancy, rising to 1,886m (6,186ft). Area:
*c.*85,000sq km (32,800sq mi).

Massine, Léonide (1896–1979) US choreographer and
ballet dancer, b. Russia. His choreography includes *Le
Soleil de Nuit* (1915), *La Boutique Fantasque* (1919) and
Three Cornered Hat (1919). He influenced the development of choreography when he created the first symphonic ballet, *Les Présages* (1933). He also performed in the
films *The Red Shoes* (1948) and *Tales of Hoffmann* (1951).

Massinger, Philip (1583–1640) English dramatist. He
wrote more than 40 plays, often in collaboration, many
of which are now lost. He is best known for his realistic
yet highly symbolic satires of domestic life, such as *A
New Way to Pay Old Debts* (1621–22) and *The City
Madam* (*c.*1632).

mass production Manufacture of goods in large
quantities by standardizing parts, techniques and
machinery. In 1798, US inventor Eli WHITNEY introduced mass PRODUCTION to produce weapons. The
assembly line, a conveyor belt carrying the work
through a series of assembly areas, was introduced in
1913 by car manufacturer Henry FORD. Many mass-production processes depend on AUTOMATION, including
ROBOTS. *See also* DIVISION OF LABOUR; FACTORY

mass spectrograph (mass spectrometer) Instrument
for separating ions according to their masses (or more
precisely, according to their charge-to-mass ratio), used in
chemical analysis. In the simplest types, the ions are first
accelerated by an electric field and then deflected by a
strong magnetic field; the lighter the ions the greater the
deflection. By varying the field, ions of different masses
can be focused in sequence onto a photographic plate or
detector and a record of charge-to-mass ratios obtained.

mastectomy In surgery, removal of all or part of the
female BREAST. It is performed to treat CANCER. Simple
mastectomy involves the breast alone; when the cancer
has spread, radical mastectomy may be undertaken,
removing also the lymphatic tissue from the armpit.

Masters, Edgar Lee (1868–1950) US poet and novelist. Although Masters published a number of volumes,
he never repeated the single success of his *Spoon River
Anthology* (1915), a series of free-verse monologues
spoken by the dead of a small Midwest town.

Masters, William Howell (1915–) US physician
who, with his psychologist wife Virginia (née Johnson)
(1925–), became noted for studies of the physiology
and anatomy of human sexual activity. Masters and
Johnson's works include *Human Sexual Response*
(1966) and *Human Sexual Inadequacy* (1970).

mastiff (Old English mastiff) Large fighting dog that
was first bred in England more than 2,000 years ago. It
has a broad, rounded head with a dark-coloured, square
muzzle and small V-shaped ears. The wide, deep-chested body is set on strong legs with large feet. The short,
coarse coat may be brown, grey or brindle. Height: to
84cm (33in) at shoulder; weight: to 95kg (210lb).

mastodon Any of several species of extinct elephantine
mammals, all of which existed mainly in the PLEISTOCENE
epoch. Mastodons had a long coat of red hair; the grinding
teeth were notably smaller and less complex than those of
modern ELEPHANTS, and the males had small tusks on the
lower as well as the upper jaw. Genus *Mastodon*.

Mastroianni, Marcello (1923–96) Italian film actor.
One of the greatest European character actors since the
1950s, Mastroianni was often associated with the films
of Federico FELLINI. Following international success in
La Dolce Vita (1960), he appeared as Fellini's alter ego
in $8\frac{1}{2}$ *(1963)* and *Intervista* (1987). He finally made his
Hollywood debut in *Used People* (1992).

masturbation Self-stimulation by manipulation of the
genital organs for pleasure, usually to ORGASM. Once
regarded as taboo, sinful or physically harmful, moderate masturbation is no longer considered abnormal.

Mata Hari (1876–1917) Dutch courtesan. Her real
name was Margaretha Geertruida Zelle. In 1917, she
was arrested in Paris as a German agent and subsequently executed. Although her conduct was suspicious, few
people now believe she was the mysterious secret agent
that the French authorities alleged.

materialism System of philosophical thought that
explains the nature of the world as dependent on MATTER.
The doctrine was formulated as early as the 4th century
BC by DEMOCRITUS. PLATO developed the contrasting philosophy of IDEALISM. The early followers of BUDDHISM
were also materialists. DIALECTICAL MATERIALISM as formulated by Karl MARX is a modern development of the
older theory. *See also* EPICURUS; MONISM; STOICISM

mathematical induction Method of proving that a
mathematical statement is true for any positive INTEGER n
by proving (1) that it is true for a base value, for example 1,
and (2) that if it is true for a value k, then it is also true for k
+ 1. If (1) and (2) hold, then it follows in a finite number of
steps that the statement is true for any positive integer n.

mathematics Study concerned originally with the
properties of numbers and space; now more generally
concerned with deductions made from assumptions
about abstract entities. Mathematics is often divided into
pure mathematics, which is purely abstract reasoning
based on axioms, and **applied** mathematics, which
involves the use of mathematical reasoning in other
fields, such as engineering, physics, chemistry and economics. The main divisions of pure mathematics are
GEOMETRY, ALGEBRA and analysis. This last deals with the
concept of limits and includes differential and integral CALCULUS. *See also* ARITHMETIC; TRIGONOMETRY

Mather, Cotton (1663–1728) Puritan minister in
colonial Massachusetts. His father, **Increase** Mather
(1639–1723) doubted the reliability of testimony at the
SALEM witch trials, and his *Cases of Conscience* (1693)
helped to stop the executions. In 1723, Cotton succeeded his father at the Boston ministry. He supported the
SALEM witch trials, though not the subsequent executions, yet was sympathetic to scientific and philosophical ideas. He was one of the founders of Yale University
and a member of the Royal Society, London.

Matisse, Henri Emile Benoît (1869–1954) French
painter, sculptor, graphic artist and designer. Having

experimented with NEO-IMPRESSIONISM in paintings such as *Luxe, calme et volupte* (1905), he developed the style of painting that became known as FAUVISM. After a relatively brief flirtation with CUBISM, Matisse turned back to the luminous and sensual calmness that typified his art. He became ill in later life, but produced one of his greatest works, the design of the Chapel of the Rosary at Venice (1949–51). Matisse also started making coloured paper cut-outs, such as *L'Escargot* (1953). His most famous sculptures include a series of four bronzes called *The Back* (1909–29).

Mato Grosso State in w central Brazil, bordered s by MATO GROSSO DO SUL, and w and sw by Bolivia; the capital is Cuiabà. First settled in the early 18th century by miners seeking gold and diamonds, it became a state in 1889. Much of the area lies on the central plateau of Brazil, and there is rainforest in the N and marshland in the sw. The w has good grazing land, and cattle rearing is the chief occupation. Rice, maize and sugar cane are grown. There are extensive mineral deposits but most of them are unexploited. Area: 881,000sq km (340,156sq mi). Pop. (1991) 2,020,581.

Mato Grosso do Sul State in sw Brazil, bordered N by MATO GROSSO, w by Bolivia, and w and s by Paraguay; the capital is Campo Grande. Early pioneers exploited the area's gold and diamonds, but there was little permanent settlement until the late 20th century. In 1979 it was created a separate state from the s part of Mato Grosso. Most of Mato Grosso do Sul lies on an extension of the central plateau of Brazil. There are vast mineral resources, including iron ore and manganese. Agriculture and livestock are important, and the main crops are peanuts, rice, beans, maize and cotton. Area: 350,548sq km (135,347sq mi). Pop. (1991) 1,778,494.

matriarchy Any society or group that is ruled by women. Matriarchal societies exist among some peoples in South America. *See also* PATRIARCHY

matrix Rectangular array of numbers in rows and columns. The number of rows need not equal the number of columns. Matrices can be combined (added and multiplied) according to certain rules. They are useful in the study of transformations of co-ordinate systems and in solving sets of simultaneous equations.

matter Any material that takes up space. Ordinary matter is made up of ATOMS, which are combinations of ELECTRONS, PROTONS and neutrons. Atoms, in turn, make up ELEMENTS, an ordered series of substances that have atoms with from one proton in their nuclei (hydrogen) to a hundred or more. All matter exerts an attractive force on other matter, called GRAVITATION. Charged particles exert an attractive or repulsive ELECTROMAGNETIC FORCE that accounts for nearly all everyday phenomena. The strong interaction force is responsible for binding the protons and neutrons in an atomic NUCLEUS, and the weak interaction is responsible for beta decay. *See also* ANTIMATTER; FUNDAMENTAL FORCES; MATTER, STATES OF; MOLECULE

matter, states of Classification of MATTER according to its structural characteristics. Four states of matter are generally recognized: SOLID, LIQUID, GAS and PLASMA. Any one ELEMENT or compound may exist sequentially or simultaneously in two or more of these states. SOLIDS may be crystalline, as in salt and metals; or amorphous, as in tar or glass. LIQUIDS have molecules that can flow past one another but that remain almost as close as in a solid. In a GAS, molecules are so far from one another that they travel in relatively straight lines until they collide. In a PLASMA atoms are torn apart into electrons and nuclei at extremely high temperatures, such as those in stars.

Matterhorn (Monte Cervino) Mountain peak in the Pennine Alps on the Swiss–Italian border. It has a distinctive pyramidal peak formed from several cirques and was first climbed (1865) by the British mountaineer Edward Whymper. Height: 4,478m (14,691ft).

Matthew, Saint (active 1st century AD) Apostle and probably one of the four evangelists of the New Testament. In the lists of the disciples given in the SYNOPTIC GOSPELS, Matthew is sometimes called Levi. Before his calling he was a tax collector working in Capernaum, a village on the Sea of Galilee, in the service of King Herod Antipas. Feast day: 21 September in the West, 16 November in the East.

Matthew, Gospel according to Saint Gospel usually placed first in the New Testament but probably written after those of St MARK and St LUKE. Written *c.*AD 70–75, it is traditionally ascribed to St MATTHEW, the tax gatherer who became one of the 12 disciples. The Gospel according to St Matthew contains more of the teachings, parables and sayings of Jesus than any other gospel. It is also the only SYNOPTIC GOSPEL written in a Jewish, rather than a Hellenistic, style and emphasizes links between the Old and New Testaments.

Matthews, Sir Stanley (1915–2000) English footballer who played for Stoke City and Blackpool. Matthews made 786 appearances, including 54 caps for England, in a professional career that spanned from 1932 to 1965. He was the first European Footballer of the Year (1956).

Mauchly, John William (1907–80) US physicist and engineer. In 1946, Mauchly and John Presper Eckert Jr (1919–95) built the first commercial general-purpose COMPUTER – the Electronic Numerical Integrator and Computer (ENIAC). Taking up 15,000sq ft and containing 18,000 electronic valves, ENIAC was bought as a military calculator by the US War Department. Their next invention, the Electronic Discrete Variable Computer (EDVAC), was able to store PROGRAMS.

Maugham, (William) Somerset (1874–1965) British novelist, short-story writer and dramatist, b. France. He achieved fame initially as a dramatist with plays such as *Lady Frederick* (1912) and *The Circle* (1921). Maugham's first successful novel was the semiautobiographical *Of Human Bondage* (1915). Other novels include *The Moon and Sixpence* (1919) and *Cakes and Ale* (1930). Maugham's experiences in British intelligence in World War 1 informs the shortstory collection *Ashenden* (1928).

Mau Mau Anti-colonial terrorist group of the KIKUYU tribe of Kenya. Members were bound by secret oath to expel European settlers from Kenya. In 1952, a state of emergency was declared following a series of attacks on settlers in the "white highlands". The violence escalated and *c.*11,000 black Africans opposed to the Mau Mau were slaughtered in reprisals. Jomo KENYATTA was imprisoned (1953–60) on suspicion of leading the violent nationalist campaign. By 1957, British soldiers had captured more than 20,000 Kikuyu, but the human and financial cost of the effort made decolonization inevitable. In 1963, Kenya achieved independence and Jomo Kenyatta was elected prime minister.

Mauna Kea (White Mountain) Dormant shield volcano in central Hawaii, USA. Mauna Kea is the highest island mountain in the world at 4,205m (13,796ft). At the snowcapped peak of the volcano stands **Mauna Kea Observatory**, the world's biggest astronomical site with the W.M. Keck 10-m (33-ft) telescope.

Mauna Loa Active volcano in central Hawaii, USA, s of MAUNA KEA. The second highest active volcano in the world, Mauna Loa has many craters. Kilauea is the largest. Mokuaweoweo is the summit crater. The greatest eruption was in 1881. Major eruptions also took place in 1942, 1949, 1975 and 1984. Height: 4,169m (13,678ft).

Maundy Thursday In the Christian liturgical calendar, the day before GOOD FRIDAY, commemorating the institution of the EUCHARIST and the washing of the disciples' feet by Jesus, described in St JOHN's Gospel.

Maupassant, Guy de (1850–93) French short-story writer and novelist. He produced one of his greatest short stories, "Boule de suif", for the collection *Les Soirées de Médan* (1880). Maupassant wrote more than 300 short stories; a number are collected in *La Maison Tellier* (1881), *Contes de la Bécasse* (1883) and *L'Inutile Beauté* (1890). His novels include *Une Vie* (1883), *Bel-Ami* (1885) and *Pierre et Jean* (1887).

Mauriac, François (1885–1970) French novelist and dramatist. His novels, *A Kiss for the Leper* (1922), *Genitrix* (1923) and *The Desert of Love* (1925), portray the futility of pursuing fulfilment through material comfort and secular love. His plays include *Asmodée* (1938). Mauriac was awarded the 1952 Nobel Prize for literature.

Mauritania Republic in NW Africa; the capital is NOUAKCHOTT. The low-lying Sahara desert covers most of Mauritania. A sandstone plateau runs N to S through the centre of Mauritania. In the SE lies the Hodh basin. The majority of Mauritanians live in the semi-arid SW region of SAHEL. Tropical savanna covers much of the rainier south. **History and politics** Berbers migrated to the region in the first millennium AD. The Hodh basin lay at the heart of the ancient Ghana empire (700–1200), and towns grew up along the trans-Saharan caravan routes. In the 14th and 15th century, the region formed part of the ancient Mali empire. Portuguese mariners explored the coast in the 1440s, but European colonialism did not begin until the 17th century, when trade in gum arabic became important. Britain, France and the Netherlands were all interested in this trade, and France set up a protectorate in 1903. In 1920, the region became a separate colony within French West Africa. In 1958, Mauritania became a self-governing territory in the French Union before achieving full independence in 1960. Mokhtar Ould Daddah was elected president and re-elected in 1966 and 1971. Mauritania became a one-party state. Devastating drought increased dissatisfaction with Ould Daddah's regime. In 1973, Mauritania withdrew from the franc zone and joined the Arab League. In 1976, Spain withdrew from Spanish Sahara; Morocco occupied the N 66% of the territory, while Mauritania took the rest. Nationalists, led by the guerrillas of the Popular Front for the Liberation of Saharan Territories (POLISARIO), began an armed struggle for independence that drained Mauritania's resources. In 1978, Ould Daddah was overthrown in a military coup, and a military committee assumed control. In 1979, Mauritania withdrew from Western Sahara, and Morocco assumed sole authority (for political developments, *see* WESTERN SAHARA). In 1984, recognition of Western Sahara's independence provoked civil unrest, and Ould Taya came to power. In 1991, Mauritania adopted a new constitution. In 1992, multiparty elections Ould Taya

was elected president. He was re-elected in 1997 after a boycott by opposition parties. Tension continues between the black African minority in S Mauritania and Arabs and Berbers in the N. **Economy** Mauritania is a low-income developing country (1995 GDP per capita, $1,540). The chief resource and leading export is iron ore. Agriculture employs 69% of the workforce. Recent droughts have forced many nomadic herdsmen to migrate to the urban areas. Farmers in the SE grow crops such as beans, dates, millet, rice and sorghum.

Mauritius Republic in the SW Indian Ocean, *c*.800km (500mi) E of Madagascar; the capital is Port Louis (on Mauritius). The country consists of the main island of Mauritius, 20 nearby islets, and the dependency islands of Rodrigues, Agalega and Cargados Carajos. The climate is sub-tropical, with up to 5,000mm (200in) of rain a year. The Dutch began to colonize the island in 1598 and named it after Prince Maurice of Nassau. In 1715, it came under the control of France. The French established sugar cane plantations and imported African slave labour. In 1810, Britain seized Mauritius, and it was formally recognized as a British colony in 1814. In 1833, slavery was abolished and Indian forced labour was used instead. In 1968, Mauritius achieved independence as a member of the Commonwealth. In 1992, it became a republic. Its vast plantations produce sugar cane; sugar and molasses are the major exports. The increase in tourism and textile production have partly compensated for the decline in the sugar market. Ethnic and class divisions, combined with economic austerity, created a divided society in the 1980s. Area: 2,046sq km (790sq mi). Pop. (2000) 1,201,000.

Maurois, André (1885–1967) French biographer, historian and novelist, b. Emile Herzog. He wrote popular histories, war reminiscences such as *The Silence of Colonel Bramble* (1918), and novels, including *Whatever Gods May Be* (1928). He is remembered mainly for his approachable biographies, including those of Shelley (1923), Byron (1930), Proust (1949) and Hugo (1954).

Maurya empire (321–185 BC) Ancient Indian dynasty and state founded by CHANDRAGUPTA (r. *c*.321–*c*.291 BC). His son, Bindusara (r. *c*.291–*c*.268 BC), conquered the DECCAN, and all N India was united under ASHOKA (r. *c*.264–*c*.238 BC), Chandragupta's grandson. After Ashoka's death the empire broke up, the last emperor being assassinated in *c*.185 BC.

mausoleum Impressive tomb. The widow of Mausolus (from whom the term derives), ruler of Caria, raised a great tomb to his memory at HALICARNASSUS (*c*.350 BC). It became one of the SEVEN WONDERS OF THE WORLD. The best-known mausoleum is the TAJ MAHAL in India.

Mawson, Sir Douglas (1882–1958) Australian geographer and Antarctic explorer. b. England. He accompanied Sir Ernest SHACKLETON on the first expedition (1907–09) to the South Pole and led the Australasian Antarctic expedition (1911–14). In 1929–31, he led a joint British, Australian and New Zealand Antarctic expedition.

Maxim, Sir Hiram Stevens (1840–1916) US inventor of the Maxim MACHINE GUN (1883). His other inventions include a smokeless powder and a delayed-action fuse. He settled in London in 1881.

Maximilian I (1459–1519) Holy Roman emperor (1493–1519), son and successor of FREDERICK III. Maximilian was one of the most successful members of the HABSBURG dynasty. He gained Burgundy and the Netherlands by marriage and defended them against France. He was less successful in asserting control over the German princes, and involvement in the ITALIAN WARS led to his defeat by the Swiss (1499). Maximilian strengthened the

---

MAURITANIA
AREA: 1,025,520sq km (395,953sq mi)
POPULATION: 2,702,000
CAPITAL (POPULATION): Nouakchott (393,325)

Habsburg heartland in Austria and, through arranged marriages, ensured that his grandson and successor, CHARLES V, inherited a vast European empire.

Maximilian, Ferdinand Joseph (1832–67) Emperor of Mexico (1864–67), brother of Emperor FRANZ JOSEPH. An Austrian archduke, he was offered the throne of Mexico after the French invasion (1862). When the French withdrew in 1867, Maximilian was overthrown by the liberal forces of Benito JUÁREZ and executed.

Maxwell, James Clerk (1831–79) Scottish mathematician and physicist, first director of the Cavendish Laboratory at Cambridge, England. His outstanding theoretical work revealed the existence of ELECTROMAGNETIC RADIATION. Maxwell used the theory of the electromagnetic field for **Maxwell's equations**, which provided a unified mathematical theory of LIGHT, ELECTRICITY and MAGNETISM. He also established the nature of Saturn's rings and completed vital work in thermodynamics and statistical mechanics. The former unit of magnetic flux, the maxwell (symbol Mx), was named after him (it has been replaced by the SI unit, the weber).
See also BOLTZMANN, LUDWIG

Maya Outstanding culture of classic American civilization. Occupying S Mexico and N Central America, it was at its height from the 3rd to 9th centuries. The Maya built great temple-cities with buildings surmounting stepped PYRAMIDS. They were skillful potters and weavers, and productive farmers. They worshipped gods and ancestors, and blood sacrifice was an important element of religion. Maya civilization declined after *c*.900, and much was destroyed after the Spanish conquest in the 16th century. The modern Maya, numbering *c*.4 million, live in the same area and speak a variety of languages related to that of their ancestors. *See also* CENTRAL AND SOUTH AMERICAN MYTHOLOGY

Mayakovsky, Vladimir (1893–1930) Russian poet and dramatist. He was the leader of the Russian FUTURISM movement and founded the journal *Left Arts Front*. Mayakovsky is often referred to as the voice of the RUSSIAN REVOLUTION. His poem *150,000,000* (1920) and the play *Mystery Bouffe* (1918) were propaganda pieces for the new Soviet Union. Mayakovsky's late work, such as the plays *Bedbug* (1928) and *Bath-House* (1930), display his disillusionment with the bureaucracy of the regime. He committed suicide.

Mayan Family of languages spoken on the Yucatán Peninsula of Mexico, Guatemala and part of Belize by the MAYA. There are several dozen of these languages, the most important being Yucatec of Mexico, and Quiché, Cakchiquel, Mam and Kekchi of Guatemala.

May beetle Alternative name for the COCKCHAFER

May Day First day of May, traditionally celebrated as a festival, the origin of which may lie in the spring fertility rites of pagan times. The Roman festival of Flora, goddess of spring, was held from 28 April to 3 May. In England, the festivities have centred on the dance around the maypole. In some countries May Day is a holiday in honour of workers and may be accompanied by a military display.

Mayer, Louis B. (Burt) (1885–1957) US film executive. In 1917 he founded a film production company, and became vice president of Metro-Goldwyn-Mayer (MGM) in 1924. During the 1930s and 1940s, Mayer was the most powerful film magnate in Hollywood.

Mayflower Ship that carried the PILGRIMS from Plymouth, England, to Massachusetts in September 1620. It carried 120 English Puritans, some from a congregation that had settled in the Netherlands, who established the PLYMOUTH COLONY in December that year.

Mayflower Compact Agreement to establish a preliminary government for the PILGRIMS. It was signed by the 41 adult male passengers of the MAYFLOWER on 21 November 1620 at sea off the New England coast. The compact bound signers to majority-rule government in the Pilgrim colony, pending receipt of a royal charter.

mayfly Soft-bodied insect found worldwide. The adult does not eat and lives only a few days, but the aquatic larvae (NYMPH) may live several years. Adults have triangular front wings, characteristic thread-like tails, and vestigial mouthparts; they often emerge from streams and rivers in swarms. The flying dun is used in fly-fishing. Length: 10–25mm (0.4–1in). Order Ephemeroptera.

Mayo County bounded to the N and W by the Atlantic Ocean, Connaught province, NW Republic of Ireland; the county town is Castlebar. A largely mountainous region, it has numerous lakes and is drained by the rivers Errif and Moy. Oats and potatoes are the chief crops and cattle, sheep, pigs and poultry are reared. Woollen milling and toy manufacturing are the main industries. Area: 5,397sq km (2,084sq mi). Pop. (1991) 110,713.

Mayotte (Mahore) French-administered archipelago in the Indian Ocean, E of the COMOROS. The two major islands are Grande Terre and Petite Terre (Pamanzi). Grande Terre includes the new capital, Mamoudzou. Mayotte was a French colony from 1843 to 1914, when it was attached to the Comoro group. In 1974, the rest of the Comoros became independent, while Mayotte voted to remain a French dependency. In 1976, it became an overseas collectivity of France. The economy is primarily agricultural; the chief products are bananas and mangoes. Area: 373sq km (144sq mi). Pop. (1991) 94,410.

Mazarin, Jules (1602–61) French statesman and Roman Catholic cardinal, b. Italy. He was the protégé of Cardinal RICHELIEU and chief minister under ANNE OF AUSTRIA from 1643. During the FRONDE (1648–52), Mazarin played off the various factions and, though twice forced out of France, emerged in control. As a former papal diplomat, he was a skillful negotiator of the treaties that ended the THIRTY YEARS' WAR.

Mazzini, Giuseppe (1805–72) Italian patriot and theorist of the RISORGIMENTO. A member of the *Carbonari* (Italian republican underground) from 1830, he founded the "Young Italy" movement in 1831, dedicated to the unification of Italy. He fought in the REVOLUTIONS OF 1848 and ruled in Rome in 1849, but was then exiled. Unlike GARIBALDI or CAVOUR, Mazzini remained committed to popular republicanism.

Mbabane Capital of Swaziland, in the NW of the country in the high veld region of S Africa. It is both an administrative and commercial centre, serving the surrounding agricultural region. Tin and iron ore are mined nearby. Pop. (1992) 42,000.

Mbeki, Thabo (1942–) South African statesman, president (1999–). He went into exile in Europe after Hendrik VERWOERD banned the African NATIONAL CONGRESS (ANC) in 1962. Mbeki was one of the leading figures in maintaining international pressure on the APARTHEID regime and, in 1990, he returned from exile to become chairman of the ANC. He succeeded Nelson MANDELA as president of the ANC (1997) and easily won the 1999 elections.

Mboya, Thomas Joseph (1930–69) Kenyan political leader. He was a founder of the Kenya African National Union (KANU), which was in the forefront of the independence movement. He served in the government of Jomo KENYATTA (1963–69). His assassination provoked rioting against the dominant KIKUYU.

ME (abbreviation of **m**yalgic **e**ncephalomyelitis) Also known as chronic fatigue syndrome and post-viral fatigue syndrome, it is a condition defined as extreme fatigue that persists for six months or more and is not relieved by rest. It ranges in severity from chronic weariness to total physical collapse. The cause of the condition is unknown.

Mead, George Herbert (1863–1931) US philosopher and social psychologist. A founder of PRAGMATISM, he was influenced by John DEWEY. His studies of the behaviour of individuals and small groups led to the sociological theories of symbolic interactionism.

Mead, Margaret (1901–78) US cultural anthropologist, curator of ethnology (1926–69) at the American Museum of Natural History. Mead's fieldwork was done in the SW Pacific, particularly Samoa, the subject of her first and most famous work, *Coming of Age in Samoa* (1928). She was primarily interested in sexuality and adolescence and helped develop the national-character approach to anthropology. Some of her early conclusions about Samoan society have been criticized for shortcomings in perspective and sampling technique.

mean (arithmetic mean) Mathematical average. It is found by adding a group of numbers and dividing by the number of items in the group. Thus, for numbers a, b, c and d, the mean is $(a + b + c + d)/4$.

meander Naturally occurring, loop-like bend of a RIVER or stream channel. As a river flows, it winds around obstacles in its path. The bend that is created is accentuated by the erosive action of the river. Meanders form on a flood plain where there is little resistance in the alluvium. They lengthen the river, thus reducing its gradient and velocity. Meanders migrate slowly downstream, depositing sediment on one bank while eroding the opposite. Sometimes they make complete loops that, when cut off, form OXBOW LAKES.

measles (rubeola) Extremely infectious viral disease of children. The symptoms (fever, catarrh, skin rash and spots inside the mouth) appear about two weeks after exposure. Hypersensitivity to light is characteristic. Complications such as pneumonia occasionally occur, and middle-ear infection is also a hazard. Vaccination produces lifelong immunity.

Meath County on the Irish Sea, Leinster province, E Republic of Ireland; the county town is Trim. A fertile, low-lying region, it is drained by the rivers Boyne and Blackwater. Cereal crops and potatoes are grown, and cattle are raised. Industries: textiles, paper-milling. Area: 2,338sq km (903sq mi). Pop. (1991) 105,370.

Mecca (Makkah) City in W Saudi Arabia, and the holiest city of ISLAM. It is the birthplace of the prophet MUHAMMAD, and only Muslims are allowed in the city. Mecca was originally home to an Arab population of merchants. When Muhammad began his ministry here, the Meccans rejected him. The flight, or HEJIRA, of Muhammad from Mecca to MEDINA in 622 marks the beginning of the Muslim era. In 630, Muhammad's followers captured Mecca and made it the centre of the first Islamic empire. The OTTOMAN Turks held the city from 1517 to 1916, finally losing their control after Arabian independence. In 1924, Mecca fell to the forces of Ibn SAUD, who later founded the Saudi Arabian kingdom. Much of Mecca's commerce depends on Muslim pilgrims undertaking the HAJJ to the Great Mosque enclosing the KAABA. Pop. (1991 est.) 630,000.

mechanical advantage (force ratio) Factor by which any machine multiplies an applied force. It may be calculated from the ratio of the forces involved or from the ratio of the distances through which they

move, as with simple machines such as the LEVER and PULLEY. *See also* EFFICIENCY

mechanical engineering Field of ENGINEERING concerned with the design, construction and operation of machinery. Mechanical engineers work in many branches of industry, including transport, power generation and tool manufacture. Achievements in mechanical engineering include the development of wind and water TURBINES, STEAM ENGINES and INTERNAL COMBUSTION ENGINES.

mechanics Branch of physics concerned with the behaviour of MATTER under the influence of FORCES. It may be divided into solid mechanics and fluid mechanics. Another classification is as STATICS – the study of matter at rest – and DYNAMICS – the study of matter in motion. In **statics**, the forces on an object are balanced and the object is said to be in equilibrium; static equilibrium may be stable, unstable or neutral. **Dynamics** may be further divided into kinematics – the description of motion without regard to cause – and KINETICS – the study of motion and force. Classical dynamics rests primarily on Isaac NEWTON'S LAWS of motion. Modern physics has shown these laws to be special cases approximating to more general laws. Relativistic mechanics deals with the behaviour of matter at high speeds, approaching that of light, whereas QUANTUM MECHANICS deals with the behaviour of matter at the level of atoms and molecules. *See also* QUANTUM THEORY; RELATIVITY

Mecklenburg-Vorpommern State in NE Germany, on the Baltic coast; the capital is Schwerin. In 1621, the region was divided into the duchies of Mecklenburg-Schwerin and Mecklenburg-Güstrow, which became part of the German empire (1817) and then free states of the Weimar Republic. In 1934, the two states were unified. In 1946 they were joined with Pomerania to form a region of East Germany. In 1990, as part of German reunification, Mecklenburg-Vorpommern was reconstituted as one of the five new states of the Federal Republic. It is mainly a low-lying agricultural state. On the coast are the Baltic ports of Rostock, Wismar and Straslund. Area: 23,170sq km (8,944sq mi). Pop. (1993) 1,843,455

Medawar, Sir Peter Brian (1915–87) British zoologist, b. Brazil. He shared the 1960 Nobel Prize for physiology or medicine with Sir Frank Macfarlane Burnet for their discovery of acquired immune tolerance. Medawar confirmed that if foreign tissue is introduced in the embryonic stages of development it may be reintroduced later without inducing a negative response from the IMMUNE SYSTEM.

Medea Daughter of Aeëtes, King of Colchis, whom she defied to help JASON retrieve the GOLDEN FLEECE. Renowned as a sorceress, she lived with Jason for many years in Corinth but fled to Athens after his desertion of her caused her to murder their children and his new wife in a jealous rage.

Medellín City in NW central Colombia; capital of Antioquia department and the second-largest city in Colombia. It was founded in the early 17th century. In recent years it has become the centre for Colombia's illegal cocaine trade. Gold and silver are mined nearby. Industries: coffee, chemicals, steel. Pop. (1997) 1,971,000.

media General term for the modern channels of public information. Traditionally, they are RADIO, TELEVISION, NEWSPAPERS and magazines, and CINEMA, but the INTERNET is increasingly accepted as a form of the media. These media disseminate information and entertainment on a wide scale, and their powers of manipulating people are the subject of much discussion and research.

median In statistics, the middle item in a group found by ranking the items from smallest to largest. In the series, 2, 3, 7, 9, 10, for example, the median is 7. With an even number of items, the MEAN of the two middle items is taken as the median. Thus in the series 2, 3, 7, 9, the median is 5.

Medici, Catherine de' *See* CATHERINE DE' MEDICI

Medici, Cosimo de' (the Elder) (1389–1464) Ruler of Florence (1434–64). With the Medici banking fortune, he led the oligarchy that was expelled from Florence in 1433 but returned to rule permanently the next year. He increased the Medici fortune, strengthened Florence by alliance with Milan and Naples and was a great patron of the scholars and artists of the early RENAISSANCE.

Medici, Cosimo I de' (the Great) (1519–74) Duke of Florence (1537–74), grand duke of Tuscany (1569–74). Under Cosimo's authoritarian rule, Florence flourished and its territory swelled with the acquisition of Siena. He was given the title of grand duke by the pope.

Medici, Lorenzo de' (the Magnificent) (1449–92) Ruler of Florence, grandson of Cosimo de' MEDICI (the Elder). In 1469 Lorenzo succeeded his father, Piero. His grip on power worried Pope SIXTUS IV who instigated a coup led by the rival Pazzi family. Lorenzo survived an assassination attempt and ruthlessly clamped down on his enemies. His patronage of RENAISSANCE artists drained the Medici coffers, so Lorenzo gained control of public funds. A notable poet, he also encouraged writers. His autocratic rule was attacked by Girolamo SAVONAROLA.

medicine Practice of the prevention, diagnosis and treatment of disease or injury; the term is also applied to any agent used in the treatment of DISEASE. Medicine has been practised since ancient times, but the dawn of modern Western medicine coincided with accurate anatomical and physiological observations first made in the 17th century. By the 19th century practical diagnostic procedures had been developed for many diseases; BACTERIA had been discovered and research undertaken for the production of immunizing serums in attempts to eradicate disease. The great developments of the 20th century include the discovery of PENICILLIN and INSULIN; CHEMOTHERAPY the treatment of various diseases with specific chemical agents) new surgical procedures; including organ transplants; and sophisticated diagnostic devices, such as radioactive TRACERS and various scanners. Alternative medicine, such as osteopathy, homeopathy or acupuncture, some of which have existed for hundreds of years, is becoming increasingly popular, and some alternative therapies are being accepted within conventional medicine.

medieval music Music produced in Europe during the later Middle Ages, *c.*1100–1400. It was dominated by Christian liturgical vocal choruses called CHANTS that were sung in polyphonic style. Secular songs were transmitted orally by travelling Saxon, French and German troubadours or MINNESINGERS. In the 14th and 15th centuries, guilds of professional musicians were formed, and musical notation began to become more sophisticated, enabling composers to transmit whole works to later generations. *See also* MOTET; MUSICAL NOTATION; POLYPHONY

Medina City in Saudi Arabia, N of MECCA. Originally called Yathrib, the city was renamed Medinat an-Nabi (Prophet's city) after MUHAMMAD fled Mecca and settled here in 622. Medina became his capital. In 661, the UMAYYAD caliphs moved their capital to DAMASCUS, and Medina's importance declined. It came under Turkish rule (1517–1916), after which it briefly formed part of the independent Arab kingdom of the Hejaz. In 1932, it became part of Saudi Arabia. Pop. (1991 est.) 400,000.

Mediterranean Sea Largest inland sea in the world, lying between Europe and Africa and extending from the Strait of Gibraltar in the W to the coast of SW Asia in the E. The Mediterranean was once a trade route for Phoenicians and Greeks, later controlled by Rome and Byzantium. In the Middle Ages, Venice and Genoa were the dominant maritime powers until the rise of the Ottoman Turks. The opening (1869) of the Suez Canal made the Mediterranean one of the world's busiest shipping routes, and the development of the Middle Eastern oil fields further increased its importance. The Mediterranean is connected to the Black Sea via the Dardanelles, the Sea of Marmara and the Bosporus, and to the Red Sea by the Suez Canal. It includes the Tyrrhenian, Adriatic, Ionian and Aegean seas. It receives the waters of several major rivers, including the Nile, Rhône, Ebro, Tiber and Po. There are *c.*400 species of fish, and tuna, sardines and anchovies are among those caught commercially. In recent years, pollution has become a major issue. Area: 2,509,972km (969,100sq mi).

medlar Fruit-bearing shrub or small tree native to S Europe and the Middle East and naturalized in central Europe and Britain. Often gnarled, it has oblong leaves and brown, apple-like fruit which are edible only at the onset of decay. Height: 4.5–7.6m (15–25ft). Family Rosaceae; species *Mespilus germanica*.

Medusa In Greek mythology a GORGON who was decapitated by Perseus on the order of ATHENA. From the wound sprang PEGASUS and Chrysaor, children of POSEIDON.

Meegeren, Hans van (1889–1947) Dutch painter and celebrated forger, especially of VERMEER paintings, such as *Christ at Emmaus* (1937). He deceived art experts for years and was discovered only via his confession in 1945.

meerkat (suricate) Any of a number of small carnivorous mammals closely related to the MONGOOSE, native to the bush country of southern Africa. It is similar in appearance to the mongoose but without the bushy tail. Length: 47cm (19in). Typical species *Suricata suricatta*.

megabyte (symbol Mb) Computing term to describe *c.*1 million BYTES. A **gigabyte** (Gb) is *c.*1,000 million bytes.

megalith (lit. huge stone) Prehistoric stone monument. Historians usually apply the term to the gigantic slabs that form many stone circles, half circles and rows in N Europe. These constructions date from the NEOLITHIC and early BRONZE AGE. One of the most well-known and complex examples is the circle at STONEHENGE (*c.*2100–2000 BC). Megaliths existed long before the first stone buildings of Mycenean Crete. *See* DOLMEN; MENHIR

Megiddo Ancient city of CANAAN. Strategically located on the route from Egypt to Mesopotamia, it was the scene of many battles, including one between the Egyptians and the Syrians in 1486 BC. It was often rebuilt, notably under the kings of ancient Israel in the 10th–9th centuries BC and after the Assyrian conquest of *c.*734 BC.

Mehta, Zubin (1936–) Indian conductor. He was musical director of the Montréal Symphony (1961–67), Los Angeles Philharmonic Orchestra (1961–77) and New York Philharmonic (1978–91). In 1977, Mehta was made artistic director for life of the Israel Philharmonic.

Meiji, Mutsohito (1852–1912) Emperor of Japan (1867–1912), whose reign saw the transformation of Japan into a modern, industrial state. Mutsuhito introduced sweeping reforms, including the abolition of feudalism, a western-style constitution, the establishment of state education and encouragement of industrial growth.

Meiji Restoration (1868) Constitutional revolution in Japan. Opposition to the shogunate built up after Japan's policy of isolation was ended by US Commodore PERRY in 1854. Pressure for modernization resulted in a new imperial government, at first dominated by former samurai, with the young Emperor MEIJI as its symbolic leader.

meiosis In biology, the process of cell division that reduces the CHROMOSOME number from DIPLOID to HAPLOID. Meiosis involves two nuclear divisions. The first division halves the chromosome number in the cells; the second division then forms four haploid "daughter" cells, each containing a unique configuration of the parent cells' chromosomes. In most higher organisms, the resulting haploid cells are the GAMETES, or sex cells, the OVA and SPERM. In this way meiosis enables the genes from both parents to combine in a single cell without increasing the overall number of chromosomes. *See also* MITOSIS

Meir, Golda (1898–1978) Israeli stateswoman, prime minister (1969–74), b. Ukraine as Golda Mabovitch. In 1906, her family emigrated to the USA, and she became active in ZIONISM. In 1921, Meir emigrated to Palestine. In 1936, she became head of the Jewish labour movement. After Israeli independence, Meir became minister of labour (1949–56) and foreign minister (1956–66). She succeeded Levi ESHKOL as prime minister. Meir managed to maintain a fragile domestic coalition while negotiating with Israel's Arab neighbours. She was forced to resign following criticism of the government's lack of preparedness for the 1973 ARAB–ISRAELI WAR.

Meistersinger German poet-musician of the 15th–16th centuries. They were organized in guilds that held competitions and awarded prizes. Generally, the songs were religious and followed strict conventions. A famous meistersinger, the cobbler Hans Sachs (1494–1576), was immortalized in the opera *Die Meistersinger von Nürnberg* (1868) by Richard WAGNER. *See also* MINSTREL

Meitner, Lise (1878–1968) Austrian physicist. She studied under Ludwig BOLTZMANN. In 1917, Meitner and Otto HAHN discovered the radioactive element PROTACTINIUM. In 1938, she was forced to flee Nazi Germany, shortly before Hahn discovered nuclear FISSION.

Mekong River in SE Asia. It rises in Tibet as the Lancang Jiang and flows S through Yünnan province, China. It forms the Burma-Laos border and part of the Laos-Thailand border and then flows S through Cambodia and Vietnam, creating a vast river delta that is one of the most important rice-producing regions in Asia. Length: c.4,180km (2,600mi).

Melanchthon, Philip (1497–1560) German theologian and educator, considered with Martin LUTHER as a founder of PROTESTANTISM. In 1930 Melanchthon wrote the AUGSBURG CONFESSION, a statement of Protestant beliefs. He also helped Luther with his German translation of the New Testament.

Melanesia Collective term for a number of island groups in the W Pacific Ocean, generally S of the equator, W of the International Date Line, N and E of Australia. It includes the Bismarck Archipelago, SOLOMON ISLANDS, New Hebrides and the TONGA group. Melanesia is one of the sub-divisions of OCEANIA. The others are POLYNESIA and MICRONESIA.

melanin Dark pigment found in the skin, hair and parts of the eye. The amount of melanin determines skin colour. Absence of melanin results in an ALBINO.

melanoma Type of skin CANCER. Melanomas are highly malignant tumours formed by melanocytes, cells in the skin that make the dark pigment MELANIN. They may also occur in MUCOUS MEMBRANES and in the eye. Untreated, they may spread to the liver and lymph nodes. Excessive exposure to sunlight has been cited as a causative factor. Treatment is usually by surgery.

Melba, Dame Nellie (1861–1931) Australian soprano, b. Helen Porter Mitchell. Initially a high coloratura soprano, she was famous in the roles of Lucia (Donizetti's *Lucia di Lammermoor*) and Gilda (Verdi's *Rigoletto*) and later for such lyric roles as Mimí (Puccini's *La Bohème*) and Marguerite (Gounod's *Faust*).

Melbourne, William Lamb, 2nd Viscount (1779–1848) British statesman, prime minister (1834, 1835–41). He entered Parliament as a Whig in 1805. He joined the House of Lords in 1828. As home secretary (1830–34) in Earl GREY's administration, Melbourne was responsible for the suppression of the TOLPUDDLE MARTYRS. As prime minister, he oversaw reform of the POOR LAW (1834) but resisted changes to the CORN LAWS. Melbourne gave Lord PALMERSTON control of foreign affairs and tutored Queen VICTORIA in statecraft. He was succeeded by Sir Robert PEEL. Melbourne's wife, Lady Caroline Lamb, is chiefly remembered for her affair with Lord BYRON.

Melbourne City and port on the River Yarra at the N end of Port Phillip Bay, SE Australia; capital of Victoria state. Founded in 1835 by settlers from Tasmania, it became the state capital in 1851 and served as the seat of the Australian federal government from 1901 to 1927. Melbourne is Australia's second largest city. A major centre of finance, commerce, communications and transport, and Australia's largest cargo-handling port, it exports wool, flour, meat, fruit and dairy produce. Manufacturing is also important. Industries: aircraft, motor vehicles, heavy engineering, shipbuilding, textiles, chemicals, agricultural machinery. Pop. (1993 est.) 3,189,200.

Mellon, Andrew William (1855–1937) US financier. He inherited a fortune, which he increased through industrial investment and banking. Later, Mellon was secretary of the treasury under three presidents (1921–32). A generous patron of the arts, He donated the funding for the National Gallery of Art, Washington, D.C.

melodrama Theatrical form originating in late 18th-century France and achieving its greatest popularity during the following century. It relied on simple, violent plots in which virtue was finally rewarded.

melody In music, a sequence of notes that makes a recognizable musical pattern. The term is most commonly used of the dominant part or voice (the "tune") in Romantic and light music, in which harmonic accompaniment is nearly always subordinate. Music featuring several melodies simultaneously is termed "contrapuntal" or POLYPHONY, and is characteristic of the late BAROQUE period. *See also* COUNTERPOINT; HARMONY

melon Annual vine and its large, fleshy, edible fruit. Melons grow in warm temperate and sub-tropical climates. The cantaloupe melon, with its rough skin, probably originated in Armenia; the smoother yellow rind honeydew, in SE Asia. The large, dark-green watermelon, with its red, watery flesh, is believed to have come from Africa. Family Cucurbitaceae.

melting point Temperature at which a substance changes from solid to liquid. The melting point of the solid has the same value as the freezing point of the liquid, so the melting point of ice, 0°C (32°F), is the same as the freezing point of water.

Melville, Herman (1819–91) US novelist. He became a sailor in 1839 and joined a whaling ship in 1841. His debut novel, *Typee* (1846), recounts his experiences among remote island natives. *Moby Dick*, an allegorical story of the search for a great whale, was written in 1851. His short story, *Billy Budd*, was published in 1924 and was the inspiration for BRITTEN's opera of the same name.

Melville's work was neglected during his lifetime, but *Moby Dick* is now regarded as a classic of US literature.

membrane In biology, boundary layer or layers inside or around a living CELL or TISSUE. Cell membranes include the plasma membrane surrounding the cell, the network of membranes inside the cell (endoplasmic reticulum) and the double membrane surrounding the NUCLEUS. The multicellular membranes of the body comprise: the mucous membranes of the respiratory, digestive and urinogenital passages; the synovial membranes of the joints; and the membranes that coat the inner walls of the abdomen and thorax and the surfaces of organs. *See also* EPITHELIUM

Memling, Hans (1440–94) (Hans Memlinc) Flemish painter, b. Germany. Memling had a flourishing workshop from which he produced a large number of portraits and religious works. His patrons included the Italians Tommaso Portinari and his wife, whom he painted in *c*.1468.

memory Capacity to retain information and experience and to recall or reconstruct them in the future. Modern psychologists often divide memory into two types, short-term and long-term. An item in short-term memory lasts for *c*.10–15 seconds after an experience and is lost if not used again. An item enters long-term memory if the item is of sufficient importance or if the information is required frequently. *See also* LEARNING

Memphis Ancient city of Egypt, s of Cairo, part of which is now occupied by the village of Mit Ra-hina. Founded in *c*.3100 BC by MENES, the city was formerly the royal residence and capital of Egypt. Material from its ruins was used by the Arabs for building Cairo.

Memphis City and river port in sw Tennessee, USA, on the Mississippi River; largest city in Tennessee. Strategically located on Chickasaw Bluff above the Mississippi, the site of Memphis was used as a French (1682), Spanish (1794), and US (1797) fort before the first permanent settlement was made in 1819. Today, it is a major transport centre and livestock market. Industries: timber, farm machinery, cotton, food processing, pharmaceuticals. Pop. (1990) 610,337.

Menander (342–292 BC) Greek playwright. He wrote more than 100 comedies of which only one survives in full. As the outstanding exponent of the New Comedy of Hellenistic times, he is regarded as the founder of the comedy of manners, his plays being concerned with domestic problems.

Mencius (*c*.372–289 BC) (Mengzi) Chinese philosopher of the Confucian school. He held that human beings are basically good but require cultivation to bring out the goodness. His teachings were recorded in the *Book of Mencius*, one of the Four Books in the canonical writings of CONFUCIANISM.

Mencken, H.L. (Henry Louis) (1880–1956) US social critic. He became a brilliantly witty and ferociously savage critic of US middle-class culture. His influence was at its height while he was editor of the *American Mercury* (1924–33). In addition to his essays and journalism, he wrote a multi-volume study of *The American Language* (1919–48).

Mendel, Gregor Johann (1822–84) Austrian naturalist. He discovered the laws of HEREDITY and in so doing laid the foundation for the modern science of GENETICS. His study of the inheritance of characteristics, such as flower colour, height of plants and texture of the seeds of garden peas, was published in *Experiments with Plant Hybrids* (1866). It was rediscovered in 1900.

mendelevium (symbol Md) Radioactive, metallic element that is the ninth of the TRANSURANIC ELEMENTS

in the ACTINIDE SERIES. In 1955, A. Ghiorso and colleagues at the University of California synthesized it by the alpha-particle bombardment of einsteinium-253. Properties: at.no. 101; r.a.m. 258; most stable isotope Md^{258} (half-life 2 months).

Mendeleyev, Dmitri Ivanovich (1834–1907) Russian chemist who devised the PERIODIC TABLE. He demonstrated that chemically similar elements appear at regular intervals if the elements are arranged in order by atomic weights. Mendeleyev classified the 60 known elements and left gaps in the table, predicting the existence and properties of several unknown elements later discovered. The element MENDELEVIUM is named after him.

Mendelsohn, Erich (1887–1953) German architect who designed the Einstein Observatory at Potsdam (1920), E Germany. perhaps the most famous example of EXPRESSIONISM in architecture.

Mendelssohn (-Bartholdy), (Jakob Ludwig) Felix (1809–47) German composer and conductor. A child prodigy, at 16 he composed an octet, and at 17 he wrote his overture to *A Midsummer Night's Dream*. His performance (1829) of the *St Matthew Passion* revived 19th-century interest in J.S. BACH. His orchestral works include a famous violin concerto (1845) and five symphonies. He also wrote much piano and chamber music. His two oratorios, *St Paul* (1836) and *Elijah* (1846), are considered to be among the greatest of the 19th century. Mendelssohn's visit to Scotland inspired his popular orchestral overture *The Hebrides* (or "*Fingal's Cave*", 1845). Typical of German romanticism, his compostions were often inspired use by extra-musical associations.

Mendes, Sam (1965–) English film and theatre director. As founder and artistic director (1992–) of the Donmar Warehouse Theatre, London, Mendes received critical acclaim for his productions of *Cabaret* (1997) and David HARE's *The Blue Room* (1999). His debut film, *American Beauty* (1999), a satire on American suburbia, was hugely successful, winning five Academy Awards, including best picture and best director.

Mendès-France, Pierre (1907–82) French statesman, prime minister (1955–56). He was imprisoned by the VICHY GOVERNMENT but escaped to London in 1941. Mendès-France enlisted in the Free French air force, and later joined General de GAULLE's government-in-exile. In 1946, he re-entered parliament. After the defeat of the French army at DIEN BIEN PHU (1954), Mendès-France became prime minister and withdrew French troops from INDOCHINA. He also prepared the way for Tunisian independence. His austere economic plans led to his downfall.

Menem, Carlos Saúl (1935–) Argentinian statesman, president (1989–99). He was imprisoned (1976–81) by the military government. Menem invoked the name of Juan PERÓN in his campaign for president. He introduced privatization, released hundreds of political prisoners and improved relations with the UK over the fate of the FALKLAND ISLANDS. He was re-elected in 1995. He was succeeded (1999) by Fernando de la Rúa.

Menes Egyptian king (*c*.3100 BC) regarded as the first king of the First Dynasty. He unified Upper and Lower Egypt, establishing the Old Kingdom with its capital at MEMPHIS. *See also* EGYPT, ANCIENT

menhir Archaeological term given to single standing stones found in w Europe. Probably of NEOLITHIC origin, they are usually tall and square in section, tapering toward the top. They are thought to have been used to mark places of religious or ritual significance. *See also* DOLMEN

Menière's disease Chronic condition of the inner EAR affecting hearing and balance. Symptoms are deafness, vertigo and ringing in the ears (tinnitus). Caused by excessive fluid in the inner ear, it occurs in middle age or later. It is generally treated with ANTIHISTAMINE drugs.

meningitis Inflammation of the meninges (membranes) covering the brain and spinal cord, resulting from infection. Bacterial meningitis is more serious than the viral form. Symptoms include headache, fever, nausea and stiffness of the neck. The disease can vary from mild to lethal.

Mennonites Christian sect founded by the Dutch reformer Menno Simons (1496–1561) and influenced by ANABAPTIST doctrines. They believe in the BAPTISM of adult believers and reject infant baptism as well as the doctrine of the real presence in the EUCHARIST.

menopause Stage in a woman's life marking the end of the reproductive years, when the MENSTRUAL CYCLE becomes irregular and finally ceases, generally around the age of 50. Popularly known as the "change of life", it may be accompanied by unpleasant effects such as hot flushes, excessive bleeding and emotional upset. HORMONE REPLACEMENT THERAPY (HRT) is designed to relieve menopausal symptoms.

menorah Sacred seven-branched candelabra that has become a symbol of JUDAISM throughout the world. It is rich in symbolic meaning. Some interpret it in terms of the seven planets, the tree of life, or the six-day creation of the universe with the centre shaft representing the Sabbath. An eight-branched menorah is used during the HANUKKAH festival.

Menorca See MINORCA

Menotti, Gian Carlo (1911–) US composer, b. Italy. His operas in modern OPERA BUFFA style include *The Telephone* (1947). Menotti won Pulitzer Prizes for his operas *The Medium* (1946) and *The Saint of Blecker Street* (1954). He has also composed operas specifically for television, such as *Amahl and the Night Visitors* (1951) and *Labyrinth* (1963).

Menshevik Moderate faction of the Russian Social Democratic Labour Party. The Mensheviks ("the minority") split from the more radical BOLSHEVIKS ("the majority") in 1903. They believed in "scientific SOCIALISM" and therefore favoured a gradual transformation of society, whereas the Bolsheviks wanted total revolution organized by a small, central group of disciplined revolutionaries. The Mensheviks were suppressed in 1922. *See also* RUSSIAN REVOLUTION

menstrual cycle (menarche) In humans and some higher primates of reproductive age, the stage during which the body prepares for pregnancy. In humans the average cycle is 28 days. At the beginning of the cycle, GONADTROPHINS (follicle stimulating hormone and luteinizing hormone) are secreted by the PITUITARY GLAND and induce the output of OESTROGEN, which stimulates the growth of an ovum (egg cell) contained in a follicle in one of the two OVARIES. At approximately mid-cycle, the follicle bursts, the egg is released (ovulation) and travels down the FALLOPIAN TUBE to the UTERUS. The follicle (now called the corpus luteum) secretes PROGESTERONE and oestrogen during this secretory phase of the cycle, and the ENDOMETRIUM thickens, ready to receive the fertilized egg. Should fertilization (conception) not occur, the corpus luteum degenerates, hormone secretion ceases, the endometrium breaks down and menstruation occurs in the form of a loss of blood. In the event of conception, the corpus luteum remains and maintains the endometrium with chorionic gonadotrophin until the PLACENTA is formed. In humans, the onset of the menstrual cycle occurs at PUBERTY; it ceases with the MENOPAUSE (around 50 years).

mental handicap Intellectual functioning that is below the average, irrespective of cause. It is usually related to congenital conditions but can arise later in life through brain damage. Assuming a normal intelligence quotient, or IQ, of 90–110, impairment is often described as borderline (IQ 68–85), mild (IQ 52–67), moderate (IQ 36–51), severe (IQ 20–35) and profound (IQ under 20).

mental health Condition of an individual whose emotional and behavioural adjustment is appropriate to his or her environment: the absence of MENTAL ILLNESS. Mental health has a social context, and modern treatment for psychological disorders tries to help people develop a more integrated relationship with their circumstances. *See also* MENTAL ILLNESS

mental disorder Any failure of MENTAL HEALTH that is severe enough for psychiatric treatment to be appropriate. Some mental disorders can be attributed to injury or organic disease of the BRAIN. Mental disorder may also be the result of a hereditary predisposition. Other disorders are psychogenic, without any clear evidence of any physiological cause. SCHIZOPHRENIA, severe DEPRESSION and manic-depressive psychoses are the most widespread of mental disorders. Neurotic disorders, which can be severe but do not often warrant prolonged stays in hospital, include persistent anxiety, PHOBIAS and obsessions. *See also* HYSTERIA

menthol ($C_{10}H_{19}OH$) White, waxy crystalline compound having a strong odour of PEPPERMINT. Its main source is oil of peppermint from the plant *Mentha arvensis*. It is an ingredient of decongestant ointments and nasal sprays and is used to flavour toothpaste and cigarettes.

Menuhin, Yehudi, Baron (1916–99) British violinist, b. USA. A child prodigy, he gave his first concert aged seven. In 1932, Menuhin recorded Elgar's violin concerto, the composer conducting. In 1942, Bela Bartók wrote his solo violin sonata for him. Menuhin was director (1959–68) of the Bath Festival and in 1963 founded the Yehudi Menuhin School for young, gifted musicians. Menuhin was knighted in 1965. He was often accompanied on the piano by his sister **Hephzibah** Menuhin (1920–81). Another sister, **Yaltah** (1922–), and Yehudi's son, **Jeremy** (1951–), are also pianists.

Menzies, Sir Robert Gordon (1894–1978) Australian statesman, the country's longest-serving prime minister (1939–41, 1949–65). He led the United Australia Party to victory in 1939 elections. In 1944, Menzies formed the LIBERAL PARTY. In the immediate aftermath of World War 2, he encouraged British and US commitment to the security of Southeast Asia and supported the ANZUS PACT and the SOUTHEAST ASIA TREATY ORGANIZATION (SEATO). Menzies supported the USA in the Vietnam War.

mercantilism Seventeenth-century trade policy advocating state intervention in economic affairs, primarily to maximize exports. Foreign trade was publicly controlled to produce the maximum possible surplus in the nation's trade balance, thus increasing the country's store of silver and gold, which constitute the "nation's wealth". Trade was controlled through tariffs on imported goods. Mercantilism was criticized by the proponents of LAISSEZ-FAIRE and FREE-TRADE.

Mercator, Gerardus (1512–94) Flemish cartographer. His huge world map of 1569 employed the system of projection now named after him, in which lines of longitude, as well as latitude, appear as straight, parallel lines.

merchant bank One of a number of UK specialist banks that offer a range of financial services primarily to corporate customers. They rose to prominence in the

18th and 19th centuries, involved in overseas trade. Now they provide an extensive range of services similar to US investment banks, and these include: operating as issuing houses, sponsoring capital issues, offering corporate advisory work, asset management and foreign exchange.

merchant navy Section of a nation's fleet concerned with international commercial shipping. Today, most international cargo is shipped in "flag-of-convenience" fleets. These lines register ships in low-tax countries, such as Liberia or Panama.

Mercury In Roman mythology, the god of commerce, merchants and thieves, identified with the Greek HERMES. Mercury had a temple on the Aventine (built in 495 BC). His festival was observed on 15 May.

Mercury Smallest of the four inner planets and the planet closest to the Sun. It has no known satellite. Very little was known about Mercury's surface until the Mariner 10 probe made three close approaches to the planet in 1974 and 1975 and returned pictures of nearly half the surface. These showed a heavily cratered, lunar-like world marked by valleys and ridges. In 1991–92 radar mapping of Mercury's polar regions revealed what may be water ice on the floors of craters permanently in shadow. There is a very tenuous atmosphere, mainly of helium and sodium, and a weak magnetic field.

mercury (quicksilver) (symbol Hg) Liquid metallic element, known from earliest times. The chief ore is cinnabar (a sulphide), from which it is extracted by roasting. The silvery element is poisonous and the only metal that is liquid at normal temperatures. Mercury is used in barometers, thermometers, laboratory apparatus, mercury-vapour lamps and mercury cells. Mercury compounds are used in pharmaceuticals. Properties: at.no. 80; r.a.m. 200.59; r.d. 13.6; m.p. $-38.87°C$ ($-37.97°F$); b.p. $356.58°C$ ($673.84°F$); most common isotope Hg^{202} (29.8%).

Meredith, George (1828–1909) English novelist and poet. His verse includes the semi-autobiographical sonnets *Modern Love* (1862). Meredith established his reputation as a novelist with *The Ordeal of Richard Feverel* (1859) and *Evan Harrington* (18961). Other novels include *Sandra Belloni* (1864), *Rhoda Fleming* (1865), *Vittoria* (1867), *The Adventures of Harry Richmond* (1871) and *Beauchamp's Career* (1876). His finest novels are *The Egoist* (1879) and *Diana of the Crossways* (1885).

merganser Any of several species of slender freshwater or marine ducks that dive for food, especially the red-breasted merganser (*Mergus serrator*), which has a hooked bill. The goosander (*M. merganser*) differs mainly in coloration. Family Anatidae.

meridian Circle that runs through the North and South Poles, at right angles to the equator. *See also* LONGITUDE

Mérimée, Prosper (1803–70) French dramatist and short-story writer. He wrote a large body of dramatic work in the 1820s but is best remembered for his historical novellas and short stories. These include the collection of short stories, *Mosaïque* (1833), and the novellas

Colomba (1841) and *Carmen* (1845), on which Georges BIZET based his opera.

meristem In plants, a layer of cells that divides repeatedly to generate new tissues. It is present at the growing tips of shoots and roots and at certain sites in leaves. In monocotyledons the leaf meristem is at the base, explaining why grasses continue to grow when the leaf tips are removed by grazing or mowing. *See also* CAMBIUM

Merleau-Ponty, Maurice (1908–61) French philosopher. A follower of Edmund HUSSERL, Merleau-Ponty contributed greatly to PHENOMENOLOGY, especially in his book *The Phenomenology of Perception* (1945). In 1945, with Jean-Paul SARTRE and Simone de BEAUVOIR, he founded the journal *Les Temps Modernes*. His later work, exploring the ambiguity of perception and experience, culminated in *The Visible and the Invisible* (1964).

Merlin Legendary magician. His origins may be traced to early Celtic folklore, although his name is usually associated with the ARTHURIAN ROMANCES as the mentor of King ARTHUR.

merlin Small, European FALCON found in hills and open moorland. Feeding on small birds, it may hover, but not as commonly as the KESTREL. Length: to 33cm (13in). Species *Falco columbarius*.

Merovingian (476–750) Frankish dynasty. It was named after Merovech, a leader of the Salian Franks, whose grandson CLOVIS (r. *c.*481–511) ruled over most of France and, converting to Christianity, established the common interests of the Frankish rulers and the already Christian population of his new kingdom. The last Merovingian king was overthrown by PEPIN, founder of the Carolingian dynasty.

Mersey River in NW England. Formed by the confluence of the rivers Goyt and Tame in the Peak District, it flows W to from a large estuary at LIVERPOOL and empties intothe Irish Sea. Length: 112km (70mi).

Merseyside Metropolitan county in NW England, formed in 1974. It lies on both banks of the estuary of the River MERSEY. The major town is LIVERPOOL. In the 19th century, shipbuilding and ship repair grew in importance, and Liverpool became one of Britain's leading ports. Industries: motor vehicles, chemicals, electrical goods. Area: 655sq km (253sq mi). Pop. (1991) 1,403,642.

mesa Large, broad, flat-topped hill or mountain of moderate height and with steep, cliff-like sides. A mesa is capped with layers of resistant horizontal rocks which may then erode to form narrower buttes.

mescaline Psychedelic drug obtained from the dried tops of the peyote cactus, *Lophophora williamsii*. In North America, mescaline is used in some Native American religious rites.

Mesmer, Franz (Friedrich Anton) (1734–1815) Austrian physician. His interest in "animal magnetism" led to his development of "mesmerism" (HYPNOSIS) as a therapeutic treatment. Ridiculed by fellow scientists, Mesmer died in obscurity.

Mesolithic (Middle Stone Age) In NW Europe the period in human cultural development following the PALAEOLITHIC and preceding the NEOLITHIC. It followed an ice age (*c.*8000 BC). As the environment changed, scrub gave way to forest and small game proliferated. A nomadic form of life became unnecessary, and human settlement was a feature of this period, as were flint tools.

meson SUBATOMIC PARTICLE, member of a subgroup of HADRONS, all of which have either zero or integral SPIN. They include the pions, kaons and eta mesons.

mesophyll Soft tissue located between the two layers of epidermis in a plant leaf. In most plants, mesophyll

---

MERCURY DATA
DIAMETER (EQUATORIAL): 4,878km (3,031mi)
MASS (EARTH = 1) : 0.055
VOLUME (EARTH = 1) : 0.056
DENSITY (WATER = 1): 5.44
ORBITAL PERIOD: 89.97 days
ROTATION PERIOD: 68.646 days
SURFACE TEMPERATURE: 427°C (800°F)

cells contain chlorophyll-producing structures called CHLOROPLASTS, which are essential to PHOTOSYNTHESIS.

Mesopotamia Ancient region between the rivers TIGRIS and EUPHRATES in SW Asia, roughly corresponding to modern Iraq. It was the setting of one of the earliest human civilizations, resulting from the development of irrigation in the 6th millennium BC and the extreme fertility of the irrigated land. The first cities were established (c.2500 BC) by the Sumerians. The first empire builders on a large scale were the people of AKKADIA under SARGON, who conquered the Sumerian cities c.2300 BC. BABYLONIA gained supremacy in the 18th century BC and was followed by others, notably the Assyrians. Later ruled by foreigners, such as Persians, Greeks and Romans, Mesopotamia gradually lost its distinctive cultural traditions. *See also* SUMERIA

mesosphere Middle shell of gases in the ATMOSPHERE between the STRATOSPHERE and the THERMOSPHERE. It rises to a height of 70km (43mi).

Mesozoic Third era of geologic time, extending from c.248 to c.65 million years ago. It is divided into three periods: the TRIASSIC, JURASSIC and CRETACEOUS. For most of the era the continents are believed to have been joined into one huge landmass called PANGAEA. The period was also characterized by the variety and size of its reptiles.

mesquite (honey mesquite) Deciduous tree common in SW USA and Mexico. Its roots may extend more than 15m (50ft), allowing it to grow in desert regions. It has small leaflets and spines. Bees make honey from the nectar of the flowers and the pods are used as fodder. Height: to 6m (20ft). Family Mimosaceae; species *Prosopis juliflora.*

Messerschmitt, Willy (Wilhelm) (1898–1978) German AIRCRAFT designer, famous for the Messerschmitt Bf-109 fighter used by the LUFTWAFFE during World War 2. Messerschmitt also designed the ME-262, the first JET-ENGINED aircraft to be used in combat (1944).

Messiaen, Olivier (1908–92) French composer and organist. His organ works, including *L'Ascension* (1933) and *La Nativité du Seigneur* (1935), are important contributions to the repertoire of that instrument. Among other compositions is the monumental ten-movement *Turangalîla-symphonie* (1949) and an opera on the life of St Francis of Assisi (1983).

Messiah (Heb. anointed) Saviour or redeemer. Specifically, the Messiah was the descendant of King DAVID expected by the Jews of ancient times to become their king, free them from foreign bondage and rule over them in a golden age of glory, peace and righteousness. It refers to the "idealized" king as having been anointed by God or his representative in the way that David and his successors were. The title "Christ", derived from the Greek version of the term Messiah, was probably applied to JESUS by his followers.

Messina Seaport and city on the Strait of Messina, NE Sicily, S Italy; capital of Messina province. It was founded by the Greeks in c.730 BC. The city was conquered by mercenaries, whose backing from Rome led directly to the first of the PUNIC WARS. From 241 BC, Messina was a free city of Rome. In the 9th century, it was conquered by the Muslim Saracen army and then by the Normans in 1061. In 1190, Messina was taken by the Crusaders and was ruled by Spain from 1282 to 1714. In 1860, it was liberated by Giuseppe GARIBALDI. In 1908, an earthquake killed more than 80,000 people and destroyed most of the city. Exports: wine, citrus fruit, olive oil, chemicals. Industries: chemicals, pharmaceuticals. Pop. (1996) 263,000.

metabolism Chemical and physical processes and changes continuously occurring in a living organism. They include the breakdown of organic matter (**catabolism**), resulting in energy release and the synthesis of organic components (**anabolism**) to store energy and build and repair TISSUES. *See also* BASAL METABOLIC RATE (BMR)

metal Element that is a good conductor of heat and electricity. Its atoms are bonded together within crystals in a unique way. Mixtures of such elements (ALLOYS) are also metals. About three-quarters of known elements are metals. Most are hard, shiny materials that form oxides. MALLEABILITY and DUCTILITY are further metallic characteristics. Some metals have very high melting points and various high-temperature applications: TUNGSTEN, with the highest melting point of all at 3,410°C (6,170°F), is employed for incandescent-lamp filaments. ALUMINIUM and IRON are the two most abundant and useful of metals. TITANIUM, although rarely seen as a metal, is more commonly distributed than the more familiar COPPER, ZINC and LEAD. Other metals of economic importance, because they can undergo nuclear FISSION, are URANIUM and PLUTONIUM.

metalloid ELEMENT having some properties typical of METALS and some normally associated with non-metals. Metalloids are sometimes called semi-metals or semi-metallic elements. Examples are SILICON, GERMANIUM and ARSENIC. Some metalloids are SEMICONDUCTORS.

metallurgy Science and technology concerned with METALS. Metallurgy includes the study of methods of extraction of metals from their ores, physical and chemical properties of metals, ALLOY production, and the hardening, strengthening, corrosion-proofing and ELECTROPLATING of metals. *See also* ANODIZING; GALVANIZING

metamorphic rock Broad class of ROCKS that have been changed by heat or pressure, or both heat and pressure, from their original nature – SEDIMENTARY, IGNEOUS, or older metamorphic. Heat is the result of volcanic activity, and pressure is the result of earth movements. Metamorphic rocks are generally hard and resistant to erosion, and are likely to form high ground. In metamorphic rocks, minerals may re-crystallize or be compressed, and the new rock may look completely different from the original sedimentary or igneous rock. Thus, the metamorphic rock SLATE is made from sedimentary SHALE, the metamorphic GNEISS from igneous GRANITE.

metamorphosis Change of form during the development of various organisms, such as the changing of a caterpillar into a moth, or a tadpole into a frog. Sometimes the change is gradual, as with a grasshopper, and is known as incomplete metamorphosis. Complete metamorphosis usually involves the more distinct stages of LARVA, PUPA and IMAGO.

metaphor Figure of speech that draws a comparison. It differs from ordinary comparisons in its inventiveness, and from a SIMILE in the complexity of the idea expressed. "Fleece as white as snow", is a simile, whereas "His political life was a constant swimming against the tide", is a metaphor.

metaphysical poetry English literary form of the 17th century, characterized by the combination of unlike ideas or images to create new representations of experience, and a reliance on wit and subtle argument. Although this method was by no means new, in the hands of such writers as George HERBERT, Andrew MARVELL and John DONNE, it infused new life into English poetry.

metaphysics Branch of philosophy that deals with the first principles of reality and with the nature of the universe. Metaphysics is divided into ONTOLOGY, the study of the essence of being, and COSMOLOGY, the study of the structure and laws of the universe. Leading metaphysical thinkers have included PLATO, ARISTOTLE, DESCARTES, LEIBNIZ, KANT and A.N. WHITEHEAD.

Metaxas, Joannis (1871–1941) Greek general and statesman, prime minister (1936–41). Metaxas fought in the BALKAN WARS (1912–13) but was dismissed for pro-German leanings during World War 1. As prime minister, Metaxas dissolved parliament and ruled as a virtual dictator. Despite fascist trappings, he led resistance to MUSSOLINI's imperialism.

meteor (shooting star) Brief streak of light in the night sky caused by a METEOROID entering the Earth's upper atmosphere at high speed from space. A typical meteor lasts from a few tenths of a second to a few seconds, depending on the meteoroid's impact speed, which can vary from c.11–70km/s (7–45mi/s). At certain times of the year there are meteor showers, when meteors are more numerous than usual.

meteorite That part of a large meteoroid (a small particle or body following an Earth-crossing orbit) that survives passage through the Earth's atmosphere and reaches the ground. Most of a meteoroid burns up in the atmosphere to produce METEORS, but c.10% reaches the surface as meteorites and micrometeorites. Meteorites generally have a pitted surface and a fused charred crust. There are three main types: iron meteorites (**siderites**); stony meteorites (**aerolites**); and mixed iron and stone meteorites. Some are tiny particles, but others weigh up to 200 tonnes.

meteorology Study of WEATHER conditions, a branch of CLIMATOLOGY. Meteorologists study and analyze data from weather ships, aircraft and satellites in order to compile maps showing the state of the high- and low-pressure regions in the Earth's atmosphere. They also anticipate changes in the distribution of the regions and forecast the future weather.

meter Instrument that measures a particular quantity. For example, a gas meter measures the amount of gas that has flowed in a certain time, and a voltmeter measures the voltage between two points in an electrical circuit.

methanal (formaldehyde, HCHO) Colourless, inflammable, poisonous gas with a penetrating odour. It is the simplest aldehyde and is produced by the oxidation of METHANOL by air. It was discovered (1867) by August von HOFMANN. Most methanal is in the form of formalin. Methanal is used in the manufacture of dyes and plastics. Chief properties: r.d. 0.82; m.p. $-92°C$ $(-133.6°F)$; b.p. $-19°C$ $(-2.2°F)$.

methane (CH_4) Colourless, odourless HYDROCARBON, the simplest ALKANE (paraffin). It is the chief constituent of NATURAL GAS, from which it is obtained. It is produced by decomposing organic matter, such as in marshes, which led to its original name of marsh gas. In the air, it contributes to the GREENHOUSE EFFECT and an increase in global temperature. Methane is used in the form of natural gas as a fuel. Properties: m.p. $-182.5°C$ $(-296.5°F)$; b.p. $-164°C$ $(-263.2°F)$.

methanoic acid (formic acid, HCOOH) Colourless, corrosive, pungent, liquid carboxylic acid. It is used to produce insecticides and for dyeing, tanning and electroplating. It occurs naturally in a variety of sources, such as stinging ants, nettles, pine needles and sweat. The simplest of the carboxylic acids, it can be produced by the action of concentrated sulphuric acid on sodium methanoate. Properties: r.d. 1.22; m.p. 8.3°C (46.9°F); b.p. 100.8°C (213.4°F).

methanol (methyl alcohol, CH_3OH) Colourless, poisonous, flammable liquid, the simplest of the ALCOHOLS. It is obtained synthetically either from carbon monoxide and hydrogen by the oxidation of natural gas, or by the destructive distillation of wood. It is used as a solvent, petrol additive, and in rocket fuel and petrol. Properties: m.p. $-93.9°C$ $(-137°F)$; b.p. 64.9°C (148.8°F).

Methodism Worldwide religious movement that began in England in the 18th century. It was originally an evangelical movement within the CHURCH OF ENGLAND, started in 1729 by John and Charles WESLEY. John Wesley stayed within the Anglican Church until his death in 1791. In 1795, the Wesleyan Methodists became a separate body and divided into other sects that were reunited with the United Methodist Church in the

▲ **metamorphosis** When common frogs mate, fertilization and egg laying occur in water (1). Within an hour, the jelly around the egg swells to produce frogspawn (2). The eggs develop (3) and produce embryos (4) that hatch as long-tailed tadpoles with external feathery gills six days after fertilization (5). Mouths and eyes develop later, and the tails become powerful means of propulsion. Hind legs are well-formed by week eight (6); meanwhile, the tadpole has changed from a herbivore to a carnivore. Via an intermediary gill and lung stage, the tadpole changes from gill- to lung-breathing, its internal lungs growing as its external gills are absorbed; the process is complete when the gills fully disappear at month three, by which time the forelegs are well developed (7). Metamorphosis is complete when the young frog loses its tail.

20th century. In the USA, the Methodist Episcopal Church was founded in 1784. Today, there are more than 50 million Methodists worldwide.

Methuselah In the Old Testament (Genesis 5:25–27), the longest-lived of all human beings; son of ENOCH and eighth in descent from ADAM and EVE. He is said to have died at the age of 969 and was the father of many children, including Lamech, the father of NOAH.

methylated spirit Industrial form of ETHANOL (ethyl alcohol). It contains 5% METHANOL (methyl alcohol), which is extremely poisonous, and enough pyridine to give it a foul taste. It is dyed purple and used as a solvent and fuel.

metre In poetry, a regular rhythmic pattern. It imposes a regular recurrence of stresses, typically dividing a line into equal units called metrical feet. The most commonly used metrical feet are anapaest, dactyl, iamb and trochee. The metre of a poem is described according to the kind and number of metrical feet per line: for example, iambic pentametres have five iambs per line.

metre (symbol m) SI unit of distance. Conceived as one ten millionth of the surface distance between the North Pole and the Equator, it was formerly defined by two marks on a platinum bar kept in Paris. It is now defined as the length of the path travelled by light in a vacuum during $1/299,792,458$ of a second. 1 metre equals 39.3701 inches.

metric system Decimal system of WEIGHTS AND MEASURES based on the METRE (m) and the KILOGRAM (kg). Larger and smaller metric units are related by powers of 10. Devised in 1791, the metric system is used internationally by scientists (particularly as SI UNITS) and has been adopted for general use by most Western countries, although the IMPERIAL SYSTEM is still commonly used in the USA and for certain measurements in Britain.

Metropolitan Museum of Art Art museum in New York City, USA. Founded in 1870, the museum has a large and diverse permanent art collection, including numerous Egyptian, Greek and Roman works. Much of the medieval collection is housed in a separate complex, The Cloisters. In addition to European sculpture, there are more than 4,600 European paintings ranging from the 15th century to the present, as well as many US paintings and sculptures. The Oriental art collection numbers 30,000 pieces.

Metropolitan Opera Company Company in New York City, USA, famous for the high standard of its productions. Operas premiered at "the Met" include *Gianni Schicchi* (1918) and *The Girl of the Golden West* (1910), both by Puccini. The Metropolitan Opera House was opened in 1883; it moved to the Lincoln Center for the Performing Arts in 1966.

Metternich, Klemens Wenzel Lothar, Prince von (1773–1859) Austrian statesman. As foreign minister (1809–48) and chancellor (1821–48), Metternich was the leading European statesman of the post-Napoleonic era. Following Austria's defeat in the NAPOLEONIC WARS (1809), he adopted a conciliatory policy towards France. After NAPOLEON I's retreat from Moscow (1812), Metternich formed the QUADRUPLE ALLIANCE (1813) that led to Napoleon's defeat. He was the dominant figure at the Congress of VIENNA (1814–15) and at subsequent conferences held under the CONGRESS SYSTEM. In 1815 Metternich secured peace in Europe and thereafter became increasingly autocratic, pressing for the intervention of the great powers against any revolutionary outbreak. He was driven from power by the REVOLUTION OF 1848.

Metz City on the River Moselle , NE France; capital of Moselle department. One of Roman Gaul's chief cities, it was burned by Vandals in 406 and by Huns in 451. After the 8th century the bishops of Metz ruled a vast empire. Made a free imperial city in 12th century, Metz enjoyed considerable prosperity. It was taken by France in 1552 but became part of Germany after the FRANCO–PRUSSIAN WAR (1871). The Treaty of Versailles (1919) restored it to France. Industries: metals, machinery, tobacco, wine, tanning, clothing. Pop. (1990) 119,594.

Mexican Revolution (1910–40) Extended political revolution that improved the welfare of the Mexican underprivileged. The Mexican Revolution was prompted by the dictatorial, elitist presidency of Porfirio DÍAZ. In 1910, Díaz, who had agreed not to run for re-election following the threat of armed revolt led by Francisco MADERO, reneged on his agreement and was re-elected. In 1911, he was forced to resign by Madero, who was subsequently elected. Madero intended to make land ownership more egalitarian, to strengthen labour organizations, and to lessen the influence of the Catholic Church. In 1913, he was assassinated by his former general Victoriano HUERTA. The repressive regime of Huerta caused massive unrest in the peasant community, who found leaders in Venustiano CARRANZA, Francisco "Pancho" VILLA, and Emiliano ZAPATA. In 1914, Huerta resigned and Carranza became president. Although some agrarian, educational and political reforms continued, it was Lázaro CÁRDENAS presidency (1934–40) that finally introduced sweeping measures involving land distribution, support of the labour movement, and improving health and education.

Mexican War (1846–48) War between Mexico and the USA. It broke out following US annexation of TEXAS (1845). The Mexicans were swiftly overwhelmed, and a series of US expeditions effected the conquest of the southwest. The war ended when General Winfield Scott, having landed at Vera Cruz in March 1847, defeated the army of SANTA ANNA and entered Mexico City on 8 September. In the Treaty of GUADALUPE-HIDALGO (1848), Mexico ceded sovereignty over California and New Mexico, as well as Texas north of the Rio Grande.

Mexico Republic in s North America. Mexico is the world's largest Spanish-speaking country. It is largely mountainous. The SIERRA MADRE Occidental begins in the NW state of CHIHUAHUA and runs parallel to Mexico's w coast and the Sierra Madre Oriental. MONTERREY lies in the foothills of the latter. Between the two ranges lies the Mexican Plateau. The s part of the plateau contains a series of extinct volcanoes, rising to Citlaltépetl, at 5,700m (18,700ft). This region includes many of Mexico's largest cities, including the capital (and world's largest city), MEXICO CITY, and GUADALAJARA. The s highlands of the Sierra Madre del Sur include the archaeological sites in OAXACA. Mexico contains two large peninsulas: the mountainous and arid BAJA CALIFORNIA in the NW, and the lowland YUCATÁN peninsula in the SE. CIUDAD JUÁREZ and NUEVO LAREDO are important cities on the border with the USA. **Climate** Mexico's climate varies greatly according to altitude. Most rain occurs between June and September, and rainfall decreases N of Mexico City. More than 70% of Mexico has a desert or semi-desert climate. Irrigation is essential for agriculture. **Vegetation** The N deserts are

MEXICO
AREA: 1,958,200sq km (756,061sq mi)
POPULATION: 107,233,000
CAPITAL (POPULATION): Mexico City (16,562,000)

abundant in plants, such as cactus, mesquite and yucca. Luxuriant rainforests exist in the s, and Mexico also has areas of tropical grassland. **History and politics** One of the earliest NATIVE AMERICAN civilizations was the OLMEC (800–400 BC). The MAYA flourished between AD 300 and 900. The TOLTEC empire was dominant between 900 and *c*.1200. But it was the AZTEC who dominated the central plateau from their capital at Tenochtitlán (modern-day Mexico City). Many splendid PYRAMIDS and temples remain from these civilizations. In 1517, Fernández de Córdoba became the first European to explore Mexico. In 1519–21, Spanish *conquistadors*, led by Hernán CORTÉS, captured the capital and the Aztec emperor MONTEZUMA. In 1535, the territory became the viceroyalty of New Spain. Christianity was introduced. Spanish colonial rule was harsh, divisive and unpopular. HIDALGO Y COSTILLO'S revolt (1810) failed to win the support of creoles. In 1821, Mexico gained independence, and General Agustín de ITÚRBIDE became emperor. In 1823, republicans seized power and, in 1824, Mexico became a republic. In 1832, SANTA ANNA became president. War with Texas escalated into the MEXICAN WAR (1846–48). Under the terms of the Treaty of GUADALUPE-HIDALGO (1848), Mexico lost 50% of its territory. In 1855, a revolution led to the overthrow of Santa Anna, and civil war broke out. Liberal forces, led by Benito JUÁREZ, triumphed in the War of Reform (1858–61), but conservatives with support from France installed MAXIMILIAN of Austria as emperor in 1864. In 1867, republican rule was restored, and Juárez became president. In 1876, an armed revolt gave Porfirio DÍAZ the presidency. Beside the period 1880–84, Díaz's dictatorship lasted until 1910. In 1911, following an armed insurrection, Francisco MADERO became president. A weak leader, Madero was toppled by General HUERTA in 1913. Huerta's dictatorship prolonged the MEXICAN REVOLUTION (1910–40) and led to US intervention. The US-backed forces of CARRANZA battled with the peasant armies of VILLA and ZAPATA. During the 1920s and 1930s, Mexico introduced land and social reforms. After World War 2, Mexico's economy developed with the introduction of liberal reforms. Relations with the USA improved greatly, although problems remain over Mexican economic migration and drug trafficking. The Institutional Revolutionary Party (PRI) has ruled Mexico continuously since its formation (1929). In 1994, the Zapatista National Liberation Army (ZNLA) staged an armed revolt in the s state of Chiapas, principally calling for land reforms and recognition of Native American rights. In 1994, Ernesto ZEDILLO of the PRI was elected president. In 1996, the government reached a peace agreement with the Zapatistas, but negotiations broke down when Zedillo failed to implement reforms. In 1999, Mexico suffered its worst floods in four decades. In 2000, the PRI was defeated for the first time in 70 years by Vicente Fox of the National Action Party. **Economy** Mexico is an upper-middle-income developing country (1995 GDP per capita, $6,400), faced with problems of unemployment, inflation, inequality and illegal emigration to the USA. Mexico's heavy borrowing on the strength of its oil reserves in the 1970s led to economic depression in the 1980s with the drop in oil prices. In June 1993, Mexico joined the Organization for Economic Cooperation and Development (OECD). In 1994, Mexico, the USA and Canada formed the NORTH AMERICAN FREE TRADE ASSOCIATION (NAFTA), the world's single largest trading bloc. In 1994, Mexico was plunged into economic crisis. Only a US$50,000 million loan from the USA prevented Mexico defaulting on its foreign debts. An austerity package of wage freezes, interest rate rises and

tax increases was introduced. Remarkably, the loan was repaid in 1997. In 1997, the economic crisis in SE Asia led to a stock market crash and a devaluation of the peso. Mexico is the world's fifth-largest producer of crude oil. Machinery and transport equipment account for 32% of exports, minerals and fuels 30%. Other manufactures include chemicals, clothing, steel and textiles. Many factories near the US border assemble goods (such as auto parts and electrical products) for US companies. Agriculture is important, contributing *c*.8% of GDP and employing 28% of the workforce. Mexico is the world's fifth-largest producer of coffee. Food crops include beans, maize, rice and wheat. Beef and dairy cattle and other livestock are raised. Fishing is also an important activity. The largest sector of the economy is services. Growing industries include forestry and tourism.

Mexico, Gulf of Gulf on SE coast of the USA and E coast of Mexico; Cuba is at the Gulf's entrance. It connects with the Atlantic Ocean through the straits of Florida, and with the Caribbean Sea through the strait of Yucatan. The Mississippi and Rio Grande rivers empty into the gulf. It is a source of shrimp and petroleum. Depth (max.): 3,878m (12,714ft). Area: 1,813,000sq km (700,000sq mi).

Mexico City (Sp. Ciudad de México) Capital of Mexico, largest city in the world, situated in a volcanic basin at an altitude of 2,380m (7,800ft), in the centre of the country. Mexico City is the nation's political, economic and cultural centre. It suffers from overcrowding and high levels of pollution and is vulnerable to earthquakes. The former AZTEC capital, known as Tenochtitlán, was destroyed by Hernán Cortés in 1521. A new city was constructed, which acted as the capital of Spain's New World colonies for the next 300 years. In 1847, during the MEXICAN WAR, the city was occupied by US troops. In 1863 French troops conquered the city and established MAXIMILIAN as emperor. It was recaptured in 1867 by Benito JUÁREZ's republican forces. Between 1914 and 1915, the city was captured and lost three times by the revolutionary forces of Emiliano ZAPATA and Francisco VILLA. The city is a major tourist centre. Pop. (1997 est.) 16,562,000.

Meyerbeer, Giacomo (1791–1864) German composer, b. Jakob Liebmann Beer. His early operas were in the Italian tradition, influenced by Gioacchino ROSSINI. His greatest acclaim, however, came in Paris, where his works laid the foundations of French grand opera. With libretti by Eugene Scribe, these operas included *Robert le Diable* (1831), *Les Huguenots* (1836) and *Le Prophète* (1849).

mezzo-soprano (middle soprano) Range of the human voice falling between SOPRANO and CONTRALTO. It was popular with 19th century opera composers, when the CASTRATO voice became less usual.

Miami City and port on Biscayne Bay in SE Florida, USA. Originally a small agricultural community, it developed quickly after 1895 when the railway was extended and the harbour dredged. Modern Miami is a popular tourist resort with luxury hotels and many sporting facilities. It is the home of many immigrants from Cuba, Haiti and other Spanish-speaking countries in the Americas. Industries: clothing, concrete, metal products, fishing, printing and publishing. Pop. (1990) 358,548.

mica Group of common rock-forming minerals characterized by a platy or flaky appearance. All contain aluminium, potassium and water; other metals, such as iron and magnesium, may be present. Micas have perfect basal cleavage. Common micas are muscovite and the biotite group. Muscovite is commonly found in coarse-grained acidic rocks, schists and gneisses, and in sedimentary rocks. The biotite micas are found in a wide range of igneous and metamorphic rocks, but more rarely in sedimentary rocks.

Michael, Saint One of the four archangels mentioned in the Bible, the others being GABRIEL, RAPHAEL and Uriel. In the Old Testament, Michael is the guardian of Israel and the highest of the archangels. In the New Testament Book of Revelation, he is said to have thrown down the Dragon (Satan). His feast day is 29 September (Michaelmas). He is given prominence also in ISLAM.

Michael (1921–) King of Romania (1927–30, 1940–47). He succeeded his grandfather as a child, surrendered the throne to his father in 1930, and regained it when his father abdicated (1940). In 1944, Michael backed the overthrow of the fascist rule of Ion ANTONESCU, whereupon Romania joined the Allies in World War 2. He was forced to abdicate when the communists gained power.

Michelangelo Buonarroti (1475–1564) Florentine sculptor, painter, architect and poet. He was one of the outstanding figures of the High RENAISSANCE and a creator of MANNERISM. He spent five years in Rome where he made his name with a statue of *Bacchus* (1497) and the *Pietà* (1499, now in St Peter's). In 1501, he returned to Florence where he carved the gigantic *David*, which symbolizes the new-found confidence of the Florentine Republic. In 1505, Pope JULIUS II called him to Rome to carry out two substantial commissions. The first, a magnificent tomb for Julius I, ended in disaster due to lack of funds from the Pope's heirs. The other, a vast painting for the Sistine Chapel ceiling (1508–12), was Michelangelo's most sublime achievement. He added *The Last Judgment* later (1536–41). Among Michelangelo's other great (unfinished) works are the Medici Chapel and the Biblioteca Laurenziana, both for the Church of San Lorenzo in Florence. For the last 30 years of his life, Michelangelo concentrated on architecture. He created the magnificent cathedral of ST PETER'S, Rome, but died before completing it.

Michelson, Albert Abraham (1852–1931) US physicist, b. Germany. In 1887, he conducted an experiment with Edward Morley to determine the velocity of the Earth through the ETHER, using an INTERFEROMETER of his own design. The negative result of the Michelson-Morley experiment prompted G.F. FITZGERALD to suggest that the length of objects change due to this sort of motion and led to the theory of RELATIVITY. In 1907 Michelson became the first US scientist to win a Nobel Prize.

Michener, James (1907–97) US writer. He won a Pulitzer Prize (1948) for his first collection of short stories, *Tales of the South Pacific* (1947). With *Hawaii* (1959), Michener established a pattern of panoramic novels, which he continued in later works such as *Chesapeake* (1978), *Texas* (1985) and *Caribbean* (1989).

Michigan State in N central USA, bordered by four of the GREAT LAKES; the capital is LANSING. The largest city is DETROIT. Michigan is made up of two peninsulas separated by the Straits of Mackinac, which connect lakes Michigan and Huron. The Upper Peninsula has swampland on the NE lakeshore and mountains in the W. The Lower Peninsula has most of Michigan's population. First settled by the French in the 17th century, the region was ceded to Britain after the SEVEN YEARS' WAR. The British finally left the area in 1796, and Michigan became a US territory in 1805, achieving full statehood in 1837. The opening of the Erie Canal (1825) aided its growth, but the real industrial boom came with the development of the motor vehicle industry in the early 20th century.

Copper and iron ore are mined and timber is a valuable resource. The Lower Peninsula is forested and mineral deposits include oil, gypsum, sandstone and limestone. In the S cereal crops are cultivated and livestock rearing is important. Industries: motor vehicles, primary and fabricated metals, chemicals, food products. Area: 150,544sq km (58,110sq mi). Pop. (2000) 9,938,444.

Michigan, Lake Third-largest of the five GREAT LAKES of North America, and the only one entirely within the USA. Discovered by the French in 1634, it is connected to Lake Huron by the Straits of Mackinac. The St Lawrence Seaway opened up the lake to international trade. Chicago is on the SW shore. Area: 57,757sq km (22,300sq mi).

microbiology Study of microorganisms, their structure, function and significance. Mainly concerned with single-cell forms such as VIRUSES, BACTERIA, PROTOZOA and FUNGI, it has immense applications in medicine and the food industry. Microbiology began in the 17th century with the invention of the microscope, which enabled scholars to view microorganisms for the first time. Pioneers include Robert HOOKE, Anton van LEEUWENHOEK and Louis PASTEUR. *See also* BIOTECHNOLOGY

microcomputer Small COMPUTER that has its CENTRAL PROCESSING UNIT (CPU) on an INTEGRATED CIRCUIT (chip) called a MICROPROCESSOR.

microeconomics Study of individual components of the economic system. It analyzes individual consumers and producers, the market conditions, and the law of SUPPLY AND DEMAND. It is one of the two major subdivisions of ECONOMICS; the other is MACROECONOMICS.

microelectronics In ELECTRONICS, systems designed and produced without wiring or other bulky components. They allow a high packing density, greatly reducing the size of component assemblies. Following World War 2, the application of such newly developed devices as the TRANSISTOR saw the beginnings of the microelectronics industry. This accelerated with the development of the PRINTED CIRCUIT. Even further reduction in size, or microminiaturization, was achieved with INTEGRATED CIRCUITS. Molecular electronics is a new development that promises to be the ultimate in size reduction.

Micronesia Group of islands located in the W Pacific Ocean, N of Polynesia. Micronesia includes BELAU, KIRIBATI, the MARIANA ISLANDS, the FEDERATED STATES OF MICRONESIA, NAURU and TUVALU.

Micronesia, Federated States of Republic in the W Pacific Ocean, consisting of all the CAROLINE ISLANDS except BELAU. The 607 islands of the republic are divided into four states: Kosrae, Pohnpei, Truk and Yap. The capital, Palikir, is on the main island of Pohnpei. The islands are widely dispersed. The economy is heavily dependent on US aid. Land use is limited to subsistence agriculture. The islands were formally annexed by Spain in 1874. In 1899, they were sold to Germany. In 1914, Japan occupied the archipelago and was given a mandate to govern by the League of Nations in 1920. In 1944, US naval forces captured the islands, and in 1947 they came under formal US administration as part of the UN Trust Territory of the Pacific Islands. In 1979, the Federated States of Micronesia came into being, with Belau remaining a US trust territory. In 1986, a compact of free association with the USA was signed. In 1990, UN trust status was annulled, and in 1991 Micronesia became a full member of the UN. Area: 705sq km (272sq mi). Pop. (2000) 110,000.

microphone Device for converting sound into varying electric currents of the same frequency. Live music performers often use a moving coil microphone, in which a coil attached to a diaphragm vibrates in a stationary magnetic field. The recording industry prefers the condenser microphone, which employs a CAPACITOR. Crystal microphones use the PIEZOELECTRIC EFFECT.

microprocessor Complex INTEGRATED CIRCUIT (chip) used to control the operation of a COMPUTER or other equipment.

microscope Optical device for producing an enlarged image of a minute object. In 1668, the first simple microscope was made by Anton van LEEUWENHOEK. The modern compound microscope has two converging lens systems, the objective and the eyepiece, both of short focal length. The **objective** produces a magnified image that is further magnified by the **eyepiece** to give the image seen by the observer. Because of the nature of the visible spectrum of LIGHT, an optical microscope can magnify objects only up to 2,000 times. For extremely small objects, an ELECTRON MICROSCOPE is used.

microsurgery Delicate surgery performed under a binocular MICROSCOPE using specialized instruments, such as microneedles as small as 2mm (0.08in) long, sutures 20 micrometres in diameter, ENDOSCOPES and LASERS. It is used in a number of specialized areas, including the repair of nerves and blood vessels; eye, ear and brain surgery; and the reattachment of severed parts.

microwave Form of ELECTROMAGNETIC RADIATION with a wavelength between 1mm (0.04in) and 300mm (12in) and a frequency range of $c.255$ to 300,000MHz. Microwaves are used for RADAR, RADIO and TELEVISION broadcasting, high-speed microwave heating (in ovens) and cellular telephones.

Midas Name of several historical Phrygian rulers and one legendary foolish king in Classical mythology. As a reward for rendering a service to a god, King Midas asked that everything he touched should become gold. Midas found he was unable to eat or drink because his food, too, was transformed. His story was told by OVID.

Mid-Atlantic Ridge Underwater topographic feature along the margin between the diverging American crustal plate on one side and the European and African plates on the other. It runs for 14,000km (8,700mi) along the middle of the Atlantic Ocean. Iceland is located on the ridge itself and was formed by the outpourings of volcanic lava.

Middle Ages Period in European history covering roughly 1,000 years between the disintegration of the Roman Empire in the DARK AGES of the 5th century and the period of the RENAISSANCE in the 15th century. The Middle Ages are sometimes divided into Early (up to the 10th century), High (10th–14th centuries) and Late Middle Ages. The Middle Ages were, above all, the age of the Christian church, whose doctrine was widely accepted in Europe, and of the social-political structure known as the FEUDAL SYSTEM. In the arts, the Middle Ages encompassed the GOTHIC period (from the 11th century), and in science and learning, the predominance of ISLAM. *See also* CRUSADES; MEDIEVAL MUSIC; SCHOLASTICISM

Middle East Geographical term loosely applied to the region that comprises the predominantly Islamic countries of the E Mediterranean, NE Africa and SW Asia. It is usually taken to include BAHRAIN, CYPRUS, EGYPT, IRAN, IRAQ, ISRAEL, JORDAN, KUWAIT, LEBANON, LIBYA, OMAN, QATAR, SAUDI ARABIA, SUDAN, SYRIA, UNITED ARAB EMIRATES and YEMEN.

Middle English Form of the English language in use from $c.1100$ until $c.1450$. This period saw the borrowing of many words from NORMAN FRENCH. Grammatical GENDER was superseded by natural gender, and the use of an Anglo-Norman writing system caused radical changes in spellings. In literature, the ARTHURIAN ROMANCES were influenced by the French TROUBADOUR tales of CHIVALRY. The "alliterative revival" in native poetry was led by LANGLAND, MALORY, GOWER and Geoffrey CHAUCER. Other forms include the MYSTERY PLAYS. *See also* ENGLISH LITERATURE

Middlesbrough Port and unitary authority on the River Tees estuary, NE England; former county town of Cleveland. During the 19th century Middlesbrough developed around its iron industry. Industries: steel, shipbuilding. Pop. (1994) 166,000

Middlesex Former county of SE England, adjoining LONDON. The area was settled by Saxon tribes in the 5th century. Throughout its history it was overshadowed by London. In 1888, it became an administrative county, losing much of its area to the county of London. In 1965, most of the county was absorbed into Greater London, the remainder going to SURREY and HERTFORDSHIRE.

Middleton, Thomas ($c.1570$–1627) English dramatist. He collaborated with Thomas DEKKER on the comedy *The Honest Whore* (1604). His own comedies include *A Chaste Maid in Cheapside* (1611) and the political satire *A Game at Chess* (1624). Middleton is chiefly remembered for his two tragi-comedies *The Changeling* (1622, co-written with William Rowley) and *Women Beware Women* ($c.1625$). Many critics

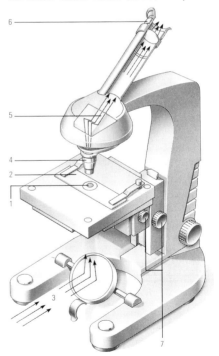

▲ **microscope** An optical microscope magnifies a sample (1) held on a slide (2). Light from below (3) illuminates the sample, which is magnified by a lens (4) that can be changed.

Complicated lenses (5) direct the image onto an eyepiece (6). The position of the sample can be altered physically by turning knobs (7) that bring the image into position and focus.

believe he wrote *The Revenger's Tragedy* (1607), traditionally credited to Cyril TOURNEUR.

Midway Islands Coral atoll in the central Pacific Ocean, *c.*2,000km (1,250mi) WNW of Honolulu, consisting of two small islands, Easter and Sand. The islands were annexed to the USA in 1867 and were made an air base in 1935. They were the scene of the Battle of Midway (1942) in World War 2. The islands are now administered by the US Department of the Interior. Area: 5sq km (2sq mi). Pop. (1995 est.) 2,000.

Midwest (Middle West) Imprecise term referring to the interior plains of the USA around the W GREAT LAKES and the upper Mississippi River valley. It usually refers to the states of INDIANA, ILLINOIS, IOWA, KANSAS, MICHIGAN, MINNESOTA, MISSOURI, NEBRASKA, OHIO and WISCONSIN. Traditionally, the Midwest has been the manufacturing heartland of the USA. The national shift to the service sector has contributed to the decline of its heavy industrial base. The Midwest is also one of the world's richest agricultural regions; the major crop is wheat.

Mies van der Rohe, Ludwig (1886–1969) US architect, b. Germany. A pioneer of MODERNISM, he began his career as an assistant to Peter BEHRENS. Mies first attracted attention in the 1920s with his unexecuted designs for glass and steel skyscrapers. His German pavilion at the 1929 International Exposition in Barcelona is regarded as one of the most pure examples of geometrical architecture. Mies was the last director (1930–33) of the BAUHAUS, moving the school to Berlin before it was closed by the Nazis. In 1938, he emigrated to the USA. Mies planned (1942–58) the new campus of the Illinois Institute of Technology, Chicago, including Alumni Memorial Hall, (1944–46). His technological aesthetic exerted a profound influence on a new generation of architects, such as Gordon BUNSHAFT, Eero SAARINEN and Philip JOHNSON. Other buildings include Lake Shore Drive, Chicago (1948–51) and the Seagram Building, New York (1958).

migraine Recurrent attacks of throbbing headache, mostly on one side only, often accompanied by nausea, vomiting and visual disturbances. It results from changes in diameter of the arteries serving the brain. More common in women, it is seen usually in young adults and often runs in families. Attacks, which may last anything from two to 72 hours, are often associated with trigger factors, such as certain foods (especially chocolate), missed meals, consumption of alcohol, fatigue, exposure to glare or use of the contraceptive pill. It can be treated, or in some cases prevented, with various drugs.

migration Any periodic movement of animals or humans, usually in groups, from one area to another, in order to find food, breeding areas or better conditions. Animal migration involves the eventual return of the migrant to its place of departure. Fish migrate between fresh and salt water or from one part of an ocean to another. Birds usually migrate along established routes. Mammals migrate usually in search of food. For thousands of years the deserts of central Asia widened inexorably and this phenomenon resulted in the human migration of pre-historic tribes to China, the Middle East and Europe. Another type of migration occurred in the 14th century when the Maoris of New Zealand left their overpopulated homes in the islands of central Polynesia.

Milan (Milano) City in NW Italy; capital of Lombardy region. It was conquered by Rome in 222 BC. It was a free commune by the 12th century and was a powerful Italian state under the Sforza family from 1447 to 1535, when it was taken by the Spanish. It was ruled by Napoleon (1796–1814) and subsequently by the Austrian Habsburgs

before becoming part of Italy in 1860. It is Italy's leading commercial, financial and industrial centre. Sights include Leonardo da Vinci's *Last Supper* (1495–98) in the Convent of Santa Maria della Grazie, a white-marble cathedral (1386–1813), and LA SCALA opera house. Industries: motor vehicles, machinery, electrical goods, textiles, clothing, publishing. Pop. (1996) 1,306,000.

mildew External filaments and fruiting structures of numerous mould-like FUNGI. Mildews are PARASITES of plants and cause substantial damage to growing crops.

Milhaud, Darius (1892–1974) French composer. In the incidental music to Claudel's translation of Aeschylus' *Orestes* (1913–22), he experimented with polytonality. He also included jazz elements in his compositions, notably *La Création du Monde* (1923). His most ambitious work was the opera *Christophe Colombe* (1930).

militia Non-standing reserve military force for use in emergencies, usually organized on a local basis. A militia typically consists of citizens who return to civilian status when the emergency is over. The name arose in Britain in the 17th century, when the obligation to provide men for service was laid upon landowners.

milk Liquid food secreted from mammary glands by the females of nearly all mammals to feed their young. The milk of domesticated cattle, sheep, goats, horses, camels and reindeer has been used as food by humans since prehistoric times, both directly and to make BUTTER, CHEESE and yogurt. Milk is a suspension of fat and protein in water, sweetened with lactose sugar.

Milky Way Faint band of light visible on clear dark nights encircling the sky along the line of the galactic equator. It is the combined light of an enormous number of stars, in places obscured by clouds of interstellar gas and dust. It is in fact the disc of our GALAXY, viewed from our vantage point within it.

Mill, James (1773–1836) Scottish philosopher, father of John Stuart MILL. He became a friend of Jeremy BENTHAM, and together they evolved the doctrine of UTILITARIANISM. Mill wrote an *Analysis of the Phenomena of the Human Mind* (1829) and, among other works, a multi-volume history of the East India Company, for which he worked.

Mill, John Stuart (1806–73) Scottish philosopher, son of James MILL. He defended EMPIRICISM and inductive LOGIC in *System of Logic* (1843). Mill is chiefly remembered for *On Liberty* (1859), a classic exposition of LIBERALISM. In *Utilitarianism* (1861), he developed Jeremy BENTHAM's theory, outlining a more humanist version of UTILITARIANISM. Mill also championed women's rights in *The Subjection of Women* (1869).

Millais, Sir John Everett (1829–96) English painter and illustrator, a founder member of the PRE-RAPHAELITE BROTHERHOOD. His pre-Raphaelite works, such as *Christ in the House of his Parents* (1850), show the Brotherhood's liking for righteous subjects. Later, Millais turned to more sentimental subjects, such as *Bubbles* (1886), used as an advertisement by Pears Soap Company.

Millay, Edna St Vincent (1892–1950) US poet. She first attracted attention for *A Few Figs from Thistles* (1920). Millay won a Pulitzer Prize for *The Harp Weaver and Other Poems* (1923). Other works include the sonnet sequence *Fatal Interview* (1931).

millenarianism Belief, widespread in Christianity until the 4th century, that Christ's second coming will bring a thousand years of peace on Earth. It has its origins in the Judaic notion of the MESSIAH and a literal translation of the Book of REVELATIONS (20). It was supplanted by St AUGUSTINE's allegorical interpretation of the kingdom of God. It was revived during the REFORMATION by sects such as the ANABAPTISTS and the MORAVIAN CHURCH. Since the 19th century, MORMONS and ADVENTISTS have professed millenarian beliefs. Some sects, such as JEHOVAH'S WITNESSES, have forecast the imminence of the second coming.

millennium Period of one thousand years. The Christian CALENDAR takes the birth of JESUS CHRIST as year 0. MILLENARIANISM holds that Christ will return to Earth to reign for 1,000 years. In the UK, celebrations for the dawning of the third millennium (1 January 2000) will be centred around the Millennium Dome, GREENWICH, s London. In computing, the so-called "**millennium bug**" is found in computer programs that are unable to compute the year 2000 as following 1999.

Miller, Arthur (1915–) US dramatist. His Pulitzer Prize-winning play *Death of a Salesman* (1949) is a masterpiece of 20th-century theatre: an egocentric salesman, Willy Loman, has unrealistic aspirations, which he struggles to articulate. *The Crucible* (1953) is both a dramatic reconstruction of the SALEM witch trials and a parable of the McCARTHY era. Miller won a second Pulitzer Prize for *A View From the Bridge* (1955). He was married (1955–61) to Marilyn MONROE, and wrote the screenplay for her film *The Misfits* (1961). *After the Fall* (1964) is a fictionalized account of their relationship. Other plays include *All My Sons* (1947) and *Playing for Time* (1981).

Miller, (Alton) Glenn (1904–44) US jazz trombonist and bandleader. During World War 2, his dance band played to servicemen all over the world. Miller composed such classic tunes as "Moonlight Serenade" and "In the Mood" (both 1939). He died as a result of "friendly fire" while flying from England to France.

Miller, Henry (1891–1980) US novelist. Miller's sexually explicit novels, such as *Tropic of Cancer* (1934) and *Tropic of Capricorn* (1939), were considered obscene, and many were banned in the USA and Britain until the 1960s. Other works include *The Rosy Crucifixion* trilogy: *Sexus*, *Plexus* and *Nexus* (1949–60).

Miller, Dr Jonathan Wolfe (1934–) English stage director. He wrote parts for, and appeared in, *Beyond the Fringe* (1961). Miller's first production for the National Theatre was *The Merchant of Venice* (1970). He has also directed definitive opera productions, notably Verdi's *Rigoletto* for English National Opera (1984). Miller was artistic director (1988–90) of the Old Vic. He writes on neuropsychology.

Millet, Jean-François (1814–75) French painter. Millet is best known for solemn, gritty scenes of rural life and labour, such as *Sower* (1850) and *The Angelus* (1859). His strengths as an artist show in his drawings, which stress the dignity of his figures without any trivializing detail.

millet CEREAL grass that produces small, edible seeds. The stalks have flower spikes, and the hulled seeds are white. In Russia, w Africa and Asia, it is a staple food. In w Europe it is used mainly for pasture or hay. Pearl millet (*Pennisetum glaucum*) grows in poor soils and is used as food in India and Africa. Height: 1m (39in). Family Poaceae/Gramineae.

Millikan, Robert Andrews (1868–1953) US physicist. His oil-drop experiment enabled him to determine the ELECTRIC CHARGE of an ELECTRON. Millikan went on to study the PHOTOELECTRIC EFFECT, verifying the equation of Albert EINSTEIN and gaining a precise value for PLANCK's constant. In 1923, he was awarded the Nobel Prize for physics.

millipede Any of numerous species of elongated, invertebrate, arthropod animals with large numbers of legs. Found throughout the world, it has a segmented body, one pair of antennae and two pairs of legs per segment, and can be orange, brown or black. All species avoid light and feed on plant tissues. Length: 2–280mm (0.2–11in). Class Diplopoda.

Milne, A.A. (Alan Alexander) (1882–1956) English writer of stories and poems for children. Milne wrote the verses in *When We Were Very Young* (1924) and *Now We Are Six* (1927), and the stories in *Winnie-the-Pooh* (1926) and *The House at Pooh Corner* (1928).

Milošević, Slobodan (1941–) Serbian statesman, president of SERBIA (1989–97), president of YUGOSLAVIA (1997–2000). In 1986, he became head of the Serbian Communist Party. As Serbian president, Milošević was confronted with the breakup of the federation of Yugoslavia. After his re-election in 1992, he gave support to the Serb populations in CROATIA and BOSNIA-HERZEGOVINA, who fought for a Greater Serbia. Milošević gradually distanced himself from the brutal activities of the Bosnian Serb leaders MLADIĆ and KARADZIĆ. In November 1995, he signed the Dayton Peace Accord with the Bosnian president IZETBEGOVIC and the Croatian president TUDJMAN to end the civil war in the former Yugoslavia. In 1996, Milošević refused to recognize opposition victories in municipal elections. In 1997, he was forced to concede some of these victories after mass demonstrations in Belgrade. In 1998, Milošević ordered Serbian forces to crush a rebellion in the province of KOSOVO, provoking NATO air attacks on Serbian military and industrial targets. In 1999, Milošević agreed to a peace plan and a United Nations' (UN) peacekeeping force was sent to Kosovo. In 2000 elections, Milošević was defeated by Vojislav KOŠTUNICA, but refused to conceded defeat until demonstrators in Belgrade had stormed the parliament building.

Milosz, Czeslaw (1911–) Polish poet and novelist, b. Lithuania. His novels, *The Valley of the Issa* (1955) and *The Usurpers* (1955), demonstrate an acute critical self-awareness. His celebrated volume of essays, *The Captive Mind* (1953), analyzes the effects of communism on writers. His poetry is collected in *Selected Poems* (1973). In 1980, he was awarded the Nobel Prize for literature.

Milstein, César (1927–) British molecular biologist and immunologist, b. Argentina. He shared the 1984 Nobel Prize for physiology or medicine for helping to develop ANTIBODIES that can be commercially produced for drugs and diagnostic tests. In 1975, he and the German immunochemist Georges Köhler developed a technique for cloning MONOCLONAL ANTIBODIES (MABs) that combat diseases by targeting their sites.

Miltiades (554–489 BC) Athenian general. He defeated the Persians in the Battle of MARATHON (490 BC). A Persian vassal who served with DARIUS I, he deserted to Athens after the Ionian revolt (499–94 BC) and was elected as a military commander. Although victorious at Marathon, his failure to take Pharos in the following season resulted in his disgrace.

Milton, John (1608–74) English poet. His first major pieces are the masque *Comus* (1634), and the pastoral elegy *Lycidas* (1637). He was committed to reform of the Church of England, and his pamphlet *Of Reformation in England* (1641) attacked episcopacy. Milton was the champion of the revolutionary forces in the English CIVIL WAR (1642–51). His *Areopagitica* (1644) is a classic argument for freedom of the press. Milton's defence of regicide in *The Tenure of Kings and Magistrates* (1649) earned him a position in Oliver CROMWELL's Commonwealth government. Blind from 1652, Milton

was forced into hiding immediately after the RESTORA-
TION (1660). *Paradise Lost*, perhaps the greatest epic
poem in English, was first published in 10 books (1667).
In 1674, he produced a revised edition in 12 books. Written in blank-verse, it relates the theological stories of
Satan's rebellion against God, and Adam and Eve in the
Garden of Eden. Its sequel, *Paradise Regained* (1671),
was published in four books, and describes Christ's
temptation. Milton's poetic drama *Samson Agonistes*
(1671) became the libretto of Handel's oratorio.

Milton Keynes Town in Buckinghamshire, s central
England. A new town, it was designed on a grid pattern
by Richard Llewelyn-Davies in 1967. Milton Keynes is
the headquarters of the Open University. The economy is
based on retail and light industries. Pop. (1994) 163,000.

Milwaukee City and port of entry on the w shore of
Lake Michigan, in SE Wisconsin, USA. It was founded
in 1836 and during the second half of the 19th century
received many German settlers. Industries: brewing,
diesel and petrol engines, construction, electrical
equipment. Pop. (1990) 628,088.

mime In drama, communication of mood, story and
idea through the use of gestures, movements and facial
expressions, with no verbal interaction. It derives from
Greek and Roman theatrical traditions. Modern mime
artists include Marcel MARCEAU.

mimicry Form of animal protection through deception.
The mimic, generally a harmless edible species, imitates
the warning shape or coloration of a "model", a poisonous or dangerous species. When coloration increases
an animal's chances of survival, it is commonly referred
to as protective coloration. **Batesian** mimicry, named
after Henry BATES, is exemplified by hoverflies, which
mimic inedible wasps. The less common **Müllerian**
mimicry, named after the German naturalist Fritz
Müller, involves two or more unpalatable species that
share a similar pattern, thus reinforcing it as a warning
to predators. A third form is **aggressive** mimicry, in
which a predatory or parasitic species resembles a harmless one, thus allowing the former to remain undetected
by its prey or host.

mimosa Genus of plants, shrubs and small trees native
to tropical North and South America. They have showy,
feather-like leaves and heads or spikes of white, pink or
yellow flowers. Family Mimosaceae. *See also* ACACIA

mina *See* MYNAH

minaret Tower of a MOSQUE from which the MUEZZIN
calls a Muslim to prayer. A mosque may have several
minarets, and they vary enormously in shape and
height. The earliest minarets were built (*c*.673) in
Egypt as low square towers; later Persian developments
included covered balconies and extensive tiling.

Minas Gerais State in SE Brazil; the capital is Belo Horizonte. It was made a province in 1822 and a state of the
republic in 1891. Located on a plateau, it has a subtropical
climate and many resorts and thermal springs. Minas
Gerais is also rich in mineral deposits, including gold,
diamonds and iron ore. Products: coffee, pasture grass,
maize, rice, cassava. Area: 586,624sq km (22,643sq mi).
Pop. (1991) 15,746,200.

mind Hypothetical faculty postulated to account for the
ability of conscious beings to think, feel, will or behave.
The mind is considered to control, or consist of, so-called
mental processes. Dualist philosophers, such as René
DESCARTES, have distinguished between mind and matter
as two totally independent entities. IDEALISM suggests that
the world is a product of the mind and dependent on experience. MATERIALISM begins with a concept of a material

world independent of experience; the mind is not separate
from the physical but derives from it. *See also* DUALISM

Mindanao Second-largest island of the PHILIPPINES, in
the S of the archipelago; DAVAO is the major port and city.
The island is forested and mountainous, rising to the
active volcano of Mount Apo, at 2,954m (9,690ft) the
highest peak in the Philippines. Islam arrived in the 14th
century, and the disparate Muslim groups united to resist
the intervention of Spain in the 16th century and the USA
in the 20th century. In the 1960s, the government encouraged Philippine colonization of the island, and the dispossessed Moros began to advocate secession from the
Philippines. In 1969, the Philippine army began a military
campaign that resulted in thousands of deaths. The
island's economy is primarily agricultural, although tin-
mining takes place around Mindanas. Area: 94,631sq km
(36,537sq mi). Pop. (1990) 14,297,000.

mine Excavation from which minerals (mainly coal and
metal ores) are extracted. Underground mines are of two
main types: shaft mines and drift mines. **Shafts** are sunk
vertically in the Earth's crust until they reach the depth of
the seams to be exploited, which are then reached by tunnels or galleries. **Drift** mines are generally shallower, the
seams being reached by a drift, or gradually sloping shaft,
which leads on to a gallery system. In **opencast** (strip)
mining, the seams are near or on the surface and are
exposed by dragline machines that dig away the topsoil.

mine Concealed explosive device detonated through
contact with individuals or vehicles. Underwater mines
are used either to protect or to blockade coastal areas.

mineral Natural, homogeneous and, with a few exceptions, solid and crystalline materials that form the Earth
and make up its ROCKS. Most are formed through inorganic processes, and more than 3,000 minerals have been
identified. They are classified on the basis of chemical
makeup, crystal structure and physical properties, such as
hardness, relative density, cleavage, colour and lustre.
Some minerals are economically important as ORES from
which metals are extracted. Some minerals, such as CAL-
CIUM and ZINC, are vital for good NUTRITION in humans
and animals. *See individual articles*

mineralogy Investigation of naturally occurring inorganic substances found on Earth and elsewhere in the
Solar System. *See* GEOCHEMISTRY; MINERALS; PETROLOGY

Minerva Roman goddess of the arts, professions and
handicrafts, whose cult is thought to have started in Etruria.
Later she was identified with the Greek goddess ATHENA.

Ming (1368–1644) Imperial Chinese dynasty. It was
founded by a Buddhist monk and peasant leader, Chu
Yüan-chang (r.1328–98), who expelled the Mongol
YÜAN dynasty and unified China by 1382. Under the
despotic rule of the early Ming emperors, China experienced a period of great artistic and intellectual distinction
and economic expansion. Decline began in the late 16th
century, and in 1644 a rebel leader took Peking (Beijing).
A Ming general summoned aid from the MANCHU, who
overthrew the dynasty and established their own.

Mingus, Charles (1922–79) US jazz bassist, composer and bandleader. His large-scale compositions and use
of over-dubbing inspired a generation of modern jazz
musicians. *The Black Saint and the Sinner Lady* (1963)
is his masterpiece.

miniature painting Term that originally meant the art
of manuscript ILLUMINATION but was later applied to very
small paintings, usually portraits. In Europe, the earliest
miniatures were produced in the late 15th century and
executed in the same materials as illuminated manuscripts. During the 18th century, miniaturists usually

painted in watercolour on ivory and sometimes worked in oils on metal. After the mid-19th century, the art of miniature painting declined in the West because of competition from PHOTOGRAPHY, but the tradition remained strong in several Islamic countries and in India.

minimal access surgery Term used to encompass operations that do not involve cutting open the body in the traditional way. Minimal access (keyhole) procedures are performed either by means of an ENDOSCOPE or by passing miniature instruments through a fine catheter into a large blood vessel. The surgical LASER is also used.

minimal art Movement in 20th-century painting and sculpture that used only the most fundamental geometric forms. It originated in the 1950s as a reaction against the chaotic emotions provoked by ABSTRACT EXPRESSIONISM.

minimalism Trend in musical composition, beginning in the 1960s, in which short melodic or rhythmic fragments are repeated in gradually changing patterns, usually in a simple harmonic context. Many minimalist composers, such as Steve REICH and Philip GLASS, were influenced by the repetitive patterns of Indian and other non-Western music.

minimum wage Lowest permissible wage, set by government. Many countries have laws decreeing that no worker may be paid less than a certain amount, which is usually calculated on a hourly rate. Such laws are designed to prevent exploitation of labour; however, they can also lead to a "pay scramble" in which some workers insist on high differentials. If the minimum is set too high, there may be a loss of jobs in some industries that cannot afford to pay the new minimum to all their employees. In the UK, national minimum wage legislation came into force in April 1999.

mining Process of obtaining metallic and non-metallic materials from the Earth's crust. Included are underground, surface and underwater methods. Mining mostly involves the physical removal of rock and earth. Any mining operation comprises four stages: prospecting, exploration, development and exploitation. In underground mining, access may be through oblique or vertical shafts or horizontal tunnels. Cross cuts are made at various levels, and the ore body is divided into blocks by vertical "rises" that connect different levels. The ore is broken up by the use of hand tools, blasting or machinery. Underwater mining uses large conveyor belts that bring to the surface many tonnes of material each minute. The parent ships sift the material and deposit unwanted material overboard. *See also* MINE

mink Small, semi-aquatic mammal of the WEASEL family, with soft, durable, water-repellent hair of high commercial value. They have slender bodies, short legs and bushy tails. Wild mink have dark brown fur with long black outer hair. Ranch mink have been bred to produce fur of various colours. They eat fish, rodents and birds. Escaped ranch mink can be a serious threat to indigenous wildlife. Length to: 73cm (29in) including the tail; weight: 1.6kg (3.5lb). Family Mustelidae.

Minneapolis City and port on the Mississippi River, next to SAINT PAUL, SE Minnesota, USA; the largest city in Minnesota. First settled in the 1840s, it developed timber and flour milling industries and is now an important processing and distribution centre for grain and cattle. Industries: farm machinery, food processing, electronic equipment, computers, printing and publishing. Pop. (1990) 368,383.

minnesinger Medieval German poet or singer of courtly love (or *minne*), similar in style to the Provençal TROUBADOURS whom they originally copied. An individual German style developed in the 14th century, and

several of the poems are considered among the best of Middle High German lyric verse.

Minnesota State in N central USA, on the Canadian border; the capital is ST PAUL. Other major cities include MINNEAPOLIS and Duluth. The terrain varies from the prairies of the S to the forests of the N. There are mountains in the E. The state is drained chiefly by the Minnesota, St Croix and Mississippi rivers. French fur traders arrived in the 17th century. The area E of the Mississippi passed to Britain after the SEVEN YEARS' WAR, then to the USA after the American Revolution. In 1803, the lands W of the Mississippi were acquired from France in the LOUISIANA PURCHASE. Minnesota was organized as a territory in 1849, acquiring statehood in 1858. Europeans settled the area during the 1880s. Wheat and maize are the major crops, and many farms raise dairy cattle. In the E there are rich deposits of iron ore in the Mesabi Range. Since the 1950s, manufacturing has replaced agriculture as the main economic activity. Industries: food processing, electronic equipment, machinery, paper products, chemicals, printing and publishing. Area: 206,207sq km (79,617sq mi). Pop. (2000) 4,919,479.

minnow Sub-family of freshwater fish found in temperate and tropical regions. It includes shiners, dace, chub, tench and bream. More specifically, the term includes small fish of the genera *Phoxinus* and *Leuciscus*. Length: 4–46cm (1.5–18in). Family Cyprinidae.

Minoan civilization (*c*.3000–*c*.1100 BC) Ancient AEGEAN CIVILIZATION that flourished on the island of CRETE, named after the legendary King MINOS. The Minoan period is divided into three parts: Early (*c*.3000–*c*.2100 BC), Middle (*c*.2100–*c*.1550 BC) and Late (*c*.1550–*c*.1100 BC). In terms of artistic achievement, and perhaps power, Minoan civilization reached its height in the Late period. The prosperity of BRONZE AGE Crete is evident from the works of art and palaces excavated at KNOSSOS, Phaistos and other sites. It was based on trade and seafaring.

Minos In Greek mythology, the son of EUROPA and ZEUS, king of Crete. He was consigned at his death to the realm of HADES to judge human souls. He angered POSEIDON who, in revenge, caused the king's wife Pasiphaë to give birth to the monstrous MINOTAUR.

Minotaur In Greek mythology, beast with the head of a bull and the body of a man, the issue of Pasiphaë, wife of MINOS, and a bull. He was confined by Minos in the LABYRINTH built by DAEDALUS. The Minotaur was killed by THESEUS.

Minsk Capital of Belarus, on the River Svisloc. Founded in *c*.1060, it was under Lithuanian and Polish rule before becoming part of Russia in 1793. During World War 2 the city's large Jewish population was exterminated by the occupying Germans. In 1991, it became the capital of the newly independent Belarus. Industries: textiles, machinery, motor vehicles, electronic goods. Pop. (1996) 1,700,000.

minstrel (jongleur) Itinerant musician and professional entertainer; more specifically, a secular musician, usually an instrumentalist. Minstrels were popular from the 12th to 17th centuries, and some were attached to courts. In the 14th and 15th centuries, their social importance was reflected in the number of minstrel guilds that were formed throughout Europe. *See also* MINNESINGER; TROUBADOUR

mint In botany, any species of aromatic herbs with a characteristic flavour, of the genus *Mentha*. It is commonly used as a flavouring in cooking, confectionery and medicines. Most species have oval leaves and spikes of purple or pink flowers. Family Lamiaceae/Labiatae. *See also* PEPPERMINT

minuet French dance fashionable at the court of Louis XIV from 1650. Graceful and precise, it is danced by couples and played in triple time. It became popular as a dance in the 18th century and was a familiar movement in the SUITES of composers such as HANDEL and MOZART.

minutemen Local MILITIA units in the AMERICAN REVO-LUTION. The first such units were formed in Massachusetts in 1774, and minutemen took part in the opening battles of LEXINGTON AND CONCORD in 1775. The name was adopted by certain extreme right-wing groups in the USA in the 1960s and was given to a class of ballistic missiles.

Miocene Geological epoch beginning *c*.25 million and ending *c*.5 million years ago. It falls in the middle of the TERTIARY period and is marked by an increase in grass-lands over the globe at the expense of forests, and the development of most of the modern mammal groups.

Mirabeau, Honoré Gabriel Riquetti, Comte de (1749–91) French revolutionary. One of the most capa-ble early leaders of the FRENCH REVOLUTION, he was instrumental in establishing the STATES GENERAL and became its leader. His goal was a parliamentary monar-chy, but his plans were frustrated by the obstinacy of both the king and the assembly.

miracle Event or occurrence that is contrary to the laws of nature and is assumed to be the result of supernatural or divine intervention. Most religions include a belief in mir-acles. The mythologies of ancient India, the Middle East, Greece and Rome abound with wonders brought about by the gods, but in Judaism, Christianity and Islam, miracles are attributed to MOSES, JESUS and MUHAMMAD.

miracle play *See* MYSTERY PLAY

mirage Type of optical illusion sometimes seen near the Earth's surface when light is refracted (bent) as it passes between cool dense air to warmer, less dense air. Mirages are most commonly seen shimmering on hot, dry roads; the shimmer is a refracted image of the sky.

Miranda, Carmen (1904–55) US film actress, dancer and singer. She was famous for her bizarre costumes, particularly her headgear, which was often fashioned from several layers of fruit. Her films include *That Night in Rio* (1941) and *Copabacana* (1947).

Mir Soviet SPACE STATION orbiting the Earth. The main part was launched in 1986. It weighed nearly 21 tonnes and had six docking ports for the attachment of scientific modules or cargo vessels. Over the years various modules have been added to enlarge the space station, which has been perma-nently manned by a succession of three-person crews. In February 2001, the ageing space station was destroyed in a controlled re-entry into the Earth's atmosphere.

Miró, Joan (1893–1983) Spanish painter and graphic artist. Early works reveal experimentation with FAU-VISM, CUBISM and DADA. His *Catalan Landscape* (1923) heralds his more mature work and a close affinity with ABSTRACT ART and PRIMITIVISM. In 1924, Miró became a member of the SURREALISM movement, producing works such as *Dog barking at the moon* (1926). His work is often playful, but the Spanish Civil War pro-voked him into creating darker, more savage images.

mirror Highly polished surface that produces an image of objects in front of it because of the laws of REFLECTION. Most mirrors are made of glass "silvered" on one side with SILVER, MERCURY or ALUMINIUM. They can be flat (plane) or curved (spherical or parabolic). **Plane** mirrors produce a virtual image that is the same size but turned sideways (left to right). **Spherical** mirrors may be con-cave (caving inwards) or convex (bulging outwards). The

image can be right-way-up or inverted, real or virtual, depending on the position of the object in relation to the focal point of the mirror; it may also be either magnified or reduced in size. A spherical mirror suffers spherical ABERRATION, which is absent in a concave parabolic mir-ror, as used in reflecting telescopes. *See also* IMAGE

miscarriage Popular term for a spontaneous ABOR-TION, the loss of a FOETUS from the UTERUS before it is sufficiently developed to survive.

Mishima, Yukio (1925–70) Japanese writer. An early novel, *Confessions of a Mask* (1949), is a semi-autobio-graphical study of homosexuality. His final work, the four-volume *The Sea of Fertility* (1965), is an epic of modern Japan. He committed ritual suicide at Tokyo's military headquarters, which he had occupied with his small, private army.

Mishnah (Heb. instruction) Collection of Jewish legal traditions and moral precepts that form the basis of the TALMUD. The Mishna was compiled (*c*.AD 200) under Rabbi Judah ha-Nasi. It is divided into six parts: laws per-taining to agriculture; laws concerning the sabbath, fasts and festivals; family laws; civil and criminal laws; laws regarding sacrifices; and laws on ceremonial regulations.

missile Unmanned and self-propelled flying weapon. BALLISTIC missiles travel in the outer atmosphere and can be powered only by rockets. CRUISE MISSILES travel in the lower atmosphere and can be powered by jet engines. GUIDED MISSILES carry self-contained guidance systems or can be controlled by radio from the ground.

Missionary Societies Organizations for the promo-tion of CHRISTIANITY among non-Christians. The first such society was established in New England in 1649. In the 18th century, both the Baptists and Methodists established societies and the 19th century saw the emergence of interdenominational and geographically specialized societies. The International Missionary Council was formed in 1921. Today, governments or agencies, such as Christian Aid, have taken over much of the Missionary Societies' work.

Mississippi State in the S central USA, on the Gulf of Mexico; the capital and largest city is JACKSON. Other major cities are Meridian, Biloxi, Vicksburg and Laurel. The land slopes W from the hills of the NE to the Delta, a fertile plain between the MISSISSIPPI and Yazoo rivers. Pine forests cover most of the S of the state as far as the coastal plain. The French claimed the region in 1682, but it passed to Britain after the SEVEN YEARS' WAR. The Territory of Mississippi was organized in 1798. In 1861, Mississippi seceded from the Union. It was a battle-ground during the American CIVIL WAR. Racial segrega-tion remained in force until the 1960s when the state became a focus of the CIVIL RIGHTS movement. Primari-ly an agricultural state, Mississippi is the leading pro-ducer of cotton in the USA; hay and soya beans are also grown. Dairy farming is of great importance. There are valuable reserves of oil and natural gas. Other indus-tries: clothing, wood products, chemicals. Area: 123,515sq km (47,689sq mi). Pop. (2000) 2,844,658.

Mississippi Principal river of the USA, second-longest national river (after the MISSOURI), *c*.3,780km (2,350mi) long. It rises in NW Minnesota and flows SE (forming many state boundaries along its course), emptying into the Gulf of Mexico via its huge marshland delta in SE Louisiana. Its chief tributaries include the Missouri, OHIO, ARKANSAS and TENNESSEE rivers. A major transport route, it is con-nected to the GREAT LAKES and the ST LAWRENCE SEAWAY (N) and the Intracoastal Waterway (E). Major ports on the river include MINNEAPOLIS, ST LOUIS, MEMPHIS and NEW

ORLEANS. In 1541, Hernando DE SOTO became the first European to discover the river. In 1682, La Salle sailed down the Mississippi to the Gulf of Mexico and gained control of the region. In 1803, it was acquired by the USA as part of the LOUISIANA PURCHASE. Since the 1950s, improvements have been made to the river's channels, enabling bulkier freight to be transported.

Mississippian Period In the USA, name given to the earlier part of the CARBONIFEROUS period.

Missouri State in central USA, W of the Mississippi River; the capital is JEFFERSON CITY. The largest cities are ST LOUIS, KANSAS CITY and SPRINGFIELD. Geographically it is divided into two parts. To the N of the MISSOURI River is prairie country, where farmers grow maize and raise livestock; S of the river are the foothills and plateaus of the Ozark Mountains. The French were the first to settle the area in the mid-18th century. In 1803, the USA acquired the region as part of the LOUISIANA PURCHASE. In 1812, the Missouri Territory was organized and became a main corridor of westward migration. In 1821, Missouri was admitted to the Union without restrictions on slavery, but when the CIVIL WAR began, sympathies were bitterly divided and there was much violence. The state remained in the Union. In the SW is a small wheat-growing area, and in the SE are the cotton fields of the Mississippi floodplain. The chief mineral resources are coal, lead, zinc and iron ore. Missouri's economy is based on manufacturing. Industries: transport equipment, food processing, chemicals, printing and publishing, fabricated metals, electrical machinery. Area: 178,446sq km (68,898sq mi). Pop. (2000) 5,595,211.

Missouri ("Big Muddy") Longest river of the USA; the major tributary of the MISSISSIPPI. It rises at the confluence of the Jefferson, Madison and Gallatin rivers in the Rocky Mountains, Montana. It then flows E through Great Falls cataracts and Fort Peck reservoir. In North Dakota it turns SE across the Great Plains, passing through OMAHA and KANSAS CITY. It joins the Mississippi River 27km (17mi) N of ST LOUIS. Sioux City, Iowa, is the head of navigation. Seasonal fluctuation in flow is a major problem, and the Missouri has seven major dams along its route. Its major tributaries are the Yellowstone and Platte rivers. The river was used as a trade route by the Native Americans for centuries before its discovery (1683) by the explorers MARQUETTE and JOLLIET. Mapped by the LEWIS and CLARK EXPEDITION (1804–06), the river was used by traders, gold seekers and pioneers as a route to the NW. Length: c.4,120km (2,560mi).

Missouri Compromise (1820–21) Effort to end the dispute between slave and free states in the USA. It permitted MISSOURI to join the union as a slave state at the same time as MAINE was admitted as a free state, preserving an equal balance between slave and free.

mistletoe Any of numerous species of evergreen plants that are semi-parasitic on tree branches. It has small, spatula-shaped, yellowish-green leaves and generally forms a large dense ball of foliage. The mistletoe taps into the branch of its host to sap its food supply, avoiding the necessity of growing roots itself. It also carries out photosynthesis, so is not entirely parasitic. Families: Loranthaceae/Viscaceae.

Mistral, Frédéric (1830–1914) French poet. In 1854, he founded the *Félibrige*, a movement to revive Provençal language and literature. Mistral's masterpiece is the epic verse *Mirèrio* (1859). In 1905, he was awarded the Nobel Prize for literature.

mistral Wind prevalent in the NW Mediterranean during the winter. It sweeps from the MASSIF CENTRAL,

down the RHÔNE valley, reaching the Rhône delta as a strong, dry wind.

Mitchell, George John (1933–) US politician and diplomat. He was majority leader of the Senate (1988–94). In 1994, Mitchell was appointed US special adviser for economic initiatives in Northern Ireland and chaired the groundbreaking Anglo-Irish committee on all-party talks and decommissioning of arms.

Mitchell, Joni (1943–) Canadian singer and songwriter, b. Roberta Joan Anderson. Her debut album was *Joni Mitchell* (1968). Mitchell fused folk melodies with confessional lyrics on albums such as *Ladies of the Canyon* (1970), *Court and Spark* (1974) and *Blue* (1971). She turned to more jazz-influenced themes on *Hejira* (1976) and *Mingus* (1979).

Mitchell, Margaret (1900–49) US novelist. Mitchell won a Pulitzer Prize for her only novel, the Civil War epic *Gone With the Wind* (1936).

Mitchell, R.J. (Reginald Joseph) (1895–1937) English aeronautical engineer. Mitchell is chiefly remembered for his design of the Spitfire fighter aircraft. He did not live to see its triumph in the Battle of BRITAIN (1940).

Mitchum, Robert (1917–97) US film actor. He won an Academy Award nomination for Best Supporting Actor in *The Story of G.I. Joe* (1945). His range was demonstrated by his relaxed insouciance in Nicholas Ray's *The Lusty Men* (1952) and his religious fanaticism in Charles Laughton's *The Night of the Hunter* (1955). Mitchum played the detective Philip Marlowe in *Farewell My Lovely* (1975) and *The Big Sleep* (1978). He appeared in two versions of *Cape Fear* (1962, 1991). Other films include *Ryan's Daughter* (1970).

mite Minute ARACHNID found worldwide, many as parasites on plants and animals. The adult has four pairs of legs with claws at the tip, and a fused head and abdomen. Length: 0.5–3mm (0.02–0.1in). Class Arachnida; order Acarina. *See also* CHIGGER; TICK

Mitford Name of six British sisters, daughters of Lord and Lady Redesdale. The most famous, **Nancy** Freeman Mitford (1904–73), was a novelist and biographer. Her first successful novel was *The Pursuit of Love* (1945), which was followed by *Love in a Cold Climate* (1949) and *The Blessing* (1951). Her sister, **Jessica** Mitford (1917–96), also wrote, protesting about snobbery, as in *The American Way of Death* (1963) and *Kind and Usual Punishment* (1973). The other two notable sisters, **Unity** Valkyrie (1914–48) and **Diana** (1910–96), turned to fascism, the former becoming a follower of Adolf HITLER in Germany and the latter marrying Sir Oswald MOSLEY.

Mithridates VI (132–63 BC) King of Pontus (120–63 BC). He attempted to extend his rule southwards but was repeatedly defeated by the Romans. He was overwhelmed by the forces of SULLA in the war of 88–85 BC and lost his kingdom in a second campaign in 83–82. He reconquered it in 74 but was defeated by POMPEY in 66 and fled to the Bosporus. He was planning an invasion of Italy when his troops mutinied, and he committed suicide.

mitochondrion Structure (organelle) inside a CELL containing ENZYMES necessary for energy production. Mitochondria are found in the CYTOPLASM of most types of cell (but not in bacteria). *See also* RESPIRATION

mitosis Nuclear division of a CELL resulting in two genetically identical "daughter" cells with the same number of chromosomes as the parent cell. Mitosis is the normal process of TISSUE growth and is also involved in ASEXUAL REPRODUCTION. *See also* MEIOSIS

Mitra (Mithra or Mithras) God who in different forms was worshipped in India, Persia and then the Roman

Empire, and whose cult was the basis of Mithraism. In Vedic mythology, Mitra was the spirit of the day, of the rain and of the sun, linked closely with VARUNA. The Persian Mitra was a popular deity of the ACHAEMENID empire, revered as the god of light and power.

Mitterrand, François Maurice Marie (1916–96) French statesman, president (1981–96). He was active in the French Resistance during World War 2, and served in the government of the Fourth Republic. In 1965, he united the parties of the left and narrowly lost the presidential election in 1974. In 1981 elections, Mitterrand defeated the incumbent GISCARD D'ESTAING. He was re-elected in 1988. Mitterrand introduced reforms, including the abolition of capital punishment, and favoured state intervention in managing the economy. In the 1980s, he gradually changed course. Nationalization ceased, and some nationalized industries returned to private ownership. He was forced further right after 1986, when he had to cooperate with Gaullist (conservative) prime minister Jacques CHIRAC. Mitterrand was a supporter of the EUROPEAN UNION (EU) and of close Franco-German relations. He was succeeded by Jacques Chirac.

mixture In chemistry, two or more substances that retain their specific identities when mixed (such as air containing oxygen, nitrogen and other gases). The identities remain separate no matter in what proportion or how closely the components are mixed. *See also* COMPOUND; SOLUTION

Mizoguchi, Kenji (1898–1956) Japanese film director. His films are often period pieces, focusing on issues of power, morality and women's rights in feudal and proto-modern Japanese society. His masterpieces are *The Life of Oharu* (1952), *Ugetsu Monogatari* (1953) and *Sansho Dayu* (1954).

Mladić, Ratko (1943–) Bosnian Serb general. In 1992, he came to international attention after civil war broke out in BOSNIA-HERZEGOVINA. As the aggressive and ruthless commander of the Bosnian Serb army, Mladić earned the sobriquet "Butcher of the Balkans". In 1996, he was formally indicted as a war criminal by the UN.

mobile Form of SCULPTURE developed by Alexander CALDER in the early 1930s and named by Marcel DUCHAMP. A mobile consists of a series of shapes (representational or abstract) cut from metal, wood, or other materials and connected by wires so that the both parts and the whole revolve freely when suspended in space. This form breaks with the traditional idea of sculpture as a static object.

Mobile City and seaport at the mouth of Mobile River, SW Alabama, USA. Settled in 1711 by the French, it was ceded to Britain in 1763 and seized by the USA in 1813. During the Civil War, it was the scene of a battle between Federal and Confederate naval forces. Industries: textiles, paper, timber, aluminium, chemicals, oil refining, shipbuilding. Pop. (1990) 196,278.

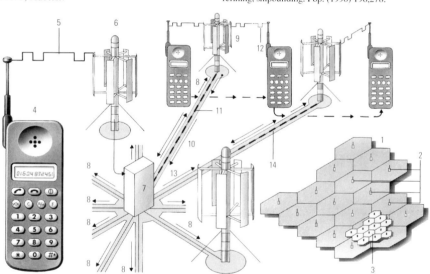

▲ **mobile telephone**
Mobile telephone networks use a system of cells (1). By having a transmitter (2) in each cell, the same frequencies can be used in each cell, allowing an enormous capacity for calls. Where there are many users, such as in the heart of a city (3), the cells are much smaller – further multiplying the number of frequencies available. A digital cellular telephone (4) sends digital information (5) to a transmitter tower (6). Digital cellular phones are better than analogue versions because they reduce background noise and interference and are more difficult to bug. The transmitter passes the message to the systems' central exchange (7). If the call is for another mobile phone, the exchange sends a message (8) to the other transmitters, which in turn send out a message to locate the receiving phone. The transmitter locating the required phone (9) sends a confirmation message to the exchange (10), which then connects the conversation (11 - dotted line). When a mobile phone moves out of range of a transmitter (12), a complicated procedure ensures the conversation can continue seamlessly. When the mobile phone's signal to the transmitter becomes weaker the exchange sends a message (13) to the transmitters in the surrounding cells to see which is receiving the strongest signal. It then transfers the conversation to that transmitter (14 - dotted line).

mobile telephone Portable radio device that connects users to the public TELEPHONE system. They operate within a network of radio cells. The first generation of telephones operated with analog signals, the second generation with DIGITAL SIGNALS. True mobile telephones (that operate from anywhere on the planet's surface by communicating directly with SATELLITES) became available in the 1990s. More recent developments to the mobile telephone involve the use of BLUETOOTH technology.

Möbius strip Shape or figure that can be modelled by giving a strip of paper a half-twist, then joining the ends together. It is of great interest in TOPOLOGY, being a one-sided surface (a line can be drawn along the strip of paper that will cover both sides, returning to the starting-point to meet itself). It was invented by August Ferdinand Möbius (1790–1868).

Mobutu Sese Seko (1930–97) Zaïrean statesman, president (1970–97), b. Joseph-Désiré Mobutu. He was defence minister under Patrice LUMUMBA. In 1960, he deposed Lumumba. In 1965, Mobutu seized power in a military coup against Joseph Kasavubu. His calls for Africanization and industrial nationalization were largely publicity stunts. The stark reality of his autocratic rule was a state founded on corruption. Mobutu amassed a huge personal fortune, while Zaïreans became increasingly impoverished. With the support of France and the CIA and the criminal activities of his security forces, Mobutu maintained his dictatorship for more than 30 years. In May 1997, he was deposed in a Tutsi-dominated revolt, led by Laurent Kabila. He died in exile.

mockingbird Any of a group of New World birds, known for imitating other birds. The common mockingbird (*Mimus polyglottos*) of the USA is typical; it is *c.*27cm (11in) long, ashy above with brownish wings and tail marked with white. Family Mimidae.

mock orange (Philadelphus or sweet syringa) Ornamental deciduous shrub native to the Western Hemisphere and Asia. It has solitary, white or yellowish, fragrant flowers. Family Hydrangeaceae; genus *Philadelphus*.

mode Classified scheme developed during the 4th to 16th centuries AD to systematize music. From the SCALE worked out scientifically by PYTHAGORAS, St Ambrose in the 4th century is thought to have devised four "authentic" modes, the Dorian, Phrygian, Lydian and Mixolydian. All the modes comprised eight notes within the compass of an octave. Pope Gregory (6th century) added four "plagal" modes, which were essentially new forms of the Ambrosian modes (Hypodorian, Hypophrygian etc.). Glareanus (16th century) added the Aeolian and Ionian modes, the basis of the minor and major scales respectively.

mode In statistics, a measure of central tendency. It is computed by determining the item that occurs most frequently in a data set. It is a quick measure of central tendency, but is not as commonly used as the MEDIAN or MEAN.

Model Parliament (November 1295) English parliament summoned by EDWARD I. For the first time, knights of the shire and burgesses (representatives of the House of COMMONS) dealt with the affairs of the nation along with the king and barons. This enlargement of the Commons' function was held to be the model for the future. They had previously merely agreed to what the king and the magnates had already decided.

modem (**mo**dulator-**dem**odulator) Electronic device for sending and receiving COMPUTER signals through a TELEPHONE system. The electrical pulses produced by a computer are fed into a modem that uses the pulses to modulate a continuous tone (carrier) by a process called

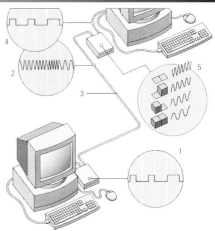

▲ **modem** A modem allows computers to communicate over telephone systems. It converts the digital signals (1) used by computers into an analogue signal (2) that travels over phone lines (3). The analogue signal is converted back into a digital signal (4) using binary code (5) which is read by the receiving computer.

FREQUENCY MODULATION (FM). At the other end, another modem extracts the pulses (demodulation), so that they can be fed into a receiving computer. The rate at which the data is transmitted is measured in BITS per second (baud). *See also* COMPUTER NETWORK; INTERNET

modern dance Dance style that began to develop during the late 19th century as a protest against classical BALLET. It is often said to have been pioneered by Isadora DUNCAN. In Europe and the USA, such innovators as Rudolph von LABAN, Ruth St Denis and Ted Shawn attempted to make dance a viable contemporary art form.

modernism In the Roman Catholic Church, movement of the late 19th and early 20th centuries that sought to adapt the Church's beliefs to developments in modern science, philosophy and history. The Modernists favoured the application of the critical method to the Bible and objected to the increasing centralization of Church authority. The movement was initially tolerated by Pope LEO XIII but condemned in 1907 by Pope PIUS X who later required all suspect clerics to take an anti-Modernist oath.

modernism Twentieth-century movement in art, architecture, design and literature that, in general, concentrates on space and form, rather than content or ornamentation. In **architecture** and design, early influences were BAUHAUS (1919–33) and individuals such as Walter GROPIUS and MIES VAN DER ROHE. Modernism developed the use of new building materials, such as glass, steel and concrete. While difficult to define and date precisely, the echoes of **literary** modernism can still be heard in late-20th-century fiction. The most recognizably distinct form is the STREAM OF CONSCIOUSNESS narrative, as evidenced in the work of Virginia WOOLF and James JOYCE's seminal novel, *Ulysses* (1922). The outstanding example of modernist poetry is the fragmentary "The Wasteland" (1922) by T.S. ELIOT. Literary modernism exhibits an increasing concern with psychological states and the subconscious. **Artists** such as PICASSO and Marcel DUCHAMP adopted new techniques of representation and worked in previously unexploited media. The movements of DADA and SURREALISM were vital to this new experimentation. In **music**, composers such as STRAVINSKY and SCHOENBERG challenged previously held notions of tonality. *See also* ABSTRACT ART; ABSTRACT EXPRESSIONISM; BLAUE REITER, DER; BRÜCKE, DIE; CONSTRUCTIVISM; CUBISM; DECONSTRUCTION; FAUVISM; FUTURISM; INTERNATIONAL STYLE; POSTMODERNISM; SUPREMATISM; VORTICISM

Modigliani, Amedeo (1884–1920) Italian painter, sculptor and draughtsman. Many of his sculptures portray elongated heads, inspired by MANNERISM and AFRICAN ART. During World War 1, Modgliani returned to painting, focusing mainly on erotic female nudes and portraits, such as *Girl with Pigtails* (1901).

modulation In physics, process of varying the characteristics of one WAVE system in accordance with those of another. It is basic to RADIO broadcasting. In AMPLITUDE MODULATION (AM), the amplitude of a high-frequency radio carrier wave is varied in accordance with the FREQUENCY of a current generated by a sound wave. For static-free, short-range broadcasting FREQUENCY MODULATION (FM) is used, in which the frequency of the carrier wave is modulated.

Mogadishu Capital and chief port of Somalia, on the Indian Ocean. Mogadishu was founded by Arabs in the 10th century. In the 16th century it was captured by the Portuguese and became a cornerstone of their trade with Africa. In 1871 control passed to the sultan of Zanzibar, who first leased (1892) and then sold (1905) the port to the Italians. Mogadishu was made the capital of Italian Somaliland. During World War 2 the city was occupied by the British from 1941. In 1960, Mogadishu became the capital of independent Somalia. During the 1980s and early 1990s, the city was devastated by civil war, its population swollen by refugees escaping famine and drought in the outlying regions. In 1992, UN troops were flown into Mogadishu to control aid distribution but withdrew in 1995 after little success. Pop. (1990 est.) 1,200,000.

Mogul Empire (1526–1857) Muslim empire in India. It was founded by BABUR, who conquered Delhi and Agra (1526). The Mogul Empire reached its height (1542–1605) under AKBAR I (THE GREAT), Babur's grandson, when it extended from Afghanistan to the Bay of Bengal and as far south as the Deccan. Religious tolerance encouraged by Akbar was reduced under his successors, JAHANGIR (r.1605–27), SHAH JAHAN (1627–58) and AURANGZEB (1658–1707). Mogul art and architecture reached a peak under Shah Jahan, builder of the TAJ MAHAL. By the death of Aurangzeb, the power of the Mogul dynasty was being supplanted by the Hindu Marathas. In 1803, the British EAST INDIA COMPANY gained control of Delhi. In 1858, the last Mogul emperor was deposed by the British after the INDIAN MUTINY. *See also* INDIAN ART AND ARCHITECTURE

Mohacs, Battle of (1526) Victory of the Ottoman Turks under SULEIMAN I (the Magnificent) over Louis II of Hungary. Louis was killed in the battle, which marked the beginning of Ottoman domination in Hungary. In a later Battle of Mohacs (1687), the result was reversed and the Turks withdrew.

Mohammed Alternative spelling of MUHAMMAD

Mohawk Iroquoian-speaking Native North American tribe of the IROQUOIS CONFEDERACY, formerly inhabiting central New York. Today, there are *c.*2,000 Mohawks. Most on two reservations in Ontario, Canada.

Mohican (Mahican) Algonquian-speaking tribe of Native North Americans, formerly inhabiting the upper Hudson valley, New York, and the area E of the Housatonic River in Connecticut. They once numbered *c.*3,000. Today, the surviving 525 Mohicans occupy the Stockbridge-Munsee Reservation in Wisconsin.

Moho (Mohorovičić discontinuity) Boundary between the Earth's CRUST and MANTLE. It is identified by a sharp increase in the velocity of seismic waves passing through the Earth, and is named after the Croatian geophysicist Andrija Mohorovičić, who first recognized it in 1909. The velocity increase is explained by a change to more dense rocks in the mantle. The depth of the Moho varies from *c.*5km (3mi) to 60km (37mi) below the Earth's surface.

Moholy-Nagy, László (1895–1946) Hungarian designer, painter and sculptor. He was a founder of CONSTRUCTIVISM. Moholy-Nagy taught with Walter GROPIUS at the BAUHAUS (1923–28) before working in Berlin as a stage designer and film-maker. He then moved to Paris, Amsterdam and London. In 1937, he emigrated to the USA and became director of the New Bauhaus.

Moi, Daniel (Torotich) Arap (1924–) Kenyan statesman, president (1978–). He was the British-appointed representative to the Kenya Legislative Council from 1958 until independence (1964). Moi succeeded Jomo KENYATTA as president. He continued his predecessor's liberal economic policies, but came under increasing international criticism for his repressive rule. He was re-elected in 1992 and 1997.

Mojave Desert Arid region with low, barren mountains in S California, USA, surrounded by mountain ranges on the N and W, and the Colorado Desert on the SE. It was formed by volcanic eruptions and deposits from the Colorado River. Area: *c.*38,850sq km (15,000sq mi).

molar One of the large back teeth of mammals, adapted for grinding and chewing food. In most herbivores,

A	O_2	H_2O	C_6H_6
B			
C			
D	$O=O$		

▲ **molecule** Molecules are groups of bonded atoms. They can be groups of the same atoms, as in oxygen (O_2), or combinations of different elements, such as water (H_2O) and benzene (C_6H_6). Molecules can be illustrated in four ways. Line one (A), the chemical formula, lists the type and number of atoms in a molecule but does not show their structure. Line two (B) is the closest representation of the actual shape of the molecule but does not detail the bonds between the atoms. Line three (C) is less realistic but does show the bonding. Line four (D) combines the chemical formula, using the abbreviations of the periodic table, and symbolic representation of the bonding structure.

the cusps (points or ridges on the top surface) are fused to form ridges for grinding plants. In adult humans there are 12 permanent molars, three on each side of each jaw.

Moldavia Historic Balkan region, between the CARPATHIAN MOUNTAINS in Romania and the River DNIEPER in MOLDOVA. Major cities in the Romanian portion include Galaţi and Suceava. Moldavia is primarily an agricultural region. Under Roman rule it formed the major part of the province of DACIA, and today's population is Romanian-speaking. In the 14th century, it became an independent principality ruled by the Vlachs; its lands included Bessarabia and Bukovina. In 1504, Moldavia was conquered by the Turks and remained part of the Ottoman Empire until the 19th century. In 1775, Bukovina was lost to the Austrians, and in 1815 Bessarabia was taken by Russia. After the Russo–Turkish War (1828–29) Russia became the dominant power. In 1856, the twin principalities of Moldavia and WALLACHIA were given considerable autonomy. Three years later they were united under one crown to form ROMANIA, but Russia reoccupied S Bessarabia in 1878. In 1920, Bessarabia and Bukovina were incorporated into the Romanian state. In 1924, the Soviet republic of Moldavia was formed, which in 1947 was enlarged to include Bessarabia and N Bukovina. In 1989, the Moldovans asserted their independence by making Romanian the official language, and in 1991, following the dissolution of the Soviet Union, Moldavia became the independent republic of MOLDOVA.

Moldova Republic in E Europe; the capital is CHISINAU. Moldova is a mostly hilly country. A large plain covers the S. The main river is the Dniester, which flows through E Moldova. The climate is moderately continental, with warm summers and fairly cold winters. Most rainfall occurs during the warmer months. Forests of hornbeam and oak grow in N and central Moldova. In the drier S, most of the region is now used for farming, with rich pasture along the rivers. **History and politics** (*for history pre-1991, see* MOLDAVIA) Following independence in 1991, the majority Moldovan population wished to rejoin Romania, but this alienated the Ukrainian and Russian populations E of the Dniester, who declared their independence from Moldova as the Transdniester republic. War raged between the two, with Transdniester supported by the Russian 14th Army. In August 1992, a cease-fire was declared. In 1994, multiparty elections were won by the former communists of the Agrarian Democratic Party. A referendum rejected reunification with Romania. Parliament voted to join the COMMONWEALTH OF INDEPENDENT STATES (CIS). A new constitution (1994) established a presidential parliamentary republic. In 1995, Transdniester voted in favour of independence in a referendum. In 1996 Russian troops began to withdraw. In 1996, Petru Lucinschi was elected president. **Economy** Moldova is a lower-middle-income developing economy (1992 GDP per capita, US$3,670). Agriculture is important and major products include fruits and grapes for wine-making. Farmers also raise livestock, including dairy cattle and pigs. Moldova has no major natural resources and has to import materials and fuels for its industries. Major manufactures include

agricultural machinery and consumer goods. Exports include food, wine, tobacco, textiles and footwear.

mole (symbol mol) SI unit of an amount of substance. This is the amount of substance that contains as many elementary units, such as atoms and molecules, as there are atoms in 0.012kg of carbon-12. A mass of one mole of a compound is its relative molecular mass (molecular weight) in grams.

mole Any of several species of small, burrowing, mainly insectivorous mammals that live in various habitats worldwide. The European mole, *Talpa europaea*, has short brown or black fur, a short tail and wide, clawed forefeet for digging tunnels. Its eyes are sensitive only to bright light. to 18cm (7in). Family Talpidae.

molecular biology Biological study of the make-up and function of molecules found in living organisms. Major areas of study include the chemical and physical properties of proteins and of nucleic acids such as DNA. *See also* BIOCHEMISTRY

molecular weight *See* RELATIVE MOLECULAR MASS

molecule Smallest particle of a substance (such as a compound) that exhibits the properties of that substance. Molecules consist of two or more ATOMS held together by CHEMICAL BONDS. For example, water molecules consist of two atoms of hydrogen bonded to one atom of oxygen (H_2O). A molecule (unlike an ION) has no electrical charge. *See also* MACROMOLECULE

Molière (1622–73) French dramatist, b. Jean-Baptiste Poquelin. An accurate observer of contemporary modern manners, he is regarded as the founder of modern French comedy. Molière's best-known comedies include *Tartuffe* (1661), *The Misanthrope* (1667), *The Miser* (1668) and *Le Bourgeois Gentilhomme* (1670). His work found favour with Louis XIV, but was unpopular with church leaders. His last play was *The Imaginary Invalid* 1673), at a performance of which he collapsed and died.

mollusc Any of more than 80,000 species of invertebrate animals in the phylum Mollusca. They include SNAILS, CLAMS and SQUIDS, and a host of less well-known forms. Originally marine, members of the group are now found in the oceans, in freshwater and on land. There are six classes: the GASTROPODS, CHITONS, univalves (SLUGS and snails), BIVALVES, tusk shells and CEPHALOPODA. The mollusc body is divided into three: the head, the foot and the visceral mass. Associated with the body is a fold of skin (the mantle) that secretes the limy shell typical of most molluscs. The head is well developed only in snails and in the cephalopods. The visceral mass contains the internal organs. The sexes are usually separate but there are many hermaphroditic species.

Molotov, Vyacheslav Mikhailovich (1890–1986) Soviet statesman, premier (1930–41) and foreign minister (1939–49, 1953–56). A loyal ally of STALIN, he became a full member of the Politburo in 1926. As foreign minister, one of Molotov's first acts was to sign the Nazi-Soviet Pact (1939) with von RIBBENTROP. His enthusiastic use of the veto in the UN Security Council contributed to the COLD WAR. He lost favour under Nikita KHRUSHCHEV and was demoted and expelled from the Communist Party in 1962. Molotov was readmitted in 1984.

Moluccas (Maluku) Island group and province in E Indonesia, between Sulawesi (W) and New Guinea (E); the capital is Ambon. The fabled Spice Islands were originally explored by Magellan in the early 16th century and later settled by the Portuguese. In the 17th century, the Dutch took the islands and monopolized the spice trade. After Indonesian independence, the S Moluccas became the focus of a movement for secession. The group

MOLDOVA
AREA: 33,700sq km (13.010sq mi)
POPULATION: 4,707,000
CAPITAL (POPULATION): Chisinau (700,000)

includes the larger islands of Halmahera, Ceram and Buru, and the island groups of Sula, Batjan, Obi, Kai, Aru, Tanimbar, Banda, Babar and Leti. Products: spices, copra, timber, sago. Area: 74,505sq km (28,759sq mi). Pop. (1990) 1,857,790.

molybdenite (molybdenum sulphide, MoS_2) Sulphide mineral, found in PEGMATITES, IGNEOUS and METAMORPHIC rocks. It is a major ore of MOLYBDENUM. It has hexagonal system tabular prisms, flakes and fine granules and is lead-grey in colour with a metallic lustre. Hardness 1–1.5; r.d. 4.7.

molybdenum (symbol Mo) Silvery-white metallic element; one of the TRANSITION ELEMENTS. It was first isolated in 1782. Its chief ore is MOLYBDENITE. Hard but malleable and ductile, it is used in alloy steels, X-ray tubes and missile parts; molybdenum compounds are used as catalysts and lubricants. It is one of the essential TRACE ELEMENTS for plant growth. Properties: at.no. 42; r.a.m. 95.94; r.d. 10.22; m.p. 2,610°C (4,730°F); b.p. 5,560°C (10,040°F); most stable isotope Mo^{98} (23.78%).

Mombasa City and seaport on the Indian Ocean, SW Kenya, partly on Mombasa Island and partly on the mainland (to which it is connected by causeway). From the 11th to 16th centuries, Mombasa was a centre of the Arab slave and ivory trades. From 1529 to 1648, it was held by the Portuguese. Taken by Zanzibar in the mid-19th century, the city passed to Britain in 1887, when it was made capital of the British East Africa Protectorate. Kenya's chief port, Mombasa exports coffee, fruit and grain. Industries: tourism, food processing, glass, oil refining, aluminium products. Pop. (1991) 600,000.

moment of a force *See* TORQUE

moment of inertia For a rotating object, the sum of the products formed by multiplying the point masses of the rotating object by the squares of their distances from the axis of the rotation.

momentum Product of the mass and linear velocity of an object. One of the fundamental laws of physics is the principle that the total momentum of any system of objects is conserved at all times, even during and after collisions.

Monaco Principality in S Europe, on the Mediterranean coast, forming an enclave in French territory near the border with Italy; the capital is Monaco-Ville. Ruled by the Grimaldi family from the end of the 13th century, it came under French protection in 1860. The chief source of income is tourism, attracted by the casinos of MONTE CARLO. There is some light industry, including printing, textiles and postage stamps. Area: 1.9sq km (0.7sq mi). Pop. (2000) 30,000.

Monaghan County in Ulster province, NE Republic of Ireland, on the boundary with Northern Ireland; the county town is Monaghan. The S and E are hilly, but the rest of the county is a fertile plain. The Blackwater and the Finn are the chief rivers. It is primarily an agricultural county, and the main crops are potatoes, oats and flax. Beef and dairy cattle are raised. Industries: linen, footwear, furniture. Area: 1,290sq km (498sq mi). Pop. (1991) 51,293.

monarchy Form of government in which one individual, whose power is usually hereditary, represents the state. There are few present-day monarchs holding absolute power. Most of those states that retain their royal families are governed by constitutional monarchies, with the sovereign performing only ceremonial functions and benefiting from few royal prerogatives.

monasticism Ascetic mode of life followed by men and women who have taken religious vows and belong to a recognized Roman Catholic or Orthodox religious order. Christian monasticism is said to have its origins

in the late-3rd-century asceticism of the desert hermits of Egypt, St ANTHONY and St Pachomius. In time, this solitary life was replaced by a communal approach, in which community members followed a strict rule. The earliest such rule in Europe was that laid down by St BENEDICT OF NURSIA in the 6th century. Monasticism still embraces community life of enclosed Christian orders, such as the CISTERCIANS and the reformed CARMELITES. There are, however, many more orders that combine asceticism with social welfare work and spiritual guidance to society at large. Spiritual leadership for a society provided through monasticism is also found in HINDUISM, BUDDHISM, JAINISM and TAOISM.

Monck, George, 1st Duke of Albemarle (1608–70) English general and diplomat. In the English CIVIL WARS, Monck fought for CHARLES I (1643–44). After his capture and imprisonment (1644–46), Monck changed sides and helped Oliver CROMWELL to quell an Irish rebellion. He was rewarded with command of the forces in Scotland (1651). Monck was a general in the DUTCH WARS. After the collapse of the PROTECTORATE, he supported the return of the RUMP PARLIAMENT. Monck led the campaign for the RESTORATION of CHARLES II.

Mond, Ludwig (1839–1909) British chemist and industrialist, b. Germany. He experimented with alkalis and developed a producer gas (a mixture of carbon monoxide and nitrogen). Mond also discovered nickel carbonyl, a gas formed from carbon monoxide and metallic nickel. Using nickel carbonyl, he developed a useful industrial method (the **Mond process**) for extracting pure nickel from its ore.

Mondrian, Piet (1872–1944) Dutch painter, co-founder (with Theo van Doesburg) of De STIJL and a pioneer of ABSTRACT ART, b. Pieter Mondriaan. Influenced by CUBISM, Mondrian developed a distinctive, geometric style, which he dubbed "neoplasticism". In 1917, he founded the art magazine *De Stijl*. Mondrian's art, such as *Composition in Yellow and Blue* (1925), informed the BAUHAUS movement and the INTERNATIONAL STYLE in architecture. In 1940 he moved to the USA where his pieces, such as *Broadway Boogie-Woogie* (1942–43), became more colourful, reflecting his interest in jazz and dance rhythms.

Monera *See* PROKARYOTAE

Monet, Claude (1840–1926) French painter. A founder of IMPRESSIONISM, Monet's piece *Impression, Sunrise* (1872) gave the movement its name. During the 1860s he studied in Paris with RENOIR, SISLEY and Bazille. The group painted directly from nature, recording the transient effects of light. Monet often painted the same scene several times, such as the *Gare St-Lazare* (1876–78) and *Rouen Cathedral* (1892–94). In 1870, he stayed with PISSARRO in London and made studies of the River Thames. In 1883, he settled in Giverny. Despite failing sight, Monet's last series, *Water Lilies* (1906–26), is his most vibrant.

monetarism Economic and monetary theory that argues that changes in monetary stability are the principal causes of changes in the economy. It asserts the importance of controlling the money supply as the means of achieving a non-inflationary, stable economy capable of supporting high employment and economic growth. This theory is associated particularly with the views of Milton FRIEDMAN, whose early work in the 1950s and 1960s stimulated the initial debate. Interest in monetarism revived in the 1970s and was extremely influential in the USA and the UK in the 1980s.

money Any type of payment that is generally accepted within an economy as a medium of exchange for goods and services. It may take many forms besides currency or cash (coins and banknotes). A large portion of the money supply may be in the form of deposits within a banking system, accessed by the use of cheques.

Mongol Nomadic people of E central Asia who overran a vast region in the 13th–14th centuries. The different tribes in the area were united by GENGHIS KHAN in the early 13th century and conquered an empire that stretched from the Black Sea to the Pacific Ocean and from Siberia to Tibet. Genghis Khan's possessions were divided among his sons and developed into four khanates, one of which was the empire of the Great Khan (KUBLAI KHAN) that included China. In the 14th century, TAMERLANE, allegedly a descendant of Genghis, conquered the Persian and Turkish khanates and broke up the GOLDEN HORDE. By the end of the century the true Mongol khanates had practically disappeared.

Mongolia Republic in central Asia; the capital is ULAN BATOR. Sandwiched between China and Russia, Mongolia is the world's largest landlocked country. High plateaux cover most of Mongolia, with the highest plateau in the w between the ALTAI Mountains and Hangai Mountains. The Altai Mountains contain Mongolia's highest peaks, rising to 4,362m (14,311ft). The land descends towards the E and S, where part of the GOBI Desert is situated. Ulan Bator lies on the N edge of a desert plateau in the heart of Asia. It has bitterly cold winters, dropping to −50°C (−58°F). Summer temperatures are moderated by altitude. Mongolia has large areas of steppe grassland. Plants become increasingly sparse to the S. **History and politics** In the 13th century, GENGHIS KHAN united the Mongolian peoples and built up a great empire. Under his grandson, KUBLAI KHAN, the Mongol empire extended from Korea and China to E Europe and Mesopotamia. The empire broke up in the late 14th century, and in the early 17th century, INNER MONGOLIA came under Chinese control. By the late 17th century, Outer Mongolia had also become a Chinese province. In 1911, the Mongolians drove the Chinese out of Outer Mongolia and established a short-lived Buddhist kingdom. In 1919, China re-established control. In 1924, the Mongolian People's Republic was established (Inner Mongolia remains a Chinese province). The Mongolian Peoples's Revolutionary Party (MPRP) became the sole political party. The revolution in ownership prompted the Lama Rebellion (1932), which saw the migration of thousands of peoples and millions of livestock into Inner Mongolia. From the 1950s, Mongolia supported Soviet policies, especially in relation to Sino–Soviet disputes. In 1961, Mongolia was accepted into the United Nations. Popular demonstrations led to multiparty elections in 1990, which were won by the MPRP. In 1992, a new constitution confirmed the process of liberalization, enshrining democratic principles and establishing a mixed economy. In 1993, President Ochirbat was re-elected, despite the MPRP refusing to endorse him as a candidate. In 1996, the Democratic Union Coalition formed the first non-communist government for more than 70 years. In 1997, Ochirbat was ousted by Natsagyn Bagabandi, leader of the MPRP. **Economy** Mongolia is a lower-middle-income developing country (1995 GDP per capita,

US$1,950). Traditional nomadic life was disrupted by communism and under forced collectivization many nomads were placed in permanent settlements, but they still remain, mainly in the Gobi Desert. In the mid-20th century, Mongolia rapidly industrialized, especially the mining of coal, copper, gold and molybdenum. Minerals and fuels now account for c.50% of Mongolia's exports. Livestock and animal products remain important. Economic development is hampered by lack of labour and poor infrastructure.

mongolism *See* DOWNS SYNDROME

mongoose Small, agile, carnivorous mammal of the CIVET family, native to Africa, S Europe and Asia. It has a slender, thickly furred body and a long, bushy tail. Mongooses eat rodents, insects, eggs, birds and snakes. Some may be domesticated, but most are highly destructive. Length: 46–115cm (18–45in). Family Viverridae.

monism In METAPHYSICS, doctrine that reality consists of a single unifying substance, or that the mental and physical are indivisible. Baruch SPINOZA saw this substance as God, while G.W.F. HEGEL believed it was the Spirit. The term was coined by the German philosopher Christian Wolf (1679–1734). Monism contrasts with DUALISM. *See also* PLURALISM

monitor Any of several species of powerful LIZARDS that live in Africa, S Asia, Indonesia and Australia, including the KOMODO DRAGON (*Varanus komodoensis*). Most species are dull-coloured with yellow markings; many are semi-aquatic. Length: to 3m (10ft). Family Varanidae.

Monitor and Merrimack IRONCLAD warships that fought an indecisive battle in Hampton Roads, Virginia, during the American CIVIL WAR. This was the first battle between ironclad ships. The *Merrimack*, which had been scuttled by the US navy, was raised by the Confederates and given armour plating. Renamed the *Virginia*, it was designed to break the Union blockade of Southern ports. The *Monitor*, a new ironclad, was designed to destroy it. The *Virginia* was subsequently destroyed by the Confederates while retreating.

Monk, Thelonious Sphere (1917–82) US jazz pianist. Along with "Dizzy" GILLESPIE and Charlie PARKER, Monk was a key figure in the development of BEBOP. In the early 1950s he formed his own band, featuring John COLTRANE. His distinctive, idiosyncratic chord structures and dissonances brought humour to the idiom. His greatest compositions, such as "'Round Midnight", "Straight No Chaser", "Epistrophy" and "Crepuscule with Nellie" have become jazz standards.

monk Member of a monastic community living under vows of religious observance such as poverty, chastity and obedience. *See* MONASTICISM

monkey Any of a wide variety of mostly tree-dwelling, diurnal, omnivorous PRIMATES that live in the tropics and sub-tropics. Most monkeys have flat, human-like faces, relatively large brains and grasping hands. They fall into two broad groups – Old World monkeys (family Cercopithecidae) and New World monkeys (Cebidae). The 60 **Old World** species include MACAQUES, BABOONS, BARBARY APES and LANGUR monkeys. They all have non-prehensile (unable to grasp) tails. They range in distribution from Japan and N China through S Asia and Africa. The 70 species of **New World** monkeys include CAPUCHIN monkeys, SPIDER MONKEYS and MARMOSETS. They are all tree dwellers, and most have grasping (prehensile) tails. They live in tropical forests of Central and South America.

monkey puzzle (Chilean pine) Evergreen tree native to the South American Andes mountains. It has tangled branches, with spirally arranged, sharp, flat leaves. The

---

MONGOLIA
AREA: 1,566,500sq km (604,826sq mi)
POPULATION: 2,847,000
CAPITAL (POPULATION): Ulan Bator (627,000)

female seeds are edible. Height to 45m (150ft). Family Araucariaceae; species *Araucaria araucana*.

monkfish (angelshark) Cartilaginous fish of the SHARK family Squatinidae. It has a flattened head with lateral gill openings, an elongated body with winglike pectoral fins and a slender tail. Monkfish are found in warmer waters of the Atlantic and Pacific oceans. It is a popular food fish.

Monmouth, James Scott, Duke of (1649–85) English noble, illegitimate son of CHARLES II. As captain general, Monmouth defeated the Scots at Bothwell Bridge (1679). Allied with the Earl of SHAFTESBURY, he became leader of the Protestant opposition to the succession of the Duke of York (later JAMES II). The discovery of a plot (1683) forced Monmouth into exile in Holland. Upon James' accession (1685), he launched a rebellion. Despite initial success, Monmouth lacked the support of the nobility and was defeated by the Duke of MARLBOROUGH at the Battle of Sedgemoor. He was executed.

Monnet, Jean (1888–1979) French economist. He was deputy secretary general (1919–23) of the League of Nations. In 1947, he introduced the Monnet Plan for the revitalization of French industry. As first president (1952–55) of the European Coal and Steel Community (ECSC), Monnet was a leading proponent of the establishment of the European Economic Community (EEC). *See also* EUROPEAN COMMUNITY (EC)

monoclonal antibody ANTIBODY produced by cells that are derived by cloning a single original parent cell. Monoclonal antibodies are all identical and have unique sequences of AMINO ACIDS in their protein make-up. They are made by fusing a normal LYMPHOCYTE with a cancerous cell derived from lymphatic tissue (LYMPHOMA) or bone MARROW (myeloma). The resulting "hybridoma" multiplies rapidly and produces large quantities of a single antibody. Monoclonal antibodies are used in highly specific VACCINES and in identifying ANTIGENS such as those involved in BLOOD GROUPS.

monocotyledon Sub-class of flowering plants (ANGIOSPERMS) characterized by one seed leaf (COTYLEDON) in the seed embryo; the leaves are usually parallel-veined. Examples include lilies, onions, orchids, palms and grasses. The larger sub-class of plants is DICOTYLEDON.

monogamy Principle that a relationship or MARRIAGE is an exclusive union between two people. It is commonly supported by legal institutions. *See also* POLYGAMY

monomer Chemical compound composed of single molecules, as opposed to a POLYMER, which is built up from repeated monomer units. For example, propene (propylene) is the monomer from which polypropene (polypropylene) is made.

mononucleosis *See* GLANDULAR FEVER

monopoly Sole supplier or producer of a product or service. A monopolistic industry has complete power over the market for its product and is able to determine levels of output and prices. In the UK, the Monopolies and Mergers Commission investigates any take-over that may impinge on competition and fair trade.

monosaccharide Sweet-tasting CARBOHYDRATE that cannot be broken down by HYDROLYSIS; a simple sugar. GLUCOSE is a monosaccharide. *See also* DISACCHARIDE; POLYSACCHARIDE

monotheism Belief in the existence of a single God. JUDAISM, CHRISTIANITY and ISLAM are the three major monotheistic religions.

monotreme One of an order of primitive MAMMALS that lay eggs. The only monotremes are the PLATYPUS and two species of ECHIDNA, all native to Australasia. The eggs are

temporarily transferred to a pouch beneath the female's abdomen where they eventually hatch and are nourished by rudimentary mammary glands. *See also* MARSUPIAL

Monroe, James (1758–1831) Fifth US President (1817–25). He fought in the American Revolution and was wounded at the Battle of TRENTON (December 1776). He was a personal friend of Thomas JEFFERSON and served him loyally in the Senate (1790–94). Monroe was governor of Virginia (1799–1802), before helping to negotiate the LOUISIANA PURCHASE (1803). He was secretary of state (1811–16) under James MADISON, before becoming president. His first term was marred by disputes over SLAVERY and resulted in the MISSOURI COMPROMISE. His foreign policy successes included an agreement with Britain on the US-Canada border, and the acquisition of Florida. He is chiefly remembered for the MONROE DOCTRINE.

Monroe Doctrine Foreign policy statement made by President James MONROE to Congress in 1823. It asserted US authority over the American continent and declared that European interference in the Western Hemisphere would be regarded as "dangerous to peace and safety" and that the USA would not become involved in the internal conflicts of Europe.

Monroe, Marilyn (1926–62) US film actress, b. Norma Jean Baker. Her films include *Gentlemen Prefer Blondes* (1953), *The Seven Year Itch* (1955), *Bus Stop* (1956), *Some Like It Hot* (1959) and *The Misfits* (1961). She attended Lee STRASBERG's ACTORS' STUDIO and married playwright Arthur MILLER in 1956. She has lived on as an icon of beauty and has consistently inspired both analysis of, and tributes to, her life.

Monrovia Capital and chief port of Liberia, West Africa, on the estuary of the St Paul River. It was settled in 1822 by freed US slaves on a site chosen by the American Colonization Society. Monrovia exports latex and iron ore; it also has warehouses and facilities for ship-repairing. Industries: bricks, cement. Pop. (1995) 962,000.

monsoon Seasonal reversal of winds, and their associated abrupt weather changes, that blow inshore in summer and offshore over nearby oceans in winter. The monsoon occurs annually in S Africa and E Asia and is centred on the Indian subcontinent where it occurs as a distinct rainy season.

monstera Genus of tropical American climbing or trailing plants with large glossy leaves that are commonly holed or deeply incised. *Monstera deliciosa* is a popular houseplant; it is often called a Swiss-cheese plant. Family Araceae.

montage (Fr. *monter*, to mount) Cinematic film-editing technique. A series of shots are cut and spliced in a particular way in order to obtain a desired narrative, structural or purely aesthetic effect. The Odessa Steps sequence in Sergei EISENSTEIN's *The Battleship Potemkin* (1925) is a classic example of montage.

Montaigne, Michel Eyquem de (1533–92) French essayist. His *Essays*, begun in 1580, touch on a wide range of subjects. They constitute an intellectual autobiography that moves from stoicism through SCEPTICISM to a mature acceptance of all that life offers.

Montale, Eugenio (1896–1981) Italian poet. In 1922, he helped to found the literary magazine *Primo Tempo*, and from 1948 was the literary editor of *Corriere della Sera*. His poetry is characteristically pessimistic in tone, such as *Cuttlefish Bones* (1925). In 1975, he was awarded the Nobel Prize for literature.

Montana State in NW USA, on the Canadian border; the capital is HELENA. Other major cities include Billings and Great Falls. The W section of Montana is dominated by the ROCKY MOUNTAINS. The E is part of the GREAT PLAINS, drained by the Missouri and Yellowstone rivers. Until the USA acquired the area in the LOUISIANA PURCHASE (1803), it was relatively unexplored. In 1852, the discovery of gold brought a rush of immigrants, and the Territory of Montana was organized in 1864. The opening of the Northern Pacific Railroad in 1883 provided a stimulus to growth and development. Sheep and cattle are raised on the plains. The principal crops (grown by means of irrigation) are wheat, hay, barley and sugar beets. The Rockies have large mineral deposits including copper, silver, gold, zinc, lead and manganese. Oil, natural gas and coal are found in the SE. Industries: timber, food processing, petroleum products; tourism is also important. Area: 381,086sq km (147,135sq mi). Pop. (2000) 902,105.

Montand, Yves (1921–91) French film actor, b. Italy. He made his film debut alongside Edith PIAF in *Star Without Light* (1946). Montand was widely acclaimed for his role in *Wages of Fear* (1953). He starred opposite Marilyn MONROE in *Let's Make Love* (1960) and made the thrillers *Z* (1969) and *State of Siege* (1973) with director Constantin Costa-Gavras. He gave commanding performances in *Jean de Florette* and *Manon des Sources* (both 1986).

Mont Blanc Highest peak in the ALPS and the second-highest peak in Europe, lying on the border between France and Italy. It was first climbed in 1786. The 11-km (7-mi) tunnel through the base of Mont Blanc (1958–62) is the longest road tunnel in the world. Height: 4,810m (15,781ft).

Montcalm, Louis-Joseph de Montcalm-Gozon, Marquis de (1712–59) French general in North America. Commander in chief of the French army in Canada (1756–59), he won several victories against the British, including the Battle of Fort Ticonderoga (1758). In 1759, he held Québec against a British siege for several months, but when the British, under James WOLFE, climbed the cliffs from the St Lawrence River to the Plains of Abraham, he was taken by surprise. Both he and Wolfe were killed in the battle.

Monte Carlo Town in N MONACO, on the Mediterranean coast. It was founded in 1858 by Prince Charles III of Monaco. Today, it is a popular resort noted for its scenery and mild climate. The Casino is a major tourist attraction. Pop. (1982) 13,154.

Montenegro (Crna Gora) Constituent republic of YUGOSLAVIA; the capital is Podgorica (formerly Titograd). The region was part of the SERBIA empire until the Turkish invasion of 1355. SERBIA was decisively defeated by Turkey in 1389, while Montenegro successfully resisted the sultan's rule. By 1500, most of the territory had been surrendered to the Ottomans. In 1799, Turkey recognized Montenegro's independence. In 1851, a monarchy was established, and in 1878 the sovereignty of the state was formally recognized. In 1910, Nicholas I assumed the title of king and sought to expel the Turks. In 1914, he declared war on Austria, and Montenegro was quickly overrun by the Austro-German armies. In 1918, he was deposed and Montenegro was united with Serbia. In 1946, Montenegro became a republic of Yugoslavia. In 1989, the local communist leadership resigned. In 1990 elections, the communists were returned to power in Montenegro, but four of the former six Yugoslav republics voted to secede from the union. Montenegro supported Serbia in the establishment of a new, Serb-dominated federation. In a 1992 referendum, Montenegro voted to remain part of the rump Yugoslav federation with Serbia. It is a mountainous region that remains industrially underdeveloped. Much of the land is barren, and agriculture is mainly centred on the Zeta Valley. Industries: tobacco, grain, stock raising, bauxite mining. Area: 13,812sq km (5,331sq mi). Pop. (1991) 615,035.

Monterrey Capital of Nuevo León state, NE Mexico. Founded in 1579, it is the heart of Mexico's iron and steel industries. Monterrey has many assembly plants for US companies. Its equable climate makes it a popular resort area. Pop. (1990) 1,069,238.

Montesquieu, Charles Louis de Secondat, baron de la Brède et de (1689–1755) French jurist and political philosopher. He first gained attention for *Persian Letters* (1721), a epistolary satire on French society. Montesquieu is chiefly remembered for his *Spirit of Laws* (1748) that compared three forms of government: republic, monarchy and despotism. He explained the evolution of societies in terms of environmental features. Montesquieu's advocacy of the separation of powers influenced the formation of the US CONSTITUTION.

Montessori, Maria (1870–1952) Italian educator who believed that preschool children, given an environment rich in manipulative materials and free from restraint, would develop their creative and academic potential. Montessori's method was adapted for use in many of the school systems in Britain and the USA.

Monteverdi, Claudio (1567–1643) Italian composer. He was the last and greatest master of the MADRIGAL. Monteverdi introduced greater dramatic power and characterization to the opera form. Many of his operas were lost: the surviving ones include *Orfeo* (1607) and *The Coronation of Poppea* (1642). He is also remembered for his *Vespers* (1610).

Montevideo Capital of Uruguay, in the S part of the country on the River Plate. Originally a Portuguese fort (1717), it was captured by the Spanish in 1726 and became the capital of Uruguay in 1828. One of South America's major ports, it is the base of a large fishing fleet and handles most of Uruguay's exports. Industries: textiles, dairy goods, wine, meat. Pop. (1996) 1,379,000.

Montezuma Name of two AZTEC emperors. **Montezuma I** (r.1440–69) increased the empire by conquest. **Montezuma II** (r.1502–20) allowed the Spaniards under Hernán CORTÉS to enter his capital, Tenochtitlán, unopposed in 1519 and subsequently became their captive.

Montfort, Simon de, Earl of Leicester (1208–65) English soldier, b. France. He distinguished himself on crusade. Resentful at being forced to cede power in Gascony to the future EDWARD I, Montfort led the rebel nobles against HENRY II in the BARONS' WAR (1263). He won the Battle of Lewes (1264) and formed a parliament. He was defeated and killed by Edward at Evesham.

Montgolfier, Joseph Michel (1740–1810) and **Jacques Étienne** (1745–99) French inventors of the hot-air balloon. In 1782, the brothers experimented with paper and linen balloons filled with hot gases collected over a fire. In November 1783, the Montgolfier brothers launched the first balloon to carry humans.

Montgomery, Bernard Law, 1st Viscount Montgomery of Alamein (1887–1976) British field marshal. As commander of the British Eighth Army in World War 2, he defeated ROMMEL and the AFRIKA KORPS at EL ALAMEIN and pursued them across North Africa. He led the invasion of Sicily and Italy. "Monty" helped to plan the Normandy landings (1944) and, under the overall command of General EISENHOWER, led the Allied forces in the initial stages. He was Deputy Supreme Allied Commander, Europe (1951–58).

Montgomery State capital of Alabama, USA, in SE central Alabama. Made state capital in 1847, in 1861 it became the first capital of the CONFEDERATE STATES OF AMERICA. It subsequently grew in importance. In the 1950s, it was the scene of the beginnings of the CIVIL RIGHTS movement. Industries: textiles, fertilizers, machinery. Pop. (1990) 187,106.

month Time taken for the Moon to travel completely around the Earth. The **sidereal** month is the time of one revolution with respect to the stars and is equal to 27.32 days. Since the Earth is in motion around the Sun, the **synodic** month – from full moon to full moon – is longer than the sidereal month and is equal to 29.53 days.

Montpelier State capital of Vermont, USA, in the N central part of the state at the confluence of Winooski and North Branch rivers. First settled in the 1780s, it was made the state capital in 1805. Industries: tourism, machinery, granite-quarrying, timber products, maple sugar and syrup, plastics. Pop. (1990) 8,247.

Montpellier City in S France, 10km (6mi) N of the Mediterranean coast; capital of Hérault department. Founded in the 8th century, it was a possession of the counts of Toulouse until the 13th century. In the 1960s, the population grew rapidly with an influx of refugees from Algeria. Industries: textiles, metal goods, wine, printed materials, chemicals. Pop. (1990) 207,996.

Montréal City on Montréal Island and the N bank of the St Lawrence River, S Québec province, Canada; second-largest city in Canada and the country's chief port. The site was settled by the French in 1642. It remained under French control until 1760 when it was taken by the British. The city's growth accelerated with the opening of the Lachine Canal in 1825, connecting it to the Great Lakes. Montréal served as the seat of the Canadian government from 1844 to 1849. Industries: aircraft, electrical equipment, rolling-stock, textiles, oil refining, metallurgy, chemicals. Pop. (1990) 1,017,666.

Montrose, James Graham, 1st Marquess of (1612–50) Scottish general. He helped compose the Covenant in support of PRESBYTERIANISM, but allied with CHARLES I in the English CIVIL WARS. Montrose's army of Highland clansmen achieved dramatic victories against the COVENANTERS at Tippermuir, Inverlochy and Kilsyth (1644), but were decisively defeated at Philiphaugh. He fled into exile in Europe. In 1650 Montrose returned but was captured and hanged.

Mont-Saint-Michel Rocky isle in the Bay of Saint-Michel, 1.6km (1mi) off the coast of Normandy, NW France. It is the site of a Benedictine abbey built in 708 by St Aubert. The base of the island is circled with ramparts, towers and bastions rising three storeys to support the Romanesque and Gothic abbey church. An island at high tide, it was linked to the mainland by a causeway in 1875.

Montserrat British dependent territory in the West Indies, a volcanic island in the Leeward Islands in the Lesser Antilles group; the capital and chief port is Plymouth. Discovered in 1493 by Christopher COLUMBUS, it was colonized in 1632 by the British. It formed part of the Leeward Island colony from 1871 to 1956, when it became a Dependent Territory. In 1996, residents in the S of the island were evacuated to neighbouring islands when a volcanoe on the island began to erupt. In 1997, increased volcanic activity prompted the British government to offer aid to the remaining islanders for rehousing in the N, or relocation to neighbouring islands. The shipping of agricultural produce, especially cotton, is the chief economic activity. There is also light industry. Area: 102sq km (40sq mi). Pop. (2000) 13,000.

Moon Natural satellite of a planet; in particular the natural satellite of the planet Earth. Apart from the Sun

it is the brightest object in the sky as seen from the Earth because of its proximity, being at a mean distance of only 384,000km (239,000mi). Its diameter is 3,476km (2,160mi). The Earth and Moon revolve around a common centre of gravity. As the Moon orbits the Earth, it is seen to go through a sequence of PHASES as the proportion of the illuminated hemisphere visible to us changes. An observer on Earth always sees the same side of the Moon because its orbital period around the Earth is the same as its axial rotation period. The surface features may be broadly divided into the darker maria, which are low-lying volcanic plains, and the brighter highland regions (sometimes called terrae), which are found predominantly in the southern part of the Moon's near side and over the entire far side. The origin of the Moon is uncertain. A current theory is that a Mars-sized body collided with the newly formed Earth, and debris from the impact formed the Moon. On 20 July 1969, Neil Armstrong became the first person to walk on the Moon. The chemical composition of material brought back from the Moon has been found to consist mainly of silica, iron oxide, aluminium oxide, calcium oxide, titanium dioxide and magnesium oxide. Lunar rocks are IGNEOUS ROCKS. The Moon has only the most tenuous of atmospheres; Apollo instruments detected traces of gases, such as helium, neon and argon. The surface temperature variation is extreme, from 100 to 400K. In 1998, it was confirmed that there was water-ice near the Moon's poles.

Moore, Bobby (Robert Frederick) (1941–93) English footballer who captained England to victory in the 1966 World Cup and won a record 108 caps (1962–70). A masterly defender, Moore played for West Ham (1968–74), captaining the team to victory in the FA Cup (1964) and European Cup-Winners Cup (1965). He ended his career at Fulham (1974–77)

Moore, Brian (1921–) Canadian novelist, b. Northern Ireland. His books examine the nature of religious and sexual guilt, and the plight of the individual when transplanted from a familiar environment. Moore's novels include *The Lonely Passion of Miss Judith Hearne* (1955), *I Am Mary Dunne* (1968), *Black Robe* (1985), *The Colour of Blood* (1987), *Lies of Silence* (1990) and *The Statement* (1995).

Moore, George Augustus (1852–1933) Irish novelist. His naturalistic novels, such as *A Mummer's Wife* (1885), *Esther Waters* (1894) and *Evelyn Innes* (1898), show the influence of Émile ZOLA.

Moore, G.E. (George Edward) (1873–1958) English philosopher. He was a professor of philosophy (1925–39) at Cambridge with Bertrand RUSSELL and Ludwig WITTGENSTEIN. Moore argued against the IDEALISM of HEGEL, defending the independent existence of the MIND and material objects. His major work, *Principia Ethica* (1903), revived British EMPIRICISM. Moore's ideas had a profound impact on the BLOOMSBURY GROUP. *See also* ANALYTIC PHILOSOPHY

Moore, Henry (1898–1986) English sculptor and graphic artist. Moore is acknowledged as one of the greatest sculptors of the 20th century. The most characteristic features of his art are hollowed-out or pierced spaces, such as *Reclining Figure* (1938). He based most of his work on natural forms, and one of his favourite themes was the mother and child. Many of his sculptures are placed in parks rather than galleries.

Moore, Marianne (1887–1972) US poet. Her verse among the most distinguished of the 20th century, with its wit, irony and wide-ranging subject matter and its highly accomplished technical discipline. Moore gained a Pulitzer Prize for her *Collected Poems* (1951).

moorhen (waterhen) Common Old World aquatic bird of the RAIL family. It has black plumage and a yellow bill, and its long toes lack the webs or lobes typical of other water birds. Length: to 32.5cm (13in). Species *Gallinula chloropus*.

Moors Name given to the predominantly BERBER people of NW Africa. In Europe the name is applied particularly to the North African Muslims who invaded Spain in 711 and established a distinctive civilization that lasted nearly 800 years. It was at its height under the Cordoba CALIPHS in the 10th–11th centuries. The Christian rulers of N Spain gradually reconquered the country, and after the ALMOHAD empire broke up in the 13th century, Granada alone survived until it fell in 1492.

moose Species of DEER found in North America and N Eurasia (when it is sometimes known as the European ELK). It is the largest of all deer. Height at the shoulder: to 1.9m (6ft); weight: 820kg (1,800lb). Family Cervidae; Species *Alces alces*.

moraine General term indicating a mound, ridge or other visible accumulation of unsorted glacial drift, predominantly TILL. **End** moraines are formed when a GLACIER is either advancing or retreating, and the rock material is dumped at the glacier's edge. **Ground** moraines are sheets of debris left after a steady retreat of the glacier.

morality play *See* MYSTERY PLAY

Moravia, Alberto (1907–90) Italian novelist. His early novels, including *The Time of Indifference* (1929) and *The Fancy Dress Party* (1940), were critical of fascism, and he was forced into hiding until 1944. Later works include *The Woman of Rome* (1947), *The Conformist* (1951) and *Two Women* (1957).

Moravia Region of the CZECH REPUBLIC, bordered N by the Sudetes Mountains, E by the Carpathian Mountains and W by Bohemia. Cities include BRNO and Ostrava. A fertile agricultural region, Moravia also has mineral resources, especially coal and iron. These helped the region's rapid industrialization in the 20th century. In the 9th century, Moravia established a large empire and adopted Christianity. In the 10th century, the empire fell and Moravia was first conquered by the MAGYARS, then subsumed into the HOLY ROMAN EMPIRE. From the 11th to 16th centuries, it was part of the kingdom of BOHEMIA. In 1526, it became Austrian HABSBURG territory and a process of Germanification was begun. In 1849, a failed revolution led to Moravia becoming Austrian crown land. In 1918, when the Habsburgs were deposed, Moravia became a part of Czechoslovakia. In 1938, S Moravia was annexed by Germany, and in 1939 Moravia became a German protectorate. Following World War 2, Moravia was restored to Czechoslovakia, and the German population expelled. In 1960, Moravia was divided into S Moravia and N Moravia.

Moravian Church Protestant church that originated in Bohemia and Moravia in the 15th century among followers of Jan HUS. In the 18th century Moravians began extensive missionary work. Several groups migrated to North America, where they founded settlements in Bethlehem, Pennsylvania and Winston-Salem, North Carolina. There are modern Moravian communities in Europe, North and South America, Africa and N India.

More, Sir Thomas (1478–1535) English scholar and statesman. He was a leading exponent of HUMANISM. More's most famous work, *Utopia* (1516), portrays an ideal state founded on reason. In 1529, More succeeded Cardinal WOLSEY as lord chancellor, despite his opposition

to Henry VIII's divorce from Catherine of Aragon. In 1532, he resigned, unhappy at HENRY VIII's break with the pope. More enraged the king by refusing to subscribe to the Act of Supremacy (1534), making the king head of the English Church, and he was executed for treason.

Moreau, Gustave (1826–98) French painter and a leading practitioner of SYMBOLISM. His pictures are sensuous and notable for his use of jewel-like colours.

Moreau, Jeanne (1928–) French film actress. She first gained recognition in Louis MALLE's films *Ascenseur pour l'Echafaud* (1957) and *Les Amants* (1958). Moreau's projection of passion, independence and vunerability was also in evidence on Michelangelo ANTONIONI's *La Notte* (1961) and François TRUFFAUT's *Jules et Jim* (1961). Other films include *Les Liaisons Dangereuses* (1960) and *Nikita* (1990). *See also* NOUVELLE VAGUE

Morgan, Sir Henry (1635–88) Welsh adventurer in the Caribbean. He led a band of buccaneers against Spanish colonies and ships, capturing and looting Panama (1671). In 1672, he was sent back to England charged with piracy but was greeted as a hero and returned to the West Indies with a knighthood as lieutenant governor of Jamaica.

Morgan, J.P. (John Pierpont) (1837–1913) US financier. Son of a rich banker, he formed what became the influential banking house of J.P. Morgan in 1871. Morgan built a vast financial and industrial empire, financing and consolidating US industries, including the giant US Steel Corporation (1901).

Morgan, Thomas Hunt (1866–1945) US geneticist. In 1933, he was awarded the Nobel Prize for physiology or medicine for the establishment of the CHROMOSOME theory of HEREDITY. His discovery of the function of chromosomes through experiments with the fruit fly (*Drosophila*) is related in his book *The Theory of the Gene* (1926).

Mörike, Eduard Friedrich (1804–75) German poet. He published several volumes of subtle lyric poetry, including *Gedichte* (1938), a collection he added to in 1848, 1856 and 1867. It ranks among the finest examples of late German ROMANTICISM. His small but influential output also includes the novel *Maler Nolten* (1832).

Morisot, Berthe (Marie Pauline) (1841–95) French painter. The leading female impressionist, Morisot was noted for her images of women and children, such as *The Cradle* (1872).

Morley, Thomas (1557–1603) English composer, organist of St Paul's Cathedral, London. He excelled at motets, compositions for the lute and MADRIGALS.

Mormons ADVENTIST sect, the full name of which is the Church of Jesus Christ of Latter-day Saints. It was established (1830) in Manchester, New York, by Joseph SMITH. Believing that they were to found Zion, or a New Jerusalem, Smith and his followers moved west. They tried to settle in Ohio, Missouri and Illinois, but were driven out. In 1844, Joseph Smith was murdered in Illinois. Brigham YOUNG then rose to leadership and in 1846–47 took the Mormons to SALT LAKE CITY, Utah.

Morocco Country in NW Africa. Morocco is separated from Europe by the narrow Strait of Gibraltar. The majority of the population live on the narrow W coastal plain, which includes the capital, RABAT, the largest city and port, CASABLANCA, and the cities of TANGIER and AGADIR. The ATLAS mountains dominate central Morocco, and Djebel Toubkal (in the Haut Atlas) is the highest peak in North Africa, at 4,165m (13,665ft). The Rif Atlas lie in the far N. Between the Atlas mountains and the coastal plain lies a broad plateau, which includes the cities of FEZ and MARRAKECH. Southern Morocco forms

MOROCCO
AREA: 446,550sq km (172,413sq mi)
POPULATION: 31,559,000
CAPITAL (POPULATION): Rabat (518,616)

part of the SAHARA Desert, which continues into the disputed territory of WESTERN SAHARA. **Climate** The Atlantic coast of Morocco is cooled by the Canaries Current. Inland, summers are hot and dry. During the mild winters (October to April) sw winds from the Atlantic bring moderate rainfall, and snow on the Haut Atlas. **Vegetation** The Sahara is barren. Forests of cedar, fir and juniper swathe the mountain slopes. The coastal plain is a fertile region. **History and politics** BERBERS settled in the area c.3,000 years ago. Jewish colonies were established under Roman rule. In c.AD 685, Morocco was invaded by Arab armies who introduced Islam and Arabic. In 711, Moroccan Muslims (MOORS) invaded Spain. In 788, Berbers and Arabs were united in an independent Moroccan state. Fez became a major religious and cultural centre. In the mid-11th century, the ALMORAVIDS conquered Morocco and established a vast Muslim empire. They were succeeded by the ALMOHAD dynasty. In the 15th century, the Moors were expelled from Spain, and Spain and Portugal made advances into Morocco. In 1660, the present ruling dynasty, the Alawite, came to power. Most of the European-held territory was reclaimed. In the mid-19th century, Morocco's strategic and economic potential began to attract European imperial interest, especially France and Spain. In 1912, Morocco was divided into French Morocco and the smaller protectorate of Spanish Morocco. Nationalist resistance was strong. ABD EL-KRIM led a revolt (1921–26) against European rule. In 1942, Allied forces invaded Morocco and removed the pro-Vichy colonial government. In 1947, Sultan Sidi Muhammad, called for the reunification of French and Spanish Morocco, but France refused and exiled the Sultan in 1953. In 1955, continuing civil unrest forced the French to accede to the return of the sultan. In 1956, Morocco gained independence, although Spain retained control of two small enclaves, Ceuta and Melilla. In 1957, Morocco became an independent monarchy when Sidi Muhammad changed his title to King Muhammad V. In 1961, Muhammad was succeeded by his son, King HASSAN II. During the 1960s, Morocco was faced with external territorial disputes (especially with Algeria) and internal political dissent. In 1965, Hassan II declared a state of emergency and assumed extraordinary powers. While the 1972 constitution reduced royal influence, Morocco remains only nominally a constitutional monarchy, and effectively the king wields all political power. In 1976, Spain finally relinquished its claim to Spanish Sahara, and the region became known as WESTERN SAHARA. Western Sahara was divided between Morocco and MAURITANIA. In 1979, Mauritania withdrew, and Morocco assumed full control of the phosphate-rich region but met with fierce resistance from independence movements. In 1993, the collapse of several coalition governments led to Hassan II's appointment of an administration. In 1994, Morocco restored diplomatic links with Israel. In 1995, Hassan II formed a new government of technocrats and members of the Entente National. In 1996, a referendum approved the establishment of a bicameral legislature, with a directly elected lower chamber. In 1997, elections a new coalition government was formed. In 1999, Hassan died

and was succeeded by his son, Muhammad VI. **Economy** Morocco is a lower-middle-income developing country (1995 GDP per capita, US$3,340). The post-independence exodus of Europeans and Jews from Morocco created an economic vacuum. The cost of war in Western Sahara further strained Morocco's scant resources. Its main resource is phosphate rock, which is used to make fertilizers. Morocco is the world's fourth-largest phosphate producer and processes 75% of the world's reserves. The principal mines are located near Khouribga. Agriculture employs 46% of the workforce. In the mountains, most agriculture is undertaken by peasant farmers or nomadic pastoralists. The chief commercial farming areas are the Atlantic coastal plains and the inland plateaux, where farming is made possible by extensive irrigation. The main crops include barley, beans, citrus fruits, grapes, maize, olives, sugar beet and wheat. Fishing is another important activity. Casablanca, the chief manufacturing city and largest port, is also a thriving tourist centre. Morocco is an important tourist destination; the annual number of visitors exceeds three million and contributes more than US$1,360 million in annual receipts. Tourism is centred on the Atlantic Coast resorts, the Atlas Mountains and the historic cities of Marrakech, Fez and Rabat. In 1996, as part of a rapidly improving infrastructure, Morocco and Spain agreed to build a tunnel linking the two countries.

Moroni Capital of the COMOROS Islands, on sw Grande Comore. Founded by Arab settlers, it replaced Mayotte as capital in 1958. Chief exports are coffee, vanilla, cacao and timber and metal products. Pop. (1988 est.) 22,000.

Morpheus In Greek and Roman mythology, the god of sleep and dreams.

morphine White crystalline ALKALOID derived from OPIUM. It depresses the CENTRAL NERVOUS SYSTEM and is used as an ANALGESIC for severe pain. An addictive drug, its use is associated with a number of side-effects, including nausea. Morphine was first isolated in 1806. *See also* HEROIN

morphology Biological study of the form and structure of living things. It often focuses on the relation between similar features in different organisms. *See also* PALAEONTOLOGY

Morricone, Ennio (1928–) Italian film composer who has scored almost 400 films. He is best known for his work with director Sergio LEONE. He wrote the scores for Leone's "spaghetti westerns", *A Fistful of Dollars* (1964), *The Good, the Bad and the Ugly* (1966) and *Once Upon a Time in the West* (1968). Other scores include *The Untouchables* (1987) and *The Mission* (1986).

Morris, William (1834–96) English artist, craftsman, writer, social reformer and printer. Associated with the PRE-RAPHAELITE BROTHERHOOD (PRB), he founded (1861) the ARTS AND CRAFTS MOVEMENT, a collection of decorators and designers influenced by medieval craftsmanship. Morris is perhaps best remembered for his wallpaper designs, which anticipated ART NOUVEAU in their use of the S-curve. In the 1880s, he became interested in socialism, writing *The Dream of John Ball* (1886–87) and *News from Nowhere* (1890). In 1890, Morris founded Kelmscott Press.

morris dance English rustic dance traditionally performed by men and probably deriving from pre-Christian rituals. It is danced to pipes, tabors and occasionally bagpipes. The dance often took place along the roads from one village to another.

Morrison, Herbert Stanley, Baron (1888–1965) British statesman, home secretary (1940–45) and deputy prime minister (1945–51). He helped found the London LABOUR PARTY and became leader of London County Council (1934–40). During World War 2, Morrison served in the War Cabinet under Winston CHURCHILL. He drafted the radical post-war programme of nationalization and social welfare reform for Clement ATTLEE. In 1955, he was defeated by Hugh GAITSKELL in the Labour leadership contest.

Morrison, Jim (1943–71) *See* DOORS, THE

Morrison, Toni (1931–) US writer, b. Chloe Anthony Wofford. Morrison's debut novel, *The Bluest Eye* (1970), established her as a major voice in AMERICAN LITERATURE. Her chronicles of African-American experience in the rural South include *Song of Solomon* (1977) and *Tar Baby* (1981). *Beloved* (1987), a powerful indictment of slavery, won a Pulitzer Prize. Other works include *Jazz* (1992). In 1993, she was awarded the Nobel Prize for Literature.

Morrison, Van (George Ivan) (1945–) Northern Irish singer and songwriter. His successful albums include *Astral Weeks* (1968) *Moondance* (1968) and *Into the Music* (1979).

Morse, Samuel Finley Breese (1791–1872) US inventor of the **Morse code**. A successful artist, he became interested in developing a practical electric TELEGRAPH in *c.*1832. His receiver was based on an electromagnet. Using a simple system of dots and dashes, now known as the Morse code, he set up the first US telegraph from Washington to Baltimore in 1844.

Morton, "Jelly Roll" (1885–1941) US jazz pianist, bandleader and composer, b. Ferdinand Joseph La Menthe. Morton played in the brothels of Storyville in New Orleans, before making some of the first JAZZ recordings (1923). Morton and his band, the Red Hot Peppers, combined blues, RAGTIME and "stomp" music on classics such as "Wolverine Blues" (1923).

mosaic Technique of surface decoration using small pieces of coloured material set tightly together in an adhesive to form patterns or pictures. The technique was employed for floor and wall decorations in ancient Mesopotamia and Greece. Roman mosaics commonly featured a central design or a portrait, surrounded by a decorative geometric border. The art developed rapidly in early Christian times, especially during the 4th–6th centuries, and continues to be used for floors, church interiors and wall decorations.

Moscow (Moskva) Capital of Russia and largest city in Europe, on the River Moskva. The site has been inhabited since Neolithic times, but Russian records do not mention it until 1147. It had become a principality by the end of the 13th century, and in 1367 the first stone walls of the KREMLIN were constructed. By the end of the 14th century, the city had emerged as the focus of Russian opposition to the Mongols. In 1610, Polish troops occupied the city but were driven out two years later. Moscow was the capital of the Grand Duchy of Russia from 1547 to 1712, when the capital was moved to ST PETERSBURG. In 1812, Napoleon I and his army occupied Moscow but were forced to flee when the city burned to the ground. In 1918, following the RUSSIAN REVOLUTION, it became the capital of the SOVIET UNION. In 1941, the failure of the German army to seize Moscow was the Nazis' first major setback in World War 2. The KREMLIN is the centre of the city and the administrative heart of the country. Adjoining it are Red Square, the Lenin Mausoleum and the 16th-century cathedral of Basil the Beatified. Industries: metalworking, oil-refining, motor vehicles, film-making, precision instruments, chemicals, publishing, wood and paper products, tourism. Pop. (1994) 9,233,000.

Moscow, Grand Duchy of Historic Russian state. Based around on the trading city of MOSCOW, it emerged from Mongol and Tatar rule in the late 15th century as the centre of a unified Russian state, defeating the principality of NOVGOROD and absorbing part of Lithuania.

Moscow Art Theatre Russian theatre, famous for its contribution to naturalistic theatre. It was founded in 1898 by Konstantin STANISLAVSKY and Nemirovich-Danchenko. The original company was composed of amateur actors from the Society of Art and Literature who were committed to adopting a more rigorous, serious and professional approach to staging as well as acting. It was at the Moscow Art Theatre that Stanislavsky developed his influential principle of "method acting".

Moselle (Ger. Mosel) River in France and Germany, Rising in the Vosges Mountains, NE France, it flows NW past Remiremont, Epinal and Toul, turning N to flow past METZ and Thionville and NE to form the Luxembourg-German border. It flows through Germany, emptying into the River Rhine at KOBLENZ. The Moselle is connected to the rivers Rhine, Meuse and Seine by canals. Grapes grown along its steep banks between Trier and Koblenz are used to make Moselle wine. Length: 545km (340mi).

Moses (active *c.*13th century BC) Biblical hero who, as a prophet and leader of the ancient Hebrew people, was the central figure in their liberation from bondage in Egypt and a formative influence in the founding of their nation-state, Israel. His story is recounted in the Old Testament books of Exodus and Numbers. Moses was an abandoned Hebrew child brought up in the pharaoh's court. As a man, Moses sought to lead the Hebrews out of Egypt, and eventually was permitted to lead the EXODUS. God (YAHWEH) revealed himself to Moses on Mount Sinai but made the Israelites wander in the desert for a further 40 years before they entered the promised land of CANAAN.

Moses, Grandma (Anna Mary Robertson) (1860–1961) US primitive painter. She only began painting when she was in her late seventies. Her scenes of country life, based on recollections from her youth, became world-famous through prints and greeting cards. Well-known examples are *Out for the Christmas Trees* and *Thanksgiving Turkey*.

Moslem *See* MUSLIM

Mosley, Sir Oswald Ernald (1896–1980) British fascist. In 1931, he formed the leftist New Party but in 1932 swung to the right and founded the virulently anti-Semitic British Union of Fascists, modelled on German and Italian FASCISM. Mosley's blackshirts engaged in confrontational marches, especially in the East End of London. His outspoken support for HITLER led to his internment during World War 2. Following the defeat of Nazi Germany in World War 2, Mosley's pernicious influence declined.

mosque Islamic place of worship. Mosques are usually decorated with abstract and geometric designs, because ISLAM prohibits representative art as the imitation of God's creation. The building's parts include a DOME, a *mihrab* (prayer niche) that shows the direction of MECCA, a MINARET, from which the MUEZZIN calls the faithful to prayer, and a *sahn* (courtyard), often with a central fountain for ritual ablution. The complex often includes a *madressa* (school). *See also* ISLAMIC ART AND ARCHITECTURE

mosquito Long-legged, slender-winged insect found throughout the world. The female sucks blood from warm-blooded animals. Some species carry the parasites of diseases, including MALARIA, YELLOW FEVER, DENGUE, viral ENCEPHALITIS and FILARIASIS. The larvae are aquatic. Adult length: 3–9mm (0.12–0.36in) Family Culicidae.

Mosquito Coast (Mosquitia) Coastal region bordering on the Caribbean Sea, c.65km (40mi) wide, now divided between Nicaragua and Honduras. A British protectorate from 1740, it was returned to its original inhabitants (the Miskito) in 1860. In 1894 it became part of Nicaragua. International arbitration awarded the N part to Honduras in 1960. The region, which consists mainly of tropical forest, swamp and lagoons, is sparsely populated.

Moss, Stirling (1929–) English Formula One racing driver. Moss won 16 Grands Prix in 66 starts and finished second four times in the world driver's championship. He retired after a serious crash in 1962.

moss Any of c.14,000 species of small, simple nonflowering green plants that typically grow in colonies, often forming dense carpets. They do not have specialized tissues for transporting water, food and minerals, although they do have parts resembling the stems, leaves and roots of the higher (flowering) plants. They reproduce by means of SPORES produced in a capsule on a long stalk. The spores germinate into branching filaments from which buds arise that grow into moss plants. Mosses grow on soil, rocks and tree trunks in a wide variety of habitats, especially in shady, damp places. *See also* ALTERNATION OF GENERATIONS; BRYOPHYTE

Mössbauer, Rudolf Ludwig (1929–) German physicist. His doctoral thesis (1958) concerned the emission of GAMMA RADIATION by radioactive nuclei within crystals (the **Mössbauer effect**). He shared the 1961 Nobel Prize for physics with the US physicist Robert HOFSTADTER. Mössbauer's discovery has been used to test Albert EINSTEIN's theory of general RELATIVITY.

Mossi People inhabiting BURKINA FASO and who are found in small numbers elsewhere in West Africa. Their traditional livelihood involves growing staple crops, including millet and sorghum.

motet Musical form prominent in all choral church music from c.1200 to 1600. In the 13th and 14th centuries, it consisted of three unaccompanied voice parts. The Renaissance motet of the 15th century, usually in four or five parts, was contrapuntal in style. PALESTRINA composed some of the purest examples of the form. After 1600, there were new developments in the form, including occasional instrumental parts and texts in vernacular languages.

moth Insect of the order LEPIDOPTERA, found in almost all parts of the world. It is distinguished from a BUTTERFLY mainly by its non-clubbed antennae, although there are a few exceptions. Most moths are nocturnal. Like a butterfly, a moth undergoes METAMORPHOSIS. It has a long, coiled proboscis for sipping liquid food, particularly the nectar of flowers. There are c.800 species

mother-of-pearl (nacre) Shiny substance lining many MOLLUSC shells. It is composed of a form of calcium carbonate deposited in layers interspersed with organic material. Diffraction of light causes the lustre and iridescence of mother-of-pearl. It is used in making buttons and jewellery, and for decorative inlay work.

Motherwell, Robert (1915–91) US painter and writer. Motherwell was a pioneer of ABSTRACT EXPRESSIONISM. Perhaps his best-known work is the series *Elegies to the Spanish Republic*. He was the editor of the influential *The Documents of Modern Art* series (1944–57).

Motion, Andrew (1952–) English writer. His collections of poems include *Pleasure Steamers* (1978), *Natural Causes* (1987) and *Of Salt Water* (1997). Other works include the biographies *Larkin* (1982), *Keats* (1998) and *Wainewright the Poisoner* (2000). He succeeded Ted HUGHES as poet laureate in 1999.

motor Mechanism that converts ENERGY (such as heat or electricity) into useful WORK. The term is sometimes applied to the INTERNAL COMBUSTION ENGINE but is more often applied to the ELECTRIC MOTOR. ROCKET engines are motors that can leave the Earth's atmosphere because they carry both fuel and oxidizer. Ion motors are in development, intended for spacecraft propulsion: a stream of ions, possibly from a nuclear reactor, is accelerated in a strong electrostatic field to produce a reaction that drives the spacecraft. *See also* AUTOMOBILE; ENGINE; FOUR STROKE ENGINE; TWO-STROKE ENGINE

motorcycle Powered vehicle, usually with two wheels. Gottlieb DAIMLER is credited with building the first practical motorcycle in 1885. It was powered by a FOUR-STROKE ENGINE. The first commercially produced model was Hildebrand and Wolfmüller's *Pétrolette* (1894). Motorcycles are classified in terms of ENGINE capacity, usually 50cc to 1200cc. Transmission of power to the rear wheel is by chain, shaft or belt. The clutch, accelerator and front brake controls are on the handlebars. Foot pedals control the gear change and rear brake. *See also* AUTOMOBILE; BICYCLE; TWO-STROKE ENGINE

motorcycle racing Sport in which motorcyclists compete on road circuits, cross-country (scrambling and trials), on grass tracks and on cinder tracks (speedway). The first organized race took place in France in 1906 from Paris to Nantes. The world championship started in 1949. The championship is organized by engine capacity: the 500cc is the premier title.

motor nerve (motor neuron) NERVE carrying messages to the muscles from the BRAIN via the SPINAL CORD. The cell bodies of some motor NERVES form part of the spinal cord. Motor nerves are involved in both reflex action and voluntary muscular control.

motor racing Competitive racing of AUTOMOBILES. The first organized race took place in 1894, from Paris to Rouen. The first Formula One Grand Prix was held in 1906. The world driver's championship started in 1950, and the constructors' trophy in 1956. The season (March–November) involves 16 Grands Prix. Formula One cars are purpose-built to strict specifications. With average speeds in excess of 240kp/h (150mph), Formula One circuits have rigorous safety procedures. Formula One is a worldwide sport which attracts major commercial sponsorship. The LE MANS 24-hour endurance race has been held annually since 1923. Other forms of motor racing include rallying and Indy car racing in the USA. Famous road races include the Monte Carlo Rally, the Paris-Dakar Rally and the Lombard-RAC Rally (first held 1927). The Indianapolis 500 was first held in 1911.

Motown Hugely successful record company whose African-American artists made a major contribution to popular music of the 1960s. Founded (1959) in Detroit, Michigan, by Berry Gordy Jr, the company's roster of artists included Smokey Robinson, Marvin GAYE and Stevie WONDER during its long and influential life. In 1988 Berry sold Motown to the MCA company.

mould Mass composed of the spore-bearing mycelia (vegetative filaments) and fruiting bodies produced by numerous fungi. Many moulds live off fruits, vegetables, cheese, butter, jelly, silage and almost any dead organic material. Roquefort, camembert and stilton CHEESES involve the use of mould. Although many species are pathogenic (disease-causing), PENICILLIN and a few other ANTIBIOTICS are obtained from moulds. *See also* FUNGICIDE; FUNGUS; SLIME MOULD

moulting Process involving the shedding of the outermost layers of an organism and their replacement.

Mammals moult by shedding outer skin layers and hair, often at seasonal intervals. Birds moult their feathers, and amphibians and reptiles their skin. In all cases the process is controlled by HORMONES. The moulting of insects and other arthropods, a process also called ecdysis, involves the resorption into the body of materials from the hard outer cuticle of the EXOSKELETON, making the cuticle more fragile. The arthropod then swells its body and bursts free from the old cuticle and slowly reforms a new one around its swollen body, increasing in size.

mound builders Name given to the Native North Americans responsible for groups of ancient earth mounds found in the Ohio and Mississippi river valleys. The mounds contain skeletons or ashes with buried ceremonial objects. Some are simple shapes, others more intricate and representing birds or snakes. The largest, the Cahokia Mound in Illinois, is c.300m (1,000ft) long and 30m (100ft) high.

mountain Part of the Earth's surface that rises steeply to at least 610m (2,000ft). They are identified geologically by their most characteristic features and are classified as FOLD, volcanic or fault-block mountains. Mountains may occur as single isolated masses, as ranges, or in systems or chains. *See individual articles*

mountaineering Sport and leisure activity of climbing mountains that gained popularity in Europe in the 18th and 19th centuries. The MATTERHORN was first scaled in 1865. In 1953, the world's highest mountain, EVEREST, was climbed by Edmund HILLARY and Tenzing Norgay. By the mid-1990s, Everest had been scaled by thousands of people – although the mountain continued to claim an average of three lives per year.

mountain lion *See* PUMA

Mountbatten, Louis, 1st Earl Mountbatten of Burma (1900–79) British admiral, great-grandson of Queen VICTORIA, uncle of Prince PHILIP. During World War 2, Mountbatten directed (1942–43) commando raids upon Norway and France. In 1943, he was appointed Allied commander-in-chief in SE Asia and led operations against the Japanese in Burma. He accepted the Japanese surrender. Mountbatten was last viceroy (1947–48) of British India, overseeing the transition to independence. He was murdered by an IRA bomb.

Mount Rushmore Mountain in the Black Hills, SW South Dakota, USA. The colossal busts of presidents Washington, Jefferson, Lincoln and Theodore Roosevelt were carved out of the granite face of Mount Rushmore by Gutzon Borglum from 1927. After his death in 1941, the work was completed by his son. Area: 5sq km (2sq mi).

mouse Any of numerous species of small, common RODENTS found in a variety of habitats throughout the world; especially the omnivorous, brown-grey house mouse (*Mus musculus*) of the family Muridae. This prolific nest builder, often associated with human habitation, is considered a destructive pest and is believed to carry disease-producing organisms. It may grow as long as 20cm (8in) overall and has been bred for use in laboratories and as a pet. Many species within the family Cricetidae are also called mice, as are pocket mice (Heteromyidae), jumping mice (Zapodidae) and marsupial mice (Dasyuridae).

mouse In computing, input device that can be operated with one hand. It is designed to fit the palm of the hand, with one or more buttons that can be pressed by the fingers of the same hand. When the mouse is moved around a flat surface, it controls the movement of a cursor or pointer on the COMPUTER screen. The cursor can be "clicked" onto icons or other responsive areas on the computer display. *See* INTERFACE *illustration*

mouth In animals, the anterior (front) end of the ALIMENTARY CANAL where it opens to the outside. In humans and other higher animals, it is the cavity within the jaws, containing the teeth and tongue.

mouth-organ *See* HARMONICA

Mowlam, Mo (Marjorie) (1949–) British stateswoman, secretary of state for Northern Ireland (1997–). While undergoing treatment for a brain tumour, her hands-on approach to mediation included meeting Loyalist paramilitary prisoners in the Maze in an attempt to win Unionist support for the Good Friday Agreement (1998). In 2000, Mowlam announced that she would retire at the next national election (due 2002).

Mozambique Republic in SE Africa. It faces the Indian Ocean. The coastline is dotted with the mouths of many rivers, including the LIMPOPO and the ZAMBEZI. The coast is fringed with swamps and offshore coral reefs. The only natural harbour is the capital, MAPUTO. The coastal plains make up 50% of Mozambique's land area. To the N of the Zambezi, the plain is narrow, while to the S it is much broader. Inland, a savanna plateau rises to highlands at the frontiers with Zimbabwe, Zambia, Malawi and Tanzania. **Climate** Mozambique has a tropical climate. The warm, south-flowing Mozambique Current gives Maputo hot and humid summers, though winters are mild and fairly dry. **Vegetation** Tropical savanna is the most widespread vegetation. Palm trees are found along the coast, and there are rainforests of ebony and ironwood. **History and politics** Bantu-speakers arrived in the first century AD. Arab traders in gold and ivory settled in coastal regions from the 10th century AD. Vasco da GAMA was the first European to discover Mozambique in 1498, and in 1505 Portugal established its first settlement. During the 16th century, Portuguese adventurers built huge, semi-autonomous plantations. In the 18th and 19th centuries, Mozambique was a major centre of the slave trade. In 1910, Mozambique formally became a Portuguese colony. Nationalist opposition increased with unfair land rights, forced labour and social inequity. The Front for the Liberation of Mozambique (FRELIMO) was founded (1961) to oppose Portuguese rule. In 1964, FRELIMO launched a guerrilla war. In 1975, Mozambique gained independence, and Samora Machel became president. Many Europeans fled the country, taking vital capital and resources. The new FRELIMO government established a one-party Marxist state. FRELIMO's assistance to liberation movements in Rhodesia (now Zimbabwe) and South Africa was countered by these white-minority regimes' support for the Mozambique National Resistance Movement (RENAMO) opposition. Civil war raged for 16 years, claiming tens of thousands of lives. In 1986, Samora Machel died and was succeeded by Joachim Chissano. In 1989, FRELIMO dropped its communist policies and agreed to end one-party rule. In 1992, faced with severe drought and famine, a peace agreement was signed between FRELIMO and RENAMO. In 1994, Chissano was elected president. In 1995, Mozambique became the 53rd member of the Commonwealth of Nations. In 2000, vast areas of Mozambique were submerged by flood waters from the River Limpopo, leaving nearly one million people homeless and shattering the nation's infrastructure.

MOZAMBIQUE
AREA: 801,590sq km (309,590sq mi)
POPULATION: 20,493,000
CAPITAL (POPULATION): Maputo (2,000,000)

Economy Mozambique is one of the world's poorest countries (1995 GDP per capita, US$810). Agriculture employs 85% of the workforce, mainly at subsistence level. In the late 1990s, the government began to make some headway in restoring the country's economy, with an annual growth of more than 10% between 1997 and 1999. Crops include cassava, cotton, cashew nuts, fruits, maize, rice, sugar cane and tea. Fishing is also important. Shrimps, sugar and copra are exported. Despite its large hydroelectric plant at Cahora Bassa dam on the River Zambezi, manufacturing is on a comparatively small scale. Electricity is exported to South Africa.

Mozart, Wolfgang Amadeus (1756–91) Austrian composer. A child prodigy on the piano, Mozart was taken by his father, Leopold, on performing tours in Europe (1762–65), during which he composed his first symphonies. In the 1770s, he worked at the prince archbishop's court in Salzburg. Masses, symphonies and his first major piano concerto date from this time. Opera was his primary concern, and in 1780 he composed *Idomeneo*, which is impressive for its rich orchestral writing and depth of expression. In the 1780s, he moved to Vienna, where he was to spend most of the rest of his life, becoming court composer to the Austrian emperor in 1787. In this decade, he composed and performed his greatest piano concertos, the last eight of his 41 symphonies and the brilliant comic operas *Le Nozze di Figaro* (1786), *Don Giovanni* (1787) and *Così fan tutti* (1790). In the last year of his life, Mozart wrote the operas *Die Zauberflöte* and *La Clemenza di Tito*, the clarinet concerto and the *Requiem* (completed by a pupil). In all, he composed more than 600 works, perfecting the CLASSICAL style and foreshadowing ROMANTICISM.

Mpumalanga Province in NE South Africa; the capital is Nelspruit. Eastern Transvaal was created in 1994 from the E part of the former province of TRANSVAAL. In 1995 it was renamed Mpumalanga. Area: 78,730sq km (30,390sq mi). Pop. (1995 est.) 3,007,100.

Mubarak, Hosni (1928–) Egyptian statesman, president (1981–). He was vice president (1975–81) under Anwar SADAT and became president on his assassination. Mubarak continued Sadat's moderate policies, improving relations with Israel and the west. In 1989, he gained Egypt's readmission to the Arab League. Mubarak has struggled to stem the rise of Islamic fundamentalism. In 1999, Mubarak was re-elected for a fourth term.

Mucha, Alphonse (1860–1939) Czech painter and designer, b. Alfons Maria. His luxurious, flowing posters are some of the finest examples of ART NOUVEAU. Working in Paris, Mucha designed sets and costumes for the actress Sarah BERNHARDT. He also designed a stained-glass window in Prague Cathedral.

Muckrakers Name given to US journalists and other writers who exposed corruption in politics and business in the early 20th century. The term was first used by Theodore ROOSEVELT in 1906.

mucous membrane Sheet of TISSUE (or EPITHELIUM) lining all body channels that communicate with the air, such as the mouth and respiratory tract, the digestive and urogenital tracts, and the various glands that secrete mucus, which lubricates and protects tissues.

mudskipper Any of several genera of amphibian-like fish of tidal swamps in Africa, Asia and Australia. It can retain moisture in its gill cavities to survive out of water when the tide recedes. With its specialized pectoral fins, it can hop on mud and can even climb trees to cling with a sucker for several hours. Length: to 20cm (8in). Family Periophthalmidae.

muezzin Person who calls MUSLIMS to prayer. In small MOSQUES, the call is given by the IMAM. In larger ones, a muezzin is specially appointed for that purpose.

Mugabe, Robert Gabriel (1925–) Zimbabwean statesman, prime minister (1980–), president (1987–). In 1961 he became deputy secretary-general of Joshua NKOMO's Zimbabwe African People's Union (ZAPU). In 1963 Mugabe was forced into exile and co-founded the Zimbabwe African National Union (ZANU). He was imprisoned by Ian SMITH's white minority Rhodesian regime, and spent the next decade (1964–74) in detention. After his release, Mugabe continued to agitate for majority rule from Mozambique. He was a leading opponent of South Africa's APARTHEID regime. In 1976, ZAPU and ZANU merged to form the Patriotic Front, which became the first black majority government. During the 1980s, Mugabe shifted away from communism. Mugabe won Zimbabwe's first multi-party elections (1990). He enforced a new constitution to allow the government to confiscate white farmers' land without compensation. After narrow re-election in 2000, Mugabe attracted international criticism for his support of the illegal occupation of white-owned farms.

Muhammad (*c.*570–632) Arab prophet and inspirational religious leader who founded ISLAM. He was born in the Arabian city of MECCA. Muhammad was orphaned at the age of six and went to live first with his grandfather, and then with his uncle. At the age of 25, he began working as a trading agent for Khadijah, a wealthy widow of 40, whom he married. For 25 years, she was his closest companion and gave birth to several children. Only one brought him descendants – his daughter FATIMA, who became the wife of his cousin, ALI. In *c.*610, Muhammad had a vision while meditating alone in a cave on Mount Hira, outside Mecca. A voice three times commanded him to "recite", and he felt his body compressed until he could hardly breathe. Then he heard the words of the first of many revelations that came to him in several similar visions over the next two decades. The revelations came from ALLAH, or God, and Muhammad's followers believe that they were passed to Muhammad through the angel GABRIEL. At the core of his new religion was the doctrine that there is no God but Allah and His followers must submit to Him – the word *islam* means "submission". Muhammad gained followers but also many enemies among the Meccans. In 622, he fled to Yathrib (MEDINA). Muslims, followers of Islam, later took this HEJIRA as initiating the first year in their calendar. Thereafter, Muhammad won more followers. He organized rules for the proper worship of Allah and for Islamic society. Muhammad also made war against his enemies. He conquered Mecca in 630. Most of the Arab tribes allied with him. In Medina, he married the woman who became his favourite wife, Aishah, the daughter of ABU BAKR, one of his strongest supporters. Muhammad is considered an ideal man, but he never claimed supernatural powers, and is not held to be divine. His tomb is in the Holy Mosque of the Prophet, Medina.

Muhammad II (1429–81) Ottoman sultan (1451–81) considered to be the true founder of the OTTOMAN EMPIRE. He captured Constantinople (1453) and made it the capital of the Ottoman Empire.

Muhammad, Elijah (1897–1975) Leader of the BLACK MUSLIMS (1934–75), b. Elijah Poole. He became leader in 1934, following the disappearance of the movement's founder, Wallace D. Fard. During World War 2 he was imprisoned for encouraging draft-dodging. The rhetorical skills of MALCOLM X gained the movement national attention, and tensions grew until Malcolm was suspended from the movement. Under Muhammad's leadership, the Muslim doctrines were codified and membership increased.

Muhammad Ali (1769–1849) Albanian soldier who founded an Egyptian dynasty. In 1798, he took part in an OTTOMAN expeditionary force sent to Egypt to drive out the French. He was unsuccessful but after the departure of the French quickly rose to power. In 1805, he was proclaimed the Ottoman sultan's viceroy. In 1811, he defeated the MAMELUKES, who had ruled Egypt since the 13th century. He put down a rebellion in Greece in 1821, but his fleet was later destroyed by the European powers at the Battle of NAVARINO in 1827. Muhammad challenged the sultan and began the conquest of Syria in 1831. The European powers again intervened, and he was compelled to withdraw.

Muhammad Ali *See* ALI, MUHAMMAD

Muhammad Riza Pahlavi *See* PAHLAVI, MUHAMMAD REZA SHAH

Mujaheddin Muslim militants dedicated to waging a holy war. The term is most used of the guerrilla fighters of Iran in the 1970s–80s and of Afghanistan in the 1980s–90s.

mulberry Any member of the genus *Morus*, trees and shrubs that grow in tropical and temperate regions. They have simple leaves, and the male flowers are catkins, while the female flowers are borne in spikes. Several species are cultivated for their fleshy, edible fruits.

mule HYBRID offspring of a female HORSE and a male ASS; it is different from the smaller hinny, which is the result of a cross between a male horse and a female ass. Brown or grey, it has a uniform coat and a body similar to a horse, but has the long ears, heavy head and thin limbs of an ass. Known since ancient times, the hardy mule is commonly used as a draft or pack animal. It is usually sterile. Height: 1.8m (5.8ft).

mule deer Game animal that inhabits the w USA from Alaska to Mexico. It is red-brown with a black-tipped white tail; the male bears antlers. It is generally solitary, but often gathers in herds in winter. Height: to 1.1m (3.5ft) at the shoulder. Family Cervidae; species *Odocoileus hemionus*.

mulla Muslim cleric well-versed in the SHARIA (Islamic law). There are no formal qualifications for a man to become a mulla, but he will usually have attended a *madressa*, or religious school.

mullein Hardy biennial or perennial plants of the genus *Verbascum*, including the common mullein (*V. thapsus*) that has 30cm (1ft) leaves and long, dense, yellow flower spikes; height: to 1.8m (6ft). Family Scrophulariaceae.

Muller, Hermann Joseph (1890–1967) US geneticist. He found that he could artificially increase the rate of mutations in the fruit fly (*Drosophila*) by the use of X-rays. He thus highlighted the human risk in exposure to radioactive material. In 1946, he was awarded the Nobel Prize for physiology or medicine.

Müller, Paul Hermann (1899–1965) Swiss chemist who was awarded the 1948 Nobel Prize for physiology or medicine for his discovery of the use of DDT as an INSECTICIDE. In 1944, DDT was successfully employed against a typhus epidemic in Naples, and for more than 20 years was the most widely used insecticide. In the 1970s, however, it was implicated as a hazard to animal life because it persists in FOOD CHAINS; its use has been banned in many countries.

mullet (grey mullet) Marine food fish found in shoals in shallow tropical and temperate waters throughout the world. Its torpedo-shaped body is green or blue and silver. Size: to about 90cm (3ft); weight: 6.8kg (15lb). Family Mugilidae.

Mulroney, Brian (1939–) Canadian statesman, prime minister (1984–93). He entered Parliament in 1983, as leader of the Progressive Conservative Party. In his first term, Mulroney signed the Meech Lake Accord (1985), which constitutionally made QUÉBEC a "distinct society". In 1987, he negotiated a free-trade treaty with the USA, which led to the 1992 NORTH AMERICAN FREE TRADE AGREEMENT (NAFTA). The status of Québec continued to vex his administration, and following defeat in a national referendum, Mulroney resigned. He was succeeded as prime minister and party leader by Kim Campbell.

multicultural education Educational settings where pupils come from different ethnic groups, and where there is a recognition of the need for all groups to express their cultural identity. Such education is designed to combat racial prejudice and stereotyping, and to promote appreciation and understanding of the culture of students' own ethnic groups and that of others.

multimedia COMPUTER system that includes text, audio (sound), and VIDEO (graphics) components. Often the user can interact with the system to interrogate it or even to control or contribute to what is happening on screen. A multimedia product is usually produced on a CD-ROM, which has the necessary high storage capacity for the audio and graphics elements. A multimedia computer must have a CD-ROM drive, together with a high-resolution colour monitor and a sound card.

multiple sclerosis (MS) Incurable disorder of unknown cause in which there is degeneration of the myelin sheath that surrounds nerves in the brain and spinal cord. Striking mostly young adults (more women than men), it is mainly a disease of the world's temperate zones. Symptoms may include unsteadiness, loss of coordination, and speech and visual disturbances. Affected people typically have relapses and remissions over many years.

Mumbai (Bombay) Largest city in India, situated on an island off the w coast; capital of Maharashtra state. In 1534, it was ceded to the Portuguese. In 1661, the British gained control of Bombay as part of Catherine of Braganza's dowry to Charles II. It was the headquarters of the British EAST INDIA COMPANY until 1858. Bombay's "Gateway to India" was the first sight many colonists had of India. After 1941, a population boom occurred as a result of immigration, rural migration and an increasing birthrate. Bombay has the largest population of PARSIS in India. The city has some fine Victorian public architecture. Bombay is a cultural, educational, trade and financial centre, and the site of the world's largest film industry. It is India's second-largest port (after CALCUTTA). Educational establishments include the University of Bombay (1857) and the Indian Institute of Technology (1958). Industries: chemicals, textiles, oil refining, motor vehicles. Exports: cotton, manganese. Pop. (1991) 9,925,891.

Mumford, Lewis (1895–1990) US sociologist and writer, best known for his essays on town planning and architecture, which include *The City in History* (1961) and *Roots of Contemporary Architecture* (1972). He also published works on a variety of subjects, including *Herman Melville* (1929) and *Renewal of Life* (1934, 1938, 1944, 1951).

mummy Human body embalmed and usually wrapped in bandages before burial. The practice was common in ancient Egypt, where religion decreed that the dead would require the use of their bodies in the afterlife. Certain other peoples, including the Incas of South America, had similar practices. *See also* EMBALMING

mumps Viral disease, most common in children, characterized by fever, pain and swelling of one or both parotid salivary glands (located just in front of the ears). The symptoms are more serious in adults, and in men inflammation of the testes (orchitis) may occur, with the risk of sterility. Children over 18 months of age can be vaccinated against the disease. One attack of mumps generally confers lifelong immunity.

Munch, Edvard (1863–1944) Norwegian painter and printmaker. He was one of the most influential of modern artists, inspiring EXPRESSIONISM. His tortured, isolated figures and violent colouring caused a scandal when first exhibited in Berlin in 1892, but his paintings inspired progressive artists to form the SEZESSION. Munch compiled a series of studies of love and death entitled a *Frieze of Life*, which included *The Scream* (1893). Other important works are *Ashes* (1894) and *Virginia Creeper* (1898).

Munich (München) City on the River Isar, S Germany; capital of BAVARIA. Founded in 1158, the city became the residence of the dukes of Bavaria in 1255. Occupied by the Swedes in 1632 and the French in 1800, Munich developed rapidly in the 19th century, when its population grew to more than 100,000. From the early 1920s, Munich was the centre of the Nazi Party. It sustained heavy bombing damage in World War 2. Industries: chemicals, brewing, pharmaceuticals, motor vehicles, food-processing, tobacco, precision instruments, tourism. Pop. (1995) 1,245,000.

Munich Agreement (September 1938) Pact agreed by Britain, France, Italy and Germany to settle German claims on Czechoslovakia. Hoping to preserve European peace, Britain and France compelled Czechoslovakia, not represented at Munich, to surrender the predominantly German-speaking SUDETENLAND to Nazi Germany on certain conditions. HITLER ignored the conditions and six months later his troops took over the rest of the country, an action that finally ended the Anglo-French policy of APPEASEMENT.

Munich Putsch (Beer hall Putsch) Attempted coup in 1923 by Adolf HITLER and the Nazi Party to overthrow the republican government of Bavaria, which began in a beer hall. The coup proved abortive, and Hitler was arrested and sentenced to five years in the Landsberg fortress, of which he served only nine months.

Munro, H.H. (Hector Hugh) *See* SAKI

Munster Province in S Republic of Ireland, on the Atlantic coast; largest of Ireland's four provinces. It includes the counties of CLARE, CORK, KERRY, LIMERICK, N and S TIPPERARY and WATERFORD. Area: 24,126sq km (9,315sq mi). Pop. (1991) 1,009,533.

muntjac Small primitive Asian DEER. It is brown with cream markings and has tusklike canine teeth and short, two-pronged antlers. There are two well-known species, the Indian muntjac or barking deer (*Muntiacus muntjak*) and the Chinese muntjac (*M. reevesi*). Height: to 60cm (24in) at the shoulder; weight: to 18kg (40lb). Family Cervidae.

muon (symbol μ^-) Negatively charged ELEMENTARY PARTICLE, originally thought to be a MESON but now classified as a LEPTON. It has SPIN $1/2$, a mass $c.207$ times that of the ELECTRON, and decays weakly into an electron, a NEUTRINO and an antineutrino. *See also* ANTIMATTER

mural Painting or other design medium applied directly to a wall; a FRESCO is a type of mural. The Egyptians,

Greeks and Romans produced murals in TEMPERA as well as fresco. In the Renaissance, mural painting was allied with architecture in efforts to create illusions of space. The 20th century has accorded more significance to the exterior mural as exemplified by the works of the Mexicans José Clemente OROZCO and Diego RIVERA. Porcelain and liquid silicate enamels are among the media used in modern murals.

Murasaki, Shikibu (978–1014) Japanese diarist and novelist. She is best known for her novel, *The Tale of Genji* (c.1000). It is one of the first works of fiction written in Japanese.

Murat, Joachim (1767–1815) French general, king of Naples (1808–15). He helped bring Napoleon to power in the coup of 1799 and married Napoleon's sister in 1800. In 1808, he was chosen to succeed Joseph Napoleon as king of Naples. A brilliant cavalry commander, Murat played an important part in NAPOLEON I's victories but in 1813 came to an agreement with the Austrians to protect his own throne. When the Austrians turned against him, he was defeated (1815) and, after an attempt to regain Naples failed, he was captured and shot.

Murcia Autonomous region in SE Spain; the capital is Murcia. It was settled in c.225 BC by the Carthaginians, who founded the port of Cartagena and the city of Murcia. The Moors captured the region in the 8th century. In the 11th century Murcia became an independent kingdom, but in the 13th century it fell under the control of Castile. Murcia is an arid, rugged province with desert vegetation. Historically, the region has been associated with the production of silk, concentrated around the city of Murcia. Area: 11,317sq km (4,368sq mi). Pop. (1991) 1,045,601.

Murdoch, Dame (Jean) Iris (1919–99) British novelist and moral philosopher, b. Ireland. She created her own genre, the philosophical love story. Murdoch's early novels, culminating in *The Bell* (1958), are short and concise. Her later novels, such as *The Black Prince* (1973), the Booker Prize-winning *The Sea, the Sea* (1978), *The Good Apprentice* (1985) and *The Book and the Brotherhood* (1987), are longer and more elaborate. Recurrent themes include the difference between sacred and profane love, and the nature of chance.

Murdoch, (Keith) Rupert (1931–) US media tycoon, b. Australia. In 1952, he assumed control of his late father's newspaper, *The Adelaide News*. Murdoch transferred his successful recipe of sensationalist journalism to British tabloid newspapers, acquiring *News of the World* (1969) and *The Sun* (1970). In 1973, he moved into the US newspaper market, acquiring the *Boston Herald* and *The Star*. In Britain, Murdoch bought *The Times* and the *Sunday Times*. In 1985, Murdoch became a US citizen. He began to diversify into other media industries, acquiring 50% of 20th Century Fox. In 1989, Murdoch launched his own satellite television network, Sky Television. He was also involved in the development of digital television.

Murillo, Bartolomé Esteban (1617–82) Spanish painter. He made his name with a series of 11 pictures showing the lives of the Franciscan saints (1645–46). His mature style is characterized by soft, idealized figures such as *Two Peasant Boys* (c.1665–75)

Murmansk City on the Kola Peninsula, NW Russia; capital of Murmansk oblast. Ice-free throughout the year, it was founded (1916) as a supply port. In 1918, Murmansk was occupied by US, British and French forces. During World War 2 it was a major port for Anglo-American convoys. Murmansk is the largest city N of the Arctic Circle and has a polar research station. Exports: fish, timber, apatite. Industries: fishing, shipbuilding, fish-canning, metal- and wood-working. Pop. (1994) 444,000.

Murphy, Eddie (1961–) US comedy film actor. His reputation established by the television series *Saturday Night Live*, he made his film debut in *48 HRS* (1982). Murphy rapidly became one of Hollywood's highest earners, following blockbusters such as *Trading Places* (1983) and *Coming to America* (1988).

Murray, (George) Gilbert Aimé (1866–1975) British classical scholar, b. Australia. He is best-known for his popular translations of Euripedes' plays *Medea*, *Bacchae* and *Electra*. Murray was also president (1923–38) of the League of Nations.

Murray Longest river in Australia. It flows 2,590km (1,610mi) from the Australian Alps in SE New South Wales through Lake Alexandrina and empties into the Indian Ocean at Encounter Bay, SE of Adelaide. It forms a large part of the border between New South Wales and Victoria. Its main tributary is the Darling. The Murray valley contains almost all the irrigated land in Australia.

Murrow, Ed (Edward Roscoe) (1908–65) US journalist. In 1935, he joined the Columbia Broadcasting System (CBS) and during World War 2 gained fame for his vivid descriptions of the Battle of Britain.

Muscat (Masqat, Maskat) Capital of Oman, on the Gulf of Oman, in the SE Arabian Peninsula. Muscat was held by the Portuguese from 1508–1650, when it passed to Persia. After 1741, it became capital of Oman. In the 20th century, its rulers developed treaty relations with Britain. Industries: fish and dates, natural gas, chemicals. Pop. (1992) 350,000.

muscle Tissue that has the ability to contract, enabling movement. There are three basic types: VOLUNTARY MUSCLE (or skeletal muscle), INVOLUNTARY MUSCLE (or smooth muscle) and cardiac muscle. **Voluntary** muscle is the largest tissue component of the human body, comprising *c*.40% by weight. It is attached by TENDONS to the BONES of the SKELETON and is characterized by cross-markings known as striations; it typically contains many nuclei per cell. Most voluntary muscles require conscious effort for contraction. A muscle whose contraction causes a limb or a part of the body to straighten (extend) is called an extensor. A muscle whose contraction causes a limb or part of the body to bend is called a flexor. **Involuntary** muscle lines the digestive tract, blood vessels and many other organs. It is not striated and typically has only one nucleus per cell; it is not under conscious control. **Cardiac** muscle is found only in the HEART and differs from the other types of muscle in that it beats rhythmically and does not need stimulation by a nerve impulse to contract. Cardiac muscle has some striations (but not as many as in voluntary muscle) and has only one nucleus per cell.

muscovite *See* MICA

muscular dystrophy Any of a group of hereditary disorders in which the characteristic feature is progressive weakening and ATROPHY of the muscles. The commonest type, **Duchenne muscular dystrophy**, affects boys, usually before the age of four. Muscle fibres degenerate, to be replaced by fatty tissue.

muses In Classical mythology, nine daughters of the Titan Mnemosyne (memory) and ZEUS. Calliope was the muse of epic poetry, Clio of history, Erato of love poetry, Euterpe of lyric poetry, Polyhymnia of song, Melpomene of tragedy, Terpsichore of choral dance, Thalia of comedy and Urania of astronomy.

Museveni, Yoweri Kaguta (1944–) Ugandan statesman, president (1986–). He worked for the government of Milton OBOTE, but was forced into exile when Idi

AMIN overthrew Obote in 1971. Museveni organized a guerrilla force, the Front for National Salvation, that succeeded in toppling Amin's regime in 1979. He was defeated by Obote in the 1980 elections, widely held to be fraudulent, and formed the National Resistance Army which overthrew the military junta in 1985. Museveni was hailed as representative of a new generation of African leaders. While imposing one-party rule, he took stringent measures to combat corruption, restore peace and reconstruct Uganda's economy through free-market reforms. In 1996, Museveni won Uganda's first presidential elections since 1980. As part of his aim to achieve regional integration, Museveni supported Laurent Kabila's successful revolt (1997) against MOBUTU SESE SEKO in neighbouring Zaïre and aided Tutsi rebels against the Hutu-minority regime in Rwanda.

mushroom Any of numerous relatively large, fleshy fungi, many of which are gathered for food. A typical mushroom consists of two parts: an extensive underground cobwebby network of fine filaments (hyphae), called the mycelium, which is the main body of the fungus, and a short-lived fruiting body (the visible mushroom). *See also* FUNGUS

music Sound arranged for instruments or voices for many purposes, exhibiting a great variety of forms and styles. It can be split into categories, including ROCK, JAZZ, BLUES, FOLK MUSIC, SOUL MUSIC, RAP, HOUSE MUSIC and COUNTRY AND WESTERN. Within classical music, there are distinct historical periods – MEDIEVAL MUSIC (1100–1400), RENAISSANCE MUSIC (1400–1600), BAROQUE (1600–1750), CLASSICAL MUSIC (1750–*c*.1800) and Romantic (*c*.1800–1900) (*see* ROMANTICISM). In the 20th century, various techniques developed, notably SERIAL MUSIC, TWELVE-TONE MUSIC and IMPRESSIONISM. Composers also experimented with ELECTRONIC MUSIC.

musical Genre of popular dramatic light entertainment exemplified by firm plot, strong songs and vivacious dance numbers. It developed at the end of the 19th century from elements of light OPERA, REVUE and BURLESQUE. The most popular musicals originated in the USA with the work of George GERSHWIN, Jerome KERN, Richard RODGERS, Oscar HAMMERSTEIN and Stephen SONDHEIM. Audiences in the 1970s responded to the works of Tim Rice and Andrew LLOYD WEBBER, including *Jesus Christ Superstar* (1971) and *Evita* (1978). Lloyd Webber's success continued with *Cats* (1981) and *The Phantom of the Opera* (1986). Successful film musicals, such as *West Side Story* (1961), *My Fair Lady* (1964) and *The Sound of Music* (1965), are generally based on stage originals. Original film musicals include *Forty-Second Street* (1933), *Meet Me in St Louis* (1944), *Singin' in the Rain* (1952) and *Gigi* (1958).

musical form Structural scheme that gives shape and artistic unity to a composition. The standard forms are binary, ternary, rondo and SONATA. Each consists of a number of musical sections or subsections. **Binary** form consists of two sections, which may be contrasted in idea, key or tempo, but which complement each other within the musical entity. **Ternary** form consists of a restatement of the first section after a middle section of contrasted material; examples are the MINUET and trio. In **rondo** form, the number of sections varies, but there is at least one restatement of the first section. **Sonata** form, as its name suggests, evolved with the sonata and is used most often for the first movement of a sonata or SYMPHONY. The exposition states (usually) two subjects, which are developed musically in the middle section, before being stated in the recapitulation.

musical notation Method of writing down music – the language of music. Staff notation defines the absolute and relative pitches of NOTES; half notes, quarter notes and so on indicate their time values.

music hall Stage for popular variety shows, originally tavern annexes, devoted to comic song, acrobatics, magic shows, juggling and dancing. The popularity of the music hall was at its height in late Victorian and Edwardian England but declined with the advent of radio and motion pictures in the 1930s. In the USA, it was known as VAUDEVILLE.

musicology Academic study of music. The term embraces various disciplines, including the study of music history, the analysis of compositions, acoustics and ethnomusicology. The study of music history began in the 18th century. Musicological research in the 20th century is responsible for the increased interest in, and performance of, early music.

Musil, Robert (1880–1942) Austrian novelist. His masterpiece is the epic novel *The Man Without Qualities* (1930–43), on the closing years of the Habsburg Empire.

musk deer Small, timid DEER of the central and NE Asian highlands. Both sexes have long, thick, bristly brown hair. The male has tusks instead of antlers and secretes musk, used in perfumes and soap. Height: to 61cm (24in) at the shoulder; weight: to 11kg (24lb). Family Cervidae; species *Moschus moschiferus*.

muskellunge Freshwater fish found in the Great Lakes, North America. A type of PIKE, it has a shovel-like bill, sharp teeth and elongated body. It eats fish, amphibians, birds and small mammals. Length: to 167.6cm (5.5ft); weight: 50kg (110lb). Family Esocidae; species *Esox masquinongy*.

musk ox Large, wild, shaggy RUMINANT, related to oxen and GOATS, native to N Canada and Greenland. Its brown fur reaches almost to the ground, and its down-pointing, recurved horns form a helmet over the forehead. When threatened, the herd forms a defensive circle round the calves. Length: to 2.3m (7.5ft); weight: to 410kg (903lb). Family Bovidae; species *Ovibos moschatus*. *See also* OX

muskrat Large aquatic RODENT (a type of VOLE) native to North America. It is a good swimmer, with partly webbed hind feet and a long, scaly tail. Its commercially valuable fur (musquash) is glossy brown and durable. Length, including tail: to 53.5cm (21in); weight: to 1.8kg (4lb). Family Cricetidae; species *Ondatra obscura* and *O. zibethica*.

Muslim (Arabic, one who submits) Follower or believer in ISLAM. A Muslim is one who worships ALLAH

▲ **muskrat** The scent of the muskrat (*Ondatra zebithicus*), from which it gets its name, comes from special glands. The animal was originally a native of North America but it has been introduced into other parts of the world and bred for its fur.

alone and holds MUHAMMAD to be the only true prophet. Today, there are *c*.935 million Muslims worldwide.

Muslim League Political organization (founded 1906) to protect the rights of Muslims in British India. The League cooperated with the predominantly Hindu CONGRESS PARTY until the 1930s when, fearing Hindu domination, it turned to independent action under the leadership of Muhammed Ali JINNAH. Although pro-British, in 1940 it called for a separate Muslim state, which was achieved when the country was partitioned at independence (1947). At first, the League dominated politics in PAKISTAN but subsequently split into rival factions.

mussel Any of several species of bivalve MOLLUSCS with thin oval shells. Marine species of the family Mytilidae are found worldwide in dense colonies on sea walls and rocky shores where they attach themselves by means of strands called byssus threads. The edible mussel, *Mytilus edulis*, is sometimes cultivated on ropes hanging from rafts. Freshwater mussels of the family Unionidae, found in northern continents only, produce PEARLS.

Musset, Alfred de (1810–57) French poet and playwright. Musset is best remembered for his poems which, after 1834, appeared in the periodical *Revue des Deux Mondes*. His four lyrics *Les Nuits* (1835–37) are the most famous of his poems. Musset's novel *Les Confession d'un enfant du siècle* (1835) is based on his love affair with George SAND.

Mussolini, Benito (1883–1945) Italian fascist dictator, prime minister (1922–43). Mussolini turned to revolutionary nationalism in World War 1, and in 1919 founded the Italian fascist movement. In 1922, the fascists' march on Rome secured his appointment as prime minister. Mussolini imposed one-party government with himself as *Il Duce* (lit. the leader), or dictator. His movement was a model for Adolf HITLER's Nazi Party, with whom Mussolini formed an alliance in 1936. Imperial ambitions led to the conquest of Ethiopia (1935–36), and the invasion of Albania (1939). Mussolini delayed entering World War 2 until a German victory seemed probable in 1940. A succession of defeats led to his fall from power. He was briefly restored as head of a puppet government in N Italy by the Germans, but in April 1945, fleeing Allied forces, he was captured and killed by Italian partisans. *See also* FASCISM

Mussorgsky, Modest Petrovich (1839–81) Russian composer, one of the "Russian Five" who promoted nationalism in Russian music. His finest work is the opera *Boris Godunov* (1868–69). Other important works include the piano work *Pictures at an Exhibition* (1874, later orchestrated by several composers) and *A Night on the Bare Mountain* (1867). After his death much of his work was edited and revised, mostly by Nikolai RIMSKY-KORSAKOV.

Mustafa Kemal *See* ATATÜRK, KEMAL

mustang Feral HORSE of the Great Plains of the USA, descended from horses that were imported from Spain. The mustang has short ears, a low-set tail and round leg bones. During the 17th century there were 2–4 million mustangs. Today, only *c*.20,000 survive in the SW USA.

mustard Any of various species of annual and perennial plants native to the temperate zone. These plants have pungent-flavoured leaves, cross-shaped, four-petalled flowers, and carry pods. The seeds of some species are ground to produce the condiment mustard. Family Brassicaceae/Cruciferae.

mutation Sudden change in an inherited characteristic of an organism. This change occurs in the DNA of the GENES. Natural mutations during reproduction are rare, occur randomly and usually produce an organism unable to survive in its environment. Occasionally the change results in the organism being better adapted to its environment and, through NATURAL SELECTION, the altered gene may pass on to the next generation. Natural mutation is therefore one of the key means by which organisms evolve. The mutation rate can be increased by exposing genetic material to ionizing radiation, such as X-rays or UV light, or mutagenic chemicals. *See also* EVOLUTION

Muti, Riccardo (1941–) Italian conductor. In 1968, he made his debut with the Italian Radio Symphony Orchestra. In 1973, Muti became chief conductor of the Philharmonia Orchestra. He was principal conductor of the Philadelphia Orchestra (1981–92) and musical director of La Scala (1986–).

Mutter, Anne-Sophie (1963–) German violinist. In 1977, Mutter made her concerto debut with the Berlin Philharmonic, having come to the notice of Herbert von KARAJAN, with whom she later recorded all the major violin concertos.

mutual fund *See* UNIT TRUST

mutualism *See* SYMBIOSIS

Muybridge, Eadweard (1830–1904) US photographer, b. Britain. After emigrating to the USA in 1852, he became a pioneer of motion PHOTOGRAPHY. From 1878, Muybridge recorded the movements of animals and people by using a series of still cameras. In 1881, he invented the Zoopraxiscope, a forerunner of moving pictures, which projected animated pictures on a screen.

Myanmar Official name of BURMA since 1989

myasthenia gravis AUTOIMMUNE DISEASE in which there is weakness and abnormally rapid fatigue of the muscles. It is a disease of young people, twice as common in women. Generally affecting the facial muscles first, it may spread to include those of the neck, trunk and limbs. It runs a protracted course, and muscle wasting may be seen in the later stages. Treatment is with drugs and, in some cases, surgery to remove the THYMUS GLAND (thymectomy).

Mycenae Ancient city in Greece, 11km (7mi) N of modern Argos, which gave its name to the MYCENAEAN CIVILIZATION. Dating from the third millennium BC, Mycenae was at its cultural peak *c*.1580–1120 BC. It was destroyed in the 5th century BC. Later restored, by the 2nd century AD it was in ruins. The ruins of the city were discovered by Heinrich SCHLIEMANN in 1874–76.

Mycenaean art Greek art of the late BRONZE AGE. The name comes from the fortress-city of MYCENAE and refers to the work of the late Helladic period (*c*.1500–1100 BC). Its greatest achievements came in the fields of architecture, which included both grand fortifications and beehive tombs, and in pottery, precious metalwork and fresco.

Mycenaean civilization Ancient BRONZE AGE civilization (*c*.1580–1120 BC) centred around MYCENAE, S Greece. The Mycenaeans entered Greece from the N, bringing with them advanced techniques, particularly in architecture and metallurgy. By 1400 BC, having invaded Crete and incorporated much of MINOAN CIVILIZATION, the Mycenaeans became the dominant power in the Aegean, trading as far as Syria, Palestine and Egypt, and importing luxurious goods for their wealthy and cultured citadel palaces. It is uncertain as to why the Mycenaean civilization collapsed, but it was most likely due to invasion by the DORIANS.

mycology Science and study of FUNGUS

mycorrhiza (FUNGUS root) Association between certain fungi and the root cells of some VASCULAR PLANTS. The fungus may penetrate the root cells or form a mesh around them. Water and minerals enter the roots via these threads. Sometimes the fungus digests organic material for the plant. *See also* SYMBIOSIS

mynah (myna or mina) Any of several species of tropical birds of SE Asia, S Africa, Australasia and the Pacific Islands; it is related to the STARLING. A natural mimic, especially the species *Gracula religiosa*, it imitates other birds. It feeds mainly on fruit. Length: to 33 cm (13in). Family Sturnidae.

myopia (short-sightedness) Common disorder of vision in which near objects are seen sharply, but distant objects are hazy. It is caused either by the eyeball being too long or the eye's lens being too powerful, so that light rays entering the eye focus in front of the retina.It is easily corrected with concave lenses in spectacles or contact lenses.

myrrh Aromatic, resinous, oily gum obtained from thorny, flowering trees, such as *Commiphora myrrha*. Known and prized since ancient times, myrrh has commonly been used as an ingredient in incense, perfumes and medicines. Family Burseraceae.

myrtle Any of numerous species of evergreen shrubs and trees that grow in tropical and sub-tropical regions, especially the aromatic shrub, *Myrtus communis*, of the Mediterranean region. Its leaves are simple and glossy; the purple-black berries that follow the white flowers were once dried and used like pepper. Family Myrtaceae.

Mysore City in Karnataka, S India. The city served as the capital of the Mysore kingdom from 1799 until 1956. It is the seat of Mysore University (1916), and has several palaces. Industries: textiles, chemicals, leather goods, cigarettes, sandalwood oil. Pop. (1991) 652,250.

mystery play (miracle play) Medieval English drama based on a religious theme. Mystery plays were originally used by the clergy to teach their illiterate congregation the principal stories of the Bible. By the 14th century, they had become a popular entertainment. Each year, the plays were performed by the various craft guilds in a town. The mystery plays from four towns have survived: Chester, York, Wakefield and Coventry.

mysticism Belief in, or experience of, a perception of reality that is elevated above normal human understanding. It may involve some form of spiritual search for unity of self with God or the universe. It is found in most major religions, and mystics may experience trances, dreams or visions. In India, mysticism has long been important in HINDUISM and is based on YOGA. Mysticism in JUDAISM is apparent in HASIDISM and the CABBALA. Mystics in the Far East have mostly been followers of TAOISM or BUDDHISM.

mythology Literally, telling of stories, but usually collectively defined as the myths of a particular culture. A myth occurs in a timeless past, contains supernatural elements and seeks to dramatize or explain such issues as the creation of the world (CREATION MYTH) and human beings, the institutions of political power, the cycle of seasons, birth, death and fate. Most mythologies have an established pantheon, or hierarchy, of gods who are more or less anthropomorphic. *See also* AFRICAN MYTHOLOGY; CELTIC MYTHOLOGY; CENTRAL AND SOUTH AMERICAN MYTHOLOGY; CHINESE MYTHOLOGY; EGYPTIAN MYTHOLOGY; GREEK MYTHOLOGY; NORTH AMERICAN MYTHOLOGY; OCEANIC MYTHOLOGY; PERSIAN MYTHOLOGY, ANCIENT; TEUTONIC MYTHOLOGY

myxoedema Disease caused by deficient function of the THYROID GLAND, resulting in fatigue, constipation, dry skin, a tendency toward weight gain and, in the later stages, mental dullness. It mostly affects middle-aged women. Treatment involves administration of the thyroid hormone, thyroxine.

N/n, the 14th letter of the alphabet, is derived from the Semitic letter nun, *which was the pictorial representation of a fish. It was adopted by the Greeks as the letter* nu *and subsequently by the Romans.*

Nabokov, Vladimir (1899–1977) US novelist, b. Russia. In 1919, he left Russia and settled in Germany. Nabokov's debut novel was *Mary* (1926). The rise of fascism forced him to flee first to France then the USA (1940). His first novel in English was *The Real Life of Sebastian Knight* (1938). Nabokov composed some of the greatest imaginative novels of the 20th century. *Bend Sinister* (1947) is a political novel on authoritarianism. His best-selling work, *Lolita* (1955), is a controversial, lyrical novel about an old man's desire for a 12-year old "nymphette". Other works include *Pnin* (1957), *Pale Fire* (1962) and *Ada* (1969).

Nader, Ralph (1934–) US consumer affairs activist and lobbyist. His book *Unsafe at any Speed* (1965) called for improved automobile design. He subsequently examined issues concerned with mining, nuclear power, meat processing and airlines. Nader unsuccessfully ran for US president as a Green Party candidate in 2000.

nadir Point on the CELESTIAL SPHERE vertically below the observer. It is diametrically opposite the ZENITH.

Nadir Shah (1688–1747) Shah of Persia (1736–47). He overthrew the Safavid dynasty and embarked upon a series of wars against neighbouring states. He invaded India, sacking Delhi, and conducted campaigns against Russia and Turkey. His ceaseless warring ruined Persia's economy, and his cruelty aroused hostility from his subjects. He was assassinated by his own soldiers.

naevus (birthmark, mole) Discoloured patch on the skin that has been present since birth.

Nagaland State in NE India; the capital is Kohima. Briefly ruled by Burma in the early 19th century, it gradually came under British control then became a separate state in 1963. The Nagas live in a tribal society with a strong separatist movement. Crops: rice, potatoes, sugar cane. Area: 16,579sq km (6,399sq mi). Pop. (1991) 439,000.

Nagasaki Port on w Kyushu island, sw Japan. In the 16th century it was the first Japanese port to receive Western ships and became a centre of Christian influence. During Japanese isolation (1639–1859) it was the only port open to foreign trade. On 9 August 1945, the inner city was destroyed by a US atomic bomb, and more than 70,000 people were killed. Sites include the Chinese Temple (1629) and Peace Park. Industries: shipbuilding and heavy engineering. Pop. (1995) 439,000.

Nagorno-Karabakh Autonomous region of Azerbaijan, between the Caucasus and Karabakh mountains. The capital is Stepanakert. During the 19th century, the region was absorbed into the Russian empire. In 1921, it was annexed to the Azerbaijan republic. In 1991, the region declared its independence, and Azerbaijan responded by imposing direct rule. The ensuing civil war claimed thousands of lives. In 1993, Armenian troops occupied the enclave, and a peace agreement was reached in 1994. The main activities are farming and silk production. Area: 4,400sq km (1,700sq mi). Pop. (1990) 192,400

Nagoya City and port on the Pacific coast, Honshu island, central Japan. Nagoya developed around its 17th-

century castle. Industries: iron and steel, textiles, motor vehicles, aircraft. Pop. (1995) 2,152,000.

Nagpur City in Maharashtra, w central India. Founded in the 18th century as the capital of the kingdom of Nagpur, it became the capital of Berar state (from 1903) and of Madhya Pradesh state (1947–56). Industries: metal goods, transport equipment, cigarettes, textiles, pottery, glass, leather, brassware. Pop. (1991) 1,624,572.

Nagy, Imre (1896–1958) Hungarian statesman, premier (1953–55, 1956). He enacted liberal reforms of the Hungarian economy and society. Under pressure from the Soviet Union, Nagy was dismissed from the Hungarian Communist Party. The Hungarian Revolution (1956) led to his reinstatement as premier. Soviet tanks crushed the uprising and handed power to János KÁDÁR. Nagy was tried and executed for treason.

Nahuatl Native American language of the UTO-AZTECAN linguistic family of the s US and Central America. Today, it is spoken by c.1 million people, mostly in Mexico.

nail In anatomy, tough KERATIN outgrowth from the fingers and toes of primates.

naiad In Greek mythology, female figure or NYMPH, identified with streams, rivers and lakes.

Naipaul, V.S. (Vidiadhar Surajprasad) (1932–) West Indian novelist and short-story writer. He was educated in his native Trinidad and at Oxford, but later settled in London. His novels include *A House for Mr Biswas* (1961), the Booker Prize-winning *In a Free State* (1971) and *A Bend in the River* (1979). His travelogues include *Among the Believers: An Islamic Journey* (1981) and *A Turn in the South* (1989).

Nairobi Capital and largest city of Kenya, in the s central part of the country. Founded in 1899, Nairobi replaced MOMBASA as the capital of the British East Africa Protectorate in 1905. Nairobi has a national park (1946), a university (1970), and several institutions of higher education. It is an administrative and commercial centre. Industries: cigarettes, textiles, chemicals, food processing, furniture, glass. Pop. (1991) 2,000,000.

Nakhichevan Autonomous republic of Azerbaijan, bounded N and E by Armenia, s and w by Iran, and w by Turkey; the capital is Nakhichevan. It became part of Russia in 1828, an autonomous republic within the Soviet Union in 1924 and, in 1991, became part of the independent republic of Azerbaijan but was subsequently disputed between Armenia and Azerbaijan. Crops: grains, cotton, tobacco, fruit, grapes. Industries include mining, silk textiles and food processing. Area: 5,500sq km (2,120sq mi). Pop. (1994) 315,000.

Namib Desert Coastal desert region of Namibia, between the Atlantic Ocean and the interior plateau. It has less than 1cm (0.4in) of rain a year and is almost completely barren. Diamonds are mined. Length: *c*.1,900km (1,200mi).

Namibia (formerly South West Africa) Republic in sw Africa. Namibia can be divided into four geographical regions. The arid NAMIB DESERT runs along the entire Atlantic coast. Inland, a central plateau, mostly between 900 and 2,000m (2,950–6,560ft), includes the capital, WINDHOEK. The highest point is Brandberg Mountain, at 2,606m (8,550ft). In the N lies an alluvial plain, which

---

NAMIBIA

AREA: 825,414sq km (318,694sq mi)
POPULATION: 2,437,000
CAPITAL (POPULATION): Windhoek (190,000)

includes the marshlands of the Caprivi Strip. To the E is the W fringe of the KALAHARI. The River ORANGE forms Namibia's S border. Namibia is a warm, arid country. Windhoek has an average annual rainfall of 370mm (15in). The N is the wettest part of Namibia, with *c.*500mm (20in) of annual rain. Grassland and shrub cover much of the interior. The Etosha National Park is a magnificent wildlife reserve. **History and politics** The nomadic SAN inhabited the region *c.*2,000 years ago. They were gradually displaced by Bantu-speakers, such as the Ovambo, Kavango and Herero. Portuguese navigators arrived in the early 15th century. Colonization began in earnest in the 19th century. In 1884, Germany claimed the region as a protectorate and subsumed it into the territory of South West Africa. Local rebellions were brutally suppressed. In 1908, the discovery of diamonds increased European settlement. During World War 1, it was occupied (1915) by South African troops. In 1920, South Africa was granted a mandate. After World War 2, South Africa refused to relinquish control. In 1966, the SOUTH WEST AFRICA PEOPLE'S ORGANIZATION (SWAPO) began a guerrilla war against South Africa. In 1968, the UN called on South Africa to withdraw. In 1971, the International Court of Justice declared that South African rule over Namibia was illegal. South Africa refused to comply and divided Namibia into bantustans (homelands). International pressure forced South Africa to promise Namibia independence. Civil war raged from 1977. In 1989, a UN Security Council peace settlement was finally implemented. In November 1989, SWAPO won multiparty elections. In March 1990, Namibia became an independent republic within the British Commonwealth. In 1990, Sam NUJOMA became president. In 1994, South Africa renounced its claim to Walvis Bay, and it was incorporated into Namibia. Nujoma was re-elected in 1994 and 1999. **Economy** Namibia is the world's seventh largest producer of diamonds and ninth largest producer of uranium (1995 GDP per capita, US$4,150). Minerals make up 90% of exports. Farming employs *c.*40% of the workforce. The main activity is cattle and sheep farming. The chief food products are maize, millet and vegetables. Atlantic fishing is also important.

Nanak (1469–1539) Indian spiritual teacher, founder and first guru of SIKHISM. Nanak preached a monotheistic religion that combined elements from both HINDUISM and ISLAM. In 1519, he built the first Sikh temple in Kartarpur, Punjab. His teachings are contained in a number of hymns in the ADI GRANTH.

Nanchang (Nan-ch'ang-hsien) City in SE China; capital of Jiangxi province. It was founded as a walled city in the 3rd century BC. A failed communist coup here in 1927 is commemorated on Army Day (1 August). Industries: rice, tea, cotton textiles, machinery. Pop. (1994) 1,169,000.

Nancy City on the River Meurthe, NE France; capital of Meurthe-et-Moselle department. It is the economic, administrative and cultural centre of LORRAINE. Nancy developed around the castle of the dukes of Lorraine and became capital of the duchy in the 12th century. The city passed to the French crown in 1766. The centre of Nancy is a world heritage site, containing elegant 18th century BAROQUE architecture built in the reign (1738–66) of Stanislaus I. Industries are based around the Lorraine iron fields. Pop. (1968) 123,428.

Nanjing (formerly Nanking) City on the River Yangtze, E China; capital of Jiangsu province. Founded in the 8th century BC, it served as the capital of China at various times. The Treaty of Nanking (1842) ended the OPIUM WAR with Britain and opened five Chinese ports to foreign trade. It was the seat of SUN YAT-SEN's presidency in 1912. In 1937, during the SINO-JAPANESE WAR, Nanking was captured by the Japanese, who massacred more than 100,000 of the population. Notable sites include the city wall and tombs of Ming emperors. Industries: iron and steel, oil refining, chemicals. Pop. (1994) 2,211,000.

nanometre (symbol nm) Unit of distance, equal to 10^{-9} metre. It is used in the measurement of intermolecular distances and wavelengths. It has superseded the ANGSTROM as the accepted unit for such measurements.

nanotechnology Micromechanics used to develop working devices the size of a few NANOMETRES. US scientists have etched an electric motor from silicon that is smaller than 0.1 mm wide and have made workable gears with a diameter less than a human hair.

Nansen, Fridtjof (1861–1930) Norwegian explorer and statesman. In 1888, he crossed the Greenland icecap on foot. In 1893, he set sail aboard the *Fram*, a ship he designed to withstand being frozen in ice so that currents would carry her to the North Pole. In 1895, Nansen and a companion left the *Fram* and set out for the Pole on foot, reaching 84° 4', the highest latitude then attained. He served (1906–08) as Norwegian ambassador in London. In 1922, he was awarded the Nobel Peace Prize for his humanitarian work for victims of the Russian famine.

Nantes City at the mouth of the River Loire, W France; capital of Loire–Atlantique department. France's seventh-largest city has been an important trading centre since Roman times. In the 10th century, it was captured from Norse invaders by the duke of Brittany. Nantes remained a residence of the dukes until 1524, and their tombs lie in the city's 15th-century Gothic cathedral. By the 18th century, Nantes had become France's largest port. During World War 2, it was a centre of the French resistance movement. Industries: shipbuilding, sugar refining, food products. Pop. (1990) 244,995.

Nantes, Edict of (1598) French decree, proclaimed by HENRY IV, establishing toleration for HUGUENOTS. It granted freedom of worship and legal equality for Huguenots and ended the Wars of RELIGION. In 1685 the Edict was revoked by LOUIS XIV, causing many Huguenots to emigrate.

Nantucket Island in SE Massachusetts, USA, 40km (25mi) S of Cape Cod in the Atlantic Ocean. Formerly a major whaling port, it is now a tourist and artist centre.

napalm (**na**phthalene **palm**itate) Gelatinous PETROLEUM used to make bombs and as fuel for flame-throwers. It was developed during World War 2 and widely used by US forces in Vietnam. When napalm hits its target, it spreads out, clinging to and burning everything it touches.

naphtha Any of several volatile liquid-hydrocarbon mixtures. In the 1st century AD, "naphtha" was mentioned by Pliny the Elder. Alchemists used the word for various liquids of low boiling point. Several types of products are now called naphtha, including coal-tar naphtha and petroleum naphtha.

naphthalene ($C_{10}H_8$) Important hydrocarbon composed of two benzene rings sharing two adjacent carbon atoms. A white, waxy solid, naphthalene is soluble in ether and hot alcohol and is highly volatile. It is used in mothballs, dyes and synthetic resins. It occurs in coal tar. Properties: m.p. 80°C (176°F); b.p. 218°C (424°F).

Napier, John (1550–1617) Scottish mathematician. He developed "Napier's Bones", a calculating apparatus that he used to invent LOGARITHMS (1614) and the present form of decimal notation.

Naples (Napoli) City on the Bay of Naples, S central Italy; capital of the province of Campania. Founded *c.*600 BC as a Greek colony, Naples was conquered by Rome in the 4th century BC. Successively ruled by the Byzantines, Normans, Spanish and Austrians, it became the capital of the Kingdom of the Two Sicilies in 1734, eventually joining the Kingdom of Italy in 1860. Notable buildings include the 13th-century Gothic cathedral, the Church of the Holy Apostles, the University (1224) and the Music Conservatory (1537). The city contains areas of great economic deprivation. Industries: textiles, leather, steel, shipbuilding, aircraft, telecommunications, tourism. Pop. (1996) 1,050,000.

Napoleon I (1769–1821) (Napoléon Bonaparte) Emperor of the French (1804–15), b. Corsica. One of the greatest military leaders of modern times, he became a brigadier (1793) after driving the British out of Toulon. In 1796, Napoleon married JOSÉPHINE de Beauharnais and was given command in Italy, where he defeated the Austrians and Sardinians (*see* FRENCH REVOLUTIONARY WARS). In 1798 he launched an invasion of Egypt, but was defeated by NELSON at the Battle of ABOUKIR Bay. In 1799, Napoleon returned to Paris, where his coup of 18 Brumaire (9 November) overthrew the DIRECTORY and set up the Consulate. As First Consul, he enacted domestic reforms such as the CODE NAPOLÉON, while defeating the Austrians at Marengo (1800) and making peace with the British at Amiens (1802). Efforts to extend French power led to the NAPOLEONIC WARS (1803–15). After the Battle of TRAFALGAR (1805), Britain controlled the seas, but Napoleon's Grand Army continued to score notable land victories at AUSTERLITZ (1805) and Jena (1806). The CONTINENTAL SYSTEM attempted to defeat Britain by a commercial blockade that led indirectly to the PENINSULAR WAR (1808–14). In 1810, after obtaining a divorce from Joséphine, Napoleon married MARIE LOUISE who bore him a son, the future NAPOLEON II. In 1812, Napoleon invaded Russia with a million-man army. Forced to retreat by hunger, more than 400,000 soldiers perished in the cold Russian winter. In 1813, Napoleon was routed by a new European coalition at Leipzig. In March 1814, Paris was captured and Napoleon was exiled to ELBA. In March 1815, he escaped and returned to France, overthrowing the BOURBON king LOUIS XVIII. The HUNDRED DAYS of his return to power ended with defeat at the Battle of WATERLOO (June 1815). Napoleon was exiled to St Helena, where he died.

Napoleon II (1811–1832) Son of NAPOLEON I and MARIE LOUISE. In 1814, he was taken by his mother to Austria, and in 1818 his grandfather, Francis I of Austria, conferred on him the title of duc de Reichstadt.

Napoleon III (1808–73) (Louis Napoleon) Emperor of the French (1852–70), nephew of NAPOLEON I. He twice attempted a coup in France (1836, 1840). Returning from exile after the FEBRUARY REVOLUTION (1848), Napoleon was elected president of the Second Republic. In 1851, he assumed autocratic powers and established the Second Empire (1852), taking the title Napoleon III. His attempt to establish a Mexican empire under the Archduke MAXIMILIAN ended in disaster, and in 1870 he was provoked by BISMARCK into the FRANCO-PRUSSIAN WAR. Defeat at Sedan was followed by a republican uprising that ended his reign.

Napoleonic Wars (1803–15) Campaigns by a series of European coalitions against French expansion under NAPOLEON I. In 1803, Britain declared war and formed the **Third Coalition** with Austria, Russia and Sweden in 1804. Napoleon defeated the Austrians at Ulm and the Russians and Austrians at AUSTERLITZ (both 1805), but the British under Admiral NELSON won a decisive naval victory at TRAFALGAR (1805). Prussia joined the **Fourth**

Coalition (1806) but was decisively defeated at Jena. Resistance to the French occupation of Portugal (1807) began the PENINSULAR WAR. In 1808, French troops were sent to quell a Spanish rebellion, but were faced by the British army led by the Duke of WELLINGTON. The **Fifth Coalition** collapsed with the defeat of Austria at Wagram (1809). In 1812, Napoleon invaded Russia. Bitter winter forced his retreat from Moscow, and much of his army died of starvation, hypothermia or were killed by the pursuing Russian forces under Mikhail KUTUZOV. Against the **Sixth Coalition**, Napoleon was defeated at Leipzig (October 1813). In March 1814, Allied forces entered Paris. While the Coalition was negotiating at the Congress of VIENNA, Napoleon escaped from exile in Elba and overthrew LOUIS XVIII. War was renewed during the HUNDRED DAYS of Napoleon's return to power and ended in his final defeat at the Battle of WATERLOO (June 1815).

Nara City on S Honshu island, Japan; capital of Nara prefecture. A centre of Japanese Buddhism, Nara was founded in 706. From 710 to 784, it acted as Japan's first imperial capital. Todaiji (East Great Temple) houses a 22m (72ft) tall bronze statue of Buddha. The 7th-century Horyuji temple is reputedly Japan's oldest building. The tomb of Jimmu, Japan's first emperor, is here. The main industry is textiles. Pop. (1993) 353,000.

Narayan, R.K. (Rasipuram Krishnaswamy) (1906–) Indian novelist and short-story writer. He won praise for his debut novel, *Swami and Friends* (1935), and has since become famous for his tragicomic representations of life in India, written in English and set in the fictional town of Malgudi. His work includes *Waiting for the Mahatma* (1955), *The Man-Eater of Malgudi* (1961), *A Horse and Two Goats* (1970) and *A Tiger for Malgudi* (1983). *Malgudi Days* (1982) is a collection of short stories, and his autobiography, *My Days*, was published in 1975. His later fiction includes *The World of Nagaraj* (1990) and *The Grandmother's Tale* (1993).

narcissism Exaggerated sense of self-importance and love of self. In PSYCHIATRY it is regarded as a personality disorder, characterized by overestimation of one's own appearance and abilities and difficulty in loving others. In PSYCHOANALYSIS it is thought to be a continuation of the infantile stage where the LIBIDO is self-directed.

Narcissus In Greek mythology, a beautiful youth who rejected the love of the nymph ECHO and was punished by being made to fall in love with his own reflection in a pond. He pined away and was turned into a flower. The NARCISSUS is named after him, as is the term NARCISSISM in psychology.

narcissus Genus of Old World, bulb-forming, garden flowers, including daffodils and jonquils. The long, pointed leaves surround yellow, orange or white trumpet-like flowers. Family Amaryllidaceae.

narcolepsy Rare disorder in which there is an irresistible tendency to fall asleep. It can happen anywhere at any time, especially if the person is engaged in monotonous activity. It is often associated with CATAPLEXY. There may also be hallucinations and sleep paralysis. It is controlled with drugs.

narcotic Any drug that induces sleep or relieves pain, especially OPIUM and its derivatives, such as HEROIN and MORPHINE. These drugs have largely been withdrawn as sedatives because of their addictive properties, but they are still used for severe pain, notably in terminal illness. Other narcotics include alcohols (such as ETHANOL) and BARBITURATES.

Narragansett Algonquian-speaking tribe of Native Americans who occupied part of Rhode Island. Once the most powerful New England group, they were almost entirely wiped out during KING PHILIP'S WAR (1675–76).

narwhal Small, toothed Arctic WHALE. The male has a twisted horn, half as long as its body, which develops from a tooth and protrudes horizontally through one side of the upper lip. Length: up to 5m (16ft). Species *Monodon monoceros*.

NASA Acronym for NATIONAL AERONAUTICS AND SPACE ADMINISTRATION

Naseby, Battle of (14 June 1645) Final battle of the first English CIVIL WAR. Royalist troops under Prince RUPERT were defeated by the Parliamentarians under Oliver CROMWELL and Thomas FAIRFAX.

Nash, John (1752–1835) English architect and town planner, an important figure in the REGENCY STYLE. Nash designed Regent's Park and Regent Street, London, enlarged Buckingham Palace, and rebuilt the Royal Pavilion, Brighton (1815–23).

Nash, Ogden (1902–71) US poet. Among his many volumes of humorous and satirical poetry are *Free Wheeling* (1931), *I'm a Stranger Here Myself* (1938) and *Everyone But Me and Thee* (1962). He also wrote the lyrics for the musical *One Touch of Venus* (1943).

Nash, Paul (1889–1946) English painter and graphic artist. Devoted to the English countryside, he was also closely in touch with European modernism. SURREALISM helped to stimulate the poetic, dream-like style of his landscapes, as in *The Menin Road* (1918) and *Landscape from a Dream* (1938).

Nash, Sir Walter (1882–1968) New Zealand statesman, prime minister (1957–60), b. England. In 1909, he emigrated to New Zealand and entered Parliament in 1929. As finance minister (1935–49), Nash helped to introduce the LABOUR PARTY'S wide-ranging social security reforms.

Nashe, Thomas (1567–1601) English pamphleteer, satirist and dramatist. In *Pierce Penniless* (1592) and subsequent pamphlets he mercilessly satirized leading Puritans. Thomas is mostly remembered for his picaresque proto-novel *The Unfortunate Traveller* (1594).

Nashville Capital of Tennessee, USA, a port on the Cumberland River. Settled in 1779, it became state capital in 1843. It is a country music centre with the home of the Country Music Hall of Fame and the Grand Old Opry. Nashville has many neo-classical buildings, two universities and a technical institute. Industries: music, publishing, machinery. Pop. (1990) 510,784.

Nasmyth, James (1808–90) Scottish inventor and engineer. He developed a foundry for making machine tools and steam-powered machines. In 1842, Nasmyth patented a steam hammer designed to forge the drive shafts originally intended for the SS *Great Britain*.

Nassau Capital of the Bahamas, West Indies, a port on the NE coast of New Providence Island. Founded in the 1660s by the British, during the 18th century it was a pirate stronghold. It is a commercial centre and popular winter tourist resort. Exports include sisal, citrus fruit and vegetables. Pop. (1992) 190,000.

Nasser, Gamal Abdel (1918–70) Egyptian soldier and statesman, prime minister (1954–56) and first president of the republic of Egypt (1956–70). In 1942, he founded the Society of Free Officers, which secretly campaigned against British imperialism and domestic corruption. Nasser led the 1952 army coup against King FAROUK. He quickly ousted the nominal prime minister General Muhammad Neguib and assumed presidential powers. In 1956, Nasser's nationalization of the SUEZ CANAL prompted an abortive Anglo-French and Israeli invasion.

He emerged as champion of the Arab world. Nasser formed the short-lived United Arab Republic (1958–61) with Syria. Nasser briefly resigned after Israel won the SIX-DAY WAR (1967). The crowning achievement of his brand of Arab socialism was the ASWAN DAM (1970).

nasturtium Annual trailing plant native to Central and South America. Cultivated as a garden ornamental, it has round leaves and spurred, trumpet-shaped flowers of yellow, salmon or scarlet. Among 80 species is the common nasturtium *Tropaeolum majus*. Family Tropaeolaceae.

Natal Former name (1910–94) of KWAZULU-NATAL

Natchez Tribe of Muskogean-speaking Native Americans of the southern Mississippi region. Today, only a handful of Natchez people survive in Oklahoma.

National Academy of Sciences US organization made up of elected members (based on original research in several fields of science). It was founded in 1863. The academy acts as an official adviser to the federal government on science and technology matters.

National Aeronautics and Space Administration (NASA) US government agency that organizes civilian aeronautical and space research programmes. NASA was established in 1958 and is the agency behind the many US successes in SPACE EXPLORATION, including the Lunar landings and the SPACE SHUTTLE. It has various departments located throughout the USA. The Lyndon B. Johnson Space Center in HOUSTON, Texas, is responsible for manned space flights. Space rockets, both manned and unmanned, are launched from the John F. Kennedy Space Center at CAPE CANAVERAL, Florida.

national anthem Music that, at an international or state ceremony, represents one specific country, usually in the form of a song or hymn. The oldest national anthem is that of Britain, "God Save The King/Queen" (1745). The French national anthem, "La Marseillaise", was composed as a marching song in 1792; the German "Deutschland, Deutschland über Alles" (1922) is sung to the music of HAYDN's *Emperor's Hymn* (1797). The US "Star-Spangled Banner" (1814) was not officially adopted until 1931. In 1977 the Australians rejected the British national anthem and, after a referendum, chose "Advance Australia Fair" as their national anthem.

National Association for the Advancement of Colored People (NAACP) US CIVIL RIGHTS organization. Founded in 1909, its objectives are "to achieve through peaceful and lawful means, equal citizenship rights for all American citizens by eliminating segregation and discrimination in housing, employment, voting, schools, the courts, transportation and recreation". Early leaders included W.E.B. DU BOIS. The NAACP set up the successful Legal Defense and Educational Fund to finance court battles over discriminatory practices. It also cooperates with other minority protection groups. Its publications include *Crisis*.

national curriculum Curriculum that is compulsory for all of a nation's schools. In the UK a national curriculum for state primary and secondary schools was introduced in 1989. Mathematics, English and science are core subjects to be studied by all pupils from 5 to 16.

National Front (NF) Extreme right-wing British political party founded in the 1960s. It has a racist doctrine advocating the repatriation of ethnic minorities irrespective of their place of birth and strongly opposing immigration. Although tainted by a neo-Nazi image, the National Front gained some support in the late 1970s, particularly in inner-city areas.

National Gallery Museum in London, which houses the largest collection of paintings in Britain. Established in 1824, it is located in Trafalgar Square. Adjoining it is the National Portrait Gallery.

National Health Service (NHS) In Britain, system of state provision of health care established in 1948. The NHS undertook to provide free, comprehensive coverage for most health services, including hospitals, general medical practice and public health facilities. It is administered by the Department of HEALTH. General practitioners (GPs) have registered patients; they may also have private patients and may contract out of the state scheme altogether. They refer patients, when necessary, to specialist consultants in hospitals. Health visitors, such as midwives and district nurses, are the third arm of the service. Hospitals are administered by regional boards, which include governors of teaching hospitals. In 1990, the Conservative government introduced the concept of the "Internal Market" into health care, establishing GP fund-holding practices and NHS Trusts independent of local health authority control. In 1997, the new Labour government announced that it would replace the internal market with primary care groups consisting of GPs and community nurses. The NHS is the largest single employer in the UK.

national insurance (NI) In Britain, state insurance scheme, founded by LLOYD GEORGE in 1911. In 1946, more comprehensive proposals by Lord BEVERIDGE formed the basis of the National Insurance Act. NI provides sickness, maternity, unemployment and child benefits as well as old-age pensions. It also contributes to the cost of the NATIONAL HEALTH SERVICE (NHS). The scheme is funded by compulsory contributions from employers and employees and is administered by the Department of SOCIAL SECURITY.

nationalism Ideology according to which all people owe a supreme loyalty to their nation and which holds that each nation should be embodied in a separate state. Nationalist sentiment, drawing upon and extolling a common culture, language and history, can be a powerful unifying force. With the possible exception of national independence movements against COLONIALISM and IMPERIALISM, nationalism is essentially conservative.

nationalization Policy of acquiring for public ownership enterprises that were formerly privately owned. Advocates of nationalization maintain that bringing essential industries under government control enhances social and economic equality. The communist states of E Europe nationalized large parts of their industry and agriculture following World War 2, and many other European states nationalized some of their major industries, such as coal, steel and transport. In the 1980s the trend was towards PRIVATIZATION. *See also* SOCIALISM

national parks Protected areas where restraint on the killing of wildlife is enforced, and forests, waters and other natural environments are preserved from commercial use. In Britain, national parks are not public property, and private land may be enclosed within the park boundaries. The first large reserve for preservation and recreation to be established was the YELLOWSTONE NATIONAL PARK, USA, in 1872. The main purpose of the famous African national parks is game preservation.

National Republican Party US political party, formed after the election of Andrew JACKSON as president (1828). Staunchly opposed to Jackson, the party supported the Bank of the United States, a protective tariff and internal improvements. Daniel Webster and Henry Clay were dedicated leaders of the party. By 1836 it had become the WHIGS.

national service *See* CONSCRIPTION

National Socialism (Nazism) Doctrine of the National Socialist German Workers' (Nazi) Party (1921–45). It was biologically racist (believing that the so-called Aryan race was superior to others), anti-Semitic, nationalistic, anti-communist, anti-democratic and anti-intellectual. It placed power before justice and the interests of the state before the individual. These beliefs were stated by the party's leader, Adolf HITLER, in his book *Mein Kampf* (1925). *See also* ANTI-SEMITISM; FASCISM

National Theatre Permanent theatre company usually subsidized by the state and housed in one venue, where national classics of drama are performed in repertory. The oldest national theatre is the COMÉDIE-FRANÇAISE in Paris, founded in 1680. The National Theatre of Great Britain, first advocated by GARRICK, only became a reality in the 1960s. Its first production, *Hamlet*, took place on 22 October 1963, at the OLD VIC theatre. In 1973, Sir Peter HALL succeeded Laurence OLIVIER as artistic director. In October 1976, new buildings designed by Sir Denys Lasdun were officially opened and comprise the Lyttleton Theatre, the Olivier Theatre and the Cottesloe Theatre. Following the departure of Richard Eyre, who succeeded Hall, Trevor NUNN became the artistic director (1996–).

National Trust British charitable organization formed in 1895 in order to permanently preserve lands and buildings of natural beauty or historic interest for the benefit of the public. In 1907 the trust was given the power to declare its land inalienable. Today, it protects *c.*420,000ha (590,000 acres) of countryside, 885km (550mi) of coastline, and owns 230 houses and gardens. The National Trust has *c.*2 million members.

Native Americans Indigenous peoples of the American continent. **North America** Native North Americans are believed to be descended from Asian peoples who crossed via the Bering Strait or the Aleutian Islands about 20,000 BC or earlier. These people spread throughout North, Central and South America and developed many distinct regional cultures with hundreds of different languages. Native North Americans may be divided into eight cultural and geographic groups: the Arctic area, the Northeastern-Mackenzie area, the Northwest Coast area, the Southwestern area, the Plains area, the California-Intermountain area, the Southwestern area and the Mesoamerican area. *See* separate articles for individual tribes. **South America** Native South Americans derived from North American groups who migrated S. Three main culture groups inhabiting distinct geographic areas are recognized: (1) Native Americans of the Andean area developed the highest cultures of the continent. After AD 1300, the QUECHUA culture dominated almost the entire region. (2) Native Americans of the Amazon Basin are mainly isolated, primitive, agricultural communities of many localized tribes. (3) Native Americans of the pampas successfully resisted INCA and Spaniard alike. In the southernmost portion of the continent, live the Tierra del Fuegans, who are now few in number.

Native Australians Indigenous peoples of Australia. Originally from SE Asia, Native Australians are thought to have colonized Australia 40,000–45,000 years ago. Before the arrival of Europeans (*c.*1788) they probably numbered more than 400,000, but many thousands died from European diseases when they were placed in reserves. All the 500 tribal groups led a nomadic life, hunting and gathering. They believe that the land is a religious phenomenon inhabited by spirits of their ancestors, which may take either human or animal form, and these beliefs are celebrated in legends, song, mime, carving and painting. In 1967, they were granted full Australian citizenship. In 1971, they were included in the census for the first time, when their numbers were c.140,000. The Aboriginal Land Rights Act (1976) and the Aboriginal and Torres Islander Heritage Protect Act (1984) have resulted today in a population of c.300,000.

Native North American art Traditional art produced by the indigenous peoples of North America. The INUIT of the Arctic area have been producing ivory carvings since prehistoric times and are also noted for their ceremonial masks (made from driftwood or whalebone). The NW region is best known for its TOTEM POLES, while in California, basket-weaving and pottery were specialties. Similar crafts were practised by the PUEBLO people of the SW, who also created remarkable prehistoric wall paintings. The painted decoration of animal hides was popular in the Great Plains, while in the Eastern Woodlands, there was a preference for copper ornaments and stone carvings.

Native North American languages Any of more than 100 languages spoken in N and Central America by descendants of the various indigenous peoples. The languages fall into many families. In the USA and Canada, they include ALGONQUIAN, ATHABASCAN and SIOUX. In the USA and Mexico, UTO-AZTECAN languages are most common, with NAHUATL the most widely spoken of these. Other language groups are Oto-Mangean in Mexico and MAYAN in Mexico and Guatemala.

Native South American languages Any of more than 1,000 languages spoken in South America by c.10–12 million people. Among the more important linguistic families are CHIBCHA, ARAWAK and GUARANÍ. Widely spoken languages are QUECHUA and Aymará, found in Peru and Bolivia.

nativity Birth of a New Testament figure as marked by a Christian feast. In general, the term refers to the birth of Jesus Christ, as described in the Gospels. These accounts relate that Jesus' birth in a stable in Bethlehem was attended by wonders – the sudden appearance of a bright star, angels rejoicing and the arrival of shepherds and the Magi to pay homage to the infant. Christians celebrate Jesus' Nativity at the festival of Christmas on 25 December. Other Nativity festivals are also held during the Church year.

NATO *See* NORTH ATLANTIC TREATY ORGANIZATION

natrolite ($Na_2Al_2Si_3O_{10}.2H_2O$) Hydrated silicate mineral, hydrous sodium aluminium silicate. It has orthorhombic system, needle-like crystals, with radiating nodules or compact fibrous masses. It is colourless or white, glassy and brittle. Hardness 5–5.5; r.d. 2.2. *See also* ZEOLITE

natterjack Small European TOAD (*Bufo calamita*). Its body is green with a thin yellow stripe down its spine. The natterjack has the loudest croak of any European toad.

natural In musical notation, an accidental sign placed before a note; it cancels a SHARP or FLAT.

natural gas Naturally occurring FOSSIL FUEL, consisting of HYDROCARBONS trapped in pore spaces in sedimentary rocks. Natural gas is the gaseous component of PETROLEUM and is extracted from OIL wells. The fossil history of gas and petroleum is the same, since they were both formed by the decomposition of ancient marine PLANKTON. Before natural gas can be used as a fuel, the heavier hydrocarbons of BUTANE and PROPANE are extracted; in liquid form these hydrocarbons are forced into containers as bottled gas. The remaining "dry gas" is piped to consumers for use as fuel. Dry gas is composed of METHANE and ETHANE.

naturalism Late 19th-century literary movement that began in France and was led by Emile ZOLA. An

extension of REALISM, it emphasized the importance of documentation. Writers sought to represent unselective reality with all its emotional and social ramifications. A major exponent of naturalistic drama was August STRINDBERG. The movement declined by the beginning of the 20th century but influenced the development of the modern US NOVEL and SOCIALIST REALISM.

natural rights Concept that human beings possess certain fundamental and inalienable rights, as described by John LOCKE. Among these rights were life, property ownership and political equality. *See* HUMAN RIGHTS

natural selection In EVOLUTION, theory that advantageous change in an organism tends to be passed on to successive generations. Changes arise out of natural genetic VARIATION, especially MUTATION. Those that give an individual organism a greater capacity for survival and reproduction in a particular environment help it produce more offspring bearing the same beneficial characteristic or trait. This theory was proposed by Charles DARWIN in his book *The Origin of Species* (1859). It is still regarded as the key mechanism of evolution.

nature-nurture controversy Debate over whether people's INTELLIGENCE, behaviour and other characteristics are influenced more by HEREDITY or ENVIRONMENT. The controversy has raised strong feelings, particularly over the question of whether intelligence is genetically fixed or the result of the way children are raised and educated. Most psychologists now believe that behavioural and intellectual traits result from a complex mix of many factors.

Nauru Island republic in the W Pacific Ocean, a coral atoll located halfway between Australia and Hawaii, and the world's smallest independent state. Nauru has rich deposits of high-grade phosphate rock, the sale of which accounts for 98% of its exports. Nauru was first explored by a British navigator, John Hunter, in 1798. In 1888, the atoll was annexed to Germany. During World War 1 Nauru was occupied by Australian forces. During World War 2 the Japanese occupied Nauru. In 1968, it became an independent republic within the British Commonwealth. Area: 21sq km (8sq mi). Pop. (2000) 10,000.

nautilus (chambered nautilus) Cephalopod MOLLUSC found in W Pacific and E Indian oceans at depths down to 200m (660ft). Its large coiled shell is divided into

▲ **nautilus** The shell is divided into c.30 compartments, but the body of the nautilus only occupies the first, and largest, chamber (1). All other chambers are self-contained buoyancy tanks filled with gas. The nautilus nevertheless is a poor shape for swimming. Water passes into the mantle (2) around its whole edge. It is expelled from the funnel (3) by the funnel muscles themselves and by the animal expanding its body in the shell. Unlike its relatives (squids, octopuses and cuttlefish), the nautilus cannot contract its mantle, which is attached to its shell.

numerous, gas-filled chambers, which give it buoyancy, with the body located in the foremost chamber. Its head has 60–90 retractable, thin tentacles without suckers, and it moves by squirting water from a funnel. Shell size *c*.25cm (10in). Family Nautilidae; genus *Nautilus*. *See also* CEPHALOPODA

Navajo (Navaho) Athabascan-speaking tribe, the largest group of NATIVE AMERICANS in the USA. Their reservation in Arizona and New Mexico is the biggest in the country. Today, the population numbers *c*.150,000.

Navarino, Battle of (1827) Naval battle off the port of Navarino (Pylos), Greece. The British, French and Russian fleets destroyed the Turkish-Egyptian fleet of IBRAHIM PASHA. The battle helped to ensure Greek independence (1829).

Navarre Autonomous region and ancient kingdom in N Spain, stretching from the River Ebro to the w Pyrenees border; the capital is Pamplona. For 400 years Navarre defended against invasions by the Visigoths, Arabs and Franks. In the 11th century, Sancho III of Navarre ruled over most of Christian Spain. In 1512, s Navarre was annexed by Ferdinand II of Aragon. The N part was incorporated as French crown land in 1589. The Spanish region has historically maintained semi-autonomous status. It is a mountainous, mainly agricultural region, producing cattle, grapes, timber, cereals, vegetables and sugar beets. Area: 10,421sq km (4,023sq mi). Pop. (1991) 519,227.

nave (Lat. *navis*, ship) Central and main area of a church or cathedral. It extends from the main entrance to the transepts and includes the main aisle. It is the area for the congregation.

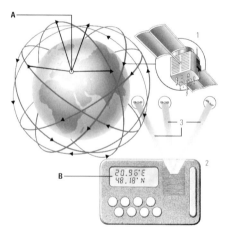

▲ **navigation** The world is ringed by 24 global positioning satellites (1) launched by the USA. At any time four are above the horizon wherever you are on Earth (A). With a receiver (2) that compares the time signals (3) from the satellite, your position can be fixed to a remarkable degree of accuracy. The receivers are now small enough to fit in the hand, and they display either longitude or latitude (B) or a grid reference. Each satellite carries an atomic clock and transmits time signals to Earth. The receiver knows exactly where each satellite should be at any given time, and, by simultaneously analyzing the time the signals from three satellites take to reach the receiver, it can compute its own position to within 10m (33ft). Aircraft and military users use a fourth satellite signal for even greater accuracy.

navigation Determining the position of a vehicle and its course. Five main techniques are used: dead reckoning, piloting, celestial navigation, INERTIAL GUIDANCE and radio navigation. The last includes the use of radio beacons, LORAN, RADAR navigation and SATELLITE navigation systems. Instruments and charts enable the navigator to determine position, expressed in terms of LATITUDE and LONGITUDE, direction in degrees of arc from true north, speed and distance travelled. *See also* COMPASS; GYROCOMPASS; SEXTANT

Navigation Acts English 17th-century statutes placing restrictions on foreign trade and shipping. The first Navigation Act (1651) declared that English trade should be carried only in English ships and was the main cause of the first Anglo–Dutch War. Later acts placed restrictions on the trade of the colonies.

Navratilova, Martina (1956–) US tennis player, b. Czechoslovakia. She dominated women's tennis in the 1980s. Navratilova won 55 Grand Slam events, second only to Margaret COURT. She won nine Wimbledon singles titles (1978–79, 1982–87, 1990). Other singles titles include the US Open (1983–84, 1986–87), French Open (1982, 1984) and Australian Open (1981, 1983, 1985). In 1981 she became a US citizen. She retired in 1994.

navy Nation's warships and auxiliary vessels and crew, organized for war at sea. The first recorded naval battle was between the Egyptians and the Sea People in *c*.1200 BC. From the 5th BC Greek city states, such as Athens and Corinth, relied on galleys to protect their Mediterranean trade routes from pirates. The Athenian victory over the Persians in the Battle of Salamis (480 BC) established Greek supremacy in the E Mediterranean. In 331 BC, Rome established the first permanent navy and it proved crucial in the PUNIC WARS. The foundations of the British ROYAL NAVY were established by ALFRED THE GREAT in the 9th century. The CINQUE PORTS were established in the 11th century. The early Middle Ages saw the development of specialized armed vessels. Spanish naval supremacy was confirmed by victory over the Byzantine fleet at the Battle of LEPANTO (1571). The Battle of TRAFALGAR (1805) marked a century of British naval superiority. In 1859, France developed the first IRONCLADS. The SUBMARINE proved a major weapon in World War 1. In World War 2, naval warfare was conducted largely by aircraft from aircraft carriers. The US Navy emerged as the world's dominant fleet. *See also* MERCHANT NAVY

Nazareth Town between Haifa and the Sea of Galilee, N Israel. According to the Gospels, it was where JESUS spent most of his childhood. Today, Nazareth is a place of Christian pilgrimage. Industries: tourism. Pop. (1990) 53,600.

Nazism *See* NATIONAL SOCIALISM

Ndjamena Capital of Chad, N central Africa, a port on the River Chari. Founded by the French in 1900, it was known as Fort Lamy until 1973. It grew rapidly after independence in 1960. It is an important market for the surrounding region, which produces livestock, dates and cereals. Industries: meat processing. Pop. (1993) 529,555.

Neagh, Lough Lake in Northern Ireland, the largest freshwater lake in the British Isles. It has many feeder channels, the largest of which is the River Bann. The lake is noted for its fishing (especially trout and eels). Area: 396sq km (153sq mi).

Neanderthal Middle PALAEOLITHIC variety of human, known from fossils in Europe and Asia. Neanderthals were discovered when a skeleton was unearthed in the Neander Valley, w Germany, in 1856. The bones were thick and powerfully built, and the skull had a pronounced brow ridge. Neanderthals are now considered a

▶ **neoclassicism** The Panthéon in the Sorbonne district of Paris was built (1755–92) by Jacques Germain Soufflot (1709–80) as a replacement for the church of St. Geneviève. It was secularized during the French Revolution and dedicated as a mausoleum for the heroes of the Revolution. Victor Hugo, Voltaire, Jean-Jacques Rousseau, Marquis de Lafayette and Emilé Zola are among those buried in the Panthéon. It exemplifies the neoclassical style. Modelled on the Pantheon at Rome (27 BC), it is cruciform in shape with a high dome in the centre. The façade is formed by a portico of Corinthian columns.

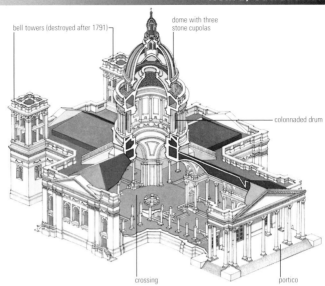

bell towers (destroyed after 1791)

dome with three stone cupolas

colonnaded drum

crossing

portico

separate species of human and not thought to be ancestral to modern humans. Neanderthals predated modern humans in Europe, but were superseded by them *c.*35,000 years ago. *See also* HUMAN EVOLUTION

Nebraska State in w central USA, in the Great Plains; the capital is LINCOLN. OMAHA is the largest city. The region was acquired under the LOUISIANA PURCHASE (1803) and was unexplored until the LEWIS AND CLARK EXPEDITION (1804). The territory of Nebraska was created in 1854. Nebraska was admitted to the union in 1867. The land rises gradually from the E to the foothills of the Rocky Mountains in the w and is drained chiefly by the River Platte, a tributary of the MISSOURI. The E half of the state is farmland. Nebraska's economy is overwhelmingly agricultural. Industries: food processing, oil, and sand, gravel, stone quarrying. Area: 199,113sq km (76,878sq mi). Pop. (2000) 1,711,263.

Nebuchadnezzar (*c.*630–562 BC) Second and greatest king of the Chaldaean (New Babylonian) empire (r.605 BC–562 BC) who had a profound effect on the lands of the ancient Middle East. He subjugated Syria and Palestine but was himself defeated by Egyptian forces in 601 BC. He occupied JUDAH, capturing JERUSALEM in 597 BC and installing the puppet king Zedekiah on the throne. Following Zedekiah's rebellion, Nebuchadnezzar destroyed the city and TEMPLE of Jerusalem and deported its population into exile in BABYLON. A brilliant military leader, he continued to follow an expansionist strategy. Nebuchadnezzar was responsible for many buildings in Babylon and, according to legend, built for his Median wife the famous hanging gardens, which became one of the SEVEN WONDERS OF THE WORLD. Biblical accounts of Nebuchadnezzar's involvement with Judah and the Jews appear principally in II Kings, Jeremiah and Daniel.

nebula (Lat. cloud) Region of interstellar gas and dust. There are three main types. **Emission** nebulae are bright diffuse nebulae that emit light and other radiation as a result of ionization and excitation of the gas atoms by ultraviolet radiation. In contrast, the brightness of **reflection** nebulae results from the scattering by dust particles of light from nearby stars. **Dark** nebulae are not luminous: interstellar gas and dust absorb light from background stars, producing apparently dark patches in the sky.

neck In vertebrates, the part of the body that connects the head and the trunk. In human beings, it contains the seven cervical vertebrae of the spinal column and, to the front, the throat or pharynx, leading to the TRACHEA and OESOPHAGUS.

Necker, Jacques (1732–1804) French financier and statesman, b. Switzerland. A Protestant banker, he was finance minister (1776–81) under LOUIS XVI. Dismissed, he was recalled to deal with a financial crisis in 1788 and advised calling the STATES GENERAL. The political demands of the Third Estate caused Necker's second dismissal, but the consequent riots, leading to the storming of the BASTILLE, forced Louis XVI to reappoint him. Unable to prevent the FRENCH REVOLUTION, he resigned in 1790.

nectar Sweet liquid secreted by flowering plants. It consists mainly of a solution of GLUCOSE, FRUCTOSE and SUCROSE in water. The glands (nectaries) that produce it usually lie at the base of the FLOWER petals but may be found also in parts of the stem or at the leaf bases. Nectar attracts insects, which help with cross-POLLINATION.

nectarine Variety of PEACH tree and its sweet, smooth-skinned, fleshy fruit. The tree and stone are identical to those of the peach. Family Rosaceae; species *Prunus persica nectarina.*

Nefertiti (active 14th century BC) Queen of Egypt as wife of AKHNATEN. Exceptionally beautiful, she supported her husband's innovative religious ideas. Her best surviving representation is a bust in the Berlin Museum.

Negev Desert region in s Israel that extends from Beersheba to the border with Egypt at Elat, and accounts for more than half of Israeli land. An irrigation network has greatly increased cultivation. The area's mineral resources include copper, phosphates, natural gas, gypsum and magnesium ore. Area: *c.*13,300sq km (5,130sq mi).

Nehru, Jawaharlal (1889–1964) Indian statesman, prime minister of India (1947–64), father of Indira GANDHI. Educated in England, he succeeded his father Motilal Nehru (1861–1931) as president of the CONGRESS PARTY in 1929. Nehru and "Mahatma" Gandhi led nationalist opposition to British rule in India. He was imprisoned nine times for non-cooperation with the British between 1921 and 1945. Nehru played a leading role in negotiations with MOUNTBATTEN and JINNAH that led to the independence of India and Pakistan. As the first prime minister of an independent India, he followed a foreign policy of non-alignment in the Cold war and became a respected leader of the Third World.

Nelson, Horatio, Viscount (1758–1805) Britain's most famous naval commander. Joining the navy aged 12, he was a captain at 20. Nelson lost an eye in action in 1794 and his right arm in 1797. Having played a notable part in the victory at Cape St Vincent (1797), he again used unorthodox tactics in the Battle of ABOUKIR Bay (1798). Nelson was killed at the moment of his greatest victory, when he destroyed the combined French and Spanish fleets at TRAFALGAR (1805). He is remembered for his courage and ability and for a long-standing love affair with Lady Emma HAMILTON.

nematode *See* ROUNDWORM

Nemesis In Greek mythology, personification of the gods' disapproval, jealousy and retribution.

neoclassicism Movement in late 18th- and early 19th-century European art and architecture. Neoclassicism grew out of the Age of ENLIGHTENMENT, whose exponents admired the order and clarity of ancient Greek and Roman art. The archaeological discoveries at Herculaneum and Pompeii, Italy, in the 1740s helped to stimulate interest in these ancient civilizations. Many of the movement's pioneers congregated in Rome, notably Johann Winckelmann, CANOVA, John FLAXMAN, Gavin Hamilton and Bertel Thorvaldsen. The most powerful neoclassical painter was Jacques Louis DAVID, whose work expressed great severity and grandeur. The concurrent GREEK REVIVAL had more superficial aims, which, in architecture, involved imitating the simplicity of ancient Greek buildings. *See artwork p.583*

neo-Darwinism Development of Darwinism that incorporates the modern insights of genetic HEREDITY with Charles DARWIN's ideas of EVOLUTION through NATURAL SELECTION.

neodymium (symbol Nd) Silver-yellow, metallic element of the LANTHANIDE SERIES. It is used to manufacture lasers, and neodymium salts are used to colour glass. Properties: at.no. 60; r.a.m. 144.24; r.d. 7.004; m.p. 1,010°C (1,850°F); b.p. 3,068°C (5,554°F); most common isotope Nd^{142} (27.11%).

neo-fascism Revival of the principles of FASCISM. Neo-fascism surfaced in Germany in the 1980s, feeding on muted social discontent and the presence of many foreign workers. In France some Jewish graves were desecrated and Swiss and Italian neo-fascism has had moderate electoral success. Neo-fascist elements are visible in the USA in certain white supremacist groups.

neo-impressionism Late 19th-century painting style, originating in France and involving the use of POINTILLISM. The style is seen at its purest in the works of SEURAT.

Neolithic (New Stone Age) Period in human cultural development following the PALAEOLITHIC. The Neolithic began *c.*8000 BC in W Asia and *c.*4000 BC in Britain. It was during this period that people first lived in settled villages, domesticated and bred animals, cultivated cereal crops and practised stone-grinding and flint mining.

neon (symbol Ne) Gaseous, non-metallic element, a NOBLE GAS. Colourless and odourless, it is present in the atmosphere (0.0018% by volume) and is obtained by the fractional distillation of liquid air. Its main use is in discharge tubes for advertising signs (emitting a bright red glow while conducting electricity) and in gas lasers,

geiger counters and particle detectors. The element forms no compounds. Properties: at.no. 10; r.a.m. 20.179; m.p. −248.67°C (−415.6°F); b.p. −246.05°C (−410.89°F); most common isotope Ne^{20} (90.92%).

Neoplatonism School of philosophy that dominated intellectual thought between *c.*AD 250 and 550. It combined the ideas of PYTHAGORAS, the STOICS, PLATO and ARISTOTLE with strains from JUDAISM, oriental religions and Christianity. Fundamental to Neoplatonism was the concept of the One, something that transcends knowledge or existence but from which are derived intelligence and the Soul. Neoplatonism's influence persisted throughout the Middle Ages and even during the Renaissance.

neo-realism Italian film movement (1945–50) that dealt with the harshness of life and death. Roberto ROSSELLINI directed the first such film *Open City* (1945), using non-professionals and real locations. Perhaps the finest example of neo-realism was Vittorio DE SICA's *Bicycle Thieves* (1948). Neo-realist writers included Alberto MORAVIA and Cesare PAVESE.

Nepal Independent kingdom in central Asia between India (S) and China (N); the capital is KATMANDU. Nepal comprises three distinct regions. A S lowland area (terai) of grassland, forests and national park is the location for much of Nepal's agriculture and timber industry. The central Siwalik mountains and valleys are divided between the basins of the rivers Ghaghara, Gandak and Kosi. Between the Gandak and Kosi lies Katmandu valley, the country's most populous area and centre for Nepal's main source of foreign currency, tourism. The last region is the main section of the Himalayas and includes Mount EVEREST. **History and politics** In 1768, Nepal was united under GURKHA rule. Gurkha expansion into N India ended in conflict with Britain. British victory led Nepal to ratify its present boundaries and accept permanent British representation in Katmandu. From 1846 to 1951, Nepal was ruled by hereditary prime ministers from the Rana family. In 1923, Britain recognized Nepal as a sovereign state. Gurkha soldiers fought with distinction in the British army during both world wars. In 1951, the Rana government was overthrown and the monarchy restored. In 1959, the first national constitution was adopted and free elections took place. In 1960, King Mahendra dissolved parliament, and the democratic constitution was replaced by village councils (*panchayat*). In 1972, King Birendra succeeded. In 1990, mass demonstrations led to the establishment of a new democratic constitution, with the king retaining joint executive powers. In 1991, multiparty elections were won by the Nepali Congress Party (NCP), led by G.P. Koirala, brother of the previous prime minister. In 1994, the United Marxist Leninist Party formed a short-lived minority government. In 1995, a coalition government led by the NCP was formed. Nepal suffered political instability under a succession of minority governments. In 1998, Koirala returned to lead a new coalition. **Economy** The most important economic activity in the Himalayas is livestock farming (especially yaks) and the growing of medicinal herbs. Nepal is an undeveloped rural country, heavily reliant on Indian trade and cooperation (1995 GDP per capita, US$1,170).

nephritis (Bright's disease) Inflammation of the KIDNEY. It is a general term, used to describe a condition

NEPAL
AREA: 140,800sq km (54,363sq mi)
POPULATION: 24,084,000
CAPITAL (POPULATION): Katmandu (535,000)

NEPTUNE DATA
DIAMETER (EQUATORIAL): 49,528km (30,707mi)
MASS (EARTH = 1): 17.2
VOLUME (EARTH = 1): 57
DENSITY (WATER = 1): 2.06
ORBITAL PERIOD: 164.8 years
ROTATION PERIOD: 16h 7m 0s
AVERAGE SURFACE TEMPERATURE: −220°C (−364°F)
SURFACE GRAVITY (EARTH = 1): 0.98

rather than any specific disease. It may be acute or chronic, often progressing to kidney failure.

nephron Basic functional unit of the mammalian KID-NEY. There are more than one million nephrons in a human kidney. Each consists of a cluster of tiny blood capillaries, cupped in a structure with an attached long, narrow tubule. Blood enters the kidney under pressure, and water and wastes are forced into the tubule. Some water and essential molecules are reabsorbed into the bloodstream; the remaining filtrate, URINE, is passed to the BLADDER for voiding.

Neptune Roman god, originally associated with fresh water but later identified with the Greek god POSEIDON and hence the sea. He was often depicted carrying a trident and riding a dolphin. His festival was in July.

Neptune Eighth planet from the Sun. The mass, orbit and position of an unseen planet had been calculated by Urbain LEVERRIER and, independently, by John Couch ADAMS. Neptune was first observed in 1846 and is invisible to the naked eye. Through a telescope it appears as a small, greenish-blue disc with very few details. The upper atmosphere is *c*.85% molecular hydrogen and 15% helium. Its predominant blue colour is due to a trace of methane, which strongly absorbs red light. Several different atmospheric features were visible at the time of the fly-by of the Voyager 2 probe in 1989. There were faint bands parallel to the equator, and spots, the most prominent of which was the oval Great Dark Spot (GDS), *c*.12,500km (8,000mi) long and 7,500km (4,500mi) wide, which is a giant anticyclone. White, cirrus-type clouds of methane crystals cast shadows on the main cloud deck some 50km (30mi) below. There are also the highest wind speeds recorded on any planet, at more than 2,000km/h (1,250mph) in places.

neptunium (symbol Np) Radioactive metallic element, the first of the TRANSURANIC ELEMENTS in the ACTINIDE SERIES. The silvery element is found in small amounts in uranium ores. Properties: at.no. 93; r.a.m. 237.0482; r.d. 20.25; m.p. 640°C (1,184°F); b.p. 3,902°C (7,056°F); most stable isotope Np^{237} (half-life 2.2 million years).

Nernst, Walther Hermann (1864–1941) German chemist who was professor at Göttingen and then at Berlin. Nernst was awarded the 1920 Nobel Prize for chemistry for his discovery of the third law of THERMO-DYNAMICS. His other important work was concerned with chain reactions in photochemistry. He wrote *Thermodynamics* (1893) and *The New Heat Theorem* (1918).

Nero (AD 37–68) Roman emperor (54–68). One of the most notorious of rulers, he was responsible for the murders of his half-brother, his mother and his first wife. Rome was burned (64), according to rumour, at Nero's instigation. He blamed the Christians and began their persecution. Faced with widespread rebellion, Nero committed suicide.

Neruda, Pablo (1904–73) Chilean poet, b. Neftalí Ricardo Reyes. He identified with the impoverished

masses and was active in politics. His poetry presents the tragedy of the human condition through surreal imagery. His best-known work is the epic *Canto General* (1950). In 1971, he was awarded the Nobel Prize for literature.

nerve Collection of NEURONS providing a communications link between the vertebrate NERVOUS SYSTEM and other parts of the body. Afferent or sensory nerves transmit nervous impulses to the CENTRAL NERVOUS SYSTEM; efferent or MOTOR NERVES carry impulses away from the central nervous system to muscles.

nerve cell *See* NEURON

Nervi, Pier Luigi (1891–1979) Italian architect. He is noted for his innovative use of concrete. Nervi first gained attention with his design for the Giovanni Berta stadium, Florence (1932). He co-designed the UNESCO building, Paris (1954–58) and the Pirelli skyscraper, Milan (1958).

nervous breakdown Popular term for a mental and emotional crisis in which the person either is unable or feels unable to function normally. It is an imprecise term and may refer to any of a range of conditions. *See also* MENTAL DISORDER

nervous system Communications system consisting of interconnecting nerve cells, or NEURONS, that coordinate all life, growth and physical and mental activity. The mammalian nervous system consists of the CENTRAL NERVOUS SYSTEM (CNS) and the PERIPHERAL NERVOUS SYSTEM.

Ness, Loch Freshwater lake in N Scotland, running SW to NE along the geological fault of Glen More. It is 38km (24mi) long and 230m (754ft) deep and forms part of the Caledonian Canal. Accounts of a Loch Ness monster date back to the 15th century, but the veracity of the legend has never been established.

nest Structure built by a living organism to house itself, its eggs or its young. Nest-builders include some invertebrates, particularly social insects, and members of all the larger groups of vertebrates. The nests of ants, bees, wasps and termites may be highly elaborate and involve tunnels, passages and chambers. The nests of fish may be simple gravel scoops or enclosed structures, sometimes made of bubbles. Birds' nests vary enormously from simple, cup-shaped arrangements of twigs and other organic materials, to woven or knotted grass or leaves; some birds scrape a hollow in the ground to make a nest, others make nest-holes in cliffs, earth banks or trees. The most highly evolved animal to make a form of a nest is probably the gorilla, which builds a new sleeping platform of leafy branches every night.

Nestorianism Christian heresy according to which JESUS CHRIST, the incarnate God, possesses two separate natures, the one divine and the other human, as opposed to the orthodox belief that Christ is one person who is at once both God and man. The heresy was associated with Nestorius, Bishop of Constantinople (d. *c*.451). It was condemned by the Councils of EPHESUS (431) and CHAL-CEDON (451). Nestorius was deposed and banished. His supporters, however, gradually organized themselves into a separate Church that had its centre in Persia (Iran). Nestorians have survived as a small community.

Netanyahu, Binyamin (1949–) Israeli statesman, prime minister (1996–99). He served as a permanent representative to the UN (1984–88). In 1993, Netanyahu became leader of the right-wing Likud Party. After the assasination of Yitzhak RABIN, Netanyahu was elected prime minister of a coalition government. His uncompromising leadership and Likud's opposition to the ISRAELI-PALESTINIAN ACCORD threatened to disrupt the peace process. In 1998, he signed a new peace agreement with

PLO leader Yasir ARAFAT. The withdrawal of the religious right from the coalition prompted fresh elections (1999), in which Netanyahu was defeated by Ehud BARAK.

netball Seven-member ball game played by women. It is a variant of BASKETBALL. Only two players of each team are allowed in the shooting circle at goal, which is the same size and height as basketball but without a backboard. The game is played chiefly in the English-speaking countries and the British Commonwealth.

Netherlands Country in NW Europe. The kingdom of the Netherlands is popularly known as HOLLAND, and with Belgium and Luxembourg forms the LOW COUNTRIES. Except in the far SE, the Netherlands is flat and *c.*40% lies below sea level. Large areas (*polders*) have been reclaimed from the sea. Dykes prevent flooding and have created IJSSELMEER. The maritime provinces contain the constitutional capital, AMSTERDAM, the administrative capital, THE HAGUE, and the cities of ROTTERDAM, DELFT, HAARLEM, LEIDEN, GRONINGEN and UTRECHT. **Climate** The Netherlands has a temperate maritime climate, with mild winters and abundant rainfall. **Vegetation** The Netherlands is very densely populated. About 66% of the land is arable or grazing land. The country is irrigated by a series of canals. **History and politics** From the 4th to 8th century, the region was ruled by the Franks. In the 10th century, it became part of the Holy Roman Empire. In the 14th and 15th centuries, trade flourished through the HANSEATIC LEAGUE. In 1477, the region passed to the Habsburgs. PHILIP II's attempt to impose the INQUISITION met with fierce resistance. In 1581, the N Protestant provinces, led by WILLIAM I (THE SILENT), declared independence. In 1602, the foundation of the Dutch EAST INDIA COMPANY marked the beginnings of empire. The mercantile class became the patrons of DUTCH ART. Following the THIRTY YEARS WAR, the Peace of WESTPHALIA (1648) recognized the independence of the N and S provinces as the United Provinces. In 1652, Jan de WITT established a republic. Trading rivalry with England led to the DUTCH WARS. The Treaty of BREDA (1667) confirmed Dutch imperial possessions. In 1672, France invaded and de Witt was murdered. The House of ORANGE re-established control under WILLIAM III (OF ORANGE). France controlled the Netherlands from 1795 to 1813. In 1815, the former United Provinces, Belgium and Luxembourg united to form the kingdom of the Netherlands under WILLIAM 1. In 1830, Belgium broke away. In 1890, Luxembourg seceded, and WILHELMINA began her long reign (1890–1948). The Netherlands remained neutral in World War 1. In May 1940, Germany invaded; most Dutch Jews were deported to Poland and murdered. Queen Wilhelmina was exiled during World War 2. ARNHEM was a vital bridgehead in the Allied liberation of Europe. In 1948, Wilhelmina abdicated in favour of her daughter, Juliana. In 1949, the Netherlands joined NATO, and Indonesia gained its independence. In 1957, it was a founding member of the European Community, and in 1958 it formed the Benelux customs union. It gave Netherlands New Guinea and Surinam independence in 1962 and 1975, respectively. It retains the islands of the NETHERLANDS ANTILLES. In 1980, Queen Juliana abdicated in favour of her daughter, Beatrix. Post-1945, the Netherlands has been ruled by a succession of coalition governments. In 1994, Wim Kok was elected prime minister. In 1998, he was re-elected as head of a centre-left coalition and led the nation into the European single currency (1999). **Economy** The Netherlands has prospered through its close European ties (1995 GDP per capita, US$19,950).

NETHERLANDS
AREA: 41,526sq km (16,033sq mi)
POPULATION: 15,829,000
CAPITAL (POPULATION): Amsterdam (718,000)

Private enterprise has successfully combined with progressive social policies. Services account for 65% of GDP and industry 30%. It is highly industrialized. Products include aircraft, chemicals, electronics and machinery. Natural resources include natural gas, but it imports raw materials. Agriculture is intensive and mechanized, employing only 5% of the workforce. Dairy farming is the leading agricultural activity. Major products are cheese, barley, flowers and bulbs.

Netherlands Antilles Group of five main islands (and part of a sixth) in the West Indies in the Caribbean Sea, forming an autonomous region of the Netherlands; the capital is Willemstadt (on CURAÇAO). The islands were settled by the Spanish in 1527 and captured by the Dutch in 1634. In 1954, they were granted internal self-government. The group includes Aruba, Bonaire, Curaçao (the largest island), Saba, Saint Eustatius, and the S half of Saint Maarten. Industries: oil refining, petrochemicals, phosphates, tourism. Area: 993sq km (383sq mi). Pop. (2000) 203,000.

nettle Any of numerous species of flowering plants of the genus *Urtica*, especially the stinging nettle (*U. dioica*), which is typical of the genus in that it has stinging hairs along the leaves and stem. It has heart-shaped serrated leaves, small green flowers and is sometimes used for medicinal or culinary purposes. The stinging agent is formic acid. Family Urticaceae.

network *See* COMPUTER NETWORK

Neumann, John von *See* VON NEUMANN, JOHN

neuralgia Intense pain from a damaged nerve, possibly tracking along its course. Forms include trigeminal neuralgia, which features attacks of stabbing pain in the mouth area, and post-herpetic neuralgia following an attack of SHINGLES.

neurology Branch of medicine dealing with the diagnosis and treatment of diseases of the NERVOUS SYSTEM.

neuron (nerve cell, neurone) Basic structural unit of the NERVOUS SYSTEM that enables rapid transmission of impulses between different parts of the body. It is composed of a cell body, containing a nucleus, and a number of trailing processes. The largest of these is the axon, which carries outgoing impulses; the rest are dendrites, which receive incoming impulses.

neurosis Emotional disorder such as anxiety, depression or various PHOBIAS. It is a form of MENTAL DISORDER in which the main disorder is of mood, but the person does not lose contact with reality as happens in PSYCHOSIS.

neurotransmitter Any one of several dozen chemicals involved in communication between NEURONS or between a NERVE and muscle cells. When an electrical impulse arrives at a nerve ending, a neurotransmitter is released to carry the signal across the specialized junction (synapse) between the nerve cell and its neighbour. Some drugs work by disrupting neurotransmission. *See also* NERVOUS SYSTEM; NORADRENALINE

neutrality Policy of non-involvement in hostilities between states. It is recognized by international law, mainly in the Declaration of Paris of 1856 and the Hague Conventions V and XIII of 1907. A state proclaiming its neutrality must be wholly impartial and refrain from helping or hindering any side.

neutralization In chemistry, the mixing, or TITRATION, of equivalent amounts of an acid and a base in an aqueous medium until the mixture is neither acidic nor basic (pH of 7).

neutrino (symbol ν) Uncharged ELEMENTARY PARTICLE with no mass or a very low mass, SPIN $\frac{1}{2}$, and travelling at the speed of light. Its existence was predicted by Wolfgang PAULI in 1930. Classified as a LEPTON, it has little reaction with matter and is difficult to detect. Neutrinos are created and destroyed by particle decays with WEAK NUCLEAR FORCE. There are three types. The **electron** neutrino is closely associated with the ELECTRON and is produced when PROTONS and electrons react to form NEUTRONS, as in the Sun. The **muon** neutrino is associated with the MUON and occurs in high-energy reactions. The **tau** neutrino is associated with the TAU particle.

neutron (symbol n) Uncharged ELEMENTARY PARTICLE that occurs in the atomic nuclei of all chemical elements, except the lightest isotope of HYDROGEN. It was identified by James CHADWICK in 1932. Outside the NUCLEUS, it is unstable, decaying with a half-life of 11.6 minutes into a PROTON, ELECTRON and antineutrino. Its neutrality allows it to penetrate and be absorbed in nuclei and thus to induce nuclear transmutation and FISSION. It is a BARYON with SPIN $\frac{1}{2}$ and a mass 1,838 times heavier than an electron.

neutron bomb NUCLEAR WEAPON that produces a small blast but a very intense burst of high-speed NEUTRONS. The lack of blast means that buildings are not heavily damaged. The neutrons, however, produce intense RADIATION SICKNESS in people located within a certain range of the explosion.

neutron star Extremely small, dense STAR that consists mostly of NEUTRONS. Neutron stars are formed when a massive star explodes as a SUPERNOVA, blasting off its outer layers and compressing the core so that its component PROTONS and ELECTRONS merge into neutrons. They are observed as PULSARS. They have masses comparable to that of the Sun, but diameters of only c.20km (12mi) and average densities of c.10^{15}g/cm^3.

Nevada State in W USA; the capital is CARSON CITY. The USA acquired the region in 1848 at the end of the MEXICAN WAR. When gold and silver were found in 1859, settlers flocked to Nevada. Much of the state lies in the Great Basin, but the SIERRA NEVADA rise steeply from its W edge. Nevada's dry climate and steep slopes have hindered the development of an agricultural economy. Hay and alfalfa are the chief crops; sheep and cattle grazing is much more important. Most of Nevada's economic wealth comes from its mineral deposits, which include copper, lead, silver, gold, zinc and tungsten. Industries: chemicals, timber, electrical machinery, glass products. It is a tourist area and, in cities such as LAS VEGAS and Reno, gambling provides an important source of state revenue. Area: 286,297sq km (110,539sq mi). Pop. (2000) 1,998,257.

New Age System of philosophy and religion that came to prominence during the late 1980s and traces its origins to a variety of sources, including oriental mysticism and new scientific ideas. The New Age movement embraces diverse issues, including feminism, astrology, ecology, spiritualism and pagan ritual, and takes a holistic approach to healing.

Newark City in NE New Jersey, USA, on the Passaic River and Newark Bay, connected to nearby NEW YORK CITY by tunnel. Founded in 1666 by the Puritans, Newark began its industrial growth after the American Revolution. It is an important commercial and financial centre. Industries: electrical equipment, paints, chemicals. Pop. (1990) 275,221.

New Brunswick Maritime province in E Canada, on the US–Canadian border; the capital is Fredericton. The region was first explored by Jacques CARTIER in 1534. It was ceded to Britain in 1713, but settlement was slow. Many loyalists entered the region from the American colonies during the AMERICAN REVOLUTION. The province of New Brunswick was established in 1784. In 1867, New Brunswick joined NOVA SCOTIA, QUÉBEC and ONTARIO to form the Dominion of CANADA. The land rises gradually from E to W and is drained chiefly by the St John and Miramichi rivers. More than three-quarters of the province is forested. The chief crops are hay, clover, oats, potatoes and fruit. Industries: timber, leather goods, pharmaceuticals, machinery. There are also valuable mineral deposits. The largest towns are St John and Moncton. Area: 73,437sq km (28,354sq mi). Pop. (1991) 723,900.

New Caledonia (Nouvelle Calédonie) French overseas territory in the SW Pacific Ocean, c.1,210km (750mi) E of Australia, consisting of New Caledonia, Loyalty Islands, Isle des Pins, Isle Bélep and Chesterfield and Huon Islands; the capital is NOUMÉA (on New Caledonia). Discovered in 1774 by Captain COOK, the islands were annexed by France in 1853. The group became a French overseas territory in 1946. In the 1980s there was a growing separatist movement. Direct French rule was imposed in 1988. Products: copra, coffee, cotton, nickel, iron, manganese, cobalt, chromium. Area: 18,575sq km (7,170sq mi). Pop. (1989) 164,182.

Newcastle upon Tyne City and port on the N bank of the River Tyne, NE England; administrative centre of Tyne and Wear. The site of a fort in Roman times, Newcastle lay at the E end of HADRIAN'S WALL. Its castle was constructed following the Norman conquest (1080). Sites include the 15th-century St Nicholas' Cathedral. It was a major wool-exporting port in the 13th century and later a coal-shipping centre. Its shipbuilding industry is in decline, but heavy engineering is still important. Other industries: pharmaceuticals, engineering, aircraft. Pop. (1994) 274,000.

Newcomen, Thomas (1663–1729) English engineer, who constructed (1712) the first practical STEAM ENGINE. It consisted of a piston moved by atmospheric pressure within a cylinder in which a partial vacuum had been created by condensing steam. Newcomen went into partnership with Thomas Savery, who had patented (1698) a pumping engine on the same principle. It was widely used to drain water from mines. The design was greatly improved by James WATT.

New Deal (1933–39) Programme for social and economic reconstruction in the USA launched by President Franklin D. ROOSEVELT and designed to restore prosperity after the GREAT DEPRESSION. It was based on massive and unprecedented federal intervention in the economy. Early measures, including extensive public works, were

▶ **nettle** Bearing both male and female flowers, the stinging nettle (*Urtica dioica*) has bristle-like stinging hairs that are long, hollow cells. The tips of these are toughened with silica, and they are easily broken off. When the plant is touched, the hairs penetrate the skin like surgical needles, the tips are lost, and the poison contained in the cells is released.

mainly concerned with relief. The New Deal encountered bitter resistance from conservatives and did not avert recession in 1937–38. Industrial expansion, full employment and agricultural prosperity were achieved less by the New Deal than by World War 2. However, the programme laid the basis for future federal management of the economy and provision of social welfare.

New Delhi Capital of India, in the N of the country on the River Yamuna in Delhi Union Territory. Planned by the British architects Sir Edwin LUTYENS and Herbert Baker, it was constructed between 1912 and 1929 to replace CALCUTTA as the capital of British India. Whereas the old city of DELHI (to the SW) is primarily a commercial centre, New Delhi has an administrative function. Industries: textile production, chemicals, machine tools, plastics, food processing, electrical appliances, traditional crafts. Pop. (1991) 301,800.

New England Region in NE USA, made up of the states of MAINE, NEW HAMPSHIRE, VERMONT, CONNECTICUT, MASSACHUSETTS and RHODE ISLAND. In 1643, the New England Confederation was set up by some of the colonies for the purposes of defence and to establish a common policy towards the Native Americans. New England was the centre of events leading up to the AMERICAN REVOLUTION. The region became highly industrialized after the WAR OF 1812 and developed as a centre of literature and learning. It was home to writers such as EMERSON, HAWTHORNE and THOREAU and the literary movement known as TRANSCENDENTALISM.

New Forest Region of forest and heathland in S England, in S Hampshire. It was established as a royal hunting ground in 1079 by William I. The forest includes many species of trees. Pigs, cattle and ponies are reared. It is a popular tourist resort. Area: c.383sq km (148sq mi).

Newfoundland Rescue and working dog originally bred by fisherman in Newfoundland, Canada. It has a massive head with a square, short muzzle, and small, triangular ears set close to the head. The full-chested, broad-backed body is set on short, strong legs, and the tail is broad and long. Height: 71cm (28in) at the shoulder; weight: 68kg (150lb).

Newfoundland and Labrador Province in E Canada, on the Atlantic Ocean, consisting of the mainland region of LABRADOR and the island of Newfoundland plus adjacent islands; the capital is ST JOHN'S (in Newfoundland). Norsemen are believed to have landed on the coast of Labrador c.AD 1000. John CABOT reached the island in 1497. The region became a British colony in 1824. It remained apart from the rest of Canada until 1949, when it became the country's tenth province. The island of Newfoundland is a plateau with many lakes and marshes. Labrador has tundra in the N, and the cold climate and lack of transport facilities have hindered economic development. There are, however, valuable mineral resources. Timber is an important industry, and the GRAND BANKS is one of the world's best cod-fishing areas. Area: 404,420sq km (156,185sq mi). Pop. (1991) 568,474.

New France Area of North America claimed by France in the 16th–18th centuries. It included the St Lawrence valley, the Great Lakes region and the Mississippi valley. Parts were lost during the Anglo–French wars of the 18th century, and the whole of New France passed to Britain in 1763.

New Frontier (1961–63) Term describing the legislative programme of US President John F. KENNEDY. It included massive expenditure on social reforms and welfare as well as ambitious new projects, such as the Peace Corps and manned space flight.

New General Catalogue (NGC) In astronomy, list of stellar clusters, nebulae and galaxies compiled (1888) by Danish astronomer Johan Dreyer, based on the observations of William HERSCHEL and his son, John. Dreyer later published two Index Catalogues (IC), bringing the number of stellar objects listed in the catalogue to c.13,000.

New Granada Historical region of NW South America forming a Spanish colonial administrative area. The capital was Bogotá. It was part of the viceroyalty of Peru in the 16th century and reconstituted as the viceroyalty of New Granada in the 18th century. The region became independent within Gran Colombia in 1819, and when Venezuela and Ecuador seceded in 1830, the remaining republic was called New Granada. The name was later changed to Colombia.

New Guinea Second-largest island in the world, part of the E Malay archipelago in the W Pacific Ocean. Discovered in the early 16th century, New Guinea was colonized by the Dutch, Germans and British during the next two centuries. In 1904, the British-administered part was transferred to Australia, and, during World War 1, Australian forces seized German New Guinea. The E half eventually achieved independence as PAPUA NEW GUINEA in 1975. The W half, IRIAN JAYA, became a province of Indonesia in 1969. The island has a tropical climate and is mountainous. Products: copra, cocoa, coffee, rubber, coconuts, tobacco. Area: 885,780sq km (342,000sq mi).

New Hampshire State in NE USA, on the Canadian border; the capital is CONCORD. The first settlement was made in 1623. Much of the land is mountainous and forested. The principal rivers are the Connecticut and the Merrimack, and there are more than 1,000 lakes. Farming is restricted by poor, stony soil and is mostly concentrated in the Connecticut Valley. Dairy and farm produce, hay, apples and potatoes are the chief products. New Hampshire is highly industrialized. There is abundant hydroelectricity. Industries: electrical machinery, paper and wood products, printing and publishing, leather goods, textiles. Area: 24,097sq km (9,304sq mi). Pop. (2000) 1,235,786.

New Haven City and port in S Connecticut, USA, on Long Island Sound. Founded by Puritans in 1638, it shared the role of capital of Connecticut with HARTFORD from 1701 to 1875. The presence of YALE UNIVERSITY (founded 1701) has made the city a cultural centre. Pop. (1990) 130,474.

Ne Win, U (1911–) Burmese general and statesman, prime minister (1958–60), head of state (1962–74), and president (1974–81). In 1943, he was appointed Chief of Staff of the Burmese army by AUNG SAN. In 1962, Ne Win seized power in a military coup. He established a military dictatorship and formed a one-party state, governed by the Burma Socialist Programme Party (BSPP). In 1988, Ne Win retired as leader of the BSPP.

New Jersey State in E USA, on the Atlantic coast, S of New York; the capital is TRENTON. Other major cities include NEWARK, ATLANTIC CITY and Paterson. Settlement began in the 1620s when the Dutch founded the colony of New Netherland (later New York). When the British took the colony in 1664, the land between the Hudson and Delaware rivers was separated and named New Jersey. The N of the state is in the Appalachian highland region; SE of this area are the Piedmont plains, and more than half the state is coastal plain. A variety of crops are grown, and dairy cattle and poultry are also important. New Jersey is, however, industrial and densely populated. Industries: chemicals, pharmaceuticals, rubber goods, textiles, electronic equipment, copper smelting, oil refining. Area: 20,295sq km (7,836sq mi). Pop. (2000) 8,414,350.

Newlands, John Alexander Reina (1837–98) English chemist. In 1864 he announced his law of octaves, which arranged the chemical elements in a table of eight columns according to atomic weight. In 1869 MENDELEYEV included the law in his own PERIODIC TABLE.

Newman, Barnett (1905–70) US painter. He was closely associated with ABSTRACT EXPRESSIONISM, but developed a distinctive kind of mystical abstraction, expressed in its earliest complete form in *Onement* (1948). Newman and Mark ROTHKO pioneered monochromatic colour field painting and the use of huge canvases.

Newman, John Henry, Cardinal (1801–90) British theologian. As leader of the OXFORD MOVEMENT (1833–45), Newman had a powerful effect on the Church of England, equalled only by the shock of his conversion to Roman Catholicism (1845). A great literary stylist, he is remembered especially for his autobiography, *Apologia pro vita sua* (1864).

Newman, Paul (1925–) US film actor, director and producer. He is known for his portrayals of independent and wryly humourous anti-heroes in such films as *The Hustler* (1961), *Hud* (1963), *Cool Hand Luke* (1967), *Butch Cassidy and the Sundance Kid* (1969) and *The Sting* (1973). Newman won an Academy Award for Best Actor in *The Color of Money* (1986). Other films include *The Hudsucker Proxy* (1994).

New Mexico State in SW USA, on the Mexican border; the capital is SANTA FE. The largest city is ALBUQUERQUE. The first permanent Spanish settlement was established at Santa Fe in 1610. The USA acquired the region in 1848 at the end of the MEXICAN WAR. It entered the Union in 1912 as the 47th state. The first atomic bomb was exploded at Alamogordo in 1945. The Sangre de Cristo Mountains in the N flank the Rio Grande, which runs N to S through the state. The terrain includes desert, forested mountains and stark mesa. In the S and SW are semi-arid plains. The S Pecos and Rio Grande rivers are used to irrigate cotton crops; hay, wheat, dairy produce and chilli peppers are also important. Much of the land is pasture. A large proportion of the state's wealth comes from mineral deposits, including uranium, manganese, copper, silver, turquoise, oil, coal and natural gas. Area: 314,334sq km (121,335sq mi). Pop. (2000) 1,819,406.

New Model Army Reformed parliamentary army in the English CIVIL WARS. Formed in 1645 by Oliver CROMWELL and Thomas FAIRFAX, it was better organized, trained and disciplined than any comparable Royalist force. After a decisive victory at NASEBY (1645), the army emerged as a powerful political force and were responsible for PRIDE'S PURGE (1648) of the LONG PARLIAMENT. The radical LEVELLER faction within the army were suppressed by Cromwell.

New Netherland Dutch colonial territory in North America, stretching from the Hudson to the Delaware River. The Dutch claim was based on the explorations of Henry HUDSON. Under charter to the Dutch West India Company, settlers founded Fort Nassau (Albany) and New Amsterdam (New York City). The last and most able governor, Peter Stuyvesant, annexed New Sweden (1655). The area was taken over by England in 1664.

New Orleans City and river port in SE Louisiana, USA, between Lake Pontchartrain and the Mississippi River. Founded by the French in 1718, it was ceded to Spain in 1763 and acquired by the USA under the LOUISIANA PURCHASE of 1803. Its industries expanded rapidly in the 20th century after the discovery of oil and natural gas. New Orleans made an important contribution to the development of JAZZ. It is also the home of the annual MARDI GRAS festival. Industries: food processing, petroleum, natural gas, oil, sugar refining, shipbuilding, tourism, aluminium, petrochemicals. Pop. (1994) 484,149.

New Orleans, Battle of Engagement fought on 8 January 1815; the last battle in the WAR OF 1812. It took place two weeks after the Treaty of Ghent was signed because news of the treaty had not reached New Orleans. The Americans under General Andrew Jackson won the battle with only 71 killed, while the British lost 2,500 lives.

Newport City and port in Narragansett Bay, SE Rhode Island, USA. Founded in 1639, it served as joint state capital with Providence until 1900. For many years it was home to the Newport Jazz Festival and the America's Cup yachting races. Tourism is the chief industry. Other industries: shipbuilding, electronic instruments. Pop. (1990) 28,227.

Newport News City in SE Virginia on the James River, 18km (11mi) NNW of NORFOLK; it comprises the Port of Hampton Roads, together with Norfolk and PORTSMOUTH. It was the scene of the CIVIL WAR naval battle between the MONITOR AND MERRIMACK (1862). It later grew in importance as a coal-shipping port. Newport News is one of world's largest shipbuilding and repair centres. Industries: food processing, metal products, building materials, textiles, paper, oil refining. Pop. (1994) 179,127.

news agency (wire service) Organization that gathers news from correspondents via telephone or satellite and sells it to NEWSPAPERS and other MEDIA. Examples include REUTERS and TASS.

New South Wales State in SE Australia, on the Tasman Sea; the capital is SYDNEY. Captain James COOK first visited the area in 1770, claiming the E coast of Australia for Britain and naming it New South Wales. It achieved responsible government in 1855, becoming a state of the Commonwealth of Australia in 1901. The Great Dividing Range separates the narrow coastal lowlands from the W plains that occupy two-thirds of the state. The River MURRAY and its tributaries are used extensively for irrigation. Wheat, wool, dairy produce and beef are the principal agricultural products. The state has valuable mineral deposits. New South Wales is the most populous and most industrialized state in Australia. Steel is the chief product. Area: 801,430sq km (309,180sq mi). Pop. (1991) 5,730,947.

newspaper Periodical publication, usually daily or weekly, conveying news and comment on current events. Handwritten news sheets were posted in public places in ancient Rome under such titles as *Acta Diurna* (Daily Events). In Europe, the invention and spread of PRINTING in the 15th century facilitated the growth of newspapers. The earliest examples were printed in German cities, soon followed by Venice, the Low Countries and other states in the 16th century. The first daily newspaper in England was the *Daily Courant* (1702). In the early 18th century periodicals such as *Tatler* and *Spectator* were founded by Joseph ADDISON. *The Times* was founded in 1785. The British government attempted to limit PRESS freedom through the introduction (1712) of a stamp duty on newspapers. It was repealed in 1855. The first tabloid, the *Daily Mirror*, was founded by Alfred Harmsworth (Viscount NORTHCLIFFE). In the late 20th century, the newspaper industry became dominated by multinational communications empires, such as Rupert MURDOCH's News International.

newt Any of numerous species of tailed AMPHIBIANS of Europe, Asia and North America. The common European newt, *Triturus vulgaris*, is terrestrial, except during the breeding season when it is aquatic and the male develops ornamental fins. Its body is long and slender, and the tail is laterally flattened. Length: to 17cm (7in). Family Salamandridae.

New Testament Second part of the BIBLE, consisting of 27 books all originally written in Greek after AD 45 and concerning the life and teachings of JESUS CHRIST. It begins with three SYNOPTIC GOSPELS (MATTHEW, MARK and LUKE), which present a common narrative of Christ's life and ministry, and a fourth gospel (JOHN), which is more of a theological meditation. The ACTS OF THE APOSTLES records the early development and spread of Christianity. Next are 21 letters (EPISTLES) addressed to specific early Church communities; the New Testament ends with the REVELATION of St John the Divine (otherwise known as the Apocalypse), which is an interpretation of history designed to demonstrate the sovereignty of God.

Newton, Sir Isaac (1642–1727) English scientist. He studied at CAMBRIDGE and became professor of mathematics there (1669–1701). His main works were *Philosophiae Naturalis Principia Mathematica* (1687) and *Opticks* (1704). In the former, he outlined his laws of motion and proposed the principle of universal GRAVITATION; in the latter, he showed that white LIGHT is made up of colours of the SPECTRUM and proposed his particle theory of light. Newton also created the first system of CALCULUS in the 1660s but did not publish it until Gottfried LEIBNIZ had published his own system in 1684. In *c*.1671, he built the first reflecting telescope. Newton was president of the Royal Society (1703–27). In 1705, he became the first person to be knighted for scientific work. Newton's theory of CELESTIAL MECHANICS remained unchallenged until EINSTEIN's theory of RELATIVITY and QUANTUM MECHANICS.

newton (symbol N) SI unit of FORCE. One newton is the force that gives a mass of 1kg an acceleration of one metre per second per second.

Newton's laws Three physical laws of motion, formulated by the English scientist Isaac NEWTON. The **first** law states that an object remains at rest or moves in a straight line at constant speed unless acted upon by a FORCE. This property is known as INERTIA. The **second** law, which enables FORCE to be calculated, states that force is proportional to the rate of change of MOMENTUM. If the mass of a body remains constant, the force F is equal to the product of mass m and acceleration a: $F = ma$. The **third** law states that every force has associated with it an equal and opposite force. *See also* MECHANICS

new town Satellite town in the UK designed to rehouse residents from a nearby large city and to create local employment. The construction of some 37 new towns began in 1946 and continued until 1975.

New Wave Term used to describe the musical successor to PUNK, following its decline in the late 1970s. Groups such as Blondie, Police, Depeche Mode, Devo and Talking Heads epitomized this more tuneful and refined style.

New York State in NE USA, bounded by the Canadian border, the Great Lakes, the Atlantic Ocean and three New England states; the capital is ALBANY. NEW YORK CITY is by far the largest city in the state. Much of the state is mountainous, the ADIRONDACK MOUNTAINS (NE) and Catskills (SE) being the principal ranges. The W consists of a rolling plateau sloping down to Lake Ontario and the St Lawrence valley. The HUDSON and its tributary, the Mohawk, are the chief rivers. Henry HUDSON discovered New York Bay in 1609 and sailed up the river that now bears his name. The NEW NETHERLAND colony was established in the Hudson valley. In 1664, it was seized by the British and renamed New York. It was one of the 13 original states of the Union. The opening

of the ERIE CANAL in 1825 was an enormous stimulus to New York's growth. Throughout US history its economic strength and large population have given it great influence in national affairs. New York is the leading manufacturing and commercial state in the USA. Industries: clothing, machinery, chemicals, electrical equipment, paper, optical instruments. Area: 127,190sq km (49,108sq mi). Pop. (2000) 18,976,457.

New York City City and port in SE New York state, at the mouth of the HUDSON River; largest city (by population) in the USA. Manhattan Island was settled in 1624 and was bought from the Native Americans in 1626 by the Dutch West India Company. New Amsterdam was founded at the S end of the island. In 1664 the British took the colony and renamed it New York. The founding of the Bank of New York by Alexander HAMILTON and the opening of the ERIE CANAL in 1825 made New York the principal US commercial and financial centre. From the CIVIL WAR, the city received a great influx of immigrants. It is made up of five boroughs: MANHATTAN, the BRONX, BROOKLYN, QUEENS and STATEN ISLAND. Monuments and buildings of interest include the STATUE OF LIBERTY, the EMPIRE STATE BUILDING, Rockefeller Center, the METROPOLITAN MUSEUM OF ART, the Museum of Modern Art, the Guggenheim Museum, Lincoln Center and Carnegie Hall. It is one of the world's leading ports and financial centres. Industries: clothing, chemicals, metal products, scientific instruments, shipbuilding, food processing, broadcasting, entertainment, tourism, publishing. Pop. (1994) 7,333,253.

New Zealand Archipelago state in the S Pacific. New Zealand consists of two mountainous main islands and several smaller ones, *c*.1,600km (1,000mi) SE of Australia. Much of NORTH ISLAND is volcanic; Ngauruhoe and Ruapehu are active volcanoes. It is noted for its hot springs and geysers. New Zealand's largest river (Waikato) and largest lake (Taupo) are both on North Island. North Island cities include the capital, WELLINGTON, and the largest port, AUCKLAND. The Southern Alps extend for almost the entire length of SOUTH ISLAND, rising to Mount COOK at 3,753m (12,313ft). South Island is famed for its glaciers and fjords. The major South Island cities are CHRISTCHURCH and DUNEDIN. Territories include the ROSS DEPENDENCY in Antarctica. COOK ISLANDS and NIUE are associated states. **Climate** The climate varies from N to S. Auckland has a warm, humid climate throughout the year. Wellington has cooler summers, while in Dunedin temperatures can dip below freezing in winter. Rainfall is heaviest on the W highlands. **Vegetation** Only small areas of original *kauri* forests survive, mainly in the N and S extremities of South Island. Beech forests grow in the highlands, and large plantations are grown for timber. Abundant sunshine is ideal for E coast vineyards. **History and politics** MAORI settlers arrived in New Zealand more than 1,000 years ago. The first European discovery was by the Dutch navigator Abel TASMAN in 1642. The British explorer James COOK landed in 1769. Trade in fur and whaling brought British settlers in the early 19th century. A series of intertribal wars (1815–40) killed tens of thousands of Maoris. In 1840, the first British settlement at Wellington was established. The Treaty of WAITANGI

NEW ZEALAND
AREA: 270,990sq km (104,629sq mi)
POPULATION: 3,662,000
CAPITAL (POPULATION): Wellington (329,000)

(1840) promised to honour Maori land rights in return for recognition of British sovereignty. In 1841, New Zealand became a separate colony. Increasing colonization led to the MAORI WARS. In 1893, New Zealand became the first country to give women the vote. In 1907, New Zealand became a self-governing dominion in the British Commonwealth. New Zealand troops fought on the side of the Allies in both world wars. In 1973, Britain joined the European Community, and New Zealand's exports to Britain shrank. Since the 1980s, it has pursued a more independent economic and foreign policy. In 1985, the Greenpeace ship, *Rainbow Warrior*, was blown up in Auckland harbour, prompting the adoption of anti-nuclear policies. Maori rights and the preservation of Maori culture remain a political issue. A 1992 referendum voted in favour of the introduction of proportional representation. After 1996 elections the National Party (NP) and New Zealand First (NZF) formed a coalition government. In 1997, Jenny Shipley became New Zealand's first woman prime minister. In 1998, the NZF withdrew from the coalition. Helen Clark formed a minority Labour administration after the 1999 elections. Maori rights and the preservation of Maori culture remain central political issues. **Economy** During the 1980s, New Zealand gradually shifted from a state-controlled economy, with a large welfare state, to a more market-oriented economy, encouraging private sector finance (1995 GDP per capita, US$16,360). The economy was badly affected by the financial crisis in SE Asia. It has traditionally depended on agriculture, particularly sheep- and cattle-rearing. New Zealand is the world's third-largest producer of sheep. Manufacturing now employs twice as many people as agriculture. Tourism is the fastest growing economic sector (1992 receipts, US$1,032 million).

Ney, Michel (1769–1815) French general, one of the most brilliant of Napoleon's commanders. He fought in the FRENCH REVOLUTIONARY WARS and the NAPOLEONIC WARS, notably at Friedland (1807) and in the retreat from Moscow (1812). In 1814, Ney urged NAPOLEON I to abdicate. He accepted the BOURBON restoration, but rejoined Napoleon during the HUNDRED DAYS and fought gallantly in the WATERLOO campaign (1815). He was subsequently executed as a traitor.

Ngo Dinh Diem *See* DIEM, NGO DINH

Niagara Falls Waterfalls on the Niagara River on the border of the USA (N New York state) and Canada (SE Ontario); divided into the Horseshoe, or Canadian, Falls and the American Falls. The Canadian Falls are 48m (158ft) high and 792m (2,600ft), wide; the American Falls are 51m (167ft) high and 305m (1,000ft) wide.

Niamey Capital of Niger, W Africa, in SW Niger on the River Niger. It became capital of the French colony of Niger in 1926. It grew rapidly after World War 2 and is now the country's largest city and its commercial and administrative centre. Industries: textiles, ceramics, plastics, chemicals. Pop. (1994) 420,000.

Nicaea, councils of Two important ecumenical councils of the Christian church held in Nicaea (modern Iznik, Turkey). The **first** was convoked in AD 325 to resolve the problems caused by the emergence of ARIANISM. It promulgated the NICENE CREED, affirming belief in the divinity of Christ. The **second**, held in 787, was summoned by the patriarch Tarasius to deal with the worship of icons.

Nicaragua Republic in Central America. Nicaragua is the largest country in Central America. The Central Highlands rise in the NW Cordillera Isabella to more than 2,400m (8,000 ft) and are the source for many of the rivers that drain the E plain. The Caribbean coast forms part of the MOSQUITO COAST. Lakes Managua and Nicaragua lie on the edge of a narrow volcanic region that contains Nicaragua's major urban areas, including the capital, MANAGUA, and the second-largest city, LEÓN. This region is highly unstable, with many active volcanoes, and is prone to earthquakes. **Climate** Nicaragua has a tropical climate, with a rainy season from June to October. The Central Highlands are cooler, and the wettest part is the Mosquito Coast, with *c*.4,200mm (165in) of annual rain. **Vegetation** Rainforests cover large areas in the E, with trees such as cedar, mahogany and walnut. Tropical savanna is common in the drier W. **History and politics** In 1502, Christopher COLUMBUS reached Nicaragua and claimed the land for Spain. By 1518, Spanish forces had subdued the indigenous population, and Nicaragua was ruled as part of the Spanish Captaincy-General of Guatemala. In the 17th century, Britain secured control of the Caribbean coast. In 1821, Nicaragua gained independence and formed part of the Central American Federation (1825–38). In the mid-19th century, Nicaragua was ravaged by civil war and US and British interference. The USA was interested in the construction of a trans-isthmian canal through Nicaragua. In 1855, William Walker invaded and established himself as the short-lived president of Nicaragua. José Santos Zemalya's dictatorial regime gained control of the Mosquito Coast and formed close links with the British. Following his downfall, civil war raged once more. In 1912, US marines landed to protect a pro-US regime and, in 1916, the USA gained exclusive rights to the canal. Liberal opposition to US occupation resulted in guerrilla war, led by Augusto César Sandino. In 1933 the US marines withdrew but set up the National Guard to help defeat the rebels. In 1934, Sandino was assassinated by Anastasio SOMOZA, director of the National Guard and official president from 1937. Somoza's dictatorial regime led to political isolation. He was succeeded by his sons, Luis (1956) and Anastasio (1967). Anastasio's diversion of international relief aid following a devastating earthquake in Managua (1972) cemented opposition. In 1979, the SANDINISTA National Liberation Front (FSLN) overthrew the Somoza regime. The Sandinista government, led by Daniel ORTEGA, instigated wide-ranging socialist reforms. The USA, anxious about the Sandinista's relations with Cuba and the Soviet Union, sought to destabilize the government by organizing and funding the CONTRA rebels. A ten-year civil war destroyed the economy and created dissatisfaction with the Sandinistas. In 1990 elections, the Sandinistas lost power to the National Opposition Union (UNO) coalition, led by Violeta CHAMORRO. Many of Chamorro's reforms were blocked by her coalition partners and the Sandinista-controlled trade unions. In 1996 elections, Chamorro was defeated by the Liberal leader, Arnoldo Alemán. In 1998, hurricane Mitch killed *c*.4000 people and caused extensive damage to Nicaragua. Plans for the deployment of US soldiers to help reconstruction efforts were approved by parliament in March 2000. **Economy** Nicaragua faces many problems in rebuilding its shattered economy and introducing free-market reforms (1995 US$2,000). Agriculture is the main activity, employing *c*.50% of the workforce and accounting for 70% of exports. Major cash

---

NICARAGUA
AREA: 130,000sq km (50,193sq mi)
POPULATION: 5,261,000
CAPITAL (POPULATION): Managua (864,000)

crops include coffee, cotton, sugar and bananas. Rice is the main food crop. It has some copper, gold and silver, but mining is underdeveloped. Most manufacturing is based in and around Managua.

Nice City on the Mediterranean coast of SE France; capital of Alpes-Maritimes department. Founded by Phocaean Greeks in the 4th century BC, Nice was conquered by Rome in the 1st century AD. In the 10th century it passed to the counts of Provence. In 1388, it became a possession of the House of Savoy. Nice was under French rule from 1792 to 1814, when it was returned to Savoy, becoming permanently part of France in 1860. It is a major centre of the French RIVIERA. Industries: tourism, olive oil, perfume, textiles, electronics. Pop. (1990) 342,349.

Nicene Creed Statement of Christian faith named after the First Council of NICAEA (325). Its exact origin is, however, uncertain. The Nicene Creed defends the orthodox Christian doctrine of the TRINITY against the ARIAN heresy. It is subscribed to by all the major Christian Churches and is widely used by them in their celebrations of the EUCHARIST. *See also* APOSTLES' CREED; ATHANASIAN CREED

Nicholas, Saint (active 4th century) Patron saint of children and sailors. According to tradition, he was Bishop of Myra in Asia Minor. Nicholas is the subject of many legends. In one he secretly gave gold to three poor girls as their dowry. From this came the custom of giving presents on his feast day, 6 December, a habit later transferred to CHRISTMAS in most countries. His name in one Dutch dialect, *Sinter Claes*, became Santa Claus.

Nicholas I (1796–1855) Tsar of Russia (1825–55). As tsar, he was immediately confronted by the Decembrist revolt, during which a secret society of officers and aristocrats assembled some 3,000 troops in St Petersburg, demanding a representative democracy. Having crushed the rebels, Nicholas ruthlessly suppressed rebellion in Poland and assisted Austria against the Hungarian REVOLUTIONS OF 1848. His pressure on Turkey led to the CRIMEAN WAR (1853–56).

Nicholas II (1868–1918) Last tsar of Russia (1894–1917). Torn between the autocracy of his father, ALEXANDER III, and the reformist policies of ministers, such as Count Sergei Witte, he lacked the capacity for firm leadership. Defeat in the RUSSO-JAPANESE WAR was followed by the RUSSIAN REVOLUTION of 1905. Nicholas agreed to constitutional government but, as danger receded, removed most of the powers of the DUMA. In WORLD WAR 1 he took military command (1915), but a succession of defeats provoked the RUSSIAN REVOLUTION (1917). Nicholas was forced to abdicate, and in July 1918 he and his family were executed by the BOLSHEVIKS.

Nichols, Mike (1931–) US stage and film director, b. Germany as Michael Peschkowsky. In 1939, his family fled to the US from Nazi Germany. Nichols began his career in theatre in Chicago. He achieved immediate success with his film debut *Who's Afraid of Virginia Woolf* (1966). Nicols won an Academy Award for best director for *The Graduate* (1967). He earned further Academy nominations for *Silkwood* (1983) and *Working Girl* (1988). Other films include *Catch-22* (1971).

Nicholson, Ben (1894–1982) English painter, one of the champions of ABSTRACT ART in Britain. Influenced by CUBISM and Piet MONDRIAN, he developed a geometric abstract style that he expressed in austere carved and painted reliefs, such as *White Relief* (1935). Nicholson later produced a series of freely abstracted still-lifes and landscapes before returning to reliefs in the 1960s. His second wife was fellow artist Barbara HEPWORTH. Nicholson was a leading member of the St Ives School.

Nicholson, Jack (1937–) US film actor and director. He gained an Academy nomination for his performance in *Easy Rider* (1969). Further nominations followed for *Five Easy Pieces* (1970) and *Chinatown* (1974). Nicholson won an Oscar for best actor in *One Flew Over The Cuckoo's Nest* (1975). He won another Academy Award for best supporting actor in *Terms of Endearment* (1983). Nicholson won a second best actor Oscar for *As Good As It Gets* (1998). Other films include *The Shining* (1980), *Reds* (1981), *The Postman Always Rings Twice* (1981), *Prizzi's Honor* (1985) and *Batman* (1989). His directorial credits include *The Two Jakes* (1990).

nickel (symbol Ni) Silvery-white, metallic element, one of the TRANSITION ELEMENTS. Its chief ores are pentlandite and niccolite. Hard, malleable and ductile, nickel is used in stainless steels, other special alloys, coinage, cutlery, storage batteries and as a hydrogenation catalyst. Properties: at.no. 28; r.a.m. 58.71; r.d. 8.90; m.p. 1,453°C (2,647°F); b.p. 2,732°C (4,950°F); most common isotope Ni^{58} (67.84%).

Nicklaus, Jack William (1940–) US golfer. He won a record 18 professional majors between 1962 and 1986, including: the US Open (1962, 1967, 1972, 1980); British Open (1966, 1970, 1978); US PGA (1963, 1971, 1973, 1975, 1980); and the US Masters (1963, 1965–66, 1972, 1975, 1986). He captained the irrepressible US Ryder Cup team (1969–81). In 1988, Nicklaus was voted "Golfer of the Century".

Nicolai, Otto (1810–49) German composer and conductor who in 1842 helped to found the Vienna Philharmonic Orchestra. His masterpiece is the comic opera *The Merry Wives of Windsor* (1849).

Nicolson, Sir Harold (1886–1968) English diplomat and writer. He is best remembered as a man of letters. The diaries he kept from 1930 to 1964 afford a fascinating glimpse of life among the ruling class. Nicolson was married to the poet and novelist Vita SACKVILLE-WEST.

Nicosia (Levkosía) Capital of Cyprus, in the central part of the island. Known to the ancient world as Ledra, the city was later successively held by the Byzantines, French crusaders and Venetians. The Ottoman Turks occupied the city from 1571 to 1878, when it passed to Britain. It is now divided into Greek and Turkish sectors. Industries: cigarettes, textiles, footwear. Pop. (1994) 194,000.

nicotine Poisonous ALKALOID obtained from the leaves of TOBACCO, used in agriculture as a pesticide and in veterinary medicine to kill external parasites. Nicotine is the principal addictive agent in smoking tobacco. *See also* CIGARETTE

Nielsen, Carl August (1865–1931) Danish composer. He developed the principle the notion of progressive TONALITY. Nielsen wrote six symphonies, of which the fourth, The Inextinguishable (1914–16), is the best known .He also composed concertos for violin, flute and clarinet, two operas, a woodwind quintet and four string quartets.

Niemeyer, Oscar (1907–) Brazilian architect. An early advocate of MODERNISM, he worked with LE CORBUSIER on the Ministry of Education and Health Building, Rio de Janeiro (1936–45). Niemeyer subsequently developed an original approach: elegant, sub-tropical luxury expressed through curving, sculptural forms. He designed (1950–60) the main public buildings in Brasília.

Niemöller, Martin (1892–1984) German Lutheran pastor. His opposition to Adolf HITLER's creation of a "German Christian Church" and his pacifist views led to his internment in a concentration camp (1938–45). Niemöller was president (1961–68) of the World Council of Churches.

Nietzsche, Friedrich Wilhelm (1844–1900) German philosopher who rejected Christianity and the prevailing morality of his time and emphasized people's freedom to create their own values. He studied classical philology and taught Greek. A friend of Richard Wagner, in *The Birth of Tragedy* (1872) Nietzsche argued that Wagnerian opera and Greek drama awakened the human spirit. In 1879, he abandoned philology for philosophy and worked out his view of the freedom of the individual over the next decade. In *Thus Spake Zarathustra* (1883–91), Nietzsche presented his notion of the *Übermensch* (superman), the idealized man, strong, positive, and able to impose his wishes upon the weak and worthless. The concept was distorted by the Nazis to justify their notion of Aryan superiority. Other works include *Beyond Good and Evil* (1886) and *On the Genealogy of Morals* (1887). In 1889, Nietzsche was declared insane.

Niger Landlocked republic in N central Africa. The N plateaux lie in the SAHARA. Central Niger contains the rugged, partly volcanic Aïr Mountains that reach a height of 2,022m (6,634ft) near Agadez. The S consists of broad plains, including the Lake CHAD basin in SE Niger, on the borders with Chad and Nigeria. The only major river is the NIGER in the SW. The Niger valley is the country's most fertile and densely populated region and includes the capital, NIAMEY. **Climate** Niger is one of the world's hottest countries. The hottest months are March to May when the harmattan wind blows from the Sahara. Niamey has a tropical climate with a rainy season from June to September. Rainfall decreases from S to N. Northern Niger is practically rainless. **Vegetation** The far S consists of tropical savanna. Buffaloes, elephants, giraffes and lions are found in the "W" National Park, which Niger shares with Benin and Burkina Faso. Most of S Niger lies in the SAHEL region of dry grassland. The Aïr Mountains support grass and scrub. The N deserts are generally barren. **History and politics** Neolithic remains have been found in the N desert. In the 11th century, Nomadic TUAREG settled in the Aïr Mountains and, by the 13th century, had established a state based on Agadez and the trans-Saharan trade. In the 14th century, the HAUSA settled in S Niger. In the early 16th century, the SONGHAI empire controlled much of Niger but was defeated by the Moroccans at the end of the century. In the early 19th century, the FULANI gained control of much of S Niger. In 1891, the first French expedition arrived, but Tuareg resistance prevented full occupation until 1914. In 1922, Niger became a colony within French West Africa. In 1958, Niger voted to remain an autonomous republic within the French Community. In 1960, full independence was achieved. Hamani Diori became Niger's first president, and he maintained close ties with France. Beginning in 1968, a succession of droughts in the Sahel killed many livestock and destroyed crops. In 1974, a group of army officers, led by Lieutenant Colonel Seyni Kountché, overthrew Hamani Diori and suspended the constitution. In 1987, Kountché died and was succeeded by his cousin, General Ali Saibou. In 1991, the Tuareg in N Niger began an armed campaign for

greater autonomy. A national conference removed Saibou and established a transitional government. In 1993, multiparty elections, Mahamane Ousmane of the Alliance of Forces for Change (AFC) coalition became president. In 1995, the collapse of the coalition led to further elections that were won by the National Movement for a Development Society (MNSD), but a military coup, led by Colonel Ibrahim Bare Mainassara, seized power. In 1995, a peace accord was signed between the government and the Tuareg. In 1999, Mainassara was assassinated by his bodyguards and Tanja Mamadou became president. **Economy** Niger has been badly hit by droughts, which have caused great suffering and food shortages, and the destruction of the traditional nomadic lifestyle. Niger's chief resource is uranium, of which it is the world's second-largest producer. Uranium accounts for over 80% of exports, most of which is exploited by the French Atomic Energy Authority. Some tin and tungsten are also mined. Other mineral resources are largely unexploited. Despite its resources, Niger is one of the world's poorest countries (1995 GDP per capita, US$750). Farming employs 85% of the workforce, though only 3% of the land is arable and 7% is used for grazing. Food crops include beans, cassava, millet, rice and sorghum. Cotton and groundnuts are leading cash crops.

Niger Major river of W Africa. It rises in the Fouta Djallon plateau in the SW Republic of Guinea and flows NE through Guinea into the Mali Republic, where it forms an extensive inland delta. It then flows in a great curve across the border into Nigeria and S into another vast delta before emptying into the Gulf of Guinea. Length: 4,180km (2,600mi).

Niger-Congo languages Group of c.1,000 languages spoken by more than 300 million people who live in Africa S of the Sahara. The main ones are BANTU (spoken in S Africa), FULANI (Guinea, Senegal and other W African countries), SWAHILI (E coast), YORUBA (primarily Nigeria) and Malinke (Mali).

Nigeria Federal republic in W Africa. Nigeria is the most populous nation in Africa. The division of Nigeria into 30 states reflects the fact that it contains more than 250 ethnic and language groups and several religious ones. It has a sandy coastline, fringed by a belt of mangrove swamps and lagoons, which includes the former capital, LAGOS. The rivers NIGER and Benue meet in central Nigeria and run S into the Niger delta where BENIN CITY is situated. North of the coastal lowlands is a hilly region of rainforest and savanna. At the foot of the great plateau of Nigeria lies the city of IBADAN. The plateau is a region of high wooded and savanna plains and includes the capital, ABUJA. In the extreme NE lies the Lake CHAD basin. In the NW lie the Sokoto plains. The Adamawa Highlands extend along the SE border with Cameroon and contain Nigeria's highest point, at 2,042m (6,699ft). **Climate** Lagos has a tropical climate with high temperatures and rain throughout the year. The N is drier and often hotter than the S, though the highlands are cooler. KANO in N central Nigeria has a marked dry season from October to April. **Vegetation** Behind the coastal swamps are rainforests, although large areas have been cleared by farmers. The plateau contains large areas of tropical savanna

---

NIGER
AREA: 1,267,000sq km (489,189sq mi)
POPULATION: 10,752,000
CAPITAL (POPULATION): Niamey (420,000)

NIGERIA
AREA: 923,770sq km (356,668sq mi)
POPULATION: 105,000,000
CAPITAL (POPULATION): Abuja (350,000)

with forested river valleys. Open grassland and semi-arid scrub occur in drier areas. To the N lie the dry grasslands of the SAHEL. **History and politics** Excavations around the Nigerian village of NOK have uncovered some of the oldest and most beautiful examples of African sculpture. The Nok civilization flourished between 500 BC and AD 200. In the 11th century, the Kanem-Bornu kingdom extended s from Lake Chad into Nigeria, and the HAUSA established several city-states. In the 15th century, the state of BENIN and the YORUBA kingdom of Oyo flourished in SW Nigeria. They were renowned for their brass, bronze and ivory sculptures. The SONGHAI empire dominated N Nigeria in the early 16th century. The Portuguese were the first Europeans to reach the Nigerian coast, and they established trading links with Benin in the late 15th century. Nigeria became a centre of the slave trade, with major European powers competing for control. The IBO established city-states built on the wealth of the trade. In the early 19th century, the FULANI captured many of the Hausa city-states. Sokoto retained its independence. The SW began a protracted civil war. In 1807, Britain renounced the slave trade, but other countries continued the practice. In 1861, Britain seized Lagos, ostensibly to stop the trade. By 1885, Britain controlled all of S Nigeria and gradually extended northwards. By 1906, Britain had conquered all of Nigeria and divided the country into the Colony (Lagos) and Protectorate of Southern Nigeria and the Protectorate of Northern Nigeria. In 1914, the two were combined. Britain ruled indirectly through colonial officials and local rulers. Cities, infrastructure and industries developed. In 1954, Nigeria was federated into three regions (N, E and W) plus the territory of Lagos. In 1960, Nigeria gained independence; it became a republic in 1963. In 1966, Ibo army officers staged a successful coup, but the regime was rapidly toppled by a Hausa-led coup. In 1967, the Ibo, increasingly concerned for their safety within the federation, formed the independent republic of BIAFRA. For the next three years civil war raged in Nigeria, until Biafra capitulated. The early 1970s were more peaceful, as Nigeria expanded its oil industry. Nigeria joined OPEC in 1971. Oil revenue created widespread government corruption and widened the wealth gap. Drought in the SAHEL killed much livestock and led to mass migration to the s. After several military coups, civilian rule was briefly restored in 1979. Following 1983 elections, the military seized power again. Between 1960 and 1998, Nigeria enjoyed only nine years of civilian government. The 1993 presidential elections, won by Chief Moshood Abiola, were declared invalid by the military government. The army commander-in-chief, General Sanni Abacha, gained power. In 1994, nationwide demonstrations prompted Abiola to form a rival government, but he was swiftly arrested. In 1995, General Abacha was given an open-ended term in office, vowing to restore civilian rule by 1998. His regime was severely criticized for human rights abuses and the suppression of opposition. In November 1995, after the execution of nine activists, Nigeria was suspended from the British Commonwealth. In 1998, Abacha died and was succeeded by General Abubakar. The death in prison of Abiola (July 1998) prompted widespread rioting. In 1999 elections, General Olusegun Obasanjo, a former military ruler (1976–79) of Nigeria, became president and Nigeria was readmitted to the Commonwealth. **Economy** Nigeria is a low-income developing country, with great economic potential (1995 GDP per capita, US$1,220). It is the world's eleventh-largest producer of crude oil, which accounts for 95% of its exports. The major oilfields are in the Niger delta and the bights of Benin and Biafra. In the 1980s, falling oil prices and mounting foreign debt caused economic recession. Agriculture employs 43% of the workforce. Nigeria is the world's third-largest producer of palm oil and palm kernels, fourth-largest producer of groundnuts, sixth-largest producer of cocoa and seventh-largest producer of rubber. Cattle rearing is important in the N grasslands, while fishing is a major activity in the S. Manufacturing is diversifying. Products include chemicals and clothing. Nigeria has some petroleum refineries, vehicle assembly plants and steel mills.

night blindness Inability to see in dim light. It is caused by disorder of certain cells in the RETINA, occurring as a result of retinal disease or vitamin A deficiency.

Nightingale, Florence (1820–1910) British nurse, b. Italy. She founded modern NURSING and became known as the "lady of the lamp" for her activities in the CRIMEAN WAR. In 1854 Nightingale took a unit of 38 nurses to care for wounded British soldiers. In 1860, she founded the Nightingale School and Home for nurse training at St Thomas' Hospital, London. In 1907, Nightingale became the first woman to be awarded the order of merit.

nightingale Migratory Old World songbird of the THRUSH family (Turdidae). The common nightingale of England and W Europe (*Luscinia megarhynchos*) is ruddy-brown with light grey underparts. The male is noted for its beautiful song. Length: *c*.16.5cm (6.5in).

nightjar (goatsucker) Insect-eating, nocturnal bird found worldwide. They have mottled grey-brown plumage and a short bill. Nightjars have a distinctive whirring cry and some species are known by the sound of their call, such as pottoo and whippoorwill. They became popularly known as goatsuckers in the erroneous belief that they fed at night on goat's milk. In fact, they eat insects in flight. Length: *c*.27cm (10.5in). Family Caprimulgidae.

nightshade Name given to various species of poisonous flowering plants, but especially to the DEADLY NIGHTSHADE (*Atropa belladonna*) and its close relatives.

nihilism Doctrine of certain Russian revolutionaries in the late 19th century. It condemned contemporary society as hostile to nature and rejected non-rational beliefs. Nihilists demanded radical reform of government and society by violent means.

Nijinsky, Vaslav (1890–1950) Russian ballet dancer and choreographer. He is often regarded as the greatest male dancer of the 20th century. In 1909, Nijinsky joined DIAGHILEV'S BALLETS RUSSES. Michel FOKINE choreographed *The Spectre of the Rose* and *Petrushka* (both 1911) especially for him. In 1912, Nijinksy choreographed himself in *The Afternoon of a Faun* (1912). His radical choreography of Stravinsky's *The Rites of Spring* (1913) outraged Parisian audiences. In 1917, Nijinsky was diagnosed as suffering from schizophrenia.

Nile Longest river in the world, flowing *c*.6,700km (4,160mi) from the Kagera headstream, E Burundi, to its Mediterranean delta in NE Egypt. The **Kagera** flows generally N before emptying into Lake VICTORIA. The **Victoria** Nile flows from Lake Victoria to Lake ALBERT in Uganda. From Lake Albert to the Sudanese border, it is called the **Albert** Nile. It continues to flow N through the s Sudanese swamps as the **Bahr el Jebel**. From Malakâl to KHARTOUM the river is called the **White** Nile. At Khartoum it converges with the **Blue** Nile. As simply the Nile, the river continues to flow N to the Egyptian border. There it flows into the man-made Lake Nasser, created by the damming of the river at ASWAN. From Aswan the river flows through LUXOR to CAIRO. N of Cairo is the Nile delta, Egypt's largest agricultural area. The Nile empties into the Mediterranean at Damietta and Rosetta. As well as supporting the agriculture of Egypt and Sudan, the Nile is used for transport, hydroelectricity and tourism.

Nile, Battle of the (1798) *See* ABOUKIR

Nimitz, Chester William (1885–1966) US admiral. He served in submarines during World War 1 and commanded the Pacific fleet during World War 2, directing operations against the Japanese at Midway.

Nin, Anaïs (1903–77) US writer, b. France. She was part of the "LOST GENERATION" of US expatriate writers in Paris during the 1920s. Nin was an early student of Carl JUNG, and her novels are all intense psychological studies. They include *The House of Incest* (1936), *Winter of Artifice* (1939) and the five volume sequence *Cities of the Interior* (1946–58). The publication of her diaries (1966–80) aroused admiration and controversy. She is particularly remembered for her erotic fiction, including *Delta of Venus: Erotica* (1977).

Nineveh Capital of ancient ASSYRIA, on the River Tigris (opposite modern Mosul, Iraq). The site was first occupied in the 6th millennium BC. It became the Assyrian capital under SENNACHERIB (r.704–681 BC). The city walls were more than 12km (7.5mi) long and contained gardens irrigated by canals. In 612 BC, Nineveh was sacked by the Medes, but continued to be occupied until the Middle Ages.

niobium (symbol Nb) Shiny, grey-white TRANSITION ELEMENT, first discovered in 1801. Its chief ore is pyrochlore. Soft and ductile, niobium is used in special stainless steels and in alloys for rockets and jet engines. Properties: at.no. 41; r.a.m. 92.9064; r.d. 8.57; m.p. 2,468°C (4,474°F); b.p. 4,742°C (8,568°F); most common isotope Nb^{93} (100%).

Nirenberg, Marshall Warren (1927–) US biochemist who found the key to the GENETIC CODE by deciphering different combinations of three nucleotide bases (called "codons") within long nucleotide chains in DNA and RNA. Each combination is coded to convert a different AMINO ACID to PROTEIN, a key process in transferring inherited characteristics. Nirenberg found he could decipher the unknown configurations by synthesizing a NUCLEIC ACID with a known base combination and then recording the amino acid that it changed to protein. He shared the 1968 Nobel Prize for physiology or medicine, with Robert W. Holley and Har Gobind KHORANA, for his part in discovering how GENES determine cell function.

nirvana Conception of salvation and liberation from rebirth in the religions of ancient India – HINDUISM, BUDDHISM and JAINISM. To Hindus, *nirvana* is extinction in the supreme being, brought about by internal happiness, internal satisfaction and internal illumination. To Buddhists, it is the attainment of a transcendent state of enlightenment through the extinction of all desires. To Jainists, *nirvana* is a state of eternal blissful repose.

nitrate (HNO$_3$) Salt of NITRIC ACID. Nitrate salts contain the nitrate ion (NO$_3^-$), and some are important naturally occurring compounds, such as saltpeter (potassium nitrate, KNO$_3$) and Chile saltpetre (sodium nitrate, NaNO$_3$). Nitrates are used as food preservers, fertilizers, explosives and as a source of nitric acid. They can be an environmental hazard.

nitric acid (HNO$_3$) Colourless liquid, one of the strongest mineral acids. Nitric acid attacks most metals, resulting in the formation of NITRATES, and is a strong oxidizing agent. It is used in the manufacture of agricultural chemicals, explosives, plastics, dyes and rocket propellants.

nitrogen (symbol N) Common gaseous, nonmetallic element of Group V of the periodic table, discovered in 1772. Colourless and odourless, it is the major component of the atmosphere (78% by volume), from which it is extracted by fractional distillation of liquid air. The NITROGEN CYCLE is an essential process for the existence of life on Earth. The main industrial use is in the HABER PROCESS, which produces ammonia for making fertilizers and nitric acid. Nitrogen compounds are used in explosives, dyes, foods and drugs. The element is chemically inert. Properties: at.no. 7; r.a.m. 14.0067; r.d. 1.2506; m.p. −209.86°C (−345.75°F); b.p. −195.8°C (−320.4°F); most common isotope N^{14} (99.76%).

nitrogen cycle Circulation of NITROGEN through plants and animals in the BIOSPHERE. Plants obtain nitrogen compounds for producing essential proteins through assimilation. Nitrogen-fixing bacteria in the soil or plant root nodules take free nitrogen from the soil and air to form the nitrogen compounds (nitrates) used by plants in ASSIMILATION (*see* NITROGEN FIXATION). HERBIVORES obtain their nitrogen from the plants, and in turn CARNIVORES obtain nitrogen by eating herbivores (*see* FOOD CHAIN). SAPROPHYTES decompose the tissue of all the organisms concerned and the nitrogen is released back into the cycle.

nitrogen dioxide (NO$_2$) Oxide of NITROGEN. It is a pungent-smelling, brown gas that readily forms dinitrogen tetroxide (N$_2$O$_4$). It is made by the action of concentrated NITRIC ACID on copper, and dissolves in water to give a mixture of nitrous and nitric acids. It is also formed by the reaction of oxygen with nitrogen monoxide. Its presence in the atmosphere from the exhaust gases of petrol engines contributes to the formation of ACID RAIN and the depletion of the OZONE LAYER.

nitrogen fixation Incorporation of atmospheric NITROGEN into chemicals for use by organisms. Nitrogen-fixing microorganisms (mainly BACTERIA and CYANOBACTERIA) absorb nitrogen gas from the air, from air spaces in the soil or from water, and build it up into compounds of AMMONIA. Other bacteria can then change these compounds into NITRATES, which can be taken up by plants. *See also* NITROGEN CYCLE

nitroglycerine Oily liquid used in the manufacture of EXPLOSIVES. It is also used in medicine (as glyceryl trinitrate) to relieve the symptoms of ANGINA.

nitrous oxide (dinitrogen oxide, N$_2$O) Colourless gas that is used as an anaesthetic or analgesic during surgical or dental operations. It is known as "laughing gas" since it produces exhilaration. It is also used in making pressurized foods.

Niue Island territory in the S Pacific Ocean, 2,160km (1,340mi) NE of New Zealand; the capital is Alofi. The largest coral island in the world, Niue was first visited by Europeans in 1774. In 1901, it was annexed to New Zealand. In 1974, it achieved self-government in free association with New Zealand. The island is prone to hurricanes and tropical rainstorms. Its economy is mainly agricultural. The major export is coconut. Area: 260sq km (100sq mi). Pop. (2000) 2,000.

Niven, David (1910–83) English film actor. Regularly cast as the reticent but urbane Englishman, he worked from the 1930s in both Hollywood and the UK. Niven gave fine performances in *Wuthering Heights* (1939) and *The First of the Few* (1942). Other films include *Around the World in Eighty Days* (1956) and *Murder by Death* (1976). He also wrote two best-selling autobiographies, *The Moon's a Balloon* (1971) and *Bring On The Empty Horses* (1975).

Nixon, Richard Milhous (1913–94) 37th US President (1969–74). He was elected as a Republican to the House of Representatives in 1946 and the Senate in 1950.

Nixon came to prominence as a member of the House UN-AMERICAN ACTIVITIES COMMITTEE (HUAC). He was vice-president under Dwight D. EISENHOWER (1953–61) but lost the presidential election of 1960 to John F. KENNEDY. In 1968, Nixon receive the Republican nomination for a second time and narrowly defeated his Democrat challenger, Hubert Humphrey. As president, he adopted a policy of détente with the Soviet Union and opened US relations with communist China. Overwhelmingly re-elected in 1972, he withdrew US troops from the VIETNAM WAR (1973). The WATERGATE affair revealed that he was personally implicated in the obstruction of justice, and he resigned to avoid impeachment.

Nkomo, Joshua (1917–99) Zimbabwean statesman, vice-president (1990–99). In 1961, he became leader of ZAPU. In 1976, Nkomo and Robert MUGABE formed the Patriotic Front in opposition to Ian Smith's white-minority government in Rhodesia. In 1982, he was dismissed from Mugabe's government, but returned in 1988.

Nkrumah, Kwame (1909–72) Ghanaian statesman, prime minister (1957–60) and president (1960–66). He was the leading post-colonial proponent of PAN-AFRICAN-ISM. In 1949 Nkrumah formed the Convention People's Party in the Gold Coast. He was imprisoned (1950–52) by the British, but released when his party won the general election. He led the Gold Coast to independence (1957) and became prime minister. In 1960, Gold Coast became the Republic of Ghana and Nkrumah was made president. Nkrumah formed a loose union with Guinea and Mali and promoted the Charter of African States (1961). Nkrumah gradually assumed absolute power and, following a series of assassination attempts, Ghana became a one-party state (1964). While on a visit to China, he was deposed in a military coup (1966).

Noah Old Testament patriarch who was the only person righteous enough to be chosen by God to survive (with his family) the destruction of the FLOOD. In Genesis 6–9, Noah built an ARK, in accordance with God's strict instructions, to carry and shelter himself, all his family, and selected animals and birds. Noah and his sons and their wives were the ancestors of the human race after the Flood.

Nobel, Alfred Bernhard (1833–96) Swedish chemist, engineer and industrialist. In 1866 Nobel invented DYNAMITE and patented a more powerful EXPLOSIVE, gelignite, in 1876. With the fortune he made from the manufacture of explosives, he founded the NOBEL PRIZES.

nobelium (symbol No) Radioactive metallic element, one of the ACTINIDE SERIES. It was first made in 1958 by bombarding CURIUM with CARBON at the University of California at Berkeley. Seven isotopes are known. Properties: at.no. 102; r.a.m. 259; most stable isotope No^{255} (half-life 3 minutes). *See also* TRANSURANIC ELEMENTS

Nobel Prize Awards given each year for outstanding contributions in the fields of physics, chemistry, physiology or medicine, literature, economics, and world peace. Established in 1901 by the will of Alfred NOBEL, the prizes are awarded annually on 10 December. The winners are selected by committees based in Sweden and Norway.

Nobili, Leopoldo (1784–1835) Italian physicist who was a pioneer in ELECTROCHEMISTRY. He generated electricity using platinum ELECTRODES in an alkaline nitrate ELECTROLYTE and devised the astatic galvanometer to measure the current.

noble gas (inert gas) HELIUM, NEON, ARGON, KRYPTON, XENON and RADON – the elements (in order of increasing atomic number) forming group 0 of the PERIODIC TABLE. They are colourless, odourless and very unreactive. They have low reactivity because their outer electron shells are complete (two electrons for helium and eight each for the rest), thus offering no VALENCE "hooks".

nocturne In music, a quiet piece endeavouring to reflect the atmosphere and mood of night-time. First used by John Field for some of his piano pieces, the title was later used by Frédéric CHOPIN. Claude DEBUSSY composed three orchestral nocturnes.

No drama Form of JAPANESE THEATRE that developed between the 12th or 13th and the 15th centuries. It was influenced by ZEN, and the actors were originally Buddhist priests. The plots were taken chiefly from Japanese mythology and poetry. With little character or plot development, the No play seeks to convey a moment of experience or insight. It is highly stylized and uses masks, music, dance and song. No was central to the development of KABUKI THEATRE.

Noether, Emmy (Amalie) (1882–1935) German mathematician. The Nazi purges of Jewish academics in 1933 forced her to seek refuge in the USA, where her main work was in the field of abstract ALGEBRA. Noether contributed significantly to the general theory of ideals and to noncommutative algebras.

Noguchi, Isamu (1904–88) US abstract sculptor. Primarily a stone carver, he was influenced by BRANCUSI, GIACOMETTI and Alexander CALDER. His works are marked by great delicacy. He created numerous sculptures for public spaces, including the Japanese garden for the UNESCO building, Paris (1956–58). Noguchi also designed ballet and theatre sets, furniture and interiors.

noise Any disturbing, often unwanted, SOUND. Experiments carried out to determine the effects of noise on workers in manufacturing industries show that it seriously affects only that output requiring mental concentration. Nevertheless, noise is often regarded as a form of acoustic pollution, and noise-abatement pressure groups have been formed to lobby for legislation. Noise is usually measured on a DECIBEL scale: conversation is generally $c.60$dB and pain starts at $c.120$dB.

Nok Ancient African civilization that flourished 500 BC to 200 AD, named after the village of Nok in central Nigeria where remains were found. Nok artists produced clay figurines that are among the first African sculptures.

Nolan, Sir Sidney Robert (1917–92) Australian painter. Nolan is famed for a series of paintings (begun in 1946) based on the life of a notorious outlaw, Ned Kelly. Other paintings that portray events from Australian history include the *Eureka Stockade* series (1949). His almost surreal landscapes express the hard, scorched majesty of the outback.

Noland, Kenneth (1924–) US painter. In the second generation of ABSTRACT EXPRESSIONISM, Noland's method draws attention to the practice of art itself. His subjects are colour and the two-dimensionality of canvas, as in *Song* (1958).

Nolde, Emil (1867–1956) German painter and graphic artist who exemplified EXPRESSIONISM. He trained as a woodcarver before turning to painting relatively late. He painted his subjects (often flowers or landscapes) with deep, glowing colours and simplified outlines, bringing the works to the borders of ABSTRACT ART. Although he was a member of die BRÜCKE (1905–07), he was essentially a solitary figure.

nomad Member of a wandering group of people who live mainly by hunting or herding. There are three broad categories of nomads. First, HUNTERS AND GATHERERS (such as NATIVE AUSTRALIANS) move in small groups at irregular interbals in search of food. Second, TRANSHU-MANCE is practised by pastoralists (such as the NUER), who often move between winter and summer pastures. Third, trader nomads (such as GYPSIES) travel widely and regularly plying their trade. *See also* PASTORALISM

nominalism Philosophical theory, opposed to REALISM, that denies the reality of universal concepts. Whereas realists claim that there are universal concepts, such as *roundness* or *dog*, that are referred to by the use of these terms, nominalists argue that such generalized concepts cannot be known, and that the terms refer only to specific qualities common to particular circles or dogs that have been encountered up to now. Nominalism was much discussed by the scholastic philosophers of the Middle Ages.

nonalignment *See* NEUTRALITY

nonconformism Dissent from or lack of conformity with the religious doctrines or discipline of an established church, especially the CHURCH OF ENGLAND. The term Nonconformist applies to all the sects of British PROTESTANTISM that do not subscribe to the principles of the established Anglican Church or the established CHURCH OF SCOTLAND. It arose in England in reaction to the Act of Uniformity (1662). Movements such as CONGREGATIONALISM and PRESBYTERIANISM, BAPTISTS and QUAKERS proliferated. Nonconformist Churches were eventually granted freedom of worship in 1689 and civil and political rights in 1828. Other Nonconformist movements, METHODISM and UNITARIANISM, were added to their ranks during the 18th century.

non-figurative (non-objective) Art that makes no attempt to represent objects from the physical world. The term comprises all ABSTRACT ART that does not rely on the appearance of the visual world for the source of its ideas.

nonjurors Clergy in England and Scotland who refused to take the oath of allegiance to WILLIAM III and MARY II in 1689. Anglo-Catholic in sympathy, they included several bishops and *c*.400 priests in England and most of the Scottish episcopal clergy.

Nootka Tribe of Native Americans living along the w coast of Vancouver Island, British Columbia. They were once expert fishermen and were the only Native Americans on Canada's Pacific coast to hunt whales.

Nono, Luigi (1924–90) Italian composer. An early follower of Anton WEBERN, he gained international recognition with the *Canonic Variations* (1950), an orchestral work based on a note series of Arnold SCHOENBERG. He composed several political works, including the antifascist opera *Intolerance* (1960).

noradrenaline (norepinephrine) HORMONE secreted by nerves in the autonomic NERVOUS SYSTEM and by the ADRENAL GLANDS. Chemically, it is related to ADRENALINE and has a similar effect on the cardiovascular system. It slows the heart rate and constricts small arteries, thus raising the blood pressure. It is used therapeutically to combat the fall in blood pressure that accompanies shock. *See also* NEUROTRANSMITTER

Nordenskjöld, Nils Adolf Erik, Baron (1832–1901) Swedish explorer and scientist. In 1878, he led the Swedish expedition in the *Vega*, which was the first ship to sail through the NORTHEAST PASSAGE.

Norfolk County of E England; the county town is NORWICH. The region was home to the ICENI tribe in the 3rd century BC. After the departure of the Romans it became part of the ANGLO-SAXON kingdom of East Anglia but was later subjugated by the Danes. In the Middle Ages, Norfolk was a centre of the wool industry. The land is generally low-lying and is used mainly for agriculture. The region is drained by the rivers Waveney, Yare, Bure and Ouse, and by the BROADS. Today, Norfolk produces cereals and root vegetables; poultry farming and fishing

are also important. Area: 5,372sq km (2,073sq mi). Pop. (1991) 745,613.

Norfolk City-port on Elizabeth River, SE Virginia, USA. Norfolk was founded in 1682; it forms the port of Hampton Roads, together with NEWPORT NEWS and PORTSMOUTH. Norfolk was almost completely destroyed by fire during the American Revolution (1776). In the Civil War it acted as a Confederate naval base. It is now the largest naval complex in the USA. Exports: coal, grain, tobacco. Industries: shipbuilding, motor vehicles, chemicals, textiles. Pop. (1990) 261,229.

Norfolk Broads *See* BROADS, NORFOLK

Norfolk Island Territory of Australia in the SW Pacific Ocean, *c*.1,450km (900mi) E of Australia. Visited in 1774 by Captain James Cook, it was a British penal colony (1788–1814, 1825–55). Many people living on Pitcairn Island, descendants of the *Bounty* mutineers, were resettled here in 1856. The chief economic activities are agriculture and tourism. Area: 34sq km (13sq mi). Pop. (2000) 2,000.

Noriega, Manuel (Antonio Morena) (1934–) Panamanian statesman and general, head of state (1983–89). In 1963, he became head of Panama's National Defense Forces. Recruited as a CIA operative by the USA, Noriega became an important backstage powerbroker. For most of the 1980s, he was effectively Panama's paramount leader, ruling behind puppet presidents. In 1987, evidence emerged of Noriega's criminal activities, and the USA withdrew its support. In 1988, he was indicted by a US court on drug-connected charges and accused of murder. In December 1989, US troops invaded Panama and installed a civilian government. Noriega surrendered to US forces and was taken to the USA for trial on corruption, drug trafficking and money laundering. In April 1992, he was sentenced to 40 years in prison.

Norman, Greg (Gregory John) (1955–) Australian golfer. He won his first European event in 1977. Norman won the British Open (1986, 1993) and the world matchplay championship (1980, 1983, 1986). Despite his huge talent, the US majors continued to elude him.

Norman, Jessye (1945–) US soprano. In 1969, she made her operatic debut at the Deutsche Oper, Berlin, as Elisabeth in Wagner's *Tannhäuser*. Norman's powerful, dramatic voice has brought her distinction both in opera and concert repertoire.

Norman architecture ROMANESQUE architectural style of the Normans in England, N France and S Italy. Characteristic buildings include the cathedrals at St Étienne and Caen in France, and Durham in England (begun 1093). The style was marked by massive proportions, square towers, round arches and little decoration.

Norman Conquest Invasion of England in 1066 by WILLIAM I (THE CONQUEROR), Duke of Normandy. William claimed that EDWARD THE CONFESSOR (d.1066) had recognized him as heir to the throne of England, and he disputed the right of HAROLD II to be Edward's successor. William's army defeated and killed Harold at the Battle of HASTINGS (1066), then advanced on London, where William was accepted as king. The ruling class, lay and ecclesiastical, was gradually replaced by Normans, and Norman institutions were imposed.

Normandy Region and former province of NW France, coextensive with the departments of Manche, Calvados, Orne, Eure and Seine-Maritime. Part of the Roman province of Gaul, it was absorbed into the Frankish kingdom of Neustria in the 6th century. In the mid-9th century it was invaded by Vikings. It was the seat of William, Duke of Normandy (later WILLIAM I), who invaded England in 1066. Normandy was recovered by the French in

1204. It was the site of the NORMANDY CAMPAIGN of June 1944. It is characterized by forests, flat farmland and rolling hills. The economy is based on livestock rearing, dairy products, fruit, cider and fishing.

Normandy Campaign Allied invasion of German-occupied France, launched on 6 June 1944 (D-DAY). Commanded by US General Dwight D. EISENHOWER, the invasion was the largest amphibious operation in history. The successful landings were the start of the final campaign of WORLD WAR 2 in W Europe.

Norman French Dialect of Old French spoken by the Normans at the time of the conquest of England (1066). In Normandy, it was the general language, but it was also used by the Normans in England where it co-existed with contemporary MIDDLE ENGLISH for about three centuries.

Normans Descendants of Vikings who settled in NW France in the 9th–10th centuries. They created a powerful state with a strongly centralized feudal society and war-like aristocracy. In the 11th century, under Robert GUISCARD and ROBERT II, they defeated the Muslims to create an independent kingdom in Sicily. In 1066 Duke William of Normandy conquered England and became WILLIAM I.

Norns In Germanic mythology, three maidens who spun or wove the fate of both mortals and gods. Their names were Urth (Past), Verthandi (Present) and Skuld (Future).

Norodom Sihanouk (1922–) Cambodian statesman, king (1941–55, 1993–), prime minister (1955–60) and head of state (1960–70, 1975–76, 1991–93). In 1955, he abdicated to become head of a socialist government in Cambodia. In 1960, Sihanouk became head of state. In 1965, he broke off diplomatic relations with the USA because of US military involvement in Indochina. In 1970, Sihanouk was deposed by Lon Nol in a right-wing military coup. In 1975, he returned from exile when the KHMER ROUGE took over, first supporting then opposing their regime. In 1979, after the Vietnamese invasion, Sihanouk formed a government-in-exile In 1991, he returned to Cambodia. In 1993, UN peacekeepers withdrew from Cambodia and Sihanouk was reinstated as a constitutional monarch. His son, Prince Ranariddh, was ousted by his co-premier, Hun Sen, in 1997.

Norse literature Literature of the Scandinavian Norsemen, written between the 9th and the 12th century. It consists mainly of mythological poetry and SAGAS. The works were set down in stone and wood and survived orally to be recorded in the 12th–14th centuries.

North, Frederick, Lord (1732–92) British statesman, prime minister (1770–82). He entered Parliament in 1754. North was lord of the treasury (1759–65) and chancellor of the exchequer (1767–70) before becoming prime minister under GEORGE III. His repressive measures against the North American colonies, particularly the INTOLERABLE ACTS, have been blamed for precipitating the AMERICAN REVOLUTION. In 1782, he formed a coalition with Charles James FOX, but was forced to resign in 1783.

North, Oliver Laurence (1943–) US marine lieutenant colonel. North was recruited as an aide to the National Security Council and was involved in several covert operations. In 1987 the Congressional committee that investigated the notorious IRAN-CONTRA AFFAIR revealed North as the central figure, and he was subsequently convicted of three criminal charges. In 1992 he was pardoned.

North America Continent, including the mainland and offshore islands N of and including Panama. **Land** North America extends N of the Arctic Circle and S almost to the Equator. To the W it is bordered by the Bering Sea and

the Pacific Ocean and to the E by the Atlantic Ocean. There are many islands off both coasts, particularly to the N in the Arctic Ocean and to the SE in the Caribbean Sea. There are two major mountain ranges: the APPALACHIANS in the E and the ROCKY MOUNTAINS in the W. Between these two ranges lie the fertile GREAT PLAINS and the Central Lowlands. In the E, a long coastal plain extends from New England to Mexico. The W coast is more mountainous. **Structure and geology** Much of Canada is an old Precambrian shield area forming a saucer-shaped depression centred in HUDSON BAY. The Appalachians also have their origins in the Precambrian era. In the W, the complex fold mountains of the Rockies and the Pacific Margin are much younger and continue into South America as the ANDES. **Lakes and rivers** Lake SUPERIOR is the largest lake in North America, 82,413sq km (31,820sq mi) and, together with MICHIGAN, HURON, ERIE and ONTARIO, makes up the GREAT LAKES. The ST LAWRENCE River forms a navigable link between the Great Lakes and the Atlantic Ocean. The longest river is the combined MISSISSIPPI-MISSOURI system. Other important rivers include the YUKON, MACKENZIE, COLORADO, COLUMBIA, DELAWARE and RIO GRANDE. **Climate and vegetation** Its geographical range means that every climatic zone is represented. In the far N, there are areas of tundra and arctic conditions. In the interior, sheltered by high mountains, there are deserts. Tropical rainforest is found in the lower areas of Central America. On much of the continent the climate is temperate. The Great Plains region is temperate, and the natural vegetation is grass, bordered by mixed and coniferous forests in the mountains to the E, W and N. **People** North America's first settlers probably arrived c.45,000 years ago from Asia by way of Alaska. By the time the Vikings arrived from Europe, c.AD 1000, NATIVE AMERICANS occupied the entire continent. European settlement accelerated after Christopher Columbus's voyage in 1492. The Spaniards settled in Mexico and the WEST INDIES. The English and French settled farther N; Swedes, Germans and Dutch also formed settlements. Europe's political and economic problems later drove larger numbers to the New World. Descendants of Spanish settlers are predominant in Mexico, Central America and some Caribbean islands. French concentrations exist in Québec province, Canada, and parts of the West Indies. In Central America and the Caribbean, European descendants are in the minority. **Economy** Much of North America benefits from fertile soil and a climate conducive to agriculture. The North American plains are one of the world's major grain and livestock-producing areas. The S area produces fruit, cotton, tobacco, coffee and sugar cane. There is also substantial industrial development. Mining is important, particularly in Canada and Mexico. **Recent history** The early 20th century saw mass emigration to the USA and Canada. The USA has been the dominant economic force on the continent throughout the 20th century. In the SPANISH AMERICAN WAR (1898) the USA emerged as a world power. In 1903, Theodore ROOSEVELT enforced construction of the PANAMA CANAL, control of which returned to Panama in 1999. The USA emerged from World War 2 as a world superpower. The ideological battle between CAPITALISM and COMMUNISM led to the COLD WAR and US involvement in the KOREAN WAR and VIETNAM WAR. Since 1994, Canada, the USA and Mexico have been linked through the NORTH AMERICAN FREE TRADE AGREEMENT (NAFTA). As the USA and Canada have developed more service-based economies, some manufacturing has transferred to Mexico. Economic inequality and instability remain major issues in Mexico. Since World War 2, many Caribbean islands have gained independence. A US trade embargo since Fidel CASTRO's revolution (1959) has crippled Cuba's economy. Central America has also been dominated by US interests and by repressive regimes and economic inequality. *Highest mountain* MOUNT MCKINLEY (Denali) 6,194m (20,321ft) *Longest river* Mississippi-Missouri 6,050km (3,760mi) *Population* 464,000,000 *Largest cities* MEXICO CITY (16,562,000); NEW YORK CITY (7,333,253); LOS ANGELES (3,448,613) *See also* individual country articles

North American Free Trade Agreement (NAFTA) Treaty designed to eliminate trade barriers between Canada, Mexico and the USA. The agreement was signed in 1992, and NAFTA came into effect on 1 January 1994. Some Latin American countries have also applied to join.

North American mythology Traditional beliefs of Native North Americans. The Native North Americans displayed a great diversity of languages and cultures, but their mythologies had many common features. Among these was the concept of heroes in the form of animal deities, such as Raven or Coyote, believed to have been the original inhabitants of the country. They brought order into the world by gaining possession of fire, wind and rain and by establishing laws and institutions. They also created mountains and rivers and other natural features. NATIVE AMERICANS had numerous gods, including the Great Spirit and the Earth Mother of the ALGONQUIANS, and the gods of thunder and wind of the IROQUOIS. Belief in protective or harmful spirits continues, and the SHAMAN plays a central part in religious life, acting as an intermediary between humans and the spirit world.

Northampton City on the River Nene, central England; county town of NORTHAMPTONSHIRE. Sites include the 12th-century Church of the Holy Sepulchre, one of only four round churches in England. In 1968, Northampton was designated as a new town. The city has long been associated with footwear industry. Other industries: engineering, leather goods. Pop. (1994) 175,000.

Northamptonshire County in central England; the county town is NORTHAMPTON. There are traces of pre-Celtic habitations as well as Roman and Anglo-Saxon settlement. The land is undulating and is drained by the rivers Welland and Nene. Much of the region is devoted to pasture, wheat growing and forestry. Products include cereals, potatoes and sugar beets. There are extensive iron ore deposits, and iron and steel industries remain important. Industries: footwear, engineering, food processing. Area: 2,367sq km (914sq mi). Pop. (1991) 578,807.

North Atlantic Treaty Organization (NATO) Intergovernmental organization, military alliance of the USA, Canada and 17 European countries. The original treaty was signed (1949) in Washington by Belgium, Britain, Canada, Denmark, France, Iceland, Italy, Luxembourg, Norway, Portugal, Netherlands and the USA. Since then, Greece, Turkey, Spain and Germany have joined. In 1999, despite Russian opposition, the Czech Republic, Hungary and Poland joined. NATO's headquarters is in Brussels. During the COLD WAR, it was the focus of the West's defence against the Soviet Union. In 1995, NATO led the International Implementation Force to enforce the Dayton Peace Accord in Bosnia-Herzegovina. In 1999, NATO launched its first military operation to prevent the genocide in the Yugoslavian province of KOSOVO.

North Carolina State in E USA, on the Atlantic coast; the capital is RALEIGH. North Carolina's coastal plain is swampy and low-lying. Its W edge rises to rolling hills,

and farther W are the Blue Ridge and GREAT SMOKY MOUNTAINS. The first English colony in North America was founded (1585) on Roanoke Island. Permanent settlers moved into the region from Virginia in the 1650s. It was the last state to secede from the Union in the Civil War. It is the leading producer of tobacco in the USA. Important agricultural products are corn, soya beans, peanuts, pigs, chickens and dairy produce. Industries: textiles, timber, fishing, tourism, electrical machinery, chemicals. Mineral resources: phosphate, feldspar, mica, kaolin. Area: 136,523sq km (52,712sq mi). Pop. (2000) 8,049,313.

Northcliffe, Alfred Charles William Harmsworth, viscount (1865–1922) British newspaper publisher, b. Ireland. He began his career as a freelance journalist but, with the help of his brother Harold, was soon publishing his own popular periodicals. In 1896, he launched the *Daily Mail*, whose concise, readable style of news presentation proved very successful. In 1905, he founded the *Daily Mirror*, the first tabloid NEWSPAPER, and in 1908 gained control of *The Times*.

North Dakota State in N central USA, on the Canadian border; the capital is BISMARCK. The region is generally low-lying and is drained by the Missouri and Red rivers. French explorers first visited the region in 1738. The USA acquired the W half of the area from France in the LOUISIANA PURCHASE (1803) and the rest from Britain in 1818 when the boundary with Canada was fixed. Dakota was divided into North and South Dakota in 1889. Wheat, barley, rye, oats, sunflowers and flaxseed are the chief crops. Cattle rearing is the most important economic activity. Area: 183,022sq km (70,665sq mi). Pop. (2000) 642,200.

Northeast Passage Route from the Atlantic to the Pacific via the Arctic Ocean. Unsuccessful attempts were made to find the passage by Dutch and English mariners from the 16th century. The complete voyage was first made by Baron NORDENSKJÖLD in 1878–80.

Northern Cape Province in SW South Africa; the capital is Kimberley. Northern Cape was created in 1994 from the N part of the former CAPE PROVINCE. Area: 361,800sq km (139,650sq mi). Pop (1994) 737,360.

Northern Ireland *See* IRELAND, NORTHERN

Northern Lights Popular name for the AURORA borealis

Northern Mariana Islands *See* MARIANA ISLANDS

Northern Province Province in N South Africa; the capital is Pietersburg. In 1994, Northern Transvaal was formed from the N part of the former province of TRANSVAAL. In 1995, it was renamed Northern Province. Area: 123,280sq km (46,970sq mi). Pop. (1994 est.) 5,201,630.

Northern Territory Territory in N central Australia bounded by the Timor and Arafura seas (N) and the states of Western Australia (W), South Australia (S) and Queensland (E); the capital is DARWIN. In 1863, it was annexed to South Australia but in 1911 was brought under the control of the federal government. In 1978, it achieved internal self-government. The territory lies mostly within the tropics. The coastal areas are flat with many offshore islands, and the region rises inland to a high plateau, the Barkly Tableland. In the mainly arid south are the Macdonnell Ranges and AYERS ROCK. Today, there is little farming but some government-aided stock-breeding. Manganese ore, bauxite and iron are mined. Area: 1,347,525sq km (520,280sq mi). Pop. (1993) 169,298.

Northern War (1700–21) Conflict in N Europe between Sweden and its neighbours. It began with an attack on Sweden by Denmark, Saxony, Poland and Russia. CHARLES XII of Sweden defeated all his opponents (1700–06), but war was renewed in 1707 when Charles invaded Russia. The Swedes were decisively defeated at Poltava (1709). Charles took refuge with the Ottoman Turks, encouraging their attack on Russia in 1710–11. At the ensuing peace treaties (1719–21), Sweden lost virtually all its northern empire.

North Island Smaller but more densely populated of the two main islands of NEW ZEALAND, separated from SOUTH ISLAND by Cook Strait. The chief cities are WELLINGTON, AUCKLAND and Hamilton. The island contains several mountain ranges, Lake Taupu (New Zealand's largest lake), fertile coastal plains and numerous hot springs. Most of New Zealand's dairy produce comes from North Island. Industries; wood pulp, paper, mining, fishing. Area: 114,729sq km (44,297sq mi). Pop. (1991) 2,553,413.

North Korea *See* KOREA, NORTH

North Pole Most northerly point on Earth; the N end of the Earth's axis of rotation, 725km (450mi) N of Greenland. Geographic north lies at 90° latitude, 0° longitude. The Arctic Ocean covers the entire area.

North Sea Arm of the Atlantic Ocean, lying between the E coast of Britain and the European mainland and connected to the English Channel by the Straits of Dover. Generally shallow, it is *c*.960km (600mi) long, with a maximum width of 640km (400mi). It is a major fishing ground, shipping route and, since 1970, an important source of oil and natural gas. Area: *c*.580,000sq km (220,000sq mi).

Northumberland, John Dudley, Duke of (1502–53) Effectively ruler of England (1549–53). He was one of the councillors named by HENRY VIII to govern during the minority of EDWARD VI. In 1553 he attempted to usurp the succession through his daughter-in-law, Lady Jane GREY, but was thwarted by popular support for the rightful queen, MARY I. He was subsequently executed for treason.

Northumberland County in NE England on the border with Scotland; the county town is Morpeth. In the 2nd century AD, HADRIAN'S WALL was built to defend Roman Britain from the N tribes. In the 7th century the region became part of the Saxon kingdom of Northumbria. The land slopes down from the CHEVIOT HILLS in the NW, and the region is drained by the rivers TYNE, Tweed, Blythe and Coquet. The county is largely rural, the chief farming activities being cattle and sheep rearing. Barley and oats are grown and forestry is important. Coal is mined in the S. Area: 5,033sq km (1,943sq mi). Pop. (1991) 304,694.

Northumbria, kingdom of Largest kingdom in ANGLO-SAXON England. Formed in the early 7th century, it included NE England and SE Scotland up to the Firth of Forth. In the age of the historian BEDE and the LINDISFARNE GOSPELS, Northumbria experienced a blossoming of scholarship and monastic culture. Its power declined in the 8th century.

North-West Frontier Province (NWFP) Province in NW Pakistan bounded by Afghanistan (N and W), located near Khyber Pass; the capital is Peshawar. Historically important during the time of Alexander the Great, in 1849 it became part of British India and was annexed to Pakistan in 1947. It is largely agricultural. Area: 106,200sq km (41,000sq mi). Pop. 10,937,000.

Northwest Passage Western route from the Atlantic to the Pacific via N Canada. Many European explorers in the 16th–17th centuries tried to find a passage through North America to the Pacific. The effort was renewed in the 19th century. The expedition of Sir John FRANKLIN, which set out in 1845, was lost with all hands, but during the search for survivors, the route was

established. First to make the passage in one ship was Roald AMUNDSEN in 1903–06.

North-West Province Province in NW South Africa; the capital is Mmabatho. North-West Province was created from the NW part of the former province of TRANSVAAL. Area: 116,190sq km (44,489sq mi). Pop. (1994 est.) 3,252,991.

Northwest Territories Region in N Canada, covering more than 33% of the country and consisting of mainland Canada N of latitude 60°N and hundreds of islands in the Arctic Archipelago. The capital is Yellowknife. Much of the N and E of the province is tundra, inhabited by INUIT and other native peoples. The HUDSON'S BAY COMPANY acquired the area under a charter from CHARLES II in 1670. In 1869, the Canadian government bought the land from the company. The present boundaries were set in 1912. In 1999, part of Northwest Territories became the INUIT land of NUNAVUT. Most economic development has occurred in Mackenzie district, which has large tracts of softwoods and rich mineral deposits. Area: 3,426,000sq km (1,320,000sq mi). Pop. (1996) 64,402.

North Yorkshire County in N England; the administrative centre is YORK. Other major towns include Scarborough, Whitby and Harrogate. In the 9th century a thriving culture was destroyed by the Scandinavian invasions. In the Middle Ages the region became noted for its many monastic foundations. In the W of the county are the PENNINES. In the E are the North Yorkshire Moors. North Yorkshire is predominantly agricultural, with dairy farming, cereals and hill sheep farming. There is some manufacturing industry. Area: 8,309sq km (3,208sq mi). Pop. (1991) 702,161.

Norway Kingdom in NW Europe, which forms the W part of the Scandinavian peninsula. Its coast is fringed by many islands and FJORDS. Many of Norway's cities lie on or near the fjords, including the capital, OSLO, and BERGEN and TRONDHEIM. The land rises steeply from the coastal lowlands to a 1,500m (5,000ft) central plateau. Europe's largest glacier field, Josdtedalsbreen, lies w of Galdhøppigen, Norway's highest point, at 2,469m (8,100ft). The plateau contains many deep valleys with lakes and rivers, such as the Glåma. The distant Arctic islands of SVALBARD and Jan Mayen are Norwegian possessions. **Climate** North Atlantic Drift gives Norway a mild climate. Most of Norway's seaports remain ice-free throughout the year. Snow covers the land for more than three months every year. In Trømso, the sun does not set from late May to late July. **Vegetation** Large areas of the rugged mountains are bare rock. Forest and woods cover *c*.27% of Norway. **History and politics** Norway's seafaring tradition dates back to the VIKINGS, who raided w Europe between the 9th and 11th centuries. OLAF II introduced Christianity in the early 11th century, but was deposed by CANUTE II of Denmark. HAAKON IV re-established unity in the 13th century. In 1319, Sweden and Norway were joined. In 1397, Norway, Sweden and Denmark were united in the Kalmar Union. For the next four centuries Norway was subject to Danish rule. Lutheranism became the state religion in the mid-16th century. In 1814, Denmark ceded Norway to Sweden. Norway declared its independence, but Swedish troops forced Norway to accept union under the Swedish

---

NORWAY

AREA: 323,900sq km (125,050sq mi)
POPULATION: 4,331,000
CAPITAL (POPULATION): Oslo (494,000)

crown. In 1905, an independent monarchy was established. Norway was neutral in World War 1. In the 1920s, Norway industrialized. In the 1930s, it adopted progressive social welfare provisions. In April 1940, German troops invaded. More than 50% of Norway's merchant fleet was destroyed in the resistance. Liberation was achieved in May 1945. In 1949, Norway joined NATO and was a co-founder (1960) of the EUROPEAN FREE TRADE ASSOCIATION (EFTA). In 1972 and 1994 referenda, Norway voted against joining the EUROPEAN COMMUNITY. In 1977, Gro Harlem Brundtland became Norway's first woman prime minister. In 1991, Olav V was succeeded by his son, Harald V. In 1996, Brundtland was replaced as prime minister by Thorbjoern Jagland. In 1997 elections, Jagland was defeated by a centrist coalition led by Kjell Magne Bondevik. In 2000, Bondevik and his minority government resigned after a vote of no confidence and Jens Stoltenberg of the Labour Party formed a new government. **Economy** Norway has one of the world's highest standards of living (1995 GDP per capita, US$21,940). Its chief exports are oil and natural gas. Oil was discovered in 1969. Norway is the world's eighth-largest producer of crude oil. Per capita, Norway is the world's largest producer of hydroelectricity. Major manufactures include petroleum products, chemicals, aluminium, wood pulp and paper. Farmland covers $c.3\%$ of the land. Dairy farming and meat production are the chief activities, but Norway has to import food. Norway has the largest fish catch in Europe (after Russia).

Norwegian Official language of Norway, spoken by nearly all the country's four million inhabitants. It belongs to the northern branch of the Germanic family of INDO-EUROPEAN LANGUAGES.

Norwich City and county town of NORFOLK, E England, near the confluence of the rivers Yare and Wensum. It was already an important market town in the 11th century. From the 14th to 19th century Norwich was the regional centre of the woollen industry. There are many fine medieval buildings, including the Norman cathedral (founded 1096). It is home to the University of East Anglia (1963). Industries: textiles, machinery, chemicals, electrical goods, foodstuffs, footwear. Pop. (1994) 130,000.

nose In human beings, other primates and some vertebrates, the prominent structure between the eyes. It contains receptors sensitive to various chemicals (sense of SMELL) and serves as the opening to the respiratory tract, warming and moistening the air and trapping dust particles on the MUCOUS MEMBRANES.

Nostradamus (1503–66) French seer and astrologer, b. Michel de Nostredame. After practising as a doctor, he began making astrological predictions in 1547. These were published in rhyming quatrains in *Centuries* (1555) and represented one verse for every year from then until the end of the world (in the 1990s). To avoid prosecution as a magician, he completely changed the order of the verses so that no time sequence was discernible.

note In music, sound of a particular pitch or frequency. The word also refers to the written symbol that represents the sound.

notochord In chordates and the early embryonic stages of vertebrates, the flexible, primitive backbone; in mature vertebrates it is replaced by the SPINE.

Notre Dame Early Gothic CATHEDRAL in Paris, France (1163–1250). One of the most daring constructions of its time, it has a wide nave and double ambulatory, and the W façade was imitated in many French churches.

Nottingham City and county town of NOTTINGHAMSHIRE, on the River Trent, N central England.

Originally a 6th-century Anglo-Saxon settlement, it is the traditional birthplace of ROBIN HOOD. The city grew rapidly in the 19th century, becoming famous for the manufacture of fine lace, cotton and hosiery. It is an important centre of communications and transport. Industries: textiles, engineering, bicycles, electronic equipment, pharmaceuticals. Pop. (1994) 285,000.

Nottinghamshire County in central England; the county town is NOTTINGHAM. The land slopes down from the E ridges of the PENNINES in the W to the lowlands of the E. The principal river is the TRENT. Wheat, barley and sugar beets are the chief crops; beef and dairy cattle are also important. There are rich deposits of coal in the county. Nottinghamshire has long been noted for its textile industries. Area: 2,164sq km (836sq mi). Pop. (1991) 993,872.

Nouakchott Capital of MAURITANIA, NW Africa, in the SW part of the country, $c.8$km (5mi) from the Atlantic Ocean. Originally a small fishing village, it was chosen as capital of Mauritania, when it became independent in 1960. Nouakchott now has an international airport and is the site of modern storage facilities for petroleum. Light industries have also been developed and handicrafts are important. Pop. (1995) 735,000.

Nouméa City and seaport in SW New Caledonia island, S Pacific Ocean; the capital of NEW CALEDONIA. Originally called Port-de-France, it was made capital of New Caledonia in 1854. Nouméa was used as a French penal colony during the later 19th century. Local mining products include nickel, chrome and manganese. Pop. (1989) 65,110.

noun Member of a linguistic class or category consisting of words that serve to name a person, place, thing or concept. In traditional grammar, nouns form one of the so-called parts of speech. Modern linguistics experts, however, tend to define them in terms of their grammatical function.

nouveau roman (Fr. new novel) Experimental fictional form. Pioneered by Alain ROBBE-GRILLET, Samuel BECKETT and Nathalie Sarraute during the 1950s, it was influenced by the work of Franz KAFKA and James JOYCE and also by film technique. It is characterized by meticulously detailed description, the avoidance of value judgments, and a consciousness of the artificiality of time sequences.

nouvelle vague Journalistic term describing the work of young French film directors between 1958 and 1961, in opposition to the contemporary conventions of French film-making. It embraced the idea that the director of a film was in effect the author (AUTEUR) of the piece. Alain RESNAIS, Jean-Luc GODARD, Claude CHABROL and Louis MALLE were among those who made personal statements through the art of CINEMA. Examples include *Les Quatre Cents Coups* (1959) by François TRUFFAUT and *A Bout de Souffle* (1960) by Godard.

nova Faint STAR that undergoes unpredictable increases in brightness by several magnitudes, apparently due to explosions in its outer regions, and then slowly fades back to normal. Novae occur in close binary systems, where one component is a WHITE DWARF and the other is a giant star. *See also* SUPERNOVA; VARIABLE STAR

Novalis (1772–1801) German romantic poet and novelist, b. Friedrich Leopold, Baron von Hardenberg. He began his major work, the mythical romance *Heinrich von Ofterdingen*, in 1799, but had not completed it by the time of his early death. His work was a significant influence on the development of German ROMANTICISM.

Nova Scotia Maritime province in SE Canada, consisting of a mainland peninsula, the adjacent Cape Breton Island

and a few smaller islands; the capital is HALIFAX. The first settlement of Nova Scotia was made by the French at Port Royal in 1605. The mainland was awarded to Britain in 1713, and Cape Breton Island was seized from the French in 1758. Nova Scotia joined NEW BRUNSWICK, QUÉBEC and ONTARIO to form the Dominion of CANADA in 1867. The land is generally low-lying, rolling country, and there are extensive forests. The principal crops are hay, apples, grain and vegetables. There are valuable coal deposits on Cape Breton Island. Fishing is very important, with cod, lobster and haddock the largest catches. Industries: shipbuilding, pulp and paper, steelmaking, food processing. Area: 55,490sq km (21,425sq mi). Pop. (1996) 909,282.

Novaya Zemlya Archipelago in the Arctic Ocean off the NW coast of Russia, between the BARENTS SEA (W) and the Kara Sea (E), and consisting of two large islands and many smaller ones. The region was first explored in the 18th century. The N island is ice-covered all the year round while the S has tundra vegetation and a sparse population that exists by trapping and fishing. Area: 81,279sq km (31,382sq mi). Pop. (est.) 400.

novel Narrative fiction, usually in prose form, that is longer and more detailed than a NOVELLA or SHORT STORY. The word is derived from the Latin word *novus* (new) and the Italian NOVELLA (a short tale with an element of surprise). The roots of the modern novel are generally traced to CERVANTES' *Don Quixote* (1605–15); its development as a major literary form can be seen in 18th-century Britain in Daniel DEFOE's *Robinson Crusoe* (1719) and Samuel RICHARDSON's *Pamela* (1740). The 20th-century has seen considerable formal experimentation, with developments such as the STREAM OF CONSCIOUSNESS technique and the NOUVEAU ROMAN.

novella Short, highly structured prose narrative. The form was developed by Giovanni BOCCACCIO in the *Decameron* (1348–53) and has proved popular since the 18th century. In modern usage, the term broadly denotes a work of prose fiction that is longer than a SHORT STORY but shorter than a NOVEL.

Novello, Ivor (1893–1951) Welsh composer, actor and dramatist, b. David Ivor Davies. He is best known as the writer of comedies and light musicals, including *The Dancing Years* (1939) and *Perchance to Dream* (1945). Novello composed the World War 1 anthem "Keep the Home Fires Burning" (1914).

Noverre, Jean-Georges (1727–1810) French choreographer and BALLET reformer. He abolished the conventional, meaningless gestures of ballet, and initiated the *ballet d'action* in which dance and story were united.

Novgorod City in NW Russia, on the River Volchov. One of Russia's oldest cities, it was supposedly founded by the Varangian prince RURIK in the 9th century. Its inhabitants were forcibly converted to Christianity in 989. It subsequently became capital of a vast territory. After a long fight for supremacy, the city was forced to submit to Moscow in 1478. In 1570 IVAN IV (THE TERRIBLE) massacred the inhabitants. It declined in importance after the founding of ST PETERSBURG. During World War 2 it suffered great destruction. Industries: distilling, foodstuffs, electrical engineering, furniture, chinaware. Pop. (1994) 233,000.

Novi Sad City in NE Serbia, a port on the River Danube; capital of the autonomous province of VOJVODINA. Industries: machinery, electrical goods, chemicals, textiles, tobacco. Pop. (1991) 179,626

Novosibirsk City on the River Ob, S Siberia, Russia. Founded in 1896 after the construction of the Trans-Siberian Railway, it grew quickly. During World War 2

it received complete industrial plants moved from war areas of the W Soviet Union. It is now a centre for scientific research. Industries: agricultural and mining machinery, metallurgy, machine tools, chemicals, textiles, foodstuffs. Pop. (1994) 1,418,000.

Noyes, Alfred (1880–1958) English poet, probably best known for his poem "The Highwayman". His works include *Drake* (1906–08), *Tales of the Mermaid Tavern* (1913) and the trilogy, *The Torchbearers* (1922–30).

Nu, U (1907–95) Burmese statesman, prime minister (1948–56, 1957–58, 1960–62). Active in the independence movement, he was independent BURMA's first prime minister. He returned to power in 1960, but in 1962 he was ousted in a military coup led by U NE WIN. After years of exile, he returned to Burma in 1980 and was later placed under house arrest.

Nuba Name for a group of several unrelated peoples inhabiting a region of S Sudan. Most Nuba peoples are farmers and many tribes cultivate terraces on rugged granite hillsides. Animal husbandry is also practised. The predominant religious rituals are closely linked to agricultural fertility rites.

Nubia Ancient state on the Upper NILE in NE Africa. It was closely associated with Egypt. At its height, Nubia extended from Egypt to the Sudan. At first ruled by Egypt, it later controlled Egypt in the 8th and 7th centuries BC. It converted to Christianity in the 6th century AD and became part of Ethiopia in the 14th century.

nuclear disarmament *See* DISARMAMENT; STRATEGIC ARMS LIMITATION TALKS (SALT)

nuclear energy ENERGY released during a nuclear reaction as a result of the conversion of mass into energy according to Albert EINSTEIN's equation $E = mc^2$. The conversion involves the binding energy of the NUCLEUS of an ATOM. Nuclear energy is released in two ways: by FISSION and by FUSION. Fission is the process responsible for the atomic bomb and for NUCLEAR REACTORS now contributing to energy requirements throughout the world. It was discovered in 1938 by Otto HAHN and Fritz Strassmann. In 1942, the first sustained nuclear CHAIN REACTION was achieved by Enrico FERMI. Fusion provides the energy for the Sun and the stars and for the HYDROGEN BOMB. It also offers the prospect of cheap energy once a method has been perfected for controlling fusion reactions. *See also* CRITICAL MASS; MANHATTAN PROJECT; NUCLEAR WEAPON

nuclear family In anthropology, term used to describe a FAMILY unit of two adults joined by a conjugal link and their children. Ideally, the nuclear family provides economic and emotional security to both the parents and children.

nuclear fission *See* FISSION, NUCLEAR

nuclear fuel Various chemical and physical forms of URANIUM and PLUTONIUM used in NUCLEAR REACTORS. Fluid fuels are required in homogeneous reactors; heterogeneous reactors use various forms of fuels – pure metals or alloys, as well as oxides or carbides. The fuel must have a high thermal conductivity, be resistant to radiation damage and be easy to fabricate.

nuclear fusion *See* FUSION, NUCLEAR

nuclear magnetic resonance (NMR) Absorption of ELECTROMAGNETIC RADIATION by certain nuclei when placed in a magnetic field. In this field the NUCLEUS, as a result of its SPIN, can have slightly different energy values. It can make transitions between these energy values, acquiring the energy by absorbing radio-frequency radiation of the appropriate wavelength. This phenomenon is used in medicine in the form of MAGNETIC RESONANCE

IMAGING (MRI), and in chemical analysis and research in nuclear physics in a method called NMR SPECTROSCOPY.

nuclear physics Branch of physics concerned with the structure and properties of the atomic NUCLEUS. The principal means of investigating the nucleus is the SCATTERING experiment, carried out in particle ACCELERATORS, in which a nucleus is bombarded with a beam of high-energy ELEMENTARY PARTICLES, and the resultant particles analyzed. Study of the nucleus has led to an understanding of the processes occurring inside stars and has enabled the building of NUCLEAR REACTORS.

nuclear reactor Device in which nuclear FISSION (and sometimes nuclear FUSION) reactions are used for power generation or for the production of radioactive materials. In the reactor, the fuel is a radioactive heavy metal: URANIUM-235, uranium-233 or PLUTONIUM-239. In these metals, ATOMS break down spontaneously, undergoing a process called RADIOACTIVE DECAY. Some NEUTRONS released in this process strike the nuclei of fuel atoms, causing them to undergo fission and emit more neutrons. These in turn strike more nuclei, and in this way a CHAIN REACTION is set up. Usually, a material called **moderator** is used to slow down the neutrons to a speed at which the chain reaction is self-sustaining. This process occurs within the reactor **core**. The chain reaction is regulated by inserting **control rods**, which contain neutron-absorbing material such as cadmium or boron, into the core. The heat generated by the nuclear reaction is absorbed by a circulating **coolant** and transferred to a boiler to raise steam. The steam drives a TURBINE that turns a GENERATOR, that in turn produces electricity. There are a variety of nuclear reactors, named after the type of coolant they use. For example, a **boiling-water** reactor (BWR) and a **pressurized-water** reactor (PWR), presently the most common type of reactor, both use water as the coolant and the moderator. In **advanced gas-cooled** reactors (AGR), the coolant is a gas – most commonly carbon dioxide. **Fast** reactors do not use a moderator, and fission is caused by fast neutrons. This type of reactor generates greater temperature and the coolant used is a liquid metal, usually liquid sodium. Sometimes called "fast-breeder" reactors, fast reactors produce ("breed") more fissionable material than they consume. Excess neutrons from the fission of a fuel such as Ur^{235}, instead of being absorbed in control rods, are used to bombard atoms of relatively inactive Ur^{238} which transmutes to the active ISOTOPE Pu^{239}. When the original fuel is spent, the plutonium can be used as a NUCLEAR FUEL in other reactors or NUCLEAR WEAPONS. *See also* ELECTRICITY SOURCES

Nuclear Test-Ban Treaty (1963) Agreement prohibiting the testing of NUCLEAR WEAPONS, signed by the Soviet Union, the UK and the USA. The Non-Proliferation Treaty (1968) was signed by the same three nations and endorsed by 59 other states. In 1994 the treaty was broken by China, who carried out underground nuclear tests. In 1995 France also broke the treaty by carrying out tests in the s Pacific.

nuclear waste Residues containing radioactive substances. After URANIUM, PLUTONIUM and other useful fission products have been removed, some long-lived radioactive elements remain, such as CAESIUM-137 and STRONTIUM-90. The storage of nuclear waste is a major environmental issue.

nuclear weapon Device whose enormous explosive force derives from nuclear FISSION or FUSION reactions. The first **atomic bombs** were dropped by the USA on the Japanese cities of HIROSHIMA and NAGASAKI in

August 1945. The bombs consisted of two stable subcritical masses of URANIUM or PLUTONIUM that, when brought forcefully together, caused the CRITICAL MASS to be exceeded, thus initiating an uncontrolled nuclear CHAIN REACTION. In such detonations, huge amounts of energy and harmful radiation are released: the explosive force can be equivalent to 20,000 tonnes of TNT. The HYDROGEN BOMB (H-bomb or thermonuclear bomb), first tested in 1952, consists of an atomic bomb that on explosion provides a temperature high enough to cause nuclear fusion in a surrounding solid layer, usually lithium deuteride. The explosive power can be that of several million tonnes (megatons) of TNT. Devastation from such bombs covers a wide area: a 15-megaton bomb will cause all flammable material within 20km (12mi) to burst into flame. A third type of weapon, the **neutron bomb**, is a small hydrogen bomb, also called an enhanced radiation weapon, that produces a small blast but a very intense burst of high-speed NEUTRONS. The lack of blast means that buildings are not heavily damaged. The neutrons, however, produce intense radiation sickness in people located within a certain range of the explosion, killing those affected within a week. *See also* DISARMAMENT; MANHATTAN PROJECT; NUCLEAR ENERGY

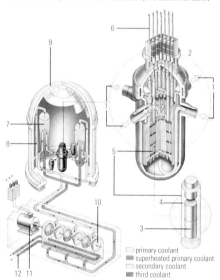

☐ primary coolant
■ superheated primary coolant
☐ secondary coolant
■ third coolant

▲ **nuclear reactor** A pressurized water reactor (PWR) is so named because the primary coolant (1) that passes through the reactor core (2) is pressurized to prevent it from boiling. The uranium-235 fuel is loaded into the reactor in pellets (3) contained by the fuel rods (4). To prevent an uncontrolled chain reaction, the fuel rods are separated by control rods of graphite (5). All the rods are loaded into the reactor from above (6). The primary coolant is heated by the fission reaction in the fuel rods and circulates into a steam generator (7) where it superheats the secondary coolant (8). The secondary coolant leaves the protective containment vessel (9) and drives turbines (10) that produce electricity through a generator (11). A third coolant loop (12) cools the secondary coolant, transferring the heat to a sea, river or lake. Reducing the temperature of the secondary coolant increases the efficiency of the transfer from the primary to the secondary coolant.

nucleic acid Chemical molecules present in all living cells and in viruses. They are of two types: DNA (deoxyribonucleic acid) stores the genetic code that functions as the basis of heredity; and RNA (ribonucleic acid), delivers these coded instructions to the cell's protein manufacturing sites. Chemically, nucleic acids are POLYMERS of NUCLEOTIDES. *See also* CHROMOSOME; ENZYME; GENE

nucleon Any of the particles found within the NUCLEUS of an ATOM: a NEUTRON or a PROTON.

nucleosynthesis Production of all the various chemical elements that exist in the universe from one or two simple atomic nuclei. It is believed to have occurred by way of large-scale nuclear reactions during cosmogenesis and is still in progress in the Sun and other stars.

nucleotide Complex, naturally occurring chemical group that contains a nitrogen base linked to a sugar and an acid phosphate. Nucleotides are the building blocks of NUCLEIC ACIDS (such as DNA and RNA). In the molecules of nucleic acids, nucleotides are linked together by bonds between the sugar and phosphate groups. Nucleotides also occur freely in a CELL as various coenzymes, such as ADENOSINE TRIPHOSPHATE (ATP), the principal carrier of chemical energy in the metabolic pathways of the body.

nucleus In biology, membrane-bound structure that, in most CELLS, contains the CHROMOSOMES. As well as holding the genetic material, the nucleus is essential for the maintenance of cell processes. It manufactures the RNA used to build RIBOSOMES. Other RNA molecules carry the GENETIC CODE from the DNA through pores in the nuclear membrane into the CYTOPLASM, where it is used as a template for PROTEIN synthesis by the ribosomes. Cell division involves the splitting of the nucleus and CYTOPLASM. Cells without nuclei include BACTERIA and mammalian ERYTHROCYTES (red blood cells). Instead of chromosomes, bacteria have a naked, circular molecule of DNA in the cytoplasm.

nucleus In physics, central core of an ATOM. Made up of NUCLEONS (PROTONS and NEUTRONS), the nucleus accounts for almost all of an atom's mass. Because protons are positively charged and neutrons have no charge, a nucleus has an overall positive charge; this is cancelled out, however, by the negatively charged ELECTRONS that orbit the nucleus. Following the discovery (1836) of RADIOACTIVITY by Henri BECQUEREL, Ernest RUTHERFORD proposed (1911) the existence of the nucleus after identifying ALPHA and BETA PARTICLES. The number of protons in a nucleus is called its ATOMIC NUMBER, while the number of nucleons is the MASS NUMBER. *See also* FUNDAMENTAL FORCE; QUANTUM THEORY; NUCLEAR ENERGY; RELATIVE ATOMIC MASS (R.A.M.); SPIN

Nuevo Laredo City in NE Mexico, on the Rio Grande, opposite Laredo, Texas, USA. Founded in 1755, it was separated from Laredo during the Mexican War (1848). It lies at the N end of the Inter-American Highway and is a rail terminus and international trade centre. Industries: cotton, livestock, natural gas, tourism. Pop. (1990) 218,413.

Nuffield, William Richard Morris, 1st Viscount (1877–1963) English AUTOMOBILE manufacturer and philanthropist. He developed low-price, mass-produced cars that revolutionized the British motor industry. In 1926 Morris produced the first MG (Morris Garage) model. In 1943, he established the Nuffield Foundation for medical, scientific and social research. In 1952 Nuffield became chairman of the British Motor Corporation (BMC), which was an amalgamation of the Morris and Austin companies.

Nujoma, Sam (1929–) Namibian statesman, president of Namibia (1990–). A founder and leader of the SOUTH

WEST AFRICA PEOPLE'S ORGANIZATION (SWAPO) from 1959, he was exiled by the South African government to Tanzania in 1960. Forced to resort to a policy of armed struggle from 1966, Nujoma controlled an army of highly effective SWAPO guerrillas. After negotiating Namibia's independence through the United Nations, he returned in 1989, when the first free elections were held. Nujoma was re-elected in 1994 and 1999.

Nukualofa Capital of Tonga, in the SW Pacific Ocean, on the N coast of Tongatabu Island. The chief industry is copra processing. Pop. (1992) 29,000.

Nullarbor Plain Vast limestone plateau in SW South Australia and S Western Australia. It is an arid, treeless plain. Area: 260,000sq km (100,000sq mi).

numbat (banded ANTEATER) Squirrel-like Australian marsupial that feeds on TERMITES. The female, unlike most marsupials, has no pouch. The numbat has a long snout and lateral white bands on its red-brown coat. Length: 46cm (18in). Species *Myrmecobius fasciatus*.

number Symbol representing a quantity used in counting or calculation. All ancient cultures devised their own number systems for the practical purposes of counting and measuring. From the basic process of counting we get the natural numbers. This concept can be extended to define the INTEGERS, the RATIONAL NUMBERS, the REAL NUMBERS and the COMPLEX NUMBERS. *See also* BINARY SYSTEM; IRRATIONAL NUMBER; PRIME NUMBER

Numbers Fourth book of the Bible and of the PENTATEUCH. Its central theme is a relation of events that took place during the Israelites' 40 years of wandering in the desert of the Sinai Peninsula in search of the Promised Land of CANAAN. Interwoven with their story is a collection of religious material, including laws concerning purification rituals and procedures for sacrificing to God.

number theory Branch of mathematics concerned with the properties of natural NUMBERS (whole numbers) or special classes of natural numbers such as PRIME NUMBERS and perfect numbers. In the 4th-century BC, EUCLID proved that the number of primes was infinite. One of the unresolved problems in number theory is to find formulae for the generation of the primes. Pierre de FERMAT in the 17th century and Leonhard EULER in the 18th century both explored aspects of number theory.

numeral Symbol used alone or in a group to denote a NUMBER. Arabic numerals are the 10 digits from 0 to 9. ROMAN NUMERALS consist of seven letters or marks.

numismatics Study or collection of coins, medals and tokens as works of art, for investment or as a source of historical information. Coins, which of course have their own intrinsic monetary value, may also preserve old forms of writing and bear portraits of eminent people. The largest coin market in the world is in London. Some numismatists also collect banknotes.

nun Woman belonging to a female religious order who has taken monastic vows (*see* MONASTICISM). Nuns may belong to either an enclosed order or one that encourages its members to work in the world for the welfare of society at large. BUDDHISM, CHRISTIANITY and TAOISM all have monastic orders of nuns. Nuns serve a preparatory period (novitiate), after which they take their final vows. For centuries, Christian nuns lived in closed orders, but in 1633 St VINCENT DE PAUL founded the Sisters of Charity, an order of nuns who work outside the convent serving the community.

Nunavut Territory in N Canada; the capital is Iqaluit. Formerly part of NORTHWEST TERRITORY, Nunavut was granted self-government in April 1999. Created as a homeland for the INUIT, its first premier was Paul Okalit.

Although subsidized by central government, the local economy is based on fishing, hunting and mining lead, zinc and coal. Area: *c*.2 million sq km (775,000sq mi).

Nunn, Trevor (1940–) English stage director. He was artistic director (1968–87) of the ROYAL SHAKESPEARE COMPANY (RSC). Nunn directed the Andrew LLOYD WEBBER musicals *Cats* (1981) and *Starlight Express* (1984). In 1996, he was appointed artistic director of the National Theatre of Great Britain.

Nur-ad-Din (1118–74) (Nureddin) Ruler of Syria. He united Muslim forces in Syria to resist the Christians of the CRUSADES. He recaptured Edessa from the Christians in 1146 and in 1154 took Damascus from the Seljuk Turks.

Nuremberg (Nürmburg) City in Bavaria, S Germany. It began as a settlement around an 11th-century castle, later becoming a free imperial city. It was a centre of learning and artistic achievement in Germany during the 15th and 16th centuries. During the 1930s, it was the location of the annual congress of the Nazi Party, and after World War 2 was the scene of the NUREMBERG TRIALS (1945–46). Today, Nuremberg is an important commercial and industrial centre. Industries: textiles, pharmaceuticals, electrical equipment, machinery, publishing and printing, motor vehicles, toys, brewing. Pop. (1995) 496,000.

Nuremberg Trials (1945–46) Trials of Germans accused of WAR CRIMES during WORLD WAR 2, held before a military tribunal. The tribunal was established by the USA, Britain, France and the Soviet Union. Ten Nazi leaders were executed (including von RIBBENTROP). GOERING committed suicide before the death sentence could be carried out. Rudolf HESS was one of six men sentenced to life imprisonment. *See also* HOLOCAUST

Nureyev, Rudolf (1938–93) Russian ballet dancer and choreographer. In 1961, while on tour in Paris, he defected from the Soviet Union. Nureyev was noted for his spectacular technical virtuosity and dramatic character portrayal. Major ballets in which he had leading roles included *Sleeping Beauty, Giselle* and *Swan Lake*, and he regularly partnered Margot FONTEYN. In 1982, he became an Austrian citizen. He died of AIDS.

Nurhachi (1559–1626) Organizer and creator of the MANCHU state in China. He welded related tribes into a powerful unit, creating the Manchu military banner organization for control and mobilization. Among other innovations, he introduced a writing system for administrative purposes.

nursing Profession that has as its general function the care of people who, through ill-health, disability, immaturity or advanced age, are unable to care for themselves. Caring for the sick was particularly emphasized by the early Christian Church; many religious orders and, later, chivalric orders performed such "acts of mercy". In the 18th century the need for reform in nursing was revealed, and by the end of the 19th century, certain principles of Florence NIGHTINGALE's teaching had been adopted in England and the USA. Today, in countries with advanced health care systems, there are many nursing specialties, with standards laid down by relevant professional bodies.

nut In botany, one-seeded fruit with a hard, woody or stony wall enclosing the seed (PERICARP). It develops from a flower that has petals attached above the OVARY (inferior ovary). Examples include ACORNS and HAZEL nuts.

nutation Oscillating movement (period 18.6 years) superimposed on the steady precessional movement of the Earth's axis so that the precessional path of each celestial pole follows the CELESTIAL SPHERE follows an irregular rather than a true circle. It results from the varying gravitational attraction of the Sun and Moon on the Earth. *See also* PRECESSION

nutcracker Crow-like bird of evergreen forests of the Northern Hemisphere. A projection inside the bill turns it into a highly efficient seed-cracker or nut-cracker. The European thick-billed nutcracker (*Nucifraga caryocatactes*) is a typical species. Family Corvidae. Length: 30cm (12in).

nuthatch Bird found mainly in the Northern Hemisphere and occasionally in Africa and Australia. It is bluish-grey above and white, grey or chestnut underneath. It eats nuts, opening them with its sharp bill. It also feeds on insects, spiders and seeds. Length: 9–19cm (3.5–7.5in). Family Sittidae.

nutmeg Evergreen tree native to tropical Asia, Africa and America. Its seeds yield the spice nutmeg; the spice mace comes from the seed covering. Height: up to 18m (60ft). Family Myristicaceae.

nutria *see* COYPU

nutrition Processes by which plants and animals take in and make use of food substances. The science of nutrition involves identifying the kinds and amounts of nutrients necessary for growth and health. Nutrients are generally divided into PROTEINS, CARBOHYDRATES, FATS, minerals and VITAMINS. *See also* DIET

Nuuk (Danish *Godthåb*) Capital and largest town of Greenland, at the mouth of a group of fjords on the SW coast. Founded in 1721, it is the oldest Danish settlement in Greenland. Industries: fishing and fish processing, scientific research. Pop. (1996) 13,000.

Nyerere, Julius Kambarage (1922–99) Tanzanian statesman, first president of Tanzania (1964–85). In 1954, he founded the Tanganyika African National Union. In 1961, Nyerere led Tanganyika to independence. In 1964, he negotiated the union between Tanganyika and ZANZIBAR that created Tanzania. Nyerere established a one-party state. His Arusha Declaration (1967) is an important statement of African SOCIALISM. In 1979, Nyerere sent troops into Uganda to help topple the regime of Idi AMIN. Under his autocratic but generally benign socialist government, Tanzania made striking progress in social welfare and education. Economic setbacks led to calls for greater democracy and he was forced to retire.

nylon Any of numerous synthetic materials consisting of polyamides (with protein-like structures) developed by Wallace CAROTHERS in the 1930s. It can be formed into fibres, filaments, bristles or sheets. Nylon is characterized by elasticity and strength and is used chiefly in yarn, cordage and moulded products.

Nyman, Michael (1944–) English composer. In his early career, influenced by John CAGE, he explored experimental music. His works include operas, notably *The Man who Mistook his Wife for a Hat* (1986), but he is best known for his film scores. These include *The Draughtsman's Contract* (1982), *Prospero's Books* (1991) and *The Piano* (1993). His accessible musical style is characterized by the repetition and variation of harmonic, melodic and rhythmic patterns.

nymph In Greek mythology, female spirit said to be a guardian of natural objects. They were identified with specific locations and commonly with trees and water.

nymph Young insect of primitive orders that do not undergo complete METAMORPHOSIS. The term is used to designate all immature stages after the egg. The nymph resembles the adult (IMAGO) and does so more closely with each successive moulting. Some examples are the aquatic nymphs of dragonflies, mayflies and damsel flies.

O/o, 15th letter of the alphabet, is derived from the Phoenician alphabet. It entered the Greek alphabet as omicron, "short o", and passed unchanged into the various languages in which it is used today.

oak Common name of *c*.600 species of the genus *Quercus*, which are found in temperate areas of the Northern Hemisphere and at high elevations in the tropics. Most species are hardwood trees that grow 18 to 30m (60–100ft) tall. Leaves are simple, often lobed and sometimes serrated. The flowers are greenish and inconspicuous; male flowers hang in catkins. The fruit is an acorn surrounded by a cup.

Oakley, Annie (1860–1926) US entertainer. She was an expert shot, eventually beating a noted marksman, Frank E. Butler, whom she married. Oakley was the star of BUFFALO BILL's Wild West Show for 17 years.

oarfish Any of several deepwater marine ribbonfish. Its long, thin body has a dorsal fin extending along its entire length. Two long oar-like pelvic fins protrude from beneath the head. Length: to 6m (20ft). Genus *Regalecus*.

OAS *See* ORGANIZATION OF AMERICAN STATES

OAS (*Organisation de l'Armée Secrète*) French terrorist group opposed to Algerian independence. It was set up in 1961 by disaffected army officers and French settlers in Algeria, when it became clear that President DE GAULLE was preparing to come to an agreement with Algerian nationalists. Acts of terrorism in France and Algeria failed to prevent Algeria's becoming independent in 1962.

oat Cereal plant native to W Europe and cultivated worldwide. The flower comprises numerous florets that produce one-seeded fruits. Mainly fed to livestock, oats are also eaten by humans. Family Poaceae/Gramineae; species *Avena sativa*.

Oates, Joyce Carol (1938–) US novelist, short-story writer and poet. Her debut book of short-stories was *By the North Gate* (1963). Oates' works, such as the trilogy of novels *A Garden of Earthly Delights* (1967), *Expensive People* (1968) and *Them* (1969), are grim chronicles of violence and deprivation in modern America. Other novels include *The Assassins* (1975), *You Must Remember This* (1987) and *We Were the Mulvaneys* (1996).

Oates, Lawrence Edward Grace (1880–1912) English explorer and soldier. He accompanied Robert SCOTT on the Antarctic expedition (1910–12). They reached the South Pole but on the return journey became weatherbound. Oates, crippled by frostbite, sacrificed his own life by crawling out into a blizzard rather than risk slowing the party down. His gallantry was in vain.

Oates, Titus (1649–1705) English author of the anti-Catholic Popish Plot (1678). He invented the story of a Jesuit plot to depose King CHARLES II. It provoked a hysterical reaction and encouraged efforts to exclude Charles' Catholic brother, the future JAMES II, from the succession.

OAU *See* ORGANIZATION OF AFRICAN UNITY

Oaxaca (officially Oaxaca de Juárez) City in S Mexico; capital of Oaxaca state. Oaxaca is an agricultural state, and coffee is the principal crop. Tourists use the city as a base for exploring its archaeological sites, such as Monte Albán. Oaxaca is renowned for its jewellery and hand-woven textiles. Pop. (1990) 213,985.

Ob River in W Siberia, central Russia. It flows NW, then NE through the lowlands of W Siberia before continuing N and then E to enter the Gulf of Ob, an arm of the Kara Sea within the Arctic Ocean. Length: 3,680km (2,300mi). With its principal tributary, the Irtysh, it is the seventh-longest river in the world: 5,410km (3,360mi).

obelisk Stone monolith that usually has a tapering, square-based column with a pyramid-shaped point. Pairs of obelisks stood at the entrance to ancient Egyptian temples, such as Karnak (LUXOR). The two Cleopatra's needles in New York City's Central Park and on London's Thames Embankment date from 1500 BC, long before CLEOPATRA's reign.

Oberammergau Village in upper Bavaria, S Germany, famous for its PASSION PLAY. The performance takes place once every 10 years, in fulfilment of a vow made by the inhabitants in 1634 during an outbreak of the plague.

Oberon In medieval folklore, the king of the fairies and husband of TITANIA. Oberon appears in Shakespeare's *A Midsummer Night's Dream* (1595). *See also* FAIRY

obesity Condition of being overweight, generally defined as weighing 20% or more above the recommended norm for the person's sex, height and build. Obese people are at increased risk of disease and have a shorter life expectancy than those of normal weight.

oboe WOODWIND musical instrument. It has a slightly flared bell and, like the BASSOON, is a double-reed instrument. The earliest true oboes were used in the mid-17th century and have been widely used since the 18th century.

Obote, (Apollo) Milton (1924–) Ugandan statesman, prime minister (1962–66) and president (1966–71, 1980–85). In 1960, he formed the Uganda People's Congress. Obote was the first prime minister of independent Uganda. In 1966, he deposed King Mutesa II of Buganda. In 1971, Obote was ousted by his army chief, Idi AMIN. He returned to power after Amin was overthrown. In 1985, Obote was again deposed in an army coup.

Obregón, Álvaro (1880–1928) Mexican statesman, president (1920–24). Obregón supported Francisco MADERO's revolution against Porfirio DÍAZ. When Madero was overthrown by Victoriano HUERTA, Obregón joined forces with Venustiano CARRANZA, "Pancho" VILLA and Emiliano ZAPATA to defeat Huerta. Widely regarded as a capable president, he enacted some notable reforms, especially in education. In 1928, Obregón was re-elected but assassinated before he could take office. *See also* MEXICAN REVOLUTION

O'Brien, Edna (1932–) Irish novelist and short-story writer. Her novels, which include the trilogy *The Country Girls* (1960), *The Lonely Girl* (1962) and *Girls in Their Married Bliss* (1964), are distinguished by their frank depiction of female sexuality. O'Brien's short-story collections include *The Fanatic Heart* (1985).

O'Brien, Flann (1911–66) Irish novelist, b. Brian O'Nolan. His first and most ambitious novel was *At Swim-Two-Birds* (1939). O'Brien wrote three other novels in English – *The Hard Life* (1961), *The Dalkey Archive* (1964) and *The Third Policeman* (1967) – and one in Gaelic, *An Béal Bocht* (1941).

O'Brien, William Smith (1803–64) Irish politician. He entered the Westminster Parliament in 1828. O'Brien supported the Act of CATHOLIC EMANCIPATION (1829). In 1843, he joined Daniel O'CONNELL's Repeal Association against the Act of UNION (1800) but left in 1846 to set up the more militant Repeal League. In 1848, O'Brien led an abortive rebellion in Ireland. He was transported to Australia and subsequently pardoned.

observatory Location of TELESCOPES and other equipment for astronomical observations. Large optical telescopes are housed in domed buildings usually situated well away from the smoke and lights of cities. Radio observatories are open sites containing one or more large RADIO TELESCOPES. The largest radio-telescope dishes have been built in natural mountain hollows: the Arecibo Observatory in Puerto Rico is 300m (975ft) across.

obsidian Rare, grey to black, glassy volcanic rock. It is the uncrystallized equivalent of rhyolite and GRANITE. It makes an attractive semi-precious stone. Hardness 5.5; r.d. 2.4.

obstetrics Branch of medicine that deals with pregnancy, childbirth and the care of women following delivery.

O'Casey, Sean (1880–1964) Irish dramatist. His early tragi-comedies, dealing with poverty and recent Irish history, such as the "Dublin trilogy" *The Shadow of a Gunman* (1923), *Juno and the Paycock* (1924) and *The Plough and the Stars* (1926), were staged at the ABBEY THEATRE. His next play, *The Silver Tassie* (1929), was more expressionistic. He wrote six volumes of autobiography. *See also* IRISH LITERATURE

Occam's razor *See* WILLIAM OF OCCAM

occult Collection of beliefs and practices involving things that are hidden or dark – that is, supposedly connected with MAGIC or supernatural forces. The term commonly describes attempts to predict, forestall or induce events by employing hidden powers, secret knowledge or external forces. In this context, the occult covers DIVINATION by all means other than by mere observation, and includes ASTROLOGY, fortune-telling, the I CHING and the CABBALA.

occupational therapy Development of practical skills to assist patients recovering from illness or injury. Therapists oversee a variety of pursuits, from the activities of daily living (ADLs), such as washing and dressing, to hobbies and crafts.

ocean Continuous body of salt water that surrounds the continents and fills the Earth's great depressions. Oceans cover *c*.71% of the Earth's surface (more than 80% of the Southern Hemisphere), and represent *c*.98% of all the water on the face of the Earth. There are five main oceans, the ATLANTIC, PACIFIC, INDIAN, ARCTIC and ANTARCTIC. They may be described by distinct region (littoral, BENTHOS, pelagic and ABYSSAL), or by depth (CONTINENTAL MARGIN, deep sea plain and deep trenches). The SEAFLOOR has a varied topography. The salt content of seawater is between 3.3% and 3.7%. Light penetrates seawater to a maximum depth of *c*.300m (1,000ft), below which plant life cannot grow. The oceans are constantly moving in currents, TIDES and WAVES. They form an integral part of the Earth's HYDROLOGICAL CYCLE and CLIMATE. They are a rich source of fossils and minerals, such as oil and gas. Marine fauna, such as fish and plankton, are a vital part of the food chain. Total area: 360 million sq km (138 million sq mi). Total volume: *c*.1.4 billion cu km (322 million cu mi). Average depth: 3,500m (12,000ft). Average temperature: 3.9°C (39°F). *See also* CONTINENTAL DRIFT; DESALINATION; SEAFLOOR SPREADING; WATER POLLUTION

Oceania Collective term applied to the islands in the central and S Pacific Ocean. It includes MELANESIA, MICRONESIA and POLYNESIA, and sometimes Australasia (Australia and New Zealand) and the Malay Archipelago.

Oceanic art Much art from Oceania involves objects used in religious rites. Among the most notable examples are the giant stone ancestor-cult figures of EASTER ISLAND, MAORI wood carvings and the carved drums, masks, stools and shields of New Guinea.

oceanic basin One of two major provinces of the deep ocean floor, lying at more than 2km (1.2mi) in depth. The mid-ocean ridges form the other province. Together they constitute 56% of the Earth's surface. The deep ocean basin is underlain by a thin basaltic crust *c*.7km (4.3mi) thick and is covered with thin sediment and dotted by low abyssal hills.

oceanic current Movement of sea water between layers of varying temperature and density. OCEAN circulation is produced by CONVECTION, with warm currents travelling away from the Equator, cooler water moving from the poles. In the Southern Hemisphere the oceanic currents move in an anticlockwise system, whereas in the Northern the system is clockwise, an effect caused by the Earth's rotation. There are *c*.50 major currents, including the GULF STREAM of the N Atlantic and the Humboldt (Peru) current off the W coast of South America. *See also* CORIOLIS EFFECT; EL NIÑO

Oceanic mythology Traditional beliefs of the native inhabitants of OCEANIA. Among the **Polynesians**, there are various accounts of the creation of the world by the celestial deity, Tangaroa (Ta'aroa). **Maui**, the most famous of the Polynesian mythic heroes, often thought of as half god and half human, is known for his cunning deeds. In **Melanesian** creation myths, the beginning of the world is seen as a movement that brings order out of chaos. In the daily life of the Melanesians, there are a vast number of unseen forces – benevolent spirits, demons, ghosts and the souls of the departed – to be dealt with by means of elaborate rituals. ANCESTOR WORSHIP is an important part of social life. The supernatural force of **mana** plays a vital role in most Oceanic mythology.

oceanography Study of the OCEANS. The major subdisciplines of oceanography include marine geology (*see* PLATE TECTONICS), MARINE BIOLOGY, marine METEOROLOGY, and physical and chemical oceanography. The science of oceanography dates from the CHALLENGER EXPEDITION (1872–76). Jacques COUSTEAU'S invention of the SCUBA aided human exploration of the seas. In 1948 August PICCARD invented the bathyscaphe.

ocelot Small cat that lives in the S USA, Central and South America. Its valuable fur is yellowish with elongated dark spots. It feeds on small birds, mammals and reptiles. Length: to 1.5m (5ft). Family Felidae; species *Felis pardalis*.

O'Connell, Daniel (1775–1847) Irish nationalist leader, known as "the Liberator". In 1823, he formed the Catholic Association. In 1828, his election to Westminster as MP for County Cork forced WELLINGTON's gov-

▲ **ocelot** A member of the flesh-eating mammal order (Carnivora), the ocelot (*Felis pardalis*) is found in Central and South America and sometimes as far N as Texas, USA. It measures from 80–147cm (31–58in) long and is grouped with all other cats in the family Felidae.

ernment to pass the Act of CATHOLIC EMANCIPATION (1829). In 1840, O'Connell founded the Repeal Association to overturn the Act of UNION (1800). In 1844, he was arrested and briefly imprisoned for sedition. O'Connell's failure to deliver significant reforms and the potato famine led to the formation of the more radical Young Ireland.

O'Connor, Feargus Edward (1794–1855) Irish Chartist leader. He was elected to Parliament in 1832. In 1837 O'Connor founded the Northern Star, the most influential newspaper of CHARTISM.

O'Connor, (Mary) Flannery (1925–64) US writer. Her first novel was *Wise Blood* (1952). Other works include *The Violent Bear It Away* (1960), and the short-story collection *A Good Man is Hard to Find* (1955). O'Connor suffered from lupus, a terminal illness.

octane number Indication of the resistance of PETROL to engine KNOCK (pre-ignition firing). The higher the number, the less likely the possibility of the fuel pre-igniting. Four-star (regular) petrol has an octane number of *c.*90. Premium grade petrols have between 95 and 96.

octave In music, the interval between any given note and another one that is exactly twice (or half) the frequency of the first and thus, acoustically, a perfect consonance. In Western music it encompasses the eight notes of the diatonic SCALE.

Octavian *See* AUGUSTUS

October Revolution *See* RUSSIAN REVOLUTION (1917)

octopus Predatory, CEPHALOPOD mollusc with no external shell. Its sac-like body has eight powerful suckered tentacles. They feed mostly on crabs and other shellfish, paralysing their prey with poison. Many of the 150 species are small, but the common octopus (*Octopus vulgaris*) grows to 9m (30ft). Family Octopodidae.

ode Lyric poem of unspecific form but typically of heightened emotion or public address. The first great writer of odes was PINDAR, but more simple were the lyrical odes of HORACE and CATULLUS. In 17th-century England it was taken up by JONSON, HERRICK and MARVELL. Representative of the more personal type are the 19th-century works of WORDSWORTH, SHELLEY and KEATS.

Odense City and port in s central Denmark. Founded in the 10th century, Odense has a 13th-century Gothic cathedral and an 18th-century palace. Industries: shipbuilding, metalworking, engineering. Pop. (1996) 184,000.

Oder Second-longest river in the catchment basin of the Baltic Sea. It rises in the NE of the Czech Republic, flows N and W through sw Poland before turning N, forming the Polish-German border and reaching the Baltic Sea. The Oder has many navigable tributaries, notably the rivers Neisse and Warta. Length: 886km (550mi).

Odessa City and port on the Black Sea, s Ukraine. A Tatar fortress was established here in the 14th century. It later passed to Poland-Lithuania and then to Turkey (1764). Brought under Russian control in 1791, it was made a naval base. Odessa was the scene of the mutiny on the battleship *Potemkin* during the RUSSIAN REVOLUTION OF 1905. Industries: fishing, whaling, shipbuilding and repairing, oil refining, metalworking, chemicals, heavy machinery. Pop. (1996) 1,046,000.

Odets, Clifford (1906–63) US social-protest dramatist. In 1931, Odets helped to organize the Group Theater. His plays include *Awake and Sing* (1935), *Waiting for Lefty* (1935) and *Golden Boy* (1937). He later moved to Hollywood, where he wrote and directed films including *The Country Girl* (1950).

Odin Principal god in Norse mythology. Identified with the Teutonic god Woden, he is considered to be the god of wisdom, culture, war and death. He lived with the Valkyries in VALHALLA.

Odoacer (*c.*433–93) (Odovacar) Chief of the Germanic Heruli people and conqueror of the West ROMAN EMPIRE. The Heruli were Roman mercenaries until 476, when they declared Odoacer king of Italy. After the Ostrogoths invaded in 489, Odoacer was murdered.

Odysseus (Ulysses) Greek hero of HOMER's epic poem, The ODYSSEY. King of the city-state of Ithaca, husband of the faithful PENELOPE, he was an astute and brave warrior. It was Odysseus who devised the stratagem of the wooden TROJAN HORSE in order to enter Troy.

Odyssey, The Epic poem of 24 books attributed to HOMER. The story of ODYSSEUS tells of his journey home from the Trojan Wars after 10 years of wandering. He wins back his wife PENELOPE and his kingdom after killing her suitors. *See also* CALYPSO; CIRCE; SIRENS

OECD Abbreviation of the ORGANIZATION FOR ECONOMIC COOPERATION AND DEVELOPMENT(OECD)

oedema Abnormal accumulation of fluid in the tissues; it may be generalized or confined to one part, such as the ankles. It may be due to heart failure, obstruction of one or more veins, or increased permeability of the capillary walls.

Oedipus In Greek mythology and literature, son of Laius (king of Thebes) and Jocasta; father of Antigone, Ismene, Eteocles and Polynices by his own mother. SOPHOCLES told how Oedipus was saved from death as an infant and raised in Corinth. He inadvertently killed his father, solved the riddle of the SPHINX and became king of Thebes. There he married Queen Jocasta, unaware that she was his own widowed mother. On discovering the truth, he made himself blind.

Oedipus complex In psychoanalytic theory, a collection of unconscious wishes involving sexual desire for the parent of the opposite sex and jealous rivalry with the parent of the same sex. Sigmund FREUD held that children pass through this stage between the ages of three and five. The complex in females is sometimes known as the Electra complex, a term coined by C.G. JUNG. The theory has been considerably modified, if not totally rejected, by most modern practitioners.

Oersted, Hans Christian (1777–1851) Danish physicist. In 1820, Oersted discovered that an ELECTRIC FIELD has magnetic properties, thus founding the science of ELECTROMAGNETISM. In 1825, he isolated metallic aluminium. The unit of magnetic field strength is named after him.

oesophagus (gullet) Muscular tube, part of the ALIMENTARY CANAL (gut), which carries swallowed food from the throat to the STOMACH. Food is moved down the lubricated channel by the wave-like movement known as PERISTALSIS.

oestrogen Female sex HORMONE. First produced by a girl at PUBERTY, oestrogen leads to the development of the secondary sexual characteristics: breasts, body hair and redistributed fat. It regulates the MENSTRUAL CYCLE and prepares the UTERUS for pregnancy. It is also a constituent of the contraceptive PILL. *See also* GONADOTROPHIN

Offaly County in the Republic of Ireland, Leinster province; the county town is Tullamore. It is mainly flat and marshy and drained by the rivers Shannon, Barrow, Brosna and Nore. The chief occupation is agriculture, particularly potatoes, cereals and cattle-raising. There is also a distilling industry. Area: 1,997sq km (771sq mi). Pop. (1991) 58,494.

Offenbach, Jacques Levy (1819–80) French composer. His reputation was founded on the brilliance of his numerous operettas, notably *Orpheus in the Underworld*

(1858). Offenbach also wrote one opera *Tales of Hoffmann* (1881), based on the stories of E.T.A. HOFFMANN.

offset Method of PRINTING widely used for high-volume publications. In the printing machine, a roller applies ink to the printing plate, which is mounted on a rotating cylinder. The image is then transferred (offset) to a cylinder with a rubber covering, called the blanket. This transfers the image to the paper. Usually, the plates are made by LITHOGRAPHY, and the process is called offset lithography. Separate plates are used for each colour.

O'Flaherty, Liam (1897–1984) Irish novelist and short-story writer. His novels, often dealing with social conditions in Ireland, include *The Informer* (1925), *The Puritan* (1931), *Famine* (1937) and *Insurrection* (1950).

Ogaden Desert region of SE Ethiopia. Inhabited chiefly by Somali nomads, it was a source of conflict between Ethiopia and Somalia for most of the 20th century. In 1977, a Somalian invasion was quickly repulsed.

Ogdon, John (1937–89) English pianist and composer. He established his strong international reputation in 1962 when he was joint winner of the Tchaikovsky Competition in Moscow with Vladimir ASHKENAZY.

O'Higgins, Bernardo (1778–1842) South American revolutionary leader and ruler of Chile (1817–23). He commanded the Chilean army against the Spanish. Defeated in 1814, he joined José de SAN MARTÍN in Argentina to defeat the Spanish at Chacabuco (1817). In 1818, O'Higgins proclaimed Chile's independence and ruled as "supreme director" for the next six years.

Ohio State in E central USA, bounded by Lake Erie in the N; the capital is COLUMBUS. Other cities include CINCINNATI and CLEVELAND. Britain acquired the land in 1763 at the end of the SEVEN YEARS' WAR. It was ceded to the USA after the American Revolution, and in 1787 it became part of the Northwest Territory. In 1803, Ohio was accepted into the Union. Mostly low-lying, the state is drained chiefly by the OHIO, Scioto, Miami and Muskingum rivers. Ohio's large farms produce hay, maize, wheat, soya beans and dairy foods; and cattle and pigs are raised. The state is highly industrialized. Its lake ports handle large amounts of iron and copper ore, coal and oil. Industries: vehicles, aerospace, transport equipment, primary and fabricated metals. Area: 106,764sq km (41,222sq mi). Pop. (2000) 11,353,140.

Ohio River in E central USA, formed at the confluence of the Allegheny and Monongahela rivers at Pittsburgh in W Pennsylvania. It flows W and then SW to join the Mississippi River at Cairo, Illinois. The Ohio River valley is a highly industrialized region, and large quantities of raw materials and manufactured goods are shipped along the river. Length: 1,571km (976mi).

ohm (symbol Ω) SI unit of electrical RESISTANCE, equal to the resistance between two points on a conductor when a constant POTENTIAL DIFFERENCE of one VOLT between them produces a current of one AMPERE.

Ohm's law Statement that the amount of steady ELECTRIC CURRENT through a material is directly proportional to the POTENTIAL DIFFERENCE across the material. Proposed in 1827 by the German physicist Georg Ohm (1787–1854), it is expressed mathematically as $V = IR$ (where V = voltage, I = current and R = resistance).

oil General term to describe a variety of substances whose chief shared properties are viscosity at ordinary temperatures, a density less than that of water, inflammability, insolubility in water, and solubility in ether and alcohol. **Mineral** oils, most notably crude oil or PETROLEUM oil, are used as fuels. **Animal** and **vegetable** oils (fatty oils or FATS) are used as food, lubricants and as a major ingredient of soap. In addition, there are ESSENTIAL OILS from plants that, unlike fatty oils, are volatile. Fatty oils can be classified into two groups: drying, such as linseed and poppy-seed oil, and non-drying, such as olive and castor oil.

oil painting Method of PAINTING that uses pigments saturated in a drying oil medium. Widely used in Europe since the 16th century, oil is still the most versatile paint medium because of its range of textures and colours.

oil palm PALM tree grown in tropical regions of Africa and Madagascar, source of oil for margarine and soap. The long, feather-shaped fronds rise from a short trunk. Height: 9–15m (30–50ft). Family Arecaceae/Palmae.

Oistrakh, David (1908–74) Russian violinist. His interpretation of the violin repertoire earned him the reputation of being the greatest violinist of his day. His son and pupil, Igor (1931–), is also a virtuoso violinist.

Ojibwa (Chippewa) Group of Algonquian-speaking Native North Americans. In the 17th century, they were constantly at war with the SIOUX, eventually driving them across the Mississippi River. Today, *c*.90,000 live in the USA and Canada.

okapi Even-toed, hoofed ruminant of African equatorial rainforests. The closest living relative of the giraffe, it is purplish in colour with striped legs. Family Giraffidae; species *Okapia johnstoni*.

O'Keeffe, Georgia (1887–1986) US painter. Her first exhibition was in 1916, and in 1924 she married Alfred STIEGLITZ. Her early works were stylized and associated with ABSTRACT ART. O'Keeffe is best known for her microscopically detailed paintings of flowers, such as *Black Iris* (1926). Her use of vibrant colour was combined with strong overtones of sexual symbolism. Many other works were more abstract.

Okhotsk, Sea of Arm of the N Pacific Ocean off the E coast of Russia, bounded E by the Kamchatka Peninsula and SE by the Kuril Islands. It is connected with the Sea of Japan by the Tatar and La Pérouse straits, and with the Pacific Ocean by passages through the Kuril Islands. It is ice-bound from November to June. The chief ports are Magadan and Korsakov, in Russia. Area: 1,528,000sq km (590,000sq mi).

Okinawa Largest island of the Okinawa archipelago, SW of mainland Japan, part of the RYUKYU ISLANDS group in the W Pacific Ocean; the major settlement is Naha. The N is mountainous, densely forested and sparsely populated. Economic activity, such as agriculture and fishing, is concentrated in the S. In the last major amphibious offensive of WORLD WAR 2, US troops landed here in April 1945 and met fierce Japanese resistance. In June 1945, Okinawa surrendered at the cost of *c*.50,000 US casualties. The island remained under US administration until 1971. The USA still maintains some bases. Area: 1,176sq km (454sq mi). Pop. (1990) 1,222,458.

Oklahoma State in central S USA; the capital is OKLAHOMA CITY. Other important cities are TULSA and Lawton. Much of the area was acquired by the USA from France in the LOUISIANA PURCHASE (1803). During Andrew JACKSON's presidency, the US Congress created the Indian Territory in the region for NATIVE AMERICANS moved by the federal government from states in the E. Cattle farmers who had settled to the W of this area organized the Territory of Oklahoma in 1889. This was merged with the Indian Territory to form the state of Oklahoma in 1907. The W of the state is part of the GREAT PLAINS. The E is hilly. The area is drained chiefly by the Arkansas and Red rivers. Wheat and cotton are the leading crops, but livestock is more important. There are many minerals, but oil and natural gas form the basis of Oklahoma's economic wealth. Area: 181,089sq km (69,918sq mi). Pop. (2000) 3,450,654.

Oklahoma City Capital and largest city of Oklahoma, USA, in the centre of the state on the North Canadian River. The area was settled in 1889. The city became state capital in 1910 and prospered with the discovery of rich oil deposits in 1928. In April 1995, a terrorist bomb killed 168 people and injured 400 others. Industries: oil refining, grain milling, cotton processing, steel products, electronic equipment, aircraft. Pop. (1990) 404,014.

okra (gumbo) Annual tropical plant with red-centred yellow flowers. The green fruit pods are eaten as a vegetable. Height: 0.6–1.8m (2–6ft). Family Malvaceae; species *Hibiscus esculentus*

Okri, Ben (1959–) Nigerian novelist. His first two novels, *Flowers and Shadows* (1980) and *The Landscapes Within* (1981), established his reputation. Okri won the Booker Prize for *The Famished Road* (1991). Its sequel was *Songs of Enchantment* (1993). Other novels include *Astonishing the Gods* (1995) and *Infinite Riches* (1998).

Olaf II (Haraldsson), Saint (995–1030) Norwegian king (1015–30) and patron saint of Norway. He introduced Christianity, but this was unpopular with a number of chiefs, who rebelled, backed by CANUTE II of Denmark. In 1028, Olaf was forced into exile and died in battle at Stikelstad. Following reports of miracles at his grave, he was canonized in 1164. His feast day is 29 July.

Olbers' paradox Why is the sky dark at night? The question was formulated (1826) by Heinrich Olbers (1758–1840). If there are an infinite number of stars, evenly distributed in space, every line of sight should end on a star, and the sky should be roughly as bright as the Sun, all over. In fact, space is not infinite. According to BIG BANG theory, the Universe is believed to have been born *c*.15,000 million years ago, and so light reaches us only from a region 15,000 million light years in radius. In addition, the light from distant galaxies is moved out of the visible spectrum by the RED SHIFT caused by the expansion of the Universe.

Old Bailey (Central Criminal Court) Court on Old Bailey Street, London. It became a CROWN COURT in 1971. The judges entitled to sit in the court include the lord mayor of London and the aldermen, as well as the recorder of London and the common serjeant.

Oldcastle, Sir John (1377–1417) English leader of the LOLLARDS. He fought in the army under HENRY IV and earned the respect and liking of the future HENRY V. A fervent supporter of the teachings of John WYCLIFFE, Oldcastle was condemned as a heretic in 1413. He escaped to lead an abortive uprising but was captured and executed.

Old Catholics Religious movement rejecting the dogma of PAPAL INFALLIBILITY, which had been announced by the First Vatican Council of 1870. In German- and Dutch-speaking Europe the Old Catholics set up churches that later united in the Union of Utrecht (1889). Since then the Archbishop of Utrecht has been head of the International Old Catholic Congress. Old Catholics have much affinity with Anglicans.

Oldenbarneveldt, Johan van (1547–1619) Dutch political leader in the Revolt of the Netherlands. With WILLIAM I (THE SILENT), he was the founder of the Dutch republic. He played an important part in arranging the union of the provinces at Utrecht (1579) and supported Maurice of Nassau as stadtholder when William was assassinated. From 1586, he was the dominant figure in Holland and, with Maurice, practically the ruler of the United Provinces. He was instrumental in securing the truce with Spain (1609), which implied Dutch

independence. He fell out with Maurice, largely over religious differences, and after an unjust trial was executed.

Oldenburg, Claes (1929–) US sculptor, a leading member of the POP ART movement. He is famous for his gigantic sculptures based on everyday objects, such as *Lipstick* (1969), and for his "soft sculptures" and pieces representing food.

Old Testament First and older section of the BIBLE, originally written in Hebrew or Aramaic, and accepted as religiously inspired and sacred by both Jews and Christians. Among Jews it is known as the Hebrew Bible. It begins with the creation, but the main theme of the Old Testament is the history of the Hebrews. In addition, there are many examples of prophetic writing, poetry and short narrative tales. It comprises the PENTATEUCH or TORAH (Genesis to Deuteronomy), the Historical Books (Joshua to I and II Kings), the Wisdom Books (Job, Proverbs and Ecclesiastes), the Major Prophets (Isaiah, Jeremiah and Ezekiel), the 12 Minor Prophets (Hosea to Malachi), and the miscellaneous collection of books known as the Writings (including Psalms and the Song of Songs). Sometimes included is a collection of books written in the final three centuries BC, known as the APOCRYPHA. The number, order and names of the books of the Old Testament vary between the Jewish and Christian traditions; texts for both are based mainly on the SEPTUAGINT. Parts of the ancient Hebrew text were found among the DEAD SEA SCROLLS. *See also* LAW AND THE PROPHETS

Olduvai Gorge Site in N Tanzania, East Africa, where remains of primitive humans have been found. Louis LEAKEY uncovered four layers of remains dating from *c*.2 million years ago to *c*.15,000 years ago. The gorge, which is 40km (25mi) long and 100m (320ft) deep, runs through the Serengeti Plain.

Old Vic London theatre. Built in 1818 as the Royal Coburg Theatre, it was renamed the Royal Victoria in 1833 and soon became known as the Old Vic. Under the management of Lilian Baylis from 1898, it was respected for its Shakespearean productions. From 1963 to 1976, it was the home of the NATIONAL THEATRE of Great Britain. The Young Vic was opened in 1970.

oleander Evergreen shrubs of the genus *Nerium*, native to the Mediterranean region. They have milky poisonous sap, clusters of white, pink or purple flowers and smooth leaves. The best-known is the rosebay (*N. oleander*). Family Apocynaceae. *See also* FRANGIPANI; PERIWINKLE

oligarchy System of government in which power is concentrated in the hands of a few who rule without the requirement of popular support and without external check on their authority.

Oligocene Extent of GEOLOGICAL TIME from *c*.38 to 25 million years ago. It is the third of five epochs of the TERTIARY period. During this time, the climate cooled, and many mammals evolved, including an ancestor of the modern horse.

oligopoly In economics, a situation of imperfect competition, which exists in an industry that contains a few firms producing similar products that are usually only differentiated by either brand or type. *See also* MONOPOLY

olive Tree, shrub or vine and its fruit, especially the common olive tree, *Olea europaea*, native to the Mediterranean region. It has leathery, lance-shaped leaves, a gnarled and twisted trunk and may live for more than 1,000 years. The fruit is bitter and inedible before processing. Height: to 9m (30ft). Family Oleaceae. *See also* OLIVE OIL

olive oil Yellowish liquid oil, containing oleic acid, obtained by pressing OLIVES. It is used for cooking, as a salad oil, in the manufacture of soap and in medicine. It contains an extremely low proportion of FATTY ACIDS.

Olivier, Laurence Kerr, Baron (1907–89) English actor and director. He was the outstanding Shakespearean interpreter of his generation. In 1930, Olivier made his film debut and quickly established himself as a romantic lead in films such as *Wuthering Heights* (1939), *Pride and Prejudice* (1940) and *Rebecca* (1940). In 1944, Olivier and Ralph Richardson became directors of the OLD VIC. He won a Special Academy Award for his directorial debut, *Henry V* (1944). Olivier's second film, *Hamlet* (1948), earned him Oscars for best actor and best picture. He starred opposite Marilyn MONROE in *The Prince and the Showgirl* (1955). Olivier was director (1963–73) of the NATIONAL THEATRE of Great Britain. He was married to Jill Esmond (1930–40), Vivien LEIGH (1940–61) and Joan PLOWRIGHT (1961 until his death).

olivine Silicate mineral, found in basic and ultrabasic IGNEOUS ROCKS. Olivines vary in composition between fosterite (Mg_2SiO_4) and fayalite (Fe_2SiO_4). It has orthorhombic system crystals and is usually olive-green. It is glassy and brittle with no cleavage. Hardness 6.5–7; r.d. 3.3.

Olmec Early civilization of Central America that flourished between the 12th and 4th centuries BC. Its heartland was the S coast of the Gulf of Mexico, but its influence spread more widely. From the 9th century BC, the main Olmec centre was La Venta. Olmec art included high-quality carving of jade and stone, notably giant human heads in basalt. The Olmec heritage can be traced through later civilizations, including the MAYA.

Olmstead, Frederick Law (1822–1903) US landscape architect. He designed Central Park, New York City (1857–61), and the Capitol grounds, Washington, D.C. (1844–92). He also laid out the grounds at the World's Fair, Chicago (1893).

Olympia Area in S Greece, the site of an ancient sanctuary and of the original OLYMPIC GAMES. Buried by earthquakes in the the 6th century AD, Olympia was not rediscovered until the 18th century. It contained some of the finest works of Classical art and architecture, including the huge temple of Zeus, which contained a giant statue of the god that was numbered among the SEVEN WONDERS OF THE WORLD.

Olympia State capital and port of entry for Washington, USA, on the S tip of Puget Sound in the SW of the state. It was made capital of Washington Territory in 1853. Industries: agriculture, food canning, beer, oysters, timber. Pop. (1990) 27,447.

Olympic Games World's major international athletic competition, held in two segments – the Summer Games and the Winter Games – from 1992 alternating so that there are two years between segments, but four years before a segment is repeated. The games were first celebrated in 776 BC in OLYMPIA, Greece, and were held every four years until AD 393, when they were abolished by the Roman emperor. The modern summer games were initiated by Baron Pierre de Coubertin and were first held in Athens, Greece, in 1896. Women did not compete until 1912. The games were cancelled during World War 1 and World War 2. Summer events include archery, track and field events, basketball, boxing, canoeing, cycling, diving, equestrian sports, fencing, hockey, gymnastics, handball, judo, rowing, shooting, soccer, swimming, volleyball, weightlifting and yachting. Winter events include the biathlon, bobsledding, ice hockey, skating and skiing. The control of the games is vested in the International Olympic Committee (IOC),

which lays down the rules and chooses venues. In 1999, the IOC was rocked by corruption scandals.

Olympus Mountain range in N Greece, on the border of Thessaly and Macedonia, *c*.40km (25mi) long. Its peak, Mount Olympus, is the highest point in Greece, at 2,917m (9,570ft). It was first climbed in 1913. In ancient Greek mythology it was considered to be the home of the gods, closed to mortal eyes.

Om (Aum) Sacred, mystical symbol representing a sound considered to have divine power by Hindus, Buddhists and other religious groups. The sound is chanted at the beginning and end of prayers and is used as a MANTRA in meditation.

Omaha Siouan-speaking tribe of Native North Americans. In the 1880s, they participated in a major political action against the US government concerning ownership of Native American lands. Today, *c*.2,000 Omaha people live in Nebraska and Oklahoma.

Omaha Port on the Missouri River, E Nebraska, USA. The area was ceded to the US government in 1854. It was the capital of Nebraska Territory from 1854 to 1867. It is a leading livestock market and meat processing centre and a major insurance centre. Pop. (1990) 335,795.

Oman Sultanate on the SE corner of the Arabian peninsula, SW Asia; the capital is MUSCAT. Oman is 95% desert. On the Gulf of Oman coast lies the fertile plain of Al Batinah and the city of Muscat. The plain is backed by the Al Hajar mountains, which rise at Jebel Sham, to 3,019m (9,905ft). In the S lies part of the barren and rocky Rub' al Khali desert ("Empty Quarter"). The sultanate also includes the tip of the Musandam Peninsula, overlooking the strategic Strait of Hormuz, and separated from the rest of Oman by the United Arab Emirates. Oman has a hot tropical climate. In Muscat, summer temperatures rise to 47°C (117°F). Parts of the N mountains have an average annual rainfall of 400mm (16in), but most of Oman has less than 125mm (5in). Date palms grow on the coastal plain and around desert oases. Grassy pasture occurs on the Al Hajar mountains and on the S coast. **History and politics** In ancient times, Oman was an important trading area on the main route between the Gulf and the Indian Ocean. Islam was introduced in the 7th century, and Muslim culture remains a unifying force. In 1507, the Portuguese captured several seaports in Oman, including Muscat. Portugal controlled maritime trade until expelled by the Ottomans in 1659. Oman set up trading posts in East Africa, including Zanzibar in 1698 and, until the 1860s, was the dominant Arabian power. The Al Said family have ruled Oman since taking power in 1741. During the 20th century, the sultanate often has been in conflict with religious leaders (imams) of the Ibahdi sect, pressing for the establishment of a more theocratic society. British colonial interference and economic inequality led to popular rebellions in the 1950s and 1960s. Insurrectionist forces continued to control much of S Oman. In 1970, Sultan Said bin Taimur was deposed by his son, Qaboos bin Said. In 1971, Oman joined the United Nations (UN) and the Arab League. Qaboos bin Said initiated the modernization of health, education and social welfare. In 1981, Oman was a founder member of the Gulf Cooperation

---

OMAN
AREA: 212,460sq km (82,278sq mi)
POPULATION: 2,176,000
CAPITAL (POPULATION): Muscat (350,000)

Council (GCC). Ties with the UK and the USA remain strong. In 1990, Oman allowed coalition forces to use its military bases during the GULF WAR. **Economy** Oman is an upper-middle-income developing country (1995 GDP per capita, US$8,140). Its economy is based on oil production. Oil was first discovered in 1964 and now accounts for more than 90% of exports. The industry attracts many migrant workers. Oil refining and the processing of copper are among Oman's few manufacturing industries. Agriculture supports 50% of the workforce. Major crops include alfalfa, bananas, coconuts, dates, limes, tobacco, vegetables and wheat. Some farmers raise camels and cattle. Fishing, especially for sardines, is also important, but Oman is reliant on food imports.

Omar (c.581–644) (Umar) Second CALIPH, or ruler, of ISLAM. He was converted to Islam in 618 and became a counsellor of MUHAMMAD. In 632 he chose the first caliph, ABU BAKR, and succeeded him in 634. Under his rule, Islam spread by conquest into Syria, Egypt, and Persia, and the foundations of an administrative empire were laid.

Omar Khayyám (active 11th century) Persian poet, mathematician and astronomer. He so impressed the Sultan that he was asked to reform the calendar. His fame in the West is due to a collection of quatrains freely translated by Edward FITZGERALD as *The Rubáiyát of Omar Khayyám* (1859).

Omayyads *See* UMAYYADS

ombudsman Official appointed to safeguard citizens' rights by investigating complaints of injustice made against the government or its employees. The office was created in Sweden in 1809. A number of other countries adopted the office from the mid-1950s onwards, including Britain in 1967. Some UK companies, such as newspapers and banks, also employ ombudsmen to handle customer complaints.

Omdurman (Umm Durmān) City on the White Nile, opposite Khartoum, NW central Sudan. It served as the military headquarters of the MAHDI during the uprising of 1884 and was captured by the British in 1898. It is the chief commercial centre of Sudan. Industries: furniture, tanning, pottery, textiles, livestock, gum arabic. Pop. (1993) 229,000.

omen Observed phenomenon that can be interpreted as a prediction of future events, either good or bad. Common omens in folk beliefs include weather changes and astronomical events, especially the sudden appearance of a comet or an eclipse.

omnivore Any creature that eats both animal and vegetable foods – examples are human beings and pigs. Omnivorous animals are characterized by having teeth adapted for cutting, tearing and pulping food.

Omsk City on the rivers Irtysh and Om, W Siberia, Russia. Founded as a fortress town in 1716, from 1918 to 1919 it was the headquarters of the anti-Bolshevik Kolchak government. It is now a major port. Industries: oil refining, chemicals, engineering, agricultural machinery, textiles. Pop. (1994) 1,161,000.

onager Fast-running animal related to the ASS, found in semi-desert areas of Iran and India. The onager is dun-coloured with a dorsal stripe that reaches the tip of the tail. Height at the shoulder: 2.9–4.9ft (0.9–1.5m). Family Equidae; species *Equus hemionus onager.*

Onassis, Jackie (1929–94) Widow of President John F. KENNEDY and Greek shipping tycoon Aristotle Onassis. She worked as a photojournalist on the *Washington Times-Herald* before marrying John F. Kennedy in 1953. During his presidential campaign, she became popular both home and abroad. His assassination (1963) in Dallas

signalled her withdrawal from the public arena. She was to give only two more interviews in her lifetime – both sealed until after her death. In 1968, she married Aristotle Onassis. The marriage was widely criticized and subsequently proved to be unhappy. When Onassis died (1975), she returned to New York and worked as an editor.

onchocerciasis (river blindness) Tropical disease of the skin and connective tissue, caused by infection with filarial worms; it may also affect the eyes, causing blindness. It is transmitted by blood-sucking blackflies found in Central and South America and Africa.

oncogene GENE that, by inducing a cell to divide abnormally, contributes to the development of CANCER. Oncogenes arise from gene mutations (proto-oncogenes), which are present in all normal cells and some viruses. *See also* GENETICS

oncology In medicine, speciality concerned with the diagnosis and treatment of CANCER.

Onega, Lake (Onezhskoye Ozero) Lake in NW Russia, near the border with Finland; second-largest lake in Europe. It drains SW through the River Svir to Lake Ladoga and has numerous inlets and islands along its N shore. The chief port is Petrozavodsk. Area: 9,610sq km (3,710sq mi).

O'Neill, Eugene Gladstone (1888–1953) US dramatist. His first full-length play, *Beyond the Horizon* (1920), won the Pulitzer Prize, as did *Anna Christie* (1921). *The Emperor Jones* (1920) was an experiment with EXPRESSIONISM. O'Neill won a third Pulitzer Prize for *Strange Interlude* (1928). His interest in Greek tragedy is evident in *Mourning Becomes Electra* (1931). In 1936, O'Neill was awarded the Nobel Prize for literature. Suffering from Parkinson's disease, he did not produce another play until *The Iceman Cometh* (1946). O'Neill won a posthumous Pulitzer Prize for *Long Day's Journey into Night* (1956).

onion Hardy, bulb-forming, biennial plant of the lily family, native to central Asia and cultivated worldwide for its strong-smelling, edible bulb. It has hollow leaves and white or lilac flowers. Height: to 130cm (50in). Family Alliaceae/Liliaceae.

on-line publishing Distribution of information for public access using COMPUTER networks instead of physical media, such as paper or CD-ROMs. Access to on-line publications may be free or allowed in return for payment. The content of on-line publications may be enhanced by the use of such features as hypertext, search facilities and multimedia. The majority of on-line publishing takes place over the INTERNET, particularly by means of the WORLD WIDE WEB (WWW).

Onsager, Lars (1903–76) US chemist, b. Norway. He was awarded the 1968 Nobel Prize for chemistry for his development of a theory of irreversible chemical reactions. Onsager developed a technique for producing uranium-235 (the basic fuel of NUCLEAR REACTORS) from uranium-238. In 1943, this technique was put into large-scale operation with the first gaseous diffusion plant at Oak Ridge, Tennessee, USA.

Ontario Province in SE Canada, bounded to the S by four of the Great Lakes (Superior, Huron, Erie and Ontario) and the USA; the capital is TORONTO. Ontario is Canada's most populous province, and other major cities include OTTAWA, HAMILTON, Windsor and London. Trading posts were established in the region during the 17th century by French explorers. The area became part of New France but was ceded to Britain in 1763. Ontario was known as Upper Canada until 1841, when it joined with QUÉBEC to form the province of Canada. In 1867, the Dominion of

Canada was created, and the province of Ontario was established. In the N is the forested Canadian Shield, with its lowlands bordering on Hudson and James bays. To the E and S are the lowlands of the St Lawrence River and the Great Lakes, where agriculture and industry are concentrated. Cattle, dairy produce and pigs are important. The chief crops are tobacco, maize, wheat and vegetables. The Canadian Shield has many mineral deposits. Industries: motor vehicles, transport equipment, metallurgy, chemicals, paper, machinery. Area: 1,068,587sq km (412,582sq mi). Pop. (1994 est.) 10,900,000.

Ontario, Lake Smallest of the Great Lakes, bounded by New York state (S and E), USA and Ontario province, Canada (S, W and N). Fed chiefly by the Niagara River, the lake is drained by the St Lawrence River. Part of the St Lawrence Seaway, it is a busy shipping route. The chief Canadian cities on the lake are Toronto, Hamilton and Kingston; on the US shore are Rochester and Oswego. Area: 19,680sq km (7,600sq mi).

ontogeny Total biological development of an organism. It includes the embryonic stage, birth, growth and death.

ontology Branch of metaphysics that studies the basic nature of things; the essence of "being" itself.

onyx Semi-precious variety of the mineral chalcedony, a form of agate. It has straight parallel bands. White and red forms are called carnelian onyx; white and brown, sardonyx. It is found mostly in India and South America.

oolith Small, spherical concretion that occurs in sedimentary rocks. Oolithic grains, up to 2mm (0.1in) in diameter, usually consist of calcium carbonate, dolomite or chamosite. Ooliths give the rounded, grainy structure to oolitic limestone.

Oort, Jan Hendrik (1900–92) Dutch astronomer. He carried out research on the structure and dynamics of stellar systems, especially our galaxy, whose rotation he confirmed in 1927. In 1950, he proposed the existence of what has come to be called the **Oort cloud** – a spherical region of space surrounding the Solar System in which comets are thought to reside.

ooze Fine-grained, deep-ocean deposit containing materials of more than 30% organic origin. Oozes are divided into two main types. **Calcareous** ooze at depths of 2,000–3,900m (6,562–12,792ft) contains the skeletons of animals, such as foraminifera and pteropods. **Siliceous** ooze at depths of more than 3,900m contains skeletons of radiolarians and diatoms.

opal Non-crystalline variety of quartz found in recent volcanoes, deposits from hot springs and sediments. Usually colourless or white with a rainbow play of colour in gem forms, it is the most valuable of quartz gems. Hardness 5.5–6.5; r.d. 2.0.

op art (optical art) US abstract art movement, popular in the mid-1960s. It relies on optical phenomena to confuse the viewer's eye and to create a sense of movement on the surface of the picture. Leading exponents include Victor Vasarély, Kenneth Noland and Bridget Riley.

OPEC Acronym for Organization of Petroleum Exporting Countries

opencast mining Stripping surface layers from the Earth's crust to obtain coal, ores or other valuable minerals. Dragline excavators strip away surface layers, and mechanical shovels distribute minerals and spoil. The minerals are carried away for grading and processing. Owners of opencast mines in some countries are required to restore the environmental quality of the land after mining has ceased.

open cluster (galactic cluster) Group of young stars in the spiral arms of our galaxy, containing from a few tens of stars to a few thousand. They are usually several light-years across. One example is the Pleiades.

Open Door US policy designed to preserve its commercial interests in China in the early 20th century. It originated in a pronouncement by the US secretary of state, John M. Hay, in 1899. At that time, China was divided into spheres of interest among European powers and Japan. The open door policy demanded that trade and traders from other countries should receive equal rights with other foreigners in China.

open-hearth process Method of producing steel in a furnace heated by overhead flames. The flames come from gas or oil burners, and oxygen may be blown through the furnace to increase its temperature. Pig iron, scrap steel and limestone are heated together. Various impurities form slag, which is removed from the surface of the molten metal. Other materials are added to the metal to produce steel of the required type.

Open University (OU) Form of British higher education, chartered in 1969 as a non-residential alternative to conventional university training, with open access. Teaching is carried out through television and radio broadcasts, as well as personal tuition and summer schools. It grants full undergraduate degrees in all faculties.

opera Stage drama that is sung. It combines acting, singing, orchestral music, set and costume design, making spectacular entertainment. The best-known opera houses include La Scala (Milan), the Opéra (Paris), the Royal Opera (London), the State Opera (Vienna), the Festspiele (Bayreuth) and the Metropolitan Opera (New York). Opera began in Italy in c.1600. The classical style evolved in c.1750; its greatest exponent was Mozart. The 19th century was dominated by Verdi and Wagner. Twentieth-century opera has been marked by a profusion of styles by composers such as Puccini, Strauss, Berg and Britten. See also opera buffa; opéra comique; opera seria; operetta

opera buffa Style of Italian comic opera that developed in mid-18th-century Naples. Light and simple in style, it introduced the elaborate finale that influenced the subsequent development of opera. An early example is La Serva Padrona (1733) by Giovanni Pergolesi.

opéra comique Style of French opera that began in the late 18th century. Its hallmarks are a witty plot involving some spoken dialogue, romantic subject matter and simple engaging music. The genre can also include tragic works, such as Bizet's Carmen (1875) and Offenbach's Tales of Hoffmann (1811).

opera seria Style of Italian opera in the 17th and early 18th centuries. The plots were usually heroic or tragic. Priority was given to virtuoso vocal display in elaborate arias. The formalism and stylization of such operas prompted a reaction that gave rise to the development of opera buffa. Examples include Mozart's Idomeneo (1781).

operetta Type of light opera involving songs, dialogue, sometimes dancing and an engaging story. Operettas developed from attempts by composers to reach wider audiences. Among these composers were Johann Strauss, Arthur Sullivan (with W.S. Gilbert) and Jacques Offenbach.

ophthalmology Branch of medicine that specializes in the diagnosis and treatment of diseases of the eye.

ophthalmoscope Instrument for examining the interior of the eye, invented by Hermann von Helmholtz in 1851.

Ophüls, Max (1902–57) German film director. His contribution was superbly realized in two masterpieces, Letter from an Unknown Woman (1948) and Reckless Moment (1949). His son, **Marcel** (1927–), is a documentary-maker. He often presents controversial issues, such as the Nuremberg trials in *The Memory of Justice* (1975) and the Bosnian war in *Veillées d'Armes* (1994).

opium Drug derived from the unripe seed-pods of the opium POPPY. Its components and derivatives have been used as NARCOTICS and ANALGESICS for many centuries. It produces drowsiness and euphoria and reduces pain. MORPHINE and CODEINE are opium derivatives.

Opium Wars (1839–42) Conflict between Britain and China. It arose because Chinese officials prevented the importation of OPIUM. After a British victory, the Treaty of Nanking gave Britain trading rights in certain ports and the grant of Hong Kong. A second, similar war (1856–60) was fought by the British and French against China. When China refused to ratify the Treaty of Tientsin (1858), Anglo-French forces occupied Peking (Beijing).

Oporto City and port on the River Douro, NW Portugal. A Roman settlement, it was occupied by the Visigoths (540–716) and the Moors (716–997) before being brought under Portuguese control in 1092. By the 17th century, it was a famous wine centre, and its PORT is still exported. Portugal's second-largest city, Oporto lies in an industrialized region. Industries: textiles, fishing, fruit, olive oil. Pop. (1991) 310,640.

opossum (possum) New World MARSUPIAL animal, the only marsupial found outside Australasia. Omnivorous tree-dwellers, they have silky grey fur (except on the long prehensile tail) and feign death when in danger. The common opossum, *Didelphis marsupialis*, grows up to 50cm (20in) long, plus a 30cm (12in) tail. Family Didelphidae.

Oppenheimer, (Julius) Robert (1904–67) US theoretical physicist. He was appointed director (1943–45) of the Los Alamos laboratory in New Mexico, where he headed the MANHATTAN PROJECT to develop the atomic bomb. In 1949, Oppenheimer opposed the construction of the HYDROGEN BOMB. In 1953, following investigations by Joseph McCARTHY, he was suspended by the Atomic Energy Commission. In 1963, he was reinstated.

opposition, leader of the In parliamentary systems, the leader of the party that is runner-up in a general election. In the UK, official recognition was given to the leader of the opposition in 1937.

optical activity Ability of some chemical compounds in solution and some crystals and transparent substances placed in an intense magnetic field to rotate the plane of POLARIZED LIGHT. Magnetic rotation of the plane of polarized light was discovered by Michael FARADAY in 1845 and is known as the Faraday effect.

optical character recognition (OCR) Technique for reading letters or numbers so that they can be input into a COMPUTER. The text to be read is scanned and the text "image" converted into a digital form. A special program then identifies the characters by their shapes.

optical disk In computing, a high-density storage device consisting of a disc on which data is recorded and read by a laser. The most common type is a CD-ROM, although an audio COMPACT DISC (CD) is also a read-only device of this kind. A recording facility is provided by a WORM disc (write once, read many), on which a computer can save data once and then read it repeatedly but not be able to change it.

optical fibre *See* FIBRE OPTICS

optical illusion Effect in which visual information is misleading or misinterpreted. Natural optical illusions are often created by light REFRACTION such as a MIRAGE of water on a hot, dry road.

optics Branch of physics concerned with the study of LIGHT and its behaviour. Fundamental aspects are the physical nature of light, both as a WAVE phenomenon and as particles (PHOTONS), and the REFLECTION, REFRACTION and polarization of light. Optics also involves the study of mirrors and LENS systems and of optically active chemicals and crystals that polarize light. *See also* POLARIZED LIGHT

option Right to buy or sell SHARES or COMMODITIES at an agreed (exercise) price by a specified date. Options may be used to speculate on an expected fall or rise in the market price, or as a guarantee against a collapse in the market. *See also* FUTURE

optometry Testing of vision in order to prescribe corrective eyewear, such as spectacles or contact lenses. It is distinct from OPHTHALMOLOGY.

Opus Dei International Roman Catholic organization of 75,000 laymen and 1,000 priests, known for its highly conservative political and religious influence. It was founded (1928) in Spain by Escrivá de Balaguer (1902–75). Its members seek to put into practice Christian values through their chosen professions. Pope John Paul II beatified de Balaguer in 1992.

oracle In ancient Greece, a priest or priestess who gave the answer of a god to questions put by individuals. The most famous was the oracle of Apollo at DELPHI. The god spoke through a priestess (Pythia), whose words were, in turn, interpreted by priests. Answers tended to be ambiguous, so that the oracle could never be said to be wrong.

Oran City and seaport on the Gulf of Oran, NW Algeria. Founded in the 10th century, it was taken by Spain from its Arab rulers in 1509. Captured by Ottoman Turks in 1708, it was retaken by Spain in 1732. Under French rule from 1831 to 1962, it developed as a naval base. It is Algeria's second-largest city. Industries: iron ore, textiles, chemicals, cereals, wine, fruit. Pop. (1994) 664,000.

Orange Longest river of South Africa. It rises in the Drakensberg Mountains in N Lesotho and flows generally W, forming the boundary between FREE STATE and CAPE PROVINCE. It continues W through the Kalahari and Namib deserts, forming South Africa's border with Namibia. It empties into the Atlantic Ocean at Oranjemund. Length: *c*.2,100km (1,300mi).

orange Evergreen citrus tree and its fruit. There are two basic types. The sweet orange (*Citrus sinensis*) is native to Asia and widely grown in the USA and Israel. The fruit develops without flower pollination and is often seedless. The sour orange (*C. aurantium*) is widely grown in Spain for the manufacture of marmalade. Related fruits include the MANDARIN, tangerine and satsuma, all varieties of *C. reticulata*. Height: to 9m (30ft). Family Rutaceae; genus *Citrus*.

Orange, house of Royal dynasty of the Netherlands. Orange was a principality in S France, which was inherited by WILLIAM I (THE SILENT) in 1544. He led the successful Dutch revolt against Spain in the late 16th century. WILLIAM III became king of England in 1689. In 1815, the son of WILLIAM V became WILLIAM I of the Netherlands.

Orange Free State Former name of FREE STATE

Orangemen Members of the Orange Society, or Orange Order. It was founded (1795) in Ulster in response to the mainly Roman Catholic, nationalist United Irishmen, and was named after the Protestant hero, WILLIAM III (OF ORANGE). His victory over the Catholic JAMES II at the Battle of the BOYNE (1690) is celebrated on its anniversary, 12 July.

orang-utan Great APE native to forests of Sumatra and Borneo. It has a bulging belly and a shaggy, reddish-brown coat. It swings by its arms when travelling through trees but proceeds on all fours on the ground.

Height: 1.5m (5ft); weight: to 100kg (220 lb). Species *Pongo pygmaeus*. *See also* PRIMATES

oratorio Form of sacred musical composition for solo voices, chorus and orchestra. The first of these compositions were presented in oratories (chapels) in 17th-century Italy. Outstanding examples are HANDEL's *Messiah* (1742) and ELGAR's *Dream of Gerontius* (1900).

orbit Path of a celestial body in a gravitational field. The path is usually a closed one about the focus of the system to which it belongs, as with those of the planets around the Sun. Most celestial orbits are elliptical, although the ECCENTRICITY can vary greatly. It is rare for an orbit to be parabolic or hyperbolic. *See also* APSIS; DECLINATION, MAGNETIC; GEOSTATIONARY ORBIT; GRAVITATION; INCLINATION, MAGNETIC; KEPLER, JOHANNES

orbital In PARTICLE PHYSICS, region around an atomic NUCLEUS in which ELECTRONS can move. There is a high probability of finding an electron in such an orbital, which can accommodate one or two electrons and has a shape and energy characterized by an atom's QUANTUM NUMBERS.

orchestra Group of musicians who play together. During the 17th century string orchestras developed out of viol consorts; in the 18th century some wind instruments were added. The woodwind section was soon established, and by the end of the 19th century the brass section was, too. Modern orchestras consist of between 80 and 120 players divided into sections: strings (violin, viola, cello, double bass and harp), woodwind (flute, oboe, clarinet and bassoon), brass (trumpet, trombone, French horn and tuba) and percussion.

orchid Any plant of the family Orchidaceae, common in the tropics. There are *c*.35,000 species. All are perennials and grow in soil or as EPIPHYTES on other plants. Parasitic and saprophytic species are also known. The flowers of many species are adapted to allow pollination only by a particular species of insect, bat or even frog. All orchids have bilaterally symmetrical flower structures, each with three sepals. They range in diameter from *c*.2mm (0.1in) to 38cm (15in). *See also* VANILLA

Orczy, Baroness (1865–1947) British writer, b. Hungary. She emigrated to England in 1880. Orczy is remembered for her adventure stories, such as *The Scarlet Pimpernel* (1905) and *The Elusive Pimpernel* (1908).

ordeal Form of trial in early medieval Europe in which the innocence or guilt of the accused, or (in Spain) the truthfulness of a witness, was established by a physical test. One method involved grasping a red-hot iron. If no scars were visible after three days, the accused was innocent.

order In TAXONOMY (biological classification), a group of related plants or animals; order is one rank below CLASS and a rank above FAMILY. For example, the tiger is of the order Carnivora (CARNIVORES).

orders, holy In the Roman Catholic, Orthodox, and Anglican churches, the duties of the clergy and the grades of hierarchical rank as outlined in the office of ORDINATION. The major orders are subdeacon, deacon, priest or bishop. The minor orders are porter, lector, exorcist and acolyte.

orders of architecture In classical architecture, style and decoration of a column, its base, capital and entablature. Of the five orders, the Greeks developed the Doric, Ionic and Corinthian. The Tuscan and Composite orders were Roman adaptations. A typical **Doric** column has no base, a relatively short shaft with surface fluting meeting in a sharp edge and an unornamented capital. The **Ionic** order is characterized by slender columns with 24 flutes and prominent spiral scrolls on the capitals. The **Corinthian** is the most ornate of the

Classical orders of architecture. A typical Corinthian column has a high base, a slim, fluted column and a bell-shaped capital with acanthus-leaf ornament.

ordination Process of consecrating a person as a minister of religion. In Christian Churches organized along episcopal lines, ordination confirms the ordinand (the individual undergoing the process) as a priest or minister in holy ORDERS. In Roman Catholic and Orthodox Churches, the rite of ordination is a SACRAMENT. In Protestant Churches without episcopal organization, ordination is carried out by ministers, ruling elders, or specially selected lay persons. In Christianity, the ban on women as full members of the clergy has persisted in some churches, notably the Roman Catholic Church. During the 20th century, however, many Protestant churches began to admit women first as deacons and later as priests and ministers. The General Synod of the Church of England agreed that there was no theological objection to women priests in 1975; but the necessary church legislation was not passed until 1992. The first women priests were ordained in 1994.

Ordovician Second-oldest period of the PALAEOZOIC era, *c*.505 to *c*.438 million years ago. All animal life was restricted to the sea. Numerous invertebrates flourished and included trilobites, brachiopods, corals, graptolites,

Doric

Ionic

Corinthian

Composite

▶ **orders of architecture**
The five main orders of architecture were first presented by Sebastiano Serlio (1475–1554) in Book IV of his treatise on architecture (1537).

Tuscan

molluscs and echinoderms. Remains of jawless fish from this period are the first record of the vertebrates.

ore MINERAL or combination of minerals from which METALS and non-metals can be extracted. It occurs in veins, beds or seams parallel to the enclosing rock or in irregular masses. *See also* MINING; SMELTING

oregano (marjoram) Dried leaves and flowers of several perennial herbs of the genus *Oreganum*, native to Mediterranean lands and w Asia. It is a popular culinary herb. Family Lamiaceae/Labiatae; genus *Origanum*.

Oregon State of NW USA on the Pacific coast; the capital is SALEM. Other major cities include PORTLAND and Eugene. Trading posts were set up in the 1790s, mainly by the HUDSON'S BAY COMPANY. From 1842, the OREGON TRAIL brought more settlers. Oregon Territory was formed in 1848 and was admitted to the Union in 1859. It is dominated by the forested slopes of the CASCADE and the Coast ranges. Between the two lies the fertile Willamette Valley. The COLUMBIA and the Willamette are the major rivers. Agricultural products include cattle, dairy produce, wheat and market garden products. Oregon produces more than 20% of the nation's softwood timber. Area: 251,180sq km (96,981sq mi). Pop. (2000) 3,421,399.

Oregon Trail Main route of US pioneers to the West in the 1840s and 1850s. It ran 3,200km (2,000mi) from Independence, Missouri, to Fort Vancouver on the COLUMBIA River in Oregon and crossed the ROCKY MOUNTAINS via South Pass. The journey took about six months.

Orestes In Greek legend, the son of AGAMEMNON and CLYTEMNESTRA, and brother of ELECTRA. He killed his mother and her lover Aegisthus to avenge their murder of his father.

Orff, Carl (1895–1982) German composer. He used deliberately primitive rhythms in his best-known works, *Carmina Burana* (1937) and *Catulli Carmina* (1943), and the opera *Trionfo di Afrodite* (1953).

organ In biology, group of TISSUES that form a functional and structural unit in a living organism. The major organs of the body include the BRAIN, HEART, LUNGS, SKIN, LIVER and KIDNEYS.

organ KEYBOARD INSTRUMENT. The player sits at a console and regulates a flow of air to ranks of pipes, producing rich tones. The organ was in use in Christian churches in the 8th century. The modern organ dates from the BAROQUE period.

organic chemistry *See* CHEMISTRY

Organization for Economic Cooperation and Development (OECD) International consultative body set up in 1961 by the major Western trading nations. Its aims are to stimulate economic growth and world trade by raising the standard of living in member countries and by coordinating aid to less developed countries. Its headquarters are in Paris, France, and it has 24 member nations including all the world's major powers.

Organization of African Unity (OAU) Intergovernmental organization. Founded in 1963, the OAU brings together all African states. It aims to safeguard African interests and independence, encourage the continent's development and settle disputes among member states. Its headquarters are in Addis Ababa, Ethiopia.

Organization of American States (OAS) Organization of 35 member states of the Americas that promotes peaceful settlements to disputes, regional cooperation in the limitation of weapons, and economic and cultural development. It was created in 1948 during an international meeting held in Colombia. The successor to the Pan American Union, the OAS works with the UNITED NATIONS (UN). Its headquarters are in Washington, D.C.

Organization of Petroleum Exporting Countries (OPEC) Intergovernmental organization established in 1960 by many of the world's major oil producing states to safeguard their interests. It was able to control oil prices in the 1970s, but its influence has waned since then, largely because of internal differences and the emergence of major oil-producing countries outside OPEC. Its headquarters are in Vienna, Austria.

orgasm Physiological culmination of sexual stimulation, marked by general release of muscular tension and waves of contractions causing climactic spasms of vaginal muscles in the female and ejaculation (the release of SEMEN) in the male.

orienteering Sport similar to cross-country running but requiring both athletic and navigational skills. Runners, leaving at timed intervals, carry a map and compass from which to locate control points around the usually 10km (6.2mi) course. The fastest to complete the course wins.

Origen (*c*.AD 185–254) Egyptian theologian and Father of the Church. In *c*.230, he was ordained at Alexandria. In *c*.250, Origen was imprisoned and tortured during the persecutions of Emperor Decius. He is chiefly remembered for his *Hexapla*, an edition of the Old Testament that favoured an allegorical interpretation of Scripture.

original sin Sin committed by ADAM and EVE for which they were expelled from the Garden of EDEN and were made mortal (Genesis 3). The sin was their eating from the tree of the knowledge of good and evil against God's strict instructions. Adam and Eve's guilt was deemed to have been passed down to their descendants through all the generations.

Orinoco River in Venezuela. Rising in the Sierra Parima Mountains in S Venezuela, it flows NW to Colombia, then N, forming part of the Venezuela-Colombia border, and finally E into the Atlantic Ocean by a vast delta. Length: *c*.2,062km (1,281mi).

oriole Two unrelated songbirds. The Old World oriole (family Oriolidae) is brightly coloured and lays eggs in a cup-shaped nest. The New World oriole (family Icteridae) has similar colouring and builds hanging nests in trees.

Orion Prominent constellation, representing a hunter. Four young stars form a conspicuous quadrilateral containing a row of three other stars representing his belt.

Orion nebula Emission NEBULA visible to the naked eye in the constellation of ORION. It is a mass of gas surrounding a quadrilateral grouping of four hot O-type stars (the trapezium).

Orissa State in NE India, on the Bay of Bengal; the capital is Bhubaneswar. After being ruled by Hindus, Afghans and Moguls, it was ceded to the Mahrattas in 1751. Occupied by the British in 1803, it was proclaimed a constituent state of India in 1950. Industries: mining, fishing, rice, wheat, sugar cane, oilseeds, forestry. Area: 155,782sq km (60,147sq mi). Pop. (1991) 31,659,736.

Orkney Islands Archipelago of more than 70 islands off the N coast of Scotland. Mainland (Pomona) is the largest; other principal islands include Hoy and South Ronaldsay. The land is a low-lying, fertile plain, and the climate is mild and wet. The islands were conquered in 875 by the Viking king Harold I. They remained Norwegian territory until 1231. In 1472, the islands were annexed by Scotland. Scapa Flow (between Mainland and Hoy) was the major British naval base in both World Wars. The economy is predominantly agricultural. Area: 974sq km (376sq mi). Pop. (1991) 19,612.

Orlando, Vittorio Emanuele (1860–1952) Italian statesman, prime minister (1917–19). He became prime minister after a succession of Italian defeats in World War 1. He represented Italy at the Treaty of Versailles. His early support for MUSSOLINI turned to opposition by 1925. After World War 2 he rejoined the Senate and ran for president (1948).

Orlando City in central Florida, USA. Orlando is one of the world's most popular tourist destinations, with theme parks including Disney World, Sea World and Universal Studios. Established in 1827 as a trading post, Orlando was incorporated as a city in 1875 and expanded with the arrival of the railway. Industries: citrus-growing, aerospace, electronics. Pop. (1990) 164,693.

Orléans, Louis-Philippe, Duc d' (1747–93) French Bourbon prince. A liberal, he was elected to the National Convention (1792) and voted for LOUIS XVI execution. When his son, the future King LOUIS PHILIPPE, defected (1793), he was arrested and subsequently executed during the REIGN OF TERROR.

Orléans City on the River Loire, N central France; capital of Loiret department. Besieged by the English during the HUNDRED YEARS WAR, it was relieved by JOAN OF ARC in 1429. During the 16th-century, Wars of RELIGION, the city was besieged by Catholic forces and held by them until the Edict of NANTES. Industries: tobacco, textiles, fruit and vegetables, chemicals. Pop. (1991) 105,111.

ornithology Study of BIRDS. Included in general ornithological studies are classification, structure, function, evolution, distribution, migration, reproduction, ecology and behaviour.

Orozco, José Clemente (1883–1949) Mexican painter. In his wash drawings, *Mexico in Revolution* (1911–16), Orozco aimed to demonstrate the futility of war. His MURALS are grand in both scale and mood, none more so than *Katharsis* (1934). His later paintings, such as *Hidalgo and Castillo* (1949), are highly emotive.

Orpheus In Greek mythology, the son of Calliope by APOLLO, and the finest of all poets and musicians. Orpheus married Eurydice, who died after being bitten by a snake. He descended into the Underworld to rescue her and was allowed to regain her if he did not look back at her until they emerged into the sunlight. He could not resist, and Eurydice vanished forever.

orphism (orphic CUBISM) Term invented (1912) by APOLLINAIRE to describe a new art form combining elements of CUBISM, FUTURISM and FAUVISM. The style was first associated with the work of Robert and Sonia DELAUNAY and its other exponents exerted considerable influence in Germany through the works of KLEE and KANDINSKY. *See also* BLAUE REITER, DER; KUPKA, FRANK

orrery Mechanical model of the Solar System. Orreries vary from simple ones with just the Earth, Moon and Sun to highly complicated representations of the whole Solar System. It is named after Charles Boyle, fourth Earl of Orrery (1676–1731), who commissioned one in 1712, although this was not the first to be made.

Ortega (Saavedra), Daniel (1945–) Nicaraguan statesman, president (1984–90). In 1963, he joined the SANDINISTAS (FSLN) and rose to become its leader in 1966. In 1979, Ortega led the revolution that toppled the SOMOZA regime and formed a socialist government. In 1984, he was elected president. The Sandinista government was destabilised by the US-backed CONTRA rebels. In 1990 elections Ortega was defeated by Violeta CHAMORRO. In 1996, he was defeated by Arnoldo Aleman.

Ortega y Gasset, José (1883–1955) Spanish philosopher and humanist. Ortega's most famous work, *The Revolt of the Masses* (1929), advocated government by an intellectual élite. Other works include *Man and*

People (1957) and *Man and Crisis* (1956). He founded (1948) the Institute of Humanities, Madrid.

orthoclase (KAlSi$_3$O$_8$, potassium aluminium silicate) Essential mineral in acidic IGNEOUS rocks and common in METAMORPHIC rocks. It has a monoclinic system of crystals and is usually white. Hardness 6–6.5; r.d. 2.5–2.6. *See also* PLAGIOCLASE

orthodontics *See* DENTISTRY

Orthodox Church, Eastern Community of *c.*130 million Christians living mainly in E and SE Europe, parts of Asia and a significant minority in the USA. The Church is a federation of groups that share forms of worship and episcopal organization, but each group has its own national head. The largest group is the Russian Orthodox Church. Although there is no central authority, member churches recognize the patriarch of Istanbul as titular head. Eastern Orthodox Christians reject the jurisdiction of the Roman pope. When Constantine moved his capital to Byzantium (Istanbul) in AD 330, a separate non-Roman culture developed. The Eastern Orthodox Christians accepted the NICENE CREED, as modified in 381. Conflicts grew between the Eastern patriarchs and Rome. In the SCHISM (1054), Western and Eastern arms of Christendom excommunicated each other's followers, and the split became irreparable when Crusaders invaded Constantinople (1204). Attempts at reconciliation in 1274 and 1439 failed. In 1962, Orthodox observers attended the Second Vatican Council. In 1963 the Eastern Orthodox Churches agreed to open dialogue with Rome.

orthopaedics Branch of medicine that deals with the diagnosis and treatment of diseases, disorders and injuries of bones, muscles, tendons and ligaments.

Orton, Joe (John Kingsley) (1933–67) English dramatist. His satirical black comedies include *Entertaining Mr Sloane* (1964) and *Loot* (1965). *What the Butler Saw* was staged posthumously (1969) after Orton's murder by his lover, Kenneth Halliwell.

Orwell, George (1903–50) British novelist and essayist, b. Eric Arthur Blair in India. His service (1922–27) with the Indian imperial police in Burma formed the basis of *Burmese Days* (1934). Other early autobiographical works include *Down and Out in Paris and London* (1933), *The Road to Wigan Pier* (1937) and *Homage to Catalonia* (1938), the latter on his experiences in the Spanish Civil War. Orwell, however, is best-known for his fictions on totalitarianism: the satirical fable *Animal Farm* (1945), and the dystopic novel *1984* (1949).

oryx (gembok) Any of four species of ANTELOPES. The male has a tuft of hair at the throat and both sexes carry long horns ringed at the base. Two species are almost extinct, but the other two survive in considerable numbers in Africa. Height: 1.2m (4ft). Family Bovidae.

Osaka City on Osaka Bay, S Honshu island, Japan; capital of Osaka prefecture. Japan's third-largest city and its principal industrial port, Osaka was intensively bombed during World War 2. It is a major transport hub. The city was the imperial capital between the 4th and 8th centuries. During the Edo Period the city became the commercial centre of Hideyoshi. Pop. (1993) 2,495,000.

Osborne, John James (1929–95) English dramatist. Osborne's play *Look Back in Anger* (1956) established him as one of the ANGRY YOUNG MEN of English theatre. His other successes included *The Entertainer* (1957), *Luther* (1961) and *Inadmissable Evidence* (1963). In *Déjàvu* (1992), Osborne revisited Jimmy Porter, the anti-hero of *Look Back in Anger*.

Oscar (officially Academy Award) Prize awarded annually since 1927 for services to the CINEMA by the

US Academy of Motion Picture Arts and Sciences. The gold-plated bronze statuettes stand 25cm (10in) high.

oscillating universe theory Variant of the BIG BANG theory in which it is suggested that the UNIVERSE passes through successive cycles of expansion and contraction (or collapse). At the end of the collapse phase, with the universe packed into a small volume of great density, it is possible that a "bounce" would occur. The universe would thus oscillate between "Big Bang" and "Big Crunch" episodes and so be infinite in age.

oscillator In physics, a device for producing sound waves, as in a SONAR or an ultrasonic generator. In electronics, an oscillator circuit converts direct current (DC) electricity into high-frequency alternating current (AC).

oscilloscope (cathode-ray oscilloscope) Electronic instrument in which a CATHODE-RAY TUBE (CRT) system displays how quantities, such as voltage or current, vary over a period of time. The electron beam that traces the pattern on the screen is moved by a time-base generator within the oscilloscope. The result is generally a curve or graph on the screen.

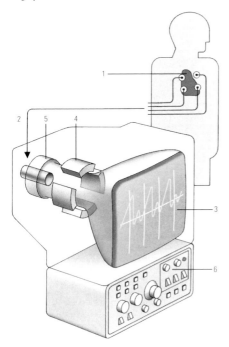

▲ oscilloscope An oscilloscope displays an electronic signal on a display in analogue form. Usually time is represented on the x-axis (horizontal) with the y-axis (vertical) recording the incoming voltage – here a heartbeat (1). The signal from the object being monitored is converted into an electrical voltage (2). That voltage is shown in visible form on the screen of a cathode ray tube

(3) similar to a black and white television. Deflector magnets (4) direct the stream of electrons from the electron gun (5). The magnets sweep the electron beam from left to right over a set period, while variations in the voltage of the external signal cause the wave pattern. The control box (6) allows the period of the x-axis and the strength of the signal displayed to be changed.

osier Any of various willows, especially *Salix viminalis* and *S. purpurea*, the flexible branches and stems of which are used for wickerwork.

Osiris In Egyptian mythology, the god of the dead. He is generally depicted wearing a feathered crown and bearing a crook and flail. Osiris was killed by his brother SETH. His sister and wife, ISIS, retrieved the corpse, and Osiris' son, HORUS, avenged his death.

Osler, William (1849–1910) Canadian physician who was the first to identify PLATELETS in the blood (1873). Osler wrote *The Principles and Practice of Medicine* (1892), the leading medical text of the time and which is still published today. Probably the most famous physician of his era, he gave his name to several medical terms, such as Osler's nodes and Osler-Vaquez disease.

Oslo Capital of Norway, in the SE of the country at the head of Oslo Fjord. The city was founded in the mid-11th century. Largely destroyed by fire in 1624, it was rebuilt by CHRISTIAN IV, who named it Christiania. In 1905, it became the capital of independent Norway, and was renamed Oslo in 1925. Industries: machinery, wood products, food processing, textiles, chemicals, shipbuilding. Pop. (1997) 494,000.

Osman I (1258–1326) Founder of the OTTOMAN EMPIRE. As ruler of the small Osmanli, or Ottoman, state in NW Anatolia (Turkey), he declared his independence of the SELJUK sultan *c*.1290. He expanded his territory in frequent wars against the BYZANTINE EMPIRE.

osmium (symbol Os) Bluish-white metallic element, one of the TRANSITION ELEMENTS. The densest of the elements, osmium is associated with PLATINUM; the chief source is as a by-product from smelting nickel. Like IRIDIUM, osmium is used in producing hard alloys. It is also used to make electrical contacts and pen points. Properties: at.no.76; r.a.m. 190.2; r.d. 22.57; m.p. 3,045°C (5,513°F); b.p. 5,027°C (9,081°F); most common isotope Os^{192} (41.0%).

osmosis DIFFUSION of a SOLVENT (such as water) through a selectively permeable MEMBRANE (one which only allows the passage of certain dissolved substances) into a more concentrated solution. Because the more concentrated solution contains a lower concentration of solvent molecules, the solvent flows by diffusion to dilute it until concentrations of solvent are equal on both sides of the membrane. Osmosis is a vital cellular process. *See also* DIALYSIS; TURGOR PRESSURE

Osnabrück City on the River Haase, Lower Saxony, NW Germany. It obtained a city charter in 1171. It was the scene of the negotiations for the Peace of WESTPHALIA in 1648. Industries: iron and steel, textiles, papermaking, chemicals, motor vehicles, machinery. Pop. (1995) 168,000.

osprey HAWK that lives beside lakes and in coastal regions of all continents except Antarctica. It has a short hooked bill, broad, ragged wings and a white head; it has brownish-black plumage on its back and a cream breast. Length: 51–61cm (20–24in). Family Pandionidae; species *Pandion haliaetus*.

Ossetia Region of the central Caucasus. The region is divided along the River Terek. **North Ossetia** is an autonomous republic within the Russian Federation, whose capital is Vladikavkaz. **South Ossetia** is an autonomous region of GEORGIA, whose capital is Tshkinvali. Ossetia is a mountainous agricultural region, producing fruit, wine and grain. North Ossetia has rich mineral deposits. Ossetia became part of the Russian empire in the early 19th century. Area: North Ossetia, 8,000sq km (3,000sq mi); South Ossetia, 3,900sq km (1,500sq mi). Pop. (1990) North Ossetia, 638,000; South, 99,800.

Ossian (Oisín) Legendary Gaelic poet, son of FINN MAC CUMHAIL. Ossian is the hero of the Fenian cycle.

ossification (osteogenesis) Process of BONE formation in vertebrates. Bone is formed through the action of special cells called osteoblasts, which secrete bone-forming minerals that combine with a network of COLLAGEN fibres.

osteomyelitis Infection of the BONE, sometimes spreading along the marrow cavity. Rare except in diabetics, it can arise from a compound fracture where the bone breaks through the skin, or from infection elsewhere in the body. It is accompanied by fever, swelling,and pain. The condition may be treated with immobilization, ANTIBIOTICS and surgical drainage.

osteopathy System of alternative medical treatment based on the use of physical manipulation to rectify damage caused by mechanical stresses. The concept was formulated (1874) by US physician Andrew Still.

osteoporosis Condition where there is loss of bone substance resulting in brittle bones. It is common in older people, especially in women following the MENOPAUSE; it may also occur in Cushing's syndrome and as a side-effect of prolonged treatment with corticosteroid drugs. There is no cure, but it may be treated with calcium supplements and a drug called disodium etidronate. HORMONE REPLACEMENT THERAPY (HRT) may help to prevent its occurrence in post-menopausal women.

ostrich Largest living bird, found in central Africa. It is flightless and has a small head and long neck. Plumage is black and white in males, brown and white in females. Eggs are laid in holes in the sand. They can reach speeds of up to 65km/h (40mph). Height: to 2.5m (8ft); weight: to 155kg (345lb). Family Struthionidae; species *Struthio camelus*.

Ostrogoths *See* GOTH

Ostrovsky, Alexsandr Nikolaievich (1823–86) Russian dramatist. He is an important figure in 20th-century Russian realism. Many of his plays deal with the life of the Russian merchant class. His masterpiece *The Storm* (1859) forms the basis of Janáček's opera *Katya Kabanova* (1921).

Oswald, Lee Harvey (1939–63) Alleged assassin of US president John F. KENNEDY, on 22 November 1963, in Dallas, Texas. Before he could stand trial, he was shot and killed in police custody by nightclub owner Jack Ruby. *See also* WARREN COMMISSION

Oswald, Saint (*c.*605–42) King of Northumbria (633–42). He became a Christian and converted his people with the help of St AIDAN. Oswald was killed in battle. His feast day is 5 August.

Othman (Uthman) (574–656) Third CALIPH (644–56), son-in-law of MUHAMMAD. He was a member of the UMAYYAD family. Othman was blamed for widespread revolts and intrigues, ending in his assassination.

Otis, Elisha (1811–61) US inventor. In 1856 Otis designed and installed the first passenger lift in a New York City department store.

O'Toole, Peter (1932–) Irish stage and film actor. His stage performances (1955) as Shylock and Hamlet exhilarated London audiences. O'Toole was nominated for an Academy Award for his first film role in *Lawrence of Arabia* (1962). Other Oscar nominations include *Becket* (1964), *The Lion in Winter* (1968), *Goodbye Mr Chips* (1969) and *The Ruling Class* (1972). His career was revived with further nominated performances in *The Stunt Man* (1980) and *My Favourite Year* (1987).

Ottawa Capital of Canada, in SE Ontario, on the Ottawa River and the Rideau Canal. Founded in 1826 as Bytown, it acquired its present name in 1854. Queen

▶ **ostrich** Africa is the home of the ostrich, the largest living bird. It is the only member of the order Struthioniformes. Several large ground-dwelling birds, the ostrich, rhea, emu and cassowary, all resemble each other quite closely but are thought to have arisen independently, and as such are examples of a phenomenon called convergent evolution.

Victoria chose it as capital of the United Provinces in 1858, and in 1867 it became the national capital of the Dominion of Canada. Industries: glass-making, printing, publishing, sawmilling, pulp-making, clocks and watches. Pop. (1991) 313,987.

otter Semi-aquatic carnivore of the WEASEL family found everywhere except Australia. Otters have narrow, pointed heads with bristly whiskers, sleek furry bodies, short legs with webbed hind feet and long, tapering tails. They feed mainly on fish. The river otter (genus *Lutra*) is small to medium-sized and spends a considerable time on land. Family Mustelidae.

Otto I (the Great) (912–73) King of the Germans (936–73) and first Holy Roman emperor (962–73). He succeeded his father, HENRY I, in Germany and defeated rebellious princes and their ally, LOUIS IV of France. Royal power was further augmented by Otto's close control of the church. In 955 he crushed the MAGYARS at Lechfeld. He invaded Italy to aid Queen Adelaide of Lombardy, married her and became king of Lombardy. In 962 he was crowned as Roman emperor (the "Holy", meaning "Christian", was added later).

Otto IV (1174–1218) (Otto of Brunswick) Holy Roman emperor (1198–1215). A member of the GUELPH family, Otto antagonized the powerful Pope INNOCENT III by his invasion of Italy against the HOHENSTAUFEN King Frederick I (later the Emperor FREDERICK II). With Innocent's support, Frederick was elected king by the German princes (1212) and supported by PHILIP II of France. Otto was defeated by Philip at Bouvines (1214) and forced to retire.

Otto, Nikolaus August (1832–91) German engineer. In 1861 he built a gas-fired engine which won a gold medal at the 1867 Paris Exhibition. Otto later built an INTERNAL COMBUSTION ENGINE based on a four-stroke cycle (also called the **Otto cycle**). This FOUR-STROKE ENGINE was the forerunner of most of today's engines.

Ottoman Empire Former Turkish state that controlled much of SE Europe, the Middle East and North Africa between the 14th and 20th centuries. It was founded by OSMAN I (r.1290–1326). He ruled a small principality in Anatolia, which he greatly enlarged at the expense of the BYZANTINE EMPIRE. The contest with the Byzantines ended with the capture of Constantinople (now ISTANBUL), which became the Ottoman capital in 1453. Under SULEIMAN I (THE MAGNIFICENT) (r.1520–66), the Ottoman Empire included the Arab lands of the Middle East and North Africa, SE Europe and the E Mediterranean. The decline of Ottoman power began before 1600, and thereafter Ottoman territory was reduced in wars with its European neighbours, Austria and Russia. After World War 1, when Ottoman territory was reduced to roughly the present Turkish borders, nationalists led by ATATÜRK deposed the last Ottoman sultan and created the modern Turkish republic (1923).

Ouagadougou Capital of Burkina Faso, West Africa. Founded in the late 11th century as capital of the MOSSI empire, it remained the centre of Mossi power until captured by the French in 1896. Industries: handicrafts, textiles, food processing, peanuts, vegetable oil. Pop. (1993) 690,000.

Ouse (Great Ouse) River rising in Northamptonshire, central England, and flowing 256km (159mi) E through East Anglia before emptying into the Wash at King's Lynn.

outback Term applied in Australia to the inland areas of the continent. In the early days of settlement, the name acquired a mythical quality as a land of adventure and opportunity that lured explorers inland. It remains an undeveloped and sparsely populated region.

ouzel (ousel) Heavy-bodied bird found in the mountains of Asia, Europe and the Western Hemisphere. The ring ouzel (*Turdus torquatus*) has black plumage with a white chest collar. Family Turdidae.

ovary In biology, part of a multicellular animal or a flowering plant that produces egg cells (ova), the female reproductive cells; in vertebrates it also produces female sex HORMONES. In women there is an ovary on each side of the UTERUS. Controlled by the PITUITARY GLAND, each ovary produces OESTROGEN and PROGESTERONE, which control the functioning of the female reproductive system. In flowering plants, the female sex cells are contained within structures called ovules inside the ovary. After FERTILIZATION the ovules develop into seeds, and the ovary develops into fruit. *See also* MENSTRUAL CYCLE; REPRODUCTION

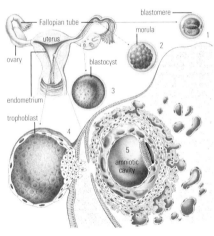

▲ **ovum** It takes about a week for the fertilized ovum to pass down the Fallopian tube and implant itself in the uterine lining, the endometrium. Within hours of conception mitosis begins with the development of a sphere of an increasing number of cells; the sphere starts as the blastomere (1) and develops into the morula (2) of about 64 cells. At this stage it changes into a hollow, fluid-containing ball – blastocyst (3) – with the inner cell mass at one end. It can now begin implantation (4). By the ninth day after conception, the blastocyst has sunk deep into the endometrium (5) and is already receiving nutrition from the mother.

overfishing Practice of catching too many marine creatures for an ecological balance to be maintained, resulting in the severe reduction in, or even disappearance of, catches of food fishes, whales and other marine animals. Overfishing has become a worldwide concern, with falling catches in most of the world's major fisheries. It remains an international problem largely because of the inability of marine law to regulate FISHING and WHALING. The term is also used of freshwater fishing, although reductions in freshwater fish stocks are more commonly the result of WATER POLLUTION.

overture Instrumental prelude to an OPERA or OPERETTA; the term now also includes an orchestral composition in its own right, usually lively in character. Famous operatic overtures were composed by MOZART, ROSSINI and WAGNER.

Ovid (43 BC–AD 18) (Publius Ovidius Naso) Roman poet. He was a great success in Rome until, aged 50, he was exiled by AUGUSTUS. Ovid's poems, mainly elegaics, fall into three categories: love poetry, such as *Amores* and *Ars Amatoria*; poems of exile, such as *Tristia*; and mythological poetry, such as his masterpiece *Metamorphoses*, written in hexameters.

ovule In seed-bearing plants, part of the reproductive organ that contains an egg cell or OVUM and develops into a seed after fertilization. In ANGIOSPERMS, ovules develop inside an OVARY. In GYMNOSPERMS, ovules are borne on the inner surface of the cone without any covering.

ovum (egg cell) Female GAMETE produced in an OVARY. After FERTILIZATION by SPERM, it becomes a ZYGOTE capable of developing into a new individual.

Owen, David, Baron (1938–) British statesman, foreign secretary (1977–79). He entered Parliament in 1966. Owen became disillusioned with the shift to the left in the LABOUR PARTY, and was one of the "Gang of Four" who formed (1981) the breakaway SOCIAL DEMOCRATIC PARTY (SDP). In 1983, he succeeded Roy JENKINS as party leader. In 1987, Owen led the small faction of SDP who rejected merger with the LIBERAL PARTY. In 1992, he retired from the Commons and was appointed as UN chief negotiator in peace talks in the former Yugoslavia.

Owen, Michael (1979–) English footballer. Owen joined Liverpool in 1996 as a forward. He played in the 1998 World Cup, becoming (aged 18) the youngest player ever to score for England.

Owen, Robert (1771–1858) Welsh industrialist and social reformer. He believed that better conditions for workers would lead to greater productivity, and put these beliefs into practice at his textile mills in Scotland. Owen attempted to establish a self-contained cooperative community in New Harmony, Indiana, USA (1825–27). His ideas provided the basis for the COOPERATIVE MOVEMENT.

Owen, Wilfred (1893–1918) English poet. His World War 1 poems, which include "Strange Meeting", "Anthem for Doomed Youth" and "Dulce et Decorum Est", are a searing indictment of war. After Owen's death in action, Siegfried SASSOON handled their publication. They form the basis of Britten's *War Requiem* (1962).

Owens, Jesse (1913–80) African-American athlete. He broke several world records for jumping, hurdling and running (1935–36). At the 1936 Olympic Games in Berlin, Owens won four gold medals, angering HITLER, who was supremely confident in ARYAN superiority. His 200m and long-jump records remained unbroken for more than 20 years.

owl Bird that is found worldwide, except at extreme latitudes. Owls have round heads, hooked bills, large eyes and long, curved talons. They are soundless in flight.

Most are nocturnal and feed on small birds and mammals. The order (Strigiformes) is divided into two families: barn owls (Tytonidae) and typical owls (Strigidae).

ox Domesticated cattle of the genus *Bos*. The term is specifically applied to castrated males used as draft animals. Many varieties of wild cattle are sometimes called wild oxen.

oxalic acid ($C_2H_2O_4$) Poisonous, colourless, crystalline organic acid whose salts occur naturally in some plants, such as sorrel and rhubarb. It is used for metal and textile cleaning and in tanning. Properties: m.p. 101.5°C (214.7°F).

oxbow Crescent-shaped section of a RIVER channel that no longer carries the main discharge of water. It is formed by contact at the neck of a MEANDER loop, leaving the loop abandoned as stagnant water and silted marsh.

Oxfam British charity formed in 1948. It attempts to alleviate suffering due to poverty or natural disaster in all parts of the world. Nearly 75% of Oxfam's overseas budget is devoted to long-term projects, including agriculture, family planning and medicine.

Oxford City and county district in S central England on the River Thames; the county town of Oxfordshire. Established as a trading centre and fort, it was raided by the Danes in the 10th and 11th centuries. During the English CIVIL WAR, the city was a Royalist stronghold. Sites include the Gothic buildings of university colleges. Industries: motor vehicles, steel products, electrical goods, printing, publishing. Pop. (1994) 121,000.

Oxford, University of Oldest university in Britain. It developed from a group of teachers and students who gathered in OXFORD in the 12th century. The first colleges, University, Balliol and Merton, were founded between 1249 and 1264. The colleges quickly increased in number and became almost autonomous. Women were not admitted until 1878.

Oxford Movement Attempt by some members of the CHURCH OF ENGLAND to restore the ideals of the pre-REFORMATION Church. It lasted from *c.*1833 to the first decades of the 20th century. The main proponents were John KEBLE, Edward Pusey and John NEWMAN.

Oxfordshire County in S central England, bounded in the NW by the COTSWOLDS and in the SE by the Chilterns, and drained by the River THAMES. The county town is OXFORD. It lies mostly within the Thames basin. The economy is based on agriculture, mainly sheep and arable farming, dairying and beef production. Industries: motor vehicles, pressed steel, light engineering. Area: 2,611sq km (1,008sq mi). Pop. (1991) 547,584.

oxidation Chemical reaction that involves a loss of one or more ELECTRONS by an atom or molecule (always part of an OXIDATION-REDUCTION reaction in which those electrons are gained by another atom or molecule). Previously, the term was more strictly applied to a reaction in which oxygen combines with another element or compound to form an oxide. Oxidation is brought about by oxidizing agents.

oxidation-reduction (redox) Chemical reaction involving simultaneous OXIDATION (a loss of one or more electrons by an atom or molecule) and reduction (a gain of those electrons by another atom or molecule). Oxidation–reduction reactions are important in many biochemical systems.

oxide Any inorganic chemical compound in which OXYGEN is combined with another element. Oxides are often formed by burning the element in air or oxygen.

oxygen (symbol O) Common gaseous element that is necessary for the RESPIRATION of plants and animals and

for combustion. Colourless and odourless, oxygen is the most abundant element in the Earth's crust (49.2% by weight) and is a constituent of water and many rocks. It is also present in the atmosphere (23.14% by weight). Oxygen can be obtained by the ELECTROLYSIS of water or fractional distillation of liquid air. It is used in apparatus for breathing (oxygen masks) and resuscitation (oxygen tents); liquid oxygen is used in rocket fuels. Oxygen is chemically reactive and forms compounds with nearly all other elements (especially by OXIDATION). Properties: at.no. 8; r.a.m. 15.9994; r.d. 1.429; m.p. −218.4°C (−361.1°F;); b.p. −182.96°C (−297.3°F;); most common isotope O^{16} (99.759%). *See also* OXIDATION-REDUCTION; OZONE

oxygen cycle Interchange of OXYGEN among agencies such as the atmosphere, the oceans, animal and plant processes and chemical combustion. The main renewable source of the Earth's oxygen is the plant process of PHOTOSYNTHESIS, wherein oxygen is liberated. Oxygen, dissolved in water, is utilized by aquatic life-forms through RESPIRATION, a process essential to most living forms except anaerobic bacteria. *See also* CARBON CYCLE

oxygen debt Insufficient supply of OXYGEN in the muscles following vigorous exercise. This reduces the breakdown of food molecules that generate energy, causing the body to overproduce lactic acid, creating a sensation of fatigue and sometimes muscular cramp. Automatic rapid breathing after exercise creates extra oxygen.

oxytocin HORMONE produced by the posterior PITUITARY GLAND in women during the final stage of pregnancy. It stimulates the muscles of the UTERUS, initiating the onset of LABOUR and maintaining contractions during childbirth. It also stimulates lactation.

oyster Edible BIVALVE mollusc found worldwide in temperate and warm seas. The European flat, or edible, oyster (*Ostrea edulis*) occurs throughout coastal waters. The pearl oyster (*Pinctada fucats*) is used to produce cultured pearls.

oystercatcher Seashore bird with a strikingly marked black-and-white stocky body and bright orange legs and beak. Oystercatchers feed on molluscs, prying them open with their long beaks. Length: 43cm (17in). Family Haematopodidae; typical genus *Haematopus*.

Ozark Plateau Mountainous upland region in S central USA, extending from SW Missouri across NW Arkansas into Oklahoma. The Boston Mountains contain the highest peaks, exceeding 610m (2,000ft). The Ozarks are a source of lead and zinc. Noted for their scenery, forests and numerous lakes, they are a popular tourist region. Area: *c.*129,500sq km (50,000sq mi).

ozone (O_3) Unstable, pale-blue, gaseous allotrope of OXYGEN. It has a characteristic pungent odour and decomposes into molecular oxygen. It is present in the atmosphere, mainly in the OZONE LAYER. Prepared commercially by passing a high-voltage discharge through oxygen, ozone is used as an oxidizing agent in bleaching, air-conditioning and purifying water. *See also* ALLOTROPY

ozone layer Region of Earth's atmosphere in which OZONE (O_3) is concentrated. It is densest at altitudes of 21–26km (13–16mi). Produced by ultraviolet radiation in incoming sunlight, the ozone layer absorbs much of the ultraviolet, thereby shielding the Earth's surface. Aircraft, nuclear weapons and some aerosol sprays and refrigerants yield chemical agents that can break down high-altitude ozone, which could lead to an increase in the amount of harmful ultraviolet radiation reaching the Earth's surface. *See also* CHLOROFLUOROCARBON (CFC)

P/p, 16th letter of the Roman alphabet, descends from the Semitic letter pe, a word meaning mouth. The letter was modified in shape by the Greeks and taken into their alphabet as pi.

paca (spotted cavy) Shy, nocturnal, tail-less RODENT of South America; it is brown with rows of white spots and has a relatively large head. A burrow dweller, it feeds mainly on leaves, roots and fruit. Length: to 76cm (30in). Family Dasyproctidae; species *Cuniculus paca*.

Pacelbel, Johann (1653–1706) German composer and organist. He wrote much organ work but his best-known composition is Canon and Gigue in D major (1695).

pacemaker (sinoatrial node) Specialized group of cells in the vertebrate HEART that contract spontaneously, setting the pace for the heartbeat itself. If it fails it can be replaced by an artificial pacemaker, an electronic unit that stimulates the heart by means of tiny electrical impulses.

Pacific Islands Former US trust territory including *c*.2,000 islands in the E central Pacific Ocean, N of the Equator, scattered over an area of more than 7,000,000sq km (3,000,000sq mi). The territory comprised the MARIANA ISLANDS (except Guam), the Federated States of MICRONESIA, the Republic of BELAU (Palau) and the MARSHALL ISLANDS. By 1994, all had ended their trusteeship status.

Pacific Ocean Largest and deepest OCEAN, covering *c*.33% of the Earth's surface and containing more than 50% of the Earth's sea water. The Pacific extends from the Arctic Circle to Antarctica, and from North and South America in the E to Asia and Australia in the W. The E Pacific region is connected with the Cordilleran mountain chain, and there is a narrow CONTINENTAL MARGIN. The ocean is ringed by numerous volcanoes, known as the Pacific "Ring of Fire". There are a number of large islands in the Pacific, most of which are in the S and W. The major ones are New Zealand and the Japan and Malay archipelagos. The average depth of the Pacific is 4,300m (14,000ft). The greatest-known depth is that of the Challenger Deep (SW of Guam in the Mariana Trench), at 11,033m (36,198ft). Most fishing in the Pacific Ocean is done on the continental margins. Crab, herring, cod, sardine and tuna are the principal catch. Area: *c*.166,000,000sq km (64,000,000sq mi).

pacifism Philosophy opposing the use of war or violence as a means of settling disputes. Elements can be found in ancient Hebrew and early Christian theology and in later Anabaptist and QUAKER beliefs. International pacifist groups were organized in the 19th century. The doctrine of "Mahatma" GANDHI was based on pacifist philosophy. *See also* CAMPAIGN FOR NUCLEAR DISARMAMENT (CND)

Pacino, Al (Alberto) (1940–) US film actor. He studied method acting at Lee STRASBERG's Actors' Studio, and made his film debut in *Me, Natalie* (1969). He appeared three times (1972, 1974, 1990) in his famed role as Michael Corleone (in *The Godfather* and its two sequels), for which he received two of his several Academy Award nominations. He finally won an Academy Award for best actor in *Scent of a Woman* (1992). Other films include *Serpico* (1973), *Dog Day Afternoon* (1975), *Scarface* (1983) and *Donnie Brasco* (1996). His directorial debut was *Looking for Richard* (1996).

paddlefish Primitive bony fish related to the sturgeon and found in the basins of the Mississippi and Yangtze rivers. Blue, green or grey, it has a long paddle-like snout. Length: 6ft (1.8m). Family Polyodontidae.

Paderewski, Ignacy Jan (1860–1941) Polish pianist, composer and statesman, prime minister (1919). He wrote a piano concerto (1888), a symphony (1907) and an opera *Manru* (1901). Paderewski was the first prime minister of an independent Poland, but retired after ten months to continue his musical career.

Padua (Padova) City in in Veneto region, NE Italy. The city is first mentioned (as Patavium) early in the 4th century BC. In the Middle Ages, Padua was a flourishing artistic centre. Ruled by the Carrara family from 1318, it came under Venetian control in 1405. In 1815, Padua passed to Austria. It played a major part in the RISORGIMENTO movement. Padua is renowned for its art treasures. Industries: motor vehicles, textiles, machinery, electrical goods. Pop. (1996) 213,000.

paediatrics Medical specialty devoted to the diagnosis and treatment of disease and injury in children.

Paganini, Niccolò (1782–1840) Italian violinist, the most famous virtuoso of his day. He enlarged the range of the violin by exploiting harmonics and mastering the art of playing double and triple stops.

Pagnol, Marcel (1894–1974) French dramatist, film director and writer. He first gained attention for the play *Topaze* (1928). Pagnol adapted for the screen his Marseilles trilogy *Marius* (1929), *Fanny* (1931) and *César* (1937). In 1946, he became the first film-maker to be elected to the Académie Française. Pagnol was rediscovered via the film adaptations of his novel *L'Eau des collines* (1963): *Jean de Florette* and *Manon des Sources* (both 1986).

pagoda Eastern TEMPLE in the form of a multi-storeyed, tapering tower. The basic design is either square or polygonal, and each storey is a smaller replica of the one beneath. The storeys often have wide, overhanging roofs, and the buildings are usually made of wood, brick or stone. Pagodas originated in India and spread with the diffusion of BUDDHISM to China, Korea and Japan.

Pahlavi, Muhammad Reza (1919–80) Shah of Iran (1941–79), son of Reza PAHLAVI. With the receipts from oil exports, Pahlavi encouraged rapid economic development and social reforms. The westernization of Iran, combined with a repressive regime and worsening social inequalities, aroused strong discontent among religious fundamentalists and others. In 1979, a theocratic revolution, led by Ayatollah KHOMEINI, forced him into exile. He died in Egypt.

Pahlavi, Reza (1878–1944) Shah of Iran and founder of the modern Iranian state. In 1921, he took part in a nationalist coup and built up a modern army as defence minister and prime minister. In 1925, Pahlavi deposed Ahmad Shah and assumed the crown. He enforced intensive social and legal reforms, crushed tribalism and ended the influence in Iran of Britain and the Soviet Union. In 1941, when British and Soviet forces occupied Iran, he abdicated in favour of his son, Muhammad PAHLAVI.

pain Unpleasant sensation signalling actual or threatened tissue damage as a result of ILLNESS or injury; it can be acute (severe but short-lived) or chronic (persisting for a long time). Pain is felt when specific nerve endings are stimulated. Pain is treated in a number of ways, most commonly by drugs known as ANALGESICS.

Paine, Thomas (1737–1809) Anglo-American revolutionary political writer. He emigrated from England to Pennsylvania in 1754. His pamphlet *Common Sense* (1776) demanded independence for the North

American colonies. He returned to England in 1787 and published *The Rights of Man* (1791–92), a defence of the French Revolution. Accused of treason, he fled to France in 1792. He became a French citizen and was elected to the National Convention but was later imprisoned (1793–94). He returned to the US in 1802.

paint Coating applied to a surface for protective, decorative or artistic purposes. Paint is composed of PIGMENT (colour) and a liquid vehicle (binder or medium) that suspends the pigment, adheres to a surface, and hardens when dry. Pigments are made of metallic compounds, usually oxides or synthetic materials. Vehicles may be oils, water mixed with a binding agent, organic compounds or synthetic RESINS. *See also* OIL PAINTING

Painted Desert Barren high plateau region in N central Arizona, USA, E of the Colorado and Little Colorado rivers. Erosion and heat have exposed bands of red and yellow sediment and bentonite clay. Area: *c*.19,400sq km (7,500sq mi).

painting Art of using one or more colours, generally mixed with a medium (such as oil or water) and applied to a surface with a brush, finger or other tool to create pictures. Paintings are among the earliest of historical records. Painting in early civilizations, such as Egypt, was largely a matter of filling in with colour areas outlined by drawing. Little Greek painting survives (apart from that on pottery). The Romans were greatly influenced by Greek art, as the fine FRESCO paintings at Pompeii and Herculaneum demonstrate. In the early Christian and Byzantine periods, traditions in mural painting and manuscript ILLUMINATION were established that were to last throughout the Middle Ages. When the humanist ideals of the RENAISSANCE took root in S Europe, the range of subjects and techniques available to the artist widened enormously. The period also saw the first use of oil paint on canvas and the beginnings of GENRE PAINTING and pure portraiture. It was also the age of PERSPECTIVE and of a more natural approach to form and composition. The great painters of the BAROQUE period added an unrivalled bravura brushwork and drama of vision. North of the Alps the Renaissance had spread more gradually than in Italy. The 17th-century Dutch painters' choice of intimate, everyday subjects was the antithesis of the grand manner characteristic of the Italian masters. By the 18th century, British painters had become established in portraiture, animal and landscape painting, although overshadowed by the great Venetian masters. The 19th century opened with the supremacy of NEOCLASSICISM challenged by the new ROMANTICISM. Both schools were superseded, first by IMPRESSIONISM and then by a succession of new movements in the late-19th and early 20th centuries. Most of these movements – IMPRESSIONISM, POST-IMPRESSIONISM, SYMBOLISM, FAUVISM, CUBISM and SURREALISM – originated with artists living in Paris. Germany was the cradle of EXPRESSIONISM and Russia contributed SUPREMATISM. In the latter half of the 20th century, the USA has produced many original movements, such as ABSTRACT EXPRESSIONISM, POP ART and OP ART.

Paisiello, Giovanni (1740–1816) Italian composer, principally of operas. As court composer (1776–84) to Catherine II (the Great) of Russia, he wrote *The Barber of Seville* (1782), which became popular throughout Europe until the version by ROSSINI superseded it.

Paisley, Ian (1926–) Northern Irish politician and cleric. In 1951, he formed the Free Presbyterian Church of Ulster. Paisley was elected to Parliament in 1970. In 1972, he formed the Ulster Democratic Unionist Party. In 1979, he was elected to the European Parliament. An outspoken defender of Protestant Unionism, Paisley briefly resigned over the ANGLO-IRISH AGREEMENT in 1985. He is a staunch opponent of the GOOD FRIDAY AGREEMENT (1998).

Paiute Shoshonean-speaking tribe of Native North Americans. They are divided into two major groups: the **Southern** Paiute (or "Digger Indians" during the Gold Rush days) who occupied W Utah, N Arizona, SE Nevada and California; and the **Northern** Paiute ("Snake Indians") who inhabited W Nevada, S Oregon and E California. Today, the Paiute number *c*.4,000.

Pakistan Republic in S Asia. The Islamic Republic of Pakistan is divided into the four provinces of BALUCHISTAN, NORTH-WEST FRONTIER PROVINCE, PUNJAB and SIND. The mountains of the HINDU KUSH extend along the NW border with Afghanistan. In N Pakistan lies the disputed territory of KASHMIR. This mountainous region is occupied by Pakistan but claimed by India. It contains the world's second highest peak, K2, at 8,611m (28,251ft), in the KARAKORAM range. At the foot of the mountains lies Pakistan's capital, ISLAMABAD, and the city of RAWALPINDI. The Punjab plains ("land of the five rivers") are drained by the River INDUS and its four main tributaries (Jhelum, Beas, Ravi and Sutlej). LAHORE lies on the border with India. The alluvial plain continues into Sind, which includes HYDERABAD and KARACHI (Pakistan's major port). Baluchistan is an arid plateau region. **Climate** Most of Pakistan has hot summers and cool winters. Rainfall is sparse, except in the monsoon season (June–October). **Vegetation** Forests grow on mountain slopes, but most of Pakistan is covered by dry grassland. **History and politics** The Indus Valley civilization developed *c*.4,500 years ago. Waves of invaders later entered the area. In the 2nd century AD, the Kushans conquered the entire region. In 712, Arabs conquered Sind and introduced Islam. In 1206, Pakistan became part of the DELHI SULTANATE. In 1526, the Sultanate was replaced by the MOGUL EMPIRE, which introduced URDU. In the late 18th century, RANJIT SINGH conquered the Punjab and introduced SIKHISM. The early 19th century saw the emergence of the British EAST INDIA COMPANY as a dominant force. The British conquered Sind (1843) and Punjab (1849). Much of Baluchistan was

▲ **pagoda** A Chinese pagoda is built on a stone podium (1). The wooden hall has a two-story elevation covered by a hipped roof (2). The first storey is overhung by eaves (3), which are supported by bracketing, as is the balcony (4). Divided into five bays, doors occupy the centre three bays (5) that are left open on the upper storey (6). The roof is wood and insulated with mud and tiles. The interior has a gallery (7) on each storey around the central wall that is the full height of the temple.

PAKISTAN
AREA: 796,100sq km (307,374sq mi)
POPULATION: 162,409,000
CAPITAL (POPULATION): Islamabad (204,000)

conquered in the 1850s. PATHANS in the NW resisted subjection, and the British created a separate province in 1901. The dominance of Hindus in British India led to the formation of the MUSLIM LEAGUE (1906). In the 1940s, the League's leader, Muhammad Ali JINNAH, gained popular support for the idea of a separate state of Pakistan (Urdu, "land of the pure") in Muslim-majority areas. In 1947, British India achieved independence and was partitioned into India and Pakistan. The resulting mass migration and communal violence claimed more than 500,000 lives. In 1947, the long-standing war with India over Kashmir began. Jinnah became Pakistan's first governor-general. Muslim Pakistan was divided into two parts: East Bengal and West Pakistan, more than 1,600km (1,000mi) apart. In 1955, East Bengal became East Pakistan, and in 1956 Pakistan became a republic within the Commonwealth of Nations. In 1958, General Muhammad AYUB KHAN led a military coup. In 1960, he became president. His dictatorship brought constitutional changes, but failed to satisfy East Pakistan's claim for greater autonomy. In 1971, East Pakistan declared independence as BANGLADESH. West Pakistani troops invaded. The ensuing civil war killed hundreds of thousands of people, and millions fled to India. India sent troops to support Bangladesh. West Pakistan was forced to surrender and Zulfikar Ali BHUTTO assumed control. In 1977, a military coup, led by General Zia-ul-Haq, deposed Bhutto. In 1978, General Zia proclaimed himself president, and Bhutto was hanged for murder. During the 1980s, Pakistan received US aid for providing a safe haven for Mujaheddin fighters in the war in Afghanistan. In 1988, Zia dismissed parliament but died shortly after in a mysterious plane crash. The Pakistan People's Party (PPP) won the ensuing elections and Benazir BHUTTO, daughter of Zulfikar, became president. Charged with nepotism and corruption, she was removed from office in 1990. The ensuing election was won by the Islamic Democratic Alliance, led by Nawaz Sharif. In 1991, Islamic law was given precedence over civil law. Sharif also faced charges of corruption and lost the 1993 elections to Benazir Bhutto. In 1996, Bhutto was again dismissed on corruption charges. Political disenchantment saw a low turnout in 1997 elections and a landslide victory for Sharif. In 1998, Pakistan became the world's seventh nuclear power. In 1999, Sharif was ousted in a military coup led by General Pervez Musharraf. There is persistent civil disorder in Sind as insurgents struggle for an autonomous province of Karachi. **Economy** Pakistan is a low-income developing country (1995 GDP per capita, US$2,230). Pakistan faces a foreign debt of US$42 billion. The economy is based on agriculture, which employs c.47% of the workforce. Pakistan has one of the world's largest irrigation systems. It is the world's third-largest producer of wheat. Other crops include cotton, fruit, rice and sugar cane. Pakistan produces natural gas and coal, as well as iron ore, chromite and stone. Major products include clothing and textiles. Small-scale craft industries, such as carpets, are also important.

palaeobotany Study of ancient plants and pollen that have been preserved by carbonization, waterlogging or freezing. Some plants have been preserved almost intact in frozen soils and in AMBER.

Palaeocene Geological epoch from c.65 to 55 million years ago. It is the first epoch of the TERTIARY period, when the majority of the DINOSAURS had disappeared and the small early mammals were flourishing.

palaeography Study of early writing. Its broad sense includes all inscriptions; more narrowly it includes only inscribed wax, parchment, papyrus or paper.

Palaeolithic (Old Stone Age) Earliest stage of human history, from c.2 million years ago until between 40,000 and 10,000 years ago. It was marked by the use of stone tools and covers the EVOLUTION of humans from *Homo habilis* to *Homo sapiens*.

Palaeolithic art Art from the PALAEOLITHIC period. Typical works are realistic cave paintings of bison, deer and hunting scenes. The best-known surviving examples are those at ALTAMIRA and LASCAUX. Other forms include portable art, such as carved animals and figurines.

palaeomagnetism Study of changes in the direction and intensity of Earth's MAGNETIC FIELD through GEOLOGICAL TIME. This is important in the investigation of the theory of CONTINENTAL DRIFT. The EARTH's polarity has reversed at least 20 times in the past 4–5 million years; earlier changes cannot at present be determined.

palaeontology Study of the FOSSIL remains of plants and animals. Evidence from fossils is used in the reconstruction of ancient environments and in tracing the evolution of life.

Palaeozoic Second era of geological time, after the PRECAMBRIAN era, lasting from 590 million to 248 million years ago. It is sub-divided into six periods: CAMBRIAN, ORDOVICIAN, SILURIAN, DEVONIAN, CARBONIFEROUS and PERMIAN. Invertebrate animals evolved hard skeletons in the Cambrian; fish-like vertebrates appeared in the Ordovician; amphibians emerged in the Devonian; and reptiles in the Carboniferous.

palate Roof of the mouth, comprising the bony front part known as the **hard** palate, and the softer fleshy part at the back, known as the **soft** palate.

Palatinate Historic state of the Holy Roman Empire, including the present German state of Rhineland-Palatinate and parts of adjacent states. It was ruled from 1156 by the counts palatine. It was a centre of the German Reformation.

Palau Former name of BELAU

Palermo City and seaport on the Tyrrhenian Sea coast of NW Sicily, S Italy; capital of Sicily. The city was founded by the Phoenicians in the 8th century BC. It passed to the Romans in 254 BC and came under Byzantine control in the 6th century AD. From the 9th to 11th centuries, it prospered under benevolent Arab rule. Captured by the Normans in 1072, it enjoyed a brief period of fame as the capital of the Kingdom of Sicily and again under the Holy Roman Emperor FREDERICK II, who established his court here. Palermo subsequently came under Spanish, then Austrian rule. It was the scene of the outbreak of the 1848 revolution in Italy and was captured by Giuseppe GARIBALDI in 1860. Industries: shipbuilding, textiles. Pop. (1996) 689,000.

Palestine Territory in the Middle East, on the E shore of the Mediterranean Sea; considered a Holy Land by Jews, Christians and Muslims. Palestine has been settled continuously since 4000 BC. The Jews moved into Palestine from Egypt c.2000 BC but were subjects of the Philistines until 1000 BC, when SAUL, DAVID and SOLOMON established Hebrew kingdoms. The region was then under Assyrian and, later, Persian control before coming under Roman rule in 63 BC. In succeeding centuries Palestine became a focus of Christian pilgrimage. It was conquered by the Muslim Arabs in 640. In 1099, Palestine fell to the Crusaders, but in 1291 they in turn were routed by the

MAMELUKES. The area was part of the OTTOMAN EMPIRE from 1516 to 1918, when British forces defeated the Turks at Megiddo. Jewish immigration was encouraged by the BALFOUR DECLARATION. After World War 1 the British held a League of Nations mandate over the land w of the River JORDAN (now once again called Palestine). In 1936, tension between Jews and the Arab majority led to an uprising. World War 2 and Nazi persecution brought many Jews to Palestine, and in 1947 Britain, unable to satisfy both Jewish and Arab aspirations, consigned the problem to the United Nations. The UN proposed a plan for separate Jewish and Arab states. This was rejected by the Arabs, and in 1948 (after the first of several ARAB-ISRAELI WARS) most of ancient Palestine became part of the new state of ISRAEL; the GAZA STRIP was controlled by Egypt and the WEST BANK of the River Jordan by JORDAN. These two areas were subsequently occupied by Israel in 1967. From the 1960s, the PALESTINE LIBERATION ORGANIZATION (PLO) led Palestinian opposition to Israeli rule, which included acts of terrorism and the INTIFADA in the occupied territories. The ISRAELI-PALESTINIAN ACCORD (1993) between Israel and the PLO led to the creation of the Palestine National Authority, which took over nominal administration of the Gaza Strip and West Bank in 1994. In 1996, Yasir ARAFAT was elected chairman of the Authority. Palestinian police were appointed to maintain security, although the Israeli army retained freedom of movement. Subsequent agreements extended the range of Palestinian self-rule, but progress was slowed by the 1996 election of Binyamin NETANYAHU as Israeli prime minister. His successor (1999–), Ehud BARAK, stated his commitment to furthering the peace process. In September 2000, violence erupted in Jerusalem following Ariel SHARON's provocative visit to a Muslim shrine. Palestinians clashed with Israeli soldiers and the fighting spread throughout the West Bank and Gaza.

Palestine Liberation Organization (PLO) Organization of Palestinian parties and groups, widely recognized as the representative of the Palestinian people. It was founded in 1964 with the aim of dissolving the state of Israel and establishing a Palestinian state. Many of its component guerrilla groups were involved in political violence against Israel and, in the 1970s, in acts of international terrorism to further their cause. Dominated by the al-Fatah group led by Yasir ARAFAT, in 1974 the PLO was recognized as a government-in-exile by the Arab League and the United Nations. In the early 1990s, PLO representatives conducted secret negotiations with Israel, culminating in the ISRAELI-PALESTINIAN ACCORD (1993). *See also* GAZA STRIP; PALESTINE; WEST BANK

Palestrina, Giovanni Pierluigi da (1525–94) Italian composer who spent most of his life in the service of the church. Palestrina wrote masses, magnificats, litanies and *c*.600 motets in four to eight or twelve parts. He also composed almost 100 secular madrigals. His works include *Missa Papae Marcelli* (1567). *See also* COUNTERPOINT

Pali Ancient Indian language in which the Buddhist canon of sacred writings was compiled in the 1st century BC. It originates from classical Sanskrit and is still the liturgical language of the THERAVADA branch of Hinayana Buddhism, which prevails in Sri Lanka, Burma and Thailand.

Palladianism Architectural style especially popular in England, derived from the work of Andrea PALLADIO. Based on Roman CLASSICISM, it emphasized symmetrical planning and harmonic proportions. Inigo JONES introduced it to England. There was a revival of Palladianism in the early 18th century. *See also* NEOCLASSICISM

Palladio, Andrea (1508–80) Italian RENAISSANCE architect. He studied Roman architecture and published his own designs and drawings of Roman ruins in *Four Books of Architecture* (1570). *See also* PALLADIANISM

palladium (symbol Pd) Shiny, silver-white metal, one of the TRANSITION ELEMENTS. It was discovered (1803) by the English chemist William Wollaston. Malleable and ductile, palladium is found in nickel ores associated with platinum. It does not tarnish or corrode and is used for electroplating, surgical instruments, dentistry, jewellery and in catalytic converters for automobiles. Properties: at.no. 46; r.a.m. 106.4; r.d. 12.02; m.p. 1,552°C (2,826°F); b.p. 3,140°C (5,684°F); most common isotope Pd^{106} (27.3%).

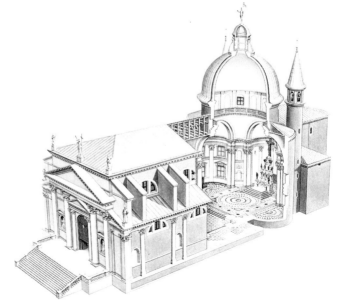

▶ **Palladio** The Redentore, Venice (1577–92), is a superb example of Italian architect Andrea Palladio's work. The whole church is raised on a podium, has a choir separated from the chancel (Palladio's innovation), an absolute minimum of non-architectural ornament, and a light, spacious interior. It was financed by the Venetian state, in fulfilment of a vow on deliverance of the city from the plague of 1575–76.

palm MONOCOTYLEDON tree found in tropical and subtropical regions. Palms have a woody, unbranched trunk covered with fibres, with a crown of large, stiff leaves. The leaves may be palmate (fan-like) or pinnate (feather-like). All palms produce DRUPES, such as DATES or COCONUTS. Palms are the source of wax, oil, fibre and sugar. Height: 60m (200ft). Family Arecacae/Palmae. *See also* LIANA

Palma (Palma de Mallorca) City and seaport on W MAJORCA island, Spain; capital of the BALEARIC ISLANDS. Under Roman rule from the 2nd century BC, Palma later became part of Byzantium before falling to the Arabs in the 8th century. Conquered by James I of Aragon in the 13th century, it was finally united with Spain in 1469. Industries: tourism, pottery, glasswork, leather goods. Pop. (1995) 315,000.

Palmer, Arnold Daniel (1929–) US golfer. He was the first player to win the US Masters four times (1958, 1960, 1962, 1964). Palmer also won the British Open (1961, 1962) and the US Open (1960). In 1968, he became the first golfer to earn more than $US1 million in prize money.

Palmer, Samuel (1805–81) English landscape painter and graphic artist, the most important follower of William BLAKE. He enjoyed his most productive period at Shoreham, Kent (1826–35), where he was the focal point for a group of artists called the Ancients. His paintings include *Repose of the Holy Family* (1824).

Palmerston, Henry John Temple, 3rd Viscount (1784–1865) British statesman, prime minister (1855–58, 1859–65). He entered Parliament as a Tory in 1807 but defected to the Whigs in 1830. As foreign secretary (1830–34, 1835–41, 1846–51), Palmerston pursued "gunboat diplomacy" in defence of British interests. As prime minister, he vigorously prosecuted the CRIMEAN WAR. In 1856, Palmerston initiated the second OPIUM WAR against China. In 1858, he ordered the suppression of the INDIAN MUTINY. Palmerston supported the Confederacy in the US Civil War but maintained British neutrality. He was an opponent of political reform. Palmerston died in office and was succeeded by John RUSSELL.

Palm Sunday In the Christian year, the Sunday before Easter. Palm Sunday commemorates Jesus Christ's triumphal entry into Jerusalem, when the people spread palm branches before him. It also marks the beginning of HOLY WEEK, the period of days commemorating his betrayal, trial and crucifixion.

Palmyra (Tadmur, City of Palms) Ancient oasis city in the Syrian Desert, central Syria. By the 1st century BC it had become a city-state by virtue of its control of the trade route between Mesopotamia and the Mediterranean. In c.AD 30, the city-state became a Roman dependency under local rule. By the 2nd century, Palmyra's influence had spread to Armenia. In 267, ZENOBIA became queen and severed the state's links with Rome. In 273, the Roman emperor Aurelian laid waste to the city. Today, visitors are attracted to its extensive ruins.

Palomar, Mount Peak in S California, 72km (45mi) NNE of San Diego. It is the site of the **Palomar Observatory** that houses the 122-cm (48-in) Schmidt telescope and a 508-cm (200-in) reflecting telescope. Palomar is administered jointly with Mount Wilson Observatory as the Hale Observatories.

Pamirs Mountainous region in central Asia, lying mostly in Tajikistan and partly in Pakistan, Afghanistan and China. The region forms a geological structural knot from which the TIAN SHAN, KARAKORAM, Kunlun and HINDU KUSH mountain ranges radiate. The climate is cold during winter and cool in summer; the terrain includes grasslands and sparse trees. The main activity is sheep herding, and some coal is mined. The highest peak is KOMMUNIZMA PIK, at 7,495m (24,590ft).

pampas Large treeless plains in S South America, situated mostly in Argentina. The humid pampas is extremely fertile; dairy farming is practised and cereals are grown. The larger dry pampas to the W, which includes the provinces of Buenos Aires, Santa Fe and Cordoba, supports mainly livestock grazing.

pampas grass Species of tall, reed-like GRASS native to South America and widely cultivated as a lawn ornamental. Female plants bear flower clusters, 90cm (3ft) tall, which are silvery and plume-like. Family Poaceae/Gramineae; species *Cortaderia selloana*.

Pamplona Ancient city in N Spain; capital of Navarre province. In 68 BC it was rebuilt by POMPEY and in AD 778 conquered by CHARLEMAGNE. In the 11th century, it was made capital of the kingdom of Navarre. In 1512, control of Pamplona passed to Ferdinand of Aragon, who united Navarre with Castile. During the PENINSULAR WAR, Pamplona was captured from the French by the Duke of Wellington (1813). Every July, in the fiesta of San Fermin, bulls are driven through the city streets. Industries: rope and pottery manufacture. Pop. (1995) 182,000.

Pan In Greek mythology, the god of woods and fields, shepherds and their flocks. He is depicted with the horns, legs and hooves of a goat. A forest dweller, he pursued and loved the DRYADS and led their dances while playing the syrinx, the reed pipes that were his invention.

Pan-Africanism Historical political movement for the unification and independence of African nations. It began officially at the Pan-African Congress (1900) in London, organized by western black leaders such as W.E.B. DU BOIS. It met five times between 1900 and 1927 and worked to bring gradual self-government to African colonial states. In 1945, the Pan-African Federation convened the sixth congress, attended by future leaders of post-colonial Africa, such as Kwame NKRUMAH and Jomo KENYATTA. It demanded autonomy and independence for African states. As independence was gained, the movement broke up and was eventually replaced (1963) by the ORGANIZATION OF AFRICAN UNITY (OAU).

Pan-Africanist Congress (PAC) Militant black South African political group. It was formed as a breakaway group of the AFRICAN NATIONAL CONGRESS (ANC) in 1959 and advocated the expulsion of all whites from South Africa. A PAC-organized demonstration against the pass laws resulted in the SHARPEVILLE Massacre (March 1960) and the subsequent banning of the PAC. It continued to pursue an armed struggle against the South African government from bases in Botswana until it was legalized in 1990 as part of the dismantling of APARTHEID.

Panama Republic on the Isthmus of Panama, connecting Central and South America; the capital is PANAMA CITY. The narrowest part of Panama is less than 60km (37mi) wide. The PANAMA CANAL cuts across the isthmus. The Canal has given Panama great international importance, and the majority of Panamanians live within 20km (12mi) of it. Most of the land between the Pacific and Caribbean coastal plains is mountainous, rising to 3,475m (11,400ft) at the volcano Barú; Panama has a tropical climate. The rainy season is between May and December.

PANAMA
AREA: 77,080sq km (29,761sq mi)
POPULATION: 2,893,000
CAPITAL (POPULATION): Panama City (452,000)

The Caribbean side of Panama has about twice as much rain as the Pacific side. Tropical forests cover *c*.50% of Panama. Mangrove swamps line the coast. **History and politics** Christopher COLUMBUS landed in Panama in 1502. In 1510, Vasco Núñez de Balboa became the first European to cross Panama and see the Pacific Ocean. The indigenous population was soon wiped out, and Spain established control. In 1821, Panama became a province of Colombia. After a revolt in 1903, Panama declared independence from Colombia. In 1904, the USA began construction of the Panama Canal and established the Panama Canal Zone. Since it was opened in 1914, the status of the Canal has been a feature of Panamanian politics. US forces intervened in 1908, 1912 and 1918 to protect US interests. Throughout the 20th century, Panama has been politically unstable, with a series of dictatorial regimes and military coups. During the 1950s and 1960s, civil strife led to negotiations with the USA for the transfer of the Canal Zone. In 1977, a treaty confirmed Panama's sovereignty over the Canal, while providing for US bases in the Canal Zone. The USA agreed to hand over control of the Canal on 31 December 1999. In 1983, General NORIEGA took control of the National Guard and ruled Panama through a succession of puppet governments. In 1987, the USA withdrew its support for Noriega after he was accused of murder, electoral fraud and aiding drug smuggling. In December 1989, he made himself president and declared war on the USA. On 20 December 1989, 25,000 US troops invaded Panama. In January 1990, Noriega was captured and taken to the USA for trial. In 1994, Pérez Balladares was elected president. In 1998, he failed in an attempt to amend the constitution in order to serve a second term. He was succeeded in 1999 by Mireya Moscoso, Panama's first woman president. **Economy** The Panama Canal is a major source of revenue, generating jobs in commerce, trade, manufacturing and transport (1995 GDP per capita, US$5,980). After the Canal, the main activity is agriculture, which employs 27% of the workforce. Rice is the main food crop. Bananas, shrimps, sugar and coffee are exported. Tourism is also important. Many ships are registered under Panama's flag, due to its low taxes.

Panama Canal Waterway connecting the Atlantic and Pacific oceans across the Isthmus of Panama. A canal, begun in 1882 by Ferdinand de LESSEPS, was subsequently abandoned because of bankruptcy. The US government decided to finance the project to provide a convenient route for its warships. The main construction took about ten years to complete, and the first ship passed through in 1914. The 82-km (51-mi) waterway reduces the sea voyage between San Francisco and New York by *c*.12,500km (7,800mi). Control of the canal passed from the USA to Panama at the end of 1999.

Panama City Capital of Panama, near the Pacific end of the Panama Canal. It was founded by Pedro Arias de Avila in 1519 and was destroyed and rebuilt in the 17th century. It became the capital of Panama in 1903 and developed rapidly after the construction of the PANAMA CANAL in 1914. Industries: brewing, shoes, textiles, oil-refining, plastics. Pop. (1995) 452,000.

Pan-American Union (PAU) Independent regional organization that existed from 1910 until 1948, when it was absorbed by the ORGANIZATION OF AMERICAN STATES (OAS). It aimed to promote international cooperation and to improve economic, social and cultural relations among the American republics. PAU was the name given to the secretariat of OAS (1948–70), but after 1970 the name Pan-American Union ceased to be used.

Panchen Lama In TIBETAN BUDDHISM, religious leader who is second in importance to the DALAI LAMA. In 1923, the ninth Panchen Lama fled to China because of disagreements with the Dalai Lama. In 1938, Bskal-bzang Tshe-brtan, a boy of Tibetan parentage, was born in China and later hailed by the Chinese government as the 10th Panchen Lama. In 1959, when the Dalai Lama fled to India, the Chinese government officially recognized him as the true leader of Tibet. In 1964, he was stripped of his power. He died in 1989. In December 1995, another Tibetan boy, Gyaincain Norbu, was selected by the Chinese government and enthroned in Beijing as the 11th Panchen Lama. He is not recognized as such by the Tibetan government-in-exile nor by the majority of the international community.

pancreas (sweetbread) Elongated gland lying behind the stomach, to the left of the mid-line. It secretes pancreatic juice into the SMALL INTESTINE to aid digestion. Pancreatic juice contains the enzymes AMYLASE, TRYPSIN and lipase. The pancreas also contains a group of cells known as the islets of Langerhans, which secrete the hormones INSULIN and glucagon, involved in the regulation of blood-sugar level. *See also* DIABETES

panda Two mainly nocturnal mammals of the family Ailuropodidae, related to raccoons and bears. The lesser or **red panda** (*Ailurus fulgens*) ranges from the Himalayas to w China. It has soft, thick, reddish brown fur, a white face and a bushy tail. It feeds mainly on fruit and leaves, but is also a carnivore. Length: 115cm (46in) overall. The rare **giant panda** (*Ailuropoda melanoleuca*) inhabits bamboo forests in China (mainly Tibet). It has a short tail and a dense white coat with characteristic black fur on shoulders, limbs, ears and around the eyes. It eats mainly plant material, particularly bamboo shoots. Length: 1.5m (5ft); weight: 160kg (350lb).

Pandora In Greek mythology, the first woman. She was created on ZEUS' orders as his revenge on PROMETHEUS, who had created men and stolen fire from heaven for

▲ **panda** The giant panda (*Ailuropoda melanoleuca*) is found in mountain forests in Sichuan, central China, and on the slopes of the Tibetan plateau. It is a rare, solitary animal that usually lives on the ground but will climb trees if pursued. Pandas spend *c*.12 hours a day feeding, mainly on bamboo shoots. An endangered species, pairs have been encouraged to breed in captivity. It is the symbol of the World Wildlife Fund.

them. When she opened a great box that she had been ordered by Zeus not to look into, all the evils of the human race flew out. Hope alone remained inside the box.

Pangaea Name for the single supercontinent that formed *c*.240 million years ago and which began to break up at the end of the Triassic period. *See also* GONDWANALAND

pangolin (scaly anteater) Any of several species of toothless insectivorous mammals, covered with horny overlapping plates, that live in Asia and Africa. It has short, powerful forelegs with which it climbs trees and tears open the nests of tree ants on which it feeds. Length: to 175cm (70in). Family Manidae; genus *Manis*.

Pankhurst, Emily (Emmeline Goulden) (1858–1928) English leader of the SUFFRAGETTE MOVEMENT. In 1903, Pankhurst set up the Women's Social and Political Union, supported by her daughters, **Christabel** (1880–1958) and **Sylvia** (1882–1960). Their militant tactics courted prosecution, and they gained further publicity in prison by hunger strikes. After World War 1, she concentrated on the employment of women in industry. *See also* FEMINISM

panpipes (syrinx) Primitive musical wind instrument, probably from Asia. Several tubes of cane, reed, bamboo or clay, of different lengths, are joined together side by side. Blown across one end, each pipe produces one note of a scale. Panpipes are associated with the Greek god Pan.

pansy Common name for a cultivated hybrid VIOLET. An annual or short-lived perennial, it has velvety flowers, usually in combinations of blue, yellow and white, with five petals. Height: to *c*.15–30cm (6–12in). Family Violaceae; species *Viola tricolor*.

pantheism Religious system, contrasted with certain forms of DEISM, that is based on the belief that God (or gods) and the universe are identical. No distinction is recognized between the creator and creatures.

pantheon Ancient Greek and Roman temple for the worship of the gods. The most famous example is the Pantheon in Rome, built by Agrippa (27 BC), rebuilt by Hadrian (*c*.AD 120), and converted into the church of Santa Maria Rotonda in the 7th century. The term was later extended to apply to a building honouring illustrious public figures.

panther *See* LEOPARD

pantomime Theatrical spectacle in Britain, with its modern origins in early-18th-century France. It has come to mean a Christmas extravaganza with music and comic actors. Popular in England by the 19th century, the "dame" figure was traditionally played by a male actor and the principal boy by a female. *See also* HARLEQUIN

Paolozzi, Sir Eduardo (1924–) Scottish sculptor and graphic artist. He created box-like, chromium-plated sculptures evocative of jazz-age amusement arcades and picture palaces. Since the 1950s, he has worked mainly on large-scale abstract sculptures such as *City of the circle and the square* (1963–66).

Papa In Oceanic mythology, both a great mother of the gods and an earth goddess. The people of Hawaii consider Papa to be an ancestress of divine origins. In New Zealand she forms part of the creation myth of the Maoris and is married to the sky god, RANGI.

papacy Office, status or authority of the pope as head of both the ROMAN CATHOLIC CHURCH and the VATICAN CITY. The pope is nominated Bishop of Rome and Christ's spiritual representative on Earth. He is elected by the College of Cardinals. There have been 265 holders of the office of pope from St PETER to JOHN PAUL II. *See also* ANTIPOPE; ORTHODOX CHURCH; PAPAL INFALLIBILITY; SCHISM

papal bull Official letter from the pope, consisting of a formal announcement. Such a document usually contains a decree relating to doctrine, CANONIZATION, ecclesiastical discipline, promulgation of INDULGENCES or some other matter of general importance.

papal infallibility Roman Catholic doctrine according to which the pope, under certain conditions, cannot make a mistake in formal statements on issues of faith or morals. It was defined in its present form, amid great controversy, at the First VATICAN COUNCIL (1869–70).

Papal States Territories of central Italy under the rule of the popes (756–1870). In the 15th century, the papal government displaced the feudal magnates who had ruled the Papal States in the Middle Ages, and imposed direct control from Rome. The territory was temporarily lost during the Napoleonic period, restored to the papacy in 1815, and annexed by the Italian nationalists during the RISORGIMENTO. The LATERAN TREATY of 1929 restored the VATICAN in Rome to papal rule.

Papandreou, Andreas (1919–96) Greek statesman, prime minister (1981–89, 1993–96). In the mid-1970s he founded the Pan-Hellenic Socialist Movement (PASOK), becoming leader of the opposition in 1977. In 1981, Papandreou became Greece's first socialist prime minister. He was re-elected in 1985. Implicated in a financial fraud, he was unable to form a government following the 1989 elections and resigned. Cleared of fraud, Papandreou was re-elected in 1993. He was succeeded by Costas Simitis.

papaya (pawpaw) Palm-like tree widely cultivated in tropical America for its fleshy, melon-like, edible fruit. It also produces the ENZYME papain, which breaks down proteins. Height: to 6m (20ft). Family Caricaceae; species *Carica papaya*.

Papeete Capital and chief port of French Polynesia in the S Pacific Ocean on the NW coast of Tahiti. It is a trade centre for the islands and a tourist resort. Its exports include copra, mother-of-pearl and vanilla. Pop. (1988) 78,814.

Papen, Franz von (1879–1969) German statesman, chancellor (1932). A member of the Catholic Centre Party, Papen resigned the chancellorship after only six months and persuaded HINDENBURG to appoint Adolf HITLER as his successor. He served (1933–34) as Hitler's vice-chancellor. As ambassador to Austria (1936–38), he pressed for ANSCHLUSS. In 1946 he was acquitted of war crimes at the NUREMBERG TRIALS.

paper Sheet or roll of compacted cellulose fibres with a wide range of uses. The word "paper" derives from PAPYRUS, the plant that the Egyptians used more than 5,500 years ago to make sheets of writing material. The modern process of manufacture originated *c*.2,000 years ago in China and consists of reducing wood fibre, straw, rags or grasses to a pulp by the action of an ALKALI, such as CAUSTIC SODA (sodium hydroxide). The non-cellulose material is then extracted and the residue is bleached. After washing and the addition of a filler to provide a smooth and flat surface, the pulp is made into thin sheets and dried.

papier-mâché (Fr. chewed paper) Method of moulding forms using paper strips soaked in a starch. The technique originated in 18th-century France. The British adopted the technique to produce a thin paperboard to make trays and mouldings, which were popular in Victorian times. It is still widely used in the production of decorative objects.

Papineau, Louis Joseph (1786–1871) French-Canadian political leader. His quarrels with Britain, which rejected his plan for greater French-Canadian autonomy, incited his followers to rebellion (1837). He escaped arrest by fleeing to the USA, then to France. Granted an amnesty (1847), he returned to Canada and was a member of the unified legislature (1848–54).

PAPUA NEW GUINEA
AREA: 462,840sq km (178,073sq mi)
POPULATION: 4,845,000
CAPITAL (POPULATION): Port Moresby (174,000)

---

paprika Popular, spicy condiment, a red powder ground from the fruit of a sweet PEPPER (capsicum) native to central Europe. Family Solanaceae.

pap test *See* CERVICAL SMEAR

Papua New Guinea Independent Commonwealth island group in Melanesia, sw Pacific, *c.*160km (100mi) NE of Australia; the capital is PORT MORESBY. Papua New Guinea includes the E part of NEW GUINEA, the Bismarck Archipelago, the N SOLOMON ISLANDS, the Trobriand and D'Entrecasteaux Islands and the Louisiade Archipelago. The land is largely mountainous, rising to Mount Wilhelm at 4,508m (14,790ft), E New Guinea. East New Guinea also has extensive coastal lowlands. Papua New Guinea has a tropical climate. The monsoon season runs from December to April. Forests cover more than 70% of the land. The dominant vegetation is rainforest. Mangrove swamps line the coast. "Cloud" forest and tussock grass are found on the higher peaks. **History and politics** The first European sighting of the island was made by the Portuguese in 1526. In 1828, the Dutch took w New Guinea (now IRIAN JAYA, Indonesia). In 1884, Germany took NE New Guinea as German New Guinea and Britain formed the protectorate of British New Guinea in SE New Guinea. In 1906, British New Guinea passed to Australia as the Territory of Papua. In 1921, German New Guinea became the League of Nations mandate Territory of New Guinea under Australian administration. In 1942, Japan captured the islands, and the Allies reconquered them in 1944. In 1949, Papua and New Guinea were combined to form the Territory of Papua and New Guinea. In 1973, the Territory achieved self-government as a prelude to full independence as Papua New Guinea in 1975. Since independence, the government of Papua New Guinea has worked to develop its mineral reserves. One of the most valuable reserves was a copper mine at Panguna on BOUGAINVILLE. Conflict developed when the people of Bougainville demanded a larger share in mining profits. In 1990, following an insurrection, the Bougainville Revolutionary Army (BRA) proclaimed independence. In 1992 and 1996, Papua New Guinea launched offensives against the BRA. The use of highly paid mercenaries created unrest in the army. In 1997, troops and civilians surrounded Parliament and forced the resignation of the prime minister, Sir Julius Chan. He was succeeded by Bill Skate. In April 1998, a permanent cease-fire was declared on Bougainville. In July 1998, a tidal wave hit N Papua New Guinea, killing more than 1,600 people. Mekere Morauta succeeded Bill Skate as prime minister in 1999. **Economy** Agriculture employs 75% of the workforce, many at subsistence level. Minerals, notably copper and gold, are the most valuable exports. Papua New Guinea is the world's ninth-largest producer of gold. Other exports include yams, coffee and timber. Manufacturing industries process farm, fish and forest products.

papyrus Stout perennial water plant, native to s Europe, N Africa, and the Middle East, and used by the ancient Egyptians to make writing material. Strips of the stem were arranged in layers, crushed and hammered to form a loosely textured, porous kind of PAPER. Height: to 4.5m (15ft). Family Cyperaceae; species *Cyperus papyrus*.

parable Short, simple story intended to convey a moral or religious message. It differs from an ALLEGORY in that it deals with events that might reasonably happen in nature. The best-known parables are those attributed to Jesus Christ in the New Testament, including the Good Samaritan and the Prodigal Son.

parabola Mathematical curve, a CONIC section traced by a point that moves so that its distance from a fixed point, the *focus*, is equal to its distance from a fixed straight line, the *directrix*. It may be formed by cutting a cone parallel to one side. The general equation of a parabola is $y = ax^2 + bx + c$, where a, b and c are constants.

Paracelsus (1493–1541) Swiss physician and alchemist. b. Philippus Aureolus Theophrastus Bombast von Hohenheim. According to Paracelsus, the human body is primarily composed of salt, sulphur and mercury, and it is the separation of these elements that causes illness. He introduced mineral baths.

paracetamol (acetaminophen) ANALGESIC drug that lessens pain and is also effective in reducing fever. It is used to treat mild to moderate pain, such as headaches, toothaches and rheumatic conditions, and is particularly effective against musculoskeletal pain.

parachute Lightweight fabric device for slowing movement through the air. Parachutes allow people to descend safely from aircraft or are used to drop cargo and supplies. The most common use is for the sport of SKYDIVING. In 1797 Jacques Garnerin made the first successful parachute jump from a balloon over Paris.

paradox In LOGIC, a self-contradictory or absurd statement that conflicts with preconceived notions of what is reasonable or possible, but which is significant when considered from the appropriate viewpoint. "This statement is not true" appears to be true if false and false if true.

paraffin (kerosene) Common domestic fuel that is mainly a mixture of ALKANE hydrocarbons. It is a product of the distillation of PETROLEUM. Less volatile than petrol, paraffin is also used as a fuel for jet aircraft. Paraffin wax is a white, translucent, waxy substance consisting of a mixture of solid alkanes obtained by solvent extraction; it is used to make candles, waxed paper, polishes and cosmetics.

Paraguay Landlocked republic in central South America; the capital is ASUNCIÓN. Paraguay is bisected by the River Paraguay. The majority of the population live between the E bank of the River Paraguay and the River PARANÁ, which forms the S border with Argentina. The S has extensive marshes. West of the River Paraguay is part of the GRAN CHACO, a flat grassy plain that extends into Bolivia and Argentina. The S is sub-tropical. Rainfall is heaviest in the SE Paraná plateau. The Chaco is the driest and hottest part of Paraguay. Paraguay is a country of coarse grass, shrub and scrub forest, with some hardwood forests. **History and politics** The earliest known inhabitants of Paraguay were the GUARANÍ. Spanish and Portuguese explorers reached the area in the early 16th century. In 1537, a Spanish expedition built a fort at Asunción, which became the capital of Spain's colonies in SE South America. From the late 16th century, Jesuit missionaries worked to protect the Guaraní from colonial exploitation and convert them to Christianity. In 1767, the Spanish king expelled the Jesuits. In 1776, Paraguay was

---

PARAGUAY
AREA: 406,750sq km (157,046sq mi)
POPULATION: 5,538,000
CAPITAL (POPULATION): Asunción (945,000)

subsumed into the colony of the viceroyalty of Río de la Plata. Paraguay declared independence in 1811. The disastrous War of the Triple Alliance (1865–70) against Brazil, Argentina and Uruguay killed more than 50% of Paraguay's population and resulted in great loss of territory. Border disputes with Bolivia led to the Chaco War (1932–35) in which Paraguay regained some land. In 1954 General Alfredo Stroessner led a successful military coup. His dictatorial regime suppressed all political opposition. In 1989, shortly after re-election for an eighth successive term, Stroessner was overthrown by General Andrés Rodríguez. In 1993 elections Juan Carlos Wasmosy became Paraguay's first civilian president since 1954. In 1996, General Lino Oviedo was imprisoned for leading an attempted military coup. In 1999, Oviedo was released by President Raúl Cubas. The assassination of the vice-president, Luis María Argaña, led to riots and the killing of four pro-democracy demonstrators. Raúl Cubas was forced to resign. He was succeeded by Luis González Macchi. **Economy** Agriculture and forestry are the leading activities, employing 48% of the workforce (1995 GDP per capita, US$3,650). Paraguay has large cattle ranches, and many crops are grown in the fertile soils of E Paraguay. Paraguay is the world's seventh-largest producer of soya beans. Other crops include cassava, cotton and coffee. Major exports include timber, coffee, tannin and meat products. In 1973, construction started on one of the world's largest dams, the Itaipú Dam on the River Paraná.

parakeet *See* PARROT

parallax Angular distance by which a celestial object appears to be displaced with respect to more distant objects, when viewed from opposite ends of a baseline. The parallax of a star (**annual** parallax) is the angle subtended at the star by the mean radius of the Earth's orbit (one astronomical unit); the smaller the angle, the more distant the star. *See also* PARSEC

parallelogram Quadrilateral (four-sided plane figure) having each pair of opposite sides parallel and equal. Both the opposite angles of a parallelogram are also equal. A parallelogram with all four sides equal is called a RHOMBUS.

Paralympic Games Sports meeting held every four years in conjunction with the OLYMPIC GAMES and in which all competitors are physically handicapped. Much of the full Olympic programme of events is staged.

paralysis Weakness or loss of muscle power; it can vary from a mild condition to complete loss of function and sensation in the affected part. It can be associated with almost any disorder of the NERVOUS SYSTEM, including brain or spinal cord injury, infection, stroke, poisoning or progressive conditions such as a tumour or motor neuron disease. Paralysis is very rarely total.

Paramaribo Capital of Surinam, a port on the River Surinam. It was founded in the early 17th century by the French and became a British colony in 1651. It was held intermittently by the British and the Dutch until 1816, when the latter finally took control until independence. Industries: bauxite, timber, sugar cane, rice, rum, coffee, cacao. Pop. (1993 est.) 200,970.

Paramecium Genus of freshwater, ciliated PROTOZOANS characterized by their streamlined "slipper" shape, defined front and rear ends, an oral groove for feeding, food vacuoles for digestion, an anal pore for elimination and two nuclei. Its stiff outer covering is studded with short, hair-like CILIA. Order Holotricha; species include *Paramecium bursaria* and *Paramecium aurelia*.

Paraná River in SE central South America. It rises in SE Brazil, flows S into Argentina, forming the SE and S border of Paraguay, and joins the River Uruguay to form

the Río de la PLATA. It is an important route for inland communications. Combined length: Paraná/Plata *c*.4,000km (2,400mi).

paranoia Term in psychology for a psychotic disorder characterized by a systematically held, persistent delusion, usually of persecution or irrational jealousy. Paranoia can accompany SCHIZOPHRENIA, manic-depressive disorder, drug or alcohol abuse or brain damage.

paraplegia PARALYSIS of both legs. It is usually due to spinal cord injury and often accompanied by loss of sensation below the site of the damage.

parapsychology Branch of psychology concerned with research into phenomena that appear inexplicable by traditional science. It involves research into EXTRASENSORY PERCEPTION (ESP), such as TELEPATHY, and precognition (perceiving future events).

parasite Organism that lives on or in another organism (the host) upon which it depends for its survival; this arrangement may be harmful to the host. Parasites occur in many groups of plants and in virtually all major animal groups. A parasite that lives in the host is called an **endoparasite**; a parasite that survives on the host's exterior is an **ectoparasite**. Many parasites, such as PROTOZOA, FLEAS and WORMS, carry disease or cause sores that may become infected. The European CUCKOO and cowbird rely on other birds to rear their young and are therefore considered "brood parasites". In **parasitoidism**, the relationship results in the death of the host.

parathyroid glands Four small endocrine glands, usually embedded in the back of the THYROID GLAND, that secrete a HORMONE to control the level of calcium and phosphorus in the blood. Overproduction of parathyroid hormone causes loss of calcium from the bones to the blood; a deficiency causes tetany (involuntary muscle spasm). *See also* ENDOCRINE SYSTEM

Paré, Ambroise (1517–90) French physician regarded by some as the founder of modern surgery. In 1537, he was employed as an army surgeon, and in 1552 became surgeon to HENRY II. Paré introduced new methods of treating wounds and revived the practice of tying arteries during surgery instead of cauterizing them.

Pareto, Vilfredo (1848–1923) Italian economist and sociologist. He studied the application of mathematics to economic theory and wrote *Manual of Political Economy* (1906). As a sociological theorist, Pareto concentrated on ruling élites and wrote *Mind and Society* (1916).

Paris In Greek legend, the son of PRIAM and Hecuba. After he chose APHRODITE as the victor in a competition among goddesses, she helped him to abduct HELEN, wife of Menelaus, King of Sparta. This kidnapping sparked the TROJAN WAR, in which he slew ACHILLES.

Paris Capital of France, on the River SEINE. When the Romans took Paris in 52 BC, it was a small village on the Ile de la Cité on the Seine. Under their rule it became an important administrative centre. Paris was the capital of the Merovingian Franks in the 5th century but subsequently declined. In the 10th century it was re-established as the French capital by the Capetian kings. In the 11th and 12th centuries, the city expanded rapidly. During the 14th century, Paris rebelled against the Crown and declared itself an independent commune. It suffered further civil disorder during the Hundred Years War. In the 16th century it underwent fresh expansion, its architecture strongly influenced by the Italian Renaissance. In the reign of LOUIS XIII, Cardinal RICHELIEU established Paris as the cultural and political centre of Europe. The FRENCH REVOLUTION began in Paris when the BASTILLE was stormed by crowds in 1789. Under Emperor NAPOLEON I the city began to assume its present-day form. The work of modernization was continued during the reign of NAPOLEON III, when Baron Haussmann was commissioned to plan the boulevards, bridges and parks. Although occupied during the Franco–Prussian War (1870–71) and again in World War 2, Paris was not badly damaged. The city proper consists of the Paris department, Ville de Paris. Its suburbs lie in the departments of the Ile-de-France region. It has many famous buildings and landmarks popular with tourists. Sites include the EIFFEL TOWER, ARC DE TRIOMPHE, the LOUVRE, NOTRE DAME and the Pompidou Centre. Paris remains the hub of France despite attempts at decentralization and retains its importance as a European cultural, commercial and communications centre. Paris is noted for its fashion industry and for the manufacture of luxury articles. Industries: motor vehicles, chemicals, textiles, clothing. Pop. (1990, city) 2,152,423; (metropolitan) 9,318,821.

Paris, treaties of Name given to several international agreements made in Paris. The most notable include: the **treaty of 1763**, which ended the SEVEN YEARS' WAR; the **treaty of 1783**, which ended the AMERICAN REVOLUTION; the **treaty of 1814**, which settled the affairs of France after the first abdication of NAPOLEON I; the **treaty of 1815**, after Napoleon's final defeat; the **treaty of 1856**, ending the CRIMEAN WAR; the **treaty of 1898**, ending the SPANISH-AMERICAN WAR and giving the Philippines to the USA; and the main international settlement (1919) after World War 1, more often called the Treaty of VERSAILLES. Also signed in Paris was the truce in the VIETNAM WAR (1973), in which the USA agreed to withdraw its forces.

Paris, universities of Collection of 13 autonomous universities, created in 1970 and known as Paris I–XIII, situated in and around Paris. Paris I–VIII replaces the original University of Paris. Each university specializes in a particular area of academic study. The original SORBONNE, which was founded in the 12th century, is the administrative centre of the universities.

Paris Commune (18 March–28 May 1871) Revolutionary government in Paris. Anger with the national government following the FRANCO-PRUSSIAN WAR provoked Parisians into establishing an independent city government. Socialists and other radicals played an important part in the Commune. Besieged by the forces of the national government, the city fell and the Commune was violently suppressed. The slaughter of an estimated 30,000 Communards alienated many French workers and encouraged revolutionary doctrines.

parity In physics, term used to denote space-reflection symmetry. The principle of conservation of parity states that physical laws are the same in a left- and right-handed coordinate system. This was regarded as inviolable until 1956, when Chen Ning YANG and Tsung-Dao LEE showed that it was transgressed by certain interactions between elementary atomic particles. Parity is also used in information theory to denote a coding method employed in message transmission to detect errors.

Park, Mungo (1771–1806) Scottish explorer. He was asked by the African Association (forerunner of the Royal Geographical Society) to investigate the course of the River Niger (1795). He explored *c*.450km (280mi) of the Upper Niger, a journey described in his *Travels...* (1799). On a second expedition (1805) he and his companions were ambushed and drowned.

Park Chung Hee (1917–79) South Korean general and statesman, president (1963–79). In 1961, he seized power in a military coup. In 1963 Park was elected president. He

was re-elected in 1967 and 1971. Park was assassinated by the head of the South Korean Central Intelligence Agency.

Parker, Alan (1944–) English film director. His debut feature, *Bugsy Malone* (1976), was followed by *Midnight Express* (1978), for which he received an Academy nomination. *Mississippi Burning* (1988) earned him a second nomination. Other films include *Birdy* (1985), *The Commitments* (1991) and *Evita* (1997).

Parker, Charlie (Charles Christopher) (1920–55) ("Bird") US JAZZ alto saxophonist. In the 1940s, Parker, Dizzy GILLESPIE, Thelonious MONK and Bud POWELL were the founders of BEBOP, a revolutionary departure in jazz. Parker's powerful improvisations inspired a new generation of jazz musicians, such as Miles DAVIS.

Parker, Dorothy (1893–1967) US poet, short-story writer and critic. She wrote three volumes of poetry, the first of which, *Enough Rope* (1926), was a best-seller. Her gift for witty epigrams is evident throughout her work.

Parkinson, Norman (1913–90) English fashion and portrait photographer. He worked for *Harper's Bazaar* (1935–40) and *Vogue* (1945–60). Awarded the CBE in 1981, he had exhibitions in London, Paris and Venice.

Parkinson's disease Degenerative BRAIN disease characterized by tremor, muscular rigidity and poverty of movement and facial expression. It arises from a lack of the NEUROTRANSMITTER, DOPAMINE. Slightly more common in men, it is rare before the age of 50. Foremost among the drugs used to control the disease is L-DOPA.

parliament Legislative assembly that includes elected members and acts as a debating forum for political affairs. Many parliamentary systems are based on the **British Parliament**. It emerged in the late 13th century as an extension of the king's council and has been housed at Westminster since that time. It is the supreme power in the country. Parliament comprises the monarch, in whose name members of the government act, and two Houses: the HOUSE OF LORDS, an upper chamber of hereditary and life peers, bishops and law lords; and the HOUSE OF COMMONS. There are 659 members of the Commons (known as "members of Parliament" or MPs), elected in single-member constituencies by universal adult suffrage. The prime minister and cabinet members are almost always members of the Commons. There is a maximum of five years between elections.

Parma City in N Italy; capital of Parma province. It was founded by the Romans in 183 BC. In the 9th century AD, it became a bishopric and in 1513 was incorporated into the Papal States. In 1545, Pope Paul III established the duchy of Parma, and until 1731 it was controlled by the Farnese family. In 1802, Napoleon conquered Parma and in 1815 handed control to his second consort, Marie Louise of Austria. Despite suffering bombing in World War 2, Parma retains many historic buildings. It is famed for its ham and Parmesan cheese. Pop. (1996) 168,000.

Parmigiano (1503–40) Northern Italian painter and graphic artist, b. Francesco Mazzola. He was a master of MANNERISM. Among his best-known works are *Madonna with St Zachary* (*c*.1530) and *Vision of St Jerome* (*c*.1527).

Parnassus Mountain peak in central Greece. In ancient times it was considered sacred to APOLLO, DIONYSUS and the MUSES, and was the site of the equally sacred Castalian spring that lies just above DELPHI, at the S foot of the mountain. Height: 2,457m (8,061ft).

Parnell, Charles Stewart (1846–91) Irish nationalist leader. In 1875, he entered the British Parliament. Parnell led the parliamentary movement for Irish HOME RULE. His filibustering tactics won the support of the FENIAN MOVEMENT. In 1879, Parnell became president of the National Land League. He was imprisoned in 1881–82. In 1886, he supported GLADSTONE's introduction of the Home Rule Bill. In 1889, his career collapsed when he was cited as co-respondent in the divorce of William O'Shea, whose wife, Kitty, he later married.

parody Work in which the characteristics of artists or their works are imitated and exaggerated for comic effect. While parody exists in music and the arts, it is most commonly associated with literature and has its roots in ancient Greece. The tendency of parody to follow hard on the heels of distinctive work means that it has often served to question, consolidate and extend original advances in form, style or subject. Among 20th-century writers who have made effective use of parody are Max BEERBOHM, James JOYCE and Stephen LEACOCK.

parrot Common name for many tropical and sub-tropical birds. Parrots are brightly coloured and have thick, hooked bills. They include BUDGERIGARS, COCKATIELS, COCKATOOS, keas, kakapos, lories, lorikeets, LOVEBIRDS, MACAWS, parakeets and others. In the wild they nest in tree holes, rock cracks or on the ground. Parrots are excellent mimics. Length: 7.5–90cm (3in–3ft). Family Psittacidae.

Parry, Sir (Charles) Hubert Hastings (1848–1918) English composer. His mastery of choral music is best shown in *Blest Pair of Sirens* (1887). He is chiefly celebrated for his setting of Blake's poem "Jerusalem" (1916).

parsec (pc) Distance at which a star would have a PARALLAX of one second of arc; equivalent to 3.2616 light-years, 206,265 astronomical units, or 3.0857×10^{13} km.

Parsi (Parsee) Modern descendant of a small number of ancient Persian Zoroastrians who emigrated to Gujarat in India from the 10th century onwards. Modern Parsis, concentrated in Bombay, follow a mixture of ZOROASTRIANISM and some Indian beliefs and practices.

parsley Branching biennial herb, native to the Mediterranean region and cultivated for its aromatic leaves used for flavouring and as a garnish. It has heads of small, greenish-yellow flowers. Height: to 0.9m (3ft). Family Apiaceae/Umbelliferae; species *Petroselinum crispum.*

parsnip Biennial vegetable native to Eurasia, widely cultivated for its edible white taproot. The plant has many leaves. The roots develop slowly until cool weather sets in, and then they mature quickly. Family Apiaceae/Umbelliferae; species *Pastinaca sativa.*

Parsons, Sir Charles Algernon (1854–1931) English engineer. In 1884, Parsons invented the first practical steam TURBINE. In 1894, he built the first turbine-driven steamship, the *Turbinia.*

Parsons, Talcott (1902–79) US sociologist. He incorporated the ideas of FUNCTIONALISM into a systematic analysis of social systems. Parsons emphasized the integrational role of social stratification. His works include *The Structure of Social Action* (1939) and *The Social System* (1931).

Pärt, Arvo (1935–) Estonian composer. His early works were written in a traditional "Soviet" style. In the 1970s, Pärt adopted a minimalist style of gradually shifting chords and note-patterns that he called "tintinnabula". Among his best-known works are *Tabula Rasa* (1977), *Cantus in memoriam Benjamin Britten* (1980) and the *St John Passion* (1981).

parthenogenesis Development of a female sex cell or GAMETE without fertilization. It leads to the production of offspring that are genetically identical to the mother. This process occurs naturally among some plants and invertebrates, such as APHIDS.

Parthenon Temple to the goddess ATHENA erected (447–432 BC) by PERICLES on the ACROPOLIS in Athens. The finest example of a DORIC ORDER temple, it was badly damaged by an explosion in 1687. Most of the surviving sculptures were removed by Lord Elgin in 1801–03. *See* ELGIN MARBLES

Parthia Region in ancient Persia, corresponding approximately to the modern Iranian province of Khorasan with part of S TURKMENISTAN. It was the seat of the Parthian empire, founded after a successful revolt against the SELEUCIDS (238 BC). Under the Arsacid dynasty, the Parthian empire extended, at its peak, from Armenia to Afghanistan. In AD 224 the Parthians were defeated by the rising power of the SASSANIDS, and the empire rapidly crumbled.

particle accelerator *See* ACCELERATOR, PARTICLE

particle physics Branch of physics that studies SUBATOMIC PARTICLES and interactions between them. Physicists now recognize more than 300 different subatomic particles. The indivisible, fundamental units of matter are known as ELEMENTARY PARTICLES. They are termed the gauge BOSON, LEPTON and QUARK. Other subatomic particles, termed HADRONS, are made up of two or more elementary particles. For example, PROTONS and NEUTRONS are made up of three quarks, and MESONS are made up of two quarks. Most subatomic particles are unstable and decay into other particles.

partridge Any of several species of gamebirds found worldwide. True partridges of Europe belong to the PHEASANT family (Phasianidae) and include the common partridge, *Perdix perdix*, which has been introduced to North America. It lives on heathland, sandy scrub and farmland, and feeds on plants and insects.

Parvati In Hindu mythology, the wife of the god SHIVA in one of her more benevolent aspects as a mountain goddess. Parvati is also the mother of the elephant-headed god, GANESH, and his brother, Skanda. She is generally depicted as a young woman.

Pascal, Blaise (1623–62) French scientist and mystic. With Pierre de FERMAT, Pascal laid the foundations of the mathematical theory of PROBABILITY. He also contributed to calculus and hydrodynamics, devising **Pascal's law** (1647). This states that the pressure applied to an enclosed fluid is transmitted equally in all directions and to all parts of the enclosing vessel. The SI unit of pressure is named after him. In 1655, Pascal retired from science to concentrate on his philosophical and religious writing. In *Lettres provinciales* (1656–57) he defended JANSENISM. Pascal's *Pensées* (1670) is a defence of Christianity.

Pashto (Pushto) One of the two major languages of Afghanistan, the other being Persian. Pashto is spoken by about 12 million people in E Afghanistan and N Pakistan. It is historically the language of the PATHAN tribes and is written in an adapted Arabic alphabet. One of the Iranian languages, it forms part of the Indo-European family of languages.

Pasolini, Pier Paolo (1922–75) Italian film director and writer. A Marxist, he wrote about urban poverty in realist novels such as *A Violent Life* (1959). Pasolini's films include *The Gospel According to St Matthew* (1964), *The Decameron* (1970) and *The Canterbury Tales* (1972). He was murdered shortly after completing *Salo* (1975).

passion In Christian theology, the suffering of JESUS CHRIST from the time of his praying in the garden of Gethsemane until his death on the cross. Passion Sunday is the fifth Sunday in LENT; PALM SUNDAY and EASTER follow.

passion flower Any plant of the genus *Passiflora*, climbing tropical plants that probably originated in tropical America, especially the widely cultivated blue passion flower, *P. caerulea*. Flowers are red, yellow, green or purple; the outer petals ring a fringed centre. The leaves are lobed and some species produce edible fruits, such as granadilla and calabash. Family Passifloraceae.

passion play Dramatic presentation of Christ's PASSION, death and resurrection, originally developed in medieval Europe. The best-known example of this tradition is still held every ten years in OBERAMMERGAU, Germany. *See also* MYSTERY PLAY

Passover (Pesach) Jewish festival of eight days, commemorating the Exodus from Egypt and the redemption of the Israelites. Symbolic dishes are prepared, including bitter herbs (*maror*) and unleavened bread (*matzot*), to remind the Jews of the haste with which they fled Egypt. It is a family celebration, at which the HAGGADAH is read. Christ's "Last Supper", at which he instituted the EUCHARIST, was a Passover meal.

pasta Food, high in carbohydrate, made from semonna derived from durum wheat. Associated with Italian cooking, it comes in a variety of shapes and sizes.

Pasternak, Boris (1890–1960) Russian novelist, poet and translator. Before the Stalinist purges of the 1930s, he published works such as the poetry collection *My Sister, Life* (1922) and the autobiographical *Safe Conduct* (1931). After the death of Stalin, Pasternak began work on *Dr Zhivago* (1957). Its themes offended officials, and he was expelled from the Soviet Writers Union; the book was not published in the Soviet Union until the 1980s. He was also compelled by official pressure to retract his acceptance of the 1958 Nobel Prize for literature.

Pasteur, Louis (1822–95) French chemist, one of the founders of MICROBIOLOGY. In 1862 his work on BACTERIA led to the "germ theory" of infection. Pasteur discovered that microorganisms can be destroyed by heat, a technique now known as PASTEURIZATION. He also found that he could weaken certain DISEASE-causing microorganisms and then use the weakened culture to provide IMMUNITY against the disease. In 1881, Pasteur produced the first VACCINES against ANTHRAX. In 1885, he produced a vaccine against RABIES. In 1885, the Pasteur Institute was founded in Paris, France.

pasteurization Controlled heat treatment of food to kill bacteria and other microorganisms, discovered by Louis PASTEUR in the 1860s. Milk is pasteurized by heating it to 72°C (161.6°F) for 16 seconds. Ultrapasteurization is now used to produce UHT (ultra-heat-treated) milk; it is heated to 132°C (270°F) for one second to provide a shelf-life of several months.

pastoral In literature, work portraying rural life in an idealized manner, especially to contrast its supposed innocence with the corruption of the city or royal court. In classical times THEOCRITUS and VIRGIL wrote pastoral poems. The form was revived during the RENAISSANCE by such poets as DANTE, PETRARCH, BOCCACCIO and SPENSER. MILTON and SHELLEY were noted for their pastoral elegies, and poets such as William WORDSWORTH and Robert FROST have been loosely referred to as pastoral poets.

pastoralism Form of subsistence agriculture that involves the herding of domesticated livestock. Societies practising pastoralism are small, restricted by the large amount of grazing land needed for each animal. Indigenous pastoralism is widespread in N Africa and central Asia. *See also* NOMAD

Patagonia Region in Argentina, E of the Andes Mountains, extending to the Strait of Magellan; the term is sometimes used to include part of S Chile. The area was first visited by MAGELLAN in the early 16th century. It was colonized in the 1880s, many of the settlers being Welsh or Scottish. Most of Patagonia is located on arid, windswept plateau land. Until recently, sheep rearing

was the main source of income. Oil production has now become important, and coal and iron ore are mined in the S. Area: 805,490sq km (311,000sq mi).

patella (kneecap) Large, flattened, roughly triangular bone just in front of the joint where the FEMUR and TIBIA are linked. It is surrounded by bursae (sacs of fluid) that cushion the joint.

patent (letters patent) Privilege granted to the inventor of a product or process. A patent excludes others from producing or making use of it for a limited period, unless licensed by the holder of the patent. *See also* COPYRIGHT

Pathans (Pashtuns) MUSLIM tribes of SE Afghanistan and NW Pakistan. They speak various dialects of an E Iranian language, PASHTO, and are composed of *c.*60 tribes, numbering in total perhaps 10 million. Formerly, they were pastoralists inhabiting the mountainous border regions, but they are now mainly farmers and are more widely spread. In their clashes with the British in the 19th century, they gained a reputation as formidable warriors. Their way of life was disrupted during the Soviet occupation (1979–89) and the subsequent civil wars in Afghanistan.

Pathé, Charles (1863–1957) French film pioneer. He produced many short films and is credited with having made one of the first long films, *Les Misérables* (1909). Through the Pathé newsreels, he helped develop the film DOCUMENTARY.

pathogen Microorganism that causes disease in plants or animals. Animal pathogens are commonly BACTERIA and VIRUSES, while plant pathogens include FUNGI.

pathology Study of diseases, their causes and their effects on the cells, tissues and organs of the body.

Patna City on the S bank of the Ganges, NE India; capital of Bihar. It was founded by the Moguls in 1541 on the site of the ancient city of Pataliputra, imperial capital of the MAURYA and GUPTA dynasties. Pop. (1991) 1,099,000.

Paton, Alan Stewart (1903–88) South African novelist and reformer. Strongly opposed to APARTHEID, he helped establish the South African Liberal Party, of which he was president (1958–68). His two best-known novels, *Cry, the Beloved Country* (1948) and *Too Late the Phalarope* (1953), raised awareness of injustices in South African society.

patriarch Head of a family or tribe, invested in certain circumstances with the status or authority of a religious leader. In the Old Testament, the term referred either to the ancestors of the human race who lived on Earth before the Flood (as recorded in Genesis 1–11) or more commonly to the ancestors of the ancient Israelites, namely: ABRAHAM, ISAAC, JACOB and Jacob's 12 sons (Genesis 12–50). Since *c.*4th century AD, the word has also been used as an ecclesiastic title for a few exalted Eastern Christian bishops.

patriarchy Social organization based on the authority of a senior male, usually the father, over a FAMILY.

patrician Aristocratic class in the ancient Roman Republic, members of the SENATE. In the early years of the republic, the patricians controlled all aspects of government and society. Under the empire the division between patricians and PLEBIANS disappeared.

Patrick, Saint (active 5th century AD) Patron saint of Ireland. Facts about his life are confused by legend. What is known of Patrick comes almost entirely from his autobiography, *Confession*. He was born in Britain into a Romanized Christian family. Abducted by marauders at the age of 16, Patrick was carried off to Ireland and sold to a local chief. After six years as a herdsman, during which period he became increasingly reliant on his Christian faith, he escaped back to Britain. In 432, Patrick returned to Ireland as a missionary of

Pope Celestine I, and established an episcopal see at Armagh. His missionary work was so successful that Christianity was firmly established in Ireland before he died. By tradition he is also said to have banished snakes from Ireland. His feast day is 17 March.

Patten, Christopher Francis (1944–) British politician and last British governor of HONG KONG (1992–97). As chairman of the CONSERVATIVE PARTY (1990–92), he helped engineer a Conservative victory in the 1992 election but lost his own seat. As governor of Hong Kong, Patten sought to preserve its political and economic institutions in the hand over to China. In 1999, he was appointed European Commissioner for External Relations.

Patton, George Smith, Jr (1885–1945) US general. In World War 1 he served with the American Expeditionary Force (AEF) in France. A controversial but highly successful officer, Patton commanded a tank corps in North Africa and the 7th Army in Sicily in WORLD WAR 2. After the NORMANDY CAMPAIGN (1944), he commanded the 3rd Army in its dash across France and into Germany. As military governor of Bavaria after the war, Patton was criticized for leniency to Nazis and was removed to command the US 15th Army.

Paul, Saint (active 1st century AD) Apostle of JESUS CHRIST, missionary and early Christian theologian. His missionary journeys among the Gentiles form a large part of the ACTS OF THE APOSTLES. His many letters (epistles) to early Christian communities, recorded in the NEW TESTAMENT, represent the most important early formulations of Christian theology following the death of Jesus Christ. Named Saul at birth, he was both a Jew and a Roman citizen, brought up in the Roman colony of Tarsus, in what is now S Turkey. He saw the teachings of Jesus as a major threat to JUDAISM and became a leading persecutor of early Christians. Travelling to Damascus to continue his persecution activities, he suddenly saw a bright light while on the road and heard the voice of Jesus addressing him. Having thus undergone his religious conversion, he adopted the name Paul and thereafter became a fluent and energetic evangelist and teacher of Christianity. In c.60, Paul was arrested after returning to Jerusalem and taken as a prisoner to Rome, where he died sometime between 62 and 68, probably suffering a martyr's execution.

Paul III (1468–1549) Pope (1534–49), b. Alessandro Farnese. As pope, he largely initiated the COUNTER REFORMATION. Paul sponsored reform, established the JESUITS (1540) and summoned the Council of TRENT (1545). He commissioned MICHELANGELO to paint the ceiling of the Sistine Chapel.

Paul VI (1897–1978) Pope (1963–78), b. Giovanni Battista Montini. He earned a reputation as a reformer as archbishop of Milan (1954–63). He continued the Second VATICAN COUNCIL, begun by John XXIII, but disappointed liberals by upholding the celibacy of priests and papal primacy, and condemning contraception.

Paul I (1754–1801) Emperor of Russia (1796–1801), son of CATHERINE II (THE GREAT). He re-established the principle of hereditary succession and instituted repressive measures to protect Russia from the influence of the French Revolution. Paul's erratic conduct and his hostility towards his son, Alexander, led to his murder by nobles and military officers.

Paul I (1901–64) King of the Hellenes (1947–64), brother and successor to George II. During his reign, he followed a pro-Western policy and received US aid to help Greece's economic recovery after World War 2. Paul was succeeded by his son, CONSTANTINE II.

Pauli, Wolfgang (1900–58) US physicist, b. Austria. His work on QUANTUM THEORY led him to formulate (1925) the EXCLUSION PRINCIPLE, which explains the behaviour of ELECTRONS in ATOMS. Pauli received the 1945 Nobel Prize for physics for his work. In 1931, he predicted the existence of the NEUTRINO and lived to see his prediction verified in 1956.

Pauling, Linus Carl (1901–94) US chemist. He applied QUANTUM THEORY to chemistry. His work on the application of WAVE MECHANICS to molecular structure led to the 1954 Nobel Prize for chemistry. In the 1950s, Pauling worked on the structure of PROTEINS, and his suggestion that DNA molecules were arranged in a helical structure anticipated the research of Francis CRICK and James WATSON. A leader in the campaign for nuclear disarmament, Pauling was awarded the 1962 Nobel Peace Prize.

Pavarotti, Luciano (1935–) Italian tenor. He made his operatic debut, as Rodolfo in Puccini's *La Bohème*, in 1961. Pavarotti toured the world many times, making his US debut in 1968. He later formed part of the popular concert grouping called "The Three Tenors", along with José CARRERAS and Plácido DOMINGO.

Pavese, Cesare (1908–50) Italian poet, novelist and translator. His translations of English and American novels had considerable influence on ITALIAN LITERATURE of the time. His work with the Resistance during World War 2 influenced his own creative writing, which includes the poem *The Political Prisoner* (1949) and the novel *The Moon and the Bonfire* (1950).

Pavlov, Ivan Petrovich (1849–1936) Russian neurophysiologist. His early work centred on the physiology and neurology of digestion, for which he received the 1904 Nobel Prize for physiology or medicine. Pavlov is best known for his studies of CONDITIONING of behaviour in dogs. His works include *Conditioned Reflexes* (1927).

Pavlova, Anna (1881–1931) Russian ballerina who made her debut in 1899. She left Russia in 1913 to tour with her own company. Pavlova excelled in *Giselle*, *The Dragonfly*, *Autumn Leaves* and the *Dying Swan*, choreographed for her by Michel FOKINE in 1905.

Paxton, Sir Joseph (1803–65) English architect and landscape gardener. Paxton designed the CRYSTAL PALACE for the Great Exhibition of 1851 in London.

Paz, Octavio (1914–98) Mexican poet and essayist. His influences ranged from Marxism to SURREALISM and oriental philosophies. His poetry was collected in translation as *The Collected Poems of Octavio Paz, 1957–1987* (1987). He also wrote essays and literary criticism, including *The Labyrinth of Solitude* (1950). Paz was awarded the 1990 Nobel Prize for literature.

pea Climbing annual plant (*Pisum sativum*), probably native to W Asia. It has small oval leaves and white flowers that give rise to pods containing wrinkled or smooth seeds, which are a popular vegetable. It grows to

▶ **peanut** The peanut (or groundnut) (*Arachis hypogaea*) is the second most important source of vegetable oil after soya beans. They are grown extensively in Georgia, which produces half the US crop, and Alabama, North Carolina, Texas and Virginia.

1.8m (6ft). Family Fabaceae/Leguminosae. *See also* ACACIA; BEAN; LEGUME; PEANUT; VETCH

Peace River formed by the confluence of the Finlay and Parsnip rivers in N central British Columbia, Canada. It joins the Slave River near Lake Athabaska. It was explored (1792–93) by Sir Alexander MACKENZIE. Length: 1,521km (945mi).

peach Small fruit tree (*Prunus persica*) native to China and grown throughout temperate areas. The lance-shaped leaves appear after the pink flowers in spring. The fruit has a thin, downy skin and white or yellow flesh, with a hard "stone" in the middle. It is eaten fresh or preserved. Height: to 6.5m (20ft). Family Rosaceae.

Peacock, Thomas Love (1785–1866) English novelist and poet. Peacock is chiefly remembered for his idiosyncratic satirical romances, such as *Nightmare Abbey* (1818), *Crotchet Castle* (1831) and *Gryll Grange* (1860–61).

peacock (peafowl) Any of several species of birds of Asia and Africa. The male is called a peacock and the female a peahen; peacock has become the common name for both sexes. The male has a 150cm (60in) tail that it spreads vertically as a semicircular fan with a pattern of eye-like shapes in order to attract a mate. The body of the male may be metallic blue, green or bronze, depending on the species. Hens lack the tail and head ornaments and are brown, red or green. In the wild, peafowl inhabit open, lowland forests, roosting in trees. Eggs are laid in a ground nest. Length of body: 75cm (30in). Family Phasianidae; genera *Pavo* and *Afropavo*.

Peak District Plateau area at the S end of the PENNINES, Derbyshire, central England. The Peak District National Park was established in 1951. The highest point is Kinder Scout, at 636m (2,088ft). Area: 1,404sq km (542sq mi).

Peale, Charles Willson (1741–1827) US painter, inventor, naturalist and father of a family of artists. In 1782, Peale opened the first US art gallery, in Philadelphia, Pennsylvania, where he exhibited his own portraits. Peale later expanded the gallery into the country's first natural history museum. His most celebrated picture is a portrait of two of his sons, *The Staircase Group* (1795).

peanut (groundnut) Annual leguminous plant *Arachis hypogaea* of the PEA family. Native to South America, it is now grown in temperate regions of the world; the major producers are China and India. In the 19th century, US scientist George Washington CARVER researched more than 300 uses for it. The seeds (peanuts) are a valuable source of protein and yield an oil used both in food (margarine) and in industry. Family Fabaceae/Leguminosae.

pear Tree and its edible fruit, native to N Asia and S Europe and grown throughout the world in temperate regions. The tree has white flowers and glossy, green leaves. The greenish-yellow, brownish or reddish fruit, picked unripe and allowed to mature, is eaten fresh or preserved. Height: 15–23m (50–75ft). Family Rosaceae; species *Pyrus communis*.

pearl Hard, smooth, iridescent concretion of calcium carbonate produced by certain marine and freshwater bivalve MOLLUSCS. It is composed of nacre, or mother-of-pearl, which forms the inner layer of mollusc shells. A pearl results from an abnormal growth of nacre around foreign matter, such as a grain of sand.

Pearl Harbor US naval base in Hawaii. On 7 December 1941, the base, headquarters of the US Pacific fleet, was attacked by aircraft from a Japanese naval task force, which had approached within range of the islands unobserved. About 300 aircraft and 18 ships were destroyed or severely damaged and c.2,400 people killed. The attack provoked US entry into WORLD WAR 2.

Pears, Sir Peter (1910–86) English tenor. A lifelong friend of Benjamin BRITTEN, he performed in many of Britten's operas, including the title roles of *Peter Grimes* (1945) and *Albert Herring* (1949), the Male Chorus in *The Rape of Lucretia* (1946) and Aschenbach in *Death in Venice* (1973). In 1948, Pears and Britten founded the Aldeburgh Festival. He was knighted in 1978.

Pearse, Patrick Henry (1879–1916) Irish writer and political figure. He headed the revival of interest in Gaelic culture, writing poems, short stories and plays. Pearse led the insurgents in the EASTER RISING (1916) and was court-martialled and executed by the British authorities.

Pearson, Lester Bowles (1897–1972) Canadian statesman and diplomat, prime minister (1963–68). A distinguished diplomatic career culminated in his appointment (1945) as head of Canada's delegation to the United Nations (UN). Pearson acted as president (1952–53) of the UN general assembly. His efforts in resolving the Suez Crisis earned him the 1957 Nobel Peace Prize. In 1958, he became leader of the LIBERAL PARTY. Pearson succeeded John DIEFENBAKER as prime minister. His term was marked by health and social welfare reforms.

Peary, Robert Edwin (1856–1920) US Arctic explorer. He made several expeditions to Greenland (1886–92), and in 1893 led the first of five expeditions towards the North Pole. He was the first person to reach the Pole (6 April 1909).

Peasants' Revolt (1381) Rebellion in England. The immediate provocation was a POLL TAX (1380). Fundamental causes were resentment at feudal restrictions and wages held down artificially, despite the shortage of labour caused by the BLACK DEATH. Led by Wat TYLER, the men of Kent marched into London, where they were pacified by RICHARD II. Promises to grant their demands were broken after they dispersed.

Peasants' War (1524–25) Rebellion of German peasants, the largest popular uprising in European history. Sparked by anger over increasing dues demanded by the princes, there was widespread pillaging in the countryside of S Germany. The peasants hoped for and needed the support of Martin LUTHER, but he rejected their charter of liberties. Some 100,000 peasants were killed.

peat Dark brown or black mass of partly decomposed plant material. It forms in bogs and areas of high rainfall, and contains a high proportion of water. Its high carbon content makes it suitable for use as a fuel. *See also* COAL

peat moss Decomposed organic matter (HUMUS) obtained from disintegrated sphagnum MOSS (bog moss). The most widely obtainable source of humus, it is dug into soil and added to compost to retain moisture. Its continuing use poses an ecological threat to peat bogs.

pecan North American tree that bears a nut resembling a small, smooth-shelled WALNUT. Valued for its flavour,

◄ **pecan** Mottled brown shells of the pecan burst apart to release the ripe nut. The pecan, a relative of the walnut, grows on large trees that are found in warm temperate parts of North America. Pecans make excellent dessert nuts.

it consists of 70% fat and is used in many desserts. Family Juglandaceae; species *Carya illinoiensis*.

peccary Omnivorous, pig-like mammal native to the sw USA and Central and South America. It has coarse, bristly hair. Collared peccaries, or javelinas (*Tayassu taja*), have dark-grey hair with a whitish collar. White-lipped peccaries (*Tayassu pecari*) have brown hair. Weight: 23–30kg (50–66lb). Family Tayassuidae.

Peck, (Eldred) Gregory (1916–) US film actor. He made his debut in *Days of Glory* (1943). Peck received Academy Award nominations for *The Keys of the Kingdom* (1945), *The Yearling* (1946), *Gentleman's Agreement* (1947) and *Twelve O'Clock High* (1950). In 1956, he finally won an Oscar for best actor in *To Kill a Mockingbird* (1962). Other films include *Spellbound* (1945), *The Gunfighter* (1950), *Moby Dick* (1956), *McKenna's Gold* (1968) and *The Omen* (1976). He starred in two versions of *Cape Fear* (1962, 1991).

Peckinpah, (David) Sam (Samuel) (1926–84) US film director. He first gained attention for *Ride The High Country* (1962). Peckinpah injected new life into the WESTERN genre with his depiction of the harsh and violent reality of the frontier. Other films include *The Wild Bunch* (1969) *Straw Dogs* (1971), *The Getaway* (1973) and *Bring Me the Head of Alfredo Garcia* (1975).

pectin Water-soluble POLYSACCHARIDE found in the cell walls and intercellular tissue of certain ripe fruits or vegetables. When fruit is cooked, pectin yields a gel that is the basis of jellies and jams.

pediment Low-pitched gable formed by the sloping eaves of a pitched roof and a horizontal cornice. The classic triangular pediment appeared in Greek temples such as the PARTHENON. Later architects developed more extravagant forms, featuring curved, broken and inverted styles over doors and windows.

Pedro I (1798–1834) Emperor of Brazil (1822–31). Son of the future JOHN VI of Portugal, he fled with the rest of the royal family to Brazil in 1807. When his father reclaimed the Portuguese crown (1821), Pedro became prince regent of Brazil and declared it an independent monarchy (1822). His reign was marked by military failure against Argentina (1825–28) and revolt in Rio de Janeiro (1831). Pedro abdicated and returned to Portugal, where he secured the succession of his daughter, Maria II, to the Portuguese throne.

Pedro II (1825–91) Emperor of Brazil (1831–89). He reigned under a regency until 1840. Pedro's rule was marked by internal unrest and external threats from Argentina and Paraguay. Slavery was abolished in 1888, and Pedro's policy was generally reformist, antagonizing the military and the rich planters. In 1889, he was forced to resign and retire to Europe, while Brazil became a republic.

Peel, Sir Robert (1788–1850) British statesman, prime minister (1834–35, 1841–46). As TORY PARTY

► **pelican** The brown pelican (*Pelecanus occidentalis*) has a large bill with a distensible pouch that it uses to catch the fish on which it feeds. It lives on the coasts of tropical and sub-tropical America.

home secretary, he created (1829) the first modern police force, the Metropolitan (London) Police. Peel was chiefly responsible for passage of the CATHOLIC EMANCIPATION Act (1829). Peel's Tamworth manifesto (1834) was a founding text of the CONSERVATIVE PARTY. He became converted to the doctrine of FREE-TRADE, and the Irish FAMINE convinced him of the need to repeal the CORN LAWS. The proposal split the Tory Party and Peel resigned. In his second term, he carried through the repeal before being finally forced from office.

peerage British nobility holding any of the following titles: baron, viscount, earl, marquess or duke. Although all titles were originally hereditary, these are now rare, and non-hereditary life peerages are more usually granted. Peers constitute the Lords Temporal section of the HOUSE OF LORDS. In 1999, legislation was introduced to abolish the right of hereditary peers to sit and vote in the upper chamber.

Pegasus (Winged Horse) Northern constellation between Andromeda and Cygnus. Three of its bright stars form the Giant Square in Pegasus with Alpha Andromedae; the brightest is Epsilon, with a magnitude of 2.30.

Pegasus In Greek mythology, winged horse. Born out of the blood of MEDUSA, it was tamed by BELLEROPHON and helped him in his battles. Later, it carried the thunderbolts of ZEUS.

Pei, I.M. (leoh Ming) (1917–) US architect, b. China. He emigrated to the USA in 1935. Pei is best-known for his simple geometrical designs for public buildings, which carefully integrate form and environment. His works include the E wing of the National Gallery of Art, Washington, D.C. (1978) and the glass and steel pyramid in front of the Louvre, Paris (1989).

Peirce, Charles Sanders (1839–1914) US philosopher. A leading exponent of PRAGMATISM, he regarded LOGIC as the foundation of philosophy. Peirce outlined his principles in a series of six articles published between 1877 and 1878. His theory of meaning influenced the development of SEMIOTICS. *See also* JAMES, WILLIAM

Peking *See* BEIJING

Pelagius (*c*.360–*c*.420) Monk and theologian, probably born in Britain, who preached the heresy of Pelagianism. In *c*.380, Pelagius came to Rome and became the spiritual guide of many clerics and lay persons. After 410, he preached in Africa, where his ideas were denounced by St AUGUSTINE, and later in Palestine. Pelagius maintained that man is master of his own salvation and rejected the idea of original sin. He countered criticisms from Augustine and St JEROME in his book *De Libero Arbitrio* (416). In 417, Pelagius was excommunicated by Pope Innocent I.

Pelé (1940–) Brazilian footballer, b. Edson Arantes do Nascimento. He scored 97 goals in 111 appearances for Brzail. Pelé led Brazil to three World Cup victories (1958, 1962, 1970). He made his last international appearance in 1971. Apart from 1975–77, when he played for the New York Cosmos, all his club games were played for Santos. Pelé scored a total of 1,281 goals. In 1997, he became Brazil's minister for sport.

pelican Any of several species of stout-bodied inland water birds, with a characteristic distensible pouch under its bill for scooping up fish from shallow water. It is generally white or brown and has a long hooked bill, long wings, short thick legs and webbed feet. Length: to 1.8m (6ft). Family Pelecanidae; genus *Pelecanus*.

pellagra Disease caused by a deficiency of nicotinic acid, one of the B group of vitamins. Its symptoms are lesions of the skin and mucous membranes, diarrhoea and mental disturbance.

Peloponnesian Wars (431–404 BC) Conflict in ancient Greece between ATHENS and SPARTA. The underlying cause was Sparta's fear of Athenian hegemony, while Athenian hostility toward CORINTH, Sparta's chief ally, provoked the Spartan declaration of war. Having a stronger army, Sparta regularly invaded Attica, while Athens, under PERICLES, relied on its navy. The Peace of Nicias (420 BC) proved temporary. Neither side kept to the agreement, and in 415 BC Athens launched a disastrous attack on SYRACUSE, which encouraged Sparta to renew the war. With Persian help, Sparta built up a navy which, under LYSANDER, defeated Athens in 405 BC. Besieged and blockaded, Athens surrendered.

Peloppónnisos (Peloponneso) Peninsula in S Greece, connected to the mainland by the Isthmus of CORINTH. The chief cities are Patras, Corinth, Pirgos and SPARTA. A mountainous region, it also included the ancient cities of Argos and Megalopolis. The peninsula was involved in the PERSIAN WARS (499–479 BC), and it was the site of many battles between Sparta and Athens during the PELOPONNESIAN WARS (431–404 BC). In 146 BC, the region fell to the Romans. Held by the Venetians from 1699 to 1718, then by the Ottoman Turks, the peninsula passed to Greece after independence. Industries: silk, fish, manganese, chromium, fruits, tourism. Area: 21,800sq km (8,400sq mi). Pop. (1991) 1,077,002.

pelota Generic name for a range of games in which a small, hard ball is hit with gloved or bare hand or with a scoop-shaped wicker racket known as a *cesta*. Enjoyed mostly in the Basque regions of Spain and France, and in South America, pelota games can be played across a net or against a wall in a two- or three-sided court known as a *fronto*. JAI ALAI is the fastest of all pelota games.

Peltier effect Phenomenon of the temperature changes at a junction where an electric current passes from one kind of metal to another. When a current passes through a thermocouple (thermometer), the temperature at one junction increases while that at the other decreases. The effect was discovered in 1834 by the French physicist Jean Charles Peltier. It is the opposite of the SEEBECK EFFECT. *See also* THERMOELECTRICITY

pelvis Dish-shaped bony structure that supports the internal organs of the lower abdomen in vertebrates. It is a point of attachment for muscles that move the limbs or fins.

penal colony Settlement to which convicted criminals were transported for imprisonment and hard labour. British convicts were sent to North America until the AMERICAN REVOLUTION, then to Australia until the mid-19th century. French convicts were transported to New Caledonia and French Guiana. Political prisoners in the Soviet Union were transported to camps in Siberia.

penance Carrying out of a specified act as a mark of sincere regret following the commission of a sin or sins. The most common penance, prescribed by a priest after ABSOLUTION, is to say a prayer at a special time.

Penang (Pinang) Island of MALAYSIA, off the NW coast of the Malay Peninsula, which (together with a coastal strip on the mainland) comprises a state of Malaysia; the capital is Penang. The island was Britain's first possession in Malaya (1786). In 1826, it united with Singapore and MALACCA, and in 1867 the group became the Straits Settlements colony. Penang joined the Federation of Malaya in 1948. Its products include rice, rubber and tin. The city of Penang is the principal port of Malaysia. Area: 1,000sq km (400sq mi). Pop. (1993 est.) 1,141,500.

penates Ancient Roman gods of the household, worshiped at home with the lares (spirits of ancestors). Originally penates were the spirits of the storeroom.

Penderecki, Krzysztof (1933–) Polish composer. His reputation was established with the *Threnody for the Victims of Hiroshima* (1960) for string orchestra. Other pieces include the *Passion According to St Luke* (1963–65), operas, and two symphonies (1973, 1980).

pendulum Any object suspended at a point so it swings in an arc. A **simple** pendulum consists of a small heavy mass attached to a string or light rigid rod. A **compound** pendulum has a supporting rod whose mass is not negligible. The pendulum was first used to regulate clocks in 1656 by Christiaan HUYGENS. Foucault's pendulum, devised by Jean FOUCAULT, swings in all directions and was used to demonstrate the Earth's rotation.

Penelope In Greek mythology, wife of ODYSSEUS. As described in HOMER's *Odyssey*, she had been married for only a year when her husband left for ten years of war and ten of wandering. Penelope remained faithful, putting off her many suitors with the promise that she would choose one when her weaving was done. By day she wove and by night she undid her work.

penguin Flightless seabird that lives in the Southern Hemisphere and ranges from the Antarctic northwards to the Galápagos Islands. Their wings have been adapted to flippers, and their webbed feet help to propel their sleek bodies through the water. Although they are awkward on land, they are fast and powerful swimmers, easily able to catch the fish and squid that they feed on. Height: to 1.2m (4ft). Family Spheniscidae.

penicillin ANTIBIOTIC agent derived from moulds of the genus *Penicillium*. The first antibiotic, penicillin was discovered by Sir Alexander FLEMING in 1928. It was synthesised and first became available in 1941. Penicillin was widely used for treating casualties in World War 2. It can produce allergic reactions, and some microorganisms have become resistant.

Peninsular War (1808–14) Campaign of the NAPOLEONIC WARS in Portugal and Spain. It began as a popular revolt in Spain against NAPOLEON I's imposition of his brother, Joseph BONAPARTE, as king of Spain. It rapidly flared into a bloody guerrilla war and British troops, led by the future Duke of WELLINGTON, landed in Portugal to support the expulsion of the French (August 1808). The major turning point was the repulsion of Massena's offensive against Lisbon (1810–11). Wellington's forces then gradually drove the French from the Iberian peninsula and, after the victory of Vitoria (1813), invaded S France. Napoleon's abdication (1814) brought the campaign to an end.

penis Male reproductive organ. It contains the URETHRA, the channel through which URINE and SEMEN pass

◀ **penguin** The royal penguin (*Eudyptes schlegeli*), like many other species of penguin, is a highly social bird. During the breeding season, colonies of up to 2 million royal penguins amass on Macquarie Island, SW of New Zealand.

to the exterior, and erectile tissue that, when engorged with blood, causes the penis to become erect. *See also* SEXUAL REPRODUCTION

Penn, William (1644–1718) English QUAKER leader and founder of PENNSYLVANIA. Penn was imprisoned four times for his advocacy of religious freedom. While in the Tower of London, he wrote *No Cross, No Crown* (1669), explaining Quaker morality. In 1681, he persuaded King CHARLES II to honour an unpaid debt by granting him wilderness land in America to be settled by the Quakers and others seeking refuge from religious persecution. The colony was named the Commonwealth of Pennsylvania in his honour.

Pennines Range of hills in N England, extending from the Tyne Gap and Eden Valley on the border with Scotland to the valley of the River TRENT. The hills are a series of highland blocks dissected by rivers such as the Tees, Aire and Ribble. The rearing of sheep is the chief occupation. Tourism and limestone quarrying are also important. The highest peak is Cross Fell, at 893m (2,930ft). A long-distance footpath, the Pennine Way, extends along the full length of the Pennines, *c.*400km (250mi).

Pennsylvania State in E USA; one of the Middle Atlantic states; the capital is HARRISBURG. The chief cities are PHILADELPHIA, PITTSBURGH and Scranton. Swedish and Dutch settlements were made along the DELAWARE River in the mid-17th century. By 1664 the area was controlled by the English, and William PENN received a charter from Charles II in 1681 for what is now Pennsylvania. It was one of the 13 original states of the Union. The DECLARATION OF INDEPENDENCE was signed and the US Constitution was ratified in Philadelphia, the national capital from 1790 to 1800. The Union victory at the Battle of GETTYSBURG in July 1863 was a turning point in the CIVIL WAR. Apart from small low-lying areas in the NW and SE, the state is composed of a series of mountain ridges and rolling hills. Farming is concentrated in the SE; the principal crops are cereals, tobacco, potatoes, and fruit and dairy products are important. Pennsylvania has rich deposits of coal and iron ore. The state, especially Pittsburgh, has long been a leading producer of steel, which today accounts for *c.*25% of the nation's output. Industries: chemicals, cement, electrical machinery, metal goods. Area: 117,412sq km (45,333sq mi). Pop. (1996) 12,281,054.

pension Money paid regularly to a retired person. Pension plans may be funded by the government, such as SOCIAL SECURITY, or by companies; both plans involve regular financial contributions by the individual for a qualifying period. *See also* NATIONAL INSURANCE (NI)

Pentagon Headquarters of the US Department of Defense, in Arlington, Virginia. The complex is made up of five concentric buildings in pentagonal form and covers 14ha (34 acres). The largest office building in the world, it was completed in 1943. The Pentagon has come to signify the US military establishment.

pentagon Five-sided plane figure. Its interior angles add up to 540°. For a regular pentagon (whose sides and interior angles are equal), each interior angle is 108°.

Pentateuch (Gk. Five scrolls) First five books of the Bible, traditionally attributed to MOSES and in JUDAISM referred to collectively as the TORAH. The Pentateuch comprises the five OLD TESTAMENT books of GENESIS, EXODUS, LEVITICUS, NUMBERS and DEUTERONOMY. Composed over a very long period (possibly 1,000 years or more), they were probably collected in their present form during the BABYLONIAN CAPTIVITY of the Jews.

pentathlon Athletic competition that originated in ancient Greece and consisting of five events. The modern pentathlon is an Olympic sport for women. Points are awarded for performances in 100m hurdles, shot put, high jump, long jump and 200m.

Pentecost Important religious festival celebrated in May or June. In Judaism, it is a festival held seven weeks after the second day of the PASSOVER, commemorating the giving of the Law to MOSES. In the Christian calendar it is also known as Whitsuntide, falling seven weeks after Easter.

Pentecostal Churches Fellowship of revivalist Christian sects, inspired by the belief that all Christians should seek to be baptized with the Holy Spirit and experience events such as speaking in tongues. Pentecostals believe in the literal truth of the Bible, and many abstain from alcohol and tobacco and disapprove of dancing, theatre and other such pleasures. The Pentecostal movement began in the USA at Topeka, Kansas, in 1901. It became organized in Los Angeles in 1906 and spread rapidly to other countries. Today, there are *c.*22 million Pentecostals worldwide. *See also* CHARISMATIC MOVEMENT

Penzias, Arno Allan (1933–) US astrophysicist, b. Germany. Penzias and Robert Wilson discovered the cosmic background radiation emanating from outer space. They detected a non-varying radio signal that is considered to be thermal energy left over from the BIG BANG. Penzias and Wilson shared the 1978 Nobel Prize for physics with Peter KAPITZA.

peony Perennial plant native to North America and Eurasia. It has glossy divided leaves and large white, pink or red flowers, and is frequently cultivated in gardens. Height: to 0.9m (3ft). Tree peonies grow in hot, dry areas and have brilliant blossoms of many colours. Height: to 1.8m (6ft). Family Paeoniaceae; genus *Paeonia*.

Pepin III (the Short) (*c.*714–68) First CAROLINGIAN king of the Franks (750–68), son of Charles Martel. In 750 he deposed the last MEROVINGIAN king, Childeric III. Pepin defeated the LOMBARDS in 754 and 756. He ceded the conquered territories (the future PAPAL STATES) to the papacy in what was known as the Donation of Pepin. He was succeeded by his son CHARLEMAGNE.

pepper (capsicum) Perennial woody shrub native to tropical America. The fruit is a many-seeded, pungent berry whose size depends on the species. Included are bell, red, cayenne and CHILLI peppers. They all belong to the NIGHTSHADE family, Solanaceae; genus *Capsicum*.

peppermint Common name for *Mentha piperita*, a perennial herb of the MINT family (Lamiaceae/Labiatae) cultivated for its ESSENTIAL OIL, which is distilled and used in medicine and as a flavouring.

pepsin Digestive ENZYME secreted by GLANDS of the STOMACH wall as part of the GASTRIC JUICE. In the presence of hydrochloric acid it catalyzes the splitting of PROTEINS in food into polypeptides.

peptide Molecule consisting of two or more linked AMINO ACID molecules. Peptides containing several amino acids are called polypeptides. PROTEINS consist of polypeptide chains with up to several hundred amino acids cross-linked to each other in various ways.

Pepys, Samuel (1633–1703) English diarist. Pepys' *Diary* (1660–69) describes his private life and contemporary English society. It includes a vivid account of the RESTORATION, the PLAGUE and the Great FIRE OF LONDON (1666). Written in shorthand, the diary was not published until 1815 and not seen in complete form until 1983.

percentage Quantity expressed as the number of parts in 100 (considered to be a whole). Fractions can be expressed as a percentage by multiplying by 100, for example, 3/4 becomes 75%.

perception Process by which the brain acquires and organizes incoming stimuli from the sensory nerves, translating them into meaningful information. *See also* EPISTEMOLOGY; MIND

perch One of two species of freshwater food fish. The European perch (*Perca fluviatilis*) is deep-bodied and greenish in colour with dark vertical banding. The North American yellow perch (*P. flavescens*) is gold-coloured with black side-bars. Weight: 1.0–2.7kg (2.2–6lb). Family Percidae.

percussion Term for any of several musical instruments that produce sound when struck. They are divided into two groups: **ideophones**, in which the whole object vibrates (such as CYMBALS, gongs and XYLOPHONES); and **membranophones**, in which a stretched skin or membrane vibrates (this group includes all DRUMS).

Percy, Sir Henry (1364–1403) English nobleman, known as "Hotspur" for his zeal in guarding the Scottish-English border. Son of the Earl of Northumberland, he supported the deposition of RICHARD II in 1399 but later quarrelled with the new king, HENRY IV. In 1403 he and his father, in alliance with Owain GLYN DŴR, launched a rebellion. They were defeated at Shrewsbury, where Percy was killed.

peregrine Crow-sized grey, black and white BIRD OF PREY. It inhabits craggy open country or rocky coastlines and marshes or estuaries. The largest breeding FALCON in Britain, it flies swiftly with prolonged glides. Length: to 48cm (19in). Family Falconidae; species *Falco peregrinus*.

perennial Plant with a life cycle of more than two years. It is a common term for flowering herbaceous and woody plants. They include the LILY, DAISY and IRIS, and all TREES. *See also* ANNUAL; BIENNIAL

Peres, Shimon (1923–) Israeli statesman, prime minister (1986–88, 1995–96), b. Poland. He was elected to the Knesset in 1959. In 1968, Peres helped found the Labour Party and became leader of the party in 1977. He held ministerial posts under Golda MEIR and Yitzhak RABIN. In 1992, losing the party leadership to Rabin, Peres played a vital role in the Palestinian peace process and was jointly awarded, with Rabin and Yasir ARAFAT, the 1994 Nobel Prize for Peace. On Rabin's assassination (1995), he returned as prime minister but was defeated in 1996 elections by Binyamin NETANYAHU. In 2000, Peres lost the presidential elections to Moshe Katsav of the Likud Party.

perestroika (Rus. reconstruction) Adopted by Soviet prime minister Mikhail GORBACHEV in 1986, *perestroika* was linked with GLASNOST. The restructuring included reform of government and the bureaucracy, centralization, and abolition of the COMMUNIST PARTY monopoly. Liberalization of the economic system included the introduction of limited private enterprise.

Pérez de Cuéllar, Javier (1920–) Peruvian diplomat, fifth secretary-general of the UNITED NATIONS (UN) (1982–91). He emerged as a successful compromise candidate following opposition to the re-election of Kurt WALDHEIM. He earned a reputation for skillful diplomacy in the cease-fire agreements at the end of the FALKLANDS WAR (1982) and the IRAN–IRAQ WAR (1980–88). He was succeeded by Boutros BOUTROS-GHALI.

performance art Events that take place before an audience but which defy the traditional definitions of DRAMA and MUSIC. Arguably originating in the USA in the 1960s, performance art is often visually oriented.

perfume Substance that produces a pleasing fragrance. The scents of such plants as rose, citrus, lavender and sandalwood are obtained from their ESSENTIAL OILS. These are blended with a fixative of animal origin, such as musk, ambergris or civet. Liquid perfumes are usually alcoholic solutions containing 10 to 25% of the

perfume concentrate; colognes and toilet waters contain *c*.2–6% of the concentrate.

Pergamum Ancient city-state on the site of modern BERGAMA, W Turkey. It was founded by Greek colonists under licence from the Persian emperors in the 4th century BC. At its peak in the 3rd–2nd centuries BC, it controlled much of W Asia Minor.

Pergolesi, Giovanni Battista (1710–36) Italian composer. His intermezzo *La Serva Padrona* (1733) became a model for Italian OPERA BUFFA. Pergolesi's *Stabat Mater* (1730) is one of the finest examples of Baroque religious music.

Peri, Jacopo (1561–1633) Italian composer. His musical drama *Dafne* (1597) is generally regarded as the first opera. His next opera, *Euridice* (1600), remains the earliest opera to have been preserved in its entirety.

perianth Outer region of a flower. The perianth includes all the structures surrounding the reproductive organs and usually consists of an outer whorl of sepals (calyx) and an inner whorl of petals (corolla).

pericarp In seed plants, the wall of a ripened fruit that is derived from the ovary wall. The tissues of the pericarp may be fibrous, stony or fleshy.

Pericles (490–429 BC) Athenian statesman. He dominated Athens from *c*.460 BC to his death, overseeing its golden age. He is associated with achievements in art and literature, including the building of the PARTHENON, while strengthening the Athenian empire and government. He initiated the PELOPONNESIAN WARS (431–404 BC) but died of plague at the outset.

peridot Gem variety of transparent green OLIVINE, a silicate mineral. Large crystals are found on St John's Island in the Red Sea and in Burma.

peridotite Heavy IGNEOUS ROCK of coarse texture composed of olivine and pyroxene with small flecks of mica or hornblende. It alters readily into SERPENTINE.

perigee Point in the ORBIT about the Earth of the Moon, or of an artificial satellite, at which the body is nearest to the Earth.

perihelion Point in the ORBIT of a planet, asteroid, comet or spacecraft at which the body is nearest the Sun.

periodic table Arrangement of the chemical elements in order of their ATOMIC NUMBERS in accordance with the periodic law first stated by the Russian chemist Dmitri MENDELEYEV in 1869. In the modern form of the table, the elements are arranged into 18 vertical columns and seven horizontal **periods**. The vertical columns containing groups are numbered I to VII (sometimes called IA to VIIA) with a final column numbered 0. The metallic TRANSITION ELEMENTS are arranged in the middle of the table between groups II and III. ALKALI METALS are in Group I and ALKALINE-EARTH METALS in Group II. Metalloids and non-metals are found from groups III to VII, with the HALOGENS in Group VII and the NOBLE GASES (inert gases) collected into Group 0. The elements in each group have the same number of VALENCE electrons and accordingly have similar chemical properties. Elements in the same horizontal period have the same number of electron shells. *See p.640* for complete table

peripheral nervous system All parts of the nervous system that lie outside the CENTRAL NERVOUS SYSTEM (brain and spinal cord). It comprises the 12 pairs of cranial nerves that principally serve the head and neck region, and 31 pairs of spinal nerves with their fibres extending to the farthermost parts of the body.

periscope Optical instrument consisting of a series of mirrors or prisms that allows a person to view the surroundings from a concealed position by changing the

KEY

atomic number	→ 43
atomic symbol	**Tc**
name of element	Technetium
relative atomic mass (r.a.m.) (most stable isotope in brackets)	[97]

Periodic Table

Columns are labelled by Group (GROUP I, II, III, IV, V, VI, VII, 0), with the transition-metal block between Groups II and III.

GROUP I	II											III	IV	V	VI	VII	0
1 **H** Hydrogen 1.00794																	2 **He** Helium 4.0026
3 **Li** Lithium 6.941	4 **Be** Beryllium 9.0122											5 **B** Boron 10.81	6 **C** Carbon 12.011	7 **N** Nitrogen 14.0067	8 **O** Oxygen 15.9994	9 **F** Fluorine 18.998	10 **Ne** Neon 20.179
11 **Na** Sodium 22.9898	12 **Mg** Magnesium 24.305											13 **Al** Aluminium 26.9815	14 **Si** Silicon 28.086	15 **P** Phosphorus 30.9738	16 **S** Sulphur 32.06	17 **Cl** Chlorine 35.453	18 **Ar** Argon 39.948
19 **K** Potassium 39.098	20 **Ca** Calcium 40.06	21 **Sc** Scandium 44.956	22 **Ti** Titanium 47.90	23 **V** Vanadium 50.941	24 **Cr** Chromium 51.996	25 **Mn** Manganese 54.9380	26 **Fe** Iron 55.847	27 **Co** Cobalt 58.9332	28 **Ni** Nickel 58.70	29 **Cu** Copper 63.546	30 **Zn** Zinc 65.38	31 **Ga** Gallium 69.72	32 **Ge** Germanium 72.59	33 **As** Arsenic 74.9216	34 **Se** Selenium 78.96	35 **Br** Bromine 79.904	36 **Kr** Krypton 83.80
37 **Rb** Rubidium 85.4678	38 **Sr** Strontium 87.62	39 **Y** Yttrium 88.906	40 **Zr** Zirconium 91.22	41 **Nb** Niobium 92.906	42 **Mo** Molybdenum 95.94	43 **Tc** Technetium [97]	44 **Ru** Ruthenium 101.07	45 **Rh** Rhodium 102.905	46 **Pd** Palladium 106.4	47 **Ag** Silver 107.868	48 **Cd** Cadmium 112.40	49 **In** Indium 114.82	50 **Sn** Tin 118.69	51 **Sb** Antimony 121.75	52 **Te** Tellurium 127.75	53 **I** Iodine 126.9045	54 **Xe** Xenon 131.30
55 **Cs** Caesium 132.905	56 **Ba** Barium 137.34	57–71 Lanthanide Series	72 **Hf** Hafnium 178.49	73 **Ta** Tantalum 180.948	74 **W** Tungsten 183.85	75 **Re** Rhenium 186.207	76 **Os** Osmium 190.2	77 **Ir** Iridium 192.22	78 **Pt** Platinum 195.09	79 **Au** Gold 196.9665	80 **Hg** Mercury 200.59	81 **Tl** Thallium 204.37	82 **Pb** Lead 207.2	83 **Bi** Bismuth 208.98	84 **Po** Polonium [209]	85 **At** Astatine [210]	86 **Rn** Radon [222]
87 **Fr** Francium [223]	88 **Ra** Radium [226]	89–103 Actinide Series	104 **Db** Dubnium [261]	105 **Ha** Hahnium [262]	106 **Sg** Seaborgium [263]	107 **Uns** Unnilseptium [262]	108 **Uno** Unniloctium [265]	109 **Une** Unnilennium [266]									

LANTHANIDE SERIES (rare earth elements)

57 **La** Lanthanum 138.9055	58 **Ce** Cerium 140.12	59 **Pr** Praseodymium 140.9077	60 **Nd** Neodymium 144.24	61 **Pm** Promethium [145]	62 **Sm** Samarium 150.36	63 **Eu** Europium 151.96	64 **Gd** Gadolinium 157.25	65 **Tb** Terbium 158.9254	66 **Dy** Dysprosium 162.50	67 **Ho** Holmium 164.9308	68 **Er** Erbium 167.26	69 **Tm** Thulium 168.9342	70 **Yb** Ytterbium 173.04	71 **Lu** Lutetium 174.97

ACTINIDE SERIES (radioactive rare earth elements)

89 **Ac** Actinium [227]	90 **Th** Thorium 232.0381	91 **Pa** Protactinium 231.0359	92 **U** Uranium 238.029	93 **Np** Neptunium 237.0482	94 **Pu** Plutonium [244]	95 **Am** Americium [243]	96 **Cm** Curium [247]	97 **Bk** Berkelium [247]	98 **Cf** Californium [251]	99 **Es** Einsteinium [254]	100 **Fm** Fermium [257]	101 **Md** Mendelevium [256]	102 **No** Nobelium [254]	103 **Lr** Lawrencium [256]

direction of the observer's line of sight. It is most commonly associated with SUBMARINES.

peristalsis Series of wave-like movements that propel food through the gut or digestive tract. It is caused by contractions of the INVOLUNTARY MUSCLE of the gut wall. The reverse process, antiperistalsis, produces vomiting.

peritoneum Strong membrane of CONNECTIVE TISSUE that lines the body's abdominal wall and covers the abdominal organs. *See also* PERITONITIS

peritonitis Inflammation of the PERITONEUM. It may be caused by bacterial infection or chemical irritation, or it may arise spontaneously in certain diseases. Symptoms include fever, abdominal pain, distension and shock. Treatment is directed at the underlying cause.

periwinkle Any of several species of trailing or erect evergreen plants that are cultivated as ground cover and for hanging baskets. Family Apocynaceae.

periwinkle (winkle) Any of several marine snails, gastropod molluscs that live in clusters along marine shores. A herbivore, it nestles in cracks among rocks. Many are edible. Length: to 2.5cm (1in). Family Littorinidæ; genus *Littorina*.

permafrost Land that is permanently frozen, often to a considerable depth. The top few inches generally thaw in the summer, but the meltwater is not able to sink into the ground because of the frozen subsoil. *See also* TUNDRA

permeability (symbol μ) In physics, ratio of the MAGNETIC FLUX density in a body to the external MAGNETIC FIELD inducing it. The permeability of free space is called the **magnetic constant** (symbol μ_0) and has the value $4\pi \times 10^{-7}$ henry per metre. The **relative** permeability of a substance (symbol μ_r) is the ratio of its permeability to the magnetic constant.

Permian Geological period of the PALAEOZOIC era lasting from 286 to 248 million years ago. There was widespread geologic uplift and periods of glaciation in the southern continents. Many groups of marine invertebrate animals became extinct during the period.

permittivity (symbol ε) In physics, the dielectric property of a material. It is the ratio of the electric flux density (displacement) in a medium to the intensity of the ELECTRIC FIELD causing it. The permittivity of free space is called the **electric constant** (symbol ε_0). The **relative** permittivity of a medium is the ratio $\varepsilon/\varepsilon_0$. It is the ratio of the CAPACITANCE of a capacitor (condenser) in which the material is the dielectric to its capacitance with a vacuum between the capacitor's plates.

Perón, Eva Duarte de (1919–52) Argentine political leader, second wife of Juan PERÓN. Known as "Evita", she administered Argentina's social welfare agencies and was the country's chief labour mediator. Eva's popularity contributed to the longevity of the Peronist regime.

Perón, Juan Domingo (1895–1974) Argentine statesman, president (1946–55, 1973–74). An army officer, he became the leading figure in the military junta (1943–46). Perón cultivated the trade unions and earned support from the poor by social reforms, greatly assisted by his wife "Evita" PERÓN. He won the 1946 presidential election and was re-elected in 1952. Perón's populist programme was basically nationalist and totalitarian. Changing economic circumstances and the death of his wife reduced Perón's popularity, and he was overthrown in 1955. He retired to Spain, but returned to regain the presidency. His second term, marked by violence, was cut short by his death.

perpendicular style Final period of English GOTHIC ARCHITECTURE, from *c.*1330 to the mid-16th century. Named after the strong vertical lines of its window tracery

and panelling, it had fan vaulting and flattened arches. *See also* DECORATED STYLE; EARLY ENGLISH; VAULT

perpetual motion Hypothetical machine that continues to work without any energy being supplied. It would require either the complete elimination of FRICTION or would violate the laws of THERMODYNAMICS.

Perrault, Charles (1628–1703) French poet and prose writer. A leading member of the Académie Française, he is best remembered for *Tales of Mother Goose* (1697).

Perry, Fred (Frederick John) (1909–95) English table-tennis and tennis player. World table-tennis champion in 1929, Perry won three successive Wimbledon tennis singles titles (1934–36). He also won the US, French and Australian titles.

Perry, Matthew Calbraith (1794–1858) US naval officer. In 1837 he commanded the first steam vessel in the US Navy, the *Fulton*. Perry also organized the first naval engineer corps. He was responsible for opening up Japan to the West (1853–54).

Persephone In Greek mythology, goddess of spring. She was the daughter of ZEUS and the Earth goddess DEMETER. When Persephone was abducted by HADES, famine spread over the Earth. To prevent catastrophe, Zeus commanded Hades to release her. He did so, and thus each year spring returns to the Earth. Persephone was known as Proserpine to the Romans.

Persepolis City of ancient Persia (Iran), *c.*60km (35mi) NE of SHIRAZ. Capital (539–330 BC) of the ACHAEMENID empire, it was renowned for its splendour. It was destroyed by the forces of ALEXANDER THE GREAT in 330 BC.

Perseus In astronomy, a prominent northern constellation. Perseus is a rich constellation, crossed by the Milky Way.

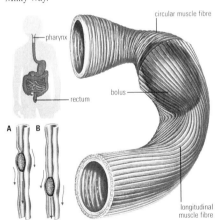

▲ **peristalsis** The digestive tract can be regarded as a long muscular tube extending from the pharynx to the rectum. The walls of the tube bear an inner, circular muscle fibre coat and an outer, longitudinal muscle fibre coat. As the ball of food (bolus) formed in the mouth enters the pharynx, a reflex action is initiated. This produces slow, wave-like contractions of the walls of the esophagus and later along the whole length of the tract. These peristaltic waves involve the contraction of the circular muscle fibres behind the bolus (A) and their relaxation in front of the bolus. Longitudinal muscles provide the wave-like action. The two functions together push the ball down the tract (B). The whole process of peristalsis is an involuntary response.

Perseus In Greek mythology, son of Danaë and ZEUS. Perseus beheaded the snake-haired gorgon, MEDUSA, turned ATLAS to stone and rescued the princess, ANDROMEDA, from being sacrificed to a sea monster.

Pershing, John Joseph (1860–1948) US general. Pershing led a punitive expedition against Pancho VILLA in Mexico (1916) before being appointed to command the American Expeditionary Force (AEF) in World War 1 (1917–19). Returning a hero, he later served as army chief of staff (1921–24). A US surface-to-surface nuclear missile is named after him.

Persia Former name of IRAN, in SW Asia. The earliest empire in the region was that of Media (c.700–549 BC). It was overthrown by the Persian king, CYRUS THE GREAT, who established the much larger ACHAEMENID dynasty (c.550–330 BC), destroyed by ALEXANDER THE GREAT. Alexander's successors, comprising the SELEUCIDS, were replaced by people from PARTHIA in the 3rd century BC. The Persian SASSANID dynasty was established by Ardashir I in AD 224. Weakened from defeat by the Byzantines under HERACLIUS, it was overrun by the Arabs in the 7th century.

Persian (Farsi) Official language of IRAN. It is spoken by nearly all of Iran's population as a first or second language. It is also widely used in Afghanistan. Persian belongs to the Indo-Iranian family of INDO-EUROPEAN LANGUAGES. Persian has borrowed from ARABIC and is written in the Arabic script.

Persian art Earliest manifestations of art in Persia (Iran) prior to the 7th-century development of ISLAMIC ART AND ARCHITECTURE. The oldest pottery and engraved seals date back to c.3500 BC. The greatest achievements of Persian art occurred during the rule of the ACHAEMENID (c.550–330 BC) and SASSANID (AD 224–642) dynasties. The former is best represented by the low relief carvings and massive gateway figures executed for the palace of Darius at PERSEPOLIS. The Sassanians excelled at metalwork and sculpture.

Persian Gulf (Arabian Gulf) Arm of the Arabian Sea between the Arabian mainland and the Asian mainland, and connected to it by the Strait of Hormuz and the Gulf of Oman. Britain had achieved supremacy in the Gulf by the mid-19th century. The discovery of oil in the 1930s increased its importance, and (after British withdrawal in the 1960s) both the USA and the Soviet Union sought to increase their influence. Tension was heightened by the IRAN-IRAQ WAR in the 1980s and the GULF WAR against Iraq in 1991. The Gulf is a major shipping and oil supply route. Area: c.240,000sq km (93,000sq mi).

Persian mythology, ancient Beliefs of the Persian people c.500 BC. The oldest Persian deity was MITRA, who was identified with the Sun. He was a god of courage and enlightenment and led the chariot of the Sun across the sky on its daily journey. Mitra was associated with Anahita, the goddess of water and of fertility. In the Zoroastrian period, he became subordinate to AHURA MAZDAH, who was worshipped by the ACHAEMENID kings of Persia as the creator and ruler of the world. Ahura Mazdah was engaged in an eternal conflict with AHRIMAN, the principle of evil. At a later period both Ahura Mazdah and Ahriman were regarded as the twin offspring of Zurvan (Time). Their cosmic struggle would end ultimately with the victory of Ahura Mazdah.

Persian Wars (499–479 BC) Conflict between the ancient Greeks and Persians. In 499 BC, the IONIAN cities of Asia Minor rebelled against Persian rule. Athens sent a fleet to aid them. Having crushed the rebellion, the Persian emperor, DARIUS I, invaded Greece but was defeated at MARATHON (490 BC). In 480 BC, his successor, XERXES, burned Athens but withdrew after defeats at SALAMIS and PLATAEA (479 BC). Under Athenian leadership, the Greeks regained territory in Thrace and Anatolia until the PELOPONNESIAN WARS (431 BC).

persimmon Any of several trees of the genus *Diospyros* that produce reddish-orange fruit that is sour and astringent until ripe. Species include the North American persimmon (*D. virginiana*) and the Japanese persimmon (*D. kaki*). Family Ebenaceae.

personality Emotional, attitudinal and behavioural characteristics that distinguish an individual. Psychologists use the term to refer to enduring, long-term characteristics of a person. Personality traits are assessed by a variety of methods, including personality tests and projective techniques. Influential theories of personality in psychology include Sigmund FREUD's PSYCHOANALYSIS, JUNG's theories of personality types, and social theories, which examine the influence of the environment on personality.

perspective Method of showing three-dimensional objects and spatial relationships in a two-dimensional image. The linear perspective system is based on the idea that parallel lines converge at a vanishing point as they recede into the distance. It was outlined in the 15th century by BRUNELLESCHI and developed by MASACCIO and UCCELLO.

perspiration *See* SWEATING

Perth City on the Swan River, SW Australia; capital of Western Australia. Founded in 1829, the city grew rapidly after the discovery of gold at Coolgardie in the 1890s, the development of the port at Fremantle, and the construction of railways in the early 20th century. Industries: textiles, cement. Pop. (1993 est.) 1,221,200.

Peru Republic in W South America. Peru can be divided into three geographical areas. Along the Pacific coast lies a narrow strip of desert. Peru's major urban areas, such as the capital LIMA, are situated beside oases. The centre is dominated by three ranges of the ANDES Mountains. In the foothills of the Cordillera Occidental lies Peru's second-largest city, AREQUIPA. The range includes Peru's highest peak, Mount Huascarán, at 6,768m (22,205ft). The Cordillera Central merges into the Cordillera Oriental, site of CUZCO and the INCA ruins of MACHU PICCHU. Between the E and W ranges lies the Altiplano Plateau, home of many lakes, including Lake TITICACA. In the E lie forested highlands and the lowlands of the AMAZON basin. **Climate** Lima has an arid climate. EL NIÑO brings infrequent violent storms. Inland, there is more frequent precipitation. The E is hot and rainy. **Vegetation** The coastal desert oases form Peru's major growing region. Mountain grassland lies on the higher slopes of the Andes. The E is a region of *selva*, tropical rainforest with trees such as rosewood and rubber. Here the major crop is coca. **History and politics** Native American civilizations developed more than 10,000 years ago. By c.AD 1200, the Inca had established a capital at Cuzco. By 1500, their empire extended from Ecuador to Chile. In 1532, the Spanish conquistador, Francisco PIZARRO, captured the Inca ruler ATAHUALPA. By 1533, Pizarro had conquered most of Peru; he founded Lima in 1535. In 1544, Lima became capital of Spain's South American empire. Spain's rule caused frequent

PERU
AREA: 1,285,220sq km (496,223sq mi)
POPULATION: 26,276,000
CAPITAL (POPULATION): Lima (6,601,000)

native revolts, such as that of TUPAC AMARU. In 1820, José de SAN MARTÍN captured coastal Peru. In 1821, Peru declared independence. Spain still held much of the interior, but Simón BOLÍVAR completed the liberation by 1826. In the War of the Pacific (1879–84) Peru lost some of its s provinces to Bolivia. The early 20th century was characterized by dictatorship and the growing gap between a wealthy oligarchy and the poverty of the native population. From 1968 to 1980, a military junta tried to carry out democratic reforms. Austerity measures, introduced by the civilian government during the 1980s, caused civil unrest. *Sendero Luminoso* (Shining Path) and the Tupac Amaru Revolutionary Movement (MRTA) have waged an insurgency campaign that has claimed more than 30,000 lives. In 1990, Alberto Fujimori was elected on a platform of tough anti-terrorist policies. In 1992, he suspended the constitution and dismissed parliament. The guerrilla movements' leaders were captured. In 1993, a new constitution was introduced. In 1995, Fujimori was re-elected. In December 1996, MRTA guerrillas captured the Japanese embassy in Lima. The four month-long siege ended when the army stormed the complex killing all the guerrillas. In 1998, Peru and Ecuador signed a peace agreement resolving a protracted border dispute. In 2000, Fujimori stood down following a series of corruption scandals and fresh elections were called for. Valentin Paniagua was appointed interim president. **Economy** Peru is a lower-middle-income developing country (1995 GDP per capita, US$3,770). Agriculture employs 35% of the workforce. Major crops include beans, maize, potatoes and rice. Coffee, cotton and sugar cane are major exports. Peru lands the world's third-largest fish catch and is the eighth-largest producer of copper ore. Since 1990 Fujimori's regime has instigated a number of free-market reforms that have reduced inflation and foreign debt.

Perugia City on the River Tiber, central Italy; capital of Perugia province. A major Etruscan city, Perugia passed to Rome in 310 BC. In the 6th century AD, it was captured by the Lombards and became a duchy. For centuries, Perugia was the scene of various power struggles before being subdued by the papacy in 1540. In 1860 it was incorporated into a united Italy. Perugia has always been the artistic centre of UMBRIA. The modern city's economy is based on tourism and commerce. It is also renowned for its chocolate. Pop. (1996) 151,000.

Perugino, Pietro Vannucci (1445–1523) Italian painter, an important figure in the art of the early RENAISSANCE. Perugino was a notable fresco painter. His *Christ Delivering the Keys to St Peter* (1481–82), painted for the Sistine Chapel, did much to establish his reputation.

Peshawar City in NW Pakistan, 16km (9mi) E of the KHYBER PASS. Brought under Muslim rule in the 10th century, it fell to the Afghans in the 16th century. Conquered by the Sikhs in 1834, it was annexed by Britain in 1849. In 1948 it became part of Pakistan. In the 1980s and 1990s it was a base for rebel groups operating in Afghanistan. The modern city is famous for handicrafts, carpets and leather goods. Industries: textiles, chemicals, paper. Pop. (1993) 1,676,000.

Pestalozzi, Johann Heinrich (1746–1827) Swiss educational reformer whose theories formed the basis of modern elementary education. His books include *How Gertrude Teaches Her Children* (1801).

pesticide Chemical substance that is used to kill insects, rodents, weeds and other pests. Among pesticides, a HERBICIDE is used for weeds, an INSECTICIDE for insects and a FUNGICIDE for fungal pests. Pesticides are usually harmful chemicals and an important factor in

their manufacture is that they should decompose after they have performed their function. Some previously common pesticides, such as DDT, have been shown to be too toxic and long-lasting, so their use is now restricted.

Pétain, Henri Philippe (1856–1951) French general and political leader. In World War 1 his defence of VERDUN (1916) made him a national hero. In 1917, Pétain was appointed commander-in-chief. He held high positions between the wars. With the defeat of France in 1940, Pétain was recalled as prime minister. He signed the surrender and became head of the collaborationist VICHY regime. He was charged with treason after the liberation of France in 1945 and died in prison.

petal Part of a flower. The petals of a flower are together known as the corolla. Surrounded by SEPALS, flower petals are often brightly coloured and may secrete nectar and perfume to attract the insects and birds necessary for cross-pollination. Once fertilization occurs, the petals usually drop off.

Peter, Saint (d. *c*.64) APOSTLE of JESUS CHRIST. He was born Simon, son of Jonas, and was a fisherman from Bethsaida on the Sea of Galilee. He and his brother, ANDREW, were called by Jesus to be disciples. Jesus gave Simon the name Peter (John 1:42). Peter was one of Jesus' closest and most loyal associates. With James and John, he witnessed the Transfiguration. While Jesus was on trial before the SANHEDRIN, Peter denied knowing him three times, just as Jesus had predicted. After Jesus' ascension, Peter was the first publicly to preach Christianity in Jerusalem. He took Christianity to Samaria. Imprisoned by King Herod, he was allegedly rescued by an angel of the Lord. In his final years, he seems to have left Jerusalem and undertaken a missionary journey. Roman Catholic theology accepts him as the first head of the Church and the first bishop of Rome, from whom the popes claim succession. His feast day is 29 June.

Peter I (the Great) (1672–1725) Russian tsar (1682–1725), regarded as the founder of modern Russia. After ruling jointly with his half-brother Ivan (1682–89), he gained sole control in 1689. Peter employed foreign experts to modernize the army, transport and technology, visiting European countries to study developments. He compelled the aristocracy and the church to serve the interests of the state, eliminating ancient tradition in favour of modernization. In the Great NORTHERN WAR, Russia replaced Sweden as the dominant power in N Europe and gained lands on the Baltic, where Peter built his new capital, ST PETERSBURG. In the E, he warred against Turks and Persians and initiated the exploration of Siberia.

Peter III (1728–62) Russian tsar (1762). During his six-month reign, he returned East Prussia voluntarily to FREDERICK II, whom he admired, thus losing all the territory that Russia had gained during the SEVEN YEARS' WAR. Peter was dethroned and murdered in a conspiracy led by the brothers Orlov and probably encouraged by his wife and successor, CATHERINE II (THE GREAT).

Peter I (1844–1921) King of Serbia (1903–21). He was brought up in exile and educated in France while the Obrenović dynasty ruled Serbia. He was elected king when his father, ALEXANDER Obrenović, was assassinated. He became the first king of the new kingdom of Serbs, Croats and Slovenes (later known as Yugoslavia) in 1918.

Peter II (1923–70) Last king of Yugoslavia (1934–41). He succeeded to the throne at the age of 11. The actual ruler was his uncle, Prince Paul, who was deposed in 1941 by a military coup. Peter ruled for a month until the invasion of the AXIS POWERS, when he fled to London. After the monarchy was abolished in 1945, he settled in the USA.

Peterloo Massacre (1819) Violent suppression of a political protest in Manchester, England. A large crowd demonstrating for reform of Parliament was dispersed by soldiers. Eleven people were killed and 500 injured.

Petipa, Marius (1819–1910) Russian BALLET dancer and choreographer. He rose to fame in 1847 as principal dancer at the Maryinski Theatre, St Petersburg, and was choreographer of the Imperial Russian Ballet (1862–1903). His *Don Quixote* (1869), *Sleeping Beauty* (1890) and *Raymonda* (1898) laid the foundations of classical ballet. *See also* KIROV BALLET

petition of right Means by which an English subject could sue the crown; in particular, the statement of grievances against the crown presented by Parliament to CHARLES I in 1628. It asserted that the crown acted illegally in raising taxation without Parliament's consent, imprisoning people without charge, maintaining a standing army, and quartering soldiers on ordinary householders. It led to the dissolution of Parliament and Charles' period of untrammelled rule.

Petőfi, Sándor (1823–49) Hungarian poet. His work includes *János the Hero* (1845) and a novel, *A Hóhér Kötele* (1845). His poetry inspired the patriots of the Hungarian revolution of 1848, in which he was killed.

Petra Ancient city in what is now sw Jordan. It was the capital of the Nabataean kingdom from the 4th century BC. It was captured by the Romans in the 2nd century AD. The city, which was rediscovered in 1812 and is the scene of extensive excavation, can be reached only through narrow gorges. Many of its remarkable, ruined houses, temples, theatres and tombs were cut from the high, pinkish sandstone cliffs that protected it.

Petrarch, Francesco (1304–74) Italian lyric poet and scholar. Most of his lyric poems, *Rime sparse*, have as their subject "Laura", a woman idealized in the style of earlier poets but seen in a more realistic and human light. Other works, which include an autobiography (1342–58), further illuminate his belief in the compatibility of classical and Christian traditions.

petrel Any of several small oceanic birds related to the ALBATROSS. Most of them nest in colonies and fly over open water, feeding on squid and small fish. They have webbed feet and tubular nostrils. Length: to 42cm (16in). Order Procellariiformes.

Petrie, Sir William Matthew Flinders (1853–1942) English archaeologist and Egyptologist. He established the system of sequence dating for excavating sites layer by layer. In 1894, Petrie founded the Egypt Research Account, later known as the British School of Archaeology in Egypt. His most important excavations were at Memphis.

petrification Fossilizing process in which organic material (such as wood) changes into stone. Petrification is caused by mineral-rich water seeping into the empty spaces of dead, buried trees or animals. Examples include the Petrified Forest, Arizona, USA.

petrochemical Chemical substance derived from PETROLEUM or NATURAL GAS. The refining of petroleum is undertaken on a large scale not only for fuels but also for a wide range of chemicals. These chemicals include ALKANES (paraffins) and ALKENES (olefins), BENZENE, TOLUENE, NAPHTHALENE and their derivatives.

petrol (gasoline) Major HYDROCARBON fuel, a mixture consisting mainly of hexane, octane and heptane. One of the products of OIL refining, petrol is extracted from crude oil (PETROLEUM). Most modern cars have high-compression INTERNAL COMBUSTION ENGINES, and the mixture of air and petrol vapour supplied to it can explode too quickly,

pushing against a rising instead of a descending piston. This effect is known as engine KNOCK, and to eliminate it many petrol manufacturers add lead(IV) tetraethyl to slow the rate of combustion. However, this additive has been found to be implicated in atmospheric pollution and causes brain damage, and so many manufacturers omit the additive and instead improve the OCTANE NUMBER of the petrol by altering the mixture of hydrocarbons.

petrol engine Most common type of INTERNAL COMBUSTION ENGINE.

petroleum (crude OIL) FOSSIL FUEL that is chemically a complex mixture of HYDROCARBONS. It accumulates in underground deposits and the chemical composition of petroleum strongly suggests that it originated from the bodies of long-dead organisms, particularly marine PLANKTON. Petroleum is rarely found at the original site of formation, but migrates laterally and vertically until it is trapped. Most petroleum is extracted via oil wells from reservoirs in the Earth's crust sealed by upfolds of impermeable rock or by salt domes which form traps. In the first stage of petroleum refining, the heavier hydrocarbons, which usually have higher boiling points than lighter ones, are distilled. The next stage is CRACKING, which breaks the heavy hydrocarbons down into more economically useful products, such as PETROL and PARAFFIN. Purification of the various products to remove impurities, such as SULPHUR and NITROGEN compounds, completes the refining process. The most versatile end products are ETHENE and PROPENE, which are widely used in the plastics and chemical industries. *See also* NATURAL GAS

petrology Study of rocks, including their origin, chemical composition and location. Formation of the three classes of rocks – IGNEOUS (of volcanic origin); SEDIMENTARY (deposited by water); METAMORPHIC (either of the other two changed by temperature and pressure) – is studied.

Petronius (d. *c.*AD 66) Roman writer, assumed author of the *Satyricon*, a humorous tale giving vivid glimpses of contemporary society. He committed suicide when accused of plotting against Emperor NERO.

petunia Genus of flowering plants of the NIGHTSHADE family that originated in Argentina, and the common name for any of the varieties that are popular as bedding plants. Most varieties derive from the white flowered *Petunia axillaris* and the violet-red *P. integrifolia*; they may be erect, shrubby or pendant. The bell-shaped flowers have five petals of almost any colour. Family Solanaceae.

Pevsner, Antoine (1886–1962) French sculptor, b. Russia, brother of Naum GABO. He was initially influenced by CUBISM, but later became a leading exponent of CONSTRUCTIVISM, creating works in bronze and other materials. In the 1930s, he concentrated on NON-FIGURATIVE structures such as *Projections in Space*. Later work include *Monument Symbolizing the Liberation of the Spirit* (1956).

Pevsner, Sir Nikolaus Bernhard Leon (1902–86) British art historian, b. Russia. His best-known works are *An Outline of European Architecture* and the monumental 46-volume series *The Buildings of England* (1951–74).

pewter Any of several silver-coloured, soft ALLOYS that consist mainly of tin and antimony. Lead was formerly used for its hardness, but because of its toxicity it was replaced by antimony. Modern pewter consists usually of *c.*92% tin, *c.*5% antimony and *c.*3% copper.

peyote (mescal) Either of two species of cactus of the genus *Laphophora* that grow in the USA. The soft-stemmed *L. williamsii* has pink or white flowers in summer and a blue-green stem. *L. diffusa* has white or yellow flowers. Peyote contains many ALKALOIDS, the principal one being MESCALINE, a hallucinogenic drug.

Pfeiffer, Michelle (1957–) US film actress. She first gained attention for her performance in *Witches of Eastwick* (1987). Pfeiffer received an Academy nomination for best supporting actress in *Dangerous Liaisons* (1988). She gained further nominations for lead performances in *The Fabulous Baker Boys* (1989) and *Love Field* (1992). Other films include *Frankie and Johnny* (1991), *Batman Returns* (1992) and *The Age of Innocence* (1993).

pH Numerical scale that indicates the acidity or alkalinity of a solution. The pH value measures the concentration of hydrogen ions. The scale (introduced in 1909) runs from 0 to 14. A solution is acidic if the pH is less than 7 and alkaline if greater than 7. *See also* ACID; ALKALI; BASE

Phaedra In Greek mythology, the daughter of MINOS and the wife of THESEUS. She fell in love with her stepson HIPPOLYTUS. When Hippolytus spurned her advances, Phaedra accused him of raping her. Theseus condemned him to death and Phaedra hanged herself.

phaeophyte Any member of the phylum Phaeophyta, which consists of the brown ALGAE. Phaeophytes are part of the kingdom PROTOCTISTA. Classified by some biologists as plants, the simple organisms belonging to this group are mostly marine, found mainly in the intertidal zone of rocky shores. They include familiar seaweeds such as *Fucus* (wracks) and *Ascophyllum* (bladderwrack). The largest, *Macrocystis*, grows to more than 100m (320ft) at up to 0.5m (18in) per day. *Sargassum* forms vast floating masses in the Sargasso Sea in the mid-Atlantic, with their own distinctive communities of animals and microorganisms.

Phaethon In Greek mythology, son of HELIOS, the Sun god. He drove his father's Sun chariot across the sky but lost control of the horses, setting the Earth on fire as he approached too close. To save the world, ZEUS struck him from the reins with a thunderbolt.

phagocyte Type of LEUCOCYTE (white blood cell) able to engulf other cells, such as bacteria. It digests them in the defence of the body against infection.

phalanger (possum) Any of *c*.45 species of mainly nocturnal, arboreal MARSUPIALS of Australasia. It has opposable digits for grasping branches, and the tail is long and prehensile. Family Phalangeridae.

pharaoh Title of the rulers of ancient EGYPT. Though loosely applied to all Egyptian kings, the title was only adopted during the New Kingdom. The pharaoh was considered divine, an incarnation of the god HORUS.

Pharisees Members of a conservative Jewish religious group, prominent in ancient Palestine from the 2nd century BC to the time of the destruction of the second TEMPLE in Jerusalem (AD 70). They were a political party opposed to the pagan influences of their Greek and Roman conquerors, but by New Testament times were largely nonpolitical. They were the founders of orthodox JUDAISM and were often in conflict with the SADDUCEES.

pharmacology Study of the properties of DRUGS and their effects on the body. *See also* PHARMACOPOEIA

pharmacopoeia Reference book listing drugs and other preparations in medical use. Included are details of their formulae, dosages, routes of administration, known side-effects and precautions. A pharmacopoeia from 1st century BC China lists more than 30 drugs. In *c*.AD 60 Dioscorides produced *De materia medica*, the first Western pharmacopoeia.

Pharos Island off N Egypt, in the Mediterranean, connected to the mainland by a causeway built by ALEXANDER THE GREAT. A lighthouse was completed by Ptolemy II in *c*.280 BC and was considered one of the SEVEN WONDERS OF THE WORLD. According to writers of the

time, it was *c*.135m (450ft) tall and its light could be seen 65km (40mi) away. It was destroyed by an earthquake in 1346. Pharos is now part of the city of ALEXANDRIA.

pharynx Cavity at the back of the nose and mouth that extends down toward the OESOPHAGUS and TRACHEA. Inflammation of the pharynx, usually caused by viral or bacterial infection, is known as pharyngitis.

phase Proportion of the illuminated hemisphere of a body in the Solar System (in particular the Moon) as seen from Earth. The phase of a body changes as the Sun and the Earth change their relative positions. The phases of the Moon are new, crescent, half, gibbous and full.

phase In physics, a stage or fraction in the cycle of an oscillation, such as the wave motion of light or sound waves. This is usually measured from an arbitrary starting point or compared with another motion of the same frequency. Two waves are said to be "in phase" when their maximum and minimum values happen at the same time. If not, there is a "phase difference", as seen in INTERFERENCE phenomenon. Phase can also refer to any one of the states of MATTER.

pheasant Gamebird of the genus *Phasianus* native to Asia, introduced into Europe and North America. PEACOCKS and GUINEA FOWL belong to the same family. Males are showy, with brownish green, red and yellow feathers; females are smaller and brownish. Length: up to 89cm (35in). Family Phasianidae.

phenol Aromatic compound group whose members each have an attachment of a hydroxyl group to a carbon atom forming part of a BENZENE ring. The simplest of the family is also called phenol or **carbolic acid** (C_6H_5OH). Phenols are colourless liquids or white solids at room temperature. They are used for such products as aspirin, dyes, fungicides and explosives, and as a starting material for nylon and epoxy resins.

phenomenalism Philosophical proposition that human knowledge is restricted to the content of mental impressions. *See also* EMPIRICISM; EPISTEMOLOGY; MIND

phenomenology School of modern philosophy founded by Edmund HUSSERL and influential in the development of EXISTENTIALISM. Husserl argued that philosophy should focus on human consciousness. Objects of consciousness (phenomena) were always mediated by the conscious mind. In contrast to EMPIRICISM or deductive LOGIC, Husserl concentrated on the description of subjective experience through intuition rather than analysis. *See also* HEIDEGGER, MARTIN; SARTRE, JEAN-PAUL

phenotype Physical characteristics of an organism resulting from HEREDITY. Phenotype is distinct from GENOTYPE, since not all aspects of genetic make-up manifest themselves.

pheromone Substance secreted externally by certain animals that influences the behaviour of members of the same species. Common in mammals and insects, these substances are often sexual attractants. They may be part of urine, or secreted by specific glands.

Phidias (*c*.490–*c*.430 BC) Sculptor of ancient Greece. During his lifetime he was best known for two gigantic chryselephantine (gold and ivory) statues, one of Athena for the Parthenon and the other of Zeus for his temple at Olympia. The Zeus was one of the SEVEN WONDERS OF THE WORLD. He also worked on the Parthenon friezes.

Philadelphia City and port at the confluence of the Delaware and Schuylkill rivers, SE Pennsylvania, USA. The site was first settled by Swedes in the early 17th century. The city was founded by William PENN in 1681. By 1774, it was a major commercial, cultural and industrial centre of the American colonies and played an important part in their fight for independence. The CONTINENTAL CONGRESSES were held in the city and the DECLARATION OF INDEPENDENCE was signed here in 1776. The CONSTITUTIONAL CONVENTION met in Philadelphia and adopted the US Constitution in 1787. Philadelphia served as capital of the USA from 1790 to 1800. Industries: shipbuilding, textiles, chemicals. Pop. (1994) 1,524,249.

Philip, Saint (active 1st century AD) One of the original 12 APOSTLES of JESUS CHRIST. Philip came from Bethsaida, on the Sea of Galilee. Christian tradition says he preached in Asia Minor and met a martyr's death. His feast day is 3 May (in the West) or 14 November (in the East). He appears to be a different person from **Philip the Evangelist**, one of the seven DEACONS who aided the apostles. According to tradition, he became bishop of Tralles, now in Turkey. His feast day is 9 June.

Philip II (Augustus) (1165–1223) King of France (1180–1223). Greatest of the French medieval kings, he increased the royal domain by marriage, by exploiting his feudal rights, and by war. His main rival was HENRY II of England. Philip supported the rebellions of Henry's sons, fought a long war against RICHARD I, and during the reign of JOHN, occupied Normandy and Anjou. English efforts to regain them were defeated at Bouvines in 1214. Philip persecuted Jews and Christian heretics, joined the Third CRUSADE but swiftly withdrew, and opened the crusade against the ALBIGENSES in S France.

Philip IV (the Fair) (1268–1314) King of France (1285–1314). Partly to pay for wars against Flanders and England, he expelled the Jews (1306), confiscating their property. Claiming the right to tax the clergy involved him in a long and bitter quarrel with Pope BONIFACE VIII. He used assemblies later called the STATES GENERAL to popularize his case. After the death of Boniface (1303), Philip secured the election of a French pope, Clement V, based at Avignon. Philip expelled the Jews from France and suppressed the KNIGHTS TEMPLAR. *See also* AVIGNON PAPACY

Philip VI (1293–1350) King of France (1328–50). First of the house of VALOIS, he was chosen to succeed his cousin, CHARLES IV, in preference to the rival claimant, EDWARD III of England. After the outbreak of the HUNDRED YEARS WAR (1337), many of his vassals supported Edward. Philip suffered serious defeats in the naval battle of Sluys (1340) and at CRÉCY (1346).

Philip II (382–336 BC) King of Macedonia (359–336 BC). He conquered neighbouring tribes and extended his rule over the Greek states, defeating the Athenians at Chaeronea (338 BC) and gaining reluctant acknowledgment as king of Greece. Philip was preparing to attack the Persian empire when he was assassinated, leaving the task to his son, ALEXANDER THE GREAT.

Philip II (1527–98) King of Spain (1556–98), king of Portugal (1580–98). In 1554, he married MARY I of England. From his father, Emperor CHARLES V, Philip inherited Milan, Naples, Sicily, the Netherlands and Spain with its empire in the New World. War with France ended at Cateau-Cambrésis (1559), but the Revolt of the Netherlands began in 1566. A defender of Roman Catholicism, Philip launched the unsuccessful ARMADA of 1588 to crush the English who, as fellow Protestants, aided the Dutch.

Philip IV (1605–65) King of Spain, Naples and Sicily (1621–65), king of Portugal (as Philip III, 1621–40). Economic and social decline in Spain continued during Philip's reign. The THIRTY YEARS WAR ended disastrously for Spain. Portugal threw off Spanish rule (1640) and maintained independence in the ensuing war. Philip supported the arts, and VELÁZQUEZ was his court painter.

Philip V (1683–1746) King of Spain (1700–46). Because he was a grandson and possible successor of LOUIS XIV of France, his accession to the Spanish throne provoked the War of the SPANISH SUCCESSION. Philip was the first BOURBON king of Spain. By the Treaty of UTRECHT (1713), he kept the Spanish throne by exclusion from the succession in France and the loss of Spanish territories in Italy and the Netherlands.

Philip, Prince, Duke of Edinburgh (1921–) Husband of Queen ELIZABETH II of Britain and Prince Consort. He was born in Corfu, the son of Prince Andrew of Greece, and educated in Britain. He became a naturalized British citizen and took the surname Mountbatten. In 1947, he married Elizabeth after becoming the Duke of Edinburgh. In 1956, he launched the Duke of Edinburgh Award Scheme to encourage the leisure activities of young people.

Philippi Ancient city of E Macedonia. It was the site of the victory of Mark ANTONY and Octavian (later Emperor AUGUSTUS) over CASSIUS and BRUTUS, the assassins of Julius Caesar, in 42 BC. Philippi became the first European city to receive a Christian mission when visited by St Paul.

Philippines Republic in SE Asia, consisting of more than 7,000 islands, of which 1,000 are inhabited. LUZON and MINDANAO islands constitute more than 66% of land area. Around Manila Bay (Luzon) lies the capital, MANILA, and the second-largest city, QUEZON CITY. The islands are mainly mountainous with several active volcanoes, one of which is the highest peak, Mount Apo, at 2,954m (9,692ft). Narrow coastal plains give way to forested plateaux. Earthquakes are common. **Climate** The Philippines has a tropical climate, with high annual temperatures. The dry season runs from December to April. Much of the rainfall is due to typhoons. **Vegetation** Mangrove swamps line many coasts. More than 33% of the land is forested. Much of the land is fertile. **History and politics** Islam was introduced in the late 14th century. In 1521, the Portuguese navigator Ferdinand MAGELLAN landed near Cebu. In 1565, Spain began its conquest of the islands. In 1571, the Spanish founded Manila and named the archipelago *Filipinas*, after Philip II. It became a vital trading centre, subject to frequent attack from pirates. In 1896, the Filipinos revolted against Spanish rule and declared independence. In the SPANISH-AMERICAN WAR (1898), the USA defeated the Spanish navy in Manila Bay. Filipinos seized Luzon. Manila was captured with US help. In the Treaty of Paris (1898) the islands were ceded to the US. From 1899 to 1902, Filipinos fought against US control. In 1935, the Commonwealth of the Philippines was established. Manuel Luis QUEZON became the first president. In 1941, the Japanese invaded and captured Manila by 1942. General MACARTHUR was forced to withdraw and US forces were ousted from BATAAN. In 1944, the USA began to reclaim the islands. In 1946, the Philippines became an independent republic. The USA was granted a 99-year lease on military bases (subsequently reduced to 25 years from 1967). In 1965, Ferdinand MARCOS became president. Marcos' response to mounting civil unrest was brutal. In 1972, he declared martial law. In 1981, Marcos was re-elected amid charges of electoral fraud. In 1983, the leader of the opposition, Benigno Aquino, was assassinated. His widow, Cory AQUINO, succeeded him.

PHILIPPINES
AREA: 300,000sq km (115,300sq mi)
POPULATION: 77,473,000
CAPITAL (POPULATION): Manila (1,587,000)

Marcos claimed victory in 1986 elections but faced charges of electoral fraud. Cory Aquino launched a campaign of civil disobedience. The USA withdrew its support for the corrupt regime, and Marcos was forced into exile. Aquino's presidency was marred by attempted military coups. In 1992, Fidel Ramos succeeded Aquino as president. At the end of 1992 the USA closed its military bases. In 1996, an agreement was reached with the Moro National Liberation Front, ending 24 years of rebellion on Mindanao. It allowed the creation of a autonomous Muslim state. In 1998, the fragile cease-fire was broken and violence continues. In May 1998, Ramos was succeeded by the former vice-president, Joseph Estrada. In 2000, Estrada was impeached over charges of financial corruption. **Economy** The Philippines is a lower-middle-income developing country (1995 GDP per capita, US$2,850). The economy was not as badly affected as others by the regional economic crisis in 1998. The devaluation of the peso and an austerity package did much to cushion the fall. Agriculture employs 45% of the workforce. It is the world's second-largest producer of rice and the world's fourth-largest producer of bananas. The raising of livestock, forestry and fishing are important activities.

Philistine Member of a non-Semitic people who lived on the S coast of modern Israel, known as Philistia, from *c.*1200 BC. They clashed frequently with the Hebrews, until decisively defeated by King DAVID. Today, the term philistine may be applied to a person indifferent to culture.

philodendron Genus of evergreen plants native to tropical America. Philodendrons have shiny, heart-shaped leaves that are sometimes split. They are popular house plants. Height: 10cm–1.8m (4in–6ft). Family Araceae.

philology Study of both LANGUAGE and LITERATURE. In addition to PHONETICS, GRAMMAR and the structure of language, philology also includes textual criticism, ETYMOLOGY and the study of art, archaeology, religion and any system related to ancient or classical languages.

philosophy Study of the nature of reality, knowledge, ETHICS and existence by means of rational inquiry. The oldest known philosophical system is the Vedic system of India, which dates back to the middle of the 2nd millennium BC or earlier. Like other Eastern philosophies, it is founded upon a largely mystical view of the universe and is integrated with India's main religion, HINDUISM. From the 6th century BC, Chinese philosophy was largely dominated by CONFUCIANISM and TAOISM. Also in the 6th century, Western philosophy began among the Greeks with the work of THALES of Miletus. Later pre-Socratic philosophers included PYTHAGORAS, EMPEDOCLES, Anaxagoras, Parmenides, HERACLITUS, ZENO OF ELEA and DEMOCRITUS. Greek philosophy reached its high point with SOCRATES, who laid the foundations of ethics; PLATO, who developed a system of universal ideas; and ARISTOTLE, who founded the study of LOGIC. ZENO OF CITIUM evolved the influential school of STOICS, which contrasted with the system of EPICUREANISM, founded by EPICURUS. A dominant school of the early Christian era was NEOPLATONISM, founded by Plotinus in the 3rd century AD. The influence of Aristotle and other Greeks pervaded the thought of Muslim philosophers, such as AVICENNA and AVERRÖES, and the Spanish-born Jew, Moses MAIMONIDES. In the work of scholastic philosophers such as ABÉLARD, Albertus Magnus, Saint Thomas AQUINAS and WILLIAM OF OCCAM, philosophy became a branch of Christian theology. Modern scientific philosophy began in the 17th century with the work of DESCARTES. His faith in mathematics was taken up by LEIBNIZ. In England, HOBBES integrated his materialist world view with a social philosophy. In the

18th-century EMPIRICISM was developed by BERKELEY and HUME. The achievements of KANT in Germany and the French Encyclopedists were also grounded in science. In the 19th century, a number of diverging movements emerged, among them the classical IDEALISM of HEGEL, the DIALECTICAL MATERIALISM of MARX and ENGELS, the POSITIVISM of COMTE, and the work of KIERKEGAARD and NIETZSCHE, which emphasized the freedom of the individual. In the 20th century, dominant movements included EXISTENTIALISM, LOGICAL POSITIVISM, PHENOMENOLOGY and VITALISM. *See also* AESTHETICS; ANALYTIC PHILOSOPHY; ENLIGHTENMENT; EPISTEMOLOGY; LINGUISTIC PHILOSOPHY; LOGIC; MATERIALISM; METAPHYSICS; PRAGMATISM; SCHOLASTICISM; UTILITARIANISM

phlebitis Inflammation of the wall of a vein. It may be caused by infection, trauma, underlying disease or the presence of VARICOSE VEINS. Symptoms include localized swelling and redness. Treatment includes rest and anticoagulant therapy.

phloem Vascular tissue for distributing dissolved food materials in plants. Phloem tissue contains several types of cells. The most important are long, hollow cells called **sieve-tube** cells. Columns of sieve tubes are joined end to end, allowing passage of materials from cell to cell. The sieve tubes are closely associated with "**companion** cells" that have dense CYTOPLASM and many MITOCHONDRIA and are thought to produce the energy needed to transport the food substances (*see* ACTIVE TRANSPORT). Phloem may also contain fibres that help to support the tissue. *See also* XYLEM

phlogiston Odourless, colourless and weightless material believed by early scientists to be the source of all heat and fire. COMBUSTION was believed to involve the loss of phlogiston. The phlogiston theory was proved erroneous when the true nature of combustion was explained by Antoine LAVOISIER.

Phnom Penh (Phnum Pénh) Capital of Cambodia, in the S of the country, a port at the confluence of the rivers Mekong and Tonle Sap. Founded in the 14th century, the city was the capital of the Khmers after 1434. In 1865, it became the capital of Cambodia. Occupied by the Japanese during World War 2, it was extensively damaged during the Cambodian civil war. After the KHMER ROUGE took power in 1975, the population was drastically reduced when many of its inhabitants were forcibly removed to work in the countryside. Industries: rice milling, brewing, distilling. Pop. (1994 est.) 920,000.

phobia Irrational and uncontrollable fear that persists despite reassurance or contradictory evidence. Psychoanalytic theory suggests that phobias are actually symbolic subconscious fears and impulses. *See also* ANXIETY

Phobos Larger of the two SATELLITES of Mars, discovered in 1877 by Asaph Hall. It is a dark, irregular body, measuring $27 \times 22 \times 19$ km ($17 \times 14 \times 12$ mi). It may well be a captured asteroid.

Phoenicia Greek name for an ancient region bordering the E Mediterranean coast. The Phoenicians were related to the Canaanites. Famous as merchants and sailors, they never formed a single political unit, and Phoenicia was dominated by Egypt before *c.*1200 BC and by successive Near Eastern empires from the 9th century BC. The Phoenician city-states, such as TYRE, Sidon and BYBLOS, reached the peak of their prosperity in the intervening period, but the Phoenicians dominated trade in the Mediterranean throughout the Bronze Age. Expert navigators, they traded for tin in Britain and sailed as far as West Africa. The Phoenicians founded colonies in Spain and North Africa, notably CARTHAGE. In 332 BC, ALEXAN-

DER THE GREAT captured Tyre and subsumed Phoenicia into the Hellenistic empire.

Phoenician mythology Beliefs current in the Phoenician city-states of the E Mediterranean c.500 BC. The most ancient god was El, revered as the father of all gods and the creator of man. Closely related to the Hebrew YAHWEH, he was a remote, benevolent deity, usually depicted as an old man, but also noted for his sexual powers. BAAL, the storm god and the god of fertility, had lightning as his weapon and defended the divine order against the ever-present menace of Chaos. Anath, the goddess of love and war, was the consort of Baal. The goddess ASTARTE was subordinate to Anath.

Phoenix Capital of Arizona, USA, on Salt River. Founded in 1870, the city expanded after the river was used to irrigate the surrounding land. Phoenix became the capital in 1889. Its dry,sunny climate makes it a popular winter resort. Industries: computer parts, aircraft, fabricated metals, textiles. Pop. (1990) 983,403.

phoenix Mythological eagle-like bird linked with Sun-worship, especially in ancient Egypt. Of gold and scarlet plumage, only one phoenix could exist at a time, usually with a life span of c.500 years. When death approached, the phoenix built a nest of aromatic plant material and was then consumed by fire. From the ashes of the pyre rose a new phoenix.

pholidota Small order of mammals, containing only one genus, *Manis*, in the family Manidae; its members are called PANGOLINS. Some species are entirely toothless and feed almost exclusively on ants and termites.

phoneme Minimum unit of significant sound; a speech sound distinguishing meaning. The phonemes /p/ and /b/ distinguish "tap" from "tab".

phonetics Study of the sounds of speech, divided into three main branches: **articulatory** phonetics (how the speech organs produce sounds); **acoustic** phonetics (the physical nature of sounds, mainly using instrumental techniques); and **auditory** phonetics (how sounds are received by the ear and processed). Linguists have devised notation systems to allow the full range of possible human speech sounds to be represented. *See also* LINGUISTICS

phosgene (carbonyl chloride, $COCl_2$) Colourless, toxic gas. It was used as a poison gas in World War 1 but is now used in the manufacture of various dyestuffs and resins. Properties: b.p 8.2°C (46.8°F), m.p. –118°C (–180.5°F).

phosphate Chemical compounds derived from phosphoric acid (H_3PO_4). The use of phosphates as FERTILIZERS can cause environmental damage.

phosphor Substance capable of luminescence (storing energy and later releasing it as light). They are used in coating inside cathode-ray tubes and FLUORESCENT LAMPS.

phosphorescence Form of luminescence in which a substance emits light of one wavelength. Unlike FLUORESCENCE, it may persist for some time after the initial excitation. In biology, phosphorescence is the production of light by an organism without associated heat, as with a firefly. In warm climates, the sea often appears phosphorescent at night, as a result of the activities of millions of microscopic algae.

phosphoric acid Group of ACIDS. **Tetraoxophosphoric** acid (H_3PO_4, formerly orthophosphoric acid) is a colourless liquid obtained by the action of sulphuric acid on phosphate rock (calcium phosphate); it is used in fertilizers, soaps and detergents. **Metaphosphoric** acid (HPO_3) is obtained by heating tetraoxophosphoric acid; it is used as a dehydrating agent. **Heptaoxodiphosphoric** ($H_4P_2O_7$, formerly pyrophosphoric acid) is formed by moderately heating phosphoric acid or by

reacting phosphorus pentoxide (P_2O_5) with water; it is used as a catalyst and in metallurgy.

Phosphoros In Greek mythology, the light-bearer. The name is synonymous with Lucifer and the morning star, VENUS. Generally portrayed as a man bearing a torch, he was the herald and harbinger of the dawn.

phosphorus (symbol P) Common, non-metallic element of Group V of the periodic table, discovered by Hennig Brand in 1669. It occurs, as PHOSPHATES, in many minerals; APATITE is the chief source. The element is used in making PHOSPHORIC ACID for detergents and fertilizers. Small amounts are used in insecticides and in matches. Phosphorus exhibits ALLOTROPY. Properties: at.no. 15; r.a.m. 30.9738; r.d. 1.82 (white), 2.34 (red); m.p. 44.1°C (111.38°F) (white); b.p. 280°C (536°F) (white); most common isotope P^{31} (100%).

Photius (c.820–91) Patriarch of Constantinople. In 858, he was elected to succeed St Ignatius of Constantinople. In 862, Pope Nicholas I declared the election invalid. In 867, Photius summoned the Council of Constantinople and withdrew from communion with Rome and denounced the Filioque clause from the Creed. He is a saint in the ORTHODOX CHURCH. His feast day is 6 February.

photocell *See* PHOTOELECTRIC CELL

photochemistry Branch of chemistry concerning photochemical reactions caused by LIGHT or ULTRAVIOLET RADIATION and those reactions that produce light. Examples include PHOTOGRAPHY, PHOTOSYNTHESIS and BLEACHING by the Sun.

photocopying Reproduction of words, drawings or photographs by machine. In a photocopying machine, a light shines on the item to be copied, and an optical system forms an image of it. Various techniques may be used to reproduce this image on paper. In a modern plain-paper copier, the image is projected onto an electrically charged **drum**, coated with the light-sensitive element SELENIUM. Light makes the selenium conduct electricity, so bright areas of the drum lose their charge. The dark areas, which usually correspond to image detail, retain their charge, and this attracts particles of a fine powder called **toner**. Electrically charged paper in contact with the drum picks up the pattern of toner powder. A heated **roller** fuses the powder so that it sticks to the paper and forms a permanent image.

photoelectric cell (photocell) Device that produces ELECTRICITY when light shines on it. It was formerly an electron tube with a photosensitive cathode, but nearly all modern photocells are made using two electrodes separated by light-sensitive semiconductor material. Photoelectric cells are used as switches (electric eyes), light detectors (burglar alarms), devices to measure light intensity (light meters) or power sources (solar cells).

photoelectric effect Liberation of ELECTRONS from the surface of a material when light, ultraviolet radiation, X-rays or gamma rays fall on it. The effect can be explained only by the QUANTUM THEORY: PHOTONS in the radiation are absorbed by atoms in the substance and enable electrons to escape by transferring energy to them.

photography Process of obtaining a permanent image of an object, either in black and white or in colour, on treated paper or film. A CAMERA is used to expose a film to an image of the object to be photographed, for a set time. In black and white photography, the film is covered on one side with an emulsion containing a SILVER halide (silver bromide or silver chloride). The silver compound is exposed, so that it reduces easily to metallic silver when treated with a **developer**. The action of the developer is to produce a black deposit of metallic silver particles on those parts of the film that were exposed to light, thus providing "negative" image. After fixing in "hypo" (thiosulphate) and washing, the negative can be printed by placing it over a piece of sensitized paper and exposing it to light so that the silver salts in the paper are affected in the same way as those in the original film. The dark portions of the negative let through the least light, and the image on the paper is reversed back to a positive. Colour photography works on a similar, but more complex, process. *See also* DAGUERRE, LOUIS JACQUES MANDE; TALBOT, WILLIAM FOX

photon Quantum of ELECTROMAGNETIC RADIATION, such as light; a "particle" of LIGHT. The energy of a photon equals the frequency of the radiation multiplied by PLANCK's constant. Absorption of photons by atoms and molecules can cause excitation or ionization. A photon may be classified as a stable ELEMENTARY PARTICLE of zero rest mass, zero charge and SPIN 1, travelling at the velocity of light. It is its own antiparticle. Virtual photons are thought to be continuously exchanged between charged particles and thus to be the carriers of ELECTROMAGNETIC FORCE. *See also* QUANTUM THEORY

photoperiodism Biological mechanism that governs the timing of certain activities in an organism by reacting to the duration of its daily exposure to light and dark. For example, the start of flowering in plants is determined by day length. *See also* BIOLOGICAL CLOCK

photosphere Visible surface of the SUN. It is a layer of highly luminous gas *c.*500km (300mi) thick and with a temperature of *c.*6,000K, falling to 4,000K at its upper level. The photosphere is the source of the Sun's visible spectrum. Sunspots and other visible features of the Sun are situated in the photosphere.

photosynthesis Chemical process occurring in green plants, algae and many bacteria, by which water and carbon dioxide are converted into food and oxygen using energy absorbed from sunlight. The reactions take place in the CHLOROPLASTS. In the first part of the process, light is absorbed by CHLOROPHYLL and splits water into hydrogen and oxygen. The hydrogen attaches to a carrier molecule, and the oxygen is set free. The hydrogen and light energy build a supply of cellular chemical energy, ADENOSINE TRIPHOSPHATE (ATP). Hydrogen and ATP convert the carbon dioxide into sugars, including glucose and starch.

phototropism Growth of a plant in response to the stimulus of light, which increases cell growth on the shaded side of the plant, resulting in curvature towards the source of light.

Phrygia Historic region of W central Anatolia. A prosperous kingdom was established by the Phrygians, immigrants from SE Europe, early in the 1st millennium BC, with its capital at Gordion. MIDAS was a legendary Phrygian king. In the 6th century BC, Phrygia was taken over by Lydia, then by Persia and later empires.

phylloxera Small, yellowish insect of the order Homoptera that is a pest on grape plants in Europe and the W USA. It attaches itself to the leaves and roots and sucks the plant's fluids, resulting in the rotting of the plant. It destroyed all of France's native root stock of *vitis vinifera*. Family Phylloxeridae; species: *Phylloxera vitifoliae*.

phylogenetics Study of the evolutionary relationships between organisms. In **molecular phylogeny**, the evolutionary distances between organisms are analyzed by comparing the DNA sequences of specific GENES. At the most fundamental level, molecular phylogeny has revealed that all known organisms evolved from a common ancestor and can be grouped into five KINGDOMS.

phylum In the systematic categorization of living organisms, a major group within the animal KINGDOM. It comprises a diverse group of organisms with a common funda-

mental characteristic. In plant classification, the analogous category is sometimes called division. *See also* TAXONOMY

physical chemistry Study of the physical changes associated with CHEMICAL REACTIONS and the relationship between physical properties and chemical composition. The main branches are THERMODYNAMICS, concerned with the changes of energy in physical systems; chemical kinetics, concerned with rates of reaction; and molecular and atomic structure. Other topics include ELECTROCHEMISTRY, SPECTROSCOPY and some aspects of NUCLEAR PHYSICS.

physical units Units used in measuring physical quantities. For example, the KILOGRAM unit of mass is defined as the mass of a specified block of platinum. Other masses are measured by weighing them and comparing them, directly or indirectly, with this. Units are of two types: **base** units that, like the kilogram, have fundamental definitions; and **derived** units that are defined in terms of these base units. Various systems of units exist, founded on certain base units. They include imperial units (foot, pound, second), CGS units (centimetre, gram, second) and MKS units (metre, kilogram, second). For all scientific purposes, SI UNITS have been adopted.

physics Branch of science concerned with the study of MATTER and ENERGY. Physics seeks to identify and explain their many forms and relationships. Modern physics recognizes four FUNDAMENTAL FORCES in nature: GRAVITATION, which was first adequately described by Isaac NEWTON; ELECTROMAGNETIC FORCE, codified in the 19th century by MAXWELL's equations; WEAK NUCLEAR FORCE, which is responsible for the decay of some subatomic particles; and STRONG NUCLEAR FORCE, which binds together atomic nuclei. The latter is some 10^{12} times stronger than the weak force and is the least understood in physics. Branches of physics include PARTICLE PHYSICS, GEOPHYSICS, BIOPHYSICS, ASTROPHYSICS and NUCLEAR PHYSICS. Physics may also be divided into six fundamental theories: Newtonian MECHANICS, THERMODYNAMICS, ELECTROMAGNETISM, STATISTICAL MECHANICS, RELATIVITY and QUANTUM MECHANICS.

physiology Branch of BIOLOGY concerned with the functions of living organisms, as opposed to their structure (ANATOMY).

physiotherapy (physical therapy) Use of various physical techniques to treat disease or injury. Its techniques include massage, manipulation, exercise, heat, hydrotherapy and electrical stimulation.

phytochrome Blue-green pigment that occurs in plant leaves. One form of phytochrome (P_R) absorbs red light and is converted by it into another form (P_{FR}) that absorbs infrared light. Normal sunlight contains more red than infrared light, so the ratio of these two forms of phytochrome provides the means by which a plant detects the difference between day and night. It also regulates certain plant activities governed by light, such as the start of the flowering period and the greening of leaves. *See also* PHOTOPERIODISM

pi (π) Symbol used for the ratio of the circumference of a CIRCLE to its diameter. It is an IRRATIONAL NUMBER, and an approximation to five decimal places is 3.14159. The ratio 22/7 is often used as a rougher estimate.

Piaf, Edith (1915–63) French cabaret singer, b. Edith Giovanna Gassion. Her small stature earned the nickname "*piaf*" (Fr. sparrow). Piaf's tragic life, which was ended prematurely by her addiction to drugs, is reflected in the emotional impact of songs such as "Non, je ne regrette rien" and "La vie en Rose".

Piaget, Jean (1896–1980) Swiss psychologist, who developed a comprehensive theory of the intellectual growth of children. Piaget's influential books include *The*

Child's Conception of the World (1926), *The Origin of Intelligence in Children* (1954) and *The Early Growth of Logic in the Child* (1964). *See also* EDUCATION

piano (pianoforte) Musical instrument whose sound is made with strings struck by hammers that are moved from a keyboard. Its invention (*c*.1709) is attributed to Bartolomeo Cristofori. Its name, from the Italian *piano* (soft) and *forte* (strong or loud), was adopted because its range of volume (as of tonal quality) far exceeded that of earlier instruments. The modern grand piano, much larger, louder and more resonant than the 18th-century piano, was developed in the early 19th century.

Picardy Region and former province of N France on the English Channel; it includes Somme and parts of Pas-de-Calais, Oise and Aisne departments. It was a French province from 1477 until the French Revolution, when it was replaced by a smaller department. Picardy was the scene of heavy fighting during WORLD WAR 1. The area is made up of the plateau to the N of Paris where wheat and sugar beets are grown; the valley of the Somme, where industrial centres such as Amiens are located; and the coast, where fishing is important. Area: 19,399sq km (7,488sq mi) Pop. 1,810,700.

picaresque (Sp. *pícaro*, rogue or knave) Term first applied to an early genre of prose fiction, such as *Don Quixote* (1615), in which a roguish hero has a series of adventures, providing the author with a means for satirical comment. In a general sense, the term is often used to refer to fiction that is episodic in structure.

Picasso, Pablo (1881–1973) Spanish painter, sculptor, graphic artist, designer and ceramicist. Art historians often divide his work into separate periods. During his "Blue" and "Rose" periods (1900–07), Picasso turned from portrayals of poor and isolated people to representations of harlequins, acrobats and dancers in warmer colours. In 1904, he settled in Paris and became the centre of a group of progressive artists and writers. In 1906, Picasso began analysing and reducing forms. The result was his spectacular canvas, *Les Demoiselles d'Avignon* (1907), which is now seen as a watershed in the development of contemporary art. The fragmentary forms in the painting also heralded CUBISM. In the 1920s, Picasso produced solid classical figures but at the same time he was experimenting with SURREALISM. He started creating more violent and morbid works, which culminated in *Guernica* (1937). Picasso's sculpture ranks as highly as his painting. He was one of the first to use assembled rather than modelled or carved materials. The most famous example is his *Head of a Bull*, *Metamorphosis* (1943), which consists of a bicycle saddle and handlebars. Picasso was also an excellent printmaker and illustrated numerous books.

Piccard, Auguste (1884–1962) Swiss physicist who explored the STRATOSPHERE and deep seas. In 1931, a hydrogen balloon carried an airtight aluminium sphere containing Piccard and an assistant to an altitude of almost 15,800m (51,800ft). This was the first ascent into the stratosphere. From 1948, he experimented with designs for a diving vessel called a bathyscaphe. In 1953, Piccard and his son, **Jacques** (1922–), descended in the bathyscaphe *Trieste* to a depth of about 3,100m (10,000ft) in the Mediterranean Sea. In 1960, Piccard and a naval officer used the same craft in the Pacific Ocean to reach a record of 10,900m (35,800ft).

piccolo WOODWIND musical instrument of the FLUTE family. About half the size of the flute and pitched one octave higher, it is played in the same way.

picketing Patrolling by striking workers outside their place of employment. The aim of the "picket line" is to persuade colleagues still working also to stop, to dissuade drivers of supply vehicles from making deliveries, and to gain publicity for their cause. There is no special law for or against pickets in the UK. Secondary or "flying" picketing (the picketing of another workplace) was made illegal following the Employment Act of 1980. In the USA, mass picketing is generally illegal. *See also* STRIKE

Pickford, Mary (1893–1979) US film actress, b. Gladys Mary Smith. Her silent films include *Poor Little Rich Girl* (1917), *Pollyanna* (1919) and *Little Lord Fauntleroy* (1921). In 1919, Pickford established the United Artists Corporation with Charlie CHAPLIN, Douglas FAIRBANKS (her husband) and D.W. GRIFFITH.

Picts Ancient inhabitants of E and N Scotland. By the 8th century, they had a kingdom extending from Caithness to Fife and had adopted Christianity. To the W and S of the Picts, invaders from Ireland had established the kingdom of Dalriada; in 843 its king, Kenneth I, also became king of the Picts, uniting the two kingdoms into the kingdom of Scotland.

pidgin Simplified form of a language, differing from other LINGUA FRANCAS by comprising a very limited vocabulary and being used for communication between people who do not speak the same language. Most pidgins in use today are based on English, French, Spanish or Portuguese, with a certain number of native words and structures added. The Pidgin English of Papua New Guinea (Tok Pisin) is an official national language.

Piedmont (Piemonte) Region of NW Italy, bounded to the N, W and S by mountains, and to the E by the Po Valley; it comprises the provinces of Alessandria, Asti, Cuneo, Novara, Torino and Vercelli. Already an important region in Roman times, it was later subject to Lombard, then Frankish rule. Under the influence of Savoy from the early 15th century, it became part of the kingdom of Sardinia in 1720. In the early 19th century, it was the focus of the movement for Italian independence, joining a united Italy in 1861. The Po Valley has some excellent farmland. Products: grain, vegetables, fruit, dairy. Industries: winemaking, motor vehicles. Area: 25,400sq km (9,800sq mi). Pop. (1991) 4,302,565.

Pierce, Franklin (1804–69) 14th US President (1853–57). He represented New Hampshire in the House of Representatives (1833–37) and the Senate (1837–42). He gained the Democratic presidential nomination as a compromise candidate and was elected in 1852. The most notable feature of his presidency was his endorsement of the Kansas-Nebraska Act (1854) that resulted in near-civil war in Kansas between pro- and anti-slavery settlers.

Piero della Francesca (1415–92) (Piero dei Franceschi) Italian painter. He was familiar with the innovations made by MASACCIO, DONATELLO, Filippo LIPPI and others. He drew their achievements together to create a monumental, deeply reflective style. His most important work is the FRESCO series depicting the *Legend of the True Cross* (*c*.1465) for the choir of San Francesco, Arezzo.

Piero di Cosimo (1462–1521) Italian painter. The pictures attributed to him are bizarre mythologies peopled by fauns, centaurs and primitive men. These paintings are sometimes comic, but he could also create moving scenes, such as *Death of Procris* (*c*.1510).

Pierre Capital of South Dakota, USA, on the Missouri River, opposite Fort Pierre. Originally the capital of the Arikara Native Americans, it was a trading settlement in the early 19th century before being established as a railway terminus in 1880. It became the permanent state capital in 1904. Its economy is based on government services and agriculture (grain, cattle). Pop. (1990) 12,906.

Pietermaritzburg City in the foothills of the Drakensberg Range, KwaZulu-Natal, E South Africa. It was founded by Boers from Cape Colony in 1838 and named in honour of their leaders Piet Retief and Gert Maritz who were killed by Zulus. Pietermaritzburg served as the regional capital of Natal from 1843 to 1994. It lies in the heart of a rich farming area. Pop. (1991) 228,500.

Pietism Influential Christian spiritual movement within Protestantism, founded in the late 17th century by the German Lutheran minister, Philipp Spener (1635–1705). Its aim was to revitalize evangelical Christianity by emphasizing spiritual issues.

piezoelectric effect Creation of positive electric charge on one side of a non-conducting crystal and a negative charge on the other when the crystal is squeezed. The pressure results in an electric field that can be detected as voltage between the opposite crystal faces. The effect has been used in record-player pickups, crystal microphones and cigarette lighters.

pig Any of numerous species and varieties of domestic and wild swine of the family Suidae. The male is generally called a boar; the female, a sow. A castrated boar is usually known as a hog. It is generally a massive, short-legged omnivore with a thick skin. Wild pigs include the wart hog, wild BOAR, bush pig and babirusa. The domestic pig (*Sus scrofa*) is reared for human consumption. For pork they are slaughtered at 70–90kg (155–200lb) and for bacon at 80–100kg (175–220kg).

pigeon (DOVE) Any of a large family of wild and domestic birds found throughout temperate and tropical parts of the world, but concentrated in S Asia and the Australian region. Pigeons have small heads, short necks, plump bodies and scaly legs and feet. Plumage is loose but thick. Homing pigeons are bred and trained for racing. Length: to 46cm (18in). Family Columbidae; typical genus, *Columba*.

Piggott, Lester Keith (1935–) English jockey. He rode his first winner at the age of 12. Piggott was champion jockey 11 times between 1960 and 1982. He rode a record nine winners of the Epsom Derby among a total of 30 English classics victories. Piggott won a career total of 4,493 races. He retired in 1996.

pigment Coloured, insoluble substance used to impart colour to an object and added for this purpose to PAINTS, inks and plastics. They generally function by absorbing and reflecting light.

pigmentation In biology, a natural chemical that gives colour to TISSUES. In humans, the skin, hair and iris are coloured by the pigment MELANIN, together with the HAEMOGLOBIN in ERYTHROCYTES (red blood cells) that also acts as a pigment.

pika Any of 12 species of short-haired relatives of the RABBIT. They live in cold regions of Europe, Asia and the W USA. Length: to 20cm (8in). Genus *Ochotona*.

pike Predatory freshwater fish found in temperate regions of Europe, Asia and North America. It has a shovel-shaped mouth, with huge teeth in the lower jaw, and a mottled, elongated body. They are voracious predators. Length: to 137cm (54in); weight: to 21kg (46lb) Family Esocidae; genus *Esox*.

pikeperch Freshwater food and game fish of Central Europe, where it includes the zander, and of North America, where it is related to the walleye and sauger. A dark olive, mottled fish, it has an elongated body and large head and mouth. Length: to 91.4cm (3ft); weight: to 11kg (25lb). Family Percidae; species *Stizostedion vitreum*.

Pilate, Pontius *See* PONTIUS PILATE

pilchard Marine food fish resembling a HERRING, found in shoals along most coasts except those of Asia.

They support a huge canning industry. The young are sometimes called SARDINES. Length: less than 45.7cm (18in). Family Clupeidae; species *Sardina pilchardus*.

pilgrimage Religiously motivated journey to a shrine or other holy place in order to gain spiritual help or guidance, or for the purpose of thanksgiving. Pilgrimages are common to many religions, particularly in the East. A Muslim should make the pilgrimage to MECCA, where devotions last two weeks, at least once in his life. This pilgrimage is known as the HAJJ. Since the 2nd century AD, Christians have made pilgrimages to Palestine, to the tomb of the apostles Peter and Paul in Rome, and to that of James in Santiago de Compostela in Spain.

Pilgrimage of Grace (1536) Major rebellion in N England against the government of HENRY VIII. The rebels were united in their opposition to Thomas CROMWELL's religious reforms, specifically the DISSOLUTION OF THE MONASTERIES. The revolt was brutally suppressed and 230 rebels were executed.

Pilgrims (Pilgrim Fathers) Group of English PURITANS who migrated to North America in 1620. After fleeing to Leiden, Netherlands, in 1608, seeking refuge from persecution in England, they decided to look for greater religious freedom by founding a religious society in America. They sailed from Plymouth, England, on the MAYFLOWER and founded the PLYMOUTH COLONY in present-day Massachusetts.

pill, the Popular term for oral CONTRACEPTIVES based on female reproductive HORMONES. They work by preventing ovulation. Two types of synthetic hormone, similar to OESTROGEN and PROGESTERONE, are generally used, although the former alone is effective in preventing ovulation; the latter helps to regulate the MENSTRUAL CYCLE. Possible side-effects include headache, HYPERTENSION, weight-gain, and a slightly increased risk of THROMBOSIS.

pilot fish Marine fish that lives in warm seas, often found swimming close to sharks, ships and other large objects. A blue fish with five to seven dark bar markings on the sides and a white tail, it feeds on smaller fish. Length: to 60cm (2ft). Family Carangidae; species *Naucrates ductor*.

Pilsen *See* PLZEŇ

Pilsudski, Józef (1867–1935) Polish marshal and statesman, instrumental in securing Poland's independence. During World War 1 he led Polish forces against Russia, hoping to establish a Polish state. After independence, Pilsudski became head of state. His attempt to create a larger Polish state during the Polish–Soviet War failed, although he inflicted a remarkable defeat on the invading Russians in 1920. Pilsudski retired in 1923, but seized power again in 1926 and established a dictatorship that lasted until his death.

pimpernel Small, trailing annual plant of the genus *Anagallis*, native to Britain and the USA. The single, small, five-petalled flowers are scarlet, white or blue. The yellow pimpernel, a creeping European plant of shady areas, is *Lysimachia nemorum*. Family Primulaceae.

Pincus, Gregory Goodwin (1903–67) US biologist who helped to develop the contraceptive PILL using synthetic HORMONES. He wrote *The Eggs of Mammals* (1936).

Pindar (522–438 BC) Greek poet known for his choric lyrics and triumphal ODES. Of the 17 volumes of Pindar's works known to his contemporaries, only 44 odes survive, written to celebrate victories in athletic games.

pine Any of various EVERGREEN, cone-bearing trees of the genus *Pinus*, most of which are native to cooler temperate regions of the world. Many have two types of shoots, some with needle-like leaves and others with deciduous, scale-like leaves. The reproductive organs may be catkins or cones. Many species are valued for soft wood, wood pulp, oils and resins. Family: Pinaceae.

pineal body Small gland attached to the under-surface of the vertebrate brain. In human beings, it has an endocrine function, secreting the hormone melatonin that is involved in daily rhythms. *See also* ENDOCRINE SYSTEM

pineapple Tropical, herbaceous, perennial plant that is cultivated in the USA, South America, Asia, Africa and Australia; also the fruit of the plant. The fruit is formed from the flowers and bracts and grows on top of a short, stout stem bearing stiff, fleshy leaves. Height: to 1.2cm (4ft). Family Bromeliaceae; species *Ananas comosus*.

Pinero, Sir Arthur Wing (1855–1934) English dramatist. His farces include *The Magistrate* (1885), *The Schoolmistress* (1886) and *Dandy Dick* (1887). Pinero is best-known for his "problem play", *The Second Mrs Tanqueray* (1893), on the social discrimination of women. Other plays include *Trelawny of the "Wells"* (1898).

ping pong *See* TABLE TENNIS

pink Common name for several genera of the pink family (Caryophyllaceae), especially the genus *Dianthus* of more than 300 species, most of which are native to the Mediterranean region. Short, herbaceous perennials, many are hardy evergreens with showy, fragrant flowers. Leaves are simple and usually opposite, and the symmetrical flowers are usually bisexual. *See also* CARNATION

Pinkerton, Allan (1819–84) US detective, b. Scotland. In 1842, he moved to the USA and became a detective in the Chicago police force. In 1850, he resigned to establish his own agency, Pinkerton's National Detective Agency. In 1861, Pinkerton organized and headed a federal intelligence service that acted throughout the Civil War, and developed into the US SECRET SERVICE.

pinna Flap of skin and cartilage that comprises the visible, external part of the EAR. It helps to collect sound waves and direct them into the ear canal.

Pinochet (Ugarte), Augusto (1915–) Chilean general and statesman, president (1973–89). He led the military coup that overthrew Salvador ALLENDE. Pinochet established a military dictatorship that enforced social control through routine torture and murder. In 1989, he was forced to permit democratic elections and was succeeded as president by Patricio Aylwin in 1990. Pinochet retained command of the armed forces until 1998. In 1998, while undergoing hospital treatment in

▶ **pine** The lodgepole pine (*Pinus contorta*) grows in W North America, reaching a height of 18m (60ft). It is a small, vigorous mountain tree that is hardy to an altitude of 3,500m (11,000ft).

England, he was arrested for crimes against humanity. In 2000, on grounds of illness, Pinochet was allowed to return to Chile, where he faced further legal action.

Pinter, Harold (1930–) English dramatist. His use of elliptical dialogue and prolonged silences induces a powerful sense of unease and menace, often reinforced by a confined setting. His second play, *The Birthday Party* (1958), was initially poorly received. Pinter gained critical praise for his next play, *The Caretaker* (1960). Other major works include *The Homecoming* (1965), *Old Times* (1971), *No Man's Land* (1975) and *A Kind of Alaska* (1982). Later plays, such as *Mountain Language* (1988) and *Moonlighting* (1993), are more explicitly political.

Pinyin System of spelling used to transliterate ideographic Chinese characters into the Roman alphabet. It is a phonetic system and was officially adopted by the People's Republic of China in 1958.

Pioneer program Series of unmanned interplanetary probes launched by the USA. In 1960 **Pioneer 5** measured distances within the SOLAR SYSTEM and studied magnetism and the SOLAR WIND. **Pioneer 10**, launched in 1972, reached Jupiter in 1973. It investigated the planet's atmosphere and magnetic field and sent back more than 300 pictures of the planet. **Pioneer 11**, launched in 1973, reached Jupiter in 1974 and Saturn in 1979, discovering two moons there. In 1978, **Pioneer Venus 1** and **Pioneer Venus 2** entered Venus' atmosphere. The first orbited the planet for 14 years before it ceased operations. The second mission impacted with the planet.

pipefish Any of numerous species of marine fish found in the shallow, warm and temperate waters of the Atlantic and Pacific oceans. Related to the seahorse, it has a pencil-like body. Its mouth is at the end of a long snout. Length: to 58cm (23in). Family Syngnathidae.

Piper, John (1903–92) English painter. His early abstract phase gave way to a commitment to neoromanticism in the 1940s. As an official war artist (1940–42) during World War 2, Piper produced striking paintings of bomb-damaged buildings. Queen Elizabeth II commissioned him to paint *Windsor Castle* (1941–42). Piper also designed the stage sets for Benjamin Britten's opera *Death in Venice* (1973) and the stained glass windows in Coventry Cathedral.

pipit (fieldlark, titlark) Any of more than 50 small, brown, inconspicuous birds that resemble LARKS in habits and appearance. They are found worldwide. The plumage of both sexes is a similar streaked brown or greyish colour, with a long, white-edged "wag" tail. Length: 15cm (6in). Family Motacillidae; genus *Anthus*.

piracy Robbery by force of arms on the high seas. Pirates usually attacked ships of all nations indiscriminately and were therefore distinguished from the crews of PRIVATEERS, who were commissioned by a particular nation to attack the shipping of certain belligerent powers. Piracy was prevalent until the 19th century.

Piraeus Seaport city in SE Greece, 8km (5mi) SW of ATHENS. Piraeus was planned *c.*490 BC and rapidly developed into the largest Greek port. It was destroyed by the Roman general SULLA in 86 BC and fell into decline. In the 19th century, following Greek independence, a process of reconstruction led to the creation of the modern naval and commercial port. Industries: shipbuilding, oil refining, textiles, chemicals. Pop. (1991) 182,671.

Pirandello, Luigi (1867–1936) Italian dramatist and novelist. His novels include *The Late Mattia Pascal* (1923). Pirandello is chiefly remembered for his plays that explore the boundaries between reality and illusion. These include *Six Characters in Search of an Author*

(1921) and *As You Desire Me* (1930). In 1934 he was awarded the Nobel Prize for literature.

Piranesi, Giovanni Battista (1720–78) Italian engraver and architect. Piranesi gained fame for his *Vedute* (1745), 137 etchings of ancient and modern Rome. The only extant building that he designed is the Church of Santa Maria del Priorato, Rome (1764–65).

piranha (piraya) Tropical, bony, freshwater fish that lives in rivers in South America. It is a voracious predator with razor-sharp teeth and an aggressive temperament. Piranhas usually travel and attack in shoals and can pose a serious threat to much larger creatures. Length: to 61cm (24in). Family Characidae; genus *Serrasalmus*.

Pisa City on the River Arno, Tuscany, w central Italy. Already an important Etruscan town, Pisa prospered as a Roman colony from *c*.180 BC. In the Middle Ages it was a powerful maritime republic but later came under Florentine domination. It is noted for the 12th century "Leaning Tower of Pisa", an eight-storey circular campanile. The bell-tower is 54m (177ft) high and is now *c*.6.5m (18ft) out of perpendicular. Industries: tourism, textiles, glass, machine tools. Pop. (1992 est.) 108,000.

Pisanello (*c*.1395–*c*.1455) (Antonio Pisano) Italian painter and medallist. Working in the INTERNATIONAL GOTHIC style, Pisanello drew detailed studies of birds, people and costumes. His medals of important people of his time are of historic value.

Pisano, Nicola (*c*.1225–*c*.1278) Italian sculptor. His first masterpiece was the pulpit for the Baptistry in Pisa (1260). In his work on the cathedral pulpit in Siena (1265–68), Pisano was aided by his son, **Giovanni** (*c*.1250–*c*.1320), whose taste in decoration was influenced by the French gothic style. Giovanni executed two other pulpits: Santa Andrea, Pistoia (1298–1301), and Pisa Cathedral (1302–10).

Piscator, Ervin Friedrich Max (1893–1966) German stage director. He developed the concept of EPIC THEATRE, which BRECHT incorporated into the work of the Berliner Ensemble. Piscator believed theatre should be a political medium. *See also* EXPRESSIONISM

Pisces (the Fishes) Inconspicuous equatorial constellation situated on the ecliptic between Aquarius and Aries; it is the 12th sign of the Zodiac.

Pisistratus (*c*.605–527 BC) Athenian ruler. He became leader of the popular party in Athens. In 560, BC he seized control of Athens by force. In 554 BC, Pisistratus was overthrown and driven into exile. In 541 BC, with support from Thebes and Argos, he regained power and ruled as "tyrant" until his death.

Pissarro, Camille (1830–1903) French painter. He was the only artist to participate in all eight exhibitions of IMPRESSIONISM (1874–86). In the 1880s, he experimented with the POINTILLISM of Georges SEURAT but abandoned it in the 1890s for a freer interpretation. His works include *Louvre from Pont Neuf* (1902).

pistachio Deciduous tree native to the Mediterranean region and E Asia. It is grown commercially for the edible greenish seed (the pistachio nut) of its wrinkled red fruit. Height: to 6m (20ft). Family Anacardiaceae; species *Pistacia vera*.

pistil Female organ located in the centre of a flower. It consists of an OVARY, a slender STYLE and a STIGMA that receives POLLEN.

pistol FIREARM held and fired in one hand. The first pistols were matchlocks, in which a glowing fuse ignited the charge; by the end of the 16th century, wheel locks and the cheaper flintlocks were also in use. The invention of the percussion cap in 1815 enabled pistol technology to advance rapidly, and Samuel COLT's revolver of 1835 was the first reliable repeating firearm. Since then pistols have become capable of automatic fire.

Piston, Walter (1894–1976) US composer. He is mainly remembered for his orchestral music, including several concertos and a number of symphonies. Piston won a Pulitzer Prize for his seventh symphony (1961). He contributed to the development of 20th-century neoclassicism in the USA.

pit bull Any of several cross-breeds of bulldog and terrier. Examples include the American pit bull terrier, bull terrier and Staffordshire bull terrier. The English bull terrier, measuring *c*.40cm (16in) at the shoulder, was originally developed for bull-baiting. The American pit bull terrier, not an official breed, is *c*.50cm (20in) at the shoulder and was bred as a aggressive watchdog. Pit bulls are very powerful and when ill-trained can be very dangerous. A few have killed people. Weight: up to 23kg (50lb).

Pitcairn Island Volcanic island in the central s Pacific Ocean forming (together with the uninhabited islands of Henderson, Ducie and Oeno) a British crown colony. First sighted in 1767, Pitcairn was settled in 1790 by mutineers from the British ship HMS *Bounty*. Some of their descendants still live on the island. The principal economic activity is the growing and exporting of fruit. Area: 4.6sq km (1.7sq mi). Pop. (1994) 56.

pitch Quality of sound that determines its position in a musical scale. It is measured in terms of the frequency of sound waves (measured in hertz) – the higher the frequency, the higher the pitch. It also depends to some extent on loudness and timbre: increasing the intensity decreases the pitch of a low note and increases the pitch of a high one.

pitchblende *See* URANINITE

pitcher plant Any of several species of INSECTIVOROUS PLANT of the tropics and sub-tropics. Insects are trapped in the vase-shaped leaves that are lined with bristles. Trapped insects decompose and are absorbed as nutrients by plant cells. The flower is usually red. Height: 20–61cm (8–24in). Family Sarraceniacea; genera *Sarracenia* and *Nepenthes*.

Pitt (the Elder), William, 1st Earl of Chatham (1708–78) British statesman, known as "the Great Commoner". He entered Parliament in 1735. Pitt was noted for his opposition to the foreign policies of prime ministers WALPOLE and Carteret and King GEORGE II. The crisis of the SEVEN YEARS' WAR (1756–63) made him effective head of the government. Widespread criticism of Pitt's dismissal (1757) brought about his reappointment

▲ **pineapple** An important cash crop in tropical regions, pineapples bear fleshy fruit that can be eaten fresh, but the majority is canned or turned into pineapple juice.

as head of the government in coalition with the Duke of Newcastle. His ministry was a brilliant one, preserving and consolidating Britain's old empire and gaining a new one. Pitt placed his main efforts on successful attempts to conquer Canada and India. In 1761, he resigned after GEORGE III refused to declare war on Spain. After the war he spoke out against the prosecution (1763) of John WILKES and the imposition of the STAMP ACT (1765) on the American colonies. The ministry he nominally headed from 1766 to 1768 was a confused and divided one. Created Earl Chatham in 1766, he retired to the House of Lords in 1768. There he spoke out against repression of the American colonies and in favour of any peace settlement that stopped short of granting independence.

Pitt (the Younger), William (1759–1806) (Pitt the Younger) British statesman, prime minister (1783–1801, 1804–06). The second son of William PITT, Earl of Chatham, he entered Parliament in 1781, became chancellor of the exchequer in 1782 and shortly after became Britain's youngest prime minister, aged 24. Pitt's reputation rests chiefly on his financial and commercial reforms in the 1780s that restored British prosperity and prestige after the disaster of the AMERICAN REVOLUTION. During his first administration, the India Act (1784), the Constitutional Act (1791) dividing Canada into French and English provinces, and the Act of UNION with Ireland (1800) were passed. Pitt resigned in the face of GEORGE III's refusal to consider CATHOLIC EMANCIPATION. In 1804, he returned to power and continued to hold office until his death. His second ministry was marked by coalition with Russia, Sweden and Austria against NAPOLEON I. Pitt stoutly defended his TORY views against his arch WHIG rival, Charles James FOX.

Pittsburgh City at the confluence of the Allegheny and Monongahela rivers, SW Pennsylvania, USA. Fort Duquesne was founded on the site by the French c.1750. Captured by the British in 1758, it was renamed Fort Pitt. Pittsburgh grew as a steel manufacturing centre in the 19th century (the industry is now in decline). Industries: glass, machinery, petroleum products. Pop. (1990) 369,379.

pituitary gland Major gland of the ENDOCRINE SYSTEM, located at the base of the BRAIN. In human beings it is about the size of a pea and is connected to the HYPOTHALAMUS by a stalk. It produces many HORMONES, some of which regulate the activity of other endocrine glands, while others control growth.

Pius IV (1499–1565) Pope (1559–65), b. Giovanni Angelo de Medici. He furthered the COUNTER REFORMATION, reconvening the Council of TRENT for its third and last session (1562–63). He also drafted the INDEX of Forbidden Books.

Pius V, Saint (1504–72) Pope (1568–72), b. Antonio Ghislieri. He was an energetic reformer of the Church and enemy of PROTESTANTISM. In 1570, Pius V excommunicated Queen ELIZABETH I of England. During his papacy, he tightened the rules of INQUISITION and succeeded in eliminating Protestantism from Italy. He was canonized in 1712. His feast day is 20 April.

Pius VII (1742–1823) Pope (1800–23), b. Barnaba Gregorio Chiaramonti. He secured the Concordat of 1801 with NAPOLEON I. After Napoleon took Rome in 1808 and annexed the PAPAL STATES in 1809, Pius excommunicated him and was removed and imprisoned until 1814. On his restoration he encouraged the reform of religious orders and education.

Pius IX (1792–1878) Pope (1846–78), b. Giovanni Maria Mastai-Ferretti. Pius fled from Rome (1848–50) in the REVOLUTIONS OF 1848 but was restored by NAPOLEON III. In 1860, the PAPAL STATES were seized by the Italian

nationalists. Pius refused to acknowledge the new kingdom of Italy, into which Rome was incorporated in 1870, and remained a voluntary "prisoner" within the walls of the Vatican until his death. He defended German Catholics from persecution by BISMARCK and defined the dogma of the IMMACULATE CONCEPTION (1854). In 1869, Pius convened the First VATICAN COUNCIL, which proclaimed the principle of PAPAL INFALLIBILITY. His pontificate is the longest in papal history.

Pius X, Saint (1835–1914) Pope (1903–14), b. Giuseppe Melchiorre Sarto. He opposed religious MODERNISM, placing several modernist books on the INDEX in 1907. Pius also condemned the separation of Church and state in France and recodified CANON LAW (a revision published posthumously in 1917). He was canonized in 1954. His feast day is 21 August.

Pius XI (1857–1939) Pope (1922–39), b. Achille Ratti. He denounced totalitarianism, both communist and fascist, though he was forced to make political compromises with fascist governments. In 1929, he signed the LATERAN TREATY with MUSSOLINI, which recognized the sovereignty of the VATICAN.

Pius XII (1876–1958) Pope (1939–58), b. Eugenio Pacelli. Fearing political reprisals, he failed to denounce the Nazis and the persecution of Jews during World War 2. He was more openly hostile to communism. On matters of doctrine, he maintained a conservative policy, although he appointed local bishops in non-Western countries and created a non-Italian majority among the cardinals. In 1997, the Vatican formal apologised for his failure to condemn ANTI-SEMITISM in Nazi Germany.

Pizarro, Francisco (c.1476–1541) Spanish *conquistador* of the INCA empire of Peru. He served under CORTÉS and led expeditions to South America (1522–28). In 1531, having gained the support of CHARLES V, Pizarro and Diego de Almagro sailed from Panama to Peru. They captured and later murdered the Inca leader ATAHUALPA, and took the capital, Cuzco, in 1534. Pizarro acted as governor of the conquered territory. In 1535, he founded the city of Lima. In 1538, he ordered the murder of Almagro. He was assassinated in Lima by Almagro's supporters.

placebo Harmless substance that has no active ingredient, given in place of actual medication. It may be psychologically effective and bring about improvement in a patient's condition. It is also used in drug trials: some subjects take placebos and others the drugs to be tested, and the reactions of the two groups are compared.

placenta Organ in mammals (except MONOTREMES and MARSUPIALS) that connects the FOETUS to the UTERUS of the mother. Part of the placenta contains tiny blood vessels through which oxygen and food are carried from the mother to the embryo via the umbilical cord and wastes are carried from the embryo to the mother's bloodstream to be excreted. The placenta secretes hormones that maintain pregnancy and is discharged from the mother's body as the afterbirth, immediately after delivery.

plagioclase Type of FELDSPAR. Plagioclase minerals occur in IGNEOUS and METAMORPHIC rocks. Off-white, or sometimes pink, green or brown, they are composed of varying proportions of the silicates of sodium and calcium with aluminium. They show an oblique cleavage and have triclinic system crystals. Hardness 6–6.5; r.d. 2.6. *See also* ORTHOCLASE

plague Acute, infectious disease of humans and rodents caused by the bacillus *Yersinia pestis*. In humans it occurs in three forms: **bubonic** plague, most common and characterized by vomiting, fever and swellings of the lymph nodes called "buboes";

pneumonic plague, in which the lungs are infected; and **septicaemic** plague, in which the bloodstream is invaded. Treatment is the administration of vaccines, bed rest, antibiotics and sulpha drugs. *See also* BLACK DEATH

plaice Marine flatfish found along the W European coast. An important food fish, it is brown or grey with orange spots. Length: to 90cm (3ft); weight: to 11.8kg (26lb). Family Pleuronectidae; species *Pleuronectes platessa*.

Plaid Cymru (Party of Wales) Welsh nationalist political party, founded in 1925 as Plaid Genedlaethol Cymru. In 1966, Plaid Cymru returned its first member to the House of Commons. It advocates Welsh independence (from the United Kingdom) within the European Union.

plainsong (plainchant) Collection of unharmonized liturgical melodies of the Western Church, traditionally performed unaccompanied. Plainsong goes back to the beginning of the Christian era. The melodies use free rhythms, and the musical "scales" they employ derive from the "modes" of ancient Greek music. In the 6th century, plainsong was reformed, supposedly at the behest of Pope GREGORY I ("the Great"). In this reformed state (known as Gregorian chant), the range of a melody is not more than five notes.

Planck, Max Karl Ernst Ludwig (1858–1947) German theoretical physicist whose revolutionary QUANTUM THEORY helped to establish modern physics. In 1900, Planck came to the conclusion that the frequency distribution of BLACK-BODY radiation could only be accounted for if the radiation was emitted in separate "packets" (quanta), rather than continuously. His equation, relating the energy of a quantum to its frequency, is the basis of quantum theory. **Planck's constant** is a universal constant (symbol h) of value 6.626×10^{-34} joule seconds, equal to the energy of a quantum of electromagnetic radiation divided by the radiation frequency. In 1918, he was awarded the Nobel Prize for physics.

plane In mathematics, a flat surface such that a straight line joining any two points on it lies entirely within the surface. Its general equation in the three-dimensional CARTESIAN COORDINATE SYSTEM is $ax + by + cz = d$, where a, b, c and d are constants.

planet Large, non-stellar body in orbit around a star, shining only by reflecting the star's light. In our SOLAR SYSTEM there are nine major planets, as opposed to the thousands of small bodies known as ASTEROIDS or minor planets. *See also* MERCURY; VENUS; EARTH; MARS; JUPITER; SATURN; URANUS; NEPTUNE; PLUTO

planetarium Domed building in which a projector displays an artificial sky in order to demonstrate the positions and motions of the Sun, Moon, planets and stars.

plankton All the floating or drifting life of the ocean, especially that near the surface. The organisms are very small and move with the currents. There are two main kinds: **phytoplankton**, floating plants such as DIATOMS and dinoflagellates; and **zooplankton**, floating animals such as radiolarians, plus the larvae and eggs of larger marine animals. They are a vital part of the food chain.

plant Any member of the kingdom Plantae, a large kingdom of multicellular organisms whose cells have cellulose cell walls and contain CHLOROPLASTS or similar structures (plastids). Plants develop from DIPLOID embryos and have a regular alternation of HAPLOID and diploid generations in their life cycles. Most plants are green and make their own food by PHOTOSYNTHESIS. A few are colourless PARASITES or SAPROPHYTES. Simple plants reproduce by means of SPORES, while more advanced plants produce SEEDS and FRUITS. Plants show a wide range of biochemistry; some produce chemicals such as ALKALOIDS,

NARCOTICS and even cyanide; others secrete substances into the soil to prevent other plants growing near them. Many of these chemicals form the bases for the development of DRUGS. Plants are classified on the basis of their morphology (shape and structure). The most important phyla are the Bryophyta (BRYOPHYTES), which includes the mosses and liverworts; LYCOPODOPHYTA (CLUB MOSSES); Sphenophyta (HORSETAILS); Filicinophyta (FERNS); Cycadophyta (CYCADS); Ginkgophyta (GINKGO); Coniferophyta (CONIFERS); and Angiospermophyta (ANGIOSPERMS). *See also* ALTERNATION OF GENERATIONS

Plantagenet English royal dynasty (1154–1485). The name encompasses the ANGEVINS (1154–1399) and the houses of LANCASTER and YORK. They are descended from Geoffrey of Anjou and Matilda, daughter of HENRY I. The name was adopted by Richard, duke of York and father of EDWARD IV, during the Wars of the ROSES.

plantain Plant with a rosette of basal leaves and spikes of tiny, greenish white flowers; it grows in temperate regions and was used for medicinal purposes. Family Plantaginaceae; genus *Plantago*. The name plantain is also given to a tropical BANANA plant believed to be native to SE Asia and now cultivated throughout the tropics. It has green fruit that is larger and starchier than a banana. It is eaten cooked. Height: to 10m (33ft). Family Musaceae; species *Musa paradisiaca*.

plant classification System devised to group PLANTS according to relationships among them. Plants are known by common names that often vary from area to area but have only one correct scientific name. *See also* TAXONOMY

plant genetics Science of HEREDITY and VARIATION in plants. Since 1900, research in GENETICS has supplied the principles of plant breeding, especially HYBRIDIZATION. The development of consistently reliable and healthy first-generation crosses (F1 hybrids) has revolutionized the growing of food crops, ornamental annuals and bedding plants. Genetic engineers grow cell and TISSUE CULTURES by the replication or cloning of sterile plant types. They also concentrate on isolating individual GENES with the aim of producing new colour varieties for traditional flowers, improving the flavour of food crops, breeding resistance to pests and herbicides, and lengthening the shelf life of harvested crops. *See also* CLONE; FOOD TECHNOLOGY; GENETIC ENGINEERING

plaque Abnormal deposit building up on a body surface, especially the film of saliva and bacteria on TEETH. It leads to CARIES and gum disease.

plasma In biology, liquid portion of the BLOOD in which the cells are suspended. It contains an immense number of ions, inorganic and organic molecules such as immunoglobulins, and hormones and their carriers. It clots upon standing.

plasma In physics, an ionized gas that contains about the same amount of positive and negative IONS. Plasma, often described as the fourth state of MATTER, occurs at enormous temperatures, as in the interiors of the Sun and other stars and in FUSION reactors.

plasmid Strand or loop of NUCLEIC ACID, containing genetic information, that can be introduced to a host cell where it will replicate independently. Plasmids are used in RECOMBINANT DNA RESEARCH.

plastic Synthetic material composed of organic molecules, often in long chains called POLYMERS, that can be shaped and then hardened. The weight and structure of the molecules determine the physical and chemical properties of a given compound. Plastics are synthesized from common materials, mostly from petroleum. CELLULOSE comes from cotton or wood pulp, CASEIN from skimmed milk, others from chemicals derived from plants. **Thermoset** plastics, such as BAKELITE, stay hard once set, while **thermoplastics**, such as POLYETHYLENE, can be resoftened by heat. New biodegradable plastics, more expensive to produce, are environmentally friendly because they eventually decompose. The first plastic was CELLULOID, invented by John Hyatt in 1869. In 1908, Leo BAEKELAND produced the first mouldable plastic industrial plastic.

plastic surgery Branch of surgery that involves the reconstruction of deformed, damaged or disfigured parts of the body. **Cosmetic surgery**, such as face-lifts, is performed solely to "improve" appearance.

plastid Type of organelle found in the cells of plants and green algae. CHLOROPLASTS and leucoplasts are two examples of plastids, which have a double membrane and contain DNA.

Plata, Río de la Estuary in SE South America formed by the junction of the rivers PARANÁ and URUGUAY at the border between Argentina and Uruguay. It was first explored by Europeans in the early 16th century. The cities of BUENOS AIRES and MONTEVIDEO lie on its S and N shores respectively. It is 270km (170mi) long and 190km (120mi) wide at its mouth. Area: c.35,000sq km (13,500sq mi).

Plataea, Battle of (479 BC) Decisive battle of the PERSIAN WARS. The Greeks under the Spartan Pausanias and the Athenian Aristides won a total victory. The Persian army was almost destroyed and its commander, Mardonius, killed. The battle ended the ambitions of XERXES to conquer Greece.

plateau Extensive, fairly flat, raised area of land. Mountains may stand up above the general level of a plateau, or it may be carved by deep river valleys or canyons to form a **dissected** plateau. An **intermontaine** plateau is completely surrounded by mountains.

platelet Colourless, usually spherical structures found in mammalian BLOOD. Chemical compounds in platelets, known as factors and co-factors, are essential to the mechanism of BLOOD CLOTTING. The normal platelet count is c.300,000 per cu mm of blood.

plate tectonics Theory or model to explain the distribution, evolution and causes of the Earth's crustal features. It proposes that the Earth's CRUST and part of the upper MANTLE (the LITHOSPHERE) is made up of several separate, rigid slabs, termed plates, which move independently forming part of a cycle in the creation and destruction of crust. The plates collide or move apart at the margins, and these produce zones of EARTHQUAKE and volcanic activity. Three types of plate boundary can be identified. At a **constructive** or divergent margin, new basaltic magma originating in the mantle is injected into the plate. The crusts are forced to separate and an oceanic ridge is formed. At a **destructive** or convergent margin, plates collide and one plate moves under the other. This occurs along oceanic trenches. The recycling of crust by subduction results in the melting of some crustal material, and volcanic island arcs (such as the islands of Japan) are produced. Material that cannot be subducted is scraped up and fused onto the edge of plates. This can form a new continent or add to existing continents. Mountain chains are explained as the sites of former subduction or continental collision. At a **conservative** margin, plates move past each other along a transform fault. Plate movement is thought to be driven by convection currents in the mantle. *See also* SEAFLOOR SPREADING; VOLCANISM

Plath, Sylvia (1932–63) US poet. Her verse includes *The Colossus* (1960) and *Ariel* (1965). The latter was published after her suicide, as were *Crossing the Water* (1971), *Winter Trees* (1971), *Johnny Panic and the Bible*

of Dreams (1977) and *Collected Poems* (1981). Plath wrote one novel, *The Bell Jar* (1963). Her most effective work is characterized by intensely personal, confessional elements. She was married to fellow poet Ted HUGHES.

platinum (symbol Pt) Lustrous, silver-white metal, one of the TRANSITION ELEMENTS. Discovered in 1735, it is chiefly found in certain ores of nickel. Malleable and ductile, it is used in jewellery, dentistry, electrical-resistance wire, magnets, thermocouples, surgical tools, electrodes and other laboratory apparatus, and as a CATALYST in catalytic converters for car exhausts. It is chemically unreactive and resists tarnishing and CORROSION. Properties: at.no. 78; r.a.m. 195.09; r.d. 21.45; m.p. 1,772°C (3,222°F); b.p. 3,800°C (6,872°F); most common isotope Pt195 (33.8%).

Plato (427–347 BC) Ancient Greek philosopher and writer who formulated an ethical and metaphysical system based upon philosophical IDEALISM. From c.407 BC he was a disciple of SOCRATES, from whom he may have derived many of his ideas about ETHICS. Following the trial and execution of Socrates in 399 BC, Plato withdrew to Megara, after which he is believed to have travelled extensively in Egypt, Italy and Sicily. He visited Syracuse in Sicily three times, in c.388, 367 and 361–360 BC, during the reigns of the tyrants DIONYSIUS THE ELDER and Dionysius the Younger. Plato sought to educate the latter as a philosopher-king and to set up an ideal political system under him, but the venture failed. Meanwhile, in Athens, Plato set up his famous ACADEMY (c.387 BC). In the Academy he taught several young people, including ARISTOTLE. In addition to being a philosopher of great influence, Plato wrote in the form of dialogues, in which Socrates genially interrogates another person, demolishing their arguments. All of Plato's 36 works survive. His most famous dialogues include *Gorgias* (on rhetoric as an art of flattery), *Phaedo* (on death and the immortality of the soul) and the *Symposium* (a discussion on the nature of love). Plato's greatest work was the *Republic*, an extended dialogue on justice, in which he outlined his view of the ideal state.

platypus (duck-billed platypus) MONOTREME mammal of Australia and Tasmania. It is amphibious, lays eggs and has webbed feet, a broad tail and a soft, duck-like bill. The male platypus has a poison spur on the hind foot. They feed on small invertebrates. Length: c.60cm (24in). Family Omithorhynchidae; species *Ornithorhynchus anatinus*.

Plautus, Titus Maccius (254–184 BC) Roman dramatist. His comedies, such as *Miles Gloriosus* (*The Braggart Soldier*, c.211 BC), were modelled on Greek originals. His plays typically combine farcical plots with amusing, low-life characters and witty dialogue. Shakespeare's *The Comedy of Errors* (1593) derives from Plautus' *Menaechmi* (*The Two Menaechmuses*).

plebeian General body of Roman citizens, as distinct from the small PATRICIAN class. In the early years of the Republic, they were barred from public office and from marrying patricians. The gulf between the two classes gradually closed. By the 3rd century BC there was little legal distinction between them.

plebiscite (Lat. *plebis citum*, decree of the people) Proposal put before the people and enacted by the people by a direct vote of an entire district or country. Plebiscites are usually concerned with matters of national importance, such as the ELECTION of a leader or choice of government.

Pléiade, La Group of seven 16th-century French poets. They were the group's leader Pierre de RONSARD, Joachim du Bellay (1522–60), Jean-Antoine de Baïf (1532–89), Rémy Belleau (1528–77), Estienne Jodelle (1532–73), Pontus de Tyard (1522–1605) and Jean

Dorat. Among the earliest writers of the French RENAIS-SANCE, they advocated French as a literary language.

Pleiades Young, OPEN CLUSTER in the constellation Taurus, popularly called the Seven Sisters. Although only six or seven stars are visible to the naked eye, there are in fact more than one thousand embedded in a reflection NEBULA. The brightest member is Alcyone, which is more than 300 times as luminous as the Sun. The cluster lies just over 400 light-years away.

Pleistocene Geological epoch that began *c*.2 million years ago, during which humans and most forms of familiar mammalian life evolved. Episodes of climatic cooling in this epoch led to the best-known ICE AGE in the Earth's history. It ended *c*.8000 BC.

Plekhanov, Georgy Valentinovich (1857–1918) Russian revolutionary. After leading populist demonstrations, he was exiled in 1880 and adopted MARXISM. He worked with LENIN until 1903 when, as leader of the MENSHEVIKS, he split with him. He returned to Russia in 1917 and died shortly after the RUSSIAN REVOLUTION.

pleura Double membrane that lines the space between the LUNGS and the walls of the chest. The fluid between the pleura lubricates the two surfaces to prevent friction during breathing movements.

pleurisy Inflammation of the PLEURA. It is nearly always due to infection, but may arise as a complication of other diseases.

Plimsoll, Samuel (1824–98) British social reformer. As a radical member of Parliament (1868–80), he was chiefly responsible for the Merchant Shipping Act (1876). This act enforced government inspection of shipping and required merchant ships to have a line, subsequently known as the **Plimsoll line**, painted on their hulls to indicate safe loading limits.

Pliny the Elder (AD 23–79) (Gaius Plinius Secundus) Roman scholar. His one major surviving work, *Historia Naturalis* (*Natural History*), covers a vast range of subjects, mixing fact and fiction.

Pliny the Younger (AD 62–114) (Gaius Plinius Caecilius Secundus) Roman administrator. The nephew and adopted son of PLINY THE ELDER, he became a senator and governor of Bythnia (*c*.112). He is best known for his correspondence with the Emperor TRAJAN, which provides a unique record of the life of a Roman gentleman.

Pliocene Last era of the TERTIARY period that lasted from 5 to 2 million years ago and preceded the PLEISTOCENE. Animal and plant life was similar to that of today.

PLO *See* PALESTINE LIBERATION ORGANIZATION

Plotinus (AD 205–270) Ancient philosopher who was the founder of NEOPLATONISM. In *c*.244, he opened a school in Rome. In essence, Plotinus conceived of the universe as a hierarchy proceeding from matter, through soul and reason, to God. His pupil and biographer, Porphyry, compiled and edited Plotinus' writings into six books of nine chapters each, known as the *Enneads*.

plough Agricultural implement used to cut furrows in soil for aeration and in preparation for sowing or planting. The first plough appeared in the NEOLITHIC period, and in the BRONZE AGE became metal-tipped wooden wedges fastened to a single handle and a beam, pulled by men or oxen. This form remained virtually unchanged until the 19th century when the mould-board was introduced in the USA. This was a curved board that turned over the slice of earth cut by the plough's blade or share.

plover Any of several species of wading shorebirds, many of which migrate long distances over open seas from Arctic breeding grounds to Southern Hemisphere wintering areas. It has a large head, a plump grey, brown or golden speckled body and short legs. Length: to 28cm (11in). Family Charadriidae; genera include *Charadrius* and *Pluvialis*.

Plowright, Dame Joan Anne (1929–) English actress. Her classical talents were mainly displayed at Chichester and the National Theatre, London, often in conjunction with her husband Laurence OLIVIER. Plowright appeared in the first performances of John OSBORNE's *The Entertainer* (1957) and Arnold WESKER's *Roots* (1959).

plum Fruit tree, mostly native to Asia and naturalized in Europe and North America, widely cultivated for its fleshy, edible fruit that has a hard "stone" at the centre. The most common cultivated plum of Europe and Asia is *Prunus domsetica*; in North America, the Japanese plum (*P. salicina*) is crossed with European varieties to give several cultivated strains. Family Rosaceae.

plumule In botany, an embryonic shoot that develops during GERMINATION of a seed.

pluralism In politics, theory that state power is wielded by a number of groups with conflicting interests, none of which is able to establish absolute authority. In philosophy, pluralism is the name given to the theory that there are many ultimate substances, rather than one, as in MONISM. Pluralism can also mean the holding of more than one office at the same time, especially within the Church.

Plutarch (*c*.AD 46–120) Greek biographer and essayist. His best known work is *The Parallel Lives*, which consists of biographies of soldiers and statesmen.

Pluto Roman god of the underworld, equivalent to the Greek god HADES. He ruled over the land of the dead and was also a god of wealth, since his realm contained all underground mineral riches.

Pluto Smallest and outermost planet of the SOLAR SYSTEM, the last planet in our Solar System to be discovered. Independently, William H. Pickering and Percival LOWELL calculated the possible existence of Pluto. The planet was eventually located in 1930 by Clyde Tombaugh within 5° of Lowell's predicted position. Pluto seems to have a mottled surface with light and dark regions and signs of polar caps. The surface is covered with icy deposits consisting of 98% nitrogen, with traces of methane and also probably water, carbon dioxide and carbon monoxide. Pluto has a single moon, Charon, which is so large that some astronomers consider Pluto/Charon as a double planet.

plutonium (symbol Pu) Silver-white, radioactive, metallic element of the ACTINIDE SERIES. It was first synthesized in 1940 by Glenn Seaborg and associates at the University of California at Berkeley by the deuteron (heavy hydrogen) bombardment of URANIUM. Plutonium is found naturally in small amounts in uranium ores. Plutonium-239 (half-life 24,360 years) is made in large quantities in breeder reactors. It is a fissile element used in NUCLEAR REACTORS and NUCLEAR WEAPONS. The element is very toxic and absorbed by bone, making it a dangerous radiological hazard. Properties: at.no. 94; r.d. 19.84; m.p. 641°C (1,186°F); b.p. 3,232°C (5,850°F); most stable isotope Pu^{244} (half-life 25,000 years). *See also* TRANSURANIC ELEMENTS

PLUTO: DATA
DIAMETER (EQUATORIAL): 2,324km (1,444mi)
MASS (EARTH = 1): 0.002
VOLUME (EARTH = 1): 0.01
DENSITY (WATER = 1): 2.03
ORBITAL PERIOD: 247.7 years
ROTATION PERIOD: 6.375 days
AVERAGE SURFACE TEMPERATURE: −230°C (−382°F)

Plymouth City and port on the Tamar estuary, Devon, SW England. In 1588, Sir Francis DRAKE set out from Plymouth to attack the Spanish ARMADA, and the MAYFLOWER sailed for America in 1620. Plymouth was severely damaged by bombing in World War 2. It has a naval base and ferry links with France and Spain. Industries: China clay, machine tools. Pop. (1994) 257,000.

Plymouth Brethren Strictly PURITAN sect of evangelical Christians, founded in Ireland in the late 1820s by J.N. Darby, an ordained Anglican. Their name comes from their having established their first English centre at Plymouth in 1831. In 1849, they split into two groups, the "Open Brethren" and the "Exclusive Brethren", and have since split further.

Plymouth Colony First colonial settlement in New England (founded 1620). The settlers were a group of *c*.100 PURITAN separatist PILGRIMS who sailed on the MAYFLOWER and settled on what is now CAPE COD Bay, Massachusetts. They named the first town after their port of departure. Lacking a royal charter, government was established by the MAYFLOWER COMPACT. During the first winter nearly half the settlers died. In 1691, Plymouth Colony became part of Massachusetts.

Plzeň (Pilsen) City in W Czech Republic. Founded in the 13th century by King Wenceslaus II, it was a focal point for Roman Catholic resistance during the HUSSITE Wars. It is a centre for heavy industry and is internationally famous for its beer. Pop. (1990) 175,000.

pneumatic Device powered by compressed air normally used to produce rotary or a reciprocating (back and forth) motion to speed up operations such as sawing, grinding, digging, hammering and riveting. The pneumatic drill used in roadworks has a reciprocating, pounding motion at speeds of between 80 and 500 revs per minute.

pneumoconiosis Occupational disease principally of miners working in confined and dusty conditions. Caused by inhaling irritants, often only as minute specks, the disease inflames and can finally destroy LUNG tissue.

pneumonia Inflammation of the LUNG tissue, most often caused by bacterial infection. Most at risk are the very young, the aged and those whose immune systems have been undermined by disease or certain medical treatments. The commonest form is pneumococcal pneumonia, caused by the bacterium *Streptococcus pneumoniae*. Symptoms include fever, chest pain, coughing and the production of rust-coloured sputum. Treatment is with ANTIBIOTICS.

pneumothorax Presence of air in the pleural space between the lungs and the chest wall. It may arise spontaneously or be caused by injury or disease. The lung is liable to collapse.

Po Italy's longest river, in N Italy. It rises in the Cottian Alps near the French border and flows E to empty into the Adriatic Sea. The Po valley is an important industrial and agricultural region, and water from the river is used extensively in irrigation schemes. Length: 650km (405mi).

Pocahontas (1595–1617) Native American princess and early colonial heroine. According to legend, she saved the life of John SMITH, leader of the JAMESTOWN colonists, when he was about to be killed by her father, POWHATAN. Captured by the colonists in 1613, she adopted their customs and in 1614 married John Rolfe. In 1616, Pocahontas and Rolfe were received at the English court. She died of smallpox in England.

Po Chü-i (772–846) Chinese poet of the T'ANG period. His social protest poetry was written in simple, everyday language.

pod Fruit of any leguminous plant, such as a PEA or BEAN. A pod is an elongated, case-like structure filled with seeds. It develops from a single CARPEL and, when ripe, splits down both sides to release the seeds. Family Papilionceae/Leguminosae. *See also* LEGUME

podiatry Treatment and care of the foot. Podiatrists treat such conditions as corns and bunions and devise ways to accommodate foot deformities.

Poe, Edgar Allan (1809–49) US poet and short-story writer. Much of his finest poetry, such as *The Raven* (1845), deals with horror in the tradition of the GOTHIC NOVEL. Other works include the poem, *Annabel Lee* (1849), and the stories *The Fall of the House of Usher* (1839), *The Murders in the Rue Morgue* (1841) and *The Pit and the Pendulum* (1843).

poet laureate Title conferred by the British monarch on a poet whose duty is then to write commemorative verse for important occasions. The first official poet laureate was John DRYDEN (1668–89). The position has been held by, among others, Robert SOUTHEY (1813–43), WORDSWORTH (1843–50), TENNYSON (1850–92), Sir John BETJEMAN (1972–84) and Ted HUGHES (1984–1998).

poetry Literary medium that employs the line as its formal unit and in which the sound, rhythm and meaning of words are all equally important. Until the modern introduction of the concept of FREE VERSE, poetry was characteristically written in regular lines with carefully structured METRES, often with RHYMES. *See also* LITERATURE; PROSE

pogrom Russian term for a destructive riot, generally applied to attacks on Jews in Russia in the late 19th and early 20th centuries. They were usually by anti-Semitic mobs and often instigated by local authorities.

poikilothermic (ectothermic) Describes an animal whose body temperature fluctuates with the temperature of its surroundings, often referred to as cold-blooded. Reptiles, amphibians, fish and invertebrates are cold-blooded. They can control their body temperature only by their behaviour – by moving in and out of the shade or orientating themselves to absorb more or less sunlight. *See also* HOMOIOTHERMIC

Poincaré, (Jules) Henri (1854–1912) French mathematician. He worked on CELESTIAL MECHANICS, winning an award for his contribution to the theory of ORBITS. In 1906, independently of EINSTEIN, Poincaré obtained some of the results of the special theory of RELATIVITY. He attempted to make mathematics accessible to the general public in such works as *The Value of Science* (1905) and *Science and Method* (1908).

Poincaré, Raymond Nicolas Landry (1860–1934) French statesman, president (1913–20) and prime minister (1912–13, 1922–24, 1926–29). An ardent nationalist and conservative, he accepted his opponent CLEMENCEAU as premier in 1917, in the cause of national unity. In 1923, he ordered the occupation of the RUHR to force German payment of REPARATIONS.

poinsettia Ornamental shrub, native to Mexico. It has tapering leaves and tiny yellow flowers centred in leaf-like red, white or pink bracts. It is a popular house plant. In its natural environment, the tree grows to *c*.5m (16ft). Height: to 60cm (2ft) when potted. Family Euphorbiaceae; species *Euphorbia pulcherrima*.

pointer Smooth-coated sporting and gun dog that was developed in the 17th century for hunting. It can be trained to indicate the direction in which game lies by standing motionless, aligning its muzzle, body and tail. It has a wide head and a strong, lean body. The short, dense coat can be white with black or brown markings. Height: to 63cm (25in); weight: to 27kg (60lb).

pointillism (Fr. *pointiller*, to dot) Technique of painting in regular dots or small dashes of pure colour, developed from NEO-IMPRESSIONISM by Georges SEURAT. From a distance, the dots create a vibrant effect.

poisoning Adverse effects of substances, either natural or synthetic, introduced into the body or produced as side-products of the organism itself. Some poisons are toxic in small doses; others work cumulatively, over longer periods. Levels of sensitivity and treatments vary.

poison ivy North American shrub that causes a severe itchy rash on contact with human skin. It has greenish flowers and white berries. Species *Rhus radicans* and *R. toxicodendron*. Family Anarcardiaceae.

Poitier, Sidney (1924–) US film actor and director. His first major role was in *No Way Out* (1950). Poitier was nominated for a best actor Academy Award for his performance in *The Defiant Ones* (1958) and became the first African-American to win a best actor Oscar for *Lilies of the Field* (1963). Other films include *Guess Who's Coming to Dinner* (1967), *In the Heat of the Night* (1967) and *They Call Me Mr Tibbs* (1970). Poitier's directorial credits include *Stir Crazy* (1980) and *Sneakers* (1992).

Poitiers City on the River Clain, w central France; capital of Vienne department and chief town of Poitou-Charentes region. Poitiers was the ancient capital of the Pictones (a Gallic tribe) and an important centre of early European monasticism. In the 5th century, the city fell to the Visigoths, who were in turn defeated by the Merovingian king Clovis I (507). Here, in 732, the Franks halted the advance of the Muslim Saracens. The Battle of Poitiers (1356) was an important English victory in the HUNDRED YEARS WAR. Industries: metallurgy, printing, chemicals. Pop. (1990) 107,625.

poker Card game believed to have originated in Europe in the 16th century. Basically a gambling game, the object is to win the pot (all the bets that are made after each card is dealt) by holding the best combination of cards (in same suit, in pairs or triples, or in numerical sequence) or by bluffing the other players into withdrawing.

Poland Republic in central Europe. It is mostly lowland, forming part of the great European plain. The N, lagoon-lined, Baltic Sea coast includes the ports of GDAŃSK and SZCZECIN and the mouths of the rivers VISTULA and ODER. There are many lakes, especially in the NE. The central plains include Poland's capital, WARSAW, and the cities of POZNAŃ, LÓDZ and LUBLIN. Poland's best farmland is in the SE Polish uplands. Beyond the cities of KATOWICE and KRAKÓW, the land rises to Mount Rysy, at 2,499m (8,199ft), in the CARPATHIAN MOUNTAINS. In the SW lies the region of SILESIA and its capital, WROCLAW. Poland has a continental climate, with warm summers and bitterly cold, snowy winters. **Vegetation** Forests cover *c.*30% of Poland. Nearly 50% of the land is arable. **History and politics** In the 9th century AD, Slavic tribes unified the region. The Piast dynasty came to power. In 1025, Boleslav I became the first king of Poland, but the kingdom disintegrated in the 12th century. In 1320, Ladislas I reunified Poland, but the dynasty collapsed under the might of the TEUTONIC KNIGHTS. The 16th-century rule of the JAGIELLO dynasty is regarded as Poland's "golden age". In 1569, Poland and Lithuania were united. In JOHN II's reign, Poland was plundered by Sweden, Russia and Turkey. JOHN III SOBIESKI restored some prestige, but his death brought division.

Following the War of Succession (1733–35), Russia dominated Polish affairs. In 1772 and 1793, Poland was partitioned between Austria, Prussia and Russia. In 1795, the defeat of a Polish revolt led to further partition, and Poland ceased to exist. The Congress of Vienna (1814–15) established a small, semi-independent Polish state based on Kraków. Polish uprisings in 1848 and 1863 against Russian dominance led to more impositions. In World War 1 Poland initially fought with Germany against Russia, but Germany occupied Poland. In 1918, Poland regained its independence. In 1920, Poland recaptured Warsaw from Russia. In 1921, Poland became a republic. The 1920s and 1930s, were a period of dictatorship and military rule. In September 1939, following a secret pact between Hitler and Stalin, Germany invaded and Poland was partitioned between the Soviet Union and Germany. Britain declared war, thus beginning WORLD WAR 2. Following the German invasion of the Soviet Union, all of Poland fell under German rule. The Nazis established concentration camps, such as AUSCHWITZ. More than 6 million Poles perished. Only 100,000 Polish Jews, from a pre-war community of more than 3 million, survived the HOLOCAUST. Polish resistance intensified. In 1944, a provisional government was established. In August 1944, the Warsaw uprising was ruthlessly crushed by the Germans. In 1945, Poland regained its independence. It lost land in the E to the Soviet Union but gained sections of Prussia from Germany. In 1949, Poland joined the COUNCIL FOR MUTUAL ECONOMIC ASSISTANCE (COMECON). In 1952, Poland became a People's Republic, modelled on the Soviet constitution. In 1955, it was one of the founder members of the WARSAW PACT. Uprisings in 1956 led to the formation of a more liberal administration, led by Wladyslaw GOMULKA. The collectivization of agriculture was reversed, and restrictions on religious worship were relaxed. In 1980, striking dockers in Gdańsk, led by Lech WALESA, formed a trade union called SOLIDARITY, which gained popular support. In 1981, General JARUZELSKI declared martial law; Solidarity was banned and its leaders arrested. In 1983, continuing recession and civil unrest led to the lifting of martial law. Following reforms in the Soviet Union, Solidarity was legalized and won free elections in 1989. In 1990, the Communist Party was disbanded, and Walesa became president. In 1995 elections, Walesa was defeated by the leader of the Democratic Left Alliance, Aleksander Kwaśniewski. In 1996, Poland joined the ORGANIZATION FOR ECONOMIC COOPERATION AND DEVELOPMENT (OECD). Poland has faced huge problems in the transition to a market economy. Elections in 1997 were won by the Solidarity Electoral Alliance (AWS), a centre-right coalition. In 1999, Poland became a member of NATO. Kwaśniewski was re-elected in 2000. **Economy** Before World War 2, Poland had a mainly agricultural economy. Under communism, industry expanded greatly. Today, 27% of the workforce is employed in agriculture and 37% in industry. Upper Silesia is the richest coal basin in Europe. Poland is the world's fifth-largest producer of lignite and seventh-largest producer of bituminous coal. Copper ore is also a vital mineral resource. Manufacturing accounts for *c.*24% of exports. Poland is the world's fifth-largest producer of ships. Agriculture remains important. Major crops include barley, potatoes and wheat. The transition to a free-market economy has doubled unemployment and increased foreign debt. Economic growth, however, is slowly returning (1995 GDP per capita, US$5,400).

Polanski, Roman (1933–) Polish actor and director. His first feature film, *Knife in the Water* (1962), was followed by *Repulsion* (1965) and *Cul de-Sac* (1966). Later

POLAND
AREA: 312,680sq km (120,726sq mi)
POPULATION: 40,366,000
CAPITAL (POPULATION): Warsaw (1,638,000)

films include *Rosemary's Baby* (1968), *Chinatown* (1974), *Tess* (1980) and *Death and the Maiden* (1994).

polar bear Large white bear that lives on Arctic coasts and ice floes. It spends most of its time at sea on drifting ice, often swimming for many miles. It preys chiefly on seals and is hunted for fur and meat. Length: 2.3m (7.5ft); weight: to 405kg (900lb). Species *Thalarctos maritimus*.

Polaris *See* POLE STAR

polarized light Light waves that have electromagnetic vibrations in only one direction. (Ordinary light vibrates in all directions perpendicular to the direction of propagation.) Three types are distinguished: plane-polarized, circularly polarized and elliptical-polarized light, each depending on the net direction of the vibrations. Polarizing sunglasses use a POLAROID material to reduce the glare from light polarized by reflection from horizontal surfaces.

Polaroid Trade name for a refracting material invented by Edwin LAND. It only transmits a certain type of POLARIZED LIGHT; all other light is absorbed. Polaroid material is used in sunglasses to reduce the glare. In 1947 Land developed a Polaroid camera that produced a finished print within one minute.

Pole, Reginald (1500–58) English cardinal, the last Roman Catholic archbishop of Canterbury. A cousin of HENRY VIII, Pole opposed Henry's divorce of CATHERINE OF ARAGON and moved to Italy during the REFORMATION. In 1554, he returned to England as papal legate to the Roman Catholic Queen MARY I. She made him archbishop of Canterbury in 1556.

pole Generally, either of the two points of intersection of the surface of a sphere and its axis of rotation. The Earth has four poles: the North and South geographic poles, where the Earth's imaginary axis meets its surface; and the north and south magnetic poles, where the Earth's MAGNETIC FIELD is most concentrated. A bar magnet has a north pole, where the magnetic flux leaves the magnet, and a south pole, where it enters. A pole is also one of the terminals (positive or negative) of a battery, electric machine or circuit.

polecat Any of several species of small, carnivorous, nocturnal mammals that live in wooded areas of Eurasia and N Africa; especially *Mustela putorius*, the common polecat. It has a slender body, long bushy tail and brown to black fur known as fitch. It eats small animals, birds and eggs. Length: 45.7cm (18in). Family Mustelidae.

Pole Star (Polaris, North Star) Important navigational star, nearest to the N celestial star. It is in the constellation Ursa Minor and always marks due N.

pole vault Field event in athletics in which contestants use a pole to swing themselves up and over a horizontal bar suspended between two uprights. The bar is progressively raised; vaulters who fail to clear a height in three attempts are eliminated. The winner vaults the highest. Pole vaulting has been an Olympic sport since 1896.

police Body of people concerned with maintaining civil order and investigating breaches of the law. The first independent police force was established in Paris, France, in 1667, becoming a uniformed force in 1829. Britain's first regular professional force, the Marine Police Establishment, was founded in 1800. In 1829, the Metropolitan Police was created by Sir Robert PEEL. The New York City Police Department was formed in 1844.

poliomyelitis (polio) Acute viral infection of the nervous system affecting the nerves that activate muscles. Often a mild disease with effects limited to the throat and intestine, it is nonetheless potentially serious, with paralysis occurring in 1% of patients. It becomes life-threatening only if the breathing muscles are affected, in which case the person may need artificial ventilation. It has become rare in developed countries since the introduction of vaccination in the mid-1950s.

Polish National language of Poland, spoken by virtually all of the country's 39 million people. It belongs to the Slavonic family of INDO-EUROPEAN LANGUAGES. Polish is written in the Roman (Latin) alphabet but with a large number of diacritical marks to represent the various Slavonic vowels and consonants.

Polish Corridor Strip of land along the River VISTULA, dividing East Prussia from the rest of Germany and providing Poland with access to the Baltic Sea (1919–39). It was created by the Treaty of VERSAILLES after World War 1, when Poland became independent. The city of GDAŃSK, near the mouth of the Vistula, was made a free city but, dominated by Germans, excluded Polish enterprise. The arrangement caused disputes between Germany and Poland, exploited by HITLER to justify his invasion of Poland in 1939.

Politburo (political bureau) Administrative and policy-making body of the COMMUNIST PARTY OF THE SOVIET UNION (CPSU). Formerly called the PRESIDIUM, it consisted of 11 or 12 full members and 6 to 9 candidate members chosen by the Party's central committee.

political correctness (PC) Ostentatiously moral attitude on contemporary issues. In the 1990s, political correctness meant conspicuously avoiding the perceived moral evils of the age – notably racial or sexual discrimination.

political party Group organized for the purpose of electing candidates to office and promoting a particular set of political principles. *See individual articles*

politics Sphere of action in human society in which power is sought in order to regulate the ways in which people shall live together. For a society to engage in politics, it must conceive of society as being in a state of perpetual change.

Polk, James Knox (1795–1849) 11th US President (1845–49). During his administration, California and New Mexico were acquired as a result of the US victory in the MEXICAN WAR (1846–48), which Polk's aggressive policy had largely provoked. He also gained Oregon through the Oregon Treaty (1846).

polka Lively Bohemian folk dance. It became fashionable in Paris in the 1940s, and thereafter in Europe and the Americas. It is often performed as a ballroom dance.

pollack (pollock) Marine food fish of the COD family found in large shoals on both sides of the North Atlantic. Coloured green with yellow or grey, it has a jutting lower jaw. Length: to 100cm (3.5ft); weight: to 16kg (35lb). Family Gadidae; species include *Pollachius pollachius* and *Pollachius virens*.

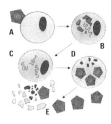

► **poliomyelitis** A viral disease that affects the human nervous system, poliomyelitis (polio) can often cause paralysis. Cells of the throat and intestines are the first to become infected. Virus absorption to the cell surface occurs (A), followed by penetration of the cell. Within the cell, the virus protein coat is shed releasing a coiled nucleic acid strand (B). Nucleic acid replication occurs (C), each new strand becoming surrounded by a protein coat (D). As many as 500 new infectious viruses are released as the cell bursts and dies (E).

pollen Yellow, powder-like SPORES that give rise to the male sex cells in flowering plants. Pollen grains are produced in the anther chambers on the STAMEN. When the pollen lands on the STIGMA of a compatible plant, it germinates, sending a long pollen tube down through the STYLE to the OVARY. During this process, one of its nuclei divides, giving rise to two male nuclei (the equivalent of male sex cells or GAMETES), one of which fuses with a female sex cell in FERTILIZATION. The other sex cell fuses with two more of the female nuclei to form a special tissue, the endosperm. In many species, this tissue develops into a food store for the embryo in the seed. *See also* ALTERNATION OF GENERATIONS; HAY FEVER; POLLINATION

pollination Transfer of POLLEN from the STAMEN to the STIGMA of a flower. Self-pollination occurs on one flower and cross-pollination between two flowers on different plants. Incompatibility mechanisms in many flowers prevent self-pollination. Pollination occurs mainly by wind and insects. **Wind-pollinated** flowers are usually small and produce a large quantity of small, light, dry pollen grains. **Insect-pollinated** flowers are usually brightly coloured, strongly scented, contain nectar, and produce heavy, sticky pollen.

Pollock, Jackson (1912–56) US painter. A leading figure in ABSTRACT EXPRESSIONISM, he began experimenting with ABSTRACT ART in the 1940s. In 1947, Pollock started pouring paint straight onto the canvas. Instead of brushes, he used sticks or knives to create surface patterns. This method is known as ACTION PAINTING. His works include *The Blue Unconscious* (1946) and *Lavender Mist* (1950).

poll tax Tax of a fixed sum imposed on all liable individuals. Such taxes were occasionally levied by medieval governments: one provoked the PEASANTS' REVOLT (1381) in England. Southern US states after the Civil War made the right to vote dependent on payment of a poll tax, a device to disenfranchise poor blacks. In 1989, a poll tax (the Community Charge) was introduced in Britain, but was withdrawn after civil disobedience.

pollution Contamination of the natural environment, generally by industrialized society. Modern industrial and agricultural methods have polluted the Earth's air, land and water mainly through manufactured toxic chemicals (such as PESTICIDES and FERTILIZERS) or the over-production of naturally occurring chemicals (such as CARBON DIOXIDE). Pesticides, such as DDT, build up in the environment and can enter the FOOD CHAIN. The excessive use of nitrate fertilizers leaches the soil and causes WATER POLLUTION through concentrated run-off. The sulphur compounds produced by burning FOSSIL FUELS causes ACID RAIN. Carbon dioxide emissions from AUTOMOBILE exhausts contributes to the GREENHOUSE EFFECT. The use of CHLOROFLUORCARBONS (CFCs) in aerosol propellants depletes the OZONE LAYER. A continuing problem is the storage of NUCLEAR WASTE. Pollution can also result from major disasters, such as CHERNOBYL, BHOPAL, or huge oil spillages from damaged tankers. Other forms of contamination include NOISE pollution. *See also* CONSERVATION; ECOLOGY; EUTROPHICATION

Pollux *See* CASTOR AND POLLUX

Pollux (Beta Geminorum) Brightest star in the constellation Gemini; a red giant. Characteristics: apparent mag. 1.15; absolute mag. 0.7; spectral type KO; distance 35 light-years.

Polo, Marco (1254–1324) Venetian traveller in Asia. In 1274 he accompanied his father and uncle on a trading mission to the court of KUBLAI KHAN, the MONGOL emperor of China. According to Marco Polo's account, he remained in the Far East for more than 20 years, becoming the confidant of Kublai Khan and travelling throughout China and beyond. His account, *The Description of the World*, became the chief source of European knowledge of China for centuries.

polo Field game played on horseback. Two teams of four players, on a field up to 182m (600ft) by 273m (900ft), each try to hit a small ball into a goal using flexible mallets. A game consists of four, six or eight chukkas (periods), each 7.5 minutes long; additional chukkas may be played to decide a game if the scores are tied. Polo originated in Persia in ancient times and spread throughout Asia. It was revived in India in the 19th century and was taken up by British army officers there. It was first played in Britain in 1868 and is also played in the USA.

polonium (symbol Po) Rare, radioactive, metallic element of group VI of the periodic table, discovered (1898) by Marie CURIE. It is found in trace amounts in URANIUM ores and may be synthesized. Properties: at.no. 84; r.d. 9.40; m.p. 254°C (489°F); b.p. 962°C (1,764°F); most stable isotope Po^{209}.

Pol Pot (1928–98) Cambodian ruler. In 1975, he led the communist KHMER ROUGE in the overthrow of the US-backed government of Lon Nol. Pol Pot instigated a reign of terror in Cambodia (renamed Kampuchea). Intellectuals were massacred and city-dwellers were driven into the countryside. Estimates suggest that *c.*2 million Cambodians were murdered. In 1979, Pol Pot was overthrown by a Vietnamese invasion. He continued to lead the Khmer Rouge. In 1997, it was reported that Pol Pot had been sentenced to life imprisonment by a Khmer Rouge court for the murder of a comrade. He died of heart failure.

poltergeist Noisy, mischievous spirit or ghost that supposedly persecutes the occupants of a house.

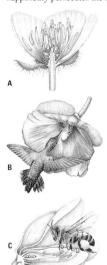

A

B

C

D

◄ **pollination** Flowers are adapted to different pollination methods. Non-specialized simple flowers, such as the buttercup (A), can be pollinated by a variety of means. Other flowers can only be pollinated by one method. There are bird-pollinated flowers, such as the hummingbird-pollinated hibiscus (B); bee-specialized flowers, including the gorse (C); and wind-pollinated flowers, such as the catkins found on the hazel (D).

polyanthus Any of a group of spring-flowering, perennial PRIMROSES of the genus *Primula*. Occurring mainly in the N temperate zone, they may be almost any colour. They have basal leaves and disc-shaped flowers, branching from a stalk to form a ball-like cluster. Height: to 15cm (6in). Family Primulaceae.

Polybius (*c*.200–*c*.120 BC) Greek historian. A leader in the Achaean Confederation, he was deported as an honoured hostage to Rome in 168 BC. He became a friend of SCIPIO AFRICANUS MINOR and accompanied him to Spain and Africa. He was present at the destruction of Carthage in 146 BC and later acted as intermediary between Rome and the Achaeans.

polychlorinated biphenyl (PCB) Any of several stable mixtures – liquid, resinous or crystalline – of organic compounds. They are used as lubricants and heat-transfer fluids. The use of PCBs has been restricted since 1973 because they are toxic and their resistance to decomposition poses a threat to wildlife.

polyester Class of organic substance composed of large molecules arranged in a chain or a network and formed from many smaller molecules through the establishment of ESTER linkages. Polyester fibres are resistant to chemicals and are made into ropes and textiles. In 1941 John Whinfield developed the first polyester, Terylene.

polyethene (polythene, polyethylene) POLYMER of ETHENE. It is a partially crystalline, lightweight, thermoplastic RESIN with high resistance to chemicals, low moisture absorption, and good insulating properties. **Low-density** polyethene (LDPE) was first produced in the 1930s. It is mainly used in the manufacture of PLASTIC bags. **High-density** polyethene (HDPE), synthesized in the 1950s, is more flexible and is used for mouldings.

polygamy MARRIAGE in which more than one spouse is permitted. More often it is used to denote **polygyny** (several wives) than **polyandry** (several husbands). Polygamy is legal and commonplace in many nations, notably many Muslim and African countries.

polygon Plane geometric figure having three or more sides intersecting at three or more points (vertices). They are named according to the number of sides or vertices: triangle (three-sided), quadrilateral (four-sided), hexagon (six-sided). A regular polygon is equilateral (has sides equal in length) and equiangular (has equal angles).

polygraph *See* LIE DETECTOR

polyhedron In geometry, three-dimensional solid figure whose surface is made up of POLYGONS. These are called the faces of the polyhedron, and the points at which they meet are the vertices.

polymer Substance formed by the union of from two to several thousand simple MOLECULES (monomers) to form a large molecular structure. Some, such as CELLULOSE, occur in nature; others form the basis of PLASTICS and synthetic RESINS. *See also* POLYMERIZATION

polymerase chain reaction (PCR) Chemical reaction, speeded up by an ENZYME, that is used to make large numbers of copies of a specific piece of DNA, starting from only one or few DNA molecules. It enables scientists to make large enough quantities of DNA to be able to analyze or manipulate it. PCR is extremely important in GENETIC ENGINEERING and GENETIC FINGERPRINTING.

polymerization Chemical combination of several MOLECULES to form straight-chain molecules, cross-linked giant molecules, or a combination of both, all called POLYMERS. It is the major industrial process in the manufacture of PLASTICS. In nature, large biochemical compounds (such as PROTEINS and NUCLEIC ACIDS) are formed by polymerization.

Polynesia One of the three divisions of OCEANIA, and the general term for the islands of the central Pacific Ocean; MICRONESIA and MELANESIA lie to the W. The principal islands in Polynesia are the Hawaiian Islands, Phoenix Islands, Tokelau Islands, the SAMOA group, EASTER ISLAND, COOK ISLANDS and FRENCH POLYNESIA. Because of their Maori population, the two larger islands of New Zealand are also usually included. The islands are mostly coral or volcanic in origin. The inhabitants show physical similarities and share common cultural and linguistic characteristics.

polynomial Sum of terms that are powers of a variable. For example, $8x^4 - 4x^3 + 7x^2 + x - 11$ is a polynomial of the fourth degree (the highest power four). In general a polynomial has the form $a_0x^n + a_1x^{n-1} + a_2x^{n-2} + \ldots\ldots\ldots + a_{n-2}x^2 + a_{n-1}x + a_n$, although certain powers of x and the constant term a_n may be missing. The values a_n, a_{n-1}, etc., are the COEFFICIENTS of the polynomial.

polyp Body type of various species of animals within the phylum Cnidaria. It has a mouth surrounded by extensible tentacles and a lower end that is adapted for attachment to a surface. It may be solitary, as in the SEA ANEMONE, but is more often an individual of a colonial organism such as CORAL.

polyp In medicine, swollen mass projecting from the wall of a cavity lined with mucous membrane, such as the nose. Some growths can be cancerous.

polyphony Vocal or instrumental part music in which the compositional interest centres on the "horizontal" aspect of each moving part rather than on the "vertical" structure of chords. The golden age of polyphonic music was the 16th century, and masters included Giovanni PALESTRINA and William BYRD. *See also* HARMONY

polysaccharide Any of a group of complex CARBOHYDRATES made up of long chains of monosaccharide (simple-sugar) molecules. GLUCOSE is a monosaccharide, and the polysaccharides STARCH and CELLULOSE are both polymers of glucose. Polysaccharides function both as food stores (starch in plants and GLYCOGEN in animals) and as structural materials (cellulose and PECTIN in the cell walls of plants and CHITIN in the protective skeleton of insects).

polystyrene Synthetic organic POLYMER composed of long chains of the aromatic compound styrene. It is a strong thermoplastic RESIN, acid- and alkali-resistant, non-absorbent, and an excellent electrical insulator.

polytetrafluorethylene (PTFE) Chemically inert, solid plastic, known also by the trade names **Teflon** and **Fluon**. PTFE is used as a heat-resistant material for heat-shields on spacecraft, as a non-stick coating on cooking utensils and as a lubricant. PTFE is stable up to *c*.300°C (572°F).

polytheism Belief in, or worship of, many gods and goddesses. The ancient Egyptian, Babylonian, Greek and Roman religions were all polytheistic, as were the religions of the Americas before the European settlement. HINDUISM is a modern polytheistic religion. *See also* ANCESTOR WORSHIP; ANIMISM; MONOTHEISM

polythene *See* POLYETHENE

polyunsaturate Type of FAT or OIL that has molecules of long CARBON chains with many double bonds. Polyunsaturated fats exist in fish oils and most vegetable oils. At room temperature, unsaturated oils are liquids and SATURATED FATS are solids. Polyunsaturates, which have low or no CHOLESTEROL content, are used in MARGARINES and cooking oils. They are considered healthier than saturated fats.

polyvinyl chloride (PVC) White, tough, solid thermoplastic that is a POLYMER of vinyl chloride. A PVC can be softened and made elastic with a plasticizer.

Easily coloured and resistant to weather and fire, PVC is used to produce a variety of products, including fibres, pipes and coatings for raincoats and upholstery.

Pombal, Sebastião José de Carvalho e Mello, Marquês de (1699–1782) Portuguese statesman. He was minister for foreign affairs (1750–56). As chief minister, Pombal was virtual ruler of Portugal from 1756 until the death of King Joseph in 1777. He increased royal power at the expense of the old nobility, the INQUISITION and the JESUITS, whom he expelled in 1759. An "enlightened despot", Pombal reformed the administration, economy, education and army, and encouraged trade with Brazil.

pomegranate Deciduous shrub or small tree native to W Asia. It has shiny, oval leaves and orange-red flowers. The round fruit has a red, leathery rind and numerous seeds that are coated with an edible pulp. Family Punicaceae; species *Punica granatum*.

Pompadour, Jeanne-Antoinette Poisson, Marquise de (1721–64) Influential mistress and confidante of LOUIS XV after 1745. A strong influence on the court, she was a great patron of the arts, befriending DIDEROT and encouraging the publication of the *Encyclopédie*.

Pompeii Ancient Roman city in Naples province, SW Italy. It was founded in the 8th century BC and ruled by Greeks, Etruscans and others before it was conquered by Rome in 89 BC. In AD 79, it was buried by the eruption of Mount VESUVIUS. The swiftness and violence of the eruption killed *c*.2,000 people and left the city covered up to six metres deep in volcanic ash, preserving possessions and houses intact until excavation began in 1748.

Pompey (106–48 BC) (Gnaeus Pompeius Magnus) Roman general. In 83 BC he fought for SULLA and campaigned in Sicily, Africa and Spain. In 70 BC, Pompey was named consul with CRASSUS and fought a notable campaign (66 BC) against MITHRIDATES VI of Pontus. In 59 BC, he formed the first triumvirate with Crassus and his great rival, Julius CAESAR. After the death of Crassus, Pompey joined Caesar's enemies, and civil war broke out in 49 BC. Driven out of Rome by Caesar's advance, Pompey was defeated at Pharsalus (48 BC) and fled to Egypt, where he was murdered.

Pompidou, Georges Jean Raymond (1911–74) French statesman, prime minister (1962, 1962–66, 1966–67, 1967–68) and president (1969–74). In 1958 he helped Charles DE GAULLE draft the constitution of the Fifth Republic. In 1961, Pompidou negotiated a settlement to the war in Algeria. He succeeded De Gaulle as president. Pompidou died in office.

Ponce de León, Juan (1460–1521) Spanish explorer. A veteran of COLUMBUS' second voyage, he conquered Puerto Rico for Spain (1508–09) and in 1513 led an expedition to explore rumoured islands north of Cuba. He reached land near what is now St Augustine, Florida, USA. In 1521, he returned with a colonizing expedition and received an arrow wound from which he later died.

pondweed Any of numerous species of a family of aquatic, perennial flowering plants of the genus *Potamogeton*, found mostly in temperate regions in freshwater lakes, but also in brackish and salt water. Most pondweeds have spike-like flowers that stick out of the water, and submerged or floating leaves. Family Potamogetonaceae.

Pontiac's Rebellion (1763–66) Native American rising against the British. Pontiac (d.1769) was an Ottawa chief who led a loose association of allies hostile to the British takeover of Québec (1760). A number of outposts in the Great Lakes region were overrun. News of the French withdrawal from North America fatally weakened the campaign, which soon collapsed.

Pontius Pilate (active 1st century AD) Roman prefect. In *c*.AD 26, Emperor Tiberius appointed him procurator (governor) of Judaea. An arrogant and cruel ruler, Pilate is noted for his order to crucify JESUS CHRIST. In *c*.AD 36, he was recalled to Rome after sanctioning the massacre of Samaritans.

Pontormo, Jacopo Carucci (1494–1557) Italian painter. He is thought to have painted *Vertumnus and Pomona* (1520–21), which shows qualities characteristic of MANNERISM. Other paintings include *The Madonna* (1518), *The Visitation* (1516) and *Deposition* (*c*.1527).

Pontus Ancient kingdom of NE Anatolia (Turkey). The coastal cities were colonized by Greeks in the 6th–5th centuries BC and retained virtual autonomy under the Persian empire. The kingdom of Pontus reached the height of its power under MITHRIDATES VI, who conquered Asia Minor, gained control of the Crimea and threatened Rome. After his defeat by Pompey (65 BC), the country was divided up under Roman rule but maintained its commercial prosperity.

pony Any of several breeds of small horses, usually solid and stocky. They are commonly used as a children's saddle horse, for show and for draught. Types include the hardy Shetland pony; the Dartmoor and Exmoor ponies of Cornwall, Somerset and Devon; the grey Highland pony; the Welsh pony; and the Welsh Cob. Height: 115–45cm (45–57in) at the shoulder.

Pony Express (1860–61) US relay mail service between Saint Joseph, Missouri, and Sacramento, California. About 25 riders changed horses at 190 staging posts on the 3,200km (1,800mi) journey. The time for the journey was ten days, less than half the time taken by stagecoach. The service gradually petered out with the introduction of the telegraph system.

poodle Breed of dog believed to have originated in Germany. Its intelligence has made it a popular pet. It has a rounded skull, a long straight body and a high-set tail, often docked. The thick, wiry coat is commonly clipped into an ornate style. The main sizes are standard, miniature and toy. Height: (standard) more than 38cm (15in) at the shoulder.

pool Form of BILLIARDS that originated in the USA. One version is played with eight single-colour balls and seven striped balls (numbered 1 to 15), plus a white cue ball, on a rectangular table with four corner pockets and two side pockets. The most popular version divides the striped balls and the single-colour balls, except the black ball (number 8), between the two players, so that the black is the last to be potted.

poor laws Legislation that was designed to relieve poverty in England. In 1601, the Poor Law Act required individual parishes to provide for the local poor via the levying of property rates. Three categories of poor were identified: vagabonds and beggars, the infirm and the "deserving" unemployed. In 1795, the Speenhamland system provided levels of poor relief based on the price of bread and the size of families. In 1834, the Poor Law Amendment Act forbade the giving of assistance to the impoverished outside of the workhouse. In the 20th century, the poor laws were finally abolished by social security legislation and the creation of the WELFARE STATE.

pop art Movement inspired by consumerist images and popular culture that flourished in the USA and Britain from the late 1950s to the early 1970s. Pop art took its ideas from comic books, advertisements, packaging, television and films. Characteristic techniques included SILK-SCREEN PRINTING and COLLAGE. Leading artists included Andy WARHOL, Roy LICHTENSTEIN, Claes OLDENBURG, Richard HAMILTON and David HOCKNEY.

Pope, Alexander (1688–1744) English poet. He first attracted attention for *Essay on Criticism* (1711), a poem in heroic couplets. Pope's reputation was established with the publication of his feminized mock epic *The Rape of the Lock* (1712–14). He collaborated with John ARBUTHNOT and John GAY on the play *Three Hours After Marriage* (1723). Pope's philosophical poem *Essay on Man* (1733–34) was complemented by the satire *The Dunciad* (1728–43). *Epistle to Dr Arbuthnot* (1735) was a stinging attack on his critics. Pope also made successful translations of Homer's Iliad (1715–20) and The Odyssey (1726–26). *See also* AUGUSTAN AGE

pope *See* PAPACY

poplar Any of a number of deciduous, softwood trees of the genus *Populus*, native to cool and temperate regions. The oval leaves grow on stalks, and flowers take the form of catkins. Some species are called cottonwoods because of the cotton-like fluff on their seeds. Height: to 60m (200ft). Family Salicaceae. *See also* ASPEN

Popocatépetl Snow-capped, dormant volcano in central Mexico, 72km (45mi) SE of Mexico City. The crater contains sulphur deposits. Height: 5,452m (17,887ft).

Popper, Sir Karl Raimund (1902–94) British philosopher of natural and social sciences, b. Austria. He proposed his theory of falsification in *The Logic of Scientific Discovery* (1934), saying scientific "truth" cannot be absolutely confirmed. In *The Open Society and its Enemies* (1945), Popper attacked the historicism of MARXISM.

poppy Any annual or perennial plant of the genus *Papaver*, family Papaveraceae, or any related plant. About 100 species of the genus exist. They have bright red, orange or white flowers, often with dark centres, with four thin, overlapping petals and two thick sepals; all produce the milky sap, LATEX. The unripe capsules of the Asian opium poppy are used to produce the drug OPIUM. Plants closely related to the true poppy include the California poppy and the Welsh poppy.

popular front Alliance of left-wing political parties. In Europe, such alliances were formed in the 1930s partly in reaction to threats from FASCISM and with the encouragement of the Soviet Union. A popular-front government came to power in France, under Léon BLUM (1936–37), and in Spain (1936), where it provoked a military revolt and the Spanish CIVIL WAR. In more recent times, revolutionary parties in many African and Asian countries have adopted the name.

porcelain White, glass-like, non-porous, hard, translucent CERAMIC material. Porcelain is widely used for tableware, decorative objects, laboratory equipment and electrical insulators. It was developed by the Chinese in the 7th or 8th century. True or hard-paste porcelain is made of KAOLIN (white china clay) mixed with

▶ **poppy** Cultivated since the Middle Ages, the opium poppy (*Papaver somniferum*) is the natural source of the drug opium and its derivatives, morphine and heroin. These are extracted from the latex of the seed pods. The seeds themselves are used as cattle food and as a source of oil. The dramatic flower makes the plant a popular garden ornamental.

powdered petuntse (FELDSPAR). Soft-paste porcelain is composed of clay and powdered glass.

porcupine Short-legged, mostly nocturnal, herbivorous RODENT with erectile, defensive quills in its back. Old World porcupines of the family **Hystricidae** have brown to black fur with white-banded quills and are terrestrial. New World porcupines of the family **Erethizontidae** are smaller with yellow to white quills and are arboreal. The largest European and African rodent, the African crested porcupine (*Hystrix cristata*), attains a length of c.80cm (31in).

pornography Visual or aural material presenting erotic behaviour that is intended to be sexually stimulating and is lacking in artistic or other forms of merit. It is often considered to be demeaning both to sexuality and to the body; many people, especially feminists, have called for a total ban. Pornographic content, however, is difficult to assess, because the response of individuals varies. There is legal CENSORSHIP in most countries, but the interpretation of the law is subjective.

porphyria Group of rare genetic disorders in which there is defective METABOLISM of one or more porphyrins, the breakdown products of haemoglobin. It can produce a wide range of effects, including intestinal upset, HYPERTENSION, weakness, abnormal skin reactions to sunlight and mental disturbance. A key diagnostic indicator is that the patient's urine turns reddish-brown if it is left to stand. There is no specific remedy, and treatment tends to be supportive.

porpoise Small, toothed WHALE with a blunt snout. Found in most oceans, the best known is the common porpoise of the Northern Hemisphere. Its body is black above and white below. Length: to 2m (7ft). Family Delphinidae; species *Phocaena phocaena*.

Porsche, Ferdinand (1875–1951) German car manufacturer who designed the Volkswagen Beetle. In 1934, Porsche produced plans for an affordable car that the Nazis named *Volkswagen* ("people's car") and promised to mass produce. In fact, production did not start until 1945. Porsche also produced sports cars.

port Fortified wine produced in the Douro Valley, N Portugal. It may be white, tawny (translucent brown) or red, and contains 17–20% alcohol. A vintage port is aged in oak casks for 15 to 20 years.

Port-au-Prince Capital of Haiti, a port on the SE shore of the Gulf of Gonâve on the W coast of Hispaniola. It was founded by the French in 1749, becoming the capital of Haiti in 1770. Industries: tobacco, textiles, cement, coffee, sugar. Pop. (1992) 1,255,078.

Port Elizabeth Seaport on Algoa Bay, Eastern Cape province, S South Africa. First settled in 1799 by the British, the city grew after the completion of the railway line to Kimberley in 1873. Exports: diamonds, fruit, wool. Industries: motor vehicles, chemicals. Pop. (1991) 853,204.

Porter, Cole (1891–1964) US composer and lyricist. His string of hit musicals for the stage included *Gay Divorcee* (1932), *Anything Goes* (1934) and *Kiss Me Kate* (1948). Porter also wrote the score for the film *High Society* (1956). His popular songs include "Let's Do It" (1928), "Night and Day" (1932) and "Begin the Beguine" (1935).

Porter, Katherine Anne (1890–1980) US writer. Her short-story collections include *Pale Horse, Pale Rider* (1939) and *The Leaning Tower* (1944). Porter's major novel was the allegorical *Ship of Fools* (1962). She won a Pulitzer Prize for her *Collected Stories* (1965).

Portillo, Michael Denzil Xavier (1953–) British politician, secretary of state for defence (1995–97). He entered

Parliament in 1984. In 1994, Portillo joined John MAJOR's cabinet as secretary of state for employment. His right-wing Euro-scepticism saw him often at odds with official CONSERVATIVE PARTY policy. Portillo lost his seat in the 1997 general election, but was re-elected in 1999 and became shadow chancellor under William HAGUE in 2000.

Portland City and port on the Willamette River, NW Oregon, USA. First settled in 1845, it developed as a major port for exporting timber and grain after 1850. It was a supply station for the California goldfields and the Alaska gold rush (1897–1900). Portland is Oregon's largest city. Industries: shipbuilding, timber. Pop. (1994) 450,777.

Portland Largest city and port in Maine, USA. Due to its deep natural harbour on Casco Bay, a settlement (Falmouth) was established here in 1632. In 1775, it was devastated by the British during the American Revolution. From 1820–32, it was state capital. The modern city is an oil terminus and shipping centre. Pop. (1990) 64,358.

Portland, William Henry Cavendish Bentinck, 3rd Duke of (1738–1809) British statesman, prime minister (1783, 1807–09). He was briefly made prime minister at the end of the AMERICAN REVOLUTION. As home secretary(1794–1801), Portland helped William PITT the Younger draft the Act of UNION (1801). His second ministry ended in a feud between CANNING and CASTLEREAGH.

Port Louis Capital of MAURITIUS, a seaport in the NW of the island. It was founded by the French in 1735. It grew in importance as a trading port after the opening of the Suez Canal. The main export is sugar. Pop. (1995) 146,000.

Port Moresby Capital of PAPUA NEW GUINEA, on the SE coast of New Guinea. Settled by the British in the 1880s, its sheltered harbour was the site of an important Allied base in World War 2. It developed rapidly in the post-war period. Exports: gold, copper, rubber. Pop. (1990) 193,242.

Port of Spain Capital of Trinidad and Tobago, on the NW coast of Trinidad. The city was founded by the Spanish in the late 16th century and was seized by Britain in 1797. From 1958 to 1962 it was the capital of the Federation of the West Indies. The city has attractive botanical gardens and is a popular tourist resort. It is a major Caribbean shipping centre. Pop. (1995) 52,000.

Porto-Novo Capital of Benin, West Africa, a port on the Gulf of Guinea near the border with Nigeria. Settled by 16th-century Portuguese traders, it later became a shipping point for slaves to America. It was made the country's capital at independence in 1960. Today, it is a market for the surrounding agricultural region. Exports: palm oil, cotton, kapok. Pop. (1994) 179,000.

portrait Likeness of a real person. Portraits as a genre represent individual people, often emphasizing particular physical, psychological or social attributes. Impressive portraits have been discovered in the art of ancient Greece, Egypt and Rome, as well as in the antique art of many other cultures. In the West, the genre came into its own in the 18th century, when the fashion for formal portraits of famous people spread from France to England. In the 20th century photographic portraits have become popular. *See also* LANDSCAPE PAINTING

Port Said City and seaport in NE Egypt at the entrance to the SUEZ CANAL. Founded in 1859 at the start of the construction of the Suez Canal, by the end of the 19th century it was Egypt's chief port after ALEXANDRIA. Industries: fishing, tobacco, cotton, textiles. Pop. (1992) 461,000.

Portsmouth City and seaport in Hampshire, S England; Britain's principal naval base. The area was first settled in the late 12th century and was already a base for warships when the naval dockyard was laid down in 1496. There are ferry link with the Isle of Wight, the Channel Islands

and France. Sites include Nelson's flagship, HMS *Victory*, and the Tudor warship *Mary Rose*. Industries: engineering, ship repairing, electronics. Pop. (1994) 196,000.

Portugal Republic on the W side of the IBERIAN PENINSULA, SW Europe. The Atlantic coastal plain includes the capital, LISBON, and OPORTO. In S Portugal lies the ALGARVE. In central Portugal, the Serra da Estrela contains Portugal's highest peak, at 1,991m (6,352ft). The TAGUS and DOURO river valleys support most of the nation's agriculture. Portugal also includes the autonomous islands of the AZORES and MADEIRA. MACAO was returned to China in 1999. Portugal has a maritime climate. Compared to Mediterranean lands, summers are cooler and winters are milder. **Vegetation** Forests cover *c.*36% of Portugal. It is the world's leading producer of cork. Olive trees are common. Almond, carob and fig trees are found in the far S. **History and politics** Visigoths conquered the region in the 5th century AD. In 711, they were ejected by the Moors. In 1139, Alfonso I defeated the Moors. In 1143, Portugal's independence was recognized by Spain. The reconquest was completed in 1249 when the Moors were removed from the Algarve. In 1385, JOHN I founded the Aviz dynasty and launched Portugal's colonial and maritime expansion. His son, HENRY THE NAVIGATOR, captured the Azores and Madeira. The reign of Manuel I was Portugal's "golden age". By 1510, Portugal had established colonies in Africa, Asia, and South America. The fall of the Aviz dynasty brought PHILIP II of Spain to the throne. For the next 60 years, Portugal was subject to Spanish control. JOHN IV established the BRAGANZA dynasty (1640–1910). In the 18th century, Marquês de POMBAL reformed Portugal's institutions and rebuilt Lisbon. JOHN VI was forced to flee to Brazil during the PENINSULA WAR (1808–14). His son, PEDRO I, declared Brazilian independence in 1822. In 1910, Portugal became a republic. In 1926, a military coup overthrew the government. In 1932, Antonio de Oliveira SALAZAR became prime minister. The terms of the 1933 constitution enabled Salazar to become W Europe's longest-serving dictator. The *Estado Novo* (New State) was repressive and the economy stagnated. In 1968, Salazar was replaced by Marcello Caetano. Failure to liberalize the regime and the cost of fighting liberation movements in Portugal's African colonies led to a military coup in 1974. In 1975, many Portuguese colonies gained independence. In 1976, a new liberal constitution was adopted. In 1986, Portugal joined the European Community, and Marco Soares became president. In 1996, Soares was replaced by Jorge Sampaio. **Economy** In 1999, Portugal became one of the 11 states to adopt the EURO. Its commitment to the EUROPEAN UNION (EU) has seen the economy emerge from recession (1995 GDP per capita, US$12,670). Manufacturing accounts for 33% of exports. Textiles, footwear and clothing are major exports. Portugal is the world's fifth-largest producer of tungsten and the world's eighth-largest producer of wine. Olives, potatoes and wheat are also grown. Tourism is a rapidly growing sector (1992 receipts, US$3.7 million).

Portuguese National language of both Portugal and Brazil, spoken by *c.*10 million people in Portugal and *c.*100 million in Brazil. In addition, another *c.*15 million people speak Portuguese in Angola, Mozambique and

PORTUGAL
AREA: 92,390sq km (35,670sq mi)
POPULATION: 9,846,000
CAPITAL (POPULATION): Lisbon (2,561,000)

other former colonies. A ROMANCE LANGUAGE, it is closely related to Spanish.

Portuguese man-of-war Colonial COELENTERATE animal found in marine sub-tropical and tropical waters. It has a bright blue gas float and long, trailing tentacles with highly poisonous stinging cells. It is not a true jellyfish: the tentacles are actually a cluster of several kinds of modified MEDUSAE and POLYPS. Length: to 18m (60ft). Class Hydrozoa; genus *Physalia*.

Poseidon In Greek mythology, god of all waters and brother of ZEUS and HADES, identified with the Roman god NEPTUNE. Poseidon controlled the monsters of the deep, created the horse (he was the father of PEGASUS) and sired Orion and Polyphemus. He is represented holding a trident.

positivism Philosophical doctrine asserting that "positive" knowledge (definite or scientific facts) can be obtained through direct experience. Positivism was first proposed by Auguste COMTE and was a dominant system of 19th-century philosophy. LOGICAL POSITIVISM was developed in the 20th century, initially by the philosophers of the Vienna Circle, as an attempt to link "positive knowledge" to the strict application of LOGIC.

positron Particle that is identical to the ELECTRON, except that it is positively charged, making it the antiparticle of the electron. It was observed in 1932 in cosmic RADIATION by Carl ANDERSON. It is also emitted from certain radioactive nuclei. Electron-positron pairs can be produced when GAMMA RADIATION interacts with matter. *See also* ANTIMATTER; ELEMENTARY PARTICLE

positron emission tomography (PET) Medical imaging technique (used particularly on the brain) that produces three-dimensional images. Radioisotopes, injected into the bloodstream prior to imaging, are taken up by tissues where they emit POSITRONS that produce detectable photons.

possum Popular name for any of the PHALANGERS of Australasia. The term is also a US word for the OPOSSUM.

post-impressionism Various movements in painting that developed (*c.*1880–*c.*1905), especially in France, as a result of, or reaction to, IMPRESSIONISM. Roger FRY invented the term when he organized the exhibition *Manet and the post-impressionists* at the Grafton Gallery, London (1910). The show revolved around the work of CÉZANNE, GAUGUIN and VAN GOGH, who are still considered to be the dominant figures in this phase of modern art.

post-modernism Originally, an architectural movement that started, in the 1970s, as a reaction to the monotony of international MODERNISM. Its exponents sought new ways to merge anthropomorphic details or traditional design elements (especially from classical buildings) with 20th-century technology. The term is no longer restricted to architecture. In literature, post-modernism is less anti-modernism than a successor to it and is characterized by works that refer to their own fictionality. In the early 1980s, the concept of post-modernism exploded into popular culture. Post-modernism is often regarded as a general cultural phenomenon rather than a particular artistic movement. *See also* DECONSTRUCTION

post-mortem (autopsy) Dissection of a body to determine the cause of death. It is to confirm a diagnosis or to establish the cause of an unexpected death.

post-natal depression Mood disorder characterized by intense sadness, which may develop in a mother within a few days of childbirth. It ranges from mild cases of the "baby blues", which are usually short-lived, to the severe depressive illness known as puerperal psychosis.

Post Office UK public corporation formed in 1969 from the General Post Office (GPO). Mail delivery, its sole function until the 19th century, is still a Post Office monopoly. Private post, at rates related to distance, was first delivered in 1635; Sir Rowland HILL's penny post of 1840 standardized the rate. The GPO set up a savings bank (1861), a telegraph service (1870) and nationalized existing private telephone companies in 1912.

post-traumatic stress disorder Anxiety condition that may develop in people who have been involved in, or witnessed, some horrific event. It is commonly seen in survivors of battles or major disasters. The condition is characterized by repeated flashbacks to distressing events, hallucinations, nightmares, insomnia, edginess and depression. As many as 10% of sufferers are left with permanent psychological disability.

potash Any of several potassium compounds, especially potassium oxide (K_2O), potassium carbonate (K_2CO_3) and potassium hydroxide (KOH). Potash is mined for use as fertilizer, because potassium is an essential element for plant growth. Potassium carbonate is used for making soap and glass, and potassium hydroxide for soap and detergents.

potassium (symbol K) Common metallic element first isolated (1807) by Sir Humphry DAVY. Its chief ores are sylvite, carnallite and polyhalite. Chemically it resembles sodium. Potassium in the form of POTASH is used as a fertilizer. The natural element contains a radioisotope, K^{40} (half-life 1.3×10^9 yr), which is used in the radioactive dating of rocks. Properties: at.no. 19; r.a.m. 39.102; r.d. 0.86; m.p. 63.7°C (146.6°F); b.p. 774°C (1,425°F); most common isotope K^{39} (93.1%). *See also* ALKALI METALS

potato Plant native to Central and South America and introduced into Europe by the Spaniards in the 16th century. Best grown in a moist, cool climate, it has oval leaves and violet, pink or white flowers. The potato itself is an edible TUBER. The leaves and green potatoes contain the alkaloid solanine and are poisonous if eaten raw. Family Solanaceae; species *Solanum tuberosum*. *See also* SWEET POTATO

Potemkin, Grigori Aleksandrovich (1739–91) Russian soldier and politician. Involved in the coup that brought CATHERINE II (THE GREAT) to power in 1762, he became her lover for a time and remained until his death the most powerful man in Russia.

potential, electric (symbol V) Energy required to transfer a unit positive electric charge from an infinite distance to a given point in an ELECTRIC FIELD. The unit of electric potential is the VOLT, and the Earth's potential is taken by convention to be zero. A battery's electric potential can make current flow in an external circuit. *See also* POTENTIAL DIFFERENCE

potential difference Difference in electric potential between two points in a circuit or ELECTRIC FIELD, usually expressed in volts. It is equal to the work done to move a unit electric charge from one of the points to the other. *See also* ELECTROMOTIVE FORCE (EMF)

potential energy Type of ENERGY an object possesses because of its vertical position in the Earth's gravitational field; also the energy stored in a system such as a compressed spring, or in an oscillating system such as a pendulum. An object on a shelf has potential energy given by mgh, where m is its mass, g the acceleration due to gravity and h the height of the shelf.

potlatch Ceremonial feast among native Americans of the NW Pacific Coast region, involving the exchange of gifts. Presents were distributed to guests with the understanding that they would be returned in kind. The scale of the gifts conferred status and prestige on the host. It was the primary means of exchanging goods and cementing alliances. The influx of European settlers led to an escalation in the scale of the potlatch and the destruction of property. The practice was banned by US and Canadian governments between 1884 and 1951.

Potomac River in the E USA. It rises in West Virginia at the confluence of the North and South Branch rivers, and flows E and SE to Chesapeake Bay on the Atlantic coast, forming the boundaries of Maryland–West Virginia and Maryland–Virginia. The river is navigable for large ships as far as Washington, D.C. Length: 462km (287mi).

Potsdam City on the River Havel, E Germany; capital of Brandenburg state. During the 18th century it was a residence of the Prussian royal family. The 1805 Peace of Potsdam strengthened the alliance between Russia and Prussia against France. The POTSDAM CONFERENCE took place here in 1945. Industries: food processing, textiles. Pop. (1995) 138,000.

Potsdam Conference (July–August 1945) Summit meeting of Allied leaders in WORLD WAR 2 held in Potsdam, Germany. The main participants were US President TRUMAN, Soviet leader STALIN and the British prime minister, at first CHURCHILL, later ATTLEE. It dealt with problems arising from Germany's defeat, including the arrangements for military occupation and the trial of war criminals, and issued an ultimatum to Japan demanding surrender.

Potter, (Helen) Beatrix (1866–1943) English children's writer and illustrator. Potter created the characters of Peter Rabbit, Jemima Puddleduck, Squirrel Nutkin and others. Her first animal stories were *The Tale of Peter Rabbit* (1901) and *The Tailor of Gloucester* (1902).

Potter, Dennis (1935–94) English dramatist. He is best known for his television plays, notably *Brimstone and Treacle* (1976), *Pennies from Heaven* (1978), *Blue Remembered Hills* (1979) and *The Singing Detective* (1986). Potter's unusual approach to dramatic form and his use of direct language often aroused controversy.

pottery Objects shaped of clay and hardened by fire or dried in the sun. The making of pottery is dependent on the plasticity and durability of clay after firing. The finished object can be divided into three categories: **earthenware**, the ordinary pottery dating from primitive times, baked at 700°C (1,292°F) or lower; **stoneware**, fired at up to 1,150°C (2,102°F), less porous, and until modern times produced more commonly in the Far East than in Europe; and PORCELAIN, fired at 1,400°C (2,552°F). After a clay pot is formed and dried, it is fired in a kiln; glaze is then applied, and the pot is refired. *See also* CERAMIC

potto Slow-moving African primate with large eyes and a pointed face; it is nocturnal and arboreal. The common potto (*Perodicticus potto*) has sturdy limbs, a short tail and a small spine. Its woolly fur is grey-red. Length: 37cm (15in), excluding the tail.

Poulenc, Francis (1899–1963) French composer and a member of Les SIX. Spontaneity and melodiousness characterize his works, which include ballets, notably *Les Biches* (1923), orchestral works, chamber music, piano music and songs. Poulenc also composed two operas

poultry Collective term for domestic fowl reared as a source of meat and eggs. CHICKENS are the most important domesticated bird in the world. They are the major source of eggs and an important meat source. These light-skeletoned birds have short, weak wings, strong legs, chin wattles and a head comb. Males are known as cocks, females as hens, and castrated males as capons. Some breeds, such as Rhode Island, Wyandotte and Plymouth Rock, are raised for meat and eggs. Others, such as White Plymouth Rock, Cornish and Rock Cornish, mainly

supply meat. Species *Gallus domesticus*. Other forms of poultry are DUCK, GOOSE, GUINEA FOWL and TURKEY.

Pound, Ezra Loomis (1885–1972) US poet and literary critic. He was a leading figure in literary MODERNISM and a founder of IMAGISM and VORTICISM. In 1907, Pound emigrated to England. His early experimental works *Exultations* and *Personae* (both 1909) established him as a leading member of the avant-garde. In 1924, Pound moved to Italy, and during World War 2 he made pro-fascist, anti-Semitic broadcasts to the USA. In 1945, he was escorted back to the USA and indicted for treason. Pound was judged mentally unfit to stand trial and confined to a mental hospital (1946–58). He spent the rest of his life in Italy. Pound's masterpiece is the epic *Cantos* (1925–60), a reconstruction of Western civilization in free verse.

pound Imperial unit of weight equal to 0.453kg. It became a unit of currency when a pound (lb) weight of silver was divided into 240 penny units. The pound STERLING has been the main unit of English currency since the Middle Ages.

Poussin, Nicolas (1594–1665) French painter who worked mainly in Rome. At first inspired by MANNERISM, he later specialized in mythological subjects. In the late 1630s Poussin turned to more elaborate Old Testament and historical themes, such as *The Eucharist* (1644–48) and *The Seven Sacraments* (1648).

poverty In economics, state of having an income so low that an individual is unable to maintain oneself and one's family at the lowest acceptable level in a society. An absolute approach defines the minimum level of income required to purchase goods and services adequate to maintain a socially acceptable standard of living. A relative approach defines poverty in relation to the rest of the community or other comparable group.

Powell, Anthony Dymoke (1905–2000) English novelist. He is best known for *A Dance to The Music of Time*, a series of 12 novels that portrays the world of the English upper classes after World War 1, beginning with *A Question of Upbringing* (1951) and ending with *Hearing Secret Harmonies* (1975).

Powell, "Bud" (Earl) (1924–66) US jazz pianist and composer. A key figure in the development of BEBOP, he played with Charlie PARKER, Charlie MINGUS, Dizzy GILLESPIE and other modern jazz masters, although mental illness limited his activity.

Powell, Cecil Frank (1903–69) English physicist. He developed a technique to record SUBATOMIC PARTICLES directly onto film. In 1947, he used this method to investigate COSMIC RADIATION and discovered a new particle, the pion (pi MESON). This discovery supported the theory of nuclear structure proposed by Hideki YUKAWA. Powell subsequently discovered the antiparticle of the pion and the decay process of kaons (K mesons). He was awarded the 1950 Nobel Prize for physics.

Powell, Colin Luther (1937–) US general. He fought in the Vietnam War and rose through the ranks to become national security adviser (1987–89). Powell was chairman of the Joint Chiefs of Staff (1989–93) during the GULF WAR. Powell served (2001–) as secretary of state under President George BUSH.

Powell, (John) Enoch (1912–98) British politician. He entered Parliament as a Conservative in 1950, and was minister of health (1960–63). Powell was dismissed from the cabinet after his "rivers of blood" speech (1968) against further UK immigration. He also opposed Britain's entry into the European Economic Community (EEC) and resigned (1974) from the Conservative Party over the issue. Powell later served as an Ulster Unionist MP (1974–89).

Powell, Michael (1905–90) English film director. Powell and **Emeric Pressburger** (1902–88) formed one of the most influential director/screenwriter partnerships in cinema history. Their collaboration began with *The Spy in Black* (1939). Their production company, The Archers, was responsible for some of Britain's cinematic masterpieces. Their wartime films, such as *The Life and Death of Colonel Blimp* (1943), *A Canterbury Tale* (1944) and *A Matter of Life and Death* (1946), were intended as propaganda pieces. Other classics include *Black Narcissus* (1946) and *The Red Shoes* (1948).

power In mathematics, number of times a number is multiplied or divided by itself. If 2 is raised to the power 3 (written 2^3, called 2 cubed, or 2 to the 3rd power) it is $2 \times 2 \times 2$ or 8. A negative power indicates a fraction: eg 2^{-3} is $1/2^3$, or 1/8. A fractional power indicates a root – the power $^1/_2$ is a square root, and the power $^1/_3$ is a cube root: e.g. 8 to the power $^1/_3$ (written 8^{l_3}) means a number (the cube root) which, when multiplied by itself three times, yields 8; the root is 2. Any number to the power 0 equals 1.

power In physics, rate of doing WORK or of producing or consuming energy. It is a measure of the output of an engine or other power source. James WATT was the first to measure power; he used the unit called HORSEPOWER. The modern unit of power is the WATT.

Powhatan (1550–1618) Chief of the Powhatan Confederacy of Native North Americans, which controlled the region of America around Jamestown at the time of the first English settlement (1607). The confederacy included *c*.30 peoples. According to legend, the colonists' leader, John SMITH, was saved from execution only by the intercession of POCAHONTAS, Powhatan's daughter.

Powys County in E central Wales; the administrative centre is Llandrindod Wells. Offa's Dyke and the later Norman castles were built as border defences by the Welsh and English. During the Middle Ages, Powys was a powerful kingdom. It is drained by the rivers Usk, Wye and Taff. Sheep and cattle are reared. Area: 5,077sq km (1,960sq mi). Pop. (1991) 117,647.

Poznań City on the River Warta, W Poland. One of the oldest Polish cities, it became the seat of the first Polish bishopric in 968. It was the centre of Polish power in the 15th–17th centuries. In 1793, it passed to Prussia. The Grand Duchy of Poznań was created in 1815 as part of Prussia, but the area reverted to Poland in 1919. Industries: metallurgy, agricultural machinery, electrical equipment, chemicals, textiles. Pop. (1996) 582,000.

praetor Public official in ancient Rome, usually translated as "magistrate". From 242 BC, two praetors were elected, serving a one-year term, usually followed by appointment as provincial governor. By the 1st century BC there were eight praetors. The office declined in importance under the emperors.

pragmatism Philosophical school holding the view that the truth of a proposition has no absolute standing but depends on its practical value or use. Primarily supported by US philosophers, it was first proposed by C.S. PEIRCE and was adopted by William JAMES and John DEWEY.

Prague (Praha) Capital of the Czech Republic, on the River Vltava. Founded in the 9th century, it grew rapidly after Wenceslaus I established a German settlement in 1232. In the 14th century it was the capital of BOHEMIA. It was the capital of the Czechoslovak republic (1918–93). It was occupied in World War 2 by the Germans and liberated by Soviet troops in 1945. Prague was the centre of

Czech resistance to the Soviet invasion of the country in 1968. Sights include Hradčany Castle and Charles Bridge. It is an important commercial centre. Industries: engineering, iron and steel. Pop. (1996) 1,210,000.

Prague Spring (1968) Short-lived political and social reorganization in Czechoslovakia. In January, Alexander DUBČEK, a liberal communist, gained power and initiated reforms intended to create "socialism with a human face". In August, Russian tanks and troops occupied Prague and imposed a Soviet-style regime.

Praia Capital of Cape Verde, a port on the S shore of São Tiago Island. It is a key point in the Atlantic telegraph cable network. A trading centre for the Cape Verde Islands, Praia exports castor oil, sugar cane, oranges and coffee. Industries: fishing, straw hats. Pop. (1995) 68,000.

prairie Region of treeless plain. The prairies of North America extend from Ohio through Indiana, Illinois and Iowa to the Great Plains and N into Canada. Others include the pampas of S South America and the steppes of central Europe and Asia.

prairie chicken Chicken-sized, pale brown GROUSE of the W USA. It has brown and black pointed tail feathers and white neck feathers. During courtship displays, the male erects his neck feathers by inflating orange neck air sacs. Species *Tympanuchus cupido*.

prairie dog Squirrel-like rodent of W North America, named after its barking cry. It has a short tail, and its fur is grizzled brown to buff. Active by day, it feeds on plants and insects, and lives in communal burrows that are interconnected to form colonies. Length: 30cm (12in). Genus *Cynomys*. *See also* GROUND SQUIRREL

praseodymium (symbol Pr) Silver-yellow, metallic element of the LANTHANIDE SERIES. It was first isolated (1885) by Carl von Welsbach. Its chief ores are monazite and bastnasite. Soft, malleable and ductile, praseodymium is used in carbon electrodes for arc lamps, and its green salts are used in coloured glasses, ceramics and enamels. Properties: at.no.59; r.a.m. 140.9077; r.d. 6.77; m.p. 931°C (1,708°F); b.p. 3,512°C (6,354°F); only one isotope Pr^{141} (100%).

prawn Any of numerous species of edible crustaceans in the order Decapoda; it is generally larger than a SHRIMP. Typical genera include *Penaeus*, *Pandalus*, *Crangon* and *Nephrops*, which includes the Dublin bay prawn. Large prawns are called scampi.

Praxiteles (4th century BC) Greek sculptor whose graceful style epitomized the ancient Greek ideal. His most famous work was the *Aphrodite of Cnidus* (*c*.350 BC).

prayer Act of thanking, adoring, conferring with or petitioning a divine power; also the form of words used for this purpose. Many religions have set forms for praying. Muslims recite prayers while facing in the direction of MECCA. In Christianity, the Roman Catholic missal contains regulated customary prayers. The Book of COMMON PRAYER plays the same role in the Anglican Communion. Prayer can also be the private devotional act of an individual using his or her own words.

praying mantis *See* MANTIS

Precambrian Oldest and longest era of Earth's history, lasting from the formation of the Earth *c*.4.6 billion years ago to the beginning of a good fossil record *c*.590 million years ago. Precambrian fossils are extremely rare, probably because the earliest life forms did not have hard parts suitable for preservation. Also, Precambrian rocks have been greatly deformed. Primitive bacteria and cyanobacteria have been identified in deposits that are more than 3 billion years old.

precession Wobble of the axis of a spinning object. It occurs as a result of the TORQUE on the spin axis, which increases as the angle of precession increases. The Earth precesses about a line through its centre and perpendicular to the plane of the ECLIPTIC extremely slowly (a complete revolution taking 25,800 years) at an angle of 23.5°. The motion of a GYROSCOPE shows precession, because the entire ring containing the spinning wheel and its axle precesses around the support pivot.

precipitate Formation of an insoluble SOLID in a LIQUID either by direct reaction or by varying the liquid composition to diminish the solubility of a dissolved compound.

precipitation In meteorology, all forms of water particles, whether liquid or solid, that fall from the atmosphere to the ground. Distinguished from cloud, fog, dew and frost, precipitation includes rain, drizzle, snow and hail. Measured by rain and snow gauges, the amount of precipitation is expressed in millimetres or inches of liquid water depth.

pre-Columbian art and architecture Arts of Mexico, Central America and the Andean region of South America before colonization. In the MAYA Classical period, beginning c.200 AD, many cities or ceremonial centres were built in Central America. Their pyramid temples were paralleled by the TEOTIHUACÁN, ZAPOTEC and Mixtec cultures, and were succeeded by TOLTEC and AZTEC civilizations in the post-Classical period (AD 900–1300). Monumental building was achieved without wheels or the use of the arch; surfaces were often decorated with dazzling patterns. In the Andean region, the early Chavin sculptures were succeeded by the Mochica, the Tiahuanaco and finally, in the 14th century, by the rich temple architecture and sophisticated engineering of the INCA. Gold-working, weaving and sculpture were other important pre-Columbian arts.

predestination Christian doctrine that a person's ultimate spiritual salvation or condemnation by God has been ordained in advance. According to this doctrine, people are at birth committed to the events of life, and their fate at death is already mapped out for them. As possible solutions to the problem of how this doctrine affects FREE WILL, three propositions have been put forward: the first is to refute the doctrine altogether (**Pelagianism**); the second is to state that God never intended to save everybody (**Predestinarianism**); and the third is to qualify the premise by seeing God's prevision as conditional and subject to possible revision depending on the will and spirituality of the individual. This last position is the solution to which most Christians adhere. The concept of predestination is also found in ISLAM. See also PELAGIUS

pregnancy Period of time from conception until BIRTH, in humans normally c.40 weeks (280 days). It is generally divided into three 3-month periods called trimesters. In the **first trimester**, the EMBRYO grows from a small ball of cells to a FETUS c.7.6cm (3in) in length. At the beginning of the **second trimester**, movements are first felt and the fetus grows to c.36cm (14in). In the **third trimester**, the fetus attains its full body weight. See also LABOUR

prehistory Term to describe the period of human cultural development before the invention of writing. See BRONZE AGE; IRON AGE; MESOLITHIC; NEOLITHIC; PALAEOLITHIC; STONE AGE

prelude In music, a preliminary movement that serves to introduce a work of which it may or may not formally be a part. It was often used as the first movement of a SUITE. The popularity of CHOPIN's piano preludes led to its associations with a short piece of an imaginative nature.

premature birth Birth of a baby prior to 37 weeks' gestation or weighing less than 2.5kg (5.5lb). Premature babies are more at risk than those born at full term and often require special care.

premenstrual tension (PMT) See MENSTRUAL CYCLE

Preminger, Otto Ludwig (1906–86) US film director and producer. He received an Academy nomination for *Laura* (1944). Preminger flouted the US film industry's censorship code with *The Moon is Blue* (1953) and courted further controversy for *The Man with the Golden Arm* (1956). Other films include *Anatomy of a Murder* (1959), *Exodus* (1960) and *The Cardinal* (1963).

premolar In the dentition of adult human beings and other mammals, the two crushing or cutting TEETH between the CANINES and MOLARS on both sides of the upper and lower jaws; there are usually eight in all.

Pre-Raphaelite Brotherhood (PRB) Name adopted in 1848 by a group of young English painters who joined forces to revitalize British art. The Pre-Raphaelites took their name from their source of inspiration: the simplicity of Italian painting before the time of RAPHAEL. The most prominent members of the PRB were Dante Gabriel ROSSETTI, John Everett MILLAIS, and William Holman HUNT. They attracted fierce criticism for their rejection of Raphael but were helped by the support of John RUSKIN. By 1853, the PRB had largely dissolved, but Rossetti maintained the name, and under his influence a second wave of Pre-Raphaelite painting began in the 1860s. It lasted well into the 20th century, and was characterized by sentimental and artificial scenes of medieval romance. See also MORRIS, WILLIAM

Presbyterianism Major form of Protestant Christianity that became the national CHURCH OF SCOTLAND in 1690. It arose in the mid-16th century from the teachings of John CALVIN in Switzerland and was taken to Britain by the Scottish religious reformer John KNOX. Ministers, occasionally called pastors, are elected by their congregations and confirmed in their office by the Presbytery, a group of ministers from the local area. Members of the Presbytery are responsible for ordaining and installing (and removing) church ministers. Once ordained, the minister carries out his work assisted by elders and trustees. Each presbytery sends delegates to a annual synod and to a General Assembly. In 1972, the Presbyterian Church of England (formed 1876) united with the CONGREGATIONAL Church of England and Wales. There are Presbyterian Churches all over the world, particularly in North America, where the Presbyterian Church (US) was formed in 1983 through the merger of several older groups.

Prescott, John Leslie (1938–) British statesman, deputy prime minister and secretary of state for environment, transport and the regions (1997–). He entered Parliament in 1970. Between 1975 and 1979, Prescott simultaneously served as a member of the European and British parliaments. In 1983, he joined the shadow cabinet. In 1994, Prescott became Tony BLAIR's deputy. His "on-the-stump" campaigning helped Labour win a landslide victory in the 1997 general election.

president Usual title for the head of a republic. In the USA the president is elected by voters (through the ELECTORAL COLLEGE) for a term of four years and not exceeding two terms. The president is supreme military commander, appoints Supreme Court justices, ambassadors and other high officials, has the authority to make treaties with foreign countries (with the advice and consent of two-thirds of the SENATE), grants pardons and vetoes legislation. Presidential power is limited by the system of checks and balances.

presidium Chief executive body of the Communist Party in the former Soviet Union and other communist states. It usually had 12–20 members who in practice were self-appointed and met under the chairmanship of the general secretary of the party. It was the name preferred between 1952 and 1966 for the POLITBURO.

Presley, Elvis Aaron (1935–77) US rock-and-roll singer. In 1953, he was signed to Sam Phillips' Sun Records in Memphis, Tennessee. In 1956, Presley took America by storm with his pelvic-thrusting performances of hits such as "Heartbreak Hotel", "Hound Dog" and "Love Me Tender". He starred in 33 highly successful film, including *Jailhouse Rock* (1957), *King Creole* (1958) and *G.I. Blues* (1960). Presley died at his Graceland mansion in Memphis of a heart attack induced by drug dependence. He has become a cult figure.

press, freedom of the Ability of NEWSPAPERS or other MEDIA forms to publish (usually political) news and opinions independent of, and unhindered by, the preferred views of government. The freedom of the press is a cherished principle of DEMOCRACY. In the USA, it is protected by the First Amendment of the BILL OF RIGHTS.

pressure (symbol Pa) In physics, the force on an object's surface divided by the area of the surface. The SI unit is the pascal; 1 pascal is equal to the pressure exerted by a force of 1 newton on an area of $1m^2$. In meteorology, the millibar (symbol mb), which equals 100 pascals, is commonly used.

Prester John Legendary ruler of a Christian kingdom in Asia or Africa in the Middle Ages. European Christians hoped to make an alliance with him against the Muslims in the age of the CRUSADES. He was often identified as the King of Ethiopia.

Pretoria City in Gauteng province, South Africa. It was founded in 1855 and named after Andries PRETORIUS. It became the capital of the Transvaal in 1860 and of the South African Republic in 1881. The Peace of Vereeniging, which ended the SOUTH AFRICAN WARS, was signed here in 1902. In 1910 it became the capital of the Union of South Africa. Pretoria is an important communications centre. Industries: steel production, car assembly, diamond mining. Pop. (1990) 1,080,187.

Pretorius, Andries (1799–1853) AFRIKANER leader in the GREAT TREK (1835) to Natal. He defeated the Zulu in 1838. Pretorius was instrumental in establishing the independence of Transvaal as the South African Republic (1852). His son, **Marthinus Wessel** Pretorius (1819–1901), served as president of the new republic (1857–71) and of Orange Free State (1959–63). In 1881 Marthinus retired after victory in the first of the SOUTH AFRICAN WARS.

Previn, André George (1929–) US conductor, pianist, and composer, b. Germany. His early career was as a jazz pianist and musical director of Hollywood film scores, for which he won Academy Awards on four occasions. Previn was principal conductor of the London Symphony Orchestra (1968–79). He was music director of the Los Angeles Philharmonic Orchestra (1986–89) and has since been a guest conductor in the USA and Europe.

Prévost d'Exiles, Antoine François (1697–1763) (L'abbé Prévost) French novelist who lived as, alternately, a Jesuit novice, soldier and forger. His most famous work is *Manon Lescaut* (1731).

Priam In Greek legend, the king of TROY at the time of the war with Greece. He had been installed as king in his youth by HERACLES, but by the time of the Ten Years War was an old man. His sons HECTOR and PARIS were killed by the Greek forces. He was killed by Neoptolemus, the son of ACHILLES.

Price, (Mary) Leontyne (1927–) US soprano. In 1961, she made a triumphant debut at the Metropolitan Opera,

New York, in Verdi's *Il Trovatore*. In 1955, Price became the first black singer to appear in a televised opera, *Tosca*.

prickly heat Skin rash caused by blockage of the sweat glands in hot, humid weather. It occurs most often in infants and obese people. It disappears as the body cools.

prickly pear CACTUS with flat or cylindrical joints. It grows in North and South America and has been introduced into Europe, Africa and Australia. The jointed pads have tufts of bristles, and the edible fruit is red and pulpy. Family Cactaceae; genus *Opuntia*.

Pride's Purge (1648) Expulsion of *c*.140 members from the English LONG PARLIAMENT. It was carried out by Colonel Thomas Pride (d.1658) on the orders of the army council. The aim was to rid Parliament of members anxious to negotiate with CHARLES I. The remnant, known as the RUMP PARLIAMENT, voted to put Charles on trial.

Priestley, J.B. (John Boynton) (1894–1984) English novelist, dramatist and critic. His criticism includes *The English Novel* (1927) and *Literature and Western Man* (1960). Priestley's novels include *The Good Companions* (1929), *Angel Pavement* (1930) and *Bright Day* (1946). Among his plays are *Time and the Conways* (1937) and *An Inspector Calls* (1945), both of which explore notions of time.

Priestley, Joseph (1733–1804) English chemist and clergyman. In 1774 Priestley discovered OXYGEN. He also found a number of other gases, including AMMONIA and oxides of NITROGEN. Priestley studied the properties of CARBON DIOXIDE and was an advocate of the later discredited PHLOGISTON theory.

primary Method used in the USA to select candidates for an election. In a **direct** primary, the commonest type, any number of party members may run and are voted for in a ballot of all the members. In an **open** primary, all the parties in an election are involved, and the voter votes for both the party and candidate of his or her choice. In a presidential election year, most US states select delegates to the national party convention in a **presidential** primary, the delegates having announced which presidential candidate they support.

primary school School that provides elementary education for children starting at compulsory school age. In the UK, primary school education starts at five, and children progress to SECONDARY SCHOOLS at 11 or 12. Primary schools cater for children throughout key stages 1 and 2 of the NATIONAL CURRICULUM.

primate Regional head of an episcopally structured church. In the Church of England, it describes the Archbishop of CANTERBURY, who is "Primate of all England", and the Archbishop of YORK, who is "Primate of England".

primates Order of mammals that includes MONKEYS, APES and HUMAN beings. Primates, native to most tropical and sub-tropical regions, are mostly herbivorous, diurnal, arboreal animals. Their hands and feet, usually with flat nails instead of claws, are adapted for grasping. Most species have opposable thumbs, and all but humans have opposable big toes. They have a poor sense of smell, good hearing and acute binocular vision. The outstanding feature of primates is a large complex brain and high intelligence. Primate characteristics are less pronounced in the relatively primitive prosimians (including tree shrews, BUSHBABIES, LORISES and TARSIERS) and are most pronounced in the more numerous and advanced anthropoids (monkeys, apes and human beings).

prime minister Chief executive and head of government in a country with a parliamentary system. He or she is usually the leader of the largest political party in PARLIAMENT. The office evolved in Britain in the 18th century, along with the CABINET system and the shift of power away from the crown towards the HOUSE OF COMMONS.

prime number Positive or negative INTEGER, excluding one and zero, that has no FACTORS other than itself or one. Examples are 2, 3, 5, 7, 11, 13 and 17. The integers 4, 6, 8.... are not prime numbers since they can be expressed as the product of two or more primes.

primitivism Russian form of EXPRESSIONISM. It developed c.1905–20 and was influenced by Russian folk art, FAUVISM and CUBISM. It was characterized by simplified forms and powerful colour, used principally to depict scenes from working-class life. MALEVICH worked in the style early in his career. Other artists include Larinov.

Primo de Rivera, Miguel (1870–1930) Spanish general. In 1923, he staged a coup with the support of King ALFONSO XIII. He dissolved parliament and established a military dictatorship modelled on the government of MUSSOLINI. He restored order and helped to end the revolt of ABD-EL-KRIM in Morocco (1926). The parlous state of the economy forced him to resign in 1930. His son, **José Antonio** (1903–36) founded the FALANGE in 1933.

primrose Any of numerous species of herbaceous, generally perennial plants of the genus *Primula* that grow in the cooler climates of Europe, Asia, Ethiopia, Java and North America. It has a tuft of leaves rising from the rootstock and clustered flowers of pale yellow to deep crimson. In Britain the name refers to *Primula vulgaris*. Family Primulaceae.

Prince (1960–) US singer-songwriter and guitarist, b. Prince Rogers Nelson. He first achieved major success with the album *Purple Rain* (1984). Other albums include *Sign O' The Times* (1987) and *Diamonds and Pearls* (1990). In 1995, a contractual dispute with his record company led to him titling himself "the artist formerly known as Prince".

Prince Edward Island Province in E Canada, an island in the Gulf of St Lawrence off the coast of New Brunswick and Nova Scotia; the capital is Charlottetown. The island was discovered by Jacques CARTIER in 1534. In the early 18th century, it was colonized by French settlers as the Ile St Jean. Ceded to Britain in 1763, it was renamed in 1799 and became a province of Canada in 1873. Fishing and agriculture are the most important economic activities. Area: 5,657sq km (2,184sq mi). Pop. (1993 est.) 131,600.

Prince of Wales *See* CHARLES, PRINCE

Princeton Borough in W central New Jersey, USA; a leading academic and research centre. Princeton was settled in the late 17th century and named in honour of William III, Prince of Orange-Nassau (1724). At the Battle of Princeton (3 January 1777) George Washington defeated the British forces. Princeton University, which is part of the Ivy League, was established in 1746. Pop. (1990) 12,016.

printed circuit Network of electrical conductors chemically etched from a layer of copper foil on a board of insulating material such as plastic, glass or ceramic. It interconnects components such as capacitors, resistors, and INTEGRATED CIRCUITS (SILICON chips). The printed circuit board (PCB) represents one stage in the miniaturization of electronic circuits.

printing Technique for multiple reproduction of images, such as text and pictures. In ancient China and Japan carved wooden blocks were inked to print pictures. From the 10th century, the Chinese used separate pieces of type, so that each page could be printed from arrangements of standard characters. In c.1403, metal type made by casting first appeared in Korea. In 15th-century Europe,

GUTENBERG and CAXTON developed the use of letterpress. In the 17th and 18th centuries, printing expanded rapidly. LITHOGRAPHY enabled printers to produce impressive colour prints. For text, stereotype printing plates were cast from the pages of type, so that the type could be re-used for setting other pages. TYPESETTING machines speeded up the process of setting up pages. In the 1820s, the invention of photography led to the development of new techniques for reproducing photographs in print, such as the HALFTONE PROCESS. More recently, production speeds have greatly increased with the application of photosetting, in which the type is set photographically on sheet film, and OFFSET printing. Today, many publications are produced using a WORD PROCESSOR to enter the text. DESKTOP PUBLISHING (DTP) allows images of the text and pictures to be arranged on screen. The computer data is used to print sheet film for each page, and the film images are transferred to printing plates.

prion Infective agent that appears to consist simply of a protein. Prions are thought to cause diseases such as CREUTZFELD-JAKOB DISEASE (CJD) and kuru in humans, BOVINE SPONGIFORM ENCEPHALOPATHY (BSE) in cattle and SCRAPIE in sheep. It is not yet understood how prions work; unlike viruses and bacteria, they do not contain DNA or RNA.

prism In mathematics, a solid geometrical figure whose ends are congruent (most commonly TRIANGLES) and perpendicular to the length, with the other faces RECTANGLES. The volume of a prism is equal to the area of the end multiplied by the length of the prism. In physics, a prism is a piece of transparent material, such as glass, plastic or quartz, in which a light beam is refracted and split into its component colours (spectrum) by dispersion.

prison Building for the confinement of criminals or people detained by the legal authorities. In most societies before the 18th century, criminals were subject to capital or corporal punishment or transportation, and prisons were places of temporary confinement only. Early prisons were usually squalid, badly organized and often brutal. During the ENLIGHTENMENT, penalties grew less harsh, and prisons developed into penal institutions: imprisonment became the punishment. Conditions

▲ **primates** Because primates have large brains, they can learn complex skills and pass them down through the generations. Chimpanzees, for example, demonstrate high intelligence in their use of tools. They have been observed using sticks to "fish" for termites. Young chimpanzees learn this by observing their parents – aged between two and three years, they manipulate sticks as a form of play, and by the time they are four, they have mastered the use of the tool.

improved in the 19th century, with emphasis on rehabilitation rather than mere punishment.

prisoner of war (POW) In international law, military personnel captured by the enemy in an armed conflict between states. Their treatment is generally expected to be humane. The terms of the first international convention on prisoners of war, signed at the Hague peace conference of 1899, were widened by the Hague Convention of 1907 and the GENEVA CONVENTION of 1949.

privateer Privately owned vessel with a government commission to capture enemy shipping. Their government licences (letters of marque) distinguished privateers from PIRATES. Crews were unpaid but were allowed to keep the booty. Privateering was at its height from the 16th to the 18th centuries. It was abolished by the Hague Convention of 1907.

private sector Part of a country's economy that is not under state control. In the private sector, capital resources and enterprises are owned by companies. The private sector is sometimes taken to include the work of individuals. *See also* PUBLIC SECTOR

privatization Transfer of state-run enterprises to private ownership. It is the opposite of NATIONALIZATION. In the 1980s policy-makers in some European countries, as well as Canada, Japan and New Zealand, maintained that economic growth would best be encouraged by governments selling nationalized industries to independent enterprises, which were then free to respond to market forces and create a more efficient and competitive company. In the early 1990s, the trend was taken up by many former Soviet-bloc countries.

Privy Council Group of leading advisers to the British monarch. It developed in the Middle Ages out of the King's Council (Curia Regis). As the CABINET system of government developed, the Privy Council became increasingly restricted in its powers. Its Judicial Committee, established by legislation in 1833, is the final appeal court for most Commonwealth countries.

probability Number representing the likelihood of a given occurrence. The probability of a specified event is the number of ways that event may occur divided by the total possible number of outcomes, assuming that each possibility is equally likely. For instance, in one throw of a six-sided die, there are six possible outcomes, and three of these result in an even number: the probability of throwing an even number is thus 3/6, or 1/2. The theory of probability was first developed (*c*.1654) by Blaise PASCAL and Pierre de FERMAT.

probate Legal term for the certification by a court of law that a document purporting to be the WILL of a person who has died is valid. The term also applies to the official copy of a will, with the certificate of validity.

probation Sentence of a COURT OF LAW on a young or first-time offender that allows the offender to remain at liberty subject to certain conditions and under the supervision of a probation officer. It is not regarded as a conviction. Breach of probation is an offence.

Procyon (Alpha Canis Minoris) Brightest star in the constellation of Canis Minor, and one of the stars nearest to the Sun. The star, known as Procyon A, has a faint white-dwarf companion, Procyon B. Characteristics: apparent mag. 0.34 (A), 10.8 (B); absolute mag. 2.6 (A), 13.1 (B); spectral type F5 (A), wF (B); distance 11.4 light-years.

Prodi, Romano (1939–) Italian statesman, prime minister (1996–98), president of the EUROPEAN COMMISSION (1999–). He led the centre-left Olive Tree Alliance to a narrow victory in the 1996 elections in Italy. Prodi skilfully managed to preserve the fragile coalition for 18 months, and his austerity measures enabled Italy to qualify for European monetary union in 1999. The Alliance collapsed after hardline communists rejected his proposals for large budget cuts. Prodi replaced Jacques SANTER as head of the European Commission after the entire Commission had resigned in the midst of a corruption scandal. Prodi sought to restore public confidence in the Commission and to prepare the EUROPEAN UNION (EU) for enlargement.

production In economics, methods by which wealth is produced. It is one of the basic principles of economics. The factors of production are land, LABOUR and CAPITAL.

profit In economics, excess of a business' income over its expenditure. In accountancy, there are two main forms of profit: **gross** profit equals receipts less all money spent directly on running the business, such as wages, rent and materials; **net** profit is gross profit less depreciation of assets and interest on loans.

Profumo, John Dennis (1915–) British politician. He entered Parliament in 1940. In 1960, Profumo joined Harold MACMILLAN's Conservative cabinet as secretary of war. In 1963, he was forced to resign after lying to the House of Commons about his affair with Christine Keeler, who was also involved with a Soviet diplomat.

progesterone Steroid HORMONE secreted mainly by the corpus luteum of the mammalian OVARY and by the PLACENTA during pregnancy. Its principal function is to prepare and maintain the inner lining (ENDOMETRIUM) of the UTERUS for pregnancy. Synthetic progesterone is one of the main components of the contraceptive PILL.

program (SOFTWARE) Set of instructions that enables a COMPUTER to carry out a task. Programs can be written in a variety of COMPUTER LANGUAGES and are stored on a magnetic DISK. To make a computer perform a particular task, a program is loaded into its RAM.

programme music (illustrative music) Music that aims to describe a scene or tell a story. Programme music is an essential concept of ROMANTICISM; perhaps the earliest example is BEETHOVEN's 6th Symphony (*The Pastoral*, 1808). SYMPHONIC POEMS by Bedřich SMETANA and Jean SIBELIUS are later instances.

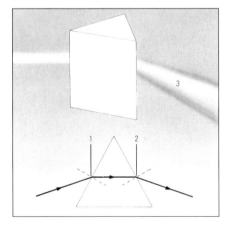

▲ **prism** When light hits a prism, it is refracted by the two surfaces it hits (1, 2). White light splits into the spectrum (3) because each of the colours of the spectrum have varying wavelengths.

For example, the short wavelengths of blue and indigo are refracted more than the colours farther down the spectrum with longer wavelengths, such as orange and red.

programming Preparation of a COMPUTER so that it can perform a specific task. Before being given DATA, a computer must be given a set of instructions, or a PROGRAM, telling it how to deal with the data. Each instruction is a single step, and all information must be in the form of binary numbers. For computer programmers, languages have been developed that make the task of programming increasingly intuitive.

Progressive Conservative Party (Fr. *Parti Progressiste-Conservateur du Canada*) Canadian political party. Formerly called the Liberal-Conservative Party (formed under John A. MACDONALD in 1854), the party adopted its present name in 1942. The Progressive Conservatives were in a minority for much of this century, only holding power under John DIEFENBAKER (1958–63) and Joe Clark (1979–80). In 1984, led by Brian MULRONEY, they returned to government with a record majority. In 1988, Mulroney won a second term though with a reduced majority. In 1993, Mulroney was succeeded by Kim Campbell but the party lost disastrously to the LIBERAL PARTY in elections later that year.

progressive education Movement that began in the late 19th century in Europe and the USA, as a reaction to traditional education. In Europe FROEBEL, PESTALOZZI and MONTESSORI were influential in the movement that aimed to educate "the whole child". In the USA, the movement owed much to the philosophy of John DEWEY. It led in some cases to what critics termed laxness and produced a "back to basics" movement.

Prohibition (1919–33) Period in US history when the manufacture, sale and transport of alcoholic drinks were prohibited. It was instituted by the 18th amendment to the US Constitution, confirmed by the Volstead Act (1919). Smuggling, illicit manufacture, corruption of government officials and police, and the growth of organized crime financed by BOOTLEGGING made it a failure. Prohibition was repealed by the 21st amendment (1933).

projection Term with various meanings in PSYCHIATRY and PSYCHOANALYSIS, but all relating to the externalization of feelings. Psychiatrists use it for the way people interpret their environment, according to their own mental and emotional state. In FREUD's psychology, the defence mechanism is described whereby people deny certain emotions in themselves but ascribe them to other people.

projector Instrument with a lens system, used to cast images onto a screen from an illuminated flat object. An **episcope** is a projector for opaque objects, such as a printed page; it uses light that is reflected from the object. A **diascope** is a projector for transparent objects, such as photographic slides and films; it uses light transmitted through the object. An **epidiascope** can project images from both transparent and opaque objects. A motion-picture, or **cine**, projector produces moving images from many frames (pictures) on a transparent film.

Prokaryotae (formerly Monera) Biological KINGDOM that includes BACTERIA and CYANOBACTERIA (formerly blue-green algae). They have more simple cells than other organisms. DNA is not contained in chromosomes in the NUCLEUS but lies in a distinct part of the CYTOPLASM called the nucleoid. They have no distinct membrane-surrounded structures (organelles). Cell division is simple, and in the rare cases where SEXUAL REPRODUCTION occurs, genetic material is simply transferred from one partner to another; there are no separate sex cells. In photosynthetic prokaryotes, PHOTOSYNTHESIS takes place on the cell membrane. At present two sub-kingdoms are recognized: ARCHAEBACTERIA and EUBACTERIA. *See also* ASEXUAL REPRODUCTION; EUKARYOTE; SYMBIOSIS

Prokhorov, Alexandre Mikhailovich (1916–) Russian physicist. He shared the 1964 Nobel Prize for physics with Nikolai BASOV and Charles H. TOWNES. Prokhorov's research in quantum electronics resulted in the development of the MASER and LASER.

Prokofiev, Sergei (1891–1953) Russian composer. His style is characterized by biting dissonances within rich harmony. Prokofiev's most popular works include the ballets, *Romeo and Juliet* (1935) and *Cinderella* (1944); the *Classical* (first) Symphony (1918); *Peter and the Wolf* (1936); and the comic opera *The Love for Three Oranges* (1921). He also composed film scores, notably *Lieutenant Kije* (1934) and EISENSTEIN's *Alexander Nevsky* (1938) and *Ivan the Terrible* (1942–45)

prolapse Displacement of an organ due to weakening of supporting tissues. It most often affects the rectum, due to bowel problems, or the UTERUS following repeated pregnancies.

proletariat Marxist term for those CLASSES of an industrial society that have no source of income other than wages. According to MARX, the proletariat is the true creator of the objects produced by industry and it would become an irresistible force when the internal contradictions of CAPITALISM weakened the authority of the FACTORY-owning BOURGEOISIE.

promenade concerts Annual concert series organized by the BRITISH BROADCASTING COMPANY (BBC) in the Royal Albert Hall, London, where inexpensive standing room is available. Such concerts originated (1833) in Paris and from 1838 were given at Drury Lane, Covent Garden, and elsewhere. The modern "Proms" began at Queen's Hall, London, in 1895, under the baton of Sir Henry Wood.

Prometheus In Greek mythology, the fire-giver. He created the human race, provided them with reason and stole fire from the gods. For this theft, ZEUS had him chained to a rock where an eagle consumed his liver for eternity. In some myths he was rescued by HERACLES.

promethium (symbol Pm) Radioactive, metallic element of the LANTHANIDE SERIES. It was made in 1941 by particle bombardment of NEODYMIUM and PRASEODYMIUM. Promethium occurs in minute amounts in URANIUM ores. The isotope Pm^{147} is used in phosphorescent paints, X-rays, and nuclear-powered batteries for space vehicles. Properties: at.no. 61; m.p. 1,080°C (1,976°F); b.p. 2,460°C (4,460°F); most stable isotope Pm^{145} (half-life 17.7 years).

pronghorn Only extant member of the family Antilocapridae, related to the ANTELOPE. It is a horned, hoofed, herbivorous animal of the W USA and N Mexico. The swiftest North American mammal, it is capable of speeds of up to 80km/h (50mph) over short distances. Height: 90cm (3ft); weight: 45kg (100lb).

propaganda Systematic manipulation of public opinion through the communications media. Many political, economic and social organizations, and pressure groups of all kinds employ some kind of propaganda. Although examples are found in ancient and early modern writings, the most effective propagandists in the 20th century have been totalitarian governments of industrialized states, which are able to control all means of public communication. In Nazi Germany, for instance, Joseph GOEBBELS was able to indoctrinate the German public.

propane Colourless, flammable gas (C_3H_8), the third member of the ALKANE series of HYDROCARBONS. It occurs in NATURAL GAS, from which it is obtained; it is also obtained during PETROLEUM refining. Propane is used (as bottled gas) as a fuel, as a solvent, and in the preparation of many chemicals. Properties: m.p. −190°C (−310°F); b.p. −42°C (−43.6°F).

propanol (propyl alcohol) Colourless ALCOHOL used as a solvent and in the manufacture of various chemicals. It exists as two ISOMERS. Normal propanol, $CH_3CH_2CH_2OH$, is a by-product of the synthesis of METHANOL (methyl alcohol). **Isopropanol** (isopropyl alcohol), $(CH_3)_2CHOH$, is a secondary alcohol that is easily oxidized into PROPANONE.

propanone (acetone, CH_3COCH_3) Colourless flammable liquid made by oxidizing propan-2-ol. It is a raw material for the manufacture of many organic chemicals and is a widely used solvent. Properties: r.d. 0.79; m.p. –94.8°C (–138.6°F); b.p. 56.2°C (133.2°F).

propeller Device for producing thrust, usually mounted on a rotating shaft. The cross-section of an AIRCRAFT propeller reveals an AEROFOIL shape. This allows it to function as a rotating wing; it generates forward thrust by producing LIFT. A ship's propeller, or screw, propels the ship through the water.

propene (propylene, C_3H_6) Colourless, aliphatic hydrocarbon, manufactured by the thermal CRACKING of ETHENE. It is used in the manufacture of a wide range of chemicals, including vinyl and acrylic resins. Properties: m.p. $-185°C$ ($-301°F$); b.p. $-48°C$ ($-54.4°F$).

property Something material that is owned. Ownership, or possession by right, is a concept strongly opposed by those who believe that all property should be held in common (the original and ideal form of COMMUNISM). Property rights, however, are absolutely essential to CAPITALISM, and virtually all societies preserve notions of how to distinguish between what is private property and what is public property. In law there is also the distinction between "real" property (such as land or real estate) and personal property (which may be transported by the owner or may have no physical existence, such as rights).

prophet Individual who is thought to be a divinely inspired messenger from a god, or is believed to possess the power to foretell future events. The classic examples of prophets were the holy men and seers who preached by the authority of YAHWEH to the Jews of the Old Testament kingdoms of ISRAEL and JUDAH. Part of the Old Testament consists of books devoted to their preachings and predictions. The term "prophet" also applied to ABRAHAM, MOSES and SAMUEL. JOHN THE BAPTIST fulfiled the role of a New Testament prophet, predicting the coming of the MESSIAH. In ancient Greece and Rome, divinely inspired prophetesses made oracular pronouncements to those who consulted them. Among Muslims, MUHAMMAD is held to be a prophet. In both Buddhist and Hindu literature, predictions occur, and many prophetic reformers have occurred in HINDUISM.

proportion Mathematical relation of equality between two ratios, having the form $a/b = c/d$. A continued proportion is a group of three or more quantities, each bearing the same ratio to its successor, as in 1:3:9:27:81.

proportional representation (PR) System of electoral representation in which the allocation of seats reflects the proportion of the vote commanded by each candidate or party. In the **single transferable vote** system, an elector ranks candidates in order of preference. In the **list system**, an elector votes of a party's entire list of candidates; the number of seats allocated to a party is determined by the number of votes for its list. The main contrast is with a majoritarian system in which representatives are elected for each of numerous single constituencies. Supporters of PR argue that it delivers more representative DEMOCRACY. Critics argue that it tends to produce coalition governments and destroys the bond between representatives and constituents. In the UK PR

was first used in 1999 ELECTIONS to the devolved Scottish assembly and the European Parliament (EP).

propylene *See* PROPENE

proscenium In the THEATRE, the front part of the stage, especially the arch, first used in the 17th-century Italian theatre to create a picture-frame effect.

prose In LITERATURE, a relatively unstructured form of language. Unlike the metrical discipline of POETRY, prose is more closely connected with the rhythms of everyday speech.

Proserpine Roman equivalent of PERSEPHONE

prospecting Search for exploitable mineral deposits using methods based on geology and mineralogy. These methods involve extensive sampling – the analysis and examination of materials taken from holes drilled at regular intervals. Other techniques include the analysis of the velocity of waves resulting from underground explosions, the measurement of variations in the Earth's magnetic field, and the detection of gravity anomalies. For radioactive minerals, Geiger counters are used. Aerial photography is a versatile method. *See also* MINING

Prost, Alain (1955–) French motor racing driver. In 1985, racing for McLaren, he became the first Frenchman to win the Formula 1 world drivers' championship. Prost was champion twice more with McLaren (1986, 1989). In 1993, he retired after winning a fourth title with Williams.

prostaglandin Series of related FATTY ACIDS with hormone-like action, present in SEMEN and liver, brain and other tissues. Their biological effects include the lowering of blood pressure and the stimulation of contraction in a variety of smooth-muscle tissues, as in the UTERUS.

prostate gland Gland in the male reproductive tract surrounding the URETHRA. It secretes specific chemicals that mix with sperm cells and other secretions to make up SEMEN.

prosthesis Artificial substitute for a missing organ or part of the body. Until the 17th century, artificial limbs were made of wood or metal, but innovations in metallurgy, plastics and engineering have enabled lighter, jointed limbs to be made. More recent prosthetic devices include artificial heart valves made of silicone materials.

prostitution Provision of sexual services for reward, usually money. Most prostitutes are women. In Britain prostitution is not illegal, but soliciting, living off the earnings of prostitution and brothel-keeping are.

protactinium (symbol Pa) Rare, radioactive, metallic element of the ACTINIDE SERIES, first identified in 1917. Its chief source is URANINITE. Properties: at.no. 91; r.a.m. 231.0359; r.d. 15.4; m.p. 1,200°C (2,192°F); b.p. 4,000°C (7,232°F); most stable isotope Pa^{231} (half-life 3.25×10^4 yr).

Protectorate (1653–59) In 1653, BAREBONE'S PARLIAMENT passed the Instrument of Government that made Oliver Cromwell lord protector. Cromwell established a state council of 11 major-generals. The Humble Petition and Advice (1657) restored some power to parliament. The Protectorate was heavily dependent on Oliver Cromwell's personal prestige and after his death (1658), his son, Richard, was lord protector for less than a year before the RESTORATION of CHARLES II.

protein Organic COMPOUND containing many AMINO ACIDS linked together by covalent, PEPTIDE bonds. Living CELLS use c.20 different amino acids, which are present in varying amounts. The GENETIC CODE, carried by the DNA of the CHROMOSOMES, determines which amino acids are used and in which order they are combined. The most important proteins are ENZYMES, which determine all the chemical reactions in the cell, and

ANTIBODIES, which combat infection. **Structural** proteins include KERATIN and COLLAGEN. **Gas transport** proteins include HAEMOGLOBIN. **Nutrient** proteins include CASEIN. METABOLISM is regulated by protein HORMONES. *See also* NUCLEIC ACID; X-RAY DIFFRACTION

Protestantism Branch of Christianity formed in protest against the practices and doctrines of the old ROMAN CATHOLIC CHURCH. Protestants sought a vernacular BIBLE to replace the Latin VULGATE and to express individual nationalism. The movement is considered to have started when Martin LUTHER nailed his 95 theses to a Wittenberg church door in 1517. His predecessors included John WYCLIFFE and Jan HUS. Later supporters included Ulrich ZWINGLI and John CALVIN. Protestants held the EUCHARIST to be a symbolic celebration, as opposed to the Roman Catholic dogma of TRANSUBSTANTIATION, and claimed that because Christ is the sole medium between God and man, his function cannot be displaced by priests. This led to an emphasis on individual contemplation of the scriptures. *See also* ANGLICANISM

Proteus In Greek mythology, a sea god, son of Oceanus and Tethys. He is depicted as a little old man of the sea. Proteus had the gift of prophecy and the ability to alter his form at will.

proteus Genus of rod-shaped BACTERIA that move by means of FLAGELLA. They are found mainly in the intestines and faeces of humans. *Proteus mirabilis* causes cystitis.

Protoctista (formerly Protista) Kingdom that includes such widely differing groups as ALGAE (including large SEAWEEDS), AMOEBAS and other PROTOZOA, SLIME MOULDS and downy MILDEWS.

proton (symbol p) Stable ELEMENTARY PARTICLE with a positive charge equal in magnitude to the negative charge of the ELECTRON. The proton was discovered (1919) by Ernest RUTHERFORD. It forms the nucleus of the lightest isotope of HYDROGEN and, with the NEUTRON, is a constituent of the nuclei of all other elements. It is made up of three QUARKS. The proton is a BARYON with a mass *c*.1,836 times heavier than the electron. The number of protons in the nucleus of an element is equal to its ATOMIC NUMBER. Protons also occur in primary COSMIC RADIATION. Beams of high-velocity protons, produced by particle ACCELERATORS, are used to study nuclear reactions. *See also* PARTICLE PHYSICS

protoplasm Term referring to the living contents of a plant or animal CELL. It includes both the NUCLEUS and the CYTOPLASM of cells.

Protozoa Phylum of unicellular organisms found worldwide in marine or fresh water, free-living and as parasites. These microscopic animals have the ability to move (by CILIA or pseudopodia) and have a nucleus, cytoplasm and cell wall; some contain CHLOROPHYLL. Reproduction is by FISSION or encystment. Length: 0.3mm (0.1in). The 30,000 species are divided into four classes: Flagellata, Cnidospora, Ciliophora and Sporozoa.

Proudhon, Pierre Joseph (1809–65) French political theorist. His anarchist theories of liberty, equality and justice conflicted with the COMMUNISM of Karl MARX. In *What is Property?* (1840), Proudhon famously argued that "PROPERTY is theft". His greatest work was *System of Economic Contradiction* (1846). *See also* ANARCHISM

Proust, Marcel (1871–1922) French novelist. Proust was actively involved in the DREYFUS AFFAIR, but asthma and the death of his parents led to his virtual seclusion from 1907. In 1912, Proust produced *Swann's Way*, the first section of a semi-autobiographical cyclical novel, collectively entitled *À la recherche du temps perdu*

(*Remembrance of Things Past*). The next instalment, *Within a Budding Grove* (1919), won the Prix Goncourt. Proust completed the series shortly before his death. Influenced by the theories of Henri BERGSON and Sigmund FREUD, *À la recherche du temps perdu* offers an extraordinary insight into the relationship between psyche and society, and the distortions of time and memory. *See also* FRENCH LITERATURE

Provençal Variety of the Occitan language, spoken in Provence, SE France. It is a ROMANCE LANGUAGE belonging to the family of INDO-EUROPEAN LANGUAGES. It enjoyed a great literary flowering as the language of the TROUBADOURS of the 12th and 13th centuries.

Provence Region and former province of SE France, roughly corresponding to the present departments of Var, Vaucluse and Bouches-du-Rhône and parts of Alpes-de-Haute-Provence and Alpes-Maritimes. The coastal area was settled *c*.600 BC by the Greeks, and the Romans established colonies in the 2nd century BC. The region came under Frankish control in the 6th century AD. It passed to the Holy Roman Empire in the 11th century. It retained its distinctive identity and language (PROVENÇAL) and was the focus of a revival of secular literature and music in the Middle Ages. It was finally united with France in 1481 and remained a province until the French Revolution. Fruit and vegetables are grown, and tourism is the major industry.

Proverbs Book of the OLD TESTAMENT, probably the oldest existing example of Hebrew WISDOM LITERATURE. The book's subtitle attributes its authorship to King SOLOMON, but in fact scholars consider that it contains material from various periods later than Solomon's time.

Providence Capital of Rhode Island, USA, a port on Providence Bay, NE Rhode Island. The city was founded (1636) as a refuge for religious dissenters from Massachusetts. It later enjoyed great prosperity through trade with the West Indies. Providence played an active role in the American Revolution. Industries: jewellery, electrical equipment, silverware. Pop. (1990) 160,728.

Proxima Centauri Nearest star to the Sun, slightly closer than the nearby star ALPHA CENTAURI. It was long thought to be part of the Alpha Centauri system, but some astronomers now believe it to be an unrelated star.

Prozac Trade name for one of a small group of antidepressants, known as selective SEROTONIN re-uptake inhibitors (SSRIs). They work by increasing levels of serotonin in the brain. Serotonin, or 5-hydroxytryptamine (5-HT), is a NEUROTRANSMITTER involved in a range of functions. Low levels of serotonin are associated with DEPRESSION. *See also* DRUG

Prud'hon, Pierre Paul (1758–1823) French painter. A favourite of two French empresses, JOSEPHINE and MARIE LOUISE, Prud'hon's elegant and emotional portraits and historical works bridged the gap between late 18th- and early 19th-century painting. His masterpiece is *Crime Pursued by Justice and Divine Vengeance* (1808).

Prussia Historic state of N Germany. The region was conquered by the TEUTONIC KNIGHTS in the 13th century. The duchy of Prussia, founded in the 15th century, passed to the electors of BRANDENBURG in 1618. From 1701, the electors took the title of king of Prussia. In the 18th century, under FREDERICK WILLIAM I and FREDERICK II (THE GREAT), Prussia became a strong military power, absorbing SILESIA and parts of Poland. After defeats in the NAPOLEONIC WARS, Prussia emerged again as a powerful state at the Congress of VIENNA (1815). In the 19th century, Prussia displaced Austria as the leading German power and, under BISMARCK, led the movement for German unity, accomplished in 1871. Comprising 65% of the new German empire, it was the leading German state until World War 1. It ceased to exist as a political unit in 1945.

Przewalski's horse (Mongolian wild HORSE) Only surviving species of the original wild horse, found only in Mongolia and Sinkiang. It is small and stocky with an erect black mane. Its red-brown coat is marked with a darker line on the back and shoulders, and by leg stripes. Height: to 1.5m (4.8ft) at the shoulder. Family Equidae; species *Equus caballus przewalskii*.

psalm Musical hymn or sacred poem. The most famous are contained in the Old Testament Book of PSALMS.

Psalms, Book of Book of the OLD TESTAMENT, consisting of 150 hymns, lyric poems and prayers. The works were collected over a very long period, at least from the 10th to the 5th centuries BC and probably achieved their final form before the 2nd century BC. Most carry titles added afterwards, and 73 are stated to have been composed or collected by King DAVID.

Pseudepigrapha Jewish writings of the period 200 BC–AD 200 that have been falsely attributed to a biblical author. The term refers more widely to almost all ancient Jewish texts that have not been accepted as canonical by the Christian Church. *See also* APOCRYPHA

psittacosis (parrot disease) Disorder usually affecting the respiratory system of birds. Caused by a bacterium, it can be transmitted to human beings, producing pneumonia-like symptoms. Treatment is with ANTIBIOTICS.

psoriasis Chronic recurring skin disease featuring raised, red, scaly patches. The lesions frequently appear on the chest, knees, elbows and scalp. Treatment is with tar preparations, steroids and ultraviolet light. Psoriasis is sometimes associated with a form of ARTHRITIS.

Psyche In Greek mythology, a beautiful mortal woman loved by EROS. She was also the personification of the soul.

psychiatry Analysis, diagnosis and treatment of mental illness and behavioural disorders. It includes research into the cause and prevention of MENTAL DISORDERS, and the administering of treatment, usually by physical means, such as drugs and electroconvulsive therapy. Some psychiatrists also use psychotherapeutic techniques.

▲ Przewalski's horse
Because it is not descended from domestic horses, Przewalski's horse (*Equus przewalski*) is the last truly wild horse. They still exist in their natural state in a small area of SW Mongolia, although the species thrives in zoos. Numbers have been reduced because they have to compete with livestock for grazing areas and water.

psychoanalysis Therapy for treating behaviour disorders, particularly NEUROSIS, based upon the work of Sigmund FREUD. Psychoanalysis is characterized by its emphasis on UNCONSCIOUS mental processes and the determination of PERSONALITY by INSTINCT, chiefly sexual development in childhood. Psychoanalytic techniques include free association and the analysis and interpretation of DREAMS. The patient expresses repressed conflicts through transference to the analyst. *See also* ADLER, ALFRED; DEFENCE MECHANISM; EGO; FROMM, ERICH; ID; JUNG, CARL; KLEIN, MELANIE; OEDIPUS COMPLEX; REICH, WILHELM; REPRESSION; SUPEREGO

psychology Study of mental activity and behaviour. It includes the study of perception, thought, problem solving, personality, emotion, MENTAL DISORDER and the adaptation of the individual to society. It overlaps with many other disciplines, including PHYSIOLOGY, PHILOSOPHY, ARTIFICIAL INTELLIGENCE and social ANTHROPOLOGY. Central areas of psychology include neuropsychology, which relates experience and behaviour to BRAIN functioning; COGNITIVE PSYCHOLOGY, which studies thought processes; SOCIAL PSYCHOLOGY, in which behaviour is studied in its social context; and DEVELOPMENTAL PSYCHOLOGY, which studies the way in which children's cognitive and emotional development takes place. Applied psychology aims to use the discipline's insights into human behaviour in practical fields, such as education and industry. *See also* BEHAVIOURISM; ETHOLOGY; GESTALT PSYCHOLOGY; LEARNING; MEMORY

psychopathic personality (antisocial personality) Personality disorder that leads to antisocial, often aggressive, behaviour. There appears to be little anxiety, guilt or NEUROSIS, and psychoanalytic theory regards this disorder as stemming from an incompletely developed SUPEREGO.

psychopharmacology Study of how DRUGS affect behaviour. Drugs are classified according to their effect: sedative hypnotics, such as BARBITURATES; stimulants, such as AMPHETAMINES; opiate NARCOTICS, such as heroin; and psychedelics and HALLUCINOGENS, such as LSD.

psychosis Serious mental disorder in which the patient loses contact with reality, in contrast to NEUROSIS. It may feature extreme mood swings, delusions or hallucinations, distorted judgment and inappropriate emotional responses. **Organic** psychoses may spring from brain damage, advanced SYPHILIS, senile DEMENTIA or advanced EPILEPSY. **Functional** psychoses, for which there is no known organic cause, include SCHIZOPHRENIA and MANIC DEPRESSION.

psychosomatic disorder Physical complaint thought to be rooted, at least in part, in psychological factors. The term has been applied to many complaints, including asthma, migraine, ulcers and hypertension.

psychotherapy Treatment of a psychological disorder by non-physical methods. It is carried out either with individuals or groups and usually involves some sort of "talking cure" and the development of a rapport between patient and therapist. Psychotherapy is often based on PSYCHOANALYSIS. *See also* GROUP THERAPY

ptarmigan Any of three species of northern or alpine grouse, all of which have feathered legs; especially the Eurasian ptarmigan, *Lagopus mutus*. The wings and breast are white in winter, but in the spring they become a mottled grey-brown. It inhabits high barren regions, feeding on leaves and lichens. Length: to 36cm (14in). Family Tetraonidae.

pteridophyte Common name for any of a group of spore-bearing VASCULAR PLANTS. *See also* TRACHEOPHYTE

pterodactyl Any of several species of small PTEROSAURS. Almost tail-less, it had a large toothed beak and flimsy membranous wings. Fossil remains show a lack of muscular development and the absence of a breast keel. It is therefore believed that pterodactyls were gliders, incapable of sustained flapping flight.

pterosaur Extinct flying REPTILE with wing membranes supported by a single, elongated finger on each side. Distributed worldwide during Jurassic and Cretaceous times, early forms had teeth and tails; later forms were tail-less and had toothless beaks.

PTFE *See* POLYTETRAFLUOROETHENE

Ptolemy I (367–283 BC) (Ptolemy Soter) King of ancient EGYPT, first ruler of the Ptolemaic dynasty, which ruled Egypt for *c*.300 years (323–30 BC). A leading Macedonian general of ALEXANDER THE GREAT, Ptolemy I was granted Egypt in the division of the empire upon Alexander's death (323 BC). In 305 BC, after many power struggles, he assumed the title of king. During Ptolemy's reign Egypt prospered through its control of trade in much of the E Mediterranean region, and his organization of land and taxes. Ptolemy established his former soldiers as settlers in Egypt, and endeavoured to unite the country through the cult of Serapis, although he also supported traditional Egyptian religion. He made his capital at ALEXANDRIA, where he created the famous library. In 284 BC, he abdicated in favour of his son, PTOLEMY II.

Ptolemy II (*c*.308–246 BC) (Ptolemy Philadelphus) King of ancient EGYPT (284–246 BC), son of PTOLEMY I. He built ALEXANDRIA into the cultural and commercial centre of the Greek world, attracting poets such as Callimachus and Theocritus, and greatly expanding the collection of books in the Library of Alexandria.

Ptolemy (AD 90–168) (Claudius Ptolemaeus) Greek astronomer and geographer. He worked at the library of Alexandria, Egypt. Ptolemy's chief astronomical work, the *Almagest*, drew heavily on the work of HIPPARCHUS. The **Ptolemaic system** is based on the geocentric world system of the ancient Greeks. His *Geography*, which provided the basis for a world map, was a definitive text until the Renaissance.

puberty Time in human development when sexual maturity is reached. The reproductive organs take on their adult form, and secondary sexual characteristics, such as the growth of pubic hair, start to become evident. Girls develop breasts and begin to menstruate; in boys there is deepening of the voice and the growth of facial hair. Puberty may begin at any time from about the age of ten, usually occurring earlier in girls than in boys. The process is regulated by HORMONES known as GONADOTROPHINS.

public health Branch of medicine that attempts to safeguard and improve the health of the population. It is involved with health promotion, the prevention or control of disease (including mass vaccination and screening programmes), health-care planning and the establishment and maintenance of acceptable standards for housing, food, water, waste disposal and air quality.

public limited company (plc) Company with limited liability whose shares are quoted on a STOCK EXCHANGE. Most companies have limited liability, which means that their owners are responsible only for the money originally invested, and not for the whole of the company's debts. Unlike a private limited company, a public limited company may have any number of shareholders.

public sector State-owned industries and services. The public sector is that part of a country's economy that "belongs" to the public and which includes state-owned institutions. These include nationalized industries (for instance, a national post office or railway) or services

▲ **pterodactyl** Living during the late Jurassic and early Cretaceous periods, the pterodactyls varied in size. The smallest specimen was the size of a sparrow (1) and the largest was the size of a hawk (2). Like the bats of today, it had a wing membrane (3) attached to an elongated fourth finger, and hind limbs and tail.

(for instance, educational or medical services) that are provided by a national government or local officials. The public sector, which is traditionally preferred by left-wing governments, is funded by public money, raised by taxes. *See also* NATIONALIZATION; PRIVATE SECTOR

public sector borrowing requirement (PSBR) Amount a government needs to borrow to cover its expenditure. A government principally raises its money by taxes and excise duties. If it has to spend more than the amount covered by these sources, it must raise the rest by borrowing. To do this, it issues short-term and long-term STOCKS and BONDS, on which it pays INTEREST. These loans form part of the national debt.

publishing Making written or illustrative material generally available by PRINTING or by electronic means. Printed publications include books, newspapers, magazines, posters and pamphlets. Electronic publishing means making material available to computer users. The publication may be made available on the INTERNET, or it may be published in the form of a computer disk known as a CD-ROM. *See also* DESKTOP PUBLISHING (DTP)

Puccini, Giacomo (1858–1924) Italian composer. His operas combine dramatic libretti with expressive music. Puccini best-known works are *La Bohème* (1896), *Tosca* (1900), *Madam Butterfly* (1904) and his last opera (incomplete at his death) *Turandot* (1926).

Pueblo Generic name for Native American tribes inhabiting the Mesa and Rio Grande regions of Arizona and New Mexico. They belong to several language families, including Tewa, HOPI and ZUNI. The multi-storey buildings of the Zuni gave rise to the legendary "Seven Cities of Cíbola" eagerly sought by the Spaniards.

Puerto Rico Self-governing island commonwealth (in union with the USA) in the West Indies, the most E island of the Greater Antilles. The capital is San Juan. Believed to have been first visited by Columbus in 1493, the island was a Spanish colony until 1898, when it was ceded to the USA. In 1952, it was proclaimed a semi-autonomous commonwealth. The decline in the sugar industry in the 1940s created considerable unemployment. Many Puerto Ricans emigrated to the USA. The island is of volcanic origin, and much of the land is mountainous and unsuitable for agriculture. The main crops are sugar, tobacco and coffee. Industries: tourism, textiles. Area: 8,870sq km (3,425sq mi). Pop. (2000) 3,836,000.

puff adder Widely distributed African VIPER. Its skin usually has yellow markings on brown. It hunts large rodents, and its poisonous bite can be fatal to humans. Up to 80 young are born at one time. Length: to 1.2m (4ft). Family Viperidae; species *Bitis arietans*.

puffball Any of a large order of MUSHROOMS (Lycoperdiales) whose SPORE masses become powdery at maturity and are expelled in "puffs" when pressed. Puffballs are stemless, and some are edible.

puffin Small, diving bird of the AUK family (Alcidae), found in large colonies in the Northern Hemisphere. The Atlantic puffin (*Fratercula arctica*) has a short neck, a triangular bill with red, yellow and blue stripes and reddish legs and feet. The puffin lays a single egg in a burrow *c*.1–2m (3.3–6.6ft) deep on a cliff. Length: *c*.30cm (12in)

pug Small dog that probably originated in China. It has a large head, a blunt muzzle and facial wrinkles. The wide-chested, short body is set on strong legs. The short coat may be grey, light brown or black with a characteristic black face. Height: to 28cm (11in) at the shoulder; weight: to 8kg (18lb).

Pugin, Augustus Welby Northmore (1812–52) English architect. Pugin and Sir Charles BARRY designed (1840–70) the HOUSES OF PARLIAMENT, London. Through his designs and writings, especially *True Principles of Pointed or Christian Architecture* (1841), he was a leading promoter of the GOTHIC REVIVAL.

Puglia (Apulia) Region in SE Italy, consisting of the provinces of Bari, Brindisi, Foggia, Lecce and Taranto; the capital is Bari. Colonized by the Greeks, it was taken by the Romans in the 3rd century BC. Conquered in turn by Goths, Lombards and Byzantines, it later formed part of the Holy Roman Empire. The region became part of Italy in 1861. Products: wheat, almonds,

figs, tobacco. Industries: iron and steel. Area: 19,357sq km (7,472sq mi). Pop. (1992 est.) 4,049,972.

Pulitzer Prize Annual US awards for outstanding achievement in journalism, letters and music. The cost is met by a trust fund left by newspaper publisher Joseph Pulitzer (1847–1911) to the trustees of Columbia University, New York City. The first prize was awarded in 1917. There are prizes for fiction, drama, US history, biography, poetry and musical composition.

pulley Simple machine used to multiply force or to change the direction of the force's application. A **simple** pulley consists of a wheel, often with a groove, attached to a fixed structure. Compound pulleys consist of two or more such wheels, some movable, that allow a person to raise objects much heavier than they could lift unaided.

pulsar Object emitting radio waves in pulses of great regularity. They were first noticed (1967) by the British radio astronomer Jocelyn Bell. Pulsars are believed to be rapidly rotating NEUTRON STARS. More than 500 pulsars are now known, flashing at rates from *c*.4 seconds to 1 millisecond.

pulse Regular wave of raised pressure in arteries that results from the flow of BLOOD pumped into them at each beat of the HEART. The pulse is usually taken at the wrist. The average pulse rate is *c*.70 per minute in adults.

pulse Any leguminous plant of the PEA family with edible seeds, such as the BEAN, LENTIL, pea, PEANUT and SOYA BEAN. The term may also refer to the seed alone. Pulses are also used for oil production. Family Fabaceae/Leguminosae. *See also* LEGUME

puma (mountain lion, cougar) Large cat found in mountains, forests, swamps and jungles of the Americas. It has a small, round head, erect ears and a heavy tail. The coat is tawny with dark brown on the ears, nose and tail; the underparts are white. It preys mainly on deer and small animals. Length: to 2.3m (7.5ft), including the tail; height: to 75cm (30in) at the shoulder. Family Felidae; species *Felis concolor*.

pumice Light rock formed when molten LAVA is blown to a rock froth by the sudden discharge of gases during a volcanic action. It is used as a light abrasive.

pump Device for raising, compressing, propelling or transferring fluids. The **lift** pump, for raising water from a well, and the **bicycle** pump are reciprocating (to-and-fro) pumps. In many modern pumps, a rotating impeller (set of blades) causes the fluid to flow. Jet pumps move fluids by forcing a jet of liquid or gas through them.

pumpkin Orange, hard-rinded, edible garden fruit of a trailing annual VINE found in warm regions of the Old World and the USA; a variety of *Cucurbita pepo*. In the USA the pumpkin is also called a squash, especially the winter pumpkin *C. maxima* and *C. moschata*. Family Cucurbitaceae.

punctuated equilibrium Theory, expounded (1972) by Stephen Jay GOULD and Niles Eldridge, that is strongly sceptical of the notion of gradual change in the EVOLUTION, as advocated by Charles DARWIN. They held that each species is in a steady state (equilibrium), which is punctuated by brief but intense periods of sudden change that give rise to new species.

Punic Wars (264–146 BC) Series of wars between ROME and CARTHAGE. In the **First** Punic War (264–241 BC), Carthage was forced to surrender Sicily and other territory. In the **Second** (218–201 BC), the Carthaginians under HANNIBAL invaded Italy and won a series of victories. They were eventually forced to withdraw, whereupon the Romans invaded North Africa and defeated Hannibal. The **Third** Punic War (149–146 BC) ended in the destruction of Carthage.

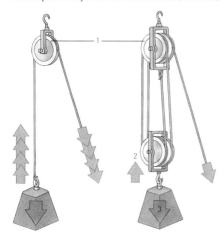

▲ **pulley** Pulleys (1) multiply the effect of a force applied. By passing the rope through four pulleys the upward pulling force (2) is multiplied four times, allowing a person to lift a weight (3) not normally portable. With four pulleys, however, the rope has to be pulled four times as far to move the weight the same distance. To move the weight up 1m (3.3ft) the rope must be pulled down 4m (13.2ft).

Punjab State in N India, bounded W and NW by Pakistan; the capital is CHANDIGARH. In the 18th century Sikhs wrested part of the region from Mogul rule and established a kingdom. In 1849, it was annexed by the British. In 1947, the Punjab was split between the new countries of India and Pakistan, the smaller E part going to India. In 1966, this was further reorganized into two states, HARYANA and Punjab, which is now the only Indian state with a Sikh majority. Apart from Chandigarh, other major cities include AMRITSAR and Jullundur. Punjab is mainly a flat plain. Much of the land is irrigated and agriculture is important. Industries: textiles, woollens, electrical goods. Area: 50,376sq km (19,450sq mi). Pop. (1991) 20,281,969.

Punjab Province in NE Pakistan, bounded E and S by India; the capital is LAHORE. It was subject to a succession of foreign conquerors, including Aryans, Greeks and the British. The province was formed in 1947, acquiring its present boundaries in 1970. The area lies on an alluvial plain, and most of the land under cultivation is irrigated. Agriculture is the chief source of income, with wheat and cotton the major crops. Industries: textiles, machinery, electrical appliances. It is Pakistan's most heavily populated province. Area: 206,432sq km (79,703sq mi). Pop. (1985 est.) 53,840,000.

Punjabi (Panjabi) Language spoken by 50 million people in the PUNJAB region of India and Pakistan. It belongs to the Indo-Iranian family of INDO-EUROPEAN LANGUAGES and is one of the 15 languages recognized by the Indian Constitution. It has similarities to HINDI.

punk Term used to describe music and fashion of the mid-1970s, characterized by raw energy and iconoclasm. Heavily influenced by US bands, such as the New York Dolls, punk was pioneered in Britain by the Sex Pistols and the Clash. Often anti-establishment, the associated fashions in dress, hair and make-up were also designed to shock.

pupa Non-feeding, developmental stage during which an insect undergoes complete METAMORPHOSIS. It generally occurs as part of a four-stage life cycle from the egg, through LARVA to pupa, then IMAGO. Most pupae consist of a protective outer casing, inside which the tissues of the insect undergo a drastic reorganization to form the adult body. Insects that undergo pupation include the many different kinds of BUTTERFLY and BEETLE and many kinds of FLY. The pupa is often called a CHRYSALIS in butterflies and moths.

pupil In the structure of the EYE, circular aperture through which light falls onto the LENS; it is located in the centre of the IRIS. Its diameter changes by reflex action of the iris to control the amount of light entering the eye.

puppet theatre Miniature stage for shows of glove puppets, marionettes, rod puppets and flat and shadow figures. Such theatres existed in ancient Egypt and in Greece in the 5th century BC, in China, Java and elsewhere in Asia, and reached their peak of popularity in 18th-century Europe.

Purcell, Henry (1659–95) English BAROQUE composer and organist. He was organist for Westminster Abbey (1679–95) and the Chapel Royal (1682–95). Purcell is chiefly celebrated for his church music. He also composed the first English opera, *Dido and Aeneas* (1689).

purgatory Place or state intermediate between HEAVEN and HELL where a soul that has died in a state of grace is purged of its sins before entering heaven. In the teachings of the Roman Catholic Church, souls that die with unforgiven venial and forgiven mortal sins go to purgatory.

Purim Ancient Jewish celebration of thanksgiving, held on the 14th day of the Jewish month of Adar (in February or March). It commemorates the deliverance of the Jews of Persia from a plot to destroy them. The story, which appears in the Old Testament Book of ESTHER, is read on this festival in all synagogue services. The gift of alms to the poor is obligatory, and the festival is imbued with a carnival atmosphere.

Puritans British Protestants who were particularly influential during the 16th and 17th centuries. They originated in the reign of ELIZABETH I as a faction within the CHURCH OF ENGLAND; their chief aim was to make it a truly Protestant Church, rather than an Anglo-Catholic one. Following the teachings of CALVIN, they were initially opposed to Anglicanism because of its preoccupation with what they considered to be "popish" practice. However, they later demanded the establishment of PRESBYTERIANISM. In the 17th century many of the parliamentary opponents of JAMES I and CHARLES I were Puritans. Among them were the PILGRIMS who emigrated to America. The English CIVIL WARS (1642–51) resulted from attempts by Puritan parliamentarians to block Charles I's policies on religious grounds. After the war, the Puritans' zenith was reached in 1653 when Oliver CROMWELL established the Protectorate. In 1660, the authority of the Church of England as an Anglican institution was re-established, although 30 years later Presbyterianism was accepted as the state-supported form of Christianity in Scotland. In England, the Puritans lived on as Dissenters. *See also* NONCONFORMISM

purpura Purplish patches on the skin due to seepage of blood from underlying vessels. Physical injury, vitamin deficiencies, some allergies and certain drugs are among the causes.

pus Yellowish fluid forming as a result of bacterial infection. It comprises blood serum, LEUCOCYTES, dead tissue and living and dead BACTERIA. An ABSCESS is a pus-filled cavity.

Pusan City on the Korea Strait, SE South Korea. It has thrived through its trading links with Japan. The Japanese modernized the city's harbour facilities during their occupation of Korea (1905–45). In the Korean War, Pusan acted as the United Nations' supply port. Pusan is the nation's leading port and second-largest city. It is an industrial and commercial centre. Industries: iron and steel, shipbuilding. Pop. (1995) 3,814,000.

Pushkin, Alexander Sergeievich (1799–1837) Russian poet and novelist. In 1820, he was exiled for his political beliefs and his folk romance *Ruslan and Lyudmila* was published. His tragedy *Boris Godunov* (1826) reveals the influence of BYRON. Pushkin's masterpiece was the verse novel *Eugene Onegin* (1833). Other works include the short story *The Queen of Spades* (1834) and

▲ **puma** A wild cat found in a variety of habitats in the New World, the puma (*Felis concolor*), gives birth to between one and six cubs. It can run at speeds of up to 48–80km/h (30–50mph).

the historical novel *The Captain's Daughter* (1836). He died in a duel with his wife's admirer.

Putin, Vladimir (1952–) Russian statesman, prime minister (1999–2000), president (2000–). He served for the KGB in East Germany until 1989, and became head of its successor organization in 1998. When Boris YELTSIN resigned in 1999, Putin became acting president. His support for the war in CHECHENIA earned him victory in the ensuing presidential elections. As president, one of his first acts was to grant Yeltsin immunity from prosecution.

Pu Yi, Henry (1906–67) (Hsuan Tung) Last Emperor of China (1908–11). Deposed after the formation of the Chinese republic, Pu Yi was temporarily rescued from obscurity to become president, later "emperor" of the Japanese puppet state of MANCHUKUO in 1932. Captured by Soviet forces (1945), he was delivered to MAO ZEDONG and imprisoned (1949–59). He later worked as a gardener in Beijing.

PVC *See* POLYVINYL CHLORIDE (PVC)

pyelitis Inflammation of the pelvis of the KIDNEY, where urine collects before draining into the URETER. More common in women, it is usually caused by bacterial infection. Treatment is with ANTIBIOTICS and copious fluids.

pygmy Member of a group of people who average less than 1.5m (4.6ft) in height. African Pygmies inhabit parts of central Africa and Democratic Republic of Congo. Asian Pygmies, often called Negritos, are found mainly in the Philippines and Malaysia. Most Pygmies are hunter-gatherers with few crafts. Their numbers are declining rapidly.

Pym, John (1584–1643) English leader of the parliamentary opposition to CHARLES I. In the LONG PARLIAMENT (1640), he took part in drafting the GRAND REMONSTRANCE (1641). Pym was one of the five members whom Charles tried to arrest in the House of Commons (1642).

Pynchon, Thomas (1937–) US novelist whose works are noted for their offbeat humour and inventiveness. They include *V* (1963), *Vineland* (1990) and *Mason and Dixon* (1997). His best-known work, *Gravity's Rainbow* (1973), won the National Book Award.

Pyongyang Capital of North Korea, in the W of the country, on the River Taedong. An ancient city, it was the capital of the Choson, Koguryo and Koryo kingdoms. In the 16th and 17th centuries, Pyongyang came under both Japanese and Chinese rule. Its industry developed during the Japanese occupation (1910–45). In 1948 it became the capital of North Korea. During the KOREAN WAR it suffered considerable damage. Industries: cement, iron and steel. Pop. (1984) 2,639,448.

pyramid In geometry, solid figure having a POLYGON as one of its faces (the base), the other faces being TRIANGLES with a common vertex. Its volume is one third of the base area times the vertical height.

pyramids Monuments on a square base with sloping sides rising to a point. They are particularly associated with ancient EGYPT, where some of the largest have survived almost intact. They served as burial chambers for pharaohs. The earliest Egyptian pyramid was a step pyramid (ZIGGURAT), built (*c.*2700 BC) for Zoser by IMHOTEP. Pyramid building in Egypt reached its peak during the 4th dynasty, the time of the Great Pyramid at GIZA. The largest pyramid in the world, it was built (*c.*2500 BC) for Khufu and stands 146m (480ft) high with sides 231m (758ft) long at the base. The largest New World ziggurat pyramid was built in TEOTIHUACÁN, Mexico, in the 1st century AD; it was 66m (216ft) high with a surface area of 50,600sq m (547,200sq ft).

Pyrenees Range of mountains in S France and N Spain, extending in an almost straight line E to W from the

Mediterranean Sea to the Bay of Biscay. They were formed in the Tertiary era. The Pyrenees contain deposits of marble, gypsum and oil, and there are extensive forests. Sheep and goat grazing is the chief farming activity. The highest point is Pico de Aneto, 3,406m (11,168ft). Length: 435km (270mi).

Pyrenees, Peace of the (1659) Treaty between France and Spain after the THIRTY YEARS WAR. France gained territory in Artois and Flanders, and PHILIP IV of Spain reluctantly agreed to his daughter's marriage to LOUIS XIV. She was to renounce her claim to the Spanish throne in exchange for a subsidy. Because Spain could not pay the subsidy, the renunciation became void, resulting in the War of Devolution.

pyridoxine VITAMIN B_6, a coenzyme in the metabolism of AMINO ACIDS in the body. Pyridoxine is found in lean meat, egg yolks, milk and fish. A deficiency can lead to anaemia, and it is also taken as a vitamin supplement by those who believe it helps ease depression.

pyrite (fool's gold) Widespread sulphide mineral, iron sulphide (FeS_2), occurring in all types of rocks and veins. It is a brass-yellow colour. It crystallizes as cubes and octahedra and also as granules and globular masses. It is opaque, metallic and brittle. Hardness 6.5; r.d. 5.0.

pyrometer THERMOMETER for use at extremely high temperatures. An optical pyrometer consists essentially of a small telescope, a RHEOSTAT (a type of variable RESISTOR) and a filament. When the telescope is aimed at a furnace or other hot object, the filament appears dark against the background. As the electric current flowing through the filament is increased slowly, using the rheostat, it grows brighter until it matches the intensity of the furnace. The amount of current is a measure of the temperature.

pyroxene Important group of rock-forming, silicate minerals. They are usually dark greens, browns and blacks. Crystals are usually short prisms with good cleavages. Hardness 2.3–4; r.d. 5.5–6.

Pyrrho (*c.*360–*c.*270 BC) Greek philosopher, founder of SCEPTICISM. Pyrrho's doctrine was that nothing can be known, because every statement can be plausibly contradicted; therefore wisdom lies in reserved judgment.

Pyrrhus (*c.*319–272 BC) King of Epirus (307–302, 295–272 BC). An able general, he fought several battles against Rome. Although he won, the cost was so heavy that victory was useless, hence the term "pyrrhic victory".

Pythagoras (*c.*580–500 BC) Greek philosopher and founder of the Pythagorean school. The Pythagoreans were bound to their teacher by rigid vows and were ascetic in their way of life. They believed in the TRANSMIGRATION OF SOULS and that numbers and their interrelationships constitute the true nature of things in the universe. Pythagoras is credited with many advances in mathematics and geometry, medicine and philosophy. The famous **theorem,** that the square of the hypotenuse of a right-angled TRIANGLE equals the sum of the squares of the other two sides, is named after him, but was already known to the Egyptians and Babylonians. His school was suppressed at the end of the 6th century, but its doctrines were revived by the Romans *c.*500 years later.

python Name of more than 20 species of non-poisonous snakes of the BOA family (Boidae), found in tropical regions. Like boas, pythons kill their prey (birds and mammals) by squeezing them in their coils. Unlike boas, pythons lay eggs. The reticulated python (*Python reticulatus*) of SE Asia vies with the ANACONDA as the world's largest snake, reaching up to *c.*9m (30ft). Subfamily Pythoninae.

Q/q, 17th letter of the Roman alphabet, derived from the Semitic qoph, *meaning* monkey. *It was taken into the Greek alphabet as* koppa. *It entered the Roman alphabet in c.AD 114 and assumed its current form c.1500.*

Qaddafi, Muammar al- (1942–) Libyan de facto head of state. In 1969, he led the coup that toppled King Idris I. As head of state, Qaddafi sought to remove all vestiges of Libya's colonial past. He shut down US and British bases, nationalized all petroleum assets, and encouraged a return to Islamic law. In 1983, Libya bombed the neighbouring state of Chad. Qaddafi has supported a number of unsuccessful attempts to bring Libya into union with other Arab countries. He also lent assistance to various international terrorist groups. In 1986, the USA bombed Libya in an attempt to stop this aid. Qaddafi survived, but one of his children was killed. In 1999, he handed over for trial two Libyans suspected of the bombing of Pan-Am flight 103 over Lockerbie, Scotland.

Qatar Sheikhdom on the Qatar peninsula in the Persian Gulf; the capital is DOHA. The low-lying land is mostly stony desert, with some salt flats. Qatar's territory includes several offshore coral islands, the most important being Habal, an oil storage and export terminal. The climate is hot and humid. A scant water supply is supplemented by desalination schemes. Forty percent of Qatar's population are Sunni Muslims, although only 25% are native Qataris, who are descended from three BEDOUIN tribes. Once a part of the Ottoman Empire, Qatar was a British protectorate from 1916 to 1971, when it achieved independence. It is an absolute monarchy. Sheikh Khalifa bin Hamad Al-Thani became emir after a coup in 1972. During the 1980s, Qatar's status was threatened by the regional dominance of Iran and Iraq, and a territorial dispute with BAHRAIN. In the GULF WAR (1991), Allied coalition forces were deployed on Qatar's territory and Palestinian migrant workers expelled because of the pro-Iraqi stance of the Palestine Liberation Organization (PLO). In 1995, the emir was overthrown and replaced by his son, Sheikh Hamad bin Khalifa Al-Thani. A coup attempt failed in 1996. **Economy** Qatar is heavily dependent on food imports. Its high standard of living (1995 GDP per capita, US$17,690) is derived from oil and gas reserves. Oil was discovered in 1939, and today it accounts for c.90% of exports and 80% of income. Oil revenue has been used to diversify the industrial base and develop agriculture. Qatar's economy is heavily dependent on immigrant labour, many from India and Pakistan. Area: 11,437sq km (4,415sq mi). Pop. (2000) 499,000.

Qattara Depression Desert basin in the Libyan Desert, NW Egypt. Impassable by armies and vehicles, it marked the S end of the British defence line at EL ALAMEIN (1942) and stopped ROMMEL's advance. It contains the lowest point in Africa, at 133m (436ft) below sea level. Area: c.18,130sq km (7,000sq mi).

QED *See* QUANTUM ELECTRODYNAMICS

Qin (formerly Ch'in) Imperial dynasty of China (221–206 BC). Originating in NW China, the Qin emerged after the collapse of the ZHOU dynasty; its founder was QIN SHIHUANGDI. The first centralized imperial administration was established, with the country divided into provinces, each under a governor. Uniformity was encouraged in every sphere, including law, language, coinage, weights and measures. The GREAT WALL took permanent shape during this period.

Qing (formerly Ch'ing) Imperial Manchurian dynasty of China (1644–1911). It was established (1636) by NURHACHI following the collapse of the MING dynasty, but it was not until the fall of Beijing that the Qing became the official ruling dynasty. The Qing emperors extended their influence. By 1800, they exercised control over an area stretching from Siam (Thailand) and Tibet to Mongolia and the River Amur. In the 19th century the dynasty weakened, following internal struggles, such as the TAIPING REBELLION, and with the increase of foreign influence, particularly after the OPIUM WARS. It ended with the abdication of PU YI in 1911 and the establishment of the Chinese republic.

Qingdao (Tsingtao) City on the Huang Hai (Yellow Sea), Shandong province, E China. Qingdao was a German treaty port (1898–1914). The Japanese occupied Qingdao in both World Wars. A US naval base (1945–49), it is now a major Chinese trade port and naval base. Industries: fishing, brewing, locomotives. Pop. (1994) 1,584,000.

Qinghai (Tsinghai) Province in NW China; the capital is Xining (Sining). Although parts of the region have long been under Chinese control, until recent times it was occupied mainly by Tibetan and Mongol nomads. It became a province of China in 1928. A mountainous region, it is the source of some of Asia's greatest rivers, including the HUANG HE, YANGTZE and MEKONG. There is farming of wheat, barley and potatoes, and stock rearing. The province is famous for its horses. Iron ore, coal, oil, salt, and potash are extracted. Area: 721,280sq km (278,486sq mi). Pop. (1990) 4,430,000.

Qin Shihuangdi (259–210 BC) Emperor of China (221–210 BC). The first emperor of the QIN dynasty, he reformed the bureaucracy and consolidated the GREAT WALL. In the 1970s excavations of his tomb on Mount Li (near XIAN) revealed, among other treasures, an "army" of c.7,500 life-size terracotta guardians.

Qom City in W central Iran. The burial place of FATIMA, her shrine is a place of pilgrimage for SHIITE Muslims. Industries: textiles, rugs, pottery. Pop. (1994) 780,000.

quadrant In plane geometry, a quarter of a circle, bounded by radii at right angles to each other and by the arc of the circle. In analytic geometry it is one of the four sections of a plane divided by an x axis and a y axis. A quadrant is also a device for measuring angles, based on a 90° scale.

quadratic equation Algebraic equation in which the highest exponent of the variable is 2; an equation of the second degree. A quadratic equation has the general form $ax^2 + bx + c = 0$, where a, b, and c are constants. It has, at most, two solutions (roots), given by the formula $x = [-b \pm \sqrt{(b^2 - 4ac)}]/2a$.

Quadruple Alliance Alliance among four states, in particular three alliances in Europe in the 18th and 19th centuries. The first was formed (1718) by Britain, France, the Holy Roman emperor, and the Netherlands against PHILIP V of Spain, after he seized Sicily and Sardinia. The second was formed (1814) by Austria, Britain, Prussia, and Russia against NAPOLEON I. After Napoleon's defeat the four partners created the CONGRESS SYSTEM. The third Quadruple Alliance (1834) consisted of Britain and France in support of Portugal and Spain, where liberal monarchies were threatened by reactionary claimants.

quail Any of a group of Old World gamebirds. The European quail (*Coturnix coturnix*), a small, short-tailed bird with a white throat and mottled brownish plumage, is found throughout Europe, Asia and Africa. The Australian quail (*Turnix velox*) is a stocky, brownish bird. They scrape for fruits and seeds and nest on the ground. The Japanese quail (*C. coturnix japonica*) is used as a source of meat and eggs in Europe and the USA.

Quakers (officially Society of Friends) Christian sect that arose in England in the 1650s, founded by George FOX. The name derived from the injunction given by early Quaker leaders that their followers tremble at the word of the Lord. Quakers rejected the episcopal organization of the CHURCH OF ENGLAND, believing in the priesthood of all believers and a direct relationship between man and the spiritual light of God. Quakers originally worshipped God in meditative silence unless someone was moved by the Holy Spirit to speak. Since the mid-19th century, their meetings have included hymns and readings. The largest national Quaker Church is in the USA, where it began with the founding of a settlement by William PENN in Pennsylvania (1681). Today, there are *c*.200,000 Quakers worldwide.

qualitative analysis Identification of the chemical elements or ions in a substance or mixture. *See also* QUANTITATIVE ANALYSIS

quango (acronym for **qu**asi-**a**utonomous **n**on-governmental **o**rganization) Any of a number of bureaux set up in Britain with government funds. They are responsible for regulating or monitoring various aspects of industrial, political, financial and social welfare. They are not directly elected, but issue reports periodically on their operational findings. There is much public debate about these bodies, resulting from their expense and lack of accountability.

Quant, Mary (1934–) English fashion designer. In 1955, she opened her first boutique, in Chelsea, London. Quant appealed to the growing youth market. Her designs, such as the miniskirt and her extensive use of vinyl, have become synonymous with "swinging" London in the 1960s.

quantitative analysis Identification of the amount of chemical constituents in a substance or mixture. Chemical methods use reactions, such as precipitation (the suspension of small particles in a liquid), NEUTRALIZATION and OXIDATION, and they measure volume (volumetric analysis) or weight (gravimetric analysis). Physical methods measure qualities such as density and refractive index (how much light is refracted by a medium).

quantum chromodynamics Study of the properties of QUARKS. To explain permissible combinations of quarks to form various ELEMENTARY PARTICLES, each is assigned a colour. Quarks are given one of the three primary colours: red, green and blue. When three quarks combine to form BARYONS, the resulting colour is always white. Antiquarks are given one of the three complementary colours: cyan, magenta and yellow. When a quark combines with an antiquark to form a MESON, the resulting colour is also white.

quantum electrodynamics (QED) Use of QUANTUM MECHANICS to study the properties of ELECTROMAGNETIC RADIATION and how it interacts with charged particles. For example, the theory predicts that a collision between an ELECTRON and a PROTON should result in the production of a PHOTON of electromagnetic radiation, which is exchanged between the colliding particles.

quantum mechanics Use of QUANTUM THEORY to explain the behaviour of ELEMENTARY PARTICLES. In the quantum world, waves and particles are interchangeable concepts. In 1924, Louis de BROGLIE suggested that particles have wave properties, the converse having

been postulated (1905) by Albert EINSTEIN. In 1926, Erwin SCHRÖDINGER used this hypothesis to predict particle behaviour on the basis of wave properties, but a year earlier Werner HEISENBERG had produced a mathematical equivalent to Schrödinger's theory without using wave concepts at all. In 1928, Paul DIRAC unified these approaches while incorporating RELATIVITY into quantum mechanics. The complete modern theory of quantum mechanics was derived by Richard FEYNMAN in the 1940s. *See also* QUANTUM NUMBERS

quantum numbers In physics, a set of four numbers used to classify ELECTRONS and their atomic states. The **principal** quantum number (symbol n) gives the electron's energy level, the ORBITAL quantum number (symbol l) describes its angular momentum, the **magnetic** quantum number (symbol m) describes the energies of electrons in a magnetic field and the SPIN quantum number (symbol m_s) gives the spin of the individual electrons. *See also* QUANTUM THEORY

quantum theory Together with the theory of RELATIVITY, the foundation of 20th-century physics. It is concerned with the relationship between MATTER and ENERGY at the elementary or subatomic level and with the behaviour of ELEMENTARY PARTICLES. According to the theory, all radiant energy is emitted and absorbed in multiples of tiny "packets" or quanta. The idea that energy is radiated and absorbed in quanta was proposed (1900) by Max PLANCK. Using Planck's work, Albert EINSTEIN quantized light radiation and explained (1905) the PHOTOELECTRIC EFFECT. In 1913, Niels BOHR used quantum theory to explain atomic structure and the relationship between the energy levels of an ATOM's electrons and the frequencies of radiation emitted or absorbed by the atom. *See also* QUANTUM MECHANICS; QUANTUM NUMBERS

quarantine Originally a 40-day waiting period during which ships were forbidden to discharge passengers or freight, to prevent transmission of plague or other diseases. Today, the term refers to any period of isolation legally imposed on people, animals, plants or goods in order to prevent the spread of contagious disease.

quark Any one of six ELEMENTARY PARTICLES and their antiparticles (antiquarks); the constituents of the HADRON group of SUBATOMIC PARTICLES. Their existence was proposed independently by Murray GELL-MANN and George Zweig in 1964. Quarks occur in one of six "flavours": up, down, top, bottom, charmed and strange. Antiquarks have similar flavours, but their charge is opposite to that of their corresponding quark. Quarks always exist in combination; free quarks cannot exist. A BARYON, such as a PROTON or NEUTRON, consists of three quarks.

quarrying Method of excavating rock from open-pit mines. Quarried rock is called stone. EXPLOSIVES are generally used in industrial quarrying. The rock, such as limestone, is shattered by detonating explosives placed in strategically drilled holes. A channelling method is used for softer rock, such as sandstone. In this process a line of holes is drilled perpendicular to the cleavage lines in the rock; wedges (plugs) are inserted into the holes and hammered until the rock is split.

quartz (SiO_2) Rock-forming mineral, the natural form of silicon dioxide (silica). It is widely distributed, occurring in igneous and metamorphic rocks (notably granite and gneiss) and in clastic sediments. It is also found in mineral veins. It forms six-sided crystals. Pure quartz is clear and colourless, but the mineral may be coloured by impurities. The most common varieties are colourless quartz (rock crystal), rose, yellow, milky and smoky. The most usual cryptocrystalline varieties, whose crystals can be seen only under a microscope, are CHALCEDONY and FLINT. Quartz crystals exhibit the PIEZOELECTRIC EFFECT and are used in electronic clocks and watches to keep accurate time. Hardness 7; r.d. 2.65.

quarter days Four days, each separated by a quarter of the year, corresponding roughly to the two equinoxes and the two solstices. From the 15th century, they were set aside for the paying of installments towards annual rents and taxes. In England and Ireland the days were Lady Day (25 March), Midsummer Day (24 June), Michaelmas Day (29 September) and Christmas Day (25 December).

quartzite METAMORPHIC ROCK usually produced from sandstone, in which the quartz grains have recrystallized. Quartzite is a hard and massive rock. It is usually white, light grey, yellow or buff, but it can be coloured green, blue, purple or black by various minerals.

quasar (quasi-stellar object) In astronomy, an object that appears to be a massive, highly compressed, extremely powerful source of radio and light waves, characterized by a large RED SHIFT. If such red shifts are due to the DOPPLER EFFECT, it can be deduced that quasars are more remote than any other objects previously identified; many are receding at velocities greater than half the speed of light. Their energy may result from the gravitational collapse of a GALAXY or from many SUPERNOVAS exploding in quick succession, although there seems to be no reason why such events should be occurring.

Quasimodo, Salvatore (1901–68) Italian poet. His first volume, *Waters and Land* (1930), established him as the leading Italian "hermetic" poet. Quasimodo was imprisoned for anti-fascist conduct in World War 2. His later poetry, such as *Day after Day* (1947), marks a shift to a poetry of social engagement. He was also a prodigious translator. Quasimodo was awarded the 1959 Nobel Prize for literature.

Quaternary period Most recent period of the CENOZOIC era, beginning *c*.2 million years ago and extending to the present. It is divided into the PLEISTOCENE epoch, characterized by a periodic succession of great ice ages, and the HOLOCENE epoch, which started *c*.10,000 years ago.

quattrocento (It. fourteen hundred) In art history, the 15th-century period of the Italian RENAISSANCE. Venice was its cultural centre and leading figures included the painters, Fra ANGELICO, Fra Filippo LIPPI, MASACCIO and UCCELLO; the architects, BRUNELLESCHI and ALBERTI; and the sculptors, DONATELLO and GHIBERTI.

Quayle, (James) Dan (Danforth) (1947–) US statesman, vice president (1989–93). He was a Republican congressman (1977–81) and senator (1981–88). In 1988, Quayle was chosen by George BUSH to act as his running mate. Quayle's tenure was marked by several public relations gaffes.

Québec (Québec) Province in E Canada; the largest province in area and second-largest in population; the capital is QUÉBEC and the largest city is MONTRÉAL. Most of the province, however, is on the Canadian Shield and is relatively uninhabited. In 1535, Jacques CARTIER landed on the Gaspé peninsula of E Canada, and in 1536 he sailed up the ST LAWRENCE River. In 1608, Samuel de CHAMPLAIN established the first settlement on the present-day site of Québec city. It served as a headquarters for the fur-traders' exploration of the interior. Following the FRENCH AND INDIAN WARS (1754–63), French Canada was ceded to Britain by the Treaty of Paris (1763). Québec retained its distinctive French culture. The Constitution Act of 1791 separated off the area w of the Ottawa River as the colony of Upper Canada (now ONTARIO). Québec became the British colony of Lower Canada. The revolt (1837) led by Louis PAPINEAU saw the appointment of the Earl of DURHAM. With the establishment of the Dominion of Canada in 1867, Québec became a province. In the late 20th century, the French-speaking inhabitants of the province intensified their demands for recognition of their cultural heritage, including complete independence. In a 1995 referendum a small majority of the population voted against independence. The lowlands by the St Lawrence River are the centre of industry and agriculture; the province's small farms provide vegetables, tobacco and dairy produce. Québec produces much hydroelectric power and timber. Copper, iron, zinc, asbestos and gold are mined. Area: 1,540,687sq km (594,860sq mi). Pop. (1991) 6,895,963.

Québec City and port at the confluence of the St Lawrence and St Charles rivers, s QUÉBEC province, Canada. It is the capital of Québec province. Samuel de Champlain established a French trading post on the site of Québec in 1608. Captured by the British in 1629, the city was returned to France and became the capital of New France in 1663. In 1763, it was ceded to Britain. The city served as the capital of Lower Canada (1791–1841) and of the United Provinces of Canada (1851–55, 1859–65) before becoming capital of Québec province in 1867. In recent years, Québec has become a focal point for Canada's French-speaking separatists. Industries: shipbuilding, paper, leather, textiles, machinery, canning, tobacco, chemicals. Pop. (1991) 167,517.

Québec Act (1774) British Act of Parliament creating a government for Québec. It set up a council to assist the governor and recognized the Roman Catholic Church and the French legal and landholding systems in the former French colony. Québec's boundary was extended south to the Ohio River, a cause of resentment among the 13 North American colonies.

quebracho South American hardwood tree, native to Paraguay. Its heartwood is *c*.30% TANNIN and is the principal source of vegetable tannin for the world's leather industry. Family Anacardiaceae. Species *Schinopsis*.

Quechua Most widely spoken of all Native South American languages, with *c*.5 million speakers in Peru, 1.5 million in Bolivia, and 500,000 in Ecuador. Originally the language of the great INCA empire, it is related to Aymará, the two forming the Quechumaran family.

Queen Anne style In art history, a British style of decorative arts (especially furniture) popular during the reign (1702–14) of Queen ANNE. The style is characterized by elegance and simplicity. Curved cabriole legs are a distinctive feature, as are inlay, veneering and lacquerwork.

Queen Anne's War *See* FRENCH AND INDIAN WARS

Queen Mother *See* ELIZABETH

Queens Largest borough of NEW YORK CITY, on the w end of Long Island, SE New York state, USA. First settled by the Dutch in the early 17th century, the area came under English control in 1664. In 1898, it became a borough of Greater New York. Queens has La Guardia and John F. Kennedy International airports and St John's University (1870). It is a residential and industrial area, and its manufacturing industries produce consumer goods for New York City. Area: 280sq km (108sq mi). Pop. (1990) 1,951,598.

Queensberry, John Sholto Douglas, Marquess of (1844–1900) British nobleman who sponsored the Queensberry rules – the basis of the rules for modern BOXING. Drafted mainly by John G. Chambers of the British Amateur Athletic Club, the Queensberry rules were standardized in 1889. In 1895, Queensberry publicly insulted Oscar WILDE because of the latter's association with his son, Lord Alfred Douglas. Wilde unsuccessfully sued Queensberry for libel and was convicted of homosexual practices.

Queen's Counsel (QC) Member of the Bar appointed to senior rank on the recommendation of the LORD CHANCELLOR (in Scotland of the Lord Justice General)

Queensland State in NE Australia; the capital is BRISBANE. Queensland was originally part of New South Wales and served as a penal colony from 1824 to 1840. In 1859, it became a separate colony and a state of the Commonwealth of Australia in 1901. Nearly 50% of Queensland lies N of the Tropic of Capricorn, and there are rainforests in the N. The GREAT DIVIDING RANGE separates the fertile coastal strip from the interior plains. Its chief crops are sugar cane, wheat, cotton and tropical fruits. Beef cattle are important. The main industry is mining, and there are are valuable mineral deposits (copper, lead, zinc, bauxite, oil and natural gas). Area: 1,727,530sq km (667,000sq mi). Pop. (1993 est.) 3,155,400.

quetzal Forest bird of Central America. The male is bright green above and crimson below with iridescent green tail plumes forming a 60cm (2ft) train. The duller female nests in a hole, often in a tree, and lays two eggs, which are incubated by both parents. Family Trogonidae; species *Pharomachrus mocinno*.

Quetzalcóatl God of CENTRAL AND SOUTH AMERICAN MYTHOLOGY, a principal deity of the TOLTECS, MAYA and AZTECS. He took the form of a feathered serpent who created humans by fertilizing bones with his own blood. Quetzalcóatl was associated with agriculture and the arts. A legend telling of his exile from his homeland is probably based on a ruler who took his name. In 1519, CORTÉS landed in Mexico on the god's birthday, and since Quetzalcóatl was expected to return in man's form, the Aztecs associated Cortés with the god.

Quezon, Manuel Luis (1878–1944) Philippine statesman, first president of the Commonwealth of the Philippines (1935–44). In 1901, he was imprisoned for his part in the revolt against US rule. After his release, Quezon became leader of the Nationalist Party and, as commissioner to the USA (1909–16), secured the passage of the Tydings-McDuffie Bill (1934) that paved the way for independence. An autocratic president, Quezon instigated administrative reforms. His strengthening of Philippine defences failed to prevent Japan's invasion. Quexon formed a government-in-exile in the USA.

Quezon City City on Luzon island, adjacent to Manila, N Philippines. Second-largest city in the Philippines, it was named after Manuel Luis QUEZON and was capital of the Philippines from 1948 to 1976. It is mainly a residential area. Industries: textiles. Pop. (1994) 1,677,000.

Quiché Mayan group of Native South Americans located in the highlands of W Guatemala. Archaeological remains show large pre-conquest population centres and an advanced civilization. Today, they are the largest Native-American group in Guatemala.

quietism Mystical Christian movement begun by the Spanish priest, Miguel de Molinos, in the 17th century. It achieved great influence in 17th-century France and in the Wesleyan movement of 18th-century Britain. Its adherents believed that only in a state of absolute surrender to God was the mind able to receive the saving infusion of grace. *See also* METHODISM; WESLEY, JOHN

quince Shrub native to the Middle East and central Asia. Its greenish-yellow fruit is used in preserves. Height: to 6m (20ft). Family Rosaceae; species *Cydonia oblonga*

Quine, Willard Van Orman (1908–) US philosopher. He was professor of philosophy at Harvard

▶ **quetzal** The resplendent quetzal (*Pharomachrus mocinno*) is a rare, perching bird found in tropical rainforests from S Mexico to Costa Rica. The Aztec and Maya worshipped the bird, associating it with the god, Quetzalcóatl. The quetzal is the national bird of Guatemala.

(1948–78). Quine was committed to philosophy as a branch of natural science. In *Two Dogmas of Empiricism* (1951), he argued for a holistic approach to EMPIRICISM, abandoning the analytic-synthetic distinction made by Immanuel KANT. In *Word and Object* (1960), Quine put forward the notion of the indeterminancy of translation. Other works include *From a Logical Point of View* (1953) and *Pursuit of Truth* (1990). *See also* LOGICAL POSITIVISM

quinine White, crystalline substance isolated in 1820 from the bark of the cinchona tree. It was once widely used in the treatment of MALARIA, but has been largely replaced by drugs that are less toxic and more effective.

quinsy Inflammation of the tonsils, caused by an abscess, often a complication of TONSILLITIS. It is generally treated with antibiotics.

Quisling, Vidkun (1887–1945) Norwegian fascist leader. A former minister of defence (1931–33), he founded the National Union Party (1933), based on the German Nazi Party. In 1940, Quisling collaborated with the invading Germans, and they set him up as a puppet ruler during their occupation of Norway. After World War 2 he was shot as a traitor.

Quito Capital of Ecuador, in the N central part of the country; it lies almost on the Equator and at 2,850m (9,260ft) above sea-level. The site was originally settled by Native Americans and was captured (1487) by the INCAS. In 1534, it was taken by Spain, and liberated (1822) by Antonio José de SUCRE. A cultural and political centre, it is the site of the Central University of Ecuador (1787) and has a notable observatory. The 17th-century cathedral is the burial place of de SUCRE. Industries: textiles, handicrafts. Pop. (1997) 1,488,000.

Qumran Ancient village on the NW shore of the Dead Sea, in the Israeli-occupied West Bank. In 1947, the DEAD SEA SCROLLS (writings of a Jewish sect that settled in Qumran *c*.100 BC–AD 68) were found in nearby caves.

R/r, 18th letter of the English alphabet. It is descended from the Semitic letter resh, *meaning* head. *It passed almost unchanged into the Greek alphabet as the letter* rho *and from there into the Roman alphabet.*

Ra (Re) In Egyptian mythology, Sun god of Heliopolis and lord of the dead. He sailed his sun boat across the sky by day and through the underworld by night. He is most often depicted as falcon-headed, with a solar disc on his head.

Rabat Capital of Morocco. In the N of the country on the Atlantic coast. Rabat dates from Phoenician times, but the fortified city was founded in the 12th century by the ALMOHAD ruler, Abd al-Mumin. In later years it became a refuge for MOORS expelled from Spain. Under French rule (from 1912) it was made the capital of the protectorate of Morocco. Industries: hand-woven rugs, textiles, food processing. Pop. (1982) 518,616.

rabbi Person qualified through study of the Hebrew Bible and the TALMUD to be the chief religious leader of a Jewish congregation and the person responsible for its education and spiritual guidance. Modern Israel has a rabbinic council with two chief rabbis, one representing the Sephardic tradition, the other representing the Ashkenazi.

rabbit Long-eared, herbivorous mammal of the family Leporidae, including the European common rabbit and the American cottontail. The common rabbit is *Oryctolagus cuniculus* and has thick, soft, greyish-brown fur. The wide variety of domesticated rabbits are also of this species. Length: 35–45cm (14–18in); weight: 1.4–2.3kg (3–5lb). *See also* HARE

Rabelais, François (1494–1553) French humanist and satirist. He is famed for his classic series of satires, now known collectively as *Gargantua and Pantagruel*. The series itself consists of *Pantagruel* (1532), *Gargantua* (1534), *Le Tiers Livre* (1546), *Le Quart Livre* (1552) and *Le Cinquième Livre* (1564). Although condemned as obscene by theologians and the Sorbonne, Paris, his books became widely popular.

Rabi, Isidor Isaac (1898–1988) US physicist, b. Austria. He was known for his work on MAGNETISM, molecular beams and QUANTUM MECHANICS. In 1944, Rabi was awarded the Nobel Prize for physics for his discovery and measurement of the radio-frequency spectra of atomic nuclei whose magnetic spin has been disturbed. This led to the development of new spectroscopic methods.

rabies (hydrophobia) Viral disease of the central nervous system. It can occur in all warm-blooded animals but is especially feared in dogs due to the risk of transmission to human beings. The incubation period varies from a week or two to more than a year. It is characterized by severe thirst, although attempting to drink causes painful spasms of the larynx; other symptoms include fever, muscle spasms and delirium. Once the symptoms have appeared, death usually follows within a few days. Anyone bitten by a rabid animal may be saved by prompt injections of rabies vaccine and antiserum.

Rabin, Yitzhak (1922–95) Israeli statesman, prime minister (1974–77, 1992–95). As chief of staff (1964–68), he directed Israeli operations in the SIX-DAY WAR (1967). He was ambassador to the USA (1968–73) before becoming prime minister. As minister of defence (1984–90), Rabin directed operations against the Palestinian INTIFADA and,

having regained leadership of the Labour Party from his colleague and rival, Shimon PERES, became prime minister for the second time. In 1993, Rabin signed the ISRAELI-PALESTINIAN ACCORD with the PALESTINE LIBERATION ORGANIZATION (PLO), promising progress towards Palestinian autonomy in the occupied territories. In November 1995, he was assassinated by an Israeli extremist.

raccoon (racoon) Stout-bodied, omnivorous, mostly nocturnal mammal of North and Central American wooded areas. Raccoons have a black, mask-like marking across their eyes and a long black-banded tail. They have agile and sensitive front paws and typically dip for food in water. The seven species include the North American *Procyon lotor*. Length: 40–61cm (16–24in); weight: 10–22kg (22–48lb). Family Procyonidae.

race Informal classification of the human species according to hereditary (genetic) differences. Different racial characteristics arose among geographically separated populations partly through environmental adaptation across many generations. However, because there is no evidence of genetic racial distinctions, anthropologists reject the term.

Rachmaninov, Sergei (1873–1943) Russian composer and pianist. Composing in the tradition of Russian romanticism, his works include songs, four piano concertos and three symphonies. His most popular works include Piano Concerto No. 2 (1901), *Rhapsody on a Theme of Paganini* (1934) and Symphony No. 2 (1907).

Racine, Jean Baptiste (1639–99) French dramatist. His early plays, such as *La Thebaïde* (1664) and *Alexandre le Grand* (1665), were influenced by contemporaries, such as CORNEILLE. Racine is regarded as the greatest tragedian of the French classical period. His major verse tragedies are *Andromaque* (1667), *Britannicus* (1669) *Bérénice* (1673), *Bajazet* (1672) and *Phèdre* (1677).

racism Doctrine advocating the superiority of one human RACE. Racism has been the avowed policy of certain regimes that, as a result, sanctioned SLAVERY and discriminatory practices, such as the ANTI-SEMITISM in Nazi Germany and the APARTHEID system in South Africa. In 1967, racism was defined by UNESCO as "anti-social beliefs and acts which are based on a fallacy that discriminatory inter-group relations are justifiable on biological grounds".

Rackham, Arthur (1867–1937) English illustrator and watercolourist whose work was inspired by the goblins, fairies and weird beasts of Nordic folk tales. Among his best-known illustrations are the ones he created for Charles LAMB's *Tales from Shakespeare* (1899).

racquets Game played by two or four people in an enclosed 18.3 × 9.1m (60 × 30ft) court. Each player uses a gut-strung racket with a circular head. A service line is painted on the front wall at a height of 2.9m (9.6ft), and a fixed wooden board, also on the front wall, extends 68.6cm (27in) up from the floor. The serve must be above the service line and must land behind a short line 24ft (7.3m) from the back wall. Games are played to 15 points.

radar (acronym for **ra**dio **d**etecting **a**nd **r**anging) Electronic system for determining the direction and distance of objects. Developed during World War 2, it works by the transmission of pulses of RADIO waves to an object. The object reflects the pulses, which are detected by an AERIAL. By measuring the time it takes for the reflected waves to return, the object's distance may be calculated, and its direction ascertained from the alignment of the receiving radar aerial. *See illustration p.686*

radar astronomy Branch of ASTRONOMY in which radar pulses, reflected back to Earth from celestial bodies in the solar system, are studied for information concerning their distance from Earth, their orbital motion and large surface features. Techniques developed for radar mapping of planetary surfaces have proved particularly important for cloud-covered VENUS.

Radcliffe, Ann (1764–1823) English novelist. Radcliffe's GOTHIC NOVELS, notably *The Mysteries of Udolpho* (1794) and *The Italian* (1797), influenced contemporaries such as BYRON and SHELLEY. Jane AUSTEN parodied her style in NORTHANGER ABBEY (1818).

Radhakrishnan, Sir Sarvepalli (1888–1975) Indian philosopher and statesman, president (1962–67). As professor of Eastern religions and ethics at Oxford (1936–52), he did much to reconcile classical Hindu philosophy with contemporary social forces. Radhakrishnan served as vice-president (1952–62) to NEHRU.

radian Angle formed by the intersection of two radii at the centre of a CIRCLE, when the length of the arc cut off by the radii equals one radius in length. Thus, the radian is a unit of angle equal to c.57.295°, and there are 2π radians in 360°.

radiation Transmission of energy by SUBATOMIC PARTICLES or ELECTROMAGNETIC RADIATION.

radiation, cosmic (cosmic rays) Streams of SUBATOMIC PARTICLES from space that constantly bombard the Earth at velocities approaching the speed of light. Primary cosmic rays are high-energy RADIATION that comes from the Sun and other sources in outer space. They consist mainly of atomic nuclei and PROTONS. When primary cosmic rays strike gas molecules in the upper atmosphere, they yield showers of secondary cosmic rays, which consist of energetic protons, NEUTRONS and pions. Further collisions yield muons, ALPHA PARTICLES, POSITRONS, ELECTRONS, GAMMA RADIATION and PHOTONS.

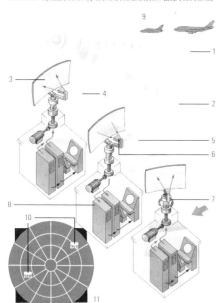

▲ **radar** A radar system locates flying objects by sending out a signal (1) and picking up signals reflected back (2). The radar dish (3) reflects the outgoing signal in an arc (4) and focuses the return signal (5) on to the receiver (6). The radar array rotates (7) to cover 360°. A computer processes the signal (8), and planes in range (9) show up as blips (10) on a screen (11).

radiation, heat Energy given off from all solids, liquids or gases as a result of their temperature. The energy comes from the vibrations of atoms in an object and is emitted as ELECTROMAGNETIC RADIATION, often in the form of INFRARED WAVES.

radiation, nuclear Particles or ELECTROMAGNETIC RADIATION emitted spontaneously and at high energies from atomic nuclei. Possible causes include RADIOACTIVE DECAY, which yields ALPHA PARTICLES, BETA PARTICLES, GAMMA RADIATION and, more rarely, POSITRONS. It can also result from spontaneous FISSION of a nucleus, with the ejection of NEUTRONS or gamma rays.

radiation sickness Illness resulting from exposure to sources of ionizing radiation, such as X-rays, gamma rays or nuclear fallout. Diarrhoea, vomiting, fever and haemorrhage are symptoms. Severity depends upon the degree of radiation, and treatment is effective in mild cases.

radio BROADCASTING or reception of ELECTROMAGNETIC RADIATION in the form of radio waves. A radio signal of fixed FREQUENCY (the carrier wave) is generated at a transmitter. The sound to be broadcast is converted by a MICROPHONE into a varying electrical signal that is combined with the carrier by means of MODULATION. FREQUENCY MODULATION (FM) minimizes interference and provides greater fidelity than AMPLITUDE MODULATION (AM). The modulated carrier wave is passed to an AERIAL from which it is transmitted into the atmosphere. At the receiver, another aerial intercepts the signal, and it undergoes "detection", the reverse of modulation, to retrieve the sound signal. It is amplified to activate a LOUDSPEAKER that reproduces the original sound. Radio waves travel at the speed of light and are transmitted not only by line-of-sight (ground waves), but also by reflection from the IONOSPHERE (sky waves). Sky waves enable long-range radio transmission. The ULTRA HIGH FREQUENCY (UHF) and VERY HIGH FREQUENCY (VHF) radio waves used to send sound and vision signals for TELEVISION penetrate the ionosphere with little reflection, and long-range broadcasting is made possible by means of artificial SATELLITES. The most efficient and commonest circuit used in radio is the superheterodyne receiver. MOBILE TELEPHONES use radio for the transmission of DIGITAL SIGNALS. RADAR transmits pulses of radio waves. The development of radio can be traced to the work of James Clerk MAXWELL. Heinrich HERTZ devised an apparatus for the transmission and detection of radio waves. In 1895, Guglielmo MARCONI gave a demonstration of the first wireless TELEGRAPH, and in 1901 he sent the first transatlantic message using MORSE CODE. In 1904, Sir John FLEMING invented the thermionic valve. In 1906, Lee DE FOREST developed the audion triode valve, which was able to detect and amplify radio waves. It remained at the heart of radio and television manufacture until the invention (1948) of the TRANSISTOR.

radioactive decay Process by which a radioactive ISOTOPE (radioisotope) loses SUBATOMIC PARTICLES from its nucleus and so becomes a different element. The disintegration of the nuclei occurs with the emission of ALPHA PARTICLES (helium nuclei) or BETA PARTICLES (electrons), often accompanied by GAMMA RADIATION. The two processes of alpha or beta decay cause the radioisotope to be transformed into a different atom. **Alpha** decay results in the nucleus losing two PROTONS and two NEUTRONS; **beta** decay occurs when a neutron changes into a proton, with an ELECTRON (beta particle) being emitted in the process. Thus, the ATOMIC NUMBER changes in both types of decay, and an isotope of another element is produced that might also be radioactive. In a large collection of atoms, there is a characteristic time (the HALF-LIFE) after which one-half of the total number of nuclei would have decayed. This time varies from millionths of a second to millions of years, depending on the isotope concerned. The activity of any radioactive sample decreases exponentially with time. *See also* CARBON DATING

radioactivity Spontaneous emission of RADIATION from an atomic nucleus. The process by which a radioactive nucleus disintegrates is known as RADIOACTIVE DECAY.

radio astronomy Study of radio waves (ELECTROMAGNETIC RADIATION with wavelengths from about 1mm to many metres) that reach the Earth from objects in space. Observations can be made using a RADIO TELESCOPE. Radio noise from the MILKY WAY was discovered in 1931 by Karl JANSKY, and the subject grew rapidly after World War 2. The number of radio sources increases with distance, demonstrating that the Universe has been evolving with time. This, combined with the discovery at radio wavelengths of the cosmic microwave background, is strong evidence in favour of the BIG BANG theory of the origin of the Universe.

radio galaxy GALAXY that emits strong ELECTROMAGNETIC RADIATION of radio frequency. These emissions seem to be produced by the high-speed motion of ELEMENTARY PARTICLES in strong magnetic fields.

radiography Use of X-RAYS to record the interiors of opaque bodies as PHOTOGRAPHS. Industrial X-ray photographs can show assembly faults and defects in metals. In medicine and dentistry, radiography is invaluable for diagnosing bone damage, tooth decay and internal disease. Using COMPUTERIZED AXIAL TOMOGRAPHY (CAT), cross-sectional outlines of the body can be obtained showing organs, blood vessels and diseased parts.

radiolaria Sub-class of PROTOZOA found in the topmost layers of the oceans. The siliceous skeleton of radiolarians forms a lattice-like structure and is so resistant to decay that great areas of the ocean floor are covered by OOZES made of nothing else. ASEXUAL REPRODUCTION is by budding or fission.

radiology Medical speciality concerned with the use of RADIATION and radioactive materials in the diagnosis and treatment of disease. *See also* RADIOGRAPHY; RADIOTHERAPY

radio telescope TELESCOPE used to collect and record radio waves from space. The basic design is the large single dish or parabolic reflector, up to 100m (330ft) in diameter. Radio waves are reflected by the dish via a secondary reflector to a focus, where they are converted into electrical signals. The signals are amplified and sent to the main control room, where there is further amplification before analysis and recording. *See also* RADIO ASTRONOMY

radiotherapy In medicine, the use of RADIATION to treat tumours or other pathological conditions. It may be done either by implanting a pellet of a radioactive source in the part to be treated, or by dosing the patient with a radioactive isotope or exposing the patient to precisely focused beams of radiation from a machine, such as an X-RAY machine or a particle ACCELERATOR. Synthesized radioisotopes are the most effective; cobalt-60 is often used as it produces highly penetrating gamma radiation. In the treatment of various types of CANCER, the radiation slows down the proliferation of the cancerous cells.

radish Annual garden vegetable developed from a wild plant native to cooler regions of Asia. Its leaves are long and deeply lobed; the fleshy root, which may be red, white or black, is eaten raw. Family Brassicaceae; species *Raphanus sativus*.

radium (symbol Ra) White, radioactive, metallic element of the ALKALINE-EARTH METALS, first discovered (1898) in URANINITE by Pierre and Marie CURIE; the

metal is present in URANIUM ores. It is used in RADIOTHERAPY. Radium has 16 isotopes that emit alpha, beta and gamma radiation, as well as heat. RADON gas is a decay product. Properties: at.no. 88; r.a.m. 226.025; r.d. 5.0; m.p. 700°C (1,292°F); b.p. 1,140°C (2,084°F); most stable isotope Ra^{226} (half-life 1,622 years).

radius In anatomy, one of the two forearm bones, extending from the elbow to the wrist. The radius rotates around the ULNA, permitting the hand to rotate and be flexible.

radon (symbol Rn) Radioactive element, a NOBLE GAS. It was first discovered (1899) by Ernest RUTHERFORD. The 20 known isotopes, which emit ALPHA PARTICLES, are present in the Earth's atmosphere in trace amounts. Radon is mainly used in medical RADIOTHERAPY. Increased levels in groundwater have been linked both to seismic activity and areas of granite rock. Chemically, it is mostly inert but does form fluoride compounds. Properties: at.no. 86; r.d. 9.73; m.p. −71°C (−95.8°F); b.p. −61.8°C (−79.24°F); most stable isotope Rn^{222} (half-life 3.8 days).

RAF *See* AIR FORCE, ROYAL

Raffles, Sir Thomas Stamford (1781–1826) British colonial administrator, founder of SINGAPORE, b. Jamaica. When Java returned to Dutch rule (1816), he bought the island of Singapore for the British EAST INDIA COMPANY (1819). Under his guidance, it developed rapidly into a prosperous free port.

rafflesia Parasitic plant native to Sumatra and Java. It grows as a PARASITE on the roots of jungle vines and has no stem or leaves. The foul-smelling, reddish-brown flowers are 1m (3.25ft) in diameter, the world's largest flowers. Family Rafflesiaceae; species *Rafflesia arnoldii*.

Rafsanjani, (Ali Akbar) Hashemi (1934–) Iranian cleric and statesman, president of Iran (1989–97). In 1979, after KHOMEINI's triumphant return from exile, he became speaker of the Iranian parliament. A leading figure in the new theocracy, Rafsanjani was acting commander of the armed forces in the final stages of the IRAN-IRAQ WAR. Following Khomeini's death, Rafsanjani became president. His presidency witnessed a slight easing of tension in relations with the West. *See also* KHATAMI, MUHAMMAD

raga (Sanskrit, colour) In Indian music, a sequence of five to seven notes that is used exclusively for the duration of a performance as a basis for improvisation. Its basic structure can be written in the form of a scale. Mood or atmosphere are created by emphasizing certain parts.

Ragnarök In Scandinavian mythology, the doom of the Gods. Heralded by bitter cold and moral decline, it signalled the end of the world and the defeat of the gods and heroes of VALHALLA by the forces of fiery destruction – giants, demons and an all-devouring wolf.

ragtime Name given to an early style of JAZZ, particularly associated with piano playing. Its essential ingredient is the constant syncopation, or "ragging", of a straightforward tune. Rags were a theme and a set of written variations. Scott JOPLIN was the most popular ragtime composer.

ragwort Any of several plants with daisy-like flowers, including the common ragwort (*Senecio jacobaea*) that bears flat-topped clusters of yellow flower heads. Height: to 1.3m (4ft). Family Asteraceae/Compositae.

rail Slender, long-legged marsh bird. Rails are shy, generally nocturnal and often emit melodious calls. They lay 8 to 15 eggs in a reed-and-grass ground nest. Length: 10–45cm (4–18in). Family Rallidae. Typical genus *Rallus*.

railway (railroad) Form of transport in which carriages (wagons or bogies) run on a fixed track, usually steel rails. Railways date from the 1500s, when wagons used in mines were drawn by horses along tracks. In 1804, Richard TREVITHICK built the first steam LOCOMOTIVE. In

1825, George STEPHENSON's *Locomotion* became the first steam locomotive to pull a passenger train. The first full passenger-carrying railway, the Liverpool and Manchester Railway, was opened in 1830. In 1830, in the USA, *Tom Thumb* was the first domestically produced steam locomotive. The first transcontinental railway was completed in 1869, when the Union Pacific Railroad from Nebraska met the Central Pacific Railroad from California in Utah. The world's first underground railway to carry passengers was the City and South London Railway in 1890. Steam locomotives are still used in India, but most countries use electric, diesel or diesel-electric locomotives. Modern developments include high-speed trains such as the Japanese "Bullet" train or the French TGV (*Train à Grande Vitesse*) that travel at an average speed of c.300km/h (185mph). **Maglev** (magnetic levitation) trains use magnetism to hold them above a guide rail. **Air** trains hover above the track by an air cushion.

rain Water drops that fall from the Earth's atmosphere to its surface, as opposed to FOG or DEW which drift as suspensions, or SNOW or HAIL which fall as ice particles. Warm air passing over the sea absorbs water vapour and rises in thermal currents, or on reaching a mountain range. The water vapour condenses and forms clouds, accounting for the usually heavier annual rainfall on windward, compared to leeward, mountain slopes. *See also* PRECIPITATION; HYDROLOGICAL CYCLE

rainbow Multicoloured band, usually seen as an arc opposite to the Sun or other light source. The primary bow is the one usually seen; in it the colours range from red at the top to violet at the bottom. A secondary bow, in which the order of the colours is reversed, is sometimes seen beyond the primary bow. The colours are caused by reflection of light within spherical drops of falling rain, which cause white light to be dispersed into its constituent wavelengths. The colours usually seen are those of the visible SPECTRUM: red, orange, yellow, green, blue, indigo and violet.

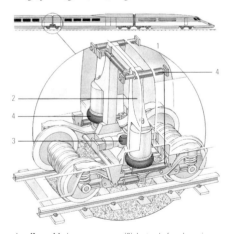

▲ railway Modern railroads feature trains, such as Eurostar shown here, with bogies that use an articulated air suspension system. This has great weight savings. The bogies (1) link the carriages, which are attached to a metal frame (2) through a ball joint (3). Instead of each carriage having a bogie at either end, there is a single suspension unit between two carriages. Dampers (4) modify articulation to improve passenger comfort. The black rings between the frame and the wheel unit are the air suspension units.

rainforest Dense forest of tall trees that grows in hot, wet regions near the Equator. The main rainforests are in Africa, Central and s America and SE Asia. They comprise 50% of the timber growing on Earth and house 40% of the world's animal and plant species. They also, through PHOTOSYNTHESIS, supply most of the world's oxygen. This is why the present rapid destruction of the rainforests (up to 20 million hectares are destroyed annually to provide timber and land for agriculture) is a cause of great concern. Also, clearing rainforests contributes to the GREENHOUSE EFFECT and may lead to GLOBAL WARMING. There are many species of broad-leaved evergreen trees in rainforests that grow up to 60m (180ft) tall. The crowns of other trees, up to 45m (135ft) tall, form the upper canopy of the forest. Smaller trees form the lower canopy. Climbing vines interconnect the various levels, providing habitats for many kinds of birds, mammals and reptiles. Very little light penetrates to the forest floor, which consequently has few plants. Rainforest trees provide many kinds of food and other useful materials, such as Brazil nuts, cashews, figs and mangosteens, as well as fibrous kapok and the drugs quinine and curare.

Rainier III (1923–) Prince of MONACO (1949–). In 1956, he married actress Grace KELLY and the couple had three children: Albert (1958–), Caroline (1957–) and Stephanie (1965–).

Rainier, Mount Peak in w central Washington, USA; the highest point in the Cascade Range. The summit of this ancient volcano is the centre of the greatest single-peak glacier system in the USA. Height: 4,395m (14,410ft).

raisin Dried, sweet, seedless GRAPE. Special varieties are grown, particularly in Australia and the w USA.

Rajasthan State in NW India on the border with Pakistan; the capital is JAIPUR. Other major cities include UDAIPUR, JODHPUR and Jaisalmer. Rajasthan was the homeland of the RAJPUTS. Rajasthan state was formed in 1950 and enlarged in 1966. The THAR DESERT in the w is inhabited by pastoral nomads. The E is part of the DECCAN plateau and wheat, millet and cotton are grown with the aid of irrigation. Coal, marble, mica and gypsum are mined. Industries: handicrafts, cotton milling. Area: 342,266sq km (132,149sq mi). Pop. (1991) 44,005,990.

Rajneesh, Shree (1931–90) (Chandra Mohan Jain) Indian religious leader who founded a religious movement in India based on what he called "loving meditation". Under Bhagwan Rajneesh's charismatic leadership, the movement spread to Europe and the USA.

Rajput Predominantly Hindi warrior caste from NW India. They became powerful in the 7th century AD, gaining control of an historic region named Rajputana. After the Muslim conquests in the 12th century, they retained their independence but by the early 17th century had submitted to the MOGUL EMPIRE. In the early 18th century, they extended their control. In the 19th century, most of their territorial gains were lost to the MARATHAS, Sikhs and the British empire. During the colonial period much of Rajputana retained its independence under local princely rule. After Indian independence in 1947, most of the princes lost their powers. *See also* RAJASTHAN

Rákóczy Hungarian family, princes of Transylvania. George I (r.1631–48) fought against Austria in defence of Protestantism during the THIRTY YEARS' WAR. George II (1621–60) allied with the Swedes to invade Poland. Francis II (1676–1735) headed a revolt against Austria in Hungary (1703) and controlled Hungary until he was defeated (1708).

Raleigh, Sir Walter (1552–1618) English soldier, explorer and writer. A favourite courtier of ELIZABETH I,

Raleigh organized expeditions to North America, including a failed attempt to found a colony. He fought in France and against Spain and sat in Parliament. On JAMES I's ascension to the throne, Raleigh was imprisoned for treason (1603–16), during which time he wrote his *History of the World*. He gained release in order to lead an expedition to Guiana in search of the gold of EL DORADO, but was betrayed to the Spanish authorities and returned to prison and later executed for treason.

Raleigh Capital of North Carolina, USA, in the E central part of the state. Founded in 1792 as state capital, it was named after Sir Walter Raleigh. It is a market centre for the cotton and tobacco trade. Industries: food processing, textiles, electronic equipment. Pop. (1990) 207,951.

RAM (random access memory) INTEGRATED CIRCUITS (chips) that act as a temporary store for computer PROGRAMS and DATA. To run a program on a COMPUTER, the program is first transferred from a MAGNETIC DISK, or other storage device, to the RAM. The RAM also holds documents produced when the program is used. Another part of the RAM stores the images to be displayed on the screen. The contents of the RAM are lost when the computer is switched off.

Rama Hero of the RAMAYANA. A chivalrous husband, obedient to sacred law, he was considered to be the seventh incarnation of VISHNU. Rama became synonymous with God.

Ramadan Ninth month of the Islamic year, set aside for fasting. Throughout Ramadan, the faithful must abstain from food, drink and sexual intercourse between sunrise and sunset. They are also encouraged to read the whole of the KORAN in remembrance of the "Night of Power", when MUHAMMAD is said to have received his first revelation from ALLAH via the angel GABRIEL.

Ramakrishna (1836–86) (Gadadhar Chatterji) Hindu spiritual teacher who taught that all religions were basically united in a common goal of union with the same God. His chief disciple, Swami Vivekananda, founded (1897) the Ramakrishna Mission in India.

Raman, Sir Chandrasekhara Venkata (1888–1970) Indian physicist. He greatly influenced the growth of science in India and founded (1946) the Raman Institute. Raman received the 1930 Nobel Prize for physics for his research on the diffusion of light and his discovery of the **Raman effect**. This states that there is a slight change in the frequency of monochromatic (single-wavelength) light that has been scattered by passing through a transparent material. This effect appears in secondary spectral lines on each side of the primary spectral line. *See also* QUANTUM THEORY; SCATTERING

Ramayana (Romance of Rama) Great epic poem of SANSKRIT LITERATURE. Written in *c*.300 BC along with the MAHABHARATA, it is ascribed to the poet Valmiki and comprises 24,000 couplets in seven books. It concerns the adventures of RAMA, his wife Sita and others.

Rambert, Dame Marie (1888–1982) British ballet dancer, teacher and choreographer, b. Poland. She was a member of DIAGHILEV's BALLETS RUSSES (1912–13). In 1920, Rambert founded her own school, which became known as the Ballet Rambert in 1935.

Rameau, Jean Philippe (1683–1764) French composer and musical theorist. His most famous opera is *Castor et Pollux* (1737), and among his other stageworks is the dramatic ballet *Les Indes Galantes* (1735).

Ramsay, Allan (1713–84) Scottish portrait painter. The Scottish counterpart of GAINSBOROUGH and Joshua REYNOLDS, Ramsay settled in London where, during 1760, he was appointed painter to George III in

preference to his rival, Reynolds. His style, graceful and Italianate, lent itself especially well to female portraiture, such as *The Artist's Wife* (1755).

Ramsay, Sir William (1852–1916) Scottish chemist. In 1894, working with Lord RAYLEIGH, he discovered ARGON in air. In 1895 Ramsay discovered HELIUM. In 1898 he isolated NEON, KRYPTON and XENON. In 1904 Ramsay was awarded the 1904 Nobel Prize for chemistry. In 1910 he found the last NOBLE GAS, RADON.

Ramses I Founder of the 19th dynasty of ancient EGYPT (r. *c*.1320–1318 BC). He was a general under Horemheb, who chose him as his successor. The great hall of the temple at Karnak was begun during his reign.

Ramses II Egyptian king of the 19th dynasty (r. *c*.1290–1224 BC). He reigned during a period of unprecedented prosperity and power. His efforts to confirm Egypt's dominant position in Palestine led to a major clash with the HITTITES at Kadesh (*c*.1285 BC). In 1269 a truce was agreed, and Ramses later married a Hittite princess. He built many splendid monuments, including the temple at ABU SIMBEL.

Ramses III Egyptian king of the 20th dynasty (r. *c*.1194–1163 BC). He defended Egypt from attacks by Libya and the Sea Peoples. Later in his reign, however, Egypt withdrew into political and cultural isolation.

Ramsey, Sir Alf (Alfred) (1920–99) English football manager and player. He was a full-back for Southampton and Tottenham Hotspur, and made 32 appearances for England (1948–53). Ramsay began his managerial career with Ipswich Town, helping them win the League Championship (1962) before managing (1963–74) the national team. He created and guided England's World Cup-winning side (1966).

Rand *See* WITWATERSRAND

Rand, Ayn (1905–82) US writer, b. Russia. In 1926, she emigrated to the USA. Her debut novel was *We the Living* (1936). Other works include *Anthem* (1938), *The Fountainhead* (1943) and *Atlas Shrugged* (1957). The last two serve as vehicles for her philosophy of objectivism, which espouses individual self-fulfilment in a capitalist society.

Rangi In the creation myth of the Maoris, the Sky god who forms such a close embrace with the Earth goddess Papa that their unborn children cannot emerge. When they are finally separated, Light and Darkness make their first appearance in the world. Rangi also figures in other OCEANIC MYTHOLOGY.

Rangoon (Yangon) Capital of Burma (Myanmar), a seaport on the River Rangoon *c*.34km (21mi) N of the Andaman Sea. The site of an ancient Buddhist shrine, Rangoon was made capital of Burma in 1886 when the British annexed the country. The scene of fighting between British and Japanese forces in World War 2, it is the country's chief trade centre. Industries: oil refining, timber, rice, iron ores. Pop. (1983) 2,458,712.

Ranjit Singh (1780–1835) Indian maharaja, founder of the SIKH kingdom of the PUNJAB. At the age of 12, he became the ruler of a small territory in NW India. He absorbed neighbouring states, and in 1799 established his capital at Lahore. In 1803, he took possession of the Sikh holy city of AMRITSAR. He established the E boundary of his kingdom on the River Sutlej. Turning his attention to the W and N, he captured Peshawar and Kashmir. His kingdom collapsed after his death.

Rank, J. (Joseph) Arthur (1888–1972) English industrialist and film magnate, chairman of many film companies. Rank promoted the British film industry when Hollywood and US film companies had a virtual monopoly.

rap Form of music that became popular during the early 1980s with bands such as Grandmaster Flash. Rap had its roots in the improvised street poetry of African-American and Hispanic teenagers in New York. The music places an emphasis on DJs who mix different tracks together, sometimes "scratching" for increased effect.

rape Plant grown for animal fodder and for its small, black seeds, which yield rape oil, used industrially as a lubricant. It has curly, blue-green leaves, small yellow flowers and slender seed pods. Family Brassicaceae; genus *Brassica*.

rape Crime of sexual intercourse without the victim's consent, often involving the use of force, implied or actual. If the victim is considered incapable of giving consent (for example because s/he is below the age of consent), this is known as **statutory** rape, and evidence of lack of consent is not required. **Marital** rape is now considered a crime in the UK.

Raphael Biblical archangel who, with MICHAEL, GABRIEL and Uriel, serves as a messenger of God. According to passages in the apocryphal Book of Tobit and the pseudepigraphal Second Book of Enoch, he is one of the seven holy angels who present the prayers of the saints to God.

Raphael (1483–1520) (Raphael Sanzio or Raphael Santi) Italian painter, one of the finest artists of the High RENAISSANCE. Born in Urbino, Raphael absorbed HUMANISM as a child. One of his most important commissions (1509) was the decoration of the four *stanze* (rooms) in the Vatican. He only completed two of these but the first, the *Stanza della Segnatura*, gave him the chance to exercise his skills to the full. The room contains two large FRESCOS, the *School of Athens* and the *Disputà*, both of which show Raphael's mastery of PERSPECTIVE. After BRAMANTE's death he became architect of St Peter's, Rome.

rare earth *See* LANTHANIDE SERIES

raspberry Fruit grown in polar and temperate regions of Europe, North America and Asia. The black, purple, or red fruit is eaten fresh or preserved. Canes, rising from perennial roots, bear fruit the second year. Family Rosaceae; species *Rubus idaeus*.

Rasputin, Grigori Yefimovich (1872–1916) Russian peasant mystic. He exercised great influence at the court of NICHOLAS II because of his apparent ability to cure the crown prince Alexis's haemophilia. Rasputin attracted suspicion because of his advocacy of sexual ecstasy as a means of religious salvation. In 1916, he was poisoned by a group of nobles, and when this failed, he was shot and drowned.

▲ **rattlesnake** Not normally aggressive, rattlesnakes try to avoid confrontation by warning of their presence. Their unmistakable and menacing rattle is produced by "bells" of hard skin on the end of the tail. The amount of venom they produce far exceeds that needed to kill the rodents that form their usual prey. They can also use it to protect themselves against large predators.

Rastafarianism West Indian religion focusing on veneration of Ras Tafari (HAILE SELASSIE I). The movement was started in Jamaica in the 1920s by Marcus GARVEY. He advocated a return to Africa to overcome black oppression. Rastafarians follow a strict diet, which forbids the eating of pork, milk and coffee.

rat Any of numerous small RODENTS found worldwide. Most species are herbivorous. The best known are the black rat (*Rattus rattus*) and brown rat (*R. norvegicus*), both of the family Muridae. They carry diseases and destroy or contaminate property and food. Both live everywhere that humans live. *See also* BLACK DEATH

ratio Number relating two numbers or two quantities of the same kind, such as two prices or two lengths, that indicates their relative magnitude. Ratios, as of the numbers 3 and 4, can be written as a fraction $\frac{3}{4}$, or with a colon (3:4).

rationalism Philosophical theory that knowledge about the nature of the world can be obtained solely by reason, without recourse to experience. Rationalist philosophers, such as DESCARTES, LEIBNIZ and SPINOZA, argued that reality could be logically deduced from "self-evident" *a priori* premises. It is usually contrasted with EMPIRICISM. In theology, rationalism holds that faith be explicable by human reason rather than divine revelation.

rational number Number representing the RATIO of two integers, the second of which is not zero. Thus, 1/2, 18/11, 0, −2/3 and 12 are all rational numbers. Any rational number can be represented as a terminating decimal (such as 1.35) or a recurring decimal (such as 18/11 = 1.636363...). *See also* IRRATIONAL NUMBER

ratite Group of large, usually flightless birds with flat breastbones instead of the keel-like prominences found in most flying birds. Ratites include the OSTRICH, RHEA, CASSOWARY, EMU, KIWI and the unusual flying tinamou.

rattan Climbing PALM native to the East Indies and Africa. Its stems can grow to 150m (500ft). They are used for making ropes and furniture. Family Arecacae/Palmae; genus *Calamus*.

Rattigan, Sir Terence Mervyn (1911–77) English dramatist. He first attracted attention with the comedy *French Without Tears* (1936). Rattigan's most popular plays include *The Winslow Boy* (1946), *The Browning Version* (1948), *Separate Tables* (1954), *Ross* (1960) and *In Praise of Love* (1973). He also wrote the screenplay for the musical *Goodbye Mr Chips* (1968).

Rattle, Simon (1955–) British conductor. He won the John Player International Conductors' Competition in 1974. In 1976, he became associate conductor of the Royal Liverpool Philharmonic Orchestra. Rattle came to international prominence as principal conductor (1980–98) and music director (1990–98) of the City of Birmingham Symphony Orchestra (CBSO). He is known for his championing of new music; the many first performances he has conducted include Toru Takemitsu's *Through the Rainbow* (1984), Mark-Anthony Turnage's *Drowned Out* (1993) and Judith Weir's *We are Shadows* (2000). Rattle made his North American début with the Los Angeles Philharmonic in 1979, later serving (1981–94) as their principal guest conductor. He is also an admired conductor of opera. Rattle was chief conductor and artistic director of the Berlin Philharmonic Orchestra (2002–).

rattlesnake Any of *c*.30 species of venomous New World pit VIPERS characterized by a tail rattle of loosely connected segments of unshed skin. It ranges from Canada to South America, usually in arid regions. Most are blotched with dark diamonds, hexagons or spots on a lighter background. They feed mostly on rodents. Length: 30cm–2.5m (1–8ft). Family Viperidae. *See also* SNAKE

Rauschenberg, Robert (1925–) US painter and graphic artist who gained recognition in the 1950s with his collages and assemblages. His works combined techniques, including dripped paint and collage, as in *The Bed* (1955). From 1955, his works juxtaposed SURREALISM with ABSTRACT EXPRESSIONISM, as in *Monogram* (1959).

Ravel, (Joseph) Maurice (1875–1937) French composer, a leading exponent of IMPRESSIONISM. His piano pieces include *Jeux d'eau* (1901), *Gaspard de la nuit* (1908) and *Le Tombeau de Couperin* (1917). Among his orchestral works are *Rhapsodie espagnole* (1907) and *Boléro* (1927). Ravel also composed the ballet *Daphnis and Chloë* (1912) and the song cycle *Shéhérazade* (1903).

raven Large bird of the CROW family found in deserts, forests and mountainous areas of the Northern Hemisphere. It has a long, conical bill, shaggy throat feathers, a wedge-shaped tail and black plumage with a purple sheen. It eats carrion or any other animal food. Length: to 68cm (27in). Family Corvidae.

Ravenna City in Emilia-Romagna, NE Italy. It was the capital of the Western Roman Empire in the 5th century AD. It was briefly capital of the Ostrogothic kingdom and then the seat of the Byzantine government in Italy. An independent republic in the 13th century, it was under papal rule from the 16th–19th centuries, becoming part of the kingdom of Italy in 1860. Industries: petroleum, natural gas, furniture. Pop. (1997) 136,000.

Rawalpindi City in Punjab province, NE Pakistan. It grew rapidly in the 18th century and became an important military base after Britain occupied the Punjab in 1849. It was interim capital of Pakistan from 1959 to 1969. Industries: iron, textiles, railway engineering, oil-refining, chemicals. Pop. (1993) 1,290,000

Rawls, John (1921–) US philosopher. His best-known work, *A Theory of Justice* (1972), is a defence of LIBERALISM and the concept of SOCIAL CONTRACT.

Ray, John (1627–1705) English naturalist whose work on plant and animal classification later influenced Carl LINNAEUS and Georges CUVIER. Ray was the first to distinguish the two main types of flowering plants as MONOCOTYLEDONS and DICOTYLEDONS.

Ray, Man (1890–1976) US photographer, painter, sculptor and film-maker. He co-founded the New York DADA movement with Marcel DUCHAMP and Francis Picabia. Ray is best known for photographs produced without a camera by placing objects on light-sensitive paper and exposing them to light. *See also* SURREALISM

Ray, Satyajit (1921–92) Indian film director. His "Apu trilogy", *Pather Panchali* (1955), *The Unvanquished* (1956) and *The World of Apu* (1959), is a poetic, humanist series of films about life in post-colonial India. Other films include *The Big City* (1963), *The Hero* (1966) and *The Visitor* (1992)

ray Any of several species of cartilaginous, mostly marine fish related to the SKATE, SHARK and CHIMAERA. Its body is flattened dorso-ventrally and extends sideways into large, wing-like pectoral fins that are "flapped" while swimming. The tail is narrow and may be whip-like or bear poisonous spines. Electric (torpedo) rays stun their prey with electrical charges of up to 200 volts. Length: 1.5m (5ft).

Rayleigh, John William Strutt, Lord (1842–1919) English physicist. His work was chiefly concerned with various forms of wave motion. Rayleigh was awarded the 1904 Nobel Prize for physics for his discovery (with William RAMSAY) of the noble gas ARGON and for work on gas densities.

rayon Fine, smooth fibre made from solutions of CELLULOSE. It was the first synthetic textile (1892). **Viscose**

▲ **ray** Found in all oceans, the various electric rays (*Dasyatis* sp.) use the electric charge they can generate both for stunning prey and warding off predators – the shock of between 35 and 60 volts may be strong enough to stun humans. They feed on smaller animals and have teeth adapted for crushing shells.

rayon, the most common, is spun-dried and has a strength approaching NYLON. **Acetate** rayon is made of filaments of cellulose ETHANOATE.

razor-billed auk (razorbill) Stocky, penguin-like seabird that lives along coastlines in the cold parts of the Northern Hemisphere. It is black and white with a white-ringed, narrow bill. Length: 41cm (16in). Species *Alca torda*.

razor shell Bivalve MOLLUSC. With a long, thin, narrow, hinged shells, this mollusc is common on beaches of the Northern Hemisphere. Family Solenidae.

Reading City in S central England, at the confluence of the Thames and Kennet rivers; county town of BERKSHIRE. The area was occupied by the Danes in the 9th century. Industries: ironware, engineering, electronics. Pop. (1994) 131,000.

reading Ability to comprehend visual symbols representing LANGUAGE, usually in the form of written or printed characters. Opinions differ over the precise physical nature of this process and over whether the language involved – phonetic, non-phonetic, or ideographic – is influential in the speed of learning and the retention of vocabulary.

Reagan, Ronald Wilson (1911–) 40th US President (1981–89). A well-known film actor, he joined the Republican Party in 1962. Reagan won a landslide victory to become governor of California (1966–74). Nominated as presidential candidate at his third attempt in 1980, he defeated incumbent Jimmy CARTER. In 1981, Reagan survived an assassination attempt. As president, he introduced large tax cuts and reduced public spending, except on defence. By the end of Reagan's second term, budget and trade deficits had reached record heights. Fiercely anti-communist, he adopted strong measures against opponents abroad, invading Grenada (1983) and undermining the SANDINISTA regime in Nicaragua. While pursuing his Strategic Defence Initiative (SDI, or "Star Wars"), Reagan reached a historic nuclear DISARMAMENT treaty (1987) with Mikhail GORBACHEV that signalled an end to the COLD WAR. The last year of his presidency was overshadowed by the IRAN-CONTRA AFFAIR. He was succeeded by his vice-president George BUSH.

realism Broad term in art history, often interchangeable with NATURALISM. Critics and historians use it to define art that tries to represent objects accurately and without emotional bias. It is also used to denote a movement in 19th-century French art, led by Gustave COURBET, against conventional subjects, focusing instead on unidealized scenes of modern life. **Superrealism** is a 20th-century movement, in which real objects are depicted in very fine detail so that the overall effect appears unreal. *See also* SOCIALIST REALISM

realism Philosophical doctrine according to which universal concepts, as well as tangible things, exist in their own right, outside the human mind that recognizes or perceives them. The idea developed from a medieval view that "universals" are real entities rather than simply names for things. Realism was thus opposed to NOMINALISM. Some philosophers rejected this view in favour of moderate realism, which held that "universals" exist only in the mind of God. *See also* IDEALISM

real number Any number that is a RATIONAL NUMBER or an IRRATIONAL NUMBER. Real numbers exclude imaginary numbers (the square roots of negative quantities). *See also* COMPLEX NUMBER

Realpolitik (Ger. politics of realism) Term first applied to the policy of BISMARCK in Prussia in 1848. It implies the pursuit of power and self-interest as the predominant principle of policy-making.

real tennis (royal TENNIS, court tennis) Medieval game played with racket and ball on a rectangular indoor court surrounded by walls, three out of four of which are surmounted by a sloping roof; there are other hazards at each end. The game was first played during the 12th century in French monastic cloisters.

Réaumur, René Antoine Ferchault de (1683–1757) French physicist. Réaumur is chiefly remembered for his THERMOMETER scale, which designates 0° as the freezing point of water and 80° as its boiling point. He wrote widely on natural history and conducted research in mining, metallurgy, fossils and insects.

Rebellions of 1837 Risings in favour of self-rule in Upper and Lower Canada (ONTARIO and QUÉBEC). In Upper Canada, the rising was led by William Lyon Mackenzie and soon fizzled out. The revolt in Lower Canada, led by Louis PAPINEAU, was more serious, and was severely suppressed. The outbreaks led to the Durham report and the union of Upper and Lower Canada (1841).

receptacle Biological structure that serves as a container for reproductive cells or organs in plants. In flowering plants, the receptacle is the enlarged end of a stalk to which the flower is attached. In ferns, it is the mass of tissue that forms the sporangium (the spore-bearing organ). In some seaweeds, it is the part that seasonally becomes swollen and carries the reproductive organs.

recession In economics, phase of the business cycle associated with a declining economy. Its manifestations are rising UNEMPLOYMENT, contracting business activity and decreasing purchasing power of consumers. Government policy, such as cuts in government spending or taxes, may be used to stimulate and expand the economy during a recession. If a recession is not checked, it can degenerate into a DEPRESSION.

recessive In GENETICS, a term to describe a form of GENE (ALLELE) that does not express itself when paired with a DOMINANT allele. Although it is part of the GENOTYPE (genetic make-up) of a HETEROZYGOTE, it does not contribute to the PHENOTYPE (physical characteristics) of the organism. It becomes expressed only when the same recessive allele form appears on both CHROMOSOMES of a HOMOZYGOTE. Recessive alleles were discovered by Gregor MENDEL, who found that a cross between pure-bred red and white flowering peas always produced red flowers in the offspring. The allele for red coloration is dominant; the allele for white is recessive. *See also* HEREDITY

Recife City and port on the Atlantic coast, NE Brazil; the capital of Pernambuco state. Originally settled by Portuguese in the 1530s, it was under Dutch occupation in the

17th century. It is now a major port and shipping centre, exporting sugar, cotton and coffee. Pop. (1991) 1,290,149.

reciprocal Quantity equal to the number 1 divided by a specified number. The reciprocal of 2 is $\frac{1}{2}$, and the reciprocal of $\frac{1}{2}$ is 2.

recombinant DNA research Branch of GENETIC ENGINEERING involving the transferral of a segment of DNA from a source organism into a host organism (typically a microbe). The transferred segment is spliced into the host's overall DNA structure, thus altering the information contained in its GENETIC CODE. When the host undergoes asexual cell division, each product cell carries a replica of the new DNA. In this way, numerous clones of the new cell can be made. *See* RESTRICTION ENZYME

recombination Process that rearranges GENES to increase genetic variation in sexually produced offspring. Recombination takes place during MEIOSIS. It is achieved by crossing over of paired CHROMATIDS. Its effect is to "shuffle" genes derived from both parents and thereby create genetic variation. Some GENETIC ENGINEERING techniques can induce recombination artificially.

Reconstruction In US history, the process of restoring the former Confederate states to the Union after the CIVIL WAR. It was the cause of fierce controversy within Congress. The relatively pro-Southern approach of President Andrew JOHNSON led to his impeachment, which failed by one vote. The Republicans were determined to establish the political and CIVIL RIGHTS of African Americans, and they succeeded in imposing the programme known as Radical Reconstruction over presidential veto. It alienated many Southern whites, and growing violence in the 1870s required the presence of federal troops. When Rutherford B. HAYES became president (1877), he withdrew the troops, Southern Republican governments collapsed, and Reconstruction was abandoned.

recorder Simple WOODWIND musical instrument, popular in Europe since the 15th century. It comprises an end-blown straight tube with eight finger holes. Modern recorders include soprano, descant, tenor and bass.

recording *See* SOUND RECORDING

rectangle Four-sided geometric figure (quadrilateral), the interior angles of which are right angles and each pair of opposite sides is of equal length and is parallel. It is a special case of a PARALLELOGRAM.

rectifier Component of an electric CIRCUIT that converts alternating current (AC) into direct current (DC). The rectifier is usually a semiconductor DIODE. *See also* ELECTRIC CURRENT

rector High-ranking clerical or educational official. In a Protestant Episcopal Church or the CHURCH OF ENGLAND, a rector is a member of the clergy who is in charge of a PARISH. In the Roman Catholic Church, a rector is a priest in charge of a congregation, religious house or college.

rectum In humans and many other vertebrates, last part of the large INTESTINE, where the faeces are stored prior to evacuation.

recycling Natural and manufactured processes by which substances are broken down and reconstituted. In nature, elemental cycles include the CARBON CYCLE, NITROGEN CYCLE and HYDROLOGICAL CYCLE. Natural cyclic chemical processes include the metabolic cycles in the bodies of living organisms. Manufactured recycling includes the use of bacteria to break down organic wastes to harmless, or even beneficial, substances. Large quantities of inorganic waste, such as metal scrap, glass bottles and building spoil, are recycled.

red admiral European BUTTERFLY with red bars on the wings and black wing-tips spotted with white. The caterpillar is dark with light sidestripes and branching spikes. Family Nymphalidae; species *Vanessa atalanta*.

red algae Taxonomic group (PHYLUM) of reddish ALGAE, the Rhodophyta. They are numerous in tropical and sub-tropical seas. Most are slender, branching seaweeds that form shrub-like masses. Some become encrusted with calcium carbonate and are important in REEF formation. Rhodophytes have red and purplish pigments that help to absorb light for photosynthesis. They also have CHLORO-PHYLL. They have complex life cycles with two or three distinct stages involving ALTERNATION OF GENERATIONS.

Red Army Army of the former Soviet Union. It was characterized by a high degree of political control and was institutionalized at all levels with a system of com-missars. During World War 2, the strength of the Red Army increased to more than 20 million men. It was renamed the Soviet Army in 1946. The Red Army was also the name of the Chinese revolutionary guard before it was formally renamed the People's Liberation Army.

red blood cell *See* ERYTHROCYTE

Red Cross International organization that seeks to alle-viate human suffering, particularly through disaster relief and aid to war victims. It is composed of more than 150 independent national societies in most countries, with central headquarters in Geneva, Switzerland. It is staffed largely by volunteers. The name comes from its symbol: a red cross on a white background. The organization is known as the Red Crescent in Muslim countries.

redcurrant Widely cultivated shrub and its small, round, red, edible fruit; it is closely related to the black-currant. Family Grossulariaceae; species *Ribes silvestre*.

red dwarf Star at the lower end of the main sequence. Red dwarfs have masses of between 0.8 and 0.08 of a solar mass. They are of small diameter, relatively low surface temperature (2,500–5,000K) and low absolute magnitude.

Redford, Robert (1937–) US film actor, director and producer. He began his career on Broadway in *Barefoot in the Park*. Redford shot to cinematic fame opposite Paul NEWMAN in *Butch Cassidy and the Sundance Kid* (1969). His popularity increased with *The Great Gatsby* (1974) and *All the President's Men* (1976). Redford won an Academy Award for his directorial debut, *Ordinary People* (1980). Other films include *A River Runs Through It* (1992) and *Quiz Show* (1994). He also established the Sundance Insti-tute, Utah, a training centre for young independent film-makers and the home of the sundance film festival.

Redgrave Name of a family of British actors and actress-es. **Sir Michael** (1908–85), also a director and writer, made major stage appearances in Shakespeare's *Hamlet*, *Macbeth* and *As You Like It*. He appeared in many films, including *The Way to the Stars* (1945) and *The Browning Version* (1951). His children are actors. **Vanessa** (1937–) frequently appears on the London stage. She won an Academy Award as Best Supporting Actress in *Julia* (1977). Other films including *Prick Up Your Ears* (1987) and *Howard's End* (1992). **Corin** (1939–) has acted on stage and television, and **Lynn** (1943–) received an Oscar nomination for *Georgy Girl* (1966).

Redgrave, Sir Steven (1962–) English oarsman. Win-ner of five gold medals at consecutive Olympic Games, the first athlete ever to do so in an endurance event. Redgrave won gold medals for Britain in the coxed fours in 1984, and in the coxless fours in 1988, 1992, 1996 and 2000. After the 2000 Olympics, Redgrave announced his retirement.

Red Guards Chinese youth movement active in the CULTURAL REVOLUTION (1966–68). They were named after the groups of armed workers who took part in the RUSSIAN REVOLUTION (1917). The Chinese Red Guards

attacked revisionists, westerners and alleged bourgeois influences. Originally encouraged by MAO, they caused severe social disorder and were suppressed after 1968.

Redmond, John Edward (1856–1918) Irish nation-alist politician. Redmond succeeded Charles PARNELL as leader of the Irish Nationalist Party in the British Parlia-ment (1891–1918). He support for the Liberals enabled the passage of the third HOME RULE Bill (1912). The EASTER RISING (1916) and the rise of SINN FÉIN weak-ened support for his reformist agenda.

Redon, Odilon (1840–1916) French painter and graphic artist. He was an exponent of SYMBOLISM. Odilon worked mainly in black and white, creating a fantasy world of weird amorphous creatures. In the 1890s he began painting mythological scenes and flower paintings in radiant colours.

Red Sea Narrow arm of the Indian Ocean between NE Africa and the Arabian Peninsula, connected to the Mediterranean Sea by the Gulf of Suez and the Suez Canal. With the building of vessels too large for the canal and the construction of pipelines, the Red Sea's impor-tance as a trade route has diminished. Its maximum width is *c*.320km (200mi). Area: 438,000sq km (169,000sq mi).

redshank Eurasian wading bird of the SANDPIPER family. It has a long slender bill, mottled grey, brown and white plumage and characteristic slender red legs. Length: to 28cm (11in). Family Scolopacidae; species *Tringa totanus*.

red shift (z) Lengthening of the wavelength of light or other ELECTROMAGNETIC RADIATION from a source, caused either by the source moving away (the DOPPLER EFFECT) or by the expansion of the Universe (cosmological red shifts). It is defined as the change in the wavelength of a particular spectral line, divided by the rest wavelength of that line. The Doppler effect results from motion through space; cos-mological red shifts are caused by the expansion of SPACE itself stretching the wavelengths of light travelling toward Earth. *See also* HUBBLE, EDWIN POWELL; RELATIVITY

reduction *See* OXIDATION-REDUCTION

redwood *See* SEQUOIA

Reed, Sir Carol (1906–76) English film director. He won Academy Awards for best picture and best director for the musical *Oliver!* (1968). Other films include *Penny Par-adise* (1938), *The Fallen Idol* (1948), *The Third Man* (1949), *Trapeze* (1956) and *The Agony and Ecstasy* (1965).

Reed, John (1887–1920) US journalist and political activist. He reported on the revolt led by Pancho VILLA in Mexico. Reed is celebrated for his account of the Russ-ian Revolution, *Ten Days That Shook the World* (1919). After helping found the US Communist Labor Party, he returned to Russia (1919), where he died.

Reed, Lou (1944–) US rock singer-songwriter and gui-tarist, b. Louis Firbank. He was a member (1965–73, 1993) of the New York avant-garde band, the Velvet Under-ground. The group's first album, *The Velvet Underground and Nico* (1967), was co-produced by Andy WARHOL. Reed's first solo album, *Transformer* (1972), featured the songs "Walk on the Wild Side" and "Perfect Day".

reed Aquatic GRASS native to wetlands throughout the world. The common reed (*Phragmites communis*) has broad leaves, feathery flower clusters and stiff smooth stems used for thatching, construction and musical pipes. Height: to 3m (10ft). Family Poaceae/Gramineae.

reed instrument Musical instrument that produces sound when an air current vibrates a fibre or metal tongue. In a CLARINET or reed organ pipe, a beating reed vibrates against a hole at the end of the tube. The OBOE and BASSOON have double-reed mouthpieces, the two tongues vibrating against each other when blown.

reef Rocky outcrop lying in shallow water, especially one built up by CORALS or other organisms.

referendum Political process in which legislation or constitutional proposals are put before all voters for approval or rejection. This direct form of voting was known in Greece and other early DEMOCRACIES. In the UK, referenda have been held over membership of the EUROPEAN COMMUNITY (1975) and DEVOLUTION for Scotland and Wales (1979, 1998).

reflection Change in direction of part or all of a WAVE. When a wave, such as a light or sound wave, encounters a surface separating two different media, it is bounced back into the original medium. The incident wave (striking the surface), reflected wave, and the normal (line perpendicular to the surface) all lie in the same plane; the incident wave and reflected wave make equal angles with the normal. *See also* REFRACTION

reflex action Rapid involuntary response to a particular stimulus – for example, the "knee-jerk" reflex that occurs when the bent knee is tapped. It is controlled by the nervous system.

reflex camera CAMERA that allows the user to view and focus through the lens of the camera. A plane MIRROR and PRISM reflect the scene through the lens onto a ground glass screen. When the photographer presses the shutter on a **single-lens reflex** (SLR) camera, the mirror flips back and light reaches the film. A **twin-lens reflex** (TLR) camera has two sets of lenses, one for viewfinding, the other for passing light directly on to the film. *See also* PHOTOGRAPHY

reflexology School of complementary medicine based on the theory that the image of the body is reflected in the foot. Modern practices are based on theories that date back as far as 3000 BC. Practitioners use foot massage to clear blockages of energy flow in the body, which cause illness.

reflexor *See* MUSCLE

Reform Acts British acts of Parliament extending the right to vote. The Great Reform Bill (1832) redistributed seats in the House of Commons to include large cities that were previously unrepresented. The second Reform Act

(1867) extended the FRANCHISE to include better-off members of the working class. The acts of 1884 and 1885 gave the vote to most adult males. Women over 30 gained the vote in 1918, and the Representation of the People Act (1928) introduced universal adult suffrage.

Reformation Sixteenth-century European movement that sought reform of the universal CATHOLIC CHURCH and resulted in the development of PROTESTANTISM. More than a revolt against the ecclesiastical and doctrinal authority of the church, it also represented a protest by many theologians and scholars against the interference of the church in secular matters and the questionable activities of the contemporary clergy, notably the sale of INDULGENCES and holy relics. In the 14th and 15th centuries, the Catholic Church had been tested by the LOLLARDS, the HUSSITES and HUMANISM. The year 1517 is often given as the starting date for the Reformation, when Martin LUTHER nailed his 95 theses to the Schlosskirche in Wittenburg, Germany. Luther's attack on the corruption of the church and the doctrines of papal supremacy, TRANSUBSTANTIATION and clerical celibacy won the support of several German princes. In Zurich, Switzerland, the Reformation was led first by Ulrich ZWINGLI and then by John CALVIN. CALVINISM was adopted in France (*see* HUGUENOTS), the Netherlands and Scandinavia. In England, the Reformation was at first more political than religious. In 1534, Thomas CROMWELL drafted the Act of Supremacy that rejected papal authority and made King HENRY VIII the head of the English Church. Under EDWARD VI Protestantism was established by the Book of COMMON PRAYER (1552). In 1559, in the reign of Elizabeth I, the CHURCH OF ENGLAND was formally established. In Scotland, the Reformation was led by John KNOX and PRESBYTERIANISM was established as the state religion in 1560. *See also* COUNTER-REFORMATION

Reformed church Any Christian denomination that came into being during the REFORMATION by separating, as a congregation, from the old universal CATHOLIC CHURCH (the Western Church). More specifically, Reformed churches are those churches that adopted CALVINISM in preference to LUTHERANISM. In the USA, the largest Reformed churches, such as the Dutch Reformed Church and the Evangelical and Reformed Church, originated from N European countries. The term is also used for a modern group that splits from its mother church, such as the Reformed Episcopal church.

refraction Bending of a WAVE, such as a light or sound wave, when it crosses the boundary between two media, such as air and glass, and undergoes a change in velocity. The incident wave (striking the surface), refracted wave and the normal (line perpendicular to the surface) all lie in the same plane. The incident wave and refracted wave make an angle of incidence, i, and an angle of refraction, r, with the normal. The index of refraction for a transparent medium is the ratio of the speed of light in a vacuum to its speed in the medium. It is also equal to $\sin i / \sin r$. **Snell's law** states that this ratio is constant for a given interface.

refrigeration Process by which the temperature in a refrigerator is lowered. In a domestic refrigerator, a refrigerant gas, such as AMMONIA or CHLOROFLUOROCARBON (CFC), is first compressed by a pump and cooled in a condenser where it liquefies. It is then passed into an evaporator where it expands and boils, absorbing heat from its surroundings and thus cooling the refrigerator. It is then passed through the pump again to be compressed. Refrigeration is also used in AIR CONDITIONING.

refugee Person who leaves his or her native land because of expulsion or to avoid persecution or war or other violent events and seeks asylum, especially in another country.

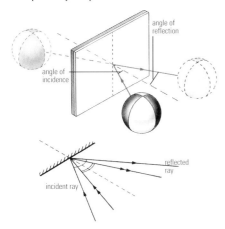

angle of reflection

angle of incidence

reflected ray

incident ray

▲ **reflection** The top diagram shows the reflection of an image in a mirror. The image reflects back with an angle of reflection the same as the angle of incidence. The image, however, appears to the eye to be behind the mirror on an extension of the angle of reflection. The bottom line drawing illustrates that the angle of reflection is always the same as the angle of incidence, whether the angle is acute or oblique.

The United Nations High Commission for Refugees (UNHCR) is responsible for the welfare of refugees.

Regency style In England, style of art and architecture fashionable when the future GEORGE IV was Prince Regent (1811–20) and during his reign. A period of great variety, it generally denotes designs that are extremely elegant and refined.

regeneration Biological term for the ability of an organism to replace one of its parts if it is lost. Regeneration also refers to a form of ASEXUAL REPRODUCTION in which a new individual grows from a detached portion of a parent organism.

Regensburg (Fr. *Ratisbon*) City and port at the confluence of the rivers Danube and Regen, Bavaria, S Germany. Founded by the Romans as Castra Regina, it was captured by Charlemagne in 788. During the 13th century, Regensburg flourished on the commercial trade with the Middle East and India and became an imperial free city. From 1663 to 1806, it was the seat of the Imperial Diet. In 1810, Regensburg was annexed to Bavaria and in 1853 was made a free port. Pop. (1993) 126,000.

reggae Form of West Indian popular music. It came into prominence in the mid-1960s, growing out of rock-steady and ska. It is characterized by a hypnotically repetitive back beat. Modern variations on the form include ragga and lover's rock. Bob MARLEY was largely responsible for bringing reggae to a worldwide audience.

Regina City in S central Canada; capital of Saskatchewan province. Founded in 1882 as the capital of Northwest Territories, in 1905 it became the capital of the newly formed province of Saskatchewan. It is an important transport centre and a distribution area for the surrounding wheat-growing region. Industries: food-processing, oil-refining, steel, engineering, motor vehicles, printing. Pop. (1996) 194,000.

Reich, Steve (1936–) US composer. A leading exponent of MINIMALISM, his works are characterized by shifting, repetitive musical patterns. Reich's compositions include *Drumming* (1971) and *The Desert Music* (1984).

Reich, Wilhelm (1897–1957) Austrian psychoanalyst, clinical assistant to Sigmund FREUD (1922–28). In the USA from 1939, he claimed to have discovered "orgone" energy, a primal force in the atmosphere. The function of the sexual orgasm was to discharge orgone energy. In 1950, he was imprisoned for fraud and died in jail.

Reichenbach, Hans (1891–1953) US philosopher, b. Germany. Associated with the development of LOGICAL POSITIVISM, he also contributed to the study of PROBABILITY and INDUCTIVE LOGIC, and the philosophy of physics, space and time. His works include *Elements of Symbolic Logic* (1947) and *The Rise of Scientific Philosophy* (1951).

Reichstag German parliament building in Berlin. Erected 1884–94, the Reichstag is where the lower legislative assembly of Germany – also called the Reichstag – met until 1933, when it was severely damaged in a fire. After the reunification of Germany in 1990, it once again served as the meeting place of Germany's parliament. A new Reichstag was constructed (1999) by Sir Norman Foster.

Reign of Terror (June 1793–July 1794) Phase of the FRENCH REVOLUTION. It began with the overthrow of the GIRONDINS and the ascendancy of the JACOBINS under ROBESPIERRE. Against a background of foreign invasion and civil war, opponents were ruthlessly persecuted and *c.*1,400 executed by the GUILLOTINE. The Terror ended with a coup on 27 July, 1794 in the National Convention, when Robespierre and leading Jacobins were arrested and executed.

Reims City on the River Vesle, NE France; a port on the Aisne-Marne Canal. CLOVIS I was baptized and

▲ **reindeer** Always found in herds, reindeer (*Rangifer tarandus*) migrate vast distances between summer and winter feeding grounds. They are adapted to both tundra and woodland. The reindeer is the only domesticated member of the deer family. It is used in Scandinavia for pulling sledges.

crowned here in 496, and it was the coronation place of later French kings. Reims is the centre of the champagne industry. Other industries: woollen goods, metallurgy, chemicals, glass. Pop. (1990) 180,620.

reincarnation Passage of the soul through successive bodies, causing the rebirth of an individual and the prolonging of his or her existence on Earth. In HINDUISM and BUDDHISM, an individual's KARMA (earthly conduct) determines the condition into which one is born in the next life. *See also* TRANSMIGRATION OF SOULS

reindeer (caribou) Large DEER of N latitudes, which ranges from Scandinavia across Siberia to North America. It has thick fur and broad hoofs, which help to spread the animal's weight on snow. It stands up to 1.4m (4.6ft) tall at the shoulders and feeds on grasses and saplings in the summer and lichens it finds beneath the snow in the winter. It is domesticated for meat and as a pack animal by the Lapps. It is the only deer in which both sexes have antlers. Species *Rangifer tarandus*.

Reinhardt, "Django" (Jean-Baptiste) (1910–53) Belgian jazz guitarist. He blended folk music with jazz and swing styles and is noted for his improvisational skill. In 1934, Reinhardt formed a quintet with the violinist Stéphane Grappelli, and they played as the "Hot Club". He also played in the USA with Duke ELLINGTON.

Reinhardt, Max (1873–1943) Austrian actor and director, b. Max Goldmann. In 1903, he gave up acting in 1903 to specialize in directing spectacular, illusionary productions that used the entire theatre as part of the set.

relative atomic mass (r.a.m.) (atomic weight) Mass of an atom of the naturally occurring form of an element divided by 1/12 of the mass of an atom of carbon-12. The naturally occurring form may consist of two or more isotopes, and the calculation of the r.a.m. must take this into account.

relative density (specific gravity) Ratio of the DENSITY of a substance to the density of water. Thus, the relative density of gold is 19.3: it is *c.*19 times denser than an equal volume of water.

relative molecular mass (molecular weight) Mass of a molecule, the sum of the RELATIVE ATOMIC MASSES of all its atoms. It is the ratio of the average mass per molecule of an element or compound to one-twelfth of the mass of an atom of carbon-12. The molecular masses of reactants (elements or compounds) must be known in order to make calculations about yields in a chemical reaction.

relativity Theory, proposed by Albert EINSTEIN, based on the postulate that the motion of one body can be defined only with respect to that of a second body. This led to the concept of a four-dimensional SPACE-TIME continuum in which the three space dimensions and time are treated on an equal footing. The **special theory**, put forward in 1905, is limited to the description of events as they appear to observers in a state of uniform relative motion. The more important consequences of the theory are: (1) that the velocity of light is absolute, that is, not relative to the velocity of the observer; (2) that the mass of a body increases with its velocity, although appreciably only at velocities approaching that of light; (3) that mass (m) and energy (E) are equivalent, that is, $E = mc^2$, where c is the velocity of light (this shows that when mass is converted to energy, a small mass gives rise to large energy); (4) the LORENTZ-Fitzgerald contraction, that is, bodies contract as their velocity increases, again only appreciably near the velocity of light; and (5) an object's sense of elapsed time expands, that is "time dilation". The **general theory** of relativity, completed in 1915, is applicable to observers not in uniform relative motion. This showed the relation of space and GRAVITATION. The presence of matter in space causes space to "curve", forming gravitational fields; thus gravitation becomes a property of space itself. This leads to such observable phenomena as the curvature of light from distant stars. The existence of BLACK HOLES is postulated as a consequence of general relativity.

relic Any object closely associated with a holy person. Sometimes the body or part of the body, relics can also be articles used by that person. Usually associated with saints, relics were greatly valued during the Middle Ages. The cult of relics was forbidden by Protestant reformers. Among Buddhist relics, the ashes of the Buddha is the most revered.

relief (It. *rilievo*, projection) Three-dimensional sculpture projecting from a flat background. In *alto-relievo* (high relief) the protrusion is great, *basso-relievo* (low relief) protrudes only slightly, and *mezzo-relievo* is between the two.

religion Code of beliefs and practices formulated in response to a spiritual awareness of existence. It may involve either faith in a state of existence after earthly death, or a desire for union with an omnipotent spiritual being, or a combination of the two. Polytheistic religions, such as those of ancient Egypt, Greece and Rome, entailed the worship of many distinct gods or personifications of nature. Many cultures classified their deities into hierarchies known as pantheons; some religions, such as HINDUISM, still have such pantheons. Other ancient religions, some of which incorporated belief in a state of existence after death, were more of a system of ethical philosophy concentrating on metaphysical contemplation (for example, BUDDHISM and TAOISM). The ancient Hebrews were among the first people to worship a single omniscient and omnipotent being, YAHWEH. The basis of their religion was a covenant or agreement that they believed had been made between Yahweh and themselves. He gave them his protection in return for their total faith and obedience. Common to all religions dominated by a single omnipotent force (such as JUDAISM, CHRISTIANITY and ISLAM) is the idea that the power is omnipresent or all places at once and that it is beyond the physical plane occupied by humans. In many religions, both monotheistic and polytheistic, sacrifice to an individual god or to God is an important element, either in propitiation, to redeem the faithful from some wrongdoing or in thanksgiving.

Religion, Wars of (1562–98) Series of religious conflicts in France. At stake was freedom of worship for HUGUENOTS, but it was also a struggle between crown and nobility. The Huguenot leaders were, successively, Louis I de CONDÉ, Caspard de COLIGNY and Henry of Navarre (later HENRY IV). The Catholic party was led by the House of GUISE. The crown, represented by CATHERINE DE' MEDICI and her sons, CHARLES IX and HENRY III, attempted to maintain a moderate Catholic line. The first three civil wars (1562–63, 1567–68, 1568–70) ended in the Treaty of St Germain (1570), which granted concessions to the Protestants. Hostilities recommenced with the SAINT BARTHOLOMEW'S DAY MASSACRE (1572). The fifth civil war (1574–76) resulted in the Edict of Beaulieu that granted freedom of worship to Huguenots. The Catholic party formed a Holy League and the edict was revoked, prompting renewed conflict. Henry III's naming of Henry of Navarre as his heir led to the War of the Three Henrys (1585–89). Henry IV emerged victorious and the Edict of NANTES (1598) extended toleration to the Huguenots.

Remarque, Erich Maria (1898–1970) German novelist, b. Erich Paul Remark. A World War 1 veteran, his best-known novel, *All Quiet on the Western Front* (1929), is a savage indictment of war. The sequel, *The Road Back* (1931), concerns Germany's post-war collapse and readjustment.

Rembrandt Harmenszoon van Rijn (1606–69) Dutch painter and graphic artist. Between 1625 and 1631, he painted many self-portraits. In 1632, Rembrandt settled in Amsterdam, becoming highly regarded as a painter of group portraits, such as the *Anatomy Lesson of Dr Tulp* (1632). By 1636, he was painting in the richly detailed BAROQUE style typified by the *Sacrifice of Abraham* (1636). In 1642, the year his first wife died giving birth to their son, Rembrandt finished his famous group portrait, *The Corporalship of Captain Frans Banning Cocq's Civic Guards* (or *The Night Watch*). By 1656, he was so deeply in debt that he withdrew from society. During these later years, Rembrandt produced some of his greatest works, such as *Jacob Blessing the Sons of Joseph* (1656) and *The Jewish Bride* (late 1660s). His works total more than 300 paintings, some 300 etchings and 1,000 drawings.

Remembrance Sunday In the UK annual commemoration of the dead in World War 1 and World War 2. After World War 1, the dead were remembered by a two-minute silence on Armistice Day, at the 11th hour on the 11th day of the 11th month, the date of the World War 1 cease-fire (1918). In 1945, it was renamed Remembrance Sunday and has been observed on the second Sunday of November since 1956.

remote sensing Any method of obtaining and recording information from a distance. The most common sensor is the CAMERA used in aircraft, SATELLITES and space probes to collect and transmit information back to Earth (often by radio). The resulting photographs provide a variety of information, including archaeological evidence and weather data. MICROWAVE sensors use radar signals that can penetrate cloud. Infra-red sensors can measure temperature differences over an area.

Remus *See* ROMULUS AND REMUS

Renaissance (Fr. rebirth) Period of European history lasting roughly from the mid-15th century to the end of the 16th century. The word was used by late 15th-century Italian scholars to describe the revival of interest in classical learning. It was helped by the fall of Constantinople to the Ottoman Turks in 1453, which resulted in the moving of classical texts to Italy. In Germany, the invention of a printing press with movable type assisted the diffusion of the new scholarship. In religion, the spirit of questioning led to the REFORMATION. In politics, the Renaissance saw the rise of assertive sovereign states – Spain, Portugal, France and England – and the expansion of Europe beyond its own shores, with the building of trading empires in Africa, the East Indies and America. The growth of a wealthy urban merchant class led to a tremendous flowering of the arts. *See also* RENAISSANCE ARCHITECTURE; RENAISSANCE ART; RENAISSANCE MUSIC

Renaissance architecture Architectural style that began in Italy in the 15th century, and spread throughout Europe until the advent of MANNERISM and the BAROQUE in the 16th and 17th centuries. Revolting against GOTHIC ARCHITECTURE, it used Roman motifs. In Italy, BRUNELLESCHI and ALBERTI studied the Roman ruins. In France, the style was first employed by Lescot, who was commissioned by FRANCIS I to work on the LOUVRE (1546). In other European countries, CLASSICAL forms were integrated with medieval motifs.

Renaissance art Style that emerged in Italy in the 15th century, heavily influenced by classical Greek or Roman models and by the new HUMANISM. In painting, the decisive differences between Gothic and Renaissance painting emerged in Florence in the early 15th century. These differences included the development of PERSPECTIVE, a new interest in composition and colour harmonies, the increasing use of secular or pagan subject matter, the rise of portraiture, constant experimentation to develop new skills and a growing concern for the expression of the individual artist. The creators of High Renaissance painting were LEONARDO DA VINCI, MICHELANGELO and RAPHAEL. The ideas of the Italian artists were taken to France and N Europe and emulated with national variations. **Renaissance literature** found an early exponent in PETRARCH; other Italian Renaissance literary figures include DANTE and MACHIAVELLI. By the 16th century, the Renaissance literary movement had reached N Europe, where it inspired much poetry and history writing and culminated, in England, in the dramas of SHAKESPEARE.

Renaissance music Music composed in Europe from *c.*1400–1600. It was mainly religious vocal POLYPHONY, usually MASSES and MOTETS. Non-religious music at this time was mainly in the form of songs – Italian and English MADRIGALS, French *chansons*, German *Lieder* – and some instrumental music for organ, clavier, lute, or for small ensembles. Composers of this period include PALESTRINA, LASSO, BYRD and GABRIELI. *See also* LIED

Rendell, Ruth Barbara, Baroness (1930–) English writer of detective fiction. Her debut novel, *From Doon with Death* (1965), introduced the character of Chief Inspector Wexford. Other Wexford stories include *Wolf to the Slaughter* (1967) and *The Tree of Hands* (1984). Rendell's psychological thrillers include *Judgment in Stone* (1977). Books published under the pseudonym Barbara Vine include *A Fatal Inversion* (1987).

renewable energy (alternative energy) ENERGY from a source that can be replenished or that replenishes itself, and is more environmentally safe than traditional energy forms such as COAL, GAS or NUCLEAR ENERGY. SOLAR ENERGY harnesses the rays of the Sun. TIDAL POWER stations use the gravitational force of the Sun and Moon on the ocean. Wave power harnesses the natural movement of the sea. The power of rivers and lakes can be tapped by damming the flow and using turbines to generate HYDROELECTRICITY. WIND POWER schemes have existed for centuries in the form of WINDMILLS. Another less well-known renewable source is the GEOTHERMAL ENERGY produced in the Earth's crust.

Reni, Guido (1575–1642) Italian painter who became the leading master of Bolognese art. His most celebrated works include *Massacre of the Innocents* (1611), *Aurora* (1613) and *Atlanta and Hippoinenes* (*c.*1625).

Rennes City at the confluence of the rivers Ille and Vilaine, NW France; capital of Ille-et-Vilaine department. During the Middle Ages, Rennes served as capital of Brittany under the Angevin dukes. In the 16th century, it became the seat of the Parliament of Brittany. The city suffered heavy bombing in World War 2. Industries: leather goods, printing, textiles, electronic equipment, motor vehicles, oil-refining. Pop. (1990) 199,396.

rennet Substance used to curdle milk in cheese-making. It is obtained as an extract from the inner lining of the fourth stomach of calves and other young ruminants, and is rich in rennin, an ENZYME that coagulates the casein (protein) of milk.

Renoir, (Pierre) Auguste (1841–1919) French painter. In 1874, he contributed to the first exhibition of IMPRESSIONISM. His masterpieces include *La Loge* (1874) and *Le Moulin de la Galette* (1876). In the early 1880s, Renoir became interested in the human figure with such works as *Bathers* (1884–87) and *After the Bath* (*c.*1895).

Renoir, Jean (1894–1979) French film director and actor, son of Pierre Auguste RENOIR. His best-known films are *La Grande Ilusion* (1937) and *La Règle du Jeu* (1939). Renoir's work is noted for its lyric response to

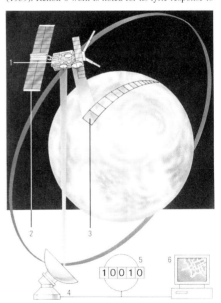

▲ **remote sensing** Remote sensing satellites (1) view the Earth from space using various sensors and cameras. The ways of looking at the Earth are divided between active and passive. Active devices, such as optical cameras and infrared scanners, pick up reflected radiation. Active instruments send out radio pulses and record the return signal. One of the strengths of active scanning is the ability to see through cloud. The satellites, powered by a solar sail (2), use orbits which take them over the whole of the Earth over a series of days (3). Images of the Earth's surfaces are beamed down to ground stations (4) and converted into digital form (5) and are converted into pictures by computers (6).

nature and humanity and for subtlety of style. Other films include *Nana* (1926), *Madame Bovary* (1934), *French Cancan* (1955) and *C'est la Revolution* (1967).

reparations War damage payments, especially those demanded by the victorious Allies from the defeated Central Powers at the Treaty of VERSAILLES (1919). The USA did not ratify the treaty and waived all reparation claims.

repetitive strain injury (RSI) Pain and reduced mobility in a limb, most often the wrist, caused by constant repetition of the same movements. The symptoms arise from inflammation of the tendon sheaths because of excessive use. RSI is an occupational disorder mostly seen in assembly-line workers and keyboard operators.

Representatives, House of *See* HOUSE OF REPRESENTATIVES

repression Process by which unacceptable thoughts or memories are kept in the UNCONSCIOUS so that they cannot cause guilt or distress. According to FREUD, it is part of the function of the EGO, whereby it controls the primal and instinctual urges of the ID. Repressed desires find an outlet in dreams and are believed to be at the root of various neurotic disorders. *See also* PSYCHOANALYSIS

reproduction Process by which living organisms create new organisms similar to themselves. Reproduction may be sexual or asexual, the first being the fusion of two special reproductive cells from different parents, and the second being the generation of new organisms from a single organism. ASEXUAL REPRODUCTION is the more limited, found mainly in PROTOZOA, some INVERTEBRATES and in many plants. By contrast, almost all living organisms have the capacity for SEXUAL REPRODUCTION. In the majority of cases, the species has two kinds of individuals – male and female – with different sex functions. Male and female sex cells (in animals, SPERM and EGG) fuse to produce a new cell, the ZYGOTE, which contains genetic information from both parents and from which a new individual develops. Alternatively, organisms may be HERMAPHRODITES, each individual of the species having male and female functions, so that when two of them mate each individual fertilizes the other's eggs. Sexually reproducing plants (or generations) are called GAMETO-PHYTE; ones that reproduce asexually, SPOROPHYTE. *See also* ALTERNATION OF GENERATIONS; POLLEN

reptile Any one of *c*.6,000 species of VERTEBRATES distributed worldwide. Reptiles are cold-blooded. Most lay yolky eggs on land. Some species – particularly SNAKES – carry eggs in the body and bear live young. The skin is dry and covered with scales or embedded with bony plates. Their limbs are poorly developed or non-existent. Those with limbs usually have five clawed toes on each foot. There are four living orders: Chelonia (TURTLES), Rhynchocephalia (TUATARA), Squamata (scaly reptiles such as snakes and LIZARDS) and Crocodilia (ALLIGATORS and CROCODILES).

republic State in which sovereignty is vested in the people or their elected or nominated representatives. A republic may also be understood to be a state in which all segments of society are enfranchised and the power of the state is limited. *See also* MONARCHY

Republican Party US political party. It was organized in 1854 as an amalgamation of the WHIG PARTY and Free-Soilers, with workers and professional people who had formerly been known as Independent Democrats, Know-Nothings, Barnburners or Abolitionists. Its first successful presidential candidate was Abraham LINCOLN (elected 1860). During the early 20th century, the Republicans were generally the minority party to the DEMOCRATIC PARTY in CONGRESS, especially in the House of Representatives. Later there was a reversal. There was a Republican

president for all but four years between 1969 and 1993. Under presidents Ronald REAGAN and George BUSH, the Republican Party seemed to have captured the popular vote until Bill CLINTON's charismatic campaign restored Democratic fortunes. In 1994, the Republicans regained control of the Senate and House of Representatives, and retained majorities in the 1998 elections. The Republicans regained the presidency in 2000, when George W. BUSH defeated the Democrat candidate, Al GORE, by an extremely narrow margin. Today, the Republican Party is considered to be more conservative than the Democratic Party.

requiem MASS for the dead sung in Roman Catholic Churches. Mozart, Verdi, Fauré and Berlioz, among others, have composed requiems.

reserves In banking, the portion of deposits that a clearing (commercial) BANK has in its physical possession at any given time to meet the withdrawal demands of its depositors. Clearing banks use only fractional reserves, limiting the amount of CAPITAL they must hold, because they do not expect all depositors to withdraw their deposits at once.

resin (rosin) Artificial or natural POLYMER that is generally viscous and sticky. **Artificial** resins include POLYESTERS and EPOXIES and are used as adhesives and binders. **Natural** resins are secreted by various plants. Oleoresin, secreted by conifers, is distilled to produce turpentine; resin remains after the oil of turpentine has been distilled off.

resistance (symbol *R*) Property of an electric CONDUC-TOR, calculated as the ratio of the voltage applied to the conductor to the current passing through it. The SI unit of resistance is the OHM. It represents the opposition to the flow of ELECTRIC CURRENT. *See also* RESISTOR

resistivity (symbol ρ) Electrical property of materials. Its value is given by $ρ = AR/l$, where A is the cross-sectional area of a CONDUCTOR, l is its length, and R is its RESISTANCE. Resistivity is generally expressed in units of ohm-metres and is a measure of the resistance of a piece of material of given size.

resistor Electrical CIRCUIT component with a specified RESISTANCE. Resistors limit the size of the current flowing. Those for electronic circuits usually consist of carbon particles mixed with a ceramic material and enclosed in an insulated tube. Resistors for carrying larger currents are coils of insulated wire.

Resnais, Alain (1922–) French film director. Resnais' early films, such as *Hiroshima mon Amour* (1959) and *Last Year at Marienbad* (1961), established him as a leading figure in the NOUVELLE VAGUE. Other films include *Providence* (1977), *My American Uncle* (1980), *Life is a Bed of Roses* (1983) and *Love Unto Death* (1984).

resonance Increase in the amplitude of vibration of a mechanical or acoustic system when it is forced to vibrate by an external source. It occurs when the FRE-QUENCY of the applied force is equal to the natural vibrational frequency of the system. Large vibrations can cause damage to the system.

resources In economics, a country's collective means of support. Economists divide resources into four categories: land, LABOUR, CAPITAL and raw materials.

Respighi, Ottorino (1879–1936) Italian composer. Respighi is best known for the symphonic poems *Fountains of Rome* (1917) and *Pines of Rome* (1924), influenced by Nikolai RIMSKY-KORSAKOV. He also composed songs, chamber music and operas.

respiration Series of chemical reactions by which complex (food) molecules are broken down to release energy in living organisms. These reactions are an essential part of METABOLISM and are controlled by ENZYMES. There are two main types of respiration: AEROBIC and ANAEROBIC. In **aerobic** respiration, oxygen combines with the breakdown products and is necessary for the reactions to take place. **Anaerobic** respiration takes place in the absence of oxygen. In most living organisms, the energy released by respiration is used to convert ADENOSINE DIPHOSPHATE (ADP) to ADENOSINE TRIPHOSPHATE (ATP), which transports energy around the cell. At the site where the energy is needed, ATP is converted back to ADP with the aid of a special enzyme and energy is released. The first stages of respiration take place in the CYTOPLASM and the later stages in the MITOCHONDRIA. *See also* KREBS CYCLE; TRANSPIRATION

respiratory system System in air-breathing animals concerned with GAS EXCHANGE. The respiratory tract begins with the nose and mouth, through which air enters the body. The air then passes through the LARYNX and into the TRACHEA. The trachea at its lower end branches into two bronchi; each BRONCHUS leads to a LUNG. The bronchi divide into many bronchioles that lead in turn to bunches of tiny air sacs (ALVEOLI), where the exchange of gases between air and blood takes place. Exhaled air leaves along the same pathway.

response, conditioned Learned pairing of a response to an artificial stimulus. In the classic experiments of PAVLOV, dogs were taught to associate the ringing of a bell with their being given food, and they began to salivate just at the sound of the bell. The dog's salivation in these experiments was the conditioned response.

Restoration In English history, the re-establishment of the monarchy in 1660. After the death of Oliver CROMWELL, his son and successor, Richard CROMWELL, was unable to prevent growing conflict. In 1659, Richard resigned, and the crisis was resolved by the march of General MONCK from Scotland. Army leaders backed down and a new Parliament was elected. From exile, CHARLES II issued the Declaration of Breda (1660), promising an amnesty to most opponents, payment of the arrears in the army's wages and religious toleration. He was invited by a new Parliament to resume the throne. The term Restoration is often extended to the period following 1660, and is especially associated with a flowering of English literature, notably in RESTORATION DRAMA. In French history, it refers to the restoration of the BOURBONS (1814–30) after the defeat of NAPOLEON I.

Restoration drama In England, plays and performances in the period following the restoration of CHARLES II, when the theatres were reopened. The drama reflected the laxity of court morals through broad satire, farce, wit and bawdy comedy. Leading dramatists included John DRYDEN and William CONGREVE.

restriction enzyme ENZYME used in GENETIC ENGINEERING to cut a molecule of DNA at specific points, in order to insert or remove a piece of DNA. There are many different restriction enzymes; each cuts the DNA at a specific sequence of bases, allowing great precision in genetic engineering.

resurrection Rising of the dead to new life, either in heaven or on Earth. JUDAISM, CHRISTIANITY and ISLAM all hold that at the end of the world there will come a Day of Judgment on which those worthy of eternal joy will be allowed to draw near to God, while those unworthy will be cast out into darkness. The term also applies to the rising of JESUS CHRIST from the dead on the third day after his crucifixion.

resuscitation Measures taken to revive a person who is on the brink of death. The most successful technique available to the layman is mouth-to-mouth resuscitation. Medical staff receive instruction in cardiopulmonary

resuscitation (CPR), which involves the use of specialized equipment and drugs to save patients whose breathing and/or heartbeat suddenly stop. *See also* FIRST AID

retail price index (RPI) Governmental measure of changing retail prices in Britain, from which the rate of INFLATION is calculated. It is based on a constant selection of goods, weighted according to their importance in a household's budget.

retina Inner layer of the EYE, composed mainly of different kinds of NEURONS, some of which are the visual receptors of the eye. Receptor cells, known as cones and rods, are sensitive to light. **Cones** respond to the spectrum of visible colours; **rods** respond to shades of grey and to movement. The rods and cones connect with sensory neurons, which in turn connect with the optic nerve that carries the visual stimuli to the brain.

retriever Sporting dog originally used to kill or cripple downed game and return it to the hunter; today it is also used to locate game and is a popular pet. The main breeds include the golden retriever and the Labrador retriever.

retrovirus Any of a large family of VIRUSES (Retroviridae) that, unlike other living organisms, contain the genetic material RNA (ribonucleic acid) rather than the customary DNA (deoxyribonucleic acid). In order to multiply, retroviruses make use of a special ENZYME to convert their RNA into DNA, which then becomes integrated with the DNA in the cells of their hosts. Diseases caused by retroviruses include the HUMAN IMMUNODEFICIENCY VIRUS (HIV) that causes AIDS.

Réunion Volcanic island in the Indian Ocean, in the Mascarene group *c.*700km (435mi) E of Madagascar, an overseas department of France; the capital is St Denis. Discovered in 1513 by the Portuguese, it was claimed by France in 1638. The island became an overseas department in 1948 and part of an administrative region in 1973. Exports: sugar, rum, maize, tobacco. Area: 2,510sq km (969sq mi). Pop. (2000) 692,000.

Reuters NEWS AGENCY that transmits international news between major cities worldwide. It originated as a service between Britain and continental Europe, using the telegraph. It is jointly owned by Australian, New Zealand and British newspapers. It was founded (1851) in London by Paul Reuter (1816–99).

Revelation (Apocalypse) Last book of the NEW TESTAMENT. It was written, perhaps as late as AD 95, by St John the Divine. In highly allegorical and prophetic terms, it concentrates on depicting the end of Creation, the war between good and evil, the Day of Judgment and the ultimate triumph of good.

Revere, Paul (1735–1818) American silversmith and patriot, famous for his ride from Charlestown to Lexington, Massachusetts. Revere made his ride on the night of 18 April 1775 to warn the colonists of Massachusetts of the approach of British troops at the start of the AMERICAN REVOLUTION. It was commemorated in LONGFELLOW's poem, "Paul Revere's Ride" (1863).

reversible reaction Chemical reaction in which the products can change back into the reactants. Nitrogen and hydrogen can be combined to give ammonia (as in the HABER PROCESS), and ammonia may be decomposed back into nitrogen and hydrogen. Such reactions yield a CHEMICAL EQUILIBRIUM.

revisionism Political theory derived from MARXISM. In 1890, Eduard Bernstein asserted that CAPITALISM was not in crisis and that the move to SOCIALISM would be a matter of peaceful evolution. This conflicted directly with orthodox Marxist belief in the inevitable collapse of capitalism. After 1945, the term was used by communist regimes to condemn political movements that threatened official party policy.

revolution Movement of a planet or other celestial object around its ORBIT, as distinct from ROTATION of the object on its axis. A single revolution is the planet's or satellite's "year".

revolution In a political sense, fundamental change in values, political institutions, social structure and leadership brought about by a large-scale, successful revolt. The totality of change distinguishes it from coups, rebellions and wars of independence, which seek to achieve only particular changes. The term is also used to indicate great economic and technical changes, such as the INDUSTRIAL REVOLUTION or the AGRICULTURAL REVOLUTION. See also AMERICAN REVOLUTION; FRENCH REVOLUTION; RUSSIAN REVOLUTION

Revolutions of 1848 Series of revolutions in European countries that broke out within a few months of each other. The general cause was the frustration of liberals and nationalists with the governing authorities, against a background of economic depression. The risings began with the FEBRUARY REVOLUTION against LOUIS PHILIPPE in France, which resulted in the foundation of the Second Republic. It inspired revolts in Vienna (forcing the resignation of METTERNICH) and among the national minorities under Austrian rule. In Germany, liberals forced FREDERICK WILLIAM IV to summon a constitutional assembly, while advocates of German unification hoped to achieve their aim in the Frankfurt Parliament. See also KOSSUTH, LOUIS; RISORGIMENTO

Revolutions of 1989 Popular risings in East European states against communist governments. Long-suppressed opposition to Soviet-dominated rule erupted spontaneously in most of the Soviet satellite states. Within months, the communists were driven from power and democratic systems installed. They were followed by the withdrawal of the constituent republics of the SOVIET UNION, which, though unwelcome in Moscow, also encountered little serious resistance.

revue Theatrical entertainment purporting to give a review, usually satirical, of current fashions, events and personalities.

Reykjavík Capital of Iceland, a port on the SW coast. Founded c.870, it was the island's first permanent settlement. It expanded during the 18th century and became the capital in 1918. During World War 2, it served as a British and US air base. Industries: food processing, fishing, textiles, metallurgy, printing and publishing, shipbuilding. Pop. (1996) 105,000.

Reynolds, Albert (1933–) Irish statesman, taoiseach (1992–94). In 1977, Reynolds entered the Dáil and soon joined the FIANNA FÁIL cabinet. In 1991, Reynolds was dismissed after trying to displace Charles HAUGHEY. Reynolds eventually succeeded Haughey as taoiseach. In ensuing elections Fianna Fáil lost their majority and he was forced into coalition with the Labour Party. In 1993, Reynolds and the British prime minister, John MAJOR, issued the DOWNING STREET DECLARATION. In 1994, the Labour Party withdrew its support, and he was forced to resign. He was succeeded as taoiseach by John BRUTON.

Reynolds, Sir Joshua (1723–92) English portrait painter and writer on art. In 1768, he became the first president of the Royal Academy (RA) and espoused the principles of the "Grand Manner" style in his annual *Discourses* (1768–90) to the Academy. These describe how painting, through allusions to classical, heroic figures, can be a scholarly activity. His masterpiece portraits are remarkable for their individuality and sensitivity to the sitter's mood, many of whom are painted in classical poses, such as *Mrs Siddons as the Tragic Muse* (1784).

rhapsody Musical term applied in the 19th and 20th centuries to orchestral works, usually performed in one continuous movement and most often inspired by a nationalist or romantic theme.

rhea Either of two species of large, brownish, flightless, fast-running South American birds resembling a small OSTRICH. They feed mostly on vegetation and insects. Height: to 1.5m (5ft). Family Rheidae.

Rhee, Syngman (1875–1965) Korean statesman, first president (1948–60) of South Korea. He was imprisoned (1898–1904) for his opposition to Japanese rule before living (1912–45) in exile in the USA. In 1919, Rhee became leader of a government-in-exile. After World War 2, he was leader of US-occupied South Korea. His presidency was marked by the KOREAN WAR. Rhee's regime became increasingly authoritarian and corrupt. After his re-election for a fourth time, accusations of vote-rigging sparked riots, and Rhee was forced to resign.

rhenium (symbol Re) Silver-white, metallic element, one of the TRANSITION ELEMENTS, which have incomplete inner electron shells. Discovered in 1925, rhenium is found in molybdenite and PLATINUM ores from which it is obtained as a by-product. It is heavy and used in alloys in thermocouples, camera flashlights and electronic filaments, and is also a useful catalyst. Properties: at.no. 75; r.a.m. 186.2; r.d. 21.0; m.p. 3,180°C (5,756°F); b.p. 5,627°C (10,160°F); most common isotope Re^{187} (62.93%).

rheostat Variable RESISTOR for regulating an ELECTRIC CURRENT. The resistance element may be a metal wire, carbon or a conducting liquid. Rheostats are used to adjust generators, to dim lights and to control the speed of electric motors.

rhesus Medium-sized, yellow-brown MACAQUE monkey of India. Short-tailed, it has a large head with a bare face, large ears, and closely spaced, deep-set eyes. Height: 60cm (2ft). Species *Macaca mulatta*.

rhesus factor (Rh factor) Any of a group of ANTIGENS found on the surface of ERYTHROCYTES (red blood cells). Rh-negative (Rh−) blood lacks the rhesus factor. Rh factor is present in c.85% of humans (Rh+). Rh incompatibility (an Rh− pregnant woman with an Rh+ fetus can give rise to ANAEMIA in newborn babies.

rhetoric Art of discourse and persuasive speaking; language, written or spoken, designed to impress or persuade. Rhetoric is valued in public speaking, but the sophistication of many of its modern techniques may have led to increased suspicion of rhetoricians – such as politicians – on the part of a better-informed public.

rheumatic fever Inflammatory disorder characterized by fever and painful swelling of the joints. Rare in the modern developed world, it mostly affects children and young adults. An important complication is possible damage to the heart valves, leading to rheumatic heart disease in later life.

rheumatism General term for a group of disorders whose symptoms are pain, inflammation and stiffness in the bones, joints and surrounding tissues. Usually some form of ARTHRITIS is involved.

Rhine (Rhein, Rhin or Rijn) Longest river in W Europe. It rises in SE Switzerland in the Swiss Alps and flows N, bordering on or passing through Switzerland, Austria, Liechtenstein, Germany, France and the Netherlands to enter the North Sea at Rotterdam. The Rhine is navigable to ocean-going vessels as far as Basel, Switzerland, and is a major transport route for some of W Europe's most industrialized areas. Length: c.1,320km (820mi).

Rhineland Region in W Germany along the W bank of the River Rhine. It includes Saarland and Rhineland-Palatinate and parts of Baden-Württemberg, Hesse and North Rhine-Westphalia. It was the scene of heavy fighting in World War 2.

rhinitis Inflammation of the mucous membrane of the nose. It may be an allergic reaction (such as HAY FEVER) or a symptom of a viral infection, such as the common cold.

rhinoceros (rhino) Massive, herbivorous mammal native to Africa and Asia. Rhinos are the second largest land mammals (after HIPPOPOTAMUSES). The largest of the five species, the central African white rhino *Ceratotherium simum*, reaches a height of 2m (1.5ft) at the shoulder. Rhinos have thick skin and poor eyesight and are solitary grazers or browsers. In the heat of the day they like to wallow in muddy pools. Now rare except in protected areas, rhinos are illegally hunted for their horns (believed to have aphrodisiac properties). Weight: 1–3.5 tonnes. Family Rhinocerotidae.

rhizoid Fine, hair-like growth used for attachment to a solid surface by some simple organisms, such as certain fungi and mosses. The rhizoid lacks the conducting TISSUES of a root.

rhizome Root-like underground stem of certain plants. It usually grows horizontally, is rich in accumulated starch and can produce new roots and stems asexually. Rhizomes differ from roots in producing buds and leaves. *See also* TUBER

Rhode Island State in NE USA, on the Atlantic coast in New England; the smallest state in the USA; the capital is PROVIDENCE. Other major cities include Warwick, Pawtucket and Cranston. The region was first settled in 1636 by people from Massachusetts seeking religious freedom. In 1663, Rhode Island was granted a royal charter. It was occupied by British troops during the American Revolution. Much of the land is forested, but there is some dairy farming. Potatoes, hay, apples, oats and maize are the chief crops, and fishing is significant. Industries: textiles, fabricated metals, silverware, machinery, electrical equipment, tourism. Area: 3,144sq km (1,214sq mi). Pop. (2000) 1,048,319.

Rhodes, Cecil John (1853–1902) South African statesman, b. Britain. In 1870, Rhodes emigrated to Natal and made a fortune in the Kimberley diamond mines. In 1880, he founded the De Beers Mining Company. He dreamed of building a BRITISH EMPIRE in Africa that stretched from the Cape to Cairo. In 1885, he persuaded the British government to form a protectorate over Bechuanaland. In 1889, he founded the British South Africa Company, which occupied Mashonaland and Matabeleland, thus forming RHODESIA (now Zambia and Zimbabwe). Rhodes was prime minister (1890–96) of Cape Colony. The discovery of his role in Leander JAMESON's attempt to overthrow Paul KRUGER in the TRANSVAAL led to his resignation.

Rhodes (Ródhos) Greek island in the SE Aegean Sea; the largest of the Dodecanese archipelago. It was colonized by the Dorians *c.*1000 BC and later conquered at different times by Persia, Sparta, Athens, Macedon, Rome and the Byzantine Empire. In 1310, the island was captured by the KNIGHTS HOSPITALLERS, who defended it against the Turks for more than 200 years. In 1522, it was taken by the Ottoman Turks. Ceded to Italy in 1912, it was awarded to Greece in 1947. The chief city is Rhodes. Products: wheat, tobacco, cotton, olives, fruits, vegetables. Area: 1,400sq km (540sq mi). Pop. (1981) 88,000.

Rhodesia Former name of a territory in S central Africa. The area was developed by Cecil RHODES. In 1923,

Southern Rhodesia became a self-governing British colony, and in 1924 Northern Rhodesia was made a British protectorate. In 1953, the two Rhodesias were united with Nyasaland (now MALAWI) in the Central African Federation. When the federation was dissolved in 1963, Northern Rhodesia gained independence as ZAMBIA. The name Rhodesia was used by Southern Rhodesia until the country achieved independence as ZIMBABWE in 1980.

rhodium (symbol Rh) Silver-white, metallic element, one of the TRANSITION ELEMENTS. Discovered in 1803, it is associated with PLATINUM, and its chief source is as a by-product of NICKEL smelting. It resists tarnish and corrosion and is used in hard platinum alloys and jewellery. Properties: at.no. 45; r.a.m. 102.906; r.d. 12.4; m.p. 1,966°C (3,571°F); b.p. 3,727°C (6,741°F); most common isotope Rh[103] (100%).

rhododendron Large genus of shrubs and small trees that grow in the acid soils of cool temperate regions in North America, Europe and Asia. Primarily evergreen, they have leathery leaves and bell-shaped white, pink or purple flowers. Family Ericaceae. *See also* AZALEA

rhodophyta *See* RED ALGAE

rhombus Plane figure with all of its sides equal in length but no right angles. A rhombus is a type of PARALLELOGRAM with diagonals that bisect each other at right angles.

Rhône River in W Europe. It rises in the Rhône Glacier in S Switzerland, runs through the Bernese Oberland, flows W to Lake Geneva and then crosses the French border. It continues S through LYON and AVIGNON to Arles, where it branches into the Grand Rhône and the Petit Rhône, which both enter the Mediterranean W of Marseilles. Length: 813km (505mi).

rhubarb Perennial herbaceous plant native to Asia and cultivated in cool climates throughout the world for its edible leaf stalks. It has large, poisonous leaves and small white or red flowers. Height: to 1.2m (4ft). Genus *Rheum*.

rhyme Identity or similarity of final sounds in two or more words, such as keep/deep, baking/shaking. Rhyme is used in POETRY to reinforce METRE. End rhymes establish verse lines, while internal rhymes emphasize rhythmic structures.

Rhys, Jean (1890–1979) British novelist, b. Dominica. Rhys is best-known for *Wide Sargasso Sea* (1966), a "prequel" to Charlotte BRONTE's *Jane Eyre* (1847).

rhythm and blues Form of popular music. It developed as an urban form of the BLUES and was also influenced by JAZZ. An energetic and relatively simple music, it was the basis of ROCK AND ROLL.

rib Projecting band-like architectural structure that supports a VAULT or ceiling and emphasizes its shape. Ribs

► **rhea** Living in open country, the flightless rhea roams the pampas of South America in flocks of up to 30. Standing tall, it can detect approaching danger even in high grass. When threatened, it can run faster than a horse.

are not always structural but may be purely decorative, as when they separate the cells of a groined vault.

rib Long, curved bones that are arranged in pairs, extending sideways from the backbone of vertebrates. In fish and some reptiles they extend the length of the spine; in mammals they form the framework of the chest and protect the lungs and heart. There are 12 pairs of ribs in humans.

Ribbentrop, Joachim von (1893–1946) German diplomat and politician. In 1932, he joined the Nazi Party and became foreign affairs adviser to Adolf HITLER in 1933. Ribbentrop negotiated the secret Nazi-Soviet Pact (1939) with MOLOTOV but steadily lost influence during World War 2. At the NUREMBERG TRIALS (1946), he was convicted of war crimes and hanged.

Ribera, José (1591–1652) Spanish painter and graphic artist. His early work, influenced by CARAVAGGIO, uses CHIAOSCURO. Ribera was also capable of expressing tenderness. His late paintings, such as *The Clubfooted Boy* (1642), are often richly coloured and softly modelled. Until the Napoleonic Wars (1803–15), he and Batholomé MURILLO were the only Spanish painters of international repute.

riboflavin VITAMIN B_2 of the B complex, lack of which impairs growth and causes skin disorders. It is a coenzyme important in transferring energy within cells. Soluble in water, riboflavin is found in milk, eggs, liver and green vegetables.

ribonucleic acid *See* RNA

ribosome Tiny structure in the CYTOPLASM of EUKARYOTE cells, involved in synthesizing PROTEIN molecules. Proteins are made up of specific sequences of AMINO ACIDS; segments of DNA, called GENES, contain the instructions for individual proteins. The DNA molecule is too large to escape from the CELL nucleus into the cytoplasm, but a "copy" is made in the form of **messenger** RNA (mRNA), and this travels to the ribosomes. Ribosomes attach themselves to the mRNA, then assemble the amino acids in the correct sequence to form a particular protein. Ribosomes are made up of proteins and ribosomal RNA. *See also* GENETIC CODE

Ricardo, David (1772–1823) English political economist. He advocated FREE-TRADE and the repeal of the CORN LAWS. Ricardo's LABOUR theory of value (that the price of commodities reflects the labour involved in their production), advanced in *Principles of Political Economy and Taxation* (1817), had a profound influence on Karl MARX.

rice Plant native to SE Asia and Indonesia, cultivated in many warm humid regions, and the main grain food for Middle and Far East countries. It provides a staple diet for half the world's population. It is an annual grass; the seed and husk is the edible portion. It is usually grown in flooded, terraced paddies with hard subsoil to prevent seepage. Species *Oryza sativa*.

Richard I (1157–99) King of England (1189–99), known as Richard the Lion-heart or *Coeur de Lion*. He was involved in rebellions against his father, HENRY II, before succeeding him. A leader of the Third CRUSADE (1189–92), Richard won several victories but failed to retake Jerusalem. Between 1192 and 1194, he was held prisoner by Emperor HENRY VI. Meanwhile, his brother JOHN conspired against him in England, while in France PHILIP II invaded Richard's territories. The English revolt was contained, and from 1194 Richard endeavoured to restore the ANGEVIN empire in France.

Richard II (1367–1400) King of England (1377–99), son of EDWARD THE BLACK PRINCE. Richard succeeded his grandfather, EDWARD III, and soon was faced with the PEASANTS' REVOLT (1381). His reign was marked by conflict with the barons. Richard's uncle, JOHN OF GAUNT, led

a council of regency until 1381. On the orders of the "lords appellant", the "Merciless Parliament" (1388) executed many of Richard's supporters. Richard reasserted control and reigned ably until he began to assume authoritarian powers. In 1397–98, he exacted his revenge on the lords appellant by having the duke of Gloucester murdered and the duke of Hereford (son of John of Gaunt) banished. In 1399, Richard confiscated Gaunt's estates. Hereford led a successful revolt and was crowned HENRY IV. Richard was imprisoned and died in mysterious circumstances.

Richard III (1452–85) King of England (1483–85). As Duke of Gloucester, he supported his brother, EDWARD IV, in N England. When Edward died, Richard became protector and had the young King EDWARD V declared illegitimate and took the crown himself. Edward and his younger brother, the "Princes in the Tower", subsequently disappeared. Richard's numerous enemies supported the invasion of Henry Tudor (HENRY VII) in 1485. Richard's death at the battle of BOSWORTH ended the Wars of the ROSES.

Richards, Viv (Isaac Vivian Alexander) (1952–) West Indian cricketer, b. Antigua. He made his test debut in 1974, and was West Indies captain (1985–91). Richards played English county cricket for Somerset (1974–86) and Glamorgan (1990–93), and in Australia for Queensland (1976–77). In 1991, he retired from test cricket. Richards is the leading West Indian run-scorer: 8,540 runs in 121 test matches, including 24 centuries.

Richardson, Sir Ralph David (1902–83) English actor. His distinguished career included fine Shakespearean and modern performances, including Harold Pinter's *No Man's Land* (1975). Richardson received Academy nominations for his film performances in *The Heiress* (1949) and *Greystoke: The Legend of Tarzan, Lord of the Apes* (1984). Other films include *Dr Zhivago* (1965).

Richardson, Samuel (1689–1761) English novelist and printer. He wrote his first work of fiction, the novel *Pamela* (1740–41), after the age of 50. It was followed by two more epistolary novels, *Clarissa* (1747–48) and *Sir Charles Grandison* (1753–54). Richardson's work prompted FIELDING's parodies *An Apology for the Life of Shamela Andrews* (1741) and *Joseph Andrews* (1742).

Richelieu, Armand Jean du Plessis, Duc de (1585–1642) French cardinal and statesman. A protégé of MARIE DE MÉDICIS and a cardinal from 1622, he became chief of the royal council in 1624. Richelieu suppressed the military and political power of the HUGUENOTS but tolerated Protestant religious practices. He alienated many powerful Catholics by his policy of placing the interests of the state above all else. He survived several aristocratic plots against him. In the THIRTY YEARS' WAR, he formed alliances with Protestant powers against the HABSBURGS. His more scholarly interests resulted in the foundation of the ACADÉMIE FRANÇAISE (1635).

Richler, Mordecai (1931–) Canadian novelist. His satirical novels, such as *The Apprenticeship of Duddy Kravitz* (1959), explore the Jewish ghetto of his native Montréal, while the experience of North Americans in the UK is wryly observed in *Cocksure* (1968) and *St Urbain's Horseman* (1971). Later novels include *Joshua Then and Now* (1980) and *Solomon Gursky Was Here* (1989).

Richmond Capital of Virginia, USA, in E Virginia, and a port on the James River. Settled in 1637, the city was made state capital in 1779. During the CIVIL WAR it was the capital of the CONFEDERATE STATES (1861) until it fell to Union forces in 1865. Industries: metal products, tobacco, textiles, chemicals. Pop. (1990) 203,056.

Richter, Burton (1931–) US physicist. In 1974, working with a very powerful particle ACCELERATOR, he discovered a new SUBATOMIC PARTICLE (psi); it is a type of MESON. Richter shared the 1976 Nobel Prize for physics with Samuel Ting, who had discovered the same particle during independent experiments.

Richter scale Classification of EARTHQUAKE magnitude established (1935) by the US geologist Charles Richter. The scale is logarithmic – each point on the scale increases by a factor of ten – and is based on the total energy released by an earthquake, as opposed to a scale of intensity that measures the damage done at a particular place.

Richtofen, Manfred, Baron von (1892–1918) German aviator. As an aviator in World War 1, he shot down 80 enemy aircraft. Von Richtofen was known as the "Red Baron". He was killed in action.

rickets Disorder in which there is defective growth of bone in children; the bones fail to harden sufficiently and become bent. Due either to a lack of VITAMIN D in the diet or to insufficient sunlight to allow its synthesis in the skin, it results from the inability of the bones to calcify properly.

Ridley, Nicholas (1500–55) English bishop and Protestant martyr. As chaplain to Thomas CRANMER, he helped to compile the Book of COMMON PRAYER (1549). In 1553, Ridley supported the Protestant Lady Jane GREY against the Catholic MARY I (MARY TUDOR). Convicted of heresy under Mary, he was burned at the stake.

Riefenstahl, Leni (1902–) German film director who was employed by Adolf Hitler to make propaganda films. Her films include *The Blue Light* (1932), *Triumph of the Will* (1934) and *Olympic Games* (1936).

Riel, Louis (1844–85) French-Canadian revolutionary, leader of the *métis* (people of mixed French and native descent) in the Red River rebellion in MANITOBA (1869–70). When it collapsed, he fled to the USA. In 1884, Riel led resistance to Canada's western policies in Saskatchewan and set up a rebel government in 1885. He was captured and subsequently executed for treason.

Riemann, Georg Friedrich Bernhard (1826–66) German mathematician who laid the foundations for much of modern mathematics and physics. He worked on integration, functions of a complex variable, and differential and non-Euclidean GEOMETRY, which was later used in the general theory of RELATIVITY.

Rietveld, Gerrit Thomas (1888–1964) Dutch architect and designer. A member of De STIJL, he was a pioneer of modern furniture design. Rietveld's most celebrated building, Schröder House, Utrecht (1924), was influenced by the paintings of Piet MONDRIAN.

rifle FIREARM with spiral grooves (rifling) along the inside of the barrel to make the bullet spin in flight, thereby greatly increasing range and accuracy over that of a smoothbore weapon. Not until the Minié rifle of 1849 were rifled weapons widely used. During the 19th century, breech-loading and magazine rifles were developed, and since World War 2, assault rifles, capable of automatic fire, have come into general use.

rift valley Depression formed by the subsidence of land between two parallel FAULTS. Rift valleys are believed to be formed by thermal currents within the Earth's MANTLE that break up the CRUST into large slabs or blocks of rock that then become fractured.

Rift Valley (Great Rift Valley) Steep-sided, flat-floored valley in SW Asia and E Africa. It runs from N Syria through the Jordan Valley and the Dead Sea and then continues as the trough of the Red Sea through E Africa to the lower valley of the River Zambezi in Mozambique. Dotted along its course are a number of lakes, including TANGANYIKA and Turkana. Length: *c.*6,400km (4,000mi).

Riga Capital of Latvia, on the River Daugava on the Gulf of Riga. Founded at the beginning of the 13th century, in 1282 it joined the HANSEATIC LEAGUE, becoming a major Baltic port. It was taken by PETER (THE GREAT) in 1710. In 1918, it became the capital of independent Latvia. In 1940, when Latvia was incorporated into the Soviet Union, thousands of its citizens were deported or executed. Under German occupation from 1941, the city reverted to Soviet rule in 1944 and subsequently suffered further deportations and an influx of Russian immigrants. In 1991, it reassumed its status as capital of an independent Latvia. Industries: shipbuilding, engineering, electronic equipment, chemicals, textiles. Pop. (1996) 826,000.

rigor mortis Stiffening of the body after DEATH brought about by chemical changes in muscle tissue. Onset is gradual from minutes to hours, and it disappears within *c.*24 hours.

Rijeka (It. *Fiume*) City on the Adriatic Sea and the Gulf of Quarnero, W Croatia. It is Croatia's major seaport. From 1779 to 1918, it served as the naval base of the Austro-Hungarian Empire. In 1919, Gabriele D'ANNUNZIO seized the city for Italy. In 1947, Rijeka returned to Yugoslavia. Industries: shipbuilding, oil refining. Pop. (1991) 167,757.

Riley, Bridget (1931–) English painter, a leading exponent of OP ART. Riley paints mostly black and white patterns, creating dazzling optical effects that cover the entire surface of the painting and create an illusion of constant movement and change. Examples include *Fall* (1963).

Rilke, Rainer Maria (1875–1926) German lyric poet, b. Prague. His first volume, *The Book of Hours* (1899–1903), was inspired by visits to Russia. During a 12-year sojourn in Paris he developed the "object poem", used in *New Poems* (1907–08); thereafter he published little until 1922, when *Sonnets to Orpheus* and his existential masterpiece, *Duino Elegies*, both appeared.

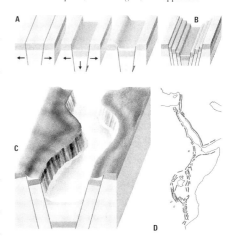

▲ **rift valley** Rift valleys are formed by tension between two roughly parallel faults (A), causing downward earth movement resulting in the formation of a *graben* (trough of land between two faults). Sometimes a number of parallel faults result in land sinking in steps (B). A typical example of a step-faulted rift valley is shown (C). A series of block faults can occur on either side of a graben, sometimes tilting in the process of creating the block-faulted rift valley. The East African Rift Valley (D) is perhaps the world's best example of this geological formation.

Rimbaud, Arthur (1854–91) French anarchic poet who influenced SYMBOLISM. He had a stormy relationship with VERLAINE, under whose tutelage he wrote *The Drunken Boat* (1871). In 1873, they separated and *A Season in Hell* appeared. Rimbaud abandoned poetry to travel, returning to Paris shortly before his death. In 1886, *Les Illuminations* was published by Verlaine as the work of the late Arthur Rimbaud.

Rimsky-Korsakov, Nikolai Andreievich (1844–1908) Russian composer, one of the RUSSIAN FIVE. His operas include *The Snow Maiden* (1881) and *The Golden Cockerel* (1907), and among his most popular orchestral works are *Sheherazade* (1888), *Capriccio espagnole* (1887) and "The Flight of the Bumblebee" from the opera, *Tsar Saltan* (1900).

ringworm Fungus infection of the skin, scalp or nails. The commonest type of ringworm is ATHLETE'S FOOT (*tinea pedis*). It is treated with antifungal preparations.

Rio de Janeiro City on Guanabara Bay, SE Brazil. Discovered by Europeans in 1502, it was later colonized by the French, then the Portuguese. By the 18th century, it was a major outlet for gold mined in the hinterland. In 1763, it became the seat of the viceroy, and from 1834 to 1960 it was Brazil's capital. The second-largest city in Brazil, Rio is its commercial and industrial centre. Its warm climate and beaches make it a popular tourist resort. There are large shanty towns surrounding the city. Industries: coffee, sugar refining, shipbuilding, pharmaceuticals, printing and publishing, engineering, textiles. Pop. (1991) 5,336,179.

Rio Grande (Rio Bravo del Norte) River in North America. It rises in the San Juan Mountains of sw Col-

orado, USA, and flows generally s through New Mexico. It forms the border between Texas and Mexico and empties into the Gulf of Mexico just E of Brownsville, Texas, and Matamoros, Mexico. One of North America's longest rivers, it is largely unnavigable and is used for irrigation and hydroelectricity. Length: *c*.3,035km (1,885mi).

riot Uncontrolled crowd violence, usually resulting in indiscriminate destruction. Most modern police forces include special riot squads. Methods of crowd control include water cannon, CS gas (tear gas), plastic bullets and, in some countries, electronic stun guns.

Risorgimento (It. resurgence) Nationalist movement resulting in the unification of Italy in 1859–70. With the restoration of Austrian and BOURBON rule in 1815, revolutionary groups formed, notably the Young Italy movement of Giuseppe MAZZINI, whose aim was a single, democratic republic. His influence was at its peak in the REVOLUTIONS OF 1848. In Sardinia-Piedmont (the only independent Italian state), the aim of the chief minister, Conte di CAVOUR, was a parliamentary monarchy under the royal house of SAVOY. Securing the support of France under NAPOLEON III in a war against Austria, he acquired much of Austrian-dominated N Italy in 1859. In 1860, Giuseppe GARIBALDI conquered Sicily and Naples. Although Garibaldi belonged to the republican tradition of Mazzini, he cooperated with Cavour, and the kingdom of Italy was proclaimed in 1861 under VICTOR EMMANUEL II of Savoy. Other regions were acquired later. Rome, the future capital, was seized when the French garrison withdrew in 1870.

river Large, natural channel containing water that flows downhill under gravity. A river system is a network of connecting channels. It can be divided into tributaries, which collect water and sediment, the main trunk river and the dispersing system at the river's mouth where much of the sediment is deposited. The **discharge** of a river is the volume of water flowing past a point in a given time. The **velocity** of a river is controlled by the slope, its depth and the roughness of the river bed. Rivers carry sediment as they flow, by the processes of traction (rolling), saltation (jumping), suspension (carrying) and solution. Most river sediment is carried during FLOOD conditions, but as a river returns to normal flow, it deposits sediment. This can result in the EROSION of a river channel or in the building up of flood-plains, sand and gravel banks. All rivers tend to flow in a twisting pattern, even if the slope is relatively steep, because water flow is naturally turbulent. Over time, on shallow slopes, small bends grow into large MEANDERS. The current flows faster on the outside of bends eroding the bank while sedimentation occurs on the inside of bends where the current is slowest. This causes the curves to exaggerate forming loops. Rivers flood when their channels cannot contain the discharge. Flood risk can be reduced by straightening the channel, dredging sediment, or making the channel deeper by raising the banks. *See also* DELTA; LEVEE; OXBOW

Rivera, Diego (1886–1957) Mexican painter, married to fellow artist Frida KAHLO. He is one of Mexico's three great 20th-century muralists (the others being OROZCO and Siqueiros). Rivera often used symbolism and allegory to depict events in Mexico's history and to express his hope for a Marxist future. His work adorns a number of public buildings in Mexico City.

Riviera Region of SE France and NW Italy on the Mediterranean Sea, extending 370km (230mi) from CANNES, France, to La Spezia, Italy. Its spectacular scenery and mild climate make it a leading tourist centre. Resorts include NICE and Cannes in France, MONTE CARLO in Monaco and San Remo and Alassio in Italy.

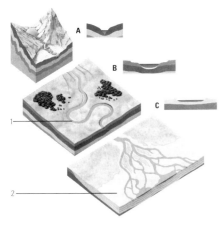

▲ **river** Young rivers (A) close to their source are fast-flowing, high-energy environments with rapid downward and headward erosion, despite the hardness of the rock over which they flow. Steep-sided, "V-shaped" valleys, waterfalls and rapids are characteristic features. Mature rivers (B) are lower-energy systems. Erosion takes place on the outside of bends, creating looping meanders (1) in the soft

alluvium of the flood plain. Deposition occurs on the inside of bends and on the river bed. At a river's mouth (C), sediment is deposited as the velocity of the river slows. As the river becomes shallower, more deposition occurs, forming islands and braiding the main channel into multiple, narrower channels. As the sediment is laid down (2), the actual mouth of the river moves away from the source into the sea or lake.

Riyadh Capital of Saudi Arabia, in the E central part of the country c.378km (235mi) inland from the Persian Gulf. In the early 19th century it was the domain of the Saudi dynasty, becoming capital of Saudi Arabia in 1932. The chief industry is oil-refining. Pop. (1994 est.) 1,500,000.

Rizzio, David (c.1530–66) Courtier and secretary to MARY, QUEEN OF SCOTS, b. Italy. The favouritism that Mary showed toward Rizzio aroused the jealousy of her husband, Lord DARNLEY, who arranged his murder.

RNA (ribonucleic acid) Chemical (NUCLEIC ACID) that controls the synthesis of PROTEIN in a cell and is the genetic material in some viruses. The molecules of RNA in a cell are copied from DNA and consist of a single strand of nucleotides, each containing the sugar ribose, phosphoric acid, and one of four bases: adenine, guanine, cytosine or uracil. **Messenger RNA** (mRNA) carries the information for protein synthesis from DNA in the cell NUCLEUS to the RIBOSOMES in the CYTOPLASM. Transfer RNA (tRNA) brings AMINO ACIDS to their correct position on the mRNA. Each amino acid is specified by a sequence of three bases in mRNA.

Roach, Hal (1892–1992) US film producer. He is best remembered for his silent comedy shorts. Co-founder of The Rolin Film Company in 1915, he encouraged Harold LLOYD, LAUREL AND HARDY and Will ROGERS.

roach European freshwater CARP found in muddy and, occasionally, in brackish waters. Colours include silver, white and green. Length: to 40cm (16in). Family Cyprinidae; species *Rutilus rutilus*.

road runner Fast-running desert CUCKOO that lives in SW USA. It has a crested head, streaked brownish plumage, long, strong legs and a long tail. It feeds on ground animals, including snakes that it kills with its long, pointed beak. Family Cuculidae; species *Geococcyx californianus*.

Robbe-Grillet, Alain (1922–) French novelist. He was the chief theorist of the NOUVEAU ROMAN. Robbe-Grillet's novels include *The Erasers* (1953), *Topology of a Phantom City* (1976) and *Djinn* (1981). He also wrote the screenplay for *Last Year at Marienbad* (1961). His critical works include *Towards a New Novel* (1963).

Robbins, Jerome (1918–98) US ballet choreographer and dancer. In 1940, he joined the American Ballet Theater. Robbins is celebrated for his choreography of Broadway musicals, including *The King and I* (1951, filmed 1956), *West Side Story* (1957, filmed 1961) and *Fiddler on the Roof* (1964, filmed 1971). From 1983 to 1990, he was joint ballet master of the New York City Ballet with Peter MARTINS.

Robert I (the Bruce) (1274–1329) King of Scotland (1306–29). He was descended from a prominent Anglo-Norman family with a strong claim to the crown. In 1296, Robert swore fealty to EDWARD I of England but in 1297, joined a Scottish revolt against the English. He later renewed his allegiance to Edward, but his divided loyalties made him suspect. After killing a powerful rival, John Comyn, Robert had himself crowned king of Scotland but, defeated at Methven (1306) by the English, he fled the kingdom. Returning on Edward's death (1307), the Bruce renewed the struggle with increasing support. In 1314, he won a famous victory over the English at BANNOCKBURN. The battle secured Scottish independence, which was finally recognized in the Treaty of Northampton (1328).

Robert II (1054–1134) (Robert Curthose) Duke of Normandy (1087–1106). The eldest son of WILLIAM I (THE CONQUEROR), he disputed Normandy and England with his younger brothers, WILLIAM II and HENRY I, and played a prominent part in the First CRUSADE (1096–99). In 1106 Robert was defeated and captured by Henry and imprisoned for life.

Roberts, Julia (1967–) US film actress. Roberts gained an Academy Award nomination for her supporting role in *Steel Magnolias* (1989). *Pretty Woman* (1990) was a massive box-office success. Other credits include *The Pelican Brief* (1993) and *Notting Hill* (1999).

Robeson, Paul (1898–1976) US actor and singer. He played the title role in Eugene O'Neill's *Emperor Jones* and Othello in Shakespeare's tragedy. Robeson is best known for his bass renditions of Negro spirituals and "Ol' Man River" in the musical, *Show Boat* (1927). In 1952, Robeson was awarded the Stalin Peace Prize, and his association with communism led to ostracism in the USA. He lived abroad from 1958 to 1963.

Robespierre, Maximilien François Marie Isidore de (1758–94) French revolutionary leader. Elected to the National Assembly in 1789, he advocated democracy and liberal reform. In 1791, he became leader of the JACOBINS and gained credit when his opposition to war with Austria was justified by French defeats. With the king and the GIRONDINS discredited, Robespierre led the republican revolution of 1792 and was elected to the National Convention. His election to the Committee of Public Safety (June 1793) heralded the REIGN OF TERROR. Ruthless methods seemed less urgent after French victories in war, and Robespierre was arrested in the coup of 9th Thermidor (27 July) 1794 and executed.

robin Small Eurasian bird, with a characteristic red-orange breast. Length: to 14cm (5.5in). Family Turdidae; species *Erithacus rubecula*. The much larger American robin (*Turdus migratorius*) is a member of the thrush family and is c.25cm (10in) long.

Robin Hood Legendary English outlaw. Medieval tradition describes him as a displaced nobleman living with his outlaw band in Sherwood Forest, near Nottingham. Robin robbed the rich and gave to the poor, fighting a running battle with the sheriff of Nottingham and the corrupt administration of King JOHN. His "merry band" included Maid Marian, Little John and Friar Tuck.

Robinson, Edward G. (1893–1973) US film actor, b. Emanuel Goldenberg. His most famous role was that of the gangster in *Little Caesar* (1930). He also played character parts in such films as *Double Indemnity* (1944) and *The Night has a Thousand Eyes* (1948).

Robinson, Edwin Arlington (1869–1935) US poet. His first volume of poems, *The Torrent and The Night Before* (1896), was followed by *The Town down the River* (1910), *The Man against the Sky* (1916) and *The Three Taverns* (1920). He was awarded the Pulitzer Prize in 1921, 1924 and 1927.

Robinson, (William) Heath (1872–1944) English cartoonist and illustrator. He is best-known for his drawings of "Heath Robinson contraptions", absurdly complicated machines for performing simple, everyday tasks.

Robinson, Jackie (Jack Roosevelt) (1919–72) US baseball player. Robinson was the first African American to play major league baseball. Signed by the Brooklyn Dodgers in 1947, he compiled a lifetime batting average of .311 before retiring in 1956.

Robinson, Mary (1944–) Irish stateswoman, president (1990–97). In 1969, she entered politics as a senator. Robinson became the Republic of Ireland's first woman president. Her stand on human rights and support for the campaign to liberalize laws on abortion and divorce gave the office a high profile. In 1997, Robinson became UN Commissioner for Human Rights.

Robinson, Sir Robert (1886–1975) English chemist. He succeeded in synthesizing the ALKALOID tropinone using three simple compounds found in plants. This led to his theory of organic molecular structure. Robinson was awarded the 1947 Nobel Prize for chemistry. He also helped in the synthesis of PENICILLIN and SEX HORMONES.

Robinson, Sugar Ray (1920–89) US boxer, b. Walker Smith. He was world welterweight champion (1946–50) and won the middleweight title five times (twice in 1951, 1955, 1957, 1958–60). Robinson lost only 19 of his 202 professional bouts.

robot Automated machine used to carry out various tasks. Robots are often COMPUTER-controlled, the most common type having a single arm that can move in any direction. Such robots are used in MASS PRODUCTION. *See also* ARTIFICIAL INTELLIGENCE (AI); AUTOMATION

Rob Roy (1671–1734) Scottish outlaw, b. Robert MacGregor. He took to banditry after his lands were confiscated by the Duke of Montrose. Rob Roy took part in the JACOBITE rising of 1715. His exploits were romaticized in Sir Walter SCOTT's novel *Rob Roy* (1817).

rock Solid material that makes up the Earth's crust. Rocks are classified by origin into three major groups: IGNEOUS ROCKS, SEDIMENTARY ROCKS and METAMORPHIC ROCKS.

rock (rock and roll) Form of popular music characterized by amplified guitars and singing, often with repetitive lyrics and driving rhythms. Rock music appealed largely to a white audience who found its forerunner, RHYTHM AND BLUES, inaccessible. It developed out of the BLUES and FOLK MUSIC of rural USA to become a major form of cultural expression in the 1960s. Rock and roll was popularized by Bill HALEY and the film *Rock Around the Clock* (1956). Its modern offshoots include heavy metal, grunge and PUNK.

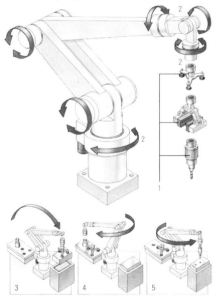

▲ **robot** A robotic arm can be programmed to use different tools (1) to carry out a variety of tasks. The arm, head, and base can all rotate (2) and can extend to reach different points. In a typical engineering setting, the robot first places the raw material into position (3). The robot then changes tools (4) before drilling the required holes (5).

Rockefeller, John D. (Davison) (1839–1937) US industrialist and philanthropist. In 1863, Rockefeller built an oil refinery in Cleveland that was incorporated (1870) into the Standard Oil Company of Ohio. On retirement, Rockefeller devoted his attention to charitable corporations, donating *c*.US$550 million. In 1913, he founded the Rockefeller Foundation.

rocket Slender, tapering MISSILE or craft powered by a rocket ENGINE. Most of its volume contains fuel; the remainder is the payload (such as an explosive, scientific instruments or a spacecraft). **Liquid-fuelled** rockets use a fuel (such as liquid hydrogen) and an oxidizer (usually liquid oxygen), which are burned together in the engine. **Solid-fuelled** rockets have both fuel and oxidizer in a solid mixture. A **single-stage** rocket has one fuel load, or several that are used simultaneously. A **multi-stage** rocket has more than one fuel load, which are ignited singly in succession as the preceding one burns out. Because rocket engines carry their own fuel and oxidizer, they can operate in outer SPACE where there is no atmosphere. They gain THRUST from the reaction (referred to in the third of NEWTON'S LAWS of motion) produced by rapid, continuous output of exhaust gases. **Chemical** rocket engines are powered by solid or liquid propellants that are burned in a COMBUSTION chamber and expelled at SUPERSONIC VELOCITIES from the exhaust nozzle. **Nuclear** engines heat fuel by RADIATION from NUCLEAR REACTOR cores. Ion engines use thermoelectric power to expel IONS. The walls of a rocket's combustion chamber and the exit nozzle must be cooled to protect them against the heat of the escaping gases, whose temperature may be as high as 3,000°C. Today, payloads are put into orbit by the SPACE SHUTTLE. Konstantin TSIOLKOVSKY is regarded as the "father of astronautics". In 1926, Robert H. GODDARD launched the first liquid-fuelled rocket. During World War 2, Wernher VON BRAUN developed the first long-range GUIDED MISSILES. After the war, Von Braun helped develop the US space programme. Saturn V, the largest rocket ever built, delivered 3.4 million kg (7.5 million lb) of thrust. *See also* SPACE EXPLORATION

Rockwell, Norman (1894–1978) US illustrator, an immensely popular painter of rural and small-town life. He was best known for the covers he created for *The Saturday Evening Post* (1916–63).

Rocky Mountains Major mountain system in W North America. Extending from Mexico to the Bering Strait, N of the Arctic Circle, the mountains form the CONTINENTAL DIVIDE. The highest point is Mount ELBERT.

rococo Playful, light style of art, architecture and decoration that developed in reaction to the BAROQUE in early 18th-century France. It soon spread to Germany, Austria, Italy and Britain. Rococo brought to interior decoration swirls, scrolls, shells and arabesques. It was also applied to furniture, porcelain and silverware. Rococo painters include WATTEAU, FRAGONARD and BOUCHER. It was superseded by the more sombre style of NEOCLASSICISM.

rodent Any member of the vast order Rodentia, the most numerous and widespread of all mammals, characterized by a pair of gnawing incisor teeth in both the upper and lower jaws. Numbering close to 2,000 species, including the RAT, MOUSE, SQUIRREL, BEAVER, DORMOUSE, PORCUPINE and GUINEA PIG, rodents live throughout the world. Most are small and light.

rodeo Sport with origins in the practical work of a COWBOY. A major entertainment in North America, its seven main events are saddle bronco (unbroken horse) riding, bareback bronco-riding, bull-riding, calf-roping, single steer-roping and team roping, and steer-wrestling.

Rodgers, Richard Charles (1902–79) US composer of BROADWAY musicals. He first worked with Lorenz Hart. Successful musicals with Oscar HAMMERSTEIN included *Oklahoma!* (1943), *Carousel* (1945), *South Pacific* (1949), *The King and I* (1951) and *The Sound of Music* (1959).

Rodin, Auguste (1840–1917) French sculptor. His first major work, *The Age of Bronze* (exhibited in 1878), caused a scandal because the naked figure was so naturalistic. His next great project was *The Gates of Hell*, unfinished studies for a bronze door for the *Musée des arts décoratifs*, Paris. It provided him with the subjects for further great sculptures, including *The Thinker* (1880), *The Kiss* (1886) and *Fugit Amor* (1897). Perhaps his most extraordinary work is the full-length bronze of Balzac, completed in 1897.

Rodrigo, Joaquin (1901–99) Spanish composer. He made his name with his *Concierto de Aranjuez* (1939) for guitar and orchestra. He also wrote concertos for violin, cello, piano, harp and flute, as well as other pieces for guitar and orchestra.

Roethke, Theodore (1908–63) US poet. His debut volume was *Opera House* (1941). Other collections include *The Waking: Poems 1933–53* (1953), which won both a Pulitzer Prize and the National Book Award.

Roger II (1095–1154) First Norman king of Sicily (1130–54). He extended his kingdom to the s Italian mainland and to the North African coast. By 1139, Roger was one of the greatest rulers in Europe and master of the Mediterranean. His kingdom became a rare example of Christian-Muslim cooperation, with a rich mixture of the two cultures. He refused to take part in the CRUSADES, instead attacking the BYZANTINE EMPIRE.

Rogers, Ginger (1911–95) US actress and dancer. Rogers is chiefly remembered for her dancing partnership with Fred ASTAIRE in film musicals, such as *Flying Down To Rio* (1933), *Top Hat* (1934) and *Swing Time* (1936). She won an Oscar for best actress in *Kitty Foyle* (1940).

Rogers, Richard (1933–) English architect. He attracted international recognition with his designs for the Pompidou Centre, Paris (co-designed with Renzo Piano, 1971–77) and the Lloyds building, London (1978–80). Rogers designs his buildings "inside-out" to allow for servicing without disrupting the interior. He designed the Millennium Dome, GREENWICH, London (1998–99).

Rogers, Will (William Penn Adair) (1879–1935) US comedian. He appeared in VAUDEVILLE and joined the Ziegfeld Follies in 1914. Through Rogers' contributions to film, radio and a syndicated newspaper column, he became known as the "cowboy philosopher".

Roget, Peter Mark (1779–1869) English scholar and physician. He helped to establish London University and is chiefly remembered for his *Thesaurus of English Words and Phrases* (1852).

role In social science, a person's perception of how to act in a given situation. For children, learning roles is central to the process of social development. Formal roles, such as teachers, doctors and police officers, help to define our behaviour in impersonal situations, while informal roles, such as husband and mother, are founded on personal relationships. *See also* STATUS

Rolland, Romain (1866–1944) French novelist and dramatist. Among his best-known works are his 10-volume novel, *Jean-Christophe* (1904–12); the pacifist essay, *Above the Battle* (1915); and the plays collected as *The Tragedies of Faith* (1913). In 1915, Rolland was awarded the Nobel Prize for literature.

roller Any of several species of Eurasian birds that roll over in flight. An occasional visitor to Britain, *Coracius*

garrulus has blue-green plumage and flies as far north as Sweden; it usually winters in Africa. Family Coraciidae.

Rolling Stones, The English rock group, formed (1962) around vocalist Mick Jagger (1943–), guitarist Keith Richards (1943–), bassist Bill Wyman (1941–) and drummer Charlie Watts (1942–). Their rebellious posturing courted great controversy and publicity and a founder member, Brian Jones (1942–69), died after a drugs overdose. Early hit singles included "Satisfaction" (1965), "Paint it Black" (1966) and "Jumpin' Jack Flash" (1968). Million-selling albums include *Beggar's Banquet* (1968) and *Exile on Main Street* (1972).

Rollins, "Sonny" (Theodore Walter) (1930–) US jazz saxophonist. Influenced by Charlie PARKER, he played with many BEBOP legends, including Max Roach, Bud POWELL, Thelonious MONK and Miles DAVIS.

Rolls, Charles Stewart (1877–1910) English car manufacturer and aviator. In 1897, he helped found the Royal Automobile Club (RAC). In 1906, Rolls and Henry Royce formed Rolls-Royce Ltd., a major manufacturer of luxury automobiles and aircraft engines. In 1910, he became the first Englishman to fly across the English Channel. Rolls was the first English casualty of aviation.

ROM (acronym for **R**ead-**O**nly **M**emory) INTEGRATED CIRCUITS (silicon chips) that act as a permanent store for data required by a COMPUTER. The contents of ordinary ROM chips are set by the manufacturer and cannot be altered by the user. The stored data is available to a computer's MICROPROCESSOR whenever it is switched on.

Romains, Jules (1885–1972) French novelist, poet and dramatist, b. Louis Henri Jean Farigoule. He was the leading exponent of unanimism, which posits a collective spirit. His works include the novel *Death of a Nobody* (1911), the comedy *Knock* (1923) and the 27-novel cycle *Men of Good Will* (1932–46), a portrait of French life in the early part of the 20th century.

Roman art and architecture Classical art and architecture of ancient ROME. Prior to 400 BC, Roman art was largely ETRUSCAN art in the form of tomb decorations, after which Greek influence became dominant. Few examples of later Roman painting have survived: the best examples are found in the Italian towns of POMPEII and HERCULANEUM. Another common art form was MOSAIC. Floors and walls were decorated mostly in elaborate geometric patterns, but mosaics were also created to depict everyday scenes, or gods and goddesses. In sculpture the Romans excelled in portrait busts and reliefs. In architecture, notable features include their adoption of the ARCH, VAULT and DOME. Fine examples include the PANTHEON and COLOSSEUM in Rome.

Roman Britain Period of British history from the Roman invasion in the reign of CLAUDIUS I (AD 43) until *c*.410. The occupation included Wales but not Ireland or most of Caledonia (Scotland). Its northern frontier was marked by HADRIAN'S WALL from *c*.130. Only the English lowlands were thoroughly Romanized, but in that region Roman rule brought a period of prosperity not matched for more than 1,000 years. Roman power disintegrated in the 3rd century. By 400, attacks from Ireland, Scotland and the continental mainland were increasing, but Roman troops were withdrawn to deal with enemies nearer home. In 410, the Emperor Honorius warned the Britons to expect no further help. Local Romano-British kings held out for more than 100 years before lowland Britain was overrun by the ANGLO-SAXONS.

Roman Catholic Church Christian denomination that acknowledges the supremacy of the pope (*see* PAPACY; PAPAL INFALLIBILITY). An important aspect of the doctrine is the primacy given to the Virgin MARY, whom Roman Catholics believe to be the only human born without sin (IMMACULATE CONCEPTION). Before the REFORMATION in the 16th century, the "CATHOLIC CHURCH" applied to the Western Church as a whole, as distinguished from the EASTERN ORTHODOX CHURCH based at Constantinople. The Reformation led to a tendency for the Roman Catholic Church to be characterized by rigid adherence to doctrinal tradition from the 16th to the early 20th century. The desire for a reunited Christendom led to a more liberal attitude in the mid-20th century. The government of the Church is episcopal, with archbishops and bishops responsible for provinces and dioceses. The centre of the Roman Catholic liturgical ritual is the MASS or EUCHARIST. Since the second VATICAN COUNCIL (1962–65), the Roman Catholic Church has undergone marked changes, notably the replacement of Latin by the vernacular as the language of the liturgy. There are *c*.600 million Roman Catholics worldwide, with large numbers in s Europe, Latin America and the Philippines.

romance (Old French *romanz*, vulgar tongue) Literary form, typically a heroic tale or ballad usually in verse. The form derives from the medieval narratives of TROU-BADOURS. The romance spread throughout Europe during the 12th century, was used in English by CHAUCER and remained popular through the 16th century.

Romance languages Indo-European languages that evolved from LATIN. They include Italian, French, Spanish, Portuguese, Romanian, Catalan, Provençal and Romansh (a language spoken in parts of Switzerland).

Roman Empire Mediterranean empire formed (*c*.27 BC) by AUGUSTUS after the assassination (*c*.44 BC) of Julius CAESAR. Its power centre was ancient ROME. The Romans adopted the culture of ancient GREECE, but their Empire was based on military power and ROMAN LAW. In terms of technology and arguably culture, Roman civilization was not surpassed in Europe until the Renaissance. By the death of Augustus (AD 14), the Empire included most of

Asia Minor, Syria, Egypt and the whole North African coast. In the 1st and 2nd centuries, Britain was conquered; in the E, Roman rule extended to the Caspian Sea and the Persian Gulf, and further territory, including DACIA (Transylvania), was added in SE Europe. The Empire was at its greatest extent at the death of TRAJAN (AD 117), when it included all the lands around the Mediterranean and extended to N Britain, the Black Sea and Mesopotamia. HADRIAN (r.117–138) called a halt to further expansion. Rome reached the height of its power during the first 150 years of imperial rule, becoming a city of grand, monumental buildings with *c*.1 million inhabitants. In the 3rd century, pressure from Germanic tribes and the Persians, plus economic difficulties, contributed to the breakdown of government. Armies in the provinces broke away from Rome. DIOCLETIAN restored order, and from his time the Empire tended to be split into E and W divisions. In 330, CONSTANTINE founded an E capital at CONSTANTINOPLE. Rome was increasingly challenged by different peoples, such as the GOTHS who sacked the city in 410. By 500, the Roman Empire in the west had ceased to exist. The Eastern or BYZANTINE EMPIRE survived until 1453.

Romanesque Architectural and artistic style that spread throughout W Europe during the 11th and 12th centuries. English Romanesque architecture includes ANGLO-SAXON and NORMAN styles. *See also* ARCH; RIB; VAULT

Romania Balkan republic in SE Europe. It is dominated by a central plateau. The CARPATHIAN MOUNTAINS run in a horseshoe-shape from N to SW and frame the region of TRANSYLVANIA. E and S Romania form part of the DANUBE river basin, the site of the capital, BUCHAREST. The Danube's delta, near the Black Sea, is one of Europe's most important wetlands. The port of CONSTANŢA lies on the Black Sea coast. The extreme W lowlands include the city of TIMIŞOARA. **Climate** Romania has hot, dry summers and cold winters. It is one of the sunniest places in Europe, with more than 2,000 hours of sunshine every year. **Vegetation** Arable land accounts for *c*.66% of Romania. Forests cover 28%. **History and politics** Modern Romania roughly corresponds to ancient DACIA, which was conquered by the Romans in AD 106. The Dacians assimilated Roman culture and language, and the region became known as Romania. In the 14th century, the principalities of WALLACHIA (S) and MOLDAVIA (E) were formed. By the 18th century, the Ottoman Empire dominated Romania. In the late 18th century, the Turkish empire began to break up. Russia captured Moldavia and Wallachia in the Russo-Turkish War (1828–29). Romanian nationalism intensified and the two provinces were united in 1861. The Congress of Berlin (1878) ratified Romania as an independent state, and in 1881 CAROL I became king. Neutral at the start of World War 1, Romania joined the Allies in 1916 but was occupied by German forces in 1917. The Allied victory led to Romania acquiring large regions, such as Transylvania. In 1927, MICHAEL became king, but surrendered the throne to his father, CAROL II, in 1930. Political instability and economic inequality led to the growth of fascism and anti-Semitism. At the start of World War 2, Romania lost territory to Bulgaria, Hungary and the Soviet Union. In 1940, Michael was restored. Ion ANTONESCU became dictator and, in June 1941, Romania joined the German invasion of the Soviet Union. During World War 2, more than 50% of Romanian Jews were murdered. In 1944, Soviet troops occupied Romania, Antonescu was overthrown and Romania surrendered. In 1945, a communist-dominated coalition assumed power, led by Gheorghe Gheorghiu-Dej. In 1947, Romania became a People's Republic. In 1952,

▲ Romanesque The enduring monuments of Romanesque architecture are the churches and cathedrals of the period. Many regional differences in style existed. Dating from the 11th century, Monza Cathedral in Lombardy, shown here, is a prime example of a central Italian Romanesque building.

The dominant feature of its façade is the striped pattern of facing material, a common motif of the Italian Romanesque – surface ornamentation was very important. The entrance is elaborated with columns, another popular design feature, with a rose window above.

ROMANIA
AREA: 237,500sq km (91,699sq mi)
POPULATION: 24,000,000
CAPITAL (POPULATION): Bucharest (2,064,000)

Romania adopted a Soviet-style constitution. Industry was nationalized and agriculture collectivized. In 1949, Romania joined the Council of Mutual Economic Assistance (COMECON) and in 1955 became a member of the Warsaw Pact. In 1965, Gheorghiu-Dej was succeeded by Nicolae CEAUȘESCU. Rapid industrialization and political repression continued. In December 1989, Ceaușescu was executed. Ion ILIESCU, a former communist official, formed a provisional government. The National Salvation Front, led by Iliescu, won elections in May 1990. In 1991, a new constitution was introduced. In 1992, Iliescu was re-elected. In 1995, Romania applied to join the European Union (EU). In 1996 elections Iliescu was defeated by Emil Constantinescu and his centre-right coalition, but was re-elected in 2000. In 1998, disputes within the coalition led to the resignation of the prime minister. In 1999 and 2000, there was a series of protests and strikes over the pace and direction of economic reforms. **Economy** Communism's over-concentration on heavy industry devastated Romania's economy (1995 GDP per capita, US$4,360). Today, industry accounts for 40% of GDP. Oil, natural gas and antimony are the main mineral resources. Agriculture employs 29% of the workforce and constitutes 20% of GDP. Romania is the world's second-largest producer of plums (after China). It is the world's ninth-largest producer of wine. Major crops include maize and cabbages. Economic reform is slow. Unemployment and foreign debt remain high.

Romanian Official language of Romania, spoken by up to 25 million people in Romania, Macedonia, Albania and N Greece. It belongs to the Romance branch of the Indo-European family. Originally written in CYRILLIC characters, Romanian has used the Roman alphabet since 1860.

Roman law System of CIVIL LAW developed between 753 BC and the 5th century AD that forms the basis of civil law in many parts of the world. Roman law was enacted originally by the PATRICIANS, then after 287 BC by the PLEBEIAN assemblies. From 367 BC, magistrates (PRAETORS) proclaimed the legal principles (*edicta*) that became an important source of law known as *jus honorium*. The emperor could also enact laws and by the mid-2nd century AD became the sole creator of laws. Roman law can be divided into two parts: *jus civile* (civil law), which applied only to Roman citizens and was codified in the TWELVE TABLES of 450 BC; and *jus gentium*, originally applying to foreigners in Rome and to others within Roman lands who were not citizens, which gradually merged into *jus civile*. Roman law was codified by the Emperor JUSTINIAN I (r.527–64) and was adapted by many later invaders.

Roman numeral Letter used by the ancient Romans and succeeding European civilizations to represent numbers before the adoption of Arabic numerals. There were seven individual letters: I (1), V (5), X (10), L (50), C (100), D (500) and M (1,000). Combinations were used to represent the numbers. From 1 to 10 they ran: I, II, III, IV, V, VI, VII, VIII, IX and X. The tens ran: X, XX, XXX, XL, L and so on up to XC, which represented 90. Modern applications include numbering the preliminary pages of a book.

Romanov Russian imperial dynasty (1613–1917). Michael, the first Romanov tsar, was elected in 1613. His descendants, especially PETER I (THE GREAT) and

CATHERINE II (THE GREAT), a Romanov by marriage, transformed Russia into the world's largest empire. The last Romanov emperor, NICHOLAS II, abdicated in 1917 and was later murdered by the BOLSHEVIKS.

Romans In the New Testament, a letter by St PAUL to the Christians of Rome, written *c*.57, probably while Paul was in Corinth. In it, he declares the universality of the saving power of God realized in the life, death and resurrection of Jesus.

romanticism Late 18th- and early 19th-century cultural movement. Its exponents valued individual experience and intuition, rather than the orderly, concrete universe of CLASSICAL artists. For this reason, romantics and classicists are often seen as opposites, but in fact they shared a belief in IDEALISM, as opposed to the exponents of REALISM and RATIONALISM. An emphasis on nature rather than science was also a characteristic. Leading European literary romantics include GOETHE, SHELLEY, BYRON, KEATS and SCHILLER. In the USA, POE, LONGFELLOW, WHITMAN, COOPER, HAWTHORNE and MELVILLE typified the style. William BLAKE was both a romantic poet and artist. Other artists include DELACROIX, Caspar David FRIEDRICH, GÉRICAULT and TURNER and the US artists of the HUDSON RIVER SCHOOL.

romanticism Period of music history lasting from *c*.1800 to 1910. It is characterized by the primacy of emotional expression and imagination, in contrast to the restrained and strict forms of the CLASSICAL era. Orchestras expanded as composers experimented with unusual and colourful orchestration to express extra-musical influences. Leading romantic composers include WAGNER, BERLIOZ, MENDELSSOHN, SCHUMANN, CHOPIN and LISZT.

Romany (Gypsy) Nomadic people and their language. Romanies are believed to have originated in N India and now inhabit Europe, Asia, America, Africa and Australia. They first appeared in Europe in the 15th century. Their nomadic lifestyle has aroused prejudice, often resulting in persecution. Their folklore is part of popular tradition. The Romany language originated in N India, and like HINDI and SANSKRIT to which it is related, it belongs to the Indo-Iranian branch of the family of INDO-EUROPEAN LANGUAGES. Many Romanies today speak it as a second language, but there is little written Romany.

Romberg, Sigmund (1887–1951) US composer, b. Hungary. He wrote the music for more than 70 operettas including *The Student Prince* (1924), *The Desert Song* (1926) and *Up in Central Park* (1945). Well-known songs include "Deep in My Heart, Dear".

Rome (Roma) Capital of Italy, on the River Tiber, W central Italy. Founded in the 8th century BC, it was probably an Etruscan city-kingdom in the 6th century BC. The Roman Republic was founded *c*.500 BC. By the 3rd century BC, Rome ruled most of Italy and began to expand overseas. In the 1st century AD, the city was transformed as successive emperors built temples, palaces, public baths, arches and columns. It remained the capital of the Roman Empire until 330 AD. It was sacked in the 5th century during Barbarian invasions, and its population (already in decline) fell rapidly. In the Middle Ages Rome became the seat of the PAPACY. In 1527, it was sacked by the army of Emperor Charles V. Rome flourished again in the 16th and 17th centuries. Italian troops occupied it in 1870, and in 1871 it became the capital of unified Italy. MUSSOLINI did much to transform Rome into a modern capital. It is home to the VATICAN CITY. Industries: tourism, pharmaceuticals, chemicals, oil-refining, engineering, textiles. Pop. (1996) 2,654,000.

Rome, ancient Capital of the Roman republic. According to tradition, Rome was founded in 753 BC by ROMULUS

AND REMUS. By 509 BC, the Latin-speaking Romans had thrown off the rule of ETRUSCAN kings and established an independent republic dominated by an aristocratic elite. Its history was one of continual expansion, and by 340 BC Rome controlled Italy S of the River PO. By the 3rd century BC, the PLEBEIAN class had largely gained political equality. The PUNIC WARS gave it dominance of the Mediterranean in the 2nd century BC, when major eastwards expansion began with the conquest of the Greek Aegean. The republican constitution was strained by social division and military dictatorship. SPARTACUS' slave revolt was crushed by POMPEY, who emerged as SULLA's successor. Pompey and Julius CAESAR formed the First Triumverate (60 BC). Caesar emerged as leader and greatly extended Rome's territory and influence. His assassination led to the formation of the ROMAN EMPIRE under AUGUSTUS (27 BC).

Rome, Treaties of (1957) Two agreements establishing the European Economic Community, now the EUROPEAN UNION (EU) and the EUROPEAN ATOMIC ENERGY COMMISSION (EURATOM). The 1957 treaty was extensively amended by the Single European Act (1986) and the MAASTRICHT TREATY (1992) but still forms the basis of the EU.

Rommel, Erwin (1891–1944) German general. He commanded tanks in France in 1940 and later led the AFRIKA KORPS in a victorious campaign in North Africa until defeated by the British at EL ALAMEIN (1942). Transferred to France in 1943, he was unable to repel the invasion of NORMANDY and was wounded. Implicated in the plot against Hitler in July 1944, he was forced to commit suicide by drinking poison.

Romney, George (1734–1802) English painter. His reputation equalled that of Joshua REYNOLDS. Romney painted more than 50 portraits of Lady Emma HAMILTON.

Romulus and Remus In Roman mythology, founders of ROME. Twin brothers, they were said to be sons of Mars. Amulius, who had usurped the throne, ordered the babies to be drowned in the Tiber. They survived and were suckled by a wolf before being found by a shepherd, Faustulus. They built a city on the site of their rescue. Romulus killed Remus during a quarrel.

Ronsard, Pierre de (1524–85) French poet and leader of La PLÉIADE. His *Odes* (1550) and *Les Amours* (1552) brought him fame and royal patronage. Other works include the incomplete national epic *La Franciade* (1572), and *Sonnets pour Hélène* (1578), some of his finest love poems.

Röntgen, Wilhelm Konrad (1845–1923) German physicist. In 1895, Röntgen discovered X-RAYS. He also did important work on electricity, the specific heats of gases and the heat CONDUCTIVITY of crystals. In 1901, Röntgen was awarded the first Nobel Prize for physics.

röntgen (symbol R) Former unit used to measure X-RAY or GAMMA RADIATION. One röntgen causes sufficient ionization to produce a total electric charge of 2.58 × 10^{-4} coulombs on all the positive (or negative) ions in one kilogram of air. The unit has been replaced by the SI unit, the GRAY (symbol Gy).

rood Large crucifix symbolizing the cross on which Christ died. It was often set up on a beam or screen dividing the NAVE from the CHANCEL in a medieval church.

rook Large European bird of the CROW family. It has glossy black plumage, except around its face. It feeds on grain and insects and has a characteristic raucous cry. Family Corvidae; species *Corvus frugilegus*.

Roosevelt, (Anna) Eleanor (1884–1962). US reformer and humanitarian, wife (and distant cousin) of Franklin ROOSEVELT. She was a supporter of social causes, including civil rights. Roosevelt served as US delegate to the United Nations (1945–52, 1961–62), and chairwoman of the UN Commission on Human Rights (1946–51).

Roosevelt, Franklin D. (Delano) (1882–1945) 32nd US President (1933–45). He served in the New York State Senate as a Democrat, as assistant secretary of the navy under Woodrow WILSON (1913–20), and was vice-presidential candidate in 1920. In 1921 he lost the use of his legs as a result of polio. He was governor of New York (1928–32) and won the Democratic candidacy for president. He was elected in 1932. To deal with the GREAT DEPRESSION, he embarked upon his NEW DEAL. He was re-elected in 1936, and won an unprecedented third term in 1940, and a fourth in 1944. When World War 2 broke out in Europe, he gave as much support to Britain as a neutral government could, until the Japanese attack on PEARL HARBOR ended US neutrality. He died in office and was succeeded by Harry S. TRUMAN.

Roosevelt, Theodore (1858–1919) 26th US President (1901–09). He was popularly known as "Teddy" and was the 5th cousin of Franklin D. ROOSEVELT and uncle of Eleanor ROOSEVELT. He gained national fame as the organizer of the Rough Riders in the SPANISH-AMERICAN WAR (1898). He became Republican governor of New York in 1899 and vice president in 1901. The assassination of President McKINLEY (1901) made him president, and he was re-elected in 1904. A vigorous progressive, Roosevelt moved to regulate monopolies through anti-trust legislation. Other radical reforms were increasingly blocked by Congress. Abroad, he expanded US power and prestige, gaining the PANAMA CANAL and taking an increasing role in world affairs. His mediation after the RUSSO-JAPANESE WAR won him the Nobel Peace Prize (1905). After retiring in 1909, he challenged his successor, President TAFT, for the presidency in 1912 as leader of his National Progressive Party (Bull Moose Party). The Republican split resulted in a Democratic victory.

Root, Elihu (1845–1937) US lawyer and statesman. He became secretary of war immediately following the SPANISH-AMERICAN WAR. Root supervised the affairs of Cuba and of the new territories of the Philippines and Puerto Rico. In 1905, he was appointed secretary of state and was awarded the Nobel Peace Prize in 1912.

root Underground portion of a VASCULAR PLANT that serves as an anchor and absorbs water and minerals from the soil. Some plants, such as the dandelion, have taproots with smaller lateral branches. Other plants, such as the grasses, develop fibrous roots with lateral branches.

root In mathematics, fractional POWER of a number. The SQUARE ROOT of a number, x, is written as either $\sqrt{x}$ or $x^{\frac{1}{2}}$. The fourth root of x may be written in radical form as $\sqrt[4]{x}$ or in power form as $x^{\frac{1}{4}}$. The fourth root of 16, for example, is 2 since $2 \times 2 \times 2 \times 2 = 16$.

root nodule Small swelling in the roots of various plants, such as LEGUMES, that contain nitrogen-fixing bacteria. *See also* NITROGEN CYCLE; NITROGEN FIXATION

rope Line made of twisted yarn or wire. Yarn used in rope-making may consist of natural or artificial fibres. Among natural fibres, HEMP is most commonly used. The fibres are first disentangled and spun into yarn, which is then twisted into strands that are laid up into rope. Commonly used artificial fibres are NYLON and polypropylene. POLYESTER rope is more expensive to make but is less easily damaged. Fine rope is called cord. Wire rope is known as cable.

Rorschach test (ink-blot test) In psychology, test used to analyze a person's motives and attitudes when these are projected into ambiguous situations. The individual is presented with 10 standardized ink blots, and interpretation is based on the description of them.

rosary Form of meditational prayer that contemplates the life of Jesus and the Blessed Virgin Mary within the Catholic and Orthodox churches. A rosary is also the string of beads on which a count may be kept of the number of prayers said.

Roscommon County in N central Republic of Ireland, in Connacht province; the county town is Roscommon. Part of the central plain of Ireland, Roscommon is generally low-lying. The Shannon is the principal river. Sheep and cattle rearing is the chief economic activity; coal-mining is important in the NE. Area: 2,463sq km (951sq mi). Pop. (1991) 51,897.

rose Wild or cultivated flowering shrub of the genus *Rosa*. Most roses are native to Asia, several to America, and a few to Europe and NW Africa. The stems are usually thorny, and flowers range in colour from white to yellow, pink, crimson and maroon; many are fragrant. The flowers are followed by false fruits called hips. There are *c*.250 species. Family Rosaceae.

Roseau Capital of Dominica, in the Windward Islands, a port on the SW coast at the mouth of the River Roseau. The city was burnt by the French in 1805 and virtually destroyed by a hurricane in 1979. Tropical vegetables, oils, spices and limes are exported. Pop. (1991) 15,853.

Rosebery, Archibald Philip Primrose, 5th Earl of (1847–1929) British statesman, prime minister (1894–95). He was foreign secretary (1886, 1892–94) under William GLADSTONE. When Gladstone retired, Queen VICTORIA called on Rosebery to become prime minister. A controversial figure, his appointment caused a split in the LIBERAL PARTY and the Conservative Party won the ensuing election. Rosebery became leader of the imperialist wing of the Liberal Party.

rosemary Perennial evergreen herb of the MINT family. It has small, needle-like leaf clusters of small pale-blue flowers. Sprigs of rosemary are commonly used as a flavouring. Family Lamiaceae/Labiatae; species *Rosmarinus officinalis*.

Rosenberg, Alfred (1893–1946) German Nazi leader, b. Estonia. He edited the newspaper of the National Socialist Party. Rosenberg's book *The Myth of the 20th Century* (1930) formed the basis of the ANTI-SEMITISM of NATIONAL SOCIALISM. In 1941, he became minister for the occupied E regions. Rosenberg was convicted of war crimes at the Nuremberg trials and executed.

Rosenberg Case (1951–53) US espionage case. A New York couple, Julius and Ethel Rosenberg, were found guilty of passing nuclear weapons secrets to Soviet agents. The trial gained international attention because many felt the couple were the victims of COLD WAR hysteria. They were the first US civilians executed for espionage.

Roses, Wars of the (1455–85) English dynastic civil wars. They are named after the badges of the rival royal houses of York (white rose) and Lancaster (red rose). Both houses were descended from EDWARD III. The Lancastrian king, Henry VI, was challenged by Richard, Duke of York, who gained brief ascendancy after the battle of St Albans (1455). The Lancastrians recovered control, but in 1460 Richard, supported by the powerful Earl of WARWICK, forced Henry to recognize him as his heir. Richard was killed months later, but the Yorkist victory at Towton (1461) put his son on the throne as EDWARD IV. In 1469, Warwick changed sides, and Edward was deposed but returned to win the decisive victory of Tewkesbury (1471). A final phase of the wars began with the seizure of the throne by RICHARD III in 1483. He was defeated and killed at BOSWORTH, when Henry Tudor (HENRY VII) won the crown with support from both houses.

Rosetta Stone Slab of black basalt inscribed with the same text in Egyptian HIEROGLYPHS, demotic (a simplified form of Egyptian hieroglyphs) and Greek script. By comparing the three versions, first Thomas Young (1818) and later Jean-François Champollion (1822), deciphered the hieroglyphs, leading to a fuller understanding of hieroglyphic writing. It is kept in the British museum, London.

rosewood Any of several kinds of ornamental hardwoods derived from various tropical trees. The most important are Honduras rosewood, *Dalbergia stevensoni*, and Brazilian rosewood, *D. nigra*. It varies from a deep, ruddy brown to purplish and has a black grain. Family Fabiaceae/Leguminose

Rosh Hashanah Jewish New Year and first day of the month of Tishri (generally in September). On this day, a ceremonial ram's horn, the *shophar* or *shofar*, is blown to call sinners to repentance – the Day of Judgment or of Remembrance. It also begins the Ten Days of Penitence that end with the Day of Atonement, YOM KIPPUR.

Rosicrucians Esoteric, secret, worldwide society, using supposedly magical knowledge drawn from ALCHEMY. The name comes from pamphlets published by Christian Rosenkreutz *c*.1615, of whom there is no other record. The modern movement has splintered into several factions.

Ross, Diana (1944–) US singer. She began her career with the vocal trio, The Supremes, whose MOTOWN hits included "Where Did Our Love Go" (1964) and "Baby Love" (1964). In 1970, Ross went solo. She was nominated for an Academy Award for her portrayal of the jazz singer Billie HOLIDAY in the film *Lady Sings the Blues* (1972).

Ross, Sir James Clark (1800–62) English explorer. He accompanied his uncle John Ross (1777–1856) on six Arctic expeditions (1819–27). In 1831, Ross discovered the North Magnetic Pole. He explored (1839–43) the Antarctic, discovering (1841) the Ross Sea.

Ross, Sir Ronald (1857–1932) British bacteriologist, b. India. Ross was awarded the 1902 Nobel Prize for physiology or medicine for his research into MALARIA.

Ross Dependency Region of Antarctica which includes Ross Island, the coast along the Ross Sea, and nearby islands. It has been under the jurisdiction of New Zealand since 1923. Area: land mass, *c*.415,000sq km (160,000sq mi); ice shelf, *c*.450,000sq km (174,000sq mi).

Rossellini, Roberto (1906–77) Italian film director and producer. His post-war films, such as *Open City* (1945), were landmarks in Italian NEO-REALISM. Rossellini made a series of films with his wife, Ingrid BERGMAN, such as *Stromboli* (1949).

Rossetti, Christina Georgina (1830–94) English poet, sister of Dante Gabriel ROSSETTI. Her most enduring work, mainly religious in content, is contained in *Goblin Market and Other Poems* (1862) and *The Prince's Progress and Other Poems* (1866).

Rossetti, Dante Gabriel (1828–82) English poet and painter. A founder member of the PRE-RAPHAELITE BROTHERHOOD, he developed a distinctive style of medieval romanticism after the group dispersed. Rossetti's lush style is evident in idealized portraits of women, such as *Beata Beatrix* (*c*.1863). His portraits were often modelled on his wife, Elizabeth Siddal. Rossetti's poetry includes *Ballads and Sonnets* (1881). He became a recluse and died of drug and alcohol addiction.

Rossini, Gioacchino Antonio (1792–1868) Italian opera composer. His comic operas, including *The Barber of Seville* (1816) and *La Cenerentola* ("Cinderella," 1817), demonstrate his wit and sense of melody. His serious operas include *William Tell* (1829).

Rosso, Il (1495–1540) (Giovanni Battista Rosso) Italian painter and decorative artist. He collaborated with Primaticcio in decorating the royal palace at FONTAINEBLEAU and helped to found the FONTAINEBLEAU SCHOOL.

Rostand, Edmond (1868–1918) French poet and dramatist. His major verse plays include *Cyrano de Bergerac* (1897), *L'Aiglon* (1900) and *Chantecler* (1910).

Rostropovich, Mstislav Leopoldovich (1927–) Azerbaijani cellist and conductor. In 1960, he gave the first London performance of SHOSTAKOVICH's First Cello Concerto. His friend Benjamin BRITTEN composed several works for him. In 1975, Rostropovich defected from the Soviet Union. He was musical director (1977–94) of the National Symphony Orchestra, Washington, D.C.

rotation Turning of a body about its axis. In the Solar System, the Sun and all the planets, with the exception of Uranus and Venus, rotate from W to E.

Roth, Philip (1933–) US novelist and short-story writer. His works often draw on his Jewish background. Roth established his reputation with the short-story collection *Goodbye Columbus* (1959). His best-known novel is *Portnoy's Complaint* (1969). Other works include *Zuckerman Bound* (1985), *Operation Shylock* (1993) and *Sabbath's Theater* (1995) and *American Pastoral* (1997).

Rothko, Mark (1903–70) US painter, b. Russia. A leader of the New York School, he developed a highly individual style featuring large, rectangular areas of thinly layered, pale colours arranged parallel to each other. Towards the end of his life, Rothko introduced darker colours, notably maroon and black. Examples of this phase can be seen in his nine paintings entitled *Black on Maroon* and *Red on Maroon* from the late 1950s.

Rothschild, Meyer Amschel (1744–1812) German financier, founder of a banking dynasty. He made his fortune in Frankfurt during the Napoleonic Wars. His five sons established branches in the financial centres of Europe. The Rothschilds were one of the chief financial powers in the 19th century, but developments in state financing reduced their influence. The family continues to be active in banking and as wine-makers.

rotifer (wheel animacule) Microscopic metazoan found mainly in freshwater. Although it resembles ciliate PROTOZOA, it is many-celled with a general body structure similar to that of a simple WORM. Rotifers may be elongated or round and are identified by a crown of cilia around the mouth. Class Rotifera.

Rotterdam City at the junction of the rivers Rotte and New Meuse, w Netherlands; chief port and second-largest city in the Netherlands. Founded in the 14th century, it expanded with the construction of the New Waterway (1866–72), making it accessible to ocean-going vessels. In 1966 the opening of the Europort harbour made Rotterdam one of the largest ports in the world. It has a large transit trade with industrial areas of Europe, in particular the RUHR. Industries: shipbuilding, petrochemicals, electronic goods, textiles, paper, clothing, brewing, oil-refining, machinery. Pop. (1996) 593,000.

rottweiler German cattle DOG. The short-backed, strong body is set on muscular, medium-length legs and the tail is commonly docked. The short, coarse, flat coat is black with brown markings. Height: to 68.5cm (27in) at the shoulder; weight: 34–41kg (75–90lb).

Rouault, Georges (1871–1958) French painter, printmaker and designer. Studying under Gustave MOREAU with MATISSE, he became acquainted with FAUVISM. A mental breakdown turned him toward more painful subjects. Rouault designed book illustrations, ceramics and tapestries, as well as the sets for DIAGHILEV's ballet, *The*

Prodigal Son (1929). From the 1930s, he concentrated on religious art, such as *Christ Mocked by Soldiers* (1932).

Rouen City in NW France, a port on the River Seine; capital of Seine-Maritime department. Already important in Roman times, by the 10th century Rouen was one of Europe's leading cities. Under English rule (1066–1204, 1419–49), it was the scene of Joan of Arc's trial and burning (1431). Badly damaged in World War 2, it was later rebuilt. Industries: textiles, flour-milling, iron, petrochemicals, perfumes, leather goods. Pop. (1990) 102,723.

roulette Game of chance in which people gamble on which of 37 numbered slots (38 in the USA) in a spinning wheel a small white ball will end up in when the wheel stops. Gamblers place their bets on a table marked out with the numbers. The bank wins all stakes if the ball stops on 0 (and 00 in the USA).

Roundheads Name given to PURITANS and other supporters of Parliament during the English CIVIL WARS. It was originally a derogatory nickname for Puritans who cut their hair short, in contrast to the ringlets of the CAVALIERS.

roundworm Parasite of the class Nematoda that inhabits the intestine of mammals. It breeds in the intestine. The larva bores through the intestinal wall, is carried to the lungs in the bloodstream and crawls to the mouth where it is swallowed. Length: 15–30cm (6–12in).

Rousseau, Henri (1844–1910) French painter, greatest of all naive painters, nicknamed *le Dounaier* (customs official). Rousseau is celebrated for his scenes from an imaginary jungle, such as *Surprised! (Tropical Storm with Tiger)* (1891) and *The Dream* (1910).

Rousseau, Jean Jacques (1712–78) French philosopher of the Age of Reason, whose ideas about society helped to shape the political events that resulted in the FRENCH REVOLUTION. He was born a Protestant in Geneva, Switzerland, and became a Roman Catholic in the 1730s. Later in his life he reconverted to Protestantism in order to regain his citizenship rights in Geneva. In 1740, Rousseau moved to Paris and devoted himself to a career as a writer and composer. In the 1740s, he contributed articles on music to the Encyclopédie of DIDEROT and won fame for his essay *Discourses on Science and the Arts* (1750). In *The Social Contract* (1762), he argued that man had been corrupted by civilization. His ideas on individual liberation from the constraints of society were developed in the novel *Émile* (1762). He described his early, wandering life in an autobiography, *Confessions*, published posthumously in 1782. *See also* SOCIAL CONTRACT

Rousseau, Théodore (1812–67) French painter, leading member of the BARBIZON SCHOOL. He was a pioneer of the open-air movement in landscape painting, and from 1836 worked in the Forest of Fontainebleau near Paris. His works include *Under the Birches, Evening* (1842–44).

rowing Using oars to propel a boat; a leisure activity and a sport. In 1900, it was unofficially included in the Olympic Games and has been a full Olympic event since 1904. Modern racing boats hold crews of two (pairs), four (fours) or eight (eights), each crew member using both hands to pull one oar (to use two oars is **sculling**). A coxswain steers for eights and directs the crew; pairs and fours may or may not have a coxswain. *See also* BOAT RACE

Rowling, J.K. (Joanne Kathleen) (1965–) English writer. Author of the bestselling Harry Potter series, *Harry Potter and the Philosopher's Stone* (1997), *Harry Potter and the Sorcerer's Stone* (1998), *Harry Potter and the Prisoner of Azkaban* (1999) and *Harry Potter and the Goblet of Fire* (2000), which relate the adventures of a young wizard. Popular with both children and adults, her books have been translated into more than 35 languages.

Rowntree, Benjamin Seebohm (1871–1954) English businessman and philanthropist. In 1889, he joined the family chocolate firm and introduced employees' pensions (1906), a five-day week (1919) and employee profit-sharing (1923). Rowntree conducted studies on urban poverty.

Royal Academy of Arts (RA) British national academy of the arts, founded by George III in 1768 and based in London. Members aim to raise the status of the arts by establishing high standards of training and organizing annual summer exhibitions. The first president was Sir Joshua REYNOLDS.

Royal Canadian Mounted Police Federal police of Canada, popularly known as the Mounties. They were organized in 1873, and opened their first post at Emerson in 1874. Active in the Red River rebellion led by Louis RIEL, the Yukon gold rush and both World Wars, today they provide police manpower in most provinces.

Royal Greenwich Observatory UK national astronomical observatory, founded at GREENWICH, London, in 1675. After World War 2 the observatory moved to Herstmonceux, Sussex, and then in 1990 to Cambridge.

Royal Marines British soldiers who serve at sea. The marines are also a mobile force that can be put ashore at any time to operate as conventional soldiers. Their first great success was the capture of Gibraltar in 1704. They played significant roles in both World Wars.

Royal Navy Fighting force that defends Britain's coastal waters and its merchant shipping. The first NAVY in Britain was assembled (878) by ALFRED THE GREAT to fight off the Viking raids. In the 16th century, Henry VII built the first specialist naval ships and established the first dockyards. The following centuries saw a struggle for naval supremacy between Britain, France and the Netherlands, culminating in the Battle of TRAFALGAR (1805). The British victory heralded the supremacy of the Royal Navy that lasted into the 20th century. Since World War 2, the role of the Royal Navy has diminished.

Royal Opera House (originally Covent Garden Theatre) Home of the Royal Opera and, from 1946, of Sadler's Wells Ballet (now the Royal Ballet). It is commonly called Covent Garden. The theatre was first opened in 1732, and the present building was completed in 1858. A modernised and rebuilt Opera House was completed in 1999. The Royal Opera traditionally performs works in the language in which they were written.

Royal Shakespeare Company (RSC) State-subsidized British theatrical repertory company, based in Stratford-upon-Avon. Originally known as the Shakespeare Memorial Company, it received a royal charter in 1961. In 1960, it established a second base in London and presented Shakespearean plays alongside other classical and contemporary pieces. The RSC also tours widely.

Royal Society British society, founded 1660 and incorporated two years later. Its aim was to accumulate experimental evidence on a wide range of scientific subjects, including medicine and botany, as well as the physical sciences. In the 20th century, it became an independent body of scientists encouraging research.

Royal Society for the Prevention of Cruelty to Animals (RSPCA) British organization established in 1824 to prevent cruelty and promote kindness to animals. The RSPCA has its headquarters at Horsham, Sussex. Its inspectors investigate cases of cruelty to animals and, if necessary, bring offenders to court.

RSI Abbreviation of REPETITIVE STRAIN INJURY

rubber Elastic solid obtained from the latex of the RUBBER TREE. **Natural** rubber consists of a POLYMER of cis-isoprene and is widely used for vehicle TYRES and other applications, especially after VULCANIZATION. **Synthetic** rubbers are polymers tailored for specific purposes.

rubber plant Evergreen FIG native to India and Malaysia. Tree-sized in the tropics, juvenile specimens are grown as house plants in temperate regions. Once cultivated for its white LATEX to make India rubber, it has large, glossy, leathery leaves and a stout, buttressed trunk. Height: to 30m (100ft0). Family Moraceae; species *Ficus elastica*.

rubber tree Any of several South American trees whose exudations can be made into RUBBER; especially *Hevea brasiliensis* (family Euphorbiaceae), a tall softwood tree native to Brazil but introduced to Malaysia. The milky exudate, called LATEX, is obtained from the inner bark by tapping. It is then coagulated by smoking over fires or chemically.

rubella *See* GERMAN MEASLES

Rubens, Peter Paul (1577–1640) Flemish painter, engraver and designer, most influential BAROQUE artist of N Europe. He began to gain an international reputation with his huge, vigorous TRIPTYCHS *Raising of the Cross* (1610–11) and *Descent from the Cross* (1611–14). He worked for many of the royal families of Europe, and his most recent commissions included 25 gigantic paintings of Marie de' Medicis and a group of more than 100 mythological paintings for Philip IV of Spain.

Rubicon Ancient name for the River Fiumicino in N central Italy. It formed the border between Italy and Cisalpine Gaul. In 49 BC, Julius CAESAR precipitated civil war by "crossing the Rubicon" into Italy with his army, hence the modern phrase meaning to take an irrevocable step.

rubidium (symbol Rb) Silver-white element, one of the ALKALI METALS. It was discovered in 1861 by Robert BUNSEN and Gustav KIRCHHOFF. The element has few commercial uses; small amounts are used in photoelectric cells. It chemically resembles SODIUM but is more reactive. Properties: at.no. 37; r.a.m. 85.4678; r.d. 1.53; m.p. 38.89°C (102°F); b.p. 688°C (1,270°F); most common isotope Rb^{85} (72.15%).

Rubik, Ernö (1944–) Hungarian architect and designer. In 1975 he patented the Rubik's Cube, a mathematical puzzle with 26 small cubes in six colours.

Rubinstein, Artur (1887–1982) US pianist, b. Poland. He made his debut with the Berlin Symphony Orchestra at the age of 12. Rubinstein is celebrated for his interpretations of CHOPIN and Spanish composers.

Rublev, Andrei (1360–1430) Russian icon painter. His most famous work is his icon of Abraham's three angels (the Old Testament Trinity, *c*.1411), which shows how Rublev moved away from the strict conventions of BYZANTINE ART and introduced a more lyrical style.

ruby Gem variety of the mineral CORUNDUM (aluminium oxide), whose characteristic red colour is due to impurities of chromium and iron oxides. The traditional source of rubies is Burma. Today, synthetic rubies are widely used in industry.

rudd (red eye) Fish related to the MINNOW. In the USA it is called pearl ROACH. Found also in Europe and N and W Asia, the rudd is a large, full-bodied fish with reddish fins. Length: to 40.6cm (16in); weight: to 2kg (4.5lb). Family Cyprinidae; species *Scardinius erythrophthalmus*.

Rudolf I (1218–91) German king (1273–91), founder of the HABSBURG dynasty. His election as king ended a period of anarchy (1250–73). Rudolf set out to restore the position of the monarchy and won the duchies of Austria, Styria and Carniola from Ottokar II of Bohemia (1278). He was never crowned emperor and failed to persuade the electors to confirm his son, Albert I, as his successor, although in 1298 Albert eventually succeeded to the German throne.

Rudolf II (1552–1612) Holy Roman emperor (1576–1612), son and successor of Maximilian II. He moved the imperial capital to Prague, which became a centre of the RENAISSANCE. Rudolf's opposition to Protestantism caused conflict in Bohemia and Hungary. A Hungarian revolt was suppressed by his brother and successor, Matthias, to whom he ceded Hungary, Austria and Moravia (1608), and Bohemia (1611).

ruff Bird of the SANDPIPER family (Scolopacidae). The male is noted for a collar of long feathers about its neck and for its antic courtship performances. The female is called a reeve. The ruff migrates across N Europe and N Asia to Africa and India. Species *Philomachus pugnax*.

rugby Ball game for two teams in which an oval ball may be handled as well as kicked. There are two forms of the game, union and league, but the purpose in each is the same: to touch the ball down in the opposition in-goal area for a try, which allows a kick at the H-shaped goal (a conversion). Kicks must pass over the crossbar between the line of the posts. Players may not pass the ball forwards or knock it forwards when attempting to catch it. The field of play is rectangular, 100m (330ft) long and 55–68m (180–225ft) wide, and play consists of two 40-minute halves. **Rugby union** is a 15-a-side game, which used to be restricted to amateurs. It is most popular in Britain, France, South Africa, New Zealand and Australia. **Rugby league** is a 13-a-side game for professionals and amateurs, played mostly in England, Australia, New Zealand and France. Recent developments are bringing about a closer affinity between the two codes.

Ruhr River in Germany; its valley is Germany's manufacturing heartland. The Ruhr rises in the Rothaargebirge Mountains, and flows W for 235km (146mi) to join the River RHINE at DUISBURG. Major cities on its banks include ESSEN, DORTMUND and Mülheim. In the 19th century, the KRUPP and Thyssen families intensively mined the region's high-quality coking coal and developed massive steelworks. The area was occupied (1923–1925) by France and Belgium in order to compel Germany to pay war reparations. In World War 2, its many armaments factories made it a major Allied target; more than 75% of the region was destroyed. The post-war decline in demand for coal led to a shift to light industry and the region regained prosperity.

Ruisdael, Jacob van (1628–82) Dutch landscape painter. Jacob brought to his paintings of the flat northern landscape an unusual breadth and accuracy. Among his many works are *Wooded Landscape* (c.1660) and *Windmill at Wijk* (c.1670).

rum Alcoholic spirit made by the fermentation of molasses and other sugar-cane products, which are then distilled. When distilled, rum is colourless, but storage in wooden casks and the addition of caramel makes it brown.

Rumford, Benjamin Thompson, Count (1753–1814) British scientist and administrator, b. USA. He discovered that HEAT is a form of motion. Rumford also introduced the standard candle, which became the unit of luminosity until 1940 (when it was replaced by the CANDELA). In 1799, he helped found the Royal Institution.

Rumi (1207–73) Persian poet, b. Jalal ad-Dinar-Rumi. A theologian and teacher whose huge body of work – some 30,000 couplets and numerous *rubaiyat* or quatrains – was inspired by SUFISM. Rumi is generally regarded as Persia's finest poet. His main work is the epic *Mathnawi* (or *Masnavi*).

ruminant Cud-chewing, even-toed, hoofed mammal. They include the OKAPI, DEER, GIRAFFE, ANTELOPE, CATTLE, SHEEP and GOAT. All except the chevrotain have four-chambered stomachs, and they are known for re-chewing food previously swallowed and stored in one of the chambers.

Rump Parliament (1648–53) Name given to the LONG PARLIAMENT in England after 140 members were expelled. Unrepresentative and quarrelsome, it was dissolved by CROMWELL in 1653. It was recalled after the collapse of the PROTECTORATE in 1659, and expelled members were reinstated.

Runcie, Robert Alexander Kennedy (1921–2000) English cleric, archbishop of Canterbury (1980–91). He was ordained in 1951 and became bishop of St Albans in 1970. In 1982, Runcie signed a pledge to move towards unity with the Roman Catholic Church during Pope JOHN PAUL II's historic trip to the UK. He was succeeded by George CAREY.

Rundstedt, Gerd von (1875–1953) German field marshal. One of Adolf HITLER's most successful army commanders, he led the Polish and French campaigns at the start of WORLD WAR 2. In 1941, Rundstedt commanded the invasion of the Soviet Union but was dismissed after being forced to retreat. He returned to active service as commander of the German forces in France. In September 1944, he directed the "Battle of the Bulge", Germany's last attempt to halt the Allied advance in the west.

runes Angular characters or letters of an alphabet formerly used by Germanic peoples in early medieval times. Also called futhark after its first six letters (*f, u, th, a, r* and *k*), the runic alphabet may have been developed by an unknown Germanic people from a N Italian alphabet.

runner In botany, a long, thin stem that extends along the surface of the soil from the axil of a plant's leaf and serves to propagate the plant. At points (nodes) along its length, a runner has small leaves with buds that develop shoots and roots and turn into small independent plants as the runner dies. Runners are produced by such plants as strawberries and creeping buttercups. *See also* ASEXUAL REPRODUCTION

Runyon, Damon (1884–1946) US writer. A newspaper columnist, he also wrote stories about colourful New York City characters, in a distinctive, slangy style. His book, *Guys and Dolls* (1932), was made into a musical.

Rupert, Prince (1619–82) British military commander, b. Bohemia and raised in the Netherlands. His uncle CHARLES I made him commander of the cavalry in the English CIVIL WAR. Rupert was undefeated until MARSTON MOOR (1644). He was dismissed after the Royalist defeat at NASEBY (1645). Rupert surrendered at Bristol. He led raids against English shipping during the PROTECTORATE period and, after the RESTORATION, he served as an admiral in the DUTCH WARS.

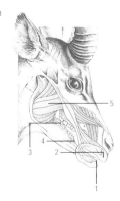

▶ **ruminant** Impalas are found in central and E Africa. Like other ruminants, they can regurgitate food in small amounts once it has been partly digested, for chewing again, reswallowing and further digestion. When grazing, an impala grasps vegetation between its incisors (1) and a hard upper pad (2) and pulls it up rather than biting it off. The molars (3) are ideal for chewing. The gap between incisors and molars (4) allows the tongue to mix food with saliva. The masseter muscle (5) moves the jaw up and down.

rupture *See* HERNIA

Rurik (d. *c*.879) Semi-legendary leader of the Varangians (VIKINGS) in Russia and first Prince of Novgorod. In *c*.862 he established his rule, a date usually taken as marking the beginning of the first Russian state. The capital was moved to KIEV under Rurik's successor, Oleg, and members of his dynasty ruled there and later in Moscow until the 16th century, eventually being replaced by the ROMANOVS.

rush Any of *c*.700 species of perennial tufted bog plants found in temperate regions. It has long, narrow leaves and small flowers crowded into dense clusters. The most familiar rush is *Juncus effusus*, found in Europe, Asia, North America, Australia and New Zealand. It has brown flowers and ridged stems. Height: 30–152cm (1–5ft). Family Juncaceae.

Rush-Bagot Convention British-US agreement of 1817 providing for disarmament of the US-Canadian border. Besides ensuring an unfortified frontier, it agreed limits for ships of the two countries in the Great Lakes.

Rushdie, (Ahmed) Salman (1947–) British novelist, b. India. His early works, including the Booker Prize-winning *Midnight's Children* (1981), were eclipsed by *Satanic Verses* (1988). This novel incited the condemnation of Islamic extremists who perceived the book as BLASPHEMY, and he was sentenced to death by Ayatollah KHOMEINI. In hiding, he wrote a number of works, including a children's book, *Haroun and the Sea of Stories* (1990), and the novel *The Moor's Last Sigh* (1995). In 1998, the Iranian government revoked the death sentence and Rushdie returned to public life. Other novels include *The Ground Beneath Her Feet* (1999).

Ruskin, John (1819–1900) English author, artist and social reformer. A strong religious conviction was the basis for his advocacy of Gothic naturalism as the best style through which to praise God. Ruskin's ideas on architecture are outlined forcefully in his books *The Seven Lamps of Architecture* (1849) and *The Stones of Venice* (three vols., 1851–53). His five-volume work, *Modern Painters* (1834–60), championed the paintings of J.M.W. TURNER. After 1851, Ruskin supported the PRE-RAPHAELITE BROTHERHOOD (PRB).

Russell, Bertrand Arthur William, 3rd Earl (1872–1970) Welsh philosopher, mathematician and social reformer. A fellow at Trinity College, Cambridge, his pupils included Ludwig WITTGENSTEIN. Russell's most influential work, the monumental *Principia Mathematica* (1910–13), written in collaboration with A.N. WHITEHEAD, set out to show how mathematics was grounded in LOGIC. In *Our Knowledge of the External World* (1914), he developed a novel approach to problems in EPISTEMOLOGY. Russell's commitment to pacifism led to his imprisonment in 1918. He supported, however, the anti-fascist aims of World War 2. Russell's *History of Western Philosophy* (1946) was a popular bestseller. In 1950, he was awarded the Nobel Prize for literature. In 1961, Russell was arrested in a demonstration on behalf of the CAMPAIGN FOR NUCLEAR DISARMAMENT (CND).

Russell, Charles Taze *See* JEHOVAH'S WITNESSES

Russell, George William (1867–1935) Irish poet, who wrote under the pen name A.E. A leading figure in the Irish literary renaissance, Russell published many collections of romantic and often mystical poetry, among them *The Divine Vision* (1904) and *Midsummer Eve* (1928).

Russell, John, 1st Earl (1792–1878) British statesman, prime minister (1846–52, 1865–66). He entered Parliament in 1813. As paymaster general, Russell introduced the Great Reform Bill (1832). He was one of the founders of the LIBERAL PARTY. Conservative divisions

over the repeal of the CORN LAWS helped Russell succeed Sir Robert PEEL as prime minister. His first administration collapsed following the resignation of his foreign secretary, Viscount PALMERSTON. Russell returned as foreign secretary (1852–55) in ABERDEEN's coalition, but retired after accusations of incompetent handling of the CRIMEAN WAR. He returned as foreign secretary (1859–65) under Palmerston and became prime minister again on Palmerston's death. His second term was curtailed by the defeat of a new Reform Bill (1866). *See also* REFORM ACTS

Russell, Ken (1927–) English film director. His first feature film was *French Dressing* (1964). Russell's adaptation of D.H. Lawrence's novel *Women in Love* (1969) gained him an Academy nomination. His reputation as the *enfant terrible* of British cinema was reinforced by *The Music Lovers* and *The Devils* (both 1971). Other films include *Mahler* (1973), *Tommy* (1975), *Valentino* (1977), *Altered States* (1980) and *Gothic* (1987).

Russia Federation in E Europe and N Asia. It is the world's largest country. The URALS form a natural border between European and Asian Russia (SIBERIA). About 25% of Russia lies in Europe, W of the Urals. European Russia contains *c*.80% of Russia's population, including the capital, MOSCOW. It is predominantly a vast plain. The CAUCASUS Mountains form Russia's SW border with Georgia and Azerbaijan, and include Europe's highest peak, Mount ELBRUS, at 5,633m (18,481ft). GROZNYY, capital of CHECHENIA, lies close to the Georgian border. The port of ASTRAKHAN lies on the shore of the CASPIAN SEA, the world's largest inland body of water. ST PETERSBURG, Russia's second-largest city, is a Baltic seaport. ARCHANGEL is the major White Sea port. European Russia's major rivers are the DON and the VOLGA (Europe's longest river). SIBERIA is a land of plains and plateaux, with mountains in the E and S. It is drained by the rivers OB, YENISEI and LENA. The industrial centre of NOVOSIBIRSK lies on the River Ob. Close to the Mongolian border lies Lake BAIKAL (the world's deepest lake). VLADIVOSTOCK is the major port on the Sea of Japan. SAKHALIN and the KURIL ISLANDS have often been a source of conflict with Japan. The KAMCHATKA PENINSULA contains many active volcanoes. **Climate** The climate varies from N to S and also from W to E. Moscow has a continental climate with cold, snowy winters and warm summers. Siberia has a much harsher and drier climate. In Northern Siberia, winter temperatures often fall below −46°C (−51°F). **Vegetation** The far N is tundra. Mosses and lichens grow during the short summer, but the subsoil is permafrost. To the S is the taiga, a vast region of coniferous forest. South-central Russia contains large areas of former steppe, most of which is now under the plough; its dark, chernozem soils are among the world's most fertile. The semi-desert lowlands around the Caspian Sea are hardy grassland. **History and politics** Traditionally, the Varangian king, RURIK, established the first Russian state in *c*.AD 862. His successor, Oleg, made KIEV his capital and the state became known as Kievan Rus. VLADIMIR I adopted Greek Orthodox Christianity as the state religion in 988. VLADIMIR and Kiev vied for political supremacy. In 1237–40 the Mongol TATARS conquered Russia and established the GOLDEN HORDE. St ALEXANDER NEVSKI became Great Khan of Kiev. In the 14th century, Moscow grew in importance, and the Grand Duchy of MOSCOW was established in 1380. IVAN III (THE GREAT) extended the power of Moscow, began the construction of the KREMLIN and completed the conquest of the Golden Horde in 1480. In 1547, IVAN IV (THE TERRIBLE) was crowned tsar of all Russia. Ivan the Terrible conquered the Tatar khanates of KAZAN (1552) and Astrakhan (1556),

RUSSIA

AREA: 17,075,000sq km (6,592,800sq mi)
POPULATION: 155,096,000
CAPITAL (POPULATION): Moscow (9,233,000)

gaining control of the River Volga, and began the conquest of Siberia. Following the death of Boris GODUNOV (1605), Russia was subject to foreign incursions and ruled by a series of usurpers. In 1613, Michael founded the ROMANOV dynasty that ruled Russia until 1917. The reign (1696–1725) of PETER I (THE GREAT) marked the start of the westernization and modernization of Russia: central governmental institutions were founded, and the Church was subordinated to the Crown. Centralization was achieved at the expense of increasing the number of serfs. Russia expanded w to the Baltic Sea, and St Petersburg was founded in 1703. Peter made it his capital in 1712. In 1762, CATHERINE II (THE GREAT) became empress. Under her authoritarian government, Russia became the greatest power in continental Europe, acquiring much of Poland, Belarus and Ukraine. ALEXANDER I's territorial gains led him into conflict with the imperial ambitions of NAPOLEON I. In 1812, Napoleon captured Moscow, but his army was devastated by the Russian winter. The Decembrist Conspiracy (1825) failed to prevent the accession of NICHOLAS I. Nicholas' reign was characterized by the struggle against liberalization. At the end of his reign, Russia became embroiled in the CRIMEAN WAR (1853–56). ALEXANDER II undertook reforms, such as the emancipation of the serfs. ALEXANDER III's rule was more reactionary, but continued Russia's industrialization, helped by the construction of the Trans-Siberian Railway. Alexander was succeeded by the last Romanov tsar, NICHOLAS II. In the 1890s, drought caused famine in rural areas, and there was discontent in the cities. Defeat in the RUSSO-JAPANESE WAR (1904–05) precipitated the RUSSIAN REVOLUTION OF 1905. Nicholas II was forced to adopt a new constitution and establish an elected DUMA (parliament). The democratic reforms were soon reversed, revolutionary groups were suppressed and POGROMS encouraged. In 1898, the Russian Social Democratic Labour Party was secretly founded , supported primarily by industrial workers. In 1912, the Party split into BOLSHEVIK and MENSHEVIK factions. Russia's support of a Greater Slavic state contributed to the outbreak of World War 1. Russia was ill-prepared for war and suffered great hardship. The RUSSIAN REVOLUTION (1917) had two main phases. In March, Nicholas II was forced to abdicate (he and his family were executed in July 1918) and a provisional government was formed. In July, KERENSKY became prime minister, but failed to satisfy the radical hunger of the SOVIETS. In November 1917, the Bolsheviks, led by LENIN, seized power and proclaimed Russia a Soviet Federated Socialist Republic. In 1918, the capital was transferred to Moscow. Under the terms of the Treaty of BREST-LITOVSK (1918), Russia withdrew from World War 1 but was forced to cede territory to the Central Powers. For the next five years, civil war raged between the Reds and Whites (monarchists and anti-communists), complicated by foreign intervention. The Bolsheviks emerged victorious, but Russia was devastated. In 1922, Russia was united with Ukraine, Belarus and Transcaucasia (Armenia, Azerbaijan and Georgia) to form the Union of Soviet Socialist Republics (USSR) (for history 1922–91, *see* SOVIET UNION). In June 1991, Boris YELTSIN was elected President of the Russian Republic. In August 1991, communist hardliners arrested the Soviet president GORBACHEV and

attempted to capture the Russian parliament in Moscow. Democratic forces rallied behind Yeltsin, and the coup was defeated. Yeltsin emerged as the major player. On 25 December 1991, Gorbachev resigned as president of the USSR, and on 31 December the Soviet Union was dissolved. The Russian Federation became a co-founder of the COMMONWEALTH OF INDEPENDENT STATES (CIS), composed of former Soviet Republics. In March 1992, a new Federal Treaty was signed between the central government in Moscow and the autonomous republics within the Russian Federation. Chechenia refused to sign, and declared independence. Yeltsin's reforms were frustrated by institutional forces, forcing him to dissolve parliament in September 1993. Parliamentary leaders formed a rival government, but the coup failed. In December 1993, a new democratic constitution was adopted. Progress in democratization and economic reform was slow. Many ethnic groups demanded greater autonomy within the Federation. In 1992, direct rule was imposed in INGUSH and North OSSETIA. From 1994 to 1996, Russia was embroiled in a costly civil war in the secessionist state of Chechenia. In May 1996, despite concern about his ill-health, Yeltsin was re-elected. In 1998, the Russian economy was devastated by the financial crisis in Southeast Asia. In March 1998, Yeltsin dismissed the entire cabinet, including the prime minister Viktor CHERNOMYRDIN. In August 1998, the stock market collapsed and the rouble was devalued by 50%. Yeltsin again dismissed the entire cabinet and was forced to appoint Yevgeni Primakov as prime minister. In 1999, Yeltsin resigned in favour of Vladimir PUTIN, who relaunched the war in Chechenia and won the 2000 elections. In 2000, Putin was widely criticised for his handling of the Kursk submarine disaster in which 118 Russian sailors died when their submarine sank in the Barents Sea.

Economy Under Soviet rule, Russia was transformed from an agrarian economy into the world's second greatest industrial power (after the USA). By the 1970s, concentration on the military-industrial complex and the creation of a bloated bureaucracy caused the economy to stagnate. Gorbachev's policy of PERESTROIKA was an attempt to correct this weakness. Yeltsin sped up the pace of reform. In 1993, the command economy was abolished, private ownership was re-introduced, and mass privitization began. By 1996, 80% of the Russian economy was in private hands. A major problem remains the size of Russia's foreign debt (1996, US$125,000 million). Industry employs 46% of the workforce and contributes 48% of GDP (1995 GDP per capita, US$4,480). Mining is the most valuable activity. Russia is rich in resources: it is the world's leading producer of natural gas and nickel, and the world's third-largest producer of crude oil, lignite and brown coal. It is the world's second-largest manufacturer of aluminium and phosphates. Light industries, producing consumer goods, are growing in importance. Most farmland is still government-owned or run as collectives. Russia is the world's largest producer of barley, oats, rye and potatoes. It is the world's second-largest producer of beef and veal.

Russian Official language of the Russian Federation and several other republics. It is the primary language of *c.*140 million people and is a second language for millions more. It is the most important of the Slavic languages, which form a sub-division of the family of INDO-EUROPEAN LANGUAGES. It is written in the CYRILLIC alphabet.

Russian architecture Architectural style that began as a regional variety of BYZANTINE ARCHITECTURE in the 10th century with the Christianization of Russia. Important centres of architectural activity developed at Kiev, Novgorod and Pskov. Early churches were built of wood. The

Cathedral of Sancta Sophia in Kiev (1018–37) was the first stone construction. The distinctive onion-shaped dome was introduced in the 12th century at the Cathedral of Sancta Sophia, Novgorod. During the 15th century, Russia was subject to a series of western European trends, and Italian architects built the KREMLIN in a Renaissance style. PETER (THE GREAT) and CATHERINE (THE GREAT) brought ROCOCO and NEOCLASSICISM to St Petersburg. In the 19th century there was a revival of medieval Russian architecture.

Russian art Paintings and sculpture produced in Russia after *c*.1000 AD, as distinct from the earlier SCYTHIAN art. In the Middle Ages, Russian art carried on the traditions of BYZANTINE ART and was primarily religious. After the fall of Constantinople (1453), Russia regarded itself as the spiritual heir of Byzantium, but its finest artworks were largely produced by foreigners. This began to change in the latter part of the 19th century, when Ilya REPIN and the Wanderers breathed new life into Russian art. This led to a fruitful period in the early 20th century, when Russia was at the heart of new developments in MODERNISM, SUPREMATISM and CONSTRUCTIVISM.

Russian Five Group of Russian composers, active during the 1860s and 1870s, who hoped to create a truly Russian style of music. They were BALAKIREV, César Cui, BORODIN, MUSSORGSKY and RIMSKY-KORSAKOV.

Russian literature Literary works of Russia until 1917, then of the Soviet Union until 1991. Thereafter the literature properly belongs to the individual republics. Russian literature has its origins in religious works dating from *c*.1000 AD. They include biographies of saints, chronicles, hymns and sermons. After the 1600s, Western influences are found. ROMANTICISM beginning in the late 1700s – dominated by Nikolai Karamzin (*Letters of a Russian Traveller*, 1790) and Alexander PUSHKIN (*Boris Godunov*, 1825) – gave way to the realism of Leo TOLSTOY (*War and Peace*, 1869), Fyodor DOSTOEVSKY (*The Brothers Karamazov*, 1879–80), Anton CHEKHOV (*Uncle Vanya*, 1899) and Maxim GORKY (*The Lower Depths*, 1902). The revolutionary feelings that dominated the early part of the 20th century witnessed a literary revival. Major figures included the symbolist poet Alexsandr BLOK (*The Twelve*, 1918) and the futurists, such as Vladimir MAYAKOVSKY. After the Russian Revolution (1917), many writers fled overseas to escape censorship. The authors who remained had to depict only favourable images of the Soviet Union. The major authors of this period were Boris PASTERNAK and Alexei Tolstoy (*Road to Calvary*, 1941). Criticism of the regime was published, however, in works by novelists Alexander SOLZHENITSYN (*One Day in the Life of Ivan Denisovich*, 1962) and Yuri Trifonov (*Another Life*, 1975) and by poet Alexander Tvardovsky. *See also* SOCIALIST REALISM

Russian Orthodox *See* EASTERN ORTHODOX CHURCH

Russian Revolution (1917) Events in Russia that resulted, first, in the founding of a republic (March) and, second, in the seizure of power by the BOLSHEVIKS (November). (In the calendar in use at the time, the two stages took place in February and October.) Widespread discontent, a strong revolutionary movement and the hardships of World War 1 forced Tsar NICHOLAS II to abdicate in March. A provisional government was formed by liberals in the DUMA (parliament), which represented only the middle classes. Its aim was to make Russia into a liberal democracy and to defeat Germany. Workers and peasants had a different agenda: greater social and economic equality and an end to the war. The provisional government faced a challenge from the powerful socialist SOVIET in Petrograd (St PETERSBURG), which in May formed a coalition government that included

Alexander KERENSKY, prime minister from July, and other socialists. The launching of a new military offensive, combined with disappointing reforms, discredited the government and the socialist parties associated with it. Meanwhile, soviets sprang up in many cities; in the countryside, peasants seized land from the gentry; at the front, soldiers deserted. In the cities, the Bolsheviks secured growing support in the soviets. In November, at the order of LENIN, they carried out a successful coup in Petrograd. The Kerensky government folded, but a long civil war ensued before Lenin and his followers established their authority throughout Russia.

Russian Revolution of 1905 Series of violent strikes and protests against tsarist rule in Russia. It was provoked mainly by defeat in the RUSSO-JAPANESE WAR (1904–05). It began on Bloody Sunday (22 January), when a peaceful demonstration in ST PETERSBURG was fired on by troops. Strikes and peasant risings spread, culminating in a general strike in October that forced the tsar to institute a democratically elected DUMA (parliament). By the time it met in 1906, the government had regained control. Severe repression followed.

Russo-Japanese War (1904–05) Conflict arising from the rivalry of Russia and Japan for control of Manchuria and Korea. The war began with a Japanese attack on Port Arthur. Russia suffered a series of defeats on land and at sea, culminating in the Battle of Mukden (February–March 1905) and the annihilation of the Baltic fleet at Tsushima (May). Russia was forced to surrender Korea, the Liaotung Peninsula and S Sakhalin to Japan.

rust In botany, group of FUNGI that live as PARASITES on many kinds of higher plants. Rusts damage cereal crops and several fruits and vegetables. They have complex life cycles that involve growth on more than one host plant.

rust Corrosion of IRON or its alloys by a combination of air and water. Carbon dioxide from the air dissolves in water to form an acid solution that attacks the iron to form iron (II) oxide. This is then oxidized by oxygen in the air to reddish-brown iron (III) oxide. Rusting may be prevented by GALVANIZING.

Ruth Eighth book of the Old Testament recounting the story of Ruth, a young Moabite widow. It tells of Ruth's decision to settle in Israelite territory and her eventual marriage to the wealthy Boaz, whereby she becomes the great-grandmother of Israel's greatest leader, King DAVID.

Ruth, "Babe" (George Herman) (1895–1948) US baseball player. He held the career home-run record (714) until 1974. Ruth's record of 60 home runs in one season (154 games) was not topped until the season was extended to 162 games.

ruthenium (symbol Ru) Silver-white, metallic element, one of the TRANSITION ELEMENTS. It was discovered in 1827 and first isolated in 1844. Ruthenium is found in PLATINUM ores. It is used as a catalyst, and its alloys are used in electrical contacts and to colour glass and ceramics. Properties: at.no. 44; r.a.m. 101.07; r.d. 12.41; m.p. 2,310°C (4,190°F); b.p. 3,900°C (7,052°F); most common isotope Ru[102] (31.61%).

Rutherford, Ernest, Lord (1871–1937) British physicist, b. New Zealand, who pioneered modern NUCLEAR PHYSICS. Rutherford discovered and named alpha and beta radiation, named the NUCLEUS, and proposed a theory of the radioactive transformation of ATOMS for which he received the 1908 Nobel Prize for Chemistry. In Cambridge, under J.J. THOMSON, he discovered the URANIUM radiations. At McGill University, Canada, Rutherford formed the theory of atomic disintegration with Frederick SODDY. At Manchester (1907), he devised the nuclear theory of the atom and, with Niels BOHR, the idea of ORBITAL electrons. In 1919, at the Cavendish Laboratory, his research team became the first to split an atom's nucleus. Rutherford predicted the existence of the NEUTRON, later discovered by James CHADWICK.

rutherfordium (symbol Rf) Synthetic, radioactive, metallic ELEMENT of the transactinide series. It has a HALF-LIFE of less than a second. It is thought to have been discovered first in 1974, but its existence was only proved in 1994, when it was officially given the name rutherfordium. The name rutherfordium had previously been used for element 104 (now known as DUBNIUM). Properties: at.no. 106

rutile (titanium dioxide, TiO_2) Black to red-brown oxide mineral, found in igneous and metamorphic rocks and quartz veins. It occurs as long, prismatic crystals in the tetragonal system and as granular masses. It has a metallic lustre, is brittle and is used as a gemstone. Hardness 6–6.5; r.d. 4.2.

Ruwenzori Mountain range in central Africa on the Uganda-Zaïre border, between lakes Albert and Edward. The highest peak is Mount Margherita, 5,109m (16,763ft). Length of range: 121km (75mi).

Ruyter, Michiel de (1607–76) Dutch naval commander. During the first of the DUTCH WARS (1652–54), he reached the rank of vice admiral. In the second Dutch War (1665–67), Ruyter commanded the fleet that defeated the English off Dunkirk (1666). In 1667, he sailed up the Medway, destroying much of the English fleet. In the third Dutch War (1672–74), Ruyter was again victorious.

Rwanda Nation in E central Africa. Rwanda is Africa's most densely populated country. It is a small state in the heart of Africa, bordered by Uganda (N), Tanzania (E), Burundi (S) and the Democratic Republic of Congo (W). The W border is formed by Lake Kivu and the River Ruzizi. Rwanda has a rugged landscape, dominated by high, volcanic mountains, rising to Mount Karisimbi, at 4,507m (14,787ft). The capital, KIGALI, stands on the central plateau. East Burundi consists of stepped plateaux that descend to the lakes and marshland of the Kagera National Park on the Tanzania border. **Climate** Rwanda's climate is moderated by altitude. Rainfall is abundant. The dry season is June–August. **Vegetation** The lush rainforests in the W are one of the last refuges for the mountain gorilla. Many of Rwanda's forests have been cleared and 35% of the land is now arable. The steep mountain slopes are intensively cultivated. Despite contour ploughing, heavy rain has caused severe soil erosion. **History and politics** Twa pygmies were the original inhabitants of Rwanda, but Hutu farmers began to settle (c.1,000 AD), gradually displacing the Twa. In the 15th century, Tutsi cattle herders migrated from the N and began to dominate the Hutu. By the late 18th century, Rwanda and Burundi formed a single Tutsi-dominated state ruled by a king (*mwami*). In 1890, Germany conquered the area and subsumed it into German East Africa. During World War 1, Belgian forces occupied (1916) both Rwanda and Burundi. In 1919, it became part of the Belgian League of Nations mandate territory of Ruanda-Urundi (which in 1946 became a UN trust territory). The Hutu majority became more vociferous in their demands for political representation. In 1959, the Tutsi *mwami* died. The ensuing civil war between Hutus and

Tutsis claimed more than 150,000 lives. Hutu victory led to a mass exodus of Tutsis. The 1960 elections were won by the Hutu Emancipation Movement, led by Grégoire Kayibanda. In 1961, Rwanda declared itself a republic. In 1962, Belgium formally recognized Rwanda's independence. Kayibanda became president. Rwanda was subject to continual Tutsi incursions from Burundi and Uganda. In 1973, Kayibanda was overthrown in a military coup, led by Major General Habyarimana. In 1978, Habyarimana became president. During the 1980s, Rwanda was devastated by drought. More than 50,000 refugees fled to Burundi. In 1990, Rwanda was invaded by the Tutsi-dominated Rwandan Patriotic Front (RPF), who forced Habyarimana to agree to a multi-party constitution. UN forces were drafted in to oversee the transition. In April 1994, Habyarimana and the Burundi president were killed in a rocket attack on their aircraft. The Hutu army and militia launched a premeditated act of genocide against the Tutsi minority, killing between 500,000 and one million Tutsis within three months. In July 1994, an RPF offensive toppled the government and created two million Hutu refugees. A government of national unity, comprised of both Tutsis and moderate Hutus, was formed. More than 50,000 people died in the refugee camps in E Democratic Republic of Congo before international aid arrived. Hutu militia remained in control of the camps, their leaders facing prosecution for genocide. The sheer number of refugees (1995, one million in Zaïre and 500,000 in Tanzania) destabilized regional politics. In 1996, UN troops left Rwanda. In 1998, former prime minister Jean Kambanda was sentenced to life imprisonment for genocide by the UN International Criminal Tribunal. **Economy** Rwanda is a low-income developing country (1992 GDP per capita, US$540). Most people are subsistence farmers. Some cattle are raised, mainly by Tutsis. Rwanda's most valuable crop is coffee, accounting for more than 70% of exports.

Ryder, Winona (1971–) US film actress, b. Winona Horowitz. She first gained attention for supporting roles in *Heathers* (1989) and *Edward Scissorhands* (1990). Ryder gained Academy nominations for her performances in the period dramas *The Age of Innocence* (1993) and *Little Women* (1994).

Ryder Cup Biennial competition in which a team of professional male golfers from the USA plays a team from Europe. The event consists of eight 18-hole foursomes, eight 18-hole four-balls and 16 18-hole singles.

rye Hardy, cereal GRASS originating in SW Asia and naturalized throughout the world. It grows in poorer soils and colder climates than most other cereals can stand. It has flower spikelets that develop one-seeded grains. It is used for flour, as a forage crop and for making alcoholic drinks. Height: to 0.9m (3ft). Family Poaceae/Gramineae; species *Secale cereale*.

Ryle, Sir Martin (1918–84) English physicist and radio astronomer. After studying radar during World War 2, he pioneered RADIO ASTRONOMY. He also catalogued radio sources, which led to his discovery of QUASARS.

Ryukyu Islands Japanese archipelago in the W Pacific Ocean, extending c.965km (600mi) between Kyushu in S Japan and Taiwan; it separates the East China Sea (W) from the Philippine Sea (E). Inhabited since early times, the islands were invaded by China in the 14th century and by Japan in the 17th century, and were relinquished by China to Japan in 1879. After World War 2, they were administered by the USA, being restored to Japan in 1972. The group includes OKINAWA, Amami and Sakishima. Agriculture and fishing are the chief occupations. Area: c.2,200sq km (850sq mi). Pop. (1984 est.) 1,161,000.

RWANDA
AREA: 26,340sq km (10,170sq mi)
POPULATION: 10,200,000
CAPITAL (POPULATION): Kigali (234,500)

S/s, 19th letter of the Roman alphabet. It is descended from the Semitic letter sin *or* shin, *meaning* tooth. *It passed into the Greek alphabet primarily as the Greek letter* sigma.

Saadia ben Joseph al-Fayumi (882–942) Jewish scholar, b. Egypt. His *Book of Beliefs and Opinions* was the first rational defence of JUDAISM. Saadia's *Book of Language* was the first systematic exposition of Hebrew grammar. Under his leadership, the Jewish Academy at Sura, Babylon, became the centre of Jewish learning. Saadia translated the Old Testament into Arabic.

Saarinen, Eero (1910–61) US architect and designer, b. Finland. He was the son of Eliel SAARINEN. His work linked with EXPRESSIONISM and the INTERNATIONAL STYLE. One of his most exciting buildings is the TWA terminal at New York's Kennedy Airport (1956–62). Other notable designs include the General Motors Technical Center in Warren, Michigan (1948–56), and the US Embassy in London (1955–61).

Saarinen, Eliel (1873–1950) Finnish architect, resident in the USA after 1923. His work had a significant impact on US architecture. In later years he collaborated with his son, Eero SAARINEN. In 1947, they won the highest award of the American Institute of Architects for their design for part of the Smithsonian Institution, Washington D.C.

Saarland State in SW Germany on the borders with France (S) and Luxembourg (W); the capital is Saarbrücken. Belonging intermittently to France, the Saar was finally ceded to Prussia after the defeat of Napoleon I in 1815. France administered the region after World War 1, but in a 1935 plebiscite 90% of the people voted to return to Germany. French forces again occupied the Saar after World War 2. Saarland finally gained the status of a West German state in 1967. The forested valley of the Saar River is occupied by blast furnaces and steel works, exploiting local coal and nearby iron ore. There is little agriculture and some market gardening. Area: 2,570sq km (992sq mi). Pop. (1989 est.) 1,054,000.

Saatchi, Maurice (1946–) British advertising executive, b. Iraq. Co-founder, with his brother **Charles**, of the advertising agency Saatchi & Saatchi. During the 1980s, the agency masterminded major advertising campaigns, including several for the Conservative Party. In 1995, the Saatchi brothers were ousted from Saatchi & Saatchi by the stockholders and formed a new agency, M. & C. Saatchi.

Sabah, Sheikh Jabir al Ahmad al- (1928–) (Jabir III) Emir of Kuwait (1977–). A member of the ruling family of Al-Sabah, a dynasty founded by Sheikh Sabah al-Awal (r.1756–72), he succeded Sabah III al Salim. When Iraq invaded Kuwait (1990), Jabir took refuge in Saudia Arabia and set up a government in exile. He returned to Kuwait in 1991.

Sabah (North BORNEO) State of MALAYSIA and one of the four political sub-divisions of the island of Borneo. Ceded to the British in 1877, it remained the British Protectorate of North Borneo until 1963, when it became an independent state of the Malaysian Federation. The terrain is mountainous and forested. The capital is Kota Kinabalu (1990 pop. 208,484). The main products include oil, timber, rubber, coconuts and rice. Area: 76,522sq km (29,545sq mi). Pop. (1990) 1,736,902.

Sabbatarianism Religious doctrine of certain Protestants that Sunday, the Christian Sabbath, should be observed as a holy day of rest. Sabbatarianism began in Britain during the Puritan interregnum (1649–60). After the Sunday Entertainments Act of 1932, which empowered local authorities to license Sunday entertainment, Sabbatarianism lost much of its force in England, but remained strong in parts of Scotland and Wales.

Sabbath Seventh day of the week, set aside as a sacred day of rest. For Jews, the Sabbath runs from sunset on Friday to sunset on Saturday. Christians set aside Sunday for their Sabbath.

Sabin, Albert Bruce (1906–93) US virologist, b. Russia. In 1957, he developed a live-virus oral VACCINE against POLIOMYELITIS. It replaced Jonas SALK'S inactivate VIRUS vaccine.

Sabines Ancient people of central Italy. They inhabited the Sabine Hills NE of Rome. After sporadic fighting, the Sabines were conquered in 290 BC and Romanized.

sable MARTEN native to Siberia. It has been hunted almost to extinction for its soft, dark-brown fur, sometimes flecked with white. Length: to 60cm (24in). Family Mustelidae; species *Martes zibellina*.

sabre-toothed tiger Popular name for a prehistoric member of the CAT family (Felidae) that existed from the OLIGOCENE period to the PLEISTOCENE period. It had extremely long canine teeth adapted to killing large herbivores. Sub-family Machairodontinae, genus *Smilodon*.

Sac (Sauk) Algonquian-speaking band of Native North Americans originally inhabiting the Saginaw Bay region of E Michigan. In the 17th century they fled to Wisconsin. In the early 18th century they merged with the remaining warriors of the Fox band. A bogus treaty forced the Sac and Fox to cross the Mississippi River into Iowa. The resultant Black Hawk War (1832) ended with the Sac and Fox settling on reservations in Iowa, Kansas and Oklahoma. Today, *c.*1,200 remain on these reservations.

saccharide Organic compound based on SUGAR molecules. Monosaccharides include GLUCOSE and FRUCTOSE. Two sugar molecules join to make a disaccharide, such as LACTOSE or SUCROSE. POLYSACCHARIDES have more than two sugar molecules. *See also* CARBOHYDRATE

saccharin ($C_7H_5NO_3S$) Synthetic substance used as a substitute for SUGAR. It is derived from TOLUENE. In 1977 it was tenuously linked with some forms of cancer in humans and is no longer widely used.

Sacco and Vanzetti Case Controversial US robbery-murder trial taken up as a cause by intellectuals, radicals and liberals in the 1920s. At the height of the Red Scare (April 1920), two men robbed and killed a paymaster and his guard in South Braintree, Massachusetts. Italian immigrant anarchists Nicola Sacco and Bartolomeo Vanzetti were convicted (1921) and executed (1927) for the crime. Their supporters claimed the verdict reflected anti-Italian, anti-radical bigotry. There is continued belief in Vanzetti's innocence, although a 1961 ballistics test suggested the fatal bullet came from Sacco's gun.

Sachs, Julius von (1832–97) German botanist. Sachs' *Textbook of Botany* (1868) was an influential synthesis of botanical data. He demonstrated the importance of transpiration and the role of CHLOROPHYLL in plants.

Sachs, Nelly (1891–1970) German-Jewish poet and dramatist. Sachs escaped from Nazi Germany in 1940 and her works, such as *In the Houses of Death* (1947) and *Later Poems* (1965), bear witness to the persecution of European Jews. Her best-known play is *Eli: A Mystery Play of the Sufferings of Israel* (1951). Sachs shared the 1966 Nobel Prize for literature.

Sackville-West, Vita (Victoria Mary) (1892–1962) English poet and novelist. She was a member of the BLOOMSBURY GROUP. Her best-known works include *The Edwardians* (1930), *All Passion Spent* (1931) and the long poem "The Land" (1926).

sacrament Symbolic action in which the central mysteries of a religious faith are enacted and which, on some accounts, confers divine grace upon those to whom it is given or administered. For Protestants there are two sacraments: BAPTISM and the Lord's Supper (*see* LAST SUPPER). In the Roman Catholic and Eastern Orthodox Churches, the sacraments are baptism, CONFIRMATION, the EUCHARIST, holy ORDERS, matrimony, PENANCE and the anointing of the sick.

Sacramento State capital of California, USA, at the confluence of the Sacramento and American rivers; seat of Sacramento County. The first settlement was established (1839) by John A. Sutter, and the California gold rush of 1848 spurred development. In 1854, Sacramento became state capital. In 1963, a 69km (43mi) deep-water channel was completed, that linked the inland port to San Francisco Bay. It is the distribution centre for the fertile Sacramento valley. Government agencies and military installations, such as the McClellan Air Force base, have contributed to the local economy. Industries: missile development, transport equipment, food processing. Pop. (1992) 382,816.

sacrifice Offering or destruction of precious objects – food and drink, flowers and incense, animals and human beings – for religious purposes. Sacrifices are made in order to maintain a relationship with a god or in the hope of winning divine favour or to atone for guilt.

Sadat, (Muhammad) Anwar (al-) (1918–81) Egpytian statesman, president (1970–81). A close associate of NASSER, he was vice president (1964–66, 1969–70) and succeeded Nasser as president. After the ARAB-ISRAELI WARS of 1973, he signed an historic Egypt–Israel peace treaty in 1979. Sadat was assassinated by Islamic fundamentalists.

Sadducees Jewish sect active in Judaea from *c*.200 BC until the fall of Jerusalem in AD 70. By the time of Jesus, the main difference between them and the PHARISEES was their refusal to recognize the oral traditions surrounding the Scriptures as part of the Hebrew Law.

Sade, Donatien Alphonse François, Marquis de (1740–1814) French novelist and playwright, and a founder of the modern French prose style. Imprisoned for sexual offences, De Sade wrote many licentious novels, among them *Justine* (1791) and *Juliette* (1797).

Safavid Persian dynasty (1501–1722) that established the territorial and Shiite theocratic principles of modern Iran. The dynastic founder, Shah ISMAIL, claimed descent from a Shiite SUFISM order, and the state adopted Shiism as the state religion. His successor, ABBAS I, accepted the Ottoman occupation of W Iran and concentrated on subduing the threat to Iran's E borders. His death created a power vacuum, and Iran's borders contracted. Shah Husayn's concentration on the capture of Bahrain enabled Afghan troops to overrun the country. His forced abdication in 1722 marked the end of Safavid rule.

Safdie, Moshe (1938–) Canadian architect, b. Israel. He is best known for his "Habitat" housing project for Montréal's Expo' 67: prefabricated cubes, stacked in various ways, formed a unified complex of apartments.

safflower Annual plant with large red, orange or white flower heads that are used in making dyestuffs. The seeds yield oil that is used in cooking and in the manufacture of MARGARINE. Family Asteraceae/Compositae; species *Carthamus tinctorius.*

saffron (autumn CROCUS) Perennial crocus, native to Asia Minor. It has purple or white flowers. The golden, dried stigmas of the plant are used as a flavouring or dye. Family Iridaceae; species *Crocus sativus.*

saga In old NORSE LITERATURE (especially Icelandic), prose narrative that relates the lives of historical figures. The sagas were written between the 7th and 14th centuries. Notable examples include the *Gísla saga*, the *Njáls saga* and the *Heimskringla* by SNORRI STURLUSON.

sage Common name for a number of plants of the MINT family (Lamiaceae/Labiatae) native to the Mediterranean region. The best known is *Salvia officinalis*, an aromatic herb used for seasoning. Height: 15–38cm (6–15in).

sagebrush Aromatic shrub common in arid areas of W North America. The common sagebrush has small, silvery green leaves and bears clusters of tiny white flower heads. Height: to 2m (6.5ft). Family Asteraceae/Compositae; species *Artemisia tridentata.*

Sagittarius (Archer) Southern constellation on the ecliptic between Scorpio and Capricorn. Rich in stellar CLUSTERS, this region of the sky also contains much interstellar matter, which obscures the central region of the Milky Way. The brightest star is Epsilon Sagittarii (*Kaus Australis*), magnitude 1.8.

sago palm (fern palm) Feather-leaved PALM tree native to swampy areas of Malaysia and Polynesia. Its thick trunk contains sago, a starch used in foodstuffs. Height: 1.2–9.1m (4–30ft). Family Arecaceae/Palmae; species *Metroxylon sagu.*

saguaro Large CACTUS native to SW North America. White, night-blooming flowers appear when the plant is 50 to 75 years old. Its red fruit is edible. Height: to 40ft (12m). Family Cactaceae; species *Carnegiea gigantea.*

Sahara World's largest desert, with an area of *c*.9,000,000sq km (3,500,000sq mi), covering nearly a third of Africa's total land area. It consists of Algeria,

▲ **sago palm** Flourishing in SE Asian freshwater swamps, the sago palm (*Metroxylon sagu*) is a primary source of carbohydrate in tropical regions. Just before flowering, the palm is cut and the pith of the trunk ground to make sago flour.

Niger, Libya, Egypt and Mauritania, the s parts of Morocco and Tunisia, and the N parts of Senegal, Mali, Chad and Sudan. It extends *c*.4,800km (3,000mi) w to E from the Atlantic Ocean to the Red Sea, and stretches *c*.1,900km (1,200mi) N to s from the ATLAS Mountains to the SAHEL. The annual rainfall is usually less than 10cm (4in), and there is very little natural vegetation. Two-thirds of the Sahara is stony desert, and the topography ranges from the Tibesti Massif (N Chad) at 3,400m (11,000ft) to the QATTARA DEPRESSION (Egypt) at 133m (436ft) below sea-level. Oases act as vital centres for water, crop farming and transport, and for the Sahara's two million inhabitants. The two main ethnic groups are the TUAREG and the Tibu. Nomads herd sheep and goats. Transport is primarily by camel and horse. Mineral deposits include salt, iron ore, phosphates, oil and gas.

Sahel Band of semi-arid scrub and savanna grassland in Africa, s of the SAHARA. It extends through Senegal, s Mauritania, Mali, Burkina Faso, N Benin, s Niger, N Nigeria and s central Chad. Over the past 30 years the Sahara has encroached on the N Sahel in the world's most notorious example of DESERTIFICATION.

Saigon *See* HO CHI MINH CITY

sailing *See* YACHT

saint Man or woman who has manifested exceptional holiness and love of God during his or her life. In the New Testament, all believers are called saints, but since the 2nd century the title has usually been reserved for men and women of outstanding merit. In the Roman Catholic and Eastern Orthodox churches, individual saints are regarded as having a special relationship with God and are therefore venerated for their perceived role as intercessors. The Protestant reformers of the 16th century abolished the veneration of saints, saying that all believers have access to God through Christ. *See also* CANONIZATION; individual saints.

St Albans Historic cathedral city on the River Ver, Hertfordshire, England. The modern city is built amongst the ruins of the Roman city of Verulamium. St Albans developed around the abbey built in 793 by King Offa to honour the martyrdom of St Albans in AD 304. The cathedral dates mostly from the 11th century. Industries: printing, clothing, tourism. Pop (1991) 77,500.

St Andrews Royal burgh and university town in Fife, on the NE coast of Scotland. It was the ecclesiastical capital of Scotland until the Reformation. The rules of golf were devised at the Royal and Ancient Golf Club. Pop. (1981) 11,400.

Saint Bartholomew's Day Massacre (24 August 1572) Mass murder of HUGUENOTS (French Protestants) on St Bartholomew's feast day. The Huguenot leaders had gathered in Paris for the marriage of Henry of Navarre (later HENRY IV). On orders from CATHERINE DE' MÉDICI, a bungled attempt was made on the life of Gaspard de Coligny. The plot's failure led to a plan for a more widespread slaughter. With the support of King CHARLES IX, the massacre began when soldiers killed Coligny and other Huguenot leaders. It soon spread and continued in the provinces until 3 October. Modern estimates suggest that *c*.70,000 people died.

St Bernard Swiss mountain dog with excellent scenting abilities used to find people lost in deep snow. It has a massive head and a dense white and red coat. Height: to 74cm (29in) at the shoulder; weight: to 77kg (170lb).

St Bernard Passes Two passes (Great St Bernard and Little St Bernard) in the Swiss Alps that link Valais, Switzerland, with Valle d'Aosta, Italy. In 1964, the Great St Bernard Tunnel was opened to traffic.

St Croix (Santa Cruz) Largest of the US VIRGIN ISLANDS, West Indies. Christiansted, on NE coast, is the chief town. St Croix was ruled by several nations until it was sold by Denmark to the USA (1917). Industries: rum, sugar. Area: 218sq km (84sq mi). Pop. (1990) 50,139.

Sainte-Beauve, Charles Augustin (1804–69) French literary critic and historian. His prolific ouput includes *Chateaubriand and His Literary Circle* (1860) and *Port-Royal* (1840–59), a history of JANSENISM.

St Elmo's fire (corposant) Electrical discharge illuminating the tops of projecting objects. It usually occurs during a storm when the strongly charged atmosphere creates a discharge between the air and an object.

Saint-Étienne City in E Central France; capital of Loire department. Saint-Étienne is a major industrial town in the Massif Central. Its textile and silk manufacture dates back to the 11th century. The city's first steel plant was built in 1815. Pop. (1990) 201,570.

Saint-Exupéry, Antoine de (1900–44) French novelist and aviator. His experiences as a pilot provided the material for his novels, which include *Southern Mail* (1928), *Night Flight* (1931) and *Flight to Arras* (1942). He is best known for his classic fable, *The Little Prince* (1943). He was killed in World War 2.

St George's Capital and port on the SW coast of GRENADA, West Indies. Founded in 1650 as a French settlement, it was capital of the British WINDWARD ISLANDS (1885–1958). Industries: rum distilling, sugar processing, tourism. Pop. (1992) 7,000.

St Germain, Treaty of (1919) Part of the peace settlement after World War 1. It established the new republic of Austria from the old AUSTRO-HUNGARIAN EMPIRE.

St Helena Island in the s Atlantic, *c*.1,900km (1,200mi) from the coast of w Africa; its capital is Jamestown (1992 pop. 1,500). It became a British crown colony in 1834 and is chiefly known as the place of Napoleon I's exile. It is now a UK dependent territory and administrative centre for the islands of ASCENSION and TRISTAN DA CUNHA. Area: 122sq km (47sq mi). Pop. (2000) 10,000.

St Helens, Mount Volcanic peak in the Cascade Range, SW Washington, USA. After remaining dormant from 1857, it erupted on 18 May 1980, killing 60 people. The 2,950m (9,580ft) summit was reduced to 2,560m (8,312ft), with a deep horseshoe crater. Two more eruptions occurred in the following two weeks, and it is predicted to erupt again in the early 21st-century.

St John of Jerusalem, Knights Hospitallers of *See* KNIGHTS HOSPITALLERS

St John's Port and capital of Antigua, in the Leeward Islands, West Indies. Industries: tourism, rum, sugar, cotton. Pop. (1992) 38,000.

St John's Provincial capital and major port of Newfoundland, Canada, on the SE coast of Newfoundland Island. Founded in 1583, it is one of the oldest settlements in North America. Industries: fishing and fish processing, iron, shipbuilding, textiles, paper. Pop. (1996) 174,000.

Saint-Just, Louis Antoine Léon de (1767–94) French revolutionary. A leading JACOBIN, he helped in the downfall of the GIRONDINS (June 1793) and was a member of the Committee of Public Safety during the REIGN OF TERROR. Saint-Just was executed with ROBESPIERRE after the coup of 9 Thermidor (27 July 1794).

St Kitts-Nevis Self-governing state in the Leeward Islands, West Indies. The state includes the islands of Saint Kitts (Saint Christopher), Nevis and Somberro. BASSETERRE (on Saint Kitts) is the capital. The islands were discovered in 1493 by COLUMBUS and settled by the English (1623) and the French (1624). Disputes over possession were settled in Britain's favour in 1783, and the islands achieved self-government in 1967. Industries: tourism, sugar, cotton, salt, coconuts. Area: 310sq km (120sq mi). Pop. (2000) 44,000.

Saint Laurent, Louis Stephen (1882–1973) Canadian statesman, prime minister (1948–57). A distinguished lawyer, he was justice minister and attorney-general (1941–46). Saint Laurent succeeded W.L. MACKENZIE KING as prime minister and leader of the Liberal Party.

Saint-Laurent, Yves (1936–) French fashion designer. An assistant to Christian DIOR, he established his own Paris house in 1961. Saint-Laurent's "chic beatnik" look epitomized 1960s Parisian style with his combination of turtleneck knitwear and skin-tight trousers.

St Lawrence Second-longest river in Canada, flowing from the NE end of Lake Ontario to the Gulf of St Lawrence, Québec. The river forms the boundary between the USA and Canada for c.180km (110mi) of its total length of 1,200km (750mi). Since the completion of the ST LAWRENCE SEAWAY in 1959, the river has been navigable to all but the very largest vessels. The St Lawrence system of canals, locks and dams generates much of the hydroelectric power used in Ontario and New York.

St Lawrence Seaway Waterway in Canada and the USA. Built in the 1950s, it connects the GREAT LAKES with the Atlantic Ocean. The St Lawrence Seaway extends c.750km (470mi) from N of Montréal down to the N shore of Lake Erie, using canals and locks that bypass the rapids along the ST LAWRENCE River. The waterway also includes the Welland Canal, which bypasses Niagara Falls. The St Lawrence Seaway allows ocean-going vessels to reach industrial lakeside ports of central North America, such as Detroit, Chicago and Toronto.

St Louis City and port in E Missouri, USA, on the Mississippi River near its confluence with the Missouri. The second-largest city in Missouri, it was founded in 1763 by the French. It was held by Spain from 1770 to 1800, returned briefly to France, and then ceded to the USA in the Louisiana Purchase (1803). Industries: mineral processing, brewing, chemicals. Pop. (1992) 383,733.

St Lucia Volcanic island in the Windward group, West Indies; the capital is Castries (1992 pop. 53,883). The island changed hands 14 times between France and Britain before being ceded to Britain in 1814. It achieved self-government in 1979. Industries: tourism, bananas. Area: 616sq km (238sq mi). Pop. (2000) 177,000.

St Mark's BASILICA in Venice. Begun in 829 to enshrine the remains of the city's patron saint, St Mark, it was restored after a fire in 976. It was later demolished and rebuilt in the 11th century in the BYZANTINE style.

St Moritz Winter-sports centre and tourist resort on Lake St Moritz, E Switzerland, at an altitude of 1,822m (5,980ft). The site of the 1928 and 1948 Winter Olympics, it is the home of the Cresta Run. St Moritz is also noted for its mineral springs. Pop. (1991) 8,700.

St Paul State capital and port of entry, on the E bank of the Mississippi River, E Minnesota, USA. It lies just E of MINNEAPOLIS, its twin city. In 1849 St Paul became capital of Minnesota territory and developed rapidly as a river port and transport centre. Today, it is a major manufacturing and distribution centre. Industries: computers, electronics, printing, automobiles. Pop. (1992) 268,266.

St Paul's Anglican cathedral in London, built (1675–1710) on the site of a medieval cathedral that had been destroyed in the Great Fire of London (1666). It was designed in a classical style by Sir Christopher WREN.

St Peter's Great Christian BASILICA in the VATICAN CITY. In 1506, Pope Julius II laid the foundation stone

on the site of an earlier structure over the supposed grave of St Peter. The church was completed in 1615 during the reign of Pope Paul V, under the architectural supervision of Carlo Maderno (1556–1629).

St Petersburg (formerly Petrograd and Leningrad) Second-largest city in Russia and a major Baltic seaport at the E end of the Gulf of Finland, on the delta of the River Neva. Founded in 1703 by PETER I (THE GREAT), the city was the capital of Russia from 1712 to 1918. It was the scene of the Decembrist revolt of 1825 and the Bloody Sunday incident in the Russian Revolution of 1905. Renamed Petrograd in 1914, it was a centre of the political unrest that culminated in the RUSSIAN REVOLUTION. The workers of Petrograd were the spearhead of the 1917 revolution, and the city was renamed Leningrad (1924). It suffered extensive damage during World War 2 and has been massively rebuilt. Renamed St Petersburg (1991) following the breakup of the Soviet Union, it enjoys federal status within the Russian Republic. Industries: shipbuilding, heavy engineering, brewing, publishing, electronics, chemicals. Pop. (1994) 4,883,000.

St Pierre and Miquelon Group of eight small islands in the Gulf of St Lawrence, SW of Newfoundland, Canada. The capital is St Pierre (pop. 5,000) on the island of the same name; Miquelon is the largest island. The group was claimed for France in 1535 and since 1985 has been a "territorial collectivity", sending delegates to the French parliament. Fishing is the most important activity and has led to disputes with Canada. Area: 242sq km (93sq mi). Pop. (2000) 6,000.

Saint-Saëns, Charles Camille (1835–1921) French composer, pianist and organist. His conservative musical style is best represented by his third symphony (1886) and his sonatas. He also wrote descriptive works, such as *Danse Macabre* (1874) and *Carnival of the Animals* (1886). His operas include *Samson and Delilah* (1877).

Saint-Simon, Claude Henry de Rouvroy, Comte de (1760–1825) French social philosopher who fought in the American Revolution. In *Du Systeme Industriel* (1820–21), he argued for an industrialized state directed by scientist-businessmen. The ideals of egalitarianism and solidarity presented in *The New Christianity* (1825) influenced SOCIALISM and the work of Auguste COMTE.

St Sophia *See* HAGIA SOPHIA

St Thomas Second-largest of the US VIRGIN ISLANDS, West Indies. Charlotte Amalie, capital of US Virgin Islands, is on the S coast. The first European to discover the island was Christopher COLUMBUS in 1493. It was first settled by the Dutch. Industries: rum, tourism. Area: 72sq km (28sq mi). Pop. (1990) 48,166.

St Valentine's Day Massacre (14 February 1929) Gangland killings in Chicago, Illinois, USA. The perpetrators were gunmen of Al CAPONE, disguised as policemen, and the seven victims were members of a rival gang of bootleggers during the PROHIBITION era.

St Vincent and the Grenadines Island state between St Lucia and Grenada, Windward Islands, West Indies. The capital is Kingstown (1991 pop. 26,233). It comprises the volcanic island of St Vincent and five islands of the Grenadine group, including Mustique. St Vincent remained uncolonized until British settlement in 1762. St Vincent was part of the British Windward Islands colony from 1880 to 1958. Self-government was granted in 1969, followed by full independence within the Commonwealth of Nations in 1979. Agriculture dominates the economy; major crops include arrowroot, bananas and coconuts. Area: 388sq km (150sq mi). Pop. (2000) 128,000.

Sakhalin (Jap. *Karafuto*) Island off the E coast of Russia, between the seas of Okhotsk and Japan. The capital is Yuzhno-Sakhalinsk (1992 pop. 174,000). Settled by Russians and Japanese in the 18th and 19th centuries, it came under Russian control in 1875. In 1905, Japan regained the S but was forced to cede it again in 1945. The island is mountainous and forested, with a harsh climate. Sakhalin has large deposits of coal and iron ore; oil extracted in the NE is piped to the Russian mainland. Industries: timber, fishing, canning. Area: 76,400sq km (29,500sq mi). Pop. (1989) 709,000.

Sakharov, Andrei Dimitrievich (1921–89) Soviet physicist and social critic. His work in nuclear FUSION was instrumental in the development of the Soviet HYDROGEN BOMB. An outspoken defender of civil liberties, Sakharov created the Human Rights Committee in 1970 and received the 1975 Nobel Peace Prize.

Saki (1870–1916) (Hector Hugh Munro) Scottish writer. His reputation rests on his short stories, among them the collections *Reginald* (1904), *Reginald in Russia* (1910) and *Beasts and Superbeasts* (1914). His novels include *The Unbearable Bassington* (1912).

Saladin (1138–93) (Salah ad-din) Muslim general and founder of the Ayyubid dynasty. From 1152, he was a soldier and administrator in Egypt. Appointed grand vizier in 1169, Saladin overthrew the FATIMIDS in 1171 and made himself sultan. After conquering most of Syria, he gathered widespread support for a JIHAD to drive the Christians from Palestine (1187). Saladin reconquered Jerusalem, provoking the Third CRUSADE (1189). His rule restored Egypt as a major power and introduced a period of stability and growth.

Salam, Abdus (1926–) Pakistani physicist who proposed (1967) a theory that unifies the electromagnetic and weak nuclear forces (*see* FUNDAMENTAL FORCES) within the NUCLEUS of an ATOM. Salam and Steven WEINBERG worked independently on the theory (now known as the Weinberg-Salam theory). After the theory was proved experimentally, the pair shared the 1979 Nobel Prize for physics with Sheldon GLASHOW, who also independently came to similar conclusions.

Salamanca City on the River Tormes, W Spain, capital of Salamanca province. It was the scene of a British victory over the French in the PENINSULAR WAR (1812) and served (1937–38) as capital for the insurgents during the Spanish CIVIL WAR. Industries: pharmaceuticals, chemicals, tanning, brewing. Pop. (1995) 167,000.

salamander Any of 320 species of amphibians found worldwide, except in Australia and polar regions. It has an elongated body, a long tail and short legs. Most species lay eggs, but some give birth to live young. The largest European species, the fire salamander (*Salamandra salamandra*), can reach a length of 28cm (11in). Order Urodela.

Salazar, António de Oliveira (1889–1970) Dictator of Portugal (1932–68). He became prime minister and assumed dictatorial powers (1932). Imposing a semi-fascist constitution (1933), Salazar held power with a powerful army and secret police, enforcing law and order at the cost of economic progress. He was sympathetic to FRANCO in Spain, remained neutral in World War 2 and subsequently sought good relations with the West.

Salem State capital of Oregon, on the Willamette River, USA. Founded in 1840 by Methodist missionaries, it was made territorial capital in 1851 and state capital in 1859. Industries: timber, paper, textiles. Pop. (1990) 112,050.

Salem City on Massachusetts Bay, NE Massachusetts, USA, 22km (14mi) NE of Boston. First settled in 1626, Salem achieved notoriety for its witchcraft trials (1692),

when 19 people were hanged. Industries: electrical products, leather goods, tourism. Pop. (1990) 38,090.

Salic law Code promulgated in the 5th century by the Salian Franks, German settlers in Gaul, which included a law that forbade daughters to inherit land. This law was cited after the 14th century as judicial ground for the exclusion of women, and those descended through the female line, from succession to the French throne. Its contravention by EDWARD III's claim to the French throne through his mother contributed to the outbreak of the HUNDRED YEARS' WAR.

salicylic acid ($C_7H_6O_3$) Colourless, crystalline solid, derivatives of which are used as analgesics (including ASPIRIN, acetylsalicylic acid), antiseptics, dyes and liniments. It occurs naturally in plants, including willow bark and oil of wintergreen.

Salieri, Antonio (1750–1825) Italian composer. As court composer in Vienna, he composed many operas (with which he made his reputation), much sacred music, and vocal and orchestral works. His pupils included Beethoven, Schubert and Liszt.

Salinger, J.D. (Jerome David) (1919–) US novelist. He achieved fame with his first book and only novel, *Catcher in the Rye* (1951). The story of a tortured teenager, it is recounted in modern speech, and its style influenced a generation of new US writers. His other works are collections of short stories, including *Franny and Zooey* (1961).

Salisbury, Robert Arthur Talbot Gascoyne-Cecil, 3rd Marquess of (1830–1903) British statesman, prime minister (1885–86, 1886–92, 1895–1902). Salisbury entered Parliament as a Conservative in 1853, and served in Benjamin DISRAELI's administration (1874–80). On Disraeli's death (1881), he became leader of the opposition to GLADSTONE's government. In each of Salisbury's terms in office, he also served as foreign secretary, guiding Britain's imperial and colonial affairs. Despite initial success, his diplomacy of "splendid isolation" resulted in the SOUTH AFRICAN WARS (1899–1902). Salisbury was succeeded by his nephew, Arthur BALFOUR.

Salish Band of Native North Americans who were formerly the principal inhabitants of parts of present-day Idaho, Montana, Oregon and Washington in the USA and British Columbia in Canada. There are two major groupings – Coast Salish and Interior Salish. Coast Salish were a fishing community, and today *c*.12,000 live on reservations in the USA and Canada. The Interior Salish lived on the plateau E of the US Coast Mountains and the Canadian Coast Range. Today *c*.20,000 remain on reservations in Canada and the USA.

saliva Fluid secreted into the mouth by the SALIVARY GLANDS. In vertebrates, saliva is composed of *c*.99% water with dissolved traces of sodium, potassium, calcium and the ENZYME amylase. Saliva softens and lubricates food to aid swallowing, and amylase starts the digestion of starches.

salivary glands Three pairs of GLANDS located on each side of the mouth that form and secrete SALIVA. The parotid gland, just below and in front of each ear, is the largest of the salivary glands and the one that becomes enlarged in mumps; the submaxillary gland is near the angle of the lower jaw; and the sublingual gland is under the side of the tongue.

Salk, Jonas Edward (1914–95) US medical researcher. In 1952, he developed the first vaccine against poliomyelitis, using inactivated poliomyelitis virus as an immunizing agent. Extensive tests of the vaccine began in 1954 and mass immunization programmes followed.

salmon Marine and freshwater fish of the Northern Hemisphere. The Pacific salmon (*Oncorhynchus*) hatches, spawns and dies in freshwater but spends its adult life in the ocean. The Atlantic salmon (*Salmo salar*) is a marine trout that spawns in rivers on each side of the Atlantic Ocean and then returns to the sea. Weight: to 36kg (80lb). Family Salmonidae.

Salmond, Alex (Alexander Elliott Anderson) (1954–) Scottish politician, national convener (1990–2000) of the SCOTTISH NATIONAL PARTY (SNP). Salmond was elected to Parliament in 1987. Despite pressing for full Scottish independence, he agreed to participate in a devolved assembly for Scotland. He resigned in 2000 and was succeeded by John Swinney.

salmonella Several species of rod-shaped bacteria that cause intestinal infections in human beings and animals. *Salmonella typhi* causes TYPHOID FEVER; other species cause GASTROENTERITIS. The bacteria are transmitted by carriers, particularly flies, and in food and water.

Salome (active 1st century AD) Daughter of Herodias and stepdaughter of Herod Antipas. She conspired with her mother to have JOHN THE BAPTIST executed.

Salon Official art exhibitions of the French Royal Academy. The term derives from the venue of the original exhibition in 1667, the *Salon d'Apollon* in the LOUVRE. The conservative nature of the institution led progressive artists to form (1863) a rival *Salon des Refusés*.

Salonica *See* THESSALONÍKI

salsa Term first used in the early 1970s for the Cuban-inspired music being produced in New York. Salsa is a percussive and brass-led big-band music. It embraces dance forms, including rumba, mambo and guaracha.

salsify (oyster plant, vegetable oyster) Hardy biennial plant with a taproot. It is grown as a vegetable and prized for its oyster-like flavour. Height: to 1.2m (4ft). Family Asteraceae/Compositae; species *Tragopogon porrifolius*.

salt Ionic compound formed, along with water, when an ACID is neutralized by a BASE. The hydrogen of the acid is replaced by a metal or ammonium ion. The most familiar salt is SODIUM CHLORIDE. Salts are typically crystalline compounds, usually soluble in water. They are formed of ions held together by electrostatic forces, and in solution they can conduct electricity.

Salt Lake City State capital of Utah, USA, 21km (13mi) E of GREAT SALT LAKE. Founded in 1847 by the MORMONS under Brigham YOUNG, it grew rapidly to become capital of the Territory of Utah (1856) and the State of Utah (1896). Salt Lake City is the world headquarters of the Mormon Church. Zinc, gold, silver, lead and copper are mined nearby. Other industries: missiles, rocket engines, oil refining. Pop. (1992) 165,835.

saluki Royal coursing dog of Egypt, perhaps the oldest domesticated breed. It was known as long ago as 7000–6000 BC. It has a long, narrow head and pendulous ears. It is one of the swiftest dogs. Height: to 71cm (28in) at shoulder; weight: to 27kg (60lb).

Salvador (Bahia) Seaport city in E central Brazil; capital of BAHIA state. Founded by the Portuguese in 1549 as Bahia, it was the capital of Brazil until 1763. Portuguese colonizers built vast sugar plantations using African slave labour, and the city is noted for its African culture. Industries: oil refining, petrochemicals, tobacco, sugar, coffee, industrial diamonds. Pop. (1991) 2,056,000.

Salvador, El *See* EL SALVADOR

Salvation Army International Christian society devoted to the propagation of the gospel among the working classes. Its origin was the Christian Revival Association founded (1865) in London by William

BOOTH. In 1878, it became the Salvation Army and the members, led by "General" Booth, were given ranks. Under the leadership of Booth's son, Bramwell, its work spread to other parts of the world.

Salween River in Southeast Asia. It rises in the Tibetan Plateau, E Tibet, and flows S through Yunnan province, cutting deep gorges through the terrain. It empties into the Andaman Sea. It forms many rapids along its course and, despite its length of *c*.2,800km (1,740mi), is navigable for only 120km (75mi) upstream.

Salzburg City on the River Salzach, NW Austria, capital of the Alpine Salzburg state. It grew around a 7th-century monastery and became part of Bavaria in 1809. It was returned to Austria by the Congress of Vienna. It is known as Mozart's birthplace and is the home of several music festivals. Industries: tourism. Pop. (1991) 144,000.

Samaria Ancient region and town of central Palestine. It was built as the capital of the N kingdom of Israel in the 9th century BC. Conquered by Shalmaneser *c*.722 BC and SARGON, Samaria was later destroyed by John Hyrcanus I and rebuilt by HEROD THE GREAT. *See also* SAMARITANS

Samaritans Descendants of the citizens of SAMARIA who escaped deportation after their kingdom was overrun by the Assyrians in 722 BC. The Jews to the south rejected them. The Samaritans call themselves "Children of Israel" (Bene-Yisreal), and their sole religious scripture is the TORAH.

samarium (symbol Sm) Grey-white metallic element of the LANTHANIDE SERIES. First identified spectroscopically in 1879, its chief ores are monazite and bastnasite. Samarium is used in carbon-arc lamps, as a neutron absorber in NUCLEAR REACTORS and as a catalyst. Some samarium alloys are used in making powerful permanent magnets. Properties: at.no. 62; r.am. 150.35; r.d. 7.52; m.p. 1,072°C (1,962°F); b.p. 1,791°C (3,256°F); most common isotope Sm^{152} (26.72%).

Samarkand City in the fertile Zeravshan valley, SE Uzbekistan. One of the oldest cities in Asia, it was conquered by ALEXANDER THE GREAT in 329 BC. A vital trading centre on the SILK ROAD, it flourished under the Arab UMAYYAD empire of the 8th century. In 1220, it was destroyed by GENGHIS KHAN but in 1370 was made the capital of the Mongol empire of TAMERLANE. Ruled by the Uzbeks from the 16th century, it was taken by the Russians in 1868, though it remained largely a centre of Muslim culture. Products: cotton, silk, leather goods, wine, tea, carpets, canned fruit, motor-vehicle parts. It is a major scientific research centre. Pop. (1993) 368,000.

Samoa Volcanic island group in the S Pacific, comprising the independent state of WESTERN SAMOA and the US-administered AMERICAN SAMOA. Extending *c*.560km (350mi), the islands are fringed by coral reefs.The majority of the population are indigenous Polynesians. The first European discovery of the islands was in 1722.

Sampras, Pete (1971–) US tennis player. In 1990, he became the youngest-ever winner of the US Open and also won the first Grand Slam Cup. He went on to win a further three US Opens (1993, 1995–96), seven Wimbledon titles (1993–95, 1997, 1998, 1999, 2000) and the Australian Open (1994, 1997).

Samson Israelite judge and Old Testament hero renowned for his great physical strength. Samson was a Nazarite, whose strength lay in his long hair. When his mistress, DELILAH, discovered this, she had his hair cut off while he slept and handed him over to the PHILISTINES. Samson regained his strength as his hair regrew, and when called upon to display his strength in the Philistine Temple of Dagon, he pulled down its central pillars and roof, killing himself and thousands of his captors.

Samuel Ninth and tenth books of the OLD TESTAMENT. Through the stories of Samuel, the prophet and judge, and of SAUL and DAVID, Israel's first two kings, they describe the transition of ISRAEL from a collection of tribes under separate chiefs to a single nation ruled through a monarchy. Historically the events belong roughly to the 11th century BC.

Samurai Member of the elite warrior class of feudal Japan. Beginning as military retainers in the 10th century, the samurai came to form an aristocratic ruling class. They conformed to a strict code of conduct, known as BUSHIDO ("the way of the warrior").

San (Bushmen) Khoisan-speaking people of S Africa. They have lived in the region for thousands of years and until recently had a hunting and gathering culture. About half still follow the traditional ways, mostly in the Kalahari region of Botswana and Namibia.

Sana'a (San'a) Capital and largest city of Yemen, 65km (40mi) NE of the Red Sea port of Hodeida. Situated on a high plateau at 2,280m (7,500ft), it claims to be the world's oldest city, founded by Shem, eldest son of Noah. During the 17th century and from 1872 to 1918, it was part of the Ottoman Empire. In 1918, it became capital of an independent Yemen Arab Republic and in 1990 capital of the new, unified Yemen. It is noted for its handicrafts. Agriculture (grapes) and industry (iron) are also important. Pop. (1995) 972,000.

San Andreas Fault Geological FAULT line extending more than 950km (600mi) through California, USA. It lies on the boundary between the North American and the eastern Pacific plates of the Earth's crust. PLATE TECTONIC movement causes several thousand EARTHQUAKES each year, although only a few are significant. The most destructive occurred in 1906: it horizontally displaced land around the fault by up to 6.4m (21ft) and killed 503 people. Notable tremors occurred in 1989 and 1994.

San Antonio City on the San Antonio River, S central Texas, USA. In 1718, Martín de Alarcón founded the mission-fort of San Antonio de Valero (the ALAMO). San Antonio became the major Spanish settlement in Texas. In 1821, the town became part of an independent Mexico. In 1835, Texas settlers revolted against Mexican rule. The Battle of the Alamo (1836) saw 187 settlers defend the fort for 13 days against 5,000 Mexican troops. The fort was captured (6 March) and all the defenders killed. After Texas became a US state in 1845, the city flourished with the arrival of the railway (1877). Industries: military, aerospace, electronics, oil refining, chemicals, financial services, tourism. Pop. (1994) 998,905.

sanctions Punitive action taken by one or more states against another stopping short of direct military intervention. Sanctions can include the cessation of trade, severing of diplomatic relations, the use of a blockade, and the breaking of cultural and sporting contacts.

sanctuary Holy or reserved part of any religious building. In a Roman temple the sanctuary was called the *adytum* or *cella*. In a Christian church, the chancel or presbytery is the sanctuary. The term also applied to a church precinct or other sacred place where a fugitive from justice could claim immunity from arrest.

Sand, George (1804–76) French novelist, b. Amandine Aurore Lucie Dupin. Romantic novels such as *Lélia* (1833) and *Mauprat* (1837) advocate women's right to independence. Her later work includes *The Haunted Pool* (1846) and *The Master Bellringers* (1853), which are masterpieces of rural life. Her autobiographical works include *A Winter in Majorca* (1842). She is also remembered for her relationships with Musset and Chopin.

sand Mineral particles worn away from rocks by EROSION, individually large enough to be distinguished with the naked eye. Sand is composed mostly of QUARTZ, but black sand (containing volcanic rock) and coral sand also occur. *See also* SANDSTONE

sandalwood Any of several species of Asian trees of the genus *Santalum*, many of which are PARASITES on the roots of other plants. The fragrant wood is used in carving and joss sticks. The distilled oil is used in perfumes and medicines. Height: to 10m (33ft). Family Santalaceae.

Sandburg, Carl (1878–1967) US poet and biographer. He was strongly influenced by Walt Whitman. His first volume of poetry was *Chicago Poems* (1916). Other collections include *Cornhuskers* (Pulitzer Prize, 1918), *Smoke and Steel* (1920), *Good Morning, America* (1928) and *The People, Yes* (1936). Sandburg also won Pulitzer Prizes for his *Complete Poems* (1950) and for the biography *Abraham Lincoln: The War Years* (1939).

sand dollar Marine ECHINODERM, similar to a STARFISH. It has a round, flattened body, a fused skeleton and five radiating double rows of respiratory feet on both sides. Species *Echinarachnius parma*.

sand hopper (sand flea) Any of several species of terrestrial crustaceans. The nocturnal European sand hopper (*Talitrus saltator*) lives on beaches near the high tide mark, emerging to feed on organic debris. Length: to 1.5cm (0.6in). Order Amphipoda; family Talitridae.

San Diego City in S California, USA, almost adjoining Tijuana on the Mexican border. In 1769, the first Spanish fort in California was founded on the site. Located on a fine natural Pacific harbour, San Diego has a huge naval base and is an important centre for scientific research (especially oceanography). Other industries: aerospace, electronics, shipbuilding. Pop. (1992) 1,148,851.

Sandinistas (Sandinista National Liberation Front) Revolutionary group in Nicaragua. They took their name from Augusto Cesar Sandino (1895–1934), who was killed for his opposition to the dominant SOMOZA family. The Sandinistas overthrew the Somoza regime in 1979 and formed a government led by Daniel ORTEGA. In power, they were opposed by right-wing guerrillas, the CONTRAS, supported by the USA. The conflict ended when the Sandinista agreed to free elections. They lost, but the Contras were disbanded and the Sandinistas remain an influential political force.

sandpiper Wading bird that breeds in cold regions and migrates long distances to winter in warm areas, settling in grass or low bushes near water. It feeds on invertebrates and nests in a grass-lined hole in the ground. Length: 15–60cm (6–24in). Family Scolopacidae.

sandstone SEDIMENTARY ROCK composed of sand grains cemented in such materials as SILICA or calcium carbonate. Most sand grains contain QUARTZ; other minerals in sandstone include feldspars and micas. Iron also occurs, which tends to give sandstones a reddish or brownish colour. Most sandstones are formed by the accumulation of river sediments on the seabed. They are then compressed and uplifted to form new lands.

San Francisco City and port in W California, USA, on a peninsula bounded by the Pacific Ocean (W) and San Francisco Bay (E), which are connected by the Golden Gate Strait. Founded by the Spanish in 1776, it was captured (1846) by the USA in the Mexican War. A gold rush (1848) swelled the town's population. Devastated by an earthquake and fire in 1906, San Francisco was quickly rebuilt and prospered with the opening of the Panama Canal. Industry developed rapidly, and it became the leading commercial city on the West Coast. Today, it comprises (with OAKLAND and SAN JOSE) the fifth-largest metropolitan area in the USA. Its mild climate and cosmopolitan feel make it a major tourist centre. Other industries: shipbuilding, oil refining, aircraft, fishing, printing and publishing. Pop. (1992) 728,921.

San Francisco Conference on International Organization (1945) Meeting that drafted the charter forming the United Nations (UN). Delegates representing 50 nations met in San Francisco from 25 April. With World War 2 ending, the Allies wanted to safeguard further peace. The UN charter was signed on 26 June.

Sanger, Frederick (1918–) English biochemist who became the first person to win two Nobel Prizes for chemistry. Sanger was awarded his first prize in 1958 for finding the structure of INSULIN. His second came in 1980 (shared with the US molecular biologists Walter GILBERT and Paul Berg) after work on the chemical structure of NUCLEIC ACID.

Sanger, Margaret Higgins (1883–1966) US social reformer, founder of the first birth-control clinic in North America (1916), in Brooklyn, New York. She advocated birth control to prevent dangerous, illegal abortions and to alleviate poverty.

Sanhedrin Ancient Jewish religious council, prominent in Jerusalem during the period of Roman rule in Palestine. The Great Sanhedrin is believed to have served as a legislative and judicial body on both religious and political issues. JESUS CHRIST appeared before the Sanhedrin after his arrest.

San José Capital and largest city of Costa Rica, also capital of San José province in central Costa Rica. Founded c.1736, it succeeded Cartago as capital of Costa Rica in 1823 and became the centre of a prosperous coffee trade. Products: coffee, sugar cane, cacao, vegetables, fruit, tobacco. Pop. (1992) 303,000.

San Jose City in W California, USA, 64km (40mi) SE of San Francisco. Founded in 1777, it was California's capital from 1849 to 1851. It is the centre of a rich fruit-growing region, but is now best known as the focal point of "Silicon Valley", the hub of the US computer industry. Pop. (1992) 801,331.

San Jose scale Scale insect introduced into California in c.1880 from E Asia. Now spread across the USA, these insects suck juices from trees and shrubs, often destroying the plants. Length: 0.1in (2.5mm). Family Diaspididae; species *Quadraspidiotus perniciosus*.

San Juan Capital, largest city and major port of PUERTO RICO, on the NE coast of the island. It has one of the finest harbours in the West Indies. Founded in 1508, the port prospered during the 18th and 19th centuries, and in 1898 was captured by the USA during the SPANISH-AMERICAN WAR. San Juan is the commercial and financial centre of Puerto Rico. Exports: coffee, tobacco, fruit, sugar. Industries: cigars, sugar refining, rum distilling, metal products, pharmaceuticals, tourism. Pop. (1996) 434,000.

San Juan Hill, Battle of *See* SPANISH-AMERICAN WAR

San Luis Potosí State in central Mexico, primarily on Mexico's N plateau; the capital is San Luis Potosí (1990 pop. 525,733). It is the chief mining state of Mexico, with mines yielding gold, copper, zinc, bismuth and (especially) silver since the 18th century. Arid conditions result in little farming, but the Pánuco River Valley produces coffee, tobacco and sugar. Area: 62,848sq km (24,268sq mi). Pop. (1990) 2,003,187.

San Marino World's smallest republic and perhaps Europe's oldest state, in the Apennines near the Adriatic Sea, NE Italy. According to legend, it was founded in the early 4th century AD. Its mountainous terrain has

enabled it to retain a separate status, becoming an independent commune in the 13th century. The economy is largely agricultural. Tourism is vital to the state's income. While San Marino has its own currency and stamps, Italian and Vatican City equivalents are widely used. There are two towns: Serraville (1991 pop. 7,264) and the capital, San Marino (1993 pop. 4,335). Area: 61sq km (24sq mi). Pop. (2000) 25,000.

San Martín, José de (1778–1850) South American revolutionary. He led revolutionary forces in Argentina, Peru and Chile, gaining a reputation as a bold commander and imaginative strategist. After defeating the Spaniards in Argentina, San Martín gained the element of surprise in Chile (1817–18) by crossing the Andes. He captured Peru (1821) after an unexpected naval attack. In 1822 San Martín surrendered his effective rule of Peru to Simón BOLÍVAR and retired to Europe.

San Salvador Capital and largest city of El Salvador in central El Salvador. Founded in 1524 near the volcano of San Salvador, which rises to 1,885m (6,184ft) and last erupted in 1917, the city has frequently been damaged by earthquakes. The main industry is the processing of coffee grown on the rich volcanic soils. Other industries: beer, textiles, tobacco. Pop. (1992) 422,570.

Sanskrit Classical language of India, the literary and sacred language of HINDUISM and a forerunner of the modern Indo-Iranian languages spoken in N India, Pakistan, Nepal and Bangladesh. Sanskrit was brought to India (c.1500 BC) by immigrants from the NW. The old form of the language (Vedic Sanskrit) gradually became simplified, achieving its classical form c.500. Sanskrit is one of the INDO-EUROPEAN LANGUAGES. Although only c.3,000 Indians are able to speak Sanskrit today, it has been designated one of India's national languages.

Sanskrit literature Classical literature of India. The two main periods in Sanskrit literature are the Vedic (c.1500–c.200 BC) and the overlapping Classical (c.500 BC–c.AD 1000). The Vedic period produced the VEDAS, the earliest works in Sanskrit literature and among the most important. Later Vedic literature includes the UPANISHADS. The early classical period contributed the MAHABHARATA and the RAMAYANA. They are significant both as literature and as Hindu sacred works. *See also* INDIAN LITERATURE

Santa Anna, Antonio López de (1794–1876) Mexican general and dictator. He was the dominant political figure in Mexico from 1823 to 1855, sometimes as president, sometimes unofficially as the result of a coup. In 1836, he led the forces that captured the ALAMO, but failed to subdue the rebellion in TEXAS. He regained power after gallant action against a French raid on Vera Cruz (1838). After his failure in the MEXICAN WAR (1846–48), he went into exile. He returned to power in 1853 but was overthrown in 1855.

Santa Cruz de Tenerife Capital of the CANARY ISLANDS and largest city in TENERIFE. Founded in 1494, it has a fine harbour and exports fruit, vegetables and sugar. Industries: oil refining, tourism. Pop. (1995) 205,000.

Santa Fe (formerly Santa Fé de Vera Cruz) City in N Argentina, capital of Sante Fé province. Founded in 1573, it was the centre of Jesuit missions and a fortification against the Native Americans. Its main exports are grain, cotton, timber, wool and cattle. Pop. (1991) 406,388.

Santa Fe State capital of New Mexico, USA, at the foot of the Sangre de Cristo Mountains. The oldest US capital city, it was founded c.1609 by the Spanish and acted as a centre of Spanish–Native American trade for more than 200 years. Mexico's independence in 1821 opened trade with the USA. Santa Fe functioned as the w terminus of the Santa Fe Trail. In 1846, US troops captured the city, and in 1850 the region became US territory, achieving statehood in 1912. Today, it is primarily an administrative, tourist and resort centre. Pop. (1992) 59,004.

Santayana, George (1863–1952) US philosopher and poet, b. Spain. After 1939, Santayana withdrew from the world, a seclusion reflected in the moral detachment of his writing. He stressed both the biological nature of the mind and its creative and rational powers. His works include *The Sense of Beauty* (1896), *The Life of Reason* (1905) and the popular novel *The Last Puritan* (1935).

Santer, Jacques (1937–) Luxembourg statesman, prime minister of Luxembourg (1984–94), president of the European Union (1994–99). Santer was a member of the Luxembourg Chamber of Deputies before being elected to the European Parliament, of which he was vice president (1975–77). In 1999, following charges of corruption, Santer and all the European commissioners resigned.

Santiago Capital of Chile, on the River Mapocho, central Chile. Founded in 1541, it was destroyed by an earthquake in 1647. Most of the city's architecture is post-1850. It is Chile's administrative, commercial and cultural centre, accounting for nearly one-third of the population. Industries: textiles, pharmaceuticals, food processing, clothing. Pop. (1995) 5,077,000.

Santiago de Cuba Second-largest city in Cuba, SE Cuba; capital of Santiago de Cuba province. Founded in 1514, it served as Cuba's capital from 1522 to 1589. The city harbour was a haven for buccaneers and was a scene of fighting in the Spanish-American War (1898). Fidel Castro's revolution against the Batista regime began here in 1953. Pop. (1994) 440,000.

Santo Domingo (formerly Cuidad Trujillo, 1936–61) Capital and chief port of the Dominican Republic, on the S coast of the island, on the River Ozama. Founded in 1496, the city is the oldest continuous European settlement in the Americas. It was the base for the Spaniards' conquering expeditions until it was devastated by an earthquake in 1562. It houses more than one-third of the country's population, many of whom work in the sugar industry. Pop. (1993) 2,135,000.

São Paulo City on the River Tietê, SE Brazil, capital of São Paulo state, located almost exactly on the Tropic of Capricorn. Founded by the Jesuits in 1554, it grew as the base for expeditions into the interior in search of minerals. It expanded in the 17th century as a trading centre for a large coffee region. While its large quantities of agricultural produce are now shipped through its port of Santos, São Paulo has become a major and diverse industrial centre attracting migrants from the interior. It is the world's fastest-growing metropolis. Pop. (1991) 9,646,185 (metropolitan area 16,567,317). São Paulo state houses up to 60% of Brazil's industry and most of its sugar production. Pop. (1991) 16,417,000.

São Tomé and Príncipe Republic in the Gulf of Guinea, 300km (190mi) off the W coast of Africa. The capital is São Tomé. The country consists of two main islands, São Tome (the largest) and Príncipe. The islands are volcanic and mountainous, the vegetation predominantly tropical rainforest. The islands were discovered (uninhabited) in 1471 and, in 1483, a settlement was established at São Tomé. In 1522, the islands became a Portuguese colony. The Dutch controlled the islands from 1641 to 1740, but the Portuguese regained control and established plantations. The official language is Portuguese and the major religion Roman Catholicism. The islands became independent when the Portuguese pulled out in 1975, ushering in 16 years of Marxist rule. Cocoa, coffee, bananas and coconuts are grown on plantations, and their export provides the main source of income. Area: 1,001sq km (387sq mi). Pop. (2000) 151,000.

sap Fluid that circulates water and nutrients through plants. Water is absorbed by the roots and carried, along with minerals, through the XYLEM to the leaves. Sap from the leaves is distributed throughout the plant.

Sapir, Edward (1884–1939) US anthropologist and linguist, b. Pomerania. His anthropological studies of Native Americans formed the basis of early linguistic anthropology. The Sapir-Whorf relativistic hypothesis argues that each language has its own unique choice of interpretations. His works include *Language: An Introduction to the Study of Speech* (1921).

sapphire Transparent to translucent gemstone variety of CORUNDUM. It has various colours produced by impurities of iron and titanium, the most valuable being deep blue.

Sappho Greek poet of the early 6th century BC. Her passionate love poetry, written on the island of Lesbos – from which the word lesbian derives – was regarded by PLATO as the expression of "the tenth Muse".

Sapporo Capital of Hokkaido prefecture, w Hokkaido, Japan. Japan's fifth-largest city, Sapporo is the industrial and cultural centre of Hokkaido. A noted winter sports resort, the city was host to the 1972 Winter Olympics – the first time the games were staged outside Europe and North America. Industries: timber, dairy-food processing, brewing, printing, tourism. Pop. (1995) 1,757,000.

saprophyte Plant that obtains its food from dead or decaying plant or animal tissue. Generally it has no CHLOROPHYLL. Saphrophytes include most FUNGI and some flowering plants.

Saracens Name applied by the ancient Greeks and Romans to the Arab tribes who threatened their borders. The name later included all Arabs and eventually all Muslims. As a term similar to "Moors", it was used by medieval Christians to denote their Muslim enemies.

Sarajevo Capital of Bosnia-Herzegovina, on the River Miljacka. It fell to the Turks in 1429 and became a flourishing commercial centre in the Ottoman Empire. Passing to the Austro-Hungarian Empire in 1878, the city was a centre of Serb and Bosnian resistance to Austrian rule. On 28 June 1914, the Austrian archduke Franz Ferdinand and his wife were assassinated here by a Serbian nationalist (an act that helped to precipitate World War 1). In 1991, Bosnia-Herzegovina declared its independence from Yugoslavia, and a bloody civil war ensued among Croatian, Bosnian and Serbian forces. Sarajevo became the focal point of the war between Bosnian Serb troops and Bosnian government forces. The city lay under prolonged siege, often without water, electricity or basic medical supplies. After the 1995 peace agreement (the Dayton Accord), it in effect became a Bosnian city, with the 1991 population figure of 526,000 drastically reduced as many Serbs fled.

Sarasvati In Hindu mythology, goddess of the arts, sciences and eloquent speech. Depicted as a beautiful young woman, she is credited with the invention of Sanskrit. She later became the consort of BRAHMA.

Saratoga, Battle of (October 1777) First American victory in the AMERICAN REVOLUTION, fought in upper New York. In the series of battles, the British were prevented from linking up with other forces at Albany and winning the Hudson valley. Surrounded, the British were forced to surrender to the Americans under Horatio GATES. The US victory persuaded the French to intervene against Britain.

Sarawak Largest state of Malaysia, in NW Borneo, comprising a highland interior and swampy coastal plain; the capital is Kuching City. Ruled as an independent state by Britain after 1841, it was made a British protectorate in 1888 and a crown colony in 1946. Sarawak became part of Malaysia in 1963, triggering a three-year dispute with Indonesia. Products: oil, coconuts, rice, rubber. Area: 124,449sq km (48,050sq mi). Pop. (1990) 1,648,217.

sarcoidosis Disorder of unknown cause characterized by enlargement of the lymph nodes and the formation of scar-like tissue in the lungs and possibly elsewhere in the body.

sarcoma Cancerous growth or TUMOUR arising from muscle, fat, bone, blood or lymph vessels or connective tissue. *See also* CANCER

sardine Small, marine food fish found throughout the world. It has a laterally compressed body, a large toothless mouth and oily flesh. Length: to 30cm (1ft). Species include the Californian *Sardinops caerulea*, South American *Sardinops sagax* and the European sardine, or PILCHARD, *Sardina pilchardus*. Family Clupeidae.

Sardinia Mountainous island of Italy, 208km (130mi) W of the Italian mainland, separated by the Tyrrhenian Sea. The only large city is Cágliari, the capital. A trading centre for the Phoenicians, Greeks, Carthaginians and Romans, Sardinia became a kingdom in 1720, and

in 1861 its king, VICTOR EMMANUEL II, became the first king of Italy. Wheat, barley, grapes, olives and tobacco are grown, and sheep and goats are reared. Salt extraction is important, and other minerals include coal, lead, magnesium, manganese and zinc. Area: 24,090sq km (9,302sq mi). Pop. (1992) 1,651,902.

Sargasso Sea Area of calm, barely moving water between the West Indies and the Azores in the N Atlantic. It takes its name from the large quantities of floating seaweed (*Sargassum*) covering its surface.

Sargent, John Singer (1856–1925) US painter. Greatly influenced by VELÁZQUEZ and HALS, he is best known for his glamorous and elegant portraits, such as *The Boit Children* (1882) and *Lord Ribblesdale* (1902).

Sargent, Sir (Harold) Malcolm (Watts) (1895–1967) English conductor. He conducted the Royal Choral Society from 1928 and the BBC Symphony Orchestra from 1950 to 1957. He was chief conductor (1948–67) of the PROMENADE CONCERTS.

Sargon (*c.*2334–*c.*2279 BC) King of Akkadia (*c.*2316–*c.*2279 BC). One of the first of the great Mesopotamian conquerors, he was a usurper who founded his capital at Agade (Akkad), from which his kingdom took its name. Sargon conquered Sumeria and upper Mesopotamia and extracted tribute from lands as far W as the Mediterranean.

Sargon (d. 705 BC) King of ASSYRIA (721–705 BC). He conquered SAMARIA in 721 BC and, according to tradition, dispersed those Israelites who became the "lost tribes" of Israel. Sargon established an imperial administration and defeated his enemies before being killed in battle against the Cimmarians.

Sark One of the CHANNEL ISLANDS of the United Kingdom, divided into Great Sark and Little Sark. Sark is part of the bailiwick of GUERNSEY, with a feudal organization dating from the late 17th century. There are no cars, and the residents pay no income tax. Industries: tourism. Area: 5.5sq km (2.1sq mi). Pop. (1991) 575.

Saroyan, William (1908–81) US novelist, short-story writer and dramatist. Saroyan followed the success of his first play, *My Heart's in the Highlands* (1939), with the Pulitzer Prize-winning *The Time of Your Life* (1939) and the autobiographical *My Name is Aram* (1940). His subsequent works were less successful, although *The Cave Dwellers* (1957) received some critical acclaim.

sarsaparilla Tropical, perennial vine of the genus *Smilax*, native to central and S America. Its roots are used to impart an aromatic flavour to medicines and drinks. The main species used are *S. aristolochiaefolia*, *S. regelii*, and *S. febrifuga*. Family Liliaceae.

Sartre, Jean-Paul (1905–80) French philosopher and writer, the leading advocate of EXISTENTIALISM. His debut novel, *Nausea* (1939), depicted man adrift in a godless universe, hostage to his own angst-ridden freedom. Sartre fought in the French Resistance during World War 2. His major philosophical work is *Being and Nothingness* (1943). After the war Sartre founded (1945) the philosophy periodical *Modern Times*. His complex relationship with Marxism is explored in *Critique of Dialectical Reason* (1960). Sartre refused the 1964 Nobel Prize for literature on "personal" grounds but is later said to have accepted it. He had a long-term relationship with Simone de BEAUVOIR.

Saskatchewan Province in W central Canada, the S half on the fertile Great Plains and the N half in the lake-strewn Canadian Shield. The principal cities are Saskatoon (1991 pop. 186,058), Regina (the capital, pop. 179,178), Prince Albert (34,181) and Moose Jaw

▲ **satellite** Four artificial-satellite orbits around the globe are illustrated. Two are equatorial: one, a geostationary satellite, orbits at 35,900km (21,500mi) (1); another has a lower orbit (2). A polar orbit, as used by remote sensing satellites, is shown running vertically around the Earth (3) and the last is an angled elliptical orbit used by communications satellites for the high latitudes of the Earth (4). The diagrams above the orbital diagram show the launching of an Intelsat communication satellite by a NASA shuttle (5) and the two main types of satellites. To prevent satellites being knocked off course by the fluctuations in the Earth's magnetic field, they remain stable in one of two ways. The first is to rotate the whole satellite, as is the case in "spinners", such as the Intelsat satellite (6). The other method is to have gyroscopes within the satellite (7).

(33,593). The first permanent white settlement was in 1774, but development was slow until the construction of the transcontinental Canadian Pacific Railroad in 1885. Saskatchewan was admitted to the Dominion of Canada in 1905. Wheat, oats, barley, rye, flax and rapeseed are grown. The province's rich mineral deposits include uranium, copper, zinc, gold, coal, oil, natural gas and the world's largest fields of potash. Most industries process raw materials, and steel is also manufactured. Area: 570,110sq km (251,700sq mi). Pop. (1991) 988,928.

Saskatchewan River in s central Canada, formed by the confluence of the North and South Saskatchewan rivers. It flows E to empty into Lake Winnipeg. With its tributaries, the Saskatchewan drains most of Canada's prairie provinces. Length: c.550km (340 mi).

sassafras Small E North American tree with furrowed bark, green twigs, yellow flowers and blue berries. Oil from the roots is used to flavour root beer. Family Lauraceae; species *Sassafras albidum*.

Sassanid (Sassanian) Royal dynasty of Persia (Iran) (AD 224–651). Founded by Ardashir I (r.224–241), the Sassanids revived the native Persian traditions of the ACHAEMENIDS, confirming ZOROASTRIANISM as the state religion. There were about 30 Sassanid rulers, the most important after Ardashir being Shapur II (309–379), Khoshru I (531–579) and Khoshru II (590–628), whose conquest of Syria, Palestine and Egypt marked the height of the dynasty's power. The Sassanids were finally overthrown by the Arabs.

Sassoon, Siegfried (1886–1967) English poet and author. His disillusionment with military service in World War 1 inspired some memorable war poetry. The semi-autobiographical trilogy *The Complete Memoirs of George Sherston* (1937) includes Sassoon's most famous novel, *Memoirs of a Fox-hunting Man* (1928).

Satan Name for the DEVIL. Satan first appeared in the Old Testament as an individual angel, subordinate to God. Gradually, however, Satan took on a more sinister role. In the New Testament, he was the devil who tempted JESUS CHRIST. Satan emerged in medieval Christian theology as the chief devil, ruler of hell and source of all evil.

satellite Celestial body orbiting a planet or star. In the Solar System, planets with satellites are Earth (1), Mars (2), Jupiter (16), Saturn (18), Uranus (15), Neptune (8) and Pluto (1). There are probably more satellites of the giant planets awaiting discovery. They vary enormously in their size, orbit, surface features and supposed origin.

satellite, artificial Man-made object placed in orbit around the Earth or other celestial body. Satellites can perform many tasks and can send back data or pictures to the Earth. Hundreds of satellites of various types orbit the Earth. They may study the atmosphere, or photograph the surface for scientific or military purposes. **Communications** satellites relay radio, television, telephone, telegraph and data signals from one part of the Earth to another. **Navigation** satellites transmit radio signals that enable navigators to determine their positions. The GLOBAL POSITIONING SYSTEM (GPS) uses satellites in this way. **Geodetic satellites** are used to make accurate measurements of the Earth's size and shape. *Sputnik 1* was the first artificial satellite, launched on 4 October 1957.

satellite television TELEVISION services transmitted to viewers via communications SATELLITES in orbit around the Earth. These satellites orbit the Equator and keep in time with the Earth's spin. As a result, each one remains above a fixed point on the Equator. Television companies beam their signals to the satellites from ground stations. The satellites retransmit the signals back to viewers'

SATURN: DATA
DIAMETER (EQUATORIAL): 120,536km (74,901mi)
MASS (EARTH = 1): 95.2
VOLUME (EARTH = 1): 744
DENSITY (WATER = 1): 0.71
ORBITAL PERIOD: 29.46 years
ROTATION PERIOD: 10h 13m 59s
AVERAGE SURFACE TEMPERATURE: −180°C (−356°F)
SURFACE GRAVITY (EARTH = 1): 1.19

dish-shaped receiving aerials. A fixed ANTENNA can receive many services from a single satellite.

Satie, Erik (1866–1925) French composer. He developed a deceptively simple style in piano pieces such as *Trois Gymnopédies* (1888). Satie also composed the ballets *Parade* (1917) and *Relâche* (1924), and a choral work, *Socrate* (1918).

satire Literary work in which human foibles and institutions are mocked, ridiculed and parodied. In Roman times a satire was a poem in hexameters, a form established through the work of Lucilius, HORACE and JUVENAL. In the Middle Ages it often took the form of *fabliaux* or bestiaries, using animal characters to illustrate typical human failings. Since Thomas MORE's *Utopia* (1516), utopian or dystopian fiction, such as ZAMYATIN's *We* (1924) and SWIFT's *Gulliver's Travels* (1726), has frequently been used as a medium for satire. Dramatists have often employed the form, as in the plays of ARISTOPHANES, Ben JONSON, MOLIÈRE, Oscar WILDE and Bertolt BRECHT.

Sato, Eisaku (1901–75) Japanese statesman, prime minister (1964–72). Sato held a number of cabinet posts (1948–64) before becoming prime minister. His term in office is notable for its foreign policy successes, such as the restoration of relations with South Korea (1965). Sato negotiated the return (1972) of OKINAWA from the USA. In 1974, he was awarded the Nobel Peace Prize.

saturated compound In organic chemistry, compounds in which the carbon atoms are bonded to one another by single COVALENT BONDS, not by the more reactive double or triple bonds. For this reason, they tend to be unreactive.

saturated fat Organic fatty compounds, the molecules of which contain only saturated FATTY ACIDS combined with GLYCEROL. These acids have long chains of carbon atoms that are bound together by single bonds only. *See also* SATURATED COMPOUND

saturated solution In chemistry, a SOLUTION containing so much of a dissolved compound (SOLUTE) that no more will dissolve at the same temperature.

Saturn Sixth planet from the Sun and second-largest in the SOLAR SYSTEM. Its famous rings are made up of particles ranging from dust to objects a few metres in size, all in individual orbits. The main rings are only about half a mile thick. VOYAGER space probes revealed the ring system to be made up of thousands of separate ringlets. Saturn has an internal heat source, which probably drives its weather systems. It is assumed to be composed predominantly of hydrogen, with an iron–silicate core about five times the Earth's mass, surrounded by an ice mantle of perhaps 20 Earth masses. The upper atmosphere contains 97% hydrogen and 3% helium, with traces of other gases. Saturn has 18 known satellites, including Titan, the only satellite in the Solar System to have a significant atmosphere.

satyr In Greek mythology, god of the woods and attendant of DIONYSUS. Sensual and lascivious, satyrs were later depicted by the Romans as goat-legged, goat-bearded men with budding horns. Satyr is also the common name for any butterfly of the Satyridae family.

Saud, Abdul Aziz ibn (1880–1953) Founder and first king of Saudi Arabia (1932–53). As leader of the Saudi dynasty, he was forced into exile in 1891 by the rival Rashid dynasty. He returned in 1902 and extended his authority, driving out the Turks and the Hashemites and founding the modern Saudi state in 1932. Ibn Saud was succeeded by his sons, **Ibn Abdul Aziz Saud** (r.1953–64) and **Faisal ibn Abd al Aziz** (r.1964–75). Saud (1902–69) acceded to the throne in 1953 but his fiscal mismanagement and personal extravagance caused a severe financial crisis in 1958. Soon afterwards his brother, Faisal (1904–75), took over all administrative powers, formally replacing him as king in 1964.

Saudi Arabia Arabic kingdom on the Arabian Peninsula, SW Asia. Saudi Arabia occupies about 75% of the peninsula. More than 95% of the land is desert. The Gulf of AQABA and the RED SEA lie off the W coast. The W coastal lands are divided into two main regions: the *Hejaz* (boundary) plain in the N includes the holy cities of MECCA and MEDINA and Saudi Arabia's main port, JIDDAH. In the S, is the *Asir* (inaccessible) highland region, which contains the country's highest point, Sawda, at 3,133m (10,279ft). The Tihama is a narrow, fertile SW coastal plain. In the centre lies the *Najd* (plateau), which contains Saudi Arabia's capital, RIYADH. The plateau descends E to the Al Hasa lowlands. This region is the centre of the Saudi oil industry, and contains Saudi Arabia's largest oasis. In the N is the Nafud Desert. The S of Saudi Arabia is dominated by the bleak Rub' al Khali (Empty Quarter), the world's largest expanse of sand. **Climate** Saudi Arabia has a hot, dry climate. The Asir highlands have an average rainfall of 300–500mm (12in–20in). The rest of the country has less than 100mm (4in) of rain **Vegetation** Grass and shrub provide pasture on the W highlands and parts of the central plateau. **History and Politics** Mecca is the holiest place in Islam. It was the birthplace of the Prophet Muhammad in AD 570, and is the site of the KAABA. In the 18th century, the Wahhabi (a strict Islamic sect) gained the allegiance of the Saud family, who formed an independent state in Nejd. With the support of the Bedouin, the Wahhabi rapidly conquered most of the Arabian peninsula. In the 1810s, the region was conquered by Turkey. Ibn SAUD laid the foundations of the modern state of Saudi Arabia. In 1902, Ibn Saud captured Riyadh and by 1906 had taken the whole of the Nejd. In 1913, the Turkish province of Al Hasa also fell. In 1920, Ibn Saud captured the Asir, and by 1925 he had conquered the Hejaz. In 1932, the territories were combined to form the kingdom of Saudi Arabia. Ibn Saud became king, ruling in accordance with the sharia of Wahhabi Islam. Oil was discovered in 1936 by the US company Arabian Standard Oil, which later became the Arabian American Oil Company (Aramco). In 1953, Ibn Saud died and was succeeded by his eldest son, King Saud, who ruled with the aid of Crown Prince Faisal. Saud's concern at the growing power of Nasser's Egypt was heightened by the overthrow of the Yemen royal family by pro-Nasser republican forces. Saud sent troops to Yemen to aid the monarchists. In 1964, Saud was overthrown, and Faisal became king. In 1970, Saudi troops were withdrawn from

Yemen. In 1971, British troops withdrew from the Gulf. Faisal supported the creation of the United Arab Emirates (UAE) and sought to increase national ownership of Saudi's oil wealth. In 1974, Saudi Arabia agreed to a 60% share in Aramco. In 1975, King Faisal was assassinated by his nephew, and Crown Prince Khalid became king. Khalid's conservatism was challenged by the growth of Islamic fundamentalism, especially in Iran. In 1979, Shiite fundamentalists captured the Great Mosque in Mecca. The rebellion was brutally suppressed. Saudi Arabia's support for Iraq in the IRAN-IRAQ WAR (1980–88) led to Iranian attacks on Saudi shipping. In 1982, Khalid died and was succeeded by Prince Fahd. In 1990, more than 1,400 pilgrims died in a stampede during the HAJJ. When Iraq invaded Kuwait in 1990, King Fahd invited coalition forces to protect Saudi against possible Iraqi aggression. Saudi air and land forces played a significant role in the Allied victory in the GULF WAR (1991). In 1996, Fahd suffered a stroke and control of the government shifted to the crown prince, Fahd's half-brother, Abdullah. In the same year, the council's president ruled out elections on Islamic grounds. Saudi Arabia has no formal constitution. It attracts much international criticism for human rights abuses, especially for its state executions and treatment of women and minorities. **Economy** Saudi Arabia is the world's largest producer and exporter of crude oil. GDP per capita (1999) US$9000. It has *c.*25% of the world's known oil reserves. Oil and oil products make up 85% of its exports. Oil revenue has been used to develop education, services, light industry, farming and purchasing of military hardware. In the mid-1980s, world oil prices slumped and many infrastructure projects were abandoned. Agriculture employs 48% of the workforce, although only 1% of the land is fertile. Crops grown in Asir and at oases include dates and other fruits, vegetables and wheat. Some nomadic livestock herders remain. Mecca is visited by more than 1.5 million pilgrims a year, making a vital addition to state revenue.

Saul First king of the Hebrew state of ancient ISRAEL (r.*c.*1020–*c.*1000 BC). He was the son of Kish, a member of the tribe of Benjamin. He was anointed by the prophet SAMUEL and acclaimed by all Israel. Through much of his reign he waged war against Israel's threatening neighbours, notably the PHILISTINES, the Ammonites and the Amalekites. He and his sons eventually died in battle against the Philistines on Mount Gilboa. The story of Saul is contained in the First Book of Samuel, the ninth book of the Old Testament.

sauna Wood-lined room in which a wood-fired stove (or an electric heater) raises the temperature to between 60 and 95°C (140 and 203°F). The sauna was originally a semi-religious exercise of the Finns.

Saussure, Ferdinand de (1857–1913) Swiss linguist, founder of modern linguistics. Saussure delivered a series of lectures at the University of Geneva between 1907 and 1911 that were published posthumously (1916) as *Course in General Linguistics*. For Saussure, language was a system of signs whose meaning is defined by their relations to each other. His work laid the foundation for STRUCTURALISM and SEMIOTICS.

savanna Plain with coarse grass and scattered tree growth, particularly the wide plains of tropical and subtropical regions. An extensive example is the savanna of the East African tableland.

Savannah City and port on the Savannah River, E Georgia, USA. The oldest city in Georgia, it was founded in 1733 and became the seat of the colonial government in 1754. During the American Revolution,

SAUDI ARABIA
AREA: 2,149,690sq km (829,995sq mi)
POPULATION: 20,697,000
CAPITAL (POPULATION): Riyadh (1,500,000)

Savannah was captured (1778) by the British and resisted all attempts at invasion until 1782. The city prospered on the tobacco and cotton trade. During the Civil War, Savannah remained a Confederate stronghold until December 1864. Savannah is a major port exporting tobacco, cotton and sugar. Industries: chemicals, petroleum, paper products, tourism. Pop. (1992) 138,908.

Savimbi, Jonas (1934–) Angolan political leader. Prominent in the struggle for independence from Portugal, he formed the National Union for the Total Independence of Angola (UNITA) in 1966. After independence (1975), the rival Popular Movement for the Liberation of Angola (MPLA) emerged as the major power and banned all other political parties. Savimbi mounted a guerrilla war against the MPLA. In 1991, President DOS SANTOS and Savimbi signed a peace agreement. Savimbi refused to recognize the 1992 re-election of Dos Santos, and civil war resumed. UNITA's dwindling support led to the Lusaka Protocol (1994). Savimbi refused the vice-presidency and fighting resumed as UNITA retained control of *c*.50% of Angola.

Savonarola, Girolamo (1452–98) Italian religious reformer. His sermons attacked the corruption and decadence of the papacy and the state of Florence. After the death of Lorenzo de' MEDICI (1494), Savonarola became spiritual and political leader of the city. His support for the invasion of CHARLES VIII of France infuriated Pope Alexander VI, who excommunicated Savonarola in 1497. Public hostility to his austere regime intensified. Savonarola was arrested and hanged for heresy.

Savoy European dynasty and ruling house of SAVOY and PIEDMONT from the 11th century, Sardinia from 1720 to 1861 and Italy from 1861 to 1946. The dynasty was founded by Humbert the Whitehanded (d. *c*.1047), the first Count of Savoy. Their seat was Chambéry, France, from 1232 to 1559, when Emmanuel Philibert relocated to Turin. The house of Savoy led the RISORGIMENTO movement, and Italy was unified under VICTOR EMMANUEL II.

Savoy Area of SE France, bounded by Lake Geneva (N), the River Rhône (W), the Dauphiné (S) and the Alps of Italy and Switzerland (E); it includes the departments of Haute Savoie and Savoie. It was part of the first Burgundian kingdom, the kingdom of Arles and, in the 11th century, the Holy Roman Empire (as a county). In 1416, it became a duchy and its area was enlarged, incorporating parts of France, Switzerland and Italy. An Italian state in the 16th century, it was part of the kingdom of SARDINIA after 1713. Savoy was annexed by France in 1792, returned to Sardinia in 1815 and finally ceded to France by the Treaty of Turin in 1860.

sawfish Any of several species of shark-like, flat-bodied RAYS that live in tropical marine and brackish waters. It has a grey or black-brown body with an elongated, saw-toothed snout resembling a flat blade. Length: to 5m (16ft). Family Pristidae; genus *Pristis*.

sawfly Any of 400 species of primitive, plant-feeding WASPS that lack a narrow waist between thorax and abdomen. Most sawflies are in the family Tenthredinidae. Length: to 20mm (0.8in). Order Hymenoptera.

Saxe-Coburg-Gotha Duchy in Saxony, Germany, whose ruling dynasty intermarried with many royal families. After Prince Albert married the English Queen VICTORIA, Saxe-Coburg-Gotha became the name of the English royal house until it was changed to Windsor in 1917.

saxifrage Perennial plant of the genus *Saxifraga* native to temperate and mountainous regions of Europe and North America. The leaves are massed at the base and the branched clusters of small flowers are white, pink, purple or yellow. Height: to 60cm (2ft). Family Saxifragaceae.

Saxons Ancient Germanic people. By the 5th century they had settled in NW Germany, N Gaul and S Britain. In Germany they were subdued by CHARLEMAGNE. In Britain, along with other Germanic tribes, known collectively as ANGLO-SAXONS, they evolved into the English.

Saxony Federal state and historic region in E central Germany; the capital is DRESDEN. Initially, it referred to the homeland of the SAXONS in NW Germany. It eventually (1815–71) comprised the Prussian province of Saxony and the kingdom of Saxony. After 1945 the province of Saxony was united with Anhalt to form the state of SAXONY-ANHALT with MAGDEBURG as its capital. From 1871 to 1918, the kingdom of Saxony was part of the German empire. In the aftermath of World War 1, the kingdom was made a state of the Weimar Republic, with Dresden as its capital. After World War 2, it joined the German Democratic Republic (East Germany). Following German reunification in 1991, it became a state in the Federal Republic of Germany. Area: 18,409 sq km (7,106 sq mi). Pop. (1993 est.) 4,608,000.

Saxony-Anhalt Federal state in S Germany, with Lower Saxony to the NW and Saxony to the SE; the capital is MAGDEBURG. Other major cities include Halle and Dessau. The history of the region coincides with that of SAXONY until 1871, when it became a state of the German empire. After World War 2, the Red Army briefly occupied the region and the district was abolished in 1952. Following German reunification in 1991, Saxony-Anhalt was reformed as a federal state of Germany. The region is mainly plains with the Harz Mountains rising in the SW of the state. Predominantly an industrial region, its major manufactures are machine and transport equipment. Area: 20,445sq km (7,892sq mi). Pop. (1994) 2,759,213.

saxophone Musical instrument with single reed, conical metal tube and finger keys. It was invented by Adolphe Sax in the 1840s. Four members of the saxophone family are commonly used today; they are the soprano (in B flat), the alto (in E flat), the tenor (in B flat) and the baritone (in E flat). They are used mostly in jazz.

Sayers, Dorothy L. (Leigh) (1893–1957) English novelist and playwright, best known for her detective

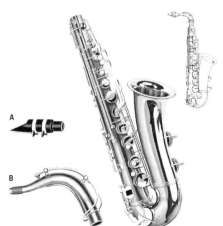

▲ **saxophone** Named after its 19th-century inventor, Adolphe Sax, the saxophone is a single-reed instrument which is usually keyed in E flat and B flat. It is shown here complete (top right) and with its mouthpiece (A) and neckpiece (B) separate.

fiction. Lord Peter Wimsey appeared in 10 books including *Whose Body?* (1923) and *Gaudy Night* (1935). She also wrote religious dramas and translated Dante.

scabies Contagious infection caused by a female mite, *Sarcoptes scabiei*, which burrows into the skin to lay eggs. It can be seen as a dark wavy line on the skin and is treated with antiparasitic creams.

scabious Plant of the genus *Scabiosa* of the TEASEL family (Dipsacaceae), native to temperate parts of Europe and Asia, and the mountains of E Africa.

Scafell Pike Highest peak in England, at 978m (3,210ft) high, part of the Scafell range in the LAKE DISTRICT.

scalar Mathematical quantity that has only a magnitude, as opposed to a VECTOR, which also has direction. Mass, energy and speed are scalars.

scale In biology, small hard plate that forms part of the external skin of an animal. It is usually a development of the SKIN layers. In most fish, scales are composed of bone in the dermal skin layer. The scales of reptiles are horny growths of the epidermal skin layer and are composed mostly of the fibrous protein KERATIN.

scale In music, term for the ordered arrangement of intervals that forms the basis of musical composition. There are many types of scale. In Western music the most important has been the seven-note diatonic scale, both in its major and minor forms. The 12-note CHROMATIC scale has a regular progression of semitones.

scallop Edible, BIVALVE mollusc. One shell, or valve, is usually convex and the other almost flat. The shell's surface is ribbed (scalloped). Most scallops have a row of eyes that fringe the fleshy mantle. Width: 2.5–20cm (1–8in). Family Pectinidae.

Scandinavia In physical geography, the N European peninsular countries of SWEDEN and NORWAY. In a broader, cultural sense it also includes DENMARK, FINLAND, ICELAND and the FAEROE ISLANDS. The climate ranges from sub-arctic in the N to humid continental in the centre and marine in the W and SW. The terrain is mountainous in the W with swift-flowing streams. In the E the land slopes more gently, and there are thousands of lakes, notably in Finland. Part of the region lies within the Arctic Circle, where tundra predominates. Denmark and S Sweden have the best farmland. A large proportion of the land is forested, there are rich mineral deposits, particularly of iron ore and copper, and fishing is still important. The largest cities are: STOCKHOLM and GOTHENBURG in Sweden; OSLO in Norway; COPENHAGEN in Denmark; and HELSINKI in Finland. Area: *c.*1,258,000sq km (485,000sq mi).

Scandinavian art Art in the Nordic countries dates back to the end of the Ice Age, when the first rock carvings were made. There was a tendency to use intricate interlacing patterns, which reached a peak in the stonework and wood-carving of the Viking period (*c.*800–*c.*1050). It was only at the end of the 18th century that artists of international standing emerged. Chief among these was Edvard MUNCH. Scandinavia has also made great contributions to the applied arts, most notably to the development of ART NOUVEAU and FUNCTIONALISM.

scandium (symbol Sc) Silver-white, metallic element of Group III of the periodic table, discovered in 1897. It is found in thortveitite. Scandium is a soft metal used as a radioactive tracer and in nickel alkaline storage batteries. Chemically it resembles the rare-earth metals of the LANTHANIDE SERIES. Properties: at.no. 21; r.a.m. 44.956; r.d. 2.99; m.p. 1,539°C (2,802°F); b.p. 2,832°C (5,130°F); most common isotope Sc^{45} (100%).

scanning In medicine, use of a non-invasive system to detect abnormalities in the body. Detectable waves (X rays, gamma rays, ultrasound) are passed through the part of the body to be investigated, and the computer-analyzed results are displayed as images on a screen.

scar Fibrous connective tissue that forms at the site of a wound or disease in any tissue of the body. Most scars develop after an injury to the DERMIS. A new EPIDERMIS is formed without oil glands, hair follicles or elastic tissue.

scarab beetle Any of several different species of broad beetles distributed worldwide. Most, including the June bug, Japanese beetle and rhinoceros beetle, are leaf chafers. A smaller group, including the DUNG BEETLE, are scavengers. Family Scarabaeidae.

Scargill, Arthur (1938–) British trade union leader. Scargill became a miner at the age of 18. He was a member (1955–62) of the Young Communist League before joining the Labour Party. In 1981, he became president of the National Union of Mineworkers (NUM). Scargill's attempt to confront Margaret THATCHER's Conservative government's programme of pit closures and anti-union legislation led to a miner's strike (1984–85). The strike split the miners' and Labour movements. In 1995, he formed the Socialist Labour Party.

Scarlatti, Alessandro (1660–1725) Italian BAROQUE composer who laid the foundations of the musical idioms that shaped music to the time of Beethoven. Scarlatti was the founder of Neopolitan opera, establishing the OPERA SERIA style. He wrote more than 100 operas, including *Mitridate Eupatore* (1707) and *Il Tigrane* (1715).

Scarlatti, (Giuseppe) Domenico (1685–1757) Italian composer, son of Alessandro SCARLATTI. A harpsichord virtuoso, he settled in Spain and is primarily known for his harpsichord sonatas, of which he composed more than 500. He is considered the founder of modern keyboard technique and the greatest Italian composer of keyboard music of the BAROQUE period.

scarlet fever (scarlatina) Acute infectious disease, usually affecting children, caused by BACTERIA in the *Streptococcus pyogenes* group. There is a red body rash, fever, vomiting and a sore throat. It is treated with ANTIBIOTICS.

scattering Deflection of ELECTROMAGNETIC RADIATION by particles. Where the particles are very much larger than the WAVELENGTH, scattering consists of a mixture of REFLECTION and DIFFRACTION, and the amount of scattering depends very little on wavelength. Where the particles are very much smaller than the wavelength, the amount of scattering is inversely proportional to the fourth power of the wavelength. Thus, blue LIGHT is scattered by small particles ten times as much as red light. ELEMENTARY PARTICLES can be scattered by atomic nuclei or other particles. It is the means by which the structure of ATOMS was discovered. Ernest RUTHERFORD's students, Hans GEIGER and Ernest Marsden, "fired" ALPHA PARTICLES through thin metal films and noted their scattering. From the results, Rutherford deduced the existence of the atomic NUCLEUS. Most knowledge of elementary particles and the discovery of new ones has been obtained by scattering experiments carried out in particle ACCELERATORS.

scepticism Philosophical attitude that asserts the limited nature of knowledge and questions the validity of SUBJECTIVE perception. The SOPHISTS were the first group of sceptics. PYRRHO's extreme scepticism argued that definite knowledge is impossible and that reality is inaccessible. Scepticism developed as a reaction to the dogmatism of STOICS. Often scepticism includes the suspension of judgement. DESCARTES set out to refute scepticism, but ended up confirming the "otherness" of external reality. It was also important in the development of EMPIRICISM. *See also* HUME, DAVID; KANT, IMMANUEL.

Scheele, Karl Wilhelm (1742–86) Swedish chemist. In 1771, Scheele discovered OXYGEN, but publication of his find was delayed and the credit went to Joseph PRIESTLEY. He made other important discoveries, including CHLORINE, GLYCEROL and a number of organic acids.

Schelling, Friedrich Wilhelm Joseph von (1775–1854) German philosopher. His early work, *System of Transcendental Idealism* (1800), attempted to develop J.G. FICHTE's science of knowledge alongside a philosophy of nature. His philosophy of IDEALISM, with its stress on the perfection of the Absolute, became the blueprint for ROMANTICISM.

Schiele, Egon (1890–1918) Austrian painter, one of the greatest exponents of EXPRESSIONISM. His characteristic paintings portray anguished or isolated naked figures whose distorted bodies reflect their mental pain. Schiele also produced landscapes and semi-allegorical pictures.

Schiller, Johann Christoph Friedrich von (1759–1805) German dramatist, historian and philosopher. His early blank verse plays, such as *The Robbers* (1781) and *Don Carlos* (1787), are classics of the STURM UND DRANG period. Schiller's aesthetic and philosophical ideas were influenced by the IDEALISM of Kant. His masterpiece is the trilogy *Wallenstein* (1800). Other historical plays include *Mary Stuart* (1801), *Maid of Orleans* (1801) and *William Tell* (1804). Schiller's "Ode to Joy" forms the finale of Beethoven's Ninth Symphony.

schism Split or division within a church, sect or other religious organization, or a breakaway from a church. Before the Protestant REFORMATION, there were two other important schisms within Christianity. The first was the split between the Eastern (ORTHODOX) Church and the Western (ROMAN CATHOLIC) Church, brought about by the two churches drifting apart over centuries and by an escalating series of disputes culminating in a complete break in 1054. The so-called GREAT SCHISM occurred in the 14th and 15th centuries and involved a split within the Roman Catholic Church itself. Various reasons, including civil war in Italy, led to the papacy transferring to AVIGNON, France, from 1309 to 1377. Rivalry grew between Avignon and Rome, with rival popes elected from 1378 to 1417. The schism was eventually resolved by the Council of CONSTANCE (1417).

schist Large group of METAMORPHIC ROCKS that have been made cleavable, causing the rocks to split into thin plates, leaving a wavy, uneven surface.

schistosomiasis (bilharzia) Visceral, venous infestation of the human body by blood flukes of the genus *Schistosoma*. Symptoms are skin eruption, inflammation, fever and often swelling of the liver. It is contracted by working or swimming in tropical water contaminated with microscopic larvae released by snail hosts. The larvae enter the body through the skin, mature in the blood and deposit eggs throughout the body. Treatment is with drugs containing antimony or with chemotherapy.

schizophrenia Severe mental disorder marked by disturbances of cognitive functioning, particularly thinking. As well as the characteristic loss of contact with reality, symptoms can include HALLUCINATIONS and DELUSIONS, and muffled or inappropriate emotions. The disorder was first identified (1808) by Eugen BLEULER. Biochemical research suggests that schizophrenia may be caused by high levels of DOPAMINE, a NEUROTRANSMITTER.

Schlegel, August Wilhelm von (1767–1845) German poet, critic and scholar. The founder and editor of the *Athenaeum*, Schlegel was one of the leading propagandists of German ROMANTICISM. His major work was *On the Language and Wisdom of India* (1808).

Schleswig-Holstein Federal state and historic region in NW Germany; the capital is KIEL. It occupies the S of the Jutland peninsula and extends from the River Elbe to the border with Denmark. The Kiel Canal links the North Sea with the Baltic. The River Eider forms the historic border between Schleswig and Holstein. In the early 12th century, the duchy of Holstein was created as part of the Holy Roman Empire, while Schleswig was made a fiefdom independent of Danish control. They were twice united under the Danish crown but not incorporated into the Danish state. In 1848, Frederick VII proclaimed the complete union of Schleswig with Denmark, the predominantly German population of both duchies rebelled, and the German Confederation occupied the two duchies. The Treaty of London (1852) re-established the duchies' personal union with Denmark. In 1863, Denmark once more tried to incorporate Schleswig into the state proper. Prussia and Austria declared war. In 1865, Schleswig was administered by Prussia, and Holstein by Austria. The resulting tension led to the AUSTRO-PRUSSIAN WAR (1866), and the Prussian victory created the state of Schleswig-Holstein. In 1920, following a plebiscite, the N part of Schleswig was returned to Denmark. In 1937, the city of Lübeck was incorporated into the German state of Schleswig-Holstein. The land is mainly flat and fertile. The region's principal economic activities are shipping and fishing, concentrated along the Baltic coast. Area: 15,738sq km (6,075sq mi). Pop. (1993 est.) 2,695,000

Schlieffen Plan German war strategy devised by Alfred von Schlieffen, chief of staff (1891–1905). It was designed for a possible war against France and Russia. An all-out attack in the W would rapidly defeat the French, enabling Germany to transfer its full force to the E against Russia, whose mobilization would be slower. A modified version was put into effect in 1914.

Schliemann, Heinrich (1822–90) German archaeologist. In 1871 his excavations in Hisarlik, Turkey, proved to be the site of the Homeric city of TROY.

Schmidt, Helmut (1918–) Chancellor of West Germany (1974–82). He became chairman of the Social Democratic Party (SDP) in 1967, and was minister of defence (1969–72) and finance (1972–74) before succeeding Willy BRANDT as chancellor. He was re-elected in 1976 and 1980 but was forced to resign.

Schnabel, Artur (1882–1951) Austrian pianist and composer who lived in the USA after 1939. Schnabel was best known as an interpreter of the classical repertoire, notably Mozart and Beethoven.

◀ **scarab beetle** The fierce-looking Hercules beetle (*Dynastes hercules*) is a type of scarab beetle. The male (shown here) can grow up to 20cm (8in) and possesses a large horn that grows up to 10cm (4in) from its head. Unlike the male, the female does not possess a horn, and its wing cases are covered in a layer of red hairs.

Schnittke, Alfred (1934–98) Russian composer. He studied (1953–58) and taught (1962–72) composition at the Moscow Conservatory. His compositions often use quotations and parodies, frequently referring to earlier musical styles or to jazz. The instrumentation is usually complex and the texture rich. Notable works include four symphonies and five concerti grossi.

Schnitzler, Arthur (1862–1931) Austrian dramatist and novelist. His plays, such as *Anatol* (1893) and *La Ronde* (1900), explore the morality of *fin de siècle* Vienna. His novella, *Rhapsody: A Dream Story* (1927) was made into a successful film, *Eyes Wide Shut* (1999), directed by Stanley KUBRICK.

Schoenberg, Arnold Franz Walter (1874–1951) Austrian composer. In early works, such as *Verklärte Nacht* (1899), he extended the chromaticism of ROMANTICISM. The song cycle *Das Buch der hängenden Gärten* (1908) and the expressionist opera *Erwartung* (1909) revolutionized modern music by abandoning traditional TONALITY. Schoenberg's form of SERIAL MUSIC, known as TWELVE-TONE MUSIC, was first employed in Suite for Piano (1923). His operatic masterpiece, *Moses und Aron*, remained unfinished at his death.

scholasticism Medieval philosophy that attempted to join faith to reason by combining theology with classical Greek and Roman thought. Scholasticism was first explored by John Scotus Erigena in the 9th century and by ANSELM OF CANTERBURY in the 11th century. Its greatest thinkers were Albertus Magnus and Thomas AQUINAS in the 13th century and DUNS SCOTUS at the turn of the 14th century.

Schongauer, Martin (1450–91) German painter and engraver. He was influenced by Netherlandish art, particularly the work of Rogier van der WEYDEN, but his style is highly individual. Perhaps his most notable engraving is *Temptation of St Anthony* (*c.*1470).

school Place of EDUCATION, usually at primary or secondary level. In Western countries there are usually several parallel school systems: one provided by the state and financed by taxpayers; one financed partly by churches in conjunction with the state or parents; and the third privately financed by parents. In the UK, the term "public school" is used of some private schools; in the USA it refers to schools subsidized by public taxes.

Schopenhauer, Arthur (1788–1860) German philosopher whose exposition of the doctrine of the will opposed the IDEALISM of HEGEL and influenced NIETZSCHE, WAGNER and others. Schopenhauer's system, described in his main work, *The World as Will and Idea* (1819), was an intensely pessimistic one.

Schröder, Gerhard (1944–) German statesman, chancellor (1998–). Schröder built a reputation for moderation as minister president of Lower Saxony, a position he held for three terms. In 1998, he was selected, over party chairman Oskar Lafontaine, as the Social Democratic Party's candiate in the general election. His success in the election brought to an end Helmut KOHL's 16 years as chancellor.

Schrödinger, Erwin (1887–1961) Austrian physicist, who formulated a quantum mechanical wave equation. He went on to found the science of quantum WAVE MECHANICS and shared the 1933 Nobel Prize for physics with Paul DIRAC. The wave equation was based on a suggestion by the French physicist Louis de BROGLIE that moving particles have a wave-like nature.

Schubert, Franz Peter (1797–1828) Austrian composer whose symphonies represent the final extension of the classical SONATA form, and whose LIEDER (songs) are

the height of ROMANTICISM. Among his more popular works are symphonies such as the Eighth ("Unfinished", 1822) and the Ninth in C major (1825). Schubert wrote more than 600 songs to the lyrics of such poets as Heine and Schiller; these include the cycles *Die schöne Müllerin* (1823) and *Winterreise* (1827). In his tragically short lifetime he also composed much chamber music, and his String Quintet (1828) is a masterpiece.

Schumacher, Michael (1969–) German racing driver. Schumacher began Formula 1 racing in 1991 and soon joined the Benetton team. He won his first Grand Prix (Belgium) in 1992. Schumacher won the world drivers' championship in 1994 and 1995. He switched to race for Ferrari in 1996 and, after narrowly missing the 1997 title, he went on to win the 2000 title.

Schumann, Clara Josephine Wieck (1819–96) German pianist and composer, wife of Robert SCHUMANN. She was an outstanding interpreter of the works of her husband and of their friend BRAHMS. She composed chamber works, piano pieces and songs.

Schumann, Robert Alexander (1810–56) German composer and leading figure of ROMANTICISM. Schumann's piano compositions include *Kinderszenen* (1838), *Carnaval* (1834–35) and *Waldscenen* (1848–49). Among his best song cycles is *Frauenliebe und Leben* (1840). His "Spring" Symphony (1841) and Piano Concerto (1841–45) are among his best-known orchestral works.

Schwarzenegger, Arnold (1947–) US actor, b. Austria. He won the Mr Universe bodybuilding title five times before turning to acting. His first major film was *Conan the Barbarian* (1982). Schwarzenegger's expressionless, almost non-verbal acting perfectly suited the robot role in the cult hit, *The Terminator* (1984). Other films include *True Lies* (1994).

Schwarzkopf, Dame Elisabeth (1915–) German soprano known for her versatility in recitals, oratorios and opera. She sang with the Berlin State Opera from 1938 to 1942 and became principal soprano of the Vienna State Opera in 1944. She made many fine recordings.

Schwarzkopf, H. Norman (1934–) US general. He served in the Vietnam War and in 1983 was deputy commander of the US forces that invaded Grenada. As supreme commander of the Allied forces in the GULF WAR (1991), he liberated Kuwait from Iraqi occupation. After retiring from the army, he published his memoirs, *It Doesn't Take a Hero* (1992).

Schweitzer, Albert (1875–1965) Theologian, musician, medical missionary and philosopher. He was born in Alsace, France, and spent most of his life in Gabon (then French Equatorial Africa), where he founded the Lambaréné Hospital in 1913. He was honoured as a scientist and humanitarian, and as an organist and an expert on J.S. Bach. He was awarded the 1952 Nobel Peace Prize.

Schwitters, Kurt (1887–1948) German DADA artist and writer. He is best known for his invention of *Merz* to denote art made from refuse. Schwitters constructed elaborate sculptures and even room interiors from such "found objects" as newspapers and tram tickets.

sciatica Severe pain in the back and radiating down the leg. It is usually caused by inflammation of the sciatic nerve or by pressure on the spinal nerve roots.

science fiction Literary genre in which reality is subject to certain transformations in order to explore man's potential and his relation to his environment; these transformations are usually technological and the stories set in the future or in imaginary worlds. The birth of the modern genre is generally dated to the US comic strip *Amazing Stories* (1926). Until the 1960s, most science fiction involved adventure stories set in space. Some writers, such as Isaac ASIMOV, explored the paradoxes contained in purely scientific ideas; others, including Ray BRADBURY, stressed the moral implications of their stories.

scientology "Applied religious philosophy" based on a form of psychotherapy called **dianetics**, which was founded in California (1954) by L. Ron HUBBARD. It advocates confrontation with, and assimilation of, painful experiences from the past to achieve true mental health. The movement is officially known as the Church of Scientology. It has aroused controversy over its methods of recruiting and keeping members.

Scilly, Isles of Archipelago of more than 140 isles and islets in the Atlantic Ocean off the coast of Cornwall, SW England. The terrain is mostly rocky. The capital, Hugh Town, is on St Mary's. Total pop. (1991) 2,900.

Scipio Africanus Major (236–183 BC) (Publius Cornelius Scipio) Roman general in the second of the PUNIC WARS. He defeated the Carthaginian forces in Spain (209 BC). Elected consul in 205, he invaded North Africa and defeated HANNIBAL at Zama (202 BC), earning the honorary surname Africanus.

Scipio Africanus Minor (185–129 BC) (Publius Cornelius Scipio Aemilianus) Roman general of the third PUNIC WAR. He took his grandfather-by-adoption's name, SCIPIO AFRICANUS MAJOR. He destroyed Carthage in 146 BC, ending the Punic Wars, and in 133 ended a long war in Spain by destroying the city of Numantia.

sclerosis Degenerative hardening of tissue, usually due to scarring following inflammation or as a result of ageing. It can affect the brain and spinal cord, causing neurological symptoms, or the walls of the arteries.

Scopes trial (1925) US court case that culminated the long anti-evolution campaign spearheaded by Fundamentalists. It upheld the constitutionality of a Tennessee law forbidding the teaching of evolutionary theory. The trial involved John Thomas Scopes, a high school biology teacher, and was a forensic battle between defence attorney Clarence DARROW and William Jennings BRYAN, who assisted the prosecution. It turned into a national circus and a public humiliation of Bryan.

Scorpius (Scorpio, scorpion) Constellation of the S sky, situated on the ecliptic between Libra and Sagittarius. The Milky Way passes through the region. The brightest star is the 1st-magnitude Alpha Scorpii (Antares).

scorpion Any of numerous species of ARACHNIDS that live in warmer regions worldwide. It has two main body sections, two eyes, a pair of pedipalps (pincers) and a long tail ending in a curved, poisonous sting. Length: to 17cm (7in). Class Arachnida; order Scorpionida.

Scorsese, Martin (1942–) US film director. His first major success was *Alice Doesn't Live Here Anymore* (1975). Scorsese often casts Robert DE NIRO in leading roles, such as in *Taxi Driver* (1976), *Raging Bull* (1980), *The King of Comedy* (1983) *Goodfellas* (1990) and *Cape Fear* (1991). Other films include *The Age of Innocence* (1993) and *Kundun* (1997).

Scotland Northern part of the main island of Great Britain, and a constituent of the United Kingdom of Great Britain and Northern Ireland; the capital is EDINBURGH. The largest city is GLASGOW. Scotland is administratively divided into nine regions and three island authorities. Its jagged coastline features many islands (including the ORKNEY and SHETLAND ISLANDS), lochs (including LOMOND and NESS) and firths. Major Scottish rivers include the TAY and CLYDE. Scotland can be broadly divided into three geographical regions: the Southern Uplands, immediately N of the English border, which are sparsely

populated, hilly moorland; the Central Lowlands, where the majority of the population live; and the HIGHLANDS, including BEN NEVIS. In prehistory, Scotland was inhabited by the PICTS. Kenneth I united the lands of the Picts and the SCOTS in AD 843. In 1174, with the development of feudalism, Scotland was made a fiefdom of England. In 1189, Richard I granted Scottish freedom, but the enmity between England and Scotland (in alliance with France) continued. EDWARD I forced the Scots to submit, only for William WALLACE to lead a Scottish revolt. ROBERT I (THE BRUCE) recaptured much Scottish land and defeated the English at the Battle of BANNOCKBURN (1314); this led to England's recognition of Scottish independence in 1328. The 15th century was characterized by internal factionalism and weak government. JAMES IV and many Scottish nobles were killed at the Battle of Flodden (1513). The Protestant REFORMATION quickly took root in Scotland via the preaching of John KNOX. In 1538, JAMES V cemented the French alliance by marrying Mary of Guise, a French Catholic. When her daughter, MARY, QUEEN OF SCOTS, assumed the throne in 1561, England supported the Scottish Protestants, and France backed the Catholics. In 1567, the Protestant faction forced Mary to relinquish the throne. Her son, James VI, assumed the Scottish crown, and in 1601 he was also crowned JAMES I of England, thereby uniting the English and Scottish thrones. The Scots opposed Charles I in the English CIVIL WAR, but the king's concessions to PRESBYTERIANISM won the support of the COVENANTERS. The GLORIOUS REVOLUTION reestablished Presbyterianism as the Scottish national church. The massacre of the Macdonald clan by WILLIAM III at Glencoe in 1692 tarnished enthusiasm for his rule, and the JACOBITE agitation prompted the constitutional union of the two crowns in the Act of UNION (1707). At CULLODEN Moor (1746) the Jacobite insurgency was finally suppressed with the defeat of the Highlanders led by Prince Charles

▲ **scorpion** The sting of the scorpion is worked by opposing muscles fixed to the base of the sting, which contract and relax, forcing the sharp tip into its prey's tissue. The poison, stored in the poison gland, is forced down and out of the tip of the sting by muscles located around the gland. There are two main types of scorpion poison. One has a local poisoning effect and is harmless to humans, the other is a powerful neurotoxin, which in some cases can cause death.

Edward STUART. (*See* UNITED KINGDOM for subsequent history) A 1979 referendum for a separate Scottish assembly was defeated, but in 1997 a referendum voted in favour of devolution and a Scottish assembly was convened in July 1999. Scotland retains its own church, education and legal system. The principal agricultural activity is the rearing of livestock; oats and potatoes are the chief crops. Coal mining and heavy industry dominated the economy of the central lowlands by the late 19th century but declined in the 1980s. The discovery of North Sea oil and natural gas in the 1970s benefited the Scottish economy. Other industries: textiles, whisky, beer, fishing. Area: 77,167sq km (29,797sq mi). Pop. (1991) 4,998,567.

Scotland Yard Name given to the headquarters in London of the Metropolitan Police, and synonymous with the Criminal Investigation Department (CID).

Scots Originally a Celtic people from N Ireland. They were Gaelic speaking. Their raids on the W coast of Roman Britain from the 3rd to the 5th century failed to establish independent settlements in Wales or NW England. In the 5th century, however, they were able to establish the kingdom of Dalriada in Pictish territory. From the 11th century the term has been applied to those people living in Scotland.

Scott, Sir George Gilbert (1811–78) English architect, prominent figure in the GOTHIC REVIVAL. He achieved a reputation with his design for the church of St Nicholas, Hamburg. Scott was involved in the restoration of Westminster and Ely Cathedrals. He designed the Albert Memorial (1862–70) and St Pancras Station, London. His son, **Giles Gilbert Scott** (1880–1960), designed the new Anglican Cathedral in Liverpool, the last major example of the Gothic revival.

Scott, Ridley (1937–) English film director. *Alien* (1979) and *Blade Runner* (1982) were seminal science-fiction offerings. *Thelma and Louise* (1991) was another genre-breaking box-office success.

Scott, Robert Falcon (1868–1912) Scottish Antarctic explorer. Scott's first expedition (1901–04), in the *Discovery*, to the South Pole ended in failure. His second expedition (1910–12) reached the Pole, but found that Roald AMUNDSEN had got there first. Beset by blizzards on their return journey, Scott and his party perished within 18km (11mi) of safety.

Scott, Sir Walter (1771–1832) Scottish novelist and poet. He began his career with a collection of old Scottish ballads, *Minstrelsy of the Scottish Border* (1802–03). The wider fame brought by "The Lay of the Last Minstrel" (1805) was consolidated by the poems, "Marmion" (1808) and "The Lady of the Lake" (1810). In 1814, he turned to historical fiction. His first novel, *Waverley* (1814), was an immediate success and was followed by a series of Scottish novels, including *Rob Roy* (1817) and *The Heart of Midlothian* (1818).

Scottish (Scots) Dialect of English traditionally spoken in Scotland and regarded by some experts as a distinct GERMANIC language. It is also called Lowland Scots (or Lallans) to distinguish it from the Scots GAELIC spoken in the Scottish Highlands. It developed from the Northumbrian dialect of EARLY ENGLISH before AD 700. Before the union of the English and Scottish crowns in 1603, the Scottish language was both a national language and an official court language. It continues as a spoken dialect in many areas and has continued to be a vehicle for a lively and vibrant literature.

Scottish National Party (SNP) UK political organization whose major aim is Scottish independence, founded in 1928. The SNP grew out of the Scottish

Home Rule Association, formed in 1886, and gained its first member of Parliament in 1945. During the 1960s, it significantly expanded its support base, gaining around 20% of the Scottish vote in most subsequent general elections. It won six seats in the 1997 elections under the leadership of Alex SALMOND and supported the Labour government's proposal for a Scottish assembly, albeit one with limited powers.

scrapie Fatal disease of sheep and goats that affects the central nervous system, causing staggering and itching. It is caused by a PRION, a slow-acting, virus-like, microscopic particle. The animal usually dies within six months of exhibiting symptoms. The disease is thought to be related to BOVINE SPONGIFORM ENCEPHALOPATHY (BSE) and CREUTZFELD-JAKOB DISEASE (CJD).

scree (talus) Heap of rock waste lying at the bottom of a cliff. It is made up of particles that have been loosened from the cliff rock by WEATHERING.

Scriabin, Alexander Nicolas (1872–1915) Russian composer and pianist. He wrote highly original piano music in which he used chords built in fourths instead of the usual major and minor triads. His most significant works include ten piano sonatas, *The Poem of Ecstasy* (1908), three symphonies and many piano pieces.

scribe Court secretary in ancient times; in JUDAISM, member of a class of scholars expert in Jewish law. From the late 6th century, the Scribes functioned as teachers and interpreters of the TORAH.

scriptures Sacred writings of a RELIGION. In Christianity, they are the books of the OLD TESTAMENT and NEW TESTAMENT, with or without those of the APOCRYPHA. It is also possible to speak of the KORAN as the scripture of ISLAM or the VEDAS as the scriptures of HINDUISM.

scuba diving Diving with the use of self-contained underwater breathing apparatus, or scuba. The equipment usually consists of tanks of compressed air connected to a demand regulator.

sculpin Any of 300 species of bottom-dwelling, usually marine, fish found in temperate and cold waters of the N Atlantic Ocean. Greyish and mottled with yellow, it has a large bony head covered with prickles. Length: to 60cm (2ft). Family Cottidae.

sculpture Art of creating forms in three dimensions, either in the round or in relief. Techniques employed include carving (in wood, stone, marble, ivory, etc.), modelling (in clay, wax, etc.) or casting (in bronze and other metals). The history of sculpture parallels that of PAINTING. The early civilizations of Egypt, Mesopotamia, India and the Far East were rich in sculpture. The Greeks developed a style of relief and free-standing sculpture. Roman sculptors were influenced by the Greeks but forsook the Greek ideal in portraiture, which they enriched with individual characterization. Medieval European sculpture was frequently a feature of ROMANESQUE and GOTHIC churches, many of which were covered with carvings. Highly stylized in the Romanesque period, this architectural sculpture became more realistic in the Gothic era. Prior to the RENAISSANCE, individual sculptors rarely achieved fame. The Florentine Renaissance was enriched by the works of such masters as GHIBERTI, DONATELLO and MICHELANGELO. High BAROQUE sculpture is exemplified in the works of the architect-sculptor BERNINI in Rome. Pierre Puget was the movement's leading exponent in France where, in the 18th century, it was superseded by NEO-CLASSICISM. This extended into the 19th century, when it was rivalled and replaced by a movement of realist sculpture, such as that of RODIN. African, Aztec and other ethnic and ancient sculpture have stimulated great modern sculptors such as PICASSO, MODIGLIANI, BRANCUSI and MOORE.

scurvy Disease caused by a deficiency of VITAMIN C (ascorbic acid). It is characterized by weakness, painful joints and bleeding gums.

Scylla In Greek mythology, a female sea monster. Once a beautiful nymph beloved of POSEIDON, she was changed by CIRCE into a long-necked, six-headed beast. She lived with CHARYBDIS beside the Straits of Messina between Sicily and Italy and devoured sailors.

Scythians Nomadic people who inhabited the steppes N of the Black Sea in the 1st millennium BC. In the 7th century BC their territory extended into Mesopotamia, the Balkans and Greece. Powerful warriors, their elaborate tombs contain evidence of great wealth. Pressure from the Sarmatians confined them to the Crimea (c.300 BC), and their culture eventually disappeared.

SDLP Abbreviation of SOCIAL DEMOCRATIC LABOUR PARTY

SDP Abbreviation of SOCIAL DEMOCRATIC PARTY

sea anemone Sessile, polyp-type COELENTERATE found in marine pools and on rocky shores. It has a cylindrical body with tentacles around its mouth; the colour varies according to species. Height: to 20cm (8in). Class Anthozoa; genera include *Tealia*, *Anemonia* and *Metridium*.

Seaborg, Glenn Theodore (1912–99) US physicist. During World War 2, he worked on the development of the atom bomb. In 1940, Seaborg and Edwin M. MCMILLAN discovered PLUTONIUM. They went on to isolate the entire ACTINIDE SERIES. Seaborg and McMillan shared the 1951 Nobel Prize for chemistry for their work on the TRANSURANIC ELEMENTS.

sea cow *See* DUGONG

sea cucumber Marine ECHINODERM found in rocky areas. It is a cylindrical animal with a fleshy body in five parts around a central axis; it has branched tentacles around the mouth. Species include the cotton-spinners (*Holothuria* sp). Class Holothuroidea.

seafloor Floor of the OCEANS. The major features of the seafloor are the continental shelf, the continental rise, the ABYSSAL floor, seamounts, oceanic trenches and mid-ocean ridges. The **abyssal** or deep ocean floor is c.3km (1.8mi) deep and is mostly made of basaltic rock covered with fine-grained sediment consisting of dust and the shells of marine organisms. Oceanic **trenches** are up to 11km (7mi) deep, typically 50–100km (30–60mi) wide and may be thousands of kilometres long. The slopes are usually asymmetrical with the steeper slope on the landward side and a more gentle slope on the side of the ocean basin. They are regarded as the site of plate subduction. Oceanic **ridges** are long, linear volcanic structures which tend to occupy the middle of seafloors; they are the sites of crustal spreading. *See also* SEAFLOOR SPREADING

seafloor spreading Theory that explains how CONTINENTAL DRIFT occurs. It proposes that the sea floor is moved laterally as new basalt rock is injected along mid-ocean ridges, and so the floor becomes older with increasing distance from the ridge. *See also* PLATE TECTONICS

sea horse Marine fish found in shallow tropical and temperate waters. It swims in an upright position and has an outer bony skeleton of plate-like rings, a mouth at the end of a long snout and a curled, prehensile tail with which it clings to seaweed. The male incubates the young in a brood pouch. Length: 3.8–30.5cm (1.5–12in). Family Syngnathidae.

seal Any of several species of carnivores, primarily marine, aquatic mammals. It feeds on fish, crustaceans and other marine animals; various species are hunted for meat, hides, oil and fur. Species of true, earless seals, such as the leopard seal (*Hydrurga leptonyx*), hooded seal (*Cystophora cristata*) and bearded seal (*Erignathus barbatus*), are included in the family Phocidae. They swim with powerful strokes of their hind flippers and sinuous movements of the whole trunk. Members of the eared family Otariidae have longer fore flippers, used for propulsion, and use all four limbs when moving on land. They include fur seals (genera *Callorhinus* and *Arctocephalus*) and species of SEA LION. Order Pinnepedia.

sea lily Crinoid ECHINODERM found in deep marine waters. Seldom seen, it has many branched arms with ciliated grooves for food collecting radiating from a tiny body disc. Spineless, it attaches itself to the ocean bottom with a stalk. Class Crinoidea.

sea lion Any of five species of SEALS that live in coastal waters of the Pacific and feed primarily on fish and squid. They have streamlined bodies and long fore-flippers for propulsion. The males of all species, except the California sea lion (*Zalophus californianus*), have manes. The largest species is the Steller sea lion (*Eumetopias jubata*); it may reach 3.3m (11ft) in length. Order Pinnepedia; family Otariidae.

seaplane Aircraft that can land on and take off from water. The first practical seaplane was built in the USA by Glenn H. Curtiss and flown in 1911. There are two main types of seaplane. **Floatplanes** have large floats that support the fuselage above the water. **Flying boats** float on their boat-shaped hulls, with small floats supporting the wings.

sea slug (nudibranch) Any of numerous species of marine gastropod molluscs related to snails and found throughout the world. They have no shells, quills or mantle cavities, and they frequent shallow water and feed primarily on sea anemones. Order Nudibranchia.

seasons Four periods of the year based on differential solar heating of the Earth as it makes its annual revolution

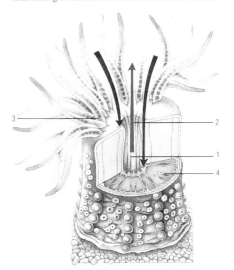

▲ **sea anemone** Having no rigid structures, the sea anemone supports itself by circulating water around its central cavity (1). Water is drawn in down siphonoglyphs (grooves) (2) at the side of the cavity and is expelled up the centre. The tentacles (3) can be withdrawn by individual retractor muscles (4).

of the Sun. The Northern Hemisphere receives more solar radiation when its pole is aimed towards the Sun in summer and less in winter when it is aimed away, whereas the opposite holds for the Southern Hemisphere. The seasons begin at the vernal (spring) and autumnal EQUINOXES and the winter and summer SOLSTICES.

sea squirt Any of numerous species of small, sac-like, marine animals with no true backbone. A sedentary creature, it constantly draws in and discharges water for food and oxygen, and can shoot out water when disturbed. Class Ascidiacea.

SEATO Acronym for SOUTHEAST ASIA TREATY ORGANIZATION (SEATO)

Seattle City and seaport in w Washington, USA, on Elliott Bay between Lake Washington and Puget Sound. Settled in 1851, it developed rapidly after the arrival of the railway (1893). Seattle served as the gateway for the Alaska Gold Rush (1897). Seattle has been an aerospace centre since William Boeing opened his first factory here in 1916. Seattle's economy has diversified in recent years. The computer company Microsoft has its headquarters here. Industries: shipbuilding, precision instruments, chemicals, lumber, fishing, tourism. Pop. (1992) 519,598.

sea urchin Spiny ECHINODERM animal found in marine tidal pools along rocky shores. Round with long, radiating (often poisonous) moveable spines, its skeletal plates fuse to form a perforated shell. Class Echinoidae.

seaweed Any of numerous and varied species of brown, green or red ALGAE, found in greatest profusion in shallow waters on rocky coasts. KELPS are the largest forms. Many species are important for the manufacture of fertilizers or food or as a valuable source of chemicals, such as iodine. Kingdom Protoctista.

sebaceous gland Gland in the skin producing the oily substance, sebum, which is secreted onto the skin and hair, making them water-repellent and supple.

▲ **secretary bird** Found in sub-Saharan Africa, the secretary bird (*Sagittarius serpentarius*) gets its name from the feathers that protrude behind its head, resembling quill pens. It is a well-known snake killer and runs after its prey, killing it by a blow from the foot followed by battering from the wings. The secretary bird is so unlike other members in the same order that it is placed in a separate family.

Sebastian, Saint (d. *c*.AD 288) Roman Christian martyr. Legend says that he was a favourite of the emperor DIOCLETIAN who, on learning that Sebastian was a Christian, condemned him to be killed by arrows. He survived and later voluntarily appeared before Diocletian, who this time had him beaten to death. His feast day is 20 January.

Sebastiano del Piombo (1485–1547) (Sebastiano Luciani) Italian painter of the VENETIAN SCHOOL. He went to Rome in 1511 to create a series of mythological FRESCOS at the Villa Farnese. Some of his best works are his portraits, such as *Clement VII* (1526).

seborrhoea Disorder of the SEBACEOUS GLANDS characterized by overproduction of sebum, resulting in red, scaly patches on the skin and in dandruff.

secant In TRIGONOMETRY, ratio of the length of the hypotenuse to the length of the side adjacent to an acute angle in a right-angled triangle. The secant of angle A (sec A) is equal to the reciprocal of its COSINE.

secession Formal separation from an organized body. The term is usually applied to the withdrawal of a political unit from the state of which it formed a part. One example is the secession of 11 Southern states from the USA to form the Confederate States of America (1861).

second (symbol s) SI unit of time defined as the time taken for 9,192,631,770 periods of vibrations of the electromagnetic radiation emitted by a caesium-133 atom. It is commonly defined as 1/60 of a minute. *See also* PHYSICAL UNITS

second coming Christian belief that JESUS CHRIST will one day return to Earth. He will sweep away the present world order, establish his kingdom, deal with his enemies and reward those who have been faithful to him.

Second World War *See* WORLD WAR 2

secretary bird BIRD OF PREY found in Africa s of the Sahara. It is pale grey with black markings and has quill-like feathers behind its ears, large wings and long legs and tail. It feeds on reptiles, eggs and insects. Height: 1.2m (4ft). Species *Sagittarius serpentarius*.

secretary of state Name for several government officers in Britain. The office dates from the 14th century, when the king's secretary was a leading adviser on matters of state. There are now secretaries of state for many departments. In the USA, the name is given to the cabinet member responsible for formulating and implementing foreign policy.

secretion Production and discharge of a substance, usually a fluid, by a cell or a GLAND. The substance so discharged is also known as a secretion. Secretions include ENZYMES, HORMONES, SALIVA and sweat.

sedative Drug used for its calming effect, to reduce anxiety and tension; in high doses it induces sleep. *See also* BARBITURATE; BENZODIAZEPINE; NARCOTIC

sedge Any of numerous species of grass-like perennial plants, especially those of the genus *Carex*, widely distributed in temperate, cold and tropical mountain regions, usually in wet conditions. Cultivated as ornamentals, they have narrow leaves and spikes of brown, green or greenish yellow flowers. Family Cyperaceae.

Sedgemoor, Battle of (1685) Defeat of the English rebellion led by the Duke of MONMOUTH against James II. An attempt to launch a surprise night attack by the untrained rebel forces ended in disaster.

sediment In geology, a general term used to describe any material that is transported and deposited by water, ice, wind or gravity. It includes material, such as lime, that is transported in solution and later precipitated, and organic deposits such as coal and coral reefs.

sedimentary rock Type of rock formed by deposition of SEDIMENT derived from pre-existing rocks, which may have been sedimentary, IGNEOUS or METAMORPHIC. Most sediment accumulates on the bed of the sea, having been dumped there by rivers, or having accumulated as dead sea creatures fall to the seafloor. This accumulated sediment is consolidated and compressed. Earth movements uplift the sediments, and they may be tilted, folded or faulted. The resulting rocks are sedimentary, and their type depends on their composition. Sedimentaries consisting of land sediment are **clastic** rocks, and are GRAVELS, SANDS, SILTS or CLAYS, according to the size of the particles. Other types of sedimentary rock include: LIMESTONE, which consists of fragments of dead sea creatures; COAL, which is accumulated vegetation; coralline, which contains large quantities of CORAL; and CHALK, which is a pure form of limestone, with very little land sediment. *See also* FAULT; FOLD

Seebeck effect Thermoelectric effect important in the thermocouple for temperature measurement. If wires of two different metals are joined at their ends to form a circuit, a current flows if the junctions are kept at different temperatures. It is the reverse of the PELTIER EFFECT.

seed Part of a flowering plant that contains the embryo and food store. It is formed in the ovary by FERTILIZATION of the female GAMETE (*see* POLLEN). Food may be stored in a special tissue called the endosperm, or it may be concentrated in the swollen seed leaves (COTYLEDONS). Seeds are the unit of dispersal of ANGIOSPERMS and CONIFERS. *See also* FRUIT; GERMINATION

Segovia, Andrés (1893–1987) Spanish guitarist who established the guitar as a concert instrument. He adapted the instrument to the complex music of modern composers and transcribed early contrapuntal music.

Segrè, Emilio Gino (1905–89) US physicist, b. Italy. In 1937, Segrè discovered TECHNETIUM, the first ELEMENT to be artificially produced. In 1940, he helped to discover ASTATINE and PLUTONIUM-239. He is, however, chiefly remembered for his discovery of the antiproton. In 1955, using a Bevatron particle ACCELERATOR, Segrè and US physicist Owen Chamberlain bombarded copper with high-energy PROTONS to produced the antiparticle of the proton. Chamberlain and Segrè shared the 1959 Nobel Prize for physics. *See also* ANTIMATTER

segregation Separation of a specific group from the rest of society on such grounds as race, religion or sex. Such separation might be enshrined in law, as in the Southern states of the USA before the CIVIL RIGHTS movement or in South Africa in the era of APARTHEID.

Seine River in N central France. It rises in Langres Plateau near Dijon, and flows NW through PARIS to enter the English Channel near Le Havre. It is connected to the rivers Loire, Rhône, Meuse, Schelde, Saône and Somme by a network of canals. With its main tributaries (Aube, Marne, Oise, Yonne, Loing and Eure), the Seine drains the entire Paris basin, and is the most important river of N France.

seismology Study of seismic waves, the shock waves produced by EARTHQUAKES. The velocity of seismic waves varies according to the material through which they pass. Primary (P) and secondary (S) waves are transmitted by the solid earth. Only P waves are transmitted through fluid zones. The movement of seismic waves is detected and recorded by seismographs.

Selassie, Haile *See* HAILE SELASSIE

Selene In Greek mythology, goddess of the Moon, daughter of Hyperion and sister of Helios (the Sun) and Eos (the Dawn). Each night she drove her chariot across the sky, as her brother Helios had done during the day.

selenium (symbol Se) Grey METALLOID element of Group VI of the periodic table, discovered (1817) by J.J. BERZELIUS. Its chief source is as a by-product in the electrolytic refining of copper. It is extensively used in photoelectric cells, solar cells, xerography and red pigments. Properties: at.no. 34; r.a.m. 78.96; r.d. 4.79; m.p. 217°C (422.6°F); b.p. 684.9°C (1,265°F); most common isotope Se^{80} (49.82%).

Seles, Monica (1973–) US tennis player, b. Yugoslavia. At the age of 16, she won her first Grand Slam title (French Open, 1990). She repeated this success in 1991 and 1992. Seles has won the Australian Open four times (1991–93, 1996) and the US Open twice (1991–92). In 1993, her career was halted when she was stabbed by a fan of her arch rival Steffi GRAF. In 1995, she resumed competitive tennis.

Seleucids Hellenistic dynasty founded (*c*.300 BC) by SELEUCUS I, a former general of ALEXANDER THE GREAT. Centred on Syria, it included most of the Asian provinces of Alexander's empire, extending from the E Mediterranean to India. War with the Ptolemies of Egypt and later the Romans, steadily reduced its territory. In 63 BC, it became the Roman province of Syria.

Seleucus Name of two kings of Syria. **Seleucus I** (*c*.355–281 BC) was a trusted general of ALEXANDER THE GREAT and founder of the SELEUCID dynasty. By 281 BC, he had secured control of Babylonia, Syria and all of Asia Minor, founding a western capital at Antioch to balance the eastern capital of Seleucia, in Babylon. He appeared to be on the brink of restoring the whole of Alexander's empire under his rule when he was murdered. **Seleucus II** (r.247–226 BC) spent his reign fighting Ptolemy III of Egypt and Antiochus Hierax, his brother and rival, losing territory to both.

Selim III (1761–1808) Ottoman sultan (1789–1807) After ending a war against Russia and Austria *c*.1791, he began a programme to westernize the state's finances and armed forces. He was assassinated during a revolt of JANISSARIES and conservatives who opposed his reforms.

Seljuk Nomadic tribesmen from central Asia who adopted Islam in the 7th century and founded the Baghdad sultanate in 1055. Their empire included Mesopotamia, Syria and Persia. Under Alp Arslan, they defeated the Byzantines at Manzikert in 1071, which led to their occupation of Anatolia. They revived SUNNI administration and religious institutions, checking the spread of Shi'a Islam and laying the organizational basis for the future Ottoman administration. In the early 12th century, the Seljuk empire began to disintegrate, and the Seljuk states were conquered by the MONGOLS in the 13th century.

Selkirk, Thomas Douglas, 5th Earl of (1771–1820) Scottish colonizer. In 1803, he established settlements in Prince Edward Island and Ontario. In 1811, he gained a controlling share of the HUDSON'S BAY COMPANY and founded the Red River Settlement in Manitoba.

Sellafield Site of a nuclear power station on the Irish Sea coast in Cumbria, NW England. Then known as Windscale, it opened in 1956. In 1957, a fire led to a serious radioactive emission. Between 1968 and 1979 it discharged over 180kg (397lb) of plutonium into the Irish Sea, the world's largest discharge of nuclear waste. The site was renamed in 1979.

Sellers, Peter (1925–80) English comedy actor. His success began in radio comedy with *The Goon Show* (1951–59). During the 1950s, he starred in various EALING STUDIOS black comedies such as *The Ladykillers* (1955) and *The Naked Truth* (1957). International recognition came in 1963 with *Dr Strangelove* and the first of

The Pink Panther series. Sellers won a best actor Academy Award for his final role in *Being There* (1979).

semantics Branch of LINGUISTICS and PHILOSOPHY concerned with the study of meaning. In historical linguistics, it generally refers to the analysis of how the meanings of words change over time. In modern linguistics and philosophy, semantics seeks to assess the contribution of word-meaning to the meanings of phrases and sentences, and to comprehend the relationship among and between words and the things they refer to or stand for.

semaphore Device or technique that communicates messages visually; a type of optical telegraph. A railway semaphore signal consists of a vertical post on which a single projecting arm is mounted, whose angle indicates "all clear" or "danger". In flag semaphore, a signaller indicates letters and numerals by the position of his outstretched arms, emphasized with flags.

semen Fluid in a male that contains SPERM from the TESTES and the secretions of various accessory sexual glands. In humans, each ejaculate is normally *c*.3–6ml by volume and contains *c*.200 to 300 million sperm.

semiconductor Substance with electrical CONDUCTIVITY between that of a CONDUCTOR and an INSULATOR. The conductivity increases as temperature increases. A semiconductor consists of elements, such as GERMANIUM and SILICON, or compounds, such as aluminium phosphide, with a crystalline structure. At normal temperatures, some electrons break free and give rise to *n*-type (negative) conductivity with the electrons as the main carriers of the electric current. The holes (electron deficiencies) left by these electrons give rise to *p*-type (positive) conductivity with the holes as the main carriers. Impurities are usually added to the semiconductor material in controlled amounts to add more free electrons or create more holes. A semiconductor junction is formed where there is an abrupt change along the length of the crystal from one type of impurity to the other. Such a *p-n* junction acts as a very efficient RECTIFIER and is the basis of the semiconductor DIODE.

Seminole Native North American band that separated from the main CREEK group in the late 18th century and fled s into Florida under pressure of wars with white settlers. Seminole involvement in wars against the USA led to the First Seminole War (1817–18). In 1832, some Seminole leaders signed a treaty agreeing to move to Oklahoma. Others opposed the move, and the Second Seminole War (1835–42) began. The war claimed 1,500 US troops and cost more than US$20 million before the Seminoles were forced to surrender and move west. Today, *c*.12,000 Seminole live in Florida and Oklahoma.

semiotics (semiology) Study of signs and symbols, both visual and linguistic, and their function in communication. Pioneers of semiotics include Charles Sanders PEIRCE and Ferdinand de SAUSSURE. Roland BARTHES and Claude LÉVI-STRAUSS developed the principles of semiotics further, into STRUCTURALISM.

Semiramis In Assyrian mythology, a queen and goddess, wife of Ninus, founder of NINEVEH. Daughter of a fish goddess and the god of wisdom, she was reared by doves. After the death of Ninus, she ruled alone, founded the city of BABYLON and led victorious armies against numerous enemies until, opposed by her son, she took the form of a dove and flew away.

Semites Peoples whose native tongue belongs to the SEMITIC LANGUAGES group. They originally inhabited an area in Arabia and spoke a common language, Proto-Semitic. Among the modern Semites are Arabs, native Israelis, and many Ethiopians.

Semitic languages Group of languages spoken by peoples native to N Africa and the Middle East and forming one of the five branches of the Afro-Asiatic language family. The Semitic languages are divided into three sub-branches: **North West Semitic** (including HEBREW, ARAMAIC and Eblaite); **North East Semitic** (consisting of Akkadian); and **Central and Southern Semitic** (including ARABIC, South Arabian and Ethiopic). Only Hebrew and Arabic have survived to develop modern forms.

Semmelweis, Ignaz Philipp (1818–65) Hungarian physician, probably the first to recognize the importance of ANTISEPTIC in preventing infection. In 1847, during a outbreak of puerperal fever, he ordered doctors at the Vienna General Hospital to wash their hands before treating a patient. His ideas were ridiculed until confirmed by Joseph LISTER.

Senate Upper house of the US legislature, which together with the HOUSE OF REPRESENTATIVES forms the CONGRESS. It is composed of two senators from each state, who are elected for six-year terms. Elections are held every other year, with about one third of the Senate elected at a time. There are usually 16 standing committees, and committee chairs retain their positions for as long as their party has a majority of the votes. The approval of a simple majority of the Senate is necessary for major presidential appointments and a two-thirds majority for treaties. The Senate can initiate legislation except on fiscal matters. Officially, the presiding officer of the Senate is the vice president, but the position is often delegated.

Senate, Roman Chief governing body of the Roman republic. It originated as a royal council under the early kings. By the 2nd century BC it controlled all matters of policy. Senators were chosen for life by the CENSORS and at first were mainly former CONSULS. They numbered 300, raised to 600 under SULLA, to 900 by CAESAR and reduced to 600 under AUGUSTUS. PLEBEIANS gained entry in the 4th century BC. Under the empire, the emperor's control of military and civil officials gradually restricted the senate to judicial matters and to the city government in Rome. Under the late empire, senatorial status was extended to the landowning elite.

Seneca (Lucius Annaeus) (AD 4–65) Roman STOIC philosopher, b. Spain. Based on Greek models, Seneca's nine tragedies, such as *Phaedra, Medea* and *Oedipus*, have had a lasting impact on European literature. His other works include 12 books of *Moral Essays* and many philosophical letters.

Seneca Most populous division of the IROQUOIS CONFEDERACY; a tribe of Native North Americans who inhabited N New York. Today, *c*.7,000 Seneca live on reservations in W New York. In 1848, the Seneca Nation was formed by the peoples of the Allegany and Cattaraugus reservations. Other Seneca live in Oklahoma, Pennsylvania and Ontario.

Senegal Republic on the NW coast of Africa. Senegal contains the continent's most westerly point, the volcanic Cape Verde, on which the capital, DAKAR, stands. It entirely surrounds The GAMBIA. The Atlantic coastline from St Louis to Dakar is sandy. Plains cover most of Senegal. The N forms part of the SAHEL. The main rivers are the Sénégal, which forms the N border, and the Casamance in the S. **Climate** Dakar has a tropical climate, with a rainy season between June and September. Temperatures are higher inland. Rainfall is greatest in the S. **Vegetation** Desert and semi-desert cover NE Senegal. Dry grassland and scrub predominate in central Senegal. The far S is a region of tropical savanna, although large areas have been cleared for farming. **History and Politics** In

SENEGAL
AREA: 196,720sq km (75,954sq mi)
POPULATION: 8,716,000
CAPITAL (POPULATION): Dakar (1,500,000)

the 6th–10th centuries, Senegal formed part of the empire of ancient GHANA. Between the 10th and 14th centuries, the Tukolor state of Tekrur dominated the Sénégal valley. The ALMORAVID dynasty of Zenega Berbers introduced Islam. In the 14th century, the MALI empire conquered Tekrur. In the early 15th century, the WOLOF established an empire. The SONGHAI empire began to dominate the region. In 1444, Portuguese sailors became the first Europeans to reach Cape Verde. Trading stations were rapidly established in the area. France gradually gained control of the valuable slave trade and founded St Louis in 1658. By 1763, Britain had expelled the French from Senegal and, in 1765, set up Senegambia, the first British colony in Africa. In 1783, France regained control of the region. In the mid-19th century France battled for control of the interior. In 1857, Dakar was founded. In 1895, Senegal became a French colony within the federation of French West Africa. In 1902, the capital of this huge empire was transferred from St Louis to Dakar. In 1946, Senegal joined the French Union. In 1959, Senegal joined French Sudan (now Mali) to form the Federation of Mali. In 1960, Senegal withdrew and became an independent republic within the French community. Léopold Sédar SENGHOR was Senegal's first post-colonial president. Following an unsuccessful coup (1962), Senghor gradually assumed wider powers. During the 1960s, Senegal's economy deteriorated and a succession of droughts caused starvation and civil unrest. In 1974, Senegal was a founding member of the West African Economic Community. In 1981, Senghor was succeeded by Abdou Diouf, and Senegalese troops suppressed a coup in the Gambia. In 1982, the two countries were joined in the Confederation of Senegambia, but the union was dissolved in 1989. From 1989 to 1992, Senegal was at war with Mauritania. In 1993 elections, Diouf was re-elected for a third term. Internal conflict continued, particularly in the S Casamance region where a secessionist movement had gathered strength. In 2000 elections, Diouf was defeated by Abdoulaye Wade of the Senegalese Democratic Party, ending 40 years of Socialist Party rule. **Economy** Senegal is a lower middle income developing country (1995 GDP per capita, US$1,780). Agriculture employs 81% of the workforce, mainly at subsistence level. Food crops include cassava, millet and rice. Senegal is the world's sixth-largest producer of peanuts, its major cash crop and export. Phosphates are Senegal's chief mineral resource, but it also refines oil. Dakar is a busy port with many industries. Fishing is an important activity.

Senghor, Léopold Sédar (1906–) Senegalese statesman and poet. He was the first president (1960–80) of the republic of Senegal. As president, he led (1974) Senegal into the West African Economic Community. His poetry, such as *Songs of the Shade* (1945), is intended for voice with musical accompaniment. Senghor was the first African to be elected to the Académie Française (1984).

Senna, Ayrton (1960–94) Brazilian racing driver. In 1984, he began racing in Formula 1. In 1985, Senna won his first grand prix. He went on to win 41 Grands Prix before dying in a crash at the San Marino Grand Prix.

senna Plants, shrubs and trees of the genus *Senna*, native to warm and tropical regions; some species grow in temperate areas. They have rectangular, feathery leaves and yellow flowers. Family Fabaceae/Leguminosae.

Sennacherib (d. 681 BC) King of ASSYRIA (704–681 BC). Son and successor of SARGON, he led expeditions to subdue Phoenicia and Palestine (701 BC) and defeated the Elamite-Chaldean alliance (691 BC). In 689 BC, he destroyed Babylon and devoted himself to rebuilding his capital, NINEVEH. *See also* ASHURBANIPAL

Sennett, Mack (1884–1960) US film director, producer and actor. Films made by his Keystone company brought fame to Charlie CHAPLIN, Mabel Normand, Fatty Arbuckle and the Keystone Kops.

senses Means by which animals gain information about their environment and physiological condition. The five senses, SIGHT, HEARING, TASTE, SMELL and TOUCH, all rely on specialized receptors on or near the external surface of the body.

Seoul (Kyongsong) Capital of South Korea, on the River Han. The political, commercial, industrial and cultural centre of South Korea, it was founded (1392) as the capital of the Yi dynasty. From 1910 to 1945, it developed rapidly under Japanese governorship. After World War 2, Seoul was the headquarters of the US army of occupation. Following the 1948 partition, it became the capital of South Korea. Seoul's capture by North Korean troops precipitated the start of the KOREAN WAR. In March 1951, Seoul became the headquarters of the UN command in Korea. In 1996, it was the scene of violent student demonstrations for reunification with North Korea. Pop. (1995) 10,229,000.

sepal Modified leaf that makes up the outermost portion of a flower bud. Although usually green and inconspicuous once the flower is open, in some species the sepals look like the PETALS.

Sephardim Descendants of the Jews of medieval Spain and Portugal. Iberian Jews followed the Babylonian rather than the Palestinian Jewish tradition and developed their own language, Ladino. After the expulsion of the Jews from Spain (1492), many settled in Ottoman parts of the Middle East and North Africa. Continuing persecution led many of them to form colonies in Amsterdam and other cities in NW Europe. Many Sephardic Jews were killed in the HOLOCAUST. *See also* ASHKENAZIM

Sepoy Rebellion *See* INDIAN MUTINY

sepsis Destruction of body tissue by disease-causing (pathogenic) bacteria or their toxins. Local or widespread inflammation may occur, possibly followed by NECROSIS, the death of tissue. Treatment is with ANTIBIOTICS.

septicaemia Term for severe SEPSIS or BLOOD POISONING

Septuagint Earliest surviving Greek translation of the Hebrew Bible (the OLD TESTAMENT), made for the Greek-speaking Jewish community in Egypt in the 3rd and 2nd centuries BC. It contains the entire Jewish CANON plus the APOCRYPHA. The Septuagint is divided into four sections: the law, history, poetry and prophets. It is still used by the Greek Orthodox Church.

sequoia Two species of giant evergreen conifer trees native to California and S Oregon, USA: the giant sequoia (*Sequoiadendron giganteum*) and the Californian redwood (*Sequoia sempervirens*). They grow to 100m (330ft). Family Taxodiaceae.

Serbia Balkan republic that, combined with the smaller republic of MONTENEGRO, forms the rump federal state of YUGOSLAVIA. The republic is bounded N by Hungary, E by Romania and Bulgaria, S by Macedonia, SW by Albania and Montenegro, W by BOSNIA-HERZEGOVINA and NW by CROATIA. It includes the provinces of Vojvodina (N) and KOSOVO (S), formerly autonomous under the Yugoslav federation. The capital is BELGRADE, and other major cities include Niš (Serbia), Novi Sad (Vojvodina),and Pristina (Kosovo). The republic can be geographically divided between the mountainous s and the fertile n plain drained by the rivers DANUBE, Sava, Tisza and Morava. Vojvodina is the principal agricultural area, producing fruit and grain. Serbia is the principal industrial area, with mining and steel manufacture. Kosovo is a poor region with large coal deposits. The area was settled by Serbs in the 7th century AD, and they adopted Orthodox Christianity under BYZANTINE rule. Serbia became the leading Balkan power until, in 1389, it was defeated by the Ottoman Turks. The Ottomans divided the territory and installed a puppet regime. In 1459, Serbia became a province of the OTTOMAN EMPIRE. The 18th-century decline of the Ottoman Empire encouraged Serbian nationalism. In 1829, Serbia gained autonomy under Russian protection. In 1867, Milan Obrenović began a war in support of a rebellion against Turkish rule in Bosnia and Herzegovina. Russia intervened to aid Serbia and, in 1878, Turkey finally granted Serbia complete independence. In 1903, King Alexander Obrenović was assassinated, and PETER I became king. In 1908, when Austro-Hungary annexed Bosnia and Herzegovina, Serbia responded by forming the Serbian League. In 1912, the alliance defeated the Turks but disintegrated into factional feuding. In 1913, Serbia defeated Bulgaria in the second Balkan War. The expansion of Serbian territory in the BALKAN WARS antagonized Austria, and the assassination of the Austrian Archduke FRANZ FERDINAND led to the outbreak of World War 1. In 1918, Serbia became the leading force in the kingdom of the Serbs, Croats and Slovenes, renamed YUGOSLAVIA in 1929. During World War 2, Yugoslavia was occupied and divided by the German army. Resistance was two-fold: TITO led the Yugoslav communist partisans, and Mihajović led the Serbian nationalists (Chetniks). In 1946, Serbia became an autonomous republic within Tito's neo-communist Yugoslavia. In 1987, President Slobodan MILOŠEVIĆ restated nationalist claims for a Greater Serbia, including Vojvodina, Kosovo and Serb-populated areas in Croatia, Bosnia-Herzegovina and Macedonia. In 1989, Serbian troops were sent to suppress Albanian nationalism in Kosovo. In 1991, Serbia prevented Croatia from assuming presidency of the federation. Croatia and SLOVENIA responded by declaring independence, and the Serbian-controlled Yugoslav army invaded. In 1991, the army withdrew from Slovenia. In 1992, a UN-brokered ceasefire was agreed between Serbia and Croatia, allowing Serbia to keep the territory it had captured. Serbian troops quickly seized nearly 75% of the newly recognized republic of Bosnia-Herzegovina and pursued a policy of "ethnic cleansing", forcibly resettling, incarcerating or killing Muslims and repopulating villages with Serbs. The UN imposed sanctions on the Serbian regime, but atrocities continued on both sides. In 1995, Bosnian Serb troops captured UN protected areas, and Western governments and NATO launched air strikes against Serb targets. Bosnia-Herzegovina and Croatia began a new offensive against Serbia and reclaimed much lost territory. The US-brokered Dayton Peace Accord (November 1995) divided Bosnia-Herzegovina into provinces. In September 1996, democratic elections were held in Serbia, but Milošević refused to recognize opposition victories. Following peaceful, mass demonstrations in Belgrade, Milošević conceded some of the Zajedno coalition victories. In 1997, Milošević resigned the Serbian presidency in order to become president of Yugoslavia. In 1998, Montenegro sought greater independence from Serbia, and fighting recommenced in Kosovo. NATO bombing of Serb positions in Kosovo took place in 1999 in response to increasing Serbian aggression. Hundreds of thousands of Kosovars fled into neighbouring countries, mainly Albania and Macedonia, to escape "ethnic cleansing". NATO's intensive bombardment devastated Serbia's economy and the Yugoslav army agree to withdraw from Kosovo in June 1999, replaced by a United Nations' (UN) peacekeeping force (K-FOR). In 2000 elections, Vojislav KOŠTUNICA replaced Milošević as president of Yugoslavia. Area: 88,361sq km (34,107sq mi). Pop. (1991) 9,778,991

Serbs Slavic people who settled in the Balkans in the 7th century and who became Christians in the 9th century. They were distinguished from Croats and Slovenes by their use of the Cyrillic, not the Roman, alphabet. Most Serbs now live in Serbia, but there are Serb minorities in Bosnia and Croatia.

serf Person legally bound to a lord. In Europe, under the FEUDAL SYSTEM, serfs had to provide labour and other services and were usually bound to the land, holding a portion for their own use. Gone from w Europe by the end of the Middle Ages, serfdom persisted in Russia and parts of E Europe into the mid-19th century.

serial music Technique of musical composition in which a work is structured on a fixed series of notes; the series is repeated in various permutations for the duration of the work. The TWELVE-TONE MUSIC of Arnold SCHOENBERG is a form of serial music.

series Mathematical expression obtained by adding the terms of a sequence. Thus, the series $1 + 4 + 9 + 16 + ...$ is formed from the sequence 1, 4, 9, 16 .... Series may be finite or infinite, and infinite series may converge. An infinite series that fails to converge is said to diverge. A series formed from increasing powers of a variable is a power series; convergent power series are used for representing many functions.

Sermon on the Mount Address given by JESUS CHRIST to his disciples and a huge crowd of other listeners on one of the hills above GALILEE. It presents many of the now familiar Christian teachings. *See also* BEATITUDES

serotonin Chemical found in cells of the gastrointestinal tract, blood platelets and brain tissue, concentrated in the midbrain and HYPOTHALAMUS. It is a VASOCONSTRICTOR and has an important role in the functioning of the nervous system and in the stimulation of smooth muscles.

serpentine ($Mg_3Si_2O_5(OH)_4$) Group of sheet silicate minerals, hydrated magnesium silicate. They have monoclinic system crystals. Usually green, they are commonly used in decorative carving. Fibrous varieties are used in asbestos cloth. Hardness 2.5–4; r.d. 2.5–2.6.

serum Clear fluid that separates out if BLOOD is left to clot. It is essentially of the same composition as PLASMA, but without fibrinogen and clotting factors.

serval (bush cat) Orange and black spotted cat found in grassy areas of sub-Saharan Africa. It has a narrow head and long legs, neck and ears. Length: body 70–100cm (30–40in); tail 35–40cm (14–16in); weight: 6.8–11.3kg (15–25lb). Family Felidae; species *Felis serval*.

Servetus, Michael (1511–53) Spanish physician and theologian. Servetus published (1531–32) his unorthodox opinions concerning the TRINITY. In medicine, he discovered that blood circulates through the lungs. Forced to flee from the INQUISITION, Servetus was unwelcome among Reformation and Catholic theologians alike. Under the orders of John CALVIN, he was arrested and tried in Geneva and burned as a heretic.

servomechanism Device that provides remote control to activate a mechanism. An input signal, such as a radio impulse or mechanical movement, is converted into a mechanical output, such as a lever or amplified hydraulic force. Some servomechanisms, such as the automatic pilot of an aircraft, incorporate a feedback mechanism that makes them independent of human control.

sesame Tropical plant native to Asia and Africa, cultivated for its oil and seeds. It has oval leaves, pink or white flowers and seed capsules along the stem. Height: 60cm (2ft). Family Pedaliaceae; species *Sesamum indicum*.

sessile In zoology, describing an animal that remains fixed in one place. Sedentary animals, such as barnacles, limpets and mussels, are usually permanently attached to a surface. The term sessile is also used to describe the eyes of crustaceans that lack stalks and sit directly on the animal's head. In botany, sessile describes any structure that has no stalk (in cases where one might be expected) and grows directly from a STEM. Examples include the acorns and leaves of some oak trees.

Sessions, Roger (1896–1985) US composer whose complex and highly individual works include a violin concerto (1935), eight symphonies, a concertino for chamber orchestra (1972) and piano and organ works.

set In mathematics, a defined collection of objects. The objects are called the elements or members of the set. The number of members can be finite or infinite, or even be zero (the **null set**). Various relations can exist between two sets, *A* and *B*: *A* equals *B* if both sets contain exactly the same members; *A* is included in, or is a subset of, *B* if all members of *A* are members of *B*; disjoint sets have no members in common; overlapping sets have one or more common members. Operations on sets produce new sets: the union of *A* and *B* contains the members of both *A* and *B*; the intersection of *A* and *B* contains only those members common to both sets.

Seth, Vikram (1952–) Indian novelist and poet. He came to attention with his award-winning travelogue, *From Heaven Lake* (1983). His epic *A Suitable Boy* (1993) is one of the longest English novels. Other works include volumes of poetry, including *All You Who Sleep Tonight* (1990), and the novel *An Equal Music* (1999).

Seth Egyptian god. Although a beneficent god in pre-dynastic Egypt, Seth became linked with darkness and was later seen as a god of evil and the rival of HORUS.

Seton, Saint Elizabeth Ann (1774–1821) US teacher and charity organizer. Seton founded (1808) the first Roman Catholic elementary school in the USA. In 1809, she founded the American Sisters of Charity. Her sainthood, the first for a native-born American, was proclaimed in 1975. Her feast day is 4 January.

setter Long-haired, hunting dog used to find game and stand on point until the hunter arrives; it also retrieves. Modern types include English, Irish and Gordon.

set theory Branch of mathematics developed by Georg CANTOR in the late 19th century. Based on George BOOLE's work on mathematical logic, it manipulates SETS of abstract or real objects rather than logical propositions. It is concerned with the properties of sets.

Settlement, Act of (1701) English parliamentary statute regulating the succession to the throne. The purpose of the act was to prevent the restoration of the Catholic STUART monarchy. It settled the succession on SOPHIA of Hanover, granddaughter of JAMES I, and her heirs, providing they were Protestants. The crown was inherited (1714) by Sophia's son, who became GEORGE I.

Seurat, Georges Pierre (1859–91) French painter, founder of NEO-IMPRESSIONISM. From 1876 to 1884, he developed POINTILLISM, which was based on the juxtaposition of pure colour dots. His paintings include *Bathing at Asnières* (1883–84) and *Sunday in Summer on the Island of La Grande-Jatte* (1886).

Seuss, Dr (1904–91) (Theodor Seuss Geisel) US children's writer and illustrator. His first book, *And to Think That I Saw It on Mulberry Street* (1937), established his style of combining doggerel verse with zany artwork. In 1957, he published *The Cat in the Hat*, the first in a series of more than 50 "Beginner" books designed to help children to learn to read.

Sevastopol (Sebastopol) Black Sea port on the SW of the Crimean Peninsula, Ukraine. Founded in 1783 by Catherine II, the city became home to the Russian Black Sea fleet and was the major strategic objective of the CRIMEAN WAR, besieged from October 1854 to September 1855. The Russians sank their own fleet to block the harbour entrance. By 1890, the city was again a working naval base. In 1995, Ukraine agreed to allow the Russian fleet to maintain its base here in return for Ukrainian ownership of 19% of the fleet. Pop. (1996) 365,000.

Seventh-day Adventists Christian denomination whose members expect JESUS CHRIST to return to Earth in person. They hold the SABBATH on Saturday and accept the BIBLE literally as their guide for living. The sect was organized formally in the USA in 1863 and today it is the largest worldwide ADVENTIST denomination.

Seven Weeks' War *See* AUSTRO-PRUSSIAN WAR

Seven Wonders of the World Group of fabled sights that evolved from various ancient Greek lists. They were, in chronological order: the PYRAMIDS of EGYPT; the HANGING GARDENS OF BABYLON; the statue of ZEUS by PHIDIAS at OLYMPIA; the temple of ARTEMIS at EPHESUS; the MAUSOLEUM at HALICARNASSUS; the COLOSSUS OF RHODES; and the PHAROS at ALEXANDRIA.

Seven Years' War (1756–63) Major European conflict that established Britain as the foremost maritime and colonial power and ensured the survival of Prussia as a major power in central Europe. The war was a continuation of the rivalries involved in the War of the AUSTRIAN SUCCESSION (1740–48). Britain and Prussia were allied, with Prussia undertaking nearly all the fighting in Europe against Austria, Russia, France and Sweden. FREDERICK II (THE GREAT) of Prussia fought a defensive war against superior forces. Only his brilliant generalship and the withdrawal of Russia from the war in 1762 saved Prussia from being overrun. Overseas, Britain and France fought in North America (FRENCH AND INDIAN WARS), India and West Africa, with the British gaining major victories. At the end of the war, the Treaty of PARIS (1763) confirmed British supremacy in North America and India, while the Treaty of Hubertusberg left Prussia in control of Silesia.

Severn Longest river in the UK, flowing 290km (180mi) through Wales and W England. It rises on Mount Plynlimon in W Wales, flows NE to Shrewsbury, turns SE and then SW to enter the Bristol Channel through a wide estuary. The Severn is connected by canal to the rivers THAMES, Mersey and Trent.

Severus, Lucius Septimius (146–211) Roman emperor (193–211). He was proclaimed emperor by his troops, who marched on Rome and persuaded the Senate to confirm him. To secure his position, Severus dissolved the Praetorian Guard, replacing it with his own men, and proclaimed himself posthumously adopted by the Emperor MARCUS AURELIUS (d.180). He divided (208) Britain into two provinces and launched a campaign to conquer Scotland. Repulsed, he died at York.

Seville Port on the River Guadalquivir, SW Spain, capital of Seville province. Ruled by the Romans from the 2nd century BC to the 5th century AD, it was taken by the Moors in 712 and served as the centre of the Moorish kingdom until conquered (1248) by Ferdinand III. Sites include a 15th-century gothic cathedral that incorporates remnants of a mosque. The port exports fruit (notably oranges) and wine. Industries: agricultural machinery, shipbuilding, chemicals, textiles, porcelain, shipping, tourism. Pop. (1995) 720,000.

Sèvres In ceramics, high-quality PORCELAIN made from 1765 to the present day at a factory in the Paris suburb of Sèvres, France. Pieces are either of soft-paste (a porcella-neous substance) or hard-paste (true porcelain).

Sèvres, Treaty of (1920) Peace treaty between Turkey and its European opponents in World War 1 that imposed harsh terms on the Ottoman sultan. The treaty, never rat-ified, was replaced by the Treaty of LAUSANNE (1923).

Seward, William Henry (1801–72) US statesman. He lost the Republican nomination for president (1860) to Abraham LINCOLN, who appointed him secretary of state. Seward succeeded in maintaining good relations with Europe during the CIVIL WAR, and his handling of the TRENT AFFAIR averted British recognition of the Confed-eracy. He was wounded in the shooting conspiracy that killed Lincoln but continued in office under Andrew JOHNSON, negotiating (1867) the purchase of Alaska.

sewing machine Machine that uses a needle to stitch material together with thread. The first basic sewing machine was invented (1846) in the USA by Elias Howe. In 1851, Isaac Merrit SINGER invented a machine for continuous stitching.

sex Classification of an organism into male or female, denoting the reproductive function of the individual. In mammals the presence of sex organs (OVARIES in the female, TESTES in the male) are **primary** sexual charac-teristics. **Secondary** sexual characteristics, such as size, coloration and hair growth, are governed by the secre-tion of SEX HORMONES. In flowering plants, the female sex organs are the CARPEL, including the OVARY, STYLE and STIGMA, and the male organs the STAMENS. Male and female organs may occur in the same flower or on sepa-rate flowers or plants. *See also* SEXUAL REPRODUCTION

sex discrimination Unequal treatment of people because of gender. This usually involves denial of eco-nomic or social opportunities and may result from preju-dice, stereotyping or social pressure. Efforts to elimini-nate sex discrimination include legislation, WOMEN'S RIGHTS MOVEMENTS and consciousness-raising groups.

sex hormones Chemical "messengers" secreted by the gonads (TESTES and OVARIES). They regulate sexual devel-opment and reproductive activity, and influence sexual behaviour. In males they include TESTOSTERONE, made by the testes; in females, the sex hormones, OESTROGEN and PROGESTERONE, are produced by the ovaries.

sextant Optical instrument for finding LATITUDE (angu-lar distance N or S of the Equator). The sextant consists of a frame with a curved scale marked in degrees, a movable arm with an ordinary mirror at the pivot, a half-silvered glass and a telescope. The instrument measures the angle of a heavenly body above the horizon, which depends on the observer's latitude. A set of tables gives the corre-sponding latitude for various angles measured.

sexual intercourse Term used to describe sexual relations between people. It is most commonly used to describe the insertion of the male penis into the female vagina. *See also* CONTRACEPTION; ORGASM; SEXUAL REPRODUCTION

sexually transmitted disease (STD) Any disease that is transmitted by sexual activity involving the trans-fer of body fluids. It encompasses a range of conditions that are spread primarily by sexual contact, although they may also be transmitted in other ways. These

include ACQUIRED IMMUNE DEFICIENCY SYNDROME (AIDS), pelvic inflammatory disease and viral HEPATI-TIS. Older STDs, such as SYPHILIS and GONORRHOEA, remain significant public health problems.

sexual reproduction Biological process of reproduc-tion involving the combination of genetic material from two parents. It occurs in different forms throughout the plant and animal kingdoms. This process gives rise to variations of the GENOTYPE and PHENOTYPE within a species. GAMETES, HAPLOID sex cells produced by MEIO-SIS, contain only half the number of CHROMOSOMES of their parent cells (which are DIPLOID). At FERTILIZATION, the gametes, generally one from each parent, fuse to form a ZYGOTE with the diploid number of chromosomes. The zygote divides repeatedly, and the cells differentiate to produce an EMBRYO and, finally, a fully formed organism.

Seychelles Republic consisting of more than 100 islands in the Indian Ocean, *c*.970km (600mi) N of Madagascar. Seychelles comprises two geologically distinct island groups: the volcanic, **Granitic** group is to the NE and includes the three principal, inhabited islands of Mahé, Praslin and La Digue. Mahé is home to more than 80% of the republic's people; Seychelles' capital, Victoria, lies on its NE coast. To the SW lies the **Outer** group of coral islands. In 1502, Vasco da Gama explored the islands and named them the "Seven Sisters". The islands were colonized in 1756 by the French, who established spice plantations worked by slaves from Mauritius. In 1794, the archipelago was captured by the British during the Napoleonic Wars and, in 1814, became a dependency of Mauritius. In 1903, the Seychelles became a separate crown colony. In 1976, they achieved full independence within the Common-wealth of Nations. In 1977, a coup established Albert René as president. In 1981, South African mercenaries attempted to overthrow the government. Continued civil unrest and another failed coup in 1987 led to the first multiparty elec-tions (1991). In 1998, Albert René was elected for a fifth term. Creole is the most widely spoken language. Tourism is the largest industry; exports include coconuts and tuna. Area: 453sq km (175sq mi). Pop. (2000) 75,000

Seyfert galaxy Class of GALAXIES that have extremely bright, compact nuclei and whose spectra show strong emission lines. About 1% of all galaxies are Seyferts. They emit strongly at ultraviolet and infrared wave-lengths and exhibit a degree of short-term variability.

Sezession Radical movement (formed 1897) of young Austrian artists who organized their own exhibitions and aligned themselves with progressive European contem-poraries. The first president was Gustav KLIMT; other members included Oskar KOKOSCHKA and Egon SCHIELE.

Sforza, Ludovico (*c*.1451–1508) Duke of Milan (1494–99). In effective control of the city-state from 1480, Ludovico tried to cement his family's power base through diplomacy and intrigue. Sforza's alliance (1494) with CHARLES VIII of France marked the start of the Ital-ian Wars. He reneged on the agreement, however, and LOUIS XII invaded Milan and dispossessed Sforza. He died a prisoner in France. Sforza is mainly remembered for his patronage of LEONARDO DA VINCI and BRAMANTE.

Shackleton, Sir Ernest Henry (1874–1922) Irish Antarctic explorer. He led an expedition (1907–09) that reached to within 155km (97mi) of the South Pole. On his second expedition (1914–16), his ship was crushed by ice and his men marooned on a small island. Shackle-ton's successful rescue mission, which he described in *South* (1919), is one of the epics of polar exploration.

shad Saltwater fish of the HERRING family that swims upriver to spawn. Shads are prized for their roe. Deep-bodied, they have a notch in the upper jaw for the tip of the lower jaw. Length: to 75cm (30in). Family Clupeidae.

shadow Area screened from a light source and therefore relatively dark. It differs in size depending on the distance between the light source and the screening object. When the light source is extended, the outline of the shadow is blurred; where the source is partly visible, there is an area of mid-shadow (**penumbra**) lying outside the darker shadow itself (**umbra**)

Shaffer, Peter (1926–) English dramatist. Following the success of *Five Finger Exercise* (1960), he wrote *The Private Ear and The Public Eye* (1962). Schaffer's plays *Equus* (1973) and *Amadeus* (1979) were both filmed.

Shaftesbury, Anthony Ashley Cooper, 1st Earl of (1621–83) English statesman. He was a member of the COMMONWEALTH council of state under Oliver CROMWELL. Dismayed by the autocracy of the PROTECTORATE, he supported the RESTORATION of CHARLES II (1660) and was rewarded with the chancellorship. Opposed to the Earl of CLARENDON, Shaftesbury became lord chancellor (1672) but was soon dismissed. His determination to prevent the succession of the Catholic JAMES II drove him to found (1673) the WHIG PARTY in opposition to DANBY. Shaftesbury's support for the duke of MONMOUTH led to his exile (1682) in Holland.

Shaftesbury, Anthony Ashley Cooper, 7th Earl of (1801–85) British social reformer. He was the chief driving force behind the acts that prohibited employment of women and young children in mines (1842) and restricted the working day to ten hours (1847).

Shah Jahan (1592–1666) MOGUL emperor of India (1628–58). Third son of JAHANGIR, he secured his succession by killing most of his male relatives. His campaigns expanded the MOGUL EMPIRE and accumulated great treasure. Though relatively tolerant of Hinduism, he made Islam the state religion. Shah Jahan was responsible for building the TAJ MAHAL and the vast ornamental chambers of the Red Fort at DELHI, which he made his capital.

Shahn, Ben (1898–1969) US painter, lithographer and photographer, b. Lithuania. His work reflected his concern with social and political injustices, notably the SACCO AND VANZETTI CASE. In the 1930s, he worked with

Diego RIVERA on murals for the Rockefeller Center, New York. He was involved with the Farm Security Administration, painting and photographing rural poverty.

Shaka (1787–1828) King of the ZULU. In *c.*1816, he claimed the throne, forming a powerful Zulu army and extending his control over all of what is now KwaZulu-Natal. Shaka maintained good relations with the white government in the Cape, but his harsh rule provoked domestic opposition and he was killed by his half brother.

Shakers (officially United Society of Believers in Christ's Second Appearing) US religious sect. Originally an offshoot of the English QUAKERS, the nickname derived from the fervour of their religious ceremonies. In 1774, Ann Lee and eight of her followers emigrated to New York. "Mother Ann" believed she was the female reincarnation of Jesus Christ. After her death (1784), the movement spread and by *c.*1850 they numbered *c.*6,000 in more than 18 communes. One of the central beliefs of Shakers is the dual (male and female) nature of the Deity. Other tenets include celibacy, sexual equality, pacifism, and the sanctity of labour. They are noted for their crafts.

Shakespeare, William (1564–1616) English poet and dramatist. By 1592, he was established in London, having already written the three parts of *Henry VI*. By 1594, Shakespeare was a member of the Lord Chamberlain's Men and in 1599 a partner in the GLOBE THEATRE, where many of his plays were presented. He retired to STRATFORD-UPON-AVON around 1613. His 154 *Sonnets*, which were first published in 1609, stand among the finest works in ENGLISH LITERATURE. The plays are usually divided into four groups – historical plays, comedies, tragedies and late romances. Shakespeare's plots are generally drawn from existing sources, such as Holinshed.

SHAKESPEARE'S PLAYS

Histories: *Henry VI (part I)* (1589–90), *Henry VI (part II)* (1590–91), *Henry VI (part III)* (1590–91), *Titus Andronicus* (1590–94), *Richard III* (1592–93), *King John* (1595–97), *Richard II* (1595), *Henry IV (part I)* (1596), *Henry IV (part II)* (1597), *Henry V* (1599), *Julius Caesar* (1599), *Troilus and Cressida* (1601–02), *Timon of Athens* (1605–09), *Antony and Cleopatra* (1606–07), *Coriolanus* (1607–08), *Henry VIII* (1613)

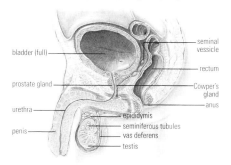

▲ sexual reproduction The male reproductive system is situated both inside and outside the pelvic region. Outside the body are the testes. They produce sperm in the seminiferous tubules. Once the sperm are matured they are stored in the epididymis. During intercourse they pass along the vas deferens to the urethra. The seminal vessicles, prostate and Cowper's glands all secrete fluids into the urethra, helping to make semen. The female reproductive organs lie solely within the pelvic girdle. The ovaries usually release just one mature egg each month, which is then transferred to the uterus via one or other of the Fallopian tubes. Embedded in the ovaries of the newly born female are several hundred thousand of the follicles that can potentially develop into eggs. Only a few hundred of them will do so, becoming mature eggs, which, when they are ripe, are caught by the fimbria at the end of the tubes, near the site where fertilization usually occurs. The woman's urinary system, unlike the male's, is separate from the genitals.

Comedies: *The Comedy of Errors* (1590–94), *Love's Labour's Lost* (1590–94), *The Two Gentlemen of Verona* (1592–93), *The Taming of the Shrew* (1592), *A Midsummer Night's Dream* (1595), *The Merchant of Venice* (1596–98), *The Merry Wives of Windsor* (1597), *Much Ado About Nothing* (1598), *As You Like It* (1599), *Twelfth Night* (1600–02), *All's Well That Ends Well* (1602–03), *Measure for Measure* (1604–05)

Tragedies: *Romeo and Juliet* (1595–96), *Hamlet* (1600–01), *Othello* (1604), *King Lear* (1605–06), *Macbeth* (1605–06)

Late Romances: *Pericles* (1607–08), *Cymbeline* (1609–10), *The Winter's Tale* (1611), *The Tempest* (1613)

shale Common SEDIMENTARY ROCK formed from mud or clay. Characterized by very fine layering, it may contain material such as FOSSILS, carbonaceous matter and oil.

shallot Perennial plant native to W Asia and widely cultivated in temperate climates. It has thin, small leaves and clustered bulbs, which have a mild, onion-like flavour. Family Liliaceae; species *Allium cepa*.

shaman Tribal witch doctor or medicine man believed to be in contact with spirits or the supernatural worlds. Shamanism is found among the ESKIMOS and NATIVE AMERICANS and in Siberia, where the term originated. African equivalents also exist. *See also* ANIMISM

Shamir, Yitzhak (1915–) Israeli statesman, prime minister (1983–84, 1986–92). He was the leader (1940–48) of the Stern Gang of Zionist guerrillas against the British mandate in Palestine. Shamir became head (1955–65) of Mossad, Israel's secret service. He was foreign minister (1980–83) under Menachim BEGIN, and succeeded him as prime minister and head of the right-wing Likud Party. In 1986, he succeeded Shimon PERES as head of a coalition government. Shamir oversaw the Jewish settlement of the WEST BANK and GAZA STRIP. In 1992, he was defeated by Yitzhak RABIN, and Binyamin NETANYAHU succeeded him as leader of Likud.

shamrock Plant with three-part leaves, usually taken to be *Trifolium repens* or *T. dubium*, the national emblem of Ireland. Legend tells that St Patrick used it to symbolize the Trinity. Family Leguminosae.

Shandong (Shantung) Province in E China. JINAN is the capital. The E part of the province is a peninsula between the Po Hai and the Huang Hai; the W is part of the HUANG HE delta. Much of the land has been reclaimed for the cultivation of wheat and cotton. Oil, coal, iron ore, salt and gold are all extracted. Fishing and silk are important industries. It is the birthplace of Confucius. Area: 153,600sq km (59,304sq mi). Pop. (1990) 84,893,000.

Shang (Yin) Early Chinese dynasty (c.1523–c.1027 BC). Successor to the Xia (Hsia) dynasty, the Shang was based in the valley of the HUANG HE (Yellow River). During the Shang period, the Chinese written language was perfected, techniques of flood control and irrigation were practised, and artefacts were made in cast bronze.

Shanghai Largest city and port in China, 22km (13mi) from the Yangtze (Changjiang) delta, SE China. By the Treaty of Nanking (1842), the city was opened to foreign trade, which stimulated economic growth. The USA, Britain, France and Japan all held areas of the city. Occupied by the Japanese in 1937, Shanghai was restored to China at the end of World War 2 and fell to the communists in 1949. Industries: textiles, steel, chemicals, publishing, rubber, farm machinery, ship-building, pharmaceuticals, financial services. Pop. (1993) 8,760,000.

Shankar, Ravi (1920–) Indian musician. He was responsible for popularizing the SITAR, and Indian music in general, in the West. Shankar founded the National Orchestra of India and was music director of All-India

Radio (1948–56). He toured Europe and the USA extensively during the 1960s and 1970s.

Shannon Longest river in the Republic of Ireland and the British Isles. It rises on Cuilcagh Mountain, NW County Cavan, and flows S through loughs Allen, Ree and Derg, S across the central plain of Ireland to Limerick and then W to enter the Atlantic Ocean. The Shannon separates Connacht from the provinces of Leinster and Munster. Length: 370km (230mi).

Shapley, Harlow (1885–1972) US astronomer who provided the first accurate model of our GALAXY. By observing CEPHEID VARIABLE stars in globular clusters, he calculated the distance to each cluster in the galaxy, obtaining a picture of its shape and size.

shares Documents representing money invested in a company in return for membership rights in the ownership of that company. Shares are expressed in monetary units. Shareholders regularly receive payment of dividends that depend on the net profit of the company. In the USA, the term stock is usually used instead of share. In the UK, although the definitions have become blurred, stocks usually mean fixed-interest securities such as those issued by governments.

sharia Traditional law of ISLAM, believed by Muslims to be the result of divine revelation. It is drawn from a number of sources, including the KORAN and a collection of teachings and legends about the life of MUHAMMAD known as the *Hadith*.

Sharjah Capital of the Sheikdom of Sharjah, third-largest of the seven UNITED ARAB EMIRATES, on the Persian Gulf, E Arabia. A British protectorate until 1971, the sheikdom is part of a prosperous oil- and gas-producing area. Pop. (1984) 125,000.

shark Torpedo-shaped, cartilaginous fish found in subpolar to tropical marine waters. They have well-developed jaws, bony teeth, usually five gill slits on each side of the head and a characteristic lobe-shaped tail with a longer top lobe. Sharks are carnivorous and at least 10 species are known to attack humans. There are about 250 living species. Order Selachii. *See also* DOGFISH; HAMMERHEAD; WHALE SHARK; WHITE SHARK

Sharon, Ariel (1928–) Israeli general and statesman. A commander in the first of the ARAB-ISRAELI WARS (1948) and the SIX-DAY WAR (1967). He was a founder (1973) of the right-wing Likud coalition. As minister of defence (1981–83) under Menachem BEGIN, Sharon was the main architect of Israel's invasion of LEBANON. He served as minister of foreign affairs (1999) under Binyamin NETANYAHU, supporting further Jewish settlement in the Occupied Territories. In 2000, he succeeded Netanyahu as leader of Likud. Later that year, Sharon's provocative visit to a Muslim shrine in Jerusalem sparked violent conflict between Israeli soldiers and Palestinians in the West Bank.

Sharpeville Black township, N of Vereeniging, South Africa, scene of a massacre (March 1960) by South African security forces. When a large crowd failed to disperse, the police opened fire, killing 67 people and wounding 186. The massacre led to greater militancy in the struggle against APARTHEID.

Shatt al Arab Channel formed by the confluence of the rivers TIGRIS and EUPHRATES, SE Iraq. It flows SE to the Persian Gulf through a wide delta. Forming the border between Iraq and Iran, its lower course was the scene of bitter fighting during the IRAN-IRAQ WAR (1980–88).

Shaw, George Bernard (1856–1950) Irish dramatist, critic and member of the FABIAN SOCIETY. Shaw transformed Victorian theatre, rejecting melodrama in favour of socially conscious drama. Although many of his plays were comedies, they expressed his radical political and philosophical ideas. *Arms and the Man* (1894) was Shaw's first publicly performed play. Plays such as *Man and Superman* (1905) and *Major Barbara* (1905) were first performed at the Royal Court, London. *Pygmalion* (1913) was turned into the musical *My Fair Lady* (1956). Other major plays include *Heartbreak House* (1920), *Back to Methuselah* (1922) and *Saint Joan* (1923). The prefaces to his plays were published separately. Shaw received the 1925 Nobel Prize for literature.

Shawnee Algonquian-speaking tribe of NATIVE AMERICANS. Their early home was along the Cumberland River in Tennessee, but today most of the 5,000 Shawnee descendants live in Oklahoma. This number includes many DELAWARE, who are closely related to them.

Shearer, Alan (1970–) English footballer. Shearer began (1988) his professional career with Southampton. A powerful striker, in 1992 he joined Blackburn Rovers. The following season, he became the first player to score 100 goals in the Premier League. In 1996, he was the leading scorer in the European Championship and moved to Newcastle for a world record transfer fee of £15 million. In 1998, he captained England's World Cup team.

shearwater Seabird related to the ALBATROSS and PETREL. Most species are brown or black with pale underparts. Shearwaters live mainly on the ocean; they feed on fish and squid and burrow nests in coastal cliffs. Length: 19–56cm (7.5–22in). Family Procellariidae.

Sheba (Saba) Ancient kingdom of s Arabia celebrated for its trade in gold, spices and precious stones. According to the Bible, the Queen of Sheba visited Jerusalem to hear the wisdom of SOLOMON in the 10th century BC.

sheep Ruminants of the genus *Ovis*, and those of the less numerous genera *Pseudois* and *Ammotragus*. Domestic sheep, *O. aries*, are now bred for WOOL, fur (karakul) and meat. Wild species are found in the mountains of Europe, Asia, Africa and North America. Family Bovidae.

sheepdog Any of several breeds of dog that were originally bred to herd and guard sheep. The term includes such breeds as the Old English sheepdog, Shetland sheepdog, COLLIE, border collie and GERMAN SHEPHERD.

Sheffield City and county district in South Yorkshire, N England. A hilly city, it lies at the confluence of the River Don and its tributaries, the Sheaf, Rivelin and Loxley. It is a major industrial centre, noted for steel and steel products. Pop. (1994) 429,000.

shell In zoology, hard protective case of various MOLLUSCS. The case is secreted by the epidermis of the mollusc and consists of a protein matrix strengthened by calcium carbonate.

shellac Purified RESIN made from the secretions of the LAC insect. Shellac is fluid when heated and rigid at room temperature. It is used in the production of adhesives, hairsprays, and varnishes.

Shelley, Mary Wollstonecraft (1797–1851) English novelist, daughter of Mary WOLLSTONECRAFT. She eloped with Percy SHELLEY in 1814 and married him in 1816. Her later works of fiction, which include *The Last Man* (1826) and *Lodore* (1835), have been eclipsed by her first novel, *Frankenstein* (1818).

Shelley, Percy Bysshe (1792–1822) English poet. A committed atheist, he was expelled (1811) from Oxford University. His radical pamphlets forced him into hiding in Wales, where he wrote *Queen Mab* (1813). *Alastor* (1816) reflects his political idealism. From 1818 he lived in Italy with his second wife, Mary SHELLEY. *The Cenci* (1819) is a five-act tragedy. The Peterloo Massacre (1819) prompted *The Mask of Anarchy. Prometheus Unbound* (1820), a four-act lyrical drama, is a masterpiece of ROMANTICISM. Smaller poems include "Ode to the West Wind" (1819) and "To a Skylark" (1820). The death of John KEATS inspired *Adonais* (1821). Shelley drowned in a boating accident.

shellfish Common name for edible shelled MOLLUSCS and CRUSTACEA. Shelled molluscs include CLAMS, MUSSELS, OYSTERS and SCALLOPS; crustaceans include SHRIMPS, LOBSTERS and CRABS.

Shenandoah Valley Part of the Great Appalachian Valley, located between the Blue Ridge and Allegheny mountains, N Virginia, USA. The Shenandoah River flows through the valley and empties into the Potomac at Harpers Ferry, West Virginia. The valley was first explored in the 1700s and was a vital route in the westward expansion of the FRONTIER. During the Civil War, it served as a supply centre for the Confederates. It was the scene of heavy fighting during General "Stonewall" JACKSON's "valley campaign" of 1862, and acted as General LEE's escape route in the ANTIETAM and GETTYSBURG campaigns. Length: 240km (150mi).

Shenyang (formerly Mukden) Capital of Liaoning province, on the River Hun, NE China. Once capital of the Qing dynasty, it was the site of the MANCHURIAN INCIDENT (1931), which served as the pretext for the Japanese invasion of Manchuria. The Japanese were responsible for the development of the city's industrial base. Today, Shenyang is China's fourth-largest city and an industrial powerhouse. Industries: aircraft, machine tools, heavy machinery, cables, cement. Pop. (1994) 3,762,000.

Shepard, Alan Bartlett, Jr (1923–98) US astronaut. In 1961, he became the first American to be launched into space. In 1971, Shepard commanded *Apollo 14* and became the fifth man to walk on the lunar surface.

Shepard, Sam (1943–) US dramatist and actor. A leader of US avant-garde theatre, he often focuses on the disjunction between contemporary US society and the American dream. Shepard won a Pulitzer Prize for *Buried Child* (1978). *True West* (1983) is a trilogy on the myth of the West. He acted in and wrote the screenplays for *Fool for Love* (1985) and *Crimes of the Heart* (1986).

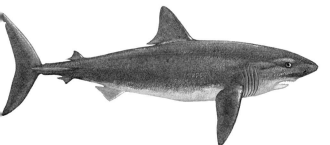

◀ **shark** The mako shark (*Isurus oxyrhyncus*) belongs to the mackerel shark family. A ferocious predator, the mako has a streamlined body that enables it to swim at speeds of more than 65km/h (40mph). Makos are found in the Atlantic, Pacific and Indian oceans and have been known to attack humans. Adults reach over 3.7m (12ft) and weigh up to 400kg (880lb).

Sheraton, Thomas (1751–1806) English furniture designer whose designs became influential through his manuals. While there are no works directly attributed to him, art historians have taken his name for a dominant style in furniture in the early 1800s.

Sheridan, Philip Henry (1831–88) Union general in the CIVIL WAR. In 1864, Sheridan was appointed commander of the cavalry corps of the Army of the Potomac and led an attack on General LEE's communications. Commanding the army of the Shenandoah, Sheridan devastated the valley. He cut off Lee's retreat and forced his surrender at APPOMATTOX Court House (1865).

Sheridan, Richard Brinsley (1751–1816) English dramatist and politician. He excelled in comedies of manners, such as *The Rivals* (1775) and *The School for Scandal* (1777). Entering Parliament (1780) as a member of the Whig Party, Sheridan became one of the most brilliant orators of his generation.

Sherman, William Tecumseh (1820–91) Union general in the CIVIL WAR. He took part in the first battle of BULL RUN and in the capture of VICKSBURG. He won the battle of Atlanta and led the "March to the Sea" from Atlanta to Savannah in 1864.

Sherpa Buddhist people who inhabit the Khumba Valley, NE Nepal. Of Tibetan origin, they are renowned for their portering of Himalayan expeditions. They cultivate cereals and potatoes and herd sheep and cattle.

Sherrington, Sir Charles Scott (1857–1952) English physiologist. He established physiological psychology with his book *The Integrative Action of the Nervous System* (1906). Sherrington shared the 1932 Nobel Prize for physiology or medicine.

sherry Fortified wine. It has a characteristic raisiny flavour produced by a special method of vinification and blending. True sherry comes from Jerez, Spain.

Sherwood, Robert Emmet (1896–1955) US dramatist. Sherwood won four Pulitzer Prizes: *Idiot's Delight* (1936), *Abe Lincoln in Illinois* (1938), *There Shall be No Night* (1940) and his memoir *Roosevelt and Hopkins* (1948). He was a speechwriter for President Franklin D. Roosevelt. Sherwood won an Oscar for best screenplay for *The Best Years of Our Lives* (1946).

Sherwood Forest Ancient royal hunting ground in Nottinghamshire, central England. Famous as the home of the legendary ROBIN HOOD, some of the original forest remains. Part of it is protected in a country park.

Shetland Islands Group of *c*.100 islands NE of the Orkneys, 210km (130mi) off the N coast of Scotland, constituting an administrative region. Settled by Norse invaders in the 9th century, the islands were seized by Scotland in 1472. The principal islands are Mainland (which has the main town of Lerwick), Yell, Unst, Whalsay and Bressay. The islands are rocky with thin soils, but oats and barley are grown in places. Fishing and livestock are important, and the islands are famous for SHETLAND PONIES. The region is also noted for its woollen clothing. More recently, oil and tourism have become major industries. Area: 1,433sq km (553sq mi) Pop. (1991) 22,522.

Shetland pony One of the smallest types of light horse. Originating in the SHETLAND ISLANDS, it makes an ideal child's mount. Height: typically 71cm (28in) at the shoulder; weight: 169kg (350lb).

Shevardnadze, Eduard Ambrosievich (1928–) Georgian statesman, president (1992–). A close ally of Mikhail GORBACHEV, Shevardnadze was Soviet foreign minister (1985–90). He oversaw the Soviet withdrawal from Afghanistan and worked on détente with the West. In 1990, Shevardnadze resigned and formed the Democratic Reform Movement. As president of Georgia, he sought Russian help to overcome supporters of the deposed leader, Zviad Gamsakhurdia. Shevardnadze escaped assassination attempts in 1995 and 1998. He was re-elected in 2000.

Shiite Followers of Shi'a, the second-largest branch of ISLAM. Shiites believe that the true successor to MUHAMMAD was ALI, whose claim to be CALIPH was not recognized by SUNNI Muslims. It rejects the *Sunna* (the collection of teachings outside the KORAN) and relies instead on the pronouncements of a succession of holy men called IMAMS. The SAFAVID dynasty in Iran was the first to adopt Shi'a as a state religion. One of the principal causes of the Iranian revolution was Shah PAHLAVI's attempt to reduce clerical influence on government. Ayatollah KHOMEINI's Shiite theocracy stressed the role of Islamic activism in liberation struggles. The largest Shiite group is the Twelve-Imaam Shiites; the other major group is the ISMAILIS.

Shikoku Smallest of the four main islands of Japan, S of Honshu and E of Kyushu. The interior is mountainous and extensively forested, and most settlements are on the coast. The principal cities are Matsuyama, Takamatsu and Tokushima. Products: rice, tea, wheat, timber, fish, tobacco, fruit, soya beans, camphor, copper. Area: 18,798sq km (7,258sq mi). Pop. (1995) 4,183,000.

Shilton, Peter (1949–) English footballer. Shilton set a record number of England caps (125) between his debut in goal (1970) and a World Cup semi-final (1990). From 1992 to 1995, he was player-manager of Plymouth Argyll. By 1997, he had made more than 1,000 league appearances.

shingles (herpes zoster) Acute viral infection of sensory nerves. Groups of small blisters appear along the course of the affected nerves. The condition can be very painful.

Shinto (Jap. way to the gods) Indigenous religion of Japan. Originating as a primitive cult of nature worship, it was shaped by the influence of CONFUCIUS and, from the 5th century, BUDDHISM. A revival of the ancient Shinto rites in the 17th century contributed to the rise of Japanese nationalism in the late 19th century. Shinto has many deities in the form of spirits, souls and forces of nature.

ship Vessel for conveying passengers and freight by sea. The earliest sea-going ships were probably Egyptian, making voyages to the E coast of Africa in *c*.1500 BC. In *c*.AD 200, extensive sea voyages were being made by Chinese ships that carried more than one mast and featured a rudder some 1,200 years before such ships appeared in Europe. In the Mediterranean region, the galleys of the Greek, Phoenician and Roman navies combined rows of oars with a single square sail, as did the Viking longboats, which were capable of withstanding violent seas. By the 14th and 15th centuries, carracks and galleons were being developed to fulfil the EXPLORATION of the New World. Fighting ships of the 17th and 18th centuries included frigates of various designs. Sailing freighters culminated in the great clippers of the late 19th century. Early in the century, the first steamships had been built. They were powered by wood- or coal-burning STEAM ENGINES that drove large paddle wheels. In 1819, the first Atlantic crossing was made by "steam-assisted sail", and this crossing soon became a regular service. By the mid-19th century, steamships were driven by propellers, or screws. Marine steam TURBINES were developed at the turn of the 19th century and gradually replaced reciprocating (back-and-forth cranking) steam ENGINES for large vessels, early examples being the ocean liners of the 1900s. Oil, rather than coal, soon became the favoured fuel for large marine engines. Diesel engines were developed in the early 1900s but were considered unreliable and did not replace steam turbines until the 1970s. Some of the newest military ships and icebreakers are fitted with nuclear engines in which heat from a NUCLEAR REACTOR drives steam turbines. *See also* AIRCRAFT CARRIER; BOAT; SUBMARINE

Shiraz Capital of Fars province, in the Zagros Mountains, SW Iran. An ancient city established near PERSEPOLIS, it was an artistic centre from the 4th century. From the 7th century it was a trade centre, and in the 9th century it developed into a place of Muslim pilgrimage. From 1750 to 1794 Shiraz was the capital of Persia. Still noted for its carpets, its other products include metalwork, textiles, cement and sugar. Pop. (1994) 1,043,000.

Shiva (Siva) Major god of HINDUISM. A complex god who transcends the concepts of good and evil, Shiva represents both reproduction and destruction. He periodically destroys the world in order to create it once more. He takes little part in the human affairs, although his wife, KALI, is actively involved in them.

shock Acute circulatory failure, possibly with collapse. Caused by disease, injury or emotional trauma, it is characterized by weakness, pallor, sweating and a shallow, rapid pulse. In shock, blood pressure drops to a level below that needed to oxygenate the tissues.

Shockley, William Bradford (1910–89) US physicist who, with his colleagues, John BARDEEN and Walter BRATTAIN, invented the TRANSISTOR. In 1947, they produced a point-contact transistor and a junction transistor. They shared the 1956 Nobel Prize for physics.

shock therapy *See* ELECTROCONVULSIVE THERAPY

shoebill stork (whale-headed stork) Tall wading bird found in papyrus marshes of tropical NE Africa. It has a shoe-shaped bill with a sharp hook, darkish plumage and long legs. It feeds on small animals. Height: to 1.4m (4.6ft). Family Balaenicipitidae; species *Balaeniceps rex*.

shogun Title of the military ruler of Japan, first conferred upon Yoritomo in 1192. The Minamoto (1192–1333), Ashikaga (1338–1568) and TOKUGAWA (1603–1868) shogunates ruled feudal Japan, although an emperor retained ceremonial and religious duties. The shogunate ended with the MEIJI RESTORATION (1868).

Sholes, Christopher Latham (1819–90) US journalist and politician who helped to develop the first commercially successful typewriter in 1867. The Remington Arms Company later purchased all rights to it.

Sholokhov, Mikhail Alexandrovich (1905–84) Soviet novelist, famous for his novel about his native land, *Tikhy Don* (1928–40), which was translated as *And Quiet Flows the Don* (1934) and *The Don Flows Home to the Sea* (1940). Sholokhov was awarded the 1965 Nobel Prize for literature.

Shona Bantu-speaking people of E Zimbabwe. Shona society is based on subsistence agriculture and is centred on small villages, abandoned when local resources are exhausted. Their culture is noted for its pottery, music and dance.

shooting Competitive sport involving FIREARMS, in which a competitor or team of competitors fires at stationary or moving targets. The three main types of shooting are rifle, pistol and clay-pigeon shooting. Within **rifle** shooting, the three basic classes of competition are for air-rifle, small-bore and large-bore rifle; all but air-rifle shooting are Olympic sports. The two main forms of **pistol** shooting, rapid-fire (or silhouette) and free shooting, are both Olympic sports. There are three disciplines of **clay-pigeon** shooting – Olympic-trench, skeet and down-the-line shooting. The first two types are Olympic sports.

shorthand System of writing, used to record speech quickly. Phonetic shorthand systems first appeared during the 18th century, and the most famous system, **Pitman's** shorthand, was published in 1837. All the sounds of the English language are represented by 49 signs for consonants and 16 signs to indicate vowels. The **Gregg** system of phonetic shorthand, widely taught in the USA, has a script based on ordinary writing.

Short Parliament (1640) English Parliament that ended 11 years of personal rule by CHARLES I. Charles was forced to summon Parliament to raise revenue through taxation for war against Scotland. When it refused his demands, he dissolved it but had to summon the LONG PARLIAMENT a few months later.

short story Prose fictional narrative, usually between 2,000 and 10,000 words, established as a separate literary form by Edgar Allan POE. A short story deals with few characters, aims for unity of effect and often concentrates on mood rather than plot. Two 14th-century works, Geoffrey CHAUCER's *Canterbury Tales* and Giovanni BOCCACCIO's *Decameron*, greatly influenced its development. Later short-story writers include Guy de MAUPASSANT, Nathaniel HAWTHORNE, Anton CHEKOV, James JOYCE, Henry JAMES, Franz KAFKA, Ernest HEMINGWAY, John CHEEVER and Raymond CARVER.

Shoshone Native North Americans of the UTO-AZTECAN LANGUAGE group. They occupy reservations in California, Idaho, Nevada, Utah and Wyoming. They were divided into COMANCHE, Northern, Western and Wind River Shoshone. Today there are *c*.9,500 Shoshone.

Shostakovich, Dmitri Dmitrievich (1906–75) Russian composer. Shostakovich's use of contemporary western musical developments in his compositions did not conform with Soviet SOCIALIST REALISM. His opera, *The Lady Macbeth of the Mtsenk District* (1934), received international acclaim but was later criticized in *Pravda*. Other works were deliberately more conventional. He composed 15 symphonies, 13 string quartets, ballets, concertos, piano music, film music and vocal works.

shot put Field event in which a competitor throws a heavy metal ball from a position close to the neck by means of a swift extension of the arm. Throughout the put, the athlete must remain inside the throwing circle. Men throw a 7.3kg (16lb) shot; women an 4kg (8lb 13oz) shot. The shot put has been an Olympic event since 1909.

▲ **ship** Worldwide expansion of Europe's trading empire during the 18th century was made possible by ships, such as the heavily armed East Indiaman like the one shown here.

shoulder In human anatomy, mobile joint at the top of the arm. It consists of the ball-and-socket joint between the HUMERUS and the SHOULDER BLADE (scapula).

shoulder blade (scapula) In vertebrates, either of two large, roughly triangular, flat bones found one on either side of the upper back. They provide for the attachment of muscles that move the forelimbs. *See also* SHOULDER

shrew Smallest mammal, found throughout the world. It is an active, voracious insectivore that eats more than its own weight daily. Family Soricidae.

shrike (butcherbird) Small perching bird found world-wide, except in South America and Australia. It dives at its prey – insects, small birds, mice – hitting them with its strong, hooked bill and then impaling them on a sharp fence post, twig or thorn. Family Laniidae.

shrimp Mostly marine, swimming crustacean. Its compressed body has long antennae, stalked eyes, a beak-like prolongation, a segmented abdomen with five pairs of swimming legs and a terminal spine. There are true, sand and pistol shrimps. Large edible shrimps are often called PRAWNS or scampi. Length: 5–7.5cm (2–3in).

Shropshire (Salop) County in W England; the county town is Shrewsbury. To the N of the River SEVERN the land is generally low-lying, and to the S it rises to the Welsh hills. Part of Mercia in Anglo-Saxon history, it became part of the Welsh Marches after the Norman Conquest. The economy is primarily agricultural. Area: 3,490sq km (1,347sq mi). Pop. (1991) 406,387.

Shrove Tuesday Day before Ash Wednesday, which is the first day of LENT. *See also* CARNIVAL; MARDI GRAS

shrub (bush) Woody perennial plant that is smaller than a TREE. Instead of having a main stem, a shrub branches at or slightly above, ground level into several stems. Its hard stem distinguishes it from an HERB. Shrubs such as rhododendrons and azaleas are popular ornamentals.

sial In geology, uppermost of the two main rock classes in the Earth's crust. Sial rocks are so called because their main constituents are silicon and aluminium. They make up the material of the continents and overlay the SIMA.

Siam *See* THAILAND

Siamese twins Identical TWINS who are born physically joined together, sometimes with sharing of organs. Surgical separation can be a complex procedure.

Sibelius, Jean Julius Christian (1865–1957) Finnish composer whose work represents the culmination of nationalism in Finnish music. He is best known for his orchestral works, including seven symphonies, a violin concerto (1903–05) and the tone poems *En Saga* (1892) and *Finlandia* (1899).

Siberia (Sibir) Extensive region of Asian Russia, extending E to W from the Ural Mountains to the Pacific Ocean, and N to S from the Arctic Ocean to the steppes of Kazakstan and the border with Mongolia. The region includes areas of tundra, taiga and steppe, almost half of it forested. Drained chiefly by the vast north-flowing rivers OB, YENISEI and LENA, and their tributaries, Siberia can be divided into five geographical areas. (1) The W Siberian plain, between the URALS and the Central Plateau, favours dairy farming, but wheat, oats, flax, potatoes, rye and sugar beets are grown. Two-thirds of the population live in the SW, where industry is concentrated in cities such as NOVOSIBIRSK and OMSK, and in the Kuznetz Basin, which has large coal deposits. (2) The Central Siberian plateau, between the rivers Yenisei and Lena. KRASNOYARSK lies on the Yenisei and the city of Yakutsk on the Lena. The region is Russia's chief producer of gold, mica, diamonds and aluminium, and forestry is an important industry. (3) The NE Siberian mountains lie to the E of the Lena. The region is sparsely populated due to the Arctic climate. Verkhoyansk is the world's coldest permanent settlement. The breeding of reindeer, fishing and seal hunting are the chief occupations. (4) The mountains of the S Trans-Baikal region form the watershed between the Pacific and the Arctic. The major city is IRKUTSK, close to Lake BAIKAL. (5) The volcanic and mountainous KAMCHATKA peninsula. The Cossacks conquered Siberia between 1581 and 1644, although the Far Eastern territory was held by the Chinese until 1860. Mining developed in the 19th century, and Siberia was used as a penal colony for political prisoners by the Russian empire and its Soviet successor. Large-scale settlement began after the construction (1881–1905) of the TRANS-SIBERIAN RAILWAY; Siberia's population doubled between 1914 and 1946. The economic development of the region was rapid. The 1960s saw the development of vast hydroelectric schemes in the Trans-Baikal region. Area: 13,807,000sq km (5,331,000sq mi). Pop. (1994) 35,605,000.

Sibyl Prophetess of Greek and Roman mythology. The Sibyl of Cumae offered nine books of her prophecies to Tarquinius Superbus of Rome. He refused her price so she began burning the books until he bought the remaining three for the price she had asked for all nine. They were consulted in times of national emergency.

Sichuan (Szechwan) Province in SW China, almost completely surrounded by mountains, and the most populous in the country; the capital is Chengdu. The E part of the region comprises the heavily populated Red Basin, the most prosperous area of China. Sichuan is China's leading producer of rice, maize and sweet potatoes. Livestock, including cattle, pigs, horses and oxen, are reared, particularly in the W. Salt, coal and iron are mined; other products include rape-oil and silk, for which Sichuan was once world famous. Area: 569,215sq km (219,774sq mi). Pop. (1990) 106,370,000.

Sicily Largest and most populous island in the Mediterranean Sea, off the SW tip of the Italian peninsula, comprising (with nearby islands) an autonomous region of Italy. The capital is PALERMO; other major cities include MESSINA. It is separated from Italy by the narrow Strait of Messina. Mostly mountainous, Sicily's Mount ETNA, at 3,340m (10,958ft), is the highest volcano in Europe. Strategically situated between Africa and Europe, from the 5th–3rd centuries BC it was a battleground for the rival Roman and Carthaginian empires and, following the first PUNIC WAR in 241 BC, became a Roman province. At the end of the 11th century, the island and S Italy were conquered by the Normans. In 1266, the throne passed to Charles of Anjou, whose unpopular government caused the Sicilian Vespers revolt (1282) and the election of an Aragónese king. In 1302, peace terms led to Aragón keeping Sicily, while S Italy became the Angevin kingdom of Naples. In 1735, the two regions were reunified under the rule of the Bourbon Don Carlos (Charles III of Spain). Centuries of centralization under Spanish imperial rule led to the crowning of Ferdinand I as King of Two Sicilies in 1816. Sicilian independence revolts of 1820 and 1848–49 were ruthlessly suppressed. In 1860, Garibaldi liberated the island, and it was incorporated into the new, unified state of Italy. Agriculture is Sicily's economic mainstay. Grain, olives, wine and citrus fruits are the principal products; tourism is also important. Sicily is one of the poorest local economies in Europe. Area: 25,706sq km (9,925sq mi). Pop. (1992) 4,997,705.

Sickert, Walter Richard (1860–1942) English painter. He inspired a circle of progressive painters to form the Camden Town Group and later the London

Group. He was a precursor of the 1950s "kitchen sink" school of drama in his rejection of "nice" subjects in favour of drab domestic interiors, sordid bedroom scenes and a spirit of desperate boredom, as in *Ennui* (*c*.1914).

sickle-cell disease Inherited blood disorder, mainly affecting black people, featuring an abnormality of HAEMOGLOBIN. The haemoglobin is sensitive to a deficiency of oxygen and it distorts erythrocytes, causing them to become rigid and sickle-shaped. Sickle cells are lost from the circulation, leading to anaemia and jaundice.

sidereal period Orbital period of a planet or other celestial body with respect to a background star. It is the true orbital period. **Sidereal time** is local time reckoned according to the rotation of the Earth with respect to the stars. The sidereal day is 23 hours, 56 minutes and 4 seconds of mean solar time, nearly 4 minutes shorter than the mean solar day. The sidereal year is equal to 365.25636 mean solar days.

sidewinder (horned rattlesnake) Nocturnal RATTLESNAKE found in deserts of the SW USA and Mexico. It has horn-like scales over the eyes and is usually tan with a light pattern. It loops obliquely across the sand, leaving a J-shaped trail. Length: to 75cm (30in). Family Viperidae; species *Crotalus cerastes*. The term also describes desert-dwelling snakes of the Old World.

Sidney, Sir Philip (1554–86) English poet, diplomat and courtier. His intricate romance *Arcadia* (1590) is the earliest example of PASTORAL in English. *Astrophel and Stella* (1591), the first English SONNET sequence, was inspired by his love for Penelope Devereux. *An Apology for Poetry* (1595) is the most important critical work of the Elizabethan era. Sidney died at the Battle of Zutphen.

Siegfried In ancient Germanic literature, hero figure who corresponds with Sigurd in Norse mythology, although accounts vary. In the story of Brunhild he is slain, but elsewhere he is generally victorious in his adventures. He plays a major part in the Germanic epic tale of the *Nibelungenlied* and in WAGNER's operatic adaptation of that tale, *The Ring of the Nibelung*.

Siemens German brothers associated with the electrical engineering industry. **Ernst Werner** von Siemens (1816–92) developed an electric telegraph system in 1849. With **Karl** (1829–1906), he set up subsidiaries of the family firm in London, Vienna and Paris. **Friedrich** (1826–1904) and **Karl Wilhelm** (later William) (1823–83) developed a regenerative furnace that led to the open-hearth process used in the steel industry.

Siena Capital of Siena province, Tuscany, central Italy. It is one of Italy's foremost tourist attractions. The town lends its name to the yellow-brown pigment sienna present in the region's soil, and the area is famous for its orange marble. Founded by the Etruscans, Siena became a commune in the 12th century. During the 13th century, it rapidly expanded to rival Florence and was the centre of the Ghibelline faction. In the mid-16th century, it fell under the control of the Medici. In art history, it is especially famed for the Sienese School of painting (13th–14th centuries). Pop. (1990) 58,278

Sienkiewicz, Henryk (1846–1916) Polish novelist and short-story writer. He glorified Poland's struggle for nationhood in the trilogy *With Fire and Sword* (1884), *The Deluge* (1886) and *Pan Michael* (1887–88). He gained international recognition with *Quo Vadis?* (1896). He was awarded the 1905 Nobel Prize for literature.

Sierra Leone Republic on the W coast of Africa; the capital is FREETOWN. **Land and climate** The coast contains several deep estuaries and lagoons, but the most prominent feature is the mountainous Freetown (or Sierra

> **SIERRA LEONE**
> AREA: 71,740sq km (27,699sq mi)
> POPULATION: 5,437,000
> CAPITAL (POPULATION): Freetown (505,000)

Leone) peninsula. North of the peninsula is the Rokel River estuary, W Africa's best natural harbour. Behind the coastal plain, the land rises to mountains, with the highest peak, Loma Mansa, reaching 1,948m (6,391ft). Sierra Leone has a wet, tropical climate, with the heaviest rainfall between April and October. Swamps cover much of the coastal areas. Inland, much of the original rainforest has been destroyed and replaced by low bush and coarse grassland. The N is covered largely by tropical savanna.

History and politics Portuguese sailors reached the coast in 1460; in the 16th century the area became a source of slaves. In 1787, Freetown was founded as a home for freed slaves. In 1808, the settlement became a British crown colony. In 1896, the interior was made a protectorate. In 1951, the protectorate and colony were united. In 1961, Sierra Leone gained independence within the Commonwealth of Nations. In 1971, it became a republic. In 1978, the All People's Congress became the sole political party. A 1991 referendum favoured the restoration of multiparty democracy, but in 1992 a military group seized power. A civil war began between the government and the Revolutionary United Front (RUF). The RUF fought to end foreign interference and to nationalize the diamond mines. Following multiparty elections in 1996, a civilian government was installed, led by Ahmad Tejan Kabbah. In November 1996, Kabbah and the RUF signed a peace agreement ending a war that had claimed more than 10,000 lives. In May 1997, a military group, led by Major Johnny Paul Koroma, seized power. The Economic Community of West African States (ECOWAS) imposed sanctions, and Nigeria led an intervention force that restored Kabbah as president in 1998. A 1999 peace treaty promised an end to a civil war that had claimed *c*.10,000 lives. UN peacekeeping troops were deployed. In 2000, the RUF rebels, led by Foday Sankoh, abducted UN soldiers and renewed their war of terror. British soldiers were deployed to strengthen the UN force. Sankoh was captured and the government took the offensive. **Economy** Sierra Leone has a low-income economy (1995 GDP per capita, US$580). Agriculture employs 70% of the workforce, many at subsistence level. Chief food crops include rice, cassava and maize, and export crops include cocoa and coffee. The most valuable exports are minerals, including diamonds, bauxite and rutile (titanium ore).

Sierra Madre Principal mountain range in Mexico, from the US border to SE Mexico and extending S into Guatemala. It comprises the Sierra Madre Occidental, Sierra Madre Oriental, Sierra Madre del Sur and the sub-range Sierra Madre de Guatemala. The ranges enclose the central Mexican plateau and have long been a barrier to E–W travel. The main range is 2,400km (1,500mi) long and *c*.16–480km (10–300mi) wide. The highest peak is Orizaba (Giltaltepetl) in the Sierra Madre Oriental, at 5,700m (18,700ft).

Sierra Nevada Mountain system in E California, USA. In the E it rises steeply from the Great Basin, while the W edge slopes more gently down to the Central Valley of California. The snow-fed rivers are used to irrigate the Central Valley and also to provide hydroelectric power. Mount WHITNEY, 4,418m (14,495ft), is the highest peak. The range is 650km (400mi) long.

Sièyes, Emmanuel Joseph (1748–1836) French statesman and revolutionary. His pamphlet *What is the Third Estate?* (1789) was highly influential at the start of the FRENCH REVOLUTION. In 1790, Sièyes became president of the States-General and helped formulate a new constitution. As a member of the Convention, he voted for the execution of Louis XVI and remained silent during the REIGN OF TERROR. In 1799, Sièyes entered the DIRECTORY but conspired with Napoleon Bonaparte (NAPOLEON I) in the coup of 18 Brumaire.

sight Sense by which form, colour, size, movement and distance of objects are perceived. It is the detection of light by the EYE, enabling visual images to form.

Sigismund (1368–1437) Holy Roman emperor (1411–37) and king of Germany (1433–37), Hungary (1387–1437) and Bohemia (1419–37). As king of Hungary, he was defeated by the OTTOMAN Turks in 1396 and 1427. In Bohemia he was challenged by the HUSSITE revolt. As emperor (crowned 1433), he was partly responsible for ending the GREAT SCHISM (1415). Sigismund secured the succession on Albert II, his son-in-law, the first ruler of the HABSBURG dynasty.

Sigismund I (1467–1548) King of Poland (1506–48). In order to resist the claims of Moscow, he formed an alliance (1515) with MAXIMILIAN I. In 1525 Sigismund made peace with the TEUTONIC KNIGHTS. He established a standing army to counter the threat of the Ottoman Empire and was a patron of Renaissance art.

Sigismund III (1566–1632) King of Poland (1587–1632) and Sweden (1592–1604). He united the JAGIELLO and Vasa dynasties. Sigismund's hostility to Protestantism led to conflict in Sweden. In 1599 he was deposed and struggled first with his uncle, CHARLES IX, then with his nephew, GUSTAVUS II. Sigismund also entered into a protracted conflict for control of Russia.

Signac, Paul (1863–1935) French painter. He was the leading writer on NEO-IMPRESSIONISM, notably in *D'Eugène Delacroix au néo-impressionisme* (1899). Signac's late paintings, such as *View of the Port of Marseille* (1905), use brilliant colour.

sign language Non-phonetic means of personal communication, using hand symbols, movements and gestures. It is used as a primary means of communication among deaf people or people with impaired hearing.

Sikhism Indian religion founded in the 16th century by NANAK, the first Sikh GURU. Combining HINDU and MUSLIM teachings, it is a MONOTHEISTIC religion, the adherents of which believe that their God is the immortal creator of the universe. All human beings are equal, and Sikhs oppose any CASTE system. The path to God is through prayer and meditation, but nearness to God is only achievable through divine grace. Sikhs believe in REINCARNATION and spiritual guidance from their guru or leader. Begun in Punjab as a pacifist religion, Sikhism became an active military brotherhood and a political force. All Sikh men came to adopt the surname Singh ("lion"). Since Indian independence, Sikh extremists have periodically agitated for an independent Sikh state, called Khalistan. In 1984, the leader of a Sikh fundamentalist revival was killed by government forces at the Golden Temple of AMRITSAR, and in retaliation Indira GANDHI was assassinated by her Sikh bodyguard. More than 1,000 Sikhs died in the ensuing riots.

Sikh Wars (1845–46, 1848–49) Two wars between the Sikhs and the British in NW India. After the death of RANJIT SINGH in 1839, disorder affected the Sikh state in the PUNJAB. When Sikh forces, including many non-Sikhs, crossed the frontier on the Sutlej River, the British declared war. After several battles involving heavy casualties on both sides, the British advanced to Lahore, where peace was agreed (1846). The conflict was renewed two years later, but superior British artillery led to a Sikh defeat at Gujrat (1849). The Sikhs surrendered, and the Punjab was annexed to British India.

Sikkim State in N India, bounded by Tibet, China (N and NE), Bhutan (SE), India (S) and Nepal (W), with its capital at Gangtok (1991 pop. 25,024). The terrain is generally mountainous, rising to Mount KANCHENJUNGA, at 8,591m (28,185ft) the world's third-highest peak. After the 17th century, Sikkim was ruled by the rajas of Tibet. It had come under British influence by 1816, and after British withdrawal from India in 1947, Sikkim became independent. Political unrest led to the country becoming a protectorate (1950) and then an associate state (1975) of India. Agriculture is the main source of income; major crops include maize, rice, barley, fruits, tea and cardamom. Tourism is a growing industry. Area: 7,096sq km (2,734sq mi). Pop. (1991) 406,457.

Sikorsky, Igor Ivanovich (1889–1972) US aeronautical engineer, b. Russia. In 1913, he built and piloted the world's first multi-motored aeroplane. He is best known for his development of the HELICOPTER.

silage Moist, green fodder used to supplement livestock feed. It is made by chopping and storing crops such as hay and lucerne (alfalfa) in airtight silos, where controlled fermentation preserves the silage for months.

Silesia Historic region in E central Europe, now mostly lying in SW Poland, with the remainder in the N Czech Republic and SE Germany. A former Polish province, it passed from Poland to Bohemia in the 14th century, became part of the HABSBURG Empire and was seized by Prussia from Austria in 1742. In World War 2, it was invaded by the Soviet Union, but in 1945 a greater part of the land was returned to Poland by the terms of the POTSDAM CONFERENCE. Upper Silesia is primarily an industrial region of mining and metals, centring on KATOWICE; Lower Silesia, with a milder climate, is more agricultural.

silica (silicon dioxide, SiO_2) Compound of SILICON and oxygen. It occurs naturally as QUARTZ and chert (which includes FLINT). Silica is used in the manufacture of glass, ceramics and SILICONE.

silicate Any of a large group of rock-forming minerals made up of SILICON and oxygen in SiO_4 units bonded to various metals. Silicate minerals, such as FELDSPAR, GARNET and MICA, form more than 90% of the material of the Earth's crust. Glass is a mixture of silicates with small amounts of other substances. Sodium silicates are used as adhesives and in the production of detergents.

silicon (symbol Si) Common, grey, nonmetallic element of Group IV of the periodic table. Silicon is found only in combinations such as SILICA and SILICATE. It is the second most abundant element in the Earth's crust (27.7% by weight). Properties: at.no. 14; r.a.m. 28.086; r.d. 2.33; m.p. 1,410°C (2,570°F); b.p. 2,355°C (4,271°F); most common isotope Si^{28} (98.21%). *See also* SILICON CHIP

silicon chip Small piece of SILICON etched to carry many tiny electric CIRCUITS. Silicon chips are at the heart of most electronic equipment. A personal COMPUTER will contain many different types of chip, most notably the MICROPROCESSOR that is the "brain" of the computer. Chips are etched, layer by layer, onto slivers of pure silicon. Each layer is "doped" to give it particular electrical properties, and the combination of different layers form components such as TRANSISTORS, DIODES and their interconnections. *See also* INTEGRATED CIRCUIT (IC)

silicone Odourless and colourless polymer based on SILICON. Silicones are inert and stable at high temperatures.

They are used in lubricants, varnishes, adhesives, water repellents, hydraulic fluids and artificial heart valves.

silicosis Chronic, occupational lung disease, caused by prolonged inhalation of SILICA dust in occupations such as mining and stone grinding.

silk Natural fibre produced by many creatures, notably the SILKWORM. The many kinds of silk cloth include crepe, satin, taffeta and velvet. Almost all silk is obtained from silkworms reared commercially; a single cocoon can provide between 600 and 900m (2,000–3,000ft) of filament. When the cocoons have been spun, the silk farmer heats them to kill the insects inside. The cocoons are then soaked to unstick the fibres, and the strands from several cocoons are unwound together to form a single thread of yarn. The Chinese were the first to use silk. Sicily was one of the first European production centres and the industry spread to Italy, Spain and France. Silk manufacturing developed in England in the 17th century. China is still the largest producer of raw silk.

Silk Road Ancient trade route linking China with Europe, the major artery of all Asian land exploration before AD 1500. For 3,000 years the manufacture of SILK was a secret closely guarded by the Chinese. Silk fetched extravagant prices in Greece and Rome, and the trade became the major source of income for the Chinese ruling dynasties. By 100 BC, the tax on the trade provided a third of all the HAN dynasty's revenue. The silk trade began to decline in the 6th century, when the SILKWORM's eggs were smuggled to Constantinople and the secret exposed. During the 13th century, European merchants (including Marco POLO in 1271) travelled along the Silk Road when it was controlled by the Mongols. In the 14th century, trade became possible via a sea route to the Far East.

silk-screen printing (serigraphy) In PRINTING, means of producing a print, generally on paper. A screen composed of a mesh of silk or artificial fibres is stretched over a wooden frame; a design is "stopped out" (painted) on the mesh, using glue, varnish, gelatin or a paper stencil. To make the print, ink is taken across the screen with a squeegee; the pressure of this pushes the ink through the unstopped areas of the mesh. Several screens may be used to build up a multi-coloured print.

silkworm Moth CATERPILLAR that feeds chiefly on MULBERRY leaves. The common domesticated *Bombyx mori* is raised commercially for its SILK cocoon. Length: 7.5 cm (3in). Family Bombycidae.

Sillitoe, Alan (1928–) British novelist and short-story writer. Sillitoe's best-known novel was *Saturday Night and Sunday Morning* (1958; filmed in 1960). *The Loneliness of the Long-distance Runner* (1959) is his most celebrated novella. Other novels include *The Open Door* (1989), *Leonard's War* (1991) and *Snowdrops* (1993).

silt Mineral particles produced by the WEATHERING of rock. These particles are carried along in streams and rivers to be deposited in the gently flowing lower reaches of rivers. When the river overflows its bank, the silt deposit forms fertile land. *See also* ALLUVIUM

Silurian Third-oldest period of the PALAEOZOIC era, 438 to 408 million years ago. Marine invertebrates resembled those of ORDOVICIAN times, and jawless fish began to evolve. The earliest land plants (psilopsids) and first land animals (archaic mites and millipedes) developed. Mountains formed in NW Europe and Greenland.

silver (symbol Ag) White, metallic element in the second series of TRANSITION ELEMENTS. It occurs in argentite (a sulphide) and horn silver (a chloride) and is also obtained as a by-product in the refining of copper and lead. Silver ores are scattered worldwide, Mexico being the major producer. Silver is used for some electrical contacts and on some PRINTED CIRCUITS. Other uses include jewellery, ornaments, coinage, mirrors and silver salts for light-sensitive materials used in photography. The metal does not oxidize in air, but tarnishes if sulphur compounds are present. Properties: at.no. 47; r.a.m. 107.868; r.d. 10.5; m.p. 961.93°C (1,763°F), b.p. 2,212°C (4,014°F); most common isotope Ag^{107} (51.82%).

silverfish (bristletail) Primitive, grey, wingless insect found throughout the world. It lives in cool, damp places feeding on starchy materials such as food scraps and paper. It gets its name from the silvery scales that cover its body. Length: 13mm (0.5in). Family Lepismatidae; species *Lepisma saccharina*.

silver nitrate ($AgNo_3$) Colourless, solid compound. It is the most important salt of silver because it is very soluble in water. Silver nitrate is used in PHOTOGRAPHY, chemical analysis, silverplating, mirrors, inks and dyes.

sima In geology, undermost of the two main rockclasses that make up the Earth's crust, so called because its main constituents are silicon and magnesium. It underlies the SIAL of the continents.

Simenon, Georges (1903–89) French novelist. His character Maigret, a Parisian police inspector, is one of the best-known creations in DETECTIVE FICTION.

simile Figure of speech comparing two things. It differs from ordinary comparisons in that it compares, for effect, things usually considered dissimilar and sharing only one common characteristic, as, for example, in the phrase "his fleece was white as snow".

Simon, Neil (1927–) US dramatist. His first play, written with his brother, Daniel, was the comedy *Come Blow Your Horn* (1961). Simon has had more Broadway hits than any other US playwright, and many of his plays have been turned into films. His major successes include *Barefoot in the Park* (1963), *The Odd Couple* (1965), *Plaza Suite* (1968), *The Prisoner of Second Avenue* (1971), *California Suite* (1976), *Brighton Beach Memoirs* (1983), *Biloxi Blues* (1984) and *Lost in Yonkers* (1991), which won a Pulitzer Prize.

Simon, Paul (1942–) US singer-songwriter. With Art Garfunkel (1941–), he formed the pop duo **Simon and Garfunkel**, whose album *Sound of Silence* (1966) sold more than a million copies. Other recordings include *Scarborough Fair* (1966), *Bookends* (1968) and *Bridge over Troubled Water* (1970), soon after which the duo split up. Simon's successful solo records include *Still Crazy After All These Years* (1975) and *Graceland* (1986).

Simpson, Sir George (c.1787–1860) Governor (1821–56) of the HUDSON'S BAY COMPANY, b. Scotland. He was instrumental in the merging (1821) of the company with the North West Company and encouraged the exploration of N Canada and Alaska. He made the company one of the world's largest fur-trading firms.

Simpson, O.J. (Orenthal James) (1947–) US football player. "O.J." was a running back for the Buffalo Bills (1969–77) and the San Francisco 49ers (1978–79). In 1973 he set a record for most yards gained rushing in a single season (2,003). In 1975, Simpson scored a record 23 touchdowns in a season. His career record of 11,236 yards gained is second in the all-time list. In 1979, he retired from football to pursue a career as a sports commentator and actor. In 1994, he was arrested on a charge of murdering his wife and her male friend. The jury found him not guilty, but in 1997 a civil jury found him liable for wrongful death, and he was fined US$30 million.

Simpson, Wallis Warfield Spencer, Duchess of Windsor (1896–1986) Wife of the Duke of Windsor, the former King EDWARD VIII of England. A US divorcee, she began her association with Edward when he was Prince of Wales. Their relationship caused controversy and resulted in Edward's abdication in December 1936. Having divorced her second husband, Ernest Simpson, she married Edward in 1937.

simultaneous equations Two or more equations that can be manipulated to give common solutions. In the simultaneous equations $x + 10y = 25$ and $x + y = 7$, the problem is to find values of x and y, such that those values are solutions of both the equations simultaneously. This can be done by subtracting the two equations to give a single equation in y, which can then be solved. Substituting the value of y in either equation gives the value of x.

sin State or instance of being or acting in a way that is contrary to the ideals of righteousness propounded by a religion. In Christianity, the seven deadly sins are anger, avarice, envy, gluttony, lust, pride and sloth. In Islam, the only sin is to deny that Allah is the only God.

Sinai Peninsula constituting a protectorate of Egypt, bounded by the Gulf of Suez and the Suez Canal (W), the Gulf of Aqaba and the Negev Desert of Israel (E), the Mediterranean Sea (N) and the Red Sea (S). It is a barren plateau region, sandy in the N, rising to granite ridges in the S, and still inhabited chiefly by nomads. The peninsula is the site of Jabal Musa (Mount Sinai). It was the scene of fierce fighting in the ARAB-ISRAELI WARS (1956, 1967, 1973). Occupied by the Israelis in 1967, it was returned to Egypt in 1982. The region is divided into two Egyptian governorates of North and South Sinai. Total area: 58,714sq km (22,671sq mi). Pop. (1991 est.) 264,000, all but 41,000 in North Sinai.

Sinatra, Frank (Francis Albert) (1915–98) US popular singer and actor. Sinatra began his career in the jazz bands of Harry James and Tommy Dorsey. His interpretations of standards, on albums such as *Songs for Swinging Lovers* (1956) and *Come Fly with Me* (1958) are definitive. Sinatra won an Academy Award for his role in *From Here to Eternity* (1953). Other films include *Guys and Dolls*, *The Man With The Golden Arm* (both 1955) and *The Manchurian Candidate* (1962).

Sinclair, Upton Beall (1878–1968) US novelist and social reformer. One of the MUCKRAKERS, Sinclair's first novel, *The Jungle* (1906), exposed conditions in the Chicago meat-packing industry. Other novels include *The Money Changers* (1908), *King Coal* (1917) and *Dragon's Teeth* (1942, part of an 11-volume *roman-fleuve* entitled *World's End*), for which he won a Pulitzer Prize.

Sind Province in S Pakistan, bounded by India (E and S) and the Arabian Sea (SW). KARACHI is the national and provincial capital. HYDERABAD is the next largest city. Sind largely consists of the alluvial plain and delta of the River INDUS. The region is hot and arid. Under Arab rule from the 7th to 11th centuries, it then came under Turkish Muslim control. Sind was part of British India (1843–1937). An autonomous province from 1937 until partition in 1947, it received many Muslim refugees from India after the creation of Pakistan. The economy is agricultural. Grain, cotton, sugar cane, fruits and tobacco are grown. Sind is famous for handicrafts. Area: 140,914sq km (54,428sq mi). Pop. (1985 est.) 21,682,000.

Sindhi Language of Pakistan and India, spoken by c.15 million people in the province of Sind, S Pakistan, and across the border in India. It belongs to the Indic branch of the INDO-EUROPEAN LANGUAGES.

sine In a right-angled triangle, ratio of the length of the side opposite an acute angle to the length of the hypotenuse. The sine of angle A is abbreviated to sin A.

SINGAPORE
AREA: 618sq km (239sq mi)
POPULATION: 3,104,000
CAPITAL (POPULATION): Singapore City (2,812,000)

Singapore Singapore is a small republic at the S tip of the MALAY PENINSULA, SE Asia. It consists of Singapore Island and 59 small islets, 20 of which are inhabited. Singapore Island is c.42km (26mi) wide and 28km (14mi) across. It is linked to the peninsula by a 1,056m- (3,465ft-) long causeway. The land is mostly low-lying. Its strategic position, at the convergence of some of the world's most vital shipping lanes, has ensured its success. **Climate** Singapore has a hot, humid equatorial climate, with temperatures averaging 30°C (86°F). Total annual rainfall averages 2,413mm (95in). Rain occurs (on average) 180 days each year. **Vegetation** Rainforest once covered Singapore, but forests now cover only 5% of the land. Today, most of Singapore is urban land. The distinction between island and city has all but disappeared. Farmland covers 4% of the land, and plantations of permanent crops make up 7%. **History and Politics** According to legend, Singapore was founded in 1299. It was first called Temasak (sea town), but was renamed Singapura (city of the lion). Singapore soon became a busy trading centre within the Sumatran Srivijaya kingdom. Javanese raiders destroyed it in 1377. Subsumed into Johor, Singapore became part of the powerful MALACCA sultanate. In 1819, Sir Thomas Stamford RAFFLES of the British EAST INDIA COMPANY leased the island from Johor, and the Company founded the city of Singapore. In 1826, Singapore, Penang and Malacca formed the Straits Settlement. Singapore soon became the most important British trading centre in Southeast Asia, and the Straits Settlement became a Crown Colony in 1867. Despite British defensive reinforcements in the early 20th century, Japanese forces seized the island in 1942. British rule was restored in 1945. In 1946, the Straits Settlement was dissolved, and Singapore became a separate colony. In 1959, Singapore achieved self-government. Following a referendum, Singapore merged with Malaya, SARAWAK and SABAH to form the Federation of MALAYSIA (1963). In 1965, Singapore broke away from the Federation to become an independent republic within the Commonwealth of Nations. The People's Action Party (PAP) has ruled Singapore since 1959. Its leader, Lee Kuan Yew, served as prime minister from 1959 until 1990, when he resigned and was succeeded by GOH CHOK TONG. Under the PAP, the economy expanded rapidly. The PAP has been criticized by human rights groups for its authoritarian social policies and suppression of political dissent. In 1997 Goh Chok Tong and the PAP were decisively re-elected. **Economy** Singapore is a high-income economy (1992 GDP per capita, US$22,770). It was one of the world's fastest growing (tiger) economies, but in 1997 was badly affected by the crisis in Asian markets. Historically, Singapore's economy has been based on transshipment, and this remains a vital component. It is one of the world's busiest ports, annually handling more than 290 million tonnes of cargo (1994). The post-war economy has diversified. Singapore has a highly skilled and productive labour force. The service sector employs 65% of the workforce; banking and insurance provide many jobs. Manufacturing is the largest export sector. Industries: computers, electronics, telecommunications, chemicals, machinery, scientific instruments, ships.

Singer, Isaac Bashevis (1904–91) US novelist and short-story writer, b. Poland. His novels of Jewish life, written in Yiddish, include *The Family Moskat* (1950), *The Magician of Lublin* (1960), *The Slave* (1962), *Shosha* (1978) and *The Penitent* (1983). Singer was awarded the 1978 Nobel Prize for literature.

Singer, Isaac Merrit (1811–75) US manufacturer, inventor of a rock drill (1839) and of a single-thread SEWING MACHINE (1852). Singer's machine allowed continuous and curved stitching.

Sinhalese People who make up the largest ethnic group in Sri Lanka. They speak an INDO-EUROPEAN LANGUAGE and practise THERAVADA Buddhism.

Sinn Féin (Gaelic, Ourselves Alone) Irish republican, nationalist party founded in 1905 by Arthur GRIFFITH. It seeks to bring about a united IRELAND. Sinn Féin became a mass party after the EASTER RISING (1916). It won 75% of the vote in the last all-Ireland election (1918) and formed an Irish assembly (the Dáil Éireann) led by Éamon DE VALERA. A two-year war of independence was fought between Britain and the IRISH REPUBLICAN ARMY (IRA), led by Michael COLLINS. The Anglo-Irish Treaty (1921) partitioned Ireland into the Irish Free State and Northern Ireland. Sinn Féin was split and the country plunged into civil war. The pro-treaty wing (FINE GAEL), led by William Cosgrave, formed a government. De Valera, leader of the anti-treaty wing, withdrew from Sinn Féin and formed FIANNA FÁIL (1926). In 1938, the remaining republican intransigents joined the outlawed IRA. In 1969, two groups emerged that mirrored the factions of the Provisional and Official IRA. "Official" Sinn Féin became the Workers Party. The Provisionals refused to recognize the authority of Dublin or Westminster. The president of Sinn Féin, Gerry ADAMS, has been elected to Westminster three times (1983, 1987, 1997). Sinn Féin signed the GOOD FRIDAY AGREEMENT (1998).

Sino-Japanese Wars Two wars between China and Japan, marking the beginning and the end of Japanese imperial expansion on the Asian mainland. The first (1894–95) arose from rivalry for control of Korea. In 1894 Japanese influence helped to provoke a rebellion in Korea. Both states intervened, and the Japanese forces swiftly defeated the Chinese. China was forced to accept Korean independence and ceded territory, including Taiwan and the Liaotung peninsula. The latter was returned after European pressure. The second war (1937–45) developed from Japan's seizure of Manchuria (1931), where it set up the puppet state of MANCHUKUO. Further Japanese aggression led to war, in which the Japanese swiftly conquered E China, driving the government out of Peking (Beijing). US and British aid was dispatched to China (1938), and the conflict merged into World War 2, ending with the final defeat of Japan in 1945.

Sino-Tibetan languages Large family of tonal, monosyllabic languages. It includes CHINESE, the Tibeto-Burman languages, the Thai languages and possibly Miao (Meo) and Yao, spoken in s China and SE Asia.

sinus Hollow space or cavity, usually in bone. Most often the term refers to the paranasal sinuses, any of the four sets of air-filled cavities in the skull near the nose.

Sioux (Dakota) Group of seven NATIVE AMERICAN tribes inhabiting Minnesota, Nebraska, North and South Dakota and Montana. In the 18th century, they numbered *c*.30,000. The largest of the tribes was the Teton. They opposed US forces in the American Revolution and the War of 1812. The tribes concluded several treaties with the US government (1815, 1825, 1851) and finally agreed in 1867 to settle on a reservation in SW Dakota.

The discovery of gold in the Black Hills and the rush of prospectors brought resistance from Sioux chiefs such as SITTING BULL and CRAZY HORSE. In 1876 they defeated General CUSTER at the Battle of LITTLE BIGHORN. The last confrontation was the Massacre at WOUNDED KNEE (1890), which resulted in the massacre of more than 200 Sioux. Today, the Sioux number more than 50,000.

siren Aquatic, tailed AMPHIBIAN of North America. The adult is neotenic (reaches sexual maturity while retaining the larval physical form). These eel-like animals have external gills, tiny forelegs and minute eyes. They have no hind legs. Length: to 92cm (36in). Family Sirenidae. *See also* SALAMANDER

sirenia Order of plant-eating, aquatic mammals with paddle-like flippers for fore limbs, no hind limbs and a horizontally flattened tail fin. Species include the DUGONG (family Dugongidae) and MANATEE (family Trichechidae). Length: 2–6m (7–20ft); weight: to 356kg (790lb).

Sirens In Greek mythology, three sea nymphs with women's heads and bird's bodies. They lived on a rocky island near the straits of Messina, home to SCYLLA and CHARYBDIS, and their beautiful singing was believed to attract sailors on to the rocks.

Sirius (Alpha Canis Majoris) Brightest STAR in the sky, situated in the N constellation of CANIS MAJOR. Its luminosity is 23 times that of the Sun. Sirius has a binary companion, Sirius B, the existence of which was deduced by Friedrich BESSEL in 1844. Sirius B is a WHITE DWARF, the first star to be recognized as such.

sirocco Hot, dry, sand-laden wind that blows N from the Sahara Desert, picking up moisture from the Mediterranean and bringing oppressive weather to that region.

Sisley, Alfred (1839–99) French painter, b. England. His early works were influenced by COROT. He met Renoir and Monet while studying with Gleyre, and his style moved towards IMPRESSIONISM. His works, which exhibit great sensitivity, include *Floods at Marly* (1876).

Sistine Chapel Private chapel of the popes in the VATICAN, painted by some of the greatest artists of RENAISSANCE Italy. It was built between 1473 and 1481 for Pope Sixtus IV. The side walls were decorated with FRESCOS by PERUGINO, Pinturicchio, BOTTICELLI, GHIRLANDAIO and Signorelli. Its most celebrated features are the ceiling, window lunettes and altar wall painted by MICHELANGELO between 1508 and 1541.

Sisulu, Walter (1912–) South African civil rights activist, a fierce opponent of APARTHEID. Sisulu became secretary general of the AFRICAN NATIONAL CONGRESS (ANC) in 1949. The ANC was declared illegal in 1961, and Sisulu, Nelson MANDELA and six others were sentenced (1964) to life imprisonment. In 1989, Sisulu was released (1989) by F.W. DE KLERK and, after the legalization of the ANC, became its deputy president (1991–94).

Sisyphus In Greek mythology, founder and king of Corinth. He was punished for trying to trick Thanatos (Death) by being condemned to the underworld to work for eternity, pushing a rock to the top of a steep hill. The rock rolled back to the base of the hill as soon as Sisyphus reached the summit.

sitar Indian stringed musical instrument with a gourd-like body and long neck. It has three to seven strings, tuned in fourths or fifths, and a lower course of 12 strings. Ravi SHANKAR is one of its greatest players.

Sitting Bull (1831–90) Native American leader, chief of the SIOUX. With others, he led the attack on General CUSTER's cavalry at the Battle of LITTLE BIGHORN (1876). In 1881 Sitting Bull was captured and imprisoned for two years. Later, he joined the Wild West Show of Buffalo

Bill. In 1890 Sitting Bull initiated a new Ghost Dance to protect Sioux braves. He was killed resisting arrest.

Sitwell, Dame Edith (1887–1964) English poet. Her anthology *Wheels* (1916) encouraged experimentalism in British verse. Sitwell contributed the words to WALTON's *Façade* (1922). She also wrote a biography of Alexander Pope (1930) and the *English Eccentrics* (1933).

Sitwell, Sir Osbert (1892–1969) English writer, brother of Dame Edith SITWELL. He wrote the words for WALTON's *Belshazzar's Feast* (1931). Sitwell is best known for his five volumes of family history, including *Left Hand, Right Hand* (1945) and *Noble Essences* (1950).

SI units (Système International d'Unites) Internationally agreed system of units, derived from the mks (metre, kilogram and second) system. SI units are now used for many scientific purposes and have replaced the fps (foot, pound and second) and cgs (centimetre, gram, and second) systems. The seven basic units are: the METRE (m), KILOGRAM (kg), SECOND (s), AMPERE (A), KELVIN (K), MOLE (mol) and CANDELA (cd).

Six, Les Collective name for six French composers who were organized as a group by Jean COCTEAU in 1917. The members were Georges Auric, Louis Durey, Arthur Honegger, Darius Milhaud, Francis Poulenc and Germaine Tailleferre.

Six-Day War (1967) Episode of the ARAB-ISRAELI WARS. Israeli forces rapidly defeated the four Arab states (Egypt, Jordan, Syria and Iraq). Israel gained control of the old city of Jerusalem, Jordanian territory on the WEST BANK (of the Jordan River), the GOLAN HEIGHTS and the SINAI PENINSULA, including the GAZA STRIP.

Six Nations *See* IROQUOIS CONFEDERACY

Sixtus IV (1414–84) Pope (1471–84), b. Francesco della Rovere. A Franciscan, he became a cardinal in 1467. Sixtus was involved in a coup (1478) against Lorenzo de' MEDICI in Florence. A series of wars between the papacy and Papal States ensued. Sixtus consented to the Spanish Inquisition but disapproved of its methods. He was a patron of Renaissance art, establishing the Vatican Library and building the Sistine Chapel (1472–81).

Sixtus V (1520–90) Pope (1585–90), b. Felice Peretti. He was a keen supporter of the COUNTER REFORMATION and served as an inquisitor. He became a cardinal in 1570. As pope, Sixtus regained the Papal States through force. He undertook a vast building programme in Rome, including the dome of St Peter's Church.

skate Flattened, food fish belonging to the RAY family, living mainly in shallow temperate and tropical waters. The pectoral fins are greatly expanded to form wing-like flaps. Length: to *c.*2.5m (8ft). Family Rajidae.

skating *See* ICE SKATING; ROLLER SKATING

skeletal muscle *See* VOLUNTARY MUSCLE

skeleton Bony framework of the body of a VERTEBRATE. It supports and protects the internal organs, provides sites of attachment for muscles, and a system of levers to aid locomotion. *See also* EXOSKELETON

Skelton, John (1460–1529) English poet. He was tutor to the young Henry VIII and took holy orders in 1498. Skelton wrote satires on the court, the clergy and Cardinal WOLSEY. His work includes the poems "Speak", "Parrot" and "Colin Clout" and the long secular morality play *Magnyfycence* (*c.*1516).

skiing Method of "skating" on snow using flat runners (skis) made of various materials, attached to ski boots; the skier also uses hand-held poles to assist balance. The principal forms of competitive skiing are Alpine skiing, ski jumping, cross-country skiing and freestyle skiing. Freestyle skiing was added to the Winter Olympic schedule in 1994; the other disciplines have been Olympic sports since 1924.

skimmer (scissorbill) Nocturnal seabird, related to the TERN. It has a thin, knife-like bill that it uses to plough the ocean surface for small animals. The lower mandible is much longer than the upper. Genus *Rynchops*. American species: *Rynchops nigra*.

skin Tough, elastic outer covering of invertebrates. In mammals, it is the largest organ of the body and serves many functions. It protects the body from injury and from the entry of some microorganisms and prevents dehydration. Nerve endings in the skin provide the sensations of touch, warmth, cold and pain. It helps to regulate body temperature through sweating, regulates moisture loss, and keeps itself smooth and pliable with an oily secretion from the SEBACEOUS GLANDS. Structurally, the skin consists of two main layers: an outer layer (EPIDERMIS) and an inner layer (DERMIS). The top layer of epidermis is made

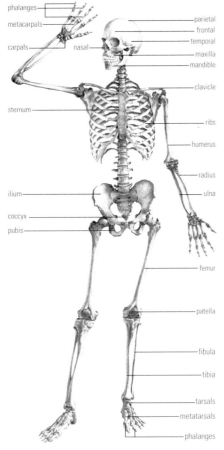

phalanges
metacarpals
carpals
nasal
sternum
ilium
coccyx
pubis

parietal
frontal
temporal
maxilla
mandible
clavicle
ribs
humerus
radius
ulna
femur
patella
fibula
tibia
tarsals
metatarsals
phalanges

▲ **skeleton** The human skeleton consists of about 206 bones divided into two broad groups, the axial and appendicular skeletons. It has three functions: it supplies support; it protects the internal organs; and, by using muscles, it gives movement. The axial skeleton, consisting of the skull, spine and rib cage, supplies the basic structure on to which the limbs, the appendicular skeleton, are joined, via the pelvic and shoulder girdles.

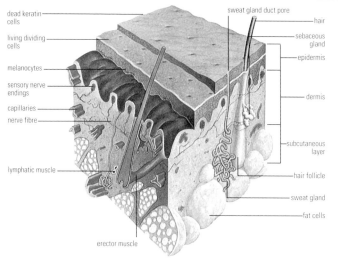

dead keratin cells

living dividing cells

melanocytes

sensory nerve endings

capillaries

nerve fibre

lymphatic muscle

erector muscle

sweat gland duct pore

hair

sebaceous gland

epidermis

dermis

subcutaneous layer

hair follicle

sweat gland

fat cells

◄ **skin** The skin consists of epidermal and dermal layers supported by a subcutaneous layer of fat cells. The epidermis is subdivided into a cornified layer of dead flattened cells, beneath which lies a granular layer containing living, dividing cells. Pigment-producing melanocytes, which colour the skin, lie below this layer. The thicker dermis consists of connective tissues in which are embedded lymphatics, nerve fibres, sensory nerve endings, capillaries, sweat glands and hair follicles. A sebaceous gland and an erector muscle accompany each follicle.

of closely packed dead cells constantly shed as microscopic scales. Below this is a layer of living cells that contain pigment and nerve fibres; they divide to replace outer layers. The dermis contains dense networks of connective tissue, blood vessels, nerves, glands and hair follicles.

skin diving *See* SCUBA DIVING

skink Common name for more than 600 species of LIZARDS found in mild and tropical regions. They have cylindrical bodies covered with shiny scales, cone-shaped heads and tapering tails. They eat small insects, plants, or other lizards. Length: to 66cm (26in). Family Scincidae.

Skinner, Burrhus Fredric (1904–90) US psychologist. He developed the concept of operant conditioning (control of behaviour by its consequences or reinforcements). His books include *Science and Human Behavior* (1953), *Beyond Freedom and Dignity* (1971) and a controversial novel about social engineering, *Walden II* (1948).

skittles Indoor bowling game, once popular in the UK but since the 1960s largely superseded by ten-pin BOWLING. Skittles is usually played by two teams with a hard flattened ball that is rolled down an "alley" to strike the nine skittles (or pins).

Skopje Capital of Macedonia, on the River Vardar. Founded by the Romans, it became the capital of the Serbian empire in the 14th century, fell to the Turks in 1392 and was incorporated into Yugoslavia in 1918. It became capital of Macedonia in 1945. Much of Skopje was destroyed in a 1963 earthquake. Industries: metals, textiles, chemicals, glassware. Pop. (1994) 540,577.

skull (cranium) In vertebrates, brain case that supports and protects the brain, eyes, ears, nose and mouth.

skunk Nocturnal, omnivorous mammal that lives in the USA and Central and South America. It has powerful anal scent glands, which eject a foul-smelling liquid, used in defence. It has a small head and a slender, thickly furred body with short legs and a large, bushy tail. The coat is black with bold white warning markings along the back. The most common species is the striped skunk, *Mephitis mephitis*. Length: to 38cm (15in); weight: 4.5kg (10lb). Family Mustelidae.

skydiving Sport in which parachutists jump from 3,500m (12,000ft) and free-fall to *c.*650m (2,000ft) before opening their PARACHUTES. Competition skydiving has events based on accuracy and events based on style.

Skye Largest island in the Inner Hebrides, off the NW coast of Scotland. The chief town is Portree. Its spectacular scenery makes it a popular vacation attraction. A bridge to the mainland was opened in 1996. Occupations include rearing livestock, weaving and fishing. Area: 1,735sq km (670sq mi). Pop. (1991) 8,139.

skylark *See* LARK

skyscraper Very tall building. True skyscraper construction, in which the metal skeleton supports both floors and walls, was introduced (1885) in Chicago, Illinois, by William Le Baron Jenney. The world's tallest skyscrapers are the twin Petronas Towers in Kuala Lumpur, Malaysia, which rise to 452m (1,483ft).

slander In law, oral defamation of a person's character made in the presence of one or more witnesses. *See also* LIBEL

slang Non-standard, vernacular idiom or vocabulary that is often full of obscure or colourful imagery. Slang differs from colloquialism in that it is short-lived. It often incorporates jargon from certain sections of the population.

slate Grey to blue, fine-grained, homogeneous METAMORPHIC ROCK, which splits into smooth, thin layers. It is formed by the metamorphosis of SHALE and is valuable as a roofing material.

Slav Largest ethnic and linguistic group of peoples in Europe. Slavs are generally classified in three main divisions: the East Slavs, the largest division, include the Ukrainians, Russians and Belorussians; the South Slavs include the Serbs, Croats, Macedonians and Slovenes (and frequently also the Bulgarians); the West Slavs comprise chiefly the Poles, Czechs, Slovaks and Wends.

slavery Social system in which people are the property of their owner and are compelled to work without pay. Slavery of some kind was common to practically all ancient societies and to most modern societies until the 19th century. Common in ancient Egyptian, Roman and Greek societies, an extreme form of slavery also existed in the Americas from the 16th century, where the need for cheap labour in European colonies was not satisfied by enslaving Native Americans or by acquiring poor Europeans as servants. This situation gave rise to the highly organized and profitable **Atlantic triangle slave trade.** Ships sailed from ports such as Liverpool with guns and other goods, which were exchanged for slaves in states on West African

▲ **sloth** Like only a few other herbivores, sloths survive on a particularly poor diet of tough leaves by means of a lifestyle that involves very little expenditure of energy. They sleep a lot and move extremely slowly. In fact, they have only half the musculature of most mammals, and their food may take a whole week to pass through the digestive system. The two-toed sloth (*Choleopus*), shown here, has two toes on its front legs and three on its back legs.

coasts. The slaves were sold in markets in the Caribbean, Brazil and North America, mainly to work on farms and plantations. On the return journey, the ships carried colonial produce from the Americas to Europe. An estimated 15 million Africans were sold into slavery. Millions more died on the voyage across the Atlantic. By the late 18th and early 19th century, slavery had been abolished throughout much of Europe. Most South American states abolished it soon after gaining independence. In the USA, slavery was one cause of the CIVIL WAR and was formally ended when the aims of the EMANCIPATION PROCLAMATION (1863) were incorporated in the 13th Amendment to the Constitution (1865). Isolated cases of slavery were discovered in China and some areas of Africa in the 1990s.

Slavic languages (Slavonic languages) Group of languages spoken in E Europe and the former Soviet Union, constituting a major subdivision of the family of INDO-EUROPEAN LANGUAGES. The main ones in use today are Russian, Ukrainian and Belorussian (East Slavic); Polish, Czech, Slovak and Sorbian or Lusatian, a language spoken in E Germany (West Slavic); and Bulgarian, Serbo-Croat, Slovenian and Macedonian (South Slavic). Some Slavic languages are written in the Cyrillic alphabet, others in the Roman.

sleep Periodic state of unconsciousness from which a person or animal can be roused. During an ordinary night's sleep there are intervals of deep sleep associated with rapid eye movement (REM) sleep. It is during this REM sleep that dreaming occurs. Studies have shown that people deprived of sleep become grossly disturbed. Difficulty in sleeping is called insomnia.

sleeping sickness Popular name of two diseases. **Trypanosomiasis** is a disease of tropical Africa caused by a parasite transmitted by the TSETSE FLY. It is characterized by fever, headache, joint pains and anaemia. Ultimately, it may affect the brain and spinal cord, leading to profound lethargy and sometimes death. **Encephalitis lethargica** is a rare, viral disease of the brain characterized by headache and drowsiness progressing to coma. It occurs in epidemic and sporadic forms and, most notoriously, was the cause of an epidemic that followed World War 1, leaving many helpless survivors.

slime mould Any of a small group of strange, basically single-celled organisms that are intermediate between the plant and animal kingdoms. During their complex life cycle they pass through several stages. These include a flagellated swimming stage, an amoeba-like stage, a stage consisting of a slimy mass of protoplasm with many nuclei, and a flowering sporangium stage.

slipped disc (prolapsed intervertebral disc) Protrusion of the soft, inner core of an intervertebral disc through its covering, causing pressure on the spinal nerve roots. It is caused by a sudden mechanical force on the spine. It leads to stiffness and SCIATICA.

sloe *See* BLACKTHORN

sloth Any of several species of slow-moving, herbivorous mammals of Central and South America. It has long limbs with long claws and spends most of its life in trees, where it generally hangs upside down. Length: to 60cm (2ft); weight: to 5.5kg (12lb). Family Brachipodidae.

Slovak Official language of the Slovak Republic, spoken by *c*.5 million people. It is closely related to Czech.

Slovak Republic (Slovakia) Republic in central Europe. It is dominated by the CARPATHIAN MOUNTAINS. The Tatra range on the N border includes the republic's highest peak, Gerlachovka, at 2,655m (8,711ft). To the S is fertile lowland, drained by the river DANUBE, on the banks of which stands the capital, BRATISLAVA. **Climate** Slovakia has a continental climate. Bratislava has average temperatures ranging from −3°C (27°F) in January to 20°C (68°F) in July, and an average annual rainfall of 600mm (24in). The highlands are much colder and wetter. **Vegetation** Forests cover 41% of the country. Evergreen trees predominate in the mountains. Arable land accounts for 31% of land use. **History and politics** Slavic peoples settled in the region in the 5th and 6th centuries AD. In the 9th century the area formed part of the empire of MORAVIA. In the 10th century, it was conquered by the MAGYARS, and for nearly 900 years the region was dominated by Hungary. At the end of the 11th century, it was subsumed into the kingdom of Hungary. In the 16th century, the OTTOMAN EMPIRE conquered much of Hungary, and Slovakia was divided between the Turks and the Austrians. From 1541 to 1784, Bratislava served as the capital of the HABSBURG Empire. The joint rule of MARIA THERESA and JOSEPH II pursued a policy of Magyarization. In 1867, the AUSTRO-HUNGARIAN EMPIRE was formed. It continued the suppression of native culture. Many Slovaks fled to the USA. In World War 1, Slovak patriots fought on the side of the Allies. After the defeat of Austro-Hungary (1918), Slovakia was incorporated into CZECHO-SLOVAKIA as an autonomous region. The Czechs dominated the union, and many Slovaks became dissatisfied. Following the MUNICH AGREEMENT (1938), part of Slovakia became an independent state, while much of S Slovenia (including Košice) was ceded to Hungary. In March 1939, Slovakia gained nominal independence as a German protectorate. In August 1939, Hitler invaded Czechoslovakia, and Slovakia became a Nazi puppet state. In 1944, Soviet troops liberated Slovakia, and in 1945 it returned to Czechoslovakia. The PRAGUE SPRING (1968) saw the introduction of a federal structure that survived the Soviet invasion. In 1989, the dramatic collapse of

---

SLOVAK REPUBLIC
AREA: 49,035sq km (18,932sq mi)
POPULATION: 5,500,000
CAPITAL (POPULATION): Bratislava (452,000)

Czech communism spurred calls for independence. Elections in 1992 were won by the Movement for a Democratic Slovakia (HZDS), led by Vladimir Mečiar. In 1993, the federation was dissolved, and the Slovak Republic became a sovereign state, with Mečiar as prime minister. The Slovak Republic has maintained close relations with the Czech Republic. In 1996, the Slovak Republic and Hungary ratified a treaty enshrining their respective borders and stipulating basic rights for the 560,000 Hungarians in the Slovak Republic. In the republic's first direct presidential elections in 1999, Rudolf Schuster of the Slovak Democratic Coalition defeated Mečiar. **Economy** Before 1948 the economy was primarily agrarian. Communism developed industry. Post-independence governments have attempted to diversify industrial ownership and production. The transition was painful: industrial output fell, unemployment and inflation rose (1995 GDP per capita, US$3,610). In 1995, the privatization programme was suspended. Manufacturing employs 33% of the workforce. Bratislava and Košice are the chief industrial cities. Major products include ceramics, machinery and steel. Farming employs 12% of the workforce. Crops include barley and grapes. Tourism is growing.

Slovenia Mountainous republic in SE Europe; the capital is LJUBLJANA. Slovenia was one of the six republics that made up the former YUGOSLAVIA. Much of the land is mountainous, rising to 2,863m (9,393ft) at Mount Triglav in the Julian Alps in the NW. Central and E Slovenia contain hills and plains drained by the rivers Drava and Sava, while W Slovenia contains the Karst region, an area of limestone landscapes. Here, surface water flows through swallow holes into deep caves, including the Postojna caves near Ljubljana, which are the largest in Europe. **Climate** The short coast has a mild Mediterranean climate, but inland the climate is more continental. The mountains are snow-capped in winter, and most of Slovenia has cold winters and hot summers. **Vegetation** Farmland covers c.35% of the land and forests another 50%. **History and politics** The ancestors of the Slovenes, the W branch of the South Slavs, settled in the area around 1,400 years ago. For most of the time from the 13th century until 1918, Slovenia was ruled by the Austrian HABSBURGS. In 1918, Slovenia became part of the Kingdom of the Serbs, Croats and Slovenes, which was renamed Yugoslavia in 1929. During World War 2, Slovenia was invaded and partitioned between Italy, Germany and Hungary, but after the war, Slovenia again became part of Yugoslavia. From the late 1960s, some Slovenes demanded independence, but the central Yugoslav government opposed the breakup of the federation. In 1990, elections were held and a non-communist coalition government was established. Slovenia declared itself independent, which led to brief fighting between Slovenes and the federal army. Slovenia did not, however, become a battlefield like other parts of the former Yugoslavia. In 1992, the European Community recognized Slovenia's independence. In 1996, a coalition government, led by the Liberal Democrats, was set up. In 1996, Slovenia applied to join the European Union (EU). In 1997, the Kucan was elected for a third term in office. **Economy** The transformation of a centrally planned economy and the fighting in

other parts of former Yugoslavia have caused problems for Slovenia. Manufacturing is the leading activity. Major manufactures include chemicals, machinery, transport equipment, metal goods and textiles. Major crops include maize fuit, potatoes and wheat.

slow-worm (blind-worm) European snake-like, legless lizard of grassy areas and woodlands. It is generally brownish; the female has a black underside. It has pointed teeth and feeds primarily on slugs and snails. Length: to 30cm (12in). Family Anguidae; species *Anguis fragilis.*

slug Mostly terrestrial, gastropod MOLLUSC, identified by the lack of shell and uncoiled viscera. It secretes a protective slime, which is also used to aid locomotion. Length: to 20cm (8in). Class Gastropoda; subclass Pulmonata; genera *Arion, Limax. See also* SEA SLUG

small intestine Part of the DIGESTIVE SYSTEM that, in humans, extends – c.6m (20ft) coiled and looped – from the STOMACH to the large INTESTINE, or colon. Its function is the digestion and absorption of food. *See also* DUODENUM; ILEUM

smallpox Formerly a highly contagious viral disease characterized by fever, vomiting and skin eruption. It remained endemic until the World Health Organization (WHO) vaccination campaign, launched in the late 1960s. Global eradication was achieved by 1980.

smell (olfaction) Sense that responds to airborne molecules. The olfactory receptors in the nose can detect even a few molecules per million parts of air.

smelt Small, silvery food fish related to SALMON and TROUT. It lives in the N Atlantic and Pacific oceans and in North American inland waters. Family Osmeridae.

smelting Heat treatment for separating metals from their ORES. The ore, often with other ingredients, is heated in a furnace to remove nonmetallic constituents. The metal produced is later purified.

Smetana, Bedřich (1824–84) Czech composer. His masterpiece, *The Bartered Bride* (1866), is one of the greatest folk operas. Among other popular works by Smetana is the cycle of symphonic poems *Má Vlast* (My Country, 1874–79), which includes the *Vltava.*

Smirke, Robert (1781–1867) English neo-classical architect, one of the chief promoters of the CLASSICAL REVIVAL in British architecture. Smirke's most famous building is the Brtish Museum, begun in 1823.

Smith, Adam (1723–90) Scottish philosopher, regarded as the founder of modern economics. His book *The Wealth of Nations* (1776) was enormously influential in the development of Western CAPITALISM. It outlined the theory of the DIVISION OF LABOUR. In place of MERCANTILISM, Smith proposed the doctrine of LAISSEZ–FAIRE: that governments should not interfere in economic affairs and that free-trade increases wealth.

Smith, Alfred Emanuel (1873–1944) US politician. He was governor of New York (1919–20, 1923–28), supporting social welfare legislation and public works projects. A candidate for the presidential nomination in 1924, he ran in 1928 but lost the election to Herbert HOOVER. He was the first Roman Catholic to become a candidate.

Smith, Bessie (1895–1937) US singer, known as the "Empress of the BLUES". In 1923, Smith made her recording debut and sold more than two million records. Her powerful voice and poignant phrasing accompanied early jazz greats, such as Louis ARMSTRONG. Smith died after being refused treatment at a whites-only hospital following a serious car accident.

Smith, David (1906–65) US sculptor. His welded sculptures often incorporate machinery parts. Smith's works are non-representational, but evoke suggestions

---

SLOVENIA
AREA: 20,251sq km (7,817sq mi)
POPULATION: 2,055,000
CAPITAL (POPULATION): Ljubljana (270,000)

of landscape or still life. From the 1950s, he worked on the *Cubi* series. These are mostly vertical constructions built up from cylinders of polished stainless steel.

Smith, Ian Douglas (1919–) Rhodesian statesman, prime minister (1964–78). He founded (1961) the Rhodesia Front Party and sought independence from Britain. In 1965, Smith's white minority regime issued a unilateral declaration of independence (UDI). Persistent international sanctions and guerrilla warfare forced his government to accept free elections (1980). Smith was defeated by Robert MUGABE's Zimbabwe African National Union (ZANU). He continued to lead white opposition.

Smith, John (1580–1631) English soldier and colonist. He was instrumental in establishing the first English colony in North America at JAMESTOWN (1607). Exploring Chesapeake Bay, Smith was captured by POWHATAN and possibly saved from death by Powhatan's daughter, POCAHONTAS. In 1608, by obtaining maize from the local people, Smith saved the colony from starvation. In 1609, he returned to England.

Smith, John (1938–94) British politician, b. Scotland. Smith entered parliament in 1970 as a Labour MP. He served in James CALLAGHAN's government and acted as shadow chancellor (1987–92). Smith was elected leader of the LABOUR PARTY in 1992. His sudden death saw a mass public outpouring of tributes. He was succeeded by Tony BLAIR.

Smith, Joseph (1805–44) US religious leader and founder of the MORMON Church of Jesus Christ of the Latter Day Saints (1830). His *Book of Mormon* (1830) was based on writings he claimed were given to him on golden plates by a heavenly messenger named Moroni. In 1830, Smith led his followers to found the New Zion. In 1844, he was jailed on a charge of treason at Carthage, Illinois, where he was murdered by a mob.

Smith, Stevie (1902–71) English poet, b. Florence Margaret Smith. She came to public notice with *Novel on Yellow Paper* (1936). Smith's witty and often pathetic poetry was collected in 1975 and includes the title poem of her 1957 volume, *Not Waving But Drowning*.

Smithsonian Institution US independent trust based in Washington, D.C. Created in 1846, the Institution funds research, publishes the results of explorations and investigations, and preserves for reference more than 65 million items of scientific, cultural and historical interest. These are housed in the nation's largest collection of museums, which include the National Gallery of Art and the National Air and Space Museum.

▲ **snail** Remarkably adept at exploring new habitats, snails originated in the sea, but over the course of millions some 22,000 species adapted to life on dry land, losing their gills and evolving air-breathing lungs. Most species of land snail of the genus *Helix*, shown here, live on the ground and are dull in coloration. A few species are arboreal: these tend to be brightly coloured. Others have returned to aquatic environments and must surface periodically to breathe.

smog Dense atmospheric mixture of smoke and fog or chemical fumes, commonly occurring in urban or industrial areas. It is most dense during temperature inversions.

Smolensk City on the upper reaches of the River Dnieper, E Russia, near the Belarus border, capital of Smolensk oblast. It was an important medieval commercial centre on the routes from Byzantium to the Baltic, and from Moscow to Warsaw. The capital of Belorussia in the 12th century, it was sacked (1238–1240) by the Mongols. During the 15th and 16th centuries it was a battleground for Polish and Russian forces. In 1812, Napoleon I seized the city and burned it in retreat from the Russian army. Occupied by Germans from 1941 to 1943, it saw some of World War 2's fiercest fighting. It is an important transport and distribution centre. Industries: linen, textile machines, timber, electrical goods, flour milling, distilling, brewing. Pop. (1994) 353,000.

Smollett, Tobias George (1721–71) Scottish novelist and surgeon. *The Adventures of Peregrine Pickle* (1751) was in a typically bawdy, PICARESQUE vein. His masterpiece is *The Expedition of Humphrey Clinker* (1771), a comic, epistolary novel.

smooth muscle *See* INVOLUNTARY MUSCLE

smuggling Illegal movement of goods or people across national or state boundaries to avoid official restrictions or taxes. Smuggling has flourished worldwide, although penalties have traditionally been high. In most Western countries it is a criminal offence punishable by a fine or prison sentence. Smugglers traffic a wide range of goods, including highly taxed luxury goods, guns and illegal immigrants. Internationally, customs authorities have been waging a constant battle against drugs smugglers.

smut Group of plant diseases caused by parasitic fungi, also called smuts, that attack many cereals. The diseases are named after the sooty black masses of reproductive spores produced by the fungi. *See also* PARASITE

Smuts, Jan Christiaan (1870–1950) South African statesman, prime minister (1919–24, 1939–48). He was a guerrilla commander during the SOUTH AFRICAN WARS (1899–1902) but afterwards worked with Louis BOTHA to establish the Union of South Africa (1910). During World War 1, Smuts suppressed a pro-German revolt, commanded British forces in East Africa and became a member of the British war cabinet. Upon Botha's death, he succeeded as prime minister. Smuts formed a second administration after James HERTZOG opposed entry into World War 2. After the war, he was defeated by the APARTHEID policies of the Nationalist Party.

Smyrna *See* IZMIR

snail Terrestrial, marine or freshwater gastropod mollusc. It has a large fleshy foot, antennae on its head, and a coiled protective shell encasing an asymmetric visceral mass. It may breathe through gills (aquatic species) or through a kind of air-breathing lung (terrestrial species), and has a radula – a rasping organ in its mouth. Some species, such as the Roman snail (*Helix pomatia*), are edible. Length: to 35cm (14in). Class Gastropoda.

snake Any of some 2,700 species of legless, elongated REPTILES forming the sub-order Serpentes of the order Squamata (which also includes LIZARDS). There are 11 families. They range in length from c.10cm (4in) to more than 9m (30ft). There are terrestrial, arboreal, semi-aquatic and aquatic species; one group is entirely marine; many are poisonous. They have no external ear openings, eardrums or middle ears; sound vibrations are detected through the ground. Their eyelids are immovable and their eyes are covered by a transparent protective cover. The long, forked, protractile tongue is used to detect odours. Their bodies are covered with scales. Poisonous snakes have hollow or grooved fangs, through which they inject venom into their prey. *See* individual species

snakebite Result of an injection of potentially lethal SNAKE venom into the bloodstream. There are three types of venomous snake: the **Viperidae**, subdivided into true VIPERS and pit vipers, whose venom causes internal haemorrhage; the **Elapidae** (including COBRAS, MAMBAS, kraits), whose venom paralyzes the nervous system; and the **Hydrophidae**, Pacific sea snakes with venom that disables the muscles. Treatment is with anti-venoms.

snapdragon Any of several species of perennial plants of the genus *Antirrhinum*, with sac-like, two-lipped, purple, red, yellow or white flowers. The common snapdragon (*A. majus*) is a popular garden plant. Height: 15–91cm (0.5–3ft). Family Scrophulariaceae.

snapper Marine food fish found in tropical waters of the Indo-Pacific and Atlantic oceans. Length: to 90cm (3ft); weight: 50kg (110lb). Family Lutjanidae.

snipe Any of several species of migratory, long-billed shorebirds found in swamps and coastal areas worldwide. It is generally mottled brown and buff. Length: 30cm (12in). Family Scolopacidae; genus *Gallinago*.

snooker Game usually for two players, played on a billiards table, using 15 red balls, 6 coloured balls – yellow, green, brown, blue, pink, black – and 1 white cue ball. Each player in turn attempts to knock a red ball into a pocket; if successful, the player may then try to pot a coloured ball; if successful again, the player may go on to another red and another colour. The turn ends when no ball is potted or when a penalty is incurred. Colours potted are returned to their positions on the table until all the reds have been potted; the colours are then potted in ascending order of values and remain off the table.

Snorri Sturluson (1179–1241) Icelandic poet and historian. His *Prose Edda* is a collection of Norse mythology and a discussion of the art of poetry. *Heimskringla*, SAGAS of the Norwegian kings to 1184, mingles NORSE LITERATURE, history and legend.

snow Flakes of frozen water that fall from clouds to the Earth's surface. Snowflakes are symmetric (usually hexagonal) crystalline structures. *See also* PRECIPITATION

Snow, C.P. (Charles Percy), Baron (1905–80) English novelist, scientist and civil servant. He is especially remembered for his lecture *The Two Cultures and the Scientific Revolution* (1959), which diagnosed a radical divide between scientists and literary intellectuals. Snow also wrote an 11-volume novel sequence, known collectively as *Strangers and Brothers* (1940–70; it includes *The Corridors of Power* (1963).

Snowdon Mountain in Gwynedd, NW Wales. Much of the area is included in the Snowdonia National Park, established 1951. Snowdon has five peaks, one of which, at 1,085m (3,560ft), is the highest in England and Wales.

snowdrop Low-growing perennial plant of the Mediterranean region, widely cultivated as a garden ornamental. The drooping, green and white, fragrant flowers appear early in spring. The common snowdrop (*Galanthus nivalis*) has narrow leaves; height: to 15cm (6in). Family Amaryllidaceae.

Soane, Sir John (1753–1837) British architect. One of the most original of all British architects, he developed his own personal style of CLASSICISM. He designed the Bank of England (1795–1827).

soap Cleansing agent made of salts of fatty acids, used to remove dirt and grease. Common soaps are produced by heating fats and oils with an alkali, such as sodium hydroxide or potassium hydroxide. Soap consists of long-chain

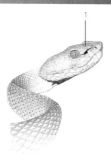

◀ snake Many snakes feed on small nocturnal mammals and must find their prey in the semi-darkness. They do so with the aid of heat-sensitive organs located in pits on the upper jaw (1). The heat sensors feed the information to the same part of the brain as the eyes. In this way snakes can "see" a thermal image of the animal super-imposed on its visual image.

molecules; one end of the chain attaches to grease while the other end dissolves in the water, causing the grease to loosen and form a floating scum. *See also* DETERGENT

soap opera Dramatic serial programme, either on radio or television, originally sponsored in the USA by companies manufacturing soap and detergents. The plot tends to revolve around family dilemmas and frequently involves melodramatic events.

soapstone (steatite) Rock with a soft, soapy or greasy texture. There are many types of soapstone but all contain a large proportion of magnesium silicate, often associated with various amounts of serpentine and carbonates. Food vessels and carvings made from soapstone have been found among the remains of prehistoric human cultures.

Sobers, Sir Gary (Garfield St Aubrun) (1936–) Barbadian cricketer, perhaps the game's greatest all-rounder. Sobers played 93 test matches for West Indies (39 as captain), scoring 8,032 runs and taking 235 wickets. He played county cricket for Nottinghamshire and, against Glamorgan (1968), became the first player to score six sixes in an over in first-class cricket.

soccer *See* FOOTBALL, ASSOCIATION

Social and Liberal Democrats (SLDP) Official name of the LIBERAL DEMOCRATS

social contract Concept that society is based on the surrender of natural freedoms by the individual to the organized group or state in exchange for personal security. The concept can be traced back to the ancient Greeks. It was developed by Thomas HOBBES and John LOCKE, and by Jean Jacques ROUSSEAU in *The Social Contract* (1762).

social democracy Political ideology concerning the introduction of socialist ideals without an immediate overhaul of the prevailing political system. Before 1914 MARXIST parties of central and E Europe termed themselves social democrats. Contemporary social democracy, however, has been invoked by those wishing to distinguish their socialist beliefs from the dogmas of Marxist parties. *See also* CHRISTIAN DEMOCRATS; SOCIAL DEMOCRATIC LABOUR PARTY (SDLP); SOCIAL DEMOCRATIC PARTY (SDP)

Social Democratic Labour Party (SDLP) Political party in Northern Ireland that leans toward SOCIALISM. It favours unification of the province with the Republic of Ireland. Founded in 1970, its leader from 1983 was civil rights activist John HUME. The party seeks to use non-violent, constitutional methods to attain its goals.

Social Democratic Party (SDP) Political party in England (1981–90), centrist in political outlook. At the general elections of 1983 and 1987, the party joined forces with the Liberal Party to create the Liberal-SDP Alliance. By the second election, however, the two parties were already in the process of merging to form the LIBERAL DEMOCRATS.

social history Branch of HISTORY focusing on the ordinary lifestyle of people in communities of all types and sizes at specific times and places. *See also* ETHNOLOGY

socialism System of social and economic organization in which the means of production are owned not by private individuals but by the community, in order that all may share more fairly in the wealth produced. Modern socialism dates from the late 18th–early 19th centuries. Many forms of socialism exist both in theory and in practice, differing over such questions as the degree of state control and the rights of individuals. With the REVOLUTIONS OF 1848, socialism became a significant political doctrine in Europe. Karl MARX, whose *Communist Manifesto* was published in that year, believed that socialism was to be achieved only through the class struggle. Thereafter, a division appeared between the revolutionary socialism of Marx and his followers, later called COMMUNISM or Marxism-Leninism, and more moderate doctrines that held that socialism could be achieved through education and the democratic process. In Russia, the revolutionary tradition culminated in the RUSSIAN REVOLUTION of 1917. From the moderate wing, social-democratic parties, such as the British Labour Party, emerged. They were largely instrumental in mitigating the effects of the market economy in W Europe through political measures and by securing social justice and welfare.

Socialist Party US political party. It was formed in 1901 by the unification of the Social Democratic Party and the Socialist Labor Party. Dedicated to the state ownership of all public utilities and important industries, its best-known leaders were Eugene V. DEBS and Norman Thomas.

socialist realism State policy on the arts, promoted by the Soviet Union from the 1930s to the 1980s. It asserted that all the arts should appeal to ordinary workers and should be inspiring and optimistic in spirit. Art that did not fulfill these precepts was effectively banned, and most serious writers, artists and composers were forced underground or into exile.

socialization Process by which a person learns and internalizes the beliefs, values and standards of behaviour acceptable to society. Socialization allows the individual to become a functioning member of his or her group. It is the means by which social continuity and cultural consistency are accomplished.

social psychology Field that studies individuals interacting with others in groups and with society. Topics include attitudes and how they change, prejudice, aggression, altruism, group behaviour, conformity and social conflict. There is some overlap with SOCIOLOGY.

social security Public provision of economic aid to help alleviate poverty and deprivation. In 1883, Germany became the first country to adopt social security legislation, in the form of health insurance. By the end of the 1920s, public social security provisions had been adopted throughout Europe. In 1909, the UK adopted an old-age pension scheme, and in 1911 LLOYD GEORGE drafted the National Insurance Act to provide health and unemployment insurance. In 1946, the National Insurance Act and the National Health Service Act were passed. In 1948, the National Assistance complemented these, and the WELFARE STATE and the NATIONAL HEALTH SERVICE (NHS) were born. In the USA, as part of the NEW DEAL, the Social Security Act (1935) was adopted.

Social Security, UK Department of UK government department responsible for the payment of universal benefits (such as child benefit), the means-testing of other benefits, and collection of NATIONAL INSURANCE contributions. It also administers the social fund and the legal aid scheme. *See also* SOCIAL SECURITY

social work Community assistance and/or care. Social workers monitor the well-being of families known to have problems and sometimes have the power to remove children from parents deemed to be dangerously violent or abusive. They may be asked to assist the police in dealing with juvenile suspects. They also help various handicapped, homeless or unemployed people.

Society Islands South Pacific archipelago, part of FRENCH POLYNESIA; the capital is PAPEETE on TAHITI. The archipelago is divided into two groups of mountainous, volcanic and coral islands. Only eight are inhabited. The larger **Windward** group includes the islands of Tahiti, Moorea, Maio and the smaller Mehetia and Tetiaroa. The **Leeward** group includes Raiatéa (the largest and site of the chief town, Uturoa), Tahaa, Huahine, Bora-Bora and Maupiti. Tourism is the most important industry, with 148,000 people visiting the islands in 1993. The economy is primarily agricultural, and the major crop is copra, with coconut trees dominating the coastal plains. The islands were first sighted by Europeans in 1607. The French claimed the islands in 1768. In 1769, the islands were visited by James COOK, who named them after the Royal Society. In 1843, they were made a French protectorate and in 1880 became a French colony. In 1946, they became a French overseas territory. The principal language is Tahitian. Area: 1,446sq km (558sq mi). Pop. (1992) 165,000.

Society of Friends *See* QUAKERS

Society of Jesus *See* JESUITS

sociobiology Study of how genes can influence social behaviour. A basic tenet of biology is that physical characteristics, such as structure and physiology, evolve through NATURAL SELECTION of those traits that are most likely to guarantee an organism's survival. Sociobiologists hold the controversial view that this selection process applies to social behaviours.

sociology Scientific study of society, its institutions and processes. It examines areas such as social change and mobility, and underlying cultural and economic factors. Auguste COMTE invented the term "sociology" in 1843, and since the 19th century numerous complex and sophisticated theories have been expounded by Herbert SPENCER, Karl MARX, Emile DURKHEIM, Max WEBER and others.

Socotra Island territory in the Indian Ocean, S of the Arabian Peninsula; the capital is at Tamridah. Strategically placed at the entrance to the Red Sea, it was taken as a protectorate by the British in 1866. In 1967, it chose to join South Yemen and is now administered by Yemen. The mountainous terrain includes peaks rising to c.1,500m (5,000ft). The economy is based on stock-rearing, but exports include tobacco, ghee, dates and myrrh. Area: 3,100sq km (1,200sq mi). Pop. 12,000.

Socrates (469–399 BC) Greek philosopher. He laid the foundation for an ethical philosophy based on the analysis of human character and motives. The son of a sculptor, he fought in the PELOPONNESIAN WARS. Information about his life and philosophy is found in the writings of PLATO, his most gifted pupil, and the historian and military leader XENOPHON, who knew him. According to these accounts, Socrates believed that moral excellence is attained through self-knowledge. For Socrates, knowledge and virtue were synonymous; immorality was founded on ignorance. His criticism of tyranny attracted powerful enemies, and he was charged with impiety and corrupting the young. Condemned to death, he drank the poisonous draft of hemlock required by law.

soda Any of several sodium compounds, especially sodium carbonate (Na_2CO_3), usually manufactured from common salt (sodium chloride, NaCl) and ammonia by the Solvay process. The anhydrous (lacking water) form is known as soda ash; washing soda is hydrated sodium carbonate ($Na_2CO_3.10H_2O$).

Soddy, Frederick (1877–1956) British chemist who was awarded the 1921 Nobel Prize for chemistry for his studies of radioactive ISOTOPES. In 1920 he revealed the value of isotopes in computing geological age. With Ernest RUTHERFORD, he worked out an explanation of RADIOACTIVE DECAY and later, with William RAMSAY, found HELIUM to be a product of URANIUM decay.

sodium (symbol Na) Common, silvery-white metallic element, one of the ALKALI METALS, first isolated in 1807 by Sir Humphry DAVY. It occurs in the sea as salt (sodium chloride) and in many minerals. Its chief source is sodium chloride, from which it is extracted by electrolysis. The soft, reactive metal is used in the manufacture of tetraethyl lead and as a heat-transfer medium in nuclear reactors. Properties: at.no. 11; r.a.m. 22.9898; r.d. 0.97; m.p. 97.81°C (208.05°F); b.p. 882°C (1,620°F).

sodium bicarbonate (sodium hydrogen carbonate, $NaHCO_3$, popularly known as bicarbonate of soda) White, crystalline salt that decomposes in acid or on heating to release carbon dioxide gas. It has a slightly alkaline reaction and is an ingredient of indigestion medicines.

sodium chloride (NaCl) Common salt. It is the major mineral component of seawater, making up 80% of its dissolved material. Sodium chloride is also the major ELECTROLYTE of living cells, and the loss of too much salt, through evaporation from the skin or through illness, is dangerous. It is used as a seasoning, to cure and preserve foods, and in the chemical industry.

sodium hydroxide *See* CAUSTIC SODA

Sodom and Gomorrah In the Old Testament, two cities S of the DEAD SEA, notorious for their carnality and vice. God could not find even ten good men within Sodom and so destroyed both it and Gomorrah with fire and brimstone. LOT and his family were allowed to escape, but Lot's wife disobeyed God's order not to look back and was turned to a pillar of salt.

Sofia (Sofija) Capital of Bulgaria and Sofia province, in W central Bulgaria, at the foot of the Vitosha Mountains. The city was founded by the Romans (as Serdica) in the 2nd century AD for its hot mineral springs. It was ruled by the Byzantine Empire (as Triaditsa) from 1018 to 1185. Sofia passed to the second Bulgarian empire (1186–1382)

and then to the Ottoman Empire (1382–1878). The city was taken by Russia in 1877 and chosen as the capital of Bulgaria by the Congress of Berlin. Industries: steel, machinery, textiles, rubber, chemicals, metallurgy, leather goods. Pop. (1996) 1,117,000.

softball Game similar to BASEBALL in which a lighter bat, a larger and softer ball and a smaller field are used. It is played by two teams of nine or ten people. The rules are close to those of baseball except for the pitching delivery (underhand) and the number of innings (seven instead of nine). Softball was originally invented as an indoor game in Chicago in 1888 and increased in popularity when moved outdoors in 1930. The sport is governed by the Amateur Softball Association, founded in 1934. The International Softball Federation coordinates competition in more than 20 nations.

software COMPUTER PROGRAM and any associated data file. The term software is used to distinguish these coded instructions and data from computer HARDWARE, or equipment. *See also* CD-ROM; MAGNETIC DISK

soil Surface layer of loose material resting on top of the rock which makes up the surface of the Earth. It consists of undissolved minerals produced by the WEATHERING and breakdown of surface rocks, organic matter, water and gases. The organic remains provide the HUMUS and the inorganic particles provide vital minerals. Soils are classified by structure and texture. The structure is determined by the aggregation of particles (peds). The four main textures of soil are SAND, SILT, CLAY and loam. Loam soils are best for cultivation, since they are able to retain more water and nutrients. Erosion and mismanagement are the chief causes of soil infertility. *See also* SOIL HORIZON

soil horizon Layer of SOIL that shows in a **soil profile** – a cross-section of the soil. Usually soil is divided into three horizons, designated A, B and C. A is the topsoil, B the sub-soil and C the bedrock. Fine particles and organic HUMUS make up the A horizon, much more inorganic material and larger particles occur in the B horizon, and the C horizon is rock.

solar cell Device that converts sunlight directly to electricity. It normally consists of a *p*-type (positive) silicon crystal and an *n*-type (negative) one. Light radiation causes electrons to be released and creates a POTENTIAL DIFFERENCE so that current can flow between electrodes connected to the two crystals. The cells are *c*.10% efficient. Solar cells are often used to power small electronic

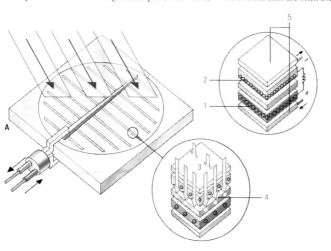

◀ **solar cell** A solar (photovoltaic) cell (A) is made up of two silicon semiconductors between metal contacts protected by a grid. One of the silicon semiconductors tends to collect positive charge (1), the other negative (2), creating a potential difference. As light photons (3) hit the *p-n* semiconductor junction between the semiconductors (4) they displace electrons, which are attracted to the positive semiconductor. The metal contacts (5) connect the two charged areas, exploiting the potential difference and creating a current.

devices such as pocket calculators. Several thousand cells may be used in panels to provide power of a few hundred watts.

solar constant Steady rate at which energy from the Sun is received from just outside the Earth's atmosphere. Its value is c.1.353 kilowatts per square metre (perpendicular to the Sun's rays).

solar energy Heat and light from the Sun consisting of ELECTROMAGNETIC RADIATION, including heat (infrared rays), light and radio waves. About 35% of the energy reaching the Earth is absorbed; most is spent evaporating moisture into clouds, and some is converted into organic chemical energy by PHOTOSYNTHESIS in plants. All forms of energy (except NUCLEAR ENERGY) on Earth come ultimately from the Sun. SOLAR CELLS are used to power instruments on spacecraft, and experiments are being done to store solar energy in liquids from which electricity can be generated.

solar flare Sudden and violent release of matter and energy from the Sun's surface, usually from the region of an active group of SUNSPOTS. Flares emit radiation across the electromagnetic spectrum. Charged particles are emitted, mostly electrons and protons and smaller numbers of neutrons and atomic nuclei. A flare can cause material to be ejected in bulk in the form of prominences. When energetic particles from flares reach the Earth, they may cause radio interference, magnetic storms and more intense auroras.

Solar System The SUN and all the celestial bodies that revolve around it: the nine PLANETS, together with their SATELLITES and ring systems, the thousands of ASTEROIDS and COMETS, meteoroids and other interplanetary material. The boundaries of the Solar System lie beyond the orbit of Pluto to include the Kuiper Belt and the Oort Cloud of comets. The Solar System came into being nearly 5,000 million years ago, probably as the end-product of a contracting cloud of interstellar gas and dust.

solar wind Particles accelerated by high temperatures of the solar CORONA to velocities great enough to allow them to escape from the Sun's gravity. The solar wind deflects the tail of the Earth's magnetosphere and the tails of comets away from the Sun.

sole Marine flatfish found in the Atlantic Ocean from NW Africa to Norway, especially *Solea solea*. A food fish, it is green-grey or black-brown with dark spots. Length: to 60cm (24in). Family Soleidae.

Solemn League and Covenant (September 1643) Agreement between the LONG PARLIAMENT and the Scots during the English CIVIL WAR. In return for Parliament's promise to reorganize the established church on a PRESBYTERIAN basis, the Scots agreed to raise an army in the north of England against CHARLES I. The Scottish help led directly to the Parliamentary victory over the Royalists at MARSTON MOOR.

solid State of matter in which a substance has a relatively fixed shape and size. The forces between atoms or molecules are strong enough to hold them in definite locations (about which they can vibrate) and to resist compression. *See also* CRYSTAL; GAS; LIQUID

Solidarity Polish organization that provided the chief opposition to the communist regime during the 1980s. The National Committee of Solidarity was founded in 1980 among shipyard workers in GDAŃSK led by Lech WALESA. Solidarity organized strikes and demanded economic improvements, but soon acquired a political, revolutionary character. Banned from 1981, it re-emerged as a national party, winning the free elections of 1989 and forming the core of the new democratic government.

solid-state physics Physics of SOLID materials. From the study of the structure, binding forces, electrical, magnetic and thermal properties of solids has come the development of the SEMICONDUCTOR, MASER, LASER and SOLAR CELL.

solipsism Philosophical theory that the mind knows nothing other than itself and that the outside world only exists in the mind of the observer. It is a form of IDEALISM.

Solomon (d.922 BC) King of Israel (c.972–922 BC), son of DAVID and Bathsheba. His kingdom prospered, thanks partly to economic relations with the Egyptians and Phoenicians, enabling Solomon to build the TEMPLE in Jerusalem. His reputation for wisdom reflected his interest in literature, although the works attributed to him, including the SONG OF SOLOMON, were probably written by others.

Solomon Islands Melanesian archipelago and nation in the SW Pacific Ocean, SE of New Guinea. The capital is Honiara (on Guadalcanal). Solomon Islands include several hundred islands spread over 1,400km (900mi) of the Pacific Ocean. The principal islands are volcanic, mountainous and covered by equatorial rainforest. The N Solomons have a tropical oceanic climate, but further S there is a longer cool season. The largest island is Guadalcanal, and other inhabited islands include Choiseul, Malaita, New Georgia, San Cristobal (Makira), Santa Isabel (Ysabel) and the Shortland islands. The vast majority of the population are indigenous Melanesians. The main languages are Melanesian dialects, but English is official. The first European discovery of the islands was by the Spanish in 1568. The islands resisted colonization until the late 19th century. In 1893, the S islands became a British protectorate, and the N was controlled by the Germans from 1895. In 1900, Germany ceded its territory to Britain. During World War 1 BOUGAINVILLE and Buka (now in Papua New Guinea) were occupied by Australian troops and were mandated to Australia in 1920. In 1942, the S islands were occupied by Japanese troops. After heavy fighting, particularly on Guadalcanal, the islands were liberated by US troops in 1944. In 1976, the Solomons became self-governing and in 1978 achieved full independence within the Commonwealth of Nations. The coastal plains are used for subsistence farming, which supports 90% of the population. Coconuts are the major products, tuna is the biggest export earner, and lumber is the main industry. Area: c.27,900sq km (10,770sq mi). Pop. (2000) 429,000.

Solomon's seal (David's harp) Perennial plants of the genus *Polygonatum*, native to cool, temperate regions of Europe and Asia. They have broad, waxy leaves and white pendant flowers. Height: to 0.9m (3ft). Family Liliaceae.

Solon (c.639–c.599 BC) Athenian statesman, poet and political reformer. In c.594 BC, during an economic crisis, he was elected archon (chief magistrate). He carried out drastic economic and constitutional reforms, laying the foundations of Athenian DEMOCRACY.

solstice Either of the two days each year when the Sun is at its greatest angular distance from the celestial equator, leading to the longest day and shortest night (summer solstice) in one hemisphere of the Earth, and the shortest day and longest night (winter solstice) in the other hemisphere. In the Northern Hemisphere the summer solstice occurs on or about 21 June and the winter solstice on or about 22 December.

Solti, Sir Georg (1912–97) British conductor, b. Hungary. He was music director of Covent Garden Opera (now ROYAL OPERA), London (1961–71); Orchestre de Paris (1971–75); and the Chicago Symphony Orchestra (1969–91). An outstanding operatic music director, he was the first conductor to record (1965) Wagner's entire *Ring* cycle.

solubility Mass (grams) of a SOLUTE that will saturate 100 grams of SOLVENT under given conditions to give a SATURATED SOLUTION. Solubility generally rises with temperature, but for a few solutes, such as calcium sulphate, increasing temperature decreases solubility in water.

solute Gaseous, liquid or solid substance that is dissolved in a SOLVENT to form a SOLUTION.

solution Liquid (the SOLVENT) into which another substance (the SOLUTE) is dissolved, or a liquid consisting of two or more chemically distinct compounds, inseparable by filtering. The amount of a solute dissolved in a solvent is called the concentration. *See also* MIXTURE

solvent Liquid that dissolves a substance (the SOLUTE) without changing its composition. Water is the most universal solvent, and many inorganic compounds dissolve in it. Ethanol, ether, propanone and carbon tetrachloride are common solvents for organic substances.

Solzhenitsyn, Alexander (1918–) Russian novelist. Sentenced to a forced labour camp in 1945 for criticizing Stalin, he was subsequently exiled to Ryazan but was officially rehabilitated in 1956. His novels include *One Day in the Life of Ivan Denisovich* (1962), *The First Circle* (1968), *Cancer Ward* (1968) and *August 1914* (1971). He was awarded the 1970 Nobel Prize for literature. Criticism of the Soviet regime in *The Gulag Archipelago* (1974) led to his forced exile to the West, from which he returned to Russia in 1994.

Somalia Republic in the E Horn of E Africa. A narrow, mostly barren, coastal plain borders the Indian Ocean and the Gulf of Aden. The capital, MOGADISHU, is also Somalia's major port. In the interior, the land rises to a plateau nearly 1,000m (3,300ft) high. In the N is a highland region. The S contains the only rivers, the Juba and the Scebeli. **Climate** Rainfall is light; the wettest regions are in the far S and N highlands. Drought is a persistent problem. Temperatures on the plateaus and plains regularly reach 32°C (90°F). **Vegetation** Much of Somalia is dry grassland or semi-desert. There are areas of wooded grassland. Plants are most abundant in the the lower Giuba valley. **History and Politics** In the 7th century, Arab traders established coastal settlements and introduced Islam. Mogadishu was founded c.900 as a trading centre. The interest of European imperial powers increased after the opening of the Suez Canal (1869). In 1887, Britain established a protectorate in what is now N Somalia. In 1889, Italy formed a protectorate in the central region and extended its power to the S by 1905. In 1896, France established a colony in modern-day DJIBOUTI. In 1936, Italian Somaliland was united with the Somali regions of Ethiopia to form Italian East Africa. During World War 2, Italy invaded (1940) British Somaliland. In 1941, British forces reconquered the region and captured Italian Somaliland. In 1950, Italian Somaliland returned to Italy as a UN trust territory. In 1960, both Somalilands gained independence and joined to form the United Republic of Somalia. The new republic was faced with pan-Somali irredentists, calling for the creation of a "Greater Somalia" to include the Somali-majority areas in Ethiopia, Kenya and Djibouti. In 1969, the army, led by Siad Barre, seized power and formed a socialist, Islamic republic. During the 1970s, Somalia and Ethiopia fought for control of the Ogaden Desert, inhabited mainly by Somali nomads. Ethiopia forced Somalia to withdraw (1978), but resistance continued, forcing one million refugees to flee to Somalia. In 1991, Barre was overthrown and the United Somali Congress (USC), led by Ali

SOMALIA
AREA: 637,660sq km (246,201sq mi)
POPULATION: 9,736,000
CAPITAL (POPULATION): Mogadishu (1,200,000)

Mahdi Muhammad, seized power. Somalia disintegrated into civil war between rival clans. The Ethiopia-backed Somali National Movement (SNM) gained control of NW Somalia and seceded as the Somaliland Republic (1991). Mogadishu was devastated by an attack from the Somali National Alliance (SNA), led by General Muhammad Aideed. War and drought resulted in a devastating famine that claimed thousands of lives. The UN was slow to provide relief, and when aid arrived, was unable to secure distribution. US marines led a task force to secure food distribution but became embroiled in conflict with Somali warlords, destroying the headquarters of General Aideed. After the deaths of UN troops, US marines withdrew in 1994. Civil strife continued, and in 1996 Aideed was killed. The Cairo Declaration (December 1997), signed by 26 of the 28 warring factions, including Ali Mahdi Muhammad and Aideed's son Hussein Aideed, held out hope of an end to factional feuding. The installation of a transitional government has been repeatedly postponed, and Djibouti has regularly acted as a peace broker. In 2000, Somalia was one of several countries in Africa threatened with serious famine. **Economy** Somalia is a low-income developing country, shattered by drought and civil war (1992 GDP, US$1,100). Many Somalis are nomadic herdspeople. Live animals, hides and skins are the major exports. Bananas are grown in the S.

Somerset, Edward Seymour, 1st Duke of (1500–52) English ruler, regent for EDWARD VI. HENRY VIII appointed him to a council of regents for the young Edward VI (r.1547–53), but he assumed supreme authority and the title of protector on Henry's death.

Somerset County on the Bristol Channel, SW England. The county is divided into five districts, with the administrative centre at Taunton (1991 pop. 93,969). Other major towns include Yeovil and Bridgewater. The region is generally low-lying in the centre and is drained chiefly by the rivers Avon, Exe and Parrett. Much of the land is given over to agriculture. Dairy farming and fruit growing are the most important economic activities, and the region is noted for Cheddar cheese and cider. Limestone is mined. Area: 3,452sq km (1,332sq mi). Pop. (1991) 460,368.

Somme, Battle of the Major WORLD WAR 1 engagement in N France along the River Somme. It was launched by Douglas HAIG on 1 July 1916. On the first day the British suffered 60,000 casualties in an attempt to break through the German lines. A trench war of attrition continued until the offensive was abandoned on 19 November 1916. Total casualties were more than one million, and the British had advanced only 16km (10mi). A second battle around St Quentin (March–April 1918) is sometimes referred to as the Second Battle of the Somme. A German offensive, designed to secure victory before the arrival of US troops, was halted by Anglo-French forces.

Somoza García, Anastasio (1896–1956) Central figure in Nicaraguan politics from 1936, when he ousted President Sacasa. Somoza created both a dictatorial government and a political dynasty; he was succeeded in office by his two sons, Luis and Anastasio. The Somoza dynasty was overthrown by the SANDINISTAS in 1979.

sonar (Acronym for **so**und **na**vigation **a**nd **r**anging) Underwater detection and navigation system. The system emits high-frequency sound that is reflected by underwater objects and detected on its return.

sonata Musical composition in several movements. In the BAROQUE era, sonatas were usually written for two melodic parts and a continuo. In the CLASSICAL period, the sonata became a more clearly defined form for one or two instruments. The movements, usually three or four in number, are in closely related keys. The first movement of a sonata is usually in sonata form, a widely used MUSICAL FORM. The second movement is generally slow in tempo and the third and perhaps fourth movements are faster.

Sondheim, Stephen (1930–) US composer and lyricist. Sondheim made his mark on Broadway in 1957 with the lyrics for *West Side Story*. His first success as a lyricist-composer was *A Funny Thing Happened on the Way to the Forum* (1962). His reputation was enhanced with works such as *A Little Night Music* (1972), *Sunday in the Park with George* (1984) and *Assassins* (1991).

Song (960–1279) (Sung) Chinese imperial dynasty (960–1279). The period is divided into the Northern (960–1126) and, after the N was overrun by Jurchen tribes, the Southern (1127–1279) Song. The Song dynasty was notable for a deliberate reduction in military might, after the initial conquests of Zhao Kuang-ying, and the development of a powerful civil service. The Southern Song, with its capital at Hangzhou, was overrun by the Mongols.

Songhai West African empire, founded in c.AD 700. In 1468 Sonni Ali captured the market city of TIMBUKTU, and the Songhai empire acquired control of most of the trade in W Africa. Sonni was succeeded by Askia Muhammad I, who further increased the Songhai stranglehold on trade routes. The empire began to disintegrate because of factional in-fighting. The Songhai peoples still control much of the trans-Saharan trade.

Song of Solomon (Song of Songs) Book of the OLD TESTAMENT, consisting of a series of love poems spoken alternately by a man and a woman. It is attributed in the Bible to SOLOMON, but was probably written in the 3rd century BC.

sonic boom Sudden noise produced by shock waves from an aircraft flying at SUPERSONIC VELOCITY. The shock waves are formed by the buildup of sound waves at the front and back of the aircraft. These waves spread out and sweep across the ground behind the aircraft, often causing a double bang. See also SOUND BARRIER

sonnet Poem of 14 lines, most often in iambic pentameter and usually employing Petrarchan or Shakespearean rhyme schemes. The Petrarchan consists of an octet and a sextet, usually with an *abbaabbacdecde* rhyme scheme. The Shakespearean, having a final rhyming couplet, is *ababcdcdefefgg*.

Sons of Liberty American colonial group. This secret organization was founded, principally in Connecticut and New York, to protest against the STAMP ACT (1765). It sought freedom and liberty in the 13 British colonies.

Sontag, Susan (1933–) US writer, critic and essayist. Perhaps best known as a critic on popular culture, as in *Against Interpretation* (1966), she has also written novels and short stories, including *The Benefactor* (1963) and *Death Kit* (1967). In more recent years, she has experimented with STRUCTURALISM, notably in her *Illness as Metaphor* (1978) and *Aids and its Metaphors* (1986).

Sophia (1630–1714) Electress of Hanover. A granddaughter of JAMES I and the widow of the elector of Hanover, she was recognized as heir to the English throne by the Act of SETTLEMENT (1701) to ensure a Protestant succession and prevent the return of the Catholic STUARTS. When she died, her son, the current elector, became king as GEORGE I.

Sophists Professional Greek teachers of the 5th–4th centuries BC. Although not a formal school, they emphasized the intellectual and rhetorical skills needed to succeed in ancient Greek society and regarded law and ethics as convenient human inventions with no basis in natural law. Serious philosophers, such as PLATO, disapproved of them.

Sophocles (496–406 BC) Greek playwright. Of his 100 plays, only seven tragedies and part of a Satyr play remain. These include *Ajax*, *Antigone* (c.442–441 BC), *Electra* (409 BC), *Oedipus Rex* (c.429 BC) and *Oedipus at Colonus* (produced posthumously). His works introduced a third speaking actor and increased the members of the chorus from 12 to 15.

soprano Highest singing range of the female human voice. The normal range may be given as two octaves upwards from middle C, although exceptional voices may reach notes higher. Sopranos have always been important in opera, with various types of soprano (dramatic, lyric or coloratura) taking different types of roles.

Sorbonne College of the University of PARIS, founded in 1253 by Robert de Sorbon (1201–74) and located in what is now the Latin Quarter of Paris. Established for the education of students of theology, it was for centuries an intellectual centre of Roman Catholic religious thought. Towards the end of the 19th century, it became purely secular.

sorcery Manipulation of the natural world by means of MAGIC. Anthropologists sometimes distinguish sorcery from WITCHCRAFT – witches claim inherent spiritual powers whereas sorcerers do not.

sorghum Tropical cereal grass native to Africa and cultivated worldwide. Types raised for grain are varieties of *Sorghum vulgare*, which have leaves coated with white waxy blooms and flower heads that bear up to 3,000 seeds. It yields meal, oil, starch and dextrose (a sugar). Height: 0.5–2.5m (2–8ft). Family Poaceae/Gramineae.

sorrel (dock) Herbaceous, perennial plant native to temperate regions. It has large leaves that can be cooked as a vegetable and small green or brown flowers. Height: to 2m (6ft). Family Polygonaceae; genus *Rumex*, especially *Rumex acetosa*.

SOS General distress signal at sea. It is a simple pattern in Morse code consisting of three dots, three dashes and three more dots. *See also* MORSE, SAMUEL FINLEY BREESE

Sosnowiec *See* KATOWICE

Sotho Major cultural and linguistic group of S Africa. It includes the Northern Sotho of TRANSVAAL, South Africa, the Western Sotho (better known as the Tswana) of BOTSWANA, and the Southern Sotho (Basotho or Basuto) of LESOTHO. Although dominating the rural territories they inhabit, the four million or so Sotho share those areas with people of other Bantu-speaking tribes. Many work and live in the urban areas and surrounding townships.

Soto, Hernando de *See* DE SOTO, HERNANDO

soul Non-material or non-tangible part of a person that is the central location of his or her personality, intellect, emotions and will; the human spirit. Most religions teach that the soul lives on after the death of the body.

soul music Form of popular music. The term designates black music that developed in the USA in the 1960s from RHYTHM AND BLUES. Soul is also used generically to describe music that possesses a certain "soulful" quality. Its influence has extended into many popular musical styles.

sound Physiological sensation perceived by the brain via the EAR, caused by an oscillating source and transmitted through a material medium as a sound wave. The velocity at which a sound wave travels through a medium depends on the ELASTICITY of the medium and its DENSITY. If the medium is a gas, the sound wave is longitudinal, and its velocity depends on the gas temperature. The velocity of sound in dry air at standard temperature and pressure (STP) is 331mps (741mph) and depends on the height above sea level. Pure sounds are characterized by PITCH, TIMBRE and intensity (the rate of flow of sound energy).

sound barrier Name for the cause of an aircraft's difficulties in accelerating to a speed faster than that of sound. When approaching the speed of sound, an aircraft experiences a sudden increase in drag and loss of lift. These are caused by the build-up of sound waves to form shock waves at the front and back of the aircraft. The problems were solved by designing aircraft with smaller surface area, swept-back wings and more powerful engines. *See also* SONIC BOOM

sound recording Conversion of sound waves into a form that can be stored and reproduced. Thomas EDISON's phonograph (1877) recorded sound vibrations as indentations made by a stylus on a revolving cylinder wrapped in tinfoil. Emile Berliner's gramophone improved the process by using a zinc disc instead of a cylinder. The volume was amplified by the addition of acoustical horns, which were replaced before World War 1 by valve amplifiers. Moulded thermoplastic records were introduced in 1901. In 1927 and 1928, patents were issued in the USA and Germany for MAGNETIC RECORDING processes. Later innovations include high-fidelity (hi-fi), stereophonic and quadrophonic reproduction. Modern recordings on COMPACT DISC (CD) usually employ laser-scanned digital signals.

Sousa, John Philip (1854–1932) US composer and bandmaster. He composed about 100 marches, including *Semper Fidelis* (1888) and *The Stars and Stripes Forever* (1896). He also composed numerous operettas, of which the most famous is *El Capitan* (1896).

sousaphone Largest BRASS musical instrument of the TUBA family. It was introduced by John Philip SOUSA to fortify the bass section of US military bands.

South Africa Republic in s Africa, the southernmost country in Africa. A narrow coastal margin includes: the Indian Ocean port of DURBAN; the dry s tablelands, Little and Great Karoo; CAPE TOWN on the CAPE OF GOOD HOPE; and part of the NAMIB Desert. The interior forms part of the African plateau. The plateau rises in the E to an escarpment more than 2,000m (6,000ft) high, on the fringe of which lies BLOEMFONTEIN. SOWETO, JOHANNESBURG and PRETORIA; all lie on the N of the escarpment. The highest peaks are in the Drakensberg range, on the E border of Lesotho. In the N lies part of the KALAHARI Desert. In the NE are the WITWATERSRAND goldfields. KIMBERLEY has the largest diamond mines. The KRUGER NATIONAL PARK lies on the border with Mozambique. The longest river is the ORANGE. **Climate** Most of South Africa is subtropical. The SW has a Mediterranean climate. Much of the plateau is arid, and the Namib Desert is almost rainless. **Vegetation** Grassland covers much of the high interior, with tropical savanna in lower areas. Forest and woodland cover only 3% of the land, and *fynbos* (scrub vegetation) is found in the Cape region. **History** The indigenous people of South Africa are the SAN. The first European settlement was not until 1652, when the Dutch EAST INDIA COMPANY founded a colony at Table Bay. Dutch AFRIKANERS (Boers) established farms, employing slaves. From the late 18th century, conflict

SOUTH AFRICA
AREA: 1,219,916sq km (470,566sq mi)
POPULATION: 43,666,000
CAPITAL (POPULATION): Cape Town (legislative, 2,350,157); Pretoria (administrative, 1,080,187); Bloemfontein (judicial, 300,150)

with the XHOSA intensified, as the Boers trekked inland. In the early 19th century, Britain gained control of the Cape. Following Britain's abolition of slavery in 1833, the Boers began the GREAT TREK. They met with fierce resistance, particularly from the ZULU kingdom. The Boer republics of TRANSVAAL and Orange FREE STATE were established in 1852 and 1854. The discovery of diamonds and gold in the 1870s and 1880s increased the pace of colonization, and Britain sought to gain control of Boer- and Zulu-held areas. The British defeated the Zulu in the ZULU WAR (1879), and Zululand was annexed to Natal (1897). In 1890 Cecil RHODES became governor of Cape Colony. Britain defeated the Boers in the SOUTH AFRICAN WARS (1880–81, 1899–1902). The Union of South Africa was formed in 1910, with Louis BOTHA as prime minister. In 1912, the AFRICAN NATIONAL CONGRESS (ANC) was founded. During World War 1, South Africa captured NAMIBIA (1915), and after the war it was mandated to the Union. In 1919, Jan SMUTS succeeded Botha as prime minister. In 1931, Smuts' successor and Nationalist Party founder (1914), James HERTZOG, realized Afrikaner ambitions as South Africa achieved full independence within the Commonwealth of Nations. Smuts regained power in 1939, and South Africa joined the Allies in World War 2. The Nationalist Party won the 1948 election, advocating a policy of APARTHEID. Apartheid placed economic, social and political restrictions on non-whites. The ANC began a campaign of passive resistance, but after the Sharpeville massacre (1960), Nelson MANDELA formed a military wing. In 1961, faced by international condemnation, Prime Minister Hendrik VERWOERD established South Africa as a republic. In 1964, Mandela was jailed. Verwoerd was assassinated in 1966 and was succeeded by B.J. VORSTER. Vorster used South African forces to prevent black majority rule in South Africa's neighbouring states. The crushing of the Soweto uprising (1976) sparked a new wave of opposition. In 1978, P.W. BOTHA was elected prime minister. During the 1970s, four bantustans (homelands) gained nominal independence. External economic sanctions forced Botha to adopt a new constitution (1984), which gave Indian and Coloured minorities limited political representation; black Africans were still excluded. From 1985 to 1990, South Africa was in a state of emergency: Archbishop Desmond TUTU pressed for further sanctions. In 1989, President F.W. DE KLERK began the process of dismantling apartheid. In 1990, Mandela was released and resumed leadership of the ANC. Clashes continued between the ANC and Chief BUTHELEZI's Zulu INKATHA movement. In 1994, the ANC won South Africa's first multi-racial elections, and Mandela became president. The homelands were reintegrated, and South Africa was divided into nine provinces. In 1995 a Truth and Reconciliation Commission, headed by Tutu, was set up to investigate political committed under apartheid. In 1999, Thabo MBEKI, who had replaced Mandela as president of the ANC (1997–), became president of South Africa. **Economy** Mining forms the base of Africa's most industrialized economy (1995 GDP per capita, US$5,030).

South Africa is the world's leading producer of gold and fifth-largest producer of diamonds. Chromite, coal, copper, iron ore, manganese, platinum, silver and uranium are also mined. Sanctions, falling gold price, and civil and industrial strife created prolonged recession. Unemployment stood at 45% (1995). Major manufactures include chemicals, iron and steel. Agriculture employs more than 33% .of the workforce. Major products include fruits, grapes for wine-making, maize, meat and sugar cane.

South African Wars Two wars between the AFRIKANERS (Boers) and the British in South Africa. The first (1880–81) arose from the British annexation of the Transvaal in 1877. Under Paul KRUGER, the Transvaal regained autonomy, but further disputes, arising largely from the discovery of gold and diamonds, provoked the second, greater conflict (1899–1902), known to Afrikaners as the Second War of Freedom and to the British as the Boer War. It was a civil war between whites; black Africans played little part on either side. In 1900, the British gained the upper hand, defeating the Boer armies and capturing Bloemfontein and Pretoria. Boer commandos fought a determined guerrilla campaign but were forced to accept British rule in the peace treaty signed at Vereeniging (1902).

South America Fourth-largest continent, the S of the two continents of America, in the Western Hemisphere, connected to North America by the isthmus of PANAMA. **Land** Off the N coast lies the Caribbean Sea, off the E the Atlantic Ocean, and the W the Pacific Ocean. It is politically divided into 12 independent nations: BRAZIL and ARGENTINA (the two largest), BOLIVIA, CHILE, COLOMBIA, ECUADOR, GUYANA, PARAGUAY, PERU, SURINAM, URUGUAY and VENEZUELA, plus the French overseas department of FRENCH GUIANA. It is c.7,640km (4,750mi) long (Punta Gallinas, Colombia, to Cape Horn, Chile) and at its widest (near the Equator) c.5,300km (3,000mi). **Structure and geology** South America's W edge towers above the rest of the continent, which slopes downwards towards the Atlantic Ocean, except for the Guiana and Brazilian Highlands. These form the continental shield. The middle of the continent is marked by a series of lowlands. The ANDES, which stretch from Colombia to Chile, contain the highest peaks of the Americas. ACONCAGUA (Argentina) is the tallest mountain outside Asia, at 6,960m (22,834ft). The ATACAMA DESERT, a coastal strip in N Chile, is the driest place on Earth. PATAGONIA is a semi-arid plateau, composed of rocky terraces to the E of the Andes. Major islands include the FALKLAND ISLANDS (a British crown colony) and the GALÁPAGOS (a territory of Ecuador). **Lakes and rivers.** Excluding Lake MARACAIBO (13,512sq km/5,217sq mi) as an extension of the Gulf of Venezuela, the largest lake in South America is Lake TITICACA, on the Peru-Bolivia border, covering 8,300sq km (3,200sq mi). Lengthy rivers combine to form three major systems that reach the Atlantic. At 6,430km (3,990mi) the AMAZON is the world's second-longest river (after the Nile). With its many substantial tributaries, it drains by far the biggest of the world's river basins. Flowing S is the PARAGUAY-PARANÁ system, and NE is the ORINOCO. **Climate and vegetation** Except in the mountains and the S, the climate remains generally warm and humid. Much of the N supports tropical RAIN-FOREST, while lowlands in the extreme N and the central region have a cover of tropical grass. The Pampas, S of the Tropic of CAPRICORN, produce temperate grasslands, but vegetation is scarce to the far SE of the mountains. In the S, pine and other temperate forests grow along the W coast. **People** Some Incas (QUECHUAS) still remain in the Andes,

as do some Mapucho (Araucanians) of Chile. But the majority of the population is mestizo (of dual Indian and European descent), except in Argentina, s Brazil, Chile and Uruguay, where the population is primarily European. Since the early 19th century many Europeans (especially Italians) and Asians (particularly Japanese) have migrated to Argentina and Brazil. Sizable black populations exist in Brazil, Colombia, French Guiana and Venezuela, descendants of slaves brought from Africa to work in the sugar cane, coffee, rubber and cotton plantations. The majority of the continent's people live in urban areas close to the coast, SÃO PAULO being by far the largest example. Latin American Spanish and Portuguese are the dominant continental languages and Roman Catholicism is the major religion. **Recent history** The early 1900s saw a number of conflicts within and between countries of the region. Notable among these were the territorial Chaco Wars (1928–30, 1932–35) between Bolivia and Paraguay. South American republics failed to become world powers until the end of World War 2, helped by the formation of the United Nations in 1945 and the ORGANIZATION OF AMERICAN STATES (OAS) in 1948, which gave them influence in international affairs. Many countries of South America have swung between military dictatorships and democratic governments, mainly caused by wildly fluctuating economic fortunes, which in turn have brought about extremes of wealth and poverty leading to unrest and instability. The periodic repressive regimes have often been the focus of international condemnation of human rights abuses. During the 1980s and 1990s, international pressure, particularly from the USA, has also been brought to bear on those governments, notably Bolivia and Colombia, that are either unwilling or unable to control the production and export of vast quantities of cocaine. **Economy** About 30% of the workforce is employed in subsistence farming, working 15% of the land, most of which is owned by Europeans. Chief exports include cash crops such as coffee, bananas, sugar cane and tobacco. The drug industry is also important: Peru and Colombia are major cultivators of coca leaves, and Colombia supplies more than 50% of the world's illegal trade in cocaine. Industrial development and mineral exploitation have been dominated by Europe and the USA. Since 1945 South American countries have sought greater economic independence, yet reliance on banking finance has often led to a burden of debt. Another drawback has been the scarcity of continental coal reserves and the dependence on petroleum, especially in Venezuela's Maracaibo region. The Guiana and Brazilian Highlands have large deposits of iron ore, and the Andes range has many copper reserves. Bolivia has large tin mines, and Brazil reserves of manganese. However, despite the industrialization of some countries, particularly Brazil, Venezuela and Argentina, most countries remain industrially underdeveloped. During the 1970s and 1980s, the rush for economic growth and industrialization was often at the expense of the continent's rainforests. Worldwide treaties in the 1990s have attempted to slow down the deforestation but with little success. Industrialization has also often been seen to exacerbate the continent's high inflation and huge debt crises. Total area: c.17,793,000sq km (6,868,000sq mi); *Highest mountain* Aconcagua 6,960m (22,834ft) *Longest river* Amazon 6,430km (3,990mi) *Population* 299,000,000 *Largest cities* São Paulo 16,567,317; Buenos Aries 11,652,050; Rio de Janeiro 5,336,179.

Southampton Port and county district in Hampshire, S England. At the head of Southampton Water and a port since Roman times, the city is Britain's principal passenger port and a major commercial port. Industries: shipbuilding, engineering, oil-refining. Pop. (1994) 214,000.

South Australia State in s central Australia, on the Great Australian Bight. The capital is ADELAIDE, home to 60% of the state's population. Other major cities include Salisbury and Elizabeth. The s coast of Australia was visited by the Dutch in 1627, the first English colonists arrived in 1836, and the region was federated as a state in 1901. The area is hilly in the E (Flinders Ranges) and the N (Musgrave Ranges), and in the W are the E parts of the Great Victoria Desert and the Nullarbor Plain. The MURRAY in the SE is the only important river, and farming is mainly confined to this area. Barley, oats, wheat, rye and grapes are the chief crops, and livestock are grazed in the N. Mineral deposits include iron ore, uranium, silver, lead, salt, gypsum, opals, coal and natural gas. Industries: heavy metals, mining, transport equipment. Whyalla has the largest shipyards in Australia. Area: 984,380sq km (379,760sq mi). Pop. (1994) 1,471,000.

South Carolina State on the Atlantic Ocean, in the SE USA; the capital and largest city is COLUMBIA. The main port is CHARLESTON. The land rises from the coastal plain to the rolling hills of the Piedmont plateau to the BLUE RIDGE MOUNTAINS in the NW. The region is drained by many rivers including the SAVANNAH, which forms most of the Georgia border. From 1633 the English were the first to settle the area permanently. South Carolina became a royal province in 1729, and a plantation society evolved based on rice, indigo and cotton. One of the original thirteen US states (1789), it was the first to secede from the Union and the first shots of the CIVIL WAR were fired at FORT SUMTER. The state was devastated in 1865 by Union troops. Major crops include tobacco, soya beans, maize, sweet potatoes and peanuts. Tourism is the state's second-biggest source of income after textiles and clothing. Area: 80,432sq km (31,055sq mi). Pop. (2000) 4,012,012.

South China Sea Part of the Pacific Ocean, surrounded by SE China, Indochina, the MALAY PENINSULA, Borneo, the Philippines and Taiwan; connected to the East China Sea by the Formosa Strait. The world's largest "sea", its chief arms are the Gulf of Tonkin and Gulf of Thailand. The rivers Si, Red, Mekong and Chao Phraya flow into it. Area: 2,300,000sq km (848,000sq mi). Average depth: 1,140m (3,740ft).

South Dakota State in the N central USA, on the GREAT PLAINS. The capital is PIERRE; the largest cities are SIOUX FALLS and Rapid City. The land rises gradually from the E to the Black Hills (featuring Mount RUSHMORE) in the W and the Badlands in the SW, with the Missouri River bisecting the state. One fifth of the area W of the river is semi-arid plain, inhabited mainly by Native Americans, and the rest is divided into large cattle and sheep ranches. French trappers claimed the region for France in the 1740s, and the USA acquired part of the land in the LOUISIANA PURCHASE of 1803. Dakota Territory was formed in 1861. The discovery of gold in the Black Hills in 1874 led to an increase in population, and the territory was divided into the states of North and South Dakota, both of which joined the Union in 1889. Agriculture is important, with livestock rearing E of the Missouri; major crops include wheat, maize, oats and soya beans. South Dakota is the largest producer of gold in the USA, but tin, beryllium, stone, sand and gravel are also mined. Industries: meat packing, food processing. Area: 199,551sq km (77,047sq mi). Pop. (2000) 754,844.

Southeast Asia Region bounded by India, China and the Pacific Ocean, and comprising BURMA, THAILAND, MALAYSIA, CAMBODIA, LAOS, VIETNAM, PHILIPPINES, SINGAPORE and INDONESIA. Area: c.4,506,600sq km (1,740,000sq mi).

Southeast Asia Treaty Organization (SEATO) Regional defence agreement signed by Australia, New Zealand, France, Pakistan, the Philippines, Thailand, Britain and the USA in Manila in 1954. It was formed in response to communist expansion in Southeast Asia. With administrative headquarters in Bangkok, Thailand, SEATO had no standing forces. Some members were unwilling to support the USA in the VIETNAM WAR, and SEATO was abandoned in 1977. The non-military aspects of the treaty were replaced by the ASSOCIATION OF SOUTHEAST ASIAN NATIONS (ASEAN).

Southey, Robert (1774–1843) British poet and prose writer, poet laureate (1813–43). His long epic poems include *Thalaba the Destroyer* (1801), *Madoc* (1805), *The Curse of Kehama* (1810) and *Roderick the Last of the Goths* (1814).

South Georgia Island in the s Atlantic Ocean, c.1,750km (1,100mi) E of TIERRA DEL FUEGO. Mountainous and arid, it rises to 2,934m (9,626ft). A British dependency administered from the Falklands, it has a research station and garrison but no permanent population.

South Glamorgan County on the Bristol Channel, s WALES. The capital is CARDIFF. The county is divided into two districts, Cardiff and the Vale of Glamorgan. The Vale of Glamorgan is fertile agricultural land, and the major economic activity is dairy farming. Cardiff is an industrial district. Industries: engineering, steel. Area: 416sq km (161sq mi). Pop. (1991) 383,000.

South Island Larger of the two principal islands that comprise NEW ZEALAND. Its chief cities are CHRISTCHURCH, DUNEDIN and Invercarguill. The Southern Alps extend the length of the island and separate the thickly forested W coast from the Canterbury Plains in the E. Cereal growing, sheep and cattle rearing, and dairying are important on the Plains, and tourism is a valuable source of income in most parts. Area: 150,461sq km (58,093sq mi). Pop. (1991) 881,540.

South Pole Southernmost geographical point on the Earth's surface. The magnetic south pole is located c.2,400km (1,500mi) from the geographical South Pole. The South Pole lies 2,992m (9,816ft) above sea level, c.480km (300mi) s of the Ross Ice Shelf.

South Sea Bubble (1720) Speculation in the shares of the English South Sea Company, ending in financial collapse. The South Sea Company was founded in 1711 for trade in the Pacific. Shares sold so well and interest was so high that in 1720 the company volunteered to finance the English national debt. The result was intensive speculation with a 900% rise in the price of shares, until the bubble burst in September 1720, bankrupting investors and closing banks. Credit for saving the company and the government was given to Robert WALPOLE.

South West Africa *See* NAMIBIA

South West Africa People's Organization (SWAPO) Political organization formed in 1960 in South West Africa (now NAMIBIA). Swapo's aim was to achieve independence for Namibia and to this end declared itself at war with South Africa. Soon after ANGOLA gained independence in 1975, SWAPO established guerrilla bases there. In 1978, these bases were attacked by South Africa. Truce talks in Geneva in 1981 failed, and in 1984 SWAPO refused to cooperate with the rival Multi-Party Conference (MCP) in drawing up a timetable for independence. When independence was achieved, SWAPO fought a general election in 1989 and gained 57% of the votes and 75% of the seats in the constituent assembly. In 1990, SWAPO leader Sam NUJOMA became president of Namibia. He was re-elected in 1994.

South Yorkshire Metropolitan county in N central England. The county is divided into four districts, with Barnsley its administrative centre. South Yorkshire's only city is SHEFFIELD. The area includes the PEAK DISTRICT National Forest and the W Pennine moors. The River Don flows E across the county. Industries: iron, steel, coal mining. Area: 1,561sq km (603sq mi). Pop. (1991) 1,249,300.

Soutine, Chaïm (1894–1943) French artist, b. Belarus. He was one of the principal expressionists in the School of Paris. He worked for years without recognition before the US collector Dr. Albert C. Barnes bought some pictures in 1923. Soutine, a depressive who disliked exhibiting his work, produced anguished and violent paintings of choir boys, animal carcasses and distorted landscapes.

sovereignty Ultimate authority, held by a person or institution, against which there is no appeal. In early modern Europe, sovereignty came to be ascribed to the absolute monarchs of the new nation states. In Britain sovereignty resides in Parliament. In most countries it now resides in "the people". Since 1945, states have agreed to pool sovereignty in certain intergovernmental organizations, such as the NORTH ATLANTIC TREATY ORGANIZATION (NATO) and the EUROPEAN UNION (EU).

soviet Russian revolutionary workers' council. Soviets appeared briefly in the 1905 revolution and again in 1917. The Petrograd (St Petersburg) Soviet, led by TROTSKY, was the leading organization in the BOLSHEVIK revolution of November 1917. In the SOVIET UNION, soviets were organized at every level from village upwards. At the top was the Supreme Soviet, the chief legislative body.

Soviet Union (officially Union of Soviet Socialist Republics) Former federal republic, successor to the Russian empire and the world's first communist state. The Soviet Union was formed on 30 December 1922 and, when dissolved on 31 December 1991, was the largest country in the world. The BOLSHEVIK regime, led by LENIN, came to power in the 1917 RUSSIAN REVOLUTION. Lenin's government survived civil war and famine (1918–22) by instituting a centralized command economy. In 1921, the New Economic Policy (NEP) marked a return to a mixed economy. In 1922, a treaty of union was signed by the republics of RUSSIA, UKRAINE, Belorussia (now BELARUS) and TRANSCAUCASIA. In 1923, a new constitution was adopted establishing the supremacy of the COMMUNIST PARTY OF THE SOVIET UNION (CPSU) and the Supreme Soviet as the highest legislative body. Lenin died in January 1924 and a power struggle ensued between TROTSKY and STALIN. Stalin emerged the victor and Trotsky was expelled in 1927. In 1928, the first Five-Year Plan was adopted. It transformed Soviet agriculture and industry. Collective and state farms were imposed on the peasantry, and industrialization was accelerated. The urban population rapidly doubled. The collectivization schemes directly led to the 1932–34 Ukraine famine, which claimed more than seven million lives. State control infiltrated all areas of society and was sometimes brutally imposed by the secret police. The systems of state control led to the creation of a massive bureaucratic administration. The murder of KIROV in 1934 led to the Stalinist purges and the wave of terror in 1936–38. The purges targeted supposed dissidents, Soviet Jews and

ethnic groups. In 1936, Transcaucasia was divided into the republics of GEORGIA, ARMENIA and AZERBAIJAN. In August 1939, Stalin concluded a non-aggression pact with Hitler. Germany and the Soviet Union invaded Poland and divided up the country. In 1940, Soviet expansion incorporated the Baltic states of LITHUANIA, LATVIA and ESTONIA into the Union. A costly war with Finland led to the formation of the Karelo-Finnish republic. On 22 June 1941, Germany invaded Russia. The 1943 failure of the siege of STALINGRAD led to the surrender of 330,000 Axis troops and was a turning-point in WORLD WAR 2. The RED ARMY launched a counter-offensive that liberated much of E Europe. World War 2 devastated the Soviet Union. It is estimated that 25 million Soviet lives were lost. The Soviet Union and the USA emerged as the two post-war superpowers. Their antagonistic ideologies and ambitions led to the COLD WAR. The Soviet sphere of influence extended into Albania, Bulgaria, Czechoslovakia, East Germany, Hungary, Poland and Romania. The importance of the military-industrial sector in Soviet politics was greatly enhanced. In 1948, the Soviet army attempted to blockade the W sectors of BERLIN. In 1949, when NATO was formed, the Soviet Union exploded its first atomic bomb. In March 1953, Stalin died and a collective leadership was installed. In 1955, the WARSAW PACT was established as the Communist counterpart to NATO. In 1956, at the 20th CPSU Congress, KHRUSHCHEV made his famous secret speech denouncing Stalin as a dictator. In October 1956, a Hungarian uprising against Moscow domination was crushed by Soviet troops. In 1958, Khrushchev won the battle for succession. He began a policy of liberalization. Economic decentralization entailed a reduction in the bloated bureaucracy. New alliances were formed with worldwide anti-colonial movements, and Khrushchev formulated a policy of peaceful coexistence with the West. The Cold War shifted into a technological battle to produce more powerful weapons of mass destruction and a "space race". In 1957, the Soviet Union launched *Sputnik 1*, the world's first artificial satellite, and in 1961 Yuri GAGARIN became the first man in space. Also in 1961, the Berlin Wall was built to divide East from West Berlin. In 1962, the CUBAN MISSILE CRISIS shattered the Cold War standoff, and the world stood at the brink of nuclear war. Khrushchev agreed to remove Soviet missiles, and catastrophe was avoided. In October 1964, Khrushchev was removed from office by a conservative collective leadership headed by BREZHNEV and KOSYGIN. They were determined to reverse his liberal reforms and improve the Soviet economy. Brezhnev ruled by consensus and brought close political associates such as ANDROPOV (KGB chief) and GROMYKO (Foreign Minister) into his politburo. He instituted cautious economic reforms and agricultural production increased dramatically. In foreign affairs, the "Brezhnev doctrine" preserved the right of the Soviet Union to intervene in Communist states to preserve international communism. On 21 August 1968, the doctrine was invoked to stem the liberalization of Czechoslovakia, and Warsaw Pact troops invaded to crush the PRAGUE SPRING. Leading dissident scientists and intellectuals, such as SOLZHENITSYN and SAKHAROV, were sent to prison or forced into exile. In 1969, an era of superpower détente began with a series of STRATEGIC ARMS LIMITATION TALKS (SALT), resulting in the signing of SALT I by Brezhnev and NIXON in 1972. In 1975, the Helsinki Accords recognized the post-war European borders. In 1977, Brezhnev was elected president and a new constitution was formed. In 1979, SALT II was signed, but the Soviet invasion of Afghanistan ended the period of détente, and the treaty was never ratified by the USA. In 1980, the USA led a boycott of the Moscow Olympics and placed new, intermediate range Pershing II missiles on European soil. The Soviet economy stagnated because of the stabilization of oil prices and its outdated manufacturing technology. Brezhnev died in 1982, and Andropov was elected leader. He began a series of far-reaching economic reforms targeting centralization, corruption, inefficiency and alcoholism. He promoted a series of advisers, including GORBACHEV, to implement the reforms. His tenure was short; he died after a mere 15 months in office. He was replaced by a hardline Brezhnevite, Konstantin Chernenko. Chernenko died 13 months later and, in March 1985, Gorbachev became CPSU General Secretary and began a process of economic restructuring (PERESTROIKA) and political openness (GLASNOST). The 1986 CHERNOBYL disaster provided the first test of glasnost. Dissidents were released, and restraints on emigration were lifted. Gorbachev began a new détente initiative, focusing on nuclear DISARMAMENT. A series of meetings with REAGAN led to the Intermediate Nuclear Forces (INF) Treaty that agreed to scrap intermediate-range nuclear missiles. The Soviet Union agreed to halt the disastrous war in Afghanistan, and all its troops withdrew by February 1989. Perestroika continued the process begun by Andropov by reducing bureaucracy and allowing a more mixed economy. The restructuring was hampered by opposition from conservatives (anxious to prevent change) and radicals led by Boris YELTSIN, urging more far-reaching policies. In March 1989, the first pluralist elections since 1917 were held, and Gorbachev was elected state president. The tide of reform swept over Eastern Europe; by the close of 1989 every communist leader in the Warsaw Pact had been overthrown. The constituent republics of the Soviet Union began to clamour for secession. In 1989, Gorbachev and BUSH declared an end to the Cold War, and the West promised economic support to the Soviet Union. In 1990, the political and economic situation worsened. The Baltic republics, KAZAKSTAN and GEORGIA, demanded independence, and ARMENIA and AZERBAIJAN fought for control of NAGORNO-KARABAKH. In March 1990, the newly elected Soviet parliament authorized the private ownership of the means of production. The central economic principle of Marxism was removed and the CPSU fractured. Boris Yeltsin resigned his membership. Amid the breakdown in federal government structures, the economy declined by 4%. In December 1990, Gorbachev gained emergency presidential powers, and the conservatives demanded action to prevent the disintegration of the Union of Soviets. Paratroopers were sent to LATVIA and LITHUANIA to prevent secession. Miners went on strike, calling for Gorbachev's resignation. SHEVARDNADZE resigned and went on to form the Democratic Reform Movement. In June 1991, a new Union Treaty was drafted that devolved power to the republics and reconstituted the federal government. It was approved by nine republics, but Armenia, the Baltic states, Georgia and MOLDOVA refused to cooperate. Also in June 1991, Boris Yeltsin was elected president of the Russian republic. In July 1991, Gorbachev attended the Group of Seven (G7) summit and signed the Strategic Arms Reduction Treaty (START), reducing the number of long-range missiles. On 18 August 1991, a coup was launched against Gorbachev by hardliners. Gorbachev was kept under house arrest, while the coup leaders assumed control of the media and sent tanks into Moscow to capture the Russian parliament and Boris

Yeltsin. The coup failed and Gorbachev was reinstated on 22 August 1991. The republics seized the opportunity to declare independence from federal control. Yeltsin emerged as the new political power broker. He banned the CPSU and seized its assets, took control of the Russian armed forces and forced Gorbachev to suspend the Russian Communist Party. Gorbachev resigned as General Secretary of the CPSU. In September 1991 the Baltic States of ESTONIA, Latvia and Lithuania were granted independence. On 8 December 1991, Russia, UKRAINE and Belarus formed the COMMONWEALTH OF INDEPENDENT STATES (CIS). By the end of December, the republics of Armenia, Azerbaijan, Kazakstan, KYRGYZSTAN, Moldova, TAJIKISTAN, TURKMENISTAN and UZBEKISTAN had all joined the CIS. On 25 December 1991, Gorbachev resigned as president and, on 31 December the Soviet Union was officially dissolved.

Soweto (South-West Township) Group of black townships of more than a million people on the outskirts of JOHANNESBURG, South Africa. Soweto attracted international attention in June 1976, when a student demonstration against the compulsory teaching of Afrikaans in Bantu schools sparked a series of riots against the APARTHEID regime. The police brutally suppressed the disturbances, killing 618 people. Comprising mostly sub-standard government housing, it remains a focus of protest. Pop. (1991 official) 597,000.

soya bean Annual plant native to China and Japan. It has oval, three-part leaves and small, lilac flowers. Grown worldwide for food, forage and oil, its seed is an important source of PROTEIN. Height 60cm (24in). Family Fabaceae/Leguminosae; species *Glycine max*.

Soyinka, Wole (1934–) Nigerian dramatist, novelist and poet. His plays include *The Lion and the Jewel* (1963), *Madmen and Specialists* (1970), *Jero's Metamorphosis* (1972) and *A Play of Giants* (1984). *The Road* (1965), *Season of Anomy* (1973) and *Death and the King's Horseman* (1975) are among his most powerful novels. He was detained without trial in 1967 during the Nigerian civil war and was not released until 1969. He was awarded the 1986 Nobel Prize for literature.

Spaak, Paul-Henri (1899–1972) Belgian statesman, prime minister or foreign minister of Belgium for most of the period 1936–66. In 1946, Spaak was the first president of the UNITED NATIONS (UN) general assembly. A strong advocate of European unity, he was a founder of the Benelux (Belgium, Netherlands and Luxemburg) union (1948) and the European Economic Community (1957). He was secretary-general of NATO (1957–61).

◄ **soya bean** Grown throughout the world, soya beans are native to China, where they were first cultivated 4,000 years ago. They were introduced into North America in 1880. Their flowers vary from white to purple. The beans themselves are yellow, brown or black. Cultivation has spread in response to the increasing demand for protein. The main cultivation areas are the USA, with more than half of world production, and the Far East.

space Boundless three-dimensional expanse in which objects are located. RELATIVITY states that space and time are aspects of one thing, known as SPACE-TIME. Also, space has a non-Euclidean GEOMETRY wherever there is a gravitational field. In another sense, space, sometimes referred to as outer space, is taken to mean the rest of the Universe beyond the Earth's atmosphere.

space exploration Using spacecraft to investigate outer space and heavenly bodies. SPUTNIK 1, launched into Earth orbit by the Soviet Union on 4 October 1957, was the first artificial satellite. Soviet cosmonauts, and their American equivalents, astronauts, orbited the Earth soon after. Unmanned space probes crash-landed on the Moon, sending back pictures to Earth during the descent. Then came soft landings, and probes made to orbit the Moon showed its hidden side for the first time. By 1968, Soviet space scientists had developed techniques for returning a Moon orbiter safely to the Earth. In 1969, the US APOLLO 11 mission became the first to place a man on the Moon. By that time, the Soviet Union had sent probes to explore Mars and Venus. **Chronology**: first space probe (Explorer 1, launched 31 January 1958); first probe to land on the Moon (Lunik 2, launched 12 September 1959); first manned spaceflight (Yuri GAGARIN, 12 April 1961); first close-up pictures of Mars (MARINER 4, received 14 July 1965); first person to walk on the Moon (Neil ARMSTRONG, 21 July 1969); first pictures from surface of another planet (Venera 2, received from Venus on 22 October 1975); first probes to land on Mars (VIKING 1 and 2 July 1976); fly-bys of VOYAGER 2: Jupiter (1979), Saturn (1981), Uranus (1986), Neptune (1989); first SPACE SHUTTLE (Columbia, launched 12 April 1981); Giotto probe (launched 1985) flew within 600km (375mi) of HALLEY'S COMET, sent back photographs and data; GALILEO project (launched October 1989) photographed the asteroids Gaspra (1991) and Ida (1993), dropped a sub-probe (1995) into Jupiter's atmosphere and provided detailed data on GALILEAN SATELLITES; Clementine probe (1994) thought to have discovered what are water-ice deposits in craters

of the Moon; Solar and Heliospheric Observatory (SOHO) probe (launched 1995) will provide data on the Sun's interior until 2000; Mars Pathfinder mission (launched December 1996) landed on Mars and deployed *Sojourner*, a "microrover", to explore and collect rock samples; Cassini space probe (launched 1997) on a seven-year journey towards Saturn.

space research Scientific and technological investigations that gather knowledge through SPACE EXPLORATION. The makeup and behaviour of stars, planets and other cosmic materials were first determined by telescopes and more recently by the HUBBLE SPACE TELESCOPE launched in 1990 by NASA. Research projects have been carried into space by artificial SATELLITES, the SPACE SHUTTLE, space stations and space probes.

space shuttle Reusable, rocket-powered US spacecraft. The main part of the shuttle, called the **orbiter** (of which four were built, *Columbia, Challenger, Discovery* and *Atlantis*), looks like a bulky jet aircraft with swept-back wings. It ferries people and equipment between the ground and Earth orbit. It takes off attached to a large fuel tank, using its own three rocket engines, assisted by two booster rockets. The boosters are jettisoned about two minutes after launch and are later recovered for reuse. Six minutes later, the orbiter's main engines cut off and the external fuel tank is dumped. Manoeuvring engines then put the craft into the required orbit. When it is time to return to Earth, these engines are used to provide reverse thrust. As a result, the craft slows down and descends into the atmosphere. It glides down and lands on a runway. The first space shuttle, *Columbia*, was launched into orbit on 12 April 1981. On mission 25 in January 1986, the shuttle *Challenger* exploded soon after launch, killing all seven on board. A leak had allowed burning gases from a booster rocket to ignite the fuel in the main tank.

space station Orbiting structure in space for use by astronauts and scientists. Space stations are more spacious than most space craft as the occupants may live there for several months before returning to Earth. Space laboratories, such as the American *Skylab* (launched

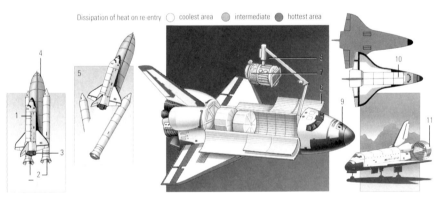

Dissipation of heat on re-entry ○ coolest area ◐ intermediate ● hottest area

▲ **space shuttle** A space shuttle flight has three parts. The first is reaching orbit. The orbiter (1) is propelled upwards from the launch platform by two solid-fuel boosters (2) and the shuttle's three engines (3) fed with liquid oxygen and hydrogen fuel from the external tank (4). After the boosters have burned out, they detach (5) and float to the surface of the Earth by parachute. The external tank detaches later and burns up in the Earth's upper atmosphere. Once in orbit the shuttle floats upside down above the Earth with its cargo bay doors (6) open to help dispel heat. Satellites (7) are launched from the cargo bay and can be retrieved with the use of an arm (8). While in orbit the shuttle manoeuvres using helium-fuelled thrusters in the nose (9). Finally, the space shuttle returns to land unpowered. The orbiter is shielded from the enormous heat that is generated on re-entering the atmosphere by ceramic tiles (10) on its outer surface. A parachute (11) slows the vehicle on the runway.

1972) and the Russian *Mir* (launched 1986), are space stations built for scientists to carry out experiments, study the Solar System and observe distant parts of the Universe, their view undistorted by the Earth's atmosphere.

space-time In RELATIVITY theory, a central concept that unifies the three space dimensions (length, breadth and height) with time to form a four-dimensional frame of reference. Durations and rates of processes depend on the relative state of motion of the observer and the system observed. In 1907, Hermann Minkowski clarified relativity theory by describing space-time in terms of a four-dimensional geometry. An event in space-time is specified by the three coordinates of space and the time coordinate. A line drawn in this space represents a particle's path both in space and time. EINSTEIN incorporated this viewpoint into his theory of relativity: in the General Theory, gravity is a distortion of space-time by matter.

Spacey, Kevin (1959–) US film actor, director and producer. Spacey's career was launched by his performances in *The Usual Suspects* (1995), for which he won a best supporting actor Oscar, and *Se7en* (1995). He made his directorial debut with *Albino Alligator* (1996). His acting success continued with *L.A. Confidential* (1997), *Midnight in the Garden of Good and Evil* (1997) and *American Beauty* (1999) for which he won an Academy Award for best actor.

spadix In some flowering plants, a spike of small flowers; it is generally enclosed in a sheath called a SPATHE. A familiar example is the CUCKOOPINT (*Arum maculatum*).

Spain Kingdom occupying 80% of the Iberian peninsula. The central Spanish regions of ARAGÓN, CASTILE-LA MANCHA and CASTILE-LEÓN form part of a vast plateau (the *Meseta*), in the centre of which lies the capital, MADRID. The plateau is drained by the rivers EBRO and TAGUS. ZARAGOZA lies on the Ebro and TOLEDO on the Tagus. The Cantabrian Mountains lie between LEÓN and the N coastal regions of GALICIA and ASTURIAS. BILBAO and PAMPLONA are the major cities in BASQUE COUNTRY. The PYRENEES form a natural border with France and extend S into NAVARRE and CATALONIA. BARCELONA lies on the Costa Brava. On the E Mediterranean coast lie the ports of VALENCIA and CARTAGENA, and the BALEARIC ISLANDS. ANDALUSIA includes the cities of SEVILLE and CÓRDOBA and Spain's highest peak, Mulhacén, at 3,478m (11,411ft), in the Sierra Nevada, close to the city of GRANADA. Many Spanish holiday resorts, such as MÁLAGA, are found on the Costa del Sol. The status of GIBRALTAR is disputed with Britain. **Climate** The *Meseta* has hot summers and cold winters. The S coast has Europe's mildest winters. Winter snowfall is heavy on the high mountains. **Vegetation** Forests cover 32% of Spain, mostly in the mountainous regions. Grassland and scrub cover much of the *Meseta*, but 30% of land is arable. **History and Politics** Iberians and BASQUES were Spain's early inhabitants. In the 9th century BC, the Phoenicians established trading posts on the S coast. In *c*.600 BC Greek merchants set up colonies. In *c*.237 BC the Carthaginian general HAMILCAR BARCA conquered most of the peninsula. By the 1st century AD, most of Spain had fallen to the Romans; it became a prosperous province. From *c*.AD 400, Germanic tribes swept into Spain. During the 5th–8th centuries, Visigoths (*see* GOTHS) controlled S Spain. In 711, the MOORS defeated the Visigoths. Spain was rapidly conquered (except Asturias and the Basque Country) and an independent Muslim state founded (756). The ALHAMBRA is testimony to the splendour of Moorish architecture. The Basques established the independent kingdom of Navarre. Asturias acted as the base for the Christian

<table>
<tr><td>SPAIN</td></tr>
<tr><td>AREA: 504,780sq km (194,896sq mi)</td></tr>
<tr><td>POPULATION: 40,667,000</td></tr>
<tr><td>CAPITAL (POPULATION): Madrid (3,030,000)</td></tr>
</table>

reconquest. In 1479, Castile and Aragón were united by the marriage of FERDINAND V and ISABELLA I. The reconquest of Granada (1492) saw Ferdinand and Isabella become rulers of all Spain. The INQUISITION was used to ensure Catholic supremacy through persecution and conversion. COLUMBUS' discovery of America (1492) brought vast wealth, and Spain became the leading imperial power. The 16th century was Spain's golden age. In 1519, Charles I became CHARLES V, Holy Roman emperor. The supremacy of the HABSBURGS was established. The extension and centralization of power was continued by PHILIP II, who gained Portugal (1580). Spanish naval power was dented by the defeat of the Spanish ARMADA (1588). During the 17th century, Spain's political and economic power declined. The War of the SPANISH SUCCESSION (1701–14) resulted in the accession of PHILIP V and the establishment of the BOURBON dynasty. CHARLES III brought the church under state control. CHARLES IV's reign ended in French occupation and the appointment of Joseph BONAPARTE as king. Spanish resistance led to the restoration of the Bourbons in 1813. Many of Spain's New World colonies gained independence. The accession of ISABELLA II resulted in civil war with the CARLISTS. A short-lived constitutional monarchy and republic was followed by a further Bourbon restoration under ALFONSO XII and Alfonso XIII. Spain remained neutral during World War 1. In 1923, PRIMO DE RIVERA established a dictatorship. He was forced to resign (1930), and a second republic was proclaimed. The Popular Front won the 1936 elections, and conflict between republicans and nationalists, such as the FALANGE, intensified. With the backing of the Axis powers, the nationalists led by General FRANCO emerged victorious from the Spanish CIVIL WAR (1936–39), and Franco established a dictatorship. Spain did not participate in World War 2. During the 1960s, most of Spain's remaining colonies gained independence. In 1975, Franco died, and a constitutional monarchy was established under JUAN CARLOS. Spain began a process of democratization and decentralization. Spain joined NATO (1982) and the European Community (EC) (1986). There is an historic tension between central government and the regions. From 1959, the militant Basque organization ETA waged a campaign of terror but announced a ceasefire in 1998. In 1977, the Basque Country (*País Vasco*), Catalonia and Galicia gained limited autonomy. In 1996 the government was forced to call early elections after allegations of complicity in an illegal anti-terrorist campaign. After 13 years in office, the Spanish Socialist Workers' Party (PSOE) was defeated. José María AZNAR formed a minority administration. He was re-elected in 2000. **Economy** Spanish economic revival began in the 1950s, based on tourism and manufacturing. It has rapidly transformed from a largely poor, agrarian society into a prosperous industrial nation (1995 GDP per capita, US$14,520). Agriculture now employs only 10% of the workforce. Spain is the world's third-largest wine producer. Other crops include citrus fruits, tomatoes and olives. Industries: cars, ships, chemicals, electronics, metal goods, steel, textiles. It lacks mineral resources. Unemployment remains high (1996, 22%).

spaniel Any of several breeds of sporting dogs that may be trained to locate and flush game, to drop for the hunter's shot and sometimes to retrieve on command. Land spaniels include the springer, cocker and toy breeds. Water spaniels are usually RETRIEVERS.

Spanish Major world language spoken as an official language in Spain, most of South America (except Brazil, French Guiana, Guyana and Surinam), all of Central America, Mexico, Cuba, the Dominican Republic and Puerto Rico. It is also spoken in a number of other countries, notably the USA and former Spanish dependencies, such as the Philippines. Its total number of speakers is more than 200 million. Spanish is a member of the Romance group of INDO-EUROPEAN LANGUAGES, but its vocabulary contains words of Arabic origin, the result of Moorish domination of Spain for many centuries.

Spanish-American War (1898) Conflict fought in the Caribbean and the Pacific between Spain and the USA. The immediate cause was the explosion of the US battleship *Maine* at Havana. Fighting lasted ten weeks (April–July). The Spanish fleets in the Philippines and Cuba were destroyed. Spanish troops in Cuba surrendered after defeat at San Juan Hill. The USA also seized Guam and Wake Island, annexed Hawaii and the Philippines and, at the Treaty of Paris, forced Spain to cede PUERTO RICO.

Spanish Armada *See* ARMADA, SPANISH

Spanish art Artistic tradition beginning with the Palaeolithic cave paintings at Altamira. Successively occupied by the Romans, Visigoths and Moors, Spain's earliest native traditions were the Mozarabic and Mudéjar styles, which blended Moorish and Christian elements. As the country was reconquered from the Moors, Spain drew closer to artistic developments in the rest of Europe. By the 16th century, it was the most powerful force on the continent, and this period coincided with the career of its first true genius, El GRECO. The most glittering era in Spanish art was the following century. The leading figures from this epoch are Diego VELÁZQUEZ, José RIBERA and Francisco de Zurbarán. In later years, Francisco GOYA was one of the greatest of the ROMANTICISM movement, and Pablo PICASSO was the dominant figure in 20th-century art.

Spanish literature One of the major early works is the epic poem *Cantar de M'o Cid* (*c.*1140). Major figures of the 14th and 15th centuries include the poet Juan Ruiz (*c.*1283–1350), the Marqués de Santilla and Juan de Mena. The most important work of fiction of the 15th century was the novel *La Celestina* (1499). French and Italian influences predominated until the 16th century. The late 16th and 17th centuries are known as the Golden Age, with the work of Miguel de CERVANTES, whose *Don Quixote de la Mancha* (1605–15) is still seen as an influential masterpiece of European literature, the poet Luis de GÓNGORA Y ARGOTE, Lope de VEGA CARPIO and the dramatist Pedro CALDERÓN DE LA BARCA. The 18th century witnessed a decline in Spanish writings, saved by the rise of ROMANTICISM. *Costumbrismo* (sketches of Spanish life and customs) flourished in the 19th century. In the early 20th century the writers of the Generation of '98 re-examined Spanish traditions. The Spanish CIVIL WAR (1936–39) drove many Spanish writers into hiding, and its reverberations can be seen in the grim realism of much of the work that followed. The theories of MODERNISM exerted an influence on formal technique and narrative style; the Generation of 1927 group of poets were also inspired by SURREALISM. Probably the most important Spanish writer of the 20th century, however, was Federico GARCÍA LORCA.

Spanish moss Common name for an epiphytic plant, not a true moss. Grown in tropical and subtropical American forests, especially on the oak of SE USA, the loose grey clumps hang from tree branches. Family Bromeliaceae; species *Tillandsia usneoides*. *See also* EPIPHYTE

Spanish Sahara Former name, from 1958 to 1975, of the WESTERN SAHARA.

Spanish Succession, War of the (1701–14) Last of the series of wars fought by European coalitions to contain the expansion of France under LOUIS XIV. It was precipitated by the death of the Spanish king, Charles II, without an heir. He willed his kingdom to the French Philip of Anjou, Louis's grandson. England and the Netherlands supported the Austrian claimant to the Spanish throne, the Archduke (later Emperor) Charles. The ensuing war marked the emergence of Britain as a maritime and colonial power. The Spanish succession was settled by a compromise in the Peace of UTRECHT, with Philip attaining the Spanish throne on condition that he renounced any claim to France, and Britain and Austria receiving substantial territorial gains. Exhaustion of the participants, especially France, helped ensure general peace in Europe until the outbreak of the War of the AUSTRIAN SUCCESSION in 1740.

Spark, Dame Muriel (1918–) British novelist, short-story writer and poet. Her collected poems and short stories were published in 1967, but she is best known for her novels, including *Memento Mori* (1959), *Girls of Slender Means* (1963), *The Mandelbaum Gate* (1965) and *Symposium* (1990). *The Prime of Miss Jean Brodie* (1961) is a portrait of a charismatic schoolmistress.

sparrow Any of a number of small FINCH-like birds that live in or around human settlements. Typical is the house sparrow. The male has a chestnut mantle, grey crown and rump and black bib. The female is duller and lacks the bib and grey rump. Sparrows feed, roost and dust-bathe in noisy, twittering flocks. Basically seed eaters, with a preference for grain, they also eat fruit, worms and household scraps. Length: 14.5cm (5.75in). Family Ploceidae; species *Passer domesticus*.

sparrow hawk Bird of prey. The European sparrow hawk (*Accipter nisus*) feeds on birds. The slightly smaller American sparrow hawk (*Falco sparverius*), often called the American kestrel, is reddish-brown and eats small animals. Length: to 20cm (12in).

Sparta City-state of ancient Greece, near the modern city of Spárti. Founded by DORIANS after *c.*1100 BC, Sparta conquered Laconia (SE Peloponnese) by the 8th century BC and headed the Peloponnesian League against Persia in 480 BC. In the PELOPONNESIAN WARS (431–404 BC) it defeated its great rival, ATHENS, but was defeated by THEBES in 371 BC and failed to withstand the invasion of PHILIP II of Macedon. In the 3rd century BC, Sparta struggled against the ACHAEAN LEAGUE, subsequently joining it but coming under Roman dominance after 146 BC. The ancient city was destroyed by ALARIC and the GOTHS in AD 395. Sparta was famous for its remarkable social and military organization.

Spartacists Members of the German political party called the **Spartacus League** that broke away from the Social Democrats during World War 1. Led by Karl LIEBKNECHT and Rosa LUXEMBURG, the Spartacists refused to support the war effort and rejected participation in the post-Versailles republican government. They instigated a number of uprisings, including one in Berlin in 1919, after which they were brutally repressed and their leaders murdered.

Spartacus (d.71 BC) Thracian gladiator in Rome who led a slave revolt known as the Third Servile (Gladiatorial) War (73–71 BC). His soldiers devastated the land and then moved s towards Sicily, where they were eventually defeated by CRASSUS with POMPEY's aid. Spartacus died in battle.

spasm Sustained involuntary muscle contraction. It may occur in response to pain or as part of a generalized condition, such as spastic paralysis or TETANUS.

spathe Broad leaf-like organ that spreads from the base of, or enfolds, the SPADIX of certain flowering plants.

speaker Presiding officer who ensures procedures are adhered to in the legislatures of various countries. In the UK the Speaker of the House of Commons presides over debates but has no other formal powers. In the US House of Representatives, the speaker is elected from the majority party by the House. Powers include the recognition of members for debate, the appointment of select and conference committees, the referral of bills to committees, and the signing of documents on behalf of the House.

spearmint Common name of *Mentha spicata*, a hardy perennial herb of the MINT family (Lamiaceae/Labiatae). Its leaves are used for flavouring, especially in sweets. Oil distilled from spearmint is used as a medicine. The plant has pink or lilac flowers that grow in spikes.

Special Branch Department within every British police force that is affiliated to MI5, the intelligence bureau within the Home Office. Its duties are to investigate and deter all activities against the nation, to protect visiting foreign rulers and dignitaries and to monitor immigration.

special education Education for children with special educational needs. It usually applies to education for students with a mental or physical disability. Some are taught in mainstream schools but with an individually designed programme. Others are taught in special schools run by the education authority or by a voluntary body, usually with the help of state funding.

species Group of physically and genetically similar individuals that interbreed to produce fertile offspring under natural conditions. Each species has a unique two-part Latin name, the first part being the GENUS name. So far, more than 1.5 million plant and animal species have been identified. *See also* BINOMIAL NOMENCLATURE; TAXONOMY

specific gravity *See* RELATIVE DENSITY

specific heat capacity Heat necessary to raise the temperature of 1kg of a substance by 1K (KELVIN) (1°C). It is measured in J/kgK (J equals joule).

Spector, Phil (1940–) US record-company executive and producer. He dominated the charts during the 1960s, producing artists such as The Crystals, The Righteous Brothers and eventually The BEATLES.

spectroscopy Branch of OPTICS dealing with the measurement of the wavelength and intensity of lines in a SPECTRUM. The main tool in this study is the spectroscope, an instrument for producing and studying the spectrum. An analysis of the spectrogram (record of the spectrum) can reveal the substances causing the spectrum, by the position of emission and absorption lines and bands.

spectrum Arrangement of ELECTROMAGNETIC RADIATIONS ordered by wavelength or frequency. The visible light spectrum is a series of colours: red, orange, yellow, green, blue, indigo and violet. Each colour corresponds to a different wavelength of light. A spectrum is seen in a rainbow or when white light passes through a PRISM.

This effect, also seen when visible light passes through a DIFFRACTION grating, produces a continuous spectrum in which all wavelengths (between certain limits) are present. Spectra formed from objects emitting radiations are called **emission** spectra. These occur when a substance is strongly heated or bombarded by electrons. An **absorption** spectrum, consisting of dark regions on a bright background, is obtained when white light passes through a semi-transparent medium that absorbs certain frequencies. A line spectrum is one in which only certain wavelengths or "lines" appear. *See* SPECTROSCOPY

speech Vocal expression of ideas and feelings, specifically intended to convey meaning. An infant's babbling is the first stage in learning to speak. Progress depends on the maturing of speech organs, the ability to hear, intelligence, learning capacity and environmental factors such as stimulation, attentive parents and reinforcement of vocalization.

speedometer Apparatus for recording the speed of a vehicle. Traditional speedometers are driven by a flexible cable connected to the transmission, which turns at a speed proportional to the road speed. Inside the speedometer the cable rotates a magnet that partly turns a spring-loaded drum to which the indicator is attached. In more modern designs, a sensor in the gearbox generates an electrical signal according to the speed of the rotation of the transmission; this signal is converted to a luminous display.

speedwell Common name applied to herbaceous plants of many species of the genus, *Veronica*, found throughout the world.

Speer, Albert (1905–81) German architect and NAZI official, a close associate of Adolf HITLER. Speer drew up the plans for Germany's autobahns and for the stadium at Nuremberg. By 1943, his authority over the war economy was second only to that of Hermann GOERING. Speer was tried in 1946 by the NUREMBERG war crimes tribunal and sentenced to 20 years in Spandau prison.

Speke, John Hanning (1827–64) British explorer of E Africa. After service in India he joined Richard BURTON in an expedition to Somalia (1854) and to the E African lakes (1856). In Burton's absence he reached Lake Victoria, which he identified as the source of the Nile.

speleology Study of CAVES and cave systems. Included also are the hydrological and geological studies concerned with the formation of STALAGMITES and STALACTITES and the influence of GROUNDWATER conditions on cave formation.

Spence, Sir Basil (1907–76) Leading British architect. He was famous for his modernist design for the new Coventry Cathedral (1951, consecrated in 1962). Other works include the Household Cavalry Barracks (1970) at Knightsbridge, London, and the British Embassy in Rome (1971).

Spencer, Herbert (1820–1903) British sociologist. He generalized DARWIN's theory of EVOLUTION, developing the idea of a natural progression from primitive to advanced societies based on survival of the fittest. Among his works are *First Principles* (1862) and *The Principles of Ethics* (1879–93).

Spencer, Sir Stanley (1891–1959) British painter. During World War 2 he was a war artist and painted a series of large pictures showing shipbuilding on the Clyde. Spencer is also known for his nude paintings, such as the so-called *Leg of Mutton Nude* (1937).

Spender, Stephen Harold (1909–95) British poet. His best verse includes the often anthologized "I Think Continually of Those Who Were Truly Great". His autobiography, *World Within World* (1951), is a powerful evocation of his time. His *Collected Poems 1928–1985* appeared in 1985.

Spengler, Oswald (1880–1936) German philosophical historian. In *The Decline of the West* (1918–22), he expounded his theory that all civilizations are subject to an inevitable process of growth and decay, concluding that Western civilization was ending. His theory had some appeal in Germany in the 1930s.

Spenser, Edmund (1552–99) English poet. His poetry includes the pastoral *The Shepheardes Calender* (1579); the sonnet sequence *Amoretti*, published with *Epithalamion* in 1595; and *Four Hymns* (1596). His masterpiece was *The Faerie Queene* (1589–96), an heroic romance and moral allegory.

sperm (spermatozoon) Motile male sex cell (GAMETE) in sexually reproducing organisms. It

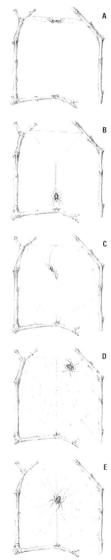

▶ **spider** When spinning its web for catching prey, the spider first casts out a thread of silk to form a horizontal strut (A). A second, drooping thread is trailed across below the bridge-line. Halfway along the second thread, the spider drops down on a vertical thread until it reaches a fixed object (B). It pulls the silk taut and anchors it, forming a "Y" shape, the centre of which forms the hub of the web. The spider then spins the framework threads and the radials, which are linked together at the hub (C). After spinning the remainder of the radials, a wide temporary spiral of dry silk is laid down, working from the inside of the web outwards (D). This holds the web together while the spider lays down the sticky spiral. This is laid down starting from the outside and is attached successively to each radial thread (E). The spider eats the remains of the dry spiral as it proceeds. The central dry spirals are left as a platform for the spider, which will often lie in wait there during the night but will retreat to a nearby silk shelter during the day.

corresponds to the female OVUM. The head of the sperm contains the genetic material of the male parent, while its tail, or other motile structure, provides the means of moving to the ovum to carry out FERTILIZATION. *See also* SEXUAL REPRODUCTION

spermatophyte Seed-bearing plant, including most trees, shrubs and herbaceous plants. It has a stem, leaves, roots and a well-developed vascular system. The dominant generation is the SPOROPHYTE. The widely accepted Five Kingdoms classification classifies seed plants in several distinct phyla: the Angiospermophyta (flowering plants), Coniferophyta (conifers), Ginkgophyta (ginkgo or maidenhair tree), Cycadophyta (cycads) and Gnetophyta (a group of cone-bearing desert plants).

sperm whale Largest of the toothed WHALES. It has a squarish head and feeds on squid and cuttlefish. Species *Physeter catodon*.

Sperry, Elmer Ambrose (1860–1930) US inventor and industrialist. He is celebrated for his improvements to the GYROSCOPE. In 1910, Sperry invented the GYROCOMPASS. He also designed other electrical devices, including a powerful searchlight. Sperry used gyroscopes in his development of autopilot systems for navigation.

sphalerite (blende) Sulphide mineral composed of zinc sulphide (ZnS), an important source of zinc. It has cubic system tetrahedral crystals or granular masses. It is white when pure, but more commonly yellow, black or brown with a resinous lustre. Hardness 3.5–4; r.d. 4.

sphere 3-D geometric figure formed by the locus in space of points equidistant from a given point (the centre). The distance from the centre to the surface is the radius, r. The volume is $(4/3)\pi r^3$, and the surface area is calculated at $4\pi r^2$.

spherical trigonometry Branch of mathematics that deals with the sides, angles and areas of spherical triangles; that is, portions of the surface of a sphere bounded by three arcs or great circles. *See also* TRIGONOMETRY

sphincter Ring of muscle surrounding a body orifice that can open it or seal it off. Important sphincters include the pyloric sphincter in the stomach and the anal sphincter.

sphinx Mythical beast of the ancient world, usually represented with the head of a man or woman and the body of a lion. In Greek mythology, the riddle of the Sphinx of Thebes was solved by OEDIPUS, so destroying her evil power. Although found throughout the Middle East, images of sphinxes were especially popular in Egypt, where thousands were built.

sphygmomanometer Instrument used to measure BLOOD PRESSURE. The device incorporates an inflatable rubber cuff connected to a column of mercury with a graduated scale. The cuff is wrapped around the upper arm and inflated to apply pressure to a major artery. When the air is slowly released, the pressure readings can be ascertained from the scale.

spice Food flavouring consisting of the dried form of various plants. Spices were used in medieval times to disguise the taste of food that was decaying and as preservatives. They also had medicinal and religious functions.

spider Any of numerous species of terrestrial, invertebrate, ARACHNID arthropods found throughout the world in a wide variety of habitats. Spiders have an unsegmented **abdomen** attached to a **cephalothorax** by a slender **pedicel**. There are no antennae; sensory hairs are found on the appendages (four pairs of walking legs). Most species have spinnerets on the abdomen for spinning silk to make egg cases and webs.

spider monkey Medium-sized arboreal (tree-dwelling) MONKEY found from s Mexico to SE Brazil. It has long, spidery legs and a fully prehensile tail. It is an agile climber, using the tail as a fifth limb. It eats mainly fruit and nuts. Genera *Ateles* and *Brachyteles*.

Spielberg, Steven (1947–) US film director and producer. The success of *Jaws* (1975) established his reputation. *Close Encounters of the Third Kind* (1977) earned him an Academy Award nomination. The "Indiana Jones" trilogy began with *Raiders of the Lost Ark* (1981). Spielberg's mastery of special effects was confirmed by *E.T. The Extra-Terrestrial* (1982). In 1984, he founded an independent production company. *Jurassic Park* (1993) is one of the highest grossing films of all time. Spielberg won a best director Academy Award for *Schindler's List* (1993), a harrowing document of the Holocaust. Other films include *Saving Private Ryan* (1998).

spin (symbol *s*) In QUANTUM MECHANICS, intrinsic angular momentum possessed by some SUBATOMIC PARTICLES, atoms and nuclei. This may be regarded by analogy as the spinning of the particle about an axis within itself. Spin is one of the quantum numbers by which a particle is specified.

spina bifida Congenital disorder in which the bones of the SPINE do not develop properly to enclose the SPINAL CORD. Surgery to close the defect is usually performed soon after birth, but this may not cure the disabilities caused by the condition.

spinach Herbaceous, annual plant cultivated in areas with cool summers. Spinach is used as a culinary herb and as a vegetable. Family Chenopodiaceae; species *Spinacia oleracea*.

spinal cord Tubular, central nerve cord, lying within the SPINE. With the brain, it makes up the CENTRAL NERVOUS SYSTEM. It gives rise to the 31 pairs of spinal nerves, each of which has sensory and motor fibres.

spinal tap (lumbar puncture) Procedure for withdrawing CEREBROSPINAL FLUID from the lumbar (lower back) portion of the SPINAL CORD for laboratory examination to aid diagnosis.

spine (vertebral column) Backbone of VERTEBRATES, extending from the SKULL to the tip of the tail (if present) and enclosing the SPINAL CORD. The human spine consists of 26 vertebrae interspersed with discs of CARTILAGE. It articulates with the skull, ribs and hip bones and provides points of attachment for the back muscles.

spinet Early musical instrument of the harpsichord family with one keyboard and one string to each note. The strings were plucked with a quill or leather plectrum.

spinning Process of making thread or yarn by twisting fibres together. The fibres may be of animal, vegetable or synthetic origin. Machines developed for mechanizing the spinning process include the spinning wheel, spinning frame (invented by Richard ARKWRIGHT), spinning jenny (invented by James HARGREAVES) and spinning mule (invented by Samuel CROMPTON). Today, large machines carry out the same basic process but at much increased speeds.

Spinoza, Baruch (1632–77) Dutch-Jewish rationalist philosopher, also known as Benedict de Spinoza. He was the son of Portuguese Jews who had been forced by the INQUISITION to adopt Christianity and had eventually fled to the relative religious freedom of the Netherlands. Spinoza argued that all mind and matter were modes of the one key substance, which he called either God or Nature. In *Ethics* (1677), he held that FREE-WILL was an illusion that would be dispelled by man's recognition that every event has a cause.

spiny anteater *See* ECHIDNA

spiraea Genus of flowering perennial shrubs native to the Northern Hemisphere. They have small flat leaves and clusters of small white, pink or red flowers. Many of the 100 species are grown as ornamentals. Height: 1.5m (5ft). Family Rosaceae.

spiritual Religious folk music, especially that associated with African-American culture. The words are generally adaptions of passages from the Bible, and the music is often in four-part harmony with certain specific features such as five-note melodies. Spirituals have influenced the development of other musical forms, such as the BLUES. *See also* GOSPEL MUSIC

spiritualism Belief that, at death, the personality of an individual is transferred to another plane of existence, with which communication from the world of the living is possible. The channel of such communication is a receptive living person called a **medium**. Spiritualism as a movement began in the USA in 1848.

spleen Dark-red organ located on the left side of the abdomen, behind and slightly below the stomach. It is important in both the lymphatic and blood systems, helping to process LYMPHOCYTES, destroying worn out or damaged ERYTHROCYTES and storing iron. Removal of the spleen (splenectomy) is sometimes necessary following trauma or in the treatment of some blood disorders.

Split Major port on the Dalmatian coast of the Adriatic Sea, Croatia. Split was held by Venice from 1420 to 1797, when it passed to Austria. It became part of Yugoslavia in 1918 and is Croatia's second-largest city. Split's industries include shipbuilding, textiles, chemicals, cement and tourism, which was severely disrupted by the wars following the breakup of Yugoslavia. Pop. (1991) 189,388.

Spock, Dr. Benjamin McLane (1903–98) US paediatrician and writer whose *The Common Sense Book of Baby and Child Care* (1946) reversed the trend in child-rearing by calling for parental warmth and understanding.

Spode, Josiah (1754–1827) British potter. He gave his name to Spode PORCELAIN, which became the standard English bone china. For this hybrid porcelain he used bone ash and feldspar in the paste as well as china clay and china stone.

Spohr, Ludwig (1784–1859) German violinist and composer. One of the most famous violinists of his day, he wrote 25 concertos for violin and other instruments, ten symphonies, many chamber works and operas, including *Zemire and Azor* (1819) and *Jessonda* (1823).

spoils system Form of US political patronage. The practice of appointing loyal members of the party in power to public offices was first referred to as the spoils system under Andrew JACKSON. It reached its height *c*.1860–80, declining after the Civil Service Act of 1883.

Spokane City and port of entry in E WASHINGTON, USA, on the falls of the Spokane River. Originally inhabited by the Spokane tribe, it began as a trading post established in 1810. Settlement began *c*.1871, and industry was spurred by the arrival of the Northern Pacific Railroad (1881). It was incorporated as a city in 1891. Industries: lumber, food processing, metal refining, mining, cement. Pop. (1990) 177,165.

sponge Primitive, multicellular, aquatic animal. Its extremely simple structure is supported by a skeleton of lime, silica or spongin. There is no mouth, nervous system or cellular coordination, nor are there any internal organs. Sponges reproduce sexually and by asexual budding. There are *c*.5,000 species, including the simple sponge genus *Leucosolenia*. Length: 1mm–2m (0.4in–6ft). Phylum: Porifera.

spontaneous combustion Outbreak of fire without external application of heat. When combustible material, such as damp hay, paper or rags, is slowly oxidized by bacteria or air, the temperature may rise to the ignition point.

spontaneous generation Belief, now discredited, that living organisms arise from non-living matter. It supposedly explained the presence of maggots on decaying meat.

Spontini, Gaspare (1774–1851) Italian opera composer. He established the style called grand opera. From 1805 he gained popularity, particularly with *La Vestale* (1807). As Generalmusikdirektor in Berlin (1820–42), he was criticized for promoting his own Italianate operas rather than German ones.

spoonbill Any of several species of wading birds, each with a long bill that is flat and rounded at the tip; species are found in tropical climates throughout the world. It has large wings, long legs, a short tail and white or pinkish plumage; it feeds on small plants and animal matter. Length: 90cm (3ft). Family: Threskiornithidae.

spore Small reproductive body that detaches from the parent organism to produce new offspring. Mostly microscopic, spores may consist of one or several cells (but do not contain an embryo) and are produced in large numbers. Some germinate rapidly, others "rest", surviving unfavourable environmental conditions. Spores are formed by FERNS, HORSETAILS, MOSSES, FUNGI and BACTERIA.

sporophyte DIPLOID stage in the life cycle of a plant or alga. Usually, the sporophyte gives rise to HAPLOID SPORES which germinate to produce a haploid generation (the GAMETOPHYTE stage) that will produce the GAMETES. In FERNS, HORSETAILS, CONIFERS and ANGIOSPERMS, the diploid sporophyte is the dominant phase of the life cycle, the plant body we usually see. In mosses and liverworts, the main plant body is the gametophyte. *See also* ALTERNATION OF GENERATIONS

sport Activities that require physical exertion and that are generally competitive between individuals or teams. The element of competition may also lie in an endeavour to outdo one's own previous best or to beat someone else's record. They are played according to specific rules. Individual sports, particularly running, jumping and wrestling, may derive from the psychological need for play; they have been common in most human societies and have been organized into competitions at least since Greek times. Team sports, on the other hand, are mostly of 18th- to 20th-century origin, although ball games such as LACROSSE were played in the Americas before Columbus landed.

sprain Injury to one or more ligaments of a joint, caused by sudden over-stretching. Symptoms include pain, stiffness, bruising and swelling. Treatment includes resting and supporting the affected part before gentle mobilization.

▶ **squirrel monkey** Found in many forested areas of South America, common squirrel monkeys (*Saimiri sciureus*) spend most of their time in the treetops, feeding on fruit and nuts as well as insects, eggs and young birds. However, they are also known to feed on the ground.

sprat (brisling) Small herring-like commercial fish found in the N Atlantic Ocean. It is slender and silvery. Length: to 12.5cm (5in). Family Clupeidae; species *Clupea sprattus*.

spring Mechanical device designed to be elastically compressed, extended or deflected. It may be used to store energy, absorb shock or maintain contact between two surfaces.

spring Natural opening for discharge of water from an underground source. Springs are an important part of the HYDROLOGICAL CYCLE. They may emerge at points on dry land or in the beds of streams or ponds. The mineral content of the water varies with the surrounding soil or rocks.

springbok (springbuck) Small, horned ANTELOPE native to S Africa; the national emblem of South Africa. The reddish-brown colour on the back shades into a dark horizontal band just above the white underside. Height: to 90cm (3ft) at the shoulder. Family Bovidae; species *Antidorcas marsupialis*.

Springfield State capital of Illinois, USA, 298km (185mi) sw of Chicago. Founded in 1818, it became state capital in 1837. It is the centre of a fertile farming area. Industries: machinery, electronics, fertilizers. Pop. (1992) 106,429.

Springsteen, Bruce (1949–) US singer-songwriter and guitarist, nicknamed "The Boss". A powerful performer, he achieved great success and influence with The E Street Band. His many albums include *Born to Run* (1975), *Born in the USA* (1984) and *Tracks* (1998).

spruce Various evergreen trees, related to firs, native to mountainous or cooler temperate regions of the Northern Hemisphere. Pyramid-shaped and dense, they have angular rather than flattened needles, and pendulous cones. The timber is used in cabinet-making, and some species yield turpentine. Height: to 50m (170ft). Family Pinaceae; genus *Picea*.

spurge Any of a widely distributed group of herbs, shrubs and trees. They exude a milky juice when cut and have small flowers surrounded by large, flower-like bracts. Some are succulent, and others are shrubs and trees. Family Euphorbiaceae; genus *Euphorbia*.

Sputnik World's first artificial SATELLITE, launched by the Soviet Union on 4 October 1957. Weighing 83.5kg (184lb) and with a radio transmitter, *Sputnik 1* circled the Earth for several months. *See also* SPACE EXPLORATION

square In geometry, rectangle with four sides of the same length. In arithmetic or algebra, a square is the result of multiplying a quantity by itself: the square of 3 is 9, and the square of x is x^2.

square root (symbol $\sqrt{}$) Number or quantity that must be multiplied by itself to give a specified number or quantity. The square root of 4 is 2, often written as. $\sqrt{4} = 2$. A negative number has imaginary square roots. *See also* IMAGINARY NUMBER

squash Any of several species of vine fruits of various shapes, all of which belong to the genus *Cucurbita*. Squashes are native to the Americas and are cultivated as vegetables. Family Cucurbitaceae.

squash Ball game played with small, round-headed rackets by two (or occasionally four) people on a rectangular, four-walled court. The wall at the front of the court is marked with three horizontal lines at different heights. The ball from the serve must land above the middle line (the cut line). Balls hitting the wall above the third line are out. The rubber ball may bounce off front, side and back walls but may bounce only once on the floor before it is struck. The object of each point is to make it impossible for the opponent to return the ball. The first player to score 15 points wins the game. It is played by both amateurs and professionals.

squid Any of numerous species of marine, cephalopod MOLLUSCS that have a cylindrical body with an internal horny plate (the pen) that serves as a skeleton. It has eight short, suckered tentacles surrounding the mouth, in addition to which there are two longer, arm-like tentacles that can be shot out to seize moving prey. Several species of giant squid (genus *Architeuthis*) may reach 20m (65ft) in length. Class Cephalopoda; order Teuthoidea.

squint *See* STRABISMUS

squirrel Any of numerous species of primarily arboreal, diurnal rodents found worldwide. Species of Eurasia, the USA and South America, such as the common grey squirrel, red squirrel and flying squirrel, are the best known. Most species feed on nuts, seeds, fruit and insects, and some eat eggs and young birds. Most have short fur and characteristically bushy tails. Family Sciuridae.

squirrel monkey Either of at least two species of small, diurnal, arboreal MONKEYS of tropical South America; it has thick, dark fur and a long, heavy tail. *Saimiri sciureus* has a cap of greyish fur; *S. oerstedi* has a black cap and reddish fur on its back. Both are gregarious and live primarily on fruit. Length: to 40cm (16in); tail: 47cm (19in). Family Cebidae.

Sri Lanka (formerly Ceylon) State in the Indian Ocean. Sri Lanka is a pear-shaped island, separated from SE India by the Palk Strait. A chain of coral islands (Adam's Bridge) almost joins the two countries. Most of Sri Lanka is low-lying. A coastal plain is fringed by cliffs and lagoons. On the sw coast lies the capital, COLOMBO. The S central core of Sri Lanka is a highland region. The highest peak is Pidurutalagala, at 2,524m (8,281ft). Nearby, Adam's Peak, at 2,243m (7,359ft), is a pilgrimage centre. The major highland city is KANDY.
Climate Western Sri Lanka has high temperatures and heavy rainfall. The N and E are drier. The monsoon season is between May and October. **Vegetation** More than 30% of Sri Lanka is tropical rainforest or woodland. The highlands are more open grassland. More than 14% of land is cultivated for tea and spice gardens, rice fields and sugar plantations. **History and Politics** The native Veddahs were forced into the mountains *c*.2,400 years ago by SINHALESE settlers from N India. Some Veddahs remain in remote regions. The Sinhalese founded Anuradhapura in 437 BC, which acted as their capital and a centre of THERAVADA Buddhism until the arrival of the Tamils in the 8th century AD. The CHOLA dynasty conquered the island in the 11th century. The Sinhalese were gradually forced S. The Portuguese landed in 1505 and formed coastal settlements. In 1658, Portuguese lands passed to the Dutch EAST INDIA COMPANY. In 1796, the British captured the Dutch colonies, and in 1802 Ceylon became a crown colony. In 1815, Britain captured Kandy. Colonial settlers developed the plantations. In 1948 Ceylon achieved self-government within the Commonwealth of Nations. In the late 1950s, following the declaration of Sinhalese as the official language, communal violence flared between Tamils and Sinhalese. In 1958, Prime Minister Solomon BANDARANAIKE was assassinated. His widow, Sirimovo BANDARANAIKE, became the world's first woman prime minister (1960). Following a brief period in opposition, she was re-elected in 1970. In 1972, Ceylon became the independent republic of Sri Lanka (resplendent island). The new republic was faced with resurgent demands for

---

SRI LANKA
AREA: 65,610sq km (25,332sq mi)
POPULATION: 19,416,000
CAPITAL (POPULATION): Colombo (684,000)

---

a separate Tamil state (Tamil Eelam) in N and E Sri Lanka. In 1983 secessionist demands spiralled into civil war between government forces and the TAMIL TIGERS. In 1987, the Sri Lankan government called for Indian military assistance. Unable to enforce a peace settlement, Indian troops withdrew in 1989. In 1993, President Ranasinghe Premadasa was assassinated. In 1994, Prime Minister Chandrika Bandaranaike Kumaratunga was elected president, and her mother, Srimovo Bandaranaike, became prime minister for the third time. Military offensives against the Tamil Tigers led to the recapture of Jaffna in 1995. The Tigers refused to accept devolution, and the war, which has claimed more than 40,000 lives, continued. President Kumaratunga was re-elected in 1999. **Economy** Sri Lanka is a low-income developing country (1995 GDP per capita, US$3,250). Agriculture employs 50% of the workforce. Sri Lanka is the world's third-largest producer of tea. It is also a leading producer of coconuts and rubber. Manufacturing has increased rapidly and contributes 67% of exports. Products include ceramics, textiles and clothes. Tourism is also important.

SS (*Schutzstaffeln*, guards unit) Chief paramilitary force of Nazi Germany. It was originally Hitler's bodyguard but expanded under HIMMLER after 1928 to become the Nazi Party militia and internal police force. With its distinctive black uniform, the SS controlled the GESTAPO and the SD (security organization). It ran the CONCENTRATION CAMPS and, from 1936, controlled the police. After the outbreak of war it formed its own fighting units, notorious for their ferocity, known as the Waffen SS.

Staël, (Anne-Louise-Germaine), Madame de (1766–1817) French writer. One of the most influential intellectual figures of her time, she published two proto-feminist novels, *Delphine* (1802) and *Corinne* (1807), but is best known for her works of social and aesthetic philosophy. They include *A Treatise on the Influence of the Passions upon the Happiness of Individuals and of Nations* (1796), a key text of ROMANTICISM.

Staffordshire County in W central England. The terrain is rolling hills with moorlands in the N. The region is drained chiefly by the River Trent. The county is primarily industrial. It includes the Potteries around Stoke-on-Trent and the Black Country, one of England's industrial hubs. Stafford (1991 pop. 117,800) is the county town. Area: 2,716sq km (1,049sq mi). Pop. (1991) 1,031,035.

stag beetle Large, brown or black BEETLE of Eurasian oak forests; the male bears large antler-like mandibles. The larvae feed on rotten wood. Length: to 8cm (3in). Family Lucanidae; species *Lucanus cervus*.

stage In the theatre, the space in which actors perform before an audience; it generally, but not always, consists of a raised platform. The traditional PROSCENIUM, first used in 17th-century Italian theatre to create a picture-frame effect, has lost some popularity in favour of more open stages.

stained glass Coloured glass used for decorative, often pictorial effect in windows. In its purest form, stained glass is made by adding metal-oxide colouring agents during the manufacture of glass. Shapes cut from the resulting sheets are then arranged to form patterns or images. These shapes are joined and supported by flexible strips of lead that form dark, emphatic contours. Details are painted onto the glass surfaces in liquid enamel and fused on by heat.

stainless steel Group of iron alloys that resist corrosion. Besides carbon, contained in all steels, stainless steels contain from 12% to 25% chromium. This makes the steel stainless by forming a thin, protective oxide coating on the surface. Most also contain nickel. Other metals and non-metals may be added to give the steel particular properties.

stalactite Icicle-like formation of CALCIUM CARBONATE found hanging from the roofs of CAVES. It is made by the precipitation of LIMESTONE out of water that has seeped into limestone caves.

stalagmite Deposit of crystalline CALCIUM CARBONATE rising from the floor of a cavern and formed by dripping water that has seeped into limestone CAVES.

Stalin, Joseph (1879–1953) (Iosif Vissarionovich Dzhugashvili) Leader of the Soviet Union (1924–53). He supported LENIN and the BOLSHEVIKS from 1903, adopting the name Stalin ("man of steel") while editing *Pravda*, the party newspaper. Exiled to Siberia (1913–17), he returned to join the RUSSIAN REVOLUTION (1917) and became secretary of the central committee of the party in 1922. On Lenin's death in 1924, he achieved supreme power through his control of the party organization. He outmanoeuvred rivals such as TROTSKY and BUKHARIN, and drove them from power. From 1929, he was virtually dictator. He enforced collectivization of agriculture and intensive industrialization, brutally suppressing all opposition, and in the 1930s he exterminated all possible opponents in a series of purges of political and military leaders. During World War 2 Stalin controlled the armed forces and negotiated skilfully during the YALTA CONFERENCE with CHURCHILL and ROOSEVELT. After the war he reimposed severe repression and forced puppet communist governments on the states of Eastern Europe.

Stalingrad *See* VOLGOGRAD

Stalingrad, Battle of (1942–43) Decisive conflict marking the failure of the German invasion of the Soviet Union during World War 2. The city (now Volgograd) withstood a German siege from August 1942 to February 1943. Total casualties at Stalingrad exceeded 1.5 million.

Stallone, Sylvester (1946–) US film actor and director. His screenplay and starring role in *Rocky* (1976) reflected his own story. Four sequels followed, three directed by Stallone. The *Rambo* trilogy developed his macho image. The 1990s saw a comeback with *Demolition Man* (1993) and *Cop Land* (1998).

stamen Pollen-producing male organ of a FLOWER. It consists of an ANTHER, in which POLLEN is produced, on the end of a stalk-like **filament**. The arrangement and number of stamens is important in the classification of flowering plants.

Stamitz Family of Bohemian musicians. **Johann** (1717–57) wrote more than 70 symphonies and many concertos – including the first known for clarinet – and was significant in establishing both these musical forms. His son, **Carl Philipp** (1745–1801), was also a virtuoso violin and viola player, and a prolific composer.

Stamp Act (1765) First direct tax levied on the American colonies by the British government. Introduced to raise revenue for the defence of the colonies, it required a special stamp on all printed material, including newspapers and legal documents. It roused widespread

opposition and led to the Stamp Act Congress (1765), at which representatives of nine colonies met in New York City and resolved that only the colonies could tax themselves. It was repealed in 1766.

standard deviation (symbol σ or *s*) In statistics, a measure of deviation of observed data or scores from the average or MEAN. A small standard deviation indicates that observations cluster around the mean, while a large one indicates that the data points are spread far from the mean. The standard deviation is equal to the square root of a quantity called the variance. The variance is the mean of the sum of the squared differences of the data points from the mean.

standard of living In economics, term that describes the material well-being of a country, group of people, or individuals, usually measured by the per capita income of the population. It can be used to compare the degree of economic development in various countries, or individuals can gauge their standard of living against the national average.

standard temperature and pressure (STP) (normal temperature and pressure) In chemistry and physics, standard conditions for measurements, especially when comparing the volumes of gases. It is a temperature of 273K (0°C/32°F) and a pressure of 1 standard atmosphere (101,325 pascals).

standing wave In physics, a wave in which the points of maximum vibration (the **antinodes**) and the points of no vibration (the **nodes**) do not move. A standing wave is formed by the interference of waves of equal frequency and intensity travelling in opposite directions.

Stanford, Sir Charles Villiers (1852–1924) Irish composer. He composed prolifically in most genres, writing ten operas, notably *Much Ado about Nothing* (1901), and seven symphonies. He is famous chiefly for his settings of the Anglican services.

Stanford-Binet scale Most commonly used English-language intelligence test for measuring a child's IQ. It was formulated at Stanford University, California, USA, in 1916, as an adaptation of the Binet Scale. *See also* APTITUDE TEST

Stanislaus I Leszczyński (1677–1766) Polish nobleman, king of Poland (1704–09, 1733–35). He became king with the support of CHARLES XII of Sweden, replacing AUGUSTUS II, but was forced to relinquish the throne to Augustus after the Swedish defeat at the battle of Poltava (1709). With French help, he regained the throne but was deposed by Augustus III, who was aided by Russia.

Stanislavsky, Konstantin (1863–1938) (Konstantin Sergeyevich Alekseyev) Russian actor, director and teacher. His theory of drama, described in *My Life In Art* (1924), stressed a naturalistic approach and the value of the ensemble, with actors making emotional contact with their characters.

Stanley, Sir Henry Morton (1841–1904) British-US explorer of Africa, b. Wales. He emigrated to the USA at the age of 16. He became a journalist and was commissioned by the *New York Herald* to lead an expedition in search of David LIVINGSTONE in E Africa. They met in 1871. On a second expedition, Stanley led a large party from the E African lakes down the River Congo to the W coast. He returned to the area (1880) as an agent for King LEOPOLD II and in 1887–89 led an expedition supposedly to rescue Emin Pasha from the Sudan and pressed on, with heavy losses, to the Indian Ocean.

Stanley (Port Stanley) Capital and chief port of the FALKLAND ISLANDS (Malvinas), on East Falkland. Originally called Port William, it became capital of the Falkland

Islands in 1843. In 1982, it was captured by the Argentinians, precipitating the FALKLANDS WAR. Pop. (1996) 2,121.

Stanton, Edwin McMasters (1814–69) US statesman. Attorney general under President BUCHANAN, he was a firm unionist and was appointed (1862) secretary of war by Abraham LINCOLN. Stanton retained his office under Andrew JOHNSON and attempted to mediate between the president and the Republican Congress over RECONSTRUCTION. Johnson's efforts to dismiss Stanton led to his own impeachment. Stanton was forced to resign after Johnson was acquitted in 1868.

Stanton, Elizabeth Cady (1815–1902) US social reformer, a lifelong worker for women's rights. She organized the SENECA FALLS CONVENTION (1848), the first public assembly in the USA for female suffrage, and was president of the National Woman Suffrage Association.

staphylococcus Spherical bacterium that grows in grape-like clusters and is found on the skin and mucous membranes of human beings and other animals. Pathogenic staphylococci cause a range of local or generalized infections, including PNEUMONIA and SEPTICAEMIA. They may be destroyed by ANTIBIOTICS, although some strains have become resistant.

star Self-luminous ball of gas, the radiant energy of which is produced by FUSION reactions, mainly the conversion of hydrogen into helium. The temperatures and luminosities of stars are prescribed by their masses. The most massive stars are about 100 solar masses (a mass a hundred times greater than the Sun). Large stars are luminous and hot, and therefore appear blue. Medium-sized stars are yellow, while small stars are a dull red. The smallest stars contain less than one-twentieth of a solar mass. *See also* BINARY STAR, STELLAR EVOLUTION

starch CARBOHYDRATE stored in many plants and providing *c*.70% of human food in such forms as rice, potatoes and cereals. Animals and plants convert it to GLUCOSE for energy (RESPIRATION). Consisting of linked glucose units, starch exists in two forms: **amylose**, in which the glucose chains are unbranched; and **amylopectin**, in which they are branched. It is made commercially from cereals, maize, potatoes and other plants, and used in the manufacture of adhesives and foods.

Star Chamber English court of the 15th to 17th centuries, named after its meeting place in Westminster. It arose as a judicial branch of the royal council, which received petitions from subjects and tried offences against the crown. It proved an honest and speedy source of justice under the early TUDORS but was used by CHARLES I to attack opponents. It was dissolved by Parliament in 1641.

starfish Any of numerous species of marine ECHINODERMS, with a central disc body and a five-rayed symmetry resulting in five to 40 radiating arms. The mouth is on the underside of the disc and the stomach can be extruded to take in other echinoderms and shellfish. Calcareous spines are embedded in the skin. Starfish move by means of tube feet, which they may also use for pulling open the bivalve molluscs on which they feed. Class Asteroidea.

Stark, Dame Freya Madeline (1893–1993) British explorer and writer. Stark travelled widely in the Middle East, especially Arabia, and gained esteem through her classics of travel literature. *The Valley of the Assassins* (1934) describes her journeys in Iran. Stark's travels in the Hadramaut (Yemen) were recorded in *The Southern Gates of Arabia* (1936).

Stark, Johannes (1874–1957) German physicist. He was awarded the 1919 Nobel Prize for physics for his discovery (1913) of the **Stark effect** (that a strong

electric field can split lines in the spectra of atoms), and for his work demonstrating the DOPPLER EFFECT. In the 1920s, Stark rejected the theory of RELATIVITY and the QUANTUM THEORY.

starling Any of several species of small, aggressive birds found throughout the world. The common Eurasian starling, *Sturnus vulgaris*, is mottled black and brown. It feeds on the ground on insects and fruit, often damaging crops. Length: to 36cm (14in). Family Sturnidae.

Star of David Six-pointed device formed by opposing two equilateral triangles. Known in Hebrew as *Magen David* or *Mogen David*, it was used as an emblem or magic sign by pagans, Christians and Muslims, and gradually found its way into JUDAISM as a cabbalistic sign. It appears on the flag of the modern state of ISRAEL.

State, US Department of US government department that conducts foreign policy. It is the oldest federal government department, created in 1789, and the secretary of state is a senior member of the cabinet.

States General National assembly composed of separate divisions, or "estates", each historically representing a different social class. In France the Assembly was divided into three estates – clergy, nobility and commoners – before the FRENCH REVOLUTION. The Dutch parliament still retains the name Estates-General.

states' rights In the USA, doctrine that the states have authority in matters not delegated to the federal government. The controversy between federal and state jurisdiction peaked with John C. CALHOUN's interpretation that a state could refuse to obey a federal law it deemed unconstitutional. This led to the Nullification Crisis (1832) and contributed to the CIVIL WAR. It was also an issue during the civil-rights movement of the 1950s and 1960s.

static electricity ELECTRIC CHARGES at rest. Electrically charged objects have either too many or too few

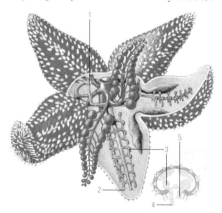

▲ **starfish** A starfish feeds by surrounding prey, pushing out its stomach through its mouth and partially digesting the food, which is then taken back into the stomach extensions. It moves by means of a water-vascular system unique to echinoderms. Water enters through the sieve plate (1) and is drawn by tiny hairs through the five radial canals into the many pairs of tube feet (2) armed with suckers. When the ampulla (3) of each tube foot contracts, water is forced into the foot (illustrated in cross-section) which extends (4) and allows attachment to the rock. Muscles in the foot then shorten it (5), forcing water back into the ampulla and drawing the animal forwards.

ELECTRONS. COULOMB's law describes the forces that charged objects have on each other and relates the force to their charge and the distance between them. Static electricity can be produced by friction. Electrons may then jump off as a spark, shocking anyone touching the object. Lightning is a larger result of static electricity. This form of electricity is studied in **electrostatics**.

statics Branch of MECHANICS that deals with the action of forces on objects at rest. Its topics include: finding the resultant (net) of two or more forces; centres of gravity; moments; and stresses and strains. *See also* DYNAMICS

statistical mechanics Branch of physics that studies large-scale properties of MATTER based on the statistical laws of large numbers. The large number of molecules in such a system allows the use of statistics to predict the probability of finding the system in any state. The ENTROPY (disorder or randomness) of the system is related to its number of possible states; a system left to itself will tend to approach the most probable distribution of energy states. *See also* THERMODYNAMICS

statistics Science of collecting and classifying numerical data. Statistics can be **descriptive** (summarizing the data obtained) or **inferential** (leading to conclusions or inferences about larger numbers of which the data obtained are a sample). Inferential statistics are used to give a greater degree of confidence to conclusions, since statistics make it possible to calculate the probability that a conclusion is in error.

Statue of Liberty Large, copper statue of a woman, standing on Liberty Island in New York Harbour. A symbol of US democracy, it was a gift from France and built to commemorate the 1876 centenary of US independence. It was designed by BARTHOLDI on an iron framework designed and built by Gustave Eiffel. The statue's correct name is *Liberty Enlightening the World*. It stands 45m (150ft) tall to the top of the torch in the goddess' raised right hand.

status In western sociology, a person's social position in a hierarchically arranged society, based on factors including lifestyle, prestige, income and education. Status can be inherited (**ascribed** status) or achieved by the acquisition of socially enviable possessions (**status symbols**), which is termed **achieved** status.

steady-state theory Cosmological theory proposed by Austrian astronomers Hermann Bondi and Thomas Gold in 1948 and further developed by Fred HOYLE and others. According to this theory, the UNIVERSE has always existed; it had no beginning and will continue forever. Although the Universe is expanding, it maintains its average density – steady-state – through the continuous creation of new matter. Most cosmologists now reject the theory because it cannot explain the cosmic microwave background or the observation that the appearance of the Universe has changed with time.

stealth technology Methods used to render an aircraft nearly invisible, primarily to radar and heat detection. To achieve "invisibility", a stealth aircraft must have sympathetic airframe design (all radar-reflecting "hard" edges smoothed away), engine exhaust dampers that mask and disperse jet efflux, and radar absorbent material that "holds" electronic emissions rather than reflecting them. The US Lockheed F-117A was the first totally stealthy aircraft to enter frontline service, in 1983, and was followed a decade later by the Northrop B-2.

steam engine ENGINE powered by steam. Steam, generated by heating water, is used to produce movement. In some engines, the steam forces pistons to move along cylinders. This results in a reciprocating (back-and-forth)

motion. A mechanism usually changes this into rotary motion. Steam LOCOMOTIVES use reciprocating engines. Steam TURBINES are engines that produce rotary motion directly by using the steam to turn sets of fan-like wheels. In any steam engine, some of the HEAT used to turn water into steam in a boiler is converted into energy of motion. The heat may be produced by burning fuel in a FURNACE, or may come from a NUCLEAR REACTOR. The first steam engine was a form of pump, used to remove water from mines. It was invented (1689) by Thomas Savery. In 1712, Thomas Newcomen invented a steam-operated pump with pistons. From the 1760s, James WATT improved on Newcomen's ideas and produced more efficient steam engines. This led to the use of steam engines to power machinery in factories. In 1884, British engineer Charles Parsons invented the first practical steam turbine. His machines were so efficient that turbines soon started to replace reciprocating steam engines in power stations.

stearic acid (octadecanoic acid, $C_{18}H_{36}O_2$) Common saturated fatty acid, often found as glyceride in animal and vegetable fats. It is used in ointments, lubricants, candles and soap. Properties: r.d. 0.85; m.p. 70°C (158°F).

Steel, Sir David Martin Scott (1938–) British politician, leader of the Liberal Party (1976–88). Steel entered parliament in 1965. In 1981, he took the Liberal Party into an electoral alliance with the newly formed SOCIAL DEMOCRATIC PARTY (SDP). In 1988, the two parties merged to form the LIBERAL DEMOCRATS, and Steel stood down in favour of Paddy ASHDOWN. He was knighted in 1990.

steel Group of iron alloys containing a little CARBON. The great strength of steel makes it an extremely important material in construction and manufacturing. The most common type is called **plain carbon** steel, because carbon is the main alloying material. This kind of steel usually contains less than 1% of carbon by weight. **Alloy** steels contain some carbon, but owe their special properties to the presence of manganese, nickel, chromium, vanadium or molybdenum. **Low-alloy** steels, with less than 5% of alloying metals, are exceptionally strong and are used in buildings, bridges and machine parts. **High-alloy** steels contain more than 5% of alloying metals. This groups includes various forms of STAINLESS STEEL

Steele, Sir Richard (1672–1729) British essayist and dramatist. He helped set the tone of public debate in his various publications, including most notably *The Tatler* (1709–11) and *The Spectator* (1711–12), which he co-founded with Joseph ADDISON. Of his plays, only *The Conscious Lovers* (1722) has won lasting acclaim.

Steen, Jan (1626–79) Dutch painter. He excelled as a painter of children, and his work includes many fine historical, mythological and religious themes. Many of his compositions depict taverns and celebrations, such as *The Egg Dance* (c.1675).

Stein, Gertrude (1874–1946) US writer and critic. She was influential in the US expatriate community in Paris. Her prodigious output includes the novel *Three Lives* (1909) and *The Autobiography of Alice B. Toklas* (1933), a fictionalized account of her life from her lover's point of view.

Steinbeck, John (1902–68) US novelist. He first came to notice with *Tortilla Flat* (1935), the success of which was consolidated by the novella *Of Mice and Men* (1937). Later novels include *Cannery Row* (1945), *East of Eden* (1952) and his masterpiece, *The Grapes of Wrath* (1939), which earned him a Pulitzer Prize and a National Book Award. He was awarded the 1962 Nobel Prize for literature.

Steinem, Gloria (1934–) US feminist leader. A campaigner for women's rights, she helped found the National Women's Political Caucus and the Women's Action Alliance (1971). She founded (1972) *Ms.* magazine, which she edited until 1987.

Steiner, Rudolf (1861–1925) Austrian philosopher and educator who helped to found the German THEOSOPHY movement. He later developed a philosophy of his own, called **anthroposophy**, which sought to explain the world in terms of people's spiritual nature or thinking independent of the senses.

Steinway German-US family of piano makers. Henry Engelhard (1797–1871) opened a piano business in Germany in 1835, emigrated to the USA in 1849 and, with his sons, founded the New York firm in 1853. It produced the first Steinway grand piano in 1856; the London branch of the firm was opened in 1875.

Stella, Frank (1936–) US painter. His work, a reaction against ABSTRACT EXPRESSIONISM, consists of basic geometric shapes set against simple backgrounds.

Stella, Joseph (1880–1946) US painter, b. Italy. He became one of the most important pioneers of modernism and an outstanding exponent of FUTURISM in North America. He is famous for his paintings of Brooklyn Bridge, such as *The Bridge* (1920–22).

stellar evolution Various phases of a STAR over its lifetime. A star can exist from thousands of years to thousands of millions of years depending on its mass. Stars form when a cloud of gas and dust collapses under its own gravity. As the cloud collapses, atoms collide and generate heat. This process continues until the heat generated is sufficient to cause nuclear FUSION reactions, converting hydrogen to helium. The reactions from the core throw out radiation, which stops further collapse. This stage (the **main sequence** phase) is the longest in a star's lifetime. Eventually the mainly hydrogen core of the star is depleted, and fusion can no longer occur. With the central energy source removed, the core collapses under gravity and heats itself further until hydrogen fusion is able to occur in a spherical shell surrounding the core. As this change takes place, the outer layers of the star expand considerably, and the star becomes either a **red giant**, or in the most massive stars, a **supergiant**. During this phase the core can reach temperatures of 100 million K, hot enough for fusion of helium to carbon. When this second process of fusion is complete, the core collapses again and heats up. In low-mass stars the temperature will not rise sufficiently for carbon fusion to take place, and the red giant looses its outer layers, leaving a WHITE DWARF. In high-mass stars, carbon fusion is initiated, converting the carbon into elements with relative atomic masses close to that of iron. At this stage no further fusion is possible, and the core collapses explosively, throwing off outer layers in a SUPERNOVA explosion. The resulting super-dense core forms either a NEUTRON STAR or BLACK HOLE.

stem Main, upward-growing part of a plant that bears leaves, buds and flowers or other reproductive structures. In VASCULAR PLANTS the stem contains conducting tissues (XYLEM and PHLOEM). In flowering plants this vascular tissue is arranged in a ring (in DICOTYLEDONS) or scattered (in MONOCOTYLEDONS). They may be modified into underground structures (RHIZOMES, TUBERS, CORMS, BULBS). Stems vary in shape and size from the thread-like stalks of aquatic plants to tree trunks.

Stendhal (1783–1842) (Marie Henri Beyle) French novelist. His first novel, *Armance*, appeared to critical scorn in 1827. In 1830, he published the first of his two great novels, *The Red and the Black*, whose ironic tones satirized Parisian contemporary society. *The Charterhouse of Parma* came out in 1839.

Stephen, Saint (977–1038) Stephen I of Hungary (r.1000–38), the first king of the Árpád dynasty. His chief work was to continue the Christianization of Hungary begun by his father, by endowing abbeys, inviting in foreign prelates and suppressing paganism. He was canonized in 1083.

Stephen (1097–1154) King of England (1135–54). A nephew of HENRY I, he usurped the throne on Henry's death in spite of an earlier oath of loyalty to Henry's daughter, Matilda. A long civil war (1139–48) began when Matilda's forces invaded. Stephen received support from most of the English barons. He was captured in 1141 but exchanged for the Duke of Gloucester, Matilda's half-brother. After the death of his son, Eustace, in 1153, Stephen accepted Matilda's son, the future HENRY II, as heir to the throne.

Stephens, Alexander Hamilton (1812–83) US statesman, vice president of the Confederacy (1861–65). A former governor of Georgia, Stephens opposed secession while upholding the right of a state to secede. As Confederate vice president, he quarreled with Jefferson DAVIS over military conscription and other matters, damaging confidence in the government.

Stephenson, George (1781–1848) English engineer, regarded as the father of the LOCOMOTIVE. He built his first locomotive, *Blucher*, in 1814. His most famous locomotive, *Rocket*, was built in 1829. It ran on the Liverpool to Manchester line, one of the many railway lines that he engineered.

Stephenson, Robert (1803–59) English engineer, son of George STEPHENSON. From 1827 Robert Stephenson managed his father's locomotive works. He built several railway lines and tubular bridges, including the Britannia Bridge over the Menai Strait, Wales.

steppe Extensive, semi-arid plains of central Eurasia. The landscape is usually flat and open with few trees. Steppes have very cold winters and warm summers, with light rainfall in the summer and little rain in the winter. The steppe comprises three zones of vegetation: the forest steppe; the grassland prairie, which is now usually cultivated; and the non-tillable steppe, which is semi-desert and fertile only after irrigation.

stereochemistry Study of the chemical and physical properties of compounds as affected by the ways in which the atoms of their molecules are arranged in space. Such arrangements can result in two or more compounds having the same numbers and kinds of atoms but differently shaped molecules, which are called **stereoisomers**. Stereochemistry also deals with optical isomerism, in which the configuration of one molecule is the mirror image of another.

stereoscope Optical device that produces an apparently three-dimensional image by presenting two slightly different plane images, usually photographs, to each eye. Some modern ones use POLARIZED LIGHT to project images that are viewed through polarized filters.

stereotyping Tendency to ascribe particular characteristics to groups of people or to individuals belonging to these groups on the basis of uncritical and oversimplified generalizations. Stereotyped judgments are often applied to members of particular races or nationalities, to members of one or the other gender or to members of particular social groups.

sterility Inability to reproduce. It may be due to INFERTILITY or, in humans and other animals, to STERILIZATION.

sterilization Surgical intervention that terminates the ability of a human or other animal to reproduce. In women, the usual procedure is tubal ligation: sealing or tying off the FALLOPIAN TUBES so that fertilization can no longer take place. In men, a VASECTOMY is performed to block the release of sperm. The term is also applied to the practice of destroying microorganisms in order to prevent the spread of infection. Techniques include heat treatment, irradiation and the use of disinfecting agents.

sterling Term for British currency, used to distinguish the UK pound from those of other currencies and also used to describe the quality and standard weight of coins. The sterling silver mark on silver (the stamp of a lion *passant*) represents a purity of more than 90%.

Stern, Isaac (1920–) US violinist, b. Russia. Stern made his debut in 1931. He has made extensive world tours and established a reputation as one of the world's leading virtuosos.

Sternberg, Josef von (1894–1969) US film director, b. Austria. He is celebrated for his sophisticated, sensual films starring Marlene DIETRICH, including *The Blue Angel* (1930), *Morocco* (1930) and *The Devil is a Woman* (1935).

Sterne, Laurence (1713–68) British novelist, b. Ireland. He achieved immediate fame for the first two volumes of the novel *Tristram Shandy* (1760–67). Sterne's playful, anarchic experiments with form foreshadowed MODERNISM. He used the persona of the parson in *Tristram Shandy* for *The Sermons of Mr Yorick* (1760–69) and *A Sentimental Journey* (1768).

sternum (breastbone) Flat, narrow bone extending from the base of the front of the neck to just below the diaphragm in the centre of the chest. The top is attached by ligaments to the collarbones and the centre part is joined to the ribs by seven pairs of costal cartilages.

steroid Class of organic compounds with a basic molecular structure of 17 carbon atoms arranged in four rings. Steroids are widely distributed in animals and plants, the most abundant being the sterols, such as cholesterol. Another important group are the steroid HORMONES, including the corticosteroids secreted by the adrenal cortex, and the sex hormones (OESTROGEN, PROGESTERONE, and TESTOSTERONE). Synthetic steroids are widely used in medicine. Athletes sometimes abuse steroids to increase their muscle mass, strength and stamina, but there are harmful side effects. Taking steroids is illegal in sports.

stethoscope Instrument that enables an examiner to listen to the action of various parts of the body, principally the heart and lungs. It consists of two earpieces attached to flexible rubber tubes that lead to either a disc or a cone.

Stevens, John (1749–1838) US engineer. He built an early screw-propelled steamer and a paddle-wheeler, the *Phoenix*, which was the first steamboat to make an ocean voyage (1809) from New York to Philadelphia. His interest later turned to railways, and he built the first US steam LOCOMOTIVE (1825). His desire to protect his many inventions led to the first US patent law (1790).

Stevens, Thaddeus (1792–1868) US political leader. As representative from Pennsylvania (1849–53, 1859–68), he was one of the fiercest opponents of slavery in Congress. Stevens successfully opposed the lenient policy of Andrew JOHNSON on RECONSTRUCTION.

Stevens, Wallace (1879–1955) US poet. A lawyer and insurance company executive, his first collection of poems, *Harmonium*, appeared in 1923. His work is rich in metaphors, and he contemplates nature and society. His early poems are often set in the tropics and reflect the lushness of their location. His *Collected Poems* (1954) won a Pulitzer Prize.

Stevenson, Robert Louis (1850–94) Scottish novelist, essayist and poet. He is celebrated for his classic children's adventure stories, such as *Treasure Island* (1883) and *Kidnapped* (1886). His later work includes historical novels, such as *The Black Arrow* (1888) and *The Master of Ballantrae* (1889), as well as the psychological novel *The Strange Case of Dr Jekyll and Mr Hyde* (1886). Stevenson spent the last years of his life in Samoa, where he wrote *The Ebb-Tide* (1894).

Stewart, Jackie (John Young) (1939–) Scottish Formula 1 motor racing driver. He retired from racing in 1973 after winning what was then a record 27 Grand Prix. In 1997, he established his own Formula 1 racing team.

Stewart, James Maitland (1908–97) US film actor famed for his gangling gait and slow drawl. Stewart's roles in the Frank CAPRA comedies *You Can't Take It With You* (1938) and *Mr Smith Goes to Washington* (1939) gained plaudits and awards. Further praise followed for his performance in *It's a Wonderful World* (1939). Stewart won a best actor Academy Award for *The Philadelphia Story* (1940) and a nomination for an Oscar for Capra's *It's a Wonderful Life* (1946). He also starred in four classic Alfred HITCHCOCK films: *Rope* (1948), *Rear Window* (1954), *The Man Who Knew Too Much* (1956) and *Vertigo* (1958). Other credits include *Anatomy of A Murder* (1959), *The Man Who Shot Liberty Valence* (1962) and *The Shootist* (1976).

stick insect Any of numerous species of herbivorous insects of the order Phasmida, which resemble the shape and colour of the twigs upon which they rest. Some lay eggs that resemble seeds. Length: to 32cm (11in). *See also* LEAF INSECT

stickleback Small fish found in fresh, brackish, and salt water. It is usually brown and green and may be identified by the number of spines along its sides and back. The male builds a nest of water plants and drives the female into it. He then watches the eggs and cares for the young. Length: 8–11cm (3–4.5in). Species include the three-spined *Gasterosteus aculeatus*. Family Gasterosteidae.

Stieglitz, Alfred (1864–1946) US photographer, editor and promoter of modern art. In 1902, he founded the Photo-Secession Group. His photographs include classic portraits of his wife, Georgia O'KEEFFE, studies of Manhattan and the cloud images known as "equivalents".

stigma In botany, the free upper part of the STYLE of the female organs of a flower, to which pollen grains adhere before FERTILIZATION.

stigmata Marks or wounds replicating those received by JESUS at the time of his trial and crucifixion. Saint Francis of Assisi is believed to have received stigmata miraculously in 1224. Stigmata have allegedly appeared on a further 330 people between the 14th and 20th centuries.

Stijl, De (Dutch, The Style) Group of modern artists that originated in Holland in 1917. They were associated with the eponymous art periodical founded by Piet MONDRIAN and Theo van Doesburg. De Stijl's aesthetic was an austere use of bold, vertical and horizontal lines, often breaking up primary colours. It was especially influential in architecture, informing the work of Gerrit RIETVELD.

Stimson, Henry Lewis (1867–1950) US statesman. He was secretary of war under President TAFT (1911–13). As secretary of state under President HOOVER (1929–33), he tried to secure international disarmament and formulated the "Stimson doctrine": that the USA would not recognize territorial changes brought about by force. He was Franklin D. ROO-SEVELT's secretary of war throughout World War 2.

stimulant Substance that increases mental alertness and activity. There are a number of stimulants that act on the CENTRAL NERVOUS SYSTEM, notably drugs in the AMPHETA-MINE group. Many common beverages, including tea and coffee, contain small quantities of the stimulant caffeine.

stingray Any of several species of bottom-dwelling elasmobranch fish that live in marine waters and in some rivers in South America. It has a flattened body, with winglike fins around the head. It has a long, slender tail. Its venomous sting is used to stun prey but can cause injury to humans. Width: to 2m (7ft). Family Dasyatidae.

stinkhorn Any of several species of foul-smelling Basidiomycete fungi. At first, it resembles a small, whitish "egg", which contains the unripe fruit body. When ripe, the receptacle elongates, rupturing the egg. It carries with it a glutinous brownish spore mass that attracts the flies that disperse the spores. Genus *Phallus*.

Stirling, James (1926–92) Scottish architect. Stirling attracted attention with the History Faculty building (1964–67) at Cambridge University and the Clore Gallery extension to the TATE GALLERY, London (1987).

stoat (ermine) Carnivorous mammal of the WEASEL family. Its slim body is *c*.30cm (12in) long, including the tail, and it has short legs and moves sinuously. It preys upon small animals in many temperate and N parts of the world. In the latter regions its fur turns from red-brown and white to white in winter, when it is known as ermine. Family Mustelidae; species *Mustela ermina*.

stock (gilliflower) Annual plant native to S Europe, South Africa and parts of Asia, cultivated as a garden flower. It has oblong leaves and pink, purple or white flower clusters. Height: to 80cm (30in). Family Brassicaceae/Cruciferae; species *Matthiola bicornis*.

stock *See* SHARES

stock exchange (stock market, securities exchange) Organized market for the buying and selling of stocks and shares issued by corporations. The stock exchange allows for the speculative purchase of stock in the hope that the price will increase and thus provide a profit to the investor, or provide dividend payment giving a fair rate of return on the investment. Stockbrokers act as the agents in the purchase and selling of stocks and shares. There are exchanges in major cities throughout the world, with the largest in New York and London.

Stockhausen, Karlheinz (1928–) German composer and theorist, the most successful exponent of ELECTRONIC MUSIC. An example of his work is *Kontakte* (1960), which uses instruments with tape. His seven-part opera, *Licht*, was begun in 1977; four parts have been completed.

Stockholm Port and capital of Sweden, on Lake Mälar's outlet to the Baltic Sea. Founded in the mid-13th century, it became a trade centre dominated by the HANSEATIC LEAGUE. GUSTAVUS I (VASA) made it the centre of his kingdom and ended the privileges of Hanseatic merchants. The city became the capital of Sweden in 1436 and developed as an intellectual centre in the 17th century. Industrial development dates from the mid-19th century. Industries: textiles, clothing, paper and printing, food processing, rubber, chemicals, shipbuilding, beer, electronics, metal, machine manufacturing. Pop. (1997) 718,000.

Stockton, Robert Field (1795–1866) US naval officer. He served in the WAR OF 1812. In 1821, he played a major role in negotiating rights to what became LIBERIA. He commanded land and sea forces in the MEXICAN WAR (1846–48), proclaiming California a US territory, and was US senator from New Jersey (1851–53).

Stockton-on-Tees Industrial town and unitary authority on the River Tees, NE England. The town developed around the world's first passenger rail service, the Stockton and Darlington Railway (1825). Industries: iron, engineering, chemicals. Pop. (1994) 157,000.

Stoics Followers of the school of philosophy founded by ZENO OF CITIUM in *c*.300 BC. Founded on the premise that virtue is attainable only by living in harmony with nature, stoicism stressed the importance of self-sufficiency and of equanimity in adversity. The philosophy was first expressed by Chrysippus in the 3rd century BC. It was introduced into Rome in the 2nd century BC, where it found its greatest adherents: SENECA in the 1st century AD; Epictetus in the 1st and 2nd centuries; and the 2nd-century emperor MARCUS AURELIUS.

Stoke-on-Trent City and county district on the Trent River, NW STAFFORDSHIRE, W central England. Stoke is the centre of the Potteries and is noted for its manufacture of china and porcelain. Pop. (1994) 257,000.

Stoker, Bram (Abraham) (1847–1912) Irish novelist. He wrote several novels and a memoir of the actor Henry Irving (1906), but he is best remembered for the classic horror novel *Dracula* (1897).

Stokowski, Leopold (Antoni Stanislaw) (1882–1977) US conductor, b. Britain. He was director of the Cincinnati Symphony (1909–12) and conductor of the Philadelphia Orchestra (1912–36). He became known for his individual interpretations and flexibility of approach.

stolon Modified horizontal underground or aerial stem growing from the basal node of a plant. Aerial stolons, also called runners, may be slender, as in strawberry, or stiff and arching, as in bramble. The stolon produces a new plant at its tip, which puts out adventitious roots to anchor itself. *See also* VEGETATIVE REPRODUCTION, TUBER

Stolypin, Peter Arkadievich (1862–1911) Russian statesman. After the Revolution of 1905, he became interior minister and then prime minister (1906–11). He introduced agricultural reforms favouring the peasants, but his conservative regime crushed political dissent and enforced

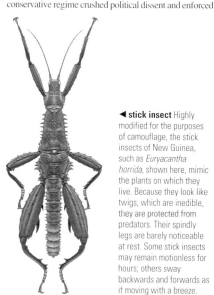

◄ **stick insect** Highly modified for the purposes of camouflage, the stick insects of New Guinea, such as *Euryacantha horrida,* shown here, mimic the plants on which they live. Because they look like twigs, which are inedible, they are protected from predators. Their spindly legs are barely noticeable at rest. Some stick insects may remain motionless for hours; others sway backwards and forwards as if moving with a breeze.

changes to reduce the electorate, ensuring a more compliant Duma. Negotiating between mutually hostile interests, he eventually antagonized the Duma, fellow ministers and the emperor. He was assassinated.

stomach J-shaped organ, lying to the left and slightly below the DIAPHRAGM in human beings; one of the organs of the DIGESTIVE SYSTEM. It is connected at its upper end to the gullet (OESOPHAGUS) and at the lower end to the SMALL INTESTINE. The stomach itself is lined by three layers of muscle and a folded mucous layer that contains gastric glands. These GLANDS secrete hydrochloric acid that destroys some food bacteria and makes possible the action of pepsin, the ENZYME that digests PROTEINS. Gastric gland secretion is controlled by the sight, smell and taste of food, and by hormonal stimuli, chiefly the HORMONE gastrin. As the food is digested, it is churned by muscular action into a thick liquid state called chyme, at which point it passes into the small intestine.

stomata In botany, pores found mostly on the undersides of leaves that allow atmospheric gases to pass in and out for RESPIRATION and PHOTOSYNTHESIS. Surrounding each stoma are two guard cells that can close to prevent excessive loss of water vapour. *See also* GAS EXCHANGE; TRANSPIRATION

Stone, Edward Durrell (1902–78) US architect. Stone achieved recognition for his use of the functional INTERNATIONAL STYLE in such buildings as the Museum of Modern Art, New York (1937–39). Later he used ornamental veils over his facades. His Kennedy Center for the Performing Arts, Washington, D.C. (1971), is distinguished by its functionalism.

Stone, Lucy (1818–93) US feminist. With others, she organized the first US women's rights convention (1850). She set up several organizations for women's suffrage and founded the *Woman's Journal* in 1870.

Stone, Oliver (1946–) US film director and screenwriter. Stone achieved commercial success with his film about the Vietnam War, *Platoon* (1987), for which he won an Academy Award for best director. Other films include *Salvador* (1986), *Wall Street* (1987), *Talk*

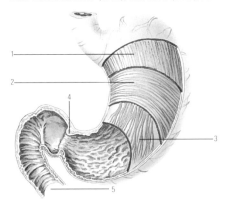

▲ **stomach** The stomach, like most of the digestive tract, is walled with involuntary muscle. The fibers of the stomach wall are built up in three layers: longitudinal (1), circular (2), and oblique (3). These muscular layers work in collaboration, producing a wavelike movement (peristalsis) and forcing food through the stomach, past the circular muscle valve sphincter (4) at the base and into the duodenum (5).

Radio (1988), *Born on the Fourth of July* (1989), *JFK* (1991), *Natural Born Killers* (1994) and *Nixon* (1995).

Stone Age Period of human evolution defined by the use of stone tools. The Stone Age dates from the earliest identifiable broken-pebble tools made by human ancestors about 2.5 million years ago. The period is generally considered to have ended when metal tools first became widespread during the BRONZE AGE. The Stone Age is usually subdivided into the PALAEOLITHIC, MESOLITHIC, and NEOLITHIC.

stonechat Small thrush found in open heath and scrubland of Europe, Africa and Asia. The plumage of the male is black, white and rust-brown. Stonechats feed on the ground on insects. Species *Saxicola torquata*.

stonefish Bottom-dwelling, marine fish that lives in tropical waters of the Indo-Pacific Ocean. It has a warty, slime-covered body and sharp dorsal spines with which it can inflict a painful, sometimes deadly, sting to humans. Length: to 13in (33cm). Family Synancejidae; species *Synanceja verrucosa*.

stonefly (salmon fly) Soft-bodied insect with long, narrow front wings and chewing mouthparts, found throughout the world. The aquatic nymphs have branched gills, and the adults, used as bait by anglers, are brown to black. Length: 5–60mm (0.2–2.5in). Order Plecoptera.

Stonehenge Circular group of prehistoric standing stones within a circular earthwork on Salisbury Plain, S England, 13km (8mi) N of Salisbury. The largest and most precisely constructed MEGALITH in Europe, Stonehenge dates from the early 3rd millennium BC, although the main stones were erected *c.*2000–1500 BC. The large standing bluestones were brought from SW Wales *c.*2100 BC. The significance of the structure is unknown.

Stopes, Marie Charlotte Carmichael (1880–1958) British pioneer of birth control. Stopes campaigned for a more rational and open approach to contraception, establishing the first birth control clinic in Britain in 1921. She wrote *Wise Parenthood* (1918) and *Contraception: Its Theory, History and Practice* (1923; 1931).

Stoppard, Tom (1937–) English dramatist, b. Thomas Straussler. His reputation was established with *Rosencrantz and Guildenstern are Dead* (1966). Plays such as *The Real Inspector Hound* (1968) and *Jumpers* (1972) confirmed his ability to combine philosophical speculation with humour. Stoppard has written plays for radio (*Artist Descending a Staircase*, 1973) and television (*Professional Foul*, 1977). Other plays include *Arcadia* (1993) and *The Invention of Love* (1997). Other writing includes the Oscar-winning screenplay for *Shakespeare in Love* (1998).

Storey, David (1933–) British novelist and dramatist. Storey's debut novel, *This Sporting Life* (1960), explored his favourite themes of class conflict and alienation. *Radcliffe* (1963) is perhaps his best-known work. Storey won the Booker Prize for *Saville* (1976). His plays include *Home* (1970).

stork Long-legged wading bird that lives along rivers, lakes and marshes in temperate and tropical regions, often nesting in colonies in trees. Usually black, white and grey, storks have straight bills, long necks, robust bodies and long broad wings. They are diurnal and feed on small animals. Length: 0.8–1.5m (2.5–5ft). Family Ciconiidae.

Stowe, Harriet Beecher (1811–96) US writer. Stowe is best known for *Uncle Tom's Cabin* (1851–52), a powerful anti-slavery novel.

STP *See* STANDARD TEMPERATURE AND PRESSURE (STP)

strabismus (squint) Condition in which the eyes do not look in the same direction. It may result from either disease of or damage to the eye muscles or their nerve supply or an error of refraction within the eye.

Strachey, (Giles) Lytton (1880–1932) English biographer and essayist. His works included *Eminent Victorians* (1918), *Queen Victoria* (1921) and *Elizabeth and Essex* (1928). He introduced a psychological dimension to modern BIOGRAPHY.

Stradella, Alessandro (1639–82) Italian composer. He lived a life of intrigue and amorous escapades, one of which led to his murder. Stradella was one of the major composers of his era, writing some 30 stage works and 200 cantatas; his 25 "sinfonias" are the earliest examples of *concerti grossi*. *See* CONCERTO

Stradivari, Antonio (1644–1737) Italian violin maker. Originally an apprentice to Nicolo AMATI, Stradivari perfected violin design. His instruments remain unsurpassed in brilliance of tone.

Strafford, Thomas Wentworth, 1st Earl of (1593–1641) English minister of CHARLES I. He became chief adviser after the death of the Duke of Buckingham, and proved an extremely capable administrator as lord president of the North (1628–33) and lord deputy of Ireland (1633–39). Charles made him an earl in 1640, but he attracted the wrath of Parliament and was executed.

Strasberg, Lee (1901–82) US theatrical director. One of the founders of the Group Theater (1931), he began teaching a "method" approach based on STANISLAVSKY'S teachings. In 1947, Strasberg and Elia KAZAN founded the ACTORS' STUDIO. As the Studio's artistic director, he was influential in shaping the careers of many leading actors, such as Marilyn MONROE and Al PACINO.

Strasbourg City in E France, on the River Ill, capital of Bas-Rhin department and the commercial capital of the ALSACE region. Known in Roman times as Argentoratum, the city was destroyed by the Huns in the 5th century. It became part of the HOLY ROMAN EMPIRE in 923 and developed into an important commercial centre, becoming a free imperial city in 1262. Strasbourg was a centre of medieval German literature and of 16th-century Protestantism. It was seized by France in 1681, regained by Germany after the FRANCO-PRUSSIAN WAR, but recovered by France at the end of World War 1. German troops occupied the city during World War 2. Its river port on the Rhine, with its good canal connections, is France's chief grain outlet. Industries: metallurgy, oil and gas refining, machinery, food processing. Pop. (1990) 252,338.

Strategic Arms Limitation Talks (SALT) Talks between the USA and the Soviet Union to limit the expansion of NUCLEAR WEAPONS. The talks began in 1969 between Lyndon JOHNSON and Leonid BREZHNEV. In 1972, Richard NIXON and Brezhnev signed SALT I. This agreement limited anti-ballistic missile systems and produced an interim accord on intercontinental ballistic missiles (ICBMs). In 1973, a second phase began with meetings between Gerald FORD and Brezhnev, and in 1974 they agreed to limit ballistic missile launchers. SALT II, signed in Vienna between Jimmy CARTER and Brezhnev, banned new ICBMs and limited other launchers. The Soviet invasion of Afghanistan meant that the treaty was never ratified by the US Senate. Nevertheless, the superpowers observed its terms until Ronald REAGAN began to increase the US nuclear arsenal. In 1986, SALT was superseded by **START (Strategic Arms Reduction Talks)** between Mikhail GORBACHEV and Reagan.

Stratford upon Avon Town in Warwickshire, central England, famous as the birthplace of William SHAKESPEARE and home of the ROYAL SHAKESPEARE COMPANY

(RSC). Industries: tourism, engineering, boatbuilding, textiles. Pop. (1992) 22,800.

Strathclyde Region in W Scotland, bounded N by the Highlands, S by the Southern Uplands and W by the Atlantic Ocean. Strathclyde is divided into 19 districts. The capital is GLASGOW; other major towns include Paisley, Kilmarnock, Clydebank and Motherwell. The industrial heartland of Scotland, it contains half of Scotland's population. Sites include Loch LOMOND, Glencoe and the islands of Mull, Arran and Bute. In the late 9th century, it was devastated by Norse raiders. It was incorporated into the Scottish kingdom in the 11th century. Industries: shipbuilding, engineering. Area: 13,529sq km (5,222sq mi) Pop: (1991) 2,248,700

stratigraphy Branch of geology concerned with stratified or layered rocks. It deals with the correlation of rocks from different localities using fossils and distinct rock types.

stratosphere Section of the Earth's ATMOSPHERE between the troposphere and the higher mesosphere. It is *c*.40km (25mi) thick and for half this distance the temperature remains fairly constant. The stratosphere contains most of the atmosphere's ozone.

Strauss, Johann (the Younger) (1825–99) Austrian composer and conductor, son of Johann Strauss (1804–49), also a conductor and composer. He became extremely popular for his waltzes, such as *The Blue Danube*, *Tales from the Vienna Woods* and *Wine, Women and Song*. Strauss also composed operettas, notably *Die Fledermaus* (1874) and *The Gypsy Baron* (1885).

Strauss, Richard (1864–1949) German composer and conductor. His SYMPHONIC POEMS, such as *Don Juan* (1888), *Till Eulenspiegel* (1895) and *Also sprach Zarathustra* (1896), use brilliantly coloured orchestration for characterization. His early operas, *Salome* (1905) and *Elektra* (1908), deal with female obsession. *Der Rosenkavalier* (1911) also uses the dramatic range of the human voice, but in a comic setting.

Stravinsky, Igor Feodorovich (1882–1971) Russian composer who revolutionized 20th-century music. His early ballets, *The Firebird* (1910) and *Petrushka* (1911), were commissioned by DIAGHILEV for his BALLETS RUSSES. The première of the ballet *The Rite of Spring* (1913) caused a riot because of its dissonance and unfamiliar rhythms. Stravinsky turned to Russian folk themes for *The Wedding* (1923) and neo-classicism in *Pulcinella* (1920). In 1939 he moved to the USA, collaborating with George BALANCHINE on the abstract ballet *Agon* (1957). He also experimented with TWELVE-TONE MUSIC.

Straw, Jack (1946–) British statesman, home secretary (1997–). Straw entered parliament in 1979. He held several shadow cabinet posts before Labour's victory under Tony BLAIR in the 1997 general election. As home secretary, he has dealt with the decision concerning the extradition of PINOCHET and the Lawrence Report (1999) into racism in the police force.

strawberry Fruit-bearing plant of the rose family, common in Europe, Asia and the Americas. It has three-lobed leaves and clusters of white or reddish flowers. The large fleshy fruit is dotted with seeds (pips). Family Rosaceae; genus *Fragaria*.

stream of consciousness Literary style in which the thought processes of characters are presented in the disconnected, illogical, chaotic or seemingly random way they might come to them, without the usual literary regard for narrative continuity or linear sequence. Edouard Dujardin's novel *Les Lauriers Sont Coupes* (1888) is generally regarded as the first example of the style in literature. The technique was also famously used by James JOYCE in his novel *Ulysses* (1922).

Streep, Meryl (1949–) US film actress. She is renowned for her attention to realistic characterization. After an Academy Award nomination for *The Deer Hunter* (1978), Streep won a best supporting actress Oscar for *Kramer vs. Kramer* (1979). Her performance as a Holocaust victim in *Sophie's Choice* (1982) earned her an Academy Award for best actress. Other credits include *The French Lieutenant's Woman* (1981), *Silkwood* (1983) and *Out of Africa* (1985). She later won Academy Award nominations for *Postcards from the Edge* (1990) and *The Bridges of Madison County* (1995).

Streisand, Barbra (1942–) US singer and actress. She achieved fame with her Broadway performance in *Funny Girl* (1964, filmed 1968). Streisand has made numerous recordings and starred in films such as *Hello Dolly* (1969) and *A Star is Born* (1976). She directed, produced and starred in *Yentl* (1983) and the *Prince of Tides* (1991).

streptococcus Genus of gram-positive spherical or oval BACTERIA that grow in pairs or bead-like chains. They live mainly as parasites in the mouth, respiratory tract and intestine. Some are harmless but others are pathogenic, causing SCARLET FEVER and other infections. Treatment is with ANTIBIOTICS.

Stresemann, Gustav (1878–1929) German statesman. He was the outstanding statesman of the WEIMAR REPUBLIC. Stresemann concluded the LOCARNO PACT (1925) and worked for a practicable post-war settlement with Germany's former enemies under the harsh terms imposed by the Treaty of VERSAILLES. He negotiated Germany's entry into the LEAGUE OF NATIONS (1926) and shared the 1926 Nobel Peace Prize with Aristide BRIAND.

stress In medicine and psychology, mental or physical strain brought on by pressures from the environment. Stress, caused by frustrating and difficult work or by family or social situations, may be a factor in many mental and physical disorders.

stress In physics, internal tension in a material. **Tensile** stress stretches an object, **compressive** stress squeezes it and **shearing** stress twists it. Fluid stresses are called PRESSURE.

strike Concerted withdrawal of labour as a form of protest. Historically, the use of strikes developed when workers collectively tried to improve conditions through TRADE UNIONS. *See also* GENERAL STRIKE

Strindberg, Johan August (1849–1912) Swedish dramatist and novelist. His major dramatic theme was subjective, psychological experience. Drawing on the insights of Henrik IBSEN and the NATURALISM of Emile ZOLA, plays such as *The Father* (1887) and *Miss Julie* (1888) take a characteristically pessimistic view of gender relations. After suffering a mental breakdown, he produced *A Dream Play* (1902) and *The Ghost Sonata* (1907), both of which prefigure the Theatre of the ABSURD and EXPRESSIONISM.

stringed instrument Musical instrument sounded by the vibration of strings. Instruments fall into different classes according to the action used to set the strings in motion: bowed, chiefly those of the VIOLIN family; plucked, chiefly the HARP, LUTE and GUITAR; and plucked and struck, such as the cittern and DULCIMER.

strip mining *See* OPENCAST MINING

stroboscope (strobe) Device that emits regular flashes of light. Stroboscopes usually have a calibrated scale from which the number of flashes per minute can be read. They are used in photography to make multiple exposures of moving subjects and in engineering to "slow down" or "stop" moving objects for observation.

stroke (apoplexy) Interruption of the flow of blood to the brain. It is caused by blockage or rupture of an artery and may produce a range of effects from mild impairment to death. Conditions that predispose to stroke include atherosclerosis and HYPERTENSION. Many major strokes are prevented by treatment of risk factors, including surgery and the use of anticoagulant drugs. Transient ischaemic attacks (TIAs), or "mini-strokes", which last less than 24 hours, are investigated to try to prevent the occurrence of a more damaging stroke.

Stromboli Volcanic island NE of Sicily, S Italy. It gives its name to a characteristic type of eruption in which molten rock is blasted out of the crater by large amounts of accumulated gas. Rising to 750m (2,460ft), the volcano is in a state of constant mild activity.

strong nuclear force One of the four FUNDAMENTAL FORCES in nature. The strongest of the four forces, it binds together protons and neutrons within the NUCLEUS of an atom. Like the WEAK NUCLEAR FORCE it operates at very short distances (a millionth of a millionth of an inch) and therefore occurs only within the nucleus. *See also* GRAND UNIFIED THEORY (GUT)

strontianite Carbonate mineral, strontium carbonate ($SrCO_3$). It has orthorhombic system, hexagonal twinned crystals, and it also occurs as massive or columnar aggregates. It can be pale green, white, grey, yellow or brown. It is found in low-temperature hydrothermal veins, often in limestone. Hardness 3.5–4; r.d. 3.7.

strontium (symbol Sr) Silvery-white, metallic element of the alkaline-earth metals in Group II of the periodic table. Resembling CALCIUM physically and chemically, it occurs naturally in strontianite and celestite and is extracted by ELECTROLYSIS. Strontium salts are used to give a red colour to flares and fireworks. The isotope Sr^{90} (half-life 28 years) is a radioactive element present in fallout, from which it is absorbed into milk and bones; it is used in NUCLEAR REACTORS. Properties: at.no. 38; r.a.m. 87.62; r.d. 2.554; m.p. 769°C (1,416°F); b.p. 1,384°C (2,523°F).

structuralism Twentieth-century school of critical thought. Ferdinand de SAUSSURE argued that underlying the everyday use of language is a language system (*langue*), based on relationships of difference. He stressed the arbitrary nature of the relationship between the **signifier** (sound or image) and the **signified** (concept). Initially a linguistic theory, structuralism was developed by Claude LÉVI-STRAUSS and Roland BARTHES into a mode of critical analysis of cultural institutions and products. It is associated especially with the notion of a literary text as a system of signs. *See also* DECONSTRUCTION; SEMIOTICS

strychnine Poisonous ALKALOID obtained from the plant *Strychnos nux-vomica*. In the past it was believed to have therapeutic value in small doses as a tonic. Strychnine poisoning causes symptoms similar to those of TETANUS, with death occurring due to SPASM of the breathing muscles.

Stuart, Charles Edward (1720–88) Scottish prince, known as "Bonnie Prince Charlie" or the "Young Pretender". A grandson of the deposed JAMES II, he led the JACOBITES in the rebellion of 1745 ("the '45") on behalf of his father, James, the "Old Pretender". Landing in the Scottish Highlands without the hoped-for backing of France, he gained the support of many clan chiefs, defeated government troops at Prestonpans, E central Scotland, and marched on London. Lacking widespread support in England, he turned back at Derby. The following year, his largely Highland force was decimated in the Battle of CULLODEN. He escaped to the continent and lived in exile until his death.

Stuart, Gilbert Charles (1755–1828) US painter. One of the foremost US portraitists of the late 18th and early 19th century, he is celebrated for three portraits of George WASHINGTON. These paintings are known as the "Vaughan" type (1795), the "Lansdowne" types (1796), and the "Athenaeum" type (1796). The last is the model for Washington's face on the one-dollar bill.

Stuart, James Francis Edward (1688–1766) British claimant to the throne, called the "Old Pretender". He was the only son of JAMES II and was proclaimed king of England by the JACOBITES on the death of his father (1701). He made two attempts to regain the throne (1708 and 1715), landing in Scotland, where support for the Stuart dynasty was greatest. On both occasions the cause was lost before James arrived. His son was Charles STUART.

Stuart, Mary *See* MARY II

Stuarts (Stewarts) Scottish royal house, which inherited the Scottish crown in 1371 and the English crown in 1603. The Stuarts descended from Alan, whose descendants held the hereditary office of steward in the royal household. Walter (d.1326), the sixth steward, married a daughter of King Robert I, and their son, Robert II, became the first Stuart king (1371). The crown descended in the direct male line until the death of James V (1542), who was succeeded by his infant daughter, MARY, QUEEN OF SCOTS. In 1603, her son, James VI, succeeded ELIZABETH I of England as JAMES I. In 1649 James's son, CHARLES I, was executed following the CIVIL WAR, but the dynasty was restored with the RESTORATION of CHARLES II in 1660. His brother, JAMES II, lost the throne in the GLORIOUS REVOLUTION (1685) and was replaced by the joint monarchy of WILLIAM III and MARY II, James's daughter. On the death (1714) of ANNE, James's second daughter, without an heir, the House of HANOVER succeeded. The male descendants of James II made several unsuccessful attempts to regain the throne, culminating in the JACOBITE rebellion of 1745.

Stubbs, George (1724–1806) English painter and engraver. Stubbs is celebrated chiefly for his book *The Anatomy of the Horse*, illustrated with his own engravings. *Horses attacked by a lion* (1770) reveals a more romantic approach.

sturgeon Large, primitive, bony fish found in temperate fresh and marine waters of the Northern Hemisphere. The ovaries of the female are the source of CAVIAR. It has five series of sharp-pointed scales along its sides, fleshy whiskers and a tapering, snout-like head. Family Acipenseridae; species Atlantic sturgeon (*Acipenser sturio*) length: to 3m (11ft), weight: to 270kg (600lb). The Eurasian freshwater sturgeon is also called beluga.

Sturm und Drang (Ger. Storm and Stress) German literary movement that takes its name from a play (1776) by F.M. von Klinger. Sturm und Drang rejected the prevailing NEO-CLASSICISM in favour of subjectivity, artistic creativity and the beauty of nature. Associated principally with the early works of Johann Wolfgang von GOETHE, Friedrich SCHILLER and Johann Gottfried von HERDER, it is seen as a precursor of ROMANTICISM. Sturm und Drang influenced HAYDN's group of minor-key symphonies.

Stuttgart Capital of Baden Württemberg, SW Germany, on the River Neckar. Now the eighth-largest city in Germany, Stuttgart was founded in *c*.950. The capital of the kingdom of Württemberg from 1495 to 1806, it had an industrial base that expanded rapidly during the 19th century. Historically, it is associated with motor vehicle construction. Stuttgart was intensively bombed during World War 2, but much of its famous architecture survived. Industries: electronics, photographic equipment, publishing, wine, beer. Pop. (1995) 588,000.

Stuyvesant, Peter (1610–72) Dutch colonial administrator. He became governor of the Caribbean islands of Curaçao, Bonaire and Aruba in 1643, and in 1647 he became director-general of all the Dutch territories, including New Amsterdam (later New York City). In 1655 he ended Swedish influence in Delaware, and ruled the colony until it was taken over by the English in 1664 and renamed New York.

style In botany, part of a FLOWER – the tube that connects the pollen-receiving STIGMA at its tip to the OVARY at its base.

Styx In Greek mythology, the river across which the souls of the dead were ferried by CHARON on their journey from the world of the living to the underworld.

subatomic particles Particles that are smaller than ATOMS or are of the types that make up atoms. They can be divided into two groups: the HADRONS, such as PROTONS and NEUTRONS, which can be further subdivided; and ELEMENTARY PARTICLES, such as QUARKS and ELECTRONS, which cannot be further divided.

sublimation Direct change from solid to gas without an intervening liquid phase. Most substances can sublimate at certain pressures but usually not at atmospheric pressure. *See also* CONDENSATION; EVAPORATION

submarine Seagoing warship capable of travelling both on and under the water. Experimental submarines were used in warfare from the late 18th century. Technical advances in the late 19th century led to the general spread of underwater craft in the world's navies. Early submarines were essentially surface ships with a limited ability to remain submerged. Once underwater, they depended on battery-powered electric motors for propulsion and, with a limited air supply, were soon forced to surface. Submerging is accomplished by letting air out of internal ballast tanks; trimming underwater is done by regulating the amount of water in the ballast tanks with pumps; and surfacing is accomplished by pumping water out of the tanks. Most modern submarines use nuclear power, which eliminates the need to surface while on operations.

submersible Small craft for underwater exploration and engineering. Modern submersibles have evolved from simple devices. Diving bells were open-bottomed craft in which people were lowered into the water. A device called the bathysphere, invented in the 1930s, was a spherical observation chamber. The bathyscaphe, invented in the 1940s by Auguste PICCARD, had a spherical chamber attached to a much larger hull, which was used as a buoyancy control device. A new generation of submersibles has evolved since the late 1950s. A typical craft has a spherical passenger capsule capable of withstanding water pressure down to *c*.3,600m (12,000ft). Attached to this is a structure containing batteries, an electric motor with propeller, lighting, a mechanical arm for gathering samples and other equipment. A support ship launches and retrieves the submersible. Some submersibles are operated by remote control from the surface. *See also* COUSTEAU, JACQUES YVES

subpoena (Lat. under penalty) In law, an order that commands a person to appear before a court or judicial officer to give evidence at a specific time and place. Failure to obey a subpoena is a criminal offense.

subsidiary In business, a company that is controlled to some extent by another corporation that holds a majority of the shares.

subsidies Government assistance to individuals or organizations to benefit the public. Subsidies are usually intended to promote growth or stability, generating higher outputs of certain products, or maintaining or reducing prices. They can be **direct** (for example, cash payments) or **indirect** (for example, when the government buys goods at artificially high prices or grants tax concessions). They are often used to protect industries by enabling them to offer more competitive prices. Commonly subsidized enterprises include agriculture, business expansion, housing and regional development.

substitution reaction Chemical reaction in which one atom or group of atoms replaces (usually in the same structural position) another group in a molecule or ion.

succession Orderly change in plant and animal life in a biotic community over a long time period. It is the result of modifications in the community environment. The process ends in establishment of a stable ECOSYSTEM (climax community).

succulent Plant that stores water in its tissues to resist periods of drought. Usually perennial and EVERGREEN, they have bodies mostly made up of water storage cells, which give them a fleshy appearance. A well-developed CUTICLE and low rate of daytime TRANSPIRATION also conserve water. Succulent plants include CACTUS, LILY and STONECROP.

sucker Any of several species of freshwater fish found mainly from N Canada to the Gulf of Mexico. A bottom-feeder similar to minnows, it has a thick-lipped mouth for feeding by suction. Length: to 26in (66cm); weight: to 12lb (5.4kg). Family Catostomidae.

Sucre, Antonio José de (1795–1830) South American revolutionary leader and first president of Bolivia (1826–28). He joined the fight for independence in 1811 and played a key role in the liberation of Ecuador, Peru and Bolivia, winning the final, decisive battle at Ayacucho (1824). With Simón BOLÍVAR's support, Sucre became the first elected president of Bolivia, but local opposition forced his resignation. He was assassinated while trying to preserve the unity of Colombia.

Sucre City in S central BOLIVIA and the legal capital of Bolivia, the seat of government being LA PAZ. Known successively as La Plata, Chuquisaca and Charcas, Sucre was renamed in 1839 after the first president of Bolivia, Antonio José de SUCRE. It is a commercial and distribution centre for the surrounding farming region. Industries: cement, oil refining. Pop. (1993) 145,000.

sucrose ($C_{12}H_{22}O_{11}$) Common, white, crystalline SUGAR, a disaccharide sugar consisting of linked GLUCOSE and FRUCTOSE molecules. It occurs in many plants, but its principal commercial sources are SUGAR CANE and SUGAR BEET. It is widely used for food sweetening and making preserves.

Sudan Republic and Africa's largest country, in NE Africa. It extends from the arid SAHARA in the N to an equatorial swamp region (the *Sudd*) in the S. Much of the land is flat, but there are mountains in the NE and SE; the highest point is Kinyeti, at 3,187m (10,456ft). The River NILE (*Bahr el Jebel*) runs S–N, entering Sudan as the White Nile, converging with the Blue Nile at KHARTOUM and flowing N to Egypt. **Climate** The climate ranges from the virtually rainless N deserts to the swamplands in the S. Khartoum is prone to summer dust storms (*haboobs*). **Vegetation** From the bare deserts of the N, the land merges into dry grasslands and savanna. Dense rainforests grow in the S. **History and Politics** The ancient state of NUBIA extended into N Sudan. In *c.*2000 BC, it became a colony of EGYPT. From the 8th century BC to

---

SUDAN
AREA: 2,505,810sq km (967,493sq mi)
POPULATION: 33,625,000
CAPITAL (POPULATION): Khartoum (925,000)

---

*c.*350 AD, it was part of the KUSH kingdom. Christianity was introduced in the 6th century. From the 13th to 15th centuries, N Sudan came under Muslim control, and Islam became the dominant religion. In 1821, MUHAMMAD ALI's forces occupied Sudan. Anglo-Egyptian forces, led by General GORDON, attempted to extend Egypt's influence into the S. Muhammad Ahmad led a MAHDI uprising, which briefly freed Sudan from Anglo-Egyptian influence. In 1898, General KITCHENER's forces defeated the Mahdists, and in 1899 Sudan became Anglo-Egyptian Sudan, governed jointly by Britain and Egypt. Opposition to colonial rule continued until independence in 1956. The S Sudanese, who are predominantly Christians or followers of traditional beliefs, revolted against the dominance of the Muslim N, and civil war broke out. In 1958, the military seized power. Civilian rule was re-established in 1964 but overthrown again in 1969, when Gaafar Muhammad Nimeri seized control. In 1972, S Sudan was given considerable autonomy, but unrest persisted. In 1983, the imposition of strict Islamic law sparked off further conflict between the government and the Sudan People's Liberation Army (SPLA) in the S. In 1985, Nimeri was deposed, and a civilian government was installed. In 1989, the military, led by Omar Hassan Ahmed al-Bashir, established a Revolutionary Command Council. Civil war between the SPLA and government forces continued in the S. Peace initiatives foundered as the SPLA split over the nature of independence from the North. In 1996, Bashir was re-elected, virtually unopposed. The National Islamic Front (NIF) dominated the government and was believed to have strong links with Iranian terrorist groups. In 1996, the UN imposed sanctions on Sudan. In 1997, an SPLA offensive, led by John Garang, made signficant advances. A South African peace initiative (1997) led to the formation of a Southern States' Coordination Council. In 1997, the USA imposed sanctions on Bashir's regim. In 1999, Bashir declared a state of emergency and dissolved parliament. Sudan's Islamicist leader, Hassan al-Turabi was dismissed in 2000. **Economy** Sudan is a low-income economy. Food shortages and a refugee crisis have added to Sudan's economic difficulties. Agriculture employs 62% of the workforce. The leading crops are cotton, millet, wheat and sesame. Nomadic herders raise livestock. Mineral resources include chromium, gold, gypsum and oil. Manufacturing industries produce cement, fertilizers and textiles. The main exports are cotton, gum arabic and sesame seeds.

sudden infant death syndrome *See* COT DEATH

Sudetenland Border region of N Bohemia (Czech Republic), including part of the Sudeten Mountains. It was largely populated by Germans, and in the 1930s Nazi-inspired agitation demanded its inclusion in Germany. Approval for its annexation was given by Britain and France in the MUNICH AGREEMENT (1938). After World War 2 it was restored to Czechoslovakia, and the German population was expelled.

Suez Canal Waterway in Egypt linking Port Said on the Mediterranean Sea with the Gulf of Suez and the Red Sea. The 169-km (105-mi) canal was planned and built in the period 1859–69 by the Suez Canal Company under the supervision of French canal builder

Ferdinand de LESSEPS. In 1875, the British government became the major shareholder in the company. In 1955, more than 120 million tonnes of merchandise passed through the canal, much of it oil. After Egypt nationalized the canal in 1956, Israeli and British forces attacked Egypt, and the canal was closed from 1956 to 1957 while repairs were carried out. It was again closed during the ARAB-ISRAELI WAR of 1967. The canal reopened in 1975. In the intervening period, many new ships, especially oil tankers, became too large to pass through the canal. Loss of revenue forced Egypt to clear and widen the waterway.

Suffolk County in E England, on the North Sea coast; the county town is IPSWICH. The land is mainly low-lying and flat, rising in the SW. The principal rivers are the Orwell, Stour and Waveney. The economy is mainly agricultural, growing cereal crops and sugar beets and rearing sheep, pigs and poultry. Fishing is in decline. Industries: food processing, farm machinery, fertilizers, finance. Area: 3,807sq km (1,470sq mi). Pop. (1991) 632,266.

suffrage See FRANCHISE

suffragette movement Women's campaign in Britain in the late 19th and early 20th centuries to win the right to vote. It began in the 1860s, and developed until the founding of the National Union of Women's Suffrage Societies in 1897. Emmeline PANKHURST founded the Women's Social and Political Union in 1903. By 1910, the movement had split into several factions, including the Women's Freedom League (founded in 1908). In 1913, Sylvia Pankhurst founded the East London Federation, which organized marches in London. Women of the age of 30 and over were given the vote in 1918.

Sufism Mystic philosophical movement within ISLAM that developed among the SHIITE communities in the 10th and 11th centuries. Sufis stress the capability of the soul to attain personal union with God. See also DERVISH

sugar Sweet-tasting, soluble, crystalline monosaccharide or disaccharide CARBOHYDRATE. The common sugar in food and beverages is SUCROSE. This is also the main sugar transported in plant tissues. The main sugar transported around the bodies of animals to provide energy is GLUCOSE. See also SACCHARIDE

sugar beet Variety of BEET grown commercially for its high SUGAR content, which is stored in its thick, white roots. Family Chenopdiaceae; species *Beta vulgaris*.

sugar cane Perennial GRASS cultivated in tropical and subtropical regions worldwide. After harvesting, the stems are processed in factories and are the main source of SUGAR. Cultivated canes are *Saccharum officinarum*. Height: to 4.5m (15ft). Family Poaceae/Gramineae.

Suharto, Raden (1921–) Indonesian general and statesman, president (1967–98). Suharto seized power from President SUKARNO, averting an alleged communist coup, in 1966. He was formally elected president in 1968 and was re-elected (unopposed) five times. Suharto ordered the invasion (1975) of East Timor. Under Suharto, Indonesia experienced rapid economic development, but his autocratic rule was criticized for frequent abuses of human rights. In 1997, economic collapse destabilized Suharto's government, and in 1998 he was ousted after widespread student rioting.

Suhrawardi, as- (1155–91) Islamic philosopher and theologian, b. Persia (Iran). He was the founder of the Ishraqi (Illuminationist) school of thought, which embraced elements from many sources, including ORPHISM, Hellenism, ZOROASTRIANISM, SUFISM and SHIITE Islam. His thinking is still in evidence in Iran today among mystical sects, such as the Nuyah. His principal work is *The Wisdom of Illumination*. He was put to death by Malikaz-Zāhir, the son of SALADIN.

suicide Deliberate act of terminating one's own life.

suite Musical form popular in the BAROQUE period, comprising a number of instrumental dances that differ in metre, tempo and rhythm but are generally all in the same key. The earliest suites date from the 16th century and usually involved only two dances, the pavane and galliard. By the 18th century, the dances had become standardized: a prelude, allemande, courante, sarabande and gigue. There was some flexibility, and the minuet, gavotte, bourrée and rondeau were often added.

Sukarno, Achmad (1901–70) Indonesian statesman, first president of independent Indonesia (1947–67). Founder of the Indonesian Nationalist Party (1927), he led opposition to Dutch rule and was frequently imprisoned or exiled (1933–42). At the end of World War 2, he declared Indonesian independence and became president of the new republic. In the 1950s, his rule became increasingly dictatorial. He dissolved the parliament, declared himself president for life (1963) and aligned himself with the communists. The failure of a communist coup against the leaders of the army in 1965 weakened Sukarno's position. He was forced out of power by the generals, led by SUHARTO, who eventually replaced him as president.

Sukkoth (Sukkat) Jewish Feast of Tabernacles, or Feast of Booths, an autumn festival that lasts for seven days. It commemorates the wandering of the Jews in the desert and their salvation through God. A *sukkat*, or simple tent of branches, is raised in the synagogue. See TABERNACLE

Sukkur City on the River Indus, Sind province, W Pakistan. It is the site of the Sukkur Barrage across the Indus, controlling one of the world's largest irrigation schemes, with canals watering more than 12 million hectares (5 million acres) of the Indus valley. Completed in 1932, the dam is 58m (190ft) high and *c*.1,500m (5,000ft) long. Industries: textiles, foodstuffs. Pop. (1991) 350,000.

Sulawesi (formerly Celebes) Large island in E Indonesia, separated from Borneo by the Makasar Strait, with Ujung Pandang (formerly Makasar, 1990 pop. 913,196) the main port and largest city. A largely mountainous and volcanic island, the highest peak is Mount Rantekombola at 3,455m (11,335ft). The first European discovery was by the Portuguese in 1512. The Dutch assumed control in the early 17th century and successfully waged war against the native population in the 1666–69 Makasar War. In 1950, it became a province of the Indonesian republic, and it is made up of four separate provinces: Utara, Tengah, Selatan and Tenggara. The population is

◀ **sugar** Sugar beets (left) and sugar cane (right) produce the same sugar – sucrose – but require completely different climatic conditions. Cane is grown as a single crop in tropical regions, whereas sugar beets form part of regular crop rotation in Europe and North and South America. Although sugar is extracted by the same method from both sources, the yield of sugar cane is higher.

primarily Malayan. Industries: fishing, agriculture. Area: 189,216sq km (73,031sq mi). Pop. (1990) 12,520,711

Suleiman I (the Magnificent) (1494–1566) Ottoman sultan (1520–66). He succeeded his father, Selim I. He captured Rhodes from the KNIGHTS HOSPITALLERS and launched a series of campaigns against the Austrian HABSBURGS, defeating the Hungarians at Mohács (1526) and subsequently controlling most of the country. His troops besieged Vienna (1529), and his admiral, BARBAROSSA, created a navy that dominated the Mediterranean and ensured Ottoman control of much of the North African coastal region. In the east he won victories against the Safavids of Persia and conquered Mesopotamia.

Sulla, Lucius Cornelius (138–78 BC) Roman dictator (82–81 BC). Elected consul in 88 BC, he defeated MITHRIDATES VI in spite of the opposition of MARIUS, Cinna and

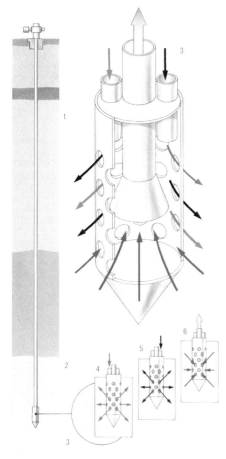

▲ **sulphur** Naturally occuring sulphur is extracted from rock formations by a method known as the Frasch process. Bore holes (1) are dug to the sulphur-rich areas (2). A specialized head (3) is dropped down the bore hole. First pressurized water at 155°C (310°F) is pumped into the rock (4) melting the sulphur. The water is followed by compressed air (5), which forces the liquid containing the sulphur to the surface (6).

their supporters in Rome. Invading Italy, he captured Rome in 82 BC and massacred his antipatrician enemies.

Sullivan, Sir Arthur Seymour (1842–1900) British composer, famous for a series of operettas written with the librettist W.S. GILBERT. They included *HMS Pinafore* (1878), *The Pirates of Penzance* (1879) and *The Mikado* (1885). Sullivan also composed one opera, *Ivanhoe* (1881), and oratorios, cantatas and church music, including many hymns, such as *Onward, Christian Soldiers*.

Sullivan, Louis Henry (1856–1924) US architect and founder of the Chicago School of architecture. The Wainwright Building in St Louis (1890) and the Transportation Building at the 1893 World's Exhibition in Chicago are counted among his best-known works.

sulphate Salt of SULPHURIC ACID (H_2SO_4). Examples include copper(II) sulphate ($CuSO_4$) and iron(II) sulphate ($FeSO_4$).

sulphonamide drug Any of a group of DRUGS derived from sulphanilamide, a red textile dye, that prevent the growth of bacteria. Introduced in the 1930s, they were the first antibacterials, prescribed to treat a range of infections. They were replaced by less toxic and more effective ANTIBIOTICS.

sulphur (symbol S) Nonmetallic element in Group VI of the periodic table, known since prehistory (the biblical brimstone). It may occur naturally as a free element or in sulphide minerals such as GALENA and iron pyrites, or in sulphate minerals such as GYPSUM. The main commercial source is native (free) sulphur, extracted by the Frasch process. It is used in the VULCANIZATION of rubber and in the manufacture of drugs, matches, dyes, fungicides, insecticides and fertilizers. Properties: at.no. 16; r.a.m. 32.064; r.d. 2.07; m.p. 112.8°C (235.0°F); b.p. 444.7°C (832.5°F). Most common isotope S^{32} (95.1%).

sulphuric acid (H_2SO_4) Colourless, odourless liquid, one of the strongest acids known. It is produced by the oxidation of sulphur dioxide (SO_2). Sulphuric acid is a major industrial chemical, used in the manufacture of many acids, fertilizers, detergents, drugs and a wide range of chemicals. Properties: r.d. 1.84; m.p. 10.3°C (50.5°F); b.p. 330°C (626°F).

Sumatra (Sumatera) Island in w Indonesia – the world's sixth-largest island. The w coast is rugged and mountainous, the Barisan Mountains rising to 3,800m (12,500ft), and nearly 60% of the lowland area is jungle. By the 7th century, India had established two states in Sumatra – Melayu and Srivijaya. The Portuguese landed on the island in the 16th century, and the Dutch followed a century later. Britain held certain parts of the island briefly in the 18th and 19th centuries, and Sumatra became part of newly independent Indonesia in 1950. The principal cities (1990 population figures) are Medan (1,685,972), Palembang (1,084,483) and Padang (477,344). The main products are oil (the largest earner), timber, rubber, tin, tobacco, palm oil, tea, coffee, sisal and rice. Mining and farming were the chief occupations, but the N is being rapidly industrialized. Sumatra now accounts for around 75% of Indonesia's total income. Area: 425,000sq km (164,000sq mi). Pop. (1990) 36,505,703.

Sumeria World's first civilization, dating from before 3000 BC, in s MESOPOTAMIA. The Sumerians are credited with inventing cuneiform writing, many familiar sociopolitical institutions and a money-based economy. Major cities were UR, KISH and LAGASH. During the third millennium it built up a large empire. In *c*.2340 BC the Semitic peoples of AKKADIA conquered Mesopotamia, and by *c*.1950 BC the civilization had disintegrated.

summer time (daylight saving scheme) System by which clocks in Britain are kept one hour ahead of GMT (Greenwich mean time) throughout the summer. Some other countries have similar daylight saving schemes.

summit meeting Name of the meeting of heads of state or their senior representatives to discuss an urgent point at issue between them. The term was first applied to the Geneva summit of July 1955, attended by Nikita Khrushchev, Dwight D. Eisenhower, Anthony Eden, Edgar Faure and Nikolai Bulganin.

Sumner, Charles (1811–74) US political leader. A passionate abolitionist, he was senator from Massachusetts (1851–74) and a leading Radical Republican during RECONSTRUCTION, supporting the impeachment of President Andrew JOHNSON.

sumo wrestling Traditional and popular sport of Japan. Pairs of wrestlers, who usually weigh more than 159kg (350lb), attempt to force each other out of a ring. The technique employs holds, trips, pushes and falls. A referee monitors the brief bout and keeps score.

Sun Star at the centre of the SOLAR SYSTEM, around which all other Solar System bodies revolve in their orbits. The Sun is a typical, average star. It consists of *c.*70% hydrogen (by weight) and 28% helium, with the remainder mostly oxygen and carbon. Its temperature, pressure and density increase towards the centre. Like all stars, the Sun's energy is generated by nuclear FUSION reactions taking place under the extreme conditions in the core. This core is *c.*400,000km (250,000mi) across. Energy released from the core passes up through the radiative zone, which is nearly 300,000km (*c.*200,000mi) thick, then passes through the 200,000km (125,000mi)-thick convective zone to the surface, the PHOTOSPHERE, from where it is radiated into space. Most of the Sun's visible activity takes place in the 500km (300mi)-thick photosphere. Above the photosphere lies the chromosphere, which consists of hot gases and extends for thousands of kilometres. Extending outwards from the chromosphere for millions of miles is the CORONA, which emits the SOLAR WIND. The solar wind and the Sun's magnetic field dominate a region of space called the heliosphere, which extends to the boundaries of the Solar System.

sunbird Tropical, nectar-feeding songbird of the Old World, often considered a counterpart of the New World hummingbird. The males are usually brightly coloured. Length: 9–15cm (3.5–6in). Family Nectariniidae.

sunburn Damage to skin caused by prolonged or unaccustomed exposure to sunlight. It varies in severity from redness and soreness to the formation of large blisters, which may be accompanied by shock. Excessive exposure to sunlight is associated with the skin cancer known as melanoma.

sun dance Important religious rite of the North American "Plains Indians". It was usually held annually in early summer and was performed around a TOTEM POLE. The sun dance was part of elaborate ceremonies held to reaffirm a tribe's affinity with nature and the universe.

Sunday, Billy (William Ashley) (1862–1935) US Presbyterian revivalist. After three years in professional baseball, he became a famous preacher at huge evangelical meetings across the country. He preached against alcohol, gaining a reputation as a temperance leader.

Sunderland County district in SE TYNE AND WEAR, NE England, at the mouth of the River Wear. Once renowned for coalmining and the biggest shipbuilding centre in the world, it now has chemicals, vehicles and furniture among its many industries. Pop. (1994) 176,000.

◄ **Sumeria** This Sumerian vessel dates from *c.*3500 BC. Clay was one of the few raw materials available to the Sumerians. The quality of their glazes and decorations were very advanced. The Sumerians were also renowned for their architecture, notably the stepped-pyramid ziggurats.

sundew Any INSECTIVOROUS PLANT of the genus *Drosera*, native to temperate swamps and bogs. Sundews have hairy basal leaves that glisten with a sticky dew-like substance that attracts and traps insects. The leaves then fold over the insect and secrete ENZYMES to digest it. Family Droseraceae.

sunfish North American freshwater fish. A popular angler's fish, similar in appearance to PERCH, it has a continuous dorsal fin containing spiny and soft rays. The 30 species range in size from the blue spotted *Enneacanthus gloriosus* (length: 8.9cm/3.5in) to the large-mouth bass *Micropterus salmoides* (length: 81cm/32in; weight: 10kg/22lb). Family Centrarchidae.

sunflower Any of several annual and perennial plants of the genus *Helianthus*, native to North and South America. The flower heads resemble huge daisies with yellow ray flowers and a central disc of yellow, brown or purple. The seeds yield a useful oil. The common sunflower (*H. annuus*) has 30-cm (12-in) leaves and flower heads more than 30cm across; height: to 3.5m (12ft). Family Asteraceae/Compositae.

Sunni Traditionalist orthodox branch of ISLAM, the followers of which are called *Ahl as-Sunnah* ("People of the Path"). It is followed by 90% of Muslims. Sunnis accept the *Hadith*, the body of orthodox teachings based on Muhammad's spoken words outside the KORAN. The Sunni differ from the SHIITE sect in that they accept the first four caliphs (religious leaders) as the true successors of MUHAMMAD.

sunspot Region in the Sun's PHOTOSPHERE that is cooler than its surroundings and appears darker. Sunspots vary in size from *c.*1,000–50,000km (600–30,000mi), and occasionally up to *c.*200,000km (125,000mi). Their duration varies from a few hours to a few weeks, or months for the very biggest. Sunspots occur where there is a local strengthening of the Sun's magnetic field.

sunstroke Potentially fatal condition caused by overexposure to direct sunlight, in which the body temperature rises to 40.5°C (105°F) or more. Symptoms include hot, dry skin, exhaustion, delirium and coma. Urgent medical treatment is required, possibly in an intensive care unit. Recovery is usual within a day or two.

Sun Yat-sen (1866–1925) Chinese nationalist leader, first president of the Chinese Republic (1911–12). In exile (1895–1911), he adopted his "three principles of the people": nationalism, democracy and prosperity. After the revolution of 1911 he became provisional president, but soon resigned in favour of the militarily powerful Yuan Shikai. When Yuan turned autocratic, Sun gave his support to the KUOMINTANG, or Nationalist Party, formed to oppose Yuan.

supercluster *See* GALAXY CLUSTER

superconductivity Electrical behaviour in metals and alloys that are cooled to very low temperatures. In a superconducting circuit, an electric current flows indefinitely because there is no electrical resistance. Research continues to develop superconductors that function at higher temperatures.

superego In PSYCHOANALYSIS, level of personality that acts as a conscience or censor. It develops as a child internalizes the standards of behaviour defined by the rewards and punishments of parents and society. *See also* EGO; ID

superfluidity Property of a liquid that has no viscosity and therefore no resistance to flow. HELIUM II – liquid helium at temperatures less than 2K ($-271°C/-456°F$) – was the first known superfluid. Helium II apparently defies gravity by flowing up slopes. It also appears to contravene the laws of THERMODYNAMICS, by flowing from a cool region to a warmer one. *See also* CRYOGENICS

Superior, Lake Lake in the USA and Canada, the largest freshwater lake in the world, bordered on the w by Minnesota, on the N and E by Ontario and on the S by Michigan and Wisconsin. The most w of the five GREAT LAKES, it is connected to Lake HURON and the ST LAWRENCE SEAWAY by the St Mary's River and the Soo (Sault Ste Marie) canals. A centre for commercial and recreational fishing, the lake is also a major commercial transport route, particularly for grain and iron ore from Duluth, Michigan, and Thunder Bay, Ontario. Area: 82,413sq km (31,820sq mi). Maximum depth: *c.*1,300ft (400m).

supernova Stellar explosion in which virtually an entire STAR is disrupted. For a week or so, a supernova may outshine all the other stars in its galaxy. After a couple of years the supernova has expanded so much that it becomes thin and transparent. For hundreds or thousands of years the ejected material remains visible as a supernova remnant. A supernova is about 1,000 times brighter than a NOVA.

superposition, law of In geology, law that states that in undisturbed layers of sedimentary deposits, younger beds overlie older ones.

supersonic velocity Velocity greater than that of the local velocity of sound. In dry air at 0°C (32°F), this velocity is *c.*330m/s (1,080ft/s) or 1,188km/h (736mph). Its magnitude is usually expressed as a MACH NUMBER. This is the ratio of the velocity of a body to the velocity of sound in a medium such as air. Any object travelling at supersonic velocity leaves behind a shock wave that a ground observer hears as a SONIC BOOM.

supersonic wave Wave set up in the air by any object moving at or above SUPERSONIC VELOCITY. At these velocities, sound waves created by the object's velocity pile up ahead of it and are released violently behind it as a shock wave. An observer on the ground sees a supersonic aircraft pass overhead before experiencing the shock wave that spreads out as a SONIC BOOM.

superstring theory Theory that attempts to explain the properties of ELEMENTARY PARTICLES and the interactions between them. It combines QUANTUM THEORY and RELATIVITY, especially to explain nuclear forces and the force of gravity (*see* FUNDAMENTAL FORCES). Superstrings are hypothetical one-dimensional objects $c.10^{-35}$m long that require a 10-dimensional universe to accommodate them. Their use in quantum calculations predicts the existence of GRAVITONS, the particles believed to be involved in gravitational interaction. *See also* UNIFIED FIELD THEORY

Suppé, Franz von (1819–95) Austrian composer. He composed 31 operettas, including *Fatinitza* (1876) and *Boccaccio* (1879). He also wrote the popular overtures *Poet and Peasant* and *Light Cavalry*.

supply and demand, law of Economic balance between goods required and produced. The law of supply indicates that, other things being equal, as the price of an item increases, suppliers are willing to produce more, and as the price decreases, producers are willing to produce less. Thus, price and quantity supplied are directly related. The law of demand states the reverse: as prices increase, consumers demand less, and as prices decrease, consumers demand more. Thus, prices and quantity demanded are inversely related.

supply-side economics Policies designed to reduce the role of governments in economic matters. The theory of supply-side economics is that production of goods and services can be stimulated by reducing taxes, thereby increasing the supply of money for investment. It also promotes governmental expenditure that generates industrial activity.

suprematism Abstract art movement launched in Russia in 1915 by Kasimir MALEVICH. Epitomized by the stark geometrical forms of Malevich's painting *White on White* (1919), suprematism had a profound influence on the development of geometrical ABSTRACT ART and CONSTRUCTIVISM.

Supreme Court of the United States US court of final appeal, the highest in the nation. Its duty is to decide and interpret the constitutionality of state and federal legislation and of executive acts. Once the Supreme Court has arrived at a decision, all lower courts must follow it in similar cases. Cases are decided by majority vote. Created by the Constitution of 1787, the Supreme Court is made up of nine justices appointed for life by the president with the advice and consent of the Senate.

Surabaja Port in NE Java, second-largest city in Indonesia and capital of East Java province. An important naval base occupied by Japan in World War 2, the city remains Indonesia's primary naval centre. A fishing and industrial port, it has shipyards, textile mills, automobile assembly plants and oil-refining. Pop. (1995) 2,701,000.

surfing Water sport in which a person lies or stands on a specially designed wooden or fibreglass board, usually 1.2–1.8m (4–6ft) long, and is propelled by the crest of a wave towards the shore.

surgery Branch of medical practice concerned with treatment by operation. Traditionally it has mainly involved open surgery: gaining access to the operative site by way of an incision. However, the practice of using ENDOSCOPES has enabled the development of MINIMAL ACCESS SURGERY using minimally invasive techniques. Surgery is carried out under sterile conditions, using local or general ANAESTHESIA.

Surinam (Suriname) Independent nation in NE South America, on the Atlantic Ocean, bordered by Brazil (S), French Guiana (E) and Guyana (W). Its capital is PARAMARIBO. Surinam is made up of the Guiana Highlands plateau, a flat coastal plain and a forested inland region. Its many rivers serve as a source of hydroelectric power. **History** The region was discovered in 1499 by Spanish explorer Alfonso de Ojeda, but it was the British who founded the first colony (1651). In 1667, it was ceded to Holland in exchange for New Amsterdam (later New York), and in 1815 the Congress of Vienna gave the Guyana region to Britain and reaffirmed Dutch control of "Dutch Guiana". It became officially autonomous in 1954, and in 1975, as Surinam, gained full independence from the Netherlands and membership of the United Nations. In 1980, the military seized control, imposing martial law and banning political parties. Guerrilla warfare disrupted the economy. In 1987, a new constitution provided for a 51-member National Assembly, with powers to elect the president. Rameswak Shankar was elected president in 1988 but was overthrown by another military coup in 1990. In 1991, the New Front for

SURINAM
AREA: 163,270sq km (63,069sq mi)
POPULATION: 497,000
CAPITAL (POPULATION): Paramaribo (200,970)

Democracy and Development won the majority of seats in the National Assembly, and their leader, Ronald Venetiaan, became president. The constitution was amended in 1992 to limit the power of the military. The 1996 general election resulted in a coalition government, led by Jules Wijdenbosch of the National Democratic Party. **Economy** Surinam's economy (1995 GDP per capita, US$2,250) depends greatly on the export of bauxite, of which it is one of the world's largest producers. The chief agricultural products are rice, bananas, sugar cane, coffee, coconuts, lumber and citrus fruits.

surrealism Influential movement in 20th-century art and literature; it evolved in the mid-1920s from Dadaism. Taking inspiration from Freudian theories of the unconscious, the surrealists used bizarre imagery and strange juxtapositions to surprise and shock viewers. Important surrealist writers include Louis ARAGON, Georges Bataille, Paul ÉLUARD and Benjamin Peret, while painters include Jean ARP, Max ERNST, René MAGRITTE, Salvador DALÍ, Joan MIRÓ and Paul KLEE. *See also* DADA

Surrey, Henry Howard, Earl of (1517–47) English poet. Like his cousin Catherine HOWARD, he died on the scaffold, a victim of the bloody power politics of HENRY VIII's court. He wrote some of the earliest English SONNETS and, with his translation of two books of the *Aeneid* by VIRGIL, introduced BLANK VERSE into English poetry.

Surrey County in SE England, bordering Greater London. From E to W are the North Downs, which slope down to the Thames Valley. The Wey and the Mole are the principal rivers. Much of the land in the W is devoted to farming, with dairy and market-garden produce, wheat and oats the chief products. Guildford (1991 pop. 122,378) is the county town. Area: 1,679sq km (648sq mi). Pop. (1991) 1,018,003.

surrogate In psychology, term used to denote a person or thing that is a substitute for another (generally the natural person or object). It may bear no physical relation to the person or object for which it is a substitute. Surrogate mothers bear children for women who are unable to conceive. *See also* IMPRINTING

surveying Accurate measurement of the Earth's surface. It is used in establishing land boundaries and the topography of landforms and for major construction and civil-engineering work. For smaller areas, the land is treated as a horizontal plane. Large areas involve considerations of the Earth's curved shape and are referred to as geodetic surveys.

Susa Ancient city in SW Iran, capital of the ELAMITES. It became an important centre under the ACHAEMENID kings of Persia, containing a palace of DARIUS I. After the conquests of ALEXANDER THE GREAT, it became the capital of a small Greek state. Among archaeological finds at Susa was the stele (stone slab) of HAMMURABI, inscribed with his code of law.

suspension Liquid (or gas) medium in which small solid (or liquid) particles are uniformly dispersed. The particles are larger than those found in a COLLOID and will settle if the suspension stands undisturbed.

Sussex Former county in SE England, on the English Channel, since 1974 divided into the counties EAST SUSSEX and WEST SUSSEX. Area: 3,773sq km (1,457sq mi).

Sussex Kingdom of Anglo-Saxon England, settled by the South Saxons under Aelle (*c.* AD 477). It was allegedly the last Anglo-Saxon kingdom to adopt Christianity (*c.*680). A number of kings of Sussex are known from the 7th–8th centuries, but at various times they were under the dominance of Mercia. Sussex was absorbed by WESSEX in the early 9th century.

Sutherland, Graham (1903–80) English painter, draftsman and printmaker. During World War 2 he was employed as an official artist to record the effects of bomb damage. After the war he concentrated on religious themes and created the celebrated tapestry, *Christ in Glory* (1962) for Coventry Cathedral.

Sutherland, Dame Joan (1926–) Australian coloratura soprano. She joined the ROYAL OPERA, London, in 1952, and her performance in the title role of Donizetti's *Lucia di Lammermoor* in 1959 earned her worldwide acclaim. She went on to perform in all the world's major opera houses before her retirement in 1990.

Sutra Sacred or authoritative text in Indian philosophy or religion. In HINDUISM, it is a concise work for use within an oral tradition. Most philosophical traditions had their own sutras, which were written down in the first few centuries of the Christian era. In Buddhism, a sutra was a sometimes lengthy sacred text dealing with a specific point of doctrine.

suttee Former Indian custom of a widow throwing herself alive on to her husband's funeral pyre. Originally confined to royalty, it was forbidden under British Rule in 1829.

Sutton Hoo Archaeological site in Suffolk, SE England. The 1939 excavation of the cenotaph of Raedwald, a Saxon King of East Anglia (d.625), was Britain's richest archaeological find. The digs revealed a Saxon rowing boat 27m (90ft) long. In the centre of the boat lay a wooden funeral chamber, containing silver plate, gold jewellry and coins and bronze armour.

Suva Seaport on the SE coast of Viti Levu Island, capital of the Fiji Islands. It is the manufacturing and trade centre, with an excellent harbour. Exports include tropical fruits, copra, gold. Pop. (1996) 167,000.

Suzhou (Soochow, Su-chow) City on the Grand Canal, Jiangsu province, E central China. It was capital of Wu kingdom in the 5th century BC, and its famous silk industry developed under the SONG dynasty in the 12th century. It has been noted since 100 BC for its many gardens, temples and canals. Industries: silk, cotton, embroidery, chemicals. Pop. (1994) 776,000.

Suzman, Helen (1917–) South African politician. Suzman was an outspoken opponent of the APARTHEID regime in South Africa for 40 years. Elected to parliament in 1953, she formed the Progressive Party in 1959 and for the next 12 years was the only member. She retired from parliament shortly after the election of Nelson MANDELA.

Svalbard Archipelago in the Arctic Ocean, *c.*640km (400mi) N of Norway, to which it has officially belonged since 1925. There are nine main islands, of which by far the largest is Spitsbergen. The administrative centre and largest settlement is Longyearbyen on Spitsbergen. Ice fields and glaciers cover more than half the land mass, although the W edge of the islands is ice-free for most of the year. The islands are an important wildlife refuge, and protective measures have saved certain mammals from extinction. Animals include polar bear, walrus and whale. Though Svalbard was discovered by the Vikings in 1194, the islands remained neglected until Willem Barents rediscovered them in 1596. During the 17th century, they were an important whaling centre, and in the 18th century the lands were hunted by Russian and Scandinavian fur traders. Large coal deposits were found on Spitsbergen at the end of the 19th century, and the area was mined by Norway, Russia and Sweden. In 1925, the islands became a sovereign territory of Norway (although more than half the population is Russian), in return for allowing mining concessions to other nations. Area: 62,000sq km (24,000sq mi). Pop. (1994) 2,906.

Svevo, Italo (1861–1928) Italian novelist and businessman, b. Ettore Schmitz. Discouraged by the failure of his first two novels, he abandoned writing to pursue a career as a lawyer until his English tutor, the young James JOYCE, read his work and urged him to persevere. Largely psychological and introspective, his novels include *A Life* (1892) and his best-known work, *The Confessions of Zeno* (1923).

Svengali Sinister character in George du Maurier's novel *Trilby* (1894), who transforms Trilby into a great singer through hypnosis. The name has become synonymous with a mentor of evil influence.

Swahili BANTU language of the Niger-Congo family of African languages. It developed as a LINGUA FRANCA and trading language in most of E Africa, becoming the official language of Tanzania in 1967 and of Kenya in 1973. It is also used in parts of central Africa. Swahili is notable for its large number of Arabic loan words and its use of the Arabic alphabet. It has a large body of literature.

swallow Any of 75 species of graceful and agile birds with long, tapering wings and a long, forked tail. The common swallow (*Hirundo rustica*), known as the barn swallow in North America, is grey-blue with a light brown underside and red throat markings; it feeds primarily on insects, which it catches in flight. Length: 20cm (8in). Family Hirundinidae.

swamp Low-lying wetland area, found near large bodies of open water. Swamps are characterized by numerous plants and animals, including rushes and sedge in N regions, and species of trees, such as the swamp cypress, in warmer S areas. Swamps can prevent flooding by absorbing flood waters from rivers and coastal regions. *See also* BOG; MARSH

swan Any of several species of graceful, white or black waterfowl that nest in N Northern Hemisphere and migrate S for winter. Three species, including the Australian Black swan, live in the Southern Hemisphere. Most have broad, flat bills, long necks, plump bodies and dense plumage. They dip their heads under water to feed on plant matter. Length: to 2m (6.5ft). Family Anatidae; genus *Cygnus*.

Swansea (Abertawe) City and county district on Swansea Bay at the mouth of the River Tawe, West Glamorgan, S Wales. The second-largest Welsh city, it is the administrative centre of West Glamorgan and an industrial city that grew with the export of coal in the 19th century. Formerly noted for its production of steel, it is now dominated by light industry. Pop. (1994) 172,000.

SWAPO Acronym for SOUTH WEST AFRICA PEOPLE'S ORGANIZATION

swastika Cross with arms bent at right angles. A mystic sign in ancient times, it appears in China, Egypt, India, Greece and among some North American peoples. Since the 1930s, it has been notorious as the emblem of German NATIONAL SOCIALISM, or the Nazi Party.

Swaziland Small, landlocked and mountainous kingdom in S Africa, bounded by South Africa (N, W, S) and Mozambique (E); its capital is MBABANE. **Land and climate** There are four land regions. In the W, the Highveld, with an average height of 1,200m (3,950ft), makes up

> **SWAZILAND**
> AREA: 17,360sq km (6,703sq mi)
> POPULATION: 1,121,000
> CAPITAL (POPULATION): Mbabane (42,000)

30% of Swaziland. The Middleveld, between 350 and 1,000m (1,150–3,300ft), covers 28% of the country, while the Lowveld, with an average height of 270m (890ft), covers another 33%. The Lebombo Mountains, the fourth region, reach 800m (2,600 ft) along the E border. The Lowveld is almost tropical, with an average temperature of 22°C (72°F) and a low rainfall of c.500mm (20in) a year. The altitude moderates the climate in the W, and Mbabane has a climate typical of the Highveld, with warm summers and cool winters. **Vegetation** Meadows and pasture cover c.65% of Swaziland. Arable land covers 8% of the land and forests only 6%. **History** According to tradition, a group of Bantu-speaking people, under the Swazi chief Ngwane II, crossed the Lebombo range and united with local African groups to form the Swazi nation in the 18th century. Under attack from Zulu armies, the Swazi people were forced to seek British protection in the 1840s. Gold was discovered in the 1880s, and many Europeans sought land concessions from the king, who did not realize that in doing this he was losing control of the land. In 1894, Britain and the Boers of South Africa agreed to put Swaziland under the control of the South African Republic (the Transvaal). At the end of the second SOUTH AFRICAN WAR (1899–1902), Britain took control of the country. In 1968, Swaziland became fully independent as a constitutional monarchy, with King Sobhuza II as head of state. In 1973, Sobhuza suspended the constitution and assumed supreme power. All political parties were banned in 1978. When Sobhuza died in 1982, his son, Makhosetive, was named as heir. In 1986, he was installed as king, taking the name Mswati III. In the early 1990s, pro-democracy demonstrations called for Mswati to reconsider the ban on political parties. In 1993 and 1998, parliamentary elections were held on a non-party basis and were not generally considered to be democratic. **Economy** Swaziland is a lower-middle-income developing country (1995 GDP per capita, US$2,880). Agriculture employs 74% of the workforce. Farm products and processed foods, including sugar, wood pulp, citrus fruits and canned fruit, are the leading exports, though many farmers live at subsistence level. Mining has declined in importance in recent years. Swaziland's high-grade iron-ore reserves were used up in 1978, and the world demand for its asbestos has fallen. Swaziland is heavily dependent on South Africa, and the two countries are linked through a customs union.

sweat gland One of many small GLANDS that open on the SKIN surface through pores and release sweat, composed mainly of water and some salt, to regulate body temperature. *See also* HOMEOSTASIS

sweating (perspiring) Loss of water, salts and urea from the body surface of many mammals as a result of the action of certain glands (SWEAT GLANDS). Sweat glands are situated in the dermis of the skin and open onto the surface through tiny pores. In humans, they are found all over the body, but in some mammals they are found only on the soles of the feet. Sweating is controlled by the nervous system and forms an important part of the body's temperature control mechanism. The evaporation of sweat cools the skin and the blood passing through capillaries close to the skin surface.

Excessive sweating must be compensated for by increased intake of water and salt.

swede Root vegetable belonging to the mustard family (Brassicaceae/Cruciferae). The large, swollen taproot may be eaten cooked as a vegetable or fed raw to animals. Height: c.30cm (12in). Species: *B. napus napobrassica*.

Sweden Kingdom on the E half of the SCANDINAVIAN peninsula, N Europe. Most of N Sweden is mountainous; its highest point is Kebnekaise in LAPLAND, at 2,117m (6,946ft). The S lowlands contain two of Europe's largest lakes, Vänern and Vättern, and Sweden's largest cities: the capital, STOCKHOLM, and GOTHENBURG. **Climate** The climate of S Sweden is moderated by the Gulf Stream. Further N, the climate becomes more severe: at the Arctic Circle, the temperature is below freezing for six months per year. **Vegetation** Forest and woodland cover c.68% of Sweden. Arable land makes up 7% and grass only 1%. **History and Politics** The earliest inhabitants of the area were the Svear, who merged with the Goths in the 6th century AD. Christianity was introduced in the 9th century. Swedes are thought to have been among the VIKINGS who plundered areas of S and E Europe between the 9th and 11th centuries. Swedes (Varangians), led by RURIK, also penetrated Russia as far as the Black Sea. In 1319, Sweden and Norway were united under Magnus VII. In 1397, Sweden, Denmark and Norway were united by the Danish Queen Margaret in the Kalmar Union. Her successors failed to control Sweden, and in 1520 Gustavus Vasa led a successful rebellion. He was crowned king, as GUSTAVUS I, of an independent Sweden in 1523. (Southern Sweden remained under Danish control until 1660.) Gustavus made the monarchy hereditary within the Vasa dynasty, and Lutheranism became the state religion. Sweden's power was strengthened by John III's marriage to the king of Poland's sister. Their son, SIGISMUND III, a Roman Catholic, came to the throne in 1592 but was deposed (because of his religion) by CHARLES IX in 1599. Charles' son, GUSTAVUS II, won territory in Russia and Poland, and further victories in the THIRTY YEARS WAR established Sweden as a European power. CHARLES XII fought brilliant campaigns in Denmark, Poland, Saxony and Russia, but his eventual defeat in Russia (1709) seriously weakened Sweden. The 18th century was marked by internal friction. Gustavus IV (r.1792–1809) brought Sweden into the NAPOLEONIC WARS. Charles XIII (r.1809–18) lost Finland to Russia in 1809, but the Congress of VIENNA granted Norway to Sweden as compensation. Industry grew in the late 19th century. In 1905, the union between Sweden and Norway was dissolved. Under Gustavus V (r.1907–50), Sweden was neutral in both World Wars. In 1946 it joined the United Nations. The current king, Charles XVI Gustavus, succeeded in 1973. In 1995, Sweden joined the European Union. The Social Democrats have been in government almost continuously since 1932. In 1994, they formed a minority government, led by Ingvar Carlsson. In 1996, Carlsson was replaced by Göran Persson, who was re-elected in 1998. The cost of maintaining Sweden's extensive welfare services has become a major political issue. **Economy** Sweden is a highly developed industrial country (1995 GDP per capita, US$18,540). It has rich iron ore deposits, but other industrial materials are imported. Steel is a major product, used to manufacture aircraft, cars, machinery and ships. Forestry and fishing are important. Livestock and dairy farming are valuable activities; crops include barley and oats.

Swedenborg, Emanuel (1688–1772) Swedish scientist, philosopher, theologian and mystic. After a glittering

| **SWEDEN** |
| AREA: 449,960sq km (173,730sq mi) |
| POPULATION: 8,560,000 |
| CAPITAL (POPULATION): Stockholm (718,000) |

scientific career, during which he wrote many books (notably on metallurgy and metaphysics), he turned to theological teaching after a spiritual crisis in the mid-1740s. In 1745 he gave up worldly learning to concentrate on religious affairs. His religious writings include *Heavenly Arcana* (1749–56), *The New Jerusalem* (1758) and *True Christian Religion* (1771).

Swedish National language of Sweden, spoken by virtually all the country's 8.7 million people. It is also spoken by many people in Finland. Closely related to Norwegian and Danish, it is a member of the northern branch of the Germanic family of INDO-EUROPEAN LANGUAGES.

Sweelinck, Jan Pieterszoon (1562–1621) Netherlands composer and organist. A famous teacher and writer of many vocal works, his most lasting influence was in his keyboard pieces: his fugues and toccatas develop genres later explored by Dietrich Buxtehude and J.S. Bach.

sweet pea Climbing annual plant native to Italy. Widely cultivated as an ornamental, it has fragrant, butterfly-shaped flowers of white, pink, rose, lavender, purple, red or orange. Height: to 1.8m (6ft). Family Fabaceae/Leguminosae; species *Lathyrus odoratus*.

sweet potato Trailing plant native to South America and cultivated as a vegetable in Japan, Russia and the Pacific. It is not related to the potato. Its funnel-shaped flowers are pink or violet. The orange or yellow, tuberlike root is edible. Family Convolvulaceae; species *Ipomoea batatas*. See also YAM.

Swift, Jonathan (1667–1745) Irish satirist and poet. He was ordained an Anglican priest in 1694 and became dean of St Patrick's Cathedral in 1713. His early works include *The Battle of the Books* (1704) and *A Tale of a Tub* (1704). His best-known work, *Gulliver's Travels* (1726), is a satire on human follies. He wrote numerous works criticizing England's treatment of Ireland, including *A Modest Proposal* (1729). His poetry includes *Verses on the Death of Dr Swift* (1739).

swift Any of several species of fast-flying, widely distributed birds. They have hooked bills, wide mouths, long narrow wings and darkish plumage. They typically feed on insects, which they catch in flight, and build nests of plant matter held together with saliva. Length: to 23cm (9in). Family Apodidae.

swimming Self-propulsion of the body through water, a leisure activity or a competitive sport. Formal competition was first introduced in 1603 in Japan. The National Swimming Association was formed in England in 1837; the Fédération Internationale de Natation Amateur (FINA), the world governing body, was formed by 1908. There are four main strokes – breaststroke, crawl (freestyle), backstroke and butterfly. Recognized race distances for men and women, established by the Fédération in 1968, range from 100m to 1,500m; there are also relay and medley races. Synchronized swimming also features at the Olympic Games and at the four-yearly world championships. Swimming is one of the disciplines of the triathlon and the modern PENTATHLON.

Swinburne, Algernon Charles (1837–1909) British poet and critic. A play, *Atalanta in Calydon* (1865), brought him fame, and his *Poems and Ballads* (1866) also won praise. Some of the poems in the collection, including "The Garden of Proserpine", are among his finest. Two further series of *Poems and Ballads* appeared in 1876 and 1889.

swing Form of JAZZ prevalent in the USA during the 1930s and 1940s. It originated in the music of small groups who played a rhythm of four even beats to the bar, as opposed to the two beats to the bar of the New Orleans style. The groups also made more use of soloists, particularly saxophonists. Larger groups, such as those of Duke ELLINGTON and Count Basie, made great use of the new possibilities. Their innovations were taken up by white musicians such as Benny GOODMAN and Glenn MILLER.

Swithin, Saint (d.862) Anglo-Saxon bishop of WINCHESTER from 852. Little is known about his life for certain. He was an adviser to the West Saxon kings Egbert and Ethelwulf. His feast day is 15 July. According to superstition, the weather on St Swithin's Day will remain for the next 40 days.

Switzerland The Swiss Confederation is a small, mountainous, landlocked country in central Europe. The JURA MOUNTAINS lie on the W border with France. The Swiss ALPS make up *c.*60% of the country. Switzerland's highest peak is Monte Rosa, at 4,634m (15,217ft). The plateau contains the cities of ZÜRICH, BASEL, LAUSANNE and BERN, and lakes GENEVA and Constance. **Climate** The climate varies with altitude. The plateau has warm summers and cold, snowy winters. **Vegetation** Grassland covers *c.*30% of the land and arable land *c.*10%. Forests cover *c.*32%. **History and Politics** Originally occupied by Celtic Helvetii people, the region was taken by Romans in 58 BC. Ruled by FRANKS in the 6th century AD, it was later divided between Swabia and Burgundy. United within the HOLY ROMAN EMPIRE, it came under HABSBURG rule in the 13th century. In 1291, the CANTONS Schwyz, Uri and Unterwalden united against the Habsburgs. Traditionally led by William TELL, the Swiss League expanded and defeated the Habsburgs (1386, 1388). The defeat of Emperor MAXIMILIAN in 1499 brought partial independence. Defeated by the French in 1515, the Swiss adopted neutrality. The REFORMATION caused religious divisions in Switzerland, but the confederation survived to achieve formal independence in 1648. The FRENCH REVOLUTIONARY WARS led to the overthrow of the oligarchy and the establishment of the Helvetic Republic (1798–1803). In 1815, the federation was fully re-established. The Congress of VIENNA expanded it to 22 cantons and guaranteed its neutrality. A brief civil war led to the constitution of 1848, turning Switzerland into one federal state. Jura, the 23rd canton, was created in 1979. A referendum (1986) rejected Swiss membership of the UN to avoid compromising its neutrality. European Community membership was similarly rejected (1992). In 1995, the ruling coalition, led by the Christian Democrats, was re-elected. In 1999, Ruth Dreifuss became Switzerland's first woman president. She was succeeded (2000) by Adolf Ogi. **Economy** Despite lacking natural resources, Switzerland is wealthy and industrialized (1995 GDP per capita, US$25,860). Manufactures include chemicals, electrical equipment, machinery, precision instruments, watches and textiles. Livestock raising, notably dairy farming, is the chief agricultural activity. Tourism is important, and Swiss banks attract worldwide investment.

swordfish (broadbill) Marine fish found worldwide in temperate and tropical seas. A food fish, it is silvery-black, dark purple or blue. Its long flattened upper jaw, in the shape of a sword, is one-third of its length and is used to strike at prey. Length: to 4.5m (15ft); weight: 530kg (1,180lb). Family Xiphiidae; species *Xiphias gladius.*

SWITZERLAND
AREA: 41,290sq km (15,942sq mi)
POPULATION: 6,762,000
CAPITAL (POPULATION): Bern (127,000)

sycamore (great maple, false plane) Deciduous tree of the MAPLE family, native to central Europe and W Asia but widely naturalized. It has deeply toothed, five-lobed leaves, greenish-yellow flowers and winged brown fruit. Height: to 33m (110ft). Family Aceraceae; species *Acer pseudoplatanus.*

Sydenham, Thomas (1624–89) English physician, often called the English Hippocrates. He initiated the cooling method of treating SMALLPOX, made a thorough study of epidemics and wrote descriptions of MALARIA and GOUT.

Sydney State capital of New South Wales, SE Australia, on Port Jackson, an inlet on the Pacific Ocean. Sydney is the oldest and largest city, the most important financial, industrial and cultural centre, and the principal port in Australia. The city was founded in 1788 as the first British penal colony in Australia. Industries: shipbuilding, textiles, motor vehicles, oil refining, tourism. The city hosted the summer Olympic Games in 2000. Pop. (1994) 3,738,500.

syllogism Logical argument consisting of three categorical propositions: two premises and a conclusion. It was devised by ARISTOTLE to establish the conditions under which the conclusion of a deductive inference is valid or not valid. A valid conclusion can only come from premises that are logically related to each other. Examples of syllogisms are as follows: All men are mortal; John is a man; therefore John is mortal (valid); All trees have leaves; a daffodil has leaves; therefore a daffodil is a tree (invalid).

symbiosis Relationship between two or more different organisms that is generally mutually advantageous. It is more accurately referred to as MUTUALISM. *See also* PARASITE

symbolism European art and literary movement. Symbolism had its origins in France in the 1880s when it arose as a reaction against the pragmatic REALISM of COURBET and IMPRESSIONISM. Its exponents wanted to express ideas or abstractions rather than simply imitate the visible world. The most powerful tendency in the movement stemmed from GAUGUIN and Émile Bernard (*c.*1888). Another less dynamic trend introduced formal innovations into traditional painting. Its chief exponents were Gustave MOREAU, Odilon REDON and Puvis de Chavannes. Outside France, BURNE-JONES and MUNCH are considered to be symbolists. In literature, the movement included a group of poets active in the 19th century who were followers of VERLAINE and BAUDELAIRE, such as the SYMBOLISTS in France and writers in English, such as POE and SWINBURNE.

symbolists Group of French poets active in the latter part of the 19th century, of whom the most famous were MALLARMÉ, VERLAINE, Corbière, RIMBAUD and Laforgue. Influenced by BAUDELAIRE, they sought to transcend reality as portrayed in the realist novel and to create poetic impressions through suggestion rather than statement. *See also* SYMBOLISM

symmetry In biology, anatomical description of body form or geometrical pattern of a plant or animal. It is used in the classification of living things (TAXONOMY) and to clarify relationships. In mathematics a symmetrical figure is one that has an exact correspondence of shape about a point, line, or plane.

symphonic poem (tone poem) Orchestral piece of the late-Romantic period that describes in music a poem, story or other extra-musical programme. The term was first used by LISZT. *Till Eulenspiegel* and *Also sprach Zarathustra* by Richard STRAUSS are the best-known examples of the genre. *See also* PROGRAMME MUSIC

symphony Large-scale musical work for orchestra. It has evolved steadily since the 18th century, when it received its first classical definition in the works of HAYDN and MOZART. A symphony usually has four movements and, in the classical tradition, has its first movement in SONATA form. The first symphonies were scored almost exclusively for stringed instruments of the violin family, but in the early 19th century the use of brass and woodwind sections had become general. Later composers of symphonies include BEETHOVEN, SCHU-BERT, SCHUMANN, BRAHMS, BRUCKNER, TCHAIKOVSKY, MAHLER, SIBELIUS and SHOSTAKOVICH.

synagogue Place of assembly for Jewish worship, education and cultural development. Synagogues act as communal centres, under the leadership of a RABBI, and house the ARK OF THE COVENANT. The first synagogue buildings date from the 3rd century BC but may go back to the destruction of Solomon's TEMPLE in Jerusalem in 586 BC.

synapse Connection between the nerve ending of one NEURON and the next or between a nerve cell and a muscle. It is the site at which nerve impulses are transmitted using NEUROTRANSMITTERS.

syncline Downward FOLD in rocks. When rock layers fold down into a trough-like form, it is called a syncline. (An upward arch-shaped fold is called an anticline.)

syncopation In music, a contradiction or breach of a regular rhythmic pattern. It is normally produced in two ways, by the momentary introduction of an accent off the regular beat of the rhythm or by placing longer notes on weak beats in a bar.

syncope *See* FAINTING

syndicalism Early 20th-century form of socialism originating in France but also influential in Spain and Italy. It proposed public ownership of the means of production by small worker groups and called for the elimination of central government.

synergism Combined effect of two drugs that is greater than the sum of the effects they would produce if used separately. This synergistic effect is not necessarily beneficial and in some cases may be dangerous.

Synge, John Millington (1871–1909) Irish dramatist and poet who was important in the Irish Literary Renaissance. He was one of the organizers of the ABBEY THE-ATRE in 1904, and his works include *Riders to the Sea* (1904), *The Well of the Saints* (1905) and *The Playboy of the Western World* (1907). *See also* IRISH LITERATURE

synodic period Interval between two successive conjunctions or oppositions with the Sun of a planet or the Moon as seen from the Earth. For the Moon, the synodic period is the time taken for a complete cycle of phases, equalling 29.53 days.

Synoptic Gospels Three of the GOSPELS of the New Testament, those of St MATTHEW, St MARK and St LUKE, which present a common account of the life of JESUS CHRIST. St Mark's Gospel is generally held to have been the model for St Matthew's and St Luke's, although most scholars believe that the latter two have gathered some material from a common source known as "Q", which no longer exists.

synovial fluid Viscous, colourless fluid that lubricates the movable joints between bones. It is secreted by the synovial membrane. Synovial fluid is also found in the

◀ **symbiosis** *Iridomyrmex* ants and the *Myrmecodia* (ant plant) benefit mutually in a symbiotic relationship. The ants feed on the sugary nectar of the plant. This is produced in nectaries (1), which develop at the base of the flower (2) after the petals and sepals have fallen off. The plant benefits from the vital minerals in the ants' defecation and waste materials (3), absorbed through the warty inner surface of the chambers (4). The ant plant is epiphytic, growing suspended from trees in upland rainforests, where the soils are often lacking in nutrients. The mineral nutrients provided by the ants supplement the plant's poor diet. As the plant grows, its stem enlarges and develops cavities that are invaded by the ants (5). These chambers do not interconnect but have separate passages to the outside (6). A complete ant colony soon becomes established in the plant.

bursae, membranous sacs that help to reduce friction in major joints, such as the shoulder, hip or knee.

syntax Branch of grammar that encompasses the body of rules governing the ways in which words are put together to form phrases, clauses and sentences in a language. The word syntax also describes the structure of a sentence produced by a writer or speaker.

synthesizer In music, an electronic instrument capable of producing a wide variety of different sounds, pitches and timbres. The modern instrument was invented by Robert Moog in 1964. Computer technology is now used to control the instrument's different functions, enabling synthesizers to replicate non-electronic sounds.

syphilis Sexually transmitted disease caused by the bacterium *Treponema pallidum*. Untreated, it runs in three stages. The first symptom is often a hard, painless sore on the genitals, appearing usually within a month of infection. Months later, the second stage features a skin rash and fever. The third stage, often many years later, brings the formation of growths and serious involvement of the heart, brain and spinal cord, leading eventually to blindness, insanity and death. The disease is treated successfully with ANTIBIOTICS.

Syracuse (Siracusa) Italian seaport city in Sicily, on the Ionian Sea; capital of Syracuse province. Founded by Corinthian Greek colonists in 734 BC, it prospered and established its own colonies, triumphing over the Carthaginians in 480 BC. It grew to become the most important Hellenic city outside Greece. Industries: tourism, petrochemicals. Pop. (1992) 127,000.

Syria Arab Republic in the Middle East. Syria is divided into two regions. The smaller, densely populated W region comprises a narrow coastal plain and several mountain ranges. The Jabal an Nusayriyah range drops sharply to the Great RIFT VALLEY in the E. In the SW, the Anti-Lebanon range contains Syria's highest peak, Mount Hermon 2,184m (9,232ft). The capital, DAMASCUS, and ALEPPO lie in fertile valleys. Eastern Syria is mainly grassy plain and contains the valley of the EUPHRATES River. In the SE, is the Syrian Desert. **Climate** The coast has a Mediterranean climate, with warm, dry summers and mild, wet winters. To the E, the land becomes drier. **Vegetation** Only 4% of Syria is forested. Farmland covers *c*.30% of Syria, grassland makes up 44%. **History and Politics** Syria's location on the trade routes between Europe, Africa and Asia has made it a desired possession of many rulers. The area, including what is now Lebanon and some of modern-day Jordan, Israel, Saudi Arabia and Iraq, was ruled by the HITTITES and by EGYPT during the 15th–13th centuries BC. Under the PHOENICIANS (13th–10th centuries BC), trading cities on the Mediterranean coast flourished. From the 10th century BC, Syria suffered invasions by ASSYRIANS and Egyptians. The ACHAEMENID empire provided stability. From the 3rd century BC, the SELEUCIDS controlled Syria, often challenged by Egypt. PALMYRA flourished as a city-state. The Romans conquered the region in AD 63. Christianity was introduced via Palestine. When the ROMAN EMPIRE split in the 4th century, Syria came under BYZANTINE rule. Arabs invaded in AD 637, and most of the population converted to Islam. The UMAYYADS and ABBASID dynasties followed. In the 11th century, Syria was a target of the CRUSADES, but at the end of the 12th century, SALADIN triumphed. MONGOL and MAMELUKE rule followed Saladin's death. In 1516, the area became part of the OTTOMAN EMPIRE. European interest in the region grew in the 19th century. During World War 1, Syrian nationalists revolted and helped Britain to defeat the Turks. After the

SYRIA
AREA: 185,180sq km (71,498sq mi)
POPULATION: 17,826,000
CAPITAL (POPULATION): Damascus (2,230,000)

war, Syria, now roughly its present size, became a French mandate territory. It achieved independence in 1944. Syria has supported the Arab cause in the Middle East and has been involved in the ARAB-ISRAELI WARS. In 1967, it lost the GOLAN HEIGHTS to Israel and in 1973 tried unsuccessfully to reclaim them. A UN-patrolled buffer zone was established in the area. It continues to be a source of considerable tension. In 1958, Syria joined the United Arab Republic with Egypt and North Yemen. Egypt's increasing power led to Syrian withdrawal from the UAR and the formation of a Syrian Arab Republic in 1961. The BA'ATH PARTY has been the ruling party since 1963. In 1970, Hafez al-ASSAD took power through a coup and was re-elected in 1971. A new constitution was adopted in 1973, declaring Syria to be a democratic, socialist state. Assad's stable but repressive regime has attracted international criticism. In the GULF WAR (1991), Syria supported the international coalition against Iraq. In 1994, Syria and Israel held talks over the Golan Heights. These talks, part of an attempt to establish a peace settlement for the entire region, received a setback when a right-wing coalition won the 1996 Israeli elections. The election of Ehud BARAK in Israel (1999) led to the withdrawal of Israeli troops from S Lebanon and Syria came under pressure to control Hezbollah forces. **Economy** Syria is a lower-middle-income developing country (1995 GDP per capita, US$5,320). Its main resources are oil, hydroelectricity and its fertile agricultural land. In 1990, crude oil accounted for 45% of exports, but Syria also exports farm products, textiles and phosphates. Agriculture employs 23% of the workforce. The chief crops are cotton and wheat. Syria is rapidly diversifying its industrial base.

Syriac Semitic language belonging to the eastern ARAMAIC group. In ancient times it was spoken in Edessa, now Urfa in SE Turkey. Because of the importance of Edessa as a centre of Christianity in the 2nd century, Syriac was adopted by the neighbouring Aramaic Christians and has been used ever since as a liturgical language by Oriental Christians of the Syrian rite. Syriac literature preserves many translations of Greek Christian texts that have not survived in the original Greek.

Szechwan *See* SICHUAN

Szent-Györgyi, Albert von (1893–1986) US biochemist, b. Hungary. He was awarded the 1937 Nobel Prize for physiology or medicine for his work on biological OXIDATION processes and the isolation of vitamin C.

Szilard, Leo (1898–1964) US physicist, b. Hungary. His early work established the relationship between information transfer and ENTROPY. Szilard devised a means of separating radioactive ISOTOPES, and suggested theories of ageing, recall and memory. He first proposed the nuclear bomb, which was developed during World War 2. In 1942, his research work with Enrico FERMI at the University of Chicago produced the first sustained nuclear CHAIN REACTION based on uranium FISSION.

Szymanowski, Karol (1882–1937) Polish postromantic composer, who did much to promote the nationalist cause in his country. His early works were in the Germanic tradition, but he later composed in a nationalist style. Szymanowski's works include two violin concertos (1917, 1933) and the opera *King Roger* (1926).

T/t, 20th letter of the Roman alphabet, is derived from the Semitic letter taw, *meaning* mark. *The original Roman letter had the same form as the modern T.*

Tabernacle Portable shrine used by the Hebrews for worship during their wanderings in Sinai. It was a rectangular tent covered with a curtain of goat's hair and a layer of animal skins and roofed with a ceiling of linen tapestry decorated with cherubs. Inside the Tabernacle, the space was divided into two rooms: the **outer** room was the Holy Place, and the **inner** was the Holy of Holies, where God was believed to be present. The Holy of Holies contained the ARK OF THE COVENANT, above which was a slab of gold believed to be the throne of God. After the Hebrews settled CANAAN, there was no further need for the Tabernacle. Eventually, its relics were transferred to the TEMPLE built by Solomon in Jerusalem. In the Christian church, a tabernacle is a receptacle in which the Blessed Sacrament is reserved for the EUCHARIST, or a recess used for spiritual contemplation.

Table Mountain Flat-topped central massif in SW Cape Province, South Africa. Often shrouded in cloud, Table Mountain looms over CAPE TOWN. Its summit is 1,083m (3,563ft) high.

table tennis (ping pong™) Table sport played by two or four people who use a rubber-covered, wooden paddle to hit a small, celluloid ball across a net 15cm (6in) high. The table is 2.7m (9ft) long and 1.5m (5ft) wide. After the serve, the ball must bounce only once on the far side of the net. If the ball misses the table or fails to clear the net, the opponent scores a point. The winner is the first player to score 21 points while leading by at least two points.

taboo (tabu) Prohibition of a form of behaviour, object, or word. A thing may be regarded as taboo if it is unclean or if it is sacred. Breaking a taboo is believed to bring supernatural retribution and often brings social ostracism or other punishment. The term originated in Tonga.

Tabriz (formerly Tauris) Capital of East Azerbaijan province, NW Iran, in the foothills of Mount Sahand, and Iran's fourth-largest city. From 1295, the chief administrative centre for the Persian empire, it was occupied by the Ottoman Turks and later held by the Russians. Tabriz's proximity to Turkey and the Commonwealth of Independent States makes it an important trading centre. Manufactured goods: carpets, shoes, soap, textiles. Pop. (1994) 1,166,000.

tachycardia Increase in heart rate beyond the normal. It may occur after exertion or because of excitement or illness, particularly during fever; or it may result from a heart condition.

Tacitus, Cornelius (AD 55–120) Roman historian. His crisp style and reliability make him one of the greatest of ancient historians. His works include a eulogy for his father-in-law, Agricola, governor of Britain. His major works, the *Annals* and *Histories*, exist only in fragmentary form.

tadpole Aquatic larva of a TOAD or FROG; it has a finned tail and gills, and lacks lungs and legs. Tadpoles of most species are herbivores, feeding on algae and other aquatic plants. During METAMORPHOSIS, legs are grown, the tail is reabsorbed, and internal lungs take the place of gills.

Taegu City in S central South Korea; capital of North Kyŏngsang province, and the country's third-largest city. Successfully defended by UN troops during the KOREAN WAR, it is the trading centre for a large apple-growing area. The main industries are textiles, including silk and synthetic fabrics. Pop. (1995) 2,449,000.

tae kwon do Korean martial art. A form of unarmed combat developed over 2,000 years in Korea, it is characterized by high, standing and jump kicks as well as punches. It is practised for sport and spiritual development.

Taft, William Howard (1857–1930) 27th US President (1909–13) and tenth chief justice of the Supreme Court (1921–30). After a distinguished legal career, he gained great credit as governor of the Philippines (1901–04) and entered the cabinet of Theodore ROOSEVELT. In 1908, Taft won the Republican nomination for president. His lack of political experience and his tendency to side with the conservatives in the REPUBLICAN PARTY against the progressives, caused increasing dissension. In 1912, Roosevelt, having failed to regain the presidential nomination, set up his own Progressive Party. With the split in the Republican vote, the Democrat, Woodrow WILSON, won the election. Taft taught at Yale Law School until 1921, when he was appointed chief justice of the Supreme Court. While chief justice, he greatly streamlined the operations of the federal judiciary.

Tagore, Rabindranath (1861–1941) Indian poet and philosopher. He wrote novels, essays, plays and poetic works in colloquial Bengali. His best-known work is *Gitanjali* (1912), a volume of spiritual poetry. In 1913, Tagore became the first Asian writer to be awarded the Nobel Prize for literature. He was knighted in 1915 but renounced the honour after the AMRITSAR massacre (1919).

Tagus (Tajo, Tejo) Longest river on the Iberian peninsula, flowing *c.*1,000km (620mi). It rises in the Sierra de Albarracin in Teruel, E central Spain, flowing generally SW for 785km (488mi), passing through Toledo, to the Spain-Portugal border. It then winds S to drain into the Atlantic at Lisbon. The Tagus estuary is one of the world's finest natural harbours.

Tahiti Island in the S Pacific Ocean in the Windward group of the SOCIETY ISLANDS, the largest in FRENCH POLYNESIA and accounting for more than half its population. Charted in 1767 by the British navigator Samuel Wallis and explored by Captain COOK, it was colonized by France in 1880. Tahiti is mountainous, rising to 2,237m (7,339ft). Its fertile soil yields tropical fruits, copra, sugar cane and vanilla. Industries: tourism, pearl fishing, phosphates. Paul GAUGUIN lived and painted here (1891–93, 1895–1901). Area: 1,058sq km (408sq mi). Pop. (1988) 115,820.

tai chi Neo-Confucian concept of the Supreme Ultimate, the intrinsic energy of the universe (*chi*). The philosophy of tai chi was developed by Chou Tun-i (1017–73) and Chu Hsi (1130–1200). *Tai chi* also refers to the most popular form of exercise in China – a martial arts-based series of slow, flowing movements designed to enhance the effective flow of *Chi* around the body. *See also* CONFUCIANISM; TAOISM

Taine, Hippolyte Adolphe (1828–93) French historian. Taine was associated with the school of philosophy known as POSITIVISM. His early writings were mainly literary studies, including a four-volume *History of English Literature* (1863–64). Influenced by the disasters of the FRANCO-PRUSSIAN WAR, Taine produced his greatest work, a reappraisal of French history, *The Origins of Contemporary France* (1876–93).

Taipei Capital and largest city of Taiwan, at the N end of the island. A major trade centre for tea in the 19th century,

TAIWAN
AREA: 35,760sq km (13,800sq mi)
POPULATION: 22,000,000
CAPITAL (POPULATION): Taipei (2,596,000)

TAJIKISTAN
AREA: 143,100sq km (55,520sq mi)
POPULATION: 7,041,000
CAPITAL (POPULATION): Dushanbe (524,000)

the city was enlarged under Japanese rule (1895–1945) and became the seat of the Chinese Nationalist government in 1949. Industries: textiles, chemicals, fertilizers, metals, machinery. Pop. (1997) 2,569,000.

Taiping Rebellion (1851–64) Revolt in China against the Manchurian QING dynasty. The fighting laid waste to 17 provinces and resulted in more than 20 million casualties. The MANCHUS never recovered their full ability to govern China.

Taiwan (officially the Republic of China) Pacific island, separated from the SE coast of the Chinese mainland by the 160km (100mi) Taiwan Strait. The republic comprises the main island of Taiwan, several islets and the Pescadores group. The terrain is mostly mountainous and forested, and the highest peak is Yu Shan at 3,997m (13,113ft). The climate is semi-tropical and subject to typhoons. In 1590, the Portuguese visited the island and named it Formosa ("beautiful"), but in 1641 the Dutch assumed full control of the island. They, in turn, were forced to relinquish control to the MING dynasty. In 1683, the ruling Chinese QING dynasty captured Taiwan and immigration increased. In 1895, it was ceded to Japan after the first SINO-JAPANESE WAR. Following the 1949 mainland victory of the Chinese Communist Party, the vanquished Nationalist KUOMINTANG government (led by CHIANG KAI-SHEK) and 500,000 troops fled to Taiwan. The new Chinese regime claimed sovereignty over the island, and in 1950 a Chinese invasion was prevented by the US Navy. The Nationalists, with continued US military and financial support, remained resolute. By 1965, the economic success of Taiwan had removed the need for US aid. In 1971, Taiwan lost its seat at the United Nations (UN) to mainland China. In 1975, Chiang Kai-shek died and was succeeded by his son, Chiang Ching-Kuo. In 1979, the US switched diplomatic recognition from TAIPEI to Beijing. In 1987, martial law was lifted. In 1988, Lee Teng-hui became president. He accelerated the pace of liberalization. In 1996, China dispatched missiles close to the Taiwanese coast, reminding the world community of its territorial claims. In March 1996, Lee won the first democratic presidential elections, but was defeated in the 2000 elections by Chen Shui-bian of the pro-independence Democratic Progressive Party, thus ending more than fifty years of Kuomintang rule. **Economy** Agriculture, fishing and forestry are important economic activities, and rice the principal crop. Spectacular economic growth from the mid-1950s was achieved primarily through low-cost, export-led manufacture of textiles, electrical goods, machinery and transport equipment (1992 GDP per capita, US$12,000).

Taiyuan City in NE China; capital of Shanxi province. The region has rich coal and iron-ore deposits, and Taiyuan is a major industrial city with iron and steel, chemical, engineering, and textile industries. Pop. (1994) 1,642,000.

Tajiki Iranian language spoken in Tajikistan and (with some TURKIC elements) in Afghanistan, S Russia, and much of central Asia. Tajiks, the native speakers of the language, constitute a minority of 30% within Tajikistan.

Tajikistan Mountainous republic in SE Central Asia. In the N is the western-most part of the TIAN SHAN range. In the E lie the snow-capped PAMIRS, including KOMMUNIZMA

PIK at 7,495m (24,590ft). The capital, DUSHANBE, lies at the foot of the central Gissar-ALTAI range. In the NW, lies part of the Fergana valley on the ancient route to SAMARKAND. In the SW, a plain extends from Dushanbe to the River Amudarya border with Afghanistan and Uzbekistan. Tajikistan is prone to earthquakes. **Climate** Summers are hot and dry in the lowlands; winters are long and cold in the mountains. Much of Tajikistan is arid, but the SE has heavy snowfalls. **Vegetation** Much of Tajikistan consists of desert or rocky mountain landscapes capped by snow and ice. **History and politics** The Tajiks are descendants of Persians who settled in the area c.2,500 years ago. Alexander the Great conquered the region in the 4th century BC. In the 7th century AD, Tajikistan was conquered by Arabs, who introduced Islam. In the 9th century, it fell to the Persian empire. The Tajik cities of BUKHARA and Samarkand were vital centres of trade and Islamic learning. In the 13th century, Tajikistan was overrun by the Mongol hordes. From the 16th to the 19th century, Uzbeks ruled the area as the khanate of Bukhara. The fragmentation of the region aided Russian conquest from 1868. Following the RUSSIAN REVOLUTION (1917), Tajikistan rebelled against Russian rule. Though Soviet troops annexed N Tajikistan to Turkistan in 1918, the Bukhara emirate held out against the Red Army until 1921. In 1924, Tajikistan became an autonomous part of the republic of UZBEKISTAN. In 1929, Tajikistan achieved full republican status, but Bukhara and Samarkand remained in the republic of Uzbekistan. During the 1930s, vast irrigation schemes greatly increased agricultural land. Many Russians and Uzbeks were settled in Tajikistan. As the pace of reform accelerated in Russia, many Tajiks began to demand independence. In 1989, Tajik replaced Russian as the official language. In 1990, the Tajik parliament declared itself the supreme sovereign body. In 1991, Tajikistan became an independent republic within the COMMONWEALTH OF INDEPENDENT STATES (CIS). In 1992, tension between the new government (consisting mainly of former communists) and an alliance of Islamic and democratic groups spiralled into full civil war. The government called for Russian military assistance, and by 1993 the Islamic-Democratic rebels had retreated into Afghanistan. Imamali Rakhmonov was appointed president. Fighting continued along the Afghan border, and the rebels made frequent incursions into Tajikistan. In 1994, a brief cease-fire enabled elections to take place. Rakhmonov was elected president amid an opposition boycott. In 1995, the civil war resumed, and the Russian air force launched attacks on rebel bases in Afghanistan. In 1995, fresh elections saw the return of the (former communist) People's Party of Tajikistan, amid charges of electoral corruption and another opposition boycott. In 1997, a peace agreement was signed formally ending the five-year civil war. In 1999, Rakhmonov was re-elected and the first multiparty parliamentary elections were held in 2000. **Economy** The poorest former Soviet republic, Tajikistan is a low-income developing country (1995 GDP per capita, US$1,920). It has faced enormous problems in the transition to a market economy. The cost of the civil war devastated its fragile economy. In 1994, Tajikistan ceded much of its economic sovereignty to Russia in return for financial and military assistance. Agriculture is the main activity. Livestock-rearing is important and cotton is the chief product. Tajikistan is rich in resources, such as hydroelectricity, oil, uranium and gold. Aluminium is the major manufactured export. Textiles are an important industry.

Taj Mahal Muslim MAUSOLEUM near AGRA, India, built (1632–54) by the Mogul emperor, SHAH JAHAN, for his favourite wife, Mumtaz Mahal. By far the largest Islamic tomb destined for a woman, it stands in a Persian water garden representing Paradise. With its bulb-shaped dome, inlays of semiprecious stones, and rectangular reflecting pool, it is among the world's most beautiful buildings.

takahe Rare, flightless New Zealand bird, related to the RAIL and gallinule. Turkey-sized, it has a heavy, curved bill, a reddish shield on the forehead, and blue-green plumage. Family Rallidae; species *Notornis mantelli*.

Talbot, William Henry Fox (1800–77) English scientist. Talbot improved on the work of Niepce and DAGUERRE by inventing the first photographic process capable of producing any number of positive prints from an original negative. *See also* PHOTOGRAPHY

talc (hydrous magnesium silicate, $Mg_3Si_4O_{10}(OH)_2$) Sheet silicate mineral. It occurs as rare tabulate crystals in a monoclinic system and as masses. It is used as base for talcum powder and in ceramics. Hardness 1; r.d. 2.6.

Taliban Radical SUNNI political movement in Afghanistan. In 1996, from their headquarters in KANDAHAR, SW Afghanistan, Taliban militia launched themselves on Afghan society, vowing to spread SHARIA (Islamic law) throughout the country. They soon captured Kabul. Taliban's philosophy is drawn from extremist theologians in Pakistan and other Arab countries.

Tallahassee State capital of Florida. First discovered by Europeans in 1539, it was the site of a Spanish mission. Tallahassee became the capital of Florida Territory in 1824. Florida State University (1857) and Florida A & M University (1887) are located here. Industries: chemicals, timber, paper, tourism. Pop. (1992) 130,357.

Talleyrand (-Périgord), Charles Maurice de (1754–1838) French statesman and diplomat. As foreign minister under the DIRECTORY (1797–99), he participated in the coup that brought NAPOLEON to power. In 1807, concerned about the growing power of Napoleon, Talleyrand resigned as foreign minister. In 1814, he negotiated the restoration of the BOURBON monarchy. As foreign minister to LOUIS XVIII, Talleyrand ably represented France at the Congress of VIENNA (1814–15). He was LOUIS PHILIPPE's chief adviser in the July Revolution (1830) and served (1830–34) as his ambassador to Britain.

Tallinn (Talin) Capital and largest city of Estonia, on the Gulf of Finland, opposite Helsinki. Founded in 1219 by the Danes, it became a member of the Hanseatic League (1285). It passed to Sweden in 1561 and was ceded to Russia in 1721. Developed in the 19th century for Russia's Baltic Fleet, it remains a major port and industrial centre. It was badly damaged in World War 2. Industries: machinery, cables, paper, textiles. Pop. (1996) 427,000.

Tallis, Thomas (*c*.1505–85) English composer of church music. In 1575, Elizabeth I granted Tallis and William BYRD a licence to print and publish music; in that year they published the *Cantiones Sacrae*, a set of motets. His church music includes a setting of Lamentations, two masses and a number of anthems. His contrapuntal skill shows in his 40-part motet, *Spem in alium* (*c*.1573).

Talmud Body of Jewish religious and civil laws and learned interpretations of their meanings. Study of the Talmud is central to orthodox JUDAISM. It consists of two elements: the MISHNA and the *Gemara*. The *Mishna* is the written version, completed by *c*.AD 200, of a set of oral laws that were handed down from the time of MOSES (*c*.1200 BC). The **Gemara**, the interpretation and commentary on the Mishna, was completed by *c*.500. The Talmud consists of short passages from the *Mishna* followed by the relevant and extensive part of the *Gemara*.

tamarind Tropical tree native to Asia and Africa. It has divided, feather-like leaves and pale yellow flowers streaked with red. The fruit pulp is used in beverages, food and medicines. Height: 12–24m (40–80ft). Family Fabaceae/Leguminosae; species *Tamarindus indica*.

tamarisk Any of a group of shrubs usually found in semi-arid areas. They are DECIDUOUS and have slender branches covered with blue-green, scale-like leaves and clusters of small, white or pink flowers. Height: to 9.1m (30ft). Family Tamaricaceae; genus *Tamarix*.

Tambo, Oliver (1917–93) South African politician, president (1977–90) of the AFRICAN NATIONAL CONGRESS (ANC). He joined the ANC in 1944. In 1960 Tambo left South Africa to organize the external activities of the ANC. During Nelson MANDELA's long imprisonment, Tambo served first as acting president (1967) then full president of the ANC. On Mandela's release, he relinquished the post. *See also* APARTHEID

tambourine PERCUSSION musical instrument much used by wandering musicians in Europe in the Middle Ages. It comprises a narrow circular frame, made of wood, with a single parchment drumhead and metal jangles attached to the sides.

Tamerlane (1336–1405) (Turkish *Timur Leng*, Timur the Lame) Mongol conqueror, b. Uzbekistan. He claimed descent from GENGHIS KHAN. By 1369, Tamerlane had conquered present-day Turkistan and established SAMARKAND as his capital. He extended his conquests to the region of the GOLDEN HORDE between the Caspian and Black seas. In 1398, Tamerlane invaded NW India and defeated the DELHI SULTANATE. He then turned toward the MAMELUKE empire, capturing Syria and Damascus. In 1402, he captured the Ottoman sultan, Beyazid I, at Angora. His death, at the head of a 200,000-strong invasion force of China, enabled the reopening of the SILK ROAD. His vast empire was divided among the Timurid dynasty.

Tamil Language spoken in S India, chiefly in the state of Tamil Nadu on the E coast, by up to 50 million people. In addition, there are *c*.3 million speakers in N SRI LANKA and *c*.1 million distributed throughout Malaysia, Singapore, Fiji, Mauritius and Guyana.

Tamil Tigers Militant TAMIL group in SRI LANKA that seeks independence from the SINHALESE majority. Located mainly in the N and E of the island, the 3 million Tamils are Hindus, unlike the Buddhist Sinhalese. In the 1980s, the Tamil Tigers embarked on a campaign of civil disobedience and terrorism. In 1986, autonomy for the Tamils was agreed by India and Sri Lanka, but no date fixed. In 1987, the Indian army was sent to restore order but withdrew in 1990, having failed to stop the violence.

Tammany Hall DEMOCRATIC PARTY organization in New York City, USA. It evolved from the fraternal and patriotic order of St Tammany, founded in 1789 and rapidly became the focal point of resistance to the Federal Party. By 1865, Tammany Hall, under William "Boss" Tweed, had become the most important voice of the Democratic Party in the city and was synonymous with the organized corruption of urban politics.

tanager Small, brightly coloured, American forest bird with a cone-shaped bill. It feeds on insects and fruit. The scarlet tanager (*Piranga olivacea*) of E North America has black on its wings and tail. Family Emberizidae.

T'ang (Tang) Chinese imperial dynasty (618–907). The early period was a golden age of China, when it was by far the largest, richest and culturally most accomplished society in the world. T'ang armies carried Chinese authority to Afghanistan, Tibet and Korea. Towns grew as trade expanded, new ideas and foreign influences were freely admitted, and the arts flourished. During the 8th century the dynasty was submerged in civil conflict.

Tanganyika, Lake Second-largest lake in Africa and the second-deepest freshwater lake in the world. It lies in E central Africa on the borders of Tanzania, Zaïre, Zambia and Burundi, in the RIFT VALLEY. Area: 32,893sq km (12,700sq mi). Depth: 1,437m (4,715ft).

tangent In TRIGONOMETRY, the ratio between the length of the sides opposite and adjacent to an acute angle within a right-angle triangle.

Tangier (Tanger) Port on the Strait of Gibraltar, N Morocco. An ancient Greek, Phoenician and then Roman port, later occupied by Moors, it was taken by the Portuguese in 1471. It was passed to England (1662), but the English abandoned it to the sultan of Morocco in 1684. Under international control from 1904 to 1956 (except during World War 2), the city then became part of Morocco. Industries: rugs, pottery, shipping, fishing, tourism. Pop. (1993) 307,000.

tango Ballroom dance originating in Buenos Aires, Argentina, in the late 19th century. Developed from the *milonga*, it was a ballroom favourite in Europe and the USA by 1915. It is characterized by quick, long strides and rapid reversals of direction on the balls of the feet.

Tanizaki, Junichiro (1886–1965) Japanese novelist and dramatist. He was influenced by classical JAPAN-ESE LITERATURE and by Charles BAUDELAIRE. His novels include *Some Prefer Nettles* (1928–29) and *The Makioka Sisters* (1943–48).

tank Tracked, armoured vehicle mounting a single primary weapon, usually an artillery piece, and one or more machine guns. Modern tanks have an enclosed, fully revolving turret and are heavily armoured; main battle tanks weigh from 35 to 50 tonnes and usually have a crew of four. Developed in great secrecy by the British during World War 1, tanks were first employed at the Battle of the Somme (1916).

tannin (tannic acid) Any of a group of complex organic compounds derived from tree bark, roots and galls, fruit, tea and coffee. Tannin is used in tanning to cure hides and make leather, in inks and dyes, and as an astringent in medicine.

tansy Any of several mostly perennial plants characterized by fern-like, aromatic leaves and clusters of yellow, button-like flower heads. *Tanacetum vulgare*, native to Eurasia, is a common weed in North America. Height: to 90cm (3ft). Family Asteraceae/Compositae.

tantalum (symbol Ta) Rare, lustrous, blue-grey metallic element. Its chief ore is columbite-tantalite. Hard but malleable, tantalum is used as a wire and in electrical components, chemical equipment and medical instruments. Properties: at.no. 73; r.a.m. 180.948; r.d. 16.6; m.p. 2,996°C (5,425°F); b.p. 5,425°C (9,797°F); most common isotope Ta^{181} (99.988%).

tantrism Collective term for religious systems within BUDDHISM, JAINISM and HINDUISM that are based on esoteric practices recorded in sacred texts called tantras. For Hindus and Jains, the tantras are post-Vedic texts that give instruction on how to fulfil worldly (sexual) desires and attain spiritual experiences. The texts contain magic spells and MANTRAS and give instructions on YOGA and meditative techniques for purifying and controlling the

TANZANIA
AREA: 945,090sq km (364,899sq mi)
POPULATION: 39,639,000
CAPITAL (POPULATION): Dodoma (203,833)

body and mind. For Buddhists, the tantras are a set of writings attributed to BUDDHA explaining how the believer may attain enlightenment. *See also* VEDAS

Tanzania Republic in E Africa. Tanzania consists of the mainland republic of Tanganyika and the island republic of ZANZIBAR. A narrow plain borders the Indian Ocean and includes the largest city, DAR ES SALAAM. The interior is dominated by a plateau between 900 and 1,500m (2,950–4,900ft). The capital, DODOMA, lies in the centre of Tanzania. The plateau is broken by the Great RIFT VALLEY, the W arm of which contains Lake TANGANYIKA. The E arm runs through central Tanzania to meet the W arm near Lake MALAWI (Nyasa). The Serengeti Plain lies on the E shore of Lake VICTORIA. In the NE lies Africa's highest peak, Mount KILIMANJARO, at 5,896m (19,344ft). **Climate** The coastal region is hot and humid, with heavy rainfall in April and May. The plateau and mountains are much less humid. Mount Kilimanjaro is permanently snow-covered. **Vegetation** Mangrove swamps and palm groves line the coast. The plateau is vast, open savanna grass or woodland (*miombo*). Tanzania's rich wildlife is protected in national parks, which cover more than 12% of the land. Only 5% of land is cultivated. **History and politics** Dr Louis LEAKEY discovered 1.75 million year-old fossils of *Homo habilis* in OLDUVAI GORGE. Around 2,000 years ago, Arabs, Persians and Chinese probably traded with coastal settlements. In 1498, Vasco da Gama became the first European to land on the Tanzanian coast. For the next 200 years, the Portuguese controlled coastal trade. In 1698, the Portuguese were expelled with the help of Omani Arabs. During the 18th century, Zanzibar was the principal centre of the E African ivory and slave trade. In 1841, the sultan moved his capital to Zanzibar. The interior of Tanganyika was opened up by new caravan routes bringing slaves and ivory to the coast for transshipment. In the European scramble for Africa, Tanganyika was subsumed into German East Africa (1887), and the sultanate of Zanzibar became a British protectorate (1890). Resistance to German colonial rule was fierce. The Germans established plantations, built railroads, and missionaries encouraged the spread of Christianity. During World War 1, British and Belgian troops occupied German East Africa (1916), and in 1919 Tanganyika became a British mandate. The British ruled indirectly, via local leaders. In 1961, Tanganyika became the first East African state to gain independence. Julius NYERERE became the first post-colonial president. In 1963, Zanzibar gained independence, and in 1964 Tanganyika and Zanzibar merged to form Tanzania, though Zanzibar retained economic sovereignty. In 1967, Nyerere issued the Arusha Declaration, an outline of his self-help (*ujamaa*) form of socialism and egalitarianism. Despite promises of decentralization, Tanzania became a one-party state. In 1977, Tanganyika and Zanzibar's ruling parties merged to form the Party of the Revolution (CCM). In 1978, Uganda occupied N Tanzania. In 1979, Tanzanian and Ugandan rebels staged a counter-attack and overthrew the Ugandan president Idi AMIN. In 1985, Nyerere retired and was succeeded by Ali Hassan Mwinyi. In 1992, Mwinyi endorsed the principle of multiparty elections. In 1995, Benjamin Mkapa became the first president to be elected in a multiparty system. In

1997, after a prolonged drought, he declared a state of famine. Mkapa was re-elected in 2000. **Economy** Tanzania is one of the world's poorest countries (1995 GDP per capita, US$640). Agriculture employs 85% of the workforce, mainly at subsistence level. Tanganyika's main export crops are coffee, cotton, tea and tobacco; Zanzibar is the world's largest producer of cloves. Diamonds are the principal mineral resource.

Tao Ch'ien (365–427) Chinese poet, one of the greatest of the Chinese tradition. His simple style distinguished his work from the ornateness of his contemporaries. His verse, which has a predominantly Taoist outlook, often extols the pleasures of nature and wine. *See also* TAOISM

Taoism Chinese philosophy and religion considered as being next to CONFUCIANISM in importance. Taoist philosophy is traced to a 6th-century BC classic of LAO TZU, the *Tao Te Ching*. The work's recurrent theme is the *Tao* (way or path). To follow the *Tao* is to follow the path leading to self-realization. *Te* (virtue) and *ch'i* (energy) represent the goal of effortless action. Taoist ethics emphasize patience, simplicity and the harmony of nature, achieved through the proper balance of YIN AND YANG (male and female principles). As a religion, Taoism dates from the time of Chang Tao-ling, who organized a group of followers in AD 142. *See also* BOOK OF CHANGES; TAI CHI

tape, magnetic Thin strip of plastic, coated on one side with a layer of iron or chromium oxide, used in audio and video TAPE RECORDERS and computers. During SOUND RECORDING, the oxide layer is magnetized by the recording head in a pattern corresponding to the input signal. During playback, the magnetized oxide particles induce an electric current almost identical to the one that produced them.

tape recorder Device which records and plays back sound on magnetically treated TAPE. Sound is transformed into electric current and fed to a TRANSDUCER, which converts it into the magnetic variations that magnetize the particles on the treated tape. *See also* DIGITAL AUDIO TAPE (DAT); MICROPHONE; SOUND RECORDING

tapestry Hand-woven, plain-weave fabric. Used for wall decoration and hangings, tapestry design is an ancient craft and a few fragments survive from 15th-century BC Egypt. The first great French woollen tapestry came from Arras in the 14th century AD. The most famous designs originated from the GOBELINS factory, Paris.

tapeworm Parasite of the genus *Taenia* that colonizes the intestines of vertebrates, including human beings. Caught from eating raw or under-cooked meat, it may cause serious disease.

tapioca *See* CASSAVA

tapir Any of several species of nocturnal, plant-eating, hoofed mammals native to forests of tropical South America and Malaysia. The tapir has a large head, a long, flexible snout, a heavy body, short legs and a tiny tail. Length: to 2.5m (7.5ft). Family Tapiridae; genus *Tapirus*.

tar Black or dark brown, complex liquid mixture of HYDROCARBON compounds, derived from wood, coal, and other organic materials. Tar, from PETROLEUM oil, is a major source of hydrocarbons for the synthesis of pharmaceuticals, pesticides and plastics; cruder tar compounds, such as pitch, are used for road surfacing and protecting lumber against rot and pests. Wood tar yields creosote and paraffin.

Tarantino, Quentin (1963–) US film director, screenwriter and actor. His debut feature, *Reservoir Dogs* (1991), established a reputation for controversial, violent and discursive films. After writing the script for *True Romance* (1993), Tarantino made *Pulp Fiction* (1994). A cult hit, featuring a cameo appearance from Tarantino, it

carried references to pop culture and film classics. Other films include *Jackie Brown* (1997).

tarantula Large, hairy wolf spider of S Europe, once thought to inflict a deadly bite that would cause madness. It spins no web, but chases and pounces on its prey. Length of body: to 2.5cm (1in). Family Lycosidae; species *Lycosa tarentula*. The name is also applied to the sluggish, dark, hairy spiders of SW USA, Mexico, and South America. Many species burrow and feed on insects. Length of body: to 7.5cm (3in). Family Theraphosidae; genera *Aphonopelma* and *Eurypelma*.

Tarawa Town on an atoll of the same name in the W Pacific Ocean, capital of KIRIBATI. Located in the N central part of the group, it is the main trade centre for the islands. Exports include copra and fish. Pop. (1990) 29,000.

tariff Tax placed on imports, calculated either as a percentage of the value of the item (ad valorem tariff) or per unit (specific duty). Tariffs may be used to discourage the import of certain types of goods or to adjust for price differentials in order to allow the home country's products to be competitive.

Tarim Basin Basin in XINJIANG region, NW China, between the TIAN SHAN and Kunlun mountain ranges. The Taklamakan Desert covers most of the region. The Turfan Depression, China's lowest point, at 154m (505ft), is in the extreme E. The River Tarim is 2,027km (1,260 mi) long; formed by the confluence of the rivers Kashgar and Yarkand, it flows E then SE into the basin.

taro Large, tropical plant native to the Pacific Islands and SE Asia and cultivated in other parts of the world for its edible, tuberous root. Family Araceae; species *Colocasia esculenta*. *See also* LILY

tarot Pack of 78 cards originating in their present form in 14th-century Italy. The cards are in two groups: the major arcana and the minor arcana. All 22 cards of the major arcana are pictorial, numbered and captioned, and are mainly used today by astrologers and fortune-tellers. The minor arcana's 56 cards are in four suits, each numbered ace to ten plus four captioned court cards.

tarpon Tropical, marine game fish. Blue and bright silver, it has a long, forked tail. Length: to 180cm (6ft); weight: to 150kg (300lb). Species include the small Pacific *Megalops cyprinoides* and the large Atlantic *M. atlanticus*.

tarragon Perennial plant with liquorice-flavoured leaves used as a culinary HERB. Family Asteraceae/Compositae; species *Artemisia dracunculus*.

tarsier Any of several species of nocturnal PRIMATES of Indonesia. They are small, squat animals with large eyes, long tails and monkey-like hands and feet. Family Tarsiidae; genus *Tarsius*.

tartan Cloth, usually woollen, with a pattern of stripes crossing at right angles. The crossbars are of different colours and widths, often on a red or green background. Tartan is associated mainly with the Highlands of Scotland. Most Scottish clans have their own, unique tartan patterns.

◀ **tarantula** The bite of the tarantula (*Aphonopelma* sp.) is not, in fact, dangerous to humans, though it is powerful enough to kill small birds, amphibians or mice. Found in SW USA and Central America, the body can be up to 7.5cm (3in) long and, including the legs, up to 25cm (10in) across.

Tartars *See* TATARS

Tashkent Largest city and capital of Uzbekistan, in the Tashkent oasis in the foothills of the TIAN SHAN mountains, watered by the River Chirchik. Ruled by the Arabs between the 8th and 11th centuries, the city was captured by Tamerlane (1361) and by the Russians in 1865. The modern city is a terminus for road, rail and air routes. Industries: textiles, chemicals, mining machinery, paper, porcelain, clothing, leather. Pop. (1996) 2,103,000.

Tasman, Abel Janszoon (1603–59) Dutch maritime explorer who made many discoveries in the Pacific. On his voyage of 1642–43 he discovered Tasmania. Tasman reached New Zealand but was attacked by Maoris in Golden Bay. He landed on Tonga and Fiji and sailed along the N coast of New Ireland. Although he circumnavigated Australia, he never sighted the mainland coast.

Tasmania Island state of Australia, separated from Victoria by the Bass Strait. The chief cities are HOBART, the state capital in the S, and Launceston in the N. Tasmania is mountainous and forested, with a temperate maritime climate. The first European discovery was made by Abel TASMAN in 1642 and it was named Van Diemen's Land. In 1777, Captain COOK visited it and claimed it for the British, who established a penal colony there. In 1825, Tasmania became a separate colony, and it was federated as a state of the Commonwealth of Australia in 1901. Mineral deposits include copper, tin and zinc. The development of hydroelectric power has stimulated the growth of manufacturing. Industries: metallurgy, textiles. Area: 68,332sq km (26,383sq mi). Pop. (1991) 452,837.

Tasmanian devil Carnivorous MARSUPIAL with a bear-like appearance, found only in the forest and scrub of Tasmania. It feeds mainly on a wide variety of animal food, including carrion. Length: to 80cm (31in). Species *Sarcophilus harrisii*.

Tasmanian wolf (thylacine) Largest carnivorous marsupial. It probably became extinct on the mainland of Australia because of relentless hunting, although a few specimens are believed to have survived in forested areas of Tasmania. It has a wolf-like appearance, but its coat is marked with transverse dark stripes on the back, hindquarters and tail. Species *Thylacinus cynocephalus*.

TASS (acronym for **T**elegrafnoye **A**gentsvo **S**ovyetskovo **S**oyuza) NEWS AGENCY of the former Soviet Union. Affiliated with press agencies around the world, it was one of the major news services used by the Western press.

Tasso, Torquato (1544–95) Italian poet and prose writer. A member of the court at Ferrara from 1565, his masterpiece, *Jerusalem Delivered* (1575), a poetic epic on the First Crusade, became a model for later writers.

▲ **Tasmanian devil** The Tasmanian devil (*Sarcophilus harrisii*) was once found on the mainland of s Australia but is now confined to remote parts of the island of Tasmania. A nocturnal marsupial, it preys on a variety of animals as well as scavenging. Very strong for its size, it is sometimes smaller than its prey.

taste One of the five SENSES responding to the chemical constituents of anything placed in the mouth. In human beings the taste buds of the TONGUE differentiate four qualities: sweetness, saltiness, bitterness and sourness.

Tatar Republic Autonomous region in the Russian Federation populated mainly by the TATARS. Tatar nationalism has its origins in the Crimean Autonomous Socialist Republic, founded in 1921. The Republic was dissolved and the entire population deported by Stalin in 1945. After the breakup of the Soviet Union in 1991, many of the 300–400,000 exiled Tatars began to return to the Crimea.

Tatars (Tartars) Turkic-speaking people of central Asia. In medieval Europe the name Tatar was given to many different Asiatic invaders. True Tatars originated in E Siberia. They were converted to Islam in the 14th century, and became divided into two groups, one in S Siberia, who came under Russian rule, the other in the Crimea, which was part of the Ottoman Empire until annexed by Russia in 1783.

Tate Gallery UK national collection of modern art. The gallery's main building at Millbank was constructed in 1897. It started as a collection of British painting and sculpture, which now ranges from the mid-16th century to the present day. A large extension was added in 1979, and in 1987 the Clore Gallery opened, containing the TURNER Bequest. There are Tate galleries in Liverpool and St Ives, Cornwall. In 2000, the Tate Gallery of Modern Art opened in the refurbished Bankside Power Station, s London. Tate Modern houses the modern, international collection.

Tati, Jacques (1908–82) French film director and actor , b. Jacques Tatischeff. His debut feature was *Jour de Fête* (1949). Tati's distinctive style of whimsical, visual humour is most apparent in *Monsieur Hulot's Holiday* (1953). He won an Academy Award for best foreign language film for *Mon Oncle* (1958). Other films include *Playtime* (1968) and *Traffic* (1971).

Tatlin, Vladimir Evgrafovitch (1885–1953) Russian sculptor. In 1913, influenced by CUBISM and FUTURISM, he instigated the ABSTRACT ART style known as CONSTRUCTIVISM. Tatlin used industrial materials such as metal, tin and glass in his work. He is celebrated for his *Reliefs*. These were innovative, three-dimensional constructions that removed pictorial illusion.

Tatum, Art (Arthur) (1910–56) US jazz pianist. Almost blind since birth, he established a standard for solo jazz piano technique. Tatum made his first recording in 1932. His reputation for technical virtuosity has endured.

Taurus (the Bull) In astronomy, northern constellation on the ecliptic between Aries and Gemini. It contains the Pleiades and Hyades stellar clusters and the Crab Nebula. The brightest star is the first-magnitude Alpha Tauri (Aldebaran).

Taverner, John (*c.*1490–1545) English composer. He composed mostly church music, notably masses and motets. His six-voice masses are complex contrapuntal structures; the smaller-scale masses are in a simpler, more restrained style. *See also* COUNTERPOINT

Tavener, John Kenneth (1944–) English composer. He achieved early success with his biblical cantata *The Whale* (1966) and has continued to compose works that are religious in character and inspiration. The opera *Thérèse* (1973–76) is a fine example of his early style. His conversion to the Eastern Orthodox Church (1977) was accompanied by a move towards a more austere musical style. *The Protecting Veil* (1987), for cello and orchestra, was inspired by a feast of the Orthodox Church.

taxation Compulsory money payments of various kinds made by members of a civil society to supply the expenditure of public authorities. Taxes are levied both on individuals and on corporations and are of two chief kinds, direct and indirect. **Direct** taxes are levied on income. **Indirect** taxes are levied on commodities and services. The fundamental purpose of taxation is to defray government expenditure on defence, social services, administration and the repayment of public debts. Taxation may also be used to reduce the inequality of income and wealth in a community; changing the rate of income tax can either reduce or increase the purchasing power of consumers by altering the level of disposable income. Indirect taxes can check the flow of imports or exports in order to alter the balance of trade.

taxonomy Organization of plants, animals and other organisms into categories based on similarities of genetic sequences, appearance, structure or evolution. The categories, ranging from the most inclusive to the exclusive, are: KINGDOM, PHYLUM, class, ORDER, FAMILY, GENUS, SPECIES, and sometimes variety. In some categories there are also sub-phyla, sub-families and so on. Ancient and extinct animals and plants are included in detailed classifications. *See also* PHYLOGENETICS; PLANT CLASSIFICATION

Tay River in central Scotland, rising in the Grampians and flowing SE to enter the North Sea through the Firth of Tay near Dundee. At 193km (120mi) it is the longest river in Scotland and has the largest drainage basin, 6,200sq km (2,400sq mi) in area. The Tay Bridge (1883–88) crosses the firth at Dundee.

Taylor, Elizabeth (1932–) US film actress, b. England. She became a child star in *National Velvet* (1944). Taylor's early mature roles include *A Place in the Sun* (1951) and *Cat on a Hot Tin Roof* (1958). She won two Academy Awards for best supporting actress in *Butterfield 8* (1960) and *Who's Afraid of Virginia Woolf?* (1966). Taylor has been married eight times, twice to Richard BURTON. She is an active campaigner for AIDS charities. Other films include *Raintree County* (1957), *Suddenly Last Summer* (1959) and *Cleopatra* (1963).

Taylor, Frederick Winslow (1856–1915) US industrial engineer who was known as the father of scientific management. Taylor developed management methods for many industries, especially steel mills.

Taylor, Zachary (1784–1850) 12th US President (1849–50). A soldier with little formal education, he fought in the WAR OF 1812. In 1845 Taylor was ordered to occupy Texas, recently annexed, which set off the MEXICAN WAR. He emerged from the war as a popular hero. Taylor won the Whig nomination for president and the subsequent election (1848) but died suddenly after only 16 months in office.

Tay Sachs disease Rare hereditary disorder causing an enzyme deficiency that results in an accumulation of fatty material in the brain. It leads to mental retardation, blindness, and death in infancy. The defective gene most commonly occurs in people of E European Jewish descent.

Tayside Region in E Scotland, bounded N and W by the Grampians and E by the North Sea. The capital is DUNDEE, and other major cities include Perth. The N of the region is mountainous and the S is low-lying farmland. It is drained by the rivers Tay, Isla, Earn, South Esk and Ericht. The economy is primarily agricultural, the major products being beef and dairy products. Area: 2,896sq mi (7,502sq km). Pop. (1991) 383,848.

Tbilisi (Tiflis) Largest city and capital of Georgia, on the upper River Kura. Founded in the 5th century AD, it was ruled successively by the Persians, Byzantines, Arabs, Mongols and Turks before coming under Russian rule in 1801. Its importance lies in its location on the trade route between the Black Sea and Caspian Sea. It is now the administrative and economic focus of modern Transcaucasia. Industries: chemicals, petroleum products, locomotives, electrical equipment, beer, wine, whiskey. Pop. (1994) 1,253,000.

Tchaikovsky, Peter Ilyich (1840–93) Russian composer. His gift for melody and expressiveness is apparent in all his works, which include nine operas, four concertos, six symphonies, three ballets and overtures. Tchaikovsky's popular ballets include *Swan Lake* (1876), *The Sleeping Beauty* (1889) and *The Nutcracker* (1892). His operas include *Eugene Onegin* (1879) and *The Queen of Spades* (1890). Other famous works include the First Piano Concerto (1875), the *1812* overture (1880) and the sixth (*Pathétique*) symphony (1893).

tea Family of trees and shrubs with leathery, undivided leaves and five-petalled blossoms. Among 500 species is *Camellia sinensis*, the commercial source of tea. Cultivated in moist, tropical regions, tea plants can reach 9m (30ft) in height but are kept low by frequent picking of the young shoots for tea leaves. The leaves are dried immediately to produce green tea and are fermented before drying for black tea. Family Theaceae.

teaching methods Varying ways of conducting instruction. Different techniques exist to convey instructional material, for example using textbooks, COMPUTER-aided instruction or AUDIO-VISUAL AIDS. Varying approaches to teaching and different teacher styles include lecturing, discussion, small-group instruction and experimental teaching. *See also* EDUCATION; LEARNING; individual educational theorists

teak Tree, native to S India, Burma and Indonesia, valued for its hard, yellowish-brown wood. Teak wood is water-resistant and takes a high polish; it is widely used for furniture and in shipbuilding. Height: 45m (150ft). Family Verbenaceae; species *Tectona grandis*.

teal Small, widely distributed river duck; many species have bright plumage. Teal dabble for food from the surface of the water. Family Anatidae, genus *Anas*.

tear gas Chemical compound known as a lachrymator, a gas or aerosol that causes an excessive flow of tears. It blinds and incapacitates temporarily without causing permanent injury.

tears Salty fluid secreted by glands that moistens the surface of the eye. It cleanses and disinfects the surface of the eye and also brings nutrients to the CORNEA.

teasel Any of several species of plants that grow in Europe, the Middle East and the USA. They are prickly plants with cup-like leaf bases that trap water. Species include fuller's teasel, whose purple flowers heads were used for carding wool. Family Dipsacaceae.

technetium (symbol Tc) Silver-grey, radioactive metallic element, one of the TRANSITION ELEMENTS. Technetium is found in the FISSION products of URANIUM and is present in some stars. It is used in radioactive tracer studies. There are 16 known isotopes. Properties: at.no. 43; r.a.m. 98.9062; r.d. 11.5; m.p. 2,172°C (3,942°F); b.p. 4,877°C (8,811°F); most stable isotope Tc^{99} (half-life 2.6 × 10^6 years).

Technicolor Trade name of the colour film process still used in the majority of motion pictures. A primitive Technicolor was first seen in 1917, and in 1933 Walt DISNEY used three-colour Technicolor for the animated film, *Flowers and Trees*. *See also* CINEMA

technology Systematic study of the methods and techniques employed in industry, research, agriculture and commerce. More often the term is used to describe the practical application of scientific discoveries to industry.

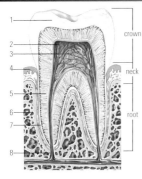

Key
1 enamel
2 capillaries, nerves, lymphatics
3 pulp
4 gum
5 dentine
6 jaw
7 cementum
8 root canal

crown

neck

root

▲ **teeth** A human tooth consists of three parts – the crown, neck and root. The crown is made up of a dense mineral, enamel, surrounding the hard dentine, which has a soft centre – the pulp; the pulp is filled with blood vessels, lymphatics, and nerves, which reach it through the root canal. The neck adheres to the gum, and the root penetrates the bone, where it is held in place by a ligament and cementum.

tectonics Deformation within the Earth's CRUST and the geological structures produced by deformation, including folds and faults. *See also* PLATE TECTONICS

Tecumseh (1768–1813) Native American leader. A SHAWNEE chief, he worked with his brother, known as the Prophet, to unite the Native Americans of the West and resist white expansion. After the Prophet's defeat, Tecumseh joined the British in the WAR OF 1812. He led 2,000 warriors in several battles and was killed in Upper Canada.

teeth Hard, bone-like structures embedded in the jaws of vertebrates, used for chewing food, defence, or other purposes. Mammalian teeth have an outer layer of hard enamel. A middle layer consists of dentine, a bone-like substance capable of regeneration. A tooth's core contains pulp, which is softer and has a blood supply and nerves. *See also* CARIES; DENTITION

Teflon *See* POLYTETRAFLUOROETHYLENE (PTFE)

Tegucigalpa Largest city and capital of HONDURAS, in the central Cordilleras. Founded in the 16th century as a mining town, it became capital in 1880. Industries: sugar, textiles, chemicals, cigarettes. Pop. (1995) 814,000.

Tehran Capital of Iran, *c*.100km (65mi) S of the Caspian Sea, in a strategic position on the edge of the plains and in the foothills of the country's highest mountains. It replaced ISFAHAN as the capital of Persia in 1788. Muhammad Reza PAHLAVI demolished the old fortifications and established a planned city. Tehran is now the industrial, commercial, administrative and cultural centre of the country. Industries: carpets, textiles, chemicals. Pop. (1994) 6,750,000.

Tehran Conference (1943) Meeting in Tehran of the British, American and US leaders (Winston CHURCHILL, Joseph STALIN and Franklin D. ROOSEVELT) during World War 2. It was the first meeting of the "Big Three."

Teilhard de Chardin, Pierre (1881–1955) French JESUIT philosopher and palaeontologist. He worked in China (1923–46) and shared in the discovery of Peking Man (a fossilized Stone-Age human). His philsosophical works, such as *The Phenomenon of Man* (1955), attempt to reconcile scientific views of evolution with Christian faith. His ideas were considered unorthodox by the church and were only published posthumously.

Te Kanawa, Dame Kiri (1948–) New Zealand opera singer of Maori origin. She first attracted attention in the role of the Countess in Mozart's *The Marriage of Figaro* at the Royal Opera House, London. In 1981, Te Kanawa sang at the wedding of Prince Charles and Lady Diana Spencer. She was made a dame in 1982.

tektite Dark, glassy objects, ranging in diameter from 20 micrometers (0.0008in) to 2mm (0.08in) (microtektites) and larger (to 10cm/4in), believed to be of either lunar origin or formed from liquefied rock during meteorite impact on Earth. They occur in limited areas, called strewn-fields, on continents and ocean floors.

Tel Aviv (Tel Aviv-Jaffa) City and port in Israel, on the Mediterranean Sea, *c*.50km (30mi) W of Jerusalem. The business, cultural, communications, and tourist centre of Israel, it was founded in 1909 as a suburb of the port of Jaffa. During the British administration of Palestine (1923–48), the town grew rapidly as Jews fled persecution in Europe. It served as the seat of the transitional government and legislature of the new state of Israel (1948–49), until the capital was moved to JERUSALEM. In 1950, it was merged with Jaffa. Industries: construction, textiles, clothing. Pop. (1994) 355,200.

telecommunications Technology involved in the sending of information over a distance. The information comes in a variety of forms, such as sounds, printed words or images. The sending is achieved through TELEGRAPH, TELEPHONE or RADIO, and the medium may be wires or electromagnetic (radio) waves, or a combination of the two. There are two basic types of message: DIGITAL SIGNALS, in which the message is converted into simple, coded pulses and then sent (as in MORSE code); and ANALOGUE SIGNALS, in which the message – for example, a human voice – is converted into a series of electrical pulses that are similar in wave form to the MODULATIONS of the original message. *See also* FAX; SATELLITE; ARTIFICIAL

telegraph Any communications system that transmits and receives visible or audible coded signals over a distance. The first, optical, telegraphs were forms of semaphore. Credit for the electric telegraph and its code is generally given to Samuel MORSE, who in 1844 inaugurated the first public line between Washington and Baltimore, USA. In 1866 the first permanently successful telegraph cable was laid across the Atlantic, and in 1875 Thomas EDISON invented a method of transmitting several messages simultaneously over the same wire.

Telemann, Georg Philipp (1681–1767) German composer. He wrote more than 40 operas, 600 overtures, and 44 settings of the Passion. His church music, of more historical importance than his operas, shows his technical mastery.

teleology Explanation of the universe, of natural phenomena, or of biological behaviour (including human conduct) by reference to an end or purpose achieved or thought to be achieved by the thing being explained. Since the advent of modern science in the 17th century, things tend to be explained as having been caused by earlier events. This cause-and-effect approach is known as **efficient causation**. In teleology, this way of thinking is reversed in an approach called **final causation**, which explains that things have developed the way they have in order to achieve the effect we now perceive or experience. In the 18th century, William Paley (1743–1805) applied a form of teleology to biological processes, explaining biological organisms as complex and ingenious machines devised by an intelligent being specifically to act in the way that they do. As a theory of morality, teleological ETHICS derives the concept of moral duty or obligation from what is good as a goal or aim to be achieved.

telepathy Form of EXTRASENSORY PERCEPTION (ESP) involving the transmission and reception of thoughts without using the usual sensory channels. Such transference has never been conclusively proved, although claims to telepathy have been extensively investigated.

telephone Instrument that communicates speech sounds over a distance by means of wires or microwaves. In 1876, Alexander Graham BELL invented the prototype that employed a diaphragm of soft iron that vibrated to sound waves. These vibrations caused disturbances in the MAGNETIC FIELD of a nearby bar magnet, causing an electric current of fluctuating intensity in the copper wire wrapped around the magnet. This current could be transmitted along wires to a distant identical device that reversed the process to reproduce audible sound. Later improvements separated the transmitter from the receiver and replaced the bar magnet with batteries. *See also* MOBILE TELEPHONE

telephoto lens CAMERA lens with a long focal length. A true telephoto LENS has a focal length longer than the physical length of the lens, as opposed to a long-focus lens, in which the focal length is equal to the physical length. For a 35mm camera, any lens with a focal length of more than *c*.80mm may be regarded as a telephoto lens. For larger-format cameras, the focal length may be as much as 1,000mm. *See also* PHOTOGRAPHY

telescope Instrument for enlarging a distant object or studying ELECTROMAGNETIC RADIATION from a distant source. **Optical** telescopes can use LENSES (refracting telescopes) or mirrors (reflecting telescopes); **catadioptric** telescopes use both in combination. The lens or mirror is the telescope's main light-gathering part (**objective**), and its diameter, known as the APERTURE of the telescope, determines its magnifying power. The point at which the objective concentrates the light from the source is its **focus**, and the distance from the focus to the objective is its FOCAL LENGTH. **Refracting** telescopes were invented by Hans Lippershey (1608) and GALILEO (1609). The main disadvantage with refracting telescopes was chromatic ABERRATION. This problem was solved in **reflecting** telescopes by combining lenses so their aberrations cancelled each other out. In 1668, Sir Isaac NEWTON built an early astronomical reflector. Modern observatories are built on mountain peaks in order to improve "seeing" and to observe INFRARED WAVES from celestial bodies. Earth-bound telescopes have limitations because the incoming radiation has to pass through the Earth's atmosphere. This ceases to be a problem with telescopes in Earth orbit, such as the HUBBLE SPACE TELESCOPE. Orbiting telescopes can also detect other types of electromagnetic radiation more easily, such as ULTRAVIOLET RADIATION, X-RAYS and GAMMA RADIATION. RADIO TELESCOPES are complex electronic systems that detect and analyze radio waves from beyond the Earth. In 1937, the first radio telescope was built by US radio engineer Grote Reber. Radio interferometers are arrays of smaller dishes that permit the investigation of even more distant radio sources. *See illustration p.810.*

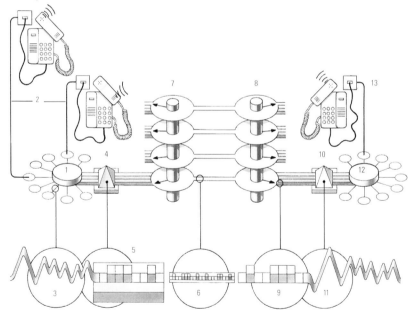

▲ **telephone** Local telephone exchanges (1) connect local calls (2), which are analogue signals (3). Long-distance calls are routed to the long-distance exchange (4) where they are converted from analogue to digital. Digital snapshots are taken of the analogue signal 8,000 times a second (every 125 microseconds) – enough information to recreate the analog signal accurately enough for the human ear. This whole process is called pulse-code modulation. Each eight-bit sample (5) is only 4 microseconds long, which leaves 121 microseconds between each one on the telephone line. To increase capacity, multiplexing combines the samples of up to 25 calls going to the same destination on the same line (6). This is done by feeding all the calls into a memory buffer (7) and then feeding them onto the long-distance line in turn. At the receiving end, the process is reversed and the combined call is again fed into a memory buffer (8), separated (9), passed to the long-distance exchange (10), where it is turned back into an analogue signal (11), and sent to the local exchange (12). From there it is routed to its final destination (13). The process happens so fast that the human ear hears a continuous voice.

teletext System for transmitting text so that it can be displayed on TELEVISION receivers. Television companies transmit the text in coded form along with the sound and vision signals. Sets are equipped to receive teletext separately and decode the text signals so that they can be displayed on the screen.

television System that transmits and receives visual images by RADIO waves or cable. A television CAMERA converts the images from light rays into electrical signals. The basis of most television cameras is an image orthicon tube. The electrical signals are amplified and transmitted as VERY HIGH FREQUENCY (VHF) or ULTRA HIGH FREQUENCY (UHF) radio waves. Typically, a television channel has a bandwidth of 5MHz (5 million cycles per second). The receiver (TV set) operates in reverse to the camera. On reception, the signals are

amplified and converted to light again in a CATHODE-RAY TUBE. Colour television has three synchronized image orthicon tubes in the camera, one for each of the three primary colours – red, blue and green. The tube of the receiver has three electron guns and the face of the tube is covered with a mosaic of fine phosphors in groups of three, each emitting only red, blue or green light when struck by a beam. These primary colours merge on the face of the screen to reconstitute the originally transmitted image. *See also* BROADCASTING; CABLE TELEVISION; RADIO; SATELLITE TELEVISION

Telford, Thomas (1757–1834) Scottish civil engineer who built roads, bridges, canals, docks, and harbours. His most notable achievements were the Caledonian Canal in Scotland and the 177m (580ft) Menai Strait suspension bridge, connecting Anglesey with mainland Wales.

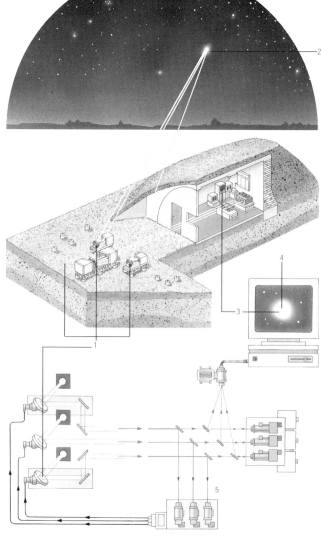

◀ **telescope** The COAST (**C**ambridge **O**ptical **A**perture **S**ynthesis **T**elescope) telescope, designed and built in Cambridge, England, is the most powerful optical telescope ever built. Instead of a single enormous reflective surface, the Cambridge telescope uses the images collected by three small and relatively inexpensive optical telescopes, and combines them to form an extremely detailed image. The three telescopes (1) are focused on a single point (2), each one producing a fractionally different picture. As the Earth rotates, the position of the telescopes alters in relation to the target star or planet. These pictures from different angles are blended together by computer equipment (3) to provide a single, highly detailed image (4). A small portion of light reflected by the telescopes is bled off (5), and used to confirm the targeting of the star as the Earth moves.

Tell, William Legendary Swiss hero, leader in the 14th-century war of liberation against Austria. For refusing to salute Albert I's steward, Gessler, he was made to shoot an arrow through an apple placed on his son's head.

Teller, Edward (1908–) US physicist, b. Hungary. He is often referred to as the "father of the HYDROGEN BOMB". In 1935, Teller left Europe and settled in the USA, where he conducted research on solar energy. During World War 2, he contributed to NUCLEAR WEAPONS research with Enrico FERMI. He was involved in the MANHATTAN PROJECT that produced the first atomic bomb. Teller was a central figure in developing and testing (1952) the hydrogen bomb. He was a supporter of Ronald Reagan's Strategic Defence Initiative (SDI) or 'Star Wars' project.

tellurium (symbol Te) Silver-white, metalloid element. It occurs naturally combined with gold in sylvanite, and its chief source is as a by-product of the electrolytic refining of copper. The brittle element is used in semiconductor devices, as a catalyst in petroleum cracking, and as an additive to increase the ductility of steel. Properties: at.no. 52; r.a.m. 127.60; r.d. 6.24; m.p. 449.5°C (841.1°F); b.p. 989.8°C (1,814°F).

Telstar First active communications SATELLITE, launched by the USA on 10 July 1962. It contained a microwave radio receiver, amplifier and transmitter for relaying telephone and television signals. It operated for about 18 weeks, failed for five weeks and then worked again for a further seven weeks before failing for good.

tempera Painting medium used extensively during the Middle Ages, made of powdered pigments mixed with an organic gum, usually made of egg yolk or egg white. Tempera dries quickly and is applied with a sable brush, one thin layer on another, so that the finished effect is semiopaque and luminous. During the 15th century, the more flexible medium of OIL PAINTING began to replace tempera.

temperance movement Campaign in the USA to wipe out the consumption of alcoholic beverages. Beginning in the late 18th century, the movement spread to Britain and Europe. In the US, it reached its peak with the ratification of the 18th Amendment (1919) that brought in PROHIBITION.

temperature In biology, intensity of heat. In warm-blooded (HOMEOTHERMAL) animals, body temperature is maintained within narrow limits regardless of the temperature of their surroundings. This is accomplished by muscular activity, the operation of cooling mechanisms, such as vasodilation, vasoconstriction and sweating, and metabolic activity. In humans, the normal body temperature is c.36.9°C (98.4°F), but this may vary with degree of activity. In so-called cold-blooded (POIKILOTHERMAL) animals, body temperature varies between wider limits, depending on the temperature of the surroundings.

temperature In physics, measure of the hotness or coldness of an object. Strictly, it describes the number of ENERGY states available to a substance or system. Two objects placed in thermal contact exchange HEAT energy initially but eventually arrive at thermal EQUILIBRIUM. At equilibrium, the most probable distribution of energy states among the atoms and molecules composing the objects has been attained. At high temperatures, the number of energy states available to the atoms and molecules of a system is large; at lower temperatures, fewer states are available. At a sufficiently low temperature, all parts of the system are at their lowest energy levels, the ABSOLUTE ZERO of temperature.

tempering HEAT treatment to alter the HARDNESS of an ALLOY. The effect produced depends on the composition of the alloy, the temperature to which it is heated, and the rate at which it is cooled. Usually, the metal is heated slowly to a specific temperature, then cooled rapidly.

Temple, Shirley (1928–) US film actress. She became a child star in films such as *Rebecca of Sunnybrook Farm* (1938) and *The Blue Bird* (1940). Temple continued to make films as a young adult but could never recapture her early success. As Shirley Temple Black, she went into politics, serving as a US delegate to the UN (1969–70), then as US ambassador to Ghana (1974–76) and to Czechoslovakia (1989–93).

temple Place of worship for Jews and members of many other religions. Temples were a grand architectural focal point in the religion and culture of ancient Egypt and the Near East. In Mesopotamia, they took the form of elaborate towers called ZIGGURATS. Greek and Roman temples, with beautifully carved statues and columns, were houses fit for the gods. In Judaism, the term refers specifically to the first and second temples built in Jerusalem. Today, Jews worship in a local SYNAGOGUE or temple.

Temple, Jerusalem Most significant shrine of the Jews, originally located on a hilltop known as Temple Mount in what is now East JERUSALEM. There have been three temples on the site. The first was built in the 10th century BC by order of SOLOMON as a repository for the ARK OF THE COVENANT. In c.587 BC, it was destroyed by Nebuchadnezzar, king of Babylon. In c.515 BC, a second temple was completed by Jewish exiles who had returned from Babylon in 537 BC. Between 19 and 9 BC, this second temple was replaced by a more elaborate structure; it was destroyed by the Romans in AD 70. Some of its ruins remain as a place of pilgrimage and prayer, known as the WESTERN WALL. Part of the ancient temple site is occupied by the DOME OF THE ROCK and al-Aqsa Mosque, both built in the late 7th century.

tempo Speed at which a piece of music should be performed, usually indicated on a score in Western music by Italian words, such as *allegro* (fast) and *adagio* (slow).

tench Freshwater food and sport fish of Europe and Asia, belonging to the carp family Cyprinidae. It has a stout, golden yellow body with small scales. Length: to 71cm (28in). Species *Tinca tinca*.

Ten Commandments (Decalogue) Code of ethical conduct held in Judaeo-Christian tradition to have been revealed by God to MOSES on Mount Sinai during the Hebrew exodus from Egypt (c.1200 BC). They represent the moral basis of the Covenant made by YAHWEH (God) with Israel.

tendon Strong, flexible band of CONNECTIVE TISSUE that joins MUSCLE to BONE. *See illustration p.812*

tendril Coiling part of stem or leaf, a slender thread-like structure used by climbing plants for support.

Tenerife Largest of the Canary Islands, Spain, in the Atlantic Ocean, 64km (40mi) WNW of Grand Canary Island. It is a mountainous island, rising to Pico de Teide at 3,718m (12,198ft). Products include dates, sugar cane, palms and cotton. Tourism is the mainstay of the economy. The main town is SANTA CRUZ DE TENERIFE. Area: 2,059sq km (795sq mi). Pop. (1991) 725,815.

Tennessee State in SE central USA between the Appalachian Mountains and the Mississippi River. The capital is NASHVILLE. Other cities include MEMPHIS, CHATTANOOGA and Knoxville. The first European discovery was by Hernando DE SOTO in 1540. The French followed a century later, but their claim was ceded to Britain in 1763, and the first permanent settlement was established in 1769. In 1796, Tennessee became the 16th state of the Union. Tennessee's enthusiastic response to the request for volunteers during the MEXICAN WAR (1846–48) earned it the nickname of the Volunteer State. During the CIVIL WAR, the state was the site of some of the bloodiest battles, including Shiloh (1862) and Chattanooga (1863). In 1866 it became the first southern state to be readmitted to the Union. Christian fundamentalism has exerted a powerful influence, and the teaching of evolution was banned from 1925 to 1967. In the E, are the GREAT SMOKY MOUNTAINS and the Cumberland Plateau. Beyond, the land slopes to the MISSISSIPPI River on the W border. West Tennessee has fertile flood plains, drained by the TENNESSEE River, that produce cotton, tobacco and soya beans. Mineral deposits include zinc and coal. Industries: chemicals, electrical equipment, foods, tourism. Area: 109,411sq km (42,244sq mi). Pop. (2000) 5,689,283.

Tennessee River in Tennessee, N Alabama and W Kentucky, USA. Formed by the confluence of the Holston and French Broad rivers, it joins the Ohio at Paducah, Kentucky, and forms part of the Alabama-Mississippi border. From 1933 the TENNESSEE VALLEY AUTHORITY (TVA) developed the river's hydroelectric potential (nine major dams) and transport facilities, along with irrigation and flood control. Length: 1,050km (652mi).

Tennessee Valley Authority (TVA) NEW DEAL agency established (1933) as part of a long-range regional planning project. An independent public corporation, it was authorized to build dams and power plants to control the TENNESSEE River and its tributaries. The success of the TVA contributed greatly to the wealth of the Tennessee valley.

tennis Racket and ball game played by either two (singles) or four (doubles) players. It is sometimes known as **lawn tennis**, despite being played on clay, concrete, shale and wood, as well as grass. The game is played on a court 23.8m (78ft) by 8.2m (27ft) for singles. For doubles play, the court is widened to 11m (36ft). It is bisected by a net 0.9m (3ft) high at the centre. On each side of the net there are two service areas marked by rectangular lines. The ball is put into play by the server, who is allowed two attempts to hit it into the opposite service court. One player serves for a complete game. If the opponent returns the ball safely, play continues until one player fails to hit the ball, hits it into the net or hits it outside the confines of the court; the opponent then wins the point. A minimum of four points is required to win a game, which must be won by two clear

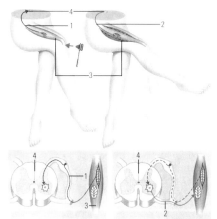

▲ **tendon** The tendon jerk is the simplest reflex action, involving only a sensory receptor neuron (1) and a motor neuron (2). Impulses, such those created by a

hammer tapping a knee, run to and from the muscles (3) and traverse only one segment of the spinal cord (4). This reflex is independent of the brain.

points. A minimum of six games must be won to win a set, which is won by either two clear games or by winning the tie-break game, played at six games all. Modern tennis evolved from REAL TENNIS in England in the 1860s.

Tennyson, Alfred, 1st Baron (1809–92) (Alfred Lord Tennyson) English poet. He became poet laureate in 1850. His massive oeuvre includes such patriotic classics as "Ode on the Death of the Duke of Wellington" (1852) and "The Charge of the Light Brigade" (1855). Tennyson also wrote deeply personal utterances, such as "Crossing the Bar" (1889) and the extended elegy for his friend Arthur Henry Hallam, *In Memoriam* (1850), often regarded as his masterpiece. Other notable works include "The Lady of Shalott", *Maud* (1855) and the Arthurian epic finally published as *Idylls of the King* (1872–73).

tenor Range of the human voice, falling below CONTRALTO and above BARITONE. It is the highest natural male voice apart from the COUNTERTENOR. In the 16th and early 17th centuries, the tenor was the most important solo voice.

tension Molecular forces associated with the boundary layer of a liquid. It makes a liquid behave as if there were a "skin" on the surface. Attractive forces in this skin tend to resist disruption, so that a needle or razor blade placed carefully on the surface floats even though its density is many times that of the liquid.

Teotihuacán Ancient AZTEC city of Mexico, *c*.50km (30mi) N of Mexico City. It flourished between *c*.100 BC and *c*.AD 700. It contained huge and impressive buildings, notably the Pyramid of the Sun. At its greatest, *c*.AD 600, the city housed at least 100,000 people and was the centre of a considerable empire.

terbium (symbol Tb) Silver-grey, metallic element of the LANTHANIDE SERIES. It is found in such minerals as monazite, gladolinite and apatite. The soft element is used in semiconductors; sodium terbium borate is used in lasers. Properties: at.no. 65; r.a.m. 158.9254; r.d. 8.234; m.p. 1,360°C (2,480°F); b.p. 3,041°C (5,506°F). Single isotope Tb[159].

Terence (*c*.190–159 BC) (Publius Terentius Afer) Roman author of comedies, noted for the elegance and urbanity of his style. He was a slave in Rome where he was educated and subsequently freed by his master, senator Terentius Lucanus. Six of his comedies survive and include *Andria* (*c*.166 BC), *Hecyra* (*c*.165 BC) and *Phormio* (*c*.161 BC).

Teresa of Avila, Saint (1515–82) (Teresa de Cepeda y Ahumada) Spanish CARMELITE nun and mystic. In 1529 she entered the Convent of the Incarnation at Ávila. From 1558, she set about reforming the Carmelite order for women, whose rules had become weakened. Under her influence, St JOHN OF THE CROSS introduced a similarly restored Carmelite order for men. Her literary works, including an autobiography and the meditative *Interior Castle* (1577), as well as her monastic reforms, led to her canonization in 1622.

Teresa, Mother (1910–97) (Agnes Gonxha Bojaxhiu) Macedonian Roman Catholic missionary. She began her missionary work as a teacher in Calcutta, India. In 1948 she left her convent in order to tend the homeless, starving and sick in the slums of Calcutta. Her Order of the Missionaries of Charity was established in 1950 and subsequently extended to other countries. She was awarded the first Pope John XXIII Peace Prize in 1971, and the Nobel Peace Prize in 1979.

terminal velocity Maximum velocity attainable by a falling body or powered AIRCRAFT. It is dependent upon the shape of the body, the resistance of the air through which it is moving, and (in the case of aircraft) the THRUST of the engines.

termite Social insect found worldwide in subterranean nests and above-ground mounds. They have a caste system, with a king and queen guarded and tended by soldiers, workers and nymphs. Wood is a common component of their diet, which is digested with the help of symbiotic protozoa or bacteria that live in the termites' intestines. Length: 0.2–2.25mm (0.08–0.9in); queens: to 10cm (4in). Order Isoptera.

tern (sea swallow) Any of several species of graceful seabirds that live throughout the world. Usually white and grey, it has a pointed bill, long pointed wings, a forked tail, and webbed feet; it dives for fish and crustaceans. Length: to 55cm (22in). Family Laridae; genus *Sterna*.

terracotta Hard, porous, usually unglazed yellow, brown or red earthenware (fired CLAY). Terracotta is used in building, sculpture and POTTERY. *See also* CERAMIC

terrapin Any of several species of aquatic TURTLES that live in fresh or brackish water in North and South America, especially the diamondback terrapin (*Malaclemys terrapin*). Length: to 23cm (9in). Family Emydidae.

terrier Any of several breeds of DOG. Originally trained to dig out game, they have been used to hunt badgers, foxes and rats. When the quarry is located, the terrier is sent down to dig it out of its burrow. Breeds include the Sealyham terrier, fox terrier and Manchester terrier. Larger breeds, such as the Airedale terrier and Irish terrier, are often used as guard and police dogs.

territory In ecology, the restricted life space of an organism. An area selected for mating, nesting, roosting, hunting or feeding, it may be occupied by one or more organisms and defended against others of the same, or a different, species.

terrorism Use of violence, sometimes indiscriminately, against persons and property for the nominal purpose of making a political statement. Intending to in-spire terror, terrorists act principally in the name of empowering political minorities and to publicize political grievances.

Terry, Dame (Alice) Ellen (1848–1928) English actress. In partnership with Henry IRVING, Terry dominated the British stage from 1878 to 1902. George Bernard SHAW created for her the role of Lady Cicely Waynflete in *Captain Brassbound's Conversion* (1900).

Tertiary Earlier period of the CENOZOIC era, lasting from 65 million to *c*.2 million years ago. It is divided into five epochs, starting with the PALAEOCENE, followed by the EOCENE, OLIGOCENE, MIOCENE and PLIOCENE. Early Tertiary times were marked by great mountain-building activity. Both marsupial and placental mammals diversified greatly. Archaic forms of carnivores and herbivores flourished, along with primitive primates, bats, rodents and early whales.

Tertullian (*c*.AD 160–*c*.220) (Quintus Septimius Florens Tertullianus) Roman writer and Christian theologian, b. Carthage. He converted to Christianity (197), later joining the Montanists, an ascetic group that was declared heretical. He used his training in law and rhetoric to develop a systematic approach to theology and the defence of Christian beliefs and practices. He helped to make Latin the official language of Christian theological writing. His works include *Apologeticus* (*Defence*) and *De anima* (*Concerning the Soul*).

terza rima In Italian poetry, a chain rhyme incorporating stanzas of three lines each (tercets). Each tercet's second line rhymes with the first and third of the next. The chain ends with a couplet or extra line added to the last tercet. This rhyme scheme first

appeared in DANTE'S *Divine Comedy* (*c*.1321), probably invented for the work.

Tesla, Nikola (1856–1943) US electrical engineer and inventor, b. Croatia. He pioneered the applications of high-voltage electricity. Tesla developed arc lighting, the first generator of alternating current (AC) and the high-frequency Tesla coil.

Test Ban Treaty (1963) Agreement signed in Moscow by the Soviet Union, the USA and Britain to cease most tests of nuclear weapons. Nearly 100 other states eventu-

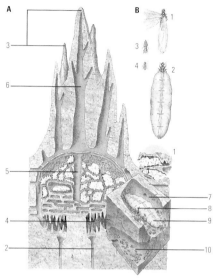

▲ **termite** Built of saliva and soil particles, termite mounds (A) dominate the African savanna. Most termites prefer to eat dead plant material that has been partly softened by fungus. This food supply is limited in dry conditions because fungi need moisture. For this reason *Macrotermes* termites create fungus chambers (1). These are combs of carton (a mixture of saliva and faecal pellets) that provide a large surface area on which the fungus grows. The fungus flourishes in the humid atmosphere of the nest as it breaks down the faeces in the carton walls. Some termite species dig deep tunnels (2) to find underground water to make sure that the nest is moist enough for the fungus to thrive. The peaks of the mound (3) act as lungs. Air seeps into the main nest from an air cellar below (4). As the fungus breaks down the faecal comb heat is generated. The hot air rises, via a large central air space (5), into the chimneys (6). The walls of the nest are porous, so carbon dioxide diffuses into the chimneys. The newly oxygenated air loses heat to the air outside and cools, sinking back to the cellar. The royal cell (7) is located in the centre of the nest, where the king (8) and the queen (9) can be protected. The workers, as well as feeding the royal couple, also remove the eggs to the brood chambers (10). There the workers lick the eggs to keep them clean. Most termite species have a variety of castes (B) or types. There are the temporarily winged reproductives (male and female) called alates (1), responsible for setting up colonies, the queen (2), the enlarged abdomen of which produces thousands of eggs, the soldier termites (3) that protect the colony, and the workers (4) that collect food, care for the queen, and serve as builders.

ally signed the treaty, although France and China continued to conduct tests in the atmosphere and underwater.

testis (pl. testes) Male sex GLAND, found as a pair located in a pouch, the scrotum, external to the body. The testes are made up of seminiferous tubules in which SPERM are formed and mature, after which they drain into ducts and are stored in the epididymis prior to being discharged.

testosterone Steroid HORMONE secreted mainly by the mammalian TESTIS. It is responsible for the growth and development of male sex organs and male secondary sexual characteristics, such as voice change and facial hair.

tetanus (lockjaw) Life-threatening disease caused by the toxin secreted by the anaerobic bacterium *Clostridium tetani*. The symptoms are muscular spasms and rigidity of the jaw, which then spreads to other parts of the body, culminating in convulsions and death. The disease is treated with anti-tetanus toxin and ANTIBIOTICS.

Tet Offensive (1968) Campaign in the VIETNAM WAR. North Vietnamese and VIET CONG troops launched attacks on towns and cities of South Vietnam. Although of little strategic value, the offensive discredited US military reports that victory over North Vietnam was imminent.

tetracyclines Group of broad-spectrum ANTIBIOTICS effective against a wide range of bacterial infections.

Teutonic Knights German military and religious order, founded in 1190. Its members, of aristocratic class, took monastic vows of poverty and chastity. During the 13th century the knights waged war on non-Christian peoples, particularly those of Prussia, whom they defeated, annexing their land. They were defeated in 1242 by ALEXANDER NEVSKI and, in 1410, by the Poles and Lithuanians at Tannenberg.

Teutonic mythology Traditional beliefs of the Germanic peoples. Much of the mythology of pre-Christian Germany and Scandinavia is preserved in two Icelandic works, the Eddas. According to the Eddas, before the creation of the world there was a land of ice and shadows called Niflheim and a land of fire known as Muspellsheim. The two lands together created the first giant, Ymir. ODIN and his brothers killed Ymir and founded the race of gods. They then created the world from parts of Ymir's body, and made the first man and woman from pieces of trees. At the centre of the worlds of gods and men stood a giant ash tree, Yggdrasil. Odin, the head of the AESIR (heroic gods), was the god of poetry and of battle. VALHALLA, a great hall in Asgard, was the resting place of warriors slain in battle. Next in line to Odin was THOR, the god of thunder, rain and fertility. Others of the pantheon included the handsome Balder and Loki, the son of a giant. The Vanir gods, regarded as less important than the Aesir, included Njörd, the sea god; his son Frey, a god of fertility; his daughter Freya, the goddess of love and magic; and Hel, the goddess of death and the underworld.

Texas State in central S USA, bounded by the Gulf of Mexico (SE), separated from Mexico by the RIO GRANDE. Major cities are HOUSTON, DALLAS, SAN ANTONIO, AUSTIN (the state capital) and FORT WORTH. The Spaniards explored the region in the early 16th century, and it became part of the Spanish colony of Mexico. By the time Mexico attained independence in 1821, many Americans had begun to settle in Texas. They revolted against Mexican rule and in 1836, after defeating the Mexican army, established the Republic of Texas, recognized by the USA in 1837. Eight years later Texas was admitted to the Union. Eastern Texas has pine-covered hills and cypress swamps; cotton and rice are the main crops, and the lumber industry is important. Cattle are raised on the plains of the Rio Grande valley from where the land rises to the Guadalupe Mountains of W Texas and the Great Plains area of the Texas Panhandle in the N. Rich oil fields are a mainstay of the state's economy. Industries: oil refining, food processing, aircraft, electronics. Area: 692,405sq km (267,338sq mi). Pop. (2000) 20,851,820.

textile Fabric, especially that produced by WEAVING yarn. The yarn is made by SPINNING natural or artificial FIBRES. Textiles are used to make clothing, curtains, carpets, sheets, blankets, towels and many other products. Powered LOOMS for spinning and weaving were introduced in the 18th century. *See also* ACRYLIC; COTTON; FLAX; LINEN; NYLON; POLYESTER; RAYON; SILK; WOOL

Tezcatlipoca AZTEC god. He appears in many different forms but is best known as the god of the night sky and summer sun. He was a protector, a creator and a harmful wizard. His cult required human sacrifice.

Thackeray, William Makepeace (1811–63) British novelist, b. India. His reputation was established with the *Book of Snobs* (1846–47). Thackeray's best-known novel is *Vanity Fair* (1847–48), a satire on early 19th-century upper-class London society. Other novels include *Barry Lyndon* (1844), *Pendennis* (1848–50), *Henry Esmond* (1852), *The Newcomes* (1853–55) and *The Virginians* (1857–59). Thackeray was the founding editor (1860–75) of the *Cornhill Magazine*.

Thai National language of Thailand, spoken by most of the population. It is closely related to Lao, spoken across the border in Laos. It belongs to the Tai family, possibly a sub-family of the SINO-TIBETAN LANGUAGES group.

Thailand Kingdom in Southeast Asia. Central Thailand is a fertile plain, drained mainly by the Chao Phraya. A densely populated region, it includes the capital, BANGKOK. To the NE lies the Khorat plateau that extends to the River MEKONG border with Laos. The NW is mountainous and includes the second-largest city, CHIANGMAI. The S forms part of the MALAY PENINSULA. **Climate** Thailand has a tropical climate. The monsoon season lasts from May to October. The central plains are much drier than other regions. **Vegetation** The N includes many hardwood trees that are being rapidly exploited. The S has rubber plantations. Grass, shrub, and swamp make up 20% of land. Arable land, mainly rice fields, covers 33%. **History and politics** The Mongol capture (1253) of a Thai kingdom in SW China forced the Thai people to move south. A new kingdom was established around Sukhothai. In the 14th century, the kingdom expanded and the capital moved to Ayutthaya. The first European contact was in the early 16th century. In the late 17th century, the kingdom was briefly held by the Burmese. European desire to acquire the brilliance of the Thai court resulted in their expulsion for more than a century; Thailand remained the only Southeast Asian nation to resist colonization. In 1782, a Thai general became King Rama I, establishing the Chakkri dynasty, which has ruled ever since. The country became known as Siam, and Bangkok acted as its capital. From the mid-19th century, Siam began a gradual process of westernization. In World War 1, Siam supported the Allies. In 1932, Thailand became a constitutional monarchy. In 1938, Pibul Songgram became premier and changed the country's name to Thailand. In 1941, Pibul, despite opposition, invited Japanese forces into Thailand. Military coups and short-lived civilian governments are characteristic of post-war Thai politics. In 1950, Bhumibol Adulyadej acceded to the throne as Rama IX. In 1957, Pibul was overthrown in a military coup. In 1992, public pressure forced elections that saw the return of civilian rule. In 1997, the prime minister resigned amid criticism of his handling of the economic

> **THAILAND**
> AREA: 513,120sq km (198,116sq mi)
> POPULATION: 63,670,000
> CAPITAL (POPULATION): Bangkok (5,572,712)

crisis. A new coalition government, led by Chuan Leekpai, was formed. **Economy** Thailand is a rapidly industrializing, developing nation (1995 GDP per capita, US$7,540). Thailand was a founder of the Association of Southeast Asian Nations (ASEAN). Manufacturing and services have grown rapidly. It is a major producer of commercial vehicles. Agriculture employs 66% of the workforce. Thailand is the world's largest producer of pineapples and natural rubber. It is also the fourth-largest producer of rice, buffalo and cassava. Thai silk is among the world's finest. Tourism is a vital source of revenue. In 1997, the economic crisis in Southeast Asia led to the collapse of its financial sector and a 20% devaluation of the baht. The International Monetary Fund (IMF) agreed to a US$17 billion rescue package.

thalamus One of two ovoid masses of grey matter located deep on each side of the forebrain. Sometimes called the sensory-motor receiving areas, they fulfil relay and integration functions in respect of sensory messages reaching the BRAIN.

thalassemia (Cooley's anaemia) Group of hereditary disorders characterized by abnormal bone marrow and ERYTHROCYTES (red blood cells). The predominant symptom is ANAEMIA, requiring frequent blood transfusions.

Thales (636–546 BC) First Greek scientist and philosopher of whom we have any knowledge. He made discoveries in geometry, such as that the angles at the base of an isosceles triangle are equal. Thales predicted the eclipse of the Sun that took place in 585 BC.

thalidomide Drug originally developed as a mild hypnotic, but whose use by women in early pregnancy until the early 1960s caused serious birth deformities. It is still manufactured for occasional use in treating LEPROSY.

thallium (symbol Tl) Shiny, metallic element of group III of the periodic table. Soft and malleable, it is obtained as a by-product of processing zinc or lead sulphide ores. It is used in electronic components, infra-red detectors and optical and infra-red glasses. Thallium is a toxic compound, and thallium sulphide is used as a rodent and ant poison. Properties: at.no. 81; r.a.m. 204.37; r.d. 11.85; m.p. 303.5°C (578.3°F); b.p. 1,457°C (2,655°F); most common isotope Tl^{205} (70.5%).

Thames Longest river in England. It rises in the Cotswold Hills, E Gloucestershire, then flows E across S England and through London to enter the North Sea at The Nore. The river is tidal up to Teddington, Surrey. Above London, it is used mainly by pleasure craft and for recreational purposes. The river is navigable for ocean-going vessels below Tilbury, Essex. The Thames Barrier (completed 1982) at Woolwich, London, controls the river's tidal system. Length: 338km (210mi).

Thanksgiving Day National holiday in the USA and Canada. Originating with the PILGRIMS in 1621, who celebrated the first harvest of the PLYMOUTH COLONY, it became an official holiday in 1863. In the USA, it is celebrated on the fourth Thursday in November; in Canada on the second Monday in October.

Thant, U (1909–74) Burmese diplomat, third secretary-general (1962–72) of the UNITED NATIONS (UN). He was acting secretary-general from 1961 before being elected in his own right. Thant helped to settle several major disputes, including the civil wars in the Congo (Zaïre) in 1963 and Cyprus in 1964.

Thar Desert (Great Indian Desert) Region in NW India and SE Pakistan, between the Aravalli Mountains (E) and the River Indus (W). The region covers parts of RAJASTHAN, GUJARAT, PUNJAB and SIND. The desert areas of Rajasthan now benefit from the Indira Gandhi Canal, 650km (400mi) long, bringing water from HIMACHAL PRADESH. Area: c.200,000sq km (77,000sq mi).

Thatcher, Margaret Hilda, Baroness (1925–) British stateswoman, prime minister (1979–90). She was perhaps the most influential British political leader since Winston CHURCHILL. Thatcher was secretary of state for education and science (1970–74) under Edward HEATH, whom she defeated for the party leadership in 1975. She defeated James CALLAGHAN to become Britain's first woman prime minister. Her government embarked on a radical free-market programme that became known as "Thatcherism". Her monetarist policies, especially cuts in public spending, provoked criticism and contributed to a recession, but her popularity was restored by victory in the FALKLANDS WAR (1982). Thatcher's determination to curb the power of trade unions provoked a bitter miners' strike (1983–84). Controversial PRIVATIZATION of national utilities boosted government revenue in a period of rapidly rising incomes, except among the poor. In 1987, Thatcher won a third term but clashed with cabinet colleagues over economic and social policy and her hostile attitude to the EUROPEAN UNION (EU). A poll tax (1989) was widely seen as unfair, and she was forced to resign. She was succeeded by John MAJOR.

theatre Building where DRAMA is staged. Its architecture has evolved gradually from early times, when ritual was most often performed in the open air. In medieval Europe, churches were used as dramatic venues. Renaissance architects, such as PALLADIO, were commissioned to design private theatres with acoustics and perspective in mind. Popular open stages evolved in Shakespearean England. By the Restoration, the PROSCENIUM arch stage had become established as the only viable form of theatre. Since World War 2, theatrical architecture has again stressed adaptability. *See also* DRAMA

theatre-in-the-round Form of theatrical presentation derived from the ancient arena stage. The audience is seated on all sides of the players, thus creating a sense of informality between the actors and the audience.

Theatre Workshop Drama company founded (1945) in London by Joan Littlewood. It staged many experimental and politically contentious plays. Several of its productions transferred to the West End, including *The Quare Fellow* (1956) and *Oh! What a Lovely War* (1963).

Thebes City-state of ancient Greece, the dominant power in Boeotia. It was allied with Persia during the PERSIAN WARS, and during the 5th century BC was continually in conflict with Athens. It reached the peak of its power under Epaminondas in the 4th century BC, defeating the Spartans at Leuctra in 371 BC and invading the Peloponnese. The city was largely destroyed after a rising against ALEXANDER THE GREAT in 336 BC.

Thebes Greek name for the ancient capital of Upper Egypt, roughly corresponding to present-day LUXOR.

theism Any of various philosophical and theological systems that profess belief in the existence of one Supreme Being, who is the creator of the universe. In most theistic systems, human beings have FREE WILL, and religious doctrines are usually based on divine revelation. *See also* MONOTHEISM; POLYTHEISM

Themis In Greek mythology, goddess of justice, daughter of URANUS and GAIA. Although one of the TITANS, she was honoured by the gods on Olympus for her wisdom and foresight. She was the mother of the Seasons and of the three FATES. Themis is depicted as a stern women bearing a pair of scales.

Themistocles (*c*.528–460 BC) Athenian statesman. He created the Athenian navy and secured the crucial victory over the Persian fleet at SALAMIS in 480 BC. Subsequently accused of conspiring with the Persians, he left Athens for Argos. A strong opponent of Sparta, his association with the former Spartan ruler, Pausanias, led to his condemnation as a traitor, but he escaped to Persia.

theocracy Government by religious leaders in accordance with divine law. Theocracies were common in non-literate societies and existed in ancient Egypt and the Orient.

Theocritus (*c*.310–250 BC) Greek poet, regarded as the father of pastoral poetry. His work, which influenced generations of later writers from VIRGIL to Matthew ARNOLD, is noted for its vivid expression and perceptive portrayal of rural life.

Theodora Name of three empresses of the BYZANTINE EMPIRE. The most famous **Theodora** (*c*.500–548) was the wife of JUSTINIAN I. A courtesan before her marriage, she had such influence that she almost ruled jointly. The second **Theodora** (d.867) ruled as regent (842–856) for her son Michael III. She expelled the iconoclasts and restored the worship of images. The third **Theodora** (980–1056) was co-ruler from 1042 and was briefly sole empress after the death of Constantine IX Monomachus (1055).

Theodoric the Great (*c*.454–526) King of the Ostrogoths and ruler of Italy. He drove ODOACER from Italy (488) and attempted to recreate the Western Roman Empire with himself as emperor. Religious differences and political rivalries frustrated his empire-building, and his kingdom was destroyed by JUSTINIAN after his death.

Theodosius I (*c*.347–395) Roman Emperor (379–95), the last to rule both Eastern (from 379) and Western (from 392) ROMAN EMPIRES. A champion of orthodox Christianity, he summoned the first ecumenical council of Constantinople (381) to solve the religious dispute over the doctrine of ARIANISM. He ended the wars with the VISIGOTHS by an agreement (382) giving them land on the frontiers in return for service in the Roman army. After 392, he briefly reunited the empire after defeating a pretender, but left the two parts separately to his sons.

Theodosius II (401–450) Eastern Roman (Byzantine) emperor (408–50). He was dominated by ministers. His armies repelled Persian invasions, and the fortifications of Constantinople were strengthened. He promulgated the **Theodosian Code** of laws (438).

theology Systematic study of God or gods. In its narrowest sense, it is the investigation or expression of the beliefs and precepts of a RELIGION. In a much broader sense, theology is intricately related to philosophical and historical studies and strives to achieve an understanding of various beliefs. Such preoccupations exercise the minds of theologians of Islam, Hinduism and most other religions, as well as Christianity.

theosophy Religious philosophy that originated in the ancient world but was given impetus in 1875 when the Theosophical Society was founded in New York by the mystic Helen Blavatsky (b. Russia) and her followers. Modern theosophy continues a mystical tradition in Western thought, represented by such thinkers as PYTHAGORAS and PLOTINUS, but is most significant in Indian philiosophy. The main aims of the Theosophical Society are to promote a spiritual brotherhood of all humanity; to encourage the comparative study of religions, philosophy and science; and to develop latent spiritual powers. Belief in the TRANSMIGRATION OF SOULS also occupies an important place in theosophical doctrine. *See also* BESANT, ANNIE

Theravada ("Doctrine of the Elders") Older of the two major schools of BUDDHISM. The doctrine originated early in the history of Buddhism as a contrast to MAHAYANA ("greater vehicle"). Theravada Buddhism stresses that sorrow and suffering can be conquered only by the suppression of desire. Desire can be suppressed only if the individual realizes that everything is always in a state of flux and the only stable condition is NIRVANA, an indefinable state of rest. This type of Buddhism is widespread in Sri Lanka and SE Asia.

Thérèse of Lisieux, Saint (1873–97) (Marie Françoise Thérèse Martin) French Carmelite nun. She entered the Carmelite convent at Lisieux at the age of 15. Later she suffered from depression and religious doubts, which she mastered by prayer. She died of tuberculosis. She chronicled her own spiritual struggle in a series of letters, *Story of a Soul* (1898). She was canonized in 1925. Her feast day is 1 October.

thermal Small-scale, rising current of air produced by local heating of the Earth's surface. Thermals are often used by GLIDING birds and human-built gliders.

thermionics Study of the emission of ELECTRONS or IONS from a heated CONDUCTOR. This is the principle on which electron tubes (valves) work. The heated conductor is the CATHODE, and the emitted electrons are attracted to the ANODE. A more modern aim for thermionics is the design and construction of thermionic power generators.

thermodynamics Branch of physics that studies HEAT and how it is transformed to and from other forms of ENERGY. The original laws of thermodynamics were conceived by observing large-scale properties of systems and with no understanding of the underlying molecular structure. The KINETIC THEORY of gases was developed in the mid-19th century. In general, the TEMPERATURE of a body is a measure of its internal energy. The three existing laws are now calculated using statistics and QUANTUM MECHANICS. The **first law** of thermodynamics, basically a restatement of the CONSERVATION law of energy, is that the change in a system's internal energy is equal to the heat that flows into the system plus the work done on the system. The two main forms of change are adiabatic and isothermal. The **second law** says that if a system is left alone, its ENTROPY tends to increase. This rules out the possibility of PERPETUAL MOTION. The **third law** states that a system at ABSOLUTE ZERO would effectively have an entropy of zero. *See also* CARNOT CYCLE; CLAUSIUS, RUDOLF; KELVIN, WILLIAM THOMSON, 1ST BARON

thermoelectricity Phenomena involving the conversion of HEAT energy into ELECTRICITY or vice versa. There are three such effects. In the SEEBECK EFFECT, a current flows if different temperatures are maintained at the junctions of a circuit containing two different metals; this is the basis of the thermocouple. The PELTIER EFFECT acts in the reverse manner, converting electrical energy to heat energy. Lord KELVIN discovered the third thermoelectric effect, called the **Thomson effect**: if the ends of a wire conductor have different temperatures, a POTENTIAL DIFFERENCE is created along the wire. If an electric current flows from the cooler to the hotter part of the wire, the effect is called the positive Thomson effect; the reverse is the negative Thomson effect.

thermometer Instrument for measuring TEMPERATURE. A MERCURY thermometer depends on the expansion of the metal mercury that is held in a glass bulb connected to a narrow, graduated tube. Temperatures can also be measured by a gas thermometer and by a resistance thermometer that measures resistance of a conductor. Common scales are the CELSIUS, FAHRENHEIT and KELVIN.

Thermopylae Strategic mountain pass in E central Greece, site of several battles in ancient times. The most famous was the defence of the pass by Leonidas of SPARTA against the Persian invasion of XERXES I in 480 BC.

thermosphere Shell of light gases between the mesosphere and the exosphere, between 100km (60mi) and 450km (280mi) above the Earth's surface. The temperature steadily rises with height in the thermosphere.

thermostat Device for maintaining a constant TEMPERATURE. A common type contains a strip of two metals, one of which expands and contracts more than the other. At a set temperature, the strip bends and breaks the circuit. As it cools, the strip straightens, makes contact, and the heating begins again once the circuit is complete.

Theseus In Greek mythology, a great hero of many adventures, the son of Aethra by Aegeus, King of Athens, or by the sea god POSEIDON. His most famous exploit was the vanquishing of the MINOTAUR of Crete.

Thespis (6th century BC) Greek writer, according to tradition, the inventor of TRAGEDY. He is also said to have introduced a character separate from the chorus, who provided dialogue by responding to the chorus' comments.

Thessalonians, Epistles to the Two of St PAUL's earliest letters, forming the 13th and 14th books of the NEW TESTAMENT. The first letter was written c.AD 50, and the second followed shortly afterward. The letters contained encouragement and pastoral guidance for the Thessalonians and neighbouring Christian communities.

Thessaloníki (Salonica) Port on the Gulf of Thessaloníki, Greece, the country's second-largest city and capital of Greek MACEDONIA. Founded c.315 BC, it flourished under the Romans after 148 BC as the capital of Macedonia. It was part of the Ottoman Empire until 1913, when it was conquered by Greece. Industries: oil refining, textiles, metals, engineering. Pop. (1991) 383,967.

thiamine VITAMIN B_1 of the B complex, required for carbohydrate METABOLISM. Its deficiency causes BERIBERI. Thiamine is found in grains and seeds, nuts, liver, yeast and legumes.

Third Reich Official name of Nazi Germany (1933–45). The first *Reich* (Ger. empire) was the HOLY ROMAN EMPIRE, the second the German empire of 1871–1918.

Third World Former term for LESS DEVELOPED COUNTRIES. "First" and "Second" world countries were those of the Western and Eastern blocs respectively.

Thirteen Colonies English colonies in North America that jointly declared independence from Britain (1776) and became the USA. They were: Connecticut, Delaware, Georgia, Maryland, Massachusetts, New Hampshire, New Jersey, New York, North Carolina, Pennsylvania, Rhode Island, South Carolina and Virginia. *See also* AMERICAN REVOLUTION

Thirty-Nine Articles (1563) Set of doctrinal formulations adopted by the CHURCH OF ENGLAND in 1571. They do not represent a creed, rather they were a compromise that enabled different interpretations of contentious issues, such as TRANSUBSTANTIATION. In such a manner they sought to establish the unity of the ANGLICAN COMMUNION. *See also* COMMON PRAYER, BOOK OF

Thirty Years' War (1618–48) Conflict fought mainly in Germany, arising out of religious differences and developing into a struggle for power in Europe. It began with a Protestant revolt in Bohemia against the HABSBURG

emperor, FERDINAND II. Both sides sought allies and the war spread to much of Europe. The Habsburg generals, Tilly and WALLENSTEIN, registered early victories and drove the Protestant champion, CHRISTIAN IV of Denmark, out of the war (1629). A greater champion appeared in GUSTAVUS II (ADOLPHUS) of Sweden, who waged a series of victorious campaigns before being killed in 1632. In 1635, France, fearing Habsburg dominance, declared war on Spain. Negotiations for peace were not successful until the Peace of WESTPHALIA was concluded in 1648. War between France and Spain continued until the Peace of the PYRENEES (1659), and other associated conflicts continued for several years. The chief loser in the war, apart from the German peasants, was Emperor FERDINAND III, who lost control of Germany. Sweden was established as the dominant state in N Europe, while France replaced Spain as the greatest European power.

thistle Any of numerous species of plants with thorny leaves and yellow, white, pink, or purple flower heads with prickly bracts. The field thistle, *Cirsium discolor*, resembles the heraldic thistle, which is the national emblem of Scotland. Family Asteraceae/Compositae.

Thomas, Saint One of the original 12 APOSTLES or disciples of JESUS CHRIST. He has been called "Doubting Thomas" because, after the RESURRECTION of Christ, he refused to believe that the risen Lord had indeed appeared to the other disciples (John 20). Only when Jesus appeared to him and allowed him to touch his wounds did he lay aside his doubts. According to Christian tradition, he took Christianity to India. His feast day is 3 July.

Thomas, Dylan Marlais (1914–53) Welsh poet and short-story writer. A self-styled *enfant terrible*, his flamboyant alcoholic lifestyle led to his early death in New York. Thomas' public persona contributed to the popularity of his powerful, meticulously crafted but often wilfully obscure verse. His first collection appeared when he was 19 years old; his *Collected Poems* was published in 1953. Many of his best short stories appear in *Portrait of the Artist as a Young Dog* (1940) and *Adventures in the Skin Trade* (1955). The "play for voices", *Under Milk Wood* (1952), is perhaps his best-known work.

Thomas, R.S. (Ronald Stuart) (1913–2000) Welsh poet. He was a clergyman for more than 40 years. Thomas' early verse is collected in *Song at the Year's Turning* (1955); it embodies his characteristic concerns with Wales and its people, and with the implications of his faith. His later work evinces a fierce distrust of the modern world.

Thomas à Kempis *See* KEMPIS, THOMAS À

Thomas Aquinas, Saint *See* AQUINAS, SAINT THOMAS

Thomism Philosophy of Saint Thomas AQUINAS, one of the major systems in SCHOLASTICISM. Aquinas blended the

► **thistle** The creeping thistle is a weed, which is common on waste and cultivated land. Like the dandelion, it is a composite. There are c.150 species of *Cirsium* whose flowers may be violet, mauve, pink, yellow or white.

philosophy of ARISTOTLE with Christian theology. Using Aristotle's concept of matter and form, he conceived a hierarchy in which spirit is higher than matter, soul higher than body, and theology above philosophy.

Thompson, Emma (1959–) English actress and screenwriter. She was married (1989–95) to Kenneth BRANAGH, and acted in his adaptations of Shakespeare's *Henry V* (1989) and *Much Ado Nothing* (1993). Thompson won an Academy Award for best actress in *Howard's End* (1991). She won a further Oscar for best screenplay for *Sense and Sensibility* (1995). Other films include *Remains of the Day* (1993) and *Carrington* (1995).

Thomson, Sir George Paget (1892–1975) English physicist, son of Sir Joseph John THOMSON. He shared the 1937 Nobel Prize for physics with Clinton Davisson for their independent work in diffracting ELECTRONS (1927). This work confirmed the wave nature of particles first predicted (1923) by Louis de BROGLIE.

Thomson, James (1700–48) Scottish poet. A precursor of ROMANTICISM, Thomson's best-known work is the four-part nature poem *The Seasons* (1730). It was used by Haydn as the basis for his oratorio (1801). Other works include the song "Rule Britannia" (1740) and the Spenserian allegory *The Castle of Indolence* (1748).

Thomson, Sir Joseph John (1856–1940) British physicist, father of George THOMSON, b. Belfast. He succeeded James Clerk MAXWELL as professor of experimental physics (1884–1919) at Cambridge. Thomson's discovery (1897) of the ELECTRON is regarded as the birth of PARTICLE PHYSICS. He established that cathode rays consisted of a stream of particles. Thomson went on to prove that the electron was negatively charged and that its mass was c.2,000 times smaller than the smallest atom (hydrogen). He was awarded the 1906 Nobel Prize for physics for his investigations into the electrical conductivity of gases. Thomson and Francis ASTON produced evidence of ISOTOPES of neon. He transformed the Cavendish Laboratory into a major centre for atomic research, attracting scientists of the calibre of Ernest RUTHERFORD. Thomson served as president (1915–20) of the Royal Society.

Thor In TEUTONIC MYTHOLOGY, god of thunder and lightning, corresponding to JUPITER. The eldest and strongest of ODIN's sons, he was represented as a red-bearded warrior, benevolent toward humans but a mighty foe of evil.

thorax In animal anatomy, part between the neck and abdomen. In mammals it is formed by the rib cage and contains the lungs, heart and oesophagus. In insects it consists of several segments to which legs and other appendages are attached.

Thoreau, Henry David (1817–62) US writer and naturalist. He was a friend of the transcendentalist Ralph Waldo EMERSON, who encouraged him to keep the journals from which he quarried much of his later work. An ardent individualist, he experimented in living a near-solitary life, rejecting materialism and finding fulfilment in observing plant and animal life. His essay *Civil Disobedience* (1849) has influenced many passive resistance movements.

thorium (symbol Th) Radioactive, metallic element of the ACTINIDE ELEMENTS, first discovered in 1828. The chief ore is monazite (phosphate). The metal is used in photoelectric and thermionic emitters. One decay product is RADON-220. Thorium is sometimes used in radiotherapy and is increasingly used for conversion into uranium-233 for nuclear FISSION. Chemically reactive, it burns in air but reacts slowly in water. Properties: at.no. 90; r.a.m. 232.0381; r.d. 11.72; m.p. 1,750°C (3,182°F); b.p. 4,790°C (8,654°F); most stable isotope Th^{232} (1.41 × 10^{10} yrs).

thorn apple Plant of the genus *Datura*, especially Jimson weed (*D. stramonium*), a poisonous, annual weed of tropical American origin. It has foul-smelling leaves and large white or violet trumpet-shaped flowers that are succeeded by round prickly fruits. Family Solanaceae.

Thorndike, Edward Lee (1874–1949) US psychologist and educator. He devised the first systematic theory of LEARNING. He carried out laboratory studies on animal behaviour, suggesting that the "law of effect" (the reinforcement principle) also applies to humans. Behaviour followed by reward tends to be repeated, whereas unrewarded behaviour tends to die away. Major works include *The Fundamentals of Learning* (1932).

Thorpe, Ian (1982–) Australian swimmer. At the 2000 Olympics in Sydney, Thorpe won a gold medal in the 400m freestyle event, beating the world record which he already held. He also anchored the gold medal winning Australian relay teams for the 4 x 100m and 4 x 200m freestyle relay events.

Thorvaldsen, Bertel (c.1768–1844) Danish sculptor. From 1797, he lived and worked mainly in Rome. Thorvaldsen's commitment to NEOCLASSICISM is evident from his *Jason* (1803). Other major works include the *Lion of Lucerne* (1819) and a monument to Byron in Trinity College, Cambridge (1829).

Thoth In Egyptian mythology, scribe of the gods. He appears as the record keeper of the dead, patron of the arts and learning, inventor of writing and as creator of the universe. Thoth is depicted as a man with the head of an ibis or as a baboon.

Thrace (Thráki) Ancient SE European country, now divided between Bulgaria, Greece and European Turkey. From 1300 to 600 BC, the Thracian lands extended W to the Adriatic and N to the Danube. By c.600 BC, Thrace had lost much of its E lands to the Illyrians and Macedonians, and the Greeks established the colony of Byzantium. In 342 BC, Philip II of Macedon conquered the country. After 100 BC, it became part of the Roman Empire. In the 7th century AD, the N of the region was conquered by the Bulgarians, and by 1300 they controlled all Thrace. From 1361 to 1453, the region was disputed between the Bulgarians and the emerging Ottoman empire, eventually falling to the Turks. In 1885, N Thrace was annexed to Bulgaria. The regions either side of the River Maritsa became known as Eastern Thrace (Bulgaria) and Western Thrace (Turkey). After World War 1, Bulgaria ceded S and most of E Thrace to Greece. The Treaty of LAUSANNE (1923) restored E Thrace to Turkey, and the region retains these boundaries. A fertile region, its main economic activity is agriculture.

threadworm (pinworm) Small ROUNDWORM of the phylum Aschelminthes. It is commonest in moist tropical regions and resembles a short length of hair or thread. It may inhabit the intestines of animals but can live and breed freely in soil. Species *Oxyurus vermicularis*.

Three Mile Island Island on the Susquehanna River near Harrisburg, Pennyslvania, USA. It is the site of a nuclear power-generating plant where a near-disastrous accident took place in March 1979. The accident involved the failure of the feedwater system that picks up heat from the system that has circulated through the reactor core, producing steam to power the turbines. Radioactive water and gases were released into the environment.

thrip Any of numerous species of slender, sucking insects found throughout the world. Species vary in colour, but most feed on plants and some carry plant diseases. Length: to 8mm (0.3in). Order Thysanoptera.

throat *See* PHARYNX

thrombophlebitis Inflammation of the walls of veins associated with THROMBOSIS. It can occur in the legs during pregnancy.

thrombosis Formation of a blood clot in an artery or vein. Besides causing loss of circulation to the area supplied by the blocked vessel, it carries the risk of EMBOLISM.

thrush Any of numerous species of small songbirds of the family Turdidae. The European song thrush (*Turdus philomelos*) is mottled brown with a lighter, speckled breast. North American species include the (North American) robin, bluebird and bluethroat. Length: to 30cm (12in).

thrush (candidiasis) Fungal infection of the mucous membranes, usually of the mouth but also of the vagina. Caused by the fungus, *Candida albicans*, it is sometimes seen in people taking broad-spectrum ANTIBIOTICS.

thrust Driving force resulting from operation of a propeller, jet engine or rocket engine. An aircraft propeller forces air backward, and jet and rocket engines expel gases backward. Thrust is produced in the forward direction in accordance with the third of NEWTON'S LAWS of motion. *See also* AERODYNAMICS

Thucydides (*c*.460–*c*.400 BC) Greek historian. A commander in the PELOPONNESIAN WARS, his *History of the Peloponnesian War* is a determined attempt to write objective history, and it displays a profound understanding of human motives.

thugs Murderous gangs in India who preyed on travellers. They were members of a secret society, who killed their victims by ritual strangulation (*thuggee*) in honour of KALI, the Hindu goddess of destruction. They were suppressed by the British in the 1830s.

thulium (symbol Tm) Lustrous, silver-white, metallic element of the LANTHANIDE SERIES. Its chief ore is monazite but thulium is as rare as gold. Soft, malleable and ductile, it combines with OXYGEN and the HALOGENS. It is used in arc lighting and portable X-ray units. Properties: at.no. 69; r.a.m. 168.9342; r.d. 9.31; 1,545°C (2,813°F); b.p. 1,947°C (3,537°F); most stable isotope Tm^{169} (100%).

thunderstorm Electrical storm caused by the separation of electrical charges in clouds. Water drops are carried by updrafts to the top of a cloud, where they become ionized and accumulate into positive charges – the base of the cloud being negatively charged. An electrical discharge (a spark) between clouds, or between a cloud and the ground, is accompanied by light (seen as a LIGHTNING stroke) and heat. The heat expands the air explosively and causes it to reverberate and produce sounds and echoes called thunder.

Thurber, James Grover (1894–1961) US humourist and cartoonist. In 1927, he became a regular contributor of essays, short stories and cartoons to the *New Yorker*. Collections of Thurber's essays and stories include *My Life and Hard Times* (1933) and *My World and Welcome to It* (1942), which includes his best-known short-story "The Secret Life of Walter Mitty" (1932).

Thuringia Historic region of central Germany. Its rulers became powerful princes with the HOLY ROMAN EMPIRE in the 11th century. In 1920, Thuringia was reconstituted as a state under the WEIMAR REPUBLIC, but it lost its separate identity in 1952. The main economic activities are manufacturing and cereal cropping. Area: 16,176sq km (6,244sq mi). Pop. (1992) 2,545,808.

Thutmose Name of four kings of the 18th dynasty in ancient EGYPT. **Thutmose I** (r. *c*.1525–*c*.1512 BC) extended his kingdom southward into NUBIA and campaigned successfully in the Near East. He was succeeded by his son, **Thutmose II** (r. *c*.1512–*c*.1504 BC), who married his half-sister, HATSHEPSUT. She ruled as regent for his son,

Thutmose III (r. *c*.1504–1450 BC). Thutmose III expanded the kingdom to its greatest extent, defeating the Mitanni kingdom on the River Euphrates and pushing the southern frontier beyond the fourth cataract of the Nile. His grandson, **Thutmose IV** (r. *c*.1425–*c*.1416 BC), continued an expansive policy but also sought to strengthen the empire by peaceful means, marrying a Mitanni princess.

thyme Aromatic garden herb of the MINT family (Lamiaceae/Labiatae), used as an ornamental plant and in cooking. Purple-flowered, it yields an oil from which the drug thymol is prepared. Height: 15–20cm (6–8in). Genus *Thymus*.

thymus gland One of the endocrine GLANDS, located in the upper chest in mammals. In childhood it controls the development of lymphoid tissue and the immune response to infection. Disorder of the thymus may be associated with autoimmune diseases (those caused by the body's own antibodies). *See also* ENDOCRINE SYSTEM

thyroid gland H-shaped gland of the ENDOCRINE SYSTEM. It lies in the base of the neck, straddling the trachea below the Adam's apple. It secretes hormones, principally THYROXINE.

thyroxine Hormone secreted by the THYROID GLAND. It contains IODINE and helps regulate the rate of metabolism; it is essential for normal growth and development.

Tiananmen Square World's largest public square, covering 40ha (98 acres) in BEIJING, China. On the S side, a marble monument is dedicated to the heroes of the revolution. A huge portrait of MAO adorns the side of the MAO ZEDONG Memorial Hall. On 4 May 1919, China's first mass public rally was held in the square, where on 1 October 1949, Mao proclaimed the People's Republic of China. In 1966, Mao made his pronouncements on the CULTURAL REVOLUTION to more than a million Red Guards assembled here. In April 1989, hundreds of thousands of citizens joined in pro-democracy demonstrations and student leaders organized hunger-strikes. On 4 June 1989, tanks and troops stormed the square. Official casualties were put at more than 200 demonstrators and dozens of soldiers. Eyewitness reports suggest thousands of deaths. The government imposed a year-long martial law and executed several student leaders.

Tianjin (Tientsin) Port and industrial city on the Hai River, NE China. The country's third-largest city, it is also N China's most important international port. Founded in *c*.300 BC, it became prominent in the late 18th century due to its strategic position en route to Manchuria. In 1860, the British and French obtained the right to use Tianjin as a treaty port. In 1900, the city came under European occupation. Because of its excellent transport links, it remains the trading centre for N China. Industries: iron, steel, heavy machinery, transport equipment, textiles, carpets. The city is administered as a special economic zone to encourage inward investment. Pop. (1993) 4,970,000.

Tian Shan (Tien Shan) Mountain range in central Asia, 2,400km (1,500mi) long, forming the border between Kyrgyzstan and Xinjiang, NW China. At their W edge, the Tian Shan ("Celestial Mountains") divide the Tarim and Junggar Basins. The range then rises to 7,439m (24,406ft) at Peak Pobeda, on the Chinese border with Kazakstan and Kyrgyzstan. The Issyk Kul in Kyrgyzstan is one of the world's biggest mountain lakes.

Tiber (Tevere) River in central Italy. Rising in the Etruscan Apennines, it flows S then SW through Rome and empties into the Tyrrhenian Sea at Ostia. The silting of the river has closed Fiumara, one of its two mouths, and its delta continues to expand; the ancient coastal port of Ostia Antica now lies 6km (4mi) inland. Length: 404km (251 mi).

Tiberius (42 BC–AD 37) (Tiberius Julius Caesar Augustus) Roman emperor (AD 14–37). He was the stepson of AUGUSTUS, who adopted him as his heir (AD 4). Initially, his administration was just and moderate, but he became increasingly fearful of conspiracy and had many people executed for alleged treason. Tiberius left Rome and spent his last years in seclusion on Capri.

Tibet (Xizang) Autonomous region in SW China. The capital and largest city is LHASA. Tibet is the highest region on Earth, with an average altitude of 4,875m (16,000ft). An historically inaccessible area, Tibet is surrounded by mountains on three sides. The Tibetan HIMALAYAS include the world's highest mountain, EVEREST. Nam Co is the world's largest natural salt lake. Many of Asia's greatest rivers, including the YANGTZE, MEKONG, HUANG HE, INDUS and GANGES have their source in Tibet, though its major river is the BRAHMAPUTRA. The area has scant rainfall, and the Brahmaputra valley is the only agricultural area and the location of the major cities. Many of the people remain nomadic pastoralists. Tibet is rich in mineral resources, such as gold, copper and uranium. The Chinese government has built internal highways and links to the Chinese provinces. The principal religion is TIBETAN

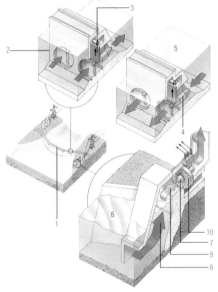

▲ **tidal power** The power of the sea can be harnessed to generate electricity. Tidal power uses a barrage (1) across an estuary or bay. The barrage contains turbines which can spin with a flow of water in either direction. As the tide comes in, gates on the barrage remain closed until a head of water has built up on the sea side of the structure (2). The gates are then opened (3) and the incoming tide flows through the barrage driving the turbines (4). As the tide falls,

the process is reversed with the gates closed until the sea has fallen below the level of water retained in the estuary (5). The second way of harnessing the power of the sea is wave power (6). The key difference is that the turbine (7) is air-driven not turned by water. As a wave hits the shore, the force of the water (8) drives air (9) through the turbine blades (10). When the water level drops, air is sucked back down through the turbine, spinning it again.

BUDDHISM. Until 1959, a large percentage of the urban male population were Buddhist monks (lamas). Tibet flourished as an independent kingdom in the 7th century, and in the 8th century Padmasambhava developed the principles of MAHAYANA Buddhism and founded Lamaism. The spiritual leaders of Lamaism (the DALAI LAMA and the PANCHEN LAMA) also acted as the country's temporal rulers. In 1206, Genghis Khan conquered the region, and it remained under nominal Mongol rule until 1720, when the Chinese QING dynasty claimed sovereignty. At the close of the 19th century the Tibetan areas of Ladakh and SIKKIM were incorporated into British India, and in 1906 Britain recognized Chinese sovereignty over Tibet. In 1912, the fall of the QING dynasty prompted the Tibetans to reassert their independence. China, however, maintained its right to govern, and in 1950 the new communist regime invaded. In 1951, Tibet was declared an autonomous region of China, nominally governed by the Dalai Lama. The Chinese government began a series of repressive measures principally targeting the Buddhist monasteries. In March 1959, a full-scale revolt against Chinese rule was suppressed by the Chinese army. The Dalai Lama managed to flee to N India (25 December 1959), and established a government-in-exile at Dharamsala. In 1965, China formally annexed Tibet as an autonomous region. The CULTURAL REVOLUTION banned religious practice, and 4,000 monasteries were destroyed. Many thousands of Tibetans were forced into exile by the brutality of the communist regime. Despite the restoration of some of the desecrated monasteries and the reinstatement of Tibetan as an official language, human-rights violations continued. Pro-independence rallies in 1987–89 were violently suppressed by the Chinese army. Area: 1,222,070sq km (471,841sq mi). Pop. (1993) 2,290,000.

Tibetan art Predominantly religious in character, Tibetan art is designed to serve the elaborate rituals of TIBETAN BUDDHISM. Artworks are anonymous, usually undated and are in the form of wall paintings or *thangkas*, which are banners, usually displayed in temples or carried in processions. *Thangkas* generally depict scenes from the life of a deity or *mandalas* (patterns used for meditation).

Tibetan Buddhism Distinctive blend of MAHAYANA Buddhism and Bonism (a pre-Buddhist SHAMANISM). It mixes meditative monasticism with indigenous folk religion and involves a system of reincarnating lamas (monks). Both spiritual and temporal authority reside in the person and office of the DALAI LAMA. King Srongtsan-gampo (b.617 or 629) sought to bring Buddhist teachers from China and India to Tibet. The Bon priests opposed the new teachings, and BUDDHISM was not thoroughly introduced into Tibet until the 8th century. Following reforms initiated by the 11th-century Indian master Atisha, four major sects emerged in Tibetan Buddhism. Of these, the Gelugpa order, to which the Dalai and PANCHEN LAMAS belong, was politically dominant from the 17th century. There are now two Gelugpa sects, the Red and Yellow monks. The Dalai Lama, a member of the latter, became revered as the "Living Buddha" and the spiritual and temporal ruler of Tibet. Each new Dalai Lama is believed to be a reincarnation of AVALOKITESVARA. The Panchen Lama heads the Red monks.

tibia (shinbone) Inner and larger of the two lower leg bones. It articulates with the FEMUR, or upper leg bone, at the knee and extends to the ankle, where its lower end forms the projecting ankle bone on the inside of the leg. *See also* FIBULA

tick Any of numerous species of wingless, bloodsucking ARACHNIDS, the most notable of which are ectoparasites of vertebrates and invertebrates. Many species carry diseases (some fatal) in wild and domesticated animals and in humans Length: to 3mm (0.1in). Class Arachnida; order Acarina.

tidal power Energy harnessed from tidal movement of the Earth's OCEANS and used by humans. It is economic only where the tidal range is greater than c.4.6m (15ft). Modern schemes involve the use of turbogenerators driven by the passage of water through a tidal barrage.

tide Periodic rise and fall of the surface level of the OCEANS caused by the gravitational attraction of the Moon and Sun. Tides follow the Moon's cycle of 28 days, so they arrive at a given spot 50 minutes later each day. When the Sun and Moon are in conjunction or opposition, the greatest tidal range occurs, called spring tides. When they are in quadrature, when the Moon is half-full, tidal ranges are lowest and are called neap tides.

Tiepolo, Giovanni Battista (1696–1770) Italian painter. His ROCOCO pictures are full of action, using light, sunny colours, with figures and objects seen in a deep, theatrical PERSPECTIVE. The peak of his career came in the 1750s when he decorated the Kaisersaal and the grand staircase of the Prince Archbishop's Palace, Würzburg.

Tierra del Fuego (Sp. Land of Fire) Archipelago separated from mainland S South America by the Magellan Strait. It consists of one large island and other smaller islands. At the S extremity of the islands lies Cape Horn. The main island is politically divided between Argentina and Chile. The islands remained undiscovered by Europeans until Ferdinand MAGELLAN's landing in 1520. They were not settled until the 1880s, when the discovery of gold and later oil attracted many Europeans, Argentinians and Chileans to the area. The indigenous population was killed by diseases brought by settlers. The mountainous terrain and harsh climate limit economic activity to sheep rearing and oil exploration. Area: 73,746sq km (28,473sq mi). Pop. (1991) 69,450.

Tiffany, Louis Comfort (1848–1933) US painter, designer, and a leader of the ART NOUVEAU style in the USA. In 1878, he formed an interior decorating firm, which by 1900 was known as Tiffany Studios. It specialized in what he termed "favrile" glass: freely shaped iridescent glasswork, sometimes combined with various metals.

tiger Large, powerful CAT found (in decreasing numbers) throughout Asia, mainly in forested areas. It has a characteristic striped coat of yellow, orange, white and black, with the chin and underparts white. Relying on keen hearing, it hunts for birds, deer, cattle and reptiles. An adult tiger will eat up to 25kg of meat in one meal. The largest tiger is the Siberian race. Length: to 13ft (4m); weight: to 230kg (500lb). Family Felidae; species *Panthera tigris*.

Tigris River in SW Asia. Rising in the Taurus Mountains of E Turkey, it flows SE through Iraq, joining the River EUPHRATES to form the SHATT AL ARAB waterway. The river is liable to sudden flooding, but there are flood-control schemes and the river irrigates more than 300,000ha (750,000 acres). It is navigable for shallow-draft vessels as far as BAGHDAD. Length: c.1,900km (1,180mi).

Tilden, Bill (William Tatem), Jr (1893–1953) US tennis player. Nicknamed "Big Bill," he was the greatest player of his day. Tilden won seven US Opens (1920–25, 1929) and three Wimbledon singles titles (1920–21, 1930). He was the first US champion at Wimbledon.

till In geology, sediment consisting of an unsorted mixture of clay, sand, gravel and boulders that is deposited directly by the ice of GLACIERS.

timber *See* WOOD

▲ **tiger** Once common in Asia, the tiger population has suffered much from hunting and the reduction of its habitat. It can leap 4m (15ft) in one bound.

timbre Characteristic of a musical sound determined by the number and intensity of the overtones (HARMONICS) produced as well as the principal (fundamental) note. Musical instruments of different types make characteristic sounds because of the different harmonics produced.

Timbuktu Town in N Mali, W Africa. It was founded by the Tuareg in the 11th century and soon became a centre of Muslim learning. The S terminus of a Saharan caravan route, it later became famous throughout Europe as a market for slaves and gold. Sacked by the Moroccans in 1591 and seized by the French in 1893, its most important trading commodity today is salt. Pop. (1992 est.) 26,000.

time Perception of a sequential order in all experience; also the interval perceived between two events. A consideration of time falls within the disciplines of physics, psychology, philosophy and biology. Until the theory of RELATIVITY was devised by Albert EINSTEIN, time was conceived of as absolute – a constant one-direction (past to future) flow. Since then the concept of time linked with distance in SPACE ("space-time") has connected time with the relative velocities of those perceiving it. For clocks at velocities approaching that of light, time expands from the point of view of a stationary observer, but it still flows in the same direction.

time scale *See* GEOLOGICAL TIME

time zone One of 24 divisions of the Earth's surface, each 15° of LONGITUDE wide, within which the time of day is reckoned to be the same. At a conference held in Washington, D.C., in 1884, the meridian of Greenwich was adopted as the zero of longitude, and zones of longitude were established. Standard time in each successive zone westward is one hour behind that in the preceding zone. *See also* GREENWICH MEAN TIME (GMT)

Timisoara City on the River Bega and Canal, W Romania. An ancient Roman settlement, it was ruled by the MAGYARS from 896, annexed to Hungary in 1010 and ruled by the Turks from 1552 to 1716. It was returned to Austria-Hungary in 1716 and passed to Romania in 1920. Events here in 1989 triggered the fall of the CEAUSESCU regime. Industries: engineering, food processing, tobacco, chemicals, textiles, machinery. Pop. (1993) 325,359.

Timor Largest of the Lesser Sunda Islands in the Malay archipelago; part of INDONESIA. The chief towns are Kupang in the W and Dili in the E. From c.1520, Portuguese spice traders began to settle on Timor. When the Dutch landed in 1620 they settled on the W side. During World War 2, the island was occupied by the Japanese. In 1950, West Timor became part of the Nusa Tenggara Timur province of the newly created Republic of Indonesia. In 1975, the Portuguese abandoned East Timor, and the colony declared its independence. Indonesia immediately invaded, and in 1976 annexed East Timor. The East Timor independence movement FRETILIN maintained resistance to Indonesian rule amid widespread reports of human rights violations. In 1999, following a vote for independence, violence erupted as pro-Indonesian militias sought to desta-bilize the country. A mountainous island, its main products are rice, coconuts, coffee, and tobacco. Area: 13,074sq mi (33,857sq km). Pop. (both provinces) (1990) 4,015,394.

timpani (kettledrums) Principal percussion instruments in a symphony orchestra. They are hemispherical vessels of copper or brass with single skins, tuned by pedals or screws and struck with sticks with hard felt heads. Military kettledrums were introduced to Europe by the Crusaders in *c*.1100.

Timur *See* TAMERLANE

tin (symbol Sn) Metallic element of group IV of the periodic table, known from ancient times. Its chief ore is cassiterite (an oxide). Soft, malleable and resistant to corrosion, tin is used as a protective coating for iron, steel, copper and other metals, and in such alloys as solder, pewter, and bronze. Properties: at.no. 50; at.wt. 118.69; sp.gr. 7.29; m.p. 449.6°F (232°C); b.p. 4,118°F (2,270°C); most common isotope Sn^{118} (24.03%).

Tinbergen, Nikolaas (1907–88) Dutch ethologist. He shared, with Konrad LORENZ and Karl von FRISCH, the 1973 Nobel Prize for physiology or medicine for his pioneering work in ETHOLOGY. Tinbergen studied how certain stimuli evoke specific responses in animals.

Tintoretto (1518–94) Italian painter, b. Jacopo Robusti. Tintoretto was the outstanding Venetian painter in the generation that succeeded TITIAN. Among his notable works are *The Finding of the Body of St Mark* (1562), *The Last Supper* (1592–94), and the huge *Paradiso* (1588–90) in the Doge's Palace, Venice. Some of Tintoretto's finest paintings are in the series of the life of Christ (1565–87).

Tipperary County in Munster province, central S Republic of Ireland. The region is part of the central plain of Ireland, but there are hills in the S; the Suir and Shannon are the principal rivers. The soil is fertile, and Tipperary is one of the country's best farming regions. The county town is Clonmel. Area: 4,255sq km (1,643sq mi). Pop. (1991) 132,772.

Tippett, Sir Michael Kemp (1905–98) English composer. His music incorporates apparently disparate musical forms and social themes of justice, pacifism and humanism. Tippett's oratorio *A Child of our Time* (1941) was a response to the 1938 Kristallnacht in Nazi Germany. His operas include *The Midsummer Marriage* (1952), *King Priam* (1962) and *New Year* (1988). Other works include the oratorio *The Mask of Time* (1982), *String Quartet No.1* (1934) and four symphonies (1945, 1957, 1972, 1977). He was knighted in 1966.

Tipu Sahib (1749–99) Indian ruler, sultan of Mysore (1782–99). He fought the MARATHA and the British in the service of his father, HYDER ALI, but concluded peace with the British in 1784. His negotiations with the French provoked a British invasion of Mysore in 1799, and Tipu was killed while defending his capital, Seringapatam.

Tirana (Tiranë) Capital of Albania, on the River Ishm. It was founded in the early 17th century by the Ottoman Turks and became Albania's capital in 1920. In 1946, the communists came to power and the industrial sector of the city was developed. Industries: metal goods, agricultural machinery, textiles. Pop. (1995) 270,000.

Tirol (Tyrol) Federal state in W Austria, bordered N by Germany and S by Italy. The capital is INNSBRUCK. The Romans conquered the region in 15 BC, and the Franks held it during the 8th century. In 1363, the province was taken by the Habsburgs. In 1805, Napoleon I awarded Tirol to Bavaria in return for its support. In 1810, Napoleon gave S Tirol to the Italians, but the Congress of Vienna (1815) reunited Tirol with Austria. After

World War 1, when S Tirol was awarded to Italy, a process of Italianization was resisted by the German-speaking inhabitants. After World War 2, S Tirol was made an autonomous Italian region. Tourists are attracted by the good skiing conditions in the Tyrolean Alps. Other economic activities are mainly agricultural. Area: 12,647sq km (4,882sq mi). Pop. (1994) 654,753.

Tirpitz, Alfred von (1849–1930) German admiral, chiefly responsible for the build-up of the German navy before World War 1. Frustrated by government cut-backs and restrictions on submarine warfare, he resigned in 1916.

tissue Material of a living body consisting of a group of similar and often interconnected cells, usually supporting a similar function. Tissues vary greatly in structure and complexity. In animals they may be loosely classified according to function into epithelial, connective, skeletal, muscular, nervous and glandular tissues.

tissue culture In biology, artificial cultivation of living TISSUE in sterile conditions. Tissue culture is used for biological research or to help in the diagnosis of diseases. It is also used a means of propagating plant CLONES. *See also* GENETIC ENGINEERING

tit *See* TITMOUSE

Titan Largest SATELLITE of Saturn, and the second largest in the Solar System, discovered by Christiaan Huygens in 1655. It is unique among planetary satellites in having a substantial atmosphere. It is composed of rock and water-ice in roughly equal proportions. The space probe Voyager 1 found no gaps in an opaque, reddish cloud layer 200km (125mi) above the surface. The atmosphere consists mostly of nitrogen, with some methane and other hydrocarbon compounds. The surface temperature is 95K, at which METHANE can exist as solid, liquid or gas, so methane may play the role that water does on Earth, forming clouds, rain and lakes.

Titania In folklore, queen of the FAIRIES and wife of OBERON. In OVID's writing she represents DIANA at the head of her nymphs. In Shakespeare's *A Midsummer Night's Dream* (1595) she quarrels with her husband over a changeling boy.

Titanic British passenger liner that sank (14–15 April 1912) on her maiden voyage. The largest vessel of her time, she was sailing from Southampton to New York when she struck an iceberg in the N Atlantic. About 1,500 people were drowned. The disaster led to international agreements on greater safety precautions at sea. In 1985, the wreck of the *Titanic* was located on the ocean floor.

titanium (symbol Ti) Lustrous, silver-grey metallic element of the TRANSITION ELEMENTS. A common element, it is found in many minerals, chief sources being ilmenite and RUTILE. Resistant to corrosion and heat, it is used in steels and other alloys, especially in aircraft, spacecraft and guided missiles where strength must be combined with lightness. Properties: at.no. 22; r.a.m. 47.90; r.d. 4.54; m.p. 1,660°C (3,020°F); b.p. 3,287°C (5,949°F); most common isotope Ti^{48} (73.94%).

Titans In Greek mythology, 12 gods and goddesses who were the sons and daughters of URANUS and GAIA. They were overthrown by the Olympians, led by ZEUS.

tithe Tax of one-tenth of income levied to support a religious institution. Tithes were prescribed in the Old Testament and were a major source of church income in medieval Europe. They were generally abandoned in favour of other sources of income in the 19th century.

Titian (1485–1576) Venetian painter, b. Tiziano Vecellio. He trained first with Giovanni BELLINI and then GIORGIONE. His reputation was established with the monumental *The Assumption of the Virgin* (1516–18). Titian combined the balance of High RENAISSANCE composition with a new dynamism, which heralded the BAROQUE. He favoured vivid, simple colours and often silhouetted dark forms against a light background. His finest mythological paintings include *Bacchanal* (*c*.1518) and the earthy *Bacchus and Ariadne* (1522–23). In 1533, Titian was appointed court painter to Emperor Charles V, and his *Charles V at Mühlberg* (1548) is one of the earliest equestrian portraits. From 1550, Titian produced erotic mythologies for Philip II of Spain, such as *The Rape of Europa* (1562). His last work was the astonishingly powerful *Pietà*, which he designed for his own tomb. Titian's oil technique was freer and more expressive than any earlier style, and he had a revolutionary influence on later artists.

Titicaca Lake in the Andes on the Peru-Bolivia border, draining s through the River Desaguader into Lake Poopó. At an altitude of 3,810m (12,500ft), it is the highest navigable body of water in the world. The constant water supply has enabled the region to grow crops since ancient times. The lake is home to giant edible frogs and is also famed for its totora reeds, from which the Uru make their floating island homes and distinctive fishing rafts. Area: 8,290sq km (3,200sq mi). Maximum depth: 280m (920ft).

titmouse (tit, chickadee) Small, stubby-bodied, and large-headed bird of open woodlands and wooded parks of the Northern Hemisphere and Africa. Most true titmice nest in self-drilled holes or abandoned woodpecker holes. Family Paridae; genus *Parus*. The long-tailed titmice and bush tits of Eurasia and w North America are larger and build closed, often hanging nests. Subfamily Aegithalinae.

Tito (1892–1980) Yugoslav statesman, b. Croatia as Josip Broz. As a soldier in the Austro-Hungarian army, he was captured by the Russians (1915) but released by the Bolsheviks in 1917. He helped to organize the Yugoslav Communist Party and adopted the name Tito in 1934. He led the Partisans' successful campaign against the Germans in YUGOSLAVIA during World War 2. In 1945, Tito established a communist government and was prime minister (1945–53) and thereafter president, although virtually a dictator. Soviet efforts to control Yugoslavia led to a split between the two countries in 1948. At home, Tito sought to balance the deep ethnic and religious divisions in Yugoslavia and to develop an economic model of communist "self-management". Abroad, he became an influential leader of the Non-Aligned Movement. As later events confirmed, his greatest achievement was to hold the Yugoslavian federation together.

titration Method used in analytical chemistry to determine the concentration of a compound in a solution by measuring the amount needed to complete a reaction with another compound. A solution of known concentration is added in measured amounts to a liquid of unknown concentration until the reaction is complete. The volume added enables the concentration to be calculated.

Titus (AD 39–81) Roman emperor (r.79–81), eldest son of VESPASIAN. In AD 70, he captured and destroyed Jerusalem after a Jewish revolt. As emperor, Titus stopped persecutions for treason, completed the COLOSSEUM and provided aid for the survivors after the eruption of VESUVIUS (79). He was succeeded by DOMITIAN.

Tlingit NATIVE AMERICAN people of the SE coast of Alaska. Famous for their totem poles (featuring stylized forms of local wildlife), they rely economically on fishing, tourism and government aid.

TNT (2,4,6–trinitrotoluene) Explosive organic compound ($C_7H_5N_3O_6$) made from TOLUENE by using sulphuric and nitric acids. Its resistance to shock (requiring a detonator to set it off) makes it one of the safest high EXPLOSIVES.

toad Any of many species of tail-less amphibians found worldwide, except Australasia. Most are short and rotund, moving with a crawling or hopping gait. Toads are differentiated from FROGS by their rougher, bumpier skin and rounder body with shorter legs. Length: 2–25cm (1–10in). Order Anura; family Bu-fonidae. *See also* TADPOLE

toadstool Popular name for the fruiting body of a FUNGUS of the class Basidiomycetae. It usually refers to inedible species and describes the stool-like appearance of the reproductive organ. It consists of a stem and a cap, on which the spores are borne on gills or in tubes.

tobacco Herb native to the Americas but cultivated worldwide for its leaves, which are dried and smoked. It has large leaves with no stalk, and white, pink or red star-shaped flowers. *Nicotiana tabacum* is the principal cultivated species. Seeds were brought to Europe in *c*.1520–30. Settlers in Virginia obtained seeds from the Spanish colonies (1612) and soon tobacco was the major crop of the Virginia colony and America's first export. Leaves are prepared for smoking by curing (drying) and then ageing. Family Solanaceae (NIGHTSHADE family). Height: 0.6–2m (2–6ft).

Tobago *See* TRINIDAD AND TOBAGO

Tocqueville, Alexis de (1805–59) French historian. Sent on a fact-finding tour to the USA by the French government, he produced *Of Democracy in America* (1835), the first in-depth study of the US political system. His later work includes *L'Ancien Régime et la Révolution* (1856).

Togo Small republic in w Africa; the capital is LOMÉ. It is divided geographically into four regions. The coastal plain is sandy; N of the coast is an area of fertile, clay soil. North again is the Mono Tableland, which reaches an altitude of *c*.450m (1,500ft) and is drained by the River Mono. The Atakora Mountains are the fourth region. The vegetation is mainly open grassland. The historic region of Togoland comprised what is now the Republic of Togo and w GHANA. From the 17th to 19th century, the ASHANTIS raided Togoland, seizing the indigenous inhabitants, the Ewe, and selling them to Europeans as slaves. As a

▶ **tobacco** Tobacco is produced mainly from the plant *Nicotiana tabacum*, which is cultivated worldwide. The leaves are removed from the plant and dried. Native Americans smoked tobacco leaves and used them medicinally, long before the arrival of Europeans in the New World.

TOGO
AREA: 56,790sq km (21,927sq mi)
POPULATION: 4,861,000
CAPITAL (POPULATION): Lomé (590,000)

German protectorate from 1884, it developed economically and Lomé was built. At the start of World War 1, Britain and France captured Togoland from Germany. In 1922, it was divided into two mandates that, in 1942, became UN trust territories. In 1957, British Togoland became part of Ghana. In 1960, French Togoland became independent as the Republic of Togo. In 1961, Slyvanus Olympio became the first president. He was assassinated in 1963. Nicolas Grunitzky became president, but in 1967 he was overthrown in a military coup, led by Ghansimgbe Eyadéma. In 1972, Eyadéma became president. In 1979, a new constitution confirmed Togo as a single-party state, the sole legal party being the *Rassemblement du Peuple Togolais* (RPT). Re-elected in 1972 and 1986, Eyadéma was forced to resign in 1991 after pro-democracy riots. Kokou Koffigoh led an interim government. Unrest continued with troops loyal to Eyadéma attempting to overthrow Koffigoh. In 1992, a new multi-party constitution was introduced and Eyadéma regained some power. In 1993, a rigged election, boycotted by opposition parties, was won by Eyadéma. In 1994, elections were won by an opposition alliance but Eyadéma formed a coalition government. In 1998, Eyadéma was re-elected in suspect elections. **Economy** The majority of the population are engaged in subsistence agriculture (1995 GDP per capita, US$1,130). Cocoa, coffee and cotton are the chief cash crops. Palm oil and phosphates are the principal exports.

Tojo, Hideki (1885–1948) Japanese statesman and general, prime minister (1941–44). He was chief of staff (1937–40) in Manchuria and minister of war (1940–41). As prime minister, he approved the attack on PEARL HARBOR and was responsible for all aspects of the war effort. In July 1944, he resigned after Japan lost Saipan. In 1945, he was arrested by the Allies, tried for war crimes, found guilty and hanged.

Tokugawa Japanese hereditary dynasty (1603–1867) that controlled Japan through the SHOGUN. The Tokugawa shogunate was established by Ieyasu Tokugawa (1543–1616) who completed the unification of Japan. They ruled through the provincial nobility (the *Daimyo*) and controlled much of Japan's wealth and farmland as well as the emperor and priests. They banned Christianity and Western trade, reviving CONFUCIANISM, and isolated Japan from the rest of the world. The regime declined during the 19th century as their isolationist policy began to crack under Western pressure, and the last Tokugawa shogun was overthrown before the MEIJI RESTORATION (1867).

Tokyo (Jap. eastern capital) Capital of Japan, on E central Honshu, at the head of Tokyo Bay. The modern city is divided into distinct districts: Kasumigaseki, Japan's administrative centre; Marunouchi, its commercial centre; Ginza, its shopping and cultural centre; the w shore of Tokyo Bay (including Kawasaki and Yokohama seaport), its industrial centre. Modern Tokyo also serves as the country's educational centre with more than 100 universities. Founded in the 12th century as Edo, it became capital of the TOKUGAWA shogunate in 1603. In 1868, the Japanese Reformation re-established imperial power, and the last shogun surrendered Edo Castle. Emperor Meiji renamed the city Tokyo and it replaced Kyoto as the capital of Japan. The 1923 earthquake and subsequent fire claimed more than 150,000 lives and necessitated the city's reconstruction. In 1944–45, intensive US bombing destroyed more than half of Tokyo, and another modernization and restoration programme began. Industries: electronic equipment, cameras, automobile manufacture, metals, chemicals, textiles. Pop. (1994) 7,894,000.

Toledo Capital of Toledo province, on the River Tagus, Castilla-La Mancha,central Spain. In the 6th century, Toledo was the capital of the Visigoths. In 1031, the Moors made it the capital of an independent kingdom. The city was fortified and acquired its enduring reputation for quality sword-making. Toledo flourished as a multi-denominational city, with Mudéjar-style synagogues, mosques and churches. In the 16th century, it became the spiritual capital of Catholic Spain and the headquarters of the Spanish Inquisition; Jews and Muslims suffered persecution, and the synagogues were converted to churches. During the Spanish Civil War, Toledo was besieged by Loyalist forces. Pop. (1991) 59,563.

Tolkien, J.R.R. (John Ronald Reuel) (1892–1973) British novelist and academic, b. South Africa. He was professor of Anglo-Saxon (1925–45) and English language and literature (1945–59) at Oxford University. Tolkien is chiefly celebrated for his novel *The Hobbit* (1937), the epic trilogy *The Lord of the Rings* (1954–55), and *The Silmarillion* (1977). These popular adventure stories are set in the fantasy world of Middle Earth.

Tolpuddle Martyrs Name given to six British farm labourers in Dorset, s England, who were convicted of a crime for forming a TRADE UNION (1834). The government was worried by the growth of organized LABOUR, but as unions were not illegal, the Dorset men were charged with taking a seditious oath. After a public outcry, they were pardoned in 1836.

Tolstoy, Leo Nikolaievich, Count (1828–1910) Russian novelist, moralist and mystic. He took part in the defence of Sebastopol during the CRIMEAN WAR (1853–56), and his unvarnished descriptions of the conflict appeared in the journal *Contemporary*. In 1862, Tolstoy married and settled down on his Volga estate, where he wrote the masterpiece *War and Peace* (1865–69), an epic account of the Napolenic Wars. Tolstoy's most popular work, *Anna Karenina* (1875–77), is a tragic love story. In his *Confession* (1879), Tolstoy outlines his conversion to an extreme form of Christian anarchism. He renounced all property and possessions and espoused total pacifism. Tolstoy's later moral works include the story "The Death of Ivan Ilyich" and the novel *The Kreutzer Sonata* (1889). *See also* RUSSIAN LITERATURE

Toltec (Nuhuatl, master builder) Ancient Native American civilization, whose capital was Tollán (Tula), Mexico. The Toltec were the dominant people in the region from AD 900 to 1200. Their architecture is characterized by PYRAMID building. Although theirs was considered a polytheistic culture, images of QUETZALCÓATL predominate. In the 12th century, the civilization was gradually supplanted by the AZTEC.

toluene (methylbenzene) Aromatic hydrocarbon ($C_6H_5CH_3$) derived from coal tar and petroleum. It is a colourless, flammable liquid widely used as an industrial solvent and in aircraft and motor fuels. Toluene is also used in the manufacture of TNT. Properties: r.d. 0.87; m.p. −94.5°C (−138.1°F); b.p. 110.7°C (231.3°F).

tomato Fruit plant native to the Americas. It was cultivated in Europe as early as 1544 but was not eaten until the 16th century because it was believed to be poisonous. Species *Lycopersicum esculentum*. The small cherry tomato is a variety (*L.e. cerasiforme*). Family Solanaceae.

Tombaugh, Clyde William (1906–97) US astronomer. In 1930, during a search based on predictions by Percival LOWELL, he discovered the planet PLUTO. He also discovered star clusters, clusters of galaxies, a comet and hundreds of asteroids. After World War 2, he developed telescopic cameras for tracking rockets after launch.

tomography Technique of X-RAY photography in which details of only a single slice or plane of body tissue are shown. *See also* COMPUTERIZED AXIAL TOMOGRAPHY (CAT)

Tomsk City on the River Tom, W central Siberian Russia; capital of Tomsk province. It was founded in 1604 by Boris Godunov and became an important trading post and gold-mining town (1824). The leading 19th-century Siberian city, it was "bypassed" by the TRANS-SIBERIAN RAILWAY and lost its leading position after 1900. Industries: electric motors, ball-bearings. Pop. (1994) 496,000.

tonality HARMONIC system that underpins most Western music from the 17th to 20th century, using the twelve major and twelve minor scales. The notes of the scale, and their corresponding chords and harmonies, have their own hierarchy around the central KEY note. *See also* ATONALITY

tone poem *See* SYMPHONIC POEM

Tonga (Friendly Islands) South Pacific island kingdom, *c.*2,200km (1,370mi) NE of New Zealand. The archipelago consists of nearly 170 islands in five administrative groups, only 36 of which are inhabited. They are mainly coral atolls, but the W group are volcanic, with some active craters. The largest island is Tongatapu, the seat of the capital, NUKUALOFA, and home to 66% of the population. The N islands were discovered by Europeans in 1616 and the rest by Abel TASMAN in 1643. During the 19th century, British missionaries converted the indigenous population to Christianity. In 1900, Tonga became a British protectorate. In 1970, the country achieved independence. The economy is dominated by agriculture, the chief crops are yams, tapioca and fish. Area: 748sq km (289sq mi). Pop. (2000) 92,000.

tongue Muscular organ usually rooted to the floor of the mouth. The tongue contains the TASTE buds and helps to move food around the mouth for chewing and swallowing; animals also use it for lapping fluids and for grooming. In humans the tongue is vital for the production of speech. *See also* SENSES

Tonkin (Tongking) Historical region of N Vietnam. It was ruled by the Chinese from 111 BC to AD 939, later becoming independent. In 1801, it was united with ANNAM and became part of the French protectorate of INDOCHINA in 1883. After World War 2, it was again occupied by the Chinese. They withdrew under French pressure, but France never fully re-established control.

tonsillitis Acute or chronic inflammation of the tonsils caused by bacterial or viral infection. Symptoms include fever, sore throat and difficulty in swallowing. Chronic tonsillitis is often treated by surgical removal of the TONSILS (tonsillectomy).

tonsils Two masses of LYMPH tissue located at the back of the throat. They have a pitted surface that easily becomes infected (TONSILLITIS).

tooth *See* TEETH

topaz Transparent, glassy mineral, aluminium fluosilicate, $Al_2SiO_4(F,OH)_2$, found in pegmatites. Its crystals are columnar prisms in the orthorhombic system . Topaz is colourless, white, blue or yellow; some large crystals are of gem quality. Hardness 8; r.d. 3.5.

tope Small SHARK that lives in British waters. It has a grey-brown body and is often found in schools or near the bottom where it feeds on small fish. Length: to 2m (6.5ft). Family Carcharinidae; species *Galeorhinus galeus*.

Topeka State capital of Kansas, on the Kansas River, 90km (55mi) W of Kansas City. It was founded in 1854 by settlers from New England and became state capital in 1861. Topeka is a major transport centre for cattle and wheat. The Menninger Clinic, world-famous for its treatment of mental illness, is located here. Industries: printing, rubber goods, steel products. Pop. (1992) 120,257.

topography Study of surfaces and their mapping, using fixed points as bases for the calculation. The result of topographic mapping is a relief MAP or a plan for construction. The terrain of a region is explored using surveyors' instruments or aerial photogrammetry. *See also* SURVEYING

topology Branch of mathematics concerned with those properties of geometric figures that are unchanged after a continuous deformation process such as squeezing, stretching or twisting. The number of boundaries of a surface is such a property. Any plane closed shape (i.e. any line that eventually comes back to its beginning, all on a single plane) is topologically equivalent to a circle; a cube, a solid cone, and a solid cylinder are topologically equivalent to a sphere. *See also* MÖBIUS STRIP

Torah (Hebrew, law) Hebrew name for the PENTATEUCH, the first five books of the OLD TESTAMENT. The Torah is the body of written Jewish laws contained within these five books. It also describes the complete Jewish Bible.

tornado Funnel-shaped, violently rotating storm extending downward from the cumulonimbus cloud in which it forms. At the ground its diameter may be only *c.*100m (310ft). Rotational wind speeds range from 160–480km/h (100–300mph). Tornadoes occur in deep low pressure areas, associated with FRONTS or other instabilities. They occur particularly in E USA.

Toronto Capital of Ontario province and Canada's largest city, on the N shore of Lake Ontario. An inland port at the mouth of the Don River, it is Canada's main banking, financial and manufacturing centre. The site was first visited in 1615 by the French explorer Étienne Brulé. In 1787, the British purchased the site from Native Americans, and the settlement of York was founded in 1793. During the WAR OF 1812 the city was twice captured by US troops. In 1834, it was renamed Toronto (Huron, meeting place), and it became the capital of Ontario province in 1867. Its development as a major distribution centre was spurred by the opening (1959) of the ST LAWRENCE SEAWAY. Toronto produces more than half of all Canada's manufacturing products. Industries: electrical equipment, brewing, printing and publishing, iron and steel, aircraft and motor vehicle manufacture. Pop. (1991) 635,395 (metropolitan area 3,893,046).

torpedo Self-propelled underwater MISSILE used by submarines, small surface warships and aircraft to destroy enemy vessels. Modern torpedoes may be launched by rocket boosters and often have internal electronic equipment for fixing the target. *See also* GUIDED MISSILE

torpedo ray *See* RAY

torque Turning effect of a force. An example is a TURBINE that produces a torque on its rotating shaft to turn a generator. The output of a rotary ENGINE, such as the familiar four-stroke engine or an electric motor, is rated by the torque it can develop. The unit of measurement is the newton meter (Nm).

Torquemada, Tomás de (1420–98) Spanish churchman and grand inquisitor. A DOMINICAN priest and confessor to King FERDINAND V and Queen ISABELLA I, he was appointed head of the Spanish INQUISITION (1483). Torquemada was noted for the severity of his judgments and punishments. He was responsible for *c.*2,000 burnings.

Torricelli, Evangelista (1608–47) Italian physicist. Assistant and secretary to GALILEO, he is credited with the first manufactured VACUUM (the Torricellian vacuum) and the invention of the mercury BAROMETER (1643).

tort In law, wrongful act or omission that can give rise to a civil action at law, other than concerning breach of contract. The law of tort includes negligence, libel, slander, trespass, false imprisonment and nuisance.

Tortelier, Paul (1914–90) French cellist. He made his concert debut in 1931. Tortelier is celebrated for his interpretations of Bach and Elgar. In 1957, he became professor at the Paris Conservatoire, where his pupils included Jacqueline DU PRÉ. His son, **Yan Pascal** Tortelier (1947–), is a noted conductor.

tortoise Terrestrial or freshwater REPTILE of the order Chelonia. All tortoises are heavily armoured and enclosed within a high, domed, bony, box-like structure called a carapace. When disturbed, tortoises pull their scaly legs, head and tail into the shelter of the shell. They live in tropical and sub-tropical regions and hibernate in temperate countries. They are slow movers, feed almost entirely on plants and live to a great age. Length: usually to 30cm (1ft). A giant species, up to 1.9m (5ft) long, lives in the GALÁPAGOS ISLANDS. *See also* TURTLE

Tory Party British political party traditionally opposed to the WHIGS. In 1670, the supporters of the Catholic Stuart monarchy were called Tories (Irish bandits) by their opponents. Under JAMES II, the Tories represented the interests of landowners and supported the royal prerogative. They maintained close links to the CHURCH OF ENGLAND and favoured an isolationist foreign policy. The Tories, led by Robert HARLEY, were at their most powerful in the reign of Queen ANNE. They were discredited by association with the JACOBITES and were excluded from power when GEORGE I acceded to the throne. In the late 18th century accusations of Toryism were levelled at independent Whigs, such as William PITT (the Younger). The Reform Bill of 1832 split the party, and the CONSERVATIVE PARTY was formed from its remnants. *See also* PEEL, SIR ROBERT; REFORM ACTS

Toscanini, Arturo (1867–1957) Italian conductor. He was musical director (1898–1901, 1906–08) at La Scala, Milan, before becoming conductor (1908–21) of the Metropolitan Opera, New York. Toscanani conducted the New York Philharmonic Orchestra (1928–36). In 1937, he founded the NBC Symphony Orchestra in New York. Toscanini returned to La Scala (1921–29), where he premièred Puccini's *Turnadot* (1926).

totalitarianism Form of government in which the state tries to acquire total control of every aspect of social and individual activity or thought, by means of controlling the mass media and suppression of opposition through the use of the police or army. The term arose in the 1920s to describe Italian FASCISM and has since been applied to Nazi Germany, the Soviet Union and many other states. *See also* ARENDT, HANNAH; AUTHORITARIANISM

totemism Complex collection of ideas held by certain primitive societies about the relationships between human beings and the animals or plants around them. The natural objects or people with which many tribal societies believe they have a kinship or mystical relationship, are called totems. Members of a totem group are prohibited from marrying others of the same group and from killing or eating their totem. Elaborate, often secret, rituals form an important part of totemistic behaviour.

totem pole Carved, painted, wooden column erected by the Native Americans of the Pacific Coast of the USA and Canada. Carved with stylized representations of real and mythical animals and men, its function is closer to that of an heraldic crest than a religious symbol. They are usually erected as roof supports, as doorways, as symbols of greeting, or as mortuary poles or grave markers.

toucan Any of 35 species of colourful, gregarious birds of the forests of tropical America, characterized by a large, colourful bill. The plumage is generally red, yellow, blue, black or orange. It feeds on fruit and berries, which may be regurgitated to feed the young. Length: 60cm (2ft). Family Ramphastidae.

touch One of the five SENSES, functioning by means of specialized nerve receptors in the skin.

Toulon Capital of Var department, on the Mediterranean coast, SE France. Toulon is France's leading naval base and its largest Mediterranean port after Marseilles. Originally known as Telo Martius, the city was a Roman naval base and an important port of embarkation for the Crusaders. In 1942, the French navy was scuttled here to prevent German capture. Industries: shipbuilding and naval repairs. Pop. (1990) 167,619.

Toulouse City on the River Garonne, S France, capital of Haute-Garonne department. Canals connect the city, the fourth-biggest in France, to both the Mediterranean Sea and the Atlantic Ocean. The capital of the Visigoths in the 5th century, it became part of the French crown lands in 1271. Toulouse is the centre of the French aviation industry. Other industries: paper, textiles, chemicals, fertilizers, armaments. Pop. (1990) 358,688.

Toulouse-Lautrec, Henri Marie Raymond de (1864–1901) French painter and lithographer. He chose a career in painting after a childhood accident left his legs permanently deformed. In *c.*1888, he began to illustrate the theatres, cabarets, music halls, cafés and brothels of the Montmartre district of Paris, such as the *Moulin Rouge* (1894) series. He was profoundly influenced by DEGAS and drew inspiration from GAUGUIN and Japanese wood-block prints. His prints depict powerfully simplified forms and their impact helped to establish the poster as a respected art form.

Tour de France Premier professional road CYCLING race in Europe. Raced over three weeks from the end of June, it travels across all types of terrain in a series of timed stages. It mostly circles France, but ventures into other countries, and ends in Paris.

Tourette's syndrome (Gilles de la Tourette's syndrome) Rare disorder of movement. It is a lifelong

▲ **toucan** The New World counterparts of the hornbills, there are some 35 species of toucans in the forest of tropical America. The large, bright bill of the Toco toucan (*Ramphastos toco*) is typical of the family and is used to reach fruit.

affliction with tics and involuntary grimaces. Involuntary sounds also frequently occur. Its cause is unknown.

tourmaline Silicate mineral, sodium or calcium aluminium borosilicate, found in IGNEOUS and METAMORPHIC rocks. Its crystals are hexagonal system and glassy, either opaque or transparent. Some are prized as gems. Hardness 7.5; r.d. 3.1.

Tours City between the rivers Loire and Cher, W central France, capital of Indre-et-Loire department. It was the seat of the French government in 1870 during the siege of Paris. A large wine market, Tours has electronic and pharmaceutical industries. Pop. (1990) 129,509.

Toussaint L'Ouverture, Pierre Dominique (1744–1803) Haitian revolutionary leader. In 1790 he took part in the slave revolt in Haiti, joined the Spaniards when they attacked the French in 1793, but fought for the French (1794) when they promised to abolish slavery. By 1801, Toussaint had gained control of virtually the whole island of HISPANIOLA. In 1802, Napoleon sought to restore French control. Toussaint was forced to surrender and died a prisoner in France. In 1804, Haiti achieved independence.

Tower Bridge Cantilever bridge over the River Thames in London, built by Sir Horace Jones between 1886 and 1894. The bridge has a pseudo-Gothic tower at each side of the river and a double-leaf mechanism that opens to provide a 76m (250ft) gap.

Tower of London English royal castle. It was begun by William the Conqueror in 1078, and was extended by later monarchs. It served various functions throughout the centuries, as residence, arsenal, prison and museum.

Townes, Charles Hard (1915–95) US physicist. In 1953, Townes invented the first operational MASER. He shared the 1964 Nobel Prize for physics with Alexsandr PROKHOROV and Nikolai BASOV.

Townshend, Charles, 2nd Viscount (1674–1738) British Whig statesman, known as "Turnip Townshend". Robert WALPOLE's brother-in-law, he helped to arrange GEORGE I's accession to the throne in 1714 and, as secretary for the Northern Department, suppressed the JACOBITE rebellion of 1715. He was forced to resign in 1730, and devoted his retirement to agricultural improvements.

Townshend Acts (1767) Series of taxes levied on the American colonies by the British Parliament. Proposed by the chancellor of the exchequer, Charles Townshend, they were to provide revenue to defray the cost of colonial government. The adverse colonial reaction ("taxation without representation is tyranny") caused the repeal (1770) of all duties except that on tea.

toxic shock syndrome Potentially fatal condition in which there is a dangerous drop in blood pressure and rapid onset of fever, diarrhoea, vomiting and muscular pains. It is caused by BLOOD POISONING arising from toxins put out by bacteria that normally reside in the body without causing harm. The syndrome is most often seen in young women using tampons during menstruation.

toxin Poisonous substance produced by a living organism. The unpleasant symptoms of many bacterial diseases are due to the release of toxins into the body by the BACTERIA. Many MOULDS, some larger FUNGI and seeds of some higher plants produce toxins. The VENOM of many snakes contain powerful toxins. *See also* POISON

toxoplasmosis Disease caused by the protozoan, *Toxoplasma gondii*, which is transmitted from animals to human beings. It produces symptoms that are mild and flu-like in adults, but it can damage the nervous system, eyes and internal organs.

Toynbee, Arnold Joseph (1889–1975) English historian. His influential though controversial *A Study of History*

(12 vols, 1934–61) emphasized the need to examine a whole civilization rather than individual nations.

trace elements Chemical elements that are essential to life but normally obtainable from the diet only in small quantities. They are essential to the reactions of ENZYMES and HORMONES.

trachea (windpipe) Airway that extends from the LARYNX to about the middle of the STERNUM (breastbone). Reinforced with rings of CARTILAGE, it is lined with hair-like CILIA that prevent dirt and other substances from entering the lungs.

tracheophyte In certain classification systems, any VASCULAR PLANT of the phylum Tracheophyta. Within this phylum are: psilopsids (leafless, rootless primitive forms, such as whisk fern), sphenopsids (such as HORSETAIL), lycopsids (such as CLUB MOSS), pteropsids (such as FERN), GYMNOSPERMS and ANGIOSPERMS.

tracheotomy (tracheostomy) Surgical procedure in which an incision is made through the skin into the TRACHEA to allow insertion of a tube to facilitate breathing. It is done either to bypass any disease or damage in the trachea or to safeguard the airway if a patient has to spend a long time on a mechanical ventilator.

trachoma Chronic EYE infection caused by the microorganism, *Chlamydia trachomatis*, characterized by inflammation of the CORNEA with the formation of pus. A disease of dry, tropical regions, it is the major cause of blindness in the developing world.

Tractarianism *See* OXFORD MOVEMENT

tractor Four-wheeled or tracked vehicle for moving and operating heavy implements, used mostly in farming and construction. The first tractors were built in the 1870s. Modern tractors have petrol or diesel engines and can haul and power a wide range of implements, including hay balers, crop sprayers and mowing machines.

Tracy, Spencer (1900–67) US film actor. Following his debut in 1930, Tracy became a leading Hollywood actor, appearing in nearly 80 films, of which nine, including *Adam's Rib* (1949), *Pat and Mike* (1957) and his last film, *Guess Who's Coming to Dinner* (1967), were with his off-screen partner Katharine HEPBURN. He won Academy Awards for *Captains Courageous* (1937) and *Boys Town* (1938).

trademark Distinguishing mark, such as a name, symbol or word, attached to goods, which identifies them as made or sold by a particular manufacturer. A trademark must be registered at the patent office to establish an exclusive right to it.

Trades Union Congress (TUC) Permanent association of UK TRADE UNIONS. The TUC was founded in 1868 to promote trade union principles. Each year it holds an annual assembly of delegates who discuss common problems. Today, the TUC has *c*.8 million members.

trade union Group of workers organized for the purpose of improving wages and conditions of work. The first trade unions were founded in Britain around the time of the INDUSTRIAL REVOLUTION. Although some craft and agricultural unions developed before industrialization, the growth of trade unionism paralleled the growth of industry. Trade unions were given restricted legality in Britain in 1825. In 1871, the Trades Union Act put the unions on a firm legal basis, and over the next 150 years, the movement grew steadily. Their rights were progressively curbed in the 1980s, through Conservative legislation under Margaret THATCHER. In the USA, the LABOUR movement had become firmly established by 1886 with the founding of the American Federation of Labor (AFL). The AFL primarily represented skilled workers, and it was not until the creation of the Congress of Industrial Organizations (CIO) in 1930 that unskilled labour gained some form of representation. The two organizations merged in 1955 to form the AMERICAN FEDERATION OF LABOR AND CONGRESS OF INDUSTRIAL ORGANIZATIONS (AFL-CIO). *See also* INDUSTRIAL RELATIONS; TOLPUDDLE MARTYRS

trade wind Steady wind that blow westwards towards the Equator from sub-tropical high pressure zones between latitudes 30° and 60° N and S.

Trafalgar, Battle of (1805) British naval victory over the French and Spanish fleets off Cape Trafalgar, Spain. It ended NAPOLEON I's plans for an invasion of England. The victory was secured by the skilful tactics of the British commander, Lord NELSON, who was killed in the battle.

tragedy Form of drama in which a noble hero (the protagonist) meets a fate inherent in the drama's action. *Oedipus Rex* by SOPHOCLES is an early example, which was unmatched until the tragedies of Christopher MARLOWE. ARISTOTLE's *Poetics* systematized tragedy and introduced such ideas as *anagnorisis* (recognition) and *catharsis* (purging of pity). *See also* AESCHYLUS; EURIPIDES; GREEK DRAMA; SHAKESPEARE, WILLIAM

Trajan (AD 53–117) Roman emperor (98–117), b. Spain. He distinguished himself as a general and administrator and was made junior co-emperor by Nerva in 97. With army support, he became emperor on Nerva's death. He conducted major campaigns in DACIA (101–102, 105–106) and against the people of PARTHIA (113–117), enlarging the Roman Empire to its greatest extent.

tranquillizer Drug prescribed to reduce anxiety or tension and generally for their calming effect. They are used to control the symptoms of severe mental disturbance, such as schizophrenia or manic depression. They are also prescribed to relieve depression. Prolonged use of tranquillizers can produce a range of unwanted side effects.

Transcaucasia Former Soviet Republic, corresponding to the three constituent republics ARMENIA, AZERBAIJAN and GEORGIA. Created in 1918 after the RUSSIAN REVOLUTION, it was re-formed in 1922 and granted full republic status in 1924. Georgia, Azerbaijan and Armenia were re-established as separate republics in 1936 and gained independence on the break-up of the SOVIET UNION in 1990.

transcendentalism School of philosophy that traced its origin to the IDEALISM of Immanuel KANT. It was concerned not with objects but with our mode of knowing objects. It spread from Germany to England, where Samuel COLERIDGE and Thomas CARLYLE came under its influence. In the mid-19th century, it spread to the USA, where it was proponents included Ralph Waldo EMERSON and Henry David THOREAU. In general, it emphasized individual (as opposed to collective) moral and spiritual responsibilities and rejected materialism, returning to nature for spiritual guidance.

transcendental meditation (TM) MEDITATION technique based partly on Hindu practice and rediscovered in the 20th century by an Indian spiritual teacher, Guru Dev (d.1958). After his death, Maharishi Mahesh Yogi introduced the technique to the West. Those who practise TM concentrate on and repeat a MANTRA over and over in order to become relaxed and achieve self-understanding. In physiological terms, TM decreases oxygen consumption and heart rate and increases skin resistance and alpha brain waves, yielding a relaxed mental state differing from sleep or hypnosis.

transducer Device for converting any non-electrical signal, such as sound or light, into an electrical signal and vice versa. Examples include MICROPHONES, LOUDSPEAKERS and measuring instruments used in ACOUSTICS.

transformer Device for converting alternating current at one voltage to another voltage at the same frequency. It consists of two coils of wire coupled together magnetically. The input current is fed to one coil (primary), the output being taken from the other coil (secondary).

transfusion, blood *See* BLOOD TRANSFUSION

transhumance Seasonal moving of livestock from one region to another. It occurs in societies living in zones with extensive climatic changes, such as in the mountainous terrain of the Arctic regions or the deserts of Central Africa. *See also* NOMAD

transistor Electronic device made of SEMICONDUCTOR material that can amplify electrical signals. The material, such as SILICON or GERMANIUM, is "doped" with minute amounts of PHOSPHOROUS, ARSENIC or ANTIMONY to produce *n*-type material, in which current is carried by negative charges, ELECTRONS; or with ALUMINIUM, GALLIUM or INDIUM to give a *p*-type material. Joining together a piece of each produces a DIODE. Sandwiching one type between two of the other produces a transistor. Transistors were first developed in 1948 by John BARDEEN, Walter BRATTAIN and William SHOCKLEY, making possible many advances in technology, especially in computers, portable radios and televisions, satellites and control systems.

transition elements Metallic elements that have incomplete inner electron shells. They are characterized by variable VALENCIES (combining power) and the formation of coloured ions. *See also* PERIODIC TABLE

Transkei Former, apartheid-created, bantustan (homeland), in CAPE PROVINCE, South Africa. In 1994, Transkei was integrated into Eastern Cape Province.

translocation In VASCULAR PLANTS, the movement of food materials in solution through the tissues from one part of the plant to another.

transmigration of souls Belief that the soul is reborn in one or more successive mortal bodies; a form of REINCARNATION. A tenet of Asian religions such as BUDDHISM, it was also accepted by the followers of PYTHAGORAS and Orphism in Greece during the 6th century BC. It is still common today in tribal religions such as that of the South African Venda.

transpiration In plants, the loss of moisture as water vapour from leaf surfaces or other plant parts. Most of the water entering plant roots is lost by transpiration. The process is speeded up in light, warm and dry conditions. The flow of water from the roots to the STOMATA is called the transpiration stream. *See also* RESPIRATION

transplant Surgical operation to introduce organ or tissue from one person (the donor) to another (the recipient); it may also refer to the transfer of tissues from one part of the body to another, as in GRAFTING of skin or bone. Major transplants are performed to save the lives of patients facing death from end-stage organ disease. Organs routinely transplanted include the kidneys, heart, lungs, liver and pancreas. Experimental work continues on some other procedures, including small bowel grafting. Many other tissues are commonly grafted, including heart valves, bone and bone marrow. The oldest transplant procedure is corneal grafting, undertaken to restore the sight of one or both eyes. In 1967, Christiaan BARNARD performed the first successful heart transplant operation. Most transplant material is acquired from dead people, although kidneys, part of the liver, bone marrow and corneas may be taken from living donors.

Trans-Siberian Railway Russian railway from Moscow to Vladivostok. The world's longest railway, the major part, E from Chelyabinsk, was built between 1891 and 1905, giving Russia access to the Pacific via a link with the Chinese Eastern Railroad in Manchuria. The total length is c.9,000km (5,750mi).

transubstantiation Belief accepted by the Roman Catholic Church that, during the prayer of consecration at the MASS (the EUCHARIST), the "substance" of the bread and wine is changed into the "substance" of the body and blood of JESUS CHRIST, while the "accidents" (the outward forms of the bread and wine) remain unchanged. The doctrine was defined at the LATERAN COUNCIL of 1215. The definition involving "substance" and "accidents" was rejected by the architects of the REFORMATION.

transuranic elements (transuranium elements) Those elements with atomic numbers higher than that of URANIUM (92), the best known of which are members of the ACTINIDE SERIES (atomic numbers 89 to 103). All transuranic elements are radioactive. Only NEPTUNIUM and PLUTONIUM occur naturally in minute amounts, but all can be synthesized. The only commercially important element in the group is plutonium, which is used in NUCLEAR WEAPONS and as a fuel for NUCLEAR REACTORS.

Transvaal Former province of South Africa. In 1994–95, Transvaal was divided into NORTHERN PROVINCE, Mpumalanga, GAUTENG and NORTH-WEST PROVINCE. The indigenous population are the Bantu-speaking Venda and Sotho peoples. In the GREAT TREK (1836), the BOERS crossed the River Vaal and began to settle the region. In 1857, the South African Republic was formed. In 1877, the British annexed the republic. In 1881, after a Boer revolt, Transvaal was again granted internal self-government under the new president, Paul KRUGER. The 1886 discovery of gold in WITWATERSRAND attracted vast numbers of Britons and Germans. The Boers imposed heavy taxation and denied political rights to the newcomers. In 1895, Leander Starr JAMESON launched an incursion into Transvaal. The "Jameson Raid" failed to ignite a full-scale rebellion, but the resultant tension between the Boers and the British led to the SOUTH AFRICAN WARS. By the Treaty of Vereeniging (1902), Transvaal became a British crown colony. In 1907, the region was again allowed self-government, and in 1910 it became a founding province in the Union of South Africa. During the 1960s, the apartheid government created separate tribal "homelands" (bantustans). In 1995, Transvaal ceased to exist as a political entity and was split into four of South Africa's nine new provinces.

Transylvania (Romanian, Beyond the Forest) High plateau region in central and NW Romania, separated from the rest of Romania by the CARPATHIAN MOUNTAINS and the Transylvanian Alps. Its major cities are CLUJ-NAPOCA, BRAȘOV and Sibiu. In AD 107 it became part of the Roman province of DACIA. It was conquered by Hungary at the beginning of the 11th century. In 1526, the ruler of Transylvania, John Zapolya, defeated the Hungarian army, and claimed the Hungarian throne as JOHN I. His claim was supported by the Turks who, following Zapolya's death in 1540, occupied Transylvania on the pretext of ensuring his son's succession. For the next two centuries Transylvania retained a semi-independent status as it played off the competing imperial claims of Turkey and Austria. During the 17th century, it flourished· as Hungary's intellectual and cultural centre, but in 1765 it became an Austrian province. Hungarian supremacy was re-established in 1867. After World War 1, Hungary ceded the territory to Romania, which embarked on a wholesale process of land redistribution and forced assimilation of other nationalities. Hungary annexed part of Transylvania in World War 2, but was forced to return it in 1947. Transylvania is the legendary home of vampires.

Trappists Popular name for the CISTERCIANS of the Strict Observance, a religious order of monks and nuns that originated in La Trappe Abbey, France, in 1664. They maintain complete silence and practise vegetarianism.

trauma Any injury or physical damage caused by some external event such as an accident or assault. In psychiatry, the term is applied to an emotional shock or harrowing experience.

treason Any act the intention of which is to overthrow the recognized government or harm the head of state. Treason is an extremely serious criminal offence and is punishable by death in many countries. In Britain, treason is defined to include the infliction of death or injury on the monarch, violation of members of the royal family, levying war against the government or giving assistance to the enemy.

Treasury UK government department responsible for national finance and monetary policy. Dating from the Norman Conquest, when the chancellor and barons exercised control of royal revenues, the Treasury developed from the office of the CHANCELLOR OF THE EXCHEQUER. It became a separate ministry in the 19th century.

Trebizond empire State established by Byzantines in the early 13th century. The Black Sea port of Trebizond (Trabzon) was founded by the ancient Greeks. When the leaders of the Fourth CRUSADE seized Constantinople in 1204, refugees established the empire of Trebizond. It prospered on trade and continued an independent existence until conquered by the Ottomans in 1461. See also BYZANTINE EMPIRE

tree Woody, PERENNIAL plant with one main trunk and smaller branches. The trunk increases in diameter each year; the leaves are evergreen or DECIDUOUS. The largest trees, SEQUOIAS, can grow to more than 110m (420ft); the bristlecone pine can live for more than 5,000 years.

treecreeper Brownish, agile bird that scurries up and down trees in cooler areas of the Northern Hemisphere. It uses its long, slightly down-curved bill to probe for insects under the bark. Length: 13cm (5in). Species *Certhia familiaris*.

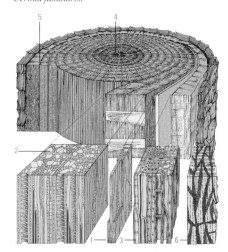

▲ **tree** Trees increase in girth by wings of new wood produced annually in temperate zones but less often in the tropics. The cambium (1) produces xylem (2) and phloem (3). They are alive but the heartwood (4) is dead. The medullary rays (5) allow the transport of food across the trunk. Bark (6) is a protective outer coating.

tree fern Tree-like FERN of the family Cyatheaceae. Tree ferns grow in tropical and sub-tropical regions, particularly moist, mountainous areas. Height: 3–25m (10–80ft). There are 600 species. Phylum Filicinophyta; genus *Cyathea*.

trefoil Any of numerous plants, such as CLOVER, with leaves divided into three parts. Bird's-foot trefoil (*Lotus corniculatus*) is a perennial used as forage. Family Fabaceae/Leguminosae.

Trent River in central England, at 274km (170mi) the country's third-longest. It rises on Biddulph Moor, Staffordshire, and flows SE through the Potteries, and then NE across central England to join the River OUSE and form the Humber estuary. Linked by canals to many industrial towns, its major modern use is the provision of water for the cooling of power stations.

Trent, Council of (1545–63) Nineteenth ecumenical council of the Roman Catholic Church, which provided the main impetus of the COUNTER REFORMATION in Europe. It met at Trent, N Italy, in three sessions under three popes (PAUL III, Julius III, PIUS IV). It clarified Catholic doctrine and refused concessions to the Protestants, while instituting reform of many of the abuses that had provoked the REFORMATION.

Trenton State capital of New Jersey, on the Delaware River. It was settled by English Quakers in the 1670s. A city monument commemorates the 1776 battle in which George WASHINGTON crossed the frozen Delaware River to defeat Hessian troops during the AMERICAN REVOLUTION. Industries: ceramics, automobile parts, plastics, rubber, steel cables, textiles. Pop. (1992) 87,807.

Trevithick, Richard (1771–1833) English engineer. In 1801, he built a steam-powered road vehicle. In 1802, Trevithick patented a high-pressure STEAM ENGINE, his most important invention. In 1803, he built the first steam railroad LOCOMOTIVE. In 1816, he went to Peru to install his steam engines in mines.

triad Chinese secret society. It existed in S China from the earliest days of the Qing empire in the 17th century until the 19th century, when the triads lent their support to the TAIPING REBELLION. Today, it is said to control Chinese organized crime throughout the world, with its chief centre in Hong Kong.

triangle Plane figure bounded by three straight lines. The sum of the interior angles totals 180°. The area is

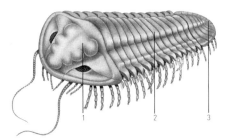

▲ **trilobite** The trilobite looked rather like today's woodlouse, being covered by a chitinous skeleton. This was divided into (1) the cephalon or headshield, which carried sensory organs and the glabella, a bump that housed the stomach; (2) the thorax, a region of articulated segments below each of which was a pair of legs; and (3) the pygidium or tail shield. Each limb consisted of a jointed organ for walking, a swimming and breathing organ and a paddle that swept food particles towards the mouth.

measured by either: (1) half the product of one of the sides and the perpendicular onto it from the opposite vertex (1/2 × base × height); or (2) half the product of two of the sides and the sine of the angle between them.

Triassic First period of the MESOZOIC era, lasting from *c*.248 to 13 million years ago. Many new kinds of animals developed. On land, the first DINOSAURS roamed. Mammal-like reptiles were common, and by the end of the period the first true MAMMALS existed. In the seas lived the first ichthyosaurs, placodonts and nothosaurs. The first frogs, turtles, crocodilians and lizards also appeared. Plant life consisted mainly of primitive gymnosperms.

tribune Official of ancient Rome. Of the various kinds of tribune, some had military functions, some political. The tribunes of the PLEBEIANS, generally ten in number and elected annually, gained an important role under the Republic. In the 2nd century BC, GRACCHUS used the office to pursue radical social reforms.

triceratops Large, horned, ornithischian DINOSAUR of the late CRETACEOUS period of w North America. The 2.4-m (8-ft) skull carried two 102-cm (40-in) horns above its eyes and a smaller horn at tip of its snout. Length: 6.1–7.6m (20–25ft); height: 2.4m (8ft); weight: 10 tonnes.

Trier, Lars von (1956–) Danish film director. Trier established his reputation with *Europa* (1991) and *Breaking the Waves* (1996), both of which attracted attention for their distinctive cinematic style based on the Dogme manifesto. *The Idiots* (1998) is emblematic of the black humour that characterizes his films and provoked widespread controversy for its treatment of disability. The musical *Dancer in the Dark* (2000) was internationally acclaimed.

Trieste City on the Gulf of Trieste, at the head of the Adriatic Sea, NE Italy. It was an imperial free port from 1719 to 1891, becoming an Austrian crown land in 1867. It was ceded to Italy in 1919, occupied by Yugoslavia in 1945, but returned to Italy in 1954. It is an important industrial and commercial centre with large shipyards. Industries: steel, textiles, petroleum. Pop. (1996) 224,000.

triggerfish Any of several tropical marine fish found in warm shallow Pacific waters, identified by a dorsal fin spine that can be erected to lodge the fish in a coral cavity, as a protection against predators. Length: to 60cm (24in). Family Balistidae; typical genus *Balistoides*.

triglyceride *See* LIPID

trigonometric function Six ratios of the sides of a right-angled TRIANGLE containing a given acute angle. They are the SINE, COSINE, TANGENT, COTANGENT, SECANT and COSECANT of the angle. These functions can be extended to cover angles of any size by the use of a system of rectangular coordinates.

trigonometry Use of ratios of the sides of a right-angled TRIANGLE to calculate lengths and angles in geometrical figures. If three sides, or two sides and the included angle, or one side and two angles of a triangle are known, then all the other sides and angles may be found.

trilobite Any of an extinct group of ARTHROPODS found as fossils in marine deposits, ranging in age from CAMBRIAN through PERMIAN times. The body was mostly oval, tapering toward the rear and was covered by a chitinous skeleton. Transverse divisions show segmentation and bear pairs of jointed limbs. Most species were bottom-crawling, shallow-water forms and ranged in size from 6mm (0.25in) to 75cm (30in).

Trimble, David (1944–) Northern Irish statesman, first minister of Northern IRELAND (1998–). He entered the British Parliament in 1990. In 1995, Trimble succeeded James Molyneaux as leader of the ULSTER UNIONIST PARTY. After the GOOD FRIDAY AGREEMENT (10 April

1998), he became first minister of the Northern Ireland Assembly. In 1998, Trimble and John HUME, leader of the nationalist SOCIAL DEMOCRATIC AND LABOUR PARTY (SDLP), shared the Nobel Prize for Peace for their efforts to find a peaceful solution to the conflict in Northern Ireland. In 2000, following the suspension of the Northern Ireland Assembly, Trimble persuaded the Ulster Unionists to accept continued power-sharing following the IRISH REPUBLICAN ARMY (IRA)'s proposal of putting their weapons beyond use, and the Assembly was reinstated.

Trinidad and Tobago Republic composed of the two southernmost islands of the Lesser ANTILLES in the SE Caribbean; the capital is PORT OF SPAIN on Trinidad. The larger island of **Trinidad** lies only 11km (7mi) off the Venezuelan coast. It is mainly low plains with coastal mangrove swamps. In SW Trinidad lies Pitch Lake, the world's largest natural source of asphalt. The Spanish colonized the island in the 16th century, but it was ceded to Britain in 1802. **Tobago** lies 30km (19mi) NE of Trinidad. The island, dominated by a mountain ridge, is heavily forested. Scarborough is the principal town. Tobago was initially settled by the British in 1616. After Spanish, Dutch and French rule, in 1803 it became a British possession. In 1883, Trinidad and Tobago were integrated into a single crown colony, becoming an independent state in 1962 and a republic in 1976. In 1990, the prime minister, Arthur Robinson, was captured and later released in an attempted coup. After 1995 elections, a coalition of the United National Congress and the Alliance for Reconstruction came to power, with Basdeo Panday as prime minister. The economy is dominated by oil and gas production, asphalt and tourism. Area: 5,128sq km (1,980sq mi). Pop. (2000) 1,484,000.

Trinity Central doctrine of Christianity, according to which God is three persons: the Father, the Son and the HOLY SPIRIT or Holy Ghost. There is only one God, but he exists as "three in one and one in three". The nature of the Trinity is held to be a mystery that cannot be fully comprehended. The doctrine of the Trinity was stated in early Christian creeds to counter heresies such as GNOSTICISM. *See also* APOSTLES' CREED; ATHANASIAN CREED; JESUS CHRIST; NICENE CREED

Triple Alliance Name given to several international alliances involving three states. They included the anti-French alliance of Britain, the Netherlands and Sweden of 1668, and the alliance of Britain, France and the Netherlands of 1717, directed against Spanish ambitions in Italy. The most recent was the Triple Alliance of 1882, when Italy joined the Dual Alliance of Austria-Hungary and Germany. In South America, Argentina, Brazil and Uruguay formed a triple alliance in the war against Paraguay (1865–70).

Triple Entente Name given to the alliance of Britain, France and Russia before World War 1. It developed from the Franco-Russian Alliance (1894), a counterbalance to the threat posed by the TRIPLE ALLIANCE of Germany, Austria and Italy. Britain became allied with France in the ENTENTE CORDIALE (1904), and the Anglo-Russian Convention of 1907 completed the Triple Entente.

triple jump In athletics, similar to the LONG JUMP with the exception that from the take-off line a contestant takes two extended leaps on alternate legs before launching into the final jump.

Tripoli Capital and chief port of LIBYA, on the Mediterranean Sea. The city was founded in the 7th century BC by the Phoenicians and developed by the Romans. From the 7th century AD, the Arabs developed Tripoli as a market centre for the trans-Saharan caravans. In 1551, it was captured by the Ottoman Turks. It was made the capital of the Italian colony of Libya in 1911, and during World War 2 it functioned as an important base for Axis forces before capture by the British in 1943. In 1986, Tripoli was bombed by the US Air Force in retaliation for Libya's support of terrorism. It is the commercial, industrial, transport and communications centre of Libya. The oases comprise the most fertile agricultural area in N Africa. Pop. (1988) 960,000.

Tripoli Mediterranean port and second-largest city in LEBANON. It was an important city of the Seleucid and Roman empires. Captured in AD 638 by the Arabs, in 1109 Tripoli was conquered by the Crusaders, who developed the city's fortifications. In 1289, it returned to Islamic rule under the Egyptian MAMELUKES. The Turks held the city until the arrival of the British in 1918, and in 1920 it became a Lebanese city. It suffered severe damage during the 1975–76 Lebanese civil war. The city remains an important centre for trade between Syria and Lebanon, and it is the terminus of the oil pipeline from Iraq. Industries: oil refining, textiles. Pop. (1991) 203,000.

triptych Painting or carving consisting of three panels, traditionally used as an altarpiece. The panels may form one picture, or the outer panels may be separate and subordinate to the central picture.

Tristan (Tristram) Hero of many medieval romances, most commonly as a knight of the Round Table in the ARTHURIAN ROMANCES. His fatal love for the Irish princess Isolde (or Iseult) is the subject of Richard WAGNER's opera, *Tristan and Isolde* (1865).

Tristan da Cunha Group of four islands in the S Atlantic Ocean, located midway between S Africa and South America. The group was discovered in 1506 by the Portuguese and annexed by Britain in 1816. In 1961, Tristan, the only inhabitable island, suffered a volcanic eruption that caused a temporary evacuation. A British dependency, it is administered from ST HELENA. Area (of Tristan): 98sq km (38sq mi). Pop. (1988) 313, all of whom live in the settlement of Edinburgh.

Triton In Greek mythology, a sea god, son of Poseidon and Amphitrite. Half-man, half-fish, he had a scaled body, sharp teeth and claws, and a forked fish tail. He had power over the waves and possessed the gift of prophecy.

triumphal arch Massive masonry structure, containing one, two, or three ARCHES covered with a flat, oblong attic. Triumphal arches were originally built by the Romans to commemorate specific victories, and in Imperial times only emperors could pass through them. They were decorated with bronze statuary and carved scenes. *See also* ARC DE TRIOMPHE

Trivandrum (Tiruvananthapuram) Seaport and resort city on the Malabar Coast, SW India, the largest city and capital of Kerala state. It served as capital of Travancore kingdom from 1745 and has an 18th-century fort, housing palaces and fine Hindu temples. Industries: tyres, tiles, plywood, titanium, textiles. Pop. (1991) 524,000.

trogon Brilliantly coloured bird of dark tropical forests in America, Africa and Asia. Trogons nest in holes in trees and feed on fruit and some insect larvae. Length: c.30cm (12in). Family Trogonidae; typical genus *Trogon*.

Trojan War War between the Greeks and Trojans, lasting 10 years. It began when PARIS, son of King Priam of TROY, kidnapped HELEN, wife of King Menelaus of Sparta. When the Trojans refused to return her, the Greeks formed an army, led by AGAMEMNON, including ACHILLES, Patroclus, Diomedes, ODYSSEUS, Nestor, the two AJAXES and Philoctetes. After nine years of fighting, the Greeks pretended to sail for home, leaving behind a large, hollow, wooden horse in which they concealed some warriors. Sinon persuaded the Trojans to bring the horse within the fortified city walls of Troy, despite the warnings of CASSANDRA and LAOCOÖN. That night, the Greeks returned and, when the concealed warriors opened the city gates, destroyed the city. HOMER wrote about the events of the war in his epic, the *Iliad*. Evidence from excavations carried out at Troy leads historians to believe that the legend reflects a real war (*c*.1200 BC) between the Greeks and the people of Troas, possibly over control of the Dardanelles and Black Sea trade.

Trollope, Anthony (1815–82) English novelist. He spent most of his life working for the Post Office and was responsible for the introduction of the pillar-box. Trollope's reputation as a writer is founded chiefly on a series of six novels, chronicling rural Victorian life in the imaginary county of Barsetshire. The series included *The Warden* (1855), *Barchester Towers* (1857) and *The Last Chronicle of Barset* (1858). His novels of the Palliser family include *Can You Forgive Her?* (1864–65) and *The Way We Live Now* (1874–75). His refreshingly modest and workman-like approach to his craft is documented in the posthumously published *Autobiography* (1883)

trombone BRASS musical instrument with a cylindrical bore, cupped mouthpiece and flaring bell. It is usually played with a slide, except for a variant which has three or four valves. The tenor and bass trombones have a range of three and a half octaves.

Trondheim City on the S shore of Trondheim fjord, central Norway, the third-largest city in Norway. Founded as Nidaros in 997, the city was the political and religious capital of medieval Norway. Until 1906, the kings of Norway were crowned in the much-restored 12th-century cathedral. Trondheim exports wood and metal products. Industries: fishing, shipbuilding. Pop. (1997) 145,000.

tropical disease Any of a number of diseases predominantly associated with tropical climates. Major tropical diseases include MALARIA, LEISHMANIASIS, SLEEPING SICKNESS, FILARIASIS and SCHISTOSOMIASIS. The infectious agents of tropical diseases include viruses, bacteria, protozoa, fungi and worms of various kinds. Many of these disease microbes are spread by insect vectors, such as MOSQUITOES.

tropics *See* CANCER, TROPIC OF; CAPRICORN, TROPIC OF

tropism (tropic response) Response in growth and orientation of a plant or a part of it in relation to a directional, external stimulus, such as light or water.

Trotsky, Leon (1879–1940) Russian revolutionary leader and theoretician, b. Lev Davidovich Bronstein. A Marxist revolutionary from 1897, he headed the workers' SOVIET in St Petersburg in the RUSSIAN REVOLUTION OF 1905. Arrested, Trotsky escaped abroad and embarked on the work that made him, with LENIN, the leading architect of the RUSSIAN REVOLUTION of 1917. He returned to Russia after the March revolution (1917), and joined the BOLSHEVIKS. As chairman of the Petrograd (St Petersburg) Soviet, Trotsky set up the Military Revolutionary Committee to seize power, ostensibly for the Soviet, actually for the Bolsheviks. After the Bolshevik success, he negotiated the peace of BREST-LITOVSK, withdrawing Russia from World War 1. As commissar of war (1918–25), Trotsky created the RED ARMY, which won the civil war and made the Bolshevik revolution safe. However, he criticized the growth of bureaucracy in the party, the lack of democracy, and failure to expand industrialization. Trotsky disapproved of Lenin's dictatorial tendencies in power. He fiercely objected to STALIN's adoption of a policy of "socialism in one country", rather than the world revolution in which Trotsky believed. He was driven from

power, from the party, and eventually from the country. In exile, Trotsky continued to write prolifically on many subjects. His ideas, although rejected in the Soviet Union, were extremely influential internationally, especially in Third World countries. In 1936, Trotsky settled in Mexico, where he was assassinated by a Stalinist agent.

troubadour Poet in the S of France from the 11th to the 14th century who wrote about love and chivalry. Their poems were sung by wandering minstrels called jongleurs. They wrote in the Provençal tongue, the *langue d'oc*, and much of their work, which was highly influential in the development of European lyric poetry, survives in songbooks.

trough In meteorology, area of low atmospheric pressure, usually an extension to a DEPRESSION. The opposite are ridges of high pressure.

trout Freshwater sport fish of North America and Europe. Also a food fish, it is commonly propagated in hatcheries. Trout move upstream to spawn. Those that migrate to the ocean between spawnings are called steelheads. Length: to 103cm (40.5in); weight: 17kg (37lb). Types include: the high mountain golden *Salvelinus aquakonita* of W North America, marked by vertical side bars; brook trout (char), *S. fontinalis*, of E North America; rainbow trout, *Salmo gairdneri*, marked by a longitudinal red stripe; large European brown trout, *S. trutta*; and cutthroat *S. clarki* of W North America. Family Salmonidae.

Troy (Ilium) Ancient city at what is now Hissarlik, Turkey, familiar chiefly through HOMER's *Iliad*. Archaeological excavation, begun by Heinrich SCHLIEMANN in the 1870s, suggests that the legend of the TROJAN WAR may be based on an actual episode. Nine cities have been detected in the archaeological strata, dating from *c*.3000 BC and reaching a peak in Troy VI (*c*.1800–1300 BC). Troy VI was ruined by an earthquake. Its successor, Troy VIIA, was destroyed, apparently by enemy attack, in *c*.1200 BC, close to the legendary date of the fall of Troy.

Troyes, Chrétien de (active 12th century) French poet, writer of the earliest extant ARTHURIAN ROMANCES. Troyes' work includes translations of OVID and the romances *Erec* (after 1155), *Cligès* (*c*.1176), and the unfinished *Perceval*, which contains the earliest known reference to the legend of the Holy Grail.

Trudeau, Pierre Elliott (1919–2000) Canadian statesman, prime minister (1968–79, 1980–84). He was minister of justice before succeeding Lester PEARSON as prime minister. Trudeau promoted the economic and diplomatic independence of Canada, reducing US influence. Aided by his French-Canadian origins, he resisted QUÉBEC separatism, imposing martial law to combat separatist terrorism in 1970. Defeated in the elections of 1979, he returned to power in 1980. Autonomy for Québec was rejected in a referendum (1980), and Trudeau succeeded in winning agreement for a revised constitution (1981).

True Levellers *See* DIGGERS

Trueman, Fred (Frederick Sewards) (1931–) English cricketer. He played (1949–68) county cricket for Yorkshire. A great fast bowler, Trueman played in 67 test matches for England (1952–65), taking 307 wickets. In 1965, he became the first bowler to take 300 test wickets.

Truffaut, François (1932–84) French film director. His first feature film was *The 400 Blows* (1959). Other films include *Shoot the Pianist* (1960), *Jules and Jim* (1961) and *Pocket Money* (1976). Truffaut won an Academy Award for best foreign language film for *Day for Night* (1973). Deeply influenced by Alfred HITCHCOCK and Jean RENOIR, and a leading member of the NOUVELLE VAGUE, Truffaut scripted or co-scripted all of his films.

truffle Any of several species of ascomycete FUNGI that grow underground, mostly among tree roots. Most are edible and are highly prized delicacies. Found in Europe, particularly France, and in parts of the USA, they are hunted with trained pigs and dogs that can scent them out. Family Tuberaceae.

Truman, Harry S. (1884–1972) 33rd US President (1945–53). He entered politics in the 1920s and won election to the Senate in 1934. In 1944, he was Franklin ROOSEVELT's running mate. Truman became president on Roosevelt's death and was faced with many difficulties abroad. He approved the use of the atomic bomb to force Japanese surrender (1945), ending WORLD WAR 2, and adopted a robust policy toward the Soviet Union during the COLD WAR. Truman approved the MARSHALL PLAN (1947), and the creation (1949) of the NORTH ATLANTIC TREATY ORGANIZATION (NATO). Lacking Roosevelt's charisma, he was expected to lose the election of 1948, but won narrowly. In the KOREAN WAR, he was forced to dismiss the US commander, General MACARTHUR. In 1952, Truman declined renomination. He was succeeded by Dwight D. EISENHOWER.

Truman Doctrine Principle of US foreign policy under President TRUMAN. It promised support for any democratic country threatened by foreign domination. In practice, application of the principle was limited. The US did not act against communist takeovers in Eastern Europe, although it did resist the invasion of South Korea.

trumpet BRASS instrument of ancient origin. It has a cylindrical bore in the shape of a flattened loop and three piston valves. It became an important ceremonial instrument in the 15th century and by the late 17th century had become standard in the orchestra.

trunkfish (boxfish) Marine fish that lives in temperate and tropical waters. Its body is almost triangular when seen from the front, with a broad flat ventral region tapering to a narrow dorsal region. Length: to 50cm (20in). Family Ostraciontidae; genus *Lactophrys*.

trust In law, situation in which one person (the trustee) holds property for the benefit of another (the beneficiary). Trusts are generally created by a legal instrument, such as a deed or a WILL.

Truth, Sojourner (1797–1883) US abolitionist. Born a slave in New York State and unable to read or write, she was freed by the New York Emancipation Act (1827). Inspired by a religious calling, she became a leading propagandist for votes for women and abolition of SLAVERY.

truth State or condition of being true. A truth is something deemed to be genuine, an accurate representation of reality or a statement that accords with proven, provable or observable facts. Defining the distinction between truth and falsity has long been a major preoccupation of philosophers and logicians. Two famous theories for determining the meaning of truth are the **correspondence** theory, which defines it as "that which corresponds with facts", and the **coherence** theory, which defines it as "that which conforms with what we have come to accept". Other theories, espoused by pragmatists, take a utilitarian view of truth, defining it as "that which it is good, useful, or helpful to believe". This evaluative concept is also important in LOGIC, where either of two truth-values can be assigned to a statement, describing as either true or false. *See also* EPISTEMOLOGY; ONTOLOGY; PRAGMATISM

trypsin Digestive ENZYME secreted by the PANCREAS. It is secreted in an inactive form that is converted into active trypsin by an enzyme in the small intestine. It breaks down peptide bonds on the amino acids lysine and arginine. *See also* ALIMENTARY CANAL; DIGESTIVE SYSTEM

tsetse fly Any of several species of blood-sucking flies that live in Africa. Larger than a housefly, it has a grey thorax and a yellow to brown abdomen. Females transmit a cattle disease. Almost 80% of flies that bite humans are males, which carry SLEEPING SICKNESS. Length: to 16mm (0.6in). Order Diptera; family Muscidae; genus *Glossina*.

Tsimshian Native American tribe resident in coastal NW British Columbia, Canada, and SE Alaska. Some groups retain elements of animist totemic religion, but the original matrilineal social organization has all but disappeared. *See also* TOTEMISM

Tsiolkovsky, Konstantin Eduardovich (1857–1935) Russian aeronautical engineer. In 1898 he became the first person to stress the importance of liquid propellants in ROCKETS. He also proposed the idea of using multi-stage rockets to overcome GRAVITATION.

tsunami (seismic sea wave) Ocean wave caused by a submarine EARTHQUAKE, subsidence or volcanic eruption. Erroneously called a tidal wave, tsunamis spread radially from their source in ever-widening circles. Tsunamis can travel across oceans at speeds of up to 400km/h (250mph) and reach heights of 10m (33ft). The eruption of KRAKATOA (1883) caused a tsunami that drowned more than 30,000 people in Java and Sumatra.

Tuareg Fiercely independent BERBERS of Islamic faith who inhabit the desert regions of N Africa. Their matrilineal, feudal society is based on nomadic pastoralism; it traditionally maintained a class of black, non-Tuareg servants. Tuareg males wear blue veils, while the women are unveiled. About half the population is no longer nomadic, and there have been demands for the Tuareg to have their own homeland.

tuatara Nocturnal, lizard-like reptile of New Zealand; remarkable for being active at quite low temperatures and for being the sole surviving member of the primitive order Rhynchocephalia. It is brownish in colour and has

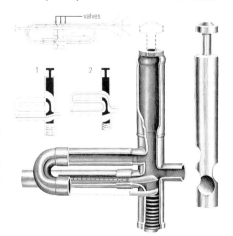

▲ **trumpet** A modern trumpet is fitted with three valves that lower the pitch of the instrument by increasing its length; this is done by means of "crooks", which are brought into play when the valves are depressed. A raised valve lets the air pass directly through (1); when the valve is depressed, the air flows through the crook (2). The first valve, nearest the mouthpiece, lowers the pitch by two semitones; the middle valve lowers it by one semitone; and the third valve, furthest from the mouthpiece, lowers it by three semitones.

an exceptionally well-developed PINEAL BODY on its head. Length: to 70cm (2.3ft). Species *Sphenodon punctatus*.

tuba Family of BRASS musical instruments, the lowest of the orchestral brass instruments. The tuba has a conical bore and a cupped mouthpiece and has four or five valves. It is held vertically with the bell pointing upward.

tuber In plants, the short, swollen, sometimes edible underground stem, modified for the storage of food, as in the potato, or as a swollen root (for example, dahlia). They enable the plant to survive an adverse season (winter or dry season), providing food for the later development of new shoots and roots.

tuberculosis (TB) Infectious disease caused by the bacillus, *Mycobacterium tuberculosis*. It most often affects the lungs (pulmonary tuberculosis) but may involve the bones and joints, skin, lymph nodes, intestines and kidneys. One-third of the world's population is infected, and up to 5% of those infected eventually develop TB. Poor urban living conditions mean that the disease is making a comeback in countries such as the USA and much of Europe, where previously it had been in decline. The BCG vaccine against tuberculosis was developed in the 1920s, and the first effective treatment drug, streptomycin, became available in 1944. However, the bacillus is showing increasing resistance to drugs, and some strains are multi-resistant.

Tubman, Harriet (1820–1913) US abolitionist. Born a slave, she escaped to the North by following the UNDERGROUND RAILROAD. She then led *c*.300 fugitive slaves, including her parents, to freedom during the 1850s and became a prominent spokeswoman for abolition.

Tubman, William Vacanarat Shadrach (1895–1971) Liberian statesman, president (1944–71). A descendant of US freed slaves who settled the country during the 19th century, he preserved Liberia's close connections with the USA, maintained prosperity and showed respect for the customs of the non-Westernized people of the interior.

TUC *See* TRADES UNION CONGRESS

Tucana (Toucan) Far southern constellation representing a toucan. Its overall faintness is redeemed by the presence of the small MAGELLANIC CLOUD and a superb globular cluster. It lies 15,000 light-years away.

Tucson City on the Santa Cruz River, S Arizona. The presidio fort of Tucson was built by the Spanish in 1776 and the city was state capital from 1867 to 1877. Today, it is better known as a foothills resort with a dry, sunny climate. It is the seat of the University of Arizona (1885). Industries: aircraft parts, electronics. Pop. (1992) 415,079.

Tudjman, Franjo (1922–99) Croatian statesman, president (1990–99). He was imprisoned twice by the Yugoslavian government for nationalist activities. In 1989, Tudjman founded the Croatian Democratic Union (HDZ) party, which helped form a coalition government in Bosnia-Herzegovina (1990). He was elected president of Croatia and retained this position during the ensuing civil war. Tudjman was re-elected in 1997.

Tudors English royal dynasty (1485–1603). Of Welsh origin, they were descended from Owen Tudor (d.1461), who married the widow of HENRY V. Owen Tudor's grandson defeated RICHARD III at Bosworth in 1485 to win the English throne as HENRY VII. The dynasty ended with the death of ELIZABETH I in 1603. *See also* HENRY VIII; EDWARD VI; MARY I; STUART

Tu Fu (712–70) Chinese poet of the T'ANG dynasty who wrote about such topics as war, corruption and patriotism. His poetry reflects his troubled personal life and laments the corruption and cruelty that prevailed at court.

tulip Hardy, bulb-forming plant of the genus, *Tulipa*, native to Europe, Asia and North Africa. Tulips have long, pointed leaves growing from the base and elongated, cup-shaped flowers that can be almost any colour or combination of colours. Family Liliaceae; genus *Tulipa*.

Tull, Jethro (1674–1741) English agriculturalist. He influenced agricultural methods through his invention (1701) of a mechanical seed drill. The drill sowed seeds in straight lines, reducing the labour involved in weeding.

Tulsa Port on the Arkansas River, NE Oklahoma, the state's second-largest city. It developed with the arrival in 1882 of the Atlantic and Pacific Railroad; the 1901 discovery of oil further accelerated development. Industries: oil refining, mining, aerospace. Pop. (1992) 453,995.

tumbleweed Plant that characteristically breaks off near the ground in fall and is rolled along by the wind. Height: to 51cm (20in). Family Amaranthaceae; genus *Amaranthus*.

tumour Any uncontrolled, abnormal proliferation of cells, often leading to the formation of a lump. Tumours are classified as either benign (non-cancerous) or malignant. *See also* CANCER

tuna (tunny) Marine fish related to MACKEREL, found in tropical and temperate seas. An important commercial fish, it has a blue-black and silvery streamlined body with a large, deeply divided tail. Length: to 4.3m (14ft); weight: to 810kg (1,800lb).

tundra Treeless, level or gently undulating plain characteristic of arctic and sub-arctic regions. It is marshy with dark soil that supports mosses, lichens and low shrubs. It has a permanently frozen sub-soil known as PERMAFROST.

tungsten (wolfram, symbol W) Silvery-grey, hard, metallic element, one of the TRANSITION ELEMENTS. Tungsten has the highest melting point of all metals and is used for lamp filaments and in special alloys. Tungsten carbide is used in high-speed cutting tools. Chemically tungsten is fairly unreactive; it oxidizes only at high temperatures. Properties: at.no. 74; r.a.m. 183.85; r.d. 19.3; m.p. 3,410°C (6,170°F); b.p. 5,660°C (10,220°F); most common isotope W^{184} (30.64%).

Tunis Capital and largest city of Tunisia, N Africa. It became the capital in the 13th century, under the Hafsid dynasty. Seized by BARBAROSSA in 1534, and controlled by Turkey, it attained infamy as a haven for pirates. The French assumed control in 1881. Tunis' port facilities were greatly improved after independence in 1956. Products include olive oil, carpets, textiles and handicrafts. The ruins of CARTHAGE are nearby. Pop. (1994) 674,100.

Tunisia Smallest country in N Africa. The NW mountain ranges are a comparatively low extension of the ATLAS Mountains. In the centre is a depression, containing the Chott Djerid salt lake. In the S lies part of the SAHARA desert. The fertile coastal lowlands include many fine Mediterranean ports, such as Bizerte and the capital, TUNIS. Kairouan is the fourth most holy city in Islam. **Climate** Coastal regions have a Mediterranean climate, with dry, sunny summers and mild winters with moderate rainfall. Rainfall decreases and temperatures increase to the S. **Vegetation** Some cork oak forests grow in the N mountains. The S plateaux are covered by steppe with coarse grasses. The Sahara is barren, except around oases. **History and politics** In tradition, the Phoenician Queen DIDO founded CARTHAGE in 814 BC. In 146 BC, the Romans destroyed the city, and the region was subsumed into the

---

TUNISIA
AREA: 163,610sq km (63,170sq mi)
POPULATION: 9,924,000
CAPITAL (POPULATION): Tunis (674,100)

Roman Empire. In AD 640, the Arabs invaded. The BERBERS slowly converted to Islam and Arabic became the principal language. In 1159, the ALMOHAD dynasty conquered Tunisia. From 1230 to 1574, Tunisia was ruled by the Hafsids. Spain's capture of much of Tunisia's coast led to the intervention of the Ottoman Empire, and the rule of Turkish governors (*beys*) continued into the 20th century. In the 16th century, Tunisia's harbours were a refuge for Barbary pirates. In 1881, France invaded and Tunisia became a French protectorate (1883). French rule aroused strong nationalist sentiment, and Habib BOURGUIBA formed the Destour Socialist Party (PSD) in 1934. Tunisia was a major battleground of the North Africa campaigns in World War 2. In 1956, it gained independence. In 1957, the *bey* was deposed and Tunisia became a republic, with Bourguiba as president. In 1975, Bourguiba was proclaimed president-for-life. He pursued a moderate foreign policy and modern domestic policies. In 1981, the first multi-party elections were held. In the 1980s, Bourguiba's failing health created a succession crisis, and he was deposed by Zine el Abidine Ben Ali in 1987. The PSD became the Constitutional Democratic Rally (RCD), and Ben Ali won a landslide victory in 1989 elections. He was re-elected in 1994. The hegemony of the RCD remains a problem for its fledgling democracy. **Economy** Tunisia is a middle-income developing country (1995 GDP per capita, US$5,000). It is the world's sixth-largest producer of phosphates. It also exports crude oil. Agriculture employs 26% of the workforce. Tunisia is the world's fourth-largest producer of olives. Other major crops include barley, dates, grapes for wine and wheat. Fishing and livestock-raising are also important. Tourism is a vital source of foreign exchange (1992 receipts, US$1,074 million). It has been an associate member of the European Union since 1969.

tunny *See* TUNA

Tupí-Guaraní Combination of two major tribes that now represents the major native cultural population in rural Brazil, Paraguay and parts of Argentina. The Tupí traditionally inhabit the banks of the lower Amazon and much of coastal Brazil south to Uruguay. The Guaraní, a more scattered grouping, once lived mainly in what is now Paraguay, but migrated into Brazil and Argentina.

turbidity current Dense current in air, water or other fluid caused by different amounts of matter in suspension. In the ocean, when sediment along the continental shelves breaks off and rushes down slope, the resulting turbidity current carves out submarine canyons and deposits distinctively bedded layers on the ocean floor.

turbine Rotary device turned by a moving fluid (liquid or gas). The modern form of water turbine is like a many-bladed PROPELLER and is used to generate HYDROELECTRICITY. In power stations that burn fuels to produce electricity, the energy released by the burning is harnessed by the blades of jet engine-like steam turbines. As they spin, the turbines turn GENERATORS that produce ELECTRICITY. Modern wind generators produce electricity when the wind turns their rotors. In gas turbines, hot gases from burning fuel turn turbines that can operate generators or other machinery.

turbocharger Device that boosts the performance of an INTERNAL COMBUSTION ENGINE. A TURBINE driven by exhaust gases compresses the fuel/air mixture before it passes through the inlet valve.

turbot Scaleless, bottom-dwelling European marine FLATFISH. It has a broad, flat body with both eyes on its gray-brown, mottled upper surface, which may also be covered in bony knobs. Length: to 1m (3.3ft). Family Scophthalmidae; species *Scophthalmus maximus*.

Turgenev, Ivan Sergeievich (1818–83) Russian novelist, dramatist and short-story writer. His novels often opposed social and political evils and attracted official disapproval. The play, *A Month in the Country* (1855), is often considered the first psychological drama of the Russian theatre. After the publication of his masterpiece *Fathers and Sons* (1862), he left Russia permanently.

turgor pressure Hydrostatic pressure generated in cells of plants and bacteria as a result of the uptake of water by OSMOSIS. Water diffuses through the semi-permeable membrane of the cell, causing it to swell; the increase in volume is resisted by the limited elasticity of the cell wall. When water is lost, a plant's cells collapse and it wilts.

Turin (Torino) City on the River Po, NW Italy, the country's fourth-largest city and capital of Piedmont (Piemonte) region. A Roman town under Augustus, Turin became a Lombard duchy from 590 to 636. From 1720 to 1861, it was capital of the Kingdom of Sardinia and a centre of the RISORGIMENTO. Damaged during World War 2, In 1997, its Romanesque cathedral was badly damaged in a fire, but the TURIN SHROUD was saved. Turin is an important industrial centre. Industries: automobiles, iron and steel, textiles, publishing, wine. Pop. (1996) 923,000.

Turing, Alan Mathison (1912–54) English mathematician. In 1937, he invented the **Turing machine**, a hypothetical machine that could modify a set of input instructions. It was the forerunner of the modern COMPUTER. During World War 2, Turing played a major role in deciphering the German "Enigma" code. In 1950, he devised the **Turing test**, that paved the way for the foundation of ARTIFICIAL INTELLIGENCE (AI). He committed suicide after being prosecuted for homosexuality.

Turin Shroud Sheet of very old linen kept in Turin Cathedral, by tradition the cloth in which the body of JESUS CHRIST was wrapped after the Crucifixion. It was photographed in 1898 when negatives were seen to show the shape of a human figure. In 1988, results of carbon dating tests revealed that the shroud had in fact been made between c.AD 1260 and 1390, well over a millennium after the death of Christ.

Turkey Country that straddles SE Europe and Asia. European Turkey (THRACE) is a small, fertile region, separated from Asia by the DARDANELLES, the BOSPORUS and the Sea of Marmara. The major city is EDIRNE. ISTANBUL lies on both continents. Anatolia (ASIA MINOR) is a mainly mountainous region, rising in the E to 5,165m (16,945ft) at Mount ARARAT. The plateau region of Central Anatolia includes the capital, ANKARA. The Mediterranean coast is a popular tourist destination. **Climate** Central Turkey has hot, dry summers and cold winters. Western Turkey has a Mediterranean climate. The Black Sea coast has cooler summers. **Vegetation** Maquis is common in Mediterranean areas. Deciduous forests grow inland, with conifers on the mountains. The plateau is mainly dry steppe. **History and politics** EPHESUS is one of the many ruins of the ancient Anatolian kingdoms of IONIA and PONTUS. In AD 330, Byzantium (Constantinople) became capital of the Roman Empire; thence capital of the BYZANTINE EMPIRE (398). In the 11th century, the SELJUKS introduced Islam, and the capital moved to KONYA. In 1435, Constantinople was captured by MUHAMMAD II, and it served as capital of

TURKEY
AREA: 779,450sq km (300,946sq mi)
POPULATION: 66,789,000
CAPITAL (POPULATION): Ankara (2,838,000)

the vast OTTOMAN EMPIRE. Defeat in World War 1 led to the sultan signing the punitive Treaty of SÈVRES (1920). Nationalists, led by Mustafa Kemal (ATATÜRK), launched a war of independence. In 1923, Turkey became a republic, with Kemal as its president. Atatürk's 14-year dictatorship created a secular, Westernized state. In 1938, Atatürk died and was succeeded by Ismet INÖNÜ. Turkey remained neutral throughout most of World War 2. In 1950, the first multiparty elections were held. A major post-war recipient of US aid, Turkey joined NATO in 1952. In 1960, a military coup led to the creation of a second republic. In 1965, Süleyman DEMIREL became prime minister. In 1974, Turkey invaded Northern CYPRUS; tension with Greece increased. In 1980, a military coup led to martial law. In 1987, martial law was lifted. In 1993, Demirel was elected president, and Tansu Çiller became Turkey's first woman prime minister. In 1995, Necmettin Erbakan of the Islamist Welfare Party (RP) became prime minister. In 1997, tension between the pro-Islamic government and the military led to Erbakan's resignation. A new secular government was formed, led by Mesut Yilmaz of the Motherland Party (ANAP). In 1998, the RP was declared illegal. In 1998, Yilmaz resigned after allegations of corruption. In April 1999, a coalition government was formed under Bülent Ecevit, leader of the Democratic Left Party (DSP). Since 1984, Turkey has been fighting the Kurdish Workers Party (PKK) in SE Turkey, Syria and N Iraq. Turkey has often been accused of violating the human rights of KURDS. In 1999, Turkey captured the PKK leader, Abdullah Öcalan. In the same year, NW Turkey was devastated by a major earthquake. In 2000, Demirel was succeeded as president by Ahmet Necdet Sezer. **Economy** Turkey is a lower-middle income developing country (1995 GDP per capita, US$5,580). Agriculture employs 47% of the workforce. Turkey is a leading producer of citrus fruits, barley, cotton, wheat, tobacco and tea. It is a major producer of chromium and phosphate fertilizers. Tourism is a vital source of foreign exchange.

turkey North American gamebird now widely domesticated. The common wild turkey (*Meleagris gallopavo*), once abundant in North America, was overhunted and is now protected. The male, or gobbler, is often bearded. Length: 125cm (50in). Family Meleagrididae.

Turkic languages Branch of the ALTAIC family of languages. Divided into six or seven separate sub-classes, Turkish is the most important. The languages are remarkable for their grammatical uniformity, structural inter-resemblances and relative lack of linguistic change.

Turkistan (Turkestan) Historic region of central Asia, inhabited by Turkic-speaking peoples. **Western** (Russian) Turkistan now consists of the republics of TURKMENISTAN, UZBEKISTAN, TAJIKISTAN, KYRGYZSTAN and S KAZAKSTAN. It mainly comprises the deserts of KYZYL KUM and Kara Kum. **Eastern** (Chinese) Turkistan comprises the Chinese region of XINJIANG and includes the TIAN SHAN mountains. **Southern** Turkistan consists of part of N Afghanistan. For nearly two centuries, Turkistan was the geographical bridge for trade between East and West. The first imperial power to control the region was PERSIA in 500 BC, but in *c.*330 BC ALEXANDER THE GREAT defeated the Persians and for the next few centuries, the region was disputed between Bactria, PARTHIA and China. Market towns developed around the oases, centres for trade and religion. In the 8th century, the Arabs conquered the region, and the local population were converted to Islam. During the 13th century, the region was controlled by the Mongols, but then fractured into small, independent khanates. In 1867, the Russian empire imposed military rule over the area, and in

---

TURKMENISTAN
AREA: 488,100sq km (188,450sq mi)
POPULATION: 4,585,000
CAPITAL (POPULATION): Ashgabat (536,000)

1918 Turkistan became an autonomous region within the SOVIET UNION. In 1924, the S part of Turkistan was divided into the republics of Uzbekistan and Turkmenistan; in 1929, Tajikistan became a republic and Kyrgyzstan followed in 1936. The N part of Russian Turkistan was incorporated into the Kazak republic, and Russian Turkistan became known as **Soviet Central Asia**.

Turkmenistan Republic in central Asia. The capital is ASHGABAT. Originally part of the Persian empire, it was overrun by Arabs in the 8th century AD. GENGHIS KHAN invaded in the 13th century, and it subsequently became part of TAMERLANE's vast empire. With the break-up of the Timurid dynasty, Turkmenistan came under Uzbek control. In the 19th century, Russia became increasingly dominant. In 1899, despite resistance, Turkmenistan became part of Russian TURKISTAN. In 1925, as part of the Turkistan Autonomous Soviet Socialist Republic, it was absorbed into the SOVIET UNION. In 1991, it achieved independence. In 1993, Turkmenistan became a full member of the Commonwealth of Independent States (CIS). In 1990, President Niyazov was elected head of state. His autocratic government prevented any political opposition to the ruling Democratic Party (formerly Communist Party). In a 1994 referendum, Niyazov's term of presidency was extended to 2002. **Economy** Almost 90% of Turkmenistan is covered by the KARA-KUM desert, parts of which are irrigated by the Kara-Kum canal. The chief crop is cotton, and there are large reserves of natural gas and oil.

Turks and Caicos Islands Two island groups of the British West Indies, including more than 40 islands, eight of them inhabited. The capital is Cockburn Town on Grand Turk Island. Discovered in 1512 by Ponce de León, the islands were British from 1766, administered via Jamaica from 1873 to 1959, and a separate crown colony from 1973. Exports include salt, sponges and shellfish. The islands' main sources of income are now tourism and offshore banking. Area: 430sq km (166sq mi). Pop (2000) 12,000.

Turku (Åbo) Finland's largest port, at the mouth of the River Aurajoki on the Baltic Sea. A Swedish settlement was established in 1157, and in 1220 it became the seat of the first Finnish diocese. It was the national capital until 1812. Fires in 1641 and 1827 destroyed much of the city. Industries: steel, shipbuilding. Pop. (1997) 167,000.

turmeric Herbaceous, perennial plant originally native to India and cultivated in SE Asia. The dried RHIZOME is powdered for use as seasoning, a yellow dye and in medicines. Family Zingiberaceae; species *Curcuma longa*.

Turner, Joseph Mallord William (1775–1851) English landscape painter. He was an associate of the Royal Academy (RA) by the age of 24, and professor of perspective at the RA from 1807 to 1838. Turner's paintings were revolutionary in their representation of light, especially on water. His style changed dramatically in his late works, such as *The Slave Ship* (1840) and *Rain, Steam and Speed* (1844), in which the original subjects are almost obscured in a hazy interplay of light and colour. His work had a profound influence on IMPRESSIONISM.

Turner, Nat (1800–31) US revolutionary. A slave in Southampton County, Virginia, he believed that he was called by God to take violent revenge on whites and win freedom for blacks. With *c*.70 followers, he was responsible for the death of more than 50 whites before the revolt was crushed. Turner was captured and hanged.

Turner's syndrome Hereditary condition in females in which there is only one X-CHROMOSOME instead of two. It results in dwarfism, infertility and developmental defects.

turnip Garden vegetable best grown in cool climates. The edible leaves are large and toothed with thick midribs. A biennial, it has a large, bulbous, white or yellow, fleshy root, which is cooked and eaten. Diameter: 8–15cm (3–6in). Height: to 55cm (20in). Family Brassicaceae/Cruciferae; species *Brassica rapa*.

turnstone Either of two species of migratory shore birds that use their curved bills to turn over pebbles in search of food; they nest on the Arctic TUNDRA. The vividly marked ruddy turnstone (*Arenaria interpres*) ranges widely in winter. Family Scolopacidae.

Turpin, Dick (1706–39) English highwayman. He engaged in many forms of robbery and was hanged for murder. Turpin became a largely fictional hero.

turquoise Blue mineral, hydrated basic copper aluminium phosphate, found in aluminium-rich rocks in deserts. Its crystal system is triclinic, and it occurs as tiny crystals and dense masses. Its colour ranges from sky-blue and blue-green to a greenish grey, and it is a popular gemstone. Hardness 6; r.d. 2.7.

turtle REPTILE found on land or in marine and fresh waters. Turtles have the most ancient lineage of all reptiles, preceding even the dinosaurs. Fossil have been found from 200 million years ago. They have a bony, horn-covered, box-like shell (carapace) that encloses shoulder and hip girdles and all internal organs. All lay eggs on land. Terrestrial turtles are usually called TORTOISES, and some edible species found in brackish waters are called TERRAPINS. Marine turtles usually have smaller, lighter shells. Length: 10cm–2m (4in–7ft). Order Chelonia.

Tuscany Region in central Italy between the Mediterranean coast and the Apennine Mountains; the capital is FLORENCE. Other cities include SIENA and PISA. Tuscany is mostly mountainous with fertile valleys. Agriculture remains the most important activity, with cereals, olives and grapes among the main products. Carrara marble is quarried in the NW, and there is mining for lead, zinc, antimony and copper in the SW. Industries: tourism, woollens, chemicals, steel, motor scooters, crafts. Area: 22,992sq km (8,877sq mi). Pop (1990) 3,528,735.

Tussaud, Madame Marie (1761–1850) French modeller, b. Marie Grosholtz. She modelled wax figures in Paris, and in 1802 went to London with her collection. In 1835, Tussaud founded a permanent waxworks museum on Baker Street, London. It has been at its present site on Marylebone Road since 1884.

Tutankhamen (*c*.1341–1323 BC) Egyptian pharaoh (r.1333–1323 BC) of the New Kingdom's 18th dynasty (1550–1307 BC). The revolutionary changes made by his predecessor, AKHNATEN, were reversed during his reign. The capital was re-established at Thebes (LUXOR) and worship of AMON reinstated. Tutankhamen's fame is due to the discovery of his tomb by Howard Carter in 1922. The only royal tomb of ancient EGYPT not completely stripped by robbers, it contained magnificent treasures.

Tutu, Desmond Mpilo (1931–) South African Anglican clergyman. A prominent anti-apartheid campaigner, he trained as a teacher before becoming an Anglican priest in 1960. Tutu was Archbishop of Cape Town (1986–96). In 1984, he was awarded the Nobel Peace Prize. Since 1995, he has chaired the Truth and Reconciliation Committee.

Tutuola, Amos (1920–97) Nigerian writer. He was a visionary, who drew on traditional tales of the YORUBA people to create a world of intermixed fantasy and reality. His works include *The Palm Wine Drinkard* (1952) and *The Brave African Huntress* (1958).

Tuvalu (formerly Ellice Islands) Independent republic in W Pacific Ocean, S of the Equator and W of the International Date Line. None of the cluster of nine low-lying coral islands rises more than 4.6m (15ft) out of the Pacific, making them vulnerable to the rising sea levels that have been predicted. Poor soils restrict vegetation to coconut palms, breadfruit and bush. The population survive by subsistence farming, raising pigs and poultry and by fishing. Copra is the only significant export crop, but more foreign exchange is derived from the sale of elaborate postage stamps. The first European to discover the islands (1568) was the Spanish navigator, Alvaro de Mendaña. The population was reduced from *c*.20,000 to just 3,000 in the three decades after 1850, by Europeans abducting workers for other Pacific plantations. The British assumed control in 1892, and it was subsequently administered with the nearby Gilbert Islands (now KIRIBATI). In 1978, Tuvalu became a separate self-governing colony within the Commonwealth. Area: 24sq km (9.5sq mi). Pop. (2000) 11,000.

Twain, Mark (1835–1910) US writer, journalist and lecturer, b. Samuel Langhorne Clemens. He took his pseudonym from the sounding calls of steamboatmen on the Mississippi, on the banks of which he was brought up. Twain was among the first to write novels in the American vernacular, such as *The Adventures of Tom Sawyer* (1876) and *The Adventures of Huckleberry Finn* (1884), which is considered to be one of the great works of US fiction. Although he tends to be categorized as a humorist, his later books, such as *The Mysterious Stranger* (1916), are often bitter and pessimistic.

tweed Rough-textured cloth, usually all wool, from which warm clothes are made. Tweed originated in Scotland but is now made in many countries. After spinning, the yarn is dyed with local LICHENS, giving the cloth its characteristic smell.

Twelve Tables Laws engraved on wooden tables representing the earliest codification of Roman law, traditionally dated 451–450 BC. Written by *decemviri* (a committee of 10), they codified the existing laws and customs of ancient Rome.

twelve-tone music (twelve-note music) SERIAL MUSIC in which the series contains all twelve notes of the CHROMATIC scale. Its introduction, in the early 20th century, is credited to Arnold SCHOENBERG. This method of composition relies not on the principle of TONALITY, in which the tonic or keynote is the focal centre, but on the relationship between the twelve notes of the chromatic scale. The composer selects the order in which the notes are to be played, and the resultant sequence is manipulated throughout the composition. Many composers have experimented with twelve-tone music; these include Anton WEBERN, Alban BERG and Hans Werner HENZE.

twins Two offspring that are born within a short time (usually minutes) of each other. In human beings, it is the most usual form of multiple BIRTH. **Identical** twins develop from a single OVUM that has divided shortly after FERTILIZATION by a single SPERM; **fraternal** twins arise from two individually fertilized ova.

two-stroke engine INTERNAL COMBUSTION ENGINE in which the operation of each piston is in two stages. In the two-stroke cycle, a piston moves up a cylinder to compress a fuel-air mixture in the top. At the same time, more of the mixture is sucked in below the piston. A spark ignites the compressed mixture, causing an explosion. This sends the piston back down the cylinder. The piston forces the fresh fuel-air mixture out from beneath it and along a transfer port leading to the top part of the cylinder. The mixture forces the exhaust gases out from the top of the cylinder. The process then repeats.

Tyler, John (1790–1862) Tenth US President (1841–45). He served in Congress (1811–16) and as governor of Virginia (1825–27). Tyler was a supporter of STATES' RIGHTS. The Whigs chose him as vice-presidential candidate with William H. HARRISON, and he succeeded to the presidency on Harrison's death (1841). He came into conflict with the nationalistic Whigs in Congress, repeatedly vetoing legislation to create a national bank. His determination to annex TEXAS bore fruit after he had left office.

Tyler, Wat (d.1381) English leader of the PEASANTS' REVOLT (1381). He was chosen as leader of the rebels in Kent, SE England, and led their march on London. Tyler was eventually killed by the lord mayor of London while parleying with RICHARD II.

Tyndale, William (c.1494–1536) English translator and religious reformer. In 1525, he started printing an English version of the New Testament in Cologne, Germany. Tyndale then began translating the Old Testament. He also wrote numerous Protestant tracts. Tyndale was eventually captured by the church authorities and burned at the stake as a heretic. His translation later provided a basis for the Authorized Version of the English BIBLE.

Tyndall, John (1820–93) Irish physicist, who correctly suggested that the blue colour of the sky is due to the scattering of light by particles of dust and other colloidal particles. By 1881, Tyndall had helped disprove the theory of SPONTANEOUS GENERATION by showing that food does not decay in germ-free air.

Tyne River in NE England. Formed at the confluence of the North Tyne (which rises in the S Cheviot Hills) and the South Tyne (which rises in Cumbria), it flows E for 48km (30mi) through Newcastle to enter the North Sea near Tynemouth. It was made fully navigable at the end of the 19th century.

Tyne and Wear Metropolitan council in NE England, formed in 1974 from parts of the former counties of NORTHUMBERLAND and DURHAM; it included the former county borough of NEWCASTLE-UPON-TYNE, its administrative centre. A highly industrialized area, its staple industries of coal mining, iron and steel production and shipbuilding declined after the 1920s. There were signs of a recovery in the 1990s based on various light industries. Area: 537sq km (207sq mi). Pop. (1991) 1,095,152.

typesetting Part of the PRINTING process. In early printing, wooden or metal type was set by hand. In hot-metal type processes, the linotype machine casts a complete line of molten type metal into a mould, and the monotype machine casts individual letters and spaces and arranges these in lines. Most type is now set using photographic or computerized processes.

typhoid fever Acute, sometimes epidemic communicable disease of the DIGESTIVE SYSTEM. Caused by *Salmonella typhi*, which is transmitted in contaminated water or food, it is characterized by bleeding from the bowel and enlargement of the spleen. Symptoms include fever, headache, constipation, sore throat, cough and skin rash.

typhoon Name given in the Pacific Ocean to a HURRICANE, a violent tropical cyclonic storm.

typhus Any of a group of infectious diseases caused by rickettsiae (small bacteria) and spread by parasites of the human body such as lice, fleas, ticks and mites. Epidemic typhus, the result of infection by *Rickettsia prowazekii*, is the most serious manifestation.

Associated with dirty, overcrowded conditions, it is mainly seen during times of war or famine.

typography Practice of designing typefaces and type styles mainly for use in printed texts. Typography is widely used in experimental, progressive art and design as well as conventional PUBLISHING. Movements that have revolutionized typography include FUTURISM, Dadaism and SURREALISM. Individuals include Eric GILL and MOHOLY-NAGY. The term also refers to the art of fine PRINTING itself. *See also* DADA; TYPESETTING

typology System of groupings that aid understanding of the objects being studied by distinguishing certain attributes or qualities among them that serve to link them together into a closed set of items.

Tyr (Tiw) In Germanic mythology, powerful sky god. He was also associated with war, government, and justice. The word Tuesday derives from Tyr's day.

tyrannosaurus Any of several species of large, bipedal, carnivorous, theropod DINOSAURS that lived during late CRETACEOUS times. Its head, 1.2m (4ft) long, was armed with a series of dagger-like teeth. The hind legs were stout and well developed, but the forelegs may have been useless except for grasping at close range. The best-known species is *T. rex*. Length: 14m (47ft); height: 6.5m (20ft).

Tyre Historic city on the coast of modern Lebanon. Built on an island, it was a major commercial port of ancient PHOENICIA. It supplied both craftsmen and raw materials, especially cedarwood, for the building of the temple in Jerusalem in the 10th century BC, and established colonies, including CARTHAGE, around the E Mediterranean. Tyre was never successfully besieged until ALEXANDER THE GREAT built a causeway linking the island to the mainland (332 BC). Ruled by successive empires, including the Romans, it was captured by the Arabs in AD 638 and destroyed by the Mamelukes in 1291. Pop. (1991) 70,000.

tyre Air-filled RUBBER and fabric cushion that fits over the wheels of vehicles to grip the road and absorb shock. The pneumatic tyre was invented in 1845 but was not commonly used until the end of the century. It consists of a layer of fabric surrounded by a thick layer of rubber treated with chemicals to harden it and decrease wear and tear.

Tyrol *See* TIROL

Tyrone Largest of the six counties of Northern Ireland, in the SW of the province. The county town is Omagh. Mainly hilly with the Sperrin Mountains in the N and Bessy Bell and Mary Gray in the S, the region is drained by the Blackwater and Mourne rivers. Cereals and root crops are grown and dairy cattle are raised. Industries: linen, whisky, processed food. Area: 3,263sq km (1,260sq mi). Pop. (1990) 153,000.

Tyson, Mike (1966–) US boxer. Known for his devastating punching power, in 1986 he became the youngest heavyweight champion in boxing history. In 1987, Tyson became the first undisputed heavyweight champion for a decade. Defeated by Buster Douglas in 1990, he was convicted of rape and sentenced to prison in 1992. Released in 1995, he regained his WBC title (1996) by stopping Frank Bruno. Later that year, he was defeated by Evander Holyfield. In a 1997 rematch, Tyson was disqualifed for biting off part of Holyfield's ear. He was fined and banned from boxing for a year. In 1999, Tyson served three months in prison for a 'road rage' assault.

Tyutchev, Fyodor Ivanovich (1803–73) Russian lyric poet and essayist. He spent much of his life abroad, an experience of exile which seems to have heightened the nationalism that infuses his work. With PUSHKIN and LERMONTOV, he was one of the dominant poetic voices of 19th-century RUSSIAN LITERATURE.

Tz'u Hsi *See* CIXI

U/u, 21st letter of the Roman alphabet. Like some other letters in the alphabet it is derived from the Semitic letter vaw, meaning hook. It was adopted by the Greeks before moving into the Roman alphabet.

Uccello, Paolo (1397–1475) Florentine painter. Celebrated as an early master of PERSPECTIVE, Uccello's works include *The Flood* (c.1450) and *The Rout of San Romano* (1454–57).

Udaipur City on Lake Pichola, Rajasthan, India. In 1586, it was made capital of the princely state of Udaipur by Udai Singh. The walled city has three palaces. It is an agricultural market and a centre for textiles. Pop. (1991) 309,000.

Uffizi (It. offices) Chief public gallery in Florence, Italy, housing one of the greatest collections of Italian paintings. The palace was built in the 16th century by Giorgio VASARI for the Grand Duke Cosimo I de' MEDICI and once housed government offices. Painters of the Florentine and other Italian schools are represented with works by Piero della Francesca, Botticelli, Leonardo da Vinci, Michelangelo, Raphael, Titian and many others, as well as Dutch and Flemish masters.

UFO Abbreviation of UNIDENTIFIED FLYING OBJECT

Uganda Republic in E central Africa. Most of Uganda consists of part of the African plateau, which slopes down from c.1,500m (4,921ft) in the S to 900m (2,953ft) in the N. In the W lies an arm of the Great RIFT VALLEY that contains Lake ALBERT and the Albert NILE. Highland regions lie in the SW and E. Much of S Uganda is made up of Lake VICTORIA, Africa's largest lake. The capital, KAMPALA, and ENTEBBE lie on the lakeside. **Climate** Uganda's equatorial climate is moderated by altitude. The wettest regions are the W mountains, especially the high Ruwenzori range. **Vegetation** Nearly 20% of Uganda is covered by lakes or swamps. Some rainforest remains in the S. Wooded savanna covers central and N Uganda. **History and politics** In c.1500, the Nilotic-speaking Lwo people formed various kingdoms in SW Uganda, including Buganda (kingdom of the Ganda) and Bunyoro. During the 18th century, the Buganda kingdom expanded and trade flourished. In 1862, a British explorer, John Speke, became the first European to reach Buganda. He was closely followed (1875) by Sir Henry STANLEY. The conversion activities of Christian missionaries led to conflict with Muslims. The *kabaka* (king) came to depend on Christian support. In 1892, Britain dispatched troops to Buganda, and in 1894 Uganda became a British protectorate. Unlike much of Africa, Uganda attracted Asian, rather than European, settlers. African political representation remained minimal until after World War 2. In 1962, Uganda gained independence, with Buganda's *kabaka*, Mutesa II, as president and Milton OBOTE as prime minister. In 1966, Mutesa II was forced into exile. In 1967, Buganda's traditional autonomy was restricted, and Obote became executive president. In

1971, Obote was deposed in a military coup, led by Major General Idi AMIN. Amin quickly established a personal dictatorship and launched a war against foreign interference, which resulted in the mass expulsion of Asians. It is estimated that Amin's regime was responsible for the murder of more than 250,000 Ugandans. Obote loyalists resisted the regime from neighbouring Tanzania. In 1976, Amin declared himself president-for-life, and Israel launched a successful raid on Entebbe airport to end the hijack of one of its passenger planes. In 1978, Uganda annexed the Kagera region of NW Tanzania. In 1979, Tanzanian troops helped the Uganda National Liberation Front (UNLF) to overthrow Amin and capture Kampala. In 1980 elections Obote was swept back into office. Amid charges of electoral fraud, the National Resistance Army (NRA) began a guerrilla war: more than 200,000 Ugandans sought refuge in Rwanda and Zaïre. In 1985, Obote was deposed in another military coup. In 1986, the NRA captured Kampala, and Yoweri MUSEVENI became president. Museveni began to rebuild the domestic economy and improve foreign relations. In 1993, the *kabaka* of Buganda was reinstated as monarch. In 1996, Museveni won Uganda's first direct presidential elections. AIDS is one of the greatest issues facing Uganda; it has the highest number of reported cases in Africa. **Economy** Civil strife greatly damaged Uganda's economy (1995 GDP per capita, US$1,4700). In 1997, it received money from the World Bank as part of a strategy to ease the debt burden of the world's poorest countries. Agriculture employs 86% of the workforce. Uganda is the world's seventh-largest producer of coffee, which accounts for 90% of exports. Cotton, sugar cane and tea are also exported.

Ugarit Ancient city in NW Syria. Inhabited as early as the 7th millennium BC, it was a great commercial power, trading with Mesopotamia and Egypt. Excavations have revealed a vast palace from the 14th century BC and many large houses filled with treasures and artifacts.

UHF Abbreviation of ULTRA HIGH FREQUENCY

Ujjain City on the River Sipra, Madhya Pradesh, W central India. It is one of the seven holy cities of India, and a Hindu pilgrimage centre. Nearby are the ruins of a city dating from the 2nd millennium BC. Pop. (1991) 362,000.

ukiyo-e Japanese paintings and woodblock prints that were prevalent in the Edo period (1615–1867). Their subject matter included people engaged in everyday activities as well as Kabuki actors. Moronobu (c.1625–95) is generally considered the originator of the true ukiyo-e print, and he gained renown for his woodcut illustrations for popular literature. Other famous printmakers include HIROSHIGE, HOKUSAI and UTAMARO.

Ukraine Independent state in E Europe. Ukraine (Borderland) is the second-largest country in Europe (after Russia). The coastal lowlands include the Black Sea port of ODESSA. CRIMEA is a peninsula region and contains the vital port of SEVASTOPOL. The River DNIEPER divides Ukraine into E and W. The capital, KIEV, lies on its banks. In the W, the CARPATHIAN MOUNTAINS rise to 2,061m (6,762ft), close to the Romanian border. The fertile central plateau is among the world's greatest producers of wheat and barley. In the E, the DONETS BASIN is one of the world's greatest industrial powerhouses. The cities of KHARKOV and Donetsk are major industrial centres. **Climate** Ukraine's continental climate is moderated by proximity to the Black Sea. Winters are most severe in the NE and the highlands. Rainfall is heaviest in summer. **Vegetation** The once-grassy central steppe is now mostly under the plough. The black, chernozem soil is especially fertile. In the N, around the Pripet marshes, are large woodlands. **History**

UGANDA
AREA: 235,880sq km (91,073sq mi)
POPULATION: 26,958,000
CAPITAL (POPULATION): Kampala (954,000)

UKRAINE
AREA: 603,700sq km (233,100sq mi)
POPULATION: 52,558,000
CAPITAL (POPULATION): Kiev (2,630,000)

and politics In ancient history, the area was successively inhabited by Scythians and Sarmatians, before invasions by the Goths, Huns, Avars and Khazars. The first Ukrainian Slavic community originated from the 4th century. In the 9th century, the N regions were united by the Varangians as Kievan Rus. The empire disintegrated under the onslaught of the Mongol hordes. In the late 14th century, Ukraine became part of Lithuania. In 1478, the Black Sea region was absorbed into the Ottoman empire. In 1569, the Lithuanian sector passed to Poland following the Poland-Lithuania union. Polish rule was marked by the enserfment of the peasantry and persecution of the Ukrainian Orthodox Church. In 1648, refugees from Polish rule (COSSACKS) completed Ukraine's liberation. Independence was short-lived due to the emerging power of Russia. A succession of wars resulted (1775) in the division of Ukraine into three Russian provinces. The nationalist movement was barely suppressed and found an outlet in GALICIA. Ukraine's industry was developed from the 1860s. In 1918, (following the Russian Revolution) Ukraine declared independence and was invaded by the Red Army, who were repulsed with the support of the Central Powers. The World War 1 armistice prompted the withdrawal of the Central Powers. A unified, independent Ukraine was once more proclaimed. The Red Army invaded again, this time with greater success. In 1921, W Ukraine was ceded to Poland, and in 1922 E Ukraine became a constituent republic of the Soviet Union. In the 1930s, Lenin's policy of appeasement was replaced by STALIN's autocratic, agricultural collectivization. It caused 7.5 million Ukrainians to die of famine. The 1939 Nazi-Soviet partition of Poland reunified the Ukraine. In 1940, it also acquired Northern Bukovina and part of Bessarabia from Romania. In 1945, it gained Ruthenia from Hungary and E Galicia from Poland. After 1945, all Ukrainian land was unified into a single Soviet republic. In 1954, the Crimea was annexed to the Ukraine. Ukraine became one of the most powerful republics in the Soviet Union, contributing 30% of total Soviet industrial output. In 1986, the CHERNOBYL disaster contaminated large areas of Ukraine. In 1990, the Ukrainian parliament declared itself a sovereign body. In August 1991, Ukraine proclaimed its independence. In December 1991, Leonard Kravchuk, a former Communist leader, was elected president, and Ukraine joined the COMMONWEALTH OF INDEPENDENT STATES (CIS). Tensions with Russia over the Crimea, the Black Sea fleet, the control of nuclear weapons and oil and gas reserves were eased by a 1992 treaty. Crimean independence was refused. In 1994 elections, Leonid Kuchma defeated Kravchuk. Kuchma continued the policy of establishing closer ties with the West and sped up the pace of privatization. In 1995, direct rule was imposed on Crimea for four months. Subsequent elections saw reduced support for pro-Russian parties. Disputes continue over the extent of the powers of the Crimean legislature. Kuchma was re-elected in 1999. **Economy** Ukraine was plunged into economic crisis by the rapid dismantling of its command economy. It is a lower-middle-income economy (1995 GDP per capita, US$2,400). Agriculture is important, and Ukraine has been called the "breadbasket of Europe". It is the world's leading producer of sugar beet and the second-

largest producer of barley. It is also a major producer of wheat. Ukraine has extensive raw materials. The Donets Basin is the world's eighth-largest producer of bituminous coal. Krivoy Rog mines are the world's fourth-largest producer of iron ore, and Nikopol is the world's leading manganese ore producer. Many of the coal mines are exhausted and antiquated technology contributes to the highest mining fatality rate in the world. Despite its hydroelectric and nuclear power stations, Ukraine is reliant on oil and natural gas imports. Ukraine's debt to Russia (1995, US$500 million) has been partly offset by allowing Russian firms majority shares in many Ukrainian industries.

Ukrainian Language spoken by c.40–45 million people in Ukraine. Significant Ukrainian-speaking communities are to be found in Kazakhstan, Poland, Romania, the Slovak Republic and Siberian Russia. Like Russian and Belorussian, Ukrainian belongs to the E branch of the Slavic family of INDO-EUROPEAN LANGUAGES.

ukulele (ukelele) Small guitar that was developed in Hawaii from the Portuguese guitar. It is shaped like a classical guitar with a wooden body, round sound hole and fretted fingerboard.

Ulan Bator (Ulaanbaatar, formerly Urga) Capital of Mongolia, on the River Tola. It dates back to the founding of the Lamaistic Temple of the Living Buddha in 1639, and it grew as a stop for caravans between Russia and China. It was later a focus for the Mongolian autonomy movement. It became the capital in 1921. Noted for its harsh climate and bleak, planned streets, it is the political and economic centre of Mongolia. Industries: textiles, food processing, building materials. Pop. (1997) 627,000.

Ulanova, Galina (1910–98) Russian ballerina. In 1944, she became the prima ballerina of the BOLSHOI BALLET. Ulanova's skill in lyrical-dramatic interpretation and the purity and lightness of her classical style earned her international recognition. Her major roles include Leonid Lavrovsky's productions of *The Red Poppy*, *Giselle* and *Romeo and Juliet*. In 1962, Ulanova retired and became a coach for the new generation of Bolshoi ballerinas

Ulbricht, Walter (1893–1973) German statesman, leader of East GERMANY (1950–71). A founder of the German Communist Party, he was forced into exile in the Soviet Union by the rise of fascism. In 1949, Ulbricht became deputy premier of the newly created German Democratic Republic (East Germany). In 1950, he became general secretary of the Communist Party. Ulbricht established close links with the Soviet Union. The repressive nature of his regime led to a rebellion in 1953, and the BERLIN WALL was built (1961) to prevent further defections to the West. In 1971, he was replaced as general secretary by Erich HONECKER.

ulcer Persistent sore or lesion on the skin or on a mucous membrane, often associated with inflammation. Ulcers may be caused by infection, pressure or chemical irritation.

Ulm Industrial city on the River Danube, Baden-Württemberg, S Germany. Founded before 800, it was an important centre of medieval Europe. The major landmark is the Gothic minster (1377) with the tallest spire in the world, at 161m (528ft). Industries: car manufacture, electrical goods, textiles, food products. Pop. (1995) 115,000.

ulna Long bone of the inner side of the forearm. At its upper end it articulates with the HUMERUS and the RADIUS.

Ulster Most northerly of Ireland's four ancient provinces, consisting of nine counties. Since 1922, six of these counties have been in Northern IRELAND, while Cavan, Donegal and Monaghan form Ulster province in the Republic of IRELAND. Area: 8,012sq km (3,094sq mi). Pop. (1991) 232,000.

Ulster Unionist Party Largest Loyalist party in Northern IRELAND. It developed in the late 19th century to defend the six northern provinces of ULSTER from Irish home rule and to maintain the union with Britain. Almost exclusively Protestant, it was the ruling party in Northern Ireland from 1922 until the imposition of direct rule from Westminster in 1972. In 1998, the Ulster Unionist leader, David TRIMBLE, became first minister of Northern Ireland.

ultra high frequency (UHF) RADIO waves in the frequency band 300–3,000MHz. UHF waves have a wavelength of c.1m (3ft) or less and are used for TELEVISION broadcasting.

ultrasonics Study of sound waves with frequencies beyond the upper limit of human hearing (above 20,000Hz). In medicine, ultrasonics are used to locate tumours, produce fetal images and to treat certain neurological disorders. Other applications of ultrasonics include the agitation of liquids to form emulsions and the detection of flaws in metals.

ultraviolet radiation Type of ELECTROMAGNETIC RADIATION of shorter wavelength and higher frequency than visible LIGHT. Wavelengths range from 4 to 400nm (nanometers). Sunlight contains ultraviolet (uv) rays, most of which are filtered by the OZONE LAYER. If the ozone layer is weakened, enough ultraviolet can reach the ground to harm living things. Excessive exposure to sunlight can cause sunburn and skin cancer in people with fair skin. Ultraviolet is used medically to sterilize equipment.

Ulysses *See* ODYSSEUS

Umayyads (Omayyads) Dynasty of Arabian Muslim caliphs (661–750). From their capital at DAMASCUS, the Umayyads ruled a basically Arab empire that stretched from Spain to India. They made little effort to convert conquered peoples to Islam, but there was great cultural exchange, and Arabic became established as the language of Islam. They were overthrown by the ABBASIDS.

umbelliferae Family of flowering plants, all of which have many small flowers borne in umbrella-like clusters (umbels) at the ends of stalks. Umbellifers are mainly herbs and shrubs. Many species are edible, including CARROT, PARSLEY, CELERY, PARSNIP, FENNEL and DILL.

umbilical cord Long cord that connects a developing FETUS with the PLACENTA. At birth, the cord is cut from the placenta, leaving a scar on the baby's abdomen known as the navel.

umbrella bird Any of three species of large tropical American birds, each with a retractile, black, umbrella-like crest, and a long, often tubular-shaped, feathered lappet (tuft) on the throat. The ornate umbrella bird (*Cephalopterus ornatus*) lives in trees and feeds on fruits. Family Cotingidae.

Umbria Region in central Italy comprising the provinces of Perugia and Terni; the capital is PERUGIA. The only landlocked region of Italy, it is traversed by the APENNINES and drained by the River TIBER. Cereal crops, grapes and olives are grown, and cattle and pigs are reared. The medieval hill towns scattered over the countryside attract tourists. Industries: iron and steel, chemicals, textiles, confectionery. Area: 8,456sq km (3,265sq mi). Pop. (1992) 814,796.

UN *See* UNITED NATIONS

Un-American Activities Committee, House (HUAC) Committee of the US House of Representatives, established in 1938 to investigate political subversion. Created to combat Nazi propaganda, it began investigating extremist political organizations. After World War 2, encouraged by Senator Joseph McCARTHY, it attacked alleged communists in Hollywood and in the federal government. It was abolished in 1975.

Unamuno, Miguel de (1864–1936) Spanish philosopher, poet and novelist. He was forced into exile (1924–30) during the dictatorship of Primo de Rivera. A precursor of existentialism, Unamuno is chiefly celebrated for *The Tragic Sense of Life in Men and Peoples* (1912).

uncertainty principle In physics, principle stating that it is not possible to know both the position and the momentum of a SUBATOMIC PARTICLE at the same time, because the act of measuring would disturb the system. It was established (1927) by Werner HEISENBERG.

Uncle Sam Symbolic figure personalizing the USA. The name was first used during the WAR OF 1812. The appearance of Uncle Sam, tall, thin and frock-coated, was developed by 19th-century cartoonists.

unconformity In geology, break in the time sequence of rocks layered one above the other. The gap may be caused by interruptions in the deposition of sediment, ancient erosion, earth movements, or other activity.

unconscious Term in psychology for that part of mental life believed to operate without the individual's immediate awareness or control. It includes memories that the person is not actually thinking about and the organizing processes underlying speech and reading. In Sigmund FREUD's system, it is the area containing the desires and conflicts of the ID. C.G. JUNG believed that part of the unconscious (the collective unconscious) contains inherited concepts, shared by all other human beings.

Underground Railroad Secret network organized by free blacks and other ABOLITIONISTS before the CIVIL WAR to assist slaves escaping from the South. It was not a railway. Although Quakers were prominent assistants (conductors), most escapees reached the North by their own efforts. One of the most prominent black conductors was Harriet TUBMAN. The major routes ran through Ohio, Indiana and w Pennsylvania. In the North escaped slaves were guided through a series of safe houses (stations) to a place of safety, often Canada.

underground railway Transport system used in urban areas. The first underground RAILWAY was opened (1863) in London, England. It was steam-powered and carried passengers between Farringdon and Paddington. Today, many cities throughout the world have underground, electrically powered railway systems for passenger transport.

Undset, Sigrid (1822–1949) Norwegian novelist. Her masterpiece, *Kristin Lavransdatter* (1920–22), is an epic trilogy set in medieval Norway. In 1928 Undset was awarded the Nobel Prize for literature.

unemployment Inability of workers who are ready, able, and willing to work to find employment. Unemployment is usually expressed as a percentage of the LABOUR force. **Cyclical** unemployment exists when the level of aggregate demand in the economy is less than that required to maintain full employment. People are laid off, and their jobs simply disappear. **Structural** unemployment exists when jobs are available and workers are seeking jobs, but they cannot fill vacancies for some reason (for example, they lack proper training or live too far away). **Technological** unemployment exists when workers are replaced by machines faster than they can find alternative employment. **Seasonal** unemployment occurs when workers are unable to find jobs at certain seasons of the year. Such workers are usually engaged in construction, agriculture or the tourist industry. **Underemployment** is inefficient use of labour. For example, an employer may keep unneeded workers on the payroll when demand falls in order to have experienced help available when demand increases.

UNESCO Acronym for UNITED NATIONS EDUCATIONAL, SCIENTIFIC, AND CULTURAL ORGANIZATION

ungulate MAMMAL with hoofed feet. Most ungulates, including cattle, sheep, pigs and deer, are members of the order Artiodactyla (with an even number of toes). The order Perissodactyla (ungulates with an odd number of toes) consists of horses, tapirs and rhinoceroses. The orders Proboscidea and Hyracoidea, collectively known as sub-ungulates, contain elephants and hyraxes.

UNICEF *See* UNITED NATIONS CHILDREN'S FUND

unicorn In mythology and heraldry, a magical animal resembling a graceful horse or a young goat with one thin, conical or helical horn on its forehead.

unidentified flying object (UFO) Any flying object that cannot readily be explained as either a man-made craft or a natural phenomenon. Reports of UFOs have been documented since ancient times. With the development of aeronautics and astronautics, the number of sightings has increased enormously. The majority of supposed UFO sightings have various rational explanations, including optical floaters (in the observer's eye), weather balloons and artificial satellites.

Unification Church International religious movement founded (1954) in South Korea by Sun Myung Moon. Its adherents are popularly known as Moonies. The movement aims to re-establish God's rule on Earth through the restoration of the family. The Unification Church is noted for its mass weddings and has been accused of cult-like practices, such as brainwashing. *See also* CULT

unified field theory Attempt to extend the general theory of RELATIVITY to give a simultaneous representation of both gravitational and electromagnetic fields. A more comprehensive theory would also include the strong and weak nuclear forces. Although some success has been achieved in unifying the ELECTROMAGNETIC and WEAK NUCLEAR FORCES, the general problem is still unsolved. *See also* GRAND UNIFIED THEORY (GUT)

Uniformity, Act of (1662) English act of Parliament regulating the form of worship in the CHURCH OF ENGLAND after the RESTORATION of the monarchy. It required all clergy to follow the Book of COMMON PRAYER. The act also required the clergy to repudiate the SOLEMN LEAGUE AND COVENANT, to forswear the taking up of arms against the Crown and to adopt the liturgy of the Church of England.

Union, Acts of Series of acts uniting ENGLAND with WALES (1536) and SCOTLAND (1707), and Britain with IRELAND (1800). In addition, the 1841 Act of Union united French-speaking Lower CANADA and English-speaking Upper Canada and established a parliament for the province. The Welsh acts incorporated Wales within the kingdom of England, provided Welsh parliamentary representation and made English the official language. The Scottish act united the kingdoms of England and Scotland forming Great Britain. Scotland retained its legal system and Presbyterian Church. In accordance with the Irish act, the Irish legislature was abolished and Ireland was given 32 peers and 100 seats in the British Parliament. The established churches of the two countries were united. *See also* DEVOLUTION; HOME RULE

Union of Soviet Socialist Republics Official name for the SOVIET UNION

Unitarianism Version of CHRISTIANITY that denies the TRINITY, accepts God as the father, and rejects the divinity of JESUS CHRIST. Originally considered a heresy, it flourished in Poland in the 16th century. Unitarianism in the 20th century has been identified with liberal politics and the movement for world peace and has taken an increasingly humanist point of view.

United Arab Emirates (UAE) Federation of the seven independent sheikhdoms of ABU DHABI, DUBAI, Ajman,

---

> **UNITED ARAB EMIRATES**
> **AREA:** 83,600sq km (32,278sq mi)
> **POPULATION:** 1,951,000
> **CAPITAL (POPULATION):** Abu Dhabi (928,000)

Ras al-Khaimah, Fujairah, SHARJA and Umm al-Qaiwain. It is bordered by the Persian Gulf (N), Oman (E), Saudi Arabia (W and S) and Qatar (NW). The terrain is flat, consisting mainly of desert. Abu Dhabi is more than six times the size of the other states put together, has the largest population, is the biggest oil producer and provides the federal capital, the city of Abu Dhabi. The other significant populations are Dubai and Sharjah. The population is almost exclusively Muslim (mostly SUNNI), though the great majority of inhabitants are expatriate workers. Formerly known as the Trucial States, the area was a British protectorate from 1892. After World War 2, the sheikhdoms were granted internal autonomy. In 1971, British troops withdrew from the Persian Gulf and the United Arab Emirates was formed. The economy is dominated by crude oil and natural-gas production, accounting for about half of its GDP. Oil was first discovered in Abu Dhabi in the early 1960s, and the 1973 increase in oil prices transformed a relatively impoverished region into one of the world's wealthiest (1995 GDP per capita, US$16,470). The UAE was part of the coalition against Iraq in the GULF WAR (1991) and joined the UNITED NATIONS (UN) and the ARAB LEAGUE the same year. Disputes over the islands of Abu Musa and Tunbs in the Persian Gulf, occupied by Iraq since 1971, continued throughout the 1990s.

United Kingdom (UK) Kingdom on the British Isles, W Europe. The United Kingdom of Great Britain and Northern IRELAND is a union of four countries. Great Britain is composed of ENGLAND, SCOTLAND and WALES. The Isle of MAN and the CHANNEL ISLANDS are self-governing UK dependencies. In 1536, England and Wales were formally united. Scotland and England were unified in the 1707 Act of UNION. (For land, climate, vegetation and separate history, *see* individual country articles) **History and politics** In the 17th century England's development of empire was combined with a financial revolution, which included the founding of the BANK OF ENGLAND (1694). Sir Robert WALPOLE's prime ministership (1721–42) marked the beginnings of CABINET government. Great Britain emerged from the SEVEN YEARS' WAR (1756–63) as the world's leading imperial power. GEORGE III's conception of absolute monarchy and resistance to colonial reform led to conflict with Parliament and contributed to the AMERICAN REVOLUTION (1775–83). William PITT (the Younger) oversaw the creation of the United Kingdom of Great Britain and Ireland (1801). The AGRICULTURAL REVOLUTION was both a cause and effect of the doubling of the population between 1801 and 1861. The INDUSTRIAL REVOLUTION brought profound socio-economic changes. The 1820s and 1830s was an era of new reform legislation, including: the Act of CATHOLIC EMANCIPATION (1829), the abolition of SLAVERY (1833), harsh new POOR LAWS (1834) and the extension of the FRANCHISE to the middle class in the REFORM ACTS. Sir Robert PEEL's repeal of the CORN LAWS (1846) marked the beginnings of FREE-TRADE and the emergence of the CONSERVATIVE PARTY from the old TORY PARTY. The LIBERAL PARTY similarly evolved out of the WHIGS. CHARTISM witnessed the beginnings of a working-class movement. The reign of VICTORIA saw the development of the second BRITISH EMPIRE, spurred on by the imperial ambitions of Lord PALMERSTON. The historic

UNITED KINGDOM
AREA: 243,368sq km (94,202sq mi)
POPULATION: 58,393,000
CAPITAL (POPULATION): London (6,966,800)

importance of trade to the UK economy was firmly established. Between 1868 and 1880, UK politics was dominated by Benjamin DISRAELI and William GLADSTONE. The defeat of Gladstone's HOME RULE Bill for Ireland (1886) split the Liberal Party. Between 1908 and 1916, Herbert ASQUITH and David LLOYD GEORGE enacted a range of progressive social welfare policies, such as NATIONAL INSURANCE and state pensions. The growing power of Germany led to WORLD WAR 1. GEORGE V changed the name of the British royal family from Saxe-Coburg to Windsor. The Allied victory cost more than 750,000 British lives. The UK was faced with rebellion in Ireland. The Anglo-Irish Treaty (1921) confirmed the partition of Ireland. The Irish Free State was formed in 1922, and the UK officially became known as the United Kingdom of Great Britain and Northern Ireland. In 1924, Ramsay MACDONALD formed the first LABOUR PARTY government. In 1931 the COMMONWEALTH OF NATIONS was founded. In 1936 EDWARD VIII was forced to abdicate in favour of GEORGE VI. Neville CHAMBERLAIN's policy of APPEASEMENT towards Nazi Germany's growing imperial ambitions ended in failure. On September 3 1939, following the German invasion of Poland, Britain declared war. From May 1940 Winston CHURCHILL led a coalition government that lasted throughout WORLD WAR 2. In 1941, the USA and the Soviet Union joined the battle against Hitler. Germany surrendered in May 1945 and Japan in September 1945. Britain had lost more than 420,000 lives, and its economy was devastated. In 1945 elections, the Labour Party was swept back into power, with Clement ATTLEE as prime minister. Attlee began a radical programme of nationalization and increased welfare provision. The MARSHALL PLAN aided reconstruction. In 1948 the NATIONAL HEALTH SERVICE (NHS) was created. The British empire was gradually dismantled, beginning with India in 1947. Most newly independent nations joined the Commonwealth. In 1949, the UK joined NATO. In 1951, Churchill returned to power. In 1952, ELIZABETH II succeeded George VI. In 1956, Anthony EDEN led Britain into the disastrous SUEZ CANAL Crisis. Harold MACMILLAN realized the importance of Europe to UK trade, and in 1959 the UK became a founder member of the EUROPEAN FREE TRADE ASSOCIATION (EFTA). In 1964, Harold WILSON narrowly defeated Alec DOUGLAS-HOME. In 1968, the British Army was deployed in Northern Ireland to prevent the violent sectarian conflict that had followed civil-rights marches. In 1971, under Edward HEATH, the UK adopted a decimal currency. In 1972, the British parliament assumed direct control of Northern Ireland. In 1973, the UK joined the European Economic Community (EEC). Deep recession led to the introduction of a three-day working week. A miners' strike forced Heath to resign. The discovery of North Sea oil and natural gas reduced Britain's dependency on coal and fuel imports. James CALLAGHAN's inability to control labour unrest led to his defeat in 1979 elections. Margaret THATCHER became Britain's first woman prime minister. Thatcher introduced MONETARISM and PRIVATIZATION. Unemployment grew as Britain attempted to switch to a more service-centred economy. The FALKLANDS WAR (1982) contributed to Thatcher's re-election in 1983. A miners' strike (1984–85) was followed by further trade

union restrictions. In 1987, Thatcher won an unprecedented third general election. Urban decay, economic inequality and an unpopular POLL TAX forced Thatcher to resign in 1990. John MAJOR signed the MAASTRICHT TREATY and won a surprise victory in the 1992 general election. He was soon forced to remove the pound from the EUROPEAN MONETARY SYSTEM (EMS). Major's administration was dogged by division over Europe and allegations of sleaze. In the 1997 general election, Tony BLAIR's modernized Labour Party formed the first Labour government for 18 years. The BANK OF ENGLAND rapidly gained independence from central government in the setting of interest rates. In September 1997, referenda on DEVOLUTION saw Scotland and Wales gain their own legislative assemblies. The Scottish assembly was given tax-varying power. The Good Friday Agreement (1998) offered the best chance of peace in Northern Ireland for a generation. In 1999, the UK contributed to NATO's military campaign in KOSOVO.
Economy The UK is a major industrial and trading nation (1995 GDP per capita, US$19,260). Despite being a major producer of oil, petroleum products, natural gas, potash, salt and lead, the UK lacks natural resources and has to import raw materials. In the early 20th century, the UK was a major exporter of ships, steel and textiles. Cars remain a major product, but the economy has become more service-centred and high-technology industries, such as television manufacture, have grown in importance. The UK produces only 66% of the food it needs and is reliant on food imports. Agriculture employs only 2% of the workforce. Scientific and mass production methods ensure high productivity. Major crops include hops for beer, potatoes, carrots, sugar beet and strawberries. Sheep are the leading livestock, and wool is a leading product. Poultry, beef and dairy cattle are important. Cheese and milk are major products. Fishing is a major activity. Financial services bring in much-needed revenue. Historic and cultural attractions make tourism a vital income source.

United Nations (UN) International organization set up to enable countries to work together for peace and mutual development. It was established (June 1945) in a charter signed in San Francisco by 50 countries. Today, the UN has 188 members, essentially all the world's sovereign states except for North and South Korea and Switzerland.
United Nations agencies Executive bodies operating on behalf of and responsible to the UNITED NATIONS (UN). They include: the FOOD AND AGRICULTURE ORGANIZATION (FAO, Rome); INTERNATIONAL ATOMIC ENERGY AGENCY (IAEA, Vienna); INTERNATIONAL LABOR ORGANIZATION (ILO, Geneva); INTERNATIONAL MONETARY FUND (IMF, Washington, D.C.); UNITED NATIONS EDUCATIONAL, SCIENTIFIC AND CULTURAL ORGANIZATION (UNESCO, Paris); United Nations High Commission for Refugees (UNHCR, Geneva); UNITED NATIONS CHILDREN'S FUND (UNICEF, New York); WORLD BANK (International Bank for Reconstruction and Development or IBRD, New York); WORLD HEALTH ORGANIZATION (WHO, Geneva); and WORLD TRADE ORGANIZATION (WTO, Geneva). For administration at its headquarters in New York, USA, the UN has a Secretariat staffed by international personnel.
United Nations Children's Fund (UNICEF) Intergovernmental organization, agency of the United Nations. Founded in 1946 (as the United Nations International Children's Emergency Fund), its aim is to assist children and adolescents worldwide, particularly in war-devastated areas and developing countries.
United Nations Educational, Scientific and Cultural Organization (UNESCO) Intergovernmental organization, agency of the United Nations. Founded in

1945, it aims to promote peace by improving the world's standard of education and by bringing together nations in cultural and scientific projects. It also gives aid to developing countries.

United Nations peacekeeping force Military personnel and their equipment placed at United Nations' disposal by member states. The function of the force is to keep the peace between warring factions anywhere in the world, as requested by the UNITED NATIONS SECURITY COUNCIL. The first UN peacekeeping forces were deployed (June 1948) in the Sinai Peninsula and Beirut. The greatest number of UN troops deployed was in Bosnia during the mid-1990s.

United Nations Security Council Council responsible for taking action against any nation or faction considered to represent a threat to the security or continued well-being of a member state. Such action can be political, economic or, as a last resort, military. The Council also has the power to hold a formal investigation into matters of common concern. There are five permanent member states: the USA, UK, France, Russia and China.

United States of America (USA) Federal republic in North America, the world's fourth largest country. The United States of America is made up of a federal district (the capital, WASHINGTON, D.C.) and 50 states (48 of which form a large block of land between Canada and Mexico). The other two states are ALASKA in NW North America, which contains the country's highest peak, Mount MCKINLEY at 6,194m (20,322ft), and the North Pacific archipelago of HAWAII. On the NE border with Canada are the GREAT LAKES. CHICAGO lies on the shore of Lake MICHIGAN. The densely populated E seaboard includes the major cities of BOSTON, NEW YORK, PHILADELPHIA and BALTIMORE. The major rivers of the E are the HUDSON, DELAWARE and POTOMAC. FLORIDA lies on a peninsula between the Atlantic and the Gulf of MEXICO and includes the city of MIAMI. The coastal plain is backed by the APPALACHIANS, including the BLUE RIDGE MOUNTAINS. The central lowlands are drained by the MISSISSIPPI-MISSOURI river system, which forms an enormous delta near NEW ORLEANS. The GREAT PLAINS gently rise to the ROCKY MOUNTAINS, which form the continental divide. Mount ELBERT is the highest peak in the Rockies. The COLUMBIA and COLORADO rivers flow into the Pacific Ocean. Between the Rockies and the Pacific coast lie plateaux, basins and ranges. The GRAND CANYON was carved out from the Colorado plateau by the Colorado River. The GREAT BASIN includes SALT LAKE CITY and desert regions, such as LAS VEGAS and DEATH VALLEY, the lowest point in the Western Hemisphere, 86m (282ft) below sea level. The Pacific seaboard, including the cities of SAN FRANCISCO, LOS ANGELES and SAN DIEGO, is fringed by mountain ranges such as the SIERRA NEVADA, which includes Mount WHITNEY (the highest peak outside Alaska). The NW CASCADE RANGE contains active volcanoes, such as Mount ST HELENS. SEATTLE lies in the foothills of the range. (*See* individual state articles) **Climate** Temperatures vary from the Arctic cold of Alaska to the intense heat of Death Valley. In the 48 states, winters are cold and snowy in the N, but mild in the S. The S has long, hot summers. Rainfall is heaviest in the NW, lightest in the SW. The Gulf of Mexico experiences violent storms. **Vegetation** Alaska contains forests of conifers. In the N states there are extensive forests, with huge redwoods along the Pacific coast, such as Sequoia National Park. In the E, the original deciduous forests only remain in protected areas, such as GREAT SMOKY MOUNTAINS National Park. The dry, central prairies merge into the high steppe of the

---

UNITED STATES OF AMERICA
AREA: 9,372,610sq km (3,618,756sq mi)
POPULATION: 266,096,000
CAPITAL (POPULATION): Washington, D.C. (567,094)

Great Plains. Large areas of the SW are desert. **History and politics** NATIVE AMERICANS arrived perhaps 40,000 years ago from Asia. Vikings, led by LEIF ERICSSON, probably reached North America 1,000 years ago but did not settle. European exploration did not begin until the discovery of the New World by Christopher COLUMBUS in 1492. In 1565, the first permanent European settlement was founded by Spain at ST AUGUSTINE, Florida. The French also formed settlements in LOUISIANA, but the first major colonists were the British, who founded JAMESTOWN, VIRGINIA, in 1607. In 1620, PURITANS landed at CAPE COD, MASSACHUSETTS, and founded the PLYMOUTH COLONY. The economic success of Massachusetts encouraged further colonization along the E coast. In 1681, William PENN founded PENNSYLVANIA. In the southern colonies, SLAVERY was used to develop plantations. During the 18th century, British MERCANTILISM (especially the NAVIGATION ACTS) restricted commercial growth. The GREAT AWAKENING and the development of higher education promoted greater cultural self-consciousness. The defeat of the French in the FRENCH AND INDIAN WARS (1754–63) encouraged independence movements. Benjamin FRANKLIN'S failure to win concessions from the British led to the AMERICAN REVOLUTION (1775–83), which ended British rule in the THIRTEEN COLONIES. George WASHINGTON, commander-in-chief of the Continental Army, became the first president. The ARTICLES OF CONFEDERATION (1777) produced weak central government and were superseded by the CONSTITUTION OF THE UNITED STATES (1787). The BANK OF THE UNITED STATES was created in 1791. US politics became divided between the FEDERALIST PARTY and the DEMOCRATIC-REPUBLICAN PARTY. In 1796, the Federalist president, John ADAMS, passed the ALIEN AND SEDITION ACTS (1798). The XYZ AFFAIR saw armed confrontation with France. In 1801 the Democratic-Republican Thomas JEFFERSON became president. Jefferson negotiated the LOUISIANA PURCHASE (1803), which nearly doubled the size of the USA. James MADISON led the USA into the WAR of 1812, which cemented the nation's independence and culminated in the MONROE DOCTRINE (1823) that sought to protect the Western Hemisphere from European interference. The MISSOURI COMPROMISE (1820) papered over the growing conflict between the commercial, industrial North and the cotton plantations of the pro-SLAVERY South. The Democratic-Republican Party became simply the DEMOCRATIC PARTY. Andrew JACKSON's presidency furthered the westward expansion of the FRONTIER. The march to the Pacific became the "MANIFEST DESTINY" of the USA. In 1841, William HARRISON became the first WHIG PARTY president. TEXAS was annexed (1845) and OREGON Territory (1846) was acquired. The MEXICAN WAR (1846–48) confirmed US gains. The 1848 discovery of gold in CALIFORNIA prompted a rush of settlers. Territorial expansion was achieved at the expense of Native Americans, who were forced onto reservations. The addition of states to the Union intensified the conflict between free and slave states. The repeal of the Missouri Compromise led to the founding of the anti-slavery REPUBLICAN PARTY (1854). In 1861, Abraham LINCOLN became the first Republican president. The southern states seceded as the CONFEDERATE STATES OF AMERICA. The CIVIL WAR

(1861–65) claimed more than 600,000 lives and devastated the country. The Union victory resulted in the abolition of slavery. The enforced RECONSTRUCTION of the South was highly unpopular. Ulysses S. GRANT's administration was plagued by corruption. In 1867, the USA bought Alaska from Russia. The late 19th century was the era of the railway, which sped industrialization and urban development. The gleaming, steel skyscrapers symbolized opportunity, and millions of European immigrants were attracted to the USA. The SPANISH-AMERICAN WAR (1898) heralded the emergence of the USA as a major world power. Hawaii was annexed. In 1902, construction started on the PANAMA CANAL. In 1917, Woodrow WILSON led the US into WORLD WAR 1. The economic boom and PROHIBITION of the roaring 1920s was followed by the GREAT DEPRESSION of the 1930s. Franklin D. ROOSEVELT's NEW DEAL attempted to restore prosperity. The Japanese bombing of PEARL HARBOR (7 December 1941) prompted US entry into WORLD WAR 2. Rearmament aided economic recovery. In 1945, Harry S. TRUMAN became president on Roosevelt's death. The use of US atomic bombs led to Japan's surrender. The USA was a founder member of NATO. Post-war tension with the Soviet Union led to the COLD WAR and spurred the space race. In order to stem the spread of communism, US forces fought in the KOREAN WAR (1950–53). In 1955, Martin Luther KING launched the CIVIL RIGHTS movement. The start of John F. KENNEDY's presidency was marred by the CUBAN MISSILE CRISIS (1962). Kennedy's assassination (22 November 1963) shocked the nation. Lyndon B. JOHNSON led the USA into the VIETNAM WAR (1965–73). Anti-Vietnam protests were coupled with civil unrest. On 20 July 1969, Neil ARMSTRONG became the first man on the Moon. In 1974, Richard NIXON was forced to resign by the WATERGATE SCANDAL. The CAMP DAVID AGREEMENT crowned Jimmy CARTER's foreign policy initiatives. The start of Ronald REAGAN's presidency (1981–89) marked the deepest recession since the Great Depression. Economic recovery brought increases in defence spending. Reagan's loosening grip on power was highlighted by the IRAN-CONTRA AFFAIR (1987–88). In 1991, after the collapse of Soviet communism, George BUSH proclaimed a "New World Order". Despite the success of the GULF WAR (1991), domestic recession led to Bush's defeat in 1992. Bill CLINTON's reform programme was largely blocked by a Republican-dominated SENATE. Despite allegations of financial and personal scandal, economic recovery led to Clinton's re-election in 1996. In 1999, Clinton survived impeachment charges and authorized the use of force against Iraq and Serbia. In December 2000, Republican George W. BUSH was declared president, narrowly defeating Democrat Al GORE, after a prolonged legal dispute over the election result. **Economy** The US is the world's largest manufacturing nation (1995 GDP per capita, US$26,980). The 1992 NORTH AMERICAN FREE TRADE AGREEMENT (NAFTA) with Canada and Mexico created the world's largest trading bloc. The USA is the world's largest farm producer. Agriculture is highly mechanized, employing only 2% of the workforce. Major products include poultry, beef and dairy cattle. Leading crops include cotton, grapes for wine, hops for beer, fruits, peanuts, maize, potatoes, soya beans, tobacco and wheat. Fishing is important. Major natural resources include oil, natural gas and coal. Timber and paper manufacture are also important. Major industries include cars, chemicals, machinery, computers and printing. California is the leading manufacturing state. Services form the largest sector, including finance and tourism (1992 receipts, US$53,361 million).

units See WEIGHTS AND MEASURE

unit trust (mutual fund) Pooled form of INVESTMENT, usually in the form of a portfolio of shares. The trust choses and manages, through fund managers, a diverse range of securities. See also STOCK EXCHANGE

universal time System of time reckoning based on the mean solar day, the average interval between two successive transits of the Sun across the GREENWICH meridian.

Universe Aggregate of all MATTER, ENERGY and SPACE. On a large scale, the Universe is considered uniform: it is identical in every part. It is believed to be expanding at a uniform rate, the galaxies all receding from one other. The origin, evolution and future characteristics of the Universe are considered in several cosmological theories. Recent developments in astronomy imply a finite Universe, as postulated in the BIG BANG theory. See also COSMOLOGY; STEADY-STATE THEORY

university Institution of higher learning. Universities grew from the *studia generalia* of the 12th century, which provided education for priests and monks and were attended by students from all parts of Europe. Bologna became an important centre of legal studies in the 11th century. Other great *studia generalia* were founded in the mid-12th century at PARIS, OXFORD and CAMBRIDGE. The first Scottish university was founded (*c*.1912) at St ANDREWS, the first Irish university at Dublin (Trinity College) in 1591. The oldest US university is HARVARD, founded in 1636. See also OPEN UNIVERSITY (OU)

unnilquadium See ELEMENT 104

unsaturated compound In organic chemistry, compound in which two or more carbon atoms are linked or bonded together with double or triple bonds. Simple examples are ETHENE and ETHYNE.

untouchables Fifth and lowest *varna* (class) of the Indian CASTE system, making up *c*.20% of India's population. The term arises from the belief among higher castes, such as BRAHMIN, that to touch *panchamas* amounts to ritual pollution or defilement. Although their pariah status and the resultant social injustice were legally abolished in India (1949) and Pakistan (1953), much discrimination remains. See also HINDUISM

Upanishads (Sanskrit, session) Texts of HINDUISM, constituting the final stage of Vedic literature. Written in prose and verse, they take the form of dialogues between teacher and pupil. They are of uncertain authorship and date from *c*.650 BC or earlier. Often referred to as the VEDANTA, the *Upanishads* speculate on reality and man's salvation. See also BRAHMANISM; VEDAS

Updike, John Hoyer (1932–) US writer. He is best known for his lyrical chronicles of Rabbit Angstrom, whose relationship crises often reflect contemporary social pressures. The tetralogy began with *Rabbit Run* (1960) and *Rabbit Redux* (1971). *Rabbit is Rich* (1981) won a Pulitzer Prize. The series was completed by *Rabbit at Rest* (1990). Other novels include *Couples* (1968) and *The Witches of Eastwick* (1984, filmed 1987). A regular contributor to *New Yorker* magazine since 1955, Updike's shorter prose includes the essay collection *Hugging the Shore* (1984) and *Forty Stories* (1987).

Upper Volta Former name of BURKINA FASO

Uppsala Medieval city in E Sweden. Its university was founded in 1477. King GUSTAVUS I (VASA) is buried in the 15th-century cathedral. Industries: machinery, building materials, pharmaceuticals, printing. Pop. (1997) 185,000.

Ur (Ur of the Chaldees) Ancient city of SUMERIA, S MESOPOTAMIA. Ur flourished in the 3rd millennium BC, but in *c*.2340 BC it was conquered by SARGON I. The

URANUS: DATA
DIAMETER (EQUATORIAL): 51,118km (31,765mi)
MASS (EARTH = 1): 14.6
VOLUME (EARTH = 1): 67
DENSITY (WATER = 1): 1.27
ORBITAL PERIOD: 84.01 years
ROTATION PERIOD: 17h 14m 0s
AVERAGE SURFACE TEMPERATURE: −214°C (−417°F)
SURFACE GRAVITY (EARTH = 1): 0.79

Akkadian period witnessed the integration of Semitic and Sumerian cultures. In c.2060 BC, the great ZIGGURAT was built by King Ur-Nammu. In c.2000 BC, much of the city was detroyed by the invading Elamites. In the 6th century BC, NEBUCHADNEZZAR briefly restored Ur as a centre of Mesopotamian civilization, but by the 5th century BC it had fallen into terminal decline.

Urals Range of mountains in Russia, traditionally marking the boundary between Europe and Asia. The range extends 2,400km (1,500mi) from the Arctic in the N to the River Ural and the Kazakstan frontier in the S. The mountains are extensively forested and the timber industry is important. The Urals' chief importance lies in their mineral deposits, which include iron ore, oil, coal, copper, nickel, gold, silver, zinc and many precious stones. These resources have given rise to the Urals industrial region. Industrial development was increased under the first two Soviet five-year plans (1929–39) and during World War 2, when many industries were moved here from W Soviet Union. The highest peak is Mount Narodnaya, rising to 1,894m (6,214ft).

uraninite (pitchblende, UO_2) Dense, radioactive mineral form of uranium oxide. Uraninite is the chief ore of uranium and the most important source for uranium and radium. The blackish, lustrous ore occurs as a constituent of quartz veins. Hardness 5–6; r.d. 6.5–8.5.

uranium (symbol U) Radioactive, metallic element, one of the ACTINIDE SERIES. It was discovered in 1789, and is now used in NUCLEAR REACTORS and bombs. The ISOTOPE U^{238} makes up more than 99% of natural uranium. Chemically, uranium is a reactive metal; it oxidizes in air and reacts with cold water. U^{235} is fissionable and will sustain a neutron chain reaction as a fuel for reactors. Uranium is used to synthesize the TRANSURANIC ELEMENTS. Properties: at.no. 92; r.a.m. 238.029; r.d. 19.05; m.p. 1,132°C (2,070°F); b.p. 3,818°C (6,904°F); most stable isotope U^{238} (half-life 4.51×10^9 years).

Uranus Seventh planet from the Sun, discovered (1781) by Sir William HERSCHEL. Uranus is visible to the naked eye under good conditions. Like all the giant planets, it possesses a ring system and a retinue of SATELLITES. Like Pluto, Uranus' axis of rotation is steeply inclined, and its poles spend 42 years in sunlight, followed by 42 years in darkness. Highly exaggerated seasonal variations are, therefore, experienced by both the planet and its satellites. In 1986 the fly-by of the VOYAGER 2 probe provided most current knowledge of the planet. The upper atmosphere is c.83% molecular hydrogen, 15% helium and the other 2% mostly methane. All 17 satellites orbit in or close to Uranus' equatorial plane. They are all darkish bodies composed of ice and rock. The main components of Uranus' ring system were discovered in 1977, and others were imaged by Voyager.

Uranus In Greek mythology, the original god of the sky, and the husband and son of GAIA, with whom he was father to the TITANS and the CYCLOPES.

Urban II (c.1035–99) Pope (1088–99), b. Odo of Châtillon-sur-Marne. He carried on the reforms begun by Pope GREGORY VII. In 1095, at the Council of Clermont, Urban preached the First CRUSADE. His work as a reformer encouraged the development of the CURIA ROMANA and the formation of the College of Cardinals.

Urban V (c.1310–70) Pope (1362–70), b. Guillaume de Grimoard. Crowned at AVIGNON, he tried in 1367 to return the papacy from Avignon to Rome. Insurrections at Rome and the Papal States forced him back to Avignon in 1370. As pope, he made a fruitless attempt to unite the Roman and Orthodox Churches.

Urban VI (1318–89) Pope (1378–89), b. Bartolomeo Prignano. The College of Cardinals declared his election invalid and appointed an ANTIPOPE, CLEMENT VII, beginning the GREAT SCHISM. Urban VI's papacy was marked by confusion and financial losses in the Papal States.

Urban VIII (1568–1644) Pope (1623–44), b. Maffeo Barberini. His reign coincided with much of the THIRTY YEARS WAR. Fearing possible domination of the papacy by the HABSBURGS, he supported France and gave little help to German Roman Catholics. An active and knowledgeable patron of the arts, he also approved the establishment of new orders.

Urdu Language belonging to the Indic group of the Indo-Iranian sub-family of INDO-EUROPEAN LANGUAGES. It is the official language of Pakistan but is used as a first language by less than 10% of the population. It is also spoken by most Muslims in India. Urdu has virtually the same grammar as HINDI, the chief difference being that Urdu is written in the Arabic script. Both derive from SANSKRIT.

urea ($CO(NH_2)_2$) Organic compound, a white, crystalline solid excreted in URINE. Most vertebrates excrete their nitrogen wastes as urea; human urine contains c.25 grams of urea to a litre. Because it is so high in nitrogen, urea is a good fertilizer.

ureter In vertebrates, the long, narrow duct that connects the KIDNEY to the urinary BLADDER. It transports URINE from the kidney to the bladder.

urethra Duct through which URINE is discharged from the bladder in mammals. In males, the urethra is also the tube through which SEMEN is ejaculated.

urethritis Inflammation of the URETHRA. It is usually due to a SEXUALLY TRANSMITTED DISEASE (STD) but may also arise from infection.

Urey, Harold Clayton (1893–1981) US chemist. He was awarded the 1934 Nobel Prize for chemistry for his isolation of DEUTERIUM, an isotope of hydrogen. Urey later isolated isotopes of oxygen, nitrogen, carbon and sulphur. During World War 2 he helped in the research that led to the production of the atomic bomb. Urey then turned to GEOPHYSICS and worked on recreating the atmospheric conditions of the primeval Earth to elucidate the origin of life.

urine Fluid filtered out from the bloodstream by the KIDNEY. It consists mainly of water, salts and waste products such as UREA. From the kidneys it passes through the URETERS to the BLADDER for voiding by way of the URETHRA.

urinogenital system Organs comprising the body's urinary and reproductive systems. The urinary system consists of the KIDNEYS, URETERS, BLADDER and URETHRA. In males, the reproductive system consists of: paired TESTES located in the scrotum; accessory glands; and the PENIS. In females, the reproductive system consists of paired OVARIES; FALLOPIAN TUBES, which provide a passage from the ovaries to the UTERUS; the CERVIX; and the VAGINA. See also SEXUAL REPRODUCTION

urology Medical speciality concerned with the diagnosis and treatment of diseases of the urinary tract in women and of the urinary and reproductive systems in men.

Ursa Major (Great Bear) Northern constellation, whose main pattern, consisting of seven stars, is known as the **Big Dipper** or **Plough**. Five of the Plough stars make up a CLUSTER.

Ursa Minor Constellation that contains the north celestial pole. Its brightest star is Alpha, the POLE STAR. The constellation's seven main stars make a pattern resembling a faint and distorted plough.

Ursula, Saint (active 4th century AD) Legendary virgin, martyr and, according to some traditions, a British princess. She was especially honoured at Cologne, where she is said to have been slain by the HUNS with her 11 (or in some reports 11,000) virgins on their return from a pilgrimage to Rome. She has become the patron of many educational establishments, including the Ursuline order.

urticaria *See* HIVES

Uruguay Republic in South America; the capital is MONTEVIDEO. The land consists of low-lying plains and hills, rising to a highest point, Mirador Nacional, which is only 501m (1,644ft) above sea level. The main river in the interior is the Río Negro. The River URUGUAY, which forms the country's w border, flows into the Río de la PLATA, a large estuary leading into the South Atlantic Ocean. Grasslands cover 77% of Uruguay and arable land *c.*7%. Uruguay has commercial tree plantations, including trees such as quebracho, whose tannin is used in tanning and dyeing. **Climate** Uruguay has a mild climate, with rain throughout the year, though droughts sometimes occur. The summer months are pleasantly warm, especially near the coast. **History and politics** The original Native American inhabitants of Uruguay have largely disappeared. Many were killed by Europeans, others died of European diseases, while some fled into the interior. The first European to arrive in Uruguay was a Spanish navigator in 1516, but few Europeans settled there until the late 17th century. In 1726, Spanish settlers founded Montevideo in order to prevent the Portuguese gaining influence in the area. By the late 18th century, Spaniards had settled in most of the country, and Uruguay became part of a colony called the Viceroyalty of La Plata, which also included Argentina, Paraguay, and parts of Bolivia, Brazil and Chile. In 1820, Brazil annexed Uruguay, ending Spanish rule. In 1825, Uruguayans, supported by Argentina, began a struggle for independence and finally, in 1828, Brazil and Argentina recognized Uruguay as an independent republic. In the 19th century, social and economic development was restricted by numerous revolutions and counter-revolutions. In 1903, following the election of Batlle y Ordóñez as president, Uruguay became a more democratic and stable country. From the 1950s, economic problems caused unrest. Terrorist groups, notably the Tupamaros, carried out murders and kidnappings. In 1972, the army crushed the Tupamaros. In 1973, a military government was established. Repressive military rule continued until 1984, when civilian rule was re-established under Julio María Sanguinetti. Economic difficulties and high foreign debts continued

---

URUGUAY

AREA: 177,410sq km (68,498sq mi)
POPULATION: 3,274,000
CAPITAL (POPULATION): Montevideo (1,379,000)

---

to threaten stability, provoking massive emigration. In 1994, Sanguinetti was re-elected president. In 2000, he was succeeded as president by Jorge Batlle. **Economy** Uruguay is an upper-middle-income developing country (1995 GDP per capita, US$6,630). Agriculture employs only 5% of the workforce, but farm products, notably hides and leather goods, beef and wool, are leading exports, while the main crops include maize, potatoes, sugar beet and wheat. The leading manufacturing industries, situated mainly in and around Montevideo, are concerned with processing farm produce. Other manufactures include beer, cement, textiles and tyres. Tourism is important.

Uruguay River in SE South America. Rising in S Brazil and forming part of the boundary between Rio Grande do Sul and Santa Catarina states, it flows SW to form the boundary between Argentina and S Brazil, and then Argentina and Uruguay. It empties into the Río de la PLATA. Length: *c.*1,600km (1,000mi).

USA *See* UNITED STATES OF AMERICA

USSR (Union of Soviet Socialist Republics) *See* SOVIET UNION

Ustinov, Peter Alexander (1921–) English actor and dramatist. His plays include *The Love of Four Colonels* (1951) and *Romanoff and Juliet* (1956). Ustinov has acted in many films, including *Billy Budd* (1962), which he also directed. In recent years he has won a reputation as an entertaining raconteur.

usury Lending of money at an excessive or unlawful rate of interest. Before the Middle Ages any payment for the use of money was regarded as usury by Christians. In the late Middle Ages reasonable interest on a loan became acceptable when the lender risked capital.

Utah State in W USA, in the Rocky Mountains. The state capital is SALT LAKE CITY, other cities include Provo and Ogden. Utah has two distinct geographical regions. To the E of the Wasatch are the peaks of the Rockies. To the W is the GREAT BASIN, which includes GREAT SALT LAKE. Utah's major settlements lie in a fertile region between Great Salt Lake and the Wasatch range. In the Pleistocene epoch, Western Utah was submerged beneath Lake Bonneville. Today, Bonneville Salt Flats are a famous site for land speed record attempts. In S Utah are spectacular canyons formed by the raging COLORADO River. The first permanent settlement was made in 1847, when Brigham YOUNG led the MORMONS into the valley of Great Salt Lake. In 1848, the region was ceded to the USA at the end of the MEXICAN WAR. Conflicts arose between federal authorities and the Church of the Latter-Day Saints, and in 1857–58 federal troops were sent to Utah. Settlement increased with the completion (1869) of the Union Pacific Railroad, and the arid land was made productive through irrigation schemes. Industry expanded rapidly during World War 2, and the post-war development of hydoelectric plants continued this process. The terrain hinders agriculture, but hay, barley, wheat, beans and sugar beet are grown. The chief farming activity is stock raising. Mining is also important: there are rich deposits of copper, petroleum, coal, molybdenum, silver, lead and gold. With many national parks and monuments, tourism is vital to the economy. Area: 219,931sq km (84,915sq mi). Pop. (2000) 2,233,169.

Utamaro, Kitagawa (1753–1806) Japanese artist, master of the UKIYO-E woodblock colour print. He excelled in depicting birds, flowers and feminine beauty. His works were strongly erotic, precise and graceful.

Ute Shoshonean-speaking tribe of Native North Americans. They were fierce nomadic warriors who engaged in warfare with other Native American tribes and hunted bison. Today, *c*.4,000 Ute live on reservations in Colorado and Utah.

uterus (womb) Hollow, muscular organ located in the pelvis of female mammals. It protects and nourishes the growing FETUS until birth. The upper part is broad and branches out on each side into the FALLOPIAN TUBES. The lower uterus narrows into the CERVIX, which leads to the VAGINA. Its muscular walls are lined with mucous membrane (ENDOMETRIUM), to which the fertilized egg attaches itself. *See also* MENSTRUAL CYCLE

utilitarianism Branch of ethical philosophy. It holds that actions are to be judged good or bad according to their consequences. An action is deemed to be morally right if it produces good results. Utilitarianism was developed by the English philosophers Jeremy BENTHAM, James MILL and J.S. MILL.

Uto-Aztecan languages Family of Native-American languages spoken in SW USA and Mexico. It includes COMANCHE of Oklahoma and SHOSHONE, spoken in some W states. In Mexico there are NAHUATL (the language of the Aztecs), Tarahumara and Mayo.

Utopianism (Gk. no place) Projection of ideal states or alternative worlds that are ordered for the benefit of all and where social ills have been eradicated. Sir Thomas MORE's *Utopia* (1516) outlines his notion of an ideal commonwealth based entirely on reason. It critically describes contemporary social existence, while prescribing a transcendent, imaginative vision of the best of all possible worlds. Enlightenment philosophers, such as Jean Jacques ROUSSEAU, portrayed a vision of a pre-feudal European Golden Age. Writers such as SAINT-SIMON, Charles FOURIER and Robert OWEN outlined ideal communities based on cooperation and economic self-sufficiency. Karl MARX and Friedrich ENGELS valued the social insights of utopianism, but rejected its unscientific analysis of political and economic realities. By the late 19th century, the utopian novel had become an established literary genre. Works such as *Erewhon* (1872) by Samuel Butler were popular and influential. The spread of TOTALITARIANISM in Europe during the 1930s encouraged **dystopian** novels, such as *Brave New World* (1932) by Aldous Huxley and *1984* (1949) by George Orwell.

Utrecht City on the River Oude Rijn, central Netherlands. Utrecht is the fourth-largest city in The Netherlands. It has been a trading centre since medieval times. It was the scene of the Peace of UTRECHT (1713). The old city includes the 14th-century St Martin's Cathedral. Utrecht is a major cultural, financial and rail centre. Industries: steel, machinery, textiles. Pop. (1996) 234,000.

Utrecht, Peace of (1713–14) Series of treaties that ended the War of SPANISH SUCCESSION. It confirmed the BOURBON King PHILIP V on the Spanish throne providing that he renounced any claim to the throne of France. Austria received the Spanish Netherlands and extensive Italian territories; Britain gained Gibraltar, Minorca and provinces of E Canada.

Uttar Pradesh State in N India, bordering Nepal and Tibet; its capital is LUCKNOW. The heartland of early Hindu civilization, it is the hub of India's Hindi-speaking region. It is by far the most populous Indian state. The region has the foothills of the Himalayas in the N and hills in the S, enclosing a low-lying plain drained by the GANGES and its tributaries. The economy is based on agriculture, mainly cereals, sugar-cane, rice and pulses, and the mining of coal, copper, bauxite and limestone. Industries: cotton and sugar processing. Area: 294,413sq km (113,673sq mi). Pop. (1991) 139,112,287.

UZBEKISTAN
AREA: 447,400sq km (172,740sq mi)
POPULATION: 26,044,000
CAPITAL (POPULATION): Tashkent (2,106,000)

Utzon, Jørn (1918–) Danish architect. He is internationally known as the designer of the much admired Sydney Opera House in Australia, completed in 1973.

Uzbekistan Republic in central Asia; the capital is TASHKENT. There are plains in the W and highlands in the E. The main rivers, the Amu Darya and Syr Darya, drain into the ARAL SEA. So much water has been diverted from these rivers to irrigate farmland that the Aral Sea has shrunk from 66,900sq km (25,830sq mi) in 1960 to 33,642sq km (12,989sq mi) in 1993. The dried-up lake area has become desert, like much of the rest of the country. Grassy steppe occurs in wetter areas, with forests on the mountain slopes. **Climate** Uzbekistan has a continental climate, with cold winters and hot summers. The W is extremely arid, with an average annual rainfall of *c*.200mm (8in), but parts of the highlands in the E have three times as much rain. **History and politics** Turkic people first settled in the area that is now Uzbekistan *c*.1,500 years ago, and Islam was introduced in the 7th century AD. In the 13th century, MONGOLS invaded the land, and in the late 14th century TAMERLANE ruled a great empire from SAMARKAND. Turkic Uzbek people invaded in the 16th century, and gradually the area was divided into states (khanates). In the 19th century Russia controlled the area, and following the Russian Revolution of 1917, the communists took over, establishing the Uzbek Soviet Socialist Republic in 1924. Under communism, all aspects of Uzbek life were controlled; religious worship was discouraged, but education, health, housing and transport services were improved. The communists also increased cotton production, but caused great environmental damage in the process. In the 1980s, when reforms were being introduced in the Soviet Union, the Uzbeks demanded more freedom. In 1990, the government unilaterally declared independence from the Soviet Union. In 1991, following the break-up of the Soviet Union, Uzbekistan became a sovereign nation. It retained its links with Russia, however, through membership of the Commonwealth of Independent States (CIS). On 29 December 1991, Islam Karimov, leader of the People's Democratic Party (formerly the Communist Party), was elected president. In 1992 and 1993, many opposition leaders were arrested. In order to avoid internal disruption, Karimov asserted that economic reform would be slow. In 1995, a referendum extended President Karimov's term in office until 2000. **Economy** Uzbekistan is a lower-middle-income developing country (1995 GDP per capita, US$6,630). The government controls most economic activity. The country produces coal, copper, gold, oil and natural gas, while manufactures include agricultural machinery, chemicals and textiles. Agriculture is important. Cotton si the main crop. Cattle, sheep and goats are also reared. Uzbekistan's exports include cotton, gold, textiles, chemicals and fertilizers.

Uzbeks Turkic-speaking people, originally from Persia, who form two thirds of the population of UZBEKISTAN. They took their name from Uzbeg Khan (d.1340), a chief of the GOLDEN HORDE. By the end of the 16th century the Uzbeks had extended their rule to parts of Persia, Afghanistan, and Chinese TURKISTAN. Their empire was never united, and in the 19th century its various states were absorbed by Russia.

V/v, 22nd letter of the Roman alphabet, is derived (as were f, u and y) from the Semitic letter vaw, meaning hook. It was identical to u in the Greek alphabet and was undifferentiated from u in English until the Middle Ages.

V1, V2 rockets (abbreviation for *Vergeltungswaffen*, Vengeance Weapons). The **V-1**s, popularly known as **doodlebugs**, **flying bombs** or **buzz bombs**, were pilotless aircraft, powered by a pulse-jet engine, with a guidance system composed of a distance-measuring device, a GYROCOMPASS and an altimeter. Launched by the LUFTWAFFE against SE England in June 1944, they carried *c*.1 tonne of high explosive. Later in 1944, England was attacked by the **V-2**, a long-range, GUIDED MISSILE carrying a 1-tonne warhead to a range of 320km (200mi), with an altitude of 95–110km (60–70mi). It was powered by a mixture of liquid oxygen and ethyl alcohol and was the precursor of post-war MISSILES.

vaccination Injection of a VACCINE in order to produce IMMUNITY against a disease. In many countries, children are vaccinated routinely against infectious diseases.

vaccine Agent used to give IMMUNITY against various diseases without producing symptoms. A vaccine consists of modified disease organisms, such as live, weakened VIRUSES or dead ones that are still able to induce the production of specific ANTIBODIES within the blood. *See also* IMMUNE SYSTEM

vacuole Membrane-bound, fluid-filled cavity within the CYTOPLASM of a CELL. Vacuoles perform various functions including the discharge of wastes from cell metabolism.

vacuum Region of extremely low pressure. Interstellar space is a high vacuum, with an average density of less than 1 molecule per cubic centimetre; the highest man-made vacuums contain less than 100,000 molecules per cubic centimetre. Evangelista Torricelli is credited with developing (1643) the first man-made vacuum in a mercury BAROMETER.

vacuum flask Container for keeping things (usually liquids) hot or cold. A vacuum flask is made with double, silvered glass walls, separated by a near VACUUM. This vessel is held in an insulated metal or plastic case. The vacuum reduces heat transfer by conduction of convection between the contents and the surroundings. The silvering on the glass minimizes heat transfer by radiation. The vacuum flask was invented (1892) by James DEWAR.

vacuum tube (electronic valve) Devices once fitted in radios, now largely replaced by TRANSISTORS. A vacuum tube contains two or more ELECTRODES. When connected to a source of electricity, the negative electrode (CATHODE) becomes heated and emits ELECTRONS into the partial vacuum inside the valve. The electrons move towards the positive electrode (ANODE). One or more intermediate electrodes, called grids, can be interposed between the cathode and the anode, to influence the rate of electron emission – that is the current flowing in the valve. A small increase in grid potential (voltage) causes a large increase in cathode current. In this way current control and amplification are possible.

Vaduz Capital city of LIECHTENSTEIN, on the right bank of the Upper Rhine. Destroyed in a war between the Swiss and the Holy Roman Emperor, it was rebuilt in the early 16th century and became a possession of the Liechtenstein family in 1712. Once a market town, it is now a major centre of international finance. The other major source of income is tourism. Pop. (1997) 5,000.

vagina Portion of the female reproductive tract, running from the CERVIX of the UTERUS to the exterior of the body. Tube-like in shape, it receives the PENIS during sexual intercourse. Its muscular walls enable it to dilate during childbirth.

valence (valency) Measure of the "combining power" of a particular element, equal to the number of single CHEMICAL BONDS one atom can form or the number of electrons it gives up or accepts when forming a compound. Hydrogen has a valency of 1, carbon 4, and sulphur 2, as seen in compounds such as methane (CH_4), carbon disulphide (CS_2), and hydrogen sulphide (H_2S). *See also* ATOMIC NUMBER; COVALENT BOND; IONIC BOND

Valencia City in E Spain, capital of the province of Valencia, situated on the River Turia. The region of Valencia comprises the provinces of Alicante, Castelló-nand Valencia. Originally settled by the Romans, the city was conquered by the MOORS in the 8th century, eventually becoming capital of the independent Moorish kingdom of Valencia. In the Spanish CIVIL WAR, it was the last Republican stronghold to fall to Nationalist forces. It is an agricultural, industrial and communications centre. Industries: electrical equipment, chemicals, textiles, shipbuilding, machinery, fruit, wine. Tourists are drawn by Valencia's many fine buildings. Pop. (1995) 763,000.

Valencia City in N Venezuela, capital of Carabobo state. It was the capital of Venezuela in 1830 when the country was proclaimed independent of Greater Colombia. It is an industrial and transport centre. Industries: textiles, paper, cement, glass, soap, furniture vehicles, brewing. Pop. (1990) 903,076.

Valentine, Saint Name traditionally associated with two legendary saints of the 3rd century: Valentine of Rome and Valentine of Interamna (modern Terni). The former was a Roman priest and physician, and the latter the Bishop of Terni. Little is known about either of them, and they may have been the same person. The martyrdom of both is commemorated on 14 February. The custom of lovers exchanging cards on St Valentine's Day possibly has its roots in the pagan Roman festival of Lupercalia, an ancient fertility rite celebrated in Rome on 15 February.

Valentino, Rudolph (1895–1926) US silent-film star, b. Italy. His smouldering blend of passion and melancholy wooed female audiences in the 1920s. Valentino's films include *Four Horseman of the Apocalypse* (1921), *The Sheik* (1921), *Blood and Sand* (1922) and *The Eagle* (1925). His early death caused hysteria among his fans.

valerian (garden heliotrope) Plant native to Europe and N Asia and naturalized in the USA. It has pinkish or pale purple flower clusters. Height: to 1.2m (4ft). Family Valerianaceae; species *Valeriana officinalis*.

Valéry, Paul (1871–1945) French poet and critic. Influenced by SYMBOLISM and MALLARMÉ in particular, Valéry's masterpiece is *La Jeune Parque* (1917). Other works, such as *Le Cimetière marin* (1920) and *Charmes* (1922), cemented his lyrical, abstract style. Valéry's *Cahiers* (1957–60) record his thoughts on a wide range of issues. In 1925 he was elected to the Académie Française.

Valhalla In Norse mythology, Hall of the Slain, where chosen warriors enjoyed feasts with the god, ODIN. It is depicted as a glittering palace with golden walls and a ceiling of burnished shields.

Valium Proprietary name for diazepam, a sedative drug in the BENZODIAZEPINE group. It is used in the treatment of anxiety, muscle spasms and epilepsy.

Valkyries In Norse mythology, war-like handmaidens of the god ODIN, who selected and conducted to VAL-HALLA those slain heroes who merited a place with him.

Valladolid City on the River Pisuerga, NW central Spain, capital of Valladolid province. The city was liberated from the Moors by Castilian kings in the 10th century. There is a 12th-century Romanesque church and a monument to Christopher Columbus, who died in the city. Valladolid's university, founded in 1346, is one of the oldest in Spain. Industries: vehicles, railway engineering, chemicals, textiles. Pop. (1995) 335,000.

Valletta Port and capital of Malta, on the NE coast of the island. It was founded in the 16th century and named after Jean Parisot de la Valette, Grand Master of the Order of the Knights of St John, who organized the reconstruction of the city after repelling the Turks' Great Siege of 1565. Notable buildings include the Royal University of Malta (1592) and the Cathedral of San Giovanni (1576). Industries: shipbuilding, tourism. Pop. (1995) 102,571.

valley Elongated, gently sloping depression of the Earth's surface. It often contains a stream or RIVER that receives the drainage from the surrounding heights. A U-shaped valley was probably formed by a glacier, a V-shaped one by a stream. The term may also be applied to a broad, generally flat area that is drained by a large river.

Valois Royal dynasty that ruled France from the accession (1328) of PHILIP VI to the death (1589) of HENRY III, when the throne passed to the BOURBONS. *See also* CHARLES VIII; FRANCIS I; LOUIS XI; LOUIS XII

Valois, Dame Ninette de (1898–) Irish ballerina and choreographer, b. Edris Stannus. She danced with Diaghilev's BALLETS RUSSES (1923–26). In 1931, de Valois founded the Sadler's Wells Ballet School that later became the Royal Ballet. She acted as director (1931–63).

Valparaíso Main port of Chile and capital of Valparaíso region, 100km (60mi) W of Santiago. Founded in 1536, the city has always been vulnerable to earthquakes. As well as Chile's chief port, it is also a cultural centre, with two universities and museums of fine arts and natural history. Industries: chemicals, textiles, sugar refining, vegetable oils, paint. Pop. (1995) 282,000.

value-added tax (VAT) Indirect tax imposed in most European countries. Introduced in Britain in 1971, it consists of a series of taxes (calculated as a percentage) levied on goods (or services) in the various stages of their manufacture until the point of sale. *See also* TAXATION

valves In anatomy, structures that prevent the backflow of blood in the HEART and VEINS. Heart valves separate and connect the two atria and ventricles, the right ventricle and the pulmonary artery and the left ventricle and the aorta.

vampire In E European legend, a corpse that lives at night and sucks the blood of the living to sustain itself. The victim in turn becomes a vampire. The monster can be killed by driving a wooden stake through its heart. Bram STOKER's *Dracula* (1897) drew on the legend of the vampire to produce a masterpiece of horror.

vampire bat Small, brown BAT that lives in tropical and sub-tropical America. It uses its sharp teeth to slice the skin of resting animals (including human beings) and then laps up their blood. Length: 7.6cm (3in); wingspan 30cm (12in). Family Desmodontidae; species *Desmodus rotundus*.

vanadium (symbol V) Silver-white, metallic element, one of the TRANSITION ELEMENTS. Discovered in 1801, the malleable and ductile metal is found in iron, lead and uranium ores and in coal and petroleum. It is used in steel alloys to add strength and heat resistance. Chemically, vanadium reacts with oxygen and other non-metals at

high temperature. Properties: at.no. 23; r.a.m. 50.9414; r.d. 6.1 at 65.6°F; m.p. 1,890°C (3,434°F); b.p. 3,380°C (6,116°F); most common isotope V^{51} (99.76%).

Van Allen radiation belts Two rings of radiation trapped by the Earth's magnetic field in the upper atmosphere. The belts contain high-energy, charged particles. The inner belt (of ELECTRONS and PROTONS) extends from *c*.1,000 to 4,000km (600–2,500mi) above the Equator. The outer belt (of electrons) extends from *c*.15,000 to 25,000km (9,000–15,000mi). It is thought that the particles come from SOLAR FLARES carried by the SOLAR WIND.

Vanbrugh, Sir John (1664–1726) English BAROQUE architect and dramatist, who worked with Sir Christopher WREN. Vanbrugh took London by storm with his witty RESTORATION comedies, *The Relapse* (1696) and *The Provok'd Wife* (1697), before turning to architecture. Blenheim Palace (1705–20) and Castle Howard (1699–1726) are among his architectural masterpieces.

Van Buren, Martin (1782–1862) Eighth US President (1837–41). He served (1821–28) in the US Senate. As Andrew JACKSON's secretary of state, Van Buren's opposition to John C. CALHOUN's idea of nullification earned him the vice-presidency (1832–36) and the Democratic nomination. An advocate of STATES' RIGHTS, his presidency was plunged into crisis by the lack of federal intervention in the economic depression (1837). In foreign affairs, Van Buren sought conciliation with Great Britain over the AROOSTOOK WAR. He was heavily defeated by William Henry HARRISON in the 1840 elections. Van Buren's rejection of the annexation of Texas and extension of SLAVERY lost him the Democratic nomination in 1844.

Vancouver City on the S shore of Burrard Inlet, S British Columbia, Canada. It is Canada's third-largest city and principal Pacific port. The area was first explored in 1792 by Captain George Vancouver. The building of the Canadian Pacific Railway allowed it to grow into the largest city on the Canadian W coast. Its excellent sea and air links make it one of N America's leading centres for transport and communication with countries of the Pacific Rim. Vancouver's beautiful harbour setting, pleasant climate and position as the terminus of both trans-Canadian railways make it a magnet for tourists. The city has two universities: British Columbia (1908) and Simon Fraser University (1963). Industries: tourism, timber, oil refining. Pop. (1991) 471,844 (metropolitan 1,602,502).

Vancouver Island Island off the Pacific coast of British Columbia, Canada. Captain Cook visited it in 1778; it became a British Crown colony in 1849, and part of British Columbia in 1866. The largest island off the W coast of N America, its interior is rugged and forested. The main city, VICTORIA, is the province's capital. Industries: timber, fishing, copper, coal-mining, tourism. Area: 32,137sq km (12,408sq mi).

Vandals Germanic tribe who attacked the Roman Empire in the 5th century AD. They looted Roman Gaul and invaded Spain in 409. Defeated by the GOTHS, they moved farther south and invaded North Africa (429), establishing a kingdom from which they controlled the W Mediterranean. They sacked Rome in 455. The Vandal kingdom was destroyed by the Byzantine general Belisarius in 533–34.

Van de Graaff generator Machine that generates high voltages by concentrating electrical charges on the outside of a hollow conductor. Positive or negative charges are sprayed onto a vertically moving belt that carries them up to a large hollow metal sphere where voltage builds up. An applied voltage of *c*.50,000 volts can generate up to 10 million volts.

van der Post, Sir Laurens Jan (1906–96) South African writer and anthropologist. He is best known for his books on the disappearing culture of the SAN bushmen of the Kalahari desert, s Africa. These works, such as *Lost World of the Kalahari* (1958), are a mix of travelogue and anthropological observation.

Van der Waals, Johannes Diderik (1837–1923) Dutch physicist. He was awarded the 1910 Nobel Prize for physics for his work on gases and the gas equation that he derived. The Van der Waals equation takes into account intermolecular attraction and repulsion, which were ignored by the KINETIC THEORY of gases.

Van der Waals forces Weak forces of mutual attraction that contribute towards cohesion between neighbouring ATOMS or MOLECULES. They are named after Johannes VAN DER WAALS.

Van Diemen's Land Original name of TASMANIA. It was discovered by Abel TASMAN in 1642 and named in honour of the governor-general of the Dutch East Indies. It became part of New South Wales in 1803, was made a separate colony in 1825, given self-governing status in 1850 and named Tasmania in 1855.

Van Dyck, Sir Anthony (1599–1641) Flemish portrait and religious painter. Van Dyck worked in RUBENS' studio before travelling abroad. His portraits of the aristocracy, such as *Marchesa Elena Grimaldi* (*c*.1625), were widely copied. In 1632 Van Dyck was invited to England by Charles I, who made him court painter and a knight. The elegance and sophistication of his depictions of the English aristocracy was the model for portraiture until John Singer SARGENT.

Vane, Sir Henry (1613–62) English statesman. A Puritan, he was briefly governor (1636–37) of Massachusetts, before returning to domestic politics. A proponent of the abolition of episcopacy in the LONG PARLIAMENT, Vane was dismissed by CHARLES I. During the English CIVIL WARS, he secured the SOLEMN LEAGUE AND COVENANT (1643) with Scotland. Vane negotiated with Charles I and was opposed to the king's execution. He was a member of the COMMONWEALTH council of state, but fell out with Oliver CROMWELL. After the RESTORATION (1660), Vane was convicted of treason and executed.

Van Gogh, Vincent (1853–90) Dutch painter, a leading exponent of EXPRESSIONISM. He was a lay preacher to Belgium coal miners before suffering a psychological crisis. Virtually self-taught, Van Gogh's early works, such as *The Potato Eaters* (1885), are MILLET-influenced studies of working-class life. In 1886 he left Holland for Paris, where his palette was transformed by POST-IMPRESSIONISM, experimenting briefly with POINTILLISM. In 1888 Van Gogh moved to Arles, Provence, where he was joined by GAUGUIN. Suffering from mental illness and depression, he cut off part of his left ear after a quarrel with Gauguin. Van Gogh's paintings from this period include the *Sunflower* series (1888) and the *Night Café* (1888). He entered an asylum at Saint Rémy, where he painted a series of intense landscapes, such as *Starry Night* (1889). These paintings are executed with heavy brushwork in heightened, flame-like colour, with passionate expression of light and emotion. Van Gogh committed suicide in Auvers. In a brief and turbulent life, he sold only one painting and was supported by his younger brother Théo.

vanilla Climbing orchid native to Mexico. The vines bear greenish-yellow flowers that produce seed pods 20cm (8in) long, which are the source of the flavouring, vanilla. Family Orchidaceae; species *Vanilla planifolia*.

Vanuatu Volcanic island group in the sw Pacific Ocean, *c*.2,300km (1,430mi) E of Australia. The group consists of 13 large islands and 70 islets, the majority of them mountainous, which form a chain *c*.725km (450mi) in length. The main islands are Espiritu Santo, Efate (which has the capital Vila, 1992 pop. 19,750), Malekula, Pentecost, Malo and Tanna. Discovered in 1606 by Pedro Fernandez de Queiros, the group was settled by the English and French in the early 1800s. Governed jointly by France and Britain as the New Hebrides from 1906, the islands became an independent republic in 1980. The inhabitants live mainly by fishing, farming and mining, with copra accounting for almost half of export earnings. Area: 12,190sq km (4,707sq mi). Pop. (2000) 206,000.

Van Vleck, John (Hasbrouck) (1899–1980) US mathematician and physicist. He studied the behaviour of electrons in non-crystalline, magnetic materials. In the 1930s, Van Vleck was the first scientist to use QUANTUM MECHANICS to explain the phenomenon of MAGNETISM. He shared the 1977 Nobel Prize for physics.

vaporization (volatilization) Conversion of a liquid or solid into its vapour, such as water into steam. Some solids (such as ammonium chloride), when heated, pass directly into the vapour state, and this is known as SUBLIMATION.

vapour pressure Pressure exerted by a vapour when it evaporates from a liquid or solid. When as many molecules leave to form vapour as return, this equilibrium is termed saturated vapour pressure.

Varanasi (Benares, Banoras) City on the River Ganges, Uttar Pradesh, N India. Varanasi is considered by Hindus to be their holiest city. Each year, it attracts millions of pilgrims who bathe in the Ganges. BUDDHA is reputed to have preached his first sermon nearby. Silk brocade, brassware and jewellery are among the city's specialist industries. Pop. (1991) 1,026,000.

Varèse, Edgard (1885–1965) French composer, a leading advocate of 20th-century experimental music. He experimented with new rhythms and timbres and dissonant harmonies in his works, which include *Hyperprism* (1923) for wind instruments and percussion and *Déserts* (1954) for tape-recorded sound. He concentrated on ELECTRONIC MUSIC after the early 1950s.

Vargas, Getúlio Dornelles (1883–1954) Brazilian statesman, president (1930–45, 1951–54). He led a successful revolt after being defeated in presidential elections. Vargas' autocratic regime was bolstered by the army. He established a corporative state, but there were few signs of economic improvement. His refusal to grant elections led to a military coup. Vargas' second term was tainted by scandal. Opposition from the right wing increased until, rather than resign, he committed suicide.

variable In mathematics, symbol used to represent an unspecified quantity. Variables are used to express a range of possible values. For example, in the expression $x^2 + x + 1$, the quantity x may be assigned the value of any real number; here x is said to be an independent variable. If y is defined by $y = x^2 + x + 1$, then y is a dependent variable because its value depends on the value of x.

variable star Star whose brightness varies with time. **Intrinsic** variables are stars that vary because of some inherent feature. In **extrinsic** variables, external factors, such as eclipses or obscuring dust, affect the amount of light reaching us from the star. *See also* MAGNITUDE

variation In biology, differences between members of the same SPECIES. Variation occurs naturally due to HEREDITY and to differences in the environment during development. *See also* ADAPTATION; EVOLUTION

variation In music, a variety of treatments upon a single theme. Successive statements of the theme are altered by such means as simple elaboration, change of KEY or change of time signature.

varicose vein Condition where a VEIN becomes swollen and distorted. Varicose veins can occur anywhere in the body but are commonly found in the legs.

varnish Solution of a RESIN or a PLASTIC that dries to form a hard, transparent, protective and often decorative coating. Varnishes may have a matt or glossy finish. Pigments are often added to colour the varnish.

Varuna In ancient Hindu mythology, the supreme ruler and possessor of universal power. He is worshipped as the upholder of moral order and is identified with the Moon.

Vasari, Giorgio (1511–74) Italian painter, architect and biographer. His fame now rests on his history of Italian art, *The Lives of the most excellent Painters, Sculptors and Architects* (1550). This lively account is the single most important document of Italian RENAISSANCE art from GIOTTO to MICHELANGELO. In architecture he is noted for his design for the UFFIZI.

Vasco da Gama *See* GAMA, VASCO DA

vascular bundle Strand of conductive tissue that transports water and dissolved mineral salts and nutrients throughout a VASCULAR PLANT. They extend from the roots, through the stem and out to the leaves. They consist of two types of tissue: XYLEM, which conducts water from the roots to the shoot and is located towards the centre of the bundle; and PHLOEM, which conducts salts and nutrients and forms the outer regions of the bundle.

vascular plant Plant with vessels to carry water and nutrients within it. All higher plants – FERNS, CONIFERS and ANGIOSPERMS – have a VASCULAR BUNDLE.

vasectomy Operation to induce male sterility, in which the tube (vas deferens) carrying SPERM from the testes to the PENIS is cut. A vasectomy is a form of permanent CONTRACEPTION, although in some cases the operation is reversible.

vasoconstrictor Any substance that causes constriction of blood vessels and, therefore, decreased blood flow. Examples include NOREPINEPHRINE, angiotensin, and the HORMONE vasopressin (antidiuretic hormone).

vasodilator Any substance that causes widening of the blood vessels, permitting freer flow of blood. Vasodilator drugs are mostly used to treat HYPERTENSION and ANGINA.

VAT *See* VALUE-ADDED TAX

Vatican City Independent sovereign state, existing as a walled enclave on the W bank of the River TIBER, within the city of ROME. It is the official home of the PAPACY and an independent base for the Holy See (governing body of the ROMAN CATHOLIC CHURCH). The first papal residence was established here in the 5th century, and it has been the papal home ever since, apart from a brief spell at AVIGNON in the 14th century. Vatican City did not achieve full independence until 1929. The world's smallest nation, its permanent population of *c*.1,000 (mostly unmarried males) includes the Pope's traditional SWISS GUARD of 100. The Commission, appointed to administer the Vatican's affairs, has its own radio service, police and railroad station and issues its own stamps and coins. The treasures of the Vatican, notably MICHELANGELO's frescos in the SISTINE CHAPEL and ST PETER's, attract huge numbers of tourists and pilgrims. The official language is Latin. Area: 0.44sq km (0.17sq mi).

Vatican Palace Residence of the pope within the VATICAN CITY. A building of more than 1,000 rooms clustered around a number of courtyards, it contains the papal apartments, the offices of the Vatican City state secretariat, state reception rooms, the Vatican Museums, the Vatican Archive and the Vatican Library.

Vatican Council, First (1869–70) Twentieth ecumenical council of the Roman Catholic Church. Convened by Pope PIUS IX to rebut various contemporary ideas associated with the rise of liberalism and materialism, it is remembered for the declaration of PAPAL INFALLIBILITY.

Vatican Council, Second (1962–65) Twenty-first ecumenical council of the Roman Catholic Church. It was convened by Pope JOHN XXIII to revive and renew Christian faith and to put the Church in closer touch with ordinary people. Among the most significant results were the introduction of the Mass in the vernacular, a greater role for lay people and a greater tolerance for other sects and other religions.

vaudeville US variety entertainment; the British MUSIC HALL is equivalent to it. Its rise and fall followed the same pattern as its European counterpart, having its heyday in the late 19th century and eventually succumbing to the popularity of the cinema.

Vaughan, Henry (1622–95) Welsh poet. After studying law, he turned to medicine and became a doctor. His METAPHYSICAL POETRY was inspired by the work of George HERBERT. Vaughan's best work draws on his religious experience, most notably *Silex Scintillans* (1650, revised 1655).

Vaughan, Sarah (1924–90) US singer. Her early work with Billy Eckstine led to the recording of "Lover Man" with Dizzy GILLESPIE. Often with full orchestral accompaniment, Vaughan sang with the bands of Duke Ellington and Count Basie. Albums include *After Hours* (1961).

Vaughan Williams, Ralph (1872–1958) English composer. His interest in English folk music is apparent in his three *Norfolk Rhapsodies* (1905–07) and *The Lark Ascending* (1914). Vaughan Williams' modal style, based on Tudor music, found its fullest expression in *Fantasia on a theme by Thomas Tallis* (1910) and *A Sea Symphony* (1909). The Tudor song "Greensleeves" appears in his opera *Sir John in Love* (1929). Works such as The *Pilgrim's Progress* (1951) and *Mass in G Minor* (1923) show the influence of the English visionary tradition. Vaughan Williams' *Sinfonia Antarctica* (1952) was based on his score for the film *Scott of the Antarctic* (1948).

vault Curved roof or ceiling usually made of stone, brick, or concrete. The simple **barrel** vault is semi-cylindrical; the **groin** vault consists of two barrel vaults intersected at right-angles; the **ribbed groin** is the same as the ordinary groin vault except that it has ribs to give the edges extra support; the so-called Gothic vault has four pointed compartments; the **fan** vault has a delicate, fan-like appearance. English masons developed the fan vault in the 15th century using tracery to make it more elaborate, as in King's College Chapel, Cambridge.

Veblen, Thorstein Bunde (1857–1929) US sociologist and economist. He wrote *The Theory of the Leisure Class* (1899), in which he introduced the idea of conspicuous CONSUMPTION. A perceptive critic of US capitalist society, he founded the institutionalist school, believing that economics must be studied in the context of social change.

vector In mathematics, a quantity that has both a magnitude and a direction, as contrasted with a SCALAR, which has magnitude only. For example, the VELOCITY of an object is specified by its speed and the direction in which it is moving; similarly, a FORCE has both magnitude and direction. Mass is a scalar quantity, but WEIGHT (the force of gravitation on a body) is a vector.

Vedanta (Sanskrit, conclusion of the VEDAS) Best known and most popular form of Indian philosophy; it forms the foundation for most modern schools of thought in HINDUISM. One of the most influential Vedanta schools was that expounded by the 7th–8th-century philosopher Sankara. This school holds that the natural world is an illusion. There is only one self, Brahman-ATMAN; ignorance of the oneness of the self with BRAHMAN is the cause of rebirth. The system includes a belief in the TRANSMIGRATION OF SOULS and the desirability of release from the cycle of rebirth. *See also* UPANISHADS

Vedas Ancient and most sacred writings of HINDUISM. They consist of a series of hymns and formulaic chants that constituted a Hindu LITURGY. There are four Vedas: *Rig Veda*, containing a priestly tradition originally brought to India by ARYANS; *Yajur Veda*, consisting of prayers and sacred formulas; *Sama Veda*, containing melodies and chants; and *Atharva Veda*, a collection of popular hymns, incantations and magic spells. The Vedas were composed between *c*.1500 and 1200 BC.

Vega (Alpha Lyrae) White, main-sequence star in the constellation of Lyra; the fifth-brightest star in the sky. Its luminosity is 50 times that of the Sun.

Vega Carpio, Félix, Lope de (1562–1635) Spanish poet and dramatist. A prolific writer, only *c*.300 of his major works survive; including the plays, *Peribáñez and the Commander of Ocaña* (*c*.1610) and *All Citizens Are Soldiers* (*c*.1613).

vegetable As opposed to ANIMAL, a form of life that builds up its tissues by means of growth using the energy of sunlight, carbon dioxide from the air, and the green pigment CHLOROPHYLL. This process is known as PHOTOSYNTHESIS. Vegetables, or green plants, also need to be supplied with water and mineral salts, which are usually present in the soil.

vegetarianism Practice of abstaining from eating meat and fish. A minority of vegetarian purists, known as vegans, further exclude from their diet all products of animal origin, such as butter, eggs, milk and cheese. Vegetarianism has a religious basis in many cultures, particularly among various Jain, Hindu and Buddhist sects.

vegetative reproduction Form of ASEXUAL REPRODUCTION in higher plants. It involves an offshoot or a piece of the original plant (from leaf, stem or root) separating and giving rise to an entire new plant. It may occur naturally, as in strawberries reproducing by runners, or artificially, as in a house plant cutting yielding a new plant.

vein In mammals, vessel that carries deoxygenated BLOOD to the heart. An exception is the pulmonary vein, which carries **oxygenated** blood from the lungs to the left upper chamber of the heart. *See also* ARTERY; VENA CAVA

Velázquez, Diego Rodriguez de Silva y (1599–1660) Spanish painter. He was strongly influenced by Venetian art and the work of CARAVAGGIO, but he quickly developed a personal style that combined NATURALISM with a deep spirituality. He painted religious works and dignified GENRE PAINTINGS, notably *The Old Woman Cooking Eggs* (1618). In 1623 Velázquez became court painter to King Philip IV of Spain. During the 1630s and 1640s he produced a series of royal and equestrian portraits. A trip to Italy resulted in the portrait of *Pope Innocent X* (1650). Towards the end of his life, Velázquez continued to paint with dazzling brushwork, culminating in *The Maids of Honour* (*c*.1656). Unknown outside Spain until the early 19th century, he came to exercise a powerful influence on European artists, especially MANET.

velocity (symbol *v*) Rate of motion of a body in a certain direction. Velocity is a VECTOR (magnitude and direction), whereas speed, which does not specify direction, is a scalar.

vena cava Main VEIN of vertebrates. It supplies the HEART with deoxygenated blood, emptying into its right atrium.

veneer Extremely thin sheet of wood or a thin sheet of a precious material such as ivory or tortoiseshell, which gives furniture or other objects the appearance of being more valuable than they are. Veneers may also be used as decorative shapes inlaid into a surface.

venereal disease (VD) Any of the diseases transmitted through sexual contact, chief of which are SYPHILIS, GONORRHOEA and chancroid. Syphilis is caused by the bacterium, *Treponema pallidum*. PENICILLIN and its derivatives can still cure syphilis in its early stages. Gonorrhoea is caused by the gonococcus bacterium and if diagnosed early may be treated with SULPHONAMIDE DRUGS.

Venetia Historic region of NE Italy, including the Veneto. Named after its ancient inhabitants, the Veneti, it was largely dominated by VENICE from the late Middle Ages. It was held by Austria from 1815 until it became part of the Italian kingdom in 1866.

Venetian School School of Italian painting that flourished in the 15th, 16th and 18th centuries. It was noted for the sumptuousness and radiance of its colour. Early Venetian masters included the BELLINI and Vivarini families, who were followed by its greatest exponents, TITIAN and GIORGIONE. TINTORETTO and VERONESE represent the transition from RENAISSANCE to BAROQUE, while TIEPOLO, CANALETTO and GUARDI revived Venetian painting in the 18th century.

Venezuela Republic in N South America. The w part of the Republic of Venezuela contains the Maracaibo lowlands, which surround the oil-rich Lake Maracaibo, and the city of MARACAIBO. Arms of the ANDES mountains extend across most of N Venezuela. Situated in this region are CARACAS and VALENCIA. A low-lying region, drained by the River ORINOCO, lies between the N mountains and the Guiana Highlands in the SE. The Guiana Highlands contain ANGEL FALLS, the world's highest waterfall, with a total drop of 980m (3,212ft). **Climate** Venezuela has a tropical climate. Lowland temperatures are always high, but the mountains are cooler and wetter. Much of the country has a marked dry season from December to April.

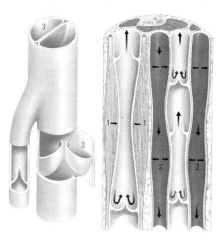

▲ **vein** Veins carry blood to the heart. The returning venous blood moves slowly due to low pressure, and the veins can collapse or expand to accommodate variations in blood flow. Movement relies on the surrounding muscles, which contract (1) and compress the vein. Pulsation of adjacent arteries (2) has a regular pumping effect. Semi-lunar valves (3) are found at regular intervals throughout the larger veins, and these allow the blood to move only in one direction.

VENEZUELA
AREA: 912,050sq km (352,143sq mi)
POPULATION: 24,715,000
CAPITAL (POPULATION): Caracas (1,824,900)

Vegetation About 34% of Venezuela is forested, with dense rainforest in the Orinoco basin and in the Guiana Highlands. Tropical savanna covers the lowlands; mountain grassland occurs in the highlands. Only *c*.4% of the land is cultivated. **History and politics** The original inhabitants of Venezuela were the Arawak and Carib Native Americans. The first European discovery was made (1498) by Christopher COLUMBUS. In 1499, Amerigo VESPUCCI explored the coastline and nicknamed the country Venezuela ("little Venice"). Spanish settlements were soon established, and German explorers, notably Nikolaus Federmann, completed the conquest. Venezuela became part of the Spanish colonial administrative area of New Granada. In the late 18th century, uprisings against Spanish rule were led by Francisco de Miranda. In 1821, Simón BOLÍVAR liberated Venezuela, and it became part of Greater Colombia, a republic that also included Colombia, Ecuador and Panama. In 1830, Venezuela became a separate state. The mid- to late-19th century was marked by political instability and civil war. Venezuela was ruled by a series of dictators: Guzmán Blanco was followed by Joaquín Crespo and then Cipriano Castro, under whom financial corruption reached new heights. Juan Vicente GÓMEZ's long and autocratic rule (1908–35) provided the stability for Venezuela to pay off its debts, helped by international interest in its rich oil-fields. In 1945, a pro-democracy military junta, led by Rómulo Betancourt, gained control. In 1948, Rómulo Gallegos was elected president, but a military coup the same year re-established a dictatorship. In 1958, popular uprisings brought a return to democracy, with Betancourt as president. Venezuela became increasingly prosperous, but left-wing uprisings, notably two revolts in 1962 (covertly supported by Fidel Castro), led to much violence. In 1976, Venezuela nationalized its oil industry, using the money to raise living standards. In 1989, Carlos Andrés Pérez became president. He introduced free-market reforms, but inflation and unemployment continued to rise. In 1992, there were two failed military coups. In 1993, Pérez resigned after charges of corruption. In 1994, Rafael Caldera became president. His austerity measures provoked civil unrest. In 1999, Hugo Chávez Frías of the Fifth Republic Movement (MVR), leader of one of the failed coups in 1992, became president. **Economy** Venezuela is an upper-middle-income developing country (1995 GDP per capita, US$7,900). Industry employs 17% of the workforce. The major industry is petroleum refining, centred around Maracaibo. The slump in oil prices during the 1980s damaged the economy. Other industries include aluminium and steel production, centred around Ciudad Guayana. Oil accounts for 80% of the exports. Other exports include bauxite, aluminium and iron ore. Agriculture employs 13% of the workforce. Major crops include bananas, coffee and maize.
Venice (Venezia) City on the Gulf of Venice, at the head of the Adriatic Sea, N Italy, capital of Venetia region. It is built on 118 islands, separated by narrow canals, in the Lagoon of Venice and joined by causeway to the mainland. Settled in the 5th century, it became a vassal of the Byzantine Empire until the 10th century. After defeating Genoa in 1381, Venice became the most important European seapower, engaging in trade in the Mediterranean and Asia. Its

importance declined in the 16th century, and it was ceded to Austria in 1797, becoming part of Italy in 1866. Venice is the site of many churches, palaces and historic buildings, and it is one of Europe's foremost attractions, drawing more than two million tourists a year. Tourism imposes a massive strain on a city already suffering from erosion, subsidence and pollution. Industries: glass-blowing, textiles, petrochemicals. Pop. (1996) 299,000.
Venn diagram In mathematics, diagrammatical representation of the relations between mathematical SETS or logical statements, named after the British logician John Venn (1834–1923). The sets are drawn as geometrical figures that overlap whenever different sets share elements.
venom, snake Toxic substance produced in the poison glands of SNAKES and injected into their victims through ducts in or along their fangs. Many venoms are dangerous, and some can be lethal unless counteracted by anti-serums. The effects of snake venom vary according to the species and the constituents of the poison. Blood coagulation, respiratory effects and haemorrhage are among the most common. *See also* SNAKEBITE
ventilation In biology, the process by which air or water is taken into and expelled from the body of an animal and passed over a surface across which GAS EXCHANGE takes place. Ventilation mechanisms include BREATHING, by which air is drawn into the LUNGS for gas exchange across the wall of the ALVEOLI, and the movements of the floor of a fish's mouth, coupled with those of its GILL covers, which draw water across the gills.
ventricle Either of the two lower chambers of the HEART.
venture capital Outside CAPITAL provided for a business. Venture capital is often needed to start up new businesses or to expand existing businesses. It is provided by investment banks and private investors.
Venturi, Robert (1925–) US architect. He argued that architectural MODERNISM was banal. Venturi's stress on the importance of "vernacular" architecture heralded POST-MODERNISM. His publications include *Complexity and Contradiction in Architecture* (1966) and *Learning from Las Vegas* (1972), in which consumer architecture is contrasted with the post-modern approach. His buildings include Gordon Wu Hall, Princeton University, New Jersey (1984), and the Sainsbury Wing of the National Gallery, London (1991).
Venus Second planet from the Sun, it is almost as large as the Earth. Visible around dawn or dusk as the so-called **morning star** or **evening star**, it is the most conspicuous celestial object after the Sun and Moon. A telescope shows the planet's dazzling, yellowish-white cloud cover, with faint markings. Venus' very high surface temperature was indicated by measurements at radio wavelengths in 1958. Space probes revealed more about the surface. A gently undulating plain covers two thirds of Venus. Highlands account for a further quarter, and depressions and chasms the remainder. Most of the surface features are volcanic in origin. The atmosphere consists of 96%

VENUS: DATA
DIAMETER (EQUATORIAL): 12,104km (7,521mi)
MASS (EARTH = 1): 0.815
VOLUME (EARTH = 1): 0.86
DENSITY (WATER = 1): 5.25
ORBITAL PERIOD: 224.7 days
ROTATION PERIOD: 243.16 days
AVERAGE SURFACE TEMPERATURE: 480°C (896°F)
SURFACE GRAVITY (EARTH = 1): 0.90

carbon dioxide and 3.5% nitrogen, with traces of helium, argon, neon and krypton. Venus has no satellites.

Venus Roman goddess originally associated with gardens and cultivation but also with the ideas of charm, grace and beauty. She became identified with the Greek goddess, APHRODITE, and hence also personified love and fertility.

verbena Genus of annual and perennial trees, shrubs and herbs, native to the Western Hemisphere. Some species are popular garden plants and have pink, red, white or purple flowers. Family Verbenaceae; there are c.250 species.

Verdi, Giuseppe (1813–1901) Italian composer. His early operas displayed an original and lively talent and a promising sense of the dramatic. Up to 1853, his masterpieces were *Rigoletto* (1851), *Il trovatore* (1853) and *La traviata* (1853). *Aïda* (1867) shows a development in style, with richer and more imaginative orchestration. With Verdi's last three operas, *Don Carlos* (1884), *Otello* (1887) and *Falstaff* (1893), Italian opera reached its greatest heights. Among other compositions are several sacred choral works, including the *Requiem* (1874).

Verdun, Battle of (February–December 1916) Campaign of WORLD WAR 1. A German offensive in the region of Verdun made initial advances but was checked by the French under General PÉTAIN. After a series of renewed German assaults, the Allied offensive on the SOMME drew off German troops, and the French regained the lost territory. Total casualties are estimated at one million.

Verlaine, Paul (1844–96) French poet. His early poetry, *Poèmes Saturniens* (1866) and *Fêtes Galantes* (1869), was influenced by BAUDELAIRE, with whom he is grouped as one of the *fin de siècle* decadents (an appellation amply fulfilled by his lifestyle). An intense relationship with RIMBAUD ended violently. While in jail (1874–75), he wrote *Songs Without Words* (1874), an early work of SYMBOLISM. Returning to Catholicism, his later poetry deals with the conflict between the spiritual and the carnal. His critical work includes the famous study *The Accursed Poets* (1884).

Vermeer, Jan (1632–75) Dutch painter, one of the most celebrated of all 17th-century Dutch painters. Early mythological and religious works gave way to a middle period featuring the serene and contemplative domestic scenes for which he is best known. The compositions are extremely simple and powerful, and the colours are usually muted blues, greys and yellows. He treated light and colour with enormous delicacy, as in the superb landscape *View of Delft* (c.1660). Towards the end of his life, Vermeer began to paint in a heavier manner, and his work lost some of its mysterious charm.

vermiculite Clay mineral. Its flakes are light and are used in plaster and insulation and as a packing material. It is also used for conditioning soil and as a starting medium for seeds.

Vermont State in New England, NE USA, on the Canadian border. The state capital is MONTPELIER; other major cities include Burlington. The Green Mountains range N–S and dominate the terrain; most of the W border of the state is formed by Lake Champlain. In 1609, Samuel de CHAMPLAIN discovered the lake, but the region was not settled permanently until 1724. Land-grant disputes with New Hampshire and New York persisted for many years. In 1777, Vermont declared its independence, retaining this unrecognized status until it was admitted to the Union in 1791. The region is heavily forested and arable land is limited. Dairy farming is by far the most important farming activity. Mineral resources include granite, slate, marble and asbestos. Industries: forestry, computer parts, tourism. Area: 24,887sq km (9,609sq mi). Pop. (2000) 608,827.

Verne, Jules (1828–1905) French novelist. He is often considered one of the founding fathers of science fiction. Verne's imaginative adventure novels include *Journey to the Centre of the Earth* (1864), *Twenty Thousand Leagues Under the Sea* (1869) and *Around the World in Eighty Days* (1873).

Verona City on the River Adige, NE Italy, capital of Verona province. The city was captured by Rome in 89 BC and still has a Roman amphitheatre. It prospered under the Della Scala family in the 13th and 14th centuries and was held by Austria from 1797 to 1866, when it joined Italy. Industries: textiles, chemicals, paper, printing, wine. Pop. (1996) 254,000.

Veronese, Paolo Caliari (1528–88) Italian painter. A member of the VENETIAN SCHOOL, he excelled at painting large scenes featuring flamboyant pageants. He also painted religious and mythological themes. The Inquisition objected to his irreverent treatment of *The Last Supper* (1573) and he had to rename it *The Feast in the House of Levi*. Other celebrated works are his frescos for the Villa Barbaro near Treviso.

veronica (speedwell) Widely distributed genus of c.250 species of annual and perennial plants of the FIGWORT family. The small flowers are white, blue or pink. Height: 7.5–153cm (3–60in). Family Scrophulariaceae.

Verrocchio, Andrea del (1435–88) Florentine sculptor and painter, b. Andrea del Cione. His training as a goldsmith gave his work a remarkable delicacy, but he is best known for his bronze sculptures. His finest works equal DONATELLO's. One of Verrocchio's most celebrated works is the equestrian statue of Bartolomeo Colleoni in Venice. His pupils included LEONARDO DA VINCI.

verruca Form of WART on the sole of the foot that is painful because it is forced to grow inward. It is due to infection with the human papillomavirus.

Versace, Gianni (1946–97) Italian fashion designer. In the 1970s, Versace set up his own company and presented his first collection in 1978. He gained a reputation for flamboyant and brightly coloured designs. In 1982, he began to design costumes for the theatre. He was murdered in 1997.

Versailles City in N France, 16km (10mi) SW of Paris, capital of Yvelines department. It is famous for its former royal palace, now a world heritage site visited by two million tourists a year. Louis XIII built his hunting lodge at Versailles. In 1682, Louis XIV made Versailles his royal seat and transformed the lodge into a palace. The architects Louis LE VAU, Jules HARDOUIN-MANSART and Robert de Cotte built the monumental palace in a French classical style. The interior was designed by Charles LEBRUN and includes the royal apartments and the Hall of Mirrors. The magnificent gardens were landscaped by André LE NÔTRE. The park also contains the Grand and Petit Trianon palaces. It was a royal residence until the French Revolution (1789). It was the scene of the signing of peace treaties after the Franco-Prussian War and World War 1. Pop. (1990) 91,030.

Versailles, Treaty of (1919) Peace agreement concluding WORLD WAR 1, signed at VERSAILLES. It represented a compromise between President Wilson's FOURTEEN POINTS and the demands of the European allies for heavy penalties against Germany. German territorial concessions included Alsace-Lorraine to France and smaller areas to other neighbouring states, as well as the loss of its colonies. The Rhineland was demilitarized, strict limits were placed on German armed forces, and extensive REPARATIONS for war damage were imposed. The treaty also established the LEAGUE OF NATIONS. It was never ratified by the USA, which signed a separate treaty with Germany in 1921.

vertebra One of the bones making up the SPINE (vertebral column). Each vertebra is composed of a large solid body from the top of which wing-like processes project to either side. The human backbone is composed of 26 vertebrae (the five of the sacrum and four of the coccyx fuse together to form two solid bones) that are held together by ligaments and intervertebral disks.

vertebrate Animal with individual discs of bone or cartilage called VERTEBRA that surround or replace the embryonic NOTOCHORD to form a jointed backbone enclosing the spinal column. The principal division within vertebrates is between FISH and partly land-adapted forms (AMPHIBIANS), and the wholly land-adapted forms (REPTILES, BIRDS and MAMMALS, although some mammals have adapted to a totally aquatic existence). Phylum CHORDATA; subphylum Vertebrata.

vertigo Dizziness, often accompanied by nausea. It is due to disruption of the sense of balance and may be produced by ear disorder, reduced flow of blood to the brain caused by altitude, emotional upset or spinning rapidly.

vervet monkey *See* GUENON

Verwoerd, Hendrik Frensch (1901–66) South African statesman, prime minister (1958–66), b. Holland. A vocal advocate of APARTHEID, he promoted the policy of "separate development" of the races. In 1961, Verwoerd led South Africa out of the British Commonwealth. He was assassinated by a white extremist.

very high frequency (VHF) Range or band of radio waves with frequencies between 30 and 300MHz and wavelengths between 1 and 10m (3–33ft). This band is used for TELEVISION and FREQUENCY MODULATION (FM) RADIO broadcasts to provide high-quality reception.

Vesalius, Andreas (1514–64) Belgian physician and anatomist. Considered to be the founder of modern anatomy, his *On the Structure of the Human Body* (1543) was the first anatomy book to make use of accurate illustrations based on dissections.

Vespasian (AD 9–79) (Titus Flavius Vespasianus) Roman emperor (69–79). A successful general and administrator, he was leading the campaign against the Jews in Palestine when he was proclaimed emperor by his soldiers. Vespasian proved a capable ruler, extending and strengthening the empire, rectifying the budget deficit, widening qualifications for Roman citizenship and adding to the monumental buildings of Rome.

vespers Evening office of the Western Church. It is a service of thanksgiving and praise, in which the liturgy consists of psalms, a reading from the Bible, the Magnificat canticle, a hymn and a collect. Celebrated in the late afternoon, it is the basis of the Anglican service of evensong.

Vespucci, Amerigo (1454–1512) Italian maritime explorer. He was possibly the first to realize that the Americas constituted new continents, which were named after him by the German cartographer Martin Waldseemüller in 1507. Vespucci made at least two transatlantic voyages (1497–1504).

Vesta In Roman religion, goddess of fire and purity, supreme in the conduct of religious ceremonies. Vesta was guardian of the hearth and patron goddess of bakers.

vestal virgin In ancient Rome, priestess of the cult of VESTA, who tended the sacred fire in the Temple of Vesta and officiated at ceremonies in the goddess' honour. The vestals remained in the service of the temple for up to 30 years under vows of absolute chastity, violation of which was punishable by burial alive.

Vesuvius (Vesuvio) Active volcano on the Bay of Naples, S Italy. The earliest recorded eruption was in AD 79, when POMPEII and HERCULANEUM were destroyed.

The height of the volcano has changed with each of the 30 or so eruptions recorded since Roman times.

veterinary medicine Medical science that deals with diseases of animals. It was practised by the Babylonians and Egyptians *c.* 4,000 years ago. In the late 18th century, schools of veterinary medicine were established in Europe.

VHF Abbreviation of VERY HIGH FREQUENCY (VHF)

vetch Any annual or perennial plant of the genus *Vicia*, native to temperate and warm areas of the world. Most are tendril climbers, with pea-like flowers, and many are grown for food, green manure or forage. Family Fabaceae/Leguminosae.

vibraphone PERCUSSION musical instrument with metal bars of different lengths that are struck with sticks or mallets to produce various notes. Tubes beneath the bars vibrate at the same frequency as the bar above and magnify the sound.

viburnum Genus of flowering shrubs and small trees, native to North America and Eurasia. All have small, fleshy fruits containing single, flat seeds. There are *c.*120 species. Family Caprifoliaceae.

vicar Priest in the CHURCH OF ENGLAND who is in charge of a parish. In the ROMAN CATHOLIC CHURCH, the term "vicar" is used to mean "representative". The pope is called the Vicar of Christ. A **vicar apostolic** was originally a BISHOP representing the pope. Today, a vicar apostolic is appointed to govern territories that have not yet been organized into dioceses. A **vicar general** is appointed by and represents a bishop in the administration of a diocese. *See also* CURATE; PAPACY

Vicente, Gil (1465–1536) Portuguese dramatist. His plays, influenced by Renaissance Italy, vividly portray Portuguese society. They include *Auto da Mofina Mendes* (*c.*1534), *Comedia de Rubena* (*c.*1521) and *Auto da Lusitania* (*c.*1532).

Vicenza Industrial city in NE Italy, 64km (40mi) W of Venice. Founded as a Ligurian settlement, it was taken by Venice in 1404 and held by Austria from 1797 until 1866, when it was united with Italy. An important rail junction, its industries include steel, machinery, chemicals, textiles, printing, glass and gold jewellery. Pop. (1996) 108,000.

Vichy government (1940–45) Regime established in France after the defeat by Germany in June 1940. Its capital was the town of Vichy, Auvergne, central France. It held authority over French overseas possessions as well as the unoccupied part of France. After German forces occupied Vichy France in November 1942, it became little more than a puppet government. *See also* LAVAL, PIERRE; PÉTAIN, HENRI PHILIPPE

Vicksburg, Siege of (1863) Fourteen-month siege by Union forces under General GRANT during the American CIVIL WAR. The capture of Vicksburg, Mississippi, on 4 July gave the Union control of the Mississippi River and split the Confederacy in two.

Vico, Giambattista (1668–1744) Italian philosophical historian. In his *New Science* (1725, revised 1730 and 1744), he advanced the arguments of historicism, that all aspects of society and culture are relevant to the study of history and that the history of any period should be judged according to the standards and customs of that time and place.

Victor Emmanuel II (1820–78) King of Italy (1861–78). In 1849 he succeeded his father, Charles Albert, as king of Piedmont-Sardinia. From 1852, guided by CAVOUR, he strengthened his kingdom, formed a French alliance, and defeated Austria (1859–61). In 1861 he assumed the title of king of Italy. Rome became his new capital after French troops withdrew (1870).

Victor Emmanuel III (1869–1947) King of Italy (1900–46). In 1922 he appointed Benito MUSSOLINI as his prime minister. Although Mussolini established a dictatorship, the king retained the power to dismiss him and eventually did so in 1943. He abdicated in 1946.

Victoria (1819–1901) Queen of Great Britain and Ireland (1837–1901) and empress of India (1876–1901). A granddaughter of GEORGE III, she succeeded her uncle, WILLIAM IV. In 1840 Victoria married her first cousin, Prince ALBERT of SAXE-COBURG-GOTHA. During her reign, the longest in English history, the role of the monarchy was established as a ceremonial, symbolic institution with virtually no power but much influence. Victoria learned statecraft from her first prime minister, Lord MELBOURNE, and was greatly influenced by the hard-working Prince Albert. After Albert's death (1861) she went into lengthy seclusion and her neglect of public duties aroused republican sentiments. Victoria's domestic popularity was restored when she became Empress of India and with the golden (1887) and diamond (1897) jubilee celebrations. Among later prime ministers, she maintained excellent terms with Benjamin DISRAELI (who astutely flattered her) but was on frosty terms with William GLADSTONE (who lectured her). Victoria reigned over an empire containing 25% of the world's people and 30% of its land. Britain's trade and industry made it the world's richest country.

Victoria State in SE Australia, bounded by the Indian Ocean, the Bass Strait and the Tasman Sea. The capital is MELBOURNE (home to more than 65% of the state population); other major cities are Geelong, Ballarat and Bendigo. The region was part of NEW SOUTH WALES until 1851, when it became a separate colony. The population increased rapidly after 1851, when gold was discovered at Ballarat and Bendigo. Victoria became part of the Commonwealth of Australia in 1901. The area is crossed by the Australian Alps and other ranges of the Eastern Highlands. Irrigation is used extensively to grow wheat, oats, barley, fruit and vegetables, while sheep and dairy cattle are also important. Brown coal, natural gas and oil are the chief mineral resources. Industries: motor vehicles, textiles, food processing. Area: 227,620sq km (87,813sq mi). Pop. (1991) 4,487,000.

Victoria Capital of the Seychelles, in the Indian Ocean. Situated on NE Mahé island, it has a deep-water harbour and is the only town of significant size in the group, acting as the administrative, commercial and tourist centre of the country. Pop. (1993) 25,000.

Victoria City on SE VANCOUVER ISLAND, capital of BRITISH COLUMBIA province, SW Canada. Founded in 1843, it developed during the gold rush of 1858. Industries: timber, paper, shipbuilding, fish processing, tourism. It also has a large naval base. Pop. (1991) 71,228.

Victoria (Victoria Nyanza) Lake in E central Africa, bordered by Uganda, Kenya and Tanzania. The second-largest freshwater lake in the world, it is the chief reservoir of the River Nile. Its long coastline provides harbours for coastal towns, notably KAMPALA, Kisumu and Mwanza. Area: 68,000sq km (26,000sq mi).

Victoria Falls Waterfalls on the River Zambezi on the border of Zimbabwe and Zambia. Formed by water erosion along a fracture in the Earth's crust, they are divided by islets into five main sections. The first European discovery was in 1855 by David LIVINGSTONE. Maximum drop: 108m (355ft); Minimum width: 1,700m (5,580ft).

vicuña Graceful, even-toed, hoofed South American mammal. The smallest member of the CAMEL family, it is humpless and resembles the LLAMA. Its silky coat is

tawny brown with a yellowish bib under the neck. Vicuña wool was used by the Inca kings and is still expensive and rare. Height: 86cm (34in) at the shoulder; weight: 45kg (100lb). Family Camelidae; species *Vicugna vicugna*.

Vidal, Gore (1925–) US novelist, dramatist and essayist, b. Eugene Luther Vidal. His debut novel, *Williwaw* (1946), drew on his experiences in World War 2. *The City and the Pillar* (1948), a frank account of homosexuality, was a bestseller. Vidal's satires include *Myra Breckinridge* (1968) and its sequel *Myron* (1974). Political novels include *Washington, D.C.* (1967) and the trilogy *Burr* (1976), *1876* (1976) and *Lincoln* (1984). Vidal also wrote the screenplay for *Suddenly Last Summer* (1958). Other works include *Hollywood* (1990) and *Live from Golgotha* (1992).

video Term used in TELEVISION and computing to refer to electronic vision signals and to equipment and software associated with visual displays. The picture component of a television signal is often referred to as the video. *See also* VIDEO RECORDING

video disc Vinyl disc coated with a reflective, metallic surfacing. On one side of the reflective surface is etched a spiral of microscopic pits corresponding to digital information that can be picked up by a laser scanner and converted electronically to video pictures and sound. Since the late 1980s, video discs have been almost entirely superseded by the smaller, more comprehensive type of COMPACT DISC (CD) called a CD-ROM. A Digital

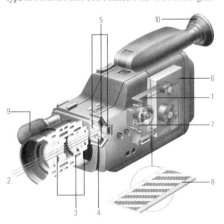

▲ videotape recording
A videotape recorder (camcorder) converts an image into an electrical signal, which can then be stored on magnetic tape (1). Light from an image (2) is focused by a series of lenses (3) and then split into its component colours by a prism (4). The red, green and blue light strike separate light-sensitive chips (5) that reproduce them in electronic form. The magnetic tape is housed in a protective case (6) that opens when inserted into the camcorder. The recording head (7) is angled and records information onto the tape in diagonal bands of magnetic particles (8). The helical scanning allows more information to be stored on a length of tape. A microphone (9) picks up sound, which is laid down in parallel to the visual information. Camcorders have a small television screen in the eyepiece (10) that allows the operator to play back and review the pictures taken. The camcorder can also be plugged directly into the television and the images played back.

Video Disc (DVD) holds 15 times as much information as a CD-ROM, and is used principally for storing computer games and feature films.

video game Game using electronically generated images displayed on a screen. High-quality graphics can produce good simulations of motor racing, football and flying. Some video games test the skill of a single player, while other games allow two or more players to compete. *See also* VIRTUAL REALITY

videotape recording Recording and reproducing sound and moving pictures using magnetic TAPE. The video recorder developed from the audio magnetic TAPE RECORDER, from which it differs in two significant respects: videotape is wider to accommodate the picture signals; and the relative speed at which the tape passes the magnetic head is greater in order to deal with the larger amount of information necessary for recording and reproducing pictures. *See artwork p.857. See also* MAGNETIC RECORDING; SOUND RECORDING

videotext General term for the different methods by which information can be brought to a television screen. Information that is transmitted by the broadcasting authority in parallel with the ordinary TV signals, and that may be screened simultaneously with or independently from other channels, is known as TELETEXT. The system that brings information to the screen from a computer databank via a telephone landline is called **videotex**.

Vienna (Wien) Capital of Austria, on the River DANUBE. Vienna became an important town when the Romans, but after their withdrawal in the 5th century it fell to a succession of invaders from E Europe. The first HABSBURG ruler was installed in 1276, and the city was the seat of the HOLY ROMAN EMPIRE from 1558 to 1806. Occupied by the French during the NAPOLEONIC WARS, it was later chosen as the site of the Congress of VIENNA. As the capital of the AUSTRO-HUNGARIAN EMPIRE, it was the cultural and social centre of 19th-century Europe under the emperor FRANZ JOSEPH. It suffered an economic and political collapse following the defeat of the Central Powers in World War 1. After World War 2, it was occupied (1945–55) by joint Soviet-Western forces. Vienna's historical buildings include the 12th-century St Stephen's Cathedral, the Schönbrunn (royal summer palace) and the Hofburg (a former residence of the Habsburgs). Industries: chemicals, textiles, furniture, clothing. Vienna is the world's third-largest German-speaking city (after Berlin and Hamburg). Pop. (1993) 1,589,052.

Vienna, Congress of (1814–15) European conference that settled international affairs after the NAPOLEONIC WARS. It attempted, as far as possible, to restore the Europe of pre-1789, and thus disappointed the nationalists and liberals. Among steps to prevent future European wars, it established the CONGRESS SYSTEM and the German Confederation, a loose association for purposes of defence. Austria was represented by METTERNICH; Britain by CASTLEREAGH; Prussia by FREDERICK WILLIAM II; Russia by ALEXANDER I; and France by TALLEYRAND.

Vienna Boys' Choir Austrian choir comprising 22 boys between the ages of eight and fourteen years. It was founded in 1498 as the choir of the court chapel. One of the world's best-known choirs, it tours regularly and makes recordings.

Vientiane (Viangchan) Capital and chief port of Laos, on the River Mekong, close to the Thai border, N central Laos. It was the capital of the Lao kingdom (1707–1828). The city became part of French INDOCHINA in 1893 and in 1899 became the capital of the French protectorate. Industries: textiles, brewing, cigarettes,

hides, wood products. It is a major source of opium for world markets. Pop. (1996) 532,000.

Viet Cong Nickname for the Vietnamese communist guerrillas who fought against the US-supported regime in South Vietnam during the VIETNAM WAR. After earlier, isolated revolts against the government of Ngo Dinh DIEM, the movement was unified (1960) as the National Liberation Front (NLF), modelled on the VIET MINH.

Viet Minh Vietnamese organization that fought for independence from the French (1946–54). It resisted the Japanese occupation of French INDOCHINA during World War 2. After the war, when the French refused to recognize it as a provisional government, it began operations against the colonial forces. The French were forced to withdraw after their defeat at DIEN BIEN PHU (1954).

Vietnam Republic that occupies an S-shaped strip of land in Southeast Asia. The coastal plains include two densely populated river delta regions: in the N, the River Red delta is the site of HANOI and HAIPHONG; in the S, the MEKONG delta contains HO CHI MINH CITY. Inland, the Annam Cordillera forms much of the boundary with Cambodia. In the NW, the highlands extend into Laos and China. **Climate** Vietnam has a tropical climate. The summer months are hot and wet with monsoon winds. The driest months, January to March, are cooler. **Vegetation** Forests cover *c*.30% of Vietnam and include teak and ebony trees. About 17% of the land is farmed. There are some mangrove swamps.

History and politics In 111 BC, China seized Vietnam, naming it ANNAM. In 939, it became independent. In 1558, it split into two parts: TONKIN in the N, ruled from Hanoi and Annam in the S, ruled from Hué. In 1802, with French support, Vietnam was united as the empire of Vietnam under Nguyen Anh. The French took Saigon in 1859 and by 1887 had formed INDOCHINA from the union of Tonkin, Annam and Cochin China. Japan conquered Vietnam during World War 2 and established a Vietnamese state under Emperor BAO DAI. After the war, Bao Dai's government collapsed, and the nationalist VIET MINH, led by HO CHI MINH, set up a Vietnamese republic. In 1946, the French tried to reassert control and war broke out. Despite aid from the USA, they were finally defeated at DIEN BIEN PHU. In 1954, Vietnam was divided along the 17th parallel, with North Vietnam under the communist government of Ho Chi Minh and South Vietnam under the French-supported Bao Dai. In 1955, Bao Dai was deposed and Ngo Dinh DIEM was elected president. Despite his authoritarian regime, Diem was recognized as the legal ruler of Vietnam by many western countries. North Vietnam, supported by China and the Soviet Union, extended its influence into South Vietnam, mainly through the VIET CONG. The USA became increasingly involved in what they perceived to be the fight against communism. The conflict soon escalated into the VIETNAM WAR. After US forces were withdrawn in 1975, Ho Chi Minh's nationalist forces overran South Vietnam and it surrendered. In 1976, the reunited Vietnam became a socialist republic. In the late 1970s, Vietnam invaded Cambodia, defeating the KHMER ROUGE government. It withdrew its troops in 1989. Vietnam's weak economy was improved in the late 1980s and 1990s with the introduction of free-market economic reforms, known as *Doi Moi*. In 1995, it became a member of ASEAN.

VIETNAM
AREA: 331,689sq km (128,065sq mi)
POPULATION: 82,427,000
CAPITAL (POPULATION): Hanoi (3,056,000)

Economy Vietnam is a low-income developing country (1992 GDP per capita, US$1,010). In 1997, its economy was badly hit by the financial crisis in Southeast Asia, and in 1998 the đông was devalued by 5%. Agriculture employs 67% of the workforce. The main crop is rice, of which it is the world's fifth-largest producer. Other crops include bananas, coffee, peanuts and rubber. Vietnam also produces oil, phosphates, and coal; natural gas resources have been found.

Vietnamese National language of VIETNAM, spoken by *c.*70 million people. It is part of the Muong branch of the Mon-Khmer sub-family of Asiatic languages and derives some of its vocabulary from Mandarin Chinese.

Vietnam War (1954–75) Conflict between US-backed South Vietnam and the VIET CONG, who had the support of communist North Vietnam. It followed the defeat of the French at DIEN BIEN PHU (1954) and the partition of Vietnam. South Vietnamese elections were cancelled in 1956 by President Ngo Dinh DIEM. HO CHI MINH denounced the action and the Viet Cong launched an insurgency. Fuelled by fear of the spread of communism, the US supported the Diem government and sent its first troops in 1961. The US received token support from its allies in the Pacific region, and North Vietnam was supplied by China and the Soviet Union. In 1963, Diem was overthrown and executed. In 1965, the US began bombing North Vietnam. As fighting intensified, US troops were committed in greater numbers: by 1968 there were more than 500,000. In spite of US technological superiority and air supremacy, military stalemate ensued. The unrepresentative South Vietnamese government, US involvement in war crimes, heavy casualties and daily TV coverage made the war highly unpopular in the USA. A peace agreement, negotiated by Henry KISSINGER and Le Duc Tho, was signed in Paris in 1973. In 1975, South Vietnam was overrun by North Vietnamese forces, and the country was united under communist rule. The war had cost 50,000 American lives, 400,000 South Vietnamese and one million Viet Cong and North Vietnamese.

Vignola, Giacomo Barozzi da (1507–73) Italian architect, who succeeded MICHELANGELO as architect of St Peter's, Rome (1567–73). His Gesú Church, Rome (1568), with its revolutionary design uniting clergy and congregation more closely, has been widely copied. His other major works include the Palazzo Farnese, Caprarola (1559), and the Tempieto di San Andrea, Rome (1550).

Vigny, Alfred de (1797–1863) French poet, dramatist and novelist. Pessimistic in tone, his work often emphasizes the lonely struggle of the individual in a hostile universe, as in the quintessential romantic drama, *Chatterton* (1853). Vigny's best poems are contained in *Poems Ancient and Modern* (1826), and his fiction includes the pioneering French historical novel, *Cinq-Mars* (1826). *See also* ROMANTICISM

Vigo, Jean (1905–34) French film director. He died tragically young of leukaemia. Vigo's anarchic debut feature, *Zéro de Conduite* (1933), was banned in France until 1945. *Atalante* (1934), his second and last feature, is an elegant amalgam of social realism and poetic lyricism, set in a dream-like Parisian landscape.

Vigo Seaport city on Vigo Bay, Galicia, NW Spain, near the Portuguese border. It was the scene of a naval battle in 1702, when an Anglo-Dutch fleet attacked Spanish galleons carrying a cargo of gold from the New World. Industries: fishing, fish processing and canning (mostly tuna and sardines), boat-building. Pop. (1995) 191,000.

Vikings Scandinavian, seaborne marauders, traders and settlers, who spread throughout much of Europe and the North Atlantic region between the 9th and 11th centuries. The remarkable Viking expansion seems to have been caused by rapid population growth and consequent scarcity of good farming land, as well as the desire for new sources of wealth. It was made possible by their advanced maritime technology that enabled them to cross N European waters in a period when other sailors feared to venture out of sight of land. They were in many respects more advanced than other European peoples, notably in metalwork. Although they first appeared in their greatly feared "longships" as raiders on the coasts of NW Europe, later groups came to settle. Swedes, known as Varangians, founded the first Russian state at Novgorod and traded via the River Volga in Byzantium and Persia. Danes conquered much of N and E England. Norwegians created kingdoms in N Britain and Ireland, founding Dublin (*c.*840) and other cities; they also colonized Iceland and established settlements in Greenland. A short-lived settlement, VINLAND, was established in North America by LEIF ERICSSON in *c.*1003. In the early 10th century, the Vikings settled in Normandy. Anarchic conditions in 10th-century Scandinavia resulted in the formation of larger, more powerful kingdoms, and Viking expansion declined. It was renewed in a different form with the conquest of England by King Sweyn of Denmark in 1013 and the Norman Conquest of 1066.

Viking space mission (1976) US space project to investigate conditions on MARS. Two spacecraft, Viking 1 and Viking 2, each attached to separate vehicles that orbited the planet, made the first successful landings on Mars. They transmitted much information to Earth, including dramatic photographs of the surface. *See also* SPACE EXPLORATION

Villa, "Pancho" (Francisco) (1877–1923) Mexican revolutionary leader. An outlaw, he later joined the forces of Francisco MADERO (1909) during the MEXICAN REVOLUTION. Villa sided with Venustiano CARRANZA for some time but later supported Emiliano ZAPATA. Angered by US recognition of Carranza's government, he murdered US citizens in N Mexico and New Mexico. In 1920 Villa was pardoned in return for agreeing to retire from politics. He was assassinated three years later.

villa Large, country house of the ROMAN EMPIRE and post-Roman period. In ancient Rome, they were the private residences of important citizens. They had spacious reception rooms, often with MOSAIC floors and sometimes even underfloor heating. Since then the term has been used to describe detached houses in a huge variety of sizes and styles.

Villa-Lobos, Heitor (1887–1959) Brazilian composer and conductor. His *Chôros* compositions were influenced by Native South American folk music and the music of Claude Debussy. Villa Lobos' range of works include operas, ballets, symphonies, religious and chamber music. His nine *Bachianas Brasileiras* are a Brazilian transcription of the music of J.S. Bach.

Villehardouin, Geoffroi de (1150–1213) French historian. He was a leader of the Fourth CRUSADE. Villehardouin's incomplete account of the crusade, *Conquest of Constantinople*, was the first historical chronicle in French.

villi In anatomy, small, finger-like projections of a MUCOUS MEMBRANE such as that which lines the inner walls of the SMALL INTESTINE. They increase the absorptive surface area of the gut. In digestion, intestinal villi absorb most of the products of food broken down in the STOMACH, DUODENUM and ILEUM.

Villon, François (1430–1463) French lyric poet, b. François de Montcorbier or François des Loges. He led

▶ **violin** Late 17th-century violin. The violin was perfected in Italy by the Amati, Stradivari and Guarneri families from 1650 to 1740. The great brilliance of violin tone soon overwhelmed the softer tones of the viols, which died out.

a troubled life after killing a priest in 1455. Villon wrote the famous *Ballad of a Hanged Man* while awaiting execution in 1462 (the sentence was later commuted to banishment). Among his other major works, which embrace a variety of forms, are *Le Petit Testament*, a satirical will in verse, and the more subtle, *Le Grand Testament*, which is in part a lament for lost youth.

Vilnius Capital of Lithuania, on the River Neris. Founded in 1323 as the capital of the grand duchy of Lithuania, the city declined after the union of Lithuania-Poland. It has been the capital under many different rulers since that time. Despite World War 2 bombing, the old city retains many of its historic synagogues, churches and civic buildings, as well as remnants of its 14th-century castle and fortifications. Industries: engineering, chemicals, textiles, food processing. Pop. (1996) 573,000.

Vincent de Paul, Saint (1581–1660) French priest. He founded the Congregation of the Mission (or Lazarists). In 1633, he helped to found the Sisters of Charity of St Vincent de Paul to minister to the sick, the old, and orphans. He was canonized in 1737.

vine Plant with a long, thin stem that climbs rocks, plants and supports. To aid their climb, vines develop modifications such as tendrils, disc-like holdfasts, adventitious roots and runners. Examples are tropical LIANA, wild GRAPE and morning glory.

vinegar Any of various types of liquid condiment and preservative based on a weak solution of ETHANOIC ACID. It is produced commercially by the fermentation of alcohol. The major type of vinegar is known as malt vinegar, which, when distilled, becomes white (or clear) vinegar. Vinegar can also be processed from cider or wine.

Vinland Region of North America settled by VIKINGS from Greenland, led by LEIF ERICSSON in c.1003. The existence of land W of Greenland had been reported a few years earlier. Leif stayed for one season only, but at least two other expeditions settled there briefly. Vinland was soon abandoned because of the hostility of local people.

viol Fretted STRINGED INSTRUMENT, played with a bow. It is held on or between the knees and, in its most usual shape, has sloping shoulders and a flat back. The six strings are tuned in fourths, in the same manner as the LUTE. A possible derivative is the modern DOUBLE BASS, which shows its ancestry by being tuned in fourths (unlike members of the violin family). Viols are still used today for the authentic performance of early music.

viola STRINGED INSTRUMENT of the VIOLIN family. It is slightly larger than the violin, and its four strings are tuned a fifth lower. It is the tenor member of a string quartet.

violet Any of c.400 species of herbs and shrublets of the genus *Viola*, found worldwide. Violets may be

annual or perennial, with five-petalled flowers that grow singly on stalks; usually blue, violet, lilac, yellow or white. Family Violaceae.

violin STRINGED INSTRUMENT. It is thought to have derived from the *lira da braccio*, a Renaissance bowed instrument, and the rebec. It was perfected in Italy by the AMATI, STRADIVARI and GUARNERI families between 1650 and 1740. The body is assembled from curved, wooden panels, the front pierced by two *f*-shaped sound-holes. Four taut strings are played by drawing a bow across them, or sometimes by plucking them with the fingers (pizzicato).

violoncello *See* CELLO

viper Any of 150 species of poisonous SNAKES characterized by a pair of long, hollow, venom-injecting fangs in the front of the upper jaw. The fangs can be folded back when not in use. The common adder (*Vipera berus*) of Europe and E Asia has a dark, zigzag band along its back. Length: to 3m (10ft). Family Viperidae.

Virchow, Rudolf (1821–1902) German pathologist. His discovery that all CELLS arise from other cells completed the formulation of the cell theory and repudiated the theories of spontaneous generation. Virchow also studied the nature of disease at a cellular level and established the science of cellular pathology.

Virgil (70–19 BC) (Publius Vergilius Maro) Roman poet. He gained a high literary reputation in Rome with the *Eclogues* (42–37 BC) and the *Georgics* (37–30), a pastoral but instructive work on farming and country life. Virgil's greatest work was the *Aeneid*, which established him as an epic poet. It relates the adventures of the Trojan hero AENEAS and echoes the themes of Homer's *Odyssey* and *Iliad*. Unfinished at his death, it was published at the command of Emperor AUGUSTUS.

virginal Musical instrument of the HARPSICHORD family. The strings, a single set running nearly parallel to the keyboard, are plucked by quills. Two keyboards, differing in size and pitch, were sometimes incorporated into the same case. Virginals were particularly popular in 16th- and 17th-century England.

virgin birth Christian doctrine teaching that JESUS CHRIST was conceived by the Blessed Virgin MARY through the power of the HOLY SPIRIT and without the involvement of a human male. That Jesus had no earthly father is a basic tenet of Roman Catholicism, all the Eastern Orthodox Churches and most Protestant Churches.

Virginia State in E USA, on the Atlantic coast, the most northerly of the "southern states"; the capital is RICHMOND. The coastal plain is low-lying. To the W the Piedmont Plateau rises to the BLUE RIDGE MOUNTAINS, and there are extensive forests. The first permanent British settlement in North America was at JAMESTOWN (1607). Virginia evolved an aristocratic plantation society based on vast tobacco holdings. Virginia's leaders were in the forefront of the AMERICAN REVOLUTION. During the CIVIL WAR, Richmond acted as the Confederate capital, and Virginia was the main battleground of the war. In 1870, Virginia was readmitted to the Union. Farming is an important part of Virginia's economy, and the chief crops include tobacco, peanuts, grain, vegetables and fruits. Dairying and poultry are also widespread. Industries: chemicals, shipbuilding, fishing, transportation equipment. Coal is the most important mineral deposit. Stone, sand and gravel are quarried. Area: 105,710sq km (40,814sq mi). Pop. (2000) 7,078,515.

Virginia Beach City on the Atlantic Ocean, SE Virginia. Site of the Cape Henry memorial cross (commemorating the first landing of English colonists, 1607), and of the oldest brick house in the USA, it is now a tourist centre with good beaches and recreational facilities. Its economy is helped by market gardening and military complexes. The population increased by c.60% between 1980 and 1992, making it Virginia's largest city. Pop. (1992) 417,061.

Virginia companies Two English companies chartered (1606) by JAMES I to establish colonies in America. The **Virginia Company of London** was to found a colony 100 miles inland from the coast between latitudes 34°N and 41°N; the **Virginia Company of Plymouth** was to establish one of the same size between latitudes 38°N and 45°N. The London Company founded the first permanent English colony in 1607, but lost its charter in 1624. The Plymouth, which was less successful, was reorganized as the Council for New England in 1620.

Virgin Islands, British British colony in the West Indies. It is a group of 36 islands that form part of the ANTILLES group; the capital is Road Town (on Tortola, the main island). First settled in the 17th century, the islands formed part of the LEEWARD ISLANDS colony until 1956. The chief economic activity is tourism. Area: 130sq km (59sq mi). Pop. (2000) 15,000.

Virgin Islands, US Group of 68 islands in the Lesser ANTILLES in the West Indies. They are administered by the US with the status of an "unincorporated territory". The chief islands are St Croix and St Thomas, which includes the capital Charlotte Amalie (1990 pop. 12,331). Spanish from 1553, the islands were Danish in 1917, when they were bought by the USA for US$25 million in order to protect the northern approaches to the newly completed PANAMA CANAL. Tourism is the biggest money earner. Industries: oil refining, aluminium, textiles, rum, pharmaceuticals, perfumes. Area: 344sq km (133sq mi). Pop. (2000) 135,000.

Virgin Mary *See* MARY

Virgo (Virgin) Equatorial constellation on the ecliptic between Leo and Libra. It lies in a region of the sky that has many galaxies and galaxy clusters. The brightest star is the 1st-magnitude Alpha Virginis, or Spica.

virology Study of VIRUSES. The existence of viruses was established in 1892 by D. Ivanovski, a Russian botanist, who found that the causative agent of tobacco mosaic disease could pass through a porcelain filter impermeable to BACTERIA. The introduction of the ELECTRON MICROSCOPE in the 1940s made it possible to view viruses.

virtual reality Use of computer graphics to simulate a three-dimensional environment that users can explore as if it were real. A virtual reality system can allow an architect to see what the inside of a building will look like before construction begins. The computer images are produced using the architect's drawings of the building. Some entertainment machines use virtual reality to simulate space-flight adventures and various ball games.

virus Sub-microscopic infectious organism. Viruses vary in size from 10 to 300 nanometers and contain only genetic material in the form of DNA or RNA. Viruses are incapable of independent existence: they can grow and reproduce only when they enter another cell, such as a bacterium or animal cell, because they lack energy-producing and protein-synthesizing functions. When they enter a cell, viruses subvert the host's metabolism so that viral reproduction is favoured. Control of viruses is difficult because harsh measures are required to kill them. The animal body has, however, evolved some protective means, such as production of INTERFERON and of ANTIBODIES directed against specific viruses. Where the specific agent can be isolated, VACCINES can be developed, but some viruses change so rapidly that vaccines become ineffective. *See also* IMMUNE SYSTEM

Visconti, Luchino (1906–76) Italian film director. His debut film *Ossessione* (1942) was a pioneering work of Italian NEO-REALISM. Other films include *Senso* (1953), *Rocco and His Brothers* (1960), *The Leopard* (1963), *Death in Venice* (1971) and *Conversation Piece* (1975). Visconti's later work is characterized by a more opulent style. He was also acclaimed for his theatre and opera work, and helped to develop the career of Maria CALLAS.

Visconti Italian family that ruled Milan from the 13th century until 1447. Ottone Visconti (c.1207–95) was appointed archbishop of Milan in 1262 and used his position to become the first Visconti *signore* (lord) of Milan. Supporters of the GHIBELLINES, the Visconti established control over Lombardy in the 14th century, and in 1349 the title of *signore* became hereditary. Visconti lordship of Milan passed to the Sforza family in 1447.

viscosity Resistance to flow of a FLUID because of internal friction. The more viscous the fluid, the slower it flows. Viscosity is large for liquids and extremely small for gases.

Vishnu Major god of HINDUISM; one of the supreme triad of gods, along with BRAHMA and SHIVA. Vishnu was mentioned as a sun god in the VEDAS (c. 1500–c.1200 BC). Over the next 1,000 years or more, his importance grew and he became an amalgam of local cultic gods and heroes. In mythology, Vishnu is worshipped as a preserver and restorer. According to Hindu tradition, he reigns in heaven with his wife, LAKSHMI, the goddess of wealth. From time to time, he comes into the world to fight evil, assuming a different incarnation each time. His incarnations have included RAMA and KRISHNA.

Visigoths *See* GOTH

vision *See* SIGHT

Vistula (Wisala) Longest river in Poland. It rises in the Carpathian Mountains of W Poland and flows NW through Warsaw, then NW through Toruń to enter the Gulf of Danzig at Gdańsk. The major waterway of Poland, it serves a large area through a tributary system. Canals link it with other important rivers both E and W. Length: 1,090km (675mi).

vitalism Philosophical theory that all living organisms derive their characteristic qualities from a universal life force. Vitalists hold that the force operating on living matter is peculiar to such matter and is quite different from any forces outside animate things. In the late 20th century, few scientists give vitalism much credence, but it has influenced many forms of alternative medicine.

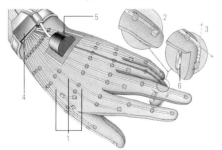

▲ **virtual reality** A data glove measures the movements of the wearer's hand allowing him/her to manipulate objects in virtual reality. Fibre-optic cables (1) detect the flexing of the hand. Light travels up and down the cables (2). When the cables are bent (3), they no longer reflect light back to the interface board (4). A position sensor (5) detects the movement of the glove in three dimensions. Fingertip padding (6) convinces the user they are touching an actual object.

vitamin Organic compound that is essential in small amounts to the maintenance and healthy growth of all animals. Vitamins are classified as either water-soluble (B and C) or fat-soluble (A, D, E and K). They are usually taken in the DIET, but today most can be made synthetically. Some are synthesized in the body. Many vitamins act as coenzymes, helping ENZYMES in RESPIRATION and other metabolic processes. Lack of a particular vitamin can lead to a deficiency disease. **Vitamin E** is important in reproduction and many other biological processes. **Vitamin D** helps the body absorb phosphorus and calcium. It is essential for the normal growth of bone and teeth. Existing in human skin (activated by sunlight), vitamin D is also found in fish-liver oil, yeast and egg yolk. **Vitamin C** (ascorbic acid) is commonly found in fruits and vegetables. It helps the body resist infection and is essential to normal metabolism. **Vitamin B** is actually a group of 12 vitamins, important in assisting the process by which energy is produced in the body (RESPIRATION). Vitamin B_1 (THIAMINE) occurs in yeast and cereals. Another B vitamin is niacin (nicotinic acid) found in milk, meat, and green vegetables. Vitamin B_{12} is needed for the formation of blood cells. It is found especially in meat, liver and eggs. **Vitamin A** (retinol), found in fish-liver oil, is important for healthy eyes. *See also* RIBOFLAVIN

Vitruvius (active early 1st century AD) Roman architect and engineer. His encyclopedic *De Architectura* (before AD 27) covers almost every aspect of ancient architecture, including town planning, types of buildings and materials. It is the only work of its type to survive from the ancient world.

Vitus, Saint (active 4th century) Italian martyr. Secretly raised as a Christian by his nurse, he was put to death during the persecutions of DIOCLETIAN. He is the patron saint of actors.

Vivaldi, Antonio (1675–1741) Italian composer. A master of the CONCERTO and a virtuoso violinist, he helped to standardize the three-movement concerto form and to develop the *concerto grosso* (a concerto for two or more solo instruments). His best-known work is *The Four Seasons* (1725). He also composed sacred vocal music and *c.*50 operas, of which 20 survive.

viviparity (vivipary) Process or trait among animals of giving birth to live young. Placental mammals show the highest development of viviparity, in which the offspring develops inside the body, within the mother's UTERUS.

vivisection Dissection of living bodies for experimental purposes. Work with laboratory animals in testing drugs, vaccines and pharmaceuticals frequently involves such dissections. The ethical issue of experimenting on living animals is a matter of controversy.

Vladimir City on the N bank of the River Klyazma, Russia. Founded early in the 12th century by Vladimir II of Kiev, it is one of Russia's oldest cities. The grand dukes of Moscow were crowned here in the 14th century. Tourists are drawn partly by three 12th-century buildings – the two cathedrals and the Golden Gate (a fortified city gate). Industries: chemicals, cotton textiles, plastics, tractors, machine tools, electrical goods. Pop. (1994) 338,000.

Vladimir I (the Great) (956–1015) Grand Duke of Kiev and first Christian ruler of Russia (980–1015). Vladimir raised an army of VIKING mercenaries in 979 and conquered Polotsk and Kiev. Proclaimed prince of all Russia, he extended Russian territories, conquering parts of Poland and Lithuania. He became a Christian and married a Byzantine princess (988). St Vladimir, as he is also called, established the Greek Orthodox Church in Russia.

Vladivostock Main port, naval base and cultural centre of SIBERIA, Russia. It is located around a sheltered harbour on the Pacific coast, 50km (30mi) from the Chinese border. Founded in 1860 as a military post, the city developed as a naval base after 1872. Vladivostock is the main E terminus of the TRANS-SIBERIAN RAILWAY. The harbour is kept open in winter by ice-breakers and is a major base for fishing fleets. Industries: ship repairing, oil refining, metal-working, timber products. Pop. (1994) 637,000.

Vlaminck, Maurice (1876–1958) French painter, graphic artist and writer. One of the leading exponents of FAUVISM, Vlaminck painted with colours squirted straight from the tube, producing exuberant landscapes, which were partly inspired by the work of VAN GOGH. In 1908 he began using darker colours and studied CÉZANNE in an attempt to give his painting more weight.

vocal cords *See* LARYNX

vocational education Instruction in industrial or commercial skills. A range of levels of vocational training and qualification are available from schools and colleges, often in collaboration with organizations concerned to improve training and quality standards in particular areas of employment.

vodka Colourless, alcoholic spirit distilled from fermented potatoes, rye or wheat. In Russia and Poland, where vodka is the national alcoholic drink, the raw spirit is subject to multiple distillation and further refining processes. Herbal flavourings are sometimes added during manufacture. It may be drunk straight or with mixers, or form part of a cocktail. A strong drink, vodka may be up to 50% alcohol by volume.

Voice of America (VOA) Radio station subsidized by the US government. It presents news, other generally factual information, and cultural programmes aimed at both English-speaking citizens of foreign countries and US troops serving abroad. VOA was originally set up by the US Office of War Information in 1943–44 to broadcast war news and propaganda. *See also* WORLD SERVICE

Vojvodina Autonomous province in N Serbia, bordered by Croatia, Hungary and Romania. The capital is NOVI SAD. From 1849 to 1860 it was the independent crown land of Vojvodina, but it was ceded to Yugoslavia in 1920. Given nominal autonomy by Belgrade in 1946, it remains firmly part of Serbia. Only *c.*50% of the population are Serbs: the rest are Hungarian (19%), Croats, Slovaks and Romanians. The province is densely populated with a fertile agricultural plain. Industries: fruit, cattle, food processing. Area: 21,500sq km (8,301sq mi). Pop. (1991) 2,013,889.

volcanism (vulcanism) Volcanic activity. The term includes all aspects of the process: the eruption of molten and gaseous matter, the building up of cones and mountains, and the formation of LAVA flows and GEYSERS.

volcano Vent from which molten rock or LAVA, solid rock debris and gases issue. Volcanoes may be of the **central vent** type, where the material erupts from a single pipe, or of the **fissure** type, where material is extruded along an extensive fracture. Volcanoes are commonly classed as active, dormant or extinct.

vole Short-tailed, small-eared, RODENT of the Northern Hemisphere. Most voles are greyish-brown, herbivorous ground-dwellers. The semi-aquatic water vole is the largest. Length: to 18cm (7in). Family Cricetidae.

Volga Europe's longest river, at 3,750km (2,330mi), in E European Russia. The river rises in the Valdai Hills, then flows E past Rzhev to Kazan, where it turns S. It continues SW to Volgograd and then SE to enter the Caspian Sea below Astrakhan. The Volga is connected to the Baltic

Sea by the Volga-Baltic Waterway, to Moscow by the Moscow Canal, and to the Sea of Azov (and the Black Sea) by the Volga-Don Canal. Many dams and hydroelectric power stations have been constructed along its course. Navigable for *c.*3,550km (2,200mi), it carries about two thirds of Russia's river freight traffic.

Volgograd (formerly Stalingrad) Major Russian inland port on the River VOLGA, the E terminus of the Volga-Don Canal. During the Civil War that followed the Russian Revolution, it was defended by Bolshevik troops under Stalin (1918–20) and was renamed Stalingrad in his honour (1925). In the winter of 1942–43 it was almost completely destroyed in a fierce battle that halted the German advance. Rebuilt after World War 2 and renamed Volgograd in 1961, it is a major rail and industrial centre. Industries: oil-refining, shipbuilding, chemicals, aluminum, steel, farm vehicles. Pop. (1994) 1,000,000.

volleyball Game in which a ball is volleyed by hand over a net across the centre of a court by two six-a-side teams. The court is 18m (59ft) long by 9m (29ft 6in) wide; the top of the net is 2.4m (8ft) high. The object of the game is to get the ball to touch the ground within the opponents' half of the court or to oblige an opponent to touch the ball before it goes directly out of court. Only the serving team can score, and failure to score loses service; 15 points wins a set, and a game is the best of five sets. Volleyball has been included in the Olympic Games since 1964.

Volstead Act *see* PROHIBITION

volt (symbol V) SI unit of electric potential and ELECTROMOTIVE FORCE (EMF). It is the POTENTIAL DIFFERENCE between two points on a conducting wire carrying a current of one ampere when the power dissipated is 1 watt.

Volta West African river, *c.*470km (290mi) long, formed by the confluence of the rivers Black Volta and White Volta at New Tamale, central Ghana. The river flows S into the Gulf of Guinea at Ada. In 1965, it was dammed at Akosombo to form Lake Volta.

Voltaire (1694–1778) French philosopher, historian, dramatist and poet, b. François Marie Arouet. He is the outstanding figure of the French ENLIGHTENMENT. Voltaire spent much of his life combating intolerance and injustice and attacking institutions, such as the Church. While in the Bastille (1717), Voltaire wrote his first tragedy *Oedipe* (1718). In 1726, Voltaire was beaten and returned to the Bastille for insulting a nobleman. While in exile in England (1726–29), he was strongly influenced by John LOCKE and Isaac NEWTON and wrote a classic biography of Charles XII of Sweden. Back in France, Voltaire wrote several tragedies and the eulogy *Philosophical Letters* (1734), which provoked official censure. Voltaire corresponded for many years with FREDERICK II (THE GREAT) and contributed to DIDEROT's *Encyclopédie*. His best-known work, the philosophical romance *Candide* (1759), was published anonymously. Other works that express his philosophy of RATIONALISM include *Jeannot et Colin* (1764) and *Essay on Morals* (1756). The *Dictionnaire philosophique* (1764) is a collection of his thoughts on contemporary matters.

voltmeter Instrument for measuring the voltage (POTENTIAL DIFFERENCE) between two points in an electrical CIRCUIT. Voltmeters are always connected in parallel with the components whose voltages are being measured. A voltmeter has a high internal RESISTANCE compared with the resistance across which it is connected. *See also* AMMETER

volume Amount of space taken up by a body. Volume is measured in cubic units, such as cm³ (cubic centimetres).

voluntary muscle (skeletal MUSCLE) In human beings and other mammals, the most plentiful of the three types of muscle comprising the bulk of the body. It is under conscious control and has a striped appearance under a microscope. *See also* INVOLUNTARY MUSCLE

vomiting Act of bringing up the contents of the stomach by way of the mouth. Vomiting is a reflex mechanism that may be activated by any of a number of stimuli, including dizziness, pain, gastric irritation or shock. It may also be a symptom of serious disease.

Von Braun, Wernher (1912–77) US aeronautical engineer, b. Germany. In World War 2 he was responsible for building the V-2 ROCKET. In 1945, Von Braun went to the USA, where he developed the Jupiter ROCKET that took the first US satellite, Explorer 1, into space (1958). In 1960, he joined the NATIONAL AERONAUTICS AND SPACE ADMINISTRATION (NASA) and developed the Saturn rocket that took astronauts to the Moon.

Vondel, Joost von den (1587–1679) Dutch poet and dramatist. Vondel struggled against the handicaps of humble birth, limited education and religious persecution to produce outstanding work based on biblical and classical sources. Of his trilogy of plays, *Lucifer* (1654), a tragedy, *Adam in Exile* (1664) and *Noah* (1667), the first is generally regarded as his masterpiece. He also wrote in various poetic genres.

Vonnegut, Kurt, Jr (1922–) US novelist. He often draws on the conventions of fantasy to satirize the horrors of the 20th century. Vonnegut's novels, such as *Player Piano* (1952), *Slaughterhouse-Five* (1969) and *Hocus Pocus* (1991), are characterized by their innovative experimentation with time sequences and narrative. He has published collections of short stories and volumes of essays. Other works include *Timequake* (1997).

Von Neumann, John (1903–57) US mathematician, b. Budapest. He left Hungary to teach at Princeton University (1930–33) and then at the Institute of Advanced Studies. In mathematics, Von Neumann helped to develop GAME THEORY. His early contribution to QUANTUM THEORY was followed by work on the atomic bomb at Los Alamos. Von Neumann is chiefly celebrated for his role in the early development of COMPUTERS. One of his first designs was used to test (1952) the first hydrogen bomb.

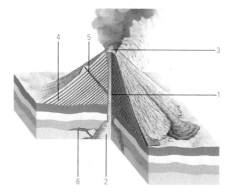

▲ **volcano** Volcanoes are formed when molten lava (1) from a magma chamber (2) in the Earth's crust forces its way to the surface (3). The classic cone-shaped volcano is formed of alternating layers of cooled lava and cinders (4) thrown out during an eruption. Side vents (5) can occur, and when offshoots of lava are trapped below the surface, laccoliths (6) are formed.

voodoo Religious belief of African origin. It is prevalent in parts of Africa but is better known as the national religion of Haiti. Adherents believe in the reincarnate qualities of **Loa**, which include deified ancestors, local gods, and Roman Catholic saints. Loa possesses the believers during dreams or ceremonies, which include dancing and hypnotic trances.

Voronezh Industrial port on the River Voronezh, W central Russia, capital of Voronezh province. Founded as a fortress in 1586, it became a shipbuilding centre under Peter I. During World War 2 the city was almost totally destroyed and most of it has been rebuilt. Industries: locomotives, machinery, synthetic rubber, oil, chemicals, food processing, television sets. Pop. (1994) 905,000.

Voroshilov, Kliment Yefremovich (1881–1969) Soviet statesman, president (1953–60). He joined the Bolsheviks in 1903 and took an military role in the RUSSIAN REVOLUTION (1917). Voroshilov was a Red Army commander in the civil war (1918–20) before becoming commissar for defence (1925–40). He commanded the Red Army on the NW front in World War 2. Voroshilov became president on the death of STALIN, but was implicated in a plot against KHRUSCHEV and resigned.

Vorster, Balthazar Johannes (1915–83) South African statesman, prime minister (1966–78). Imprisoned during World War 2 as a Nazi sympathizer, he was a staunch advocate of APARTHEID under Hendrik VERWOERD and succeeded him as prime minister and Nationalist Party leader. Vorster established Transkei as a "bantustan" and suppressed the SOWETO uprising (1976). He invaded Angola to try and prevent Namibian independence. In 1978, Vorster became president, but corruption charges forced his resignation in 1979.

vortex Eddy or whirlpool observed in FLUID motion. Vortices cannot occur in ideal (non-viscous) fluid motion, but they are important in the study of real fluids. In particular, the vortices occurring behind aerofoils are of great interest in aerodynamic design.

vorticism British art movement. Derived from CUBISM and Italian FUTURISM, it was originated in 1913 by Wyndham LEWIS in an attempt to express the spirit of the time in harsh angular forms derived from machinery. David Bomberg, Henri GAUDIER-BRZESKA and Jacob EPSTEIN were members of the movement. The term was coined by Ezra POUND.

Voysey, Charles Francis Annesley (1857–1951) British architect and designer. A key member of the ARTS AND CRAFTS MOVEMENT, he was a master of the detached middle-class house, specializing in unassuming, rustic,

rural architecture. Norney, near Shackleford, Surrey (1897) and The Pastures at North Luffenham in Leicestershire (1901) are good examples of his style.

voting Process employed to choose candidates for public office or to decide controversial issues. Early forms were by voice or sign, but the secret ballot became popular in order to eliminate the possibility of intimidation and corruption. Voters usually mark a piece of paper and deposit it in a ballot box, but in the USA voting machines, operated by polling levers, are commonly in use. *See also* DEMOCRACY; ELECTION; FRANCHISE

Voyager program SPACE EXPLORATION programme to study JUPITER, SATURN, URANUS and NEPTUNE, using two unmanned craft. In 1977, the two Voyager probes were launched 16 days apart from Kennedy Space Center at CAPE CANAVERAL, Florida. In 1979, they beamed back the first close-up pictures of Jupiter. The probes then passed Saturn and showed the structure of the planet's rings. Voyager 2 went on to study Uranus in 1986 and Neptune in 1989. Both probes have now left the Solar System.

VTOL (vertical take-off and landing) Experimental AIRCRAFT designed to perform vertical take-offs and landings while also being capable of maintaining flight speed and payload capabilities superior to those of a HELICOPTER. There are designs that permit rotation of the wing and engines from vertical for take-off, to horizontal for high-speed cruising. Another design allows for the diversion downward of the exhaust of fixed JET ENGINES, as in the highly successful Harrier jet. A third style has two separate systems of thrust for upward and forward movement.

Vulcan (Volcanus) Roman god of fire and volcanoes, identified with the Greek god HEPHAESTUS. His temples were prudently situated outside city walls. Often invoked to avert fires, he was associated with thunderbolts and the Sun.

vulcanization Chemical process, discovered in 1839, of heating SULPHUR or its compounds with natural or synthetic RUBBER in order to improve the rubber's durability and resilience.

Vulgate Oldest surviving version of the complete BIBLE, compiled and translated, mostly from Greek, into Latin by St JEROME from 382. The text was revised several times and was used universally in the Middle Ages. In 1546 it was promoted as the official Latin translation by the Council of TRENT.

vulture Large, keen-sighted, strong-flying bird that feeds on carrion. New World vultures, found throughout the Americas, include the CONDOR, turkey BUZZARD and king vulture; family Cathartidae. Old World vultures, related to eagles, are found in Africa, Europe and Asia, and include the Egyptian vulture and the griffon vulture; family Accipitridae.

vulva In human females, the external genitalia. Extending downward from the clitoris (a small, sensitive, elongated, erectile organ), a pair of fleshy lips (labia majora) surround the vulvar orifice. Within the labia majora, two smaller folds of skin (labia minora) surround a depression called the vestibule, within which are the urethral and vaginal openings.

Vyatka (formerly Kirov) City and river port on the W bank of the River Vyatka, W Russia; capital of Kirov region. Founded as Khlynov in 1174, it was annexed by Ivan III in 1489. The city was renamed Vyatka in 1780 and then known as Kirov from 1934 to 1992. It has a 17th-century cathedral. Industries: metal products, agricultural machinery, meat processing, timber, leather, furs. Pop. (1994) 491,000.

▲ **vulture** The red-headed turkey vulture (*Cathartes aura*) is a New World vulture, found from Canada to the Magellan Strait. It has a sharply hooked bill with fleshy seres across the top, through which the nostrils open. Because it is not as strong as other birds of prey, it feeds chiefly on carrion or on helpless animals, which it can spot from a great distance.

W/w, 23rd letter of the Roman alphabet, and like f, u, v and y, derived from the Semitic letter waw, meaning hook. The Greeks adopted waw into their alphabet as the letter upsilon. In Anglo-Saxon times, it appeared as VV.

Waco City on the Brazos River, central Texas; settled as a ferry-crossing in 1849. In 1993, 80 members of the BRANCH DAVIDIANS religious sect died during a confrontation with federal authorities, who had four agents killed. Industries: cotton, grain, tyres, paper, furniture, clothing, cottonseed oil products, glass, aircraft parts. Pop. (1996) 108,000.

Wagner, Richard (1813–83) German composer. His works consist almost entirely of operas, for which he provided his own libretti. Early operas include *Der fliegende Holländer* (1843), *Tannhäuser* (1845) and *Lohengrin* (1850). With *Tristan and Isolde* (1865) and the four-part *Der Ring des Nibelungen* (1851–76) the genius of Wagner is fully displayed. His rich, chromatic style lends emotional depth, and a web of LEITMOTIFS propels the drama. Other operas include *Die Meistersinger von Nürnberg* (1868) and the sacred stage drama, *Parsifal* (1882).

Waikato Longest river in New Zealand, in central and NW North Island. It rises from Lake Taupo in the central highlands and flows NNW into the Tasman Sea. The river is navigable for 130km (80mi) of its 425-km (264-mi) course.

Wailing Wall *See* WESTERN WALL

Waitangi, Treaty of (1840) Pact between Britain and several New Zealand MAORI tribes. The agreement protected and provided rights for Maori, guaranteeing them possession of certain tracts of land, while permitting Britain formally to annex the islands and purchase other land areas. *See also* MAORI WARS

Wake Island Largest of three small coral islands, known collectively as Wake Island, enclosing a lagoon in the W Pacific Ocean. The atoll was discovered by the Spaniards (1568) and later named by the British in 1796. It was annexed by the USA (1898) and became a naval base, captured by Japan (1941) and recaptured in 1945.

Waksman, Selman Abraham (1888–1973) US microbiologist, b. Russia. He was awarded the 1952 Nobel Prize for physiology or medicine for his discovery (1943) of the antibiotic streptomycin. He developed techniques for extracting antibiotics from various microorganisms and discovered new ones, including neomycin.

Walcott, Derek (1930–) Caribbean poet and dramatist. He has written many plays, including *Henri Christophe* (1950), *Drums and Colors* (1961), *O Babylon* (1978) and *Viva Detroit* (1992), but is perhaps best known as a poet. The first volume of his verse was published in 1948; it was collected in 1986. Other volumes include *Omeros* (1989). He was awarded the 1992 Nobel Prize for literature.

Wald, George (1906–) US biologist. He shared the 1967 Nobel Prize for physiology and medicine for being "one of the world's greatest authorities on the biochemistry of perception". He studied visual pigments and the effect of light on these pigments. Wald was an outspoken critic of US policy in Vietnam. He later criticized DNA research and nuclear safety.

Waldemar IV (1320–75) (Waldemar Atterday) King of Denmark (1340–75). He restored the Danish kingdom after a century of disintegration by a mixture of force,

diplomacy and persuasion. In 1367, his enemies, including the HANSEATIC LEAGUE, united to drive him Denmark. He regained the throne at the Peace of Stralsund (1370).

Waldenses Small Christian sect founded in the 12th century. It had its origins in the "Poor Men of Lyons", the followers of Peter WALDO of Lyons. The Waldenses renounced private property and led an ascetic life. They repudiated many Roman Catholic doctrines and practices, such as INDULGENCES, PURGATORY and MASS for the dead, and denied the validity of SACRAMENTS administered by unworthy priests. The movement flourished briefly in the 13th century, but active persecution extinguished it except in the French and Italian Alps. Persecution continued until the Waldenses received full civil rights in 1848. In the later 19th century, many Waldenses emigrated to the Americas.

Waldheim, Kurt (1918–) Austrian statesman and diplomat, fourth secretary general of the United Nations (1972–81). He succeeded U THANT as secretary general, but proved to be a weak appeaser of the major powers. Waldheim's tenure was tainted by revelations of his Nazi war record, and he was replaced by PÉREZ DE CUÉLLAR.

Waldo, Peter (1140–1218) French religious reformer after whom the WALDENSES are named. He sent out disciples, known as Poor Men, to read to the common people from the Bible. He preached without ecclesiastical authorization and was excommunicated.

Wales Constituent member of the UNITED KINGDOM, occupying a broad peninsula in W Great Britain; the capital is CARDIFF. Another major city is SWANSEA. **Land and climate** In the N, lies Wales' highest peak, Snowdon, at 1,085m (3,560ft). ANGLESEY lies off the NW coast. The Black Mountains lie in the SE. The border regions and coastal plains are lowlands. The principal rivers are the SEVERN and Dee. On average, Cardiff experiences twice as much annual rainfall as London. **History** The Celtic-speaking Welsh stoutly resisted Roman invasion in the first centuries AD. St DAVID introduced Christianity in the 5th century. In the 10th century, political power was centralized. In the 11th century, the English conquered the border counties and established the Welsh Marches. In 1282, Wales was conquered by the English Norman King Edward I, and in 1301 Prince Edward (later Edward II) became Prince of Wales. In the early 15th century, OWAIN GLYN DWR led spirited resistance against English rule. The accession of the Welsh TUDOR dynasty to the English throne paved the way for the Act of Union (1536) of England and Wales. Wales supported the Royalist cause in the English Civil War. In the late 19th century, Wales became the world's leading producer of coal. Rapid industrialization brought social problems, including unemployment and poverty. From the 18th century, Wales had been a centre of nonconformism, and Calvinism injected new life into Welsh nationalism. In 1996, the Welsh Nationalist Party (Plaid Cymru) won its first seat in the Westminster Parliament and in 1997 a referendum voted for a devolved Welsh assembly in Cardiff. The maintenance of a distinct Welsh culture has been strengthened by the teaching of Welsh in schools. **Economy** North Wales is predominantly agricultural, with the world's greatest density of sheep. Dairy farming is also important. Tourism is important in the coastal region of GWYNEDD. The S valleys and coastal plain are Wales' industrial heartland. The drastic late 20th-century decline of its traditional heavy industries of coal and steel (only one working mine remains) has been only partly offset by investment in light industries, such as electronics. Area: 20,761sq km (8,016sq mi). Pop. (1994) 2,913,000.

Wales, Prince of *See* CHARLES (PRINCE OF WALES)

▲ **walrus** A unique relative of the seal, the walrus (*Odobenus rosmarus*) is assigned a family of its own. It is a gregarious animal and has a tough hide and a thick fat layer that helps protect against cold as well as the tusks of other walruses.

Walesa, Lech (1943–) Polish statesman and labour leader, president (1990–95). In August 1980, he organized SOLIDARITY, an independent, self-governing trade union. A general strike took place, and in December 1980 Polish administrators agreed to give workers the right to organize freely. In 1981, the government outlawed Solidarity, and Walesa was interned until late 1982 as part of the government's effort to silence opposition. In 1983, he was awarded the Nobel Peace Prize. Following reforms in the Soviet Union, Solidarity was legalized and won free elections in 1989. In 1990, the Communist Party was disbanded and Walesa became president.

Walker, Alice (1944–) African-American writer. Her volumes of poetry include *Revolutionary Petunias and Other Poems* (1973). Walker won a Pulitzer Prize for her epistolary novel *The Color Purple* (1982). Other works include *In Search of My Mother's Garden* (1983).

Walker, William (1824–60) US adventurer in Central America. In 1853, he led an armed band that attempted to seize land in Mexico. He made a similar invasion of Nicaragua in 1855, with US business support, and set himself up as president (1856) but was expelled in 1857. In 1860, he made a sortie into Honduras but was captured and shot.

wallaby Any of various medium-sized members of the kangaroo family of MARSUPIAL mammals, occurring chiefly in Australia. All species are herbivorous, feeding in open grassland at night. They move fast in a series of leaps, using both strong hind legs simultaneously, balanced by the tail. Length: head and body 45–105cm (18–41in); tail 33–75cm (13–30in). Family Macropodidae. *See also* KANGAROO

Wallace, Alfred Russel (1823–1913) English naturalist. He developed a theory of NATURAL SELECTION concurrently with, but independent of, Charles DARWIN. Wallace wrote *Contributions to the Theory of Natural Selection* (1870) outlining his theory of EVOLUTION.

Wallace, Sir William (1270–1305) Scottish nationalist leader. He led resistance to the English king, EDWARD I. Wallace defeated an English army at Stirling Bridge (1297). The English were driven from Scotland, and Wallace pursued them over the border. He was confronted by Edward with a large army at Falkirk in 1298 and was defeated. He went into hiding, but was eventually captured (1305) and executed.

Wallachia (Walachia, Valahia) Historic region in Romania, formerly the principality between the River Danube and the Transylvanian Alps. It is said to have been established in 1290 by Ralph the Black, vassal of the king of Hungary, from whom the region secured temporary independence in 1330. It came gradually, however, under the domination of the Turks, whose suzerainty was acknowledged in 1417. Wallachia and MOLDAVIA became protectorates of Russia under the Treaty of Adrianople (1829)

and by their union formed the state of ROMANIA in 1859. An important agricultural region, it has been developed industrially since World War 2. Industries: oil, chemicals, heavy machinery. Area: 76,599sq km (29,575sq mi).

Wallenstein, Albrecht Eusebius Wenzel von (1583–1634) German general. During the THIRTY YEARS' WAR (1618–48), he was commander of the armies of the Holy Roman Empire, winning a series of victories in the late 1620s, but losing the Battle of Lützen (1632). Wallenstein was later convicted of treason, dismissed and then assassinated.

Waller, Fats (1904–43) US jazz pianist and composer, b. Thomas Waller. He wrote many successful tunes, including "Honeysuckle Rose" and "Ain't Misbehavin'".

wallflower Any of several species of PERENNIAL plants of the genera *Cheiranthus* and *Erysimum*, a few sweet-scented, that are commonly cultivated in Europe and the USA. The European wallflower, *C. cheiri*, has lance-shaped leaves, and red, orange, yellow, or purple flowers. Height: to 90cm (36in). Family Brassicaceae/Cruciferae.

Wallis, Sir Barnes Neville (1887–1979) English aeronautical engineer and inventor, best known for his invention of the bouncing bomb during World War 2. After the war, he designed the first swing-wing aircraft.

Wallis and Futuna French territory in the S Pacific Ocean, W of Samoa. The territory is made up of two small groups of volcanic islands, the Wallis Islands and the Hoorn Islands. The principal islands are Uvea, Futuna and Alofi, with Uvea containing 60% of the population and the capital of Mata-Utu (1983 pop. 1,000). Timber is the main export. The French took the islands in 1842 and in 1959 they became an overseas territory. The islands' economy is based on subsistence agriculture of copra, cassava, yams, taro and bananas. Pop. (2000 est.) 26,000.

Walloons French-speaking people of S Belgium, as opposed to the FLEMISH-speaking people of the N. They inhabit chiefly the provinces of Hainaut, Liège, Namur and S Brabant. Today, they number *c*.3,000,000.

Wall Street Centre of the business district of NEW YORK CITY which, together with Broad Street and New Street, houses many US and overseas banks and brokers, as well as the New York Stock Exchange. It has become the international symbol of US finance.

walnut Deciduous tree native to North and South America, Europe and Asia. It has smoother bark than HICKORY, to which it is related, and is grown for timber, ornament and nuts. Height: to 50m (165ft). Family Juglandaceae; genus *Juglans*.

Walpole, Horace, 4th Earl of Orford (1717–97) English writer. His Gothic house near London represents a milestone in architectural taste; his bizarre novel *The Castle of Otranto* (1764) established a parallel fashion for the Gothic in literature. Walpole's reputation rests on his letters, which provide a portrait of Georgian England.

Walpole, Sir Robert, 1st Earl of Orford (1676–1745) British politician. Although he resigned as chancellor of the exchequer in 1717, after developing the first sinking fund, he restored order after the SOUTH SEA BUBBLE crisis in 1720. He returned as chancellor of the exchequer and first lord of the Treasury in 1721. He was forced to resign in 1742 because of opposition to his foreign policy.

walrus Arctic mammal; it has a massive body and a large head. Its tusks, developed from upper canine teeth, may reach 1m (39in) in length and are used to rake up the seafloor in search of molluscs and to climb on to ice floes. Length: to 3.7m (12ft). Family Odobenidae; species *Odobenus rosmarus*.

Walsingham, Sir Francis (1532–90) English statesman, a leading minister of ELIZABETH I. He was a zealous Protestant, who set up an efficient intelligence system, based on bribery, to detect Catholic conspiracies. Walsingham produced the evidence that led to the conviction and execution of MARY, QUEEN OF SCOTS.

Walter, Hubert (d.1205) English statesman. As bishop of Salisbury, he joined RICHARD I on the Third CRUSADE and later negotiated his ransom. Appointed archbishop of Canterbury and chief justiciar (1193), he was virtual ruler of England in Richard's absence.

Walter, Bruno (1876–1962) German conductor. After a series of conducting posts in Europe, he went to the USA in 1939. From 1947 to 1962, he was primarily associated with the Metropolitan Opera Company, New York.

Walter, Thomas Ustick (1804–87) US architect. In 1851, he was appointed to plan extensions to the CAPITOL at Washington, D.C. Walter also designed the interior of the Library of Congress.

Walther von der Vogelweide (1170–1230) German poet, considered the greatest MINNESINGER of the Middle Ages. He produced poems of enduring immediacy, such as the popular "Unter den Linden".

Walton, Ernest Thomas Sinton (1903–95) Irish physicist. Walton shared the 1951 Nobel Prize for physics with John COCKCROFT for their development (1929) of the first nuclear particle ACCELERATOR. In 1931, they produced the first artificial nuclear reaction without radioactive isotopes, using high-energy protons to bombard lithium nuclei.

Walton, Izaak (1593–1683) English biographer and author. His lives of Donne (1640), Sir Henry Wotton (1651), Richard Hooker (1665), George Herbert (1670) and Bishop Sanderson (1678) are the first truly biographical works in English literature. His most famous work, however, is *The Compleat Angler* (1653).

Walton, Sir William Turner (1902–83) English composer. His orchestral works include *Portsmouth Point* (1926) and the comedy overture *Scapino* (1941). He wrote *Crown Imperial* (1937) and *Orb and Sceptre* (1953) as coronation marches for George VI and Elizabeth II. His most widely known works are the jazz-oriented *Façade* (1923), the oratorio *Belshazzar's Feast* (1931) and the opera *Troilus and Cressida* (1954).

waltz Dance performed by couples to music in triple time. A graceful ballroom dance, it became fashionable in the early 19th century, having developed from s German folk dances, such as the *Ländler*.

wampum Beads made by Native Americans from the shells of molluscs. They were an important currency in trade with other bands and early European explorers. Wampum were coloured either purple or, more commonly, white. They were also used for the ornamentation of necklaces or belts.

wandering jew Common name for some creeping plants of the genus *Tradescantia* in the spiderwort family.

Wang Ching-wei (1883–1944) Chinese nationalist leader. A close associate of SUN YAT-SEN and one of the founders of the KUOMINTANG, he led the leftist wing of the party in 1925 in opposition to CHIANG KAI-SHEK (1926). He was prime minister (1932–35) and headed the puppet government set up by the Japanese in 1940.

Wang Mang (33 BC–AD 23) Emperor of China. He overthrew the HAN dynasty and proclaimed the Hsin (New) dynasty in AD 8. Opposition from landowners and officials forced him to withdraw his reforms, and his one-emperor dynasty, which divides the Former Han from the Later Han, ended in his assassination.

Wankel rotary engine Gasoline engine with rotors instead of pistons. German engineer Felix Wankel invented the engine in the 1950s. Each triangular rotor turns inside a casing. Gaps between the casing and rotor form three crescent-shaped combustion chambers. Each chamber goes through a sequence of events similar to those in a FOUR-STROKE ENGINE with pistons.

WAP *See* WIRELESS APPLICATION PROTOCOL (WAP)

wapiti (elk) Large DEER of North America, closely related to the Old World red deer. It is grey-brown with a whitish rump and dark, brown-black legs, head and neck; its antlers may span 1.5m (5ft). Height: to 1.5m (5ft); length: to 2.5m (7.5ft). Family Cervidae; species *Cervus canadensis*.

war Military combat between large communities, nations and/or groups of nations. All-out (nuclear) war between major powers using modern weapons would undoubtedly result in what is known as "mutually assured destruction" (MAD). Other forms of war include civil war, in which factions within one state or community struggle between themselves for supremacy, and guerrilla war, in which partisan forces harass occupying or government troops by surprise attacks. *See also* DISARMAMENT

warbler Numerous birds of two families, one in the Old World (Sylviidae) and the other in the New World (Parulidae). Old World warblers include the hedge sparrow and tailorbird. Most New World warblers have brighter plumage.

Warburg, Otto Heinrich (1883–1970) German biochemist who was awarded the 1931 Nobel Prize for physiology or medicine for his discovery of respiratory

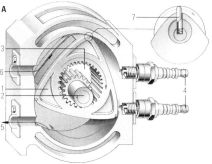

▲ Wankel rotary engine

A rotary engine, such as the Wankel (A), compresses and ignites a petrol/air mixture with a spark plug like a conventional combustion engine but does so with a rotating three-sided cylinder (1) not a straight-line action. The explosion of the fuel/air mixture drives further rotation, continuing the process and driving a crankshaft (2) passing through the centre of the cylinder. (3) The movement of the piston sucks air into the cylinder (so valves are not needed) and compresses the mixture as it continues to turn. The spark plugs (4) then ignite the mixture, which expands, rotating the piston and driving the crankshaft. The burned fuel is expelled through an outlet (5) as the piston turns, pulling in more air to repeat the process (6). The seals (7) at the edge of the piston's faces are important in creating the vacuum needed to pull in the fuel/air mixture and in compressing the mixture. A complete cycle is shown (B).

ENZYMES. He made significant contributions to the understanding of the mechanisms of cellular respiration and energy transfer, and of PHOTOSYNTHESIS.

war crimes Violations of international laws of WAR. The modern conception of war crimes followed the atrocities committed in World War 2, resulting in the NUREMBERG TRIALS. *See also* GENEVA CONVENTION

Warhol, Andy (1928–87) US painter, printmaker and film-maker, innovator of POP ART. He achieved fame with his stencil pictures of Campbell's soup cans and his sculptures of Brillo soap pad boxes (1962). In 1965, Warhol gave up art to manage the rock group "The Velvet Underground". He continued to make controversial films that often had a voyeuristic quality.

warlords Rulers who hold local authority by force of arms. The term is applied, in particular, to regional military leaders in China in the late 19th and early 20th centuries.

warm-blooded *See* HOMOIOTHERMIC

War of 1812 (1812–15) Conflict between the USA and Britain. The main source of friction was British maritime policy during the NAPOLEONIC WARS, which included the impressment of sailors from US vessels and the interception of US merchant ships. Difficulties on the border with Canada also contributed. In 1811, President James MADISON reimposed the Nonintercourse Act on trade with the British. The USA was ill-prepared for war and an invasion of Canada failed. Stephen DECATUR restored US pride. Victory on Lake Erie (September 1813) enabled US forces, led by William H. HARRISON, to force British troops back across the Canadian border. The possible secession of New England was raised by the HARTFORD CONVENTION and the end of the NAPOLEONIC WARS (1814) freed more British forces. They imposed a naval blockade and captured Washington, D.C., burning the White House. A US naval victory on Lake Champlain, however, ended the British threat to New York. With the war at stalemate, John Quincy ADAMS and Henry CLAY led US negotiations that resulted in the Treaty of Ghent (24 December 1914). Andrew JACKSON's victory at New Orleans occurred after the signing of the treaty.

Warren, Earl (1891–1974) US politician and jurist. He was governor of California (1943–53) and an unsuccessful Republican candidate for vice president (1953). Appointed as chief justice (1953–69) of the US Supreme Court by President EISENHOWER, he began the "Warren Revolution" that lasted until his retirement. Some of his court's noteworthy cases include: Brown v. Board of Education of Topeka (1954); *Engel v. Vitale* (1962), which prohibited prayers in public schools; and *Miranda v. Arizona* (1966), which made it obligatory that a suspect be informed of his rights, be provided with free state counsel, and be given the right to remain silent. *See also* WARREN COMMISSION

Warren, Robert Penn (1905–89) US poet, novelist and critic. A member of the Fugitives, a group of Southern agrarian poets, he co-edited the *Southern Review* with Cleanth Brooks. Warren won Pulitzer Prizes for his volumes of poetry, *Brother to Dragons* (1953), *Promises* (1957), and *Now and Then* (1978). His most famous work is the Pulitzer Prize-winning novel, *All the King's Men* (1946). In 1986, he became the first US poet laureate.

Warren City in SE Michigan. Essentially a suburb of DETROIT, it ranks as the state's third-largest city. Industries: automobile parts, steel, electrical equipment, plastic mouldings, tools, dyes. Pop. (1992) 142,404.

Warren Commission (1963–64) US presidential commission that investigated the assassination of President KENNEDY. It was headed by Earl WARREN. After taking evidence from 552 witnesses, it concluded that the act

had been committed by Lee Harvey OSWALD, acting alone. Denial of conspiracy was not universally accepted.

Warrington County district in N Cheshire, England; created in 1974 under the Local Government Act (1972). Area: 176sq km (68sq mi). Pop. (1996 est.) 189,000.

Warsaw Capital and largest city of Poland, on the River VISTULA. Its first settlement dates from the 11th century. In 1596, it became Poland's capital and developed into the country's main trading centre. From 1813 to 1915, it was controlled by Russia, and during World War 1 it was occupied by German troops. In 1918, it was liberated by Polish troops and was restored as capital of Poland. The 1939 German invasion and occupation of Warsaw marked the beginning of World War 2. In 1940, the Germans isolated the Jewish ghetto, which contained 500,000 people, and when the Red Army liberated Warsaw, they found only 200 surviving Jews. After the war, the old town was reconstructed. Warsaw is a major transport and industrial centre. Industries: steel, automobiles, cement, machinery. Pop. (1996) 1,638,000.

Warsaw Pact Agreement creating the Warsaw Treaty Organization (1955), a defensive alliance of the Soviet Union and its communist allies in Eastern Europe. It was the equivalent of Western Europe's NORTH ATLANTIC TREATY ORGANIZATION (NATO). Its headquarters were in Moscow, and it was controlled by the Soviet Union. Attempts to withdraw by Hungary (1956) and Czechoslovakia (1968) were crushed. It was dissolved after the collapse of the Soviet Union (1991).

Wars of the Roses *See* ROSES, WARS OF THE

wart Raised and well-defined small growth on the outermost surface of the skin, caused by the human papilloma virus. It is usually painless unless in a pressure area, as with a VERRUCA.

wart hog Wild, tusked PIG, native to Africa. It has brownish-black skin with a crest of hair along the back. Height: *c.*76cm (2.5ft) at shoulder; weight: 90kg (200lb). Family Suidae; species *Phacochoerus aethiopicus.*

Warwick, Richard Neville, Earl of (1428–71) English magnate, known as "the Kingmaker", who held the balance of power (1461–64) during the Wars of the ROSES. Breaking with EDWARD IV, Warwick changed sides and restored HENRY VI to the throne in 1470. Edward returned with fresh troops, and Warwick was defeated and killed at the Battle of Barnet.

Warwick, Sir Robert Rich, 2nd Earl of (1587–1658) English naval officer and colonialist. He was given the patent to administer Massachusetts in 1628 and Connecticut in 1631. He was a leader of the Puritan opposition to CHARLES I. As lord high admiral (1643–45), he secured the navy for the Parliamentarians in the CIVIL WARS.

Warwickshire County in central England. The land is gently rolling, rising to the Cotswold Hills in the S, and is drained by the River Avon. Cereals are the main crop, dairy cattle and sheep are raised. The county town is Warwick (1992 pop. 116,299). Area: 1,981sq km (765sq mi). Pop. (1991) 484,287.

Washington, Booker T. (Taliaferro) (1856–1915) US educator and black leader. Born a slave, he gained an education after the Civil War and became a teacher. In 1881, he organized Tuskegee Institute in Alabama for blacks. He advocated self-help, education and economic improvement as preliminaries to the achievement of equality for blacks, and he believed in compromise with white segregationists. He had considerable influence among whites as a spokesman for black causes.

Washington, Denzel (1954–) US film actor. His first major role was in *Cry Freedom* (1987). He was chosen by Spike LEE to play the lead roles in *Mo' Better Blues* (1990) and *Malcolm X* (1992). Other credits include *Philadelphia* (1993), *Pelican Brief* (1993) and *Devil in a Blue Dress* (1995).

Washington, George (1732–99) Commander in chief of the Continental army in the AMERICAN REVOLUTION and first president of the USA (1789–97), b. Virginia. He fought with distinction in the FRENCH AND INDIAN WARS and was a member (1759–74) of the house of burgesses. In 1775, Washington was chosen as commander in chief by the CONTINENTAL CONGRESS. With victory achieved, he resigned (1783) but was recalled from retirement to preside over the CONSTITUTIONAL CONVENTION at Philadelphia (1787). In 1789, Washington was elected, unopposed, as president of the new republic. He was unable to heal the divisions between his secretary of state, Thomas JEFFERSON, and his secretary of the treasury, Alexander HAMILTON. The FEDERALIST PARTY and the DEMOCRATIC REPUBLICAN PARTY emerged from this split. In 1793, Washington was reelected. His second administration was dominated by Federalists, and the Jeffersonians criticized John JAY's negotiation of peace terms with Britain. In 1796, Washington declined a third term as president. In his *Farewell Address* (17 September 1796), Washington warned against the geographical divisions encouraged by the party system and advised the nation to steer clear of "permanent alliances" with foreign nations. He spent the rest of his life on the family estate at Mount Vernon.

Washington State in the extreme NW USA, bounded on the N by British Columbia, Canada, E by Idaho, S by Oregon and W by the Pacific Ocean. The state capital is OLYMPIA, and the largest city is SEATTLE. In the NW is the navigable PUGET SOUND, along which lie Washington's major industrial and commercial cities. Its physiography and climate are dominated by the CASCADE RANGE, which crosses the state from N to S. Mount RAINIER and Mount ST HELENS are notable peaks in the range. The coastal region to the W of the range is one of the wettest areas of the USA and has some of the densest forest in the world; the region to the E of the Cascades is mostly treeless plain with low rainfall. An important wheat-producing area, the plateau is heavily dependent on various irrigation schemes. The COLUMBIA RIVER is one of the world's best sources of hydroelectricity and is also used for irrigation. The Spanish discovered the mouth of the Columbia River in 1775, and in 1778 Captain COOK established the area's fur trading links with China. In 1792, George Vancouver mapped Puget Sound and Robert Gray sailed down the Sound to establish the US claim to the region. The claim was strengthened by the LEWIS AND CLARK EXPEDITION (1805) and the establishment of an American Fur Company trading post at the mouth of the Columbia by John Jacob ASTOR in 1811. From 1821 to 1846, the region was administered by the HUDSON'S BAY COMPANY. In 1846, a treaty with the British fixed the boundary with Canada, and in 1847 most of present-day Washington State became Oregon Territory. In 1853, Washington Territory was created. Exploitation of its forests and fisheries attracted settlement, and Washington was admitted to the Union in 1889. Washington is the leading producer of apples in the USA. The largest mineral deposits are magnesium and aluminium ores. Industries: food processing, timber, aluminium, aerospace, computer technology. Area: 172,431sq km (66,581sq mi). Pop. (2000) 5,894,121.

Washington, D.C. Capital of the USA, on the E bank of the POTOMAC River, coextensive with the District of Columbia and bordered by Maryland (NE and SE) which gave up land occupied by the district, and Virginia (W and S). The site was chosen as the seat of government in 1790, and the city was planned by the French army engineer Pierre Charles L'Enfant. Construction of the WHITE HOUSE began in 1793 and of the Capitol the following year. CONGRESS moved from Philadelphia in 1800. During the WAR OF 1812, the city was occupied by the British and many public buildings were burned (1814), including the White House and the Capitol. Washington is the legislative, judicial and administrative centre of the USA. Washington has severe social problems; many of its large black population live in slum housing. Pop. (1996) 543,000.

Washington, Treaty of (1871) Agreement settling a number of disputes involving the USA, Britain and Canada. The most serious was the question of the ALABAMA CLAIMS, which was submitted to international arbitration. US–Canadian disputes over fisheries and the border were also resolved.

wasp Any insect of the stinging Hymenoptera order that is neither a bee nor an ant. The common wasp (*Vespa vulgaris*) has a yellow body ringed with black. Adults feed on nectar, tree sap and fruit. Length: to 3cm (1.2in). Family Vespidae.

Wassermann, August von (1866–1925) German bacteriologist. He made important contributions to immunology, the best known of which was his development of a diagnostic test for SYPHILIS, the Wasserman test.

watch *See* CLOCK

water (H_2O) Odourless, colourless liquid that covers about 70% of the Earth's surface and is the most widely used SOLVENT. Essential to life, it makes up *c.*60–70% of the human body. It is a compound of hydrogen and oxygen with the two H–O links of the molecule forming an angle of 105°. This asymmetry results in polar properties and a force of attraction (hydrogen bond) between opposite ends of neighbouring water molecules. These forces maintain the substance as a liquid, in spite of its low molecular weight, and account for its unusual property of having its maximum density at 4°C (39°F). Properties: r.d. 1.000; m.p. 0°C (32°F); b.p. 100°C (212°F). *See also* DESALINATION

water beetle Aquatic BEETLE of several families. **Whirligig** beetles (family Gyrinidae) skim around the surface of water, feeding on small insects. **Water scavenger** beetles (family Hydrophilidae) feed on water plants. Their larvae are fierce predators. **Predaceous diving beetles** are the most numerous water beetles. They are black, brown or greenish and can remain underwater for long periods. They prey on snails and fish.

water boatman (water bug) Aquatic insect found worldwide. Its body is grey to black, oval and flat, with fringed, oarlike hind legs. Length: about 15mm (0.6in). Order Hemiptera; family Corixidae. The carnivorous "backswimmers" of the family Notonectidae are also sometimes called water boatmen.

waterbuck (waterbok) Large, gregarious, coarse-haired ANTELOPE, native to Africa S of the Sahara, and the Nile Valley. There are six species. Length: 1.4–2.1m (4.5–7ft); height: 1.1–1.5m (3.6–4.9ft) at the shoulder. Family Bovidae; genus *Kobus*.

water buffalo (carabao) Large OX, widely domesticated in much of the tropical world; it is feral in some parts of India. Height: to 1.8m (6ft) at the shoulder. Family Bovidae; species *Bubalus bubalis*.

watercolour Paint that is made from a pigment ground up with a water-soluble gum, such as gum arabic; also, a PAINTING that is rendered in this medium.

watercress Floating or creeping plant found in running or spring waters. The succulent leaves, divided into small, oval leaflets, have a pungent flavour and are used in salads and soups. The clustered flowers are white. Height: 25cm (10in). Family Brassicaceae/Cruciferae; species *Nasturtium officinale*.

water cycle *See* HYDROLOGICAL CYCLE

waterfall Point in the course of a river at which the water drops perpendicularly. The site of a waterfall usually indicates an outcrop of rock that is particularly resistant to erosion. *See* ANGEL FALLS; NIAGARA FALLS

water flea Any of numerous species of small, chiefly freshwater branchiopod crustaceans, especially those within the genus *Daphnia*, which are common throughout the world. Order Cladocera. *See also* CRUSTACEA

Waterford County in Munster province, S Republic of Ireland, on the Atlantic Ocean. It is a mountainous region, drained chiefly by the rivers Blackwater and Suir. The raising of beef and dairy cattle and sheep is the chief agricultural activity. Industries: fishing, food processing, tanning, glassware. The county town of Waterford (1991 pop. 40,300) is an important port for the whole of S Ireland. Area: 1,838sq km (710sq mi). Pop. (1991) 91,624.

waterfowl Aquatic birds, including species of DUCK, GOOSE and SWAN, found throughout most of the world. Large flocks migrate from cool nesting grounds to warm winter homes. All have short bills, short legs and dense plumage underlaid by down. Order Anseriformes.

Watergate affair (1972–74) US political scandal that led to the resignation of President NIXON. It arose from an attempted burglary of the Democratic Party's national headquarters in the Watergate building, organized by members of Nixon's re-election committee. Evidence of the involvement of the administration provoked investigations by the Senate and the Justice Department, which ultimately implicated Nixon. He was pardoned by his successor, Gerald FORD but his closest advisers (Halderman, Erlichman, and Mitchell) were convicted.

water glass (Na_2SiO_3) Viscous form of sodium silicate. It dissolves in water and was traditionally used to preserve eggs. Water glass is used in the manufacture of silica gel and cement and is employed in petroleum refining.

water hyacinth Aquatic herb native to the American tropics. It has swollen petioles that float in water and spikes of violet flowers. Family Pontederiaceae; species *Eichhornia crassipes*.

water lily Any of about 90 species of freshwater plants, widely distributed in temperate and tropical regions. They have leaves that float at the surface and showy flowers of white, pink, red, blue or yellow. Family Nymphaeaceae; genera *Nymphaea*, *Nuphar*, *Nelumbo*, and *Victoria*. *See also* LOTUS

Waterloo, Battle of (1815) Final engagement of the NAPOLEONIC WARS, fought *c.*20km (12mi) from Brussels, Belgium. Allied forces were commanded by the Duke of WELLINGTON against Napoleon's slightly larger French forces. Fighting was even until the Prussians under Marshal Blücher arrived to overwhelm the French flank, whereupon Wellington broke through the centre. The battle ended Napoleon's HUNDRED DAYS and resulted in his second, and final, abdication.

watermelon Trailing annual VINE, native to tropical Africa and Asia and cultivated in warm areas worldwide. Its edible fruit has a greenish rind, red flesh and many seeds. Family Cucurbitaceae; species *Citrullus lanatus. See also* GOURD

water moccasin (cottonmouth) Venomous, semiaquatic SNAKE, native to the swamps of SE USA. It is a

pit VIPER, closely related to the COPPERHEAD. Adults have broad, brown bands along their bodies. When threatened, it bares its white mouth. They feed on warmblooded animals. Length: to 1.5m (5ft). Family Viperidae; species *Agkistrodon piscivorus*.

water pollution Contamination of water by harmful wastes. The chief source of water POLLUTION is **industrial waste**. Toxic chemicals, such as POLYCHLORINATED BIPHENYL (PCB), are discharged as effluent and cannot be disinfected with CHLORINE. In addition, the burning of fossil fuels causes ACID RAIN. Untreated or partially treated **sewage** is another source of water pollution. Sewage treatment is unable to prevent the spread of viruses and some phosphorus-based detergents that cause EUTROPHICATION. Agricultural chemicals and wastes, such as PESTICIDES and FERTILIZERS, are another major cause of pollution. Once pollution has affected GROUND WATER it spreads more rapidly. Oil spills and ocean dumping are major causes of marine pollution.

water polo Game devised as an aquatic form of FOOTBALL. It is played by two teams of seven people in a pool. At each end of the pool is a net-enclosed goal defended by a goalkeeper. It has been an Olympic event since 1900.

water power *See* HYDROELECTRICITY

water-skiing Leisure activity and competitive sport in which a person skis across the surface of water while being towed by a motorboat. In **slalom**, skiers are towed several times through a series of staggered buoys. In **jumping**, each skier must ski up and over a wooden ramp. For the **tricks**, skiers devise their own 20-second routines of complex manoeuvres.

water table In geology, level below which the ground is saturated. The height of the water table moves up or down depending on rainfall. Water located below the water table is called GROUND WATER.

Watson, James Dewey (1928–) US geneticist and biophysicist. He is known for his role in the discovery of the molecular structure of deoxyribonucleic acid (DNA), and he shared the 1962 Nobel Prize for physiology or medicine with Francis CRICK and Maurice Wilkins. Watson later helped to break the GENETIC CODE of the DNA base sequences and found the ribonucleic acid (RNA) messenger that carries the DNA code to the cell's protein-forming structures.

Watson, John Broadus (1878–1958) US psychologist, founder of BEHAVIOURISM. His work did much to make psychological research more objective and influenced B.F. SKINNER's theory of operant conditioning.

Watt, James (1736–1819) Scottish engineer. In 1765, he invented the condensing STEAM ENGINE. In 1782, Watt invented the double-acting engine in which steam pressure acted alternately on each side of a piston. With Matthew Boulton, he coined the term "horsepower". The unit of power is called the WATT in his honour.

watt Unit of power in the SI system of units. A machine consuming one JOULE of energy per second has a power output of one watt. One horsepower corresponds to 746 watts. A watt is also a unit of electrical power, equal to the product of voltage and current.

Watteau, Jean-Antoine (1684–1721) French painter. His admiration for RUBENS' series *The Garden of Love* inspired his development of the category of *fêtes galantes*. These ROCOCO works, notably *The Embarkation for Cythera* (1717), combine elements of masquerade and COMMEDIA DELL' ARTE to create an aristocratic fantasy. They are pervaded by a sense of melancholy.

Watts, George Frederick (1817–1904) British painter and sculptor. He produced complicated, moralistic allegories such as *Hope* (1886). Watts' best-known sculpture is an equestrian statue called *Physical Energy* (1904).

Waugh, Evelyn Arthur St John (1903–66) English novelist. Waugh established his reputation with *Decline and Fall* (1928). *Vile Bodies* (1930), *A Handful of Dust* (1934) and *Put Out More Flags* (1942) reflect inter-war, British upper-class life, while *Brideshead Revisited* (1945) is informed by the Roman Catholicism to which he was converted in 1928. Other major works include the *Sword of Honour* trilogy: *Men at Arms* (1952), *Officers and Gentlemen* (1955) and *Unconditional Surrender* (1961).

wave In oceanography, moving disturbance travelling on or through water that does not move the water itself. Wind causes waves by frictional drag. Waves not under pressure from strong winds are called swells. Waves begin to break on shore or "feel bottom" when they reach a depth shallower than half the wave's length. When the water depth is *c*.1.3 times the wave height, the wave front is so steep that the top falls over and the wave breaks.

wave In physics, carrier of energy from place to place. Waves are caused by disturbances that result in oscillation. These oscillations then spread out (propagate) as waves. The velocity depends on the type of wave and on the medium. ELECTROMAGNETIC waves, such as light, consist of varying magnetic and electric fields vibrating at right angles to each other and to the direction of motion; they are **transverse** waves. Sound waves are transmitted by the vibrations of the particles of the medium itself, the vibrations being in the direction of wave motion; they are **longitudinal** waves. Sound waves, unlike electromagnetic waves, cannot travel through a vacuum and cannot undergo polarization. Both types of waves can undergo REFLECTION, REFRACTION and give rise to INTERFERENCE phenomena. A wave is characterized by its WAVELENGTH and FREQUENCY, the VELOCITY of wave motion being the product of wavelength and frequency. *See also* POLARIZED LIGHT; WAVE AMPLITUDE; WAVE FREQUENCY

wave amplitude Peak value of a periodically varying quantity. This peak value may be either positive or negative as the quantity varies either above or below zero.

wave dispersion Alteration of the refractive index of a medium with wavelength. It occurs with all ELECTROMAGNETIC waves but is most obvious at visible wavelengths, causing light to be separated into its component colours. Dispersion is when light passes through a refracting medium, such as a PRISM, and forms a SPECTRUM. Each colour has a different wavelength, and so the prism bends each colour by a different amount. *See also* REFRACTION

wave frequency Number of oscillations or wave cycles produced in 1 second, measured in HERTZ. It can be calculated from the wave VELOCITY divided by WAVELENGTH. By QUANTUM THEORY, the frequency of any ELECTROMAGNETIC RADIATION is proportional to the energy of the component photons.

wavelength (symbol λ) Distance between successive points of equal phase in a WAVE. The wavelength of water waves could be measured as the distance from crest to crest. The wavelength of a light wave determines its colour. Wavelength is equal to the wave VELOCITY divided by the WAVE FREQUENCY.

wave mechanics Version of QUANTUM MECHANICS developed in 1926 by Erwin SCHRÖDINGER. It explains the behaviour of electrons in terms of their wave properties. Although quickly superseded by a more complex formulation by Paul DIRAC, it is still widely used.

wax Solid, insoluble substance of low melting point. It is mouldable and water-repellent. Animal and vegetable waxes are simple LIPIDS consisting of esters of fatty acids. Mineral waxes include PARAFFIN wax made from petroleum. Waxes are used in the manufacture of lubricants, polishes, cosmetics and candles, and to waterproof leather and coat paper.

wax myrtle Large, evergreen shrub or tree that grows on the E coast of the USA and in the West Indies. Its fragrant leaves are spotted with brown and the plant bears inconspicuous small green flowers. Height: up to 11m (35ft). Family Myricaceae; species *Myrica cerifera*.

waxwing Any of a few species of small, grey-brown birds with distinctive black markings on the head, a small crest and characteristic red or red-and-yellow waxy tips on the secondary wing feathers. They are found in the forests of Eurasia and North America and feed on berries and fruit. Length: to 20cm (8in). Family Bombycillidae; genus *Bombycilla*.

Wayne, Anthony (1745–96) American Revolutionary general. He was called "Mad Anthony Wayne" because of his daring tactics. In 1777, he was made brigadier general and joined George WASHINGTON's army. He led a division at the Battle of Brandywine, fought at Germantown, and wintered with Washington at Valley Forge. In 1779, Wayne led the successful night attack on Stony Point, New York. He also fought in the Siege of YORKTOWN and occupied Charleston. In 1792 he became commander in chief in the Northwest Territory and defeated the Ohio tribes in the Battle of Fallen Timbers (1794). Wayne secured the Treaty of Greenville (1795), the first to recognize Native American title to US lands.

Wayne, John (1907–79) US film actor, b. Marion Michael Morrison. His first major success was in the Western *Stagecoach* (1939), directed by John FORD. Wayne won a best actor Academy Award for *True Grit* (1969). Other films include *She Wore a Yellow Ribbon* (1949), *The Man Who Shot Liberty Valance* (1962) and *The Shootist* (1976).

Waziristan Arid and mountainous region in North-West Frontier province, NW Pakistan, on the Afghanistan border. It is divided into N and S Waziristan. In the N, Wazir tribes live in fortified mountain villages and farm the fertile valleys. In S Waziristan, the semi-nomadic Mashud tribes live in tent camps and graze their livestock on the hills. Waziristan became an independent territory in 1893. In 1947, it was incorporated into Pakistan, but with the support of Afghanistan it has struggled to create an independent Pushtu state. Area: 11,585sq km (4,473sq mi). Pop. (1981 est.) 545,000.

weak nuclear force (weak interaction) One of the four FUNDAMENTAL FORCES in physics. It causes radioactive decay. The weak nuclear force can be observed only in the subatomic realm, being of very short range. It is weaker than the ELECTROMAGNETIC FORCE and the STRONG NUCLEAR FORCE (the strongest of the forces), but stronger than GRAVITATION.

weasel Any of several species of small, carnivorous, mostly terrestrial mammals of Eurasia, N Africa, and North and South America. Most species have small heads, long necks, slender bodies, short legs, and long tails. Reddish-brown with light coloured underparts, some species turn completely white in winter. Weasels are fierce predators, eating eggs and rodents and often attacking much larger animals and domestic poultry. Length: 50cm (20in) overall. Family Mustelidae; Genus *Mustela*.

weather State of the atmosphere at a given locality or over a broad area, particularly as it affects human activity. Weather refers to short-term states (days or weeks) as opposed to long-term CLIMATE conditions.

weather forecasting *See* METEOROLOGY

weathering Breakdown and chemical disintegration of rocks and minerals at the Earth's surface by physical and chemical processes. In **physical** weathering in cold, wet climates, water seeping into cracks in the rock expands on freezing, so causing the rock to crack further and to crumble. Extreme temperature changes in drier regions, such as deserts, also cause rocks to fragment. **Chemical** weathering can lead to a weakening of the rock structure by altering the minerals of a rock and changing their size, volume, and ability to hold shape. Unlike EROSION, weathering does not involve transportation.

Weaver, Sigourney (1949–) US actress, b. Susan Alexandra Weaver in New York. Highly respected and adept actress whose stardom came about through the fiercely independent but emotionally charged Ripley character first seen in *Alien* (1979). The range of her acting also extends to the romantic *The Year of Living Dangerously* (1983), the comic *Ghostbusters* (1984) and the political thriller *Death and the Maiden* (1994).

weaverbird Any of several species of short-billed, often yellow-and-black, finch-like birds that weave complex nests from grass and leaves. Weaverbirds are gregarious insect-eaters of hot, dry areas. The African *Ploceus cucullatus* knots strands of grass together. Length: to 22cm (7.5in). Family Ploceidae.

weaving Process of making fabric by intertwining two sets of threads. A loom is threaded with a set of warp threads. The weft thread is wound round a shuttle and passed between the warp threads, which are separated according to the desired pattern. A reed keeps the woven rows tightly packed.

Webb, Beatrice (née Potter) (1858–1943) and **Sidney** (1859–1947) British social historians and politicians. Sidney Webb was one of the founders of the FABIAN SOCIETY. They founded the London School of Economics (1895) and the *New Statesman* magazine (1913).

Weber, Carl Maria von (1786–1826) German composer, conductor and pianist. He helped establish a German national style in his operas *Der Freischütz* (1821) and *Euryanthe* (1823). He composed concertos and chamber and piano music, including *Invitation to the Dance* (1819).

Weber, Max (1864–1920) German sociologist. He advanced the concept of "ideal types", generalized models of social situations, as a method of analysis. In his book *The Protestant Ethic and the Spirit of Capitalism* (1904–05), Weber put forward the idea that CALVINISM was influential in the rise of capitalism.

weber (symbol Wb) SI unit of magnetic flux. In a circuit of one turn, one weber produces an ELECTROMOTIVE FORCE of one volt as it is reduced to zero in one second. It is named after the physicist Wilhelm Weber (1804–91).

Webern, Anton von (1883–1945) Austrian composer. His *Passacaglia* (1908) was written using late-romantic tonality. Influenced by his teacher, SCHOENBERG, he adopted atonality, as in the *Six Bagatelles* (1913), and then TWELVE-TONE MUSIC, such as his symphony (1928).

Webster, John (1580–1634) English dramatist whose reputation rests upon his two great tragedies: *The White Devil* (*c*.1612) and *The Duchess of Malfi* (1614). Both plays explore the theme of revenge using macabre language.

Wedekind, Frank (1864–1918) German dramatist. He was a precursor of EXPRESSIONISM and a major influence on BRECHT. His plays include *Spring Awakening* (1906) and *Lulu*, which appeared in two parts: *Earth-Spirit* (1902) and *Pandora's Box* (1905).

wedge In mechanics, an example of the inclined plane. It is used to multiply an applied FORCE while changing its direction of action. For example, if a metal or wooden wedge is driven into a block of wood, a force is exerted by the wedge at right angles to the applied force and greater than it.

Wedgwood, Josiah (1730–95) English potter. He pioneered the large-scale production of pottery at his Etruria works near Stoke-on-Trent, and became famous for his creamware. Wedgwood is best known for his jasper ware, which gave expression to the contemporary interest in the revival of classical art.

weed Uncultivated or unwanted plant. Weeds are a threat to commercial crops because they compete for water and sunlight and harbour pests and diseases.

weedkiller *See* HERBICIDE

Weelkes, Thomas (*c*.1575–1623) English madrigal composer and organist. Almost 100 of his madrigals have survived, the finest being sets of five- and six-part madrigals.

weevil Any of numerous species of beetles that are pests to crops, especially the numerous snout beetles (time weevils), with long, down-curved beaks for boring into plants. Family Curculionidae, the largest in the animal kingdom.

weever Any of four species of small fish that commonly bury themselves in sand in European and Mediterranean coastal waters. Poison spines on the dorsal fin and gill covers can inflict a painful sting. Family Trachinidae; genus *Trachinus*.

Wegener, Alfred Lothar (1880–1930) German geologist, meteorologist and Arctic explorer. In *The Origin of Continents and Oceans* (1915), he first proposed the theory of CONTINENTAL DRIFT.

weight Force of attraction on a body due to GRAVITATION. An object's weight is the product of its MASS and the gravitational field strength at that point. Mass remains constant, but weight depends on the object's position on the Earth's surface, decreasing with increasing altitude.

weightlessness Condition experienced by an object when the force due to GRAVITATION is neutralized. Such an object is said to have zero gravity and no weight; it floats and cannot fall. Weightlessness can be experienced in space and during a free fall. The adverse effects

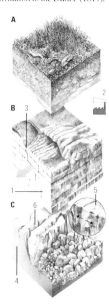

► **weathering** Weathering is the breakdown of rock in place. It occurs in two main ways: physical (A and C) and chemical (B) and usually in combination. At the surface, plant roots and animals break down rock, turning it into soil (A). In chemical weathering (B), soluble rocks such as limestone (1) are dissolved by ground water. Acid rain caused by sulphate pollution (2) also attacks the rock. Both heat and cold can cause physical weathering (C). When temperatures drop below freezing, freeze-thaw weathering can split rocks such as granite (4). Water that settles in cracks and joints during the day expands as it freezes at night (5). This expansion cleaves the rock along naturally occurring joints (6).

on the human body of prolonged weightlessness (hydrogravics) include decreased circulation of blood, less water retention in tissues and loss of muscle tone.

weight lifting Exercise or sport in which weights at the end of a bar are lifted over the head. Competitions are conducted according to weight classes that range from bantamweight to heavyweight. In a weight-lifting competition, each participant uses three standard lifts known as two-hand press, clean-and-jerk and snatch. The competitor who lifts the greatest combined total of weights wins. It has been an Olympic event since 1920.

weights and measures Agreed units for expressing the amount of some quantity, such as capacity, length or weight. Early measurements were based on body measurements and on plant grains. In 1799 France introduced the metric system, in which the unit of length, the METRE, was taken as one ten-millionth of the distance from the equator to the North Pole. A LITRE was the volume occupied by one KILOGRAM of water. *See also* SI UNITS

Weil, Simone (1909–1943) French philosopher and writer. In the late 1930s she had the first of several mystical experiences that drew her to the Roman Catholic Church. During World War 2, Weil became an activist in the French Resistance. Most of her works were published after her death, and include *Gravity and Grace* (1947) and *Waiting for God* (1951).

Weill, Kurt (1900–50) German composer. He is best known for his satirical operas, which include *Der Protagonist* (1926) and the *Rise and Fall of the City of Mahagonny* (1927), the latter with a libretto by Bertolt BRECHT. *The Threepenny Opera* (1928) was a modern version of John Gay's *Beggar's Opera*, again with a libretto by Brecht. In 1935,Weill emigrated to the USA and wrote several Broadway musicals, including *Street Scene* (1947) and *Lost in the Stars* (1949). His wife, Lotte LENYA, was a notable interpreter of his works.

Weimar City in the state of Thuringia, E central Germany. Founded in 975 and chartered in 1348, the city was capital of the Saxe-Weimar duchy from 1547 to 1918. In the 18th century, Weimar was the literary capital of Europe. The 19th century witnessed a gradual artistic decline. In 1919, the German National Assembly convened here to establish the WEIMAR REPUBLIC, and Walter GROPIUS founded the BAUHAUS. Pop. (1991) 59,100.

Weimar Republic (1919–33) Popular name for the republic of Germany created after World War 1. It was named after the city of WEIMAR, where the constitution was drawn up (1919). It was hampered by severe economic difficulties. The Weimar constitution was suspended after Adolf HITLER became chancellor, and the republic was superseded by the THIRD REICH.

Weinberg, Steven (1933–) US physicist who in 1967, independently of Abdus Salam, proposed a theory that unifies the ELECTROMAGNETIC and WEAK NUCLEAR FORCES between subatomic particles – now known as the electroweak force. Later experiments proved the Salam-Weinberg hypothesis to be true. In 1979, they shared the Nobel Prize for physics with Sheldon Glashow. *See also* GRAND UNIFIED THEORY

Weir, Peter Lindsay (1944–) Australian director. His early films *Picnic at Hanging Rock* (1975) and *The Last Wave* (1977) demonstrated a fascination for the power of the natural world that would be a theme in later works, compounding his ever-growing reputation with films such as *Gallipoli* (1981), *Witness* (1985), *Dead Poets Society* (1989) and *Fearless* (1993).

Weismann, August (1834–1914) German biologist. His essay discussing the germ-plasm theory, *The Continuity of the Germ Plasm* (1885), proposed the immortality of the germ line cells as opposed to body cells. It was influential in the development of modern GENETICS.

Weiss, Peter (1916–82) Swedish dramatist, b. Germany. His reputation was established with *Marat/Sade* (1934). Other plays include *The Investigation* (1965) and *Trotsky in Exile* (1970).

Weizmann, Chaim (1874–1952) Zionist leader and chemist, first president of Israel (1948–52). He was born in Russia and became a British subject in 1910. Weizmann was instrumental in securing the BALFOUR DECLARATION (1917). He served as president of the World Zionist Organization (1920–31, 1935–46).

welding Technique for joining metal parts, usually by controlled melting. Several welding processes are used. In **fusion** welding, the parts to be joined are heated together until the metal starts to melt. On cooling, the molten metal solidifies to form a permanent bond between the parts. Such welds are usually strengthened with filler metal from a welding rod or wire. In **arc** welding, an electric arc heats the work and filler metal. In **oxyacetylene** welding, heat is provided by burning ethyne gas in oxygen. In resistance or **spot** welding, the heat is generated by passing an electric current through the joint. In brazing and soldering, the temperature used is sufficient to melt the filler metal, but not the parts that it joins.

welfare state Description of a state that takes responsibility for the health and subsistence of its citizens. Limited forms of welfare·were introduced by Western governments in the late 19th century, such as Germany. Comprehensive policies were introduced after World War 2, such as in the UK. *See also* SOCIAL SECURITY

well Shaft sunk in the Earth's CRUST through which water, oil, natural gas, brine, sulphur or other mineral substances can be extracted. Artesian wells are sunk into water-bearing rock strata, the AQUIFERS, from which water rises under pressure in the wells to the surface.

Welland Ship Canal Canal that connects Port Weller on Lake Ontario with Port Colborne on Lake Erie, SE Ontario, Canada. It forms a part of the ST LAWRENCE SEAWAY. The first canal was completed in 1829 but was greatly improved between 1912 and 1932. There are eight locks along its length of *c.*44km (27mi).

Welles, (George) Orson (1915–85) US actor and director. His first film, *Citizen Kane* (1940), earned him an academy award for best screenplay. As an actor, he starred in *The Third Man* (1949). Welles directed and acted in *The Lady of Shanghai* (1948) and *Touch of Evil* (1958). Disenchanted with Hollywood, he went into self-imposed exile in Europe, directing *The Trial* (1963), *Chimes at Midnight* (1966) and *The Immortal Story* (1968). Welles' vivid radio dramatization (1938) of H.G. WELLS' *War of the Worlds* caused mass panic and hysteria.

Wellington, Arthur Wellesley, Duke of (1769–1852) British general and statesman, prime minister (1828–30). He was knighted for his defeat of the Marathas in India (1803). In 1809, Wellesley became commander of allied forces in the PENINSULAR WAR. He gradually drove the French army back over the Pyrenees. Wellington's victory at the Battle of Toulouse (1814) precipitated NAPOLEON I's abdication. Wellesley was created the duke of Wellington. While representing Britain at the Congress of VIENNA (1814–15), he learned of Napoleon's escape from Elba. Wellington resumed command of allied troops and, with the Prussian General von Blücher, defeated Napoleon at the Battle of WATERLOO (1815). In 1819, he became a Tory cabinet minister. As prime minister, Wellington grudgingly accepted the passage of the

Act of CATHOLIC EMANCIPATION (1829). He served as foreign secretary (1834–35) under Sir Robert PEEL.

Wellington Capital of New Zealand, in the extreme S of North Island on Port Nicholson, an inlet of Cook Strait. First visited by Europeans in 1826, it was founded in 1840. In 1865, it replaced Auckland as capital. Wellington's excellent harbour furthered its development as a transport and trading centre. Much of the city's manufacturing industry (textiles, clothing, transport equipment and machinery) is located in outlying suburbs. Pop. (1996) 329,000.

Wells, H.G. (Herbert George) (1866–1946) English writer. His reputation was established with the science fiction novels *The Time Machine* (1895), *The Invisible Man* (1897) and *The War of the Worlds* (1898). Later novels, including *Love and Mr. Lewisham* (1900), *Kipps* (1905), *Tono-Bungay* (1909) and *The History of Mr. Polly* (1910), draw on experiences more directly related in his *Experiment in Autobiography* (1934). *Ann Veronica* (1909) and *The New Machiavelli* (1911) reflect his interest in sociology and politics as a member of the FABIAN SOCIETY. Wells also wrote a number of short stories.

Welsbach, Baron Carl Auer von (1858–1929) Austro-Hungarian chemist who discovered the rare-earth elements NEODYMIUM and PRASEODYMIUM. He is best known for his 1885 invention of the gas mantle, which produces a bright, incandescent light from a gas flame.

Welsh (*Cymraeg*) Language of Wales. It is spoken by less than 19% of the Welsh population, chiefly in the rural north and west. It belongs to the Brittonic sub-branch of the Celtic family of INDO-EUROPEAN LANGUAGES and is closely related to BRETON and CORNISH. It survives more strongly than most other CELTIC LANGUAGES.

Welsh National Party *See* PLAID CYMRU

Welsh pony Light saddle-horse known in Wales since Saxon times. Usually a child's mount, it has the physique of a miniature coach horse. Height: to 1.2m (48in) at the shoulder; weight: to 225kg (500lb).

Welty, Eudora (1909–) US short-story writer and novelist. Her works are set often in her native Mississippi. Welty's short-story collections include *A Curtain of Green* (1941) and *The Golden Apples* (1949). Her novels, firmly in the Southern Gothic tradition, include the Pulitzer Prize-winning *The Optimist's Daughter* (1972). Her autobiography is *One Writer's Beginnings* (1984).

welwitschia (tumboa) Plant that grows in the sandy regions of SW Africa. It produces only two leathery leaves that split into many ribbon-like strands up to 1.2–1.8m (4–6ft) long. Welwitschia may live up to 2,000 years. Cone clusters – actually small flower spikes – are borne each year on both male and female plants. Division Gnetophyta; species *Welwitschia mirabilis*.

Wembley Complex of sports stadiums in Wembley, NW London. The outdoor Empire Stadium, with its twin towers, built for the 1924 Empire Exhibition, is used for the finals of the FA Cup, Football League Cup and Rugby League Cup, as well as England's home international football matches. In the nearby Empire Pool, a covered arena, ice shows and pop concerts share the facilities with boxing, show-jumping and other sports. In 1996, Wembley was granted funding for a complete rebuild to make it the official National Sports Stadium. The last match was played under its twin towers in 2000.

Wenceslas, Saint (907–29) Prince of Bohemia and patron saint of the Czechs. In *c*.925 he overthrew his mother who, as regent, persecuted Christians. He continued the Christianization of the country which, together with his submission to the Germans, aroused opposition. He was killed by his brother and successor, Boleslav I.

Wenceslaus (1361–1419) King of the Germans (1378–1400) and king of Bohemia (1378–1419) as Wenceslaus IV. He succeeded his father, CHARLES IV, as emperor but was never crowned. Wenceslaus' neglect of German affairs angered the princes, who deposed him (1400) in favour of Rupert. He enabled his half-brother, SIGISMUND, to become (1387) king of Hungary. In Bohemia, Wenceslaus supported the reforms of Jan HUS.

Wentworth, William Charles (1793–1872) Australian journalist and politician. In 1824, he founded the *Australian* newspaper, which he used to promote the cause of self-government for the Australian colonies. His activism was the most important factor leading to the granting of self-government by the British Parliament in 1842.

werewolf In folklore, a person who changes into a wolf at night but reverts to human form by day. Some werewolves can change form at will; in others the change occurs involuntarily under the influence of a full moon.

Werfel, Franz (1890–1945) Austrian dramatist, novelist, and poet. His religious, historical and modernist dramas include *The Trojan Women* (1915), *Paulus Among the Jews* (1926) and *Jacobowsky and the Colonel* (1943). *The Forty Days of Musa Dagh* (1933), *Embezzled Heaven* (1939), *The Song of Bernadette* (1941) and *Star of the Unborn* (1946) are among Werfel's most famous novels. His popular expressionist poetry, found in *The Friend of the World* (1911) and *Each Other* (1915), expressed his love for mankind.

Wergeland, Henrik Arnold (1808–45) Norwegian poet and patriot. Much of his short life was devoted to working for Norwegian cultural independence from Denmark. Such works as *Creation, Man and Messiah* (1830) and "The English Pilot" (1844) helped establish his reputation as Norway's national poet.

Werner, Alfred (1866–1919) Swiss chemist. He was awarded the 1913 Nobel Prize for chemistry for his coordination theory of VALENCE in which he correctly suggested that metals have coordinate bonds that make ISOMERS possible in inorganic compounds.

Wertheimer, Max (1880–1943) German psychologist. Wertheimer was a founder of GESTALT PSYCHOLOGY. His early work concerned visual perception. Later, he attempted to apply Gestalt principles to cognitive and educational problems.

Wesker, Arnold (1932–) English dramatist. His childhood in the East End of London is recollected in the trilogy *Chicken Soup with Barley* (1958), *Roots* (1959), and *I'm Talking about Jerusalem* (1960). His experiences in World War 2 are the subject of *Chips with Everything* (1962). His later work includes *The Old Ones* (1972) and *The Wedding Feast* (1974).

Wesley, Charles (1707–88) English evangelist and hymn-writer, brother of John WESLEY. In 1735, he was ordained and in 1738 experienced an evangelical conversion. Wesley wrote nearly 6,000 hymns, including "Hark! the Herald Angels Sing" and "Love Divine, All Loves Excelling".

Wesley, John (1703–91) English theologian and evangelist, founder of METHODISM. With his brother Charles WESLEY, he founded (1729) the Holy Club at Oxford. In 1735, the brothers travelled as missionaries to the USA, but John returned in 1737. In 1738, during a Moravian meeting, Wesley underwent a personal, religious experience that laid the foundation upon which he built the Methodist movement. Wesley's *Journal* (1735–90) records the extent of his itinerant preaching.

Wessex Anglo-Saxon kingdom established in Hampshire, SW England. Traditionally founded by Cerdic (r.519–534), by the beginning of the 9th century it had extended its territory to include much of s England. Egbert became overlord of all England, but his successors lost much of the kingdom to the Danes. ALFRED THE GREAT ensured that Wessex was the only English kingdom to escape Danish conquest.

West, Benjamin (1738–1820) US painter. He settled in Britain, where he became historical painter to George III and a leader of NEO-CLASSICISM. Two of his best-known paintings are *Death of Wolfe* (1771) and *Penn's Treaty with the Indians* (1772).

West, Mae (1893–1980) US stage and film actress. She began her career in burlesque. Her first film was *Night After Night* (1932). Her overt sexuality and use of double entendre in *She Done Him Wrong* and *I'm No Angel* (1933) led to increased censorship in the movie industry. Other films include *Go West, Young Man* (1936) and *My Little Chickadee* (1940).

West, Nathanael (1903–40) US novelist, b. Nathan Wallenstein Weinstein. He wrote four novels: *The Dream Life of Balso Snell* (1931); *Miss Lonelyhearts* (1933), a grimly comic story about a columnist for the lovelorn; *A Cool Million* (1934); and *The Day of the Locust* (1939), a tale of false dreams and failed lives in Hollywood, where West spent his last years as a scriptwriter.

West, Dame Rebecca (1892–1983) English novelist and critic, b. Cicily Isabel Fairfield. She is best known for her first novel, *The Return of the Soldier* (1918), the story of a shell-shock victim. Her political works include *The Meaning of Treason* (1949) and a two-volume study of Yugoslavia, *Black Lamb and Grey Falcon* (1942). West also wrote psychological novels such as *The Thinking Reed* (1936) and *Birds Fall Down* (1966). Her last work was *1900* (1982).

West Bank Region w of the River JORDAN and NW of the Dead Sea. Under the United Nations plan for the partition of Palestine (1947), it was designated an Arab district. It was administered by Jordan after the first ARAB-ISRAELI WAR (1948) but captured by Israel in the SIX DAY WAR of 1967. In 1988, Jordan surrendered its claim to the Israeli-occupied West Bank to the PALESTINE LIBERATION ORGANIZATION (PLO). Under the terms of the ISRAELI-PALESTINIAN ACCORD (1993), limited autonomy in the West Bank was conceded to the newly formed Palestinian National Authority (PNA). Difficulties created by the growth of Israeli settlements, security disputes, Palestinian terrorism, and the accession (1996) of a Likud government in Israel threatened to disrupt progress towards total Israeli withdrawal.

West Bengal State in NE India bordering Nepal, Bhutan and Sikkim (N), Bangladesh and Assam state (E), the Bay of Bengal (S) and Bihar and Orissa states (W). The state capital is CALCUTTA. It was formed in 1947 after the independence of India and Pakistan, and the partitioning of the former British province of BENGAL into Hindu West Bengal (India) and Muslim East Bengal (East Pakistan). In 1950, West Bengal absorbed the state of Cooch Bihar. In the 1970s, political instability was caused by Muslim-Hindu disputes, large immigration from newly created BANGLADESH and Naxalite disturbances. The state is highly industrialized and its cities (notably Calcutta) attract male migrants from neighbouring states. Industries: vehicles, steel, fertilizers, chemicals. Agricultural products: rice, fish, jute, oilseeds, tea, tobacco. Area: 88,752sq km (34,258sq mi). Pop. (1991) 68,077,965.

Western Type of popular fiction and film, native to the USA, featuring "cowboys" and sometimes "Indians" in a Wild West setting. It first appeared in the form of short stories and novels in the "pulp" magazines of the late 19th century. Owen Wister's *The Virginian* (1902) is perhaps the defining influence on the form, and Zane Grey its most prolific exponent. *The Squaw Man* (1914), one of the first Hollywood Westerns, set a trend for a whole new breed of movie cowboy such as Tom Mix, Roy Rogers, Gene Autry and "Hopalong" Cassidy. Famous Westerns include *Stagecoach* (1939), *High Noon* (1952) and *Shane* (1953). Television hits included *Gunsmoke* (1955–75). More recent examples of the genre have re-evaluated the treatment of Native Americans by settlers.

Western Australia State in Australia, bordered by the Timor Sea (N) the Indian Ocean (W and S), South Australia state and the Northern Territory (E). The capital is PERTH, and other significant cities are Mandurah, Kalgoorlie, Bunbury and Fremantle, Perth's ocean port. Though Western Australia was first visited by Dirck Hartog in 1616, settlement did not begin until 1826, when a penal colony was founded. The first free settlement was in 1829. By far the largest state in Australia, it was governed by New South Wales until 1831, becoming a state of the Commonwealth of Australia in 1901. The climate is mainly tropical or subtropical, and more than 90% of the land is desert or semi-desert. Only the sw, which enjoys a temperate climate, is permanently settled. Swan River is the state's only significant water source. The raising of sheep and cattle is the principal agricultural activity, but cereals, fishing and forestry are also important. Western Australia is the country's major gold-producing state, and there is also mining for iron ore, coal, nickel, uranium, bauxite, phosphates, oil and natural gas. Industry is still expanding, and wine became a major earner during the 1980s. Area: 2,525,500sq km (975,095sq mi). Pop. (1991) 1,586,393.

Western Cape Province in sw South Africa, bounded by the Indian Ocean (S) and Atlantic Ocean (W). The capital is CAPE TOWN. Other major towns include Simonstown and Stellenbosch. Formerly part of CAPE PROVINCE, Western Cape was founded in 1994. Its chief physical features are Table Mountain (1,088m, 3,566ft high) and the rugged Swartberg Range (maximum height 2,326m, 7,627ft). Robben Island was the site of an offshore prison used to house political prisoners during the APARTHEID era. The main economic activity is agriculture, with fruit and tobacco growing, dairy farming and sheep rearing. There is also an important fishing industry, and an offshore gas field is exploited in Mossel Bay. Industries: chemicals, machinery, metal goods, textiles. Area: 129,390sq km (50,500sq mi). Pop. (1993) 3,620,200.

Western European Union (WEU) Defence alliance consisting of most of the European members of the NORTH ATLANTIC TREATY ORGANIZATION (NATO).

Western Isles *See* HEBRIDES

Western Sahara (formerly Spanish Sahara) Desert territory on the Atlantic coast of NW Africa, bordering Morocco (N), Algeria (NE) and Mauritania (E and S). The capital is El Aaiún. The territory comprises two districts: Saguia el Hamra in the N and Río de Oro in the S. The population is composed of Arabs, BERBERS and pastoral nomads, most of whom are SUNNI Muslims. The first European discovery was in 1434, but the area remained unexploited until the 19th century, and even then Spain controlled only the coastal area. In 1957, a nationalist movement overthrew the Spanish, but in 1958 the Spanish regained control of the region and merged Saguia el Hamra and Río de Oro to form the province of Spanish Sahara. In 1963, large phosphate deposits were discovered. In 1973, the Polisario Front began a guerrilla war that forced Spain to withdraw in 1976. Within a month, Morocco and Mauritania had partitioned the country. Polisario (backed by Algeria) continued to fight for independence, unilaterally renaming the country the Saharawi Arab Democratic Republic. In 1979, Mauritania withdrew, and Morocco assumed full control. In 1982, the Saharawi Republic was granted membership of the Organization of African Unity (OAU) and, by 1988, controlled most of the desert up to the Moroccan defensive line. Fragile ceasefires were agreed in 1988 and 1991. An estimated 200,000 Saharawis live in refugee camps, mostly in Algeria. Area: 266,769sq km (102,680sq mi). Pop. (2000) 228,000.

Western Samoa Independent island republic in the s Pacific Ocean, encompassing the w half of the SAMOA island chain. It comprises the two large volcanic and mountainous islands of Savai'i and Upolu, the smaller islands of Manono and Apolima, and several uninhabited islets. The capital, Apia (on Upolu), has 66% of the total population. The cradle of Polynesian culture, the islands became a German protectorate under the terms of an 1899 treaty, but in 1914 New Zealand seized them and they were administered by New Zealand from 1920–61 under a League of Nations mandate and then a United Nations trusteeship. Resistance to New Zealand rule led to a plebiscite and, in 1962, Western Samoa became an independent state within the Commonwealth. Under a friendship treaty, New Zealand handles relations with governments outside the Pacific zone. The Polynesian population is employed mainly in subsistence agriculture, and the chief exports are coconut oil, taro and copra. Area: 2,840sq km (1,097sq mi). Pop. (2000) 171,000.

Western Wall (Wailing Wall) Place in Jerusalem sacred to all Jews. It is a remnant of a wall of the great TEMPLE destroyed by the Romans in AD 70 and is the focus of many pilgrimages.

West Glamorgan County in s Wales on the Bristol Channel; the administrative centre is SWANSEA. Tourists are attracted by the rugged Gower Peninsula. Area: 820sq km (317sq mi). Pop. (1991) 361,428.

West Indies Chain of islands encircling the Caribbean Sea and separating it from the Atlantic Ocean. They extend from Florida to Venezuela. Geographically they are divided into three main groups: the BAHAMAS and the Greater and Lesser ANTILLES. Most islands are now independent, but were formerly British, Spanish, French or Dutch possessions. The indigenous population was killed by the colonial powers, who fought for possession of the islands. The islands were transformed by the introduction of sugar cane in the 17th century, fuelling the slave trade from Africa. *See* individual country articles

Westinghouse, George (1846–1914) US engineer and inventor. The best known of his hundreds of inventions was the air brake (1868), which made high-speed rail travel safe. In 1886, he formed the Westinghouse Electric Company for the transmission of electricity.

Westmeath County in Leinster province, N central Republic of Ireland. It is mainly low-lying, with many lakes or loughs and is drained by the rivers SHANNON, Inny and Brosna. The county town is Mullingar. Area: 1,763sq km (681sq mi). Pop. (1991) 61,880.

West Midlands Metropolitan county in central England. It is divided into seven council districts: BIRMINGHAM (the administrative centre), COVENTRY, Dudley, Sandwell, Solihull, Walsall and Wolverhampton. Area: 899sq km (347sq mi). Pop. (1991) 2,551,671.

Westminster, City of Part of the LONDON borough of Westminster since 1965. From 785, Westminster was the site of a monastery upon which EDWARD THE CONFESSOR built WESTMINSTER ABBEY. Parliament met in Westminster Palace until a fire in 1834 led to the building of the HOUSES OF PARLIAMENT (1840–68). Pop. (1991) 174,718.

Westminster, Statutes of English acts of the reign of EDWARD I. The first (1275) and second (1285) statutes enshrined Edward's overhaul of English law. A further statute of 1290 is sometimes called the third statute of Westminster. The Statute of Westminster of 1931 granted autonomy to the dominions in the British Empire.

Westminster Abbey Gothic church in London, originally the abbey church of a Benedictine monastery (closed 1539). In 1050, EDWARD THE CONFESSOR began to build a Norman church on the site. In 1245, Henry III began work on the present structure. The Lady Chapel, dedicated to Henry VII, is a fine example of the PERPENDICULAR STYLE. The two western towers were built (1722–45) by Sir Christopher WREN and Nicholas HAWKSMOOR. The 19th century restoration was managed by Sir George Gilbert SCOTT. It is cruciform in plan. Since William of Conqueror, most English monarchs have been crowned in the abbey. It is the burial place of 18 monarchs. Poets' Corner lies in the south transept.

Weston, Edward (1886–1958) US photographer. In 1932, he helped form the influential *64 group*. Weston's style of "straight photography" was sharp and direct, emphasizing the texture and forms of the natural world.

Westphalia Historic region of w Germany between the rivers Rhine and Weser. From 1180, it was a duchy under the archbishops of Cologne. Briefly a kingdom during the NAPOLEONIC WARS, it became a province of Prussia in 1816.

Westphalia, Peace of (1648) Series of treaties among the states involved in the THIRTY YEARS WAR. Peace negotiations began in 1642, and meetings were held in cities of Westphalia. In Germany, the peace established the virtual autonomy of the German states and diminished the authority of the Holy Roman emperor. It also established the ascendancy of France, the power of Sweden in N Europe and the decline of Spain.

West Point US military post on the w bank of the Hudson River, SE New York. The site of several revolutionary forts, it has served as the headquarters of the US Military Academy since 1802.

West Sussex County in SE England; the county town is Chichester. Other towns include Crawley and Worthing. Area: 2,016sq km (778sq mi). Pop. (1991) 702,290.

West Virginia State in the Appalachian Mountain region, E central USA. The capital is CHARLESTON. The land is mountainous and rugged. West Virginia has two narrow projections: the Northern Panhandle extends N between Ohio and Pennsylvania; and the Eastern Panhandle cuts E between Maryland and Virginia. Harpers Ferry lies on the bank of the Potomac River, which forms much of the state's E border. The Ohio River forms most of its w border. In 1727, Germans established the first settlement at New Mecklenburg (Shepherdstown). Settlers crossing the Appalachian and Allegheny mountains led to the last of the FRENCH AND INDIAN WARS (1754–63). The region was then part of Virginia, but political and economic disagreements, especially over slavery, arose between western Virginians and the dominant E. When Virginia seceded from the Union in May 1861, there was much opposition in the w, and it was admitted to the Union as West Virginia in 1863. Hay, tobacco, maize and apples are the principal crops, but West Virginia also has rich mineral deposits and is the leading US producer of bituminous coal. Some 65% of the land is forested. Industries: glass, chemicals, steel, machinery, tourism. Area 62,629sq km (24,181sq mi). Pop. (2000) 1,808,344.

West Yorkshire County in N central England. It is divided into the districts of BRADFORD, Calderdale, Kirklees, LEEDS and Wakefield (the county town). Area: 2,036sq km (786sq mi). Pop. (1991) 2,013,693.

wetland Ecosystem where the water table lies close to the surface for much of the year. Wetlands include bogs, marshes, swamps and fens. There are both saltwater and freshwater wetlands. Coastal wetlands are said to contain a greater concentration of flora and fauna than any other ecosystem. They are also ecologically valuable as regulators of flooding and the water cycle. Many of the world's wetlands have been drained for farming or housing.

Wexford County in Leinster province, SE Republic of Ireland. The land is mostly low-lying. The chief river is the Slaney. Wexford is primarily an agricultural county. The county town is Wexford (1991 pop. 9,500). Area 2,351sq km (908sq mi). Pop. (1991) 102,069.

Weyden, Rogier van der (1400–64) Netherlandish painter. In 1436, he became official painter to the city of Brussels, where he lived for the rest of his life. His finest works include *Deposition* (before 1443), and he excelled at inventive compositions.

whale Any of several species of large aquatic mammals; it has a fish-like body with paddle-like flippers and a tail flattened horizontally into flukes for locomotion. It spends its whole life in water. Two main groups exist: toothed whales and baleen whales. Toothed whales (Odontoceti) have simple teeth and feed primarily on fish and squid. They include the bottle-nosed whale, SPERM WHALE and BELUGA. Baleen whales (Mysticeti), including the right whale, BLUE WHALE and California grey whale, have no teeth but carry comb-like plates of horny material (baleen or whalebone) in the roof of the mouth. These form a sieve, through which the whales strain krill on which they feed. Order Cetacea. The order also includes DOLPHINS and PORPOISES. *See also* WHALING

whale shark Largest species of SHARK; it lives in tropical waters throughout the world. Brownish to dark grey with white or yellow spots and stripes, this docile, egg-laying fish often travels near the surface. Length: 9m (30ft). Family Rhincodontidae; species *Rhincodon typus*.

whaling Industry involved in the pursuing and catching of WHALES for their oil and flesh. The modern whaling era began in the 1850s with the development of harpoons with explosive heads; after 1925 ocean-going factory ships were sent to the Antarctic. Since then most larger whale species, including the blue whale, have been hunted to near-extinction. In 1986, the International Whaling Commission (IWC) agreed a moratorium on commercial whaling. Whaling for "scientific purposes", by Japan, Iceland and Norway, continued. In 1990, Norway claimed that whale numbers were high enough to sustain hunting; public opposition, however, remains strong.

Wharton, Edith Newbold (1862–1937) US novelist. She is best known for *Ethan Frome* (1911), a grim portrait of New England farm life, and her polished anatomies of New York society, *The House of Mirth* (1905) and *The Age of Innocence* (1920), for which she became the first woman to be awarded a Pulitzer Prize for fiction.

wheat CEREAL grass cultivated in the Middle East since 7000 BC; it is now grown worldwide. It is used for BREAD, PASTA, cake and pastry flour. Wheat is also used in the preparation of MALT, dextrose and ALCOHOL. Family Poaceae/Gramineae.

Wheatstone, Sir Charles (1802–75) English physicist and inventor. In 1843, with William Cooke, he improved the Wheatstone bridge, a device for measuring electrical resistance. In 1837, they patented an electric TELEGRAPH. Wheatstone also invented the harmonica.

wheel Circular structure that revolves around a central axis. Before the wheel was invented, heavy loads were sometimes moved by rolling them on logs or on rounded stones. More than 5,000 years ago, sections of tree trunks were cut to form the first wheels for carts. Spoked wheels were introduced several hundred years later. Eventually, the wheel was used in simple machines, such as the waterwheel and potter's wheel.

wheel and axle Machine based on the principle that a small force applied to the rim of a wheel will exert a larger force on an object attached to the axle. The MECHANICAL ADVANTAGE, or force ratio, is the ratio of the radius of the wheel to that of the axle.

whelk Edible, marine GASTROPOD found on seashores. It has a coiled shell with a smooth rim and a notch at the end. Family Buccinidae. Length: 13–18cm (5–7in).

Whig Party One of the two major US political parties from 1834–54. It was a coalition party and had the support of eastern capitalists, western farmers and southern plantation owners. The party elected two presidents, William Henry HARRISON in 1840 and Zachary TAYLOR in 1848. The issue of slavery split the Whigs, however, and the REPUBLICAN PARTY emerged from its disintegration in 1854.

Whigs Semi-formal parliamentary grouping in the UK from the late 17th to the mid-19th century. The word Whig was used by the TORY supporters of JAMES II for politicians who wished to exclude the Duke of York from the throne. The Whig Party thus became those people who promoted the GLORIOUS REVOLUTION of 1688 and who applauded the HANOVERIAN SUCCESSION of 1714. Between 1714 and the accession of George III in 1760, the Tories were so discredited by association with the JACOBITES that most politicians became Hanoverian Whigs, even in opposition to a Whig ministry. In the reign of GEORGE III, Toryism gradually reasserted itself. Whiggism became the party of religious toleration, parliamentary reform and

▲ **whale** Among the largest and most intelligent animals that have ever lived, whales all belong to the order Cetacea. The beluga whale (*Delphinapterus leucas*, A) is an Arctic species and travels in schools of many hundreds. It grows to 4.25m (17ft). The pilot whale (*Globicephala* sp., B) is found in most oceans except the polar seas. They migrate between cold and warm waters depending on the season. The Californian grey whale (*Eschrichtius glaucus*, C) is confined to the North Pacific. From the N seas they migrate S in winter to breed in the shallow, warmer seas off Baja California and South Korea. They feed on plankton, which they strain from the water by means of baleen plates (1). They grow to 9m (30ft).

opposition to slavery. From the appointment of PITT as prime minister in 1783 until 1830, the Whigs remained in opposition (with one brief exception). They then returned to office under Lord GREY, passing the Great Reform Act of 1832. By the mid-19th century, they had come to be replaced by, or known as, the Liberal Party.

whinchat Small Eurasian THRUSH that commonly inhabits grassy coastal areas in England. It has a brown, mottled back with a white rump and distinctive red breast. The dark head is clearly marked by a white eye-stripe. Length: to 13cm (5in). Species *Saxicola rubetra*.

whip UK government officer whose duty is to see that government supporters attend debates and vote in divisions. It is also the name for the notices that they send to members of Parliament. There are also opposition whips.

whiplash Neck injury that results when the head is jerked rapidly backwards and then forwards. It occurs most often in car accidents when the car is hit from behind. Neck muscles and ligaments are injured, causing pain and stiffness.

whippet Sporting dog that was originally bred in England for racing and hare coursing. It is capable of running at speeds of 56km/h (35mph). Height: to 56cm (22in) at the shoulder; weight: to 11kg (24lb).

whippoorwill *See* NIGHTJAR

whirligig beetle *See* WATER BEETLE

whirlpool Circular motion of a fluid. Whirlpools in rivers occur in regions where WATERFALLS or sharp breaks in topographic continuity make steady flow impossible. *See also* VORTEX

whisky Alcoholic spirit made by distilling fermented cereal grains. Scotch whisky and Irish whiskey are both distilled from barley that has been allowed to sprout, then roasted, and finally "mashed" and distilled. In the USA, corn and rye are used to produce bourbon whiskey (corn) and rye whiskey. After distillation, refined whisky spirit is 70–85% alcohol by volume; all whiskies are, therefore, heavily diluted. Almost all whiskies are blended.

whist Card game for four people. The aim is to accumulate "tricks" – sets of cards, one from each player, in which the player of the highest-value card "takes the trick". The object of ordinary whist is to amass more tricks than any other player. Other whist games include contract whist, in which players specify how many tricks they will make, and solo whist, in which one player contracts to make tricks. *See also* BRIDGE

Whistler, James Abbott McNeill (1834–1903) US painter and etcher who lived and worked in England from 1859. He was a precursor of ABSTRACT ART. For Whistler, the artist's duty was to select elements from nature to create a harmonious composition that, like music, existed for its own sake. His most famous painting is the portrait of his mother, entitled *Arrangement in Gray and Black* (1872). Other works include *Chelsea: Nocturne in Blue and Green* (c.1870). He also produced some 400 plates of etchings.

Whitby Coastal town in N Yorkshire, England. St Hilda founded an abbey here in 657 which was destroyed by the Danes in the 9th century. In c.663 the **Synod of Whitby** was held at the abbey. The subsequent break with the Celtic church placed the English church in line with mainstream European Christian theology.

White, Gilbert (1720–93) British naturalist. He held curacies at Selborne in Hampshire, devoting himself to the study of natural history around his parish. His famous *The Natural History and Antiquities of Selborne* (1789) consists of letters to his fellow naturalists.

White, Patrick (1912–90) Australian novelist, b. Britain. His novels, concerned with Australian history and identity, include *The Tree of Man* (1955), *Voss* (1957) and *Riders in the Chariot* (1961). Later novels include *The Eye of the Storm* (1973), *A Fringe of Leaves* (1976) and *The Twyborn Affair* (1979). In 1973, White became the first Australian to win the Nobel Prize for literature. His autobiography is *Flaws in the Glass* (1981).

white ant *See* TERMITE

white blood cell *See* LEUCOCYTE

white dwarf High-density type of star about the size of the Earth but with a mass about that of the Sun. White dwarfs are of low luminosity and gradually cool down to become cold, dark objects.

white-eye Common name for a group of arboreal songbirds found mainly in tropical forests in Africa, Asia, and Australasia. They are usually small and green with a prominent ring of white feathers around the eyes. They have pointed bills and extensible tongues for feeding on fruits. Length: to 12.5cm (5in). Family Zosteropidae.

Whitefield, George (1714–70) English evangelical preacher, an important figure in early METHODISM. In 1738 he made his first visit to America. Whitefield's stirring, open-air sermons contributed to the GREAT AWAKENING. He broke away from John WESLEY to form the Calvinistic Methodist Church.

whitefish (cisco, lake herring) Any of several species of freshwater food fish that live in Eurasia and the USA. It is silvery with large scales and a small mouth. Length: to 150cm (59in); weight: to 29kg (63lb). Family Salmonidae.

Whitehead, A.N. (Alfred North) (1861–1947) English philosopher and mathematician. In his "philosophy of organism" he attempted a synthesis of modern science and metaphysics. The system is presented in his *Process and Reality* (1929). His three-volume *Principia Mathematica* (1910–13), written in collaboration with Bertrand RUSSELL, is an important work in the study of LOGIC.

Whitehorse Capital of Yukon Territory, Canada. It lies on the Alaska Highway and the w bank of the Yukon River. The town developed during the Klondike gold rush (1897–98). Pop. (1991) 17,925.

White House Official residence of the US president, WASHINGTON, D.C. It was designed in the neo-classical style by James Hoban in 1792, and completed in 1800. After being burned down by the British in 1814, it was rebuilt, and the porticoes were added in the 1820s.

white shark (great white shark) SHARK found in tropical and sub-tropical waters; it is the most aggressive of sharks. It has a crescent-shaped tail and saw-edged triangular teeth; it is grey, blue or brown with a white belly. Length: to 11m (36ft); weight: to 2,200kg (7,000lb). Family Isuridae; species *Carcharodon carcharias*.

white whale *See* BELUGA

Whitgift, John (1530–1604) English churchman. In 1583, he became archbishop of Canterbury. Whitgift tried to maintain a middle course in the REFORMATION, upholding the recently established doctrine of the CHURCH OF ENGLAND and strongly opposing the Puritans.

Whitlam, (Edward) Gough (1916–) Australian statesman, prime minister (1972–75). In 1967, Whitlam became leader of the Australian Labour Party. His government ended compulsory conscription and relaxed Australia's stringent immigration laws. In 1975, Whitlam was dismissed by the governor general, an action that highlighted Australia's constitutional relationship with the UK. In December 1977, after a crushing defeat in the general election, Whitlam resigned as party leader.

Whitman, Walt (Walter) (1819–92) US poet. In 1855, he published, at his own expense, *Leaves of Grass*, a volume of 12 poems that included "Song of Myself". In 1856 and 1860 Whitman published enlarged editions of the work. *Drum-Taps* (1865), which draws on his experience of medical service in the Civil War, and *Sequel to Drum-Taps* (1865–66), which includes his famous elegies to Abraham Lincoln, "When Lilacs Last in the Dooryard Bloom'd" and "O Captain! My Captain!", were both incorporated into a much-expanded 1867 edition of *Leaves of Grass*. Whitman's use of free verse, symbolic association and colloquial language represents a major transition in AMERICAN LITERATURE.

Whitney, Eli (1765–1825) US inventor and manufacturer. Whitney invented (1793) the COTTON GIN, which revolutionized cotton culture in the South and turned cotton into a profitable export. After 1798, he manufactured muskets at a factory in New Haven, Connecticut, which was one of the first to use mass-production methods.

Whitney, Mount Highest peak in the US (excluding Alaska), at 4,418m (14,495ft). Situated on the E edge of SEQUOIA NATIONAL PARK, it is part of the Sierra Nevada range in E California.

Whittington, Dick (Richard) (1358–1423) English merchant. He became wealthy dealing in fine cloth and was lord mayor of London on several occasions (1397–1420). Whittington is, however, best known as the subject of a legend about a poor boy who makes his fortune with the aid of his cat.

Whittle, Sir Frank (1907–96) English inventor. In 1930, he patented the first turbojet (gas turbine) engine for aircraft. Whittle developed the engine while a test pilot in the Royal Air Force (RAF), but he was refused government support until the outbreak of World War 2. By 1941, his first jet plane was flying, and the first jets entered service with the RAF in 1944. *See also* JET ENGINE

whooping cough (pertussis) Acute, highly contagious childhood respiratory disease. It is caused by the bacterium *Bordetella pertussis* and is marked by spasms of coughing, followed by a long-drawn intake of air, or "whoop". It is frequently associated with vomiting and severe nosebleeds. Immunization reduces the number and severity of attacks.

Whorf, Benjamin Lee (1897–1941) US linguist and anthropologist. Whorf and Edward SAPIR developed the Sapir-Whorf hypothesis, which states that "the structure of language influences thought processes and our perception of the world around us".

whortleberry *See* BILBERRY

Wichita City in S central Kansas, at the confluence of the Arkansas and Little Arkansas rivers. Established (1864) as a trading post, it developed with the arrival of the Chisholm Trail and the railway (1872). It was incorporated in 1886. A cattle town and later a wheat centre, its growth was spurred by the discovery of oil (1915) and the development of the aircraft industry (1920). It is the largest city in the state. Industries: aviation, railway workshops, oil refining, grain processing, meat-packing. Pop. (1996) 320,000.

Wicklow County in Leinster province, E Republic of Ireland; the county town is Wicklow. The terrain is dominated by the Wicklow Mountains. The Liffey, Slaney and Avoca are the chief rivers. Sheep and cattle are reared and cereals grown. The scenery attracts many tourists. Area: 2,025sq km (782sq mi). Pop. (1991) 97,265.

Wieland, Heinrich Otto (1877–1957) German chemist who was awarded the 1927 Nobel Prize for chemistry for his research into BILE acids. He showed

them to have a STEROID skeleton and thus found that they were structurally related to CHOLESTEROL.

Wiener, Norbert (1894–1964) US mathematician and originator of CYBERNETICS. He contributed to the development of the COMPUTER and to feedback systems that control the behaviour of humans and machines.

Wiesbaden City on the River Rhine at the foot of the Taunus Mountains, W central Germany; the capital of Hessen lande. Founded in the 3rd century BC and later a Roman spa town, the city is still famous for its mineral springs. Wiesbaden was capital of the Duchy of Nassau from 1806 to 1866, when it passed to Prussia. Industries: metal goods, chemicals, cement, plastics, tourism, publishing. Pop. (1996) 266,000.

Wiesel, Elie (1928–) US novelist, b. Romania. The sole family survivor from the Nazi concentration camp at Auschwitz, he became a US citizen in 1963. His work is an attempt to ensure that the HOLOCAUST is not forgotten. Wiesel won the 1986 Nobel Peace Prize. His first three accounts of concentration camp survivors, *Night* (1958), *Dawn* (1960) and *The Accident* (1961), are collected as *The Night Trilogy*. Other novels include *The Town Beyond the Wall* (1962) *A Beggar in Jerusalem* (1968), *The Fifth Son* (1985) and *The Forgotten* (1989).

Wight, Isle of Island and county off the S coast of England, separated from the mainland (Hampshire) by the Solent. Newport is the county town. The island's mild climate and coastal scenery make it a popular tourist destination. Cowes, the major port, is a famous yachting centre. Area: 318sq km (147sq mi). Pop. (1991) 124,577.

Wigner, Eugene Paul (1902–95) US physicist, b. Hungary. During World War 2, he worked on the MANHATTAN PROJECT. Wigner was the first physicist to apply group theory to QUANTUM MECHANICS. He discovered the law of conservation of parity. For his work on the structure of the atomic NUCLEUS, Wigner shared the 1963 Nobel Prize for physics.

wigwam Shelter used by Native North Americans of the E woodlands area. Wigwams were made from bark, reed mats or thatch spread over a pole frame, and should not be confused with the conical, skin-covered tepees of the Native Americans of the Plains.

Wilberforce, William (1759–1833) English social reformer. In 1780, he was elected to Parliament. In 1785, he was converted to evangelicalism. Wilberforce led the ABOLITIONIST cause in Parliament for more than 20 years. His campaign led to the abolition of the slave trade in 1807, but Wilberforce continued to work for abolition throughout the British empire. His works include *A Practical View* (1797).

Wilbur, Richard (1921–) US poet laureate (1987–88). His first volume was *The Beautiful Changes* (1947). Wilbur won two Pulitzer Prizes for *Things of This World* (1956) and *New and Collected Poems* (1988).

Wilde, Oscar (1854–1900) (Oscar Fingal O'Flahertie Wills) Irish dramatist, poet, prose writer and wit. A leader of the AESTHETIC MOVEMENT, he wrote only one novel, *The Picture of Dorian Grey* (1891). His short-story collections include the *Happy Prince and Other Tales* (1888). Wilde is best known for his drama, which combines social criticism with epigrammatic wit. His plays include *Lady Windermere's Fan* (1892), *A Woman of No Importance* (1893), *An Ideal Husband* (1895) and his masterpiece, *The Importance of Being Earnest* (1895). In 1895, Wilde was convicted of homosexual practices and sentenced to two years' hard labour. While in prison, he wrote *The Ballad of Reading Gaol* (1898).

wildebeest *See* GNU

Wilder, Billy (1906–) US film director and screenwriter, b. Germany. His partnership with Charles Brackett began with comedy scripts, such as *Ninotchka* (1939). *Double Indemnity* (1944) is a classic FILM NOIR. Wilder won Academy Awards for best director, best picture and shared the best screenplay prize with Brackett for *The Lost Weekend* (1945). Their last collaboration, *Sunset Boulevard* (1950), also earned them an Oscar for best screenplay. His solo career proved just as successful, with films such as *The Seven Year Itch* (1955) and *Some Like it Hot* (1959). Wilder won further Academy Awards for best picture and best director for *The Apartment* (1960).

Wilder, Thornton Niven (1897–1975) US dramatist and writer. He received the Pulitzer Prize for his second novel, *The Bridge of San Luis Rey* (1927), which examines the role of destiny in the death of five travellers when a bridge collapses near Lima. Other novels include *The Woman of Andros* (1930), *Heaven's My Destination* (1934) and *The Eighth Day* (1967). He won further Pulitzer Prizes for his plays *Our Town* (1938) and *The Skin of Our Teeth* (1942).

Wilhelmina (1880–1962) Queen of the Netherlands (1890–1948). She helped keep the country neutral in World War 1 and often intervened in political affairs. During World War 2, she led the government in exile in England and became a symbol of Dutch independence. In 1948, she abdicated in favour of her daughter, Juliania.

Wilkes, Charles (1798–1877) US naval officer and explorer. In his circumnavigation of the world (1838–42), Wilkes explored the South Seas and proved that ANTARCTICA was a continent. Wilkes Land is named after him. In the TRENT AFFAIR, he almost brought Britain into the Civil War on the Confederate side.

Wilkins, Maurice Hugh Frederick (1916–) English biophysicist. He shared the 1962 Nobel Prize for physiology or medicine with James D. WATSON and Francis CRICK for his X-ray diffraction studies that helped to determine the molecular structure of DNA.

Wilkinson, Sir Geoffrey (1921–) English chemist. He shared the 1973 Nobel Prize for chemistry with Ernst Fisher for their independent research on organometallic compounds of transition metals. In these compounds, the metallic atom is "sandwiched" between two carbon rings.

Wilkinson, James (1757–1825) American general. He served in the AMERICAN REVOLUTION but was forced to resign (1778) because of his role in the Conway Cabal. In 1784, Wilkinson moved to Kentucky and joined a conspiracy with the Spanish governor of Louisiana to gain trade monopolies for himself and to give Kentucky to Spain. Returning to the army, he was quickly dismissed after failing to capture Montreal in the WAR OF 1812.

will In law, a clear expression of intent by a person (the testator) concerning the disposal of his or her effects after death. The testator must be of sound mind and legal age, and the will must be witnessed by two competent people who are not beneficiaries. It may be altered or revoked by the testator at any time, with due legal process.

Willemstadt Capital of NETHERLANDS ANTILLES, on Curaçao Island, West Indies. The city is a free port, exporting oil from Venezuela and coffee. Oil refining and tourism are major industries. It has the largest dry dock in the Americas. Pop. (1995) 119,000.

William I (1797–1888) King of Prussia (1861–88) and emperor of Germany (1871–88). He was regent for his brother, FREDERICK WILLIAM IV, from 1858. His suppression of revolution in 1848–49 earned him a reputation as a reactionary, but as king he displayed sensible pragmatism and followed the advice of his chief minister, Otto von BISMARCK. William supported the unification of Germany but accepted his proclamation as emperor reluctantly, fearing a reduction in Prussia's status.

William II (1859–1941) Emperor of Germany (1888–1918). He modelled himself on his grandfather, WILLIAM I, but lacked his good sense. In 1890, he dismissed BISMARCK and assumed leadership of the government. His aggressive foreign policy, including the construction of a navy, antagonized Britain, France and Russia. Many regard his policies as largely responsible for the outbreak of World War 1 (1914). During the war, William was exclusively concerned with military matters. He abdicated after the armistice (November 1918).

William I (the Conqueror) (1027–87) King of England (1066–87) and Duke of Normandy (1035–87). Supported initially by Henry I of France, he consolidated his position in Normandy against hostile neighbours. On the death of EDWARD THE CONFESSOR, he claimed the English throne, having allegedly gained the agreement of King HAROLD in 1064. He defeated and killed Harold at the Battle of HASTINGS (1066) and subsequently enforced his rule over the whole kingdom. He rewarded his followers by grants of land, eventually replacing almost the entire feudal ruling class, and intimidated potential rebels by rapid construction of castles. He invaded Scotland (1072), extracting an oath of loyalty from Malcolm III Canmore, and Wales (1081), although he spent much of his reign in France. He ordered the famous survey known as the DOMESDAY BOOK (1086).

William II (Rufus) (1056–1100) King of England (1087–1100). He was the second surviving son of WILLIAM I (THE CONQUEROR). His elder brother, Robert Curthose (Robert II), was Duke of Normandy, and William had to crush revolts by Anglo-Norman lords in Robert's favour. He invaded the duchy twice, and in 1096 Robert mortgaged it to him to raise cash for the First Crusade. He invaded Scotland, later killing Malcolm III (1093), and subdued Wales (1097). He was killed hunting, allegedly, though improbably, by accident.

William III (of Orange) (1650–1702) King of England, Scotland and Ireland (1689–1702). He was born after the death of his father, William II, Prince of Orange, and succeeded him as ruler in effect of the United Provinces (Netherlands) in 1572. In 1677, he married MARY, daughter of JAMES II of England, and following the GLORIOUS REVOLUTION (1688), he and Mary, strong Protestants, replaced the Catholic James II. They ruled jointly until her death in 1694. In 1699, he organized the alliance that was to defeat the French in the War of the SPANISH SUCCESSION. Never popular in England, William approved the BILL OF RIGHTS (1689) and other measures that diminished the royal prerogative.

William IV (1765–1837) King of Great Britain and Ireland and elector of Hanover (1830–37). Third son of GEORGE III, he succeeded, unexpectedly, aged 65 after a long career in the navy. Nicknamed "Silly Billy", he was well-meaning though unkingly. He assisted the passage of the Great Reform Bill (1832) by creating new peers to give the government a majority in the House of Lords.

William I (1772–1843) First king of the Netherlands (1815–40) whose kingdom included Belgium and Luxembourg. He fought in the French Revolutionary and Napoleonic Wars. His forceful government offended liberals and Roman Catholics, and a revolution in Belgium (1830) was followed by Belgian independence (1839). Compelled to accept a constitution restricting his powers, he abdicated in favour of his son, William II.

William I (the Lion) (1143–1214) King of Scotland (1165–1214). He succeeded his brother Malcolm IV and forged what was later called the "Auld Alliance" with France. Captured by the English during an attempt to regain Northumbria, he was forced to swear fealty to HENRY II (1174). He regained Scotland's independence from RICHARD I in return for a cash payment towards the Third Crusade in 1189. William the Lion established the independence of the church under the pope and strengthened royal authority in the north.

William I (the Silent) (1533–84) Prince of Orange, leader of the revolt of the Netherlands against Spanish rule. In 1572, he became the leader of a broad coalition in the Low Countries that opposed Spanish rule on the principle of religious tolerance. It broke down in 1579, when the Catholic s provinces, seeking reconciliation with Spain, broke away. William continued as stadholder of Holland and leader of the N provinces until he was assassinated in Delft.

William of Occam (1285–1349) English scholastic philosopher. Contributing to the development of formal LOGIC, he employed the principle of economy known as Occam's Razor; that is, a problem should be stated in its most basic terms. As a Franciscan monk, he upheld ideals of poverty against Pope John XXII and was excommunicated. In 1328, he was imprisoned in Avignon, France, but he escaped and fled to Munich, where he later died.

Williams, Ralph Vaughan *See* VAUGHAN WILLIAMS, RALPH

Williams, Roger (1603–83) English Puritan minister. In 1631, he emigrated to the Massachusetts Bay colony. His radical politics and theology antagonized the Puritan authorities, and he was expelled (1635). In 1636, Williams founded PROVIDENCE, the first settlement in RHODE ISLAND, on land purchased from the Narragansett. He returned to England and acquired a charter. Williams served (1654–57) as president of Rhode Island colony.

Williams, Tennessee (Thomas Lanier) (1911–83) US dramatist. His first Broadway play, *The Glass Menagerie* (1945), was awarded the New York Drama Critic's Circle Award. He received Pulitzer Prizes for *A Streetcar Named Desire* (1947) and *Cat on a Hot Tin Roof* (1955). His other plays include *Suddenly Last Summer* (1958), *Sweet Bird of Youth* (1959) and *The Night of the Iguana* (1961). Many of his plays were set in the South, in a cloying and repressive environment that reflected the plight of the characters.

Williams, William Carlos (1883–1963) US poet. His deceptively simple style incorporates colloquial American. Williams' early work shows the influence of IMAGISM. His most monumental achievement was *Paterson* (1946–58), a five-volume epic of American life as seen in the microcosm of a New Jersey city. His *Pictures from Brueghel* (1962) won a posthumous Pulitzer Prize and his *Collected Poems* appeared in 1986–88.

Williamsburg Historic city in SE Virginia, USA. It lies on a peninsula between the James and York rivers. Founded in 1633, Williamsburg was capital of Virginia from 1699 to 1779. The Virginia Resolution for American Independence was passed in the city in 1776. The Battle of Williamsburg (1862) was part of the PENINSULAR CAMPAIGN in the Civil War. In 1926, John D. Rockefeller Jr. provided for the restoration of the colonial city. Today, it is a major tourist site. Pop. (1990) 11,530.

will-o'-the-wisp (Jack-o'-lantern) Mysterious light sometimes seen at night in marshy areas. It is thought to be due to the spontaneous combustion of METHANE.

willow DECIDUOUS shrub and tree native to cool or mountainous temperate regions. It has long pointed leaves, and flowers borne on catkins. Familiar species include the weeping willow (*Salix babylonica*), with drooping branches, and pussy willow (*S. caprea*) with fuzzy catkins. Family Salicaceae.

willow herb *See* FIREWEED

Wilmington City in N Delaware, USA, at the junction of the Delaware and Christina rivers and Brandywine Creek. The first settlement in Delaware (1638), Wilmington was founded by Swedes. It was later enlarged by Dutch and British settlers and became the state's largest city. It is an important industrial centre with shipyards, railway shops and chemical manufacturing plants. Pop. (1992) 72,411.

Wilson, Sir Angus (1913–91) English novelist, short-story writer and critic. Wilson's characteristic fictional territory is the satire of English middle-class life. His best known novels include *Hemlock and After* (1952), *Anglo-Saxon Attitudes* (1956), and *No Laughing Matter* (1967). He was knighted in 1980.

Wilson, August (1945–) African-American playwright. He has written a series of plays that chronicle the black experience in the 20th century, including *Ma Rainey's Black Bottom* (1984). He has won two Pulitzer Prizes for *Fences* (1987) and *The Piano Lesson* (1988).

Wilson, Charles Thomson Rees (1869–1959) English physicist who invented the Wilson cloud chamber used to study radioactivity, X-rays and cosmic rays. It uses water droplets to track ions left by passing radiation. For this invention, he shared the 1927 Nobel Prize for physics with Arthur COMPTON.

Wilson, Edmund (1895–1972) US literary critic and writer. He was editor of *Vanity Fair* (1920–21), associate editor of *The New Republic* (1926–31) and regular critic for *The New Yorker* (1944–48). His highly influential critical work includes *Axel's Castle* (1931) on SYMBOLISM; *To the Finland Station* (1940) on the origins of the Russian Revolution; and *Patriotic Gore* (1962) on the literature of the Civil War

Wilson, Sir (James) Harold (1916–95) (Baron Wilson of Rievaulx) British statesman, prime minister (1964–70, 1974–76). Wilson entered Parliament in 1945. In 1951, he resigned from Clement ATTLEE'S cabinet. In 1963, Wilson succeeded Hugh GAITSKELL as Labour leader. In 1964, he won a narrow general election victory. His administration was faced with Rhodesia's unilateral declaration of independence and domestic recession. Wilson was forced to impose strict price and income controls and devalue sterling. In the 1970 general election, he was defeated by Edward HEATH. Conflict between Labour's left and right wing over nationalization and membership of the European Economic Community (EUROPEAN COMMUNITY) threatened to divide the party. In 1974, however, Wilson returned to power at the head of a minority Labour government. In 1976, he unexpectedly resigned and was succeeded by Jim CALLAGHAN. In 1983, he was made a life peer.

Wilson, (Thomas) Woodrow (1856–1924) 28th US president (1913–21). As governor of New Jersey (1910–12), he gained a reputation as a progressive Democrat. In 1912, he unexpectedly gained the Democratic nomination. The split in the Republican vote between TAFT's REPUBLICAN PARTY and Theodore ROOSEVELT's PROGRESSIVE PARTY handed Wilson the presidency. His "New Freedom" reforms included the establishment of the FEDERAL RESERVE SYSTEM (1913). Several amendments to the US CONSTITUTION were introduced, including PROHIBITION (18th, 1919) and the extension of the FRANCHISE to women (19th, 1920). The MEXICAN REVOLUTION brought instability to the s border, and Wilson

▶ **wind** Onshore winds (A) generally occur during the day. The land is heated by the Sun, causing the air over it to rise. As the warm air rises it is replaced by cooler air overlying the sea. At night, because the land loses heat more quickly than the sea, air flows down hillsides out to sea, where the air is relatively warmer, generating offshore breezes (B).

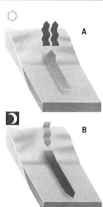

ordered John PERSHING's intervention. Wilson's efforts to maintain US neutrality at the start of WORLD WAR 1 aided his re-election in 1916. The failure of diplomacy and continuing attacks on US shipping forced Wilson to declare war (April 1917) on Germany. His FOURTEEN POINTS (January 1918) represented US war aims and became the basis of the peace negotiations at the VERSAILLES peace conference (1919). Wilson was forced to compromise in the final settlement but succeeded in securing the establishment of the LEAGUE OF NATIONS. Domestic opposition to the League was led by Henry Cabot LODGE, and the Republican-dominated Senate rejected it. In October 1919, Wilson suffered a stroke and became an increasingly marginal figure for the remainder of his term.

Wiltshire County in central s England. Trowbridge is the county town. Dominated by Salisbury Plain and the Marlborough Downs, much of this rural county is given over to agriculture. Tourists are attracted by the county's many historic sites: STONEHENGE and Avebury Hill are England's oldest monuments, built more than 4,000 years ago. Swindon, the main manufacturing centre, is one of the fastest-growing cities in England. Industries: textiles, farm machinery, food processing, electrical goods. Area: 3,481sq km (1,344sq mi). Pop. (1991) 564,471.

Wimbledon Popular name for the All England Lawn Tennis Championships played annually at the All England Club, Wimbledon, sw London. It is the world's leading grass-court championship. It was first held in 1877 and was open only to amateurs until 1968. The championships have been held at the present site since 1922.

winch Drum that turns to pull or release a rope, cable or chain. A winch is used to raise, lower or pull heavy loads. The device may be motor-driven or operated by hand.

Winchester County town of Hampshire, on the Itchen River, s central England. It became capital of the Anglo-Saxon kingdom of WESSEX in 519 AD. During the reign of ALFRED THE GREAT, it was capital of England. Despite the growth of London, Winchester retained its importance as a centre of learning and religion throughout the medieval period. Much of the old city remains, including the ruins of a Norman castle. Pop. (1991) 96,386.

wind Air current that moves rapidly parallel to the Earth's surface. (Air currents in vertical motion are called updrafts or downdrafts.) Wind direction is indicated by wind or weather vanes, wind speed by ANEMOMETERS and wind force by the BEAUFORT WIND SCALE. Steady winds in the tropics are called TRADE WINDS. MONSOONS are seasonal winds that bring predictable

rains in Asia. Foehns (föhns) are warm, dry winds that are produced by compression accompanied by temperature rise as air descends the lee of mountainous areas in the Alps; a similar wind called CHINOOK exists in the Rockies. SIROCCOS are hot, humid Mediterranean winds.

Windhoek Capital and largest city of Namibia. In 1892, it was made the capital of the new German colony of South-West Africa. In 1990, Windhoek became capital of the independent Namibia. It is an important market for karakul sheepskins. Industries: diamonds, copper, meat packing. Pop. (1995) 190,000.

wind instruments Musical instruments that are sounded by blowing, which sets the air inside them vibrating. They may be classified into two types: WOODWIND and BRASS.

windmill Machine powered by the wind acting on sails or vanes. Windmills were built in the Middle East in the 7th century. The idea spread to Europe in the Middle Ages. Their use was widespread during the INDUSTRIAL REVOLUTION, but declined with the development of the STEAM ENGINE in the 19th century. *See also* RENEWABLE ENERGY; WIND POWER

window In computing, a rectangle visible on the screen of a computer that displays what is stored in part of the machine's memory or some other storage device. A window may show text, graphics or other work in progress.

windpipe *See* TRACHEA

wind power Harnessing of wind energy to produce power. Since the 1970s, advanced aerodynamic designs have been used to build wind turbines that generate electricity. The largest of these, on Hawaii, has two blades, each 50m (160ft) long, attached to a 20-storey high tower. Individual turbines are often grouped in strategic locations (wind farms) to maximize the generating potential. Wind power is a cheap form of RENEWABLE ENERGY but cannot as yet produce sufficiently large amounts of electricity to provide a realistic alternative to fossil fuel and nuclear power stations. *See also* WINDMILL

Windsor, Duke of *See* EDWARD VIII

Windsor Castle English royal residence, 32km (20mi) w of London. It was founded by WILLIAM I to defend the Thames valley. Much renovated, it retains the appearance of a medieval fortress.

wind tunnel Chamber in which scale models or full-size vehicles are tested in a controlled airflow. Some wind tunnels can reproduce extreme conditions of wind speed, temperature and pressure. Structures are tested to check that winds cannot set up destructive vibrations.

Windward Islands Southern group of the Lesser ANTILLES islands, SE West Indies. They extend from the Leeward Islands to the NE coast of Venezuela. The principal islands are MARTINIQUE, GRENADA, DOMINICA, ST LUCIA, ST VINCENT AND THE GRENADINES group. The islands, volcanic in origin, are generally mountainous and forested. Crops include bananas, spices, limes and cacao, but tourism is the leading industry. The islands were inhabited by the indigenous Carib until colonization began in the 17th century. The next two centuries witnessed a struggle for control between France and Britain. Britain came to control all the islands, except Martinique.

wine Alcoholic beverage made from the fermented juice (and some solid extracts) of fruits, herbs and flowers – but classically from the juice and skins of grapes. The three standard grape wine colorations are white, red and rosé, depending on the grape used and whether, and for how long, the grape skins are left on. For **white** wine, the grapes are fermented without the skin; for **red** wine, the whole grape is used; for **rosé** wine, the skins are removed after fermentation has begun. Dry wines are fermented until all the sugar has turned to alcohol; sweet wines are fermented for less time so that some sugar remains. Champagne is bottled while it is still fermenting. Table wines contain 7–15% alcohol by volume; fortified wines, such as SHERRY, contain added BRANDY, giving a 16–23% alcohol content.

Winfrey, Oprah (1954–) US television talk-show host. She worked as a news reporter before hosting the "A.M. Chicago Show" in 1984. Renamed "The Oprah Winfrey Show", it enjoyed great success. She also received an Academy Award nomination for Best Actress in the film *The Color Purple* (1985). Other films include *Beloved* (1998).

wings In biology, specialized organs for flight that are possessed by most birds, many insects and certain mammals and reptiles. The forelimbs of a bird have developed into such structures. Bats have membranous tissue supported by the digits ("fingers") of the forelimbs. Insects may have one or two pairs of veined or membranous wings.

Winnebago Native American band that in the 1820s and 1830s ceded its tribal lands in sw Wisconsin and nw Illinois to the US government. Linguistically part of the Siouan language group, the tribe's 3,000 members live mostly in reservations in Nebraska and Wisconsin.

Winnipeg Capital of Manitoba, Canada, at the confluence of the Assiniboine and Red rivers, in the far s of the province. Founded in 1812 by the HUDSON'S BAY COMPANY, the town grew after the completion of the Canadian Pacific Railroad (1882) and is now the major city of the Canadian prairies. It has one of the largest wheat markets in the world and vast flour mills, grain elevators and food-processing plants. Pop. (1996) 667,000.

Winnipeg, Lake Lake in s central Manitoba province, the third-largest in Canada. It was used extensively by early fur traders and explorers in the 18th century. Fed by the Red, Saskatchewan and Winnipeg rivers, and drained by the Nelson River to Hudson Bay, it is believed to be a remnant of the glacial Lake Agassiz. Area: 24,514sq km (9,465sq mi).

Winthrop, John (1588–1649) Puritan colonist and theocratic governor of the MASSACHUSETTS BAY COLONY. As governor, he led 700 colonists to Salem (1630) and later to Charlestown and Boston. He was governor for 12 years (1630–34, 1637–40, 1642–44, 1646–49) and also served as president of the New England Confederation.

wire Strand of metal made by drawing a rod through progressively smaller holes in metal dies. The drawing process toughens STEEL, so that a CABLE made from steel wire is much stronger than an undrawn steel rod of the same diameter. Copper and aluminium wires are used to make electric cables. If flexibility is important, each conductor is made of several fine strands of wire.

Wireless Application Protocol (WAP) Set of telecommunication rules to standardize the way that wireless devices, such as MOBILE TELEPHONES and radio transceivers, can be used for Internet access, including ELECTRONIC MAIL and the WORLD WIDE WEB. WAP provides a common technology to enable a user to communicate with all the various makes and models of wireless devices. There are four 'layers' to WAP technology: the application environment, the session layer, the transport layer and the transport security layer.

wireworm Long, cylindrical larva of the click beetle of n temperate woodlands. It is generally brown or yellow and is distinctly segmented. Most species live in the soil and may cause serious damage to the roots of cultivated crops. Family Elateridae. *See also* MILLIPEDE

Wisconsin State in the n central USA, sw of the GREAT LAKES and e of the Mississippi River. MADISON is the state capital and MILWAUKEE the largest city. The land is rolling plain that slopes gradually down from the n. There are numerous glacial lakes. The French claimed the region in 1634. Wisconsin was an important centre in the fur trade and was ceded to Britain at the end of the FRENCH AND INDIAN WARS (1763). In 1783, it was ceded to the USA. Settlement increased after the Black Hawk War (1832) ended Native American resistance. The Territory of Wisconsin was established in 1836 and admitted to the Union in 1848. Wisconsin is the leading US producer of milk, butter and cheese, and the chief crops are hay, corn, oats, fruit and vegetables. The state's most valuable resource, however, is timber: 45% of the land is forested. Mineral deposits include zinc, lead, copper, iron, sand and gravel. Industries: farm machinery, brewing, tourism. Area: 145,438sq km (56,154sq mi). Pop. (2000) 5,363,675.

wisdom literature Collection of writings and sayings in the Hebrew Bible. From the Old Testament it includes the Books of Proverbs, Ecclesiastes and Job, and the Song of Solomon, and from the Apocrypha it includes the Books of Ecclesiasticus and the Wisdom of Solomon.

wisent *See* BISON

wisteria Genus of hardy, woody vines, native to North America, Japan and China. They have showy, fragrant, pendulous flower clusters of purplish-white, pink, or blue. Family Fabaceae/Leguminosae.

witchcraft Exercise of supernatural occult powers, usually due to some inherent power rather than to an acquired skill, such as sorcery. In Europe it originated in pagan cults and in mystical philosophies such as GNOSTICISM, which believed in the potency of both good and evil in the universe. In some societies, the belief in spirits is associated with attempts to control them through witchcraft for harmful or beneficial ends.

witch doctor See SHAMAN

witch hazel Shrubs and small trees of the genus *Hamamelis*, native to temperate regions, mostly in Asia.

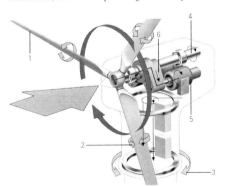

▲ **wind power** A wind generator converts the energy of the wind into electricity. Three-bladed variable-pitch designs are the most efficient. Variable pitch means the attitude of the blades (1) can be changed. By altering the pitch (2) of the blades they can generate at maximum efficiency in varying wind conditions. The whole rotor assembly rotates (3) into the wind. The blades turn a prop shaft (4) that links to a generator (5) through gearing (6). The largest wind farms have thousands of linked turbines and can produce the same power as a fossil-fuel power station.

They bloom in late autumn or early spring. The common witch hazel (*Hamamelis virginiana*) has yellow flowers. Family Hamamelidaceae.

witness Legal term referring to a person who testifies in court to facts within his/her knowledge. In most western legal systems, a witness is usually required to take an oath swearing truthfulness prior to testifying, and he/she is then first examined (questioned) by the party who offers him/her and then cross-examined by the opposing party.

Witt, Jan de (1625–72) Dutch political leader. A republican and opponent of the House of Orange, he became grand pensionary and effectively head of government in 1653. He defeated the English in the second DUTCH WAR (1665–67). In 1672, he resigned after a French invasion and the accession of WILLIAM OF ORANGE as stadholder.

Wittenberg Town on the River Elbe, Sachsen-Anhalt state, E central Germany. Founded by Frederick III, its university became the cradle of the Protestant REFORMATION during the time Martin LUTHER and Philip MELANCHTHON were teaching there. Today, it is primarily a mining and industrial centre, producing chemicals, rubber goods and machinery. Pop. (1993) 47,200.

Wittgenstein, Ludwig (1889–1951) Austrian philosopher. His masterwork, *Tractatus Logico-philosophicus* (1921), influenced LOGICAL POSITIVISM, positing the strict relationships between language and the physical world. After 1929 he criticized this hypothesis, and these second thoughts were posthumously published in *Philosophical Investigations* (1953), in which he claimed that language was only a conventional "game" in which meaning was affected more by context than by formal relationships to reality.

Witwatersrand (Rand) Series of parallel mountain ranges more than 1,500m (5,000ft) high, forming a watershed between the Vaal and Olifant rivers, in S former TRANSVAAL, NE South Africa. The region extends *c*.100km (62mi) E and W of Johannesburg. Gold was first discovered in 1884. Witwatersrand produces about one third of the total world output of gold.

Wodehouse, P.G. (Sir Pelham Grenville) (1881–1975) English novelist and short-story writer. He began his career writing lyrics for musicals by, among others, Cole PORTER and George GERSHWIN. Wodehouse wrote more than 100 humorous books set in genteel Edwardian society. His most enduring creations are Bertie Wooster and his valet Jeeves, who first appeared in *The Man with Two Left Feet* (1917). During World War 2, his ill-advised radio broadcasts from Berlin outraged British public opinion. In 1955, he became a US citizen.

Woden *See* ODIN

Wöhler, Friedrich (1800–82) German chemist who first isolated ALUMINIUM and BERYLLIUM and discovered calcium carbide. In 1828 his synthesis of UREA (from the inorganic substance ammonium cyanate) was the first synthesis of an organic chemical compound from an inorganic one; it contributed to the foundation of modern organic chemistry.

Wolf, Hugo (1860–1903) Austrian composer, generally regarded as one of the finest composers of *Lieder*. He produced five "songbooks" setting poems by Mörike (1888), Eichendorff (1888–89), Goethe (1888–89), Spanish authors (1889–90) and Italian poets (1891, 1896), the last two in German translation.

wolf Dog-like, carnivorous mammal, once widespread in the USA and Eurasia, especially the grey wolf (*Canis lupus*), which is now restricted to the USA and Asia. It is powerfully built with a wide head and neck, muscular limbs, large feet and a deep-chested body; the tail is long and bushy. It has earned a reputation for savagery and cunning from attacks on livestock and human beings. Length: to 2m (6.6ft), including the tail. Family Canidae.

Wolfe, James (1727–59) British general. He commanded the force that captured Quebec by scaling the cliffs above the St Lawrence River and defeating the French, under MONTCALM, on the Plains of Abraham (1759). This victory resulted in Britain's acquisition of Canada. Wolfe's death in action made him a hero.

Wolfe, Thomas Clayton (1900–38) US writer. His reputation rests on his sequence of four sprawling autobiographical novels, *Look Homeward, Angel* (1929), *Of Time and the River* (1935), *The Web and the Rock* (1939) and *You Can't Go Home Again* (1940).

Wolfe, Tom (Thomas Kennerley) (1931–) US journalist and novelist. Wolfe established his reputation with his "New Journalism" essays on US counter-culture, such as *The Electric Kool-Aid Acid-Test* (1968). His first novel, *The Bonfire of the Vanities* (1987), was set in New York and was a biting satire on the materialist society. *A Man in Full* (1998) was nominated for a National Book Award.

wolffish Voracious fish that lives in the N waters of the Atlantic Ocean. It is brown or grey with long fins along its back and belly, and powerful jaws and teeth. It is valued as a food fish in Iceland, where its skin is made into leather. Length: 91cm (3ft). Family Anarhichadidae; species *Anarhichas lupus*.

wolfram *See* TUNGSTEN

wolframite (iron-manganese tungstate) Black to brown mineral, (Fe,Mn)WO$_4$. It is the chief ore of the metal TUNGSTEN. It occurs as crystals in the monoclinic system or as granular masses. It is found in quartz veins and pegmatites associated with granitic rocks and also in hydrothermal veins. Hardness 5–5.5; r.d. 7–7.5

Wolfram von Eschenbach (1170–1220) German poet. His only complete work is the Middle High German epic *Parzival*. A masterpiece of medieval literature, it introduced the Grail legend into German.

Wollongong City and port in New South Wales, Australia, 65km (40mi) S of Sydney. The area was settled in 1815, and Wollongong became a major exporter of grain and coal, and a large iron and steel centre. Port Kembla has Australia's biggest steelworks. Other industries: chemicals, textiles, copper. Pop. (1993) 249,000.

Wollstonecraft, Mary (1759–97) English writer. Her *Vindication of the Rights of Women* (1792) was FEMINISM's first great work. She was the mother of Mary Wollstonecraft SHELLEY.

Wolof People of Senegal who speak a language belonging to the W Atlantic group of the NIGER-CONGO family. In the 15th century, a Wolof empire dominated West Africa and traded in slaves with the Portuguese. They were converted to ISLAM in the 18th century.

Wolsey, Thomas (1475–1530) English cardinal and statesman, lord chancellor (1515–29). After the accession of HENRY VIII (1509), Wolsey became archbishop of York (1514) and then cardinal and lord chancellor. As chancellor, he controlled virtually all state business. Wolsey's attempts to place England at the centre of European diplomacy ended in failure. Despite becoming papal legate (1518), his ambition to become pope was never realized. Domestically, he made powerful enemies through his method of raising taxes through forced loans, his conspicuous wealth and his pluralism. Wolsey gave HAMPTON COURT PALACE to Henry VIII, but his failure to obtain the king a divorce from CATHERINE OF ARAGON brought about his downfall. Thomas MORE replaced Wolsey as chancellor. Charged with high treason, he died before his trial.

wolverine Solitary, ferocious mammal, native to pine forests of the USA and Eurasia, the largest member of the WEASEL family. Dark brown, with lighter bands along the sides and neck, it has a bushy tail and large feet. Length: 91cm (36in); weight: 30kg (66lb). Species *Gulo gulo*.

womb *See* UTERUS

wombat Either of two species of large, rodent-like marsupial mammals of SE Australia and Tasmania. Both species are herbivorous, primarily nocturnal and live in extensive burrows. The common wombat (*Vombatus ursinus*) has coarse black hair and small ears. The hairy-nosed wombat (*Lasiorhinus latifrons*) has finer, grey fur, and large ears. Length: to 1.2m (4ft). Family Vombatidae.

women's rights movement Broad term for the international movement that began in the early 19th century and which promotes and works for the equality of women. Originally concentrating on women's suffrage, the movement has since worked for equality of employment opportunity and pay; freedom from unjust social, political and theological expectations; and an awakening of physical, intellectual and emotional awareness for women. *See also* FEMINISM; SUFFRAGETTE MOVEMENT

Wonder, Stevie (1950–) US SOUL singer and songwriter, b. Steveland Judkins Morris. Blind from birth, Wonder played the harmonica, keyboard, guitar and drums. In 1961, he joined MOTOWN Records. His first record was *Little Stevie Wonder* (1962). Other albums include *Talking Book* (1972), *Innervisions* (1973), *Songs in the Key of Life* (1976) and *Hotter Than July* (1980).

Wood, Sir Henry Joseph (1869–1944) British conductor. He conducted the London PROMENADE CONCERTS from 1895–1944. The concerts are now named after him.

wood Hard substance that forms the trunks of trees; it is the XYLEM which comprises the bulk of the stems and roots, supporting the plant. Wood consists of fine, cellular tubes arranged vertically within the trunk, which accounts for its grain. The relatively soft, light-coloured wood is called **sapwood**. The non-conducting, older, darker wood is called **heartwood** and is generally filled with RESIN, gums, mineral salts and TANNIN. The two chief types are softwoods from CONIFERS, such as PINE, and hardwoods from deciduous species, such as OAK. Wood is commonly used as a building material, fuel, to make some types of PAPER, and as a source of CHARCOAL, CELLULOSE, ESSENTIAL OIL, LIGNIN, tannins, dyes and SUGAR.

woodchuck (groundhog) MARMOT found in North America from Alaska to the Gulf States, having grizzled black-brown hair. Using its sharp front teeth and short, strong legs, it digs burrows. It feeds heavily in autumn before hibernating. The woodchuck eats plants, often becoming a garden pest. Length: 61cm (2ft); Weight: to 6.3kg (14lb). Species *Marmota monax*.

woodcock Any of five species of reddish-brown shorebirds that nest in cool parts of the Northern Hemisphere and winter in warm areas. Both the Eurasian *Scolopax rusticola* and American *Philohela minor* insert their long, sensitive, flexible bills into swampy ground to find worms. Length: to 34cm (14in). Family Scolopacidae.

woodcut Oldest method of printing, using designs carved into wood. The carving produces a negative image, the carved areas representing blank spaces while the flat areas retain the ink. Woodcuts were invented in China in the 5th century AD and became popular in Europe in the Middle Ages.

wood engraving Print made by incising a design on the flat, polished (cross-grain) transverse section of a block of hardwood. Textural and linear effects can be achieved by varying the pressure and direction of the

cutting strokes. This technique developed from the less-sophisticated WOODCUT in 18th-century England.

wood louse (sowbug) Terrestrial, isopod crustacean found in damp conditions worldwide. It has an oval, segmented body, feeds mainly on vegetable matter, and retains its eggs in a brood pouch. Length: 20mm (0.75in). Order Isopoda; Genus *Oniscus*.

woodpecker Tree-climbing bird found nearly worldwide. Woodpeckers have strong pointed beaks and long protrudable tongues, which in some species often have harpoon-like tips for extracting insect larvae. They have two toes pointing forward, and black, red, white, yellow, brown or green plumage; some are crested. The tail is stiff and helps to support the bird's body when pressed against a tree trunk. Family Picidae.

Woods, "Tiger" (Eldrick) (1975–) US golfer. He won the US amateur championship three times (1994, 1995, 1996) before turning professional. In 1997, Woods became not only the youngest player to win the Masters, but also the first African-American to do so. In 1999, he won the US PGA Championship in 1999. In 2000, Woods won the US and British Opens.

Woodstock Name given to a music festival held between 15 and 17 August 1969, near Bethel, SW of Woodstock, New York, USA. Forced to shift from the original location because of residents' protests, *c*.450,000 people arrived for the free outdoor concert. It was a celebration of both the music and aspirations of the hippie generation.

Woodward, Robert Burns (1917–79) US chemist. He was awarded the 1965 Nobel Prize for chemistry in recognition of his synthesis of a number of complex organic substances, including quinine, cholesterol, cortisone, strychnine, lysergic acid, reserpine, chlorophyll and tetracycline.

woodwind Family of musical wind instruments that are traditionally made of wood but now often metal. They are played by means of a mouthpiece containing one or two reeds. The FLUTE and PICCOLO, however, are exceptional in that they are played by blowing across a hole. Other woodwind instruments include the CLARINET (single reed) and the OBOE, COR ANGLAIS and BASSOON (all double reed). SAXOPHONES are also part of the woodwind family.

woodworm (furniture beetle) Larva of various species of beetles that burrow in wood. Woodworms can cause extensive damage. Their presence can be detected by holes in wood from which the adult beetles have emerged. Genera include *Anobium* and *Lyctus*.

▲ **woodpecker** The ivory-billed woodpecker (*Campephilus principalis*) is the largest of the North American woodpeckers and is one of the rarest birds in the world. It is believed to be nearly extinct now; any that remain are thought to inhabit swamp forests in SE USA and Cuba. Native American chiefs once adorned their belts with its bill and plumes, but tree felling has now removed most of the big trees in which it breeds.

wool Soft, generally white, brown or black animal fibre that forms the fleece (coat) of sheep. Wool is also the name of the yarns and textiles made from the fibres after spinning, dyeing and weaving. The fibres, composed chiefly of KERATIN, are treated to remove a fat called lanolin, which is used in some ointments.

Woolf, Virginia (1882–1941) English novelist and critic. Her novels, which often use the STREAM OF CONSCIOUSNESS style associated with MODERNISM, include *Mrs Dalloway* (1925), *To the Lighthouse* (1927), *Orlando* (1928) and *The Waves* (1931). *Between the Acts*, her last novel, was published posthumously. A member of the BLOOMSBURY GROUP, her long essay *A Room of One's Own* (1929) is a key text of feminist criticism. Her critical essays, including *Modern Novels* (1919) and *The Common Reader* (1925), are integral to modern literary theory.

Worcester County town of Worcester, on the Severn River, w central England. There is a cathedral dating from the 13th and 14th centuries. The Battle of Worcester (1651) was the last engagement of the English CIVIL WAR. Industries: Royal Worcester porcelain, Worcester sauce, shoes. Pop. (1991) 81,700.

word processor COMPUTER system used for compiling and printing text. The system may be designed just for this purpose, in which case it is called a dedicated word processor. More common is a general-purpose personal computer running a word-processing program. Text typed on the keyboard is displayed on the screen. Any errors are easily corrected before a "printout" is produced. The text can be stored on a magnetic disk for future use.

Wordsworth, William (1770–1850) English poet. He collaborated with Samuel Taylor COLERIDGE on *Lyrical Ballads* (1798). The collection concluded with his poem "Tintern Abbey". Wordsworth's preface to the second edition (1800) outlined the aims of English ROMANTICISM, which through the use of everyday language enabled "the spontaneous overflow of powerful feelings". Critics derided his style. In 1799, he and his sister Dorothy moved to the Lake District; his poetry was always bound up with a love of nature. *The Prelude*, a long autobiographical poem, was completed in 1805, but only published posthumously in 1850. After *Poems in Two Volumes* (1807), which includes "Ode: Intimations of Immortality", it is generally recognized that his creativity declined. In 1843 he succeeded Robert SOUTHEY as poet laureate.

work In physics, energy transferred in moving a force. It equals the magnitude of the force multiplied by the distance moved in the direction of the force. If the force opposing movement is the object's weight mg (where m is the object's mass and g is the acceleration due to gravity), the work done in raising it a height h is mgh. This work has been transferred in the form of POTENTIAL ENERGY; if the object falls a distance, the KINETIC ENERGY at the bottom of the fall equals the work done in raising it.

Works Progress Administration (WPA) Former US government agency created (1935) under Franklin ROOSEVELT'S NEW DEAL policy to stimulate national economic recovery. Billions of dollars were contributed to the scheme in which work programmes provided jobs for the unemployed. About two million people were registered on WPA rolls at any one time between 1935 and 1941.

World Bank (International Bank for Reconstruction and Development (IBRD)) Intergovernmental organization based in Washington, D.C. A specialized agency of the UNITED NATIONS since 1945, its role is to make long-term loans to member governments to aid their economic development. The major part of the Bank's resources are derived from the world's capital markets.

World Council of Churches International fellowship of Christian churches formed (1948) in Amsterdam, Netherlands. Its aim is to work for the reunion of all Christian churches and to establish a united Christian presence in the world. The headquarters of the council are in Geneva, Switzerland. Its membership consists of some 300 churches. The Roman Catholic Church is not a member but has been sending observers to assemblies of the World Council of Churches since 1961.

World Cup Worldwide competition for national association FOOTBALL teams, held every four years. The winner receives the Jules Rimet trophy. Qualifying rounds take place over the previous two years on a geographical league basis. The finals are organized by the Fédération Internationale de Football Associations (FIFA), football's governing body. Only the winners of each group, the host nation, and the previous winner automatically qualify for the finals. There are also world cup competitions in other sports, notably rugby, cricket and hockey.

World Health Organization (WHO) Intergovernmental, specialized agency of the UNITED NATIONS. Founded in 1948, it collects and shares medical and scientific information and promotes international standards for drugs and vaccines. WHO has made major contributions to the prevention of diseases such as malaria, polio, leprosy and tuberculosis, and the eradication of smallpox. Its headquarters are in Geneva, Switzerland.

World Trade Organization (WTO) Body sponsored by the UNITED NATIONS to regulate international TRADE. The WTO was established on 1 January 1995 to replace the GENERAL AGREEMENT ON TARIFFS AND TRADE (GATT). The WTO took over GATT's rules with increased powers to regulate agriculture, clothing and textiles, intellectual property rights and services.

World War 1 (1914–18) (Great War) International conflict precipitated by the assassination of the Austrian Archduke Francis FERDINAND by Serbs in Sarajevo (28 June 1914). Austria declared war on Serbia (28 July), Russia mobilized in support of Serbia (from 29 July), Germany declared war on Russia (1 August) and France (3 August), and Britain declared war on Germany (4 August). World War I resulted from growing tensions in Europe, exacerbated by the rise of the German empire since 1871 and the decline of Ottoman power in the Balkans. The chief contestants were the Central Powers (Germany and Austria) and the Triple Entente (Britain, France and Russia). Many other countries were drawn in. Ottoman Turkey joined the Central Powers in 1914, Bulgaria in 1915. Italy joined the Western Allies in 1915, Romania in 1916 and, decisively, the USA in 1917. Russia withdrew following the RUSSIAN REVOLUTION of 1917. In Europe, fighting was largely static. After the initial German advance through Belgium was checked at the MARNE, the Western Front settled into a war of attrition, with huge casualties but little movement. On the Eastern Front, the initial Russian advance was checked by the Germans, who overran Poland before stagnation set in. An Anglo-French effort to relieve the Russians by attacking GALLIPOLI (1916) failed. Italy and Austria became bogged down on the Isonzo front. Campaigns were also fought outside Europe, against the Turks in the Middle East and the German colonies in Africa and the Pacific. At sea only one major battle was fought, at JUTLAND (1916). German submarines proved highly effective against Allied merchant ships in the Atlantic, but the naval blockade of Germany caused severe food shortages and helped end the war. An armistice was agreed in November 1918, and peace treaties were signed at VERSAILLES (1919). The war introduced new weapons, such as tanks, poison gas, airplanes and depth charges. Casualties were high: *c*.10 million people were killed.

World War 2 (1939–45) International conflict arising from disputes provoked by the expansionist policies of Germany in Europe and Japan in the Far East. During the 1930s APPEASEMENT failed to check the ambitions of Adolf HITLER's regime in Germany. Having made a defensive pact with the Soviet Union (August 1939), Germany invaded Poland, whereupon Britain and France declared war (3 September). In 1940 German BLITZ tactics resulted in the rapid conquest of Denmark, Norway, the Low Countries and France (June). Inability to gain command of the air prevented a German invasion of Britain (*see* BATTLE OF BRITAIN), although bombing devastated British cities, and German submarines took a heavy toll of British merchant shipping. Italy, under MUSSOLINI, having annexed Albania (1939) and invaded Greece (1940), joined Germany in 1941. Germany invaded Greece, where the Italians had been checked, and Yugoslavia. In June 1941, the Germans, violating the pact of 1939, invaded the Soviet Union, advancing to the outskirts of Moscow and Leningrad (St Petersburg). Italian defeats by the British in North Africa also drew in German troops, who threw back the British. In the Pacific, the Japanese attack on PEARL HARBOR (December 1941) drew the USA into the war. Japan rapidly overran SE Asia and Burma, but the Battle of MIDWAY (June 1942) indicated growing US naval and air superiority. From 1942, the tide in Europe turned against Germany. Defeat at STALINGRAD (January 1943) was followed by a Soviet advance that drove the Germans out of the Soviet Union by August 1944. Defeats in North Africa in 1942–43 led to the Allied invasion of Italy, forcing the Italians to make peace (September 1943). German troops then occupied Italy, where they resisted the Allied advance until 1945. In June 1944, Allied forces invaded NORMANDY, liberated France, and advanced into Germany, linking up with the Soviets on the River Elbe (April 1945). Germany surrendered in May. Japan continued to resist but surrendered in August after the USA dropped atomic bombs on Hiroshima and Nagasaki. Estimates of the numbers killed in World War 2 exceed 50 million. The great majority of the dead were civilians, many murdered in the HOLOCAUST. Politically, two former allies, the USA and the Soviet Union, emerged as the dominant world powers.

Worldwide Fund for Nature (WWF) International organization, established (1961) in Britain as the World Wildlife Fund. It raises voluntary funds for the conservation of endangered wild animals, plants and places. Its headquarters are in Bland, Switzerland.

World Wide Web (WWW) Name given to a series of COMPUTER NETWORKS that can be accessed via local servers, which in turn are serviced by telephone lines. It consists of a network of sites that users can access via the INTERNET to retrieve or post data. Web documents may include text, graphics and sound, and have hypertext that the user can click on to access further related information from other Web documents.

worm Any of a large variety of wriggling, limbless creatures with soft bodies. Most worms belong to one or other of four main groups: ANNELIDS, FLATWORMS, nematodes (ROUNDWORMS) and ribbon worms.

Worms Industrial town on the River Rhine, in Rhineland Palatinate, w Germany. In the 5th century it became the capital of the kingdom of Burgundy. It was made a free imperial city in 1156. Worms was annexed to France in 1797 but passed to Hesse-Darmstadt state in 1815. The French occupied the city from 1918 to 1930 and much of it was destroyed during World War 2. Today, it is a centre of the wine industry. Pop. (1991) 77,430.

Worms, Concordat of (1122) Agreement between the Holy Roman emperor, Henry V, and Pope Calixtus II settling the investiture conflict, a struggle over the control of church offices. The emperor agreed to the free election of bishops and surrendered his claim to invest them. They were, however, to pay homage to him as feudal overlord for their temporal possessions.

Worms, Diet of (1521) Conference of the Holy Roman Empire presided over by Emperor CHARLES V. Martin LUTHER was summoned to appear before the Diet to retract his teachings. Luther refused to retract them, and the Edict of Worms (May 25, 1521) declared him an outlaw. The Diet was one of the most important confrontations of the early REFORMATION.

wormwood Genus (*Artemisia*) of aromatic bitter shrubs and herbs, including common wormwood (*A. absinthium*), a European shrub that yields a dark green oil used to make absinthe. Family Asteraceae/Compositae.

Wounded Knee, Massacre at (1890) Last engagement in the conflict between Native Americans and US forces. Fearing a rising by the Sioux, US troops arrested several leaders. Chief SITTING BULL was killed resisting arrest. Another group was arrested a few days later and brought to Wounded Knee, South Dakota. A shot was fired, and the troops opened fire. About 300 people, including women and children, were killed.

Wren, Sir Christopher (1632–1723) English architect, mathematician and astronomer. He designed more than 50 new churches in the city of London based on syntheses of CLASSICAL, RENAISSANCE and BAROQUE ideas; the greatest of these is ST PAUL'S Cathedral. Among his many other works are Chelsea and Greenwich Hospitals, London, and the Sheldonian Theatre, Oxford.

wren Small, insect-eating songbird of temperate regions of Europe, Asia and most of the New World. Many species have white facial lines. The typical winter wren (*Troglodytes troglodytes*) has a slender bill, rounded wings, upright tail and dark brownish plumage; length: to 10cm (4in). Family Troglodytidae.

wrestling Sport in which two opponents try to throw each other to the ground or secure each other in an unbreakable hold, by means of body grips, strength, and adroitness. The two major competitive styles are **Greco-Roman** (most popular in continental Europe), which permits no tripping or holds below the waist, and **free-style** (most popular in the USA and Britain), which permits tackling, leg holds and tripping. A match consists of three periods of three minutes each; points are awarded for falls and other manoeuvres. Professional wrestling is mostly orchestrated entertainment. Wrestling originated in ancient Greece and has been part of the modern Olympics since 1904. *See also* SUMO WRESTLING

Wright, Frank Lloyd (1869–1959) US architect, regarded as the leading modernist designer of private housing. He worked as an assistant to Louis SULLIVAN in the Chicago School of architecture before his first independent design in 1893. His distinctive "organic" style of low-built, prairie-style houses was designed to blend in with natural contours and features. Influenced by JAPANESE ART AND ARCHITECTURE, Wright's open-plan approach to interiors was highly influential. His use of materials and mechanical construction techniques was radical.

Notable buildings include Robie House, Chicago (1909); "Fallingwater", Bear Run, Pennsylvania (1936–37); and the Guggenheim Museum, New York (1946–59).

Wright, Richard (1908–60) US novelist. His novels include *Native Son* (1940), which describes the life of an African-American youth in white-dominated Chicago; and *Black Boy* (1945), an account of the author's boyhood in the South. He also wrote short stories.

Wright brothers US aviation pioneers. Wilbur Wright (1867–1912) and Orville Wright (1871–1948) assembled their first aircraft in their bicycle factory. In 1903, Orville made the first piloted flight in a power-driven plane at Kitty Hawk, North Carolina. This flight lasted just 12 seconds and attracted little attention. In 1909, they established the Wright Company in New York.

writing Process or result of making a visual record for the purpose of communication by using symbols to represent the sounds or words of a language. Writing systems can be **ideographic** (using signs or symbols that represent concepts or ideas directly rather than the sound of words for them); **pictographic** (in which a picture or sign represents the meaning of a word or phrase); **syllabic** (in which signs represent groups of consonants and vowels); or **alphabetic** (in which symbols stand for individual speech sounds or certain combinations of sounds). The Chinese dialects have long made use of ideographic symbols. Ancient Egyptian HIEROGLYPHICS and CUNEIFORM scripts from Mesopotamia were originally pictographic. The LINEAR SCRIPTS of ancient Crete and Greece are syllabic, as is the modern Japanese Katakana. The Phoenicians were the first to use a phonetic system, with an ALPHABET of signs representing speech sounds. The Greek and Roman alphabets in use for most modern non-Asiatic languages are descended from the Phoenicians.

Wroclaw (Breslau) Industrial city and port on the River Oder, sw Poland. It is the capital of lower Silesia. Originally a Slavic settlement, it was destroyed by the Mongols in 1241, rebuilt by the Austrians from 1526, and ceded to Prussia in 1741. It developed as a trade centre in the 19th century and became part of Poland with the Potsdam Conference. Wroclaw is Poland's fourth largest city. Industries: machinery, electrical equipment, textiles, paper, timber, chemicals. Pop. (1996) 643,000.

Wuhan City and river port in central China, at the confluence of the Han and Yangtze rivers. It is the capital of Hubei province and the fifth-largest city in China. The town developed as a treaty port following the 19th-century OPIUM WARS and grew with the arrival of the railway and China's first modern iron and steel plants in 1891. Wuhan itself was formed in 1950 after the merger of three cities (Hankow, Hanyang and Wuchang) and is now the industrial and commercial hub of central China. Wuhan has China's largest cotton mill. Industries: textiles, iron, steel, heavy machinery, cement. Pop. (1994) 3,520,000.

Wundt, Wilhelm (1832–1920) German psychologist. He established the first laboratory for experimental psychology in 1879 at Leipzig and did much to convince early psychologists that the mind could be studied with objective, scientific methods. His major publication is *Principles of Physiological Psychology* (1873–74).

Wyatt, Sir Thomas (1503–42) English poet and courtier, a pioneer of the English SONNET. He was popular at Henry VIII's court although, as an alleged former lover of Anne BOLEYN and friend of Thomas CROMWELL, he was briefly imprisoned in 1536 and 1541.

Wycliffe, John (1330–84) English religious reformer. Under the patronage of JOHN OF GAUNT, he attacked corrupt practices in the church and the authority of the pope, condemning in particular the church's landed wealth. His criticism became increasingly radical, questioning the authority of the pope and insisting on the primacy of scripture, but he escaped condemnation until after his death. His ideas were continued by the LOLLARDS in England and influenced Jan HUS in Bohemia.

Wyeth, Andrew Newell (1917–) US painter. His best-known painting is *Christina's World* (1948). He was trained by his father, the illustrator, N.C. Wyeth. His son, James (1946–), is also a noted artist.

Wyler, William (1902–81) US film director. Wyler won three best director and best picture Academy Awards: *Mrs Miniver* (1942), *The Best Years of Our Lives* (1946) and *Ben-Hur* (1959). Other credits include *Jezebel* (1938), *Wuthering Heights* (1939), *The Little Foxes* (1941) and *Roman Holiday* (1953).

Wyndham, John (1903–69) English novelist. He is remembered for his science-fiction "disaster" novels, such as *The Day of the Triffids* (1951). Other works include *The Kraken Wakes* (1953), *The Chrysalids* (1955) and *The Midwych Cuckoos* (1957).

Wyoming State in the NW USA, rectangular and bounded by Montana (N), South Dakota (E), Colorado (S), Utah (SW) and Idaho (W). Wyoming has the nation's smallest state population. The state capital and largest city is CHEYENNE. Other important centres are Casper and Laramie. The landscape is dominated by mountains and 4 million hectares (10 million acres) of forest. The ROCKY MOUNTAINS cross the state from NW to SE. To the E of the Rockies lie the rolling grasslands of the Great Plains, and the centre of the state is also high plains country. The N of the state is primarily tall grass plain where bison roamed and were hunted by the CROW and then the SIOUX. The area is fertile farmland and cattle-ranch country. Yellowstone National Park is the nation's oldest and largest national park, occupying the entire NW corner of Wyoming. From the tops of the mountain ranges flow many rivers, including the North Platte and the Snake. Following the LOUISIANA PURCHASE (1803), by 1846 the USA had acquired the entire territory through treaties. Later 19th-century development was linked to the fur trade and westward migration along the OREGON TRAIL. The 1860s marked the first dramatic arrival of new settlers: the Bozeman Trail was opened (1864), gold was discovered in S Wyoming (1867), and the railway was completed (1868). By the end of the 1870s, the Native American population had been pacified and placed on reservations. The next 20 years were marked by a rise of vigilante groups to deal with cattle rustlers and outlaws, and in 1890 Wyoming became the 44th state of the Union. While cattle ranching and sheep and wheat farming remain important to the economy, Wyoming is primarily an oil-producing state. Oil was discovered in the 1860s, and in 1993 output totalled 87.7 million barrels. Other important mineral resources include coal and uranium. Area: 253,596sq km (97,913sq mi). Pop. (2000) 493,782.

Wyszynski, Stefan (1901–81) Polish Roman Catholic cardinal. As Primate of Poland from 1948, he protested against the communist attacks on the church during the trial of Bishop Kaczmarek of Kielce. In 1952, Pope Pius XII appointed him cardinal. Wyszynski was imprisoned from 1953 to 1956. In 1957, he was allowed to go to Rome to receive the honour of a cardinal's hat. In the early 1980s, he played an active mediating role between Solidarity and the government.

X/x, 24th letter of the Roman alphabet. It is believed to have developed from the Semitic character, samekh. *A letter resembling the modern* X *existed in the Greek alphabet,* chi.

x-chromosome One of the two kinds of sex-determining CHROMOSOME; the other is the Y-CHROMOSOME. In many organisms, including humans, females carry two x-chromosomes in their DIPLOID cell nuclei, whereas males carry one x- and one y-chromosome. Non-sexual characteristics are also carried on the x-chromosome – for example, the genes for one form of colour blindness and for haemophilia. See also GENETICS; HEREDITY

Xenakis, Yannis (1922–) Greek composer. Xenakis studied music under Arthur HONEGGER and Olivier MESSIAEN and also trained as an architect. Some of his work is TWELVE-TONE MUSIC, and he has been a pioneer of the use of computers and mathematical models in the compositional process. His compositions include *Metastasis* (1954) and *Stratégie (1962)*.

xenon (symbol Xe) Gaseous, nonmetallic element, one of the NOBLE GASES. Discovered in 1898, xenon is present in the Earth's atmosphere (about one part in 20 million) and is obtained by fractionation of liquid air. Colourless and odourless, it is used in light bulbs, lasers and arc lamps for cinema projection. The element, which has nine stable isotopes, forms some compounds, mostly with FLUORINE. Properties: at.no. 54; r.a.m. 131.30; r.d. 5.88; m.p. −111.9°C (−169.42°F); b.p. −107.1°C (−160.8°F); most common isotope Xe^{132} (26.89%).

Xenophanes of Colophon (*c.*560–*c.*478 BC) Travelling Greek poet and philosopher. He proposed a version of pantheism, holding that all living creatures have a common natural origin. His work survives only in fragmentary form.

Xenophon (*c.*430–*c.*354 BC) Greek historian. He studied with SOCRATES, whose teaching he described in *Memorabilia*. *Anabasis*, an account of his march with a Greek mercenary army across Asia Minor in 401–399 BC in support of a pretender to the Persian throne, is his best-known work. Other works include a history of Greece from 411 to 362 BC.

xerography Most common process used for PHOTOCOPYING.

xerophyte Any plant that is adapted to survive in dry conditions, in areas subject to drought or in physiologically dry areas such as saltmarshes and acid bogs, where saline or acid conditions make the uptake of water difficult. Succulents such as cacti (see CACTUS) have thick fleshy leaves and stems for storing water. Other adaptations include the ability to reduce water loss by shedding leaves during drought or having waxy or hairy leaf coatings or reduced leaf area.

Xerxes I (519–465 BC) King of Persia (486–465 BC). Succeeding his father, DARIUS I, he regained Egypt and crushed a rebellion in Babylon before launching his invasion of Greece (480 BC). After his fleet was destroyed at the Battle of Salamis (480), he retired. The defeat of the Persian army in Greece at the Battle of Plataea (479) ended his plans for conquest. He was later assassinated by one of his own men. *See also* PERSIAN WARS

Xhosa (Xosa) Group of related BANTU tribes. The Xhosa moved from E Africa to the vicinity of the Great Fish River, S Africa, in the 17th and 18th centuries. In 1835 they were defeated by the Europeans, after which they came under European rule. In culture they are closely related to the ZULU. The 2.5 million Xhosa live in the Transkei and form an important part of South Africa's industrial and mining workforce. Xhosa is the most widely spoken African language in South Africa.

Xiamen Seaport city in Fujian province, SE China. As Amoy, it flourished in the 19th century after being declared an open port by the Treaty of Nanking (1842). It gained extra strategic importance after the communists took control of the Chinese mainland (1949). In 1981 Xiamen was granted the status of special economic zone, accelerating its role as the centre of growing "unofficial" trade between China and Taiwan. Pop. (1994) 459,000.

Xian (Sian, formerly Changan) Capital of Shaanxi province at the confluence of the rivers Wei and HUANG HE, NW China. Inhabited since 6000 BC, from 255 to 206 BC it was the site of Xianyang, the capital of the QIN dynasty. The elaborate tomb of the dynastic founder, emperor QIN SHIHUANGDI, is a world heritage site and major tourist attraction. Xian was the focus for the introduction of Buddhism to China, and in 652 the Big Wild Goose pagoda was built here. In the following centuries it became a major centre for other religious missionaries. It is an important commercial centre of a grain-growing region. Industries: cotton, textiles, steel, chemicals. Pop. (1994) 2,115,000.

Xingu Brazilian river, rising in central Mato Grosso state. It flows N for 1,980km (1,230mi) and empties into the River Amazon at its delta. It courses through rain forest and is navigable only in its lower reaches. The area focused international attention on the plight of Native Americans when a government proposal to dam the Xingu meant the flooding of tribal land. The dam and hydroelectric scheme was completed in December 1994 at a cost of US$3.2 billion.

Xinjiang (Mandarin, new frontier; Sinkiang or Chinese Turkistan) Autonomous region in NW China, bordered by Tajikistan, Kyrgyzstan and Kazakstan (N and W), Mongolia (E) and Kashmir and Tibet (S). The capital is Ürümqi. The region includes the Dzungarian Basin to the E and the Tarim Basin to the W. The ALTAI, TIAN SHAN and Kunlun mountains frame the region to the N, W and S respectively. First conquered by the Chinese in the 1st century BC, the region changed hands many times in the following centuries. From the 13th to 18th centuries it was loosely controlled by the Mongols. In 1756 the QING dynasty became the leading power in the region. It was made a Chinese province in 1881. It is a predominantly agricultural region growing wheat, cotton, maize, rice, millet, vegetables and fruit; livestock rearing (particularly sheep) is also important. The area is rich in minerals, including oil, copper, zinc, gold and silver. Industries: iron and steel, chemicals, textiles. Area: 1,647,435sq km (636,075sq mi). Pop. (1990) 15,370,000.

X-ray astronomy *See* ASTRONOMY

X-ray crystallography Use of X-RAYS to discover the molecular structure of CRYSTALS. It uses the phenomenon of X-ray diffraction, the scattering of an X-ray beam by the atomic structure of a crystal, and has been used to reveal the structure of crystalline DNA.

X-rays ELECTROMAGNETIC RADIATION of shorter wavelength, or higher frequency, than visible light, produced when a beam of ELECTRONS hits a solid target. X-rays were discovered (1895) by Wilhelm RÖNTGEN. They are normally produced for scientific use in X-ray tubes. Because they are able to penetrate matter that is opaque to light, X-rays are used to investigate inaccessible areas, especially of the body. *See also* RADIOGRAPHY

xylem Transport TISSUE of a plant, which conducts water and minerals from the roots to the rest of the plant and provides support. The most important cells are long, thin, tapering cells called **xylem vessels**. These cells are dead and have no cross-walls; they are arranged in columns to form long tubes, up which water is drawn. As water evaporates from the leaves (TRANSPIRATION), water is drawn across the leaf by OSMOSIS to replace it, drawing water out of the xylem. This suction creates a tension in the xylem vessels, and the side walls are reinforced with rings or spirals of LIGNIN, a rigid substance, to prevent their collapsing. Tiny holes in the walls of the xylem vessels, called pits, allow water to cross from one tube to another. In trees, the xylem becomes blocked with age, and new xylem forms towards the outside of the trunk to replace it. The core of dead, non-functioning xylem remains an essential part of the support system. *See also* PHLOEM; VASCULAR BUNDLE

xylophone Tuned PERCUSSION instrument. It is made of hardwood bars arranged as in a piano keyboard and played with mallets. The modern xylophone normally has a range of four octaves, extending from middle C upwards.

XYZ Affair (1797–98) Diplomatic incident that strained US relations with France. President John ADAMS sent three representatives to renegotiate the French-US alliance of 1778, which had given way to hostility after the signing of JAY'S TREATY (1794). Three French agents, known as X, Y and Z, demanded bribes and a loan before negotiations began, causing an uproar in the USA and the recall of its commissioners.

Y/y, 25th letter of the Roman alphabet. It was derived from the Semitic letter vaw, *meaning* hook. *It was adopted by the Greeks as* upsilon, *before passing into the Roman alphabet as Y and V.*

yacht Boat used for sport and recreation, powered by sail or motor. Sailing yachts, which are usually fore-and-aft rigged, vary from 6m (20ft) to more than 30m (100ft) and include cutters, schooners, ketches, sloops and yawls. Those fitted with diesel or petrol engines are usually classified as cruising, or motor yachts. Although most are used for vacationing and cruising, yachting has been an international sport since 1851, when the Royal Yacht Squadron (formed at Cowes, England, in 1812) offered a silver cup as a prize for a race of 97km (60mi) around the Isle of WIGHT. The race was won by the schooner yacht, *America*, owned by the members of the New York Yacht Club (organized 1844); it has since been known as the AMERICA'S CUP. The Admiral's Cup is an international race held biennially since 1957 at Cowes. The Observer Single-Handed Transatlantic Race has been held every four years since 1960. The Olympics have competition in seven yachting categories.

Yahweh Personal name of the God of the ancient Israelites of the Old Testament. God revealed His name to MOSES when He called to him out of the burning bush at Mount Horeb (Sinai) (Exodus 3:14). In Hebrew, it was made up of four consonants, YHWH, and was apparently related to the Hebrew verb "to be". Most English translations render it as "I am". *See also* JEHOVAH

yak Large, powerful, long-haired ox, native to Tibet, with domesticated varieties throughout central Asia; it inhabits barren heights up to 6,100m (20,000ft). Domesticated varieties are generally smaller and varied in colour; they breed freely with domestic cattle. Wild yaks have coarse, black hair, except on the tail and flanks, where it hangs as a long fringe. The horns curve upwards and outwards. Height: to 1.8m (6ft) at the shoulder. Family Bovidae; species *Bos grunniens*.

Yakutia (officially Republic of Sakha) Constituent republic of the Russian Federation, NE Siberia. The capital is Yakutsk. The region is bounded by the Laptev and East Siberian seas (N) and the Stanovoy Range (S). It is the largest Russian republic and one of the coldest inhabited regions, with more than 40% of the territory within the Arctic Circle. The principal rivers are the LENA, Yana, Indirka and Kolyma. One-third of the population is Yakut, a Turkic-speaking people who settled in the Lena basin from the 13th–15th century. They are noted bone carvers, iron workers and potters. The area was colonized by Russia during the 17th century, and many Yakuts were forcibly converted from shamanism to Christianity. A republic of the former Soviet Union (1922–91), Yakutia became a member of the new Russian Federation in 1992. Agriculture is only possible in the S. The major industry is diamond mining and processing. Other important minerals are gold, silver, lead and coal. Timber is an important industry in the taiga regions. Area: 3,100,000sq km (1,200,000sq mi) Pop. (1994) 1,060,700.

Yale University Institute of higher education in New Haven, Connecticut. USA Founded in 1701 in Branford, Connecticut, it operates several colleges for the study of arts, science and social science, as well as professional schools and a graduate school. Its current charter dates from 1745. It is a member of the IVY LEAGUE.

Yalow, Rosalyn (1921–) US biochemist. In the 1950s, she found that some people who received INSULIN injections developed ANTIBODIES against the HORMONE. Yalow discovered that insulin, labelled with radioactive iodine, combined with the antibodies; from this she developed radio-immunological tests to detect and measure the amount of insulin present. She shared the 1977 Nobel Prize for physiology or medicine for her development of a method of detecting PEPTIDE hormones in the blood.

Yalta Conference (February 1945) Meeting of the chief Allied leaders of WORLD WAR 2 at Yalta, Crimea, S Ukraine. With victory over Germany imminent, ROOSEVELT, CHURCHILL and STALIN met to discuss the final campaigns of the war and the post-war settlement. Agreements were reached on the foundation of the UNITED NATIONS, the territorial division of Europe into "spheres of interest", the occupation of Germany, and support for democracy in liberated countries. Concessions were made to Stalin in the Far East in order to gain Soviet support against Japan.

yam Any of several species of herbaceous vines that grow in warm and tropical regions; also the edible large, tuberous roots of several tropical species. The plant is an annual with a long, climbing stem, lobed or unlobed leaves and small clusters of greenish, bell-shaped flowers. The SWEET POTATO is also sometimes called a yam. Family Dioscoreaceae; genus *Dioscorea*.

Yamasaki, Minoru (1912–) US architect. He is famous for designing the Lambert-St Louis Municipal airport terminal (1953–55), USA, which is noted for its concrete vaults. Yamasaki was the chief architect of the World Trade Center (1962) in New York City.

Yamoussoukro Capital of IVORY COAST since 1983. Originally a small Baouké tribal village and birthplace of Ivory Coast's first president Félix HOUPHOUËT-BOIGNY, it has developed rapidly into the administrative and transport centre of Ivory Coast. Yamoussoukro's Our Lady of Peace Cathedral (consecrated by Pope John Paul II in 1990) is the world's largest Christian church. Pop. (1990) 120,000.

Yamuna (Jumna) River in N central India. It rises in the Himalayas and flows S and SE. The Yamuna's confluence with the GANGES at ALLAHABAD is one of the most sacred Hindu sites. The TAJ MAHAL lies on its bank at AGRA. Navigable for almost its entire length, the Yamuna was once an important trade route and is now primarily used for irrigation. Length: *c*.1,380km (860mi).

Yang, Chen Ning (1922–) US physicist, b. China. With Tsung-Dao LEE, he studied the decay of K MESONS, which seemed to break down in two different ways, and in 1956 they concluded that in these weak interactions PARITY need not be conserved. In 1957, they shared the Nobel Prize for physics.

Yangtze (Chang Jiang) River in China, the longest in Asia and third longest in the world. Rising in the Kunlun Mountains in NE Tibet, it flows 6,300km (3,900mi) through the central Chinese provinces to the East China Sea near Shanghai. It was joined to the HUANG HE (Yellow River) by the Grand Canal in 610. Navigation becomes difficult at the spectacular Yangtze Gorges, between CHUNGKING and Yichang, but after Yichang (site of the huge Gezhouba Dam) it enters the fertile lowlands of Hubei province. The Yangtze and its main tributaries traverse one of the world's most populated areas, providing water for irrigation and hydroelectricity, and it is China's most economically important waterway. The Chinese government's controversial Three Gorges dam scheme E of Fengjie, destined to take 15 years to complete, will create a reservoir *c*.600km (375mi) long, displacing *c*.1.2 million people.

Yanomami Native American tribal group living chiefly in the rainforests of N Brazil and S Venezuela. Traditionally semi-nomadic hunter-gatherers, during the 1980s and 1990s they lost much of their land to road builders, logging companies and gold prospectors, causing the population to fall to *c*.18,000. Their plight raised international concern.

Yaoundé Capital of Cameroon, W Africa. Located in beautiful hills on the edge of dense jungle, it was founded by German traders in 1888. During World War 1 it was occupied by Belgian troops, and from 1921 to 1960 it acted as capital of French Cameroon. Since independence, it has grown rapidly as a financial and administrative centre. The city also serves as a market for the surrounding region, notably in coffee, cacao and sugar. Pop. (1992) 800,000.

yard Imperial unit of length equal to 3 feet. 1 yard (yd) equals 0.9144m.

Yaroslavl (Jaroslavl') City and river port on the Volga, W central Russia; capital of Yaroslavl oblast. The oldest town on the Volga (founded 1010 by Yaroslavl the Great), it was capital of Yaroslavl principality when absorbed by MOSCOW in 1463. From March to July 1612 it served as Russia's capital, and still boasts many historic buildings. It is a major rail junction. Industries:

linen, diesel engines, construction equipment, oil refining, petrochemicals, plastics. Pop. (1994) 631,000.

yaws (framboesia) Contagious skin disease found in the humid tropics. It is caused by a spirochaete (*Treponema pertenue*) related to the organism causing SYPHILIS. Yaws, however, is not a SEXUALLY TRANSMITTED DISEASE (STD) but is transmitted by flies and by direct skin contact with the sores. It may cause disfiguring bone lesions.

y-chromosome One of the two kinds of sex-determining CHROMOSOME, the other is the X-CHROMOSOME. Many male organisms have one x- and one y-chromosome in their DIPLOID cell nuclei. SPERM cells contain either an x- or a y-chromosome, and since female ova (egg cells) always contain an x-chromosome, the resulting offspring is either XY (male) or XX (female). The y-chromosome is smaller than the x- and contains fewer GENES.

year Length of time taken by the Earth to circle once around the Sun in its ORBIT. It is defined in various ways, such as the sidereal year, which is timed with reference to the fixed stars. *See also* SIDEREAL PERIOD.

yeast Any of a group of single-celled microscopic FUNGI found worldwide in the soil and in organic matter. Yeasts reproduce asexually by BUDDING or FISSION. Yeasts are also produced commercially for use in baking, brewing and wine-making. They occur naturally as a bloom (white covering) on grapes and other fruit.

Yeats, W.B. (William Butler) (1865–1939) Irish poet and dramatist, often cited as the greatest English language poet of the 20th century. In 1094 he and Lady Gregory founded the ABBEY THEATRE, Dublin, as an Irish national theatre. Yeats' plays *On Baile's Strand* (1905) and *Cathleen Ni Houlihan* (1902) were on the first bill, the latter often regarded as the beginning of the renaissance in IRISH LITERATURE. Yeats' early poetry, collected in *The Wanderings of Oisin, and Other Poems* (1889), betrays the influence of mysticism. His unrequited love for Maud Gonne inspired him to produce more directly nationalistic statements. The poetry in *Responsibilities* (1914) acted as contemporary social commentary. Following the creation of the Irish Free State, Yeats served (1922–28) as a senator. His mature poetry includes *Michael Robartes and the Dancer* (1921, which contains "The Second Coming"

► **yam** Commercially important in E Asia and in tropical America, the yam (*Dioscorea* sp.) produces thick, starchy rhizomes, often weighing up to 13.6kg (30lb). These are a valuable food source and form part of the staple diet of many people worldwide, especially in Africa.

and "Easter 1916") and *The Tower* (1928, which contains "Sailing to Byzantium"). Yeats received the 1923 Nobel Prize for literature.

yellow fever Acute, infectious disease marked by sudden onset of headaches, fever, muscle and joint pain, jaundice and vomiting; the kidneys and heart may also be affected. It is caused by a VIRUS transmitted by mosquitoes in tropical and sub-tropical regions. It may be prevented by vaccination.

yellow hammer (yellow bunting) Small Old World finch known for its pair formation ceremony, in which males and females drop and pick up small inanimate insects before mating. Species *Emberiza calandra*.

yellowlegs Two species of American shore birds named for their long yellow legs. Both have black and white markings and white underparts. They nest in summer in N North America, laying four buff or brown eggs, and fly S as far as Chile in winter. Once over-hunted, they are now protected species and their numbers have increased. Family Scolopacidae; species *Tringa melanoleuca* (greater yellowlegs), *Tringa flavipes* (lesser yellowlegs).

yellowthroat Small New World WARBLER, especially *Geothlypis trichas*, which has a brownish back, yellow throat, and, in the male, a black facial mask. The yellow-throated warbler (*Dendroica dominica*) is a wood warbler.

Yeltsin, Boris Nikolayevich (1931–) Russian statesman, first democratically elected president of the Russian Federation (1991–). He was Communist Party leader in Ekaterinburg (Sverdlovsk) before joining (1985) the reforming government of Mikhail GORBACHEV, becoming party chief in Moscow. His blunt criticism of the slow pace of PERESTROIKA led to demotion in 1987, but his immense popularity gained him election as president of the Russian Republic in 1990. His prompt denunciation of the attempted coup against Gorbachev (August 1991) established his ascendancy. Elected president of the Russian Federation, he presided over the dissolution of the Soviet Union and the termination of Communist Party rule. Economic disintegration, rising crime and internal conflicts, notably in Chechnia, damaged his popularity, and failing health reduced his effectiveness. Nevertheless, he was re-elected in 1996. In 1998, Yeltsin twice sacked the entire cabinet, including the prime minister, in the face of economic crisis in Russia. In 2000, Yeltsin stepped down in favour of Vladimir PUTIN, and was granted immunity from prosecution.

Yemen Republic on the SE tip of the Arabian peninsula. Much of Yemen's interior forms part of the Rub al Khali (Empty Quarter) desert. The desert is bisected by a central plateau. A narrow coastal plain borders the Red and Arabian seas. The Arabian coastal plain includes ADEN, the former capital of South Yemen, and the fertile Hadramaut valley. The W plain is backed by highlands that rise to more than 3,600m (12,000ft) near the capital SANA'A. **Climate** Most of Yemen is hot and rainless, except during the monsoon month of August. The highlands are the wettest part of Arabia, and the temperature is moderated by altitude. **Vegetation** Palm trees grow along the coast. Plants such as acacia and eucalyptus flourish in the interior. Thorn shrubs and mountain pasture are found in the highlands. The Rub al Khali (Empty Quarter) is a barren

desert. **History and politics** The ancient kingdom of SHEBA (Saba) flourished in present-day S Yemen between *c*.750 BC and 100 BC. The kingdom was renowned for its advanced technology and wealth, gained through its strategic location on important trade routes. The region was invaded by the Romans in the 1st century BC. Islam was introduced in AD 628. The Rassite dynasty of the Zaidi sect established a theocratic state that lasted until 1962. The FATIMIDS conquered Yemen in *c*.1000. In 1517, the area became part of the OTTOMAN EMPIRE and largely remained under Turkish control until 1918. In the 19th century, the Saudi Wahhabi sect ousted the Zaidi imams, but were in turn expelled by IBRAHIM PASHA. In 1839, Aden was captured by the British. In 1937, Britain formed the Aden Protectorate. Following the defeat of the Ottomans in World War 1, Yemen was ruled by Imam Yahya of the Hamid al-Din dynasty. In 1945, Yemen joined the ARAB LEAGUE. In 1948, Yahya was assassinated. Crown Prince Ahmed became imam. From 1958 to 1961, Yemen formed part of the United Arab Republic (with Egypt and Syria). A 1962 army revolution overthrew the monarchy and formed the Yemen Arab Republic. Civil war ensued between republicans (aided by Egypt) and royalists (aided by Saudi Arabia and Jordan). Meanwhile, the Aden Protectorate became part of the British Federation of South Arabia. In 1967, the National Liberation Front forced the British to withdraw from Aden and founded the People's Republic of South Yemen. Marxists won the ensuing civil war in South Yemen and renamed it the People's Democratic Republic of Yemen (1970). Border clashes between the two Yemens were frequent throughout the 1970s and erupted into full-scale war (1979). In 1990, following lengthy negotiations, the two Yemens merged to form a single republic. Yemen's support for Iraq in the GULF WAR (1991) led to the expulsion of 800,000 Yemeni workers from Saudi Arabia. A coalition government emerged from 1993 elections, but increasing economic and political tensions between North and South led to civil war in 1994. The South's brief secession from the union ended with victory for the Northern army. In 1995, agreement was reached with Saudi Arabia and Oman over disputed boundaries. Yemen clashed with Eritrea over the Hanish Islands in the Red Sea until a mutually acceptable agreement had been reached by 1998. In 1998, four hostages were killed in an attempted rescue. President Saleh was decisively re-elected in 1999. In 1999, several British citizens were arrested on terrorist charges. **Economy** Civil strife has devastated Yemen's economy, seriously damaging the country's infrastructure, such as the oil refinery at Aden. Yemen is a low-income developing nation (1992 GDP per capita, US$2,410). In 1995, inflation and unemployment stood at over 50%, forcing Yemen to borrow from the INTERNATIONAL MONETARY FUND. Agriculture employs 63% of the workforce, mainly at subsistence level. The major economic activity is livestock-raising, principally sheep. Crops include sorghum, wheat and barley. Oil extraction began in the NW in the 1980s. Natural gas is also exploited.

Yenisei (Yenesey) River in central Siberia, Russia. Formed by the confluence of the Bolshoi Yenisei and the Maly Yenisei at Kyzyl, it flows for 4,090km (2,540mi) W then N through the Sayan Mountains and across Siberia, forming the W border of the central Siberian plateau, emptying into the Yenisei Gulf on the Kara Sea. A large hydroelectric station has been built at Krasnoyarsk. The river is a source of sturgeon and salmon. It is a shipping route, although some of its sections are frozen in winter. When the river is combined

YEMEN
AREA: 527,970sq km (203,849sq mi)
POPULATION: 13,219,000
CAPITAL (POPULATION): Sana'a (972,000)

with the Angara (its major tributary), it is the world's fifth longest river, at 5,550km (3,445mi).

Yerevan Capital of Armenia, on the River Razdan, s Caucasus. One of the world's oldest cities, it was capital of Armenia as early as the 7th century (though under Persian control), and was a crucial crossroads for caravan routes between India and Transcaucasia. It is the site of a 16th-century Turkish fortress and a traditional wine-making centre. Industries: chemicals, plastics, cables, tyres, metals, vodka. Pop. (1994) 1,254,000.

Yerkes Observatory Observatory of the University of Chicago, at Williams Bay, Wisconsin, USA. It was founded by George Ellery HALE. Its main instrument is a 1m (40in) refractor, opened in 1897 and still the largest in the world.

Yersin, Alexandre Émile John (1863–1943) French bacteriologist. In 1894 he discovered (1894) the PLAGUE bacillus in Hong Kong. In 1896 Yersin developed a serum against it. He is also reputed to have introduced the rubber tree into Indochina.

Yevtushenko, Yevgeny (1933–) Russian writer. During the 1960s, he headed a new wave of nonconformist, modern Soviet poetry. Rejecting SOCIALIST REALISM, Yevtushenko's rhetorical poetry anticipated GLASNOST in its examination of Soviet history. His most famous work, "Babi Yar" (1961), was a direct indictment of Soviet anti-Semitism. Other works include *Precocious Autobiography* (1963) and *The Bratsk Station* (1965).

yew Any of a number of evergreen shrubs and trees of the genus *Taxus*, native to temperate regions of the Northern Hemisphere. They have stiff, narrow, dark green needles, often with pale undersides, and poisonous red, berry-like fruits. Height: to 25m (80ft). Family Taxaceae.

Yiddish Language spoken by Jews living in central and E Europe and other countries (including the USA) with Jewish communities. It first developed in w Europe in the 10th and 11th centuries and was taken E with migrating Jews. It is a variety of German, with many Hebrew, Aramaic, French, Italian and Slavic words added. It is written using the Hebrew alphabet.

Yin Alternative transliteration of the SHANG dynasty

yin and yang Interaction of two complementary forces in the universe, as described in the Chinese philosophy of TAOISM. *Yin* and *yang* are two cosmic energy modes comprising the *Tao* or the eternal, dynamic way of the universe. Earth is *yin*, the passive, dark, female principle; heaven is *yang*, the active, bright, male principle. All the things of nature and society are composed of combinations of these two principles of polarity, which maintain the balance of all things. The hexagrams of the I Ching *see* BOOK OF CHANGES) embody *yin* and *yang*.

YMCA Abbreviation of YOUNG MEN'S CHRISTIAN ASSOCIATION

yoga (Sanskrit, union) Term used for a number of Hindu disciplines to aid the union of the soul with God. Based on the *Yoga-sutras* of Patañjali (written at about the time of Christ), the practice of yoga generally involves moral restraints, meditation and the awakening of physical energy centres through specific postures (*asanas*) or exercises. Devoted to freeing the soul or self from earthly cares by isolating it from the body and the mind, these ancient practices became popular in the West during the second half of the 20th century as a means of relaxation, self-control and enlightenment.

yogurt (yoghurt, yoghourt) Semi-solid, cultured dairy food, fermented by bacteria. Pasteurized milk is inoculated with a culture of *Streptococcus acidophilus* and *Lactobacillus bulgaricus* and incubated to achieve a sourish acidity. Yogurt originated with nomadic tribes in Central Asia and became popular in the Balkans as a drink. It then spread throughout Europe and the USA as a creamy, custard-like product, often sweetened and flavoured with fruit.

Yogyakarta (Jogjakarta) City in s Java, Indonesia. Founded in 1749, it is the cultural and artistic centre of Java. Capital of a Dutch-controlled sultanate from 1755, it was the scene of a revolt (1825–30) against colonial exploitation. During the 1940s it was the centre of the Indonesian independence movement and, in 1949, acted as the provisional capital of Indonesia. Its many visitors are drawn by the 18th-century palace, the Grand Mosque, the religious and arts festivals, and its proximity to the BOROBUDUR temple. The major industry is handicrafts. Pop. (1995) 419,000.

Yokohama Port and major industrial city on the w shore of Tokyo Bay, SE Honshu, Japan. Japan's main port for many years, it is now the country's second largest city. It grew from a small fishing village to a major Japanese port after opening to foreign trade in 1859. It served as Tokyo's deep-water harbour and was a vital silk-exporting centre. The city has been rebuilt twice: once after the devastating earthquake in 1923 and again following intensive Allied bombing during World War 2. Many of the modern port and industrial facilities have been built on land reclaimed from the sea. Industries: iron, steel, shipbuilding. Pop. (1995) 3,307,000.

yolk Rich substance found in the eggs or ova of most animals, except those of placental mammals. It consists of fats and proteins and serves as a store of food for the developing embryo.

yolk sac Membranous, sac-like structure in the eggs (ova) of most animals. It is attached directly to the ventral surface or gut of the developing EMBRYO in the eggs of birds, reptiles and some fish, and contains YOLK. The term also refers to an analogous sac-like membrane that develops below the mammalian embryo. It contains no yolk but is connected to the umbilical cord.

Yom Kippur (Day of Atonement) Most solemn of Jewish holy days. It is the last of the Ten Days of Penitence that begin the New Year. On this day, set aside for prayer and fasting, humanity is called to account for its sins and to seek reconciliation with God. Yom Kippur is described as the SABBATH of Sabbaths, because the break from work is almost complete, and Jews must abstain from food, drink and sex. *See also* ROSH HASHANAH

York City and county district in NORTH YORKSHIRE, N England. Located at the confluence of the rivers Ouse and Foss, it was an important Roman military post, an Anglo-Saxon capital, a Danish settlement and then the ecclesiastical centre of the North of England. York Minster cathedral dates from the 13th century. Tourists are attracted by York's old buildings and museums. Industries: engineering (including rail workshops), confectionery, precision instruments. Pop. (1994) 107,000.

York, Archbishop of Second-highest office of the CHURCH OF ENGLAND. The acts of the Council of Arles (314) mention a bishop of York, but the early Christian community in York was destroyed by Saxon invaders. The uninterrupted history of the present see began with the consecration of Wilfrid as bishop of York in 664. York was raised to the dignity of an archbishopric in 735, when Egbert was given the title PRIMATE of the Northern Province. The archbishop is now called Primate of England (the Archbishop of CANTERBURY is Primate of all England).

York, House of English royal house, a branch of the PLANTAGENETS. During the Wars of the ROSES, rival claimants from the houses of York and LANCASTER contended for the crown. The Yorkist claimant, Richard, duke of York, was a great-grandson of EDWARD III. His son gained the crown as EDWARD IV. The defeat of Edward's brother, RICHARD III, by HENRY VII in 1485 brought the brief Yorkist line to a close. *See also* TUDORS

Yorkshire *See* NORTH YORKSHIRE, SOUTH YORKSHIRE and WEST YORKSHIRE

Yorkshire terrier Small, long-haired dog originally bred in Lancashire and Yorkshire, England, in the 19th century. It has a small head with a short muzzle and small, V-shaped, erect ears. The compact body has a short, straight back and is set on short legs, which are hidden under the coat. The tail is commonly docked. The straight, fine, silky coat is generally black and tan. Height: to 20cm (8in) at the shoulder; weight to 3kg (7lb).

Yorktown, Siege of (1781) Last major military campaign of the AMERICAN REVOLUTION. Trapped on the peninsula of Yorktown, Virginia, 7,000 British troops under Lord CORNWALLIS surrendered to superior US and French forces, after attempts to relieve them had failed.

Yoruba People of SW Nigeria of basically Christian or Islamic faith. Most are farmers, growing crops that include yams, maize and cocoa. Many live in towns built around the palace of an *oba*, or chief, and travel daily to their outlying farms.

Young, Brigham (1801–77) US religious leader, founder of Salt Lake City. An early convert to the Church of Jesus Christ of Latter-Day Saints (MORMONS), Young took over the leadership when Joseph SMITH, the founder, was killed by a mob in 1844. Young held the group together through persecutions and led their westward migration (1846–47) to Utah, where he organized the settlement that became Salt Lake City. He was governor of Utah Territory (1850–57).

Young, Lester Willis (1909–59) US jazz saxophonist. A major jazz influence, with his characteristically cool and melodious improvisations, he made his name playing tenor saxophone with Count BASIE's band. His abilities also extended to the alto saxophone and clarinet, and he made many guest appearances, including work with Benny Goodman and Dizzy Gillespie.

Young, Neil (1945–) Canadian singer-songwriter and guitarist. Inspired by the diverse influences of folk, country and rock, he has worked with Crosby, Stills and Nash, as well as solo. His recordings include *After the Goldrush* (1970), *Harvest* (1972), *Rust Never Sleeps* (1979) and *Arc-Weld* (1991).

Young Men's Christian Association (YMCA) Christian association for young men established in London (1844) by George Williams. Its aim is to develop Christian morals and leadership qualities in young people. Clubs were soon formed in the USA and Australia, and the world alliance of the YMCA was formed in Geneva in 1855. Women were accepted as members in 1971. *See also* YOUNG WOMEN'S CHRISTIAN ASSOCIATION

Young, Thomas (1773–1829) English physicist and physician. Young revived the wave theory of light first put forward in the 17th century by Christiaan HUYGENS. He helped present the Young-Helmholtz theory of colour vision and detailed the cause of ASTIGMATISM. He studied elasticity, giving his name to the tensile elastic (Young's) modulus. Young was also an Egyptologist who helped decipher the ROSETTA STONE.

Young Turks Group of Turks who wished to remodel the OTTOMAN EMPIRE and make it a modern European state with a liberal constitution. Their movement began in the 1880s with unrest in the army and universities. In 1908 a Young Turk rising, led by ENVER PASHA and his

chief of staff Kemal ATATÜRK, deposed Sultan Abdul Hamid II and replaced him with his brother, Muhammad V. Following a 1913 coup d'etat, Enver Pasha became a virtual dictator. Under Kemal Atatürk, the Young Turks merged into the Turkish Nationalist Party.

Young Women's Christian Association (YWCA) Christian association for young women, the counterpart of the YMCA. Two groups were founded simultaneously in 1855 in different parts of England, and the associations merged in 1877. The YWCA provides accommodation, education, recreation facilities and welfare services to young women. It has local branches in more than 80 countries.

Ypres, Battles of Several battles of World War 1 fought around the Belgian town of Ypres. The first (October–November 1914) stopped the German "race to the sea" to capture the Channel ports, but resulted in the near destruction of the British Expeditionary Force. The second (April–May 1915), the first battle in which poison gas was used, resulted in even greater casualties, without victory to either side. The third (summer 1917) was a predominantly British offensive. It culminated in the Passchendaele campaign, the costliest campaign in British military history, which continued until November.

Ysaÿe, Eugène (1858–1931) Belgian violinist, conductor, teacher and composer. He became professor of music at the Brussels Conservatory of Music in 1886 and later conductor of the Cincinnati Symphony Orchestra (1918–22). His compositions, mainly for the violin, are in a post-romantic style.

ytterbium (symbol Yb) Silver-white, metallic element of the LANTHANIDE SERIES. It was first isolated in 1828. Its chief ore is monazite. The shiny, soft element is malleable and ductile and is used to produce steel and other alloys. Properties: at.no. 70; r.a.m. 173.04; r.d. 6.97 m.p. 824°C (1,515°F); b.p. 1,193°C (2,179°F); most common isotope Yb^{174} (31.84%).

yttrium (symbol Y) Silver-grey, metallic element of group III of the periodic table. First isolated in 1828, it is found associated with lanthanide elements in monazite sand, bastnaesite and gadolinite; it resembles the LANTHANIDE SERIES in its chemistry. Yttrium was found in lunar rock samples collected by the Apollo 11 space mission. Its compounds are used in phosphors and communications devices, such as colour televison picture tubes and superconducting ceramics. Properties: at.no. 39; r.a.m. 88.9059; r.d. 4.47; m.p. 1,523°C (2,773°F); b.p. 3,337°C (6,039°F); most common isotope Y^{89} (100%).

Yüan (1246–1368) MONGOL dynasty in China. Continuing the conquests of GENGHIS KHAN, KUBLAI KHAN established his rule over China, eliminating the last SUNG claimant in 1279. He returned the capital to Beijing and promoted construction and commerce. Chinese literature took new forms during the Mongol period. Native Chinese were excluded from government, and foreign visitors, including merchants such as Marco POLO, were encouraged. Among the Chinese, resentment of alien rule was aggravated by economic problems, including runaway inflation. The less competent successors of Kublai were increasingly challenged by rebellion, culminating in the victory of the MING.

Yucatán State in the N part of the Yucatán Peninsula, SE Mexico. Its capital is Mérida. The terrain is low-lying, covered in places with scrub and cactus thickets. Once the centre of the MAYA civilization, Yucatán was conquered by the Spanish in the 1540s. The region is a major producer of henequen (sisal hemp used for cordage). Other products: tobacco, sugar, cotton, tropical fruit.

Fishing is important along the coast. Area: 38,508sq km (14,868sq mi). Pop. (1990) 1,362,940.

yucca Genus of *c*.40 species of succulent plants native to the s USA, Mexico and the West Indies. Most are stemless, forming a rosette of leaves, or have a trunk. The clusters of flowers are white, tinged with yellow or purple. The leaves are poisonous. Height: to 10m (33ft). Family Liliaceae.

Yugoslavia Federal republic, SE Europe, now consisting of SERBIA and MONTENEGRO. The rump Yugoslav federation has not gained international recognition as the successor to the Socialist Federal Republic of Yugoslavia created by Josip TITO. In 1991, the federation began to disintegrate when SLOVENIA, CROATIA and MACEDONIA declared independence. In 1992, BOSNIA-HERZEGOVINA followed suit. A narrow coastal strip on the Adriatic Sea includes Montenegro's capital, Podgorica. The interior of Montenegro consists largely of barren karst, including parts of the DINARIC ALPS and the BALKAN MOUNTAINS. KOSOVO is a high plateau region. Serbia is dominated by the fertile lowland plains of the DANUBE, on whose banks lie the capital BELGRADE and the N city of NOVI SAD. (*See* individual country/republic articles for pre-1918 history and post-independence events.) **Climate** The coastal Mediterranean climate gives way to the bitterly cold winters of the highlands. Belgrade has a continental climate. **Vegetation** Forests cover *c*.25% of the republic, while farmland and pasture cover more than 50%. **History** Serbian-led demands for the unification of South Slavic lands were a major contributing factor to the outbreak of WORLD WAR 1. In 1918, the "Kingdom of Serbs, Croats and Slovenes" was formed under the Serbian king, PETER I. In 1921, he was succeeded by ALEXANDER I. In 1929 Alexander formed a dictatorship and renamed the country Yugoslavia. PETER II's reign was abruptly halted by German occupation (1941) in World War 2. Yugoslav resistance to the fascist puppet regime was stout. The main resistance groups were the communist partisans led by Tito and the royalist *chetniks*. In 1945, Tito formed the Federal People's Republic of Yugoslavia. In 1948, Yugoslavia was expelled from the Soviet-dominated Cominform. Tito adopted an independent foreign policy. In domestic affairs, agricultural collectivization was abandoned (1953), and new constitutions (1963, 1974) devolved power to the constituent republics in an effort to quell unrest. Following Tito's death in 1980, the country's underlying ethnic tensions began to re-surface. In 1986, Slobodan MILOŠEVIĆ became leader of the Serbian Communist Party. In 1989, he became president of Serbia and called for the creation of a "Greater Serbia". Federal troops were used to suppress demands for autonomy in Albanian-dominated Kosovo. In 1990 elections, non-communist parties won majorities in every republic, except Serbia and Montenegro. Serbian attempts to dominate the federation led to the formal secession of Slovenia and Croatia in June 1991. The Serb-dominated Federal army launched a campaign against the Croats, whose territory included a large Serbian minority. A ceasefire was agreed in January 1992. The European Community (EC) recognized Slovenia and Croatia as separate states. Bosnia-Herzegovina's declaration of independence in March 1992, led to a brutal civil war between Serbs, Croats and Bosnian Muslims. In April 1992, Serbia and

Montenegro announced the formation of a new Yugoslav federation and invited Serbs in Croatia and Bosnia-Herzegovina to join. Serbian military and financial aid to the Bosnian Serb campaign for "ethnic cleansing" led the United Nations to impose economic sanctions on Serbia. The threat of further sanctions prompted Milošević to sever support for the Bosnian Serbs. In 1995, Milošević signed the Dayton Peace Accord, which ended the Bosnian war. In 1996, local elections, the Serbian Socialist (formerly Communist) Party was defeated in many areas. In early 1997, massive and prolonged public demonstrations in Belgrade forced Milošević to acknowledge the poll results. Later in 1997, Milošević resigned the presidency of Serbia in order to become president of Yugoslavia. In Montenegro, tension remains high between pro- and anti-independence factions. In 1998, fighting erupted in Kosovo between Albanian nationalists and Serbian security forces. In 1999, following the forced expulsion of Albanians from Kosovo, NATO bombed Serbia and Montenegro. In September 2000, Vojislav KOSTUNICA, leader of an opposition coalition (Democratic Opposition of Serbia), won the presidential elections, despite attempts by Milošević's supporters to sabotage election results. The high court annulled the election, prompting mass demonstrations in Belgrade in October. The parliament building and radio-television station were occupied and Milošević was forced to concede defeat. **Economy** Yugoslavia's lower-middle income economy has been devastated by civil war and economic sanctions (1992 GDP per capita, US$4,000). Hyperinflation is one of the greatest economic problems. The war has also seen a collapse in industrial production. Natural resources include bauxite, coal and copper. Oil and natural gas are exploited from the N Pannonian plains and the Adriatic Sea. Manufacturing: aluminium, cars, machinery, plastics, steel and textiles. Agriculture remains important.

Yukawa, Hideki (1907–81) Japanese physicist. In the 1930s, he proposed that there was a nuclear force of very short range (less than 10^{-15} m) strong enough to overcome the repulsive force of protons and that diminished rapidly with distance. In 1949, he was awarded the Nobel Prize for physics for his prediction of the existence of the MESON.

Yukon Fourth-longest river in North America, deriving its name from a Native American word meaning "great", It rises at Lake Tagish on the border of British Columbia and flows N and NW through the Yukon Territory into Alaska. It then flows SW to the Bering Sea. It was a major transportation route during the KLONDIKE GOLD RUSH. Navigable for *c*.2,858km (1,775mi) of its 3,185km (1,980mi) course three months each year, it is ice-bound from October to June.

Yukon Territory Territory in the extreme NW of Canada, bounded by the Arctic Ocean (N), Northwest Territories (E), British Columbia (S) and Alaska (W). The capital and largest town is Whitehorse. In the N the region consists of Arctic waste and is virtually uninhabited. Further S there is spectacular mountain scenery with lakes and coniferous forests. The region is drained chiefly by the YUKON and MACKENZIE rivers. The climate is harsh, with freezing winters and short summers. The region, then part of Northwest Territories, was first explored by fur traders from the HUDSON'S BAY COMPANY after 1840. The KLONDIKE GOLD RUSH brought more than 30,000 prospectors in the 1890s. In 1991 the Canadian government recognized the land claim of the indigenous Yukon (First Nation) Native Americans. Farming is extremely limited, but a few cereal crops and vegetables are grown in the valleys. The principal activity is mining, with major deposits including lead, zinc and gold. There is also a healthy forestry industry. With a small manufacturing

---

YUGOSLAVIA
AREA: 102,173sq km (39,449sq mi)
POPULATION: 10,761,000
CAPITAL (POPULATION): Belgrade (1,168,454)

base, tourism plays an important part in the economy. Area: 483,450sq km (186,675sq mi). Pop. (1991) 27,797.

Yunnan (South of the Clouds) Province in S central China, bounded by Laos and Vietnam (S) and Burma (W); the capital is Kunming. Its remote, mountain location enabled Yunnan to retain an independent status until conquered by the Mongols in 1253. In 1659, it became a province of China, and it was captured by Chinese communist forces in 1950. Yunnan is divided, along ethnic lines, into eight autonomous districts that are home to many of China's minority nationalities. It is renowned for the rich diversity of its wildlife, particularly rare plant species. Agriculture is restricted to a few plains, with rice the major crop. Its valuable mineral resources include deposits of tin, tungsten, copper, gold and silver. Mining and timber are the main industries. Area: 436,200sq km (168,482sq mi). Pop. (1990) 36,750,000.

Yurok Native American tribe formerly residing around the estuary of the Klamath River, California, and speaking an Algonquian language. Reduced in number to fewer than 1,000, the group is now mainly scattered along the N Californian coast.

YWCA Abbreviation of YOUNG WOMEN'S CHRISTIAN ASSOCIATION

Z/z, 26th and last letter of the Roman alphabet. It is derived from the Semitic letter, zayin, which then passed into Greek as the letter zeta where it assumed its present form.

Zacharias, Saint (d.752) (Zachary) Pope (741–52). He strengthened the Holy See and achieved a 20-year truce with the LOMBARDS. Along with St BONIFACE, Zacharias established cordial relations with the FRANKS by supporting the accession of PEPIN III (THE SHORT) to the Frankish throne.

Zacharias Variant spelling of ZECHARIAH

Zagreb Capital of Croatia, on the River Sava. Founded in the 11th century, it became capital of the Hungarian province of Croatia and Slavonia during the 14th century. The city was an important centre of the 19th-century Croatian nationalist movement. In 1918 it was the meeting place of the Croatian diet, which broke all ties with Austria-Hungary. It later joined a new union with Serbia in what was to become Yugoslavia. In World War 2, Zagreb was the capital of the Axis-controlled puppet Croatian state. Wrested from Axis control in 1945, it became capital of the Croatian Republic of Yugoslavia. It was damaged in 1991 during the Croatian civil war. Following the break-up of Yugoslavia in 1992, Zagreb remained capital of the newly independent state of Croatia. It is the industrial and manufacturing heart of Croatia. Industries: steel, cement, machinery, chemicals. Pop. (1991) 726,770.

Zagros Mountain range in S and SW Iran, extending c.900km (560mi) from the borders with Turkey and Armenia almost to the Persian Gulf. The topography varies from rugged peaks in the N to ridges and fertile valleys in the central region (producing cotton, tobacco and fruits) and lowland marshes and rock in the S. One of the world's most productive oilfields is located in the W foothills. Zard Kuh is the highest peak, at 4,548m (14,921ft).

zaibatsu Large industrial conglomerates in Japan formed after the MEIJI RESTORATION (1868). Headed by powerful families, such as Mitsui and Mitsubishi, they came to dominate the Japanese economy in the early 20th century. Though broken up during the US occupation after 1945, they subsequently reformed and reclaimed their dominant position.

Zaïre See CONGO, DEMOCRATIC REPUBLIC OF

Zaïre River See CONGO

Zambezi River in S Africa. Rising in NW Zambia, it flows in a rough "S" shape through E Angola and W Zambia. It turns E to form part of the Zambian border with Namibia and the entire border with Zimbabwe (including the VICTORIA FALLS). It crosses the widest part of Mozambique and turns SE to empty into the Indian Ocean. There is great potential for the generation of hydroelectricity along the river's course, and it has two of Africa's biggest dams: Kariba (Zambia-Zimbabwe) and Cabora Bassa (Mozambique). Length: 2,740km (1,700mi).

Zambia Landlocked republic in S central Africa. Most of the country consists of a highland plateau between 900m and 1,500m (2,950ft and 4,920ft) high. The ZAMBEZI and Luangwa river valleys are the only low-lying areas. In the NE, the Muchinga Mountains rise above the flat plateau. The highest peak, at 2,067m (6,781ft), lies close to the Lake TANGANYIKA border with Tanzania. Lake Mweru lies on the border with Zaire. Lake Bangweulu lies in the marshlands of Northern Province. The Zambezi forms Zambia's entire S border with Botswana and Zimbabwe. The spectacular VICTORIA FALLS and the man-made Lake Kariba lie on its banks. **Climate** Although Zambia lies in the tropics, temperatures and humidity are moderated greatly by altitude. The rainy season lasts from November to March. Rainfall is greatest in the N. **Vegetation** Grassland and wooded savanna cover much of Zambia. There are also several swamps. Evergreen forests exist in the drier SW. **History and politics** In c.800 AD, Bantu-speakers migrated to the area. By the late 18th century, Zambia was part of the copper and slave trade. In 1855, the Scottish explorer David LIVINGSTONE made the first European discovery of Victoria Falls. In 1890, the British South Africa Company, managed by Cecil RHODES, made treaties with local chiefs. The area was administratively divided into NW and NE RHODESIA. Local rebellions were crushed. Intensive mining of copper and lead saw the development of the railway in the early 1900s. In 1911, the two regions were joined to form Northern Rhodesia. In 1924, Northern Rhodesia became a British Crown Colony. The discovery of further copper deposits increased European settlement and the migration of African labour. In 1946, mineworkers formed the first national mass movement. In 1953, Britain formed the federation of Rhodesia (including present-day Zambia and Zimbabwe) and Nyasaland (now Malawi). In 1963, following a nationwide campaign of civil disobedience, the federation was dissolved. In 1964, Northern Rhodesia achieved independence within the Commonwealth of Nations as the republic of Zambia. Kenneth KAUNDA, leader of the United Nationalist Independence Party (UNIP), became Zambia's first president. Zambia was faced with problems of national unity, European economic dominance, and tension with the white-minority government in Rhodesia. Following his re-election in 1968, Kaunda established state majority holdings in Zambian companies. Zambia supported the imposition of economic sanctions on Rhodesia. In 1972, Kaunda banned all opposition parties; he won the uncontested 1973 elections. In 1990, a new multiparty constitution was adopted. The Movement for Multiparty Democracy (MMD) won a landslide victory in 1991 elections. The MMD leader, Frederick Chiluba, became president. In 1993, Chiluba declared a state of emergency. Legislation excluded Kaunda from contesting the 1996 presidential elections. Chiluba was resoundingly re-elected following a UNIP boycott. The government faced charges of electoral fraud. In 1997, a military coup was crushed. Kaunda was arrested and a state of emergency proclaimed. In 1998, Kaunda was freed and the state of emergency lifted. In 2000, there were a number of border skirmishes with Angola. **Economy** Zambia is the world's fifth largest producer of copper ore, which accounts for 80% of exports (1995 GDP per capita, US$930). It is also the world's second largest producer of cobalt ore. Zambia also mines lead, zinc and silver. Zambia's dependence on mineral exports constitutes a structural imbalance. The MMD's introduction of free market reforms and privatization has seen a large influx of aid and the reduction of national debt. Agriculture employs 38% of the workforce. Maize is the chief food crop. Cash crops include cassava, coffee, sugar cane and tobacco.

Zamyatin, Yevgeny Ivanovich (1884–1939) Russian novelist and dramatist. He was censored both by the pre-revolutionary tsarist authorities and by their revolutionary Bolshevik successors. Zamyatin was an early exponent of the dystopian novel in the form of his most famous work, *My*, an attack on Soviet society and politics, written in 1924 but not published in the Soviet Union until 1989. He was permitted to emigrate in 1931 and died in Paris.

Zanzibar Island region of TANZANIA, in the Indian Ocean off the E coast of Africa; the capital is ZANZIBAR. The first European discovery was by Vasco da Gama in 1499, and the Portuguese quickly established colonial rule. In the late 17th century, it came under the control of the Omani Arabs. It developed into the major centre of the East African ivory and slave trade. The slave trade was halted in 1873, and in 1890 the sultanate of Zanzibar was made a British protectorate. In 1963, it became an independent state and a member of the British Commonwealth. Tension between the Arab ruling class and the indigenous Africans (who formed the majority of the population) led to the overthrow of the sultanate. In 1964, Zanzibar and Tanganyika merged to form the United Republic of Tanzania. Zanzibar retained control over domestic affairs. During the 1980s and 1990s, conflict developed between secessionist and mainland centralist forces. In 1993, a regional parliament for Zanzibar was established. The two largest population groups are the indigenous Hadimu and Tumbatu. The major religion is Sunni Muslim, and the main language is Swahili. The chief export is cloves, and the biggest industry is fishing. Area: 1,660sq km (641sq mi). Pop. (1988) 375,539.

Zanzibar City in Tanzania, on the W coast of Zanzibar Island. The sultan of Oman transferred his capital here in the early 19th century, and the city flourished as a base for commercial activities (notably the slave trade). Its importance has declined with the rise of competing ports, but it remains a centre of East African trade. Industries: cloves, citrus fruits, chilies, copra, mangrove bark, clove oil, soap, coconut oil and hand crafts. Pop. (1988) 157,634.

Zapata, Emiliano (1880–1919) Mexican revolutionary leader. Of peasant origin, he became leader of the growing peasant movement in 1910. His demands for radical agrarian reform, such as the return of *haciendas* (great estates) to native Mexican communal ownership, led to the MEXICAN REVOLUTION. In pursuit of "Land and Liberty", he

ZAMBIA
AREA: 752,614sq km (290,586sq mi)
POPULATION: 12,267,000
CAPITAL (POPULATION): Lusaka (982,000)

opposed, successively, Porfiro DÍAZ, Francisco MADERO, Victoriano HUERTA and (with Pancho VILLA) Venustiano CARRANZA. His guerrilla campaign ended with his murder.

Zaporizhzhya City on the River DNIEPER, SE Ukraine. The area was settled in the 16th century by Zaporozhye Cossacks, leaders of the Ukrainian nationalist movement. In 1770 Zaporizhzhya was founded as a fortress, and in 1775 the Russian army of Catherine II forced the removal of the Cossacks. In the early 19th century, the fortress became a town, known as Aleksandrovsk until 1921. Zaporizhzhya consists of the old city and a new industrial area, development of which began in the 1930s with the construction of the Dneproges dam and a large hydroelectric plant. It is now one of the Ukraine's leading industrial complexes. Industries: aluminium, iron and steel, motor vehicles, chemicals. Pop. (1996) 882,000.

Zapotec Native American group that inhabits part of the Mexican state of Oaxaca. The Zapotec built great pre-Columbian urban centres at Mitla and Monte Albán and fought to preserve their independence from the rival Mixtecs and Aztecs until the arrival of the Spanish.

Zappa, Frank (Francis Vincent) (1940–93) US rock musician and composer. Classically trained and a technical virtuoso on the guitar, Zappa and his group, The Mothers of Invention, produced closely edited recordings such as *Freak Out* (1966) and *We're Only In It For The Money* (1967). A prolific and innovative composer, he drew on a wide variety of styles, often courting controversy with his subject matter.

Zaragoza (Saragossa) City on the River Ebro, NE Spain; capital of Zaragoza province and Aragón region. The city was taken by the Romans in the 1st century BC and by Moors in the 8th century. In 1118 it was captured by Alfonso I of Aragón, who made it his capital. It was the scene of heroic resistance against the French in the Peninsular War (1808–09). The city is an important commercial and communications centre. At the heart of an agricultural region, it acts as a distribution point for wine, olives and cereals. Industries: heavy machinery, textiles. Pop. (1995) 608,000.

Zarathustra *See* ZOROASTER

Zaria Historic walled city in Kaduna province, N central Nigeria. Originally one of the seven HAUSA city states and a centre of the slave trade, Zaria was taken by British forces in 1901. It is now a trade centre for the surrounding agricultural region, trading especially in cotton, peanuts, palm oil and sugar. Industries: bicycles, textiles, cigarettes, hides, printing, handicrafts. Pop. (1996) 379,000.

Zatopek, Emil (1922–2000) Czech athlete, b. Moravia. Zatopek's tortured, lolling racing style first brought major success at the 1948 Olympic Games, when he won a gold medal in the 10,000m and a silver medal in the 5000m. At the next Olympics (1952) in Helsinki, Zatopek became the first (and only) athlete to win all three endurance races (5000m, 10,000m and the marathon). From 1948 to 1954 (a total of 38 races), he remained undefeated over 10,000m.

Zealots Jewish sect, active in opposition to Roman rule at the time of JESUS CHRIST and after. They refused to agree that Jews could be ruled by pagans, led resistance to the Roman census of AD 6, pursued a terrorist campaign and played an important role in the rising of AD 66. Their activities continued into the 2nd century.

zebra Any of three species of strikingly patterned, striped, black-and-white, equine mammals of the grasslands of Africa; the stripes are arranged in various patterns, according to species. It has long ears, a tufted tail and narrow hooves. Height: to 55in (140cm) at the shoulder. Family Equidae; genus *Equus*.

zebu (Brahman cattle) Numerous, domestic varieties of a single species of OX, native to India. Zebu have been used extensively in Asia and Africa and have been introduced to the New World as livestock. Species *Bos indicus*.

Zechariah (Zachariah, Zacharias) Any of several biblical personalities. One of the most significant was a Jewish prophet of the late 6th century BC. He prophesied the rebuilding of the TEMPLE in JERUSALEM by the Jews who had returned from exile in BABYLON. In the Book of Zechariah, the 11th book of the 12 minor OLD TESTAMENT prophets, he described visions of four horsemen patrolling God's world, four horns symbolizing the destruction of Israel's enemies and six other night visions prefiguring the coming of God in judgment. Many of Zechariah's images were taken up in the REVELATION of St John the Divine. The other important Zechariah was the priest mentioned in the GOSPEL according to St LUKE (Luke 1) as the father of St JOHN THE BAPTIST. Zechariah was visited by the angel GABRIEL, who foretold the birth of John to Zechariah's wife, Elizabeth. For doubting Gabriel's prophecy, Zechariah was struck dumb until the time of John's circumcision.

Zedekiah Any of several biblical personalities, most notably the last King of Judah (597–586 BC). Placed on the throne as a puppet king by NEBUCHADNEZZAR, king of Babylon, he could not stave off the Babylonian capture and destruction of JERUSALEM. He was captured while trying to escape the city, blinded and deported to Babylon.

Zedillo, Ernesto (1951–) Mexican statesman, president (1994–). In 1971, he joined the Institutional Revolutionary Party (PRI). In 1994, Zedillo ran for president after the PRI's candidate, Luis Colosio, was assassinated. He received just over 50% of the vote. He promised to combat unemployment and tackle the failing economy. Within a few months, however, he was forced to devalue the peso, despite his earlier successes in government finance.

Zeeman, Pieter (1865–1943) Dutch physicist. He shared the 1902 Nobel Prize for physics with his teacher, Hendrik LORENTZ, for their 1896 discovery of the ZEEMAN EFFECT. Zeeman also detected the magnetic fields at the surface of the Sun.

Zeeman effect In physics, effect produced by a strong magnetic field on the light emitted by a radiant body; it is observed as a splitting of its spectral lines. It was first observed in 1896 by Pieter ZEEMAN. The effect has been useful in investigating the charge/mass ratio and magnetic moment of an ELECTRON.

Zeffirelli, Franco (1923–) Italian theatre, opera and film director. He worked at London's Covent Garden on *Cavalleria rusticana*, at Stratford-upon-Avon on *Othello* and on Broadway on *The Lady of the Camellias*. Renowned for their sumptuous and rich production, his films include *The Taming of the Shrew* (1966), *Romeo and Juliet* (1968) and *Brother Sun and Sister Moon* (1973). His major success, *Jesus of Nazareth* (1978), was originally made for television.

Zemin, Jiang *See* JIANG ZEMIN

Zen Japanese school of BUDDHISM, initially developed in China, where it is known as Ch'an. Instead of doctrines and scriptures, Zen stresses mind-to-mind instruction from master to disciple in order to achieve *satori* (awakening of Buddha-nature). There are two major Zen sects. **Rinzai** (introduced to Japan from China in 1191)

emphasizes sudden enlightenment and meditation on paradoxical statements. The **Soto** sect (also brought from China, in 1227) advocates quiet meditation. In its secondary emphasis on mental tranquillity, fearlessness and spontaneity, Zen has had a great influence on Japanese culture. Zen priests inspired art, literature, the tea ceremony and the NO DRAMA. In recent decades, a number of Zen groups have emerged in Europe and the USA.

Zend-Avesta (AVESTA) Sacred book of ZOROASTRIANISM. The word *Zend* means tradition or commentary.

zenith In astronomy, point on the CELESTIAL SPHERE that is directly overhead. The zenith distance of a heavenly body is the angle it makes with the zenith. It is diametrically opposite the NADIR.

Zeno of Citium (*c.*334–*c.*262 BC) Greek philosopher and founder of the STOICS. He attended lectures by various philosophers before formulating his own philosophy. Proceeding from the CYNIC concept of self-sufficiency, he stressed the unity of the universe and the brotherhood of men living in harmony with the cosmos. He claimed virtue to be the only good, and wealth, illness and death to be of no human concern.

Zeno of Elea (*c.*495–*c.*430 BC) Greek philosopher. A disciple of Parmenides, he sought to reveal logical absurdities in theories of motion and change, using paradoxical arguments.

zeolite Group of aluminosilicates containing sodium, calcium or barium and loosely held water that can be continuously expelled on heating. Some zeolites occur as fibrous aggregates, whereas others form robust, nonfibrous crystals. Zeolites vary in hardness from 3 to 5 and in relative density from 2 to 2.4.

Zephaniah (active *c.*630 BC) OLD TESTAMENT prophet. He was named as the author of the Book of Zephaniah, the ninth of the 12 books of the Minor Prophets. He condemned Israel's religious and political corruption and stressed the certainty of God's judgment against Israel.

Zeppelin, Ferdinand, Count von (1838–1917) German army officer and inventor. He served in the armies of Württemburg and Prussia. While an observer with the Union army during the American Civil War, he made his first balloon ascent. In 1900, he invented the first rigid airship, which was called Zeppelin for him.

Zernike, Frits (1888–1966) Dutch physicist. In 1935, he developed the phase contrast microscope, in which objects being viewed (often living-cell biological specimens) take on a different colour from their surroundings. For this work, he received the 1953 Nobel Prize for physics.

Zeus In Greek mythology, the sky god, lord of the wind, clouds, rain and thunder. He is identified with the Roman god JUPITER. Zeus was the son of Rhea and Cronus, whom he deposed. Zeus was the supreme deity of the Olympians. He fathered huge numbers of children by his wives and others, often seducing goddesses, nymphs and mortal women by taking the form of an animal.

Zhao Ziyang (1918–) Chinese statesman who played a leading part in China's economic modernization. Zhao joined the Chinese COMMUNIST PARTY in 1938 and during the 1960s acted as party secretary of Guangdong province. He was dismissed by MAO ZEDONG during the CULTURAL REVOLUTION, but rehabilitated and restored to his post in 1971. In 1975, he was appointed party secretary of Sichuan province. Zhao introduced radical economic reforms that vastly improved industrial and agricultural production. In 1980, he was made premier. In 1987, LI PENG replaced him as premier and Zhao became general secretary. With the support of DENG XIAOPING, his liberal economic reforms moved China towards a market economy. In 1989, Zhao was dismissed from office and placed under house arrest for advocating negotiation with the pro-democracy demonstrators in TIANANMEN SQUARE.

Zhejiang (Chekiang) Province in SE China, S of the Yangtze River and on the East China Sea; the capital is Hangzhou. It was the centre of the Sung dynasty in the 12th and 13th centuries. Many of Zhejiang's cities were razed during the Taiping Rebellion (1850–65). A mountainous region, it is one of China's most populous areas and includes the Zhoushan Archipelago. The province was designated a special economic zone to encourage inward capital investment. The major river is the Qiantang. Mount Tianmu is on the tourist and pilgrimage trails. Over one-third of the region is pine or bamboo forest. The chief crops are rice and tea. Major industries include silk production and fishing. Area: 101,830sq km (39,300sq mi). Pop. (1990) 40,840,000.

Zheng Ho (1371–1435) Chinese admiral, explorer and diplomat, known as the "three-jewelled eunuch". Between 1405 and 1433, Zheng Ho led seven naval expeditions across the China Sea and the Indian Ocean to gather treasures and unusual tributes for the Imperial court. His voyages reached as far W as the Persian Gulf, visiting ports in SE Asia, India, East Africa and Egypt. His voyages prepared the way for Chinese colonization of SE Asia.

Zhengzhou (Chengchow) City in E central China, 16km (10mi) S of the Huang He (Yellow) River; capital of Henan province. Capital of the Shang dynasty before 2000 BC, it has a walled city from that time. The present city grew with the railway (1898) to become the main rail junction of E China. Industries: cotton, food processing, agricultural tools, thermal power. Pop. (1994) 1,324,000.

Zhou Chinese dynasty (1030–221 BC). After the nomadic Zhou overthrew the SHANG dynasty, Chinese civilization spread to most parts of modern China, although the dynasty never established effective control over the regions. The Late Zhou, from 772 BC, was a cultural golden age, marked by the writings of CONFUCIUS and LAO TZU. It was a period of rising prosperity. As the provincial states grew in power, the Zhou dynasty disintegrated.

Zhou Enlai (1898–1976) Chinese statesman. Zhou was a founder of the Chinese COMMUNIST PARTY. As a member of the Communist-KUOMINTANG alliance (1924–27), he directed the general strike (1927) in Shanghai. When CHIANG KAI-SHEK broke the alliance, Zhou joined the LONG MARCH (1934–35). He was the chief negotiator of a renewed peace (1936–46) with nationalist forces. After the establishment of a communist republic, Zhou became prime minister (1949–76) and foreign minister (1949–58). Although publicly supportive of the CULTURAL REVOLUTION, he protected many of its intended victims.

Zhu De (1886–1976) Chinese communist military leader. Zhu helped to overthrow (1912) the QING dynasty. In 1922, he met ZHOU ENLAI and joined the Chinese Communist Party. In 1928, Zhu joined forces with MAO ZEDONG and led his section of the Fourth Red Army on the LONG MARCH (1934–35). Commander in chief during the Second Sino-Japanese War, he retained the post after the establishment of a communist republic (1949). Zhu held several important party posts before being denounced during the CULTURAL REVOLUTION.

Zhukov, Georgi Konstantinovich (1896–1974) Soviet military commander and politician. In World War 2, he led the defence of Moscow (1941) and defeated the German siege of Stalingrad and Leningrad (ST PETERSBURG) (1943). In 1945, he led the final assault on Berlin. After STALIN's death, he became defence minister (1955). Although supportive of Nikita KHRUSCHEV's reforms, he

was removed from office in 1957. He was rehabilitated in the 1960s, receiving the Order of Lenin in 1966.

Ziegler, Karl (1898–1973) German chemist. He shared the 1963 Nobel Prize for chemistry with Giulio Natta for research into POLYMERS. Ziegler discovered a technique that used a resin with metal ions attached as a catalyst in the production of POLYETHYLENE. He also researched aromatic compounds and organometallic compounds.

ziggurat Religious monument originating in BABYLON and ASSYRIA. It was constructed as a truncated, stepped PYRAMID, rising in diminishing tiers, usually square or rectangular. The shrine at the top was reached by a series of ramps. Ziggurats date from 3000–600 BC, and the one at UR still stands.

Zimbabwe Landlocked republic in S central Africa. It consists mainly of a plateau 900 to 1,500m (2,950 to 4,900ft) high, between the rivers ZAMBEZI and LIMPOPO. The principal land feature is the High Veld, a ridge running from NE to SW. HARARE lies on the NE edge of the ridge. BULAWAYO lies on the SW edge. The Middle Veld is the site of many large ranches. Below 900m (2,950ft) is the Low Veld. Highlands lie on the E border with Mozambique. **Climate** The sub-tropical climate varies according to altitude. The Low Veld is much warmer and drier than the High Veld. November to March is mainly hot and wet. Winter in Harare is dry but cold. **Vegetation** Wooded savanna covers much of Zimbabwe. The Eastern Highlands and river valleys are forested. There are many tobacco plantations. **History and politics** Bantu-speakers migrated to the region in AD 300. By 1200, the SHONA had established a kingdom in Mashonaland, E Zimbabwe. GREAT ZIMBABWE was the capital of this advanced culture. Portugal formed trading links in the early 16th century. In 1837, the Ndebele displaced the Shona from W Zimbabwe and formed Matabeleland. In 1855, David LIVINGSTONE made the first European discovery of VICTORIA FALLS. In 1888, Matabeleland became a British protectorate. In 1889, the British South Africa Company, under Cecil RHODES, was granted a charter to exploit the region's mineral wealth. Native revolts were crushed, and the area became Southern RHODESIA (1896). In 1923, it became a British crown colony. European settlers excluded Africans from participation in the government and economy. In 1953, Southern Rhodesia, Northern Rhodesia (now Zambia) and Nyasaland (Malawi) became a federation. In 1961, Joshua Nkomo formed the Zimbabwe African People's Union (ZAPU). In 1963, the federation dissolved and African majority governments were formed in Zambia and Malawi. Southern Rhodesia became simply Rhodesia. Robert MUGABE formed the Zimbabwe African National Union (ZANU). In 1964, the white nationalist leader Ian SMITH became prime minister. Nkomo and Mugabe were imprisoned. In 1965, Smith made a unilateral declaration of independence (UDI) from Britain. The UN imposed economic sanctions. In 1969, Rhodesia became a republic. In 1974, Nkomo and Mugabe were released. Smith's refusal to implement democratic reforms intensified the guerrilla war waged by ZAPU and ZANU rebels against the Smith government (aided by South Africa's apartheid regime). The 1979, Lancaster House Agreement established a timetable for full independence. ZANU won a decisive victory in 1980 elections, and Robert Mugabe became prime minister. In 1982, Nkomo was dismissed from the cabinet. Mugabe was decisively re-elected in 1985. In 1987, ZANU and ZAPU merged. The post of prime minister was abolished as Mugabe became executive president. In 1988, Nkomo became vice president. Despite the formation of an opposition party, the Zimbabwe Unity Movement, Mugabe was

ZIMBABWE

AREA: 390,579q km (150,873sq mi)
POPULATION: 13,123,000
CAPITAL (POPULATION): Harare (1,189,000)

easily re-elected in 1990. In 1991, ZANU-PF abandoned Marxism. In 1996, Mugabe was elected for a fourth term. In 1999, there were calls for greater democracy. In the run-up to elections in 2000, many white-owned farms were forcibly occupied by supporters of Mugabe. **Economy** Zimbabwe is a low-income developing country (1995 GDP per capita US$2,030). The post-independence emigration of most of the white population removed vital capital. The government's redistribution of land to the African population via compulsory purchase schemes has been tainted by government corruption. Agriculture employs 70% of the workforce. Zimbabwe is the world's largest exporter of tobacco. Other cash crops include cotton, sugar and beef. Maize is the main food crop. It has valuable mineral resources, especially around the Great Dyke, a low ridge that crosses the High Veld. Mining accounts for 20% of exports. Zimbabwe is the world's fourth largest producer of asbestos and fifth largest producer of chromium ore. Gold and nickel are mined. In 1990, the government began to introduce free market reforms. The restructuring of the command economy has resulted in high unemployment. National debt remains an economic problem.

zinc (symbol Zn) Bluish-white, metallic element of Group II of the periodic table, known from early times. Chief ores are SPHALERITE, smithsonite and calamine. Zinc is a vital trace element, found in erythrocytes (red blood cells). It is used in many alloys, including brass, bronze and soft solder. It is corrosion-resistant and used in galvanizing iron. Zinc oxide is used in cosmetics, pharmaceuticals, paints, inks, pigments and plastics. Zinc chloride is used in dentistry and to manufacture batteries and fungicides. Properties: at.no. 30; r.a.m. 65.38; r.d. 7.133; m.p. 419.6°C (787.3°F); b.p. 907°C (1,665°F); most common isotope Zn^{64} (48.89%).

Zinoviev, Grigori Evseyevich (1883–1936) Russian revolutionary. A self-educated lawyer, Zinoviev joined the BOLSHEVIKS in 1903, and was active in the RUSSIAN REVOLUTION OF 1905. He was a close collaborator of LENIN in exile (1908–17). In the RUSSIAN REVOLUTION (1917), Zinoviev voted against seizing power but remained a powerful figure in ST PETERSBURG and was appointed head of the COMMUNIST INTERNATIONAL in 1919. Though he sided with STALIN against TROTSKY in 1922, Zinoviev was later expelled from the party and eventually executed. The "Zinoviev letter" (1924), urging the British Communist Party to revolt, may have contributed to the subsequent electoral defeat of the Labour government, but has since proved to be a forgery.

Zinnemann, Fred (1907–97) US film director, b. Austria. Zinnemann won his first Academy Award for the short film *That Mothers Might Live* (1938). He moved into commercial features, winning his second Oscar for the western *High Noon* (1952). Zinnemann won a third award for *A Man For All Seasons* (1966). Other films include *From Here to Eternity* (1953) and *Julia* (1978). His autobiography, *A Life in the Movies*, was published in 1992.

zinnia Genus of chiefly annual plants native to North and South America. Most garden zinnias are varieties of *Z. elegans*, which has flower heads of all colours but blue and green. Height: to 91cm (3ft). Family Compositae.

Zion Hill in E Jerusalem, Israel. Zion was originally the

hill on which a Jebusite fortress was built. It now refers to the hill on which the TEMPLE was built. It is a centre of Jewish spiritual life and symbolic of the Promised Land.

Zionism Jewish nationalist movement advocating the return of Jews to the land of Zion (Palestine). Though it represents a desire expressed since the Jewish DIASPORA began in the 6th century BC, the modern Zionist movement dates from 1897, when Theodor HERZL established the World Zionist Congress at Basel, Switzerland. In 1917, it secured British approval for its objective in the BALFOUR DECLARATION, and Jewish immigration to Palestine increased in the 1920s and 1930s. In 1947, the United Nations voted to partition Palestine between Jews and Arabs, leading to the foundation of the state of ISRAEL.

zircon Orthosilicate mineral, zirconium silicate ($ZrSiO_4$), found in IGNEOUS and METAMORPHIC rocks and in sand and gravel. It has prismatic crystals. It is usually light or reddish brown but can be colourless, grey, yellow or green. It is used widely as a gemstone because of its hardness and high refractive index. Hardness 7.5; r.d. 4.6.

zirconium (symbol Zr) Greyish-white, metallic element, one of the TRANSITION ELEMENTS. Zirconium was discovered in 1789 by the German chemist Martin Klaproth. Its chief source is ZIRCON. Lunar rocks collected during the Apollo space missions show a higher content of zirconium than Earth ones, and zirconium exists in meteorites and stars, including the Sun. Chemically similar to titanium, it is used in ceramics and in alloys for wire and absorption of neutrons in nuclear reactors. Properties: at.no. 40; r.a.m. 91.22; r.d. 6.51; m.p. 1,852°C (3,366°F); b.p. 4,377°C (7,911°F); most common isotope Zr^{90} (51.46%).

zither STRINGED INSTRUMENT. It consists of a resonator in the form of a wooden box, with 30 to 45 strings stretched over it. Some of the strings are stretched over a fretted board for melody; the rest and for accompaniment. The melody strings are plucked with the fingers or a plectrum.

zodiac (Gk. circle of animals) Belt on the CELESTIAL SPHERE that forms the background for the motions of the Sun, Moon and planets (except Pluto). The zodiac is divided into twelve **signs** that are named after the constellations they contained at the time of the ancient Greeks: Aries, Taurus, Gemini, Cancer, Leo, Virgo, Libra, Scorpio, Sagittarius, Capricorn, Aquarius and Pisces. The constellations inside the Zodiac do not now correspond to those named by the ancients, because PRECESSION of the Earth's axis has meanwhile tilted the Earth in a different direction. To modern astronomers, the zodiac has only historical significance. *See also* ASTROLOGY; ASTRONOMY

Zola, Émile Edouard Charles Antoine (1840–1902) French novelist. He became widely known following the publication of his third book, the novel *Thérèse Raquin* (1867). For the next quarter of a century, he worked on what became the Rougon-Macquart sequence (1871–93), a 20-novel cycle telling the story of a family during the Second Empire; it established his reputation as the foremost exponent of the naturalistic school of fiction. The sequence includes his famous novels *The Drunkard* (1877), *Nana* (1880), *Germinal* (1885) and *The Human Animal* (1890). In 1898 he wrote a famous letter, beginning "*J'Accuse*", which denounced the punishment of Alfred Dreyfus. This led to a brief exile in England and, after his death, the vindication of Dreyfus, a hero's return. *See also* DREYFUS AFFAIR

Zollverein German customs union formed in 1834 by 18 German states under Prussian leadership. By reducing tariffs and improving transport, it promoted economic prosperity. Nearly all other German states had joined the Zollverein by 1867, despite Austrian opposition. It was a major step towards the creation of the German empire (1871).

zoo (zoological gardens) Public or private institution in which living animals are kept and exhibited. Organized public zoos, sometimes called menageries or aquariums (for fish), have been operating for more than 500 years in Europe. Today, most zoos are run by non-profit oganizations or zoological societies. They are organized for public recreation, as well as for scientific and educational purposes. The emphasis is on conservation of endangered species and exhibiting animals in natural settings.

zoology Study of animals; combined with BOTANY, it comprises the science of BIOLOGY. It is concerned with the structure of the animal and the way in which animals behave, reproduce and function, their evolution and their role in interactions with humankind and their environment. There are various sub-divisions of the discipline, including ANATOMY, TAXONOMY, ECOLOGY, PALAEONTOLOGY and zoogeography (the distribution of animals). ANTHROPOLOGY is an extension of zoology. *See also* EMBRYOLOGY; GENETICS; MORPHOLOGY

zoonosis Any infection or infestation of VERTEBRATES that is transmissible to human beings.

zooplankton Animal portion of the PLANKTON. It consists of a wide variety of microorganisms, including COPEPOD and larval forms of higher animals. It is an important constituent of the ocean's food chain. There are few levels or areas of the ocean that have no zooplankton.

Zoroaster (*c.*628–*c.*551 BC) (Zarathustra) Ancient Persian (Iranian) religious reformer, founder of ZOROASTRIANISM. At the age of 30, he saw the divine being AHURA MAZDAH in the first of many visions. Unable to convert the petty chieftains of his native region, Zoroaster travelled to E Persia, where he converted the royal family in Chorasmia (now in Khorasan province, NE Iran). By the time of Zoroaster's death (tradition says that he was murdered while at prayer), his new religion had spread to a large part of Persia. Parts of the AVESTA, the holy scripture of Zoroastrianism, are believed to have been written by him.

Zoroastrianism Religion founded by ZOROASTER in the 6th century BC. It was the state religion of PERSIA from the middle of the 3rd century AD until the mid-7th century. Viewing the world as being divided between the spirits of good and evil, Zoroastrians worship AHURA MAZDAH as the supreme deity, who is forever in conflict with Ahriman, the spirit of evil. They also consider fire sacred. The rise of Islam in the 7th century led to the decline and near disappearance of Zoroastrianism in Persia. Today, the PARSI comprise most of the adherents of Zoroastrianism, which has its main centre in BOMBAY, India.

Zsigmondy, Richard Adolf (1865–1929) Austrian chemist who won the 1925 Nobel Prize for chemistry for his work on COLLOIDS. While employed at a glass manufacturing company (1897–1900), he discovered a water suspension of gold and proposed that the shape and size of colloids could be deduced from the way in which the particles scatter light. To aid such studies, he developed the ultramicroscope with Heinrich Siedentopf in 1903.

Zulu BANTU people of S Africa, living mainly in KWAZULU-NATAL. They are closely related to the Swazi and the XHOSA. The Zulus have a patriarchal, polygamous society, with a strong militaristic tradition. Traditionally cereal farmers, they possessed large herds of cattle, considered to be status symbols. In the 19th century, under their leader SHAKA, they fiercely resisted colonialism. The predominant religion is now Christianity, although ethnic religions are still common. They are organized politically into the INKATHA movement under Chief Mangosutho BUTHELEZI.

Zululand Historic region of South Africa, now part of KWAZULU-NATAL.

Zulu War (1879) Conflict in South Africa between the British and the ZULU. Fearing a Zulu attack, the Afrikaners of Transvaal requested British protection. The British high commissioner demanded that the Zulu king, Cetewayo, disband his army. He refused, and the Zulu made a surprise attack at Isandhlwana, killing 800 British. Lacking modern weapons, the Zulu were checked at Rorke's Drift and decisively defeated at Ulundi.

Zuni PUEBLO Native Americans who live on the Zuni reservation in w New Mexico, USA. The present pueblo is on the site of one of the seven Zuni villages discovered by Marcos de Niza in the early 16th century, and identified as the mythical Seven Cities of Cibola. In 1540, CORONADO sacked the villages, and following a revolt in 1680, the Pueblo abandoned the site for fear of Spanish reprisal. Modern Zuni maintain their traditions and skills.

Zurich City on the River Limmat, at the NW end of Lake Zurich, in the foothills of the Alps, N Switzerland; it is the country's largest city. Conquered by the Romans in 58 BC, the city later came under Alemanni and then Frankish rule. It became a free imperial city in 1218 and joined the Swiss Confederation in 1351. In the 16th century, it was a focal point of the Swiss REFORMATION. Ulrich ZWINGLI founded Swiss Protestantism at Zurich's cathedral in 1523. In the 18th and 19th centuries, the city developed as a cultural and scientific centre. It has the Swiss National Museum and many old churches. Zurich is the commercial hub of Switzerland, and has numerous banking and financial institutions. Industries: motor vehicles, machinery, paper, textiles, electrical products, printing and publishing, tourism. Pop. (1996) 344,000.

Zwingli, Ulrich (1484–1531) Swiss Protestant theologian and reformer. He was ordained as a Roman Catholic priest in 1506, but his studies of the New Testament in ERASMUS's editions led him to become a reformer. By 1522 he was preaching reformed doctrine in Zurich, a centre for the REFORMATION. More radical than LUTHER, he saw communion as mainly symbolic and commemorative. He died while serving as a military chaplain with the Zurich army during a battle against the Catholic cantons at Kappel.

Zworykin, Vladimir Kosma (1889–1982) US physicist and inventor, b. Russia, a pioneer of TELEVISION. In 1929 he joined the Radio Corporation of America (RCA), becoming its director of electronic development and a vice president (1947). Zworykin and his colleagues developed the iconoscope, the forerunner of the modern television camera tube, and the kinescope, a CATHODE-RAY TUBE for television sets. In 1928, he patented a colour television system. He also invented the ELECTRON MICROSCOPE and developed a secondary emission multiplier for a sensitive radiation detector. He received (1967) the National Medal of Science for his inventions and contributions to medical research.

zygote In sexual reproduction, a cell formed by fusion of a male and a female GAMETE. It contains a DIPLOID number of CHROMOSOMES, half contributed by the SPERM, half by the OVUM. Through successive cell divisions, the zygote develops into an EMBRYO.

Zyuganov, Gennady (1944–) Russian politician. He moved up the Soviet Communist Party hierarchy in the 1970s and 1980s, taking positions dealing with ideology and propaganda. In 1993, he became chairman of the executive committee of the reconstituted Russian Communist Party and was elected to the State Duma (the lower house of the Russian parliament). In the 1995 parliamentary elections, the Communist Party gained the largest number of votes. Zyuganov mounted a strong challenge in the 1996 presidential elections, but was defeated by a coalition of Boris YELTSIN and Aleksander LEBED.

CONVERSIONS

Length
1 inch (in)	= 2.54 centimetres (cm)
	= 25.4 millimetres (mm)
1 foot (ft)	= 0.3048 metre (m)
1 yard (yd)	= 0.9144 metre
1 mile (mi)	= 1.6093 kilometres (km)
1 centimetre	= 0.3937 inch
1 metre	= 3.2808 feet = 1.0936 yards
1 kilometre	= 0.6214 mile

Area
1 square inch	= 6.4516 square centimetres
1 square foot	= 0.0929 square metre
1 acre	= 0.4047 hectare
1 square mile	= 2.5899 square kilometres
1 square centimetre	= 0.155 square inch
1 square metre	= 10.7639 square feet
1 hectare	= 2.471 acres
1 square kilometre	= 0.3861 square mile

Volume
1 cubic inch	= 16.3871 cubic centimetres
1 cubic foot	= 0.0283 cubic metre
1 cubic yard	= 0.7646 cubic metre
1 cubic centimetre	= 0.061 cubic inch
1 cubic metre	= 35.3147 cubic feet
1 cubic metre	= 1.3030 cubic yards

Capacity
1 UK fluid ounce (fl oz)	= 0.02841 litre (l)
1 US fluid ounce	= 0.02961 litre
1 UK pint (pt)	= 0.56821 litre
1 US pint	= 0.47321 litre
1 UK gallon	= 4.546 litres
1 US gallon	= 3.7854 litres
1 litre	= 35.1961 fluid ounces (UK)
	= 33.814 fluid ounces (US)
	= 1.7598 pints (UK)
	= 2.1134 pints (US)
	= 0.22 gallon (UK)
	= 0.2642 gallon (US)
1 US cup	= 8 fluid ounces
1 UK pint	= 1.2 US pints
1 UK gallon	= 1.2009 US gallons
1 US pint	= 0.83 UK pint
1 US gallon	= 0.8327 UK gallon

Weight (avoirdupois)
1 ounce (oz)	= 28.3495 grams (g)
1 pound (lb)	= 0.454 kilogram (kg)
1 UK ton	= 1.016 tonnes
1 US ton	= 0.9072 tonne
1 gram	= 0.0353 ounce
1 kilogram	= 2.205 pounds
1 tonne	= 0.9842 UK ton = 1.1023 US tons
1 UK ton	= 1.1199 US tons
1 US ton	= 0.8929 UK ton

Temperature
°Celsius to °Fahrenheit: ×9, ÷5, +32
°Fahrenheit to °Celsius: −32, ×5, ÷9

CONVERSIONS

Energy (work, heat)
1,000 British thermal units (Btu)	= 0.293 kilowatt hour
100,000 British thermal units	= 1 therm
1 UK horsepower	= 550 ft-lb per second
	= 745.7 watts
1 US horsepower	= 746 watts

Nautical length and speed
UK nautical mile	= 6,080 feet
International nautical mile	= 6,076.1 feet
	= 0.9994 UK nautical mile
1 knot = 1 UK nautical mile per hour = 1.15 mph	

Petroleum
1 barrel = 34.97 UK gallons = 42 US gallons
= 0.159 cubic metres

Precious stones
1 troy ounce	= 480 grains
1 metric carat	= 200 milligrams

Type sizes
72 1/4 points	= 1 inch
1 didot point	= 0.376 mm
1 pica em	= 12 points

SI UNITS

The *Système International d'Unités* is the worldwide standard system of units used by scientists. Originally proposed in 1960, it is based on seven basic units.

Measurement	Unit	Symbol
Basic units		
Length	metre	m
Mass	kilogram	kg
Time	second	s
Electric current	ampere	A
Thermodynamic temperature	kelvin	K
Amount of substance	mole	mol
Luminous intensity	candela	cd
Supplementary units		
Plane angle	radian	rad
Solid angle	steradian	sr
Derived units		
Frequency	hertz	Hz
Force	newton	N
Pressure, stress	pascal	Pa
Work (energy, heat)	joule	J
Power	watt	W
Electric charge	coulomb	C
Electromotive force	volt	V
Electric resistance	ohm	Ω
Electric conductance	siemens	S
Electric capacitance	farad	F
Inductance	henry	H
Magnetic flux	weber	Wb
Magnetic flux density	tesla	T
Illuminance	lux	lx
Luminous flux	lumen	lm
Radiation exposure	röntgen	r

PLANET EARTH

Mean distance from the Sun	149,500,000km (92,860,000mi)
Average speed around the Sun	108,000km/h (66,600mph)
Age	c.4,500,000,000 years
Mass	5,975 million million million tonnes
Density	5,515 times that of water
Volume	1,083,207,000,000cu km (260,000,000,000cu mi)
Area	509,450,000sq km (196,672,000sq mi)
Land surface	149,450,000sq km (57,688,000sq mi) = 29.3% of total area
Water surface area	360,000,000sq km (138,984,000sq mi) = 70.7% of total
Equatorial circumference	40,075km (24,902mi)
Polar circumference	40,008km (24,860mi)
Equatorial diameter	12,756km (7,926mi)
Polar diameter	12,714km (7,900mi)

LARGEST ECONOMIES

Country	GNP*
USA	7,903.0
Japan	4,089.1
Germany	2,179.8
France	1,465.4
UK	1,264.3
Italy	1,157.0
China	923.6
Brazil	767.6
Canada	580.9
Spain	555.2
India	427.4
South Korea	398.8
Netherlands	389.1
Australia	387.0
Mexico	368.1

* Gross National Product in US$ billions (1998)

LARGEST ISLANDS

	sq km	sq mi
Europe		
Great Britain [8]	229,900	88,700
Iceland	103,000	39,800
Ireland	84,400	32,600
Novaya Zemlya (N)	48,200	18,600
Sicily	25,700	9,900
Sardinia	24,090	9,300
Asia		
Borneo [3]	743,000	287,400
Sumatra [6]	425,000	164,000
Honshū [7]	230,800	89,100
Sulawesi	189,200	73,000
Java	126,500	48,800
Luzon	104,700	40,400
Mindanao	95,000	36,600
Hokkaidō	83,500	32,200
Sakhalin	76,400	29,500
Sri Lanka	65,600	25,300
Africa		
Madagascar [4]	587,000	226,700
Socotra	3,100	1,200
Réunion	2,510	969
North America		
Greenland [1]	2,175,000	840,000
Baffin Island [5]	507,500	195,900
Victoria Island [9]	212,200	81,900
Ellesmere Island [10]	196,200	75,800
Cuba	110,860	42,800
Newfoundland	96,000	37,100
Hispaniola	76,500	29,500
Jamaica	11,000	4,200
Puerto Rico	8,900	3,400
South America		
Tierra del Fuego	47,000	18,100
Falkland Island (E)	6,800	2,600
Oceania*		
New Guinea [2]	885,800	342,000
New Zealand (S)	150,500	58,100
New Zealand (N)	114,700	44,300
Tasmania	68,300	26,400
Hawaii	10,450	4,000

* Geographers consider Australia to be a continental landmass

LARGEST INLAND LAKES AND SEAS

	Location	sq km	sq mi
Europe			
Lake Ladoga	Russia	17,700	6,800
Lake Onega	Russia	9,600	3,700
Saimaa system	Finland	8,000	3,100
Vänern	Sweden	6,500	2,100
Asia			
Caspian Sea [1]	W. Central Asia	371,000	143,000
Aral Sea* [6]	Kazakstan/ Uzbekistan	33,640	13,000
Lake Baikal [9]	Russia	31,500	12,200
Tonlé Sap	Cambodia	20,000	7,700
Lake Balkhash	Kazakstan	18,400	7,100
Africa			
Victoria Nyanza [3]	East Africa	68,000	26,000
Lake Tanganyika [7]	Central Africa	33,000	12,700
Lake Malawi [10]	East Africa	29,600	11,400
Lake Chad	Central Africa	26,000	10,000
Lake Turkana	Ethiopia/Kenya	8,500	3,300
Lake Volta†	Ghana	8,480	3,250
North America			
Lake Superior [2]	Canada/USA	82,400	31,800
Lake Huron [4]	Canada/USA	59,600	23,010
Lake Michigan [5]	USA	58,000	22,300
Great Bear Lake [8]	Canada	31,800	12,280
Great Slave Lake	Canada	28,400	11,000
Lake Erie	Canada/USA	25,700	9,900
Lake Winnipeg	Canada	24,500	9,500
Lake Ontario	Canada/USA	19,700	7,600
Lake Nicaragua	Nicaragua	8,000	3,100
South America			
Lake Titicaca‡	Bolivia/Peru	8,300	3,200
Lake Poopó	Peru	2,800	1,100
Australia			
Lake Eyre§	Australia	9,300	3,600
Lake Torrens§	Australia	5,800	2,200
Lake Gairdner§	Australia	4,800	1,900

* Shrinking in area due to environmental factors; until the 1980s it was the world's 4th largest
† Artificial lake created by Akosombo Dam (1966)
‡ Lake Maracaibo, in Venezuela, is far larger at 13,260 sq km (5,120 sq mi), but is linked to the Caribbean by a narrow channel and therefore not an "inland" lake
§ Salt lakes that vary in size with rainfall

OCEANS

Ocean	Area			Average depth		Greatest known depth		
	sq km	sq mi	%	m	ft		m	ft
Pacific	166,000,000	69,356,000	49.9	4,300	14,100	Mariana Trench	11,033	36,198
Atlantic	82,000,000	32,000,000	25.7	3,700	12,100	Puerto Rico Trench*	8,650	28,370
Indian	73,600,000	28,400,000	20.5	4,000	13,000	Java Trench	7,725	25,344
Arctic	13,986,000	5,400,000	3.9	1,330	4,300	Molloy Deep	5,608	18,399

*7th deepest trench in the world; 8 of the deepest 10, including 1-6, are in the Pacific Ocean

HIGHEST MOUNTAINS

	Location	m	ft		Location	m	ft
Europe				Mt Kenya	Kenya	5,200	17,058
Elbrus*	Russia	5,633	18,481	Ruwenzori	Uganda/Zaïre	5,109	16,763
Mont Blanc[†][‡]	France/Italy	4,810	15,781				
Monte Rosa[‡]	Italy/Switzerland	4,634	15,203	**North America**			
also				Mt McKinley (Denali)[‡]	USA (Alaska)	6,194	20,321
Matterhorn (Cervino)[‡]	Italy/Switzerland	4,478	14,691	Mt Logan	Canada	6,050	19,849
Jungfrau	Switzerland	4,158	13,642	Citlaltépetl (Orizaba)	Mexico	5,700	18,701
Grossglockner	Austria	3,797	12,457	Mt St Elias	USA/Canada	5,489	18,008
Mulhacen	Spain	3,478	11,411	Popocatépetl	Mexico	5,452	17,887
Etna	Italy (Sicily)	3,340	10,958	*also*			
Zugspitze	Germany	2,962	9,718	Mt Whitney	USA	4,418	14,495
Olympus	Greece	2,917	9,570	Tajumulco	Guatemala	4,220	13,845
Galdhopiggen	Norway	2,468	8,100				
Ben Nevis	UK (Scotland)	1,343	4,406	**South America**			
				Aconcagua[#]	Argentina	6,960	22,834
Asia[§]				Ojos del Salado	Argentina/Chile	6,863	22,516
Everest	China/Nepal	8,848	29,029	Pissis	Argentina	6,779	22,241
K2 (Godwin Austen)	China/Kashmir	8,611	28,251	Mercedario	Argentina/Chile	6,770	22,211
Kanchenjunga[‡]	India/Nepal	8,586	28,169				
Lhotse[‡]	China/Nepal	8,516	27,939	**Oceania**			
Makalu[‡]	China/Nepal	8,481	27,824	Puncak Jaya	Indonesia (W Irian)	5,029	16,499
Cho Oyu	China/Nepal	8,201	26,906	Puncak Trikora	Indonesia (W Irian)	4,750	15,584
Dhaulagiri[‡]	Nepal	8,172	26,811	Puncak Mandala	Indonesia (W Irian)	4,702	15,427
Manaslu (Kutang)[‡]	Nepal	8,156	26,758	Mt Wilhelm	Papua New Guinea	4,508	14,790
Nanga Parbat	Kashmir	8,126	26,660	*also*			
Annapurna[‡]	Nepal	8,078	26,502	Mauna Kea	USA (Hawaii)	4 205	13 796
also				Mauna Loa	USA (Hawaii)	4,169	13,678
Kommunizma Pik	Tajikistan	7,495	24,590	Mt Cook (Aorangi)	New Zealand	3,764	12,349
Ararat	Turkey	5,165	16,945	Mt Kosciusko	Australia	2,228	7,310
Fujiyama (Fuji-san)	Japan	3,776	12,388				
				Antarctica			
Africa				Mt Tyree	—	4,965	16,289
Kilimanjaro	Tanzania	5,895	19,340	Vinson Massif	—	4,897	16,066

* Caucasus Mountains include 14 other peaks higher than Mont Blanc, the highest point in non-Russian Europe
† Highest point is in France; the highest point wholly in Italian territory is 4,760m (15,616ft)
‡ Many mountains, especially in Asia, have two or more significant peaks; only the highest ones are listed here
§ The ranges of Central Asia have more than 100 peaks over 7,315m (24,000ft); thus the first 10 listed here constitute the world's 10 highest mountains   # Highest mountain outside Asia

LONGEST RIVERS

	Outflow	km	mi		Outflow	km	mi
Europe				**North America**			
Volga	Caspian Sea	3,750	2,330	Mississippi-Missouri[4]	Gulf of Mexico	6,050	3,760
Danube	Black Sea	2,859	1,770	Mackenzie	Arctic Ocean	4,240	2,630
Ural	Caspian Sea	2,535	1,575	Missouri	Mississippi	4,120	2,560
				Mississippi	Gulf of Mexico	3,780	2,350
Asia				Yukon	Pacific Ocean	3,185	1,980
Yangtze [3]	Pacific Ocean	6,300	3,900				
Yenisey-Angara [5]	Arctic Ocean	5,550	3,445	**South America**			
Huang He [6]	Pacific Ocean	5,500	3,400	Amazon [2]	Atlantic Ocean	6,430	3,990
Ob-Irtysh [7]	Arctic Ocean	5,410	3,360	Paraná-Plata	Atlantic Ocean	4,000	2,400
Amur [10]	Pacific Ocean	4,400	2,730	Purus	Amazon	3,350	2,080
Mekong [9]	Pacific Ocean	4,180	2,600				
				Australia			
Africa				Murray-Darling	Southern Ocean	3,750	2,830
Nile [1]	Mediterranean	6,700	4,160	Darling	Murray	3,070	1,905
Congo (Zaïre) [8]	Atlantic Ocean	4,670	2,900	Murray	Southern Ocean	2,575	1,600
Niger	Atlantic Ocean	4,180	2,600	Murrumbidgee	Murray	1,690	1,050

LARGEST CITIES

UN estimates for "urban agglomerations", which take no account of administrative boundaries.

City	Country	1994 Est.	2015 Proj.
Tokyo-Yokohama	Japan	26,518,000	28,700,000
New York	USA	16,271,000	17,600,000
São Paulo	Brazil	16,110,000	20,800,000
Mexico City	Mexico	15,525,000	18,800,000
Shanghai	China	14,709,000	23,400,000
Mumbai	India	14,496,000	27,400,000
Los Angeles	USA	12,232,000	14,300,000
Beijing	China	12,030,000	19,400,000
Calcutta	India	11,485,000	17,600,000
Seoul	S. Korea	11,451,000	13,100,000
Jakarta	Indonesia	11,017,000	21,200,000
Osaka-Kobe-Kyoto	Japan	10,585,000	10,600,000

WORLD POPULATION

Date	Millions	Date	Millions	Date	Millions
2000BC	100	1800	900	1970	3,700
1000BC	120	1850	1,250	1980	4,450
1	180	1900	1,620	1990	5,245
1000	275	1920	1,860	1995	5,735
1250	375	1930	2,070	2000*	6,100
1500	420	1940	2,300	2050*	11,000
1650	500	1950	2,500		
1700	615	1960	3,050		

United Nations "medium" estimates

KINGS AND QUEENS OF ENGLAND AND BRITAIN

Years	Monarch	Age*	R'd†	Years	Monarch	Age*	R'd†
KINGS AND QUEENS OF ENGLAND				1413-22	Henry V	34	9
West Saxon Kings (House of Cerdic)				1422-61	Henry VI#	49	39
802-839	Egbert‡	—	37				
839-858	Ethelwulf	—	19	**House of York**			
858-860	Ethelbald	—	2	1461-83	Edward IV¶	40	21
860-866	Ethelbert	—	6	1483	Edward V	12	2m
866-871	Ethelred I	—	5	1483-85	Richard III	32	2
871-899	Alfred (the Great)	52	28				
899-924	Edward (the Elder)	55	25	**House of Tudor**			
924-939	Athelstan (the Glorious)	45	15	1485-1509	Henry VII	52	23
939-946	Edmund I	25	6	1509-47	Henry VIII	55	37
946-955	Edred	32	9	1547-53	Edward VI	15	6
955-959	Edwy (the Fair)	18	3	1553	Jane (Lady Jane Grey)**	16	9d
959-975	Edgar (the Peaceful)	32	16	1553-58	Mary I (Mary Tudor)	42	5
975-978	Edward I (the Martyr)	17	3	1558-1603	Elizabeth I	69	44
978-1016	Ethelred II (the Unready)	47	38				
1016	Edmund II (Ironside)	2	7m	**KINGS AND QUEENS OF BRITAIN**			
				House of Stuart			
Danish Kings (House of Denmark)				1603-25	James I (VI of Scotland)	58	22
1016-35	Canute (Cnut)‡	40	19	1625-49	Charles I	48	23
1035-40	Harold I (Harefoot)	23	4	1649-60	Commonwealth††		
1040-42	Hardecanute (Harthacnut)	24	2	1660-85	Charles II	54	24
				1685-88	James II	67	3
West Saxon Kings (restored)				Interregnum 11 December 1688 to 12 February 1689			
1042-66	Edward II (the Confessor)	61	23	1689-1702	William III	51	13
1066	Harold II (Godwinesson)	45	10m	[and to 1694	Mary II	32	5]
				1702-14	Anne	49	12
House of Normandy							
1066-87	William I (the Conqueror)‡	60	20	**House of Hanover**			
1087-1100	William II (Rufus)	41	12	1714-27	George I (Elector of Hanover)	67	13
1100-35	Henry I (Beauclerc)	67	35	1727-60	George II	76	33
1135-54	Stephen§	53	18	1760-1820	George III	81	59
				1820-30	George IV	67	10
House of Anjou (Plantagenets)				1830-37	William IV	71	7
1154-89	Henry II (Curtmantle)	56	34	1837-1901	Victoria	81	63
1189-99	Richard I (the Lionheart)	42	9				
1199-1216	John (Lackland)	48	17	**House of Saxe-Coburg and Gotha**			
1216-72	Henry III	65	56	1901-1910	Edward VII	68	9
1272-1307	Edward I (Longshanks)	68	34				
1307-27	Edward II	43	19	**House of Windsor ‡‡**			
1327-77	Edward III	64	50	1910-36	George V	70	25
1377-99	Richard II	33	22	1936	Edward VIII§§	77	10m
				1936-52	George VI	56	15
House of Lancaster				1952-	Elizabeth II	—	—
1399-1413	Henry IV	47	13				

* On death † Duration of reign in years (m = months, d=days) ‡ Became ruler by conquest § Son of William's daughter Adele and Stephen, Count of Blois; sometimes given as the monarch of the House of Blois # Deposed March 1461, restored October 1470, deposed April 1471, and killed in Tower of London May 1471 ¶ Acceded March 1461, deposed October 1470, restored April 1471 ** Edward was forced to name Lady Jane as his successor and a Council of State proclaimed her Queen; Mary, proclaimed Queen by the Council, had Jane beheaded in 1554 †† 1649-53 Council of State; 1653-58 Oliver Cromwell, Lord Protector; 1658-60 Richard Cromwell (son), Lord Protector ‡‡ Name changed from the German Saxe-Coburg and Gotha on 17 July 1917 (during World War 1) §§ Abdicated at the age of 42

UK PRIME MINISTERS

Years	Prime Minister	Party	Years	Prime Minister	Party
1721-42	Sir Robert Walpole	Whig	1866-68	Earl of Derby	Conservative
1742-43	Earl of Wilmington	Whig	1868	Benjamin Disraeli	Conservative
1743-54	Henry Pelham	Whig	1868-74	William Gladstone	Liberal
1754-56	Duke of Newcastle	Whig	1874-80	Benjamin Disraeli	Conservative
1756-57	Duke of Devonshire	Whig	1880-85	William Gladstone	Liberal
1757-62	Duke of Newcastle	Whig	1885-86	Marquis of Salisbury	Conservative
1762-63	Earl of Bute	Tory	1886	William Gladstone	Liberal
1763-65	George Grenville	Whig	1886-92	Marquis of Salisbury	Conservative
1765-66	Marquis of Rockingham	Whig	1892-94	William Gladstone	Liberal
1766-67	Earl of Chatham*	Whig	1894-95	Earl of Rosebery	Liberal
1767-70	Duke of Grafton	Whig	1895-1902	Marquis of Salisbury	Conservative
1770-82	Lord North	Tory	1902-05	Arthur Balfour	Conservative
1782	Marquis of Rockingham	Whig	1905-08	Henry Campbell-Bannerman	Liberal
1782-83	Earl of Shelbourne	Whig	1908-15	Herbert Asquith	Liberal
1783	Duke of Portland	Coalition	1915-16	Herbert Asquith	Coalition[§]
1783-1801	William Pitt[†]	Tory	1916-22	David Lloyd George	Coalition[§]
1801-04	Henry Addington	Tory	1922-23	Andrew Bonar Law	Conservative
1804-06	William Pitt[†]	Tory	1923-24	Stanley Baldwin	Conservative
1806-07	Lord Grenville	Whig	1924	Ramsay MacDonald	Labour
1807-09	Duke of Portland	Coalition	1924-29	Stanley Baldwin	Conservative
1809-12	Spencer Perceval	Tory	1929-31	Ramsay MacDonald	Labour
1812-27	Earl of Liverpool	Tory	1931-35	Ramsay MacDonald	National#
1827	George Canning	Tory	1935-37	Stanley Baldwin	National#
1827-28	Viscount Goderich	Tory	1937-40	Neville Chamberlain	National#
1828-30	Duke of Wellington	Tory	1940-45	Winston Churchill	Coalition
1830-34	Earl Grey	Whig	1945-51	Clement Attlee	Labour
1834	Viscount Melbourne	Whig	1951-55	Winston Churchill	Conservative
1834-35	Sir Robert Peel	Tory	1955-57	Anthony Eden	Conservative
1835-41	Viscount Melbourne	Whig	1957-63	Harold Macmillan	Conservative
1841-46	Sir Robert Peel	Conservative	1963-64	Alec Douglas-Home	Conservative
1846-52	Lord John Russell[‡]	Whig	1964-70	Harold Wilson	Labour
1852	Earl of Derby	Conservative	1970-74	Edward Heath	Conservative
1852-55	Earl of Aberdeen	Peelite	1974-76	Harold Wilson	Labour
1855-58	Viscount Palmerston	Liberal	1976-79	James Callaghan	Labour
1858-59	Earl of Derby	Conservative	1979-90	Margaret Thatcher	Conservative
1859-65	Viscount Palmerston	Liberal	1990-97	John Major	Conservative
1865-66	Earl Russell[‡]	Liberal	1997-	Tony Blair	Labour

William Pitt the Elder   †William Pitt the Younger   ‡Lord John Russell later became the Earl Russell

§ *Coalition governments; Lloyd-George was Liberal   # National Coalition governments; Chamberlain was Conservative*

SOUTH AFRICAN LEADERS

Until the Republic of South Africa left the Commonwealth in 1961 the Governor-General performed the role of President, and until 1984, when the prime ministership was abolished, the presidential function remained largely non-political.

Years	Prime Minister	Party
1910-19	Louis Botha	South Africa Party
1919-24	Jan Christiaan Smuts	South Africa Party
1924-39	James Hertzog	National
1939-48	Jan Christiaan Smuts	United
1949-54	Daniel Malan	National
1954-58	Johannes Strijdom	National
1958-66	Hendrik Verwoerd	National
1966-78	Johannes Vorster	National
1978-84	Pieter Botha	National

Years	President	
1989-94	F.W. de Klerk	National
1994-99	Nelson Mandela	ANC
1999-	Thabo Mbeki	ANC

NEW ZEALAND PRIME MINISTERS

Years	Prime Minister	Party
1949-57	Sidney Holland	National[†]
1957	Keith Holyoake	National
1957-60	Walter Nash	Labour
1960-72	Keith Holyoake	National
1972	John Marshall	National
1972-74	Norman Kirk	Labour
1974	Hugh Watt[‡]	Labour
1974-75	Wallace Rowling	Labour
1975-84	Robert Muldoon	National
1984-89	David Lange	Labour
1989-90	Geoffrey Palmer	Labour
1990	Michael Moore	Labour
1990-96	Jim Bolger	National
1997-99	Jenny Shipley	National
1999-	Helen Clark	Labour

† *Formed from merger of Reform Party and United Party in 1936*   ‡ *Acting Prime Minister*

US PRESIDENTS

No.	President	Years	Party	Age*
1.	George Washington	1789-97	Federalist	57
2.	John Adams	1797-1801	Federalist	61
3.	Thomas Jefferson	1801-09	Dem-Rep	57
4.	James Madison	1809-17	Dem-Rep	57
5.	James Monroe	1817-25	Dem-Rep	58
6.	John Quincy Adams	1825-29	Dem-Rep	57
7.	Andrew Jackson	1829-37	Democrat	61
8.	Martin Van Buren	1837-41	Democrat	54
9.	William H. Harrison†	1841	Whig	68
10.	John Tyler	1841-45	Whig	51
11.	James K. Polk	1845-49	Democrat	49
12.	Zachary Taylor†	1849-50	Whig	64
13.	Millard Fillmore	1850-53	Whig	50
14.	Franklin Pierce	1853-57	Democrat	48
15.	James Buchanan	1857-61	Democrat	65
16.	Abraham Lincoln‡	1861-65	Republican	52
17.	Andrew Johnson§	1865-69	Nat. Union	56
18.	Ulysses S. Grant#	1869-77	Republican	46
19.	Rutherford B. Hayes	1877-81	Republican	54
20.	James A. Garfield‡	1881	Republican	49
21.	Chester A. Arthur	1881-85	Republican	51
22.	Grover Cleveland	1885-89	Democrat	47
23.	Benjamin Harrison	1889-93	Republican	55
24.	Grover Cleveland	1893-97	Democrat	55
25.	William McKinley‡	1897-1901	Republican	54
26.	Theodore Roosevelt	1901-09	Republican	43
27.	William H. Taft	1909-13	Republican	51
28.	Woodrow Wilson	1913-21	Democrat	56
29.	Warren Harding†	1921-23	Republican	55
30.	Calvin Coolidge	1923-29	Democrat	51
31.	Herbert Hoover	1929-33	Republican	54
32.	Franklin D. Roosevelt†	1933-45	Democrat	51
33.	Harry S. Truman	1945-53	Democrat	60
34.	Dwight D. Eisenhower	1953-61	Republican	62
35.	John F. Kennedy‡	1961-63	Democrat	43
36.	Lyndon Johnson	1963-69	Democrat	55
37.	Richard Nixon¶	1969-74	Republican	56
38.	Gerald Ford**	1974-77	Republican	61
39.	Jimmy Carter	1977-81	Democrat	52
40.	Ronald Reagan	1981-89	Republican	69
41.	George Bush	1989-93	Republican	64
42.	Bill Clinton	1993-2000	Democrat	46
43.	George W. Bush	2000-	Republican	54

*At inauguration; Kennedy was the youngest, Reagan the oldest † Died in office and succeeded by the vice president ‡ Assassinated in office and succeeded by the vice president § A Democrat, Johnson was nominated vice president by Republicans and elected with Lincoln on a National Union ticket # Born Hiram Grant ¶ Resigned in face of impeachment proceedings following the Watergate scandal ** Born Leslie Lynch King

BOOKER PRIZE

Year	Author and title
1987	Penelope Lively Moon Tiger
1988	Peter Carey Oscar and Lucinda
1989	Kazuo Ishiguro The Remains of the Day
1990	A.S. Byatt Possession
1991	Ben Okri The Famished Road
1992	Michael Ondaatje The English Patient
	Barry Unsworth Sacred Hunger
1993	Roddy Doyle Paddy Clarke Ha Ha Ha
1994	James Kelman How Late It Was, How Late
1995	Pat Barker The Ghost Road
1996	Graham Swift Last Orders
1997	Arundhati Roy The God of Small Things
1998	Ian McEwan Amsterdam
1999	J.M. Coetzee Disgrace
2000	Margaret Atwood The Blind Assassin

AUSTRALIAN PRIME MINISTERS

Years	Prime Minister	Party
1900-03	Edmund Barton	Protectionist
1903-04	Alfred Deakin	Protectionist
1904	John Watson	Labor
1904-05	George Reid	Free Trade
1905-08	Alfred Deakin	Protectionist
1908-09	Andrew Fisher	Labor
1909-10	Alfred Deakin	Fusion*
1910-13	Andrew Fisher	Labor
1913-14	Joseph Cook	Liberal
1914-15	Andrew Fisher	Labor
1915-17	William Hughes	National Labor
1917-23	William Hughes	Nationalist
1923-29	Stanley Bruce	Nationalist
1929-32	James Scullin	Labor
1932-39	Joseph Lyons	United Australia†
1939	Earle Page	Country
1939-41	Robert Menzies	United Australia†
1941	Arthur Fadden	Country
1941-45	John Curtin	Labor
1945	Francis Forde	Labor
1945-49	Joseph Chifley	Labor
1949-66	Robert Menzies	Liberal
1966-67	Harold Holt	Liberal
1967-68	John McEwen	Country
1968-71	John Gorton	Liberal
1971-72	William McMahon	Liberal
1972-75	Gough Whitlam	Labor
1975-83	Malcolm Fraser	Liberal
1983-91	Bob Hawke	Labor
1991-96	Paul Keating	Labor
1996-	John Howard	Liberal-National‡

* Protectionist-Free Trade Alliance
† Became the Liberal Party in 1944 ‡ Coalition

INDIAN PRIME MINISTERS

Years	Prime Minister	Government
1947-64	Jawaharlal Nehru	Congress
1964	Gulzari Lal Nanda	Congress
1964-66	Lal Shastri	Congress
1966	Gulzari Lal Nanda	Congress
1966-77	Indira Gandhi	Congress
1977-79	Morarji Desai	Janata
1979-80	Charan Singh	Coalition
1980-84	Indira Gandhi	Congress (I)
1984-89	Rajiv Gandhi	Congress (I)
1989-90	V.P. Singh	Coalition
1990-91	Chandra Shekhar	Janata
1991-96	P.V. Narasimha Rao	Congress (I)
1996-97	H.D. Deve Gowda	Coalition
1997-98	Inder Kumar Gujral	Coalition
1998-	Atal Bihari Vajpayee	BJP

UN SECRETARIES-GENERAL

Secretary-General	Country	Tenure
Trygve Lie	Norway	1946-53
Dag Hammarskjöld	Sweden	1953-61
U Thant	Burma	1962-71
Kurt Waldheim	Austria	1971-81
Javier Pérez de Cuéllar	Peru	1982-92
Boutros Boutros Ghali	Egypt	1992-96
Kofi Annan	Ghana	1997-

2000 SUMMER OLYMPIC GAMES (SYDNEY) GOLD MEDALLISTS

ATHLETICS	Men	Country	Women	Country
Track events				
100 metres	Maurice Greene	USA	Marion Jones	USA
200 metres	Konstantinos Kenteris	Greece	Marion Jones	USA
400 metres	Michael Johnson	USA	Cathy Freeman	Australia
800 metres	Nils Schumann	Germany	Maria Mutola	Mozambique
1,500 metres	Noah Ngeny	Kenya	Nouria Merah-Benida	Algeria
5,000 metres	Millon Wolde	Ethiopia	Gabriela Szabo	Romania
10,000 metres	Haile Gebrselassie	Ethiopia	Derartu Tulu	Ethiopia
Marathon	Gezahgne Abera	Ethiopia	Naoko Takahashi	Japan
100m hurdles	—	—	Olga Shishigina	Kazakhstan
110m hurdles	Anier Garcia	Cuba	—	—
400m hurdles	Angelo Taylor	USA	Irina Privalova	Russia
3,000m steeple	Reuben Kosgei	Kenya	—	—
20km walk	Robert Korzeniowski	Poland	Liping Wang	China
50km walk	Robert Korzeniowski	Poland	—	—
4 × 100m relay	[Drummond/Williams/ Lewis/Greene]	USA	[Fynes/Sturrup/Davis-Thompson/Ferguson]	Bahamas
4 × 400m relay	[Harrison/Pettigrew/ Harrison/Johnson]	USA	[Miles-Clark/Hennagan/ Jones/Colander-Richardson]	USA
Field events				
High jump	Sergey Kliugin	Russia	Yelena Yelesina	Russia
Long jump	Ivan Pedroso	Cuba	Heike Drechsler	Germany
Triple jump	Jonathon Edwards	Germany	Tereza Marinova	Bulgaria
Pole vault	Nick Hysong	USA	Stacy Dragila	USA
Javelin	Jan Zelezny	Czech R.	Trine Hattestad	Norway
Shot put	Arsi Harju	Finland	Yanina Korolchik	Belarus
Discus	Virgilijus Alekna	Lithuania	Ellina Zvereva	Belarus
Hammer	Szymon Ziolkowski	Poland	Kamila Skolimowska	Poland
Multi-discipline				
Heptathlon	—	—	Denise Lewis	GB
Decathlon	Erki Nool	Estonia	—	—
SWIMMING	**Men**	**Country**	**Women**	**Country**
50m freestyle	Anthony Ervin	USA	Inge de Bruijn	Netherlands
100m freestyle	P. van den Hoogenband	Netherlands	Inge de Bruijn	Netherlands
200m freestyle	P. van den Hoogenband*	Netherlands	Susie O'Neill	Australia
400m freestyle	Ian Thorpe*	Australia	Brooke Bennett	USA
800m freestyle	—	—	Brooke Bennett	USA
1,500m freestyle	Grant Hackett	Australia	–	
100m breaststroke	Domenico Fioravanti	Italy	Megan Quann	USA
200m breaststroke	P. van den Hoogenband	Netherlands	Agnes Kovacs	Hungary
100m backstroke	Lenny Krayzelburg	USA	Diana Mocanu	Romania
200m backstroke	Lenny Krayzelburg	USA	Diana Mocanu	Romania
100m butterfly	Lars Froelander	Sweden	Inge de Bruijn*	Netherlands
200m butterfly	Tom Malchow	USA	Misty Hyman	USA
200m medley	Massimiliano Rosolino	Italy	Yana Klochkova	Ukraine
400m medley	Tom Dolan*	USA	Yana Klochkova*	Ukraine
4 × 100m freestyle relay	[Thorpe/Klim/ Callus/Fydler]*	Australia	[Thompson/Shealy/ Torres/van Dyken]*	USA
4 × 200m freestyle relay	[Thorpe/Klim/ Kirby/Pearson]*	Australia	[Arsenault/Munz/ Benzo/Thompson]	USA
4 × 100m medley relay	[Krayzelburg/Moses/ Crocker/Hall]*	USA	[Bedford/Quann/ Thompson/Torres]*	USA

New world record